# THE NEW STANDARD ENCYCLOPEDIA OF ART

# THE NEW STANDARD ENCYCLOPEDIA OF ART

## Architecture · Sculpture · Painting
## Decorative Arts

*Based on the Work of*

LOUIS HOURTICQ

*Member of the Institute of France*

*and*

*Translated Under the Supervision of*

TANCRED BORENIUS, Ph.D., D.Lit.

*Durning-Lawrence Professor of the History of Art*
*in the University of London*

*Fully Revised Under the Supervision of*

J. LEROY DAVIDSON *and* PHILIPPA GERRY

*With the Assistance of the*
*Staff of the Index of Twentieth-Century Artists College Art Association*
*New York City*

TWO VOLUMES IN ONE

*DeLuxe Edition*

GARDEN CITY PUBLISHING CO., INC.

NEW YORK

GARDEN CITY PUBLISHING CO., INC.
1939

# *List of Halftone Plates*

Captions refer to page groups. Plates are numbered in lower right-hand corner and appear in their numerical order.

## VOLUME I



## VOLUME II

# *Preface*

THE purpose of this encyclopedia is to bring together in compact and accessible form the pertinent facts of the whole history of art. In order to do this it has been necessary to make what may at first seem arbitrary and inconsistent selections. Each contributor has judged the suitable form required by his material. Thus, in material which has been as intensively studied as Italian Renaissance art, special attention has been given to individual artists and the framework of documentary evidence upon which study of their work is based. On the other hand in such fields as Chinese and Japanese art, the scientific study of which in the West is still in its infancy, general articles have been written to provide a broad foundation upon which the student can build. Between these two extremes there is considerable variation, subjects having been handled in the way which would best serve the needs of the student. No arbitrary system has been attempted. For instance, cities which are of fundamental art-historical importance have been treated as units, whereas in other cities leading monuments have been indexed as special articles.

This encyclopedia is based upon the French work by Louis Hourticq, translated under the direction of Tancred Borenius, Ph.D., D.Lit., Durning-Lawrence Professor of the History of Art in the University of London. The editors have subjected the text to copious revision and have included many new fields of art history which had not been investigated at the time of the original publication.

Selected bibliographies have been given as a guide to further research, and books which themselves contain important bibliographies have been stressed. In addition to these, significant recent publications, including periodical literature, have been cited. The student's attention is called in particular to such standard and exhaustive publications as Thieme-Becker's *Kunst-Lexikon*, the *Reallexikon der Vorgeschichte*, Pauly-Wissowa's *Real-encyclopädie der classischen Altertumswissenschaft, The Index of Twentieth Century Artists,* and the various specialized and national encyclopedias. For new material, appearing currently, the reader is referred to *The Art Index*, and the *Internationale Bibliographie für Kunstwissenschaft.*

The editors wish to express their appreciation to those who have made this encyclopedia possible. To Audrey McMahon of the College Art Association in particular a word of thanks is due for her constructive criticism and unfailing assistance. Special mention should be given to Martha Davidson for editorial collaboration. The editors are also grateful to the staff of specialists which has contributed to the enterprise.

The staff has included: Milton Brown, Ancient Near East; Lillian Canfield, Greek and Roman art; Samuel Caumen, Architecture; J. LeRoy Davidson, Far East; Martha Davidson, Persian Miniature Painting; Florence Diamond, Byzantine and Egyptian art; Michael Fooner, Jewish art; Philippa Gerry, Italian proto-Renaissance and Renaissance painting and sculpture; Dr. Robert Goldwater, Oceanic and Negro (African) art; Dr. Julius Held and Lucy Hernady, Flemish, Dutch and German painting and sculpture; Dr. Herbert J. Spinden, America (Archæology); Herbert Weissberger, Spanish painting and sculpture. The material on contemporary American artists has been supplied by the Index of Twentieth Century Artists of the College Art Association.

J. L. D. and P. G.

*New York,* 1 July, 1937

AN ARTIST'S STUDIO IN THE RENAISSANCE: The Florentine sculptor Baccio Bandinelli and his pupils, after an engraving by Enea Vico.

# A

**AACHEN.**—See Aix-la-Chapelle.

**ABACUS.**—A square block which crowns the capital of a column or of a pillar.

**ABA-NOVÁK (Vilmos).**—Contemporary Hungarian painter. He was born in Budapest in 1894. After completing secondary school he attended the School for Drawing Instructors. During the World War he served in the Hungarian army and then got a position as assistant at the Polytechnic School in Budapest. His first exhibition was in 1922; two years later he sold a painting to the Museum of Fine Arts. In 1927 he became a member of the KUT (New Society of Fine Arts) and in 1929 he won the Grand Prix of the Szinnyei Merse Society and was elected a member of the Munkácsy Guild. His foreign exhibitions include a showing in Zürich in 1923 and since 1929 frequent participations in the galleries of Rome, Milan, Venice, New York and the Carnegie Internationals of 1931 and 1935 in Pittsburgh. It was the scholarship to Rome, which he won in 1929, that brought about his change of style and technique. While in Italy he became interested in the fresco technique and colouring of the Primitives; he abandoned painting with oils and developed an unusual style and skill in handling tempera. His paintings of this period show the influence of the perfect colour harmony which dominates the Italian landscape. He was equally impressed and influenced by the contemporary art of France and the paintings of his countryman Károly Ferenczy. Aba-Novák manifests his *joie de vivre* and his native sparkling Hungarian spirit in his lively bright colours and his choice of subject matter, which is dominated by episodes of Hungarian folk-life, landscapes, circuses and genre paintings. In his realistic treatment of these topics he seems to recreate the temperament of the Hungarian peasants: their deep and troubled sorrow as well as their gallantry, humour and buoyant spirit. He is a meditative and logical, as well as an inventive artist; he receives great satisfaction in creating clear, well-composed patterns of brilliant and pure local colours. The tempera paints are especially suited to render his dynamic light effects. For a small church in Hungary he has done a series of frescoes of *Christ and the Apostles* in the original Byzantine tradition.

BIBLIOGRAPHY: Catalogue, *International Exhibition,* College Art Association, New York, 1933. Catalogue, *Exhibition of Paintings by Vilmos Aba-Novák and Béla Iványi-Grünwald,* E. & A. Silberman Gallery, New York, 1935.

**ABBATE (Nicolo dell').**—Italian painter, born at Modena, but associated with the school of Bologna (1512-1571). He went to Bologna in 1547. In 1552 he was already in France with Primaticcio, helped him with the decorations of Fontainebleau, and there died. Most of his works have been lost. As far as can be judged by those which remain, he had a pleasing style. In the Poggi Palace, now the University of Bologna, there is a frieze by him, and in the Palazzo Leoni a Birth of Christ.

**ABBAYE-AUX-DAMES.**—See Caen.

**ABBAYE-AUX-HOMMES.**—See Caen.

**ABBEVILLE (France).**—The *Church of St. Wulfran* was begun in 1488 and finished in 1663. It is in the Flamboyant Gothic style. The church has a magnificent façade, which is richly decorated with sculptures, and is divided vertically into three parts by buttresses, and into three parts, horizontally, by string-courses. Three fine doorways, with deep voussoirs and gables, are adorned with statues, several of which were carved by P. Leureux in 1502. The central doorway is the most remarkable.

**ABBEY (Edwin Austin).**—American painter (1852-1911). He was born in Philadelphia 1st April 1852, the son of a family of French, English and Irish ancestry. He was always fond of sketching and began taking drawing lessons when he was fifteen years old. He studied with Isaac L. Williams and soon entered the Pennsylvania Academy of Fine Arts where he was in the class of Christian Schussle. In 1871 he became an illustrator for the publishing house of Harper and Brothers and assisted other members of the staff in the creation of new drawings or the revision of old sketches. For a short time he was a free-lance illustrator and then began working again for Harper's and Scribner's, finding his most appealing subjects in the life of the 17th and 18th centuries in England. In 1877 he was sent to England for some pictures of the Shakespeare country and soon decided to make it his permanent home. He illustrated some books of which the most important was the *Selections from the Poetry of Robert Herrick,* published in 1889. That same year he won an award for his drawings in the Paris Exposition and the next year he received his great commission for the murals in the new Boston Public Library. For twelve years he worked on this series of scenes for the story of the Quest of the Holy Grail, searching for the proper costumes, accessories and background features for the story, which he placed in France in the 12th century. In 1902, the year of the dedication of these murals, he was highly honoured by being requested to do the official picture of the coronation of King Edward VII. Some years later he was selected to do some murals for the State Capitol at Harrisburg, Pennsylvania, but these were unfinished at the time of his death 1st August 1911. Though essentially an illustrator Abbey never rose above that category even in his murals, which stretch along from one episode to the next. Due to his ability to draw fine lines his pen sketches were much more successful than those which he attempted in wash. Throughout his whole life he was influenced by Millais and Rossetti and their confrères and patterned his work after them, particularly in regard to the careful archæological research which preceded his many historical compositions.

BIBLIOGRAPHY: E. V. Lucas, *Edwin Austin Abbey, Royal Academician,* 1921.

**ABBOTT (Lemuel Francis).**—English painter (1760-1803), pupil of Francis Hayman. A good portrait painter, especially noted for his vigorous portraits of Lord Nelson.

**ABSIDIOLE.**—See Apsidiole.

**ACANTHUS.**—A leaf-form much used as a basis for classic ornament. See Capitals.

**ACHAEMENIAN.**—See Persia—Art.

**ACROPOLIS OF ATHENS.**—The Acropolis of Athens comprises a hill which dominates the town for 80 metres, on a space of about three hectares. The earliest settlement of Athens took place here. The primitive Cyclopean wall (the most extensive portion being exactly south of the Propylæa) comprises the oldest masonry present on the Acropolis. It dates from prehistoric times. In turn, the Acropolis contained the royal residence, the citadel, and then the temples of Athena, protectress of the town.

The excavations of 1885 laid bare the site of the original wall of the Acropolis. This prehistoric wall composed of Cyclopean masonry was a massive rampart, measuring 4 metres, 50 thick, by 10 metres high, composed of great blocks of rough stone relieved by some ashlars and mortar. It followed the contours of the natural rock but to a considerable extent within the later wall. This prehistoric wall is known as the Pelasgicum, or Pelargicum,—the name probably referring to the Pelasgian settlers mentioned by Herodotus.

A postern gateway at the northeast corner and at the foot of the ancient palace was reached by a staircase of twelve steps, cut in the rock. The prehistoric wall enclosed the royal quarters, the altar of Athena Polias, and some private dwelling-places of the Eupatrides. Under the foundations of the Hekatompedon, the Old Temple of Athena to the north of the Parthenon, were discovered some traces of a royal palace, which does not seem to have been very large. At the western end of the Acropolis stood the great fortress of "Nine Gates," the Enneapylum. Later constructions have destroyed practically every trace of it. The Athenian tyrants, the Peisistratids in particular, erected new buildings on the Acropolis. They built a very fine Propylon at the western entrance. It is they probably who surrounded the old Hekatompedon with a Doric peristyle and adorned it with new sculpture. The east pediment now had a scene representing the battle of the gods and the giants (replacing the old scene, probably one depicting episodes from the Labors of Heracles). In the centre of the new pediment Athena was shown with the recumbent figure of the giant Enceladus. The scene of the west pediment (which replaced the older archaic figures of serpents and gods) is unknown. Both the earlier and later pedimental groups reveal traces of paint. It is not yet certain whether the older Hekatompedon before its remodelling was a temple in antis, having two columns between the pilasters of the longer sides, or one of amphiprostyle having four columns across each end. It was about the sixth century B.C. that the Greeks began to erect on their Acropolis statues in tufa of young men and maidens (kouroi and korai) a certain number of which are in the Acropolis Museum. The Peisistratids levelled the slope of the entrance of the Acropolis in such a way that chariots could ascend it. The old door became a Propylæa, 11 metres in width, and 30 metres 50 in length. The Acropolis was covered with beautiful buildings, dating from many centuries, when the Lacedæmonians besieged it, in 510 B.C., and Hippias had to surrender. His house and many others, were razed to the ground. The invaders respected the temples and other buildings. Nevertheless, the head of the democratic party, Cleisthenes, wishing to surpass the gifts of the tyrants, decided to build a new temple to Athena. This was the first thought of the Parthenon. A free site was found a little to the south of the Hekatompedon. He levelled it, and enlarged this space to the ledge of the rock by means of a terrace held together by masonry in tufa. The works were stopped by the Persian wars (490 B.C.).

After the battle of Marathon, the Athenian conquerors at once thought of building the temple, which had been planned by Cleisthenes. Aristeides enlarged the site of the temple, a base of three steps was constructed, then the stylobate. The building must have been in the Doric style, peripteral, with interior arrangements like those of the Hekatompedon, and all of Pentelic marble. The work was in progress when the Second Persian war interrupted it. In 480 B.C., when the people sought refuge in Salamis, the abandoned town of Athens was invaded by the Persians who attacked the Acropolis.

The priests of Athena, assisted by some citizens, barricaded themselves within the sacred wall to defend their temples, but, guided by a spy or an Athenian traitor, the Persians succeeded in misleading their watch, made a surprise entry, massacred the defenders, overturned and set fire to all the monuments.

Shortly afterwards, in 479 B.C., the Athenians, victorious over the Persians, turned their attention to resurrecting the ruins of their Acropolis. Themistocles constructed a new wall, 4 metres in thickness by 5 in height, on the foundations of the old Pelasgic wall. The Athenians worked hurriedly, often making use of such material as the fallen stones of earlier buildings. After Themistocles, Cimon continued the work of rebuilding or reënforcing the south wall of the Acropolis. Things were in this state when, in 467 B.C., Pericles came into power.

Pericles had grand schemes for the restoration of the Acropolis; he wanted to rebuild all the old temples. Enormous sums of money were collected. It was his great good fortune to meet an artist of genius who could understand and, in a marvellous way, materialise these schemes. Phidias (*see this name*), then famous throughout Greece became coadjutor in the work. Prior to this period he made the colossal Athena of bronze which stood in the open on the Acropolis. His famous Athena Lemnia must have been modelled considerably later, probably c. 447 B.C. This statue, so highly praised by Lucian, also stood upon the rock of the Acropolis which was to be adorned with the purest wonders of Greek art. These were: the pedestal and altar of Victory Apteros (from 460 to 450), the Parthenon (from 447 to 438), the Propylæa (from 437 to 432); and then, after Pericles, the Erechtheum and the temple of Victory Apteros.

The Acropolis of the 5th century had its entrance at the West, like the former ones; it was a slope 23 metres wide; the Sacred Way was in the middle, and formed a bend from North to South as far as the Propylæa. It was paved, and grooved in the middle to allow the sacrificial animals to be led in more easily. A branch road which broke away from it in front of the Propylæa led to a staircase which ascended directly to the pyrgos (pedestal in the form of a tower) of the Temple of Victory Apteros. On the lower part of the incline was the guard-house which kept watch on the buildings night and day.

*Propylæa.* The Propylæa was built at the threshold of the Sacred Hill. It was a majestic and elegant portico, and it formed a monumental entrance to the Acropolis. The architect, Mnesicles, began the construction when the Parthenon was finished, in 437. The work lasted five years, and cost 2012 talents. The building is entirely in Pentelic marble. Mnesicles had conceived his plan on a vast scale, but was obliged to reduce it, especially in the South aisle, for want of money, and because of objections of the priests of the Temple of Victory Apteros. They were opposed to the building, at the South, of an aisle as wide as the corresponding one to the North. In spite of the lack of symmetry, the Propylæa has at all times excited admiration. The architect had to overcome great difficulties in building this monument (which measures 47 metres in width by 30 metres in length) on an unequal foundation of rock. The Propylæa is composed of a central entrance-way, and two aisles. The central Propylæa is 18 metres 20 wide; it is adorned with a portico, amphiprostyle, with six Doric columns resting on a stereobate of three steps; these columns are 8 metres 53 high, including the capitals. The flutes, hollowed out in twenty grooves, are 1 metre 60 in diameter at the base, and 1 metre 20 at the top. A wall, pierced with five doorways, divided the width of the vestibule (which was 24 metres long) into two. The part contained between these doors and the western portal was divided into three aisles by two ranges of three Ionic columns which supported the roof. In the middle of the central aisle passed the Sacred Way. The formation of the hill had forced Mnesicles to place the base of the East portico on a level higher, by 1 metre 50, than that of the West portico. The columns being all the same height, the roofing is consequently higher above the East portico, and independent of that of the vestibule. The façade was decorated with a Doric entablature and with a pediment which may have been painted. Of the interior Ionic columns, nothing remains but some capitals. The ceiling was painted blue. There was a gutter beneath the pavement of the middle aisle.

The aisles extended from each side of the western façade, at a lower level. They were not symmetrical. According to Mnesicles' plan, they were to be of equal importance, and to have two vast lateral porticos, which were intended to shade processions. But only the north aisle was built according to the original plan. This is the better preserved; it rests on a stereobate with a bed of chalk and marble; the walls are perfectly constructed and joined together. It is composed of a vestibule of three Doric columns "in antis," and of a rectangular room (10 by about 8 metres), called the Pinakothek, because it contained paintings, many of which were by Polygnotus. Pausanias has described these paintings.

The south aisle, much smaller than the other, is formed by a room, 8 metres by 4, enclosed by a wall on the east and south sides, by three Doric columns on the north, and, on the west, by an open façade which was divided by a central pillar. See Pl. 1, Vol. I.

*The Temple of Victory Apteros.* On the same level as the Propylæa, the Temple of Victory Apteros (or Athena Nike) occupied the same site as a bastion belonging to the primitive walls. From here, according to the legend, Ægeus watched for the return of his son Theseus. When he sighted the black sail of the ship, the sign of death, he threw himself from the top of the rampart. The goddess of the new sanctuary was Victory Apteros ("the Wingless Victory"), who, unable to fly away, must remain for ever protectress of the Athenians.

The architect Callicrates was ordered between 460 and 450 to build the temple of Victory Apteros but the actual building was not carried out until a number of years later. The pedestal of the temple, built in the form of a tower, or pyrgos, measures 8 metres in height. Begun before the Propylæa, this pedestal was found to be too high, and too wide; therefore it had to be altered, and put on a level with the entrance portico. Some time passed between the construction of the pedestal and of the temple; it was not until about 426 that the work of the building was undertaken. The temple of Athena Nike still existed until almost 1687, when it was pillaged and destroyed by the Turks who used its members to restrengthen the fortification wall. It was restored in 1835 by Ross, Schaubert and Hansen. They recovered all the fragments and succeeded in reconstructing the building exactly as it was originally. The temple is built on the pyrgos, the three upper courses of which are adorned by votive offerings. It is in Pentelic marble, amphiprostyle tetrastyle. It is very small, and consists of a cella (4 metres 20 wide by 3 metres 78), preceded by an Ionic portico with four columns. These columns are 4 metres high; their shafts are formed from a single block of marble. The two façades are alike. The cella opened by three doors two of which were closed by bronze gratings. The entablature consists of an architrave in three courses, above which runs a frieze, decorated with sculpture. Parts of the frieze were taken to England by Lord Elgin and are now in the British Museum. Terracotta copies later replaced these missing portions. The sculptures on the Eastern side show us an assembly of the gods: Athena crowning Victory, and at the north and south sides a contest of Greeks and Persians. Probably these sculptures were not executed before about 420 B.C. The work is of great delicacy, and the beautiful, supple figures are very skillfully sculptured. It is an art not far removed from the mature style of Phidias.

All around the temple, serving as a parapet to the pyrgos, is a balustrade decorated with bas-reliefs; these bas-reliefs are among the most exquisite works of Greek sculpture of this period; they probably date from about 406 B.C., after the triumphs of Alcibiades, and well express the feelings of pride and enthusiasm which must have animated the victors. The balustrade (32 metres long and 1 metre high) exposed to Athenian gaze a whole series of Victories, symbols of their successes. The well-known fragments which remain are in the Acropolis Museum. Most important of all is the "Victory fastening her sandal," an exquisitely graceful figure, clad in light drapery. This and the "Victory decorating a trophy" and the "Victories leading a bull to the sacrifice" are among the most beautiful works of Greek sculpture. Phidias rendered the nobility and charm of female figures and the undulating folds which draped them without disguising the perfection of their bodily forms. These works are very likely by a follower of Phidias.

Between the temple and the Propylæa was the Altar of Victory Apteros where the sacrifice was made at the time of the great Panatheniac celebrations, and a statue of the threefold goddess, Hecate, by the hand of Alcamenes. To go from the Propylæa to the Parthenon, one had to follow the Sacred Way, which was bordered by a series of statues, votive monuments and grave-stones, of which only traces now remain, and of which nothing is known, except from the description of Pausanias. Within the sacred enclosure of Athena Hygieia (goddess of health) were many and various buildings; a little further was a bronze statue of Athena, the work of Pyrrhos, of which some traces of the base are left. A kind of esplanade, the "Brauronion," sacred enclosure of Artemis Brauronia, contained a portico, 8 metres wide, the little room of the goddess, with the archaic "hedos" (cult statue) and a statue by Praxiteles. Near the west end of the Brauronion is today to be found the marble base of the bronze "Wooden Horse" sculptured by Strongylion. Where the horse was originally located we do not know. Between the Propylæa and the Erechtheum lies a marble base (about five and one-half metres square). Whether this is the base of the bronze statue of Athena Promachos made by Phidias, sometime before 467 is a matter of conjecture.

The Sacred Way was also adorned with the bronze quadriga, erected in 506 B.C., to commemorate one of the Athenian victories. To the south, on an esplanade higher than that of the Brauronion, stretched the precincts of Athena Ergane (the worker) in which the workmen of Athens came to deposit their offerings. The edifice built in this precinct does not seem to have been a temple. It is generally recognized as having been a repository for bronzes. Some archæologists hold that this was in the southeast corner of the Acropolis, and that the building in the precinct of Athena Ergane was the Opisthodomos of the Parthenon, which was separated from the temple. To the east of the precinct, a stairway cut in the rock leads to the terrace of the Parthenon. Not far from the Parthenon, in a space today surrounded by a railing, was the statue of Gæa supplicating Zeus; at the side statues of Timotheus and Conon.

The Sacred Way went around the northeast corner of the Parthenon and led to the entrance of the temple.

*The Parthenon.*—The Parthenon is the marvel of the Acropolis, and the masterpiece of Attic art. Pericles entrusted the building to the best artists. Ictinus and Callicrates were the architects. Phidias made the gold and ivory statue of Athena which stood in the cella. The controlling thought of the builders was the creation of a fitting home for the magnificent statue of the goddess Athena. The name of "Parthenon" means "dwelling of the virgin."

The work, begun c. 447 B.C., was finished c. 438 B.C. The Parthenon is a temple of the octostyle peripteral type, and built of Pentelic marble. Time has given the marble a rich golden patina which seems to be due to a lichen. The temple, the total height of which is 21 metres, rests on a base, above which there is a stereobate consisting of three marble steps.

The inner temple or secos, a rectangle of 59 metres long by 21 metres 72 wide, rests on a pedestal of two steps, placed on the stylobate. It is bounded on the two façades by a portico of six columns, and on the sides by a wall ending "in antis." It was divided into four parts: the pronaos, the cella, and the Parthenon proper (so-called), and the opisthodomos.

The pronaos, at the east, leads into the peristyle by a bronze staircase; it was shut off by high iron gateways between the columns; and the west wall was pierced by a door by which one entered the cella. It was in the pronaos that guard was kept over the rich presents which were offered to the goddess.

The cella was a hundred feet, or 32 metres 84 in length, by about 20 in width; the walls were, it is believed, coloured a dull red. A Doric peristyle of 9 columns divided it into three aisles, the middle one being just about 10 metres wide, the other two 3 metres 25. An upper colonnade carried the roof. The floor was paved with marble. In its length the cella was divided into three parts by marble screens. The statue of the goddess appears to have been placed in the last division. One can still see the place on the ground near the second screen. The cella was separated from the Parthenon proper by a plain wall.

This actual Parthenon, or apartment of virgins, was a room probably reserved for young girls on days of celebration. It was 19 metres wide by 13 metres 37; in the middle, four Ionic columns supported the roof. The back wall was pierced by a door (which was closed by a railing), which communicated with the opisthodomos.

The opisthodomos was enclosed by railings; it possibly contained the treasures of the goddess; or else it was a room where the treasurers of the temple came to count the contents of the silver caskets. It was terminated by the western peristyle.

In style the Parthenon is modified Doric. The columns of the façades are eight in number, instead of the standard six; and the proportions of the building are changed because the architect did not lengthen the sides on account of this; the rectangle approaches a square more nearly than is usual. The metopes of the exterior frieze are decorated with sculptures all the way around, while those of strictly Doric temples were not decorated on the façades. The Doric *secos* is "in antis" with two columns; here, the antes are omitted and there are six columns, an arrangement which allows of better interior lighting. The secos is also, because of this, more spacious, particularly the cella. The interior of the Parthenon is divided into four parts, whereas the pure Doric temple contains only three: pronaos, cella and opisthodomos. The true Parthenon is an innovation. A final violation of the Doric style consists in all sides of the secos being decorated with an Ionic sculptural frieze, instead of with a constant alternation of triglyphs and metopes. Every detail of the Parthenon was weighed and considered. Every part was designed to fulfil a special purpose, and to contribute to the harmony of the whole. Above all, the Parthenon was to be a home worthy of the colossal statue of Athena. It had to be a temple large enough, and high enough, to hold a statue 12 metres high; the figure of the goddess must be visible from all sides, and be properly lighted; the cella and its divisions must not appear crushed by its proportions. Athena was truly at home. It was of her that Ictinus and Callicrates thought continuously while they elaborated the plan of the Parthenon. This statue, one of the wonders of Attic art, was unfortunately destroyed.

The Parthenon, conceived and executed under the direction of the most brilliant Greek sculptors, gave a large space to their work. The decoration of the friezes, metopes and pediments is one of the greatest marvels of fifth century Greek art. Many artists had a share in it. On the Eastern pediment was sculptured "The Birth of Athena," fully armed by the side of Zeus. This pediment is in a bad state of preservation, having suffered from the construction of a Byzantine apse, and especially from the hands of Lord Elgin, who pulled down the most beautiful pieces and transported them to London. Scarcely anything remains on the pediment but some heads, two of the "Horses of the Sun," and one of the "Horses of Selene." With the help of certain documents, the arrangement of the figures can be reconstructed in imagination. Zeus occupied the middle, seated upon his throne; Hephæstus was behind, holding the hatchet which had cleft the skull of the father of the gods; before Zeus, Athena, fully armed, warlike, was being crowned by Victory. Gods and goddesses, sitting, and reclining in such a way that their pose harmonised properly with the shape of the pediment, completed the assembly. In the left angle Helios was rising from the sea with his horses. Then came the beautiful reclining male figure traditionally named the Theseus. Immediately behind this male figure is the group of two sitting female figures, sometimes regarded as Demeter and Persephone and sometimes as "the Hours." Hurrying toward this group is a figure usually known as Iris, the messenger of Zeus, but this identification is to be questioned. To the right of the central group are three seated female figures, frequently known as the Fates, which are universally famous for their beauty.

The western pediment represented the dispute of Athena and Poseidon for the possession of Attica. Poseidon held the trident with which he struck the ground, thus causing water to gush forth, which was symbolised by a prancing horse. Athena brandished her lance, which caused an olive-tree to spring up when she had hit the earth with it. This olive-tree, which gave her the victory, stood between the two rivals. Behind them were their chariots, that of Athena led by Niké and Hermes, that of Poseidon by Amphitrite and Iris; and these were followed by gods and heroes. Of these masterpieces, there remain in position only two figures in the north-west angle, perhaps Cecrops and Pandrosas, and one figure of a crouching woman in the opposite angle. The other fragments are in the British Museum. The Acropolis Museum has a reconstruction of the pediments, according to Furtwängler, and some fragments and casts of the sculptures (room VIII, of the Parthenon).

The exterior frieze, in the Doric style, comprised 92 metopes; very few remain in position and these are much damaged: fifteen metopes are in London, one in the Louvre. They are the work of many artists, and their quality is unequal. Athena was the inspiration behind all the subjects. The goddess is not always represented, but she helps her people in the rough combats, and it is she who gives them the victory. The western metopes represent the fight of the Athenians against the Amazons; those to the east, incidents in the war of the gods against the giants; the south side shows the combat of Lapiths and Athenians against the Centaurs; and to the north are other warlike scenes. All these sculptures made a much grander effect when they stood out against coloured backgrounds, some traces of which remain; it is believed that the backgrounds of the pediments were blue, and those of the metopes red. The draperies were painted as well; many accessories, crowns, acroteria, sceptres, bridles of chargers were in gilt metal, which shone in the sunlight.

The most celebrated sculptures of the Parthenon are those of the Ionic frieze which surrounds the cella for a length of 160 metres, at a height of about 12 metres above the stylobate. It represents the most characteristic episode of the worship of Athena, the procession of the great Panathenaic Festival. Every four years a train of young Athenian maidens, escorted by a party of people, formed a solemn procession to the Acropolis to offer an embroidered robe to the statue of the Goddess which was shut up in the Erechtheum. This festival Phidias represented on the frieze of the cella; most of it is in London; half of the remainder of the east side, are in the Acropolis Museum, and eight figures of this same side are in the Louvre. With the exception of three figures, nothing is left on the Parthenon itself but the west frieze. Phidias did not execute the sculptures, but he had control of the work, and probably designed most of them. The Panathenaic festival unfolded itself on the four sides of the frieze; more than 350 people are represented, and more than 125 horses. First, on the west face, are the preparations for the procession, youths putting on their festal garments and slaves bridling the horses; the first chariots move forward, horses prance, a herald tries to form the train. Then the procession begins to move, led by the priests and magistrates; it goes forward in double file, one on the north side, the other on the south, to meet on the east front; there the festival ends, by the giving up of the embroidered peplos in which the archon and his wife clothe the goddess, under the benevolent eyes of the Olympian divinities. The workmanship, and the happy blending of details of familiar life with majestic attitudes fill the spectator with wonder. The train of young girls is full of simplicity and noble grace; they are dressed in softly falling drapery, and walk with lowered eyes. Just as in the pediments, one finds here the work of many artists, of unequal ability; but the effect of the whole is harmonious.

Time and vandalism have mutilated the masterpiece of Ictinus and Callicrates. It remained almost intact, when, in 1687, the Doge, Morosini, accompanied by a German prince, laid seige to Athens and blew up a powder-magazine installed on the Parthenon, and then deliberately destroyed the whole of one part of the building. All the cella and the frieze, six columns of one of the porticos and eight of the other lay in ruins; the pediment sculptures were taken down so clumsily that they fell and were broken. Soon, other mutilations continued the work of destruction. An Englishman, Lord Elgin, having obtained, in 1815, the authority of the Turkish government to "remove some blocks of stones with figures and inscriptions," transported to London a large part of the frieze, the pediment sculptures, some capitals, and some fragments of the cornice; he pulled down the metopes of the Doric frieze. The English government bought the whole for the British Museum. This method of enriching the British Museum provoked violent protests. Lord Elgin alleged, for his defence, that the example had been set him by France. In 1787, the Comte de Choiseul had, in fact, carried off a fragment of the frieze, but this unique fragment had been detached for a long time, and in taking it, he did not cause other damage.

The Parthenon still stands proudly, and alone, in the midst of ruin. The interior of the temple has completely disappeared, and likewise the roof. The western façade is the best preserved, although the pediment has lost its sculptures, and the frieze some of its metopes.

Fragment of the Panathenaic Frieze. (Louvre.)

*Erechtheum.*—After he had built the Parthenon, Pericles thought of building the Erechtheum, but death prevented him from realizing that part of his plan. It was Nicias who, about 421 B.C., decided to build the Erechtheum on the spot immediately adjoining the Old Hekatompedon on the north. Erechtheus was a heroic character, personifying the water of the earth; his worship was soon confused with that of Poseidon, god of the sea. Whether an earlier temple dedicated to his worship existed on the same spot as the Erechtheum has not yet been decided by the archæologists. Only Pausanias, who describes the beautiful temple at great length, Plutarch and Heliodorus use the term Erechtheum. Therefore the name may have come into use only in later times.

The first works, begun c. 420, were interrupted by the war with Sicily, and resumed in 409. Philocles was made the architect. Three years after, the temple suffered from fire, together with the Hekatompedon: the damage was repaired in 395. In 27 B.C. the Romans made some ill-considered additions; then the Christians converted it into a Church; and the Turks, into a harem. But the greatest damage was caused, first, by Lord Elgin's removal of the sculpture, and then by the siege of the Acropolis at the time of the War of Independence. In 1842, a Frenchman, Piccard, was entrusted with the restoration of the Caryatid portico; in 1902, the reconstructors began to add the roof, and to set up some columns and the entablature of the northern portico.

If the Parthenon is the masterpiece of the Doric style, the Erechtheum is one of the most graceful creations in the Ionic style. The difficulties of construction were considerable: limited space and an uneven surface of the rock. The building was required to hold both the treasures and idols of the various divinities—the water of Erechtheus, the serpent, the old symbol of Athena, the sacred olive and the tomb of Cecrops. Possibly the present monument does not represent more than one part of the original plan. The Erechtheum is composed of a double cella, or rather of one large cella which is divided into two by a plain wall, and of three porticos. The east portico has six Ionic columns of 6 metres 80 in height, and ¾ metre in diameter at the base, resting on a marble stereobate with three steps; one of these columns was taken away by Lord Elgin. Below the architrave runs a frieze of blue Eleusinian marble on which the sculptures representing a festal procession were carved. Today these are almost entirely destroyed. This portico was entered by the cella of Athena Polias, a rectangular chamber of 9 metres 83 by 7 metres 30, which contained a reproduction of the primitive statue, or xoanon, of Athena, which the Persians had destroyed. The statue was the object of the principal worship of the Athenians; a gold lamp burned before it day and night. The purpose of the Panathenaic Procession, which took place every four years, was to attire this statue with a magnificent embroidered peplos. A stairway of twelve steps led to the north side. The northern portico or entrance porch surmounted the door of the Erechtheum proper, the cella of Erechtheus. This, with the Caryatid portico, is one of the wonders of the Erechtheum. It is composed of six Ionic columns, slender and graceful —there being four to the façade and one to each side; a blue Eleusinian marble frieze surmounts the architrave; the ceiling and large door were decorated with sculpture. This porch sheltered one of the sacred signs of the worship of Poseidon, the three holes that the trident of the god had hollowed in the Acropolis rock, at the time of his dispute with Athena. In the middle of the north porch, was the sacrificial altar. The entrance door which leads from the north porch into the west cella is a masterpiece of Ionic decoration. Although it has suffered from time and mutilations, it may still be admired. The finely chiselled railings have disappeared, as well as the gilded rosettes. The decoration of the lintel with palm-leaves and rosettes was done in 27 B.C. with much less care than is to be found in the original work. The north porch, as already stated, gave access to the cella of the Erechtheum. This cella, according to the majority of authorities, was bounded behind by a wall which separated it from the cella of Athena and was three metres lower than its neighbour, owing to variations in the ground level. It was 11 metres long. A colonnade divided it into two parts. The part adjoining the cella of Athena, or naos, probably contained the altars of Poseidon-Erechtheus, and Hephæstus. Under the pavement stretched the crypt, where the sacred serpent was kept. The second part covered a cistern which held the water which had gushed forth when Poseidon-Erechtheus had struck the earth with his trident. The great door of the northern portico opens on this second part of the cella.

The western façade connected the northern portico with that of the Caryatids. It was composed of four columns standing on a plain wall of 3 metres 75 in height, which extended between the columns, to a third of their height. This façade was restored by the Romans in the first century before Christ. They changed the columns into half-columns, and made a wall, pierced by three windows, as high as the architrave. It was this arrangement that was adopted in 1910 for the restoration of the façade. It is near the north-west corner of this façade that the Pandroseum, which held the sacred olive tree and the altar of Zeus, is regarded by many archæologists to have been located.

The Caryatid portico, or Hall of the Maidens, is the most famous part of the Erechtheum. Backed by the western façade, it is directly opposite the north portico. It owes its originality and beauty to the famous Caryatids, or statues of young maidens, which take the place of columns. Two metres 60 high, the six figures (four in front, and one on the return of each side), stand on a pedestal, 2 metres 60 high and about 4 metres wide. They are clad in long, pleated tunics which reveal the proud, vigorous forms of their bodies; their arms hang downward; their hair is thrown back; the head of each supports a capital, decorated with egg-and-dart moulding, upon which rests the architrave. The motif of the Caryatid had been borrowed from the temples of Delphi, the Treasury of the Cnidians and that of the Siphnians. According to tradition, the model of these beautiful, strong maidens, with broad chests, and shapely backs, had been taken from Caryia (Laconia), whence the name of "Caryatids." The artist who executed the Caryatids of the Erechtheum has not, then, the credit of their invention, but he has carried to perfection the use of a motif already known. See Pls. 20, 21, 23, Vol. I.

Bibliography: Benté, *L'Acropole d'Athènes.* Paris, 1853-54, 2 Vols.—Bohn, *Die Propyläen der Akropolis zu Athen,* 1882.—Collignon and Boissonnas, *Le Parthénon.* Paris, 1911.—Dickens, *Catalogue of the Acropolis Museum.* Cambridge, 1912.—D'Oge, *The Acropolis of Athens.* London, 1918.—Gardner, Ernest A., *A Handbook of Greek Sculpture.* London, 1920.—Gardner, Ernest A., *Six Greek Sculptors.* London, 1910.—O. Jahn and A. Michælis, *Arx Athenarum a Pausania descripta,* 1917.—Michælis, *Der Parthenon,* 1871.—Perrot and Chipiez, *Histoire de l'Art.* Vol. VIII, 1903.—Schrader, *Archäische Marmor Sculpturen in Akropolis Museum zu Athen.* Vienna, 1909.—Weller, Charles Heald, *Athens and Its Monuments.* New York, 1913.—Wiegand, *Die archäische Poros-architektur der Akropolis zu Athen,* 1904.

**ACROTERIA.** — Ornaments in marble or terra cotta which crowned the angles of the pediments of Greek temples.

**ADAM (Robert).** — Scottish architect (1728-1792), born at Kirkcaldy; visited Italy in 1754-58 and made a profound study of the remains of classical architecture, notably the ruins of Diocletian's palace at Spalato on which in 1764 he published a work; on his return to England he quickly rose to fame and in association with his brothers (of whom James was the most gifted) carried out a large number of architectural commissions all over England in a neo-classical style, extending his attention also to the design of furniture. The quarter in London known (from the Adam brothers) as Adelphi is perhaps his most famous creation. Among famous country seats built by him are Harewood House, near Leeds and Kedleston Hall, near Derby.

Bibliography: Alfred T. Bolton, *The Architecture of Robert & James Adam.* London, 1922.

**ADAMS (Herbert).**—American sculptor, born 1856, much influenced by the Italian Renaissance, as may be seen for instance in his numerous female portrait busts.

**ADAMS (Wayman).**—Contemporary American painter. He was born in Muncie, Indiana, 23rd September 1883. He showed talent for drawing as a child and from 1905 to 1909 attended classes at the John Herron Art Institute in Indianapolis where he worked under William Forsyth. In 1910 he went to Italy and studied with William Merritt Chase in Florence. Two years later he was in Spain working under the able direction of Robert Henri. Although he did at that time make sketches of street scenes in Spain, and later in Chinatown in San Francisco, and in New Orleans, he is best known for his portraits. He has been successful, since he has the faculty of quick and keen observation together with rapid execution. His portraits are usually completed in one sitting and they present a frank and open portrayal of the subject from an objective viewpoint. His single portraits include such well-known names as Joseph Pennell, Booth Tarkington, James W. Riley, and Jerome Myers. He won the Thomas R. Proctor prize of the National Academy of Design in 1914, the Frank G. Logan medal of the Art Institute of Chicago in 1918, a silver medal at the Sesqui-Centennial Exposition in Philadelphia in 1926, and the gold medal of the Holland Society of New York in 1933. Examples of his work are in the John Herron Art Institute in Indianapolis, the Art Institute of Chicago, and the Los Angeles Museum of History, Science and Art.

Bibliography: Frank J. Mather, Jr., Charles R. Morey, William J. Henderson, *The American Spirit in Art,* The Pageant of America, Vol. 12, 1927.—Rilla Evelyn Jackman, *American Arts,* 1929.

**ADELPHI.**—See Adam (Robert).

**ADYTUM.**—The innermost sanctuary or shrine in an ancient temple.

**ÆGINA.**—*1. The Temple of Aphaia.*—Late archaic Greek temple dating from the earlier 5th century, B.C., famous because it is the most perfectly developed of the late archaic Greek temples, and because of its sculptures.

ÆGINA: WEST PEDIMENT OF THE TEMPLE OF APHAIA. (Restoration by Charles Garnier.)

It was first thought that this was a temple of Zeus, then, of Athena; but the excavations of 1907 brought to light a dedication to Aphaia, patron-goddess of Ægina. Destroyed during the Persian wars, it was probably rebuilt after 480 B.C., and dedicated anew to Aphaia.

The temple stands on a plateau, 66 metres long and 40 wide, surrounded by an enclosing wall. It is of limestone, in Doric peripteral style, with six façade columns, and twelve side ones. Twenty-nine columns are still standing on a stereobate of three steps. Several are cut from a single block of stone. They measure 5 metres 25 in height and the diameter of the base is 0 m. 29. The greater part of the architrave is still in position.

The interior shows traces of the walls of the cella, and the position of a double colonnade which divided it into three parts. Staircases gave access to the side galleries. Traces of red paint remain on the central part of the cella. On the other hand, no fragment of the metopes has been found. A stone incline led to the pronaos. In front of this, on the outside terrace, was the altar, from which a paved pathway led to the propylæa.

The pediments, of Pentelic marble, were decorated with celebrated sculptures. These sculptures were discovered at the beginning of the 19th century. The excavations were undertaken in 1811 bv a group of English, German and Danish scholars and artists. Seventeen statues were found, of which two smaller ones are simply decorative figures. The other fifteen decorated the two pediments. In 1812, they were bought for the sum of 10,000 Venetian sequins by the Prince Royal of Bavaria, the future Ludwig I. They were sent to Rome, where they were restored under the direction of the Danish sculptor Thorwaldsen. In 1830, they were set up in Munich, in the Museum of Sculpture, which was built by the architect von Klenze.

The two pediments represent similar subjects. In the middle, a warrior falls at the feet of Athena; on either side are combatants. According to the interpretation of the German archæologist, Brunn, the east pediment group represents a battle between Heracles and the Trojans—one of his companions, Oikles, having fallen in the fray, the hero is represented fighting the Trojans for the possession of his body. The western pediment represented the Trojan war: Ajax and Teucer contend with Aeneas and Paris for the body of Achilles. The scene may represent the combat round the body of Patroclus. These identifications remain problematical. The recalling of the Homeric conflicts at this date, was an allusion to the recent struggles between Europe and Asia. All these sculptures date from a little after the Persian wars, between 480 and 470. At this time the most famous Æginetan sculptor was Onatas. It is, therefore, probable that either he or his pupils had a hand in these figures, especially those of the eastern pediment, which seem to be freer in treatment.

Onatas was famous for his bronze statues, and it is not difficult to see the very strong influence that bronze statuary must have had on the sculptors who made the marble figures of the Æginetan temple. The figures are so independent of each other that archæologists still discuss their relative positions. "The sculptors of Ægina," said Collignon, "owe their remarkable qualities to practice in bronze work. They are masters in the art of statuary. How daringly they scorn artificial means for securing the balance of their statues! Standing, reclining or kneeling, they have the solidity and assurance of figures cast in bronze." Moreover, in spite of traces of a certain archaic rigidity, the Æginetan sculptures render bodily movement admirably. The attitudes are correct and varied; those of the archers kneeling and aiming their arrows, and those of the soldiers, wounded and fallen, are particularly admirable. Each of these individual movements corresponds to other movements, thus making a remarkably balanced composition. The modelling is nervous but restrained, without refinements or subtleties. The planes are simplified, but certain details are closely studied,—for instance, the modelling of a knee, with some large vein running under the skin, and details of the armour. The most archaic parts of the work are the faces, which are stretched into a kind of rigid grin, known as the "Æginetan smile."

The Æginetan sculptures were formerly relieved with bright colours, especially on the cuirasses and tunics. Athena's hair was painted a reddish brown, and there was a blue band on her curls. Red coloring relieved details of the faces, garments and armour. Certain bronze accessories were added to the stone figures. The whole stood out against the blue background of the pediment.

*2. The Temple of Aphrodite*, situated in the town itself, has been completely destroyed. Only the shaft of one column remains. It was a Doric peripteral temple, built at the beginning of the 5th century, on the site of an earlier temple, three rooms of which were discovered. This first temple itself covered traces of a pre-Mycenean habitation, with tombs underneath the paving.

See Greece; also Pls. 19, 22, Vol. I.

BIBLIOGRAPHY: Collignon, *Histoire de la sculpture grecque,* Vol. I, p. 287, et seq.—Joubin, *La sculpture grecque entre les guerres médiques et l'époque de Périclès*. Paris, 1901.

**ÆMILIA.**—See Emilia.

**AERTSEN (Pieter).**—Surnamed Peter the Long, Dutch painter, born at Amsterdam in 1503, went to Antwerp in 1525; there he was made a master in the Guild in 1535, then he returned to Amsterdam in c. 1555 where he died in 1575. He executed many mediocre religious paintings, and represented scenes that are well-observed, rustic, and of a spicy gaiety. Among these last are: *People Flirting* (Antwerp), *The Kitchen* (Copenhagen), *The Beer-Shop* and *The Market* (both in Vienna), and *The Dance of the Eggs* (Amsterdam).

BIBLIOGRAPHY: Sievers, J., *Pieter Aertsen*. Leipzig, 1908.

**AGABITI or AGAPITI (Pietro Paolo).**—Marchigian painter, sculptor in terra cotta and architect. Born c. 1470, in Sassoferrato; died c. 1540 in Cupramontana. Influenced by Venetian School, mainly Cima; and by the Umbrians. Earliest known work 1497, Pinacoteca, Padua, Madonna with Peter and Sebastian. Works to be found mainly in Sassoferrato, Jesi, and Cupramontana.

BIBLIOGRAPHY: A. Anselmi, *Pittori Marchigiani*. Florence, 1904.—*Miscell. Stor. Art. di Sassoferrato*, Florence. 1905, pp. 15-23 (bibliog.)

**AGASIAS (son of Dositheus).**—Greek sculptor of the first century

AGASIAS: BORGHESE GLADIATOR. (Louvre.)

B.C., who signed the famous statue called the *Borghese Warrior* (or *Fighting Gladiator*) of the Louvre Museum.

**AGISANDROS.**—See Laocoön.

**AGORA.**—Open meeting place for the transaction of business. See Athens.

**AGOSTINO D'ANTONIO di DUCCIO.**—Sculptor and Architect. Born, Florence, 1418. His earliest known works are the four small reliefs, representing scenes from the life of St. Geminiano, on the façade of the Cathedral at Modena, 1442, which show the influence of Donatello. In 1446, in Florence, he was accused of theft and was forced to fly to Venice. Alberti, in 1447, entrusted him with the interior decoration of the Tempio Malatestiano at Rimini, and he worked there until 1454, with Bernardo Ciuffagni and Simone di Giovanni Ferrucci da Fiesole under his direction. In 1455, in Rimini, he executed a relief now in the Museo Lapidario of the Brera in Milan and probably also a Medallion in the Museo Civico, Rimini. In 1557 he went to Perugia to design the façade of the Chiesa di S. Bernardino, for which he used as model Alberti's façade of S. Andrea at Mantua. Rich sculptural decoration makes it Agostino's most notable creative achievement, and it is signed and dated 1461. In 1459 he had been commissioned to do a large altarpiece for the Church of S. Domenico in Perugia, which he carried out partly in painted and unglazed terracotta, partly in colored majolica. In 1463 he received a commission from the Florentine Opera del Duomo for a large statue, payment for which was made in the same year; and in 1464 another such sculptural commission which he transferred to Bartolommeo di Piero da Settignano, called Baccellino. Michelangelo afterwards took over this last roughly hacked block of marble and carved from it his David.

Agostino later did in Florence the tabernacle for the Church of the Ognissanti, a Resurrection of Christ in terracotta for a chapel of the Church of the SS. Annunziata, a Madonna-relief (now in the Opera del Duomo), and probably a Crucifixion now in the Museo Nazionale. In Rome he executed a tabernacle for the Church of S. Agostino. In 1473 he obligated himself to build for the Opera del Duomo of Perugia a chapel, which was finished in 1474. In 1475 he worked on a Maestà for the ceiling of the same cathedral, of which fragments remain in the Cathedral itself, in the adjoining Chiostro della Canonica, and in the Museum at Perugia. In the same year he undertook the Porta di S. Pietro, designed in full Renaissance style, in collaboration with the Perugian Polidoro di Stefano, and after his death in 1480 with another master-worker. The façade design is a free rendering of the Tempio Malatestiano; unfinished, it still lacks the originally planned pinnacles. The year of Agostino's death is not known, only that in 1498, his widow was remarried.

BIBLIOGRAPHY: Vasari-Milanesi.—Gaye, *Carteggio,* I, 196; II, 454, 465, 466.—Campori, *Art. ital. stran. negli stati estensi.* Modena, 1855, p. 207.—Rumohr, *Italien. Forschungen.* Berlin, 1872, I, 31; II, 278, VI, 372 ff.—Ad. Rossi, *Prospetto cronol. d. vita e d. opere di Agostino d' Antonio* (from Gior. d. erudiz. artist.), Perugia, 1874.—Yriarte, *Agostino di Duccio,* Paris, 1883.—W. Bode, *Florent. Bildhauer der Renaiss.* Berlin, 1902.—Perkins, *Tuscan Sculptors,* I, 200.—M. Reymond, *La sculpture florentine du 15 siècle.*

**AGOSTINO di GIOVANNI and AGNOLO di VENTURA.**—Sculptors and architects of Siena. Trained in the school of the Pisani, these two masters were active in Tuscan and Umbrian cities in the first half of the trecento. Their best-known work, signed and dated 1330, is the tomb of Bishop Guido Tarlati in the cathedral at Arezzo, a bold compositional innovation, weak in the execution of certain details, no doubt due to the lesser powers of their assistant, Giovanni di Agostino, son of Agostino di Giovanni.

Other works attributed to them are: Arezzo, the lunette-statues over the side-portal, an Enthroned Madonna between two angels and two holy bishops; Arezzo, in the interior of the cathedral, the wall-tomb of Pope Gregory X (died in 1276); Pistoia, Duomo, tomb of Cino de' Sinibaldi, 1337; Pistoia, Duomo, tomb of Bishop Ricciardi, 1343; Volterra, Duomo, relief-fragments from Arca S. Ottaviano, 1320 (attribution Venturi); Siena, among other works statues of a Prophet, a Deacon, an Angel, and a Virgin Annunciate in the Opera del Duomo; Florence, tomb of Gastone della Torre, in the Cloister of Sta. Croce.

Agostino di Giovanni is mentioned as dead in 1350, and no work or mention of Agnolo di Ventura exists after the middle of the century. Documentary records of the two run between 1310 and 1350 and apply chiefly to their architectural activity in Siena, Arezzo, and elsewhere. Agostino di Giovanni: 1330, in partnership with son Giovanni, Tarlati Tomb, Arezzo; 1331, arches Palazzo Communale, Siena; 1331-32, in partnership with son Giovanni, Chapel for Simone and Jacopo Ghini in Pieve di S. Maria, Arezzo; 1336, Veste Massa di Maremma; 1339, again in Siena working on the Palazzo Communale and also on the Torre del Mangia, collaborated on the water-system for the Campo, which was opened in 1343; 1340, active on the façade of the Palazzo Sansedoni, Siena.

Agnolo di Ventura: 1325, delivered plans for Porta S. Agata or de' Tufi, Siena; 1327, delivered plans for the Porta Romana or di S. Martino, Siena; 1333, returned opinion (with other masters) on the Duomo, Siena; 1334, built with Guidone di Pace the Castello di Grosseto.

Bibliography: Milanesi, *Docum. Sen.* I, 200-206, 231 ff.—Borghesi e Banchi, *Nuovi Doc. Sen.*, p. 17, Arte Toscana, p. 19.—Milizia, *Mem.* II.—*Atti e mem., etc., per le prov. Modenesi e Parmensi*, ser. III, vol. I, Pte. I, pp. 1-70.—A. Venturi, *Storia*, etc., IV, 66, nota 1, p. 367 ff.—Albert Brach, *Nic. u. Giov. Pisano*, 1904, pp. 96-100.

**AGOSTINO (VENEZIANO).**—His real name was Agostino Musi, and he was a Venetian engraver, whose works show poor talent. However, his *Apollo Belvedere* has documental interest, and his *Skeleton* is a strange work, not entirely devoid of power. It may have inspired Callot's Portrait of Barbarossa, which had some influence on French portrait painters of the 17th century.

Bibliography: Thode, *Die Antiken in den Stichen Marc-Anton's A. Veneziano's und M. Dente's.* Leipzig, 1881.—A. M. Hind, *A History of Engraving and Etching.* London, 1923.

**AGRIGENTUM.**—A town in Sicily today known as Girgenti. It was founded in 581 by the Dorian colonists established in Gela, and it rapidly became a flourishing city. The rich citizens built, on the north and southern mountain ranges of the town, some magnificent temples of which the imposing ruins are still partly standing. The buildings have suffered from wars, destructions, and especially from earthquakes.

Agrigentum: Temple of Hera Lacinia.

*Temple of Hera Lacinia.*—This temple (41 metres by 19 metres 53) dominates the landscape. It is built on a platform to give it greater prominence. It dates from 470 B.C., and is in the Doric style, hexastyle peripteral (with 6 columns to the façade, and surrounded by columns on each side). Of these there remain 25 standing, and nine broken ones. They are 6 metres, 44 high, with a diameter of 1 metre 29, and have 16 flutes.

Agrigentum: Temple of Concord.

*The Temple of Concord.*—This building was constructed a little later than the temple of Hera Lacinia, and dates from 440 B.C. It belongs to the same Doric style and has the same number of columns at the front and sides. It is much better preserved: the columns are all standing, and the building, frieze, and pediments, as well as the architecture, are also preserved. The openings in the wall of the cella were made in the Middle Ages when the temple was converted into a church.

See Pl. 19, Vol. I.

*The Temple of Heracles* c. 510, B.C.—This monument (73 metres 40 by 27 metres 56) is found near the Temple of Concord; it is hexastyle peripteral, with 6 columns to the façade and 15 at the side. The cella, which was later divided into three parts, contained a statue of Asclepius (Palermo Museum); the famous picture by Zeuxis, representing Alcmena, was found here, according to the ancients.

*Temple of Asclepius.*—This vanished temple may probably be the ruins that one finds in a dwelling near the meeting of the Acragas and Hypsa rivers. It contained the statue of Apollo by the Greek sculptor. Myron.

*Temple of Zeus Olympios.*—Much admired by Greek historians who have left us the description of it; it dates from the first half of the 5th century. It is completely in ruins. It measured 113 metres 45 by 56 metres 30,—enormous dimensions; it was Doric pseudo-peripteral (only one range of columns), with 7 half-columns to the façade and 14 at the side. The proportions of these half-columns, which in the interior formed pilasters, are colossal; they measure 16 metres in height, including the capital; their diameter is 3 metres 48. The cella was 92 metres long; it was decorated with 38 Atlantes or telamons (statues of men supporting an entablature or a motif of architectural decoration). (See Atlante.) One of these Atlantes is restored and measures 7 metres 75 in height. They were placed either above the pilasters, supporting the carpentry of the roof, or in between the columns, their heads at the same height as the capitals of the columns supporting the architrave, their feet resting on a projection of the wall which formed a pedestal. Sculptures adorned the pediments; on the east is represented the battle between the gods and giants; and on the other, the taking of Troy.

*Temple of Castor and Pollux.*—The ruins of the Temple of Castor and Pollux lie near to those of the temple of Zeus. Of it there remain four columns supporting an angle of the entablature; a fragment of the architrave, of the Doric frieze, and of the pediment. The temple was in the Doric style, peripteral hexastyle, with 34 columns; it was built about 250 B.C.

Outside of the Acropolis and of the town was a small temple of Demeter and Persephone, dating from the 5th century. It has completely gone to ruin.

Bibliography: Serradifalco, *Le antichita della Sicilia,* 5 Vols. Palermo, 1834-1842.—Hittorf and Zanth, *Architecture antique de la Sicile,* 1 Vol. 1870.—Koldewcy and Puchstein, *Die grieschiche Tempel in Unter italien und Sicilien,* 2 Vols. Berlin, 1899.

**AGRIPPA (Pantheon of).**—See Pantheon of Agrippa.

**AIGUES - MORTES.** — Aigues-Mortes owed the beginning of its prosperity to St. Louis. The King

Aigues-Mortes: The Watchman's Gate.

wanted to possess a port on the Mediterranean. To defend it he built the tower of Constance. His son, Philippe le Hardi, built the town and the surrounding ramparts, which remain intact. It has been said that these fortifications were built on the model of those of Damietta. The tower of Constance stands isolated, outside the walls, by the north-west corner. A moat, now filled in, formerly surrounded it. It is a great circular mass (37 metres high, and 20 metres in diameter) pierced by some narrow loopholes in the walls, which are 6 metres in thickness. It contains a circular, vaulted guard-room, a little oratory, and the "Salle des Chevaliers." The ramparts round the town form a rectangle of more than 1600 metres in length; the walls are formed of large stones, carefully dressed, about 7 metres high, with battlements and isolated machicolations, near the gates. Fifteen towers protect them. These fortifications are the work of the Genoese, Boccanegra.

See Pl. 51, Vol. I.

**AIX - EN - PROVENCE.**—The Cathedral of St. Sauveur, built in the 11th century, preserves the famous picture of *The Burning Bush* by Nicolas Froment. The Church of St. John, 13th century, contains the tombs of the Counts of Provence. There are also the Archbishop's Palace, the staircase of which is decorated with marble bas-reliefs by Puget; the Hôtel Thomassin Saint Paul (now the Academy); and the School of Arts and Crafts, built by Vauban.

**AIX - LA - CHAPELLE.** — The Cathedral is a complex of buildings. The oldest and most important part is the famous Minster (796-804), which was the palatine chapel of Charlemagne and remains the outstanding monument of the Carolingian period. A rude imitation of the 6th century Byzantine church of S. Vitale at Ravenna, Italy, it consists of a central octagonal structure in four storeys covered by an octagonal cloister vault and ringed by a groin-vaulted aisle with an unvaulted tribune on the second storey. The columns were imported from Ravenna; sixteen of them are incongruously placed within the span of the topmost arches. A tower porch on the west side has two cylindrical stair turrets. The square eastern termination was replaced, in the 14th century, by a Gothic choir larger than the original chapel. Other accretions to the group mask the original building. These include the Gothic cloisters and four small chapels. The Cathedral contains famous relics: the 4-metres wide copper-gilt "crown of light" given by Frederick Barbarossa; the throne given in 1011 by the Emperor Henry II; the antique sarcophagus in which Charlemagne was originally buried; and the casket in which his remains now rest.

Bibliography: P. Frankl, *Die frühmittelalterliche und romanische Baukunst,* Potsdam, 1926.—E. Gall, *Karolingische und Ottonische Kirchen,* Magdeburg, 1930.

**AJANTA.**—See India.

**AKEN (Jerome van).—See** Bosch.

**AKKAD (Agade).**—See Sumerian Art.

**ALAMANNA (Pietro).**—Painter of Ascoli. Active from 1470 to 1498. Pupil of Carlo Crivelli whose style conditioned his own. Influenced also by Antoniazzo Romano. A master of small talent.

Bibliography: Ricci, *Memorie storiche,* etc., I, 218, 219, 229, 230.—Orsini, *Guida di Ascoli,* p. 45, 61.—Cantalamessa, *Memorie intorno ai letterati ed artisti ascolani,* Ascoli, 1839, p. 115.

**ALBANI (Francesco).** — Bolognese painter (1578-1660). He was an amiable, gracious painter, whose paintings show a happy disposition. A follower of Annibale Carracci, he only borrowed from him what was charming and rural and that is why he is called the "Anacreon of painting." He spent some time in the towns of Querzuola and Meldola to be nearer to nature, but he enlivened his rural impressions with the flowers of his mythological imagination. Garlands of cherubim blossom in these peaceful countrysides.

Albani was the favourite of princes, and his quarrels with Guido Reni did not succeed in darkening his life. His career as a painter began at Bologna where he did a *Birth*

# STONE ARCHITECTURE

ARCHITECTURE, *which is the most important of all the arts, was not the first to appear. In fact it can only develop in a society which is already strongly established, because it represents collective work, discipline, and hierarchy, not to mention mechanical knowledge and perfected tools. Architecture is conditioned above all by material; there are some nations which have ignored or disregarded stone. The Mediterranean civilisations, on the contrary, commenced to build with stone; they depended on the work of the mason and the skill of the architect.*

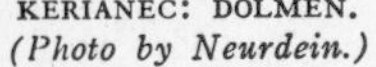

KERIANEC: DOLMEN.
*(Photo by Neurdein.)*

MYCENAE: LION GATE.
*(Photo by Boissonnas.)*

ATHENS: EAST PORTICO OF THE PROPYLÆA.
*(Photo by Boissonnas.)*

THE principal requirement of all architecture lies in the observation of the laws of equilibrium; the placing of a horizontal board on vertical supports. The prehistoric dolmen with its crude and barbaric aspect, already belonged to the family of monuments which later are illustrated by Greek temples and Gothic churches. The adjustment of the stone is less exact and less clever, but it compensates for this by the might expressed in its mass. The admirable Doric entablature on the colonnade is only a refined inheritance of the primitive dolmen, but the architect understands better how to apply the laws of gravity.

CARCASSONNE: RAMPARTS, STAIRWAY OF THE GATE OF AUDE.
*(Photo by Hachette.)*

POITIERS: APSE OF ST. HILAIRE.
*(Photo by Neurdein.)*

COUTANCES: TOWER AND LANTERN OF THE CATHEDRAL.
*(Photo by Hachette.)*

THE adaptation of stone to the necessities of construction, and the ease with which the problems of balance are solved, are the foundation for the development of decorative forms. It is not the artist's imagination alone which is responsible for the invention of the loveliest themes of art; they spring from a combination of thought and material. Most motifs of our plastic art, Greek or Gothic, were discovered by architects who thought "in stone"; most of the motifs of architecture result from an adaptation of stone to the requirements of the function. Many ornaments are merely atrophied organs.

CHAMBORD: THE GREAT STAIRCASE.
*(Photo by Neurdein.)*

FLORENCE: PALAZZO RICCARDI.
*(Photo by Brogi.)*

BORDEAUX: WELL OF THE STAIRCASE OF THE GREAT THEATRE.
*(Photo from l'Architecte.)*

FINALLY, when architects became masters of their material, they began to take more liberties. They began looking for difficulties since it gave them pleasure to solve them dexterously; or, for the sake of visible structure they made a form of architecture without any ornament, a work of incomparable elegance. The building assumes a different appearance according to the architect's treatment of the stone. According to the way it is carved, the stone presents a more or less luminous surface and assumes a different color. By a carved stone one can date a monument.

# BRICK ARCHITECTURE

*Brick architecture was employed early in such countries as Chaldea, where there was no stone for building purposes. They built immense monuments by piling up sun-dried bricks. Those monuments have disappeared; the making of brick, however, has been maintained and perfected. Due to its characteristic nature, brick did not lend itself to the basic elements of construction, which are found in Egyptian architecture, the column and the entablature. The architects were obliged to devise another method of roofing, namely, that of the vault. The lightness of this method of construction makes it a comparatively simple one.*

MISTRA: CHURCH OF THE PANTANASSA.
*(Photo by Millet.)*

ALBI: TOWER OF THE CATHEDRAL.
*(Photo by Hachette.)*

GRANADA: ALHAMBRA, HALL OF THE TWO SISTERS.
*(Photo by Anderson.)*

SIENA: PALAZZO PUBBLICO.
*(Photo by Alinari.)*

PAVIA: CERTOSA.
*(Photo by Brogi.)*

PARIS: PLACE DES VOSGES.
*(Photo by Hachette.)*

The use of brick has developed a decorative system different from that developed by the use of stone. Stone decoration is plastic and sculptural, brick is picturesque through its color which compensates for sculptural poverty. Architects have known how to use it in different ways, whether they have used again the forms invented by stone architecture, or have drawn an ornamentation from the adjustment of the bricks, or were content to contrast the red brick against the white stone work. The classical architects, good students of Greek art, have always considered brick as a less noble material than stone. But its simplicity pleased the bourgeoisie.

# WOOD ARCHITECTURE

*Wood architecture is less durable than stone architecture and men have generally deserted it for masonry, because wood is continually threatened by fire in a civilisation where fire is in constant use. However, a wooden house has been preferred to a house of masonry in countries like Japan, where earthquakes are frequent. The very old wooden structures have disappeared because of their fragility, but it is evident that the men who were capable of erecting the colossal menhirs had the necessary tools to construct wooden shelters.*

PEIPING: PAVILION IN THE GARDEN OF THE SUMMER PALACE.

SIBERIAN HUT.
*(Photo by Underwood and Underwood.)*

TYROLEAN CHALET.

TELLEMASKEN: CHURCH.

For various reasons wooden architecture has been maintained in many countries, because of the ease with which wood can be worked and because it is readily obtained, and also perhaps because of its decorative qualities; because wood is a light and very resistant material it can be made into bold and elegant forms. The Chinese and Japanese have used it in a remarkable manner. In heavily forested countries, as in the northern regions, the houses generally are of wood. In this type of house the roof dominates the walls which sustain it. The trunks of trees, from which is fashioned the framework of immense beams, are not as well adapted to the building of walls.

EVRON: THE MARKET.
*(Photo from Archives photographiques.)*

REIMS: OLD TIMBERWORK OF THE CATHEDRAL.
*(Photo by Baudet.)*

Scaffolding is made for the construction of roofs; as in the Chinese pavilions or in the European markets, the wooden construction may consist merely of roofs supported on pillars. These market-halls have an air of grandeur; by the radiation of their beams which support the roof, they imitate the principle of branches which spread out from the central trunk. In this combination of beams which support each other and are tangent to each other, there is a play of strength which is the forerunner of the ribs in the ogival arches and the flying buttresses. Thus the archæologists have been able to see in the Gothic cathedral a realisation in stone of the idea originated by a carpenter.

# STONE SCULPTURE

*SCULPTURE is the most spontaneous of the arts; it needs only a little material, such as stone, earth, or wood, and an instrument for carving. Sculpture is an art of all ages; it never ceased except when it was forbidden for religious reasons. As the simple procedure of this art and its most frequent model, the human body, do not vary with the passing of time, sculpture is not only the most universal but it is also the most intelligent of all the arts; it is the most naturalistic and the least conventional. Among the differences between the various schools one has, first of all, to observe the differences in material.*

BUST OF KHONSU. MUSEUM OF CAIRO.

HEAD OF GUDEA FROM THE EXCAVATION OF DE SARZEC. LOUVRE.
*(Photo by Hachette.)*

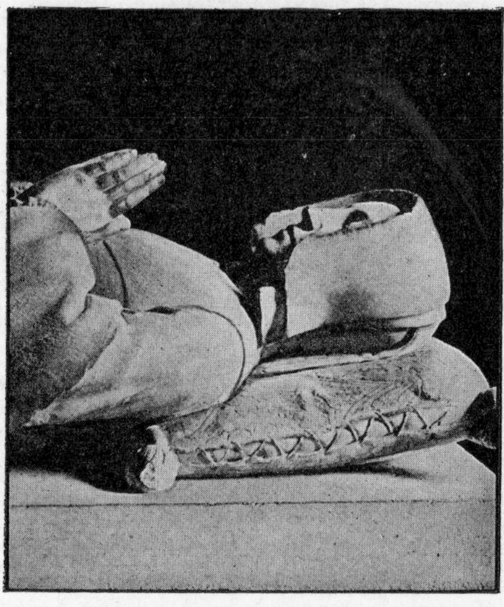

BUST FROM ELCHE. LOUVRE.
*(Photo by Hachette.)*

CHARTRES: CHRIST OF THE ROYAL PORTAL OF THE CATHEDRAL.
*(Photo by Giraudon.)*

TOMB OF ROBERTE LEGENDRE. LOUVRE.
*(Photo by Hachette.)*

EACH school of sculpture had its own preference of material. The Egyptians and the Chaldeans, who above all wanted to create indestructible figures, worked readily with very hard stone such as granite, sandstone, and diorite, and the choice of these materials inspired to a certain degree the style, the positions, and the type of the modelling. The artists of the Middle Ages, whether they worked with a finer or coarser grained limestone, conceived form in a different manner. The sculpture of the east portal of Chartres is of hard limestone which lends itself to fine chiseling; here the artists took pleasure in sharpening it to a cutting edge. The sculptor of Roberte Legendre, who worked with coarse grained stone, was trying for more simplified modelling.

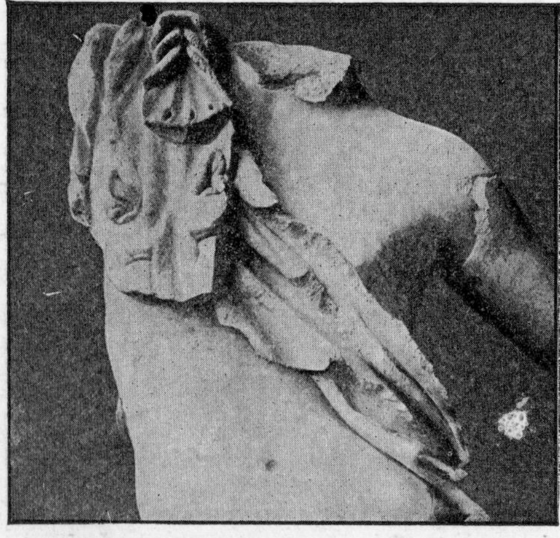

GREEK SCULPTURE: FAUN. LOUVRE
*(Photo by Hachette.)*

MICHELANGELO: SLAVE. LOUVRE.
*(Photo by Hachette.)*

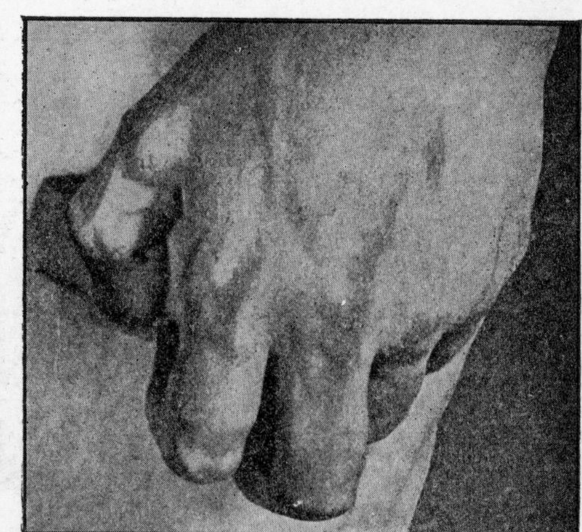

PUGET: LEFT HAND OF THE HERCULES. LOUVRE.
*(Photo by Hachette.)*

MARBLE is the finest stone of all, lending itself to the delicacies of modelling. Having a slightly transparent quality, it allows the sunlight to penetrate, which makes it particularly qualified to imitate the skin and to suggest the living quality of the flesh. Because of this, marble is the best medium for nude sculpture. It is with marble that the Greeks have given human shape to pagan deities. When, in the Renaissance pagan art took its place next to Christian art, it could do so only because marble had been adopted by the sculptors. One could not conceive of Apollo or Aphrodite sculptured in granite.

# SCULPTURE: BRONZE AND WOOD

*Bronze, an alloy of copper and tin, was used at an early age. Men had bronze weapons before they discovered the use of iron. Iron replaced bronze in many ways, but for statuary bronze remained the favorite metal because of the simplicity of its casting, its resistance, and the beauty of its patina. With it the sculptor is able to make more hollowed out contours of figures than with stone. Some of the thin silhouettes of Greek sculpture are a translation of bronze figures into marble. The darkness of the shadows contrasted with the highlights of the edges gives to the bronze modelling a vibrant look. The rough appearance of the marble, on the other hand, dulls and weakens this.*

PERSIAN LION. LOUVRE.
*(Photo by Hachette.)*

PETER VISCHER: HIS PORTRAIT, TOMB OF ST. SEBALD. NUREMBERG.
*(Photo by Stich.)*

GHIBERTI: DOOR OF THE BAPTISTERY. FLORENCE (DETAIL).
*(Photo by Anderson.)*

ROME: PUGILIST. NATIONAL MUSEUM.
*(Photo by Anderson.)*

BARYE: TIGER AND KID. LOUVRE.
*(Photo by Hachette.)*

Wood sculpture was done at an early age, no doubt, from the time that man had flint tools for carving. Wood sculpture, however, is easily destroyed, except in Egypt where the soil preserved all that was confined in it. Wood carving and the necessity of reckoning with texture leads the sculptor to choose forms which are neither like those of stone, nor like those of bronze. Wood, first of all because of its visible grain, is opposed to the fine nuances of modelling; wood sculpture is usually finished off by a coat of paint, which is a protection against humidity and against dryness.

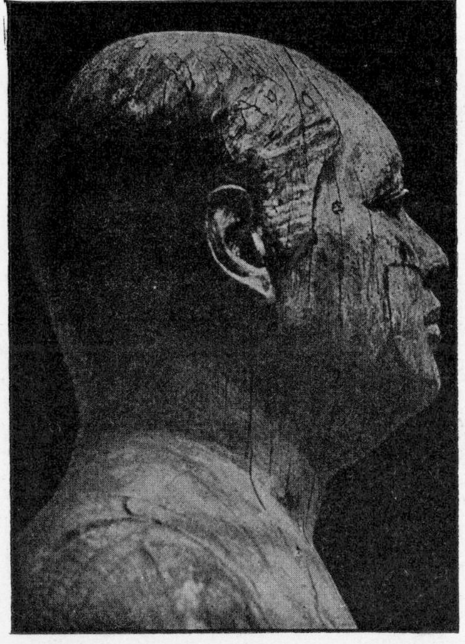

SHEIKH-EL-BELED. MUSEUM OF CAIRO.

JACQUES DE BAERZE: ADORATION OF THE MAGI. MUSEUM OF DIJON.
*(Photo by Neurdein.)*

MADONNA OF NUREMBERG.
*(Photo by Giraudon.)*

# BAKED CLAY (TERRA COTTA)

*Clay was first used by architects of countries who, like the people of Mesopotamia, were deprived of stone. They had to content themselves with drying clay in the sun, and these dried bricks piled on top of each other resulted in the formidable constructions of Babylonia, whose memory tradition has preserved for us. The Asiatics have remained to this day particularly able in the art of ceramics. It is they who taught us how to cover these bricks with a material which, when heated to a high temperature, will become a brightly coloured glaze. The whole art of pottery was derived from the glazed bricks of ancient Persia.*

STONEWARE VASE FROM JAPAN, MUSÉE DES ARTS DÉCORATIFS, PARIS.
*(Photo by Hachette.)*

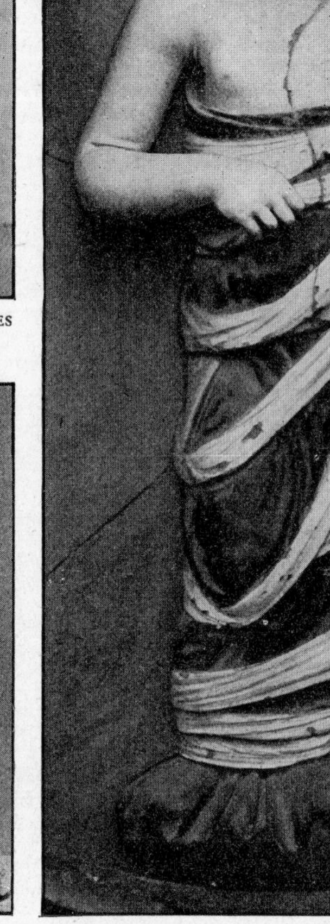

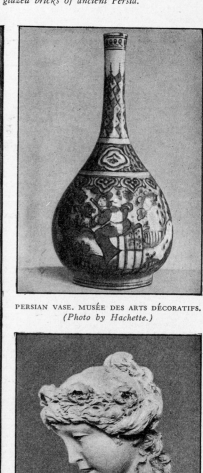

PERSIAN VASE. MUSÉE DES ARTS DÉCORATIFS.
*(Photo by Hachette.)*

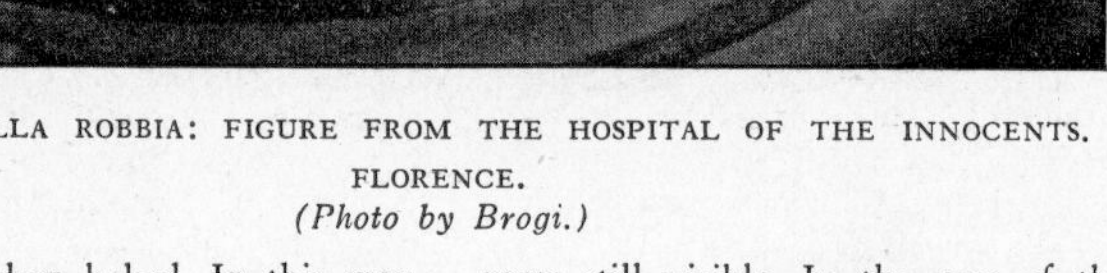

FIGURE FROM TANAGRA. LOUVRE.
*(Photo by Hachette.)*

ANDREA DELLA ROBBIA: FIGURE FROM THE HOSPITAL OF THE INNOCENTS. FLORENCE.
*(Photo by Brogi.)*

CLODION: BACCHANTE. LOUVRE.
*(Photo by Hachette.)*

The soil, a particularly malleable substance, hardens when baked. In this way it is capable of giving all the service which is expected of stone sculpture, and has the added advantage that many replicas can be made from the same mould. Clay modelling is such that when the object leaves the artist's hand—as for example in the work of Clodion—it seems as if the impression of his thumbs were still visible. In the case of the work of the della Robbias the figures are covered with a coloured glaze after removal from the mould. The figurines from Tanagra were also coloured, but with water colours, which are not well preserved after several centuries.

DELAHERCHE: STONE-WARE. MUSÉE DES ARTS DÉCORATIFS, PARIS.
*(Photo by Hachette.)*

CARRIÈS: FIGURE. PALAIS DES BEAUX-ARTS, PARIS.

DECOEUR: VASE. MUSÉE DES ARTS DÉCORATIFS.
*(Photo by Hachette.)*

Terra cotta may be used for sculpture; but it is most frequently used in the making of vases; the simplicity of the material and method results in an art of never ceasing usefulness. Depending on its shape and kind of glazing, a piece of pottery may become an exquisite object of art, even though it is of no practical use. Modern potters have rediscovered the technique of the Persian and Japanese craftsmen, the transformation of clay by heat. The most important relics left behind by civilisations are remnants of pottery. All peoples have played a part in the history of ceramics.

*of the Virgin* in Sta. Maria del Piombo. He continued the decoration of the Fava Palace with the series of the *Adventures of Æneas.* He next went to Rome, and it was there especially that his energy was employed in the splendid palaces which he then decorated. He carried out many works in collaboration with Annibale Carracci and Domenichino, such as those which were painted for the Aldobrandini Chapel and which are now in the Doria Gallery. They are remarkable especially for their beautiful landscapes which are worthy forerunners of those of Poussin. *The Virgin and St. Joseph Seeking Shelter* and *The Assumption* are attributed to Albani.

He helped Annibale Carracci with the frescoes which are now in Madrid and Barcelona, carrying out Carracci's drawings.

He worked with Domenichino in the decoration of the mansion of Bassano di Sutri, where he painted a *Fall of Phaeton* in the middle of the ceiling, among other mythological scenes. He decorated a loggia of the Palazzo Verospi. He worked at the Quirinal with Guido Reni. He decorated the vault of the Chapel of Santa-Maria della Pace with an *Assumption.*

Bibliography: E. Ravaglia, *Il fanciullo dell' arte dell Albani.* Bologna, 1908.—G. Rouches, *La Peinture bolognaise à la fin du XVI siècle.* Alcan, 1913.

**ALBERTI (Leone Battista).**—Florentine architect (1404-1472). One of the most cultured spirits of the Renaissance and a versatile genius. He was the first to undertake a scientific investigation of the laws of perspective. His book, *De Re Aedificatura,* influential in ideating the style of the High Renaissance, shows his classical and antiquarian tendencies as effectively as do his buildings. He was essentially a theorist and amateur and executed only the plans for his designs, leaving the actual building to others.

The Palazzo Rucellai, built according to his plans by Bernardo Rossellino, shows the addition of classical orders to the traditionally astylar Florentine palace exterior.

San Francesco at Rimini, designed for Pandolfo Malatesta, replaces a Gothic church. The façade, which is unfinished, derives from the Roman Arch of Augustus in the same town. The building is surrounded by arcades resembling triumphal arches.

Alberti also designed the chapel beside the Rucellai Palace (1467), the façade of Santa Maria Novella (1456-1470), for which he did some beautiful volutes, and the choir of the Annunziata (1470, disfigured afterwards by a baroque decoration), in the same church.

He was called to Mantua in 1470 by the Gonzaga family for whom he designed the churches of San Sebastiano and Sant' Andrea (1472-94). The latter building (see Plate 5, vol. 2) is a landmark in Renaissance architecture and represents an intermediary phase between early churches like Santo Spirito in Florence and the more monumental structures of the 16th century. The great innovation here is the substitution of heavy piers carrying a barrel vault for the arcades on columns and the flat ceilings of the earlier 15th century.

Bibliography: W. J. Anderson, *Architecture of the Renaissance in Italy* (5th ed.). New York, 1927.

**ALBERTINELLI (Mariotto).**—Florentine painter (1474-1515). He was a pupil of Piero di Cosimo, also

Albertinelli (Mariotto). (After Vasari.)

studied in the studio of Cosimo Rosselli with Fra Bartolommeo, whose friend and collaborator he remained. Before 1500 they had already worked together on a *Last Judgment* in Santa Maria Nuova. Albertinelli's original masterpiece by which he is well-known is the *Visitation* of the Uffizi (1503). At the Pitti Palace, there is a *Holy Family* by him; in the Accademia, a *Trinity* (1500) a *Virgin Enthroned with Saints* and an *Annunciation* (1510), much retouched. They are well designed, and well painted. The *Crucifixion* in the principal room of the Certosa di Galuzzo (1505) is more striking.

The usual signature of the two painters when they worked in collaboration was a monogram representing two circles interlaced

**ALBI (France).**—The Cathedral (St. Cécile) is a magnificent building in red brick. It has a porch enriched with sculptures. It was built from 1282 to 1397, beside an old building, which, in accordance with the wishes of the Bishop of Albi, Bernard de Castanet, was destroyed after the construction of the new one. This prelate—who spent his life fighting against the Albigensian heretics, and still more against those of his wealthy subjects whose fortunes might be confiscated to the profit of his church!—realised the need for an impregnable Cathedral: hence the fortress-like character of the edifice. The plan is very simple. An immense vaulted hall (the widest in France), without side aisles or transepts, has an apsidal end and a series of side chapels separated by internal buttresses. A rich, flamboyant rood-screen separates the choir from the nave; it entirely surrounds the choir, forming as it were a second church surrounded by an ambulatory. The screen is richly adorned with sculptures which are not all of equal merit, but the work was certainly directed by an excellent artist. It dates from the 15th century. If not of Burgundian origin, the sculptures of Albi are evidently related to this school. This appears not only in the workmanship, but in the thickset proportions of the figures.

The western façade is dominated by a formidable looking square tower; and the high walls of the Cathedral are reinforced with turrets, and pierced with long, narrow windows. The richly carved entrance porch, the architecture of which contrasts strangely with the severity of the Cathedral walls, is on the south side of the building.

See Pls. 2, 48, 50, Vol. I.

**ALCAMENES.**—A Greek sculptor who was thought by Pliny to be a pupil of Phidias. He was the sculptor of a figure of Hecate which was set up on the Pyrgos beside the Temple of Athena Niké at Athens. He is said to have originated the three-fold type of Hecate in which she is represented by three distinct bodies set back to back. A little younger than Phidias he worked until the end of the 5th century. Pliny considered him to be the greatest Attic sculptor after Phidias. Among his works he mentions: a *Dionysos* in an Athenian theatre; the *Hephaistos* of the Hephaisteion; an *Ares* near the Areopagus; an *Asclepius* at Mantinea. His masterpiece was a statue of Aphrodite Ourania, which was celebrated in ancient times. Lucian composed a lively eclogue on it (portrait Dialogues, nos. 4 and 6). Modern archæologists are trying to identify sculptures which might have been inspired by the statues of Alcamenes. Collignon thinks that the *Aphrodite* of the Louvre, called "Aphrodite of Frejus," is among those figures which are most likely to be copies of those of Alcamenes. The figure in the Louvre is still near to the style of Phidias. The numerous copies or imitations in marble and terra cotta prove that the type was widespread. According to certain archæologists, the *Discobolus* of the Vatican was a copy of a famous bronze statue by Alcamenes. The *Mars Borghese* of the Louvre was also derived from a model created by Alcamenes.

Bibliography: Collignon, *Histoire de la Sculpture Grecque, II.* Paris, 1896.

**ALCANTARA (Bridge of) (Spain, prov. of Caceres).**—This ingeniously constructed and magnificent bridge crossing the river Tage was built during the reign of Emperor Trajan in 105-106 by the architect Julius Caius Lacer. It is 71 m. high measured from the bed of the river to the top of the triumphal arch erected in the center, a height rarely surpassed by Roman structures. Due to military reasons the bridge occasionally suffered damage and had to be restored at various times. The most important restorations were made in the reigns of Emperor Charles V in 1543 and Queen Isabel II in 1859.

Bibliography: Marqués de Lozoya, *Historia del arte hispanico.* Barcelona, 1931. Vol. I.

**ALCAZAR.**—See Seville.

**ALDEGREVER (Heinrich).**—German engraver and painter; born c. 1502, and died probably about 1558. He worked in Soest in Westphalia. His style shows a marked influence from Nüremberg engravers of the school of Dürer. Among his works one finds: *The Labours of Hercules, Marcus Curtius,* or *Pyramus and Thisbe*; *The History of Joseph,* the *Parable of the Wicked Rich Man,* and the *Wedding Dancers.*

Bibliography: H. W. Singer, *Die Kleinmeister.* Bielefeld, 1908.—L. Rosenthal, *La Gravure.* Paris, Laurens, 1909.—Zschelletschky, H., *Das graphische Werk Heinrich Aldegrevers.* Strassburg, 1933.

**ALDOBRANDINI (marriage scenes of).**—An antique painting which bears the name of Cardinal Aldobrandini, who bought it, in Rome, when it was discovered, in 1606, on the site of the old gardens of Mycenæ. It is now in the Vatican Museum. It is a picture of fair size (2 metres 60 in width by 1 metre 20 in height). It represents marriage scenes, and is one of the rare paintings that has come down to us from classic times, and one of the most important.

See Pl. 28, Vol. I.

**ALEGRETTO NUZI.**—Painter of Fabriano. The most important 14th-century painter of the Marches. Probably came as a young man to Florence, where his name is found in 1346 in the register of the Compagnia di S. Luca. Influenced by the followers of Giotto, in particular by Bernardo Daddi and Maso di Banco. Active in Fabriano and Macerata. Earliest still existing work a triptych, Madonna and Child, Donors and Saints, in the Vatican Pinacoteca, signed and dated 1365. A Madonna with saints in the Municipio, Apiro, is signed and dated 1366. A triptych, Madonna, saints and angels, in the Duomo at Macerata, is signed and dated 1369, and there is a Madonna Enthroned in Urbino, 1372. Alegretto died in 1373. Most of his work is to be found in Fabriano, where, in the church of S. Domenico, there are frescoes attributed to him.

His color-scale is high-pitched, with gold, red, and rose predominating. He reflects the miniature tendency, employing rich decorative accessories and figured brocades.

His pupils were Francescuccio Ghissi, Antonio and Gentile da Fabriano, perhaps also Lorenzo and Jacopo Salimbeni da Sanseverino.

Bibliography: Vasari-Le Monnier, III.—Crowe and Cavalcaselle.—Colasanti, *Italian Painters of the Marches.*

**ALENIS (Tommaso de).**—Painter of Cremona, active 1500-1515, friend and imitator of Galeazzo Campi, influenced by Perugino and Francia. Earliest work, 1500, in Bignami Collection, Casal Maggiore. Signed and dated Adoration, 1515, in the Municipio, Cremona.

Bibliography: Crowe and Cavalcaselle, *Gesch. d. italien. Malerei,* VI, 517.—*Nuova Antologia,* Vol. 138, fasc. 21, pp. 5-14; Vol. 130, fasc. 16, pp. 629-653.

**ALEOTTI (Giambattista), called L'Argenta, from the name of his native town near Ferrara.**—Architect at Ferrara and Parma (1546-1636). He worked first at Ferrara in the service of the Duke Alfonso II and the magistracy. His principal works were the façade of the Jesuit Church of San Carlo, and the Teatro degli Intrepidi, which was unfortunately destroyed by a bomb in 1679. His most admired work is the great Farnese Theatre at Parma, built from 1618 to 1619, which is a remarkable adaptation of the classical theatre to modern methods of representation, and where we find the Palladio's arrangement (see this name) of two tiers of boxes.

Bibliography: D. Bandi, *Giambattista Aleotti architetto.* Argenta, 1878.—Glanco Lombardi, *Il Teatro Farnese* in Archivio Storico delle Provincie Parmesi, Vol. IV. Parma, 1909.

**A L E S S I (Galeazzo).**—Italian architect, born in Perugia, who worked chiefly at Genoa (1512-1572), and gave the town its most beautiful palaces. He had the same importance there that Sansovino had in Venice, or Palladio at Vicenza, and his name is always associated with the nobility, and magnificence of the Genoese Renaissance. He received his first instruction from G. B. Caporali and from Giulio Dante. But when he went to Rome he was captured by the genius of Michelangelo and fell entirely

Alessi (Galeazzo): Doria Palace, Genoa.

under his influence. On his return to his birthplace, he built the Citadelle Pauline, and made the plans of

Alessi (Galeazzo): Marino Palace, Milan.

various churches. But it was in Genoa that he found the most propitious soil. His signature is found there from 1549. He built the Church, the Hospital and the Presbytery of Santa Maria in Carignano. Bramante's idea of a Greek cross (which was not carried out at St. Peter's), was a bugbear to architects. Galeazzo succeeded in realising it, and finished each angle by a high tower which, however, somewhat spoils the effect of the dome. But it was an imposing novelty, if not very harmonious. He then attacked the great thoroughfare, la Strada Nuova, which he straightened (now the Via Garibaldi), and on which he built his wonderful palaces. These were the Cambiaso, the Parodi (built for Franco Lercaro from 1567 to 1581), the Spinola, the Doria, the Adorno, the Serra, and possibly the Rosso Palaces—all large palaces of pleasant proportions, and at the same time with an elegance in the smallest details which seems at times to foretell the Baroque. Bosses, friezes, sometimes painted decorations on the façades, courtyards with columns, balconies, cornices, charming loggias, large vestibules, beautiful staircases, and all manner of rich conceits, are there found united. He was particularly happy in conveying an impression of space which did not exist, and in opening out effects of perspective from one courtyard to another across several buildings.

Still other palaces, and houses in the neighbourhood of Genoa were created by him, and it was to him the Genoese turned when, in 1567, they wished to raise a dome to the Cathedral.

To complete his embellishment of the town, Alessi made esplanades, piers, and a great portico opening on to the Mediterranean, as simple as the art of Bramante on the land side, and of an almost Baroque richness on the side which faced the sea.

The architect of Genoa worked also at Milan, where he built the elegant Marino Palace (1558) for a Genoese trader, and designed the rich façade of Santa Maria, near Santo Celso (1569-1572). At the Certosa of Pavia he made the beautiful tomb of Giovanni Galeazzo Visconti.

He worked at Bologna, at Parma, where he built the Jesuit College (now the University), and at Assisi, where he raised the dome of Santa Maria degli Angeli; he also designed the dome for the Escorial.

**ALEXANDER (Francis).**—American painter (1800-1881), ceased his art comparatively early in life, but was for a while a noted portrait painter in Boston.

Bibliography: Charles H. Coffin, *History of American Painting*. New York, 1907.

**ALEXANDER (John White).**—American painter (1856-1915). He was born in Allegheny, Pennsylvania, 7th October 1856 and was brought up in that city by his grandparents. He went to work as a messenger boy for the Atlantic and Pacific Telegraph Company and soon became the ward of the president, Colonel Edward J. Allen. At the age of eighteen he joined the illustrators' staff of Harper and Brothers and three years later had saved enough money to finance a European trip for further art study. He found the rules too strict in the Munich Academy so moved on to Pölling in Bavaria, where he lived and painted with such men as Frank Currier, Joseph DeCamp, Walter Shirlaw and others. Later he spent some time with Duveneck in Florence and with Whistler in Venice. During his leisure moments he was at work making illustrations for the *Century* and *Harper's Magazine*. In 1890 he went to Paris for his health, remaining there for the next eleven years, during which time he became a member of the Société Nationale des Beaux-Arts on his merit as a portrait painter. About 1901 Alexander returned to the United States and, although never very strong physically after his illness of 1887, he continued painting portraits and figure studies as long as he was able. He tried his hand at murals, doing a series regarding the iron industry for Carnegie Institute in Pittsburgh, and the *Evolution of the Book* for the Library of Congress in Washington. He was the president of the National Academy of Design for several years and at one time on the board of the Metropolitan Museum of Art. His work shows the influence of the French masters of that time as well as a decorative sense derived from the Orient, and examples of his art may be found in the leading museums of the United States.

Bibliography: *Address of Mr. John G. Agar—and Resolutions Adopted at the Testimonial to John W. Alexander,* 1916.—W. L. Harris, *John White Alexander; His Influence on American Art and Industry,* n. d.—J. W. McSpadden, *Famous Painters of America,* 1916. —J. C. Van Dyke, *American Painting and Its Tradition,* 1919.—*Catalogue of Paintings, John White Alexander Memorial Exhibition,* Carnegie Institute, Pittsburgh, March, 1916.

**ALEXANDRIA.**—See Greece (Sculpture; Terra-cottas).

**ALFANI (Domenico).**—Italian painter, born at Perugia about 1480, died about 1553. He worked in Perugino's studio, where he knew Raphael. The influence of these two masters can be seen in his pictures, the *Madonna* of the Gregoriano College, in Perugia, the *Holy Family* (in Pinacoteca of Perugia) and the *Madonna with Saints* (Cathedral of Città della Pieve). About 1529, the Florentine, Rosso, coming to Perugia, taught him the Florentine manner. The soft tenderness of Perugino was replaced by more severe and precise drawing. One can note the change in his later works, the *Adoration of the Magi* (Sant' Agostino), and the *Virgin between St. John and a Saint* (1532).

His son, Orazio (1510-1583), also a painter, worked under his direction, often in collaboration. It is sometimes difficult to distinguish his work from that of his father. Among the paintings which can be attributed to him are: the *Holy Family* (Uffizi), the *Mystic Marriage of St. Catherine* (Louvre), *Christ Crucified* (San Francesco, Perugia), and in collaboration with his father, the *Virgin with Saints* (Perugia), etc.

Bibliography: Rossi Scotti, *Guida di Perugia,* 1867.—Bonacci Brunamonti, *Pietro Perugino e l'arte umbra.*—Lupatelli, Storia della pittura in Perugia, p. 43, 49, 51, 53.—Mariotti, *Lettere pittoriche perugine,* pp. 241-250.

**ALGARDI (Alessandro).**—Bolognese sculptor and architect (1602-

Algardi (Alessandro): Tomb of Leo XI, St. Peter's, Rome.

1654). He worked chiefly in Rome and imitated his contemporary, Bernini, without having his talent and originality, and holding more closely to tradition. His most remarkable work is perhaps the immense bas-relief representing Attila and St. Leo, with many figures in high-relief in front of a landscape and complicated architecture, which he placed at the base of the altar to St. Leo, in St. Peter's. He is also the author of the memorial to Leo XI in the same church, and of the statue of Innocent X which one can compare with that of Urban VIII by Bernini, in the Palazzo dei Conservatori. As an architect, it was his majestic façade of the Church of Sant'Ignazio that secured his fame.

He made the plans of the beautiful gardens of the Villa Panfili.

He also carved some ivory crucifixes.

**ALGIERS.**—See Moslem Art; Timgad.

**ALHAMBRA.**—See Granada.

**ALIENSE (Antonio Vassillacchi) of Milo.**—Venetian painter; died in 1629. A follower of Veronese, of Titian and of Palma. To him are due: *The Coronation of Baudouin,* at Constantinople; the *Taking of Brescia,* and the *Visit of the Magi,* which are in the Doge's Palace; the *Arrival in Venice of Catherine Cornaro,* of the Museo Civico; the *Easter of the Hebrews,* in the Church of the Pietà.

**ALJAFERIA.**—See Saragossa.

**ALKEN (Henry).**—English painter and engraver (1784-1851), specialized in sporting subjects.

Bibliography: Walter Shaw Sparrow, *Henry Alken.* London, 1927.

**ALLEGRI (Antonio).**—See Correggio.

**— (Pomponio).**—Parmese painter (1521-1593), son of Correggio, without originality or talent.

**ALLORI (Alessandro).**—Florentine painter (1535-1607), pupil of Bronzino. He especially affected Michelangelo, exaggerating his style. In the Annunziata of Florence there is a copy by him of the *Last Judgment* in the Sistine Chapel. He painted some frescoes in the Cappella Gaddi of Santa Maria Novella.

**— (Cristofano or Cristoforo).**—Florentine painter (1577-1621), a mannerist painter who enjoyed representing scenes of passion and sensuality. His *Judith* is in the Pitti Palace.

**ALLSTON (Washington).**—American painter (1779-1843), pupil of Benjamin West in London, visited Paris and Italy 1804-1809, subsequently again in London 1811-1813 (elected A.R.A. 1817), the remainder of his life in America. An important figure in the early history of American painting; much influenced by the Venetian school and the author of several large and ambitious compositions of scriptural subjects.

**ALTAMIRA (Caves of) (Spain).**—Located near Santillana del Mar (prov. Santander) these caves with their prehistoric rockpaintings were discovered in 1876 by Marcelino Sautuola. His discovery met with skepticism, if not with frank disbelief, on the part of foreign historians who held the rockpaintings to be apocryphal. But in 1902 with the discovery of the cave of Font-de-Gaume (Dordogne, France) Sautuola was fully vindicated. With other rupestral paintings of the South of France and Spain those of Altamira belong to the so-called Franco-Cantabrian school. They are of the Soloutrean-Magdalenian period—that is of the last phases of the paleolithic age. The representations (which are in color) include animals of various kinds with bulls and bisons predominating, but there are also paintings of horse, boar and deer. In one of the caves there is a human head engraved into the rock. In some instance these early artists took advantage of the formation of the rock tracing the contours around its natural salients and lending thereby to the paintings the effect of colored bas-relief. Altamira yielded also finds of various utensils.

Bibliography: *Enciclopedia universal ilustrada europeo-americana.* Barcelona, 1905-30, Vol. IV, art. *Altamira.*—H. Alcalde del Rio, *Las pinturas y grabados prehistoricas de la provincia de Santander*. 1906.—H. Obermayer. *Fossil man in Spain*; New Haven (publ. for Hisp. Soc. of Am. by Yale Un. Press), 1925.—H. Breuil and H. Obermayer, (foreword by the Duke of Berwick and Alba, Engl. text by M. E. Boyle), *The Cave of Altamira at Santillana del Mar*. Madrid (The Hisp. Soc. of Am. and the Academia de la Historia), 1935.

**ALTARPIECE.**—This is the name given to the picture placed behind the altar in churches. Hardly any altarpieces appear before the Romanesque period. They are of stone, silver, ivory, and silver gilt. On them were painted, in compartments or panels, scenes from the life of Christ and the Virgin. One of the most famous is the *Pala d'oro,* of St. Mark's, Venice, a Byzantine work of the end of the 11th century or beginning of the 12th century. It is goldsmith's work, embellished with enamels. The enamelled altarpiece of Klosterneubourg, made in 1181, by the sculptor Nicholas de Verdun, is a remarkable work. The artist there represented the life of Christ in fifty-one compartments. Many old churches, and museums, contain altarpieces carved in stone or wood. Altarpieces were often used as portable altars, and for this purpose painted ones were preferred, being light and easy of transport. The Middle Ages have bequeathed us a considerable number of painted altarpieces, triptychs and polyptychs. Among the most famous may be mentioned: the *Adoration of the Lamb*, by the brothers Van Eyck (see Eyck in Ghent); *La Maestà*, of Duccio (see this name), in Siena; the *Altarpiece of the Last Judgment*, by Rogier Van der Weyden (see this name), in Beaune; the *Altarpiece of the Virgin*, by Mantegna (see this name), in San Zeno, Verona.

**ALTDORFER (Albrecht).**—German painter (1480-1538) of the Danube School; also architect of the town of Ratisbon. His chief works are: the *Holy Family at the Fountain* (1510, Berlin Museum); St. Florian altarpiece (1518); the *Birth of the Virgin* (about 1520, Munich Pinacothek); *Suzanna Bathing* (1526, Pinacothek, Munich); and the *Battle of Arbeles* (1529). Altdorfer left beside a number of engravings and wood cuts many of which are in colour: the best known is the *Beautiful Virgin of Ratisbon*. He is one of the first painters who studied landscape for its own sake, not merely as a background for the figures, and he painted it with the minuteness of a miniaturist.

BIBLIOGRAPHY: Friedländer, *Altdorfer, der Maler von Regensburg*. Leipzig, 1891.—Sturge Moore, *Altdorfer*. London, 1900.—Hildebrandt, *Die Architektur bei A. Altdorfer*. Strassburg, 1908.—Tietze, H., *A. Altdorfer*. Leipzig, 1923.

**ALTICHIERO da ZEVIO.**—Painter from Zevio near Verona. Founder of the Veronese School, and of the first importance in the development of North Italian painting. Born c. 1330, died c. 1395. Developed under the influence of Giotto but at once manifested a dominant and original personality. His so-called partnership with Avanzo is rather the relationship of master and pupil.

Frescoes: Padua, Sant' Antonio, Capella di S. Felice (after 1370); Padua, Oratorio di S. Giorgio, begun 1377; Padua, Eremitani, Capella Dotti; Verona, Capella Cavalli, after 1390.

Although Altichiero was strongly influenced by Giotto, his emphasis upon interior space, and his intermingling of figures and architecture are most un-Florentine. His narrative loquacity, fondness for genre, and love of color and detail indicate an esthetic conception essentially opposed to that of the great Florentine with his austere moral force, and make him a forerunner of Jacopo Bellini and Carpaccio.

His richly animated narrative style soon found imitators: to the south there are traces in Parma and Bologna and deep into Umbria; to the north beyond Treviso.

BIBLIOGRAPHY: E. Förster, *Die St. Georgskapelle zu Padua*. Berlin, 1841 (Italian ed. Selvatico. Padova, 1846).—Gonzati, *La Basilica di S. Antonio di Padova*. Padova, 1852. I, p. 178 ff, 273 ff.—Schubring, P., *Altichiero und seine Schule*. Leipzig, 1898.

**AMADEO (Giovanni Antonio) (called also Omodeo).**—Lombard architect and sculptor, born in Pavia 1447. Pupil of Michelozzo.

One of his earliest works is the signed doorway connecting the small cloister of the Certosa at Pavia with the transept of the cloister church, in which may be seen a combination of the old Lombard tradition with Renaissance Tuscan forms derived from his master. This Tuscan influence is deepened in the Cappella Colleoni built in Bergamo, 1470-75, the earliest example in Lombardy of a building in the Tuscan Renaissance style. The tombs of Medea Colleoni and her father Bartolommeo, famous condottiere, in this chapel, date from the same period.

AMADEO (GIOVANNI ANTONIO): CERTOSA DI PAVIA.

In his later works Amadeo is strongly affected by Mantegazza, by Northern forms and the school of Padua. The reliefs for the pulpit of the Cathedral of Cremona date from 1482; the tomb of the holy martyr Orialdus, at Cremona, from 1484 (fragments exist still in the Cathedral); and the sculptural work on the Ospedale Maggiore, Milan, from 1490. Here his part is difficult to distinguish because of later working over. In 1491, Amadeo undertook the decoration of the façade of the church at the Certosa of Pavia, in collaboration with Mantegazza. An obvious difference in style between the lower and upper halves of the façade shows that other architects did the less harmonious upper half. In 1492-94 he built the Palazzo Bottigelle. His work on the Tiburio of the Duomo, Milan, was finished in 1497; and the sarcophagus of St. Lanfrancus in the church of this saint near Pavia dates from 1498.

BIBLIOGRAPHY: G. Frizzoni, *G. A. Amadeo*. Rome, 1873.—G. A. Meyer, *Oberitalien. Frührenaiss.*, 1900, II.—R. Majocchi, *G. A. Amadeo*. Pavia, 1903.—F. Malaguzzi-Valeri, *G. A. Amadeo*. Milan, 1905.—Mongeri, *L'Arte in Milano*, pp. 102, 126f, 128, 131f, 139f, 151f, 226, 396.

**AMALTEO (Pomponio).** — Venetian painter (1505-1584), pupil and son-in-law of Pordenone, whose manner he copied in the frescoes which he painted in the Friuli, at Treviso, and the Choir of the Church of the hospital of San Vito (1535).

**AMBER.**—A yellowish translucent resin, found in the Baltic Sea area, which has been used for carvings since prehistoric times. Darkens with age to a reddish brown.

**AMBERGER (Christoph).**—German painter (c. 1500-1561) of the school of Augsbourg. A good portrait painter, his best works are portraits of Charles V (1532), and of Sebastian Münster (both in Berlin Museum), the Dombild of the Cathedral of Augsbourg, and *Christ with the Wise and Foolish Virgins*; St. Anne, Augsbourg, 1560.

**AMBOISE.**—The Château of Amboise, one of the most beautiful in France, is built on a height which commands the meeting of the Loire with the river Amassi, and upon which had been built successively Gallic, Romanesque and feudal edifices, of which nothing remains. In 1431, Charles VII confiscated the Château of the Comte d'Amboise, and Charles VIII undertook the complete reconstruction of the buildings in 1491. He set Italian artists to work. After him, Louis XII and Francis I continued the work. The Château was preserved in perfect condition until the time when Roger Ducos, to whom Napoleon I gave it, perpetrated most unfortunate mutilations. Since this time only two blocks of square buildings which lean on an enormous round battlemented tower, called the Tour des Minimes, remain. The oldest of these blocks, known as the "Logis du Roi," is that which faces the Loire; it is in the Gothic style, with an open gallery, pinnacled buttresses, and windows with pointed arches in the roof. It dates from the time of Charles VIII; as does a little gallery situated behind the Tour des Minimes. The other block of buildings, at right angles to the "Logis du Roi," had been built under Louis XII, with pilasters, columns and Italian decoration; it is higher. The big Chapel belonging to the Château and the old "Logis" of the Queen have disappeared. But the lovely Chapel of St. Hubert remains, with its lace-like decoration and its beautiful bas-reliefs, representing the Vision of St. Hubert, and the Legend of St. Christopher. By the side of the valley stands the curious Hurtault tower.

AMBOISE: THE CHÂTEAU.

**AMBROGIO di BALDESE.**—Florentine painter. Born 1352; died 1429. In 1386, he painted frescoes in the Bigallo, Florence, in collaboration with Niccolò di Pietro Gerini; in 1387 a tabernacle for Alberto Arnoldi's Statue of the Madonna for the Bigallo; from 1411 to 1412 frescoes at S. Francesco, Prato, in collaboration with Niccolò di Pietro Gerini and others; in 1415 frescoes on the ceiling and one wall of the Capella dell' Oratorio. Milanesi gives additional documentary notices for the years 1389, 1409, and 1412.

BIBLIOGRAPHY: Vasari-Milanesi, Vol. I.—Rivista d'Arte, 1904, pp. 229-232.—Rassegna d'Arte, IV, p. 177ff.

**— da Predis.**—Lombard painter (1450-1520). Pupil of Leonardo da Vinci. He painted under his master's supervision the *Virgin of the Rocks* in the National Gallery, London, a copy of Leonardo's composition in the Louvre.

**— of Fossano.**—See Bergognone.

**AMBROSIAN LIBRARY.**—See Milan.

**AMBULATORY.**—Passageway around an apse.

**AMERICA (Archæology).**—*Aboriginal Civilizations.*—The Redman reached America by way of Siberia and Alaska probably as recently as four or five thousand years ago—although some enthusiasts for antiquity would double or even quadruple this estimate. He brought with him the polished stone axe, typical tool of the northern or forest neolithic of Europe and Asia, and carried it to lands' end in both Americas. Also he brought other tools of non-agricultural nomads, such as the bow and arrow, harpoon, fire-drill, needle and thread, etc. He had clothing, basketry, and simple boats and was accompanied in his wanderings by the dog. But it seems he brought neither pottery nor domesticated plants to America although both may have existed in southerly regions of Asia and Europe at the time of his departure. Racially the Indian is predominantly Mongolian but various physical strains are discernible. His language, from the first, was probably extremely diversified. While it has often been pointed out that migration into the New World via the Siberia-Alaska route may have kept up for centuries, one group after another entering America, it does not appear that any immigrating group was on a cultural plane higher than the neolithic. Nor does it seem likely that America received any ingredients of population or culture by ocean voyages across either the Pacific or the Atlantic.

*Problem of Parallelisms in Culture.*—However, there are most important parallelisms in art, ceremony and social structure between civilizations of the eastern and western hemispheres and it should be understood that one school of anthropologists accepts such parallelisms, *ipso facto*, as a kind of proof of diffusion while another and numerically larger school demands data on transmission. Even the more romantice group has its scientific rationale which dismisses as unworthy of credence all plots formed on the sunken continents of Atlantis and of Mu, on voyages of St. Brendon, and on the identification of Quetzalcoatl with St. Thomas.

The important consideration in matters of diffusion and independent invention concerns the roots of ideas widely implanted in the mind of man during the early stages of culture and also the controls over apparent spontaneity which lie in uniform sensory mechanisms and thought processes—or, let us say, the reasons why man behaves like a human being. It seems that deep in the mind of the first American immigrant the idea was already established that graphic and plastic art might be an instrument of magic, and that magic, in turn, might be an instrument of social service. According to primitive animistic philosophy every physical entity in the world possesses a spiritual counterpart and the common corollary is that control can be secured over any living creature or any state of nature by means of representative design. Whether or not the philosophy of animism and the procedure of sympathetic magic can be traced to the first query on "what becomes of

COARSE POTTERY OBJECTS FROM FLORIDA. (Moore Collection.) (After Beuchat, *Manuel d'archéologie américaine,* A. Picard, edit.)

personality when a man dies," the fact is incontrovertible that animism was broadly accepted in ancient America and that art was broadly used for the defensive and aggressive purposes of magic.

However, it appears that agriculture was independently invented and developed in a central region of

FUNERAL MOUND WITH SEVERAL TOMBS. (Caldwell County, North Carolina.) (After Beuchat, *Manuel d'archéologie américaine,* A. Picard, edit.)

America and that the advantages of an assured food supply led to a recapitulation in the New World of the civilizing processes and results observed in the Old World. No domesticated food plants were common to the eastern and western hemispheres until distributions were made by Europeans in the recent epoch of world exploration. Actually the independent evolutions of high civilizations out of stabilized economy do not take precisely the same pattern in America that they take in the eastern continents. Pottery making without the wheel was independently invented in America and loom weaving without the treadle. Metallurgy shows the independent invention in America of the lost wax process in casting. The architecture of the Mayas shows independent invention of lime as a building material made by burning limestone, and independent uses of it in stucco work and fresco painting. The list of striking parallels might be carried much farther, but nowhere in America was there any application of the wheel to traction, (indeed, the only American wheel is the disk of the spindle whorl) and while the completely distributed neolithic stage was succeeded in several places by an eneolithic stage, as in southern Alaska, northern Canada, the Mound Area and perhaps also the West Indies, and while advanced metallurgy was distributed from Peru to Mexico with true bronze and numerous alloys, the dates for these ascending stages do not agree, even roughly, with those given for similar stages in the Old World. The most brilliant period of the Mayas was passed in complete ignorance of metals yet these Mayas possessed a remarkable science of astronomy and a system of writing numbers well in advance of anything then known in the Old World. The concept of zero is perhaps a thousand years older in American mathematics than it is in Asia or Europe. Granting a common start at the neolithic plane of culture we conclude that at least one family of civilizations arose in the Old World and at least one other completely independent family of civilizations arose in the New World.

*The Earliest American Archeology.*—With man entering and spreading over America as a non-agricultural nomad his earliest remains must be expected in situations of temporary residence. Archeologists now regard the Folsom and Yuma flints, found along the eastern flanks of the Rocky Mountains and the western edges of the Great Plateau, as the earliest cultural remains in America which can be isolated as types. Belief in their considerable antiquity comes from the fact that in several instances contact has been established between these lance heads and the bones of extinct animals, which are known, however, to have survived the last glaciation. The Folsom and Yuma blades are superb examples of chipping, greatly superior to any pre-neolithic work of the Old World, and there is no good reason for considering them pre-neolithic in America. No sites yielding mesolithic tools have been found in the New World while crude tools which resemble paleoliths are dismissed as such because they do not occur in the required geological strata. On the other hand the technique of the Folsom and Yuma flints is consistently developed into a wider range of shapes by recent Indians. While ground stone axes have not been found as yet in association with the early flints, other specimens made by the grinding technique have been found.

It was once thought that the most remote manifestations of man's industry in the New World would be excavated from the shell heaps which dot the eastern and western shores of North and South America from the Aleutian Islands to Tierra del Fuego. However, these are obviously of varying ages and do not correspond archeologically to the Danish kitchen-middens. Some are old as can be seen from great trees growing upon them, from shells now locally extinct, and from lower layers consolidated into solid masses, while others are recent, containing post-Columbian objects. Like all refuse heaps the shell mounds are important for stratigraphic study.

Typological antiquity in tools and manner of life is found among many tribes of the New World who live beyond the limits of agriculture or who for some reason or other have failed to accept it. Actually about half of the territory of the New World is held by such retarded peoples, or was so held until recent years. Most of the Indians of Canada fall in the non-agricultural group, as do those along the Pacific coast of the United States beyond a line from the upper Missouri River to the head of the Gulf of California. Other lowly Indians live back from the coast in eastern Brazil, and in Argentina and Chile below 35° south latitude. But no considerable group of American Indians is without art and not infrequently tribes commonly regarded as backward in the general political sense manufacture objects of great beauty and technical perfection.

The forest nomads belonging to the Athabascan and Algonkin language groups who inhabit the interior of Alaska and Canada lead a precarious life. They are divided into small hunting bands, a condition which deters ceremonialism. Yet they embroider their clothing with porcupine quills and dyed moose hair in pleasing patterns and paint their bodies with designs intended to flatter animals and increase the game supply. Since securing glass beads in trade they have shown skill in color-mosaic patterns. Their sinew work in snow shoes and carrying nets is technically excellent. The somewhat more favorably situated tribes who

OCTOPUS VASE FROM CHIMBOTE. (After Beuchat, *Manuel d'archéologie américaine,* A. Picard, edit.)

inhabit the Rocky Mountain plateau exemplify capable but retarded peoples, living until recently on a purely neolithic plane of culture.

*The Semi-Nomadic Eskimo.*—Before the plane of sedentary villages and towns dependent upon agriculture is reached we find a stage which may be called semi-nomadic. Fairly permanent houses are constructed for winter habitation or even for the year round if the food quest permits. The Eskimo have long led such a life, transportation by boat and sledge making it possible for them to do their hunting at some distance. At the same time they may wander seasonally and change the location of their villages after a term of years. Cultural sequence has now been demonstrated for the Eskimo who seem to have adjusted their life to hunting sea mammals after reaching America. Their Old Bering Sea culture, datable a thousand or fifteen hundred years ago, shows decorative art of fine quality on hunting gear of walrus ivory. It seems that the pictographic style is recent and therefore fails to give a link with paleolithic art of the Old World as some have argued. The eastern Eskimo make minor carvings and their tools and boats have excellent lines.

*Wood Carvers of the Northwest Coast.*—Along the Northwest Pacific Coast a rather high social evolution is explained by an assured food supply with the salmon as the principal item. The art of several tribes belonging to different language stocks is fairly homogeneous in symbolic content and in general style. Various animals appear as helpers of man and as clan patrons, according to mythological relations. Very often the pattern of sympathetic magic is followed in the choice of animals and birds designed to aid in common pursuits and vicissitudes. The sea raven is painted on boats to protect against mishaps and the killer whale is appealed to when great sea mammals are hunted, as also the thunder bird who is supposed to kill whales by hurling a

STONE JAGUAR FOUND IN MEXICO. (After Beuchat, *Manuel d'archéologie américaine,* A. Picard, edit.)

lightning lance. In the strange forms of design which the Northwest Coast Indians have devised a single typical feature may carry the essential realism in a body overlaid with supernumerary faces and eyes.

*The Basket Makers.*—While excellent baskets are found among the Aleuts of the Aleutian Islands as well as in southern Alaska, a more intensive development begins in British Columbia and extends south across Washington, Oregon and California, also reaching inland to the continental divide but with lessening importance back from the coast and the large streams. This craft is a reflection of the importance of wild crops, such as edible roots, acorns, berries and dry seeds of many sorts, in the economic life of non-agriculturalists who also obtain some of their food by hunting and fishing. In the northern part of this area imbricated basketry is found, this term applying to a peculiar method of overlaying wide flat coils by a method of looping ribbon-like colored filaments. Along the Columbia River flexible bags are made by twining string from Indian hemp and a different overlay called false embroidery is employed. In California both twined and coiled basketry occurs, the Indians of this region being famous for their remarkably even and skillful workmanship. In the Pueblo area, which centers in New Mexico and Arizona, there is an ancient basket culture underlying one of later pottery making which followed the introduction of agriculture.

*The Archaic Civilization.*—The advanced cultures of the New World were made possible by the domestication of an important series of indigenous American plants and it appears that the first taming of some of these took place on the plateau of Central America and southern Mexico. There resulted the Archaic civilization marked by village life and the development of the ceramic and textile arts—American style. It seems that the agricultural level is superimposed over one in which man was semi-nomadic, gathering food in natural gardens. This is difficult to isolate because polished stone tools and implements of chipped flint continued in use side by side with pottery, and without much change in forms. A change came over religious art owing to new emphasis on plant cultivation as against hunting and fishing. Perhaps agriculture was first of all woman's business; at any rate there is clearly indicated an association of the fertility of Mother Earth with the female fetishes. The most striking products of the Archaic civilization are figurines of women frequently nude and gravid. While some of these have children in their arms it seems more likely that they do not represent maternity magic pure and simple but rather fecundity in an extended sense. It is not impossible that the use of the female fetish was part of the culture complex introduced from the Old World; at least there is a remarkable parallelism in female hunting and fertility fetishes in the eastern and western hemispheres both before and after agriculture. Male figures are less frequent but they also can be connected with the same magical concept.

The plastic art of the Archaic civilization was developed along highly characteristic lines and the spread of agriculture can be postulated on the spread of this art, first over arid regions and secondly penetrating into humid regions. Typical products of the Archaic civilization are traced from the Central American and Mexican highlands far into South America and also northward into the southwestern part of the United States, objects found in Ecuador, for instance, being closely comparable with those from Mexico. Animal motives are almost completely neglected at least until an upper plane has been reached. The ordinary decoration on pottery often follows textile forms and is generally geometric without much probability that the patterns had significance.

TWIN VASES FROM THE REGION OF PACHACAMAC. (After R. d'Harcourt, *La Céramique ancienne du Pérou.* A. Morancé, edit.)

In some regions the Archaic civilization was replaced at a rather early date by much more involved arts, which reflect the rise of priestcraft and political administration. In other regions the early art of farmers developed along the lines laid down at its inception, with a gradual enrichment in motives. A good example of this is seen in the art history of the Pueblo Indians now pretty accurately dated by dendrochronology. Here the early thesaurus of designs on baskets was carried over into pottery, it being unlikely that the majority of the patterns were symbolically significant. Female fetishes are found only at the very beginning of pottery making, and there are vessels which represent ducks, possibly a sympathetic water magic. Gradually, however, designs change until it is the obvious intention to picture clouds, lightning, falling rain, etc. The rich symbolism which now distinguishes Pueblo ceramics seems to have made its appearance after 1500 A.D. when communication was established with Mexico. It is possible, however, that it had its birth in a ceremonial life, indifferently reflected in decorative designs during early stages of development. Space does not permit a discussion of the stylistic sequences observed in Pueblo art history or a fuller treatment of the marginal manifestations of the Archaic civilization.

*The Maya Civilization.*—The Maya civilization which resulted from the carrying of agriculture down into the wet lowlands of eastern Central America is far and away the leading demonstration in ancient America of art and science. It probably had humble origins about 800 B.C. when the attention of agriculturalists was first directed toward astronomy. Figurines of the archaic style were used until about the beginning of the Christian Era after which we note the emergence in art of a series of beast gods who gradually became composite and are then humanized. One godhead formed on the serpent had to do with rain and all phenomena of the darkened sky; another formed on the jaguar had to do with the sun and the revealed sky of the stars and planets. Other bird and animal divinities are pictured as well as the composite monsters who symbolize a joining of natural powers.

The dated monuments of the First Empire of the Mayas cover 727 years beginning at 98 B.C. and running to 629 A.D. During this time there is a rich development of ceramic art in plastic and polychrome, splendid lapidary products in jade, stone monuments which take the form of stelae and deal with priests and rulers holding religious objects and richly costumed, and temples which illustrate a fine art in architecture. Many of these monuments carry inscriptions and from an analysis of the dates and numbers it appears that Maya art had much to do with astronomy and with cosmic theories.

Also, thanks to the dates, we are able to measure very accurately the rate of artistic change, first the development out of an archaic style, second the duration of the fine style and the rapidity with which flamboyancy makes itself felt. The earliest sculptured figures of men show the profile presentation in low relief, next the front view presentation develops from a low relief stage into the full round, thirdly emphasis is again placed on the profile treatments but with a growing improvement in foreshortening. True portraiture does not appear till the sixth century. The greatest of the First Empire cities in which these tendencies are to be noted are Tikal, Uaxactun, Copan, Quirigua, Yaxchilan, Piedras Negras and Palenque. These may be the capitals of separate city states. The rulers are spokesmen of the gods who suffer apotheosis and sit on celestial thrones.

A collapse of the Maya First Empire was followed by an Intermediate Period in which architecture was kept alive in a small central area, even developing definite style which differs from that of the First Empire or of the Second Empire which began about 960 A.D. It seems, however, that during the Intermediate Period the minor arts of the Mayas were maintained over a much wider territory and that the pottery continued to follow the tradition of earlier times but with gradual change and deterioration.

The Second Empire witnessed the building of cities in northern Yucatan including Chichen Itza, Uxmal, Labna, Kabah, etc., sometimes on sites which may have been used in First Empire times. Now the architectural forms, while magnificent, have their own new quality. They show a use of grotesque faces in decoration as well as frets and applied decorative columns. Columns in wide doorways and for the support of vaulting were introduced about 1200 A.D. by the Toltec conquerors. The last of the great Maya cities were abandoned about 1450 and some rebuilding on the East Coast of Yucatan began about 1500 A.D.

*Lesser Civilizations Influenced by the Mayas.*—As a result of the Maya demonstration a series of lesser civilizations arose on the periphery of the Maya territory, each producing fine art with a new national ingredient, but also largely containing Maya conventions. To the north are found the Olmec, Totonac and Huaxtec cultures along the gulf coast of the state of Vera Cruz. The Zapotecs and Mixtecs occupied the Isthmus of Tehuantepec and the State of Oaxaca. The Toltecs seem to have had their first headquarters at Teotihuacan in the Valley of Mexico, later conquering a wide empire which collapsed about 1220 A.D. Afterwards the Aztecs began their career in the alley of Mexico but the extent of their cultural dominance only extends from about 1400 to 1520. In all of these minor centers we find pyramids, and rather splendid stone sculptures together with richly diversified art in pottery, in jewelry and in illuminated manuscripts. Among the most striking ruins mention should be made of Monte Alban and Mitla, the Zapotec capitals, Tajin, great city of the Totonacs, and Teotihuacan and Xochicalco which exemplify the Toltec rule.

Under the Toltecs trade and conquest were carried far afield. Evidences of cultural influences are found at some of the Pueblo towns in New Mexico and it appears that the Mound culture of the eastern United States was pretty profoundly modified by introduced ideas following, however, an early autochthonous development largely concerned with the cult of the dead. Pyramids for use as temple platforms occur over about a third of the Mound area and the art of the southern districts shows the intrusive Toltec cults of Eagle Men in connections with war and the apotheosis of warriors.

South of the Maya area comes the Chorotegan area with diversified pottery and some stone sculptures which follow Maya conventions rather closely. The effort to show that these sculptures precede the earliest Maya work rests on errors in comparison; instead they date from a rather late period (about 1100-1200 A.D.) although lesser works of greater age doubtless exist. It appears that gold was introduced into Mexico from South America via the Chorotegas in the two or three centuries which preceded the coming of the Spaniards.

*The Andean Civilizations.*—Passing from Panama southward along the Andes a chain of civilizations is encountered. It seems that all of these rise as it were from the cultural platform of the earlier Archaic civilization. But in addition to the earlier food plants a number of new domestications must be noted, especially important being the potato of Andean origin. Agriculture gave the peoples receiving it the opportunity to develop their several abilities influenced by special elements in their environment. Peru, for example, possessed three wool-bearing animals, a circumstance which led to the great enhancement of textile art among them. It has long been a question to what extent the Andean civilizations are connected with those of Central America. Giving every play to the spontaneous florescence of native abilities there are some things not easily invented. For instance, in Peru we find the Sun conventionalized as a humanized jaguar very like the jaguar sky god of the sun and planets found among the Mayas. This similarity is reenforced by pictures of the sun-disk in both areas which has four serpent rays. Certainly no such ideas were pictured on the Archaic horizon and when other jaguar sun subject matter is found at San Augustin of Colombia and at Esmeraldas in Ecuador we may decide that cultural infiltration actually is proved. The closest Maya similarities appear at Huarez, Recuay, and Chavin in Peru, at Tiahuanaco in Bolivia and at Catamarca in Argentina. On a later level the Eagle Men of the Toltec war cults reach northern Peru.

In Colombia special centers of art are found in the Quimbaya territory along the Cauca River, in Chibcha territory in the highlands near Bogota, etc. In Venezuela interesting art is found in the vicinity of Merida and Maracay. Reference has already been made to San Augustin on the headwaters of the Magdalena in southern Colombia where many fine statues have been unearthed. Other stone sculptures of considerable merit occur in western Ecuador together with rich products in pottery and golden jewelry. The word Peru is employed archeologically to cover a great area extending south from Ecuador. We should understand that before the unifying conquests of the Incas this territory was broken up into several regions, each boasting its own peculiarities in design. In the north along the coast was the Chimu culture, the Tiahuanaco center was on the highlands near Lake Titicaca and the Paracas-Nasca-Ica center was on the southern coast near the Chincha Islands. It is the textiles of Peru which deserve first attention. Peru sets world standards for diversity and fineness of weaving. The subject matter of textile decoration is largely religion with composite monsters in first place but there are examples of geometric designs executed in fast and brilliant colors. Also the metal work, shell mosaic, lacquer work and other crafts are superbly illustrated by finds in Peruvian graves. As regards dates authorities disagree widely.

*Southern South America.*—As we

pass southward out of the tropics over the plains of Argentina and finally to the forested southern tip of the New World the life of the Indians becomes much more like that of northern North America. The Tehuelche have been compared to the tribes of our Great Plains. They make skillful use of the horse, which they acquired from the Spaniards, and hunt the guanaco and the rhea with whirling bolas. We know from the archeology of northern Argentina that a considerable influence from the great Andean civilization was felt rather far south but actually we have little data on the pampas region. In Tierra del Fuego the primitive Yahgan use decorative designs in body painting, albeit very simple ones. Their culture is low but apparently superior to that of the Botocudos of Brazil, and has been described as safely on the neolithic plane.

*Eastern South America.*—East of the Andes the numerous tribes inhabiting the forest and grass land territories drained by the Orinoco, the Amazon and La Plata rivers, sometimes produced pottery, basketry, feather ornaments and carved wooden objects of considerable artistic merit. Among these tribes the widely distributed Arawak group gets credit for the best work; next come the Tupi-Guarani, who inhabit the Atlantic coast and the banks of large rivers. Nearer the Andes the Pano, Betoya and Jivaro languages are spoken by numerous politically independent tribes with similar forest culture. The Carib tribes have a bad name as raiders and cannibals. Perhaps their first homes were on poor strips of land between southern tributaries of the Amazon but if so, they greatly enlarged their holdings by warfare. It seems pretty certain that they dispossessed agricultural groups of Arawaks from Venezuela compelling them to flee to the West Indies.

But in the eastern parts of South America are found several Indian groups much more primitive than the Caribs. There are the lowly Ges of the Matto Grosso region in southern Brazil and the even more primitive Botocudo who inhabited semi-desert regions in eastern Brazil. These Indians go about entirely naked, build only wind breaks for shelter and their tools and ornaments are of the simplest order. They wear large wooden disks in lips and ears—whence they get their name Botocudo which is Portuguese for a barrel bung.

Rafael Karsten's *Civilization of the South American Indians* is a book largely devoted to the thesis that the ceremonies, personal ornaments, and the designs applied to pots and baskets by the Indians of Amazonia constitute a body of prophylactic magic, the major purpose being to ward off diseases and misfortunes which emanate from spirits of the dead. Other writers, such as Koch-Grunberg and Von den Steinen, explain this Indian art as purely esthetic. It is clear, however, many designs reached in a formal manner in one technique are carried over into other techniques. For instance designs reached by the interplay of structural elements in twilled basketry—a very fundamental Amazonian art—are carried over into painted pottery. Of course such designs might also possess from the first, or acquire in the course of time, symbolical significance.

The most impressive products of Amazonian art are the enormous burial urns found on the Island of Marajo in the mouth of the great river. These generally have two large faces looking in opposite directions, partly modelled and partly painted, with curiously conventionalized hands below the faces in a welter of geometric scrollwork. Urn burial extends from the Caribbean Sea across eastern South America to Argentina; some urns are plain but many are decorated with painted and plastic figures which doubtless had religious import. A newly found area in which the plastic side of pottery ornamentation is astonishingly developed has its center at Santarem on the Amazon. Like the work at Marajo it is pre-Columbian.

Petroglyphs deeply engraved on granite boulders at waterfalls and rapids are an important type of artistic expression in northern South America. Sometimes the strange conical disguises still used in Indian ceremonies are pictured. Also the modern Indians have a gruesome skill in preparing the heads of their enemies as trophies.

*The West Indies.*—The West Indies were peopled at a rather late date in the pre-Columbian period by Arawak tribes who previously had resided in the Amazon and Orinoco valleys. They had reached the Greater Antilles and the Bahamas by way of the Lesser Antilles, bringing in agriculture, pottery making and other arts. The religion of the West Indian peoples is called zemi-ism, the zemi being a grotesque idol partly human, partly animal, which the Spaniards promptly identified with the Devil. Actually the principal animal motive entering into the strangely conventionalized art of the Taino, who inhabited Porto Rico, Santo Domingo and Cuba, is the bat. Among their strange cult objects are beautifully carved stone rings like horse collars. Also there are triangular stones intended to be placed with one point upward as can be seen by the pose of the animal figure whose head and feet decorate the other two points, and richly decorated stools made of wood or stone.

It is doubtful whether any important contacts had been established in pre-Columbian times between the West Indies and Florida. It seems, however, that the rich Taino culture had risen in the midst of humbler arts, distributed over central and eastern Cuba where the Siboney lived, among the Lucayos of the coral islands where Columbus had his landfall, in Jamaica and the long chain of the Lesser Antilles whose inhabitants are generally known as the Inyeri. Everywhere, however, there seems to have been pottery, beautifully shaped axes, often of jade, and a considerable use of shell for tools and ornaments.

Bibliography.—The bibliography of American Indian art is so extensive that only a few general works can be listed here. Many technical treatments are published by learned societies, including museums and universities. In the United States the publications of the Bureau of American Ethnology, the National Museum, the Smithsonian Institution, the Carnegie Institution of Washington, the Peabody Museum of Harvard University, the Field Museum, the American Museum of Natural History, and the University of California are outstanding. In Canada there are archeological and ethnological papers under the School of Mines. In Mexico they are mostly under the Secretary of Public Education and the National Museum. In Ecuador there is the National Academy, and in Argentina, the University of La Plata. The national museums of Brazil, Argentina and Peru have published important material. Also there are scientific serials such as the American Anthropologist, Zeitschrift für Ethnologie, Internationales Archiv für Ethnographie, the Journal of the Anthropological Institute of Great Britain and Ireland, etc. J. W. Fewkes, *A Prehistoric Island Culture Area of America.* 34th Annual Report of Bureau of American Ethnology. Washington, 1912-1913.—P. E. Goddard, *Indians of the Northwest Coast.* Handbook of American Museum of Natural History. New York, 1924.—M. A. Harrington, *Cuba before Columbus.* Contributions of Museum of the American Indian. New York, 1921.—D. Jenness, *The American Aborigines.* Toronto, 1933; *The Indians of Canada.* Ottawa, 1932.—T. A. Joyce, *South American Archaeology.* London, 1912.—A. V. Kidder, *Southwestern Archaeology.* New Haven, 1924.—S. K. Lothrop, *Pottery of Costa Rica and Nicaragua.* New York, 1926.—A. P. Maudslay, *Biologia Centrali Americani.* Archaeology. 4 vols. London, 1889-1902.—P. A. Means, *The Ancient Civilizations of the Andes.* New York, 1931.—E. Nordenskiold, *Comparative Ethnographical Studies.* Goteborg, 1918-1930; *L'Archéologie du Bassin de l'Amazone.* Ars Americana. Paris, 1930.—M. Schmidt, *Kunst und Kultur von Peru.* Berlin, 1929.—H. C. Shetrone, *The Mound Builders.* New York, 1930.—H. J. Spinden, *Ancient Civilizations of Mexico and Central America.* Handbook of American Museum of Natural History. New York, 1928.—C. C. Willoughby, *Antiquities of the New England Indians.* Peabody Museum, Harvard University. Cambridge, Mass., 1935.—C. W. Wissler, *The American Indian.* New York, 1917.

**AMERICAN INDIAN ART.**—See America.

**AMERIGHI (called Il Caravaggio).**—See Caravaggio.

**AMIENS.**—The Cathedral of Notre Dame is one of the biggest and one of the most remarkable Gothic buildings in France. It was begun in 1220, according to the plans of Robert de Luzarches; in 1238, the nave and façade were finished. The rest was completed in 1270, with the exception of the chapels (1292-1376), the upper parts of the façade, and the towers (15th and 16th centuries). The façade is pierced with three fine porches, covered with statues and bas-reliefs in the purest Gothic style. The middle porch shelters the famous statue known as the "Beau Dieu d'Amiens" (on the pier); to right and left, in the medallions, are figures of Virtues and Vices, the Arts and Crafts, and two fables—the *Fox and the Crow*, and the *Wolf and the Swan.* On brackets are statues of the Apostles; and in the arches, 150 statues representing the celestial hierarchy; on the jamb of the door are figures of the Five Wise Virgins and the Five Foolish Virgins; in the tympanum, the *Last Judgment* and at the top of the gable, *St. Michael.* On the pier of the right-hand porch, or the Porch of the Virgin, is a statue of Mary crushing a Monster, with a human head; below, Adam and Eve, and their Expulsion from the earthly Paradise. On the sides: the *Annunciation, Presentation at the Temple, Visitation, Queen of Sheba, Solomon,* etc.; on the tympanum: *the Death and Assumption of the Virgin.* On the pier of the left-hand portal is represented St. Firmin trampling Idolatry underfoot. On the sides: the bishop saints of Amiens and the surrounding district, the signs of the Zodiac, and the Labours of the Months. In the tympanum, the Invention and Glorification of the relics of St. Firmin. Above the porches, is a gallery of columns, surmounted by a gallery of the Kings of Judah, ancestors of the Virgin, 22 huge statues. A stage higher is a magnificent rose window. The two towers are connected by the gallery called the *"Ringers' Gallery"*; they are of unequal height and differently deco-

Amiens: The Cathedral.

Amiens: Cathedral, the month of February.

Amiens: Central Porch of the Cathedral.

rated in the upper part. The side of the northern one is ornamented with a double row of statues, between the windows (saints and kings). In the north doorway of the transept, a statue dedicated to St. Firmin, a glazed tympanum, surmounted by a magnificent rose-window. The south transept doorway has the famous statue of *"la Vierge*

AMIENS: CHARLES V.

*dorée"* (on the pier), formerly gilt. On the sides are statues of saints and priests; sixty statues of angels, apostles, prophets, etc., are on the voussoirs; in the tympanum relics of saints were discovered; above, an admirable statue of the dying Christ between the Virgin and Saint John. Above the porch is a gallery and rose-window. The timber *flèche* (spire) measures 112 metres 70; it is decorated with colossal statues of saints. The interior of the Cathedral

AMIENS: LINTEL OF THE SOUTH PORTAL OF THE CATHEDRAL.

(143 metres long; 65 metres 25 wide at the transept; 42 metres 30 high) is remarkable for the grandeur of its proportions, and for the daring height of the vault, which is supported by 126 pillars of wonderful lightness: it is one of the highest in the world. The Cathedral is divided into three aisles, with chapels, choir and ambulatory; the high arcades measure almost half the total height, and are surmounted by a string-course of foliage, and a triforium. At the entrance to the nave are copper tombs of the two bishop founders of the building. The choir contains 110 stalls which are admirably carved (1508-1519) with 400 subjects from the Old Testament and the Life of the Virgin. It is surrounded by a screen with rich, flamboyant arcading; and beautiful carvings representing the Legends of Saints Firmin and Saulve, and the History of John the Baptist (1531). The Chapels, the transepts and the side-aisles contain a great many sculptures, tombs and bas-reliefs.

See Pls. 47, 53, Vol. I.

**AMIGONI (Jacopo).**—Venetian painter (1675-1752). He worked chiefly in Germany, England and Spain.

**AMMANATI (Bartolommeo).**—Florentine architect and sculptor (1511-1592). A pupil of Jacopo Sansovino at Padua, and a follower of Michelangelo. He imitated the great master, but his style was more mannered and less energetic. He followed the tradition of the Renaissance and its beautiful, finely-proportioned buildings, also tending towards a luxurious style which savours of the Baroque. His Florentine palaces are many, at once homely and sumptuous, always with the classical courtyard with columns; and often decorated with "graffiti" (Palaces Vitali, Pucci and Guigni). His contribution to the Pitti Palace made him famous. We may admire the gargoyles and the lions' heads which he placed at the ground-floor windows (about 1568), and the large courtyard with pillars (1558-1570). Nevertheless, that of the Collegio Romano is more successful.

In Florence, he designed the cloisters of San Spirito, with alternate arches and entablature (1564), a part of the Jesuit Church of San Giovannino (1579), the graceful Bridge of Santa Trinità, and the large fountain in the Piazza della Signoria with a huge Neptune, called "il Biancone." In Rome, he built the Ruspoli Palace (1586), and the Fontana della Vigna of Pope Julius; at Lucca, several palaces; at Volterra, the beautiful courtyard of the Bardia di Monaci.

As a sculptor, he is responsible for the Mausoleum of the parents of Gregory XIII in the Campo Santo of Pisa, and for the tomb of Cardinal Antonio del Monte in San Pietro in Montorio, in Rome.

**AMMANN (Jobst).**—Engraver and woodcut designer, born in Zurich, in 1539; died at Nuremberg in 1591. He is not very interesting except on account of the documentary value of his prints, which show a strong Italian influence. He left a mediocre series of etchings of eighty Bavarian princes, a large *Allegory of Commerce* on wood; but the best of his work is a series of *Trades* and *Costumes.*

BIBLIOGRAPHY: C. Becker, *Jobst Ammann.* Leipzig, 1854. *"L'Allégorie des Arts,"* of Jobst Ammann,. facsimile. Munich, 1889.

**AMMON (Temple of).**—See Egypt (Architecture); Luxor.

**AMPHIPROSTYLE.**—A temple having columns across both front and rear, but not along the sides.

**AMPHORA.**—A terracotta vase, in use among the Greeks and Romans, usually rather high, tapering inward at the base and having two handles at the neck. Undecorated amphorae were used for storing wine, grain, etc. The decorated amphorae were given as prizes. The Panathenaic amphorae (on which Athena was depicted) were given as prizes to the victors in the Panathenaic Games. These amphorae have an unusually dilated body and taper sharply inward at the foot.

PANATHENAIC AMPHORA. (Louvre.)

See Pl. 27, Vol. I.

**AMPULLA.**—Globular flask, usually with two handles.

**ANACREON OF PAINTING.**—See Albani.

**ANATOLIA.**—See Byzantine Art.

**ANATOMY LESSON (The).**—See Rembrandt; also Pl. 38, Vol. II.

**ANCONA.**—An altarpiece with many sections; polyptych.

**ANCY-LE-FRANC (Yonne—France).**—This village possesses a château, built according to the plans of Primaticcio and of Serlio, finished in 1622. It is composed of four blocks of buildings, with pavilions at the angles, surrounding an inner courtyard.

**ANDALUSIAN ART.**—See Pl. 33, Vol. I.

**ANDREA BRIOSCO.** — See Riccio.

**ANDREA di BARTOLO.**—Sienese painter, son of Bartolo di Fredi, and close follower of his father. Active from 1389 to 1426. He is known to have worked in the Duomo in Siena; and in 1389 with his father and Luca di Tommè did the altarpiece for the Chapel of the Compagnia dei Calzolai; in 1398 two panels in the Cappella S. Giacomo; in 1405 (or 1406) paintings with the story of S. Vittorio in this chapel. Two signed pictures in S. Domenico are also mentioned.

A signed triptych by Andrea is in the Pieve Museum at Buonconvento, with an Annunciation, Magdalen and St. Anthony Abbot; and a signed altarpiece with the Assumption of the Virgin, discovered by Förster in the House of the Castragani in Fano. A large group of pictures is associated with his name.

BIBLIOGRAPHY: Milanesi, *Doc. Sen.* I, 41, II, 26, 36, 383.—Milanesi, *Arte Toscana,* p. 48.—Annales archéol. XXV, 277, 279, 282.—Brogi, *Invent. gen., etc., della prov. di Siena* (1897), p. 44.—Rassegna d'arte, 1906, pp. 35-36.

**— da BOLOGNA.**—No work or document referring to this painter exists in Bologna, unless he may be identified with a certain Andrea di Guido mentioned in 1382, a miniature painter, which identification does not seem possible. Active chiefly in the Marches in the latter half of the trecento, his art was probably derived from that of March masters. Two signed and dated works by him, an altarpiece in the Museum at Fermo, 1368; and a panel with the Madonna and Child in S. Agostino, Pausula, 1372, bear out this conclusion, and distinguish him from Bolognese painters in the ornament, the wealth of decorative details, the rich stuffs with flowers in the gold-engraving of the backgrounds, in the haloes, and in the general compositions.

In Assisi (San Francisco, lower church), in Atri, and in Offida, are frescoes attributed to him.

BIBLIOGRAPHY: Crowe and Cavalcaselle, *Storia di pitt. ital.*—Calzini, Rassegna bibl. d. arte ital. VIII, 8-10.—C. Ricci, Emporium, marzo, 1906.

**— del CASTAGNO.**—See Castagno.

**— di CIONE.**—See Orcagna.

**— da FIRENZE.**—Florentine painter, probably to be identified with Andrea di Bonaiuto, mentioned in Florentine documents from 1343-1377. Influenced by the School of Orcagna.

"Andreas de Florentia" received in 1377 from Luca Orselli, foreman at the Duomo in Pisa, a quittance payment for frescoes with the story of S. Raniero in the Camposanto, Pisa. Since Antonio Veneziano had painted in 1384-1387 the lowest row of this fresco-cycle, the only ones with which Andrea is concerned are the three upper, to be found on the south wall of the Camposanto, unfortunately in a very bad state.

With these frescoes are associated, on the basis of stylistic evidence, the famous decorations of the Cappella Spagnuoli, adjoining Sta. Maria Novella in Florence. The chapel was built in 1350, through the patronage of Buonamico di Lapo Guidalotti, and when Guidalotti made his testament in 1355 the paintings were as yet unfinished. Andrea's richly detailed narrative style, with its repudiation of plastic space, is brilliantly representative of the non-Giottesque tendency in Florentine painting and exerted considerable influence upon contemporary and succeeding painters.

BIBLIOGRAPHY: Vasari-Milanesi, I, 553.—Bonaini, *Memorie inedite, etc.,* Pisa, 1846, pp. 104-106, 141.—Crowe and Cavalcaselle.—J. B. Supino, *Il Camposanto di Pisa.* Florence, 1896. —A. Venturi, *Storia, etc.,* V, 724, 725, 777-816.

**— di GIUSTO.**—Tuscan painter of the beginning of the 15th century, who was without originality and imitated in turn Lorenzo Monaco, whose pupil he was, Bicci di Lorenzo, Fra Angelico and Masaccio, with whom he collaborated at Pisa in 1426.

**— di LUIGI D'ASSISI.**—See L'Ingegno.

**— PISANO.**—See Pisano.

**— da MURANO.**—Venetian painter, mentioned 1462-1502. Pupil of Bartolommeo Vivarini and strongly influenced by Giovanni Bellini. His chief work is the high altar of S. Maria in Trebaseleghe, near Padua, begun in 1484, and there is a triptych by him in the Venice Academy.

BIBLIOGRAPHY: M. Caffi, *Andrea da Murano,* in Arch. Veneto, XXIII, pte. II, 1887, pp. 331-336. —L. Venturi, *Le Origini della pittura Veneziana.* Venice, 1907.—Testi, *Storia d. pitt. veneziana,* II, 530-547.

**— di NICCOLO di GIACOMO.**—Sienese painter, born 1440-50 and mentioned until 1514. Pupil of Matteo di Giovanni Bartoli; worked with Giovanni di Paolo in 1470 for the Ospedale della Scala in Siena, and painted in the same year a tabernacle for the Compagnia di S. Bernardino; 1477, frescoes with the life of S. Bernardino on the façade of the Oratorio di Sta. Lucia. In 1488 he executed an altarpiece for the high altar of the Collegiate Church of Casole and in 1490 he worked in the Chapel of the Compagnia della Santissima Trinità in Siena. With Paolo di Urbano he painted a chapel of the Duomo at Massa.

The signed Madonna and Saints in the Accademia at Siena is from the year 1500, and the Crucifixion in the same gallery from 1502.

BIBLIOGRAPHY: Milanesi, *Doc. Sen.,* II, 425, III, 5, 40, 296.—Milanesi, *La scrittura di artisti italiani,* tav. 84.—F. Brogi, *Invent. gen., etc., della prov. di Siena,* 1897, indices p. 645. —C. Ricci, *Il Palazzo Pubblico di Siena e la Mostra antica arte Senese.* Bergamo, 1904, pp. 66, 71, 72.—Berenson, Rassegna d'arte, IV, 153, V, 103.

**— del SARTO.**—See Sarto.

**ANDREANI (Andrea).**—Italian engraver of Mantua, towards the middle of the 16th century. Active 1584-1610. He engraved with much skill, on wood, the *Triumph of Religion,* by Titian, the *Triumph of Julius Caesar,* some scenes from the pavement of Siena Cathedral, and a quantity of engravings after contemporary painters.

**ANDRON.**—In antiquity, the men's quarters in a house or establishment.

**ANDROUET du CERCEAU.**—A family of French architects of whom Jacques Androuet, called du Cerceau (16th century), architect of the King, is the best known. He stayed in Italy, where he engraved many prints representing the monuments of Rome, the restoration of buildings, plans, and architectural subjects. He also worked a great deal in France. His two volumes, which appeared in 1576 and 1579, on the "Plus excellents bastiments de France," contain the most valuable information regarding the buildings of Paris and the great Châteaux of the Renaissance.

His son, Baptiste (about 1544-1590), and Jacques II Androuet (died in 1614), were, like him, architects to the King. Then the same title passed to their grandson, Jean Androuet (died after 1649), who built the Hôtel de Sully and began the Pont au Change. Jacques Androuet's sister married Jean de Brosse, and their son was the famous architect Salomon de Brosse. The family Androuet du Cerceau still had many architects, Jean II (1623-1644), Paul, Guillaume, and Jean III, whose parentage is not exactly known.

**ANET.**—A remarkable château, built about 1548, by Philibert Delorme, for Diane de Poitiers, and burnt in the Revolution. A beautiful entrance door remains, which opens between walls with Doric columns, surmounted by a coping which supports a group of sculpture, a stag attacked by two dogs. Then the left wing is decorated with Ionic pilasters and turrets at the angles. and a Chapel decorated by Jean Goujon. The *Diana* of Jean Goujon (Louvre) was sculptured to adorn the Château of Anet.

ANET: THE CHÂTEAU.

See Pl. 27, Vol. II.

**ANGELICO (Fra Giovanni da Fiesole) (Guido di Pietro da Mugello).**—Born in 1387 in Vicchio di Mugello; died in Rome 1455. Florentine fresco, panel, and miniature painter.

Fra Giovanni, with his brother, entered the order of preaching monks in 1407, at the Dominican Cloister in Fiesole, but was sent to Cortona to serve his novitiate in the branch cloister there. He took his vows in 1409, but it is not known if he stayed longer in Cortona or returned at once to Fiesole. He may have been among the fugitives from the latter monastery who took refuge first in Foligno, then in Cortona, during the schism that followed the choice of Pope Alexander V. Fra Giovanni's name is not mentioned in the records of the order during this period of wandering but, in any case, he would have been in the monastery at Fiesole from 1418 to 1436.

In 1436 the Dominican monks of Fiesole took up residence in the Cloister of San Marco in Florence, assigned to them by Cosimo and Lorenzo de' Medici. The cloister, which was in a ruined state, was entirely remodelled after designs by Michelozzo in 1439, and in 1441 was completed the restoration and decoration of the Church of S. Marco. The fresco-decoration was largely entrusted to Fra Giovanni and his pupils, and this, as well as the numerous altarpieces which he painted at the same time for other Florentine churches made him famous throughout Italy. In 1445 he was called to Rome by Pope Eugene IV.

The chapel which Fra Giovanni decorated for Eugene IV was afterwards demolished, but his work was continued after Pope Eugene's death for the new pope, Nicholas V, for whom he painted the lives of SS. Stephen and Lawrence, with the assistance of Benozzo Gozzoli, in 1447-49.

Between the painting of the first and second chapels in the Vatican, Fra Giovanni was absent from Rome at Orvieto, where he was commissioned to paint in the Chapel of S. Brizio in the Duomo. He took to Orvieto as helpers Benozzo, Giovanni d'Antonio da Firenze, and Giacomo di Poli, and he afterwards employed Pietro di Niccolà of Orvieto. The frescoes were begun on June 15, 1447, but Fra Giovanni returned to Rome without completing them, to resume his work in the Vatican.

In 1452, he was again in Fiesole, as Prior of the Cloister. He rejected a request from the Municipality of Prato to fresco the Cappella Maggiore in the Duomo there, and the commission was then given to Fra Filippo Lippi. After sixty-eight years of a life consecrated to art and piety, he died in Rome in 1455, and in honor of his religious virtues was named "Beato Angelico." His burial place is in Santa Maria sopra Minerva.

Who Angelico's master was remains a matter of supposition. Baldinucci and Rossini both cite Gherardo Starnina, but this is most unlikely. He was very probably the pupil of Lorenzo Monaco; certainly his style is derived from Lorenzo's linealism and lyricism, and his types from the shop-formulas of this master.

His earliest works may be those still preserved in Cortona in the Churches of S. Domenico and del Gesú (Museo): a triptych with Madonna and four saints, an Annunciation, and two predellas, one of which, with scenes from the Life of the Virgin, seems to belong to the Annunciation-altar in this Church; the other, with representations of St. Dominic, might have belonged to an altar in S. Domenico.

Three frescoes remain of those which Angelico painted for the Cloister at Fiesole, and which therefore are to be dated before 1436: the Crucifixion in the Sacristy of the Monastery at Fiesole, that in the Louvre, and the Madonna between Dominic and Thomas Aquinas in Leningrad.

To this period also belong the Madonna painted for the High Altar of the Cloister Church of S. Domenico, Fiesole, much restored and repainted in 1501 by Lorenzo di Credi (transferred to the Uffizi); the Annunciation in Madrid; the two Coronations of the Virgin, one in the Uffizi, one in Paris; and several Last Judgments, among them those in Florence, Berlin, and the Galleria Nazionale in Rome.

In the Museum in Perugia is a polyptych, Madonna and Saints, from the dismantled altar of S. Domenico, Perugia, dating from 1437. Two predella panels from this altar are in the Pinacoteca Vaticana.

The contract for the tabernacle of l'Arte dei Linaiuoli (Madonna, Saints, and Musical Angels, now in the Museo di S. Marco, Florence) was made in 1434, but the work was not finished until 1443.

The frescoes in the cloister, corridors, and cells of St. Marco date between 1439 and 1445 and provide the first opportunity to study on a wide scale Fra Angelico's developing fresco style, evolving out of the miniature tradition into greater breadth and plasticity. In his wall-paintings and in the panels contemporary with them, his early Gothicism yields to Renaissance forms in composition, architecture, and landscape, and his figures depart from their original immateriality under the powerful and omnipresent influence of Masaccio. This development culminates in the strong plastic organization and genuine monumentality of the frescoes of the Studio of Nicholas V in Rome.

Fra Angelico's activity was by no means limited to fresco and panel painting; a prolific school of miniature illuminators worked under his guidance and may be studied exhaustively in the manuscripts preserved at S. Marco. In common with most notable painters of the quattrocento he had many pupils and imitators whose works today frequently are attributed, sometimes through lack of exact knowledge and sometimes for less excusable reasons, to the hand of the master himself.

BIBLIOGRAPHY: Vasari-Milanesi.—E. J. Förster, *Leben und Werke des Fra Giov. Angelico.* Regensburg, 1859.—T. Goodwin, *Life of Fra Angelico.* London, 1861.—A. Rio, *De l'art chrétien.* Paris, 1864.—V. Marchese, *Memorie dei più insigni pittori scultori e architetti Domenicani.* Bologna, 1879.—E. Müntz, *Les arts à la cour des papes.* Paris, 1898. —M. Wingenroth, *Beiträge zur Angelico-Forschung,* Repert. f. KW., 1898.—Supino, J. B., *Beato Angelico.* Florence, 1901.—Douglas, Langton, *Fra Angelico.* London, 1901.—E. Schneider, *Fra Angelico da Fiesole.* Paris, 1924 (bibliog.).—Schottmüller, Frida, *Fra Angelico da Fiesole* (Klassiker der Kunst), 1924.—Papini, Roberto, *Fra Giovanni Angelico.* Bologna, 1925.

**ANGELUS (The).**—See Millet (J. F.); also Pl. 55, Vol. II.

**ANGERS (David d').**—See Pl. 51, Vol. II.

**ANGERS (Maine-et-Loire; France).**—The *Château,* built by Louis XI, and rebuilt several times, looks like a fortress with its massive rampart towers.

The *Cathedral* (Saint Maurice) dates from the 12th and 13th centuries. It has stained glass of the period, and magnificent tapestries of the 14th century. The *Church of the Holy Trinity,* in the Romanesque style, dates from the 12th century. Of the great Abbey of St. Aubin (6th century) only one tower remains.

**ANGOULÊME.**—The 12th-century Cathedral of St. Pierre of Angoulême (begun 1105) is an instance of the remarkable Byzantine-inspired domed Romanesque churches of Acquitaine. As opposed to St. Front at Périgueux, it is a Latin cross in plan with an undivided nave in three compartments, each compartment being covered with a dome on pendentives. The crossing has a dome in two shells mounted on a drum. The south transept tower was destroyed in 1569. The north transept tower is modern. The eastern termination is an apse with radiating chapels. The

ANGOULÊME: THE CATHEDRAL.

façade, indiscreetly restored in the 19th century by Abadie, is the familiar type of the Romanesque of the west of France, and has remarkable 12th century Romanesque sculptures representing the Second Coming.

See Pl. 44, Vol. I.

BIBLIOGRAPHY: Biais, *La Cathédrale d' Angoulême,* "Collection des Chefs d'œuvre."—H. Labbé de la Mauvinière, *Poitiers et Angoulême.* "Collection des Villes d'art célèbres."

**ANGUISSOLA (Sofonisba).**—Woman painter of Cremona (1528-1625). She was a pupil of Bernardino Campi, oldest of a whole family of painters, and taught her sisters Elena, Minerva, Lucia, Europa, and Anna-Maria. Sofonisba Anguissola was very famous, especially for her portraits. The self-portrait, which is in the Museum of Naples, has an attractive seriousness. She was called to the Spanish court where, at the height of her success, she married Don Fabrizio de Moncade. He moved to Sicily. But after his death she accepted the hand of a captain of a galley so that he would bring her back to Italy.

**ANGKOR-VAT (Cambodia).**—See Cambodia and Indo-China; also Pl. 35, Vol. I.

**ANNUNCIATION (The).**—Announcement of the incarnation, made by the Angel Gabriel to the Virgin Mary. For a study of the iconography of the Annunciation, see David M. Robb, Art Bulletin, XVIII, No. 4, December, 1936.

**ANSANO di PIETRO.** — See Sano di Pietro.

**ANSUINO da FORLI.**—Italian 15th-century painter whose signature is found on one of the frescoes in the Cappella di S. Agostino in the Eremitani at Padua, where he painted scenes from the Life of St. Christopher. Mentioned as having assisted Fra Filippo Lippi when the latter painted in the now-destroyed Cappella del Podestà, Padua. Influenced by Florentine art, especially Donatello.

BIBLIOGRAPHY: Schmarsow, *Melozzo da Forlì,* pp. 302-5.—Kristeller, *Mantegna,* p. 74 ff.—Moschini, *Della pittura in Padova,* p. 37.—Lazzari, *Not. della opere d'arte nella raccolta Correr.* Venice, 1859, p. 12.

**ANTELAMI (Benedetto).**—Italian sculptor, active 1177-1233. Most important North-Italian master of the Romanesque period.

The signed relief of 1178 (Bearing of the Cross) in the wall of the Baiardi Chapel of the Duomo in Parma is this master's earliest recorded work. In Borgo San Donnino, the Duomo, there are sculptures which indicate a style intermediate between this first and the series begun in 1196 in the Baptistry, Parma. An extensive system of decoration, these latter are in wonderful harmony with their architectural setting. Representations of the Months, similar to those included among the Baptistry sculptures in Parma, are to be found on the façade of the Cathedral in Cremona, where Antelami probably worked also. After 1219 he was active in Vercelli, where he did a Crucifixion of St. Andrew for the great portal of S. Andrea. In 1233 he executed an equestrian statue of Podestà Oltrado da Tresseno for the Palazzo della Ragione, Milan.

BIBLIOGRAPHY: Lopez, *Il Battistero di Parma.* Parma, 1864.—G. B. Toschi, *Le sculture di Benedetto Antelami a Borgo San Donnino,* in Archiv. Stor. dell' Arte, 1888.—Schmarsow, *San Martino von Lucca.* Berlin, 1890.—A. Venturi, *Storia, etc.,* III, 1903.

**ANTENOR.**—Greek sculptor. This artist is the only one of the

ANTENOR: STATUE. (Acropolis Museum.)

Attic sculptors of the 6th century, mentioned by the ancients, who has left us one authentic work. In the excavations of the Acropolis at the end of the 19th century, the base of a votive statue was discovered bearing the following inscription: "Néarchos, the doorkeeper, has dedicated this to Athena, as the first-fruits of his work; Antenor, son of Eumares, made the statue." Pliny (H. N. 35, 56) tells us that this Eumares was a painter. He attributes to him the innovation of differentiating the sexes in painting. His son Antenor was a sculptor at the time of the Peisistratids. In the Acropolis Museum one can restore in mind the statue signed by him. This figure reproduces the inimitable type of "Korai" of the old Parthenon. It is one of the most remarkable of the series. Some technical refinements set it apart—for instance, the workmanship of the eyes which were made of a vitreous paste "encased in a bronze shell of which the barbed edges imitated eye-lashes" (Collignon). This work belongs to the last third of the 6th century.

The most important work of Antenor was the bronze group, representing the slayers of Hipparchus, Harmodius and Aristogiton. They killed Hipparchus in 514. The monument was consecrated in 510. This group of the *Tyrannicides* was set up on the highway which led from the Agora to the Acropolis. But in 480, at the time of the pillage of Athens, Xerxes carried it off to Ecbatana, and it was not restored to the Athenians until after 280, by Antiochus, son of Seleusus. In the interval, from the year 477, until Hellenistic times two other sculptors, Critius and Nesiotes, had replaced Antenor's group by a new work which doubtless reproduced as nearly as possible the work which had been carried away by the Persians.

The two memorials have both disappeared. Nevertheless, several works have come down to us which probably give some idea of the appearance of the Tyrannicides group: for instance, on a Panathenaic amphora, on several Attic tetradrachmes, on lead counters, in a bas-relief decorating a marble seat found in Athens. All these scenes happen to be upon objects which have a certain official character; and in fact the representation of the downfall of the tyrants was, for the Athenians, a civic theme often reproduced.

Finally, in the Museum of Naples, there is a marble group of two figures which is certainly a copy dating from the time of the Tyrannicides. The sculptor has shown some respect for the archaic original of his model; he has reproduced the parallelism of the poses. Some modern restorations have only succeeded in spoiling its character; for instance, the head of one of the young men is in a much later style.

From which of the two groups was the work in Naples copied? Because the composition is so bold and vigorous, it seems improbable, from what we know of the extant works of Antenor and his associates, that it could belong to their cycle. It is, however, completely in accordance with Attic art at the beginning of the 5th century, in which Critius and Nesiotes appear to have played an important part.

BIBLIOGRAPHY: Collignon, *Histoire de la Sculpture grecque,* Vol. I, p. 368 et seq.—Joubin, *La Sculpture grecque.* Paris, 1901.

**ANTHEMIUS OF TRALLES.**—See Constantinople; Saint Sophia.

**ANTOINE (Jacques - Denis).**—1733-1801. Architect of *"La Monnaie,"* Paris. Several architects com-

ANTOINE (JACQUES-DENIS): THE MINT, PARIS.

peted, in 1768, for the construction of this building: Moreau, Boullée, Barreau. Antoine's plan was chosen solely because of his superiority, for the young architect, unknown until then, was not recommended by any person of influence. The *Mint,* finished in 1775, excited general admiration. The following year the artist was received at the Academy. He worked next at the reconstruction of the *Palais de Justice,* which was damaged by fire in 1776; the large flight of steps is owing to him, and various work in the interior. He also made the plans of the *Chapelle Saint-Nicholas-des-Champs,* the *Hôtel Jaucourt* (rue de Varenne), the *Hôtel de Maillebois* (rue du Bac), the *Hôtel de la rue d'Enfer* (now Deufert-Rochercau), where Madame de Châteaubriand later installed the "Maison de Marie-Thérèse," the *Hôtel de la Monnaie* at Berne, the *Church des Filles Saint-Marie,* at Nancy, the façade of the *Hôtel de Ville* at Cambrai, and various plans of private residences. After the suppression of the Académie Royale, during the Revolution, Antoine was nominated a member of the Institut, in 1799.

**ANTOKOLSKI.**—The most popular Russian sculptor of the second half of the 19th century. His fame spread also abroad. He was, however, only a very skilful craftsman without great originality, and very academic. He represented chiefly national heroes, and in that respect may be compared with the historical painter, Paul Delaroche. His chief works are *Jermak, Nestor* and *Socrates,* and his best production is, undoubtedly, the figure of Ivan the Terrible.

**ANTONELLO da MESSINA,** rare and unique talent of the Italian Renaissance, was born in Messina, Sicily, in 1430, the son of a sculptor. His painting was much admired by his contemporaries and he is mentioned by early writers whose conflicting accounts of his schooling and attainments have contributed to the confusion of later commentators. Necessarily a study of Antonello must be based upon those facts of his life which are substantiated by documentary evidence: In 1455, he marries, in Messina; in 1457 is commissioned to paint a banner for Reggio in Calabria and is recorded as hiring a helper; in 1460 he is living in Calabria; but 1461-65 is again in Messina. In 1473-74, Antonello is again mentioned in Messina; nothing is known of his activity during the intervening period. To this 1473-74 Messina interval belong the triptych for San Gregorio in Messina, now in the Messina Gallery, and the Syracuse Annunciation. In 1475-76 he is in Venice, where he paints an altarpiece for S. Casciano, which no longer exists; and is active in Milan in the service of the reigning duke. In November of 1476 he is back in Messina; in 1478 recorded as undertaking work for Randazzo, and he dies toward the middle of February of 1479.

Who Antonello's master was is not known, and there is no evidence for his supposed journey to the Netherlands, nor for his introduction of the oil technique into Venice. However Bartolommeo Vivarini painted in oil in Venice already in 1473, whereas there is no proof that Antonello arrived there until 1474.

Dated works by Antonello run between 1465 and 1478: the Salvator Mundi in the London National Gallery is of 1465; the Messina Gallery polyptych, Madonna, Gregory and Benedict and Annunciation, is of 1473; as is also the Piacenza Christ Crowned with Thorns. The Berlin male portrait is dated 1474 and the Paris Condottiere 1475. To the period of these two portraits belongs the frescoed Annunciation at Syracuse; and 1475 is also the date of the magnificent Antwerp Crucifixion. The Turin, Museo Civico (formerly Trivulzio) portrait follows, in 1476; and the London Crucifixion in 1477. To Antonello's latter period belongs the undated St. Jerome in the National Gallery.

BIBLIOGRAPHY: Vasari-Milanesi.—Morelli-Lermolieff, *The Borghese and Doria-Pamfili Galleries; The Galleries of Munich and Dresden; The Berlin Gallery.*—Crowe and Cavalcaselle.—G. di Marzo, *Di Antonello da Messina e dei suoi congiunti, studi e documenti,* Palermo, 1903.—G. La Corte-Cailler, *Antonello da Messina, Studi e ricerche con documenti inediti.* Messina, 1903.—A. D'Amico, *Antonello d'Antonio, Le sue opera e l'invenzione della pittura ad olio.* Messina, 1904. —L. Venturi, *Le origini della pittura veneziana.* Venice, 1907, 213 ff.

**ANTONIAZZO ROMANO.**—Antoniazzo Aquilio, Roman painter active 1460-1508, influenced by Perugino and more strongly by Melozzo da Forlì. Painted at Rome with Melozzo from 1460. In 1464 he was commissioned to paint frescoes in the Santi Apostoli in the Chapel of Sant' Angelo and in the Chapel of Sant' Eugenio, but these have not been preserved. The principal works which have come down to us are a picture, dated 1467, in San Francesco at Subiaco, the *Madonna Enthroned* in a niche of the "Civica Quadreria" of Rieti, signed, another in the Louvre, the *Madonna* in the Corsini Gallery and the *Madonna with the Wheel*, in the Vatican, the *Annunciation* in Santa Maria sopra Minerva (c. 1489), inspired by that of Melozzo in the Panthenon.

From 1480 to 1481 he helped Melozzo in the decoration of the Papal Library, and after the departure of that master, he seems to have still worked at the Vatican as an assistant of Perugino. He died about 1508.

BIBLIOGRAPHY: Bernardini, *Alcune opere di Antoniazzo Romano in Roma*. "Rassegna d'Arte." 1909.—M. Ciartoso, *Nota su Antoniazzo Romano*.

**ANTONIO da FABRIANO.**—Active 1450-85. Developed under the influence of Lorenzo Salimbeni and the Vivarini. Works by him are to be found in Fabriano, including frescoes of 1480 in S. Domenico; and in Jesi, Sassoferato, Urbino and elsewhere.

**— da FAENZA.**—Marchigian painter, active c. 1500-30, influenced by Melozzo da Forlì and Lotto.

**— da FERRARA (A. di Guido Alberti).**—Painter, born in Ferrara between 1390 and 1400, lived in Urbino. Antonio married in Urbino in 1423, his brother-in-law being Matteo Gennari, a painter, from whom he may have had some instruction. His wife died in 1432 and Antonio married again. Until 1435 he is mentioned in the book of Entrate e Spese, from 1439-1445 in that of the Brotherhood of Sta. Maria della Misericordia. In 1449 he is referred to as dead. His daughter was the mother of Timoteo Viti.

Much of Antonio's work has been lost in the course of time. There are signed frescoes of 1437 in the old chapel of Talamello near Pesaro. Crowe and Cavalcaselle follow Pungileoni in believing that Antonio worked in 1438 in the Palazzo del Paradiso in Ferrara. Frescoes by him of 1435-40 in the Cappella de' Signori in S. Francesco, Urbino, have been largely destroyed; a few traces remain in the Campanile. In the Gallery at Urbino there are thirteen panels that originally formed the altarpiece that Antonio painted for the Bernardine monks, the central panel of the Madonna signed and dated 1439. Another panel by this master depicting a Risen Christ was found by Calzini in 1897 under a worthless painting in a room near the Sagrestia de' Zoccolanti, and is also to be found in the Urbino Gallery.

BIBLIOGRAPHY: Vasari, *Vita di Agnolo Gaddi*.—Pungileoni, *Elogio Storico di Timoteo Viti*, Urbino, 1835, p. 81-87.—Crowe and Cavalcaselle.—Calzini, *Urbino e i suoi monumenti*, 1897, p. 135-37.—Scatassa in Rass. bibl. dell' arte ital. I, 196-197, VI, 13, IX, 53-63.—H. Thode, Archiv. stor. dell' arte I, 137-141.

**— da TRENTO.**—Italian engraver, born at Trent, at the beginning of the 16th century. Active in Bologna. Parmigianino was possibly his master. Vasari mentions four of his works: the *Virgin with the Roses*, the *Martyrdom of St. Peter*, the *Liburtine Sibyl*, and a *Nude Man Asleep*.

BIBLIOGRAPHY: Bartsch, *Le peintre-graveur*, Vol. XII.

**— VENEZIANO.**—Painter, probably from Venice, active in Tuscany in 1370-88. In 1370 he received with Andrea Vanni payment for paintings in the Duomo of Siena (Milanesi, Doc. I, 305); in 1374 he is found in Florence on the register of the Arte dei Medici e Speziali; and in Pisa, from 1384-1387, he received payments for the three lower paintings with the legend of S. Ranieri in the Camposanto. Unfortunately these frescoes are in very bad state. Another fresco, also in bad state, attributed to the master is the Last Judgment in a tabernacle at Torre degli Agli in the environs of Florence. The panel paintings of Antonio Veneziano have been gathered together by Richard Offner (*op. cit.* below).

The master's style developed out of that of Taddeo Gaddi, with the later influence of Bernardo Daddi and the Sienese.

BIBLIOGRAPHY: Vasari (ed. Lemonnier, II, 171 ff.; ed. Milanesi I, 661 ff.).—Milanesi, *Doc. Senesi*, I, 305.—Tanfani Centofanti, *Provincia di Pisa*, 1881, n. 33, and *Notizie di artisti*, 1897, pp. 34-40, 441-42.—Frey, *Il Codice Magliabecchiano*, 1892, pp. 253, 259.—Ciampi, *Not. sul Campo Santo in Pisa*, 151.—Rosini, *Descr. delle Pitture del Campo Santo*. Pisa, 1816, pp. 80-98.—C. Bernasconi, *Antonio Veneziano*. Verona, 1862.—Crowe and Cavalcaselle, *Storia*, II, 209-228.—J. B. Supino, *Il Camposanto di Pisa*, 1896.—Schubring, *Altichiero und seine Schule*, 1896, p. 129.—Venturi, L., *Le origini della pittura veneziana*. Venice, 1907.—Offner, *Studies in Florentine Painting*, 1927, pp. 67-81.

**— da VITERBO.**—Umbrian painter, active 1478-1509, a follower of Pintoricchio and Perugino. There are frescoes by him in the Duomo at Orvieto, and in Rome and Viterbo.

**ANTWERP.**—The most famous building is the Cathedral of Notre Dame, begun in 1352 and completed in 1518. The choir was added in 1550. The Guild Houses, the Hôtel de Ville, and the Plantin Museum date from the 16th century. The Royal Museum has a fine collection of paintings, including many from the early Flemish school. See Rubens; also Pls. 11, 49, Vol. I.

**— SCHOOL OF.**—See Matsys (Quentin); also Pl. 24, Vol. II.

**APELLES.**—The most famous of the 4th century Greek painters was Apelles. He was born in all probability at Colophon (370 B.C.) in Ionia and studied in the neighboring Ephesus. He continued his education at Sicyon.

He soon became famous, and Philip called him to the Macedonian Court, where he became the friend of his son, Alexander, who, when he became king, made Apelles his official painter, and forbade, by royal ordinance, that any other artist should paint his portrait. Apelles reproduced the features of his royal friend, many times. One of the most beautiful portraits was that of Alexander holding a thunder-bolt, which was found in the temple of Artemis, at Ephesus. The right hand which holds the thunder-bolt is particularly fine, and is so powerfully rendered that one almost expects to see it come out of the frame. Another portrait represents Alexander on horseback, also at Ephesus. The king, on seeing this portrait, did not express the admiration which the artist expected, but his horse, at the sight of the horse painted on the canvas, began to neigh. The artist turned to Alexander, exclaiming, "See, your horse knows more about painting than you do!" or perhaps "Your horse recognises you better than you recognise yourself." Other portraits represent heads of the king, surrounded by gods and victories. Apelles also painted the chief people of the court. Among the best was the portrait of Antigone, which he painted in profile because this prince was blind in one eye, and the artist did not want either to represent the diseased eye, nor to make it appear sound; the equestrian portrait of Clitus. Other portraits include that of Archelaus, of the beautiful Pancaspe, Alexander's mistress, of Menander, King of Caria, and of Gorgosthenes, the famous tragic actor. Apelles executed all these portraits with a fidelity and concern for exactitude hitherto unknown. He enjoyed, not only the royal favour, but the admiration and friendship of everyone he met. The sweetness of his character, his kindliness and generosity contrasted with the immense pride and arrogance of Zeuxis and Parrhasios. As long as Alexander lived he resided at the Court of Macedonia. When he had lost his protector and friend, he went to the Court of Ptolemy I, in Alexandria. There he met the painter, Antiphilos, who, through jealousy, slandered him, and excited the king's anger against him. He, however, soon perceived his mistake and offered Apelles a huge sum of money. From this time dates the famous picture of *Calumny*, described by Lucian. Here, the master expressed all his knowledge of human nature, and of the evil passions which leave their mark on the face; a series of allegories express their psychological intent clearly and with inimitable vigour. After his sojourn in Egypt, Apelles worked in Rhodes, in Athens, and in the island of Cos. In Rhodes he made the acquaintance of a painter of great talent, Protogenes, who was not as yet very well known, and lived in poverty. A pretty anecdote tells us how the two artists became acquainted. Apelles, staying in Rhodes, betook himself to the studio of Protogenes. He was out, and the servant asked the visitor his name. On an easel was stretched a canvas, ready for painting. Apelles went up to it without saying a word, and there drew with a paint-brush a line of remarkable delicacy. Protogenes, when he saw it, recognised the touch of the master, drew in his turn a line still finer, and sent it to Apelles, who returned a little later, and painted, between the two lines, a portrait so fine that Protogenes admitted himself beaten. Apelles helped greatly in making Protogenes known and appreciated.

In this second part of his life, the master painted mythological and symbolical pictures: *Artemis in the Midst of a Band of Young Girls, Heracles, Charity, Bronte* (the thunder), *Astrape* (the lightning), *Keraunobolia* (the thunder-bolt), *Fortune*, and his admirable *Aphrodite Anadyomene* (Venus rising from the waves), whose praises rang in ancient times. It is said that he was inspired to the subject by the courtesan, Phryne, who, at the close of an Eleusian festival, undressed herself and, her hair floating over her shoulders, plunged into the sea, in front of the assembled Greeks. The supple body of the goddess was rendered with a grace and elegance which delighted the eyes of a people who loved fair forms. Apelles willingly painted the figure of Aphrodite in her dazzling nudity. Towards the end of his life he wished to paint for the last time the goddess of love and beauty, for the town of Cos. Death did not allow him to finish his masterpiece. He could only execute an admirable head and shoulders of a drawing so perfect that no painter could be found who dared to finish the picture.

The greatness of Apelles lay probably, first of all, in his own genius, evidenced in the particular grace that marked his work. Both his design and his modelling were brought to a high point of perfection.

BIBLIOGRAPHY: Brunn, *Geschichte der griechischen Künstler*.—Overbeck, *Die antiken Schriftquellen zur Geschichte der bildenden Kunst bei den Griechen*.—H. Houssaye, *Histoire d'Apelle*. Paris, 1868.—Woermann, *Die malerei des Alterthums*. Leipzig, 1878.—P. Girard, *La peinture antique*.

**APHAIA (Temple of).**—See Ægina.

**APHRODITE.**—See Venus.

**APOLLO BELVEDERE.**—Famous Greek statue which was discovered at the end of the XVth century, near the Ferrate Grotto, on an estate of Cardinal Giuliano della Rovere. When he became Pope, under the name of Julius II, the former Cardinal had it removed to the Vatican Palace, where it still is today. It underwent some restorations by a pupil of Michelangelo, the sculptor Montorsoli, who repaired the right forearm and the left hand. Despite the fact that there are remains of a bow in the left hand, the god does not seem to be actually represented in the act of shooting. The ease with which the right hand moves backward implies the intention of no particular action at all unless it be that of just having let fly his arrow. The statue is a marble copy of a bronze original. The metallic-like rendering of the hair and the great thin expanse of garment which hangs from the left arm, clearly indicating a bronze prototype, conclusively prove this fact. The left arm is extended and the glance of the god follows in the same direction. The impression is given of an archer who has just shot an arrow and is watching the path of its flight. The Apollo of the Pergamene frieze, although offering strong contrast to this statue, should be observed for analogies. It is difficult to assign the Apollo Belvedere to any precise school and period. Other copies taken from the same original exist. Therefore the original must have been a very familiar work. The character of the style and the theatrical posture link it to the Hellenistic period. Because of the over refinement of the modeling it may well be regarded as a reaction against the realistic tendency of the time present in Pergamon and elsewhere. In the Apollo Belvedere generalization and lack of individualistic traits have removed the work completely from the realistic world. See Pl. 25, Vol. I.

BIBLIOGRAPHY: Collignon, *Histoire de la Sculpture Grecque*; Vol. II,

p. 316 et seq.—Furtwängler, *Meisterwerke der griech. Plastik*, p. 660 seq.

**— DIDYMUS.**—See Pl. 20, Vol. I.

**— OF DELOS.**—See Pl. 20, Vol. I.

**— OF TENEA.**—This statue is the best preserved of all the early works found in the Peloponnesus, dating about 550-540 B.C. It is now in the Sculpture Museum of Munich. It forms a striking contrast to the massive Argive statues and may well have been executed in one of the islands. This Apollo resembles the *Apollo of Thera* very closely, and is partly a reproduction of it, though showing greater ability. The significance of the statue is uncertain. There is some evidence that it was placed above a grave as an effigy of the deceased.

The execution is extremely careful: the curled hair falls on the shoulders and frames the oval face, the nose is pointed, the eyes protrude; the chin is large and strong, and the mouth has a smiling expression. The face as a whole expresses a wide-awake intelligence. The modelling of the torso shows some insufficiencies: the shoulders are too slanting, the thorax is badly indicated; the abdomen is too flat and contracted, the legs seem a little stiff; nevertheless, they are the part which is the best modelled, especially from the knees to the feet, which are drawn with great delicacy. The weight of the body is carried equally on the two legs, although one of the two is slightly advanced. The sculptor remained bound to the frontal aspect of the figure, and did not know how to make the torso supple by making it rest on one hip more than on the other. Such as it is, this image of a youth is one of the best examples of the 6th century of this sculptural type, from which the vigorous figures of youths and athletes are derived. The Museum of Athens has a virile statue, very like this in style. It was found in Attica. See Pl. 20, Vol. I.

Bibliography: Perrot, *Histoire de l'art*, Vol. VIII, p. 400 seq.

**— OF THERA.**—This *Apollo*, found on the Island of Thera, belongs to a group of figures with which archæologists reconstruct the primitive school of statuary of the *Cyclades*. Nothing remains of it but the legs. The modelling is very rounded, but this does not allow of more than a recognition of the influence of wooden sculpture. It is still, however, very archaic in type. It very likely belongs to the end of the 7th century, or to the beginning of the following one.

**APOXYOMENUS.**—See Lycippus.

**APPIAN WAY.**—See Pl. 29, Vol. I.

**APSE.**—The end of the church, behind the choir, round or polygonal in shape. By extending the meaning, one may speak sometimes of a square apse.

**APSIDIOLE.**—Small or secondary apse, especially as distinguished from a larger one in the same church.

**APT (Ulrich).**—Ulrich Apt the Elder, German painter of the early 16th century, Swabian school of Augsbourg, author of a *Crucifixion* (1517, Museum of Augsbourg).

Bibliography: Buchner, E.-Feuchtmayr, K., *Augsburger Kunst der Spätgotik und Renaissance*. Augsburg, 1928.

**APTEROS (Nike).**—See Acropolis of **Athens.**

**AQUAMANILE.**—Basins of copper or bronze, in use in the Middle Ages, intended to hold liquids. They served especially as ritual vases, for ablutions. The name of aquamanile is sometimes also given

Aquamanile. (Museum of Cordova.)

to bronze ewers; Arabic art produced some very beautiful examples in the form of animals.

**AQUATINT.**—See Engraving.

**ARABESQUE.**—Properly speaking, this is decoration made of combinations of interlacing lines, either straight or curvilinear and in the form of stars, polygons, etc., which characterizes Arabic art. But the term "arabesque" is also used for decorations combining winding lines with ornamental leaves, garlands, vases, fragments of architecture, fantastic animals, as well as elements borrowed from the human figure. In this last case, one ought rather to speak of "grotesque" (see this word), since Arabic art excluded the human figure. The most famous arabesques are those of the Loggia of the Vatican, by Raphael, those of Fontainebleau, and those of the Château of Blois (for the most part repainted in the 19th century, but faithfully restored).

Bibliography: *The Encyclopædia of Islam*. Leyden, 1913. Vol. I, art. *Arabesque* by E. Herzfeld.—*The Encyclopaedia Britannica,* 14th ed. London-New York, 1929. Vol. II, art. *Arabesque*.

**ARABIAN ART.**—See India; Moslem Art; etc.

**ARALDI (Alessandro).**—Parmese painter, 1460-1528. Mediocre, he scarcely painted anything but imitations of Raphael, Mantegna, Leonardo, etc. But he showed some gifts as a decorator in the charming ornamentation in the cloisters of San Paolo at Parma, beside the room where Correggio's frescoes are.

**ARCANGELO di COLA da CAMERINO.**—In 1416 in Città di Castello he painted a fresco of St. Mary Magdalen in the Palazzo Communale; in 1420 he matriculated in the Arte de' Medici e Speziali in Florence; in 1421 he executed a panel for the chapel of the Bardi family in Chiesa S. Lucia. He settled in Rome, probably in order to do paintings for Pope Martin V in the Church of S. Giovanni in Laterano.

Bibliography: Vasari-Milanesi, II, 294.—Moreni, *Not. istor. dei contorni di Firenze*.—Gaye, *Carteggio,* 1839-40, II, 377.—Gualandi, *Mem. orig. Bologna,* 1884.—Frey, *Loggia de' Lanzi,* Berlin, 1885, p. 363.—Margherini-Graziani, *L'arte a Città di Castello,* 1897, pp. 73, 182.—Ricci, *Mem. Stor.* I, 175-80.—Santoni in Nuova Rivista Misena, 1890, No. 12; *Catal. degli uomini illustri di Camerino*.—Feliciangeli, *Sulla vita di Giov. Boccati da Camerino,* S. Severino, 1906.

**ARCH OF AUGUSTUS.**—See Nîmes; Perugia.

**— OF CONSTANTINE.**—See Rome.

**— OF TITUS.**—See Rome; also Pl. 29, Vol. I.

**— OF TRAJAN.**—See Timgad.

**ARCHES (Triumphal).**—See Pl. 29, Vol. I.

**ARCHITRAVE.**—Lowest division of the entablature; the main beam that rests on the abacus on the capital of the columns; epistile.

**ARCHIVOLT.**—Band of concentric mouldings which decorates the arch of a façade. This band may be

Archivolt.

formed of a single row or of many, with or without decoration.

**ARETINO.**—See Spinello Aretino.

**ARETIUM.**—See Ceramic.

**ARGOS (School of).**—See Polyclitus.

**ARIOSTO OF PAINTING.**—See Dosso Dossi.

**ARDELL (James Mac).**—English engraver (1710-1765). He was a pupil of John Brooks, and used almost exclusively the "black manner." Examples: *Moses on the waters of the Nile,* after Van Dyck; the *Assumption of the Virgin,* after Murillo; *Tobias and the Angel,* after Rembrandt; and also a great number of portraits, among them those of Rubens (1752), of George Duke of Buckingham, of Rachel Countess of Southampton, after Van Dyck; and Benjamin Franklin, after Wilson. With Earlom, Green, and Watson, he forms part of the group of engravers whom Reynolds guided in the reproduction of his works.

Bibliography: G. Goodwin, *James MacArdell*. London, 1903.

**ARLES.**—Owing to its geographical position, at the place where

Arles: The Roman Theatre.

the Rhone divides, Arles soon became an important centre. Under Roman domination, it became a military colony and a flourishing town, as the monuments of this period prove. The *Arena,* or amphitheatre, could hold 25,000 spectators; the large axis measures 69 metres 40, the small one 39 metres 63. The monument is formed of two tiers of 60 superimposed arcades, the first of the Doric order, the second of the Corinthian order. The steps and the interior have been destroyed, and in the Middle Ages houses were built there.

*The Theatre,* which is much more damaged, was surrounded by three tiers of arcades. Its statues and marbles have been carried off or destroyed. In 1651, excavators discovered there the famous statue, known as the Venus of Arles, which was given to Louis XIV, and is now in the Louvre. All that remains of the building are three arcades, two columns, a doorway, the marble pavement, some steps and the proscenium. It held 16,000 people.

Arles: Tympanum of St. Trophime.

There are only some scraps of the forum left, and scarcely more of the Cemetery of Alyscamps, famous from Roman times and throughout the Middle Ages. The local tradition says that Christ appeared during the consecration of the Cemetery by St. Trophime. The most influential families of the neighbourhood were buried here in magnificent tombs. Churches and chapels were built there. The number and beauty of all those buildings gave rise to legends and to a 12th century "chanson de gestes," which relates of two battles by Guillaume d'Orange with the Saracens. In the 16th century the people of Arles began to despoil their cemetery of its richest monuments, to offer them to princes. And all that remains of Alyscamps is a

Arles: Cloister of St. Trophime.

vast field and some remains of chapels and tombs.

*St. Trophime,* formerly St. Etienne, is a Romanesque church, partly rebuilt from 1421 to 1450. The most remarkable part is the doorway, which was begun about 1221, and ornamented with statues of Apostles, separated by granite columns; in the tympanum is a figure of Christ surrounded by the symbols of the Evangelists. The Cloisters of St. Trophime are formed of four arcaded galleries with columns of white marble with sculptured capitals and carvings on the corner pillars. See Pls. 44, 46, Vol. I.

The *Hôtel de Ville* was built according to the plans of Mansart. The clock tower is surmounted by a statue of Mars.

**ARMENIA.**—See Moslem Art.

**ARMS (John Taylor).**—Contemporary American etcher. He was born in Washington, D. C., 19th April 1887. He studied architecture at Princeton University and later at the Massachusetts Institute of Technology under Despradelles.

Two years after graduating from the latter college he entered the employ of Carrère and Hastings as a draftsman and some time after that he was a member of the firm of Clark and Arms. He served in the United States Navy during the World War and shortly after its close began to take up etching as his profession. He studied for a time with Ross Turner, D. A. Gregg, and Felton Brown. His great interest was and still is architecture, particularly that of the Gothic period. Other subjects which interest him are street scenes of European villages and some views of the Venetian canals. He was the illustrator for two books written by his wife, Dorothy Noyes Arms, on "Churches of France" and "Hill Towns and Cities of Northern Italy." His etchings are characterised by a delicacy of shading, keen and close rendition of architectural details as on cathedral façades, a distinct unity of conception and beauty of design. He is a facile worker with many plates to his credit for the number of years which he has practised this graphic art. He won the Mrs. Henry F. Noyes prize at the exhibition of the Society of American Etchers in 1931 and the Member's prize in the show of the Chicago Society of Etchers in 1932. In 1930 he was elected to associate membership in the National Academy of Design and he is now the President of the Society of American Etchers.

BIBLIOGRAPHY: Cynthia Eaton, *John Taylor Arms, Aquatinter,* Goodspeed's Monographs, 1923.—*John Taylor Arms,* American Etchers, Vol. 5, 1930.

**ARNOLFO di CAMBIO (from Colle di Val d'Elsa).**—Documentary sources on the life of the great Florentine architect are so few that his activity has been the subject of widely varying conjecture. Karl Frey (in Thieme-Becker) has advanced the theory that the architect Arnolfo di Cambio is to be distinguished from the sculptor Arnolfo di Firenze, but modern scholarship tends to merge the two personalities into one, thus according with earlier literature. However the problem awaits further investigation.

For Arnolfo di Cambio but two dates are known: in 1300 a document records (Gaye I, 445; Frey, Loggia dei Lanzi, p. 192) that the Signorie of Florence granted him freedom from the tax raised for the building of the Duomo in recognition of his outstanding performance in church building; and in 1302 he is dead. His birth date is not known, but as his mother was still living when the first document was filed it is to be assumed that he was not of a great age. Where, when, and with whom he studied architecture are not known. A Gothic builder, not in the Northern sense but in the Tuscan sense, his work was modified by pre-existing tendencies. With certain Gothic elements and using the basilica tradition, Arnolfo evolved a space style of specifically Florentine stamp, distinguished in its characteristic powerful personality from those of his predecessors and contemporaries.

He is known to have been the designer of Sta. Croce, begun in 1295, the building of which he supervised until his death. How much was completed by that time is not known, but his plans probably were carried out in toto. The building was finished c. 1330. Arnolfo also was the designer of the Duomo of Florence, originally known as Sta. Maria Reparata, since 1412 called Sta. Maria del Fiore. The cornerstone of the Duomo was laid in 1296, but it was not finished until well into the 15th century. Further architectural works by Arnolfo are not certain; he was possibly the architect of Sta. Maria Maggiore and Sta. Trinità, both of which precede Sta. Croce in type.

For the sculptor, Arnolfo di Firenze, whom Mr. Frey would separate from Arnolfo di Cambio, but who may be identical with him, more documentary information is available. Although his birth and death dates are unknown, he was certainly a pupil of Niccolò Pisano, and is so mentioned when in 1267 he was busy on the pulpit for the Duomo of Siena, Niccolò's second masterwork after the Pisan altar. In 1277 it is evident that he had been working for some time in Rome in the service of Charles I of Anjou, but his activity there is not specified. In 1277 he was called to Perugia with Niccolò and Giovanni Pisano to work on the fountain for the Duomo. However, it is not known if he went to Perugia at that time, or what he did if he did go. A document of 1281 indicates payment to him for twenty-four days' work and travel-fare from Perugia to Rome and back, but the payment does not necessarily imply artistic activity and may refer to an improvement of the water-system.

The following sculptural works are known by inscription: the tomb of Cardinal de Braye in S. Domenico di Orvieto (the Cardinal died in 1284); the tabernacle in San Paolo fuori le Mura, finished in 1285 (with one Petrus); the altar-tabernacle of 1293 in Sta. Cecilia in Trastevere; and the tomb of Pope Boniface VIII.

BIBLIOGRAPHY: See Cicognara, *Stor. di Scult.* for older literature.—Crowe and Cavalcaselle, *Stor. d. pitt.,* I.—Vermiglioli, *Dell' acquedotto e della fontana maggiore di Perugia,* etc., 1827.—Frey, *Loggia dei Lanzi.* Berlin, 1884.—Venturi, *Storia,* etc., III, 888; IV, 1 ff.

**ARPINO (Il Cavaliere d').**—Giuseppe Cesari, il Cavaliere d' Arpino. Roman painter (1568-1640). Born in Rome, where, under the patronage of Pope Gregory XIII, he did some decorations at the Vatican, and a large *Canonization of Saint Francis and Saint Paul.*

He worked in the Lateran, in San Lorenzo, in San Lorenzo in Damaso in the Aldobrandini Chapel, in Santa Maria-in-Via, in the Villa Aldobrandini of the Frascati. He was commissioned by the Roman Senate to paint subjects from Roman history in the Palazzo dei Conservatori.

BIBLIOGRAPHY: Vasari-Milanesi, IV, p. 149 f.—De Pagave, Vita di C. Cesariano, pub. C. Casati, 1878.

**ARRAS.**—In Arras, the Germans destroyed two masses of remarkable building, the most complete of their kind in France—the Grande Place, and the Petite Place.

The Grande Place, which extended over two hectares, was surrounded with old houses, mostly of the 17th century, in the Flemish style, with arcades and decorated gable-ends. Some were older (the Chapel of the Templars, 13th century); others had courts with sculptured façades. Many still bore the name and the signs of other days—"Le Chapeau vert," "La Cloche," "Le Monton d'Argent," "le Heaume," "le Chaudron," "le Fer à Cheval."

The Petite Place was in the same style as the Grande Place, with houses of the same period, decorated with devices—such as the unicorn, etc. One side of the Place was occupied by the magnificent Hôtel de Ville, surmounted by a belfry, built at the opening of the XVIth century by Jacques Caron, restored, and partly rebuilt by Mayeur in 1858 to 1866. The façade was formed of seven Gothic arcades, surmounted by richly decorated windows, and by a high roof with skylights. Framing the building were two graceful wings in the Renaissance style (that of the right, modern, had been built to match the other). The belfry was a magnificent construction built from 1463 to 1554, 75 metres high, and ending in a ducal coronet in cast-iron and a colossal lion in the same material (partly rebuilt in the 19th century).

ARRAS: THE GREAT SQUARE.

Until their destruction, these two squares had never changed their appearance; an order of Philippe II obliged the owners to restore or rebuild the houses in the same style.

**ARRAS (Tapestry).**—See Tapestry.

**ARROTINO (L'), or "the Knife-Grinder."**—A famous antique statue, representing a Scythian slave crouching and sharpening a knife; it is in the Uffizi, in Florence. Other copies of this motive have also come down to us from antiquity. Certain archæologists have thought that this figure belonged to some picturesque group such as the sculptors of the Alexandrian period loved to create. In this case, this figure was part of some scene, like that of the supplicating Marsyas being flayed by Apollo. From antiquity, too, have come down to us some figures of Marsyas hanging from a tree; to complete the group one has only to imagine a figure of Apollo. The *Arrotino* has been much admired for the vigour of its muscles, and often copied by modern artists.

**ARTEMIS.**—Greek goddess of the chase, associated with the moon; identified with Diana by the Romans. See Greece.

**— OF DELOS.**—See Pl. 20, Vol. I.

**ASHLAR.**—Hewn or squared stone.

**ASPERTINI (Amico).**—Bolognese painter (c. 1474-1552), a pupil of Ercole Roberti, follower of Costa and Francia. He travelled a great deal, gathering at random a great number of models, which afterwards allowed him to make quick adaptations. Also his fertility was inexhaustible. Vasari says that there was not one church or one street in Bologna that had not some trace of his hand. But many of his paintings have disappeared. There remains at Lucca his decoration of a chapel of San Frediano, which was much esteemed. In Bologna there are frescoes by him in S. Giacomo Maggiore, Sta. Cecilia, and S. Martino Maggiore.

**ASPETTI (Tiziano).**—16th-Century Venetian sculptor from Padua. Pupil of Jacopo Sansovino. Author of a figure of *Atlas* in the Library of St. Mark, of a *Moses* and *St. Paul* on the façade of San Francesco della Vigna, and of several sculptures in the Santo of Padua.

**ASSISI (Italy).**—Assisi is the town of Saint Francis and one of the greatest artistic monuments in Italy.

The Convent of the Franciscans was begun in 1228, two years after the death of Saint Francis (1182-1226), who founded this Order in 1208. From afar, one sees this building set up on the hill, where it is secured by enormous substructures, altered in 1475. To this convent belong the two superimposed churches, which were built over the tomb of Saint Francis.

The *Lower Church,* begun in 1228, continued by Filippo di Campello, was finished in 1253. It is a nave surmounted by four large ribbed arches, supported by semicircular arcades, with transept, apse, and adjoining Gothic chapels from the beginning of the 14th century. The Renaissance porch dates from 1488. An extraordinary group of great painters have contributed to its fresco decoration. In the right transept there is a Madonna Enthroned attributed to Cimabue, and in the Chapel of the Magdalen scenes from the life of this saint by a follower of Giotto. Followers of this master also painted the Glory of St. Francis and the Allegories over the tomb of Francis, the Legend of Nicholas and the Madonna in the Chapel of the Sacrament. In the Chapel of St. Stanislas there are further Giottesque frescoes, attributed to Maso di Banco. In the crypt are five frescoes from the New Testament and five from the life of St. Francis by the painter known as the St. Francis Master.

But the Florentines were not the sole contributors to the artistic enrichment of the great Franciscan foundation. In the left transept are a Madonna with Francis and John, a Crucifixion, Scenes from the Passion, the Stigmatization of Francis and other frescoes by Pietro Lorenzetti; and in the Chapel of St. Martin, Scenes from the Legend of Martin by Simone Martini. In the Chapel of St. Catherine, representations of the life of that saint are attributed to Andrea da Bologna, as well as frescoes in a passage between chapels in the right nave.

The Upper Church, finished in 1253, also has famous frescoes: In the transept and choir are a Crucifixion, three scenes from the Life of the Virgin, and four Evangelists (on the ceiling) by Cimabue. On the north wall are scenes from Genesis by Torriti and his followers and by the Roman school; and on the south wall scenes from the Life and Passion of Christ by the school of Cimabue, by a follower of Rusiti, and by the Roman school. The Ascension on the entrance wall is by the great leader of the Roman school of painting, Pietro Cavallini. Also on the wall of the Upper Church is the great St. Francis series which has occasioned such volumes of speculation among art historians. The first and last three frescoes in the series have been identified as by the painter of the altarpiece representing St. Cecilia in the Uffizi Gallery and known as the St. Cecilia Master. The rest are to be attributed to painters of the Roman school.

The town of Assisi also possesses the Church of Santa Maria della Minerva, whose portico of Corinthian columns was perhaps the work of the brothers Caesius, of the time of Augustus; the Cathedral San Rufino, finished in 1140, with a façade decorated with three rose-windows; and the Church of Santa Chiara, in the Gothic style, built about 1260 by Filippo da Campello, with frescoes of the school of Giotto.

At the side of the town is the Church of Santa Maria degli Angeli (begun in 1569 by G. Alessi, finished in 1640) which is surmounted by a lofty dome. It was built over the oratory of St. Francis.

**ASSYRIA.**—*Art.*—Assyria was originally inhabited by the Sumerians, but some time prior to Sargon of Akkad, the Assyrians, a mixed race connected ethnologically with the tribes of North Syria and linguistically with the Akkadians, invaded the Tigris Valley. During the second millennium they were constantly at war; dominated first by the Akkadians and then by the Kassites. The Assyrian Empire emerged about the year 1000 B.C. and continued down to the fall of Nineveh, 612 B.C. It was prolonged under Chaldean rule down to the time of the Persian invasion under Cyrus, 539 B.C.

During the period prior to the rule of Assurnasirpal, Assyrian art was slowly forming. When the Assyrians migrated to the Mesopotamian region they found and assumed the already developed art of the Sumerians, but invested it with their own cultural character. There are two early reliefs, one in terracotta, the other in stone, which although iconographically related to Sumer are none the less Assyrian in style. The enameled-tie technique of this period is closely related to Egypt and the Mediterranean and the seal style to Syro-Hittite rather than Sumerian art.

The art of Assyria began its great era with the reigns of Assurnasirpal (885-860) and Shalmaneser II (860-825) and reached its zenith under Assurbanipal (668-626) declining under the Second Babylonian Empire.

*Architecture.*—We owe our knowledge of Assyrian architecture as well as art to the excavations of Layard at Nineveh (Kuyunjik) and Nimrud (Kalakh) and of Place at Khorsabad. Assyrian architecture achieved its completest expression in the palace complex. Although the Assyrians were not as limited by the lack of wood and stone as were the Sumerians they constructed their buildings almost completely of sun-dried brick, except for the substructure and the decorative facings. The outstanding constructional feature of the Assyrian building was the vault which is continued in the East down to modern times as an indigenous type. Because of the scarcity of wood and stone a columnar style was never developed. We can imagine the appearance of these vaulted and domed buildings from a relief of the time of Sennacherib found at Nimrud. The palace itself was a fortress and was contiguous with the town fortifications making it accessible from both the exterior and interior of the town. It consisted of rectangular units grouped around a series of courtyards and divided as are modern eastern palaces of India, Persia and Turkey into a Seraglio containing the king's quarters and court, a Harem containing the women's quarters, and a Khan containing the offices and servants' quarters. The rooms and long corridors were probably vaulted and the walls partially decorated with alabaster reliefs. The façade, faced with glazed tile and sculpture, was the most imposing feature of the structure. The arched entrances were flanked by colossal winged human-headed bulls. The palace proper could be entcred either through these gates or by means of the lateral ramps which were used for vehicles. The Zigurat or temple was part of the palace complex. See *Zigurat*.

Group of Buildings: Kouioundjik (Nineveh). (Layard, *Monuments,* pl. 17.)

View of an Assyrian Palace. (Layard, *Monuments,* pl. 40.)

The important architectural monuments begin with the moving of the capital from Nineveh to Nimrud about 880 B.C. by Assurnasirpal who rebuilt the city, constructing a canal, a city wall and a large palace. Shalmaneser III (859-824) rebuilt the fortifications of Assur with a double wall, giving the inner command of the outer, a construction which became the subsequent type of city fortification. In Khorsabad the great palace of Sargon has been excavated and serves as a model for our conception of Assyrian building. Nineveh contains the remains of three palaces, those ot Sennacherib (705-681), Esarhaddon (681-668) and Assurbanipal (668-626).

Khorsabad: Single gate. (Perspective view after the scale drawing by Thomas.)

The Assyrian building depended for its effect upon the bold massing of block-like units, upon the flat bare wall with intervals of flashing color and friezes of alabaster and upon the dominating height of the ziggarat. It was a mixture of brutal power and delicate refinement.

For the palaces, see *Babylon, Nimrud.*

Bronze Lion from the Palace of Sargon, Khorsabad. (Louvre.)

*Sculpture.*—Assyrian sculpture begins with the eleventh century with a bas-relief cut in the natural rock near one of the sources of the Tigris during the reign of Tiglath-Pileser I, c. 1060. But in reality Assyrian sculpture begins with the buildings of Assurnasirpal at Nimrud. Most Assyrian sculpture is confined to bas-reliefs which covered the palace walls. Among the figures which appear most frequently is the winged human-headed bull as guardian of the gate. This type can be traced to early Sumerian seal-cylinders and it is only reasonable to assume that similar figures were an important element of Sumerian architecture. This monster is a composite figure with human head, wings, and a bull or lion's body. Statues in the round are extremely rare and in those extant examples fully clothed.

The subjects which recur constantly in the palaces of Nimrud, Nineveh and Khorsabad are the events in the king's life. The sculptors represented him variously occupied—directing building operations, dispensing justice, hunting wild beasts, commanding his army, contending in battle or sacrificing to the gods. Around the king are shown his officers, soldiers and servants. These bas-reliefs have a strong narrative character especially in the later periods. Some of these may appear monotonous to us due to the multiplication of formula-figures, a characteristic of all Assyrian art which apparently tried to impress by an endless repetition. They are circumscribed also by traditionalism in the rendering of space and the figure. The figures are always in one plane with no attempt at perspective although there is an overlapping of figures in later works. The single figure was conceived diagrammatically with profile head and feet, and frontal shoulders. Similar conventions are to be seen in the treatment of arms and hands. The human types are restricted to single formula with social rank designated by size, dress, beard and hair. The facial type is consistent throughout, with curved nose, flaring nostrils, heavy eyebrows, curled beard, thick lips, high cheek bones and bulging

Assurbanipal in his Chariot. (Louvre.)

Assurbanipal Hunting. (British Museum.)

eyes. The development of Assyrian bas-relief sculpture as a whole is from a hierarchical and formal symbolism to a naturalistic narrative.

Hunting Dogs of Assurbanipal. (British Museum.)

The reliefs of Assurnasirpal's palace at Nimrud are extremely flat, with single large symbolic figures covering the entire vertical surface and repeated in endless horizontal rows. The large mass of the body is simple and monumental while the details are chiseled with extreme precision. The characters do not take part in a narrative action but are performing ritualistic acts. The mixture of facile execution and formalized posture and gesture points to an archaistic art whose origin is probably in the highly developed art of Sumeria. The script explaining the scenes is cut indiscriminately across the surface and figures. The limestone statue of Assurnasirpal with its powerful simple mass and its very fine rendering of details in hair, beard and dress is reminiscent of the Sumerian works of Gudea; the Assyrian is more impressive but has not the beauty or fineness of the earlier work.

The two major works of the time of Shalmaneser III (859-824) belong

Wild Goats. (British Museum.)

to the transitional period. The bronze repousse gate-bands from Balawat employ the formal repetition of the previous period but the narration of a royal military campaign presented problems of naturalistic representation which destroyed the symbolic art of Assurnasirpal. Landscape is already suggested but still in an abstract manner, while the figures continue to follow each other in single file. The "Black Obelisk" presents the homage of Jehu, Omrite of Israel in a heraldic and symbolic manner.

The reliefs of Sargon at Khorsabad are of softer alabaster and in their major characteristics are a reversion to the art of Assurnasirpal, except for a greater slenderness of proportion and refinement of modeling, losing thereby a goodly measure of the latter's impressive power. Under Sennacherib naturalism clearly comes to the fore; the figures become smaller in relation to the surface, the scenes become more crowded, the action becomes more animated. There is an increased interest in naturalism and genre. Instead of a processional repetition there is the beginning of the unified scene with a natural locale rather than an abstract space. In general both the reliefs of Sargon and Sennacherib are higher than those of Assurnasirpal.

The greatest products of Assyrian sculpture are the reliefs of Assurbanipal from Nimrud. Here the scenes are highly developed and complicated in movement and composition. There is no longer any repetition but instead a very fertile invention of naturalistic incident. In those depicting his Arabian campaign we see struggling groups, charging horsemen, overturned char-

Hunting the Wild Ass. (British Museum.)

iots, slaughtered men, and in general all the blood and thunder of war. The hunting scenes contain a remarkable realism in the description of animals—dogs, horses, mules and lions. They have all the variety of spirited action. The background is again clear and abstract. Against this bare surface the fine animal silhouettes create noteworthy pictures. The "Dying Lioness" of this series with its tragic and doomed power is worthy of its fame. The Banquet Scene of Assurbanipal and his wife, with its exquisite rendering of the overhanging vine, of costume and furniture is a fine work but it lacks the vitality of the more virile subjects. In the sculpture of this period the art of Assyria reached its height. The

Lion and Lioness in a Park. (British Museum.)

richness of invention, the fineness of execution, together with an ornamental archaism produced a style never again equalled.

In the succeeding dynasty, the Second Empire of Babylon, under Nebuchadnezzar, there was a fabulous revival of culture and art. Babylon was rebuilt with unsurpassed pomp and sumptuousness. However the only monument excavated is the Ishtar Gate, forty feet high and completely covered by an enameled-brick relief. This brilliantly colored surface is constructed of single non-autonomous bricks, a technique new to this time. Although achieving a greater richness of color this art is a stylized and devitalized form of the previous high period.

The outstanding characteristics of Assyrian sculpture are its impressive power, its brutality, its realism and its refined execution.

*Minor and Industrial Arts.*—The seal-cylinders develop from very rudimentary designs to complicated narratives, after the introduction of the drill, but they never equal the beauty and intricacy of the earlier Sumerian seals.

If one judges of it by the remains of the oldest Assyrian tombs of Warka and of Mougheir, metallurgy was already strongly advanced in the early times of the Sumerian civilisation. According to the excavations of Botta, Layard and Place, the Sumerians seem to have made great use of iron. They used it before the Egyptians. Now, to reduce iron needs an industry already well advanced. The Sumerians and the Assyrians were near to the legendary country of the Chalybes, near the Caucasus, where the ancients placed the origin of metallurgy. Iron was used for arms and agricultural instruments; bronze for luxury objects.

The finest metal work comes from the Lake Wan region where many pieces of bronze were found; a bull's head, a sphinx and a round repoussé shield. The bronze bowls from Nimrud were probably imported from Phoenicia. After the time of Sennacherib bronze casting became common.

The prophets of Israel often inveighed against the luxury of Babylon. Sometimes one can reconstruct some of the pieces of royal furniture of Sumer and especially of Assyria, thanks to the numerous picture documents which are found in the Assyrian bas-reliefs. Wood, metal, bronze or gold, and ivory enriched luxurious furniture. Ivory, from India or Africa, was used in the making of many small objects. Some ivories, of very able workmanship, are in the British Museum; here, too, are quantities of small objects—toilet articles, arms, fragments of all kinds, from which the luxury trade of Assyria is known.

Finally, though nothing remains of Assyrian textiles, we learn from the bas-reliefs what the materials in which the wealthy people clothed themselves must have been like. In fact, the bas-reliefs show the embroidered ornamentation, which adorned the stuffs, very clearly. The decoration strongly recalls that of the bronze vases. Geometric design combines with lively figures. Parallel bands mingle with rosettes, palm-leaves, and animals or men confronting each other, or facing towards a sacred tree. These motifs continued beyond the Assyrian world. They were found very much later among the Persians, whence they passed into our western art.

Bibliography: Botta, P. E. and Flandin, E., *Monuments de Ninive.* 1849-50.—Layard, A. H., *Nineveh and Babylon.* 1857.— Place, V., *Ninive et L'Assyrie.* 1867-1870.—Perrot, G. and Chipiez, C., *History of Art in Chaldaea and Assyria* (trans.). 1884.—Heuzey, L. A., *Les Origines Orientales de l'Art.* 1891-1915. Olmstead, A. T. E., *History of Assyria.* 1923.—Schaefer, H. and Andrae, W., *Die Kunst des Alten Orients.* 1925. —Contenau, G., *Manuel d'Archeologie Orientale.* 1927-31.—Hall, H. R. H., *Ancient History of Near East.* 8th ed. 1932.

**ASSYRIAN (Temple).**—See Zigurat.

**ASTRAGAL.**—Relief moulding, which separates the shaft of the Ionic column from the capital.

**ATHENA LEMNIA.**—See Acropolis of Athens; also Pl. 20, Vol. I.

**— OF THE PARTHENON.**—See Acropolis of Athens; also Pl. 23, Vol. I.

**ATHENODOROS.**—See Laocoön.

**ATHENS.**—Legend attributes to the Cecropids the foundation of Athens. From the 16th Century B.C. the Acropolis rock was inhab-

Embroidery from the Upper Part of an Assyrian King's Cloak.

ited. Of this primitive civilisation, contemporary with the Mycenean period, there remain fragments of a wall, and some traces of a royal palace or megaron, discovered under

Assyrian Carved Plaque. (After Perrot and Chipiez.)

the foundations of the Hekatompedon. Between the time from the end of the seventh to the beginning of the sixth century B.C. the Hekatompedon or "Old Temple" was erected. It was dedicated to Athena. That the Hekatompedon was destroyed by the Persians is generally agreed. (See Acropolis of Athens).

Acropolis Museum, Athens: Head of Kore.

Soon the Acropolis was covered with those marvellous buildings, some of which have come down to us, defying the ravages of centuries and the vandalism of men. (See Acropolis of Athens.)

On the slopes of the Acropolis, the Athenians built several monuments. To the north, they fitted up some caves as sanctuaries. On the southern slope, they built the

Choragic Monument of Lysicrates (see Lysicrates), the Theatre of Dionysos, the monument of Thrasyllos (destroyed during the war of

Greek Vase Painting.

1826), the Asclepieum, the Odeon of Herodes Atticus, and the Stoa of Eumenes.

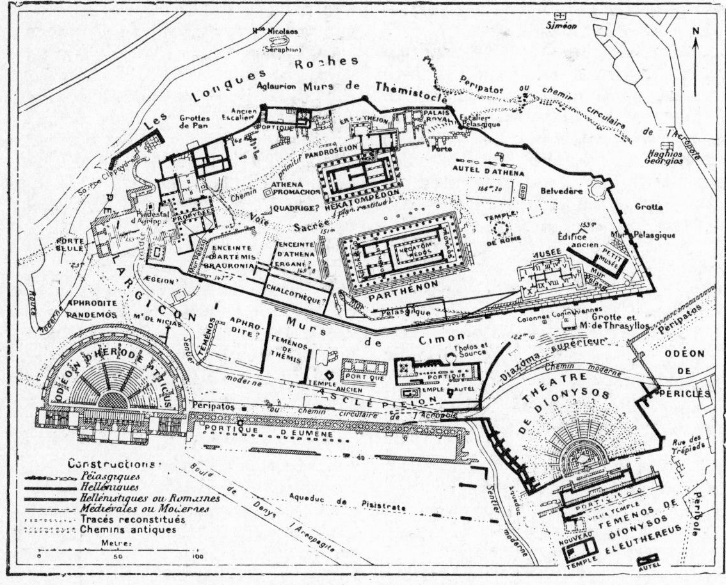


Athens: Plan of the Acropolis.

To the north stretches the cemetery, and the pottery market (agora—open meeting place for the

Athens: Reconstructed View of the Acropolis.

transaction of business), the Dipylon, the Theseum, etc.

To the east of the agora, in the quarter where the merchants have their shops, is the Roman agora (built about 12 B.C.), which communicated with a small square in the middle of which is the "Tower of the Winds," also known as the Horologium of Andronicus, who built it for measuring time internally by a water-clock, and externally by sundial; while the roof, in the form of an inverted pyramid, was formerly provided with a weather-vane. The building, on a stylobate of three steps, is octagonal, and its eight sides face the more important points of the compass. Every side bears the name of a wind (Boreas, Kaikias, Apeliotes, Euros, Notas, Lips, Zephyrus, Skyron) and is accompanied by a figure in bas-relief.

Parallel to the agora, is the Portico of Hadrian, or, more exactly, the Library of Hadrian, of which some ruins are left—some walls and columns, which formerly surrounded the magnificent buildings which the Emperor Hadrian had built in this town, which was one of his favorite abodes. Pausanias has left a description of it in which he praises the portico of a hundred columns of Phrygian marble. The Arch or Gate of Hadrian is elegantly surmounted by a small building, with columns bearing a pediment—the whole in Pentellic marble. Near this arch stand the columns of the Olympieum, finished by Hadrian which was the largest

Athens, Acropolis: Victory and Heifer.

Athenian temple (107 metres 75 in. length). It contained a colossal statue of Olympian Zeus in gold and ivory. To the south of the Olympieum in the bed of the Ilissus, a single rock is bathed by the little cascades of Callirrhoë Fountain, the sacred source whence water, needed for the rites of worship, was taken.

Athens: The Parthenon. (Southwest corner.)

As for the Panathenaic stadium, (begun about 33 B.C., finished later by Herodes Atticus, later still ruined by builders who used its marbles) it has been restored; it was set up again in 1895 by a wealthy amateur, M. Averof, for the Olympic games.

Acropolis: Dispute of Athena and Poseidon.

All the buildings that we have enumerated, contained treasures of sculpture, statues and bas-reliefs. A great part of those which have been found are now in the museum.

See Pls. 19, 30, Vol. I.

Bibliography: G. Fongere, *Athenes*, Series, "Villes d'artcélèbres." Paris, 1912. C. H. Weller "Athens and its Monuments," New York, 1913.

Athens: The Parthenon. (Northeast corner.)

**ATHENS.**—Medieval Architecture. See Byzantine Architecture, Middle Period, Greek School.

**ATHOS (Mt.).**—See Mount Athos.

Athens: Tower of the Winds.

**ATLANTE.**—Statue of a male figure corresponding to a Caryatid. The name "Atlante" comes from Atlas, the giant who carried the sky on his shoulders. They are also called "telamons" (word derived from Greek). While the Caryatids (statues of women) are nearly always clothed, and their pose is calm and noble, the Atlantes are always nude and their attitude expresses violent effort.

**ATREUS (Treasury of).**—See Mycenæ.

**ATRIUM.**—Originally the central room of a Roman house in which the hearth was built. As houses grew larger the hearth and kitchen were removed to more distant locations, leaving the atrium to serve as a formal reception room and official center of family life. The atrium was a court with a marble basin or cistern (*impluvium*) in the middle, with an opening in the roof (*compluvium*) directly above it to let in the rain.

**ATTICA.**—See Greece (Sculpture; Terra cottas).

**AUBIN.**—See Saint-Aubin.

**AUDENARDE.**—Old Flemish town which formerly produced famous tapestries. It has a magnificent Hôtel de Ville in the third (late) Gothic style, built in 1525 by Van Peede and G. de Ronde.

AUDENARDE. (City Hall.)

**AUDRAN (Gérard).**—French engraver, born at Lyon, 2nd August 1640; died in Paris, 26th July 1703. He was first the pupil of his father, the first Claude Audran, then of his uncle, Charles. From the first period of his life date some engravings signed G. Audran, which are generally attributed to him, but which might be the work of his uncle, Gérard, or of his brother, Germain. Audran next went to Paris where he became acquainted with Le Brun and engraved the *Triumph of Constantine,* in four plates, after this painter (1666). Wishing to go and study the Italian masters on their own soil, he was given the means for it by Colbert, at the request of Le Brun, and spent three years in Rome. There he copied some paintings, made many drawings from the antique, and some engravings after Raphael (the Genii of the ceiling of the Farnesina, in 14 plates) and after Domenichino (*David Dancing before the Ark, Esther and Ahasuerus, Judith Showing the People* the *Head of Holophernes*). He also engraved a fairly large number of portraits, among them those of Dr. Samuel Sorbière, of Clement V, and of the secret chamberlain, Jordan Hilling. During the whole of this period, he perfected himself in the art of drawing; he took to combining on the same plate, engraving, etching and dry-point, and when he returned to France, recalled by Colbert, he had acquired the manner which he used in the big engravings to which he owes his fame.

On his return, Le Brun obtained for him accommodation at the Gobelins, the title of Engraver in Ordinary to the King, and the commission of engraving his *Battles of Alexander,* in four plates of exceptional dimensions. Into this work, to which he devoted eight years, Gérard Audran put the whole measure of his talent, and it is these engravings which have made him one of the masters of the French school. He likewise engraved *Pyrrhus Saved,* after Poussin; and became a member of the Académie Royale de Peinture, 31st March 1674. In 1675 he paid a visit to Rome and there engraved the *Cardinal Virtues,* after Domenichino. Afterwards, he set up his studio in Paris, rue Saint-Jacques, at the sign of the Deux Piliers d'or, and there became publisher of engravings (1680).

Among his best known works, one might mention: the *Martyrdom of St. Proteus*; the *Martyrdom of St. Lawrence*; the *Chariot of the Sun,* after Le Sueur; the *Plague of Ægina,* after Mignard; and the *Triumph of Truth,* after Poussin, which is considered his masterpiece, and one of the masterpieces of engraving.

He has left a work entitled: *The Proportions of the Human Body,* measured according to the most beautiful figures of antiquity (30 engravings; published in 1683; reproduced in 1855). Among his numerous pupils, the most distinguished were Duchange, Dorigny, Desplaces, Nicolas Henri Tardieu.

BIBLIOGRAPHY: Vivant-Denon, *Noticè sur Gérard Audran.*—M. Gatteaux, *Considérations sur la gravure en taille-douce et sur Gérard Audran.* Paris, 1850.—G. Duplessis, *Notice sur G. Audran.* Lyon, 1858.—P. de Bandricourt, *Le peintre—gravure français,* Vol. II.—Vicomte H. Delaborde, *La gravure,* p. 202 et seq. Paris.—Passeron, *Notice sur Gérard Audran.*—Edm. Michel, *Les Audran, peintres et graveurs.* Orléans, 1884 (genealogical essay).

**AUGSBURG.**—City of Bavaria. During the Renaissance it was the centre of a school of painting which included Burgkmair and the elder Holbein.

**AUGUSTUS (Arch of).**—See Nîmes; Perugia.

**— (Palace of).**—See Rome.

**AUTUN.**—Autun (ancient Augustodunum) was very prosperous under Roman domination. Destroyed in 270, it was rebuilt by Constantine Chlore in 307 and became one of the residences of the Burgundian princes and of the first Dukes of Burgundy. The town is interesting because of the beautiful remains of Roman monuments. Of the ancient Roman theatre, hardly anything remains but the site, where one can see the shape, under the talus, and some vestiges of the foundations. The Porte St. André is composed of two large arcades, crowned by a gable of six little arcades; on the exterior side, a decorated projection with a tower was converted into the Church of St André. The Porte d'Arroux (Porta Senonica, Porte de Sens), is formed of two large arcades, two little ones for pedestrians, and a gallery of ten arcades, three of which have been demolished. It is built of superimposed stones without cement. The name of "the Temple of Janus" was given, in the 16th century, to some beautiful Roman ruins on the right bank of the Ternin.

AUTUN: THE LAST JUDGMENT. (Tympanum of the cathedral.)

The Cathedral of Saint-Lazare, built from 1120 to 1178, was restored at the end of the 15th century by Cardinal Rolin, who added some chapels and the central tower, with its beautiful *flèche.* Like other Burgundian Romanesque churches, including the great abbey church at Cluny, Autun was roofed by a barrel vault above a clerestorey. The crossing had an octagonal lantern and there were low western towers. There was much use of fluted pilasters. The sculpture is famous, particularly the *Last Judgment* of the tympanum, by Master Gilbert.

**AUVERGNE (Churches of).**—See Pl. 44, Vol. I.

**AVANZO (Jacopo).**—Paduan painter of the 2nd half of the 14th century, pupil and collaborator of Altichiero. Formerly thought to have come from Verona, due to confusion with another painter, Jacopo da Verona, who painted in Padua also.

BIBLIOGRAPHY: See literature on Altichiero, and Giuseppe Gadego, *Il pittore Jacopo da Verona,* 1355-1442, Treviso, 1906.

**— (Jacopo da Bologna).**—Bolognese painter of the trecento, contemporary with Vitale, Simone and Cristoforo da Bologna. A small signed Crucifixion by him is in the Galleria Colonna, Rome. Also in the Academy in Venice is a signed panel, dated 1367. There are two other panels in the Bologna Pinacoteca. Jacopo also had a share in the frescoes finished in 1404 in the Chiesa di Mezzarata, near Bologna; under one of these appears the signature "Jacobus fecit."

BIBLIOGRAPHY: A. Brach, *Giotto's Schule in der Romagna,* p. 95 ff.

**AVIGNON.**—Probably built by the Phœnicians of Marseilles, Avignon was a flourishing town under Roman domination. None of her Roman buildings remain. The materials of which they were composed were used for other buildings in the 12th and 13th centuries. *The Cathedral,* the *Bridge,* and the *Abbey of St. Rulf* date from the 12th century.

AVIGNON: PALACE OF THE POPES.

The *Cathedral of Notre Dame des Doms* was built towards the middle of the 12th century. There is a fine porch to the façade; and over the door are remains of frescoes by Simone Martini of Siena (14th century), representing, in the tympanum, Cardinal Leccano at the feet of the Virgin, and, on the pediment, God the Father and two angels. Over the choir is a magnificent dome, the lantern of which is ornamented with columns of Corinthian pattern. A beautiful Romanesque chair served as the Papal Throne. The Cathedral also contains the tomb of John XXII (restored in 1825 and 1840); and a statue of St. Peter, by Puget.

*The Palace of the Popes* is both a palace and a fortress. Externally it is composed of rough walls, flanked by six square towers, and defended by arcades with machicolations. The general plan of this immense building is very irregular: buildings were added according to the needs of defence. It was the second of the Avignon Popes, John XXII, who began to build, but nothing remains of his work, for his successor had it destroyed. This Pope, Benedict XII, and his successor, Clement VI, built the present Palace. From the pontificate of Benedict XXII, date the Tour de la Camagne, the Papal chapel, the "salle brûlée," the cloisters, and the Towers Trouillas, des Anges, de la Glacière and Saint-Jean. Clement VI built the Tour Saint-Laurent, the magnificent Audience Chamber, the principal entrance, and the new Papal chapel, in a bold Gothic style. Clement VI, less austere than Benedict XII, had the Palace decorated with sculptures and paintings. The most celebrated of these decorations were in the Audience Chamber, which had beautiful frescoes attributed to Simone Martini, who came to Avignon in 1338, and died before he had finished the paintings. They have largely perished. Only the Prophets which decorate a part of the vault remain. Fine frescoes are to be found also in the Chapelle Saint-Martial, by Matteo Giovanetti, in the Tour de la Garde-Robe (artist and period unknown), and in the Chapelle Saint-Jean.

Not content with having built a solid fortress for their residence, the Popes encircled the town with a girdle of ramparts, five walls of little stones carefully put together, with machicolations and crenellations and flanked with square towers and round towers at equal distances. These fortifications were begun by Clement VI, continued under Innocent VI (from Saint-Roch to Saint Lazare), and under Clement VII (from Saint Roch to the Porte de l'Ouille, round towers). The ramparts were restored by Viollet-le-Duc, and, in our own time, new gateways have been let in, and those of Ouille and Imberts destroyed.

**— (School of).**—See Pl. 4, Vol. II.

**ÁVILA (Spain).**—*The Ramparts.*—The fortified walls, built in the last years of the 11th century, form an irregular quadrangle of well over one mile, with 88 granite towers, nearly all half cylindrical, and eight gateways. It is one of the finest mediæval fortifications.

*The Cathedral of San Salvador* was begun in 1091, modified in 1252, and restored in 1280 and in 1290. The monumental doorway, added in the 16th century, is decorated with mediocre sculptures.

The northern doorway, decorated with statues and bas-reliefs of the 14th century, is, on the contrary, of great interest. The church is divided into nave and two aisles. The nave and transept are very high. The apse, with its double ambula-

tory, its crown of chapels, the bays of the "Capilla Mayor," is a robust model of Romanesque architecture. This apse, built in the 13th century, with archaic forms on a new and learned plan, is enclosed in an enormous fortified tower, as in a cupboard. The "Capilla Mayor" contains a fine altar-piece (scenes from the Life of Christ), painted from 1499 to 1508, by Pedro Berruguete, Juan de Borgona and Santa Cruz.

*The Church of San Vicente* is situated outside the city walls. It is a very fine example of 12th century Romanesque architecture in Spain. The fine western façade has a thirteenth century portal with two doors, the pillars of which are decorated with statues of Apostles, in the Burgundian style. The south doorway, dating from the 12th century, is decorated with statues some of which—such as the *Annunciation* —recall the statues on the porch of the Abbey of Vézelay. San Vicente has Cistercian nave vaults: the interior consists of three aisles, a transept, and three apses, in the Romanesque and transitional style. The tomb of St. Vincent and his two sisters is a magnificent 12th century sarcophagus, supported by delicate little columns, and ornamented with remarkable reliefs representing the Martyrdom of the Saints, under a flowery Gothic canopy (1465).

See Pl. 2, Vol. II.

**AZAY-LE-RIDEAU.**—The Château of Azay-le-Rideau takes its name from Hugues le' Rideau, owner of the fief in the 13th century. It was built by Gilles Berthelot and his wife Phillipe Lebès, whose initials can be read on the friezes, from 1518 to 1529. Francis I, after having confiscated it from Gilles Berthelot, lived in it often, and there set up his coat of arms, the salamander, and his motto:

Azay-le-Rideau: The Château.

"Ung seul désir." The château is built on a very simple plan: two blocks of buildings are united at a right angle. The exterior façades are unostentatious, with round turrets, and a large round tour; the façades looking on to the court-yard are pierced with high windows—those of the top storey have a pediment. The entrance doorway and façade are richly decorated with columns, pilasters, friezes, pediments and armorial bearings. It is thought that the work was directed by Etienne Rousseau, an architect of the district. Azay-le-Rideau has simple elegance and harmonious proportions, and is built in pleasing white stone.

**AZTEC ART.**—See America (Archæology).

**AZULEJO (Der. from Arab azuleich, a small burnished stone).** —Spanish term for undecorated or decorated, monochrome or polychrome glazed tile. The repertory of ornament includes mainly geometric, floral, vegetable, animal, armorial and sometimes epigraphic motifs. From the late 15th century onward religious subjects were depicted. Toward the end of the 18th century the representation of human figures in picturesque contemporary costumes was introduced. Azulejos are and were usually employed for pavements and wallfacings, but sometimes also purely decoratively on the exterior of buildings as for instance those designed in 1504 by Francisco Nicoluso Pisano for the archivolt of the portal of the Convent of Santa Paula in Seville. Though it is assumed that azulejos were introduced in Spain under the Almohades dynasty, as early as in the 12th century, the first datable examples in Southern Spain are of the 14th. During the 14th and 16th centuries tile manufacture flourished in Andalusia, principally in Seville, as well as in Eastern Spain, Valencia and Catalonia, imitating probably Valencian models, produced a series of white and cobalt-blue tiles, known as rajolas, remarkable on account of their technical execution and variety of ornament. Noteworthy are the azulejos with lustre decoration for which there was a constant demand in other countries during the 14th and 15th centuries. In the 16th centuries the fabrique of Talavera produced tiles decorated in blue and yellow which were to influence the tile production of Mexico. The manufacture of Azulejos subsists until the present day, Talavera de la Reina, Valencia and Triana, a suburb of Seville, being reputed for the excellence of their kilns.

Bibliography: *Enciclopedia universal ilustrada europeo-americana.* Barcelona, 1905-1930, Vol. VI, Art. *Azulejo.*—J. Gestoso y Perez, *Historia de los barros vidriados sevillanos desde sus origenes hasta nuestros dias.* Seville, 1913.—J. Font i Gumá, *Rajolas* valencianas i catalanas. Vilanova y Geltrú, 1905.—L. Williams, *The arts and crafts of older Spain,* Vol. II. London, 1907. —E. Atlee Buttler, *Spanish majolica in the coll. of the Hispanic Society of America,* Hispanic notes and monographs. New York, 1915.—A. W. Frothingham, *Catalogue of hispano-moresque pottery in the coll. of the Hisp. Soc. of Am.,* Hispanic notes and monographs. New York, 1935.—Burlington Magazine Monographs, No. 2, London, 1927: R. R. Tatlock and others, *Spanish Art;* A. van de Put, *Ceramics.*

# B

**BAALBEK.**—A small Syrian town, built on the ruins of the old Heliopolis. Occupied successively by the Greeks, the Romans and the Arabs, it possesses famous ruins of buildings erected by these divers

Baalbek: Temple of Bacchus.

civilizations. A Roman wall, 4 kilometres long, surrounds the town, the Arabs added a crenellated wall with towers. There are imposing ruins of Greek temples. Of the largest, the Temple of Jupiter, probably dating from the Augustan age (89 metres by 49), there remain only six columns, in the midst of enormous blocks of stone. The small temple of Bacchus (83 metres by 36) still has its cella intact, also a large number of columns, with a part of the frieze, the cornice and the roof. The round temple, very ornate, is in a good state of preservation. See Pl. 30, Vol. I.

Bibliography: Dawkins and Wood: *The Ruins of Baalbek.*—Cassas, *Voyage pittoresque en Syrie.* Paris, 1799.

**BABYLON.**—There is no ancient Asiatic town which has a greater renown and of which fewer traces remain. It is this which gives it such an atmosphere of romance. In the confused mass of overturned bricks which marks its site on the banks of the Euphrates, it is impossible to trace the plan of this old capital of Chaldea. But excavations have never been carried out there with such method and persistence as at Nineveh or Khorsabad. It seems now that the old town of Babylon, or royal city, had been surrounded by a rampart of 13,000 metres, that this rampart was square in shape, and that the walls faced the cardinal points. To the north was the Temple of Belus; in the centre, the royal Palace, with its hanging gardens. Around this central town, a second town developed, much more vast, of which the perimeter was, according to Herodotus, 480 stadia, that is to say nearly 55 kilometres, three times the size of present-day Paris. Herodotus had visited the town at a time of its decadence; the ramparts, especially, had been destroyed by the Persians. "The houses are of three and four storeys," he says, in speaking, doubtless, of the royal city, "the streets are straight, and intersected by others which lead to the river. Facing this, they have made, in the wall built along by the river, little bronze gates by which one descends to its banks. There are as many of them as there are cross-roads." It is not known for certain whether a tunnel united the two banks of the Euphrates; but it is known, on the other hand, that a stone bridge crossed the River, which was not less than 180 metres in width and 4 to 5 metres in depth. Ctesias saw Babylon a century after Herodotus. His statement coincides in the main with that of his predecessor, although it seems sometimes to have a certain exaggeration. In fact, Ctesias gives a circumstantial description of Nineveh which, in his time, was absolutely destroyed. Xenophon, when he passed quite close to the ruins of Nineveh, did not mention any important ruin. Herodotus makes out that the enclosing walls of Babylon were 200 royal cubits high, that is to say, 104 metres 50. Perhaps he exaggerates a little; but doubtless he is not far wrong, because he gives, as the width of this wall, 50 royal cubits (26 metres); now at Khorsabad the wall was 24 metres. These thick brick walls must have resisted the use of battering rams which the Assyrian bas-reliefs show us were used in the besieging of towns. The walls were crenellated and machicolated, and each gateway was flanked by two towers.

See Assyrian Art, Sumerian Art.

**BACCHIACCA.** — Francesco d'Ubertino, called Bacchiacca. Florentine painter, 1494-1557. A follower of Perugino and Franciabigio. His was essentially a small, decorative art, in which he displayed much imagination and grace. In addition to his paintings, which are widely scattered in public and private collections, the Uffizi in Florence possesses tapestries after his designs.

**AGNOLO (Baccio d').**—Florentine architect and sculptor (1462-1543). One of the most important architects during the flowering of the Renaissance in Italy. He imitated Cronaca, with more simplicity. The Serristori and Bartolini palaces are by him; also others, less well-known, such as the Palazzo Levi, and the Palazzo Roselli del Turco. He built the Campanile of San Spirito, and reconstructed that of San Miniato (1518). Some designs on the pavement of the Duomo are attributed to him.

**BACCIO BIGGIO (Nanni di).**—Florentine sculptor of the end of the 16th century. Follower of Michelangelo.

**— DELLA PORTA.**—See Bartolommeo (Fra).

**BACHOT (Jacques).**—French sculptor. Born about 1470, died about 1540. One of the masters of the flourishing Champagne school at the beginning of the 16th century. In 1500, he worked at Joinville, on the lower parts of the tombs of the Bishop of Metz, of Charles de Lorraine, of the Seigneur of Joinville, Ferry II, and of his wife, the Queen of Sicily: these monuments were destroyed in 1793. In 1506, he was commissioned to decorate, with *Virtues,* the sarcophagus of the tombs of the Ponchers (Louvre), for which the recumbent figures were sculptured twenty years afterwards by Guillaume Regnault of Touraine. Bachot made several statues for the Churches in Troyes. About 1525 he returned to Lorraine; for the Church of St. Nicholas-du-Port he made a *St. Nicholas* which is preserved, and especially a *Deposition,* which was famous for a long time. There were two sculptors of Troyes who bore the name of Bachot and were doubtless relations of Jacques: Marc, born about 1480, and Yvon, born about 1490.

BACHOT (JACQUES): THE VIRTUES. TOMB OF THE PONCHERS. (Louvre.)

**BACKHUYSEN (Ludolf).**—Dutch painter, 1631-1708. Author of seascapes, which show us the sea in tempestuous mood, with great gusts of wind and high waves.

**BACON (Peggy).**—Contemporary American graver and illustrator. Miss Bacon was born in Ridgefield, Connecticut, 2nd May 1895. Both of her parents were painters and she came naturally into an artistic inheritance. She studied under many different masters, gaining information and experience from such painters as Jonas Lie, John Sloan, Kenneth Hayes Miller, George Bellows, and Randall Davey. Three trips abroad taught her to observe the human traits which are characteristic of people all over the world. She married Alexander Brook, the well-known artist, and together these two have steadily climbed to the first ranks of their profession. Miss Bacon is the author of many children's stories, some of which appeared in the *Delineator*. Others were published in book form, including *The Lion-hearted Kitten and Other Stories, The Terrible Nuisance and Other Tales,* and *Mischief in Mayfield,* each illustrated in her own inimitable way. In addition to these she has written books of poetry and contributed to the *Americana Magazine* and the *New Yorker*. But perhaps better known are the many etchings and drypoints that she has made, giving brilliant insight into human affairs and peculiarities in a few well-disposed lines both sensitive and expressive. She has also used pastel to depict some well-known persons, particularly a few of the art critics that have written about her work, including Royal Cortissoz, Henry McBride, Heywood Broun, and Forbes Watson. These caricatures of the critics narrowly escaped being satirical, but what was omitted from the portraits was touched upon in the accompanying word pictures describing the subjects. She won an award at the Sesqui-Centennial Exposition in Philadelphia in 1926, and in 1934 was the recipient of a Guggenheim Fellowship. Outstanding examples of her work may be seen at the Metropolitan Museum of Art and the Whitney Museum of American Art in New York City.

BIBLIOGRAPHY: William Murrell, *Peggy Bacon,* Younger Artists Series, 1922.—For other bibliographical information see *The Index of Twentieth Century Artists* for October, 1934.

**BADAJOZ (Juan de).**—One of the most prominent architects of 16th century Spain and an adherent of Renaissance forms. In 1512 he superintended the work on the Cathedral of Leon. The fact that he was consulted in connection with the Cathedrals of Salamanca, 1512 and 1522, and of Seville, 1513, is proof of the high esteem in which he was held. He is known for the façade of San Marco of Leon, for the main chapels of the collegiate church of San Isidoro in the same city and for his designs and plans for the cloister of the Benedictine monastery of S. Zoil at Carrion de los Condes. A. Byne and M. Stapley say that this cloister, profuse in sculptural decoration, "has a typically Spanish note, —a sculpturesque conception of architecture, restless, but a marvel of execution."

BIBLIOGRAPHY: Thieme-Becker, 1908, Vol. II.—A. Byne and M. Stapley, *Spanish architecture of the sixteenth century.* New York, 1917.

**BADILE (Antonio).**—Painter of Verona (1518-1560). Pupil of Caroto.

**BAERTSON (Albert).**—Belgian painter, born in 1866.

**BAGDAD.**—See Moslem Art.

**BAGNACAVALLO (Bartolomeo Ramenghi, called).**—Bolognese painter, 1484-1542. Pupil of Francia. He went to Rome, and made a special study of Raphael, of whose works his are a striking imitation. (See the *Circumcision* in the Louvre, painted for the Corollo Chapel, at San Giacomo.) After his return to Bologna, he painted a great number of decorations in various churches, particularly at the Convent of San Michele in Bosco. A "Mannerist" painter of slight inspiration.

**BALDACHIN.**—A kind of canopy, in wood, metal or marble, decorated with sculpture and set up over an altar, throne, or doorway.

**BALDINI (Baccio).**—Italian Engraver (1436?-1487?). A certain number of rather dissimilar engravings have been attributed to him, and probably the works of several unknown artists have been grouped under his name. He may have helped Botticelli in three copperplate engravings of the *Monte Sancto di Dio* of Bettini (Florence, 1477), and in the 19 plates for the edition of the *Divine Comedy* (Florence, 1481).

BIBLIOGRAPHY: H. Delaborde, *La Gravure en Italie avant Marc-Antoine,* 1883.—L. Rosenthal, *La Gravure.* Paris, 1909.—A. M. Hind, *A History of Engraving and Etching.* London, 1923.

**BALDOVINETTI (Alesso).**—Painter and mosaicist, born in Florence 1425, died 1499. His school training is not indicated by documentary evidence, and little is known of his earliest activity. He probably was employed as a helper on the decoration of the church of S. Egidio in the Hospital of S. Maria Nuova, where Domenico Veneziano was working from 1439 to 1445 and Castagno from 1451. In 1448 Baldovinetti is listed among the members of the guild of painters in Florence. We know that in 1460 he received a small payment for figures at the high altar of S. Egidio and that in 1461 he finished a Story of the Virgin begun by Domenico.

His earliest extant work is the *Nativity* in the SS. Annunziata, 1460-62. Even in its ruined condition it reflects the special characteristics of his maturer art, particularly in the landscape, which was to be developed so notably in his Louvre Madonna. In 1463 he drew five heads and a *Nativity* for the intarsias in the sacristy of the Duomo. From 1466-73 date the Annunciation and Evangelists and fathers of the Church in the Portuguese Chapel in S. Miniato. The frescoes in the choir of Sta. Trinità, begun in 1471, are almost effaced. His altarpiece for Sta. Trinità, a Trinity with saints and angels, also of 1471, is now in the Academy. He was active in his later years at mosaic, and throughout his life, in common with most of his contemporaries, at the painting of chests, shields, banners, and designs for glass. In 1481 he executed a composition for a window at S. Agostino, Arezzo.

On stylistic grounds, few pictures are associated with his documented works, among which are three Madonnas, one in the Uffizi, one in the Louvre, and one in the Jacquemart-André, Paris; a *Crucifixion,* much damaged, in S. Marco; an *Annunciation* in the Uffizi; a *Resurrected Christ* in S. Pancrazio; and the profile portrait of a lady in the National Gallery, London. Three small pictures by Baldovinetti in the Museum of S. Marco, *The Marriage at Cana, Baptism,* and *Transfiguration,* belong to the series that Fra Angelico did for the sacristy of the SS. Annunziata and are dated 1448.

BIBLIOGRAPHY: G. Pierotti, *Ricordi di Alesso Baldovinetti.* Lucca, 1868.—Repert. f. Kst. w. XXV, 1902, p. 393 (Fabriczy, *Dokumente f. Annunziata-Fresko*); XXVIII, 1905, p. 540 (Fabriczy, *Memoriale des Francesco Baldovinetti*).—Berenson, *Study and Crit. of Ital. Art,* 1902.—H. Horne, Burlington Magazine, II, 1903, pp. 22, 167, *A Newly Discovered "Libro di Ricordi" of Alesso Baldovinetti;* VIII, 1905, p. 51 (Altar in S. Ambrogio).—Emilio Londi, Alesso Baldovinetti. Florence, 1907.

**BALDUCCI (Matteo).**—Umbro-Sienese painter, active first part of 16th century. Pupil of Pacchiarotto, assistant of Pintoricchio.

**BALDUNG GRIEN (Hans).**—1480-1545. German painter, pupil of Dürer, lived at Strassburg.

His best-known work is the high-altar of the Cathedral of Freiburg (Breisgau), executed from 1512 to 1516, which represents the Coronation of the Virgin, and, on the wings, the Annunciation, the Visitation, the Nativity, and the Flight into Egypt. He also painted two allegories (Basle Museum), representing Luxury and Death; and the *Adoration of the Magi* (Berlin Museum).

Hans Baldung, who knew Grünewald, sought like him for effects of dazzling and strange light; but his colour is harder, less mellow. The surname of Grien (grün, green) was given to him from the frequent use of the colour green in his pictures.

See Pl. 26, Vol. II.

BIBLIOGRAPHY: Terey, *Die Gemälde H. Baldungs.* Strassburg, 1896-1900.—Baumgarten, *Der Freiburger Hochaltar*—Strassburg, 1904. —Escherich, M.: *H. Baldung Grien-Bibliographie.* Strassburg, 1916.—Curjel, H., *H. Baldung Grien.* Munich, 1923.

**BALEN (Hendrik Van).**—Flemish painter (Antwerp, 1575-1632). He imitated Velvet Breughel with whom he often collaborated; he painted charming little figures in Breughel's landscapes. His colour is brilliant and a little commonplace. His best pictures are the *Rape of Europa* (Vienna), of which the landscape and the flowers are by Breughel; a *Diana at the Chase,* Dresden; and the *Banquet of the Gods,* Munich.

**BALL (Thomas).**—American sculptor (1819-1911), of Boston, author of numerous works, including many public monuments, of which the equestrian statue of Washington in the Public Gardens, Boston, is the most notable.

**BAMBINI (Niccolò).**—Venetian painter (1651-1736). He contributed, with Padovanino and Pietro Liberi, to the lightening of the gloomy colours used by painters during the period of decadence which succeeded Titian and Veronese, and prepared the way for the delightful colours of Tiepolo.

**BAMBOCHADE.**—Picture representing a gay or grotesque scene of family life; derived from the name of an Italian artist, Bamboche (Bamboccio), who made such scenes popular.

**BANCHI (Francesco di Antonio).**—Florentine painter, active middle of 15th century, pupil of Lorenzo Monaco.

**BANDINELLI (Baccio).**—Florentine sculptor (1488-1560). He emulated passionately the glory of Michelangelo. His lines and forms strive after the fine, tormented movements of the great master, but do not attain to Michelangelo's aesthetic realization. Bandinelli was the son of a worthy goldsmith who worked for the Medici. But after he had received his first teaching from his father, he turned towards monumental sculpture, in the grand manner. He worked in the studio of Francesco Rustici. So enthusiastic was he, that he made the peasants on his father's farm, at Pizzi di Monte near Prato, strip and pose for him. One of these first works was a colossal *Hercules* which became the subject of a derogative sonnet by Benvenuto Cellini.

BACCIO BANDINELLI: BAS-RELIEF. (Cathedral Museum, Florence.)

Some other works of Bandinelli's youth were a *Mercury,* sent to the King of France, which has disappeared, a *St. Peter* in the Duomo of Florence, an *Orpheus* which is an imitation of the *Apollo Belvedere,* a *Birth of the Virgin,* at Loreto, and a copy of the *Laocoön.*

His group of *Hercules and Caius* is especially well-known. It was ordered by the Medici as a fellow to Michelangelo's David on the Piazza della Signoria. The figure of Hercules looms like a huge butcher against the soft Florentine sky. The block of marble which had first of all been chosen by Michelangelo from the quarries of Carrara to make a *Samson*, and which had the misfortune to fall into the Arno (in trying to flee from the cruel hand of Bandinelli, according to Cellini), ended by being shaped into this monstrous body. The group caused so much criticism that its author appealed to the ducal tribunal. However, they left it in position, and it still attracts attention today.

In spite of his reputed ill-nature, he managed to keep the favour of the great. Pope Clement VII ordered from him the tomb which he made for Santa Maria sopra Minerva, statues of St. John the Baptist, St. John the Evangelist, St. Peter, and St. Paul, besides bas-reliefs representing the Coronation of Charles V and the Reception of Francis I. Cosimo de' Medici ordered a monument to his father Giovanni delle Bande Nere; and today the fierce condottiere can be seen on the Piazza San Lorenzo, on top of a monumental pedestal.

Bandinelli made an *Adam and Eve* for the high-altar of the Duomo (now on the Bargello), a *Dead Christ* for Santa Croce, a *God the Father*, which is in the cloisters of the same church, statues of Leo X, Giovanni de' Medici, of Duke Alexander for the Hall of the Five Hundred, and some decorations for the Pitti Palace.

He boasted that the art of design would die with him.

**BAPTISTERY.**—A little church or chapel, built near a large church, where baptism was given. The buildings are often round. The most famous are those of Florence (doors by Ghiberti and Andrea Pisano), Padua, Pisa, Parma, Ravenna, Rome (San Giovanni Laterano). France, less rich than Italy, possesses some baptisteries, at Poitiers (see Poitiers), Aix, Le Puy, etc.

**BARBARI (Jacopo de').**—Venetian painter and engraver (1440-50—1511-15), worked first in Venice, (until the end of the fifteenth century) subsequently in Germany, where he was known as Jacob Walch; eventually court painter to Margaret of Austria, Regent of the Netherlands. More important than his few surviving pictures are his engravings which from their signature, the wand of Mercury, used to be given to the "Master of the Caduceus."

Bibliography: Tancred Borenius, *Four Early Italian Engravers*, London, 1923.

**BARBIERE (Domenico del).**—Known as Domenichino Fiorentino. —See Domenichino.

**BARBIERI (Francesco).**—See Guercino.

**BARBIZON SCHOOL.**—A group of French painters who worked at Barbizon, in the Forest of Fontainebleau. They found their subject matter in the local landscape which they reproduced naturalistically. They included Daubigny (1817-1878), Dupré (1812-1889), Diaz (1808-1876), Millet (1814-1875), and, for a time, Corot (1796-1875).

**BARGELLO (The).**—See Florence.

**BARI (Italy).**—S. Nicola, c. 1088-1132. A Benedictine abbey church built to house the relics of St. Nicholas of Myra, brought to Italy in 1087. It is large, wide, and high, with a triapsidal choir raised over a crypt accessible by descending aisle staircases. Norman influence may be seen in the use of a high triforium between the clerestorey and the arcade on almost classical columns. The nave has a timber roof; the aisles are groin-vaulted. The façade is wider than the church and has two towers. S. Nicola was an influential design, determining the later style of Romanesque Apulia, as in the Cathedral of Trani, and was even the model for the Piedmontese Cathedral of Modena.

**BARKER (Thomas).**—English painter (1769-1847), known from the city in which he long resided as "Barker of Bath." Studied in Italy 1790-93. A painter of assimilative tendency but not without talent, especially as a colourist; specialized in scenes from passing life and landscapes.

**BARLACH (Ernst Heinrich).**—Contemporary German sculptor. He was born 2d January 1870 in Wedel, near Hamburg, Germany. He grew up in Schönberg and Ratzeburg and in 1888 went to Hamburg where he began to study art at the Hamburg School of Arts and Crafts. In 1891 he was attending classes given by Robert Diez at the Dresden Academy and somewhat later he went to Paris to work. He was early influenced by the work of Daumier and Rodin, but after a trip through the southern part of Russia in 1906 he returned to Germany full of enthusiasm for Russian wood carvings. He is primarily a wood carver although he has worked also in porcelain, terra cotta and bronze. His subjects are taken from the daily life of the peasants who in their expressions of joy or sorrow become symbolic figures that represent the emotions of all mankind. They are individuals struggling hopelessly against the unalterable ways of Fate. All are poor folk depicted in a realistic manner, dressed in sombre clothes or great flowing capes, now shown alone or in groups, but in the latter case always giving the impression of isolated figures not held together by any common tie of affection. Barlach is also the author of several portrait busts which give a very individualised treatment of the face. He has done quite a number of book illustrations, both drawings and woodcuts for *Arme Beter*, *Die Echten Sedemunds*, *Blaue Boll*, *Der Findling*, Schiller's *Lied an die Freude*, Goethe's *Walpurgisnacht* and *Die Wandlungen Gottes*. Other books that he has made lithographs for include *Der tote Tag*, *Die Sündflut* and *Der Kopf*. Barlach is the creator of the War Memorial in Güstrow Cathedral, and made some figures for the Magdeburg Cathedral and the Deutsches Theatre in Berlin. Examples of this artist's work may be found in the museums of Berlin, Cologne, Dresden, Munich, Vienna, and Detroit.

Bibliography: Carl Dietrich Carls, *Ernst Barlach, das plastische, graphische und dichterische Werk*, 1931.—*Ernst Barlach, ein Selbsterzähltes Leben*, 1928.—Reinhold von Walter, *Ernst Barlach, eine Einführung in sein plastisches und graphisches Werk*, c. 1929.

**BARNA (or Berna).**—Sienese painter, of the trecento. Barna did frescoes in S. Agostino, Siena, which are now destroyed, as are those he executed in Sto. Spirito in Florence and various churches of Cortona and Arezzo. He was in Arezzo in 1369. He is best known to us today through his fresco-cycle in S. Gimignano. Vasari says that it was here in 1380 that he met his death through a fall from the scaffold. Various panels are attributed to Barna on stylistic grounds.

Bibliography: Vasari-Milanesi, I, 647-651.—Baldinucci, *Not. d. prof. d. disegno*, 1767, II, 192 ff.—W. Rothes, *Die Blütezeit d. Sien. Malerei*. Strassburg, 1904.—A. Venturi, *Stor. d. Arte Ital.*, V, 1907, 740 f.

**BARNABA da MODENA.**—Painter from Modena, resident in Genoa in 1367 where he painted the Madonna now in the Gallery at Frankfurt, signed and dated. Probably worked in Liguria and Piedmont until 1380; and was called to Pisa to work on the frescoes in the Camposanto, which, however, he did not execute. The Madonna in Berlin is of 1369; that in Turin of 1370; the panel in London with the Coronation of the Virgin, Trinity, Madonna, Crucifixion, and twelve Apostles of 1374; the Madonna in Alba, the Church of S. Giovanni Battista, of 1377; and the Madonna in the Church of SS. Cosma e Damiano in Genoa, of 1383.

Bibliography: Alizeri, *Not. dei prof. del disegno in Liguria* (1870-80), I, p. 129 ff.—A. Venturi, *La R. Gall. Estense in Modena*, 1883; *Storia d. Arte Ital.*, V, 1907, 948 ff. —Suida, *Genua*. Leipzig, 1906.

**BARNARD (George Grey).**—Contemporary American sculptor. He was born in Bellefonte, Pennsylvania, 24th May 1863. He was interested in natural history as a boy and learned to do taxidermy so that he might preserve his specimens to act as his models. His youth was spent in Muscatine, Iowa, where he was apprenticed to a local jeweller where he learned to make good letters and the rudiments of engraving. At the age of eighteen he entered the Art Institute of Chicago where he stayed nearly two years. Then he left for Paris to study at the École des Beaux-Arts in the Atelier Cavelier. He learned to work directly in stone and how to realise the fullest potentialities of his material. Soon he opened his own studio at Vaugirard near Versailles and gradually the piece *Two Natures* took shape. It was exhibited in the Salon of the Champs de Mars in 1894 and caused much comment by the heroic size of the two figures and the broken contour line of the group as a whole. On the merit of that piece he was elected to associate membership of the Société Nationale des Beaux-Arts. He returned to the United States in 1896 and established himself in New York City. In 1902 he was commissioned to do work for the new State Capitol at Harrisburg, Pennsylvania. He completed only two entrance groups for it, working on the job in France, and when the scandal broke concerning the work he was obliged to pay his assistants in his own money. To raise the necessary amount he went to the far corners of the country, collecting and digging out odd fragments of Gothic art; some of these he sold to meet the necessary obligation. The rest formed the nucleus of his famous Cloisters collection which is now the property of the Metropolitan Museum of Art. Barnard executed the *Hewer* and the more celebrated *Lincoln*. A replica of this statue is now in Manchester, England, which is very gaunt and lean when compared to St.-Gaudens' figure. His work has been compared to that of Rodin with the large elemental figures used, often half hewn from the solid block of stone, though occasionally the force and vigour of his forms recall the work of Michelangelo. Since the close of the World War he has formulated an idea for a gigantic Rainbow Arch to commemorate the fallen dead but it has reached only the plaster stage. Early in 1935 he had a retrospective exhibition of his work which included some of the figures for this memorial as well as models and sketches of his earlier successful works.

Bibliography: C. H. Caffin, *American Masters of Sculpture*, 1903.—Kineton Parkes, *Sculpture of To-day*, 1921.—Lorado Taft, *The History of American Sculpture*, 1930.—Lorado Taft, *Modern Tendencies in Sculpture*, 1921.

**BAROCCIO (Federigo).**—Italian painter (1528-1612) was born at Urbino, and worked chiefly in his native town, at Pesaro, in Rome, Milan (1592-1608), and Genoa (where he left a beautiful *Crucifixion*, commissioned by the Doge Matteo Senarega). He was influenced especially by Correggio in his search after enveloping light. He accentuated effects of light and shade rather too artificially. But he often uses charming colours, sometimes fresh and cheerful, sometimes subdued, all uniting pleasantly in very choice harmonies.

**BARONZIO (Giovanni da Rimini).**—Giottesque painter of the Romagna, influenced also by Cavallini. Died before 1362. Two dated pictures by him are in the Mercatello, Urbino, a Crucifix of 1344; and a polyptych in the Urbino Gallery of 1345. Frescoes by him or related to him are in Ravenna, Rimini, Tolentino and Jesi, and a considerable group of panels have been attributed to him.

Bibliography: Rossini, *Storia della pittura*, II, p. 63.—C. Tonini, *Rimini nella Signoria de' Malatesta*, IV, p. 389 f.—Calzini, *Urbino e i suoi monumenti*, 1897, p. 31; and in L'Arte, IV, 1901, p. 364.—A. Brach, *Giottos Schule in der Romagna*. Strassburg, 1902.—J. Hermanin, *Gli affreschi di G. Baronzio e dei suoi seguaci in Tolentino*, in Bollettino della soc. filol. romana, 1905, No. 7, p. 65.

**BAROQUE.**—A style of architecture, painting, and sculpture typical of the seventeenth century. Its chief characteristics are heaviness and unrest, attained through additive forms, broken contours, and recessive modelling and space. A heavy chiaroscuro is often used by painters of this style.

**BAROZZI (Jacopo).**—See Vignola.

**BARRIAS (Louis Ernest).**—French sculptor. Paris (1841-1905). Son of a painter on china, and brother of a talented painter, Felix Barrias. In spite of the example of his father and his brother, he preferred sculpture to painting, and entered the studio of the sculptor Cavelier, where he acquired a technical knowledge—rare in his day—of the chasing and engraving of bronze. From Cavelier's studio, he entered the atelier of Jouffroy, at the École des Beaux-Arts, after having been through the studio of the painter Cogniet where he made a special study of drawing. He obtained the Grand Prix de Rome in 1865, with the bas-relief of the *Foundation of Marseille*. When the War of 1870 broke out, he was in Rome and there finished *The Oath of Spartacus*, which he exhibited at the Salon in 1872. After the first reverses of the war, he returned to France and joined in active service on the Marne, returning to Paris with the rank of lieutenant. As soon as peace came, he married, and resumed his hardworking existence. The great success of the *Spartacus* at the Salon of 1872 (Tuileries Gardens) encouraged him, and brought

BARRIAS (LOUIS ERNEST): THE FIRST FUNERAL. (Petit Palais, Paris.)

him a first medal and numerous orders. In spite of these commissions, he found time to undertake a large group, the *First Funeral* (1876), which he kept for two years, and which is his most characteristic work, showing best his qualities of charm and correctness, of knowledge and of feeling. Its success at the Salon was enormous, both with the public and with the artists who

BARRIAS (LOUIS ERNEST): NATURE UNVEILING HERSELF. (Musée du Luxembourg, Paris.)

decided to give their colleague the Medal of Honour (Petit Palais). After this success, Barrias proved the elasticity of his talent by the execution of picturesque works such as the *Bernard Palissu* (1880—Place Saint-German-des-Prés), and *Mozart as a Child* (1883, Luxembourg), and bronzes, of a grace, elegance and style that well expressed his temperament. Then he returned to large works, and made one after another, the *Defence of Paris* (Rond-point de Courbevoie), the *Defence of Saint-Quentin* (Saint-Quentin), the *Memorial to French Soldiers*, at Tananarivo, and, finally, the *Victor Hugo Monument* in Paris. In all these works the action is expressed clearly, concisely, correctly; with some literary pretension, and a certain vague allegory: it is a plastic language comprehensible to all, the good popular style of statuary in public squares.

An excellent portraitist, Barrias left a number of busts; a beautiful bronze on the tomb of Anatole de la Forge (1893), in Père-Lachaise; a polychrome marble statue of *Nature Disrobing* (1899, Luxembourg), and a statue of Jeanne d'Arc as a prisoner (Bonsecours, at Rouen), which is dramatic and resolute.

BIBLIOGRAPHY: Lafenestre, *Œuvres de Barrias*. Paris, 1908.

**BARRY (Sir Charles).**—English architect, 1795-1860. After having travelled a great deal, and studied the buildings of numerous countries —Greece, Asia, France, Italy, Egypt —he began to work about 1820. His first works, churches, chapels, public buildings, attracted attention. In 1834 a competition took place for the rebuilding of Westminster Palace, which had been destroyed by fire, and Barry was chosen for the work. He performed it in a way to

BARRY (SIR CHARLES): PORCH OF THE CATHEDRAL OF WESTMINSTER.

excite general admiration. In 1840 he designed, in the Gothic style, the Houses of Parliament, finished in 1860. He was buried in Westminster Abbey.

BIBLIOGRAPHY: Alfred Barry: *The Life and Works of Sir Charles Barry*. London, 1867.

**BARTHOLDI (Frédéric-Auguste).**—French sculptor, 1844-

BARTHOLDI: STATUE OF LIBERTY, NEW YORK.

1904. Born at Colmar, he first of all studied architecture in this town; then he went to Paris to join the painting classes at Ary Scheffer's studio; and then he studied sculpture, with Soitoux.

His inspiration was towards the grandiose — monumental fountains (at Colmar, Bordeaux, Washington), and statues of large dimensions. The two works which made his name famous are the *Lion of Belfort*, and *Liberty Lighting the World* (New York). The War of 1870 inspired the magnificent figure of the *Lion of Belfort*, cut in the grey-red rock which bears the château of Belfort (22 metres long by 11 metres high). The plaster model was cast in bronze and is to be found on the Place Denfert-Rochereau. The Statue of Liberty (33 metres high) dominates the New York harbour; there is a reduced copy on the Pont de Grenelle, Paris. Bartholdi worked a great deal for Colmar (Statue of Rapp, of Martin Schongauer, fountain, the *Alsatian Vigneron*); and for America (statue of Lafayette, the *Times of Peace*, the *Four Stages of the Christian Life*). To him are due also the plans of the Palais de Longchamp, at Marseille, and many other monuments, statues and busts.

BIBLIOGRAPHY: Lefebvre, *L'œuvre de Bartholdi*. Paris, 1876.

**BARTHOLOMÉ (Paul Albert).**—French sculptor and painter. Born

BARTHOLOMÉ: DETAIL OF THE MONUMENT TO THE DEAD.

at Théverval, 1848. He was taught by Barthélemy Menn in Geneva; he then passed through Gérôme's studio, in Paris, but he did not stay there. He wanted to devote himself to painting. In 1879, he exhibited a *Portrait of a Woman*, and a study, *A l'Ombre*. He contributed to Salon after Salon, and sent portraits, pastoral scenes, and interiors, the *Refuge*, *Old Men Resting*, the *Last Ears of Corn*, etc. Then, in 1887, he gave up exhibiting, and did not appear again until 1890, in the Salon of Sculpture. For several years, he showed isolated figures of a funeral character, remarkable for their twofold aspect, the individual note and the symbolic sentiment. In 1895, all these figures reappeared together, grouped into one composition called the *Monument to the Dead*, which was a great success, and was ordered by the Government and the city of Paris to be placed in the cemetery of Père-Lachaise (1899). This work made Bartholomé's name famous. Other smaller works, clever and expressive —statuettes, busts, monuments— only confirmed this success (*Little Girl Weeping*, bust of Mme. X, both in the Luxembourg). At the moment when sculpture, democratic and socialistic, was following a passionate, human course, Bartholomé had the originality to revert to the past ideal, and at the same time to express the terror of life confronted with death in a language quite new. and very modern. In the heart of Paris, in the courtyard of the Carrousel, is a statue representing the heroism of Paris during the war.

See Pl. 52, Vol. II.

**BARTLETT (Paul Wayland).**—American sculptor (1865-1925). He

BARTLETT (PAUL WAYLAND): EQUESTRIAN STATUE OF LAFAYETTE, PARIS.

was born in New Haven, Connecticut, 24th January 1865, the son of Truman Howe Bartlett, the art critic and sculptor who for a time was the teacher of modelling at the Massachusetts Institute of Technology. Young Bartlett went to live in France with his mother while still a boy and at the age of fifteen entered the École des Beaux-Arts in Paris. There he worked under Cavelier and Frémiet and began to devote himself to the modelling of animals. He collaborated with many artists of human figures for groups requiring both animals and persons. In 1895 he was honoured by the French government by being made a member of the Legion of Honor. After that time Bartlett made frequent visits to the United States where he made statues of Columbus and Michelangelo for the rotunda of the Library of Congress in Washington. He also executed some figures for the façade of the New York Public Library, the pediment of the House of Representatives wing of the Capitol in Washington, and with John Quincy Adams Ward the pediment sculptures for the New York Stock Exchange. In 1908 his great equestrian statue of Lafayette was unveiled in the courtyard of the Louvre in Paris. It was his masterpiece and expressed very adequately the spirit of that national hero. Mr. Bartlett was also the creator of a number of statues in different cities in the eastern part of the United States and his last commission was a portrait statue of Blackstone, a gift from the United States Bar Association to the British Bar Association. He died of blood poisoning in Paris 20th September 1925. His work has been compared to that of Rodin in the use of intelligent figures boldly grouped in simple and unified masses or single figures dignified and heroic in their representation.

BIBLIOGRAPHY: C. H. Caffin, *American Masters of Sculpture*, 1903.—Lorado Taft, *History of American Sculpture*, 1930.—Lorado Taft, *Modern Tendencies in Sculpture*, 1921.

**BARTOLO di FREDI BATTILORI.**—Sienese painter of the trecento, about 1330-1410. Follower of Lippo Memmi and the Lorenzetti, influenced by Barna. Best to be known through fresco-cycles in S. Gimignano, those in the Collegiata from the Old Testament, to be dated, according to Vasari, in 1356, which would make them the earliest frescoes of the city. The Birth and Dormition of the Virgin in S. Agostino, S. Gimignano, are some ten years later. Bartolo di Fredi painted two dated altars, both in Montalcino, of 1382 and 1388. In 1353 he had a workshop with Andrea Vanni, and he was the Master of Andrea and Taddeo di Bartolo.

BIBLIOGRAPHY: Brogi, *Inventario . . . della Provincia di Siena,* 1897. —A. Venturi, *Storia dell'arte ital.,* V, 744; *Miscell. stor. d. Valdelsa,* XIV, 194-211, XV, 1-18, 57.—O. Sirén in L'Arte, IX, fasc. V.

**BARTOLOMMEO (Fra).**—Bartolommeo Pagholo del Fattorino, called Baccio della Porta, and then, when he became a monk, Fra Bartolommeo. Florentine painter (1475-1517), who shows the transition between the style of the 15th and that of the 16th century. He charms by his sincerity, his pious seriousness, his pure colours, but he did not escape the degenerative influences which surrounded him, far removed in feeling from the pure and powerful aesthetic feeling of the quattrocento.

A pupil of Piero di Cosimo, he afterwards succumbed to the universal influence of Michelangelo and Leonardo.

An early work, the striking profile of Savonarola (which is in the Convent of San Marco), with the aquiline nose and thin lips, which, under the severe hood, remind one that the monks were not all as gentle as Fra Angelico, has an energetic and decorative beauty which resembles that of the Primitives.

Bartolommeo became one of the most fervent disciples of Savonarola. He was saddened by the tragic events that surrounded him. After the death of his friend, he was consecrated as priest, and took the habit of the Dominicans (1500). He only took up his paint-brushes again after several years and on the entreaties of his prior. He then (1506) painted for the Badia, that suave *Apparition of the Virgin to St. Bernard* (now in the Academy of Florence).

Like Angelico, Fra Bartolommeo would paint only for God. With the simplicity of earlier times, he wrote under his altar-pieces "Orate pro pictore," and he used pure, bright colours to express his sentiments the better. But times had moved forward. The grave disciple of Savonarola fought against the abuse of science; he did not want to dress the Virgin like a princess, but he could not resist drawing perspective effects with which he had become acquainted, to show off new beauties.

Fra Bartolommeo was the friend of the young Raphael. Being the elder, he gave him advice and ideas, but soon the precocious genius came to react, in his turn, on the more timid, less gifted painter. The *Virgin* of San Marco, and that in the Corsini Gallery (painted for Angelo Doni, and dating from 1516) resemble Raphael's Madonnas. They probably went to Rome together, and the pious monk let himself be seduced by beauty of a sculptural and powerful character. In Venice, where he also went, it is said in 1508, he was influenced by the soft, warm character of Venetian art. He there painted a *St. Magdalen* and a *St. Catherine*, for the monks of the Convent of St. Peter Martyr, at Murano. The Virgin which he painted for Lucca Cathedral shows chiefly the influence of the charming Madonnas of Giovanni Bellini and of Carpaccio.

In Florence, he worked in his convent with the monk Fra Paolino. In 1509, he undertook a collaboration with Mariotto Albertinelli, which lasted until 1512.

From the same period date a great many of his pictures to which Albertinelli perhaps contributed: the *Marriage of St. Catherine* (1511, Louvre); the *Virgin of Ferry Carondelet* (1512, Cathedral of Besancon); the *Madonna and Saints* (1512, Uffizi). He produced much during his last years, trying to express his pious sentiments with scholarly arrangements and softer modelling.

He died at only forty-two years of age, of fever, on the 6th October, 1517.

BIBLIOGRAPHY: Vasari-Milanesi, IV, 175.—Crowe and Cavalcaselle, III, 434 ff.—E. Frantz, *Fra Bartolommeo della Porta,* 1879.—Leader Scott, *Fra Bartolommeo,* 1881.—Fritz Knapp, *Fra Bartolommeo,* 1903.

**— DELLA GATTA (Piero d'Antonio Dei).** — Umbro - Florentine painter, 1448-1502, influenced by Piero della Francesca and Signorelli.

**— SUARDI.**—See Bramantino.

**— VENETO.**—Venetian painter of the 16th century (worked from 1502 to c. 1535). A pupil of the Bellini influenced by Venetian and Lombard schools.

**— VIVARINI.**—See Vivarini.

**BARTOLOZZI (Francesco).**—Italian painter and engraver (1728-1813). In Venice he was the pupil of Joseph Wagner; then he went to London in 1764, and there received a pension from King George III. This artist was very celebrated and had considerable influence on English and French engravers, who, following his example, adopted to a great extent the stipple method. But none equalled him in the use of this method, in which he was expert. In 1802, he left London for Lisbon, where he was nominated Director of the National Academy of Fine Art.

He left more than 700 engravings, among them: *Clyte* (after Annibale Carracci); *Venus, Cupid and a Satyr* (after L. Giordano); *St. Jerome* (after Correggio); portraits of Lord Clive, of Lord Thurlow; of Rosalba, and facsimiles of drawings by Holbein in George III's Collection. Bartolozzi lived expensively, and he has been accused of having often, when pressed by need of money, signed engravings executed by pupils, and only finished or retouched by him.

BIBLIOGRAPHY: S. Redgrave: *Dictionary of Artists of the English School.*—H. Delaborde, *La gravure,* p. 246 et seq.

**BARTON-ON-HUMBER (England).**—*St. Peter's.* The town, late 10th century, is post-Danish Anglo-Saxon, with Anglo-Saxon long-and-short stripping joined by arcuation in the first stage and mitreing in the second. The church behind is Gothic.

**BARTSCH (Jean Adam Bernard).**—Viennese engraver. 1757-1821. He engraved some original compositions, and some plates after the 16th century masters, Dürer and Burgkmair. He was the author of an excellent book, "Le Peintre Graveur" (21 vols.), which is full of technical details, bibliographies, and iconographical studies.

**BARYE (Antoine Louis).**—French sculptor. Born in Paris, 24th September, 1796; died 25th June, 1875. Son of a Parisian goldsmith. Bosio and Gros were his masters. The former had but little influence on this obscure student; but the painter of *Jaffa* exercised an influence on his young pupil such as Delacroix felt, without having joined Gros's studio.

From 1819 to 1824, when he was not even eligible for the Prix de Rome, Barye had no success. In 1823 he had to have recourse to industry as a means of livelihood, and he entered the shop of the goldsmith Fauconnier as an assistant; and the future sculptor of wild beasts made jewels and invented models for trinkets. For Fauconnier, for whom he worked until 1828, Barye executed sixty little models of animals, of very small size, which are unsigned. Of these rare pieces, an example is a little *Stork Perched on a Tortoise.* The young artist constantly visited the Jardin des Plantes. He observed the life of the great captive wild-beasts, which his powerful imagination restored to the liberty of vast spaces. Barye's taste for nature studies in the Jardin des Plantes was to decide the whole of his work. Wishing to know all about his models, he followed natural history courses, and plunged into the reading of Cuvier and of Lacepède. Barye was thirty-one years old before he won the approval of the public (in the Salon of 1827: busts of a young girl, and of a young man). But still this was not with one of his favourite subjects. He sent a figure, a *St. Sebastian,* to the Salon of 1831, which was remarked upon, and at last a group of animals, *Tiger Devouring a Crocodile,* which was commented upon with surprise and animation, and gained a second medal. If the Salon of 1831 drew attention to Barye, his appearance at the Salon of 1833 created a great impression. The *Lion Crushing a Serpent* aroused both fury and admiration. Besides this work, he also exhibited a bust of the Duke of Orleans, and numerous groups or statuettes. Moreover, he exhibited several water-colours. The little bronze paper-weights have a lively quality; while, as for the water-colours, their quiet austerity won for them little success. Nevertheless, Barye gained from this discussion, in attracting attention and obtaining the good-will of the "Court." The Duke of Orleans, especially, accorded him his approval, and ordered the famous Epergne. In the same year, the *Lion with the Serpent* was bought by the state, and its author decorated with the Legion of Honour.

Barye's contributions to the Salon of 1824 were less numerous. They included: the *Dead Gazelle*; an *Elephant; Panther Devouring a Gazelle; Stag Surprised by a Lynx;* and another series of water-colours. The artist did not win a medal, and they pretended to confuse his exhibits with those of one Fratin. Rebuffed, Barye seems thenceforth to have withdrawn from exhibitions, just as he had, in his youth, given up official competitions. He did, however, send a small piece to the Salon of 1835, a *Tiger,* in stone, which is now at Lyon. In 1836, he again sent one of his most beautiful works, the admirable *Lion in Repose,* also a series of little bronzes which the jury rejected "en bloc," under the ridiculous pretext that this was not sculpture, but goldsmith's work. Deeply wounded, Barye took no part in the Salons for many years. He only reappeared there in 1850, but then with exceptional brilliance.

Absorbed in his dream of independence, Barye engaged in one of the most disastrous adventures of his life. Haunted by the desire to sign his name only to perfect pieces, he decided himself to practice the profound studies which he had made in the technical processes of casting and of carving. He put himself at the head of a foundry. But Barye understood nothing of commerce. When, after the revolution of 1848, his money-lenders exacted a complete repayment, the artist found it impossible to pay. Then the creditors turned, legally authorized to lay hands on all Barye's models. The unfortunate artist found himself at over fifty years old, ruined, and more desperate than at the beginning of his career. It was not until about 1857 that Barye, possessed at last of an undoubted fame, and having found, if not fortune, at any rate some relief, managed to free himself from his creditors, and was able to repossess himself of his models.

The revolution of 1848 ruined the plan of M. Thiers, who dreamed of commissioning Barye to make a colossal group, which was to be placed on the Arc de Triomphe. He was nominated by the Government as temporary keeper of the gallery of casts and head of the cast-room in the Louvre, but two years later this office was suppressed and the artist had to retire.

At the Salon of 1850, Barye reappeared with the admirable group, *The Centaur and Lapith* (Louvre). This work, long contemplated, gave him the prestige which was owing to him. The state bought this magnificent work, but this was in order to send it far from Paris to the Museum of Puy. This was another disappointment for Barye. Two years after (1852) the artist exhibited the *Jaguar Devouring a Hare* (Louvre), where the wild beast betrays something of the reptile nature, with its working jaws, and its whole body quivering with murderous hunger. In 1854 Barye saw his wishes fulfilled. His friends obtained for him the position of Professor of Drawing at the Museum. Without seeking them, honours came to him at last. On the occasion of the Universal Exhibition of 1855, he was awarded the grand medal in the section of bronzes, and was made an officer of the Legion of Honour. The official sculptors began to admit his superiority in animal sculpture, but this was not through a spirit of justice, but a means of relegating Barye to the first rank of artists "of the second order." One of the first figures which put him among the finest artists of his day, was the beautiful *Theseus and the Minotaur,* executed when the artist had given up exhibiting at the Salons. And one sees this powerful serenity again in the *Centaur and the Lapith.* In the *Three Graces;* the *Juno,* and the *Minerva* there is a feeling for feminine beauty, unexpected in this austere sculptor of wild life.

See Pl. 5, Vol. I; Pl. 51, Vol. II.

BIBLIOGRAPHY: T. Silvestre, *Histoire des Artistes vivants.* Paris, 1855.—Gustave Plauche, "Barye." *Revue des Deux-Mondes,* July, 1851. —Arsène Alexandre, *A. L. Barye,*

1889.—Ballu, *L'œuvre de Barye,* 1890.

**BASAITI (Marco).** — Venetian painter of the end of the 15th century, and of the beginning of the 16th (c.1740-c.1530), of Dalmatian or Albanian origin. A pupil of Alvise Vivarini, he has a lively sense of beautiful, bright colours, but little originality. A prolific painter, his works are well scattered.

See Pl. 14, Vol. II.

**BASHKIRTSEFF (Marie).**— Russian woman painter. She was very popular in France about 1880. Her art resembles that of Bastien-Lepage. She is noted also for numerous pastel portraits, which resemble the style of Manet; several are in the Luxembourg Museum, also one of her most characteristic paintings, entitled *The Meeting,* which represents a group of children chatting in the street.

**BASILICA.**—Originally buildings which served as meeting places for

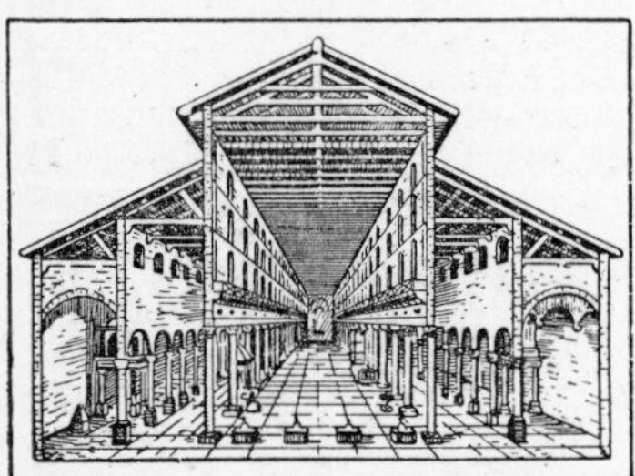

Rome, Basilica of Old St. Peter's.

tribunals, the Exchange, and conversation. The first basilica (Porcia) was a simple shelter, set up by Cato (185 B.C.). After him the emperors, or wealthy individuals, built sumptuous edifices. The basilicas were in the form of a long rectangle, divided by columns into three naves. They were surrounded by walls, or left open, and were entered by a portico. Among the most famous must be mentioned the basilicas Æmilia, Constantine, and Julia, in the Roman forum.

The term basilica also refers to a type of church plan which originated in Early Christian times. In plan, the Early Christian basilica had a nave and two or more side aisles, the aisles being separated from the nave by colonnades or columnar arcades terminating at the bema in an arch of triumph. The nave was higher than the aisles and was illuminated by a clerestorey and covered by a trussed timber roof. Behind the altar at the crossing, or containing the altar, was the semicircular apse with the cathedra in the rear. Sometimes the bema projected north and south to form rudimentary transepts, giving the basilica the form of a T. Basilicas were often preceded by a narthex and atrium. By extension, the word refers also to all later churches of Latin cross plan.

**BASSANO (Francesco da Ponte, the older).**—Venetian painter (c. 1475-1539). Follower of Montagna. Father of Jacopo Bassano.

**— (Francesco da Ponte, the younger).**—Venetian painter (1548-1591). Son and close follower of Jacopo Bassano.

**— (Jacopo da Ponte, called).**— Venetian painter (1510-1592). A native of the town of Bassano from which he derived his name. Having received his first education from his father Francesco, he went to Venice where he became the pupil of Bonifazio. But he was not long in returning to his native country, to remain there until the end of his long life in the calm and love of nature. He had no need of fêtes, of illuminated serenades on the Grand Canal, and of pleasures amid brocades and gold. Fields and woods, and the blue distances of the mountains were enough for him. He occupies a place apart from the painters of his own day, ignoring dazzling and highly-coloured beauties, but penetrating intimately the sweetness of the simple things which surrounded him, painting landscape for its own sake, as other artists did later on. His canvases are little genre pictures. The sacred legends take on the reality that he saw around him. There, one sees the animals that he loved in the green fields where he walked, the inn kitchens where he found refreshment in pewter jugs, among the cat, the dog and the chickens; and as he understood the charm of simple objects, he painted them carefully, like jewels. In certain of his pictures, he became vigorous and dramatic, using strong contrasts of light and shade. One might say that he was a forerunner of Rembrandt and Velazquez. He taught his four sons, of whom two, Francesco and Leandro, worked with him.

Bassano's many works are in Venice, in Bassano, in Vicenza, in London, Florence, Madrid, Vienna, and a large number of other places.

Bibliography: P. M. Tua: Contributo all'elenco *delle opere dei Pittori da Ponte,* in Bollettino del Museo civico di Bassano, 1907.—E. Zottmann: *Zur Kunst der Bassani.* Strasbourg, 1908.—G. Gerola: *Il primo pittore bassanese. Francesco da Ponte il Vecchio,* in Bollettino del Museo civico di Bassano, 1907.—Un nuovo libro sull' Arte dei Bassani (*id:* 1908).

**— (Leandro).**—Venetian painter (1558-1623). Son and close follower of Jacopo Bassano.

**BASTIANI (Lazzaro).**—Venetian painter of the end of the 15th century. Born about 1430, died in 1512. A pupil of Bartolommeo Vivarini, he was strongly influenced by the Bellini. He was much esteemed in his own day, and certainly prepared the way for the beautiful representations of Venice which Carpaccio has given us in his large compositions.

He is mentioned in documents from 1449. He must have had several schemes for mosaics for St. Mark's, and for the choir of Ferrara Cathedral (where one sees the signature: "Lazzaro pictor"), and have painted several portraits of the Doge for the Ducal Palace.

The principal pictures attributed to him are: a *St. Veneranda,* painted for the Church of Corpus Domini in Venice, signed (probably about 1460-1470); a *St. Anthony Preaching in a Tree,* above *St. Bonaventura* and *St. Leo,* in the Venice Academy, signed (about 1470); the *Last Communion of St. Jerome* and the *Funeral of the Saint,* painted for the Brotherhood of St. Jerome, and now in the Venice Academy (about 1470); a picture in the Cathedral of San Donato of Murano (1484); another in the Lochis Gallery at Bergamo (1490); the *Miracle of the Holy Cross,* painted the Scuola of St. John the Evangelist, now in the Venice Academy (1486-1500); an *Annunciation,* in the Civic Museum of Venice; and another in the Museum of Klosterneubourg, in Austria.

**BASTIEN-LEPAGE (Jules).**— (Damvillers, Meuse, 1848; Paris, 1884.) After having, throughout his youth, learned to draw under the direction of his father, a simple amateur, he was sent to the College of Verdun, where his Professor of Drawing, M. Fouquet, noticed him, and advised him to devote himself to painting. He finished his classes, received his diploma of Bachelor of Arts, and went to Paris. Obliged to earn his living, he entered the postal service, and at the same time studied at the École des Beaux Arts, in the atelier of Cabanel. But, at the end of some months, worn out by this over-work, he gave up the Administration, and contented himself with living on a modest pension which he received from his Department. This was in 1867. But 1870 came. He went on active service during the war, fought as a skirmisher, and was wounded. When peace came, Bastien-Lepage returned to Cabanel's atelier, and, while pursuing his studies at the school, made his first appearance at the Salon (1873) with a little allegorical composition, *Spring.* The portrait of his grandfather (of the following year, 1874) is very remarkable in its feeling of open-air and its sincerity. The *Spring Song,* a little fantasy in the vein of the *Spring,* passed almost unnoticed. But in 1875, the *Communicant,* in her white veils, and the portrait of M. Hayem (Luxembourg) show his lively personality and strong feeling. The same year he entered for the Prix de Rome, and obtained a second prize with the *Annunciation to the Shepherds.* The day after the judging, it is said that some of his competitors, or in any case admirers, who protested against the judgment, placed a palm against the frame, indicating that he deserved the Grand Prix. The following year the crowd again bore him to the École des Beaux-Arts in front of his competition picture, *Priam at the Feet of Achilles,* which in spite of its fine qualities was not classical enough to receive the Prix, which was awarded to Wencker. But it did not matter. Bastien-Lepage was already celebrated. He painted numerous portraits, all very fine: Wallon (1876, Louvre), and his father and mother (1877), as scrupulous and naïve as a primitive. To these life-size portraits, he added little portraits, precious and precise as those of Clouet: his brother, Emile Bastien-Lepage, architect; and André Theuriet; Sarah Bernhardt; Mme. Juliette Drouet; Maurice Fenaille; the Prince of Wales—all alike intimate and profound. At the same time, he painted large canvases. *Les Foins* (1878, Luxembourg): in a mown meadow, a peasant woman sits, dreaming, in front of a man who lies stretched out on his back, asleep. It is somewhat in Millet's style, but everything is drawn with great care, the landscape, the figures, the garments, with special attention to portraiture, by which the work gains a lively accent of individual character. His way of seeing the open-air in too much evenness of tone, without accents either of colour or of shade, gives a flat appearance, which does not strengthen the drawing, which is, nevertheless, very firm, and the modelling very close. But nature has this appearance sometimes, and Bastien-Lepage renders it with much truth and expressive intensity. The same qualities reappeared the following year, in the *Potato Gatherers* (Luxembourg). In the Salon of 1880, he exhibited *Joan of Arc Listening to the Voices* (New York Museum), in which he emphasised the contrast of the scarcely visible apparition in the midst of a very realistic landscape. In spite of its fine qualities, this picture was much discussed and, on the whole, not liked. So it went out of France, and the artist found it hard to console himself on seeing it go to America. The *Beggar* (1881), *Père Jacques* (1882), and *L'Amour au Village* return to the simple rustic note. Next the artist was going to London to paint some of the street types—chimney-sweepers and flower-girls. But a terrible illness seized him, and he died at thirty-four years of age.

**BASTILLE (The).**—See Paris.

**BATALHA (Portugal).**—Monastery in the Flamboyant style, dating from the early 15th century. A tomb chapel, which was never completed, was added in 1500.

Batalha: Royal Cloister.

**BATTAILLE (Nicolas).**—See Tapestry.

**BAYEUX (France).**—The *Cathedral* of Notre Dame was consecrated in 1077, in the presence of William the Conqueror and Queen Matilda. Partly destroyed by fire, in 1105, which left standing the Romanesque nave arcades and the crypt, the reconstruction of the edifice was accomplished during the 12th, 13th and 14th centuries. In the 15th century was built the famous tower covered with a metallic dome, which was destroyed by fire in 1676, and rebuilt in the early 18th century. The interior of the Cathedral is superb in its height, and in the lightness of the half-Romanesque, half-Gothic nave, with its high windows.

The *Museum* contains the celebrated "tapestry" of Bayeux, which is more interesting from the point of view of history than of art. It is a long band, over 70 yards long and more than half a yard wide, embroidered in colours on a white ground. Legend has it that it was worked by Queen Matilda, but it is really of Anglo-Saxon workmanship, and represents the Norman Conquest of England. It traces various

BATALHA: UNFINISHED CHAPEL. OUTER DOOR.

episodes, from the departure of Harold to the Battle of Hastings. The crude figures are amusing in their naïvete, and give valuable information about the costumes and armour of the time (623 persons, 202 horses, 52 dogs, 505 various animals, 37 buildings and ships).

BIBLIOGRAPHY: J. Vallery-Radot, *La Cathédrale de Bayeux.*—F. F. L. Birrell, *Guide to the Bayeux Tapestry*. London, 1921.

**BEAL (Gifford).**—Contemporary American painter. He was born in New York City 24th January 1879. He studied art under William Merritt Chase and at the Art Students' League under Frank V. DuMond and Henry W. Ranger. Although early known as a marine painter he is now connected with figure studies of people who seem to be on a perpetual holiday. They include scenes of garden parties, views of circus life and some landscapes. All are typically American in treatment with strongly balanced compositions enhanced by the use of brilliant colours. They are characterised as good studies of line and rhythm with a feeling for groups seen through the encircling atmosphere. All form pleasant patterns of light and colour presented in vivid and direct methods which tend to add to the sense of reality. His summers are spent at Provincetown or Gloucester, Massachusetts, where he can glimpse and sketch the coast, the throngs on the beaches, or street scenes where busy people hurry by, intent on their own affairs. Gifford Beal won a gold medal at the Panama-Pacific Exposition in San Francisco in 1915, the gold medal of the National Arts Club in 1918, and the first Altman prize at the National Academy of Design exhibition in 1931. Examples of his work are found in the Metropolitan Museum of Art, the Art Institute of Chicago, and the Syracuse, New York, Museum of Fine Arts.

BIBLIOGRAPHY: Frank J. Mather, Jr., Charles R. Morey, William J. Henderson, *The American Spirit in Art*, The Pageant of America, Vol. 12, 1927.—Eugen Neuhaus, *The History and Ideals of American Art*, 1931.—Duncan Phillips, *A Collection in the Making*, 1926.

**BEARDSLEY (Aubrey).**—English draughtsman (1872-1898), an artist of very precocious development, whose brilliant drawings, mainly done as illustrations for books, belong to the most characteristic examples of certain highly artificial artistic tendencies of the 'nineties and have had an enormous influence. Specially famous are his illustrations to *The Yellow Book, The Savoy, The Rape of the Lock, Lysistrata* and *Volpone.*

BIBLIOGRAPHY: Robert Ross, *Aubrey Beardsley*. London, 1909.

**BEAULIEU.**—See Pl. 46, Vol. I.

**BEAUNE (Côte d'or, France).** Beaune possesses the famous *Hôtel Dieu* (or *hospital*), founded in 1443 by the Chancellor Rollin and his wife Guigone de Salins. The hospital has large timber-roofed wards (still used for the sick). Built round a courtyard, the hospital has a steep sloping roof, with high dormer-windows. This roof covers an open gallery which runs round the building.

In the Museum of Beaune is the famous altarpiece, attributed to Roger van der Weyden (see this name) representing the Last Judgment.

See Pl. 29, Vol. II.

**BEAUNEVEU (André).**—French painter and sculptor, of the 14th century, born at Valenciennes. He worked first for several Flemish towns, and then settled in Paris. Charles V ordered several statues from him, portraits of himself and of John the Good, Philippe VI, and Jeanne de Bourgoyne. But it was chiefly the King's brother, the Duc de Berry, who gave Beauneveu work, making him his "maître des œuvres de taille et de peinture." It was for this prince that the artist made the twenty-four miniatures representing apostles and prophets which illustrate a manuscript in the Bibliothèque nationale (No. 13,091), the "Psaultier du duc de Berry."

**BEAUVAIS (France).**—The *Church of St. Etienne* was begun early in the 12th century, and from this period date the nave and transept which are in the Romanesque style. A fine rose-window in the North transept represents the Wheel of Fortune. The Choir is Gothic (begun in 1506). It has magnificent windows (the *Last Judgment*; the *Tree of Jesse*, etc.).

*The Cathedral* (St. Pierre), conceived by too bold architects, was never finished. It would have been the vastest of all the Gothic churches. As it is, it was never completed westward of the choir and transepts. Begun in 1227, the choir was built in 1272, but the pillars were spaced too widely for the great height, and twelve years later the building fell. The number of pillars and buttresses had to be doubled; then the work was left until 1500. From 1500 to 1548, the transept was built. An open-work spire over the crossing collapsed in 1573, and was never rebuilt. The building is extremely high, being 157 ft. 6 ins. to the vault—the highest in Europe. The transepts end in flamboyant Gothic façades.

See Pl. 47, Vol. I.

The *Palais de Justice*, the old episcopal palace, was built in the 12th, 14th and 16th centuries, on the Gallo-Roman walls of the town. The rampart walls are supported by strong buttresses (14th century).

**— MANUFACTORY.**—See Tapestry; also Pl. 44, Vol. II.

**BEAUX (Cecilia).**—American painter, born 1863 in Philadelphia, settled since 1891 in New York, a noted portrait painter in a vigorous, effective style.

**BECCAFUMI (Domenico).**—Domenico Meccherino, surnamed Beccafumi. Sienese painter (1485-1551) of the decadence. His "graffiti" for the pavement of Siena Cathedral are pretentious, and lack the beauty of those of the beginning of the century. He studied Raphael and Fra Bartolommeo and painted with Sodoma in the oratory of San Bernardino.

**BECCARUZZI (Francesco).**—Venetian painter of the middle of the 16th century. Born at Conegliano. A pupil of Cima and Pordenone who influenced him. His numerous works are described by Ridolfi. The principal ones are at Conegliano, at Venice (where there is a *St. Francis Receiving the Stigmata*, of 1545, in the Academy; and at Treviso.

**BECKET'S CROWN.**—See Canterbury.

**BEECHEY (Sir William).**—English painter (1753-1839). Born at Burford, Oxfordshire. He became famous as a portraitist. He was elected an Associate of the Academy in 1793, and the same year became regular painter to Queen Charlotte. In 1798, he executed an equestrian portrait of George III, which caused a sensation. The same year he was knighted, and made an Academician. The National Gallery only possesses one work of William Beechey: the portrait of the sculptor, Joseph Nollekens, which is considered to be happiest of his pictures. At Dulwich, the portrait of John Philip Kemble is still much admired. One of his finest works is in the Louvre—a portrait group, entitled *Brother and Sister.*

BIBLIOGRAPHY: W. Roberts, *Sir William Beechey.*

**BEGARELLI (Antonio).**—Terra cotta sculptor of Modena. 1498?-1565. He did not make isolated figures to adorn monuments or façades, but veritable pictures to be placed in niches, the figures of natural size giving an illusion of living people.

BEGARELLI (ANTONIO): DESCENT FROM THE CROSS, SAN FRANCESCO, MODENA.

Moreover, he did not try to heighten his effects by the use of colour, and, in spite of the frenzied movement of cloaks and veils, he often succeeded in being restrained enough to be effective.

His most important works are the great *Descent from the Cross*, in San Francesco; the *Lamentation*, in San Pietro, where the kneeling Virgin is supported by St. John, and, in the same church, a group representing the Virgin in the clouds, and, in the four arms, Saints (begun in 1553, and finished by his nephew, Lodovico), six statues also in San Pietro. Other statues at San Benedetto, near Mantua (1559) show that he was less successful with isolated figures than with scenes full of movement. There is a little *Presepio*, in Modena Cathedral.

BIBLIOGRAPHY: G. Franciosi, *Dell'animo e dell'arte di Antonio Begarelli.* Modena, 1879.

**BEGAS (Reinhold).**—German sculptor, pupil of Rauch (1831-1911). He is the principal representative of that naturalistic school, more or less mixed with academicism, which sprang up at Munich in reaction against the neo-classicism which ensued from the theories of the great æsthetic, Winckelmann, and of which the chief artists were Daunecker, Tück, Rauch and especially Schadow. The only work of Begas that we have in the classic style is his memorial to Schiller, in Berlin. His best works are his busts, in which he allowed himself to be influenced by real life. He had numerous pupils, of which the most noted were Koft (1827), F. Schaper (1841), and Eberlein (1847), etc.

**BEHAM (Barthel).**—German painter and engraver, born in 1502. In 1525, he was exiled from Nuremberg, together with his brother and G. Pencz, for revolutionary activities. He spent part of his life in Italy, where he died in 1540. He had a delicate sense of beauty of form, and was naturally ready to receive Italian influence. He left an *Apollo and Daphne, Lucretia, Cleopatra,* scenes representing ancient combats—all works in which it is difficult to trace the artist's origins. But the *Virgins*, especially the *Virgin at the Window*, have intimacy and simple feeling. One must also mention a large and vigorous portrait of Charles V, engraved in 1531.

BIBLIOGRAPHY: Rosenberg, *Sebald und Barthel Beham.* Leipzig, 1875. —Seibt, *Hans Sebald Beham und seine Zeit.* Frankfort, 1882.—H. W. Singer, *Die Kleinmeister.* Bielefeld, 1908.

**— (Hans Sebald).**—German engraver, born in 1500; died in 1550. He frequently copied the engravings of his brother, Barthel Beham (see this name) but only dulled their qualities. He was always torn between his German origin and the influence of Italy. He painted a *Dido*, and a *Cleopatra*, which borders on the grotesque; on the other hand, the *Labours of Hercules*, the *Planets*, and the *Arts*, the table top in the Louvre, often show a happy imagination. But the artist's most spontaneous works are the *Village Weddings*, a series of little scenes, ably and strongly drawn, with a rough, and often coarse, gaiety.

BIBLIOGRAPHY: Rosenberg, *Sebald und Barthel Beham.* Leipzig, 1875. —Seibt, *Hans Sebald Beham und seine Zeit.* Frankfort, 1882.—G. Pauli, *Hans Sebald Beham.* Strasbourg, 1901.—H. W. Singer, *Die Kleinmeister*. Bielefeld, 1908.

**BEHISTUN (Persia).**—A mount situated near Ecbatana, in ancient Media. This mount formed a colossal cliff on the side of which successive kings of Persia carved bas-reliefs and engraved inscriptions. The celebrated monument, known as the "inscription of Behistun," is situated about 50 yards above the valley. Below a relief (which shows the king as conqueror of his enemies, worshipping his god), Darius, son of Hystapes, engraved, in the thirteenth year of his reign, an account of the rebellions which followed his accession, of their suppression, and of the punishment which followed. The inscription is written in the three dialects usual to the king's scribes. The Persian text numbers 416 lines. The surface on which the inscription is engraved measures 45 metres in width and 30 metres in height.

The text has been translated and studied by Ménant: *Les Achéménides et les Inscriptions de la Perse*, pp. 102-126.

**BEHRENS (Peter)** 1868— .—German architect and pioneer in the development in the late 19th and early 20th centuries toward the modern style of architecture, noted for his frank use, at an early date, of steel, glass, and concrete. Among his better known buildings are the Turbine Factory for the AEG, Berlin, 1909; the German Embassy, Leningrad, 1912; and the Factory and Office Building of NAG, 1915.

**BELEM (Portugal).**—Monastery in the Flamboyant style, dating from 1517.

See Pl. 50, Vol. I.

BELEM: THE TOWER.

**BELFORT (The Lion of).**—The celebrated *Lion*, sculptured from 1875 to 1880, by Bartholdi, in red sandstone (22 metres long by 11 metres high) is cut in the rock itself. (See Bartholdi.)

**BELFRY.**—The belfry is the wooden structure which, inside a tower, supports the bells. The name is also used to refer to a clock-tower.

**BELLANO (Bartolommeo).**—Sculptor and architect in Padua. His birth and death dates are not certain; he was born c. 1435, and died c. 1496. He was perhaps a pupil of Donatello when the latter was in Padua, 1443-53. Bellano's earliest known work is a marble relief of the Madonna, Child and Angels, from the André Collection, Paris, signed and dated 1461. In 1466 a Perugian document refers to him as "de Florentia," indicating that he had passed some time in Florence, where he evidently took part in the execution of the pulpit of S. Lorenzo. It was due to a summons of Pope Paul II that he was called to Rome and Perugia in 1466, as architect of the Vatican Palace. He was active also on the Palazzo di S. Marco, where he executed a bust of the Pope. In 1467 his statue of the Pope for Perugia was finished and installed in a niche by the side of the side portal of the Duomo (the statue was melted down for coinage in the 18th century). In 1469 he returned to Padua and undertook the marble enframing of the reliquary shrine in the sacristy of the Santo. This work, still showing Donatellesque characteristics, was finished in 1472.

Bellano apparently went next to Venice, from which city he was sent in 1479 with Gentile Bellini to Constantinople to work for Mohammed II. It is not known how long he stayed there, or if he visited Venice again on his way back. In 1484 he had been for some time active in Padua and had finished one of twelve bronze reliefs for the Choir of S. Antonio; from 1485-88 nine more reliefs were completed (the last two were carried out by Briosco). In 1491 Bellano undertook a large bronze work, still preserved in two pieces in S. Francesco, Padua, the tomb of Pietro Roccabonella, professor at the University of Padua (finished 1498 according to the inscription).

A large number of works are attributed to him on stylistic grounds.

BIBLIOGRAPHY: Vasari-Milanesi, II, 363 ff., III, 368.—Scardeonius, *De antiqu. urbis Patav.*, 1560, p. 374.—Portenari, *Felicità di Padova*, 1623, pp. 401, 446.—Morelli, *Notizia*, p. 13.—Cicognara, *Stor. d. scult.*, pp. 132.—Gonzati, *Basil. di S. Antonio*, I, 60 f., 133 ff., 262; II, 168.—Pietrucci, *Biogr. d. art. padovani.*—Perkins, *Les sculpt. ital.*, II, 250 f. —Bode, *Florentin. Bildhauer der Renaiss.; Italien. Plastik*, pp. 79, 134 ff.; *Ital. Bronzen*, pp. 303 ff., 670.—Venturi, *Storia d. arte ital.*, VI.

**BELLECHOSE (Henri).**—Flemish painter, originally from Brabant. He worked in Burgundy, and, in 1415, became painter to Jean san Peur, Duke of Burgundy, for whom he painted a large number of escutcheons, standards, banners, etc.; and then he finished the *Last Communion and Martyrdom of St. Denis* (Louvre), begun by Malouel. This picture represents Christ on the Cross, in the middle; to the left, the saint is seen shut up in a tower, and someone is giving him the Host; to the right, the executioner, surrounded by a crowd, hacks off the head of the martyr. Certain details lead one to think that the artist was acquainted with Italian works.

Some paintings executed by him for the Church of St. Michel at Dijon, have disappeared. There is a *Martyrdom of St. George* (Louvre), which is attributed to Bellechose, but it is much feebler in execution, and cruder in style. At one time of his life, Bellechose was head of a very prosperous studio, but misfortune overtook his last years. The works of the Van Eycks began to come to the fore, eclipsing the fame of the older painters. Bellechose died before 1444.

See Pl. 4, Vol. II.

**BELLEGAMBE (Jean).**—Born about 1470; died about 1533. Flemish painter, born at Douai. Little is known of his life. From 1504 until his death, he lived in his native town, a comfortable citizen and a noted painter. His first known work is a series of mural paintings for the choir of St. Amé (1509); then the *Altarpiece of St. Maurand* (1525-1530); the *Altarpiece of the Immaculate Conception* (wings in Douai Museum), and the *Death and Miracles* of *St. Dominic*. His most famous work is the *Anchin Altarpiece* (Notre Dame, Douai), made by command of an abbé of Anchin. It is a magnificent polyptych whose parts have been put together again after having been scattered. The central panel represents the Holy Trinity. The colours are clear, bright, and harmonious; and one can understand his being called the "Colour Master." Another very fine work is the *Bathing in the Blood of Christ*, in Lille Museum. The Cathedral of Arras has two magnificent triptyches: the *Adoration of the Magi*, and the *Crucifixion*; and Berlin Museum, a *Last Judgment*. Bellegambe liked to express dogma in painting.

There were several painters among his sons and descendants (Jean, Vaast, etc.).

BIBLIOGRAPHY: A. Wauters, *Jean Bellegambe de Douai*. Brussels, 1862. —Dehaisnes, C., *La vie et l'œuvre de Jean Bellegambe*. Lille, 1890.

**BELLINI (Gentile).**—Venetian painter, 1429-1507. Son and pupil of Jacopo Bellini, who may have called him Gentile because of his admiration for Gentile da Fabriano. His name, inscribed on an altar piece of the Santo in Padua proves that he worked there with his father. The organ doors of the Opera di San Marco, which represents Saints Mark, Theodore, Jerome and Francis, he must have painted about 1464. Then he worked with his brother, Giovanni, very little younger than himself, and they remained associated until about 1472.

After the period of a set, Byzantine style, which held sway longer in Venice than anywhere else, the period of Renaissance flowering was given extraordinary impetus by the achievements of the Bellini family, led by Jacopo (see page 31), whose scientific researches were of the highest importance for the sixteenth-century development of Venetian art.

Padua had become an active centre, rich in masterpieces, those of Mantegna in particular, and many Venetians came there for inspiration.

Although Venice was continually visited by artists from the North, who imported their methods of painting, Vasari attributes, to Antonello da Messina (1475, 1476) the introduction of oil painting into Italy. It must have been known earlier. But certainly it was used more and more in imitation of the North. The great innovation of Gentile Bellini was the use of this method, employed in little Flemish pictures, for large mural decorations which, until then, the Italians had painted in fresco. In their hands, the oil medium was made to express the warmth and pageantry of Venetian life.

In 1465, Gentile painted and dated an altarpiece, representing Lorenzo Giustiniani, now in the Venice Academy. In 1466, he was commissioned for two canvases for the Scuola di San Marco, that are now lost. In 1474, he was nominated official painter of the Republic of Venice, and was charged with the restoration of pictures in the Grand Council. In 1479, Mahomet II, a strange man, who interested himself in the study of religions, philosophy and art, asked for a Venetian painter, and Gentile Bellini had the good fortune to be sent to Constantinople, which haunted the imagination of more than one Italian painter. Of this period, there remains a portrait of his master, which is in the National Gallery. The fine nose, extremely long, dips sharply downwards to the black beard, while the dark, round eyes are piercing as the eyes of a bird, and the pale skin beneath the bright turban adds to the Oriental character of this portrait. Mahomet must have been very proud of his painter, for he gave him the title of Bey. Bellini brought back a large number of drawings.

On his return from Constantinople, in 1480, Gentile Bellini continued, with his brother, to restore the pictures in the Grand Council Hall, and to add new ones, which were later augmented by works of Carpaccio, Titian, Tintoretto, Veronese, etc. In 1577, a fire destroyed the whole of the great decoration.

But it was above all for the "Scuole" for those religious associations, which, under the patronage of a great saint, had so much influence on Venetian life and art, that Gentile devoted his talent. There he could represent the great processions which he watched and enjoyed in the sunshine; and he gives us a real sense of great ceremonies, under a large sky, and amid varied architecture.

The body known as the Scuola di San Giovanni Evangelista, which had already commissioned decorations from Jacopo Bellini, now required his son, Gentile, to decorate the walls of its "Antisala." Lazzaro Bastiani, Carpaccio and Mansueti contributed works also which represented the Miracles of the Reliquary of the Holy Cross, possessed by the Scuola. Gentile's *Procession on the Piazza San Marco* (1496) is now in the Venice Academy. The procession unfolds itself in front of the subdued gold of the church, the clergy in white, red and black robes. The artist's patience was unwearied in giving to the majestic ceremony all the fulness of detail which pleased him.

A second picture (1500), also in the Academy, represented a Miracle of the Holy Cross. The relic suddenly falls into the canal while the procession is crossing a little bridge. Immediately several priests, and citizens plunge into the water and swim to bring it back, but it escapes them, and only when Andrea Vendramino, the "guardian" of the Scuola, tries to rescue it does it glide gently to meet him, and into his hand. The great lady, kneeling on the quay in the foreground, is Catarina Cornaro, of whom there is also a portrait by Gentile at Budapest.

The third picture (1501), likewise in the Academy, represents the cure of Piero di Lodovico by a candle which had touched the relic.

In 1492, Gentile proposed to redo the decoration of the Scuola di San Marco, which had been destroyed by fire, but he did not begin it until 1504. He did this work, he said, by an inspiration "more divine than human." He painted the *Preaching of St. Mark at Alexandria* (Brera Gallery, Milan), and this time he had the very occasion to use the notes he had made at Constantinople. St. Mark's becomes St. Sophia, the whole Venetian piazza is transformed by being filled with white, bare Arab horses, veils of Dalmatian women; turbans take the place of the clergy's surplices, and giraffes and camels walk among the spectators.

But Gentile was not able to finish his work. He entrusted the fulfilment of it to his brother, Giovanni, and died in February, 1507.

See Pl. 16, Vol. II.

**— (Giovanni).**—About 1430-1516. Important Venetian painter, who helped to create the magnificent, richly coloured style of Venice. Giovanni represents the whole of the great movement from the primitive style to that of the finished Renaissance. Though still tender and re-

# FRESCO PAINTING

*There are many ways of using colour; each constitutes a different technique of painting. One of the simplest, used since antiquity, has been maintained to the present day. To it we owe the masterpieces of the Middle Ages and of the Renaissance. It is known as* alla fresca, *that is, done freshly. It consists of painting with water colour on a wall, the top layer of which is still damp. The plaster and colour dry simultaneously, the colour penetrates the top layer and becomes part of the wall. This is a quick procedure and not expensive. The grand manner of the Italians was determined by this rapid, large scale painting.*

GIOTTO: PIETÀ. MADONNA OF THE ARENA CHAPEL. (PADUA.)
*(Photo by Alinari.)*

TIEPOLO: CLEOPATRA. FRESCO IN THE PALAZZO LABIA, VENICE.
*(Photo by Anderson.)*

RAPHAEL: PLATO AND ARISTOTLE IN THE SCHOOL OF ATHENS. VATICAN, ROME.
*(Photo by Brogi.)*

Fresco painting was done very differently in the fourteenth century by Giotto than in the sixteenth century by Raphael, or in the eighteenth century by Tiepolo. But at all times the painters had to obey the exigencies of this technique: to paint rapidly without any possibility of correcting or retouching; to see on a large scale; to seek a general harmony rather than the precision of rendering. Fresco painting makes the artist use his imagination rather than letting him rely on his copying ability. This is why Italian artists were more original than the Flemish masters, who, painting in oils, practiced the "after nature" method. Fresco painting is a form of decorative art, while oil painting is best adapted for portraits, landscapes, and still-lifes.

# PAINTING: TEMPERA AND PASTEL

DISTEMPER *painting—referred to as* tempera *by the Italians—uses colour mixed with a substance which has the consistency of the white of eggs. The painters of the Middle Ages used this on panels of white wood, or on wood covered with gold leaf. This technique retains the purity and softness of the colours. It is the method employed by the religious painters. Its luminosity like a flame or the azure of the sky, gives to the pictures of the fourteenth and fifteenth centuries a soft and tender aspect, like the images in stained glass windows and missals. The tender Madonnas of Fra Angelico are the loveliest examples of tempera painting.*

STEPHAN LOCHNER: MADONNA (MUSEUM OF COLOGNE).
*(Photo by Nohring.)*

SIMONE MEMMI: ST. JULIETTE. FLORENCE.
*(Photo by Alinari.)*

ENGUERRAND CHARONTON: VIRGIN. VILLENEUVE-LÈS-AVIGNON.
*(Photo by Langlois.)*

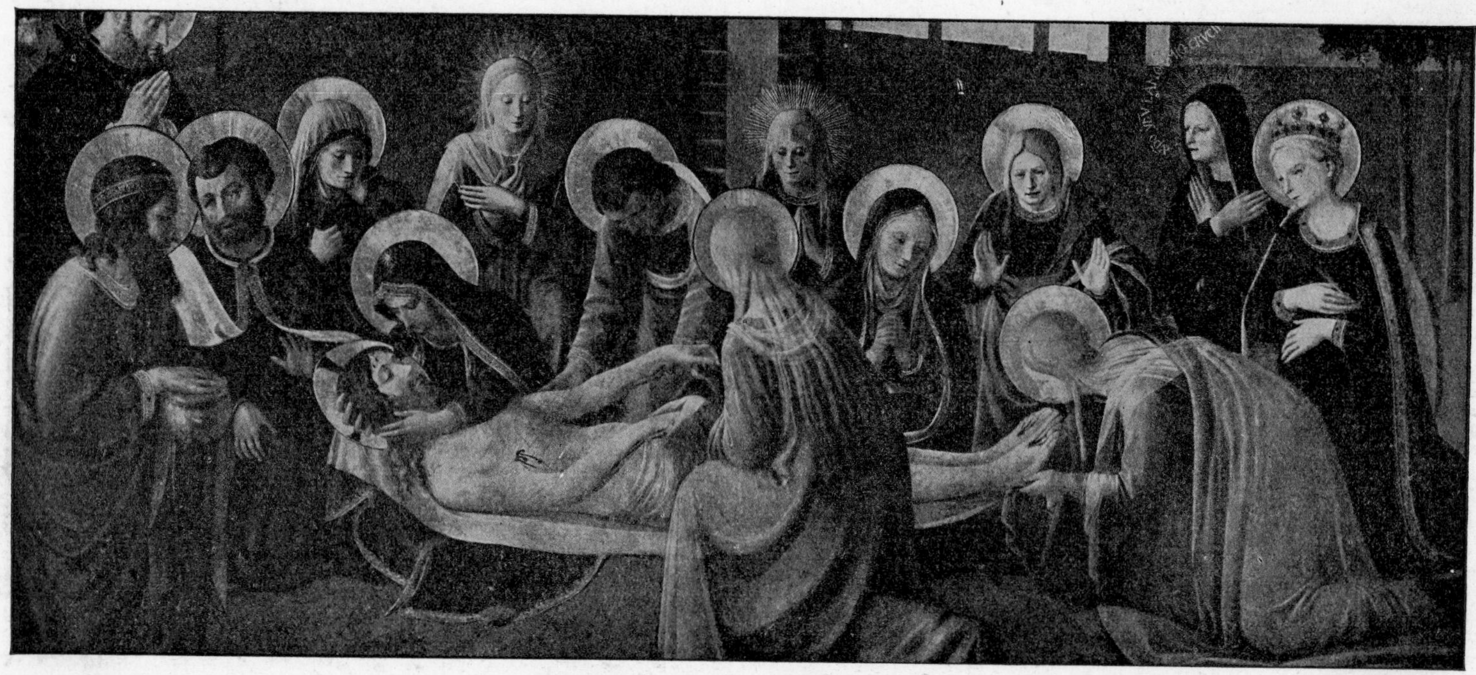

FRA ANGELICO: THE ENTOMBMENT. FLORENCE.
*(Photo by Alinari.)*

PASTEL—Pastel is a dry-paint process. The artist works with coloured chalk. This method does not have the permanence of other techniques, but it presents a charming lightness. Above all, the coloured chalk with which one paints reflects a nervous vivacity which liquid or paste media can achieve only to a very small degree. In a pastel, the spirit of the execution adds to the expression of the fact. The painting, benefiting by the charm and lively qualities of the colour, preserves the abstract grace of the sketch. The societies which liked to read the quick thoughts of an expressive face liked portraits in crayon or pastel.

LAGNEAU: DRAWING. LOUVRE.
*(Photo by Hachette.)*

CHARDIN: HIS PORTRAIT, PASTEL. LOUVRE.
*(Photo by Hachette.)*

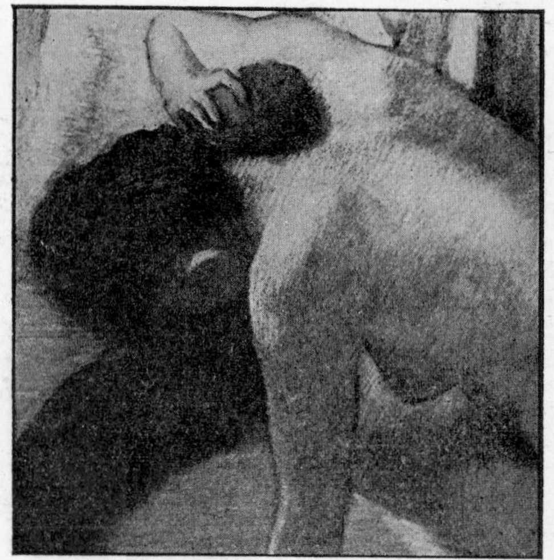

DEGAS: PASTEL. LOUVRE.
*(Photo by Hachette.)*

ligious like the old painters of the school of Murano, he profited from the example of his family, and from his early Paduan period where he was formed under the influence of Donatello and his own brother-in-law, Andrea Mantegna.

Very little is known of his life, which, except for some time spent in Padua, was probably passed entirely in Venice. He was born a little after his brother, Gentile, and they worked together in their father's studio, helping him with the execution of his large historical paintings, and his rich processional banners. Mantegna married their sister in 1453. They went to Padua when he had covered the walls of the Eremitani with superb frescoes. But in the midst of all the influences which they received, they each remained essentially Venetian.

Giovanni's name is first mentioned in 1459. There is a regrettable lack of sure dates for the first third of his life, and of dated works up to the year 1487. But in the early group can be placed those pictures which bear the strong imprint of Mantegna and of Donatello. To this earliest period belong a number of Madonnas: those of the Johnson Collection, Philadelphia; Trivulzio Collection, Milan; Metropolitan, New York (from the Davis Collection); Berlin Museum (1177); Museo Civico, Venice (formerly Frizzoni Collection); also the Blood of the Redeemer, National Gallery, London; the Transfiguration in the Museo Civico, Venice, and the Crucifixion in the same place. In all this group the forms are hard, the contours sharply drawn, the folds angular, and the endency towards stylization of type not so obvious. He is still more draughtsman than painter; Mantegna's influence appears in the landscape, the rock-formation, the dress, and the antique reliefs in the London picture. The culmination of this Mantegnesque period is the Agony in the Garden, also in London.

Giovanni Bellini's later Madonnas (1465-70) show fuller head-forms, wider hands, as for instance the Madonna dell' Orto, Venice; that in the Brera; that in Bergamo; and the Madonna with the standing Child in the Venice Academy. The masterpieces of this period include the altarpiece in Pesaro, deeper in character and purer in form, with, in the predella, a most happy disposition of figures in landscape; also the Pietà in the Vatican (top to the Coronation in Pesaro); the Transfiguration in Naples; and the Risen Christ in Berlin.

Authenticated dates of Giovanni's life are as follows: in 1460 he was helping his father in Padua; in 1464 he painted two pictures for the Scuola di S. Girolamo in Venice; in 1471 maintained an atelier with his brother. In 1472 he executed the grisaille-paintings in the Scuola della Carità; and in 1479 was intrusted, instead of Gentile, with the maintenance of the paintings in the Grand Council Hall. In 1483 he is mentioned as having been freed from the payment of guild fees. In 1492 he is active with a corps of helpers, Cristoforo Caselli da Parma, Lattanzio da Rimini, Marco Marziale, Bissolo, and Vincenzio da Treviso. In 1507 he declared himself able to undertake the three unfinished compositions left by Alvise Vivarini.

It is to be lamented that none of Giovanni's historical pictures in the Council Hall have survived, so that there is nothing from which we can determine their nature. He must have here mastered the oil technique in which his later large altarpieces are carried out. Of the Enthroned Madonna with ten Saints and three angels which was burned in 1867 with Titian's Peter Martyr, three inferior reproductions remain.

Two dated altarpieces remain from his middle period and show his gifts in full maturity. Both are of 1488: the great triptych in the Frari, Venice; and the Madonna with Saints and the Doge Barberigo in Murano. In this period, from 1475 to 1500 may be placed also: the Madonna with the Child Blessing, of which there are two versions, one in the Galleria Morelli, Bergamo; and the other in Kaiser-Friedrich, Berlin; the Madonna degli Alberelli, of 1487, in the Venice Academy; the Madonna with Catherine and the Magdalen and the Madonna with Paul and George, both in the Venice Academy; and the Madonna and Cherubim, also in the Venice Academy; the Madonna and Child with the Apple, in the National Gallery, London. Several small poetic pictures fall within this group, including the Allegory in the Uffizi, and the five Allegories in the Venice Academy.

From 1500 until Giovanni's death in 1516 date his large altars, in oil, in which landscape plays a dominant part and the old tradition of draughtsmanship has given way to a fully realized technique of pure painting. These include the Baptism in Vicenza, Sta. Corona; the 1505 altarpiece of Sta. Zaccaria; the 1507 Madonna in Landscape of S. Francesco della Vigna (in 1507 also he finished Gentile's picture for the Scuola di S. Marco and Alvise Vivarini's for the Council Hall); the 1510 Madonna in the Brera; the 1513 Madonna in S. Giovanni Cristosomo (his last great altarpiece). From 1514 dates the Feast of the Gods in the Widener Collection, Philadelphia (trees on the right by Titian); and from 1515 the Lady at her Toilet in Vienna.

**— (Jacopo).**—Great innovator and great intellect of the Renaissance, Jacopo Bellini exercised a profound influence not only upon the art of Venice but upon that of all of North Italy. He was born c. 1400 and was a pupil of Gentile da Fabriano, was also influenced by Pisanello and the Florentines.

The dates of Jacopo's life are few, as are also his extant paintings. His originality, his scientific knowledge, and the extraordinary breadth of his interests are best to be realized from his two great sketch-books, one of which is in the British Museum, the other in the Louvre. His genius might be compared to that of Leonardo in that his passion for research and for aesthetic problems far outweighed his interest in the practice of painting.

Jacopo was probably in Florence with his master, Gentile da Fabriano, in 1423, although it has never been definitely established that the Jacopo there mentioned was he. In 1424 he is referred to in his father's testament, in Venice. In 1436, he executed a Crucifixion for the Duomo of Verona, which was destroyed in 1759; and in 1437 he is mentioned as among the confratelli of the Scuola Grande of S. Giovanni Evangelista. In 1441 he triumphed over Pisanello in a competition for a portrait of Lionello d'Este; in 1443 he was again in Venice; and in 1453 he married his daughter Nicolosia to Andrea Mantegna. In 1456 he is paid for the figure of Lorenzo Giustiniani above his tomb; in 1460 he painted in Sant' Antonio in Padua, Cappella Gattamelata, aided by his sons, Gentile and Giovanni. In 1465 he executed paintings for the Scuola di S. Giovanni Evangelista; and in 1466 finished two pictures for the Scuola di S. Marco, and was commissioned for five more pictures. (The Scuola burned in 1485.) In 1471, Anna, his widow, makes her will.

Bibliography: Bellini family: Vasari, III.—Ridolfi, I, 34-38.—Paoletti, *Raccolta di documenti inediti per servire alla storia della pittura veneziana,* I, 1894.—Crowe and Cavalcaselle, V, 99-198.—Berenson, *Venetian Painters,* 1897, p. 81.—L. Venturi, *Le origini della pittura Veneziana,* 1907, pp. 118-167, 323-397.—Gronau, Georg, *Jacopo, Gentile u. Giovanni Bellini,* Künstlermonographien; and *Die Künstlerfamilie Bellini,* Leipzig, 1909.—Testi, *Storia della pitt. veneziana,* II, 1915, pp. 143-294. Literature on Jacopo is given in Rivista d'Arte, IV, 1906, p. 23; also Corr. Ricci, *Jacopo Bellini e i suoi libri e disegni,* Florence, 1908; and V. Golubew, *Les dessins de Jacopo Bellini au Louvre et au British Museum,* Brussels, 1908. For Giovanni, see Roger Fry, *Giovanni Bellini,* London, 1900; and Georg Gronau, *Giovanni Bellini,* 1930.

**BELLOTTO (Bernardo).**—Called Canaletto after his uncle, Antonio Canaletto, Venetian painter (1720-1780). Worked first in Venice and elsewhere in Italy; from 1747 onwards lived exclusively abroad (Dresden, Vienna, Petersburg, Warsaw, where he died as court painter to the King of Poland). A topographical painter of great talent even if not on the same level as his uncle.

**BELLOWS (George Wesley).**—American painter and graver (1882-1925). He was born in Columbus, Ohio, 12th August 1882, the descendant of a long line of American ancestors. Even as a child it was recognized that he possessed an unusual talent. After his graduation from Ohio State University he went to New York to study painting with Robert Henri. He also worked for a time with Kenneth Hayes Miller and H. G. Maratta. Soon he was showing his pictures in the large annual exhibitions and in 1909 he was elected an associate member of the National Academy of Design, a great honour, since he was then only twenty-seven years old. The following year Bellows became an instructor of life and composition classes at the Art Students' League in New York. The subjects for his paintings were drawn from the members of his family and friends, scenes of various sports including prize fights, the exciting world of the circus, and the gay holiday crowds at the seashore. About 1916 he took up the study of lithography and succeeded in popularising that branch of the graphic arts which had been neglected in this country. In 1918 and 1919 he again taught at the Art Students' League and about the same time at the Art Institute of Chicago. When he died 8th January 1925 he left behind him a great quantity of work—paintings, drawings, and lithographs—more than many other artists have produced over a longer period of time. He saw clearly and rendered truthfully the playtime occupations of the American people. His portraits are characterised by a sympathetic and revealing interpretation of the personality of his sitters. While not a great colourist he was able to bring about certain emphasis and concentration by a few judiciously placed bits of bright colour as for example in the *Edith Cavell,* a very strong piece of anti-war propaganda. The lithographs display the artist's ability to express himself through the medium of tonal values in a clear representation of themes similar in scope to those used in his paintings. He received many prizes during his lifetime and his work is to be found in most of the large museums of this country, including the Boston Museum of Fine Arts, the Metropolitan Museum of Art and the Corcoran Gallery of Art in Washington.

See Pl. 62, Vol. II.

Bibliography: *George Bellows, His Lithographs,* compiled by Emma S. Bellows, 1928.—*The Paintings of George Bellows,* compiled by Emma Louise Bellows, 1929.—George W. Eggers, *George Bellows,* 1931.—For other bibliographical material on this artist see *The Index of Twentieth Century Artists* for March, 1934.

**BENEDETTO da MAJANO.**—See Majano.

**— da ROVEZZANO.**—Florentine sculptor and architect, born 1474 in Pistoia, died after 1552 in Vallombrosa near Florence. While inheriting the beautiful Florentine tradition, he aimed at greater realism, combined with imposing effects. He accentuates reliefs to produce strong shadows and is not afraid of a certain roughness. But his sculpture betrays the fact that art was already becoming academic. His chief works are: tomb of Piero Soderini, in the Carmine, Florence (1510); the beautiful marble altar in Santa Trinità (1552), probably made from decorative pieces of an earlier (1506) altar of Giovanni Gualberto, of which there are other pieces in the Bargello; the tomb of Oddo Altoviti (d. 1507) at the Church of SS. Apostoli; the chimney-piece of the palazzo Rosselli del Lureo, in the Bargello; and a statue of *St. John the Evangelist* (1512) in the Duomo of Florence.

Benedetto da Rovezzano: Tomb of Piero Soderini, The Carmine, Florence.

He was active in England where he worked (c. 1524-1529) on a tomb for Cardinal Wolsey, which was afterwards appropriated by Henry VIII. It was stripped of its bronze decoration under the Commonwealth, and the marble sarcophagus is still in St. Paul's, the burial-place of Nelson.

In 1543, Benedetto was once more in Florence.

**BENEVENTO (South Italy).**—This is a very old town which, according to tradition, was founded by Diomedes or by a son of Ulysses and Circe. From the Roman period, there remain some ruins of an ancient *theatre*, and an arch of triumph dedicated to Trajan, and known as the *Porta Aurea*. It is a magnificent monument, in a good state of preservation. It was formerly surmounted with a chariot with a statue of Trajan. It is covered with bas-reliefs representing scenes from the life of this emperor.

The *Cathedral* dates from the 11th and 12th centuries, and is decorated with antique bas-reliefs in marble.

**BENOZZO GOZZOLI.**—(Benozdi Lese di Sandro). Florentine painter, 1420-1497. First trained as a sculptor, as is indicated by the document of 1444, in which he contracts to work under Ghiberti on the second doors of the Baptistry in Florence. In 1447 he was Fra Angelico's assistant in Rome, and he went with his master to Orvieto, remaining there after Angelico returned to resume his work for the Pope. In 1449, Benozzo also is back in Rome, working on the Chapel of Nicholas V, where certain frescoes and decorations reveal his hand. Other works by him in Rome are the fresco of St. Anthony of Padua with Donors and Angels and the Madonna Enthroned at San Domenico e Sisto: a Madonna Giving the Girdle to Thomas (polyptych) in the Vatican; and, near Rome at Sermoneta, Church of Sta. Maria, the Madonna in Glory.

Benozzo worked alone at Montefalco from 1450 to 1452, painting in the Church of San Fortunato frescoes of a Madonna, Saints and Angels; a Madonna and Angel; and a S. Fortunato Enthroned. In the choir of San Francesco, Montefalco, there are frescoes of scenes from the Life of Francis by him.

In 1453 he was in Viterbo, frescoing the Cloister of Santa Rosa. These frescoes, now destroyed, are recorded for us only through copies in the form of tinted drawings. In 1456 he executed the altarpiece for the Collegio Gerolimiano in Perugia, a Madonna and Saints, now in the Gallery in that city. In 1458 he appears again in Rome.

The year following Benozzo undertook the commission for which he is most noted, the frescoes in the Chapel of the Riccardi Palace in Florence. Here, in his richly decorative Procession of the Magi, he included many portraits, among them studies of members of the Medici family.

Of the same period of Benozzo's development is the Madonna, Saints, and Angels (1461) in the National Gallery London. From 1464 to 1467 Benozzo was working in San Gimignano, where in the choir of S. Agostino there are frescoes by him of the Life of Augustine, in the execution of which he was assisted by pupils. In the Museo, in the Collegiata, and at Monte Oliveto near San Gimignano, are other works by Benozzo, dated during this interval.

In 1468 he began the large frescoes with scenes from the Old Testament of the Camposanto at Pisa, finished in 1484.

Many other works, scattered over the world, are attributed to Benozzo Gozzoli; in addition to painting, he decorated banners, standards and coats of arms. Through a document of 1497 we know that in that year he was one of a group of painters who judged Alesso Baldovinetti's frescoes in Sta. Trinità. In the same year he retired to Pistoia, where he died on the 4th of October 1497 and was buried in San Domenico.

Bibliography: Vasari-Milanesi, III, p. 45.—Gaye, *Carteggio*, I, pp. 191, 209, 271.—Zanobi-Bicchierai, *Alcuni documenti artistici*, Florence, 1855, Nos. III, VI.—Alb. Chiappelli, *Arch. stor. italiano*, S.V.t. XXXIV, p. 146 ff.—Crowe and Cavalcaselle, *Storia, etc.*, VIII, 1-143.—Benvenuti, *Gli affreschi di Benozzo Gozzoli nella Cappella del Palazzo Riccardi*, Florence, 1901.—A. Venturi, *Beato Angelico e Benozzo Gozzoli*, L'Arte, 1902.—Berenson, *Florentine Painters*, 1905, p. 105; same author, *Drawings of Flor. Painters*, I, p. 6; II, p. 25.—Ricci, *Benozzo Gozzoli*, Riv. d'Arte, Vol. I, 1904.—U. Mengin, *Benozzo Gozzoli*, Paris, 1909.

**BENSON (Ambrosius).**—Flemish painter of the first half of the 16th century. Probably of Lombard origin, he went to live in Bruges, in 1519; was there received as a master and died c. 1550. He submitted to Gerard David's influence, together with the influence of Italian Art. To him is attributed the *Deipara Virgo*, or Virgin announced by Prophets (Antwerp Museum), signed with the letters A. B., and inspired by a picture of the *Deipara Virgo* of St. Jacques, Bruges. Other works given to him are: a head of a Sibyl, wrongly held to be the portrait of Jacqueline of Bavaria; another *Sibyl* (Hainauer Collection, Berlin); the *Life of St. Anne* (Prado), a polyptych in five leaves, from Segovia; a triptych, signed A. B., found at Avila; a *Holy Family* (Nuremberg Museum); a *Madonna Between Two Saints* (Martin Le Roy Collection, Paris); a *Magdalene Reading* (Martin Le Roy Collection); a *Repose in Egypt* (Palazzo Durazzo, Genoa), and some portraits.

Bibliography: Bodenhausen, *G. David und seine Schule*, Munich.—Fierens Gevaert, *Les Primitifs Flamands*. Vol. v. p. 160.—Friedländer, M. J., *Altniederl. Malerei*. Vol. XI.

**— (Frank Weston).**—Contemporary American painter.

He was born in Salem, Massachusetts, 24th March 1862. From 1880 to 1883 he studied at the art school of the Boston Museum of Fine Arts and then went abroad for further instruction. For two years he worked at the Académie Julian in Paris under Boulanger and Lefebvre. He returned to the United States in 1885 and for the next two years taught at the Portland, Maine, School of Arts. He then went back to Boston and opened his own studio there. For some years he was an instructor in drawing at the Boston Museum of Fine Arts. He did figure pieces and some portraits, very often placing the subject in the open air so that he might study the effect of the sunlight upon his model. His wife and daughters were his models in his pictures, where they were treated with charming sentiment, very appealing in the figure arrangements and the delightful attitude represented. Other pictures depicted the joys of the fisherman or some still lifes which are characterised by the same delicacy of treatment and care for design. Mr. Benson is also the creator of many etchings which deal largely with studies of wild geese and ducks, the fowl that delight the sportsman. All have a spontaneous quality and linealistic character with the lovely patterns of the natural flying formations of those birds or the grace of a single one as it wings its way above the earth. He has tried his hand at mural decorations also, as may be seen in the *Graces* and the *Seasons* for the Library of Congress in Washington. He won a gold medal in the Corcoran Gallery exhibition of 1919, another at the exhibition of the Philadelphia Watercolor Society in 1924 and another gold medal at the Sesqui-Centennial Exposition in Philadelphia in 1926. Examples of his work are in the Corcoran Gallery in Washington and the Worcester Art Museum.

Bibliography: Lorinda M. Bryant, *American Pictures and Their Painters*, 1920.—Samuel Isham, *The History of American Painting*, 1927.—Pauline King, *American Mural Painting*, 1902.—Eugen Neuhaus, *The History and Ideals of American Art*, 1931.

**BENTLEY (John F.).**—British architect, 1839-1902. Designer of many collegiate and ecclesiastical monuments, but best known for the Roman Catholic *Cathedral of Westminster*, London, a huge church based upon the Byzantine-like Romanesque of Périgord, resembling the Cathedral of Angoulême.

**BENTON (Thomas Hart).**—Contemporary American painter. He was born in Neosho, Missouri, 15th April 1889. Both his father and his grandfather were prominent in national politics and he spent much of his youth in Washington, D. C. He started drawing sketches for a Joplin, Missouri, newspaper at the age of sixteen and later attended classes at the Art Institute of Chicago. In 1908 he went to Paris to continue his art education and remained there about five years, assimilating various influences of the younger men. Upon his return to the United States he painted movie sets and did some camouflage work for the United States Navy during the war. Later he travelled around the country making sketches and gathering ideas for use in some future mural depicting the life and customs of the different sections of the United States. He was able to employ the results of this study of regional conditions in the decorations for the New School for Social Research in New York City. Different phases of American industry were included along with a representation of the leisure-time occupations in any large American city. Two other important mural projects have since been completed by this artist: the *Arts of Life in America* for the Whitney Museum of American Art in New York City and the *History of Indiana* for the Indiana Building at the Century of Progress Exposition in Chicago in 1933. This mural was later moved to the War Memorial in Indianapolis for a permanent setting.

Aside from his murals Mr. Benton has executed many single paintings which include portraits and genre subjects. He has made illustrations for books and magazines and has taught classes at Bryn Mawr and Dartmouth and more recently at the Art Students' League in New York City. His art is characterised by plastic figures reminiscent of the Italian Renaissance, defined by strong rhythmical outlines and strengthened by a use of vivid colours.

See Pl. 63, Vol. II.

Bibliography: For a complete bibliography see *The Index of Twentieth Century Artists* for April, 1935.

**BENVENUTO (Gian Battista).**—Called l'Ortolano. Ferrarese painter, active first quarter of 16th century, influenced by Ercole Grandi, Dosso, and Garofalo.

**— di GIOVANNI.**—School of Siena, 1436-1518, a pupil of Vecchietta, influenced by Francesco di Giorgio.

His earliest work is the Annunciation in Volterra, S. Girolamo, signed and dated 1466. From 1470 date the ruined frescoes in the Spedale, Siena; the Nativity and predella, Volterra; and the Annunciation at Sinalunga, S. Bernardino. In 1475 he signed and dated a triptych in S. Michele Arcangelo, at Montepertuso. The signed triptych in the National Gallery, London, is of 1479. From 1483 dates the pavement from his designs in the Duomo of Siena; and the Madonna, Saints and Angels, with Pietà, in S. Domenico, Siena. In 1491 he dated and signed the Ascension now in the Academy, Siena; and in 1497 the Madonna and Saints at Torrita, Sta. Flora, which he executed with Girolamo di Benvenuto. The Sinalunga, Sta. Lucia, Madonna with Saints and Angels, on which he was assisted, is of 1509.

Bibliography: Vasari-Milanesi, III, 18.—Milanesi, *Doc.*, II, 344, 366, 378, 382, 387, 420; III, 46, 79; also *Discorsi*, 119, 130, 131; also *Scrittura degli artisti*, I, 77.—Crowe and Cavalcaselle.—Berenson, *Central Italian Painters*, 1900, p. 134.

**BERCK-HEYDE (Gerrit).**—Dutch painter, of Haarlem (1638-1698). He painted chiefly towns, houses, churches, squares, canals and bridges, first at Haarlem, and then at Cologne, and Heidelberg. To him are due the *Hotel de Ville at Haarlem*, the *Market Place*, the *Fish Market* (Haarlem), etc. He painted charming houses, bathed in light, and people chatting or moving about the streets.

**— (Job).**—Dutch painter, of Haarlem (1630-1693). He worked at Haarlem, Cologne and Heidelberg. In his *Painter's Studio* (Haarlem), it is said one can recognise the figures of Hals, of Wouwermann, of himself and that of his brother, Gerrit. He painted architectural and genre scenes.

**BERETTINI (Pietro).**—See Pietro da Cortona.

**BERGAMO (Italy).**—In the "old town" stands the Church of *Santa Maria Maggiore*, a Romanesque building, dating from 1137. The doorways have porches with columns resting on the backs of lions, sculptured by Campione. Near the church is the *Colleoni Chapel*, in the Renaissance style, the work of Amadeo (or Omodeo), 1470-1476. The façade was restored in the 18th century. The *Cathedral* was built by Scamozzi, in 1614. The *Accademia Carrara* contains an interesting collection of pictures.

**BERGOGNONE.**—See Borgognone.

**BERLAGE (Hendrik P.) 1856—.**—Dutch architect and designer of the Bourse, Amsterdam, 1898-1904; the Dye Works, Hochst, 1912; and the Christian Science Church, The Hague, 1914.

BIBLIOGRAPHY: J. Havelear, *Dr. H. P. Berlage.* 1927 (?).

**BERLINGHIERI (Barone).**—Lucchese dugento painter, brother of Bonaventura Berlinghieri. He contracted for various wall-paintings in Lucca 1240-1244; in 1254 executed a Crucifix for the Pieve at Casabasciana; in 1282 a Madonna with S. Andrew; and, 1284, a Crucifix for S. Alessandro Maggiore.

**— (Berlinghiero).**—Painter in Lucca, mentioned in a document of 1228 as born in Milan. Father of Barone, Bonaventura and Marco Berlinghieri. He painted the Crucifix for the monastery of Sta. Maria degli Angeli, Lucca, which is signed "Berlingerius me pinxit." Crosses in the Palazzo Venezia, Rome, and S. Maria Assunta at Villa Basilica (1230) are attributed to him.

**— (Bonaventura).**—Mentioned in Lucca 1240, 1243, and 1244, but the only sure existing work by him is the St. Francis panel in S. Francesco in Pescia, signed and dated 1235. In 1266 he is mentioned as about fifty years old.

BIBLIOGRAHY: Berlinghieri family: Ridolfi, *Sopra i tre più antichi pittori lucchesi,* Atti del R. Acc. lucchese, XIII, Lucca, 1845.—Crowe and Cavalcaselle, Douglas ed., I, p. 140.—M. Salmi, *Una tavola primitiva nella chiesa di S. Francesco a Pescia,* Rivista d'Arte, VII, 1910, fasc. 3-4.—B. Khvoshinsky e M. Salmi, *I pittori toscani dal XIII al XVI secolo,* I, Rome, 1912, p. 27.—O. Sirén, *Toskanische Maler,* p. 37.—Sandberg-Vavala, *La Croce Dipinta Italiana.*—V. Marle, *Italian Schools,* etc., I, 319-323.

**BERNA.**—See Barna.

**BERNARDINO BETTI.**—See Pinturicchio.

**— de' CONTI.**—Painter of Lombardy, c. 1490-1522. Pupil of Leonardo da Vinci.

**— di MARIOTTO.**—Umbrian painter, active 1497-1566, pupil of Fiorenzo di Lorenzo, influenced by Signorelli and Crivelli. Several pictures by him are in the Museo of Perugia.

**BERNINI (Gian Lorenzo Bernini).**—Architect and sculptor of Rome (1598-1680). The greatest representative of the Baroque style. His father was a Florentine painter and sculptor. But he was born in Naples and his taste for striking sights and animated gestures might be ascribed to the theatrical atmosphere he breathed on coming into the world. He was educated in Rome, however, arriving there in 1605 at the age of seven; and it is in Rome that most of his works are to be seen. With his buildings, colonnades and many fantastic fountains he gave to Rome a new and striking character.

At the age of fifteen Bernini had already received a commission for four statues for the Casino of Cardinal Scipio Borghese (now the Casino Rospigliosi). He represented Aeneas and Anchises, David throwing the stone, the Rape of Proserpine, Apollo and Daphne. These four groups are now in the Villa Borghese. Although still a little timid in comparison with the life and spirit of his later works, his gifts already made themselves felt. Under Bernini's chisel, the marble became supple and obedient, and he made it seem to quiver with life. His *Apollo* recalls the *Apollo Belvedere.* But the smooth, warm flesh of *Daphne* stirs convulsively as, in

BERNINI: TOMB OF URBAN VIII, ST. PETER'S, VATICAN, ROME.

its transformation, the raised arms take on the form of leafy branches.

Bernini made a statue representing Truth, which is at the entrance of a bathing-establishment in the Corso. The figure is merely graceful, dimpled and coquettish. But the face of the Blessed Albertina, dying, on a sculptured mattress, has a haunting smile (Church of San Francesco, Ripa).

BERNINI: ST. THERESA. SANTA MARIA DELLA VITTORIA, ROME.

The *St. Theresa* of Santa Maria della Vittoria is his masterpiece in sculpture. The little saint swoons in front of the angel, who aims at her the arrow of love. With closed eyelids and half-open mouth, she lets fall her hand, and faints amidst a tumult of drapery and clouds. Golden rays fall on her, from heaven. This kind of thing evidently pleased Urban VIII, for he became Bernini's patron and, after the death of Maderna (1629), commissioned him to direct the work of St. Peter's. The chief part of the building was finished. The nave was enlarged, but the Pope wanted it decorated, and Bernini did it sumptuously, adorning the building with different coloured marbles, as though he wished to do a kind of painting in sculpture, adding bronze and gold, false curtains in stucco, immense baby angels, large restless saints jutting out from their niches and destroying all the calm of the basilica by their enormous proportions and

BERNINI: APOLLO AND DAPHNE. (Museum of Villa Borghese, Rome.)

frenzied movements. The size of the building can no longer be easily appreciated because of the figures and ornaments which encumber it.

The baldachin over the High Altar, which was commissioned in 1624, but which was not finished till nine years later, is the striking example of this restless architecture. The twisted columns support the undulating canopy, while above angels perform circus exercises.

At the end of the church, Bernini put his great orchestra round the throne of St. Peter, hiding the old ivory underneath.

He hollowed out three passages in the piers which support the dome, for the ceremonious display of relics. He made the elaborate tomb of Urban VIII (d. 1644). The bronze figure of the Pope has neither the calmness of death, nor even simplicity, but, while in the act of blessing, his pontifical robes are disturbed and restless. *Charity* and *Power* on either side are fine strong figures, with smooth marble forms and elaborate garments. Their children are robust and chubby. But in the midst of this wealth of life, the

BERNINI: FONTANA DEL MORO, ROME.

fearful skeleton of *Death* appears, to inscribe the name of Urban on a black marble tablet.

Not less remarkable are the tombs of Alexander VII and of Clement IX. Bernini finished the decoration of the Pauline Chapel, opened the Sala Ducale, constructed the beautiful Scala Regia for the Popes to pass in pomp through the Ionic columns. Finally he built the celebrated colonnade which unrolls its Tuscan order in an immense semicircle in front of St. Peter's: 284 columns; 88 great pilasters, forming three large galleries; 162 gigantic saints, making lively silhouettes on top of the balustrade—never could one conceive of grander sentinels to guard the entrance to the Papal Church.

Beside such magnificence, the other Roman Churches seemed poor. He clothed their unadorned beauty with gold, marble and stucco, and added statues and balancing angels, especially in the sanctuaries, which were no longer worthy of religion of these worldly times. Bernini succeeded in changing the character of several of these forsaken churches. Santa Mariá del Popolo was enriched among others. There he put statues of Daniel and Habakkuk in the Chigi Chapel. He built Sant'Andrea on the Quirinal (1678) in an elliptical form. He contributed to the Palazzo Barberini.

He gave Rome a new appearance especially by his wonderful fountains. In the open air, under the vast blue sky, and in golden sunshine, he was freer to give reign to his fantastic imagination. Water springing up among rockwork was the essence of his choice. In the Piazza Navone, he surrounded it with a world of figures—four huge *Rivers,* and the *Continents* emerging from an enormous rock with the animals of their countries. The burlesque *Triton,* breathing into a shell, in the Piazza Barberini, and the one who is filling a fantastic ship, in the Piazza di Spagna, are entertaining figures. It was still after his designs that Niccolò Salvi erected the Trevi fountain.

On the Sant'Angelo Bridge he put up the statues of five graceful, though dreamy, angels holding instruments of the Passion.

Throughout the whole of his long life, Bernini was a universal artist, and while he built his enduring monuments of stone and bronze, he was not above organising fêtes, with canvas and cardboard decorations, accumulating complicated platforms and erections, effects of water and lighting, and so forth. There is a decoration of his in the studio of mosaics of the Vatican. There are caricatures by him in the cabinet of engravings of the Galleria Nazionale, in the Palazzo Corsini. It is said that he painted more than 200 pictures. He even illustrated the sermons of the Jesuit Oliva.

His influence, which was immense, was felt especially in France, where he spent some time, called there by Louis XIV. It is seen in the works of Legros, Houdon, Puget, etc.

**BERRUGUETE (Alonso).**—Born toward 1490 at Paredes de las Navas—died 1561 at Toledo. Though he was a painter as well as a sculptor, Alonso de Berruguete owes his great fame to his works executed in sculpture. It is believed that he left for Italy 2 or 3 years after the death of his father, the painter Pedro Berruguete (d. 1502), who, probably, was also his first teacher. Vasarı mentions him; he worked under

Michelangelo and Bramante. For the latter he made copies of the Laocoön group which was discovered in 1506. Bertaux says that he was destined to remember throughout his life this group of antique martyrs together with Michelangelo's titans. In 1520 Berruguete returned to Spain and was appointed to the rank of a court-painter by Emperor Charles V. But this appointment proved unsatisfactory, and after unsuccessful attempts to receive from the Emperor a favorable consideration of his claims, he established an atelier of his own at Valladolid. He prospered during the succeeding years.

Berruguete is the author of various sepulchral monuments. His first commission upon his return from Italy included a tomb for one of the chapels of the Monastery of Santa Engracia (destroyed in 1808) of Saragossa. His last work was the tomb of Cardinal D. Juan de Tavera (begun in 1554—more or less finished at the time of his death) in the hospital of San Juan Bautista, also called de Afuera, of Toledo.

However Berruguete's powers are most characteristically revealed in his woodcarvings and alabaster sculptures executed for the Cathedral of Toledo as well as in a number of gilded and polychromed wooden retablos with their decorated architectural encadrements enclosing statues and groups. Of the choir-stalls of Toledo Cathedral those on the right or Epistle side—are by Berruguete whereas the other half is the work of Felipe Bigarny also called Felipe de Borgoña. Both masters began work on the choir-stalls after 1539. After Bigarny's death (1543) Berruguete was given the contract previously awarded to his former collaborator, namely the execution of the episcopal chair and also with "the crowning feature of the west end and trascoro, . . . a transfiguration of large size, made of alabaster and encircled by gilded wood . . ." (finished 1548). Of his retablos the fragments of the high altar of the church of the monastery of San Benito of Valladolid—now in the museum of that city, are perhaps among his best known works. D. Manuel Gomez Moreno says that in the little figure of San Sebastian Berruguete obtained a perfect model, and one unmatched for its perception of beauty in all the range of his art.

The first of his retablos was ordered for the church of the monastery La Mejorada (1526) and is now at Olmedo. After pointing out the defects manifest in this altarpiece as, for instance, those of a technical nature or a failing in anatomical rendering, Gomez Moreno passes on to say: ". . . he sets everything aside in his striving after features of the dramatic passion which stirs within him, without formulas, without types, overflowing with fertile invention almost misplaced. At first these perversions offend, but afterwards they become understandable; they obsess us, and the suggestive effect pleases." Though during the succeeding years Berruguete's work underwent a process of modification the dramatic passion stirring within him always left its imprint upon his works.

Bibliography: *Enciclopedia universal ilustrada europeo-americana; Barcelona* 1905-1930; vol. VIII, art. Berruguete (Gonzalez Alonso). —M. Dieulafoy, *La statuaire polychrome en Espagne,* 1908.—*Thieme-Becker,* vol. III, 1909; art. *Berruguete, Alonso.*—A. Michel, *Histoire de l'art;* vol. IV, part 2. Paris, 1911.—E. Bertaux, *La Renaissance en Espagne et Portugal.*—A. Calvert, *Sculpture in Spain,* 1912. —R. de Orueta y Duarte, *Berruguete y su obra. Madrid,* 1917.—J. Agapito y Revilla, *La obra de los maestros de la escultura vallisoletana;* 1920-1929.—Tübinger Forschungen zur-Archaeologie und Kunst. G. Weise, *Spanische plastik aus sieben Jahrhunderten,* vol. II, parts 1 and 2, Reutlingen 1927; vol. III, part 2, Reutlingen, n. d.—Manuel Gomez-Moreno, *Renaissance sculpture in Spain.* Florence (Pantheon) 1931. —*Junta de ampliación de estudios é investigación es cientificas. Centro de estudios historicos,* El museo nacional de escultura de Valladolid; 1933.—M. E. Gomez-Moreno, *Breve historia de la escultura española.* Madrid, 1935.—*El arte en España,* M. Gomez-Moreno, Valladolid. Barcelona, n. d.

**BERTOLDO di GIOVANNI.**—Florentine bronze sculptor of the

Bertoldo di Giovanni: Pietà. (Louvre.)

15th century, pupil of Donatello and teacher of Michelangelo. Died 1491 in the Medici Villa at Poggio a Caiano at a great age; his birth date was approximately 1420 or even earlier. It is not impossible that Bertoldo was also a stone sculptor and in a rather unclear letter to Lorenzo de' Medici of 1469 he speaks also of architecture and perspective.

He may have assisted Donatello in Padua (1443-1453), which would explain the Bellerophon group having been in Paduan private possession, in the Alessandro Cappella; and would also explain his having been commissioned to do two reliefs for the choir-screen of the Santo, a commission afterwards turned over to Bellano. In any case, he took part in the execution of Donatello's pulpit at S. Lorenzo (1461-1466).

He was patronized by the Medici, as was Donatello, and like him had a room in the Palace in the Via Larga. In 1485 he accompanied Lorenzo to Morba. When at the death of Clarice Orsini, the Villa near S. Marco was made a museum of the Medici collections, Bertoldo was given the directorship of it and the newly organized art school. This academy came to a sudden end in 1494, but in its short life its pupils included Michelangelo, Torrigiani, Granacci, and Bugiardini.

Sure works by Bertoldo are the Bellerophon and Pegasus, now in Vienna; the medal of Sultan Mohammed II, after the portrait by Gentile Bellini; and the Battle Relief in Florence, Museo Nazionale. Innumerable other works have been collected under his name by various critics.

Bibliography: Vasari-Milanesi, II, 416, 423, 425; IV, 257; VI, 201; VII, 141-142.—Gulandi, *Lettere,* I, 14.—Milanesi, *La scrittura, etc.,* I, 60.—Morelli-Frizzoni, *Notizia d'opera d. disegno, etc.,* p. 39.—Müntz, *Les collections des Medicis* (Inventory of 1492, pp. 84, 96).—Bode, *Florent. Bildhauer der Renaissance; Italien. Bonzestatuetten der Ren.* I, pp. 13-15; *Renaissance Skulptur Toskanas,* p. 132-137.—M. Reymond, *La Sculpture florentine,* III, 42-46.—A Venturi, *Stor. d. arte ital.,* VI, 1908, pp. 342 f., 435, 494-521.—Burckhardt, *Cicerone,* 1909.

**BERTUCCI (Giovanni Battista).**—Painter of Faenza, active 1503-16, influenced by Perugino and Costa.

**BERVIC.**—French engraver, 1756-1822. Pupil of J. G. Wille, he derived from his master the taste for regular cutting, for a faultless but limited technique. His productions are not numerous but he had a considerable influence, which was felt during the whole of the first half of the 19th century. Bervic was held, in his day, to be one of the greatest engravers who had ever existed, and honours were heaped upon him. When, after the suppression of the Academy at the Revolution, the popular and republican Society of Arts was formed (on the proposal of Sergent), Bervic was chosen to take part. In 1803, he attained to the Institute, and resided there until the end of his life, the uncontested master of engraving.

**BESANÇON (Doubs, France).** The most interesting buildings are:

Besançon: The Black Gate. (Porte Noire.)

The *Porte Noire* (formerly Porte de Mars), with antique reliefs.

The *Cathedral* (St. Jean), 12th century, partly rebuilt in the 18th century.

The *Palais Granvelle,* built in the first half of the 16th century. It now contains the Museum, the Academy of Sciences and several administrations.

The *Hôtel de Ville* (1565-1573) was restored in 1911.

**BESNARD (Paul Albert).**—French painter (1849-1934). He was born 2d June 1849 in Paris, the son of an artist who had been a pupil of Ingres. His mother was a miniaturist and it was she who was the boy's first instructor. He was always interested in drawing and at the age of seventeen he entered the École des Beaux-Arts, working in the atelier of Cabanel. Later he was in the studio of Cornu who had been a pupil of Ingres, but his most important work was done outside school hours. In 1874 Besnard won the Prix de Rome and the next five years were spent studying in Rome. There he met and married Miss Charlotte Dubray, a sculptor, and in 1879 they moved to London. In England he executed some important portraits, including those of General Wolseley and Sir Barthe Frere, and also made some landscape studies. His first important commission for some mural paintings came in 1883, when he received an offer to do panels for the School of Pharmacy of the University of Paris. These paintings were strongly influenced by the work of the Pre-Raphaelite Brotherhood, but they also reflected the academic tradition of his early training. That same year Besnard and his wife left England and returned to live in Paris, where he continued his work, which at that time fell halfway between true academicism and impressionism. In 1890 he did some decorations for the Salon des Sciences in the Hotel de Ville in Paris, an allegorical theme of the benefits of science for mankind. From 1897 to 1901 he was engaged on some panels for the chapel of the Hospital Cazin-Perrochaud at Berck as partial payment for the curing of his child at the institution. He also did mural decorations for the Petit Palais, a ceiling for the Théâtre-Français, and some panels for the Salle des Mariages in the Mairie of the First Arrondissement, all of which were in Paris. He made trips to Algiers and Hindustan, where he sketched the people and street scenes full of the colour of the native life. In 1912 Besnard was elected to membership in the Académie des Beaux-Arts and the following year he succeeded Carolus-Duran in the management of the Villa Medici in Rome, which position he retained until 1919. In that year he became the director of the École Nationale des Beaux-Arts, the leader of the state school of art. Beside his mural decorations and paintings of figures, landscapes and some portraits Albert Besnard did some book illustrations for novels, including *L'Affaire Clemenceau* and *La Dame aux Camélias.* He died in Paris 4th December 1934, one of the last of the academic painters of the older generation.

Bibliography: Albert Besnard, *Sous le Ciel de Rome,* 1925.—Albert Besnard, *La Tour, la Vie et l'Œuvre de l'Artiste,* 1928.—Camille Mauclair, *Albert Besnard, l'Homme et l'Œuvre,* 1914.—Gabriel Mourey, *Albert Besnard,* 1906.—Hans W. Singer, *Zeichnungen von Albert Besnard,* 1914.

**BETHLEHEM.**—*Church of the Nativity,* 330 A.D. A great five-aisled Constantinian basilica, now much restored, erected over the supposed birthplace of Christ. It had an atrium and a narthex. Monolithic debased Corinthian columns support the high nave wall. The trefoil choir concentrates attention upon the crossing, supposedly the actual site of the Nativity.

**BETTO (Bernardino di).**—See Pinturicchio.

**BEUKELAER (Joachim).**—Flemish painter, born in Antwerp about 1530, master of the Guild in 1560; died c. 1573. Pupil and nephew of Aertsen, whose rustic, popular "genre" he imitated. His best paintings are: the *Game Merchant* (Vienna), the *Fishmonger's Stall* (Munich), the *Market* (Munich), the *Game Market* (Stockholm), and a whole series of *Ecce Homo,* which are chiefly scenes of market-gardeners (three in Stockholm).

**BEVERLEY.**—Municipal borough in East Riding, Yorkshire, England. The *Church of St. John the Evangelist,* Beverley minster, is a fine example of Early English architecture. Most of the exterior is in the Decorated style. The Church of St. Mary's is in the Decorated and Perpendicular style.

See Pl. 49, Vol. I.

**BIANCHI-FERRARI (Francesco).**—Painter of the school of Modena, born in 1457, settled in Modena in 1481, died in 1510. Influenced by Cosimo Tura and Ercole Roberti; here is an expressive roughness in the *Crucifixion* of the Este Museum, Modena. The *Annunciation,* in the same Museum, was left unfinished at his death. He is credited with a *Virgin Enthroned between St. Jerome and St. Sebastian,* in St. Peter's at Modena.

**BIANCO (Bartolommeo), or Baccio del Bartolommeo di Como.**

Bianco (Bartolommeo): The University Palace, Genoa.

—Genoese architect. Died about 1656. Pupil of Galeazzo Alessi. His style was less grandiose than that of his master, as may be seen in his fine University buildings, and his monumental vestibule in the Palazzo Durazzo-Pallavicino (in collaboration with Tagliafico), and the Palazzo Balbi-Senarega.

**BICCI di LORENZO.**—Florentine painter, 1373-1452, pupil of his father Lorenzo di Bicci, influenced by Gentile da Fabriano and Lorenzo Monaco.

The earliest recorded date for Bicci di Lorenzo is 1414, at which time he was at work in the church at Porciano in the Casentino. In 1416 he colors and gilds candlesticks in the Bigallo, Florence. From 1420 to 1446 he is documented with great regularity, and a document of 1424 proves he was sculptor as well as painter, in that he executed for the church of S. Egidio reliefs in terra-cotta. From the tax statements, Bicci's activity must have been enormous, and this assumption is confirmed by the large number of paintings extant which show his hand.

Among his dated works are the following: 1414, Porciano, triptych, Annunciation, four Saints; 1423, Empoli, Madonna Enthroned; 1427, Florence, Corner Via Serragli and Via S. Monaca, tabernacle, Madonna Enthroned; 1430, Porta S. Giorgio, Madonna with Saints George and Leonard; 1430, Vertine, Chianti, Parish Church, triptych; 1433, Parma, Madonna; 1434, Florence, S. Trinità, Cappella Compagni, Coronation and Saints; 1435, Bibbiena, Casentino, triptych, Madonna and four Saints; 1440, Legnaia, S. Arcangelo, Annunciation; 1445, Empoli, S. Stefano, altarpiece, Nicholas of Tolentino. Frescoes by Bicci are in Arezzo, Lastra a Signa, among others.

Bibliography: Vasari-Milanesi, II. —G. Poggi, *Rivista d'arte,* V. 1907.—Poggi, Supino e Ricci, *Il Bigallo,* p. 50.—O. Sirén, *L'Arte,* 1913, p. 216.—M. Logan Berenson, *Rassegna d'arte,* 1915, p. 209.

**BIERSTADT (Albert).**—American painter (1830-1902). He was born at Solingen near Düsseldorf on the Rhine but came to the United States as a young child. He grew up in New Bedford, Massachusetts, and decided that he would like to become a painter. He went back to Germany and studied at Düsseldorf under Achenbach and Lessing. He also made a trip to Rome where he remained for a time, but in 1857 he returned to the United States to live. His great opportunity came the following year when he made a cross-country trip with a surveying expedition. He was much impressed with the height of the Rocky Mountains and the wonders of the Yosemite Valley and tried to set down his reactions in the meticulous and detailed style of the Düsseldorf school. A very exact topographical study of these locations was made which today strikes us as being very photographic and descriptive rather than touched by the artistry of genius. He always chose the romantic aspects of the scenery and tried to endow them with the correct air of mystery which was at that time the popular approach to landscape painting. He made several trips to Europe and in 1867 was given the award of the Legion of Honor. During his later years he devoted his time to the painting of wild animals similar in character to the bird studies of Audubon. He died 18th February 1902.

Bibliography: Samuel Isham, *History of American Painting,* 1927. —H. T. Tuckerman, *Book of the Artists,* 1867.

**BIGALLO (The).**—See Florence.

**BIGORDI.**—See Ghirlandaio (Domenico).

**BIRON (Dordogne, France).**—The most famous château of Péri-

Biron: The Château.

gord, a collection of buildings in various styles. The oldest part is a 12th century keep, in ruins. The greater part dates from the 15th century.

**BISCUIT.**—Said of pottery and porcelain before it has received a covering. A "biscuit" is also a statuette, a little group in fine pottery or porcelain, without glaze or paint. The pottery biscuits are made chiefly at Luneville and at Saint Clément on the models of Cyfflé, called "terres de Lorraine." Biscuits of soft porcelain, and of hard porcelain, are of the glories of Menneny, of Niderviller, of Vincennes and of Sèvres. The greatest sculptors of the 18th century made models for it, and the rather finikin grace which was the ideal of that period, is nowhere expressed more completely than in these fragile figures.

**BISSOLO (Francesco).**—Venetian painter, active from the end of the 15th century until he died in 1554. A pupil of Giovanni Bellini, whose modelling of forms is soft, with bituminous shadows. He signed a beautiful *Coronation of St. Catherine of Siena,* which takes place in the calm of a golden evening. It is now in the Academy of Venice, from St. Peter Martyr of Murano.

**BLACK MANNER.**—See Engraving.

**BLAKE (William).**—English painter and engraver (1757-1827), an artist possessed of powers of highly original and abstruse imagination which are reflected in his remarkable poetical production. Much of his work as an artist was done for the purpose of book illustration: particularly celebrated are his illuminated engravings for his poems, *Songs of Innocence,* 1787, and his engravings for Young's *Night Thoughts,* 1797, and for the *Book of Job,* 1825. An extensive collection of paintings and engravings by him may be studied at the National Gallery, Millbank.

Bibliography: A. G. B. Russell, *The Paintings and Drawings of William Blake.* London, 1909.

**BLAKELOCK (Ralph Albert).**—American painter (1847-1919). He was born in New York City 15th October 1847. He was the son of a physician but preferred music and painting to the practice of medicine. He studied for a while at Cooper Union Institute but was otherwise a self-taught artist. He made tight pictorial compositions copied exactly and minutely from nature. Many of his pictures portray episodes in the lives of the American Indians, but the figures seem dwarfed in the great expanses of scenery as they pitch their camps or build their canoes amid the quiet and solemnity of the deep forest. Others of his pictures are exclusively landscapes, some of the most beautiful being studies of moonlight with great dark masses of trees in the foreground silhouetted against a luminous sky. He also painted figure studies, marines, and some flower pieces, all of which are characterised by a mood of quiet melancholy. The technique of his work is interesting by the layers of paint put on over fresh varnish, smoothed down and gone over with transparent paint to produce an opaque effect and depth in the composition.

Blakelock's career was one of many privations and financial hardships which reflected in his paintings. The uncertainty of an income and the attendant worry caused him to lose his sanity. He was committed to an asylum in Bennington, New York, in 1899. There he remained until 1916 when his condition had improved enough to enable him to be released. During the period of his confinement his paintings became of note in the art world. He was elected to full membership in the National Academy of Design in 1916, and from exhibitions an adequate income was available for his family. The improvement in his mental condition in 1916 proved only temporary. He could not paint and his mental worries returned. He went back to the asylum in 1918 and died at a camp in the Adirondacks 9th August 1919. His poetic treatment of nature has been compared to the work of Albert P. Ryder, but it is extremely different in the minute treatment of nature as compared with the broad masses and surfaces in the work of Ryder. His interest in the American Indians followed a trip to the West where he came into intimate relations with them. His pictures include natural objects which stand out like silhouettes, unreal as the dreams th[illegible] and this unreality is[illegible] the strong contras[illegible] shade which are [illegible] Among his best wo[illegible] tioned *Sunset* and [illegible] in the National [illegible] Washington, D. C[illegible]

Bibliography [illegible] field, *Ralph A.* [illegible]

**BLANCHE** [illegible] French painter, [illegible] Pupil of Gervex and [illegible] was early distinguished [illegible] style which recalls the [illegible] lish painters of the 18t[illegible] with more decided colour [illegible] nervous drawing. In this sty[illegible] he made very personal, [illegible] painted chiefly portraits, somet[illegible] groups, more often individuals. H[illegible] also painted some fine still-life groups. Thanks to the freshness and variety of the execution his work forms a gallery of contemporary notabilities, full of interest, in spite of the monotony in the kind of art which he practised. The *Thaulow Family* (Luxembourg Museum), *Cottet* (Brussels Museum); *Maurice Barrès; Debussy; Rodin; Mme. Rauray* (Lyon Museum); *Child lying down* (Dieppe Museum); *Portrait of a Lady* (Munich); *Little Girl with a Straw Hat* (Rouen), etc.

**BLARENBERGHE (Louis Nicholas van).**—1716-19—1794. Son of a Fleming, he studied Flemish and Dutch paintings. He was much influenced by Van der Meulen, and, like him, painted sieges (chiefly those of the Marshall of Saxe, Fribourg, Mons, Namur, Berg-op-zoom, Ghent, Brussels, etc.), battles, and harbour views. His pictures of sieges, as well as views of some European capitals, are at Versailles.

**BLASHFIELD (Edwin Howland).**—American mural painter (1848-1936). He was born in New York City 15th December 1848. With the advice of William Morris Hunt he went abroad to study in 1867. He worked in Paris under Léon Bonnat and also got some help from Gérôme and Chapu for the next three years. In 1870 he spent some time in Florence and Belgium and then returned to his own studio in Paris. About 1881 he went back to New York City but in 1887 he went abroad with his wife to do magazine articles for *Scribner's* and the *Century* on medieval and Renaissance art. They travelled to England, Egypt, Greece, Italy and France where Mrs. Blashfield wrote the articles and he did the illustrations. In 1892 he was invited to help decorate the Manufacturers' and Liberal Arts Building for the Columbian Exposition in Chicago. It was the first of his long series of mural decorations. After that he executed murals for the dome of the Library of Congress, the Court House in Baltimore, the State Capitols of Minnesota, Iowa, and Wisconsin, the public library in Detroit, the Assembly Hall of the College of the City of New York, the Citizens' Bank in Cleveland, and the Federal Building in that same city. With Mrs. Blashfield he wrote *Italian Cities* and with the further assistance of A. A. Hopkins edited Vasari's *Lives of the Painters.* Some years later he wrote *Mural Painting in America.* He was the recipient of many awards, including the gold medal for distinguished service given by the National Academy of Design in the early part of 1934. His work is charl draughtsman- rawing through schemes, and is for the buildings s by its presence. ctober 1936.

nda M. Bry- es and Their uline King, ting, 1902.— ss, Architec- tions, 1900. History and t, 1931.

.—Flemish painter ury. Little is known was born perhaps at nd died after 1550. He prolific, and is chiefly s a landscape painter. He e little compositions of trees, ocks, towns, drawn with exquisite delicacy, in pure, deep tones, from which figures clad in bright colours stand out. He signed them with an owl, which he took as his emblem ("Owl" or "Tawny-owl" was the nickname of the people of Bouvignies). He is often called the "Master of the Owl."

He knew Patinir, and probably visited Italy, especially Venice, where he is credited with: *Dante's Hell* (Doges' Palace); the *Temptation of St. Anthony* (Correr Museum); the *Tower of Babel* (Academy); and the *Preaching of St. John* (late Manfrino Gallery). Almost all the European Galleries, except the Louvre, have pictures attributed to Bles: the *Adoration of the Magi* (Munich); the *Holy Family* (Basle); the *Pilgrimage to Emmaus* (Vienna). He collaborated with a number of contemporary artists, often painting the landscapes of their pictures.

Bibliography: J. Helbig, *L'Art Mosan;* Brussels, 1906.—H. Béquet, *Henri Bles, artiste bouvinois* (Ann. of the Soc. arch. of Nauner; 1863-1866).—Woermanor, *Gesch. der Malerei.* Vol. II.

**BLOEMAERT (Abraham).**—Dutch painter, 1564-1651, who studied in Paris and worked at Utrecht. His best known pictures are *Niobe* (1591, Copenhagen); and *Lazarus* (1607, Munich).

Bibliography: Delbanco, G., *Der Maler A. Bloemart.* Strassburg, 1928.

**BLOIS (Loir-et-Cher, France).**—Magnificent château, built by the Comte de Chatillon who sold it to the Duke of Orleans, at the end of the 14th century. The château was begun in the 13th century ("Grande Salle des Etats"), was continued in the 15th century, and added to by Louis XII and Francis I. The buildings are grouped round an irregular courtyard. One enters the courtyard by a passage through the buildings erected by Louis XII (A.D. 1503). Over the doorway is an equestrian statue of this King. On entering the great courtyard the Renaissance building of Francis I (1515-1530) is on the right. The façade is famous for its open spiral staircase adorned with statues. Some interesting chimney-stacks are decorated with reliefs of salamanders—ubiquitous emblem of Francis I. Gaston d'Orléans, who came into possession of the Château of Blois in 1626, added a wing, built by François Mansart. Its stately formality contrasts with the early Renaissance work. This is that part of the château which faces the visitor on entering the courtyard.

Blois: The Château. Wing of Louis XII. Side Facing the Court.

Blois: The Château. Wing of Francis I. Side Facing the Court.

The Château of Blois was the scene of many historic events, the most famous being the assassination of the Duke of Guise, in 1588. See Pl. 27, Vol. II.

**BLONDEEL (Lancelot).**—Flemish painter, of 16th century. Born at Poperinghe in 1496. A mason before he became a painter, he was received in July, 1519, as a master of the Guild of St. Luke. He chiefly designed cartoons for tapestries, sculpture, and goldsmith's work, and showed considerable fantasy and spirit. He abused details taken from Italian art—garlands, cupids, arabesques. He painted a *St. Luke Painting the Virgin,* in the Museum of Bruges; a *Legend of Sts. Cosmo and Damiano,* 1523, inspired by Raphael (St. Sauveur, Bruges); a *St. Peter* (Brussels Museum), and the design of the famous chimney of Franc de Bruges. He died in 1561.

Bibliography: Friedländer, M. J., *Altniederländ. Malerei,* Vol. XI.

**BLONDEL (François).**—French architect. Born: Ribemont, 1618; died: Paris, 1686. Son of a professor of mathematics, François first received a scientific education. In 1652, he accompanied a son of the Secretary of State, Loménie de Brienne, with whom, according to the custom, he made a tour of Europe. The stay in Rome inspired Blondel with a taste for architecture, to which, however, he never devoted himself entirely. In 1659, the king dispatched him on a diplomatic mission to Constantinople, and he took the opportunity to visit the East and Egypt. Later, he saw the West Indies.

Blondel (François): Porte St. Denis, Paris.

His first work dates from 1665: the construction of the Pont de Saintes, which he crowned with a triumphal arch. In 1666, he, together with the ingenious Clerville, made the plans of Rochefort, and there built the arsenal. Then he taught the Dauphin mathematics, while he was professor at the Royal College. A member of the Academy of Science since 1669, he was one of the first eight members of the Academy of Architecture, at the time of its foundation on the 31st December, 1671. He there exercised the functions of Director, and was the uncontested head of it until his death.

The king, who had commanded him to make a plan of buildings to be set up in Paris, conferred upon him the titles of "Seigneur des Croisettes" and "Seigneur de Gaillardon," on the occasion of his work on a cannon.

The chief work of Blondel, "Le Cours d'Architecture," appeared in 1675. To have an idea of Blondel's knowledge, one must add "L'Architecture française" (1673), "La Résolution des quatre principaux problèmes d'architecture" (1673), "L'Art de fortifier les places," "L'Art de jeter les bombes" (1685), "Le Cours de mathématiques" (1683), "La Comparaison de Pindare et d'Homere," "L'Histoire du Calendrier romain" (1682).

Blondel was a theorist, and he built little apart from the Porte St. Denis. He speaks of architecture in terms of mathematics, and geometry. He had travelled a great deal, and only conceived of architecture through Vitruvius, Palladio, and Vignola; but he brought it round chiefly to arithmetic.

To understand the entirely classical thought of Blondel, one must hear him speak of his masterpiece in his "Cours d'architecture": "And since the whole world is agreed that there is nothing more beautiful among the remains of antiquity than Trajan's Column, than the obelisques which have been transported from Egypt to the city of Rome, and remains of the rostral column that is still to be seen on the Capitol, I wanted the ornament of the Porte St. Denis to be composed of parts copied from these beautiful originals."

Blondel put his theories into practice by applying the Egyptian pyramid to the Roman arch, and, with the collaboration of Girardon and of Michel Anguier, decorating his triumphal arch with abstract figures, perfectly subordinated to the architecture.

**BLOUET (Guillaume Abel).**—French architect. Born at Passy (Seine), 6th October, 1795. Died in Paris, 17th May, 1853. In 1821, he won the Grand Prix de Rome by a "Palais de Justice."

In 1848, Blouet, having been nominated architect of the château of Fontainebleau, carried out important restoration work in this royal residence.

**BOBOLI GARDENS.**—See Florence; Tribolo.

**BOCCACCINO (Boccaccio).**—Painter of Cremona (1467?-1525?). Born at Ferrara, son of Antonio, an embroiderer, he went to work in Venice (1496), where he studied under Alvise Vivarini and was influenced generally by the Venetian School; and after having been to Genoa, and to Milan, where he was imprisoned for killing his wife for adultery, at Ferrara, he settled in Cremona (1505), where he was the founder of the 16th century school. One of his best known pictures is the *Virgin Surrounded by Saints,* of the Academy, Venice, a beautiful Holy Conversation in front of a wide landscape. One might also mention the *Virgin Enthroned,* in San Guiliano, Venice. With several collaborators, he decorated the interior of the Cathedral of Cremona (1515-1518).

**BOCCADOR (Domenico di Cortona, known as Il).**—Italian architect, born at Cortona. Died about 1549. He worked in France for Louis XII and Francis I. According to documents, he was one of the earliest architects of the Château of Chambord. His chief title to fame is the Hôtel de Ville, of Paris, begun in 1533. (The present Hôtel de Ville was built in 1871).

Boccador: City Hall, Paris.

Bibliography: Leroux de Lincy, *Histoire de l'Hôtel de Ville de Paris.* Paris, 1846.

**BOCCATI (Giovanni, da Camerino).**—Active in Umbria third quarter of the 15th century, influenced by Lorenzo Salimbeni, Piero della Francesca and the Florentines. He is well represented in the Museum at Perugia.

Bibliography: Feliciangeli, *Sulla vita di Giov. Boccati da Camerino.* San Severino, 1906.

**BOCHOLT (Franz von).**—German engraver of the 15th century. Nothing is known of the life of this artist, who signs himself F. V. B. It is only known that he worked between 1455 and 1480. He left fifty engravings, among them the *Judgment of Solomon,* the *Virgin with the Infant Christ, Christ on the Cross,* and some copies of Engravings by Martin Schongauer.

Bibliography: Bartsch, *Le Peintre-Graveur,* Vol. IV.— Passarant, *Le Peintre-Graveur,* Vols. I and II. —Willshire, *Catalogue of the Early Prints in the British Museum: German and Flemish schools,* 1883, Vol. II.

**BÖCKLIN (Arnold).**—Swiss painter, 1827-1901. Born in Basle. He studied first at Düsseldorf, and then, in 1848, went to Paris, where he witnessed the Revolution. From 1850 to 1862, he stayed in Munich and in Rome. From 1862 to 1866, he executed various copies of the Villa by the Sea, of which two examples are to be seen at the Schack Gallery, in Munich. In Basle, from 1866 to 1871, he gave himself up to fresco, and carried out three important compositions for the house of M. Sarasin and for the town museum. From then Böcklin seems to have found himself more completely. His style became broader, and he won a technical ability that he had not had before these efforts. The *Ride of Death*, the *Pilgrims of Emmaus*, and the *Furies and the Murderer* (Schack Gallery) have a powerful effect and intense colour. About the same time, he modelled some busts of his contemporaries, but in such a spirit of satire that he made enemies and had to leave his native town. He went to Munich (1871-1874), to Florence (1874-1885), to Zurich (1885-1892). He was strongly influenced by Botticelli's *Primavera*, and the triptych of Hugo van der Goes in Florence. His compositions became more simple, and his taste for bold colour was singularly subdued. It was at this time that he painted the *Isle of the Dead*. In Zurich, he painted portraits, idyls, historical and mythological pictures, such as the *Play of the Wave*, in the Munich picture gallery. He died at Florence, in 1901.

See Pl. 59, Vol. II.

**BOECKHORST (Jan van).**—Flemish painter, 1605-1668. Pupil of Jordaens. The author of pictures of churches, and a mythological picture, *Herse Presenting Herself at the Temple of Minerva* (Vienna). He painted the figures of four fine still-lifes of Snyders (Hermitage Museum).

**BŒOTIA.**—See Greece (Sculpture).

**BOICHOT (Guillaume).**—French sculptor, 1735-1814. Pupil of the school of Dijon, gifted with a pleasing imagination. His bas-relief, the *Triumph of Temperance* (Dijon Museum) is a harmonious and supple work. He made the bas-reliefs of the Arc de Triomphe du Carrousel, Paris.

Boichot (Guillaume): "The Rivers." (Bas-relief of the Arc de Triomphe du Carrousel, Paris.)

**BOILLY (Louis Léopold).**—French painter and lithographer. Born at La Bassée, 1761; died in Paris, 1845. Son and pupil of Arnould Boilly, a sculptor in wood, he began his career in Arras as a provincial painter, and executed a number of portraits. When he went to Paris, in 1787, he was already master of his art—a minute, painstaking art, which rivalled the Flemings. He painted large scenes of the Revolution and the Empire, and represented, with the same smooth and brilliant brush, heroic incidents and familiar scenes. This little master had a very strong sense of the grotesque but none of the tragic. Boilly drew faithfully the people at public shows—urchins, haranguers, rag-gatherers, cocoa-nut sellers, and soldiers on the spree. He watched the sights of the boulevard, the entrance to little shows, the interior of cafés, the walks of the Jardin-Turc. He studied billiard players, chess players, types of Petite Provence—the *Distribution of Provisions in the Champs-Elysées* (Petit Palais), and the *Arrival of Diligences in the Courtyard of the Coaching Office* (Louvre). But this anecdotal painter seems very cold when he deals with dramas of the revolutionary period. He is neat, polished, and cold and never stirring. Thus when, about 1817, lithography came into wider circulation in France, Boilly gave up painting without regret, and took to lithography. His *Grimaces* have no other interest than details of costume, and a certain quaintness.

As a caricaturist, Boilly's humour is heavy; as an artist, his work is mediocre, and often very dull. His paintings and lithographs are, however, valuable for the information they give about the fashions, manners and types of his day.

Bibliography: H. Harrisse, *L. Boilly*. Paris, 1898.

**BOLDINI (Giovanni).**—Italian portrait painter (1842-1931). He was born in Ferrara 31st December 1842, the son of Antonio Boldini who was himself a painter. Even as a small child Giovanni Boldini was fond of drawing and it was his custom to visit Schifanoia to see the frescoes of Francesco Cossa and Cosimo Tura there and to try his hand at copying them. When he was about eighteen years of age he went to Florence and entered the Academy, studying under Stefano Ussi and Enrico Pollastrini, but he soon left to work by himself. He travelled throughout Italy, stopping at Naples and later at Monte Carlo and Venice, where he was strongly influenced by the paintings of Tiepolo. When Boldini was twenty-six years of age he went to Paris and then returned in a short time to Florence. There he met Sir Cornwallis West who induced this young artist to come to London. Almost from the first his work was a success and orders began to arrive. It became the fashion to have one's portrait painted by Boldini, as later it was the custom to have the family painted by John Singer Sargent. But in 1872 Boldini left London and went to live in Paris. There he made many studies of one particular model, Bertha, in the guise of a midinette, lying at her ease in a hammock or sitting pensively with a letter. His paintings showed the influence of Watteau and Fragonard in the choice of subject matter and its treatment. He made trips to the theatre to see the famous actresses and painted some of them, including the famed Eleonora Duse, in their favourite rôles. In 1876 he went to Holland, where he became interested in the work of Frans Hals, and then went on to Germany, making some landscape studies in the region of Versailles, some pastels and also flower studies. In the company of Degas he travelled to Spain and later went to Morocco and in 1897 made a short trip to the United States. His eyes grew bad in his later years and he was forced to give up his painting. He died early in January, 1931, when his type of painting was no longer the vogue, and instead the new forces of cubism and futurism were making the high points of conversation in artistic circles. Perhaps his best-known portraits of men are those of James McNeill Whistler and Robert Montesquiou. With the ladies he was more successful in capturing a likeness as in the portraits of the Infanta Eulalia, the dancer, Lina Cavalieri, Princess Martha Bibesco and the early one of the Duchess of Marlborough. Every painting was filled with luxurious surroundings, and accessories and the subjects of his compositions were always endowed with an air of elegance and refinement. There was no moral attached to his pictures, but he did manage to suggest the character of his model in spite of the fashionable settings and the elaborate dress of the period. There are a sparkle and verve to his paintings of women which outlive the period when they were first shown.

Bibliography: Cardona, *Vie de Jean Boldini*, 1931.

**BOLOGNA (Italy).**—Bologna, one of the oldest towns in Italy, has, throughout the centuries, been more celebrated for its University and its scholars, than for its artists. It has a curious aspect, with its streets lined with high arcades, its palaces and numerous churches. The oldest buildings are the famous *Leaning Towers Asinelli and Garisenda*, dating from 1109 and 1110, respectively.

Bologna: Basilica of San Petronio.

Bologna: Leaning Towers Asinelli and Garisenda.

Bologna: Fountain of Neptune.

*San Petronio* is one of several old churches. It was begun in 1390. Its large doorway is of special interest, for it is decorated with splendid statues and reliefs by Jacopo della Quercia.

Bologna also possesses many interesting civil buildings. The oldest, the *Palazzo della Podestà*, built in 1201, was rebuilt in the late 15th century in the Renaissance style. The *Fountain of Neptune*, by Giovanni da Bologna, is a charming construction, built 1564-1566, from the plans of Laureti.

**— (School of).**—See Pls. 15, 22, Vol. II.

**BOLTRAFFIO (Giovanni Antonio).**—Lombard painter (1467-1516), imitator of Leonardo da Vinci.

**BONAGUIL (Lot-et-Garonne, France).**—Magnificent ruins of a 15th century Château.

See Pl. 51, Vol. I.

Bonaguil: The Tower.

**BONASONE (Guilio).**—Italian painter and engraver. Born about 1500; died after 1574. He left a great many engravings after Raphael, Michelangelo, Parmegiano, Primaticcio, Guilo Romano, and after his own designs. Nothing is known of the life of this artist, who shows very profoundly the influence of Marcantonio.

Bibliography: Bartsch, *Le peintre graveur*, Vol. XV.—G. Duplessis: *Histoire de la gravure*.

**BONATZ (Paul) 1877-.**—German architect and leader in the pre-War modernist movement. He is best known for his solid and dignified Railway Station, Stuttgart, 1913.

**BONE (Muirhead).**—Contemporary Scotch painter and etcher. He was born 23d March 1876 in Patrick, a suburb of Glasgow. He went to evening classes at the Glasgow School of Art, studying architecture, learning the fundamentals of building construction and something of the laws of aerial perspective. Soon his interest in drawing outweighed his desire to become an architect. He studied the etchings of Meryon and Whistler and tried his hand at their methods of pictorial expression. At first he made some lithographs and later he turned to the production of etchings. He attended some sessions of a life class and after that time made a few figure studies, although the majority of his plates are devoted to landscapes. Around 1900 he was at Ayr, but later he settled in London, where his first exhibition was held at the Carfax Gallery early in 1902. Later he travelled throughout Great Britain, doing his best work in the region of Glasgow and the scenes along the Clyde River. His drawings illustrated stories and articles in many magazines, including *Scots*

*Pictorial*, the *Yellow Book, North British Daily Mail, Architectural Review*, and the *Pall Mall Magazine*. He also did the drawings for his wife's books, including *Provincial Tales* and *Children's Children*. During the war he was at the front making pictorial records of the devastated regions, the machines of war and the munition factories, the peaceful landscapes of the section around Loos and Ypres before they were ruined by the shell fire, and the men of the British army engaged in the grim business of war or at rest. They were not representations of the horror of war as others pictured it but rather the scenes before and after the actual conflict. Muirhead Bone is one of the original members of the Society of the Twelve and is a member of the International Society of Painters and Gravers and the New English Art Club.

BIBLIOGRAPHY: Campbell Dodgson, *Etchings and Dry Points by Muirhead Bone, 1898-1907*, 1909.—*Glasgow, Fifty Drawings by Muirhead Bone*, 1911.—*Munition Drawings, by Muirhead Bone*, 1917.—*The Western Front, Drawings by Muirhead Bone*, 1917. 2 Vols.—*With the Grand Fleet, by Muirhead Bone*, 1917.

**BONFIGLI (Benedetto).**—Perugian painter (active 1445 to 1496). Perhaps a pupil of Boccatis, influenced by Florentines. In the Cappella dei Priori of Perugia, he executed frescoes representing scenes from the lives of Bishop Louis of Toulouse and Hercolanus. The work was begun in 1454, and was judged in 1461 by Filippo Lippi who was not content with it. Bonfigli was discouraged and left it. He only took it up again in 1469, and had not time to finish it before his death (1496). Perugia contains numerous other works by him.

**BONHEUR (Rosa).**—French woman painter. Born in Bordeaux, 1822; died at By, near Fontainebleau, 1899. A pupil of her father, she very quickly won a great reputation as an animal painter. Her first success, *Ploughing in the Nivernaise* (Luxembourg), was followed by the *Horse Market* (1853—Tate Gallery). Her works are very numerous, and are to be seen chiefly in English and American collections. The artist was greatly appreciated in England, and she stayed there a long time. In France, she settled in the neighbourhood of Fontainebleau, at By, near Thomery, where she worked until her death, surrounded by animals who served her as models. Her very conscientious talent tended to a truthfulness of construction and movement, but not to much variety. Her colouring is cold, and her design, monotonous. The best of Rosa Bonheur's work are the simple studies that she planned for her pictures. But her faults escaped a people fond of animals, who only saw truth of attitude and forms, and neatness and honesty of work. Thus the popularity, and even the glory of Rosa Bonheur were firm and undisputed in her own day. The future will probably be more severe, for honesty is not enough in art.

**BONIFAZIO VERONESE (de' PITATI).**—Painter of the Venetian school, born in Verona, 1487-1553. Went to Venice at the age of twenty-eight, was a pupil of Palma Vecchio, and his niece married Antonio Palmea, his master's nephew. He was one of the most brilliant painters of his day, creating, under the pretext of religious scenes or allegories, the most astonishing compositions, enlivened by pages, singers, cavaliers and charming ladies and rich in color. All this voluptuousness is not dream-like, but transports us into a real world. Thus he has a predilection for *Holy Conversations* in which the Saints come and walk upon the earth (in the Palazzo Giovanelli, Venice, in the Louvre, in the National Gallery, in Padua, Leningrad, The Vatican, Copenhagen, and in the Gardner Collection in Boston).

It was he who decorated the Palazzo Camerlenghi on the Rialto. We may also mention, among his numerous works: the *Massacre of the Innocents*, the *Judgment of Solomon*, and the *Christ Enthroned Surrounded by Saints*, (in the Academy of Venice).

BIBLIOGRAPHY: G. Ludwig, Bonifazio dei Pitati. *Jahrbuch d. königl. preuss. Kunstsamml.* 1901.

**BONINGTON (Richard Parkes).** English painter, 1801-1828. Born in the village of Arnold, near Nottingham. He went to Paris at the age of 15. His artistic education was entirely in France, chiefly in the Louvre. He studied industriously at the École des Beaux-Arts, and in the studio of Gros, which was then the favourite "rendezvous" of all young painters with revolutionary tendencies. Nevertheless, he paid repeated visits to England, which explains the undeniable influence of Constable. In the Salon of 1822, he exhibited his first landscapes, of Normandy and Picardy. In 1824, he went to Italy. On his return he exhibited some Venetian marine paintings at the Salon, and some little historical scenes which won him the gold medal, an honour which was accorded to Constable at the same time. In 1827, he exhibited in England, at the Royal Academy, a marine painting, *Henry III, King of France*, and the *Grand Canal in Venice, with the Church of Santa Maria della Salute*. Unhappily, when he was in Normandy with the landscape painter, Paul Huet, he was stricken with consumption. Knowing himself doomed, he returned to London, where he died.

This young master, who died at the age of twenty-seven, was a painter of genre subjects, of landscapes, and of seascapes, a watercolourist and a lithographer. English by birth, and French by education, he seems at first to be one of the most seductive adepts of the romantic movement in France, but, in reality, he possessed all the qualities essential and peculiar to the England of his day. Bonington was a fine painter of sea- and landscape. His views of Venice are very beautiful, and his paintings of corners of France have rare delicacy of colour. He rendered the most varied and opposite aspects of nature with the same mastery: his springtime landscapes and his sunsets are justly famous. As for his lithographs of Paris, these are masterpieces of observation: here one feels Constable's influence.

**BONNARD (Pierre).**—Contemporary French painter. He was born 30th October 1867 at Fontenay-aux-Roses, near Paris. He studied painting at the Académie Julian in Paris under Bouguereau and Robert-Fleury. After a year spent at the École des Beaux-Arts he left to join with the younger artists of the group known as the Independents. He exhibited his work in their Salon after 1891. While much of his early output was of a decorative nature, such as panels, posters and stage settings, he began to devote himself exclusively to paintings about 1903. His artistic style shows the influence of Degas, Renoir and the Japanese printmakers, particularly in the use of a brilliant colour scheme. The colour determines the outlines of the figures and the pattern of the composition, drawing the whole into a luminous harmony. His subjects include landscapes, interiors usually adorned with some figures and some still lifes. All are treated in an impressionistic manner with the outlines melting together into a misty pattern, which method often hides the deficiencies of the modelling of the human figures. Bonnard has done a number of book illustrations, including some for Claude Terrasse's *Solfège*, Longus' novel *Daphnis und Chloë*, Paul Verlaine's *Parallèlement*, André Gide's *Le Prométhée mal enchaîné* and Octave Mirabeau's *La 628-E8*. He is also the author of some lithographs in *Figaro* and *L'Estampe Originale*. His winters are spent in the Midi and his summers at Vernon, near Paris. He has held one-man shows at the Galerie Drouet and the Galerie Bernheim and in 1906 showed his work with the Berlin Secession. His pictures are to be found in the leading museums of France and some have made their way into the private collections in Europe and the United States.

BIBLIOGRAPHY: Gustave Coquiot, *Bonnard*, 1922.—André Fontainas, *Pierre Bonnard*, 1928.—François Fosca, *Bonnard*, 1919.—Claude Roger-Marx, *Pierre Bonnard*, 1924.—Charles Terrasse, *Bonnard*, 1927.—Léon Werth, *Bonnard*, 1919.

**BONO da FERRARA.**—Painter, pupil of Pisanello in Verona and later of Squarcione and Mantegna in Padua, under whose (Mantegna's) leadership he painted with Ansuino da Forlì and others (before 1450) in the Chapel of S. Cristoforo in the Eremitani. The fresco of St. Christopher with the Christ-child is signed OPUS BONI.

Documents tell us that Bono da Ferrara worked 1450-52 for the Este Court in Migliaro and Belfiore and in 1461 in the Duomo of Siena. The only sure panel by him is the small St. Jerome in the National Gallery, which is signed.

BIBLIOGRAPHY: Frizzi, *Mem. per la storia di Ferrara*, 1791-1809, V, 323 f.—Baruffaldi, *Vite de' pitt. etc., Ferrar.*, 1846, II, 560 ff.—Laderchi, *La pitt. Ferrar.*, 1856, pp. 33-36.—Kristeller, *Mantegna*, 1902.—M. Logan Berenson, Rassegna d'arte, 1907, p. 53 f.—L. Testi, *Storia d. pitt. venez.*, 1909, pp. 442, 460.

**BONONE (Carlo).** — Ferrarese painter, 1569-1632. A good follower of the Caracci. He is known chiefly for his decorations in the Church of Santa Maria in Vado, in Ferrara.

**BONSIGNORI (Francesco).**—Veronese painter, c. 1452-1519, influenced by the Bellini, Mantegna and by Costa.

**BONVICINO.**—See Moretto da Brescia.

**BONVIN (François).**—French painter, 1817-1887. He is the painter of interiors, and familiar scenes. His precise little pictures, lively in colour and painted with a sure, painstaking brush, remind one of the interiors of the little Dutch masters. Like them, he shows us modest apartments, dining-rooms, parlours, kitchens where housewives are sewing, polishing copper, or busying themselves with casseroles. For instance: *Men Drinking at an Inn; A Cook at her Stove; Servant at the Fountain; Nuns making Jam;* the *Workroom*, etc.

BIBLIOGRAPHY: J. Clarétie, *L'Art et les artistes contemporains*.

**BORDEAUX.**—See Pl. 1, Vol. I.

**BORDONE (Paris).**—Venetian painter, 1500-1571. Born in Treviso, and died in Venice. A pupil of Titian, and also influenced by Giorgione or Palma. There are several works by him in the Cathedral and in the picture gallery of his native town: a *Holy Family*, an *Adoration of the Shepherds*, etc. His best known and most admired picture is in the Academy of Venice. It is the *Fisherman Returning the Ring to the Doge* after he has received it miraculously from St. Mark during a night at sea. It has a most wonderful effect of full, dazzling light, under the great arcades of marble palaces, amid the gay, brocaded company, while the old man mounts the wide steps towards the magnificent Doge.

Paris Bordone was also very well known as a portrait painter, and if he is really the author of the beautiful *Lovers*, in the Brera Gallery, which expresses deep and intense feeling, he is certainly a very fine painter. A very prolific painter, his works may be found in museums all over the world.

BIBLIOGRAPHY: L. Barlo and G. Biscaro, *Della Vita e delle opere di Paris Bordon.* Treviso, 1900.

**BORGHESE GLADIATOR.**—See Agasias.

**— (Villa).**—See Rome.

**BORGIA ROOMS.**—See Vatican.

**BORGLUM (John Gutzon de la Mothe).**—Contemporary American sculptor. He was born in Idaho 25th March 1867. He copied the works of the old masters as a boy and studied at the San Francisco Art Association under Virgil Williams, but got more influence from William Keith, a California landscape painter. About 1890 he went to Paris where he worked at the Académie Julian. He made a short trip to Spain before returning to the United States, where he worked in California with his younger brother, Solon Borglum. But in 1895 he went back to Europe, this time to London, where he remained until 1901. He was doing both painting and sculpture at this time and in 1898 did some murals for the Queen's Hotel in Leeds. After his return to the United States he did some murals for the Midland Hotel Concert Hall in Manchester, England. But he was turning more and more to the work in sculpture in which he has made his present reputation. From his Danish father who delighted in wood-carving young Gutzon had early acquired a liking for thinking in the plastic medium. His first works in sculpture were gained from his own experience and included such pieces as the *Mares of Diomedes* and some other horse studies. His early influence was the realism of the Italian Renaissance but soon the idealism of Rodin and Whistler succeeded it and his works became more impressionistic and simplified. He did some apostles in the Cathedral of St. John the Divine, the Sheridan Monument in Washington, and the Lincoln Monument in Newark. For a time he was

# OIL PAINTING

*Oil painting has been the favourite medium of European painters since the Renaissance. It is preferred to other media because of its flexibility: oil paints lend themselves to almost anything. Their softness matches that of tempera. It is possible to imitate with them the largeness of the fresco; with them nature can be imitated better than with either of the other two media. Because of its enamel-like transparence it is good for rendering chiaroscuro effects.*

JAN VAN EYCK: THE CANON VAN DER PAELE. BRUGES.
*(Photo by Bruckmann.)*

TITIAN: PORTRAIT. DETAIL OF THE MADONNA OF THE PESARO FAMILY. VENICE.
*(Photo by Anderson.)*

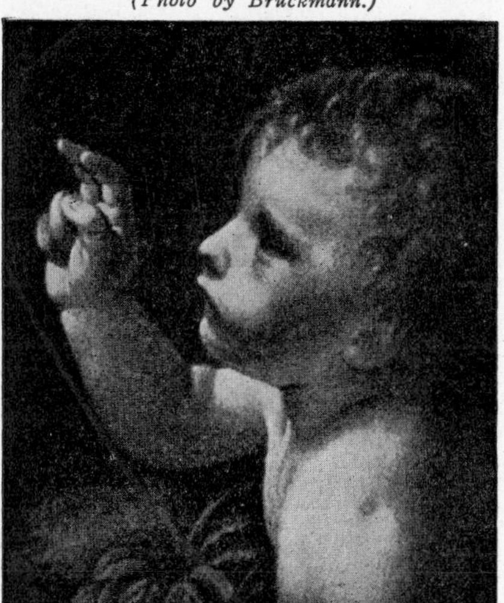

LEONARDO DA VINCI: THE INFANT JESUS. LOUVRE.
*(Photo by Hachette.)*

VELASQUEZ: MENIPPUS. PRADO, MADRID.
*(Photo by Anderson.)*

RUBENS: HEAD OF A CHILD. DETAIL FROM THE MARRIAGE OF MARIE DE MÉDICIS. LOUVRE.
*(Photo by Hachette.)*

Choosing, as an example, the face as painted in oil in different schools, the variety of effects which this procedure takes from nature becomes evident. Jan van Eyck, one of the principal initiators of this art, rendered the details of the skin; da Vinci, by using transparent mysterious shadows, tried to create the infinite modelling of a child's head; Titian, with his passionate colouring, rendered the profundity and serenity of life in the flesh; Rubens played with the lustrous reflections on fair skin; Velasquez expressed in a few rapid strokes the essential characteristics of his model, the expression, the flesh, the light, the atmosphere.

FRAGONARD: NYMPHS BATHING. LOUVRE.
*(Photo by Hachette.)*

Finally, oil painting is such a supple art, that many artists have become virtuosi. In the works of Tintoretto, Velasquez, Rubens, one can feel that the artist sometimes subordinates nature for the pleasure derived from exercising his skill. Fragonard was one of these jugglers to whom art was merely a game without accidents or difficulties. In a composition like this, one may follow the movements of his playful brush. There are other painters, like Rembrandt, to whom the execution of a painting does not seem quite as amusingly vivacious; they are not, however, less capable as technicians. But with them the brush, instead of playing, seems to be working hard.

# GLASS

*Glass is basically silica, transformed by smelting. The heat makes a glassy paste which is transparent and impermeable. Glass may be coloured; it may be blown into vases of a variety of shapes. Glass was known to the Egyptians who sometimes gave coloured glass eyes to their statues; they also made jewelry by placing coloured glass in a gold setting. The Orientals used glass a great deal. Modern glass blowers still go back to the ancient methods and technique.*

LAMP FROM A MOSQUE: ARABIC ART. LOUVRE.
*(Photo by Hachette.)*

GALLÉ: GLASS VASE. MUSÉE DES ARTS DÉCORATIFS, PARIS.
*(Photo by Hachette.)*

PALERMO: PULPIT OF THE CATHEDRAL DECORATED WITH GLASS MOSAIC.
*(Photo by Alinari.)*

RAVENNA, SAN VITALE: THE EMPRESS THEODORA.
*(Photo by Alinari.)*

MOSAIC AFTER L. O. MERSON. (PASTEUR INSTITUTE.)
*(Photo by Hachette.)*

Coloured glass made two procedures of painting possible; both are admirably adaptable for decorative purposes: mosaic and stained glass. Mosaic was especially dear to Byzantine art. Christianity in the Near East found a way to reconcile the decorative customs of the Orient (enamel covering the architecture) with the iconesque exigencies of Christianity (to represent the human figure). Mosaicists paint with the tiny cubes of coloured glass ingeniously placed together in a fashion imitating the shape and colour of living forms. This procedure gives the appearance of fixedness to figures and the quality of indestructibility to the composition. These ancient paintings congealed themselves in the rigidity of this magnificent jewelry—of crystallised life.

CHARTRES: CHRIST ON THE CROSS, STAINED GLASS WINDOW OF THE CATHEDRAL.
*(Photo by Houvet.)*

CHARTRES: THE VISITATION, STAINED GLASS WINDOW OF THE CATHEDRAL.
*(Photo by Houvet.)*

CHARTRES: ROLAND AT RONCEVAUX, STAINED GLASS WINDOW OF THE CATHEDRAL.
*(Photo by Houvet.)*

In stained glass windows the coloured pieces of glass, instead of being placed on a wall as in mosaic, are placed in frames open to the light. The pieces are cut down and adjusted to form figures; they are set in leads, which, besides forming the basic structure of the windows, accentuate the contours of the glass pieces. More delicate details are added by painting on the glass. But the art of stained glass, whose splendor of color and light is unsurpassed, cannot attain the expressive power of oil painting or fresco.

connected with the great project for depicting the leaders of the Confederacy on the side of Stone Mountain near Atlanta, Georgia, but there was much discussion concerning the plan as a whole and the financial outlay, which led to his dismissal. At present he is engaged in the portrayal of some of the most famous men of our country on the side of Mount Rushmore, South Dakota.

Bibliography: George Henry Chase and Chandler Rathfon Post, *A History of Sculpture,* 1925. —Kineton Parkes, *Sculpture of Today,* 1921.—Chandler Rathfon Post, *A History of European and American Sculpture,* 1921.—Lorado Taft, *The History of American Sculpture,* 1930.

**— (Solon H.)**—American sculptor, born in 1868, brother of the preceding, specializing in subjects drawn from the life of the cowboys and Indians and the animal world of America (*Lassoing Wild Horses,* Cincinnati Museum, *On the Border of the White Man's Land,* Metropolitan Museum of Art, etc.). He died in 1922.

**BORGOGNONE.**—Ambrogio of Fossano, in the province of Cunco, called Borgognone or Bergognone, (working from 1480-1523). Painter of the Milanese school, pupil of Foppa.

Borgognone's most important work is the decoration of the Certosa of Pavia. He was called there in 1488, and he was employed as both painter and architect. He devoted all his energies and all his piety to the decoration of the bare walls of the beautiful church, and of the wonderful convent which was to become a jewel-case for the works of so many artists. His frescoes there range in date from 1490 to 1509 and contain numerous portraits of the Visconti family.

Of his other work, the greater part is in Milan: in the Brera, Ambrosiana, and Poldi Pezzoli, and in various churches. An important and vigorous work is the *Way to Golgotha,* with Carthusian monks (in Pavia). In the background of this, we see the Certosa in various stages of construction.

Borgognone also occupied himself with stained glass and marquetry. In 1498, he went to Lodi to paint the apse of the Incoronata, on which he represented a *Coronation of the Virgin,* now destroyed. Later, he painted the *Life of Mary,* in four panels, in the Chapel of the Virgin, with buildings already in the style of the 16th century (1498-1500).

In 1514, he was recalled to Pavia by the Prior of the Certosa, to do restoration work.

In San Sempliciano, at Milan, he again painted a *Coronation of the Virgin* (1517).

In the Carrara Gallery, at Bergamo, there are several pictures by him. Likewise at San Spirito, a large altarpiece in several compartments, all in gold and dark brown (1508).

His last work, dated 1522, is an *Assumption,* painted for the Church of Nerviano (now in the Brera). At this period, after all the progress which had been made in painting, while Leonardo da Vinci was working under his very eyes, Borgognone still created works which owe their beauty to his simplicity of outlook.

Bibliography: L. Beltrami, *Ambrogio Fossano, detto il Bergognone.* Milan, 1895.

**BORROMINI (Francesco).**—Roman architect and sculptor, 1599-1669. The most restless, accentuated and exaggerated of the creators of the Baroque style. His very exaggerations gave him a wide influence, and his works are rich in fantasy and skill.

Borromini (Francesco): Santa Agnese, Rome.

The walls of his façades curve, undulate, swell, like a moving sea. There are no straight, horizontal lines. In him can first be seen the achievement of one aim of Baroque art: the blending of architecture with sculpture, sculpture with painting, so that one cannot tell where one leaves off and another begins, and the whole ensemble assumes a unity which can be achieved in no other way.

In the Piazza Navona, the Church of Sant'Agnese (built with Carlo Rainaldi, 1625-1650), he reproduced Bramante's design for St. Peter's, but he seems to have been seized with a kind of nervous frenzy in the execution of it: the façade rounds itself to the segment of a circle, the angle towers form an ellipse, and little Chinese bell-turrets rest on top of them.

When he went to build a church for the Barberini, Sant'Ivo, near the Sapienza, he did not forget the bee on their arms. He wanted the whole building, by its form and decoration, to recall the insect! Then he crowned the whole with strange spiralling forms.

In San Carlo alle Quattro Fontane, the feverish undulation has no limit, and does not allow of a single quiet line. Nevertheless, in spite of its sinuous movement it is always elegant.

In these Baroque churches, sculptures appear in unexpected places, and the polychromy of the sumptuous marbles adds to the magnificent effect. All this richness recalls, in one way, the old Byzantine magnificence.

Pope Innocent X ordered Francesco Borromini to continue the work of San Giovanni Laterano, about 1650, and he planned the interior of it, in one nave and four aisles.

Bibliography: Corrado Ricci, *Baroque Architecture and Sculpture in Italy.* Stuttgart, 1926.

**BOSCH (Jerome).**—Dutch painter. Born, between 1450 and 1460; died, 1516. His real name was Jerome van Aken (from Aix-la-Chapelle, where his family originated). He was born at Bois-le-Duc, where he worked until his death. Bosch is the Dutch name of Bois-le-Duc. He began his career by designing stained-glass and cartoons for tapestries. One of his first pictures is the *Last Judgment,* painted for Philippe le Beau. His work is very varied. He painted religious pictures, scenes with devils, allegories, and genre pieces.

His chief religious pictures are: *Ecce Homo* (Escorial); the *Walk to Çalvary* (Ghent), with a crowd of sinister figures surrounding Christ; the *Adoration of the Magi* (Prado), with a beautiful, varied landscape; and the *Martyrdom of St. Julia* (Vienna).

From scenes of the Last Judgment, representing the supplications of the damned, Jerome Bosch took his "devilries" which are the most curious of his works, and which so pleased the gloomy, tormented soul of Philip II of Spain, and were imitated by a whole school. With the realism and precision of the best Flemish masters, the painter combined heads, limbs, wings and paws to form the most fearful monsters: little bodies of men with fishes' heads; toads with men's faces swarming in the midst of huge, terrible insects, riding on household utensils, dressing themselves in funnels, and arming themselves with impossible instruments.

Jerome Bosch ignored all proportion, and his scenes of hell give an impression of nightmare. The most famous of these fantastic pictures are: the *Seven Deadly Sins* (Escorial); the *Temptation of St. Anthony* (Lisbon, Ajuda Palace—several European museums possess copies); the *Hay Waggon* (Escorial), the *Prodigal Son* (Rotterdam), and engravings of works which are lost.

His genre pieces, the "drolleries," represent popular scenes, such as the *Quack* (Prado), the *Juggler* (Museum of Saint-Germain-en-Laye), and the *Masquerade* (or *Shrove Tuesday*). These paintings are full of a satirical spirit, with picturesque or amusing details. The drawing is clear, precise and spirited, and the colour lively and transparent.

See Pl. 24, Vol. II.

Bibliography: Lafond, P., *Hieronymus Bosch, son art, son influence, ses disciples.* Bruxelles, 1914.—Friedländer, M. J., *Altniederl. Malerei.* Vol. V.—Sir Martin Conrow, *The Van Eyck and their Followers.* London, 1921.

**BOSCOREALE (Italy).**—Roman town, situated 4 kilometres from Pompeii, destroyed by the eruption of Vesuvius in 79. It was excavated in 1894. Utensils, such as large earthenware vases were discovered; and the "treasure of Boscoreale"—94 pieces of silver work (which are in the Louvre). In some villas, interesting paintings were found. These villas were richly decorated and had several rooms.

Bibliography: A. Héron de Villefosse, *Le Trésor de Boscoreale.*

**BOSIO (François Joseph, Baron).**—French sculptor (1768; 1846). A pupil of Pajon, he soon became the rival of Chaudet, and, like him, one of the upholders of the neo-classical style. He was often commissioned to make busts of the Emperor, of Empresses and imperial princesses. Elegance of form, pleasing expressions and delicacy of workmanship are qualities of his work. One can see their beginnings in *Love Seducing Innocence* and in *Aristo,* and one sees a striving after energy in *Hercules Fighting Achelous.* Bosio's work recalls the antique, while certain figures, such as *Salmacis* and *Hyacinthe,* are afflicted with cylindrical limbs, and faces whose expression is so slight that it is stupid. As for his portraits, which contributed more than anything else for Bosio's success, we cannot explain their vogue by anything we find in them (Cf. *Napoleon,* at Amiens, and at Versailles; *Davout* and *Lauriston,* at Versailles). Apart from the bust of Josephine, in the Museum of Dijon, which is refined and animated, they are conventional, lifeless and cold. The *Henry IV as a Child* (marble,

Bosio: Statue of Louis XIV, Paris.

in Pau Museum; silver, at Versailles) is, however, rather pleasing. Also due to Baron Bosio are twenty bas-reliefs on the Vendôme Column; the bronze chariot which surmounts the Triumphal Arch of the Carrousel, and symbolises the Restoration; the *Louis XIV Triumphant,* of the Place des Victoires; the statues of *France* and *Fidelity* which adorn the memorial to Malesherbes (entrance-hall of the Palais de Justice); and the *Death of Louis XVI,* the marble group which decorates the Expiatory Chapel.

Bibliography: L. de Loménic, *M. Bosio.* Paris, 1844.

**BOSRĀ (Syria).**—Roman Bostra. *Cathedral,* 512 A.D., dedicated to SS. Sergius, Bacchus, and Leontius. One of the outstanding monuments of southern Syria, Bosrā shows a plan cognate with that of S. Vitale, Ravenna. Eight elbow piers form a central octagon, about which is a circular annular aisle in alternate triangular and rectangular compartments. De Vogüé's drawing incorrectly shows squinches above the piers; the wall merely warps forward to form a circular opening, which could not have originally been domed. Four angle niches fill out the annular aisle to a square. At the east are three apses separated by two pastophoria.

**BOTH (Jan).**—Dutch painter, 1610-1652. Pupil of Blomaert. He travelled in Italy, where he much admired the works of Claude Lorrain, and, like him, painted sunsets, but less ably. His landscapes are more complicated than those of Lorrain: he liked to accumulate details, rocks, ravines, and cascades. Most of his works are in the Museums of Rotterdam and Brussels, and in England.

**SANDRO BOTTICELLI (Alessandro di Mariano Filipepi).**—Florentine painter, 1444-1510. The critical fate of Botticelli contributes one of the most interesting chapters to the history of taste. Singled from among his contemporaries, who were misunderstood by later generations because they were ignored by them, Botticelli was in his turn misunderstood and vulgarized by sentimental adulation. The "mood" of

Botticelli, interpreted not in its own terms, but in those of his Pre-Raphaelite admirers, has long obscured the critical estimate of the great Florentine.

The pupil of Fra Filippo Lippi, Botticelli inherited from his master the lineal and lyrical tradition of Lorenzo Monaco, as opposed to the plastic force and directness of statement of such painters as Masaccio and Castagno. He was of course profoundly influenced, as was virtually every Florentine painter of the quattrocento, by the Florentine preoccupation with plastic form, but his own gift was of an essentially different nature, one related to the older Gothic style and to that of the painters of Siena.

Fra Filippo's influence is to be seen in his pupil's early Madonnas, none of which are dated, but which form a group by themselves through stylistic affinities. In 1470 Botticelli was commissioned to paint the figure of *Fortitude* for the Mercatanzia of Florence, beside the *Virtues* of the Pollaiuoli (executed by Piero and pupils). Now in the Uffizi Gallery, it is his earliest dated work. It is followed by the St. Sebastian in the Berlin Museum, of 1473.

In 1474 Botticelli was called to Pisa to paint an *Assumption of the Virgin* in the Duomo, but left the work unfinished. In 1478 he was working for the Medici, with other artists, already in favor with the great family with whom he maintained his connection throughout its political upheavals, as one of the familiars of Lorenzo Magnifico and later of Pierfrancesco de' Medici. Portraits of members of the Medici family, notably that of Giuliano, appear in the *Adoration of the Magi* in the Uffizi (c. 1477) and the figure at the extreme right is probably a self-portrait of the painter. In style, metallic in its modelling and showing the influence of Verrocchio, this great *Adoration* is related to that of the *St. Sebastian* in Berlin, the *Adoration* in London (1477-1478), and the portrait of the *Man with the Medal* in the Uffizi.

In 1478, Botticelli painted the effigies of the Pazzi conspirators, later destroyed. The three portraits of Giuliano de' Medici, who was assassinated in this conspiracy, in Berlin, Bergamo, and Lugano (Thyssen Collection), supposed to have been done about this time, are not by the master himself but by his shop.

Probably in 1480 Botticelli painted the fresco of St. Augustin in the Ognissanti, typical of his work in its intensity and angularity. A contract of 1481-1482 dates the period of his activity in the Sistine Chapel in Rome, where there are three frescoes of episodes from the Life of Moses. Here the hardness of the Augustin begins to give way to an easy swinging lyricism, bodies entirely unfunctional (as Pollaiuolo's, for instance, are functional) related in an exquisite decorative harmony. In 1482 he returned to Florence, to collaborate with Ghirlandaio and Perugino in the Palazzo della Signoria. Of his work there nothing is known. In 1483 he was employed by Lorenzo Magnifico for the decoration of the Villa Spedaletto, Volterra. In 1485 he painted for the Bardi Chapel the *Madonna between St. John the Baptist and St. John the Evangelist* now in the Berlin Museum.

The famous *Spring*, now in the Uffizi, the date of which is not certain, Botticelli painted to adorn the Villa di Castello, acquired in 1477 by Lorenzo de' Medici. With its foliated background and rhythmically interweaving line, it contributed to a decoration further enriched by the painter's other great mythological panel, *The Birth of Venus* of about 1485 (Uffizi).

The frescoes in the Louvre, much impaired by time, once contributed to the decoration of the Villa Lemni, and probably represent Lorenzo Tornabuoni with the Liberal Arts and Giovanna Tornabuoni with the Virtues. They date from 1486.

To Botticelli's late period (c. 1490), in which his style is looser, more mystical and pictorial, belongs the portrait of Lorenzo Lorenzano in the Johnson Collection in Philadelphia, an extraordinarily modern work, freed from traditional portrait rendering and highly personal. *The Coronation of the Virgin* in the Uffizi comes also from this period, as well as *The Lamentation* in Munich, and the altarpiece of the Virgin, Child and Saints in the Uffizi, works which reflect the excessive emotionalism of the period of his growing adherence to the passionate teachings of Savanarola.

About the end of the century he illustrated the Divine Comedy for the Medici (Berlin, Vatican). In 1491 he is mentioned in documents, which state that he, with other artists, had been consulted in regard to the façade of the Duomo in Florence. The following year he was commissioned to decorate the Chapel of St. Zanobius with mosaics. His last Medici commission was in 1497 and it was in 1501 that he painted *The Madonna Adoring the Child* in the National Gallery.

Botticelli died in 1510 and was buried in the Ognissanti on the 17th of May.

See Pl. 12, Vol. II.

Bibliography: Vasari-Milanesi.—Borghini, *Riposo*, 1787.—Baldinucci, *Not. dei prof. d. disegno*. Florence, 1845.—Crowe and Cavalcaselle.—Frey, *Il codice Magliabecchiano; Libro di Antonio Billi*. Berlin, 1892.—C. v. Febriczy, *Il codice dell' anonimo Gaddiano* (in Arch. Stor. Ital., 1893).—Ulmann, *Sandro Botticelli*, 1893.—J. B. Supino, *Sandro Botticelli*, 1903.—Gebhart, *Sandro Botticelli et son époque*. Paris, 1907.—Herbert Horne, *Sandro Botticelli*, 1908.—W. v. Bode, *Botticelli* (Klassiker der Kunst).—Yashiro, *Sandro Botticelli*, 1929.—L. Venturi, *Sandro Botticelli*.

(See Van Marle, *Italian Schools*, etc., XII, p. 14 ff., for additional literature.)

**BOTTICINI (Francesco).**—Florentine painter, 1446-1498, pupil of Neri di Bicci, influenced by Castagno, Cosimo Rosselli, and Botticelli; worked with Verrocchio.

Botticini was apprenticed to Neri di Bicci in 1459. In 1469 he is mentioned as one of a commission to estimate the value of a painting by Neri. In 1473 he had executed one of his pictures of the *Archangel Raphael* and in 1484 the order was placed for the altar for the Compagnia di S. Andrea della Veste Bianca for the Pieve, Empoli (now in the Gallery, Empoli), which was delivered in 1491. The Sto. Spirito altar, Sta. Monica and Nuns, is dated 1483.

Botticini's early style shows his derivation from Neri; later it gradually evolves toward the fuller forms of Verrocchio and the greater grace of Botticelli.

Bibliography: Vasari-Milanesi, IV, 245-247.—Milanesi, *Nuov. Doc. dell' arte tosc.*, 1901, p. 132.—Mesnil in Gazette des Beaux Arts, 1902, I, 205, and Rivista d'Arte, III, 1905, pp. 39-42.—Berenson, *The Drawings of Florentine Painters*, 1903, I, 41 ff.—Crowe and Cavalcaselle, Douglas ed., 1911, IV, p. 293.—Ernst Kuhnel, *Francesco Botticini*. Strassburg, 1909.

**BOUCHARDON (Edme).**—French sculptor, born at Chaumont

Bouchardon.

(1698-1762). Son of Jean Baptiste Bouchardon, architect and sculptor who worked at Chaumont, Langres, and Dijon for the decoration of several churches. He worked under his father's direction, from 1715 to 1721; then he continued his studies in Paris, in the studio of Guillaume I. Coustou. In 1722, he competed for the Prix de l'Académie Royale, and obtained the first prize. The subject of the competition was *Gideon Choosing his Soldiers by Observing the Way They Drank.* The following year he entered the French Academy in Rome, and acquired a passion for antique art. He copied the finest marbles, and began to execute busts. He was immediately a great success; commissions showered upon him. Bouchardon, nominated a member of the Academy of St. Luke in Rome, enjoyed himself so much in this city, full of remains of antiquity, that he was in no hurry to return

Bouchardon (E.): Detail of the Fountain in the Rue de Grenelle, Paris.

to France. At the end of nine years, the Duc d'Antin, the King's Superintendent of Buildings, wrote to the Director of the Academy that it was not "for the enrichment of foreign countries that the King spent so much on his Academy in Rome." The Director was ordered to make Bouchardon understand the necessity of returning. He was no doubt eloquent, for Bourchardon returned to France, in spite of the regrets of his Roman patrons and friends.

He carried out some fine work in Rome: a statue of *Hercules*, more than life-size (1730); the *Sleeping Fawn* (1732) was sent to France and is now in the Luxembourg Gardens; the *Fawn with a Kid*, in marble, after the antique, and the *Flute-Player*, bought by Frederick the Great, are in Berlin; and some busts, among them those of Pope Clement XII, Cardinal de Polignac and Madame Wleughels.

Bouchardon (E.): Love. (Louvre.)

On his arrival in Paris, Bouchardon was given accommodation in the Louvre and several commissions by the Duc d'Antin. The relations of patron and protégé were not without some annoyances. Bouchardon wanted large subsidies; the Duc d'Antin was an economist, found his sculptor "difficult," and did not hide from him that "it is never the custom for the king to pay in advance." But he appreciated the artist's talent, knew that he was not rich, and that he could not raise the large sums necessary, and he ended by "paying in advance." The first commission was the statue of Louis XIV, ordered in 1733, for which the plaster model only was executed. Bouchardon was associated with the Comte de Caylus for whom he designed the en-

Bouchardon (E.): Bronze Model for a Statue of Louis XV. (Louvre.)

graved stones of the Cabinet du Roi, which Caylus reproduced in engraving, and this collaboration did not prevent the nomination of the artist to the post of designer of the king's medals in the Académie des Inscriptions (1736). He had already made several works for the king and for individuals, among them some busts and medallions of Louis XV and the Dauphin; some charming groups, the god Proteus and dolphins led by cupids, in the "Fountain" of Neptune at Versailles; statues of angels and saints for various churches (St. Sulpice, among others); then the city of Paris commissioned him to make the famous Fountain in the Rue de

Grenelle. The first stone was laid by Turgot, Provost of merchants. Bouchardon worked on it from 1739 to 1745. The monument, of vast dimensions for two thin streams of water, measures 29 metres in length by 11 metres 60 in height. A fine marble statue representing the City of Paris, and seated on a pedestal, occupies the middle, between two reclining figures, the *Marne* and the *Seine*, under a pediment supported by four columns. On each side in niches are stone figures of the Four Seasons, and above, bas-reliefs representing Children's Games in these various seasons. The inscription of dedication still exists, engraved in black marble; that which bore the name of the author and aldermen has disappeared. Bouchardon carried out the whole of this tremendous undertaking by himself, only assisted by his own workers. The architects and sculptors who had hoped for a collaboration criticised the work, but the public took no notice of them, and the aldermen were so satisfied with it that, after they had paid the sculptor the sum promised, they gave him, apart from this, a pension of 1500 livres. They also had a studio built for him in the Roule quarter. The plaster models of the *Seasons* are in the Museum of Chaumont; those in terra cotta of the *City of Paris*, the *Seine* and the *Marne* are in Dijon Museum; and a series of drawings are in the Louvre. In 1745, Bouchardon became a member of the Académie Royale, with a little marble statue, *Christ Bearing the Cross* (Louvre). Until then Bouchardon had only known the admiration of the public. He made his name also by the *Cupid Making a Bow out of Hercules' Club* (Louvre), finished in 1744. The statue was put in Versailles, but the natives had nothing but criticism for this thin, nervous youth, so different from the plump cupids which people the galleries. In spite of the objections of artists, who appreciated its pure, classic style, *Cupid* left the Palace of Versailles and was relegated to the Château of Choisy. There were, however, some amateurs who appreciated it, since in 1750, the author was begged to make a copy. In 1748, the city of Paris, wishing to put up a monument in honour of Louis XV, gave Bouchardon the commission for an equestrian statue of the King. This statue, in bronze, executed from 1748 to 1757, adorned the Place Louis XV (Place de la Concorde) until 1792, when it was melted down. The artist had made several designs which were submitted to the king. Louis XV decided upon one, which is probably the horse in the Museum of Besançon. Louis is represented on horseback, in Roman attire, on a pedestal decorated with bas-reliefs representing the king giving Peace to Europe, and the king seated in a chariot led by Victory. Bouchardon could not finish his work. When he was near death, he chose Pigalle to finish the bas-reliefs. When the statue was finished, and carried with great ceremony to the Place Louis XV (17th February, 1763), the procession passed in front of Bouchardon's house, and three guns were fired in front of his residence, in honour of the great artist. The Museums of the Louvre and Versailles possess bronze reproductions of this statue, the work of Pigalle and Vassé.

Besides his sculptured works, the artist left a collection of 60 engravings, the *Cries of Paris* (1746), a miscellany engraved by Caylus which shows in an amusing series all the little peripatetic trades of the period.

Bouchardon was a fine designer. His sculpture does not reflect the taste of his contemporaries for light sparkling work. He studied a great deal, and loved the antique, the simplicity and elegance of which he imitated, perhaps a little coldly. He makes a link between Le Brun and David, whom he resembles much more closely than his contemporaries, Falconet and Le Moyne. He is one of the finest sculptors of the 18th century.

See Pl. 45, Vol. II.

BIBLIOGRAPHY: D'Argenville, *Vie des fameux sculpteurs.*—L. Gouse, *La Sculpture française,* 1895.—E. Jofibois, *Notice sur Edme Bouchardon, sculpteur.* 1837.

**BOUCHER (François).**—French painter, 1703-1770. He was born in the heart of Paris (rue de la Verrerie, in the parish of St. Jean en Grève), the 29th September, 1703. Little is known of his father Nicolas, or of his mother, Elizabeth Lemesle; the former had the title of master painter. A true Parisian, he must have passed his childhood in the midst of the daily sight and chants of street merchants, for he left quick sketches of them, in a series called the *Cries of Paris.* He was about seventeen years old when he entered the studio of François Le Moyne. According to his own saying, he had nothing to do but pass the time away. However, there is no doubt that the works of this master, even without "direct teaching," exercised a strong influence on him.

*Venus Ordering Vulcan to Make Weapons for Æneas,* a picture which he painted in 1732 (Fontainebleau), entirely proclaims this model, notably in the mixture of brownish and gold tones in the god's flesh, which recalls very nearly those used in the *Hercules* of the other painter (Louvre, Salle La Caze). His resemblance to him in his early works has caused erroneous attributions.

FRANÇOIS BOUCHER.

From Le Moyne's studio, Boucher went to that of the father of Laurent Cars, the engraver, who, trading in "thèses," taught him the art of composing these sorts of decorative show-cards, then much used, which he designed in this name; afterwards, he, in his turn, showed extraordinary ability for this kind of work. At the same time he was commissioned by M. de Julienne, the old friend of Watteau, to engrave, after this artist, a portion of a series called "Faces of Different Characters." Not yet being "accepted" by the Académie Royale, although he had already taken a first prize there for painting, but in a hurry to make himself known to the public, Boucher took advantage of a fine morning, on the day of Fête-Dieu in 1725, and the permission which had been granted him, and exhibited some pictures on the Place Dauphine, which did not pass unnoticed. Two years afterwards, though this visit cannot be explained by a place at the Académie de France, nor by any official position, he was in Rome with Carle Van Loo and his two nephews, François and Louis Michel, where he chiefly admired Pietro da Cortona, Benedetto Castiglione and Giovanni Lanfranco, all masters who staged large compositions. If he did not go to Venice, he none the less knew Tiepolo and possessed an important collection of his drawings. On his return to Paris he was "accepted" by the Académie (24th November, 1731).

From the following year dates the first signed painting of his that has come down to us, that of *Renaud et Armide* (Louvre). In these first two known examples of his work, Boucher colour is still rather dull, but in his pink and white female forms, modelled in full light, he already shows himself to be the painter of light, voluptuous compositions.

Before examining Boucher's talent in its different phases, we must mention his marriage in the Church of Saint Roch, in 1733, to the pretty Marie Jeanne Buseau, then seventeen years old. Closely connected with her husband's works, she transposed them into miniatures, and, above all, as we learn from their contemporaries who were unanimous in paying homage to her beauty, she took the place of model. La Tour made a portrait of her in 1737, and Roslin in 1761.

Boucher is essentially a decorator. It is as a decorator that he chiefly appeals, and, in his own day, exercised the greatest influence. One finds this quality in all his work. He began by being commissioned, in 1734, to paint the four pretty grisailles which may still be seen in the Queen's apartments at Versailles —*Charity, Abundance, Fidelity* and *Prudence.* From 1737 to 1740, he collaborated with Parrocel, Natoire, Trémolières, Carle Van Loo and Restout in the decoration of the palace which was built by Delamaire for the Prince de Soubise, on the site of the old Hôtel de Guise. One can still see some of his compositions there: the *Three Graces Capturing Cupid;* the *Education of Cupid by Mercury; Aurora and Cephalus,* and especially—above the door, in the Prince's old apartments, on the ground-floor of the hôtel—the *Venus Descending from Her Car to Enter the Bath,* in which this "painter of the graces" shows all his seductive qualities. In 1741, when the Cabinet des Médailles was moved from Versailles to the Bibliothèque du Roi (Bibliothèque Nationale), in Paris, he competed with four panels for the decoration of this new installation.

The royal tapestry-weavers naturally profited by the inexhaustible fecundity of his charming scenes. Oudry, director of the Beauvais enterprise since 1734, applied to Boucher, who, among other motifs, provided notably that of the See-Saw with a lively surounding of palm-leaves.

At the same time, he indulged the fashion which then raged for things Chinese and made a series of designs to be carried out in "tapestry" (Besançon Museum has some specimens of these designs). The success of his collaboration made Oudry take him to the Gobelins, where he was given the management of this other factory. On the death of Oudry, in 1755, Boucher was nominated Inspector of the Factory, and became the great purveyor of it.

One of the most active stimulants to his bent for decoration was the taste of Madame de Pompadour. A good part of his career was devoted to working for her, especially in her château of Bellevue. As a result Boucher became associated with the "little brother" of the marquise, Abel Poisson de Vandière; he became "Director and General Manager of Buildings," and then the all-powerful of Marigny. He received a pension, and was given a studio in the Louvre. About 1752, he worked at Fontainebleau. He was entrusted with one of the most important paintings, that of the Council Hall. There he painted the Sun beginning his course and chasing away the night, surrounded by the Seasons, represented by children, which is still in position, and shows us Boucher with all his genial instinct for decoration.

He was facile in all kinds of work. He painted portraits. His charming *Woman with a Muff* (Louvre; Salle La Caze) shows us that his capricious talent could not rise above the level of fantasy. He painted Madame de Pompadour several times. At the Louvre, too, is his *Déjeuner.* Had he paused more often to paint interiors, he would have given us delightful glimpses at the life of the 18th century. Then he painted himself as a landscape painter working in his studio. The necessity of finding backgrounds for his cartoons for tapestries made him turn his thoughts to country scenes. He used them when he was working for the Beauvais factory. Certainly, his scenery could not generally be applied to anything very positive. It lends distance to the picture by a conventional bluish colour; and gives a very artificial conception of nature, which was most justified in the decoration of the Opera House, with which Boucher was charged on several occasions. Nevertheless, these landscapes, free from heavy, brownish tones, have a quality of lightness and serenity which appeals to the French instinct.

Boucher loved bright shining things. Thus, he collected precious stones and rich shells which, we learn from his friend, Wille, he arranged on glass tables to lighten still more their pearly, iridescent reflections. Nothing inspired him so much as to paint a feminine nude in full light.

He died on the 30th May, 1770, having borne the title of First Painter to the King. He had two sons who made a name in art, Deshays and Beaudouin. There is a portrait of him in the Louvre by the Swedish pastelist, Lundberg, and there is one at Versailles by another Swede, Roslin.

See Pls. 44, 47, Vol. II.

BIBLIOGRAPHY: Goncourt, *L'Art au XVIII<sup>e</sup> siècle,* Vol. I.—André Michel, *François Boucher.* (Collection des artistes célèbres.)—Gustave Kahn, *Boucher.* (Collection des grands artistes.)

**BOUDIN (Eugène).**—French painter, 1824-1898. Of very humble origin, he went to Paris with a pension from the town of Havre, and entered the École des Beaux-Arts. His first picture (1859) represented the Pardon of St. Anne, Palud. He devoted himself exclusively to landscapes of Brittany, Normandy and Holland. He painted them in foggy weather, under watery skies. He hardly used any colours but greys and blacks, but with his delicate perception and deft handling, he distributed the values very skilfully, hollowed out sails, designed masts and spars, made a play of light, and gave a choppy effect to the waves. He is much valued among connoisseurs, and his little canvases are found in many private collections. Certain titles are: *The Beach near Trouville* (1864); a *Concert in the Casino of Deauville* (1865); *Reunion on the Beach* (1866); *Low-Tide,* and *The In-coming Tide* (1869); the *Road of Brest* (1870); *Rotterdam* (1877); the *Meuse at Rotterdam,* and the *Pilot-boat* (1888), etc.

**BOUGUEREAU (Adolphe William).**—French painter, 1825-1905, who achieved popular but not critical success. His best known pictures include *The Birth of Venus* and *La Vierge Consolatrice.*

**BOULLE (André Charles).**—1642-1732. Famous French cabinet-maker. Admitted to the Académie de Saint Luc, first cabinet-maker to the King (Louis XIV), accommodated in the Louvre in 1672. He made magnificent furniture, of the greatest richness, after his own designs, and more often after those of Le Brun. Boulle's furniture is inlaid with bronze, copper, tortoise-shell, the whole forming ornamental designs which are both elegant and sumptuous in effect. Of these numerous pieces, tables, bureaux, chests of drawers, wardrobes, etc., made for Louis XIV, the Dauphin and the Court, relatively few have come down to us. This delicate inlay work needed much care, and restoration. There are examples of it in the Louvre, in the Mazarine Library, in Windsor Castle, in the Wallace Collection, etc. Boulle had a big studio, in which his sons worked. Charles Cressent was among his best pupils. See Furniture (Seventeenth Century).

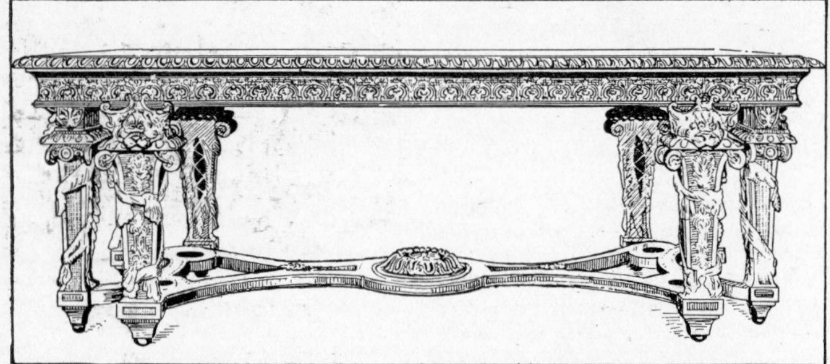

Boulle (André Charles): Inlaid table. (Museum, Versailles.)

Bibliography: Asselineau, *André Boulle, ébéniste de Louis XIV,* 1855.—De Champeaux, *Le Meuble,* Vol. II.

**BOURDELLE (Emile-Antoine).**—French sculptor (1861-1929). He was born in Montauban 30th October 1861, the son of a cabinetmaker from whom he learned the rudiments of woodcarving. After some training by a local art teacher he entered the École des Beaux-Arts in Toulouse, where he worked under the direction of Brassine and Larroque. In 1884 he went to Paris, where he entered the École Nationale des Beaux-Arts and took instruction from Falguière. He left the École des Beaux-Arts in 1889 and for a while worked in the atelier of Dalou. From there he went to help in the studio of Auguste Rodin as an assistant, and a short time later he opened his own studio, where he could work out his own theories of sculpture, which were at variance with those practised by Rodin. Bourdelle drew his inspiration from figures done in the archaic Greek style and also those done at the height of the Gothic era. He was concerned with the architectural character of his sculpture and chose very often mythological or symbolic subjects, which he expressed in statues of heroic size. Such were the *Hercules* and the *Dying Centaur,* conceived and executed with a great feeling for simple masses and only a few essential details. He did some reliefs, including the frieze and cartouches for the Théâtre des Champs-Élysées and another frieze for the Opera House at Marseilles. For the city of Buenos Aires he created the equestrian statue of General Alvéar, accompanied by the four symbolic figures of Eloquence, Right, Force and Victory, and in Paris was erected his monument to Adam Mickiewicz with the group of the Épopée Polonaise in memory of the Polish poet. But he also made small bronzes of dainty figures, recalling the works done in France in the 18th century, and he painted some mural panels for the interior of the Théâtre des Champs-Élysées, showing evidence of the various sides of his genius. Bourdelle made some book illustrations, including those for Emile Pourvillon's *Cezette,* Flaubert's *Légende de St.-Julien l'Hospitalier* and Clemenceau's *Demosthène.* He died 1st October 1929 at Le Vesinet, a respected and renowned artist famous not only in his own country but also in many foreign countries throughout the world. His heroic figures were undoubtedly classic in inspiration, but they were timeless and full of the power and vigour which only Bourdelle could instill in the marble. They were true to nature, but they were also the expression of a strong emotion permanently and adequately depicted. Besides his work in sculpture Bourdelle tried his hand at pastels, oil paintings, gouaches, watercolours. He was a tireless worker and for a time was the instructor of an art course given at the National Factory of Gobelin tapestries and also was a professor at the Grande Chaumière. He was the creator of a number of war memorials, including the *Virgin of Alsace* and some portrait busts—all displaying a vigour of expression and an excellent insight into human character. With his death there passed from France the last of the great classic artists.

Bibliography: André Fontainas, *Bourdelle,* 1930.—Emile-François Julia, *Antoine Bourdelle,* 1930.—Sàndor Kémeri, *Visage de Bourdelle,* 1931.—Charles Léger, *Antoine Bourdelle,* 1930.—Daniel Marquis-Sébie, *Le Message de Bourdelle,* 1931.

**BOURDICHON (Jean).**—French painter, about 1457 to 1521. Next to nothing is known of his life. From registers and receipts we learn that he worked for four kings of France. For Louis XI, he made a manuscript ornamented with "histories," and a "pourtraict" in parchment of 24 paintings, each containing a boat with several young ladies and sailors. For Charles VIII he painted standards, a portrait of the king and queen, and a large picture of Our Lady, with the Annunciation and the Nativity. For Francis I, he painted a portrait of St. François de Paule, which he presented to the Pope, and a portrait of the king. All these works have disappeared. The only work of Bourdichon that we possess is an illustrated manuscript in the Bibliothèque Nationale, the *Grandes heures d'Anne de Bretagne,* painted in 1508. The miniatures of this precious collection are arranged in a series of 63 large paintings, each of which fills an entire page, and 350 borders and text ornaments. In these little pictures, one feels the first influence of Italian art. Bourdichon is no longer content with Flemish exactitude. One sees a striving after the beautiful and elegant in the faces of his Madonnas and saints. In him we find the subjects of Fouquet and the iconography of the Middle Ages; and Flemish saints, side by side with their Italian sisters, share their sweetness and tenderness.

See Pl. 4, Vol. II.

Bibliography: E. Muntz, *La Renaissance en France et en Italie sous Charles VIII.*

**BOURDON (Sébastien).**—French painter, born at Montpellier in 1616, of Calvinist family. Of an extremely versatile temperament, and, like a true Southerner, having an alert mind and able hand, Bourdon went early in life to paint in Paris, in Bordeaux and in Toulouse, where, reduced to expedients, he became a soldier. Regrets came quickly, and his captain set him free. The young artist then went to Rome. There he earned a mean livelihood by painting scenes of low life. This stay among Roman artists taught him to cover his canvas very rapidly. However, as the result of a quarrel he had to flee from the Papal City, and from Venice he made for France again.

Bourdon wished to revisit his birthplace, Montpellier. There he was commissioned to decorate the Chapter House of the Cathedral, and in three months he painted the *Downfall of Simon the Magician,* a vast picture, full of figures. On being severely criticised by a colleague, Sébastien boxed his ears, and left Montpellier. He returned to Paris, where he painted the *Martyrdom of St. Peter,* for Notre Dame, and, in 1648, contributed to the foundation of the Academy of Painting, which admitted him on a level with twelve older painters. Then, although married, he resumed his wandering career.

Christine of Sweden ordered him to Stockholm, where he painted portraits of the Queen and her gentlemen. At the end of three years Bourdon returned to Paris, where great works awaited him—landscapes, "bambochades," vast decorations, portraits: he refused nothing. He decorated the walls of the Hôtel de Bretonvilliers, and painted the *Story of Phaeton,* doubtless his finest work, but which we can only judge from engravings by his pupils.

His last years were absorbed in incessant labour. He was unable to finish the decoration of the rooms in the Tuileries, with which Louis XIV had commissioned him, and which was done by his pupil and rival Nicholas Lovi. Bourdon was fifty-five years old when a violent fever caused his death in May, 1671.

This favoured artist was not often more than an imitator. In Rome, he took to Claude Lorrain. His works show a strange mixture of various influences. The Flemings, Venetians and Bolognaise impressed him equally. His ideas of design were classical, and he carried Poussin's doctrines to an extreme. He declared that "to avoid falling into the trivial . . . one should early be familiar with beautiful antiques, so that it becomes such a habit that one could, if one wished, draw them even from memory." But one has only to look at his *Julius Caesar before the Tomb of Alexander,* or his *Solomon Sacrificing to Idols* (both in the Louvre) to be convinced that he had no understanding of the spirit of ancient art.

He never composed like Poussin and never attained to the picturesqueness of the little northern masters, but he shows himself a brilliant and charming improviser in such pictures as the *Presentation to the Temple,* and the *Halt of the Bohemians* (both in the Louvre).

His portraits, enveloped in smoky shadows, like Caravaggio's, have more personality. There one feels a sensitive hand, thoroughly southern, and a remarkable quickness in grasping individual characteristics. The Museum of Montpellier contains fine portraits by Bourdon; and at Versailles there is one of Fouquet, subtle and sensitive, characteristic of this curious, intelligent financier whose pomp threatened the rising sun of Louis XIV.

See Pl. 39, Vol. II.

Bibliography: Ch. Ponsonhailhe, *Sébastien Bourdon, sa vie et son œuvre.* 1891.—Kuhnholtz, *Samuel Boissière de Montpellier.*

**BOURGES (Cher, France).**—The *Cathedral* (St. Étienne) is one of the most magnificent early Gothic churches in France. It was begun in 1190, by Archbishop Henri de Sully. He executed only a part of the crypt. The Cathedral was built in the 13th century. It is remarkable for the absence of transepts, and for its shortness compared with its width. It has five aisles, in different heights. The façade has five deeply recessed doorways, corresponding to the five aisles, which are approached by a flight of steps. The most splendid of these doorways is the central one, the tympanum of which is carved with three tiers of reliefs, representing the *Last Judgment*—a subject frequently seen over the portals of French Cathedrals. At the bottom is the *Resurrection of the Dead*;

above this we see the *Weighing of Souls*, while angels welcome the blessed to Paradise, and demons drag the damned to the mouth of hell; above, the figure of Christ is surrounded by the Virgin, St. John and four angels. The sculptures—like those of the other tym-

Cathedral of Bourges, Stained Glass: The Lepers.

pana—were formerly painted and gilded. They date from about 1275. In spite of clumsy restorations, they form an admirable whole—the most complete that we possess. The two western towers are of unequal height. That of the north (the *Tour du Beurre*, or *Butter Tower*) is in the flamboyant Gothic style. . . . The exterior view from the East reveals an imposing array of double flying-buttresses over the aisles. Bourges Cathedral possesses a wealth of stained-glass. Its series of 13th century windows are among the most beautiful in France. High up in the choir are figures of prophets and apostles, glowing in splendid colours. Few of the windows date from the 14th century, only the western "rose" (1390). The windows of the chapels of nave and choir belong to the 15th and 16th centuries.

See Pls. 48, 53, Vol. I.

The *House of Jacques Cœur* was built by a merchant prince round a central courtyard and has seven turret stairs. The finest mediæval town residence in France, it was finished about 1455, and is in a perfect state of preservation.

See Pl. 52, Vol. I.

Bibliography: Amédée Boinet, *Les sculptures de la Cathédrale de Bourges*. Paris, 1912.

**BOUTS (Albert).**—Flemish painter, second son of Thierry Bouts. Born about 1460, died in 1548. He was far from having his father's talent. His colour is harsh, and his drawing lacks correctness. He painted an *Assumption of the Virgin* (Brussels Museum) for the Lady Chapel of St. Pierre, at Louvain. The author of this picture was for a long time known as "The Master of the Assumption." The *Assumption* is the central panel of an altarpiece. The left wing depicts the Donor, and the right wing probably one of his uncles. The landscapes are the happiest parts. The figures are rather displeasing, and the attitudes stiff. *The Last Supper*, inspired by that of Thierry Bouts in its composition, is very inferior to it in handling and colour. A little picture, *Jesus in the House of the Pharisee* (Brussels Museum) reproduces, inversely, the picture by Thierry Bouts, representing the same subject. At Brussels there is also a *St. Jerome*. Other works by Albert Bouts, the *Nativity*, and a pretty *Holy Family*, are in Antwerp.

**— (Thierry—also called "Dierik" or "Dirk").**—Flemish painter. Born at Haarlem, about 1410. We know little of his earliest years. He worked in Holland, probably under the influence of Jan Van Eyck, who had stayed for two years at The Hague. About 1448, he married a young girl of rich family, in Louvain, and settled in this town, where he led a wealthy life, until his death. About 1468 he was elected official painter to the town of Louvain, and received a commission for four large compositions concerning the administration of Justice, of which two only were carried out. He died in 1475, leaving two daughters and two sons, one of whom, Albert Bouts, was an appreciated painter.

Thierry Bouts is one of the best of the primitive Flemish painters. Without having the powerful genius of a Van Eyck, or the dramatic feeling and fervour of a Van der Weyden, he was an excellent painter, able, sincere, and a fine landscapist; his palette is brilliant. His figures are, however, inexpressive and placid. He loved to represent great dramatic scenes, but the people taking part in his scenes of horror or fear, almost always have perfectly calm faces. He may have been the pupil of Roger van der Weyden.

His earliest known work is a Portrait of a Man (National Gallery), which is dated 1462. About 1465, he painted, perhaps ordered by Gérard de Smet, a *Martyrdom of St. Erasmus* for the Church of St. Pierre, Louvain, where the work is still to be found. The central panel shows us the scene of martyrdom. The Saint is stretched on a bed of torture; and through an incision in his abdomen the executioners wind out his intestines. The subject certainly is frightful; but it is difficult to feel very moved, for the martyr endures his agony without a gesture or expression of suffering; four persons in rich attire follow the scene with interest, but without the least trace of horror or pity. The scene is set in a luminous, tender landscape. On the wings are *St. Jerome* and *St. Bernard.*

Perhaps the most beautiful work of Bouts is the *Last Supper*, the central piece of a big polyptych, finished between 1464 and 1468, for the Collegiate Church of Louvain. The polyptych has suffered many vicissitudes, but since the war, all the panels have been restored to the Church of St. Pierre, in Louvain.

The arrangement and attitudes of the figures were evidently taken from representations of old Mystery plays. As usual, the figures are passive. The whole is, however, remarkable for beauty of colour, and truth of drawing.

From the same period dates the *Christ in the House of the Pharisee*, Berlin. The Christ recalls that of the *Last Supper*. On the left, the Donor is kneeling; and on the right, the Magdalene spreads her ointment on the feet of Christ.

On the 20th May, 1468, Bouts was commissioned to paint two large compositions for the Hôtel de Ville. One of them, the *Last Judgment* has disappeared. The second, the *Legend of Otho*, was not finished; it was meant to include four pictures, but death prevented the artist from painting the two last, and he only carried out the two fine paintings, now in Brussels Gallery: the *Unjust Sentence of the Emperor Otho*, and the *Emperor Otho repairing his Injustice*. Originally, both decorated the great hall of the Town Hall of Louvain. After being greatly admired, they were so much despised that even the name of the artist was forgotten. In 1827, the aldermen sold them to William I, who presented them to the Prince of Orange. They were afterwards re-bought by Nieuwenhuys, who, in 1861, sold them to Leopold, King of the Belgians, for the Brussels Gallery, where they are now. A professor of Louvain University, Jan van Haecht, provided the subjects. In the first picture, the Emperor Otho is about to condemn an innocent man, on the false evidence of his wife. The second picture shows the widow of the victim, who undergoes victoriously the "trial by fire"; the criminal empress condemned to death by her husband, is bound to a stake and burned alive. The figures in the drama are of exaggerated height, and too thin in their close-fitting doublets and long, trim robes. They appear interested and sad, but without indignation against the guilty, or pity for the condemned.

Other works by Bouts are the *Martyrdom of St. Hippolytus*, in the Church of St. Sauveur, Bruges, with portraits by Hugo Van der Goes; the triptych of Granada, and various *Madonnas* in the Museums of Berlin, Antwerp, Florence and Frankfort, as well as the *Adoration of the Kings*, in Munich.

See Pl. 60, Vol. I.

Bibliography: Arnold Goffin, *Thierry Bouts*. Collection des grands artistes des Pays-Bas, 1907.—E. Van Even, *Thierry Bouts dit Thierry de Haarlem, 6 lettres à Monsieur Wauters*, 1864.—A. Wauters, *Notre première école de peinture, T. Bouts et ses fils*. Brussels, 1863.—Fierens-Gevaert, *Les Primitifs flamands*. Brussels, 1908—Max J. Friedländer, *Altniederländische Malerei*, Vol. III.

**BRADFORD-ON-AVON (England).**—*St. Lawrence*. An Anglo-Saxon church of about 700, tiny in scale and consisting of four small interpenetrating rectangular shed-like structures, one forming the nave, two the north and south porches, and the easternmost the apse. The rectangular apse is an Anglo-Saxon feature.

**BRAEKELEER (Henri de).**—Belgian painter, 1840-1888. Pupil of Leys. A very able painter, who left large historical compositions for familiar subjects. He painted charming little interiors, labourers working, drinkers seated round the table, and old men in the chimney corner. A pleasing warm light brightens humble utensils and poor dwellings. His *Tavern* (Antwerp) shows very well the scope of his talent.

See Pl. 59, Vol. II.

**BRAHMAN ART.**—See India-Art.

**BRAMANTE (Donato).**—Italian architect and painter, 1444-1514. The inaugurator of the High Renaissance in architecture, he occupies the place in the history of building occupied by Raphael or Michelangelo in the history of painting or sculpture.

We do not know exactly where Bramante was born. Some say at Urbino, others in the neighborhood of Castel Durante, others, with more authority, give the little country place of Fermignano the honour of his birth.

In Urbino, where he received his training, there was already an architect of genius, Luciano Laurana, who may have been Bramante's

Bramante: Cancelleria, Rome.

master, and certainly influenced him profoundly. The elegant Ducal Palace of Urbino, a model of Renaissance architecture, was being built while Donato was growing up.

But it was not only his native place that influenced him. He travelled, and from his work we can see that he admired the buildings of Perugia, Ancona, Rimini, Mantua, Ferrara, Venice, etc. He knew and certainly admired Mantegna, in Padua. Finally, it was Leone Battista Alberti who must have had the greatest influence on him, through a mutual admiration of classical design.

Bramante: Court of the Belvedere. (Vatican Museum, Rome.)

In the first place he was probably a painter and continued to be one, not only in his pictures and frescoes, but in his buildings, where he created illusionistic bas-reliefs and bosses to imitate sculpture, and applied to architecture effects of colour and of values which really belong to painting.

Unfortunately there only remain a few examples of his painting, properly speaking: some decorations of houses in Milan—those of the Fontana, for instance, with his elegant frieze of putti; the warriors and famous men, among which are *Heraclitus Weeping* and *Democritus Laughing*, painted for the Casa dei Panigarolo, now at the Brera (figures in a large style, with abundant hair, recalling those of Melozzo da Forlì, but not very lifelike, in front of rich architectural motifs); the fine *Christ at the Column* in the Badia of Chiaravalle; the impressionistic figure of Argo, a powerful apparition, in spite of its missing head, which was discovered in 1894 on a wall of the Castello of Milan, and which has been much discussed; also four angels, which are probably still at the Certosa of Pavia—such are the painted works which are generally attributed to him, not to speak of many drawings in Milan, Venice, Paris, Berlin, Lille, etc., and several engravings.

In 1472, just after the death of Alberti, Bramante came to Mantua, where he undoubtedly studied Alberti's masterpiece, the Church of

Sant'Andrea. The effects of this study can be seen in Bramante's early designs for St. Peter's.

It was at Milan that he began creating his masterpieces. He arrived there about 1474, and remained in Lombardy until 1499, interrupting his work sometimes to go to Liguria, Tuscany, and Rome. In Milan, where he was still unknown, he found interest in San Lorenzo, the Cappella Portinari of Michelozzo, the Cathedral, and the Castello Sforzesco, then being built, and the Certosa of Pavia, in the neighbourhood; while he made the modest decorations of the Casa delle Fontane (Corso Venezia), and of the door of the Casa Mozzanica (now the Villa Serbelloni, at Trino, near Angera) with two Corinthian pilasters framing an arch which rests on two smaller pilasters.

He soon made a more important work in the façade of the Cathedral of Abbiate Grasso (1477).

In 1479, he was busy with Santa Maria presso San Satiro, and he did not finish the work until about 1498. Here the master aimed at make-believe effects. The church is built on the site of an older building. It has an octagonal sacristy (now the baptistery) of great beauty; and is notable for a curious chancel designed in perspective to simulate a choir.

In the courtyard of the Casa Pozzobonelli, also, he was able to give reign to his inventive genius. The elegant columns are well proportioned for the small size of the space, but, in order to allow the arches to reach the height of the usual first storey, the fine capitals have cubes placed on top of them, decorated with medallions and large acanthus leaves. The whole courtyard is remarkable for its harmony and exquisite sobriety.

Although documents are lacking to prove it, it is thought that he must have collaborated at the Cathedral of Como, for the elegant exterior doorway on the right side (1491) seems to be by him, besides the windows and a magnificent cornice. In the semi-circular space of the door, there is a division into compartments arranged in rays around the lunette, which is one of his personal characteristics.

His contribution to the Duomo of Pavia is more doubtful; but, in the building of the ciborium of Milan Cathedral he was certainly consulted (1486, 1488, 1491). He was always a marvellous inventor, in whom new ideas surged without very often allowing him time to realise the old—so much so, that he sometimes handed over his plans to others. The light of the created idea stimulated him more than the fulfilment of the project—the cold, immobile realisation in his heavy material, and it was enough for him to construct in his mind what he could not build upon the earth. That is why many buildings in Lombardy, begun on his designs, were only finished after his death. Thus the Church of Santa Maria di Canepanova at Pavia, a development of the Sacristy of San Satiro, and a prelude to St. Peter's, founded in 1492, was not consecrated until 1564.

Bramante had now a great reputation and the favour of Ludovico il Moro, who gave him important orders. He must have worked from 1492 to 1499 at Santa Maria delle Grazie. There he built the elegant doorway with a semi-circular canopy, and, above all, he was responsible for the choir, the transept, and the dome, of which at least the lower part was executed under his direction. There one sees the fine boldness, so characteristic of the Renaissance. Above the tribune, which recalls Santa Maria del Fiore, in Florence, by its three semi-circular apses, he raised a great sixteen-sided drum; and by his skillful decorations and shaded frames, he built up to the immense dome, surrounded by a pierced gallery. Here one enjoys particularly the polychromy of diverse materials, the pale rose of brick mixed with the white of marble among the cornices and medallions. The cloister, with its play of colour, is a delightful work. That of the Canonica of Sant'Ambrogio (from 1492, and unfinished in 1499) with the same designs and the same proportions, is perhaps still more perfect.

Bramante built the Ponticella del Castello (1495), the Palazzo di Cecilia Gallerani (now Broletto—there remains only a pleasing courtyard), the Castello di Vigevano, with the large entrance tower (finished in 1492), the loggia of a courtyard, very happy in proportions, but now, unfortunately, walled-in, and a vestibule; and he also did the painted decorations of the Palazzi which surround the grand Piazza.

At Piacenza, are attributed to him two cloisters and the courtyard of San Sepolcro, and the extraordinary Church of San Sisto. The sanctuary of Santa Maria di Piazza in Busto Arsizio, is in his style. It appears to have been finished from his plans after his death (1517).

In 1499, he returned to Rome, where, except for short travels, he remained. In 1509-1510, he worked in Loreto. Rome formed his mind. There he could contemplate in turns the harmonious proportions of the Pantheon or of the Theatre of Marcellus, and the immensity of the Coliseum or the Thermæ of Caracalla. These wonderful sights inspired him to new creations, which were the natural developments of his work in Lombardy, made grander by the influence of Rome.

In painting, he decorated the façade of San Giovanni in Laterano, and represented a Madonna and Saints in the portico of San Paolo (according to Vasari; these paintings have been destroyed). But he soon devoted himself entirely to architecture.

Until now all his work had been in the Early Renaissance style of Lombardy, famous for its wealth of ornament in carved marble or in terra cotta. But, in 1501, he finally synthesized the High Renaissance style of the early 16th century in Rome. Il Tempietto, in the cloisters of S. Pietro in Montorio, inspired by small circular Roman temples, is the tiny masterpiece which has the distinction of being the first building in the new style. A study for the dome of St. Peter's, the building has a round cella surrounded by a Doric colonnade; above is a handsome balustrade about a drum with niches; a panelled dome and heavy finial crown the building.

In the courtyard of the Palazzo della Cancelleria in Rome, one again finds the influence of the Canonica of Sant'Ambrogio and the interior of San Satiro. The interior of the Church of San Lorenzo in Damaso is characteristic of Bramante. But Rome caused him to replace rose coloured brick by grey Travertine, and the severity of the classic orders appealed to him more and more.

In the limited space in which he had to build the cloisters of Santa Maria della Pace (1504), he succeeded—by means of large pillars, reinforced with columns of the Ionic order, in the lower arcade, and pilasters and columns alternating in the second stage (the columns raised above the arcades—an innovation)—in giving the impression of large cloisters, severely classical, but with Tuscan grace.

His fame grew. It equalled that of Giuliano da San Gallo. Cultured, refined, a poet, and at the same time a great architect, Bramante won favour with Julius II, who, in 1504, ordered him to enlarge Santa Maria del Popolo, the church of the della Rovere family.

The vast spaces of the Vatican were the Mecca of his genius. What emotion he must have felt when the Pope asked him for plans!—a day too passionately desired perhaps, for the jealousy and famous quarrel between the two great artists, Michelangelo and Bramante, especially embittered Bramante, who helped to kill his rival's fine scheme for the tomb.

Neither was Bramante able to carry out his plans. His immense Vatican, with palace, gardens, colonnades, church, a colossal whole, rhythmically proportioned, was to evoke, and perhaps surpass, the grandeur of the imperial forums. It was a superhuman conception, and not to be realised. But these works, which never came into being, are as celebrated as any others, and as impressive.

Bramante began by surrounding the first cortile (the cortile of San Damaso) with graceful and simple loggie. Then he planned the court of the Belvedere, building to the right and to the left two large buildings, 300 metres long, parallel to Innocent VIII's palace. At the end of an impressive perspective effect (unfortunately cut short later by the Braccio Nuovo), he built the Palazzo di Chinsura, with an enormous semi-circular niche in the middle, which seems like half of a superb temple, behind the antique marble "pigna," which is placed there like an altar.

He also made the staircase which descends into the gardens in spirals.

But the church itself, the great Papal Church of the world, which was to be built on the site of the old Basilica, and which had already been begun according to the plans of Leone Battista Alberti and of Giuliano da San Gallo (see article on St. Peter's), fascinated Bramante's brain. It was on account of this that he broke with Michelangelo; and he must have thrilled with the joy of triumph when he won in his competition with Giuliano da San Gallo.

He began his work enthusiastically in 1506, at the age of sixty-two. His colossal scheme was a Greek cross, with a semi-circular apse at the end of each of the equal arms, a tower at each angle of the square which contained the cross, and a dome over the crossing of the arms. Thus, like stars round a sun, the four little domes surrounded the big central one, which had a colonnaded drum and was crowned by a lantern. The old Basilica still stood intact in the shade of the great new buildings, as though hidden in the humility of age.

This symmetrical plan was a summary and fulfillment of Bramante's thought, which contained both Lombard and Roman forms. The tendency toward buildings of the central type, a tendency always present in North Italy, where Byzantine influence lingered, was characteristic of the High Renaissance. In the use of many piers, carrying barrel vaults into which the dome was broken at the crossing, we see the influence of Alberti's Sant'Andrea at Mantua. The great Basilica seems to belong at the same time to antiquity, the Middle Ages, and the East, as though to embarrass all worldly aspirations, a marvellous, impossible symbol which was not to find realisation, and which we can only see in Bramante's designs, in the background of Raphael's *School of Athens*, in some frescoes in the Vatican Library, and especially in the bronze medal of Caradosso. A copy of this was placed by the Pope at the bottom of the ditch, hollowed to receive the first stone of one of the piers which support the dome (18th April, 1506).

The work was begun. Three other gigantic piers were raised. They were united by four immense arches. The South arm of the cross was built, one of the little domes was raised. And then the great architect died (14th March, 1514). The project died, too. Rivalries began over his ashes, and when, after some years, Bramante's ideas were taken up again, they had paled. They were altered and weakened, and dominated by the Baroque. From a Greek cross, the building was changed to a basilica, whose western end steadily increased to over twice the originally planned length, so that the huge dome, built by Michelangelo and Della Porta, can be seen only from the side and rear. But beneath the flood of light, from the vast dome, which widens into the four great arms, unfortunately unequal, something of the great artist's spirit survives, in spite of the alterations that have been made in his designs.

Classical art inspired Bramante. He studied it and understood it, like Leone Battista Alberti. He also followed Umbrian and Lombard models. But his mind was intensely original. He had a great many pupils.

See Pl. 7, Vol. II.

BIBLIOGRAPHY: L. Pungileoni, *Memorie intorno alla vita e alle opere di Dounino o Donato Bramante.* Rome, 1836.—Carlo Casati, *I capi d'arte di Bramante di Urbino nel Milanese.* Milan, 1870.—H. de Geymüller, *Les projets primitifs pour la Basilique de Saint-Pierre de Rome, par Bramante, Raphael, etc.* Paris, 1875-1880.—*Bramante et la Restauration de Sainte-Marie-des Grâces à Milan.* Paris, 1887 (extract from La Gazette Architecturale).—W. von Seidlitz, *Bramante in Mailand* Jahrbuch der K. Preus. Kunst Samm. Berlin, 1887, Vol. IV.—L. Beltrami, *Bramante poeta.* Milan, 1884.—*Bramante e la Ponticella di Lodovico il Moro.* Milan, 1903.—Corrado Ricci and L. Beltami, *Gli affreschi di Bramante e la Sala dei Maestri d'arme.* Milan, 1902.—G. Carotti, *Le Opere di Leonardo, Bramante e Raffaello.* Milan, 1905.

**BRAMANTINO (Bartolommeo Suardi).**—C. 1460-1536. Architect and painter of Milanese school, close follower of Bramante.

**BRANCUSI (Constantin).**—Contemporary sculptor. Born in Roumania in 1876, he studied art in Bucharest until 1902, and in 1904 went to Paris where he was a pupil of Mercié at the Ecole des Beaux-

Arts. From 1906 on he worked in Rodin's atelier and was a member of the circle of Guillaume Apollinaire. In 1908 Brancusi carved *The Kiss*, the most abstract sculpture of this period representing two primitive block-like figures. The *Sleeping Muse* of 1910 still shows Rodin's influence, but the *New-Born* five years later, is already the highly polished egg-shape which is the essential form of most of the artist's later works. Magic or mythological inspiration is the basis of many of his sculptures. This symbolism is combined with the most modern technique, the understanding and adaptation of materials, and the extreme simplification of forms approaching the purely geometric conception, but still remaining organic with subtly modulated surfaces. Brancusi is equally sensitive in handling wood, bronze, marble, stone, glass, steel, etc. The slender, glossy *Bird in Space*, 1925 (Mus. Modern Art, N. Y.), traverses dynamically through space; this momentary action is caught with equal skill in several other bird and fish compositions, while lyric potentiality emanates from heads like *Leda* or *Mlle. Pogany*. Brancusi exhibited in Paris, Berlin, New York; The Art Inst. Chicago, as well as many notable collections in America and Europe include his sculpture.

Bibliography: Adlow, *Brancusi, drawing and design,* 1927; Pound, *Brancusi,* 1921.

**BRANGWYN (Frank).**—Contemporary English painter. He was born at Bruges, Belgium, 12th May 1867, the son of parents who were of English and Welsh ancestry. His father was a reproducer of mediæval cloths and vestments, following in the tradition of William Morris. The family returned to London in 1875 and there young Brangwyn began to work in his father's office making architectural designs. Later he did some details of tapestries for William Morris and some cartoons for his workroom. His real training came from the drawings and sketches that he brought back from his travels. He worked in Kent, Sandwich and other rural districts of England, drawing the fishermen and their simple cottages, and then worked his way back to London on a schooner watching and learning the routine of the sailors and the structure of the masts and sails, which information he was later able to utilise in his pictures. Trips to Asia Minor, Tunis, Tripoli, Constantinople and the Black Sea soon followed. Later he went to Russia, South Africa and Madeira, sketching and always making notes planning for the future. His first great commission was for some murals in Skinners' Hall, done between 1904 and 1909. Other orders for murals soon came in, for two overmantels in Lloyd's Registry, frescoes for the Royal Exchange, depicting modern commerce, decorations for the offices of the Canadian National Grand Trunk Railway in London, panels for the Chapel of Christ's Hospital in West Horsham and many others. He did some historical panels for the New Court House in Cleveland, Ohio, murals for the Panama-Pacific Exposition in San Francisco in 1915, a panel, *Canada's War Record,* for the Parliament Building in Winnipeg and murals for the new State Capitol in Jefferson City, Missouri. In addition to these murals Brangwyn has done some mosaics, including those for the apse decoration of St. Aidan's Church in Leeds, and working after the manner of William Morris he designed tables, chairs and cabinets, made cartoons for tapestries and a few for stained glass. Although some of his work has dealt with religious topics much of his art deals with the life and industry of the present time. It is the product of an intelligent observer who is impressed by the drama of human life. Basing his themes on actual facts as he has seen them the artist is able to present a convincing picture which is shown in a large composition, simplified to suit its position as a mural decoration and yet capable of expressing the sentiment of the artist in its individual treatment of the theme. From the time when Frank Brangwyn's first picture was accepted by the Royal Academy in 1885, when he was only eighteen years of age, he has had a most successful career as a painter and mural decorator. He is known for his work outside of England, as witness the number of murals that he has executed in the United States and Canada, of which the most recent is the group of panels for Rockefeller Center in New York City.

Bibliography: Frank Brangwyn and Hayter Preston, *Windmills,* 1923.—Frank Brangwyn and Walter Shaw-Sparrow, *A Book of Bridges,* 1915.—*Frank Brangwyn,* with notices by Steinlen, Richepin and Verhaëren, 1929.—Herbert Furst, *The Decorative Art of Frank Brangwyn,* 1924.—A. S. Levetus, *Frank Brangwyn, zwanzig graphische arbeiten,* n. d.—Frank Rutter, *The British Empire Panels Designed for the House of Lords, by Frank Brangwyn,* 1933.—Malcolm C. Salaman, *Frank Brangwyn,* 1924; 1932 (Modern Masters of Etching).—Walter Shaw-Sparrow, *Frank Brangwyn and His Work,* 1915.

**BRAQUE (Georges).**—Contemporary French painter. He was born at Argenteuil in 1881. He was the son of a painting contractor and early showed an active interest in art. He first became prominent when he exhibited his work at the Salon des Indépendants. He has been called one of the early exponents of Fauvism and was one of the founders of the Cubistic movement which has had such an important bearing upon modern art. From an expression of actual facts he advanced to the creation of more striking compositions by freeing himself from the restrictions and taboos of old outworn artistic conventions. In an attempt to express the dynamic character of the world around us he built up pictorial compositions composed of simple architectonic forms divided arbitrarily into smaller parts, each treated as a separate unit. His pictures show the influence of Cézanne with the attempt to suggest depth, but his method differs from that of Cézanne in that he depicts his objects in a flat way. He seeks to show the ultimate reality of nature which is perfect as contrasted with the imperfect appearances that we are accustomed to. His usual themes are still lifes although he has done some landscapes and a very few figure subjects. Besides his work in oil he has tried some experiments with papier maché and the addition of small bits of paper and fabrics to his canvases. He has done some book illustrations, including woodcuts for *Le Piège de Meduse* by Erik Satie and others for *Les Fâcheux* by Diaghilew. Examples of his work may be seen in the Musée du Luxembourg in Paris as well as in many other European museums and in the Art Institute of Chicago, the Columbus, Ohio, Gallery of Fine Arts and the Gallery of Living Art in New York.

Bibliography: Bissière, *Georges Braque,* 1920. — Carl Einstein, *Georges Braque,* 1934.—Maurice Reynal, *Georges Braque,* 1924.

**BRASS.**—See "Dinanderie."

**BRAURONION.**—See Acropolis of Athens.

**BRAY (Jan de).**—Dutch painter, of a family of painters. Died in 1697. He worked at Haarlem. His chief pictures are in the Museum of this town. He painted historical pictures which have no particular distinction, and some excellent Corporation pictures, such as the *Regents of Haarlem,* which are among the best portraits of the Dutch school. The faces are admirably studied and rendered.

**BREA (Ludovico).**—Piedmontese painter, c. 1443-1523, influenced by local Franco-Flemish tradition, and by Foppa, with whom he worked on the altarpiece of Santa Maria di Castello of Savona (1490). There is a *Coronation of the Virgin* by him in Santa Maria de Castella of Genoa (1513), and a *Crucifixion* in the Palazzo Bianco (c. 1481), but Ludovico worked chiefly in Nice where he is well represented. He was the most important of many painters in his family, and of all the painters of Nice.

**BREENBERGH (Bartholomeuf).**—Dutch painter born in Deventer (1599-before 1659). He chiefly painted ruins.

**BREGNO (Andrea) or Andrea da Milano.**—Italian sculptor, 1421-1506. Born in Osteno, on the Lake of Lugano. He worked chiefly in Rome. and he is one of the most important Roman sculptors of the Renaissance. He shows himself a Lombard by his qualities of nobility and serious grace, and by something rather heavy, too. He worked in collaboration with Mino da Fiesole and Giovanni Dalmata.

Certain of his more important works are:

The tomb of Cardinal Lebretto (died 1465), in Santa Maria in Aracœli, a sarcophagus of Roman form.

The tomb of Tibaldi (d. 1466) in Santa Mariasopra Minerva.

The monument of Cardinal Coca (d. 1477), in the same church. one of the finest tombs by Andrea Bregno, with a delicate polychromy.

In Santa Maria del Popolo, the tomb of Gomiel, Bishop of Burgos, and the large altar of Cardinal Roderigo Borgia (1473).

The tomb of Pietro Riario (d. 1474), in the Santi Apostoli.

And that of Cristoforo della Rovere (d. 1479), again in Santa Maria del Popolo.

He also worked in Siena, where he made the altar of the Piccolomini in the Cathedral (1481-1485) and Viterbo, where he made the Tabernacle for the Church of the Madonna della Quercia (1490) in the neighbourhood.

**BRERA.**—See Milan.

**BRESCIANINO (Andrea del).**—Painter of Siena, active 1507 until after 1525, probably pupil of Pacchia, influenced by Raphael and the Florentines.

**BREUGHEL (The).**—Family of Flemish painters. The oldest was Peter Breughel (see this name), who had two sons, Jan Breughel, known as "Velvet Breughel" (see this name), and Peter II, known as "Hell-fire Breughel" (1564-1638). This nickname of "Hell-fire" came from his predilection for scenes of the nether regions and devils, and effects of burnings and flames, as can be seen in his best pictures: *The Burning of Sodom,* the *Burning of Troy,* the *Deliverance of Souls from Purgatory, Aeneas in Hades, Orpheus in Hades,* the *Temptation of St. Anthony,* etc.

"Hell-fire" Breughel had a son, Peter III Breughel (1589?), a mediocre painter; while Jan, or "Velvet," Breughel had two—Ambroise Breughel (1617-1675), and Jan II Breughel (Antwerp, 1601-1678) who imitated his father without having his talent: there are pictures by him, signed and dated, in Dresden and Munich.

Velvet Breughel had, also, three daughters who all married painters: Catherine, wife of Borrekens; Paschasie, wife of Kessel; and the beautiful Anne, who married David Teniers II, by whom she had a son, David Teniers III (1638-1685), who also had a son, David Teniers IV (1672-1731).

It was Jan II Breughel (the Young), the elder of Velvet Breughel's children, who had the most numerous posterity, five sons, likewise all painters but without great talent: Jan Peter (1628-?), Abraham (1631-?), Philip (1635-?), Ferdinand (1637-?), and Jan Baptiste (1647-?), whose children were not artists.

On the other hand, the grandson of Velvet Breughel, Jan Kessel (son of Jerome Kessel and Paschasie Breughel) had six sons, of whom five were painters: Gaspard, Jan Baptiste (1670-1719), Abraham (1672-1720), Ferdinand (1648-1696) and Jan (1654-1708).

**— (Peter).**—Flemish painter, also known as Breughel "the Droll" or "Peasant Breughel." (He himself spelled his name "Bruegel.") His name is that of a village in Brabant where he was born about 1525. He studied in Antwerp, with P. Coecke, then with J. Cock, and he went to Italy in 1551. He returned to Antwerp in 1553, and ten years later settled in Brussels, where he died in 1569. From his marriage with the daughter of P. Coecke, he had two sons, Peter (called Hell-fire) and Jan (called Velvet). He always lived a peaceable, busy life. He was much admired by his contemporaries, and especially appreciated by the Emperor Rodolphe, who bought, at a considerable price for those days, all the works now in the Museum of Vienna.

Breughel is the painter of peasants. He studied them with an inexhaustible interest in all their occupations. We find them in his work, not caricatured but as they are in reality, worthy rustics, loving noisy festivals and copious meals,—rough, peace-loving fellows who enliven beautiful country scenes. His very personal technique had not submitted to the influence of any master. He drew with great delicacy and precision, sincerely reproducing his homely models. But what gives him his especial charm is his colour. We find daring, lively tones placed side by side, without transition, bright colours on a background of snow. It is a pleasure to follow the fantasies of his whimsical brush, in the little motley figures which fill his landscapes. His palette has a richness of tone unknown until then, from bright fresh shades to exquisite half-tones. He varied infinitely his reds, browns, and yellows, which have a brightness and clearness which gives all his panels a sense of gaiety.

We only possess a small number of his works. They might be classed into three categories, according to their subjects: village scenes, devilries, and religious pictures.

The first have won him the name of "Peasant" Breughel; no one has expressed the life of the people better. The *Village Wedding* (Vienna) shows us worthy country folk enjoying themselves. The red caps and garments of variegated colours are brushed in with rapid strokes. In the *Kermesse* (Vienna) there are, again, the deep, reddish brown shades that the artist loved. *The Hunters* (Vienna) shows us a beautiful landscape of thick snow, against the whiteness of which the dark shapes, made by the figures of men and dogs, stand out.

A gentle, melancholy poetry pervades the *Return of the Herds* (Vienna): the figures in the foreground are in subdued tone, while a fine silvery light brightens the landscape in the distance. Very different is the impression that we get from the *Peasants' Battle* (Dresden). Then in the *Land of Cockayne*, painted in 1567 (Munich), which illustrates an old Flemish tale, roast pigs, bearing in their sides the knife to carve them, run eagerly to offer themselves to hungry youths.

But life does not consist only of eating and drinking, dancing and laughter. So Breughel reminded his friends the peasants, and he tried to teach them to live wisely. They must see their business clearly. "When the blind lead the blind both fall into the ditch." In *The Blind Leading the Blind* (Naples) there are not two, but six blind men who go groping, and stumbling, connected by the same cord, which is about to cause their downfall. There is a replica of this composition in the Louvre.

*The Bird-Catcher* (Vienna) was also inspired by an old proverb. A countryman passes and sees a nest in a tree. He points to it with his finger. But a smart, agile child has already climbed the tree and robbed the nest. "Who sees a nest, sees it; who takes it, has it." Breughel was very fond of these amusing, moral subjects. His lighthearted work has a satirical side, of which the sting is hidden under the whims of a rich imagination. If the artist had not submitted to the influences of any of his masters, he had, on the contrary, studied and greatly admired Jerome Bosch. He painted scenes of devils, and witchcraft, fantastic incidents, which entertained, and frightened a little, the good Flemings of the 16th century. Among his best pictures of this kind are the *Battle of Lent against Carnival* (Vienna), with droll and spirited details, and the *Tower of Babel* (Vienna), which is being built in a beautiful Flemish landscape.

Biblical scenes inspired in Breughel original compositions: *The Bearing of the Cross* seems more like a joyful throng of peasants in holiday dress than a walk to Calvary. The *Massacre of the Innocents* is a little more moving. In the depth of winter, the soldiers of Herod—hardened Flemish warriors—have sacked the village which slept under a coat of snow; and in this bright and cheerful setting, the carnage begins in a pretty square of red and yellow houses. The soldiers perform their pitiless task in the midst of groaning, beseeching parents.

Breughel observed nature closely, and rendered it faithfully and delicately. The snow effects which recur in many of his pictures have a clarity which is emphasised again in the charming notes of houses painted in red, brown, and even in egg yellow, and sky-grey. His distances have exquisite half-tones, which melt into a fine silvery light. The Autumn landscapes, such as the *Return of the Herds,* have warm tints and soft lighting.

Breughel the Elder is the last of the great Flemish painters who derived all their inspiration from their native soil. After him, artists studied the great Italian masters, who much influenced their technique and the subject of their pictures.

See Pl. 24, Vol. II.

BIBLIOGRAPHY: E. Michel, *Les Breughel.* Paris, 1892.—Bastelaer, *Peter Breughel.* Brussels, 1905.—Romdahl, Pieter Breughel d. ä. und sein Kunstschaffen, *Jahrb. der Kunsthistor.* Samml., Vienna, 1904.

**— (Jan).**—Flemish painter, surnamed Velvet Breughel. Son of Peter Breughel the Droll, he was born in Brussels in 1568, and went early to Antwerp where he lived until his death, in 1625. He never left it, except for a short visit to Italy. His numerous qualities of heart and spirit won him all sympathies, among others that of Rubens, who several times painted the figures in his landscapes. He had two sons, eight grandsons, and four great-grandsons, all painters.

Breughel chiefly painted little panels in which he displayed much skill, and a graceful poetic imagination. His colour is enamel-like. Certain details, over-analysed, give a worried effect to the whole. Nature, landscapes, flowers, plants inspired charming works with velvety shades, and deep, bluish distances.

His works are numerous and varied. He touched all kinds. The Museums of Madrid (52 pictures), Munich (41 pictures), Dresden (33 pictures) and Milan (29 pictures) are especially rich in his paintings.

First, he painted numerous pictures which had been ordered from him by the Archbishop of Milan, during history in Italy, and which are in the Ambrosian Library. One of the best is *Daniel in the Lions' Den.* On his return to Antwerp he executed fifty pictures (Madrid) for the Archdukes Albert and Isabella, which are his best productions, such as the *Five Senses,* and the *Four Elements.* Then historical scenes: the *Battle of Arbela* (Louvre); the *Preaching of St. Norbert* (Brussels); little genre pictures, such as the *Fish Market* (Munich), etc.; the *Earthly Paradise* (Doria Gallery, Rome) shows us animals, admirably painted, in a beautiful pasture. In *Christ Stilling the Tempest,* the waves are well rendered. Breughel excelled in painting flowers: the *Flora* (Palazzo Durazzo, Genoa) and the *Garland* (Munich) have bright, velvety colours. He was also very skillful in the painting of accessories, furniture, arms, glittering cuirasses. We can admire a whole collection in the *Venus and Cupid in an Armory* (Madrid). Breughel is the first of a whole series of little masters who produced quantities of admirable and elegant works, but often lacking simplicity and rightness of colour.

BIBLIOGRAPHY: Tolnai, K., *Die Zeichnungen P. Breugels.* München, 1925.—Tolnai, K., *P. Bruegel, l'ancien.* Bruxelles, 1935.—Friedländer, M. J., *P. Bruegel.* Berlin, 1921.

**BRIDGE OF SIGHS.**—See Venice.

**BRÎLL.**—Family of Flemish painters of the 16th century. The best known are Matthew (1550-1583), and especially Paul (see below).

**— (Paul).**—Flemish painter, 1554-1626. He studied in Rome, which did not prevent his remaining a true Fleming by the sincerity and finish of his execution. Among his best work are *Christ Casting out a Devil* (Munich), a little panel on copper, made in 1601; the *Mountain Landscape* (1608—Dresden); and some decorations for churches and palaces (Palazzo Rospigliosi, Rome; house of St. Cecilia, Vatican; Santa Maria Maggiore, Rome). There are some pretty landscapes, some fine as miniatures, others in large compositions, in the Ambrosiana, Milan.

BIBLIOGRAPHY: Mayer, A., *Das Leben u. die Werke von Matth. und Paul Brill.* Leipzig, 1910.

**BRIOSCO (Andrea).**—See Riccio (Andrea).

**— (Benedetto).**—Lombard architect and sculptor of the 15th century. Pupil of Amadeo. He worked chiefly in Milan, particularly in the Cathedral. In 1499, he took his master's place at the Certosa of Pavia, where he made the main doorway. At the end of his life, he felt the modernising influence of the school of Leonardo da Vinci.

**BRITISH MUSEUM.**—See London.

**BRIXWORTH (England).**—*Anglo-Saxon church,* c. 670. As opposed to most pre-Romanesque English churches, Brixworth has the round apse and columnar division into nave and side aisles of the Christian Roman basilica. The scale is tiny and the workmanship crude, as in all barbarian architecture.

**BROEDERLAM (Melchior).**—Flemish painter from the end of the 14th to the beginning of the 15th century. Originally from Ypres. He became painter and valet de chambre to the Duke of Burgundy in 1385. He worked chiefly at Ypres, and it was there that he painted the exterior wings of two sculptured altarpieces, ordered by the Duke of Burgundy, for the Chartreuse of Champmol (near Dijon). The wings, finished in 1399, were much admired. One of these altarpieces has come down to us (Dijon). On one of the wings is painted, in distemper, the *Annunciation* and the *Visitation*; on the other, the *Presentation at the Temple* and the *Flight into Egypt.* The delicate, minute painting, full of little details, shows the influence of the miniaturists.

See Pl. 4, Vol. II.

**BROGNIART (A. T.).**—Parisian architect, 1739-1813. His best known design is the Bourse.

**BRONZE.**—See Assyria and Chaldea; Byzantine Art; China; Greece; Prehistoric Archæology; etc.

**BRONZI (Il).**—See Ghiberti.

**BRONZINO (Agnolo).**—Florentine painter (1503-1572). A mannerist, Bronzino was the pupil of Pontormo, and an imitator of Michelangelo. His numerous pictures in Florence, particularly the frescoes in the Palazzo Vecchio (1545-64) and that of 1565-69 in San Lorenzo, are academic or artificial scenes, empty, forced and pretentious.

But cold and unoriginal as this painter was, he shows himself an excellent portraitist. His grave figures, as though sculptured in fine marble, have at once power, distinction and life. Perhaps the most striking is that fair Lucrezia Pucci Panciatichi (Uffizi), so straight in her heavy and magnificent violet robe, which sets off the pallor of her beautiful soft hands, while above her swan-like neck her refined, transparent face has a fixed, serious look. The portrait of Cosimo de' Medici (Uffizi) has character, too, in the noble sobriety of his cuirass. But how rich and majestic is the dress of the Duchess Eleonora of Toledo (Uffizi), how distinguished are her hands. How lifelike, too, is the little Don Garcia de' Medici (also in the Uffizi), a fat, merry little prince, happy in his splendid surroundings, with his goldfinch, which it appears he could suffocate if he had a mind to do it. One involuntarily compares Bronzino with Holbein.

BIBLIOGRAPHY: Arthur McComb, *Agnolo Bronzino,* Cambridge, Mass, 1928.

**BROOK (Alexander).**—Contemporary American painter. This artist was born in Brooklyn, New York, 14th July 1898. He painted even as a child and in 1915 entered the Art Students' League in New York City. For four years he worked there under John C. Johansen and Kenneth Hayes Miller. He married Miss Peggy Bacon, who is well known for her prints and book illustrations. He has been connected with the Whitney Studio Club in an executive capacity and for some time was an instructor at the Art Students' League. Between the years of 1929 and 1931 he received important prizes in the annual exhibitions held at the Art Institute of Chicago, Carnegie Institute in Pittsburgh, and the Pennsylvania Academy of Fine Arts in Philadelphia. In 1931 he was awarded one of the Guggenheim Fellowships in Painting. He is the author of a number of articles in magazines which deal in a lucid way with the peculiarities of the styles of the various schools of contemporary art. His own work is characterised by certain aspects of mysticism treated in a very individual manner with brilliant patches of colour emphasising the dull tones which are usual in his compositions. Examples of Mr. Brook's paintings may be found in the Albright Art Gallery at Buffalo, the Art Institute of Chicago, the Whitney Museum of American Art in New York City, and the Corcoran Gallery of Art in Washington.

BIBLIOGRAPHY: William Murrell, *Alexander Brook,* 1922.—Forbes Watson, *Alexander Brook,* c. 1930.—Edward Alden Jewell, *Alexander Brook,* 1931.—For a complete bibliography see *The Index of Twentieth Century Artists* for February, 1934.

**BROSAMER (Hans).**—German engraver of the 16th century, who left some charming engravings in which the Italian influence dominates: *Bathsheba,* the *Kiss* (1549), the *Lay of Aristotle,* and a *Book of*

# IRON

*Since man has learned to use iron, he has above all utilised it for making weapons and tools. With the aid of iron he has been able to work other materials: stone, wood, or soil. But iron may also become the material for a work of art. Iron may be shaped with a mallet when it is melted by heat. The blacksmith, with the aid of a hammer stretches, flattens, twists, and moulds the red-hot bar of iron. The number of objects thus manufactured is limited, but wrought iron work can have great beauty; on a simple balcony it may add charm and elegance to the most modest façade of a building.*

FORGED IRON GRATING: SPANISH WORK. LOUVRE.
*(Photo by Hachette.)*

Iron is well adapted for gratings. Its resistance makes it favourable for the execution of enclosures, which must serve as an obstacle but at the same time must not obstruct the view or intercept the light.

FORGED IRON GATE OF THE GALLERY OF APOLLO. LOUVRE.
*(Photo by Hachette.)*

This comes from the château of Maisons. These symmetrical shapes of classic art were adopted, and to achieve a more regular design the chiseler finished the work of the blacksmith.

BORDEREL: GATE. ROBERT GRANET, ARCHITECT.
*(Photo by Borderel.)*

ANTWERP: THE WELL ATTRIBUTED TO QUENTIN MATSYS.
*(Photo by Neurdein.)*

NANCY: IRON GATES OF LAMOUR.
*(Photo by Hachette.)*

PARIS: HINGE OF A DOOR OF NOTRE DAME. THIRTEENTH CENTURY.
*(Photo by Hachette.)*

The blacksmith attached to a central panel branches twisted with a mallet, and to these he added flower-like pieces. This sheaf of iron binds together the panels of the door.

PARIS: IRON GATE OF THE PALACE OF JUSTICE.
*(Photo by Neurdein.)*

In this masterpiece of forged iron the artist has transposed into metal the decorative style of the Louis XVI period. Contemporary artists can shape iron equally well into the forms used today.

EDGAR BRANDT: UMBRELLA-HOLDER.
*(Photo by Brandt.)*

By its inherent qualities iron is easily adaptable to certain shapes. If the iron is hammered while red-hot, certain shapes can be obtained with ease, while others are scarcely compatible with the possibilities of iron. The decorations of the flamboyant style and the rococo style of the eighteenth century seem to be the best suited for forged iron work. From the end of the Middle Ages and from the eighteenth century there are left a number of gratings, balconies, and fences, which with few exceptions are works of art. Among the most famous is the Well of Antwerp, attributed to Quentin Matsys, and the gates of Lamour at Nancy, which are among the masterpieces of decorative work of the era of Louis XV.

# ENGRAVING

*Engraving is a form of painting by printing; most frequently the printing is done with black ink. The picture is cut into wood or on copper. In wood the drawing is in relief, like the letters of the printing press. The strokes are cut into copper, and these hollows when filled with ink, retrace the design on paper. The results depend on the depth of strokes engraved with the burin on the copper plate. The beauty of the engraving depends on the skill of the draftsman.*

RAPHAEL: JUDGMENT OF PARIS, LINE ENGRAVING, BY MARCANTONIO RAIMONDI.
*(Photo by Hachette.)*

CLAUDE MELLAN: PEIRESC, LINE ENGRAVING.
*(Photo by Hachette.)*

ALBRECHT DÜRER: ST. JEROME IN HIS CELL, LINE ENGRAVING.
*(Photo by Hachette.)*

REMBRANDT: CHRIST HEALING THE SICK, ETCHING. MUSÉE DE CONDE, CHANTILLY.
*(Photo by Hachette.)*

Etching is engraving on a copper plate; it is done with acid biting out parts of the metal. The artist draws on a copper plate which is covered with a ground: the needle exposes the metal. The acid, when poured on the plate, bites into the copper wherever it was exposed. This procedure is much more flexible than the burin method; it also results in effects of translucence which equal those of oil painting. The etchings of Rembrandt are characterised by the same poesy and mystery as his paintings. Etching may give the objects a sharp contour as well as soft, shady effects. The plate may also be redone with the burin.

ALBRECHT DÜRER: THE VISITATION, WOODCUT.
*(Photo by Hachette.)*

OUTAMARO: WOMAN AT HER TOILET, WOODCUT.
*(Photo by Giraudon.)*

GAVARNI: GRISETTES, LITHOGRAPH.
*(Photo by Hachette.)*

In wood cutting the sketch stays in relief and the artist cuts around it. The lines are heavier than in copper engraving. The 18th century Japanese were wood engravers. But by successive printings which superposed various coloured inks, they made prints which are like paintings. In lithography the engraver draws with a crayon on stone. The acid bites out the stone where the crayon has not touched it. The drawing remains in relief, ready for the printing, and can thus be reproduced with great accuracy.

*Vases*, containing a set of models for goldsmith's work.

BIBLIOGRAPHY: H. W. Singer, *Die Kleinmeister*—Bielefeld, 1908.—L. Rosenthal, *La Gravure*. Paris, Laurens, 1909.

**BROU (Ain, France).**—One kilometre from Bourg is the Church of Brou, one of the artistic wonders of France. In 1480, Marguerite de Bourbon, wife of the Duc Philippe, made a vow that she would build a magnificent monastery if her husband, wounded in the hunt, recovered his health; but she died three years later, and her sister-in-law, Margaret of Austria, carried out her idea, in memory of her husband, Philibert le Beau. The first architect chosen by Margaret of Austria was Jean Perréal, and Michel Colombe was the sculptor. They only worked for one year, and were replaced by the Flemish architect Van Boghem, and the Swiss sculptor Konrad Meyt. The church, composed of a nave and side aisles, possesses magnificent carvings. The rood-screen is a marvellous lacework of stone, composed of three flattened arches. The choir contains three celebrated tombs. That of Philibert le Beau is isolated in the middle of the choir. The Duke is there represented twice. He lies, clad in his armour, surrounded by angel genii, his head turned towards the tomb of Margaret, his wife. The figure is in white marble, lying on a black marble slab, which is supported by pillars, richly decorated with riches and figures of Sibyls. Below is a second black marble slab, with the Duke represented in his shroud. The tomb of Margaret of Austria, his wife, has a marble canopy, and is decorated with a profusion of delicate sculptures. The princess is also represented twice—in Court dress, and in a winding-sheet. The tomb of Marguerite de Bourbon is also richly decorated.

Brou Church is famous chiefly for the extraordinary wealth and delicacy of the carvings on these three tombs, which abound in exquisite details.

**BROUWER (Adriaen).**—Flemish painter (1605-1638). Born in Oudenarde, he went to Holland early in life, and entered the studio of Frans Hals. In 1631, he was made a master of the Guild of St. Luke, in Antwerp. In company with his friend, the painter Craesbeeck, he lived a most restless life, frequenting taverns, station-houses, gambling-dens; drinking, smoking, and singing in company with the worst scamps of Antwerp, who were his chosen models. It is said that this life of adventure and debauchery cut short his life.

In spite of his premature death, Brouwer left many masterpieces. A good colourist, like other Flemings of his day, he differed from them in his technique. He is less minute, and more spirited. From his passage through the studio of Hals, he kept a love of rapid work, and for abundant, thick paint which he applied with a sure, bold brush. The faces are lively; and the figures, too, painted with broad, vigorous brush strokes, have incomparable liveliness and expression. His art is well calculated to make us interested in his models, a drunken crew of shouting drinkers. *The Drinker* (also called *Taste*) in the Staedel Institute, Frankfort, raises his glass to his large open mouth, his eyes screwed up, and his whole face grimacing. The *Smoker* (Louvre) is very amusing. In all these pictures of drunken, brutalized types, with brandy-blossomed faces, Brouwer painted the sordid garments with a richness of colour worthy of the richest brocades. *The Village Inn* (Amsterdam) shows us a fine collection of them. They are not always on the best of terms. In the *Brawl* (Dresden) they fall on one another, armed with chairs or knives, mad with drunken rage. Others, in the *Station-House* (Munich) are absorbed in a game of cards.

Brouwer's only disciple was his friend, Craesbeeck, who joined him in these tavern adventures, studying and painting the same models, but with less talent.

See Pl. 35, Vol. II.

BIBLIOGRAPHY: W. von Bode, *Adriaen Brouwer*, Berlin, 1924.

**BROWN (Ford Madox).**—English painter, 1821-1893. Born in Calais, of English parents. He first studied in the studio of Van Hauselaer in Ghent. He next spent two years with Baron Wappers, at the Academy of Antwerp, and travelled in France and Italy. He had a tenacious will and a deep love of truth. He said: "I put truth above originality, and desire above all to be truthful, from which comes truth."

At the Belgian school, of which the Baron Leys was the head, he learned respect for document, the art of staging his scenes correctly, the charm of archaism, and of the historically picturesque. He had a romantic soul and worshipped heroism.

Brown's compositions were inspired by historical, religious or legendary events. Among the most interesting are: *The Dream of Sardanapalus,* the *Widow's Son,* the *Death of Sir Tristram,* the *Honeymoon of King Rene, Cromwell at St. Ives, Romeo and Juliet, Christ Washing Peter's Feet, Chaucer at the Court of Edward III,* and *Cordelia.* In a series of mural paintings in Manchester Town Hall, he recalls the famines of the prosperous city. He made a quantity of cartoons of decorative frescoes, stained glass and furniture which testify to his great activity. He also illustrated a number of famous books, particularly the works of Shakespeare. But to have an idea of how fine an artist Brown was, one must consider his *Work* and the *Last of England.* The one, which dates from 1857 is now in Manchester Gallery; the other (1855) is in Birmingham. Mr. Percy H. Bates says: "The first idea of the *Last of England* came to Madox Brown during a journey to Gravesend, to say good-bye to the sculptor, Thomas Woolner, who was leaving for Australia. And as Brown himself was thinking of a voyage to the Indies, it occurred to him to fix on canvas the feelings and emotions stirred by these departures for a new land. And so he painted himself, his wife and his child in the guise of emigrants—the wife full of sadness, looking for the last time on the dear face of her native soil." With regard to this work, Brown himself wrote: "Without heeding the art of any other people or country, I have tried to render the scene as it would be seen. I thought it necessary to imitate the minuteness of detail which would be visible in the same conditions of full daylight, in order to accentuate the intimate emotion of the subject." These means of expression are indeed those which the Pre-Raphaelites, with their profound love of nature, adopted. They sometimes pushed too far this care of microscopic detail and infinitely close searching after "truth."

The picture of *Work,* now in the Manchester Gallery, represents "an episode of communal life." From the point of view of execution, this work has been "carried to a pitch of perfection almost disconcerting. One is bewildered before the minute care, the conscientiousness, and even the tenderness with which the smallest parts have been studied and drawn." One finds there, too, a moral symbolism which is the very background of the Pre-Raphaelite doctrine.

However, the painting is clear enough without borrowing its significance from literary elements. It has been justly said of this work that: "in colour it is a pure precious stone; in significance, a sermon and a hymn of praise; in conception, the creation of a great brain; in execution, the work of a master."

Brown had an immense influence on the artistic movement of his day, and on the following generation. He also played an important moral part in the formation of the Pre-Raphaelite Brotherhood.

See Pl. 58, Vol. II.

BIBLIOGRAPHY: Chesneau, *Historie de la Peinture Anglaise.*—R. I. La Sizeranne, *Le Préraphaélitisme.*—G. Monzey, *D. G. Rossetti et les préraphaélites Anglais.*

**BROWN (Henry Kirke).**—American sculptor (1814-1886). He was born 24th February 1814 in Leyden, Massachusetts, where his parents lived on a farm. His first attempts at art were made in imitation of a travelling silhouette-cutter whom he had seen in the vicinity. His people thought so highly of his talent that he was apprenticed to the famous portrait painter, Chester Harding. In 1836 Brown moved to Cincinnati with the idea of opening a studio, but instead became interested in sculpture. He wanted to go to Italy to study, but because of financial reasons the trip was delayed. However, he continued to work in clay and plaster and finally in stone. In 1842 he and his wife sailed for Italy and there he went on with his work in the classic style then at the height of its popularity. Four years later he opened a studio in New York and became quite successful with his execution of portrait busts, relieving the monotony by some studies of American Indians. He is chiefly remembered today for his three equestrian statues: General Washington in Union Square, New York, General Winfield Scott and General Nathaniel Greene in Washington, D. C. His inspiration for the horses of these statues was the equestrian statues of the Italian Renaissance, particularly the *Gattamelata* of Donatello and the *Colleone* of Verrocchio. Henry K. Brown died in Newburgh, New York, 10th July 1886. His most famous pupil was John Quincy Adams Ward who continued to work in the pseudo-classic manner of the American school as it was trained in Italy at that time.

BIBLIOGRAPHY: S. G. W. Benjamin, *Art in America,* 1879.—C. H. Caffin, *American Masters of Sculpture,* 1903.—Jas. Lee, *The Equestrian Statue of Washington in Union Square,* 1864.—Lorado, Taft, *History of American Sculpture,* 1930.—H. T. Tuckerman, *Book of the Artists,* 1867.

**BRUGES.**—The most important place in Western Flanders, was formerly a flourishing town of 200,000 inhabitants. It is much impoverished now, but has kept its mediaeval character more than any other Belgian town. The Dukes of Burgundy lived there in the 15th century, and the finest masterpieces in the town date from this period.

BRUGES: CHIMNEY IN THE MAGISTRATE'S HALL IN THE HOUSE OF THE FRANC, BRUGES.

Among the chief buildings are: *St. Sauveur,* in the first Gothic style. The exterior is heavy; the interior, elaborately decorated, contains a great many works of art.

*Notre Dame,* in the first pointed style of the 12th and 13th centuries, with an elegant annex in the third Gothic style, contains many pictures, and in one chapel the tombs of Charles the Bold and his daughter.

The *Chapel of the Holy Blood* is

BRUGES: THE SQUARE AND THE BELFRY.

a little edifice in two storeys. The lower building dates from the 12th century; the other from the 15th. The doorway, added in the 16th century, is in the Flamboyant style, like the staircase.

The *Hospital of St. John,* 12th century, the door of which is surmounted by a Gothic bas-relief, possesses Memling's masterpieces, among them the famous *Shrine of St. Ursula.*

The *Market Buildings* (13th century; rebuilt in 1561 by Dieriex) are surmounted by a fine *Belfry.* The "tour des halles," of the 13th century, is in two low, and heavy stages, upon which is a third stage, very high and slender.

The *Hôtel de Ville*, begun by J. Roegiers in 1376. A fine building in the Gothic style decorated with turrents, and forty-eight inches containing statues of the Counts of Flanders.

The *Hôtel Grunthunse*, built in 1465 of stone and brick, contains a museum of lace and antiquities.

— **(School of).**—See Pl. I, Vol. II.

**BRUNELLESCHI or BRUNELLESCO (Filippo di Ser Brunellesco).**—Florentine architect, engineer and sculptor. 1377-1446. One of the chief creators of the Renaissance style. Sometimes still Gothic, but much absorbed by the antique, and eager for novelty, he marks the transition between the Trecento and the Quattrocento. It was he, above all, who stated, solved and taught, even to his dear and celebrated friend, Donatello, the great problems of perspective geometry and foreshortening. He pointed out how the forms of ancient Rome could be imitated and adapted. And after him something was changed in the taste of artists and princes, which brought forth quite a new flowering of buildings and marbles on Italian soil.

His father, Ser Brunellesco, intended him to be a notary or a doctor. But he wished to be a goldsmith. He early applied himself to perspective of which he was passionately fond. And he loved above all things to discuss art with his friend Donato, who became the great Donatello.

Brunelleschi: San Lorenzo, Florence.

In their early youth, perhaps in 1401, perhaps a little later, an amusing competition took place between them, characteristic of their different personalities. Donatello asked his friend to give him his opinion about a crucifix which he was finishing, and of which he was very proud. Filippo, very frank, told him that it seemed to him that he had crucified a peasant, and not Jesus Christ who was the most perfect man ever born. "Then take some wood and try to make one yourself," said Donatello, amicably, but a little humiliated. This Brunelleschi did; and when Donatello saw his *Christ* he was dumbfounded. Vasari tells how he dropped the eggs and other provisions he was carrying. When Brunelleschi exclaimed, laughing: "What shall we dine on if you upset everything, Donato?" His friend could only reply: "For my part, I have had enough for this morning. To you it is given to make the figure of Christ; to me, only peasants."

The *Christ* in Santa Maria Novella, in coloured wood, still has the character of the Trecento, with emaciated body, and pitiful figure, with closed eyelids and head bent on the shoulder in an inert gesture of suffering. The peasant, on the contrary, in the shade of Santa Croce is not suffering. In comparison with Donatello, Brunellesco remained faithful to the traditional ideal.

But the affable, benevolent artist who sought the society of virtuous men, was of a passionate disposition. His part of the competition for the second door of the Baptistery of Florence (executed about the same time as the Crucifix, 1402) is almost brutal in feeling. Abraham hurls himself towards his prey like a gale of wind. The little body of his son is twisted like a tree in a tempestuous blast. But out of the sky comes an angel, like a ray of sunlight to still the storm (Bargello, Florence). The composition is tumultuous. The servants, symbols of the pagan world, it has been said, bend down in foreshortened positions. The whole scene is full of purpose and life-like expression; but it is still somewhat archaic.

Brunelleschi: Sacrifice of Abraham. (National Museum, Florence.)

See Pl. 8, Vol. II.

Ghiberti was proclaimed the winner, with Brunellesco, who, however, did not want a divided triumph and left Ghiberti the reward—the task of making the whole door.

It has been said that in anger and to escape human rivalries, Brunellesco left for Rome, with his friend Donatello, immediately after the competition (L'Anonimo and Vasari). As a matter of fact, Donatello was among Ghiberti's assistants in 1403; and Brunellesco himself was registered among the Florentine goldsmiths in 1404. It is, then, more likely that the journey to Rome had taken place before the competition, and that the artist had already profited from the lessons of the antique when he made his *Sacrifice of Abraham*. Donatello, however, would have been very young (born in 1386). At all events, one day, fleeing the plague, the two friends left together for the Eternal City, where they wandered in the vast Campagna, among the immense ruins, and followed their dreams amid the broken marbles. Brunelleschi there discovered a magnificent mission—that of resurrecting the great dead and recalling to life the forms of bygone days. He resolved to be, above all, an architect, leaving sculpture to Donatello and Lorenzo Ghiberti.

Naturally, he thought a great deal about the problem that occupied the attention of so many Florentines of his day. He wanted to unite the four arms of The Duomo of Florence by a dome. Since the death of Arnolfo di Cambio no one had dared to undertake it. When the Guild of Wool Merchants decided to call a meeting of architects to decide what could be done (1418), while all were considering how to overcome the great difficulties, Brunelleschi advised them to give up Arnolfo's plan. He returned to Rome, probably at this time, secretly preparing all the plans for the vast undertaking, drawing all the antique buildings.

Then there was a great council in Florence. A great number of architects took part in it, and each one suggested something more extravagant and ridiculous than the other. One citizen of the Republic was inspired by the proceedings to suggest that a huge pile of dirt be built up in the cathedral with pennies distributed at intervals and that the dome be built upon this pile. The natural cupidity of the Florentines would supposedly supply the agency by which the dirt would then be removed.

Because he promised to complete the dome without using centering, Brunelleschi was commissioned with the work, which lasted from 1420 to 1434. The octagonal lantern was only finished in 1462, according to his designs. The solution, which consisted of raising the dome without any frame work, won the admiration of everyone. His idea was to raise a polygonal drum, and to make two domes fitting one into the other. Perhaps the influence which he received in Rome has been exaggerated. No progress is made suddenly, by a single artist, and no doubt he already had a model to encourage him in the Baptistery of Florence. But he succeeded in raising the most immense of domes, both wide and high.

Brunelleschi was also the author of the cornice of the nave of the Cathedral of Florence, and of the three little tribunes at the sides of the dome.

Brunelleschi: Dome of the Cathedral of Florence.

The Pazzi Chapel, which he built in 1429, in the Cloisters of Santa Croce, also had a great influence on the development of Renaissance architecture. The charming dome in cup form, as well as the portico with a semi-circular vault, was a model for his successors.

The Ospedale dei Innocenti (begun in 1419), has a very simple, very elegant beauty, and gives the first example of windows surmounted by a pediment.

Above all in San Lorenzo, the Church of the Medici, Brunelleschi shows himself the great inaugurator of Renaissance architecture. This is the early Renaissance style of church like an Early Christian basilica in conception and execution except for the succession of vaulted lateral chapels, the dome at the crossing, and the complication of the east end. The tombs of the Medici are in the New Sacristy of this church.

San Spirito was built according to his plans, but only after his death. To him are also attributed the second cloister of Santa Croce, one of the most beautiful of its time, the plans of the Badia of Fiesole and of the Pitti Palace, and a great number of more ornate and delicate buildings, such as the Palazzo Quaraetsi.

Among his sculptures are: a *St. Mary Magdalen*, made for San Spirito (destroyed), a gilt marble figure for Santa Maria del Fiore, sculptured with Donatello, and the wooden model for the pulpit of Santa Maria Novella, which was clumsily executed by Buggiano.

See Pl. 5, Vol. II.

Bibliography: Frey, *Vita di Filippo di ser Brunelleschо Scritta da anonimo contemporaneo autore*—Berlin.—*Architecture of the Renaissance from Brunelleschi to Michelangelo*, The Hague, 1925.—Alessandro Chiapelli, *Gli Scultori Florentini del Quattrocento. Nuova Antologia*, 16th July 1899.—E. Maclagan, *Italian Sculpture of the Renaissance*, Cambridge, 1935.

**BRUSASORCI (Domenico).**—Painter of Verona, c. 1516-1567, pupil of Caroto. The great majority of his works are still to be found in Verona.

**BRUSH (George de Forest).**—Contemporary American painter. He was born in Shelbyville, Tennessee, 28th September 1855. He studied at the art school of the National Academy of Design and in the 1870's at the École des Beaux-Arts under Gérôme. Upon his return to the United States he made a trip west to Montana where he came into intimate contact with the Crow, Shoshone and Arapahoe Indians. These American natives formed the subjects of his first pictures. The best known of this series is *The Sculptor and the King*, where the humble craftsman of a carved relief waits silently for the approval of his sovereign. The figures are well rounded and solid, definitely standing away from the background. Others of these Indian pictures depict hunters returning with their game, sending their canoes along the rivers with swift and silent strokes of the paddle, or engaged in the household tasks in their camps.

Later Brush turned to intimate studies of his wife and children, clad in simple draperies and treated after the manner of the Italian Renaissance. All exhibit the sentiment of the Florentine work of the 15th century and the polished technique of that period. The mothers have faces which reflect a melancholy and age-old weariness and sadness, while the children are delightfully appealing with their wistful dreamy faces and shy gestures. These pictures show a delight in linear rhythms and the warm mellow tones which were used by the Italians, managing to capture some degree of the spirit which moved the old masters to the heights of their expression. Examples of his work are in the Metropolitan Museum of Art, the Museum of Fine Arts in Boston, and the Pennsylvania Academy of Fine Arts in Philadelphia.

BIBLIOGRAPHY: Charles H. Caffin, *American Masters in Painting,* 1902. —Charles H. Caffin, *Story of American Painting,* 1907.—Royal Cortissoz, *American Artists,* 1923.—Catherine Beach Ely, *The Modern Tendency in American Painting,* 1925.—Sadakichi Hartmann, *History of American Art,* Vol. 1, 1902.—Samuel Isham, *The History of American Painting,* 1927.—Eugen Neuhaus, *The History and Ideals of American Art,* 1931.—S. C. Kaines Smith, *An Outline of Modern Painting,* 1932.

**BRUSSELS (Belgium).**—The Gothic Church of *St. Gudule* is an interesting building (1220 to 1273). The vault and windows are later (1350 to 1450). The windows have fine glass.

See Pl. 49, Vol. I.

The *Grand' Place* is one of the most remarkable squares that has come down to us from mediæval times. The *Hôtel de Ville* is a large and noble 15th century Gothic building. Houses belonging to the various corporations or guilds (such as the *Maison des Charpentiers,* and the *Maisons des Archers*) add to the curious and picturesque effect of the Grand' Place.

See Tapestry.

**BRUYN (Bartholomeus).**—German painter, of Cologne, c. 1493-1555. He worked first in the Flemish manner and then in that of the Italians. He is the author of several portraits in Cologne Museum—the *Burgomaster, Arnold von Brauweiler*; the *Woman with the Necklace*; and, in the same Museum, an *Adoration of the Magi,* and *Saint Ursula.*

BIBLIOGRAPHY: Firmenich-Richartz, E., *B. Bruyn und seine Schule.* Leipzig, 1891.

**BRYGOS.**—See Greece (Vases).

**BUCCHERO NERO.**—See Ceramic.

**BUCKINGHAM PALACE.**—See London.

**BUDDHA, BUDDHISM, etc.**—See China; India; Indo-China; Japan Art.

**BUGIARDINI (Giuliano).**—Florentine painter. 1475-1554. He studied in the studio of Domenico Ghirlandajo where he had Michelangelo as a comrade. But he was never more than a conscientious imitator without any originality. His *Mystic Marriage of St. Catherine* is in Bologna Museum.

**BULFINCH (Charles).**—American architect. (1763-1844.) A Harvard graduate, he designed the Massachusetts State House, 1795, a building influenced strongly by Chambers' Somerset House in London. He also designed many fine houses in Boston; Bulfinch Crescent (now destroyed), Boston; University Hall, Cambridge; and the Hall of Representatives in the Capitol, Washington. He began as an academic late Renaissance architect, but his later work is neo-classic.

**BULLANT (Jean).**—See Champmol; Tuileries.

**BUNCHO (Tani).**—An eclectic Japanese painter (1765-1842), especially known for his landscapes in the Chinese style.

**BUONACCORSI (Piero).**—See Perino del Vaga.

**BUONCONSIGLIO (Giovanni).**—called Il Marescalco. Painter of Vicenza—the most important after Bartolommeo Montagna, whose follower he was. Died in 1537.

BIBLIOGRAPHY: Tancred Borenius, *The Painters of Vicenza.* London, 1909.

**BUON.**—Italian architect and sculptor of the 12th century. He built the Campanile of the Piazzo San Marco, in Venice, about 1150. He also built the Castel Capuano of Naples.

**— (Bartolommeo).**—Venetian architect and sculptor of the 15th century. Died about 1465. Imitator of the Renaissance style in Venice, he might be compared to Jacopo della Quercia. Son of Giovanni Buon (see). He is chiefly famous for the beautiful Porta della Carta of the Doges' Palace (1440-1443), for the old Procuratie, the Scuola di San Rocco, and the cella of the Campanile of San Marco. In the town gilded by the sun over the sea, and caressed by the iridescent waves of the Lagoons, sculpture came to be particularly magnificent. It had no longer Roman grandeur and gravity, nor quiet grace, as under Tuscan skies. Bartolommeo Buon felt that architecture should be adorned with wreaths, pierced with numerous windows, lightened with little columns, and made infinitely rich, almost aerial, in this place of dreams.

BUON: CAMPANILE OF ST. MARK'S, VENICE.

**— (Giovanni).**—Venetian architect and sculptor. Born about 1360. Originally from Bergamo. He worked with his sons, Bartolommeo and Panteleone, especially on the façade of the Doges' Palace, and on the Ca d'Oro (1424-1430). They are still Gothic in character, but they show a pleasing facility of execution. Their doorways in Venice, are very decorative and rich, such as the famous Porta della Carta of the Doges' Palace, with the noble Doge kneeling before the proud Lion (1438), and the beautiful figures of Temperance, Strength, Prudence and Charity. Giovanni died in 1442, and Bartolommeo finished the work alone. He came to be more famous than his father, and to be the real founder of the Renaissance in Venice.

**BURCHFIELD (Charles E.).**—Contemporary American painter. He was born 9th April 1893 in Ashtabula Harbor, Ohio. After his father's death the family removed to Salem, Ohio, and there he grew up and went to work as an accountant for an auto parts company. In 1912 he secured a scholarship for the Cleveland School of Art where he studied under Henry G. Keller. Gradually his own individual style developed, characterised by strong rhythmic lines and weird, rather dreamlike subjects. He made a trip to New York City where some of his work was placed on exhibit at the Sunwise Turn Bookshop. Following a period spent in an Army training camp in 1918 his subject matter became more conventional and realistic. In fact it almost reached a point where it was not far from true satire. Most of the scenes depicted relics of Victorian architecture, lending an air of formal respectability to the midwest communities and also the false-front stores peculiar to that region. However, he did retain the gloomy and mysterious colour schemes of his early work for the majority of his more recent pictures. A notable example is the oil *November Evening,* at the Metropolitan Museum of Art in New York, where heavy black clouds hang low over the scene, adding a touch of mystery to an otherwise commonplace subject.

From 1921 to 1929 he was a designer for the wallpaper firm of M. H. Birge and Sons in Buffalo, but since then he has devoted himself almost exclusively to his painting. The greater part of his work is done in watercolour, but he has also made a few compositions in gouache and oil. In 1929 he was awarded the Jennie Sesnan Gold Medal at the annual exhibition of the Pennsylvania Academy of Fine Arts. Examples of his work may be found in the Fogg Art Museum at Cambridge, Massachusetts, the Cleveland Museum of Art, the Whitney Museum of American Art in New York, and the Phillips Memorial Gallery in Washington, D. C.

See Pl. 63, Vol. II.

BIBLIOGRAPHY: For a complete bibliography see *The Index of Twentieth Century Artists* for December, 1934.

**BURGKMAIR (Hans).**—German painter (1473-1531), of the Swabian School of Augsburg. Pupil of Schongauer and the Venetians. The *Coronation of the Virgin* (Augsbourg Gallery), painted in 1507, shows the scene in a fine Renaissance setting; the *Madonna of the Grapes* (1509, Germanische Museum), is a kind of adaptation of the Venetian style; *Esther and Ahasuerus* (1528, Munich) is a decorative picture, well composed.

Burgkmair left a series of numerous engravings: the Allegorical Triumph, drawn for the Emperor Maximilian, illustrations of Teuerdank and of Weisskunig, and the famous *Death the Exterminator* (1510).

BIBLIOGRAPHY: Burkhardt, A., *Hans Burgkmair d. Ä* Leipzig, 1934.

**BURGOS (Spain).**—The *Cathedral* (1221-1285), has two western towers with open-work spires, and a richly treated central lantern or "Cimborio." "The interior has elaborate triforum tracery, and massive piers, rebuilt to support the high Cimborio when it was finished in 1567. The choir is in the usual Spanish position west of the crossing." The side chapels are very large; and the Capilla del Condestable (1487) is especially remarkable for the richness of its detail.

See Pl. 49, Vol. I.

The *Arco de Santa Maria* is one of the most interesting monuments of Burgos. It was begun in 1536, in honour of Charles V. The Arch is flanked with two half towers, surmounted by four turrets, and decorated with sculpture. Its beauty is questionable, but it is certainly an original conception.

**BURGUNDY (Churches of).**—See Pl. 44, Vol. I.

**— (Dukes of).**—See Champmol; Dijon.

**— (School of).**—See Sluter (Claus); also Pl. 4, Vol. II.

**BURIN.**—See Engraving.

**BURNE-JONES (Sir Edward Coley).**—English Pre-Raphaelite painter born in Birmingham, 28th August 1833, and died 1898. His family came originally from Wales. He spent seven years at King Edward's College; and then he went to Exeter College, Oxford, to read Theology. Rossetti, who was there painting his frescoes, had an irresistible attraction for the young man. Until then, Burne-Jones had not given himself up to any artistic pursuit, but he showed some drawings to the master, which, in spite of their lack of skill, expressed such power and poetry, that Rossetti, struck with admiration, allowed him to paint, in the Debating Hall of the University, a subject taken from the Legend of King Arthur, the *Death of Merlin.* Burne-Jones gave up Theology, and became an intimate friend of Rossetti, who accompanied him to London.

He then designed a number of stained glass windows for the Cathedral, Oxford. In 1864, he exhibited his first painting *The Merciful Knight,* which was soon followed by the triptych *"Pyramus and Thisbe,"* and by the picture entitled *The Evening Star,* a gleaming landscape. None of his works attracted attention. The little painting called *Phyllis and Demophoon,* which he exhibited in 1870, was even judged improper because of the sensual expression of the nymph, and for several years Burne-Jones ceased to exhibit at the Royal Academy. For seven years his name did not appear in the Catalogue. In May 1877, the painter Sir Coutts Lindsay founded the Grosvenor Galleries, to allow artists to exhibit elsewhere than at the Academy. Burne-Jones reappeared, and from then he was highly thought of, stirring an even greater admiration than that which Rossetti had aroused. The Grosvenor Gallery, where he then exhibited, was considered as the "Temple of the Æsthetic." There a worship was given to Burne-Jones comparable to that which Wagner was given in Bayreuth. It was only with the greatest difficulty that the visitor could see his work, for the crowd which gathered to admire it. In 1884, he exhibited *King Cophetua and the Beggar Maid,* one of his best known works. The whole work is full of an indescribable emotion, and there is also fine colour and a unique richness of tone.

In Burne-Jones' work one sees a strange mixture of austere mysticism and of idealism. He was not only inspired by the classical antique, but the Christian legends and the Bible. One of his principal works symbolises the Creation of the World. It is composed of six panels, in each of which an angel holds a sphere in which are seen the stars, the waters, the trees, the animals and, finally, man and woman as God created them.

On a picture entitled *Spousa di Libano* are the words from the Song of Solomon: "O north wind; and comest thou south; blow upon my garden, that the spices thereof may flow out." The Betrothed wears an ample blue robe. She walks pensively along the river bank, where white lilies bloom, while figures symbolising the North and South winds break impetuously through the air. Besides his preferences for Homer and the Bible, Burne-Jones had a passion for the Troubadours and the "chansons de gestes," for the fantastic adventures of Chivalry, the legends of Arthur and the Enchanter Merlin, and the Knights of the Round Table.

In other paintings, Burne-Jones simply expresses his thought by a group of young figures, making a beautiful work by composition, linear subtlety rarity and refinement of colour and graceful attitudes. The *Golden Stairs* exhibited in 1878, is one of the most characteristic works in this vein (Tate Gallery).

His decorative works must also be noted. He painted rich decorations in the Byzantine style for the English Church in Rome. In England, where there is little space in the Churches for mural paintings, stained glass is in great favour. Burne-Jones was a master in this art. He was deeply imbued with mediaeval forms, and created a new style of painting on glass. In his painted compositions, one again finds these long, vertical figures which recall the stained-glass figures. It is easy to recognise the models that inspired him in all these works—Pompeii, Ravenna, Giotto, Etruscan vases, Giorgione, Perugino, and above all Botticelli.

There is something mannered and artificial in this art, and "it would have been lost with the rapidity of an exotic plant, if its author had not been an accomplished Englishman." In these legends he discovered analogies with the passions and ideas of his own day, while he entirely renewed the spirit of the old stories. His figures are of a very personal type. He transformed the severe, rigid charm of the Quattrocento into a sentimental melancholy.

According to Rossetti's enthusiasm: "the work of Burne-Jones is a unique work, not only in English art, but in the art of all countries and all time." Apart from the works already spoken of, we may mention the following: *The Jurage of Wex*, the *Song of the Niebelung* (1856), *St. George and the Dragon*, the *Fairy Rosamond, Chaucer's Dream, Love disguised as Reason* (1870), *Phyllis* (1870), the *Garden of the Hesperides, Love Among the Ruins* (1871), the *Sleeping Beauty in the Wood,* the *Wheel of Fortune, Faith, Hope and Charity,* the *Hours, Pygmalion and the Statue* (1879), the *Siren, Vespertina Quies* (1888), the *Depths of the Sea* (1893).

See Pl. 58, Vol. II.

**BURROUGHS (Bryson).**—American painter, (1869-1934), pupil of Luc-Olivier Marson in Paris, practising a style of heroic and romantic figure composition, definitely reminiscent of certain aspects of French nineteenth century painting. Curator of Paintings, Metropolitan Museum of Art, New York.

**BUSI (Giovanni).**—See Cariani.

**BUSON (Yosa).** — Japanese painter, 1716-1783, born at Kyoto. Reputedly followed the style of Sakaki Hyakusen (d. 1753). Influenced especially by late Ming artists. By 1775 developed an independent style characterized by simplicity at times poetic and broad ("poetic sketches"), at times realistic. He was the master of Goshun.

**BUSTI (Agostino).** — Architect and sculptor, of Lombardy. About 1480-1548. Graceful and unaffected at the beginning of his career, he quickly became a mannered virtuoso, lacking character. His work suffers from excessive ornamentation. His monument to Gaston de Foix, ordered by Francis I in 1515, and never finished, won him a great reputation. Fragments of it are in the Brera and the Ambrosiana, Milan, and in Turin Museum. He was one of the many sculptors of the Certosa of Pavia.

**BUTINONE (Bernardino).**—Milanese painter from Treviglio, active 1454-1507. Pupil of Foppa, collaborator of Zenale, with whom he executed the 1485 polyptych in S. Martino, Treviglio.

**BUTTRESS.**—Reinforcement of a wall in order to offset a lateral thrust. There are two kinds of buttresses: strip or pier buttresses and flying buttresses. See Flying Buttress.

**BYZANTINE ARCHITECTURE.** — Byzantine architecture emerged as a developed style only in the first Golden Age, the 6th century, but had previously been in process of gestation in Italy, Egypt, North Africa, Syria, Mesopotamia, Anatolia, and Greece. Contributions from all these regions were fused in Constantinople, then the center of the known world, forming a new synthesis under the directing energy of the Emperor Justinian. The dome was the prime Byzantine solution of the problem of transforming the light, flimsy, and inflammable timber-roofed Early Christian church into a vaulted fireproof structure. Accordingly, the basilican type, which retained its popularity in the West, was, in the East, supplanted by the type of building with a central vertical axis or accommodated to the central type. Inasmuch as the dome was used to cover a square area, pendentives were employed to effect a transition from square in plan to round in plan. A pendentive is a spherical triangle which effects such a transition. The structural principle of the dome on pendentives was contributed to Constantinople by the region of Anatolia. There trade routes from Syria and from Mesopotamia joined to form a single trunk line extending from Antioch, in extreme northern Syria, to Constantinople. Anatolia combined impulses from Syria and from Mesopotamia to create the domed basilica. The low masonry dome covering a square area seems originally to have been developed in Sasanian Mesopotamia. The earliest domed basilica known is the 5th century church of S. Thekla, Meriamlik. There is doubt that the contemporary church at Kodja Kalessi was domed. It is worthy of note that two Anatolians were the architects of Santa Sophia.

The flat, crisp Byzantine carved decoration, in which the plane is carved into, as opposed to the plastic decoration of classical architecture, is also of Eastern origin. Its beginning can be seen in the 2nd century monuments at Baalbek, in Syria, and in the 3rd century Arch of the Silversmiths in Rome, and the late 3rd and early 4th century palace of Diocletian at Spalato, Dalmatia, both constructed by Syrians. The marble of the Proconnesus was used for this decoration in buildings at Constantinople.

Brick was the most common Byzantine building material, and was used with thick mortar joints often higher than the bricks themselves. The result was a flexible, elastic domed and vaulted construction whose uneasy, shifting loads required the interposition of an impost block between the capital of a column and the spreading mass of masonry above. After the 5th and 6th centuries the functions of the capital and the impost block were usually combined in a single wide-spreading capital. Columns and frames were usually of stone. In interiors the brick was plastered or covered with a placaging of marble or with mosaic in glass or stone.

*Early Period.*—Pre-Justinian architecture was basilican, in brick, with trussed timbered roofs, as in *St. John Stoudion*, Constantinople, 463, and the slightly later *St. Demetrius*, Thessalonika.

Several types of buildings were employed in the First Golden Age. *St. Irene,* Constantinople, built in 532 and rebuilt in 740, is a domed basilica of Anatolian origin. *S. Sophia,* Constantinople, 532-537 is a magnificent great church of the same type, and the unquestioned masterpiece of the period. The central, peri-apsidal type of church developed from such pagan examples as the Pantheon and the Temple of Minerva Medici, Rome, may be seen in *SS. Sergius and Bacchus,* Constantinople, 527, and *S. Vitale,* Ravenna, 526-547. A third type is the Greek cross plan with a dome over the center and over each of the four arms. The *Church of the Holy Apostles,* Constantinople, 536-546, destroyed in the 15th century, was such a building. We know it now only through a manuscript in the Vatican and through such derivatives as the Second Golden Age church of *S. Marco,* Venice.

There was important building in the First Golden Age outside the orbit of Constantinople, notably in Armenia. In Armenia there was a vigorous and native development in stone which we find reflected later in the Pro-Romanesque of Spain and France, as at S. Miguel de Tarrasa and Germigny-des-Près. In plan the Armenian churches of the period are square with four apses having Greek crosses inscribed within the square, the domes being supported on four columns in the center of the church. On the exterior the domes are many-sided pyramids. Such buildings are *S. Hripsime,* Walarshapat, 618, and the *Cathedral at Edgmiadzin,* 640-666.

*Middle Period.*—Byzantine architecture of the Middle Period is smaller in scale than that of the First Golden Age. There is much more exterior decoration consisting of patterned brick sometimes combined with freestone. The typical building of the Second Golden Age is in plan square on the ground storey and a Greek cross in the clerestorey. A dome, now on a drum, appears over the center. Smaller domes in the angles between the clerestorey arms are hidden by the roof. *La Nea,* the palatine chapel of Basil I, built before 886, set the type for Second Golden Age church design. La Nea has since been destroyed. The *Myralaion,* Constantinople, 10th century, demonstrates the type.

*Greek School.*—There were variations from the usual Constantinople type in Greece. In Athens, under Armenian influence, cut stone was used on the exterior, and angle domes were often omitted, as in the tiniest of cathedrals, the *Metropolitan,* and the *Church of the Kapnikarea,* both 12th century. The church of *Daphni,* and *St. Luke of Stiris,* Hosios Loukos, both 11th century, are heavier in proportion than is usual in the second Golden Age, have squat sixteen-sided drums, and have squinches instead of pendentives. The middle and late period monastery churches at Mt. Athos, notably the *Great Lavra, Chilandari, Simopetra,* and *Vatopedi,* preserve the earlier type of the *Kilisse-Djami,* Constantinople, being basilicas with a dome on four columns. They show even more Armenian influence than their supposed prototype, however, in their frequent lateral exedrae.

*Armenia.* — Armenian architects were active and original in the 10th and 11th centuries. *Akthamar,* 10th century, is entirely cut stone, with flat, crisp sculpture of Persian origin. The 11th century of architecture of Armenia is very close to that of Persia, as in the multiple ribs and compound piers of the *Cathedral of Ani.*

*Late Period.*—The fundamental type did not change under the Paleologi. The domed basilica with four columns became more popular. Constantinople, being poverty-stricken, was no longer the center. Most building was done in Russia and the Balkans. (See Russian Art.) Although there were no changes in plan, there were profound changes in elevation. The vertical rhythm, possibly under the influence of contemporary Western Gothic, was sharply accented. The four angle domes appear on the exterior above elongated drums. Roofs curve over the barrel vaults through which the

MISTRA: ST. DEMETRIOS OR THE METROPOLE.

domes are broken, and vertical exterior strips are added. Balkan examples are the 14th century churches of *Ravanitsa, Gracanica* and *Manassija*. *Hagia Sophia* at Trebizond is the same type. After the fall of Constantinople in 1453, and the final collapse of the Eastern Empire eight years later, the Byzantine tradition was preserved in the Turkish architecture of the Suleimans and the later architecture of Russia. (See Russian Architecture.)

BIBLIOGRAPHY: J. A. Hamilton, *Byzantine Architecture and Decoration*. London, 1934.

**BYZANTINE ART.** — In 326, Constantine commenced the building of a new city, Nova Roma, on the site of the ancient Greek city, Byzantium, which was to be known as Constantinople. In 330 the capital of the Roman Empire was moved to it, thus officially demonstrating that the center of gravity of the Roman Empire was now in the East. At the same time (325), Christianity was established as the state religion, and the Emperor placed at the head of the Church. Byzantine art includes all the art which is associated with the Byzantine Empire and the Orthodox Church established at this time. Though the church art has persisted to the present, the creative period is usually considered to have ended with the capture of Constantinople by the Turks in 1453.

The Byzantine or East Roman Empire (the split between the Eastern and Western Empires occurred in 395) was not a mere continuation of the old Roman Empire with the substitution of Christianity for Paganism. This is clearly revealed in the art. For the purposes of classification, it has become customary to recognise two main sources, the Western or Hellenistic and the Oriental. The distinction is a useful one, though the use of geographical terms is misleading. Hellenistic traditions existed not only in Rome and Alexandria, but also in all the leading cities of the former Roman provinces in the East. These traditions not only underwent an evolution when applied to the new subjects of this period, but were also used in a more or less pure form as an anti-monastic expression. Meanwhile, native cultures in the former provinces flowered under the popular Christian movement. Both sources were occasionally perfectly fused, as is the case of the miniatures in the *Vienna Genesis*. Byzantine art was once considered a degenerate form of Antique art. Today, it is recognised as an independent expression, having its own character, intentions and æsthetic appeal.

The Byzantine Empire originally included all the provinces of the Roman Empire; gradually these were lost to the invading Barbarians. In spite of the difficulties with the Slavic invaders from the North, their eventual adoption of the Orthodox Christian Religion extended Byzantine art to the North. A different situation was created by the invasion of the Arabs and Turks, since these adopted the Muslim religion. In 638, Syria and Palestine, and in 645 Egypt were lost to the Byzantine Empire. In 1040, the Turks conquered Asia Minor. Soon after this, the Crusades commenced with their disastrous effects upon the Byzantine Empire. When the Latin Empire was established in 1204, it seemed that Byzantine history was at an end. However, under the Paleologues (1261-1453) the Christian part of the former Empire was reunited, and the reduced Byzantine Empire enjoyed a last Renaissance. The final split between the Roman Catholic and the Orthodox Church did not occur until 1054. Consequently, Byzantine art is also found in Rome. Parts of Italy, such as Ravenna, Venetia, and Sicily were under Byzantine domination.

*Art Periods.*—As a result of the various crises through which the Byzantine Empire passed, the art did not constantly flourish. The chief periods are:

1. THE EARLY PERIOD. This includes the pre-Justinian period, and the Justinian period (518-610) which is known as the FIRST GOLDEN AGE.
2. THE SECOND GOLDEN AGE (Macedonian Dynasty, 867-1025). The Iconoclastic Controversy occurred between the First and Second Golden Ages.
3. THE FOURTEENTH CENTURY (Paleologue Dynasty, 1261-1453).

*Iconoclasm.* — Since representational art constituted one of the main supports of Paganism, Christianity was opposed to it in the beginning. This position was supported by the opposition to image worship in the Old Testament. After the triumph of Christianity this opposition diminished. Art was used in the first church buildings to lend them an appearance of great magnificence. Towards the end of the fourth century, decoration was considered insufficient, and art was called upon to "remind those who cannot read the Holy Scriptures of the beautiful deeds of those who have faithfully served the true God, and arouse in them the desire to imitate their conduct" (St. Nil). Iconoclasm, however, was not dead. In the eighth century the government and the central church authorities found it expedient to revive the controversy in their attack upon the power of the monasteries. The first edict against images was issued by Leo III in 726. The Iconoclastic Council of 753 went further, and anathemised all those who made images. Precious manuscripts, mosaics, frescoes and sculptures were destroyed. In 787 the ban was lifted, only to be imposed again in 815. Finally, in 843, iconoclasm was fully defeated.

*Character of Byzantine Art.*—Byzantine art underwent marked changes during its history. However, there are certain tendencies which are constant for most of its history. These are dependent to a great extent upon the nature of the Orthodox Catholic Religion, though it must not be forgotten that the Imperial court also influenced art. In most of Byzantine art there is a great emphasis upon luxury and ornament. Decorative values are never neglected, even when the main interest is moralistic. There is a tendency towards the elimination of real or cubic space. This expressed itself in various ways. First, paintings and mosaics are preferred to sculpture, while in sculpture, very flat relief is used. Second, in painting, backgrounds and even groundlines are omitted, and forms express no bulk. This elimination of spatial restrictions is further emphasised by the use of dazzling light effects. Brilliant colors and gold were used for mosaics. In sculptured ornament, the stone was treated in a manner to create a play of light and dark. The costly materials, such as gold, precious stones and silks, not only expressed gorgeousness, but also this interest in light effects. In religious art, there is a constant increase in the use of hieratic formulae. This interest in fixed and formal arrangements has its counterpart in ornament, where there is a tendency to reduce natural forms to patterns.

THE EARLY PERIOD.—*Mosaics.*—The most magnificent art of Byzantium is its mosaics. Just as it is true that the architecture cannot be considered apart from the light and color effects or the rhythms introduced by the mosaics, so it is true that these must be considered in connection with church architecture. In *St. Apollinare Nuova* (Ravenna) of the early sixth century, the procession of martyrs emphasises the axis of the church and introduces a rhythmical movement towards the altar. In the Baptistry of the Orthodox, which is a round building, there is a procession of apostles in the dome, which makes the dome appear to rotate, and thus makes it independent of the structure of the building. The mosaics are not limited to panels, but cover the entire interiors. The result is to make the walls lose their character as limiting agents and to create an extensive new world. The mosaics of *San Vitale,* also in Ravenna (540-550) are especially famous for the representation of Emperor Justinian and Empress Theodora, each attended by their court followers. Though the heads of these figures have qualities of portraiture, there is little modelling, and an emphasis is placed upon the pattern of the gorgeous costumes. The poses and the composition are already hieratic. In this single church, organised into a unified system of decoration, there is the most varied subject matter, representations of the symbols of the dogma, church history, a very interesting cycle devoted to early sacrifice and the glorification of the "lamb", and the majesty of the court. In this art, there is a curious mixture of mysticism and realism. A much greater naturalism exists in the earlier cycles of mosaics. In the *Tomb of Galla Placida* (Ravenna, second half of the fifth century) the representation of the Good Shepherd, though still very close to Hellenistic traditions, already shows a first step in the transformation of the naturalism of antiquity towards the more hieratic Byzantine expression.

RAVENNA: THE EMPEROR JUSTINIAN AND HIS TRAIN. MOSAIC OF SAN VITALE.

Unfortunately, little remains of the mosaics in the East. The finest series were discovered in *St. Demetrios* in Salonika. Unfortunately, these were partially destroyed in a fire in 1917. Choricius of Gaza has described extensive series, such as in the *Church of the Holy Apostles,* which have disappeared.

After the Justinian period mosaic art commenced to decline. The lower walls of *St. Apollinare in Clase* (Ravenna, 672-677) are weak imitations of the earlier period.

*Sculpture.*—There is little stone monumental sculpture. Hellenistic traditions, however, are responsible for a small amount of it, particularly on tombs. In the Berlin Museum there is an imposing relief from the end of a sarcophagus which comes from Asia Minor, known as the *Christ of Psamatia*. Though it is closely related to early Christian sarcophagi, the portico in which Christ and the two followers stand, is decoratively treated in the lace effect characteristic of Byzantine art. Other sarcophagi showing figures in a colonnade or portico are from Sidamara, Konia and Selefkeh, all in Asia Minor.

According to literary sources imperial sculpture existed in Constantinople. Mentions are made of equestrian statues of Theodosios, his sons and of Justinian. These have all been destroyed. On the other hand, a few portraits still exist of empresses (Ariadne, wife of Anastasios, died 548; Theodora, wife of Justinian), which bear a resemblance to the style found in the four porphyry emperors in Venice (c. 300 A.D.). In the Museum of Budapest there is a gilt bronze head, probably of Constantius II (361 A.D.) which is very striking in its use of flat simple planes. Apparently, in both mosaics and sculpture there is a preference for simplified forms, the frontal pose, and over large eyes.

Stone carving, however, was extensively used to decorate the interior of churches. Capitals of columns, pilasters, and mouldings were covered with patterns derived chiefly from vines and rosettes. These, instead of being modelled plastically, were flat and carved into the marble to form contrasts of light and dark. The effect is like that of embroidery (San Vitale). Frequently, there is not even an obvious pattern, but the entire surface is pierced to form a shimmering lacy effect. (SS. Sergius and Bacchus). It has been suggested that the origins of this art are to be sought in Syria. Mshatta, once believed to be a Syrian building, but now known to be Muslim,

SALONICA: ESKI-DJUMA. CAPITAL.

has walls which are covered with luxurious ornament. Though the building is Muslim, the stone carvers were most likely Syrians.

*Ivories.*—Ivory was in great demand for liturgical instruments and objects of luxury. It was the practice of newly elected consuls of Constantinople to send souvenirs of their accession to their friends and the emperor, in the form of a diptych. These consular diptychs show the consul wearing the insignia of office, either presiding at the Circus, or receiving the felicitations of his friends. There is a fairly com-

Magnus Diptych. (Bibliothèque Nationale.)

plete series in existence, commencing in 487 with the *Diptych of Boethius,* and ending in 541 with the *Diptych of Basil.* These diptychs are not very remarkable as works of art, but they are invaluable in giving a picture of the evolution of style during this period. The best represent Anastasius (517), Magnus (518) and Philoxenus (525). Not all official ivory carving was of low value. The *Barberini Ivory* (Louvre) which probably represents Justinian is of very high quality. It shows a mixture of Hellenistic and Christian iconography. The victorious emperor is shown receiving a crown from Victory, while above, two angels present the medallion of the blessing Christ. It has been suggested that the diptychs were made in Constantinople, while the Barberini Ivory was made in Alexandria.

There is evidence that the finest of the early ivories were made in Alexandria. A number of very fine pyxes, in which the style is very close to the Hellenistic, are probably Alexandrian. Among the most interesting church objects which belong to the Alexandrian School, is the *Trivulce Ivory* (Milan) containing scenes at the Holy Sepulchre. Even here, the style varies considerably from the Hellenistic. On the other hand, the *Lipsanoteca* in Brescia remains very close to it. Attention should also be directed towards the very beautiful ivory of the *Archangel Michael* in the British Museum, which belongs to this school.

The masterpiece of early Byzantine ivory carving is unquestionably the *Episcopal chair of Maximian,* which was probably executed during Justinian's reign. The front surface is the most remarkable part. Here, there are five large plaques, representing John the Baptist, and the four evangelists. These are contained in a magnificent and luxurious frame of vines, deer and peacocks. The other bas-reliefs, which are drier in execution, represent the Joseph story and the life of Christ. The origins of the chair have been disputed. Elements have been assigned to Alexandria, Syria and Palestine.

*Miniatures.*—The illustration of manuscripts originated in Alexandria, where, under the Ptolemies, precious books were ornamented with miniatures. When Constantine called the Alexandrine savants to his capital, they brought not only their learning, but also their books. In contrast to the more monumental forms of art, miniature painting enjoyed greater tolerance. It alone was creative during the sterile periods of court art. The study of the evolution of miniatures is complicated by the fact that efforts were made at later dates to make authentic copies of early manuscripts. Thus the *Paris Psalter* (Bibl. Nat. gr. 139) is a tenth century copy which may reflect either a classical revival in style of this period, or it may be a careful copy of a much earlier style.

In general, the miniatures may be divided into two groups, religious and secular, which roughly correspond to the Hellenistic and oriental categories. Examples of the secular and Hellenistic group are the *Vatican Virgil,* the *Vienna Dioscorides* (contains one distinctly sixth century miniature of the second category) and the *Cosmas of Indicopleustes.* (This contains along with miniatures of a Hellenistic type, others related to the art of the early Christian catacombs and contemporary mosaics.) The most important non-secular manuscript to be added to this group is the Josuah Roll, which was probably executed in the sixth or seventh century after an earlier Alexandrian model.

The great masterpieces of miniature art are found among the religious manuscripts where works of exquisite æsthetic sensitivity have been found. The *Vienna Genesis,* illustrated by five different hands, with an indisputable Hellenistic base, is, however, so completely transformed, that there is no question, but that in types, method of narration and conception, this is oriental art. Other manuscripts which belong to this group are the *Codex Rosanensis* (end of 6th Cent.), the *Sinope Fragments,* and the *Rabula Gospels.* The *Rosanensis* is more monumental in conception than the *Vienna Genesis.* The scenes of *Christ before Pilate* and *Pilate and the Jews* which also contains the *Death of Judas,* reveal a highly dramatic and emotional art. The *Sinope Fragments* is very similar in style to the *Rosanensis.* The *Rabula Gospels* is very different. It is interesting, not so much for its artistic worth, as for its relations to mosaics and types which have been found on the Monza ampoules. Another manuscript to be added to this group is the *Cotton Bible,* which was destroyed in a fire in 1731. This is very close to the Hellenistic type, and is important because of its relations to the mosaics of the north of St. Marks in Venice. The place of origin of these various manuscripts has been disputed. There were probably a number of centers.

*Painting.*—Little remains of the great cycles of paintings in the churches of the period of Justinian. Apart from the *Frescoes of Bawit* (Egypt) and a few others found in Cappadocia, nothing remains but the memory of their existence. Choricius, to whom we owe the description of the *Church of St. Sergius of Gaza,* relates the character of the frescoes in this church in great detail. The monumental and historical style rather than the Hellenistic picturesque style was apparently used. The subjects were taken from the New Testament. The Bawit frescoes are interesting to students because of their kinship to early Spanish Romanesque painting.

The Second Golden Age.—*Introduction.*—During the long intermission between the first and second golden age few monuments of art were created. It is very likely that the Byzantine artists, being unable to work at home because of the Iconoclastic controversy, went to Italy. In Rome there are a number of examples of Byzantine art. The most outstanding cycles of frescoes and mosaics are found in St. Agnesa, the Oratory of Pope John VII, the cemetery of Cocodilla (catacomb frescoes), St. Sabas and St. Maria Antiqua. The secular art produced in the Byzantine Empire was chiefly in the Hellenistic style. In addition to these, there are stone bas-reliefs, showing fantastic animals which bear some resemblance to Romanesque types. These animals are in very flat relief, are treated decoratively, and are usually combined with some foliage (Cf. relief from Salonika).

*Mosaics.*—The art of the Second Golden Age has a new character. It is more religious and more emotional. Much greater attention is accorded Mary than had formerly been

Communion of the Apostles: Mosaic of St. Sophia at Kiev. After Diehl: *Manuel d'Art Byzantin.* (A. Picard, edit.)

the case. Subjects capable of arousing strong emotional responses, such as the Crucifixion, the Last Judgment and the Dormition of the Virgin are represented. The ending of iconoclasm signified the victory of the monastic party, and with it, the domination of the church in art. In the selection and arrangement of

The Virgin before the Priests. Mosaic at the Kahrie-Djami. After Diehl: *Manuel d'Art Byzantin.* (A. Picard, edit.)

scenes for church interiors, a rigid order was usually followed. Instead of the earlier narrative or chronological sequence, a hieratic one was used. Art was no longer intended to teach a moral, but to be a revelation. In order to accomplish this, the iconography was enriched and transformed, Christ the Pantocrator, and not the gentle Shepherd, is placed in the highest point of the church, the dome. The second position of honor, the apse, is dedicated to the Virgin, while the Last Judgment is placed on the West or exit wall. Two scenes which are now regularly represented, the Descent into Limbo and the Dormition of the Virgin, along with the 12 feasts of the Church and single representations of holy figures are placed on the nave walls. According to descriptions, the Nea of Basil I was decorated according to this system. Other churches with mosaic cycles are St. Luke (Phocis), St. Sophia (Kiev), Nea Mone (Chios), St. Sophia (Salonika) and Daphni (near Athens).

Daphni belongs to the end of the eleventh century. The figures are arranged in exquisite rhythms. In contrast to the earlier mosaics of this period, these are more delicate and tender. The earlier ones were more powerful. The recently uncovered mosaics of St. Sophia (Istanbul) belong to the ninth and tenth centuries.

During the eleventh and twelfth centuries, several magnificent mosaic cycles were created in those parts of Italy which were under Byzantine domination. These have a marked resemblance to the mosaics of Daphni, but they are more descriptive and narrative. This is particularly true of the cycles in Venice and Torcello. The outstanding Sicilian mosaics are in Cefalua and Palermo (Capella-Palatina, Martorana, and Monreale).

*Miniatures.*—In the manuscripts of the Second Golden Age, ornamentation plays a rather large rôle. Initial letters, for example, which has been emphasised formerly only by a difference in size and color, are now formed of braided vegetable motives, and even of birds, fishes and human forms. The most elaborate designs are found in the Can-

The Vision of Ezekiel. Manuscript of Gregory of Nazianzum. (Bibliothèque Nationale.)

on Tables. In these, in addition to the antique and oriental motives appear Muslim and Persian designs.

Two systems of illustration are used in the manuscripts of the ninth and tenth centuries: marginal illustrations in the theological manuscripts which have a popular character, and full page illustrations in the court or "aristocratic" ones. In the *Chludoff Manuscript* (Moscow) which belongs to the first type, the compositions and the postures are dramatic and have an appearance of "realism." An interesting development in the iconography of this type is the prosaic illustration of figurative language. For example, the verse ". . . And his enemies shall lick the dust" (Psalm 72, 9) is rendered by showing the enemy, with a long protruding tongue, literally licking the dust. Other Psalters of this type, are the *Barberini* (Vatican) and the *Stoudion* (British Museum) *Psalters*. In contrast to these are the "aristocratic" manuscripts, such as the *Paris Psalter* (Bibliothèque Nationale, gr. 139) where the Hellenistic style is copied. The large number of secular books which were illustrated at this time are in the same style. Among these are the *Theriaca of Nicandre*, the *Treatise of Apollonius of Citium* and the *Manuscript of Oppien*.

One book, in great favor, was *The Homilies of Gregory Nazianzenus*. The most impressively illustrated copy, Paris, 510, has two distinct styles which are occasionally even placed on the same page. One is the picturesque antique type, characteristic of court art, while the other is a new monumental type, related to the mosaics of the period.

Towards the beginning of the eleventh century, all the illustration undergoes a marked change. The variety and spontaneity previously found disappear. The art takes on a disciplined theological character. This new miniature style became the foundation for the monumental art of the last Renaissance in the fourteenth century. A typical example is the *Menologium of Basil II* (976-1025) in the Vatican Library.

*Frescoes.*—Few frescoes of this period have survived. Recently, a series has been uncovered in Cappadocio, which is interesting for its iconography. Byzantine frescoes have also been found in Italy (St. Blaise, near Brindisi) and in Russia (area around Novgorod, in twelfth and thirteenth century churches).

*Sculpture.*—If sculpture was neglected during the first period, it practically disappeared after the Triumph of the Images. However, the art of stone working continued in ornamental flat sculpture. There are a few figures of beautiful modelling, such as the reliefs of the Virgin Orante in Constantinople (discovered in 1922) and in the Church of St. Maria in Porto (near Ravenna).

*Ivories.*—Ivories continued to be the main expression of sculptured

Harbaville Triptych. (Fragment, Louvre.)

art. Several small caskets, such as the one in the National Museum of Florence, depend entirely upon antique models for style and subject matter. Others are of a more liturgical nature. The plaque representing the seated Virgin, which was formerly in the Stroganoff Collection and is now in the Cleveland Museum, is one of the masterpieces of this art. The subject is treated with majesty and power. Later ivories, such as the relief showing Christ crowning Romanus and Eudocia (c. 945) and the *Harbaville Triptych*, have a figure style which is more delicate and graceful, and resembles the style of the Daphni mosaics.

The Fourteenth Century.—After the terrible ordeal of the Crusades, the country was reunited under the Paleologues, and Byzantium enjoyed an intense intellectual life of which art was part. The art of this late period was no longer marked by the use of luxurious materials. Frescoes replaced mosaics, and became the most important vehicle of art expression. Church art was particularly active in Russia, Servia, Bulgaria, and Roumania. In these countries, as well as in Macedonia, and particularly in Mistra (capital of the Paleologues) and Mount Athos, there are very important fresco paintings.

*Frescoes.*—The frescoes in fine, rich colors covered all the available wall space. The walls were usually divided into five horizontal zones. The compositions in these zones were small and very varied. The single figures which had played a large rôle in the eleventh century mosaics practically disappeared. The subject matter became much richer, both the Bible and Apocryphal texts being freely drawn upon. Details from popular life were also used to supply realism to the scenes. The Baptism, for example, is no longer limited to the two main actors, but groups of people who are resting and bathing in the Jordan are added. The art is not only more picturesque, but it is also more dramatic and emotional. In the scene of the Crucifixion, the body of Christ is shown sagging under its own weight, and the Virgin, completely overcome with grief, faints at the foot of the cross. The mystical writings of the Pseudo-Bonaventura, popular in Italy and France, were derived from Byzantine sources of this date.

Piece of Silk. (Hanover, Kestner Museum.) After Diehl: *Manuel d'Art Byzantin*. (A. Picard, edit.)

The fresco painters are divided into two main schools, the Cretan and the Macedonian. Extensive cycles by artists of the Macedonian School have been found in Serbia, in the churches of Studenica, Nagoicino, Gracanica, Matejic, Lesnovo, etc. These have been signed with Greek names. The most famous of these paintings have been found in Athos, where the somewhat mysterious Panselino of Thessaly worked. The paintings of the Macedonian School may owe some of their inspiration to Syria, while the gestures of tenderness may come from Siena.

The Cretan School was more varied and subtle in expression than the Macedonian School. The forms are more refined and have greater nobility in their poses. The compositions are clearer, and at the same time, there is much more minutiae than in the Macedonian examples. The great masterpiece of this school

Textile of Byzantine Manufacture, Eighth Century. (Musée historique des tissus, Lyon.)

is the *Peribleptos* at Mistra. In the 16th century, Teofane from Crete rivalled Panselino in working at

Tunic Belonging to Charlemagne. (Sacristy of St. Peter's, Rome.)

Athos. He decorated the churches of Lavra, Stavronikita, Dionisio and Dochiario. The Pantassa at Mistra, executed during the fifteenth century, also belongs to the Cretan School.

La Pala d'Oro. (Fragment, St. Mark's, Venice.)

The very fine icons painted by the Cretan School can be attested by those in the Russian Museum in Leningrad.

*Gold, Silver, Enamels, Textiles.*—Among the great Byzantine works of art, mention must also be made of the extremely fine textiles, enamels and gold and silver vessels. These are among their most original creations. In all of this work there is an accent on wealth and luxury. Since the materials were costly and admired, their own particular qualities were never destroyed. The color, texture and luminosity of the materials were emphasised.

In the sixth century silk weaving became a Byzantine industry. The cloths of Byzantium were highly prized throughout its history. They did not deteriorate even when the Empire was impoverished. Beautiful "historiated" cloths come from the necropolises of the sixth century of Antinoe and Akhnin in Egypt. The textiles of the East are characterised by more brilliant colouring and the use of stylised symmetrical forms. Persia undoubtedly influenced the Eastern designs. Byzan-

The Marriage of David. Silver Plate from Cyprus. (Pierpont Morgan Collection.) After Diehl: *Manuel d'Art Byzantin*. (A. Picard, edit.)

tine textiles were highly prized in the West, where they were used for liturgical and imperial purposes. Magnificent examples exist in the principal cathedral treasures and in the Sancta Sanctorum, Rome.

Among the enamels, an art industry developed by Byzantium, the most outstanding are the *Pala d'Oro* of St. Marks (11th-12th Cent.), and the *Triptych of Kakouli* in Georgia (11th Cent.). Many icons in the St. Mark's Treasury are decorated with enamels. Enamels were used for liturgical instruments, as for example the stauroteche (reliquary containing a fragment of the true cross). An outstanding example is the *Limburg Staurotecre* of the tenth century.

*Goldsmith Work.* — The finest metal work was produced during the Second Golden Age. Of the earliest period, the most interesting objects are the ampoulae from Monza. The diffusion of Palestinian elements, particularly in iconography is ascribed to these little vessels. Early silver plates from Syria are of outstanding quality. The Kouchakji Collection in New York has a very interesting example from Antioch, which is probably of the fifth century. Particularly interesting are the Cyprus plates, containing scenes of the hunt, pastorals, and the Bible. These are from Kerynia and are divided between the British Museum and the Metropolitan Museum (New York).

*Conclusion.*—While it is true that Byzantine art too often copied earlier works, still this must not be interpreted to mean that the Byzantine artists lacked imagination. Byzantine art was in the main, highly inventive. It dominated the art of both the East and West during the Middle Ages, and it played a very important part in the evolution of Western art. Byzantine art created monuments of superlative quality, but even that art which appears to lack high æsthetic quality is exceedingly important in understanding the history of art and culture.

Bibliography: Anthony, *A History of Mosaics*, 1935.—Breasted, *Oriental Forerunners of Byzantine Painting*, 1924.—Byron & Rice, *The Birth of Western Painting*, 1931.—Dalton, *Byzantine Art and Archeology*, 1911.—Dalton, *Early Christian Art*, 1925.—Ch. Diehl, *L'art chretien primitif et l'art Byzantin*, 1928.—Ch. Diehl, *Manuel d'art Byzantin*, 2 ed., 1925.—Ch. Diehl, *La Peinture Byzantine*, 1933.—Diez & Demus, *Byzantine Mosaics in Greece*, 1931.—Glueck, *Die christliche Kunst des Ostens*, 1923.—Hamilton, *Byzantine Decoration*, 1934.—Hauttmann, *Die Kunst des Fruehen Mittelalters*, 1929.—Kondakoff, *Histoire de l'art byzantin*, 2 vols., 1886-1891. —Millet, *Le Monastere de Daphni.* —Millet, *Monuments Byzantins de Mistra*, 1910.—Morey, *Christian Art*, 1935.—Muratoff, *La pittura bizantina*, 1928.—Pierce & Tylor, *Byzantine Art*, 1926.—Sherrill, *Mosaics in Italy, Palestine, Syria, Turkey and Greece*, 1933.—Strzygowski, *Origin of Christian Art*, Eng. ed., 1923.—Rice, *Byzantine Art*, 1935.—Whittemore, *Mosaics of St. Sophia at Istanbul*, 1933.

**BYZANTIUM.**—See Constantinople; Miniature.

# C

**CABANEL (Alexandre).**—French painter, 1823-1889, born at Montpellier; noted for portraits.

**CABINET.**—Of Eastern origin, the cabinet was much used during the 17th century, in Italy, Spain,

French Cabinet by Boulle (André Charles).

France and other northern countries, as an elegant and precious piece of furniture. It was intended to hold jewelry and other small, valuable objects. Originally it was a kind of little coffer, placed on a table, which opened by a flap, a form adhered to for a long time in Spain. However, with a great complication of inner drawers, pigeon-holes and niches, the cabinet became essentially a little cupboard, the upper part having two doors, and the lower being reduced to two or more supports in front with a solid back and base. Spanish and Portuguese cabinets are generally decorated with plaques of open gilt and ironwork. Those of Florence are in walnut or, more generally, ebony, enriched and even overladen with fine stone columns, with gold and silver inlaying on a shell background and fine mosaics. Those of Naples are usually inlaid with mother-of-pearl and ivory on an ebony background. Milanese cabinets, more subdued, are ornamented with ivory arabesques engraved on the same background of ebony. All over Italy, a certain number of cabinets were entirely painted. In Milan and Florence they were even made of iron repoussé work, damascened and inlaid with gold and silver.

The cabinets of Germany and the Netherlands are usually of ebony with bas-reliefs and undulated edges, decorated inside with fine paintings, sometimes signed by the best Flemish and Dutch painters.

In France, until the great André Charles Boulle stamped them with his individuality, the cabinets had little originality. They were either imported from Italy, Germany or the Netherlands, or they were made in Paris by cabinet-makers from these countries, or were more or less copied from foreign models. The fashion for them disappeared at the beginning of the 18th century. But the famous jewel-cases of Marie Antoinette, by Schwerdfeger, and of Marie Louise, by Jacob Desmalter, are in reality nothing else but cabinets.

In the 18th century, large Chinese and Japanese folding screens, with numerous leaves, were also called "cabinets."

**CAEN (Normandy, France).**—Caen owes its oldest buildings to William the Conqueror, Duke of Normandy and King of England. Of the old ramparts, almost nothing remains. The enormous feudal château, partly ruined, is used as a barracks. But William and his wife, Queen Matilda, left more glorious monuments than these—the famous Churches of the Holy Trinity (*Abbaye-Aux-Dames*) and of St. Etienne (*Abbaye-aux-Hommes*).

The *Abbaye-aux-Hommes*, built by William the Conqueror, was consecrated in 1077, although not finished until 1290. The western façade is severe in style, and flanked by two square towers, crowned by octagonal spires. The Abbaye-aux-Hommes has no fewer than nine spires "giving the vertical expression which became characteristic of Gothic architecture." The east end has a "chevet" ("a term applied to a circular or polygonal apse when surrounded by an ambulatory off which are chapels")—a characteristic feature of French mediaeval churches. The interior is vast, and majestic in its simplicity. Arcades and windows have round arches (Romanesque); and "the nave vaulting illustrates the difficulties of spanning an oblong compartment without the aid of the pointed arch. Here, two bays are comprised under one vaulting compartment, which is approximately square." . . . The resulting system is known as "sexpartite" vaulting. This method was superseded by the introduction of the pointed arch (Gothic style). The Abbaye-aux-Hommes thus shows an interesting transition from Romanesque (or Norman, as the style is called when it refers to English buildings of the same period—11th and 12th centuries) to Gothic. "The thrust of this nave vault is counteracted by a semi-barrel vault over the triforium gallery, protected externally by a timber roof, thus forming, as it were, a concealed flying buttress."

The *Abbaye-aux-Dames*, built under the direction of Lanfranc, was consecrated in June, 1066. With its proud outlines and simple, massive appearance, it has the air of a fortress. The plan is very simple. Behind a façade, pierced with three semi-circular doorways—the two side ones are in the bottom stage of strong flanking towers—is a Romanesque nave, with a sexpartite vault, and side aisles. As in the Abbaye-aux-Hommes, the massive walls have slightly projecting buttresses. There is a square tower over the crossing. The pillars have carved capitals, some of them very rich and fantastic. Caen possesses other interesting churches; and the Hôtel d'Ecoville, a Renaissance building (1535-1541).

Bibliography: H. Prentont, *Caen et Bayeux*. Paris, 1909.

**CAFFIERI (The).**—They belonged to an Italian family, which

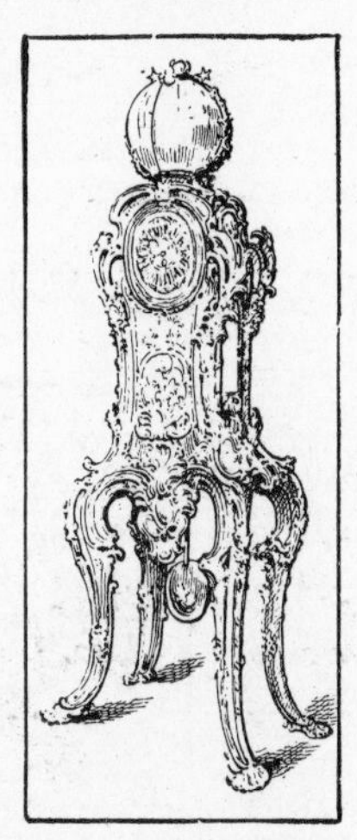

Caffieri (Philippe): Engraved Copper Clock.

settled in France during the 17th century, of which several members occupied the position of master sculptor of the King's ships, which was handed on from father to son.

Philippe Caffieri, the first of the name (1634-1716), exercised this capacity under Louis XIV. He was, at the same time, associated with the great works of Charles Le Brun, and, in fact, became connected with this family by his marriage. Jacques Caffieri (1678-1755), fifth son of Philippe, sculptor and founder, worked a great deal for the royal houses. He made the bronzes which decorate the clock of Passemant (thus called from the name of the clock-maker), in the Château of Versailles. Of sculpture, his busts include a bronze of the Baron de Bezenval—a foretaste of that lively feeling for reality which gives so much savour to the work of the most illustrious of his sons.

**— (Philippe),** 1714-1777.—Fifth son of Jacques, was a sculptor and founder like his father. He was commissioned, notably, to make bronze substitutes for the silver cross and chandeliers of Claude Ballin on the High Altar of Notre Dame, Paris, since the expenses of the latter wars of Louis XIV had necessitated payment of these into the royal melting-pot. The cross and chandeliers were, in their turn, destroyed during the Revolution. He also made similar objects for Bayeux Cathedral, where they are still to be found and show the decorative elegance of his art. These may be copies of the old pieces of Notre Dame, Paris.

**— (Jean Jacques),** 1725 - 1792.—The most famous of Jacques Caffieri's sons. He was a sculptor only and unlike his two predecessors, did no bronze casting. He had access to the Académie Royale and had lessons from J. B. Lemoyne after he had passed through the teaching of his father who inculcated the taste for nature and truth. While still only a pupil of the Academy, he made a bust of Lanquet de Gergy, curé of St. Sulpice, his parish church, the man for whom Michel Ange Slodtz built the solemn tomb which is still to be seen in one of the chapels of the church. In 1748, he won the Grand Prix for sculpture, and went to Rome. He stayed nearly two years beyond the three regular years, giving proof of remarkable skill and rapidity of execution in works of a decorative character—such as in the Trinity above the High Altar of the French Church of St. Louis.

On his return to Paris, he was "accepted," in 1757, and two years later received at the Académie Royale, on the presentation of a marble figure personifying a river (Louvre), a work in which the movement is perhaps more picturesque than truly plastic, but showing a particular suppleness in the rendering of flesh.

It is not these works, however (which fail in invention), that best show his talent, but the simple bust for which his father, sculptor of the portrait bust of the Baron de Bezenval, had so well prepared him. There he showed keen talent and spirited execution as a portraitist. His busts (such as those of the sculptor Van Cleves, and the astronomer Pingré, in the Louvre) show fine, powerful workmanship, which suggests the effects of that profession of bronze founding practised by his relatives. Since he had a great liking for the theatre, where

# PREHISTORIC ART—CAVE DRAWINGS

*These forms of art were recently revealed to us in places where they have been since the Glacial Period. The most beautiful and most significant works were found in the southwest of France (Dordogne-Pyrénées). It is impossible to set their date accurately. They are placed in the period when the glaciers moved down the valleys of Europe, when men lived by hunting and fishing and dwelt in caves.*

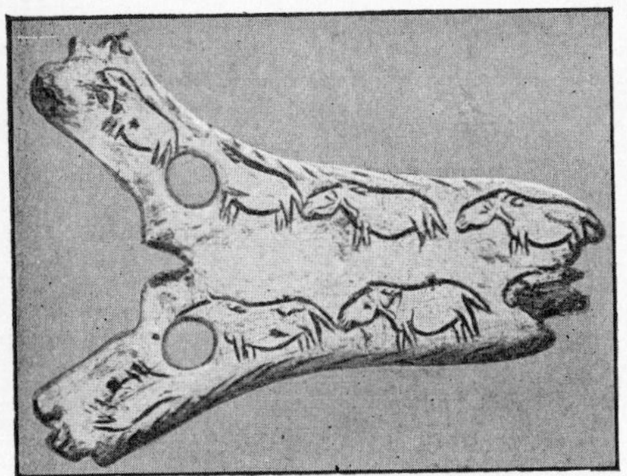

ENGRAVED BONE, CAVERNE DE LA MADELEINE (DORDOGNE). (BRITISH MUSEUM.)

STATUETTE OF A BISON MADE FROM REINDEER ANTLER. GROTTE DE LA MADELEINE (DORDOGNE).

ENGRAVED REINDEER BONE, CAVERNE DE LORTHET (HAUTES-PYRÉNÉES). (MUSEUM, ST.-GERMAIN.)

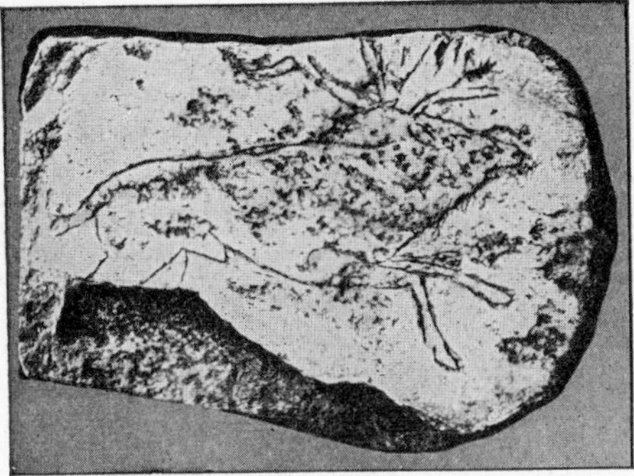

GALLOPING REINDEER, ENGRAVED ON FLAT STONE (INDRE). (MUSEUM, ST.-GERMAIN.)

GROUP OF TWO BISONS, CAVE OR TUC D'AUDOUBERT (ARIÈGE).

DETAIL OF A STAFF OF REINDEER ANTLERS (THAINGEN, NEAR SCHAFFHAUSEN): GRAZING REINDEER.

## Sculpture and Engraving

With knives and pointed flint they engraved reindeer antlers and carved bones. It is astounding that their art is so far from mere groping. Each drawing is a spirited characterisation of an animal and its movements. The outlines of the reindeer are amazingly accurate. One, while walking, is grazing with its snout in the grass; others are galloping; and the engraver must have noticed the stamping of their thin and brittle hoofs.

HORSE PAINTED IN BLACK. (INSTITUT DE PALÉONTOLOGIE HUMAINE.)

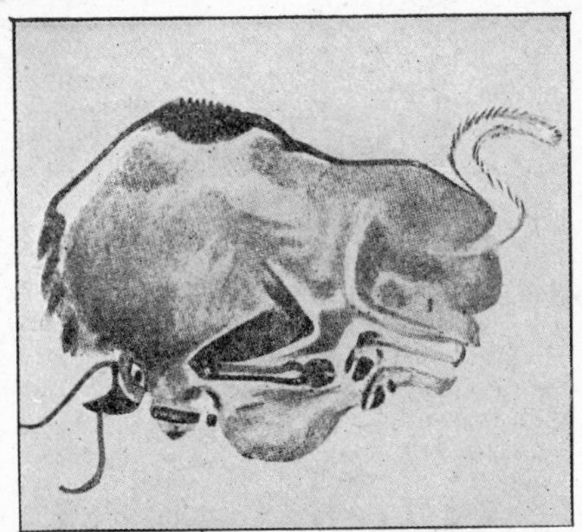

BISON PAINTED ON THE WALL, CAVE OF ALTAMIRA (SPAIN). ("L'ANTHROPOLOGIE," MASSON EDIT.)

LARGE COLOURED REINDEER. (INSTITUT DE PALÉONTOLOGIE HUMAINE.)

GROUP OF BISON, MAMMOTHS, REINDEER, AND HORSES. (INSTITUT DE PALÉONTOLOGIE HUMAINE.)

## Paintings

Finally, on walls of obscure caves which are accessible with difficulty, there have been deciphered paintings of animals. The colours are earthen, ochre and black. In these a very rudimentary form of art was discovered, but nevertheless very well applied. The drawing of the bison with his four hoofs off the ground in a bounding position, has been cited as one of the most expressive pictures in the history of art.

# MEGALITHIC MONUMENTS

*These Megalithic monuments, which were preserved due to their massiveness, date from very different periods. There are some, the oldest, which belong to the polished stone age, the Neolithic period. Man had no other tools than hatchets of flint. These early monuments were probably tombs. They are the first attempts at architecture. They present, even if not a highly developed plastic sense, at least a use of the mechanical arts, and also a form of social organisation. Monuments like these, which presuppose that large stones were transported for large distances, had to be constructed by a well-organised group of men. On the other hand, it does not seem that the people cared to engrave these stones. They used them as nature had formed them.*

KARNAC: THE AVENUE OF MÉNEC.
*(Photo by Neurdein.)*

SCULPTURED MENHIR. ST.-SERNIN (AVEYRON).

DOLMEN CALLED THE PLANK OF PIARRE. ÎLE D'YEU.
*(Photo from Section Photo des Beaux-Arts.)*

DOLMEN MADE INTO A ROMAN BUILDING. ST.-GERMAIN-DE-CONFOLENS.

TRILITHS OF STONEHENGE, NEAR SALISBURY.
*(Photo by Spooner.)*

At Stonehenge, in England, a very impressive megalithic unit, is the transition between the shapeless dolmen of the stone ages, and architecture of well thought-out structure which resulted from the use of iron tools. The blocks are already squared off, forming a circle of triliths, each composed of two vertical stones supporting a lintel. Greek and Egyptian architects employed the basic power of these rudimentary structures. They could only have been done by people who owned bronze tools. During the era when they were erected, in the Orient, Egypt, and Asia, men had been building for a long time monuments of perfect structure, richly decorated.

he made many friends, his most important work consists of busts of great French playwrights. The foyer of the Opera possessed his busts of Lulli, Quinault and Raineau, but these unfortunately were destroyed by fire. The Théâtre Français possesses many busts, all of which are signed and dated, but apart from this they could not fail to be recognised as his work: Piron (1775), Pierre Corneille, Quinault and La Fontaine (1779), La Chaussée and Thomas Corneille (1782), the famous Rotrou (1783), J. B. Rousseau (1787), De Belloy (1788). There are also busts by Caffieri in the Bibliothèque St. Geneviève. The Institute possesses full-length statues of Pierre Corneille (1779), of which the plaster model is in Rouen, and of Molière (1787).

His masterpiece is the *Rotrou* of the Comédie Française. "It is indeed the head of an inspired *poet,*" writes M. Jules Guiffrey in his work on the Caffieri, "and at the same time the type of the accomplished, almost delicate, 'cavalier.' . . . But words cannot describe the intense vitality and expression of all the features, especially of the eyes and mouth."

See Pl. 45, Vol. II.

At the Académie Royale, Jean Jacques Caffieri was pupil-teacher. He was also a member of the Academies of Rouen and of Dijon. With his sensitive, jealous disposition, he suffered a good deal in seeing his fame eclipsed by that of Houdon. He even entered into competition with him on several occasions, notably when he, too, reproduced the features of Voltaire, of Rousseau and of Franklin, which gave Houdon the inspiration for some of his best work. But Caffieri was among the first to bring back a feeling for nature and realism to French sculpture, and in this he prepared the way for his young and genial rival.

Bibliography: Jules Guiffrey, *Les Caffieri,* 1876.

**CAHORS (Lot, France).**—The *Fontaine des Chartreux* and the *Porte de Diane* date from the Roman era. The *Cathedral,* built in the 11th century, is in the Romanesque style, surmounted with domes. The North doorway has some fine 12th century sculptures. The *Palace of John XXII* is a strong, heavy building of the 14th century. The *Bridge* over the Lot is celebrated. Its arches support three square towers with machicolations.

**CAIRO (Egypt).**—The town is composed of a modern town and an Arabic town, quite distinct from each other. The Arabic town has kept its old appearance, with its narrow passages, terraced houses and innumerable minarets and domes. The mosques—about four hundred —are very rich buildings. The best known are the Mosque of Sultan Hassan, 140 metres long, with a dome and two minarets and a door 38 metres high, dating from 1356; and the Mosque of Tulun, etc. The public fountains are often very graceful. The town gates are sometimes surmounted with crenellated towers. Near the town is an ancient necropolis, the "Tombs of the Caliphs," which encloses the mortuary mosques of Sultans and tombs of persons once famous.

*Mosque of Ibn-Tulun.* See Moslem Architecture, Syro-Egyptian School.

*Mosque of Sultan Berkuk.* See Moslem Architecture, Syro-Egyptian School.

See Moslem Art.

Cairo: Mosque of Sultan Hassan.

Bibliography: P. Coste, *L'Art Arabe ou les Monuments du Caire.* Paris, 1826.—G. Migeon, *Le Caire.* Paris, Laurens.

**CALAMIS.**—Attic sculptor of the beginning of the 5th century, contemporary with Cimon. He is the artist who best personifies the transition between the Persian wars and the reign of Pericles. It has even been said that he played a similar part in his relationship to Cimon, as Phidias, to Pericles. Pausanias tells us that he joined with Onatas in making the chariot ordered by Hieron of Syracuse, in commemoration of his Olympic victory in 468. He was also the sculptor of a statue of Aphrodite, consecrated by Callias, which crowned the Propylea, at the entrance to the Acropolis. A base, bearing a dedication by Callias, was found on this spot, and no doubt it was that belonging to the Aphrodite of Calamis. He seems to have worked between the years 480-460, or at most from 490 to 450.

Old writings have preserved a record of a certain number of works by Calamis: a statue of Apollo; a votive offering of the Agrigentans, at Olympia; an *Athena Nike,* dedicated by the Mantinians, at Olympia; a gold and ivory *Asclepios,* for Sicyonia; for the Spartans, a statue of Hermione at Delphi; for the town of Apollonia du Pont, a colossal bronze statue of Apollo, which was later carried off to Rome by Lucullus; for the Tanagrans, a statue of Dionysos, in Parian marble; a *Hermes* carrying a ram (Criophoros).

His most admired work was the statue of Aphrodite, set up on the Acropolis under the name of Sosandra, highly praised by Lucian. He speaks of "her proud, modest smile, and the light, graceful arrangement of her garments." The ancients also greatly admired his talent as an animal sculptor. He was considered to be one of the finest masters, preceding the classic period, and doubtless it was his work which so many archaistic sculptors of the time of Hadrian took as model. His abilities were very varied, for he worked on marble, bronze and chryselephantine sculpture.

Bibliography: Collignon, *Histoire de la sculpture Grecque,* Vol. I. Paris, 1902.—Lechat, *La Sculpture attique avant Phidias.* Paris, 1905.—Ernest Gardner, *A Handbook of Greek Sculpture.* London, 1920.

**CALIARI (Paolo).**—See Veronese.

**CALISO.**—See Temperelli.

**CALLCOTT (Augustus Wall).**—English painter, 1779-1844. He studied under Hoffner. He entered the Royal Academy in 1797, and made his début with some portraits. But he found his bent in landscape and marine painting. He painted the sea admirably. In technique, he sometimes recalls Claude Lorrain. In 1837, he attempted figure painting, with two important works: *Raphael and La Fornarina,* and *Milton Dictating his Poems to his Daughters.* He was knighted sometime after the exhibition of these two canvases.

Among his works must be mentioned: the *Mouth of the Tyne* (belonging to Mr. W. Ridley), and a *View of the Thames* (Marquis of Landsdown). The National Gallery possesses nine pictures of which the most remarkable is the *Old Jetty at Littlehampton.* South Kensington possesses ten paintings, among them *Slender* and *Anne Page.*

**CALLICRATES.**—See Acropolis of Athens.

**CALLIMACHUS.**—Greek sculptor of the end of the 5th century B.C. Old writings allow us to catch a glimpse of his originality. He made a lamp which burned night and day in the cella of Athena Polias, in the Erechtheion. Pausanias, and Vitruvius (Vol. IV, 1, 10) admired especially the refinement and perfection of his work. He is said to be the first sculptor to use the running drill in marble in order to achieve deep lines in the folds of drapery and in the modelling.

In addition to a statue of Hera at Plataea only one other work of sculpture by Callimachus is mentioned: a group of dancing maidens, possibly those who danced at the festival of Artemis at Caryae.

**CALLOT (Jacques).**—French engraver, born in Nancy in 1592; died

Callot (Jacques). (Uffizi, Florence.)

in 1635. He learned drawing in his childhood with the engraver Crocq, and was afterwards the pupil of Claude Henriet, painter to the Duke of Lorraine. He fled from his father's house, with a band of gipsies in order to go to Rome; but in Florence, where he went to the studio of Canta Gallina, some merchants from Nancy recognised him, and brought him back to his father. He succeeded in escaping a second time, but was taken in Turin. He was then allowed to go to Rome, where he arrived in 1609, at the age of sixteen. He soon found a place with an obscure French practitioner, called Thomassin, who had a shop for the sale of religious engravings, and had not the least talent. Callot there accomplished some modest work, and familiarised himself with the burin; but, after a dispute with his master, he went to Florence, where he was well received by the Grand Duke Cosimo II. Callot was not yet, however, very skillful. He engraved the *Purgatory,* after B. Poccetti, his patron, and the set of the *Battles of the Medici.*

He then entered the service of the architect Giulio Parigi, a curious man, who busied himself with various things—mathematics, architecture, the organisation of fêtes—and who perceived Callot's bent, and urged him to study nature. With Parigi, Callot learned etching, which suited his spontaneity infinitely better than engraving. At the same time he contrived to replace the soft varnish used until then, by the hard varnish used by the mu-

Callot: A Character of the Italian Comedy.

sical instrument makers. He was thus able to give his work more refinement and distinctness, and to represent a crowd of little figures in a restricted space. He did this very successfully in the plates of the *War of Love,* which suggest the fêtes given in 1615, in the Piazza Santa Croce, and of the *Nautical Fête* on the Arno in 1619. About the same time he engraved scenes from the tragedy of "Soliman," which show that vivacity and sureness of touch which distinguish his work. In these first works is seen his taste for picturesque rags and ostentatious attire. For him there were only great lords and beggars, and the ordinary spotless costume of the bourgeoisie does not seem to have attracted him in the least. This tendency comes out distinctly in the series of *Caprices,* finished in 1617. Behind a figure—gentleman, fine lady, beggar, or strolling comedian—placed in the foreground, are street scenes, fêtes or Florentine landscapes.

The well-known plate of the *Impruneta,* the great Florentine fair, dates from 1620. The innumerable groups there represented are all different, and interesting. The artist had then attained wonderful mastery. A tradition (related by M. Rosenthal) has it that "Callot, examining his plate, noticed, in the moment of printing, that it showed an unpleasant blank in one corner, and he at once drew new incidents on the copper, with the same ease as he had done on paper."

From this time, Callot's influence was considerable. Among the Italian artists who tried to imitate him were Cantarini, Benedetto Castiglione, Canta Gallina, his old master, and, above all, Stefano della Bella, who in his admiration even tried to turn himself into a Frenchman, and took the name under which he is generally known, of Etienne de la Belle.

On the death of Cosimo II, the grants which he made to artists were done away with, including that of Callot. He was then rich enough to live comfortably, but he resented some ill humour in it, and could hardly bring himself to ask leave to return to Lorraine, whither the Duke Charles IV called him. At this period he published the series of the *Nobility*, and that of the *Beggars*, which fully reveal his fantastic bent and which are among his most popular works. The sets of the *Gobbi* and the *Balli*, from earlier drawings, come a little later. *Combats de la Barrière* (1627) is the last work of his first period. He then bade farewell to the actors of the Commedia dell'Arte and to brilliant fêtes, and only engraved scenes of warfare, dramatic pictures of the horrors of war, and some religious compositions.

The Infanta Elizabeth Claire Eugénie made him come to Belgium, and he engraved for her the *Siege of Breda*. Richelieu, put on his guard by this engraving, presented the author of it to Louis XIII, who ordered engravings of the *Siege of Saint Martin de Ré* and of the *Siege of La Rochelle*. But, after the Siege of Nancy, in 1633, Richelieu wished him to draw from that a fellow to the Siege of La Rochelle. Callot replied to the Cardinal's envoy that he "would rather cut his thumb off than obey." Then, realising that he had definitely lost the royal favour, he retired to Nancy, where he engraved the tragic scenes of the *Miseries of War*. There he represented relentlessly terrible scenes, which he had perhaps witnessed, or which had been described to him—peasants tortured and robbed, convents laid waste, marauders executed, burned, shot, hanged. No description by historians could make one realise better the horror of this age, so brilliant in appearance, but in which the people had, in the regions devastated by war or simply occupied by the armies, to endure suffering beyond words. A new Callot is revealed to us, very different from that of the first period. About this, M. Delaborde has written so justly and precisely that we cannot do better than quote him here. "Callot," he says, "gave himself up freely to his fancy, and seemed to have only seen in art a means of amusement, in the people, a pretext for caricatures, and in imaginative and even sacred subjects the chance to invent grotesque figures. Like another satirical Frenchman, Mathurin Régnier, who had preceded him to Rome, he favoured vulgar types, beggars, dwarfs, and the dissolute. And the works of these two men have too often a bad savour. They represent degraded objects with an almost repulsive realism. All the same, the vigour of expression does not always degenerate into cynicism, and the accuracy of the pictures is not always shameful. Both Régnier and Callot had the secret of saying precisely what was necessary to make their thoughts clear, even when they resulted from the most fanciful inspiration. One may reproach them for having cared too little to raise the standard; but one cannot deny them the merit of having painted blackguards of all kinds in a firm, concise style, and of having given, each in his language, a definite and truly rational form to this art of satire."

It must be remarked, however, that this appreciation does not perhaps take sufficiently into account the last works of Callot. Beneath this taste for "beggars and dwarfs" he hides a deep pity, a strange tenderness, which had free expression in the *Miseries of War*; it is there that the untiring visionary, the frank debauchee, shows his pitiful and generous nature.

Callot engraved a certain number of religious pictures. During his last years, he gave more time to them, and when he died, in 1635, he had finished the *Temptation of St. Anthony*, a large composition from a plate engraved in Florence, five years previously. Of other works of the same kind, the *Massacre of the Innocents*, and the *Martyrdom of St. Sebastian*, are very fine; but generally his tendency to realism hampered him greatly, and his religious engravings are the least interesting part of his work.

Bibliography: Delaborde, *La Gravure*. Paris, 1882.—Elise Voiard, *Jacques Callot*. Paris, 1841.—Edouard Méaume, *Recherches sur la Vie et les Ouvrages de Jacques Callot*, 2 vols.; Nancy. 1860.—Marius Vachon, *Jacques Callot*. Paris, 1886.—Bouchot, *Jacques Callot*. Paris, 1889.—L. Alvin, *Le Séjour de Callot à Bruxelles*. Brussels, 1861.—Paul Plan, *Jacques Callot*. Brussels, 1910.—Edmond Bruwaert, *Jacques Callot*. Paris ("Les Grands Artistes").

**CALVAERT (Denis).**—Flemish painter, 1540-1619. He was born in Antwerp and went to Bologna about 1560, at the time when the Bolognese school was developing. There he became the master of Guido Reni, Albani and Domenichino, who admired his brilliant colour and fresh realism, whilst the study of Italian painting influenced his way of interpreting profound sentiments, passions and religious exaltation. These qualities are found in his *Saints Francis and Dominic*, in his seductive *Danae* (Lucca), in the *Annunciation* (Church of St. Dominic, Bologna), the *Souls in Purgatory* (Bologna), *Paradise* (Bologna), the *Martyrdom of St. Lawrence* and the *Virgin and St. Apollonia* (Reggio).

**CAMBIASO (Luca).**—Genoese painter, 1527-1585. One of the most important of the Genoese school. His precocity and fecundity are celebrated, for he painted important pictures at fifteen years of age, and he produced so much that it has been said that he had two right hands. He was chiefly influenced by Perino del Vago. He went to Florence, Rome, and other towns to study the masters, and he thus acquired a considerable skill. He painted Madonnas who recall beautiful, calm Genoese women and serious, noble Saints, in the midst of large masses of trees and lights (several pictures in the Cathedral of Genoa, the *Madonna* of the Adorna Palace, a *Madonna* in the Uffizi). The *Entombment* in Santa Maria di Carignano, in Genoa, is particularly fine in its energetic and expressive simplicity. In the *Presentation at the Temple*, in San Lorenzo, the painter aims at effects of richness and grandeur, after the manner of Veronese.

Perhaps he collaborated in the decorations of San Matteo, and, above all, he contributed to the famous decoration of the Escorial, where he painted a *Paradise* which was much admired.

**CAMBIO (Collegio del).**—See Perugia.

Angkor-Vat: North porch of the gallery of the first floor.

**CAMBODIA (Indo-China).**—Famous for grandiose ruins (Angkor-Vat, Angkor Thom, and Phnom Penh) of the former empire of Cambodia and for prehistoric ruins of an earlier Khmer civilisation. See Indo-China. See Pl. 35, Vol. I.

Angkor-Vat: North gallery, Deity in a chariot.

Lintel from the Temple of Bayon. (Musée Guimet.)

**CAMBRIDGE (England).**—University town with many colleges. *King's College* (15th century) possesses a magnificent chapel in the Perpendicular style, with a splendid fan-vault and decoration of Tudor roses. Most of its windows date from the early 16th century. *St. John's College* (1511) "may be taken as typical of the plan of Oxford and Cambridge Colleges, although they vary in size and layout." Library, chapel, hall and students' chambers are ranged round a square courtyard. The master's lodge and other buildings enclose adjacent courtyards.

See Pl. 50, Vol. I.

The Church of *St. Sepulchre* (the *Round Church*) is the oldest circular church in the country.

**CAMEO.**—A cameo is an agate (onyx, sardonyx or chalcedony) sculptured in relief, in which the colours, varied by the layers, and the vignettes produced by their transparency, are used to shade the various parts of the work. There are cameos in two, three and four layers. Others, much less precious and less artistic, are cut in shells. Many antique cameos have been re-used several times in the course of centuries either for jewels, or for the decoration of ciboria, chalices, and other sacred objects, for precious bindings, cups, comfit-boxes, ewers, mirrors, etc.

**CAMERON (Sir David Young).**—Scottish painter and etcher, born 1865. Elected member of the R. A., 1920. Has devoted himself specially to the interpretation of Scottish landscape, in his paintings no less than in his etchings.

Bibliography: F. Rinder, *D. Y. Cameron's Etchings*. Edinburgh, 1908.

**CAMPAGNA (Girolamo).**—Venetian sculptor, about 1550-1623. One of the best pupils of Jacopo Sansovino. His able works are often a little mannered, according to the taste of his age. His principal works are the *Pietà* of the Church of San Giuliano, in Venice, a beautiful figure of Christ supported by two angels; the four half-kneeling Evangelists who support the Saviour on a golden globe, in San Giorgio Maggiore; the St. Mark and St. Francis on the high-altar of the Redeemer; a *St. Sebastian*, in San Lorenzo; some statues in San Tommaso; a *Virgin*, in San Salvator; two huge "Atlantes" in the style of Zecca. He also made portrait statues.

Campagna (Girolamo): Pietà. (San Giuliano, Venice.)

**CAMPAGNOLA (Domenico).**—Italian painter and engraver. Probably born in Padua, about 1482, he still worked there in 1562. The date of his death is unknown. Almost nothing is known of his life: some make out he was a relative of Giulio Campagnola; others say that he was only a pupil of Giulio, whose name he kept, as was often the case. The only certainty is that he worked in Padua when Titian was painting in the Scuola del Carmine and in the Scuola del Santo (1511). On the back of a drawing, in the Crozat Collection, are these words, written by Domenico Campagnola: "In 1511, we were painting some frescoes in the Scuola del Carmine in company with Titian; and we entered the Scuola di Padova together on the 24th September of the same year." Another drawing bears a note in Titian's handwriting, telling us that Titian and Domenico worked together on the decoration of the façade of the Palazzo Cornaro, in Padua. Beyond these data, one is reduced to conjectures, and the obscurity which rests on the life and work of this artist encourages to hazardous attributions. He tried to imitate Titian in his drawings and engravings, and it is somewhat difficult to distinguish the work of the master from that of his imitator. Owing to this, charming motifs of mountain landscape have sometimes been attributed to Campagnola, and it is sometimes supposed that there may have been a collaboration between Titian, painting the figures of his pictures, and Campagnola, painting the sky and the landscapes—a free hypothesis for which there is no serious reason. Also, Campagnola's name has been brought up together with those of Titian, Giorgione and Sebastiano in the disputes over the attributions of pictures of the Venetian school of the beginning of the 16th century.

Campagnola's painted works are the frescoes of the Scuola della Santa representing the Miracle of the Ass, the Resurrection of the Drowned Child, and some frescoes and pictures which have disappeared, and some little water-colour landscapes on canvas, mentioned by Michiel.

Among his signed copper engravings are: *Christ Healing the Sick, Pentecost*, the *Virgin Surrounded by Saints*, the *Beheading of a Saint, Venus*, the *Shepherd and the Old Warrior*, the *Shepherd Musicians*, the *Battle*. His wood engravings include: the *Massacre of the Innocents, Landscape with St. Jerome, Landscape with Children, Landscape with Two Men and their Children, Landscape with the Fruiterer*.

— **(Giulio).**—Italian engraver, son of Girolamo Campagnola. Born in Padua about 1482. The date of his death is not known. It is sometimes said that he painted, but one cannot cite any picture by him. He was a poet, sculptor, musician and a very able engraver. He made copper engravings of pictures by Bellini, Dürer, Mantegna, Titian, and owing to his stippling technique was able to express Titian's and Giorgione's depth and softness of colour. We have about sixteen engravings by Campagnola. Among the best known is the *Rape of Ganymede*.

Bibliography: Tancred Borenius, *Four Early Italian Engravers*. London, 1923.

**CAMPANA (Pedro or Pierre de Kempeneer).**—Spanish painter, of Brussels origin, 1503-1580. He was brought up in the school of Michelangelo, and lived for a long time in Seville, where many of his pictures decorate the churches. His chief work is a *Descent from the Cross* (Seville Cathedral, 1549), painted for the Church of Santa Cruz, where, according to Cean Bermudez, it won the admiration of Murillo, in the following century. The people, who are lowering Christ's body from the Cross, recall strangely the bearded prophets of the Sistine, while in the group of holy women one again sees the attitudes of Michelangelo's grief-stricken Virgins. This majestic composition, with its strange energy and violent colour, deeply impressed the indigenous painters by its severe and scholarly character. The *Purification*, also in Seville Cathedral, is less robust and original.

**CAMPANILE.**—Bell tower, especially one built separate from a church. See Giotto; Florence; Pisa; etc.

**CAMPHUYSEN (Govaert).**—Dutch painter and engraver, 1624-1672. He is the best known of a family of Dutch painters, among which Raphaël Camphuysen (1598-1657) is distinguished as a good landscape painter. Govaert Camphuysen, his younger brother, was his pupil. He worked in Amsterdam and in Stockholm. He painted landscapes and animals, and may have influenced Paul Potter. His best known works are of stable interiors, and of shepherds with their flocks. They are to be seen in the Museums of Amsterdam, Cassel, Lille, Leningrad, Brussels, and Sweden.

**CAMPIN (Robert).**—Flemish painter of the 15th century. Born c. 1375; died April 1444. About 1406, he settled in Tournai, and in 1410 became town painter. Some critics identify him with "the Master of Flémalle." His last dated painting is from 1438, stylistically a very late work, probably his last. (See Flémalle.)

**CAMPO SANTO.**—See Pisa.

— See Bellotto.

**CANALETTO (Antonio Canale, called).**—Venetian painter, 1697-1768. Son of a theatrical decorator, he went to Rome where he studied perspective, and made drawings of ruins and landscapes. When he returned to Venice, he painted it unceasingly, and represented it more satisfactorily than anyone else had done. His pictures which are to be seen in nearly all the museums of Europe, have not the luminosity of modern paintings. But they show an endeavour to express effects of sunlight and delicate mists, which was quite new in his time, and, above all, a sincerity and love of nature for its own sake which puts him among the first great landscape painters. Among his best known works are: *The Imperial Ambassador presenting himself at the First Audience in the Doges' Palace*, in the Sormani Collection, Milan; and *The Scuola di San Rocco*, in the National Gallery. He worked in England between 1746 and 1755.

Bibliography: A. Moureau, *Antonio Canale, dit Canaletto*. Paris, 1894.—V. Uzanne, *Les Canaletto*. Paris. H. Finberg, in the Warpole Society's ninth annual volume, 1921.

**CANDIA.**—See Crete.

**CANDIDO (Pietro).**—Florentine sculptor of the 16th century. From his real name Pieter de Witte, we gather that he was of Flemish origin. He studied in Italy, and went to Munich where he was the head of the artistic production of Bavaria. He made the celebrated tomb of Louis I of Bavaria (Munich, Frauenkirche), and the statues and fountains of the Residenz (Munich).

Bibliography: Steinbart, K., *Die Niederländ. Hofmaler der bayrischen Herzöge*. Marburger Jahrbuch, 1928.

**CANO (Alonso).**—Spanish painter and sculptor. Granada, 1601-1667. His father, "asemblador" or maker of altar-pieces, first taught him his trade, and then sent him to Seville, where he entered the studio of Don Juan Martinez Montañes, a sculptor of high repute. He also followed the courses of the Academy of Painting which Don Francesco Pacheco had opened; it was there that he made the acquaintance of Velázquez, of whom he became the intimate friend. To finish his artistic education, Alonso

Cano (Alonso): St. Bruno. (Carthusian convent, Granada.)

Cano also worked a great deal from the antique statues in the Casa de Pilatos. From this period date the two altar-pieces of St. Paul (Seville) which it is said he designed, carved, gilded and painted all by himself. He was then scarcely 26 years old. Another early work is an *Immaculate Conception* placed on the door of the convent of this name, a second belongs to the parish of San Andrès, and some less important statues. The parish church of Lebrija then commissioned him to make an altar-piece, the paintings of which are by the Fleming, Pablo Legote, and for which Cano made a statue of the Virgin and Child. In these early works, the young artist shows a keen feeling for classical beauty in his studies from the antique. Naturally delicate in his carving, with very noble religious feeling, graceful in his representations of the Virgin and Saints, more virile in his figures of Christ and of ascetic Saints, Cano's painting has distinguished qualities, such as pure, firm drawing but is much less vigorous in expression than are his sculptured works. His colour, entirely influenced by Flanders and Venice, sometimes lacks accent. A. L. Mayer says that, as a painter, Cano was, in spite of his ability, only a second-rate talent, a versatile man, but not a genius.

It is surprising, to contrast the Italianised and restrained paintings of Cano with the embittered and passionate character which all his biographers give him. Coming to Madrid 1637, following a quarrel with the painter Llano y Valdés, in the course of which the latter was seriously wounded, Cano found a warm friend in Velázquez. He gave him work at the palace, got him nominated painter to the Royal Household, and chosen to teach drawing to the heir to the throne, the Infante Don Balthazar Carlos. During this, his first residence at Court which extended from 1637 to 1644, Cano produced numerous paintings.

It is said, without much foundation, that Alonso Cano was obliged to leave Madrid in 1644 on the charge of having killed his wife, and was forced to seek a refuge in the monastery of Porta-Coeli near Valencia, where he left numerous works such as those for that monastery as well as for the churches of San Juan de Ribera and San Francisco of Valencia.

In 1648 we see him again at Madrid; in that year he executed a triumphal arch for the celebration of the entry of Queen Marianne. This monument, influenced by Borromini, showed many innovations; because of his treatment of the entire problem, Cano is sometimes called the forerunner of the baroque architect Churriguera.

In 1652 he requested a position as Canon of Granada Cathedral, which was quickly granted, on condition that the artist take orders in the course of the year. Don Alonso Cano did not hurry in the least to fulfil his agreement, and the chapter deprived him of his prebend (1656). But, thanks to the bishop of Salamanca, who conferred minor orders on him, these difficulties were smoothed away. After coming into possession of his benefice (1658), Cano enjoyed it peacefully until his death. The oeuvre of Alonso Cano is considerable. There are very fine examples in the museums of Berlin, Munich, Dresden and in the Hermitage. The Spanish gallery, formed by Louis Philippe, has two especially remarkable pictures by this master, the *Ass of Balaam*, and the *Virgin and Child*. There are also numerous works of his in Spain; we only cite the *Purisima Concepción* in the Cathedral of Granada, a *Madonna and Child* at Seville Cathedral, the *Madonna of the Rosary* at Malaga, and a painting representing two Visigothic Kings at the Prado Museum, which he executed, during his first sojourn at the capital, for the sala de comedias of the Royal Castle.

Alonso Cano preferred his statues to his pictures. Certainly the painter was inferior to the sculptor. His best sculptures are in wood, generally painted. Among the most important are: in Seville, apart from the works already specified, the statues of Saint Theresa and St. Anne, in the College of St. Alberto; in Madrid, a *Crucifixion* for the Benedictines of Montserrat; in Valencia, another *Crucifixion* for the altar of the Socos; in Malaga, an *Immaculate Conception* for the Church of the Incarnation. The *St. Bruno* (half life size) in the Chartreuse of Granada enjoyed a well deserved reputation in Spain. The *Soledad* (moral solitude, deprivation of affection) of Santa Ana, in Granada, reproduced the famous *Virgin*, which Cano painted for the Cathedral under this name, in relief.

Noteworthy are his statues of the Holy Virgin and the bust of Adam on the triumphal arch of the Capilla Mayor of Granada Cathedral. The same cathedral possesses also a bust of St. Paul, the *Virgin with a Rosary*, gracefully modelled, a *St. Bruno*, different from that of the Chartreuse, of a moving asceticism. The Church of San Juan de Dios has a fine *Head of St. John the Baptist*. In Murcia, in the Church of St. Nicholas, is a little *St. Anthony* which might be thought his masterpiece, if one did not know his famous *St. Francis of Assisi*, which is now in a private collection in Paris. Nothing is so impressive or expresses Spanish mysticism better than this ascetic figure, clad in a miserable, torn garment, inspired with divine love. This figure is certainly previous to the year 1662-1663, when Pedro de Mena carved his *St. Francis of Assisi*, which was long attributed to Cano, for the Cathedral of Toledo.

The teaching of this master, who had numerous pupils, both sculptors and painters, created in Granada an artistic centre which had a certain activity for half a century. In sculpture, his best pupils were Pedro de Mena and José de Mora; and, in painting, Alonso de Mesa, Miguel Geronimo Cieza, Sebastian de Herrera Barnuevo, Pedro Atanasio Bocanegra, Ambrosio Martinez, Sebastian Gomez, and Juan Nino de Guevara.

See Pl. 23, Vol. II.

BIBLIOGRAPHY: P. Lefort, *La sculpture espagnole*. Paris, 1901.—*Enciclopedia universal ilustrada europeo-americana*. Barcelona, 1905-30; vol. xi art. *Cano (Alonso)*.—*Thieme Becker*, 1911, vol. V, art; *Alonso Cano*, by M. v. Boehm.—O. Schubert, *Geschichte des Barock in Spanien*, 1908.—*Jahrbuch der kgl. preuss. Kunstsammlungen* XXX, Beiheft, XXXI; *Alonso Cano und die Kunst von Granada*, by A. L. Mayer.—A. L. Mayer, *Geschichte der spanischen Malerei*, 1922.

**CANOVA (Antonio).**—Italian sculptor, 1757-1822. Born in Possagno, near Treviso, he arrived in Rome in 1779. He studied Raphael, Mengs, Winkelmann, and wished to return to the simplicity of classical art. He remodelled Italian sculpture, his cold white marbles showing a reaction against the Baroque style. His group of *Theseus and the Minotaur* made his name, and he became the chosen artist of popes and princes, for whom he made several masterpieces, always perfect, pure, frigid. His nude figures, which emulate the *Apollo Belvedere*, have a snow-like beauty which does not belong to nature. His naked *Napoleon*, in the Court of the Brera Palace, Milan, looks like a powerful circus athlete. He was more successful in the *Venus and Adonis* (1795, for the Marquis Salsa Berio of Naples), or in the charming *Paulina Borghese as Venus*, half-reclining and half-nude (Villa Borghese, 1805), or even in the statue of the Emperor's mother, Madame Letitia, as a seated Agrippina.

CANOVA, BY GIRODET. (Louvre.)

CANOVA: PAULINE BORGHESE. (Villa Borghese, Rome.)

His funeral monuments are rigid and serious, and contrast with the warm movement of the Baroque tombs like a block of ice (tomb of Pope Leo XII, the grave of the Stuarts, or the kneeling figure of Pope Pius VI, in St. Peter's).

He died in Venice.

BIBLIOGRAPHY: A. d'Este, *Memorie di Antonio Canova*. Florence, 1864.—Cicognara, *Storia della Scultura*.

**CANTARINI (Simone).**—Called Simone da Pesaro, or Il Pesarese. Painter and engraver. Born in Pesaro; died in Venice (1612-1648).

He was an imitator of Guido Reni, with whom he worked in Bologna. Afterwards he went to study Raphael in Rome; and then travelled in the service of the Duke of Mantua.

His chief pictures are in the Museums of Bologna, Dresden, Milan, Madrid, Paris, Munich, etc.

**CANTERBURY (England).**—*Cathedral.*—"The choir, of great interest, was erected by William of Sens, on the model of Sens Cathedral, after the destruction of Anselm's Norman choir (1170). Work carried on under William the Englishman. Original Norman work of singular interest." At the extreme east is a curious chapel known as "Becket's Crown." There are extensive crypts, and wide transepts. The nave and central tower are in the Perpendicular style; and there are Perpendicular cloisters on the north. The *Church of St. Martin* is very ancient. Roman bricks are built into the walls.

See Pl. 49, Vol. I.

**CAPELLE (Jan van de).**—Dutch painter (1624-1679). A friend of Rembrandt. He painted fine seascapes. Outstanding representative of the new coloristic trend in Dutch painting after the middle of the 17th century. Paintings in London, Glasgow, Amsterdam, Antwerp, Berlin, Stockholm.

**CAPITAL.**—The upper part of the column which includes the whole of the ornament between the shaft and the architrave or the fall of the arch. It can be very simple and reduced to the abacus, the slab on which falls the weight, or very ornate with mouldings and decorations of geometric patterns, plants, animals and figures. The oldest capitals are those of Egypt and the East. In Egypt one finds, apart from the simple abacus, the bell-shaped capital, decorated with various motifs; the lotus-shaped capital, having the form of the bud of the lotus flower; and the capital with the head of Hathor. Certain of these Egyptian capitals go back to the 13th century before Christ.

The Assyrian and Phœnician capitals resemble those which were to appear later in Greece. They already had the Doric echinus (or neck-moulding), and the Ionic volute, as can be seen in the bas-reliefs of the Palace of Sagon (8th century before Christ).

Persian art produced very curious capitals, often several metres in height. Those of the Palace of the Achæmenides at Persepolis (6th century B.C.) are decorated at the top with crouching bulls whose heads support the architrave.

The Greeks carved the most perfect capitals of ancient times. The form of these capitals distinguishes the Greek orders.

The impost capital was much used in Santa Sophia. The impost is a kind of curtailed and inverted pyramid, of which the base is uppermost, and which is placed between the capital and the spring of the vault. But often the impost is transformed in such a way as to form the whole column; the carvings on these impost capitals have only slight depth.

It is impossible to enumerate here the many types of Romanesque and Gothic capitals. According to the region, and the stone employed, they are more or less sculptured. Antique elements still figure there, but to this are added decorations of geometric ornaments, plants, animals, and figures representing scenes taken from the Old and New Testaments.

The Mussulmans, to whom the representation of live beings is forbidden, could only decorate their capitals with geometric ornaments. The two types which they generally used are composed, one of little pointed niches, arranged in corbels one above the other, and the other of a basket of leaves placed under the abacus and above the mouldings.

See Byzantine Art (First Period: Architecture).

The Renaissance naturally reverted to the use of the ancient capital, and imitated its most varied forms, adding various details according to the artist's fancy. Since then sculptors have always made use of the classical or mediæval types, only varying the decoration or combining, more or less successfully, motifs suggested by geometry, botany, the human figure or the animal kingdom.

BIBLIOGRAPHY: Viollet-le-Duc, *Dictionnaire de l'Architecture française*. Paris, 1867.—Chipiez, *Histoire critique des ordres Grecs*. Paris, 1876.—*Dictionnaire des antiquités grecques et romaines*.

**CAPORALI (Bartolommeo).**—Umbrian painter, c. 1420- c. 1505. Collaborator of Bonfigli, pupil of Benozzo Gozzoli, influenced by Umbrian painters.

**CAPPADOCIA (Frescoes of).**—(Asia Minor). Recently discovered in the ruins of monastic establishments. Mortuary chapels and underground churches have been discovered, the interior walls of which were entirely covered with mural paintings. Among the groups of Churches of Gueureine and Soghanli, there are hundreds which are fairly well preserved. The oldest doubtless belong to the 8th or 9th century, and are painted directly on the rock; these are simple ornamental motifs. Most belong to the 10th and 11th centuries, and are painted on a coating of plaster. The greater part of these frescoes are of a popular character, painted by copyists. They represent, in fact, all the known models of Christian iconography. There is not much variety in colour; but the works have great interest in being "almost the only specimens of Byzantine painting in the Macedonian period, and like pale, distant reflections, of what was a great art." We only mention the subjects of the best-preserved—the gospel cycle, the feasts of the church, episodes in the life of Christ, preceded by scenes from the life of the Virgin. The arcades are covered with long processions of saints. The founders of the church are often represented offering their work to Christ; drawn like true portraits, these figures are particularly interesting owing to their facial expressions and details of costume. Among the Bible scenes, subjects from the Apocrypha have a special place. As for the order, this follows the principles of the 6th century. The frescoes of the three chapels in the form of a Greek cross of Gueureine, are the most remarkable of the whole Cappadocian group. They doubtless belong to the 10th or to the beginning of the 11th century, and show an art superior to that of all the other mural paintings discovered there up to the present. The colour is attractive, and the shades numerous; the figures of prophets, especially that of Daniel, are living and natural; the draperies are harmonious, and the attitudes and faces (of pure Oriental type) have no longer the archaic and conventional character which is general in Cappadocia.

BIBLIOGRAPHY: G. de Jerphanion, *Une nouvelle province de l'art byzantin; les églises rupestres de Cappadocie*. Paris, 1925.

**CARADOSSO.** — Cristoforo Foppa, called Caradosso, goldsmith and sculptor, of Lombardy and Rome. Born about 1452 in Brianza; died in 1527. One of the most famous medallists of his day. The influence of Rome (where he stayed a long time at the Papal Court) drew him from the Lombard style, and gave him a grandeur and at the same time a freshness almost Florentine. His frieze for the baptismal Chapel of San Satiro in Milan—a garland of playing children, interrupted with medallions containing busts—is at once decorative and realistic. Owing to their resemblance to this work, and to a coffer in the Museo Nazionale, Florence, the following might also be attributed to him: two bronze doors of the reliquary of San Pietro in Vincoli, with the arms of Sixtus IV and of Giulio della Rovere, and some scenes from the life of St. Peter (1477).

**CARAGLIO (Giovanni Jacopo).**—Italian engraver, born in Verona at the beginning of the 16th century; died in Parma about 1570. He went to Rome to study under Marc-Antonio; and, in 1526, he engraved the *Gods of Mythology*, after Rosso, in eight plates. Then, after Rosso and Perino del Vaga, the *Loves of the Gods*, also in eight plates. He also left behind a *Holy Family* and a *Combat of a Roman with a Barbarian*, after Raphael, and a great many varied engravings. Caraglio was one of Marc-Antonio's best pupils, and some have even attempted to attribute some of his works to his master.

BIBLIOGRAPHY: Bartsch, *Le Peintre-Graveur*, Vol. XV.—H. Delaborde. *Marc-Antoine*. Paris, 1888.

**CARAVAGGIO (Michelangelo Amerighi da).**—Painter of the Roman school. Born in Caravaggio, near Milan, 1569-1609. He aimed at realism, and violent naturalism, in reaction against the pompous and wearisome style of the "Mannerists" which then flourished and made such artists as the Cavaliere d'Arpino and Federigo Zuccaro successful. His passionate, fantastic nature aimed at tragic, gloomy effects, and he spent his life combating the cold Bolognese school.

Son of a mason, he went to Milan to learn painting, but we do not know who was his master. Next, in Venice, he studied Giorgione, Titian and Veronese. Then he went to Rome where Michelangelo's *Pietà* won his greatest admiration. There he experienced great poverty, but he also began to be successful in his large pictures of sacred sub-

Caravaggio.

jects. He painted the *Flight into Egypt* and the *Magdalen* of the Doria Gallery. In 1591, he finished the decoration of the Contarelli Chapel in the French Church of St. Louis, where he painted *St. Matthew Writing* (altar picture), *Christ calling St. Matthew*, and the *Martyrdom of St. Matthew*. He placed his religious scenes in a realistic setting, and was not afraid of giving them a popular character which sometimes became vulgar. Raphael, in his decoration of the Loggia of the Vatican, had suggested this style, which is very different from the moving and decorative compositions of the Quattrocento, but he retained a moderation and beauty which Caravaggio lost in pushing naturalism to the extreme and painting violent effects.

However, Caravaggio loved the common people, and experiments. His rough, energetic nature made him flee from worldly considerations, and even from the tyranny of cultured people. He enjoyed painting scenes of everyday life and chose such subjects as fortune-tellers, card-players, and strolling musicians.

He attempted new and extraordinary lighting effects, by hanging his lamps in unexpected places, and thus obtaining contrasts between deep shadows and sharp lights. And so he arrived at those gloomy, intense effects which are his chief characteristic. The *Death of the Virgin*, in the Louvre, is one of many scenes the tragedy of which he emphasizes by his use of light and shade.

The *Entombment* (Vatican) is one of his best works (about 1598).

Caravaggio's life was crowded with passionate episodes. He had adventures of all kinds: duels, imprisonments, flights, etc. His life ended in misery, like that of Annibale Carracci. Both had striven against the "Mannerists." But he whose nervous paint brush had represented the most realistic, sometimes even ugly, scenes, and who prepared the way for the terrible energy of Ribera, had a more tragic death. He died in the fierce sunshine of the open campagna. He was in Naples, where he had gone to obtain pardon after escaping from prison. The ship which he should have taken put to sea without him, with all his possessions on board. Stripped of everything, he endeavoured to return to Rome on foot, in the burning heat of a brilliant summer. Arriving at Porto Ercole, he fell, and never rose again.

Bibliography: Gabriel Rouchès, *La Peinture bolonaise à la fin du XVIe siècle*. Alcan, 1913.

**CARCASSONNE.**—The town is divided into two parts: the new town, on one of the banks of the Aude, without artistic interest; and the "cité," the old, mediæval town which rears its towers, ramparts and buildings on an isolated hill. Owing to its situation, which commands the gap between the Pyrenees and the Cevennes, Carcassonne had to be prepared to resist numerous attacks. In the 5th century, the Romans began the construction of this magnificent fortified wall which surrounds the whole town and which Viollet-le-Duc restored in 1850, at the moment when the government was thinking of its demolition. After the Romans, the Visigoths continued the work. Then from the 11th to the 17th century, the ramparts underwent enlargements and modifications of such a kind that one can there study the different phases of military architecture over a period of nearly ten centuries.

Carcassonne: View from the east.

Carcassonne: Towers of the Visigoths and of the Inquisition.

The ramparts are composed of two walls, separated by a space of from 7 to 8 metres wide. The exterior wall measures 1500 metres; it is composed of a series of advance works, with crenellated walls, protected by a wide ditch. The interior wall is enormous, measuring 1100 metres, and fortified by numerous towers (52 for the two walls), and the most ingenious contrivances to resist sieges. In the Middle Ages, the city was impregnable. Several of the towers contain wells, ovens, prisons. No other European town from this period possesses a system of defense so formidable and so complete.

From Roman times, scarcely more remains than the bases of towers, which were afterwards used by the Visigoths and architects of the 13th century. The Visigoths built the Tower of Samson, on a square base, and the upper parts of the Tour du Moulin-du-Connétable, of the Tour du Moulin-d'Avar, of the Tour de la Chapelle (on a Roman base), the Tour de St. Laurent, and the Tour de St. Serrin (Roman base; masonry renewed in 13th century). Most of the other towers date from the 13th century, from the period of Philippe le Hardi and St. Louis. The tower of the Inquisition contains a prison (13th century); the tower of St. Nazaire (13th century) contains an oven and a well—this tower alone would have been able to withstand a siege. Two towers with vaulted compartments, served as the magazine for the garrison. The Tour du Trésor, built by Philippe le Hardi, has walls 4 metres thick, and is 21 metres high.

Inside these ramparts is the old town. The finest buildings are: the Château Comtal, a vast building, defended with wide moats and great round towers (11th to 17th century); and the Church of St. Nazaire, with an old Romanesque, barrel-vaulted nave, of which the oldest parts date perhaps from the end of the 8th century. The transept and choir are 13th century; the tower and doorway are Romanesque.

See Pls. 1, 51, Vol. I.

**CARIANI (Giovanni Busi, called).**—Painter of the Venetian school (1480?-1550?), born in Fulpiano in the neighbourhood of Bergamo, he worked chiefly in Venice. A follower of Giovanni Bellini and of Palma Vecchio, he also imitated Giorgione's style. He is most fully represented at Milan and Bergamo, although other paintings by him are widely scattered.

**CARMONTELLE.**—French draughtsman, 1717-1806. Author of a collection of pencil drawings, with washes of colour in distemper. There are about seven hundred portraits by him, now scattered in various collections.

Bibliography: A. Portalis, *Les Dessinateurs d'illustrations au XVIIIe siècle*.

**CARNAVALET (Hôtel).**—See Paris.

**CAROLUS-DURAN.**—French painter (Lille, 1837-1917). At the age of eight, he entered the Academy of Painting of his native town. When he was fifteen he left, having already worked hard and learned a great deal in order to go to Paris (1853), to draw at the Swiss Academy, to study the masters in the Louvre, and to paint in his student's room. Returning to Lille in 1858, he obtained a new pension from his department, which gave him the right to spend several years in Rome. There he studied the old masters, and then shut himself up for six months in the Convent of St. Francis, at Subiacco. He there painted the *Evening Prayer*, which drew attention to him at the Salon of 1865. He returned to Paris in 1866, and won great success at the Salon with *The Assassinated* (Lille Museum) a work which is remarkable for its qualities of energy, colour, and setting, which shows the influence of Courbet. But the young artist then went to study Velázquez in Spain, and his admiration for the master of the Prado moderated his first passion, and softened the tones of his palette. In 1869, Carolus-Duran painted two pieces, at once brilliant and reserved: the *Lady with the Glove* (Luxembourg Gallery), and *Madame Feydeau* (Lille Museum), portraits entirely modern in feeling, which stand high among the works of the fashionable artists of that day, which are generally insipid, laboured and commonplace. After the war of 1870—in which he played his part—he continued to win successes at the Salon: the *Seaside* (1873), *Portrait of Madame Criozette on Horseback*, *Emile de Girardin* (1875, Lille Museum), *Comtesse de Vandal* (1879), *Madame de Pourtalès*.

Thenceforth Carolus-Duran became a favourite portrait painter. He had an alert, clever way of posing a head in full light, against a red plush background. His art became free from its first influences and very personal and fresh. But his attempts at large compositions were a mistake. He never recaptured the vigour and drama of *The Assassinated*. He even lost his qualities of harmonious colour and good composition in pictures such as the ceiling in the Louvre, the *Glory of Marie de Medicis* (1878) and the *Triumph of Bacchus* (1889). But every time he turned to portraiture, or to the dimensions of a portrait, his freshness and skill reappeared: the *Old Lithograph* (1903), the *Spanish Sponge Merchant* (1904). He painted some distinguished landscapes. President of the Société Nationale des Beaux-Arts, and for several years Director of the French Academy in Rome, Carolus-Duran was one of those portraitists who, like Rubens and Van Dyck, were men of action and of affairs as well as masters of their art.

**CAROTO (Giovanni Francesco).**—Veronese painter, c. 1480-1546. A pupil of Liberale. He worked in Mantegna's studio. He was an untiring worker, fairly able, but lacking in originality. Having developed within the Veronese school, he turned to the more supple art of Raphael. He has been nicknamed the Proteus of painters. Among his best works are: the frescoes of St. Euphemia, the frescoes of Santa Maria in Organo, and the *Virgin in Glory*, in San Fermo (all in Verona). He worked in partnership with his brother Giovanni, whose work is difficult to distinguish from his.

Bibliography: Crowe and Cavalcaselle, *History of Painting in North Italy*.

**CARPACCIO (Benedetto).**—Venetian painter of the beginning of the 16th century. Son of Vittorio Carpaccio, whom he imitated. He emigrated to Istria, about 1545. There are, by him, a *Coronation of* *the Virgin*, dated 1537, and several other pictures in Capodistria.

— **(Pietro).**—Venetian painter of the beginning of the 16th century. Son of Vittorio Carpaccio. No picture can be attributed to him with certainty.

— **(Vittore) or Vittorio Scarpaza.** —Venetian painter of the end of the 15th and beginning of the 16th

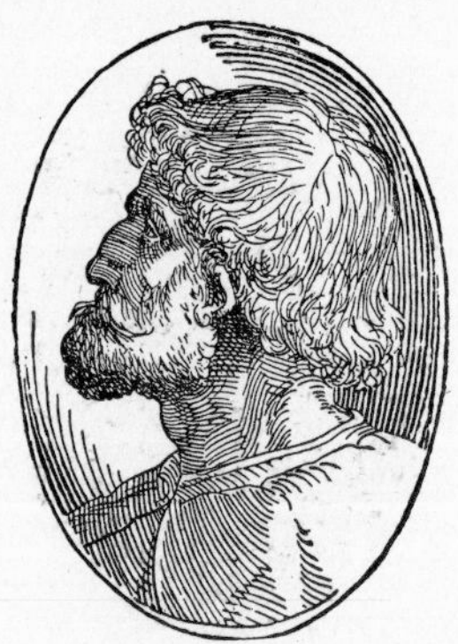

CARPACCIO.

century, famous for the richness and fancy with which he represented Venetian life. He was born in Venice about 1455. His family originated from the Island of Mazzorbo, and not from Istria, as it is often said.

In spite of the progressive period in which he lived and all the lessons which he received, Carpaccio was, like his master Lazzaro Bastiano, not very scientific in dealing with forms in perspective, but he had a lively feeling for beauty of colour.

It has been supposed that Carpaccio went to the East, since many of his works have Oriental settings, exotic buildings, and Turkish costumes. But so long a voyage must have been for him, as for many others, an impossible dream. He did not have the opportunity of Gentile Bellini, who was invited to Constantinople by Mahomet II (1459), and he could only have been inspired by the studies which the latter brought back. Also he must have copied the drawings of Renwich which illustrated the work of Breydenbach, *Peregrinatio in Terram Sanctam*, which was printed in Mayence in 1486. In a drawing in the British Museum, a landscape sketch for the Departure of the Betrothed, the so-called Port of Ancona is the Port of Rhodes, copied in the drawing of Renwich, as Mr. Sidney Colvin noticed. If one follows the comparison, one finds other details throughout Carpaccio's work, coming from the same source: The Tower of Candia, the Temple of Jerusalem, the Tower of the Church of the Holy Sepulchre, the pyramids of Giseh, Eastern women, Saracens, palm-trees, etc. . . . But the East so inspired Carpaccio that, from cold, indistinct engravings, he created animated scenes of Venetian life.

Little is known of Vittorio Carpaccio's life, beyond what can be gathered from his works. He is mentioned in documents in 1472, 1486, and as no longer living in 1526. In 1501, he was everywhere in demand to decorate palaces, scuole, chapels, and in 1507 he worked in the Council Hall of the Doge's Palace with Gentile Bellini, where he painted the great picture of Pope Alexander III, celebrating Mass in St. Mark's, which was unfortunately destroyed by fire in 1677. We also know that in 1501 he was invited to judge Giorgione at the Fondaco dei Tedeschi.

Carpaccio is above all celebrated for the decorations of the scuole. These were religious brotherhoods (under the patronage of various saints) which had altars in the churches, but also built reunion halls which were richly decorated. There it was that Gentile Bellini and Carpaccio found a wonderful opportunity to exercise their skill in oil painting, which they had admired in Northern artists.

Carpaccio began by the decoration of the Scuola di Sant'Orsola (1490-1515). He there represented the History of St. Ursula, which was a pretext for rich compositions showing ambassadors, princes, members of the Loredan family, patrons and benefactors of the Scuola, and crowds of people and even animals coming and going on the sunny piazzi, among rich buildings, and splendid ships. Perhaps it was inspired from the remains of frescoes by Tommaso da Modena, in Santa Margherita Treviso (now in the museum). Carpaccio's scenes, which now adorn a room of the Accademia of Venice, represent: the Christian King Maurus receiving the ambassadors of the pagan King Colon, who come to ask the hand of his daughter, Ursula, and the reflections of father and daughter; the reply of King Maurus who says that Ursula wishes first to make a pilgrimage to Rome with her eleven thousand maidens; the return of the ambassadors to King Colon; the departure of the pagan prince who also wishes to make the pilgrimage, and his meeting with Ursula; the dream of St. Ursula; the meeting in Rome of the betrothed and Pope Ciriaco; the arrival at Cologne; the martyrdom, burial, and apotheosis of the Saint.

In 1502, the Scuola di San Giorgio degli Schiavoni gave him a commission, and he painted: *St. Jerome and the Lion, St. Jerome's Study;* the *Death of St. Jerome*; *St. George and the Dragon* (there is a copy of this fine work in San Giorgio Maggiore, 1516); the *Triumph of St. George*; *St. George Baptising the Gentiles, with King Aia and his court;* the *Miracle of St. Tryphon*; and, finally, to the left and right of the altar, the *Calling of St. Matthew*, and *Christ in the Garden of Olives.* The order of the pictures has been changed, but, except for that, they can be admired in their own place.

In the Scuola degli Albanesi, he in 1504, began a series of scenes from the Life of the Virgin, which is now scattered: the *Birth of Mary* (in the Lochis Gallery, of the Academy of Bergamo), the *Presentation in the Temple* (for which there are drawings in the Library of Windsor, and in the Uffizi), the *Marriage of the Virgin* (Brera, Milan); the *Annunciation* and the *Death of Mary* (Venice—another *Death of the Virgin* in Ferrara Museum, is later), and the *Visitation* (Venice).

For the Scuola di San Stefano, he painted an altarpiece, with St. Stephen in the middle, and St. Augustine and St. Anthony of Padua, or St. Nicholas of Tolentino, on each side, and five large decorations: the *Consecration of Seven Deacons* (1511, now in the Berlin Museum), the *Preaching of St. Stephen* (1520?, now in the Louvre), the *Dispute Among the Doctors* (1514, in the Brera), and the *Stoning of St. Stephen* (1515, now in the Gallery of Stüttgart). This last, very brownish, is not as good as the others.

The Scuola of San Giovanni Evangelista was the richest and most important of the scuole and contained a precious relic of the Holy Cross (see Gentile Bellini). There Carpaccio painted (about 1494) the Patriarch of Grado, Francesco Quirini, freeing a man possessed with a devil, by means of the reliquary.

The Christ with the Instruments of the Passion, painted for San Pietro Martiro, Udine (1496), is very fine. The thin, suffering body reveals a sense of plastic beauty which recalls certain suffering, tender figures of Giovanni Bellini, as these recall, also, the stiff corpse, stretched out peacefully in the *Entombment* of the Berlin Museum.

In 1510, Carpaccio painted an altarpiece for San Giobbio, Venice, which represents the presentation of Jesus to St. Simeon. It is now in the Accademia and is one of his best known pictures. The charming little angel musicians were repeated endlessly by copyists.

We have as well a great many drawings by Carpaccio, especially in the Uffizi: a Donor, an *Adoration of the Magi*, a *Circumcision*, a *Presentation of the Virgin at the Temple*. In the Louvre and in Dresden are drawings of the Madonna.

Towards the end of his life, his style became drier and his colours more crude. He lost that diffused golden light which added charm to the variety of his compositions. He received fewer and fewer commissions in Venice, for his glory was eclipsed by Giorgione and Titian. But the walls of the scuole keep, for the pleasure of future generations, pictures of the Venice of former days, more rich and living than those of Gentile Bellini.

See Pl. 14, Vol. II.

BIBLIOGRAPHY: G. Ludwig and Pompeo Molmenti, *Vittorio Carpaccio*. London, 1901.—P. G. Molmenti, *The Life and Works of Vittorio Carpaccio*. 1907.—G. Fiocco, *Carpaccio*. 1931.

**CARPATHIUS (Victor).**—See Michele da Verona.

**CARPEAUX (Jean Baptiste).**—French sculptor. Born: Valenciennes,

CARPEAUX: MODEL OF FLORA. (Louvre.)

1827; died: Courbevoie, 1875. Son of a poor mason of Valenciennes, Carpeaux began his career under difficulties, but from his youth he showed a pride which faced obstacles, and an obstinacy which difficulties only stimulated. He went to Paris with his family, and at the age of fifteen entered the Petite École in the Rue de l'École de Médecine, of whom Belloc was the head, and later Lecoq de Boisbaudran. There, he was the comrade of the future artists, Charles Garnier, the architect, and the sculptors, Chapu and Carrier-Belleuse. Charles Garnier wrote later: "Carpeaux was then a swaggering youth, rather undisciplined but solid at his work." He tried to earn his bread at the same time as he was studying drawing, and was employed as a porter at the Halles. Soon he came to modelling statuettes, and selling little models. A group of Two Goats brought him 15 francs. For two vases he was paid 15 francs and two eight pound loaves. He ended by working for a founder at the rate of two francs a day. . . . In 1844, he was received at the École des Beaux-Arts, and in 1845, he obtained a pension of 600 francs from the "département du Nord."

The following year he went to ask the advice of Rude, the sculptor of the *Marseillaise*, on the Arc de Triomphe de l'Etoile. For eight months, Carpeaux attended the master's Studio, until Rude (who knew himself to stand in a bad light with the Institute because of his independence) urged him to choose a more influential teacher, and one more capable of helping him to win the Prix de Rome. The young artist applied to Duret, member of the Institute. He won medals in the "concours de l'École," and several times entered for the Rome competition: in 1848, 1849, 1850, 1851. In 1852, he won the second prize. The same year, he sent a bas-relief to the Salon—the *Muses of the Countryside Inspiring a Poet*, which he signed with a pseudonym, Ernest Blangy. It was accepted. In 1853, he again entered, without result; but in 1854, his efforts were crowned with success and he received the Grand Prix with *Hector Imploring the Gods in Favour of his Son Astyanax.* The work is rather insignificant. Nevertheless in Rome, Carpeaux began to reveal himself. He lived in the streets and museums, inspired equally by the present and the past. His independence and eccentricity at once drew upon him the thunder of the Administration. The director of the Villa Medici, the painter Schnetz, complained of him incessantly. "Since he came here he has done nothing like anyone else." He wanted to make an *Ugolino with his Children*, an unclassical subject, and exceeding the proportions allowed. Schnetz cited the regulations. Carpeaux became infuriated, went to Paris, saw the minister, showed him a drawing of his scheme, passionate and full of promise, obtained from him authority to execute the *Ugolino* and even to remain in Rome beyond the usual limit. The finished work was unanimously praised. The princess Borghese, descendant of the princess Peschiera, friend of Michelangelo, fainted in the studio at the sight of the Ugolino, saying to the young master: "After three centuries, the genius of Michelangelo is resting on you."

On his return to Paris, Carpeaux was invited to the court of Napoleon III and to the receptions of Compiègne. He was given a studio in the Orangery of the Tuileries, gave lessons in drawing and modelling to the Prince Imperial, executed the bust of the Empress Eugénie and the statue of the Prince Imperial with his dog, Nero. Official commissions were added to these works. He was asked for a bas-relief for the pavilion of the Tuileries Palace (*Flora*), and a group destined for the façade of the Opera House (*The Dance*). The *Flora* was much admired, and won the artist the cross of Chevalier of the Legion of Honour (1866), but *The Dance* was not at first understood. The most indulgent called it "bad taste." Others were scandalised, and cried out that it was drunken and bacchanalian.

The public affected alarm, and talked of "an outrage to modesty," and on the night of the 27th or 28th August 1869, a bottle of ink was thrown at the group, which was entirely splashed. Its removal was discussed. The sculptor Gunery even received the commission to make another to replace it. However, *The Dance* was not moved. Some years later, there was still more talk of removing it, but this time to preserve it from inclemencies of the weather. After throwing ink at it, the Parisians wanted to protect it from dust and rain.

In April 1869, some months after this scandal, Carpeaux married the daughter of the General, Vicomte de Montfort. He had three children: Charles Carpeaux, who died at Saïgon, in 1904; Louis Carpeaux, a captain in the Colonial Army; and Madame Clement-Carpeaux, a sculptress. Meantime, the war of 1870 broke out. The artist remained in Paris during the siege of the capital, observing and drawing, while his wife cared for the wounded. When, after the siege, the Commune broke out, the young family went to England.

On this return, Carpeaux made one of his most remarkable works, the Fountain of the Luxembourg, which was exhibited at the Salon of 1872 under the title of *The Four Corners of the Earth Supporting the Globe*. In spite of its quality, this group was refused by the city of Paris. Carpeaux meant the figures to be in marble and the globe in gilt bronze. Without listening to him, the group was cast entirely in bronze. The artist was ignored when he asked that the figures should be patined according to racial colour. Then the master's brilliant career was suddenly arrested by illness.

If he had never enjoyed peace of heart and mind, he had at least until then had bodily health. He did not seem to fear sickness and a premature death, when, suddenly, in 1872, he fell ill. Clumsy operations aggravated his condition. During an operation for stone, a probe cut the bladder, and cancer set in. The illness increased his natural nervousness. After long months of suffering, he died in 1875, at Courbevoie, near Paris, at the Château of Bécon, when staying with his friend, Prince Stirbey.

Chief works: *Ugolino* (Garden of the Tuileries); *Flora* (Pavilion of the Tuileries); busts of Gérôme, Dumas "fils," Charles Garnier, Napoleon III (Louvre); the Empress Eugénie, statue of the Prince Imperial and his dog Nero; *Neapolitan Shell-fisher* (Louvre).

Always and everywhere drawing, Carpeaux left numerous sketches. He also painted very lively impressions of worldly life and of the life of officialdom. In the Museum of Versailles is a drawing of Napoleon III in his coffin; and, in the Louvre, a *Ball at the Tuileries* (painting).

Carpeaux, whom his contemporaries accused of realism, and who seemed to them a revolutionary, held to the robust tradition of French sculpture, and recalls the great artists of the 18th century, Houdon, Clodion and Pajou. Like them, he gave a quivering grace to bronze and to marble, but to the grace of the 18th century, he added a new note of vigour and impetuosity which is personal. He seemed a revolutionary, and he was so in that he broke away from the coldness of the so-called classical sculpture of his contemporaries, who, inspired by the school of David, were at a stand still in an unchanging and false imitation of the antique. His habit of sketching gave him an ease and brilliancy which he kept in the handling of the clay. He was an alert kneader, with freshness of touch, and he created the course which little by little transformed not only sculpture itself but also relations of painting and sculpture. Before Carpeaux, the laws which David had imposed still regulated painting, and the ideal of which was dominated by the pure and lofty rigidity of sculpture. Carpeaux had the daring to reverse this and to give his statues the movement and vibrating modelling of painting. And as clay was better adapted to this expressive treatment, he adopted a thumb technique which soon became a technique of pellets, and even of sponges. Sculpture now imitated painting, whereas, from the beginning of the 19th century, painting had imitated sculpture. It resulted in there being more "colour" in the modelling, and more life in the movements. And since bronze is the material which best expresses the form and colour of modelling, Carpeaux excelled in bronzes. Marble seems to demand a restraint, and severity of handling, which were less congenial to him. His imitators exaggerated his manner fatally, and in the end sculptors did not know how to treat their material, and they gave up the practise of skilful, objective treatments. With rare exceptions, this was the fault of sculptors of the second half of the 19th century.

The masterpieces of Carpeaux are, then, his fine bronzes, his *Fontaine de l'Observatoire*, his numerous busts, and above all the *Ugolino*, which, shortly before his death, he mentioned as his favourite work.

See Pl. 52, Vol. II.

**CARRACCI (Agostino).**—Bolognese painter and engraver (1557?-1602), of the celebrated Carracci family. He was the literary one of the group of three painters, loving knowledge, and seeking general culture with a spirit of curiosity, resembling that of Leonardo. He was patient and a little slow, like Ludovico, sad, careful,—very different from his brother Annibale who was always ardent, careless and very gifted, which often caused rivalries between them, amounting to quarrels. Already in his childhood, Agostino suffered from his father's reproaches, in comparison with the praises which were given to Annibale. His retentive memory stifled all ease of invention and spontaneity.

CARRACCI (AGOSTINO.) (Uffizi, Florence.)

He had his part, however, in the great reformatory movement of the Carracci Academy, and his pictures, especially the large religious scenes, were, like those of the others, models for centuries to come.

He studied with Fontana and Passerotti. Then his father sent him to Domenico Tibaldi to learn engraving. It is uncertain whether he also studied with the Dutch engraver Cornelius Cort. In any case, he also studied with the sculptor Alessandro Minganti, "the unknown Michelangelo," as Ludovico Carracci called him. He worked hard, and engraved the works of a great many painters, and soon he even received commissions from Venice. His *Crucifixion*, after Tintoretto, had a great success. He often returned to Venice. It has been reckoned that he made three hundred and fifty engravings, for the most part very interesting, with accentuated blacks and whites, and he certainly gained energy in practicing this technique.

Agostino had made his brother, Annibale, come to him in Venice. They went together to Parma, and then back to Bologna (1582). When the Carracci Academy was founded by Ludovico, Agostino took charge of all that concerned general culture and theory. He organised courses on perspective, architecture, and anatomy, with the help of the doctor, Lanzoni. He gave instruction in the choice of subjects and methods of composition.

Agostino painted with his brother Annibale and his cousin Ludovico in the Fava Palace (1584); in the Gessi Chapel at San Bartolommeo (the *Nativity* is attributed to him); in the Magnani Palace (where he painted various scenes, and made a fine chimney-piece, with the date 1592); in the Sampieri Palace (1593-1594), (*Hercules and Atlas*, and *Hercules and Cacus*). It was he who chose and ordered the subjects, which he took from his store of mythology.

He went to Rome shortly after Annibale (1595), and worked with him there on the large and splendid decoration of the Farnese Palace. All the glory for the invention and richness of this work certainly belongs to his brother. Nevertheless, he contributed some successful scenes. The one of Aurora carrying off Cephalus in her chariot is perhaps more cold and incorrect than Annibale's paintings, but there is a certain power in the soft forms, like those of a large cumulus, of the heavy white horses which bear away the gods, who are themselves like beautiful clouds, to heaven.

However, quarrels between the two brothers increased, and were embittered by Annibale's passionate character. Agostino preferred to leave Rome. He was sent to Parma by Cardinal Odorado Farnese, who gave him an introduction to his brother the Duke of Parma. The Duke commissioned him to decorate one of the apartments of the Palazzo dei Giaroini. He began some scenes symbolising Love, which he was unable to finish. During this period, too, he painted the *Assumption* of the Bologna Gallery. It is said that, feeling himself ill and on the point of death, he retired into a Capuchin Monastery to do penance. He died on the 22nd March 1602, in Parma.

The best known picture of Agostino Carracci is the *Last Communion of St. Jerome* (Bologna Gallery), afterwards imitated by Domenichino.

**— (Annibale).**—Bolognese painter, 1560?-1609, the most celebrated of the Carracci family.

CARRACCI (ANNIBALE.) (Uffizi, Florence.)

Ludovico (see under his name) was chiefly the founder and organiser of the Carracci Academy. Agostino (see) was the most learned. Annibale was the best painter, the most gifted, the most passionate. He adds a liveliness and intensity even to the figures he borrowed from the old masters.

CARRACCI (ANNIBALE AND AGOSTINO): HALL IN THE FARNESE PALACE, ROME.

The son of a tailor, he was born at Bologna. Annibale Carracci like his brother, Agostino, was taught painting by their cousin, Ludovico. They entered the studio of Domenico Tibaldi together. On leaving the school, at the age of eighteen, Annibale painted his first works—*A Crucifixion*, for San Niccolo di San Felice, and a *Baptism of Christ* for San Gregorio. But envy rose against him. No doubt because he had been too successful, he was reproached for being too realistic, trivial, lacking in nobility, and, with more justification, with having copied studio models. His cousin, Ludovico, seeing the ill-feeling against him in Bologna, sent him to Parma (1580), and from there he went to Venice to join his brother, Agostino. This was an opportunity, since he made his first acquaintance with Correggio and Titian.

When he returned to Bologna with Agostino (1582), they began a collaboration which lasted a long time.

The decoration of the Fava Palace (1584), under the direction of Ludovico, was one of their most important works. Agostino, who had studied literature and mythology, chose the subjects. Annibale did most of the painting. In the first room, they represented the Legend of the Argonauts, with large landscapes, and animals, separating the various scenes by figures of the gods. Thus the building of the ship Argo recalls that of Noah's ark. In the second and smaller room they represented subjects borrowed from Virgil. They were successful, but rivals continued their criticisms, attacking especially Annibale's realism, and calling his angels "skinned cats," "gattucci scorticati."

It was at this time that the Carracci, wishing to triumph over their enemies, opened an Academy (1585-1595), alongside the many literary academies that then reigned. Annibale taught there, especially technique.

During this period, Annibale painted an *Assumption* for the Brotherhood of Saint Roch, in Reggio. (1587—Dresden Museum); and a *Pietà* for the Capuchins of Parma (Parma Museum); the *Assumption,* of Bologna Museum, the *Madonna with St. John, St. Catherine, and St. John the Evangelist* (Bologna Museum), the *Madonna Appearing to St. Catherine and St. John,* and the *Resurrection* (Louvre); and *St. Roch distributing Alms* (Dresden Museum).

The Carracci painted together the decoration of the Gessi Chapel in San Bartolommeo (the *Adoration of the Magi,* and the *Circumcision* have been attributed turn about to Annibale and Ludovico), and the more important decoration of the Magnani Palace, where they represented the history of Romulus and Remus. The scenes are separated by atlantes, but instead of "grisailles" as in the Fava, there are marble statues with golden children holding garlands of coloured fruit. They are most likely by Annibale. According to critics, Annibale was the author of scenes 1, 3, 6, 7, 9, 11, 14; Ludovico painted scenes 2, 4, 10 and 12 and Agostino was responsible for scenes 5 and 18. Agostino made a chimney-piece, decorated with a fine picture by Annibale, with the date 1592.

They next (1593-1594) painted, in fresco, the ceilings and mantelpieces of three large rooms in the Sampieri Palace. Annibale painted the ceiling —the *Way of Virtue* and a *Giant Struck by Lightning.* The diffused orange light contrasts with the reds and whites, and with the bright blues.

About 1595, Annibale left for Rome, whither he was shortly followed by Agostino. It seemed to them that they could no longer find enough work to do at Bologna, where Ludovico remained as head of the school. They wanted to extend their fame and increase their wealth; and Cardinal Odorado gave them a good opportunity, by calling upon them to decorate a new room in the Farnese Palace.

It was the time of great changes in Rome, in the expanding of the Jesuit and Baroque style, the flowering of volutes, and the glitter of complicated fountains. Churches, colleges and tombs multiplied in the reign of Clement VIII Aldobrandini (1592-1605). Annibale was so enthusiastically attracted by the antique that he gave up making his own designs. He reproduced endlessly the *Laocoon,* or the *Hercules* in the Cortile of the Farnese Palace.

First he painted a *Canaanite Woman Prostrate before Christ,* which is now lost, for the Chapel of the Palace. Then he transformed a *St. Catherine,* painted for Reggio into a *St. Margaret* for St. Catherine of Fungari. The *Christ Triumphant* in the Pitti Palace which has bright, pure colours like those of Correggio, must also belong to this time.

The decoration of the Farnese Palace was most important. Monsignor Agucchi, a learned priest, gave the subjects. In a small apartment, known as the Camerino, the paintings represent the *Triumph of Virtue over Vice, Hercules between Virtue and Pleasure,* the *Repose of Hercules,* and *Hercules Supporting the World.* In the lunettes: *Ulysses and the Sirens, Ulysses and Circe, The Legends of Amphonus and Anapus,* and *The Death of Medusa.* These scenes were separated by stucco garlands and "putti."

But it was in the great gallery that Annibale Carracci's masterpiece was achieved. It is not only each particular scene which is so successful; the whole gives an infinitely rich and decorative impression. This gallery still reveals, especially when lit up in the evening, an admirable pagan festival.

There is a whole collection of drawings in the Louvre, which show Annibale's different schemes, and hesitations. Sometimes he was inspired by Tibaldi's decoration in the Poggi Palace, sometimes by the Sistine Chapel. Especially, he tried to find a means of connecting the frieze with the vault. In the final execution, he painted a false stone framework, supported by atlantes, to which the compositions seemed to be attached. He multiplied garlands, ornaments, grotesques, "putti," "ignudi," imitating those of Michelangelo. The subjects, inspired by Ovid and Theocritus, were as it were an apotheosis of refined and sensuous love. The largest composition, in the middle of the ceiling represents the Triumph of Bacchus and Ariadne.

For his four years' work, Annibale only had five hundred crowns. He had always been original, disorderly, wild and solitary. He fell out with his brother, who left Rome. He retired into a little house of the Quirinal where he shut himself up in his melancholy and rage.

However, some time later he took up his brush again to paint a *Birth of the Virgin* for Duke Cesar d'Este (1606). Gout prevented him from finishing his picture. Albani came near to look after him, and he made some designs for the Spanish Church of St. James, which the pupil executed. But the illness gained ground. In 1609, more melancholy than ever, he dragged himself to Naples, where he found neither death nor health, which he wished for alternately. He went back to Rome, where, in his almost wretched house, he died, on the 15th July 1609, at the age of forty-nine. His nephew Antonio Carracci laid his body in state in the Pantheon, beside Raphael's tomb, as he had wished, awaiting the splendid funeral.

Among his last works were:—

The *Domine Quo Vadis,* of the National Gallery—dramatic, in the rapid stride of Christ and the frightened gesture of St. Peter, before a gloomy, ruined landscape.

The *Three Marys,* of Castle Howard, shows a moving lamentation round Christ's body.

*Christ and the Woman of Samaria* (Vienna) has a very fine landscape, a large simple countryside, in shade around the figures of the pretty, fair woman and the gentle Christ who talks to her while she comes to draw water from the well.

The *Pietà* (Louvre), ordered by the Mattei family for San Francesco, in Ripa, is rather like Domenichino.

Annibale did a considerable amount of work, and there are a great number of his paintings in the Museums of Europe.

See Pl. 22, Vol. II.

— **(Antonio).**—Bolognese painter (1583-1618), son of Agostino Carracci. Always ailing, he died young, and carried out only a very few works in the style of the Carracci. The most important is the decoration of the Chapel of St. Charles in San Bartolommeo, where he represented the Passion of Christ, and scenes from the life of St. Charles. There is a *Deluge* by him, in the Louvre, with groups of Michelangelesque nudes.

— **(Ludovico).**—Bolognese painter (1555-1619).

The eldest of the Carracci, who led the others in a reaction against the anæmic mannerism of the imitators of Raphael and Michelangelo, to a new eclectic style; and who founded the Academy. He was descended from a family of artisans of Cremonese origin. He began his career by studying painting in the studio of Prospero Fontana. But he was so slow and dull that he was nicknamed "il bue," the ox, and he ended by leaving the master who was dissatisfied with him. He went to Venice, where Tintoretto discouraged him even more. But he energetically persevered. He loved work, and his application made up for his lack of gift and spontaneity. He studied and copied without ceasing. He went to Florence where he studied Andrea del Sarto thoroughly, to Parma for a better knowledge of Correggio and Parmigianino, and to Mantua for the sake of Giulio Romano and Primaticcio. Returning to Bologna in 1578, he was also inspired by the two Bolognese painters, Bagnacavallo and Tibaldi. He collected a great many documents from which his two cousins, Annibale and Agostino, to whom he taught painting, profited.

Carracci (Ludovico). (Uffizi, Florence.)

He founded the famous Academy of the Carracci (1585). Annibale taught the technique of painting, and corrected sketches. Agostino, the learned one, taught perspective, architecture and anatomy with the assistance of the doctor, Lanzoni, and controlled discussions. Living models had a very important place, and he also had a great many casts, which the pupils copied. They had competitions, and exhibitions. But, especially, they codified the art of painting, just as the *Accademia della Crusca* fixed the language, and, besides artists, a great many students, and learned men flocked to the Carracci Academy, which was given the name of *Accademia dei Desiderosi* or *degli Incamminati.* There is a sonnet, attributed to Agostino, addressed to Niccolo dell'Abbate, in which their principles are expressed. He recommends classical design, Umbro-Venetian adornments, the colour of Lombardy, Michelangelo's force, the truth and naturalism of Titian, the pure style of Correggio, Raphael's symmetry, Tibaldi's discretion, Primaticcio's invention, and a little of Parmigianino's grace! This eclecticism was a reaction against the superficial and empty facility of such painters as Vasari and Federigo Zuccaro. At the same time, appeared the treatise of Lomazzo in which he describes an ideal picture, and the type of Adam and Eve. Adam was drawn by Michelangelo and painted by Titian; Eve was drawn by Raphael and painted by Correggio.

It was a period when there seemed nothing more to invent, and that the best means of preventing art from dying out was to make, as it were, a grammar of the great masters' works. In default of inspiration, there would, nevertheless, be perfection.

A method of the same kind gave prescriptions for rendering physical states and moral sentiments. A whole repertory of types was created—the old man, the sick man, the beggar, etc.—and facial expressions, representing pain, joy, ecstasy, pity, horror, etc. Pupils had only to choose the wares which they wanted for their works. The representation of religious sentiment became fixed, as though preparing for the period of Jesuit fervour. A whole art of pious images was created, which still exists today.

The Carracci worked day and night, cutting short their meals in order to carry out all their plans for their Academy. So much labour could not be without some fruit. For a moment, declining art raised its head a little, in this serious and studied perfection. Fortunately, one of the Carracci, Annibale, added to all this legislation the temperament of a true artist. But after this last flame, blind obedience to well made codes led to the death of art, just as certainly as did the passive and superficial imitation of the followers of Raphael and Michelangelo.

Ludovico, who was fat and majestic and a serious steady citizen, directed his Academy admirably. But his painting was cold. The *Madonna degli Scalzi* and the *Madonna delle Convertite* (Bologna Gallery), bathed in a soft, idealised light, are among his most successful works. The following may be mentioned:—the *Preaching of St. John* (1592, Bologna Gallery); the *Vision of St. Hyacinth* (Louvre); a *Last Supper* and a *Vision of St. Peter,* in San Michele in Bosco; the *Marriage of the Virgin* (in the Gallery of Cento); the *Preaching of St. Anthony* (Brera Gallery, Milan); and *Christ in Limbo* and the *Apostles at the Tomb of Mary,* in the Church of Corpus Domini, Bologna.

With his cousins, Annibale and Agostino, he painted in the Fava Palace (1584); in the Gessi Chapel, in St. Bartolommeo; in the Palazzo dei Diamanti; in the Palazzo Magnani; and in the Palazzo Sampieri (1593-1594).

After a short journey to Rome, in 1602, he did not leave Bologna any more. With his pupils, he decorated the Cortile of San Michele in Bosco (1604-1605) with scenes from the lives of St. Benedict and St. Cecilia. Unfortunately, we can only judge what these paintings must have been like, from engravings by Giovanini and by Zanotti. The scene representing the burning of the

# EGYPTIAN ARCHITECTURE

*EGYPTIAN architecture is an architecture of temples and tombs, characterized by massive power and durability. The Egyptians built for eternity; their tombs were forts protecting the remains of their dead. The most celebrated ones are the three famous pyramids of Gizeh which were built to preserve the mummies of famous Pharaohs. Some of these pyramids, which were very flat, form a regular necropolis in the lower valley of the Nile; they are called mastabas. Even though the most ancient of relics of human civilisation, they are the best preserved.*

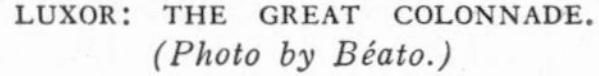

LUXOR: THE GREAT COLONNADE.
*(Photo by Béato.)*

FAÇADE OF THE GREAT SPEOS OF IPSAMBUL.
*(Photo by Oropesa.)*

CLERESTORY OF THE HYPOSTYLE HALL, KARNAK.
*(Photo by Béato.)*

## The Egyptian Temple

IN THE Egyptian temple the entablature is carried on powerful columns. The pyramidal walls were of indestructible solidity made of huge shaped stones fitted together without mortar. The columns have wide capitals in the form of a bell-shaped flower, compact like a lotus bud or in the shape of the head of the goddess Hathor. Some temples were built in rocks; the great Speos of Ipsambul is the most remarkable of the underground temples. The plan of the underground temple is the same as of the one above ground.

PYLON OF THE TEMPLE AT EDFU.
*(Photo by Béato.)*

PRONAOS AND TERRACES OF THE TEMPLE OF EDFU.
*(Photo by Noniger.)*

COURT AND PORTICOES OF TEMPLE OF EDFU.
*(Photo by Béato.)*

## The Egyptian Temple

ONE enters the temple through the pylon, a colossal door surmounted by a cornice and flanked by two rectangular walls with slanting sides. Then one crosses the peristyle court and the hypostyle halls, where the ceiling rests on the columns: finally one reaches the deep and secret sanctuary, the home of the god. Only the court was open to the public; commoners were not admitted to the interior of the sanctuary or naos. The temple of Horus at Edfu is the most perfect existing Egyptian temple. It dates from the time of Alexander the Great.

PHILAE BEFORE THE COMPLETION OF THE ASSUAN DAM.
*(Photo by Béato.)*

THE PAVILION OF NECTANEBO AT PHILAE.
*(Photo by Béato.)*

THE PAVILION OF TRAJAN AT PHILAE.
*(Photo by Béato.)*

## The Egyptian Temple

ONE of the outstanding monuments is the temple of Philae, admired equally for its picturesque location as well as its well preserved state. It was started at the time of the Ptolemies and was continued under Roman domination. Nectanebo constructed a pavilion which marked the landing place on the island to the travellers ascending the river. Augustus had a kiosk erected at the northern point of the island, also unfinished, which is wrongly known as the Kiosk of Trajan. In this last example, the Egyptian architecture shows less massive structure and a more cheerful aspect.

# EGYPTIAN SCULPTURE

*The sculpture of the Egyptians is closely associated with their religious beliefs and rites. The most ancient tombs preserved besides the mummies, a statue of wood or stone, which was a likeness of the deceased. In this we may see their precaution to assure a future life for the body, one which is even better than the embalmed mummy. It is not only in Egyptian art that we find likenesses prepared to help man fight against death. Often other figurines were placed near the statue to keep it company and to serve it after death.*

SEATED SCRIBE, LOUVRE.
*(Photo by Hachette.)*

SHEIKH-EL-BELED. CAIRO.
*(Photo by Brugsch.)*

THE BREWER. CAIRO.
*(Photo by Brugsch.)*

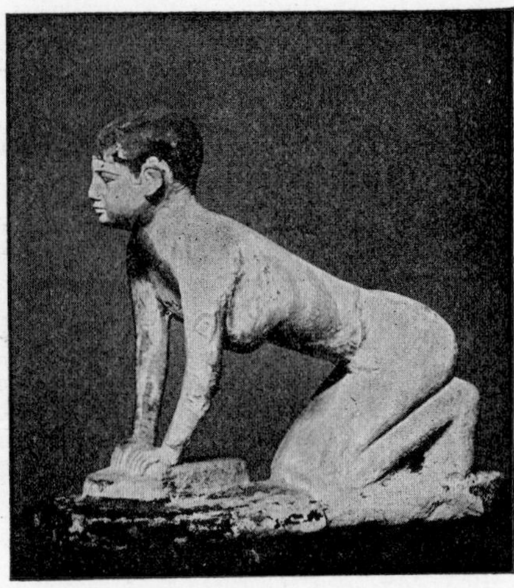

WOMAN GRINDING WHEAT. CAIRO.
*(Photo by Brugsch.)*

## Portrait Statues

We cannot trace the origin of Egyptian sculpture. It was already developed when it appeared. The earliest figures are sometimes the most realistic. Some types are very striking: Kaapirou, the Sheikh-el-Beled, carved of wood, is especially alive. The Seated Scribe in the Louvre is attentive to the sentence he expects to write down. All these sculptures present their models in characteristic attitudes.

MAN AND WIFE SEATED. CAIRO.
*(Photo by Brugsch.)*

ONE OF THE TRIADS OF MYCERINUS. CAIRO.
*(Photo by Brugsch.)*

THOTHMES AND HIS MOTHER. CAIRO.
*(Photo by Brugsch.)*

SENEFERU THE GREAT OF CAIRO.
*(Photo by Brugsch.)*

SUKHATPOU. LOUVRE.
*(Photo by Brugsch.)*

## Religious or Royal Statues

But if a group of sculptures in Egypt was characterized by utter naturalism, this character was often hampered by the care for style or the religious respect for tradition. Thus all these statues of men or gods, carved in granite or diorite, are done in uniform types. The Egyptian sculptors gave only a few close gestures to their figures. They always rendered the body in a symmetrical way expressing repose rather than motion. These unchangeable beings seem to have been made to resist the wear of passing centuries.

HEAD OF CANOPE. CAIRO.
*(Photo by Brugsch.)*

BUST OF AMON, KARNAK.
*(Photo by Legrain.)*

BUST OF KHONSU. CAIRO.
*(Photo by Brugsch.)*

PRINCESS NEFERT. CAIRO.
*(Photo by Daumas.)*

## Egyptian Portraits

The rare originality of Egyptian sculpture lies in the fact that it could develop equally well in two such different ways as portraiture and style. With each carved figure the artists tried to reach the heights of simplification and impeccable purity of form. At the same time an intense feeling of life is embodied in this geometric perfection. Individual types are certainly recognizable. Their great immobility fascinates us. The Egyptians seem to have projected everything into eternity, but even after forty centuries the life and art of ancient Egypt seem near to us.

Monastery was perhaps Ludovico's masterpiece.

He next executed three large pictures for the Cathedral of Piacenza: the *Assumption of the Virgin,* and the *Apostles Finding a Rose instead of the Body of Mary* (Parma Museum), and *St. Martin Dividing His Cloak* (which remains in place). Then he painted the large religious pictures which are now in the Bologna Gallery: the *Transfiguration,* the *Overthrow* and the *Conversion of St. Paul.* He began to paint more and more quickly, and groups of nude figures, and exaggerated gestures, multiplied without ceasing.

His last works were painted in Bologna Cathedral, where on the vault of the Chapter House, he represented St. Peter, and the Virgin and Apostles mourning the Dead Christ, and in the principal chapel, an *Annunciation.*

Thus his last days were filled with a melancholy and bitterness which perhaps hastened his end. He died on the 13th November 1619.

See Pl. 22, Vol. II.

BIBLIOGRAPHY: Tietze, *Annibale Carraccis Galerie im Palazzo Farnese und Seine römische Werkstatte,* Annual of the Museums of Vienna, 1906.—Gabriel Rouchès, *La Peinture bolonaise à la fin du* XVI° *Siècle.* Paris, 1913.

**CARRARA (Accademia).**—See Bergamo.

**CARREÑO de MIRANDA (Juan).**—Spanish painter. Born in Avilés (Asturias) 25th March 1614; died in Madrid, September 1685. He was early taken to Madrid by his father D. Juan Carreño de Miranda.

In 1653, Carreño began large frescoes in the churches in Madrid, and collaborated with Francisco Rizi in Toledo Cathedral. Carreño's high position began especially after the death of Velázquez and of his patron, Philip IV. The new King, Charles II, nominated him Painter of the Royal Household, 11th April 1671. Carreño made a number of portraits of Charles II.

In his very complicated, and very numerous compositions, this artist always shows himself to be skilful, versatile, an able draughtsman, and a harmonious colourist. Some of his religious paintings as for instance that of San Sebastian in the Prado Museum of Madrid (1656) show the influence of Van Dyck; in others reminiscences of Titian are visible. As a portrait painter, where he shows himself at his best, Carreño resembles Velázquez. In his youth he made many copies after the master of "Las Meninas." Famous are his portraits of the Queen-Mother Maria Anna (Madrid, Prado; Munich, Alte Pinakothek; Vienna, Hofmuseum; Richmond, England, Collection Cook), of the Duke of Pastrana (Madrid, Prado), of Charles II of Spain (Berlin, Kaiser Friedrich Museum), etc.

Carreño, whom Charles II "loved extraordinarily," died in September 1685, and was buried in the vault of the Royal Monastery of San Gil. Mateo Cerezo was his best pupil.

BIBLIOGRAPHY: A. de Beruete y Moret, *The Madrid School of Painting.* Madrid, 1909.—*Thieme-Becker,* Vol. VI; Leipzig, 1912, art. *Carreño de Miranda.*—A. L. Mayer, *Geschichte der spanischen Malerei;* Leipzig, 1922.

**CARRÈRE (John Merven).**—American architect (1858-1911). He was born in Rio de Janeiro 9th November 1858 of French and Scotch parentage. He first studied in Switzerland at the Institute Breitenstein at Grenchen and even then he liked to draw pictures of houses. He was then sent to the École des Beaux-Arts where he worked with Robert Laisne and Ginain and was awarded his government diplôme in 1882. The following year he came to the United States and was employed by McKim, Mead and White in New York City. There he met again Thomas Hastings, whom he had known at the École des Beaux-Arts, and soon those two set up the partnership of Carrère and Hastings which was to execute so many fine buildings in the United States. Among the most notable structures that they designed were the Alcazar and Ponce de Leon hotels in Saint Augustine, Florida, the Jefferson Hotel in Richmond, Virginia, the Mail and Express Building in New York—all done in the style of the French Renaissance. Carrère was chairman of the board of architects of the Pan-American Exposition at Buffalo in 1901 and helped with the St. Louis Exposition in 1904. Later buildings designed by the firm include Woolsey Hall at Yale University in New Haven, the approaches to the Manhattan Bridge in New York City, the Senate and House office buildings in Washington, and the New York Public Library. Simplicity of plan and beauty of exterior and interior characterised their plans, most of which were derived from the style of the French Renaissance. Carrère died after an automobile accident 1st March, 1911, but the work of the firm continued in the same tradition begun by its founders.

BIBLIOGRAPHY: Thomas Hastings, *John Merven Carrère, New York Architect,* Vol. 5, May, 1911, memorial number devoted to Carrère.—Francis S. Swales, *John Merven Carrère,* London Architectural Review, Vol. 29, pp. 283-293.—*The Work of Messrs. Carrère and Hastings,* Architectural Record, Vol. 27, January, 1910, pp. 1-120.

**CARRIERA (Rosalba).**—Woman painter of Venice, 1675-1758. Her pastel portraits are charming, elegant, facile and soft. The Venetian ladies whom she painted, tranquilly display all their grace, their enchanting or melancholy smile, their light powder and their fresh complexions. The best portraits are in the Dresden Gallery. Her own portrait is in the Venice Academy.

**CARRIER-BELLEUSE.**—French sculptor, 1824-1887. He began to exhibit at the Salons in 1857. His works were almost at once a success. The most important are:—*Undine* (1864); the well-known *Angelica* (1866); *Phoebe Sleeping* (Luxembourg); *Psyche Abandoned;* the *Nymph* of the fountain of the Place du Théâtre-Français; and busts of Renan, Jules Simon, and Mademoiselle Croizette. He also applied himself to decorative art, and in this capacity, was nominated Director of the art works of the Sèvres factory. The Musée des Arts Decoratifs possesses numerous drawings of Carrier-Belleuse.

**CARRIÈRE (Eugène).**—French painter. Born: Gournay-sur-Marne, Seine-et-Oise, 1849. Died: Paris, 1905. Brought up in Alsace, he finished his studies in Strasbourg, and did not think anything about painting until, at the age of nineteen, he went to settle in Saint-Quentin, where he saw La Tour's pastels in the Museum. They made a great impression on Carrière, who resolved to devote himself to painting. He went to Paris to begin his studies at the École des Beaux-Arts, when the war of 1870 broke out. He was made prisoner at Neuf-Brisach, taken to Dresden as a captive, during which time the visit to the Museum was like a ray of sunlight. On his return to Paris, he entered the studio of Cabanel and worked there from 1872 to 1876, without submitting to the influence of his master. He had a more fruitful teaching in studying the old masters in the Louvre. In 1876, he exhibited a Portrait of a Woman and from then he sent to the Salon regularly. Married, and father of a large family, he used the members ceaselessly as models. He also painted some portraits: Portrait of Mademoiselle Stern (1877), Portrait of M. Musset (1878).

In 1879, a *Young Mother Nursing Her Child* (Avignon Museum) was his first success. But for several years, he continued to work without becoming really well known. Other works were: the *Nymph Echo* (1880), *Grandfather and Grandson* (1881), *Two Friends or the Child With a Dog* (1884), the *Sick Child* (Museum of Montagis, 1885), and the *First Veil* (Toulon Museum, 1886). Without establishing his personality, his way of "enveloping" forms, was already apparent by the time the Portrait of M. Devillez appeared, which attracted attention to the young painter, and gave him the sympathy of artists. It represents a young sculptor, dabbling with a ball of potter's clay, while a large greyhound caresses his leg. The painting is almost monochrome, and the modelling by planes is in a very misty atmosphere. In this canvas Carrière expresses a grace and youthful charm, which he lost later. His touch became broader and more sure, he became simpler and more serious, but he never had more freshness and delicacy.

In the following years, other portraits appeared as well as pictures: *Portrait of Jean Dolent; Woman at her Toilet* (1888); Portraits of Alphonse Daudet, Verlaine, Berton, Geoffroy; *Maternity* (1892, Luxembourg), *The Family* (1893, Luxembourg). Carrière had now found himself. He transformed his subjects into decorative compositions, but in execution he was still the concise artist in these canvases which are, after all, his most personal work. He was a painter of Motherhood. Taking his wife and children as models, he painted them at all ages. He made studies of babies, little girls, and older children. The mother always dominates the group, often with an uneasy, sad expression. The father is never seen. However, Carrière represented him in some portraits, in those of Dolent, of Séailles, of Daudet, but this father always seems distressed, and the daughter seems destined for the part of Antigone. His execution is precise. His work has an almost monochrome surface, although he really covered his canvas with a reddish underpainting which he alone prepared. Owing to the thick "atmosphere" of the pictures, the backgrounds, still visible in Carrière's early compositions, have disappeared, and a well-known critic complains that "there is a smoking chimney in the artist's ideal."

Until the end of his life Carrière was keenly discussed, attacked and defended. In the midst of these clamours, he went on progressing in his work. He painted some large compositions, very sensitive and of great decorative unity: the Hôtel de Ville, Paris; Amphitheatre of the Sorbonne; Théâtre Populaire in Belleville (belonging to M. Gallimard, 1895); the *Crucifixion* (1897, Luxembourg).

Carrière was a painter of volume. He was preoccupied with masses, and their position in the light. He had a sense of sculpture, as Rodin understood it. He saw, not in terms of contour, but in terms of form.

As his career advanced, the faces of his figures expressed a painful sadness. All art is a confession. The master undermined by an incurable illness painted in a sick, restless eagerness to accumulate numerous works for his family. He made some good lithographs which chiefly reproduce his portraits and pictures.

**CARRUCCI (Jacopo).**—See Pontormo.

**CARTHAGE.**—See Phœnician (Art).

**CARYATID.**—The sculptured figure of a woman, sometimes isolated, but generally used as a support to a building, in place of a column. The most famous Caryatids are those of the Erechtheum, on the Athenian Acropolis.

See Acropolis of Athens.

**CASA BUONARROTI.**—See Florence.

**CASELLI da PARMA, (Christoforo).**—Venetian painter, active c. 1488 until he died in 1521. Influenced by Giovanni Bellini and Antonello da Messina. His chief works are a triptych of 1495 in the sacristy of the Salute, Venice; and three dated paintings in Parma: the *Madonna with the Baptist, Hilary, and Angels* of 1496-1499 in the Museum; the *Adoration of the Magi,* in S. Giovanni Evangelista, of 1499; and a monochrome tondo in the Duomo, of 1507.

**CASORATI (Felice).**—Contemporary Italian painter. He was born 4th December 1886 at Novara, in the Piedmont district. He grew up in Padua and there studied law, finishing his studies in 1907. That same year he began to paint and exhibit some of his work in the Venice International Exhibition. The next three years he spent in Naples, where he came in contact with the work of Pieter Brueghel, whose allegorical subjects interested him. Previously he had been under the strong influence of the rich colouring of Titian and to this he now added a maze of allegory and symbolism. From 1911 to 1915 Casorati lived in Verona, where he became interested in cubism and its continuation as futurism. He was particularly impressed by the compositions of Kandinsky and tried to simplify his own compositions with some thought for stylization and the treatment of the surface of the paintings. About 1915 he moved to Turin and there he remained until 1920, at which time he removed to Venice. It was during this visit that he saw for the first time a painting by Cézanne, whose style became the model for his work from that time on to the present. He attempted to portray solid forms in correct perspective blocked out in realistic colour with a very naturalistic effect. Soon he tried experiments in the shadings of light and its relation to the objects which it touched, modelling his figures with an eye to the balance of the masses and a preoccupation with the use of inclined planes and some foreshortening. He has done a number of figure studies and some very individualized portraits, including those of the lawyer *Gualino*, and one of a woman, *Silvana Cenni.* In these portraits there is a tendency on the part of the artist to use open backgrounds behind his figures, and the faces are endowed with a calmness which almost rivals that of the Italian Renaissance master, Piero della Francesca. Casorati is an example of an artist whose stylistic development has gone from the realistic and lyrical through a mild form of cubism and then back to nature. He has painted some stage decorations, including those for the theatre of Gualino in Turin, and stage settings for *La Vestale* of Spontini, which was produced in Florence in 1933, and for *Orpheus* by Monteverdi, which was given in the Opera House in Rome in 1934. Pictures by this artist are to be found in the museums of Turin, Venice, Milan, Florence, Rome, Buenos Aires, Moscow and Berlin.

Bibliography: Raffaello Gialli, *Felice Casorati,* 1925.—Piero Gobetti, *Felice Casorati,* 1923.

**CASSATT (Mary).** — American painter and graver (1845-1926). She was born in Allegheny City, Pennsylvania, which is now part of Pittsburgh, 22d May 1845. While a young girl she passed some time in France but returned to the United States, where she began to study at the Pennsylvania Academy of Fine Arts in Philadelphia. Despite her father's opposition she decided to become a painter and accordingly left her home in 1868 to go abroad for further study. After that time with the exception of a few short visits she made her home abroad, living most of her life near Paris. She pursued her art education in Parma, in Spain, and in Antwerp, coming under the successive influences of Correggio, Velazquez, and Rubens. From 1872 to 1874 her work was exhibited at the Paris Salon, but in 1875 and again in 1877 the jury refused to hang her pictures. After that she never made another attempt to enter that annual exhibition, but instead displayed her work with the Impressionist group. She was introduced to that company by Dégas and there she came into contact with Manet, Renoir, Cézanne and the other leaders of that movement. The style of Dégas was particularly influential in forming Miss Cassatt's treatment of pictures of motherhood. In 1893 she was chosen to decorate the north tympanum of the Woman's Building at the Columbian Exposition in Chicago, one of the first public commissions to be given to a woman artist. She was offered many prizes but declined the majority of them, although she did accept the French award of Chevalier of the Legion of Honor. Her later years were clouded by the loss of her sight, but she tried to maintain a lively interest in the affairs of the day and current art trends with which she was not in sympathy. She died after a long illness on 14th June 1926, at her villa at Mesnil-Théribus, Oise, a suburb of Paris.

Her most popular theme was the intimate relationship between a mother and her child as seen in the occupations of different hours of the day under varying circumstances. The racial types of the figures are French, but the appeal of the subject matter is universal. In all the media that she used—oil, pastel, etching and the colour-print—she was able to express in simple linear compositions the characters of the drama of human life.

See Pl. 62, Vol. II.

Bibliography: Achille Ségard, *Un Peintre des Enfants et des Mères, Mary Cassatt,* 1913.—Edith Valerio, *Mary Cassatt,* 1930.—Forbes Watson, *Mary Cassatt,* American Artists Series, 1932.—For other material see *The Index of Twentieth Century Artists* for October, 1934.

**CASTAGNO, ANDREA del (Andrea di Bartolommeo di Simone).** —Born in Castagno in the valley of the Mugello, in 1410. Vasari states that he was brought to Florence and educated by Bernardetto de' Medici, and the story is not at all unlikely since this member of the Medici family had an estate near Andrea's birthplace.

The documented dates on Castagno's activity are scanty and not particularly helpful for his artistic evolution. His tax declaration of 1430 indicates that at the time he was very poor. In 1442 he was in Venice, where he signed the frescoes in the church of S. Tarasio adjacent to S. Zaccaria, with a certain Francesco da Faenza. In 1444, back in Florence, he received payment for a drawing of the Descent from the Cross for one of the windows in the cupola of the Duomo. In 1449-1450 he executed for the church of S. Miniato fra le Torri a panel of the Assumption with S. Miniato and Emilian, now in Berlin. In 1450 he was partner to a contract for frescoes in the church of S. Egidio, where Domenico Veneziano and Baldovinetti also worked. In 1456 he painted a fresco, now lost, in the SS. Annunziata. 1456 is also the date of his equestrian fresco of Niccolò da Tolentino in the Duomo. He died in 1457.

In addition to the extant works among those mentioned above (the 1442 frescoes in S. Zaccaria, Venice; the Deposition window after his design in the Duomo; the Berlin Assumption; and the Niccolò da Tolentino), Castagno is credited with the following works: In the Castagno Museum, S. Apollonia, in Florence, there are his magnificent *Last Supper*, the *Nine "Worthies,"* Boccaccio, Petrarch, Dante, Queen Thomyris, the Cumæan Sibyl, Niccolò Acciajuoli, Farinata degli Uberti, Filippo Scolaro, and Esther; two Crucifixions; an *Entombment*; a *Resurrection*; and a *Dead Christ with Angels.* In the SS. Annunziata are still to be found his *Trinity with St. Jerome* and his *Christ and St. Julian.* There is a *Crucifixion* in London; a painted shield representing David in the Widener Collection, Philadelphia; and in Washington, in the Mellon Collection a male portrait, remarkable both for its extraordinary quality and for the fact that it is the earliest three-quarter Florentine portrait which remains, and exercised an enormous influence over the further development of the outward-facing portrait form.

Castagno realizes to a marked extent the specifically Florentine genius, an intense expression of will, a statement of plastic actuality, a conflict between physical mass and limited, tangible space, a substantive simplification, a tight organization and power of modelling, which make him a notable figure in the direct Florentine evolution from Giotto to Michelangelo.

Bibliography: Vasari-Milanesi, II. —Richa, *Chiese fiorentine,* IV, p. 69. —Gaye, *Carteggio,* I., p. 562.—Poggi, *Il Duomo di Firenze,* pp. 145, 227.—W. Waldschmidt, *Andrea del Castagno.* Berlin, 1900.—H. Horne, *Andrea del Castagno,* Burlington Magazine, VII, 1905, pp. 66, 222.—O. Gigoli, *L'arte di Andrea del Castagno,* Emporium, XXI, 1905, p. 114.—Poggi, *Degli affreschi di Andrea del Castagno nella cappella di San Giuliano della SS. Annunziata,* Rivista d'arte, IV, 1906, p. 24.—C. Gamba, *Una tavola di Andrea del Castagno,* Rivista d'arte, VII, 1910, p. 25.—Fiocco, *Andrea del Castagno a Venezia,* L'Arte, 1921, p. 85; and *Andrea del Castagno at Venice,* Burlington Magazine, XL, 1922, p. 11.

**CASTELFRANCO (Italy).**—Little town, celebrated as the home of Giorgione, the "Master of Castelfranco." The Cathedral contains one of his masterpieces, *The Virgin With St. Francis and St. Liberale.* The old city was surrounded by ramparts with towers which are well preserved and the finest ornament to the town.

**CASTELLANI.**—Family of Roman goldsmiths. They made pieces of jewelry, derived from Etruscan work, in charming taste, and with an ability comparable to the work of the finest goldsmiths.

The most famous examples of their work are the two gold swords presented to Napoleon III and to Victor Emmanuel II.

**CASTIGLIONE (Balthazar de).** —Italian courtier and author, 1478-1529; subject of a remarkable portrait by Raphael.

See Pl. 19, Vol. II.

**— (Giovanni Benedetto).**—Italian painter and engraver, 1616-1670, born at Genoa. Chief work animals and still life.

**— (Giuseppe).** — Jesuit brother and missionary at court of China in eighteenth century. Forced to learn Chinese methods of painting, he combined Far Eastern technique with Western perspective.

**CATACOMBS.**—See Early Christian Art; Rome.

**CATE (Ten).** — Contemporary Dutch painter, well-known in Parisian circles. He is the author of small pictures in oil and pastel, and has an extremely crisp and lively touch.

Cate is chiefly known for his seascapes which seem inspired by the watercolours of Jongkind.

**CATENA (Vincenzo di Biagio).** —Venetian painter, active from 1495 until death in 1531. Perhaps a pupil of Cima, Catena was strongly influenced by Giovanni Bellini and the general development of Venetian painting during his period. An altarpiece in Sta. Maria Mater Domini, Venice, is from 1420. Other works by him are in Venice, Vienna, London, New York, and elsewhere.

**CATERINO VENEZIANO.**—Mentioned 1362-1382, a Venetian painter working in the Byzantine tradition but subject to Giottesque influences.

In 1367 Caterino worked with Donato da S. Vitale on a *Crucifix* for S. Agnese in Venice (no longer existing); and in 1372, with the same painter, he executed a *Coronation of the Virgin* now in the Quirini-Stampalia Collection, Venice. His lost altarpiece for San Giorgio Maggiore was dated 1374; and the *Coronation* now in the Venice Academy is from 1375. Also in the Venice Academy is an undated but signed triptych, a *Coronation of the Virgin with St. Lucy and Nicholas of Tolentino.*

Bibliography: Paoletti, *Archit. e scultura in Venezia,* p. 98.—Testi, *Storia della pitt. venez.,* I, p. 236.

**CATHEDRAL OF FRANCE (National).**—See Reims. For other Cathedrals see under their own names and under cities and towns where they are located.

**CATLIN (George).** — American painter (1796-1872), specialized in subjects for the life of the Red Indians (examples in the United States National Museum, Washington.)

**CATTANEO (Danese).**—Venetian sculptor of the 16th century. A pupil of Jacopo Sansovino. He contributed to the decoration of the Libreria Vecchia.

**CAVALLINI (Pietro).**—Roman painter and mosaicist, lived about 1250-1330. The factual evidence for this most important artist and head of the Roman school is very scant. In a document of 1273 there is mention of a "Petrus dictus Cavallinus de Cerronibus," which may or may not refer to Cavallini. In 1291 he signed the mosaics in Sta. Maria-in-Trastevere, Rome, and in 1308 he received a salary in Naples from the King.

In addition to the Sta. Maria-in-Trastevere mosaic series, the frescoes in Sta. Cecilia, Rome (probably 1293, in which year Arnolfo di Cambio was also working there); the fresco in S. Giorgio in Velabro, Rome (soon after 1295—that is to say soon after Jacopo Stefaneschi became Cardinal-deacon, he being the brother of Cavallini's patron, Bertholdo Stefaneschi who ordered the mosaics in Sta. Maria-in-Trastevere); and the *Ascension* on the entrance wall of the Upper Church of St. Francis at Assisi are attributed to Cavallini. Various other attributions have been made from time to time, including the frescoes in S. Maria in Donna Regina in Naples; and those in S. Giovanni Laterano and S. Maria in Aracœli, Rome.

Bibliography: Lorenzo Ghiberti, *Comment.,* II (ed. Frey), cap. IX; cf. *Cod. d. Anon. Gaddiano* (ed. Fabriczy, XVII, 17.—Vasari-Milanesi, I, 537 ff.—Baldinucci-Ranalli, I, 167, ff.—Titi, *Ammaestr. di pitt., etc., di Roma,* 1686, pp. 14, 36, 43, 52; *Descriz. d. pitt., etc., in Roma,* 1763, pp. 9, 44, 65, ff, 194.—D. Salazaro, *Pietro Cavallini.* Naples, 1882.—F. Hermanin, *Gli affreschi di Pietro Cavallini a S. Cecilia in Trastevere.* Rome, 1902.—Crowe and Cavalcaselle, Douglas ed., I, 201 ff, II, 312, III, 281.—A Venturi, *Storia d. arte ital.,* III, 888; IV, 91.—Van Marle, *Italian Schools,* I. 505 ff.—Morey, *Lost Mosaics and Frescoes of Rome.*

**CAVAZZOLA (Paolo).**—1486-1522. Venetian painter, pupil of Domenico Morone, the most important of the whole school at this time, who was inspired by the Venetians and by Raphael.

**CAVE DRAWINGS.**—See Pl. 13, Vol. I.

**CAZIN (Jean Charles).**—French painter (Saurer, Pas-de-Calais, 1841—Le Lavandou 1901). Son of a doctor he was educated at the College of Boulogne where he became an intimate friend of the two brothers Coquelin, the future actors of the Théâtre Français. The artistic gifts which he early showed were encouraged by his family, who sent him to Paris to follow the courses in drawing at the "Petite École," of the rue de l'École de Médecine, which was directed by Lecoq de Boisbaudran. He noticed Cazin's ability, guided him, and gave him a taste for teaching; for three years, the artist taught drawing at the special school of architecture of M. Trilat. But, naturally unstable and versatile, Cazin left Paris to work in solitude, and to paint on the borders of the forest of Fontainebleau. In 1868 Lecoq de Boisbaudran, who had not forgotten him, obtained for him the curatorship of the Museum of Tours and the directorship of the school of drawing there. To help the young director, he wrote him a series of letters which were published under the title of "Letters to a Young Teacher." Cazin set himself enthusiastically to work, when the war of 1870 awakened his taste for adventure. He left Tours in 1871, and went to England to found a school, with the painter Legros. The enterprise came to nought. Not discouraged, Cazin, who had always been interested in ceramic and who had attempted a little pottery in his youth, made decorative vases and utensils which were a great success.

But he did not forget painting and while appearing to hesitate to devote all his time to it, he did not cease to study it. In 1874 he left London and went to Italy with the sole aim of studying the old masters. He returned in 1875, crossed France, stopped in his native country, and went to Antwerp for some months to follow the course of the Academy of painting. He was then 34 years old. On his return to Boulogne, he sent a simple study, painted of the quays, the Dockyard, to the Salon. Its success made him decide to settle in Paris. From then he exhibited regularly at the Salon, and every year he awakened among both artists and public, interest, surprise, and sympathy. His art, at once very simple and very refined, changed the outlook of art-lovers. The equal importance given to the figure and to the landscape seemed odd, and was in any case expressed in a new way. Cazin was mentioned for his *Flight into Egypt* (1877), and won a first medal with *Ishmaël*, which was bought by the state, for the Luxembourg Museum. But after the *Souvenir de Fête* (1881), and *Judith* (1883) he again disappeared, drawn away by his taste for solitude and travelling; he revisited Holland, Flanders, and Italy. When he returned in 1888, his art seemed transformed by his increasing taste for realism. Until the end of his life he only painted landscapes, corners of villages at nightfall—very personal in feeling and with great charm of colour. Principal works: *Death Chamber of Gambetta* (Luxembourg); *Souvenir de Fête à Paris* (Galliera Museum); *Tobias* (Lille Museum); *Hagar and Ishmaël* (Luxembourg); *End of the Day* (Lyon); *Judith,* and *The Departure* (collection of Mrs. Potter-Palmer).

Cazin recalls both Millet and Puvis de Chavannes. Less bitter and less severe than Millet, he lacks his most delicate harmonies. Less ideal and less decorative than Puvis de Chavannes, he held more closely to reality. At the beginning of his career he used Biblical subjects in modern decorations with figures taken from contemporary life. This rendering of the Bible, which caused astonishment, was not new. Rembrandt had thus interpreted his *Disciples at Emmaus*, and his *Good Samaritan*. Cazin also studied Poussin's harmony of figures and landscape, the unity of emotion in his actors, and his intimate poetry. But in this kind of painting, he struck only one note: the tender, humble and sad. The cast-out Hagar weeps; Tobias longs to heal his father; Judith goes forth to sacrifice for her country; the Virgin and Joseph flee into Egypt. When some landscape impressed him, he endeavoured to evoke an historical or legendary scene. The importance of landscape increased and soon he painted nothing else: *The End of the Day, Souvenir de Fête,* and his career ended in the simple reproduction of the familiar places where his life passed. The figures disappeared. He painted landscapes of the Pas-de-Calais, and Seine-et-Marne. The teller of tales became a rustic poet. The landscape was no longer used as a setting for a subject: it was itself the subject, and, in accordance with the feeling in all his work, he chose a poor countryside in melancholy evening light. By reason of this melancholy, and by his sense of poetry, and the newness of his cloud effects, Cazin recalls Corot.

Bibliography: L. Bénédite, *Cazin.*

**CECCARELLI (Naddo).**—Painter of Siena, pupil of Lippo Memmi, active middle of 14th century.

**CEFALÙ (Sicily).**—The *Cathedral* was begun in 1145 by King Roger of Naples. The King was Norman and there are many Norman features in the building. The Cathedral contains beautiful 12th century Byzantine mosaics. There are Moorish elements as well.

**CELLA.**—See Greece (Architecture).

**CELLINI (Benvenuto).**—Florentine sculptor and goldsmith, 1500-1571. One of Michelangelo's pupils who is celebrated not because he imitated his master, but because he knew how to do something else, and became the greatest goldsmith of his age. His name suggests marvels of elegance and richness—bronze, silver and gold, soft forms with shining reflections, the graceful curves of animals, chimeras and plants, expressed in a supple, sensitive modelling. But it suggests also, besides all this sumptuous art, an extraordinarily wild, proud, quarrelsome life, and a glitter of knife-blades. Cellini is as famous for his graphic memoirs as for his works. They must be read for a knowledge of the customs of his time.

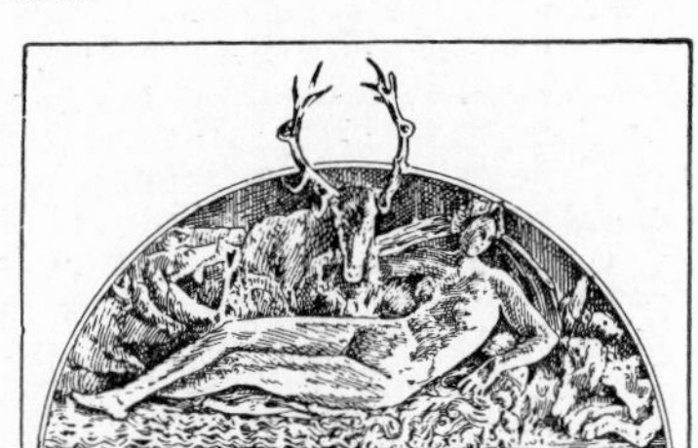

Cellini (Benvenuto): Diana. (Louvre.)

To prove his noble birth, he relates that his family went back to a lieutenant of Julius Cæsar, Florentius of Cellino, who founded Florence, and set up his camp near the city of Fiesole. His childhood passed in the midst of harpsichords, lutes, and harps, which his father made. He studied the goldsmith's art, chiefly with Antonio di Sandro. But while still young, he began that life of adventures which never found him long in the same place. He went to Pisa, to Siena, to Bologna, to Rome. He was exiled, and returned. The first time he went to Rome was to copy the antique. He set out on horseback with his friend Tasso, stayed with one Firenzola and worked fairly seriously for a time. But one day when he was collecting pebbles on the beach of Ostia, he was attacked by pirates. He freed himself by his bravery. Opportunities of using his sword were not lacking. Fêtes, masked-balls, banquets, his love for the beautiful Pantasilea, were, together with his skirmishes, the background of a life which his work enriched with silver candlesticks, golden vases and table services, enamels, girdle-clasps, and metals, which were ordered from him by the rich Roman Cardinals. (Some cameos at Chantilly, in the Bibliothèque Nationale, Paris; and in Vienna, are attributed to him.) He killed the Constable de Bourbon during the Siege of Rome (1527). Seeking refuge in the Castle of Sant'Angelo, he spent terrible days which seem in keeping with his fiery temperament. Later, he wounded the Prince of Orange. Thus in the turbulent Italy of those days, he lived through a thousand dangers, killed, loved, and worked.

Besides his lively memoirs, he left reliquaries and seals. The stamp of the seal of Hippolyte d'Este is in the Lyon Museum: the figures are crowded, but the whole is still elegant (1539).

In 1540, Benvenuto Cellini left for France in order to work near Francis I. Until then, he had only travelled for adventure. He now went to live and work in the smiling tranquillity of Fontainebleau.

He had artists of all countries to help him, and two chosen pupils, Pagolo and Ascanio. Above all, he had the admiring protection of the king.

The famous gold salt-cellar was originally part of the royal treasure of France. From there it passed to the Archduke Ferdinand of Austria, then to the collections of the Château of Ambres, and the Museum of Vienna. In reality, Cellini had begun it for his protector, the Cardinal of Ferrara. But he finished it for Francis I. It is an extraordinary and magnificent jewel. Earth and ocean are represented by the supple figures of a woman and a man, facing and balancing each other, surrounded by crowded, symbolic details.

The *Nymph of Fontainebleau*, a bronze bas-relief, which is now in the Louvre, was made for the gardens of Fontainebleau, and for a long time adorned the entrance-door of the Château d'Anet. A little stiff and dry, the long-limbed figure is admirably adapted to the middle of the tympanum, which is surmounted by the high antlers of a stag.

In the end Cellini fell out of favour at the court of Francis; and the hostility of the Duc d'Etampes caused him to leave in 1545. Nevertheless, he had made his influence felt in France.

He returned to Florence, where he sought the patronage of Cosimo de' Medici.

The *Greyhound*, a bronze bas-relief in the Bargello, is attributed to him. It has the decorative silhouette of Pisanello. Certainly the new goldsmith had, like the old artist, a predilection for animals, and one finds a great many dogs, roebucks, wild boars, etc., in his work, besides chimeras and monsters, for his imagination often led him to other worlds than ours.

Towards the end of his life, he took chiefly to sculpture, and one finds a great many schemes and rough models from his studio, but few definite works remain. We no longer have the *Leda with her Four Children,* nor the group of *Apollo and Hyacinth,* cut in a block provided by Bandinelli, nor the bust or statue of the Duchess Eleonore, nor the *Ganymede*; nor have we the wax models for a *Virgin,* for a *Hercules Killing Antæus,* and for a *Neptune* made for a competition in which Ammanati carried off the prize. Nevertheless, we may still see the bronze bust of Cosimo de' Medici which is in the Bargello, and the famous *Perseus* (1553), in the Loggia dei Lanzi. There is a rough model for this statue in the Bargello—a little different, calmer and taller, than the finished bronze. The work lasted for years. One must read the pathetic account of it in the artist's memoirs—how the marvellous figure finally emerged from the turmoil of its dramatic casting. The young Perseus is pitying his victim, while triumphantly and cheerfully holding aloft the bloody head: the pedestal has charming statuettes in niches, and fine bas-reliefs. The one representing Perseus delivering Andromeda is like strange, lyrical music. The whole is strong, perfect in execution, rich and harmonious. What distinction beside the works of his jealous rival, the terrible Bandinelli! They both competed with each other in making a Crucifix. That of Cellini is now in the Escorial, having been offered to Philip II by the Grand Duke Francis. It is beautiful and calm and very moving, and seems far removed from petty disputes of the world. But the carving of the figure of the Christ did not abate Bandinelli's jealousy. One day he tried to poison Cellini.

Cellini (Benvenuto): Gold salt-cellar. (Museum, Vienna.)

The great goldsmith, who took orders in 1558, and was afterwards released from his vows, ended by marrying, and having children. He died of pleurisy on the 14th February, 1571, and was buried with great ceremony in the Annunziata.

**CENNINO di DREA CENNINI di VAL D'ELSA, commonly known as CENNINO CENNINI.**—Florentine painter born c. 1370 in Colle di Valdelsa. Supposedly for 12 years a pupil of Agnolo Gaddi, certainly trained in the Giottesque tradition. There is no extant work by Cennino Cennini, but he is widely known for his valuable "Trattato della Pittura," which explains the principles and technique of the Giottesque school.

BIBLIOGRAPHY: *Il Libro dell'Arte o Trattato della Pittura, di Cennino Cennini da Colle di Val d'Elsa.* Florence, Le Monnier, 1869.

**CERAMIC.**—Ceramic is the art of shaping, baking and decorating all kinds of objects for use or purely for decoration, made of a plastic material with a clay base; with the exception of terra cotta sculpture, which belongs rather to statuary modelled by hand and not cast.

*Classification.*—Two main groups must be distinguished: (1.) Pottery, and (2.) porcelain.

(1.)—Ceramic belonging to the first group is:—

(a.) Comparatively soft, and absolutely opaque. (b.) It is permeable. (c.) Its glaze (enamel, varnish, or glaze) adheres to the paste and does not become one with it. (d.) It is baked at a rather low temperature.

(2.)—Ceramic of the second group is:—

(a.) Hard, and more or less translucent. (b.) It is impermeable, and sonorous. (c.) Its glaze becomes one with the paste and could not be separated from it. (d.) It is baked at a high temperature.

*Non-Vitreous Ceramics.*—If these are not covered with any varnish

FRAGMENTS OF LARGE VASES OF THE MYCENÆAN PERIOD. (Louvre.)

or enamel, like the prehistoric potteries or the little figures in "terre de Lorraine," they are *terra-cottas.* If they have a thin lustre, colourless or black, they are *lustre ware.* When the clay is covered with a transparent enamel (uncoloured or coloured) it is known as *glazed-pottery.* Instead of a transparent glaze, the clay may be covered, to modify its colour, with a clay artificially coloured and kept in water, called "slip."

*Tin-enamelled* pottery, made of clay, the natural colour of which is hidden under an opaque enamel (white or coloured), which contains lead and tin.

*Vitreous Ceramics.*—One kind of vitreous ceramic has a base of ordinary clay, and under a certain thickness is opaque: this is known in French as *grès.* Another kind, with a base of kaolin, and translucent, is *hard porcelain. Soft porcelain* is an artificial product, the elements of which are similar to those which compose glass. They are baked at a very low temperature. English soft porcelain contains a certain proportion of clay.

Ceramics are moulded by turning and casting.

The baking is done in a clay oven, heated with wood or coal. The degree of heat used depends upon the nature of the porcelain. Hard porcelain requires great heat (over 1400 degrees); whereas soft porcelain needs only a small fire.

The methods of decoration are very numerous: incision, clay reliefs added on, inlays of coloured clay, slips, coloured enamels, underglaze painting (applied with a brush on the raw piece after a first baking, and before it has received its enamel), over-glaze painting (applied after enamelling; and baking of enamel;—the piece then passes into a muffle-kiln—the colours then vitrify, by incorporating superfi-

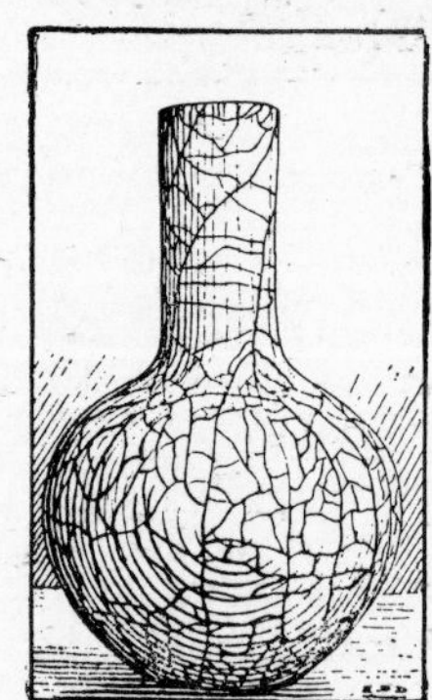

CRACKLED VASE. (Musée Cernuschi.)

cially with the softened enamel). Gilding is always made on the glaze, in the muffle-kiln.

A piece of ceramic is "crackled" when the enamel is covered with a net-work of little splits, produced by an unequal expansion and contraction of the clay and its glaze in the process of heating. The "crackling" sometimes constitutes the only decoration to a piece of pottery. If the net-work is very fine it is not "crackled," but "speckled."

*Technique.*—The material employed in ceramic is clay (usually supplemented with various elements) which is baked, and generally has a vitreous coating, called the *glaze.*

Clay is used because of its plasticity. It has both sufficient plasticity to allow of its being modelled, and, at the same time, enough cohesion of its elements for the modelled piece to retain its form, and not to break under its own weight.

During the drying, the evaporation of the tiny drops of water included in the mass produces a considerable shrinkage, which may be as much as 20% of the original size. The advantage of this is to facilitate its withdrawal from the mould. But it has the serious inconvenience of nearly always producing cracks in the baking, and

WINGED BULL FROM SUSA. (Louvre.)

even in the drying. The shrinkage may be reduced by mixing the clay with substances which cannot absorb water; these particles constitute a kind of formless net-work in the mass, and support it during the baking and drying. The best substance for this purpose is clay (of the same kind which is being used) baked to a very high temperature, and pounded into minute grains. The preparation of this is costly, and as a rule silica is used.

Once dried and baked, the clay is porous, owing to "voids" left by the evaporation of the water. These "voids" may comprise as much as 30% of the whole volume. Sometimes the ceramic may be left in this porous state (if, for instance, it is to be used as a filtre). Generally, however, impermeability is preferred, and this is achieved by mixing the clay with flux, which has the property of fusing, vitrifying, and filling the voids. Mica, felspar, phosphate of lime, or finely powdered glass may be used. But the presence of the flux increases the risk in fabrication: if it is heated too little the flux does not vitrify, and the clay remains porous; if it is heated too much, it runs and the shape of the piece is spoiled. In spite of all precautions, the waste may be as much as 50%, and this is one of the reasons for the high price of porcelain.

HYDRIA: HECTOR'S DEPARTURE. CORINTH. (Louvre.)

Whatever kind of glaze is used, it is important that its capacity for expansion should be equal or slightly superior to that of the clay.

The decoration of ceramic may be realised by three different methods: (a.) the clay may be painted, with a brush, with solutions of metallic nitrates in glycerine; (b.) the glaze may be coloured directly by the incorporation of metallic salts; or (c.) the decoration may be drawn by means of infusible albuminates and silicates. The ornamentation may be done by hand, by the application of rubber stamps, or transfers.

STATUE OF A WOMAN. (Terra cotta from Tanagra. Louvre.)

Some of the materials used for ceramic have been known from furthest antiquity. Others are almost modern. But what most varies in the different ages are the methods used for decoration, and the nature of the glazes employed.

*Ceramics in Antiquity.*—Glazed and enamelled pottery existed in *Egypt* and *Chaldea* from very early

SILENUS. (Greek terra cotta figure, Louvre.)

times. We have indicated how the glaze could be produced naturally in certain conditions. The Egyptians were able to procure it at will, and they coloured it a greenish blue by means of oxide of copper, and a violet blue by means of oxide of cobalt. The earth they used was not very plastic, was baked at a high temperature, and became extremely durable. In this way they made the statuettes which have been discovered in their tombs. In the Memphite period an enamel was used with which they made the eyes of statues, and covered utensils. Enamel was also used in architectural ornament. In *Chaldea,* the same methods were used, but they were largely applied to raiment. A great many remains of enamelled articles have been brought to light in the region which extends between the Indus and the Euphrates; and some fine pieces have been discovered in Khorsabad. In Susa, the winged bulls were made of baked clay, mixed with straw before being baked. The carbonization of the straw takes the heat to the centre of the piece. The frieze of lions in the palace of Artaxerxes Mnemon is made of clay, cleaned with vitreous quartz, which takes enamel well. The contours are made by the application of thin partitions of clay, which separate the colours, and prevent the mixing of the enamels.

In *Greece,* on the contrary, enamelling was quite unknown, and glazing was never practised. Pottery was made of a soft clay. In the *Mycenæan* period (16th to 10th century B.C.) surfaces were decorated by means of chevrons, in alternate bands, of a blackish or dark red colour, which contrasted with a background of natural colour, pink, red or dark grey, according to the time of baking. The decoration is not obtained by means of metallic oxides, but with a paint brush charged with a fluid paste of coloured clay. Towards the end of this period (11th and 10th century B.C.), the piece was often entirely submerged in a mixture of white clay, and, then, after drying the surface was scraped away from the background, and the decoration obtained.

It was only about the 8th and 7th century B.C. that incised decoration, common with the Dorians and Ionians, appeared. About the same time there appeared in Corinth the famous potteries with black figures on a red ground, which were succeeded by red figures on a black ground. The clay is composed half of silica, an important quantity of albumin, and a little lime. It is wetted to obtain a uniform background, and then the figures are drawn with a paint brush. The nature of the lustre on this pottery is disputed. It is attributed either to a kind of glaze, the process of which has been lost, or to polishing. The Greek vases were twice baked.

Statuette of a woman. (Terra cotta from Tanagra, Louvre.)

In *Etruria* a black pottery (which is sometimes called "bucchero nero") was made, and decorated with reliefs. It was composed of very fine clay, with which was incorporated a good proportion of lampblack. In appearance, it is very like bronze. The figures are sometimes gilded, on the black background.

Under the *Roman Empire*, the demand for Etruscan pottery continued, but about the second century blackened clay was replaced by a very fine red earth, which was covered with a darker varnish. The chief centre was Arretium (Arezzo). Here, there were found, besides a great number of finished vases, the moulds which were used for their fabrication, and from which the process can be reconstructed. The mould was of clay. While it was still fresh, ornaments (already modelled and baked) were applied. Then it was baked at a very high temperature. Handles, feet or spouts were added separately to the cast pieces.

However, throughout antiquity, methods were used which are still employed today. Pottery was "turned," or modelled on a circular, horizontal plate, in rotation. This allowed of modelling by hand.

Faïence panel from the Pavilion of Forty Columns, at Ispahan (Persia). (Louvre.)

The methods practised in Arretium were imported into Gaul by the Roman conquest, and were developed in such a way that Gallo-Roman products soon supplanted those of Arretium.

Whilst Italian ceramic was thus evolving, the Greeks gradually came to use relief-decoration, and then they began to make terra cotta statuettes. Such is the origin of the little figures from Tanagra and Myrina (4th and 3rd centuries B.C.). . . .

Funeral stele of Hegeso. (Dipylon cemetery, Athens.)

*Oriental Ceramics.*—Moslem art developed in Persia, and, about the 14th century, reached Turkestan and India. Building involved the use of small materials arranged in corbels, which were hidden under a mosaic of enamelled pottery. A peculiarity is the use of colours obtained by reduction: a metallic oxide is reduced by oven heat, and brought to the state of pulverous metal. Thus a light and superficial metallization is produced, which gives beautiful reddish-brown tones, such as those seen on pottery wrongly known as Spanish-Mooresque (the Moors in Spain only applied a process which came to them from the East).

In Samarkand, in Turkestan, there still exist important architectural decorations in enamelled clay: the Medressehd (schools of theology) have façades and domes covered with turquoise blue, white and yellow enamel.

Persian influence spread to Egypt, as may be seen in the Mosque of Sultan Hassan, in Cairo, built between 1356 and 1358. From there, the methods spread westward, and the Medersa (School of Advanced Studies) of Tlemcen has a door covered with ceramic in geometric designs, which follows oriental technique very closely.

*Ceramics in the West.*—In the East almost the only material available for building and decoration is clay. In the West, on the contrary, enamelled clay has nothing like the same importance that it has in the East, in the covering of buildings. It is only used for partial decoration. The chief examples are to be found in Spain, in buildings erected under Moorish domination, such as the Alhambra, in Granada.

In Italy and France, baked clay was used fairly often in the construction of walls and vaults, but enamelled clay was only used for pavements. In Italy, brick buildings are covered internally with enamelled mosaic, or polished marble, but not with enamelled ceramic. It is only in modern times that we find attempts to apply enamelled clay to architectural decoration.

Bernard Palissy: Fecundity. (Oval platter of faïence, Arts Décoratifs.)

We have seen how the "Roman" pottery of Arretium was implanted and developed in Gaul. After the barbarian invasions, there was a return to the use of coarse materials, and uncouth incised decoration. About the 11th and 12th centuries, potters began to make vessels in finer clay, grey, with short necks and "fat" bodies. About the 12th century, in countries where clay was to be obtained, there seems to have been an attempt to varnish pottery, especially tiles. Two kinds of clay were used, white and red. The varnish of oxide of lead being reddish yellow in colour, and fairly transparent, these two kinds of clay became, after varnishing and baking, yellow and reddish brown.

Bernard Palissy: Large coarse platter of faïence. (Arts Décoratifs.)

These were all the elements of decoration. Small pieces were made in various shapes, which fitted like marquetry, according to a determined design. To obtain two colours on the same piece, the ornament was kept hollowed out, by means of a stamp or cast, and then the hollow was filled with clay of another colour.

Tin-enamelled pottery appears to have been introduced into Europe by way of Italy. It is supposed that the name of "Majolica" (see this word) which is often given to it, comes from that of the Island of Majorca, and an indication of its origin has been sought for there.

Sèvres porcelain vase.

However that may be, from the 15th to the 17th century, Italy applied to pottery and even to buildings, such subjects in moulded terra cotta as decorated arches and tympana. In this connection may be mentioned the figures of angels in the big cloister of the Certosa of Pavia, and the busts in high relief on the cornice of the little cloister. In the middle of the 15th century, Luca della Robbia thought of covering these potteries with stanniferous (tin) enamels (e.g., in San Miniato, Florence). In some figures, the flesh parts are not covered, and retain the red colour of the terra cotta.

Sèvres porcelain vase. (Arts Décoratifs.)

Beside the opaque tin-enamels of Luca della Robbia and his school, those of Palissy show a very different tendency. The glaze is transparent, and, moreover, the enamels are allowed to mingle in the baking, and this partial confusion results in those unexpected and charming colourings which make Palissy pottery so attractive. His celebrated dishes are known as "rustic ware."

About the same period, in the reign of Henri II, appeared the fine, pipe-clay pottery of Saint Porchaire and of Oiron. A fine white clay received an arabesque decoration, by inlays of bands of red or black. The glaze is amber-coloured, and transparent.

About the middle of the 16th century, studios for the making of ceramic already existed in Rouen, whence came white pottery with blue or polychrome decorations, radiating round a central ornament or arabesque. Nevers was another centre of pottery-making. Here, a glaze,

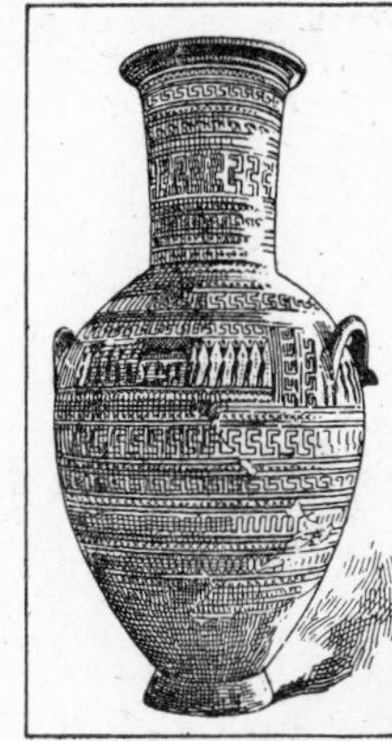

Attic vase from the Dipylon cemetery, Athens. (National Museum.)

coloured blue by cobalt, was used, and on this enamels were applied which, blending with the glaze, produced grey designs.

Dutch pottery, and especially Delft pottery, did not come into fashion until the 18th century. Beautiful coloured enamels were used on fine clay.

FRAGMENT OF A GREAT CRATER. (Dipylon, about ninth-eighth century B.C.)

At the same time, England produced fine opaque white ceramic, which, thanks to Wedgwood and his imitations of antique medallions, enjoyed a fleeting success.

"China" was unknown to the ancients. It appeared in China about the 10th century, and attained its perfection in the 15th century. In France, attempts were made to imitate it, about the 17th century. In 1761, a German potter sold the process of hard porcelain to the Sèvres manufacturers, who continued to make experiments. . . . Pottery manufactories opened in other countries, but none of them attained the perfection of the Sèvres products. Nevertheless, the royal factory of Copenhagen should be noted. From the end of the 19th century it has produced remarkable white porcelain, with blue-grey decoration; and, more recently, has turned out figures of animals, which are very delicate in form and colour, and deserve the success they have obtained.

See Pls. 6, 26, 27, 34, 37, Vol. I; Pl. 31, Vol. II. Also see China-Art.

BIBLIOGRAPHY: Burton and Hobson, *The Marks of Pottery and Porcelain.* London, 1908.—L. Magne, *Le décor de la terre.* Paris, Laurens, 1913.—Forrer, *Geschichte der Europaischen Pliesen Keramik.* Strassburg, 1901.—S. Vogt, *La Porcelaine.* Paris, 1893.—E. Hannover, *Pottery and Porcelain,* ed. by Bernard Rackham. London, 1925.

**CERANO (Il).**—See Crespi (Giovanni).

**CERES (Temple of).**—See Paestum.

**CEREZO (Mateo).**—Spanish painter (Burgos, 1635—Madrid, 1685). His father, himself a painter, taught him the rudiments of his art, and then, about 1650, when the young Mateo had reached his fifteenth year, he sent him to Madrid to study in the studio of Juan Carreño. From 1655 to 1665, Cerezo worked with great success in Madrid. Herrera el Mozo trusted to his collaboration for the execution of the dome of the Chapel of Our Lady of Atocha. A brilliant and delicate colourist, now inspired by Van Dyck, now by the Venetians, especially by the older Titian, but a mannered draughtsman with a taste for floating draperies, Cerezo was then at the height of his power. He painted a great many *Crucifixions* and *Magdalens,* among which is that in the Museum of The Hague.

Cerezo also executed "bodegones" or still-lifes as well as genre scenes of which, however, none are known today. He is praised for his painting of *Christ in Agony* at Burgos Cathedral (chapter room): "the figure of the Lord is modelled in warm color tonalities, and interesting is the treatment of the landscape with a phantastic city and snow-covered mountains in the background." In A. L. Mayer's opinion Cerezo's *St. John the Baptist* in the gallery of Cassel is one of his best creations. The large composition of *Christ at Emmaus,* painted for the Convent of the order of the Augustinos Recoletos of Madrid (1672) was one of his last works; it is now only known to us through the etching of José de Castillo (1778).

BIBLIOGRAPHY: A. de Beruete y Moret, *The School of Madrid.* London, 1909.—*Thieme-Becker,* vol. VI, Leipzig, 1912; art. *Mateo Cerezo* by A. L. Mayer.—A. L. Mayer, *Geschichte der spanischen Malerei.* Leipzig, 1922.

**CERTOSA.**—Carthusian monastery.

**— MAGNI.**—Lombard painter of the end of the 15th century and beginning of the 16th century. Follower of Cesare da Sesto. There is a *Holy Family* by him, in the Brera.

**CESARE da SESTO.**—Lombard painter, 1477-1527. Pupil of Leonardo da Vinci, he was hardly more than an imitator. He has a rather gracious, but unoriginal *Virgin* in the Brera Gallery, Milan.

**CÉZANNE (Paul).**—French painter. Aix-en-Provence, 1839-1906. Son of a banker, he studied law in Aix, then went to Paris to meet Zola, who had been his comrade at college and remained his best friend. In spite of his family, he decided to study painting, and frequented the studios. He was refused as a student at the École des Beaux-Arts. He studied and admired the old masters in the Louvre. But, of an excessive sensibility and shyness, he became frightened and discouraged by the competition of Parisian life, and he returned to Aix, confused and full of doubts. But in 1863, he returned to Paris, became intimate with Pissarro and Manet (whom he encouraged Zola to defend in the papers), and joined the young group of Impressionists, whose complicated and anti-traditional theories he did not, however, adopt. Rejected every year, he sent perseveringly to the Salon which he called with a mixture of irony and ingenuity, "le Salon de M. Bouguereau." In 1879, he left Paris, and returned to Aix, where he lived an isolated and almost uncivilised life. Only towards the end of his life, he made brief sojourns in Paris, and short trips to Belgium and Holland. He did not go to Italy. Even in his native town, he became a kind of foreigner. Misunderstood, despised, flying from inspection, followed by jests and stones, he painted for the joy of painting, caring nought for success, or even for personal souvenirs, for he often forgot his paintings, which his relatives would go and look for afterwards in the woods. Zola himself, who loved him much, and who often thought of him in writing his novel of the life of painters, "L'Œuvre," did not understand him either, and almost denied him. For twenty years, he lived absolutely unknown. It was with difficulty that some old Parisian friends came to know that he was still living, and working arduously. Finally, in 1895, a dealer, M. Vollard, exhibited in his shop in Paris fifty of his canvases—rough, forbidding, restricted in subject and primitive: "still lifes" of fruit in dishes and on cloths; heavy, massive landscapes; strange, distorted and clumsy nudes; strong, uningratiating portraits. These paintings frightened most people; but some paused and were influenced. Maurice Denis, Vaillard, and Gauguin recognised in Cézanne a master, and like him approached nature with a desire to realise her essential forms and pure colours. Cézanne, shy and misanthropic, never attempted to found a school, and denied several of his disciples, such as Gauguin, whom he accused of distorting his thought. Indeed, he had numerous false pupils, who thought they were following him by imitating his awkwardness and his subjects, drawing clumsily, and painting more clumsily still. But his influence on the new generation is undeniable.

He said: "When colour is richest, form is in its plenitude." He also said: "I want to make of Impressionism something solid and durable, like the art of the museums." Which shows that he wished to rebuild pictorial solidity by reaction against excessive analysis, and the abuse of reflections and decomposition in colour of impressionism. He considered himself, however, to be an initiator, a kind of "primitive" pointing out a new road: "I am the Primitive of the way I have discovered."

BIBLIOGRAPHY: Elie Faure, *Paul Cézanne.*—Roger Fry, *Cézanne.*—L. Venturi, *Cézanne.* 1937.

**CHAISE-DIEU (La) (Haute-Loire, France).**—The Church of St. Robert (begun, 1344) contains interesting frescoes representing the *Dance of Death.* The figures are painted in yellow and ochre, on a red ground.

**CHALDEA.**—See Assyria.

**CHALGRIN (Jean François).**—French architect (Paris, 1739-21st

CHALGRIN: ARC DE TRIOMPHE DE LA PLACE DE L'ÉTOILE, PARIS.

January, 1811). He belonged to a family of honest Parisian bourgeois. In 1758, he won the Grand Prix of the Academy of Architecture, and a King's pension to live for three years in Italy. On his return from Rome, he built the hôtel of the Duc de La Vrillière (rue Saint Florentin). In 1770, Chalgrin was admitted to the Royal Academy of Architecture, and in 1799, to the Institut. As King's architect, and first architect of the Comte de Provence, Chalgrin built numerous edifices in Paris, among them: the northern tower, the baptismal chapel, and the organ case of the Church of St. Sulpice, the Church of St. Philippe du Roule, the Meeting Hall of the Directoire, then of the Senate, the grand staircase of the right wing of the Luxembourg, the gardens, of which he extended; the new hall (since altered) of the Odeon; and, finally, his chief work, l'Arc de Triomphe de l'Etoile, begun in 1806, raised 5 metres at the time of his death, and of which the conception of the whole does him great honour. Chalgrin had numerous pupils, among them Goust, de Gisors, Viel and Percier.

**CHAMBIGES (Pierre).**—See Fontainebleau.

**CHAMBORD (Loir-et-Cher).**—The most famous of the châteaux of

CHAMBORD: LANTERN OF THE CHÂTEAU.

the Loire. Its plan is as simple as it is original. The central part is built round a famous double staircase, in spirals which overlap one above the other, in such a way that a person going up would not meet one who was descending. From this staircase as centre, stretch, in the form of a Greek cross, four vast halls or "salles des gardes," which each abut on a large tower, 20 metres in diameter. These towers are united by blocks of buildings. Two of them stand out on the façade. The roof is of extreme richness. The towering skylight, which crowns the spiral staircase, is a forest of chimneys, turrets, and windows, delicately carved. This keep forms the central part of a vast quadrilateral of low buildings, which has towers at the four angles.

Francis I began the château in 1519, and chose the site, on the banks of the Cosson, in a woody countryside. The work was carried out by Pierre Nepveu, known as Trinqueau, Denis Sourdeau and Jean Gobereau, on plans inspired by Domenico di Cortona, called Boccador. Francis I died before the completion of Chambord, which was finished by Henry II. Louis XIII and Louis XIV stayed there several times, and effected certain restorations.

See Pl. 1, Vol. I; Pl. 27, Vol. II.

**CHAMPAGNE SCHOOL.**—See Bachot.

**CHAMPAIGNE (Philippe de).**—Painter, born in Brussels (1602-1674). At twelve years of age, he was placed with a Brussels painter, named Bouillon, then with another, called Bourdeaux, and he worked for the landscape painter, Fouguières. In 1621, Champaigne set out for Rome, but he stopped in Paris and studied there under mediocre artists, and painted the portrait of "Jansenius," whose austere doctrine he adopted.

The young Fleming put his native realism to the service of the Port Royal. About 1623, he came to feel the nobler influence of Nicolas Poussin. He was engaged on the decoration of the Luxembourg, by Duchesne, painter of Marie de' Médicis; and, in 1628, on the death of Duchesne, he was given his position, and married his daughter.

Commissioned by the queen-mother and by Richelieu to paint sacred and profane decorations, which add nothing to his fame, Champaigne soon became on intimate terms with the chief Jansenists, with Lemaistre and his brother, Lemaistre de Sacy, the same who translated the Bible in the Bastille, with the powerful Arnauld family, and especially with Arnauld of Andilly, "l'ami universel," whom he painted three times. Finally, about 1636, he made the acquaintance of the Abbé of Saint Cyran, the intimate friend and inspirer of Jansenius.

His reputation grew; the Cardinal posed for him several times. Champaigne's serious realism gives his portraits a naturalism which was very rare at that period. There is no straining after allegory, and no display of pomp, save that of the prelate's costume, the severe folds of which envelop the thin, haughty figure of the powerful minister. Portraying Richelieu as he saw him, Champaigne expressed all the dignity of his model (Louvre). Much more than the portrait of Louis XIII, still more than that of the painter by himself (both in the Louvre), the portrait of the Cardinal shows, with singular force, the characteristics of the individual, of the age, and of the artist's talent.

Although always faithful to his native realism, Champaigne, owing to his living in France and especially in the society of the Port Royal, felt keenly the moral preoccupations of contemporary French society.

His *Dead Christ* (Louvre) is so corpse-like that one is almost tempted to believe the absurd story, according to which the painter assassinated his model in order to have in front of him a dead and wounded body; but it is enough to contemplate this livid mysteriously lighted figure, and the face of the Crucified, hidden in shadow, to dispel the fears of the credulous. One is not surprised to learn that sometimes the Jansenist artist deserted his principles to revere the image of Christ the Victim.

This rigid and ascetic faith, so far removed from that of a Le Sueur or of a François de Sales, we again find in those fine portraits of the persecuted—"la Mère Angélique," Saint Syran, Arnauld d'Andilly, Antoine Arnauld—which are so natural and so energetic. There, far more than in his large religious compositions, in his cartoons for the Louvre, and still more than in his *Last Supper*, we see the healthy and dignified piety of Champaigne. It is the very vigour of this sentiment which makes the *Portraits of La Mère Catherine, Agnès Arnauld and of Sœur Catherine Sainte Suzanne* (Louvre), a pure masterpiece. This Sœur Sainte Suzanne was Champaigne's own daughter, healed as though by a miracle. The father represented his daughter reclining on the very chair in which she had suffered so much. The Mère Catherine is kneeling in front of the invalid, and a ray of light illuminates her. There is no ornament or allegory; only on the bare, white-washed wall can be read Philippe de Champaigne's acknowledgment, perpetuating the memory of this wonderful recovery. The folds of the dresses are straight and simple as the faith of these two nuns, who have pale hands, colourless lips, and expressions more meditative than ecstatic. It is a work not only of great piety, but very human in its appeal.

As an academician, Champaigne must have been the only one to attempt to react against the formidable teaching of Poussin. It was hard enough to uphold the rights of nature and life against LeBrun. This grave, dignified life, so full of works, ended in Paris, on the 12th August, 1674.

Bibliography: Stein, *Philippe de Champaigne et ses relations avec Port Royal*, in Réunion des Sociétiés des Beaux Arts des departements, 1891.—Gazier, *Philippe et Jean-Baptiste de Champaigne*, 1893.

**CHAMPENOISE (School of Sculpture).**—A school of sculpture at the end of the 15th and during the 16th century. Its history shows the passing from the Gothic to the Renaissance period, and the progress of Italianism. Its centre was Troyes. Many works have come down to us, but most of them are anonymous. The figure of St. Martha (Church of St. Urbain, Troyes) is one of the finest works of the school.

**CHAMPLEVÉ.**—See Enamel.

**CHAMPMOL (Chartreuse de).**—The Chartreuse of Champmol was

Champmol: Doorway of the old Carthusian Convent.

founded in 1383, by Philippe le Hardi, Duke of Burgundy, who wished to have his tomb and those of his descendants placed there. The greatest artists of the day worked there, Claus Sluter, Jean de Marville, Jacques de Baerze, etc., and they made a wonderful building. The Revolution destroyed this masterpiece of art, of which there remain only the tombs of the Dukes of Burgundy, now in Dijon Museum; altarpieces (Dijon Museum); the doorway of the old church, used for the chapel of the establishment, and the *Well of Moses* (see Sluter). On the chapel doorway is a pleasing statue of the Virgin and Child, statues of Philippe le Hardi and his patron, St. John the Baptist, and of his wife, Marguerite of Flanders, with St. Catherine.

**CHAMPS ÉLYSÉES.**—See Paris.

**CHANG SENG-YU.**—C. 502-557, Chinese painter, active during Liang dynasty.

**CHANTILLY.**—The Château of Chantilly is composed of two parts: the little château or "capitainerie," built about 1560 by Jean Bullant, for the High Constable of Montmorency, and the large château,

Chantilly: The Château.

modern, built from 1876 to 1882, by the architect Daumet, for the Duc d'Aumale on the site of the old château destroyed in the Revolution. After the execution of Henri de Montmorency, this old château came into the hands of Henri II de Bourbon Condé, in 1632. It was inhabited by the great Condé, who there lived an ostentatious life and entertained the king with splendid fêtes. There, at a banquet to Louis XIV, occurred the suicide of the cook, Vatel, as told by Madame de Sévigné. The most famous authors of the period, Racine, Boileau, Molière, La Fontaine, Fénelon, etc., frequented the residence of the great Condé. The Duc d'Aumale, the last heir of the Condé, bequeathed the Château of Chantilly to the Institute of France, after having restored it and enriched it with a magnificent collection which is there preserved.

The park was designed by Le Nôtre, about 1663. A part of the park, the "jardin de Silvie," encloses the "maison de Silvie," a pretty hunting rendezvous, built in the 17th century.

Among the masterpieces kept in the Musée Condé of Chantilly must be mentioned: Raphael's *Vièrge d'Orléans* (1507), and his *Three Graces* (1500); *Esther and Ahasuerus*, by Filippino Lippi; and forty miniatures, by Jean Fouquet, painted from 1452 to 1460, for the Book of Hours of Etienne Chevalier, treasurer of Charles VII. These paintings are collected together in a little room, called the Sanctuary, which also houses the famous manuscript known as *Les Très Riches Heures du Duc de Berry*. Many schools are represented in the Condé Museum. The French school, by Philippe de Champaigne, Poussin, Rigaud, Largillière, Prud'hon, Watteau, Gros, Delacroix (*The Two Foscari*), Ingres (*Stratonice, Venus Anadyomene, Madame Devauçay*), Meissonier, Fromentin (*Falcon Hunt*), Corot, Detaille, etc. The Italian school is represented by Giotto, Fra Angelico, Botticelli, Pollaiuolo, Perugino, Raphael, Francia, Vinci, Palma Vecchio, Titian (*Ecce Homo*), Tiepolo, etc. The Flemish school, by Van Ostade, Ruysdaël, Teniers, etc., etc.

Chantilly possesses some fine grisailles on which, according to Palustre, Jean le Pot represented the Story of Psyche, after cartoons by Michel Coxcie. This glass had been executed for the Château of Ecouen, which also belonged to the Condé family.

See Pl. 31, Vol. II.

**CHAO MENG-FU.**—1254-1322, Chinese painter and official during Yuan dynasty. Received posthumous title of Duke of Chou. Famous for paintings of horses. See China—Art.

**CHAO PO-CHU.**—Chinese painter of twelfth century. He followed the "blue and green" style of Li Ssu-hsun. See China—Art.

**CHAPU (Henri).**—French sculptor, 1833-1891. *St. Joan Listening to the Voices* is one of his most popular works.

See Pl. 52, Vol. II.

Bibliography: O. Fidière, *Chapu.*

**CHARDIN (Jean Baptiste Siméon).**—French painter, 1699-1779. This artist's work had no other theme than the reproduction of his own peaceful existence, the horizon of which hardly stretched beyond his own courtyard and the quiet rooms of his house, representative of innumerable French interiors of his day.

Chardin (Siméon). (Pastel by La Tour, Louvre.)

Such a quiet, gentle existence was for a long time hidden in the neighbourhood of the Rue de Seine, in one of those narrow abodes which only the order and discretion of the Parisian housewife can make habitable. Chardin was born in this quarter, on the 2nd November, 1699, second son of a father who was a master joiner, maker of billiard-tables, by appointment to the king, and of a mother whose name was Jeanne Françoise David. Yielding to his desire to be a painter, he joined the studio of the Academician Cazes, the best reputed studio. The teaching was on conventional lines, and suggested later this reflection: "At seven or eight years of age we are given a pencil. We begin to draw according to example, eyes, noses, mouths, ears, and then feet and hands. When we have long been round-shouldered over the drawing-book, we are placed in front of Hercules, or a torso, and you will never know the tears that this Satyr, Gladiator, Venus di Medici, and Antaea have caused. . . ." In several of his little pictures, he shows the pupil engaged in this way, copying an antique subject.

He added: "After having wearied out the days, and spent nights by the lamp in front of inanimate nature, we are presented with living nature, and suddenly the work of preceding years seems to be reduced to nothing. . . . They keep us five or six years in front of the model, before they deliver us to our own bent, if we have one. . . ." It was his second master, Noël Nicholas Coypel, who gave him this surprise of "leaving him to his bent": a hunter's gun, to be reproduced in its true lighting, was the self-revealing occasion. Henceforward his eyes were open to the most immediate realities. One day, a surgeon-barber having ordered a sign, or rather a picture to be placed as a ceiling over the front of the shop, he had the idea of representing that everyday street scene: a gaping crowd round an accident; he showed a dentist, wounded by his adversary, being carried to the surgeon; the periwigged commissionaire makes a formal statement, and a Sister of Charity helps the wounded man. . . . The picture painted in a lively manner, would make passers-by stop. Chardin's next feat again had the street for audience. At one of the "Expositions de la Jeunesse," which took place in the open air, on the Place Dauphine, during the morning of Corpus Christi, he exhibited (1728) his famous painting of the *Skate*, whose warm execution can be admired in the Louvre. One might say that this opened the doors of the Academy to him straight away: he had only to add its fellow, the *Buffet*, which is in the same room. Not only was he "accepted," but he was at the same time made a member. To sound the feeling of Academicians, Chardin displayed his pictures in a room without making their author known. Largillière, who, besides his preoccupations as a portraitist, had a very sensitive eye for the art of still-life, and held an important place at the Academy, passed by there, and thought that these paintings were Flemish pieces.

Chardin's first marriage was of short duration (four years). On his wife's death he was left with two children, a boy and a girl. To this time belong his first pictures of family scenes, such as the *Grace*, which alternated with his simple paintings of still-life. Chardin then lived in the rue Princesse, always in the neighbourhood of his original house, while one of his brothers carried on the paternal trade of joiner in the same street.

In 1744, after nine years of widowhood, he married a well-to-do widow of thirty-seven, Françoise Marguerite Pouget, of whom there is an engraving by Laurent Cars, and perhaps also a picture in the Carnavalet Museum, attributed to Aved, which strongly resembles the model in the engraving, and represents her at her spinning-wheel. At the Academy, Chardin was promoted to the position of adviser, and, owing to his instinct for order and economy, he was shortly afterwards given charge of the treasury. Three years later, in 1759, he achieved the still more delicate position of "tapissier du Louvre," which consisted in arranging the pictures according to periods. Critics of the day pay homage to the taste, tact and impartiality which he showed in this difficult task, and to the example of moderation he gave. "Gentlemen, be indulgent," he advised. "Among all these pictures, find the worst, and know that, even to do so badly, two thousand unfortunate ones have broken their paint-brushes between their teeth in despair—Lemoine said that he needed thirty years' practice to do a sketch worth preserving, and Lemoine was no fool. If you take my advice, you will be indulgent." These services were rewarded, from 1757, by the grant of a pension of five hundred livres, to which another of two hundred was added a little later. He practiced his attentive, peaceful art until he was eighty years old. He died on the 6th December, 1779, a little neglected, it is true, by the new generation, but giving them the example of an astonishing challenge to the attempts of age, by the three pastels in the Louvre, in which he has represented himself and his old companion.

Chardin charms us by the inimitable quality of his execution. "O Chardin," Diderot wrote of him, "you paint not with white or red or black, but with the very substance of the objects you represent, with air and light." And the best of Chardin's successors, Goncourt and Decamps, repeated in despair to Mariette, "Chardin's whites! I can't find them!" Now, as formerly, his workmanship excites curiosity, and makes one try to discover its secrets.

In the first place, we know from Mariette that he did not make sketches or studies on paper, which explains the rarity of his drawings. He worked directly from nature. Seen from near by, he often arrived at what, states a contemporary critic (Lacombe, Salon of 1753), "looked, at first, only like a kind of mist, which seemed to envelop all the objects." In a final operation the master blended his colours. The result of this finishing process is a softening of light-and-shade, and a repetition of the equal lighting effect which generally characterises his pictures. But artists and critics have attempted to discover what is hidden behind that which has been called "a kind of mist blown on to the canvas, a light foam cast there." They have recognized that the artist has more than once adopted the means of the juxtaposition of tones, but with a restraint and discretion that make them only felt by the eye curious to penetrate the mystery of an art as subtle as it is attractive. Even in his own day, it was said: "See how all is confused, and smooths itself out. . . . Thick coats of paint are applied one on top of another, and the effect of the bottom layer shows on the uppermost one" (Diderot).—"He places his colours one close to another, almost without mixing them, in such a way that his work has a slight resemblance to mosaic." (Journal of J. G. Wille).—"These are not finished touches. . . . It is rough and uneven." (Letter to the Marquise de S. P. R., Paris, 1738.)

Chardin's technique is, indeed, exceedingly complex, owing to the multiplicity of his touches which are as much relative to reflections as to the atmosphere. His themes have little variety, but his observation is insatiable. Within his little world, the sight of things gave him a thousand surprises, which kept his artistic soul busy. It was to these intimate emotions that he alluded when he said to his pupils: "One designs with colours; one paints with feeling." His most famous works are: in the Louvre—*The Busy Mother, Grace, Menu de Maigre, Menu de Gras, The Housewife, Child with a Teetotum, The Monkey Antiquary, The Copper, The Skate,* and several "still-lifes," his own portrait and that of his wife, in pastel; *The Dead Hare* (Stockholm); *Provisions for Convalescence* (Liechtenstein Gallery, Vienna); *Le Négligé* (Stockholm); *The House of Cards* (Leningrad); *The Governess* (Liechtenstein Gallery, Vienna). The chief European museums, and many private collections, possess works by Chardin, and the subjects are always akin to those here mentioned.

See Pl. 8, Vol. I; Pl. 46, Vol. II.

Bibliography: Goncourt, *L'art au XVIII^e siècle,* 1873, Vol. I.—Charles Normand, *Chardin,* 1901; Collection des Artistes célèbres.—Gaston Schefer, *Chardin,* 1904. Collection des grands Artistes.—Edmond Pilon, *Chardin.* Collection des Maîtres de l'Art.—H. E. A. Furst, *Chardin,* 1911.

**CHARIOTEER OF DELPHI.**—This bronze statue was discovered in the excavations of Delphi. It formed part of a considerable group: a chariot harnessed with four horses, a charioteer or aurige, standing on the chariot by the side of his master, and one or two servants in attendance on each side of the horses. The whole rested on a stone base, and on the anterior side was engraved a metrical inscription in two verses only the final hemistich of which can be read. It tells us that the work had been consecrated by a certain Polyzalos, to Apollo Pythea. The characters of the second line being archaic Sicilian, it has been plausibly concluded that this Polyzalos was the brother of the tyrants of Syracuse, Gelon, Hieron and Thrasybulus and that his offering at Delphi could not have been after the year 468 B.C. It is thought, too, that it may have been consecrated earlier, in 477, on the occasion of the victory of Gelon in the Pythian games. As Gelon died before he could offer his votive statue, Polyzalos, his brother, took over this task.

The *Charioteer* is standing, the right leg perhaps slightly bent. The right fore-arm is raised, the hand holding the reins. He is clad in a long chiton, caught in by a girdle, and falling in long grooved pleats. The head, like the hand and the two feet, has been executed with extreme refinement by an artist who cared greatly for truth. The eye is made more lifelike by the brightness of enamel. A slight asymmetry in the face makes the realism still more striking. The only mark of archaism is in the rather rigid regularity of the folds of the dress. The sculptor has no more progress to make in the modelling of the nude; but he is not yet free enough to treat the drapery with suppleness. It is asked to which artist one must attribute this masterpiece. The most illustrious names of the period are those of Calamis, Pythagoras, and Onatas; but one does not know to which group of statuary the *Charioteer* ought to belong. Some compare it to the works of Argos; those who contest the existence of this school insist upon the resemblance which exists between the head of the *Charioteer of Delphi* and those of certain painted figures by Euphronios, the Attic vase painter.

See Pl. 20, Vol. I.

Bibliography: Homolle, *Monuments Piot,* 1897.

**CHARLEMAGNE.**—See Aix-la-Chapelle.

**CHARLET (Nicolas Toussaint).**—French painter and lithographer (Paris, 20th December, 1792-29th December, 1845). Son of a Republican dragoon and a mother who was enthusiastic for Imperial glories. Charlet was taught by Gros in 1817 when the quite recent invention of lithography gave him the chance to reveal himself. "Horace Vernet's soldiers were conventional . . . the soldiers of Scribe; those of Charlet were the only real ones." This saying of a hero of the Empire was true. Charlet did not try to dramatise, and his work shows something of the glamour of childhood. One day, as a child, he had caught a glimpse of the Emperor in a procession; a momentary image which made a lasting impression on his mind. He enlarged, idealised, and reconstructed it, and finally drew that unforgettable figure which he transmitted to his successors, to Bellangé, and Raffet, and which no one since has dared to change.

In 1820, during a visit which they made together to London, Charlet introduced Géricault to lithography. But it was not until about 1822 that Charlet began to come to the fore. He then published an album of lithographs of children, which showed his tendencies: Parisian irony mixed with an amiable satire, reminiscences of the art school translated into frank sketches, and adorned with a delightful inscription. Later, he became attracted by Napoleonic incidents, not at all those relating to his great deeds, but to the homelier side of his campagne, to the yarns of the old soldier who has been on the spree, and of the other old warrior, who is argumentative, sceptical and cold. There is a touch of sentimentality in the scenes. At a time when princes were visiting churches and deserting the camps, these frolics of victorious soldiers came as satire to the eyes of officers of the old régime.

From the technical point of view, Charlet was an incomparable virtuoso. His drawings on stone have the quality of water-colour. He attempted all methods of lithography: pencil, pen, wash, and the black manner. But his pencil works were his masterpieces, for here everything is thought out and defined, and the composition is better and simpler.

Under the July monarchy Charlet was preoccupied with "great works" in order to earn the approval of the Institute, and he neglected lithography a little for painting. *The Retreat from Russia* (Lyon Museum), and *Crossing the Rhine* (Versailles) show that Charlet was in fact a painter. His *Grenadier* (Louvre) is a vigorous painting, of a workmanship that yields nothing to his fine lithographs. Charlet died in Paris on the 29th December, 1845.

Bibliography: A. Dayot, *Charlet et son œuvre.* Paris.

**CHARONTON (Enguerrand).**—French painter of the 15th century, born in the neighbourhood of Laon. He settled in Avignon, about 1447, and there painted two very beautiful pictures, the *Virgin of Sorrows,* for the Cadart family, painted in 1452 with the collaboration of Pierre Villate (Chantilly), and the *Coronation of the Virgin,* painted in 1453, for the altar of the Chartreuse of Villeneuve-lès-Avignon, and which is now in the "hospice" of that town.

See Pl. 8, Vol. I; Pl. 4, Vol. II.

**CHARTRES (Cathedral).**—There have been several churches on the site of the Cathedral. The first, built in the 4th century by Bishop Adventus, was destroyed in 743. The second was burned in 858 by Danish pirates. Bishop Gislebert, desirous to repair the disaster immediately, built the crypt of the 9th century, known as the Cave of St. Lubin, which still exists. Another fire having destroyed the church, in 1020, Bishop Fulbert rebuilt the cathedral. From this period—11th century—dates the large crypt, composed of two parallel galleries separated by a space above which is the nave. In 1194, a fire destroyed the whole edifice with the exception of the crypts, the two towers and the narthex. The rest was rebuilt from 1194 to 1220. Later.

# EGYPTIAN PAINTINGS AND BAS-RELIEFS

*Egyptian art seems to serve the purpose of prolonging life after death by protecting the mummies in an indestructible tomb. It also strives to furnish this eternal prison with all the necessities of life, and to populate it with all the personages whose services will be useful and agreeable to the deceased. This explains why the sides of the sarcophagi and the walls of the tombs are covered with active figures. The Pharaohs had their deeds carved in bas-reliefs also on the walls of temples. These bas-reliefs, which are in most cases hollowed out reliefs, are conceived in the same way as a painter's composition.*

DETAIL OF THE HEAD OF A WOMAN. TOMB OF GEMNIKAI.

THE SACRIFICIAL BULL ROPED BY THE KING. ABYDOS.

BAS-RELIEF FROM THE TEMPLE OF EDFU.
*(Photo by Béato.)*

CROUCHING PEASANT. (AFTER CHAMPOLLION.)

THE HIPPOPOTAMUS HUNT IN THE TOMB OF TI.
*(Photo by Hachette.)*

THE NORTH WALL OF THE FIRST CHAMBER IN THE TOMB OF NAKHT.
*(Photo by Béato.)*

Egyptian sculpture is characterised by the so-called "frontality"—it never shows any other movement than that of the arms or legs. The painters and sculptors of bas-reliefs have never been surpassed in the art of painting with linear contours. They ignored roundness and the depth of space. With all these characteristics of design the profiles were submitted to a number of distortions resulting from the absence of the third dimension, and the impossibility of rendering details in perspective. Other curious conventions included the replacing of depth by exaggerating height, and with the images at all times done flat instead of in perspective. The objects are superposed instead of receding in the distance.

WRESTLERS AT BENI-HASSAN. (DETAIL.) (AFTER CHAMPOLLION.)

THE GEESE OF MEIDUM, CAIRO MUSEUM.
*(Photo by Brugsch.)*

As soon as one takes for granted the characteristics of Egyptian painting, one can only admire the elegance of the silhouettes and the decorative qualities of these designs. Despite their geometric regularity they possess an extraordinary suppleness in rendering the most varied kinds of movements. The positions of the wrestlers of Beni-Hassan succeed each other endlessly without the artist's repeating the same hold twice, and all of them are equally amusing due to their clarity and accuracy. When the Egyptians painted animals, the pictures were characterised by a frank naturalism; conventionalization is less apparent, and their lifelike quality is the more obvious. These famous geese are certainly painted without restraint.

# SCULPTURE OF ASSYRIA AND CHALDEA

*Unlike Egypt, Asia did not leave us many important monuments of architecture. The palaces of Babylonia and Nineveh, built of crude brick, have fallen, and of the large cities only hills are left in the desert, the tellos. But excavators have unearthed sculptures which decorated the palaces of the Assyrian kings of Nineveh. Other generally mutilated statues were found in Chaldea and near Susa among the ruins of forgotten cities.*

THE QUEEN NAPIR-ASU. LOUVRE. *(Photo by Hachette.)*

HEAD FROM TELLO. LOUVRE. *(Photo by Hachette.)*

KING GUDEA. LOUVRE. *(Photo by Hachette.)*

HEAD FROM TELLO. LOUVRE. *(Photo by Hachette.)*

ROYAL STATUE FROM TELLO. LOUVRE. *(Photo by Hachette.)*

## Chaldea

These statues were excavated by de Sarzec and Morgan at Tello (lower Chaldea), and in ancient Susa. The statue of Queen Napir-Asu is of bronze, and the modelling of her hands as well as of her dress is interesting to observe. Other fragments of diorite come from Tello and represent the Chaldeans of twenty centuries before Christ. King Gudea's portrait appears frequently; standing or sitting he has his hands folded. The heads, hands, details of costume are of a clear-cut precision, but the positions and the drapery remain rigid.

WINGED BULL. LOUVRE. *(Photo by Hachette.)*

WINGED GENIUS. LOUVRE. *(Photo by Hachette.)*

ASSURBANIPAL. LOUVRE. *(Photo by Hachette.)*

STONE LION. LOUVRE. *(Photo by Hachette.)*

## Assyria

The Assyrians have left us many pieces of sculpture, the most important of which came from Khorsabad, the royal Assyrian palace near Nineveh. This sculpture, in bas-relief or in the round, represents royal personages, servants, religious characters, winged genii, and finally the famous winged bulls with human heads, which are the *Cherubim*, cited by the prophets in the Bible. These fantastic animals were placed before the palace entrance as protectors. Assyrian sculpture is characterised by the precision of rendering detail and an impression of force.

WOUNDED LIONESS. BRITISH MUSEUM. *(Photo by Hachette.)*

THE LION HUNT. BRITISH MUSEUM. *(Photo by Hachette.)*

LION VOMITING BLOOD. BRITISH MUSEUM. *(Photo by Hachette.)*

HUNTING SCENES. BAS-RELIEF FROM NINEVEH. BRITISH MUSEUM. *(Photo by Hachette.)*

## Assyrian bas-reliefs

The Assyrian royal palaces were decorated with bas-reliefs depicting the life-history of the king. In these bas-reliefs we find characteristics which are accepted by all sculptors, especially for the rendering of scenery and the human figure. But in portraying animals the Assyrians are unsurpassed. They caught the characteristic movements of animals as they ran, fought, or turned back wounded and roaring. The lioness that drags her wounded hind-limbs, the lion that withdraws vomiting blood, are masterpieces which no modern art has surpassed.

some details of decoration were added, and the upper part of the northern tower.

Chartres: The Cathedral.

Chartres Cathedral is one of the most magnificent Gothic buildings of France, as remarkable for its enormous and majestic proportions, as for the wonderful series of

Chartres: The Cathedral. (South portal.)

statues and sculpture which adorns it. The façade is formed by a triple doorway, known as the *Portail Royal*, surmounted by three large stained glass windows, above which

Chartres: The Cathedral. (North porch.)

is a magnificent "rose," and then a gallery of kings. It is flanked by two famous towers. This façade, which seems a little restricted between the towers, was formerly wider and situated further back, serving as a façade to the old narthex. It was brought forward, stone by stone, to the present position. The *Portail Royal*, of Romanesque architecture, is decorated with magnificent Romanesque statues, representing the life of

Chartres: Choir Stall. (Fragment.)

Christ: in the central tympanum, Christ enthroned in a nimbus with the four symbols of the Evangelists; in the southern tympanum, the Nativity, etc.; in the northern tympanum, the Ascension. The large statue-columns represent kings, queens and personages belonging to the family of Christ. The capitals of the columns have charming bas-reliefs of subjects taken from

Chartres: Pythagoras. (Moulding of inner row of voussoirs, Royal Portal.)

the New Testament. The lintels and bends of the arches are also decorated with a multitude of figures —apostles, angels, elders of the

Chartres: West portal, the Annunciation.

apocalypse, signs of the Zodiac, the labours of the months, etc. The three windows of the façade are enriched with precious 12th century glass, the middle one showing the life of Christ in twenty-nine pictures; the southern one tells the story of the Passion; and the one to the north has a Tree of Jesse, in marvellous colours. The large rose-window measures 14 metres in diameter. The two towers are of very different architecture. The northern tower, the oldest, was finished about 1150, but the fine flamboyant Gothic spire which crowns it, was built in the 16th century by Jean Texier, known as de Beauce. It is 115 metres high. The southern tower, 12th century work, is a masterpiece of architecture. with its bold spire, the base of which is surrounded with beautiful "lucarnes."

The extremities of the transept have two magnificent porches. The south porch was executed between 1224 and 1230, and has a triple portal. The pier of the middle doorway has a statue of Christ blessing, and below figures (probably of the donors of the statue). At the sides are figures of the twelve Apostles; and in the tympanum, Christ between the Virgin and St. John, with angels; and a quantity of bas-reliefs in the arches and on the lintel. The two other doorways of the south porch are also peopled with statues, the left-hand one with martyrs, and the right-hand one with confessors. The porch which shelters these three doorways is also decorated with pillars, bas-reliefs, statues, and medallions, treated with charming sincerity and simplicity.

The northern porch, begun about 1230 (thus very near in date to the southern one), is still finer. It, too, shelters three doorways. On the pier of the middle doorway is a statue of St. Anne holding the Infant Virgin. On either side are statues of saints, and on the lintel and tympanum, scenes from the life of the Virgin. The two other doorways have scenes from the Old and New Testaments; and the bends of the arches, and lintels, are crowded with sculptures. The sculptures of the porch itself, too, are more sup-

Chartres: Tympanum, the Annunciation to the Shepherds. (Façade, portal on the right side.)

ple and able than are those of the south porch; the pillars and columns are most elegant, and are decorated with large statues of kings and queens. which have often been taken for kings and queens of France, but which most probably represent those of Judah. The arcades of the porch are decorated with charming little statues, and with four figures of kings seated in niches.

The interior of the cathedral has a magnificent nave with side aisles. Above the arcades is a triforium, above which is a stage of windows, 7 metres high, and rose-windows. The high vaults exert a formidable thrust, which is counterbalanced by the powerful buttresses, and three tiers of flying-buttresses. The interior decoration is very simple, and consists of carved capitals and keystones, and a magnificent stone choir-screen begun by Jean de Beauce in 1514 and finished in the 17th and 18th centuries. It has two hundred statues, divided into forty scenes, surmounted with richly carved canopies. The scenes represent the life of the Virgin and Christ. They are due to several sculptors, including Jean de Beauce, François Marchant, Thomas Boudin, Simon Mazières, etc. A wonderful rood-screen was destroyed about 1763.

The stained-glass of Chartres Cathedral makes a magnificent whole. In the upper windows are immense figures of saints, very simple in design, strongly accentuated, and made to be seen from a distance. In the aisle windows, the glass, in beautiful medallions, represents scenes from the Bible and from the lives of saints. Most of the glass dates from the first half of the 13th century.

See Embroidery; Stained Glass; also Pls. 4, 10, 46, 48, 53, Vol. I.

Bibliography: René Merlet, *La Cathédrale de Chartres*.—Emile Niale, *L'art Religieux du XIIIe siècle in France*, 1902.—Étienne Houret, *La Cathédrale de Chartres*, 1919.—R. C. Lasteyrie de Saillant, *L'architecture religieuse en France à l'epogue gothique*, 1926.

**CHASE (William Merritt).**—American painter (1849-1916). He was born in Williamsburg, Indiana, 1st November 1849. The family moved to Indianapolis in 1861 where young Chase was employed to wait on customers in his father's shoe store. But he did not enjoy business life and soon with his parents' consent entered the studio of Benjamin Hayes in Indianapolis. In a short while he went to New York to study with J. O. Eaton and remained there for the next two years. Then he returned to his new family home in St. Louis and began to paint still-life subjects and flower pieces. Soon he wanted further instruction in painting and determined to go to Munich.

In 1872 with the financial assistance of some friends he was able to go and soon was enrolled in the Royal Academy in Munich, taking instruction from Karl von Piloty and A. Wagner. Other American students there at that time included Frank Duveneck, Walter Shirlaw and Frank Currier, who later became well known in the field of art. Chase won many prizes there and absorbed completely the dark brown technique which was characteristic of the school. After leaving Munich he accompanied Duveneck and Twachtman to Venice where he came under the influence of Tintoretto. In 1877 he returned to the United States and settled in New York City in the famous Tenth Street Building. He became an instructor in the newly formed Art Students' League and remained with that school for the next eighteen years, teaching also at the Pennsylvania Academy of Fine Arts and the Brooklyn Art School. His vacations were spent abroad, travelling and sketching with Robert Blum in France, Spain, Italy and Holland. On one of these European trips he met and painted the portrait of James McNeill Whistler, the famous American artist.

He married Miss Alice Gerson in 1886 and moved to Brooklyn where he did some landscapes of Prospect Park. About 1891 he began giving lessons at his summer home in the Shinnecock Hills region of Long Island and in 1896 he started the Chase School of Art. Later he took pupils abroad to study and copy the works of the old masters and in 1914 he held classes at Carmel, California. In the fall of 1916 he was taken ill and went to Atlantic City to recuperate. But instead he grew worse and returned to New York to die on the twenty-fifth day of October of that year. He is chiefly remembered for his studies of still life today, but he was also the painter of a large number of portraits and landscapes. As a teacher he was quick to criticise but also as quick to recognise true artistic talent in his pupils, who included Irving R. Wiles and Charles Hawthorne. For ten years he was the president of the Society of American Artists, an organisation devoted to the more progressive tendencies of American painting. He was the recipient of many awards and examples of his work are to be found in the leading museums of the United States.

Bibliography: Katharine Metcalf Roof, *The Life and Art of William Merritt Chase,* 1917.—*Paintings by William Merritt Chase, N.A., L.L.D.,* 1927.—For other material see *The Index of Twentieth Century Artists* for November, 1934.

**CHASSÉRIAU (Théodore).**—French painter. Born in Samana, South America, 1819; died in Paris, 8th October, 1856. He was scarcely more than ten years old when Ingres admitted him to his studio. The child soon became Ingres's favourite pupil. "Never speak to me of that child," said the old master later, when someone mentioned Chassériau, whose desertion he felt keenly. On Ingres's departure for Rome, Chassériau was left to work alone, with a view to exhibitions. He exhibited for the first time at the Salon of 1836, the *Return of the Prodigal Son* (La Rochelle Museum), and *Cain,* pictures which show the influence of Ingres. The *Cain* won a third class medal. He was not yet sixteen. In spite of this official encouragement, Chassériau only exhibited one picture in the following three years—*Ruth and Boaz,* in the same style, and the critics hardly took any notice of it. Travels in the south of France, and then in Belgium and Holland had a marked influence on the formation of his art. When he reappeared at the Salon of 1839, with a *Venus* and a *Susanna* (Louvre), Chassériau was hailed by independent criticism as one of the young masters of the new French school. The artist's personality already shows itself. The form of his figures remained antique, but this antique character was expressed with a dreamy, passionate grace, that was quite modern. The Hebraic type of *Susanna,* which Gustave Moreau retained, appeared in all her oriental purity. The *Susanna* and the *Venus* began a series of women, unique in art. They became less idyllic, but they always bore the original stamp of the painter, a special kind of beauty which makes them a race apart.

In 1840, Chassériau went to Italy. He then painted the sublime portrait of Lacordaire (Louvre), in retreat at Santa Sabina, an ardent, passionate figure, enframed by the cloister arcade, whose solemn gaze is illumined by a mystic fire. It is a magnificent painting, broadly handled, and the dark colour harmonises well with the romantic eloquence of the preacher of Notre Dame. Chassériau was won to the cause of the young school, and when he left Rome he had broken, morally, with his master, who, however, received him kindly. He then wrote on the subject of Ingres: "He has lived his years of power, and he has no comprehension of the ideas and of the changes which are taking place in present-day art; he is completely ignorant of all the latest artists. For him, it is very well; he will remain as a recollection and a reproduction of certain ages of the art of the past, without having created anything for the future. My aims and ideas are not at all similar." He returned to Paris, and still hesitated. His *Andromeda Bound to the Rock* (Salon of 1841), and his *Women of Troy Weeping by the Sea* (Salon of 1842) show Pompeian influence. Chassériau always retained feeling for the antique. The enchantments of romantic colouring never made him lose his sense of form and line.

The most important and most original work of his youth dates from this time. In 1843, Chassériau exhibited the admirable portrait of his *Two Sisters* at the Salon, and finished decorating the Chapel of St. Mary of Egypt, in St. Merry, a delightful work in which Chassériau has given a very beautiful, draped silhouette to the repentant sinner. By an inexplicable mixture of the sacred and profane, the young artist's oriental imagination has illustrated the Golden Legend of this pious courtesan, with a flowery sense of poetry.

After the *Apollo and Daphne* and the *Othello* series, Chassériau exhibited the *Caliphe of Constantinople* (Salon of 1845, Versailles), which completed the break with Ingres. Baudelaire then outlines, not without injustice, the dualism of Chassériau's uneasy personality: "The position he wishes to hold, between Ingres, his master, and Delacroix, is somewhat ambiguous to everyone, and embarrassing for himself." Ali-Hamed, Caliphe of Constantinople, became the painter's friend, and Chassériau accepted his invitation and went to Algeria the following year (1846). For three months, in the height of summer, he toured the three provinces, and mixed with the staff of African generals. The East, which was to be discovered by Decamps, Marilhat and Delacroix, had a decided influence on the dazzled Chassériau. The sun of Islam revealed colour to him; and the passionate painter of beautiful African Jewesses was far from the angelic poet who had sung of St. Mary in the Chapel of St. Merry. The East of Chassériau, however, is not at all that of Delacroix. The vision of the antique never ceased to haunt him. Paul de Saint-Victor discerned: "Théodore Chassériau remained Greek even in this Mohammedan East. To the women of the harems, he gave the nobility of Virgins of the Gynæcea; and the Arab's burnoose he arranged like the drapery of saints."

From Algeria, Chassériau brought back numerous studies and three large compositions: *The Jews' Sabbath in Constantinople, Arab Horsemen Carrying away their Dead,* and *Arab Horsemen Injuring Themselves Before Battle.* The *Jews' Sabbath,* refused by the Salon of 1847, reappeared triumphantly at the Salon of the following year, owing more to public clamour than to the approval of the jury. At the same time, Chassériau finished the paintings which he had begun in 1844 on the staircase of the Cour des Comptes. Unfortunately the fire of 1871 completely destroyed this work, so important in the history of French art and decorative painting. The little that remains of it, some fragments in the Louvre, show analogies between Chassériau's art and the frescoes of Pompeii. The friezes, the grisailles, the large allegorical figures, show a grandiose and noble inspiration worthy of the best classics. Maurice Denis could write on this subject: "The mural tonality of the colour, as well as the arrangements of the groups, and even the action of some of the figures, had a decided influence on Puvis de Chavannes."

At the Salon of 1850 appeared one of Chassériau's most seductive works, *A Bather Asleep near a Spring,* given to Avignon Museum by the model herself, the celebrated Alice Ozy. In 1853, he exhibited one of the most animated paintings of this second period, the *Tepidarium* (Louvre), which many consider his masterpiece. It is certainly one of the most voluptuous manifestations of this sensual and refined art. There is a reminiscence of Greek sculpture in these figures of bathers, drying themselves, stretching luxuriously, or clothing themselves with a careless grace. But there is much of what Baudelaire called "modernité" in the models, and a taste for romantic colour—greenish yellows, dull mauves, harsh greens, and lacquer red—shows itself in the long cloaks in which the bathers wrap themselves.

In his last years, the painter, as though warned by a secret instinct of the nearness of death, abandoned these romantic subjects, and became grave and reflective. He executed the paintings for the baptismal Chapel of St. Roch, and for the dome of St. Philippe-du-Roule, *Vercingetorix Defending his Country* (Clermont Museum): and when death overtook him, he was working on a *Nativity.* His decorations for St. Roch and St. Philippe-du-Roule, too obviously inspired by Delacroix, are far from equalling the charm of the Chapel of St. Mary of Egypt, in St. Merry. Feasts of colour are out of place in the mural painting of churches, which should, above all, be quiet in tone for the sake of the architecture, touch the spirit and the heart, and strike the eyes without dazzling them. This is no doubt why, in spite of their great ability, *St. Philip Baptising a Eunuch of Queen Candace, St. Francis Xavier Baptising the Gentiles* (St. Roch), and the *Descent from the Cross* (St. Philippe-du-Roule), fail to move us as do the decorations in the Chapel of St. Mary of Egypt.

This precocious artist died prematurely, 8th October, 1856. He was scarcely thirty-seven years old. His restless genius, which had doubtless not yielded all its measure, was not left, however, to influence strongly the following generations. Nevertheless, Gustave Moreau, Ary Renan and Puvis de Chavannes owed much to the painter of *Susanna,* and the decorator of St. Merry and the Cours des Comptes.

See Pl. 57, Vol. II.

Bibliography: Théophile Gautier, *Portraits contemporains.* Paris, 1874. —Valbert Chevillard, *Théodore Chassériau.* Paris, 1893.—Henry Marcel, *Chassériau.* Paris, 1912.

**CHÂTEAU.**—The word denotes a fortified residence, placed on a

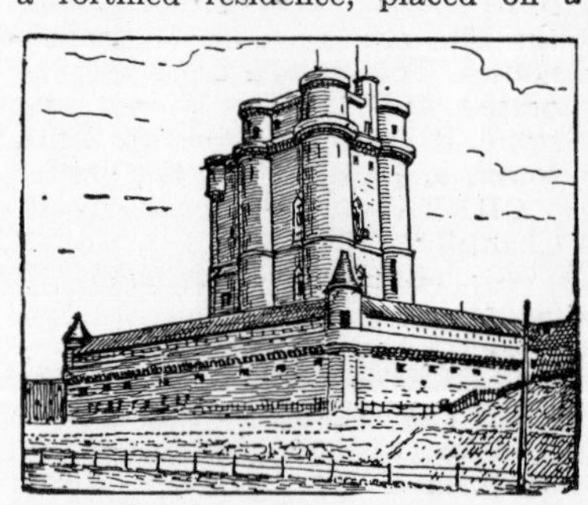

Vincennes: The Château.

height or in a strategic position. In the middle of the apartments, already protected by crenellated walls, and moats, and machicolated towers, was the keep, a massive tower of which the walls were often several yards in thickness, and where the inhabitants of the château took refuge in case of attack. These buildings were the fortified châteaux or castles, of the Middle Ages. In France the most celebrated are the Château of Coucy, Château Gaillard, the Château of Vincennes, the Louvre, and Château Porcien. The use of artillery, which overcame these strong walls, and the growth of royal splendor, led to the ruin of the fortified châteaux, and many were razed to the ground. The great lords replaced them by gayer, more comfortable dwellings, which in the Renaissance, and since, were often true works of art, such as Azay-le-Rideau, Anet, Blois, Chenonceaux, Chaumont, Chambord, Chantilly, Écouen, Saint-Germain, and the Louvre. These Renaissance châteaux still preserve all the elements of the old feudal châteaux, such as moats and crenellated walls, but these became lighter and only served for ornament. The château must be distinguished from the palace. The palace has no longer any of the elements of the feudal château. It is an enlarged "maison des champs," more or less beautiful, built for great lords, rich financiers, or for the king. It has neither towers, nor crenellated walls, nor machicolations, even as ornament. Such are the Palaces of Versailles, Fontainebleau, Compiègne and Vaux, which are, however, often, but incorrectly, called châteaux. These palaces appeared in the 17th century.

See Pl. 27, Vol. II.

**CHAUMONT (Haute-Marne).**—The Church of Saint Jean-Baptiste dates from the 13th century. The choir and lateral chapels were added later. The *Tour Hautefeuille,* an 11th century keep, is the chief relic of a château of the counts of Champagne.

See Pl. 27, Vol. II.

**CHELLIAN EPOCH.**—See Prehistoric Archæology.

**CH'EN JUNG.**—Chinese painter of the thirteenth century. Famous as a painter of dragons. An exceptional painting in the Museum of Fine Arts, Boston, seems to be well attributed to him. See China—Art.

**CHENONCEAUX** (Indre-et-Loire, France).—One of the most charming of the French Renaissance châteaux. It is picturesquely situated on a bridge over the Cher. See Pl. 27, Vol. II.

**CHESTER** (England).—The town is very interesting, for it has to some extent kept its mediæval appearance. Its city walls, fortified with towers, remain; its streets have covered arcades, dating from the 16th century, and old timbered houses. The cathedral, in the Decorated style, is built of red sandstone. It has a Perpendicular central tower, and cloisters on the north.

**CHEVALIER** (Étienne).—See Chantilly.

**—** (Guillaume Sulpice).—See Gavarni.

**CHEVET.**—See Caen.

**CHIAROSCURO.**—An Italian term which denotes a method of painting with deep shadows emphasizing the modelling and atmosphere, thus creating a pictorial design through light and dark areas.

**CH'IEN HSUAN.**—1235-1290. Chinese painter of the Yuan dynasty. He followed the style of the academic school of Sung. The finest painting attributed to him is a hand scroll depicting birds, flowers, and insects which is now in the Detroit Inst. of Arts. See China—Art.

**CHINA—ART.** Neolithic and Aeneolithic ?3000 B.C.-?1500 B.C.—The earliest Chinese art known begins in the neolithic period. As yet, no paleolithic artifacts have been discovered, although the skull of the "Peking Man" shows that China was inhabited at a very early period and indicates pre-neolithic cultures, still unknown.

J. G. Andersson, the leading discoverer and excavator of pre-historic Chinese sites, has defined six different cultures within his finds. Although it is still uncertain whether the groups isolated by Andersson show only a chronological evolution or whether they represent different groups of peoples, nevertheless, there does seem to be a temporal sequence.

The earliest of these cultures is the *Ch'i Chia*, named by Andersson after one of the find-sites in Kansu. Polished stone utensils were found as were three types of pottery: 1) a grey ware, impressed with mat and basket patterns; 2) a grey ware with regular designs impressed on collar, handles and body of the vessels; 3) a light, greyish-yellow ware, with elegant shapes, high collars and large handles.

The second stage is called *Yang Shao* after the original find in Honan. Quantities of the same type pottery were also found in Kansu. The pottery of this stage is generally recognized to be the most beautiful. A comparison of the shape of the Yang Shao vessels and their ornamentation with the well dated pottery of Annau and the Indus Valley finds of Mohenjodaro and Harappa, permits us to assume a relationship among the three cultures and to date the Chinese material about 2800 B.C. The designs painted on the pottery consist of spirals, the double ax-head, ovals (interpreted as cowrie shell motifs), and the death-pattern, so called by Andersson because of its restriction to burial sites in Kansu. This pattern consists of a red band bordered by an unpainted narrow strip, along which run black bands with saw-like dentations projecting toward the red band. An unusual motif resembling a highly conventionalized human figure or deity appears on one jar. Other objects peculiar to this culture are pottery representations of human heads surmounted by snakes and decorated by wavy lines which have been called fertility symbols. Bone objects are frequently found at this stage, and in the cave deposit of Sha Kuo T'un a small marble animal figurine which was discovered may belong to the Yang Shao period.

The third period, *Ma Chang*, appears to be little more than a degeneration of the Yang Shao culture. One new element appears in the decoration of the pottery, i.e., a design with finger-like projections at the apex of triangular motifs. These "fingers" may be further conventionalizations of the stylized figure on the Yang Shao jar.

Stage four, *Hsin Tien*, is the first of the cultures to contain metal. The pottery of Hsin Tien is softer than that of either Yang Shao or Ma Chang. For the first time a concave foot appears. The designs are usually arranged in horizontal registers, and consist of geometric patterns, essentially the continuous meander and the spiral, and sketchy renderings of human figures, animals, and birds.

Group five, *Ssu Wa*, is less unified but is composed mainly of large unpainted urns with saddle mouths. The bulbous legged tripod (*li*), later a common bronze form, has also been found in this group.

In the sixth stage, *Sha Ching*, among other artifacts, there were found copper arrowheads, cowrie shells, and turquoise beads, materials which point to a date later than that of the other cultures. The pottery is coarse and sometimes painted with a red slip or with designs of highly stylized birds similar to those found on pottery from Susa.

The durations of these cultures and their terminating dates are still a matter of conjecture. The presence of highly complicated bronzes of the Shang dynasty, some certainly as early as 1500 B.C., would tend to preclude a date much after 2000 B.C. On the other hand, the provincial location of these cultures gives us reason to expect that they persisted as late as the first millennium B.C. Certainly the meander pattern on the Hsin Tien pottery has close relationships to some of the decorations on Shang bronzes, and this pottery must have been a close forerunner of the bronzes.

Shang Dynasty ?1766 B.C.-?1122 B.C.—According to the orthodox system of Chinese reckoning, the Shang dynasty began in 1766 B.C. and ended in 1122 B.C. Modern research has shown a general agreement in accepting the latter date as approximately correct, although no evidence has appeared to substantiate the beginning date, nor the dates of the legendary Hsia dynasty which preceded the Shang.

Recent excavations at An-yang in Honan, the Shang capital toward the end of the dynasty, have revealed the general soundness of Chinese traditions which until the third decade of the twentieth century were considered pious fabrications by most Western scholars. Large finds of inscribed bones used for oracular purposes were found, as were carved jade and bone, marble sculpture, bronze utensils and vessels, and remnants of painting on beams from tombs. The bronzes have always been considered objects of the greatest value and veneration in China, not only because of their aesthetic merit, but even more for the historical inscriptions which they bear, often cast into the surface.

Even the very earliest of these bronze vessels show an extremely high state of development. On account of their advanced technique some scholars have deduced that China learned the art of bronze casting from the West, but too little is known about pre-Shang China to venture such an hypothesis. There is enough material to presume an indigenous growth. Copper was found within the Hsin Tien culture which preceded the earliest known bronzes probably by five hundred years. Even within the Shang dynasty a development can be traced. Both *cire-perdue* and open mould casting were used. Some vessels which seem to have employed the more primitive open mould casting also perpetuate forms of pre-Shang cultures along with other features which indicate an early Shang date.

A clear development can be traced in Shang bronzes starting from a large group of vessels with an almost flat surface, into which the decoration seems to be incised. This type of decoration, probably derived from a wood-carving art which has disappeared, is also represented in objects of other media from the An-yang site: bone, marble, and an impressed white pottery. Decorative motifs take the form of meander patterns, round and angular spirals, and highly conventionalized zoomorphic forms which include most commonly: the bull's head, the cicada, a lizard-like dragon, birds, and less commonly, the stag's head and other animal representations. Floral motifs never appear.

Some of the "incised" bronzes are inlaid with a dark pigment, possibly lacquer. Later, as the bronze caster realized the potentialities of his material he not only incised his wax model, but built it up into several layers of relief, until by the end of the Shang period the vessels achieved a sculptural solidity with numerous projections which give them a fortress-like appearance. At this time animals of convincing organic expression make their appearance on the vessels, beside the abstract zoomorphic forms already noted. This greater naturalism of the animal forms has been attributed to Scythian influence, but now it is known that these vessels pre-date Scythian art. Primitive naturalism in a lingering state has also been given as an explanation, but such naturalism is not found in earlier bronzes. The explanation rests on a purely technical basis. Whenever the flat, highly abstract forms were reproduced in the high relief of the protuberances characteristic of this period, the forms became more naturalistic. The flat pattern is inherently more abstract than the three dimensional form, and the transference brought about a naturalism that was entirely fortuitous. It was under the influence of this fortuitous naturalism of the high relief, that the craftsman further developed the style, until it appeared in low relief also, in conjunction with the abstract animal forms that had preceded it. It is important to note in connection with this change that the older decoration persisted independently, as we find in all Chinese art. Although we may sometimes find the beginning of a style in China, it is more difficult to find the terminus because the same style continues to exist for long periods alongside later styles.

By the end of the Shang dynasty, ceremonial bronzes were codified into almost all the types that later literature discusses. Chief among these are: (1) the *li*, the bulbous-legged tripod, also found in neolithic pottery, (2) the *ting*, a solid legged tripod, (3) the *lei*, a cauldron-like vessel, (4) the *hsien*, a steamer with a colander top and a tripod base, (5) the *ku*, a narrow trumpet-formed beaker, (6) the *tsun*, a large beaker, sometimes square, (7) the *ho*, a covered tripod pouring vessel, (8) the *i*, a casket-shaped vessel, (9) the *chio*, and the *chueh*, three legged libation cups. Other forms exist and frequently combinations of two types obscure exact classifications.

Jades and bone carvings reflect the same changes noted in the bronzes. Marble sculptures in relief and in the round have been found at An-yang. The largest sculpture is about three feet high. Slots in the back of most of the specimens indicate an architectural use. The repertoire of the stone sculpture comprehends human and animal forms reproduced in an organic, if conventionalized naturalism, upon which is superimposed a geometric tracery.

The most important type of pottery found in the Shang excavations is a fine white ware, impressed with the same geometric and zoomorphic patterns found on early bronzes. Some of the sherds show a dancing figure with three claw-like fingers, reminiscent of motifs on Yang Shao and Ma Chang vessels. Fragments of a polished black pottery have also been discovered. One of these pieces bears a decoration of small naturalistic animals in low relief.

Architecture becomes an art for the first time in this period. Neolithic houses had been limited to beehive-shaped pits, about ten feet in diameter, roofed with timbers which were covered with sod or thatched. Shang architecture shows a great advance and utilizes the basic principles still adhered to in China. A terrace of closely pounded earth was constructed as a foundation for the building. Upon this base wooden pillars supported a gable roof. Stones and bronze discs prevented the pillars from sinking into the earth. Three rows of these pillars supported the roof, one row at each side and one row supporting the ridge-pole. The material, as in modern China, was wood and the roof thatched. Halls have been found as large as ninety-two by twenty-six feet. The building was decorated with carvings, sculpture, and paintings, and may have been surrounded by a courtyard.

Chou Dynasty 1122 B.C.-249 B.C.—The Chou dynasty has been divided into three historical periods: Early (or Western) Chou, 1122 B.C.-722 B.C.; Middle Chou (or Period of the Spring and Autumn Annals), 722 B.C.-481 B.C.; and Late Chou (or Period of the Warring States), 481 B.C.-249 B.C. According to orthodox Chinese chronology, the Chous overthrew the Shang dynasty in 1122 B.C. Although a more barbaric people, they continued the arts of their predecessors, the craftsmen of the previous rulers doubtless supplying their needs.

*Bronze.*—Little change is apparent between the earliest Chou bronzes and those from the end of the Shang period. The evolution already noted continues. The decoration becomes more baroque, with more emphasis placed on the projections. Flanges become more prominent and flamboyant. Dated inscriptions on vessels show that this style persisted until the end of the

Large bronze bowl. Chou dynasty. (Musée Cernuschi.)

tenth century B.C. But in the tenth century a new trend appears. Workmanship becomes heavier and more coarse. Zoomorphic forms become so degenerated that they are barely recognizable. The vessels lose their sculptural form and adopt utilitarian forms which are seemingly devoid of all ceremonial significance. The end of this development is reached in the sixth century B.C. This date is noteworthy in that it concurs with the lifetime of Confucius whose philosophy embodied a reaction against the contemporary decadence, and an appeal for a return to ancient customs.

The sixth century witnessed a technical renaissance in China, but in contrast to the strength of the Shang and early Chou vessels a rococo virtuosity is for the first time introduced into China. Superimposed upon essentially utilitarian shapes, small snail-like spirals are found, curving in agitated movements over the surface, while fantastic animals in high relief serve as handles or hooks.

Bronze Buddha. (Musée Cernuschi.)

The belt-hook introduced into China at this time, points to Siberian contacts and raises the question as to whether the so-called Scythian animal style originated in China; whether, on the contrary, it was brought into China at this time from Siberia; whether it came to both countries from a third; or whether it was created independently in each culture. From weapons found at Minussinsk in Siberia it is known that China had influential contact with northern civilizations as early as the Shang dynasty. But it is likely that the answer to the question of Sino-Siberian relationships is complex and that no one theory can be sustained with the material now available.

*Jade.*—Jade, during the late Chou period (often called the Period of the Warring States), again follows the sumptuous style of decoration found on the bronzes of this period. Jade is used at this time (as it probably had been earlier), for official insignia, funeral gifts, and personal adornment. Even ceremonial cups have been found made of this precious stone. The workmanship at this time is unexcelled. The material is worked, in a most delicate and refined manner, into the same spirals and fantastic animals found on the bronzes. Other jades often represent human figures and domestic animals in a simplified naturalism achieved by broad planes and sharp angles.

Peiping Temple of the Summer Palace.

*Sculpture.*—Besides these small jade pieces, sculpture of the period is known only from small bronze figurines said to have come from Loyang, the Chou capital at that time. These display a lively naturalism, of a somewhat primitive cast. Slightly later is a fantastic animal (in the Stoclet Collection, Brussels), which displays on a large scale the same elements already indicated on the bronze vessels.

*Architecture.*—Little is known about architecture of the Chou dynasty, but it probably carried on the Shang style, for the architecture of the succeeding Han dynasty was a further development of this earliest style of Shang.

*Pottery.*—Pottery continues to take a subordinate place during the Chou dynasty. The only true ware that can be definitely assigned to the period is a coarse mat-marked type, possibly used only by peasants. Another kind has been found, which is inlaid with glass-paste and seems to be one of the innovations of the age.

*Mirror.*—Another artifact attains importance at this time. This is the Chinese mirror. Made of bronze it is highly polished on the side used for reflection while the reverse is decorated with the same patterns found on ceremonial bronzes. The shapes are generally round, although the square mirror is not uncommon. In the center of the back is a round knob through which a silk cord was passed. No mirrors have yet been discovered which can be dated earlier than the sixth century B.C., but after that time they became one of the most common articles and were used either as toilet accessories or as magic funeral gifts.

Ceremonial bronzes continued to be the most important expression of Chou art up to the end of the dynasty. In the fifth and fourth centuries B.C., the agitated surface of the bronzes became flattened out, and the animal decoration so abstract that it hardly recalls its zoomorphic beginnings. At the same time naturalistic animals in high relief were placed on the vessels in conjunction with the abstract pattern in the same relationship already noted in late Shang bronzes, where naturalistic animals were superimposed on abstract zoomorphic patterns.

In the fourth and third centuries B.C. bronzes inlaid with gold and silver became popular. The inlay, at times geometric, at times naturalistically illustrating legends of Taoist inspiration, was executed in a refined niello technique.

Han Dynasty 206 B.C.-A.D. 220.—The Han dynasty unified a China that had been torn by conflicting feudal states toward the end of the Chou dynasty, and had suffered the destruction of much of its literature under the short lived Ch'in dynasty (221-206 B.C.). A period of geographical, political, and artistic expansion followed. Silks from China were sold in Rome, and Chinese generals carried the imperial power as far west as the Pamirs.

*Painting and Calligraphy.*—Painting as an art may have existed as early as the Shang dynasty, despite the orthodox tradition that the brush was invented in 206 B.C. by Meng Tien. The tradition probably refers to a refinement of the brush at that time, for the pictorial ideograms of the Shang dynasty clearly depict the brush. Literary sources mention paintings of the sixth century B.C., but it is not until the Han period that painting appears as a great art.

Chinese painting is derived from calligraphy which in China ranks with the greatest of the arts. In calligraphy, not only is the relationship of each stroke to another carefully considered, but the power and beauty of the individual stroke are stressed. So important is this art, that excellent writing is an integral part of scholarship, and painting is considered in relationship to calligraphy, as we consider engineering in relation to pure science. The national reverence for the art of writing is evident as early as the Han period. Scraps of paper with calligraphy have been found at the outermost borders of China, where Han soldiers whiled away the hours in the occupation of the scholar.

The effect of this art upon Chinese painting cannot be overestimated. The same materials were used: the brush and the Chinese ink, which is compounded basically of charcoal and glue and then mixed with water. When colors were used water remained the vehicle. The coloring materials were mainly vegetable dyes, although lapis-lazuli and malachite were also used. Most painting was done on paper and silk, again the same materials used by the calligrapher. The painter working with such media was severely limited in his methods. The absorbent silk or paper retained the color once the brush stroke had been made, and no correction was possible. Thus the painter had to have a sure command of his technique, and a clearly formulated vision of his completed work before he could hope for success. The necessity of long years of practice in order to achieve the purely technical proficiency of the calligrapher intensified the relationship to writing. The rhythmic and suggestive interplay of line became the most important consideration of the artist. Representation was subordinated to the interpretation of reality through the medium of the brush stroke.

*The Six Canons of Hsieh Ho.*—The "Six Canons," formulated by Hsieh Ho in the sixth century, have served ever since, in various interpretations, as a credo for Chinese painting. Although the cryptic form of the text admits of different translations, the general meaning as given by R. L. Binyon is clear. In Hsieh Ho's order the rules are: 1) Rhythmic Vitality, or Spiritual Rhythm expressed in the movement of life, 2) The art of rendering the bones or natural structure by means of the brush, 3) The drawing of forms which answer to natural forms, 4) Appropriate distribution of colors, 5) Composition and subordination, or grouping according to the hierarchy of things, 6) The transmission of classic models.

During different periods of Chinese history the weighting of the individual rules seems to have changed considerably, and it is quite possible that the emphasis on the brush stroke which forms the backbone of contemporary art criticism in the Far East, might have been subordinated to other factors in earlier periods. A résumé of Chinese painting, from the few early examples which have come down to us to the comparatively large group of seventeenth and eighteenth century paintings, shows an ever-increasing tendency towards virtuosity of brushwork.

*Tomb Engravings.*—Beyond literary evidence the only means we have of knowing Han painting is the evidence of decorations

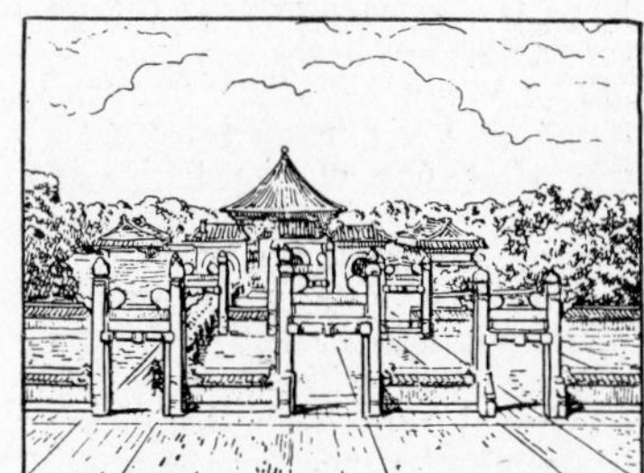

Imperial tomb, near Chi-Men, China.

on lacquer and pottery, and of stone engravings probably based on paintings. These fragmentary remains testify to a highly developed if still archaic art. The stones from the tombs of *Wu Liang Tzu* (A.D. 147) are cut in a series of superimposed registers which illustrate scenes of Confucian filial piety and from Taoist and historical tradition. Perspective is usually rendered by placing the distant figures above those in the foreground; but overlapping is also found as is foreshortening. The three-quarter view is achieved by combining a somewhat distorted front view of the face with a profile, a method which, however, shows no trace of a primitive groping, but rather of a completely developed formula. The aesthetic interest is found mainly in the curving linear contours. These are broken only by incised lines completing the details of the figures. A striated background sets off the figures which are highly polished. Landscape is used symbolically only in so far as it is an integral part of the story.

POU-T'AI, GOD OF GOOD LUCK. (Musée Cernuschi.)

In the *Chu Wei* tombs, dating from about the first century A.D., the decoration is entirely incised, and is probably an even closer approximation of painting. These engravings represent scenes from the burial ceremonies and contain some very life-like portraits.

A third group of Han tomb engravings comes from *Shao Tang Shan*. These combine the techniques noted in the first two and belong to the same tradition.

*Paintings on pottery and lacquer.* These add little more to our knowledge but display some of the actual brush work.

Chinese lacquers have been excavated from the sites of the Chinese colony at Lo-lang in Korea and Noin Ula in Mongolia. Inscriptions on these objects indicate dates from 85 B.C. to A.D. 71, and many bear the name and location of the factory where they were made in Ssuchuan. Through stylistic anal-

AVENUE OF TOMBS, NEAR CHI-MEN, CHINA.

ogies with reliefs, lacquers, and other potteries that are known to be Han the painted pottery vessels and tiles are dated in the same period. These painted decorations show that at this early date the Chinese artist had already become a master of the brush stroke, and could build convincing figures and compositions with a great economy of means. Subject matter rarely consists of more than decorative patterns, but there are some objects which bear figure compositions. Of these three of the most important are: 1) the painted tile in the Museum of Fine Arts, Boston, 2) a lacquer box from Lo-lang which carries fluid representations of Shih Wang Mu and other Taoist divinities, and the date A.D. 70, 3) a basket from Lo-lang with human representations painted on panels. The subject matter of the Boston tile is the most puzzling. Obviously a lintel, and probably part of a tomb decoration, it shows figures of men and women some of whom lead animals. The scene has been variously described as a hunt, or the preparations for some kind of game. However, a ram's skull in high relief at the top of the tile indicates the possibility that the scene represents a skull sacrifice. A stone stele of the same period in a Chinese collection also bears a similar skull and corroborates this theory, which if correct, adds to our very fragmentary knowledge of Chinese religious beliefs in the Han period.

*Sculpture.*—At this time sculpture begins to take an important place among the arts in China. Besides the engraved stones already discussed, there are several other important groups of Han sculptures. In Ssuchuan, the Segalen-Lartigue Mission discovered a number of commemorative pillars in stone but imitating a wood technique. These are covered in high and low relief with mythological scenes and symbols which in their cutting and in the "drôlerie" of their representations bear witness of an almost virtuoso quality.

A problem of the period is the sculpture in full round at the tomb of *Ho Chu Ping* (d. 117 B.C.). Although the tomb was built shortly after the death of Ho Chu Ping, contemporary records do not mention the sculpture. However, the representation of a large horse trampling a barbarian, although in full round, is seen best from the side and gives the impression of a bas-relief, while the oblique cutting of some of the other animal figures resembles that of late Chou and Han jades.

Sculpture of the period can also be seen in the tomb figurines which are usually of pottery but sometimes of lacquered wood. Statuettes and models buried with the corpse included representations of servants, attendants, horses, dogs, and even houses and furniture, which would permit the deceased to enjoy in the after-life all that he had been accustomed to use in his past. These figures show a lively, if crude naturalism which can be explained by the frequently perfunctory workmanship on the *ming chi* or funerary gifts which were required to have imperfections. Utilitarian art is represented by a group of small bronze bears about six to eight inches long. They were probably used as furniture supports and exhibit the same free naturalism that is found in the figurines. The broad treatment of planes also links them with a group of horse heads in jade and pottery.

An important type of Han sculpture was used to line the "spirit path," the avenue leading to the tomb. Many of the animals from the tomb of Ho Chu Ping were used for this purpose. Frequent among this group are winged lions and chimeras. Osvald Sirén has contributed a valuable study of these animal representations which allow a continuity of development to be traced from the Han dynasty through the succeeding centuries. Sometimes actual lions as contrasted to fantastic were depicted, as at the tomb of *Wu Liang Tzu,* but from the fourth to the sixth centuries winged lions and chimeras (or kylins) were favored. In general the development is from a clumsy, if powerful and convincing naturalism in Han times to a stylized representation with dramatic force. A series of dated examples from the fifth and sixth centuries shows a gradual change toward this more spirited concept. In the sculptures created toward the end of this development, the proportions of the body are destroyed in the elaboration of the component parts of the body. Heads become enormous and terrifying. Chests swell in huge curves, and the body itself becomes tense with latent movement. The concentrated strength of the best of these sculptures shows signs of over-elaboration in some of the later representations and the decline can be followed into the T'ang dynasty.

*Architecture.*—Although, as a result of the use of wood for most architecture in China no actual Han buildings survive to this time, pottery models, representations in stone engravings, and sculptured stone pillars based on wooden prototypes, permit a reconstruction of the general characteristics of the buildings of this period.

As we have noted, wood was the chief material of construction, although a legend illustrated on the Wu Liang Tzu reliefs shows an assassin plunging a dagger into a column supposedly made of bronze or copper. Whether metal columns actually were used in the royal palaces during the Ch'in dynasty as described in the story or whether the column was merely wood sheathed in a thin covering of metal is not known. However, wood was in general use and Chinese architecture as we know it today was already defined. The main features of Chinese architecture are: the location of the buildings within a compound which has a central axis running from north to south, the arrangement of the buildings one behind the other within the compound, and the construction of the buildings with a large roof supported on a series of brackets surmounting wooden columns.

The basis of the Chinese building has already been noted in the discussion of art in the Shang dynasty, but one important development appears in the Han period. Previously the roof was supported by two rows of columns at each side and a third row under the ridge pole. In the Han dynasty a system of brackets was developed which supported cross beams which in turn supported the roof. Since all the weight of the building is carried by the columns the walls in such a scheme of construction serve no other purpose than to enclose space within the building.

Tile roofs were known at least as early as Han times. Large quantities of green glazed tiles with moulded designs of this period have been found. The roof with the upturned corners so typical of China seems to have appeared during this period. Some of the pottery models show houses with upturned eaves. Many theories have been advanced to account for the peculiar shape of the Chinese roof but none can be supported with any certainty. Perhaps the best is that as the roof became larger the upturned corners offered a means of shortening the large overhanging projections at the ends.

*Ordos Bronzes.*—Another type of art that is usually ascribed to the Han period is found in the northern part of China where the large bend in the Yellow River forms the Ordos region. From this district have come a series of plaques based on belt buckles that show close resemblances to the art of contemporaneous Siberia. It is strange, however, to find that motifs belonging to Sarmatian art and to the art of Minusinsk which are never combined on the Siberian steppe, are here united at the Chinese frontier. Although these pieces are usually considered to date from the Han period, Dr. Alfred Salmony believes that degenerated forms were still being made as late as the tenth century.

*Pottery.*—Pottery attains more prominence during the Han dynasty. A soft green glaze, in its present state frequently iridescent from long burial, is most common. Less usual are brown and black glazes. Chief among the potters' works at this time are the tomb figurines mentioned above. Large pottery vessels are also common. These adopted the shapes of bronze prototypes. Most prevalent were the so-called "hill jars" and large wine containers of the *hu* type. The "hill jars," sometimes with perforated tops for incense, sometimes with solid tops, all bear mythological scenes and representations of the Taoist Holy Mountain.

*Bronze.*—At the same time that this period saw the beginning of a continuous development that was to lead to the finest ceramic art the world has yet produced, it witnessed the decline of bronze casting as a great art. Mirrors remained the only bronze form to show a creative impulse—an impulse which was visible only in the changing types of decoration applied to the mirror and the continued excellence of craftsmanship. This art remained vital throughout the T'ang dynasty (618-906) and persisted in a slightly weaker form during the Sung dynasty (1179-1368).

*Lacquer.*—Lacquer is also important in the Han dynasty. Besides the painted boxes already mentioned, furniture and various utensils were coated with this resinous varnish which was used in many colors, although red seems to have predominated. Lacquer was also employed for the decoration of mirrors, sometimes as inlay, sometimes as a base upon which thin silver sheets were applied.

THREE KINGDOMS AND SIX DYNASTIES A.D. 221-589.— At the break-up of the Han dynasty in A.D. 221, China once more passed through a period of anarchy and internal strife. The periods of the Three Kingdoms (221-280) and the Six Dynasties (220-589) carried on Han traditions and witnessed the growth of Buddhism which brought with it new art forms and which transformed others.

*Buddhism.*—Buddhism was probably introduced into China as early as the first century A.D., but it was not until the fifth century that it began to spread with tremendous rapidity all over China. Periodic persecutions and outbreaks of iconoclasm have destroyed most of the earliest monuments, but a few bronze statues of the early fifth century enable us to glimpse the beginnings of this art. There also remains the sculpture of the cave temples of Yun Kang, the first of a series of monuments which permit us to trace Buddhist sculpture from its rise to its decay.

*Sculpture.*—The earliest Buddhist sculptures show close relationships to the art of central Asia—an art which in its turn had derived from the Graeco-Buddhist art of Gandhara in northwestern India. In most of these statues the human form is felt only as a cubic mass which supports the drapery. The drapery itself is a degenerated schematization of Gandharan drapery, but it soon develops a pure archaic formula which is entirely Chinese. The heads have a typical "archaic smile" and are devoid of any passing emotion. This absence of emotion is not necessarily due to the artists' inability to render facial expression, but on the contrary, is a definite part of the concept of a Buddhist statue. The Buddhas or the Bodhisattvas who are represented are timeless and unchanging; for the sculptor to convey a temporal or human attitude would be to misinterpret the icon. It is well to note in this connection that at slightly later periods when the disciples of Buddha are portrayed they are more lifelike in appearance since they represent humans who have not yet attained enlightenment.

*Yun Kang.*—The most important monuments remaining from the fifth century are the cave temples cut into the soft sandstone cliffs at Yun Kang, near Ta Tung, Honan. The majority of the statues date from 470 to 494, when the work was discontinued, following a change of the imperial residence to Lo-yang. In general the figures in these caves have the block-like forms noted above, with the serrated folds of the drapery forming a geometric border at the bottom and edges of the robe. In addition to these archaic and Chinese sculptures, there is another group peculiar to Yun Kang. This is composed of Hindu rather than Buddhist divinities, and the fluid forms suggest the possibility that Indian sculptors actually worked at Yun Kang side by side with the Chinese craftsmen.

*Lung Men.*—At Lung Men, near Lo-yang, another group of caves was commenced soon after the arrival of the court in that city. The hard limestone of the locality was a better medium for the sculptor than the soft stone of Yun Kang. The forms become more elegant, elongated and graceful. The folds of the drapery swing in taut, flame-like curves from the hips. The narrow-waisted bodies frequently have the "S" curve which is so common in Gothic sculpture. The taut draperies reflect a style suited to bronze rather than stone and it is probable that statues cast in bronze played an important part in determining the style of this period.

*Bronze.*—Traditions tell of Buddhist priests returning from India with small bronze statues which, no doubt, served as models for the Chinese worker. Even more important was the custom among the Toba Tatars, the founders of the Wei dynasty (386-557), which specified that a Wei prince had to cast an acceptable statue before he could attain to the kingship. The emphasis on metal craft among the Weis was probably due to the importance of the blacksmith among their nomadic ancestors. Whatever the reason, the finest of the small bronze altar-sets made during the sixth century evince the caster's ability to develop the malleable qualities of his material to the greatest aesthetic potentialities. Dated inscriptions on many of these bronzes offer a sound basis for a chronology of Chinese sculpture during the sixth century. This period witnessed a change from the archaism at the beginning of the century, with highly stylized drapery and stiff almost cubistic figures, to a softer, more naturalistic drapery and a more human rendering of the figure. By the middle of the century the drapery generally loses the sharp flame-like folds, although the geometric formula is retained in a looser manner. In the Northern Ch'i dynasty (550-577) a new development appears. The silhouette instead of broadening towards the bottom because of the winged drapery, now becomes vertical and a tendency towards flatness in the figure is replaced by a cylindrical volume.

SUI DYNASTY (589-618).—This transition was climaxed in the Sui dynasty when the silhouette was reversed and the figure tapered from the rather wide shoulders down to the ankles, although at times the older style was suggested by flowing scarfs at the feet. It is in the short span of the Sui dynasty too, that Chinese sculpture changed from the hieratic abstraction of the archaic periods to a more personal art in which the sculptor seems interested in aesthetic problems to the detriment of more profound concepts. Parallels in Western art might be found between Cimabue and Botticelli, or between Romanesque and late Gothic sculpture. Nevertheless, some of the best of Chinese sculpture dates from this period, for when the artist combined his new formal problems with the older religious intensity, he created works unsurpassed in China. Elegance, without the elaboration which was to detract from much of the later sculpture is the keynote of this period. So fine is a large proportion of these works that one questions the usual Chinese tradition that the sculptors who made these works were merely artisans. The high standards realized in many of these works, on the contrary, raises the question as to whether the Confucian literati who wrote the histories were guilty of errors of omission. Certainly it is known that Chinese and Korean sculptors who worked in Japan at that time were signally honored with the imperial favor.

*Tien Lung Shan.*—Another important group of sculptures dating from the middle of the sixth century are found in the caves of Tien Lung Shan. Many of these statues show that a new wave of Indian influence arrived during the Sui period, which was to affect the sculpture of the following T'ang period.

*Painting.*—Painting during the fifth and sixth centuries seems to have developed at an equally rapid pace. It was at the beginning of the sixth century that Hsieh Ho's Six Principles had been formulated, but important painters and calligraphers are known to have worked long before that time.

VASES, MING AND CH'IEN LUNG DYNASTIES.

In the British Museum there is a painting attributed to *Ku K'ai-chih* who lived during the second half of the fourth century. The painting itself has been so greatly repaired that it is impossible to say definitely whether the picture is actually by Ku K'ai-chih or whether it is a somewhat later copy. However, there is no doubt that the painting is certainly in the style of the period. The history of the painting can be traced over a long period, and its style forms a logical link between Han painting as we know it from rock engravings and T'ang. Its importance is further increased by the fact that it is the only secular painting of an early period. The painting consists of a series of isolated scenes illustrating a didactic essay, *The Admonitions of the Instructress in the Palace.* One scene, however, at the end of the scroll, depicts a hunter aiming his bow at a mountain which is filled with animals, and may refer to Yu, the archer hero of Chinese mythology. The pictures are painted in fine lines and filled in with colored washes. The figures have a dignified simplicity and show a high degree of sophistication in their graceful poses and subtle groupings.

VASE DECORATED WITH DRAGON, CH'IEN LUNG DYNASTY.

MING DYNASTY. (Grandidier Collection.)

Especially highly developed is an almost cinematographic movement in one picture which shows a group of servants carrying a palanquin. In the Freer Gallery of Art in Washington, D. C., is another painting at one time attributed to Ku K'ai-chih. This work, *The Nymph of the Lo River,* is a long, horizontal landscape, which although probably not painted before the eleventh or twelfth century, contains many elements of composition which are found in early paintings. Chief among these is the method of breaking up the long, horizontal composition into individual cell-like units. This method is also used in some of the earliest wall paintings in the Caves of the Thousand Buddhas at Tun Huang.

*Tun Huang.*—This city on the westernmost border of China, in Kansu, was the last Chinese outpost on the important trade route through Turkestan. The cave temples were begun in 366, but Buddhist persecutions from 444 to 446 probably were the cause of the destruction of the earliest monuments. The problem of dating the paintings which stretch over several centuries and are still being made today, is crucial to the study of Chinese painting. In an intensive research of the material Martha Davidson has presented a chronology which, by comparisons with well-dated sculptures, by use of inscriptions, and by stylistic analyses, shows a continuous development of painting within the caves. Throughout the Wei period she finds strong influences of the art of Turkestan, especially of Qyzil.

FIGURE WITH DRAGON, MING DYNASTY.

Three caves are dated before 500, 111a, 111, and 103 (Pelliot's cave numbers). In these, the wall paintings merely give a tapestry-like effect. Caves 110, 135, 129, 101, 137b, belong to the period from 500 to 550. The wall space is divided in these caves in an advanced manner. A horizontal register appears as the predecessor of the *makimono* (the Japanese term that is generally used for the horizontal scroll-type painting common in the Far East; when vertical, the scroll is called a *kakemono*). Cave 110 is the earliest to have the composition broken up into cell-like units by mountains which recede diagonally. Animals, disproportionately large, fill the spaces. The painting has the same fleeting rhythms found in the contemporary sculptures and in the paintings in Korea (see *Korea Art*). In cave 135 three superimposed registers appear; the mountains congeal, forming valleys which enclose separate scenes. Space and time within these paintings are additive rather than continuous. Although there is unity within each cell, proportions are still unreal, and the cells are united only by decorative arrangements.

At this time we are able to recognize one of the fundamental principles of Chinese painting—the treatment of perspective. The Far-Eastern artist has never been interested in the so-called scientific perspective of the West. Instead he has manipulated his two-dimensional surface in whatever manner best suited his purpose, and for his purposes he developed conventions which are neither more naïve nor more arbitrary than those used by European artists. Two main types are important. One prefers a high and moving station point which gives a "bird's eye" view of the scene. This is used mainly for narrative and secular painting (including landscapes) and is especially well adapted to story-telling since it permits descriptions of large areas. Although this type of perspective is used for the scene in general, figures and individual objects within the picture are shown on the eye level in order that they may be the more easily recognized. Were they drawn according to the same conventions used in the landscape, whole figures would appear only as heads. In this type of perspective, lines which recede into the picture plane do not converge in depth as in Western paintings but are either parallel or converge toward the spectator. The second type of perspective is used in hieratic Buddhist paintings. In these the most important figures are placed in a central position and painted on a much larger scale than the less important figures. All significant lines converge upon a vanishing point along a central axis which bisects the chief figure. A system of dominant and recessive colors coordinates with this method in creating the imposing power of the divinity. It also is an aid in modeling form in space.

T'ANG DYNASTY, 618-906.—The T'ang dynasty continued and brought to a blossoming many of the arts of the previous centuries. Later caves at Tun Huang show a steady development of painting while adhering to the same formulae mentioned above. As the artist became more conscious of his powers he enlarged the single cell of his horizontal painting until he could expand it both horizontally and vertically so subtly that the framing hills led the eye of the spectator to the next section rather than restraining it. At this time too, the hieratic painting became more fixed. In general it represents the heaven of the Mahayana Buddhists. A large hieratic representation dominates the wall, while around it are scenes from the *Jatakas* painted in the narrative style.

Chinese historians have frequently considered the T'ang era as the Golden Age of China. Many of the greatest painters worked at that time, and although we have no certain works by any masters of the period, later literature, copies, and a few paintings possibly of the period testify to the soundness of the analysis. Early in the seventh century we are told of *Wei-ch'ih I-seng* an artist from Khotan in Chinese Turkestan, who painted at the Imperial court. It is interesting to notice that this "western" artist was especially famous for the plastic modelling of his figures.

Another important painter of this period was *Yen Li Pen* (died 673) whose style is known through numerous copies and a possible original in the Museum of Fine Arts, Boston. The figures in the Boston scroll are constructed with the same massive dignity and simplicity that is found in slightly later paintings in Japan and Turkestan. In Japan, an Imperial storehouse, the Shosoin, which was closed in the eighth century contains paintings on lutes and screens dating from that time. If these are not by Chinese artists they surely reflect the same æsthetic. Sweeping lines, monumental grace, and dignified spacing, express the power of an age of unrivalled territorial expansion and imperial magnificence.

*Landscape Painting.*—Landscape as an independent art form seems to date from this period. *Li Ssu-hsun* has been named the father of the northern school of landscape painting, a category which has no geographical meaning and is probably little more than a late division created by hair-splitting scholars. In general it is taken to mean the brightly colored landscapes with blue, green, and gold, in contrast to the monochrome style of the southern school. The distinguishing factors are not always very clear for a certain hardness of drawing often is considered a characteristic of the northern school, and many monochrome paintings are grouped in that category because of their brushwork. A large number of brilliantly colored paintings are connected with the name of Li Ssu-hsun and his son *Li Chao-tao*. It is unlikely that any of these works, which are frequently pictures of palaces, even date from the period. There is, however, in the Palace Museum in Peiping a landscape which has been assigned by Dr. Ludwig Bachhofer with good reason to the eighth century. In its coloring and style this painting shows relationships to the traditional "Li" type while its spatial concepts are closely related to those in wall paintings from Tun Huang dating from the eighth century.

*Wang Wei,* born at the end of the seventh century, is considered the founder of the monochrome style of landscape. His work is known only through traditional copies and engravings on stone after early copies. Whether Wang Wei really created the characteristic monochrome landscape with its suggestive veil of mist, is questionable. This style seems to have matured during the tenth century, although traces of it appear as early as the ninth century at Tun Huang. However, Chinese tradition has generally been correct in regard to the broader phases of art history, and it may be that one day evidence will be found corroborating Wang Wei's nomination as the creator of the finest and most typical painting in China.

The third great painter of this epoch was *Wu Tao-tzu* whose works, like those of his contemporaries, have vanished. Innumerable legends have clustered about his name; these tell us that he was appreciated for the powerful sweep of his brush strokes, and the grand conceptions of his figures. Equally at home in Buddhist religious painting or secular landscape, he has remained the ideal of all later artists. Even the late copies that have survived until now reflect strong compositions that are built up by broad calligraphic strokes.

Other important painters mentioned by the historians are: *Han Kan,* famous for his horses; *Chou Fang* whose style is preserved in some excellent Sung copies; *Lu Tan Wei;* and *Chang Seng-yu.* In Japan there still exists a set of Buddhist paintings by *Li Chen* which were brought to Japan in 803 by the great Buddhist priest, Kobo Daishi. These paintings are drawn with thin even strokes, the so-called "iron wire" technique. They are representations of the Buddhist patriarchs, and have the monumentality of the period and the spiritual simplicity demanded by the subject.

*Sculpture.*—Sculpture during the T'ang dynasty continued the path traced for it in the preceding centuries. At the beginning of the seventh century, the forms still retain some of the slender strength of six century sculpture. Under a new wave of Indian influence, however, the figures soon became more baroque. Costume becomes more elaborate at the expense of structural qualities, and the figures acquire exaggerated "S" curves. In some of the works of this time, however, a sensuous, fluid rhythm, derived from Indian prototypes offers a seductive charm to the spectator weary of archaic detachment. This new approach to form is reflected in the portrait figures which develop at this time. A set of life-sized figures of Lohans, now scattered in museums throughout the world, are examples of this new realism in glazed pottery, while stone statues of monks and semi-secular personages manifest this same realism, which is also apparent in the mortuary figurines at this time. These figurines contrasted to the stylized and heraldic Wei pieces are highly developed naturalistic in form, although the running glazes of brown, cream, green, and less commonly blue, make no attempt to reproduce reality. The careful workmanship found in the best of these is further evidence of the sumptuousness of the age, as is their large size.

*Ceramic.*—For the first time, one might say, ceramics become an independent art. Up to this time the potter had on the whole, contented himself with copying forms derived from bronze casting. But in the T'ang period forms appear which are pottery conceptions, although the close relationship with Sassanian Persia caused the potter to sometimes copy Near Eastern metal forms.

High-fired glazes make their appearance at this time and among these the beginnings of the famous celadon greens can be found. New forms like those in sculpture and painting prefer strength to sweetness. Glazes are applied boldly and a clear definition of structure is emphasized in form and decoration.

Meanwhile toward the end of the dynasty, sculpture tended to become more and more baroque, until the creative spirit seems to be overpowered by mere elaboration. An increasing heaviness plus a tendency toward sweetness which culminated during the following Sung dynasty (960-1279) places sculpture with rare exceptions, in the class of craftsmanship rather than art. T'ang types are perpetuated with so little variation that it is at times almost impossible to make stylistic distinctions between T'ang originals and later copies.

Wood as a medium becomes common during the T'ang period, and this, too, probably contributed to the decline of the art, for Chinese sculpture never seems to have had the understanding for this material that Japanese sculpture had.

(See Japan—Art.)

*Architecture.*—Architecture during the T'ang dynasty carried on the same practices that had originated in Han times. In general the only change that occurs is in the direction of greater elaboration. Many buildings in Japan which date from the eighth century and which may even have been built by Chinese workmen show us the style of the period. The innovations are chiefly found in the more complex bracketing systems, which, while structurally necessary, became the most important æsthetic element at this time. Since most of the buildings were constructed of wood, few have survived the ravages of fire and decay. A series of pagodas dating from the sixth centurv, however, proves that structures in stone and brick did little more than adapt those materials to the principles derived from wooden architecture. The pagoda was probably introduced into China with the advent of Buddhism, and is really nothing else than the Chinese concept of the Buddhist *stupa.* (See India—Art.) But square, round, and octagonal, they have become an integral part of the Chinese landscape, with their series of roofs rising gracefully to the sky.

Architecture until the Yuan period continued to multiply the structural advantages of the bracketing systems, but from that time on no real innovations were made. The complex systems became burdened with decorative additions but no fundamental characteristics were added.

FIVE DYNASTIES 906-960.—With the fall of the T'ang dynasty in 906, China once more went through a period of internal struggle. This period which lasted until 960 is called under the general name of the Five Dynasties. At the same time another dynasty held control of part of China until 1125, under the title of Liao. Despite this political unrest, the arts flourished.

*Painting.*—The monochrome landscape, traditionally the invention of Wang Wei in the T'ang period, reached its full stature in the tenth century. In this type of landscape, generally painted entirely in the black Chinese ink (*sumi*) but sometimes relieved by light colors, the artist aimed at suggestion in order to interpret the grandeur of nature. When human figures appear they are dwarfed into insignificance by the power of the scene, or else they merely serve, as the Greek chorus, to share the emotions with the spectator. For in these works the spectator must participate actively and create in his mind what the artist has suggested with brush and ink. For it is always the cumulative power of the brush stroke that serves to stir the spectator, and if modern Chinese criticism now overemphasizes the brush stroke, it is because of the knowledge that in the great paintings of the past the means served the end so well. However, brushwork was a means to an end. In modern criticism it is treated as though it were an end in itself.

Highly advanced as these paintings are, they are built on primitive formulae. Usually in one corner of the foreground is a rock, hill, or tree which serve as repoussoirs. Mountains and hills in the distance are separated by indefinite layers of mist. Space is suggested, neither defined nor continuous. Paintings attributed to this early period of landscape painting are few, but those which seem to have the best claim to such a date are austere in strength. Chief among the Five Dynasties landscape painters were *Tung Yuan,* the priest *Chu-jan,* and *Huang Ch'uan,* who is said to have introduced the method of painting without outlines (boneless painting). *Kuan Hsiu* who lived at this time is noted for his paintings of Arhats, whom he portrayed as weird-looking ascetics. A group of paintings of this type in Japan has long been associated with his name and may be by his hand.

SUNG DYNASTY, 960-1279. *Painting.*—The Sung Dynasty reunited China for a short time, but in 1127 the empire was divided by barbarian invaders who came from the north and seized control of northern China. The Sung court retreated to a new capitol at Hang Chou. During the first part of the period, the so-called Northern Sung, painting continued to flourish under imperial patronage. Only a few originals but many later copies which maintain the style of Sung artists enable us to reconstruct the art of this age of splendor. Majestic landscapes by *Kuo Hsi* with, as the descriptions tell us, "mountains like cumulous clouds" have the restrained exuberance of a master sure of his own ability to control a capricious medium. *Fan Kuan* (c. 990-1030) painted in a more quiet mood and was noted for his snow scenes. It is perhaps well to mention that although Chinese critics have been in the habit of placing painters into categories such as "horse painters," "bird and flower painters," or "bamboo painters," the artists themselves practiced more than one type. As a consequence good, and frequently bad paintings of a specialized subject are almost always ascribed to the leading artist who "painted" that subject. Thus most dragon pictures are attributed to *Chen Jung* for Chen Jung is "famous for his dragon paintings."

Perhaps the most important painter of the northern Sung period was *Li Lung-mien,* also called Li Kung-lin, who lived from about 1040 to 1106. First known for his horse pictures, he later became a painter of Buddhist subjects and the acknowledged founder of a new style. A series of pictures of the Five Hundred Arhats in the Museum of Fine Arts, Boston, by *Lin Ting-kuei* and *Chou Chi-ch'ang* reproduce the style generally attributed to Li. Simple but sensitive lines build up the figures while the contours are filled with clear washes of delicate color.

But all the painters were not creators of new styles. *Chao Po-chu* continued the brightly colored landscape tradition of Li Ssu-hsun, but invested it with a delicate suggestivity which was probably foreign to the earlier master. The Imperial Academy fostered painting under a series of art-loving emperors. *Hui Tsung,* the last of Northern Sung emperors, was himself an important painter and encouraged the development of a highly detailed transcription of nature. The Chinese artist, however, never copied a model, but after close study and meditation painted from memory which he modified by his academic formulae. Some of the leading painters of the Academy were, *Li An-chung, Li Ti,* and *Mao I.*

*Mi Fei* (1051-1107) was also one of the few innovators among the painters. He developed a manner of painting in large blobs of ink which produced an impressionistic effect. The style was perpetuated by his son *Mi Yu-jen.*

After the removal of the court to Hang Chou, painting loses a great measure of its power. Instead of the rugged landscapes of early Sung, the artist seems to have sought escape from disaster by depicting the softer and more serene aspects of nature. Paintings by *Li T'ang, Hsia Kuei,* and the Ma family, *Ma Yuan, Ma Lin,* and *Ma Kuei,* are characteristic of this change. In them we find less of the rugged aspects of nature. Even when a tempest is represented, it lacks the inherent power found in the calmest moments portrayed by the earlier masters. But if the Southern Sung painters are less strong, they have their own kind of beauty. Never before had paintings been so imbued with repose. Wide spaces of unpainted silk or paper suggest infinite space reaching beyond the layers of mountains that are shuffled one behind the other.

However, at the same time another school was flourishing in China. The *Ch'an* (Japanese "Zen") sect of Buddhism had to a great measure superseded the more formal religion. Its doctrine required no formulae, no set prayers, no sculpture, no intermediary between the believer and the Buddha. Enlightenment came only through revelation, a revelation which might result at any time from the most slight accident, although meditation was practised. The influence of this sect without doubt hastened the decline of sculpture through the decline of patronage, as it also changed the direction of painting. The Ch'an painters gave up the older hieratic pictures used in ceremonies no longer observed. Instead they painted pictures with a didactic purpose of another sort. Scenes representing Ch'an legends, illustrating the lives of former Patriarchs and showing the accidental manner in which they had received enlightenment, were portrayed with a sketchy technique that retained all the accidental spontaneity of the incident. So in contrast to the sweet and sophisticated art of the court, in the Ch'an monasteries there developed an art at once personal and universal, which retained only an amazing technical facility employed to abbreviate reality in the effort to constantly increase the suggestivity of the painting. Two great painters of the thirteenth century dominate this school. These are *Mu Ch'i* and *Liang K'ai,* who had been a member of the academy. The first painted in broad soft strokes and wet washes, the second usually with a jagged splintered line. They were the predecessors of a line of priest-painters, which was to create a school of painting in Japan equal to their own.

*Ceramics.*—Only one other art was of great importance in Sung China. Ceramics at this time reached a position never surpassed before or after. During the preceding Five Dynasties high-fired glazes had advanced in perfection. Two important types of glaze were first made at that time. One was the *pi se* (secret color) ware, also known as Yueh ware, after the site of its manufacture. The actual place of manufacture was recently discovered in Chekiang and a sherd was found which bears a date corresponding to 978, the earliest date so far found on Chinese pottery. The glaze on these vessels is a grey or olive green. The other ware for which the Five Dynasties were known was the Ch'ai ware with the color of "the sky after rain." It was also thin and resonant. Although attempts have been made to relate the description with known Sung potteries, the type has not yet been definitely isolated. The production of these and related wares continued throughout the Sung dynasty and in some instances even later. Closely connected with the types already mentioned are a large group of monochrome glazes loosely known as "celadons." These are usually described in the Chinese texts by the word *ching* which may mean either blue or green. Most well known are the celadons made at Lung Ch'uan which gave its name to them. The color of these varies from a lettuce-green to a grey or blue-green. It is not only the subtlety of tone that is pleasing in these ceramics but also the texture which is thick and waxy. The so-called Northern celadon is a darker, olive green, and shows close relationships to some of the Korai potteries of Korea (see Korea—Art). Another of the famous types of this period was the Ju ware, which has been identified with a ware known for some time under the term *ying ch'ing.* The glaze on these potteries is generally a faint blue-green which at times attains a rare delicate intensity. Similar to the *ying ch'ing* ware is the Ting Yao (ware). In the best Ting, the ware is finely potted and the glaze milky white. An inferior kind of Ting is the *t'u ting,* less finely potted and covered with a thicker glaze that is frequently crackled. Bowls of the Ting and *ying ch'ing* types usually have a silver rim round the mouth to protect the thin material. The shapes of all these types are graceful and elegant. Unlike the T'ang potteries the units of the vessels are not emphasized but flow into one sophisticated shape. Decoration is confined in most instances to incised or moulded designs which are usually floral patterns. In the Lung Ch'uan celadons the design sometimes appears on the unglazed biscuit which is raised on a moulded relief above the glaze.

Other wares of the period are Ko Yao (Elder Brother's) a grayish glaze usually crackled, Chun Yao with a blue glaze splashed with red and purple transmutation colors which are sometimes so controlled that recognizable fish or birds are used as decoration. Another pottery found is sometimes called Chun, sometimes identified with Kuan (the Imperial ware). The shapes are in most cases jardinières or shallow saucers and are covered with a rich, deep purple glaze relieved by red mottling.

Another group of Sung potteries are commonly designated by the Japanese term of *temmoku.* These are covered with black glazes, sometimes streaked with brown or mottled in what is called "like the breast feathers of a partridge" or lined with brown and called "hare's fur." The site of these wares, in Fukien, has recently been discovered. Other variations in glazes include the so-called "oil spots" and deep plum colors. The Fukien group is known as Chien Yao after the kiln site, while a similar type ware is known as Honan *temmoku* from its northern provenance, and frequently includes painted designs and an all-brown glaze. Tea bowls form the most common types. Vases are not rare. The great beauty of this type is due to the thick glaze which forms lustrous pools wherever it is permitted to thicken.

The last important type of Sung pottery is the Ts'u Chou ware. The base is a hard stoneware, usually buff or gray. The shapes and method of decoration are almost impossible to catalogue. Incision, and painting are the most common techniques, but frequently the glaze is scraped away leaving the biscuit showing, or else part of slip is removed giving variety to the surface. The glaze is usually cream colored, but blue, green, and a dark brown are also found. Painted Ts'u Chou pieces are also known.

YUAN DYNASTY (1280-1368).—The Yuan dynasty unified China again, this time under foreign rulers—the Mongols. Many of the officials and scholars refused to serve the Mongol rulers and left the court to live in semi-banishment in provincial districts. As a result most of the arts suffered. Ceramics were less carefully made and merely perpetuated the Sung techniques in poorer quality. Sculpture had already declined under the Sungs and the only innovation under the Yuans was a further exaggeration of form. Yet it must not be thought that this was a barbarous period. It was the magnificent China of which Marco Polo wrote, and far superior in civilization to contemporaneous Europe.

*Painting.*—Painting, however, continued to develop. The situation was favorable to the growth of that art. On the one hand it had been freed from the academic shackles of the Imperial Academy. On the other hand the Ch'an Buddhist painting had, through its violent destruction of accepted aesthetic, cleared the way for new forms without having substituted an art that could have a general appeal over a long period. The leading Yuan painters turned back not to their immediate predecessors, but to the classic models of T'ang and the Five Dynasties. *Chao Meng-fu* (1254-1322) became famous for his paintings of horses, supposedly under the inspiration of Han Kan, but perhaps as much under the attraction of the Mongol horsemen. Other painters shunned the court. *Huang Kung-wang* (1264-1354), *Wang Meng* (d. 1385), *Wu Chen* (1280-1354), and *Ni Tsan* (1301-1374) were considered by later ages to be the "Four Masters" of the Yuan dynasty. Of the four Ni Tsan was the most conservative, painting the quiet scenes of the academic Sung painters. The other three artists painted landscapes in which every brush stroke reveals the powerful, latent energy of the forces of nature. Instead of the indefinite space of Sung painting, clear articulation of land and water form a more tangible composition. The Sung ideal had gone and the bitter reality is expressed in the more rugged landscapes of these painters.

Other Yuan painters, however, continued to paint in the older manner. The best of these, *Ch'ien Hsuan,* ranks with the greatest of the Sung painters in his accurate and poetic transcription of insects, birds and flowers.

MING DYNASTY, 1368-1644.—*Painting.*—In 1368 a popular revolution overthrew the foreign Mongol dynasty, and China was once more united under the rule of native sovereigns until 1644. The Ming dynasty turned to indigenous art for its models, and during the first part of the period painting returned to Sung models. As numerous copies and literary references show, Ma Yuan and Hsia Kuei became the idols of the age. But for some reason the creative impulse which had enabled the Yuan artists to transform their models into a new and living art, was missing. Painting degenerated

# GREEK TEMPLES

*Greek temples sum up the efforts of Greek architecture. This art was formed during the seventh and sixth centuries B.C. and the archaeological discoveries permit us to follow, theoretically, its formation from the old Mycenaean* megaron *up to the marble temple of the classical era. The explanation of its origin by the transformation of wooden architecture to a stone architecture gives a better account of each detail and aspect of this building; it is not the result of an abstract effort of imagination. It is the finishing touch of a technique which seeks and finds its answer in the perfect equilibrium between the law of gravity and the resistance of the support.*

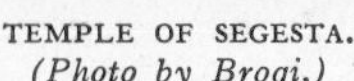

TEMPLE OF SEGESTA.
*(Photo by Brogi.)*

AGRIGENTUM: TEMPLE OF CONCORD.
*(Photo by Brogi.)*

PAESTUM: TEMPLE OF NEPTUNE.
*(Photo by Alinari.)*

The temples of Sicily and of Greece are the best preserved ones of antiquity. They represent the Doric temple of the sixth century which has already achieved perfect form. The cella is surrounded by an independent peristyle. At Segesta only the peristyle was built. The powerful columns carry a heavy entablature. In architecture as in sculpture the sixth century tries to express strength, and to make it more obvious, it gives great thickness to the columns and additional height to the entablature. These Doric temples are somewhat like the archaic Apollos, where strength is manifested by muscular exaggeration.

HERAEUM OF OLYMPIA. (SOUTH-EAST VIEW.)

RUINS OF CORINTH AND ACROCORINTH.
*(Photo by Boissonnas.)*

TEMPLE OF ÆGINA.
*(Photo by Boissonnas.)*

In the columns from Paestum and Ægina one can see the evolution of the Doric order. The shapes have become more delicate, but they retain their austere sobriety. Even when only a few columns remain standing, a fragment of an architrave resting on the capitals suffices to show how the purity of form results from the relation between force and the masses. Of the Heraeum at Olympia there is nothing left but the stereobate and a part of the columns. The plan of the building is that of an archaic temple, and Pausanias tells us that in his time one of the columns was still of wood.

ATHENS: THESEUM.
*(Photo by Alinari.)*

ATHENS: CHORAGIC MONUMENT OF LYSICRATES.
*(Photo by Alinari.)*

ATHENS: OLYMPIEION OF HADRIAN.
*(Photo by Alinari.)*

Besides the sanctuaries of the Acropolis: the Parthenon, the Erechteion, the Temple of Nike Apteros—Athens had other temples, including the Theseum, in reality a temple of Hephaistos. This Hephaisteum, somewhat more recent than the Parthenon, is likewise in the Doric style, but it is especially well preserved. The Temple of Olympian Zeus, started under Pisistratus, was finished only in the time of Hadrian by a Roman architect. Only a few of the colossal columns remain. The choragic monument of Lysicrates, which is well preserved, is a delightful example of the Corinthian style of the fourth century B.C.

# GREEK SCULPTURE BEFORE PHIDIAS

SCULPTURE *did not possess from the start a completely realistic aspect, or one of perfect beauty. During the seventh and sixth centuries B.C. it went through a long period of transition. After contact with the Egyptian and Asiatic Schools which was stopped during the conquests, Greek sculpture overcame the difficulties due to the hardness of material, and triumphed over the restraint of tradition. Thus from marble and bronze they created bodies which have the plastic refinement and the suppleness of the human flesh. One can follow the process of slow advance toward maturity in a progressive series of archaic sculptures where movement is apparent in the limbs before it can be seen in the graceful torsos.*

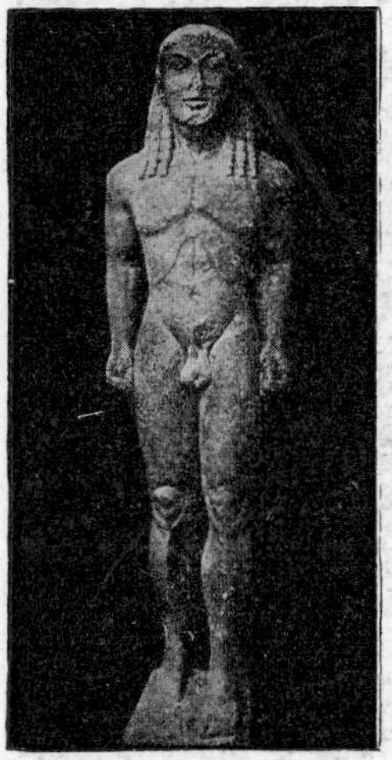

STATUE BY POLYMEDES OF ARGOS. DELPHI.

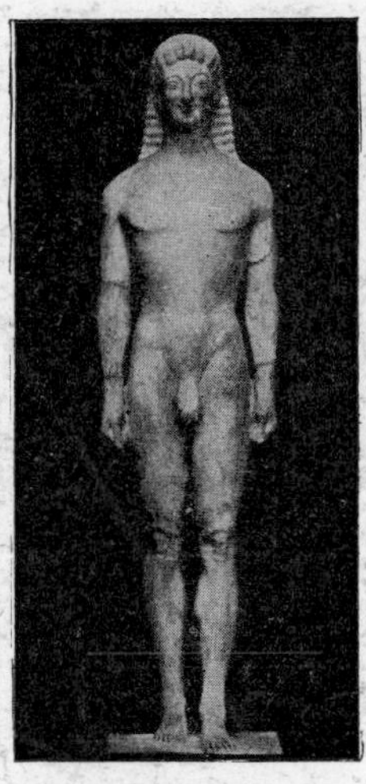

APOLLO OF TENEA. GLYPTOTHEK, MUNICH. *(Photo by Bruckmann.)*

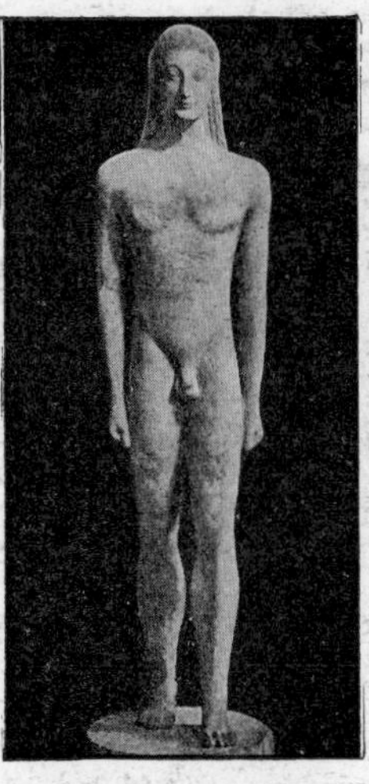

APOLLO OF MELOS. NATIONAL MUSEUM, ATHENS. *(Photo by Alinari.)*

ARTEMIS OF DELOS. MUSEUM OF ATHENS. *(Photo by Giraudon.)*

HERA OF SAMOS. LOUVRE. *(Photo by Hachette.)*

NIKE OF ARCHERMOS. NATIONAL MUSEUM, ATHENS.

CHARIOTEER OF DELPHI. *(Photo by Alinari.)*

DISCOBOLUS OF MYRON. NATIONAL MUSEUM, ROME. *(Photo by Anderson.)*

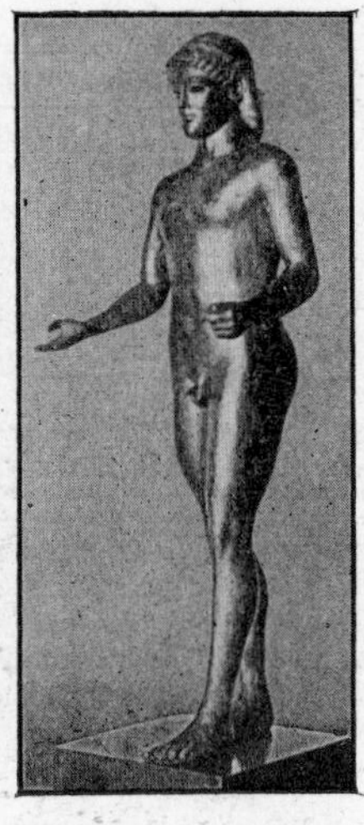

DIDYMEAN APOLLO OF PIOMBINO. LOUVRE. *(Photo by Hachette.)*

ARCHAIC FIGURE. OLD PARTHENON. ATHENS. *(Photo by Alinari.)*

HEAD OF A CARYATID. CNIDIAN TREASURY, DELPHI. *(Photo by Giraudon.)*

XOANON STATUE. *(Photo by Alinari.)*

SCULPTORS employed two main types of models: the nude male athlete and the draped female figure. These two types were first characterized by the inert rigidity of the stone block from which they were hardly separated. Before stone sculpture these figures were done in wood and these archaic stone sculptures recall the wooden figures which served as their models. One can follow the awakening of life in this inert rigidity, the motion of the legs, the arms, the pattern of the thorax, the abdomen, the rigid smile on the face, and the subtle rendering of the flowing drapery.

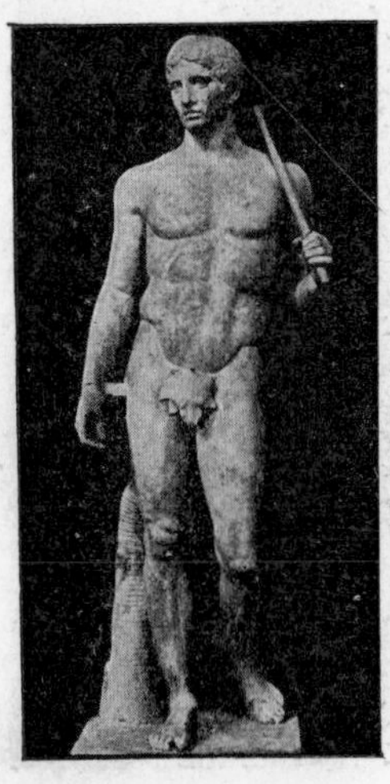

DORYPHORUS. NATIONAL MUSEUM, NAPLES. *(Photo by Alinari.)*

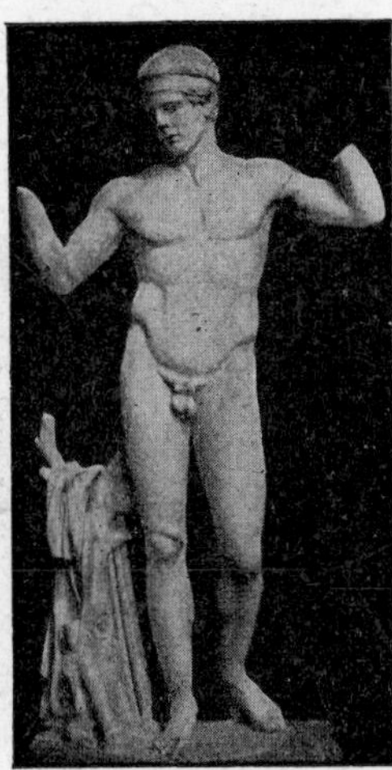

DIADUMENOS. REPLICA OF A STATUE BY POLYCLITUS. ATHENS. *(Photo by Alinari.)*

IDOLINO. ARCHAEOLOGICAL MUSEUM, FLORENCE. *(Photo by Brogi.)*

ATHENA LEMNIA. RESTORATION OF THE MUSEUM OF DRESDEN.

NIKE OF PAIONIOS. MUSEUM OF OLYMPIA. *(Photo by Tamme.)*

STYLE OF POLYCLITUS. WOUNDED AMAZON. MUSEUM OF BERLIN. *(Photo by Bard.)*

## Polyclitus

GREEK sculptors were the first to show the articulations of the spine, to balance the thorax on the pelvis, and to turn the head on the shoulders. During the second half of the fifth century Greek sculpture was at the height of its power. It equalled the human body in its grace and elegance. At this period Polyclitus created the statue of Doryphorus, a vigorous athlete "with square muscles," whose nonchalant solidity has often been imitated. Polyclitus, contemporary of Phidias, was the master of the Dorian school.

# THE ACROPOLIS OF ATHENS

*The most ancient cities were nearly always citadels, fortified cities, built on elevated places. It was in these that the people of the plains protected their most precious belongings, the statues of gods and their treasures. The Acropolis of Athens thus dominates the plain where the* demes *of Attica are scattered. As urban life assumed more importance, the civic centre moved from the hill to the plain. During historic times the Acropolis was mostly composed of sanctuaries. The Acropolis of Pericles suffered several pillages, because it became a fortress during the wars between the Turks and Venetians.*

ATHENS: THE ACROPOLIS.
*(Photo by Alinari.)*

## The Acropolis of Pericles

After the Persian invasion and destruction of Athens, during the wars with the Medes, the Athenians, who finally defeated the barbarians, used all their resources to reconstruct the city. On their Acropolis the new Parthenon soon arose, as well as the Erechteion, and the Temple of Nike Apteros. Pericles was the statesman who gave the impulse; Ictinos and Mnesicles were the architects; but the name of Phidias should be remembered above all. He was the great director who inspired and unified the whole.

PARTHENON: SOUTH PERISTYLE.

PARTHENON: WEST AND NORTH SIDES.

THE PROPYLÆA.

## The Parthenon

This is the temple of Athena, which sheltered the famous statue of the goddess executed by Phidias in ivory and gold. The Parthenon is of the Doric order, but the columns are so slender that the architect could place eight on the façade, as in the Ionic temples. The entablature is in the Doric style, but at the top of the wall of the cella under the colonnade there runs a frieze carved like an Ionic entablature. The Parthenon has suffered much at the hands of time and man; it has been temple, mosque, church; half destroyed, it remains the sanctuary of an immortal culture. The Propylæa led to the terrace of the Acropolis.

TEMPLE OF NIKE APTEROS.

THE ERECHTEION.

PORCH OF THE CARYATIDS.

## The Erechteion

On the Acropolis of Athens there is not only the temple of Athena, but also the sanctuary of Erechtheus, the ancestor of Attica. This temple, called the Erechteion, is of a complex structure; it sheltered an image of Athena, the statue to which, every four years, the entire population carried with great pomp the veil embroidered by young Athenian girls. The Erechteion has a porch on which the entablature is supported by graceful caryatids. The Temple of Nike Apteros, or Wingless Victory, stands near the Propylæa where it was rebuilt. These small Ionic temples represent a less formal type of art than their great forerunner, the Parthenon.

# DECORATIVE SCULPTURE PRIOR TO THE PARTHENON

*Next to sculpture which depicted the nude athlete type or the draped woman, Greek art also produced decorative sculpture, generally destined for the ornamentation of temples. This sculpture, found in the friezes and metopes, is not completely separated from the walls of the buildings; the figures are more or less protruding reliefs. However, in the pediment the sculpture is always in the round, and the figures are separate, but these statues never show the same rigid aspect as did the archaic ones. These sculptors had a superficial knowledge of positions in profile, movements of forms, and foreshortening.*

WOMAN BURNING INCENSE. THRONE OF VENUS.
*(Photo by Anderson.)*

BIRTH OF VENUS. THRONE OF VENUS (THE LUDOVISI THRONE). TERME MUSEUM, ROME.
*(Photo by Anderson.)*

FLUTE PLAYER. THRONE OF VENUS.
*(Photo by Anderson.)*

GROUP OF GODS. FRAGMENT OF THE FRIEZE OF THE TREASURY OF THE CNIDIANS AT DELPHI.
*(Photo by Giraudon.)*

DELPHI: GIGANTOMACHY.
*(Photo by Giraudon.)*

DELPHI: BATTLE OF THE GREEKS AND THE TROJANS.
*(Photo by Giraudon.)*

The famous bas-relief known as the Ludovisi Throne, represents, possibly, Venus Anadyomene arising from the waves, supported by the two Horae of Spring; to the left is a matron burning incense, to the right a courtesan playing a flute. The work is exquisite but still slightly reminiscent of the archaistic style. In the bas-reliefs of the frieze of the Treasury of the Cnidians the profile positions, the squat figures, and the exaggerated muscular activities, are characteristic of archaism; but the attitudes of the seated gods show the incomparable elegance which is later present in the gods of the frieze of the Parthenon.

FIGURES FROM THE PEDIMENT OF THE TEMPLE OF ÆGINA. GLYPTOTHEK, MUNICH. *(Photo by Bruckmann.)*

PEDIMENT OF THE TEMPLE OF ZEUS AT OLYMPIA. *(Photo by J. Bard.)*

The pediments of the Temples of Olympia and Ægina date from the middle of the fifth century. At Ægina one is still conscious of archaism: neither the placing of the figures nor the subject presented are absolutely determined. The sculpture at Olympia is larger and is composed of groups having lovely movement and rhythm; the vehemence of movement is admirably controlled within the frame of the pediment, which shows the fight between the Centaurs and the Lapiths. An Apollo, like Athena in the Æginetan pediment, dominates the conflict and tries to appease the combatants.

largely into copying. Figure pieces are one of the few creative types developed at this time. These are sweet rather than powerful, and even at their best carry within them the seeds of quick decay. *T'ang Yin* and *Ch'iu Ying* in the sixteenth century were the leaders of this type of painting.

The dangers of technical virtuosity, always inherent in the methods of Chinese painting were realized for the first time at this period. In order to avoid too obvious technical displays the literati developed a new technique called "ink flinging." Broad brush strokes gave a superficial appearance of carelessness to the works of "gentlemen painters" who did not wish to be confused with the growing class of professional artists. At times the brush was given up and the painting done with the fingers. For authority this group turned, toward the end of the dynasty, to the Yuan painters in whose powerful brush work they found precedents. Innumerable copies of the "Four Masters" of Yuan as well as quotations from their writings supplant the earlier appreciations of the Sung masters. But wherever the Yuan painters had always subordinated the brush stroke to the whole, the line itself became the end in the "literary man's" painting. *Tung Ch'i-ch'ang* (1555-1636) was the leading critic of this movement as well as one of its most important painters.

*Ceramics.*—Ceramics continued to hold its position as a creative art during the Ming period. Porcelain had been made at least as early as the Sung dynasty, but pottery had predominated. In the Ming dynasty the situation was reversed. Technical discoveries encouraged a greater use of porcelain. The subtle glazes of Sung were displaced in favor of combinations of bright colors. Painting in a cobalt blue may have originated in Sung times, but the superior surface of the porcelain in the later period caused it to be used extensively. Three reigns, Hsuan Te (1426-35), Cheng Te (1506-21), and Chia Ching (1522-66) were especially noted for the fine blue caused by the mixture of the imported "Mohammedan blue" from the Near East. Another of the unique glazes of Ming was the under-glaze copper red of the Hsuan Te period. In this type a tawny red design was set off against a pure white background.

Polychrome wares were made both with the use of under-glaze colors and by over-glaze painting. Various shades of green, red, yellow, aubergine, and blue were used. The so-called three color ware (*san ts'ai*) of Ming was made in either pottery or porcelain and sometimes has more than the required three colors. The selection of colors was made from a palette consisting of blue (turquoise or violet), aubergine, yellow, and white. The designs often in striking floral patterns are often formed by cloisons of clay or by incised lines to prevent the glazes from running. Monochromes such as the well-known *sang de boeuf* were made in the Ming period, as were some of the finest enamel on biscuit, both of which were carried on with consummate success in the following dynasty.

*Sculpture.*—Beyond pottery figurines there is no sculpture in Ming times that shows any creative force. The spirit path leading to the tombs of the Ming emperors at Nan K'ou, Chihli, shows how sterile the art had become through its continued repetition of classic models.

*Architecture.*—Architecture likewise shows no advance. During this period the structural use of bracketing systems was destroyed by their continued elaboration which left parts of the building an over-carved mass of writhing rococo ornament.

CH'ING DYNASTY.—The later Ming art had reflected a decadent court given up to pleasure and dissipation. In 1644 an invasion of Manchus from the north once more set a foreign dynasty upon the throne. Under a series of extremely able emperors China began to regain a measure of the political and artistic prestige she had lost during the decline of the Ming regime.

*Painting.*—No great innovations were made but a good quality was generally sustained. A group of able painters followed in the footsteps of Tung Ch'i-ch'ang in their admiration for the Yuan masters. They were known as the "Four Wangs" as a parallel to the earlier "Four Masters." *Wang Yuan ch'i* (1642-1715) possibly the greatest of the Four, has made many copies of paintings by Huang Kung-wang and it is in these that the change in temper can be seen between the two periods. A series of horizontal cross strokes which give a vibrating, impressionistic effect take the place of the static and eternal quality felt in the works of Huang. It is the difference between Degas and Giotto, paralleled in China. In the eighteenth century *Giuseppe Castiglione,* a Jesuit missionary at the court of the emperor Ch'ien-lung, was forced to learn the Chinese method of painting, and became a great favorite of the emperor. Painting under the name of Lang Shih-ning, he combined Western and Eastern methods and had some influence on a group of artists. Painting from the eighteenth century to the fall of the dynasty in the revolution of 1912 made no progress. Academic copying maintained an even standard, but the increased virtuoso quality of the "literary man's" painting and the influence of poor Western painting at the end of the nineteenth century hastened a decline, which only now has begun to show signs of an upward trend.

*Porcelain.*—Porcelain of all the arts showed the greatest vitality during the Ch'ing dynasty. The great factories at Ching-te Chen provided quantities of material for the imperial use. During the reign of the Emperor *K'ang-hsi* (1662-1722) some of the monochrome porcelains achieved new perfections. The *Lang yao* types continued the Ming monochromes and the *sang de boeuf,* cherry, and strawberry reds yield no precedence to their Ming prototypes. One of the most famous glazes of the period was the peach bloom, pinkish-red with green fleckings and sometimes creamy patches. During the *Yung-cheng* period (1723-35) pale blue and gray glazes, frequently crackled, supplanted the richer hues of the preceding era. It was at this time that the *flambé* glazes, reds streaked with blue, first appeared. At the beginning these effects were accidental, but by the *Ch'ien-lung* period (1736-95) they were controlled and became usual. During the Ch'ien-lung period too, a virtuosity in the use of unusual shades and imitations of other materials led to bad taste in some of the colors such as the magenta or the mustard yellow.

Blue and white porcelain of the K'ang-hsi period is unsurpassed in the purity of the blue, which attains rich depths without becoming black. Later it loses its intensity and becomes paler although fine examples were made until the middle of the nineteenth century. Polychrome pieces of the K'ang-hsi period were often carried out in the *famille verte* colors: green, yellow, red and violet blue. The colors were applied in over-glaze enamels, sometimes upon a white glaze, sometimes directly upon the biscuit, forming the famous *émaille sur biscuit.* The same colors were frequently used in this manner against a black background forming the much sought after and often forged, *famille noir* porcelains. These combinations lost much of their popularity during the succeeding eras and were supplanted to a large extent by the *famille rose* palette in which a pinkish rose took the place played formerly by the green.

Numerous other fine types were produced, until 1853 when the factories at Ching-te Chen were destroyed in the T'ai-p'ing rebellion. The white pottery of Fukien (*blanc de Chine*) still flourishes but China's supremacy in the art of ceramics has not yet emerged from the blow it received through the destruction of the leading factories and the consequent dispersion of highly skilled workmen.

*Minor arts.*—The minor arts (including jade and lacquer work) carry on old traditions, but they have for the first time in China become "minor arts." For their revival we shall probably have to wait until China has been able to assimilate those features of Western culture, which are best suited to her peculiar traditions.

BIBLIOGRAPHY: General: O. Siren, *A History of Early Chinese Art,* 1929-1930.—Early Periods: J. G. Andersson, *Children of the Yellow Earth,* 1936.—H. G. Creel, *The Birth of China,* 1936.—B. Karlgren, *Yin and Chou in Chinese Bronzes,* in Bulletin of Mus. of Far Eastern Antiquities, Stockholm, No. 8.—J. L. Davidson, *Toward a Grouping of Early Chinese Bronzes,* Parnassus, April 1937. Painting: O. Sirén, *A History of Early Chinese Painting,* 1933.—P. Pelliot, *Les Grottes de Touen-houang,* 1914-24. Sculpture: O. Siren, *Chinese Sculpture from the 5th to the 14th Century,* 1925.—Chavannes, *Mission archéologique dans la Chine septentrionale,* 1909-15. Ceramic: H. L. Hetherington, *The Early Ceramic Wares of China,* 1922.—R. L. Hobson, *The Wares of the Ming Dynasty,* 1923; *The Later Ceramic Wares of China,* 1923. Miscellaneous: A. Salmony, *Sino-Siberian Art,* 1933. Periodicals: Kokka, Revue des Arts Asiatiques, Artibus Asiae, Ostasiatische Zeitschrift, Bulletin of Museum of Far Eastern Antiquities (Stockholm), T'oung Pao.

**CHING HAO.**—Chinese painter of the tenth century. One of the earliest masters of the monochrome landscape. See China—Art.

**CHINON (Indre et Loire, France).**—Extensive ruins of an old castle, where Joan of Arc met the Dauphin (Charles VII).

**CHIOS (School of).**—See Greece (Sculpture).

**CHIPPENDALE (Thomas).**—English cabinet-maker and furniture designer (1718-1779), the son of a joiner of Ottley, Yorkshire, named John Chippendale. By 1727 he was settled in London where, from about 1750 until his death, he was the most fashionable representative of his craft. In 1754 he published a collection of his designs in a book entitled *The Gentleman and Cabinet-Maker's Director.*

BIBLIOGRAPHY: Oliver Brackett, *Thomas Chippendale.* London, 1924.

**CHIRICO (Giorgio de).**—Contemporary Italian painter. He was born 10th July, 1888 at Volo, Greece, of Italian parents. For two years he studied at an art school in Athens and then spent about a year and a half at the Academy in Munich, learning the fundamentals of painting. For some time he worked in the museums in Italy, absorbing much of the style of the old masters, particularly those who worked in the Quattrocento during the first part of the Italian Renaissance. From 1911 to 1915 he lived in Paris, where he met such people as Picasso and Reynal and unconsciously became influenced by their experiments in cubism. From 1915 to the end of 1924 he was in Italy working in Rome and Florence, perfecting his artistic style. Late in 1924 he moved to Paris, where he has since lived, painting his very individual and striking compositions. He is one of the founders of the art movement called Surrealism, where the literary significance of the painting takes precedence over the study of the objects for their form and colour values. Four distinct stages of development may be studied in the work of de Chirico up to the present time. His first period while he was under the influence of the early Italian masters shows a predilection for great wide open spaces like those of Uccello and Piero della Francesca, with some bits of classic architecture in a ruined state seen under a strange light and often in peculiar perspective, suggesting loneliness and desolation on the part of the artist. His next development took place under the influence of the Munich Academy with some resemblances to the work of Böcklin and Hans von Marees in the combinations of the antique with German symbolism. It was at this time that he did a series of self-portraits with classic busts seen in silhouette behind his head. The true stage of Surrealism began with his removal to Paris in 1924. Strange figures dressed in classic garb, but more like mannequins than real people, holding queer combinations of temples and antique shrines on their laps, series of gladiators and some scenes of horses alone or in pairs beside the seashore began to appear. The so-called human figures had no features but only spherical heads decorated with a few lines not placed in any realistic relation. These figures were not real people and could not be connected with any literary allusions, but were merely the creation of the fertile imagination of the artist. All recalled the decay of the classical civilisations, since they included some ruined bits of architecture such as might be the fruits of an archeological expedition. There was no possible intercommunication between these figures; each was an isolated entity, the product of its creator to express his emotion. The last stage of de Chirico's style came after 1929, when he began to show an influence of the work of Renoir, Rubens and even Delacroix, and tried to instill into his compositions some measure of vitality and reality, but as one critic has put it, instead of becoming live figures his mannequins were as petrified and stiffened figures, no more real than in any of his previous compositions. This artist has also tried his hand at stage decoration, doing some settings for Pirandello's *La Giarra,* which was given by the Swedish Ballet in Paris in 1925, for the ballet *Morte di Niobe* by Alberto Savinio, which was performed in Rome in 1926, and for *Le Bal* given by the Ballet Russe in 1929. He is the author of *Hebdomeros,* some poetry and art criticism for magazines and was the editor of some of the Valori Plastici series of monographs. His work may be seen in the museums of Rome, Chicago, Buffalo, Moscow and in the Barnes Foundation collection at Merion, Pennsylvania.

BIBLIOGRAPHY: Pierre Courthion, *Giorgio de Chirico,* 1926.—*Dodici Opere di Giorgio de Chirico,* 1919.—Waldemar George, *Chirico,* 1928.—Boris Ternovetz, *Giorgio de Chirico,* 1928.—Roger Vitrac, *Georges de Chirico,* 1927.

**CH'IU YING.**—c. 1522-1560. Chinese painter, known for his figure paintings and landscapes. See China—Art.

**CHO DENSU (or Min Cho).**—A Japanese painter (1352-1431), working partly in the style of the Takuma school but greatly influenced by Chinese artists of the Yuan period (1280-1368) from whom he learned to give to his realistic portraits (e.g. *The Hundred Rakan* in the Tofuku-ji, Kyoto) bold freedom of colors and brush stroke which swells and decreases with great power. He also learned to shade along contour lines to give depth.

**CHODOWIECKI (Daniel Nicolas).**—Painter and engraver of Polish family. Born at Danzig in 1726; died in Berlin in 1801. He learned oil painting at the Academy of Rode. His first engraving (1756) attracted attention, and the vignettes which he made for the Almanach of the Academy of Arts of Berlin established his reputation. The most important part of his work consists of the innumerable illustrations which he made from this time. He engraved more than 4000 subjects—*Don Quixote, Roland,* and *Clarissa Harlowe,* besides large engravings, such as *Bidding Farewell to His Family* (1767), after his own picture, and *A Painter's Work Room* (1771). Chodowiecki became rector of the Berlin Academy in 1764, and director in 1797.

BIBLIOGRAPHY: R. Portalis, *Le dessinateur d'illustrations.*—Jacobi, *Catalogue de l'œuvre gravé de Chodowiecki.* Berlin, 1814.—W. Engelmann, *Catologue des estampes de Chadowiecki.* Leipzig, 1857.—Kaemmerer, *Chadowiecki.* Bielefeld, 1897.

**CHOKI. Sometimes called, by an incorrect reading of his name, Nagayoshi.**—Japanese painter and colour-printer, working 1785-1805. A pupil of Sekiyen, he was first inspired by Kiyonaga, but he felt especially the influence of his fellow-pupil, Utamaro, from whom, however, he seems only to have taken the faults. He is generally less good as a colourist, and mediocre as a draughtsman, always excepting certain plates which are altogether unrivalled, such as: *The Hunt with Fire-flies; Sunset,* and *Women Boating on the Sumida.*

**CHOU FANG.**—c. 780-810, Chinese painter. Surviving copies of his paintings portray various scenes of court life, in a simple, monumental style. See China—Art.

**CHRISTIAN ART.**—See Early Christian Art.

**CHRISTUS (Petrus).**—Flemish painter. Born about 1410, at Baerle, in Flanders. In 1444, he obtained the right of citizenship in Bruges, where he lived until his death, in 1472. Among the pictures which are certainly by him are the *Portrait of a Man* (Verulam Collection, England), painted in 1446; a painting of 1449, which belonged to the Goldsmiths' Guild of Antwerp; represents *St. Eloi Receiving a Betrothed Couple* (Philip Lehman Collection, New York), is a charming interior scene which introduces us into the intimacy of a goldsmith's shop. Seated at his counter, St. Eloi is visited by two lovers who have come to buy rings. In 1452, the artist painted the diptych of the Berlin Museum, representing the Last Judgment (left wing), and the Annunciation (right wing, upper part), and the Nativity (right wing, lower part). The *Last Judgment* recalls the one in New York, attributed to Hubert Van Eyck, but it has not its amplitude and depth of feeling. Originality is not the dominant characteristic of Petrus Christus.

Signed and dated 1447 is the *Madonna and Saints* in Frankfort.

Works generally attributed to Christus, but unsigned, are: *Portrait of a Young Woman,* said to be Lady Talbot (Berlin); *Portrait of a Young Man* (National Gallery), which is very superior in workmanship to the preceding and is reminiscent of the Van Eyck, and the *Madonna with the Carthusian Monk* (Berlin).

Critics are almost unanimous in giving to Christus a magnificent picture in the Brussels Gallery, a *Pietà,* which would be his masterpiece. It is dependent upon the Master of Flémalle and probably an early work of Christus.

The Duke of Anhalt's Collection (Woeritz) possesses a very moving, even tragic, *Calvary.*

See Pl. 59, Vol. I.

BIBLIOGRAPHY: Friedländer, *Altniederländ. Malerei.* Vol. I.

**CICOGNARA (Antonio).**—Ferrarese painter, active 1486-1500, follower of Tura and Cossa.

**CIGOLI (Ludovico Cardi da).**—Florentine painter (1559-1613). Pupil of Alessandro Allori.

**CIMA (Giovanni Battista, called Cima da Conegliano).**—Venetian painter, c. 1459-c. 1517. Pupil probably of Giovanni Bellini.

Cima is mentioned in 1473 and 1489 in the tax-lists of Conegliano, and is first mentioned in Venice in 1492, when he contracted to paint an altar for S. Giovanni in Bragora, representing the Baptism, finished in 1494. In 1493 he signed and dated the Madonna and Saints in the Duomo, Conegliano. In 1516, he is again mentioned in Venice as a painter, but in the same year he reappears in Conegliano, where he closes an agreement for an altarpiece with the Abbess of Sta. Maria Mater Domini.

Cima's earliest extant picture for which we have a sure date is the 1489 Madonna with SS. Jerome and James in Vicenza, painted in tempera. Also early are the polyptych in Olera in the Parish Church, and the Madonna with Saints and worshippers in the Brera, formerly S. Giovanni Battista at Oderzo. From 1495 is the Annunciation in Leningrad; from 1496 the much-damaged Madonna at Sta. Maria della Grazie, Gemona; from 1496-99 the Madonna and Child with six Saints in the Academy, Venice; from 1499 the polyptych in the ex-Convento della Crocifissione at Miglionico; from 1502 the Helen and Constantine in S. Giovanni in Bragora, Venice; 1502-04 the London Incredulity of Thomas; from 1504 the Madonna in Este, Chiesa degli Zoccoli.

The high point of Cima's art is its maturity at the period of Giorgione and the young Titian. His gift, and the originality of his personality are more evident in his small secular pictures, many of them classic in theme, than in his large and more conventional altars.

BIBLIOGRAPHY: Vasari-Milanesi, III, 645.—Ridolfi, *Maraviglie,* ed. II, Vol. I, p. 100 f.—Crowe and Cavalcaselle.—Morelli, *Die Gal. zu Berlin.*—Berenson, *Venetian Painters,* p. 104 ff.—V. Botteon e A. Aliprandi, *Ricerche intorno alla vita e alle opere di Giambattista Cima,* Conegliano, 1893. — Burckhardt, *Cima da Conegliano,* 1905.

**CIBORIUM.**—A free standing canopy, usually supported by four columns, over a high altar.

**CIMABUE (Cenni di Pepo).**—Florentine painter. Cimabue, a most debated figure, enjoys a fame largely due to the estimation in which he was held by his contemporaries, rather than to an exact knowledge of his activities. Dante states that he was the most celebrated painter of his time, and his opinion has been echoed by later commentators, but very little is known of the facts of the master's life.

In August, 1301, Cimabue followed Master Francesco as director of the mosaic work at Pisa and remained until January 1302, receiving ten soldi a day, the next best paid artist receiving only four soldi. He must have had a high reputation if this commission went to a Florentine instead of to a native Pisan. The St. John is the only part of this mosaic that was executed by him.

A Roman document of 1272, in the archives of Sta. Maria Maggiore, mentions as a witness "Cimmabove pictore de Florencia." In 1301 he is charged with the execution of a picture for the church of the hospital of Sta. Chiara in Pisa, and referred to as "Magister Cenni dictus Cimabu pictor condam pepi de florentia de populo sancti Ambrosii." In the same year he receives a partial payment. In 1302 he is named as a member of the Compagnia de Piovuti in Pisa.

In addition to the St. John in the mosaic mentioned above, which is the only documented work by the master, the following works are attributed to Cimabue on stylistic evidence: In Assisi, the Upper Church, transept and choir, the Crucifixion, three scenes from the Life of the Virgin, and four Evangelists (on the ceiling); in Florence, Uffizi, the Madonna Enthroned (from Sta. Trinità), and in Sta. Croce, Museo, a Crucifix; in Paris, Louvre, the Madonna Enthroned (from San Francesco, Pisa).

BIBLIOGRAPHY: Vasari-Milanesi, I, 247; Vasari-Frey, I, 389 ff.—Ghiberti (ed. Frey).—*Codice Magliabecchiano* (ed. Frey), p. 49.—Ciampi, *Not. ined. d. Sagrestia Pistoiese,* 1810.—Strzygowski, *Cimabue und Rom,* 1888.—Gius. Fontana, *Due doc. ined. rig. Cimabue,* Pisa, 1878.—Villani (ed. C. Frey), *Libro di Billi,* p. 73, 1892.—Tanfani-Centofanti, *Not. di artisti, etc., Pisani,* 1897.—Crowe and Cavalcaselle, Douglas ed., I, 178 ff.—Venturi, *Storia d. arte ital.,* V, 1907.—Aubert, D., *Maler. Dekoration d. S. Francescokirche in Assisi, ein Beitr. z. Lösung der Cimabue-Frage,* 1907.—Van Marle, *Italian Schools,* I, 1923, p. 453 ff.

**CIMON.**—See Acropolis of Athens.

**CINTRA (Palace of).**—See Lisbon.

**CIRCIGNANI (Cristoforo).**—See Pomerancio.

**CIST.**—A sepulchral chest or chamber.

**CIVERCHIO (Vincenzo) da CREMA.**—(1470?-1544). Brescian painter; pupil of Foppa, influenced by Leonardo.

**CIVITALI (Matteo).**—Italian sculptor, architect and engineer of Lucca (1436-1501); active in Lucca, Carrara, Pisa, Sarzana, and Genoa, and, from stylistic evidence, in Florence. He probably was formed in the shop of Antonio Rossellino, and later collaborated with him.

Among his earliest works is the tomb of Pietro Noceto (d. 1457), in Lucca Cathedral, partly copied from the monument of the Cardinal of Portugal, by Antonio Rossellino.

Of his Altar of the Holy Sacrament, of Lucca Cathedral (1473-1476), only two angels, which were to the right and left of the Tabernacle, remain.

The *Madonna della Tosse,* in Santa Trinità, Lucca, is of 1480. It was formerly in the Cloister of S. Ponziano.

CIVITALI (MATTEO): FAITH. (National Museum, Florence.)

From 1481, Matteo took to architecture, and he made a charming little "tempietto" for Lucca Cathedral, to hold the precious Crucifix, adored under the name of "Volto Santo." His most important monument is the altar of Saint Regulus (in the cathedral), which is very ornate and complicated, and which, following Jacopo della Quercia, has two rows of figures.

In 1480 he had been commissioned to execute a number of altars (perhaps 22), and friezes, capitals, and decorative fragments, for the Duomo of Pisa. Payments for completed work are registered in 1486-88. He made the tomb of San Pelegrino dell'Alpe (1489), that of San Romano di Lucca (1490), the pulpit of Lucca Cathedral (1494), holy-water vessels for the same

Duomo (1498), and a statue of St. George (1500, destroyed). He was engaged on the fortifications of Lucca, built bridges, and even printing-works.

He went to Genoa, where he decorated the Chapel of San Giovanni, in the Duomo. The statues in niches, representing Adam, Eve, Habakkuk and Zacharia, are by him.

See Pls. 5, 9, Vol. II.

Bibliography: Charles Yriarte, *Matteo Civitale*. Paris, 1886.—F. Burger, *Geschichte d. Florent. Grabmals*, 1905.—A Venturi, *Storia d. arte ital.*, 1908, pp. 693-706.

**CLAPEROS (Anton).**—Spanish sculptor; Catalonian school. In 1450, he made the proud young *St. George* in the Cloisters of the Cathedral of Barcelona. He executed simple terra cotta statues for the Apostles' doorway, at Gerona.

**CLERESTORY.**—That part of a building which rises above the roofs of the other parts and contains windows for lighting the interior.

**CLERMONT - FERRAND (France).**—The town is composed of two "cités"—Clermont and Montferrand.

Clermont possesses the interesting Romanesque Church of *Notre*

Clermont-Ferrand, Notre Dame du Port: Capital.

*Dame du Port* (12th century), and a *Cathedral* in dark grey stone, dating largely from the 14th century.

The town of Montferrand has some interesting old houses (the houses of *Adam and Eve*, and *St. Christopher*). The place now has the aspect of a sordid village.

See Pl. 44, Vol. I.

Clermont-Ferrand, Notre Dame du Port: Tympanum of the south doorway.

**CLÉSINGER (Jean-Baptiste, called Auguste).**—French sculptor. Born in Besançon, 20th October, 1814; died in Paris, 5th January, 1883. After a restless youth in Florence, where he lived, he sent a work to the Salon for the first time in 1843—the bust of the Vicomte de Valdahon, which passed unnoticed. Two years after, he returned to Paris, and exhibited busts of Weiss, the librarian of Besançon, and of the Duc de Nemours (Besançon

Clésinger: Cleopatra. (F. Barbedienne, edit.)

Museum). But his first great success was at the Salon of 1847, with the *Woman Bitten by a Serpent*. The trivial realism of this marble figure, for which a pretty actress of the Odéon served as model, was admired.

About this time, Clésinger who was working on a bust of George Sand (Comédie-Française), married her daughter, Solange Gabrielle Dudevant. The marriage, celebrated in May, 1847, could not have been very happy. It ended in 1852, and a separation was pronounced against the sculptor. In 1848, Clésinger exhibited a *Reclining Baccante* which won him a first class medal. At the time of the Revolution, he showed himself very enthusiastic for the new régime. He sculptured for the Government a large bust of *Liberty*, and a colossal statue of *Fraternity*, which was erected in the Champ-de-Mars. In 1850, he finished the monument to Chopin (Père-Lachaise), two busts of Rachel, those of Théophile Gautier, of Arsène Houssaye, and of Pierre Dupont. The same year, he approached religious sculpture. The boudoir pathos which animates the *Pietà* and the *Last Supper*, of St. Sulpice, is unbearable when thus associated with sacred things. On the other hand, the marble statue of *Tragedy* (Théâtre de l'Odéon) was much discussed at the Salon of 1852. Two years later, Clésinger began an equestrian statue of Francis I, of colossal proportions. This statue, placed in one of the Louvre courtyards in 1856, only remained there until the end of the year.

This failure decided the artist to leave France. He set himself up in Rome, where he dazzled Italian society with his ostentation. From Rome, he sent a veritable cargo of work to the Salon of 1859: two marble statues, a *Zingara*, and a *Sappho*; a *Roman bull*, in marble; marble busts of Christ, of Charlotte Corday, and of a Roman (Louvre); moreover, he sent a large painting, inspired by Michelangelo, and representing Eve tempted during her sleep, and two mediocre landscapes of the Roman campagna. In 1861, appeared his group of *Cornelius and His Children;* in 1863, a *Seated Faun*, and a *Bacchante*. In 1864, Clésinger returned to Paris; on the 15th August the Emperor made him an officer of the Légion d'Honneur. The same year, he exhibited a statue of Caesar, and a *Fight Between Two Roman Bulls* (Museum of Marseilles), in red marble. From this period dates the purchase of the marble statue of George Sand seated (Théâtre Français). In 1869, Clésinger exhibited a *Cleopatra*, but one can only admire the precious stones and enamels with which it is laden. At the end of his life, he obtained an important commission from the Administration des Beaux-Arts,—four equestrian statues, representing Marceau, Kléber, Hoche and Carnot, which were to decorate the façade of the École Militaire. Only the first three were finished. Clésinger died suddenly in Paris from an attack of paralysis.

**CLEVE (Joos van), or Joos Van der Beke.**—Flemish painter, born in 1491, died in 1540, whose name was long forgotten, and recovered in recent researches. Perhaps he was a pupil of Jean Joest, in Calcar. In any case, he knew his trade when he arrived in Antwerp, where he was admitted to the Guild in 1511; he was senior of it in 1519 and 1525. It is generally admitted that he is the "Master of the Death of Mary," so called because two pictures of this subject (Cologne and Munich Galleries), commissioned, in 1514, of Joos van Cleve, by Nicaise Hackenay (an officer of the Emperor Maximilian) are attributed to him. Other works attributed to Van Cleve are: the two wings, in the Louvre, painted in 1507, representing Adam and Eve; his portrait and that of his wife (Uffizi), which was attributed to Matsys; *Holy Family* (Brussels); two *Adorations of the Magi* (Antwerp, and San Donato, Genoa); *Virgin and Child* (Vienna); two *Calvaries* (Naples, and Weber Collection, Hamburg); the *Annunciation* (Kleinberger Collection, Paris); a fine portrait, called the *Man with the Beautiful Hand* (Munich); a magnificent and famous portrait of a professor or preacher, wrongly said to be of Knipperdoling. All these pictures showed Van Cleve to be a fine colourist, and an able, sincere portrait painter, on whom Matsys' influence certainly had a refining effect.

Bibliography: Baldass, L, *Joos van Cleve*. Vienna, 1925.—Friedländer, J. M., *Altniederl. Malerei*. Vol. IX.—C. Justi, Jahrb. der Königl. Preuss. Kunstsamm, 1881.—Hulin de Loo, *Van Cleve et le Maître de la Mort de Marie identifiés* (Catalogue critique de l'Exposition de Bruges, 1902).

**CLIFF DWELLINGS (American).**—See America (Archæology).

**CLOACA MAXIMA.**—See Forum (of Rome).

**CLODION (Claude-Michel, called).**—French sculptor, 1738-1814.

Clodion: Bacchante. (Terra cotta.)

This modeller of charming terra cottas did not debase great subjects by applying them to industrial art. He was born at Nancy in 1738, the tenth child of a family of sculptors. His father, Thomas Michel, was a sculptor as well as a restorer. His mother belonged to the Adam family. It was his maternal uncle, Lambert Sigisbert Adam, author of the principal group of the Fountain of Neptune at Versailles, who taught him the rudiments of his art. Afterwards he studied under Pigalle.

In 1759, he won the Grand Prix de Rome, and went to Italy in 1762. He remained there for nine years. Attracted by antique fragments, he prolonged his stay in Rome well after the duration of the pension of the French Academy, and already he took to that kind of little modelling, which was to make his name. On his return to Paris, he was "accepted" by the Académie Royale, in 1773, but with that ended his ambition to achieve academic honours, and he never did more than execute his "morceau de réception." Clodion was not, however, incapable of succeeding in sacred sculpture, as is proved by a charming *Saint Cecilia*, which is not without religious character, and was commissioned from him, with a bas-relief, for Rouen Cathedral, where the two works are still to be seen; also, a very fine figure of Montesquieu, now kept in the Institut, which was ordered from him by the superintendent of buildings to make part of a series of great Frenchmen. But he had to specialise in that kind of sculpture which, after a brilliant success, the requirements of amateurs demanded. This success was due to a *Triumph of Galatea*, a long bas-relief measuring ten metres, which he exhibited at the Salon of 1779. From then, he was commissioned by one (the Baron de Besenval) for the decoration of a bathroom and the whole of a gallery; by another (the Princesse de Condé, abbess of Remiremont) for that of a Court of Honour in a house still existing—No. 12, rue Monsieur,—and known under the name of Hôtel de Chambrun. In this last residence, notably, are admirable chains of children and young satyrs frolicking round a goat and holding garlands, playing round a panther and holding bunches of grapes. Terra cotta was the most suitable medium for his talent, being the one that lent itself the best to elastic modelling. His faunesque fantasies were in demand for medallions and statuettes to put over clocks. The Cluny Museum has two very beautiful examples, dating from 1783. To meet all the orders, he was helped by three of his brothers, and, besides this, he employed a certain number of practical workers: a studio was devoted to the industrial reproduction of his works.

During the Revolution, he returned to Nancy, his native town, where he modelled figures for the Niderwiller works. He returned to Paris under the Directory, but he was quite forgotten there, and one is rather astonished to hear of his exhibiting at the Salon of 1801 (among others, a *Deluge Scene*, a group of three life-size figures). He exhibited again at the Salon of 1810. But this was no longer Clodion. He gave way to the taste of the day, and abandoned his nymphs and satyrs. Having succeeded in attracting attention again, he received some commissions, including that of a Cato for the Senate.

He died of pneumonia in 1814, at the age of seventy-five, having known, in old age, the sadness of a solitary hearth, which made him pay dearly for the unrestraint of a life which had only too well corresponded to the licence of his works.

In 1781, when over forty, he married the daughter of Pajou, Catherine Flore, who was scarcely sixteen. But their life together was of short duration, and during the Revolution their bond was completely broken by divorce.

See Pl. 6, Vol. I; Pl. 45, Vol. II.

Bibliography: H. Thirion, *Les Adam et Clodion*, 1885.

**CLOISONNÉ.**—See Enamel.

**CLOUET (François).**—French painter. Often called Janet or Jeannet, from the name of his father, Jean or Janet Clouet. Born at Tours, about 1516; died about 1572. Pupil of his father, he inherited his title of "Painter to the King," in 1540, and he lived in the royal household under François I, Henri II, François II, and Charles IX. In this capacity, he had to take the cast of the features of François I, on the death of that prince (1547), and direct the funeral decorations, banners, standards, etc.; and again, on the death of Henri II (1559). He was much appreciated at court and executed numerous portraits of the royal family. His work is less well known to us than his life. There are but two signed pictures in oil by François Clouet: the portrait of Pierre Cutte (1562) in the Louvre; and the figure-group in the Cook Collection. All other attributions are based on conjecture. Drawings in the Paris Bibliothèque Nationale, the Musée Condé at Chantilly, and the British Museum are helpful in identifying his completed works.

The full-length portrait of Henri II in the Uffizi is attributed to F. Clouet, also the portrait of Charles IX in Vienna (a miniature version of this is in the Louvre). Among other portraits thought to be by his hand are: the bust-portrait of Charles IX in Vienna, and the miniature portraits of Charles IX and Catherine de' Medici, also in Vienna; the bust-portraits of Henri II at Versailles and in the Pitti in Florence; and the Mme. de Roannais, and Elisabeth of Austria in the Louvre.

Bibliography: Leon de Laborde, *La Renaissance des Arts à la Cour de France*. Paris, 1855.—Grandmaison, *Les arts en Touraine*, 1870. —Alphonse Germain, *Les Clouet*. Paris, Laurens.

**— (Jean, called Janet).**—This painter, although of foreign, probably of Flemish, origin, worked in France from some time before 1516. Scarcely anything is known of his life, except that he was court painter under Louis XII and François I, that he lived most of the time in Tours, coming to court to make the sketches and drawings from which he afterwards painted his pictures. He was a portraitist, and also made small decorative works for furniture. There is no portrait that can be given with certainty to Jean Clouet rather than to his son François; the only one which documentary evidence gives to him, that of Oronce Finé, has disappeared.

In this obscurity, the "manner" of the two artists being difficult to distinguish, the more archaic portraits are generally ascribed to Jean Clouet—the *François I* of the Louvre, a very detailed work in spite of its large size, two portraits of Guillaume de Montmorency (Louvre, and Lyon Museum), and drawings of A. Gouffier, Robert de la Marck, Guillaume Gouffier, Tournon, Odet de Foix, and Anne de Montmorency (Chantilly). Perhaps Jean Clouet also executed the miniatures of a manuscript of the Bibliothèque Nationale, *The Gallic War*, in 1519,—portraits of Claude d'Urfé, Henri Albert, and Catherine de'Médici. In speaking of the work of Jean Clouet, one may mention his brother, Clouet de Navarre, of whom it is only known that he was painter to Marguerite d' Angoulême, sister of François I. The problem of the distribution of works between the Clouets, father, brother, and son, is not nearly solved.

Bibliography: Alphonse Germain, *Les Clouet* ("Collection des Grands Artistes." Paris).

**— de NAVARRE.**—French painter, brother of Jean Clouet, called Janet. He was in the service of Francis I's sister, Marguerite de Navarre. Nothing is known of his life, or his work. A portrait of Saint Gelais, in the Louvre, is attributed to him.

**CLUNY (Hôtel de).**—See Paris.

**CNIDUS.**—See Demeter.

**— (Venus of).**—See Praxiteles.

**CNOSSUS.**—See Crete.

**COCHIN (The).**—French engravers. Charles Nicholas Cochin, known as Cochin the Elder (1688-1754), a member of the Académie Royale, was the interpreter of the greatest paintings of the first half of the eighteenth century, notably those of Watteau and Chardin; but seeing the growing talent of his son, he made himself his collaborator and engraved several of his compositions. In 1713, he married Louise Magdeleine Horthemels, who also engraved, and was able, in her turn, to translate some of her son's works. Charles Nicolas Cochin, known as Cochin the Younger, the most famous of the whole family, was born in 1715. Having studied with his father, he became the pupil of an Académie painter, Dulin, who then had a great reputation. His bent was rather towards etching than engraving, and towards facetious subjects in preference to religious themes. He frequented the studio of the engraver Le Bas, whose Voltairian spirit pleased him. Certain remarkable plates, such as those representing the principal fêtes given in honour of the marriage of Madame Première to the Infant Don Philip, opened the doors of the Académie to him, and he was "accepted" in 1741. (It was not until ten years later that he exhibited the engraving which conferred on him the title of Academician.) His reputation grew, and he was in request to fulfil all kinds of commissions: headings, flower-work, tail-pieces, addresses, invitation cards, frontispieces, historical scenes, and portraits. He is sometimes rather heavy and monotonous but inexhaustibly ingenious. He was a friend of Madame de Pompadour, to whom he taught etching and engraving; and she, wishing her young brother, Abel Poisson, the future Marquis de Marigny, to rise to the position of Superintendent of Fine Art, sent him to Italy with the accomplished engraver (December 1749). Cochin brought back numerous pencil drawings which appeared under the title of *Voyage en Italie* (1758). From that time, honours rained upon him. He was promoted to the rank of chevalier of the Order of St. Michael, succeeded Charles Coypel as Keeper of Drawings, and Lépicié (1752), as historical secretary to the Académie (1755). He was the intimate adviser of Marigny, and, under him, fulfilled the functions of a veritable Director of Fine Art. He engraved the series of French ports, which had been commissioned from Joseph Vernet; also the fine series representing the principal events in the reign of Louis XV, which shows his powers of composition. At the same time, owing to his extraordinary power of seizing a likeness, especially in profile, he had many commissions for portraits. In fact, it might be said that Cochin left a whole gallery of the celebrities of his day. He died on the 29th April, 1790, at the age of seventy-five. Besides his *Voyage en Italie*, he left a certain number of other interesting writings: *The Arts in Italy, The Effect of Light in Painting*, etc. He took a lively part in the art criticism of the day.

Bibliography: A. Tardieu, *Notice sur les Tardieu, les Cochin*, etc. Arch. de l'Art français, Vol. IV.—Portalis de Béraldi, *Les Graveurs du XVIIIe siècle*, Vol. I².—E. Bocher, *Catalogue descriptif et raisonné de l'œuvre de Cochin.*—S. Rocheblave, *Les Cochin*. Collection des Artistes célèbres.

**COELLO (Claudio).**—Born between 1630 and 1635 at Madrid, died there in 1693. His father, Faustino Coelho, who moved from Lisbon to Madrid, stood in high repute on account of his works in bronze. Claudio's first teacher was Francisco Rizi. Later on he entered into close relations with Carreño de Miranda who permitted him to copy the masterworks in the Royal castles, where he studied the paintings by Titian, Rubens and Van Dyck. The technique of fresco painting he probably learned from Ximenez Donoso who had spent several years in Italy.

Coello and Donoso combined in the execution of immense frescoes in churches and public buildings. Together they made the designs and paintings for the triumphal arches, on the occasion of the entry into Madrid of Marie Louise of Orleans, first wife of Charles II. Having executed the frescoes of the dome of the College of Augustines, at Saragossa, in 1683, Claudio returned to Madrid, and became court painter, in 1684; in 1686 he succeeded Francisco Herrera el Mozo as "pintor de camara."

In 1691, Claudio also became painter of Toledo Cathedral. But the following year, Luca Giordano arrived in Madrid, and all the favour which Coello had enjoyed, left him.

It is said that Claudio Coello realizing that he could not compete with his rival, gave up painting and finally died of grief.

The best preserved of his many frescoes are those of the ceiling of the Vestiario of Toledo Cathedral (1671). The condition of those at the College of the Augustinian fathers of Saragossa (1683) leave much to be desired. His most famous painting probably is the altar-panel on canvas of the sacristy of the Escorial called *La Sagrada Forma*. It represents, in the presence of Charles II and numerous personages, the transport of a miraculous Host to a chapel adjoining the sacristy. "With its many vivid portraits and the unique representation of space—the architectural motifs giving the illusion of a continuance of the architecture of the sacristy—this painting makes us recognize that in Claudio Coello we see the last important painter of the glorious school of Madrid."

Of Claudio Coello's canvases the Prado Museum at Madrid possesses an Apotheosis of St. Augustine very sumptuous in color (1664), also other representations of religious subjects like S. Domingo de Guzman, Sta. Rosa de Lima, the Virgin amid various Saints and allegorical figures, etc. At the Städelsche Institute at Frankfurt-a.-M. there is a half-length portrait of Charles II of Spain, and a portrait of D. Juan de Alarcón was formerly in the Beruete collection at Madrid. Other paintings of his are owned by various museums in Europe. The drawings for his *La Forma Sagrada* at the Escorial are in the Biblioteca Nacional at Madrid.

Bibliography: Aureliano Beurete y Moret, *The School of Madrid.* London, 1909.—*Thieme Becker*, Vol. VII, Leipzig, 1935; art. *Claudio Coello* by A. L. Mayer.—A. L. Mayer, *Geschichte der spanischen Malerei*. Leipzig, 1922.

**COGNIET (Leon).**—French painter, 1794-1880, born in Paris.

**COIMBRA (Portugal).**—The *Old Cathedral* or *Sé Velha* was built in the 12th century. It is a solid Romanesque building, the walls of which are crenellated and pierced with semi-circular openings.

The *Mosteiro de Santa Cruz*, begun at the end of the 15th century, has a fine doorway.

**COLA D'AMATRICE.**—Central Italian painter, active at Ascoli first half of 16th century. Influenced by the Umbrians and by Michelangelo.

**COLE (Thomas).**—American painter (1801-1848). He was born 1st February 1801 at Bolton-le-Moor in Lancashire, England. He was educated at Chester and there worked in a textile factory designing patterns. In 1819 with his family he came to the United States and in Philadelphia took up the production of wood engravings. After a short trip to the West Indies he joined the family in Steubenville, Ohio. He then tried his hand at designing wallpaper and travelled for a time as an itinerant portrait painter. The winter of 1823 he spent in Philadelphia studying at the Pennsylvania Academy of Fine Arts and soon afterward he moved to New York City. From that city he made short trips up the Hudson, painting views of the scenery along the river and the wooded slopes of the Catskill Mountains. In 1826 he was elected to full membership in the National Academy of Design and three years later he made a journey to England. There he stayed until 1831, painting rural landscapes and exhibiting his work at the Royal Academy. Then he went on to France and Italy where he visited the artistic centers of Genoa, Florence, Rome and Naples before returning to his home in New York. His earlier work had been realistic and done in the manner of the Hudson River School, but after his sojourn abroad he adopted the romantic tradition then popular in France. Another trip to Europe in 1841 took him to England, France, Switzerland, Italy and Germany, providing rich material for his brush. When he was back again in New York he continued painting in the same vein scenes of the Adirondacks and in 1847 he recorded his impressions of Niagara Falls. He died 11th February 1848, leaving unfinished a series of religious pictures of which only the *Pilgrim of the Cross* was completed. A series entitled *The Course of Empire* may be seen at the New York Historical Society.

BIBLIOGRAPHY: Louis L. Noble, *Life and Works of Thomas Cole,* 1856.

**COLEMAN (Glenn O.).**—American painter (1887-1932). He was born in Springfield, Ohio, 18th July 1887 and spent his youth in Indianapolis, where his early training was received. In 1905 he came to New York City, where he studied with William Merritt Chase, Robert Henri, and Everett Shinn. He painted many scenes of lower Manhattan, the Brooklyn Bridge section and Chinatown, using the knowledge gained from living in or near those sections. Most of his work was done in New York City, where he lived continuously except for one short trip to Cuba and several to Canada. Though an uncompromising realist his early work was filled with human interest tinged with humour and melancholy. It was a personal view of the growing metropolis trying to capture its various moods even at the sacrifice of some plastic values. As his art grew stronger and more assured it veered away from the human touches and the views became of greater significance and more structural in the careful planning of the forms and the interrelation of the various planes. His early pictures were characterised by a sketchy quality with attendant darkness of colour and uncertainty of the forms, but with his development of the formal units he began to use brighter colours to emphasise the structural character of his work. He died suddenly at Long Beach, Long Island, 8th May 1932. Some of his earlier drawings he had transferred into striking prints toward the close of his life and these were similar in treatment and scope to his oils of the later period. Examples of his paintings and prints are in the Detroit Institute of Arts, the Musée du Luxembourg in Paris, and the Phillips Memorial Gallery in Washington, D. C.

BIBLIOGRAPHY: C. Adolph Glassgold, *Glenn O. Coleman,* American Artists Series, 1932.—For a complete bibliography see *The Index of Twentieth Century Artists* for December, 1935.

**COLISEUM.**—The most famous amphitheatre in the world, built in Rome, between the Palatine and the Esquiline, by the Flavians on the site of an artificial lake belonging to the gardens of the golden house of Nero. It originally bore the name of the Amphitheatre of the Flavians. Begun by Vespasian, it was finished by Titus. It was given the name of Coliseum in the 8th century, probably after the colossal statue of Nero. Titus celebrated the dedication, in the year 80, to inaugurate the games which lasted a hundred days.

In the Coliseum took place combats of wild beasts and gladiators, representations of naval battles, and games of all kinds. In the 8th century, two earthquakes destroyed a part of it; and another part was used as a fortress by the Frangipani. From the 15th to the 17th century, architects used it as a quarry for building. In the 19th century it was consolidated. The exterior of the Coliseum is built of blocks of travertine, formerly tied together with iron clamps; the interior is built of tufa and bricks. It is in four storeys: an arcaded ground-floor with Doric columns, a first storey with arcades with Ionic columns, a second arcaded storey with Corinthian columns, and lastly a walled storey with Corinthian pilasters, higher than the others and surmounted with staffs to fix the ropes of the awning. Under every arcade was a statue. The circumference of the building is 524 metres; the arena measures 86 by 54 metres. It accommodated 50,000 spectators. Two boxes were reserved for the emperor and great dignitaries; above the arena, on a platform, the vestals and senators took their places. The people sat on the steps. The women sat on a large platform between the second and third stage. The steps were reached by the eighty lowest arcades, and a whole system of passages and "vomitoria," and staircases. Beneath the arena were the dens and cages where the wild animals were kept. This gigantic construction was finished in ten years. The Romans worked quickly and solidly, putting together the arcades without cement, keeping them in place by their method of cutting the blocks of stone. The interior vaults are concrete masonry, in stone and cement, which is one with the wall. Roman cement has proved to be almost indestructible; and the Coliseum has always typified the power of ancient Rome.

See Pl. 29, Vol. I.

**COLLEONI.**—See Venice; Verrocchio; also Pl. 9, Vol. II.

**COLLEONI CHAPEL.**—See Bergamo.

**COLOGNE.**—From the 12th century, Cologne was an important artistic centre. In painting, its most famous representative is Lochner (see this name). It is rich in Romanesque and Gothic buildings.

*S. Maria im Kapitol,* a Romanesque Church, 1047; the choir is of trefoil formation and has a trefoil ambulatory. The vaults are not Romanesque but Gothic.

*St. Martin the Great,* of the 12th century, also possesses a choir with a trefoil apse, surmounted by a powerful square tower.

The *Church of the Holy Apostles* is a fine Romanesque building; the exterior is decorated with an elegant gallery with little columns.

*St. Gereon,* in the Romanesque style, has a very curious plan. It is formed of a little narthex, a round nave, and a very long choir. Cologne has yet other Romanesque Churches, of less importance.

See Pl. 45, Vol. I.

Cologne *Cathedral* was begun about 1248. The choir was built from 1248 to 1322; the transept and the towers from 1322 to the end of the 15th century. The building was then left until 1815. The nave and towers were built from 1815 to 1880, but in accordance with the old plans. The choir is Gothic, copied so exactly from that of Amiens Cathedral that probably the architect, Gerard de Rile, was French. In any case, Gerard de Rile worked in Amiens until the moment that Cologne Cathedral was begun. Over a first stage of sombre architecture, the triforium and clerestory form an immense field for stained glass. The choir is in five aisles, like those of French Cathedrals. In the 14th and 15th century the towers were built (without their spires); and then for four centuries a large empty space lay between the choir and the towers. In the 19th century, eager propaganda brought about the resumption of the work; "the building of Cologne Cathedral is a matter of honour for Germany," declared the King of Bavaria. It was then that the nave, with its five aisles, was built, and the two spires, which are 157 metres high. The interior is 144 metres long; 61 wide; 45 high. Cologne Cathedral has great unity of style, because it was largely executed in the 19th century by architects who calculated its proportions, but this makes it a cold imitation of the true Gothic style.

COLOGNE: APOSTLE FROM THE CATHEDRAL.

See Pl. 49, Vol. I.

The *Town Hall* is composed of a belfry, in ornate Gothic style, and several buildings of different styles, of which the loggia, of the 16th century, is a charming Renaissance construction, the work of Wilhelm Vernuycken.

COLOGNE: CITY HALL.

The *Gürzenich* was built about 1450 by Johannes von Büren. Cologne possesses many mediaeval houses. The most interesting is the *House of the Templars,* 13th century.

BIBLIOGRAPHY: P. Clemen, *Die Kunstdenkmäler der Stadt Köln.* Dusseldorf, 1906.—Korth, *Köln im Mittelalter.* Cologne, 1891.—Hoelscher, *Köln am Rhein.* Cologne, 1903.—Louis Réau, *Cologne,* Collection des Villes d'art célèbres. Paris.—W. Pinder, *Deutsche Dome des Mittelalter,* 1921.

**— (Schools of).**—See Pl. 3, Vol. II.

**COLOMBE (Jean).**—French painter of the 15th century who lived chiefly at Bourges. He worked in 1467, for the wife of Louis XI, and in 1486 was "illuminator of books" to the Duke of Savoy. For this prince, he finished the miniatures of the Apocalypse (Escorial), and added some miniatures to the *Très Riches Heures du duc de Berry.*

**— (Michel).**—French sculptor, born about 1430, died in 1512. He was doubtless of Breton origin, born in the neighbourhood of Léon, but he lived chiefly in Touraine, and his art is that of a master of the Loire. Very little is known of the early part of his career, which was no doubt the most fruitful. His art, which heralds that of the Renaissance, was formed in the midst of the Gothic period. He settled at Tours in 1473 and executed several works which have not come down to us: a bas-relief, for the Abbey of St. Michel en l'Herm, representing St. Michael on horseback, piercing a furious wild boar with his lance by the side of Louis XI praying (the first idea of the St. George); a plan for the tomb of Louis XI (1473-1474); and a plan for the tomb of Louis de Rohault, Bishop of Maillezais (1480). His position in Tours was considerable. He worked for the municipality from the time of the entry of Louis XII in 1500. He then executed, at the age of seventy, the first of his works that have come down to us, the Louis XII medal; decided and simple in drawing, it is a masterpiece of realism, and has an ugliness which was probably very lifelike.

COLOMBE (MICHEL): ST. GEORGE FIGHTING THE DRAGON.

From 1502 to 1507, he worked at the tomb of Duke François II of Brittany (died in 1488) and of his wife, which was set up by order of their daughter in the Carmelite Church of Nantes, taken to pieces in 1791, and transported to the Cathedral in 1817. The general ordering of the work, its architecture, belongs to Jean Perréal, who was a kind of artistic director of Charles VIII and Louis XII. Colombe was helped by his nephew, Guillaume Regnault, and by Jean de Chartres in the marble work. At the four corners are four life-size figures of women, representing the cardinal virtues. The tomb is an important and composite work, in which are concentrated all the problems of technique and aesthetics offered by French sculpture of this period: in its plan, in its combinations of coloured marble, in certain Italian motifs, it introduces the Renaissance. At the same time, it is traditional: Colombe accepted foreign elements, but he worked in the French style, equally removed from Italianism and from the exaggerated realism of his French and Flemish predecessors.

Colombe received many commissions in the latter part of his career; but all these works, except one, have disappeared. He made an altarpiece for High-Altar of the Carmelite Church of Nantes, where the tomb of François II was; a sepulchre for St. Sanolin de la Rochelle (1507-1510); an altarpiece for St. Saturnin of Tours. In 1508, Georges d'Amboise ordered the bas-relief of *St. George and the Dragon* (Louvre) for his Chapel of Gaillon. It is a picturesque work. The marble frame, decorated with arabesques, is by an Italian who worked far from Colombe, in Gaillon itself. In 1511, he was commissioned to make the tombs of Philibert of Savoy, of Margaret of Austria, and of her Mother, Marguerite de Bourbon, for the Church of Brou, which was built by Margaret of Austria. This tremendous undertaking he accepted at the age of eighty. He executed a rough model, but the disgrace of Jean Lemaire and Jean Perréal caused him to lose this commission, which was given to Flemish artists. He is mentioned again in July, 1512. He probably died soon afterwards, in any case, before 1519.

Michel Colombe's art dominates sculpture at the beginning of the 16th century. His influence is found in all the works of the Loire region. It was maintained, thanks to the master's pupils, especially to Guillaume Regnault. The studio existed until about 1530. From it came such works as the *Vierge d'Olivet*, the tomb of the children of Charles VIII, certain parts of the tomb of the Cardinals of Amboise, in Rouen, and of the tomb of Louis XII, in St. Denis; and outside the Loire region, where all these works were executed, Colombe's art spread in the Ile-de-France, in Normandy, in Champagne, in Burgundy, and in the Bourbonnais, with Jean de Chartres as its chief representative. But the great movement of the "détente" was stayed by the progress of Italianism. The Justes, installed in Tours itself, were at the height of prosperity. Then the court deserted Touraine, and Orléans and Blois succeeded Tours, with Martin Cloître, Bomberault, Marchand. Colombe's school disappeared about 1530.

See Pl. 28, Vol. II.

Bibliography: Paul Vitry, *Michel Colombe et la sculpture française de son temps.* Paris, 1901.—L. Courajod, *Leçons professées à l'Ecole du Louvre,* Vol. II, 1901.

**COLOMBIA.**—See America (Archæology).

**COLUMBARIUM.**—The Latin word "columbarium" means pigeon-hole. In ancient times people who were not rich enough to build themselves tombs, placed urns, which contained the ashes, in little niches arranged in tiers in the walls of a large room—the columbarium or pigeon-hole. The largest was that of Augustus' wife, Livia, which was built for her slaves. It contained 3,000 places.

**COMBOURG (France).**—Feudal château, where Chateaubriand lived as a child. The oldest part, the thick north tower, was built in 1016.

**COMPIÈGNE (France).**—Compiègne possesses some old churches (15th and 16th century); and a château, which was almost entirely built under Louis XV, by the architect Gabriel. It was finished in 1786. See Pl. 29, Vol. II.

**CONCORD (Temple of).**—See Agrigentum.

**CONCORDE (Place de la).**—See Paris; also Pl. 43, Vol. II.

**CONDÉ, MUSÉE.**—See Chantilly.

**CONDER (Charles).**—English painter (1868-1909), an artist of charming and delicate fancy, favouring the medium of water colour on silk, and particularly happy in his designs for fans.

Bibliography: F. Gibson, *Charles Conder.* London, 1914.

**CONFUCIUS (Temple of).**—See Peiping.

**CONINXLOO (Cornelis Van).**—Flemish painter, of the Brussels school, born about 1500. He worked from 1529 to 1558. There are two pictures by him in Brussels Museum—the *Legend of Mary Magdeleine,* painted in 1537 for Jan Teughel, and the *Genealogy of Mary,* with its excess of architectural ornament. He headed the so-called "School of Frankenthal."

Bibliography: A. J. Wauters, *Cornelius van Coninxloo et le Triptyque de l'abbé de Tuegele.*—Plietzsch, E., *Die Frankenthaler Maler.* Leipzig, 1910.

**— (Gilles van).**—Flemish painter of fine landscapes, 1544-1607. The Lichtenstein Gallery, Vienna, possesses two of the best.

**CONQUES (Avignon).**—A poor little village which possessed one of the richest abbeys in France, of which there remains the magnificent *Church of St. Foy,* a large Romanesque edifice, built from 1030 to 1060. On the tympanum of the principal doorway is a representation of the Last Judgment. The walls are hollowed out to hold sarcophagi of the 12th and 13th centuries.

The *Treasury* of Conques is famous for its objects of goldsmiths' work, which date from the 10th to the 16th centuries, and especially for the statue of St. Foy in gold and precious stones (10th and 11th centuries).

**CONSTABLE (John).**—English painter, 1776-1837. Born at East Bergholt, a pretty little village, fourteen miles from Sudbury, where Gainsborough was also born. His father was a miller, very comfortably off. Observation of the sky is a professional habit among millers, and it is said that this attention was not without its influence on the future artist, for no one before him studied and rendered atmospheric effects so perfectly. In London, he undertook the most varied work, copying Reynolds, and composing religious pictures, such as *Christ Blessing Little Children.* He also studied Ruysdael, whose works in the National Gallery made a profound impression on him. In 1802, he exhibited at the Royal Academy for the first time, where he was henceforth represented every year, until his death: he sent about 104 paintings there. In 1803, he wrote to his old friend, Dunthorne: "There is almost nothing at the exhibition worth stopping to look at; there is room for a painter of nature." He then left London, and in 1804 worked quite alone among the oak-trees and solitudes of Helmington Park. "For all painting" he said, "is nothing else but feeling." From this time he painted the places dear to his youth, the smiling valleys, harvests, the verdant Suffolk woods, thatched cottages, churches, picturesque farms, canals, windmills, manors, always showing a predilection for orchards, villages, the ploughed earth, and for all that shows a toiling, active humanity. A glimpse of meadow, a lock, a clump of thick trees were enough for him. Constable is one of the first modern landscape painters to aim at independence and truth. In his youth, he copied Claude Lorrain, Rubens, Ruysdael, Teniers, and Wilson with extraordinary ability. He was one of the first to paint summer foliage green, and rosy morning light in its most intense colours. He noticed how leaves glistened in the sunshine, and how light walls were dazzling as snow. In his day, there was much raillery about "Constable's snow." But his pictures never sold. Yet he was already famous in France, and in 1824 he won a gold medal at the Salon of Paris. His pictures inspired Delacroix to take down his entry to the Salon and to repaint with greater light the background scene of his *Massacre of Chios,* which he did in four days. Later, his influence on the Barbizon masters and on Manet is seen. In fact, the problem of "plein air" which the old school had left unsolved, seemed to be completely answered by Constable. The artist is admirably represented in the English galleries. In the National Gallery: *The Corn-field;* the *Farm in the Valley.* At South Kensington: *Salisbury Cathedral, Hampstead Heath, Dedham Mill.* In the Diploma Gallery, Burlington House: the *Leaping Horse.* The gallery owns about 500 examples—oil-paintings, sketches, water-colours, pencil drawings—which were given by the artist's daughter.

See Delacroix. Bibliography: André Fontainas, *Constable.* New York, 1927.

**CONSTANTINE (Arch of). (Rome).**—The largest and best preserved of the Roman triumphal arches. It was built by Constantine in 312 A.D. It has three arches; and a long inscription dedicates it to "the divinity" without stating that this divinity was probably Christ, the God of Constantine, and not the pagan deities of Maxentius, whom Constantine had vanquished. Many of the sculptures which decorate it are very poor (those dating from the time of Constantine, and representing assemblies and battles). Other rectangular bas-reliefs and medallions come from a triumphal arch of Marcus Aurelius and from buildings in Trajan's Forum, and are much superior to the others.

**CONSTANTINOPLE.** — Until the 4th century A.D., Constantinople bore the name of Byzantium. It was founded in 667 B.C. by the inhabitants of Megara and Argos, passed under the dominion of the Romans who built magnificent monuments, which were mostly destroyed by earthquakes and fires. Constantine made it the capital of his Roman Empire in the East, and there founded a new city, much bigger than the old one, in 330 A.D. He gave it its present name of Constantinople, filled it with buildings, and the most wonderful art treasures which he carried off from the Greek cities, Asia Minor and Sicily. The chief buildings, which have all disappeared, were the Hippodrome, which was adorned by the famous horses of St. Mark's, which had been brought away from Chios. For a long time it was the centre of the life of the city, which had a passion for chariot races and often organised contests in its Hippodrome. Of all the splendours which were gathered here, there remain only an obelisk, 30 metres high, brought from Egypt, under Theodore II, the Column of Constantine, and the Column of Serpents. The Forum occupied one of the hills of the town; on its site is the burned column in red porphyry. The Baths of Zeuscippe, built by Constantine, were perhaps the most sumptuous in the Roman Empire.

Constantinople: Mosque of the Sultan Ahmed and the Hippodrome.

Constantinople: Mosque of the Sultan Bayezid.

The successors of Constantine continued to embellish the city, building churches, baths, aqueducts, palaces. The Imperial Palace, of which nothing remains, was of unheard-of splendour. Around it were eight other palaces, almost equally luxurious.

Of the buildings of Constantinople which have come down to us, the most famous is *St. Sophia* which has recently been turned into a museum of Byzantine art. It was built on the site of a church of Constantine, destroyed by fire, in the reign of Justinian (6th century), by the architects Anthemius of Tralles and Isidorus of Miletus. The plan is 71 metres wide. A huge dome on pendentives crowns it, and is supported inside by four strong piers. This audacious dome, destroyed in 558, by an earthquake, was rebuilt by Isidorus's nephew who made it still higher. The interior was rich and colourful as an Eastern fairy-tale. It was a treasure-house of marbles, precious metals, golden mosaics, golden ornaments, and the altar-table was covered with gold and enriched with precious stones; the very floor was of marble inlaid with plaques of gold and silver. These riches have disappeared, stolen by the divers conquerors who took possession of the city. The magnificent mosaics which, forming a part of the building, could not be removed, were whitewashed by the Turks, since the Koran forbids the representation of human figures, but are now being uncovered.

The city has many other mosques —those of the Little St. Sophia, built by Theodora, of Kachrieh, and the Mosque of Ahmed, etc. The seraglio is a vast collection of palaces, gardens, kiosks, surrounded by a strong crenellated wall. Many of the buildings perished in a fire in 1865. The Sultans have had other palaces built in various quarters of the city, such as the Palaces of Yldiz, Tchiragon, Dolma Bagcheh, etc. Other large, grandiose edifices were built in the 19th century, but they have little artistic interest.

*St. Irene.* See Byzantine Architecture, Early Period.

*"La Nea."* See Byzantine Architecture, Middle Period.

*Monastery of St. Myralaion.* See Byzantine Architecture, Middle Period.

*Kilisse Djami* (St. Theodore). See Byzantine Architecture, Middle Period.

See Byzantine Art; Architecture; also Pl. 58, Vol. II.

Bibliography: H. Barth, *Constantinople.* Paris, Collection des Villes d'Art célèbres.

**CONTUCCI (Andrea).**—See Sansovino.

**COPLEY (John Singleton).**—Early American painter (1738-1815). He was born presumably in Boston, Massachusetts, in 1738 and very shortly afterward his father died in the West Indies, where he was in business. His mother remarried in a few years, this time Mr. Peter Pelham. Pelham was by trade an engraver who taught portrait painting as a side line, and probably young Copley received his first instruction from his stepfather. When he was still in his teens he was filling commissions for portraits in that community and in 1766 one of his pictures was exhibited in London. At that time Benjamin West wrote urging the young artist to come abroad to try his skill. Copley did not accept this invitation at once, but continued painting in Boston, helped in his work by the social connections of his wife. During the winter of 1771 and 1772 he travelled to New York and Philadelphia, where he added to his reputation by painting more portraits. He set out for England in 1774 and there made the acquaintance of West and Sir Joshua Reynolds, the leader of the English school. But he did not stop there immediately, going instead to Italy to visit the important art centres and copy the work of the old masters. The next year the threat of war was so strong that he sent for his wife and family to join him in London. From that time on he lived in England, painting the portraits of the nobility and also doing some historical compositions. Perhaps the best known of these is the *Death of Lord Chatham* which had a great vogue at the time it was painted. Later in life he was less successful in disposing of his work and worried over financial conditions. Although he expressed the wish to return to America he never did so. After suffering two strokes of paralysis he died 9th September 1815 and was buried at Croydon, England. In spite of his long residence abroad he is generally considered with the American school of painting inasmuch as his early training and most characteristic works were done in this country.

See Pl. 61, Vol. II.

Bibliography: Martha Babcock Amory, *The Domestic and Artistic Life of John Singleton Copley,* 1882.—Frank W. Bayley, *Five Colonial Artists of New England,* 1929.—Frank W. Bayley, *The Life and Works of John Singleton Copley,* 1915.—Frank W. Bayley, *A Sketch of the Life and a List of Some of the Works of John Singleton Copley,* 1910.—*John Singleton Copley,* Masters in Art Series, December, 1904.—*Letters and Papers of J. S. Copley and Henry Pelham, 1739-1776,* 1914.—Augustus Thorndike Perkins, *A Sketch of the Life and Some of the Works of John Singleton Copley,* 1873.

**COPPO di MARCOVALDO.**—Painter, born in Florence 1225-30, mentioned in 1260 in the "Libro di Montaperti" as one of the combatants in the battle of Montaperti.

His first known work is the Madonna in the Chiesa dei Servi, Siena, dated 1256, signed "Coppus de Florentia me pinxit," later overpainted by a follower of Duccio. In 1265 Coppo painted frescoes in the Cappella S. Jacopo in Pistoia, with which he was again busy in 1269 (not preserved). In 1274 he and his son Salerno were commissioned to do a Christ on the Cross with the Madonna and John for the choir, and a Christ on the Cross and a St. Michael for the high altar of the Duomo in Pistoia, of which there still remains in the sacristy a Crucifix with Scenes of the Passion. The last mention of his work for the Pistoia Cathedral is in 1276.

In Sta. Maria Maggiore in Florence there is a panel with a relief sculpture in wood of the Madonna, surrounded by painted scenes by Coppo.

Bibliography: Vasari-Milanesi.—Crowe and Cavalcaselle, Douglas ed., I.—Venturi, *Storia d. arte ital.,* V, 1906.—Bacci, in L'Arte, III, 1900, p. 32, republ. in *Doc. tosc. per la stor. dell'arte,* II, 1912 (with further literature).—Van Marle, *Italian Schools,* I.

**COPTIC ART.**—See Byzantine Art (in Egypt).

**COQUES (Gonzales).**—Flemish painter, 1618-1684. Pupil of P. Breughel III. He was the painter of the aristocracy of his day, which won him the name of "the little Van Dyck." He had his elegance, but he put his models in a different setting—less sumptuous, more familiar. He arranged them in groups, in a garden or on a terrace. He only painted the figures, leaving his pupils to carry out the backgrounds, landscapes or buildings, and the accessories. He was very successful. As in the case of Van Dyck, the English Court monopolised the artist, and nearly all his works are in England. His finest works are: the *Verhelst Family* (Buckingham Palace), the *Prince of Orange and his Family* (Leicester Collection), *Charles I,* the *Archduke Leopold, David Teniers* (Bridgewater Gallery), *Luc Faydherbe* (Berlin).

**CORBEL.**—Projecting stone used as a support.

**CORBUSIER (Le).**—See Jeanneret-Gris.

**CORDOVA.**—See Moslem Art.

**— (Great Mosque of).**—See Moslem Art; also Pl. 33, Vol. I.

**— (Spain).**—The *Great Mosque* was the centre of Islam in the West. It is the largest mosque in the world, after the Caaba of Mecca. It was begun by the Caliph Abd-el-Rahman, in 786. It was enlarged by successive rulers, especially in the 10th century. "The enclosed portion alone occupies a larger area than any Christian cathedral, consisting of nineteen aisles running north and south, with thirty-three bays to each aisle, supported on a labyrinth of 1,200 many-coloured columns, and approached from the open court by nineteen bronze doors. . . . The magnificent interior is ablaze with the jasper, porphyry, and the coloured marbles of its columns, sometimes supporting three superimposed tiers of Saracenic arches. . . ." (Banister Fletcher, *A History of Architecture*).

**CORINTH.**—See Greece; also Pl. 19, Vol. I.

**CORINTH, LOVIS.** — German painter (1858-1925). His work formed a transition between Impressionism and Expressionism.

**CORINTHIAN ORDER.**—See Capital; Greece (Architecture).

**CORNELISZ (Cornelis).** — Of Haarlem, 1562-1638. Leader of the first Haarlem school of mannerists. Painted mythological, allegorical and historical subjects and portraits. Many of his compositions were engraved by Goltzius, de Gheyn, Matham, Saenredam and others. He seems to have influenced even Frans Hals with regard to his group portraits.

Bibliography: Stechow, W., *Elseviers Geillustreerd Maandschrift,* 1935.

**CORNELISZ VAN OOSTSANEN (Jacob).**—Dutch painter and draughtsman for woodcut. Born in Oostsanen before 1470, died in Amsterdam in 1533. He probably is to be identified with the painter Jacob of Amsterdam. His best known pictures are: the *Adoration of the Trinity* (Cassel Museum); several *Adoration of the Magi* (Utrecht, Vienna); some *Crucifixions; Salome* (The Hague Museum), painted in 1524; *Saul and the Witch of Endor* (Amsterdam); the *Virgin Enthroned, with Angels* (Berlin); the *Virgin and Child* (Antwerp).

He is a precise, minute painter, whose compositions seem uninspired by strong religious emotion.

Bibliography: Steinbart, K., *Jacob Cornelisz v. Amsterdam.* Strassburg, 1922.—Friedländer, M. J., *Altniederl. Malerei.* Vol. XII.

**CORNELIUS (Peter).**—German painter, 1783-1867. Son of the Director of the Academy of Düsseldorf. He was first one of the group of the Nazarenes. But he was not content with admiring the Pre-Raphaelites. He studied the school of Raphael, Michelangelo, and the antique. He resurrected the art of fresco painting. He collaborated in the decoration of the Casa Bartholdi and painted, under the influence of Overbeck, a *Holy Family,* and a *Flight into Egypt.* On his return to Germany in 1821, he was asked to fill his father's position as Director of the Düsseldorf Academy. The King of Bavaria, Louis I, gave him commissions in Munich, where "he tried to create a whole world of thought and science, and to give complete expression to the national genius." Such works are his fresco in the Sculpture Museum, where, under the guise of the Olympian gods, he tried to represent life and the forces of nature, and his *Last Judgment,* in the Church of St. Louis. He made these "exercises in the manner of Michelangelo," as Muther calls them, "worthy counterparts to the Raphaelesque compositions in which the master's thought, exaggerated and deformed, immediately turns into pathos; and they are the products of an age that knew more about philosophy than painting." Then there are the compositions which Cornelius executed for the King of Prussia, Frederick William, who called him to Berlin, in 1841, when he fell out with the King of Bavaria on the subject of the execution of his *Last Judgment*: the cartoons, inspired by Signorelli, which he designed for the decoration (which was never realised) of a Campo Santo; and the frescoes which he made, after sketches by Schinkel, on the staircase of the old museum. If the artist's work is open to criticism, one must, nevertheless, admire the grandeur of his conceptions, the nobility of his spirit, the high ideal he had of art, and the eagerness with which he tried to realise it. In his drawings for Goethe's "Faust" (1810-1816, in the Staedel Museum), he tries to attain a purely German ideal, with Dürer's definition of form. It is not an exaggeration to say that he sometimes reached it there.

**CORNICE.**—Upper or crowning part of an entablature; applied also to any crowning projection.

**CORNY (Héré de).**—1705-63. See Nancy.

**COROT (Jean Baptiste Camille).**—French painter. Paris, 17th July, 1796, to 22nd February, 1875. Camille Corot was born in the Rue du Bac, Paris. His mother had a dress shop there, and his father did the accounts. Camille was put out to nurse near the Isle Adam until he was four years old, was sent to board in the Rue de Vaugirard from seven to eleven, and then completed his studies at the College of Rouen and in a school of Poissy, until he was nineteen. From then, the young man lived with his parents. His father, who had acquired some means in the fashion business, placed Camille as a salesman with a cloth merchant. But Corot only thought of painting. Freed from the counter after five years of probation, assured of receiving a little income from his parents, Corot went to ask his first lessons from Michallon. The latter, however, died prematurely at the end of the same year (1822), having advised his pupil above all "to look at nature, and reproduce it simply, with the greatest care." With Victor Bertin, who was his master after Michallon, Corot was initiated into the beauties of historical landscape. For three years, he followed Bertin, and never freed himself completely from the influences he came under at that time. Much later he exhibited at the Salon such pictures as *Homer and the Shepherds* (1845) and *Dante and Virgil* (1859). He was not combative, he did not take any part in the attack on the defenders of historical landscape While the school of classical landscape was in favour with the jury, he did not hesitate to submit compositions which at least seemed to respect their essential principles—this, however, he did quite naturally, and without forcing himself in the least.

On leaving Bertin's studio, Corot made his first journey to Italy. In Rome, his comrades much appreciated his jovial humour, but very little, his talent of painting. They found him too servile to nature, and lacking in style. Caruelle d'Aligny alone paid homage to the originality of his vision.

This first journey had a great influence on Corot. He freed himself from a good many of the school theories which oppressed him. An echo of Claude ennobles such studies as the *Basilica of Constantine* and the *Arch of Narni* (both in the Moreau-Nélaton Collection), and the *Coliseum* and the *Forum*, which Corot bequeathed to the Louvre.

After three years' absence, Camille Corot returned to Paris, and went to live with his parents. They tempted him in vain to marry. His love of wandering, which sent him to all parts of France, twice to Italy, to Holland, and to England, his exclusive passion for painting and nature, prevented his ever marrying. Corot had been received at the Salon of 1827 with a certain good-will. From 1831, Delécluze, Jal and Peisse noticed the unity of conception common to Edouard Bertin, d'Aligny and Corot. Delécluze saw in "this brotherhood of talent, the foundations of a school of landscape painters." This did not prevent Corot from being accused of "awkwardness, inability, and inadequacy." He was reproached, as Paul de Saint Victor still reproached him in 1867, with being "a most imperfect practitioner." The traveller was treated as an improviser, but he it was who said: "I see how severely one must follow nature, and not be content with hasty sketches. . . . There must be no indecision in anything." Corot was not only exposed to the sarcasm of the classicists: his quiet colour put him out of favour with the romantics. "The two first things to study are form, and then value. To me, these two things are the most serious considerations in art." How could this lover of form be accused of scorning it? Why in his woodland scenes do we no longer find the detail dear to the Dutch artists? Why have the Italian buildings and Picardy willows so little precision in their outlines? Because —and it is this which made the modest Corot a forerunner—form itself must bow to feeling. "In our search for truth and exactitude of form, let us never forget to give it that atmospheric envelopment which impressed us." Corot strove for "envelopment" long before the Impressionists. Favoured by effects of dawn and twilight, he came to represent objects according to their appearance. "Water in art," he taught, "is truth to nature bathed in the impression which its appearance has given us." Who kept Claude Monet from making such a precept his own?

Much is said about Corot's "two styles." It is customary to say of a composition which reveals the master's classical leanings: "it is in Corot's first style"; while an impression of morning or of evening is said to show his "second style." Moreau Nélaton has done justice to this specious classification: "Corot's chief claim to glory is, on the contrary, having persevered to the end in a love of truth, and in a conscientious endeavour to express it. The only difference is that, contrary to most men, years made his hand more skilful, and his vision keener. So, too, the nymphs and eclogues which made his late reputation are in germ in the more or less historical landscapes, in which, from about 1830 to 1850, he softened classical formulæ with a certain vaguely romantic sentiment." One has only to compare the two pictures, *Chartres Cathedral*, and the *Church of Marissel*, which are side by side in the Musée des Arts Decoratifs, and of which one was painted at the beginning and the other at the end of the painter's career, to see that they both express, by the same means, the same quality of emotion.

Corot never completely disarmed the attacks of the critics, and the hostility of the judges. In 1838, he found Gustave Planche on his side; but in 1842, on exhibiting the severe and harmonious *Site d'Italie* (Avignon Museum), and the fresh *Verger* (Semur Museum), Corot was subjected to the worst reproaches of Delécluze and Peisse. In 1843, his *Fire of Sodom* was rejected. But the outcry of his friends was so clamorous that the following year the *Sodom* appeared at the Salon. Nevertheless in 1846 two of his canvases were again refused. The Revolution of 1848 freed Corot, with Rousseau and many others, from the whims of the jury. One can then appreciate the esteem in which he was held, more perhaps on account of the kindness and nobility of his character than for the superiority of his talent. Sincere manifestations of sympathy supported his election as a member of the jury. His reputation increased. He was then sixty years old. Pupils came to him, and his studio was full of admirers. In 1861, Delécluze criticised his *Orpheus* harshly. But the number of writers who took his part increased each day. Champfleury was among the first, also Baudelaire, the great prophet who, after praising Corot from the time of the battles of 1846, showed, in 1859, the fallacy of the opinion that the artist of the *Souvenir d'Italie* (Louvre) was ignorant of the grammar of his art: "His work must be understood, for with him there is no slurring-over, but an infallible severity of harmony. Moreover, he is one of those rare artists, perhaps the only one, who has kept a profound feeling for construction, who observes the value of each detail in the whole, and, if it is allowable, to compare the composition of a landscape with the construction of the human body, who always knows where to put the bones, and what size to make them. One feels that Corot drew simply and broadly, which is the only way of amassing quickly a great deal of precious material." And further on Baudelaire extolled Corot's excellent teaching, "solid, illuminating, methodical," and, among his numerous pupils, praised the melancholy Lavieille.

At the Salon of 1865, where he exhibited the *Lac de Némi* and the *Bacchante Detaining Love*, the master achieved such a success that his admirers, all the adversaries of official art, thought that the time had come to present him with the "médaille d'honneur." This was furiously resisted; and Cabanel was awarded the supreme prize for his Portrait of the Emperor.

In 1867, at the time of the Universal Exhibition, Corot met with the same tenacious, blind hatred. While several of the large prizes went to Cabanel, to Gérôme, to Meissonier, and first medals to Bida, to Plis, and to Robert Fleury, the poet of *Morning* and *Evening* only obtained a medal of the second class. In 1872, he met with the same lack of success. The lovely *Souvenir de Mortefontaine* only won him three votes; and the "médaille d'honneur" was given to Gérôme.

Official encouragements were not more prodigal than the honours awarded by the jury. During his long career he only obtained two commissions: one for the Town of Paris—a panel, for the Church of St. Nicholas du Chardonnet, representing the Baptism of Christ, which has fine classical feeling; the other for the State—a cartoon for Beauvais (now in the Louvre), which was never put in position. In the course of fifty years uninterrupted production, shown at the Salons by more than two hundred works, the State only bought six of his canvases. Two of them are in the Louvre, the *Souvenir de Mortefontaine*, and the *Danse des Nymphes* (1851), which has a silvery, dawn-like freshness, with trembling foliage, through which is seen the country, and poetic bands of nymphs and fauns celebrating the return of the sun. Then there are three in other parts of France: the *Little Shepherd*, in Metz (1840); the *Bani du Berger*, in Donai (1848); and *Christ in the Garden of Olives*, in Langres (1849). Many of Corot's works were bought for local galleries. Thus the *Shepherd's Star*, one of his most beautiful paintings, has been in Toulouse since 1864; a *Landscape* at Dunkerque since 1865; *Souvenir de Ville d'Avray* at Le Mans since 1867; etc.

Apart from the three pictures acquired or commissioned by the State, all the rest of Corot's works in the Louvre have been given or lent: two by Corot himself, a dozen by Thomy Thierry, one by Lallemand, thirty-six by Moreau Nélaton; and finally the Chauchard Collection has added more than twenty-five pictures to these.

Apart from the Louvre, the best gallery in which to study Corot is that of Reims, where there are at least sixteen canvases by the master.

Corot's childlike soul was touched not only by the lights and soft colours of dawn and twilight: he loved the human form, and frequently painted nude figures in his soft countryside, *Wounded Eurydice*, the *Bacchante with a Panther*, the *Nymph lying on the Sea-shore*, the *Danse des Nymphes* (Glasgow), recalling the pure grace of the model, and the silvery delicacy of flesh of Prud'hon's figures. Both artists had a profound admiration for Correggio. The *Young Girl with a Mandolin*, the *Femme au Capulet* (Lyon Museum), the *Femme à la Perle* (Louvre), the portraits of himself, such as the very beautiful one in the Uffizi, and many paintings of friends, have only been appreciated of recent years.

Corot was an indefatigable traveller. His paintings include: the *Belfry of Donai, Chartres Cathedral*, the *Port of La Rochelle*, the *Arras Road*. He had already painted views of the hill cities of Tuscany (e.g., *Volterra*, in the Moreau Nélaton collection); and his treatment of the damp, atmospheric effects of France, was ennobled by deep and sensitive feeling.

How was Corot able to keep that lightness and freshness which is so eminently characteristic of his work? By leaving the canvas at the first attempt, and freeing his palette from thick, earthy and bituminous colours. Otherwise, colour did not count very much with him. Once his pictures were composed, his masses indicated, his values precise, colour was only a detail. This palette was quite personal, but he attached little importance to it. White, which he instinctively mixed with his colours, gave his foliage a pearly tint. He often brushed his canvas with light "scrubbings," especially in the leafy parts, to give his trees a quivering look, which he expressed better than any other painter.

Until 1874, Corot never really felt suffering; then the death of his sister affected him deeply, and his strong life declined. He died on the 22nd February, 1875, in his "appartement" in the Faubourg Poissonnière.

See Pl. 55, Vol. II.

Bibliography: Alfred Robaut, *L'œuvre de Corot* (remarks by Moreau Nélaton). Paris.—Maurice Hamel, *L'œuvre de Corot*. Paris.—Gustave Geffroy, *Corot*. Paris.—E. Moreau Nélaton, *Corot*. Paris.—P. Cornu, *Corot*. Paris, 1911.

**CORREGGIO (Antonio Allegri).** —Antonio Allegri, known as Correggio, the name of the town where he was born. Famous Parmese painter (1494-1534), whose very original work had considerable influence, almost comparable to that of Raphael or of Michelangelo. The details of his childhood are uncertain. His uncle, Lorenzo Allegri, must have taught him the first principles of the art of painting. And his next master was probably Antonio Bartolotti, surnamed Tagnino degli Anceschi (d. 1525), head of the school of Correggio. He may have worked at Modena with Bianchi Ferrari, and at Bologna with Francia. He visited Mantua and Parma. He doubtless did not go to Rome, but he saw Mantegna, Leonardo da Vinci; and the *Sistine Madonna* of Raphael made him exclaim: "Anch'io sono pittore!" He certainly knew how to paint the learned, complicated foreshortenings of Michelangelo.

On his return to Correggio (1514) his work was much admired, and he was probably commissioned to work at the Palazzo dei Signori. To this period belongs, no doubt, the large altarpiece, painted for San Francesco, which is in the Dresden Gallery, still very Venetian in character. But very soon his individuality showed itself, and it was of a rare and precious quality. Correggio sang praises to light, while the savants around him discoursed on perspective. He created angels, which Vasari likened to celestial rain, and transformed the world into music.

His grace was different from that of Raphael, his voluptuous colour was not that of Titian, his "morbidezza" was other than Leonardo's. For his joyous, ethereal lyricism softened his forms, brightened and gladdened his tones, and put enchanting gleams into his light and shade. Sometimes in his attempt to make his figures supple, his drawing became incorrect. The soft bodies became strangely swollen, like that of Venus borne by cupids in the Louvre drawing, or that of the so-called *Antiope* who is sleeping in such an uncomfortable position. But he always rendered light with an exquisite transparence.

"In his *Leda* and his *Venus*," Vasari says, "Correggio put such

*Phidias was the artistic genius in charge of the great projects of Pericles for building a new Athens from the ruins left by the wars with the barbarians. By his contemporaries he was admired mostly as a sculptor. His most famous works have disappeared: the two statues of Athena which were on the Acropolis (one on the road used for processions, the other in the temple); also the statue of Zeus, in gold and ivory, which he made for the temple of Olympia towards the end of his life when he was exiled by the Athenians. His types of Zeus and Athena were retained by other ancient sculptors.*

FIGURES FROM THE EAST PEDIMENT OF THE PARTHENON. BRITISH MUSEUM. *(Photo by Hachette.)*

THE "THREE FATES," EAST PEDIMENT OF THE PARTHENON. BRITISH MUSEUM. *(Photo by Hachette.)*

## Pediments of the Parthenon

It was Phidias and his assistants who finished the monument of Ictinos by animating it with figures and bas-reliefs. The pediments adorned with large statues tell two legends dear to the Athenians: the dispute between Poseidon and Athena, and the birth of this goddess. The best preserved figures come from the latter composition. All that was left of these statues is now in London. In these marble bodies life was so profoundly rooted that even in mutilation it lightens the mass of the stone.

PARTHENON: THREE DIVINITIES. *(Photo by Hachette.)*

PARTHENON: YOUNG ATHENIANS. *(Photo by Hachette.)*

PARTHENON: KNIGHTS. *(Photo by Hachette.)*

## The Frieze of the Parthenon

The famous frieze of the Parthenon represents the people marching in great ceremony to bring to the goddess a veil embroidered by the young Athenian girls. The gods, priests and their servants, young girls, citizens, and knights are done in flat relief. Their beauty lies above all in the balance of postures and the rhythm of the silhouettes. The slow movement of the march of the virgins, the gallop of the small Attic horses, the majesty of the seated Olympians present a softer rhythm accompanying the motions of life than can be found anywhere else. This frieze spreads over the wall of the cella, behind the colonnade.

NIKE FASTENING HER SANDAL, ATHENS. *(Photo by Hachette.)*

HEAD OF APOLLO. TERME MUSEUM, ROME. *(Photo by Giraudon.)*

HEAD OF ARTEMIS. LABORDE COLLECTION. PARIS. *(Photo by Giraudon.)*

ATHENA PARTHENOS. ATHENS. *(Photo by Alinari.)*

## School of Phidias

Phidias did not make all the figures of the pediments and metopes of the Parthenon himself. With him worked a large school, of which he was the guiding spirit. He represents one of the most beautiful phases of Greek art, the one in which sculpture finally conquered the stiffness of material to render softness and life. At this point sculpture is still idealistic, rendering pure beauty rather than resemblance to the individual. This sculpture fixed the types of Athena and Zeus, and one can picture these famous statues which have disappeared, by some antique replicas and by some preserved fragments.

# SCOPAS AND PRAXITELES

*Phidias was a contemporary of an artist much admired by the Greeks, namely, Polyclitus, whose style can be reconstructed only by guess-work. He was succeeded by a new generation of sculptors, of whose style we can judge somewhat by the descriptions of historians, and by the few pieces which are more or less identified. This generation succeeds the age of idealism and imagination, a phase of art closer to the simplicity of nature. Little by little the somewhat abstract and stiff figures of Phidias became more like flesh and blood, expressing human sentiments. The two best known names of this generation, at the beginning of the fourth century, are Scopas, a sculptor of Paros, and the Athenian, Praxiteles.*

EIRENE AND PLOUTOS. MUNICH.
*(Photo by Bruckmann.)*

HEADS OF THE SCHOOL OF SCOPAS. ATHENS AND FLORENCE.
*(Photo by Hachette.)*

MAUSOLUS. BRITISH MUSEUM.
*(Photo by A. Richgitz.)*

## Scopas

As often happens in Greek sculpture, one has to be acquainted with the life of the ancients to be able to reconstruct their style; such is the case with the famous statues of Scopas. The ancients mention his statues of Pothos and Himeros, Desire and Passion. It seems that this artist gave a less serene expression to his figures than Phidias. He worked, no doubt, on the celebrated Mausoleum of Halicarnassus. This has been destroyed, but some of its ruins were found in the walls of a Frankish fortress. To him are attributed certain statues expressing passion, by the vivacity of their attitudes, by their facial animation, or by the sadness and revery of their expression.

APOLLO SAUROKTONOS. LOUVRE.
*(Photo by Alinari.)*

HERMES OF OLYMPIA, BY PRAXITELES.
*(Photo by Alinari.)*

VENUS OF ARLES. LOUVRE.
*(Photo by Hachette.)*

CAPITOLINE VENUS.
*(Photo by Anderson.)*

ARTEMIS OF GABII. LOUVRE.
*(Photo by Hachette.)*

## Praxiteles

Praxiteles was the creator of a Hermes cited by Pausanias, which was excavated at Olympia. He is the originator of the familiar type of a youth leaning on his elbow, engrossed in thought, Hermes, a satyr or Apollo. It was also Praxiteles who created the nude female goddesses. His Venus emerging from the water was supposedly inspired by the noted Phryne. Judging from his Hermes, one can understand how the ancients saw in him the sculptor of human flesh. He rendered in marble the warmth of the flesh, the softness of the hair, the moistness of the eyes. We find again the elegance and charm of his goddesses in the small figures of terra cotta which were found at Tanagra.

# GREEK SCULPTURE AFTER THE FIFTH CENTURY

*Two methods are used in the study of ancient sculpture: the documentary method by means of which the most celebrated names are made known to us, and the method in which the preserved works are directly studied. Our task consists most frequently in attempting to apply the research of historians to museum pieces. But the majority of the latter are none the less anonymous. The most famous extant statues are almost always by an unknown master. We can rarely date them with certainty. Most of the statues mentioned by ancient historians are known to us only by what they have told us about them.*

VICTORY OF SAMOTHRACE. LOUVRE.
*(Photo by Hachette.)*

VENUS DE' MEDICI. FLORENCE.
*(Photo by Brogi.)*

DIANA THE HUNTRESS. LOUVRE.
*(Photo by Hachette.)*

VENUS DE MILO. LOUVRE.
*(Photo by Hachette.)*

APOLLO BELVEDERE. VATICAN.
*(Photo by Brogi.)*

These statues, all famous, are of an uncertain date, with the exception of the *Victory of Samothrace* which commemorated a naval battle of the year 306 B.C. The *Venus de' Medici* is derived from the type of Venus created by Praxiteles. The *Diana the Huntress* and the *Apollo Belvedere* with their elegance and their somewhat theatrical attitude seem to resemble it. The *Venus de Milo*, the pride of the Louvre, preserves the secret of its origin. Because of its serene beauty, it appears to date from the fourth century; by virtue of its naturalism, it seems more recent. It is undoubtedly the work of a master.

FIGHTING GLADIATOR. LOUVRE.
*(Photo by Hachette.)*

THE WRESTLERS. UFFIZI, FLORENCE.
*(Photo by Brogi.)*

NIOBE AND HER DAUGHTER. UFFIZI, FLORENCE.
*(Photo by Brogi.)*

Each of these works is the subject of discussion. The violence of the attitudes and the pathetic quality of the expressions indicate the Hellenistic period. Greek statuary followed an evolution which we observe in other schools: rigid archaism, classic certainty, then naturalism, the portrait and the expression of violent passions. It is not unlikely that the *Fighting Gladiator* is a copy of a lost original by Lysippus and the Niobid group a replica of a work by Scopas.

LAOCOÖN AND HIS SONS. VATICAN.
*(Photo by Brogi.)*

ATHENA OVERCOMING A GIANT. BERLIN.
*(Photo by Brogi.)*

THE FARNESE BULL. NAPLES.
*(Photo by Brogi.)*

## Hellenistic Sculpture

After Alexander, Hellenism penetrated Asia and was influenced by that contact. It is apparent in the sculpture of picturesque and dramatic groups made perhaps in imitation of painting. There were art centres at Pergamon, Rhodes and Tralles. The frieze of giants was executed at Pergamon; the Laocoön came from Rhodes; the Farnese Bull from Tralles. In all these works, Asiatic exuberance dominates Attic moderation.

# GREEK TERRA COTTA FIGURINES

*The art of terra cotta is one of those which furnish archaeology with the most figurines, since in spite of their fragility, these small objects have come down to us through the ages in their entirety. Clay modelling is one of the most natural and most spontaneous of technical methods. By means of baking, this malleable clay is hardened and it perpetually preserves the shape into which the thumb has so easily impressed it. Terra cotta thus contributes for most civilisations a popular and familiar transcription of large sculpture. Greek terra cotta sculptures are the most charming; they achieve the most unaffected naturalism and attain the most refined beauty.*

PLOWING. LOUVRE.
*(Photo by Hachette.)*

KNEADING DOUGH. LOUVRE.
*(Photo by Hachette.)*

WAR CHARIOT. LOUVRE.
*(Photo by Hachette.)*

## Archaic Terra Cotta Sculpture

The sculpture of figurines, by virtue of the flexibility of its material, escapes from the limitations which encompass large statuary and prevent it from attaining the suppleness and the familiarity of life. The hands which have modelled these very picturesque, lifelike and typical groups are not those of a great master. They are only the fantasies of an improvising artist who, without pretension, amused himself with the caricature-like silhouettes which he modelled. The minor arts of Greece thus reveal to us a familiar and popular realism; this gift of observation is the source of the plastic genius. One already has found it in the art of Crete.

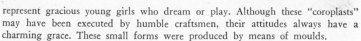

TANAGRA FIGURINES. LOUVRE.
*(Photo by Hachette.)*

The most celebrated group of terra cotta figurines which antiquity has left to us are those discovered in the tombs of Tanagra in Boeotia. These statuettes destined originally without doubt to accompany the dead in the tomb most often represent gracious young girls who dream or play. Although these "coroplasts" may have been executed by humble craftsmen, their attitudes always have a charming grace. These small forms were produced by means of moulds.

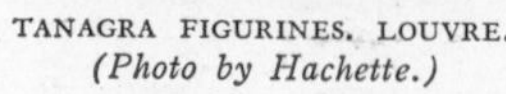

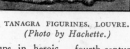

TANAGRA FIGURINES. LOUVRE.
*(Photo by Hachette.)*

Some of these figurines are very like miniature copies of groups in heroic sculpture. But most often they are directly inspired by nature. One must not compare these figures to the ivory statuettes of the Middle Ages which reproduced large figures of monumental sculpture on a small scale. With a few exceptions the types are original. One may study here the female costume of the Athenians in the fourth century B.C. The remains of polychromy which are extant add to the realism of the imitation. And that does not prevent one from recognising the contemporaries of figures by Praxiteles and Scopas: the types of the head, headdress, movements and folds of draperies.

morbidezza that one seems to see not a painting, but real flesh."

These subtle tints, flushed with reflections, are harmonies in themselves, independent of what they represent. The colours and light are in themselves themes, a means of expression which he added to that of the scenes which they envelop. Correggio had no need of material details to enrich his work. What need had he of complicated buildings, sumptuous costumes, balanced crowds? Landscapes sufficed, for over them are large, clear skies on which clouds seem to float like swans on a blue lake. Draperies are better than all clothing, for they have more folds for the sunshine to play upon. The painter's joyous melody needed no rhythmic processions. What interested him were the smiles and caresses of light.

Vasari said that, looking at the smile of one of Correggio's children, one could not help smiling, too. That of his Virgins and Saints is more dreamy; their smile recalls slightly the characteristic smile of Leonardo's figures. It is, however, different—more spiritual and less ironical perhaps, and more tender and less melancholy. Correggio was no thinker, scrutinising the problems of life and seeing in it disillusionment.

Already, in his first works, his style and qualities are apparent in the *Rest in Flight* (Uffizi), still a little heavy and awkward, as in the *St. Francis Altarpiece* (Dresden), but above all in the *Marriage of St. Catherine* (1517, Louvre), where the caress of the child is so delicate as he passes the ring on to the rosy finger of his charming spouse, as though in play. There are replicas of this delightful picture in Naples, and in the Hermitage Museum.

In 1518, he was commissioned, by Giovanna di Piacenza, to decorate a part of the Convent of St. Paul, in Parma, of which she was the abbess. There he represented Diana, over the fire-place, and the frieze of Graces, Fortune, Adonis, etc., and on the ceiling, among an exquisite vine arbour, through which the blue sky can be seen, delightful cupids, holding emblems of the hunt, are painted both richly and lightly, and are exceedingly decorative. The impression of spring-like freshness which this decoration gives to the whole of the large hall is not easily forgotten, and many princes claimed this pagan decoration for palaces which were not convents. This *Pergola* of St. Paul was the source of innumerable decorations in the following centuries.

In 1519, Correggio returned to his little native town, where he married Gerolama Merlini. He had four children, three daughters and a son, Pomponio, who became a painter. But his happiness did not last long, for his wife died ten years after, about 1529.

Shortly after his marriage, he settled in Parma. There he painted a new and important work: the decoration of the dome of San Giovanni Evangelista (1524-80), with a *Christ in Glory*, surrounded by the Apostles. This fresco has been much retouched, but it shows a lack of form in the soft, elegant figure of the foreshortened Christ. In the semi-dome of the choir, he painted a *Coronation of the Virgin*, which was unfortunately destroyed in 1584. The original of the principal group is, however, in the Library of Parma, and some copies in the Museum give us an idea of the other parts. Aretusi repainted the ceiling with the same subject. Over a door, a fine *St. John the Evangelist*, by Correggio, remains.

Finally, from 1520 to 1524, Correggio painted another large decoration—an *Assumption* on the octagonal dome of Parma Cathedral. His brush, which had acquired more and more mastery, seems by now to have wings. Among diaphanous nudes are innumerable clusters of angels, in voluptuous confusion in pearly grey and pale yellow clouds —a tangle of legs and arms.

This work was not finished happily. In his sorrow he left Parma, and returned to Correggio. His wife was dead. He had not had the success he counted on. He was discouraged. But Gonzaga of Mantua and Isabella d'Este, who much appreciated him, ordered pictures from him, and it was for them that he set to work, now painting chiefly mythological works—the fair *Danaë*, in the Borghese Gallery, with her subtle smile at Cupid who comes to tease her; *Antiope*, in the Louvre, who is perhaps only a nymph, unless she is Venus, but who is, at any rate, gazed at by a satyr; and *Io and Jupiter*, which is in the Vienna Gallery, as well as a *Leda*, a *Rape of Ganymede*, etc.

It is said that at the end of his life Correggio was in the greatest distress. In any case, he was not rich, and his death, which occurred five years after that of his wife, passed unnoticed (15th March, 1534). His grave is unknown.

It was while he was working on his large decorative frescoes in Parma that Correggio painted his finest pictures.

The *Madonna of St. Jerome* (Parma Gallery) was ordered in 1523, and painted about 1527-1528. Its tenderness and caressing tints are admirable, and the figure of the Magdalen has a haunting charm. The *Madonna della Scodella*, in the same gallery, belongs to the same period, and was taken from a youthful picture, the *Flight into Egypt*. The painter now possessed all the means of expression, and here he painted figures bathed in light, in front of a dark forest.

Among other works in Parma must be mentioned the *Martyrdom of Saint Placidus, and St. Flavia*, etc. (1520-24), in a beautiful landscape full of light and shade, a *Descent from the Cross*, and the *Madonna della Scala*, a fresco which is, unfortunately, damaged.

His chief works scattered in other towns are: the *Nativity* (or *Holy Night*), commissioned in 1523, finished in 1530; the *Madonna with St. Sebastian* of 1525, both of which are at Dresden; the *Madonna dell' Latte*, in the Hermitage Museum, Leningrad; the *Madonna* of Frankfort Museum (1517); the *Virgin with Christ*, and the little *Saint John* (Madrid); the *Ecce Homo* (National Gallery); and the *Virgin and Child* in the Uffizi.

The tender charm and spiritual grace of Correggio was as much sought after as Titian's voluptuousness. From him the Carracci took one of the chief means of extending their influence. Innumerable motifs of the rococo, and the fluttering baroque angels recall the caressing touch of the painter of Correggio.

See Pl. 22, Vol. II.

Bibliography: C. Ricci, *Antonio Allegri da Correggio*. London, and Berlin, 1896.—J. Mayer, *Correggio*. Leipzig, 1871.—G. Gronau, *Correggio*. Stuttgart, 1907.

**CORSINI PALACE.**—See Florence.

**CORTILE.**—Small court, surrounded by the walls of a building or group of buildings.

**CORTONA (Domenico di).**—See Boccador.

**CORTONA, PIETRO da.**—See Pietro.

**COSIMO ROSSELLI.**—Florentine painter of the 15th century, born in 1439. He lacks the individuality of the other great painters of his day. He borrowed here and there, and so developed the solid ability of a good painter who knew his craft and followed the fine traditions of his century, but he was wanting in originality. He began to learn painting in the studio of Neri di Bicci, at fourteen years of age; and his *Glory of St. Anne* (1471, Kaiser Friedrich Museum), as well as the *"Annunciation"* in the Louvre (1473), which can perhaps be attributed to him, show the influence of this first master. *The Adoration of the Magi* (Uffizi) was somewhat influenced by Benozzo Gozzoli; the *St. Barbara* (Uffizi) by Pollainoli.

In 1476, he painted the *Taking of the Habit* and the *Vision of San Filippo Benizzi*, in the cloister of the Annunziata, Florence, with the heads not very lifelike but rather beautiful.

The chief event of his life was his journey to Rome to paint in the Sistine Chapel in company with Ghirlandajo, Botticelli, Piero Francesco Dei, and Diamante. Vasari relates how, feeling himself poor both in imagination and drawing, in comparison with the others, he told himself that in hiding his defects under a superabundance of ultramarine and other bright colours, he would dazzle Pope Sixtus IV, who understood very little about art, and win the prize. And, in fact, when all the works were uncovered, the other artists greeted Cosimo's paintings with mocking laughter, but the Pope declared that he had shown himself to be the best painter.

He showed some progress in the *Procession of the Holy Sacrament*, in Sant'Ambrogio, Florence (1485). His frescoes in Lucca Cathedral have fine landscape with a gleam of light behind the town and cypress trees; those in San Francesco are much injured, and the Virgin, in the marriage scene, has a doll-like air.

In 1486, together with his pupil, Fra Bartolommeo da San Marco, he painted eight pictures, in the dormitory of Sant'Ambrogio, which are now lost.

Then, about 1505, he executed two pictures for Santa Maria Maddalena dei Pazzi, one of which is the monumental *Madonna* of the Accademia of Florence. Among other paintings attributed to him is a Portrait of a Man in the late Spiridon Collection in Paris. He was the master of Piero di Cosimo, who was much greater and more interesting than he.

**COSMATI (The).**—Two separate families of Roman mosaicists bore this name, one, James and Cosmas, called Cosmas I, working at the beginning of the 13th century on the façade of S. Tommaso in Formis and in the narthex of the Cathedral of Civita Castellana, where there is a half-length Christ signed by James and dated 1210.

The second family, headed by Cosmas, known as Cosmas II, was active in the latter half of the century. Cosmas' signature appears on a pillar of the Sancta Sanctorum, rebuilt by Pope Nicholas III (1277-80). Cosmas II's son Giovanni signed two monuments in Rome; one of 1296 in memory of Bishop Durand of Mende in the church of Sta. Maria sopra Minerva, the other, 1299, in memory of Cardinal Gonsalve Rodriguez in Sta. Maria Maggiore.

Bibliography: *Die Genealogie der Cosmati*, Jahrb. der Preuss. Kunstsamml., 1885.—A. Milani, *I cosidetti Cosmati*, Arte e Storia, XVIII, Feb. 1889.—G. Boni, *The Roman Marmorari*. Rome, 1893.—G. Giovannoni, *Note sui marmorari romani*, Arch. della Soc. Rom. di Stor. Patr., 1904, p. 11.

**COSSA (Francesco del).**—Ferrarese painter, born in Ferrara, 1435; died in Bologna, 1477. A pupil of Tura, he was strongly influenced by the Florentines and especially by Piero della Francesca.

Cossa is mentioned first in a Ferrarese document in 1456 as working in Vescovado, where he did for the high altar a Pietà in three half-length figures. In 1470 he wrote to Duke Borso d'Este that he had finished the frescoes in the Schifanoia Palace, Ferrara, and complained of poor treatment and inadequate payment. Evidently this did not result in any particular improvement, since it was a very short time after that Cossa removed to Bologna, where he found new patrons in the Bentivoglio, whose palace he decorated with frescoes that are unfortunately now destroyed. In 1472 he was commissioned by Giovanni II Bentivoglio to restore a fresco of the Madonna in the Chiesa Madonna del Baraccano. Around this fresco he did frescoes of St. Lucia and St. Catherine. From 1474 dates the Catanei altar, the Madonna with Petronius, now in the Bologna Pinacoteca. His last work was the frescoes in the family chapel of Garganelli in S. Pietro, destroyed in 1606 (finished by Ercole Roberti after Cossa's death in 1477 of the plague).

A very limited number of works by Cossa have come down to us. From his Ferrarese period dates an altar originally in S. Domenico in Ferrara and now dispersed among the National Gallery, London (Vincent Ferrer); the Brera, Milan (SS. John and Peter); and the Vatican (Predella with miracles of Vincent Ferrer). The Dresden Annunciation is considered to be the earliest work of his Bolognese period; and his late activity is represented by the Autumn in Berlin. In the Kress Collection in New York there are two very fine Cossa panels.

Bibliography: Masini, *Bologna perlustr.*, 1666, p. 213.—G. A. Scalabrini, *Mem. stor. d. Chiese di Ferrara*, 1773.—Lamo, *Graticola di Bologna*, 1844.—Baruffaldi, *Vite d. pitt. ferr.*, ed. 1844.—Laderchi, *La pitt. ferrar.*, 1856; *Sopra i dip. d. Pal. Schifanoia*, 1840.—Cittadella, *Not. rel. Ferrara*, 1864; *Ric. e doc. int. alla vita di Cosimo Tura.*—A. Venturi, *L'Arte a Ferrara nel periodo di Borso d'Este*, Riv. Stor. Ital., 1885, p. 591 f.; *I primordi del rinascim. artist. a Ferrara*, 1884.—Gruyer, *L'art ferrarais*, 1897.—Berenson, *No. Ital. Painters of the Renaissance*, 1907, p. 60 f., 201 f.—Gardner, *The Painters of Ferrara*, 1911.—A. Venturi, *North Italian Painting of the*

*Quattrocento,* 1931?.—Roberto Longhi, *Officina Ferrarese,* 1936.

**COSTA (Lorenzo di Ottavio).**—Painter, school of Ferrara-Bologna, born probably in Ferrara, 1460; died in Mantua, 1535. Costa received his training in Ferrara, not in Florence as Vasari claims, but there are no documents bearing on his Ferrarese activity.

In 1483 he is mentioned in Bologna, among other painters, as working on the painting of the Bentivoglio Palace, which was destroyed in 1507. In 1488 he signed *The Enthroned Madonna with the Bentivoglio* family (fresco) in S. Giacomo Maggiore, Bologna; in 1490 the *Triumphs of Death and Fame* on the left wall of the same chapel. Other frescoes, now destroyed, painted for the Bentivoglio family are mentioned by Gozzadini. From this time on, Costa's works follow in a steady progression: 1491, the signed and dated *Madonna Enthroned with James and Sebastian* in the Bologna Pinacoteca (tempera on canvas); 1492, the *Madonna and Four Saints* in S. Petronio, Capella Baciocchi (oil on canvas, signed and dated); 1496, the *Madonna Enthroned with Petronius and Thecla,* Bologna Pinacoteca, painted for the Chiesa S. Thecla (no longer existing); 1497, the *Madonna, Four Saints, Two Angels,* in S. Giovanni in Monte (date of commission given by Vasari as by Jacopo Ghedini in that year); 1499, the *Adoration of the Magi* in the Brera, predella to Francia's Nativity altar in the Bologna Pinacoteca, and additional panels of this altar, also by Costa, in the choir of the Misericordia in Bologna (Resurrected Christ between figures of the Annunciation); 1499, Costa undertook contract with Nicola Pisano for the fresco painting of the choir of the Cathedral in Ferrara, work which apparently was never begun; 1501, the *Coronation and Six Saints* on the high altar of S. Giovanni in Monte; 1502, the *St. Petronius Enthroned with Francis and Dominic* in the Bologna Pinacoteca; 1503, Costa was in Rome for a short time as a member of a delegation from the Bolognese Senate; 1504, the signed *Pietà* in Berlin; 1505, the signed and dated *Sposalizio* in the Bologna Pinacoteca (from SS. Annunziata), and the polyptych in the National Gallery, signed and dated (from the Oratorio delle Grazie, Faenza); 1506, frescoes in the Oratorio di Sta. Cecilia; 1506, the *Assumption* in S. Martino Maggiore, Bologna (execution only in part by Costa, assisted by Chiodarolo); 1506-7, went to Mantua to paint for the Gonzaga family (the commission from the Gonzaga had been given him in 1504 for the Court of Isabella d'Este, now in the Louvre); 1507-09, busy with the painting of the Palazzo di S. Sebastiano, now destroyed (during this period he executed several portraits, one of the Marchese, one of his daughter Eleonora, one of her mother Isabella); 1510, he was for a short time in Bologna to do a portrait of Isabella's son, Federigo; 1511-12, the *Kingdom of Comus,* now in the Louvre; 1519, directed the painting of the new palace in Marmirolo; 1520, portrait of the humanist, Mario Equicola; 1522, signed and dated *Investiture of Federigo Gonzaga* in the Collection of Prince Clary-Aldringen, Teplitz, Czechoslovakia; 1525, S. Andrea, Mantua, *Enthroned Madonna and Saints.* Costa was ill during his last years, and was succeeded as court painter by Giulio Romano in 1524.

BIBLIOGRAPHY: Vasari-Milanesi, III, 131.—C. Cittadella, *Catal. istor. de' pitt., etc., ferrar.,* 1782, I, 83.—G. Gozzadini, *Mem. p. la vita di Giov. II Bentivoglio.* Bologna, 1839, pp. 40, 80 f., 146, 148, 237.—M. Gualandi, *Mem. orig.,* 1840 ff., I, 52; III, 8.—G. Baruffaldi, *Vite de' pitt. e scult. ferraresi,* ed. 1844, I, 27.—C. Laderchi, *La pitt. ferrarese,* 1856, p. 39.—A. Bertolotti, *Artisti in relaz. coi Gonzaga.* Modena, 1885, p. 26.—G. Campori, *I pittori degli estensi nel sec. XV.* Modena, 1886, pp. 50, 57.—Crowe and Cavalcaselle.—Berenson, *Study and Criticism of Italian Art.* London, 1901, p. 27 f., 30, 33, 35, 40; 2nd ser., 1902, pp. 18-20; *North Italian Painters of the Renaissance.* London, 1907, pp. 67 f., 202 f.—E. C. Gardner, *The Painters of Ferrara,* 1911.—Roberto Longhi, *Officina Ferrarese,* 1936.

**COSWAY (Richard).**—English painter (1742-1821), chiefly known as a miniature painter but also a painter of portraits on a life-size scale. Elected A.R.A. 1770, R.A., 1771. His wife Maria (1759-1838) was also an artist (painter and etcher).

BIBLIOGRAPHY: G. C. Williamson, *Richard Cosway.* London, 1905.

**COTES (Francis).**—English painter (1725-1770), pupil of George Knapton; an excellent portraitist, both in oils and in pastel. He was one of the foundation members of the Royal Academy in 1768.

**COTMAN (John Sell).**—English painter (1782-1842), one of the principal artists of the Norwich School, distinguished by his fine sense of colour and his gifts as a designer—qualities which are apparent both in his oil pictures and water colours.

**COTTET (Charles).**—French painter, from Le Puy, Haute-Loire, 1863. Cottet was taught by Maillard, Roll, and Puvis de Chavannes. Little by little, his style became very personal: austere, heavy, opaque, lacking spiritual grace, and harmonious colour, but capable of warm, deep notes. He travelled much, and visited Algeria, Egypt, Italy, Spain, Ireland, Palestine and Constantinople. He brought back expressive studies of old Spanish walls, Venetian canals, Arab markets, and Savoy mountains. A thoughtful, temperamental artist, his execution was lively and concise. His colour was sometimes very hot, sometimes grey; but the foundation of it was always very dark. The whole is striking on account of its massive roughness. His most resounding success reveals him entirely: *Au Pays de la Mer.* This triptych shows, on one side, those who are departing, and, on the other, those who remain, and in the middle is the farewell feast (Luxembourg Gallery). In this strain, Cottet painted a series under the title of "Mournings," then fine landscapes and scenes of the life of mariners, large pictures, some nudes and some portraits.

Finally, the artist produced some very remarkable and very personal etchings (in the collection of the Ducet Library).

**COUCY-LE-CHÂTEAU (Aisne; France).**—The ruins of the château and its famous keep, the broadest tower in the world, were completely razed to the ground during the war. The walls were more than 7 to 10 metres thick.

See Pl. 51, Vol. I.

BIBLIOGRAPHY: Viollet-le-Duc, *Description du château de Coucy.*—Lefèvre-Pontalis, *Le château de Coucy.* Paris.

**COURBET (Gustave).**—French painter. Born at Ornans, 1819; died

COURBET.

at La Tour de Peilz, near Vevey, Switzerland, 1877. After having studied law, in accordance with the wishes of his family, Courbet took up painting under the direction of an artist of Besançon, Flageoulot, and, in Paris, joined the studios of Steuben, and then of Hesse (1839). He preferred to study the old masters in the Louvre. In 1844, he sent to the Salon his self portrait, *Courbet with a Black Dog,* which was accepted, and the *Wounded Man,* which was rejected, and is now, by an irony which became frequent, in the Louvre. It was refused again in 1846, together with the *Man with a Pipe* (Montpellier Gallery). In 1848, he sent six pictures to the Salon; but it was only in 1849 that he attracted attention for the first time with *L'Après Diner à Ornans* (Lille Gallery). In a dark interior, three people, seated at table, listen to a violin player. Its breadth of touch, and fine qualities were not understood by a certain public, and the picture raised as much indignation as praise. Nevertheless, *L'Après Diner* was acquired by the State, and he was given the second medal. In the following year the *Funeral at Ornans* (Louvre) created more discussion. The artist was accused of deriding death, and caricaturing the figures. One cannot say whether his critics refused to see qualities of colour and execution, which out-weighed certain weaknesses and certain vulgarities, which were perhaps intentional. If so Courbet was certainly mistaken in repeating them in his succeeding works, through a desire to shock the bourgeois. It is, nevertheless, true that in the midst of the insipidity of the painters who were appreciated in his day, Courbet introduced a note of energy and freshness. What surprised others, and perhaps himself, was that, after all, his "enveloped" style and fresh palette recalled the best traditions of the old masters. On the other hand, he was a revolutionary, in proving that the picture painted directly from nature, and stripped of literary intention, had a right to be painted on the same scale as historical or "subject" pictures. Courbet was mistaken in putting forward these theories in a provocative and pretentious manner, with a ridiculous and affected contempt for Raphael and all the classical masters. On the other hand, the jeers of his critics often reached the height of absurdity. The discussion about him at least made his exhibitions in Dijon, Besançon, Munich and Frankfort, successful. But in Paris the enthusiasm of his partisans did not avail to stifle the attacks of his enemies. The fuss was renewed in 1852, over the *Village Maidens;* in 1853, over the *Bathers* (Montpellier Gallery); in 1855, over the *Meeting,* known as *Bonjour, Monsieur Courbet,* in which the artist represented himself greeted by the amateur, Bruyas (Montpellier Gallery. Rejected, at the Universal Exhibition in 1855), he exhibited his work independently. At this time, he painted an important composition: the *Studio:* a realistic allegory, showing a period of seven years of very artistic life. There he represented himself painting a landscape surrounded by his friends and his models. This pretentious work, which, in spite of some good passages, is not equal to the *Funeral,* lent itself too easily to ridicule to be spared. But nothing shook Courbet's confidence. He even enjoyed the outcry he caused. Among his next pictures were: a portrait of Prud'hon, studies of landscapes, and animals, especially deer, the *Wave* (Louvre), one of his best paintings in spite of its heavy treatment, due to the use of the palette knife, and the *Siesta during the Haymaking.* In 1863, his desire to scandalise won him another refusal "to outrage religious morality" with the *Retour de la Conférence,* an enormous canvas, showing drunken curés. But he went much further. In 1870, urged by the journalists who surrounded him and dominated him, without his being aware of it, he refused the Cross of the Legion of Honour, and, in 1871, he became associated with the Communist movement. With the intention of safeguarding the interests of artists and the works in museums, he formed the Federation of Artists, but he also inspired the overthrow of the Vendôme column. On the return of order, he was condemned to six months' imprisonment, for the usurpation of office and the destruction of a public monument. He had, moreover, to pay 323,000 francs for the rebuilding of the column. Ruined, exposed to the hatred of the triumphant political party, and, it must be said, of independent people, disgusted by the horrors of which the Commune had been the cause, he went to Switzerland, to the Tour de Peilz, near Vevey, on the shore of the Lake of Geneva (1873). A brave man at heart, and at the same time a child full of vainglory and vanity, he suffered terribly from the general disgrace, and had not the energy to bear it patiently and to await the acclamation which was to come, as it comes for so many others—late. The following years were a long agony. He still painted, but he exhibited no more, the last work he sent to the Salon, in 1872, having been, at the proposal of Meissonier, rejected without examination. He died poor, and almost deserted, in 1877.

Courbet began the reactionary movement against the insipidity of the classicists descended from David and Ingres. This is his true merit. Beneath the characteristics of a revolutionary, he was a great realist in the manner of Rembrandt, of Tintoretto, of Frans Hals. He fell short by reason of his heaviness, opaqueness, black tones, the use of bitumen, and the employment of a palette knife, which was a dangerous example and misled his imitators. But, at his best, he painted freshly, with a sense of form, and superb confidence.

Courbet made some very fine copies after Rembrandt, which remain in his family at Ornans. To the pictures mentioned, we add: the *Hammock* (1844, in the Collection of the Prince de Wagram); the *Sleeping Lace-Maker* (Montpellier); portrait of Baudelaire (Louvre); *Woman with a Parrot* (Bordet Collection, Lyon).

See Pl. 56, Vol. II.

**COURT.**—A family of Limousin enamellers. The last of whom one can trace anything lived in the 16th century. The initials I D C, or I C, which are found on certain pieces could belong to one of the two—Jean Court, or Jean Courteys. To Jean Court, called Vigier, is attributed a cup offered to Mary Stuart by Francis II, and some other pieces. To Jean Court II are attributed a large *Descent from the Cross*, in the Dutuit Collection; a large oval plate, in the same collection; and some plates, with Biblical scenes, in the Louvre. These pieces are among the finest productions of the 16th century.

Suzanne Court signed the fine plates with scenes of the Wise and Foolish Virgins, and of the Queen of Sheba, in the Louvre.

Bibliography: P. Lavedan, *Léonard Limousin et les émailleurs français*. Paris, 1913.—René Jean, *"Les Arts de la Terre,"* 3rd part: "L'Émaillerie." Paris, 1911.

**— (Jean de).**—French enameller of the 16th century. The Wallace Collection has a plaque by him, representing Marguerite of France as "Minerva" (1555). It is not known whether he should be identified with the "Jean de Court," called "Vigier," who signed a very fine cup in the Malcolm Collection, and perhaps also with a Jean de Court, who was painter to King Charles IX in 1572.

**COURTEYS (The).**—Limousin enamellers, of whom the most interesting is Pierre I^er^ Courteys, who painted between 1540 and 1570. Three other enamellers bore the same name, and few attributions are certain. Nevertheless, a cup, representing the Judgment of Paris and the Triumph of Diana, have the signature, P. Courteys, 1544.

Pierre Courteys left numerous plates and dishes, nine large plaques in half relief for the Château of Madrid (they are now in the Cluny Museum), and an altarpiece, composed of sixteen plaques, which is in the Louvre.

Bibliography: René Jean, *Les Arts de la Terre,* 3rd part: "L'Émaillerie." Paris, 1911.—P. Lavedan, *Léonard Limousin et les émailleurs français*. Paris, 1913.

**COURTOIS (Jacques).**—French painter and engraver. Born at Saint Hippolyte (Doubs) in 1621; died in Rome, in 1676. This painter of battles lived in Italy for a long time. Towards the end of his life, he became a Jesuit. He then painted pictures of holy subjects. His *Cavalry Charging* (Louvre) is exceedingly spirited.

There are many of his works scattered in European galleries.

**COUSIN (Jean).**—French painter, born at Soucy, near Sens. About 1500-1590. He was geometrician, designer, painter, sculptor and writer. In 1563, he made the decorations for Charles IX's entry into Sens. The only authentic picture which we possess by him is the *Last Judgment* in the Louvre. The drawing shows Florentine influence, but his figures are reduced to the size of miniatures, and the composition is very complicated. His portrait is among the resurrected, to the left. Modern criticism gives Cousin an importance he was very far from having in his own day. He is sometimes considered the first great painter of the French Renaissance. Rather, he was a theorist; the first of modern art critics. His book on perspective, containing engravings by him, and book on portraiture, very learned, and re-edited in the succeeding centuries, prove how closely he studied Michelangelo, and the Florentines. Five portraits of the Bovyer family (Bovyer Collection) are often attributed to him, without proof. Other critics only leave him two, that of J. Bovyer, and that of his own daughter; but very likely he did not paint any of them.

Jean Cousin worked on the tomb of Admiral de Chabot (Louvre), but he certainly did not make the fine figure of the Admiral. To him is also attributed the painted glass of the Sainte Chapelle, Vincennes, and of Sens Cathedral. There is no proof that he was responsible for more than the designs in the Library of the Institute.

Bibliography: Firmin Didot, *Études sur Jean Cousin,* 1872.—J. Guiffrey, *La Famille de Jean Cousin, peintre et verrier du XVI^e^ siècle.* — Montaiglon, *Jean Cousin a-t-il été sculpteur,* Arch. de l'art français, 1881.

**COUSINS (Samuel).**—English engraver, 1801-1887. He was trained by W. Reynolds. Among his engravings may be mentioned: Portrait of Lord Aberdeen, after Lawrence; *The Tithe,* after Landseer; and *The Daughter of Saragossa,* after Wilkie. Cousins was admitted to the Royal Academy in 1835, and became Professor in 1855.

**COUSTOU.**—Family of French sculptors. The father, François Coustou (died in 1690), carved in wood. He married the sister of the sculptor Coysevox, and was the father of the celebrated sculptors, Nicolas and Guillaume Coustou, and grandfather of Guillaume II Coustou.

Coustou (Nicolas), by Largillière.

**—(Nicolas).**—Famous French sculptor (1658-1733), eldest son of François Coustou, born in Lyon. He studied in the studio of Coysevox, his uncle. He won the Prix de Rome in 1682, with a bas-relief. In Rome, he copied the statue of the Emperor Commodius as Hercules (Park of Versailles). He became a member of the Académie Royale in 1693. After making statues of religious subjects, such as the *Prophets* and the *Guardian Angel* (Chapel of St. Jerome, Invalides), *St. Joseph and St. Augustine,* for a convent of Moulins, and an allegorical figure of *Valour* for the tomb of the Maréchal de Créqui (Church of the Jacobins, Paris), he devoted nearly ten years (1700-1710) to the embellishment of the Château of Marly, for Louis XIV.

Nicolas Coustou executed some admirable works: *The Seine* and *The Marne* (Tuileries); *A Resting Huntsman* (Tuileries); two *Nymphs,* and a *Cæsar* (Louvre); *Diana and Endymion, Mercury and Argos, Apollo and Daphne* (Tuileries); and *Tritons, Shepherds, Sphinx,* and *Children.*

He next worked with his brother, Guillaume, at the *Vow of Louis XIII,* in Notre Dame, Paris. His part of the work is the figure of the Virgin holding Christ.

From 1713 to 1715, he made a statue of the Maréchal de Villars, a *Saint Denis,* and a figure of *Minerva* holding a medallion of the Prince of Conti.

For Lyon, his native town, he made a personification of the Saône seated on the back of a Lion, and a Trophy with Minerva, both in bronze (about 1720).

In the last years of his life, he carved some busts—Colbert, d'Argenson, Bignon, and the statue of the Cardinal de Janson (Beauvais). He had a King's pension and was Professor of the Académie Royale.

Bibliography: Cousin de Condamine, *Éloge historique de M. Coustou, sculpteur ordinaire du Roy,* 1737.—A. Jal, *Dict. crit. de Biogr. et d'hist.* Paris, 1867.

**— (Guillaume).**—French sculptor, 1677-1746, brother of Nicolas Coustou. He studied in the studio of Coysevox, his uncle, and won the Prix de Rome in 1697. On arrival in Rome, he was unable to obtain a place of King's pensioner in the academy—it is not known why. Obliged to earn his living, he decided to go to Constantinople, when a friend, Frémin, introduced him to Pierre Legros, who commissioned the young artist for a bas-relief.

Coustou (Guillaume): Marie Leczinska. (Louvre.)

On his return to France he became a member of the Académie, and taught there from 1706 to 1738. He worked for the King at the decorations of Versailles and of Marly. His best known works are: bas-reliefs and stone statues for the Chapel of Versailles (*St. Jerome, St. Augustine,* a *Pietà, Angels,* etc.); *Daphne* (Tuileries); *Louis XIV on horseback,* a bas-relief (restored by Cartier) on the door of the Invalides; the *Rhone,* a magnificent bronze group which, with the *Saône* of his brother Nicolas, decorated the pedestal of the statue of Louis XIV in the Place Bellecour, in Lyon; it is now in the Vestibule of the Hôtel de Ville, of Lyon. Also, *Louis XIII Offering His Sceptre and Crown to the Virgin* (choir of Notre Dame, Paris); the statue of Cardinal Dubois (Saint Roch), which figures on his tomb; *Marie Leczinska* (Louvre); the *Meeting of the Ocean and the Mediterranean;* and, finally, the work which is his chief title to fame, the *Horses of Marly,* two groups which figured on either side of the horse-pond of Marly, and which are now at the entrance to the Champs Elysées. The artist worked on them from 1740 to 1745.

See Pl. 45, Vol. II.

Bibliography: L. Gonse, *Les Chefs d'œuvre des Musées de France.*—D'Argenville, *Vie des fameux Sculpteurs.*

**— (Guillaume II).**—French sculptor, 1716 to 1777, son of Guillaume Coustou. After studying at the French Academy, in Rome, he worked with his father on the famous *Horses of Marly.* His chief individual work is in Sens Cathedral—the allegorical tomb of the Dauphin Louis and of the Dauphine Marie Josèphe de Saxe (1766 to 1777). His art was influenced by the paternal tradition, and still has all the characteristics that belonged to French art, at the beginning of the 18th century, which was always decorative and graceful.

**COUTANCES (La Manche France).**—Town of Normandy, famous for its Cathedral of Notre Dame dating from the 13th century.

See Pls. 1, 48, Vol. I.

**COUTURE (Thomas).**—French painter. Senlis, 1815-1879. He studied under Gros and Delaroche, and, having won a second Prix de Rome, he was able to complete his studies at the Villa Médicis.

In 1841, his *Prodigal Son* was noticed; but the *Thirst for Gold* (1844, Toulouse Museum) scored a great success with the public, although the work was feeble in design, colour and modelling. This first success was followed by the *Romans of the Decadence* (1847—Louvre) which won Couture the name of a great artist. This enormous canvas represents, in the middle of a room, surrounded by columns and statues, Romans reclining on couches in disorder and drunkenness, after a banquet. The figure of a woman in the middle of the picture recalls one of the Parthenon figures. In one corner two personages — philosophers — stand apart, grave and sad. After having been, on the whole, much admired, this picture is now judged, somewhat severely, as being conventional, lacking character and of commonplace execution.

Then he painted an official picture, the *Baptism of the Prince Imperial,* which does not do him any credit; and in St. Eustache, he painted a Chapel of the Virgin, which finished by discouraging him.

Renouncing his art, he retired into the country where he died, embittered, alone, and quite forgotten.

This artist, who was not without

a certain technical facility, began with too much confidence and suddenly lost it. For a time he was the teacher of Manet who soon rebelled against his academism. He left only two good pictures, a *Wandering Minstrel*, dating from his youth (1843), and a *Falconer* (1855). High-spirited and a great talker, he wrote a book of criticism *Entretiens d'atelier* ("Studio Conversations"). See Pl. 57, Vol. II.

**COX (David).**—English painter, 1783-1859. He was born in Birmingham, son of a village blacksmith. After a short stay in London, he went with his family to Hereford, and later to Harborne, near Birmingham. The scrap of landscape he saw from his windows was almost his only field for study. He learned from Constable that a painter may spend his life in one little place and that nature provides inexhaustible themes. His *Treatise on Landscape Painting*, written in 1814, tells us how he understood his art.

**COYPEL (Noël).**—French painter, 1628-1707. He worked for some time in the Louvre, and in the Tuileries, under the direction of Errard. Then Le Brun called him to Versailles where he executed one of the richest ceilings, that of the Salon de Marbre. In the arrangement of the cornice, as a faked balustrade, on which curious spectators are leaning, he imitated Le Brun's inventions in the Ambassadors' Stairway. The most personal works of Noël Coypel are those of a good pupil of Poussin: *Solon Defending His Laws, Trojan Giving Public Audiences* (Louvre). Late in life (about 1704), he had the chance to make a large, monumental painting in the Invalides. His fresco, the *Assumption of the Virgin*, is the work of a singularly vigorous old age.

**— (Antoine).**—French painter, 1661-1722. Son and pupil of the

Coypel (Antoine), self-portrait.

above, he went to Italy early in life, his father having been made Director of the Academy in Rome. Bernini and Maratte encouraged his efforts. Unfortunately, the influence of this last was profound. It is too clearly seen in his figures which, to use Voltaire's word, "grimace" with Italian intensity.

Antoine Coypel returned to France at the age of nineteen. He was just twenty when the Academy of Painting opened its doors to him. For the vault of the Chapel at Versailles, he painted the *Eternal Father in Glory*—an able composition, but lacking in religious inspiration. Then he made a sumptuous decoration for a theatre, representing Esther fainting before Ahasuerus (Louvre). This is already characteristic of the historical painting of the 18th century—picturesque, brilliant and facile.

In 1714, the Academy nominated A. Coypel director. The next year the Duke of Orleans, who had become Regent, gave him the new gallery of the Palais Royal to decorate. Walls and ceilings were gay with an operatic *Æneid* in pleasant colours; and, the times not being very severe, ladies of the Court enjoyed seeing themselves in the guise of goddesses, scantily clad, and gracious.

The Regent was so pleased with Coypel's work that in 1719, he presented him with a carriage, and a pension of fifteen hundred pounds. Moreover, he asked him to give him some painting lessons.

Coypel's influence on the art of his day was considerable. The Académie des Inscriptions asked him to make the designs for the medals of Louis XIV, which it was ordered to strike. He composed Twenty Discourses on Painting (Paris—Collombat, 1721).

Bibliography: Pierre Marcel, *La Peinture française au début du XVIIIe siècle*. 1906.

**— (Charles Antoine).**—French painter, 1694-1752. Son of Antoine, like him, Painter to the King and Director of the Academy, he was the last of this dynasty of Coypel, which succeeded Le Brun and Mignard in their official functions. He had a leaning for genre subjects, and, like all the historical painters of his time, he brought "grand" themes to that measure. In the Church of St. Merri is a *Supper at Emmaus* by him, which is chiefly attractive for its harmonious colour. He affected the tones of the

Coypel (Charles Antoine): (Tapestry from the series of "Don Quixote"). Entrance of the Shepherdesses.

school of Rubens, thus conforming with the tendencies of his father, who preferred Flemish realism to Italian idealism. He is particularly happy in scenes with children, or in comic compositions taken from Cervantes or from Molière. The Château of Compiègne has twenty-five little pictures by him, of the adventures of Don Quixote. The drawings after Molière are very much in the master's spirit. He himself was endowed with the sense of comedy, and he wrote several plays for the Italian theatre, which were never printed.

Bibliography: Pierre Marcel, *La Peinture française au début du XVIIIe siècle*. 1906.

**COYSEVOX (Antoine).**—French sculptor. Lyon, 1640—Paris, 1720.

Coysevox, by H. Rigaud.

He went to Paris in 1657 and studied with the sculptor Louis Lerambert. He stayed in Alsace, and in Lyon, and finally settled in Paris in the year 1677: he was then thirty-seven. From that time he was associated with all the great decorative works at Versailles, being first of all employed on secondary tasks: statues for the façade of the château, trophies on the grand staircase, and ornaments in the Galerie des Glaces. Already, however, he had made busts of Le Brun and of the King (1681). In 1683, with the equestrian bas-relief of Louis XIV (Salon de la Guerre), he began

Coysevox: Bust of Mansart.

more important works, and his reputation was established. If the paintings in this salon are unworthy of Le Brun, the mural sculptures proclaim Antoine Coysevox's mastership. The large oval bas-relief, representing the King galloping over his conquered enemies, is a very lively work. In the same Salon, on the frames of the four doors, motifs in gilded metal enframing the monogram of the King, show Coysevox's skill at ornamentation.

The same year, 1683, the artist collaborated with Tuby in a group of *France Triumphant*; he carved the delightful *Nymph with a*

Coysevox: The Garonne. (Versailles.)

*Shell* (the original is now in the Louvre), which is very youthful and very French in its interpretation of the antique; he made portraits of Michel and of Maurice le Tellier, and of the Queen Marie Thérèse. In 1685, he worked on the tomb of Colbert, in Saint Eustache.

In 1686, he made the *Crouching Venus*, and the bust of Louis XIV (Dijon). In 1689, he sculptured the Louis XIV in Roman dress (Musée Carnavalet); and in 1692 he made the monumental tomb of Mazarin (Louvre), destined for the Chapel of the Collège des Quatre Nations.

Coysevox now worked for Marly. He executed two winged horses, one bearing Fame, and the other Mercury. These works are now at the entrance to the Gardens of the Tuileries. The tendency towards realism, which is indicated in his admirable busts, is manifest in the equestrian statue of Louis XIV, for which he was commissioned by States of Brittany; he studied the finest horses in the King's stables, he consulted equerries about the attitudes and movements of horses, he even dissected in order to understand better the play of muscles and bones.

He worked at Sceaux for Colbert, of whom he left a fine, melancholy bust (Versailles). At Petit Bourg, of the residence of the Duc d'Antin, he sculptured that delightful figure of Adélaïde de Savoie, Duchess of Burgundy, "passing through the woods with her dogs," in the guise of Diana (Louvre). The work quivers with life and tenderness, and one feels that this time, more than ever, Coysevox was in love with his task.

One thing should be noted. What gives Coysevox's statues so much value is the fact that the artist made them entirely himself. He alone carved and finished them.

He made innumerable busts—those of: Louis XIV, Colbert, Mansard, Le Brun, Le Nôtre, the Cardinal de Bouillon, Louis XV, etc., etc. All have a nervous distinction. Beneath the periwig and the lace jabot, the types are always strongly and finely marked. But finest of all is the bust of Condé. Nothing is more vivacious than this bronze. There indeed is the keen expression —the beak-like nose—the restless neck of the conqueror of Rocroy. This bust, one of the finest in all French sculpture, might well be considered as the masterpiece of Antoine Coysevox.

Coysevox died in Paris in 1720, at the age of eighty-one, "having worked till the age of eighty with the same ardour."

See Pl. 41, Vol. II.

Bibliography: Fermeltuis, *Éloge de Coysevox*. Paris, 1721.—H. Jouin, *Antoine Coysevox*. Paris, 1883.—Stanislas Lami, *Dictionnaire des Sculpteurs français*. Paris, 1908.

**COZENS (John Robert).**—English painter (1752-1797), son and pupil of Alexander Cozens (born in Russia, died 1786); visited the continent in 1776-1779 and again in 1782. His water colour landscapes entitle him to a very high rank in the English water colour school. Constable, who admired him greatly, said of Cozens that he was "all poetry." He is well represented in the Victoria and Albert Museum. During the last three years of his life he was insane.

**COZZARELLI (Giacomo).**—Sienese architect and sculptor, 1453-1515. Pupil of Francesco di Giorgio, with whom he worked on the ceiling of the Osservanza. He made a great many statues of saints, some in terra cotta, some in wood.

His chief statues are a *St. John the Evangelist*, in the Opera del Duomo of Siena; a *St. Vincent*, in Santo Spirito; a *St. Nicholas*, in Sant'Agostino; a *St. Sigismond* in terra cotta, in the Church of the Carmine; and the terra cotta *Pietà* in the Museo Artistico Industriale in Rome.

According to a tradition, he built the Palazzo Magnifico, in Siena, and other buildings.

— **(Guidoccio).**—Sienese painter, 1450-1516. Assistant and follower of Matteo di Giovanni.

**CRACKLE WARE.**—See Ceramic.

**CRAESBECK.**—Flemish painter, born at Neerlinter (Brabant), about 1605; died at Brussels before 1661. He went to Antwerp about 1631, and there set up as a baker. He was very fond of painting, was intimate with Brouwer, and frequented the taverns with him. He imitated his style and, with much less talent, painted scenes of drinkers, smokers, and beggars. His two best pictures are: *Craesbeck Painting a Portrait* (Louvre), and *Craesbeck Painting a Group* (Arenberg Collection, Brussels).

**CRAM (Ralph Adams).**—Contemporary American architect. He was born 16th December 1863 at Hampton Falls, Minnesota. He was educated at the Phillips Academy, Exeter, N. H., and the Westford, Massachusetts, Academy. He learned the rudiments of architecture by working in the office of Rotch and Tilden in Boston and then spent two years as the art critic of the *Boston Transcript.* In 1889 with Charles Francis Wentworth he formed the firm of Cram and Wentworth. Three years later Bertram Goodhue joined them and the firm was then known as Cram, Wentworth and Goodhue. After Wentworth's death it became Cram, Goodhue and Ferguson and when Goodhue resigned from the firm in 1914 it took on its present name of Cram and Ferguson. Cram's desire was to find some architecture more suited to modern American conditions than the Richardson Romanesque which was then prevalent. He found his solution in the English Gothic style as it would have developed logically but for the break caused by the Reformation. It was not an attempt to make exact copies of medieval architecture but rather to try to revive the exact spirit of the buildings as they were adapted to various conditions of living. Quite naturally his greatest field has been that of religious architecture, where modern American churches are constructed after models of the Gothic era whether found in England, France, or Spain. These include St. Thomas' Church in New York, the chapel of Princeton University, and parts of the Cathedral of St. John the Divine in New York. He also adapted Gothic architecture for scholastic structures, where it has become known as "collegiate Gothic." Among the buildings erected in this style are some of the buildings of the United States Military Academy at West Point, New York, and the Graduate College at Princeton University. The firm of Cram and Ferguson has also made structures in other architectural styles, such as Sweetbriar College which is Colonial; Rice Institute at Houston, Texas, which is modified Byzantine; and the National Life Insurance Building in Montpelier, Vermont, which is classic. Other buildings designed by this firm include Phillips Academy at Exeter, New Hampshire, Wheaton College at Norton, Massachusetts, and the Federal Building in Boston. Mr. Cram is the author of a number of books on architecture and related subjects, which include *The Ruined Abbeys of Great Britain* and *The Substance of Gothic.* He is a Fellow of the American Institute of Architects and a member of the National Institute of Arts and Letters.

BIBLIOGRAPHY: *Ralph Adams Cram, Cram and Ferguson,* Contemporary American Architects Series, 1931.

**CRANACH (Lucas).**—German painter, 1472-1553. The name of Cranach represents less the personality of Lucas Cranach than an atelier composed of Lucas Cranach, his two sons and of numerous apprentices. It is very difficult to pick out his own productions.

We know almost nothing of the first thirty years of his life. He may have been his father's pupil. In 1503, he went to Austria, and painted the first works we know to be by him: the portrait of St. Reuss (Germanic Museum); the *Crucifixion* (1503, Munich Gallery); and the *Repose in Egypt* (1504, Berlin Gallery) which is one of his most charming pictures—a fresh idyll, in a mountainous landscape, with fluttering, light-winged angels. The colour is tender, lively and gay.

In 1505, Cranach went to live at Wittenberg, and entered the service of the Elector of Saxony, Frederick the Wise. For him, he painted frescoes, which are now lost; the triptych of the *Marriage of St. Catherine* (1508, Dresden); and a fine *Venus* (1509, Leningrad). The *Family of the Virgin* (1509, Frankfort Gallery) is one of the last works that can be attributed to him personally.

CRANACH (LUCAS).

After 1510, many of the pictures which came out of his studio were executed by his sons, especially by Hans Cranach who worked much from 1520 to 1537, and by his apprentices. Hans was probably responsible for the numerous little pictures representing Venus and other mythological divinities clad in a transparent gauze scarf and a collar. One of the best known is the *Venus,* in the Frankfort Gallery, a pale, slender little form, with a sly look, and an awkward pose. Cranach's atelier, which sent out these little nudes, also delivered pious pictures to the Reformers, portraits of Luther and his family, and edifying pictures, illustrating verses of the Bible.

Lucas Cranach was not a great artist. He lacks grace; his drawing is soft, often incorrect; and his colour, hard. He succeeded best in his portraits, which are very able.

See Pl. 26, Vol. II.

BIBLIOGRAPHY: Flechsig, *Cranachstudien.* Leipzig, 1900.—Michaelson, *Lucas Cranach.* Leipzig, 1902.—Friedländer, M. J.—Rosenberg, J. *Die Gemälde von Lucas Cranach.* Berlin, 1932.

**CRATER.**—See Greece (Vases).

**CRAWFORD (Thomas).**—American sculptor (1813-1857), a prolific worker in many fields, prominently associated with the decoration of the Capitol at Washington, for which he did the *Armed Liberty,* in bronze, surmounting the dome; the sculptures of the pediment of the Senate Wing; and the pair of bronze doors of the Senate Portico, the bas-reliefs of which symbolize the terrors of war contrasted with the blessings of peace.

**CRAWHALL (Joseph).**—Scottish painter (1860-1913), noted for his skillful renderings of subjects from animal life which betray the influence of the French Impressionists and of Japanese art. He is but sparingly represented in public collections.

**CRAYER (Gaspard de).**—Flemish painter, 1585-1669. Contemporary of Rubens, to whom he owed a great deal. He imitated his boldness, the attitudes of his figures, his brilliant colour. He worked with wonderful facility, but he lacked dramatic power.

His works are very numerous. Many are to be found in the churches of Brussels, and other Belgian towns. Among the best, we mention: a *Madonna with Saints* (Church of Alost); *St. Theresa Receiving a Necklace from the Hands of the Virgin* (Vienna); a *Virgin with Saints* (Antwerp); the *Plague of Milan* (Nancy): the *Assumption* (Brussels); and an equestrian portrait of Philip IV, executed during a visit to Madrid, and which may be that in the Uffizi, attributed to Velázquez.

**CRAYON ENGRAVING.**—See Engraving.

**CREDI (Lorenzo di).**—Florentine painter, born 1459-60, according to a fiscal declaration by his mother in 1480-81, in which she states his age to be twenty-one.

In 1480, Credi is mentioned as working with Verrocchio on a salary of twelve florins a year; and from 1478-85, he collaborated with his master on the execution of the altarpiece for the Cathedral of Pistoia. In 1486, there is further mention of activity in Verrocchio's workshop and the regard in which Verrocchio held his pupil is indicated by his will of 1488 in which he makes Credi his executor and heir (the will was contested by Verrocchio's brother), and expresses the wish that Credi be commissioned to finish his Colleoni monument (Credi passed this commission over to Giovanni d'Andrea di Domenico and it was afterwards carried out by Alessandro Leopardo).

In 1491, Credi is one of the members of a commission to judge the plan for the façade of the Duomo; in 1494 the altarpiece was ordered for the Cappella Mascalzoni in the church of Castello, later called S. Maria Maddalena de' Pazzi, which is now in the Louvre. In 1498 he was asked to give an opinion on the cupola of the Duomo; in 1501, he restores the panel by Fra Angelico in S. Domenico, Fiesole, adding the landscape and throne; in 1504, he gives an opinion as to the site of Michelangelo's David; in 1505, judges, with Perugino and Giovanni delle Corniole, the mosaic competition between Davide Ghirlandaio and Monte di Giovanni; in 1507, with Albertinelli and others estimates the Vision of St. Bernard by Fra Bartolommeo; in 1508, paints the wood crucifix by Benedetto da Majano for the Duomo. In 1510 there is a document of payment for the *Madonna and Four Saints* painted for the Spedale del Ceppo in Pistoia, now in Sta. Maria delle Grazie (also del Letto); and in 1510 the *St. Bartholomew* in Or San Michele and the *Adoration of the Shepherds,* formerly in Sta. Chiara, now in the Uffizi, were mentioned by Albertini, as having been done before this date. In 1513, Credi was arbiter in a disagreement between Davide Ghirlandaio and the Operai di SS. Annunziata; in 1514 his opinion was requested regarding paintings by Ridolfo Ghirlandaio in the Palazzo Vecchio; and in 1517, he was asked to estimate the value of a sculpture for the Duomo by Baccio Bandinelli. In 1524, Credi restored the Hawkwood equestrian by Uccello and the Niccolò da Tolentino by Castagno in the Duomo. In 1531 he retired to the hospital of Sta. Maria on a pension, and made his will. He died in 1537.

A rather monotonous and uninspired painter, Credi was an extraordinary technician. His numerous works scattered through the museums and collections of the world are nearly all in perfect state.

BIBLIOGRAPHY: Vasari-Milanesi, IV.—Gualandi, *Memorie,* VI, p. 185. —Gaye, *Carteggio,* I, 367, 372.—Crowe and Cavalcaselle.—Morelli, *Italian Painters, Critical Studies of Their Works.* London, 1882.—Berenson, *Florentine Painters.*—A. Venturi, *Storia d. arte ital.,* VII, I, 797. —Van Marle, *Italian Schools,* XIII, p. 269 ff.

**CRESPI (Daniele).**—Milanese painter, c. 1590-1630. Pupil of Gian Battista, and of G. C. Procaccini. An imitator of the Carracci. The *Last Supper* (Brera) is his best-known picture. He painted in the Certosa of Pavia and in the Ducal Palace, Milan. He died of the plague.

— **(Giovanni, or Gian Battista, known as "il Cerano," because of his birth-place in the province of Novara).**—Milanese painter, 1557-1633. He studied in Venice and in Rome. Then he went to Milan, where he became court painter, and directed the Cathedral works (from 1629). There are numerous frescoes and altarpieces by him in Milanese churches and galleries.

— **(Giuseppe Maria), known as Lo Spagnuolo.**—Bolognese painter, 1665-1747. He worked chiefly in Venice, in an elegant manner, with transparent, silvery colours.

**CRESSENT (Charles).**—See Furniture (Eighteenth Century).

**CRESWICK (Thomas).**—English landscape painter, 1811-1869.

**CRETE.**—At the beginning of the 20th century, sensational discoveries were made by archæologists excavating in the island of Crete. For a long time it had been thought that the civilisation, which the excavations of Troy, Mycenæ and Tiryns had revealed, existed between 2000 and 1000 B.C., and had its centre in Crete, the country of the Keftiu of the Egyptians, the Kaphtor of the Bible. Proof of this has been established by the recent discoveries, especially those of Sir Arthur Evans, at Cnossus (since 1898), and those of Halbherr, at Phaestos. It is now known that this island was, before the year 3300 B.C., in the neolithic period, inhabited by a Mediterranean race, different from that of the Acheans which we know through the sculptures and paintings of Mycenæ. This race then mingled with Asiatic races—with the people of Asia Minor—Hittites, Carians, Lycians, Philistines—and also with African peoples, Egyptians and Lybians. Among the objects brought to light by the excavations, many are Asiatic importations. About 2000 B.C., the population and the art of Crete included elements of various origin, as though the part played by this island was, owing to its geographical situation, that of uniting the various continents.

Cretan civilisation appears to have been very brilliant from the 20th to the 15th centuries B.C. There are many traces of this in history and legend. The Greeks made many allusions to King Minos and his palace with the labyrinth. It was Minos who founded the Cretan Empire, subdued the whole of the island, and extended his authority afar in the islands and to the borders of continents. He founded colonies in Asia, in Sicily, and as far as Gaul. To this brilliant period belong, no doubt, the events which one can try to unravel in the legends of Daedalus, Icarus, the Minotaur, Theseus, etc. It seems that this Minoan civilisation was different from, and opposed to, that of the inhabitants of Greece. The Achaeans first invaded Crete about 1400 and burned the Palace of Cnossus. A second invasion, that of the Dorians in the 11th century, brought about the ruin of the Cretan Empire. Homer called Crete the island of a hundred towns, which is explained by the old subdivision of the Empire of Minos. From that time, Crete never recovered her independence, and her civilisation is mingled with Hellenism.

It was only at the end of the 19th century that the enfranchisement of Crete, until then under the control of Turkey, made archæological excavations possible. As a result of excavations on the Island, it became clear that the Mycenæan civilisation, revealed by the work of Schliemann, had its origin in the Cretan civilisation.

The most important of these excavations are those of Sir Arthur Evans, at Cnossus; those of the Italian Mission, at Phaestus; those of the French School, at Lato; and finally those of the Americans at Gournia, Vasiliki and Palaikastro.

*Cnossus.*—This central town on the southern side of the island, was the residence of King Minos about the 18th century before our era.

There, Sir Arthur Evans brought to light the foundations of an immense palace. The plan of this palace, with its irregular façades, recalls those of Assyrian and Sumerian palaces. It is separated from the external world by huge, strong walls. Nevertheless, it is not fortified, as were the Acropolises of Mycenæ and Tiryns. The rooms opened into interior courts. The masonry is of ashlar with earth mortar; the foundations are of stone. Wood is used also. Floors and ceilings were plastered with cement; and walls were covered with stucco, and painted with frescoes. The angles of the walls were protected by woodwork. The columns which supported the wooden roofs were, like the Mycenæan columns, of wood and narrower at the bottom than at the top. On the whole, then, the method of construction is the same as at Mycenæ and Tiryns: cut stone at the base; walls of light materials, and a great deal of wood for the upper parts.

The plan of the palace is not easy to explain. However, it is believed that, as in the Asiatic palaces, it was divided into several different quarters: in the west wing were the royal apartments, and storerooms; the south-west wing enclosed the sanctuaries; the eastern wing was chiefly for women, and domestic servants; but there seems to have been women's apartments in other quarters of the palace also.

Among the oldest parts revealed by Sir Arthur Evans, must be mentioned: at the north-west, deep secret dungeons, which doubtless served as prisons; the throne-room, which was decorated with paintings, and which still has a throne of sculptured stone, though the forms indicated that this is the copy of a wooden one. Near the King's apartments, all along a corridor, 50 metres in length, are shops or treasuries—nineteen long, narrow cells. In some of these were still found large earthenware jars, made to contain oil, wine or vegetables. Everywhere is engraved the sign of the double axe, the significance of which we shall see later. On the walls of these cells are traces of fire.

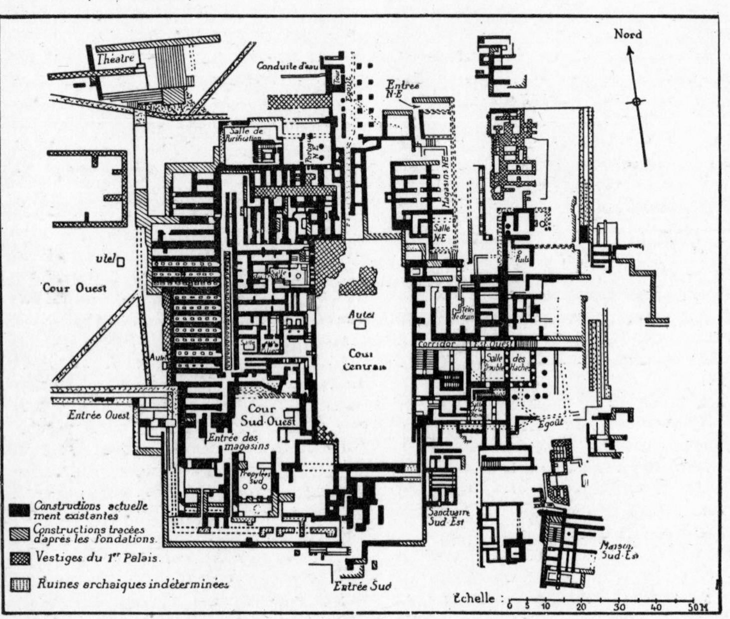


Plan of the Palace of Phaestos. Crete.

In the south wing was discovered a domestic sanctuary, a "chapel with idols or palace gods, with a tripod, small figures, double axes, and consecration horns, placed on three shelves of clay and sand." Near by is a sacred bath for the use of the priest before the ceremony.

In the east wing, or women's quarter, is a child's bathroom, and next to the large court, a lavatory with a drain.

A hundred metres away stood a villa, a kind of terrace in a garden, which was reached by an exterior staircase. The ground floor formed a large room, measuring 11 metres 50 by 4 metres 55, with a niche for the King's throne.

In a neighbouring Minoan town, over a hundred tombs were found cut into the rock. Near Candia, on the plateau of Isopata, was found a royal tomb with a dome, which dates from the 15th century before our era, and which is perhaps the legendary tomb of Idomeneus, grandson of Minos. Like the Mycenæan tombs, it is composed of an avenue or dromos, a quadrangular vestibule, and a vaulted, rectangular chamber. But the vault has fallen.

Some statuettes were found, which are now exhibited in the Cnossus Museum. They show Egyptian origin, which proves the relations between Crete and Egypt about the year 2000 B.C. Statues of women in enamelled porcelain represent priestesses; they wear dresses cut very low, with a very tight waist, and a high tiara on their heads. These little votive figures are among the most curious found at Cnossus. A very life-like bull's head in painted plaster is also noteworthy, also vases decorated with reliefs. One of these vases, found at Phaestus, is in black steatite, and is known as the *Harvesters' Vase.* The bas-relief figures which decorate it represent reapers or haymakers carrying long pitchforks. They walk in procession, preceded by three singers of Libyan type, and a sistrum player. They wear caps and short drawers. The work is amazingly truthful and animated.

But the fragments of painting have awakened still more interest by their astonishing vivacity. These remains of frescoes generally represent religious ceremonies. One, for instance, shows a group of women, seated on a bank, under some trees. The modernism of the dress and the attitudes are surprising. This lively sketch shows us an art which is entirely different from the hieratic art of Asia. Even the costume and the way the hair is arranged show that we are already in Europe, even in a Europe already modern. On the other hand, a figure of a vase-bearer, of life-size, is painted in the reddish colour that the Egyptians used for men's flesh, and has a more stylised silhouette, with wide shoulders and a narrow waist. The bull is often in evidence both in the painting and sculpture of Cnossus. One composition shows a bull-fighting scene, which recalls the one discovered at Tiryns. A bull is thrown at a gallop; a man, jumping over the beast, makes a dangerous leap; behind, a woman, painted in yellow according to the Egyptian convention (just as the man is painted in red), seems to await the moment of his touching the ground; while another woman in front of the animal seems ready to jump in her turn.

We may also mention a funeral urn found at Phaestus (Hagia Triada), which belongs to the same style and the same period as the works of Cnossus. It dates from the end of the 14th century. It is decorated with paintings, representing religious scenes. There are divinities and priestesses in chariots drawn by other divinities and griffins. On one of the sides is represented a funeral sacrifice of a bull, whose blood flows into a vase. All round are priestesses in ritual costume, with the accessories which have a part in this religious scene. On another side one sees three men bearing their offerings to the dead, who is represented standing near a tree, before the door of a tomb in the Mycenæan style.

The Harvesters' Vase.

Finally, in the Palace of Cnossus frequent representations of the double axe were discovered. In neolithic times there may have been a religious cult centering around stone axes. This axe is called, in the Carian tongue, "labrys." It has been suggested that the name of "labyrinth" was derived from it. The Palace of Cnossus was, then, the Palace of the double-axe or labyrinth. The word had another meaning for the Greeks, by reason of the extreme complexity of its plan. Its twistings and turnings, and, moreover, the bull-worship which seems to have been practised there, suggested to the Greeks the legends of the Labyrinth, of the Minotaur, of Ariadne, and of Theseus guided by the thread of Ariadne. This fabulous animal, the Minotaur, half man and half bull, recalls a time when the Cretans still gave their divinities the forms of animals.

Certain archæologists have not only seen, at Cnossus, signs which link this civilisation to that of Greece and of Egypt; they believe they have found elements which prove its kinship with the beliefs of the peoples of Europe, such as the cult-buckle in the form of a figure "8" which recalls the buckles of the Palians in Rome, and even the double axe, which sends us back to a prehistoric worship in the neolithic age.

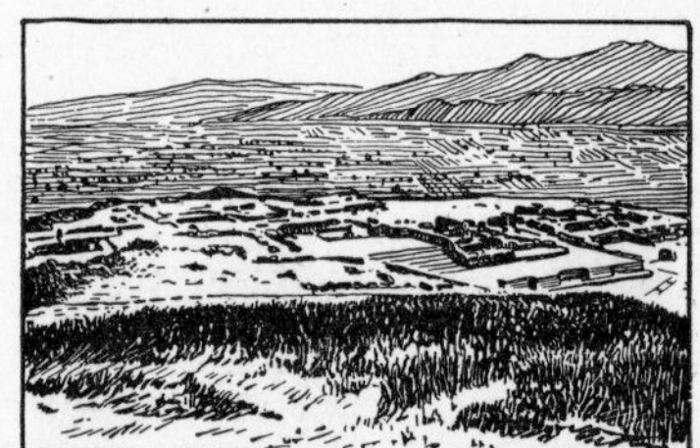

Palace of Phaestus, bird's-eye view.

*Phaestus.*—Phaestus is one of the oldest towns of Crete. It is mentioned by Homer. Its foundation was attributed to Minos. A palace has been discovered there, which has been investigated since 1900 by the Italian mission of Halbherr and Pernier. There, as at Cnossus, several layers of architectural ruins can be distinguished. Above the neolithic constructions, are the remains of a palace, dating from the 20th century, B.C., and above this remains of another palace which as built on the ruins of the preceding one, about the 16th century. hough more regular, and of less ast proportions, the plan seems to eproduce that of Cnossus. It was uilt of finer materials. The palace uildings enclose a vast court, of 6 metres 50 by 22 metres 30. On he west was the official quarter, cut 1 two by the principal entrance, which separated the guest-rooms, ellars and workshops from the state partments. The entrance was by he west gateway (one column in he middle, in the Cretan manner), nd penetrated into a vast hall which led into the interior court, nd communicated with the storeooms. These storerooms, as at nossus, are adjacent cells opening nto the same corridor. Staircases ed to a large state apartment. The orth wing was the private quarter r gynæcium; it is separated from he state apartments by a large eristyle, placed on a higher level. The rooms of the gynæcium opened n to a small interior court. Of the hird wing, on the east, nothing is eft but the remains of serviceooms, cisterns, tiny courtyards and veranda. The objects which were ound in the Palace of Phaestus are xhibited in the Museum of Candia.

*Hagia Triada*.—Not far from the Palace of Phaestus, Halbherr and Pernier also explored a palace nown as the Villa of Hagia Triada, which was no doubt built by some vassal prince of the Kings of Phaestus. Here again the superimposed buildings of two periods are distinguishable: a first palace of very complicated plan seems to date from the 18th century. It is composed of two blocks of buildings, placed at right angles. Here were found some of the most precious works of Minoan art that have come down to us, in particular three steatite vases, including the famous Reapers' Vase (see above), frescoes, clay tablets, and candelabra. All these objects are now in the Museum of Candia. This palace was destroyed at the time of the invasion of the Achaeans, about 1450.

The remains of a more recent building, dating from the end of the 15th century, were also recognised. These are the foundations of a large building of the Mycenæan period, a megaron, or temple. In the neighbourhood were discovered the remains of a straggling village, and, 100 metres away, a domed tomb, and a small square hold which contained the rectangular, painted sarcophagus, which is in the Candia Museum.

Also at Dikté, statuettes, double axes, and fragments from the Minoan and Mycenæan periods, were found in the sacred cave, discovered in 1883, and which was the centre of the worship of Mother Earth (Dictynna) and of the Cretan Zeus, before the arrival of the Dorians.

The excavations of Lato, conducted by Sir Arthur Evans, and by the French School, led to the discovery of an important collection of ramparts, houses, shops and temples from the 6th to the 3rd centuries B.C. In the village of Gourina, American excavations from 1901 to 1904 uncovered a town, "a very Minoan Pompeii, dating from 1700 to 1500 B.C."

All these recent discoveries have laid bare a Cretan civilisation anterior to the civilisation of Mycenæ, which is derived from it. Archæologists are not at all in agreement concerning the origin of this civilisation. Perhaps the greatest light will come to us from its inscriptions which cannot yet be read. The characters are almost Egyptian, according to Sir Arthur Evans. Monsieur Salomon Reinach, on the other hand, thinks they appear Greek, and hence European. This last opinion tends to attach Minoan civilisation to European progress after the neolithic age. Nevertheless, it is very difficult to consider this Cretan civilisation as absolutely independent of Egypt and of Sumer. Until more is known, it must be assumed that Crete received various influences, but that she added to them her own genius. There was, then, an original Cretan civilisation, which expanded in numerous directions. The Mycenæan civilisation was doubtless imported from Crete.

Bibliography: Burrows, *Discoveries in Crete*. 1907.—Mosso, *Palaces of Crete*. 1907.—Lagrange, *La Crete ancienne*. 1908.—Dussaud, *Les civilisations préhelléniques dans le bassin de la mer Elgée*. 1910.—A. Mosso, *The Dawn of Mediterranean Civilisation*. 1910.—Sir A. J. Evans, *The Palace of Minos, a comparative account of the successive stages of a Cretan civilization, etc.* 1921.

**CRIBLÉE.**—See Engraving.

**CRISTOFORO (Tommaso di).**—See Masolino.

**CRIVELLI (Carlo).**—Venetian painter, born 1430-35; died 1495; active in Venice and in the Marches.

Carlo Crivelli is first mentioned in Venice in 1457, at which time he was brought before the Venetian courts on a charge of adultery. It may be that he left Venice immediately after this incident, for he is not recorded in any Venetian documents and he evidently spent considerable time in Padua, whose school exercised a profound influence upon his style. From records and from the dispersion of his paintings it is obvious that he spent most of his maturity as an itinerant painter through the small towns of the Marches, where his art was very highly appreciated and had a widely extended influence upon the development of local schools, even into Umbria.

His activity in the Marches begins with a polyptych of 1468 ordered for Massa Fermana. In 1470 he was in Fermo; and in 1473 he was entrusted with paintings in the Duomo of Ascoli. He was still in Ascoli in 1478 and appears there again, according to a document, in 1484. In 1487 he was back in Fermo; and from 1486-88 he produced an ancona (unidentified) for the Chiesa di S. Lorezo di Castello in Palmiano. From 1488 dates the altarpiece for the Church of S. Pietro degli Osservanti in Camerino. In 1490 Crivelli was raised by Ferdinand II of Capua to the rank of *Miles*, a title which he proudly adds to his signature on the paintings following this date. On the *Madonna della Candeletta* in the Brera (c. 1498) appears the even prouder title *Eques laureatus*.

In the Museum in Verona is a signed *Madonna*, chief work of his Venetian period; another early work is the signed *Pietà with St. Jerome and a Martyr* in Berlin. The works which follow his Paduan period are: the 1468 ancona with predella in the Municipio at Massa Fermana; the 1470 *Macerata Madonna*; the 1476 altarpiece in thirteen compartments (the Madonna only is of 1476, other figures later) painted for S. Domenico, Ascoli; the 1477 *Beato Giacomo della Marca* with two donors now in Paris; the 1481 polyptych in the Vatican, in the execution of which he was assisted, particularly by Vittorio Crivelli; the 1482 *Vatican Madonna* and the *Brera Madonna* of the same date; the 1485 *Boston Pietà*; the 1486 *London Annunciation*. Among his late works, signed "Miles," are: the 1490 *London Madonna with Sebastian and Jerome*, the *Madonna della Rondine*, formerly in S. Francesco at Matelica; the 1491 *Madonna with Francis and Sebastian and a Donor* in London; the 1492 *Madonna in Ecstasy* in London, from S. Francesco, Rimini; and the 1493 *Brera Coronation*, chief work of his late period. After 1493 are the previously mentioned Madonna della Candeletta, signed "Eques laureatus"; and side pieces of four Saints, in a damaged condition, in the Venice Academy.

Bibliography: C. Ridolfi, *Le Marav. dell Arte*, 1648, 2, p. 49.—Tullio Lazari, *Ascoli in Prospettiva*, 1724, pp. 11, 12, 74, 76, 87, 89.—Bald. Orsini, *Descriz. di Ascoli*, 1790, pp. 7, 40, 44, 61, 70, 171, 183, 184, 214.—Em. Cicogna, *Iscriz. Venez.*, 1827, II, 411-12.—Cantalamessa-Carboni, *Dei letterati ed. art. ascol.*, 1830, p. 115 ff.—Ricci, *Memor. istor. della Marca di Ancona*, 1834, I, 205 ff.—Crowe and Cavalcaselle.—Berenson, *Venetian Painters of the Ren.*, 1894, 191 f.—G. Rushforth, *Carlo Crivelli*, 1900.—Berenson, *Study and Crit. of Ital. Art*, 1901, I, 101 ff.—L. Venturi, *Le origini della pitt. venez.*, 1907, p. 187 ff.—Testi, *Storia d. pitt. venez.*, II, 555-691.

**— (Vittorio).**—Venetian painter, possibly the brother, and certainly the pupil and close imitator of Carlo Crivelli. Active according to documents in the Marches from 1481 to 1501.

Vittorio's chief work is the *Torre di Palme*, S. Agostino, polyptych, formerly attributed to Carlo (1487). In 1489 he signed and dated the *Monte San Martino Madonna del Pozzo*; and from 1490 dates the polyptych in Monte San Martino. More of Vittorio's pictures have remained in the Marches than of Carlo's; they are to be found at Massa Fermana, Monteprandone, Ripatransone, San Elpidio a Mare, San Elpidio di Monsanpietro, San Severino.

Bibliography: For literature see Carlo Crivelli.

**CROME (John).**—English painter (1769-1821), known as "Old Crome." He was the founder of the Norwich school of landscape painting. Norwich was his native town, and he lived there all his life. He was completely isolated from contemporary England. He did not know the name of Turner, or Wilson, or perhaps even Gainsborough. His work was uninfluenced by his contemporaries. He earned his living by giving drawing lessons in the rich families of the neighbouring country; and he thus had a chance of seeing many Dutch pictures, the only works which had a part in forming his talent. Towards the end of his life, he became acquainted with Paris. Crome painted Norfolk scenes with great sincerity: oak-trees beaten by the storm, old woods, fishermen's huts, lonely ponds, and misty swamps. To every tree he gave its own character. Some of his oaks are wonderfully expressive.

Crome began as a labourer, and died a humble citizen. His leisure was passed in the society of sailors, shopkeepers and artisans. In 1805, he founded in Norwich, far from all academies, a society of artists which gave annual exhibitions. Cotman, the young Crome, Stark and Vincent are the principal representatives of this vigorous Norwich school, and through them the name of this town became as well known as Delft and Haarlem had been formerly.

**CROMLECH.**—See Dolmen.

**CRUICKSHANK (George).**—English draughtsman (1792-1878) famous for his many vivid political cartoons and also as a prolific and imaginative book illustrator.

Bibliography: G. W. Reid, *Descriptive Catalogue of the Works of G. C.* London, 1871.

**CSÓK (István, or Stephen).**—Hungarian painter, born in 1865. He studied with Székely in 1883, in 1886 he went to Munich to Lotz and two years later we find him in Paris in the atelier of Bouguereau and Robert Fleury. His early works as *Communion* (1890) are reminiscent of Bastine-Lepage's naturalism; but soon he became interested in impressionism and *Orpheus* (1894) already shows his *Plein-air* tendencies and the impressionistic technique. It was also during this time that he painted several historic compositions as *Elizabeth Báthory*, a psychological study of a dramatic and strained situation. After 1896, as a member of the Nagybánya art colony in Hungary, his style changed, for a short while he continued to paint in the impressionistic vein and then he was converted to the methods of the Fauves. Despite his experiences in the World War, and other hardships, he still sees the world in rosy colors. Lightness of touch and a sense of humor are present in all of his later works. He paints the apotheosis of the female nude and glorifies the Hungarian country-side. Csók can reproduce the French elegance, wit and finesse with remarkable skill, on the other hand he can recreate the Hungarian rural atmosphere with equal ability, as seen in *Godfather at Breakfast*. His formerly glowing colors have become more mellow and silvery, the erstwhile erotic mood is more melodious, and the former bravura of technique has recently also subsided. He is represented in several museums and private collections.

Bibliography: Genthon, *Uj magyar festömüvészet*, 1935.

**CTESIPHON (Mesopotamia).**—*Palace*. Sassanian, 6th century A.D., now in ruins. It was an oblong block, with a great central catenary vaulted room. The vault was buttressed on either side by walls of masonry, which divided the lateral areas into many rooms. The vault appeared on the façade as a great arch, which was flanked on either side by ranges of blind arcades and colonnades. The construction was of brick. Also known as the *Tag-i-Kisra*.

**CUBISM.**—Movement begun around 1910 by Picasso and Braque in revolt against representational art, especially that of the Impressionists. Its object is to convey ideas through abstract forms based upon architecture and three-dimensional geometry. See Braque; Léger; Picasso.

**CUVILLIÈS (François de) 1698-1768.**—German architect and author of the Nymphenburg, Munich; Amalienburg; and the Archbishop's Palace, Munich.

**CUYP (Aelbert).**—Dutch painter, 1620-1691, of Dordrecht. Cuyp composed large, well-balanced pictures, with solidly painted figures which stand powerfully against backgrounds of golden light. He was equally happy in his renderings of the tranquil life of the fields, honest citizens and lively cavaliers.

Among his best pictures are: the *Promenade* (Louvre) of Dordrecht citizens, with a luminous background; *Moonlight on the Sea* (late Six Collection, Amsterdam), a wonderful nocturne; *Landscape* (Louvre), with cows grazing and, again, a golden light; *Dapple-grey Horses* (Rotterdam), which Burger said prevented Géricault from sleeping; a *Cock and a Hen* (Rotterdam); the *Mussel-Eater* (Rotterdam), a pretty genre scene; the *Storm* (Louvre); and *View of Dordrecht* (Amsterdam).

See Pl. 37, Vol. II.

**CYLIX.**—Greek drinking cup with two handles.

**CYPRUS.**—The island of Cyprus was probably the first colony

Coin from Cyprus.

founded by the Phœnicians, who were the great travellers and traders of antiquity. Throughout its history, however, it has been subject to alien influences, Greek as well as Phœnician. Its oldest monuments are tombs, which were discovered for the first time by Di Cesnola, in the region of Idalium and Alambra. They have the form of an oven; in them the bodies were placed on a bench, without being enclosed in a coffin, and near to them were put quantities of objects —vases, statuettes, utensils of all kinds in engraved or painted pottery. The oldest tombs are those of Alambra; the objects found are very coarsely made. They belong to the eleventh century B.C. Near the village of Athieno, which is sometimes thought to be the site of the

Limestone Stele from Cyprus. (Metropolitan Museum of Art, New York.)

famous temple of Golgoi, some tombs, built about the sixth century, contained sarcophagi decorated with sculpture, and some sculptured steles, of a much more refined art, which had felt the influence of Greece. One of the finest Cyprian steles, or grave-stones, is in the Metropolitan Museum.

Greek and Latin poets sang of the marvels of the temples which the Cyprians had raised to their goddess, Astarte. The temples of Paphos, Amathonte, Idalie and Golgoi were famous throughout the ancient world. Now we scarcely know where they stood. We have, however, some information about the temple of Paphos, which was the most famous of all. Tacitus relates how Titus marvelled at the riches accumulated in the temple; and from a Greek coin we can picture its appearance. In front of the building is a semi-circular court. The façade was formed of a sort of pylon, flanked, on either side, by a portico on a terrace. The temple measured 67 metres long by 50 metres wide. Behind the façade was probably a court, surrounded with porticoes, in which was placed the figure of the goddess. This is the conjecture, very probable, of G. Perrot. Other archæologists have spoken of a cella, and a pronaos, like the Greek temples, but this cannot be proved. As for the statue of the goddess, the beautiful and divine Astarte, it was a simple conical stone, and the head and arms are difficult to distinguish.

Cyprian sculpture, although derived from Phœnician sculpture, has certain differences. In Cyprus, two races mingled, the Syrians and the Greeks, these last being much finer artists than the Phœnicians. Moreover, the soil of Cyprus provided her sculptors with a stone very much easier to carve than the coarse limestone of Syria. The drawback to this stone is its lack of resistance. Almost all Cyprian statues have their contours blunted. One of the characteristics of Cyprian sculpture is the flattening of the human form. Statues are only modelled in the front; the back, almost flat, was placed against a wall.

The artists of Cyprus made many statuettes in bronze and clay. They were inspired by Assyrian art, then by Egyptian art, and, above all, by Greek art, but with more independence than the Phœnicians. The Cyprian style, properly called, is very close to the archaic Greek style, especially in the drapery. The oldest little Cyprian figures come from the town of Alambra. They represent either the goddess of love and fruitfulness, or the god of force, a kind of Hercules, of which the colossus of Amathonte is the most famous. There, too, groups of little figures were found, most of

Vase from Cyprus. (Eugene Piot Collection.)

which are in the Metropolitan Museum.

Cyprian glyptics show no originality: the carved stones represent Egyptian scarabs and Assyrian motives.

On the other hand, in ceramics they produced works far superior to those of the Phœnicians—painted vases of strange, complicated shapes. Some of them represent the bodies of animals or of human beings. Hardly more than two colours were used, a dark brown and a soft red.

# D

**DADDI (Bernardo).**—Florentine painter. The first authentic date of the activity of Bernardo Daddi is that of his matriculation in the guild of Medici e Speziali in the register covering the years 1312-1320; and is mentioned again in the roll for 1320-1353. The signed and dated triptych in the Uffizi, the *Madonna with Matthew and Nicholas*, is of 1328, and is followed by the 1332 signed and dated panel in the Florence Academy, the *Madonna with Peter, Paul, and Angels;* and the 1333 dated tabernacle in the Bigallo, Florence, the *Madonna with Saints and Donors.* In 1335 Daddi is mentioned in the Archivio de' Contratti, and this year is also the date recorded for the altar of San Bernardo. Of 1338 was the lost altarpiece representing three Dominican Saints, once in Sta. Maria Novella. In 1339 Daddi is referred to as one of the "Chonsiglieri" of the Compagnia of S. Luca. 1340 is the date of the lost panel in the choir of Sta. Maria a Quarto; and 1341 that of the high altar in Sta. Maria a Quarto. There is a document of payment recorded, in 1347, from the Compagnia d'Or San Michele for "la detta tauola di nostra donna in prestança." In this same year Daddi is mentioned in the Archivio de' Medici e Speziali, Cod. VIII. In 1348 he did the signed and dated polyptych in the Collection of Major Gambier Parry, Highnam Court, Gloucester, a Crucifixion, eight Saints, etc. His testament is of this year, and he probably died in 1348.

Bernardo Daddi was a master of the greatest importance. A successor of Giotto in time, he inherited little of his bulk or his essentialism. He was a painter of supreme lyrical inspiration, mobility and sweetness, who leaned to the Sienese and the Gothic rather than to Giottesque plastic organization, borrowing as much from Siena as from contemporary sculpture. His miniature exquisiteness and delicacy exercised a profound influence over Florentine painting, an influence which persisted in the School of Orcagna until the end of the century.

He was himself the master of a large school, and works by his pupils and imitators are habitually attributed to Bernardo's own hand. Dr. Richard Offner, in his definitive work on Daddi, has isolated the following works as by the master:

Altenburg, Museum, Crucifixion and tabernacle with the Madonna and Child with Saints and Angels, Nativity, and Crucifixion; Bayonne, Musée, part of a tabernacle, *Annunciate Virgin*; Crespina, S. Michele, the *Archangel Michael*; Florence, Sta. Croce, Cappella Pulci-Berardi, frescoes depicting the *Martyrdom of Saints Stephen and Lawrence*; Florence, Or San Michele, Madonna and Child and eight Angels; Florence, Academy, the 1332 Madonna; Florence, Bigallo, the 1333 tabernacle; Florence, Uffizi, the 1328 triptych; Highnam Court, the 1348 polyptych; London, Buckingham Palace, predella-scene, *Marriage of the Virgin;* Naples, Muséo Nazionale, Madonna and Child and four Saints; New Haven, Jarves Collection, predella-scene, *St. Dominic's Vision of SS. Peter and Paul;* New York, Griggs Collection, two panels, scenes from lives of Virgin Martyrs; New York, Georges Wildenstein, *Scene from the Life of St. Barbara;* Paris, Musée des Arts Decoratifs, predella-scene, *St. Peter Martyr Stopping Runaway Horse;* Pisa, Museo, two scenes from the life of St. Cecilia; Ponte a Mensola, Berenson Collection, *Madonna and Child;* Posen Museum, predella-scene, *St. Dominic Rescuing Sailors;* Prato, Galleria, predella, seven scenes from *Legend of Holy Girdle*; Rome, Vatican, eight panels, *Martyrdom of St. Stephen and Removal of His Relics;* Verona, Pinacoteca, *Crucifixion.* The New Haven-Paris-Posen predella probably formed part of the lost Dominican altarpiece, painted in 1338 for Sta. Maria Novella.

Bibliography: Vasari-Milanesi, I, p. 459 ff.—Passerini-Milanesi, *Giornale del Centenario di Dante,* 1865. —Milanesi, *Nuova Antologia,* 1870. —Frey, *Loggia dei Lanzi,* 1885, pp. 61, 315.—Bode, 1888, Gazette des Beaux Arts, I, p. 199.—Milanesi, *Nuovi Documenti,* 1893, pp. 30-31, 49.—Schmarsow, 1897, *Festschrift z. Ehren d. Khst. Inst. zu Florenz,* p. 168 ff.—Vitzthum, *Bernardo Daddi.* Leipzig, 1903.—Crowe and Cavalcaselle, Douglas ed., II, 1903, p. 177 ff.—Siren, *Giotto and Some of His Followers,* 1917, p. 157 ff.—Offner, *A Corpus of Florentine Painting, Bernardo Daddi,* 1930.

**DAGNAN-BOUVERET (Pascal Adolphe Jean).**—French painter, 1852-1929; pupil of Gérôme; influ-

# GREEK VASES

*Greek vases furnish a double interest. First, they are admired for the beauty of their proportions; the potters who made these shaped them in the same refined way that the sculptors shaped the much-admired graceful sweep of the Doric capitals. The Greeks, unlike the Asiatics, did not seek richness of decoration in the material itself or in the metamorphosis of the material by fire. The decoration is of neat sobriety: black glaze on a red ground; the beauty rests in the quality of the design. The great difference between European and Asiatic art lies in the fact that European art seeks expressive form, while Asiatic art prefers richness of material.*

MYCENAEAN VASE. MUSEUM, MARSEILLES.

DECORATED CUP, SIXTH CENTURY. BIBL. NAT. *(Photo by Hachette.)*

AMPHORAE OF THE SIXTH CENTURY. LOUVRE. *(Photo by Hachette.)*

OINOCHOË. LOUVRE.

AMPHORA, SIXTH CENTURY, WITH RED FIGURE DECORATION.

CUP WITHOUT A FOOT: SILENUS AND MAENAD. LOUVRE. *(Photo by Hachette.)*

CUP OF THE FIFTH CENTURY WITH RED FIGURE DECORATION.

EOS CARRYING THE BODY OF MEMNON. (DOURIS.) LOUVRE.

SKYPHOS: BRISEIS RETURNED TO HER FATHER. (HIERON.) LOUVRE.

THESEUS AND THETIS. (EUPHRONIOS.)

Vases preceding the fifth century were decorated with black figures on a red ground. The vases of the fifth century are generally covered with a black glaze, and the isolated figures show the red of the baked clay. The painter-designer ingeniously adapted his live figures to the surfaces but he was so interested in design, that he sacrificed life for ornamentation. These painters often signed their compositions. The paintings reflect the style of Polygnotos.

FUNERAL SCENES DECORATING WHITE LEKYTHI OF ATTICA (LOUVRE).

The white lekythi of Athens deserve special mention. These graceful vases with their tall bodies and slender necks were meant for funerals. They were placed next to the dead, and contained perfume; they were not meant for constant use, so they could be fragile in nature, and the lighter baking allowed the use of a soft polychromy which could not be used with the ordinary vase. The scenes usually represent entombments, or visits to the dead. The colour-scheme may give us an idea of what the murals of Polygnotos might have been like, since these compositions were conceived for a flat surface.

# ANCIENT PAINTING

*The ancients were just as proud of their painters as of their sculptors, and they tell us more often of their paintings than of their sculptures. While a part of the sculpture survived, the paintings have disappeared almost entirely. We can judge of them only by the paintings on Greek vases, and those in the Etruscan tombs of the archaic period before the fifth century. Works of a later date done by the most famous masters were preserved by the cataclysm of Pompeii, and some fragments have been unearthed in the buried houses of ancient Rome, and in the ruins of Egyptian sarcophagi. The masterpieces, however, are missing.*

THE TORTURING OF IXION, POMPEII.
*(Photo by Alinari.)*

MERCURY AND ARGUS, HOUSE OF LIVY, ROME.
*(Photo by Alinari.)*

SACRIFICE OF IPHIGENIA, POMPEII.
*(Photo by Brogi.)*

## Paintings of Pompeii

The murals of Pompeii or of the house of Livy in Rome show us how much painting was dominated by sculpture during antiquity. The compositions resemble groups of statues; each figure is separately modelled, and is constructed to resemble marble or bronze. All that is not sculptural—light and landscape—is of less importance than the play of muscles or the pattern of drapery. The picture representing the *Sacrifice of Iphigenia* is perhaps the famous painting of Timanthos where we can see Agamemnon hiding his face to weep. This pose became emblematic of him.

MARRIAGE SCENE, CALLED THE ALDOBRANDINI MARRIAGE, VATICAN, ROME.
*(Photo by Alinari.)*

This picture is called the *Aldobrandini Marriage*, as it belonged to the Aldobrandini family after it was unearthed early in the seventeenth century. We assume that it is a Roman copy of a lovely Greek work of the fourth century B.C. In the center is the bride, clad in white, listening to final bits of advice; to the right is the groom. On either side young women prepare a bath, chanting an epithalamium. The composition recalls a bas-relief. Poussin copied it, and it exercised a visible influence on his style. Some of the figures are reproductions of famous statues.

PORTRAITS FROM FAYOUM.
*(Photo by Hachette.)*

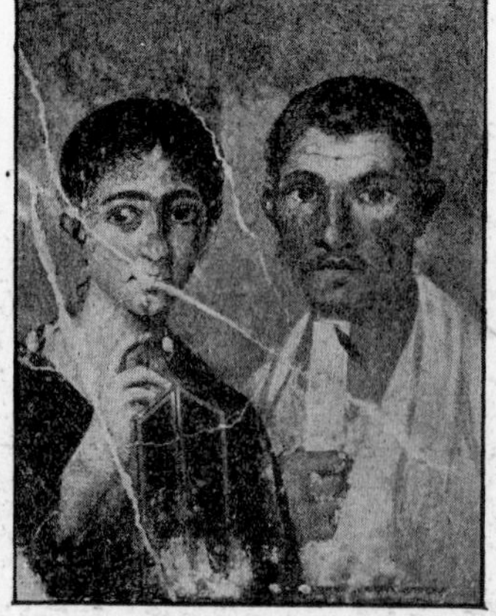

PASQUIUS PROCULUS AND HIS WIFE, POMPEII.
*(Photo by Alinari.)*

PORTRAITS FROM FAYOUM.
*(Photo by Hachette.)*

## Roman and Egyptian Portraits

Romans always painted portraits; at the end of antiquity they tried to reproduce the traits of the human face. At Pompeii, some of these ancient faces look at us with eyes full of life. The portraits of Fayoum are fragments from sarcophagi found in Egypt; they are far from masterpieces, but they evoke better than sculpture the men of antiquity. Thus one can see the rise of this stiff type of painting, which later passed into the Byzantine art, showing faces with enormous eyes and a stupid expression.

# ANCIENT ROME

*The role that the Romans play in the history of art is not as important as that of the Greeks. The Romans did not invent much: we attribute to them neither a new plan for a temple, nor a decorative style, nor even a truly new way of handling the plastic arts. The role of Rome in the political history of the world was more important; as an empire it received impressions in the field of art from its subjects. Rome accepted, seemingly, the forms of Greece, and adapted them. Thus its role in the history of art is primarily to propagate Hellenism to all parts of the Roman Empire. Without the strength of Rome, Hellenism probably would have remained localized, instead of becoming of such universal importance that it covered the Empire.*

ROME: THE APPIAN WAY.
*(Photo by Brogi.)*

ROME: THE FORUM, VIEW OF THE CAPITOLINE HILL.
*(Photo by Brogi.)*

## The Country and the City

For many centuries Rome remained the capital of the Mediterranean world. The highways led from there to all the frontiers of the Empire, that is, to the ends of the then known world. The distances were measured from the milestone placed in the Forum next to the Temple of Saturn (the colonnade on the right in the picture). The aqueducts, now broken, which traversed the desert country brought water from the Appennines to the cities. The monuments of Rome, destroyed during the Middle Ages, have again been brought to light by modern excavators.

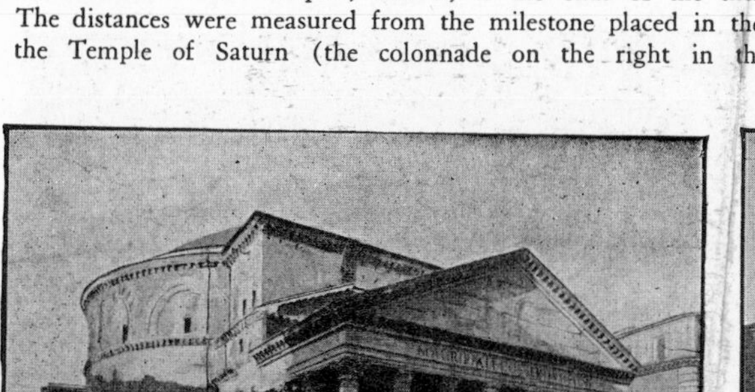

THE PANTHEON. ROME.
*(Photo by Brogi.)*

ARCH OF TITUS.
*(Photo by Brogi.)*

FORUM OF TRAJAN.
*(Photo by Maurel.)*

## Temples and Triumphal Arches

The most beautiful monuments preserved from ancient Rome show how the Romans used Greek art to embellish their own edifices. The Pantheon, dating from the time of Agrippa, with its circular form and domed roof, shows no Greek influence; the approach to it is, however, a peristyle with columns. The entablature and pediment are of the Ionic and Corinthian orders. An arch shows no Greek influence, nor did the Greeks employ the vault, but these arched doorways which one can find in ancient Etruscan cities are framed by Greek columns. The triumphal arches and commemorative columns were built to glorify the Emperors.

BASILICA OF CONSTANTINE.
*(Photo by Alinari.)*

THE BASE OF THE PALATINE.
*(Photo by Maurel.)*

THE COLISEUM.
*(Photo by Maurel.)*

## Roman Masonry

The Romans were skillful masons. The solidity of their gigantic edifices is not due to well-cut and well-adjusted stone blocks, as in the Greek temples, but to a conglomeration of ashlars set into indestructible cement. The advantages of this method are its solidity, and its ability to make large monuments possible. With time these ashlars wear off; wealthy Romans covered them with marble.

# DIFFUSION OF ROMAN ART

*The Roman Empire, by uniting the ancient civilisations under the same law, propagated a uniform art in the Mediterranean world. The Roman took with him his styles and his methods. He superintended the building of comfortable cities with temples, triumphal arches, baths, circuses, and amphitheatres. In different countries his roads traversed the empire, and were maintained during the Middle Ages as highways of commerce. Often aqueducts passed over valleys and brought water to the cities. These great enterprises of Roman genius contributed to the evolution of mediaeval and modern Europe.*

ARENA OF NÎMES.
*(Photo from Mon. Hist.)*

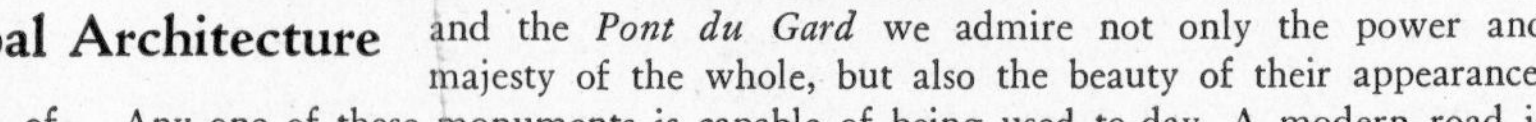

PONT DU GARD.
*(Photo by Hachette.)*

## Municipal Architecture

Among the famous Roman monuments are those of southern France. Arles has the most important ruins of the Gallo-Roman period, while Nîmes has several buildings in a much better state of preservation: the *Arena*, the *Maison Carrée*, and the *Pont du Gard*. In the *Arena* and the *Pont du Gard* we admire not only the power and majesty of the whole, but also the beauty of their appearance. Any one of these monuments is capable of being used to-day. A modern road is built on the lower level of the aqueduct.

REIMS: GATE OF MARS.
*(Photo by Courleux.)*

TRIUMPHAL ARCH AT ORANGE.
*(Photo by Neurdein.)*

NÎMES: MAISON CARRÉE.
*(Photo by Neurdein.)*

## Greek and Roman Architecture

Roman architecture is characterised first of all by its type of masonry: an ashlar of pebbles, with layers of brick and rows of shaped stones. But this makes up merely the body of the building. To adorn it, the Romans borrowed from Greek architecture. On the façades they framed the openings with columns or pilasters, which supported entablatures and pediments. The Greek orders were carried out in Roman masonry. The Romans of the empire preferred from among the Greek orders those which seemed the richest.

ATHENS: TEMPLE OF HADRIAN.
*(Photo by Alinari.)*

TEMPLE OF BAALBEK. (SYRIA.)

TRÈVES: THE BLACK GATE.
*(Photo by Frith.)*

## Roman Art in the Empire

In Greece and the Orient the Romans had to cope with far-removed and long-lived traditions. Greece and Asia had not yet declined, and Roman art had to accommodate itself to local customs. But in the west, in Spain, at the other end of the Empire, the Roman genius could express itself unhampered in military monuments and public works. At the frontier of Germany the Empire accumulated its defense, and the Rhine valley will carry forever the traces of Roman dominance.

enced by Bastien-Lepage and Holbein.

**DAHL (Michael).**—Anglo-Swedish painter (1659-1743). A native of Stockholm, and trained there, he settled in England in 1688, and was much employed as a portrait painter by Queen Anne and the English aristocracy.

BIBLIOGRAPHY: W. Nisser, *Michael Dahl and the Contemporary Swedish School of Painting in England.* Upsala, 1927.

**DALI (Salvador).**—Contemporary Spanish painter. He was born 11th March 1904 in Figueiras, in the district of Catalonia. For a time he attended classes at the Academy of Fine Arts in Madrid, but because of his advanced ideas concerning art and art teaching he was soon asked to leave. Shortly thereafter he went to Paris to work independently and there met and was influenced by the work of the younger artists who were leaders of the new art movements. His present artistic style developed after successive stages of impressionism, divisionism, futurism, constructivism, scientific cubism, magical realism, and abstract irrationalism to surrealism. With some influence of cubism he began subordinating the objects of reality to the literary associations which they brought up in his mind. He was an interpreter rather than a mere imitator of things seen in nature. It was an objective vision as seen by the mind rather than by the eyes, a mind which did not permit of any intervention of will or any attempt to suggest the pictorial side of the composition. His early works were very plastic, like those of Severini, but gradually the poetry of the situations became the important thing, although he did not relinquish the realistic approach to his subject. His pictures are now explained by him as paranoiac dreams, which explanation has come after a study of Freudian psychology. All things are realistic, but the combinations are weird, as if the painter had some inspiration from the work of Hieronymus Bosch, the Dutch painter of the 17th century who delighted in painting phantasmagoria such as his many versions of the Temptation of St. Anthony. Dali's work is eminently of the 20th century in its connotations and the objects therein, portrayed in a clear and revealing light so as to leave no doubt in the mind of the spectator as to his meaning. Beside his paintings Dali has collaborated with Luis Bunuel in the scenarios of two surrealist films: *Le Chien Andalou* and *L'Age d'Or* and illustrated *Les Chants de Maldoror* by the Comte de Lautréamont. He is the author of some articles on surrealism and the book *Babaoua.* In January, 1935, he lectured at the Museum of Modern Art in New York City, his subject being *Surrealist Paintings: Paranoiac Images,* an attempt to explain the motives of his paintings which were on display there at the same time.

BIBLIOGRAPHY: A. Breton, *Le Surréalisme et la Peinture.*—R. Crevel, *Dali ou l'Antiobscurantisme,* 1931.

**DALLIN (Cyrus E.).**—American sculptor, born in 1861, specialized in Indian subjects, among his best known works being the *Medicine Man,* Fairmount Park, Philadelphia, and the *Signal of Peace,* Lincoln Park, Chicago.

**DALMAU (Luis).**—Spanish painter. His birthplace is unknown. He is mentioned for the first time in Valencia in 1428, where he bore the title of Painter to the King's Household, concurrently with Anton Guerau. In September, 1431, he received a hundred gold florins from the treasurer of Alphonso V, to cover the expenses of a journey in the service of the monarch to Flanders, where he arrived a few months later. One may assume that he was sent on this trip in order to study under Jan Van Eyck at Bruges where he also would have seen the famous polyptych of the brothers Van Eyck delivered for the Chapel of the Vydt family at Ghent on May 6, 1432. The date of Dalmau's return to Spain is not known, but it is known that he resided at Barcelona in 1443, when the councillors chose him as "the best and most apt painter who could be sought and found," to paint the altarpiece of their chapel. After signing his large picture, in 1445, Luis Dalmau remained in Barcelona, where he seems to have been occupied with rather modest work, until 1460, when trace of him is lost.

Of this career of thirty years, the only known authentic work which remains is the *Altarpiece of the Virgin of the Barcelona Councillors,* which is now in the Municipal Museum, in its old oak frame, carved by Francesch Gomar. Here one sees St. Andrew and St. Eulalia presenting the five town councillors to the Virgin. The town magistrates are characterized with singular power. This picture, of which the Predella has been lost, shows that Dalmau was a most exact pupil of Jan Van Eyck. "Although one has to give credit to Dalmau for his ambition to approach Jan Van Eyck in this master's objectivity, his work yet seems to be hard and dry. His was only a very estimable—not a great—talent whose importance does not lie in his artistic personality but in the rôle of an intermediary between Flemish and Catalan art" (A. L. Mayer). Dalmau did not dare to attempt the Van Eycks' technical methods but used *tempera.*

See Pl. 2, Vol. II.

BIBLIOGRAPHY: D. S. Sanpere y Miguel, *Los Cuatrocentistas Catalanes.* Barcelona, 1905-1906.—E. Bertaux, *Les Primitifs espagnols. R.A.A.M.,* 1906-1909.—A. Michel, *Histoire de l'Art,* Vol. III, 2nd part. —E. Bertaux, *Peinture espagnole au XIV^e et au XV^e siècle.* Paris, 1908.—L. Tramoyeres y Blasco, *Luis Dalmau.* Cultura esp., 1907. *Thieme-Becker,* Vol. VIII, Leipzig, 1913. Art. *Luis Dalmau* by A. L. Mayer.— A. L. Mayer, *Gesch. der span. Malerei.* Leipzig, 1922.—Ch. R. Post, *A hist. of Span. painting,* Cambridge, Mass., 1935. Vol. VI, Parts I and II.

**DALOU (Aimé Jules).**—French sculptor. Paris, 1838-1902. He was the son of a working glover, an ardent republican, who transmitted his love of the people and of work. While attending the Communal school, the little Dalou made sketches and dabbled with modelling clay. By chance, Carpeaux, still a young student of the École des Beaux-Arts, noticed these attempts and persuaded his parents to send their son to the Petite École, now the École des Arts Decoratifs. While he received, at the Petite École, the teaching of Lecoq de Bois Baudran, whose name is associated with the beginnings of the careers of almost all the best French artists of this period, he was not forgotten by Carpeaux, who took him to his studio, and gave him an excellent training. From the age of fifteen, he gained admission to the École des Beaux-Arts and joined Duret's classes, not, for that reason, leaving Carpeaux whom he always considered as his master. At the Petite École, he had been the comrade of Legros and Fantin-Latour; he was at the École des Beaux Arts at the same time as Barrias. His keenness struck his colleagues, who said "Dalou lunches off a pennyworth of cheese, and a leaf of Plutarch." But he had to earn his pennyworth of cheese. He worked

DALOU.

for clock-makers, engaged himself as modeller to a naturalist, where he earned three or four francs a day. In the evenings, he still found time to go and draw at the Swiss

DALOU: THE EMBROIDERER.

Academy. His friends did not forget him: and hating to see him absorbed by work unworthy of him, they found him work in the Hôtel Païva, which brought him into notice as well as assuring his living. In 1866, while still young, he married. Owing to his devotion, his great character and his intelligence, his wife had a deep and precious influence on his career. The War of 1870 broke out at the time when he won his first success at the Salon with *The Embroiderer,* a mixture of charm and realism which already heralded the talent he developed later.

At the end of the Commune, Dalou had to retire to England, with his wife and child. Thanks to his friend Legros, who was already settled in London, he soon became known and appreciated by English amateurs. He modelled a series of statuettes which bear out the qualities of his *Embroiderer*: the *Peasant Woman* (Sir Coutts Lindsay), and *The Shepherdess,* or *The Rocking-Chair* (Duke of Westminster), the group of the Queen of England (Windsor), and numerous busts. Although he did not know English, he became teacher of modelling at the Royal College of Art. This enabled him to visit Belgium, where Rubens' works gave him a knowledge of himself by revealing a temperament which was akin to his own. Henceforth his art developed in a particular direction, and his works kept traces of the deep impression which the sight of Rubens' paintings had made. Another artist, unknown in France, although French, Roubillac, an eighteenth century sculptor, who only lived in England, where his works abound, also influenced Dalou, by showing him how

DALOU: GROUP FROM THE TOMB OF THE ENGLISH QUEEN'S CHILDREN. (Windsor.)

sculpture could be made lively and vivid and more akin to painting. He was at this stage when the Municipal Council of Paris opened a competition for the erection of a monumental statue of the Republic. Dalou at once set to work. The subject enchanted him. He wrote to his friends: "The monument shall be in the style of Louis XIV, the style I respect above all others." His model, exhibited in Paris, made a stir owing to its power and originality, but it was much criticised. The enemies of all innovation remarked: "This is not sculpture! It is painting!" Dalou only received a "mention," but the Municipal Council voted that Dalou's monument was to be acquired by the city, and set up in Paris.

In the course of 1879, Dalou obtained permission to return to Paris, and he settled in a modest "appartement" in the Avenue du Maine, where he remained till the end of his life, and set about the great work which was to occupy him for eight years, the Monument of the Republic. This colossal work did not absorb Dalou: he continued to produce other works while perfecting this one. Such was the *Fraternity* (Petit Palais), a bas-relief worthy to put beside the *Diogenes* and *Alexander* of Puget, and perhaps Dalou's best work. Conceived in England, it only appeared in France in 1883, with his statue of *Mirabeau Answering Dreux Baézé* (Chambres des Députés). In the *Mirabeau* the figures are full of life and colour; in the *Fraternity* they are grouped easily, and both movements are lively and expressive. A symbolical idea could not be more clearly explained. The correct, broad, brilliant and distinguished treatment make it one of the finest pieces of French sculpture. All one can criticise is a certain uniformity of execution and interest. Dalou had acquired the qualities he admired. He makes one think of Rubens and the great masters of the century of Louis XIV, but he is somewhat lacking in breadth of touch, and, in fact, simplification of decorative unity.

In the *Triumph of the Republic*, he glorified Work by old symbols.

DALOU: TRIUMPH OF THE REPUBLIC. (Place de la Nation, Paris.)

He wanted to represent realistic actions and gestures; and workers of town and country and sea. This piece, which occupied him for a long time, only ended in sketches for the Workers' Monument (Petit Palais), and in a statue, the *Peasant* (Luxembourg). He died without finishing his task. Absorbed by his success, and the commissions which came to him, he had no time to fulfill his dream of becoming the sculptor of the people.

DALOU: MONUMENT TO DELACROIX. (Luxembourg Gardens, Paris.)

To works already mentioned may be added, the Memorial to Delacroix (Luxembourg Gardens); *Silenus* (Luxembourg Gardens); the tomb of Blangin (Père Lachaise); the tomb of Victor Noir (Père Lachaise); the memorial to Alphand (Avenue du Bois de Boulogne), where Dalou represented himself among the figures; bust of Vacquerie (Théâtre Français), etc.

BIBLIOGRAPHY: M. Dreyfous, *Dalou*. 1903.

**DAMASCENE.**—A method of decorating steel by the process of watering which can be controlled so that regular designs are formed. The method was originally applied in the famous Damascus blades.

**DAMASCUS.**—See Pl. 34, Vol. I.

**— (Great Mosque of).**—See Moslem Art; also Pl. 33, Vol. I.

**DANCE OF DEATH.**—See Holbein (Hans, the Younger).

**DANNAT (William T.).**—American painter, born 1853, studied in Paris under Carolus Duran and Munkacsy, won fame in the eighties with a series of scenes from Spanish life; adopted subsequently a more "decorative" method (*La Robe Rouge*, Luxembourg, Paris, 1889). Also a much patronized portrait painter.

**DANNECKER (J H. von).**—German sculptor. 1758-1841. The most representative of that transition period of Neo-Classicism, of which Winckelmann formulated the principles. Dannecker is the sculptor of the *Ariadne*, in the Bethmann Collection, Frankfort. He made an expressive bust of his friend, the poet Schiller.

**DANTI (Vicenzo).** — Florentine sculptor, 1530-1576. He shows a mingling of Roman influence and of the influence of Andrea Sansovino whose *Baptism of Christ*, above Ghiberti's second door to the Baptistry of Florence, he finished. The *Beheading of St. John*, over Andrea Pisano's door, is his own. His other chief works are: the bronze relief of the *Adoration of the Serpent*, in the Bargello; an *Allegory*, in the Boboli Gardens; and a statue of Pope Julius III in Perugia Cathedral.

**DAPHNI (Monastery of), near Athens.**—Its church (11th century) has a square-in-cross plan preceded by a narthex, and has a dome on a sixteen-sided drum. Its Byzantine mosaics are of great beauty, suffering, however, from earthquakes and restoration.

**DARET (Jacques).**—Painter of Tournai; born c. 1404. In 1418, he joined the studio of Robert Campin. In 1432, he became a master, and was nominated Provost of the Guild. Summoned to Arras, in 1441, to design cartoons for tapestries, he stayed there until 1453. The following year he went to Lille to help with the town decoration on the occasion of the celebrations of the "Vœu du Faisan." In 1468, he was in Bruges to take part in, and perhaps even to direct the decorations for the marriage of Charles the Bold. No signed works have come down to us. Parts of an altarpiece which he executed in 1433-35 for the abbot of St. Vaast in Arras are preserved in Berlin.

BIBLIOGRAPHY: Friedländer, M. J., *Altniederl. Malerei*, Vol. II.

**— (Jean).**—Flemish painter and engraver. Born in Brussels, in 1613. Died in Aix, in 1668. He had lived there for thirty years. Like other of his compatriots, this painter's native naturalism was modified by his contact with Provence. Many of his paintings are in Aix and Marseille.

**— (Pierre).**—French painter and engraver. Born in Paris, about 1604; died in the Château of la Luque, near Dax (Landes) in 1678. He made numerous engravings after Jacques Blanchard, Simon Vouet, Guido Reni, and wrote a treatise on engraving.

**DAUBIGNY (Charles François).** —French painter. Born in Paris, February, 1817. Died at Auvers-sur-Oise, February, 1878. His father, a pupil of V. Bertin, exhibited at the Salons landscapes of the surroundings of Paris. He gave his son his first lessons. Then Charles Daubigny worked with Delaroche; then he made the traditional journey to Italy, and stayed there a year. Throughout his life, Daubigny was little attracted to places which evoked memories of lectures or of museums. To the studied composition of historical landscape painting, Daubigny always preferred "the real country, where an honest manure-

DAUBIGNY: SPRING. (Louvre.)

heap is not out of place." Hence his predilection for open-air study.

On his return from Italy, he took up illustration for a living. He made excellent woodcuts, notably the *Ashes of Napoleon I Being Brought Back to Paris*. He made his début as a painter at the Salon of 1838, with a view of Notre Dame

DAUBIGNY: THE BANKS OF THE OISE. (Louvre.)

of Paris, now lost, which was followed, in 1840, by a *St. Jerome in the Desert*, accompanied by a view of the Val d'Oisans. At the same time, he exhibited etchings which are distinguished by their vigour of effect, and breadth of execution. The interest of Daubigny's first original etchings is that one can trace from them the development of his conception of landscape, and follow his progress along the path of realism. (See *Stormy Weather, Les Petits Cavaliers, Moonrise in the Valley of Andilly*.) All these studies show direct, sincere vision.

At the Salon of 1848, Daubigny made his real début before critical opinion. He showed a series of small landscapes—*View of the Environs of Chinon, By the Cousin, near Avallon* (Louvre, Moreau Nélaton Collection), etc. In the latter canvas, nature is well represented, but memories of historical landscape give it a certain dryness and stiffness. *Les Iles vierges à Bezons* (Avignon Museum), of the Salon of 1851, brings us back to more familiar places of the Ile-de-France. Daubigny exhibited two pictures at the Salon of 1852—*Harvest* and *View from the Banks of the Seine at Bezons*, and the former, especially, was considered to be one of the most important works of the young landscape painters.

At the Salon of 1857, Daubigny revealed his powers. Three works he exhibited were unanimously recognised as masterpieces: *La Grande Vallée d'Optevoz* or *La Mare* (Louvre), *Spring* (Louvre), and *Sunset*.

Two years later he exhibited *Le Pré des Graves à Villerville* (Marseille), the first important canvas of the series of Normandy landscapes; and the very fresh and charming *Bords de l'Oise* (Bordeaux). The great success of this picture established Daubigny as the painter of river banks.

For several years Daubigny had been living on the banks of the Oise. To make a still closer acquaintance with nature, the artist built a kind of cabin on a barge, transported his materials there, and thus let himself float on the Oise or the Seine. The washerwomen on the banks called this craft "le Botin" ("the little box").

After his brilliant success at the Salon of 1859, Daubigny was commissioned to decorate the entrance hall and stairway of the Ministry of State (now the Ministry of Finance). He executed four large decorative panels. In those of the entrance hall, he represented stags and herons in the middle of a forest. For the staircase, he chose a view of the Flora's Pavilion and a perspective of the garden of the Prince Imperial.

From 1861, Daubigny's style changed. Criticism and the public were bewildered, and soon hostile. The forerunner of Impressionism had appeared.

In *Les Vendanges de Bourgogne* (Salon of 1863; Louvre), which raised heated discussions, and which Daubigny considered as one of his most important works, the new method was seen. "Here," observed J. Lafenestre, "special study disappears; the exactness of local representation matters little; art dominates, and fidelity of imitation has comparatively little interest."

The careful building up of his landscapes, in spite of the swiftness of the direct studies, is well seen in *Les Bords de l'Oise*, his favourite theme, the composition of which recalls *The Ford* of Claude Lorrain. The tragic and vigorous *October* (Amsterdam Gallery), with its astonishing simplicity of means, appeared in the year 1868, when the outcry of the realists was at its height. During the Commune, the artist retired to London, whence he brought back the beautiful *Thames at Erith* in the Thomy Thiéry Collection. He went to Holland and painted the *Windmills at Dordrecht*.

Suffering from rheumatism and asthma, Daubigny was near the end when he painted his *Moonlight*, of the Mesdag Museum, at The Hague (Salon of 1877). This time the success was unanimous. This *Moonlight* sums up satisfactorily Daubigny's last style, the seeking for sentimental impression, at the expense, if necessary, of design, and by a large, free technique.

BIBLIOGRAPHY: Fr. Henriet, *C. Daubigny*. Paris, 1875.—Jean Laran, *Daubigny*. Paris, 1912.

**DAUMIER (Honoré Victorin).** —French painter and lithographer. Born at Marseille, February, 1808; died, Valmondois, February, 1879. The little Honoré Daumier was not seven years old when his father, a glazier-poet, took him to Paris, to put him in the way of earning his own living early in life. He was not a success either as an usher's clerk or as an employee in a bookshop, and eventually his parents had to yield to his desire to study art. Alexander Lenoir gave the young man his first drawing lessons.

But the doctrines which Lenoir taught were too academic ever to influence this student of real life. Daumier soon left the studio and took to sauntering about Paris, watching the innumerable types of people. But he could not live forever in this way, and so he asked one of his friends, Ramelet, to find him a means of earning a living. This mediocre painter taught him the rudiments of lithography, then at the height of fashion. At the same time—about 1828—Daumier followed, as assiduously as he was capable of doing, the courses of the Académie.

Daumier. (Bibl. Nat.)

Daumier's first lithographs, published by "La Silhouette," are not very interesting.

A new dawn broke on France, during which arose a young generation jealous for liberty and justice. The July Government had given the Press a dangerous liberty, and the Republicans seized this weapon. Articles and discussions, riots and meetings of secret societies, were less dangerous to the Orleans régime than were the lithographs of Traviès, of Decamps, of Grandville, those fierce caricatures which made the whole of France laugh at the expense of "the Order of Things" ("L'Ordre des Choses"). Republican in spirit, Daumier took the offensive, and devoted himself to that ideal of liberty and justice which was never extinguished in him. He gained access to the firm of Aubert. From henceforth his fortune as a lithographer was assured. His first political plates are already very vigorous. One of them, *Le Patrouillotisme chassant la Patriotisme du Palais Royal* attracted the attention of Philipon, the caustic editor of *La Caricature,* who enrolled Daumier under his banner, by the side of Grandville, Henry Monnier, Traviès, Raffet, Pigal, Eugène Lami and Decamps. From that time the government of Louis-Philippe began to lose its meekness. The *Allegory of the Pear,* at which the king was the first to laugh, seemed less amusing to his ministers, and condemnations rained on *La Caricature.*

Daumier (Honoré): Rue Transnonain, April 15, 1834. (Bibl. Nat. Est.)

In this atmosphere of battle appeared the plate of the *Gargantua,* signed H. Daumier. The rather coarse allegory attracted the Parisian crowd to the shop-front of Aubert's firm. As a result he was imprisoned for six months and fined 500 francs. When Daumier was released he was more ardent than ever. He had already made several remarkable attempts at characterisation. In the *Masques of 1831,* published 1832, the lithographic technique was a little soft, but the design was already sculptural. The suppleness which was lacking in the *Masques* was discovered in the series of "Busts," which began finely with those of Charles de Lameth and the elder Dupin. But how much superior to the "Busts" was that relentless *Galerie des illustrations de la bourgeoisie parlementaire,* which Daumier made on coming out of prison! All the noted politicians of the day are portrayed with magnificent vigour and rare penetration.

The murders of the Rue Transnonain (15th April, 1834) inspired Daumier with one of his most terrible masterpieces. He represents a workman's room, at sunrise. To the right, in the foreground, near an overturned chair, lies the head of an old woman. Against a disarranged bed, a man, clad only in a blood-stained shirt, is stretched out, the eyes are closed, the mouth half-open. His left fist is clenched; and the muscular legs are set wide apart. The man has fallen on a small child. In the shadow, in the background, lies the body of a woman, the head of whom disappears in obscurity. The struggle is over; the soldiers have left; but this solitary hour is even more tragic than the moment of the massacre. It is a powerful declamation against civil war. This plate appeared in a collection entitled "Association mensuelle lithographique," which had before published three of Daumier's plates, including the celebrated lithograph, *Enfoncé, Lafayette!*

Daumier: The Trouble-makers.

The well-known *Ventre Législatif* shows all the ugliness, pettiness, and physical and moral deformities of humanity, gathered on the ministerial benches. The personnel of the July Monarchy is here analysed in a way that is at once very minute and very broad.

The disturbances had peopled the prisons with rioters, and with wounded. One of Daumier's plates (1834) shows Louis-Philippe talking to a judge before the pallet of one who is lying in agony. "This one," the king is saying, "can be set at liberty—he is no longer dangerous."

In 1835, *La Caricature* was suppressed, and Daumier's part in politics under the July Monarchy came to an end. He then devoted himself exclusively to "Le Charivari." There appeared *The Bathers,* a striking representation of monstrosities; *The Blue Stockings* (1844), and *Les Divorceuses* (1848), are bitter satires against certain types of women. Most often Daumier returns to his favourite model, to that honest, mediocre person of whom he has left unforgettable portraits,—the little Parisian "bourgeois." Daumier loved the theatre. To his understanding of stage conventions, and his critical sense we owe the curious *Physionomies tragico - classiques* (1841) and the *Physionomies tragiques* (1851). "Daumier looked for the comic almost exclusively in the plastic distortion of persons supposed to be models of beauty." But here his mirth was frank, and without bitterness.

Daumier: The Print-Lover. (Palais des Beaux-Arts, Paris.)

In his attacks on the "gens de justice" he went to work differently. Here he was aggressive, biting, cruel. He shows barristers, with lordly gait, and insolent mien; advocates, shrivelled with envy; seated defendants, hardened and cynical; and deaf, somnolent old magistrates, on whom rests the charge of judging other people very like themselves. Later, Daumier expressed this seething world of the Law Courts in painting, and his paintings were as satirical as his lithographs.

He painted scenes from Don Quixote and La Fontaine, buffoons, scenes from Molière, interiors of third-class railway compartments, and a whole world of amateurs, advocates and washerwomen. The influence of the Dutch masters shows itself in the light and shade, the simplification of line, the transparence of masses, and the precious quality of his greens and reddish browns, bathed in luminous half-tones.

Daumier's water-colours are as fine as his oil paintings. (In the Louvre, and the galleries of England and Germany have important examples). They are rather touched-up drawings than pure water-colours.

Not content with lithography and painting, Daumier attempted sculpture, such as the two magnificent bas-reliefs of *Les Emigrants.*

Towards the end of his life Daumier became almost blind, and was no longer able to make lithographs. His paintings and water-colours accumulated and either did not sell, or sold very badly. The old master died in February, 1879, at Valmondois, in a little house, which he owed to the generosity of Corot. Since then, full justice has been paid to Daumier; and the reputation of this profound observer will grow still more.

Bibliography: Baudelaire, *Curiosités esthètiques.* Paris.—Champfleury, *Histoire de la Caricature moderne.* Paris.—Arsène Alexandre, *Daumier, sa vie et son œuvre.* Paris, 1888.—Henry Marcel, *Daumier.* Paris.—L. Rosenthal, *Daumier.* Paris, 1912.—Raymond Escholier, *Daumier.* Paris, 1924.—E. Klossowski, *Honoré Daumier.* Munich, 1923.

**DAVID (Gerard).**—Flemish painter, of Bruges. Very celebrated in his day, he was forgotten for a long time. The researches of James Weale have restored to him the admiration which is due to the last great painter of the Bruges school. Gerard David was born about 1460, at Oudewater. He settled in Bruges about 1483, was there admitted into the Guild of St. Luke. and in 1496 married Cornelia Cnoop, daughter of the senior goldsmith, who was a fine miniaturist, a talent which their daughter inherited. In 1501, he became head of the guild. He died on the 13th August, 1523. He was buried in the Church of Notre Dame, near the door of the tower. From his first period date: *Birth of Christ* (Budapest); the *Nativity* (late Kaufmann Collection); a fine *Adoration of the Shepherds* (Uffizi, Florence); a *St. Jerome* (Salting Collection, London); and a *Crucifixion* (National Gallery, London) the wings of which are in the Antwerp Museum. These wings, remarkable for their vigour, for the individual types of the faces, and for their composition, represent Jewish Judges and Roman Soldiers, and St. John and the Holy Women.

Some of David's early works were done under Memling's influence, as the three *Madonnas* of Madrid (Traumann Collection), of Bruges (Béthune Collection), and of Berlin. Other works from this period are a *Tree of Jesse* (Lyon Museum), a *Pietà* (Johnson Collection, Philadelphia), the *Adoration of the Kings* (Munich), perhaps executed with the help of Jan Prevost. Darmstadt Museum possesses a *Virgin* attributed to David, which is probably a copy of a lost original.

In 1488, David was commissioned with the first work mentioned in contemporary writings. Nothing of this remains. According to the transaction, the artist was to paint the iron grilles of the windows of the house of one Jean de Gros, where the Emperor Maximilian of Austria was held captive. Among his first important works are two pictures representing the execution of justice, commissioned by the magistrates of Bruges in February, 1498. The first, the *Judgment of Cambyses,* shows an unjust judge, Sisamnes, arrested by order of Cambyses. The second picture, the *Punishment of Sisamnes,* shows a cruel scene, in which, however, the actors do not seem to be very deeply moved, except the sufferer, who grinds his teeth, while the executioners flay him alive.

To about the same time belongs the fine *Adoration of the Magi* (Brussels), which was long attributed to Van Eyck, and then to Mabuse, but which is certainly by Gerard David. The work has rich, warm colour, exquisite grace, and a mystic, tender poetry.

The *Last Judgment,* which the artist executed in 1498, for the Hôtel de Ville of Bruges, has disappeared; but from the following years various fine works remain to us, such as *The Marriage at Cana* (Louvre); a *Bishop with Three Saints* (National Gallery); the *St. Catherine Altarpiece* (National Gallery); *St. Jerome* (Staedel Institute); *God the Father and Two Angels* (Schickler Collection, Paris); the three wings of an altarpiece (Brignole Museum, Genoa); *St. Michael* (Vienna); the *Annunciation* (Sigmaringen); and, finally, the two famous pictures which are perhaps his masterpieces: the altarpiece of Jean des Trompes; and the altarpiece of Rouen. The altarpiece of Jean des Trompes, or the *Baptism of Christ* (Bruges), was commissioned by a citizen of Bruges, of that name, in 1502, and finished in 1507. The central panel shows Christ standing in the Jordan; St. John, grave and austere, is pouring out the water of baptism, while an angel, in a richly embroidered mantle, guards Christ's clothing. On the wings is the donor's family—the father and his sons under the pro-

DAVID (GERARD): JEWISH JUDGES. (Museum, Antwerp.)

tection of St. John the Baptist, and his first wife and four daughters under the protection of St. Elizabeth of Hungary. On the exterior of the wings, is the donor's second wife, Madeleine Tordier, and her daughter, with the Magdalen. The other masterpiece, perhaps even finer, is the *Virgin Surrounded by Saints* (Rouen Gallery), painted in 1509 for the Carmelites of the Convent de Sion, Bruges, who kept it until the monastery was closed in 1785. The work was then sold. It went to Paris, and was given to Rouen in 1803. The Virgin and saints are grouped against a background which, neither landscape nor hangings, probably represents the wall of a room. Some of the figures are idealised; others are evidently portraits. The whole is simple and noble in composition, harmonious and brilliant in colour.

In 1515, David visited Antwerp, and could there admire the fine decorative works of the younger school, but his work did not gain by their influence. His last productions are inferior in colour, colder and duller; and the attitudes of the figures, sometimes more dramatic, are often awkward and agitated. One must except certain charming *Madonnas* (such as those of Brussels, Genoa, Strassburg, Madrid), in which grace is allied to simplicity. Other pictures of this fourth period are: a *Golgotha* (Genoa); the *Adoration of the Kings* (perhaps not by David), and a *Pietà* (National Gallery); *Rest on the Flight into Egypt* (Kauer Collection); *Holy Family,* of which the attribution is much disputed (Church of Notre Dame, Bruges); *Virgin and Child* (Palazzo Communale, Genoa); and the wings of a lost triptych, and a *St. Michael* (Vienna).

Gerard David has been considered not only a great painter, but an excellent miniaturist. It is known that he had a studio for miniature work, but no certain work of his in this medium has come down to us.

See Pl. 1, Vol. II.

BIBLIOGRAPHY: Bodenhausen, *Gerard David und seine Schule.* Munich, 1905.—J. Weale, *Gerard David, Painter and Illuminator.* London, 1895; *Portfolio,* 1895.—Fierens-Gevaert, *Les Primitifs flamands.* Brussels, 1909.—M. J. Friedländer, *Altniederländische Malerei,* Vol. VI, 1928.

— **(Jacques Louis).**—French painter. Born in Paris, 30th August, 1748; died in Brussels, 29th December, 1825. His father was killed in a duel when the child was eight years old.

François Boucher, a friend of the family, noticed David's gift for drawing; but, being too old to teach himself, he arranged for him to study with Vien, the apostle of Neo-Classic reform. With Vien, David made rapid progress. After unsuccessful attempts, he finally, in 1774, won the Prix de Rome, with his *Stratonice.*

DAVID (LOUIS): SELF-PORTRAIT. (Louvre.)

David left for Rome in 1775, with his master, Vien, elected Director of the French Academy. In spite of his studies with Vien, the ideas of François Boucher influenced the young man. "The antique will not seduce me," he declared; "it lacks

DAVID (LOUIS): HELEN AND PARIS. (Louvre.)

spirit, and does not move one." But the results of the excavations at Pompeii and Herculanium, the publications of Winckelmann and of Agincourt, and a visit to Naples with Quatrenière de Quincy, determined David's evolution, and the opening of a great Neo-Classical movement, of which Rome was the centre. One of the first works he sent to Paris was a *Patroclus* (Cherbourg Gallery).

David left Rome in 1780. Pupils came to him, and included Wicar, Fabre, Deberet, and Germain Drouais. In 1782, he married. Then the young master painted the picture which assured his position as leader of a school: *The Oath of the Horatii* (Louvre). Its success was tremendous. Princes, cardinals and amateurs invaded his studio. Nevertheless, the *Horatii* shows the artist

DAVID (LOUIS): M. SÉRIZIAT. (Louvre.)

still falling in with the ideas of his time: the figures are not represented nude. He confessed to Drouais, "For the moment, I am not sure enough of myself to attempt such a difficult thing."

He was a success in Paris. Despite the jealousy of Academicians, who hung his *Horatii* very badly, he won the favour of the public.

The following year (1786), he sent from Rome the *Death of Ugolino* (Valence Museum).

From now, David was the master of a recognised school. Pupils flocked to his studio, as well as his most famous contemporaries. His *Socrates Drinking the Hemlock* (Metropolitan Museum of Art, New York), for which André Chénier indicated the gesture, met with a triumphant acceptance. Reynolds declared it was the greatest artistic effort since the Sistine Chapel and the decorations of Raphael.

This mania for the antique did not, however, prevent David from praising the colour of the Flemings, especially Rubens. And, to distract himself from grief for the death of Drouais, he spent part of the year of 1787 in Brussels and Antwerp. Flemish influence, and doubtless that of Boucher, is evident in *Paris and Helen* (Louvre), which is brighter in colour than usual. His *Brutus returning home after the putting to death of his sons* (Louvre), which he sent to the Salon of 1789, with the *Paris and Helen,* moved people very differently. Archæological detail has been minutely studied. The statue of Rome, and the head of Brutus, were copied from the antique. The desolate figure of one of Brutus' daughters revolutionised feminine fashions: ladies gave up powdered coiffures and arranged their locks in the Roman style. Furniture was made according to David's design, by the well-known cabinet-maker, Jacob. But people in general cared nothing for these archæological researches. What moved then was the subject itself, the political bearing of the work, which glorified the sternest of Republican judges.

Pushed into the Revolutionary party by this sudden popularity, and by his hatred of the Academy, David threw himself into it with bitter frenzy. During the period 1789-1792, the painter was not, however, inactive. He executed some of his finest portraits, those of the Marquis and Marquise de Sorcy-Thelusson, and of her sister, Madame d'Orvilliers. At the end of 1790, the Constituent Assembly commissioned him to represent the *Oath of the Jeu de Paume.* It is not known if this picture was ever finished, but the completed drawing aroused enthusiasm in the 1791 Salon. David was then only half through his career. His talent was in full bloom. Thanks to him, historical painting recovered simplicity, not, unfortunately, without some stiffness. But the artist forgot his theories, and let himself be carried away by the general heightened feeling.

But it was in his intimate portraits that Louis David's naturalistic tendency expressed itself. He could be graceful, or tragic. He was equally happy in rendering the voluptuous grace of Madame Vigée Lebrun (Rouen), the honest repose of the *Gérard Family,* and the horror of the assassinated *Marat* (Brussels).

David's best portraits are those of Monsieur and Madame Sériziat (Salon of 1795); those of *L'Homme rouge,* the Ambassador of the United Provinces; the delightful sister of Eugene Delacroix, Madame de Verninac; the charming portrait of Madame Récamier (Louvre) which David left unfinished. He considered these works as belonging to an inferior art, chiefly useful for bringing painters an immediate income. *The Sabines* (Louvre) absorbed him.

This vast canvas was finished at the end of 1799. Curiosity was extreme as to who were the models. It was known that professional models had been rejected as not being noble enough. Three young ladies in the best society posed for the painter.

At this time, David painted the *Bonaparte au mont Saint Bernard* (Versailles).

From 1800, the first Consul took the old Jacobin into his favour. Sometimes he visited his studio, and took him over Paris, to give his opinion on changes he thought of making in the city. He was made first painter to the Emperor Napoleon. The portrait of Pius VII, which he then painted, is a masterpiece of patient observation (Louvre).

Four events announced the coming of Napoleon to the throne: the Coronation and Enthroning of the Emperor, the Distribution of the Eagles, the Reception of the Emperor at the Hôtel de Ville. David was commissioned to make their memory permanent. Only the *Coronation* (Louvre), and the *Distribution of the Eagles* (Versailles) were completely carried out. In these two masterpieces David shows his skill in dealing with vast compositions. In the *Coronation* each figure has been studied separately, drawn nude first, and clothed afterwards. In spite of its classic composition, the hundred and fifty portraits show considerable realism. Nothing reveals better the power of the Emperor and the display of his court than this huge canvas, which shows

Napoleon crowning Josephine, with a theatrical gesture, in front of the helpless Pope and a crowd, whose faces express respect or envy. It is a learned composition proudly conceived.

The *Distribution of the Eagles* is inferior. David gave his mania for introducing figures taken from sculpture full play. Thus he has clothed Giovanni da Bologna's *Mercury* as one of the hussars who is swearing fealty to the Emperor. But the general enthusiasm did not suffer from these strange minglings, and the picture appealed strongly to the war passions of the time.

At the Hundred Days, David was one of the first to greet Napoleon; and he was one of the first, too, to sign the additional acts, excluding the Bourbons from the throne. The vengeance of the royal government was not slow. In 1816, those who had signed the additional acts were condemned to exile. At sixty-seven years of age, David went into exile with dignity.

In Brussels, which he chose for residence, he had a great welcome. Unfortunately, the master aged. The decadence, which had already shown itself in *Leonidas* (Louvre), was only accentuated in *Cupid Leaving Psyche, The Wrath of Achilles,* and above all in *Venus and the Graces Disarming Mars* (1824). David's rhetoric now dressed itself in more lively colours. Flemish influence reasserted itself, but his modelling became weaker.

The storms of the Revolution and Empire were over. In France, the star of the first painter of the Emperor paled. The Romantics were coming to the fore. David's most faithful friend, Gros, was attacked for his devotion to the exiled master, who was seized with paralysis, and died on the 29th December, 1825.

As in the case with most of the masters of the French school, David was governed by intellectual theories. No artist, setting aside Poussin, had a higher ideal of painting. His influence on his time was tremendous. His pupils included: Gros, Gérard, Ingres, Girodet, Riesener, Isabey, Granet and Rude. In a sense, his artistic Empire was universal. Not only did he restore painting to noble ends, but he also organised brilliant fêtes, and revolutionised the costume, furniture, and decoration of his time.

It is in this aspect of director of Republican art that it is fitting to judge Louis David.

See Pl. 49, Vol. II.

BIBLIOGRAPHY: Renouvier, *L'Histoire de l'Art pendant la Révolution.* Paris, 1863.—F. Benoît, *L'Art français sous la Révolution et l'Empire.* Paris, 1897.—Spire Blondel, *L'Art pendant la Révolution.* Paris. —M. Dreyfous, *Les Arts et les Artistes pendant la Période révolutionnaire.*—Delécluze, *Louis David, son école et son temps.* Paris, 1855. —J. David, *Le Peintre, Louis David.* Paris, 1880.—Charles Saunier, *Louis David.* Paris.—L. Rosenthal, *Louis David.* Paris.—Richard Continelli, *Jacques-Louis David.* Paris, 1930.

**DAVIDSON (Jo).**—Contemporary American sculptor. He was born 30th March 1883 in New York City, of Russian extraction. His boyhood was spent in the East Side in the tenement district. At the age of sixteen he won a scholarship for study at the Art Students' League and for the next three years attended classes there. Uncertain, perhaps, of the merit of his art he turned from it and entered the Yale School of Medicine. But he became attracted by the clay modelling done in the Yale School of Fine Arts and made up his mind to become a sculptor. He returned to New York City and there worked in the studios of George de Forest Brush, the painter, and Hermon A. MacNeil, the sculptor. In 1907 he went to Paris and there entered the École des Beaux-Arts. Like many other young pupils he rebelled against the academic traditions and classic tendencies of that school. He gave up his classes there and tried to support himself by selling his pictures and some sculpture. Fortunately he was saved from much privation by some friends who secured a Hallgarten scholarship for him. This gave him a steady income and he was able to make a walking trip to Switzerland, noting and sketching the various people he came in contact with. Upon his return to Paris he put the peasants and others that he had seen into plastic compositions. Later he turned to portrait sculpture, the field which has made him famous. One of his largest commissions was the one at the close of the World War for the making of bronze busts of the military and political leaders of the Allies. In this group he made studies of President Wilson, General Pershing, Colonel House, Field-Marshal Haig, Marshal Joffre and Marshal Foch. Any one of these may be taken as a typical work highly realistic in treatment with a psychological analysis hinted at but not emphasised. More recently he has attempted heads of terra cotta tinted in the colours of life, which have been quite successful. While the majority of his subjects have been men he has done a few heads of women, but with less striking results. Among his latest works is a head of President Franklin D. Roosevelt, excellently characterised and remarkable for its fidelity to nature.

BIBLIOGRAPHY: For a complete bibliography see *The Index of Twentieth Century Artists* for August, 1935.

**DAVIES (Arthur Bowen).**—American painter (1862-1928). He was born in Utica, New York, 26th September 1862. His youth was spent sketching scenes along the Mohawk Valley, where he lived, trying to portray the trees and skies and the distant hills exactly as he saw them. He took drawing lessons from a local man, Dwight Williams, who urged him to try for more accuracy and breadth in his work. In 1878 the family moved to Chicago and there he did clerical work for the Board of Trade, but also worked under Roy Robertson at the Chicago Academy of Design. Two years later he went to Mexico as a civil engineer and there was impressed by the old Spanish religious art. Back again in Chicago he studied at the Art Institute of Chicago under Charles Corwin. About 1886 A. B. Davies came to New York City and worked at the Gotham Art Students and the Art Students' League. For a few years he did magazine illustrations for *St. Nicholas,* but was displeased by the criticism and gave up that position to devote himself exclusively to painting. He lived on a farm at Congers, New York, painting and hoping for better luck until William Macbeth, the art dealer, became sufficiently interested in his work to fit him up a New York studio. About 1893, with the financial aid of Benjamin Altman, A. B. Davies went abroad to work. He went to Italy and there came to understand something of the sentiment of Giorgione, as may be seen in his pictures dating from that period. His work was admired and compared in its idyllic character to that of Watteau, yet how different it is in the maze of symbolism and reality. He came out of seclusion long enough to arrange the famous Armory Show of 1913 in his position as President of the Society of Independent Artists, and then returned to his painting to experiment somewhat with a form of Cubism. He was a friend and patron of younger artists and amassed quite a collection of modern works of art when he had sufficient funds at his disposal. In 1916 he won the first Clark prize and the Corcoran Gold Medal at the biennial exhibition in Washington, D. C. He made some mural decorations for the home of Miss Lizzie P. Bliss and a few years later two panels for the International House. He suffered a severe heart attack in 1923 but soon recovered and turned his attention to sculpture and tapestry designs for the Gobelin factory. He passed part of each year in Italy and there he died in Florence 24th October 1928, alone and almost unknown. The news of his passing did not reach his family until some weeks later. His art was poetic fancy and symbolism disguised as reality—strange figures in mysterious landscapes or delightful children sporting in wooded glens. He was a careful draftsman, making many studies of the figure before actually incorporating it into his composition. Some of these figure drawings were made into etchings and lithographs later, retaining the delicacy of touch and accuracy of details. Typical examples of his work are the *Unicorns* in the Metropolitan Museum of Art and *Four o'Clock Ladies* in the Phillips Memorial Gallery.

See Pl. 62, Vol. II.

BIBLIOGRAPHY: *Arthur B. Davies; Essays on the Man and His Art,* 1924.—Frederick Newlin Price, ed., *The Etchings and Lithographs of Arthur B. Davies,* 1929.—Royal Cortissoz, *Arthur B. Davies,* American Artists Series, 1931.—*Catalogue of a Memorial Exhibition of the Works of Arthur B. Davies,* Metropolitan Museum of Art. New York, 1930.

**DAVIOUD (G.).**—1823 - 1881, French architect and designer of the Trocadéro, Paris.

**DE BROSSE (Jehan).**—Family of French architects who lived in the 16th and 17th centuries. The oldest, Jehan de Brosse, was architect to Margaret of Valois, wife of Henry IV, about 1580.

— **(Salomon).**—French architect, son of Jehan de Brosse (about 1562-1626). The greatest architect of the early 17th century, he first designed various works for Henry IV. In 1614, he became architect to the king and to the queen-mother. In this capacity, he was entrusted with the building of the Palais du Luxembourg (then, the Palais Médicis), in 1615, for Marie de Médicis who was desirous to have a palace which recalled the Palazzo Pitti, in Florence. Salomon de Brosse's building is less severe than the Florentine palace, and built on a French plan, opening on to a beautiful garden, which he designed himself. It is simple and elegant, with high roofs and large windows. The building was afterwards enlarged. The Medici fountain, which he also designed, is still as he conceived it, but differently placed. To bring water to the Palais Médicis and neighbourhood, de Brosse built the aqueduct of Arcueil. In 1618, he began the construction of the entrance hall of the Palais de Justice, twice burnt, but restored in the original style.

DE BROSSE (SALOMON): THE LUXEMBOURG, PARIS.

DE BROSSE: MEDICI FOUNTAIN. (Luxembourg Gardens, Paris.)

De Brosse planned various other buildings, such as the Parlement of Rennes, and several private houses.

He had a son, Paul de Brosse, who was king's architect, from 1615 to 1625, and who worked on the Cathedral of Troyes.

See Pl. 39, Vol. II.

BIBLIOGRAPHY: Ward, W. H., *Architecture of the Renaissance in France,* 1926.

**DEBUCOURT (Louis Philibert).**—French painter, designer and engraver. 1755-1832. He attended Vien's studio, but he was too wayward and fault-finding to submit for long to the severe teaching of the forerunner of Neo-Classicism. In 1781, he exhibited some mediocre paintings, which have none of the interest of his later aquatints. In 1785, Debucourt inaugurated that series of well-known plates, works of painting and engraving of current topics, which are admirable in their resourceful colouring, and show remarkable technical skill.

To Debucourt is due the spreading of the process of successive impressions. The first plate gives the values, the picture in black and white, and the three copper plates give the primary colours, red, blue and yellow. Green is obtained by two superimposed impressions of these last two colours. Debucourt was certainly master of this method. In 1786 appeared his masterpiece, the *Bride's Minuet*, and 1787, the *Promenade du Jardin du Palais Royal*. In the same year were published those little marvels of grace and spirit, the *New Year Morning*, the *Broken Pitcher*, and the *Promenade de la Galerie du Palais Royal*, a delightful picture of Parisian life, at the time of the decline of the monarchy. In 1788, appeared the *Bouquets* or *Grandmama's Birthday*; in 1789, the *Wedding at the Château*; and in 1792, the famous *Public Walk of the Garden of the Palais Royal*, completed the series of little works.

Under the Directoire, Debucourt recovered a little of his spirit; but he was soon surpassed by Carle Vernet, and, from the early days of the Empire, he lost little by little all the qualities of his art.

BIBLIOGRAPHY: Portalis and Béraldi, *Les graveurs du XVIII<sup>e</sup> siècle*. Paris, 1880.—E. and J. de Goncourt, *L'Art du XVIII<sup>e</sup> siècle*. Paris, 1883.—Société pour l'étude de la gravure française (1920), Debucourt Exhibition (Catalogue with articles by Dacier, Vuaflart and Hèrold).

**DECAMPS (Alexander Gabriel).** —French painter, 1803-1860. Brought up in a secluded valley in Picardy, "in order to be early acquainted with the hard life of the fields," the little Decamps had no ideas outside cottage gardens when he went to Paris. Seeing him already beginning to scribble, his father, who was a painter, taught him the rudiments of his art; after which he went to the studio of Abel de Pujol. He soon left him, and attempted lithography. His personality quickly showed itself. What biting humour there is in his thrusts at Charles X!

Decamps showed himself for the first time as a painter at the Salon of 1827. He exhibited a *Lapwing Shooting*.

His *Turkish Patrol* discovered the East to the West, and brought all the young artists to his side. But it proclaimed other influences than those of the East. His *Ronde de Nuit* recalls Rembrandt. But no doubt the painter's natural irony urged him to the grotesque.

Nevertheless, from 1834, Decamps gave high-sounding titles to his pictures, such as *Samson* (1845).

In his art, sentiments and ideas are subordinated to the representation of skirmishes, incendiary campagnes, curious costumes, and overturned temples. In fact "absolute indifference" was characteristic of Decamps, who was a far better representative than Delacroix of the doctrine "art for art's sake." He painted oriental scenes, landscapes, "genre" subjects, illustrations to the Bible, the gospels, and classical antiquity, and his work proves that it is possible to be a fine painter without making an intellectual appeal. His most serious themes are only pretexts for painting. Thus in a hideous torture scene (1839), Decamps sees only a magnificent spectacle. He strikes us with his radiant harmonies of blue sky, sunbaked walls, and swarming crowds. All details interested him, such as the texture of materials, and of fortifications. He delighted in the play of sunlight. But what he cared for most was neither the open air, nor exact representation, nor diversity of colour, nor subtlety of atmosphere, but the quality of materials.

DECAMPS: CHILDREN AT THE FOUNTAIN. (Musée Condé, Chantilly.)

The ironic side of his art pleased the public. Nor were familiar subjects less congenial to the painter of the rowdy scene of Turkish boys coming out of school (Musée des Arts décoratifs).

Strangely enough, Decamps greatly admired Ingres' painting. Ill health, melancholy, a belated feeling for the great truths of art, and the consciousness of what he had never attained, brought about a kind of decadence in Decamps' work. His work became monotonous. On the 22nd August, 1860, at Fontainebleau, he was kicked by a horse, and died a few hours afterwards.

BIBLIOGRAPHY: Baudelaire, *Salons de 1845, de 1846*. Paris, 1862.—Charles Clément, *Decamps*. Paris. —Adolphe Moreau, *Decamps et son œuvre*. Paris.

**DEGAS (Edgar).**—French painter. Paris, 1834-1917. Son of a banker, pupil of the Lycée Louis-le-Grand, he was studying law, when he saw some of Ingres' works, and resolved to devote himself to painting. In 1855, he entered the École des Beaux Arts, and the next year he went to Rome to study the Italian masters. On his return to Paris, he continued these studies in the Louvre. Until 1865, he worked in a dry academic style. These early efforts did not reveal the independent spirit he afterwards showed. After the War of 1870, he visited America. His *Comptoir de Cartons à la Nouvelle Orléans* (Pau) is dry, precise and minute, and still recalls his studies of the old masters. But in 1874 he exhibited, with the Impressionists, some portraits and scenes of dancing.

It is sometimes asked whether Degas was an Impressionist. He did not make use of "division of tone" at all, and at first sight he does not seem to be one of them. Nevertheless, his handling, his unexpected foreshortenings, his reflections, the originality of his lighting effects, his concise drawing, his daring freshness of movement, allow him to be classed among them. They always counted him as one of their most faithful colleagues, and to him they owed the saying, which affirmed their influence: "They deride us, but they pick our pockets!" He became a tireless chronicler of contemporary life: slender jockeys on lank horses; round-faced washerwomen; women at their toilet; anæmic dancers. The deformities he shows are not exaggerated. He is sincere and caustic, that is all. His colour is refined and silvery. His handling, masterly and attractive. He used all methods—oil, tempera, pastel—and sometimes he combined them all on the same paper or canvas.

DEGAS: THE DANCER. (Musée du Luxembourg.)

The man himself was original—solitary, independent, enthusiastic for painting, and contemptuous of honours. His sayings, like his art, were caustic and concise. One of his pictures, *Dancers at the Bar*, he sold to Rouart for five hundred francs, though at the sale it had reached the sum of four hundred and thirty-five thousand francs. "I'm a horse that runs big trials," he said, "but I'm satisfied with my ration of oats."

Blind, and unable to paint any longer, he ended his life alone in his studio in Montmartre.

Among his works which include some of the finest paintings of the nineteenth century must be mentioned: *The Star Dancer* (Luxembourg); *Robert le Diable* (South Kensington); *Dancer Fastening her Sandal* (Luxembourg); *Café, Boulevard Montmartre; Dancers* (Lerolle Collection); *Woman at her Toilet* (Luxembourg).

See Pl. 8, Vol. I.

BIBLIOGRAPHY: Lemoisne, *Edgar Degas*. Paris, 1913. — P. Jamot, *Degas*, 1924.—P. Lafond, *Degas*, 1918.—J. Meier-Graefe, *Degas*, 1923. —*Degas*, Cat. Phil. Mus., Exhib. 1936.

**DEINEKA (or Deyneka, Alexander).**—Contemporary Russian painter and graver. He was born in Kursk in 1899, the son of a railway man. He spent his early childhood roaming about in the fields with his comrades until he entered school. He showed a particular aptitude for mathematics and for drawing. He wanted to become an engineer, but could not afford the necessary education. At the age of sixteen he was sent to the Kharkov Art School, where he was forced to wander a great deal in the relatively new and untested "isms." From Pestrikov he received training in classical drawing. As his father was not fond of artists, he did not give any pecuniary aid to his son, and the young man had to get along as best he could. In 1918 he went to Kursk, preparing for the exhibition commemorating the anniversary of the October Revolution; his contribution was his first monumental work. He also taught at the People's Commissariat of Education. About this time he began to inculcate cubism to Kursk, which was received with enthusiasm among the workers, but shocked the citizens. In 1921 he was sent to Moscow to study in the State Higher Art and Technical Studio, working under the guidance of Favorsky. In 1924 he was employed on the staff of the magazine *Atheist on the Bench*, doing lithographic work. In the same year the OST society was organised, of which group he became a member. In their first exhibit he presented his *Miners* and a year later *At the Erection of New Shops*, but due to his dissension with the leaders he resigned from the society in 1928. He illustrated the book, *In the Fire*, by Henri Barbusse and also a number of children's books. He did poster designs and participated in a number of exhibits in the U.S.S.R., Austria, France, Switzerland, Sweden, Greece, Germany and the United States. Since 1930 he has worked in the IZOGUIZ as a consultant on posters and is also teaching in the Polygraphic Institute. In the *Russian Rivera* Deineka shows the type of the new Russian factory worker and the machine age in his own original way. His art embodies the spirit of his time; he seizes these new aspects of life and develops a new style to treat most suitably these motives. A sincere artist, he rejoices in fine pattern and rhythms; he is a firm draftsman and shows strength in his structural compositions. The topics include sports, factory and peasant scenes; there is often the rendering of interrupted motion, and the background frequently assumes the importance of the figures and machines in the foreground. He paints with oils, watercolour and inks; the colours are always moderate and subdued.

BIBLIOGRAPHY: Paul Ettinger, *Alexander Deineka*, Cicerone, Vol. 20, 1928.

**DELACROIX (Ferdinand Victor Eugène).**—French painter, 1798-1863. His father, a very distinguished man, was minister of the French Republic at the time of Eugène's birth. He died at Bordeaux in 1805. A high-spirited child, Delacroix, at nine years of age, went to the Lycée Imperial (now Louis-le-Grand), in Paris.

In 1816, he entered Guérin's studio, and the École des Beaux Arts. He began a period of severe study, drawing incessantly from the antique and from the Italian masters, in the Louvre. He made a masterly copy of the Christ Child in Raphael's *"Belle Jardinière."* Then, under the influence of Géricault, who, already well known, had returned to the studio to study the living model, he painted men and horses from nature. In 1819, he painted a *Virgin*, for the Church of Orcemont, strongly Raphaelesque. And in 1821, he painted, for a convent in Nantes, a *Vierge du Sacré Cœur*, which Géricault had been asked to execute; but, as he was already ill, he entrusted the task to his young comrade.

The *Dante and Virgil* (Louvre) was an important work in Delacroix's career, and also in the history of the French school. It won a great success in the artistic world,

Delacroix: Self-portrait. (Louvre.)

and its qualities of powerful modelling and romantic feeling were a challenge to the staleness of the Davidian school. In this picture, the artist was obviously under the influence of Géricault, whom he watched hour by hour painting the *Raft of the Medusa*.

Delacroix: Jewish Wedding. (Louvre.)

Two years later, in 1824, *The Massacre of Chios* (Louvre) showed all his originality. The whole of Europe was following intensely the desperate struggle for Greek independence. No scene could be more moving and bolder than the episode he depicted here. The *Massacre* was finished and placed in the Louvre, where the annual exhibitions were then held, when Delacroix saw some of Constable's pictures at the Salon. He was so struck by them that he had his picture taken down, repainted it, and, in four days, completely changed its colouring. "This scene, the horror of which, the convulsive drawing, the violent colour and the passionate brush work," which constitute one of the masterpieces of modern art, raised the indignation of the classicists and the enthusiasm of the young painters. The Administration proved its intelligence and eclecticism by buying the *Massacre of Chios* for the relatively high price of 600 francs.

The same Salon of 1824 revealed the evolution made in the art of portrait and landscape painting by Thomas Lawrence and John Constable. Delacroix, whose admiration for the latter never abated, at once seized the occasion to go and study English painting. His sojourn in London (May to August, 1825), during which he met Thalès Fielding and Bonington, had an influence which was manifest in the *Christ in the Garden of Olives* (Church of Saint Paul Saint Louis), and especially in the *Death of Sardanapalus*, which was received at the Salon of 1827, at the same time as *Marino Faliero* (Wallace Collection), and nine less important pictures, among them the fine *Still Life* of the Moreau Nélaton Collection (Louvre), which is very English in colouring. The *Sardanapalus on His Pyre* (Louvre) was not among them; some critics find there too much of "the machinery of the fifth act of an opera."

The self-portrait, known under the title of the *Man in the Green Waistcoat* (1829; Louvre), recalls Baudelaire's words: "Everything about him was energetic, but the energy was the result of nerves and willpower; physically, he was frail and delicate."

Delacroix had long been without governmental favours, when he was commissioned, almost simultaneously, by the Duc d'Orléans (Louis Philippe) for a *Cardinal Richelieu Saying Mass at the Palais Royal* (destroyed in 1848); and by the Duchesse de Berry, for *King John at the Battle of Poitiers*.

In 1831, Delacroix sent eight pictures to the Salon, among them one of his favourite works, *The Murder of the Bishop of Liége*, which was acquired by the Duc d'Orléans, and the admirable *Tiger Cub Playing with Its Mother* (Louvre).

Attached to the diplomatic mission of the Comte de Mornay, Delacroix disembarked at Tangiers in January, 1832. From Tangiers, the mission went to Mekinez, where it was officially received by the Sultan. Then it returned to Tangiers, and Delacroix embarked for the south of Spain. He returned to Paris in August.

Various water-colours, in the 1833 Salon, recalled this journey. And in that of 1834, a *Road in Mekinez*, and *Algerian Women in Their Apartment* evoke the hot-house atmosphere of the harem.

*A Jewish Marriage* (1841, Louvre) was unfortunately altered by the use of bitumen, but it is still full of colour and life.

The July Monarchy made important acquisitions of Delacroix's work. The *Death of Charles the Bold* or the *Battle of Nancy* (Nancy Museum), the *Portrait of Rabelais* (Chinon Library), *St. Sebastian and the Holy Women* (Church of Mantua), the *Battle of Taillebourg* (Versailles Museum), and the *Entry of the Crusaders into Constantinople* (Louvre) were bought by the State. The two last-mentioned compositions, of vast proportions, were two masterpieces.

These official purchases were, however, very badly paid, and did not lessen the severity of the jury with regard to Delacroix. The Salon of 1834 refused two works, that of 1836, a *Hamlet in the Graveyard;* that of 1839, *Tasso on His Bed in Prison, An Arab Camp* and *Ben Abou by a Tomb*. In 1840, *The Justice of Trajan* (Rouen), perhaps his finest work, was only accepted by a majority; and, in 1845, the *Education of the Virgin* was rejected.

In 1833, Thiers ("the only man in a position to be useful, who lent me a hand," wrote Delacroix later) commissioned him to paint four allegorical figures—*Agriculture, Industry, War,* and *Justice*—for the Salon du Roi, in the Chambre des Députés. The Salon du Roi was not finished until 1838. The same year Delacroix was commissioned to decorate the Library of the Chambre, a tremendous undertaking. On the five domes, including twenty pendentives, Delacroix painted the history of ancient civilisation from the myth of Orpheus to the invasion of Attila. The colossal task took him nine years, and was finished at the same time as the decoration of the Library of the Chambre des Paris (now the Senate), for which he had been commissioned in 1845. Of smaller dimensions, the subject of this decoration is taken from an incident of the fourth song of the "Inferno," where Dante meets Homer, Horace, Ovid and Lucian in the Elysian Fields.

Nothing gives us a higher opinion of Delacroix than do these vast decorations—the first restless and brilliant, the second, reposeful. The colour, in which reds, greens and violets predominate, makes a full, vibrating harmony. As Fromentin says, in his analysis: "Delacroix's colour has something subtle and intellectual about it, a quality which is very rare in all schools. It is always the garment which expresses the thought. . . . It is essentially a language."

In this respect, the pathetic *Pietà*, in the Church of Saint Denis du Saint Sacrement, is very characteristic. Again, this gift is magnificently displayed on the ceiling of the Galerie d'Apollon. The success of this Louvre ceiling had an unhoped-for result; for the first time, Delacroix's works were sought after.

Delacroix's two last pictures were *Botzaris Surprising the Turkish Camp*, and the *Collection of Arab Taxes*, showing that at the end of his life, his thoughts turned again to the struggle for Greek independence and to that vision of the East which had inspired and delighted his youth.

It is hard to believe that the author of so many vast undertakings was a valetudinarian, whose health required the greatest care, and who often interrupted his work to go to Valmont, to Dieppe, to Nohant to visit George Sand, to Angerville, and for various seasons to Eaux-Bonnes, to Vichy, to Ems, etc. In 1838, he went to Belgium and Holland. His hoped-for visit to Italy never took place. He died in Paris in 1863.

Since the publication of Delacroix's Correspondence, his "Journal" has given a very high opinion of that vast intelligence and ever quick sensibility. There, far more than in his articles on Raphael, Michelangelo, Puget, Poussin, Gros, "The Question of Beauty," etc., published in the *Revue de Paris*, in the *Revue de Deux Mondes*, etc., appear his exceptional gifts as a writer, his developed sense of musical criticism, as well as his receipts for painting. For Delacroix, however, this minutely worked-out palette was never more than the servant of the spirit.

Delacroix has been reproached for his incorrect drawing. But such a painter could not have drawn otherwise. He had a horror of inertia: everything is in action. As André Michel has truly remarked: "All uninspired work was impossible to him; he was like the serpent in the hand of Python, and, more than once, it is in apparent faultiness that one finds the most convincing proof of the sincerity of his emotion, and the power of his genius."

He translated the vague aspirations of his contemporaries into an original, intense language, the strength of which reveals a master painter, a man of powerful imagination, and tenacious will, of deep conviction, and acute sensibility. This is the man and the artist who, in the last analysis, we find behind all the works of Eugène Delacroix.

See Pl. 53, Vol. II.

Bibliography: Théophile Silvestre, *Histoire des Artistes Vivants.* Paris.—Baudelaire, *Curiosités esthétiques; L'Art romantique.* Paris. —E. Chesneau, *Peintres et sculpteurs romantiques.* Paris.—A. Robaut and Chesneau, *L'Œuvre de Delacroix.* Paris, 1885.—Correspondance de Delacroix, published by Barty. Paris.—*Journal d' Eugène Delacroix*, published by Paul Flat and R. Piot. Paris, 1894.—Henry Marcel, *La Peinture française au XIXe* Siècle. Paris, 1905.

**DELAROCHE (Hippolyte, called Paul).**—French painter, 1797-1856. After having lessons in landscape painting with Waterlet, Paul Delaroche joined Gros's studio. There he met Charlet, Bonington, Roqueplan, Bellangé, Eugène Lami.

He made his début with a large picture of *Josabeth Saving Joas*, which he exhibited at the Salon of 1822. At the Salon of 1824, his cold *Jeanne d'Arc* hung beside Delacroix's *Massacre of Chios*, and Delaroche was hailed as a compromise between academic staleness and romantic disorder. What Casimir Delavigne did for Victor Hugo, Paul Delaroche was to become for Delacroix.

His *Death of Elizabeth* (1827), with its array of brilliant materials, is like a bazaar. This large painting, treated as a decoration, is not put to shame by its proximity, in the Louvre, with Deveria's *Birth of Henry IV*. If there is less movement in the design, there is the same riot of colour, and the same facility of execution.

Delaroche.

The historical novel was very popular; and Delaroche realised his bent and opportunity.

His *Cromwell Opening the Coffin of Charles I* (Nîmes) is awful in its realism. The *Children of Edward* (Louvre), exhibited at the same Salon of 1831, a rosy glimmer coming from outside emphasises the horror of the approaching drama.

*The Death of the Duke of Guise* (Chantilly), exhibited in 1835, is perhaps his best work. The execution is sure, and the faces are finely observed.

Delaroche, who had become a member of the Institut in 1832, was elected Professor of the École des Beaux Arts. He visited Italy with Edouard Bertin and Henri Delaborde. On his return he married Louise Vernet, daughter of Horace Vernet.

Guizot's work on the English

revolution inspired him with two pictures, of poor execution—*Charles I Insulted by Cromwell's Soldiers* and *Stafford Walking to His Execution.* Unfortunately, on his aiming at a higher type of painting in his *Saint Cecilia* (Salon of 1837), his critics made such cruel thrusts that he resolved not to exhibit any more.

On being commissioned to decorate the dome of the École des Beaux Arts, Delaroche became merely anecdotal. Detail abounds but no grace. Its success was prodigious. This illustrator of historical scenes was an intelligent and spirited portrait painter. The types are very human, and very ably characterised, such as the portraits of Guizot, Salvandy, Rémusat, François Delessert, and Prince Adam Czartoryski.

A great sorrow—the death of his

DELAROCHE: THE CHILDREN OF EDWARD. (Louvre.)

young wife—struck Delaroche towards the end of his life. To this, no doubt, was due the melancholy of his last compositions. *The Young Martyr* (Louvre) is perhaps the only really inspired work that Delaroche has left us. It has a soft, sad light which is genuinely touching. His last works, the *Return from Golgotha* and *The Crown of Thorns*, have a mournful poetry.

See Pl. 54, Vol. II.

BIBLIOGRAPHY: Henri Delaborde, *Notice sur Paul Delaroche.* Paris, 1857.

**DELFT.**—A town in Holland, famous for its pottery. This art of ceramic was brought to Holland, to Delft especially, in the 16th century, by German potters. It flourished chiefly in the 17th century. The Dutch, who were great navigators and traders, brought back pottery, from the Far East, which was such a success in Europe that they soon came to imitate it. The Delft pottery makers used a particular glaze which gave the colours a special brilliance, and which was only applied over them. We cannot enter here into the details of fabrication. It is enough to say that the process allowed of very perfect decoration. Domestic utensils, vases, plates, cups, etc., were produced, and tiles which are veritable pictures, reproducing landscapes of the painters. In the 18th century this industry lost its importance, through the rivalry of English porcelain, and most of the Delft factories disappeared.

**DELHI.**—See Moslem Art (Indian School).

**DELLA PORTA (Giacomo).**—Italian architect, 1541-1604, and a practitioner of the early Baroque. Circa 1573 he designed the façade of the Gesù, Rome (see Rome), and in 1575 the Università della Sapienza. Between 1585 and 1590 he reconstructed Michelangelo's dome for St. Peter's, raising its height 16 feet in order to assure stability.

**DELLO DI NICCOLÒ DELLI.**—Tuscan painter and sculptor, born c. 1404, who lived chiefly in Spain. He was in Seville in 1442; was made a knight by the King of Aragon and Castille; returned to Florence in 1446; and was back in Spain in 1448, where he was active until 1464. Probably to be identified with the painter called in Spain Nicolao Florentino, who died in 1471 in Valencia. A number of works in the old Cathedral of Salamanca are attributed to him.

**DELORME or DE L'ORME (Philibert).**—French architect, born at Lyon, 1510-1570. He was one of the greatest architects of the French Renaissance. Unfortunately, many of his works have disappeared or have been transformed, but his style has much freedom such as his use of the "French Order." His father taught him the elements of architecture, and then sent him to Italy. There he studied and admired the Roman works of antiquity and of the Renaissance, but his individuality was not overpowered by studying these foreign works. He always prided himself on being a "bon Lyonnais," and he never followed in the wake of the Italian masters whom the French Kings called to their court.

On his return from Italy, he went first to Lyon, where the Cardinal du Bellay procured him work which kept him there several years. He next gave him the building of the Château de Saint Maur les Fossés (in Paris) showing advanced knowledge of Renaissance principles in addition to attracting the attention of Francis I, who, in 1545, gave him the title of "Master Architect and General Director of Buildings and Fortifications." In this capacity, he built, for Diane de Poitiers, the Château d'Anet (1548), one of the most sumptuous in France. This Château, finished under Henri II, has been partly destroyed. Only one wing and the chapel remain. Thanks to Du Cerceau, we know the plan of the whole. It had decorative sculpture by Gonjou and Cellini.

DELORME (PHILIBERT). (Bibl. Nat.)

In 1548, Philibert was given the title of "Inspector of the Royal Buildings of Fontainebleau," where Primaticcio was executing and directing the decorations.

Henri II ordered him to construct new buildings to the Louvre. The King, or rather, Catherine de' Medici had grandiose schemes which their architect was not able to carry out entirely. He built the façade of the Tuileries, on the garden side, in a quiet, elegant and imposing style. This building, spacious and low-lying, was transformed under Louis XIV, and destroyed in 1870, together with the whole Tuileries wing.

At the same time, Philibert de l'Orme was occupied with the building or transformation of various parts of the king's Châteaux—Saint Germain, Fontainebleau, Vincennes, etc.—and making plans for private châteaux and houses.

DELORME (PHILIBERT): CHAPEL OF THE CHÂTEAU OF ANET.

On the death of Henri II, in 1559, he lost the royal patronage. His protectrice, Diane de Poitiers, was chased from the court, and Catherine de' Medici, who could not forgive the architect for having built the magnificent Château d'Anet for her rival, took away his commission as "Inspector of Building" and gave it to his adversary, Primaticcio, having thereafter only the Tuileries and minor works for de l'Orme's designs.

BIBLIOGRAPHY: Blomfield, R., *Studies in Architecture,* 1905; pp. 124-90.

**DELPHI (Greece).**—The excavations at Delphi brought to light

DELPHI: THE SANCTUARY.

the great Temple of Apollo wherein the Delphic Oracle was situated (built between 370 and 330 B.C.). Descent to the Temple was made

DELPHI: THE HOLY ROAD AND THE GREAT ALTAR.

by five or six terraces, connected by the Sacred Way, which descended in sharp bends from one stage to another. The Sacred Way was lined with votive monuments given by the various Greek states. The only ones of which important fragments remain are the *Treasuries of the Sicyonians and of the Athenians.* Interesting sculptured metopes from the former have come down to us. The foundations of the Treasury may still be seen, and there is a reconstruction of its façade in the Museum of Delphi.

Almost the entire series of met-

DELPHI: FRIEZE OF CNIDIAN TREASURY.

opes from the Treasury of the Athenians has been recovered, though many of them are in a fragmentary condition. They represent the labours of Theseus and

DELPHI: THE LABOURS OF HERCULES. METOPE. Sixth century B.C. (Louvre.)

the labours of Heracles. Many of the sculptures have great delicacy and precision of workmanship (6th or early 5th century, B.C.). Most of the metopes are in the Museum of Delphi (e.g., Athena and Theseus). The relief showing Heracles and the Stag is, however, in the Louvre.

**DELPHI.**—See Charioteer of Delphi; Greece (Sculpture); also Pl. 22, Vol. I.

**DEMETER of CNIDUS.**—Famous Greek statue discovered at Cnidus, and transported to the British Museum. This seated figure of Demeter mourning for her lost

DEMETER OF CNIDUS. (British Museum.)

daughter Persephone has often been compared to the "Mater dolorosa" of later art; but in the Greek work, the grief expressed is so restrained that the beauty of the features and the repose of the figure are retained. Only the deep-set eyes give intense expression to the face. The work probably belongs to the 4th century

# POMPEII AND TIMGAD

*The eruption of Vesuvius in 79 A.D. buried Pompeii in ashes and preserved for us an example of a city of antiquity. Everywhere else the Greek and Roman cities were transformed by the passing of centuries. Pompeii is revealed to us as it was at the moment that it was buried by the lava of the volcano. Only the wooden parts were destroyed, but the excavations have brought to light the walls, the columns and the flaggings in the same condition they were in during the first century A.D. The life that the inhabitants of this city led at that time can be imagined without much effort.*

POMPEII: HOUSE OF ARIADNE.
*(Photo by Brogi.)*

POMPEII: HOUSE OF THE VETTII.
*(Photo by Brogi.)*

POMPEII: HOUSE OF ARIADNE.
*(Photo by Brogi.)*

## The Pompeian House

The street side of the Pompeian house was closed, while the inside opened on roofless courts. Through the vestibule one entered the *atrium.* Next one reached the *peristyle,* around which there was a covered gallery, its roof supported by columns; around this were the chambers; the most important was the dining room. These brick houses were covered with stucco and coloured plaster. The garden, with flowing water in the pools, was enlivened with small statues. Pompeii was not large, but it was quite wealthy.

POMPEII: INTERIOR OF THE HOUSE OF THE VETTII.
*(Photo by Brogi.)*

MOSAIC REPRESENTING THE BATTLE OF ISSUS, MUSEUM OF NAPLES.
*(Photo by Alinari.)*

## Pompeian Decorations

The Pompeian house has suffered so little that it shows us its mural decorations in perfect condition. It is only through these mural paintings that we can reconstruct for ourselves the painting of antiquity. We think that we can recognise some of the compositions by great masters who were mentioned by contemporary historians. Painting, like sculpture, did not believe in repetition. These decorations are frescoes, painted with tempera, encaustic, or mosaic; with the exception of the encaustic, all these paintings have survived from the ancient time.

POMPEII: THE STREET OF TOMBS.

POMPEII: THE MACELLUM AND THE ENTRANCE TO THE FORUM.

TIMGAD: VIA DECUMANUS MAXIMUS.

## The Ancient City

The houses in Pompeii seem new, since the city was rebuilt a short while before the eruption. But the flaggings of the streets show signs of the wear of centuries, and indicate a period prior to the Roman conquest. The plan of these cities is symmetrical; the streets meet at right angles as in a Roman camp. The roads are wide, often bordered by sidewalks. The Roman cities in Africa, which have long been abandoned and are half destroyed, recall the time when this desert was fruitful soil, the granary of Italy.

# GREEK AND ROMAN PORTRAITS

*Greek sculpture was not designed for the same purpose as Egyptian sculpture: to represent the individual traits of a human being. Its history shows the development and the softening of the human form, and the creation of idealised types, mostly of the figures of the gods.*

PERICLES. (*Photo by Rischgitz.*)

EURIPIDES. (*Photo by Brogi.*)

LYSIAS. (*Photo by Alinari.*)

SOCRATES. (*Photo by Brogi.*)

DEMOSTHENES. (*Photo by Brogi.*)

PTOLEMY. (*Photo by Alinari.*)

ALEXANDER. (*Photo by Brogi.*)

ARATUS. (*Photo by Alinari.*)

HOMER. (*Photo by Coolidge.*)

UNKNOWN GREEK. (*Photo by Alinari.*)

## Greek Portraits

Despite the basic idealism of Greek art, it also engaged in portraiture. This did not occur before the complete maturity of their plastic art. The busts of the fourth century B.C., were restricted largely to the representations of famous personages.

UNKNOWN ROMAN. (*Photo by Brogi.*)

UNKNOWN ROMAN. (*Photo by Alinari.*)

SO-CALLED PORTRAITS OF CATO AND PORCIA. (*Photo by Brogi.*)

UNKNOWN ROMAN. (*Photo by Alinari.*)

JULIUS CAESAR. (*Photo by Alinari.*)

AUGUSTUS. (*Photo by Brogi.*)

NERO. (*Photo by Brogi.*)

UNKNOWN ROMAN WOMAN. (*Photo by Anderson.*)

AGRIPPINA. (*Photo by Hoffmann.*)

MARCUS AURELIUS. (*Photo by Brogi.*)

ANTINOÜS. (*Photo by Brogi.*)

UNKNOWN ROMAN WOMAN. (*Photo by Hoffmann.*)

CARACALLA. (*Photo by Brogi.*)

CONSTANTINE. (*Photo by Brogi.*)

## Roman Portraiture

The Romans were good portraitists even before they came into contact with Greek art. During the Empire art played an important part in the cult of the Emperors Official portraits were copied in the provinces, and there are many in existence. Executed at the end of the Empire the inert and stupid bust of Constantine reveals the decadence of the plastic arts at that time.

# MOSLEM ARCHITECTURE

*Moslem architecture skilfully utilizes the resources and adopts the local customs of Islam. The same Arab genius is recognized in the immense empire from Spain to Persia, in Egypt and Asia Minor. The most typical Arabic building is the mosque, the temple for prayers. These very numerous mosques are from different periods and of different types; all of them, however, consist of at least one hall, covered by a flat roof or by vaults. The Arabs nearly always use light materials for construction, preserving the Asiatic taste for precious colors. Their architecture is polychromatic.*

CAIRO: MOSQUE OF AMRU.

JERUSALEM: MOSQUE OF OMAR (VIEW OF THE WHOLE).
*(Photo by Courtellemont.)*

DAMASCUS: GREAT MOSQUE.
*(Photo by Gervais-Courtellemont.)*

## Asia Minor

The Mosque of Omar at Jerusalem is one of the oldest examples of Arabic art. It is built on the rock where, according to tradition, Abraham made his sacrifice. The graceful dome covering the sacred ground is characteristic of the Arabic style; it is not spherical but starts as a cylinder and ends in a point. The Mosque of Amru at Cairo is of the early type previous to the domed style; it is covered by a flat roof which rests on arcades supported by columns. The nave of the mosque is usually preceded by a court with a fountain for ablutions before prayer.

CAIRO: MINARET OF THE BORDEINI MOSQUE.

MOSQUE OF ISPAHAN.
*(Photos by Gervais-Courtellemont.)*

CAIRO: MIHRAB AND MINBAR OF MOSQUE OF SULTAN HASSAN.

## Persia

Persia adopted Mohammedanism, and under the defined form of Arabic architecture one can find here some trace of ancient Persian art. The immense door with the broken arch, in the Mosque of Ispahan, is an obvious imitation of the palace of Ctesiphon which is in ruins today. The vaults and Arabic domes originated in Persia; architecture with enamelling flourished there. The mosque can be recognised from afar by its minarets. In the interior one sees the mihrab, a niche which indicates the direction of Mecca, and the minbar, an elevated chair from which the Koran is read.

CORDOVA, MOSQUE; NAVE, SIDE AISLES, MAKSOURA, MIHRAB.
*(Photo by Lacoste.)*

SEVILLE, ALCAZAR; INNER DOOR.
*(Photo by Lacoste.)*

GRANADA, ALHAMBRA: COURT OF THE LIONS.
*(Photo by Laurent.)*

## Andalusia

Early in the seventh century the Arabs conquered Africa and landed in Europe; they retained Spain until the fifteenth century. They made Andalusia one of the most flourishing Islamic provinces. The mosque of Cordova is, after the one in Mecca, the largest one in the Moslem world. It has small arches which are superposed with great imagination above a forest of a thousand columns, remnants of the tradition of ancient temples in Spain and in Africa. The Alhambra at Granada, the last work of the Moslems before they left Spain, is of light architecture, brilliant and fragile in its decoration, composed in blue, white, and gold.

# MOSLEM DECORATIVE ART

*The Arabs were always decorators and ornamenters. There were many reasons why they did not practice sculpture and the figurative arts. For them art was never, as for the ancient Greeks and for the modern Europeans, an imitation of nature. The human body is not included in their vocabulary of decoration, and even the plants, when they appear, are quickly changed into a geometric design. Even in their architecture the Arabs displayed their main interest, the decoration of surfaces with vari-coloured enamel and carved plaster, making their palaces and mosques into gigantic jewels.*

MOUCHARABIEH, OR PIERCED WOOD GRATING. CAIRO.

HALL OF THE AMBASSADORS AT THE ALCAZAR, SEVILLE.

DOOR TO THE APARTMENT OF MARIA PRADILLA AT THE ALCAZAR.

INLAID WOODEN DOOR, EGYPT, FIFTEENTH CENTURY.

INLAID AND CARVED WOOD.

MOUCHARABIEH, WOODEN WINDOW GRATINGS. CAIRO.

DOOR WITH SMALL PANELS. (MUSEUM OF FEZ.)

DETAIL OF CARVED WOODEN DOOR, EGYPT, FIFTEENTH CENTURY.

BRONZE COVERED DOOR. FEZ.

BARBERINI VASE, THIRTEENTH CENTURY. (LOUVRE.)

COPPER PLATE. ALGIERS, THIRTEENTH CENTURY.

EWER WITH INLAID WORK. (R. KOECHLIN COLLECTION.)

FORGED IRON HINGE. MECKNÈS.

VASE PAINTED ON WHITE ENAMEL. (MUSEUM OF FEZ.)

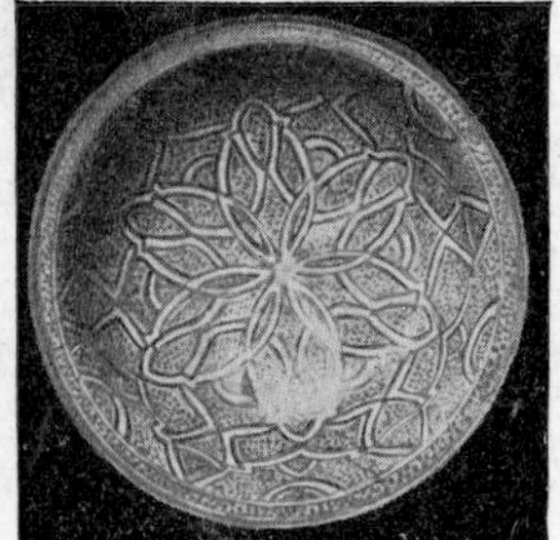

THREE PLATES FROM DAMASCUS. (MUSÉE DE CLUNY.)

BUTTER DISH. (MUSEUM OF FEZ.)

In decorative art the material is even more important than in naturalistic art. The material, by its inherent qualities, constitutes the essential part of the decoration, and the craftsman's work is to know the secrets of handling it. The Arabs were masters in this. They knew what to do with baked clay (enamel painting with soft or harsh colours), with rugs (intense and harmonious colours), with wood (inlaid work with geometric patterns), with metal (hammered iron, repoussé, chiseled and incrusted copper), with ivory, leather, etc. . . . Arab art will always remain as an example of skilful technique and ingenious decoration.

B.C., and shows the influence of the sculptor, Scopas.

See Ceres.

**DEMUTH (Charles).**—Contemporary American painter (1883-1935). He was born in Lancaster, Pennsylvania, in 1883. In 1903 he began to study painting at the Pennsylvania Academy of Fine Arts under Anschutz and Chase. Four years later he went abroad to study for a year and again in 1912 he was in Europe, working at his painting. Upon his return to the United States he made some illustrations for different books, including Émile Zola's *Nana*, Henry James' *The Turn of the Screw* and *The Beast in the Jungle*. About the same period, that is, in 1919, he made some drawings of actors and actresses, inspired perhaps by the work of Fantin-Latour, done in strongly contrasted colours with very expressive contours. Probably best known are his watercolours of studies of flowers, each species carefully characterised with remarkable precision and a feeling for the essence of its existence. Also he is the author of city vistas in oil, watercolour, and tempera, tinged with his characteristic delicacy of touch and sensitive approach to his subject and influenced by the geometric order of Cubism. He received the silver medal at the Sesqui-Centennial Exposition in Philadelphia in 1926, and examples of his work may be seen in the Columbus, Ohio, Gallery of Fine Arts, the Whitney Museum of American Art in New York, and the Phillips Memorial Gallery in Washington. He died 23 October 1935 in Lancaster, Pennsylvania.

Bibliography: Albert E. Gallatin, *Charles Demuth,* 1927.—William Murrell, *Charles Demuth,* 1931.—For other articles see *The Index of Twentieth Century Artists* for July, 1935.

**DENIS (Maurice).**—French Symboliste painter, born 1870. Influenced by Gauguin, this artist returned to the archaism of the primitives. His design is simple, and the figures, flatly painted, and occupied with pious acts and mystic rites, are set in calm, luminous landscapes. The very fresh colour is often charming, but the forms are often badly drawn and the archaism seems artificial. The collection of the painter Lerolle has some early works by Maurice Denis. The paintings in the Church of Le Vésinet are the best expression of his talent. We may also mention the decoration of the hôtel Rouché, and the ceiling of the Théâtre des Champs Elysées.

Bibliography: Desfossès and Mithouard, *Maurice Denis au Vésinet,* 1903.

**DENNER (Balthazar).**—German painter, 1685-1749. His pictures are painted with great minuteness and show the most insignificant details.

**DENON (Dominique Vivant, baron).**—French designer and engraver, 1747-1825. Lively, amiable, and elegant, Denon had a brilliant and varied career as a writer, diplomat and artist. His first success as a draughtsman was the famous *Déjeuner de Ferney*, in which he represented Voltaire, unknown to him. Voltaire was not satisfied with his portrait: "It looks like a crippled monkey," he said. Denon executed many engravings. The best known are *Le Serment du Jeu de Paume, Republican Costumes*, and numerous portraits. He followed Bonaparte to Egypt, and drew the buildings there. In 1804, he was nominated "Directeur Général des Musées," and urged Napoleon to bring masterpieces from conquered countries to put in the Louvre. The Louvre collections owe him much.

**DEOATO ORLANDI.**—Painter, mentioned 1288-1301. A Crucifix in the Gallery at Lucca is signed and dated 1288 (originally in the Church of S. Cerbone outside Lucca); and a five-part panel with half-figures of the Virgin and Saints, which bears a signed inscription and the date 1301, is in the Gallery at Pisa.

Bibliography: M. Ridolfi, *Sopra i tre più antichi dipintori lucchesi,* in Atti e Mem. d. R. Accad. lucchese, XIII, 1845, 370 ff.; *L'arte in Lucca,* 1882.—Crowe and Cavalcaselle, Douglas ed., I, p. 142.—A. Venturi, *Storia d. arte ital.,* V, 1907, 18, 92, 206.—Van Marle, *Italian Schools, etc.*

**DERAIN (André).**—Contemporary French painter. He was born at Chatou, near Paris, 10th June 1880. At first he showed an interest in engineering, but soon his thoughts turned toward painting and with the advice and counsel of his friend and fellow townsman, Maurice de Vlaminck, he went to Paris to study. For a time he was at the Académie Julian and later he worked with Eugene Carrière. Then he came in contact with the works of Matisse and the leaders of the Fauvism movement. During this time he was working under the influence of van Gogh, Gauguin, and Cézanne, but in 1913 he showed a tendency toward cubism, making his pictures more schematic and the treatment of the figures more simple with the least amount of details. His colours showed some influence from the colour schemes of the Gothic era and the Italian primitives such as Giotto and Cimabue. Together with Vlaminck he displayed an interest in art history, trying to reconcile the classic and medieval traditions, yet preserving a certain amount of independence in his style. During the period of the war Derain came under the spell of the art of Auguste Renoir. His figures took on a three-dimensional character and showed a direct contact with nature interpreted with a freshness and poetry of conception. He was attempting an objective view of nature depicted by analogies and allusions, which reflected his vast knowledge of the art of other ages; but his own style rose above mere imitation. It has a very definite character of its own where the forms are concentrated and decorative, arranged with a view to the harmony and coherence of the whole composition. Derain has illustrated *A la Santé du Corps* by Maurice de Vlaminck, *Le Nez de Cléopâtre* by G. Gabory, and *Les Plaisirs et les Jeux* by V. Muselli as well as many other books.

Bibliography: Adolphe Basler, *André Derain,* 1929.—Carlo Carrà, *André Derain,* 1924.—Elie Faure, *André Derain,* 1923.—Daniel Henry, *André Derain,* 1920.—André Salmon, *André Derain,* 1929.

**DÊR TERMÂNÎN.**—6th century monastery of North Syria. The church is an important example of the Early Christian architecture of Syria, is basilican in plan, with a façade consisting of a galleried porch between dwarf towers. Some believe that this design was instrumental in the ideation of the great Romanesque and Gothic façades of Western Europe.

**DERUET (Claude).**—French engraver (1588?-1660). About 1620, he was working with Claude Lorrain. He then went to the Court of Louis XIII and painted the large *Allegory*, in the Museum of Versailles. He etched a series of plates—*The Triumph of Charles IV*.

**DESIDERIO da SETTIGNANO.**—Florentine sculptor in marble, wood, and terra cotta, born 1428 in Settignano, near Florence; died 1464 in Florence.

It is not known with whom Desiderio studied; Vasari calls him a pupil of Donatello, but since Donatello left Florence for ten years in 1443, an actual apprenticeship is unlikely. He was, however, unquestionably influenced by Donatello's forms.

A tax statement of 1457 indicates that he shared a workshop with his older brother Geri. In 1453 he had been mentioned on the rolls of the guild of maestri di pietra; his largest and best-known work, the tomb of Carlo Marsuppini in Sta. Croce was executed in 1455 or shortly after. In 1461 he took part in the competition for the Oratorio of the Madonna della Tavola in the Orvieto Duomo, with Giuliano da Maiano and Verrocchio. The commission was carried out after 1464 by the Sienese sculptor Giovanni di Meuccio. To Desiderio's last year, 1464, belongs the tabernacle in the Chapel of the Sacrament in S. Lorenzo (partially altered in 1677). The original form of the ciborium in S. Pier Maggiore has been even more tampered with. According to the description of Bocchi-Cinelli it must originally have resembled that of Benedetto da Maiano in S. Domenico, Siena.

Among his more important works are the marble chimney in the Victoria and Albert, London, and the wood-sculpture of Sta. Maria Maddalena in Sta. Trinità (begun by Desiderio, finished by Benedetto da Maiano). Many other works, reliefs, busts, etc., are attributed to him on stylistic grounds.

Desiderio represents the second generation of Florentine Renaissance sculptors, in that the monumentality and functional expressiveness of Donatello yield place with him to an elegant and charming refinement of forms, types, and decorative motifs.

Bibliography: Vasari-Milanesi, II, 483; III, 107-113; VIII, 87.—Milanesi, Giorn. stor. degli arch. tosc., VI, 14-15.—Fabriczy, Jahrb. d. k. preuss. Kstsamml., XXIV, 1903; XXVIII, 1907; Repert. f. Kstwiss., III, 1880.—v. Geymüller and v. Stegmann, *Archit. der Ren. in Tosk.,* 1885 ff.—M. Reymond, *La Sculpt. Flor.,* III, 1899, 63-76.—W. Bode, *Denkmäler der Ren. Skulptur Tosk.,* 1892 ff., pp. 91-97.—W. Burger, *Das florent, Grabmal,* 1904, pp. 142-50, 188-89.—Venturi, *Stor. dell'arte ital.,* VI, 1908.—W. Bode, *Florent. Bildhauer,* 1910, pp. 176-229; *Die ital. Plastik,* 1911, pp. 94-98.

**DESPIAU (Charles).**—Contemporary French sculptor. He was born at Mont-de-Marsan 4th November 1874. When he was seventeen years of age he went to Paris and there studied at the École des Arts Décoratifs under Louvrier de Lajolais, and for a while he worked with Hector Lemaire, who had been a pupil of the sculptor Carpeaux. Two years later Despiau entered the École des Beaux-Arts, where he received instruction from Barrias for the next three years. He left the school finally because of the strict academic training which did not suit his way of thinking about sculpture. It was a long hard climb for recognition and he added to his income by tinting postal cards. For a time he was an assistant to Auguste Rodin and from him he gained some of the master's classical interpretation of the human figure. From 1901 on he exhibited his work in the annual show of the Société Nationale des Beaux-Arts, showing at first portrait busts and figures in modern dress and much later studies of the nude. He is primarily known for his busts, which have an impersonal character strangely objective rather than any intimate interpretation of the individual. The contours have a smooth almost classic quality and the modelling in general has a very blond appearance, but the result of the whole is most pleasing, endowed as it is with some of the passion and life which Despiau learned from his contact with Rodin. Many of his subjects are women and young girls and he has been particularly successful in his interpretation of feminine characteristics. Despiau has done some portraits of men, which are on the whole less penetrating and happy in their conception, and he has also made a few full-length nude figures, but these are distinctly in the minority. He has executed many sketches in sanguine of the human figure in various attitudes, which are chosen for their possibilities for future modelling in stone. He is the creator of the War Memorial at his birthplace, Mont-de-Marsan, and has illustrated *Les Heures Claires*, a book by Émile Verhaëren. His work was first introduced to New York in 1927 and since then he has become a great favourite with the American public. He is a Chevalier of the Legion of Honor and his *Eve* is in the Musée du Luxembourg in Paris. Concerning his work the critic Deshairs has said: "He aspires spontaneously to a calm, but always living harmony." Examples of his work in the United States are in the Buffalo Fine Arts Academy, the Detroit Institute of Arts and the John Herron Art Institute in Indianapolis.

Bibliography: Adolphe Basler, *Despiau,* 1927.—Leon Deshairs, *Charles Despiau,* 1930.—Claude Roger-Marx, *Charles Despiau,* 1922.

**DESPORTES (Alexandre François).**—French painter, 1661-1743.

Desportes (François): Self-portrait. (Louvre.)

He was born in Champagne, son of a rich labourer. He first studied in Paris, with a Flemish painter, of the name of Nicasius, who had been a pupil of Snyders. Some Polish gentlemen took him for a visit to their country, where he stayed for two years, and painted the portraits of the King and Queen. On his return to Paris, he became a painter of hunting scenes to Louis XIV. He was pensioned, and lived in the Louvre. We learn that he was a man as simple in his ways as he was sincere in his art. Perhaps the other painter of the hunt, Oudry, had more ability, but Desportes certainly had more charm. He was a member of the Académie Royale from 1699. He died, at an advanced age, in 1743.

BIBLIOGRAPHY: *Mémoires inédits sur les Membres de l'Académie royale.* Paris, 1854.

**DETAILLE (Edouard).**—French painter of military scenes, 1848-1912, born in Paris; imitator of Meissonier.

**"DEUTSCH."**—See Manuel (Nicolas).

**DEWING (Thomas W.).**—American painter, born 1851, studied in Paris under Boulanger and Lefebvre, noted as a painter of figure subjects of much delicacy and charm.

**DE WINT (Peter).**—English painter (1784-1849), one of the most talented representatives of the school of English water colour painting of his time. Elected Associate of the Old Water Colour Society in 1810 and a Member in 1811.

BIBLIOGRAPHY: M. Hardie, *Peter de Wint.* London, 1929.

**DIAMANTE (Fra).**—Florentine painter, born in 1430 at Terranuova, Val d'Arno. He became a Carmelite monk and the first reference to his artistic activity is in 1452 when he is mentioned as assisting Fra Filippo Lippi in Prato. In 1463, Fra Diamante was recalled to Florence by his ecclesiastical superiors and jailed. The document does not record the nature of his offense. Shortly after he left the Carmelite order and entered that of Vallombrosa; in 1466 he became chaplain of the Convent of Sta. Margherita in Prato. In 1468 he went to Spoleto with his master, Fra Filippo, and finished the frescoes there after the latter's death in 1469. His hand can easily be distinguished in the Spoleto decorations, his style, though dependent on that of Lippi, being clearly recognizable.

In 1470 Fra Diamante was back in Prato, painting in the Palazzo Pubblico; but his stay there must have been short, since in 1472 he is listed in the Corporation of S. Luca in Florence. A document of payment of 1481 indicates that he was among the artists employed in the decoration of the Sistine Chapel, Rome, and because of the size of his wages causes us to assume that his share was considerable. In 1493 Fra Diamante became prior of the Convent of S. Pietro di Gello in Volterra. The record of his career closes on a lugubrious note, for in 1498 he was again in prison. The date of his death is unknown.

Fra Diamante's style is best to be studied at Spoleto, where certain of the frescoes are by him alone; and at Prato, whose gallery contains several of his works.

BIBLIOGRAPHY: C. F. Baldanzi, *Relazione della pittura di Fra Filippo nel coro della cattedrale di Prato,* 1835, p. 50.—Ulmann, *Fra Filippo und Fra Diamante als Lehrer Botticellis,* 1890.—Steinmann, *Sixtinische Kapelle,* I, p. 202.—Mendelsohn, *Fra Filippo Lippi,* 1909.

**DIAMOND PALACE.**—See Ferrara.

**DIANA.**—See Artemis.

**— THE HUNTRESS.**—See Pl. 25, Vol. I.

**— (Temple of).**—See Nîmes.

**DIANA (Benedetto), or Benedetto Rusconi.**—Venetian painter of the end of the 15th century, and beginning of the 16th (about 1482 to 1525). He was a pupil of Lazzaro Bastiani and a follower of the Bellini. The majority of his works are in Siena.

**DIAZ de la PEÑA (Narcisse Virgile).**—French painter. Born in Bordeaux, 1808; died in Mentone, 1876. Son of a political Spanish refugee, Diaz went to Paris early. He was ten years old and an orphan when a Protestant minister, living at Bellevue, took him. He began painting in a Parisian porcelain factory, in company with Jules Dupré, Raffet and Cabat, but he disliked smooth, "finished" painting. Souchon and Sigalon gave him advice, but he heeded nothing but his own romantic passion. He painted scenes of the East, which he had only seen across the footlights. Then came his procession of Dianas, Venuses, and Cupids. Diaz did not draw his figures. He sketched them quickly with his brush, employed the palette-knife, used pure colours, exaggerated the impasto, and placed his tones on the canvas by degrees, as though he were making a bouquet. He was a fastidious colourist, and his best paintings are certainly his landscapes, which he painted from nature in the forest of Fontainebleau. With a keen sense of effect, Diaz often painted stones and moss and mists, and flecked sunlight filter through the rich leafiness of trees (*Hunter and Dogs,* in the Thomey Thiéry Collection, Louvre;

DIAZ DE LA PEÑA: FAIRY WITH PEARLS. (Louvre.)

and in the Chauchard Collection: the *Forest of Fontainebleau,* and *The Road*). Apart from his landscapes, his best pictures are: *Bohemians on Holiday, Two Rivals* (Louvre), *The End of a Fine Day, The Gifts of Love, The Spell, Love Disarmed.*

BIBLIOGRAPHY: Théophile Silvestre, *Histoire des Artistes Vivants.* Paris.

**DICKINSON (Preston).**—American painter (1891-1930). He was born in New York City in 1891. His art education was gained in some time spent at the Art Students' League, but much of his real inspiration came from careful study of the old masters at the Louvre between the years 1910 and 1915. He also made some trips to Canada to gain information to use in his pictures. Most of his influence came from a study of the works of Cézanne and the designs of Japanese printers. His pictures were composed of delicate and carefully planned organisations with a nice feeling for design and related planes. His art reflects the restlessness of his nature, always seeking Utopia and never quite ready to admit the good points of this life. Impersonal though his pictures were they showed a good sense of colour and harmony of tones. In general, Dickinson seemed to be striving to recreate the world in accordance with his own ideas, but his art was lacking in substance though excellent from a technical standpoint. He won a bronze medal at the Sesqui-Centennial Exposition at Philadelphia in 1926. Late in the year of 1930 Preston Dickinson died in Spain. His pictures are to be found in the Brooklyn Museum, the Buffalo Fine Arts Academy, the Detroit Institute of Arts, and the Phillips Memorial Gallery in Washington, D. C.

BIBLIOGRAPHY: C. J. Bulliet, *Apples and Madonnas,* 1927.—Samuel Kootz, *Modern American Painters,* 1930.—Eugen Neuhaus, *The History and Ideals of American Art,* 1931.—Duncan Phillips, *A Collection in the Making,* 1926.

**— (William).**—English engraver. Born in London, in 1746; died in Paris, in 1823. He left chiefly portraits, such as those of Madame de Talleyrand, after Gérard; of Lord Grosvenor, after B. West; and of Garrick, after E. Pisie.

**DIDYMEAN APOLLO.**—See Pl. 20, Vol. I.

**DIETRICH (Chr. W. E., also known as "Dietricy").**—German painter, 1712-1774. He copied the Dutch masters.

**DIEZ (Pedro).**—See Plateresque.

**DIJON (France).**—Among the many old buildings of Dijon are:—the *Cathedral* (late 13th century): the *Church of Notre Dame* (13th century), which is unique of its kind in that its façade is composed of three tiers of arcades (a feature often found in Italian Romanesque churches—e.g., Pisa); the *Palace of the Dukes of Burgundy,* now the Hôtel de Ville (12th century; largely rebuilt in the 17th century). The Hôtel de Ville houses a rich Museum, which contains the famous tombs of the Dukes of Burgundy—Philip the Bold, and Jean sans Peur. At Champmol (near Dijon) is the celebrated *Well of Moses* by Claus Sluter (see Sluter).

See Pl. 54, Vol. I.

**"DINANDERIE."**—Brass ware, made especially in Dinant (Belgium). There were, however, important manufacturies in other towns—Tournai, Brussels, Bruges, Bouvignies. These workshops produced not only objects such as vases, pitchers, basins, etc., but articles of such large dimensions as baptismal fonts, lecterns and candelabra, which were often decorated with remarkable sculptures. The Church of St. Barthélemy, Liége, possesses baptismal fonts, executed in 1112 by Lambert Patras of Dinant. Their shape, and the twelve figures of oxen which bear them, recall the "bronze era" of the Temple of Jerusalem. The Dinant workshops produced chiefly small pieces, delicately sculptured.

The names of some of these masters have come down to us: Jehan Josès, of Dinant (14th century);

DIJON: NOTRE DAME.

Guillaume le Fèvre, of Tournai (15th century); Nicolas Josès, who worked at the Court of Burgundy for Philip III, "the Bold"; Jacques de Germes, who executed the tombs of Louis le Mâle and of his wife.

Western Germany, also, had similar workshops, and Holland had very flourishing manufacturies, in the 15th, 16th, and 17th centuries.

BIBLIOGRAPHY: J. Tavenor-Perry, *Dinanderie,* London, 1910.

**DIOCLETIAN.**—See Rome.

**— (Palace of).**—See Spalato; Byzantine Art (First Period: Architecture).

**DIOSCORIDES.**—See Byzantine Art (Miniatures of Illustrated MSS.).

**DIPTYCH.**—Among the Romans

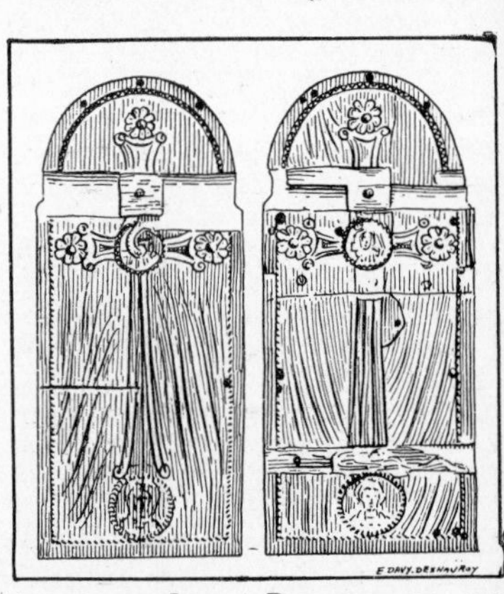

BYZANTINE IVORY DIPTYCH, OF THE TENTH CENTURY. (Treasury of the Cathedral of Halberstadt.)

this word signified two tablets joined by a hinge which closed them like a book. The inner face was covered with a coat of wax on which they wrote with a point; and the external faces were often decorated with sculptures in wood or ivory. In the Middle Ages many diptychs were produced, but it was then the inside panels and not the outside which were decorated, often with paintings. Devotional figures—Madonnas, scenes from the Passion, etc.—transformed the diptych into a kind of portable altar. Sometimes the number of panels was increased, and the diptych then becomes a triptych (3 panels), or a polyptych (several panels). The diptych varies greatly in size, from small Byzantine ivories to large painted altarpieces.

**DIPYLON POTTERY.**—See Greece (Vases).

**DISCOBOLUS.**—See Myron; also Pl. 20, Vol. I.

**DISTEMPER.**—A painting medium similar to tempera but with a glue size used as base instead of an egg size as in tempera.

**DIVINO (El).**—See Morales.

**DIX (Otto).**—Contemporary German painter. He was born at Unterhaus, near Géra in Thuringia, in 1891, the son of a farmer whose ancestors had been miners. From 1905 to 1910 he was an assistant to a mural decorator and then he went to Dresden, where he entered the School of Arts and Crafts and later attended classes at the Academy, working under Karl May. He fought all during the war and then went back to the Dresden Academy, where he stayed from 1919 to 1921. The next four years he spent in Düsseldorf and then in 1926 he moved to Berlin. He was selected as a professor at the Academy of Düsseldorf and in 1931 was named a member of the Prussian Academy. His early style was based on the art of the Quattrocento, but after the war he passed through a period of disillusionment, when he showed in his paintings a bitter dislike of war and biting satire of the hypocrisy of the human race. This period in his work has been compared with the spirit seen in the writings of Erich Remarque, especially his book *All Quiet on the Western Front.* It was at this time that he displayed his love of exact realism and his close spiritual affinity with the works of earlier German masters such as Albrecht Dürer, Hans Holbein, Matthias Grünewald and Baldung Grien and a kindred feeling to the sentiments expressed by Goya in his satiric views of Spanish court life. Dix made many paintings and etchings of his war experiences, which were not softened for the benefit of the general public—scenes of horror and destruction that he remembered and painted for future generations to look at and consider. Aside from these war pictures of the years immediately succeeding the conflict, Dix painted the humble German peasantry and the bourgeoisie with a satiric and barbed realism, nudes, figure studies and portraits. Much of his work concerns the grotesque and fantastic part of the population, faces such as look out of some early Flemish paintings and yet are still to be found if we do but use our eyes. Since the rise of Hitler he has tempered his eye and his hand to conform with the restrictions against "modern" art. All are done with an objective vision and surely exemplify the best of the New Realism (Neue Sachlichkeit) movement. His paintings are in many museums in Europe and America where his *Child with Doll* is in the Museum of Modern Art in New York.

Bibliography: P. F. Schmidt, *Otto Dix, Holzschnitte,* 1922.—P. F. Schmidt, *Otto Dix,* Radierwerk, 1921.—Willi Wolfradt, *Otto Dix,* 1924.

**DOAN.**—Japanese painter. One of the masters of the 16th century. He was a Buddhist priest; a great imitator of Sesshu and, like him, he visited China. His works show a strong Chinese influence. Some have come to Europe.

**DOGES' PALACE.**—See Venice; also Pl. 6, Vol. II.

**DOLCI (Carlo).**—Florentine painter, 1616-1686. Over-sentimental painter of soft expressions, of heads raised heavenward, of eyes bathed in tears and ecstasy, of pearly flesh. His *Magdalen* and his *Ecce Homo* are in the Corsini Gallery, in Rome.

**DOL-EN-BRETAGNE (France).**—The Cathedral (St. Samson) is in the Norman Gothic style (13th century).

**DOLMEN.**—A circle of monoliths, usually inclosing a sepulchral monument; an ancient structure consisting of a large flat stone laid as a roof across two or more upright stones.

See Pls. 1, 14, Vol. I.

**DOMENICHINO (IL).**—Domenico Zampieri, Bolognese painter, 1581-1641. He began his education as a painter at Bologna with the Fleming, Denis Calvaert, but he then went to the Academy of the Carracci, and remained faithful to this serious teaching and considered eclecticism. At the beginning of his activity, he imitated the Carracci, especially Annibale, with whom he often worked. He went to Rome early in life, and there assisted in the Palazzo Farnese by painting two pictures, representing the *Legend of Perseus,* eight little mythological scenes, and the scene of the *Maiden and the Unicorn.* His style became more individual. His "realism" was conventional. He has been called a quattrocentist strayed into the 17th century, on account of the sincere fervour with which he tried to paint the human soul. But they are peculiarly cold and unconvincing souls that inhabit his noble or melodramatic forms, and they tend to be wearisome. In his large compositions, well done, well drawn, well painted as they are, we look in vain for decorative harmonies capable of moving us.

In San Gregorio at Celio in Rome, he painted a *Martyrdom of St. Andrew,* which enjoyed a great reputation (1608). In the Farnese Chapel of the Abbey of Grottaferrata, he made an important decoration (1610) with the histories of St. Nilus and of St. Bartholomew. He there represented himself as a page in green (these frescoes were restored in 1819 by Camuccino). In the French Church of St. Louis, he painted the story of St. Cecilia (1616-1617). In Sant' Andrea della Valle, he painted the Evangelists in the pendentives (1623) and frescoes on the vault of the apse; in Sant'Onofrio, scenes from the life of St. Jerome; in San Pietro, in Vincoli, a *Deliverance of St. Peter* and an *Adoration of the Shepherds,* now at Dulwich; in the Farnese Palace, a *Venus Finding the Body of Adonis,* to decorate a loggia, now destroyed; in the Castle of Bassano di Sutri, the ceiling of a room, with the legend of Diana; in the Villa Aldobrandini dei Frascati, paintings now lost, representing the *Story of Apollo,* with very small figures in a big landscape (engravings by Landon); in Santa Maria in Trastevere, a ceiling; in the Palazzo Costaguti, a ceiling, etc.

There are pictures by him in a great many museums. The most important are the *Communion of St. Jerome,* in the Vatican (1614); the *Guardian Angel,* Naples (1615); the *Pietà,* Louvre; the *Ascension of the Magdalen,* Leningrad; the *Hunt,* in the Borghese Gallery; and the *St. Cecilia,* Louvre.

See Pl. 22, Vol. II.

Bibliography: L. Serra, *Domenico Zampieri detto il Domenichino.* Rome, 1909.

**DOMENICO DEL BARBIERE.**—See Domenico (Fiorentino).

**— di BARTOLO.**—Sienese painter, from Asciano; born c. 1400; died before 1447.

In 1428 Domenico is first mentioned in the corporation of painters in Siena; and in 1434 the Operai of the Duomo pay him for a sketch of the Emperor Sigismond, which may have been used for the representation of that monarch on the pavement of the Duomo. From 1435-39 dated the frescoes of *The Lives of SS. Ansanus, Victor, Sabinus, and Crescentius* in the sacristy of the Duomo; and from 1437 the lost altarpiece for S. Agostino at Asciano. In 1441 Domenico is recorded as having done scenes from the *Legend of Tobias* in the hospital of Siena, assisted by Luciano da Velletri. These no longer exist. From 1443-44 date the extant frescoes in the Ospedale della Scala, in the execution of which he was aided by Priamo della Quercia. During the same period he worked on a *Coronation of the Virgin* for the hospital. Domenico died before 1447.

His absolutely authentic works are few and include the following, all three of which are signed and dated: the 1433 *Madonna* in the Academy of Siena; the 1437 *Madonna* in the Johnson Collection, Philadelphia; the 1438 polyptych in the Gallery at Perugia.

Bibliography: Vasari-Milanesi, II.—Milanesi, *Doc. . . . Senese.* I.—H. J. Wagner, *Domenico di Bartolo Ghezzi, Das Dompaviment v. Siena und seine Meister,* V. Göttigen, 1897-8.—Van Marle, *Italian Schools, etc.,* IX, 1927.

**— FIORENTINO.**—Known in France as "Domenico del Barbiere." Italian sculptor who worked in France, particularly in Troyes, in the middle of the 16th century. He was one of the artists who came to France after 1530, in the following of Rosso and Primaticcio. He was employed in the Château of Fontainebleau from 1537 to 1540, with Jean Leroux, called Picart, who remained his colleague.

In 1541, he was in Troyes. To the brilliant school of Champagne sculpture, which had been developing from the beginning of the century, he brought the influence of the classical art of Michelangelo, and the elegance of the Fontainebleau school. In this respect, he is singularly interesting. No doubt he was attracted by the Champagne artists who worked at Fontainebleau, such as the Juliots and, perhaps, François Gentil. He made the acquaintance of Primaticcio, whom Francis I had made Abbot of St. Martin-ès-Aires of Troyes, and worked with him in the Château of Polisy (1544). He received a great many commissions from the town and clergy of Troyes. Numerous works, which have disappeared, were attributed to him in the Churches of St. Pantaléon, St. Pierre and of the Jacobins. From 1549 to 1555, he executed, with his son-in-law, Gabriel Favercau, the rood-screen of St. Etienne, of which four declamatory bas-reliefs remain in the Church of Bar-sur-Seine, and, in the Church of St. Pantaléon of Troyes, two statues of Faith and Charity, in a learned, ample style, which soon became fashionable in Champagne, and gave birth to painful, academic pictures, such as the *Christ at the Column,* in St. Nicolas, Troyes.

Domenico's chief work is the tomb of Claude de Guise and his wife, in St. Laurent of Joinville, executed after 1550, in collaboration with Jean Picart, called Le Roux. In 1793, four ornate statues, two caryatides, and two bas-reliefs were destroyed. But much remains of it: in the Mairie of Joinville are two caryatides (*Justice* and *Temperance*); in the Museum of Chaumont, two bas-reliefs (the charity and justice of the Duke); in the Louvre, two bas-reliefs (the battles and triumphs of the Duke) an escutcheon, and two funeral genii.

In 1560, Domenico, on his return to Fontainebleau, carved nine wooden statues for the Queen's garden. In 1561, he made the fine lower part of the funeral monument of Henry II (see article on Pilon). He was one of the artists chosen by Primaticcio for the tomb of Henry II, which was chiefly Germain Pilon's work. Domenico died shortly after 1566. He was famous also as a painter and engraver.

Domenico Fiorentino: The Victory of Claude de Guise. (Louvre.)

Bibliography: Koechlin et Marquet de Vasselot, *La Sculpture à Troyes et dans le Champagne méridonale au XVI siècle.* 1900.

**— di MICHELINO.**—Florentine painter of the school of Angelico; born 1417; died 1491.

In 1450 Domenico finished the gonfalcon started by Lorenzo di Puccio for the Compagnia di Sta. Maria delle Landi. A document of payment of 1466 records the extant panel of Dante in the Duomo, Florence, which was estimated on its completion by Neri di Bicci and Baldovinetti. In 1473 there is mention of certain figures of Saints in the cupboard of the Compagnia di S. Zanobi.

It is the Dante of 1466 which forms the basis for the artistic reconstruction of Domenico di Michelino; a number of attributions have been made to him on grounds of stylistic similarity.

BIBLIOGRAPHY: Vasari-Milanesi, II. —Gaye, *Carteggio,* II.—Berenson, *Drawings of the Florentine Painters,* 1903.—Van Marle, *Italian Schools, etc.*, X, 1927.

— **VENEZIANO.** — Florentine painter, probably of Venetian origin, born c. 1400; died 1461. One of the rarest talents of the quattrocento, whose influence upon later painters was profound, most notable in the case of his great pupil, Piero della Francesca. The origins of Domenico's style are difficult to determine. A great master, his painting is highly personal and does not reveal its school origins. Although an innovator in the specifically Florentine sense, his enchanting grace results from the fusion of Florentine and northern elements.

In 1438 Domenico wrote from Perugia to Piero de' Medici, asking to be recommended to his father Cosimo for the execution of an altarpiece (Gaye, Carteggio, I, p. 36). He speaks of the activity of Fra Filippo Lippi and Angelico, indicating a familiarity with Florentine artistic circles. From 1439 to 1445 he worked on frescoes in the choir of S. Egidio in the hospital of Sta. Maria Nuova (no longer existing), Bicci di Lorenzo and Piero della Francesca being mentioned as his assistants (Crowe and Cavalcaselle. Douglas ed., IV, 1911, p. 140, n. 1). It is mentioned in this document that Domenico painted in oils. In 1448 there is a record of two coffers for the marriage of Marco Parenti and Caterina Strozzi; in 1455 Domenico rents a house in Florence and passes judgment on a picture by Pesellino; in 1461 he dies.

Two signed pictures are left to us: the Uffizi altarpiece, painted for the Church of Sta. Lucia de' Magnoli; and a fresco fragment of the Madonna in London. Predella panels from the former altarpiece are scattered: Berlin, the *Martyrdom of St. Lucy;* Cambridge, England, the Fitzwillian Museum, the *Miracle of St. Zenobius;* Kress Collection, New York, the panel of *St. Francis Receiving the Stigmata;* Carl Hamilton Collection, New York, *St. John in the Desert.* The second signed work is the detached fresco fragment, formerly adorning the tabernacle of the Canto de' Carnesecchi near Sta. Maria Novella, now in the National Gallery. It represents the *Madonna Enthroned.*

In addition to these there are several other pictures by Domenico: the Berlin *Adoration of the Magi* (tondo); a Madonna in the Berenson Collection, Florence; a Madonna in the Kress Collection; two Saints in fresco, London; the fresco of *St. Francis and St. John the Baptist* on the wall of the nave of Sta. Croce, Florence.

The two Olivieri portraits, one in the Rockefeller Collection, New York, the other in the Mellon Collection, Washington, are products of Domenico's school.

BIBLIOGRAPHY: Vasari-Milanesi, II. —Gaye, *Carteggio,* I.—Crowe and Cavalcaselle, Douglas ed., IV, 1911. —Berenson, *Florentine Painters;*. and *Drawings of Florentine Painters,* II.—Venturi, *Storia,* etc., I, VII. —Bode, Jahrb. d. preuss. Kunstsamml., IV, 1883, 89 ff.; XVIII, 1897, 187 ff.—Schmarsow, Report. f. Kunstw., XVI, 1893, 159; L'Arte, XV, 1912, 9 ff., 81 ff.—Van Marle, *Italian Schools, etc.*, X, 1928, 308 ff.

**D O N A T E L L O.**—Florentine sculptor, 1386-1466. One of the greatest sculptors of all time, Donatello's influence upon his own and succeeding generations, not only in Florence but throughout Italy and, indeed, throughout Europe, is incalculable. It is extremely fortunate that there is so much factual evidence of his activity, because to it is related the whole Florentine Renaissance evolution.

His master is unknown; nor is there any document which proves the youthful trip to Rome with Brunelleschi to study the antique

DONATELLO: THE MARZOCCO. (National Museum, Florence.)

mentioned by Vasari, although Vasari's story is confirmed by Antonio Manetti, Donatello's and Brunelleschi's most intimate friend. If the expedition took place it must have occurred before 1406, at which time Donatello is first mentioned in Florence.

In 1406 he received the commission for two statues of Prophets for the Porta della Mandorla, statues which still exist as evidence for his early style. These were followed in 1408 by a commission for a colossal statue of brick and stucco for the buttress of the Tribuna, a work no longer in existence. From the same year dates the commission for the statue of the Evangelist, now in the left aisle of the Duomo. In 1411, Donatello was charged to execute the St. Mark on the exterior of Or San Michele; in 1415 he and Brunelleschi were to make a marble statue to be overlaid with gilded lead for the Duomo; in 1416 the marble David was taken from his workshop to its place in the Piazza Signoria (now in the Bargello); and from the same year dates the St. George for Or San Michele (now in the Bargello; the relief of St. George Slaying the Dragon is still on the exterior of Or San Michele, beneath a copy of the St. George). The commission for the Marzocco was of 1418; that of the St. Louis for Or San Michele (in Sta. Croce) of the same year; and in 1418 Donatello also executed a model in competition for the cupola of the Duomo.

In 1419 Donatello received the commission for the Tomb of John XXIII (in the Baptistry, the bronze figure only by Donatello); in 1420 the Marzocco was paid for; in 1421 he and Il Rosso were commissioned to execute a statue of Abraham for the Campanile (still in place, but not carried out by Donatello); and in the same year these two artists were charged to complete the statue of Moses for the Campanile begun by Ciuffagni (still in place, but not by the hand of Donatello). In 1422 the two heads of Prophets for the Porta della Mandorla were paid for; and four statues by Donatello were placed on the Campanile. In 1423 the Operai del Duomo, Orvieto, commissioned a gilded bronze statuette of the Baptist to surmount the font in the cathedral (now in Berlin); and in the same year Donatello was paid for the statue of St. Louis, and for the tabernacle which he had created to enframe Verrocchio's Christ and St. Thomas on the exterior of Or San Michele. In 1425 he took Michelozzo into partnership; and from the same year dates the Banquet of Herod for the font in the Duomo of Siena (still in place). In 1426 he contracted to make a sepulchral slab for the tomb of Giovanni Pecci; and in 1426-27 executed the Bust of S. Rossore, Pisa. In 1427 he and Michelozzo undertook the monument of Rinaldo Brancacci (relief of the Assumption of the Virgin now in the Naples Museum). The next year they received the commission for the Prato pulpit. A document of payment for Faith and Hope, figures for the Siena font, is also recorded in 1428. In 1430 payment is made to Donatello, Michelozzo and Brunelleschi for engineering work in the military camp near Lucca. In 1432-33, a commission is recorded for the sepulchral slab of Giovanni Crivelli; and in the latter year Pagno di Lapo Portigiani is dispatched to Rome to remind Donatello of the Prato pulpit, work on which has apparently not been proceeding fast enough to suit the Prato authorities. In 1433 Donatello receives the commission for the Cantoria. In the next year he competes with Ghiberti for the design of a windows in the Duomo; and in the same year the commission for the Prato pulpit is renewed, difficulties evidently having been smoothed out. Also in 1434 Donatello and Luca della Robbia receive the commission for a colossal head for the decoration of the cupola. From 1437 dates the commission for bronze doors for the Sagrestia Vecchia, Duomo, but in the same year this commission is transferred to Luca della Robbia and Michelozzo. In 1438 Donatello is charged to make the wax model for an altar to be executed by Luca della Robbia for the chapel of St. Paul in the Duomo. In 1442 there is the commission for an equestrian statue of Alfonso of Aragon to commemorate his conquest of Naples.

The next year, 1443, is most important in the great sculptor's chronology, for it is then that he goes to Padua, where he was to remain for the better part of the next ten years. From 1443-44 dates the Crucifix of the Santo in Padua; from 1446 the commission for ten reliefs of Angels and four Symbols of the Evangelists for the altar of the Santo; in 1446 he begins the statue of Gattamelata and in the same year receives the commission for the four reliefs of the Miracles of S. Antonio. In 1450 the completed altar of the Santo is dedicated (dismantled in the 17th century; now reconstructed to approximate original form). 1451 finds him in Ferrara and in the same year he receives from Modena commission for a gilded bronze equestrian statue of Borso d'Este (never carried out). Also from 1451 dates the wooden statue of the Baptist, still in place in the Church of the Frari, Venice. In 1453 the completed Gattamelata statue is uncovered to the public.

In 1457 he is commissioned by the Signoria, Siena, to make a statue of Goliath and another statue for the altar of S. Maria delle Grazie. From the same year dates the bronze statue of the Baptist still in the Duomo in Siena; and in 1457 he makes models for the bronze doors of the Siena Duomo. About 1460 he receives the commission from Cosimo de' Medici for decorations in S. Lorenzo, Florence, consisting of two pulpits, a Cantoria, four figures of Evangelists. The Cantoria in general resembles that of the Duomo differing from it in its proportions. The two pulpits were executed on Donatello's designs, and were finished by pupils, probably by Bertoldo, long after the master's death. The order to complete them was not given until 1515. Up to that time they were probably in the Academy of which Bertoldo was director, and may have influenced its students, of which the most noted was Michelangelo. These are Donatello's last recorded works; his death is registered in 1466, and there is a description of the majesty of his funeral and the universal honor paid him as one of the great men of Florence. Donatello had been for years the friend of Cosimo de' Medici, who not only admired his genius but felt for him the warmest personal affection. His great talent, the nobility of his character and the generous warmth of his personality won him a place in Florentine society attained by few artists of his period, a period in which the artist was still a craftsman, and of humble social station.

DONATELLO: BUST OF NICCOLÒ DA UZZANO. (National Museum, Florence.)

In addition to the extant works among those mentioned above, numerous works are attributed to Donatello, among which are the following: the Crucifix in Cappella dei Bardi, Sta. Croci, Florence; the

Campanile figures (see 1422) of the Zuccone or Job, Jeremiah, Habakkuk, and the *Baptist*; the *Poggio* on the Duomo; the bust of Niccolò da Uzzano, in the Bargello, one of the most dramatic portraits in existence; and several renditions of the Baptist, that in the Palazzo Martelli, those in Berlin, in the Louvre, and in the Bargello. The Magdalen, in wood, in the Baptistry, Florence, is connected stylistically with the later Baptists.

BIBLIOGRAPHY: R. Eitelberger von Edelberg, *Donatello, seine Zeit und seine Schule,* Quellenschriften für Kunstgeschichte. Vienna, 1875.—Reymond, *Donatello,* 1890.—A. G. Meyer, *Künstler Monographien,* 1903.—Frida Schottmüler, *Die Gestalt des Menschen in Donatello's Werk.* Zurich, 1904, and *Donatello, Ein Beitrag, etc.,* 1906.—*Tat. Munich* 1904.—Paul Schubring, Klassiker der Kunst. Stuttgard and Leipzig, 1907.—Bertaux, Les maîtres de l'Art.—Maud Cruttwell, *Donatello,* 1911 (with further literature).—Hans Kauffmann, *Donatello: Eine Einführung in sein Bilden und Denken.* Berlin, 1935; reviewed by U. Middeldorf in the Art Bulletin, December, 1936.

**DONATO di SAN VITALE.**—Trecento painter of Venice, collaborator of Caterino, first mentioned in 1344; died before 1388, when his wife makes her testament as a widow.

In 1367, Donato receives payment, together with Caterino, for a cross in S. Agnese. In 1372, he signs with Caterino the *Coronation* now in the Quirini-Stampalia Collection. From 1374 and 1382 date two testaments, in which he signs himself painter of San Vitale.

BIBLIOGRAPHY: B. Cecchetti, Arch. Veneto, XXXIII, 412; XXXIV, 208.—P. Paoletti, *Raccolta di doc.,* I, 7.—G. Ludwig, Jahrb. d. k. pr. Kunstsamml., XXIV.—L. Testi, *Storia d. pitt. venez.,* I, 1909, 237 ff.

**DONJON.**—See Keep.

**DONZELLO (Piero and Ippolito).**—Neapolitan painters, of the 15th century; they were brothers. They have been thought to have been pupils of Antonio Solario, called Lo Zingaro.

**DORÉ (Gustave).**—French draughtsman and painter. Born in

DORÉ (GUSTAVE): ILLUSTRATION FOR DON QUIXOTE OF LA MANCHA.

Strassburg, 1833; died in Paris, 1882. Gifted with extraordinary facility, Gustave Doré, from the age of sixteen, contributed to the *Journal pour Rire*. His production was considerable. Unfortunately he has frequently suffered from the translation of his drawing by the engraver, a translation which was too often a travesty. But when his drawing is well reproduced, it has qualities of chiaroscuro and fantasy which no other illustrator possesses to the same degree. His imagination was as marvellous as it was fertile. The gaiety of his work made him an admirable illustrator of Rabelais (1872), and of *Les Contes Drolatiques* of Balzac (1865). But serious, calm subjects were not congenial, and his illustrations to the *Bible* (1865), and to the *Fables of La Fontaine* (1867), are less good. But he found himself again in *The Divine Comedy* (1861-1868), and in *Don Quixote* (1861) which gave scope to his fancy. They are not much esteemed in France, but they were appreciated in England. His drawing is often feeble, and his colour acid (the *Rebel Angels*; the *Titans*; the *Death of Orpheus*; the *Martyrs*; the *Downfall of Paganism*, etc.). But he painted some fine landscapes of mountains (*A Lake in Scotland,* in the Collection of M. Germain). At the end of his career. he devoted himself to sculpture. The only notable work of this kind he left is the monument to Alexandre Dumas "père" (Place Malesherbes, Paris).

**DORIA PALACE.**—See Genoa; Rome.

**DORIC ORDER.**—See Capital; Greece (Architecture).

**DORYPHORUS.**—See Polyclitus; also Pl. 20, Vol. I.

**DOSSI (Battista).**—Italian painter, died in 1548. Brother of Giovanni Dosso Dossi, with whom he worked a great deal. He was chiefly a landscape painter, and a decorator. He painted landscape backgrounds to his brother's pictures. He also designed cartoons for tapestry—the *Story of Hercules,* and the *Metamorphoses.*

**DOSSO DOSSI (Giovanni Luteri, called).**—Ferrarese painter. About 1479-1542. He may have been a pupil of Costa. But he was influenced chiefly by the great Venetians. His landscapes and mysterious distances must have been inspired by Giorgione and Titian. He was called the Ariosto of painting. Not only was he actually the friend of the poet who celebrated him in his *Furioso,* but he imitated the elegant and subtle heroism in his paintings. His *St. George* and *St. Sebastian* are in the Brera Gallery, Milan. *Circe,* in the Borghese Gallery, seated in front of a warm, wide landscape, is at once haughty and seductive. The principal paintings of Dosso Dossi are in the Galleries of Ferrara (notably, a large altarpiece with six compartments), and of Modena.

**DOU (Gerard).**—Dutch genre and portrait painter of Leyden, Apr. 7, 1613-Feb. 9, 1675. A slow and fastidious painter, he was a pupil of Rembrandt, in Leyden (1628-31). In the 50-60s he travelled in Germany and to Haarlem; there are several extant works dated in Munich. He then opened a studio and painted for nobility and royalty. In his early works one may detect the same model as used by Rembrandt; his paintings have the same golden tonality as those of his master, but unlike Rembrandt, he copied every minute detail with the most exacting technique. After 1640 Dou's style changed. The influence of Rembrandtesque chiaroscuro, and idealized realism disappear. Two types of compositions may be distinguished: The portrait, mostly self-portraits (famous one in Amsterdam), in which the model is framed by an arched window and illuminated artificially. Dou was the originator of this, later so popular, type of portrait composition. His other paintings were genre-scenes mostly of indoor life. The typical paintings show a large interior with numerous small figures, including the old and sick; despite the spotless interiors there is an artificial disorder illuminated by a concentrated lighting. This pseudo-realism of his compositions may be compared to the pseudo-democracy of the Dutch republic at that time. There is a finely blended colorharmony with occasional brilliant spots. His most famous paintings are *Young Man* (Hague), and *Dropsical Woman* (Louvre).

BIBLIOGRAPHY: Hofstede, *Holländische Maler,* 1907, I.—W. Martins, *Life and works of Gerard Dou,* 1902.

**DOUANIER (Le).**—See Rousseau (H. J.).

**DOUGHTY (Thomas).**—American landscape painter (1793-1856). He was born in Philadelphia, Pennsylvania, 19th July 1793, and at an early age was apprenticed to learn the leather business. He had a few lessons in drawing, but was otherwise self-taught when he decided some time later to be a painter by profession. He worked in Boston for a while and also travelled to Paris and London. His most characteristic works were done in the United States. They were stiff and precise after the manner of the Hudson River school but at the time they were painted they were popular. He sketched calm and peaceful river scenes along the Hudson and the Delaware, but also did some of the banks of the Thames and the Seine. He died in New York City 22d July 1856. Examples of his work may be seen in the Metropolitan Museum of Art, the Pennsylvania Academy of Fine Arts, and the Corcoran Gallery in Washington, D. C.

BIBLIOGRAPHY: H. T. Tuckerman, *The Book of the Artists,* 1867.—William Dunlap, *The History of the Rise and Progress of the Arts of Design in the United States,* 1918.

**DOURIS.**—See Greece (Vases).

**DOWNMAN (John).**—English painter (1750?-1824), pupil of Benjamin West; elected A.R.A. 1795. Chiefly known for his coloured portrait drawings, many of which have great gracefulness and charm.

BIBLIOGRAPHY: G. C. Williamson, *John Downman.* London, 1907.

**DRESDEN.**—Dresden does not possess interesting buildings dating from earlier than the Renaissance. Nothing is left of the early castle whose buildings were transformed in the 16th century (east wing, and west tower), by Hans Dehn, in the style of the Italian Renaissance; and in the 17th century, the Electors embellished their palace, as well as the chapel. The architecture was again much modified after 1890.

Dresden was most flourishing during the reign of Frederick Augustus II (1694-1733). He built the "Zwinger," an elegant construction in the Rococo style, begun in 1711, and never finished (Pöpplemann, architect). The Frauenkirche (Bähr, 1722) is another interesting building, and the Royal Gallery contains famous paintings, notably Raphael's *Sistine Madonna.*

BIBLIOGRAPHY: G. Servières, *Dresden,* Collection des villes d'art. Paris.—O. Richter, *Geschichte der Stadt Dresden.* Dresden, 1900.—P. Schumann, *Dresden.* Leipzig, 1909.

**DREUX (France).**—The Chapel Royal was begun in 1816 by the Duchess of Orleans. The glass was made from designs by Ingres.

The Hôtel de Ville dates from the first half of the 16th century.

**DREVET (Claude).**—French engraver, nephew of Pierre Drevet, 1697-1781. He left only 14 engravings, of which five are portraits after Rigaud.

**— (Pierre).**—French engraver, 1663-1738. He was first the pupil of Germain Audran, in Lyon, and then of Gérard Audran, in Paris. He engraved chiefly Rigaud's pictures. His finest engravings are the portraits of: Louis XIV, Louis XV, the Comte de Toulouse, and the Duc de Villars.

**— (Pierre Imbert).**—French engraver. 1697-1739. He was the son of Pierre Drevet, and left some fine portraits: Adrienne Lecouvreur, Samuel Bernard, and especially one of Bossuet, after Rigaud, which is his masterpiece. He died insane, as the result of sun-stroke. He left only 33 engravings, all remarkable.

BIBLIOGRAPHY: A Firmin Didot and G. Pawlowski, *Les Drevet.* Paris, 1876.

**DROLLING (Martin).**—Flemish painter. Born in Oberhergheim, 1752; died in Paris, 1827. Little is known of his life. Pupil of an obscure painter of Selestat, he went to Paris, and exhibited little intimate scenes, inspired by the Dutch, which still interest us. There is much domestic calm in the *Kitchen* (Louvre).

The painter has irreproachable sincerity, but lacks spirit. One looks in vain for the half-carelessness of a Teniers, or the lively accents of a Metsu.

Orleans Museum possesses two pictures by Martin Drolling: a *Kitchen Interior,* and the *Woman and the Mouse.*

**DROUAIS (The).**—They were descended from a family of Pont Audemer. The first to make a name as a painter was Hubert Drouais (1699-1767). After receiving lessons from an artist monk of Rouen, he went to Paris to study with François de Croy, and was received at the Academy on showing his portraits of the painter Christophe (in the École des Beaux Arts) and of the sculptor Lemoyne (now in the Louvre). He also painted miniatures, and even confined himself to this kind of work, during the second period of his career. His tender, rosy tones pleased the public. His works are scarce. He had, however, a "clientèle" of ladies of fashion, and painted four of the celebrated beauties of the day. Hubert Drouais lacked much individuality.

His son, François Hubert Drouais (1727-1775) was trained by Boucher, whose pleasing colour, mannered poses and operatic landscape backgrounds he imitated. He was the most superficial of the portrait painters of Louis XV's reign, and, in fact, characteristic of that artificial period. He was the chosen painter of women. He painted their dresses, chiefly pink, with exquisite modulations of colour. He painted the Pompadour in her old age (Orléans Gallery), but he was more particularly the painter of Madame Dubarry, whom he painted as *Flora*, in hunting costume (engraved by Beauvarlet), and, in a garment, the lightness of which evoked a scandal at the Salon of 1771, as a vestal virgin. He was also the fashionable painter of children. He painted them in grape-gatherers' costume, in mountain dress, and dancing at the end of a ribbon (thus, the children of the Duc de Bouillon); beside the Comte d'Artois, aged six, sits his sister Clotilde, future queen of Sardinia, in Amazon style, on a goat (Louvre). The picture of a little scholar carrying his portfolio of drawings under his arm which was shown at the Salon of 1755, under the title of *Le Petit Polisson*, was an extraordinary success. It is, in fact, in these portraits, that he shows the most charm and fancy. His fragile, superficial art is one of the most refined of the 18th century. To give more purity to his colour, he used, especially in his painting of flesh, an under painting of white. The care he took as to the choice of colours and their quality promised his pictures long preservation. François Hubert Drouais had a son, Germain Jean, who became David's chosen pupil, and rose among his contemporaries like an infant prodigy. But the fevers from which he suffered in Rome proved fatal, and he died in 1788, at the age of twenty-five.

Bibliography: P. Dorbec, *Revue de l'Art ancien et moderne*. 1904, Vol. II.—C. Gabillot, *Gazette des Beaux Arts*. 1905, Vol. II; 1906, Vol. I.

**DRY POINT.**—See Engraving.

**DU BOIS (Guy Pène).**—Contemporary American painter and critic. He was born in Brooklyn, New York, 4th January 1884, the son of Henri du Bois, a literary and music critic. He studied at the Chase School under Carol Beckwith, William M. Chase, Frank V. DuMond, Robert Henri, and Kenneth H. Miller. In 1905 he went to Europe, where he worked under Steinlen. When he returned to the United States the next year he began writing for various periodicals and newspapers. He was art critic on the *Evening Post*, assistant to Royal Cortissoz on the art criticism for the *New York Tribune*, and wrote articles on fine art for *Vogue* and *Hearst's Magazine*. For about seven years he was the editor of *Arts and Decoration*. He is also the author of monographs on Edward Hopper, Ernest Lawson, George B. Luks, John Sloan, and William J. Glackens. He is sincere in his criticism but is slightly more inclined toward idealism than the realism evident in his own paintings.

Although much of his time has been taken up with the writing of art criticisms du Bois has continued his painting. He depicts scenes of city life, glimpses of nightclubs and restaurants and some outdoor scenes. His figures are solidly built and have well-rounded compact forms. They stand out before a vaguely sensed background of scenery which never obtrudes on their consciousness. All are studies of contemporary life often treated a bit on the satirical side as in the famous *Waiter!* While the majority of his work are figure pieces he has done some portraits, including *Jeanne Eagels as "Sadie Thompson" in "Rain"* and *Robert W. Chandler*, both of which are in the Whitney Museum of American Art in New York City. He is also well represented in the collection of the Phillips Memorial Gallery in Washington, D. C.

Bibliography: Royal Cortissoz, *Guy Pène du Bois*, American Artists Series, 1931.—For other articles see the *Index of Twentieth Century Artists* for November, 1934.

**DUBOIS (Paul).**—French sculptor and painter, 1829-1905. His

Dubois (Paul): Tomb of General Lamoricière. (Cathedral of Nantes.)

father was a notary. Through his mother, he was descended from the great sculptor Pigalle. He sometimes signed himself Dubois-Pigalle.

After studying law in Paris with the intention of becoming a notary like his father, he entered the studio of the sculptor Toussaint, at the age of twenty-six, and at the same time studied in the studio of the painter Picot. His progress was rapid. In 1859, he went to Italy. He saw Genoa, Pisa, Rome, Naples, but he was chiefly impressed by the closely-observed and sensitive draughtsmanship of the Florentine masters. This was the influence that he brought back with him to France. The fruits of this sojourn, which had lasted five years, appeared at the Salon of 1863. The *St. John* (Luxembourg), and the *Narcissus* (Luxembourg), made a sensation in the artistic world. By these works, Dubois became the inspirer of a kind of neo-Florentine school which was responsible for several good French sculptors at the end of the 19th century. He married, and settled in the Rue d'Assas, Paris, in the studio which he kept till his death. If these works of the artist were respected, they were followed by a really popular one, *The Florentine Singer* (1863—Luxembourg), which won him the Medal of Honour, and became one of the best known statues through reproduction and small bronzes. In the Salon of 1867, Dubois exhibited the *Virgin and Child* (Church of the Trinity), which is reminiscent of Luca della Robbia. The artist, incapable of abandoning himself to facile work, was conscientious and fastidious in the extreme, but apt to stop short before carrying his works as far as he might have done.

His next exhibit to the Salon was a simple nude, *Eve* (Petit Palais). Dubois also showed himself to be a talented painter. In the same Salon (1876), the portrait group of his children placed him among the best portrait painters, and so many commissions came to him that his friends feared he would neglect sculpture.

Dubois (Paul): Meditation. (Tomb of General Lamoricière at Nantes.)

But Dubois was given the commission for the tomb of Lamoricière (Nantes Cathedral), for which he made in turn statues representing *Military Courage, Charity, Faith,* and *Civil Courage*. To these followed: the equestrian statue of the Constable of Montmorency (Chantilly); the *Jeanne d'Arc* (Place St. Augustin, Paris); tomb of the Duc d'Aumale (Dreuse); and *Alsace and Lorraine* (Nancy), a group on which he was still working at the time of his death. To these works must be added about forty remarkable busts of Baudry, Heuner, Pasteur, Bonnat, Duc d'Aumale, Legouvé, Saint Saëns, Gounod, etc.

In painting, Dubois executed about 70 portraits. His modelling is of great refinement; his colour has a tendency to monochrome. His work has a certain "sameness" and insignificance. It lacks breadth and power, but it is, nevertheless, graceful and refined in feeling.

Dubois was modest, hard working, and unspoiled by honours. He accepted the directorship of the École des Beaux Arts, and devoted twenty-seven years of his life to it.

See Pl. 52, Vol. II.

**DUCCIO di BUONINSEGNA.**—Sienese primitive painter, whose influence profoundly affected the development of the Sienese school, and of Italian painting in general.

In 1278 Duccio is mentioned as decorating twelve chests for the municipal archives, and in 1279 the cover of an account book. In 1280 he pays a fine of 100 livres for an unspecified offense—the first comment upon his character, attested to ever more forcibly by the documents which follow. In 1285 he contracted with the Confraternity of Sta. Maria Novella, Florence, to execute a painting of the Virgin. Book-covers are mentioned in the years 1285, 1286, 1291, 1293, and 1295. In the last year he is requested to give his opinion regarding the site of a fountain, and in this year he is again fined. In 1298 Duccio sat on the "Radota," a committee assisting the town council. The next year he refuses to swear fidelity to the Capitano del Popolo; the difficulty evidently persisted for in 1302 the Capitano fines him 18 livres 10 soldi. Three small fines are listed for 1302, all for non-payment of debts, and at the end of the year he is fined 5 livres for causing a public disturbance. Also in 1302 he receives 48 livres for a Maestà with predella for the altar of the chapel of the Town Hall.

In 1304 Duccio is mentioned as the owner of a "mountain of vines." From 1308 dates the contract for the large Maestà now in the Opera del Duomo, Siena, the predella of which is dispersed in several museums and collections. In 1310 he is urged to hurry the work upon it; in 1311 it is finished and is received, according to contemporary chronicles, with great popular rejoicing. In 1319 Duccio died, probably insolvent, since his widow and seven children refused their heritage.

The single authenticated work of Duccio's which has come down to us is the great Maestà of 1311. The scattered predelle are to be found in the following places: Berlin, *Nativity with two Prophets;* London, *Annunciation, Christ Healing the Blind, Transfiguration*; Mackay Collection, New York, *Christ Calling the Children of Zebedee;* Frick Collection, New York, *Temptation of Christ;* Rockefeller Collection, New York, *Christ and the Samaritan Woman, The Raising of Lazarus*. The rest of the predelle are in the Opera del Duomo, Siena.

The fact that this masterpiece of Duccio's dates from the very end of his activity makes the attribution of further works a particularly difficult problem, since it must be assumed that a considerable development took place in his style. Already in 1285 Duccio had been commissioned to execute a major altarpiece, and not in Siena but in Florence, which would indicate that he was then well known as a painter. Critics have attempted to identify this Maestà of 1285 with the famous *Rucellai Madonna,* in Sta. Maria Novella, Florence, subject of controversy for many years. It was traditionally ascribed to Cimabue, an assumption based upon the statement of Vasari who tends to give to every work of high quality a Florentine origin. The picture is quite obviously not by Cimabue, and few critics persist in attributing it to him. It is much closer to Duccio, but shows, on the other hand, certain affinities to the art of Cimabue and stylistic differences from the style of Duccio as we know it in the Siena Maestà. Art historians are by no means agreed as to whether these differences can be due to the twenty-three years which would separate it from the Maestà if it is the picture painted by Duccio in 1285; or whether it must be attributed to a painter working between Cimabue and Duccio, but more Sienese than Florentine.

A number of further pictures are attributed to Duccio on stylistic grounds.

Bibliography: Vasari-Milanesi, I. —Milanesi, *Doc. per la stor. dell' arte senese*, I, 1854.—A. Linsini, Bull. sen. di stor. patr. V, 1898, 20 ff. — R. Davidsohn, Repert. f. Kstwiss., XXIII, 900, pp. 313-14.—Ghiberti, *Commentarii* (ed. Frey, 1886; ed. Schlosser, 1911).—Crowe and Cavalcaselle, Douglas, 1903, I, III.—Venturi, *Storia dell' arte ital.*, V, 1907.—E. Jacobsen, *Das Trecento in der Gemäldegal. zu Siena,* 1907, p. 21 ff.—Berenson, *Central Ital. Painters,* 1908.—C. H. Weigelt, *Duccio di Buoninsegna*, 1911.—Van Marle, *Recherches sur l'iconographie de Giotto et de Duccio,* Strassburg, 1920; Italian Schools, etc., II, 1 ff.

**— (Agostino di).**—See Agostino.

**DU CERCEAU.**—See Androuet du Cerceau.

**DUCREUX (Joseph).**—French portrait painter, 1737-1802. Pupil of La Tour. In 1769, he was ordered to the court of Vienna to paint the portrait of the future Dauphine Marie Antoinette, who, when she came to the throne, conferred on him the title of Painter to the Queen, and was even the godmother of one of his daughters. He was not a member of the Academy where, it is said, he had enemies owing to the frankness of his naturalism. But, to judge from the number of oil and pastel portraits which he made of his contemporaries, his work was not less in demand for that. He portrayed Revolutionary figures—Robespierre, Couthon, Saint Just, Boissy d'Anglas; and Louis XVI during his captivity in the Temple, and Bailly on the eve of his execution. Under the Directory, he painted celebrated beauties, such as Madame Récamier. He often painted self-portraits. Like his master, La Tour, he amused himself in painting himself in various and comic positions.

Bibliography: Prosper Dorbec, *Gazette des Beaux Arts,* 1902.

**DUGHET (Gaspard).**—Known as Le Guaspre, and Gaspard-Poussin. French painter. Born in Rome, 1613, died in Rome, 1675. Son of a Parisian, Jacques Dughet, who had settled in Rome, Gaspard Dughet was sixteen years old when Poussin married his sister. Gaspard had already covered his books with able pen and ink studies. On the advice of his brother-in-law, he spent three years scouring the Roman campagna, and studying its noble sites. The young man seemed to add an ideal grandeur to the realism of Poussin's school; but one soon tires of the rather unreal magnificence of his sites of his monotonous buildings, and majestic forests.

However that may be, at the age of twenty, Gaspard was among the most esteemed painters of his day. After a short visit to Castiglione, Gaspard took his way across the Sabine mountains, which he represented in so many of his pictures. His landscapes appealed so much to the Romans, and his compositions reminded them so vividly of the artist who inspired them that the artists of Rome joined the name of his master to that of Gaspard or Guaspre. According to his biographers, although Gaspard-Poussin painted a magnificent *View of Damascus,* he never left Italy. He only visited Naples, Perugia and Florence. He arrived in Florence when Pietro di Cortona was painting the Loggie of the Pitti Palace, and on the request of this painter, he decorated one of the apartments of the palace with a large fresco landscape. When he returned to Rome, Claude Lorrain's works filled him with so much admiration that, in spite of his age and celebrity, he studied at the school of this painter of sunlight.

There is one kind of painting in which Gaspard-Poussin excelled, and seemed quite original. He was the first painter who thought of representing storms, and for two centuries he has been unsurpassed in expressing the confusion and poetry of the countryside beaten by storm. These paintings are now mostly in the English galleries.

Towards the end of his life, Gaspard, who had earned a big fortune, but had not known how to keep it, became infirm. The necessity of remaining inactive produced a profound melancholy. He died on the 25th May, 1675, leaving innumerable pictures. The Louvre has several pictures by Gaspard-Poussin, but it is chiefly in the Fabre Museum of Montepellier and in Italy that he is most abundantly represented. He was an able painter, but he lacked the highest qualities of emotion and thought.

**DUJARDIN (Karel).**—Dutch painter and etcher. About 1622-1678. He first studied with Berghem, and then went to Italy. He lived a very chequered life, spending a great deal of money. In France, he married an elderly widow who was very rich, and took her back to Holland. In 1674 he returned to Italy, where he ended his life.

His chief works are: a group-portrait of the Regents of the Amsterdam Prison (Amsterdam); the *Charlatans* (Louvre); *Calvary* (Louvre), and several landscapes.

He also left etchings of landscapes and of animals.

Bibliography: Blanc, *Histoire des Peintres.*

**DU MONSTIER (Daniel).**—French painter, 1574-1646. Son of Cosme Du Monstier, painter to the king. He left some very fine portraits, generally executed with red and black chalk, or with pastel, such as the magnificent portrait of the Duke of Longueville (1632), which is remarkable for its sure and supple execution (Louvre).

**— (Nicolas).**—French painter and engraver. Pupil of his father, Daniel, he was received at the Academy, in 1665, with the portrait of Errard.

**DÜNWEGGE (or Duenwege, Victor and Heinrich).**—German painters (brothers) active end of the 15th and beginning of the 16th century. School of Westphalia. Their most important works are the *Examples of Justice* (Town Hall of Wesel), and the Triptych of the Domenican Church, Dortmund, painted in 1521.

**DUOMO.**—An Italian cathedral. —See Florence; Milan; Pisa; etc.

**DUPRÉ (Giovanni).**—Italian sculptor, 1817-1882. He worked first with his father, a sculptor in wood, in Siena; and then went to Florence to study in Bartolini's studio. The first work he exhibited, the *Dead Abel,* was a great success. The jury had, in the first instance, refused it, saying that the young sculptor had simply cast a model. But Bartolini protested, and demonstrated on the model that his proportions were not absolutely the same as those of the sculpture, and the work was received, and much admired.

Dupré sculptured chiefly mythological allegories and religious subjects: *Giotto and St. Anthony* (Uffizi); the *Dying Sappho*; the *Child Bacchus*: the *Triumph of the Cross,* and the *Deposition*; the fine *Pietà* in the cemetery of Siena, one of his most moving works; and the bas-reliefs of the base of the Egyptian cup, in Rome. His most popular work in Italy is the Monument of Cavour (Turin, 1872).

**— (Guillaume).**—French sculptor and engraver of medals. Born between 1575 and 1580; died 1647. He was a Protestant, and married a daughter of Barthélemy Prieur, himself a Protestant. From 1604 to 1639 he was "controller general of the figures on coins." In the art of the medallion, this master equalled the Italians of the 15th century. The individuality of each physiognomy is expressed with singular energy and sincerity. The division of the medal into front and reverse gave Dupré scope to express both his sense of realism and classicism. The allegories on the back are drawn in a broad, firm style.

Among his numerous productions we may mention: the large medal of Henri IV and Catherine de Médicis; those of Pierre Jeannir (1618), a pure masterpiece; of Louis XIII (1623), with the image of Justice on the back; of the Doge, Antonio Memmo; of Brulart de Sillery (Apollo on the reverse); of Henri de Maleyssie (1631). In the Louvre, the bust of Nicolas de Vic shows Dupré's strong qualities of naturalistic art.

Bibliography: Freury, *Guillaume Dupré.* Paris, 1883.

**— (Jules).**—French painter, 1811-1889. Son of a china manufacturer, he would not carry on the paternal trade. Nature was his best master. From 1831, he sent some studies to the Salon, which were rather weak, but which had a certain sincerity: they were views of Haute Vienne, of Montmorency and of the Isle Adam. In 1835, a view of the neighbourhood of Abbeville was noteworthy; and the following year, the *Sunset* showed that he was in full possession of his art. A visit to England contributed to his taste for broad harmonies and fine colour. He painted seascapes which are perhaps rather heavy. He was inspired by the Landes, and ended his days in the Isle Adam, the watery landscapes of which provided the subjects for his last paintings. Robust forms and powerful masses abound in his pictures, but the gloomy scale of colour he adopted, combined with the mass of his material, too often deprived his works of all impression of lightness.

*Morning* (Louvre) has poetic charm; and pictures in the Thomy Thiéry and Chauchard Collections show how admirably he painted oak-trees. *The Large Oak,* in the Louvre, shows that Dupré cared for the effect above everything, simplifying his composition and pruning his landscape, to give the old oak-tree its full value. A picture of this kind recalls rather the composed landscapes of the classicists than the nature studies of Rousseau. Two pictures with oak-trees in the Chauchard Collection show us his predilection for these heroic trees with their twisting branches. But his finest picture in this collection, and perhaps in the Louvre, is the *Vanne.*

Dupré formulated his doctrine in striking precepts, sometimes even by paradox. "Nature is the pretext," he was fond of saying, "art is the end."

See Pl. 55, Vol. II.

**DUQUESNOY (François).**—Known as "François Flamand." Flemish sculptor, 1594-1643. He first worked with his father, and then finished his studies in Italy. In Flanders he was a friend of Rubens; in Rome he became intimate with Poussin. Both influenced him. His first works were a fine marble group *Venus and Cupid,* a large statue of the Virgin, an *Apollo* and a *Mercury.* He made a charming bas-relief of Children Playing with a Goat for the Cardinal Barberini. He had a special talent for carving the chubby forms and grace of childhood. Pope Urban VIII commissioned him to make the statue of St. Andrew which decorates one of the supports of the dome of St. Peter's: he worked there for seven years. He also decorated the baldacchino of St. Peter's. He left other works—tombs, bas-reliefs (among them the well-known *Silenus Asleep,* and *Sacred Love Overcoming Profane Love*), a statue of Bacchus, in marble, a *Concert of Cherubim,* and *Children Playing.*

His talent brought him to the notice of Richelieu, who, on the advice of Poussin, called him to Paris to create a school of sculpture there. Duquesnoy at once set out, but he did not reach the end of his journey. He fell ill at Livourne, and died there. He was not fifty years of age.

Bibliography: Fétis, *Notice sur Duquesnoy.* Brussels, 1856.

**DÜRER (Albrecht).**—Celebrated German painter and engraver, 1471-

Dürer (Albrecht): Self-portrait. (Museum, Munich.)

1528. We know his life from his own writings: *The Family Chronicle, Letters from Venice,* and *The Journal of a Visit to the Low Countries.* He was born in Nuremberg in 1471. His father was a goldsmith, and intended his son for the same trade; but when the child showed a desire to learn painting, he sent him to be apprenticed to Wolgemut, in 1486. Before this date, the young Dürer had already drawn a portrait of himself in pencil (1484—in the Albertina), and a *Madonna* between two angel musicians (1485). From the point of view of technique the years of apprenticeship were very profitable to the artist, but it does not appear that Wolgemut, who was a mediocre painter, exercised a great influence on his development.

On leaving his studio, in 1490, Dürer worked in Basle, perhaps also in Strassburg, and later in Venice (1490-1494). From this period dates the portrait of himself at the age of twenty-three, one of the finest and most expressive of Dürer's self-portraits. On his return to Nuremberg, he married, and for many years led a hard-working existence to support his family. He made some pen and ink copies after Mantegna, and then set up as a painter. Probably it was Frederick the Wise who commissioned him to make the Triptych of Dresden, a work much influenced by Italian art, but also showing German sentimentality. The *Men Bathing* and *Women Bathing* (Bremen Museum) show early attempts of the artist to render the human body (1496). In 1498, came the self-portrait (Madrid), then those of Hans and Elizabeth Tucher. The same year, he published the *Apocalypse according to St. John,* wood-engravings, in fifteen large plates, a powerful work, of grave and fantastic inspiration, in which the engraver expresses himself vigorously and precisely. The most famous of the plates of this series shows the *Four Horsemen*—the archer, the two kings, and Death—galloping over everything in their way.

Dürer, who is so vigorous in this vision of the Apocalypse, was also a fervent lover of nature. He

DÜRER (ALBRECHT): THE FOUR HORSEMEN. (Wood Engraving illustrating the *Apocalypse of St. John.*)

painted fresh water-colours of the surroundings of Nuremberg, pools, glades, the meadow of Haller, *the Little Mill* (Louvre), the *Wire-factory* (Berlin); Views of Nuremberg (Berlin, Bremen), the *Village* (Bonnat Collection).

Dürer expresses himself best in his drawings and engravings. There is still a hardness of execution in

DÜRER (ALBRECHT): DESTINY.

the *Offers of Love* (1496), *the Promenade, the Turkish Family,* and the *Four Witches.* The *Prodigal Son,* more supple in modelling, has, for a background, a picturesque corner of an old village, with steep roofs. *The Large Hercules,* also called the *Effects of Jealousy* (c. 1500), shows us a large, sturdy body, with protruding muscles. The large *Fortune,* or *Nemesis,* is a magnificent conception. Fortune, strong and severe Nemesis, with long, unfolded wings, stands on a ball, which floats above the picturesque village of Klausen, the little houses of which are huddled together at the meeting place of two torrents; in one hand she holds the cup for the prudent; in the other, the bridle for the proud. The heavy figure of an ungraceful matron, with protruding stomach and plump thighs, rather expresses the inevitability of fate than careless destiny. The *St. Hubert* is one of Dürer's best known copper engravings (c. 1500-03). *Adam and Eve* (1504) is a close study of the nude, for which the artist made numerous researches in his preoccupation with

DÜRER (ALBRECHT): ADAM AND EVE. (Engraving on copper.)

the ideal proportions for the human body, a preoccupation which was suggested to him by the Venetian painter, Jacopo de' Barbari, who was living in Nuremberg from 1500 to 1504, and who made Dürer acquainted with copies of antique statues. Dürer's oil paintings of this period are not as important as his engravings. *The Baumgartner Altarpiece* (Munich) is, however, famous for the portraits of the donors, Lucas and Stephan Baumgartner, represented standing, in armour, on a black background.

In 1506, Dürer paid a second visit to Venice, during which he painted the *Feast of the Rosary,* for the Fondaco dei Tedeschi (the picture, much damaged by clumsy restorations, is in the Convent of the Premonstrants of Strahow, in Prague). The Italians, who greatly admired Dürer's engravings, accused him of not being able to paint. "Now they all confess that they have never seen finer colour," wrote Dürer, after he had painted the *Feast of the Rosary.* The Portrait of Dürer by himself (Munich) shows Italian influence; the serious countenance, with very wide-open eyes, framed by long curly hair, is certainly not a faithful portrait. The artist has tried to build up the face geometrically. The same concern is seen in the *Adam and Eve* of the Prado (1507), and in the researches of perspective in the *Martyrdom of Ten Thousand Christians under King Sapor* (Vienna), finished in 1508. In the same museum is preserved the large picture of *All Saints Adoring the Trinity,* painted for M. Landauer in 1511. In 1512, after his *Madonna with a Lily* (Prague) and his *Virgin with a Pear* (Vienna), Dürer gave up painting for a long time, and returned to engraving, his favourite means of expression.

Two of Dürer's woodcut series depict the Passion of Christ: one, the *Large Passion,* finished in 1510, contains some plates executed in 1498; the other, the *Small Passion,* was completed in 1511. The same subject was treated in a cycle of sixteen engravings, finished in 1513. A large group of wood-cuts, done partly in the years 1502-05, partly in 1510, depict the *Life of the Virgin.*

In 1513 and 1514, Dürer made three famous copper engravings: *The Knight, Death and the Devil,*

DÜRER (ALBRECHT): THE KNIGHT, DEATH AND THE DEVIL. (Engraving on copper.)

*Melancholy* (considered by Professor Panofsky to be a spiritual self-portrait), and *St. Jerome in his Study.* The knight, strong and resolute, passes proudly on his way, scorning Death who holds out an hour-glass, and the horrible demon who accompanies him. Melancholy, a winged woman, seated and weary, symbolises the despair of unavailing curiosity, and contrasts with the happy serenity of faith, which St. Jerome typifies. *The Triumph,* executed for the Emperor Maximilian, is an ambitious composition, in wood-cuts. The *Book of Hours,* full of spirited drawings (Munich), was also made for the Emperor.

In 1520, Dürer visited the Netherlands, where he was triumphantly welcomed. He learned a great deal from the Flemish masters. He appreciated their precision, and realism, and, like them, he set to work to paint portraits: *Head of an Old Man* (Louvre); *Portrait of an Unknown Man* (Prado, 1521); portraits of two Nuremberg citizens; the well-known portraits of Jerome Holzschuher (Berlin, 1526) and of J. Muffel (Berlin). His engraved portraits include those of the Elector Frederick the Wise, W. Pirckheimer (his close friend) and Erasmus. Finally, the *Four Apostles* (Munich), a diptych, are the artist's most powerful creations. On one side, the active disciples, St. Paul and St. Mark, on the other side, the gentle, meditative face of St. John, and the paternal one of St. Peter.

The *Four Apostles* was Albrecht Dürer's last work. He spent the last two years of his life in publishing his theoretical writings. Dürer kept the fantastic imagination and sensibility of the primitives, together with a certain Gothic brutality; but the Renaissance gave him a taste for analysis and philosophy and a lucidity of spirit which restrained his other qualities.

See Pl. 12, Vol. I; Pl. 26, Vol. II.

BIBLIOGRAPHY: Sir Martin Conway, *The Literary Remains of Albrecht Dürer.* London, 1889.—M. Thausing, *A. Dürer.*—H. Wölfflin, *Die Kunst Albrecht Dürers.* Munich, 1905.—V. Scherer, *Dürer,* Klassiker der Kunst, Vol. IV.—T. D. Barlow, *A. Dürer, His Life and Work.* London, 1923.—M. J. Friedländer. *A. Dürer der Kupferstecher und Holzschneider.* Berlin, 1919.—Campbell Dodgson, *Albrecht Dürer,* The Masters of Engraving and Etching. London, 1926.—Kurth, W., *The Complete Woodcuts of A. Dürer.* London, 1927.—Tietze, H., *Der junge Dürer.* Augsburg, 1928.

**DURHAM (England).**—Durham possesses the finest Norman Cathedral in England. It dates from the 12th and 13th centuries. The west front is flanked by two square towers. Its interior is very harmonious.

See Pl. 49, Vol. I.

**DÜSSELDORF (School of).**—See Lessing.

**DUVENECK (Frank).**—American painter, sculptor, graver and teacher (1848-1919). He was born in Covington, Kentucky, 9th October 1848, the son of Bernard Decker, but changed his name when his mother married Squire Duveneck. He was, as a boy, an assistant to an ecclesiastical decorator gilding altars, carving frames, etc. In 1870 he went to the Munich Academy to study and carried off many of their prizes during his three years' stay. He then returned to Cincinnati to paint portraits and do odd jobs for church decorations, but in 1875 he again went to Munich. This time he stayed two years, then spent a year at Venice. That same year, 1878, he opened an art school in Cincinnati and soon had over fifty pupils. Included among them were DeCamp, Blum, and Twachtman. But at the end of 1879 Duveneck went to Venice and there he was followed by some of his pupils who enjoyed his gay comradeship and teaching. He did some etchings of the Venetian canals about 1880, which were very fine and received much commendation. He was married in 1886 and when his wife died two years later he designed her memorial, a reclining figure in bronze, of which a replica is in the Metropolitan Museum of Art. He then returned to the United States and began teaching at the Cincinnati Art Academy, where he continued in that position for most of his later years. He did not paint much then, but was content to teach the younger generation how to become independent and individual artists without the stigma of convention of any particular school or period. His own flashing strokes were reminiscent of the work of Hals, and other influences of Rubens and Rembrandt were apparent in such works as the *Laughing Boy* and *Squire Duveneck.* His work is best represented in the Cincinnati Museum, to which he left his large collection of drawings that had accumulated during his lifetime.

See Pl. 61, Vol. II.

BIBLIOGRAPHY: *Frank Duveneck, 1848-1919,* published by the Cincinnati Museum Association, 1919. —Norbert Heermann, *Frank Duveneck,* 1918.

**DUVET (Jean).**—French engraver. Born in Langres in 1481, died after 1561. He was long known under the name of "the Master of the Unicorn." He had first learned the goldsmith's craft; then, inspired by Mantegna and Ghissi, he took to engraving. It is not known whether he went to Italy to see their works or whether he merely handled some of their engravings. He was strongly influenced by the Italian school, especially by Leonardo da Vinci.

# HINDU ARCHITECTURE

*Hindu architecture manifests itself primarily by its variety, caused by the diversity of beliefs and of races mingled together on the peninsula of India. Some Buddhist monuments in the northwestern part show the influence of Western art. The Mohammedans imported their elegant mosque architecture, but the most characteristic monument is the pagoda-like tall pyramid composed of numerous superposed and set back stories—perhaps a descendant of the Chaldean ziggurat.*

DELHI: MAUSOLEUM OF HUMAYUN.

GWALIOR: ONE OF THE JAINA TEMPLES ON THE CITADEL.

LAHORE: THE ESPLANADE AT BADSHAHI MOSQUE.

THE DILWARA: JAINA TEMPLE ON MOUNT ABU.

CONJEVARAM: THE GREAT TEMPLE OF SIVA.

TANJORE: TEMPLE OF SIVA. THE ENCLOSURE AND THE GOPURAMS (GATEWAYS).

THE SEVEN PAGODAS BETWEEN PONDICHERRY AND MADRAS. SIVA TEMPLE.

FATEHPUR-SIKRI: THE RED SANDSTONE PALACE AND THE MOSQUE.

GWALIOR: THE ENAMEL-DECORATED TOWERS OF THE PALACE OF MAN-MANDIR.

ANGKOR-VAT: ONE OF THE CORNER TOWERS OF THE CENTRAL MASS.

ANGKOR-VAT: PRINCIPAL FAÇADE.

ANGKOR-VAT: NORTH-WEST CORNER OF THE SECOND FLOOR GALLERY.

## The Monuments of Angkor

Among the most outstanding monuments of Hindu art one must consider those of Cambodia and in particular the group of temples of Angkor. Their carved decoration, of an unforgettable richness, seems to vie in exuberance with the irresistible vegetation which climbs over them, at certain points practically obliterating them. The numberless figures which animate this architecture illustrate the ponderous dogmas and the intricate poetry of India.

# CHINESE AND JAPANESE ARCHITECTURE

THE TEMPLE OF THE CLASSICS AT PEIPING.

THE TEMPLE OF THE HEAVENS AND ITS TRIPLE MARBLE BALUSTRADE AT PEIPING.

PAVILION OF THE SUMMER PALACE AT PEIPING.

TOWER OF THE LONG-HOA PAGODA.

TRIUMPHAL ARCH ALONG THE YUN-NAN-SEN ROAD AT CHAOTUNG.

WAY OF THE ROUNDS ON THE GREAT WALL.

A GATE AT SAN-HO.

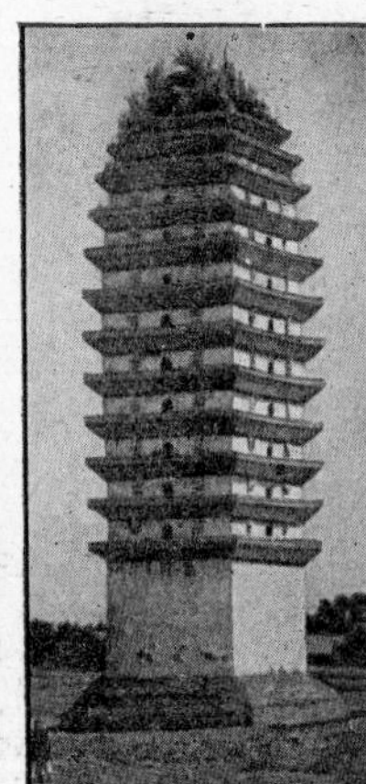

TOWER OF YUN-NAN-SEN.

## China

The Chinese were powerful builders as the famous Great Wall of China, the most gigantic monument executed by human hands, proves. But what characterises this architecture above all, to be seen in the pagodas as well as in the decorative monuments, is the permanence of the characteristics of work in wood. We find again the traces of carpentry in many architectural forms. One of the picturesque traits of these buildings is the importance and the form given to the roof. The Chinese loved to superpose roofs (the number of them is a sign of dignity) and to raise their corners like tents which are open to the light.

ENTRANCE TO THE TEMPLE OF CHIOU-IU.

TORII (GATE) OF MIYAJIMA.

A TEMPLE AT KOYA-SAN.

THE PARK OF NARA, ANCIENT CAPITAL OF JAPAN.
*(Photo by Kudo.)*

## Japan

The architecture of the Japanese is apparently related to that of China. But it is distinguished from it by its lightness and its picturesque qualities. In their homes as in their temples, the Japanese preferred light wood construction to heavy masonry. The frequency of earthquakes in these volcanic isles justifies this preference. Furthermore, the Japanese keenly felt the picturesqueness of their rocky and twisted landscapes. Their light architecture is built on hilly ground thick with forests somewhat in the manner of Alpine chalets. They readily associated the worship of nature with their religious ceremonies.

# CHINESE AND JAPANESE MISCELLANEOUS ART

*It was largely through trinkets that Europeans became acquainted with the art of China and Japan. These small objects fascinate us first because they are exotic and difficult for us to understand. The highly colored porcelains of seventeenth and eighteenth century China were at first the goal of western collectors. Their taste later changed in favor of the more simple and elegant ceramics of the Sung period. It is only in comparatively recent years that the greatness and monumental qualities of the ritual bronzes of the Shang and Chou dynasties has been understood in the West.*

*Japan has suffered even more than China from an unintelligent appreciation of its minor arts. The conscious simplicity of pottery for the tea ceremony, the masculine art of the armorer, the dignified productions of the early lacquerers, have been overlooked and preference given to the technical ingenuity of late periods.*

CHINESE VASE. MUSÉE DES ARTS DÉCORATIFS. *(Photo by Hachette.)*

CHINESE PORCELAIN VASE. MUSÉE GUIMET. *(Photo by Hachette.)*

BRONZE YU, EARLY CHOU DYNASTY. METROPOLITAN MUSEUM.

CHINESE VASE. MUSÉE DES ARTS DÉCORATIFS. *(Photo by Hachette.)*

CHINESE PORCELAIN VASE. K'ANG-HSI DYNASTY. MUSÉE GUIMET.

KOUAN-TI. CHINESE GOD OF WAR. BRONZE. *(Photo by Hachette.)*

BIRD: BRONZE, SEVENTEENTH CENTURY. MUSÉE DES ARTS DÉCORATIFS. *(Photo by Hachette.)*

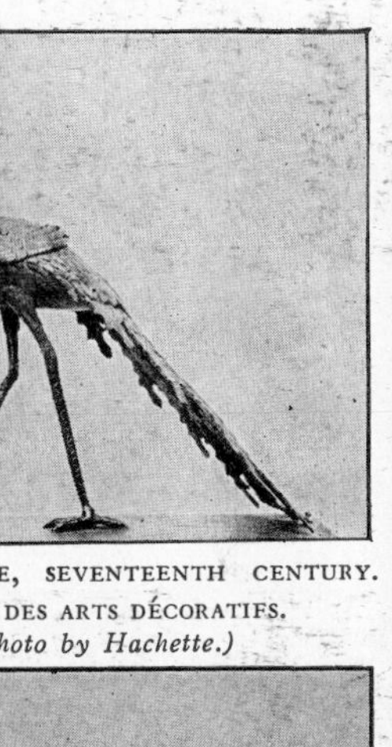

SWORD GUARD, MOMOYAMA PERIOD. FOGG ART MUSEUM.

TENAGA, THE MAN WITH THE LONG ARMS. BRONZE. *(Photo by Hachette.)*

JAPANESE LACQUER, EIGHTEENTH CENTURY. MUSÉE DES ARTS DÉCORATIFS. *(Photo by Hachette.)*

PERSONAGE ON A BULL. MUSÉE DES ARTS DÉCORATIFS. *(Photo by Hachette.)*

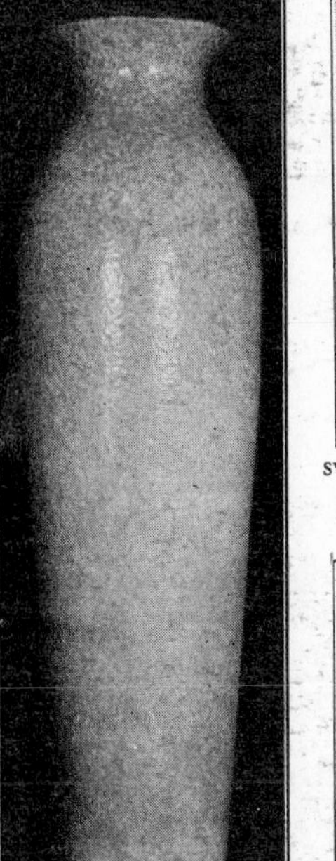

TING YAO. SUNG DYNASTY. *(Photo Yamanaka)*

TEA CEREMONY BOWL, JAPAN, DATED 1779. WILLIAM ROCKHILL NELSON GALLERY OF ART.

JAPANESE LACQUER, EIGHTEENTH CENTURY. MUSÉE DES ARTS DÉCORATIFS. *(Photo by Hachette.)*

FLUTE PLAYER. POTTERY. MUSÉE CERNUSCHI. *(Photo by Hachette.)*

JAPANESE SATSUMA VASE. MUSÉE DES ARTS DÉCORATIFS. *(Photo by Hachette.)*

LARGE PLATE. MUSÉE DES ARTS DÉCORATIFS. *(Photo by Hachette.)*

SATSUMA PORCELAIN VASE. MUSÉE DES ARTS DÉCORATIFS. *(Photo by Hachette.)*

RITUAL BRONZE VASE. EARLY CHOU DYNASTY. COLLECTION C. T. LOO.

# BUDDHIST ART

*Buddhist art is of Indian origin as was the religion of Buddhism. But, if the religious inspiration was Indian, discoveries have proven that its sculpture was at times derived from Hellenic influences. Actually, in the northwestern part of India, at Gandhara, in the first centuries of The Christian era there flourished a sculpture whose style was Greek and whose iconography was Buddhist. But the forms were very quickly adapted to the Indian style.*

JIZO BOSATSU. JAPANESE, WOOD, THIRTEENTH CENTURY. *(Photo by Giraudon.)*

BUDDHIST GUARDIAN, FUJIWARA PERIOD. WORCESTER ART MUSEUM.

AMIDA BUDDHA. WOOD, JAPAN, TWELFTH CENTURY. *(Photo by Hachette.)*

PORTRAIT OF TOKIYORI. LACQUERED WOOD, SIXTEENTH CENTURY JAPAN. LOUVRE. *(Photo by Hachette.)*

WOODEN BUDDHA. LOUVRE. *(Photo by Hachette.)*

BODHISATTVA KSITIGARBHA. TENTH CENTURY, TUN HUANG. MUSÉE GUIMET. *(Photo by Hachette.)*

BUDDHIST STELE, CHINA EARLY SIXTH CENTURY. COLLECTION CITY ART MUSEUM, ST. LOUIS.

JIZO BOSATSU, SCHOOL OF KOSE KANOAKA. LOUVRE. *(Photo by Hachette.)*

FUGEN MOUNTED ON AN ELEPHANT. JAPANESE PAINTING, TOKYO MUSEUM.

HEAD OF BODHISATTVA.

HEAD OF BUDDHA.

CAMBODIAN ART

BODHISATTVAS. TENTH CENTURY, TUN HUANG. *(Photo by Hachette.)*

One may follow the development of Buddhist art in all the Asiatic regions which were penetrated by the preaching of Buddha; in Tibet, Turkestan, China, Korea, Japan, Siam and Cambodia. Everywhere one finds the image of Buddha seated upon a lotus flower, eyes lowered, under the spell of an inner ecstasy, the image of happiness obtained by the renunciation of the world. It is this attitude of idealized repose in the impersonal representations of the various deities that underlies all manifestations of Buddhist art. Only in the semi-secular portraits of priests does the human character of individuals appear.

But he differs from them in his way of entirely covering his plate with figures and ornaments which are all given the same importance, so that nothing stands out from the whole. But in spite of these faults, Duvet had an original imagination, the like of which is only found in the nineteenth century artists, Blake, Dante Gabriel Rossetti and Gustave Moreau. In this spirit were conceived a *Marriage of Adam and Eve*, where the Almighty is officiating, in the midst of angels; an *Annunciation*; and some allegories: the Royal Majesty, and a Portrait of Henry II. A series, incomprehensible to us, is entitled the *History of the Unicorn*. It is thought that it may be an allusion to the history of Henry II and of Diane de Poitiers.

Jean Duvet's most extraordinary work is the series of the Apocalypse which he published in 1561, at the age of eighty. The interpretation is entirely original. "It has the literal crudeness of Dürer: the angel whose feet were columns of fire, the sword and flames exhaled by God, are presented without reticence, but with a marvellous plastic sense. As for the Four Horsemen, they might be compared with the most famous page of the German Apocalypse, and yet they are totally different."

Jean Duvet has long been unjustly forgotten. His originality, his creative power, and his sense of form make him the greatest French engraver of the 16th century.

Bibliography: L. Rosenthal, *La Gravure*. Paris, Laurens, 1902.—E. J. de Laboulaye, *Étude sur la vie et sur l'œuvre de J. Duvet*. Paris, 1884.

**DYCK.**—See Van Dyck.

**DYING GAUL.**—See Pergamum.

# E

**EAKINS (Thomas Cowperthwait).**—American painter (1844-1916). He was born in Philadelphia, Pennsylvania, 25th July 1844, the son of a family descended from Scotch, Irish, Dutch, and English pioneers. After his graduation from the public school there he began studying at the Pennsylvania Academy of Fine Arts, copying antique casts in the usual manner. But young Eakins did not like that method of training and took some courses in anatomy at Jefferson Medical College in order to find out more of the makeup of the human body. When he was twenty-two he set out for Europe to study more of painting and its methods. In Paris he worked under Jean Léon Gérôme but soon went to Spain where he was influenced by the paintings of Ribera and Velazquez. Upon his return to the United States in 1870 he opened a studio as a portrait painter but attracted very few commissions. Six years later he became an instructor in the life and anatomy classes at the Pennsylvania Academy of Fine Arts. But his rough criticisms and the teaching of anatomy from a living model found disfavour and he was forced to resign his post in 1886. For a short time he taught at the Art Students' League of Philadelphia but it was the end of his career as an instructor in the methods of painting. He continued making realistic portraits but was unable to sell very many due to the almost photographic likenesses that he executed. In his later years some of his work won public recognition and he received a medal at the Columbian Exposition of 1893, honourable mention at the Paris Exposition of 1900, and gold medals at the Pan-American Exposition of 1901 and the St. Louis Exposition of 1904. He was elected to full membership in the National Academy of Design in 1902. After an illness in 1910 he was unable to do any more painting and he died at his home in Philadelphia 25th June 1916. As has been the case with many other artists his work began to be acknowledged widely throughout the country after his death and today he is recognized as one of America's outstanding Realists, second perhaps to none save Winslow Homer. His native city of Philadelphia organised a large memorial exhibition and the collection of the Pennsylvania Museum of Art, in that city was enriched by a gift of sixty paintings from his widow in 1930.

See Pl. 62, Vol. II.

Bibliography: Lloyd Goodrich, *Thomas Eakins, His Life and Work*, 1933.—For a complete bibliography see *The Index of Twentieth Century Artists* for January, 1934.

**EARLE (Ralph).**—Early American painter (1751-1801). He was born 11th May 1751 in Shrewsbury Massachusetts, and presumably spent his youth there. In 1774 he was painting pictures in New Haven, Connecticut, and the following year as an itinerant painter visited the battlefields of Lexington and Concord. He painted pictures of those historic spots which were widely spread throughout the colonies when engraved by Amos Doolittle. During the winter of 1776-1777 Earle was living in New Haven, but three years later he was established in London. There he studied with Benjamin West, became a member of the Royal Academy and married again, leaving his first wife and family in America. In the late 1780's he returned to America, deserting his second wife, and travelled as an itinerant painter through New York, Connecticut and Massachusetts. He died about 16th August 1801 in Bolton, Connecticut, the victim of over-indulgence. He was the brother of James Earle, the painter, and the father of Ralph E. W. Earle by his second marriage. The younger Ralph Earle became quite well known as a painter and married the niece of President Jackson.

Ralph Earle's paintings rank with the best work done in Colonial America. Although uneven in style they usually managed a good facial resemblance and a detailed treatment of the clothes and other accessories. Among his best works are the two portraits of *William* and *Mary Carpenter* which are now in the Worcester Art Museum. These young children are depicted with smiling faces done in the characteristic cool flesh tones, dressed in their quaint costumes and posed informally in armchairs against flat decorative backgrounds which seem modern in their treatment. However, he generally uses the typical 18th century backgrounds, posing the figures in an open landscape very like contemporary English works.

See Pl. 61, Vol. II.

Bibliography: William Dunlap, *The History of the Rise and Progress of the Arts of Design in the United States*, 1918.—H. T. Tuckerman, *The Book of the Artists*, 1867. —*Bulletin of the Worcester Art Museum*, July, 1916, January, 1917.

**EARLOM (Richard).**—English engraver. Born in London in 1743; died in 1822. He was the pupil of Cipriani, and used alternately, the "black manner," etching, and the needle. He left portraits: Rubens and his wife returning from the Hunt, Rembrandt, Rembrandt's Wife, etc., but his most important work is the facsimile,—not very faithful, however,—of two hundred drawings by Claude Lorrain, belonging to the Duke of Devonshire.

Bibliography: Wessely, *Critical Catalogue of the Work of Earlom*. Hamburg, 1889.

**EARL'S BARTON (England).**—*Tower*, late 10th century. An example of the post-Danish period of Anglo-Saxon architecture, when towers were the most important features of churches. These towers had no buttresses and were decorated in Anglo-Saxon long-and short work, possibly in imitation of the pilaster-strips of Lombardy. At Earl's Barton the strips are crossed and mitred in the third stage. The belfry openings consist of an arcature on balusters, a treatment typical of England in this period.

**EARLY CHRISTIAN ART.**—Christian art grew as a scion from the art of the Roman and Hellenistic civilization and hence, while falling heir to the previous culture was essentially different.

*The Catacombs.*—Christian art, at its beginning, was an exclusively funereal art, and only showed itself in the catacombs (underground cemeteries). The name "catacomb" is Latin, and in the Middle Ages was given to the only cemetery which remained open, that of San Sebastiano, "ad catacombas." Catacombs are frequent along the road outside of Rome, especially the Via Appia. They were known to the Romans before the persecutions, and the term cemetery (in Greek, "sleeping places"), symbolized the Christian aspirations. Underground burial was already an Oriental custom. But while among the Orientals, the vault was secured in a way to insure its inviolability forever, with the Christians, on the other hand, only the tombs were closed, and the vault which enclosed them was left open to all who came to pray near the dead. The catacombs grew until they became veritable subterranean cities. It has been calculated that they could not have covered less than 1000 kilometres. In the first century appeared the first catacombs around Rome, along the consular roads that led into the country. They are all devised on the same plan, which, in the first instance, hardly differed from pagan architecture. They were open to the sky, with a brick façade bearing the name of the master, then a court surrounded by porticoes (the atrium), preceding a room (trilinium), where the early Christians, in commemoration of the Last Supper, took the evening meal and exchanged the kiss of peace. At the back was the fountain for ablutions. All this exterior part of the catacombs has disappeared. Next came a gentle slope leading underground, covered with stucco and having at the two sides, niches for the sarcophagi which were later buried in the earth when more room was needed. From this central way branched off an infinite number of other galleries, peopled with the dead. Even the walls enclosed tombs. These galleries are high, but very narrow (from two to three feet). The roof is flat or arched, and lit by a kind of round or square chimney, through which the sarcophagi were let down. Owing to the necessity for enlarging the cemeteries indefinitely, superimposed galleries were dug out, —to five, but the length and number of these depended upon the nature of the soil. The entrance was commonly at the bottom of a slope containing tombs to prevent flooding.

Religious emblems and objects, fixed into the cement, served as a guiding-mark to families to recognise their respective dead. The architectural work is the work of the "fossores," a corporation of architects and workmen.

The ordinary burial niche was called the *sepulchrum* or *locus* and was an oblong receptacle in the side of a wall. A more distinguished type was the *arcosolinum* which had the opening from above, usually under an arch. This type allowed several bodies to be buried together. The ordinary chambers were called *cubicula*, those including tombs of martyrs, *cryptae*. A *hypogeum* was a private chamber. Burial near martyrs was desired, and relics such as parts of saints' bodies or even objects which had been near to the tombs of saints became highly prized. The religious life of the Christians centered in the catacombs and consequently the fourth century witnessed a development of church organization with resulting changes in the underground structure to accommodate more people and a different type of church service. The *agape* was the first Christian feeding of the poor, but later, when it became merely riotous feasting, it had to be given up. With the coming of Alaric in 410, underground burial ceased, although the catacombs were not deserted. By the sixth century, much of the city of Rome had become depopulated, and hence there was less objection to burial within the city walls. Moreover, much cemetery construction was carried on above ground in the fifth and sixth centuries. The seventh century was the period of great pilgrimages from the North, during which time relics went sky-high in value. During the eighth and ninth centuries the Campagna became unsafe, and a wholesale translation of the bodies of saints took place, resulting in a dilapidation and destruction of the cemeteries. Finally the names of actual sites of burial were forgotten. Catacombs are found throughout the Christian domain of this time. Of the famous examples near Rome, San Callisto on the Appian Way has eight hundred sepulchres which can still be counted, and was once the burial place of the popes. That of San Valentino was one of the smallest.

*Basilicas.*—That the very earliest churches were houses is proved

Rome: Basilica of Saint Paul's Outside the Walls.

by the atrium surrounded by columns, which preceded them. The famous basilica of St. Pudenziana, in Rome, is supposed to have been originally a private oratory in the house of the senator Pudens. But the innumerable pagans who were converted to Christianity after the Edict of Milan, forced the Christians to build churches to shelter the congregations. By the 4th century, the liturgy had taken a form already well-defined. Each one of the classes of the ecclesiastical hierarchy had its particular part. The bishop, seated behind the altar, presided over the Assembly, surrounded by priests, deacons, and sub-deacons; in front of the clergy a place was kept for a choir of singers; then came the faithful: on one side, men, and on the other, women, among whom virgins and widows had a special place; finally, the catechumens (those who have not received baptism) and penitents were near the doorway, for these were not allowed to take part in the singing, and had to leave the church when the celebration of the sacred office began. The buildings consecrated for worship had, then, to fulfil many definite needs, which accounts for the almost unique plan adopted for the construction of basilicas from the 4th century. The Greco-Roman basilica, otherwise called the Latin basilica, was, then, the one which the faithful adopted in Italy, and sometimes in the East, and in Africa. The plan is precisely described by Bréhier: "In front, a square courtyard, surrounded by walls, and having on three sides at least porticoes supported on columns, serves as the entrance to the church: this is the 'atrium.' In the middle is a fountain for ablutions (cantharus). Here the penitents, who were deprived of taking part in divine celebration, assembled. The form and proportions of this courtyard are the same as those of the 'peristylium.' The church, properly called, has much the same arrangement as the civil basilicas. There is a long nave, divided into aisles by ranges of columns which support the wall, on which are built the trusses of a frame-work which is either visible or hidden by a ceiling. These naves were lit by *clerestory* windows at the top above the *triforium* gallery level. To each aisle there is always a corresponding special door. Sometimes a transversal nave, the transept, gives the church the form of a cross. Beyond the transept is a square space more or less developed—the choir. Finally, the basilica is terminated by a vaulted niche—the apse." In Rome, there remains only one basilica dating from the 5th century, that has not been entirely restored; that is, Santa Maria Maggiore. All the others, such as San Giovanni di Laterano, San Pietro, San Paolo-fuori-le-Mura, Santa Sabina, San Lorenzo-fuori-le-Mura, San Clemente, and Santa Maria Antica, were entirely altered, or destroyed and rebuilt. It is the same in Milan, where the church of Sant'Ambrogio only possesses one apse from the 4th century; and in Naples, in the basilicas of Santa Restituta and of the Savior. The *martyrium* of San Felice, in Nola, which includes five basilicas, is the most important buildings known of this period. Nevertheless, it is entirely restored. The existence of this new type of building already developed, and its simultaneous appearance in all parts of the Christian domain as soon as the peace of the Church was proclaimed, indicates its constant development during the persecution. The plan was determined by the form of service, and took shape during the first worshipping in the catacomb chapels and in Roman houses. The form of the actual building came to be an enlargement of the Roman house, influenced by the structure of Roman basilicas. Lack of any decoration, and the emphasis on the longitudinal axis as a processional path show the difference between the Christian basilica and the buildings which immediately preceded it.

*The Baptistery.*—It was in the East that the Christians built the first buildings with a central plan and covered with a dome, which served as sepulchres for the martyrs, whence the name of *martyrium*. They are of Hellenistic origin, and were inspired by pagan monuments consecrated to heroes. The use of brick allowed lighter, organically

Rome: Baptistery of San Giovanni in Laterano.

built, walls. Their use spread in the West, where they were made smaller and became baptisteries. In the East, the usual plan of the martyrium is, according to Bréhier, "an octagon, surmounted by a conical dome which is applied on little angle trumpets, or by an octagonal dome which fits the form of the plan." In Egypt, Clédat has discovered more than a hundred of these dome-covered buildings the plan of which must have served the origins of Byzantine art. In the West, few baptisteries or *martyria* have survived. Among the most famous must be mentioned in Rome, the baptisteries of the Vatican and of San Giovanni Laterano, the mausoleum of St. Helena and of Santa Constanza, very well preserved and containing famous mosaics, and of Santo Stefano Rotundo; in Ravenna, the baptistry of the Orthodox, that of Gallia Placidia; in Naples, the baptistery built by Bishop Sotter against the apse of Santa Restituta.

*The Sarcophagi.*—The sarcophagi are the only remains of Christian art where one can study the sculpture of the period, for monumental sculpture does not exist. They are of great interest, in showing the influence of Roman art in their decoration. They are in marble, stone, terra cotta or in porphyry according to the social rank of the deceased, and are of exactly the same form as the Roman sarcophagi; that is, a rectangular chest, sometimes rounded at the ends and surmounted by a cover, either flat or in the form of a roof. Before the peace of the Church, the necessity for the Christians to hide their religion forced them to buy, for their sarcophagi, slabs of marble prepared for the unconverted. They contented themselves with choosing those which recalled as little as possible their pagan origin or else they bought finished sarcophagi which they placed in the holes in such a way that the sculptured side was against the wall; or again, they covered the sculptured face with a coating of lime. After the Edict of Milan, these sarcophagi often served to support the altar, or were placed at the back of the apse. Very few Christian sarcophagi can be attributed to the period anterior to the Edict of Milan. The oldest go back to the 4th century, except perhaps that of Livia Primativa which is supposed to belong to the 2nd century. But the oldest Christian sculpture that is known is the tomb belonging to the Priory of Gayolle (Provence). The decoration is a curious mixture of purely Christian elements, such as the Good Shepherd and the Orante (see Early Christian Painting), and pagan elements, such as the sun surrounded by seven rays and a seated figure holding a long sceptre. The figures are short and thick-set. Nearly all the 4th century sarcophagi come from Rome which sent them long distances or sent her artists to teach in Naples, Milan, Arles, and in Spain. They are fairly easily classified: the simplest, or those bearing only a single decorative composition (such as the image of the Good Shepherd) are the earliest. In the 5th century, the pastoral scenes of pagan art were sometimes used, mingled with religious motifs, as on the large sarcophagus in the Lateran Museum, on which one sees three statues of the Good Shepherd surrounded by little cupids. The adventures of Jonah (sarcophagus in the Lateran Museum) and the crossing of the Red Sea form the principal motif of the sarcophagi of Pisa and Arles. In the most elaborate sarcophagi, the sides are divided into compartments by means of columns, and trimmed with figures; at other times, the sarcophagus is divided into two superimposed tiers, as on the sarcophagus of the Lateran Museum, which has scenes from the Old and the New Testament. Many sarcophagi have medallions with bas-relief portraits of the dead, sometimes husband and wife. Like the painters, the sculptors relate the history of our first parents: the Creation, the Deluge, the Sacrifice of Abraham, etc., etc.; then the Birth of Christ, manger scenes (which appear for the first time on a sarcophagus in the Lateran Museum), sarcophagi decorated with historical scenes, representing Christ before Pilate, Pilate washing his hands, scenes from the Passion, Christ teaching the Apostles, are documents of great value. In the Church of St. Honorat, in Arles, a single tomb depicts the whole history of Christ; at Fermo, a sarcophagus tells the whole story of the life of St. Peter. All these compositions, which express religious fervour, are sprinkled with pagan elements, such as Victories, Cupids and Genii. Christ was even represented with the attributes of Prometheus.

Painting. — *The Catacombs.* — Painting appeared from the age of the catacombs. The first elements of decoration were figures engraved in line, among the inscriptions, on the marble, stucco, or terra cotta, which sometimes covered the walls of the catacombs. When one realises the difficulty of working in this darkness, and in a deleterious atmosphere, one is not surprised to find the first Christian paintings halting and clumsy. Moreover, the walls, pierced here and there with openings and niches, hampered design, and did not encourage artists to arrange their figures with real ingenuity. All the catacomb paintings were executed like frescoes. In the first place the stucco is covered with a coating on which, before it is dried, the figures are drawn with an iron point or with a light brush outline. The figures are in three colours: yellow, red and green on a white background—very mellow in the first and second centuries, cruder from the third century. The chief interest of Early Christian painting is in its creation of Christian iconography: gestures, features, attitudes and garments which became characteristic of the figures of the new religion. From the very first the artist gives his personages beardless faces and Roman dress. Attributes sufficed to identify them: Jonah and his whale, Daniel and the lions, Noah and the dove, etc. The pure figure of the Orante (or praying one) was created to represent the immortal soul. At the beginning, it personified the immortal image of the dead, under the features of a young girl, simply dressed, and praying near the tomb. This attitude of prayer became the common gesture of all Christian figures, such as Noah, Daniel, Isaac, etc. The most beautiful Orante figures were in the cemetery of Priscilla, and on the famous ceiling of the vault of Lucina. Near the immortal soul they had to represent God, the Saviour of this soul, and they created the image of the Good Shepherd and the Lamb. Sometimes the shepherd had a sheep on his left and on his right. Then the scene expanded, and into the heavenly pastorals, they put sheep, and sometimes men clad in white raiment, listening to the voice of the divine shepherd. In the crypt of Lucina (2nd century) the representation of the mystery of the Eucharist appeared for the first time, in a pastoral scene. One of the very earliest Christian frescoes, in the cemetery of Domitillia represents the Celestial Banquet, an allegory which was often repeated in the catacombs. From the 2nd century the iconography of the catacombs takes for subject, scenes from the Old and New Testament: the Ark of Noah, the Sacrifice of Isaac, Moses striking the Rock, Job seated on a mound of Stones, David brandishing his Sword, Suzanna and the Elders, Daniel in the Lions' Den. The favourite allegory of the Christian catacombs is the story of Jonah; it provided the subject for more than forty different compositions. All this Christian iconography was perpetuated down to the Middle Ages. The figure of Christ, which at the beginning only appears in the allegory of the Good Shepherd, does not seem to have been rendered until the 4th century. Only three scenes from the life of Christ were used as a theme by the first catacomb painters: the Resurrection of Lazarus (cemetery of Callixtus), the Healing of the Paralysed Man, and the Miracle of the Loaves (cemetery of Priscilla). The Virgin Mary is represented for the first time in the 4th century.

In the cemetery of Priscilla may still be seen one of the most beautiful frescoes of Christian art: Isaiah prophesying before the Virgin and Child. After the peace of the Church, portraits of the deceased, as well as allegories, were executed: the dead is represented in an attitude that had been familiar in life, and with the attributes of his calling; or else the compositions represented scenes from daily life: diggers, coopers, bakers, the distribution of corn, etc.

The art of the basilicas had an influence upon the iconography of the catacombs. From the fourth century, one begins to notice, still under disguise, it is true, the image of the Cross. In the crypt of Santa Cecilia (5th century) is a Latin cross between two sheep. In large compositions the influence of mosaic is incontestable, as can be judged from the scene of Christ teaching and giving the Law. Jesus is not yet of the "historical type, bearded and serious" as in the mosaics, but the saints are painted according to the formulae adopted by the mosaic artists: St. Peter and St. Paul on either side of Christ; St. Protus and St. Hyacinthe presenting an "Orante" to Christ; St. Petronilla welcoming the matron Veneranda to Paradise. Finally there are the portraits of Saints Policamus, Sebastianus, and Curinus, painted in the 5th century, in the tomb of Santa Cecilia, in the cemetery of Callixtus. As for the Virgin, she was only represented in the Basilicas after the peace of the Church.

*The decoration of Basilicas.*—A prodigious artistic activity followed the peace of the Church. Until then, art was developed in shade and mystery; now it became one of the manifestations of the general delight and the servant of the official worship. A new taste for splendour and magnificence appeared from the first in the interior decoration of the basilicas. Painting was there subordinated to mosaic. Until then only marble mosaic had been used. This was no longer used except for the pavement and was substituted for that enamelled mosaic which Ghirlandaio described as "painting for eternity." Blue and gold predominate, and the colour is of an intensity, and brilliance which painting could not then pretend to equal. The type of Christ was definitely fixed: the Good Shepherd became the Lamb of the Apocalypse. From then, the chief scenes were taken from the Gospels, or from the Apocalypse. The first Constantine mosaics were executed on the vault of the mausoleum of Santa Constanza. The composition recalls very strongly the pictures of the bath-rooms of pagan houses, also some of the allegories dear to the catacomb artists. From the same period date the apsidal compositions, which are the masterpieces of Christian mosaic work. That of Santa Pudenziana was covered with mosaics, half marble and half enamel. The marble inlay has disappeared, and the enamel has suffered a good deal. Nevertheless, it is the most perfect expression of that ideal of beauty which Christian art set forth. In Santa Maria Maggiore, the mosaic consecrated to the history of the Virgin still exists. In 1823, medallions containing portraits of the Popes (498) were still to be admired in San Paolo fuori-le-Mura. If one can judge from the remains of a Baptistery in Naples, the campagna adopted the same mode of decoration. In Ravenna, in the wonderful Baptistery of the Orthodox, the central subject is the Baptism of Christ. In Asia Minor and in Syria, remains of mosaics again reveal the unity of art throughout the Christian world.

*The Minor Arts.*—For a long time, the Christians kept up the custom of burying their dead with certain objects which had surrounded them when alive. On the other hand, they used these objects for the Mass, or at wedding breakfasts. Gilt vases have been discovered in great numbers; they are formed from two discs united together by fusion, and they have inscriptions, or scenes from the Old and New Testament, portraits of the deceased, and scenes from public life. The Museum in Florence possesses bronze lamps from the Roman

Ravenna: Interior of Sant' Apollinare Nuova.

catacombs which are very beautiful; they were placed in little hollow niches by the side of the tomb. In certain children's tombs, toys have been found; in others, domestic objects. To form an exact idea of the Christian basilicas one must picture them enriched with precious knickknacks, rare stuffs, and rich furniture. In the Vatican is still to be found the ivory throne of St. Peter (6th century), on the panels of which are carved Biblical scenes. The altars were covered with gold and silver inlay, sometimes with precious stones. The Basilica of San Giovanni Laterano possesses seven of them in silver. Silk materials were used for curtains for the interior of the Basilica or used to the altar-table; sometimes they covered the relics of martyrs. No religious figures are found on these materials, for they were made in Persia, the only centre for the making of woven silks at this period, and have representations of animals facing each other, archers, and in a word,

Ravenna: Baptism of Christ. (Orthodox Baptistery.)

all the familiar elements of Saracenic art. Relics of saints were enclosed in precious caskets of sculptured ivory or goldsmith's work, which recall the sarcophagi. Milan possesses the famous silver casket containing relics of the apostles of the church of San Nezaro (382), on the sides of which are the Virgin presenting the Child to the Shepherds, Daniel defending Susannah against the Elders, and the three young Hebrews delivered to the flames, and, on the cover, Christ in the midst of the Apostles. On the "Lipsanoteca," the ivory casket, in Brescia, (which doubtless also contained relics) are scenes from the Passion. The glasses, with gold backgrounds, from the catacombs, of which we have previously spoken were for every-day use in the basilicas, as well as the lamps which became more and more richly decorated. The Church of Ravenna received from Galla Placidia a gold lamp, on which was engraved a portrait. The terra cotta lamps, decorated with allegorical images, were only used in Africa. The manuscript Bibles dating from the 4th and 5th centuries have a much greater interest in that one there finds all the themes exploited by the painters, and it seems that they were inspired by them. Texts from the Bible and the Gospels were inscribed on parchment from the beginnings of Christianity; but it was only after the peace of the Church that miniaturists began to enrich every page. Miniature is "par excellence," a pagan art; and for a long time profane figures were mingled with religious symbols. It is extremely difficult to date the manuscripts, and Byzantine art generally claims them. Nevertheless, the celebrated Bible of Quedlimburg is undoubtedly of the 4th century, as may be judged from the character of the drawings that remain, but the painting has quite disappeared. The Genesis of Vienna, and the Joshua (Vatican Museum), where the whole story of the Jews entering the Promised Land is represented, are of the 5th century. These manuscripts, enriched with miniatures, were kept in wonderful boxes of goldsmith's work, or of ivory, which are veritable works of art: the Gospel of Theodelinda, in the Monza Treasury, is of gold, and the ivory covers are identical with diptychs (double tablets), the interior of which were inscribed with the names of people to be specially mentioned in prayers. These ivory tablets are carved all over. Generally, the composition is divided into two, or several compartments, and the scenes are of Christian iconography. In Milan, an ivory book-binding represents, in three compartments, the Annunciation, the Massacre of the Innocents, and the Adoration of the Magi; another, the Resurrection. There, as in all the artistic manifestations of budding Christianity, one can see links which unite ancient and Christian art.

See Pl. 41, Vol. I.

Bibliography: Ch. Diehl, *Manuel d'Art byzantin.*—W. Lowrie, *Monuments of the Early Church,* 1923.—L. Bréhier, *Les basiliques chrétiennes.*—A. Michel, *Histoire de l'Art,* Vol. I.—Dom Leclerc, *Manuel d'Archéologie chrétienne.* Paris, 1907.—A. L. Frothingham, *The Monuments of Christian Rome.* London, 1908.—Morey, *Christian Art,* 1935.

**EAST (Alfred).**—English painter (1849-1913), studied in Glasgow and Paris; elected A. R. A. in 1899 and R. A. in 1913. One of the most noted landscape painters of the English school of his period.

**ECHMOUNAZAR (Tomb of).**—Phœnician tomb (Louvre), enclos-

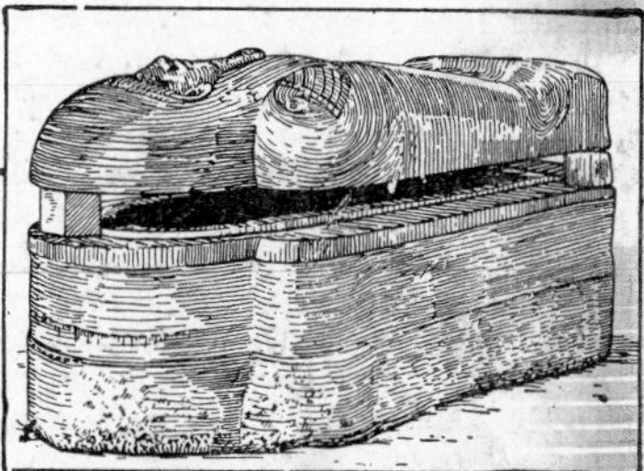

Sarcophagus of Echmounazar. (Louvre.)

ing the anthropoid sarcophagus of a king of Sidon. This sarcophagus was made in Egypt, probably about the beginning of the 4th century B.C. It is distinguished from others of the same kind by a long inscription and absence of colour.

Bibliography: Perrot and Chipiez, *Histoire de l'Art,* Vol. III.

**ECHINUS.**—See Capital.

**ECKERSBERG (Christopher Wilhelm).**—Danish painter, 1783-1853. He was the master of 19th century Danish painting. A pupil of David in Paris, and friend of Thorwaldsen, he fell under the influence of classicism. To this period of his life belongs the famous Portrait of Thorwaldsen, now in the Academy of Fine Art in Copenhagen. There, already, are the astonishing qualities of precision and observation which became his characteristics. Later, he broke away completely from his first influences, and his historical and religious pictures show a new stage in his development. His landscapes, and especially his seascapes, are masterly. In them he expresses his passion for exactitude, assisted by a calm, powerful will. In this way, Eckersberg painted portraits, some of which are real masterpieces. His influence was enormous on nearly all the painters of the mid-nineteenth century.

**EDELFELT (Albert).**—Finnish painter, 1854-1905. He lived for a long time in Paris, where he painted his best works. Nevertheless, he never broke the intimate bonds which united him with his native land, and he is thus one of the most representative of Finnish painters. He was strongly influenced by Bastien-Lepage and by Dagnan Bouveret. Two of his paintings, now in the Luxembourg, recall these two masters—one, the *Preaching on the Sea-shore,* and his fine, frank portrait of Pasteur. Edelfelt contributed energetically to the development of the decorative arts in his country, together with Gallén, Engberg, Blomstedt, the brilliant escort of Count Louis Sparre who had given the lead, by creating a workshop of industrial art in Borgå.

**ÉDELINCK (Gérard).**—Flemish engraver. Born in Antwerp, 1640; died in Paris, 1707. He was a contemporary of the pupils of the engraver-followers of Rubens, and like them, Gérard Edelinck distinguished himself before he came to Paris by the vigour of his workmanship and his skill in obtaining effects. Once in France, Édelinck added to these Flemish qualities the perfect taste of Nanteuil and the brilliance of François de Poilly, his neighbours at the Gobelins. Gifted with a quick intelligence, Édelinck soon became one of the leading engravers of the day. He assimilated, and sometimes improved, the style of painters whose works he reproduced. In interpreting the works of Le Brun, Édelinck changed neither the matter nor the manner; he only gave them more naturalism, as when he engraved for Rigaud, whose pomp and exaggeration he transformed into rich liveliness. His talent, at one moment so brilliant, could also reproduce the serenity of the portrait of Philippe de Champaigne, the object, it was said, of the painter's predilection, and one of the masterpieces of engraving. Édelinck died in 1707, leaving to his two brothers and his son Nicolas, who, all three, had been his pupils, a wisely regulated fortune.

Bibliography: H. Delaborde, *Gérard Édelinck,* 1886.

**EDFOU (Nubia, Egypt).**—Possesses the best preserved temple of the Egypt of the Ptolemies (Saïte age. See under Egypt). It was begun in 237 B.C.

**EDGMIADZIN.**—See Byzantine Architecture, Early Period, Armenia.

**EECKHOUT (Gerbrand van den).**—Dutch painter and engraver, 1621-1674. Pupil of Rembrandt, whose way of painting he imitated. The subjects of his pictures are often, like those of his master, scenes taken from the Bible. He also painted portraits. Among his best works are: *Anne Consecrating Her Son to the Lord* (Louvre); the *Continence of Scipio* (Lille); *Children in a Park* (Leningrad); the *Family of Darius* (Leningrad); the *Resting Huntsman* and the *Woman Taken in Adultery,* both in Amsterdam. Five etchings and a number of drawings are known by the master. He also published several books with ornamental engravings.

**EGAS (Enrique de).**—Spanish architect and sculptor, and son of the important Fleming Anequin de Egas. His dates of birth and death are 1455-1534. In architecture he is an exponent of the detailed, ornamental, and exuberant plateresque style of Late Gothic and Early Renaissance, a style formed of commingled Gothic, Moorish, and Renaissance elements and having the appearance of goldsmith's work. In this style he designed the Colegio de Sta. Cruz, Valladolid, 1480; the Hospital Real, Santiago de Compostela, 1501-1510; the Hospital de Sta. Cruz, Toledo, 1494-1516; and the Hospital Real, Granada, finished 1536. He also made plans for the Cathedral of Granada, which was built by Diego de Siloé after Enrique de Egas was removed from the office, 1525.

**EGYPT—Art.**—Egyptian art has been discovered only recently. Formerly, Egyptian painting, pottery or sculpture were regarded either as historical documents, or curiosities, but not as objects possessing aesthetic values. The post-impressionistic movements in modern art have broadened the receptivity to aesthetic expressions, so that now Egyptian art, lacking in naturalism, is no longer viewed as an aberration. However, it would be incorrect to interpret Egyptian art in terms of "pure art." All of the monumental art was created either for the Egyptian state or church. The primary function of art was to fulfill religious or political requirements.

In analysing Egyptian art, care must be taken not to make hasty generalisations, which might be invited by its unified character. During a period lasting over two thousand years, from about 3000 B.C. when Egyptian art emerged, to the first millennium, when Egypt came under foreign domination, the art changed very little. Consequently, it has become customary to speak of the conservative nature of the Egyptians, or of their "eternal" nature. It is true that there are no breaks in the history of the art (even when long gaps exist in our knowledge of the history of the country), and that the aesthetic and stylistic formulae changed very little. However, it must be obvious that the Egyptians were not born an old civilisation. The early Egyptians, who formed the art, were as independent and vigorous as any pioneering people. One cannot imagine a more radical change than that which occurred between 3300 and 3000 B.C.

Thebes: The two colossi of Memnon.

The major art of Egypt was devoted to the religious cult, which was bound up with the ritual of the dead. Even the state art had this character, since the king was divine. His temple was usually associated with his tomb. Under these conditions, it is not surprising that the art was conservative. On the other hand, the popular art shows a great deal of freedom. The popular art probably formed the basis for Coptic art during the Christian period. The only revolution in religion in old Egypt, the substitution of the cult of Aten for Amun (Amarna period) resulted in a very striking modification of the art.

Gizeh: The great Sphinx.

*History.*—Ancient Egypt extended along the two sides of the Nile, from the Sea to the First Cataract. During periods of expansion this area was advanced further South to include Nubia, and East and West to include Lybia and Sinai. The ancient kingdom, however, suffered from internal dissension. Actually, it consisted of two kingdoms, known as Upper and Lower Egypt (South Nile and Delta regions), and the rulers assumed the title, King of Upper and Lower Egypt. Sometime around 3400 the first unity was effected, and Egypt entered history. Twice this unity was broken, and each time a "dark age" occurred. These interludes divide the history into three distinct groups of dynasties:

Thebes: The Atlantes of the Ramesseum.

- Old Kingdom (3200-2270) Dynasties I-VI
- Middle Kingdom (2100-1700) Dynasties XI-XIII
- Empire (1555-1090) Dynasties XVIII-XX.

Father and child. (Museum, Cairo.)

Further excavations are bringing the dark ages to light. (Dy. VII-X; XIV-XVII.) Indeed, not so long ago, even the Middle Kingdom was almost a complete blank. After the XX Dynasty the period of Egyptian decline began and the country fell under the domination of various foreign powers: Ethiopia, Lybia, Persia and Greece.

*The Art.—Introduction.*—Figures in Egyptian sculpture are constructed in vertical and horizontal planes. The axis of the figure is always absolutely perpendicular. The two sides are not necessarily symmetrical, but they are always balanced. The King will be shown with one foot advanced (this involves no shift in weight), and it is common to have one arm bent over the chest. All sculpture is designed to be seen only full face or profile, but never at an angle. The sculptor's approach to his material proves this. Unfinished works have been found which show that the sculptor marked his rectangular block off into proportional squares. On each surface of the block he outlined the view which was appropriate to it (profile, full-face and top-view) and then cut away the rock.

Woman grinding corn. (Museum, Cairo.)

Ipsambul: The two colossi of the south side.

Queen Teje. (Museum, Cairo.)

In flat relief and painting, the Egyptians used a unique system for the representation of the human form. The head is placed in profile, though the eye is full, the shoulders and upper torso are also in full view, while the waist and lower limbs are again in profile. The same variation in full and profile views is found in all forms. Two rules are probably operative. The first is to show each part in its most characteristic aspect. The advantage is that clarity and precise descriptions are achieved. Schaefer compares Egyptian methods of representation to a carpenter's blue print. The second rule, is to show each part in its flattest aspect. This has an aesthetic advantage in maintaining the plane of the wall. Though perspective was not used, spatial relationships were indicated. Figures in the foreground blocked out those which were behind them, and occasionally, more distant figures were placed on a higher ground level. Usually, however, all figures are placed on the same ground line, even when they are directly in back of each other. Important figures, however, were never blocked. Thus, the king and queen sitting side by side appear to be placed in file. Within the Egyptian system, the artists showed remarkable skill in the representation of action.

Weh-eb-re, Twenty-sixth dynasty. (Louvre.)

The artist prepared the wall for reliefs by marking it off into proportional squares. Though the modelling was usually very summary, occasionally it was exquisite. After the figures were cut, the stone was carved in flat colors. When the walls were rough, they were covered with stucco, and then painted. The fresco process was not used. The paint, consisting of pigment and a gum was applied to the dry walls. In a typical relief or wall painting, the wall is divided into several horizontal zones. The figure of the king or nobleman, however, occupied several zones, and was thus many times the size of the other figures.

Egyptian architecture, as all other Egyptian art, is characterised by an appearance of perfect static con-

Bas-relief of the victory of Seneferu at Sinai.

trol. Houses do not grow by accretion, as is the case of ancient Cretan architecture, which is very picturesque, but are planned within a rectangular space. Floor plans are not symmetrical, though individual chambers usually are. The chief buildings which have survived are the temples and tombs. These were built of large blocks of granite. The system of architecture was that of the column and lintel. The lintels were placed directly on the columns. Though the vault was known, it was not used (brick grave at Katta). The roofs were perfectly flat, since there was no rainfall.

No orders were followed as in Greek architecture. A single chamber might even have more than one type of column. Various forms

Cat on the watch. (After H. Carter.)

of column were used. At a very early date, the square monolith was used, and in the third dynasty, we find a column which resembles the Doric. It is known as "protodoric." Most of the columns are derived from natural forms. The lotus blossom and bud, the palm leaf and papyrus blossom are the chief forms. The capital is based upon the flower form and the shaft represents a collection of stems (or reeds). Leaves are often indicated at their bases. The columns are painted, and sometimes have inscriptions and compositions engraved upon them. Inscriptions and flat reliefs or paintings cover the entire interior space. Rooms were occasionally painted symbolically, the ceiling being the heavens, the walls, the landscape, and the floor the earth. The front exterior walls were also sculptured in flat relief.

In the tombs of the nobility, scenes of the deceased's daily life were represented. In the Temple of the king, the public chambers were covered with scenes depicting his exploits, while cult scenes were placed in the private sanctuaries.

*Prehistory.*—Egypt enters history with the founding of the Old Kingdom. Because of the lack of any certain dating, the entire prehistory has been divided for convenience into eighty stages. New finds are given their proper position in this scale of eighty. Consequently, the prehistory can be ordered consecutively. The oldest stone age culture (Badari) has been placed at the thirtieth level, while the First Dynasty is placed at the eightieth. There may be about two thousand years between these two levels, but that is not certain.

At Badari small female figures have been found which are slightly steatopygic, with small pointed breasts and an emphasis upon the phallic triangle. There seems to be no relation between them and later Egyptian figures, and yet, Badari may be the dawn of Egyptian culture. Among the most interesting of the prehistoric finds are the cosmetic plates in animal form. Very

Amenhotep IV and the Queen. (Museum, Berlin.)

elaborate cosmetic plates have been found in the First Dynasty. The most finished of all Stone Age instruments have been found in Egypt, thus indicating the possibility of a continuous tradition of superb workmanship from the early

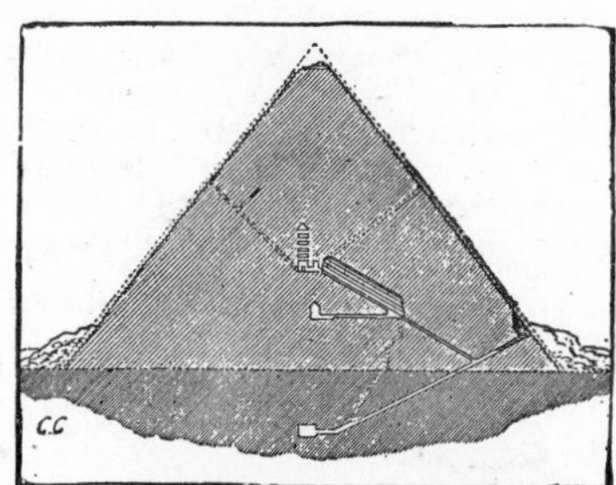

Cross-section of a pyramid.

Stone Age through the entire history of the ancient Empire.

As we climb the scale of Egyptian prehistory, and enter the stages 70 to 80, true Egyptian features begin to appear, such as amulets, the holy falcon, and the Hathor head. In Kom-el-Ahmar (Hierakonpolis) a mural has been found which possesses not only Egyptian features of a later period, but also Mesopotamian features. The University Museum of Philadelphia has a superb door base from Kom-el-Ahmar which is of granite and was used as a pivot for a stone door. It represents a prisoner with his arms tied behind his back. The rotation of the door, pivoted in his back must have been intended as torture. At Gebel-el-Arak a slate tablet representing the victory of an Egyptian king has been found (now in the Brit. Museum). It is in the form of a cosmetic plate, and is in many respects similar to the plate of King Narmer of the First Dynasty. The defeated enemy is represented being led away by the falcon gods. The dead or wounded are in contorted poses being ravaged by beasts of prey.

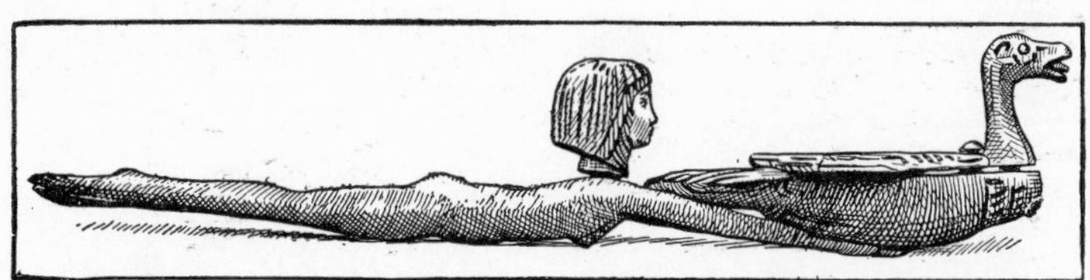

Perfume spoon in the shape of a swimmer. (Museum, Cairo.)

*Early Dynastic History* (*Dynasties I-II*).—Egyptian history (the age of written records) commences with King Narmer. In the Berlin Museum there is an excellent ape in alabaster which bears his name. His victory slate has all the essential formulae of Egyptian art, with its ordering of spatial relationships, clarity of representation and flat treatment of the human form. This slate is also inscribed. Two other kings of this early period are identified on monuments. One is Wenefes-Djet, represented by a beautiful relief of the falcon, and the other is Semeses-Semerchet, whose name is inscribed on a cliff relief in Sinai, showing his victory over the local tribes. The work is crude, but the character is Egyptian.

The tombs of the pre-dynastic

Royal head in glass. (Egypt, thirteenth dynasty.)

period were shaft graves. These are elaborated at this period. Several rooms are constructed underground, and a small flat building is erected over the shaft. Because of their bench-like appearance, the Arabs called them mastabas, and this is the name now applied to these tombs. The earliest mastabas were constructed of sundried brick. A striking exception to the typical mastaba is the tomb of King Menes (Narmer), where the chambers are contained in the upper construction of the mastaba instead of being underground. Furthermore, the wall, instead of being smooth, is indented in the Mesopotamian manner.

Though no dwellings have survived, some indication of their form is given by the hieroglyph for the word house. These indicate two types, a long house with an entrance on the short side (symbol ht) and the open court, with an entrance on the broad side (symbol pr).

*Old Kingdom* (*III-VI Dynasties*).—Real Egyptian history begins with King Zoser and his remarkable minister Imhotep of the Third Dynasty.

*Sculpture.*—The first figures in in the round express a virility and dynamic strength associated with archaic art in Greece. The Seated Man in Naples, the Shipbuilder in the British Museum and several in the Metropolitan Museum, though lacking in refinement, possess both power and freshness. In the earlier works, the stone is not cut away, and the figures have a very block like character. But in the famous scribe in the Louvre or the so-called Sheik el-Beled, one is no longer aware of technical difficulties. The figures express joy, confidence and strength. A different character is found in the figures of the kings. Here, majesty and power replace youthful strength (Khafre, Ranofer).

Small figures, such as Woman Grinding Wheat, which were placed in the graves and intended to represent the servants of the deceased are free and realistic in their treatment.

*Reliefs.*—The Egyptians had no painting, properly speaking, but painted reliefs. The first great monument in relief is carved in wood. It represents Hesire and was found in his mastaba at Saqqara. It is beautifully modelled, showing the bony structure and musculature of the face, limbs and breast. The body conforms to the peculiar Egyptian system, in which the lower torso is in profile, the shoulders in full face, and the head in profile. The bas-reliefs of the Old Kingdom, and especially those of the Fifth Dynasty were never surpassed. In these reliefs, carved on the walls of the mastabas and pyramids, all the essential activities of Egyptian life were represented, such as caring for the flocks, fishing, hunting, marketing, exchange, the practice of the crafts, pleasures such as feasts, trips up the Nile, and finally cult practices. While warfare is not shown in the early period, the capture of prisoners and the bringing of tribute are represented. All of these bas-reliefs were originally painted. In the sacrificial chamber of Mereb in Giza there is painting without relief, but this is unusual. The most beautiful and complete series of reliefs were found in the Mastaba of Ti (Saqqara). Though conventionalised forms were used, the artists never failed to find a very happy expression for any activity, whether it is the muscular exertion of rowing, or girls engaged in extravagant dances.

*Architecture.*—The mastabas became more elaborate during this period. The tomb of the King, however, underwent a radical change. Instead of the flat construction of the mastaba, a pyramid was placed over the grave shaft, and the cult chambers were contained in two new buildings, the Temple and Gate-house. The first known pyramid was built for Zoser by Imhotep. It is not constructed, like the later pyramids, according to a well engineered plan giving the pyramid a monolithic character, but consists of five steps. The most famous pyramids are at Gizeh. Of these Chefren's is the finest (Khafre). It consists of three separate buildings, a temple, gate-house and pyramid. The gate-house has two entrances flanked by sphinxes, which lead into a broad but shallow court. This, in turn, leads by a narrow passage to a large double pillared court which is "T" shaped. Along the walls once stood twenty-three statues of the King. There are a few store rooms at the side, and a narrow passage leads to the pyramid. The walls are exceedingly thick, and the exterior plan is a rectangle into which the rooms seem to have been carved. The famous Sphinx of Gizeh is the guardian of Chefren's temple grounds.

In the Fifth Dynasty, the plan became more elaborate, and the three units were more closely united. Sahure's temple (Saqqara) is reached by a long corridor which leads into a pillared court. Around it are numerous store rooms. Through a devious passage one reaches the Holy sanctuary. The pyramid rises immediately in back.

*The Middle Kingdom (XI-XIII Dynasties).*—The Sixth Dynasty ended in civil war, and to the disasters of civil war were added the crises of foreign invasion. The Nubians attacked in the South and the Semites in the North. Order began to prevail in the Ninth Dynasty, but not until the Eleventh, does art begin to reach the level it had achieved during the Old Kingdom (one hundred seventy years after the end of the Sixth Dynasty). The Temple of King Mentuhotep III is the first monument expressing the power of the new era. There are not many objects known of the Eleventh Dynasty. The Metropolitan Museum has a very fine small wooden figure of a woman carrying a basket of fruit. The beginnings of a new style can also be seen in the relief on the stone sarcophagus of Princess Kawit (Cairo) where there is a new feeling for subtle outlines accompanied by a more rigid and hieratic style than is to be found in the Old Kingdom.

*Sculpture.*—In the Twelfth Dynasty the art flowers once again. The portrait heads of Sesostris III (MacGregor Coll.: Berlin Museum; Carnavron Coll.) must be considered among the world's masterpieces. In contrast to the optimism and joy found in the works of the Old Kingdom, we find pessimism and intellectual suffering. Art such as this can only arise in a matured and rich culture. Sesostris III was followed by Amenemhet III. The sphinx statue of this king, in which a human mask is given to the lion is one of the most majestic works in Egyptian art. The artists successfully expressed the consciousness of power and the need for watchfulness. The expressions found in sculpture can be verified by the superb literature of this period with its emphasis upon personal feeling, social fear and pessimism. Egypt is no longer a young country ready for conquest in every field, but one which already has a long history of civilisation and conquest, and is faced with the problem of maintaining itself. This does not imply that the period of progress was past, but it helps to explain the formality and sense of tragedy which is to be found in the art.

The art work is never stereotyped, but is rich in new expressions and new solutions. One strange type of figure introduced at this time, is what we might call, the figure squatting in a cube. The cloak of the figure is arranged around his squatting form in such a way that he appears to be sitting in a cube, with only his head emerging. In contrast to this "closed" form, we also find figures in which the extreme frontality is partially forsaken, so that one shoulder is pushed slightly forward (wooden figure of Enemachet, Berlin). In the smaller figures, which are always freer, there is also a richer expression than in the Old Kingdom, as for example, the very intriguing figure of a woman nursing her child (Isis and Horus). The Metropolitan Museum has a very fine collection of small figures of striking realism, which represent warriors, herdsmen, rowers, etc., practising their professions.

*Flat Relief.*—There is a greater emphasis upon action now than had appeared in the Old Kingdom. Sesostris I, for example, is shown marching towards the god Min (University College, London) instead of standing before him. The tenseness of his musculature is consistent with the greater tension of this period. The artists also show a great preference for sunken relief, which also adds to the appearance of constraint. The use of sunken relief throws a shadow on the figures, and thus gives them an appearance of rounder modelling. Some of the art work shows a great deal of freedom. Thus at Mer, there is a remarkably emaciated herdsman shown leading his flocks. Excellent painting was also done during the Middle Kingdom, as can be seen in the rock-cliff tombs of Beni Hasan. In the tomb of the nobleman Chnemhotep there is a very beautiful series depicting every phase of contemporary life. The animals and birds represented in landscape settings are particularly noteworthy.

*Architecture.*—Through the excavations of a complete town, which Flinders Petrie conducted at Kahun, we have some knowledge of the dwellings of the Middle Kingdom. Three classes of houses were found which obviously corresponded to three strata of society. Some of the houses had such small narrow chambers that it seems inconceivable that they were even used for sleeping purposes. These were in the majority. Then there were very similar houses which were roomier. Finally, there was a third type, in a separate quarter of the town which were palatial. In one of these better dwellings or palaces, near the tomb of Sesostris II, there are three courts. One of these was difficult to reach, and was therefore most likely the harem. The floor plan is exceedingly complicated, the rooms are not symmetrical in shape, and there isn't even a central axis to the house. However, like the earlier temples, the rooms were fitted into a regular rectangle. The streets ran North-South and East-West and were perfectly regular. The poorer houses also consisted of several chambers which were not arranged in any obvious order. A somewhat different type house for the poorer classes is indicated by the numerous clay models found in the tombs. According to these the typical house is in the form of a box, with windows and a door.

The temple of Mentuhotep is picturesquely set against the wall of the cliff. (The burial chamber of the King is carved into the rock.) It is in three stories. The actual temple is in the second story which is reached by a ramp. On top of this is the projection of the pyramid. The main assembly room has one hundred forty octagon pillars. It forms a broad corridor around the base of the pyramid.

The Middle Kingdom dynasties maintained themselves for four hundred years, but in the last century of this period the country was greatly weakened. During the Fourteenth and Fifteenth Dynasties the Hyksos, a Semitic people, ruled in the North. They are known as the Shepherd Kings and apparently assumed the habits of the country. Meanwhile, the South remained independent, and local rulers were established in Thebes. Finally, the Theban rulers successfully ousted the Hyksos, and reunited Egypt. It has been suggested that the expulsion of the Hyksos is related to the Bible account of the Exodus of the Jews.

*The Empire.*—The new era commencing with the Eighteenth Dynasty in 1555 is known as the Empire or New Kingdom. In contrast to the two other main periods, Egypt is now no longer a kingdom, but an empire which dominates the political and economic policies of the Near East. The borders are extended to include Upper (South) Nubia and the lands to the East and West of the Nile. Syria and Palestine are Egyptian provinces. During the Eighteenth Dynasty, King Amenophis IV tried to institute the worship of Aten instead of Amun. This religion was more universal than the older cults, but it was also more mystical. As a result, art which was used primarily in the service of religion, underwent important changes. These changes left their imprint upon subsequent art, even after the religion had been rejected. After Amenophis IV who took the name of Ikhnaten, Tutankhamen ruled for a few years. His death brought the Eighteenth Dynasty to an end. Beginning with this date, the slow decline of Egypt can be traced. During the Nineteenth and Twentieth Dynasties, known as the Ramessides, Egypt maintained its position as the most important single power, but autochry was beginning to replace world trade. In the meantime, the power of the priests grew. Finally, at the beginning of the twelfth century, the Amun priest had full control of the government, and the swift decline commenced.

*Sculpture.*—Egyptian art had always been characterised by fine craftsmanship, but this period is distinguished from the preceding ones by a still greater refinement of form. The increased aesthetic sensitivity is revealed not only in the elegant objects of everyday use, and the smooth flowing outlines of figures, but also in the increased number of representations of the enjoyment of sensuous delights, such as smelling the fragrance of flowers or listening to music. Costumes also change. Instead of the single sheath, they are elaborately pleated and draped.

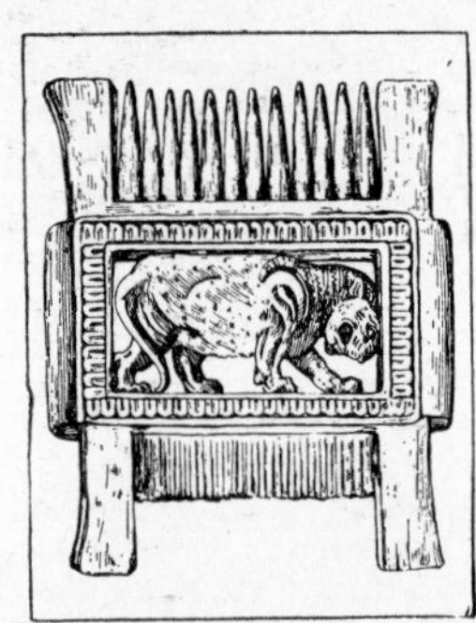

Comb. (Louvre.)

Some of the changes instituted by Amenophis IV are already heralded in the works of his father's reign. Two outstanding portraits of the pre-Amarna period are of Queen Hatshepsut and her brother Thutmosis III. The figures are exceedingly similar. They express confidence and power, but are lacking in the fine psychological character of the portraits of the Middle Kingdom. Ikhnaten's (Amenophis IV) portraits are strikingly dissimilar to all other Egyptian art. Egyptian portraiture had taught the beauty of realism, but Ikhnaten made a cult of the worship of ugliness. It is probably incorrect to consider the extremely ugly representations of the King as examples of portraiture. They were more likely conscious distortions which were related to the mystic character of the new sun worship. Ikhnaten is represented as a scrawny figure, with a tremendously long face, and an exaggerated big belly, suggestive of pregnancy. (Karnak figures in Museum of Cairo.) His children are invariably represented with malformed heads. Yet, accompanying this extreme ugliness, the members of the royal family are shown as exquisitely beautiful. (Queen Nefritite, Berlin Museum; Cairo Museum.) In University College, London, there is a tiny torso, only six inches in length of one of the princesses which is of great beauty and delicacy. Many of the Amarna sculptures were found in the workshop of the sculptor, Thutmosis.

Ikhnaten not only introduced new art styles, but also new subjects based on the cult of love. The Berlin Museum has a small statue of him kissing his daughter.

*Flat Reliefs and Painting.*—The very impressive series of paintings in the grave of Nakht of the early Eighteenth Dynasty shows the increased interest in aesthetic expressions. One of the most impressive scenes is that of the three girl musicians. Each wears a lotus blossom and a perfume cone on her head. Both of these become regular features. The girls, one of whom is nude, are beautifully grouped. Landscapes now become very common. In Queen Hatshepsut's Temple at Der el Bahari, there is a series of relief scenes depicting the expedition to Punt. One scene is a landscape of Punt with its tall palms and sycamores. Another unusual landscape scene was found in a Theban grave (now in British Museum). It shows a garden pool, filled with fish, and surrounded by trees. The pool is in "bird's-eye view."

ARMCHAIR. (Museum, Cairo.)

The Egyptians seem to have been moving towards a new feeling for space at this period. Figures are grouped together in such a way that they seem to have freedom in space (the musician girls already referred to in the Tomb of Nakht). The bird's-eye view of the garden, with trees placed horizontally and vertically to indicate that they surround the pool, also indicates a broader perspective. A scene of a bird hunt, also from Thebes, and now in the British Museum, is less a conceptual rendering of such a scene, as an attempt to express descriptively the true luxuriance of life along the Nile. Even such a motive in it, as the boat bending down a reed indicates spatial relationships. The system of horizontal stripes is also frequently discarded. For example, in the lion hunt on Tutankhamen's chest, the animals are placed freely in the open field, and not in zones. The Amarna period has occasionally been called the Egyptian Baroque. In some ways this is justified. Not because of the exaggeration of forms, which is the usual interpretation of "baroque," but because of the interest in personal emotion, and in landscape. Instances of emotional expression are the "Wailing Women," a wall painting in the Tomb of Ramose (an official of Ikhnaten) and the grief stricken mourners in the funeral procession from a tomb in Memphis of the Nineteenth Dynasty.

A compromise with this Baroque tendency is found in the stone reliefs in the Metropolitan Museum (New York City) of the sacrifices of Sethos I and Rameses I. There is an expression of calmness and restraint in these which is in contrast to the emotionalism of the preceding works. However, there is a softness and prettiness in them which reduces their power. Not all the later Empire work has this softer character. The Hunt in Medinet-Habu of Rameses III (1198-1167) has a magnificent treatment of the wounded beasts. A painted wooden tablet (Cairo) is also worth mentioning because of its resemblance to Early Christian art. It is a landscape scene, in which a hillside is represented by conventional striations. A woman sits at the top of the hill mourning before the houses of the dead. There are several levels in this composition, which is in conformity with the attempt to represent space.

*Architecture.*—The architecture of the Empire has a more orderly character than that of the Middle Kingdom. The houses of Amarna are no longer labyrinths, like those of Kahun, but are well planned. However, they are also more picturesque. Gardens form an important part of the homes of the wealthy, and except for a small part of the town, where serf labor lived, the streets are not aligned as regularly in Amarna as in Kahun.

The temples of the Empire follow a regular plan, though this may be greatly elaborated. The Temple of Chons in Karnak may be considered the model. It was reached by a long alley of stone goats. The front wall of the Temple consists of two pylons, with a central entrance. The first three chambers all have a monumental character and are intended for the public. These are the full width of the building, and must be passed through in order to reach the back half of the building. The first chamber is a shallow pillared court. A ramp leads from it to the second chamber which is in the form of a basilica and is lighted by a clerestory. This in turn opened upon a third pillared court, which we may call the pronaos. A smaller chamber containing the sanctuary of the god, the royal chamber and store rooms are in the back of the pronaos. There is a marked vertical axis in these plans. Peristyle temples were also used, but these are in ruins. Examples are, the small temple of Thutmosis III at Karnak; the temple at Medinet-Habu and the South Temple at Wadi Halfa. In the late period, the temples dedicated to the midwife gods were peristyle. (Dendera, Edfu, Philae.) In addition to the basilica temple of Chons at Karnak, other temples of that type are the large temples of Amun and Mut in Karnak and the Temple of Luxor. Occasionally, the landscape dictated a different ordering. Thus in Nubia, where the cliffs are very close to the river edge, it is necessary either to build into the cliffs (Garf Husen) or to place the parts at right angles to each other (Abydos). Rameses II's temple at Abu Simbel is carved into the living rock. More than half the buildings which are now standing in Egypt were built during the sixty-seven year reign of Rameses II. The temple at Abu Simbel is particularly remarkable because of the huge figures carved into the rock. Rameses II has been attacked as suffering from gigantism. However, the very size of the figures at Abu Simbel, sixty-five feet high, gives them an appearance of majesty. His portrait (Turin Museum) is a beautiful piece of work, and proves that technique was still at a very high level.

*The Late Period.*—Beginning with the Twenty-first Dynasty, Egypt declines (1090). After the control of the priests of Amun, the power passed into the hands of various foreign rulers. However, for one brief period, from 663-525, an Egyptian house ruled. This period is known as the Saitic, after Psammetich of Sais, founder of the dynasty. It is characterised in art by imitation of Fifth Dynasty forms. The Ethiopian rulers of the preceding period had also tried to reconstruct the ancient glories of Egypt. However, there is little difficulty in recognizing the lateness of this work. The refinement of form proves the conscious effort at archaism. Some of the figures have a smiling expression which suggest early Greek art. It is, however, oversweet, soft and unpleasant. Under the Ethiopians, several remarkable portraits were made. As for example, the high official with negroid features from the Temple of Mut in Karnak or the portrait of Metemhet.

Magnificent realistic portraits have been found which are placed at a later date (c. 400 B.C.). These emphasise the bony structure of the head, and are beautiful examples of economy. (As for example, the Green Head in the Berlin Museum.) The tradition for portraiture is undoubtedly Egyptian. It was found at a very early period, and continues into Roman times in the painted portraits of Fayoum.

The effect of Alexander's conquest (332 B.C.) was not beneficial for Egyptian art. Imitations of ancient Egyptian art and Greek art continue side by side. In addition, there is a hybrid art which is decidedly unpleasant, in which Greek figures are dressed in Egyptian forms and vice versa.

BIBLIOGRAPHY: K. Baedeker, *Egypt and the Sudan.* Leipzig, 1929.—Ch. Boreux, *L'art egyptien,* 1926.—J. H. Breasted, *Ancient Times,* 2 Ed., 1935.—Brunton & Caton-Thompson, *Badarian Civilisation,* 1928.—J. Capart, *Primitive Art in Egypt,* 1905.—J. Capart, *Lectures on Egypt Art,* 1928.—U. G. Childe, *The most ancient East,* 1929.—N. de G. Davies, *The tomb of Nakht at Thebes,* 1917.—H. Fechheimer, *Die Plastik der Aegypter,* 1922.—H. Fechheimer, *Kleinplastik,* 1922.—H. Frankfort, *Mural Painting of El Amarna,* 1929.—A. P. Laurie, *The materials of the painters craft in Europe and Egypt,* 1911.—G. Maspero, *Manual of Egyptian Archaeology,* 1914.—M. A. Murray, *Egyptian Sculpture,* 1930.—Reisner, *Naga ed Der.*—F. Petrie, *Arts and crafts of ancient Egypt,* 1910.—*Social Life in ancient Egypt,* 1923.—*Decorative patterns of the ancient world,* 1931.—Quibbel, *Hierakonpolis,* 1900-02.—E. D. Ross, *The art of Egypt through the ages,* 1931.—H. Schaefer, *Von aegyptischer Kunst,* 2 Ed., 1922.—H. Schaefer, *Die Kunst Aegyptens* (Propylaen, Kunstgeschichte, Vol. 2), 1925.—A. Scharff, *Grundzeuge der aegyptischen Vorgeschichte,* 1927.—W. Worringer, *Egyptian art,* 1928.

**EIFFEL (A. G.).**—French engineer (1832-1923) whose researches in structural steel design were instrumental in ideating the modern style of architecture. His popular fame rests on the tower which he designed for the Paris World's Fair of 1889 and which bears his name.

**EISEN (Charles).**—French painter and engraver, 1720-1778. He was born in Valenciennes, son of François Eisen, a painter of scènes galantes, who came to live in Paris. In 1753, there appeared by him the "First book of a work containing different decorative and ornamental subjects," which is, according to Goncourt, "like a complete album of Rococo sketches." In 1770, he illustrated the "Baisers" of Dorat with vignettes; but his best known vignette-work is the decoration of the edition of "Fables" by La Fontaine, known as the "édition des fermiers, généraux." The "galant" drawings of Charles Eisen are not very distinguished, but of great ability. His paintings are very rare. After the death of Louis XV, the taste of amateurs turned away from his vignettes, and he went to Brussels to end a life which was in harmony with the usual licence of his compositions.

**ELCHE (Bust of).**—This masterpiece, the artistic origins of which are much disputed, was discovered in 1897 in Elche, formerly Ilice, an important Greek and Roman city on the South Eastern shore of Spain.—It is now in the Louvre.—In some quarters it is believed that this bust may have been part of a full-length statue similar to an Iberian statue, also of a woman, found at the Cerro de Los Santos (prov. Albacete) and now in the Museo Arqueológico of Madrid. The bust is of calcareous stone and measures 53 cm. in height. Much of the old polychrome is still intact (brown, mauve, pink, blue, yellow, carmine red; see col. reprod. in *Lozoya,* I). Dieulafoy says of this bust: "enormous wheel-shaped ear-pendants, a head-dress recalling

BUST FOUND AT ELCHE (SPAIN). (Louvre.)

the sarmat, a fine Phœnician necklace, and in addition the style of the sculpture and the ethnical type of the face determine the face and the origin of this bust. It must be a work of the second half of the Vth century B.C. by a native sculptor who had come under the dual influence, 1) that of Greece filtering through the Phocaeans (a Greek tribe) and the colonies succeeding each other along the coasts of Catalonia, and 2) that of Phœnicia which made its way from Carthage and the trading posts established in the South of Spain." S. Reinach's famous verdict on the Lady of Elche is: "Spanish on account of the modèle and garments, —Phœnician, perhaps, because of the jewelry,—but Greek, purely Greek, in style." R. Carpenter agrees with S. Reinach's opinion as to a Greek authorship and expresses his own; that an Ionic workman established in Spain may have done the work and marshals as evidence the strikingly close proximity of facial measurements between the bust and a Greek head, namely that of the Chatsworth Apollo. The Chatsworth head is dated by Furtwängler 465-460 B.C., and R. Carpenter allowing "for retardation attendant upon work in the provinces at a distance from the centre of artistic growth" is prone to date the Lady of Elche between 460-450 B.C. Again the Marquess of Lozoya believes the author to be a native artist, who already knew of Greek art—then in its apogee—but who because of local traditionalism clung to hieratic types. The same author furthermore points out that the facial type (in agreement with Reinach) is typical of that still surviving in the regions of Murcia and Valencia and that the adornment is not only similar to treasure finds made in Spain but recalls certain features in their general aspect—such as the peineta or Spanish high comb, or the filigree jewelry, which are still in use in those areas today. The same author emphasizes the fact that in the back of the bust there is a circular orifice which may have reference to an ancient rite. This orifice has been found also on several statues coming from the island of Ibiza.

Bibliography: *Monuments Piot,* Vol. IV, 1897.—Pierre Paris, *Promenades archéologiques en Espagne.* 1st series, Paris, 1910. 2nd series, Paris, 1921.—J. R. Mélida, *Busto anteromano descubierto en Elche,* Revista de archivos, Bibl. y Museos. Madrid (3a época) 1897; Vol. 1.—T. Reinach, *La Tête d'Elche au Musée du Louvre,* Révue d'Études grecques, 1898.—Rhys Carpenter, *The Greeks in Spain,* Bryn Mawr Notes and Monographs, VI. Bryn Mawr College, 1925.—Marqués de Lozoya, *Historia del arte hispanico.* Barcelona, 1931; Vol. 1.

**ELGIN (Lord).**—See Acropolis of Athens.

**ELIASZ (Nicolas).**—Dutch painter, c. 1590-c. 1655. He may have been the pupil of C. van der Voort. He worked in Amsterdam. He painted the Portraits of Cornelius de Graef, and of his wife Catherine Hooft (Berlin); the portraits of Martin Ray, and his wife, and the four Governors of the Spinhuis, as well as paintings of Corporations, banquets, etc. (all in the Amsterdam gallery). His works represent the style of portrait-painting in Amsterdam before Rembrandt's arrival.

**ELLIOTT (Charles Loring).**—American painter (1812-1868). He was born at Scipio, New York, 12th October 1812. He began making sketches as a child and soon was making architectural drawings for his father, who was an architect. His father disapproved of his son's desire to be an artist, but in 1834 allowed him to go to New York City to study painting. A letter of introduction to John Trumbull led him to work under that artist in the American Academy for a time, but there also he was urged to try architectural drawing. Disappointed at such rebuffs he left Trumbull and went to study with John Quidor. He remained with him for several years and then set himself up as an independent artist. For several years he travelled through central and western New York State as an itinerant portrait painter and as he went from town to town his artistic ability and skill grew accordingly. In 1845 he returned to New York City and there opened his own studio and was quite successful for the rest of his life. Among those he painted were John Ericsson, Matthew Vassar, James Fenimore Cooper and some of the contemporary artists, including F. E. Church and Asher Brown Durand. He was elected an associate member of the National Academy of Design in 1845 and became a full-fledged academician some years later. One of his portraits was sent abroad to the Paris Exposition of 1866 as a typical example of American art of that period. He died in Albany, N. Y., 25th August 1868, a successful painter to the last.

Although he never studied in Europe his style compares favourably with the work of his contemporaries. He was able to achieve good likenesses of his subjects and specialised mostly in heads or bust portraits. The few full-length pictures reveal an inadequacy of treatment of the figure and draperies as accessories to the picture.

Bibliography: C. H. Caffin, *The Story of American Painting,* 1907. —Samuel Isham, *History of American Painting,* 1927.—H. T. Tuckerman, *Book of the Artists,* 1867.

**ELLORA.**—An Indian village. famous for its monuments, and rock-cut temples, and its great monolithic temple—twenty Buddhist and Brahmin temples. The Vicwakarman cavern (8th century B.C.) encloses a famous image of Buddha. The most celebrated of all these monuments is the Kaïlasa (about 1000 B.C.), cut in a single block of rock, which includes a vast courtyard (225 metres long), in the centre of which are porticoes, columned halls, obelisks, and towers, which form the temple. The walls are covered with bas-reliefs of personages representing the gods, and scenes from the Ramayana.

**ELMES (H. L.).**—Neo-classic British architect (1815-1847) who designed St. George's Hall, Liverpool, based on the tepidarium of the Baths of Caracalla in the interior, with a pedimented and colonnaded exterior.

**ELSHEIMER (Adam).**—German painter (1578-1610), also known as "Adamo Tedesco." He studied with a pupil of Grünewald in Frankfort, and then in Rome. His small mythological or religious pictures include the *Flight into Egypt* (Munich), the *Good Samaritan* (Louvre), *Philemon and Baucis* (Dresden), etc. He loved night effects, and placed the scenes of his pictures in beautiful Roman landscapes.

Elsheimer was the master of Peter Lastman, who was the master of Rembrandt.

Bibliography: Bode, W., in Studien zur Geschichte d. holl. Malerei. Brunswick, 1883.—Weizsäcker, H., in Thieme-Becker.—Drost, W., *Adam Elsheimer und sein Kreis.* Potsdam, 1933.

**ELY (England).**—Cathedral, 1107-1362. One of the largest of English cathedrals, Ely is a latin cross in plan, with Norman nave and transepts built between 1107 and 1137. The nave is still covered by the Norman timber roof, which has 19th century decoration. Before the nave is the Lancet Galilee porch, 1198-1215. Adjoining the North Transept is the Decorated Lady Chapel. The huge octagonal lantern at the crossing is also Decorated. The choir is Lancet. The west façade retains the central Norman tower, as wide as the nave, and the projecting southwest screen with two turrets. The corresponding northwest turreted screen has been destroyed.

**EMBROIDERY.**—The art of embroidery consists of producing ornaments or figures, by means of needle and thread, on the surface

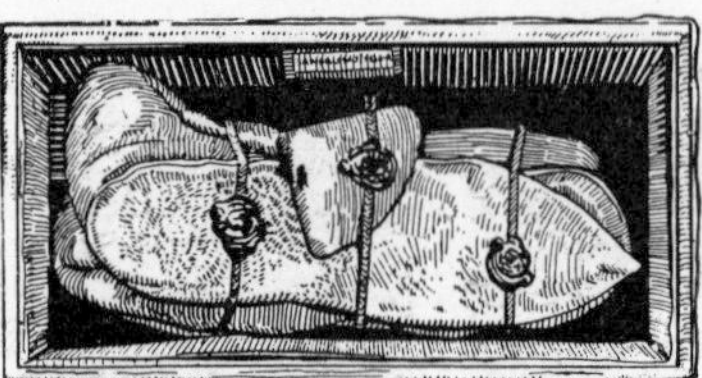

Sandals of St. Césaire, Notre Dame de la Majeur, Arles.

of a textile which serves as a base. This base may be linen, velvet, silk or satin; or it may be net, and then the result is filet-embroidery, the origin of lace. Finally a strong canvas may be covered with single or crossed stitches called "gros point," "petit point" and Hungarian embroidery.

St. Césaire's Chasuble, Notre Dame de la Majeur, Arles.

There are essential differences between embroidery and lace. In embroidery a foundation is always necessary, and the embroidery is applied to it. In lace the ornament is fashioned independently, and afterwards joined together. In woven textiles the tissue and decoration are produced at the same time by the crossing of the threads in the process of weaving.

Embroidery may well be the oldest of the arts. Homer speaks of it, and it has been mentioned by writers of all periods and all countries. It has always been an important feature in costume, and in the 17th and 18th centuries it was also used for furniture. It has largely been used to decorate sacerdotal vestments, which have always been remarkable for their richness; and this has resulted in the disappearance of the finest pieces, which were destroyed (in France) either at the time of the wars of religion, or at the Revolution;—in one case owing to religious passion; in the other, for the sake of the gold and silver which adorned them.

To embroider the material (which forms the base), a needle holding a thread (of wool, cotton, linen, silk, gold or silver) is passed through it. The part of the thread which remains on the surface of the stuff, between two pricks of the needle, is the "stitch." If the stitch is too long, and there is a risk of it catching and breaking, it is fixed on the stuff, here and there, by means of narrow little stitches; this practice is applied especially to gold, and the stitch is then called a couch stitch. Threads of coloured silk may be passed over the gold thread, to modify the lights: this is embossed, satin or shadow stitch.

Embroidery began to hold a very important place in Byzantium, under the inspiration of Asiatic luxury, and thanks to the facility with which embroiderers could procure silk. Its importance grew at the time of the Roman emperors, but no work of this period has come down to us, and a study of embroidery must begin with Byzantine work.

*The Byzantine Embroideries.*—It is generally admitted that the tunic

Priestly Vestments of Thomas à Becket, Cathedral of Sens.

and pallium of St. Césaire, Archbishop of Arles, from 501 to 542, are the oldest Byzantine embroideries we possess. These vestments, kept in Notre Dame de la Majeur, near Arles, are decorated with blue hares on a yellow background, and yellow hares on a red background. There is the monogram of Christ, in red silk, and various ornaments. In Ravenna, there are embroideries of a slightly later period; and others in the Cathedral of Aschaffenburg; and in the Cluny Museum (vestments of Morard, Abbé of St. Germain-des-Prés). Chartres preserves the Virgin's veil, which was said to have been sent to Charlemagne by Nicephore, in 803. But the finest work we possess is the dalmatic, said to have belonged to Pope Leo III, which is in the Vatican: it dates from the end of the 10th or beginning of the 11th century. It is decorated with a "Glory" of Christ, on a deep blue background, with a pattern of foliage and Greek crosses, surrounded by a circle, worked in gold and silver. Other beautiful embroideries of the same period are in the treasury of Bamberg Cathedral, and in Sens Cathedral (a cap said to

# CHINESE AND JAPANESE PAINTING

*CHINESE painting was executed in water colour upon silk. It is of extreme lightness and is generally free from the sculptural solidity of European painting. For this reason the Chinese artist is an admirable painter of atmosphere. Long before the masters of Holland or Fontainebleau, Chinese landscape painters of the twelfth century expressed the poetry of nature using their brush with a breadth which has not been excelled.*

CHINESE PAINTING, FOURTEENTH CENTURY. WILLIAM ROCKHILL NELSON GALLERY OF ART.

CHINESE LANDSCAPE, SUNG STYLE. WILLIAM ROCKHILL NELSON GALLERY OF ART.

CHINESE PAINTING BY EMPEROR HUI TSUNG, SUNG DYNASTY. *(Photo Champeau)*

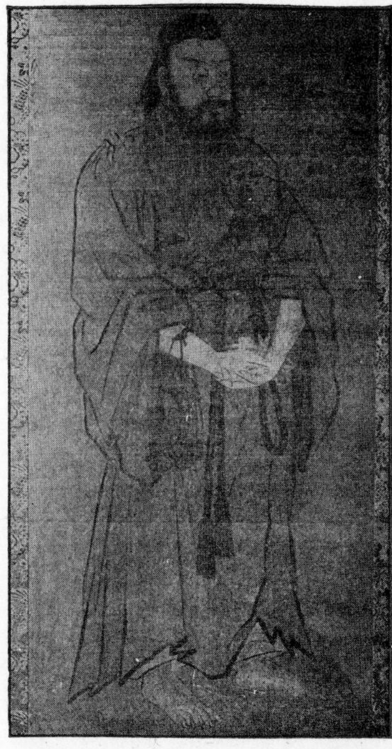

PERSONAGE OF THE MING DYNASTY. COLLECTION OF MME. LANGWEILL. *(Photo by Giraudon.)*

SESSON: LANDSCAPE WITH BOAT. (From Kokka-Tokyo.) *(Photo by Giraudon.)*

OKYO: PUPPIES. (From Kokka-Tokyo.) *(Photo by Giraudon.)*

HOKUSAI: MAN PLAYING WITH A DOG. (From Kokka-Tokyo.) *(Photo by Giraudon.)*

MOTONOBU: ROCKY LANDSCAPE. (From Kokka-Tokyo.) *(Photo by Giraudon.)*

SESSON: BIRD. (From Kokka-Tokyo.) *(Photo by Giraudon.)*

PRIEST, FUJIWARA PERIOD. (From Kokka-Tokyo.) *(Photo by Giraudon.)*

KANO MASANOBU: LANDSCAPE WITH BOAT. (From Kokka-Tokyo.) *(Photo by Giraudon.)*

## Japanese Painting

THE Japanese practice painting with the same methods and obtain the same effects as their Chinese masters: figures in pure and flat colours, neatly set forth, landscapes in Chinese ink, in light grisaille. But they are cleverer and gayer, and as their observation is livelier, less mixed with revery, their skill of execution easily develops into a more ingenious virtuosity.

# THE JAPANESE PRINT

*The Japanese print, which flourished from the eighteenth century until the middle of the following century, fills an altogether original and particularly brilliant chapter in the history of engraving. It translates the subject scarcely diminishing the effect of the original painting. It can do this because water colour painting is made up of precise lines and flat tones. Moreover, wood engraving can easily reproduce linear drawing; it can also reproduce colour effects by means of impressions of coloured inks placed one upon the other.*

KWAIGETSUDO: COURTESAN.
(H. Vever Collection.)

MASANOBU: BOAT RIDE ALONG THE SUMIDA.
(H. Vever Collection.)

HARUNOBU: COUPLE IN THE SNOW.
(H. Vever Collection.)

## Masanobu-Harunobu

The first coloured wood engravings done by hand date from the end of the seventeenth century. Then the system of successive impressions by means of colour plates was thought out. As for the drawing, it reproduces the beautiful linear patterns of Japanese painting. In these very supple curves which the engraver's knife was able to set apart, we must recognise the initial trace furnished by the brush. This type of engraving very quickly specialised in the representation of small scenes of popular and worldly life and particularly the lives of the higher classes; the most favoured subject was that of female figures in supple draperies.

SHARAKU: ACTOR IN NOBLE'S COSTUME.
(Collection of R. Koechlin.)

SHARAKU: ACTOR IN WOMAN'S COSTUME.
(Musée des Arts Décoratifs.)

KIYONAGA: A TERRACE AT THE SEASHORE.
(H. Vever Collection.)

UTAMARO: WOMAN NURSING HER CHILD BEFORE A MIRROR.
(H. Vever Collection.)

## Kiyonaga and Utamaro

The golden age of the Japanese print is represented by the work of Kiyonaga. He was the elegant historian of lovely women. More than any other Japanese, he established his figures in well-balanced compositions caring more for rhythm than for movement. Utaramo was perhaps the most refined of these linear draftsmen and we immediately recognise the long pale countenances of his fair women and their swaying attitudes. Sharaku was a satirist who amused himself with the grimaces of actors.

HOKUSAI: CRANES IN THE SNOW.
(Collection of H. Vever.)

HOKUSAI: HALT AT THE INN.
(Collection of G. Marteau.)

HIROSHIGE: THE BRIDGE IN THE RAIN.
(British Museum.)

## Hokusai and Hiroshige

Hokusai and Hiroshige were among the last arrivals in the great family of Japanese engravers. Hokusai was the first engraver known to Europeans and has remained the most popular. He was the master of pictures of movement taken from life; our impressionists owe much to him. Hiroshige was an admirable landscape painter whose vision is close to our own. With the spirited ingenuity of his engraving craft—strokes and specks—he understood how to attain the poetry of the old Chinese and Japanese masters.

# EARLY CHRISTIAN ART

*When Christianity was introduced at Rome in opposition to the state religion, its principles were discussed and fostered by services held in the catacombs. It is there that one must seek the first traces of the new religion. It manifests itself primarily in the inscriptions carved on the walls of the sarcophagi and in the paintings which decorate the galleries of the subterranean cemeteries. Christianity does not fill a great place in sculpture; just the same, the art of sarcophagi carved in bas-relief continued. After the Edict of Constantine which made a state religion of Christianity, the Church was set up in magnificent basilicas, of which the oldest extant examples are at Rome.*

PAINTINGS OF THE CATACOMBS:
1. PARADISE, THE GOOD SHEPHERD AND THE ORANTE.
2. VIBIA LED INTO PARADISE.
*(Photo by Wilpert.)*

THE GOOD SHEPHERD. LATERAN MUSEUM.
*(Photo by Anderson.)*

1. THE SARCOPHAGUS OF ORESTES.
2. "THEOLOGICAL" SARCOPHAGUS. LATERAN MUSEUM.
*(Photos by Brogi and Anderson.)*

## Paintings and Bas-Reliefs

Painting was one of the favourite means of expression of Christianity from its origin. It served to translate in symbolic form the beliefs of the new religion. The *orante* was a figure connected with prayer and the content of the prayer was almost always a request for eternal happiness in Paradise. The only statue permitted by Christianity was the image of the Good Shepherd, symbol of Christ gathering in the souls. Upon the sarcophagi, the sculptures, sometimes preserving the pagan style, treated Christian themes, often episodes from the life of Christ.

CHRIST AND THE APOSTLES. ROME. S. PUDENZIANA.
*(Photo by Anderson.)*

THE CHRIST. ROME, SS. COSMO E DAMIANO.
*(Photo by Anderson.)*

## Mosaics

Under the half-domes of the apses the basilicas offer magnificent compositions in mosaics. This decorative process was widely developed by the Byzantines. Among the most beautiful mosaics in Rome we must include Santa Pudenziana which dates from 390 and that of SS. Cosmo e Damiano which is of the sixth century. In the first, types, costumes and style are close to ancient Rome; the latter reveals the Byzantine East.

BASILICA OF SAN PAOLO-FUORI-LE-MURA. ROME.
*(Photo by Alinari.)*

BASILICA OF SAN LORENZO-FUORI-LE-MURA. ROME.
*(Photo by Alinari.)*

## Basilicas

When, under Constantine, Christianity became the official religion it abandoned the Catacombs and installed itself in grandiose basilicas. These basilicas are very different from the pagan temples inasmuch as they are a great deal larger. They are also built of light materials. In the interiors there is an extraordinary richness: mosaics, marbles, monolith columns, gilt wood ceilings. . . . At Rome, many of these basilicas were constructed outside the walls, that is to say beyond the protecting wall of the city, whence comes their appellation.

# BYZANTINE ARCHITECTURE

*Byzantine architecture is the heir of eastern constructions characterised by the use of brick and the vault. The most frequently used vault is the dome, which is adapted to the Greek cross plan by means of pendentives which allow the transition from the square plan of the church to the circular base of the dome. This architecture is still Asiatic due to the nature of its decoration: the mosaics which recall the enamel work of ancient Chaldea and which permit, on the other hand, the representation of themes from the cycle of the Gospels. It is a decoration admirably suited to the architecture and it is also pleasing to the eye.*

TOMB OF GALLA PLACIDIA, RAVENNA.
*(Photo by Alinari.)*

SANTA SOPHIA (EXTERIOR).
*(Photo by Sébah and Joaillier.)*

SANTA SOPHIA (INTERIOR).
*(Photo by Sébah and Joaillier.)*

## Santa Sophia of Constantinople

This church is one of the most beautiful of architectural monuments. Justinian wished to build a colossal edifice. The architects were named Anthemius of Tralles and Isidore of Miletus. The principle of the monument consists of an enormous dome upon pendentives; it is buttressed on two sides by two semi-domes and on the other two sides by powerful piers. The decoration in its richness, the sculpture of the capitals, the polychrome marbles and mosaics, are equal in power to the construction.

CHURCH OF MONREALE.
*(Photo by Alinari.)*

CHURCH OF ST. THEODORE, ATHENS.
*(Photo by Giraudon.)*

LA MARTORANA, PALERMO.
*(Photo by Alinari.)*

## The Second Byzantine Golden Age

After the Iconoclastic controversy, Byzantine art experienced a Renaissance in the ninth and tenth centuries. In architecture this Renaissance saw the erection of a large number of churches of elegant proportions which sometimes anticipate the Romanesque architecture of the West. It is at this time that the plan of the Greek cross becomes fixed and generalized. The dome which covers the crossing of the two naves is raised upon a drum which gives the exterior silhouette of the building more lightness. These buildings spread even as far as western Europe and one may class St. Mark's at Venice among the buildings of this type.

KHARIE-DJAMI, CONSTANTINOPLE.
*(Photo by Sébah and Joaillier.)*

THE PERIBLEPTOS, MISTRA.
*(Photo by Millet.)*

THE PANTANASSA, MISTRA.
*(Photo by Millet.)*

## The Renaissance of the Fourteenth Century

Before undergoing the final assault of the Turks, Byzantine civilisation experienced a last flowering in the course of the fourteenth century. The architecture of this time, though it was less grandiose and less rich than in the two preceding periods, is no less charming, animated, and picturesque; it shows how much Byzantine art preserved its vitality in its somnolent backwardness. It is at Mistra near ancient Sparta that the most important and the most instructive group of monuments from this period are preserved. After this last flowering, the Byzantine spirit was confined to the arts of the monasteries.

have belonged to St. Thomas of Canterbury, etc.).

*Western Embroideries.*—In the monasteries, particularly at St. Gall,

Tapestry of Queen Matilda. (Museum, Bayeux.)

there were, from the early Middle Ages, schools of embroiderers who worked the vestments and materials which were used for altar decoration. At the same time, similar work was being done by lay persons, such as the chasuble which the wife of Hugh Capet offered to the Church of St. Martin of Tours and the one she made for St. Denis.

The vestments, which were used at services, were covered with extremely rich embroideries. There was the *cope*, or cape, which was used outside the church, during processions. The *chasuble* was worn by the priest while saying Mass, while the deacon wore the *dalmatic*. The *mitre*, or bishop's headgear, had a horizontal band at its base, the *circulus*, which was surmounted in front by a little decorated panel, the *titulus*. The symbolic gloves, and even the shoes, were generally decorated with embroidery.

In the 11th and 12th centuries, silk was only used for the grounds, the decoration being worked almost exclusively in gold and pearls. During the 12th century the subjects were composed of volutes, foliage,

Alms-bag of the thirteenth century. (Musée de Cluny.)

and animals derived from the East: all this decoration was as large as possible. The imitation of nature did not appear until the end of the 12th century, and then feebly: until then, leaves, animals and human figures were of conventional design. The figures, isolated or grouped, are placed under arcades or in compartments, and are often accompanied by a name or inscription.

In the 13th century, floral ornament was developed: lilies, roses, tree leaves, the oak and ivy, came to be studied more and more closely from nature. Sometimes subjects are set in foliage, sometimes in an architectural framework, inspired by Gothic windows. As with the other arts, embroidery freed herself from traditional forms, and became more supple. The figures were more natural, and, in the corners of certain works, even portraits of the donors are attempted.

During the 14th century, an industry of civil embroidery sprang up (no example has come down to us), which led to the creation of workshops in the large towns. Religious embroidery profited from the rapid progress due to this popularising of embroidery: portraits of donors became more and more numerous, and all work tended to become more realistic. Vegetable decoration was always used, but the number of plants reproduced now became very varied. Finally, heraldry makes its appearance.

During the following centuries, the same evolution was followed, but embroidery decreased in importance: weaving and tapestry came to the fore. Under the influence of the Renaissance, embroiderers attempted to rival the painters, imitating and copying pictures, even of landscapes and buildings in perspective. By degrees the decoration of religious vestments approached that of civil costume, and in the 17th century, the same decoration was applied to either. In the 18th century, brocade was much in favour, and from that time the importance of embroidery became less and less.

We will now glance at some of the most celebrated European embroideries.

*Germany.*—The German embroideries of the 10th and 11th century show marked Byzantine influence, as in the mantle of Otto III, decorated with Visions of the Apocalypse. Treves, and the Treasury of Open possess chasubles, one of which was offered to Pope John XVIII (1003-1009), by St. Stephen, King of Hungary; the other, dating from 1031, served at the coronation of the kings of Hungary. These works were made in Hungary, but by workers of Queen Gisele, wife of St. Stephen, from her native country of Bavaria. Byzantine influence then became slighter, as the antependium of Rupersberg shows (Museum of the Cinquantenaire, in Brussels), or the altar-cloth, preserved in the convent of Goesz, in Styria, which was made in the middle of the 13th century. The Cluny Museum possesses an altar-cloth from the hospital of Malines, representing scenes from the life of St. Mark and St. John. Here, one observes the couch stitch, which was frequently used in German work.

In the 14th and 15th centuries Cologne also produced gold and silver embroideries, in satin stitch, and known as "Opus Coloniense." A fine altar-frontal in this style, and representing the Coronation of the Virgin, under graceful arcades, is preserved in the Church of Kloster Kamp. The Cologne workshops also produced orphreys—wide bands, for the adornment of vestments—woven in tapestry on an upright loom, and then embroidered in relief. Examples may be seen in the Church of St. Cecilia, in Cologne, and in the Cluny Museum.

We may also mention a wool embroidery on linen, representing twenty-six scenes from the story of Tristram and Yseult. This was worked about 1380, and comes from a convent in Wurtzbourg. It is now in Erfurt Cathedral.

*England.*—The origin of English embroideries may be established by comparison with early English manuscripts. The Cathedral of Sens possesses the liturgical vestments of Thomas à Becket, who, it appears, took them to France when he had to flee from England to escape the wrath of Henry II. In the 13th and 14th centuries, English embroidery (often known as "Opus Anglicorum") is always on linen, the ground being completely covered with the decoration, often in gold and colours, in zig-zag or lozenge patterns, as in the cope of Darocca (Madrid), the Sion Cope (Victoria & Albert Museum, London), and the copes of Agnani and Bologna. St. Bertrand de Comminges possessed two copes, of early 14th century work, one with Passion scenes embroidered in silk on a gold ground, and the other with scenes from the life of the Virgin, embroidered in gold on a red ground. Finally, in the 15th century, England produced quantities of embroidered ornaments — six-winged angels, two-head eagles, stars, lilies and other flowers—which were appliqued on to velvets. (Examples in the Museums of Lyon and Cluny.)

*Italy.*—Milan and Florence possessed important studios of embroidery from the 14th century. From Florence came the gonfalon of Santa Fosca, preserved in Torcello, near Venice, and dating from 1266; it has four figures, the bodies of which are embroidered in silver thread, but the heads are painted. In the Duomo of Florence are embroidered pictures, representing scenes from the life of St. John the Baptist, which seem to form part of a series, the cartoons for which were executed by Antonio Pollaiuolo between 1469 and 1487. In the 16th century, the influence of Italy spread throughout Europe. Modelling was attempted by means of graded tints. Sometimes even touches of paint were added. In Venice, embroidery with coloured beads was attempted, but this work is not pleasing, and the weight of the glass beads makes the material base undurable. One of the most remarkable productions of Italian embroidery is in the Cluny Museum.

Hebrews Adoring the Golden Calf. (Italian embroidery, Musée de Cluny.)

It is an oval medallion, representing the Israelites adoring the Golden Calf, and Moses receiving the Table of the Law, the cartoon for which was furnished by Raphael, at the request of Francis I.

*Spain.*—Spanish embroidery was for a long time in the oriental style. It is distinguished by the application of velvet on to a satin ground, by the importance given to gold (often in large plaques studded with pearls), and especially by the use of spangles of gold, silver, or polished steel, which had no doubt been invented by the Moors. In the 15th century, the introduction of German and Italian embroideries profoundly modified this style. In the Cathedrals of Toledo and Valencia are remarkable embroideries of the 15th and 16th centuries, among which is the tent of Ferdinand and Isabella, which must be a little previous to 1488. One of the most famous works of Spanish art is the Mantle of the Virgin of the Sagrario, in Toledo. It was offered to the Cathedral at the beginning of the 17th century by Cardinal Sandoval, and is entirely covered with fine pearls.

*Flanders.*—From the 13th century, Flanders produced fine embroideries, the artistic merit of which is not inferior to that of her masterpieces of painting and sculpture. Vienna Museum possesses sacerdotal ornaments, executed before 1430, decorated with figures of saints worked in silk on a gold ground. The embroideries in Berne Museum are also of Flemish origin, and were acquired by the Swiss under Charles the Bold, in 1470, at the Battle of Granson. In the Museum of Brussels is a gold embroidered altar-cloth, with scenes of the Last Supper, the Marriage of Cana, the Pilgrims of Emmaus, etc. (between 1615 and 1647).

*France.*—In the Cathedral of Sens, there is a piece of fine linen on which is embroidered an Assumption, with oval medallions enclosing a praying figure accompanied by two angels. Below, eight little figures are placed vertically, and two horizontally. An inscription indicates the subject, and the form of the letters makes it supposed that this embroidery belongs to the Merovingian period, and doubtless from the beginning of the 7th century: this is the oldest embroidery known.

Of more certain date is the work incorrectly known as the "Bayeux tapestry," possibly made in England, which is in the Museum of Bayeux.

It was not until after the Crusades that the art of embroidery began to develop in France, to satisfy the luxurious tastes which the Crusaders brought back with them from the East. Many embroidered garments of this time have armorial bearings, which were often embroidered separately, and then sewn on to the stuff. This method was sometimes used for the heads of figures, while the bodies were simply embroidered on the ground.

The embroideries of the 13th century are characterized by the arrangement of the subjects under pointed arches. The altar-cloth of St. Bertrand de Comminges has five figures of apostles under arcades, and the red satin chasuble of Reims Cathedral, which dates from before 1299, recalls the form of the door paintings.

From the 14th century, the Museum of Chartres possesses a triptych representing Christ supported by the Virgin and St. John. Of the same period, must be mentioned the altar-cloth of Narbonne which is of silk, not embroidered, but painted, and the mitre of the Old Temple (in the Archives Nationales), of white silk, decorated with paintings in black.

In the 15th century, embroidery was used for all articles of dress, even for shoes and gloves. Charles VII organized an atelier of embroiderers at Blois; Louis XI summoned Italian workers to Tours; Charles VIII brought them back from Italy, and pattern books, printed in Lyon, Paris and Venice, soon spread abroad the decorative subjects which were used.

During the 16th century many complicated refinements of workmanship were practised, but they were so costly that they soon had to be given up. At the end of the century, some very rich ornaments were for the Order of the Holy

Spirit, founded by Henri III in 1578; the canopy, the chapel altar-cloth, and the Knight's mantles may be seen in the Cluny Museum.

Under Louis XIV, embroidery played a more important part than ever, and the king employed several embroiderers, for himself alone. Soon, however, brocades came into fashion, and this resulted in the complete decadence of embroidery.

BIBLIOGRAPHY: Bertaux, Trésors d'églises. *Mélanges d'archéologie et d'histoire,* 1897.—G. Migeon, *Les arts du tissu,* 2nd part. Paris, 1909.

**EMILIA.**—Ancient Æmilia, a division of Italy.

See Pl. 22, Vol. II.

**EMPIRE STYLE.**—See Furniture; also Pl. 44, Vol. II.

**ENAMEL.**—Enamel is obtained by the fusion, at high temperature, of a mixture of silica, borate of soda, oxide of lead, minium, and nitrate of soda, or potash, commonly called nitre or saltpetre. The substance thus obtained is called flux, and is simply a crystal; in this state, it is colourless and transparent. It can be coloured by the addition of metallic oxides, as is done for glass. By adding oxide of tin, it can be made opaque; in the absence of any other colouring, it then has the appearance of china.

RELIQUARY IN THE SHAPE OF A HEAD. From the region of Limoges, end of the thirteenth century. (Louvre.)

The enameller reduces the flux to a very fine powder, mixes the necessary proportion of metallic oxide which corresponds to the colour desired, and adds a slightly gummed water to obtain a thick paste, which he places on the surface to be decorated. The piece is passed into an oven, the enamel melts and adheres closely to the metal. Other coats of enamel can be superimposed, by putting the piece into the oven each time; but, in this case,

HEAD OF ST. MARTIN. (Louvre.)

more and more fusible enamels must be used, and the temperature of the oven must be maintained at a degree which liquefies the last layer of enamel, but not the preceding ones. It may be pointed out, simply, that the temperature required for the fusion of enamel depends almost exclusively on the proportion of oxide of lead that it contains.

Enamel is usually applied on gold, silver, or copper. The difficulty is to prevent the various adjacent enamels from mingling during the firing, which would destroy the design,—unless, however, the enameller tries (as he sometimes does) to profit from this mingling to obtain unexpected colours and decoration. But, generally, when it is desired that the design should be kept very clear, and the colours very fresh, the enameller has recourse to various processes on the distinction of which the whole classification of enamels is based.

(1.) *Cloisonné* enamel.—Thin soldered compartments (or even simply compartments coloured with resin and gum) may be applied on to the surface to be decorated. These are the little divisions on which the enamel is to be placed. The enamel is then called "cloisonné." This process is long and delicate, but it survives all damage to the metal which serves as a support. It is used chiefly when the enamel is to be applied to gold or silver.

(2.) *Champlevé* enamel.—When, however, the metal is of mediocre value, it is more expedient to take a thick plaque of it, and to raise, with a burin, all the part that is to be enamelled, only leaving the line of the design. A plaque thus prepared is called champlevé.

(3.) *Relief* enamel.—Enamels in relief are obtained by the applica-

PROCESSIONAL CRUCIFIX DECORATED WITH ENAMELLED FIGURES IN RELIEF. (Limoges, twelfth century, Musée de Cluny.)

tion of enamels on to plaques of metal in bas-relief or high-relief.

(4.) *Painted* enamel.—The process known as "émaux peints" consists in the application of vitrified enamels on to a level surface. There are various forms of painted enamels. The plaque may be covered with a coat of flux or white opaque enamel, on which the subject is then painted with a paste of coloured enamels, the modelling being achieved by superposition of tones; or else the plaque is covered with several coats of various coloured enamels, so that by scraping the surface the colour desired can be recovered. This process ("enlevage") was seldom used except with two coats of enamel, in the grisailles of the 16th century. A coating of opaque white enamel was applied to a coating of black, which, slightly transparent, gave a general greyish tone; then, by "enlevage," or removing of the upper coat, the shadows and drawing were indicated, and the lights were re-added by further layers of

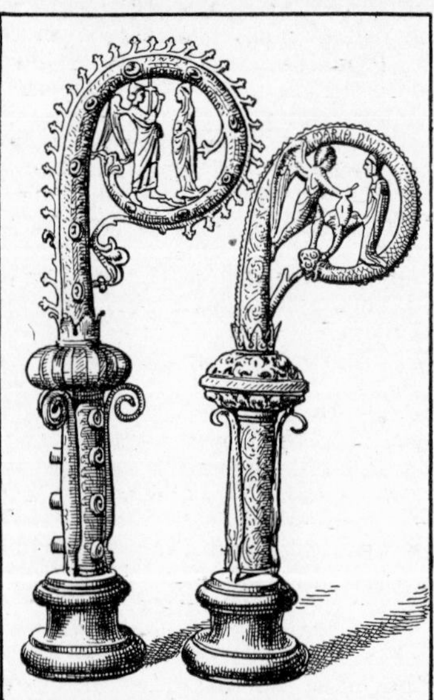

CHAMPLEVÉ ENAMELLED COPPER CROSIERS. (Limoges, thirteenth century, Louvre.)

white. Or, finally, the design was painted with vitreous colours on a blue, white or black background, like a water-colour: this method was employed chiefly in the 17th and 18th centuries.

(5.) Enamels "cloisonnés à jour."—The panel was not soldered on to a metal plaque, but remained independent. It was placed in an iron mould or framework, reproducing the shape of the object that was desired, and of which the sides and background were covered with a very thin coat of clay, to prevent the enamel from adhering to the metal. The enamels once added, as in ordinary cloisonné, it was heated, and the plaque, separated from the iron mould or framework, had the appearance of a very small piece of stained glass.

RELIQUARY DECORATED WITH ENAMELLED FIGURES. (From Limoges, National Museum, Florence.)

(6.) Enamels *"en résille."*—These were made sometimes in France in the 17th century, but chiefly in the East, and particularly in India. The designs were pushed back (repoussés) on a gold plaque, which thus showed the pattern in relief on one side and hollow on the other. The reverse was covered with a colourless enamel, which filled in the hollows; on the other side were then laid coloured enamels, which were fixed by firing. The two faces of the plaque were then applied to the grindstone, so as to make the repoussé and reserved surfaces disappear, and all that was left was an enamel set in a plaque of crystal.

*Origins.*—It is not quite certain whether the Egyptians thought of

A CAVALRY BATTLE. (Enamel work by Jean Pénicaud, Louvre.)

applying enamel hot on to the metal; but the profound knowledge they had of glass-making and of clay-enamelling makes it probable. Nevertheless, most of the objects that have been discovered are simply decorated with enamels worked

SAMSON AND DELILAH. (Enamel work by Jean Pénicaud, Louvre.)

separately and set in compartment when cold.

As to Greece and Rome, nothing seems to have been known about enamelling metals.

But there have been found in Germany, England, France and even in the Caucasus, pieces of champlevé enamels anterior to the 3rd century, of which the Asiatic origin is evident. It seems that champlevé enamels are of Asiatic, and, more exactly, of Persian, origin.

The art of enamelling was very widely developed in Byzantium. Nothing harmonised better with the mosaic decorations which covered the walls and vaults of the churches than gilded and enamelled altars, and reliquaries, and all the pieces of goldsmith's work used for religious ceremonies, enriched with bright enamels. The finest Byzantine work was produced in the 10th and 11th centuries, and it was in full decadence, in the 12th and 13th centuries, when Limoges was creating its most brilliant work.

Among the most beautiful pieces of Byzantine work that have come down to us must be mentioned a fragment of a reliquary, in cloisonné enamel, which the Emperor Justinian gave to the Monastery of St. Radegonde, in Poitiers; a reliquary of the True Cross (now in the Church of Limbourg-sur-la-Lahn) which was made between 911 and 948; and, above all, the famous *Pala d'Oro,* in the Church of St. Mark's, Venice. This is an altar screen (3 metres 48, long, and 1 metre 40, high), which was ordered in Constantinople by the Doge Pietro Orsoleo, about 976; enlarged between 1205 and 1209; and restored in 1343. Kondakov believes the medallions date from the 10th century. Venice possesses many other Byzantine enamels, most of which have come from the taking of Constantinople in 1204. Finally must be mentioned two crowns of investiture, sent by the Eastern Emperors to the kings of Hungary. One, only fragments of which remain, dates from about 1046; the other, which is the famous crown of St. Stephen, was made in 1074.

*The Middle Ages, in the West.*—During the Carolingian period, enamel is only an accessory of goldsmith's work, and, whatever may be its origin, the production shows characteristics indicating the persistence of Byzantine influence, and the fact that, at this period, enamel work was practiced exclusively in the monasteries; it was thus from the beginning of the 9th century until the end of the 11th, and even, for France, until almost the first years of the 12th century. From this period of mediocre work, the few pieces which remain are in cloisonné. Examples include: (a.) a reliquary, made between 785 and 807, from the Church of Herford, in Westphalia, and now in the Museum of Industrial Art of Berlin; (b.) the reliquary of St. Nicolas of Agaune; (c.) that of the Treasury of Utrecht; (d.) the Paliotto of St. Ambrogio of Milan, with a border of cloisonné enamels, the work of Wolvinius, at the beginning of the 9th century; (e.) the Iron Crown of the Monza Treasury, which has cloisonné enamels of blue, white and green; and (f.) reliquaries from the 10th century, in the Bibliothèque Nationale.

About the end of the 11th century, the old process of champlevé was rediscovered, and enamel work took on a new life. Gold which, until then, had been used to support the cloisonné enamels, was replaced by copper; and enamels, now less expensive, spread quickly, and large schools formed, such as that of the Rhine, the Meuse, and of Limoges.

(1.) The Rhine School.—This school seems to have had centres in Cologne (the Benedictine Abbey of St. Pantaleon; the workshop of Frederick, monk of St. Pantaleon; and, finally, the works known as the Shrine of St. Anno), and branches in Trier, Verdun and Coblenz. This second branch produced, among other famous enamellers, the celebrated Nicolas of Verdun, author of the Klosterneuburg altarpiece, executed in 1181, and of the Shrine of the Church of St. Nicolas of Tournai (1205).

(2.) School of the Meuse.—Possessed an important atelier in the diocese of Liége, and one of its masters was Godefroy de Claire. The works of the Meuse school are, however, very like those of the Rhine School.

(3.) Limoges.—Enamel work attained its height in Limoges. It is often asked why French enamel work became localised in the Limoges country. Pierre Lavedan, in his learned study of Léonard Limosin and the French enamellers, remarks that the country was always noted for its richness in precious metals, that gold mines were even exploited, and that the memory of this is preserved in the names of certain localities, such as Laurière and l'Aurance. Lead, iron, tin and copper were also found. This abundance of primary materials is, by itself, enough to explain why this region became the real enamel country.

Limoges work, also, may be divided into two periods: the ecclesiastical period, and the lay period.

Few works have come down to us from the ecclesiastical period. The production was attached chiefly to three monasteries: St. Foy of Conques, St. Martial of Limoges, and Grandmont.

St. Foy was, in the 10th century, one of the most frequented places of pilgrimage. People went to pray before the statue of St. Foy, a stiff, primitive image with an enormous head, covered with precious stones, and credited with countless miracles. All the monks of St. Foy were artists, painters, sculptors, poets or musicians. Very likely it was at Conques, a little after 1107, that the champlevé technique was rediscovered.

St. Martial of Limoges does not seem to have had an atelier of enamel workers, but it possessed a very rich library for the period, and an atelier of miniaturists. Now it was from the miniaturists that the enamels almost always took their subjects, and from this point of view the monastery of St. Martial was most important.

The Abbey of Grandmont did not possess an atelier for enamel work, either, but its part was not less important. The Grandmontians were, from the origin of the order, the most austere and the poorest imaginable, and its rule, which dates from 1076, was extremely rigorous. But in the 12th century, there was a relaxation of these severities, and the order of Grandmont became very rich. It built a church which was finished in 1166 or 1168, and for which they ordered a high-altar of gilded copper and enamel, with four columns, and representations of "the stories of the Old and New Testament, and the thirteen apostles" (the thirteenth is St. Matthew, who replaced Judas), "the whole to be adorned with little stones, and made as rich as may be for the money." Only a few fragments survive, these marvels having been destroyed in the French Revolution.

The art of enamel work became secularised about the beginning of the 13th century. The enamellers constituted a distinct body, but formed part of that of the goldsmiths, known as the Corporation des Dauradiers et Argentiers. It possessed a mark, and the right to destroy any object imported into Limoges and not reaching the prescribed standard. In their hands, enamel work became somewhat commercialised, and they used rather hasty methods. Thus they seem to have worked their relief ornaments, which formerly had been carved in the mass, and soon these methods were applied to figures as well. Hence they could no longer compose scenes, but only isolated figures or groups of a rudimentary simplicity: a Christ on the Cross, or a Christ on the Cross between two apostles, and other variations of similar themes. In the Cluny Museum are many of these little figures, which were fixed on the article by means of nails.

Limoges enamels then came to be in demand all over Europe, and it was to profit from this that they had recourse to such regrettable methods. A multitude of enamelled objects were made, chiefly for church use: Crucifixes, crosses, reliquaries, and especially shrines, rectangular boxes, covered with a roof of two inclined planes, decorated at the top with a copper ridge, cut into with a key-hole shaped pattern, which is peculiar to the Limoges shrines. But some of the works produced at the beginning of this commercial outburst are admirable, notably the Ciborium (Louvre), signed by G. Alpais.

Classification of Champlevé Enamels.—The great number of champlevé enamels makes it convenient to class them in categories, according to certain characteristics. Certain similarities of method make it possible to determine the part of each atelier. It is generally impossible to put an artist's name to any one piece. Limoges enamels can be divided into two main groups: those with enamelled figures on a plain background, and those with plain figures on an enamelled background.

The first of these groups can perhaps be divided again. It includes, in fact, pieces with uniform backgrounds, pieces with backgrounds scattered with stars, pieces decorated with uncut polished gems, and pieces with backgrounds of vermiculated work, that is to say, with cast foliage decoration. These latter are very numerous, and M. Marquet de Vasselot divides them into four series, according to the shape of their frames—flower-form, semi-circular, four-leafed, and separate pieces.

In the same way, the group of figures "réservées" (or left plain) on an enamelled background subdivides into pieces with blended colours, and pieces with separate colours. Pierre Lavedan remarks that the first which generally date from the 13th century have two combinations of colours of which the order is invariable—one series is yellow gold, yellowish green, dark green, black and red; and the other series is white-gold, pale blue, dark blue, black and red. These two scales of colour were applied either in concentric circles, the red being in the centre, or in large palmettes. In both cases deep blue is used for the background. Most of the shrines in the Cluny Museum were made like this, and the plaque of the Death of the Virgin, which is in the Louvre.

As to the pieces with separate colours, the backgrounds are entirely covered with enamel, or with backgrounds on which engraved motifs, such as flowers, are reserved.

Examples.—The oldest examples are to be found in the Treasury of Conques, which possesses, notably, the Reliquary of Pépin d'Aquitaine (9th century); the statue of St. Foy (10th century); and the copper chest of Boniface (13th century), which is one of the earliest pieces of champlevé. In the Cluny Museum there are the Adoration of the Magi, and the Meeting of St. Nicholas and St. Étienne de Muret, which are enamelled figures on "réservé" backgrounds, absolutely uniform, like that of enamelled mosaics: these two plaques come from the Abbey of Grandmont. Near them is the celebrated and admirable Christ in Majesty, seated in a mandorla, between the four symbols of the Evangelists: here the body is enamelled, and the flesh "réservée."

In the middle of the 13th century, the fashion passed for enamelled figures on a reserved background. Enamel becomes an accessory: it was used for backgrounds, and the figures were engraved or carved. The first style had lasted from about 1107 to 1240; the second was prolonged until the decadence of champlevé.

The finest pieces with enamelled figures are those with foliage backgrounds, which appear about 1170; the most famous is the Shrine of Guisel. There is an example of this technique in the Louvre: a shrine, bearing a Christ in Majesty between two apostles.

When Limoges enamels took on a really commercial character, most of the pieces produced had reserved figures on backgrounds of dark enamel—*e.g.*, the Death of the Virgin, in the Louvre. From this time date a great many shrines, to which the same method was applied, as may be seen in the Cluny Museum, notably in a shrine decorated with a whole series of little episodes from the life of Christ.

In the 14th century, the enameller is no more than the goldsmith's assistant, and beautiful as certain works of this period are—such as the Ciborium of G. Alpais,—one feels that the day of champlevé has passed. Translucent enamel on relief begins to appear.

It is thought that the process of enamelling on relief comes from Italy. In Limoges it was hardly attempted; and enamellers' workshops sprang up rather in the North of France and in Paris. It was the northern workshops that produced the beautiful statuette of the Virgin (1339), which comes from the Abbey of St. Denis, and is now in the Louvre. Nevertheless, it is from Limoges that the admirable bands ornamented with birds, which decorated the Chef de St. Martin de Sondeilles, have come down to us.

*The Renaissance.*—The vogue for enamel on relief did not last long, and about the end of the 15th century, the workshops of Limoges recovered their old success, with painting on enamel. Two processes were employed successively—one, which might be called "painting in enamel," by means of paste enamels, applied with a spatula, which was the original method; and the other, which is really "enamel painting," by which vitrifiable colours are placed, with a paint-brush, on a background of enamel. This was only used in the 17th century, and later.

In the 16th century, the enamellers borrowed their subjects not from the miniaturists, but from the masters of painting and engraving, thus following the same evolution as the painters on glass. Sometimes they are taken from the Books of Hours of Simon Vostre, sometimes, from Martin Schongauer, Dürer, and the painters of Fontainebleau.

Italy does not appear to have had any influence on the origins of painted enamels in France, and in this connection may be mentioned two plaques, in Poitiers, representing a man and a woman, whose costumes suggest the date of 1450. It may also be remarked that a coloured glass of St. Pierre du Queyroix, is signed by a Pénicaud, and has touches of enamel: the method of treating glass had only to be transferred to metal for painted enamels to be invented. Nevertheless, the subsequent influence of Italy on painted enamels, through the School of Fontainebleau, is undoubted, and it is notable that Jean Fouquet asked the Italian Filarete to teach him the technique of painted enamel (see the fine cameo self-portrait of Jean Fouquet, in the Louvre).

The first painted enamels of Limoges cannot be given any certain attribution. From inscriptions on some of the pieces, a certain number of works, anterior to the beginning of the 15th century, and the earliest painted enamels, have been grouped under the name of Monvaerni. In 1503, we find the first dated and signed work—the Christ on the Cross, by Nardon Pénicaud. We now enter the big, classical period of Limoges enamels, which extends from the beginning of the 16th century until about 1580, and includes such artists as the Pénicaud, Léonard Limosin, Pierre Reymond, the hypothetical master Kip, Martin Didier, the Noylier, Pierre Courtey, and the Court. Then the decline set in. Artists became more and more commercial, and it is with difficulty that in the 17th century, one quotes the names of Laudin and Petitot, who were painters rather than enamellers.

See Pl. 30, Vol. II.

Bibliography: Bourdery, *Léonard Limosin et son œuvre.* Limoges, 1895.—Bourdery and Lachenaud, *Léonard Limosin,* peintre de portraits. Paris, 1897.—Demartial, *Les émaux peints. Les Primitifs, l'école de Monvaerni.* Limoges, 1910.—Kondakov, *Histoire et Monuments des émaux byzantins.* Frankfort, 1892.—F. de Lasteyrie, *Des origines de l'émaillerie limousine.* Limoges.—Marquet de Vasselot, *L'orfèvrerie et l'émaillerie aux XIII<sup>e</sup> et XIV<sup>e</sup> siècles,* in L'Histoire de l'Art, André Michel, Vol. III, 2nd part. Paris, 1906.—Marquet de Vasselot, *Les émaux limousins à fond vermiculé.* Paris, Leroux, 1906.—Molinier, *L'évolution des Arts humains du au VIII<sup>e</sup> XII<sup>e</sup> siècles,* Vol. I, 2nd part, 1905.—Pierre Lavdan, *Léonard Limosin et les émailleurs français.* Paris, 1913.—René Jean, *Les Arts de la terre,* 3rd part: *l'Émaillerie.* Paris, 1911.—M. Chamot, *English Mediæval Enamels.* London, 1930.

**ENCAUSTIC PAINTING.**—In encaustic painting, heat was applied to soften the medium, a mixture of resin, wax, and color in the form of small cylinders. The softened color-mixture was then applied with a spatula. This process was employed by the Greeks and Egyptians and was perhaps used for the murals at Pompeii and Herculaneum.

**ENGELBRECHTSEN (Cornelius).**—Dutch painter, 1468-1533. He was born in Leyden, and worked there all his life. We possess very few of his works: most of them were probably destroyed in the 16th century, at the time of the Reform in Holland. Two altarpieces have come down to us: one represents a Calvary (from the Convent of Marienpool), and the other the Deposition from the Cross, with the Seven Sorrows of Mary, in medallions (both Lakenhal, Leyden). They are not inspired by profound religious feeling. It is the little pictures which attract by their refined colour and execution.

Carel van Mander mentions, as Engelbrechtsen's masterpiece, a triptych, now lost, of which the centre represented the Lamb of the Apocalypse, and which decorated the Church of St. Peter, of Leyden.

Bibliography: Franz Dulberg, *Die Leydener Malerschule.* Berlin, 1899.—Taubel, *L'Art Chrétien en Flandre et en Hollande.*—Friedländer, M. J., *Altniederländische Malerei,* Vol. X.—Gavelle, E., *C. Engelbrechtz.* Lille, 1929.

**ENGRAVING.** — technique. — The object of engraving is the reproduction of a certain number of copies of a drawing, in black and white, or in colours. The methods used for engraving in black and white may be classed into two groups: (I.) In one case the wood or metal block is attacked in such a way as to leave in relief only the outline of the drawing and the strokes which form the modelling; then, by means of a roller, the reliefs only are inked, the hollows showing white on the proof: this is known as *relief engraving.* (II.) Or, on the other hand, the plate is cut wherever black is intended to show on the print: the hollows are inked in with a pad, and the plate is carefully wiped. The proof gathers the ink which has remained in the hollows. This is *intaglio engraving.*

The first proof of an engraving rarely satisfies the artist, whose method does not make it easy for him to see the value of his work in the course of its execution. Then there are retouches, and a second proof is necessary to appreciate the effect. It is by retouching after retouching, proof after proof, that the artist achieves his original conception. These experimental proofs (known as "first proof," "second proof," etc.) are very interesting, as they allow us to follow and study the development of the work. It sometimes happens that a first proof has a vigour and expression which the finished work does not possess in the same degree.

I. *Relief Engraving.*—Engravings in relief have generally been executed in *wood.*

The engraver begins by placing his design on the block. Originally the drawing was traced directly on to it; but nowadays it is generally transferred, or conveyed by a photographic method, which has the advantage of preserving the modelling intact. Then, with a tool, the wood is dug away wherever the print is to show white, and the blacks are left in relief. The artist, as already explained, is guided by taking proofs; which show the various "states" of his work. The block is often cast by electrotype, and prints are taken on the metallic block thus obtained—for wood wears down too quickly under the press for a very great number of copies to be taken from it. About the end of the 15th century an attempt was made to substitute copper and steel for wood, but the process is long and fatiguing; and has only been retained for the making of bank-notes, marking stamps, etc.

Mantegna: Triumph of Caesar. (Detail from a cartoon at Hampton Court.)

II. *Intaglio Engraving.*—This is generally made on copper, sometimes on steel. The processes of intaglio engraving are fairly numerous.

(a) *Manière criblée* (white line engraving).—The earliest metal blocks were made by means of the rudimentary method of white line engraving: the copper block was riddled with little holes, irregularly

Dürer: The Nativity (1504). (Engraving on copper.)

spaced, to each one of which there was a corresponding white. These were obtained with a burin, or with

Maximilian I, emperor of Germany. (After Lucas van Leyden.)

little punches shaped like a star or fleur-de-lys, etc. This method is fairly easy, but clumsy, and it was soon abandoned.

(b) *The Burin.*—This is the name given to a tool formed of a quadrangular steel shaft, with a bevelled end, and a wooden handle. The name of the tool (burin) also serves to denote the works which are executed with it.

This type of engraving is made on plates of copper, on brass or steel. The plate is carefully prepared, and then beaten on an anvil with a steel hammer. Next the main lines of the drawing are traced on the copper with a dry point; or the plate may be covered with a varnish which the point penetrates. In the latter case, an acid bath suffices to indicate, on the copper, the first drawing. In either case, the work is continued with the burin, by means of long or short strokes, parallel, crossed or recrossed, dots, and little lines. The most delicate works are then finished with "dry point," a steel needle with a handle. Burin engraving presents great difficulties, and demands extreme sureness of hand, as it cannot easily be retouched. This method was for a long time considered to be the noblest form of engraving, and it was especially appreciated in the second half of the 17th century.

(c) *Etching.*—In this method the plate is covered with a varnish which is impervious to acids. This is spread over the slightly warmed copper, by means of a cotton pad,

Rembrandt: The artist's father (1630).

covered with silk. Then the plate is fired in a smoky flame to tint the varnish, which becomes a brilliant black. The lines of the drawing are then transferred on to the varnish, which is attacked with a needle in such a way as to expose the copper wherever a black line is desired. The plate is then edged with a thick border of soft wax so as to form a hollow into which acid may be poured. When the exposed parts of the plate seem to have been sufficiently bitten by the acid, it is thoroughly washed, the varnish is removed by heating, and a first proof is taken ("first state"). As this may indicate, the work is retouched, by recovering the whole plate with varnish, and again going over the unsatisfactory parts. The burin is often useful for improving lines, of which the edges may be rather irregular after the acid "biting." Some etchers, however, have achieved remarkable effects from this very irregularity and slight blur. Anyhow, the point is sometimes useful in delicate work; and a little instrument, the burnisher, allows slight modifications or alterations to be made.

(d) *Stippling.*—This is a process in which the blacks are obtained by the juxtaposition of little points, more or less close together, which are marked with the burin, with the dry-point needle, by means of etching, or with a graver which is struck with a hammer. Hence the name "*hammer engraving*" is sometimes given to this method.

Stippling was invented in the 17th century by the Dutch engraver Lutma. At the end of the 18th century, Bartolozzi produced stippled engravings inked in several colours. About the same time, Carolini Watson thought of combining the "black manner" with stippling, and by this means obtained some very delicate effects.

(e) *The "black manner."*—The "black manner" was invented in 1642, in Amsterdam, by Louis de Singen. For some time he kept his method a secret. Then he entrusted it to Prince Rupert, who divulged it in England, where, under the name of "mezzotint," it was widely used by the engravers of the second half of the 18th century.

In the *black manner*, a uniform surface is first obtained by means of an instrument called the "cradle"—a kind of wheel which is rolled over the copper in several directions. Then, if the plate were inked, and a proof taken, it would come off entirely black. Then, with a burnisher, the engraver breaks into the surface to make his design, and repolishes the plate wherever he wishes to obtain the whites. This method may be compared with that of opaque water colour on black paper.

(f) *Aquatint* was invented by J. B. Le Prince (1734-1781). The background is mechanically engraved by various processes: (i) The plate may be varnished with a slightly drying varnish, which is sprinkled very regularly with fine, dry salt. When the varnish has set, the plate is warmed in water, and the salt dissolves and leaves the copper exposed. The plate is then bitten with acid, and to each grain of salt corresponds a little hollow in the surface of the copper. (ii) Another method is to put the plate horizontally in a box in which is blown a thin dust of resin. A gentle heating makes the grains of resin adhere to the metal, and the plate is then attacked with acid as in the previous case. (iii) Still another method is to wash the copper with oil, and sprinkle it with flower of sulphur. The metal, lightly corroded, now has a clotted, unpolished appearance. The work is continued by means of acids.

(g) *Crayon Engraving* was invented by J. C. François (1717-1769), and practised by Demarteau of Liége. François drew on the plate with a little wheel which cut away the varnish. Continuing with different rollers, and touching up certain parts with the burin, he finally gave to his work the illusion of having been executed in crayon. In other engravings, he used different methods.

BOSSE (ABRAHAM): THE ROYAL PALACE. (Bibl. Nat.)

In England, another method was used: The plate is covered with a mixture of drying varnish and pork fat. Then tracing-paper is laid over it, and the drawing is gone over with an ivory point. Wherever the point presses, the varnish comes away and sticks to the paper. The plate has now only to be "bitten" by acid.

These various methods all disappeared with the coming into practice of lithography.

(h) *Colour Engraving.*—The earliest attempts at this process were made in the 17th century, especially in England. At first only one block was used. It was not until later that the Frenchman, Le Blond (1670-1741) thought of preparing three blocks, one for blues, another for reds, and a third for yellows. Colours were superimposed in certain places to produce intermediary effects. Dagoty, in 1753, had the idea of using a third block to give blacks. All these blocks were prepared in accordance with the method used in the "black manner." The result tended to be heavy in effect. Descourtis and Janinet replaced the "black manner" aquatint. Nowadays, heliography is generally employed.

III. *Mechanical Engraving.*—Various machines for engraving have been invented, by Conté, to engrave parallel and equally spaced lines; and by Collas, to reproduce blocks in relief. So ingeniously were they made, that they have been replaced by the methods we are about to describe, which are often extremely simple, and give very interesting results.

IV. *Electrical, Chemical, and Electro-chemical Engraving.*— The electric current allows a metallic deposit to be obtained on a wooden block, which has been previously covered with a conductor, generally with a graphite base. In this way a metal proof is obtained, from which an almost indefinite number of prints can be taken, and, when it is worn, it can easily be replaced by another. This is the process of *electro-typing*. There are also other methods.

The *chemical* methods allow, for instance, that the plate, after being attacked by acid according to the usual method, may be attacked a second time, after it has been stripped, but varnished in the hollows. The action of the acid consumes the raised parts, and the hollows, not attacked, end by standing out in relief.

The method can be varied.

V. *Engraving by the Action of Light.*—After the invention of photography, attempts were made to utilise the action of light to obtain, directly, true *clichés gravés*. Cuvelier, in the middle of the 19th century, thought of coating a sheet of glass with an opaque mixture of white lead and printing ink. He drew with a point on this surface, as in etching. The needle left a transparent line, and a print was taken from the block on paper sensitive to light. Corot engraved many such plates, but the method soon fell out of favour.

True relief plates, allowing of printing by the ordinary processes, were sought. The methods employed may be grouped in three categories: those which give a relief-plate; those which give an intaglio (the design hollowed out); and, finally, collotype.

Relief-plates are obtained in transferring a drawing or print on to a zinc plate. This is then attacked with acid, and the plate is "bitten" away, except at the places where it is inked. This method, which was due to Gillot, who was granted a patent in 1850, bears the name of *gillotage* (French), and is still used for cheap illustration. Originally only line drawings could be produced by this process: half-tones and shadows were represented uniformly by black strokes. Later, these were modelled over a thin net, which is called an "American grill." The darks are thus decomposed into an infinite number of little adjacent black points, more or less thickly interspaced, and this gives the whole scale of values.

SAINT-AUBIN: THE CONCERT. (Engraving on copper, Bibl. Nat.)

The methods which produce the concave blocks are designated under the names of heliography, photogravure, etc. They are all based on the fact that certain substances undergo a change in their physical or chemical nature under the action of light.

HISTORY.—*The Origins.*—Engraving, in the narrow sense of the word, is a comparatively modern invention. The ancients used it for their seals and cylinders, but it seems certain that they never used it except to stamp soft materials, such as wax, and that they never thought of applying ink in order to obtain a black and white print. The idea of using engraved wood blocks was first thought of for the decoration of materials, and a piece of fourteenth century linen, on which the story of Œdipus is represented is the oldest engraving we have, and there is no need to attribute the invention of this process (as Vasari does) to the Florentine goldsmith, Finiquerra. This attractive legend must be given up, and it must be admitted that engraving was not the invention of a moment, but, rather, that it is the result of slow elaboration. It cannot even be said in what country this evolution was accomplished. One of the oldest engravings we possess, the *St. Christopher* of 1423 has been attributed to the Netherlands, Germany, and Italy. Other pieces date perhaps from the end of the 14th century, but their origin and date are too uncertain for us to be able to accord the priority to any one of these countries. Some of these early works are of special interest: they are known as xylographs, and have an inscription engraved on the same plate as the drawing. They show very clearly the part engraving played in the discovery of printing, and, although their origin is not exactly known, they may probably be attributed to the Netherlands. These works were very successful, and some of them were printed several times; such as the *Bible of the Poor*, *Ars Moriendi*, *Speculum Numanae Salvationis*, the *Apocalypse* and the *Life of the Virgin*.

*Engraving to the End of the 17th Century.*—In *Italy* copper was always preferred to wood, and engravings are treated as simple drawings. Nearly all the early examples show the strong influence of Botticelli. It is supposed that he himself engraved the series of Prophets, and Sibyls, a part of the illustration of Dante. Other works were engraved from his designs by unknown artists, whose production is grouped arbitrarily under the name of Baccio Baldini. Such may be the series of *Planets*, the *Labyrinth* and the *Allegory of Urbanity*. At the same time were working Antonio Pollaiuolo, who engraved the *Combat of Centaurs*, and Robetta, who was inspired, more or less, by Filippino Lippi, and sometimes copied Dürer.

Besides the slightly dry grace of the Florentines, Mantegna's engravings are grave and powerful. Among them are: *Christ between St. Andrew and St. Longinius*, the *Flagellation*, the *Entombment*, and, above all, the *Triumph of Cæsar* (the engraving of which seems to be anterior to the cartoons kept in the Orangery, at Hampton Court), and the *Combat of the Marine Gods*. The drawing of the figures is sure and precise, and the modelling is obtained by oblique patchings, sometimes simple zigzags which do not attempt to follow the form. Mantegna founded no real school, although he had imitators and copiers, such as Zoan Andrea, who, while he reproduced faithfully his master's work, did not disdain to imitate, even to the signature, the engravings of Dürer, who had arrived in Venice. Under this double influence were formed such artists as Giulio Campagnola, Benedetto Montegna, and Jacobo dei Barbari, who was for a long time known as the "Master of the Caduceus."

In the following century, the engraver was in full possession of his technique, but he suffered from the general weakening of art, for which the overwhelming superiority of Michelangelo and Raphael was partly responsible. The great name of this period is that of Marc Antonio Raimondi, a Bolognese, who settled first in Venice, where he counterfeited Dürer, and then in Rome, where Raphael made him his regular engraver. Marc Antonio created interpretative engraving, and was the first to give the general composition of a picture by totally different means from those employed by the painter. He lacked great imagination, and was rather an intelligent and skillful craftsman than an original artist. His pupils were many, but mediocre. They include Agostino Veneziano and Marco Dento di Ravenna; and they engraved after Raphael, Giulio Romano, Bandinelli, Franz Floris, and others. They were succeeded by still more mediocre engravers, and Giorgio Ghisi and Diana Scultori are only mentioned as marking the transition between the school of Marc Antonio and that of the Carracci.

All the Carracci (see this name) were engravers, but Agostino is the most important. Through Passarotti, Procaccino and especially through his master, D. Tibaldi, he was imbued with the tradition of Marc Antonio. He transformed it into the taste of his own day, and, under the influence of the broad and facile works of the Dutchman, Cornelius Cort, and thanks also to the great Venetian painters, he acquired an ample and magnificent manner, from which emotion is absent, and of which only the rhetoric is sincere and spontaneous.

In *Germany* the success of engraving was extreme from the middle of the 15th century.

We know little of the earliest masters. Certain engravings can be grouped together, owing to similarity of workmanship, but the names of the artists escape us, and so they have to be designated from some peculiarity, under such appellations as the "Master of the Game of Cards," and "Master E. S.," who is a very fine artist, in whom delicacy and care associate rather strangely with a certain childish awkwardness. Among his chief works are a *Virgin on a Human Crescent, Mary of Einsiedeln,* and the *Child Jesus in His Bath.* They already reveal the characteristics which German art always retained —notably, strong realism, and an indifference to ugliness which differentiates the northern schools from those of Italy.

At the time when "Master E. S." was producing his most remarkable works, which date from 1466, an artist of genius suddenly appeared. This was Martin Schongauer (born in Kulmbach in 1456, died in Colmar in 1491). Among his works must be mentioned: the *Death of the Virgin,* the *Bearing of the Cross,* the *Adoration of the Kings.* Towards the end of his short life, he gave up representing great scenes, and generally engraved isolated figures, such as St. Lawrence, St. Stephen, and the Apostles. Except in the Passion scenes, emotion is absent, but the line is always of perfect purity and distinction, the modelling is strong and the composition learned. Martin Schongauer had considerable influence in France, in the Netherlands, and even in Italy. In Germany, his imitators were as mediocre as they were numerous. They include: Glockenton, Wenceslas of Olmütz, Master B. M.; only one, Master L. C. Z., reveals, in a *Temptation of Christ,* an interesting personality.

If Dürer several times gave up painting, he remained, on the contrary, always faithful to engraving, which made him famous throughout Europe. In his youth he learned the goldsmith's craft, which may partly account for his skill in the use of the burin. He seems never to have done any wood-engraving himself, but to have handed his designs to careful craftsmen to reproduce. Holbein seems to have had the same contempt for wood-engraving. Two influences dominated Albrecht Dürer in his early work: that of Martin Schongauer, whose work he had seen at Colmar in 1491; and that of Mantegna, two of whose engravings he copied, when he visited Italy in 1494. Masterpieces succeeded one another: the *Great Fortune,* the *Death and the Knight,* the *Three Genii,* etc. In seeking for new methods, Dürer thought of combining drypoint with the burin, and attempted etching, in the *Holy Family,* and *St. Jerome,* and etching on iron in the *Canon* (1516). Dürer was a profound thinker. His engravings are no mere illustrations of an anecdote, or representations of a mythological or biblical scene. There is always a hidden symbol; sometimes the idea is everything, and the symbol is personified as in *The Knight, Death and the Devil,* or in the tragic and despairing *Melancholy.*

Holbein himself seems never to have engraved. The blocks of the *Alphabet of Death* and the *Shadow of Death* were executed by Hans Lutzelbürger. It is a poem of Death, ever-present and threatening — an interpretation of the gloomy fear which tortured men of the 15th and beginning of the 16th centuries.

At the same time Waechtlin, known as "Pilgrim," also called the "Master of the Crossed Staves," used cameo, in two blocks, which he is said to have invented, and which passed to Italy where Ugo da Carpi perfected it. It was the method used by two German artists, Hans Baldung Grün; the Bavarian, Altdorfer, and Lucas Cranach. The last-named was chiefly a painter, but he used the burin a little, and designed a great deal for wood-engraving.

This was the great period of German art. Upon the pupils of Dürer, Holbein, Cranach and Grün, the influence of Italy and of Marc Antonio was fatal; and feeble eclecticism replaced originality. Barthel Beham (1502-1540) was able to assimilate the Italian manner, but his brother, Hans Sebald Beham, in spite of considerable talent, sometimes attained the grotesque. Georg Penez, Brosamer and J. Binck continued in the same direction; whereas Aldegrever (1502-1558) happily saved himself by recovering the tradition of his master Dürer.

Nevertheless, etching on iron, which had been invented by Albrecht Dürer, was practised, not unsuccessfully, by the brothers Hopfer —Jerome, Lambert and Andrew—of Augsburg, who engraved plates in the manner of the old xylographs, the appearance of which was more or less reproduced by iron etching. Simultaneously, Hirschvogel (1503?-1552) and Lautensack (1524-1563) revived etching—the former, in its pure form; the latter, combined with burin-engraving.

During the second half of the 16th century, technique became facile and varied. Works were abundantly and carelessly produced. It was the end of German engraving, considered as a fine art. It is, however, necessary to mention Theodore de Bry (1528-1598), a Fleming who settled in Frankfort, and Wendel Dieterlin, of Strassburg (1541-1599) who made the plates for an "Architectura" (1593).

In *Flanders and the Netherlands* we find the origins of engraving wrapped in the same obscurity, as in Italy or Germany. It is unknown, for instance, who was the delicate and charming "Master of 1480," author of *The Youth and Death* and of the *Lovers.* It is only at the beginning of the 16th century that we find ourselves in full daylight, with the great name of Lucas van Leyden, whose earliest work seems to be *Mahomet and the Monk Sergius,* and bears the date 1508. Lucas van Leyden, contemporary and friend of Dürer, had none of the latter's profundity of thought; but his technical ability is admirable. He was the first who thought of indicating distance by fine, shallow lines; and thus the planes of even his most complicated compositions are clearly distinguished. From 1509, the date of his *Passion* series, he produced some very fine works, mostly of religious subjects—the *Conversion of St. Paul, The Return of the Prodigal Son,* and very many others. After 1520, under the influence of Dürer, he attacked scenes of everyday life, and ceased to represent those wide spaces which he rendered so well. From this period date: the *Musicians,* the *Dairy,* and the *Portrait of Maximilian.* After 1528, he was led away by Marc Antonio. To this period belong his Venuses, Virtues, Mars and Venuses —completely decadent works. Besides Lucas van Leyden, certain other artists, of various merits, must be mentioned. These are Dirck Jacobz Vellert (called "Dirck von Staren," or the "Master of the Star"), S. Cornelius Matsys (of Brussels), Alaert Claeissins (of Amsterdam), and Lambert Suavius.

The Spaniards had imported into Antwerp that liking for pious images which possesses Catholic countries. Veritable workshops were opened in Antwerp, and their production soon flooded the whole of Catholic Europe. A deep "split" was made between Spanish Flanders and independent Holland, which is expressed even in the art of engraving. The very method differed. Flanders preferred burin-engraving; Holland favoured etching.

In Flanders, engraving enjoyed a period of magnificent prosperity, thanks to Rubens. This great painter saw in engraving only the means of reproducing and of making known his pictures. He entrusted the task first to Cornelius Galle, then to J. A. Mathau and Jan Muller, both pupils of Goltzius. He was not satisfied with their work, and he then employed a Frenchman, Michel Lasne; next he tried a Dutchman, Peter Soutman, and, finally, he met Lucas Vosterman, likewise a Dutchman, and gave the task to him. Vosterman devoted himself entirely to Rubens, and lived with him in his house in Antwerp. From the co-operation of these two artists, the one guiding, the other acting, resulted some admirable engravings. Unfortunately the association did not last long. Vosterman, who had an irritable temper, broke with Rubens, and went to England; but he left behind him pupils, one of whom, Paul Pontius, nearly equalled his master. Rubens then employed Pontius, summoned two Dutchmen, the brothers Utuyma, better known under the name of their native place, Bolswert, and thus created under his direction a veritable workshop of reproduction. At the same time Christopher van Jegher undertook similar works, but he worked in wood-engraving.

Etching was practised not without some ability by two pupils of Rubens, Theodore Van Thulden and Lucas Van Uden, but it would scarcely be worth mentioning if Van Dyck had not produced some very fine engravings, notably *Titian and His Mistress,* and the famous and moving *Christ with a Reed.*

After Rubens and Van Dyck, Flemish engraving falls into insignificance, just when, in Holland, Rembrandt reached his maturity. Dutch engravers who preceded him are of comparatively little importance compared with the masters who now took to etching. Ruysdael, in the ten plates he left, shows astonishing skill, and Rembrandt was as great an etcher as he was a painter. It is almost superfluous to mention the celebrated works which the whole world admires—such as the *Hundred Guilder Print, Christ Healing the Sick,* the *Return of the Prodigal Son,* and the tragic engraving of the *Three Crosses.* Contemporary with Rembrandt were many good Dutch engravers: Jan van Goyen, Everdingen, Waterloo, Berchem, Paul Potter, A. van der Velde, Adrian van Ostade, and others. About the end of the century, Jan Luyken, who illustrated the Bible, and Romyn van Hooghe, a confused chronicler, mark the decadence of the period. The only exception was that of a pupil of Rembrandt, Bol, who applied his master's methods with discretion.

In *France* the origins of engraving are not better known than elsewhere, and it is only towards the end of the 15th century that we find some precise data. At this period, engravers devoted themselves exclusively to book-illustration, for which they either made original drawings, or imitations or copies of Martin Schongauer, and Albrecht Dürer. The engravers' names are unknown, and only those of the publishers and printers have come down to us. Engraving had to rival the art of miniature painting, which artists such as Fouquet and Bourdichon had brought to such perfection. Engravings were conceived in such a way as to allow of colouring, which was not, however, always applied. Some works show an endeavour to retain the aspect of xylographs which had been very successful. Among these are the *Dance of Death* (1485), and the *Shepherds' Calendar* (1491). These were popular books. More luxurious works show an attempt to imitate miniatures (e.g., *La Mer des Histoires,* printed 1488-'89). Finally, a number of extraordinary *Books of Hours* were published. In the 16th century, wood-engraving, which alone had been employed till then, gave place to copper-engraving, which remained in use until the following century. Paris and Lyon remained the chief centres of production, but they had very different tendencies. Paris yielded to Italian influence, with Goffroy Tory, an elegant and learned artist who dominated this period. Before him, Jean Cousin should be mentioned, were the attribution to him of certain engravings not so uncertain. Various anonymous works are very remarkable, such as the *Dream of Polyphiles* (1546), which may pos-bly be attributed to Jean Cousin or Jean Goujon. Lyon produced works with little illustrations, such as the *Apocalypse*, and the *Loves of Cupid and Psyche*. In Lyon were published, in 1538 and 1539, the *Shadows of Death*, and the *Images of Death*, of Holbein. They had considerable influence on the engravers of Lyon, especially on the first of them, Bernard Salomon, known as Little Bernard, who seems to have lived from 1508 to 1561.

Copper-engraving was practised rather late and clumsily. It was over-influenced by the many fine works which had already been produced in neighbouring countries. Noël Garnier made awkward copies of Dürer or Georg Penez, while others, such as Étienne Dupérac, or Nicolas Beatrizet, went and settled in Italy and ceased to belong to the stream of French art. Only Jean de Gourmont and Claude Corneille, of Lyon, submitted in a less servile way to the lessons of Italian art, in some little engraved illustrations. Near them, we must also recall the names of Georges Reverdy (who, owing to his love of Italianism, was called Cesare Reverdino), and especially Jean Duret, of Langres (1481-1561), a remarkable artist who, inspired by Mantegna and Leonardo da Vinci, produced works which are strange, and often incomprehensible, to us.

Other artists submitted to the Italian influence, through the school of Fontainebleau: Jean Chartier, of Orleans, René Boyvin, of Angers, and Étienne Delanne.

During the troublous period of the Wars of Religion, the art of engraving came to a standstill, and was only resumed when Henri IV had restored peace and quiet. Wood-engraving disappeared almost completely.

During the first part of the 17th century, some artists made engraving their sole means of expression (such an one was Callot, 1592-1635); others saw it only as a means of popularising their pictures (the greatest of these was Claude Lorrain). With Callot may be mentioned Abraham Bosse and Israel Silvestre. The group of painter-engravers is bigger. It includes: Simon Vouet, Eustache Le Sueur, Le Brun, Sébastien Bourdon, and Laurent de la Hyre. Poussin himself never engraved, but around him may be grouped some interpreters: Jean Pesne, le Guaspre, and Francisque Millet (1643-1680).

In the second half of the 17th century, after 1660, approximately, engraving, like the other arts, came under royal discipline. To this period belong Claude Mellan, Pierre Daret, his pupil, and Robert Nanteuil, who was practically official portrait engraver.

New methods make their appearance in the 18th century. There were attempts to render the haziness and softness of the drawings of Watteau and Boucher, and to imitate the light rubbings of pencil on full-grained paper, J. C. François (1717-1769) invented "crayon engraving." Bounet discovered "pastel engraving."

The school of David reacted against all these artifices. The graceful, lively productions were sacrificed, sometimes even destroyed, and for a time the only productions which seem to have been respected were those of J. G. Wille (1715-1807), whose success was unprecedented.

*England* produced, in the 18th century, a certain number of excellent engravers, who almost all worked in mezzotint, for which the rage in other European countries was short: older methods were preferred, which were more difficult and allowed a display of virtuosity. In England, on the other hand, engraving was still in its infancy, and the simple method was quickly adopted. Up to this time English engravers had been very rare, and one can only mention Wengel Hollar (who was born in Prague, but lived and worked in England under Charles I and Charles II), and an unequal engraver, Faithorn (1616-1691).

The "black manner" was first used by some Dutch engravers, settled in England: Gerard Vaick, Blolelingh, and Verkolje (1650-1693). The Englishmen who practised it were Bernard Lens (1659-1725), Isaac Becket and John Smith: this was the first period of engraving in the "black manner."

In the second half of the 18th century, Reynolds gave a strong impetus to the art of engraving. A host of interpreters grouped themselves round him, as formerly round Rubens. J. MacArdell and R. Houston were the first, and were soon joined by James Watson and J. R. Smith, and so many others that it would be impossible to name them all. When Reynolds died, other engravers attached themselves to his successors, modifying their style according to the character of the master whom they reproduced, and forming that English school, the unity of which is not incompatible with great suppleness and perfect adaptability.

At the same time burin-engravers and etchers were also working. The greatest artist of this school was the satirical painter, Hogarth.

Outside England and France, these were no schools of engraving at this time. Nevertheless, some talented artists deserve to be mentioned: Chodowiecki (a Pole, settled in Germany), the Swiss poet, Cessner, Volpato and Morghen, in Italy. The Italian engraver of genius, Giovanni Battista Tiepolo (1693-1770) stands apart. Besides a tedious *Adoration of the Magi*, he left some series of *Caprices* and *Fantasies*, the mystery of which has not yet been pierced. Tiepolo inherited something of his father's rare qualities. Among other works, he left twenty-seven variations of the theme of the "Flight into Egypt." After these artists must be placed Canaletto and Piranesi, whose fancy often seems demented and sometimes has almost the quality of genius.

*Later Engraving*.—After the Revolution, it was no longer the French kings and nobles who were the patrons of engraving, but the anonymous multitude. There was a growing popular demand for all kinds of images. During the revolutionary period there were working certain noteworthy but cold artists: Descourtis, Duplessis-Berteaux, Cochin, Tardieu, Roger. But they are all eclipsed by the Spaniard Goya (1746-1828), the author of remarkable *Caprices, Proverbs*, and *The Horrors of War*. In England, Gillray produced mediocre political engravings, and William Blake did some moving engravings for his poems.

In France, interpretive engraving was not very brilliant during the 19th century.

Géricault was one of the first to show what could be done with lithography. Goya gave him an impetus by the publication, in Bordeaux, of four plates of the *Tauromachie* (1828), and Delacroix, under the influence of Géricault, drew from them, with admirable results. Lithography was now in great favour, and it is only possible to mention here the best artists who practised it: Bonington, Louis Boulanger, Prud'hon, Ary Scheffer, Horace Vernet, Decamps, Daumier and Gavarni.

Etching, forgotten for the moment, reappeared with: Tony Johannot, Nanteuil, Bresdin, Chassérau and, later, Rousseau and Corot.

Finally, the original wood-engraving returned to favour. Colour-engraving was practised by Manet and Toulouse-Lautrec. In 1889, Raffaelli attempted to produce colour engravings on copper, in spite of the difficulties of the process, which was adopted by Henri Guérard, Charles Maurin, Mary Cassatt and Madame Marie Gautier.

To bring this incomplete survey to the end of the 19th century, certain artists who practised book-illustrating must be included. Tony Johannot and Porret opened this path with *The Story of the King of Bohemia and his Seven Castles*, by Charles Nodier. Then came *Molière* by Tony Johannot; the *Tales of Perrault* and *Paul et Virginie*, by Camer. Books illustrated with wood-engravings ("wood-cuts") multiplied. Horace Vernet illustrated a work on *Napoleon*; Héliodore Pisan (1822-1890) engraved Gustave Doré's drawings for Rabelais, "Don Quixote," and the Bible.

See Pl. 12, Vol. I.

BIBLIOGRAPHY: Fraipont, *Les procédés de reproduction en creux et en lithographie*. Paris, 1902.—A. Marty, *L'impression et les procédés de la gravure au XX<sup>e</sup> Siècle*. Paris, 1906.—Köhler, *Old and Modern Methods of Engraving*. Boston, 1894.—K. Robert, *Traité de la gravure de l'eau forte*. Paris, 1891.—Duchâtel, *Traité de lithographie artistique*. Paris, 1893.—M. P. Verneuil, *Le procédé de gravure en trois couleurs* (Art et Décoration, 1908).—Duplessis, *Histoire de la gravure*. Paris, 1881.—André Michel, *Histoire de l'Art*. Paris.—Max Osborn. *Der Holzschnitt*. Bielefeld, 1905.—Bryan, *Dictionary of Painters and Engravers* (5 vols.). London, 1903-1905.—G. Rosenthal, *La Gravure*. Paris, Laurens, 1909.—Courboin, *L'eau forte* (Art et Décoration, 1906).—A. M. Hind, *A History of Engraving and Etching*, 1923.

**ENGSTRÖM (Albert)**.—Swedish painter, born in 1869. Well-known and very popular caricaturist. His book is sometimes of a precise, familiar realism, and sometimes shows a lively or sardonic fancifulness. The artist gave full rein to his fancy in his collaboration with the humourist paper, *"Le Strix,"* where every week his satirical pen amused Stockholm at the expense of Stockholm.

**ENTABLATURE**.—Architecturally treated area resting upon the capitals of the columns in classical architecture, and supporting the pediment. Divided into architrave, immediately above the capitals; frieze; and cornice, the projecting mouldings.

**ENTASIS**.—Slight convexity in the shaft of a column, as in the Doric columns of the Parthenon.

**EPHESUS (Temple of Artemis)**.—See Greece.

**EPSTEIN (Jacob)**.—Contemporary sculptor who, though born in the United States, lives in England and is often classified as an English artist. He was born of Russo-Polish parents in New York City in 1880, and studied for a while at the Art Students' League, learning the technique and fundamental characteristics of sculpture. When he was twenty-two years old he went to Paris to enter the École des Beaux-Arts. In his spare time he studied in the Louvre, working from the statues of the earliest dynasties of Egypt and he was also somewhat influenced by the sculpture of Rodin, feeling particularly the classic features therein embodied. In 1905 he moved to London, England, where he has resided ever since, and in 1908 he received his first important commission. It was for eighteen figures to decorate the building of the British Medical Association in the Strand and in them he displayed the characteristics which have become a part of all his later work. His inspiration was from the works of the past, but it was interpreted with a new and fresh vision free from any academic conventionalism. At first these figures were assailed as being too revolutionary, but they remained in situ and now are forgotten in the criticisms which have arisen concerning the more recent works of this sculptor. In 1912 came the Oscar Wilde Memorial in Père Lachaise Cemetery in Paris, showing a strong influence from the winged bulls of ancient Assyria in the disposition of the group. His standing bronze of the *Christ*, executed about 1919, came in for its share of criticism because of the stark realism and austerity of the figure, which was very different from the usual sentimentalised versions of the same subject. But perhaps the most adverse criticism came with the unveiling of the W. H. Hudson Memorial in Hyde Park, the figure *Rima* representing a sort of bird woman shown in a very distorted form of reality. This bas-relief received many times a coat of tar and feathers and much space was devoted to it in current periodicals, and even now occasionally one hears of a new attack upon it. The distortion of the human figure was something that the average onlooker could not understand from a realistic viewpoint and the fact that it was much more decorative and conformed to the architectural setting did not count with the general public. More recent pieces of sculpture by Epstein which have stirred the curiosity and criticism of the English people are the *Day* and *Night*, colossal figures which adorn the façade of St. James Park Station, the marble *Genesis*, a study of a pregnant woman symbolic of the eternal motherhood of humanity, and the *Christ*, which appeared in the spring of 1935, a peculiar block-like interpretation of the Saviour with the crown of thorns. Aside from these symbolic figures and groups Epstein is also the author of a number of portrait busts, including studies of Paul Robeson, Ramsay MacDonald and many of Mrs. Epstein, all of which show a very individual treatment of the facial characteristics of these people, which are extremely realistic and very strong and vital portraits. Needless to say these have evoked only admiration and the supposition that the other figures by Epstein are done for exhibitionism and to arouse comment. But a better explanation seems that the distortion is used to gain an effect in some cases to strengthen the architectural character of the pieces and in others to make more clear the expression of a strong emotion. Everything is done with an eye to the utmost simplicity and only the most important details are included, which tends to clarify his work and to raise it above the stratum of those dated works of less capable sculptors. Examples of his work are in the Tate Gallery, London, the Brooklyn Museum and the Metropolitan Museum of Art in New York.

See Pl. 64, Vol. II.

BIBLIOGRAPHY: L. B. Powell, *Jacob Epstein,* 1932.—*The Sculptor Speaks, Jacob Epstein to A. L. Haskell,* 1931.

**ERECHTEION or ERECHTHEUM.**—See Acropolis of Athens.

**EREMITANI (Church of the).**—See Padua.

**ERLACH (Johann Bernard Fischer von).**—Austrian architect, 1658-1723, whose architecture, although Baroque in conception, shows here and there, in classical borrowings, the same academic spirit which made him the first modern historian of architecture. His best known buildings are in Vienna, and include the Palace of Prince Eugene, 1703, and the Church of S. Carlo Borromeo.

**ERRI (Family of the).**—Painters of Modena, at the end of the 15th and beginning of the 16th centuries. The most important are Agnolo and Bartolommeo, who were the authors of the fine altarpiece which is in the Museo d'Este of Modena (1462-1466). They also painted frescoes in the Abbey of Nonantola and in the Palazzo di Borso d'Este, at Sassuolo. They show the influence of Francesco Cossa.

**ES or ESSEN (Jan Van).**—Flemish painter (1596-1666). He was a painter of still-life, much esteemed in his day. Born 1587 or 1589; died after 1648, in Amsterdam.

**ESCORIAL or ESCURIAL (The), or, more precisely, San Lorenzo.**—Begun in 1563 by Juan Bautista of Toledo, and finished in 1584 by Juan de Herrera, this royal monastery was founded by Philip II, in fulfilment of a vow made to St. Lawrence, on whose feast-day he had fought the siege of St. Quentin.

THE ESCORIAL.

Thus the building is in the form of a grill (206 metres by 161), the instrument of the saint's martyrdom. The handle is represented by the palace, and the feet are represented by four towers, 55 metres high. The edifice is built entirely of bluish grey granite, from Guadarrama. There are 16 towers, 1110 exterior windows, 1600 interior windows, 1200 doors and 86 staircases. The plan of the church was modelled after that of St. Peter's, Rome, but it shows Philip II's austere and inflexible nature in its geometric design. Philip's own room was next to the church to facilitate his frequent worship. The palace is decorated by pictures of many famous artists. When referring to Philip II's part in the planning and building of the Escorial, Karl Justi says: "The Escorial is an example of desire coupled with inability to perform. The divine spark of genius was lacking in Philip II's enterprise. He had the misfortune to belong to an age which was inspired neither by creative force nor by taste. It was singularly incapable of producing a monument of the highest religious art. The whole was given a stiff geometric design, and, though contemporaries and admirers praised the noble simplicity and majesty of the style, it seems to us now of a repelling bareness. The restless and incessant surveillance of the royal director, his often mistaken criticism, his grieved way of cutting down suggested plans, the forms of which seemed to him too rich or too pretentious; all this, and many other circumstances, must have paralysed creative enthusiasm. . . . The spirit of severe etiquette which Philip imposed on the Spanish court, and which acted so deplorably on the mental forces of his successors, is expressed in his work, which seems to regard us with an almost petrifying power of fascination. The only charm of the Escorial is that it forms an integral part of the surrounding landscape, a feature which was not foreseen by its builders."

BIBLIOGRAPHY: J. R. Mélida, *The Escorial,* 1925.

**ETCHING.**—See Engraving.

**ETRUSCAN ART.**—The Etruscans, whose origin is unknown, settled in Italy long before the foundation of Rome, about the 11th century B.C. They inhabited the country between the Tiber and the Arno, and then conquered a large part of the peninsula where they were masters, until the power of Rome extended to Etruria. In the 3rd century B.C. the Etruscan federation succumbed under the attacks of Rome.

The creations of this civilization occupy an important place in the artistic history of the Italian peninsula. Unlike the Villonovian civilization which preceded it, and which appears to have been indigenous, the Etruscan civilization is a foreign importation: of mingled Eastern and Greek elements. The form of the earliest Etruscan tombs, the tumuli, was taken from Asia Minor; and the objects found in these tombs are copied from those which the Phœnicians exported. It is possible, but not certain that the Etruscans were of Lydian or of Phrygian origin. In any case, they had commer-

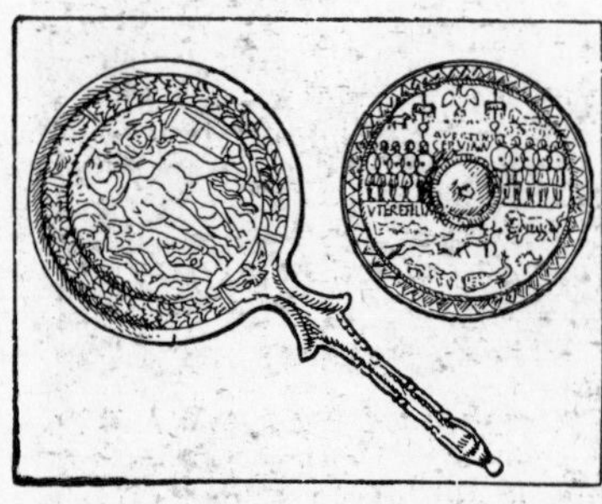

ETRUSCAN MIRROR AND ROMAN MEDALLION OF THE SECOND CENTURY. (Bibliothèque Nationale.)

cial relations and customs in common with these countries. Their oldest works are bronze utensils and jewels, ornamented with rosettes and fantastic animals, borrowed from the East. The duration of this style varied in different centres. In most, it was replaced by the Hellenic civilization. From the 7th century B.C., Etruria was in communication with Greece, and it was from the Greek colonies that the painted vases, known as "Etruscan vases," came. Most of those discovered in the tombs of Etruria came from Greece; others were copied in Italy, by Greek or Etruscan artists. We will not, therefore, stop to describe them here. The methods of fabrication and of decoration are those of the Greek vases (see Greece: vases). The Etruscans made great use of these vases, and funereal vases have been found by the thousands in their tombs.

ETRUSCAN SARCOPHAGUS CALLED THE "LYDIAN TOMB." (Louvre.)

Of the Etruscan architecture few remains are left except ruins of walls, which resemble the Pelasgic defences, and the famous "cloaca maxima" of Rome, a large vaulted sewer, which still exists as the Tarquins built it. It is known that the temples included the same elements as the Greek temples, with a slightly different plan, and that wood was used instead of stone.

The Etruscans were poor sculptors. They lacked marble and Greek models, and, in fact, the need for statuary was not felt in a country where the buildings were of wood, and where religion did not require the faithful to represent the numerous Olympian gods. Stone was hardly carved at all except for the representation of divinities of an archaic type, and some animals, such as the sphinx and lion, imitations of Asiatic or Greek models, and for rather clumsy bas-reliefs. On the other hand, the sculptors were able bronze-workers, and they have left some excellent statues (the She-Wolf, of the Capitol; the Child with a Bird, of the Vatican, etc.).

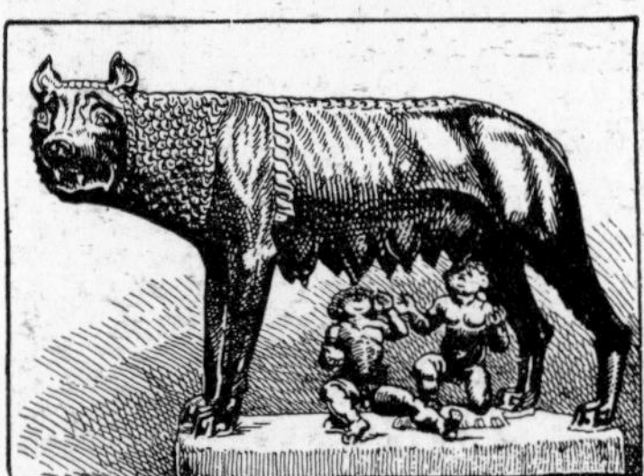

THE WOLF OF THE CAPITOL. (Rome.)

The true originality of Etruscan art is to be found in ceramic sculpture, clay statues. The Etruscans put them everywhere—on their temples, buildings and sarcophagi. The earliest being completely destroyed, we can only picture this art by the covers of sarcophagi, which are decorated with bas-reliefs, and with reclining figures. These are not very artistic works, and the execution leaves much to be desired. The artists were chiefly concerned with rendering the individuality of the dead, so that the gods should make no mistakes. The features, details in the arrangement of the hair, and familiar jewels, are most carefully rendered. On the other hand, it mattered little that the legs were too long or too short, the arms badly attached, and the attitude impossible. The bas-reliefs on the sides of the sarcophagi, generally very clumsy, show us scenes of everyday life—games, sacrifices, banquets, ceremonies, or incidents in the life of the deceased.

Painting had a more prosperous destiny than architecture or sculpture. It was easier to borrow Greek models from the scenes painted on the vases, and to reproduce them in fresco on the walls of tombs. Most examples of these come from the town of Corneto Tarquinia. The oldest date from the 5th century B.C.; the latest from the 3rd century. M. Martha divides them into three groups:—(1.) The archaic style, poor in colour, with figures of men or of animals, drawn in profile in red, yellow or black, on a greyish background. (Tomb of Campana, at Veii; painted bricks of Corneto, Chiusi, etc.) The subjects are those of the funereal vases. (2.) The severe style—still clumsy, but more correct in drawing. The figures are more animated, the faces are slightly modelled, the drapery more supple, sometimes transparent, and the colours more numerous. The subjects are death scenes, funereal dances, feasts of the dead, and, on the friezes, episodes of the hunt and of games. (3.) The free style: subjects and technique now change. Scenes from Greek or Etruscan mythology replace funereal scenes on the sides of tombs. Among the most famous are the paintings on the Grotto dell'Orco (Corneto), representing a Descent into Hades, and the François tomb (Vulci), representing Achilles killing Trojan prisoners on the tomb of Patroclus. The painters of this period have acquired more ability. They know how to represent their figures full face, or in profile, how to model the forms, and how to render the play of features, and bold attitudes; and their acquaintance with perspective allowed them to compose in several planes. However they never attained to the formal mastery of the Greeks or to the grace and harmony of Greek work.

The Etruscans cultivated the industrial arts—silver and bronze medals, engraved stones in the form of the Egyptian scarab, jewels, etc.

See Ceramic.

BIBLIOGRAPHY:—J. Martha, *L'Archéologie étrusque et romaine.* —Noël des Vergers, *L'Etrurie et les Etrusques.*—O. Muller, *Die Etrusker.* —Dennis, *The Cities and Cemeteries of Etruria.* London.

**ETTY (William).**—English painter, 1787-1849. Born in York. In London he became the pupil of Fuseli, at the Royal Academy. Then he joined Lawrence's studio, where he remained for a year. Few artists have had such unfortunate and difficult beginnings. Every year from 1820, he sent pictures to the Royal Academy, which rejected them. He left London, and visited Venice, Florence, Rome and Naples, where he studied the Venetian masters enthusiastically, especially Titian. The first work he painted

# BYZANTINE PAINTING

*There is no Byzantine sculpture and scarcely any statuary. Christianity imposed on the Greco-Roman world the exclusion of statues because they had been so closely associated with the pagan cults. It was a victory of the Asiatic spirit which is decorative and colourful over the Greek and European spirit which is sculptural. The visual habits of the ancient world were transformed: instead of divine representations in the forms of sculptured marbles men became accustomed to the flat forms of painting. The sense of relief and naturalism inherent in sculpture was replaced by care for ornament and love of colour.*

THEODORA AND HER COURT. MOSAIC OF SAN VITALE, RAVENNA.
*(Photo by Giraudon.)*

PROCESSION OF SAINTS. MOSAIC IN SANT'APOLLINARE NUOVO, RAVENNA.
*(Photo by Alinari.)*

## Byzantine Mosaics

Mosaic work consists of placing little cubes of stone or coloured glass together to make pictures. This decoration has the advantage of being unchangeable. The Byzantines preferred it to painting because it is richer and can be made in a mechanical way. Even in the most beautiful mosaics of the time of Justinian there is, in spite of the Greek heritage, an extraordinary lack of plastic sentiment.

THE CRUCIFIXION. MOSAIC FROM DAPHNI.
*(Photo by Millet.)*

THE ENTRY OF CHRIST INTO JERUSALEM. MOSAIC FROM DAPHNI.
*(Photo by Millet.)*

THE PROPHET ISAIAH BETWEEN NIGHT AND THE DAWN. MINIATURE; PSALTER, BIBL. NAT., PARIS.
*(Photo by Catala.)*

DEATH OF THE VIRGIN. MOSAIC FROM PALERMO.
*(Photo by Brogi.)*

## The Second Byzantine Golden Age

During this period which almost corresponds to the Romanesque period, Byzantine art, after the Iconoclastic controversy, had a renaissance when it showed a plastic sentiment more evident than at the time of Justinian. In any form that we may consider, mosaic, fresco or miniature, Byzantine painting was characterised by more elegance, if not by the correctness of ancient drawing. We can see how lively the art still is in its Christian iconography but it lacks freshness and youth.

CHRIST CROWNING ROMANUS AND EUDOXIA. IVORY, BIBL. NAT.
*(Photo by Hachette.)*

BARBERINI IVORY. LOUVRE.
*(Photo by Hachette.)*

CONSULAR DIPTYCH. BIBL. NAT.
*(Photo by Hachette.)*

THE HOLY WOMEN AT THE TOMB. GOLD REPOUSSÉ WORK, LOUVRE.
*(Photo by Hachette.)*

## Byzantine Ivories

Statuary is not a part of Byzantine art; but bas-relief sculpture was much practiced because it is, like painting, a decorative complement for architecture. The Byzantines who got from the Asiatic peoples the taste for precious things and fine materials, practiced sculpture in ivory which is in comparison to monumental sculpture as miniatures are to great paintings. These little plaques teach us of the history of plastic art. From this period which has left so few monuments they form a transition from Greco-Roman drawing to the Byzantine style.

# FRENCH ROMANESQUE ARCHITECTURE

*ROMANESQUE architecture covers the period of the eleventh and twelfth centuries. It is usually of a monastic origin and character. The Romanesque churches are distinguished from the earlier basilicas by the substitution of stone vaults for ceilings of wooden rafters. The exclusive use of stone in the construction of Romanesque buildings has protected them from destruction by fire. But the weight of the vault forced the architects to give to their buildings squat proportions; it led to the perfecting of their system of equilibrium and they soon discovered the method of ribbed groins which carried the vault while distributing the weight equally; the Gothic cathedral continued and completed the development of the Romanesque church.*

ARLES: ST. TROPHIME. PORCH.
*(Photo by Neurdein.)*

VÉZELAY: CHURCH. NAVE.
*(Photo by Neurdein.)*

ST. GILLES (GARD): CHURCH. FAÇADE.
*(Photo by Neurdein.)*

## Provence and Burgundy

ROMANESQUE architecture has different characteristics according to its location. It dates from a time when there was no national unity; each province had its unique architecture. Provence was more under the influence of Rome than the other parts of France.

TOULOUSE: ST. SERNIN. APSE.
*(Photo by Hachette.)*

SAINT-NECTAIRE: CHURCH.
*(Photo by Neurdein.)*

CLERMONT-FERRAND: NOTRE DAME DU PORT. NAVE.
*(Photo by Neurdein.)*

## Auvergne and Languedoc

AUVERGNE is one of the provinces whose original appearance has been kept throughout the ages. The natives preserved the excellent traditions of the Romanesque builders. They faced their churches with hard granite; these churches were ingeniously contrived and show a rustic elegance in perfect harmony with the landscape. The types of architecture spread far, particularly towards Languedoc, Toulouse, and northern Spain. On the other hand, the Moslem art of Spain crossed the Pyrenees and we may see its influence in the churches of Le Puy.

POITIERS: NOTRE DAME LA GRANDE. FAÇADE.
*(Photo by Hachette.)*

PÉRIGUEUX: CATHEDRAL. NAVE.
*(Photo by Neurdein.)*

ANGOULÊME: CATHEDRAL. FAÇADE.
*(Photo by Hachette.)*

## Poitou and Perigord

THE Romanesque churches of the west, in Poitou and Saintonge, are far from the perfect and solid structures that Auvergne made in its native granite. They are of limestone which is soft and easy to work; the sculptors carved the façades of these churches like ivory caskets. One of the original features of certain churches of the southwest: Périgueux, Angoulême, Cahors, is that they are covered by vaulted domes like the Byzantine churches. St. Front at Périgueux does not possess the richness of St. Mark's in Venice, but it reproduces its plan, proportions and the method of construction. Byzantine influence shows in the details of the sculptured and painted decorations.

on his return, in 1823, *Pandora Crowned by the Seasons*, was at once accepted at the academy, of which he became an associate, and then a member in 1828.

His work is sometimes mannered, and his colour wanting in harmony. But he sometimes shows a fine decorative sense, which recalls Titian, whom he had admired so much in his youth. Some of his nudes are admirable: their flesh is velvety and healthy, and they could stand comparison with the finest pieces of Rubens. As Etty tells us in his autobiography, he had an excessive taste for moral compositions. But his chief works are hymns of youth and pleasure. They are entitled *Duo* and *The Lute Player*. Etty is very well represented in the national museums: *Cupid and Psyche* (South Kensington), *Bathing Woman* (National Gallery); *The Tempest* (Manchester Gallery). We may also mention three studies of the nude, in the Metropolitan Museum, New York; and a free interpretation of a *Venus* by Titian, in the Royal Scottish Academy.

**EU (Seine-Inférieure).**—Church of St. Laurent.—A fine Gothic

Eu: Church of St. Laurent.

building of the 12th and 13th centuries. Its nave buttresses prop at the level of the triforium which is high and almost completely suppressed. This construction allows a double arcade in the nave, and a double window height—a system also employed at Rouen.

There is also a château at Eu, much of which is recent construction, however, since a fire in 1902.

**EUPHRONIS.**—See Greece (Vases).

**EUSEBIO da SAN GIORGIO.**—Umbrian painter active 1492-1540. He worked in 1501 with Fiorenzo di Lorenzo; and in 1508 with Pinturrichio. He is the author of two *Adorations of the Magi*, one in S. Pietro, Perugia, of 1508, the other in the Gallery, Perugia, of 1505, and of three Madonnas in the same gallery.

Evora: Doorway in the cloister of Loyos.

**EUTHYCRATES.**—Greek sculptor, son of Lysippus who, according to old writings, seems to have been his father's faithful follower.

**EVANS (Sir Arthur).**—See Crete.

**EVERDINGEN (Allart Van).**—Dutch landscape painter, 1621-1675. He seems to have introduced Scandinavian scenery into Dutch painting. He went to Sweden in the 1640's, and it is through him that Jacob van Ruisdael was inspired to his landscapes of rocks and waterfalls. Many drawings, signed with the monogram AVE are in existence.

Evora: Temple of Diana.

Bibliography: O. Granberg, *A. van Everdingen och Lans norska landskap*. Stockholm, 1902.

— **(Cæsar Van).**—Dutch painter, 1616-1679. About 1648, he settled in Haarlem, where he painted portraits. His best known pictures are *Diogenes Searching for a Happy Man* (The Hague), two large pictures representing members of the Civic Guard (Town Hall of Alkmaar), *Flora, Pomona and Bacchus with Cupid* (Dresden).

Evora: Porch of San Francisco.

Évreux: The Cathedral. South Transept.

Bibliography: Schneider, A. von, *Die niederländischen Manieristen*. Marburg, 1933.

**EVORA (Portugal. Temple of).**—This Roman temple dates from the 1st or 2nd century B.C., and has Corinthian columns.

**EVREUX (Eure).**—Fine Cathedral, in which all styles are represented from the 11th to the 18th centuries. The lower end of the nave is Romanesque, the upper end, the choir and the tower at the crossing are Gothic. The remarkable north doorway dates from the 16th century. The main portal, with its two unequal towers, belongs to the Renaissance. There is some magnificent 15th century glass in the Chapel of the Virgin, and in the apse.

Exeter: The Cathedral.

**EVRON.**—See Pl. 3, Vol. I.

**EXETER.**—Exeter Cathedral was begun in the 12th century, and rebuilt in the 13th and 14th centuries. It is one of the finest examples of the "Decorated" style of English architecture.

— **(Cathedral of).**—The cathedral (begun in 1186) has a cruciform plan, barrel vaulting and two western towers, from French influence. Moorish motifs survive.

**EYCK.**—See Van Eyck.

**EZRA.**—See Zorah (es-Zorah).

# F

**FABRITIUS (Barent).**—Dutch painter (1624-1673). His painting is strongly influenced by Rembrandt. The chief works, bearing his signature, are: *St. Peter in the House of Cornelius* (Brunswick Museum); the *Birth of St. John the Baptist*, and the *Adoration of the Shepherds* (National Gallery); *Mercury and Argus*, and *Abraham visited by Angels* (Cassel); the *Family Meal*, and the *Alchemist* (Stockholm).

Bibliography: Valentiner, W. R., *The Art Bulletin*, 1932.

— **(Carel).**—Dutch painter, of Delft (1614-1654). He studied in Rembrandt's studio. Almost nothing is known of his life, which was short, for he perished at the age of forty in the explosion of the powder-magazine of Delft. His works, therefore, are few. He is a charming artist, and one of Rembrandt's best pupils. His admirable *Portrait of a Man*, in the Museum of Rotterdam, was for a long time attributed to Rembrandt himself, and it was not before his signature was discovered that it was given to Fabritius. He left some delightful pictures: *The Sentinel* (Museum of Schwerin), and several portraits of men, in the Museums of Munich, Berlin, and Cologne. The *Family Group*, which was considered to be his masterpiece, was destroyed in the fire of the Rotterdam Museum.

Bibliography: Hoftede de Groot, *Vermeer and Fabritius*, 1906-1908.—Valentiner, W. R., *The Art Bulletin*, 1932.

**FADINO (Il).**—See Alenis.

**FADRUSZ (John).**—Hungarian sculptor. Most important of the modern school, he was born in Pozsony in 1858, died in Budapest, 1903. As a young boy he was a skilled woodcarver, but received no real artistic education until a stipend was given to him in 1884 to study sculpture in Vienna with Tilgner. The first work he exhibited, *Christ on the Cross*, 1892, (Szeged, marble copy in London,) brought him a national award and immediate success and fame. He was engaged to execute a number of historical and portrait sculptures; among these the equestrian statue of *Empress Maria Theresa*, 1896, may be called his *chef d'oeuvre*. Another equestrian statue, *King Mathias I.* (Kolozsvár), won the Grand Prix in Paris. Inspired by the equestrian statues of Donatello and Verocchio, Fadrusz works in the highest neo-classic tradition. He endows his monumental and powerful works with the new nationalistic spirit, creating purely Hungarian types in a somewhat glorified manner, thus evoking irresistible patriotism in the onlooker. One of the most expressive and forceful sculptors of his century, he is responsible for a number of monumental statues of Hungarian and Austrian statesmen.

**FAES (Peter van der).**—See Lely.

**FAÏENCE.**—Word derived from Faenza, Italy, used specifically to denote a fine tin-glazed pottery, but sometimes applied to any kind of glazed earthenware.

See Majolica.

**FAITHORNE (William), the Elder.**—English painter and engraver (1616-1691). Exiled for supporting the cause of Charles I, he went to France, where he received lessons from Robert Nanteuil. He engraved some portraits and cards, and wrote a treatise on the art of engraving (1662). He was the first notable English engraver.

BIBLIOGRAPHY: L. Fagan, *Descriptive Catalogue of the Engravings of Faithorne.* London, 1888.

**FALCONET (Étienne Maurice).**—French sculptor (1716-1791). Pu-

FALCONET.

pil of J. B. Lemoyne. His education made him familiar with dead languages, and enabled him to edit chapters of Pliny concerning art. He also published his own very independent theories. For instance, he considered antique sculpture inferior to the work of Puget, who, he said, had more feeling for drapery, and the softness of flesh. But he only knew antiques through

FALCONET: PYGMALION AND THE STATUE. (After Sèvres porcelain.)

debased Roman copies. He held that they were particularly weak in equestrian representation, and he did not share the general admiration for the famous horse of Marcus Aurelius. The Empress of Russia, Catherine II, gave him the chance to put his ideas into practice, by commanding him to make a colossal equestrian statue of Peter the Great in St. Petersburg (1776). An immense block that had been successfully extricated from a marsh served for the pedestal of the statue, which is still standing; and represents Peter the Great, majestically calm, controlling his spirited horse. The horse's attitude is striking in its novelty and boldness. His pupil, Mademoiselle Collot, who became his daughter-in-law, helped him with this work. His inventions were sometimes purely theatrical, as, for instance, the *Assumption* of St. Roch (disappeared since the Revolution), above which was a celestial glory, illuminated by transparently shaded lights. Nowadays, we chiefly remember him as the author of the Bathing Girl (1757—Louvre) and of graceful little subjects, made to be reproduced in Sèvres china.

See Pl. 45, Vol. II.

BIBLIOGRAPHY: Notice bv Lévêque, preceding *Les Œuvres d'Etienne Falconet, Statuaire.* Lausanne, 1785, 5 vols.—St. Lami, *Dictionnaire des sculpteurs français.*—L. Réau, *Falconet,* 1922.

**FALCONETTO (Giovanni Maria).**—Architect and painter of Verona (c.1468-c.1534), who worked chiefly in Padua, where he is one of the best representatives of the architecture of his age. As he was a painter at the same time, and excelled in representing buildings in his frescoes, he understood how to decorate his buildings, how to combine effects of colour with white stucco and with gold. An example is the fine vault of white stucco, slightly gilded, of the Chapel of the Saints in Sant' Antonio of Padua, which was commissioned in 1533. In 1524 Falconetto built for Cornaro in Padua the Loggia and the Casino; 1528 the Porta San Giovanni; 1530 the Porta Savonarola, all of which bear his signature. His frescoes in the Duomo of Verona were painted about 1503. Other signed frescoes by him are in the Biagio Chapel of S. Nazaro e Celso, in Verona. Pictures attributed to him are in the Pinacoteca.

**FALGUIÈRE (Jean Alexandre Joseph).**—French sculptor and painter. (Toulouse, 1831-Paris, 1900). He went to Paris when quite

FALGUIÈRE: ST. VINCENT DE PAUL. (Pantheon.)

young, and entered the École des Beaux Arts, in the atelier of Jouffroy. He won the Prix de Rome in 1859. At that time he made two charming works, which are among his best: the *Winner of a Cock Fight* (1864, Luxembourg), and *Tarcisius, Christian Martyr,* also called the *Little Martyr* (1867, Luxembourg). The first shows the alert grace of a Frenchman, influenced by Florence; and the second attains mysticism without insipidity. He shows the same qualities in *Lamartine* (1878, Mâcon); and *St. Vincent de Paul* (1879, Panthéon). He then began to exhibit paintings at the Salon: the *Wrestlers* (1875), etc. His colour shows more facility than study. Utter neglect of technique foredoomed these pictures to prompt destruction. His sculpture, on the contrary, though sometimes careless and vulgar, shows more understanding and conscientiousness. We may mention: *Music* (1889); *Dancer; Eve;* monument to Admiral Courbet (Abbeville,

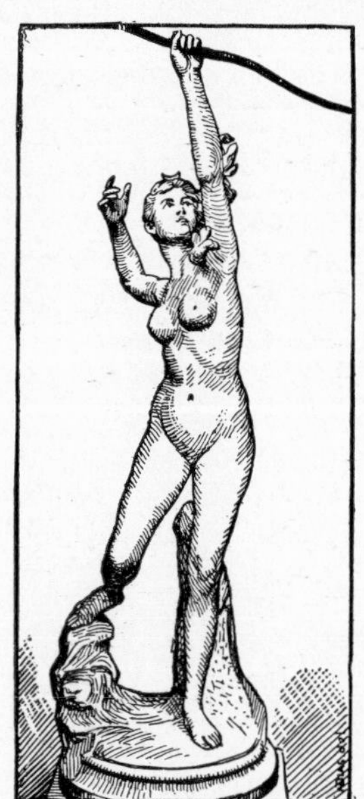

FALGUIÈRE: DIANA.

1890); monument to Lafayette (Washington); monument to Bizet; statue of Cardinal Lavigerie (Panthéon); bust of the Baronne Daumesnil, etc. Towards the end of his career, the artist made a series of female nudes, which he called Diana, Juno, etc.; these are original works, which show some of the nervous grace of his beginnings, with more realistic accents. The public wrongly accused him of vulgarity, but this was only because he was enslaved by convention, and looked for the usual, classical types. Falguière designed a colossal group,

FALGUIÈRE: BUST OF THE BARONESS DAUMESNIL. (Musée du Luxembourg.)

representing the Triumph of the Republic, to be placed on the Arc de Triomphe de l'Etoile. The work was placed there in 1881, displeased, and disappeared in 1886, without leaving any regrets.

See Pl. 52, Vol. II.

**FAN K'UAN.**—Chinese landscape painter of the Five Dynasties and Early Sung periods. Known as a painter of snow scenes.

See China—Art.

**FANTIN-LATOUR (Ignace Henri Jean Théodore).**—French painter. Born in Grenoble, 1836; died in Buré (Orne), in 1904. He went to Paris, at the age of fifteen, and studied at the Petite École in the Rue de l'École de Médecine. He also copied in the Louvre, especially Titian and Veronese, copying the *Marriage of Cana* five times. In 1859, he sent three portraits to the Salon: a self-portrait (Grenoble); the portrait of his Sister, and the portraits of his two Sisters (Madame V. Koltz's Collection). All these pictures being rejected, he exhibited them in Bouvin's studio, in the Rue St. Jacques. As a result of this exhibition, Fantin-Latour became acquainted with Courbet, Manet and their friends, but he did not come under the influence of the new school. Fantin-Latour combined the temperament of a realistic painter, with the soul of a poet. He only cared to copy objects which "composed well." He never painted any landscape from

FANTIN-LATOUR: THE RHEINGOLD. (Musée du Luxembourg.)

nature, because he said that sunlight and clouds were too ephemeral, and could not be copied. Nevertheless, his idealism often transported him into the world of fiction and allegory. Towards the end of his life especially, he drew fantastic compositions, pastels, lithographs and oil paintings, inspired by the great masters of music, interpreting them in tender, vaporous colour, too often rather weak: *Tannhäuser* (1886); the *Damnation of Faust; The Rheingold* (1888); *Immortality* (1889), etc. Fantin-Latour is seen at his best in his portraits, which are quite superior, and original. He painted himself and his friends, grouping them in such pictures as *Homage to Delacroix* (1864); the *Toast to Truth* (1865); *Round the Piano* (Adolphe Julien Collection), etc. *Homage to Delacroix* (Moreau Nélaton Collection) shows Baudelaire, Manet, Whistler, Champfleury, Duranty, etc., grouped round the great painter. *The Corner of the Table* (1872) unites certain poets—Verlaine, Rimbaud, Blémont, Jean Aicard, Ernest d'Hervilly, Valade and Pelletan. As well as pictures, which by their composition, recall the pictures of the Dutch Guilds, he painted smaller, more intimate groups: portrait of Mr. and Mrs. Edwin Edwards (1875, National Gallery); the Dubourg Family; the Drawing (1879)—pictures which have a simple charm, and an extraordinary quietness and distinction. His isolated portraits, less numerous, are also quite remarkable: Portrait of Manet (1867); portrait of Lerolle (Lerolle Collection).

Finally, Fantin-Latour painted still-life, especially flowers. Here, his power and gentleness, precision of construction and refinement of colour, are remarkable. His colour is subdued and greyish in tone, but warmed with bright touches. Owing to his delicate reflections, the light seems to tremble on faces and objects. As he never exaggerated this, his work has an atmospheric quality which, combined with great fidelity of pose and expression, gives a profound impression of truth and intimacy. We seem really to know the subjects of his portraits, such as his sister-in-law, Mademoiselle Dubourg, whom he often painted. She haunts the memory as though one had really seen and spoken to her.

BIBLIOGRAPHY: René Ditte, *Fantin-Latour.*

**FARINATI (Paolo).**—Veronese painter, 1522-1606, a pupil of Giolfino.

**FARNESE BULL.**—See Pl. 25, Vol. I.

**— PALACE.**—See Pl. 7, Vol. II.

**FARNESINA PALACE.**—See Rome; also Pl. 7, Vol. II.

**FAUVE.**—Term meaning "wild beast" applied to a group of expressionistic painters who exhibited at the Salon of 1906. These include Matisse, Vlaminck, Van Dongen, Braque, and Friesz.

Characteristics are broad patterns of decorative color used in large unbroken areas chained by heavy outlines.

See Casorati; Matisse; Vlaminck.

**FAYUM (Portraits of).**—Portraits from Fayum, a province of Middle Egypt. They are by Greek artists, who painted the portrait of the dead on wood. The portrait was then held in place by the wrappings. These works, which were found in the tombs of Egypt, were executed between the 2nd and the 5th century A.D., and are now scattered in various museums (London, Paris, Florence, Leningrad, Gizeh). Most of them are not of great artistic value. "In spite of the sincerity of the painting, traces of the conventional and commonplace type of decadent sculpture remain: the nose is too wide, the lips thick, the forehead round, and, above all, is a placidity which appears stupid in faces which are not beautiful . . . each has its particular ugliness: here a bony nose and hollow cheeks, there a round, clean-shaven face. Roman types are often found—such as Lucius Virus, dark and curled, and heads of empresses with large, placid eyes (made to seem larger through the use of cosmetics), which seem to herald the Byzantine type." (L. Hourticq.)

PORTRAIT FROM FAYUM (EGYPT). (Found in a mummy case, Louvre.)

Nevertheless, these images, often clumsy, give us an idea of what must have been the masterpieces of the best artists. Many have a realism which makes one feel that they must have been good likenesses. They are almost all portraits of young people, which makes it supposed that they were painted, not at the time of death, but in youth or in mature age. Or the artist may have painted them after the subject's decease, recalling youthful characteristics, in the Egyptian way.

These portraits of Fayum set before us a Graeco-Egyptian society; and also reveal to us the Greek method of painting. Most of them are encaustic painting, some in distemper; a few combine the two methods.

See Pl. 28, Vol. I.

BIBLIOGRAPHY: Graul, *Die antiken Porträtgemälde aus den Grabstätten des Faijum.* Leipzig, 1888.—Wilchen, Die hellen. Porträte aus El. Faijum. *Jahrb. Deuk. d. arch. Inst.*, 1889.

**FEI (Paolo di Giovanni).**—Pupil of Bartolo di Fredi and Andrea Vanni.

In 1372 Fei is mentioned as a member of the city government; in 1395 he is at work for the Cathedral, paints a St. Paul in the Choir, a St. Ansanus on a tabernacle; in 1397 he is paid for further paintings; and in 1398, 1399, and 1400, he executes images of SS. Peter, Paul, Boniface, and Savinus. In 1400 he is again working in the Cathedral; in 1408 is mentioned as active in the Chapel of the Passion; and in 1409 does figures of SS. Peter and Paul for Sta. Maria della Scala. The last mention of his activity is of 1410, when he paints four Saints in the Chapel "dei Maestri."

But two authentic works are left: a signed polyptych in the Academy, Siena, a Madonna and Saints; and the figures of 1409 in Sta. Maria della Scala, which is closed to the public. A very prolific painter, his attributed works are numerous. He was the master of Sassetta.

BIBLIOGRAPHY: Milanesi, *Doc. . . . senese,* I.—Crowe and Cavalcaselle, Douglas ed., III.—F. M. Perkins, Burlington Magazine, August, 1903. —Berenson, Burlington Magazine, Nov., 1903. — Langton Douglas, Nineteenth Century and After, Nov., 1904.—Van Marle, *Italian Schools, etc.,* II, 1924.

**FELIPE DE BORGOÑA.**—See Berruguete.

**FERENCZY (Kárely, or Charles).** —Hungarian painter, 1862-1917. He was born in Vienna of Hungarian parents. He studied art in Naples, 1886, Paris, 1887, and from 1893 to '95 in Munich where he joined the group of Hollósy. In 1896 he returned to Hungary and together with Hollósy founded the famous art colony at Nagybánya where he taught for many years. Ferenczy has often been called the Hungarian Manet. While at the Academie Julian in Paris, he adopted Bastien-Lepage's strict naturalistic point of view which he counteracted with his deeply poetic feeling. While in Munich, he assimilated the analytic and synthetic methods of approach. His early works as *Joseph Sold by His Brothers,* still shows the religious theme, and is characterized by simple monumentality and unity of action. The calm objective mood is entoned by the barren background. From 1896 on, his style underwent a considerable change; his art became exceedingly personal and spontaneous, his naturalistic conception was achieved through a synthetic approach. Ferenczy shows delight in the country surrounding him and interest in atmosphere and rendering pure vivid colors. Clean, transparent shadows, bold value contrasts and a consciousness of tectonic qualities are always present. He is one of the few painters who were in search of type rather than the individual, and yet he never failed to grasp the salient qualities of the individual sitters. His technique is one of broad brushstrokes and a fairly heavy impasto. The *Woman Pressing* is comparable to Degas's works in catching the significance in fleeting gesture. In his later works his color became richer and more sonorous. He illustrated a number of books and was the recipient of several medals and awards.

BIBLIOGRAPHY: Lázár, *13 magyar festö,* 1912.—Malonyay, *Fiatalok,* 1906.

**FERNANDES.**—See Hernandez.

**FERRARA (Italy).**—A flourishing town in the Middle Ages, under the government of the d'Este family, especially under Duke Ercole I, who enlarged the town, and made wide, straight roads.

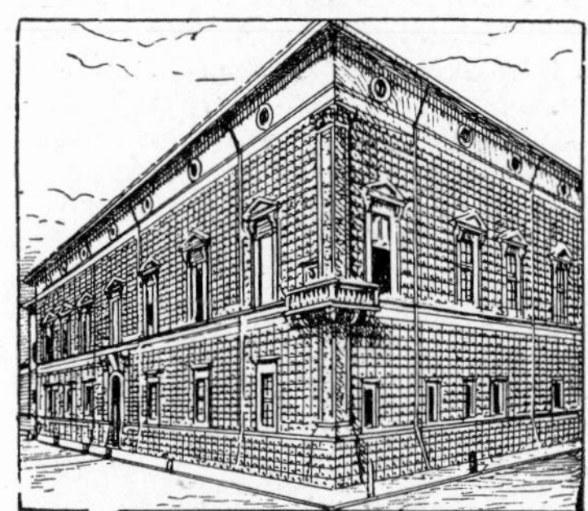

FERRARA: PALAZZO DE' DIAMANTI.

The oldest building in Ferrara is the Cathedral, begun in 1135, in the Lombard Romanesque style; continued in the 13th and 14th centuries. It has a fine façade with three stages of arcades.

The Castello, surrounded by a moat, is an old feudal fortress, flanked by four square towers. Built by B. da Novara, it was rebuilt after a fire in 1554. The interior is decorated with frescoes of the school of Dosso Dossi.

The Palazzo Schifanoia, begun in 1391, and finished by P. Benvenuti in 1466-1469, is noted for its frescoes, painted about 1470 by Francesco del Cossa and the Ferrarese School.

The Palazzo dei Diamanti (Diamond Palace) is so called because it is built with stones cut in facets. The building is severe in character. It was built by Rossetti about 1492, finished in 1567, and decorated by the sculptor, G. Frisoni of Mantua. It contains a picture gallery.

San Francesco is also the work of Rossetti, and was built from 1492 to 1530. Decorated with frescoes by Garofalo.

San Benedetto, built by G. and A. Tristani, about 1550, in the Renaissance style.

**— (School of).**—See Pl. 15, Vol. II.

**FERRARI (Antobello).**—See Melone.

**— (Defendente).**—Painter Piedmontese School, active c. 1510-1535. Pupil of Macrino d'Alba and of Gian Martino Spanzotti. Influenced by Franco-Flemish art. A prolific painter, he is widely represented, but the greatest part of his production is to be found at Turin and in the vicinity.

**— (Gaudenzio).**—Painter 1481?-1546. He is associated with the Lombard school, of which he is one of the most interesting artists. He was born in Valduggia in Piedmont, and had his first teaching in Vercelli. His activity extended throughout Piedmont and Lombardy. Besides Tuscan and Umbrian traditions, he was influenced by Leonardo. He died in Milan.

He left numerous works, which are rich in colour and have heavy shadows.

His best-known works are in the Sanctuary of Varallo: in San Gaudenzio is a fine altarpiece in six compartments, with the *Mystic Marriage of St. Catherine,* a *Pietà* and saints. In Santa Maria delle Grazie, on the road from the Sacro Monte, are frescoes representing the Life of Christ, and the Passion (1513). In Santa Maria di Loreto, an *Adoration of the Magi,* on the doorway. And, finally, in the sanctuary, all the chapels of which have terra cotta figures, or frescoes, recalling Christ's walk to Calvary, the fine procession of the Magi, the Crucifixion and Pietà (1523) are by the hand of Gaudenzio.

He also contributed to the decoration of another famous sanctuary —that of the Beata Vergine, in Saronno, where there are frescoes by Luini. There, he painted a concert of angels on the dome (1535-36).

For San Cristoforo of Vercelli, he painted a fine altarpiece, with a Virgin in an orchard, and a St. Christopher. For Como Cathedral he painted a Marriage of the Virgin, and a Flight into Egypt, tempera paintings. He also painted a large altarpiece (1514, restored) for San Gaudenzio of Novarra; and dramatic frescoes for Sant'Ambrogio of Milan.

He is well represented in other Milanese Churches and in the Brera, Castello, and Poldi-Rezzoli, as well as at Turin and elsewhere.

BIBLIOGRAPHY: Ethel Halsey, *Gaudenzio Ferrari.* London, 1904.

**FETI (Domenico).**—Italian painter (1589-1624). Pupil of Lodovico Cardi. He first worked in Mantua, at frescoes which have now disappeared. He then settled in Venice. He painted a great deal, and left numerous religious pictures, although his vigorous, rather commonplace, talent would seem to have lent itself better to realistic scenes. His best works are: *Melancholy* (Louvre), a powerful painting, in the style of Caravaggio; *Nero* (Louvre), where strength becomes brutality. The same may be said of the *Guardian Angel* (Louvre), and the *Workers of the Vine* (Pitti Palace), *Meditation,* and the *Good Samaritan*. The naturalist school, and, especially Courbet, greatly admired Feti.

**FEUERBACH (Anselm).**—German painter (1829-1880). He studied in Düsseldorf, in Antwerp, in Paris with Couture; and then visited Venice and Rome. His pictures owe their seduction partly to the beauty of the figures, and partly to the colour which is sometimes very luminous, and sometimes in a greyish harmony, which is very decorative. His chief works are: *Hafiz at the Fountain*, *Medea* (Mannheim Gallery), *Iphigenia* (Stuttgart Museum), the *Judgment of Paris* (Hamburg), the *Banquet of Plato* (National Gallery of Berlin); and *Dante in Ravenna*, and the *Contest of Amazons* (Nuremberg).

Bibliography: Allgeyer, J., *Anselm Feuerbach*. Berlin, 1904.—Uhde-Bernays, A. F., *Anselm Feuerbach*. Leipzig, 1914.

**FIELDING (Anthony Vandyke Copley).**—English painter (1787-1855); a pupil of John Varley and one of the leading English water colour painters of his time. Elected an Associate of the Old Water Colour Society in 1810 and a Member in 1812.

**FILARETE (Antonio di Pietro Avellino, called).**—Florentine sculptor and architect. Born, Florence, c. 1400; died, Rome, c. 1469. He

Filarete: Detail of the door of St. Peter's, Rome.

was full of theories, and wrote a treatise on architecture. His reputation rests on the bronze door of St. Peter's, Rome, executed for Eugene IV (attributed by Vasari to Somoni). He arrived in Rome when Donatello was there, but had not sufficient natural gift to profit deeply from his example. He began his door in 1433, and was twelve years working on it. These bas-reliefs, which represent, at the top, the Saviour and the Virgin, then St. Paul and St. Peter giving the keys to the little kneeling Pope, and, below, the Judgment of St. Paul and the Martyrdom of St. Peter, are far from attaining mastery of form. There is a conscious attempt to render the surroundings, especially to represent the buildings of Rome. But the figures are coarse, and the drapery lacks variety and movement. There is an accumulation of details, but no effect of intensity. The decorations on the frame, however, show a very charming fancy.

In 1447, he was accused of having stolen some relics, and was driven out of Rome. In Venice, where he took refuge, he made a processional cross for the Cathedral of Bassano. In Milan, where he entered the service of the Duke Francesco Sforza in 1451 he was engaged chiefly on architectural works in the Castello, in the Ospedale Maggiore, and so forth. He made a medal, in honour of his master, which is in the Municipal Museum. Various sculptural works are attributed to Filarete.

Bibliography: Lazzaroni and Munoz, *Filarete scultore e architetto del secolo XV*. Rome, 1908.

**FINIAL.**—Knot, bunch of foliage, or other ornament which tops a pinnacle, gable, canopy, or frame in Gothic architecture.

**FINIGUERRA (Tommaso or Maso).**—Florentine draughtsman and crafts worker, 1425-1464, who made designs for inlaid work in the sacristy of the Duomo and to whom are attributed several figure drawings in the Uffizi and illustrations for a chronicle of subjects from the Old Testament, now in the British Museum.

Finiguerra was trained as a goldsmith and may have worked with Ghiberti on the bronze doors of the Baptistry. In 1449 Baldovinetti makes a cast of a niello plate by Finiguerra. In 1451, 1452, and 1457 Finiguerra's activity as a goldsmith is mentioned. He had a shop with Antonio Pollaiuolo; is mentioned in 1459 by Giovanni Rucellai as a drawing master, working with Antonio Pollaiuolo in the Rucellai palace, among other artists such as Fra Filippo, Giuliano da Maiano, Verrocchio, Domenico Veneziano, Castagno, and Uccello.

Baldovinetti colored the five drawings that Finiguerra sketched and Giuliano da Maiano executed in wood-inlay for the Sacristy of the Duomo. The inlay of the Annunciation is still in the Sacristy; that of St. Zenobius and two Saints is in the Opera del Duomo.

Bibliography: Vasari-Milanesi, I, 209; III, 287, 288; V, 395, 443, 444, 446.—v. Rumohr, *Untersuchung über d. Gründe d. Annahme dass M. di Finiguerra, etc.* Leipzig, 1841.—Berenson, *Drawings of Florentine Painters*, I, 31; II, 129; Gazette des Beaux Arts, ser. III, Vol. XXIII, p. 170.—Colvin. *Florentine Picture Chronicle*.—Hind and Colvin, *Cat. of Early Ital. Engr. in the British Museum*.—A. M. Hind, *Short Hist. of Engraving*, 1908.—Venturi, L'Arte, II, 1899, 112.—Van Marle, *Italian Schools, etc.*, XI.

**FIORENZO di LORENZO.**—Umbrian painter, born in Perugia c. 1445; died in the same city before 1525.

In the guild registers of 1463-69 Fiorenzo is mentioned as a painter; and in 1472 he became Prior of the guild. In the same year he received a commission for a double-sided triptych for S. Maria Nuova in Perugia, the price to be paid being set at 200 fiorini. This painting was the cause of protracted negotiation, for in 1487, Fiorenzo renounced his right to paint the back sides of the panels and accepted a reduction in price to 100 fiorini, and in 1491 a new arrangement was made, since the painter had apparently not held to the specifications, and 30 fiorini were added to the price, the delivery date being set at 1493. This altarpiece is probably to be identified with sixteen pictures now in the Perugia Pinacoteca, from S. Maria Nuova, which are reunited in a triptych. They include: a Madonna Enthroned in the Clouds, two Angels and four Saints; God the Father; and Fathers of the Church. This reconstructed altarpiece is stylistically close to Fiorenzo's signed Peter and Paul of 1487 from S. Francesco al Prato.

Other documentary notices of his activity apply to works now lost; attributions to him rest upon those two mentioned above.

Bibliography: Vasari-Milanesi.—J. Carlyle Graham, *The Problem of Fiorenzo di Lorenzo*. Perugia, 1903.—Siegfried Weber, *Fiorenzo di Lorenzo* (Zur Geschichte des Auslands No. 27). Strassburg, 1904.—W. Bombe, *Gesch. der Perug. Malerei*. Berlin, 1912.—E. Jacobsen, *Umbr. Malerei* (Zur Gesch. d. Ausl. No. 107). Strassburg, 1914.

**FIRST ROMANESQUE STYLE.**—See Romanesque.

**FIRUZ-ABAD (Mesopotamia).**—*Palace*, c. 450 A.D. An important relic of Sasanian Persian civilization. An oblong block with a great arched entrance with blind arcades on either side. Beyond were three compartments, linked transversely and covered by domes, and a court. The construction is crude. Squinches permitted the transition from the square halls to the round dome.

**FISCHER von ERLACH (John Bernard).**—Austrian architect, 1656-1723. Chief architect of the Austrian court. He was responsible for important buildings in Vienna and in several towns, among them the Castle of Schönbrunn, a part of the Imperial Palace, other palaces for Austrian princes and several churches in Vienna.

**FLAMBOYANT.**—Term applied to the late Gothic style of architecture which is characterised by flame-like curves and the ogee arch.

See Pl. 50, Vol. I.

**FLAMENG (François).**—French painter, 1856-1923. Son and pupil of the good engraver, Léopold Flameng, the artist passed through the studios of Cabanel and J. P. Laurens. He made his appearance at the Salon when very young, in 1875, and was soon noticed. His first pictures represent large, historic scenes, skillfully and picturesquely composed. He then painted military scenes. His best works are the mural decorations of the Sorbonne. In his last years, Flameng devoted himself exclusively to portraits of women, whom he painted in the style of the 18th century, showing great suppleness and grace in his assimilation (Empress of Russia, Grand Duchess Xenia, Queen of the Belgians and her Children, etc.).

**FLAMOND (François).**—See Duquesnoy.

**FLANDERS (Juan of).**—Spanish painter, of Flemish origin. In 1506 he was commissioned to paint twelve panels for the Cathedral of Palencia. The Royal Palace of Madrid has fourteen of the forty-six panels executed by Juan of Flanders for Isabella. They are delicate works, which were much admired by Albrecht Dürer. Although very near to Gerard David in style, Juan was much influenced by Castillian colouring.

**FLANDRIN (Jean Hippolyte).**—French painter. Born in Lyon, 1809; died in Rome, 1864. He became a member of the Institute in 1853. Hippolyte Flandrin is one of the best-known pupils of Ingres. He decorated the Church of Ainay with paintings which recall Roman mosaics; those in St. Paul of Nîmes, with a procession of Virgins, show the Byzantine idea; and those in the Chapel of St. Jean, of St. Séverin, Paris, are remarkable for harmoniously proportioned figures and naïve quality of design.

His creations, always noble and pure, are never indifferent. But his carefully studied drapery, for instance, wearies: it lacks spontaneity. Some of his landscapes are worthy of Puvis de Chavannes, and there is considerable grace in some of his frescoes in St. Germain-des-Prés, Paris.

Flandrin (J. H.).

The modesty of his study of a *Young Girl* (Louvre), with the profile hidden, is very touching. We may also mention the self-portrait, and the portrait of Napoleon III (both in Versailles).

See Pl. 54, Vol. II.

Bibliography: J. B. Poncet, *Hippolyte Flandrin*. Paris, 1864.—Amaury Duval, *L'Atelier d'Ingres*. Paris.—L. Flandrin, *H. Flandrin*. Paris, 1903.

**FLAXMAN (John).**—English sculptor, 1755-1826. He is celebrated both for his sculptured works, and for a remarkable series of drawings illustrating literary works. The son and brother of modellers, he acquired the taste for the antique in the paternal workshop, where he saw copies and casts. He was extraordinarily precocious, and exhibited terra cottas at the age of twelve, and a *Death of Cæsar* at the age of fourteen, after which he became a pupil of the Royal Academy. In the competition for the gold medal in 1772, the public expected his success, but Reynolds, head of the jury, awarded the prize to a mediocre sculptor. Flaxman continued to exhibit fine pieces of sculpture: *Pompey; Hercules in the Garment of Nessus* (1778); *the Death of Cæsar; Prometheus;* the tomb of Mrs. Morley (Gloucester Cathedral), a charming work, executed in 1786. The following year he went to Rome where he stayed seven years, and was a great success. He much admired the antique, and made many drawings from statues. His drawing is remarkably able and pure. He was commissioned to make forty-eight drawings to illustrate the Iliad and the Odyssey. This work (1793-1795) made its author famous throughout Europe, and was so successful that he was asked for a new series of thirty drawings for Æschylus, and for a hundred and nine for Dante. These drawings are admirably composed, and the elegance of the figures often recalls the harmony of the Greek vase paintings. He became a member of the Academies of Florence, and of Ferrara, and then returned to England in 1794, where he made the memorial to Lord Mansfield (Westminster). In 1800, he became a member of the Royal Academy. His reputation grew, and commissions came from all parts. Among his best works are: *Mercury and Pandora, Resignation, Maternal Love, Cupid and Psyche, Raphael* and *Michelangelo*, several tombs (Benson, Skinner, Reynolds), statues of Pitt, and Moore, and the Nelson memorial, at Westminster; and, finally, the famous *Shield of Achilles*, which represents figures of men and animals according to the description in the Iliad. This shield was cast in silver, and sung by Goethe.

Flaxman died, covered with honour and glory, at the age of seventy-one. His last years were saddened by the death of his wife (1820), who was associated with all his works. Besides sculpture and drawing, he left some critical works, ten lessons given at the Royal Academy, some of lectures on sculpture, and some anatomical studies.

BIBLIOGRAPHY: W. G. Constable, *John Flaxman*, London, 1927.

**FLÈCHE.**—A slender spire, especially one rising above the intersection of the nave and transepts of a church.

**FLÉMALLE (Bertholet).**—Flemish painter (1614-1675). Worked in Paris for Maria de' Medici, and in his native town Liège. He painted many mythological and sacred scenes and a great number of portraits. The influence of Poussin is evident in his style.

**— (Master of).**—Nothing is more obscure than the personality of the "Master of Flémalle." He was first known under the name of the "Master of the Mouse-trap," from a detail in the *Annunciation*, one of the wings of his principal picture; then under the name of the "Master of Mérode," from the name of the owner of "the *Annunciation*" and, finally, he was called the "Master of Flémalle." Flémalle is the name of a Belgian village between Liége and Namur, where there is an abbey in which, according to a German critic (Tschudi), the paintings in the Städel Institute, Frankfort, were discovered. It is not certain that these paintings came from the Abbey of Flémalle, and the name

FLÉMALLE (MASTER OF): THE BAD THIEF. (Museum, Frankfort.)

given to the artist is thus the most hazardous of the three. As to what was the real name of the "Master of Flémalle," the consensus of opinion now favours the story that it was Robert Campin of Tournai (1375-1444), the master of Roger van der Weyden and Jacques Daret.

The most important work of the Master of Flémalle is the famous triptych of the *Annunciation* (Mérode Collection, Brussels). The middle panel represents the Annunciation. In a pleasing Flemish room, full of familiar furniture and details, the Virgin, clad in a red dress, with an ample red mantle, is seated very low near a round table, so absorbed in reading her missal that she does not notice the entrance of the angel Gabriel. On the left wing, St. Joseph, a peaceful old man with a white beard, is patiently making mouse-traps, having exhibited a sample of his trade on the window-ledge. In this intimate picture the artist shows the charm of simple, everyday life.

In the Staedel Institute (Frankfort) are the works which won the artist the name of the Master of Flémalle. They come from the old house of the Knights of Jerusalem, in Flémalle, and from part of an altarpiece of the Virgin, of which the central panel has disappeared. The two wings represent, in life size, a St. Veronica, and a Virgin and Child. Both stand on a flowery sward, against an oriental tapestry. St. Veronica, richly clad, holds the handkerchief with which she wiped the face of Christ. The Virgin is decidedly the most beautiful of all those attributed to the artist. She holds the Child with a tender, protecting gesture, and her figure is full of a sad sweetness and divine purity. On the reverse of these wings is a *Trinity*, in "grisaille," which inspired the two paintings of the Brussels Gallery, and of the Communal Museum of Louvain, which may be by an imitator of the Master of Flémalle, Colin de Coter.

Also in the Staedel Institute is the *Good Thief*, attributed to the artist, a fragment of an altarpiece. The central panel represented a *Descent from the Cross*, of which we gain an idea from the mediocre copy in Liverpool. This *Descent* strongly recalls the one in the Berlin Museum, which has been attributed to the Master of Flémalle. The arms of Bruges figure on the Liverpool copy, and, on the other hand, one of the pictures of the Church of St. Sauveur of Bruges reproduces certain figures of the *Descent*, which proves that the lost original was in Bruges.

The "Somzée Madonna" (National Gallery) is after that of Frankfort, the most beautiful of the Virgins attributed to the Master of Flémalle. The young mother, seated on a little bench in front of a fire, protected by a fire-guard, is preparing to feed the child. Through the window one sees a town, with a little "place." Here, again, is the intimate charm of the *Annunciation*.

The *Virgin in Glory* in the Museum of Aix gives us quite a different impression. Here, the Virgin is enthroned in the sky, on a seat decorated with sculpture. Her features recall those of the "Somzée Madonna," but the expression is pleasanter. The attribution of this graceful work to the Master of Flémalle is much disputed, as is that of diverse *Madonnas* in various European countries (Richmond, Leningrad, Brussels).

The Prado Museum possesses two wings of an altarpiece, generally attributed to the Master of Flémalle, of which the middle panel has disappeared. On one is painted the portrait of Heinrich Werle, superior of the Convent of Osnabruck; on the other, a young, fair-haired St. Barbara is seated on a bench, with her back to the fire, deep in a Book of Hours. The painting bears the date 1438.

*The Marriage of the Virgin* (Prado) is also attributed to the artist, though without much certainty. The composition, divided in two, shows, on one side, the Betrothal; on the other, the Marriage. Still more doubtful is the *Legend of St. Joseph* (Church of Hoogstraeten), which is generally thought to be the copy of a lost original.

The *Adoration of the Shepherds*, in the Museum of Dijon, is, on the other hand, almost unanimously given to the Master of Flémalle. It is a charming work, full of attractive details. Grouped round the little Christ are a fair, graceful Madonna, kneeling on the folds of her wide blue mantle: a venerable St. Joseph, who holds a candle, sheltering the flame with the hollow of his hand; two midwives, three shepherds, and angels. In the background is a beautiful landscape, with houses, trees, hills, and steep rocks.

The Master of Flémalle did not have the influence of a Van Eyck or of a Roger Van der Weyden. His works have, however, often been copied. Mysticism and pathos are not his dominant qualities. He is not an artist of genius; but a painter of great talent, and solid technique.

See Pl. 59, Vol. I.

BIBLIOGRAPHY: Winkler, F., *Der Meister v. Flémalle u. Roger van der Weyden.* Strassburg, 1913.—M. J. Friedländer, *Die Altniederländische Malerei*, Vol. II., 1924.—Renders E., *La solution du Problème v. d. Weyden, Flémalle, Campin.* Bruges, 1931.

**FLORENCE.**—The prosperity of Florence and its extraordinary ar-

FLORENCE: PALACE OF THE PODESTÀ, CALLED THE BARGELLO.

tistic development date from the end of the middle ages. From the 13th to the 16th centuries, the town became covered with buildings —churches and palaces—built and decorated by the greatest artists of Italy, for an intelligent people, sensitive to all forms of beauty.

The oldest, and one of the most famous buildings in Florence is the *Baptistery*, which dates from the 7th and 8th centuries. It is an octagonal building, surmounted by a dome, decorated with coloured marble, replaced about 1200, and mentioned by Dante in the Purgatorio. The Baptistery is famous for its bronze doors. The oldest were executed between 1330 and 1336, by Andrea Pisano, who represented the Life of St. John, and the eight cardinal virtues. For the second doors, there was a competition in which Ghiberti, Brunelleschi and Jacopo della Quercia competed. Ghiberti carried off the prize, and sculptured twenty scenes of the Life of Christ. Above this doorway is a *Preaching of St. John the Baptist*, by Rustici.

Of the third doors (Ghiberti), Michelangelo said that it was worthy to be the gate of Paradise.

FLORENCE: FAÇADE OF THE CATHEDRAL.

Here are ten Biblical scenes, enframed in superb sculptures.

The interior of the Baptistery contains mosaics, many times restored, the tomb of Pope John XXII, and a wooden statue of the Magdalen, both works by Donatello.

The *Church of the Santi Apostoli* is a Romanesque basilica which, according to an inscription, was founded by Charlemagne. The doorway was decorated by Benedetto da Rovezzano.

FLORENCE: THE BAPTISTERY.

The *Piazza della Signoria* was the centre of the political and economic life of Florence, from the 14th century.

The *Palazzo Vecchio* (Old Palace) was begun in 1298, and finished in 1314, on the plans of Arnolfo di Cambio. The interior was transformed in the 15th century, and the buildings enlarged by Vasari, Buontalenti, etc. It is a severe feudal castle, pierced with some windows, crowned with crenellations, and surmounted by a high square tower (94 metres high). The courtyard of the palace was restored by Michelozzo in 1454, in the Renaissance style. In the middle is a statue of a Child with a Dolphin, by Verrocchio. The interior has magnificent rooms, such as the Hall of the Five Hundred, built by Cronaca, which was to have been decorated by Leonardo da Vinci and Michelangelo, but this decoration was never carried out, and was replaced by frescoes by Vasari, and his pupils. The Hall of the Five Hundred has a fine ceiling, perhaps the original work of Michelozzo.

The *Duomo*, or Santa Maria del Fiore, was begun in 1296 by Arnolfo di Cambio, and continued by Giotto, and by Andrea Pisano. After 1357, the Cathedral was enlarged and the three apses finished. In 1418 the competition for doming the crossing was won by Brunelleschi whose huge and famous octagonal dome, built between 1420 and 1434, now crowns the Cathedral. The lantern was finished more than thirty years later from a model left by Brunelleschi. The façade is modern.

FLORENCE: LOGGIA DEI LANZI.

The Cathedral is a huge hall with aisles nearly as high as the nave, no triforium, oculi in the clerestory, and bare doming vaults springing from piers which already prophesy the Renaissance. The principles of Gothic, as elsewhere in Italy are completely misunderstood, and indeed, even negated.

One of the side doorways was decorated by Piero di Giovanni Tedesco (1395-1399), another door, by Nicola d'Arezzo, in 1408. In the interior are numerous statues by Donatello (St. John the Evangelist) Ghiberti (Shrine of St. Zenobius), Michelangelo (unfinished Pietà), etc. Cartoons for the stained glass were made by Ghiberti, Donatello and Paolo Uccello. The dome is covered with paintings by Vasari (1572) and Zucchero.

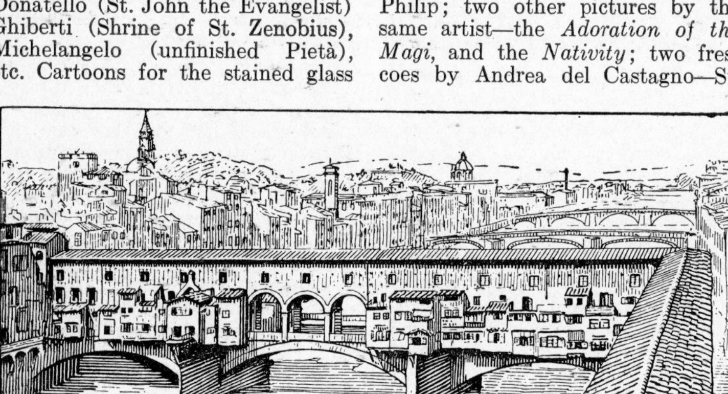

FLORENCE: PONTE VECCHIO.

The *Campanile*, at the side of Santa Maria della Fiore was begun by Giotto in 1334, and continued by Andrea Pisano and F. Talenti (84 metres high). It is richly decorated with coloured marbles and statues by the best artists: St. John the Baptist, the "Zuccone," Jeremiah, Habakkuk, and the Sacrifice of Abraham, by Donatello; prophets, sibyls, and exquisite bas-reliefs, by Andrea Pisano (perhaps conceived by Giotto), and by Luca della Robbia. These bas-reliefs represent the Seven Cardinal Virtues, the Seven Sacraments, the Seven Beatitudes, the Seven Works of Mercy, and the Progress of Civilization through the ages.

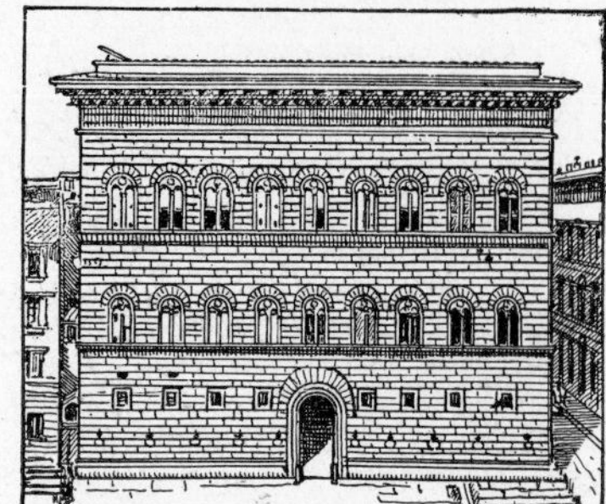

FLORENCE: THE STROZZI PALACE.

The *Museo dell'Opera del Duomo* contains works of art of the Cathedral and Baptistery. The most famous are the singing-galleries, decorated with reliefs, one by Luca della Robbia (with ten groups of children, singing and dancing, 1431-1440), and one by Donatello (with dancing "putti"). Other works include a bas-relief by Agostino di Duccio, an *Annunciation* by Nicola d'Arezzo, and an Execution scene, by Verrocchio.

The *Bargello*, begun in 1255, as the palace of the Podestà, is a powerful freestone building, pierced with narrow windows, crowned with crenellations and surmounted with a tower. It contains an incomparable collection of which the greatest treasures are the bronzes and marbles by the great Florentine artists of the Renaissance. It is the best place in the world to study 15th century Florentine sculpture.

The *Church of the Annunziata*, built in 1250, was enlarged and decorated from 1444 to 1460, by Michelozzo, who was the designer of the porch. The interior contains famous frescoes, painted by Andrea del Sarto, about 1510, representing five scenes from the life of St. Philip; two other pictures by the same artist—the *Adoration of the Magi*, and the *Nativity*; two frescoes by Andrea del Castagno—St. Julian praying, and St. Jerome; and Baldovinetti's ruined Nativity; and, in the cloisters, a fine fresco by Andrea del Sarto—the *Madonna del Saco*.

*Santa Maria Novella,* begun in 1278, was finished after 1350 by Talenti. The façade is early Renaissance and was executed in 1456 after the designs of L. B. Alberti. Here Alberti united the nave and side aisles, as expressed on the façade, with consoles. This treatment had a great influence on Manneristic and Baroque churches in Rome in the late 16th and 17th centuries notably on the Church of the Gesù by Vignola and Della Porta. The interior is similar to that of the Cathedral of Florence. The church contains many artistic treasures: a fresco by Masaccio, representing the Trinity; The Rucellai Madonna; frescoes by Filippino Lippi, painted in 1502 (*St. John the Evangelist Raising Drusana,* etc.); famous frescoes by Ghirlandaio and School, 1490, representing scenes from the life of the Virgin, scenes from the life of St. John the Baptist, and the Coronation of the Virgin; the Crucifix, in wood, made by Brunelleschi, in a competition with Donatello; frescoes in the Strozzi Chapel, the *Last Judgment, Paradise* and *Hell,* Nardo di Cione. In the cloisters are frescoes, by Paolo Uccello, in a very bad state of preservation. The Chapter House, known as the Spanish Chapel, built in 1355, is decorated with frescoes by Andrea da Firenze.

The Church of the *Badia* was built in 1285, perhaps by Arnolfo di Cambio, and was remodelled in the early 15th century by Brunelleschi.

The *Convent of San Marco,* dating from the 13th century, was transformed from 1437 to 1443 by Michelozzo, and decorated with exquisite frescoes by Fra Angelico. The corridors and cells have quantities of paintings, among the most famous being a large *Crucifixion,* a *Coronation of the Virgin,* and an *Annunciation.* Fra Bartolommeo, who lived in the convent, also painted some fine frescoes there and a portrait of Savonarola, who preached and stayed in the convent. The Church of San Marco, built in 1290, has been restored many times.

*Santa Croce* is perhaps the richest of the Florentine churches and the least Gothic of Gothic churches. Begun in 1294 by Arnolfo di Cambio, its façade was only added in 1857. The interior (117 metres long) is decorated with magnificent frescoes. The Peruzzi Chapel has frescoes by Giotto, representing scenes from the lives of St. John the Baptist and St. John the Evangelist; and the Bardi Chapel also has famous frescoes by Giotto, representing scenes from the life of St. Francis of Assisi (see Giotto). The choir has mural paintings by Agnolo Gaddi—the *Discovery of the Holy Cross,* saints and evangelists (see Gaddi). In the Castellani Chapel, too, are frescoes by Agnolo Gaddi, in a bad state of preservation, showing incidents from the lives of St. Nicholas, St. John the Baptist, St. John the Evangelist, and St. Anthony. The Baroncelli Chapel has remarkable frescoes by Taddeo Gaddi, scenes from the Life of the Virgin. In the Pulci-Berardi Chapel are frescoes of the martyrdom of SS. Stephen and Laurence by Bernardo Daddi; and in the Bardi di Vernio Chapel frescoes of the story of Pope Sylvester and the Emperor Constantine by Maso di Banco. In the nave of the church is Domenico Veneziano's famous fresco of SS. Francis and John the Baptist.

Santa Croce is equally rich in sculpture. There is a famous marble pulpit, by Benedetto da Majano, with five very fine bas-reliefs and charming statuettes (see Majano); the Annunciation, by Donatello; the tomb of Leonardo Bruni, by Rossellino; a marble tabernacle, by Mino da Fiesole (Medici Chapel); a Crucifix in wood, executed by Donatello in a competition with Brunelleschi (whose Crucifix is in Santa Maria Novella); the superb tomb of Marsuppini, by Desiderio da Settignano; the tomb of Galileo, by Foggini; and the tomb of Michelangelo, executed in 1570, from Vasari's design. The cloisters of Santa Croce, built by Arnolfo di Cambio, have modern tombs.

*Or San Michele* (1336-1412) is both a church (ground-floor), and a lecture hall (first floor). Each guild placed a statue of its patron on the exterior. These include *St. Luke,* by Gian da Bolonga; *St. John the Baptist,* by Ghiberti; *St. Mark,* by Donatello; *St. Stephen,* by Ghiberti; *St. Matthew,* by Ghiberti and Michelozzo; a copy of the famous *St. George,* by Donatello; *Christ and St. Thomas,* by Verrocchio, etc. The church contains a remarkable marble tabernacle by Orcagna.

*The Bigallo* (home for foundlings) is an elegant Gothic construction, 1352-1358, built for the "Capitain di Santa Maria." It contains a *Virgin,* by Alberto di Arnoldo (1361), and a triptych by Bernardo Daddi.

The *Ponte Vecchio* was built about the same time. It has had rows of jewelry shops, since the 14th century, and the gallery which unites the Uffizzi to the Pitti Palace passes over it.

On one side of the Piazza della Signoria is the famous *Loggia dei Lanzi,* completed by 1382. This is a vaulted porch, with large semi-circular arcades. The Loggia was executed by Benci di Ciore and Talenti, with sculptural decoration by G. d' Ambrogio and J. di Piero. There are several celebrated sculptures under this loggia, including the *Rape of the Sabines,* by Gian da Bologna (1583); *Perseus,* Benvenuto Cellini's masterpiece (1553), and *Judith and Holophernes,* by Donatello (about 1440).

The *Spedale degli Innocenti* (Foundling Hospital) was begun by Brunelleschi in 1419, and finished in 1451, by F. della Luna. The arcaded façade is decorated with charming medallions of children in enamelled terra cotta, by Andrea della Robbia (see Robbia). The interior contains a *Virgin* in bas-relief by Luca della Robbia, and an *Adoration of the Magi* by Ghirlandaio.

The *Palazzo Riccardi,* formerly the *Palazzo Medici* is one of the many magnificent quattrocento Florentine palaces. It was built by Michelozzo about 1440. The apartments centers about the arcaded court. On the exterior the palace is grim and fortress-like, a quality characteristic of the Florentine palace. The only decoration consists of the fenestration of the piled-up three storeys, the magnificent great cornice proportioned to the whole building, and the rustication of the masonry. The rustication is very heavy on the ground storey; on the second storey the rustication is less heavy, consisting merely of the drafting of the joints; the top storey is in ashlar masonry. The same progression occurs in the size of the stones, from large at the bottom to small at top.

Michelangelo filled in the ground storey openings with tabernacle windows in the fourth decade of the 16th century. The palace was enlarged in the 18th. The Chapel is decorated with frescoes, painted by Benozzo Gozzoli from 1459 to 1463. They represent the journey of the three kings, and include a great many portraits of the Medici family. Near the windows are paintings of angels in the Earthly Paradise. The large banqueting hall has a ceiling decorated by Luca Giordano.

See Pl. 1, Vol. I.

The *Pitti Palace* was begun 1435. A rich Florentine citizen, Luca Pitti, desirous of surpassing the magnificence of his enemies the Medici, erected this powerful building, by Luca Fancelli, from plans by Brunelleschi. He was unable to complete the work which was not finished until 1549 for Cosimo dei Medici, the owner of the palace. The whole has an effect of grandeur and robustness, with its enormous blocks of hewn stone. In the 17th century, the architect Parigi built the two parts which lengthen the façade (205 metres). The two wings are of the 18th century. The Pitti Palace contains a magnificent gallery of paintings collected by the Medici. Round the palace stretch the Boboli Gardens, designed in 1550 for Cosimo de' Medici, by Tribolo, then by Buontalenti and Gian da Bologna.

The *Palazzo Quaratesi,* formerly Palazzo Pozzi, was begun about 1445, it is said by Brunelleschi. Finished 1462 to 1470, by G. da Majano.

The *Palazzo Rucellai* was designed by L. B. Alberti. It is noteworthy for the application of superimposed orders to the traditionally astylar exterior of the Florentine palace, a treatment indicative of the strength of Alberti's classicism.

The *Palazzo Strozzi* is the finest of the Florentine palaces. Its façade is composed of three storeys separated by stone string-courses, and is built in naïvely rusticated large blocks of stone. The building is crowned with a magnificent cornice, the work of Cronaca, who continued this palace which was begun in 1489 by Giuliano da San Gallo, for the famous Strozzi family.

During the same period, several churches were being built in Florence. *Santa Maria del Carmine,* built at the beginning of the 15th century, was largely destroyed by fire and rebuilt in 1782. The *Brancacci Chapel* of the old church was saved. This is decorated with remarkable frescoes by Masaccio, Masolino and Filippino Lippi (see these names), mainly representing scenes from the life of St. Peter.

*San Lorenzo,* built in the 11th century, was enlarged and rebuilt after 1425, according to the plans of Brunelleschi. It is in the form of the ancient basilicas, with three naves, and a ceiling instead of a vault. There is a dome over the crossing. A very fine annunciation by Fra Filippo Lippi is in the Martelli Chapel. The old sacristy, built by Brunelleschi, from 1421 to 1428, in the Renaissance style, with a dome, is decorated with carvings by Donatello. It contains the tomb of Piero dei Medici by Verocchio. But the glory of San Lorenzo is the new sacristy, built from 1521-1534, by Michelangelo. The Cardinal Giulio dei Medici (who became Pope Clement VII in 1523) designed it to be the mausoleum of his family. The architecture is very simple: a square building surmounted by a dome. Of all the tombs and sculptures foreseen in the plans, Michelangelo only executed those of Giulianno and Lorenzo dei Medici, works which are among his masterpieces.

The Library of San Lorenzo, which communicates with the Church, was begun about 1523, from designs by Michelangelo, to shelter the Greek and Latin manuscripts gathered together by the Medici. Michelangelo designed the ceiling, the desks, and the staircase.

*Santo Spirito,* begun about 1436, from plans by Brunelleschi, was finished in 1482. It has a fine campanile, the work of Baccio d'Agnolo. The sacristy, built by Cronaca, and, probably, by Giuliana da Sangallo, shelters a *Virgin with Saints* by Filippino Lippi, and a *Virgin* by Donatello.

The *Pazzi Chapel,* built in 1429, by Brunelleschi, is decorated with a charming frieze of angels' heads by Donatello and Desiderio da Settignano. The interior in the form of a Greek cross surmounted by a surbased dome, is decorated with sculptures by Luca della Robbia, representing the Evangelists and Apostles.

The *Cenacolo di Foligno* is decorated with a vast fresco of the *Last Supper,* by Perugino. The *Cenacolo di Sant' Appollonia* encloses frescoes by Andrea del Castagno, including his superb Last Supper.

The cloisters of the *Scalzo,* a pleasing Renaissance construction possesses remarkable frescoes in brown cameo, by Andrea del Sarto and Franciabigio, representing scenes from the life of St. John the Baptist and allegorical figures.

The *Ognissanti,* built in 1554, and rebuilt in 1627, has frescoes by Ghirlandaio and Botticelli. The refectory contains a fine *Last Supper* by Ghirlandaio.

The *Uffizi Palace* was built from 1560 to 1574, by Vasari. It possesses a fine portico of arcades (modern statues), and houses one of the richest picture galleries in the world.

The *Casa Buonarotti* contains a collection of Michelangelo's sketches and drawings.

The *Corsini Palace* has a rich picture gallery.

After the 16th century, the artistic prosperity of Florence declined. The Popes called her best artists to Rome.

See Pl. 5, Vol. II.

**FLORENTINE PRIMITIVES.** —See Pl. 12, Vol. II.

**— SCULPTURE.**—See Pl. 9, Vol. II.

**FLÖTNER (Peter).**—German artist of the Nüremberg school (1485-1546). He was sculptor, architect and decorator. He is responsible for the fountain in the market-place of Mayence (1526), the decoration of the Tucher House and of the Hirschvogel House (Nüremberg, 1533 and 1534), a statuette of Adam (Vienna), medal portraits and statuettes of allegorical subjects.

BIBLIOGRAPHY: Lange, K., *Peter Flötner, ein Bahnbrecher der deutschen Renaissance.* Berlin, 1897.

**FLYING BUTTRESS.**—In Gothic Churches, the pressure of the rib-vaulting is localised. So much force is exerted that builders of the Gothic period contrived to counterbalance this outward thrust by means of exterior props of diverse forms. These spring from an ordinary buttress to meet the distant bearing-surface, and are designed to check the line of thrust of the vault. These supports are called "flying-buttresses."

**FOGOLINO (Marcello).**—Venetian painter (records between 1510 and 1548); influenced by Bartolommeo Montagna and Pordenone. Worked at Vicenza in the Friuli and at Trent.

**FONTAINE (Pierre François Léonard).**—French architect (1762-1853). In 1785 he went to study in Rome. His stay there strongly influenced his development. In 1786 he was joined by his friend Percier who had won the Prix de Rome. Fontaine returned to Paris first,

FLYING BUTTRESS.

and in 1790 Percier went to live with him in the Rue Montmartre. The cabinet-maker, Jacob, asked the two young architects to design the furniture for the Convention. Percier and Fontaine tried to return to the antique style. Their attempt was so successful that they soon accepted commissions from goldsmiths, jewellers, and carpet makers. This kind of work pleased

FONTAINE AND PERCIER: ARC DE TRIOMPHE DU CARROUSEL. (Paris.)

Percier, but Fontaine, who was more inclined to architecture, wanted to try his fortune in London. On his return, in 1793, he became, with Percier, director of the decorations of the Opera.

Their work of restoration and embellishment of Saint Cloud and Malmaison won them the favour of the First Consul. The first sign of Napoleon's approval was their nomination as architects of the Tuileries of the Louvre. Unfortunately, the restorations of the Imperial Palace absorbed so much time and money, that nothing remained for the original works.

The masterpiece of Percier and Fontaine is the Arc de Triomphe du Carrousel, which they built during the Imperial period, which was inspired by the arches of Constantine and Septimius Severus.

Percier died in 1838. Fontaine survived him fifteen years.

BIBLIOGRAPHY: F. Halévy, *Souvenirs et portraits.* Paris, 1861.—Maurice Fouché, *Percier et Fontaine.* Paris.

**FONTAINE.**—See Swebach-Desfontaine.

**FONTAINEBLEAU (Château of).**—This château is associated with the name of Francis I, who gave it its present appearance. But long after him the kings of France delighted to stay in this charming spot, on the edge of the beautiful forest. The oldest document we possess concerning this château is a charter of Louis VII, dated from 1169, which proves that the kings of France had already lived in this place. The oldest part is the Oval Court, around which were the residential quarters. Of it there remains the large tower, which contains the "room of St. Louis." About 1527 the buildings were in a very bad state, and Francis I decided they must be demolished, with the exception of some towers, and entrusted the plan of the new château to Gilles Le Breton. The building was begun in 1528, under Gilles Le Breton, who built the façade of the White Horse Court (which received this name from the cast of the horse of the statue of Marcus Aurelius, in Rome, and which was later called the Cour des Adieux in remembrance of Napoleon I), the gallery of Francis I, the gallery of Henry II, the new Chapel St. Saturnin, and the peristyle of the Oval Court. The remainder of the buildings were finished by Pierre Chambiges and Pierre Girard, called Castoret, but it is difficult to know exactly what is due to each.

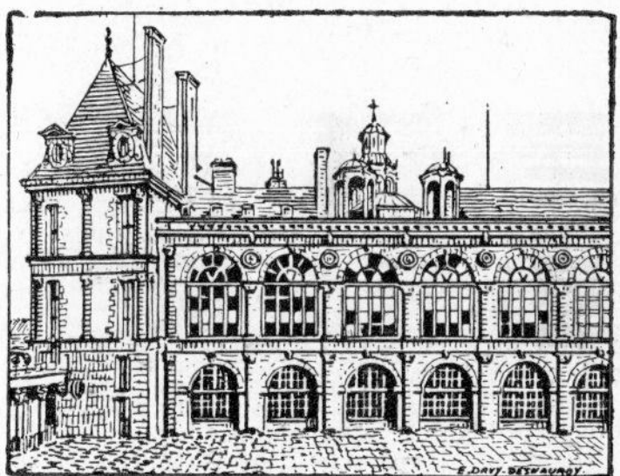

FONTAINEBLEAU (PALACE OF): SECTION FACING THE OVAL COURT.

Francis, who was content with a simple exterior, had the apartments sumptuously decorated in the Italian style. The decoration was entrusted to two Italian artists, Rosso, of Florence and Primaticcio, of Bologna. Rosso went to France in 1531, and worked there until his death ten years later. He executed the decoration, stucco and painting, in the Francis I gallery. The paintings form a series of thirteen pictures, of allegorical and mythological subjects. The stuccos which enframe them are better preserved, and show great richness of invention. The whole is magnificent. Rosso was naturally not able to execute all this decoration himself. Like Primaticcio, he employed numerous painters. Primaticcio worked at Fontainebleau from 1533 to 1570. On the death of Rosso, he took over the decoration of the work. Most of his pictures have disappeared, and those which remain have been retouched.

Francis I also employed Benvenuto Cellini, the famous goldsmith. He collected rare manuscripts and works, and pictures by the most famous Italian masters. He bought *Mona Lisa* by Leonardo, *St. Michael* and *St. Margaret* by Raphael, *Charity* by Andrea del Sarto, etc.

This magnificent palace was not neglected by Francis's successors. Henry II realised a scheme of his predecessors, by having a ball-room built, by Philibert de l'Orme, who was the author of the entrance doorway and the celebrated chimney.

Needless to say, the greatest attention was paid to the designing of gardens and to the decorating of them with statues.

Fontainebleau was then neglected for a time, until Henry IV restored it. From his reign date the Cour des Offices, and some pavilions; also the door of the Baptistery in the Oval Court. Martin Fréminet decorated the Chapel, and the gardens were adorned by the brothers Francine, who built fountains and canals.

FONTAINEBLEAU (PALACE OF): THE COUR DES ADIEUX, AND THE STAIRCASE IN THE SHAPE OF A HORSESHOE.

FONTAINEBLEAU: ARMCHAIR DESIGNED BY DAVID. (Throne room.)

After Henry IV, the kings continued to inhabit Fontainebleau from time to time, and to adorn the rooms and gardens. A whole school of painting kept up the tradition of the school of Fontainebleau. But, generally speaking, after the time of Louis XIV, who preferred Versailles, Fontainebleau ceased to be the principal residence of the Court when it left Paris.

Under Napoleon it recaptured its old splendour. The Cour du Cheval Blanc was enlarged and became the court of honour. On the groundfloor are the Emperor's bed-room, the library, and the apartments of Josephine. Later, in 1810, Napoleon inhabited the first floor, where is the "Cabinet d'Abdication" with the table on which (according to King Louis-Philippe) he signed the act of abdication.

After the fall of the Empire, the palace was restored.

See Pls. 27, 44, Vol. II.

BIBLIOGRAPHY: Ducerceau, *Les plus excellents bâtiments de France.* —Palustre and Molinier, *Les architects de Fontainebleau.*—Penor and Champollion-Figeac, *Monographie du palais de Fontainebleau.*—L. Dimier, *Fontainebleau.*

— **(School of).**—When Francis I had decided to make Fontainebleau his favourite residence and to build there a palace worthy of royalty, he summoned numerous artists. France provided good architects, Gilles Le Breton and Pierre Chambiges, but she had no painters capable of producing vast decorations, and so Francis had to send for Italian artists. Leonardo da Vinci came, but only to die in France. It was Rosso and Primaticcio who founded the school of Fontainebleau. They imported the Italian style of painting, the art of painting large fresco figures in architectural decorations, such as stucco columns and bas-reliefs. A host of painters, mostly Italian, worked under these two masters, but most of their paintings have disappeared. Those which remain have been so badly restored that it is difficult to find the original touch of the artist. Rosso painted vigorous bodies in studied compositions. Primaticcio painted with more charm and grace. French painters of the time did not show much aptitude for this kind of decoration, and the example of the great Italian painters was not followed for a long time. It was less a school than a colony of painters that they founded. Fontainebleau was, however, the place where young French and Flemish artists went to study the new methods of decorative painting, and to copy Rosso and Primaticcio.

See Pl. 55, Vol. II.

BIBLIOGRAPHY: L. Dimier, *French Painting in the Sixteenth Century.* London, 1904.

**FONTAINE DES INNOCENTS.**—See Paris.

**FONTANA (Domenico).**—Italian architect, 1543-1607. At the age of twenty he went to Rome where he was soon noticed by Cardinal Montalto for whom he executed a Chapel in Santa Maria Maggiore, and a little palace. On becoming Pope, under the name of Sixtus V, the cardinal gave his protégé the title of pontifical architect, and charged him with setting up in the Piazza of St. Peter's the great obelisk which had been brought from Egypt by Caligula. The difficulties of the work and the enthusiasm with which Fontana's success was greeted may be read about in contemporary chronicles. He had to accomplish this kind of work several times, for the obelisk of Santa Maria Maggiore, of San Giovanni Laterano, and for the one near the Porta del Popolo; also for the transport of the statues of Castor and Pollux, of the Therme of Diocletian, and of statues of St. Peter and St. Paul on two columns. He built the Vatican Library, and the aqueduct of Aqua Felice. On the death of his patron, Fontana lost all credit at the pontifical court, and was even accused by envious rivals of having embezzled money intended for his works. He left Rome, and, in Naples, became architect to the King of the two Sicilies. He there built the royal palace (re-built since), and carried out various ingenious works. He wrote a book: *Del modo tenuto nel trasportare l'obelisco Vaticano,* and *Delle fabriche fatte da N. S. Papa Sixto V.* (Rome, 1589.)

FONTANA (DOMENICO): THE ROYAL PALACE AT NAPLES.

— **(Lavinia).**—Woman painter, 1552-1602. Daughter of Prospero Fontana.

— **(Prospero).**—Bolognese painter, 1512-1597. Pupil of Francucci da Imola. Imitator of Raphael. He went to France to help Primaticcio at Fontainebleau. He worked in Genoa, and in Rome. His chief work is a *Baptism of Christ* (1566), for the Poggi Chapel, in San Giacomo Maggiore. He was the master of the Carracci.

**FONTEVRAULT (Maine-et-Loire).**—A little town which dates from the creation of the celebrated Abbey, founded by Robert d'Arbrissel in 1099. The church (1101 to 1119) is in the Romanesque style and has been many times restored. It was surmounted by domes of which only one still exists. This church, which was formerly in the domains of the Plantagenets, enclosed their tombs with their statues. The tombs have been destroyed. Of the statues there remain those of Henry II and his wife Eleanor, of Richard Cœur de Lion and Isabella of Angoulême. The Abbey possesses a fine Romanesque cloister, and an interesting kitchen.

FONTEVRAULT: THE ABBEY.

BIBLIOGRAPHY: Courajod, *Sépultures des Plantagenets à Fontevrault.*

**FOPPA (Cristoforo).**—See Caradosso.

**FOPPA (Vincenzo).**—Born in or near Brescia, between 1427 and 1430; died 1515-16 in Brescia. Founder of the Lombard school of the 15th century; influenced by the Paduan and Venetian schools.

Foppa's earliest dated picture is of 1456, the *Crucifixion* in the Carrara Gallery, Bergamo. In this same year he is mentioned in Brescia as the father of a family and is recorded as moving to Pavia. In 1467 he bought a house in Pavia and received the citizenship of that city at the request of Galeazzo Maria Sforza. However the next year he is again referred to in Brescia, as a householder. In 1481 he was a citizen of Milan, where he enjoyed a close relationship with the ducal house through the reigns of Francesco and Galeazzo Maria Sforza. During these years Foppa had been intermittently active in Genoa, which he visited for the first time in 1461, to execute frescoes in the Cappella di San Giovanni Battista of the Duomo. Having left this work unfinished he returned to Genoa in 1471, 1477, 1478, 1481, 1487-90. In 1489 he was temporarily imprisoned there. (The Genoa frescoes no longer exist.) Foppa was generally active in Pavia, Milan, Brescia and Bergamo. He kept his dwelling in Pavia until 1490, then returned to Brescia where he received for five years an annual pension.

Style criticism of Foppa's painting is dependent upon his signed works which include the Crucifixion mentioned above; a *St. Jerome* in the Carrara Gallery in Bergamo; a *Pietà* in Berlin; a polyptych with Giuliano della Rovere as Donor, of 1490, in S. Maria di Castello, Savona. A fresco now in the Brera, Milan, a *Madonna with the Baptist and Evangelist,* is dated 1485; and the Savona altarpiece with Manfredo Fornari is dated 1489.

BIBLIOGRAPHY: Toesca, *La pitt. e miniat. nella Lombardia.*—Berenson, *North Italian Painters,* 1907.—C. Jocelyn Ffoulkes and R. Maiocchi, *Vincenzo Foppa of Brescia.* London and New York, 1909 (with bibliography and documents).

**FORAIN (Jean-Louis).**—French etcher and lithographer (1852-1931). He was born in Reims 23d October 1852, the son of a house painter. He started copying the work of the old masters in the museums and at the age of fifteen became the pupil of Jacquesson de la Chevreuse, a painter of historical scenes. In 1867 he entered the École des Beaux-Arts, but remained there only a short time because he disliked the academic method of instruction. At that time he entered the atelier of Carpeaux, the sculptor, learning the technique of modelling and doing further drawings of the figure. His evenings were spent in the Print Room of the Bibliothèque Nationale, copying the prints of Holbein, Rembrandt and Goya. He made drawings after bits of life that he observed on the streets of Paris and also did some paintings of still life and flowers, but soon turned his interest to etchings and watercolours. In 1879 he exhibited his watercolours in the fourth exhibition of the Impressionists along with the work of Cassatt, Degas, Monet and Pissarro, and again the next year he showed his pictures with that group. He made drawings for many magazines, including the *Scapin,* the *Cravache, Parisien, Chat Noir, Vie Moderne* and later his sketches were a regular feature in the *Courrier Français, Figaro, Echo de Paris, New York Herald, Vie Parisienne* and many other publications. In 1889 he published his own illustrated journal *Fifre* and in 1898 he tried another magazine called *Psst!* His first interest was in the portrayal of popular actresses and entertainers, but later he turned his talents to the political cartoons. In 1908 he made a series of studies dealing with Biblical subjects, in which his pictorial method changed from the cruel biting lines of satire to a more suave treatment of the human figure bathed in light instead of the dark shadows of his early work. His work was done from memory and always there was a touch of melancholy and sadness even in the gayest compositions. His lithographs showed a fine command of chiaroscuro giving ef-

# ROMANESQUE ARCHITECTURE OUTSIDE OF FRANCE

*ALTHOUGH it was in close harmony with the Byzantine civilisation which was then at the peak of its glory, Romanesque art remained the heir of Roman art. It flourished wherever Roman culture had spread, with the exception of the territories which had surrendered to Islam. There were Romanesque schools as far as the Rhenish frontier, in England, in Italy and in Spain. One of the characteristics of this art is that it displayed regional and national features at the time when they were beginning to develop. There is in the Romanesque epoch no artistic style as well defined as in the Gothic era.*

TOURNAI: CATHEDRAL.
*(Photo by Nels.)*

AIX-LA-CHAPELLE: CHAPEL OF THE PALACE.
*(Photo by Busch.)*

COLOGNE: ST. GEREON.

## Northern Schools

ROMANESQUE art is by nature more southern, because it expresses the civilisation of the high Middle Ages which is of Roman and oriental origin. But it followed the monastic civilisation in its conquests; the Rhine was Romanesque because of the military occupation at the time of the Roman empire. Aix-la-Chapelle, the city of Charlemagne, before the Romanesque era benefited by its importance as his capital; the emperor built there an edifice in imitation of Byzantine architecture in which some ancient columns were used rather clumsily.

MILAN: ST. AMBROSE.
*(Photo by Brogi.)*

PARMA: CATHEDRAL.
*(Photo by Alinari.)*

FLORENCE: SAN MINIATO.
*(Photo by Brogi.)*

PISA: BAPTISTERY AND CATHEDRAL.
*(Photo by Brogi.)*

## Italy

IN ITALY, Romanesque art has not the charm of an art in an early phase of development. It simply continues the architecture of the Latin basilicas. Italian Romanesque churches, if they were finished before the Gothic epoch, are covered by ceilings and timberwork. The vault which characterises French Romanesque art is lacking. Marble decoration often gives to Italian architecture an original character.

LEÓN: CATHEDRAL.
*(Photo by Dieulafoy.)*

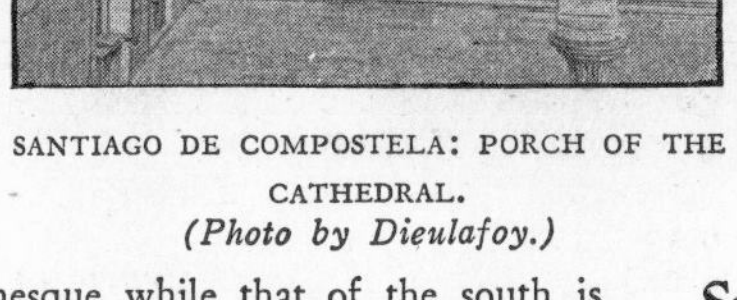

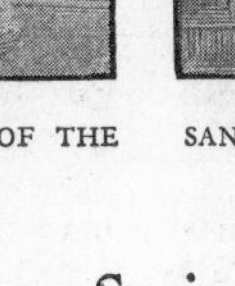

SANTIAGO DE COMPOSTELA: PORCH OF THE CATHEDRAL.
*(Photo by Dieulafoy.)*

SANTIAGO DE COMPOSTELA: NAVE OF THE CATHEDRAL.
*(Photo by Dieulafoy.)*

ZAMORA: PORCH OF THE CATHEDRAL.
*(Photo by Dieulafoy.)*

## Spain

THE art of northern Spain is Romanesque while that of the south is Moslem. The churches extend as far as Avila and the mosques as far as Toledo. These two architectures express in stone monuments the battle between Christianity and Islam: the poem of the Chanson de Roland transferred into stone. These Romanesque churches seem to have come from France. We recognise the influence of Cluny, of Toulouse and the schools of the southwest. The pilgrims of St. James went from Tours to Compostela spreading the germs of their national architecture along the route.

# ROMANESQUE SCULPTURE

*R*OMANESQUE *sculpture was preceded by many centuries without any sculpture. Sculpture was considered as allied to a religion of false gods, and up until the end of the eleventh century, Christian iconography had only painted figures, greatly influenced by Byzantine models. At first the Romanesque sculptors tried to put into relief these old flat figures. The work showed the ingenuity of a developing art and the senility of ancient models; it also showed an effort to reanimate the subjects of the reliefs.*

SOUILLAC: PROPHET.
*(Photo by Hachette.)*

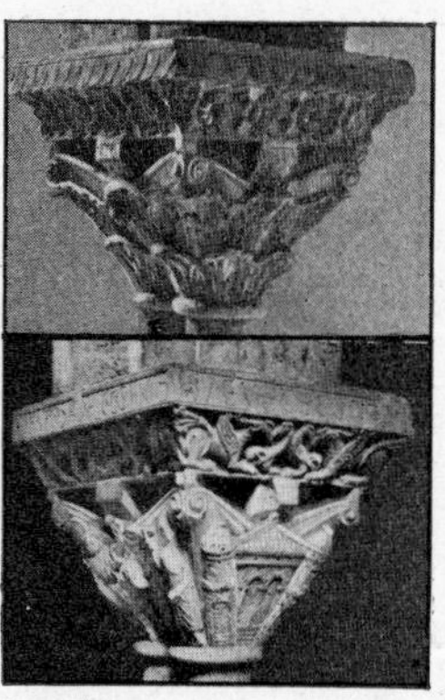

MOISSAC: CAPITAL.
*(Photo by Hachette.)*

VÉZELAY: TYMPANUM. CHRIST AND THE APOSTLES.
*(Photo by Brisdoux.)*

VÉZELAY: CAPITAL.
*(Photo by Neurdein.)*

TOULOUSE: ZODIAC.
*(Photo by Hachette.)*

ROMANESQUE sculpture was exclusively a sculpture of bas-reliefs; the bas-relief is a transition between painting and statuary. These bas-reliefs answer two necessities; they act as decoration to enrich the architecture; and they represent sacred figures and so act as instruction. We easily recognise the models that inspired their creators. Those in Provence and at Toulouse, copied the monuments of ancient statuary; others at Vézelay and Autun seem to have translated into bas-reliefs Byzantine miniatures; sometimes monsters carved in the stone seem to come from a barbarian imagination.

MOISSAC: TYMPANUM. CHRIST IN GLORY.
*(Photo by Hachette.)*

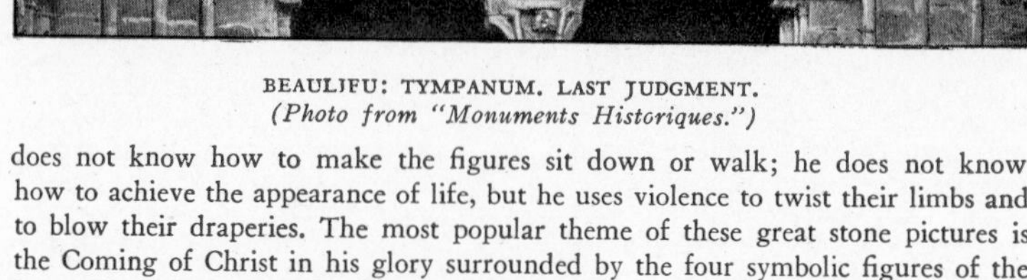

BEAULIFU: TYMPANUM. LAST JUDGMENT.
*(Photo from "Monuments Historiques.")*

IT IS on the capitals, the voussoirs, and especially in the tympanums of the porches that the sculptural decoration of the Romanesque period is to be found. These tympanums, of Vézelay and Autun in Burgundy, of Moissac, Beaulieu and Conques in Languedoc, are magnificent works despite their barbaric character. The sculptor is struggling against the rigidity of the forms; he does not know how to make the figures sit down or walk; he does not know how to achieve the appearance of life, but he uses violence to twist their limbs and to blow their draperies. The most popular theme of these great stone pictures is the Coming of Christ in his glory surrounded by the four symbolic figures of the Evangelist inspired by the book of Revelation.

ARLES: APOSTLE.
*(Photo by Neurdein.)*

CHARTRES: ROYAL PORTAL.
*(Photo by Gallas.)*

ARLES: ST. TROPHIME.
*(Photo by Neurdein.)*

THE Royal Portal of the cathedral of Chartres is one of the most beautiful works of art in the world. There the Romanesque bas-relief becomes statuary; the figures are separate from the wall; they are restrained to the lines of the architecture but they have an independent existence. This porch marks a unique moment in the history of plastic art: the moment when statuary is already in possession of the forms of life, yet remains closely associated with the architecture from which it is disengaging itself. After this the statues gain more liberty; soon they will become free and independent of architecture.

fects of depth and atmosphere which could not be obtained in his etchings. After the war Forain went into retirement and returned again to his paintings, but his technique as an engraver coloured his work and gave an element of sharpness to his compositions. He died in Paris 11th July 1931, the most eminent etcher of his generation, best remembered for his political satires and his commentaries of human life exposing the ironies of circumstance and the tyrannies of present-day conventions and methods of jurisprudence. He was a member of the Académie des Beaux-Arts and president of the Société des Dessinateurs Humoristes.

Bibliography: Marcel Guerin, *Jean-Louis Forain, Catalogue Raisonné de l'Œuvre Gravé de l'Artiste*, 1912, 2 Vols.—Charles Kunstler, *Forain*, 1931.—Malcolm C. Salaman, *J. L. Forain*, 1925.

**FORTUNY (Mariano).**—Spanish painter, 1838-1874. He devoted himself to anecdotal representation, which he carried out with a sense of the picturesque which won him his reputation.

**FORUM (of Rome).**—The Roman forum, which was the centre of the life of ancient Rome, occupies the valley which extends between the Capitol and the Palatine. It was certainly not here that the earliest inhabitants of Rome assembled, for the water which came down from the neighbouring hills made it marshy. The Etruscans, who settled in this valley, undertook the work of draining it. They constructed a canal which carried the marshy water to the Tiber. This canal was the "Cloaca Maxima," which had a barrel vault (several times restored under Augustus and Agrippa) and the mouth of which can still be seen in the Tiber. From the same period dates the Tullianum, a subterranean prison, composed of two superimposed rooms.

Rome: The Tiber and the Cloaca Maxima.

The Forum was then used as the market place. Another small square, the Comitium, was the meeting place and was used for audiences of justice. Soon the Romans began to erect civil and religious buildings. The forum became the centre of the life of the town. It served the most various uses: meetings of the people, funeral ceremonies of patricians, contests of gladiators, and triumphs of victorious generals who passed by the Via Sacra on their way to the Capitol. Cato, Cæsar and Augustus enlarged and adorned it, and throughout antiquity it was covered with the most splendid buildings. In the Middle Ages many buildings were transformed into Churches or destroyed; and for centuries marbles, bronzes and columns were taken from the forum for the construction of the palaces or fortresses that the nobles built on the Palatine. In the 12th century, it was a confusion of rubbish. In the 15th century gardens covered the ruins. At the time of the Renaissance, in the 16th century, excavations were made for the recovery of antique statues, but the most important work, which laid bare the remains of old buildings, dates from the 19th century.

The buildings discovered on the forum were erected at various periods between the 6th century B.C. and the 7th century of our era. Perhaps the oldest is the so-called tomb of Romulus, which one enters by descending a stairway.

Among the most famous buildings are:—

*The Temple of Vesta.*—This circular temple is surrounded by columns, and the remains of an entablature. The existing architectural fragments date from its final restoration by Julia Domna, the consort of Septimius Severus (3rd century, A.D.).

The *Atrium of Vesta*, or the Palace of the Vestals, dates from about the first century of our era.

Of the *Temple of Saturn*, eight columns still stand on their high base. It was dedicated in 497 B.C., and housed the public treasure.

The *Temple of Castor and Pollux* was dedicated to these gods c. 484, B.C. (according to tradition) in recognition of the succour they had given to the Roman armies in the battle of Lake Regillus, against the Latins. Only the foundations, a part of the entablature, and three fine marble columns, with Corinthian capitals, remain. These fragments date mostly from the Augustan period.

Triumphal arch of Septimius Severus. (Forum.)

The *Temple of Concord*, consecrated, according to tradition, in 367 B.C., was built to celebrate the end of the wars between the plebeians and patricians. It was rebuilt and transformed by Tiberius in 7 B.C.

The *Basilica Julia* was probably begun in 54 B.C., was rebuilt and enlarged by Augustus, burned in the 3rd century, and restored in the 5th century. The present brick pillars replace the old ones which were used in the fifteenth century, in the building of the Giraud Palace.

The *Triumphal Arch of Septimius Severus* was built in 203 A.D. in honour of the Emperor's victories against the Arabs.

The *Church of Santa Maria Antiqua* was built in the 5th century inside a building that was perhaps the library of the Temple of Augustus.

The *Column of Phocas*, built in 608 A.D., in honour of Phocas, is the last ancient monument in the forum. Only the base dates from the 7th century. The column belonged to an earlier building.

In the middle of all these buildings runs the Sacred Way, which formerly passed under the arches of triumph, between rows of statues and buildings, and led to the Temple of Jupiter on the Capitol.

See Pl. 29, Vol. I.

Bibliography: Hoffbauer and Thédenat, *Le Forum romain et la Voie sacrée. Aspects successifs des Monuments depuis le IVe siècle jusqu'à nos jours.* Paris, 1905.—C. Hülsen, *Le Forum romain, son histoire et ses monuments.* French translation by J. Carcopino. Rome, 1906.—H. Thédenat, *Le Forum romain et les Forums impériaux.* Paris.—L. Homo, *La Rome antique.* —Platner and Ashby, *A Topographical Dictionary of Ancient Rome.* London, 1929.

**— (of Trajan).**—See Rome; also Pl. 29, Vol. I.

**FOSTER (Myles Birket).**—English painter (1825-1899), one of the most celebrated English water colour painters of his time; elected in 1860 Associate and in 1862 Member of the Old Water Colour Society.

Bibliography: H. M. Cundall, *Birket Foster.* London, 1906.

**FOUQUET (Jehan).**—French painter, of Tours, about 1416- about 1480. Little is known of his life. He early became an able portrait painter, and travelled in Italy, for about 1445 he painted the portrait of Pope Eugène IV (disappeared). On his return to France, he was patronised by Etienne Chevalier, treasurer of Charles VII and then of Louis XI, for whom he worked a great deal. Fouquet, one of the greatest of the French primitives, was completely forgotten for two centuries after his death, and has only lately been given the place he deserves. His oldest works are a Bible (Bibliothèque Nationale), decorated with 150 miniatures, and a striking portrait of Charles VII (Louvre). He probably painted these two works before his journey to Italy, in 1445. Later, about 1458, he painted for Etienne Chevalier, the miniatures of two manuscripts: "Les Cas des Nobles hommes et femmes malheureux" (Munich), of which he only executed the nine large compositions at the end of each book; and the famous "Book of Hours of Etienne Chevalier," which has gone through many vicissitudes. The pages decorated with miniatures, after being cut out and sold, have been gathered together by collectors. There are forty in the Museum of Chantilly, one in the Louvre, and one in the Cabinet des Estampes. For the same patron, Fouquet painted a diptych which was in Notre-Dame-de-Melun, and which, after having disappeared, was found, the two parts separated: one of the wings represents the Donor and his patron Saint Stephen (in Berlin), and the other Virgin surrounded by angels (Antwerp). From the same period, about 1460, dates the fine portrait of Juvénal des Ursins (Louvre). In 1465, on the command of the Duc of Nemours, Fouquet finished the nine miniatures of a manuscript of the "Antiquitées des Juifs" of Josèphe (Bibliothèque Nationale), which is perhaps the most remarkable of his works.

Fouquet's art is rather that of an observer than of an inventor; and he shows some difficulty in placing scenes of the ancient Jews or of martyrs, in appropriate surroundings. From Italy, Fouquet brought back architectural and decorative motifs, which he sometimes mixed curiously with Romanesque and Gothic patterns. He is more akin to the Flemings than to the Italians, but is less precise than the one, and less idealistic than the other.

See Pl. 58, Vol. I; Pl. 4, Vol. II.

Bibliography: Vallet de Viriville, *L'Œuvre de Jehan Fouquet*, 1856.—E. Müntz, *La Renaissance en Italie et en France au temps de Charles VIII.*—P. Durrieu, *Mélanges de l'Ecole de Rome*, Vol. XII.—H. Bouchot. *Gazette des Beaux-Arts*, 1890. Vol. II.—Trenchard Cox, *Jehan Fouquet.* London, 1931.

**FOUNTAINS ABBEY.**—The first Cistercian monastery in England, founded 1135, now in ruins. It was a complete monastic establishment with a convent church begun in 1147 but with the choir replaced 1120-47 and the Chapel of Nine Altars added at the East to change the plan from a Latin to an archiepiscopal cross. A Perpendicular tower was added in the early 16th century before the north transept.

**FRAGONARD (Jean Honoré).**—French painter, 1732-1806. He was

Fragonard.

born at Grasse. He was the son of a linen draper, and he began his career as a scrivener's clerk, but because of his artistic bent, he was allowed to study in Paris. After six months with Chardin, he studied under Boucher, who was more congenial to his artistic temperament. He won the Prix de Rome in 1752. On his departure for Italy, Boucher gave him this memorable advice: "My dear Frago," he said, "you are going to see Michelangelo and Raphael, but let me tell you this in friendly confidence—if you take to that kind of painting seriously, you are lost." He took this advice to heart, and in Italy chose Cortona and Tiepolo for his masters. For a time he imitated them. Then he became acquainted with Hubert Robert, who had recently come to Rome, and with the Abbé of Saint-Non, who was an engraver, and who invited the two young artists to stay in his Villa d'Este in Tivoli, where, owing to important relatives, he had the right to stay. Fragonard spent two years in this enchanting place of antique ruins, high pastures and falling cascades.

As Fragonard wished to become a member of the Académie Royale he had to paint historical or mythological scenes. An opera by Roy suggested his subject: *Coresus, the High-priest of Bacchus, Sacrificing Himself to Save Callirhoe*. This picture, exhibited in 1765, is now in the Louvre. It shows Italian influence, but also the artist's own delicate sense of colour. Fragonard felt, however, that these ambitious representations were little in accordance with his natural spontaneity. Subjects such as *The Visit*, *The Fountain of Love*, and *Bathing Women* were more in sympathy with his bent, and they sold well.

Nevertheless, Fragonard was also asked for large decorative works. La Guimard, in 1771, entrusted to his inspiration the drawing-room of her house, in the Chaussée d'Antin, which was known as the Temple of Terpsichore. But a misunderstanding which arose between the dancer and her painter put a stop to the work, which was finished, not by Fragonard, but by David, who was then at the beginning of his career, and had as yet no idea of breaking with the light taste of the century.

FRAGONARD: TWO WOMEN CHATTING. (Louvre.)

Fragonard made five compositions for the little pavilion of Louveciennes. These became celebrated as the "Fragonards of Grasse," but some years ago they were sent to America. It is not known why they remained in the possession of the painter who, during the French Revolution, took them to his native town, where he entrusted them to the care of friends. In these works he shows the greatest delicacy. In them he develops the theme of *the Progress of Love in the Hearts of Young Girls*. First comes the *Rendezvous* where, in the guise of shepherdess and shepherd, one recognises the favourite and her royal lover. Then follow *the Pursuit*, *Souvenirs*, and *the Lover Crowned* by the young girl, under the eyes of the painter, who is engaged in perpetuating this solemn scene with his pencil. Finally, there is the *Deserted*, to which Fragonard returned twenty years later, but which he never finished. This is a scene of disillusionment, which shows the girl fallen at the foot of a statue of *Amour*, who laughingly indicates on a dial the hour of happiness, which never returns.

In 1769, Fragonard married; and his choice of subjects reflects the fact. His young wife, Marie-Anne Gérard, presented him with a daughter (who died young), and then with a son (who also became a painter). Marie-Anne's youngest sister, Marguerite Gérard, who made a name for herself as a painter of familiar scenes, and her young brother, who studied engraving, joined their household. Here were those elements of scenes of childhood and family groups, which suggested to the painter his pictures of *Little Girls with Black Dogs*, *The Jealousy of Childhood*, *Happy Motherhood*, etc. Moreover, the household settled in Vaugirard, which was then true country, and Fragonard returned to the observation of nature which had already inspired him at the Villa d'Este. But his work was now more rustic, even realistic, in character, and betrays the influence of the Dutch painters.

This family and rural existence was interrupted when one of the keenest and richest of his patrons made a journey to Italy, taking with him his favourite painter. Madame Fragonard accompanied her husband, and the party, which included a governess and servants, not forgetting the cook, crossed the South of France, embarked at Antibes, for Genoa; visited Naples and Rome, and returned by way of Vienna, Dresden, Leipzig, Frankfort and Strassburg. After eleven months of wandering, Fragonard's portfolios were full of drawings which the financier would not give up to their author, even preferring, it is said, to pay him the pretty sum of thirty thousand pounds.

On his return to Paris, Fragonard soon obtained, like all artists in favour, a lodging and studio in the Louvre. At the outbreak of the Revolution, he would have been ousted from this position, had it not been for his avowed republicanism, and for the support of David. He tried to conform to the taste of the day by painting some subjects of Roman history, and by sending his son to be a student of David. Nevertheless the position was precarious and, seeing himself threatened with the same poverty as so many of his fellow painters, he retired with his wife to Grasse, where hospitality was offered to him by an old family friend, Maubert, whose heirs came into possession of the "Fragonards of Grasse."

When "Frago" returned to Paris under the Directory, although he was only sixty-four years of age, he was considered as a little old man. At the Louvre he was known as "le petit papa Fragonard." He did not do much more work. The evacuation of the Louvre was ordered by Imperial decree, and Fragonard went to live in the Rue Grenelle-Saint-Honoré. One summer day, on his return from the Champ-de-Mars, he stopped to take an ice at a café, was seized with a congestion, and died (2nd August, 1806).

Fragonard was certainly influenced by Boucher and, like him, employed the bright, pearly colours, such as Tiepolo used; but he was also indebted to diverse other painters—to the Venetians, whose warm, strong browns he borrowed; to northern masters, such as Rubens, whose influence is clearly seen in his *Sleeping Bacchante* and *Women Bathing*, in the Louvre; to the Dutch masters; and to the sentimentalities of Greuze. Nevertheless, all these influences were subordinated to his own adventurous personality. His admirable sepias have a feeling for the open air, and a very luminous quality.

See Pl. 9, Vol. I; Pl. 47, Vol. II.

BIBLIOGRAPHY: Goncourt, *L'Art au XVIII[e] s.*, Vol. III.—R. Portalis, *Fragonard*, 1888.—V. Tosz, *Fragonard*, 1901.—P. de Nolhac, *Fragonard*, 1906.—C. Mauclair. *Fragonard*, Collection des grands artistes.

**FRANCESCA or FRANCESCHI.**—See Piero.

**FRANCESCO D'ANTONIO del CHERICO.**—Florentine miniaturist who collaborated between 1453 and 1469 on antiphonaries with Filippo di Matteo Torelli, and between 1463 and 1471 with Zanobi Strozzi on antiphonaries for the Cathedral of Florence.

**— dei FRANCESCHI.**—Venetian painter, active middle of the 15th century, close follower of Giambono.

**— di GENTILE da FABRIANO.**—Umbrian painter, active second half of the 15th century, pupil of Antonio da Fabriano, influenced by the Bellini and other Venetian painters.

**— di GIORGIO MARTINI (in full, Francesco Maurizio di Giorgio Martini Pollaiuolo).**—Sienese painter, sculptor, architect, engineer and theoretician; born 1439 in Siena; died 1502 near Siena. With Jacopo della Quercia, one of the most important and universal personalities of the Sienese school.

Francesco di Giorgio was a pupil of Vecchietta, and a partner of his relative Neroccio until 1475. Their most important collaborative work was the 1472 panel of the *Coronation of the Virgin* in the Siena Academy, painted for Monte Oliveto Maggiore near Siena (predella, scenes from the *Life of Benedict*, is in the Uffizi and is largely by Neroccio). Much of Francesco di Giorgio's painting dates from this period of his close connection with Neroccio. Among his finest works is the *Nativity* of 1467 in S. Domenico, Siena.

In 1477 he was called by Federigo da Montefeltre to Urbino as architect for fortifications. He was active there until 1482, contributing to the decoration of the Ducal Palace; and executing various reliefs: the *Pietà* now in Sta. Maria del Carmine, Venice, was originally done at the order of Federigo for the Congregazione della Croce in Urbino (Federigo and his son Guidobaldo kneel at the right); the *Baptism of Christ* in Perugia Università; and the London *Discordia* relief.

In 1482 he returned to Siena, directed the enlargement of the Church of San Francesco, then built the *Madonna del Calcinaio* in Cortona. From 1484 dates the *City Hall* in Ancona; and from 1486 the *Municipal Palace* of Jesi. In the same year he is again in Urbino. In 1489 Francesco di Giorgio undertook the creation of two bronze angels for the high altar of the Duomo in Siena. In 1490 he was in Milan to give an opinion on the cupola of the Duomo. There he met Leonardo and went with him to Pavia, where they gave their views upon the Duomo there. Then for the third time Francesco di Giorgio went to Urbino; afterwards to Bracciano; and in 1491 to Naples by way of Rome. He was in Naples during the siege by Charles VIII of France and the abdication of Alfonzo II. In 1495 he is mentioned as helping with the fortifications. In 1497 he returned to Siena, cast the aforementioned bronze angels, and became chief architect of the Duomo. A new model for the choir of this cathedral is his last work.

The reconstruction of the Osservanza near Siena (after 1485) Francesco di Giorgio left to his pupil Giacomo Cozzarelli. In his thirty-year activity he fortified about one hundred places, in addition to his sculptural, architectural, and painting achievements; and produced the *Trattato dell' architettura civile e militare*, in five books.

BIBLIOGRAPHY: Vasari - Milanesi, III.—C. Promis, *Vita di Francesco di Giorgio*, etc. Siena, 1841.—Francesco di Giorgio Martini, *Trattato, etc.*, published by C. Saluzzo. Turin, 1841.—Milanesi, *Doc. . . . senese*, 1854, II, III.—Brogi, *Invent. . . . prov. di Siena*, 1897.—Borghesi e Banchi, *Nuovi doc. . . . senese*, 1898.—Pini-Milanesi, *Scrittura, etc.*, I.—F. Donati, *Biogr. e opere di Francesco di Giorgio*. Siena, 1903.—Crowe and Cavalcaselle.—Otto Stein, *Die Architekturtheoretiker der Ital. Ren.* Karlsruhe, 1914.—P. Schubring, *Die Plastik Sienas im Quattrocento*, 1907, Kstgesch. Gesellsch. Berlin, Sitzungs-Ber., VII, 1915 and Monatsh. f. Kstwiss., IX, 1916, 81ff.

**— dai LIBRI.**—Veronese painter, c. 1450-c. 1514, influenced by Mantegna.

**— NAPOLETANO.** — Lombard painter of the 15th and 16th century. A follower of Leonardo da Vinci.

**— da TOLENTINO.**—Umbro-Marchigian painter, active early decades of the 16th century, perhaps a pupil of Agapiti.

**— TORBIDO.**—Called "Il Moro di Verona," 1483-1565. Painter of Verona. He chiefly painted portraits.

**— D'UBERTINO.**—See Bacchiacca.

**FRANCHESCHINI (Marcantonio).**—Bolognese painter (1648-1729). An able painter, who painted in the great Council Hall of Genoa, which was unfortunately destroyed by fire. Some decorations by him remain in the Law Courts, in Bologna.

**FRANCHEVILLE or FRANQUEVILLE (Pierre).**—French sculptor, 1548-1618. He eventually became the pupil and then the associate of his compatriot, Jean de Donai, known as Gian da Bologna, and, like him, settled in Italy. His works include: two colossal statues of Jupiter and Janus, in the courtyard of the Grimaldi Palace, Genoa; statues of St. Ambroise, of St. Stephen, and of the four Evangelists, in Genoa Cathedral (1585); in Florence, five statues in the Nicolini Chapel, Santa Croce, and numerous statues and busts. In Pisa, where he lived for several years, he executed various works which won him the rights of citizenship.

He won fame in France in the last years of the 16th century, and Henry IV gave him a lodging in the Louvre in 1601. Francheville then executed large statues of *Mercury*, *David* (Louvre), groups of *Time* and *Truth*, and of *Saturn carrying off Cybele* (Tuileries Gardens).

Bibliography: Courajod, *Leçons*, Vol. III.

**FRANCHOYS (Pierre).**—Flemish painter, 1606-1654. His portraits have something of the charm and elegance of Van Dyck. Most of his pictures have disappeared. There remain one in Frankfort, one in Lille, one in Dresden and one in Cologne.

**FRANCIA (Francesco di Marco di Giacomo Raibolini).**—Bolognese painter and goldsmith, born c. 1450 in Bologna; died 1517. Influenced by Costa, with whom he collaborated, and by Ercole Roberti.

Francia matriculated in the goldsmiths' guild in 1482; numerous documents refer to his activity in this craft, but no works have been preserved of those authenticated in the records. However certain pieces in the Bologna Gallery are attributed to him. He was known also as a medallist and maker of coins.

In 1486 he is listed in the goldsmiths' guild as a painter; from 1492 dates the London *Madonna with an Angel*, formerly in the Mond Collection; from 1494 the Bologna *Madonna, Saints and Bartolommeo Felicini* (from Sta. Maria della Misericordia); 1495 the Budapest *Holy Family* (painted for Jacopo Gambara); 1499, the Bologna, S. Giacomo Maggiore, Bentivoglio Chapel, *Madonna, Four Saints and Four Angels;* and the Bologna Pinacoteca *Nativity and Saints with Anton Galeazzo Bentivoglio* (from S. Maria della Misericordia; the date is given in the predella painted by Costa, now in the Brera); 1500, the Leningrad *Madonna with Two Saints and Two Angels* (from S. Lorenzino delle Grotte, Bologna, painted for Lodovico de Calcina); and the Bologna Pinacoteca *Annunciation and Four Saints* (from the high altar of SS. Annunziata); 1502, the Berlin *Madonna in Glory and Six Saints* (painted for Sta. Cecilia in Modena); 1505, the Bologna, Palazzo Communale, fresco, the *Madonna del Terremoto;* 1506, the Bologna, Oratory of S. Cecilia, frescoes, the *Life of St. Cecily;* 1509, the Dresden *Baptism;* 1510, the New York, Metropolitan Museum, portrait of Federigo Gonzaga as a boy; 1513, the Vienna *Madonna and Two Saints;* 1515, the Parma Gallery *Madonna and Four Saints and the Infant Baptist* (painted for the Frati dell' Annunziata); and the Turin Pietà.

A large number of altarpieces signed by Francia exist, many of them in part shop work.

Bibliography: Vasari - Milanesi, III.—Gualandi, *Intorno a Francesco Francia in Opere*, 1880, III.—J. Cartwright, *Mantegna and Francia.*—Crowe and Cavalcaselle.—G. Lipparini, *Francesco Francia*. Bergamo, 1913.—Venturi, *Stor. d. arte ital.*, VII, III, 1914.—A. Foratti, *Note su Francesco Francia*. Bologna, 1914.

**— (Giacomo).**—Italian painter, about 1487 to 1557, son of Francesco Francia. He worked with his father and with his brother Giulio. His works include a *Virgin in Glory* (Berlin, 1525) and the *Holy Conversation* (Bologna, 1526).

**— (Giulo).**—Bolognese painter. Son of Francesco Francia, and brother of Giacomo with whom he was associated.

**FRANCIABIGIO (Francesco di Cristofano Giudini or Giudici, called).**—Florentine painter, from Milan, 1482-1525. Pupil of Mariotto Albertinelli and Piero di Cosimo. He chiefly imitated Mariotto and Andrea del Sarto with whom he often worked. He contributed to the frescoes of the Annunziata for Florence, representing there a *Marriage of the Virgin*, of 1513. His portraits of young men in the Uffizi, in the National Gallery and in the Museum of Berlin are perhaps his best works.

The *Triumph of Hercules*, in the Uffizi, is a decoration for a marriage chest.

Bibliography: Crowe and Cavalcaselle, *History of Painting in Italy*, ed. T. Borenius, Vol. VI.

**FRANCKE (Master).**—German painter of the 15th century, active in Hamburg. Together with Konrad von Soest, the leading representative of the so-called fluent style of the early 15th century. The following works are preserved: A picture of the *Man of Sorrows* (imago pietatis) in Leipzig and another with the same subject in Hamburg; nine fragments from the Thomas altarpiece of 1424, Hamburg; an altarpiece with the *Legend of St. Barbara* in Helsingfors, Finland, from the church in Nykyrko. His style is decidedly derived from western sources, particularly from the Paris school of miniature-painting of around 1400.

Bibliography: Lichtwark, *Meister Francke*. Hamburg, 1899.—Martens, Bella, *Meister Francke*. Hamburg, 1929.

**FRARE.**—See Bianchi-Ferrari.

**FRAZEE (John).**—American sculptor (1790-1852), worked in New Jersey and New York City, producing portrait busts (examples in the Boston Athenaeum).

**FREIBURG (Germany).**—*Cathedral* c. 1250-1513. Freiburg is a Gothic church with a huge single western tower with a spire almost 400 feet high completed in 1270. The choir is 14th and 15th century Gothic.

**FRÉMIET (Emmanuel).**—French sculptor, 1824-1911. Nephew and pupil of Rude, his beginnings were, nevertheless, modest and difficult. He had a preference for the study of animals. His works include: a colossal *Gorilla* (which was refused by the Salon of 1859 on account of its realism and twenty-nine years later, in 1888, won a medal of honour), *Gaulish Horseman* (1864), and *Roman Horseman* (1867), *Sea-horses* and *Dolphins*, *Stone-Age Man*, the *Grand Condé*, *Charles V*, and *Joan of Arc* (an equestrian statue, erected on the Place des Pyramides, in Paris).

Frémiet: A chief of the Gauls. (Museum, Saint-Germain.)

See Pl. 52, Vol. II.

**FRENCH (Daniel Chester).**—American sculptor (1850-1931). He was born in Exeter, New Hampshire, 20th April 1850. His father and grandfather were prominent in legal affairs, but even as a small boy he was interested in modelling. His youth was spent in Concord, Massachusetts, where his talent was recognised and encouraged by May Alcott, whose sister Louisa won literary fame. In 1870 young French entered the studio of John Quincy Adams Ward, the famous sculptor. He also studied anatomy with Dr. William Rimmer and had some drawing lessons with William Morris Hunt. Although a young man he was given the important commission of executing a memorial for the battle of Concord Bridge. The result was the *Minute Man* which was dedicated at the centennial of the first encounter of the Revolutionary War.

Shortly before that time French went abroad to study in Italy. He worked in Florence under Thomas Ball, making figures after the classic tradition of that era. In two years' time he returned to the United States where he worked in Washington, Concord and Boston. But in 1886 he made another trip to Europe at which time he studied under Léon Glaize in Paris. After his marriage to his cousin, Mary Adams French, in 1888 he settled permanently in New York City. Slowly the number of his commissions grew until he was one of the most important sculptors of the country. He executed groups for the Columbian Exposition at Chicago in 1893, made an equestrian statute of George Washington for Paris and created many single figures and groups for public buildings and memorials throughout the country. He made other trips abroad when he showed his work at the Paris Salon and in 1910 he was made a Chevalier of the Legion of Honor. For about thirty years he was a trustee of the Metropolitan Museum of Art, during part of which time he was the Curator of Sculpture of that institution. He was also a trustee of the Russell Sage Foundation and the Tiffany Foundation.

In 1922 when he was over seventy years of age he was selected to make the characterisation of President Lincoln for the Lincoln Memorial in Washington. He succeeded in rendering a masterful picture of the wartime President, bowed down by his sorrow and yet retaining his dignity and the majesty befitting his office. Mr. French continued working up until the time of his last illness in the summer of 1931. He died 7th October of that year at his summer place at Stockbridge, Massachusetts. His work is characterised by anatomical accuracy, fidelity of representation and a fine sense of the colouristic values of the composition. Outstanding examples of his skill are the *Milmore Memorial* in Boston, the *Melvin Memorial* in Concord, Massachusetts, and the *Memorial to Alice Freeman Palmer* at Wellesley College.

Bibliography: Mrs. Daniel Chester French, *Memories of a Sculptor's Wife*, 1928.—Adeline Adams, *Daniel Chester French, Sculptor*, 1932.—For other articles see *The Index of Twentieth Century Artists* for May, 1935.

**FRESCO.**—The method of fresco painting consists of the use of water-colours on the fresh plaster of a wall ("fresco" is the Italian word for "fresh"). The damp plaster absorbs the colour. This very simple process is extremely difficult in execution. It exacts a great many precautions in preparation, and great sureness and dexterity in performance. As the preservation of the painting depends on the wall which supports it, this should be favourably placed without risks of damp and without materials likely to contain saltpetre. The upper coat of the wall, which is to receive the colour, is a mixture of slaked lime and fine sand, put there at the last minute and covered with colours before it dries. Thus the painting must be done quickly and not retouched. After a first coat of this plaster has been spread on the wall and has received the design of the complete composition, the whole subject is then divided into parts that the artist thinks he will be able to finish in one day. The ground is, at the last minute, covered with a second coat of plaster of such dimensions as the artist can paint then and there.

Fresco was admirably treated by artists of the Italian school from its beginnings until the time of Raphael. Cennino Cennini, a Florentine artist of the Renaissance, wrote a very complete treatise on his technique, which includes all the receipts for painting in use in his day: *Il Libro dell'Arte*, or *Il Trattato della Pittura.* (English translation by Lady Herringham, 1899.)

See Pl. 7, Vol. I.

**FRITH (William Powell).**—English painter (1819-1909), studied in the Royal Academy School. He is especially noted for his populous figure subjects—such as *The Derby Day* (1858; National Gallery, Millbank), *Ramsgate Sands* (1854; Buckingham Palace) and *The Railway Station* (1862; Holloway College)—which preserve a wonderfully accurate and vivid picture of Mid-Victorian England, while by no means deficient in strictly pictorial qualities. He was elected a full Member of the Royal Academy in 1852.

**FROMENT D'UZÈS (Nicolas).**—French painter of the 15th century. He was born at Uzès, and worked for King René of Anjou. The only two works that we know for certain to be by him are a *Resurrection of Lazarus* (Uffizi), painted in 1461, and the famous triptych of the *Burning Bush* (1475) which is in Aix Cathedral. That this is the work of a disciple of the Flemish school is seen by the realism and precision of the faces and landscapes. The types and costumes even recall the Van Eycks. The same qualities are seen in a diptych in the Louvre, representing King René and Jeanne de Laval.

See Pl. 4, Vol. II.

Bibliography: G. Lafenestre, *Nicolas Froment*, Revue de l'Art ancien et moderne, Vol. II.

**FROMENTIN (Eugène).**—French painter and littérateur, 1820-1876. He went to Algiers, and painted pictures inspired by his travels. He also wrote novels, and finally, after a journey to Belgium and Holland, in 1876, he wrote *Maîtres d'autrefois*, which is considered one of the masterpieces of art criticism of the 19th century. In spite of these four volumes, Fromentin considered himself a painter rather than a writer, but nowadays the author of *Maîtres d'autrefois* is much more esteemed than the painter of *The Quarry* (Louvre), *Les Femmes Fellahs* (Louvre), etc.

FROMENTIN (EUGÈNE): THIRST. (Collection of M. Jacques Normand.)

**FUGA (Ferdinando).**—Florentine architect, 1699-1780. He worked in Rome, and followed the example of Bernini. He built the Corsini Palace (1729-1732), worked in the

FUGA: SANTA MARIA MAGGIORE, ROME.

Quirinal Palace, and made the façade of Santa Maria Maggiore, an example of return to the façade in two orders (1743).

**FULDA (Germany).**—Benedictine monastery, 803. One of the few preserved Carolingian basilicas. It is above the remains of an 8th century abbey church. Fulda is one of the earliest examples of the western apse which was used in Carolingian, Ottonian, and Romanesque Germany in conjunction with the usual eastern apse.

**FULLER (George).**—American painter (1822-1884). He was born 17th January 1822 on his father's farm at Deerfield, Massachusetts. His maternal grandfather was a painter by inclination and one of his mother's brothers was a professional painter and a sister did miniatures. His parents thought that George should go into business, so when he was old enough he went to work in a grocery. He also tried selling shoes and helping with a railroad survey in the midwest. With his half-brother he travelled through northern New York as an itinerant portrait painter. In the winter of 1841-1842 he studied with Henry Kirke Brown, the sculptor, at Albany and later he worked at the Boston Artists' Association for some time. Five years later he entered the art school of the National Academy of Design in New York and remained in that city until 1859. In 1860 he travelled in Europe to Paris, Florence, Rome, Venice and England, where he met Holman Hunt and Dante Gabriel Rossetti. His father had died in 1859 so he was forced to return home to manage the farm. For the next fifteen years he was primarily a farmer, his main interest being in the tobacco crop, which product is widely cultivated in the fertile valley of the Connecticut river. In 1875 the price of tobacco declined sharply and the Fullers had to think of some other way to earn a living. Mr. Fuller had done some painting at odd moments and he sent the canvases to Boston for exhibition. The results were most encouraging so he set up a home in Boston and began exhibiting regularly in the large annual shows. The poetic mood of his landscapes and figure pieces such as *Winifred Dysart* appealed to the general public and his last years were spent in comfort. While an exhibition of his work was being shown in Boston he caught pneumonia and died 21st March 1884 at his home in Brookline, Massachusetts.

BIBLIOGRAPHY: Josiah B. Millet, ed., *George Fuller, His Life and Works,* 1886.

**FUNGAI (Bernardino).**—Sienese painter, born c. 1460; died 1516 in Siena, probably a pupil of Giovanni di Paolo.

His earliest known painting is the *Assumption* in San Girolamo, Siena, of 1487; the *Coronation of the Virgin* in the Church of the Servi, Siena, is of 1500; the *Coronation* in the Academy of Siena of 1512. Undated pictures by Fungai include: the *Assumption* in the Siena Academy; the *Coronation* in Fontegiusta; the frescoes in the Istituto dei Sordi Muti, Siena.

BIBLIOGRAPHY: Vasari-Milanesi, VI. —Milanesi, *Doc. . . . senese,* III.—Borghesi e Banchi, *Nuovi documenti, etc.*—Crowe and Cavalcaselle. —L. Olcott, *Guide to Siena,* 1903.

**FURINI (Francesco).** — Florentine painter, 1604 to 1516. He painted *The Creation of Eve* (Pitti Palace), *David and Abigail* (Capponi Palace), and several mythological figures in the Corsini Palace.

**FURNITURE.**—*Egypt.*—As with many of the other arts, the oldest documents and remains come from

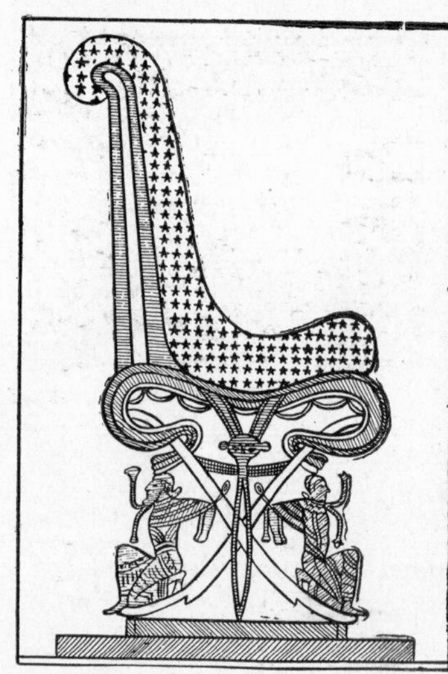

CHAIR FROM THE TOMB OF RAMESES III.

Egypt. The Egyptians practised sculpture in wood, and their furniture industry gained from the ability which they thus acquired. Numerous articles of furniture were preserved in the tombs, and have come down to us intact. All the great museums possess some of them, notably the Louvre, from the common stool to luxurious articles, decorated with inlays of "ebon and ivory," and brightened with vivid colours. Subjects derived from local fauna were used—feet of the lion, bull, or gazelle; and, for the elbow-seats, heads of gazelle or ibex. Like sculpture, the art of furniture, in Egypt, remained subservient to priestly rules, which kept it unchanged for centuries, and yielded nothing to the influence of Greek art, which was introduced by the Ptolemies.

*Asia.*—Assyrian furniture was more original, more varied, but, at the same time, cruder. It can only be reconstructed from the bas-reliefs, for owing to the climate, which is damper than that of Egypt, no piece of old Assyrian furniture has been preserved. We have only the wide bands of beaten copper (in the British Museum) which adorned and strengthened the doors of the royal palaces, like the iron hinges of our cathedrals. According to descriptions, principally those of Herodotus, the Assyrians seem to have attached chief importance to the richness of their materials, and in the royal palaces were seen beds, chairs and tables made of solid gold. Such valuable furniture was too great a temptation to thieves to survive the centuries.

*Greece.*—Eastern influence seems to have predominated in Greece, until the time of the Persian Wars. According to Homer, beds, tripods and chairs were made of chased bronze, and gold and silver vases were magnificently worked. Pausanias speaks of a cedar-wood coffer, adorned with bas-reliefs of gold and ivory, which was offered by Cypselus, King of Corinth, to the Treasury of Olympia. Some fragments, which seem to date from the 4th century B.C., were found in tumuli, in Koul-Oba, on the coast of the Bosphorus, and were taken to Leningrad (Hermitage Museum).

*Rome.*—The art of furniture as practised by the Romans is well known to us, at least in its most brilliant manifestation, since the excavations of Pompeii. There were found fairly well preserved beds, the frames of which were made of light wood, painted red. Wooden strips or copper thongs formed the support for mattress and cushions. These beds are decorated with inlays of silver on a bronze field. Bronze chairs were also discovered —backless, and probably not very comfortable. Drawings on vases show us the existence of other chairs, in wood, with a sloping back, but none of these have been found. There are also metal table-supports, the tops of which, probably in wood, have disappeared. They are all delicately chased, and a certain support with three feet (Naples Museum), the circular gallery of which is supported by winged sphinxes, was imitated by French artists of Louis XVI's reign. Mention must also be made of fine candelabras and seats of inlaid bronze, and of the bronze baths in the thermal establishments.

When Roman art was destroyed by the invasion of barbarians, and Constantine established his capital in Byzantium, Greek and Roman artists flocked to the centre of the Eastern Empire, and, under Asiatic influence, a luxurious art grew up and flourished. Unfortunately, the very richness of the work of this period destined it to destruction, and what has come down to us consists largely of ivories and enamels.

THE MIDDLE AGES.—It was not until the 13th century that a real furniture industry was established in France. Throughout this century a great quantity of chests were made. These were very important articles of furniture, serving, as they did, as trunks, wardrobes and seats. Some of them are covered with curious paintings. The finest articles of furniture of the period are the choir-stalls in churches, such as those of Notre Dame (Paris), of the Cathedral of Poitiers, and of the Church of Saint Andoche of Saulieu.

Of 14th century furniture, little remains.

The following century, on the other hand, bequeathed us a great many articles. This was the great period of wood carving, which was used for the decoration of churches, and houses. In the Museum of Orléans is a coffer, destined to receive the sacred vessels, offered to the Church of Saint Aignan by Louis XI, probably in 1461. It is ornamented with arcades, and in its design shows all the architectural tendencies of the day. Wood carvers were inspired by the work of architects, and at no other period do we find more harmonious agreement between the lines and decoration of the building, and those of the furniture which embellished it.

RENAISSANCE.—*France.*—In the 16th century, under Italian influence new tendencies appeared. Important schools were formed, the productions of which may be fairly easily distinguished—that of Normandy (where Jean Goujon began his career), and those of Picardy, Champagne, Lorraine, Touraine (which clearly show the influence of the Italian artists of Amboise), of the Ile-de-France, of Burgundy, Lyon, Auvergne, Toulouse and, finally, the school of the "Midi."

The Louvre and the Cluny Museums possess some very fine sixteenth century works, such as a cupboard front made from an openwork panel from the Château of Gaillon; a marriage chest, of the school of Tours, from the Château of Loches. It is supported on the paws of a lion, and decorated at the corners with caryatides. The carved panels of Fontainebleau (period of Francis I), and the choir stalls of the old Collegiate Church of Champeaux, near Melun, must also be mentioned. But examples of this period, which may be seen in many of the large museums, are very numerous, and all of them are remarkable.

The *German* school was less influenced by the Italians than were the French wood-carvers and furniture-makers. It aimed at solidity rather than refinement and purity of line. Many of the models were designed by Wenderlin Dietterlin (1550-1599). German production became more and more debased, and disappeared completely during the Thirty Years' War.

In the *Netherlands* many very fine works in sculptured wood were produced. This work suited the patience and application of the Flemings. Italian influence here was disastrous, and resulted in a hybrid style, which did not last. Antwerp, however, continued for a long time to be famous for her finely carved cupboards and ebony cabinets.

The *Italians*, who played such an important part in the evolution of European art, employed very different methods from those used in

Riesener: Commode.

France and other countries. Instead of giving value to the material by large carvings, they tried to conceal the wood under mosaics, paintings, and inlaid plaques of rare substances. They used original processes:—"tarsia," the inlay of coloured woods; "scagliolia," where the cut-out parts were filled in with a coloured paste; the "laboro alla certosa," employed in Lombardy—tree trunks of various colours, juxtaposed and mounted, are cut into thin slices, and these leaves are then inlaid in the panels. In Florence, furniture was valued chiefly for the paintings with which some of the best artists covered it. The "cassoni," or marriage chests, were often real masterpieces.

*Spain* submitted for a long time to Moorish traditions. It was not until the 15th century that she opened her gates to foreign influences. She produced and exported a great many cabinets, which were

Oak chest of the fifteenth century with window compartments and coil motifs.

placed on a stand with four supporting columns, and called "Vargueños" in Spain. They were decorated with bands and stamped lock-plates, of gilt ironwork.

*England* possesses the most magnificent timber roofs. Among the most famous are those of the Hall of Westminster Palace (recently restored), and of the great Hall, Hampton Court Palace. There are many others, at Oxford and elsewhere.

Pieces of English furniture of this period show great technical skill.

*Seventeenth Century.*—The beginning of the 17th century was an experimental period, and it is not characterised by any personal style. The schools of the Renaissance had reached their decline, although the influence of their refined technique was still felt. Between them and the schools which characterise the reign of Louis XVI, attempts were made which are often interesting, but not co-ordinated. The piece of furniture which was then most in favour was the cabinet, which replaced the great carved cupboards and heavy dressers of the Renaissance. Their origin is not clearly known. Spain produced and exported a great number, at the time when they also appeared in Venice, which took them from the East. The fashion spread, and each country adapted the cabinet to its own taste, and to its own technique. *Spain* and *Portugal* made them of rare woods and ivories from their colonies. Those produced in Toledo were the most famous. The plaques of gilded ironwork which decorate them generally bear the two lions of Aragon. Those of Portugal are frequently decorated with mosaics on wood, and the design is treated with Hindu subjects.

In *Italy,* Florence adorned her cabinets with designs made of hard stones; while Milan preferred ivory; Venice, inlays of mother-of-pearl and coloured glass; and Naples favoured mother-of-pearl inlaid in shell. The Cluny Museum, Paris, possesses a fine Venetian cabinet which represents the front of a palace, crowned with a gallery of inlaid copper.

*Germany* also produced a great many cabinets, most of which came from Nuremburg and Augsburg. These first show Italian influence, then they came to be made almost entirely of ebony, ornamented with shell, or with paintings. In the Cluny Museum may be seen a cabinet of German origin, with bas-reliefs representing scenes from Roman history, and another decorated with caryatides and lions' heads.

In *France*, Flemish and German cabinets were the fashion. Then the influence of Mazarin inspired amateurs with a taste for Italian furniture. However, in the Palace of Fontainebleau may be seen two fine ebony cabinets, which are Flemish in character, although they were executed in France. There are others in the Cluny Museum. The pieces which were made in France are seldom trimmed with paintings.

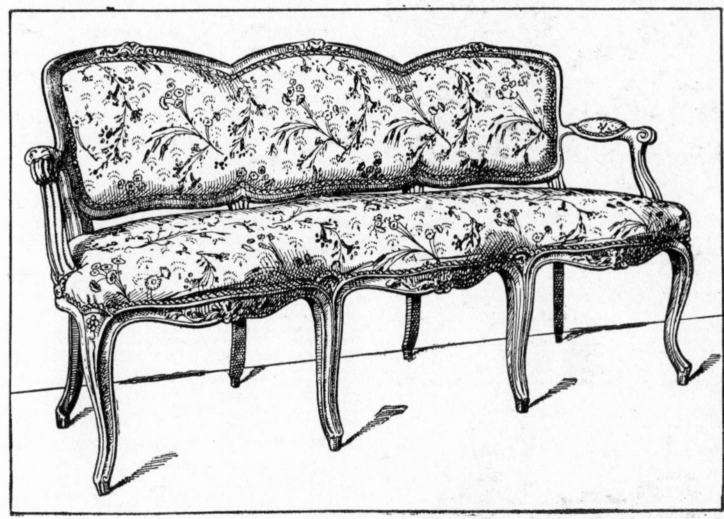

Louis XV sofa of gilt wood.

During the reign of Louis XIII, furniture was somewhat neglected. Tables and chairs with twisted columns, beds covered with materials, octagonal and square mirrors—all these were common, and show little aesthetic aim. It needed the powerful impulse given by Louis XIV, and the appearance of artists such as André Charles Boulle, to bring about a renewal of the art of furniture in France. The name of Boulle often appears in the royal accounts, after 1673. He made numerous pieces of furniture for the royal residences, among others a marquetry table of brass inlaid into tortoiseshell, with ebony panels, a marquetry chest for the Dauphin, and a large sideboard for a "salon" of Marly. Of Boulle's work, the Bibliothèque Mazarin possesses two commodes of brass marquetry in tortoiseshell; and Fontainebleau, a clock in the same style. Boulle's furniture has ornaments of gilt bronze, in which he reveals his ability as a sculptor. His favourite method came into fashion again under Louis XVI, but none of the furniture made at this period, in the style of Boulle, can be compared with the master's own work. Some of the finest of Boulle's furniture may be seen in the Wallace Collection (London). The examples in the Louvre have suffered restorations and modifications which have often disfigured them.

Small cabinet by Boulle.

Around Boulle, a whole school of cabinet-makers arose, which practised marquetry of brass and tortoiseshell. In this connection, the following names should be mentioned: Pierre Poitou, Jacques Sommett, Jean Normant, Jean Oppenordt, Martin Dufause, and Claude Bergerat.

Nevertheless, other craftsmen continued to carve furniture in plain wood, as had been done in the preceding period. To them we owe those fine pieces of sculptured furniture, often gilt, which harmonised so well with the luxurious Court of Louis XIV. One of the masters of this art was the Italian, Philippe Caffieri (see this name). Antoine Lepautre had a great influence on all these sculptors, and most of the carved furniture of this period was executed from his engravings.

*Eighteenth Century.*—This pompous type of furniture scarcely survived the reign of Louis XIV, and under the Regency, a lighter and more graceful style was evolved, thanks to the influence of Robert de Cotte, who was chiefly a carver of wood-panelling, and who made the carved woodwork in the choir of Notre Dame, Paris.

The chief master in the art of furniture-making in the time of the Regency was Charles Cressent. In his work, ebony ceases to play an important part, and the chief importance is given to bronze ornaments, often inspired by the engraver, Gillot. This characterises the furniture of the time of Louis XV. Among the many artists working in this period were Jacques Caffieri (fifth son of Philippe Caffieri) and his son. All Jacques' pieces are remarkable for their grace and purity of line.

Towards the end of Louis XV's reign, ebony returned to favour, and bronze work was gradually dropped. Jean François Oëben made numerous pieces in marquetry for Madame de Pompadour, and ordered bronzes from Philippe Caffieri, then at Duplessis; but in these works bronze is only an accessory, instead of being essential, as in the works of Cressent or of Jacques Caffieri.

During the 18th century a special form of decoration was used for furniture. It was known as "Vernis Martin." For a long time, since the

Norman oak wardrobe with griffon feet.

reign of Louis XIV, many attempts had been made to discover the secret of Oriental lacquers. In experimenting to this end, Martin discovered his celebrated varnish ("vernis"). It was first used for carriages and Sedan-chairs, but it soon came to be used for furniture and panelling. A few examples of it remain, at any rate in France, for the Château of Sans-Souci contains a room decorated with "Vernis Martin," perfectly preserved, which

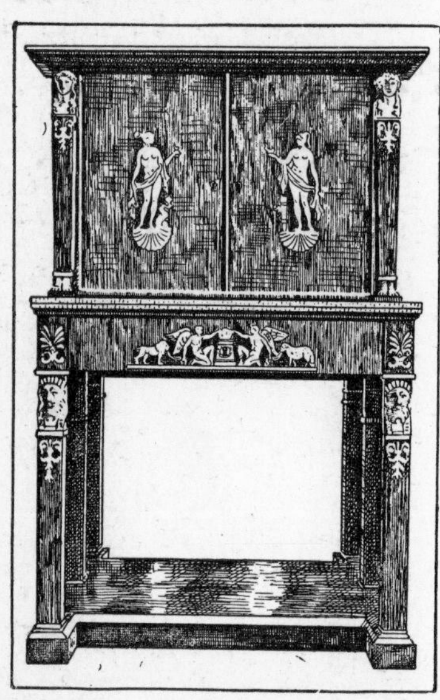

Whatnot of mahogany with dull gilded bronze ornaments.

gives a complete idea of the effects that could be obtained by this very delicate process. In the Cluny Museum there is a carriage, a sledge, and some panels from carrying-chairs, in "Vernis Martin." Robert Martin, the head of the family, and the inventor of the varnish, owes his fame to the art with which he painted little scenes—pastorals, allegories, and little "galant" pictures—on a background strewn with golden spangles, on a field of blue or green. The decorating which he, or his descendants, achieved for the royal palaces of France soon disappeared, for want of upkeep; but a fair amount of furniture has remained, such as the commodes in the Palace of Fontainebleau, and some fine panels in the Carnavalet Museum, Paris. After Martin, other lacquer-workers settled in Paris, but their work was of more commercial than artistic value. Chevalier, Aubert and Pierre de Neufmaison must, however, be mentioned.

The discoveries at Pompeii brought into fashion the imitation of the antique. This tendency, which was apparent in the last years of Louis XV's reign, became more definite under Louis XVI. The new school produced furniture with pure, simple lines, of the style known as "Louis XVI," and had as its leader Jean Henri Riesener (1735-1806), who had been a pupil of Oëben, and married his widow. His works are very numerous, and are remarkable for their quiet grace of line, and for the delicacy of their designs in marquetry, and for their bronzes. There are admirable examples at Fontainebleau, in the Mobilier National, Trianon, the Louvre, and elsewhere.

*Empire.*—During the Reign of Terror the ruthless fury of a nation under mob-law did not spare the most beautiful objects of art which

Dufrène: Mahogany secretary.

were associated with a hated aristocracy. Furniture especially suffered. The Revolution was the death-blow to Rococo ornament. In the transition days before the style known as "Empire" had become fixed, there is exhibited in art a feeling which suggests the deliberate search after new forms and new ideas.

Napoleon himself fostered the classic spirit. Furniture, like everything else, had to be in the Greek or Roman style. The pleasing curves of the Rococo gave place to straight, severe lines. Furniture became more massive, and was smothered with sculptured brasses copied from antique ornaments—heads of lions, griffins, and sphinxes, the bay-leaf, caryatids, etc. The graceful simplicity of Louis XVI yielded to a wealth of decoration that was not always in the best taste. Corners, which were gently rounded in the preceding period, now had an austere sharpness. Under the influence of David, Percier and others, furniture was made which is chiefly curious on account of its archæological inspiration.

A few years later, a version of this Empire furniture, despoiled of its

Ruhlmann: Waxed macassar commode, with ivory marquetry.

bronzes and luxuries, found its way into middle-class homes, and became the ungraceful furniture of the Louis-Philippe period, which had no other merit than that of being solidly and "comfortably" built.

The Second Empire was barren of invention. Furniture-making was now a decadent art, in spite of the efforts of such artists as Fourdinois. Massive embellishments and heavy gildings replaced the nervous refinements of the preceding century. Cabinet-making fell into a state of barbarity.

*The Contemporary Period.*—It was not until the end of the 19th century that an effort was made to produce a new style. The "modern style" which, from 1895 to 1902, had some success with de Feure and Colonna, was hardly more than a praise-worthy attempt to break down chronic ugliness. It introduced twisted, absurd lines. The only reason for its existence was to escape from monotony, and to create something which would be neither of Louis XV, nor yet of Louis XVI, for which there was awakening an admiration which has been increasing down to the present day. The "modern style" was soon played out, and gave place to various experiments. Some imitated Japanese art; others, English or Austrian styles. Gradually, a steadying of aim was produced, and thanks to Gaillard, Selmersheim, Dufrêne and Plumet, a genuine "modern style" evolved. Well-proportioned furniture is made, and, in accordance with the spirit of the times, stress is laid on practicability. There is a liking for rare woods; for simple, harmonious lines; and unobtrusive carving. Thus it is in France, anyway. In England, lines tend, on the whole, to be squarer and sharper. In Vienna, modern furniture is heavy. In Belgium, curves are more abrupt and often startling. The influence of such artists as Jallot, J. Dampt and Alexandre Charpentier is considerable.

Bibliography: A. de Champeaux, *Le Meuble.* Paris, 1885.—R. de Félice, *Le Meuble français du Moyen âge à Louis XIII; Le Meuble français sous Louis XIV et la Régence; Le Meuble français sous Louis XV; Le Meuble français sous Louis XVI et sous l'Empire.*—Léon Moussinac, *Le Meuble français moderne.* Paris, 1925.—F. Roe, *Old Oak Furniture.* 1905.—W. E. Mallett, *An Introduction to Old English Furniture.* 1906.

**FUSELI (Henry).**—English painter, 1741-1825. He was of Swiss origin, but by education and character may be considered as an Englishman. About 1770, he travelled to Italy. In 1782, he exhibited the *Nightmare* at the Royal Academy, where he became a professor in 1799. A great part of his career was devoted to teaching and his most important pupil was William Blake. Many of his works were inspired by the poems of Milton and Shakespeare. In spite of qualities of composition and a certain knowledge of drawing, these pictures are melodramatic and declamatory. His best works are *Titania and Bottom,* taken from "A Midsummer Night's Dream," and *The Dream of Queen Katherine* (Victoria and Albert Museum).

**FYT (Jan).**—Painter of Antwerp, 1611-1661. A pupil of Snyders, he equalled and perhaps even surpassed, his master. Like him, he painted animals, still-life, and hunting scenes. His colour is very bright, and he paints details of plumage and peelings with a care and sincerity that is entirely Flemish. His best works include: *The Eagle's Feast* (one in Antwerp, and one in Cologne), *Dogs Fighting a Bear* (Munich), *Game and Fruit* (Schleissheim Gallery, Vienna), and *Still-Life* (Berlin).

# G

**GABBIANI (Antonio Domenico).**—Italian painter, 1652-1726. He worked in Sustermans' studio, in Venice. On his return to Florence, his native town, he founded an Academy which was very successful. We possess a good many works by him, including frescoes in the Corsini Palace, *Dance of Cupids* (Pitti Palace), *Christ in the House of Simon* (*Dresden*), etc.

**GABLE.**—Vertical end of a roof (usually triangular) from the cornice

TYPES OF GABLES.

or eaves to the ridge of the roof; also the end wall of a building as distinguished from the front or rear walls. A *gable roof* is one which forms gables at either end or at several ends.

**GABRIEL (Jacques Ange).**—French architect (1690-1782), son of Jacques Gabriel, who was also an architect. He succeeded his father as Inspector General of Buildings. The construction of the Louvre had been abandoned for more than half a century. He took up the work again, and in 1755 he had to restore Perrault's colonnade, which was threatened in several places. He was then commissioned with the decoration of the Place Louis XV now the Place de la Concorde. The two colonnaded buildings in this square and the École Militaire are among his important works. A triumph of the refined, elegant, classical, and academic style of Louis XVI which succeeded the capricious rococo style of Louis XV is the Petit Trianon. The Aile Gabriel at Versailles, next to J. H. Mansard's Chapel, is that portion built of an extremely ambitious project. Its pavilions are almost identical with those in the buildings in the Place de la Concorde.

GABRIEL (J. A.): MILITARY SCHOOL, PARIS.

See Pl. 43, Vol. II.

**GADDI (Agnolo).**—Florentine painter, pupil of his father, Taddeo Gaddi.

In 1369 Agnolo is employed for the decoration of the Vatican. From 1370 to 1380 his name appears several times on the tax registers of Florence; and in 1380 he creates designs for the plastic decoration of the Loggia de' Lanzi. From 1383 to 1386 he designs and colors statues of Faith, Hope, Prudence, and Charity, executed in stone by Jacopo di Piero Guidi and Piero di Giovanni. In 1385 he is active in Prato, in connection with Francesco Marco Datini. He is mentioned as a member of the S. Luca corporation in 1387, and in the same year he designs and paints a statue of an Apostle for the façade of the Cathedral, carved by Giovanni di Tedesco. In 1390 he makes with Giuliano d'Arrigo a design for a wood equestrian of Pietro Farnese to be placed over one of the lateral doors of the Duomo; and he is paid for two statues of St. John. In 1391 Agnolo presses Datini for payment of the services he has extended to him. Evidently the matter is settled for in 1393 Agnolo returns to Prato, where the same Datini provides him with household utensils. In 1395, mention is made of four figures of Apostles for the façade of the Duomo; and in 1396 he is paid for sketches of six Saints for the windows of the Duomo. In the same year the extant frescoes in the Cathedral at Prato, the *Legend of the Virgin and Her Girdle*, are finished (various payments had been made to Agnolo during 1395). In 1396 the painter died while working at San Miniato al Monte.

The frescoes in Sta. Croce of the Legend of the True Cross attested as having been painted by Agnolo Gaddi in a document of 1395, but the date of their execution is not given.

BIBLIOGRAPHY: Vasari-Milanesi, I.—Frey, *Loggia dei Lanzi*.—Crowe and Cavalcaselle.—Poggi, *Il Duomo di Firenze*. Berlin, 1909.—Sirén, *Giottino*.—Khvoshinsky and Salmi, *I pittori toscani*.—J. B. Supino, Rivista d'Arte, V, 1907.

**— (Gaddo).**—Florentine mosaic worker, of the end of the 13th and beginning of the 14th century. Vasari says that he finished the mosaics of the façade of Santa Maria Maggiore, Rome, and others in the Lateran, left unfinished by Torriti in 1308. No work is to be attributed with certainty to Gaddo.

**GADDI (Taddeo).** — Florentine painter, the son of Gaddo Gaddi, mosaicist, and traditionally a pupil of Giotto, according to Cennino Cennini, whose contemporary testimony is reliable, and to Vasari who records a signature on a painting (now lost) in which Taddeo speaks of himself as Giotto's disciple.

From 1332-38 date the frescoes in the Baroncelli Chapel, Sta. Croce, Taddeo's most extensive and most famous achievement. The small triptych in the Berlin Museum is of 1334. In 1341-42, Taddeo received payment for paintings in San Miniato al Monte. From the latter year date the frescoes in S. Francesco, Pisa, of which but a few figures remain. About 1347 he is mentioned in the register of S. Giovanni fuoricivitas, Pistoia; and in 1353 there is record of a document of payment for work done there (the altarpiece involved is still in the church). In 1353, Taddeo painted in a chapel of the SS. Annunziata; and from 1355 comes the signed and dated *Madonna* in the Uffizi. In 1352 and 1365 Taddeo buys property in Florence; in 1359, 1363, and 1366 he is one of a commission to supervise the construction of the Cathedral. His matriculation in the corporation of painters in Florence does not take place until 1366, which must also have been the year of his death, since in that year his wife is mentioned as a widow.

The following works are among those attributed to Taddeo Gaddi: Florence, Academy, Lunette, *Madonna;* Florence, Academy, panels, small scenes of the *Life of Christ* and *Life of Francis;* Pistoia, S. Giovanni Fuoricivitas, polyptych; Florence, Sta. Felicità, polyptych; S. Martino a Mensola, altarpiece; Florence, S. Miniato, vault of crypt, *Prophet;* S. Lorenzo alle Rose, *Virgin and Child;* Worcester, Massachusetts, Philip Gentner Collection, *St. John Evangelist.*

BIBLIOGRAPHY: Vasari-Milanesi.—v. Rumohr, *Italienische Forschungen*, 1827, Schlosser ed. Frankfurt, 1920.—Crowe and Cavalcaselle, Douglas ed., II.—M. Wehrman, *Taddeo Gaddi*, Gymnascal Programm. Stettin, 1910.—O. Sirén, *Giotto and Some of his Followers*, I.—I. Maioni, *Fra Simone Fidati e Taddeo Gaddi*, L'Arte, 1914, p. 107.—R. Offner, L'Arte, 1912, p. 116; *Studies in Florentine Painting*, 1927, pp. 59-66.

**GAETANO.**—See Pulzone.

**GAGGINI (Domenico di Pietro).**—Genoese sculptor and architect, died 1492. His most important work in Genoa is the façade of the Chapel of S. Giovanni Battista in the Duomo (begun 1448). In Naples the Triumphal Arch of Alfonso of Aragon, and the decoration of the Sala del Barone of Castelnuovo are attributed to him. To escape the plague, Gaggini returned to Palermo (1463), which he had visited already, and where he probably designed the side portal of St. Agostino (c. 1484) among other works. A partnership with Francesco Laurana has been suggested.

GAGGINI: CHAPEL OF SAN GIOVANNI. (Cathedral of Genoa.)

He died in 1492, and was buried in San Francesco.

**— (Giovanni).**—Genoese sculptor of the 15th century. His bas-reliefs are rich and decorative. The five figures of *St. George*, of the Danovaro Palace (formerly Doria), and of the Victoria and Albert Museum, London, are specially admirable. He carried out many decorations in the Genoese churches (1449-1495).

**GAILLARD (Château).**—See Pl. 51, Vol. I.

**GAILLON (Eure).**—The Château of Gaillon was formerly one of the finest in France. It was built by the Cardinal of Amboise, after 1502, and at the end of the 16th century, the Cardinal of Bourbon had it enlarged. Nothing remains of it now, except ruins, which serve as a prison, and the magnificent doorway, which has been transported to the courtyard of the École des Beaux Arts, Paris.

GAILLON: THE CHÂTEAU.

**GAINSBOROUGH (Thomas).**—English painter, 1727-1788. He was born at Sudbury, in the county of Suffolk. His mother was known as a flower painter. At the age of fourteen, he was sent to London, where he entered the studio, first of a French engraver, and then of a deplorable painter of historical scenes. At eighteen, he returned to his native place, where he married almost at once. He and his wife settled in Ipswich, where they lived for twelve years. He painted numerous portraits, but was interested chiefly in landscape. In 1758, he moved to Bath. Meantime the number of clients grew daily, and twice he had to change his residence for a larger house. Gainsborough exhibited regularly at the Royal Academy. Lord Pembroke's admirable collection of Van Dycks, the finest pictures that the master had painted in England, excited his enthusiasm. He copied them unceasingly, "professing for this artist a tender, humble, and respectful admiration, until his last breath." He painted his most admirable portraits, and such pictures as *The Horse-Pond* and *Forest Landscape at Sunset*. These poetical works make one feel that Gainsborough might be considered even greater as a landscape painter than as a portrait painter, and that, in any case, he well deserves to be called "the father of English landscape." "I am tired of portraits," he once said. "I would like to take my viol-de-gamba, and go and live in some peaceful village, where I could paint landscapes and enjoy the last part of my life in tranquillity and well-being. But these fine ladies, with their cups of tea, their balls,

Gainsborough.

and their husband-hunting cheat me out of my last ten years."

While executing his wonderful landscapes, he painted portraits of General Wolfe, Lady Grosvenor, Field Marshal Seymour Conway, John Campbell, Captain Augustus Harvey, Lord Rivers, Lady Sussex, Mr. Nuthall, Mrs. Sheridan, Mrs. Tickell, Georgiana Spencer and the Duchess of Devonshire—that is to say, nearly all his masterpieces. In 1774, he settled in London, where all the famous people of the day—statesmen, actors, soldiers, lawyers and great lords and ladies—frequented his studio. From this period date the portraits of Master Buttal (the "Blue Boy"), Lady Mulgrave, William Pitt, Mrs. Ley-

Gainsborough: The Duke and Duchess of Cumberland.

bourne, Mrs. Moodey and her Children, Mrs. Fitz Herbert, Miss Sukey Trevelyan, Lady Sheffield, Mrs. Siddons, George Canning, Dr. Johnson and the Baillie family. Gainsborough, unlike Reynolds, was a creature of instinct. He studied but little, and showed little curiosity outside art. He loved music, and was essentially a man of feeling. He only painted from nature under the influence of direct emotion. He had none of the assurance and tranquil premeditation of Reynolds. He had an instinctive love for colour, as for sound. "I am lost as soon as I pretend to reason," he said. He thought that his attitude on meeting Sir Joshua Reynolds had not been what it ought to have been, and the painter of *Perdita* wrote to the painter of *Nelly O'Brien*: "Dear Sir Joshua, I write today to tell you from a sincere

Gainsborough: Princess Elizabeth.

heart that I have always sincerely loved and admired Sir Joshua Reynolds."

Reynolds came to him, and they parted with these words of Gainsborough: "We will all go to Heaven and Van Dyck will be of the party." Shortly afterwards, on the 2nd August, 1788, he died. "His works have a peculiar charm and tenderness, and a touch of melancholy that can hardly be attributed to all his sitters. Rather this emanates from himself, and it is apparent in his portraits as it is in his landscapes."

*The Blue Boy* was painted to show that Reynolds was mistaken in the statement he made at the Academy that blue could not be used as the dominant colour in a portrait, and that strong tones should be placed in the middle of a composition. *The Blue Boy* is painted according to principles which are exactly opposite to those which Reynolds pronounced. The portrait of Mrs. Siddons is conceived in the same spirit, with the same skilful harmonies, but with more warmth. The portraits of Miss Graham, and of the Duchess of Devonshire, and, above all, that adorable *Perdita*, embody all his gracefulness and melancholy. The latter is a harmony of silver and opal colourings of indefinable charm. The chief reproach that can be made against Gainsborough's work is that his drawing is often soft and negligent.

His chief works are scattered as follows:—

In the National Gallery: eleven pictures, including the portrait of Mrs. Siddons, the portrait of Edward Opin, *The Horse-Pond* and *The Hay-Waggon*.

In the National Gallery of Edinburgh: Portrait of Mary Graham.

In Dulwich Gallery: the portraits of Mrs. Sheridan, the Duke of Westminster, the family of George III, Nancy Parsons, etc.

See Pl. 48, Vol. II.

Bibliography: Sir W. Armstrong, *Thomas Gainsborough*, 1899 (new edition, 1905).—W. T. Whitley, *Thomas Gainsborough*. 1915.—H. Stokes, *Thomas Gainsborough*, 1925.

**GALILEI (Alessandro).**—Florentine architect, 1691-1736. A pupil of Bernini. He designed the façade of the Church of the Florentines in Rome, San Giovanni dei Florentin, for which Michelangelo made many designs which were lost. He also made that of the Lateran (1734), where a pompous but rectilinear style, prophetic of neo-classicism, replaces the picturesque curves of the Baroque.

**GALLE.**—Family of engravers, of Antwerp, of the end of the 16th and beginning of the 17th century. They made reproductions of a great many second-rate artists. One of them, Cornelius, made the first engraving after Rubens.

**GALLEGO (Fernando).**—Spanish painter who was born c. 1440-45 and probably died shortly after 1507. To judge from his surname, Gallego, who is regarded as the most important of north-west Castilian painters of the second half of the 15th century, was a native of Galicia. "In spite of this master's essential independence, strong elements of Flemish influence are dominant in him. . . . If one had to name the Northern painter who exerted the strongest influence on Gallego it would be Dirk Bouts." Gallego's first work known to us is the altar ordered by Cardinal Juan de Mella for the Chapel of San Ildefonso of Zamora Cathedral. On the central panel (signed Fernandus Galecus) the Virgin surrounded by angels and saints is seen handing the miraculous chasuble to the Saint. In spite of repaintings, the enamel-like quality of the picture remains, and in the heavy embroidered capes, studded with pearls and gems, Gallego rivals the magnificence and preciseness of the Flemish masters. A. L. Mayer states that about contemporary with this altarpiece—which does not show yet the Master at his height—are the paintings of the chapel of St. Anthony of the New Cathedral of Salamanca. Among the later works of this artist special mention must be made of the fine *Pietá* in the collection of E. Weibel at Madrid. Highly important is the discovery made by Gómez-Moreno that the great altar dedicated to St. Catherine in the Old Cathedral of Salamanca was painted by a Francisco Gallego. This Francisco, perhaps a relative, perhaps even a son of Fernando, received two payments for his work in 1500. The center panel of the altar of San Lorenzo of Toro, representing Christ Enthroned, had been displaced in the 18th century by a wooden statue. It was found in Paris by D. Pablo Bosch and is now in the Prado Museum. Like the altar it is ascribed to Francisco Gallego.

Fernando Gallego's authorship of the panels from the Cathedral of Ciudad Rodrigo in the Sir Herbert Cook Collection at Richmond has been disputed. The last documentary mention we have of Fernando is in connection with the "Tribuna" of the Chapel of the University of Salamanca (1507).

Bibliography: *Boletín de la Soc. Castellana de Excurs.*, VI (1913-14).—M. Gómez-Moreno, *La capilla de la universidad de Salamanca.—Thieme-Becker*, Vol. XIII, Leipzig, 1920. Art. *Gallegos (Fernando)* by A. L. Mayer.—*Enciclop. univ. ilustrad. europeo-americana*, Vol. XXV, Barcelona (Espasa) 1924, Art. *Gallego (Fernando)*.—A. L. Mayer, *Gesch. der span. Malerei*. Leipzig, 1922.—*Catálogo monumental de España*. M. Gómez-Moreno, Provincia de León, 2 vs. Madrid, 1925; Id., Provincia de Zamora. Madrid, 1927.—*Archivo español de arte y arqueologia*, III, 1927.—M. Gómez-Moreno and F. J. Sánchez Cantón, *Sobre Fernando Gallego*. Abridged catalogue of the pictures at Doughty House, Richmond, Surrey, in the Coll. of Sir H. Cook, Bart. London, 1932.—R. C. Post, *A History of Spanish Painting*, Vol. IV. Cambridge, Mass. (Harvard Univ. Press) 1933.

**GALLERY OF KINGS.**—See Reims.

**GAMBARA (Lattanzio).**—Painter of Brescia of the 16th century. Pupil of Romanino. He contributed paintings to the large nave of Parma Cathedral (about 1570). He made a good many decorations in Brescia.

**GANDARA (Antoine de La).**—French painter, born of foreign parents. Paris, 1862. He chiefly painted portraits of ladies, such as *The Woman with a Rose, The Lady in Green, Sarah Bernhardt* (1895). La Gandara also painted views of Paris.

**GANDHARA.**—See India.—Art.

**GARBO.**—See Raffaellino del Garbo.

**GARGOYLE.**—To prevent the rain water from dripping down the walls of buildings, and damaging the lower parts, the Gothic architects placed gargoyles at the gutters of the roof to eject the water into the street. In the execution of these gargoyles the Gothic architects gave free play to their imagination, and achieved the most fantastic and varied forms. The study of Gothic gargoyles reveals a very interesting aspect of mediaeval sculpture.

**GARISENDA.**—See Bologna (It.).

**GARNIER (Charles).**—French architect, 1825-1898. He worked a great deal in Rome, and then in Greece, where he made a remarkable restoration of the Temple of

Garnier (Charles): The Opera House, Paris.

# GOTHIC CATHEDRALS—FRANCE

*The French Gothic cathedrals were built in the thirteenth century after the beginning of the reign of Philip Augustus until the end of the reign of St. Louis. This architecture started in the Île de France; its blossoming and its expansion correspond to the establishment of a powerful French monarchy. At the same time these churches express the activity and wealth of the common people. While the Romanesque art spread all through western Christianity as the local product of each country and province, the Gothic art is* opus francigenum.

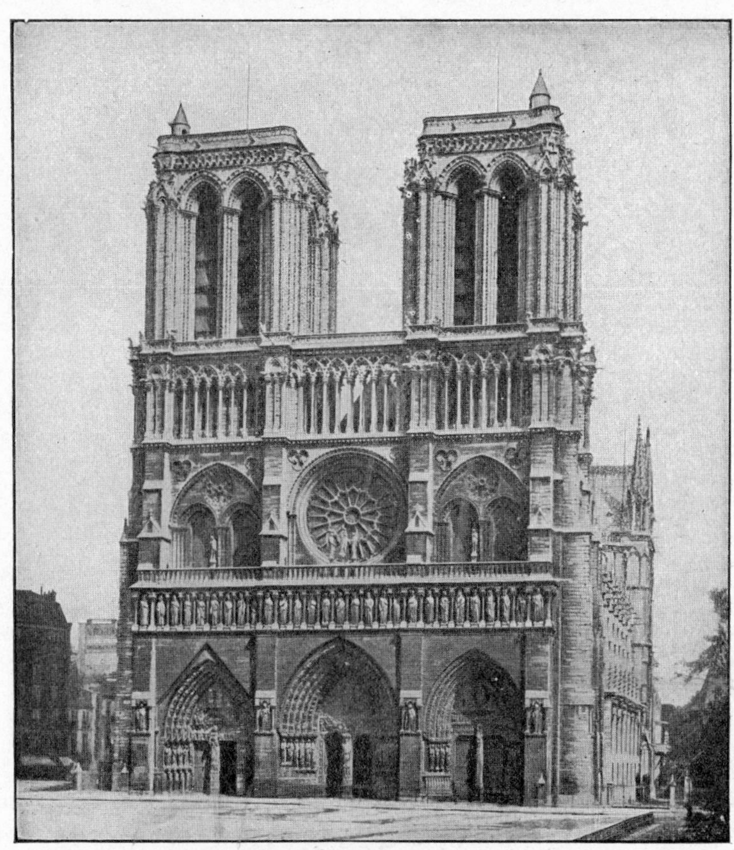

PARIS, NOTRE DAME: FAÇADE.
*(Photo by Hachette.)*

REIMS, CATHEDRAL: FAÇADE.
*(Photo by Neurdein.)*

Notre Dame in Paris is the oldest sister of Notre Dame in Reims. To compare the two façades is to mark two very different times in the evolution of the Gothic style. At Paris, the style is still severe, the lines of the architecture strongly marked constituting the only decoration. The two horizontal galleries and the vertical piers divide this façade into regular quadrilaterals which frame the bays here boldly carved out. At Reims, this bareness of the architecture is covered by tracery: the porches are surmounted by gables; the piers are topped by pinnacles; the towers are pierced and the horizontal lines are hidden by the ascending movement of the mouldings, the arches and the spires.

BEAUVAIS: CHOIR OF THE CATHEDRAL.
*(Photo by Hachette.)*

REIMS: NAVE OF THE CATHEDRAL.
*(Photo by Neurdein.)*

AMIENS: NAVE OF THE CATHEDRAL.
*(Photo by Hachette.)*

The Gothic cathedral was conceived by architects who wished to construct beautiful naves. In designing the mouldings of the vault and the columns, the forces which play in the building and make its balance, they handled stone so that it seems to be without weight. The nave of Amiens is the most beautiful in the world; no part of Gothic architecture shows more lightness and size in the spring of its arch. The nave of Beauvais, still more bold in design, has never been finished. That of Reims which shields the relics of the kings of France was very much damaged in the last war.

# GOTHIC CATHEDRALS—FRANCE

*The Gothic cathedrals, although they were all constructed on the same principles, with ogival arches and flying buttresses, show very different appearances. They do not resolve themselves, like the Greek temple, to certain types with unchangeable proportions. Each cathedral has a marked individuality. Some are more admired for their naves (Amiens), others for their façades (Reims), their porches (Bourges), their apses (Le Mans), or their spires (Chartres).*

NOTRE DAME, PARIS: APSE.
*(Photo by Hachette.)*

CATHEDRAL OF CHARTRES.
*(Photo by Neurdein.)*

CATHEDRAL OF COUTANCES: FAÇADE.
*(Photo by Hachette.)*

As each cathedral has its own physiognomy, it is the typical monument of each city, and we sum up the memory of a city in its cathedral. Notre Dame in Paris presents views equally elegant in the façade, the profile and the apse. Notre Dame in Chartres, admirable above all for the number of statues and its well preserved stained glass, shows on its Romanesque façade two bold spires, the one thin and sharply pointed dating from the twelfth century, the other more ornamental dating from the beginning of the sixteenth century. The cathedral of Coutances is one of the best constructed monuments of the Middle Ages.

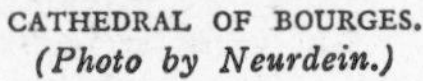

CATHEDRAL OF BOURGES.
*(Photo by Neurdein.)*

CATHEDRAL OF NOYON.
*(Photo by Neurdein.)*

CATHEDRAL OF LE MANS.
*(Photo by Hachette.)*

The cathedral of Bourges, famous for the five porches of its façade, has the peculiarity of not being crossed by a transept. The cathedral of Noyon belongs to a transitional style; like Notre Dame in Paris it contains both the slightly heavy simplicity of the Romanesque style and the more delicate and graceful lines of the Gothic art. The cathedral of Le Mans attaches a choir of the most beautiful Gothic style to a Romanesque nave. From this choir radiate deep apses like little chapels. The central apse is supported by flying buttresses which are separated from the main building and rest their weight upon multiple piers. Like the cathedral of Chartres, it has preserved an admirable display of stained glass.

CATHEDRAL OF STRASBOURG.
*(Photo by Lévy.)*

CATHEDRAL OF ALBI.
*(Photo by Hachette.)*

CATHEDRAL OF RODEZ.
*(Photo by Hachette.)*

The Gothic style, spreading from the Île de France throughout the whole kingdom, then into the whole of Christianity, accommodated itself to the customs and materials of each region. In Brittany, the churches of modest proportions put their luxury into the fine pierced clock towers. In southern France, the Gothic art did not adopt all its innovations; the flying buttresses were avoided most of the time. St. Cécile of Albi, in brick, resembles slightly a defiant fortress, but in the interior the decoration is of an exuberant richness. The cathedral of Rodez is flanked by a very beautiful tower and has a curious façade with no door.

Jupiter at Ægina. On his return to Paris, he built the *Opera House* (1860-1875), in the grandiose style of the Baroque Revival.

**GAROFALO (Benvenuto Tisi da).**—Italian painter. Ferrara, 1481-1559. Friend and pupil of Dosso Dossi, he was one of the most appreciated painters of the Ferrarese school. He was a conventional imitator of Raphael. His best pictures are in Rome, in various galleries, and in Ferrara, Gallery and churches.

**GASPARD - POUSSIN.**— See Dughet.

**GASTANO (Il).**—See Pulzone.

**GATTAMELATA.**—See Donatello; also Pl. 8, Vol. II.

**GATTI (Bernardino, called Il Sojaro).**—Italian painter of Cremona, 1495-1575. Influenced by the Venetians and by Correggio. There is a *Nativity* by him in San Pietro of Cremona, and decorations at the Madonna della Steccata of Parma.

**— (Fortunato).**—Bolognese painter, 1596-1651.

**GAU (F. C.).**—Parisian architect, 1790-1853. With Ballu, he designed the Church of Ste. Clothilde, Paris, in the Gothic Revival style.

**GAUDIER-BRZESKA (Henri).**—French sculptor (1891-1915). He was born at St. Jean de Braye in the Loiret 4th October 1891, the son of Joseph Gaudier, a carpenter. When he was a boy of fourteen years he won a scholarship for an art school in London and two years later he won another which enabled him to study at University College, Bristol, England. For a while in 1908 he was working in a contractor's office in Cardiff, Wales, spending his spare time making pictures of birds and animals at the local zoo. The next year he was sent to Germany by the University College to continue his art studies. He travelled through Holland to Nuremberg and Munich, where he gained some ideas from the examples of the old masters that he saw. To add to his income he made some fake masterpieces, copying the work of Rembrandt especially. Gaudier returned to Paris in 1910 and there met Sophie Brzeska, the Polish woman with whom his future was to be linked so definitely. It was drawing near the time when he would be called upon to serve his tenure of three years in the French army, which was required of every French citizen. Gaudier decided to evade this military life and taking with him Miss Brzeska he left for England to live there during the remainder of his life. The two, Henri Gaudier and Sophie Brzeska, joined their names together and lived as brother and sister. About this time Gaudier-Brzeska took up sculpture as his particular metier, working in a very simplified style which had in it some of the elements of Negro and Peruvian art. To support himself he worked as a clerk and a designer of advertising material, spending his leisure moments working on his carving. He tried working directly in stone, attempting to see the figure in the whole before chiselling it out into some more definite shape. He made some bas-reliefs of animal studies which were among his more successful pieces. There are a few portrait busts from his hand, but many more were destroyed because they did not come up to the standard that he had set for himself. He fought in the World War and was killed in the battle of Neuville St. Vaast 5th June 1915.

Bibliography: Horace Brodzky, *Henri Gaudier-Brzeska*, 1933.—*Drawings from the Note-books of Henri Gaudier-Brzeska*, 1919.— H. S. Ede, *Savage Messiah*, 1931.—Ezra Pound, *Gaudier-Brzeska, A Memoir*, 1916.

**GAUGUIN (Eugène Henri Paul).**—French painter (1848-1903). Paul Gauguin, as he is generally known, was born in Paris 8th June 1848, the son of a French father and a Spanish mother. When he was only three years old the family went to Lima, Peru, to live with his mother's people. She was the daughter of Flora Tristan, the writer of many Socialist pamphlets. His father died just as they landed in South America and the boy and his mother returned to France in 1855. Gauguin joined the merchant marine and in 1865 made a trip with them to Rio de Janeiro. A few years later he was in the French navy which was cruising in the north Atlantic around Greenland and the North Cape. After the close of the Franco-Prussian War he began to work in the banking house of M. Bertin, painting in his spare time for amusement. They were academic works and showed the influence of Delacroix and Courbet. Soon he became interested in the pictures of the Impressionists, especially those of Pissarro, and tried to model his paintings in that new technique. In 1883 he gave up his business to devote his entire time to painting and with his family moved to Rouen and later to Brittany. His wife was the daughter of a Danish minister and soon they found themselves unable to go on living together. Gauguin left his wife and went back to Paris and although he went to foreign countries later in life he never divorced his wife, sending her money occasionally or some paintings to sell for him. In 1887, accompanied by Charles Laval he set out for Martinique, but the climate was too much for his health and his friend nearly died of yellow fever. He returned to Paris later that year and soon was devoting his time to the making of ceramics and some sculptured figures. The next year was the occasion of his sojourn in Arles with Vincent van Gogh, when Gauguin tried to give van Gogh some of the fundamentals of impressionism. Then followed another interlude in Brittany, at which time the *Christ Jaune* and the *Lutte de Jacob et de l'Ange* were painted, showing the inclusion of Breton types and all painted with a simplicity and almost primitive quality. In 1891 he left Paris for Tahiti with a letter from the French government giving him permission to paint and work where he chose. He had always longed for freedom from the conventions of society and now here was his chance. He lived as much as possible like the natives, even taking to himself a native wife. But in 1893 he returned to Paris to try to sell some of his pictures so that he might go back to the tropics to spend the rest of his life. However, his pictures did not sell very well and he grew discouraged at his reception in France. Instead of being the hero of the hour he was almost forgotten and the interest of the people lay in the pictures of younger artists who had remained in France. His leg was broken in a scuffle and never properly healed; but in February, 1895, Gauguin sailed again for the South Seas, still seeking an artistic Utopia. He worked for a while as a shipping clerk in the Board of Public Works in Papeete, but his health was broken from a lingering illness and he grew steadily weaker. In 1900 he made a short trip to the Marquesas Isles and there had his own little hut and life seemed brighter for a while. However, his eyes were failing and after an attack of influenza he died 6th May 1903 and was buried there in the land where he had sought for peace and quiet for so long. Gauguin's art is characterised by the use of brilliant colour and very simplified forms of the human figures. His pictures are decorative and recall in their synthesis and feeling of repose the early Italian primitives. They were painted from memory and many of his later subjects were given Tahitian titles although there was usually no direct use of their symbolism or legends as subject matter. As has been mentioned before Gauguin also tried his hand at sculpture, in marble, wood, clay and paste, ceramics, lithographs, etchings and stained glass. He was the author of *Avant et Après* and *Noa Noa* which tell of his existence in the islands of the south Pacific, which has so often been called the earthly paradise. His pictures may be seen in many European museums and the Boston Museum of Fine Arts, the Art Institute of Chicago and the Worcester Art Museum in the United States.

Bibliography: Arsène Alexandre, *Paul Gauguin, sa Vie et le Sens de son Œuvre*, 1930.—Wilhelm Barth, *Paul Gauguin*, 1929.—Beril Becker, *Paul Gauguin, the Calm Madman*, 1931.—Anthony Bertram, *Paul Gauguin*, 1930.—Charles Chasse, *Gauguin et le Groupe de Pont-Aven*, 1921.—Maurice Denis, *Theories, 1890-1910, du Symbolisme et de Gauguin vers un Nouvel Ordre Classique*, 1920.—Jean Dorsenne, *Vie Sentimentale de Paul Gauguin*, 1927.—John Gould Fletcher, *Paul Gauguin, His Life and Art*, 1921.—Pierre Girieud, *Paul Gauguin*, 1928.—*The Intimate Journals of Paul Gauguin*, 1936.—Charles Kunstler, *Gauguin, Peintre Maudit*, 1934.—*Lettres de Paul Gauguin à Georges-Daniel de Monfried*, 1918, edited by Victor Segalen.—Charles Morice, *Paul Gauguin*, 1920.—Robert Rey, *Gauguin*, 1924.—Jean de Rotonchamp, *Paul Gauguin, 1848-1903*, 1925.—Erich Wiese, *Paul Gauguin*, 1923.—R. Burnett, *The Life of Paul Gauguin*, 1937.

**GAVARNI (Guillaume Sulpice Chevalier, called).**—French lithographer, 1804-1866.

He contributed to "La Mode" such works as "La Loge à l'Opéra," illustrating the amusing fashions of the day, which he had every opportunity of studying at the salons and balls which he frequented. Later he enlarged his field of observation, but his drawing tended to become weaker.

Unfortunately for him, Gavarni founded a paper called the "Journal des gens du Monde." After nineteen numbers had appeared, the paper foundered, involving Gavarni in its disaster. Worried by creditors, and disillusioned, he expressed his horror of business men in a series of engravings which were published in the "Charivari."

About 1837, he represented the *Deceits of Women*, and returned to the same subject in his *Letter-box.*

A few years later he enriched his technique, but his types of men and women hardly varied, and he continued to exaggeratc.

Gavarni spent three years in Great Britain (1848 to 1851), but the change did not renew his vitality. His "bag-pipers" and "Scottish washerwomen" are pleasant works, but nevertheless proclaim the decadence of his art. His water-colours are heavy and spiritless.

Gavarni: Waltzing couple. (Bibl. Nat.)

Towards the end of his life he gave up lithography for mathematics.

See Pl. 12, Vol. I.

Bibliography: E. and J. de Goncourt, *Gavarni, l'homme et l'œuvre.* Paris, 1871.—Eugène Forgues, *Gavarni*, Les Artistes Célèbres. Paris, 1912.

**GAY (Walter).**—American painter, born 1856, died 1937. Studied under Leon Bonnat and Benjamin Constant in Paris where he settled. Specially noted for his sensitive and intimate renderings of interiors, generally without figures.

**GEBHARDT (E. von).**—German painter of the Düsseldorf school, who was born in 1838. He was one of the revivers of religious painting. His best known pictures are: the *Entry of Christ into Jerusalem*, the *Last Supper*, the *Resurrection of Jairus' Daughter*, which are in the National Gallery of Berlin, and the *Crucifixion*, in the gallery of Hamburg.

**GEERTGEN TOT SINT JANS (or Gerard of Haarlem).**—Dutch painter. Born in Leyden about 1465; died in Haarlem about 1490. His best known works are two pictures in Vienna, which originally formed an altarpiece (one is a *Lamentation over Christ*, and the other, *Julian the Apostate Causing the Bones of St. John the Baptist to be Burned*); the *Resurrection of Lazarus* (Louvre); a *Madonna* (Berlin); the *Adoration of the Magi* (Amsterdam, and Prague); *St. John the Baptist in the Desert* (Berlin); *The Holy Kinship* (Rijks Museum, Amsterdam); a little *Virgin* (Milan); and a *Nativity* (formerly von Kaufmann Collection, Berlin, now in the National Gallery, London).

See Pl. 60, Vol. I.

Bibliography: M. J. Friedländer, *Altniederländische Malerei.*

**GEEST (Wybrandt de).**—Dutch painter, 1590-1650. He married Rembrandt's sister-in-law, but he does not seem to have been influenced by her famous relative. One of his best pictures is the portrait of a little girl, in Amsterdam.

**GELDER (Aert van).**—Dutch painter, 1645-1727. Pupil of Rembrandt.

BIBLIOGRAPHY: Lilienfeld, K., *A. de Gelder*. Haag, 1914.

**GENGA (Girolamo).**—Umbro-Romagnol painter, 1476-1551; pupil of Signorelli, influenced by Raphael.

**GENNARI (Benedetto, the Elder).**—Bolognese painter (1570-1610), of Cento, near Ferrara. He may be considered as the founder of the school of this little town, which was attached to the school of Bologna, and had Guercino as its celebrity. His *David* is in the Pitti Palace. The *Virgin in the Clouds Appearing to St. Nicholas of Bari* (Bologna Gallery) is a striking example of the elegant, declamatory art, which was so much sought after.

**GENOELS (Abraham).**—Florentine painter, 1640-1723. He worked chiefly in Paris, where he acted several times as Le Brun's assistant in details of cartoons for tapestries, made for the Gobelins.

**GENOA (Italy).**—Marvellously situated on the Mediterranean, with

GENOA: THE CATHEDRAL.

rich marble palaces built at the time of the Renaissance. The architect Galeas Alessi planned several of these buildings. Amongst the finest and oldest is the *Ducal Palace*, built in the 13th century, for the doges of Venice. From this period there

GENOA: PORTA PILA (1633). (Attributed to Bartolommeo Bianco.)

remains the "torre del popolo." The building was transformed in the 16th and 17th centuries. The *Municipal Palace* is decorated with frescoes. The *Palazzo Russo* takes its name from the red colour of its façade. It may have been built by Alessi. It contains a fine picture gallery. The *Palazzo Bianco*, built from 1565 to 1569, was also named from its colour, and has a collection of pictures. The *Durazzo Pallavicini Palace* has a superb 18th century staircase, and contains a picture gallery. The *Palazzo Doria*, built in the 16th century, transformed in 1529 by Montorsoli, is decorated with frescoes by Perino del Vaga, a pupil of Raphael. The *Palazzo Balbi Senarega*, built in the 17th century by Bianco, has a fine courtyard surrounded by a Doric colonnade, and a picture gallery. The *Royal Palace* is remarkable for the beauty of its apartments.

Genoa also possesses fine Churches. The *Cathedral San Lorenzo*, begun in 985, was transformed in 1100, in the Romanesque style, and then, in 1307, in the Gothic style.

GENOA: THE DUCAL PALACE.

In 1567 Alessi added a Renaissance dome. The façade is in black and white marble, alternately. The carvings on the central doorway date from the 13th century; and those on the side doorways from the 13th and 14th centuries. Near to the Cathedral are 12th century Romanesque cloisters of the 12th century. *Sant'Ambrogio* is a rich building in the Jesuit style, built in 1589. *Santa Maria di Carignano*, begun in 1552, from plans of Alessi, was finished in 1660. His design was inspired by St. Peter's, Rome.

**GENRE PAINTING.**—Realistic depiction of scenes from every day life.

See Pl. 36, Vol. II.

**GENTILE da FABRIANO.**—Born c. 1360-70 in Fabriano; died 1427.

The great Gothic painter and founder of the school of painting in the Italian Marches is first mentioned in 1408, when he executes an altarpiece for Francesco Amadi, for which he was so well paid that he must have had by that time a high reputation. About 1410 his name appears in a list of painters in Venice in Mariegola della Scuola di S. Cristoforo. Gentile's profound influence upon the development of Venetian painting, and in particular upon the Bellini, dates from this Venetian sojourn. In 1414-19 he decorated a chapel in Brescia for Pandolfo Malatesta. His work there was probably intermittent. In 1419 he went to Rome at the request of the Pope Martin V, but is recorded the next year as having returned to Fabriano. In 1421 Gentile's name appears on the register of the Corporation of S. Luca in Florence, and in 1422 on that of the Medici e Speziali. In 1423 he painted the altarpiece with the *Adoration of the Magi* that Palla Strozzi ordered for Sta. Trinità; signed and dated, it is now in the Uffizi, one predella panel, of the *Presentation in the Temple*, in the Louvre. During this Florentine period Gentile may have had as assistant Jacopo Bellini. In 1424-25, Gentile was in Siena, where he painted the *Madonna of the Notaries*, in 1424, on the corner of the Via del Casato, mentioned by contemporary chroniclers. From 1425 dates the Quaratesi altar, at one time in S. Niccolò in Florence, now dispersed (the *Madonna* in the National Gallery of London, on loan by H. M. the King; four lateral Saints in the Uffizi; four scenes from the *Legend of St. Nicholas* in the Vatican). Of 1425 also is the extant fresco of the *Madonna* in the Duomo at Orvieto. From 1426-27, Gentile was again in Rome, where he received payments for paintings in S. Giovanni Laterano (no longer existing). He died in 1427.

In addition to those mentioned above, two authentic works of Gentile's remain, both signed: the *Coronation* in the Brera, probably from an early period in his career; and the *Madonna* in the Jarves Collection, New Haven, Connecticut.

Gentile da Fabriano is the most notable exponent in Italy of that richly decorative, lineal style known as International Gothic—international because it appeared, with inevitable local school differences, all over Europe, as a last manifestation of the exquisite and chivalric Gothic spirit, in contradistinction to the vigorous new plasticity, the functional realism, of the Renaissance. Gentile's style found followers in Italy, not only in Venice and in his native Marches, but even in Florence, birthplace of Renaissance rationalism.

BIBLIOGRAPHY: Vasari - Venturi (Lives of Gentile and Pisanello), 1896.—L. Cust and H. Horne, *The Quaratesi Altarpiece*, in the Burlington Magazine, 1905, p. 470.—Crowe and Cavalcaselle, Douglas ed. —L. Venturi, *Origini della pitt. venez.*, 1907.—Testi, *Storia della pitt. venez*, I, 1909.—Berenson, *Central Italian Painters*, 1909.—A. Colasanti, *Gentile da Fabriano*. Bergamo, 1909.—R. Sassi, *La famiglia di Gentile da Fabriano*, Rassegna Marchigiana, 1923, p. 21.—P. Lugano, *Gentile da Fabriano e l'ordine di Montoliveto*, Rivista di storia benedettina, XVI, 1925.—A. Colasanti, *Italian Painters of the Marches*.

**GÉRARD (François Pascal Simon).**—French painter, 1770-1837.

GÉRARD: MARIA-LETITIA BONAPARTE, MOTHER OF NAPOLEON I. (Museum of Versailles.)

He spent the first ten years of his life in Rome. In 1780, his father returned to France, bringing his family with him. François finally became a pupil of David.

His portrait of Isabey holding his daughter's hand (Louvre) appeared at the Salon of 1796. This work shows Gérard at his best, and as a very fine portrait painter. Unfortunately, the lively, facile portraits which followed did not always justify the promise of this remarkable work. He painted an enormous number of portraits.

Other pictures include: *Psyche Receiving the First Kiss of Love* (Louvre), which shows all his faults of mannered grace and cold colouring; the *Battle of Austerlitz* (Versailles); the *Entry of Henry VI into Paris, Achilles Taking up His Arms after the Death of Patroclus*, etc.

See Pl. 50, Vol. II.

**— (Marguerite).**—French painter, 1762-1837. Sister-in-law of Fragonard. She painted a certain number of graceful scenes, and then tried to develop her talent on the same lines as Boilly. She studied the Dutch masters, notably Terborch, and strove to equal his perfect execution of materials and details of furniture.

**GERARD OF HAARLEM.**—See Geertgen Tot Sint Jans.

**GÉRICAULT (Jean Louis André Théodore).**—French painter, 1791-

GÉRICAULT.

1824. Géricault studied under Carle Vernet, and then under Guérin, at whose studio he made the acquaintance of Delacroix and other Romantic painters. It is strange to find the studio of the painter of *Dido* sheltering such romanticism. Guérin had little encouragement for the young Géricault, who was an enthusiastic admirer of Rubens, of warm colours, and bold forms. He advised him to give up painting. Géricault merely renounced Guérin's lessons and finished his own studies at the Louvre.

GÉRICAULT: THE STABLE. (Louvre.)

One of his earliest paintings is the vigorous *Officer Charging*, which must have made a strange impression amid the coldly classical art of the day!

*The Wounded Cuirassier* (Louvre) was exhibited at the Salon of 1814.

Géricault studied all kinds of horses. He painted nervous, rearing battle-horses, thin race-horses (such as Gros and Carle Vernet painted), and heavy cart-horses.

In 1817 Géricault went to Italy, and was greatly impressed by Michelangelo's frescoes.

On his return to Paris he painted the *Raft of the Medusa*. For this tragic picture, Géricault made severe studies, even visiting hospitals to observe the effects of suffering.

The appearance of the *Raft of the Medusa* (Louvre) at the Salon of 1819, was an event. We cannot imagine how such a subject must have shocked both artists and public of the day. The work (which reveals the influence of the Sistine Chapel) was generally found detestable. The robustness of handling, and trivialities of realism (which the younger generation was to foster) were regarded as defying both good taste and good sense.

In 1820, Géricault went to England, where someone persuaded him to exhibit the *Medusa*. Its success in London brought Géricault twenty thousand francs. This visit to England was ultimately to have as great an influence on the artist as his journey to Italy.

His impressions of England, green landscapes under a watery sky, racecourses and stables, are expressed by means of nervous painting and fresh colour. Even more than Carle Vernet, it was Géricault who introduced the race-course into French art, thus inaugurating a "genre" which was after popularized by engraving and lithography.

When he returned to France, Géricault was already suffering from an accident with a horse and subsequent unwise exertions, resulted in his being unable to move for many months. He died in his father's house in 1824.

At the sale of his pictures, his friend Dedreux Dorcy and the Comte de Forbin succeeded in saving his *Medusa*, which speculators talked of cutting to pieces.

Géricault died just before the battle between Romanticism and Classicism began, for although his youthful work betrayed a vigorous temperament, it could scarcely be considered as a declaration of war. This broke out some months after his death, with Delacroix's *Massacre of Scio*.

See Pl. 53, Vol. II.

BIBLIOGRAPHY: L. Rosenthal, *Géricault*. Paris.—C. Clément, *Géricault*, 1879.

**GERINI.**—See Lorenzo di Niccolò Gerini and Niccolò di Pietro Gerini.

**GERMAIN (The).**—Family of Parisian goldsmiths. The eldest is François Germain. His son, Pierre Germain (1647-1684), worked for Louis XIV, under LeBrun. Thomas Germain, his son (1673-1748), goldsmith-sculptor, executed many objects for Louis XV and for foreign courts. Most of his work was melted down for the sake of the precious metal, but some religious objects are kept in the Church of St. Roch, of Lisbon. François Thomas Germain (1726-1791), son of the preceding, was likewise king's goldsmith, and lived in the Louvre. He was much appreciated, and worked with a rapidity which equalled his skill. Among his most famous pieces are the magnificent silver epergnes, made for Elizabeth of Russia in 1760.

**GERMANIC MUSEUM.**—See Nuremberg.

**GERMIGNY-LES-PRÈS (801-886).**—An important building of the Carolingian period. Like the East Christian monuments from which it derives ultimately, although there is a strong possibility of immediate derivation from pre-Romanesque of Spain, it has an interior divided into nine square compartments by four central supports from which proceed arches carrying diaphragm walls. The dome covering the central compartment is modern. An apse is centered on each of the four walls. The horseshoe plan of the apses points to a Spanish source.

**GERNRODE (Germany).**—St. *Cyriacus*, 961-1050. Rebuilt 12th century. An Ottonian abbey church, basilican in plan, with a triapsidal choir and a large atrium.

**GÉRÔME (Jean Léon).**—French painter, 1824-1904. He painted historical and genre scenes, and pictures of animals. His pictures are striking and facile in their "mise en scène," correct in drawing, and conscientiously archæological. He favoured anecdotal scenes of historical events. He was a great popular success. But the dryness of his style, the dryness of his composition, drawing and colour alienated amateurs at a time when taste was turning towards freer, more synthetic painting. Some critics preferred his sculpture, remarking that his precision, at times excessive in his painting accorded better with a more material art.

GÉRÔME. (After A. MOROT.)

GÉRÔME: EQUESTRIAN STATUE OF BONAPARTE. (Gilded bronze, Musée du Luxembourg.)

BIBLIOGRAPHY: Charles Moreau Vauthier, *Gérôme, l'homme et l'artiste*, Paris, 1906.

**GERONA (Spain).**—*Cathedral*, 1312-1733. A masterpiece of the late Gothic of Catalonia, and closely related to the Gothic of the south of France, as the Cathedral of Albi. The 15th century nave is undivided, and is covered by one wide vault, the widest in all Europe. The baroque façade was begun 1607.

**GERVEX (Henri).**—French painter, born 1852. He showed promise at the beginning, but his later work is often unequal and inferior, in spite of good portraits such as that of Alfred Stevens (1884). His pictures entitled *Satyr Playing with a Bacchante* and *Members of the Jury of the Salon* 1885) are in the Luxembourg Gallery.

**GESSO.**—Prepared plaster mixed with a binding material and used as a background for paintings or relief work.

**GESELLIUS (Herman).**—Contemporary Finnish architect. Gesellius can hardly be mentioned apart from Lindgren and Saarinen. These three were the authors of the Finnish Pavilion at the Paris Exhibition, in 1900. One of their most characteristic buildings is the curious Château of Merijoki.

**GHENT.**—An old Flemish town which has largely kept its ancient character. Among its finest buildings are: *St. Bavon*, a Gothic church of which the crypt was founded in the 10th century and became, later, the Church. The Chapels are in flamboyant Gothic style. One of them contains the masterpiece of Hubert and Jan Van Eyck, the *Adoration of the Lamb*.

The *Château des Comtes*, rebuilt in the 12th century; it still has remains of the old keep, and a fine Romanesque gallery. The Château has been recently restored.

GHENT: CHÂTEAU DES COMTES.

The *Hôtel de Ville* is a fine Gothic building. Most of it dates from the 15th century; the north façade from the 16th, and the eastern façade from the 17th century. The interior contains fine rooms and a Gothic staircase, restored by Viollet-le-Duc.

**GHIBERTI (Lorenzo).**—Florentine bronze and stone sculptor, goldsmith, architect, painter and writer; born in Florence 1378; died 1455.

GHIBERTI (LORENZO): DOOR OF THE BAPTISTERY OF S. GIOVANNI, DETAIL. (Florence.)

Ghiberti learned the goldsmith's trade with Bartoluccio di Michele. In 1400 he went to the Romagna to escape the plague in Florence, and painted, as helper of another painter, frescoes in the castle of Carlo Malatesta, which no longer exist. On his return to Florence he took part, with six Tuscan sculptors (Brunelleschi, Simone da Colle, Niccolò Spinelli d'Arezzo, Jacopo della Quercia, Francesco di Valdambrino and Niccolò Lamberti), in the competition for the doors of the Baptistery, and won with his relief of the *Sacrifice of Isaac* (now in the Museo Nazionale, Florence). In 1403 he received the commission, with Bartoluccio di Michele. In 1424 the doors were finished, and Ghiberti left Florence, again to escape the plague, this time going to Venice. In 1425 he was charged to execute his second doors for the Baptistry, known as the *Paradise Doors*. These were finished in 1452, his helpers including: Bartoluccio di Michele, Donatello, Bernardo Ciuffagni, Michelozzo, and Paolo Uccello.

He was accepted in the goldsmiths' guild in 1409; in that of the painters in 1423; and in the stonemasons' guild in 1427.

Additional bronze works by Ghiberti include: the 1414 statue of *John Baptist* for Or S. Michele, signed and dated; reliefs for the font of S. Giovanni in Siena, for which the commission was given in 1417, work on which was begun in 1424, and which were cast and gilt in 1427; the *St. Matthew* for Or San Michele, commission 1419, model 1420, finished 1422; the 1423 tomb slab for Fra Leonardo Dati in S. Maria Novella; the 1428 reliquary shrine, *SS. Hyacinth, Protus and Nemesius*, for Sta. Maria degli Angeli, Florence (commission from Cosimo de' Medici; stolen and sold during the French occupation; pieces reassembled; now in the Museo Nazionale); the 1428 *S. Stefano* for Or S. Michele, and the reliquary shrine of *S. Zenobius*, of the same date, in the Duomo. In 1428 he receives the commission for the shrine in Venice, in 1434 purchases bronze for the shrine, in 1437 is reminded to finish it, in 1439 is given a new commission, the reliefs of the small sides being not yet finished, and in 1444 the work is completed.

GHIBERTI (LORENZO): DOOR OF THE BAPTISTERY OF S. GIOVANNI, DETAIL. (Florence.)

In 1450 Ghiberti was working on the small doors for the tabernacle of Bernardo Rossellino in S. Maria Nuova (S. Egidio), Florence. Statuettes of a caryatid and a saint are in Berlin, in the Kaiser-Friedrich Museum.

His works in marble include: the tomb slab for Lodovico degli Obizi (died 1424); and that for Bartolommeo Valori (died 1427), both in S. Croce; and the design for the tabernacle enclosing Fra Angelico's Linaiuoli Madonna, in the Museo S. Marco.

Many Madonnas, small sculptural compositions and goldsmith's articles are attributed to Ghiberti. No goldsmith's article mentioned in contemporary documents is still extant.

Ghiberti was active also as an architect, and from 1404 to 1436 took part in various commissions to advise on the Duomo, submitted models, and engaged in competitions for its design. He designed a number of the windows of the Cathedral.

In his writings, *I Commentarii,* Ghiberti describes works of art in various cities which he must have visited himself: Siena (1416-17), Pisa, Massa, Volterra, San Gimignano, Cortona, Pistoia, Perugia, Rome, Naples.

BIBLIOGRAPHY: Ghiberti, *Commentarii* (Julius v. Schlosser, *Lorenzo Ghibertis Denkwürdigkeiten,* including *I Commentarii*), 1912.—Vasari-Milanesi, II.—Charles Perkins, *Ghiberti et son École.* Paris, 1886.—Burckhardt-Bode, *Cicerone,* 1910.—Bode, *Florent. Bildhauer der Renaiss.,* 1910; and *Die ital. Plastik* (Handbücher der K. Museen). Berlin, 1911.—P. Schubring, *Die ital. Plastik des Quatrocento,* Burger's Handbuch f. Kstwiss., 1919.

**GHIRLANDAIO (Benedetto).**—Florentine painter, brother of Domenico Ghirlandaio, born in 1458; died 1497.

In 1480 his father states of his son that he had abandoned miniature painting on account of weak eye-sight, but that he still made sketches for paintings. In 1494 Benedetto went to France, but returned the same year. In 1495, he was commissioned with his father to execute a window for Pisa, a *Coronation of the Virgin.*

Benedetto is a very nebulous figure, and nothing is known of his activity save the rather meagre evidence furnished by a signed picture in the Church of Aigueperse in Auvergne, a *Nativity,* in very poor state, almost effaced and more northern in forms than one would expect from a brother of Domenico.

BIBLIOGRAPHY: Vasari-Milanesi VI.—Fabriczy, Repert. f. Kunstwiss., XI, 1888, p. 95.—Warburg, Rivista d'arte, 1904, p. 85.—J. Guiffrey, *La Nativité de Benedetto Ghirlandaio.*—Francovich, *Benedetto Ghirlandaio.*

**— (Davide).**—Florentine painter and mosaicist, brother of Domenico Ghirlandaio, born in Florence in 1452; died 1525. A mosaicist active for the Cathedrals of Orvieto, Siena, and Florence. A signed and dated (1496) mosaic, *Madonna and Child,* is in the Musée Cluny. The only documented painting by Davide is a panel of *St. Lucy with a Donor* in the Cappella Rucellai in S. Maria Novella (1484). A large number of works are attributed to Davide. For dates of his collaborative activity with Domenico, see Ghirlandaio, Domenico.

BIBLIOGRAPHY: Vasari-Milanesi, VI, 531ff.—Crowe and Cavalcaselle, Douglas ed., IV and VI.—Borghesi-Banchi, *Nuovi doc. senesi.*—Tanfani Centofanti, Not. di Art. etc., pisani, 1897.—Fumi, *Duomo di Orvieto,* 1891.—Bacci, *Doc. toscani,* II, 1912, 113ff.—Poggi, *Un quadro di Davide Ghirlandaio in S. M. Novella,* Miscell. d'arte, 1903; *Duomo di Firenze,* 1909 (Ital. Forsch. of Kst. Inst. in Florence II).—Berenson, *Drawings of Florent. Painters,* 1903; *Cat. of the Johnson Coll., Ital. Paintings,* 1913.

**— (Domenico, also called Girlandaio or with his family name Bigordi).**—Born in Florence in 1449, according to documents of 1457 and 1480 in which his grandfather and his father Tommaso state his age and abode. Died in Florence 1494. Baldovinetti was one of Domenico's masters, according to the latter's *Ricordi,* and Domenico's painting likewise shows the influence of Verrocchio.

His first mention as an artist, and his earliest dated works still extant are from 1475, in which year he finished the frescoes in the Chapel of Sta. Fina, in San Gimignano. In the same year he was called to Rome where he was active, with Davide, his brother, in the library of Pope Sixtus IV. In 1476, he executed with Davide a *Last Supper* for Don Isidoro del Sera in the Monastery of Passignano. The next year he was again in Rome, working in the burial chapel of Giovanni Francesco Tornabuoni, of which decoration nothing remains. From 1478-79 he receives payments for two *Madonnas* and a *Coronation* for the large hall of the Opera del Duomo of Pisa; and in the latter year he is back in Florence where he executes, with assistants, a fresco in the Badia at Settimo. *The Last Supper* and the *St. Jerome* in the Ognissanti, Florence, date from 1480. In this year and the next he was working with Davide in the Church of S. Donato a Polverosa, executing a *Last Supper* which was destroyed in 1530; and from 1481 dates his activity with Botticelli, Cosimo Rosselli and Perugino in the Sistine Chapel, where he did the extant frescoes of the *Calling of Peter and Andrew* and single figures of *Popes* (1482). In 1482-83, Domenico received payments in Florence for the large fresco of the *Glory of St. Zenobius,* in the Palazzo Vecchio. The frescoes in the Sassetti Chapel, Sta. Trinità, representing scenes from the *Legend of Francis* are of 1485, and the *Adoration of the Shepherds,* right of the choir, is of the same date. From 1486 to 1490, Domenico was busy with the frescoes in the Choir of Sta. Maria Novella, made on the order of Giovanni Tornabuoni to replace those by Orcagna destroyed by leakage. The execution of these frescoes is chiefly from the hands of assistants. In 1486 he finished the extant *Coronation* for the monks of S. Gerolamo of Narni, in which he was also assisted. The *Adoration of the Magi* in the Spedale degli Innocenti was finished by Bartolommeo di Giovanni; and in the same year Domenico and Davide received as apprentice Michelangelo Buonarroti, aged thirteen. In 1490 Domenico and Davide were commissioned by the del Palco Convent near Prato to paint a *Madonna Enthroned with SS. Francis, Bonaventura, Anthony of Padua and Bernardino of Sienna;* and in the same year they worked on the mosaic *Annunciation* (extant) over the Porta della Mandorla of the Duomo of Florence; decorated, in Florence, the doors for the organ of the Cathedral of Pisa; and painted a *Visitation* for the Church of Sta. Maria de' Pazzi, on the order of Giovanni Tornabuoni. In 1491 Domenico was requested to submit a cartoon for a mosaic in the vault of the Chapel of S. Zenobi, with Botticelli and Gherardo and Monte di Giovanni, the latter two being charged with the commission. From 1492 dates the *Christ in Glory with Two Saints* at Volterra; and in the same year Domenico undertook paintings for the Duomo in Pisa, partial payment for which was made over to his heirs after his death. His work there included restoration of the Cimabue mosaic in the apse. Domenico died of plague in 1494, leaving his two brothers and his son Ridolfo, then eleven.

Among the works attributed to Domenico Ghirlandaio are a series of notable portraits, a form to which he was particularly well suited because of his vigorous and sincere realism. Domenico was not a highly imaginative painter nor a great innovator, but he has left an extraordinarily vivid record of his time and its great personalities. The portraits among the Sassetti Chapel frescoes are among the finest of the quattrocento.

BIBLIOGRAPHY: Vasari-Milanesi, III.—Bacci, *Doc. toscani,* II, 1912, p. 113 f.—Baldinucci, *Not. de' profess. del disegno.*—Bigazzi, *Iscriz. e mem. della città di Firenze.*—Borghini, *Riposo.*—Gaye, *Carteggio.*—Fabriczy, L'Arte, IX, *Mem. sulla chiesa di S. Maria Maddalena.*—Landucci, *Florentiner Tagebuch.*—Malaguzzi, Arch. stor. dell'Arte.—Tanfani Centofanti, *Not. di artisti, etc., Pisani.*—Manni, *Vita di Domenico del Ghirlandaio, Raccolta di opuscoli, etc., del P. Calogera.* Venice, 1751.—Steinmann, *Ghirlandaio,* 1897.—Michel, *Hist. de l'art,* III, 1907.—G. S. Davies, *Ghirlandaio.* London, 1908.—Crowe and Cavalcaselle, Douglas ed., IV, 1911, VI, 1914.—Venturi, *Storia, etc.,* VII, I.—Küppers, *Die Tafelbilder des Domenico Ghirlandaio,* 1916.

**— (Ridolfo).**—Florentine painter, 1483-1561. Son of Domenico Ghirlandaio. Eclectic painter, pupil of Piero di Cosimo and Granacci, and imitator of many of his contemporaries, chiefly of Raphael. He is particularly well represented in Florence, where there are several excellent portraits.

**GHISLANDI (Vittore).**—Also called Fra Paolotto or Fra Galgavio, from the name of his convent. Bergamese painter, chiefly known for his portraits. 1655-1743.

**GHISSI (Francescuccio di Cecco).**—Marchigian painter, follower of Alegretto Nuzi; active 1359-1389.

From 1359 is the signed and dated *Madonna of Humility* in San Domenico, Fabriano; and from 1374 the signed and dated *Madonna* in San Salvatore, Montegiorgio.

**GIAMBONO (Michele di Taddeo).**—Painter and mosaicist in Venice, first mentioned in Venice in 1420; still living in 1462.

The Academy, Venice, owns two works by Giambono: a five-part altarpiece from the Scuola del Crocifisso, signed; and a *Coronation of the Virgin* from S. Gregorio (painted in 1447 for the high altar of S. Agnese). This last, a tempera painting, is, according to documentary evidence, a copy of the altarpiece by Giovanni d'Alemagna and Antonio Vivarini in S. Pantaleone, and bears the false signature "Joannes et Antonius di Murano" and the date 1440.

BIBLIOGRAPHY: L. Venturi, *Le origini della pittura veneziana,* 1907.—Testi, *Storia d. pitt. venez.,* II, 1915.

**GIAN da BOLOGNA.**—Gianbologna. Florentine sculptor, 1524-1608. Born in Donai, he was educated at Antwerp, and did not go to Italy until 1551. There, he copied antiques, and was taught by Michelangelo. He left Rome in 1553, and settled in Florence with the patronage of the senator, Vecchietti.

He loved great masses of boldly cut white marble, and agitated forms, and he imitated the powerful athletes of his master. With him, however, the drama is on the surface. The tormented flesh no longer expresses the soul within, but only serves for extraordinary and complicated forms.

GIAN DA BOLOGNA: FOUNTAIN, BOBOLI GARDENS, FLORENCE.

His first statue was a *Venus* (1558), bought by the Grand Duke Francesco. Then he competed for the fountain of the Piazza della Signoria, without success, however. (The graceful sea gods are, nevertheless, of his school.) Together with Tommaso Laureti, he made a fountain dominated with a colossal *Neptune* (1563) for Bologna.

It is chiefly in the beautiful Boboli Gardens that his gifts for grand effects and bold movements are displayed. He must have had a large part in designing the rhythmic and fantastic terraces and avenues. His *Venus* hides herself under a grotto, and his statue of Abundance stands out among the green. A dark avenue of cypress trees, lit with statues, leads to the famous fountain of a little island, "l'Isoletto," where a colossal *Neptune* is surrounded by three river gods, urns and monsters. Figures of bathers cluster round another fountain.

At the Villa Petraja he repeated this theme of the Bather. At Pratolino, he made an enormous figure of the Apennine.

In the charming *Mercury* of the Bargello (1564) he attained the greatest lightness of effect. The figure seems to lift itself into the air in the most effortless way. But the large groups in the Loggia dei Lanzi, the *Rape of the Sabines* and *Hercules Overcoming the Centaur Nessus,* overwhelm us by their forced gesticulations.

To mention some of the rest of Gianbologna's chief works, there are: his *Virtue Triumphing over Vice* (Bargello); several bronze statuettes; the rather insignificant *St. Luke* of Or San Michele; altar statues in Lucca Cathedral; reliefs on the door of Pisa Cathedral; his own funeral chapel at the Annunziata, with columns in niches; and the Chapel of Sant' Antonio in San Marco, with an entrance formed by two simple arches on columns. He made two equestrian statues, the large one of Cosimo I, which is in the Piazza della Signoria, and the Ferdinando I, in the Piazza d'Annunziata.

Gianbologna is one of the foremost sculptors of his own day. By his accomplished and vigorous art he is the heir of Michelangelo;

evertheless, his work is facile, orldly and ostentatious, and he ave to art an impulse which was ot arrested and which led to the xtravagancies of the Baroque peiod.

See Pl. 18, Vol. II.

BIBLIOGRAPHY: Desjardin, *La Vie t L'œuvre de Jean Bologne,* 1883.

GIAN DA BOLOGNA: VIRTUE. (National Museum, Florence.)

**GIANPIETRINO (Gian Pietro Rizzi, known as).**—Lombard painter active at the beginning of the 16th century. Follower of Leonardo da Vinci.

**GIBBONS (Grinling).**—English sculptor (1648-1721), much patronised by Charles II, a very skilled woodcarver, of whose art many of the mansions of England contain excellent specimens. The fine bronze statues of Charles II at Chelsea Hospital and of James II in St. James Park are also by him.

BIBLIOGRAPHY: H. A. Tipping, *Grinling Gibbons,* London, 1914.

**GIBBS (James), 1682-1754.**—One of the foremost British architects of the Georgian Period. His *St. Martin-in-the-Fields,* London, a parish church with a pedimented front and a great western tower and steeple, is based upon the previous London parish churches of Wren. He also designed the *Radcliffe Library,* Oxford, 1737-1747; *St. Mary-le-Strond,* London, 1714-1727; and the *Senate House,* Cambridge, 1722-1730.

**GILBERT (Cass).**—American architect (1859-1934). He was born in Zanesville, Ohio, on November 24, 1859 and when he was nine years old the family moved to Saint Paul, Minnesota. He displayed an interest in architecture early in life and in 1876 entered the employ of an architect in Saint Paul. Two years later he became a pupil of Professor Eugène Létang at the Massachusetts Institute of Technology. There he won a prize offered by the American Institute of Architects in 1879 and that same year was appointed to a post on the United States Coastal Survey. In the early part of 1880 he made a tour of England, France and Italy studying the historic and contemporary styles of architecture of each country. That fall he obtained a position in the office of McKim, Mead and White and worked especially as the assistant of Stanford White. For a while he was in the Baltimore branch of that firm but in 1882 he returned to Saint Paul and there went into partnership with James Knox Taylor, an association which lasted for the next ten years. One of the buildings designed by that firm was the Endicott Building in Saint Paul. Gilbert won the competition for the design of the new State Capitol for Minnesota and also planned the Capitol buildings for Arkansas and West Virginia. The structure most often connected with his name is the Woolworth Building in New York which was built about 1911. This "skyscraper" as it came to be styled was one of the first buildings of that type covering a relatively small space but extending upward to a height of several hundred feet. It was conceived in the Gothic style, with the emphasis on the vertical lines of the main mass which is topped by a tower. Other buildings planned by this architect include the public libraries in Detroit and New Haven, the Army Supply Base in Brooklyn, the New York Life Insurance Company Building and some of the buildings at Oberlin College. He was one of the founders of the Architectural League of New York and a member of the Commission of Fine Arts during the administrations of Presidents Taft and Wilson. He was a consulting architect at the time of the construction of the George Washington Bridge across the Hudson River from New York to Fort Lee. One of his last commissions was for the design of the new United States Supreme Court Building in Washington. He died at Brockenhurst, England on May 17, 1934.

BIBLIOGRAPHY: *Cass Gilbert, Reminiscences and Addresses,* 1935.—Francis B. Swales, *Cass Gilbert,* Pencil Points, VII (1926), pp. 583-598.

**GILLOT (Claude).**—French painter and engraver, 1673-1722. He was Watteau's master, until the latter's difficult character obliged them to separate. Nevertheless, he introduced his pupil to those subjects to which Watteau added the charm of his own imagination and sentiment. Gillot made a series of etchings entitled *Le Lire des Scènes Comiques.*

**GILLOTAGE.**—See Engraving.

**GILLRAY (James).**—English draughtsman and engraver (1757-1815), the leading political cartoonist of his time.

BIBLIOGRAPHY: *The Works of James Gillray the Caricaturist.* Ed. T. Wright. London, 1873.

**GIOCONDA (La).**—See Leonardo da Vinci; also Pl. 17, Vol. II.

**GIOCONDO (Fra).**—Italian architect of Verona, 1435-1515. One of the most celebrated at the beginning of the Renaissance. He occupied himself with all the arts, as well as with botany and philology. He discovered the letters of the younger Pliny. The Palazzo del Consiglio (1476-1493) is probably his work. His innovation was to place statues on the roof, over the façade. This treatment later attained great popularity. To him has been attributed the Fondaco dei Tedeschi, in Venice. Vasari says that he made a much finer plan for the courtyard of the Doges Palace than that which was adopted. After Bramante's death, Pope Julius II entrusted him with the control of the works of St. Peter's.

**GIOLFINO (Niccolò).**—Italian painter, of Verona. 1476-1555. He was a pupil of Liberale and is best represented in Verona. Among other works by him are two *Madonnas* in the Museo Civico, *Christ with Saints,* and the *Story of a Dominican Saint* (Saint'Anastasia), and the *Bearing of the Cross* and *Resurrection* (San Bernardino).

BIBLIOGRAPHY: Crowe and Cavalcaselle, *History of Painting in North Italy,* ed. T. Borenius, Vol. II.

**GIORDANO (Luca.)**—Neapolitan painter, 1632-1705. A pupil of Pietro da Cortona, whose faults he exaggerated. He was also a pupil of Ribera. He was a very rapid worker. The scenes of *Judith* and the *Brazen Serpent* on the vaulting of San Martino, Naples, were finished in forty-eight hours. *St. Francis Xavier Baptising Savages* (Naples Gallery) was finished in three days.

GIORGIONE. (Portrait after Vasari.)

**GIORGIONE (Giorgio Barbarelli).**—Venetian painter, 1478-1510. One of the most important masters of the Venetian school.

Very little is known about Giorgione and his case is much disputed. Even the dates of his birth and death are uncertain, but it is supposed that he died of the plague in 1510.

He was probably the pupil of Giovanni Bellini, and Titian must have worked with him. They both painted frescoes in the Fondaco dei Tedeschi (Giorgione in 1508).

Only four pictures can be certainly given to Giorgione:

1. *The Virgin of Castelfranco* (1504).
2. The picture known as *The Storm,* in the Giovanelli Gallery (Venice) (1515).
3. *The Three Philosophers* (Vienna), probably finished by Sebastiano del Piombo.
4. *Venus* (Dresden).

This last, which was formerly in the Casa Marcello, in Venice, has long passed for a copy by Sassoferrato, and indeed it has the character of a study and can hardly be taken as the example of a personal style. The soft, luminous flesh and beautiful landscape are admirably painted.

The *Castelfranco Altarpiece,* ordered about 1504 by the Condottore Tuzio Costanzi, for his family chapel in the Cathedral, shows a Bellini-like Virgin between St. Liberale and St. Francis. She is seated on a high throne. Behind her is an exquisite landscape, glowing in mellow light. The modelling is soft, and the calm figures are remarkable for their graceful, slightly hesitating outlines. It is a serene and beautiful picture.

*The Storm,* from the Giovanelli Palace, is a more striking development. The dark clouds seem to threaten torrents of rain, and quite a modern feeling for nature pervades the trembling trees. It is no longer the stylised landscape of the primitives, the rhythmic decoration which formed a background to religious scenes. Nature herself—her shadows and lights, her winds and thunder—inspired the artist. Few works make us feel so strongly the tremor of reality. The subject of the picture is unknown. But the figures, who appear to have no connection with each other are unimportant compared with their natural surroundings. Human beings in a landscape setting also characterises the *Three Philosophers* of Vienna. The picture apparently represents Evander pointing out to Æneas the future grandeur of Rome.

The other pictures which are attributed to Giorgione have all been disputed.

The bust of *Christ Bearing His Cross* (Gardner Collection, Boston) is considered to be one of his earliest works.

The *Madonna between St. Anthony and St. Roch,* in the Prado Museum, formerly attributed to Pordenone, has been given to Giorgione by Morelli. But this is also ascribed to Titian. The *Pala San Giovanni Crisostomo,* attributed to Giorgione by Vasari, was then given to Sebastiano del Piombo. The picture of St. Mark calming the tempest (Venice) has perhaps been given to Giorgione with more reason, but it is also attributed to Palma Vecchio and to Paris Bordone.

*The Concert,* also known as *The Three Ages,* in the Pitti Palace has also borne the name of Giorgione.

GIORGIONE: THE CASTELFRANCO ALTARPIECE. (Detail.)

Finally, the celebrated *Concert champêtre* (Louvre), subject of protracted argument, is now generally considered to be by Giorgione. Giorgione's works are poems to nature, whose mellowing influence he was one of the first to feel, and to express in paint.

See Pl. 16, Vol. II.

BIBLIOGRAPHY: Herbert Cook, *Giorgione.* London, 1907.—Ludwig Justi, *Giorgione.* Berlin, 1908.—Lionello Venturi, *Giorgione e il giorgionismo.* Milan, 1913.—Georges Dreyfous, *Giorgione.* Paris, 1914.—Louis Hourticq, *La jeunesse de Titien.* Paris, 1920.

**GIOTTINO (Giotto di Maestro Stefano).**—A nebulous Florentine painter known only through literary evidence and not through any existing work which can be proved to be by his hand. He matriculated in the guild of S. Luca in 1368; and in 1369 was among the painters working for Urban V in the Vatican, as a helper of Giovanni da Milano and Agnolo Gaddi. He had a son named Stefano who died in 1404. The Anonimo Gaddiano calls him a pupil of Gaddi, but confuses works attributed to him with those attributed to Maso (di Banco); and this confusion has persisted down to the present. Vasari, Billi, Albertini, all give to him numerous works, none of which can be ascribed to him with certainty.

BIBLIOGRAPHY: Vasari-Milanesi.—Müntz, *Le Giottino à Rome,* Archives des Arts, 1896.—Schubring, *Giottino,* Jahrb. der K. preuss. Kstsamml., 1900, p. 161.—Crowe and Cavalcaselle, Douglas ed., II, 1903. —Sirén, *Giottino.* Leipzig, 1908.—Schlosser, *Das Giottinoproblem und die mod. Stilkritik,* Kstgesch. Jahrbuch d. K. Zentr.Komm., V, 1910, 192ff.—Suida, *Maso u. Giotto di Maestro Stefano,* Repert. f. Kstwiss., XXVII, 1905, 481-90; Monatsh. f. Kstwiss., XII, 1914, 1ff.

**GIOTTO DI BONDONE.**—It is highly characteristic of Vasari, who was far more a literary man than a critic, that his most fabulous tales were born out of necessity, that he spun out his most richly imaginative accounts when he was dealing with artists about whom few facts were available. This is particularly true whenever the artist in question was a great figure, in which case Vasari's anxiety to create a worthy background far exceeded his interest in mere historical accuracy. Indeed historical accuracy has but recently become a virtue. Thus it is necessary to strip from his life of Giotto much that is pure legend, originally intended to add dignity to a personality who was considered even by his immediate contemporaries to be a very great man. Dante spoke of him as the man who "hath the cry" in his day; Petrarch and Boccaccio hail him as the reviver of art; Villani ranks him higher than any of the masters of antiquity; and anecdotes about him appear in Sacchetti's Novelle.

GIOTTO: RESURRECTION OF LAZARUS. PADUA.

Giotto was born in 1266, probably in Colle, Commune of Vespignano, to the north of Florence. He died in Florence in 1337. His birth date is vouched for by Antonio Pucci, a younger contemporary, who in a rhymed version of Villani's Chronicle, called the *Centiloquio,* states that he was seventy years old at the time of his death. Documents of 1329-1330, and 1331 mention his birthplace and his father's name (Davidsohn, *Die Heimath Giottos, etc.,* p. 374). Various stories of his youth were popularized by Vasari, that of his having been a shepherd boy whose drawings upon stones attracted the attention of Cimabue, and so forth. The most credible of the early accounts is that which appears in a 14th century commentary on Dante, namely that Giotto's father apprenticed him to a wool merchant but that he spent so much time in the studios of painters that on Cimabue's suggestion he was allowed to follow the painter's craft (Vasari-Milanesi, I, p. 371, n. 1).

In 1312 Giotto's name is inscribed in the guild of Medici e Speziali (Frey, *Loggia dei Lanzi,* pp. 72, 319), and in the years 1311, 1312, 1314, 1320, 1321, 1325, 1326, he is mentioned as living in Florence in the quarter of Sta. Maria Novella.

In addition to these documents of Florentine residence, there are a few records which point to Giotto's activity. A notice in the archives of St. Peter's, Rome, written in 1342, refers to the death of the Cardinal Jacopo Gaetano Stefaneschi a short time previously, stating that he had had an altarpiece made in St. Peter's by the famous painter Giotto at the same time as the so-called Navicella mosaic, but gives no definite date for either. The mosaic is so altered by restoration that it is valueless for the criticism of Giotto's art. Contemporary literary authorities state that he decorated with three frescoes a loggia at the Lateran Basilica in Rome at the great jubilee of 1300.

No actual document connects Giotto with his masterwork, the fresco-decoration of the Arena Chapel in Padua, but his authorship is mentioned in two trecento accounts, the Chronicle of Riccobaldo of Ferrara and the Dante Commentary of Benvenuto da Imola. The Arena Chapel was founded in 1303, according to an inscription; and was consecrated in 1305. It is not certain that the frescoes were finished at the time of the consecration, but they must have been completed soon after. The Ferrarese Riccobaldo mentioned above cites activity of Giotto's in the year 1305 in Rimini, Assisi, and Padua, which is unsubstantiated by documents. In 1312 a Rinuccio di Puccio del Mugnaio donates money to Sta. Maria Novella, Florence, to supply oil for a lamp to burn before a crucifix he is having made by Giottus Bondonis de Florentia (Vasari-Milanesi, I, 394).

A document of 1318 indicates that Giotto was not then living in Florence but gives no clue as to his whereabouts (Crowe and Cavalcaselle, Italian ed., I, 506, note). In 1330, a Neapolitan document signed by King Robert of Anjou describes Magister Joctus de Florentia as a member of his household (Crowe and Cav., Ital. ed., I, 546) and a record of a lawsuit of 1332 establishes Giotto's presence in Naples at that time.

In 1334 Giotto is made Magnus Magister of Florence, and Capomaestro for the Duomo, city fortifications, and other works. The cornerstone of the Campanile, for which Giotto made the original design, was laid in 1334, and the two lower storeys were completed in his time. Critical opinion has reached no final conclusion as to how much of the Campanile, either of its architectural form or its sculptural decoration, can be attributed to Giotto and how much to Andrea Pisano who succeeded Giotto as Capomaestro.

The *Ognissanti Madonna,* now in the Uffizi, was attributed to Giotto by Ghiberti and all other Florentine sources; and a *Dormition of the Virgin* is referred to by both Ghiberti and Vasari as among the pictures Giotto painted for the Ognissanti (Berlin Museum). Giotto's other great work in Florence, the frescoes of the *Legend of Francis* of the Bardi Chapel in Sta. Croce, could not have been done before 1317, due to the date of completion of the chapel.

Two existing pictures bear Giotto's signature but are hardly to be considered as by his own hand: the *Stigmatization of St. Francis* in the Louvre; the polyptych in the Bologna Pinacoteca. In a period when painting was a craft to be performed to the satisfaction of the patron, not a personal statement of the painter to be bought for its originality, a signature had a far different meaning from that which it has today. Masters of the trecento and quattrocento frequently affixed their signatures to works in the execution of which they had been largely assisted by pupils and even to works which were mere productions of their school and which they had never touched.

The most debated Giotto problem has been that of the frescoes at Assisi, whole series of which have been attributed to Giotto, but which are probably divided between the Roman school from whom his style was evolved and his own pupils. There are many Giottesque frescoes at Assisi, but none which are unmistakably by the master's hand.

The origins of any really great artist are difficult to delineate. Certain form elements of Giotto's painting can be traced to his predecessors: to Cimabue, to Pietro Cavallini and the Roman school, and to Giovanni Pisano. But although Giotto's style is of traditional development, it is a great style by virtue of individual genius, the power of a personality great enough to materialize and give form to an amazingly vigorous emerging culture. Giotto's Florentine intellectualism, his stark statement, his dramatic balance and essentialism and the plastic existence of his figures, his purity of vision were attributes of a gift too exalted to be attained by either his contemporaries or his immediate followers. But he had given form to a specifically Florentine spirit, and after almost a century of artists had played variations upon Giotto's forms, the Florentine spirit was reembodied in another great innovator, Masaccio.

BIBLIOGRAPHY: Vasari-Milanesi.—Ghiberti, *Commentarii,* C. Frey, *Vita di Lorenzo Ghiberti,* etc. Berlin, 1886.—Crowe and Cavalcaselle, Italian ed.—Berenson, *Florentine Painters of the Ren.* London, 1898; 3rd ed. 1908.—Moschetti, *La Cappella degli Scrovegni.* Florence, 1904.—Venturi, *Storia d. arte ital.,* 1907, V.—Rintelen, *Giotto und die Giotto-Apokryphen.* Munich, 1912, 2nd ed., 1925.—O. Sirén, *Giotto and Some of His Followers.* Cambridge, Mass., 1917.—J. B. Supino, *Giotto.* Florence, 1920.—C. Carrà, *Giotto.* Rome, 1924.—Weigelt, *Giotto,* 1925. —Kleinschmidt, *Die Basilika San Francesco in Assisi.*—Toesca, *La pittura fiorentina del trecento.* Verona, 1929.

**GIOVANNI ANTONIO.**—See Pordenone.

**— d'ALEMAGNA (Zuan da Muran).**—Venetian painter. It is impossible to determine where Giovanni was born (perhaps in Augsburg), or exactly when he came to Venice. He died after 1450. Data on his career are confused by the existence of several painters called Giovanni d'Alemagna in Venice of the period.

In 1447 one Giovanni Dotto orders from Giambono a picture which is to be similar to that painted in 1444 in the Chapel of the Ognissanti in S. Pantaleone by "Ser Joannes Theothonicj pictoris." In 1448 a Paduan document refers to the contract for the fresco painting of the Cappella Ovetari which he executed with Antonio Vivarini. Additional documents of 1449 and 1450 are concerned with this chapel. There are various contemporary records of works destroyed or lost. His collaboration with Antonio Vivarini began in 1441 and they evidently executed about fifteen works together, of which few remain. These include the frescoes mentioned above; three "pale" in the Church of S. Zaccaria, Cappella di S. Tarasio, Venice, of 1443; the *Coronation of the Virgin* in the Church of S. Pantaleone, of 1444; and the 1446 *Madonna and Child with Four Holy Fathers of the Church* (from the Scuola Grande della Carità) in the Venice Academy.

BIBLIOGRAPHY: L. Testi, *Storia d. pitt. venez.*

**— di BARTOLOMMEO CRISTIANI.**—Pistoiese painter, mentioned 1366-98.

In 1367, he worked in S. Salvatore, Pistoia; and in 1370 signed the extant altarpiece in S. Giovanni fuorcivitas. In 1377-78 he painted figures of *Virtues and Fathers of the Church* in the portico of the Cathedral; in 1381-82 worked with Antonio di Borghese in the Campo Santo of Pisa. In 1396-98 he executed frescoes in the Church of "Disciplina dei Rossi."

The only existing authenticated works by Giovanni are the S. Giovanni altar and fragments of the frescoes in the Cathedral portico. Among the paintings attributed to him on stylistic grounds are a polyptych in the Acton Collection, Florence, and a *Madonna* in the Griggs Collection, New York.

BIBLIOGRAPHY: Crowe and Cavalcaselle.

**— del BIONDO dal CASENTINO.**—Florentine painter, influenced by the Gaddi and by the School of Orcagna.

Giovanni del Biondo is first mentioned in Florence in 1356 (Gaye, *Carteggio*). In 1360 he painted for the Franciscans at Sta. Sofia at Castelfiorentino a now lost five-part altarpiece with Francis, John Evangelist, Sophia and Verdiana (Giacomini), signed "Giovanni Biondi fiorentino" and dated. In 1392 he painted the extant signed and dated altarpiece at Figline (Della Valle and Poggi-Gamba), with the inscription "Giovanni del Biondo la fe." The Siena Academy tabernacle with the Madonna and small Crucifixion is signed and dated 1377.

Giovanni del Biondo is stylistically identified with the master of the Rinuccini altarpiece in Sta. Croce, Florence, of 1379; and a large number of works have been attributed to him.

BIBLIOGRAPHY: Vasari-Milanesi, I, 669 ff.—Gaye, *Carteggio,* I, 508.—L. Giocomini, *Vita di S. Verdiana.*

'lorence, 1692, p. 323; cf. Arte e Storia, XXIV, 1905, 41.—G. della Valle, *Lett. Senesi s. le B. Arti,* 782 ff., II, 119.—Gamba and Poggi n Rivista d'Arte, V, 1907, 22-28.—Suida, *Florent. Maler d.* 14 *Jahrh.* 905, 45 ff., 50; Monatsh, f. Kstwiss., 'II. 1914, 4.—R. Offner, *Italian Primitives at Yale University.* 1927, . 18 ff.

**— DA BOLOGNA.**—See Gian da Bologna.

**— BONSI.**—Florentine painter, known through a signed and dated 1370) polyptych in the Vatican, depicting the *Virgin Enthroned between SS. Onuphrius, Nicholas, Bartholomew, and John Evangelist.* He s mentioned in 1366 among the addresses of the Operai of the Duomo of Florence.

**— di FRANCESCO (Master of he Carrand Triptych).**—The Master of the Carrand Triptych was an identifying name given to a personality whose works had been gathered together because of stylistic affinity, since proved by Toesca (Rassegna d'Arte, 1917, p. 1) to be identical with one Giovanni di Francesco, by whom we possess a documented work: the lunette of *The Eternal and Angels* over the entrance of the Loggia degli Innocenti in Florence (1459).

Bibliography: Toesca, *op. cit.*—Horne, Burlington, VIII, 1905, pp. 50, 189.—Weisbach, *Pesellino.*—Berenson, *Italian Pictures,* 1932.—Van Marle, *Italian Schools,* etc., X, p. 383-393.

**— FRANCESCO da RIMINI.**—Umbrian painter mentioned by Marcello Oretti in his Memorie as the author of two panels dated 1459 and 1461, and mentioned in the legal records of 1462 in Bologna. He died in 1470.

The two works are: 1459, the *Madonna Enthroned,* signed and dated, in S. Domenico, Bologna; and the *Madonna and Two Angels,* signed and dated, in the National Gallery, London. Giovanni Francesco's hand has been recognised in a number of other pictures.

Bibliography: Ricci, Rass. d'Arte, II, 1902, 134; III, 69, VII. 102; *Art in Northern Italy,* 1910, p. 314.—Crowe and Cavalcaselle, Douglas ed., V, 225.

**— da MILANO (Giovanni di Jacopo di Guido da Caversaccio or Giovanni da Como).**—Giovanni da Milano is mentioned first as a foreign painter's helper in Florence; in 1363 he becomes a member of the Arte de' Medici e Speziali, and a tax statement of the same year indicates that he owned property in Florence. In 1365 he applies to the Capitani of Or San Michele for an extension of time for the frescoes he is painting in the Rinuccini Chapel of Sta. Croce. In 1366 he receives Florentine citizenship. In 1369 he paints in the Vatican, Rome; of his work there nothing remains, and it is not entirely certain that the documents refer to him.

In addition to the part of the fresco-decoration of the Rinuccini Chapel executed by Giovanni there is a signed polyptych in Prato, a *Madonna with Saints* and predella; and a *Pietà,* signed and dated 1365, in the Florentine Academy. A number of other pictures have been attributed to him.

Bibliography: Vasari-Milanesi, I.—Milanesi, *Nuovi doc. d. arte toscana,* 1901, p. 58; Giorn. stor. d. archivi tosc., VI, 65.—Rumohr, *Ital. Forschungen,* 1827, II.—Crowe and Cavalcaselle, Douglas ed., III, 1908.—Suida, *Florent. Malerei d. Trecento.* Strassburg, 1905.—Venturi, *Storia,* etc., V, 1907.—Sirén, *Giottino,* 1908.—Toesca, *Pitt. e. Miniatura nella Lombardia,* 1812.—R. Offner, *Studies in Florentine Painting,* 1927, 119 ff.

**— ORIOLO.**—Italian painter (working c. 1440-1473-74), "pictor publicus" at Faenza in 1461. The National Gallery possesses by him a signed portrait of Leonello d'Este.

**— di PAOLO.**—Sienese painter, c. 1403-1482. Close follower of Sassetta.

In 1423 a "Giovanni di Paolo di Poggio" is mentioned, and 1426 is the date on the panel of the *Madonna* in the Propositura of Castelnuovo. In 1428 Giovanni is listed in the Corporation of Sienese painters; in 1441 his name is recorded as rector of this organization. In 1446, with Fruosino di Nofrio he receives payment for paintings executed at the main entrance of the Cathedral and for gilding a Madonna; and in the next year, with Sano di Pietro he receives payment for an altarpiece for the Confraternity of S. Bernardino. This same year the Università e Arte di Pizzicaiuoli order from him the *Presentation in the Temple* now in the Gallery of Siena, specifying that it be finished before 1449. Giovanni is remunerated in 1450 for two books he illuminated for the Ospedale della Seala. From 1465-75 there are various payments for works in the Church of Sta. Caterina at Fontebranda. In 1480 Giovanni marries, at the age of 78, and in 1482 he makes his will.

In addition to the extant pictures mentioned in the documents above, there are certain other sure panels by Giovanni: the 1427 Frankfurt, Robert von Hirsch Collection, *Madonna and Cherubim;* the 1436, Siena, Church of the Servi. *Madonna of Mercy;* the 1440, Siena, Archivio di Stato, *Pietro Alessandrino Enthroned,* a book-cover; and the Siena Academy *Crucifixion* of the same year; the 1445, Siena, S. Andrea, *Coronation of the Virgin;* the 1453, Siena, Academy, triptych, with *Nicholas Enthroned and Saints;* the 1457 Castiglione Fiorentino two panels of a triptych, with the *Virgin and Child and St. Catherine;* and the 1463 Pienza *Madonna and Four Saints with Pietà.*

Bibliography: Milanesi, *Doc. . . . Senese,* I.—Borghese e Banchi, *Nuovi doc.... senese,* 1898.—Jacobsen, *Der Quattrocento in Siena.*—V. Romea, *Nuove opere di Giovanni di Paolo,* Rassegne d'arte senese, XVIII, 1926, p. 72.—Van Marle, *Italian Schools,* etc., IX, 1927.

**— PISANO.**—See Pisano.

**— dal PONTE (Giovanni di Marso).**—Florentine painter, of a rather reactionary temperament, perhaps a pupil of Spinello, and influenced by Lorenzo Monaco; born in 1385.

In 1408 Giovanni dal Ponte is listed in tthe Compagnia di S. Luca; in 1422 painted a cassone for Ilarione de' Bardi; in 1424 was imprisoned for debt for eight months; in 1427-33 occupied a studio with Smeraldo di Giovanni; and from 1429-30 worked for the Capitani of Or San Michele. In 1434 he executed the extant frescoes in the Scali Chapel of Sta. Trinità.

Bibliography: *Umili pittori fiorentini al principio del Quattrocento,* L'Arte, 1904.—H. P. Horne, *Giovanni dal Ponte,* Burlington, IX.—C. Gamba, *Giovanni dal Ponte,* Rassegna d'Arte, 1904; and *Ancora di Giovanni dal Ponte,* Rivista d'Arte, 1906.

**— da UDINE (Giovanni de' Ricamatore; or di Nanni; known as Giovanni da).**—Venetian painter, 1487-1564. He was born in Udine, where he probably stayed until 1508. In Venice, he was a pupil of Giorgione; went to Rome and fell under the influence of Raphael, who chose him for the largest share in the decoration of the Loggia of the Vatican. Raphael entrusted him with the ornamental parts of the Hall of the Pontiffs (Vatican), of the Farnesina, and of the Villa Madama. He had a great many commissions.

Giovanni da Udine: Vault from the Hall of the Pontiffs. (Vatican, Rome.)

He returned several times to his native Udine. But he was always recalled to Rome by the Popes to design and paint their banners and canopies.

Giovanni da Udine: Stained glass of the Laurentian Library. (Florence.)

In Florence he decorated the Medici Palace, Michelangelo's chapel, and the Laurentian Library. In Cividale and in Venice he also designed a great many decorations. He died in Rome in 1564, and was buried in the Pantheon, near Raphael, whom he so greatly admired.

**GIOVANNINO DI GRASSI.**—Painter and sculptor of Lombardy. Probably born in 1340, died in 1398. He was in Milan from 1389. There is a very interesting collection of drawings by him in the Library of Bergamo.

**GIOVENONE (Girolamo).**—Painter of the School of Vercelli, c. 1490-1557. Follower of Gaudenzio Ferrari.

**GIRARDON (François).**—French sculptor, 1628-1715. For more than thirty years nearly all his works were made under the direction or according to designs of Le Brun. He was kept very busy, in the "Galerie d'Apollon," from 1664 to 1671, and in the Tuileries, at about the same time. In 1672, Girardon began the high reliefs of the gate of St. Denis, finished by Michel Anguier. In 1694, he made the tomb of Richelieu. The arrangement is harmonious. On a tomb of antique design, partly covered with a rich cloth, the Cardinal is half reclining, supported by Religion. On the right, two little tomb genii bear the Cardinal's arms. At the foot of the tomb, the figure of Learning is in tears.

Girardon: Tomb of Richelieu. (Church of the Sorbonne, Paris.)

After 1685, Girardon was the leading sculptor of his time. He designed numerous public statues, notably for the Invalides. He made the colossal equestrian statue of Louis XIV, in Roman attire with a wig, destined for the future Place Vendôme. The group representing the Rape of Proserpine (Versailles), finished in 1699, already announces, in spite of reminiscences of Giovanni da Bologna and of Bernini, the voluptuous grace of the 18th century.

See Pl. 41, Vol. II.

Bibliography: Pierre Francastel, *Girardon.* Paris, 1928.

**GIRAULT (Charles Louis).**—French architect, born in 1851. He built the Petit Palace or Palais des Beaux-Arts, Paris.

**GIRGENTI.**—See Agrigentum.

**GIRODET DE ROUCY TRIOSON (Anne Louis).**—French painter, 1777-1824. A pupil of David. He won the Prix de Rome in 1789.

In his *Sleep of Endymion* (Louvre) the chief figure is copied from the antique bas-relief Endymion, in the Villa Borghese, but the rays of silvery light, caressing the sleeping body, belong to Girodet himself.

Other pictures include *The Deluge* (1806), and *The Funeral of Atala* (Louvre).

See Pl. 50, Vol. II.

BIBLIOGRAPHY: Quatremere de Quincy, *Éloge de Girodet.* Paris.

**GIROLAMO di BENVENUTO di GIOVANNI del GUASTA.**—Sienese painter, born 1470, son and pupil of Benvenuto di Giovanni; died before 1524. His early works,

GIRAULT: LE PETIT PALAIS, PARIS.

done in Benvenuto's studio, reveal him as a close but inferior follower of his father.

**— da CREMONA.**—North Italian painter, chiefly of miniatures, active 1467-1483, influenced by Mantegna and Liberale.

**— di GIOVANNI da CAMERINO.**—15th century, Umbrian. Probably the pupil of Giovanni Boccati di Camerino. His chief works are in Camerino, in the Brera Gallery, Milan, and in Monte San Martino (1473). He was influenced by the Venetian school.

**— dai LIBRI.**—Veronese painter, 1474-1556. Pupil of Domenico Morone and then of Bartolommeo Montagna.

**— da SANTA CROCE.**—Painter of Bergamo and Venice, active 1503-1556; follower of the Bellini.

**— di Tommaso da Treviso.**—Painter of Treviso, 1497-1544. Eclectic painter, influenced by Titian, Raphael, Parmigianino and others.

**GIRTIN (Thomas).**—English painter (1775-1802), a friend and contemporary of J. M. W. Turner, and doubtless the most gifted among the English water colour painters of his generation. He is well represented in the Victoria and Albert Museum.

BIBLIOGRAPHY: Randall Davies, *Thomas Girtin's Water-Colours.* London, 1929.

**GIULIANO MAJANO.** — See Majano.

**GIULIO ROMANO.** — Roman painter, 1492-1546. The most individual and powerful of Raphael's followers, influenced by Michelangelo. He was probably Raphael's assistant in the frescoes of the Stanza d'Eliodoro, and of the Stanza dell'Incendio (Vatican).

His work includes frescoes in the ducal palace of Mantua (*Story of Diana;* and the *Trojan War*).

His art was well adapted to tapestry, and he made a great many cartoons—compositions which are always colossal, and uneasy (e.g. the *History of Romulus and Remus*).

His easel pictures include many Madonnas, and he shows some skill in portraiture. On the whole, however, his work is mannered, and pretentious.

BIBLIOGRAPHY: D'Arco, *Istoria della Vita e delle opere di Giulio Pippi Romano.* Mantua, 1842.

**GIUNTA PISANO.** — Dugento painter of Pisa, mentioned in documents of 1229, 1241 and 1255 (Bacci). In 1255 "Juncta Capitaneus pictor" swore fidelity to the Archbishop Federigo Visconti. Two signed works of his exist: a Crucifix in Sta. Maria degli Angeli; and one in SS. Raniere e Leonardo of Pisa (formerly S. Ana). Rossini read Giunta's signature on an entirely repainted Crucifix still in the Museo Civico, Pisa. Record of a fourth signed Crucifix, formerly in S. Francesco, Assisi, is given by Da Morrona.

BIBLIOGRAPHY: Da Morrona, *Pisa illustr.,* 1792.—Crowe and Cavalcaselle, Douglas ed., I, 1903.—A. Venturi, *Stor. d. arte ital.,* V, 1907; *Basilica di Assisi,* 1908.—Weigelt, *Duccio di Buoninsegna.* Leipzig, 1911.—P. Bacci, *Juncta Pisanus pictor,* Bollettino d'arte del Minist. della Pubbl. Instr., 1922, 145.

ROMANO (GIULIO): THE ABDUCTION OF PROSERPINA. (Drawing, Museum of the École des Beaux-Arts.)

**GUISTO D'ANDREA MANZINI.**—Florentine painter, son of Andrea di Giusto, born 1440; died 1497, a pupil of Neri di Bicci for two years, and of Fra Filippo for one year. Giusto assisted Benozzo Gozzoli in 1465-68, helping on the frescoes in S. Agostino, San Gimignano, and Certaldo. A document of 1466 establishes his authorship of the frescoes in the portico of Sta. Maria at Peretola, entirely repainted. Many works are attributed to Giusto without any particular foundation because there is no recognizable authentic painting from which his style may be judged.

**— di GIOVANNI di MENABUOI (Called Guisto fiorentino or padovano).**—Florentine painter in Padua, died before 1393.

From 1363 is the signed and dated *Madonna Terzaghi,* formerly in Milan, now in Pisa; and from 1367 the signed and dated altar wing, the *Coronation and Scenes,* in London. In 1370 Giusto finished frescoes in the Cappella Cortellieri near the Eremitani in Padua. He was granted Paduan citizenship in 1375 through Francesco il Vecchio da Carrara, and in 1376 finished the fresco-decoration of the Battistero, Padua (extant) for Fina Buzzaccarina, wife of the above Francesco. In 1382 Giusto completed the fresco-decoration for the Cappella Sel. Luca Belludi in Sant' Antonio, Padua, for the de Conti family. He acquired land in Padua in 1387, and sometime between this year and 1393 he executed part of the decoration of the Chapel of St. Louis of France in S. Benedetto, which was finished in 1394 after his death.

The early works of Giusto di Menabuoi are strongly Florentine and Giottesque; his later style was one of fuller and softer forms, developed perhaps under the influence of Siena. Additional works in Padua are attributed to him.

BIBLIOGRAPHY: Vasari-Milanesi, III.—Crowe and Cavalcaselle, Hutton ed., II.—J. v. Schlosser, *Giustos Fresken in Padua u. die Vorläufer der Stanza d. Segnatura,* in Jahrb. d. Ksthist, Samml. d. ah. Kais., XII, 1896.—Venturi, *Storia d. arte ital.,* V, 1907.—Testi, *Pitt, venez.,* I, 1909. —Moschetti, *Padova,* 1927. — R. Longhi, *Frammenti di Giusto di Padova, in Pinacoteca,* I, 1928-29.

**GLACKENS (William J.).**—Contemporary American painter. He was born in Philadelphia, Pennsylvania, 13th March, 1870. After graduating from the Central High School he joined the staff of *The Philadelphia Record* as an artist. The next year he was working for the *Philadelphia Press* and later he was on the staff of the *Philadelphia Ledger.* In his spare time he was studying at the Pennsylvania Academy of Fine Arts where he continued to work until 1895. He then went to Paris for a year and upon his return to New York worked as an illustrator on both the *New York World* and the *New York Herald.* He also did illustrations for periodicals, especially *McClure's Magazine,* which publication sent him to Cuba for the duration of the Spanish-American War to make sketches of the high-lights of the campaign. Later he became associated with *Scribner's* and the *Saturday Evening Post,* doing many illustrations for those publications. In 1906, accompanied by his wife, the former Edith Dimock, he returned to Paris where he produced a number of dry points and paintings. His early paintings were in dark colou[rs] where the feeling for form dom[i]nated the whole, but soon a stro[ng] sense of the colour values was add[ed] to enrich the forms. His later wo[rk] is done in light and vivid colou[rs] wherein the forms are modelled [in] an impressionistic method compar[a]ble to Renoir and Pissarro. In 19[..] he was elected to full membersh[ip] in the National Academy of D[e]sign. He has received many award[s] including the Temple Gold Med[al] at the annual exhibition of t[he] Pennsylvania Academy of Fi[ne] Arts in 1924 and the Carol H. Be[ck] Gold Medal in the exhibition of t[he] same association in 1933. Exampl[es] of his work are in the Columbu[s] Ohio, Gallery of Fine Arts, t[he] Whitney Museum of American A[rt] in New York and the Phillips M[e]morial Gallery in Washington, D. C.

BIBLIOGRAPHY: Forbes Watso[n], *William Glackens,* The Arts Mono[graphs], 1923.—Guy Pène du Bo[is], *William Glackens,* American Ar[t]ists Series, 1931.—For other mate[rial] see *The Index of Twentiet[h] Century Artists* for January, 193[.]

**GLADIATOR (Borghese).**—Se[e] Agasias.

**— (Fighting).**—See Pl. 25, Vol. [.]

**GLASS.**—See Stained Glass; als[o] Byzantine Art; Korean-Art; Egypt[ian] Moslem Art; Phœnician Art; et[c].

**GLAZE.**—See Ceramic.

**GLEANERS (The).**—See Mille[t] (J. F.).

**GLOCKENDON.** — Nurember[g] family of engravers and illumina[tors].

*Albert the Elder* engraved severa[l] pieces after Martin Schöngauer.

*Georges the Elder,* born in Nu[]remberg, died in 1514. None of hi[s] works has come down to us.

*Georges the Younger* was th[e] painter of the "Glockendon Missal" in the Nuremberg Library (1530-42).

*Albert the Younger* was famou[s] as a glass-painter and enamel worker. He was living in Nurem[]berg in 1553.

*Nicholas the Elder,* died 1534. Th[e] Library of Ashraffenburg has [a] missal dated from 1524 which is il[]lustrated in a very remarkable man[]ner, after Martin Schöngauer, Al[]brecht Dürer, and Lucas Cranach. Other missals, kept in various li[]braries, also contain very fin[e] miniatures by this artist.

**GLOUCESTER (England).**—Magnificent *Cathedral,* built in th[e]

GLOUCESTER: THE CATHEDRAL.

11th century, by the Normans; partly rebuilt in the 14th century, in the "perpendicular" style (choir). The cloisters of Gloucester Cathedral are most remarkable in England.

See Pl. 50, Vol. I.

**GLYPTOLOGY.** — See Greece, Engraved gems.

**GOBBO (Il).**—See Solari (Christoforo).

# GOTHIC CATHEDRALS OUTSIDE OF FRANCE

*Gothic architecture was born in the Île de France during the last third of the twelfth century and it was fully developed in the young kingdom from the time of Philip Augustus to St. Louis. It was from the Île de France that it spread across France, across the whole of Christianity as far as Cyprus and the Holy Land where it was carried by the Crusades. In the west it spread over the whole of Christian Europe where it was used extensively until it yielded to the architecture of the Renaissance in the sixteenth century. At this time the Gothic art was still called the French style,* opus francigenum.

CANTERBURY.
*(Photo by Valentine.)*

BEVERLEY
*(Photo by Valentine.)*

DURHAM.
*(Photo by Valentine.)*

YORK.
*(Photo by Frith.)*

## English Cathedrals

Gothic architecture developed in England at almost the same moment that it appeared in France. Also archæologists have been able to prove that the cathedral of Durham was chronologically the first edifice vaulted with ogival arches. However, it seems that this vault had to be restored and was constructed later than the rest of the building. The English cathedrals have a powerful and majestic appearance; they seem severe because they are not animated by the decoration of statues and windows of stained glass.

LEÓN.
*(Photo by Garcier.)*

SEVILLE.
*(Photo by Laurent.)*

BURGOS.
*(Photo by Lévy.)*

## Spanish Cathedrals

Spain possesses several of the most beautiful cathedrals in the world: Burgos, Toledo, Seville, and León. We can compare these buildings with the French cathedrals. In the Romanesque era and in the Gothic epoch, the cathedrals of France and Spain were of a very similar nature despite the barrier of the Pyrenees. It is, in particular, the Burgundian style that we recognise very often in the peninsula, without doubt because of the role that the people from Cluny played in the peninsula; but the Spanish temperament and devotion have strongly marked this architecture which is of French origin.

BRUSSELS: ST. GUDULE.
*(Photo by Neurdein.)*

COLOGNE.
*(Photo by Lévy.)*

ULM.
*(Photo by Lévy.)*

ANTWERP.
*(Photo by Neurdein.)*

## Rhenish and Flemish Cathedrals

The Gothic architecture spread toward the north and the east, in the Rhine valley, in Flanders and southern Germany. This Christian art of the Middle Ages covered a territory which corresponds almost to the ancient Roman Empire. And these Germanic regions of Christianity, being farther from the center of Romanesque art, received later than other countries the light of the Renaissance. That is why the Gothic art seemed to the first Romanticists to be Germanic and dominated by fantasy rather than reason.

# FLAMBOYANT GOTHIC

*This term* flamboyant *serves to designate the final stage of the Gothic art. The word which calls up the figure of a flame characterises the undulations of the mouldings in the long windows of the nave and apse and the rose windows. But there are also many other aspects of this decorative style. Gothic architecture in its evolution obeyed an internal principle which suppressed all useless material so as to contain in the masonry only the elements strictly necessary for equilibrium. In a short time only a skeleton from the slightly massive body of the Romanesque cathedral was left.*

LOUVIERS: PORTAL OF THE CHURCH.
*(Photo by Hachette.)*

ROUEN: ST. MACLOU.
*(Photo by Hachette.)*

ALBI: PORTAL OF THE CATHEDRAL.
*(Photo by Hachette.)*

VENDOME: CHURCH OF THE TRINITY.
*(Photo by Hachette.)*

## France

It was only at the end of the fifteenth century, that is, a short time before the birth of a new style, that of the Renaissance, that the flamboyant style flourished. It is an ornamental style and not a new method of architecture. It developed to the extreme the principles of Gothic construction, the slenderness of forms, the multiplication of mouldings, the replacement of plain surfaces by small columns and stone lacework. In the interior, the ribs of the vaults branched out; on the exterior, gables, pinnacles and spires increased in number. This flamboyant style added some precious details to the great cathedrals, but we do not owe to it any truly important monument.

GLOUCESTER: VAULT OF THE CLOISTER.
*(Photo by Valentine.)*

CAMBRIDGE: CHAPEL OF KINGS COLLEGE.
*(Photo by Valentine.)*

OXFORD: THEOLOGICAL SCHOOL.
*(Photo by Giraudon.)*

## England

One of the original features of the English Gothic style was in the boldness of its vertical lines. Like the Norman architecture to which it is closely related, English architecture liked lofty buildings, a tendency which is clearly affirmed by the multiplication of vertical lines. This became the *perpendicular style*, the last form of the English Gothic art, in which we can see only an excess of stiffness and regularity. In the design of the vaults, the architects multiplied the fan-shaped ribs. It is in the old colleges of Oxford that we can admire the last stage of Gothic art.

MILAN: CATHEDRAL.
*(Photo by Brogi.)*

BELEM: THE CLOISTER.
*(Photo by Hachette.)*

VERONA: SCALIGER TOMB.
*(Photo by Alinari.)*

## Spain and Italy

The Gothic style did not penetrate as far into Italy as it did in the other parts of the Christian world. Here this architecture ran against more lively reminders of the classical period. Also the Renaissance, that is, the return to antique models, began in Italy. However, some famous monuments like the cathedral at Milan bear witness that Italian art sometimes surrendered to the power of the Gothic art. Elsewhere the Romanesque art passed directly to the Renaissance without crossing the Gothic period. In Spain and Portugal, the final exuberant richness of the Gothic decoration combined easily with the ornamentation of the Renaissance.

**GOBELINS (The).**—See Tapestry.

**GODEFROY de CLAIRE.**—12th century goldsmith, born in Huy, Belgium. He went to St. Denis, in the middle of the 12th, but none of his works remain there. He is the author of the foot of the cross of St. Bertin (Museum of St. Omer), which reproduces, in little, the gold cross of St. Denis, a wonderful piece of goldsmith work, which he made, but which has been destroyed. He made precious pieces of work, enriched with enamels, two shrines (Huy) a reliquary (Haran) and a shrine of St. Heribert (Deutz).

Bibliography: O. von Falke and H. Frauberger, *Deutsche Schmelzarbeiten des Mittelalters.* Frankfort.—E. Mâte, *L'art religieux au XII^e siècle.* Paris.

**GOES (Hugo van der).**—Flemish painter. Probably born about 1440 at Goes in Zeeland. In 1467, he

Goes (Hugo van der): Pietà. (Kunsthistorisches Museum, Vienna.)

was admitted into the Guild of Painters in Ghent. In 1476, he retired into the monastery of Rouge Cloître, near Brussels. After some years he became afflicted with madness, imagining that he was damned. He died in 1482.

There are few authenticated works by Hugo van der Goes. Critics are almost unanimous in ascribing to him the following: (1) a small diptych in the Kunsthistorisches Museum, Vienna, representing *Adam and Eve* drawn with great delicacy, and a finely composed *Pietà*.

(2) A *History of Abigail,* unfortunately lost, which was painted over the chimney-piece of an old house. There are many copies of it, which give an impression that this was a majestic work, well composed, concisely drawn, and of rich colour. Copies are in Brussels, Musée des Arts Décoratifs; Prague, Novak Collection; Wiesbaden, Collection of Dr. Hülseman.

(3) *The Death of the Virgin* (Bruges) dates from the last years of the painter and expresses an intense and contorted emotion, profoundly dramatic.

(4) Two portraits of donors on the wings of the Altarpiece of the Martyrdom of St. Hippolytus, attributed to Dirk Bouts (Bruges).

(5) The artist's masterpiece, and his only authenticated picture, is the Portinari Altarpiece, also known as the *Adoration of the Shepherds* (Uffizi, Florence), painted about 1475 for Tommaso Portinari, the agent for the Medici in Bruges. On one wing is represented the donor with his two sons, accompanied by St. Thomas and St. Anthony; and, on the other, the donor's wife and daughter and St. Margaret and St. Mary Magdalen.

Other works by the master are an *Adoration of the Magi,* from the Monforte Monastery in Spain, now in Berlin; an *Adoration of the Shepherds* (Berlin); the *Virgin and St. John* (Oxford), with figures in tempera; a *Holy Family* (Brussels); fragments of paintings in the Berlin Gallery; the *Holy Family* (Brussels) and other works in Frankfurt, Holyrood Castle, and the Walters Gallery, Baltimore.

The artist also painted a great many pictures which can only be judged by copies.

See Pl. 60, Vol. I.

Bibliography: Sir Martin Conway, *The Van Eycks and Their Followers.* London, 1921. M. J. Friedländer, *Altniederländische Malerei.*

**GOGH (Vincent van).**—Dutch painter (1853-1890). He was born 30th March 1853 in the town of Zundert in Brabant. At the age of sixteen he was an assistant in The Hague branch of the Goupil Galleries, which were under the management of his uncle. When he was twenty years of age he was sent to the London branch of that firm and in 1875 he was associated with the Paris establishment. As he grew older Vincent van Gogh was becoming more engrossed in a study of religion. He wanted to become a preacher and for a time helped in a Methodist school in Isleworth. In 1877 he began his intensive study for the Church. For a year he was in Amsterdam and then in the School for Missionaries in Brussels. At length he was allowed to go as a missionary to the mining town of La Borinage in Belgium, where he stayed for about two years, but he was dismissed because he gave his belongings to the poor, feeling that by that action he was acting closer to the true principles of Christianity, though degrading himself in the eyes of the Church. However, he continued to live on there, drawing for the first time and finding therein a sort of solace for his pains. He copied the work of Millet and strove to model his work on that artist's productions to catch the true spirit of the peasants and their sordid existence. In 1880 he went to The Hague and there gained some instruction from Mauve, and three years later he moved to Drenthe, where he painted some landscapes and figure pieces. The year 1885 found him living at home again in Nuenen in Brabant, a period when his style was changing from mere illustration to a direct study of nature as may be seen in the *Potato Eaters.* True, his colours were muddy and dark and the picture showed some influence of the work of Delacroix, but there was a touch of distinction in this study of Dutch peasants engaged in their homely feast.

The end of that year van Gogh went to Antwerp and there entered the Academy, copying heads, still lifes and casts from antique models. In 1886 he went to Paris and there lived with his devoted brother Theodore, who was in the Goupil Galleries. There Vincent learned to know the work of Rembrandt and met the leaders of the new Impressionist group, including Henri de Toulouse-Lautrec and many others. He was strongly impressed by their use of light colours and tried to paint a few flower studies, using a much more delicate palette. From Gauguin he learned of the pictures of Pissarro and he also absorbed some baroque feeling which made itself evident in the wavelike lines of his foliage and trees. For a while he tried to imitate the pointillistic method of Seurat, but soon decided that he could not restrain himself to such a minute technique and went back to his own personal manner, alternating streaks and dots of colour in a very pleasing harmony. Early in the year of 1888 van Gogh went south to Arles to find peace from the hurry and bustle of Paris and there for almost the first time in his life he found contentment. He painted the orchards in their spring flowering, the rolling meadows and the tall cypresses. Some of the people in the village, including Roulin the postman and his family, were depicted in brilliant colours in a high degree of naturalism. At this time were painted the well-known compositions *L'Arlesienne* and *La Berceuse.* But all seemed incomplete and soon van Gogh invited Gauguin to join him, hoping to form an artist colony there. It was not a happy thought and soon they quarrelled on account of Gauguin's overbearing personality and his scepticism of the good qualities of human nature. Vincent van Gogh had always been high strung and nervous and the shock of this misunderstanding was enough to destroy his sanity. He had numerous attacks of insanity, during one of which he cut off his own ear. At other times he was weak but sane and then he continued his painting as long as his strength held out. He was in an asylum in St. Remy near Arles and then in May, 1890, he was in the care of a doctor in Auvers. There he committed suicide and died 29th July 1890, putting to rest a spirit that during life had always been troubled and restless, always seeking peace and quiet—an object which he had finally attained. Examples of his work may be seen in the Municipal Museum in Amsterdam as well as many other European museums, and in the United States in the Art Institute of Chicago and the Phillips Memorial Gallery in Washington. In the fall of 1935 a comprehensive exhibit of his work was opened at the Museum of Modern Art in New York City. It proved to be the most popular display ever staged by that institution. Subsequently it visited a number of other cities in the United States and everywhere awakened beholders to an interest in the life and work of the artist.

Bibliography: Alfred Bader, *Künstler-Tragik: Karl Stauffer, Vincent van Gogh,* 1932.—Anthony Bertram, *Vincent van Gogh,* 1930.—Peter Burra, *Van Gogh,* 1934.—Paul Colin, *Van Gogh,* 1925.—Gustave Coquiot, *Vincent van Gogh,* 1923.—Victor Doiteau and Edgard Leroy, *La Folie de Vincent van Gogh,* 1928.—Victor Doiteau and Edgard Leroy, *Vincent van Goghs Leidensweg,* 1930.—Théodore Duret, *Van Gogh, Vincent,* 1919.—Florent Fels, *Vincent van Gogh,* 1928.—*Further Letters of Vincent van Gogh to His Brother, 1886-1889,* 1929.—Waldemar George, *Van Gogh,* 1927.—Roch Grey, *Vincent van Gogh,* 1924.—G. F. Hartlaub, *Vincent van Gogh,* 1930.—Karl Jaspers, *Strindberg und Van Gogh,* 1926.—Fritz Knapp, *Vincent van Gogh,* 1930.—H. Kroeller-Mueller, *Vincent van Gogh, 1853-1890,* 1927.—J.-B. de la Faille, *L'Epoque Française de Van Gogh,* 1927.—J.-B. de la Faille, *L'Œuvre de Vincent van Gogh,* 1928, 4 Vols.—*Letters of a Post-impressionist,* being the familiar correspondence of Vincent van Gogh, edited by A. M. Ludovici, 1912.—*Letters of Vincent van Gogh to His Brother, 1872-1886,* with a Memoir by his sister-in-law, J. Van Gogh-Bonger, 1927, 2 Vols.—*Lettres de Vincent van Gogh à Emile Bernard,* 1911.—Julius Meier-Graefe, *Vincent van Gogh,* 1922.—Kurt Pfister, *Vincent van Gogh,* 1922.—Louis Piérard, *The Tragic Life of Vincent van Gogh,* 1925.—Charles Terrasse, *Van Gogh,* 1931.—Charles Terrasse, *Van Gogh, Peintre,* 1935.—Hans Tietze, *Vincent van Gogh,* n. d.—E. Du Quesne van Gogh, *Personal Recollections of Vincent Van Gogh,* translated by K. S. Dreier, 1913.—J. Van Gogh-Bonger, *Briefe an seinen Bruder,* 1914.—*Vincent van Gogh,* Museum of Modern Art, New York, 1935.

**GOODHUE (Bertram Grosvenor).**—American architect (1869-1924). He was born in Pomfret, Connecticut on April 28, 1869. From his mother he inherited a love of drawing and soon turned his attention to architecture. At the age of fifteen he entered the employ of Renwick, Aspinwall and Russell in New York and there he studied and drew plans for the next seven years. In 1889 he obtained a position as draftsman with the Boston firm of Cram and Wentworth and two years later he became a partner in that firm which upon the death of Wentworth became known as Cram, Goodhue and Ferguson. Goodhue was primarily interested in the adaptation of the Gothic style to modern usage especially for churches and schools. In the early 1890's he made a trip to Europe and at other times he visited Canada, Mexico, Persia and China where he was much impressed by the beauty and romantic aspect of Oriental architecture. About 1903 the firm received the contract to design the new buildings for the United States Military Academy at West Point. The Gothic style was chosen and Goodhue was chiefly responsible for the chapel which conveys a sense of space and lofty height akin in a small measure to the old world cathedrals. The firm was dissolved in 1913 and after that time Goodhue remained in New York where he formulated the designs of Saint Thomas's Church and Saint Bartholomew's which combines the Byzantine and Romanesque styles. The plans for the exposition at San Diego in 1915 were done in the Spanish Colonial style and some Oriental influence is to be seen in his design for the Los Angeles Public Library. But as he grew older his viewpoint changed and his later works were done in accord and sympathy with the ideals of the younger generation of architects. He was preoccupied with simple masses and unbroken lines and tried out his theories in the War Memorial at Kansas City, the new State Capitol at Lincoln, Nebraska and the National Academy of Sciences Building in Washington. Perhaps the most striking of these is the Capitol at Lincoln which is characterized by widespread low masses from the center of which rises a tower unadorned except by the simplest of buttresses. Goodhue besides his career as an architect was also the designer of some book covers, title pages and even some fonts of type including the well known Cheltenham. His memories of his foreign travels were perpetuated by sketches of significant and interesting bits of architecture as well as drawings of dream-like vistas conceived in the workings of his vivid imagination. He died while still in the prime of life on April 23, 1924.

Bibliography: *A Book of Architectural and Decorative Drawings by Bertram Grosvenor Goodhue,* 1914.—M. Schuyler, *The Works of Cram, Goodhue and Ferguson, 1892-1910,* Architectural Record XXIX (1911), 1-112.—Charles Harris Whitaker, editor, *Bertram Grosvenor Goodhue—Architect,* 1925.

**GOLTZIUS (Hendrik).**—Dutch engraver, of Haarlem, 1558-1617. He published a series of six plates, on which he imitated the style of Dürer, Lucas van Leyden, Raphael, Bassano, Barocci, and Parmigianino.

His engravings show a remarkable technical virtuosity. They were made after compositions by Spranger, Cornelisz, and other artists, but frequently also from his own designs. He also did wood-cuts, some of which are printed in several colors.

Bibliography: O. Hirschmann, *H. Goltzius,* (Meister der Graphik, Vol. 7, 1919; same author, *H. Goltzius als Maler*. Strasbourg, 1916.

**GONTARD (Karl von).**—German architect, 1731-1791. Author of the Neues Palais, Potsdam, 1765-1769.

**GOSHUN.**—Japanese painter. Born in Kyoto in 1741; died in 1811. He combined the naturalistic style of Okyo with the Chinese style and formed the Shijo school which became very popular. Embroiderers, lacquer-workers and carvers borrowed their finest models from him. His favourite subjects were flowers and animals.

**GOSLAR (Germany).**—*Kaiserhaus,* 1040.

**GOSSAERT (Jan).**—See Mabuse.

**GOTHIC ARCHITECTURE.**—Gothic is that style of architecture characteristic of the late Middle Ages, from about 1150 to 1500 and after in Northern Europe, from about 1200-1400 in Italy. The style was more general and international than the more purely local syntheses of the various Romanesque styles, but the architecture of the Ile de France and surrounding regions is generally recognized to embody the most complete expression of Gothic ideas, the Gothic of Italy the least complete.

The fundamental principle of Gothic is to immaterialize the solid parts of a church through a vertical treatment and through elimination of all structure which can possibly be eliminated. The development of the ribbed groin vault was a necessary condition for the existence for Gothic, for in such, a vault thrust is not continuous but is concentrated at the four corners. The exterior flying buttress, characteristic of developed Gothic, enables walls to be eliminated between the points where thrust is concentrated and permits the replacement of wall by glass. The development of Gothic vault construction involved the pointing of arches, the most easily recognized differentium of the style, for pointed arches are uncommon in Romanesque architecture.

The structural innovations which permitted the synthesis of Gothic occurred prophetically in the Romanesque churches of Normandy and the Ile de France. The Abbot Suger of St. Denis, in the middle of the 12th century united all those elements in the first expression of the Gothic style.

The chronology of the style is as follows: Transitional, 12th century; High Gothic, 13th; Flamboyant Gothic, 14th and 15th. Among the great High Gothic cathedrals of the Ile de France and surrounding provinces are Chartres, Laon, Le Mons, Bourges, Paris, Amiens, and Reims. Some of these have Transitional and Flamboyant features, for the great medieval cathedrals were built over long periods of time.

**GOTHIC CATHEDRALS.**—See Pls. 47, 48, 49, 50, Vol. I.

**— CIVIL MONUMENTS.**—See Pl. 29, Vol. II.

**— ENAMEL.**—See Pl. 30, Vol. II.

**— IVORIES.**—See Pl. 55, Vol. I.

**— SCULPTURE.**—See Pl. 2, Vol. II.

**GOUJON (Jean).**—French sculptor; born between 1510 and 1514; died between 1564 and 1568. His life and work are still not well known, in spite of many researches, and of the fact that he was the first really celebrated French sculptor.

Jean Goujon.

From his arrival in Paris, about 1543, he worked with Pierre Lescot at the decoration of the rood-screen of St. Germain d'Auxerrois. This work, which is very Italian in character, is preserved in the Louvre, with the exception of some cherubs' heads. Between 1545 and 1547, Goujon worked in the Château of Ecouen, perhaps as architect. He made the monumental Chapel Altar, now in Chantilly. He was probably responsible for several decorative carvings in the château, notably the Wingèd Victory on the chimney-piece of the large hall.

Goujon (Jean): Nymphs. (Bas-relief from the Fountain of the Innocents, Paris.)

In 1547, Goujon furnished several plates (academic figures, caryatids, friezes, etc.) for the first French edition of Vitruvius. His preface and illustrations show a profound knowledge of antique art.

Henceforward Goujon was in the king's service, and nearly all his works were made in collaboration with Lescot. He was probably the author of the sculpture on the Hôtel Carnavalet, Paris. The entrance doorway is decorated with a figure of Abundance, and, on the side of the courtyard, with a figure of Authority.

The *Fontaine aux Nymphes,* now known as the *Fontaine des Innocents,* was built between 1547 and 1549, at the corner of the Rue St. Denis and the Rue aux Fers, Paris. It was rebuilt and isolated, in the 18th century. Goujon decorated it with bas-reliefs. Between the pilasters of the arcade are five large figures of nymphs, holding urns (three were added in the 18th century, of which two are by Pajou). Over each arcade, are children and dolphins; and below three were bas-reliefs, representing Nymphs of the Seine, Tritons and Nereids (now in the Louvre).

Goujon (Jean): Diana the huntress. (Bas-relief from the Château d'Anet, Musée de Cluny.)

Tradition attributes to him part of the decoration of the Château of Anet. He is still credited with sculpture in the chapel (Angels bearing instruments of the Passion, etc.), as well as the *Fountain of Diana.* In this work (now in the Louvre) Goujon did not attempt a portrait of Diane de Poitiers. It is a charming mythological figure, reminiscent of certain drawings and stuccos by Primaticcio.

The decoration of the Louvre occupied Goujon from about 1549. On the ground-floor of Lescot's façade, he surrounded the oval windows with six allegorical figures, representing History and Truth, War and Peace, the Glory of the King and Fame, executed in the style of the Nymphs on the Fontaine des Innocents. He made the four caryatids, his most classical work.

From 1562, we lose trace of Goujon. He was a Protestant, and had to leave France. He settled in Bologna, where he died, between 1564 and 1568.

Goujon preserved those traditions of taste and restraint which characterise French sculpture, adopting the firm, long forms of the School of Fontainebleau. He recovered the technical perfection of the 15th century Florentines. But, above all, he contributed to the first triumph of classicism in France, through his taste for mythology and the antique.

See Pls. 27, 28, 31, Vol. II.

Bibliography: Paul Vitry, *Jean Goujon,* Les Grands Artistes, 1909.

**GOYA Y LUCIENTES (Francisco José).**—Spanish painter 1746-1828. This great painter and great man was born on March 30, 1746, at Fuendetodos, a poor Spanish village near Saragossa. When scarcely fourteen years old he worked at Saragossa as an apprentice in the studio of José Luzan y Martinez. Later on he continued his studies at Madrid under the guidance of his countryman, Francisco Bayeu. To complete his artistic education, he went to Rome. The paintings of the sojourn in Italy—genre scenes and a picture representing Hannibal gazing from the Alps at Italy (1771), which won for him the second prize in a competition held by the Academy of Parma—are lost.

In the fall of 1771 we meet with Goya at Saragossa, where he was active until 1774. The frescoes of the Cathedral de la Virgen del Pilar, as well as those in the Carthusian Church of Aula Dei near Saragossa, date from this stay. Critics agree that these frescoes betray a strong influence of Tiepolo.

About 1775 Goya settled in Madrid, whither his reputation had preceded him. He was then twenty-nine years old. The following year he married Josefa Bayeu, sister of his friend, Francisco Bayeu. Of the numerous children of this marriage, only one, Francisco Javier, survived. Shortly after his return from Italy (1776) Goya was commissioned to do cartoons for the Royal Tapestry looms of Santa Barbara, which was then under the management of "Madrid's artistic dictator, Raphael Mengs." By 1778 he had delivered twenty cartoons; these and the following were really painted canvases, some of which were destined to serve for the tapestries decorating the El Pardo Palace near Madrid. A second series was begun in 1786 for the bedroom of the Infante D. Gabriel Anthony in the royal apartment of the Monastery of El Escorial, and a third series for the King's study, at the same place, was finished in 1791. A. L. Mayer recommends Cruzada Villamil's fundamental research into the subject of Goya's tapestries and also gives in his *Francisco de Goya* (London-Toronto, 1924) a convenient list in chronological order of the designs executed, their designation, date of production, numbers of tapestries completed, etc. There are forty-five designs altogether, all depicting popular scenes, as may be seen from the titles of those listed: *The Picnic on the Banks of the Manzanares* (1776); *Sunshade, The Flying Kites* (1778); *The Earthenware-Venders of Valencia, The Swing* (1779); *The Woodcutter* (1780); *The Fallen Mason, See-saw, The Jumping Jack* (El Pelele), (1791). The aforementioned author says:

"Goya took some time to get accustomed to this kind of work. He had to consider the technique of tapestry-weaving before all else, to avoid as far as possible accentuating any depth of perspective and to renounce all marked gradations of colour value. . . . In the first designs he did not avoid these faults: the finished Gobelins prove that they were thoroughly altered by the workmen. In this case the weaver's arbitrary alterations can be understood; in other cases . . . corrections were not founded upon impossibility of execution. In these works Goya's individual style slowly makes itself felt. . . . The energy with which Goya seized upon and executed his subjects, his unusually strong accentuation of the Spanish national characteristics, the use he made later of social scenes depicting not the sunny side, but the sadder elements in the life of the working-people and the pains he took to free himself as much as possible from the foreign influence in the rendering of these scenes, all combine to give significance to his series of tapestry cartoons."

In 1778 Goya had made eleven large etchings after paintings by Velázquez, of whom he later said that, with Rembrandt and Nature, he was one of his three masters. The *Blind Street Singer* was made in the following year.

In 1779 Goya was presented at Court; however, his petition, tendered in the same year, to be nominated court painter, was not granted. Yet in 1780 he was elected member of the Académia de Bellas Artes de San Fernando of Madrid, on which occasion he presented a canvas to that society representing a *Crucifixion* (now in the Prado Museum). In the same year, Goya went to Saragossa in connection with the frescoes of the cupola of the Cathedral. Continuous differences with his brother-in-law, Francisco Bayeu, who supervised the works, as well as with the commission in charge of them, led to a definite break in 1781, and Goya returned to Madrid. (The studies in oil for the projected frescoes of the cupola are preserved in the museum of the cathedral.) It has been said that the years from 1781 to 1785 were his worst, and that because of fatigue he produced very little in 1784. His father died in 1781, his sister a year later; his

Goya, by Vincent Lopez.

mother came to live with him in 1783, but left the following year. During this period he executed various religious pictures: for instance, the altar piece for San Francisco el Grande of Madrid (1782-84) representing San Bernardino of Siena preaching to a King of Aragon; and the paintings, no longer there, for the Colegio of Salamanca. He was befriended then by the Ex-Cardinal Infante D. Luis of Bourbon, who with his morganatic wife was a patron of the arts. At the palace at Arenas de San Pedro, Goya was the object of their princely hospitality. The portraits of his patron and the latter's family were formerly at the Palace of Boadilla del Monte and are now said to be in Italy. According to A. Beruete y Moret, the year 1783 is of significance to students of Goya as a portrait-painter, for this year "is the first date in which we can bring into line portraits of importance executed by him." Among them the best is held to be that of Count Floridablanca, Minister of Charles III (Coll. Marqués de Martorell, Madrid). It is a full-length portrait of the Count standing in his room, another figure in the background, and that of the painter himself in the left foreground, offering a canvas to the Minister. Beruete states that various portraits of the same sitter are derived from this one, which, though seemingly inspired by the art of Mengs, shows strong personal notes which Mengs would not have approved. The portrait of little Manuel Osorio (Jules Bache Coll., N. Y.) with its brilliant colours and realistic rendering of the cats looking fiercely at the magpie depicted in the left corner of the painting, was probably finished about three years later.

While in 1785 he was again refused the position of court painter, the Académia de San Fernando raised him to the rank of subdirector. About 1785 a new chapter in Goya's life seems to begin. A. L. Mayer says that ". . . just as one does not observe genius in the creations of the young Beethoven, so the early works of Goya impress one as a harmless gay andante. . . . There is nothing . . . to forecast the future creator of the *Desastres de la guerra* . . . whereas from 1777 until 1785 his paintings show brownish red flesh tones, those of 1786 are already tuned to a silvery grey, the flesh tones also becoming more tender." This applies also to the delightful *Pradera de San Isidro*, a view of Madrid as seen on the Saint's feast-day from the southern bank of the Manzanares River, with camping figures in the foreground (Prado Museum, Madrid, 1788-91?). Also the Spanish critic, F. J. Sánchez Cantón, finds 1785 as "the beginning of an important stage in the life of Goya which one may call the hour of optimism; his brilliant, luminous paintings, opulent in form and colour expressing the joy of his spirit. He was then at the beginning of his maturity. . . . The painter himself calls his situation enviable. His works were widely solicited and he was able to choose the commissions most agreeable to him." Finally with 1785 begins his activity for the Duke of Osuna, which was to last until 1799 and which produced portraits, genre scenes on wood or metal, decorative paintings, etc. Mayer makes the reservation that not all portraits of this and the successive years are of evenly high quality, as, for instance, those of the directors of the Banco de San Carlos, now owned by the Bank of Spain (1785-89). (Beruete points out that these portraits, together with documents preserved, afford valuable material because of establishment of dates, identification of personages, and prices paid.) Among the earliest of the group of portraits betraying the new phase in Goya's artistic orientation are those of the Duke and Duchess of Osuna. Of that of the Duchess (formerly Coll. Bauer, Madrid) Sánchez Cantón says that it is painted with the precision and minuteness of a French pastel representing the characteristic type of the *portrait élégant*. Well known is the group portrait of the same ducal family in the Prado Museum (1787). ". . . Unequal in construction and strength . . . the most salient quality of this canvas is its total effect without any hardness of outline, just as reality presents itself to our view. He tries, as Velázquez has done . . . to draw with line and to paint with paint—not to reproduce the things, but the sense of things within ourselves" (Beruete). The picture representing Charles III hunting (1786, Prado Mus.) shows in spite of a close dependence on Velázquez a distinct note of its own, especially in the colour. (Other portraits of the King in Bank of Spain and Palace of Duke of Fernan-Nuñez, Madrid.) From this period also dates Goya's self-portraits (Conde de Villagonzalo, Madrid) with the artist standing with his palette at the easel placed against a window through which light is entering. Among the religious paintings of this period are the pictures of the Church of Santa Ana at Valladolid (1787); the *Kiss of Judas* of Toledo Cathedral (main sacristy, 1788-89); *St. Francis of Borgia Taking Leave*, ordered by the Duchess of Osuna, a descendant of the Borgia family, for the family chapel of Valencia Cathedral, "which shows a surprising technical advance" (1789). Others are lost.

In 1790 he travelled to Valencia and Saragossa (portraits of the writer and architect, Ramon Pignatelli, and of his beloved friend, Zapater, the latter in the Widener collection at Philadelphia). In the fall of 1791 he again visited Saragossa. In 1792 he was gravely ill, and in the following year left for Andalusia to recuperate in a milder climate. It was during this illness that he contracted his deafness which was to become worse with the advancing years. A number of wash-drawings in India-ink are believed to date from this Andalusian journey, some of them having been discussed by Sánchez Cantón (*Los dibujos del viaje a Sanlúcar*) and others, on the occasion of their purchase by the Met. Mus. of Art, N. Y., by H. B. Wehle (*Met. Mus. Bull.*, February, 1936). Some of these drawings supposedly refer to the Duchess of Alba, whose name—whether justifiably or not—is a favourite topic with biographers and has often been linked to that of the painter. In 1799 he was finally awarded the position of First Court Painter, coveted by him for many years and vacant since 1795, date of the death of Francisco Bayeu. In his aspiration to achieve this distinction he was generously supported by Manuel Godoy, later Principe de la Paz, the favourite of Queen Maria Louisa and powerful Minister of Charles IV. Goya painted various portraits of Godoy and of his wife, the Countess of Chinchón, daughter of Goya's former patron, the Ex-Cardinal Infante de Bourbon. Of Godoy's portraits the one considered the most important is that at the Ac. de S. Fernando, representing the Prince in company of his adjutant, with horses in the background and a banner in the left foreground (shortly after 1800). Dear to critics is the seated full-length picture of the Countess, formerly at Boadilla del Monte and now in Italy (1800).

In spite of the interruption caused by the master's illness, the period from 1790 until the end of the century was one of greatest activity. A prolific output of portraits, the famous frescoes of the Hermitage of San Antonio de la Florida, picturesquely situated on the banks of the Manzanarez River, genre paintings and, finally, the famous series of etchings called *Los Caprichos*, fall in this period.

In 1790 he finished the portraits of Charles IV and his Queen (Madrid, Prado Museum, and Capodimonte). The portrait of Sebastian Martinez, lawyer and art-collector of Cadiz, at the Met. Mus. of Art, bears the date of 1792. For the Duchess of Alba and her husband, the Duke-consort Marqués de Villafranca, Goya executed various portraits (portraits of the Duke: Chicago, Chas. Deering Coll., c. 1790; portrait with the Duke standing at a clavichord, Madrid, Condesa de Niebla, 1795-96. Of the Duchess: portrait owned by the Duke of Berwick and Alba and until the outbreak of the civil war at his Palace de Liria at Madrid, 1795; a replica of the Palace de Liria portrait in the Chas. Deering Coll. at Chicago; the Duchess dressed as a *Maja* in the Hisp. Soc. of Am., N. Y., 1797; etc.).

Contemporary with the portrait of 1794 of D. Felix Colon (in 1924 at Madrid, R. Traumann Coll.) is the first of the two portraits of the famous actress Doña Maria del Rosario Fernández, known as La Tirana (Madrid, Conde de Villagonzalo); the other (Acad. de S. Fernando) with "its flesh tones of a truth coming very near to perfection" (Beruete), dates from 1799. During 1794 Goya also painted the beautiful portraits of Da. Tadea Arias de Enriquez (Madrid, Duquesa de San Pedro de Galatino) and of the Marquesa de Solano (Paris, Coll. Beistegui). Beruete considers the last-mentioned portrait, as well as that of Bayeu (in the opinion of Mayer painted perhaps in 1796, after Bayeu's death) in their scheme of grey the most advanced in technique and in the handling of tones of this phase of their painter's style. Also Mayer, after stating that "the portraits of the '90's are with few exceptions distinguished by a very high level of achievement" and that "it is difficult to say which should be mentioned as the best . . . in their general rendering, which is free and delicate," passes on to award the prize to that of Bayeu. "It is perhaps the best expression up to date of Goya's ideal conception of the art of portraiture, but the later full-length portrait of the *Man in Grey* in the Bishoffsheim collection in Paris—probably a picture of Goya's son, Francisco Javier—attains a like degree of perfection." In 1797 he made another portrait of Zapater (Durand-Ruel, Paris). The portrait of the Marqués de Bondad Real (N. Y., Hisp. Soc. of Am.) is dated 1799, and Mayer is right in pointing out that if it were not for this evidence the picture would have to be dated earlier, which, however, does not signify a relapse into an earlier style, but rather the preference for such a style by the sitter. The same critic places between 1795-1800 the portraits of the bull-fighter Pedro Romero, in the A. Sachs collection, N. Y., as well as that of Juan de Villanueva, builder of the Prado Museum, now preserved in the Acad. de S. Fernando.

Commissions for portraits of the royal couple followed those executed in 1790 (see above). A number of these portraits originally ordered for various governmental departments can now be seen in the Prado Museum. In 1799 Goya painted the King and Queen as colonels of the Regiment of the

Life Guards (the Queen on horseback); another portrait of the Queen in a black mantilla (Munich, Alte Pinakothek); and an equestrian picture of Charles IV (Madrid, formerly Royal Palace and Prado Mus.). However, Goya's universally best-known rendering of the monarchs is probably the group portrait depicting the entire royal family as well as the painter himself (Prado). In this painting, with its superbly ruthless characterization, the silver-grey tones give way to a mass of brilliant colours. . . . "explained by the showy dresses of the court . . . the richest combination that has ever issued from any palette" (Beruete). At the Prado Museum and elsewhere (for instance, N. Y., Met. Mus., Infanta Maria Luisa and her child) are preserved the study portraits for this large composition which "were painted on canvas with a red preparation."

That some of the portraits, beginning with the end of the eighteenth century, are reminiscent of contemporary English masters was already noticed during Goya's lifetime. Goya, knowing that rumours were circulating that he had spent a few months in England, jokingly dated one of his letters to Zapater from London. Mayer believes that such a similarity is not a question of technique and characterization, but of composition. And also that the importation into Spain of English engravings or mezzotints, and perhaps the works by the Italian artist Pompeo Battoni, who was popular in England, and whose works found their way to Spain, may account for it. Among these pictures, and adducing their English parallels, Mayer cites: *Marquésa de Pontejos,* c. 1790 (A. Mellon Coll., Washington, D. C.); *Melendes Valdés* (1797, Barnard Castle, Bowes Museum); *Jovellanos* (1798, Madrid, Marqués de Villemajor); *Joaquina Candado* (1803, ? Valencia Museum).

There seems to be a divergence among critics whether or not to identify five cabinet paintings at the Académia de S. Fernando of Madrid (the *Bullfight, Lunatic Asylum, Tribunal of the Inquisition, Carnival Scene, Procession of Flagellants*) with cabinet paintings mentioned in a letter of 1794 to his friend Yriarte. But it remains significant that Goya in this letter says, among other things, that he felt the need to make "observations" of his own, a freedom not enjoyed while executing portrait commissions. Of a number of pictures of this period, including those supposed to represent the Duchess of Alba (as, for instance, the *Conversación galante,* Madrid, Marqués de la Romana) Mayer writes: "Here we learn to know Goya as the great master of sharp, merciless, vivid characterization; as a master of impressionism who knew how to seize light and movement; we see here his capacity to create, out of the momentary experience of the eye, works of everlasting importance without the loss of that charm of the eighteenth century which he"—at that time and sometimes later—"gave to his portraits and genre pictures." The six so-called scenes of witchcraft for the small palace of the Duke of Osuna near Madrid, called La Alameda, date from 1798. Contrary to other critics, Sánchez Cantón believes that the *Maja desnuda* (the unclothed Maja) and the *Maja vestida* (the clothed Maja) should be assigned to the year 1800. The popular belief that these two *Majas* represent the Duchess of Alba has been dispelled through the story told by Goya's grandson to D. Federico Madrazo. "But, forgetting the problem of identification, the *Maja desnuda* is one of the greatest nudes in the history of painting. How much Manet must have learned from this canvas for his Olympia!" (Sánchez Cantón). The various paintings known as the *Majas on the Balcony* seem still to be in need of accurate chronological classification. The version at the Met. Mus., N. Y. formerly Infante D. Sebastian de Bourbon; Duke of Marchena; Mrs. O. Havermayer is believed to have been painted in 1810.

The frescoes of the Hermitage of San Antonio de la Florida, "these worldliest of all church frescoes," were done in 1798 with the help of Asencio Juliá. "In this shrine which was visited chiefly by a suburban public and which the lower classes loved, Goya has kept his art as popular as possible. . . . The men, women, and children watching the miracle appear to have been drawn from the inhabitants of the district. It seems to be a tumultuous mob. . . . The marked accentuation of the popular element, the conspicuous setting forth of simple national costume, and the spread of a large *Manton* over the balustrade, are characteristically Spanish. . . . Yet . . . they recall the peculiar illusionistic decorative paintings of northern Italy which found their classic expression in Correggio's paintings at Parma. Who knows if he did not in his Parmese days make notes of Correggio's paintings in the Cathedral?" (A. L. Mayer.)

The first edition of the *Caprichos,* consisting of eighty plates, appeared in 1799, although an edition of seventy-two plates had already been announced two years earlier. The first edition was made under Goya's supervision and is in reddish tones. The plates he sold later to the Crown. Ch. H. Caffin (*The Print Collector's Quarterly,* vol. V; 1935) comments that the *Caprichos* "represent the most spontaneous expression of Goya's temperament and of his attitude toward the life and society of his day. It is in this set that the creative quality of [his] imagination is most demonstrated. He could not only summon visions from the void, but clothe them in convincing shape. Whether he stretched some human type to the limit of caricature or invested it with attributes of bird, beast, or reptile . . . or created a hybrid monster, he had the faculty of giving it an actuality that makes it seem reasonable."

Among the portraits by Goya one may generally distinguish between two classes: the *portrait intime* and the *portrait de salon.* Male *portraits intimes* painted after the turn of the century are, for instance, those of the actor D. Isidoro Maiquez (1807, Prado Mus.) and of the singer Mocarte (1806, N. Y., Mr. Archer Huntington). These were the portraits of his friends, of his own people, and are the expression of psychological concentration, in contrast to the *portraits de salon,* where internal values have partly to give way to external details like costume, pose, gesture, etc. Among these *portraits de salon* may be mentioned the magnificent picture of the Cónde de Fernán Nuñez (Madrid, Duque de Fernán Nuñez), that of the Marqués de San Adrian (Madrid, Marqués de San Adrian) and that of Da. Isabel Cobos de Porcél (1806, London, National Gallery). (Sánchez Cantón, *passim.*) The superb portraits of the Marqués and Marquésa de Castelfort were painted in 1805 (Montreal, heirs of Sir William van Horne). Mayer states that the free brushstroke and fragrant delicacy noticeable in the masculine portraits of the close of the century has been replaced by a rich impasto technique. Towards 1808, a tendency to introduce slightly blackish-grey hues in the flesh tints become apparent, with which elaborate costumes often form a peculiar contrast (for instance, in the portrait of D. Pantaleón Perez Nenin Madrid, D. Pedro Labat y Arrizabalaga, which is considered to be Goya's finest military portrait).

The series of six small paintings telling the entertaining narrative of the arrest of Maragato, the bandit, through the monk Pedro de Valdivia, are of the year 1806 (Chicago, Art Inst., M. A. Ryerson Coll.). Sánchez Cantón believes that from this period date a number of drawings of a social-satirical nature, as well as those depicting a series of nine grotesque visions. Most of them are outlined in India-ink, their sobriety bespeaking a technical progress over the sketches for the *Caprichos.* The opinion that Goya intended to use these drawings in the future for etchings seems convincing. A number of paintings in the collection of the Marqués de la Romana, Madrid, belong to the first decade of the century, or shortly after, as, for instance, *The Robber's Case,* 1808-12; *Bandit and a Woman,* 1808-13; *Murder by Brigands,* 1803-13; *The Plague Terror,* 1810-13. (Dates by Mayer.)

The events of the year 1808 were of far-reaching effect on the destiny of Spain and of many Spaniards. Too well known to dwell upon in detail are the facts of Charles IV's abdication in favor of his son Ferdinand VII; his later retraction of this step; and finally Napoleon's clever exploitation of the situation in placing his brother Joseph upon the throne of Spain. Among those (called Afrancesados) hospitable to the change in dynasty, expecting from it liberty and reform, was Goya. On the other hand, there was a large element hostile to the intrusion of foreigners and foreign ideas. Brewing discontent fanned by events bound to irritate Spanish pride and sensitiveness led to open revolution in Madrid on May 2nd. Quiet seemed to have settled again over the capital when Joseph made his second entry in 1809. By giving proof of his desire to be a good monarch, he gained adherents (Josefinos) during the succeeding years. (Von Loga, *passim.*) In 1808, Goya visited Saragossa (portrait of General Palafox, Madrid, Prado); in the following year he made another trip to the Aragonese capital, which by then had passed through its second siege. Justly deserving of their universal fame are the two canvases in the Prado Museum, one depicting the bloody battle between the rebelling populace and Mameluke cavalry at the Puerta del Sol at Madrid, and the other the nocturnal scene of the shooting down of citizens by foreign soldiers. (Sketch for the first of the two canvases owned by Marqués de Casa-Torres, Madrid, that for the other by Hisp. Soc. of Am., N. Y.) Especially in the latter, Goya's superior intelligence and genius as a painter are revealed. How many artists have failed in their effort to render similar subjects producing merely trivially detailed narratives. "Not a glorious uprising nor the great national deed has here been exalted, but the bestial brutal aspect of these fights . . . the dull sense of duty and the last outcry of the condemned facing the firing-squad." Goya's reactions to the horror of war experienced at Madrid, on his travels to Saragossa, and later, have come down to us in his dramatic, scornful *Desastres de la Guerre* (The Disasters of War), a series of etchings (1810-13), of which the first complete edition (title page, explanatory page, and eighty plates in two sets of four albums each) appeared in 1863, Goya himself having only made a few impressions. This edition, as well as others, and also some of the other graphic *œuvres* of Goya's were printed by order of the Académia de Bellas Artes de San Fernando of Madrid at the Calcografia Nacional.

Among the portraits done during the French reign and subsequent War of Independence may be cited those of D. José Manuel Romero, Spanish Minister of Joseph Bonaparte (c. 1809; Chicago, Chas. Deering Coll.); Ferdinand Guillemardet, French envoy to Madrid, a picture which was probably familiar to Delacroix (1798; Louvre); General Guye (1810; N. Y., Mr. Marshall Field); the three portraits of the Duke of Wellington (1812; Stratfieldsaye and Duchess of Leeds). To these should be added the portrait of Victor Guye, the French general's nephew (N. Y., Mr. Ch. B. Harding) which is another among Goya's paintings attesting to his love for and keen understanding of children. About 1810 he painted the *Allegory of the City of Madrid,* replacing later on the picture of Joseph Bonaparte with a cartouche bearing the inscription "2 de Mayo." Other portraits of Joseph Bonaparte have been lost. Outstanding, not only for treatment of form and colour but for characterization as well, is the portrait of the Canon Juan Antonio Llorente, historian of the Inquisition (c. 1810; Berlin, Kaiser Friedr. Museum).

With the conclusion of the Peninsular War and the liquidation of the Napoleonic Empire, Ferdinand VII regained his throne in 1814. In spite of Goya's previous affiliations, Ferdinand retained him as a court painter, since Goya's prestige as an artist was such that he could not be dispensed with. In the same year Goya, close to seventy, retired to the house he owned in the outskirts of Madrid, called La Quinta del Sordo. In the opinion of Mayer, the frescoes, most of which, transferred to canvas, have been donated to the Prado Museum, may be dated around 1815. In these paintings (*Manola, Pilgrimage to the Miraculous Wall of San Isidro, The Fates, Two Old Men Belabouring Each Other with Clubs, Saturn Devouring His Children,* etc.) which Goya painted for his own pleasure we see that "they are the most important evidence of his artistic ideal in his old age. Here we recognize the impulse to monumentality, to immensity of form . . . simplification, omission of all detail, and concentration of colour. A greater simplification of colour can hardly be imagined; black, white, brown;

and yet a richness has been attained, unsurpassed even by Daumier's creations, which objectively and subjectively resemble these works. Here the lonely master is at his best. . . . He recalls his dreams of the night and his spiritual visions of the day. . . ." In other compositions produced after 1815 Goya took motives of an earlier period but rendered them in an entirely new fashion. To this series, for instance, belong the *Majas on the Balcony* (Paris, M. Gronet) and the *Majas on a Walk* (Lille, Mus. Gronet). In contrast to the monumental effect of the *Smithy* (c. 1820; H. Frick Coll., N. Y.) are such colourful paintings as the *Fantastic Rock* (Met. Mus., N. Y.), the *Carneval* (formerly Coll. Nemes, Munich), the *Maypole* (Kaiser Fried. Museum, Berlin) . . . (Mayer).

"The portraits of about 1814 denote striving for monumentality, as shown in his figure compositions . . . the colour becomes simpler, the tones grey, the mood melancholy. Various of the portraits of Ferdinand VII demonstrate this change" (for instance, that in uniform with horses in the background in the Prado, and a variant of this, painted a few years later, preserved at the Consejo Supremo de Guerra at Madrid). "The most characteristic portrait is that of the Duke of San Carlos (Saragossa, Direccion del Canal Imperial de Aragon, 1815; study for the head in the Coll. of Conde de Villagonzalo, Madrid; a smaller version of the Saragossa portrait was owned by the late Marqués de la Torrecilla, Madrid). It is interesting to note that Goya prepared his canvas for the study of the Duke in a fashion much resembling that of his earlier years (style of about 1800) as suitable to his study of a courtier. On the other hand, the dark grounding of other portraits is expressive of the master's inclinations during these years, in accordance with his tendency to deaden his colours working from dark to light, and thus producing greater effects with fewer colours. . . . Deep blue is the colour on which Goya concentrated in this later time." In the portrait of the Duchess of Abrantes (1816, Madrid, Conde Quinta de la Enjarada) "Goya enriched the painter's handicraft with a new technique producing greater unity by disjointed strokes of the brush . . . though he did not use this new technique in all his later works." Four years later he painted the portrait of the architect Tiburcio Pérez (N. Y., Met. Mus.), which "marks a new phase in Goya's development as a portrait-painter by its free-and-easy attitude, perhaps only surpassed in one other portrait, that of Ramon Satué (1823—Amsterdam, Rijksmuseum). The portrait of Da. Maria Martinez de Puga (1824—H. Frick Coll., N. Y.) reaches beyond Manet's paintings to Munch's art of portraiture." (Mayer).

Keeping pace with his artistic evolution are two series of etchings: the *Tauromaquia* (Bullfight) and the *Disparates*, the latter also known under the name of *Proverbios* (Proverbs). *Tauromaquia*: of the first edition, 1815, made under the supervision of Goya, only very few copies are known. In the second edition by the Calcografia Nacional a portrait of Goya was added to the thirty-three plates and one explanatory page of the first edition. The third edition by E. Loizelet at Paris, c. 1875, was increased by a fanciful title page and seven hitherto unpublished plates. With two exceptions these "etchings are done in aquatint which has been more fully used to secure the desired effect than in the *Desastres*. Beruete says rightly that Goya has reproduced things which in our own days have been made visible by means of the photographic camera" (Mayer). *Proverbios*: The first edition, lithograph title-page and eighteen plates, made by the Calcografia Nacional, appeared in 1864. W. M. Ivins, Jr. (*Bull. Met. Mus.*, 1911), writes of the *Proverbios* that they are "the most amazing etched pictures by any artist who has worked since the time of Rembrandt." Speaking generally on Goya's achievements in the graphic arts, the same authority observes that it is "architectonic, organic, functional . . . it is discovered to be the product of a new mating of nature and geometry, inspired by a wider and more penetrating observation of the former and a more extended and imaginary use of the latter. . . . For sensitiveness to the beauty of the human body, for curious research in the esthetic inversion, the beauty of the hideous, Goya stands alone. . . . Who except Hokusai has expressed in black and white, weight, the heaviness of tired bodies, the leaden fall of a woman's unconscious arm . . . as this Spaniard? . . . Who has ever made motion so moving? . . . His every line is kinetic, he does not relate motion, he exhibits it." And conclusive are Mr. Ivins' statements that "on the purely technical side—the broad massing of light and shade, the ability to tell a tale with the simplest means, the instinctive choice of the pictorially dramatic detail—Rembrandt and Goya stand alone. On another side that is purely technical . . . Goya is the only one who has availed himself of all the possibilities of aquatint—the only one who has used the medium with audacity and resolution and success; the only one who has dared use it to express powerful, fundamental things." According to Mayer, three of Goya's etchings surpass those so far discussed. The *Landscape with Two Trees*, the *Landscape with Waterfall*, the *Giant* are said not only to represent the most accomplished achievements in the realm of etching, but they belong to the most monumental works of art of all times.

In 1817 Goya had visited Seville. The picture of *SS. Justa and Rufina* (Seville, Cathedral), recognized principally for its technical excellence, marks a renewed activity in sacred subjects, culminating in the *Communion of St. Joseph of Calasanz* and the *Prayer at the Mount of Olives* (1819, Madrid, Escuelas Pias de S. Antonio Abad), which are spoken of as his most inspired religious paintings. In 1819 he was gravely ill, narrowly escaping death. It is supposed that in 1823 with the beginning of the "white terror" brought about by Ferdinand VII, Goya was suspected and had to take refuge in the house of a friend. The following year he was granted leave of absence on the ground of the advisability of taking the waters at Plombières. Via Bordeaux he travelled to Paris, returning again to Bordeaux. At Paris he painted the portraits of his friend, J. M. Ferrer and wife, and also a bullfight scene, the *Picador* (Marquésa de Baroja, Biarritz). His request from Bordeaux in 1825 for a prolongation of his leave was granted. In 1826 he returned to Madrid to apply personally for permission to stay abroad without having to renounce his salary. Ferdinand granted this petition under the condition that Goya would have his portrait painted by Vicente Lopez (Prado). Accompanied by his grandson Mariano he returned to Bordeaux, where, surrounded by Spanish friends of whom those who were poor partook of his hospitality, he spent his last years. He died there on April 16, 1828.

"Almost blind, working with double spectacles or with a magnifying glass, Goya went on drawing and painting till the end of his life." The *Milkmaid of Bordeaux* (Madrid, Conde de Alto Barcilés), the portrait of D. Santiago Galos (1826—Dr. Barnes, Overbrook, Philadelphia), that of D. Juan Muguiro (1827—Condesa de Muguiro, Madrid) with the sitter "dressed in blue that looks almost black," and a number of drawings (Prado and Coll. Gerstenberg, Berlin), are among his last works. According to Sánchez Cantón, he left us his last will in the unfinished portrait of D. José Pio de Molina (1828—Coll. M. Reinhardt, Winterthur). Among Goya's last works of note are his lithographs. As far as we know, he was already interested in this new art in 1819—*Woman Spinning* and *The Duel*—and he continued practicing at Bordeaux. Best known are probably the four bullfight scenes, the *Toros de Bourdeos*. Also here he excelled. ". . . Without doubt he was by nature a great lithographer, the greatest that we yet know. . . ." (J. Copley, *A Print Lover's 100;* see also von Loga and others).

It has been argued that Goya left no school behind him. But be this as it may, he stands at the head of a movement, the beats of which are felt in increasing rather than diminished measure until the present day. Dwelling on the works of the older Goya, Sánchez Cantón exclaims: "What prescience! they betray that they are among the distinct precursors of Cézanne, though the latter may never have seen these pictures of the last period." In *Goya, the First Modern* (a study embodying also a psychological biography of Goya), A. P. McMahon has dealt with the various aspects of Goya's importance in the development of modern painting. Specific reference is made in this article to artists such as Delacroix, Géricault, Manet, Odilon, Redon, Munch, Klinger, Cézanne, Daumier, Picasso, and Matisse.

Why Goya is regarded as the first modern painter has also been answered by the same author. He says, for instance, that "Modernity is not all of Goya but arising out of him. His modernity, judged technically, is to be seen in his persistent experimentalism. . . . He transcended what were sincerely believed the limitations of his media as vehicles of expression. In the field of decoration he succeeded in superimposing something national and contemporary on eighteenth-century French and Venetian painting. . . . Into the accepted conventions of portrait-painting he injected two elements: He focussed attention sometimes on characterization, and again he exhibited the impressionist's joy in the light that reflects colour. . . . He produced arbitrary methods which were condoned in his own time because of adventitious circumstances. But it was these unesthetic qualities which enabled them to survive and stimulate the modern movement."

(*Note.* Dates and localities in this article are mainly those as given in the catalogue of A. L. Mayer's *Francisco de Goya*, 1924. Since publication of that work, ownership of a number of the paintings cited may have changed. No precise information is at present available on the fate of works of art which, prior to the outbreak of the Civil War—July, 1936—have been in Spain.)

Bibliography: *General and Biographical Works*: F. Zapater y Gómez, *Noticias biograficas*. Saragossa, 1868 (Biography founded upon Goya's correspondence with D. Martin Zapater, the author's uncle).—L. Matheron, *Goya*. Paris, 1858.—V. Carderera y Solano, *Francisco Goya*. Gazette des B. A., 1863. —C. Yriarte, *Goya. . . .* Paris, 1867.—Conde de la Viñaza, *Goya, sus tiempos, su vida, sus obras*. Madrid, 1887.—A. F. Calvert, *Goya, an Account of his Life and Works*. London, 1908.—G. Lafond, *Goya y Lucientes*. Paris, 1910.—A. Beruete y Moret, 3 vols.: I. *Goya, pintor de retratos*, II. *Composiciones y Figures*, III. *Goya, grabador*. Madrid, 1915. (Vol. I. English trans.: *Goya as Portrait Painter*. London, 1922). —V. von Loga, *Francisco de Goya*. (2nd ed.) Berlin, 1921—A. L. Mayer, *Geschichte der span. Malerei*. (2nd ed.) Leipzig, 1922.—id., *Francisco de Goya*. London-Toronto, 1924 (valuable bibliographical leads).— ibid., art. *Goya y Lucientes* in Thieme Becker, Vol. XIV. Leipzig, 1921 (valuable bibliographical leads).—A. P. McMahon, *Goya, the first Modern* (in *The Arts*, Vol. 10, 1926).—*Junta organizadora del centenario de Goya*. Zaragoza, 1927-28 (various monographs dealing with different aspects of Goya's times, life, and art).—J. Ezquerra del Bayo, *La Duquesa de Alba y Goya*. Madrid, 1928.—*Arte Español*, 1928-29 (articles by various authors on occasion of Goya's centenary).—F. J. Sánchez Cantón, *Goya*. Paris, 1930.

*Graphic art* (see also above, under General Works): L. Lefort in Gaz. des Beaux Arts, XXII (1867); XXIV, XXV (1868).—J. Hofmann, *Francisco de Goya*, (critical catal.). Vienna, 1907.—V. von Loga, *Goya's seltene Radierungen und Litographien*. Berlin, 1907.—id., *Francisco de Goya, Meister der Graphik*, Vol. IV.—L. Delteil, *La Peintre graveur illustré;* Vols. XIV, XV. —A. P. McMahon, *Goya as a master of lithography*, in International Studio, Vol. 86, 1927.—F. Boix, *La primera edicion de los Caprichos*, Arte Español, 1929.—P. Vindel, *Los Caprichos; la Tauromaquia; los Desastres de la Guerra; los Proverbios de D. Francisco Goya. . . .* Madrid, 1928.—Bull. Met. Mus. of Art, N. Y.; 1911, 1918, 1924, 1928, 1933, 1935, (W. M. Ivins, Jr.); 1936 (A. H. Mayor).

*Drawings* (see also above, under General Works): G. D'Achiardi, *Les dessins de D. Francisco de Goya au musée de Prado*. 3 vols., Rome, 1908.—V. von Loga, *Goya's Zeichnungen* in Die graph. Künste, XXXI. Vienna, 1908.—F. Boix. *Los dibujos de Goya*. Madrid, 1922.—id., *Catal. general ilustr. Exposicion de dibujos orignales 1750-1850*. Madrid (Soc. amigos de arte), 1922. —F. J. Sánchez Cantón, *Los dibujos del viaje à Sanlúcar.* Madrid, 1928. —F. J. Sánchez Cantón, F. Boix, *Goya, cien dibujos inéditós.* Madrid, 1928.—A. L. Mayer, *Francisco Goya,* Ausgewählte Handzeichnungen. Berlin, (Prophylaen-Verl.) n.d.—H. B. Wehle, in Bull. Met. Mus. of Art. *An album of Goya's drawings,* N. Y., Feb., 1936.

*Tapestries:* G. Cruzada-Villaamil, *Los tapices de Goya.* Madrid, 1870. —*"Tapestries and carpets from the palace of the Pardo woven at the Royal Manufactory of Madrid,"* N. Y. (Hisp. Soc. of Am.), 1917.—F. J. Sánchez Cantón, E. Tormo Monzó, *Los tapices de la casa del Rey N. S.* Madrid, 1919.

*Exhibitions: Museo del Prado, Madrid;* Centenario de Goya, Exposicion de pinturas, Abril-Mayo, 1928. Foreword by E. Tormo y Monsó. — *Bibliothèque Nationale. Paris,* 1935. Goya, exposition de l'oeuvre gravée, de peint., de tapiss. et de 110 dessins du Mus. du Prado. (Cat. by J. Adhemar).—*Metrop. Mus. of Art, N. Y.;* Francisco Goya, his paintings, drawings and prints; Jan.-March, 1936.—*California Palace of the Legion of Honor, San Francisco;* Exhibition of paintings, drawings, and prints by F. Goya. June-July, 1937.

**GOYEN (Jan van).**—Dutch painter, 1596-1656. A prolific landscape painter whose works are characterised by a delicate sense of atmosphere, and generally carried out in a quiet greyish-brown tone. He also produced five engravings.

Bibliography: Hopstede de Groot, *Catalogue of Dutch Painters,* Vol. VIII.

**GOZZOLI (Benozzo).**—See Benozzo Gozzoli.

**GRACANICA (Serbia).**—See Byzantine Architecture, Late Period.

**GRADO (Italy).**—*Cathedral,* 571-586. An early Christian basilica in Istria, connected stylistically with the contemporary architecture at Ravenna, as S. Apollinare Nuovo.

**GRAFFIONE (Giovanni di Michele Scheggini da Larciano).**—Painter, born in Florence, 1455; died there 1521.

In 1468 Graffione was apprenticed to Piero di Lorenzo Zuccherini; in 1484 he worked with Baldovinetti, receiving five payments for painting the centre of the panel of *The Madonna, Saints and Angels* in Sant' Ambrogio. In 1491 he was a member of a commission to judge plans for the façade of the Cathedral of Florence; and in 1503 and 1508 he appears on the register of the Compagnia di San Luca. Certain attributions have been made to Graffione through stylistic analogies to the 1484 Madonna.

Bibliography: Vasari-Milanesi, II.—H. Horne, *Il Graffione,* Burlington Magazine, VIII, 1905.

**GRAFFITO.**—Literally, a scratching; applied to rude inscriptions and drawings.

**GRAFLY (Charles).**—American sculptor, born 1862, of Philadelphia, specializing in allegorical and symbolical subjects (*Symbol of Life, From Generation to Generation,* etc.).

**GRANACCI (Francesco).**—Florentine painter, 1469-1543, pupil of Credi and of Ghirlandaio, whose assistant he was; influenced by Michelangelo and Raphael.

**GRANADA.**—The *Alhambra.*—After the decisive conflict of Navas de Tolosa (1212), the taking of Cordoba (1226), and of Seville (1248), by St. Ferdinand, all that remained of splendor in Mussulman Spain was concentrated in the state of the Sultans of Granada.

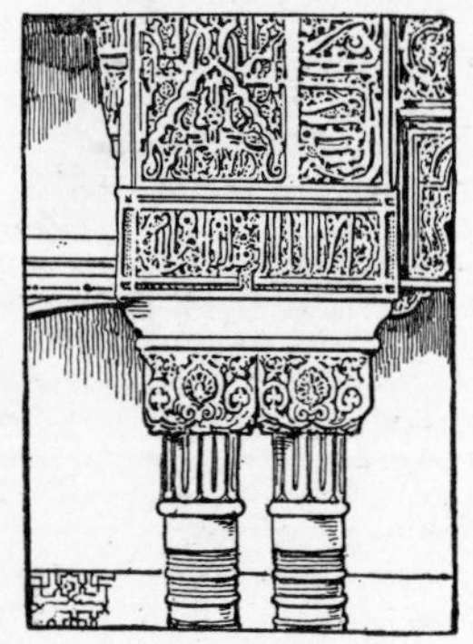

Granada: Capital from the court of Lions. (Alhambra.)

The Alhambra, which the Nasserides built and fortified as their residence, stands at the top of a hill. The whole fortress includes, at the South and at the bottom of the hill, the "Torres Bermejas" (Vermilion Towers), mentioned from 864 under the name of Medinet el Hamra (the Red Town), and then, on the plateau, the Alcazaba and the Alhambra, properly called. The Alcazaba, which is the oldest part of the palace, is on the west. (Dieulafoy has noted curious analogies between the Alcazaba and the famous Château Gaillard, where the principles of oriental poliorcetics—the art of conducting sieges—were first applied in the west). After Yusuf I built a palace outside the Alcazaba, the fortress of Mohammed became an outwork. Besides this, Yusuf completed the existing ramparts, including the Puerta Judiciaria and the Puerta del Vino. His successor, Mohammed V (1354-1391), built the "Patio de los Arrayanes" or "de la Aberca," and the sumptuous palace of which the Court of Louis is the centre. This famous courtyard is surrounded with openwork tympana and slender little columns crowned with exquisitely carved capitals. In the middle stands the fountain, with strange stiff lions, of a hieratic style.

After the downfall of the Mussulman power, Ferdinand and Isabella took great interest in the Alhambra. By their command, the Count of Tendilla restored the interior decoration of the palace, and strengthened the walls.

In 1526, Charles V built a new Palace to which a great many annexes of the old Alhambra were sacrificed. This palace, begun in 1526, by Pedro Machuca, in the Italian Renaissance style, was continued after his death (1550) by his son, Luis, who died in 1572. The work languished at the end of the 16th century, and definitely ceased in the next century.

See Pls. 2, 33, Vol. I.

*Cathedral.* The type church of the Griego-Romano style, as the Early Renaissance Spanish manner succeeding the plateresque was called. The plan is like that of a Gothic church—a great hall filled with three rows of supports carrying vaults—but the decorative detail is classical, correct, and antiquarian. Enrique de Egas planned the church in 1523; the present conception of the interior is due to Diego de Silaé, who took it on from then, without, however, altering the plan. Alonso Cano designed the façade in the 17th century.

**GRANDE CHARTREUSE (France).**—The monastery of the Grande Chartreuse was founded in the 11th century by St. Bruno. In 1132, it was destroyed by an avalanche, and rebuilt a little later. The buildings were several times destroyed by fire. In 1676, after a final disaster, the monastery was rebuilt as it now exists, and occupied by monks of the Chartreuse until 1903, when they were expelled.

The monastery stands high in the mountains amid grand and lovely scenery.

**GRANDI (Ercole di Giulio Cesare).**—Ferrarese painter, c. 1463-1531, a pupil of Ercole Roberti, influenced by the Ferrarese school in general and by Mantegna.

**GRANDMONT (Abbey).**—See Enamel.

**GRANET (François Marius).**—French painter, born in Aix-in-Provence in 1775. Died 1849. He went to Paris on foot, and studied in David's studio until, for want of money, he had to leave the school. He then studied in the Louvre. In 1802, he was able to go to Rome, where he painted the *Choir of the Church of the Capucins,* which was very successful at the 1819 Salon. He was a very refined painter.

*The Death of Sodoma* and the *View of the Coliseum* (both in the Louvre) do not give any idea of his resourceful talent. He should be judged by his pictures in the Museum of Aix. The Louvre, however, has a rich collection of Granet's drawings. These reveal the artist's qualities of taste and intimacy even better than do his paintings, which are sometimes rather heavy.

**GRANT (Duncan).**—English painter, born 1885, one of the most gifted of the more "advanced" members of the contemporary English school of painting. An artist of rare sensitiveness, he is represented in the National Gallery, Millbank, by two works, *The Queen of Sheba* and *Lemon Gatherers.*

**GREAT WALL OF CHINA.**—The oldest remains of Chinese architecture. Parts date from the end of the third century B.C. to the sixteenth century A.D. It extends for 500 to 600 leagues and is the most formidable work ever undertaken by the hand of man. It was destined to defend the empire from foreign invasions. At times it is 20 feet high, and 12 feet thick.

**GRECO (Theotocopulos, Domenicos or Theotocopuli Domenico, surnamed El, 1541-1614).**—Thanks to Señor de San Román's discovery of two signed documents new light has been shed on the formerly much debated date of El Greco's birth: On the occasion of his lawsuit with the *Hospital de Santa Caridad* of Illescas the painter declared twice, in 1606 (Oct. 31st and Nov. 4th) that he was 65 years old. It has, therefore, been assumed that he was born in 1541.

That he was a native of Crete, then under the sovereignty of Venice, is primarily known from a number of pictures which are signed in Greek characters Domenichos Theotokopoulos, Kres (the Cretan) . . . as for instance the *Healing of the Blind* at Parma, the *San Mauricio* at the Escorial, etc. But the more explicit information that he came from Candia, the island's capital, appears for the first time in the first document definitely mentioning the painter, namely in Julio Clovio's letter to the Cardinal Nepote Alessandro Farnese. On November 16th, 1570, the miniature painter wrote that "there has arrived in Rome a young man from Candia, a disciple of Titian, who in my opinion is a painter of rare talent; among other things he has painted a portrait of himself, which causes wonderment to all the painters in Rome. I should like him to be under the patronage of your Illustrious and Reverend Lordship, without any other contributions towards his living than a room in the Farnese Palace for some little time, until he can find other accommodation. I therefore beg and pray you to have the kindness to write Count Lodovico, your Majordomo, to provide him with some room near the top in the said Palace . . ." (transl. by Calvert). From this letter then we learn that as a pupil of Titian, El Greco must have been in Venice. This information were it not implied in this letter would also be suggested by the Venetian note discernible in El Greco's paintings and chiefly in those of his early period.

We do not know when he left Rome, why he went to Spain or when he arrived there. The often advanced theory that the ultimate purpose of his journey was to obtain important commissions from Philip

Greco (El): The Holy Family. (Wames Collection, Budapest.)

II, plausible as it seems, has never been supported by any proof whatsoever. Another theory advanced by students, that he received the commission for the Convent Church of Santo Domingo el Antiguo of Toledo, seems, considering various circumstances, more convincing but has not been substantiated either. When, on occasion of a lawsuit, he was asked what had brought him to Spain, El Greco refused to answer this question. "Sometime before 1577 . . . El Greco came to Spain. In that year we find him at work in Toledo, engaged in decorating the then new church of Santo Domingo el Antiguo as we know from the date 1577 after his signature upon the central picture of *The Ascension* in the retablo of the said church. . . . The commission for the *Espolio* for Toledo Cathedral was also given in 1577, the year in which Greco finished his first Spanish work *The Ascension,* and it is presumable that it was the success of this work which led the chapter to employ him to work for the cathedral. . . . On July 2nd he received the payment of 400 reales on account for the work" (Calvert). From now on data concerning his life and activities are not wanting. (Since the appearance in 1908 of Sr. Cossio's profound study, more facts have become known on El Greco's life and character. Much of the additional information is due to the indefatigable research done by Sr. D. Francisco Borja de San Román.)

He had a son, Jorge Manuel, from Jeronimo de las Cuevas but it is not known whether he was married to her. Jorge Manuel, more competent as an architect than as a painter, was his father's assistant. In matters of business El Greco relied very much on his servant, Francisco Preboste, an Italian by birth, and also a painter. In the various lawsuits concerning his paintings, he never lacked in generous support given to him by high ecclesiastics, individuals of standing, or artists. Pacheco (see *Pacheco*) who visited El Greco in 1611 tells us that he "was a student of many things, a writer on art, a great philosopher given to witty sayings, a sculptor and architect, as well as a painter. Pacheco speaks of much work that he saw, and in particular of a cupboard in which were models of clay, and of a collection of small paintings the originals of all those that he painted during his life-time. The painters talked on many subjects, . . . they discussed the value of colour and its supreme quality in painting; they spoke of Michelangelo and his failure as a colourist. . . . Pacheco summed up his impression of the old master in the significant saying: *He was in all things as singular as in his paintings*. We have the eulogistic sonnets of Paravicino and Gongora. Nor will it do to overlook Juseppe Martinez, who though not Greco's contemporary, doubtless heard him discussed by others who knew him: *. . . he earned many ducats, but spent them in too great pomp and display in his house, to the extent of keeping paid musicians to entertain at meal times, etc. . . .*" (Calvert, passim). Of greatest interest on El Greco's more intimate life are two inventories. One, telling us of his belongings, was drawn up during his life-time. Another lists those of his son and sole heir, Jorge Manuel, in 1621. Since among the latter there can be traced a great number of things that were his father's, this second document completes the first one. San Román and Cossio have made penetrating comments on these finds; especially as regards El Greco's library and unsold paintings. (The library included 19 books on architecture, 27 in Greek, 67 in Italian and 17 in *romance*, which probably means in Spanish.)

An entry in the records of the Church of Santo Tomé informs us that he died on April 7th, 1614, that the funeral services were held in that church, and that he was buried in Santo Domingo el Antiguo.

The signatures appearing on his canvases are signed in Greek characters—those of the earlier years in mayuscles, the later ones in minuscles. Some of these signatures as well as others in Latin characters affixed to documents are reproduced in Cossio's little volume published in 1914.

"The earliest pictures by El Greco, the dates of which are definitely known from signatures or contemporary inventories, are the *Healing of the Blind* at Parma (1571-1574); the two versions of the *Cleansing of the Temple* in the Cook Collection at Richmond (1571) and in the museum at Minneapolis (1571-1576), and the small *Sinai* picture (1571) in a private collection in Hungary. These pictures allow us to place in these years of activity a number of other paintings such as two copies after Titian; his earliest *Annunciation*; a small copy after Correggio's *Night*; the *Adoration of the Shepherds* (Coll. Willumsen, Copenhagen); the *Flight into Egypt* (formerly in the Gorostiza Coll., Bilbao); the *Pietà* (Hispanic Society, New York); etc. The afore mentioned *Cleansing of the Temple* of the Minneapolis Museum (formerly Yarborough Coll., London) acquires special historical interest due to the presence of the portraits appearing in the right corner of Titian, Michelangelo, Julio Clovio, and a fourth, which perhaps may be identified with Raphael. Of non-religious pictures the two variants of the *Boy Lighting a Coal* (Private Coll., New York, 1570-1573; Museum, Naples, 1574-1576) and the portrait of *Julio Clovio* (Naples, Museum, 1571-1573), as well as the signed *Anastagi* portrait in the Frick Coll. of New York belong to this period" (A. L. Mayer). Señor Cossio also assigns one of the examples of the so-called *Proverb* to the period between 1571-1576 (Paris, Cherfils Coll.). This canvas then would be the first of the series of the genre scene in which a woman blows on a coal and candle, while a man and an ape are watching her with interest. In all these paintings a relationship, varying in degree, with a number of contemporary Italian artists can be seen.

Indeed, the chapter of El Greco's artistic evolution while in Italy is as significant as it is complicated. Of his Venetian stay Sr. Cossio states that "here one has to look for the different influences which contributed toward the formation of the artist, upon his virtues as well as upon his defects. They were active on a genuine and primitive fund of local creto-byzantine traditions, . . . and upon a vigorous personality more inclined to revolt than to submit with servilism." As regards to Titian's influence on El Greco the same authority says: "Titian was his material teacher. El Greco acquired from him technique, the secret of art, . . . received his advice and perhaps copied some of his pictures. But the true Titianesque spirit never became incarnate in him, neither then nor later." Lately, A. L. Mayer has examined the two-sided problem not only of El Greco's indebtedness or lack of indebtedness to Titian but also to other Italian artists or their immediate forerunners. Recalling El Greco's compositions of this period one will in the main agree with that student's opinion that "as much as we may recognize the relationship with definite Italian masters and pictures, we, nevertheless, make the important observation of a wilful transformation of their art into his own. Such a transformation was surely not intentionally activated by the artist but rather surged from unconscious and innate currents within him. In spite of the fact that the rendering of naturalistic details occupied him down to his late Spanish period, he was in discord with Venetian and Spanish sensualism. This led from the beginning toward an un-European sublimation. Everything becomes two-dimensional and we feel the note of dematerialization. We observe this precisely in those pictures where the artist, above all, seems to attach himself as a copyist—crude as this may sound, to Titian, Correggio, and Bassano. . . . Never are the silhouettes of the figures, in the Italian sense, sharply defined. There is rather a curious connection between them and the background which instead of being neutral is also treated as a living mass; thus the figures and backgrond become woven into one homogeneous fabric."

Mayer also discusses more specifically the problem of influence in regard to such artists as Michelangelo, Veronese, Tintoretto, Correggio, the Bassanos, as well as Raphael and Julio Clovio. "It would seem natural that among the Venetian painters, Paolo Veronese made the least impression on the young Greek. Certainly his pictures must have appeared banal to him. Nevertheless, a number of figures in El Greco's early paintings are reminiscent of some of Veronese's. The love for cool harmonies, especially in the employment of blue, is purely a commonly shared predilection. . . . Certainly, he must have admired the energy of a Tintoretto, though his energy may have impressed him as rather uncouth . . . for in contrast to this master, all of El Greco's figures, even those living in a tangible world, appear to have their origin in a world of vision. Yet, what must have attracted the Greek are Tintoretto's compositions, their originality, and their dramatic rendering. More than anyone else, he understood the musical quality, the rhythm of these creations. Without copying that master, he found here special encouragement for his own complicated compositions. . . . After that teacher of drama, he could have received many a valuable stimulus from the older Michelangelo's fresco-compositions." The Italian memories still discernible in El Greco's earlier Spanish paintings are becoming with time fainter, while his genius asserts itself in all its personality and freedom.

The earliest of his Spanish pictures are the nine canvases painted for the High-altar and the lateral altars of the Convent Church of Santo Domingo el Antiguo of Toledo (1577-79) and the *Espolio* (Christ Despoiled of his Raiments) for the sacristy of the Cathedral. Not all of the nine paintings are still at Santo Domingo. The *Ascension of the Virgin*, which occupied the central panel of the High-altar, dated in Greek letters 1577, is in the Art Institute of Chicago, and others, among them the *Trinity*, are in the Prado. The *Ascension of Christ* with the half-length portrait of Don Diego de Castilla, the painter's patron, is "full of elements of the contemporary manneristic style. At the same time there becomes evident the painter's striving after a supernatural note in the rendering of happenings that took place on earth. . . . The *St. John the Evangelist* (Prado) holds one's attention because of the dignified treatment of the folds. The hands in their slenderness and studied position are already very frank documents of El Greco's typical style." In the *Espolio* (1577-1579), the red of Christ's mantle, also reflected in the armour of the Roman captain, is of the strongest expression—almost like the blare of a trumpet. Other examples of this scene from El Greco's hand are known, the most mature conception probably in the Pinakothek of Munich (not later than 1584), but neither in force of expression nor in colour are they surpassed by the Toledo version. From the point of view of technique and rendering of form, the *Crucifixion* at the Louvre (1579-1580) and the *San Sebastian* of Valencia Cathedral can be linked to the abovementioned paintings. The action in the *Crucifixion* is placed against a blue sky torn by ragged clouds. The portraits in the lower corner remind one of the Anastagi portrait. (A. L. Mayer, passim.)

The portrait of the sculptor Pompeo Leoni (Coll. Stirling-Maxwell, Keir in Scotland) is supposed to have been painted in 1578. A. L. Mayer attaches importance to El Greco's friendship with that Italian sculptor, as he believes that Leoni was instrumental in introducing the Cretan to Philip II. This monarch used to demand a trial piece from the painters before giving them commissions. That the picture known as the *Dream of Philip II* at the Escorial had such a purpose seems convincing. (However, on grounds of technique and style this painting is dated by Sr. Cossio toward 1600. The name of the *Dream of Philip II* appears for the first time in the catalogue of paintings at the Escorial of 1857. Cossio agrees with its author that the theme has been taken from St. Paul (Phil. II, 10) and like Titian's *Glory of Charles V* represents rather a *Glory of Philip II*, which would be an additional argument supporting his theory that this picture was painted after 1598, the date of Philip II's death.) This painting must have pleased the King for according to a letter of 1580 to the Prior of the monastery of the Escorial, El Greco had received the order for the well-known *St. Mauritius and the Theban Legion*. This picture, now in the chapter room of the Escorial was originally intended to adorn one of the altars of the monastery's church. It was finished in 1584 and, as we are informed by Father Siguenza, rejected by Philip II. Romulo Cincinnati was ordered to replace it with another composition of his own. El Greco then had to abandon all hope of receiving further royal favors, which instead the monarch granted to painters whose names are almost forgotten.

Señor Cossio stresses the point that the *San Mauricio* was begun shortly after El Greco had finished the *Espolio* for the Toledo Cathedral and, probably, while he was still engaged with the altar paintings for Santo Domingo of Toledo. This observation is of consequence for the *San Mauricio* is not only a typical but the first example of a new form of expression sought by the artist and the most significant one of his extravagant manner which was to shock so many people. . . . The reminiscences of Italian formulas still manifest in other of his paintings are not found here. It is a work of greater originality; the starting point of a new series of productions. . . .

No wonder it disappointed Philip II. Instead of depicting the death of the saint, the artist chose the great moment in the story when San Mauricio was persuading the entire legion to suffer a heroic death. The narrative is divided into two parts, namely, the larger area of the foreground where the saint surrounded by his officers is represented. In the other part, secondary in time and distance, San Mauricio is seen in the supreme moment consoling his soldiers while he stretches out his hands to receive their heads. Above in the heavens, appear two groups of angels with musical instruments and the attributes of martyrdom. The attitude of the personages in the first plane; the fidelity to Spanish facial types and Spanish landscapes; the intensity, coldness and crudity of light inundating the entire painting and impeding the onlooker from realizing fully the harmonious half-tones or the vigorous colours of the dress of the martyrs, angels and banner, were strange and dangerous novelties. They brought about the victory of Spanish realism, and the emphasis on a nervous and daring concept intent on breaking the classic moulds of light and colour (Cossio, passim).

Among the paintings of the middle period, there are a number of important canvases that relate themselves because of style, colour, and intensity of expression to the *San Mauricio*: the *Baptism*, the *Resurrection*, the *Crucifixion*, and the *Annunciation*. The *Baptism* is definitely known to have come from the College Church of Doña Maria de Aragon of Madrid (1596-1600). With the exception of the *Annunciation* which is in the museum Balaguer of San Geltrú, these paintings are in the Prado. Cossio and Mayer disagree on the dates, Cossio being inclined to date them in the decade of 1584-1594, whereas Mayer places them in the nineties and the *Resurrection* even possibly as late as 1603.

Probably the most renowned of El Greco's paintings is the *Burial of the Count of Orgaz* in the Parish Church of Santo Tomé at Toledo. Although it does not show so markedly the characteristics of paintings of the same period, for instance as does the *San Mauricio*, it belongs to his middle period. The contract for this painting was signed on March 18, 1586, with the stipulation that it should be finished on Christmas of the same year. The date of 1578, inscribed on the handkerchief of the young page with the torch, has repeatedly created confusion among critics. In the dating of the picture we must be guided by the above mentioned contract.

The iconographical repertory of the *Burial of the Count of Orgaz*, which sometimes has been wrongly interpreted, may be briefly described as a composite scene representing the burial of the count and the ascension and judgment of his soul. "There are thirty figures in this composition of living portraits. . . . Seven figures comprise the central group, which is admirably composed of bending forms around the supine count, they emerge from the gloom in flashes of splendid colour—gold, white, and steel blue. The inward interpretation of life—Spanish life—seems to summarize the entire impression of that passionate, conscious individualism, characteristic of Greco and of Spain. In the count in armour, with the livid face of death, in the cowled monk and the two robed priests, we see expressed the fervid piety of a people who have felt themselves in mystical communion with God. In the St. Augustine, splendid in ecclesiastical robes, is the magnificent opulence of the Catholic Church; in the young warm beauty of St. Stephen and the lovely acolyte are the full joy and rich colour which the East has left in Spain. Then behind are the mourners—a long row of vivid portrait heads seen against a dark background, and illuminated by the light which flickers from a few torches. These heads dominate the picture, they are the types unchanged in Castile today. . . . The magnificent white-bearded head, seen in profile, is Antonio Covarrubias" (Calvert, passim).

The action of the lower portion is carried above by the figure of an angel ascending with the soul of the deceased toward Christ. The more sombre colour intonation of the burial scene gains in light as the composition leads upward to the haloed figure of the Lord. Christ is seen in the company of winged hosts, the Apostles, and other personages. Below Him are the figures of St. Mary and St. John, who intercede for the soul of the Count. (Don Gonzalo Ruiz, Governor of Orgaz died in 1323. He was a charitable man; he rebuilt the Church of Santo Tomé in 1300. According to a legend, St. Augustine and St. Stephen descended from heaven to carry his body to the sepulchre.)

Stephan Bourgeois (Art News, Dec. 1, 1934) stressed the point that El Greco's gift for concentration is one of the main properties of his Byzantine equipment. His power of concentration is psychologically, for instance, as in all of his portraits, evident in the burial scene, and is also felt in the dynamically dramatic action above.

Señor Cossio characterizes the last period of El Greco's art as "the spring having come to the extreme limit of its tension." Mayer, discussing the paintings of the Church de la Caridad of Illescas, which ushers in this last style (1603-1606, all in situ with the exception of the *Marriage of the Virgin*) comments that: "A specially marked distortion of proportions, the small heads with their consciously contorted features, especially the slanting mouths, are characteristics of the last period. Equally typical is the highest imaginable tension felt in the nervousness of the light, which is generously sprinkled over the entire picture. Refinement of technique distinguishes the smaller paintings, whereas in the larger ones is an art which tells rapidly and audaciously the entire story in broad and free treatment. These later works are all feverish; everything is tender . . . a fabric of sparkling brush strokes. . . ."

In the *Ascension of the Virgin* (San Vicente de Toledo) El Greco's tendency to elongate, visible in the body of the Virgin being carried to heaven, heightens the sense of the upward sweeping movement. The ecstasy which is the keynote of the picture seems even to have transcended to the flowers in the foreground. Their richness of colour, as well as that of the flowers of the *San Mauricio*, have always delighted critics and induced them to recall the splendor of Byzantine mosaics.

In the ardent style of this period are also the *Baptism* (Hospital de San Juan Bautista, Toledo); the *Adoration of the Shepherds* (Metropolitan Museum, New York); the *Pentecost* (Prado, Madrid); etc.

A unique subject among El Greco's repertory of biblical scenes is one taken from the Book of Revelations, namely the *Opening of the Fifth Seal* (Zuluoga coll., Zumaya). "This picture toned to blues and yellows is one of the most fantastic and monumental creations of the painter. The sweep and ecstasy of the painting have never been attained by any other artist."

In a systematic study of El Greco as a landscape painter, his renderings of the cosmographical elements of earth and sky should also be considered in canvases where they seem less important. For the modelling of earth, that is terrain, and clouds, the often sharply contrasting use of light and colour and the dramatic aspect of the whole are characteristic of his art and temperament (for instance, in the various versions of the *Agony in the Garden* and of the *Crucifixion*, in those of *St. Francis* and *St. Jerome in the Wilderness*, etc.). Secondary, yet more than a merely indispensable, accessory to the subject, are the landscape and city view in such canvases as *San José* (Santa Magdalena, Toledo, 1599-1602), *St. Martin and the Beggar* (Charles Deering Coll., Chicago, 1599-1604), etc.

In the *Laocoön* (Charlottenburg, E. Fischer Coll., 1606-1610) the importance given to figures and landscape is equally distributed, and finally, landscape for its own sake appears in the incomparable canvases depicting the city of Toledo. Cossio says that there are none of the Italian antecedents for the *View of Toledo* (Met. Mus., N. Y.), which exist for the so-called *Panorama of Toledo* preserved in the Casa del Greco (c. 1609). ". . . this is a work probably commissioned by the Municipality, in which the main protagonist is the city itself. It is sort of an architectural perspective, a geographic statistical document, and a topographical city-plan with legends and observations in the left to explain it. And in spite of the scientific intention the whole is enveloped in a delicate ambient of art. . . . The *View of Toledo* on the other hand is a purely artistic creation. It is a sombre painting. . . . The monuments seem to be made of lead, the horizon is black and the sky tormented. The dark green of the water, trees and ground transform the banks of the river Tage, sometimes smiling and at other times placid and clear, into a tenebrous vale. Yet El Greco does not sin here against truth; corresponding to his temperament, he exalts what he sees" (Cossio, passim).

It may be admissible to call portraits some of El Greco's renderings of sacred personages. In the *St. Simeon* (after 1600, A. M. Huntington Coll., New York) or in the *San Ildefonso in His Study* (c. 1603-1605 Illescas, Church of the Hospital de la Caridad) the note of individuality is so striking as to dismiss the notion of a traditional formula. And, although the repeated use of one model turned them eventually into a type, the same may be said of his *St. Jerome as Cardinal* (Frick Gallery, New York; Lehman Coll., New York; Musée Bonnat, Bayonne; etc.). Yet it is in his astounding portraits that the faculty to describe personality with his brush is brilliantly revealed. "The necessity of submitting to nature ties here the hands of the artist. . . . Expression, drawing and colour are correct. But there is also strongly manifested the indelible personal accent which El Greco gave to the essential traits of the sitters. Melancholy and austere dignity. . . . The most magnificent and splendid of all his portraits is that of Fernando Niño de Guevara, the Inquisitor (1600-1601, Metropolitan Museum, New York). This picture takes equal rank with the most important portraits of other schools . . ." (Cossio, passim). Among the portraits, less sumptuous but equally penetrating, may be cited: *Diego Covarrubias* (Greco Museum, Toledo, 1596-1600); *Antonio Covarrubias* (Greco Museum, Toledo, 1594-1600); *Self-Portrait* (Metropolitan Museum, New York, c. 1609); *Jeronimo de Cevallos* (Prado, Madrid, 1608-1612).

It is sometimes believed that El Greco was the architect of a number of buildings. Cossio has established the error of the various attributions involved. We know of his architectural activity only from the altars of Santo Domingo of Toledo; of San José, also at Toledo; of the church of the Caridad at Illescas; of the church at Titulcia; and the altar for the Hospital of San Juan Bautista at Toledo (founded by Cardinal Tavera, and also known as the *Hospital de Afuera*).

Among his sculptures, the foremost is probably the *Virgin Presenting the Chasuble to St. Ildefonso*, a group designed for the architectural frame of the *Espolio* (Sacristy of the Toledo Cathedral, 1585-1587). It has been debated whether he executed or only designed the eight Apostles for the Church of the Hospital of San Juan Bautista of Toledo. The statue of the *Christ Resurrected* for the same church he finished in 1598.

Although he was a Greek by birth, and only arrived in Spain after having spent the formative years of adolescence and early manhood in Italy, El Greco is generally considered a Spanish painter, by Spaniards even more so than by others. Which then are the elements in the art of this foreigner that appealed to Spaniards? "Partly the Venetian note in his art, for the Spanish painters were more attracted by the art of Venice than by any other." There are, however, more profound ties of kinship between El Greco and his adopted country. More important than "*how* he painted is the question of *what* he painted. Through the contents of his representations, the treatment of *motifs*, the grasping of expression he reached the heart of Spaniards. The truthfulness of his portraits, his comprehension of Spanish religiousness as well as understanding for Spanish character, the passionate love for the beauty of Spanish landscapes made him the last great hispanized foreigner, the last of a long lineage of artists who had imigrated from foreign countries and absorbed the spirit of Spain . . ." (A. L. Mayer). As regards to Spanish religious sentiment, it is commonly known that the 16th century witnessed the height of Spanish mysticism. Nowhere, "in a shorter span than that of a century, and to a smaller extent before and after that epoch, did there proceed such an outpouring of the heart of love (for God), such a torrent of devotion and incidentally such a wealth of literary treasure, as has surely never been surpassed in Christian Europe" (Peers). In the *Burial of Count Orgaz* as well as in most of El Greco's numerous renderings of sacred subject and personages, his contemporaries may well have felt that they were shown their own spiritual visions. Not only was the artist receptive to Spain, but Spain had definitely cast her spell over him thus making the Greek a son of her own.

"An artist as fundamentally an individual as El Greco could not have founded a school, he could only have had imitators. His son's qualifications as a painter are revealed through the mediocre copies after his father's paintings (*Espolio*, Prado). Tristan and Mayno who are usually singled out as his pupils aimed at different ideals; they were consistent champions of chiaroscuro and belong to a new and completely different era" (Mayer). Sr. Cossio states that El Greco's only pupil was Velázquez, and Beruete says "that the study of the works of El Greco taught Velázquez to employ his fine grays in the flesh colours and enriched his palette by a number of new colours." El Greco as a universal teacher has come into his own in our times, many of the moderns finding in him their inspiration as well as a con-

# MILITARY ARCHITECTURE

*The military architecture of the Middle Ages was of its kind as admirable as the religious architecture. But as it belonged to a regime, the feudal system, which was destroyed by the monarchy, the monuments associated with this regime disappeared at the same time as it did. The châteaux-forts were cannonaded by the king, then destroyed by his order. As for the civic ramparts, most of them were razed to let the growing cities expand. Their sites have been transformed very often into promenades. For cities which have a very long history, like Paris, it is easy to recognise the traces of their successive enclosures.*

LES ANDELYS: CHÂTEAU GAILLARD.
*(Photo by Hachette.)*

AIGUES-MORTES: RAMPARTS.
*(Photo by Neurdein.)*

CHÂTEAU OF COUCY BEFORE ITS DESTRUCTION.
*(Photo by Bertrand.)*

The first châteaux-forts were of a very simple architecture, like the famous Château Gaillard, constructed by Richard the Lion-hearted to bar Philip Augustus from Normandy. The ramparts of Aigues-Mortes, which are well preserved, were built by St. Louis and his son to protect the port of the king of France on the Mediterranean; behind these walls, there is a very well-planned system of defense. The tower of Coucy was one of the most powerful dwellings of the thirteenth century; its great turret was destroyed in the last war. In all these constructions there is the same system of defense: an enclosure composed of towers joined by a curtain of walls, and in the interior, the turret.

CHÂTEAU OF PIERREFONDS (OISE).
*(Photo by Neurdein.)*

CHÂTEAU OF BONAGUIL (LOT-ET-GARONNE).
*(Photo by Perret.)*

RAMPARTS OF CARCASSONNE.
*(Photo by Hachette.)*

At the end of the Middle Ages, the old château was very much improved. It was no longer only a fortress; in this fortress there was a true palace, whose skylights and heights topped the curtain of walls. The château of Pierrefonds is the most skillful type of these feudal dwellings; it was reconstructed by Viollet-le-Duc. Bonaguil sought to adapt itself for a war of artillery. As for the ramparts of Carcassonne, of very different dates, from the Gallo-Roman time to the end of the Middle Ages, they present one of the most astonishing aspects of mediæval France. Such a fortress reveals the importance of the thoroughfare which it commands.

CHÂTEAU OF ARQUES.
*(Photo by Hachette.)*

TOWER OF LANGEAIS.
*(Photo by Neurdein.)*

RAMPART OF VILLENEUVE-LÈS-AVIGNON.
*(Photo by Hachette.)*

The ruins of châteaux and ramparts are among the most suggestive monuments of the Middle Ages; it is by them that we must imagine the life of long ago. Even today, mutilated as they are, since they have regained little by little the aspect of the soil from which they were taken, they form a part of the historic landscape; the village, which nestles at their foot, or in the interior of the enclosure, was protected or suppressed by this powerful military architecture; and very often after the fall of the feudal system and the destruction of the useless ramparts, the modern houses were constructed with the debris of the old fortresses. The villagers went into the ruins of the château as into a quarry.

# MEDIAEVAL URBAN ARCHITECTURE

*The oldest and most important monuments are the religious structures and the châteaux-forts. The architecture shows that in the old French society, the first places were for the church and feudalism. However, especially in the southern provinces, there existed at the height of the Middle Ages, the remains of the Gallo-Roman municipal civilisation and, at the close of the twelfth century, in the north, powerful communal governments were established. To this bourgeois civilisation the forms of architecture correspond: ramparts, city halls, mansions, and houses of which rare examples remain.*

CORDES (TARN): HOUSE OF THE MASTER OF THE HOUNDS.

LYON: THE HOUSE OF THE SINGERS.
*(Photo by Neurdein.)*

ST. GILLES: ROMANESQUE HOUSE.
*(Photo by Neurdein.)*

## Southern Houses

SOUTHERN France retains a Romanesque appearance. It received more strongly the influence of the Latin spirit, and it has remained a country of beautiful buildings. In the province of Languedoc many of the little towns have, besides their churches, some monuments dating from the twelfth or thirteenth centuries; these have been preserved no doubt because of their beauty and because they are distinguished from other buildings by their careful masonry and their decoration. The most important group of Gothic houses preserved in France is at Cordes in the region of Albi in Languedoc. In Italy, these monuments preserved from the Middle Ages are frequently found.

BAYEUX: OLD HOUSE.
*(Photo by Neurdein.)*

LISIEUX: OLD HOUSE.
*(Photo by Neurdein.)*

ROUEN: OLD HOUSE.
*(Photo by Neurdein.)*

## Northern Houses

IN THE north, the light architecture of clay and visible timberwork was preferred to stone. It seems that the men of these regions were carpenters more than masons. These wooden houses have not the resistance of buildings of masonry; however, some very old ones are preserved in Flanders and Normandy. They have a picturesque charm, by reason of their pointed gables and their visible timbers which enrich the ornamentation. Though modest, they seem to us to possess an urban look after which the Romanesque buildings seem rustic.

BOURGES: MANSION OF JACQUES COEUR.
*(Photo by Neurdein.)*

ROUEN: PALACE OF JUSTICE.
*(Photo by Hachette.)*

PARIS: HÔTEL DE CLUNY.
*(Photo by Hachette.)*

## Mansions

FRANCE of the Middle Ages is not the country of beautiful city halls like Flanders or Italy. This is because the monarchy could not tolerate the independence of municipal life. In retaliation, at the end of the Middle Ages, the rich bourgeoisie installed themselves in cities in charming mansions, some of which have been preserved. The mansion is different from the château; it is located between a court and a garden. It was begun on the eve of the Renaissance; the return of classic antiquity did not stop its growth but transformed its appearance.

firmation of their own ideals.

(Dates or localities indicated in this article are those given by either Cossio or Mayer.)

BIBLIOGRAPHY: M. Menendez y Pelayo, *Historia de las ideas esteticas en España*, Vol. II. Madrid, 1883-1891.—M. B. Cossio, *El Greco*. Madrid, 1908, 2 Vols.—M. B. Cossio, *Lo que se sabe de la vida Greco*. Madrid, 1914.—A. Calvert & G. Hartley, *El Greco*. New York, 1909.—F. San Román y Fernandez, *El Greco en Toldeo*. Madrid, 1910.—E. Bertaux, *Notes sur le Greco* in Revue de l'art ancien et moderne, XXIX, p. 401; XXXII, p. 401; XXXIII, p. 29. 1911, 1912, 1913.—M. Barres, *Greco ou le secret de Tolede*. Paris, 1912.—G. Beritens, *Aberacciones del Greco cientificamente considerados*.—Madrid, 1913.—H. Kehrer, *Die Kunst des Greco*. München, 1914.—N. Sentenach y Cabañas, *Tecnica pictorica del Greco*. Madrid, 1916.—A. L. Mayer, *Gesch. der Span. Malerei*, 2nd ed., 1922.—*Domenico Theotocopuli—el Greco*. München, 1926.—*El Greco*. Berlin, 1931.—E. du Gue Trapier, *El Greco*, Hisp. Soc. of Am., 1925.—E. A. Peers, *Studies of the Spanish Mystics*, 2 Vols. London, 1927.—J. F. Willumsen, *La jeunesse du peintre El Greco*. Paris, 1927.—F. San Román y Fernandez, *De la Vida del Greco in Archivio Español de Arte y Arquelogia*, III, p. 139.—R. Byron, *Greco; the Epilogue to Byzantine Culture* in the Burlington Magazine, LV, p. 160, 1929.—J. A. Merediz, *La transformación española de "El Greco."* Madrid, Ed. Plutarco S. A., 1930.—J. Pla Cargol, *El Greco*. New York, 1930.—J. Babelon, *Greco* in Gazette des Beaux Arts, XVII, pp. 299-314. Paris, 1937.—Thieme-Becker, *Künstler-Lexikon* (art. on Theotokopulos to appear after 1936).

**GREECE.**—BRONZES.—From earliest times, the Greeks made considerable use of bronze. We will not, under this heading, discuss the statues of gods and others, made by the greatest masters, but only small objects, such as statuettes, plaques and toilet articles.

Greek artists executed many small bronze figures intended for various uses. Some were intended to adorn the interior of temples, others were votive offerings.

The oldest Greek statuettes in bronze, date from the 7th century B.C. They were discovered in Dodona, on the site of the temple of Zeus. They have all the ungainliness and stiffness of primitive art, allied with a care for truth and exactness, which characterises the art of Greece.

The influence of the greatest masters of sculpture—Myron, Lysippus and Phidias—appeared in later statuettes, which often reproduce the types and attitudes of masterpieces, such as the *Marsyas* of Myron, and the *Poseidon of* Lysippus.

During the Hellenistic period, charming statuettes were produced, which tended to show more and more conscious grace.

The excavations at Pompeii brought to light a quantity of bronze statuettes, made by Greek artists, to adorn Roman houses. Many of them are remarkable for their elegance and refinement.

VASES.—The various European museums contain over 20,000 painted vases, on the sides of which are innumerable scenes taken from the mythology and life of the Greeks.

The earliest pottery was not, however, discovered on Greek soil, but in Tuscany, at the end of the 17th century. It was wrongly called Etruscan until Winckelmann proved that it was of Hellenic origin.

We will consider Greek ceramics under the twofold aspect of *form* and *painting*.

DANCING FAUN. (National Museum, Naples.)

(1) *Form.*—Greek ceramic offers a great variety of forms, which answered to the various uses for which the potteries were destined. It would be difficult to give a special name to each, but most of them can be included in a methodical classification, thanks to the researches of Panofka and others who sought for the true names of the Greek vases. We mention the ones most frequently employed.

The *amphora* is more or less egg-shaped. It is terminated below by a foot in the form of a truncated

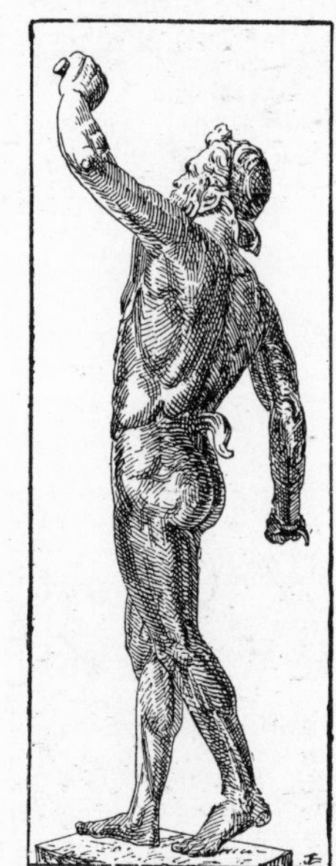

DANCING SATYR. (Bibl. Nat.)

cone; and above by a neck, which is united to its rounded part by two handles. Its size varies. Some are very large, and richly decorated; these may have served as ornaments. Most are of medium size, and were made to contain oil and wine.

The *crater* is very broad, with a wide mouth, and two handles, which are often low down. It served to contain a mixture of oil and wine. It is much higher and wider than the amphora.

The *oxybaphon* resembles the crater, but its handles are attached higher on the body of the vase and the mouth is less wide.

NARCISSUS. (National Museum, Naples.)

The *kelebe* resembles the two others, but it becomes narrower towards the top to form a neck, to which the upper part of the handles are attached. The lower part of the handles are fixed to the main body.

GREEK MIRROR OF BRONZE.

The *stamnos* is more or less the same shape; but the handles, instead of joining the neck, are fixed to the upper part of the jar's curve.

The long-necked forms include the hydria, the kalpis and the pelike:—

SMALL AMPHORA. AMPHORA OF THE PELIKE SHAPE. LECYTHOS. (Louvre.)

The *hydria* has three handles instead of two—one large handle, and two much smaller. This very convenient pitcher has several variants: the *kalpis*, the handle of which is much lower; and the *pelike*, which only has two handles.

Some very large vases served for storing different liquids. Others, more handy, were used as decanters. Among these latter the most graceful is the *oinochoë*, which is small, terminated by a low base, and with a single handle. The mouth is peculiarly formed in three lobes, recalling a trefoiled leaf. The *lecythus*, a vase for ointments, oils, etc., has, in its usual form, a high cylindrical body, a single handle and small mouth. The white-ground lecythus

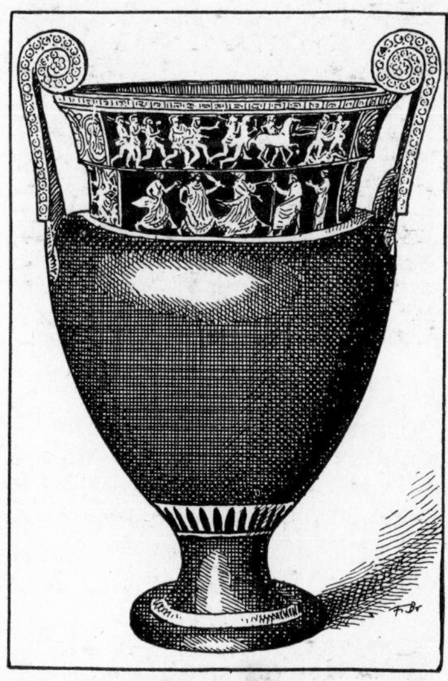

LARGE CRATER WITH VOLUTE HANDLES. (Louvre.)

with polychrome decoration, is the most famous variety, and was used as a funeral offering. The *cylix* was a two-handled drinking cup, having a shallow bowl, resting on a stem and foot. It was a great favorite with the vase-painters.

We have only mentioned the most usual forms of vases. The Greeks designed many other kinds, which were very varied. Some of them even imitated animal forms.

(2) *Vase Paintings.*—The ceramic industry, developing for several centuries, naturally underwent many changes, especially from the point of view of decoration.

The history of vase painting may be divided into six periods:—

(1) Ægean period (Hissarlik, Crete, Mycenæ) from about 2200 to 1500 B.C.; and the Mycenean period, from 1500 to 1100 B.C.

(2) The Geometric period—about 11th to 8th century B.C.

(3) The period of the Ionian and Corinthian styles—7th to 6th century B.C.

(4) Black figures on a red ground.
(5) Red figures on a black ground; and figures on a white ground—6th to 4th century.
(6) Vases of Italy.

(1) *Ægean period.*—The Ægean civilisation is that of the different peoples who inhabited the basin of the Ægean Sea. The oldest of all was that of which remains have been found at Hissarlik, on the site of ancient Troy. The potteries discovered there were made before the Trojan War. Their execution is extremely primitive. The vases represent the human figure, and are decorated with drawings.

The ceramists of Cnossos (Crete) made vases decorated with geometric patterns, and then with ornaments adapted from the vegetable kingdom.

Mycenean ceramics recall Cretan work in many particulars, to which indigenous elements were added.

(2) *The Geometric period.*—The brilliant Mycenean period was arrested by the Dorian conquest, which brought in its wake another, less advanced, civilisation, of which the Dorians were not, perhaps, the inventors, but which they spread throughout Greece—in Cyprus, in Bœotia, in the islands, and above all, in Athens. It prospered in such a measure in this last-named town that the general name of "Dipylon vases" is given to vases made from the 11th to the 8th century B.C. It is, in fact, in the necropolis of Dipylon that the finest examples of these vases, the large funeral amphoræ, have been discovered. Through the whole evolution of vase painting, methods remained much the same. The painter used the natural red color of the clay, and a black obtained from a black varnish which vitrifies in baking. Sometimes he added a reddish brown colour to his figures; and, at other times, before beginning to paint, he covered the clay with a coat of white.

In Dipylon pottery, the figures are black or reddish brown on a red ground. The decoration is chiefly geometric. It includes linear ornaments, and plants, men and animals in stylised form. Parallel bands with geometric patterns surround the vases. The execution of the silhouettes of men and animals is very clumsy, certain parts of the body, such as the thighs, being greatly exaggerated. The subject most frequently represented is the funeral ceremony, with its train of mourners, and chariots drawn by lean, stiff-legged horses. Another subject favoured by the decorators of the period is that of naval combats.

To this stiff, angular style, succeeded the style known as the Ionian, and the Corinthian style.

(3) *The Ionian and Corinthian styles.*—The style which was in circulation in the Ionic countries took on the richness of decoration which characterised Mycenean ceramic. It was inspired by the Eastern arts, and introduced new subjects—volutes, lotus flowers, and palm leaves; fantastic animals, sphinxes, human-headed bulls, and winged horses. The Ionian painters used a slightly different technique from that generally employed by the Greeks from the 11th to the 6th century.

(4) *Black figured vases.*—This was not really a new style. The potteries of the 8th century, the Dipylon vases, were already decorated with black silhouettes. But for two centuries the style suffered changes due to the imitation of Ionian, Corinthian or Oriental methods and subjects. To funeral scenes there succeeded joyous subjects, choruses of dancers, and athletic contests. But the Attic ceramists did not progress as did those of Ionia and Corinth. In the 6th century, under the government of Peistratus, Athens began to take a lead, which was soon no longer disputed. On the whole, art was ennobled. We no longer find, in Attic black-figured vases, the varied colours and pleasing appearance of the Ionian vases; but the figures are drawn with scrupulous fidelity, and with an endeavour to portray noble attitudes. During the 6th century, ceramists traced their drawing on the red clay ground, and filled the hollows with black varnish. This was the method employed during the Geometric period. Only the decorators were now more skilful, and traced their contours more carefully. On the black coating, still fresh, they drew with a dry point, so that the red earth ground reappeared where it touched. The fine lines thus produced showed the forms, and indicated the muscles and folds of the dress. The most remarkable work of this period is the François vase in the Etruscan Museum, in Florence, made by the potter Ergotimos and the painter Clitias. It is a large crater (about a yard and a half in circumference), made about 570 B.C. "It is a kind of illustrated Greek Bible, including nearly 250 figures of animals, and 128 inscriptions, in about a dozen compositions." . . . All these figures are grouped in six zones, or bands, encircling the vase.

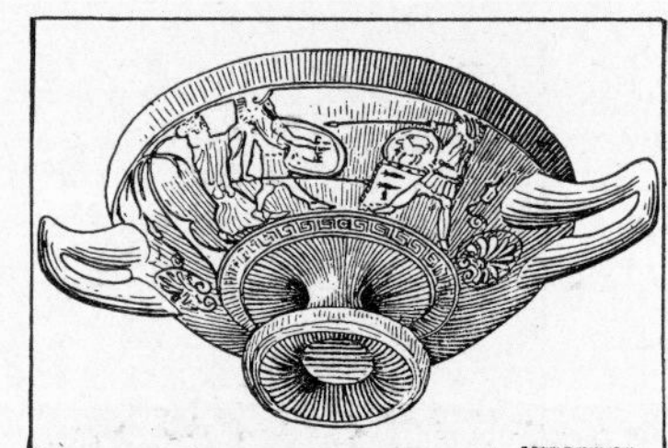
Cup of archaic shape. (Louvre.)

Small oinochoë. Amphora. Attic drinking cup in the form of an eagle's head. (Louvre.)

The ceramists who made the black figured vases preferred vases of large size—craters, amphoræ, hydriæ.

The panathenaic amphoræ, which were presented to winners in the games, are very numerous. Many of them have been found in the towns of Greece, Italy, and Africa. These amphoræ are provided with a lid, decorated in the same way. One side of the vessel shows Athena armed, ready for the contest. The goddess is framed by two columns, surmounted with an owl. Along the columns are writings telling in whose honour the amphora is offered. The other side depicts the contest.

About the middle of the 6th century painting, apart from vase decoration, began to develop. Eumaros perfected the old monochrome painting, distinguishing, by the use of white, figures of women from those of men. His successor Simon of Cleone about 530 or 520 introduced innovations, which had considerable influence on vase painting. He varied the attitudes, distinguished different planes, softened the folds of garments, and replaced the monochrome painting, which was practised in the preceding centuries, by polychrome decoration. This transformation in the art of painting resulted also in changes in vase painting.

(5) *Red-figured Vases.*—The beginning of the 6th century, about 520, saw a great change. The black glaze which previously covered the figures now surrounded them. This produced an effect which seems much more natural. Many potters did not like the change, and continued for some time to make ceramics according to old methods. Nevertheless, red-figure vases were, in the end, universally adopted, except for panathenaic amphoræ, the decoration of which had to conform to tradition. The interchange in the part played by the two colours, important as it may be, was not the only contribution made to the rapid progress of ceramic painting. We must also remember the influence of fresco painting, which refined the taste of purchasers, and gave valuable instruction to the makers. The latter, in their endeavour to reproduce the pure-lined figures which they admired in the frescoes of Cimon and Polygnotus, had to change their technique in order to perfect their drawing.

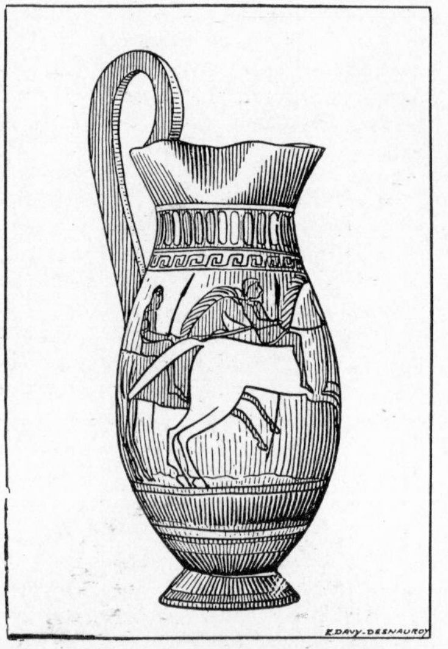
Oinochoë with elongated handle and trefoil spout. (Louvre.)

Fragment of the design of a large funerary crater from Dipylon.

François vase. (Etruscan Museum, Florence.)

The paint-brush, in replacing dry-point, gave greater freedom to the artist. The ability with which Greek vase painters of the 5th century drew with a brush, without retouching their supple figures is quite remarkable. Progress was rapid. Painters soon abandoned the silhouette which only allowed of profile views, and portrayed their figures in all positions—profile, full-face, and three-quarter. They attempted daring foreshortenings, often successfully; they learned not to draw the front view of an eye in a profile face; and to render the softness of materials which follow the movements of the body.

Decorated amphora. (Louvre.)

During the 5th century, the most usual forms of vases were amphoræ, hydræ, craters, and more especially cups of varied shape. They were decorated with subjects

LARGE SKYPHOS WITH LARGE RING-LIKE HANDLES. (Louvre.)

taken from everyday life—the toilet, banquets, dances and physical exercises. The red-figured vases may be divided into two large groups—(1) Those of severe style (about 520 to 460 B.C.), and (2) those of

CRATER FROM DIPYLON. (Louvre.)

the free style (460 to 430 B.C.). The "severe style" owes its name, not so much to a certain archaism of draughtsmanship, as to strict ability of composition. Among the painters of this group, *Epictetos* seems to have excelled in the familiar kind. He worked in the last years of the 6th century, and we

CRATER WITH RED FIGURE DECORATION. (Louvre.)

possess many works signed by him. He sometimes represented mythological subjects, but he preferred familiar scenes, and was not afraid to portray realistic details. *Epilykos,* his contemporary, painted the same subjects, and youths playing games. *Pamphaios* was a potter whose signature is found on many vases which were painted by other hands. *Pheidippos, Psiax,* and *Praxias* belong to the same period.

The most illustrious painters of the "severe style" were working between 500 and 460 B.C. With them, ceramics attained their fullest glory. These three artists are Euphronios, Douris, and Brygos.

*Euphronios* was perhaps the greatest of all. He was potter and painter, and directed a studio where the most perfect pieces were made. Euphronios represented with equal success the calm, noble attitudes of goddesses and the clumsy movements of foot soldiers. One of his finest works is a cylix in the Louvre, representing the *Exploits of Theseus.* On the exterior is the contest against Procrustes, against the bull of Marathon, against Cercyon, and against Sciron. The most delightful scene is that which occupies the bottom of the cup. Theseus, defied by Minos to bring him back his ring which has fallen into the sea, descends to the abode of the goddess Amphitrite. Three little fishes suffice to tell us that this is the watery kingdom. The young hero, clad in a short, transparent tunic, extends his hand gracefully and timidly, to receive Minos' ring. Athena, a gracious, noble figure, accompanies her protégé, and leans slightly towards Amphitrite.

LARGE CRATER. (Signed by the painter Euphronios, it bears also the name Leagros, Louvre.)

This celebrated cup is not signed "Euphronios painted it," but "Euphronios made it"—the potter's mark. Thus it is possible that it was not actually painted by his own hand, although he probably conceived the scene and supervised its execution. The same applies to many of the works of Douris and Brygos. Very different is the Crater of Anteas (Louvre). Here strength predominates over grace, in Euphronios' scene of the *Contest between Hercules and Anteas.* The two adversaries, heavy, muscular figures, fight under the eyes of the gods who frame the composition with symmetrical gestures. The

ZEUS ABDUCTING A WOMAN. (Cup attributed to Douris, Louvre.)

artist has signed, as painter, three works: the Crater of Anteas, the Cylix of Geryon (Munich) and the psykter of Leningrad. His style evolved: archaic at first, it became more supple, and enabled him to give free rein to his imagination. Most archæologists give Euphronios first place among the ceramists of his time. Furtwängler, on the contrary, prefers Euthymides. The latter is undoubtedly a fine artist, but he was limited, and retained the older methods. Despite the proud announcement on a vase signed by him: "Euphronios could not do better," Euthymides is far from rivalling Euphronios.

CRATER FROM ORVIETO. (Louvre.)

Most of the vases which we possess signed "painted by" (as opposed to "made by," the potter's mark) are the work of *Douris.* Like Euphronios and Brygos, he was potter and painter, and head of a studio. We can study his work from twenty-eight vases, decorated by his hand. His style is sometimes archaic, dry and stiff, with the

VASE FROM RUVO. (Naples.)

symmetrical composition dear to the "black figure" painters. Other vases show him to have been a skilful decorator, varying pleasantly the attitudes of his supple, alert figures. In this disconcerting artist, "one must recognise a lively, spirited, and capricious personality." Douris, as Pottier remarks, "is a warning to all those who, on the single inspection of an unsigned vase, think they can name the author." The richest collection of Douris' vases is in the Louvre. The finest of them is the cup, showing *Eos Carrying the Body of His Son Memnon,* killed by Achilles, while Aurora, goddess of the dawn, bends sadly over the rigid body. A vase in London depicts the *Exploits of Theseus.* Another, in Vienna, has the *Dispute of Ulysses and Ajax* for the arms of Achilles.

Douris seems to have preferred warlike subjects, contests of soldiers, and athletes, and exploits of heroes.

ALEXANDER THE GREAT. (Antique cameo, Bibl. Nat.)

A charming work by him shows us *Zeus Carrying off a Woman* (Louvre).

*Brygos* worked about the middle of the 5th century. All the works which he signed have the statement "Brygos made it"; none, "Brygos painted it." Thus he may have been the author of the whole work, pottery and decoration, or he may have entrusted the painting to a collaborator. The latter supposition is probably the true one. The painter generally employed by Brygos appears to have been Onesimos, who painted the fine cup of Perugia, representing the *Death of Troilos,* and a cup in Munich, representing the *Combat of Lapiths and Centaurs.* There are discrete attempts at polychromy—touches of gold and red in certain details.

PELOPS AND HIPPODAMIA. (Cameo, Bibl. Nat.)

The most celebrated works signed by Brygos are the *Taking of Troy* and *Briseis and Phœnix* (?) which decorate two cups, in the Louvre. No artist had yet attained expression of pathos as is seen in this composition. All the attitudes are remarkable for their expression of power and emotion. A celebrated cup in London, shows us Iris and Hera attacked by Satyrs.

*Hieron* was head of another studio. We possess 25 vases signed by him. He employed several painters, who favoured amorous scenes, dances and banquets as subjects for decoration.

Many other artists whose names have not come down to us decorated the sides of vases. They became more and more skilful in overcoming difficulties, and in giving suppleness to their figures.

The ceramists of the 4th century B.C. did not limit themselves to representing small scenes with a few figures. They tended to imitate mural painting, and made complicated compositions. Owing to the restrictions of their medium, this imitation could not, however, be carried very far, and soon vase-painting fell out of demand, and disappeared.

THE APOTHEOSIS OF TIBERIUS. (Cameo from Vienna, in the Imperial Cabinet, Vienna.)

Before this happened, there developed in the 4th century, two different types of ceramic industry: one produced vases with figures in relief, the other, vases with a white ground.

The former are less numerous. Among the most famous is the Hydria of Cumes (Hermitage), with a black ground.

The vases with a white ground are, on the contrary, numerous. This process was not, it is true, new. The Rhodians had used it from the 7th century. In the 6th century, Nicosthenes introduced it into Attica, and it rapidly became popular. The white-ground process consisted of covering the clay with a coat of

ONYX BUST OF CONSTANTINE. (Bibl. Nat.)

white colour, upon which the figures were painted. These figures were first silhouettes, filled in with black, which stood out in contrast to the white ground. The painter then drew in details; and, finally, coloured them in different hues—the same, probably, as those employed by Polygnotus or Zeuxis. The line used is not comparable to that on the red figure vases; it is lighter, more varied, sometimes of extreme delicacy, sometimes firmer and broader. The hair is often suggested by a faint red; garments are mauve, yellow, pink or brown.

Ceramists decorated a number of vases and cups in this way. Euphronios signed one representing a young girl turning to drink to a young man (Berlin), which is very delicate in workmanship. The British Museum possesses the beautiful cylix of *Camiros*. On the bottom is painted the goddess Aphrodite seated on a swan with wings outspread. The ceramist *Sotades* made exquisite cylices, which are also in the British Museum. These works have a more graceful and delicate appearance than the red-figured vases, but the method of their fabrication, which precluded baking at a high temperature, made them fragile objects, and impractical for the purposes for which they were intended. For this reason, Greek ceramists soon gave up making them for utensils, such as cylices

GREEK SILVER COINS. (Luynes Collection, Bibl. Nat.)

and amphoræ; and reserved them for the lecythus, a funeral vase which was filled with perfume and left in tombs, and which was used exclusively in Attica. The lecythi with a white ground are among the most exquisite productions of Greek ceramic. Their form is elegant and pleasing; and the paintings which adorn them, always of a funeral character, have a melancholy grace which is moving without being depressing. There are no agonising farewells, or scenes of violent grief, but rather graceful or touch-

GREEK SILVER COINS. (Luynes Collection, Bibl. Nat.)

ing banquets which recall the reunion of the departed with his family, and not the separation. The subjects of such paintings are naturally rather restricted. The most frequent are: the deceased reposing on his bed, with his friends standing round; the offering at the "stele," uniting near the tomb the family of the deceased, who advance in double file, each bearing a gift; sometimes the departed is represented as a small winged figure, flying round the tomb. The funeral toilet is the occasion of gracious scenes, and was used chiefly for women. The deceased is represented as surrounded by her servants who present perfumes, and jewels she had loved; she, lifting her veil, seems still to live, and amuse herself by choosing from her gifts. Another frequent subject was the arrival of Charon in his barque, coming for the dead who await him on the bank. Always there is the same delicate feeling which frees these funeral objects from all terrifying or too-realistic associations.

Vase painting on a white ground reached the height of its perfection in the 4th century, when the "red figured" vases declined rapidly.

TETRADRACHMA OF THE TIME OF ALEXANDER.

Soon, however, the white lecythus went the same way. The public no longer admired the small figures in flat colours which seemed primitive and old-fashioned compared to those of mural painting. Thus, gradually, the ceramic industry disappeared in Greece. See Pl. 27, Vol. I.

BIBLIOGRAPHY: Collignon and Couve, *Catalogue des vase peints du Musée d'Athènes*.—Murray, *White Athenian Vases*. — Ernst Buschor, *Greek Vase-Painting;* translated into English by G. C. Richards, with a preface by Percy Gardner. London, 1921.

ARCHITECTURE:—*The Greek Orders*.—The Greek orders are the different systems employed by architects for the construction and decoration of their buildings. There are three Greek orders: (1) the Doric, (2) the Ionic, and (3) the Corinthian.

(1) *The Doric Order* is the oldest. To understand its origins, one must recall the arrangement of the "megaron" of the Mycenean palace, in which one finds future Doric elements. The "megaron" was the name given to the hall of honour of the royal palace. At Mycenæ, as at Tiryns, this hall was in the form of a long rectangle. The walls were prolonged "in antes" from each side and enclosed a vestibule (the *prodomos*).

Two columns adorned the entry between the antes. The walls of the original megaron were in stone. To support the roof, wooden columns were used, on a stone base. All the Doric principles are contained in these elements. They underwent changes in detail in the construction of the Doric temple. The megaron becomes the *cella* (the hall which sheltered the xoanon or statue of the divinity); the prodomos became the *pronaos;*

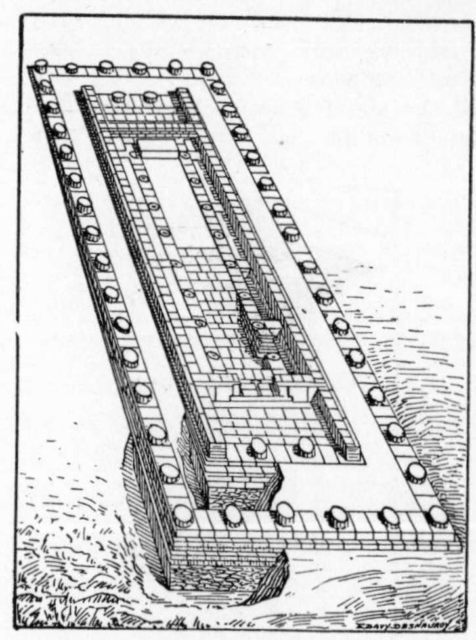

PLAN IN PERSPECTIVE OF THE HERAION OF OLYMPIA.

the *opisthodomos* was formed of a second megaron backing the first. The two columns at the entrance became the colonnade of the façade. The temple is entirely surrounded by a colonnade. The columns of the inside of the temple and those of the external colonnade were entirely independent. These two parts of the building are only united by the roof. On the other hand, the influence of the interior of the tem-

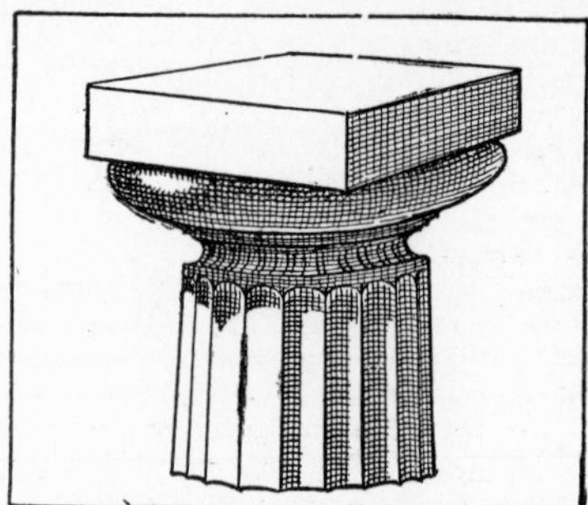

DORIC CAPITAL. (Paestum.)

ple on the number of columns used for the façade, must be recognised. With the exception of the Parthenon, Temple G T at Selinus and two or three other examples, Doric temples always have six columns. They are *hexastyle peripteral* (six columns to the façade, and surrounded by a colonnade). According to this theory of the origin of the Doric order (from the Mycenean palaces), the earliest Doric temples were wooden constructions. Another important theory is that of its derivation from the rock-cut tombs of Beni-Hassan in Egypt.

The Doric temple reached the height of its perfection in the 5th century B.C. The Parthenon is its most glorious creation.

We will now consider the different parts of the Doric building.

The *Doric column* stands without a base directly on a stylobate, usually of three steps; including the capital, its height is from 4 to 6½ times the diameter at the base. The circular shaft, diminishing at the top, is fluted (generally about 20 flutes, but the number varies in different buildings). The shaft was generally slightly convex in profile (called the entasis) in order to counteract the concave appearance which results from straight-sided columns. The columns of the earliest temples were cut from a single block (such as those of the ancient temple of Corinth, and of the temple of Artemis in Syracuse). But when the height of the buildings increased, the difficulties involved in cutting and transporting monolithic columns became too great, and the shaft was divided into several cones or "drums," which were

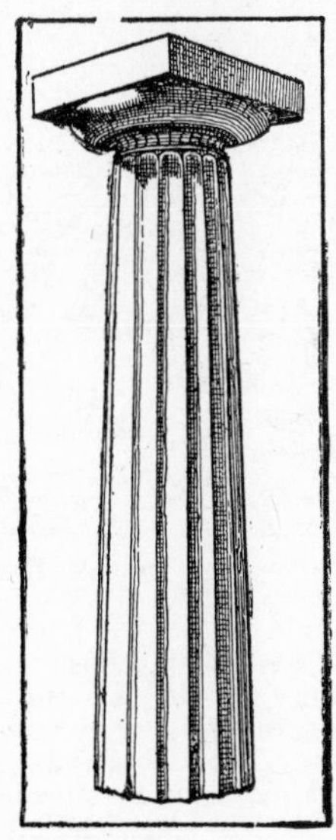

Geometric elevation of the Doric column.

superimposed in position. Architects took infinite pains to cut each drum accurately, to fit the place for which it was intended. Finally, the column appeared as regular as if it had been cut from a single block of stone.

The shaft ends in the "hypotrachelium," formed of three grooves in archaic examples, and later of one groove, and above it is the "trachelium," or necking. The capital consists of annulets (or horizontal fillets, 3 to 5 in number), echinus (which is curved, and varies greatly in outline) and abacus (a square, unmoulded slab).

Doric capitals were never decorated.

The columns which surrounded a temple were placed with the utmost forethought and precision. In the Parthenon all the columns lean very slightly towards the interior of the building—so slightly that the effect

Metope of the temple of Selinus.

is scarcely perceptible (the inclination is 4 centimetres in the large temple of Paestum). Further, the columns were not placed at the same distance from each other. Generally the space between the middle columns is greater than that between the angle columns. There is, however, no fixed rule.

*The Doric entablature* is supported by the columns. It has three main divisions: architrave, frieze, and cornice.

The architrave is the principal beam. It is composed of long blocks of stone, each of which rests on the half of two capitals. In the smaller temples each block was the thickness of the architrave; but in the large temples, two or three blocks had to be superimposed to attain the desired thickness. It has considerable depth and its vertical face is in one plane (in the Ionic and Corinthian orders it is usually stepped in three planes). The upper part has a flat moulding, called the tenia, and under this, at intervals corresponding to the triglyphs, is a narrow band, called the regula, with six guttae, or small conical drops.

The frieze is formed of a series of triglyphs and metopes which alternate. The former have three upright channels, and are placed at equal distances apart. They come immediately over the centre of each column, and there is generally one over the space between the columns. The metopes, or square spaces, between the triglyphs were often ornamented with groups of fine sculpture. Following Vitruvius, many archæologists have maintained that the metopes were, originally, open spaces.

door; in other temples it was quite separate. Four columns generally supported the roof. The opisthodomos was usually the treasure chamber.

This division into three parts is the most usual arrangement in the Doric temples. Several sanctuaries, however, possessed a fourth chamber, where men could go to consult the oracle. Some of the earliest Doric temples also possessed a fourth room, but it was not open to the public. It was, on the contrary, the most sacred part of the temple, the *adytos*, where only the priests penetrated. It contained the statue of the god. In this case, the cella, dispossessed of its statue, became simply the hall of offerings (e.g., temples of Selinus and Paestum).

No Greek temple has retained its roof, and among the ruins no single piece has been discovered which can, with certainty, be said to have formed part of one. It seems certain that the ceiling of the cella was always of wood.

*Colour.*—The Greeks made great use of colour for their temples and civic buildings.

The process of polychrome decoration was transformed in the 6th century. Instead of applying the colour directly on to the building in tufa and stucco, architects had re-

West pediment of the Temple of Zeus at Olympia. (Restoration.)

The cornice is the upper or crowning part of the entablature. It supports the roof and the pediments, and shelters the frieze and architrave, since it juts out some distance beyond them. The underside of the cornice has an inclination corresponding to the slope of the roof, and has flat blocks or mutules which suggest the ends of sloping rafters. On each mutule are carved three rows of six little cones, called guttae, like those under the triglyphs.

The *pediment* is a triangular space above the cornice. Placed over the façade of Greek temples, it offered an important field for sculpture.

*Interior arrangement of the Temple.*—The Greek peripteral temple is divided into two distinct parts: one, open to the people, comprised the external peristyle, the *peristasis*, or external portico.

The interior part, or *secos*, is divided into three parts. First, the pronaos, or entrance vestibule, formed by the prolongation of the cella walls, and closed by columns united by railings; a central door communicated with the *naos* or *cella*, which was the most sacred part of the temple, since it was the abode of the divinity. In most of the temples the cella was divided lengthwise into three aisles by a double row of columns. The columns supported an architrave which in Doric buildings is surmounted by a Doric frieze. It is not known whether there was a gallery, but no traces of a staircase have been found.

The third division of the temple is the *opisthodomos*. Sometimes it communicated with the cella by a

course to coloured terra cotta. Later, when the beautiful marble temples were built, the colour was mixed with wax and applied to the marble. It seems that only the upper parts of buildings were decorated with colour. The entablature, furthest from the eyes had most need of being accentuated in its details. Colour put in relief various parts of frieze, architrave and cornice.

Under the burning sky of Greece, the brilliance of white marble would have tired the eyes by its extreme brightness, and blotted out architectural detail. The addition of colour thus robbed the building of none of its harmony, but, on the contrary, softened the effect of the whole, and enhanced the beauty of details of sculpture. Red was used for parts of the architrave, and the lower moulding of the cornice. Blue served for the triglyphs, and the mutules. The guttae were often yellow, or gilt. The metopes were left white, unless they were sculptured, in which case the background was painted red or blue. This method was, however, varied. To judge from the fragments of polychrome architecture which have been found, it seems that bright, bold colours produced the most successful effects. But colour has long almost entirely disappeared from the Greek temples.

Among the most celebrated of the Doric temples are:—

In Greece: The Heraeum, Olympia (c. 620 B.C.). Temple of Apollo, Corinth (c. 540 B.C.). Temple of Zeus, Olympia (c. 465 B.C.). The Theseum, Athens (421 B.C.). The Parthenon, Athens (447 B.C.). Temple of Apollo, Bassae (450 B.C.). Temple of Apollo, Delos, first building period, c. 450 B.C.; second building period, c. 300 B.C.

In Sicily and South Italy:—The Temple GT at Selinus (c. 530 B.C.). Three temples at Paestum (540-460 B.C.). Three temples at Agrigentum (530-440 B.C.). Temple of Athena, Syracuse (c. 470 B.C.).

(2) *The Ionic Order.*—The Greeks called the Doric order the masculine order because all parts of the Doric order contributed to give an impression of vigour, solid strength and robust austerity. The Ionic order is distinguished for opposite qualities, and they called it the feminine order. It is graceful, refined and supple. The forms have lost their stern simplicity, and details of architecture are enriched with varied ornamentation, which is still, however, in very pure taste.

The Ionic order was born in eastern Greece, in the Greek towns of Asia Minor, the home of the Ionians. They were inspired by Oriental art, which their genius completely transformed.

Unfortunately none of the earliest temples in Asia Minor remain, and it is impossible to reconstruct their plan. We must look to Attica to find the plan of Ionic buildings. The Ionic temple had not always, like the Doric temple, a simple plan, as may be seen by two of the most celebrated Ionian temples—the Temple of Nike Apteros, and the Erechtheum (see Acropolis of Athens).

*Ionic columns* are relatively more slender and taller than the Doric column. They are, including capital and base, usually about nine times their lower diameter in height. The flutes are deeper, narrower, and more numerous than in the Doric order. There are scarcely ever fewer than 24 of them. The moulded base usually consists of an upper and lower torus, divided by a scotia and fillets.

The Ionic order is especially remarkable for its original capital. It is separated from the shaft by the astragal (moulding), above which is a band decorated with designs of palm-leaves or water-lilies. "The capital consists of a pair of volutes or spirals, about two-thirds the diameter in height, on the front and back of the column, connected at the sides by the cushion, and on the front and back by an echinus moulding carved with the egg-and-dart and a bead moulding. The treatment of the capital of the angle columns, in which it was necessary to show the volutes on two adjacent faces, was very skilfully effected."

This brief description merely indicates the chief elements of the Ionic column as it was used in the fine Attic temples of the 5th century.

*The Ionic entablature* consists of architrave, frieze and cornice. The architrave is "usually formed as a triple fascia, in three planes like superimposed beams." The frieze was often decorated with a band of continuous sculpture. The frieze did not, however, appear until the classical period of the 5th century. In the early Ionic entablature, such as is found on the façades of tombs from Asia Minor, there was no frieze—the cornice was placed directly on the architrave.

The cornice usually had dental ornament, and was surmounted by a corona and cyma recta moulding.

Among the most celebrated Ionic buildings are:—

Archaic Temple of Artemis,

Ephesus (c. 560 B.C.). Temple of Hera, Samos (c. 525 B.C.). Temple of the Ilissus, Athens (c. 448 B.C.). Temple of Nike Apteros, Athens (c. 426 B.C.). The Erechtheum, Athens (c. 421 B.C.).

(3) *The Corinthian Order* is later than the Doric and Ionic orders and was less used by the Greeks. In general arrangement, the buildings follow the Ionic order. The Corinthian Order is distinguished by the form of its capital. The Greeks had a legend which explained the capital's origin. In the town of Corinth a little girl died, and her nurse placed on her grave a basket filled with the things she had loved, and covered it with a tile. When the spring came, an acanthus which was growing there surrounded the basket with its leaves. The sculptor, Callimachus, struck by its beautv, was inspired to create a new capital, which he probably made in metal.

Charming as is the story, it is prosy historical fact that the Corinthian capital existed before Callimachus, who but perfected its forms. It is composed of a kind of basket or inverted bell-like form, the lower part of which is surrounded by two tiers of eight acanthus leaves. From between the leaves of the upper row rise other elongated leaves and volutes which support the abacus. Each side of the moulded abacus is curved outwards to a point at the angles.

The Corinthian entablature bears a general resemblance to the Ionic, but with additional mouldings.

ATHENS: THE PARTHENON. (East façade.)

Corinthian examples include:—

Temple of Apollo, Bassae (c. 450 B.C.). Choragic Monument of Lysicrates, Athens (334 B.C.). The Temple of Zeus Olympius (later Olympieum), Athens (c. 170 B.C.). Tower of the Winds, Athens (c. 100 B.C.). See Pl. 19, Vol. I.

SCULPTURE.—The principal works of archaic Greek sculpture may be grouped under three main headings: (1) The group of Ionian sculpture; (2) that of Dorian sculptures; and (3) the Attic group.

(1) *The Schools of Ionia; Asia Minor and the Ægean Islands.*—According to Pliny, the Islands of Naxos and Chios contested the honour of having produced the earliest sculptors in marble. A monument bears witness to the great antiquity of the *school of Naxos*—the base of a statue found in Delos, which bears an inscription. It is the oldest signature of a Greek artist that we have and it is that of a native of Naxos, Iphikartides.

Among the oldest statues of this school must be mentioned two statues—an "Apollo" from Thera (National Museum, Athens), and an "Apollo" from Melos (Athens).

TEMPLE OF THE NIKE APTEROS RESTORED. (Ionic order.)

They probably date from the 7th century, and testify to the great antiquity of the Naxian school (to which they are closely related in style). The Naxians seem to have had a taste for colossal statues. At Delphi, they set up one of the most conspicuous of all the monuments —a huge Sphinx mounted on an Ionic column of very primitive form. "The marble of Naxos, like that of the sister island of Paros, was a favourite material with early sculptors, and may have contributed to an early development of sculpture in the island."

*The school of Chios* which is said to have continued in one family for four generations, is mentioned on an inscribed base found at Delos, which contains the names of Mikkiades and his son Archermos. Near this base was found an early winged figure which may have stood upon it, and which may be the work of these two artists. It is a draped female figure intended to be in rapid flight. The arms are broken, but one was raised, and the other rested in front of the hip. The legs are separated and bent at the knee. These features, and the wings, convey the idea of flight. In spite of the vivacity of the attitude, the artist only really considered the frontal aspect of his figure—a characteristic of primitive sculpture. "Although the design is probably based on an already existing decorative type (small bronzes), its translation into marble and its execution on a much larger scale really amounts to an original invention." The flat, linear treatment of the

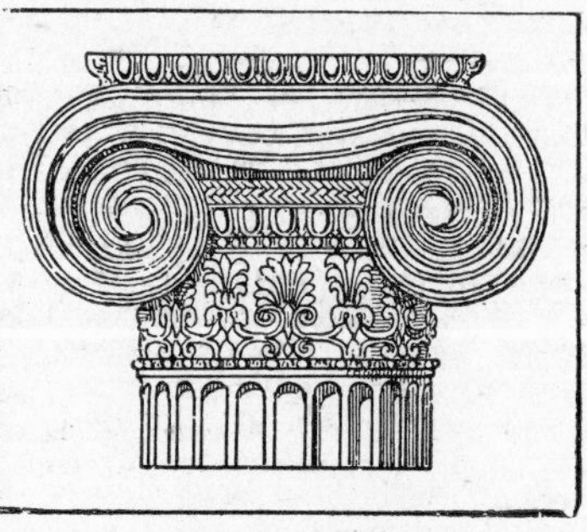

IONIC CAPITAL FROM THE ERECHTHEUM.

hair follows a system often met with in archaic works. "The face is angular; the eyeballs project; and the mouth in a strong but simple curve runs up at the corners into a band of flesh that curves

CORINTHIAN CAPITAL FROM THE TEMPLE OF BASSAE.

round it both above and at the sides." Similar treatment is seen in the Apollo of Thera, and other early statues.

The island of *Samos* played an important part in the early progress of sculpture. The artists of this island seem to have practised working in bronze from very early times; and by the second half of the 7th century the bronze technique was already very advanced. Although Samos specialised in bronze, the only important work that has come down to us from this ancient school is a work in marble—the statue of Hera, which is in the Louvre. The lower part of the body is a mere circular column from which the feet project at the bottom. It seems to prove that the figure was derived from some old xoanon, cut in a shaft of cylindrical wood. The folds of the drapery are indicated by a conventional system of parallel lines. The peculiar type of this Hera of Samos finds a striking analogy in two statues which have been found on the Athenian acropolis, but are not of Attic work. One, like the Hera, lacks the head. Its position is precisely similar to that of the Samian figure. The second similar figure has its head preserved, though the body is lost below the waist. As in the other figures, one arm holds a fruit close to the breast, while the other is pressed close to the side.

(1) *Ionia.*—Two sites in Ionia have yielded important remains of archaic sculpture—these were two centres of worship, which therefore attracted those dedications which offered most opportunities for the energy of the sculptor in early times. These are the Temple of Apollo at Branchidae, near Miletus and the temple of Artemis at Ephesus.

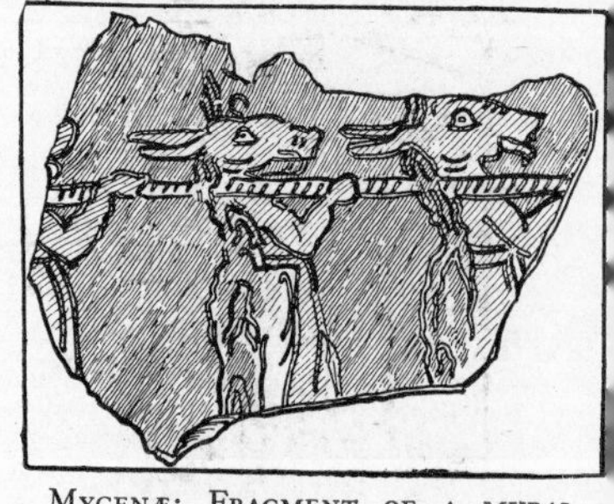

MYCENÆ: FRAGMENT OF A MURAL PAINTING.

At Branchidae many of the statues which lined the Sacred Way have survived. Most of these are now in the British Museum; some are in the Louvre. All the figures are seated in the same stiff attitude on square seats. They date from about 550 B.C., but some appear to be a little earlier, and some rather later, and there are corresponding differences in style—thus in the later examples, the drapery is more elaborately arranged and more carefully rendered, and there is some attempt to reveal the forms of the body through the drapery which envelopes them. But they are still clumsy and heavy.

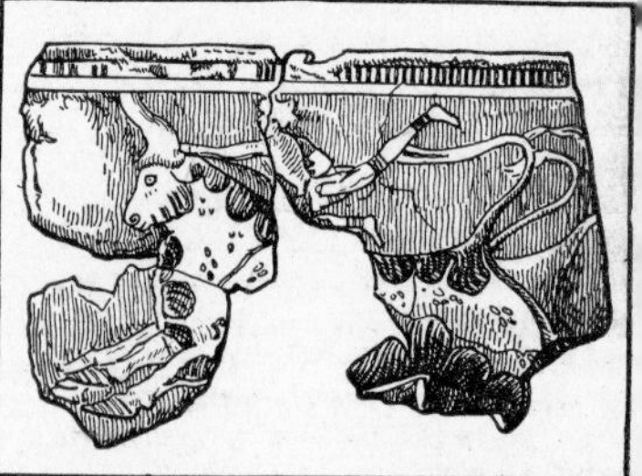

FRAGMENT OF A FRESCO FROM TIRYNS, DISCOVERED BY SCHLIEMANN.

The most interesting sculptures of the temple at Ephesus "formed bands of relief round the columns of the temple, most of which were dedicated by Croesus. We are thus enabled to date these reliefs approximately, because the reign of Croesus lasted from c. 560 to c. 546 B.C." Their style may best be judged from the restored drum in the British Museum.

SARCOPHAGUS OF KLAZOMENAE: DETAILS OF THE DECORATION.

*Asia Minor.*—The great example of Lycian art of this period is the Harpy tomb, brought from Xanthos to the British Museum. It has very interesting bas-reliefs on its four sides and is in general more oriental than Greek.

Ionian civilisations were brutally interrupted by the Persian conquests, and the plastic arts had not time to reach their full development.

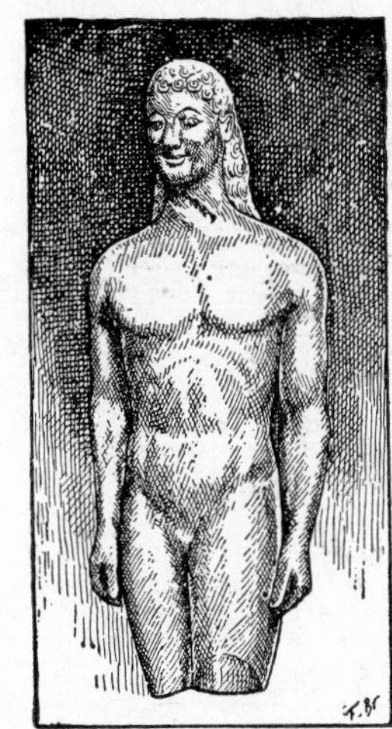

Apollo of Thera, at Athens.

(2) *Dorian Sculpture*.—If one passes over the most archaic works—consisting of small bronze ornaments discovered in the excavations of Olympia—the earliest works of sculpture of the continent which must be noted are those of the Cretan artists, Dipoinos and Scyllis, who, according to tradition, landed in The Peloponnesus in the middle of the 6th century. None of their works has survived. Those works which have come down to us from this time can be grouped most clearly according to a geographical classification, thus: (a) The Peloponnesus; (b) greater Greece and Sicily; (c) Central Greece, and (d) Ægina.

(a) The Peloponnesus.—The discoveries made at Delphi have brought to light many interesting monuments—two nude statues, and some bas-reliefs found in the ruins of the Sicyonian Treasury. The nude figures are of square, heavy build, with large heads, expressionless faces, and large, flat eyes. They are valuable as examples of early Argive work. The remains of sculptural metopes from the Sicyonian Treasury are among the earliest architectural sculptures we possess, and date from the earlier part of the 6th century B.C. "The relief is bold, but there is not much of that refinement of detail which we see later in the athletic art of the same region." The subjects include Europa on the Bull, and soldiers returning from a raid.

Paestum: The Basilica.

At Olympia, several heads were found, among them a colossal head of Hera, which is primitive and uncouth in workmanship. In spite of the large flat eyes, the clumsy attachment of the ears, the heavy nose, and the simple curve of the mouth, thus producing the "archaic smile" in its most primitive form, the head is full of life Two heads of Zeus are much more advanced in style. The pediment of the Treasury of Megara at Olympia was probably the work of a Megarian sculptor. It represents the contest between the gods and giants and probably dates from the middle of the 6th century B.C.

At the end of the 6th century and the beginning of the 5th century, begin to appear names of great artists concerning whom the ancients have bequeathed us some information, such as Kanachos of Sicyonia, and Ageladas of Argos. Unfortunately, none of their works have survived, and we can only imagine the Zeus of Ageladas and the Apollo of Kanachos from medals which reproduce their general aspect, or from works (such as the charming *Apollo of Piombino*, in the Louvre) which seem to give a reduced likeness of these works, already refined though still rather dry in style, which preceded the art of Phidias.

Preparations for a race and a war dance. (Sarcophagus.)

(b) *Sicily and Greater Greece*.—Sicily and Greater Greece were colonised by the Dorians in the course of the 8th century B.C. These countries always remained in close relationship with the Peloponnesus. They were faithful to the Olympic festivals, and several "treasuries" were built in the sanctuary of Olympia, offered by the people of Metapontum, Syracuse, Sybaris and Gela. History has preserved the name of one sculptor of Rhegium—Clearchos.

If one neglects certain very archaic works, the first sculptures which must be mentioned are the metopes from the temples of Selinus. Three of these metopes are in a fairly good state of preservation. They represent: Perseus cutting off the head of the Gorgon in the presence of Athena; Heracles carrying the Cercopes head downwards, one at each end of a pole; and a chariot with four horses, seen full face, with a figure on each side of the charioteer.

A second series of metopes, slightly later, and showing different influences, include one of Europa on the Bull. A third series is considerably later, and represents scenes from a gigantomachy.

These interesting metopes from Selinus are now preserved in the Museum of Palermo.

(c) Bœotia.—Bœotian sculpture is represented by a large series of "Apollos" of varying quality, but all characterised by a certain heaviness and passivity of type, and monotony of pose.

(d) Ægina.—Ægina was distinguished from the 6th century for its bronzes.

Anatas was the most celebrated of the early Æginetan sculptors. It may be that he is represented by a very characteristic work of the school—a bronze head of a bearded man, found on the Athenian Acropolis.

It is, however, from the sculptures which decorated their temple that the work of the Æginetan sculptors can now best be studied. They are preserved in Munich (casts in the British Museum). Although they are of marble, the sculptures from the Ægina pediments, give very precise indications of the particular style created by these sculptors in bronze. The figures are still rather stiff in treatment; but it is none the less evident that these sculptors could model the human body with considerable skill, and could vary the attitudes. (For a study of these figures, see *Ægina*.) The Æginetan school was arrested in its development by the collapse of political independence. The results of its researches enriched the great neighbouring school of Attica.

(3) *Attica*.—To judge from archæological discoveries, the Attic school is far from seeming to be the most precocious in Greece. Nor does the primitive sculpture of Attica seem to have fallen under foreign influence. The oldest sculpture we have dates from the end of the 7th century, and shows very clearly the influence of the technique of sculpture in wood. One of the earliest sculptural examples is a pediment representing *Heracles Attacking the Hydra* (Acropolis Museum, Athens). Other pediments and bas-reliefs also represent the deeds of Heracles. There is, for instance, the contest of Heracles and the marine god, Triton—it is in high relief, and made of rough limestone. The archaic character of the work is evident in the faces, with their large, staring eyes. These groups have retained a good deal of their colour.

The first notable marble work was, like the coloured limestone groups, of an architectural character. It belonged to the early temple of Athena, and represents *Athena Triumphing over a Giant*. This group probably belonged to the central part of a pediment, but the rest cannot be reconstructed. As was the case with all sculpture of the time, certain details of the costume and figure were picked out in colour. Judging from the refinement of the workmanship, these figures appear to belong to the end of the 6th century.

Our knowledge of early Attic art has been revolutionised by a series of female draped statues found on the Acropolis of Athens. They were evidently overturned by Persian invaders. The figures probably represent worshippers of Athena, who dedicated themselves symbolically to the goddess. "These statues may seem at first to be but monotonous repetitions of the same type," but "they are not really very like each other, much less identical." Within limits, "every one shows the most remarkable individuality of treatment." One of the chief attainments of the early Attic school was the elaboration and detail in the arrangement and treatment of drapery. "Here, as throughout the history of archaic art in Greece, freedom and accuracy of work in detail precedes any general advance towards freedom of type and of composition." These female figures are in the Acropolis Museum, Athens.

The Acropolis Museum contains other figures, such as statuettes of Athena, and figures of men. The earliest marble statue on the Acropolis represents a man carrying a calf over his shoulder. As examples of two later developments of the male and female types of statues may be mentioned the upper part

Apotheosis of Heracles at Assos. (Louvre.)

of a very fine draped female figure, and the head of a youth. These are, however, considerably more advanced in style, and probably date from just before the Persian Wars.

The soil of Attica has also yielded a certain number of tombstones with reliefs, the most celebrated of which is known as the Stele of Aristion, the work of Aristocles. It belongs to the last years of the 6th century, and represents a warrior in profile, holding a staff. In spite of archaisms—such as the incorrect drawing of the hands, and the representation of the eye as if in full face—the grace and dignity of the whole is very impressive. "Aristocles may be classed as the most representative of the early Attic masters, who aimed at grace and delicacy of detail, at expression in the face, at harmonious effect generally, without any daring innovations or violent departures from the simple types of archaic art" (E. Gardner).

Before passing to the 5th century, reference must be made to sculptures from the temple of Apollo and the Treasury of the Athenians at Delphi. These sculptured metopes appear to be the work of attic sculptors (e.g. *Athena and Theseus*; *Heracles and the Stag*).

See Pls. 20, 22, Vol. I.

*The Fifth Century* (B.C.).—The brilliant victory which ended the Persian wars (465 B.C.) is a con-

THE HARPY TOMB AT XANTHOS.

venient date to divide the archaic masters from those of the classical epoch. "The common danger had drawn the various Greek cities together, and the deliverance from that danger was celebrated by common offerings to the gods." Political unity resulted in a closer association of the various artistic

ACTAEON BEING DEVOURED BY HIS DOGS. (Heraeum of Selinus.)

schools. Athens became the powerful Ionian centre. In the Peloponnesus, Argos was the artistic capital. In this town we find the most representative artists of the Dorian

ZEUS AND HERA. (Metope of the Heraeum of Selinus.)

school. Their genius radiated throughout the Peloponnesus, as far as Sicily and greater Greece.

Themistocles and then Cimon dreamed of rebuilding Athens from its ruins. Cimon did great things—he built a Theseum, c. 475 B.C. (The building which today goes under this name belongs, however, to c. 428 B.C. This building is usually held to be the Temple of Hephaestus mentioned by Pausanias.) In addition he began works on the Acropolis, which were completed under Pericles. Among the great artists of the time were Hegias, Calamis, Micon, Critios and Nesiotes—but they are only known to us through the old writers and inscriptions. Lucian's description of the style of Hegias, Critios and Nesiotes is borne out by the famous statues of "Harmodius and Aristogiton" (copy of this group in Naples). Their works, he says, are "concise, sinewy, hard, exact and strained in their lines."

The sculptures from Olympia (see Olympia) probably belong to the School of the Peloponnesus.

In the middle of the 5th century we come to the great names of Greek sculpture—Myron, Lycippus, Polyclitus, and Phidias (see these names). Myron is the creator of the famous type of *Discobolus*; Polyclitus, with his *Doryphorus*, fixed a "canon" of proportion which was long observed by Greek sculptors; Phidias is the immortal artist who organised the artistic work of Athens, directed the sculptural decoration of the Parthenon, and created the types of Athena and Zeus with his two famous chryselephantine statues of the Parthenon and the temple of Olympia.

In the second half of the 5th century may be placed a certain number of votive bas-reliefs or tomb-stones which cannot be attributed to any definite artist. Among the noblest of these works is the relief found at Eleusis (National Museum, Athens) representing the boy *Triptolemus between Demeter and Persephone*. There are many copies of a very beautiful relief of *Hermes, Orpheus and Eurydice*. The finest of these is in the Museum of Naples, and shows very clearly the influence of the reliefs of the Parthenon. Yet another relief is known as the *Mourning Athena* (Acropolis Museum, Athens). It represents the goddess with her head bent leaning on her spear, while in front of her is a plain slab like a stele. It has been

FIGHT OF HERACLES AND THE TRITON. (Louvre.)

suggested with much plausibility that the goddess is represented as mourning over a list of some of her chosen warriors who have fallen in battle. The simplicity and directness of this figure are very impressive.

*The Fourth Century* (B.C.).—The best Attic masters of the early fourth century are Cephisodotus (author of an *Eirene*, of which there probably exists a copy in Munich), and Demetrios (who, according to Lucian, made portraits). Also at the beginning of the fourth century must be placed a certain number of sculptures which were executed under the influence of the Attic school: the groups discovered at Delos (among them *Boreas Carrying off Orithyia*, in the Athens Museum); and the remains of pediments from the Temple of Aesclepius at Epidaurus (the most important being *Combats of Greeks and Amazons*—same museum).

Then a certain number of Ionian monuments must be mentioned, such as the friezes of Trysa, and the Nereid monument (see).

THE SPINARIO. (Rome.)

The two greatest masters of the first half of the fourth century are Scopas (of Paros) and Praxiteles (of Athens). (See these names.)

Bryaxis and Leochares were coworkers on the Mausoleum at Halicarnassus (see Mausoleum).

The most famous sculptor of the second half of the fourth century is Lycippus (see), the author of a new "canon" which replaced that of Polyclitus by substituting taller and more graceful forms for the heavier proportions of Polyclitan art.

The chief characteristic which distinguishes Greek art of the 4th century from that of the 5th is the growth of individualism. "Phidias embodied in his great statues a noble conception of the permanent and immutable character of the deity, his power and his benignity. Scopas and Praxiteles seem rather to realise the gods as individuals of like passions with ourselves, to express their varying moods and phases of character or emotion, and to draw subtle distinctions of personality" (Ernest Gardner). It follows that while Phidias might devote all his energy to the artistic expression of his ideal, the later sculptor, who aimed rather at expressing moods and shades of character, would pay more attention to the appearance of his statue and the effect it produced, than to the perfection of its actual form. As opposed to the idealism of the 5th century, there was, in the 4th century, a tendency towards realism and impressionism. And no 5th century work reveals to us as wonderfully as does the *Hermes* of Praxiteles, how the Greek sculptor could render, in marble, the texture of flesh, or the folds and material of drapery.

*The Hellenistic Period.*—After the death of Alexander, his empire crumbled into small kingdoms of

DEMETER, TRIPTOLEMUS AND KORE. (Bas-relief from Eleusis.)

which the capitals, Pergamon, Antioch, Seleucia and Alexandria were the centres for which artists deserted the old Greek towns, divested of their ancient power. The chief patrons of artists were the Greek princes, heirs of Alexander. "Under the influence of a kind of Asiatic exoticism, the happy balance which the Hellenic genius had for so long maintained, tended to break. There was, as it were, an invasion of new taste, which valued chiefly brilliance, facility and theatrical display" (Collignon). During this period art became more naturalistic: sculptors observed nature more closely; certain erotic types appear, which had previously been

THE VICTORY OF SAMOTHRACE. (Louvre.)

disdained and more familiar subjects were treated. The Hellenistic period falls roughly between the death of Alexander (323 B.C.) and the conquest of Greece by the Romans (155 B.C.). It is during this period that many archæologists place the execution of such beautiful works as the *Victory of Samothrace* and the *Venus of Melos* (both in the Louvre). That the

# FRENCH SCULPTURE OF THE THIRTEENTH CENTURY

In the *last third of the twelfth century sculptors freed statuary from the bas-relief, but the sculptors remained the decorators of the cathedrals. The most beautiful groups of Gothic statuary are at Notre Dame in Paris, at Chartres, Reims and Amiens.*

CHARTRES: FIGURES. *(Photo by Hachette.)*

QUEEN. LOUVRE. *(Photo by Hachette.)*

CHARTRES: FIGURE. *(Photo by Hachette.)*

REIMS: CAPITAL. *(Photo from Mon. Hist.)*

REIMS: CAPITAL. *(Photo from Mon. Hist.)*

CHARTRES: ST. THEODORE. *(Photo by Hachette.)*

AMIENS: VIERGE DORÉE. *(Photo by Hachette.)*

AMIENS: BEAU DIEU. *(Photo by Hachette.)*

In passing from the first figures of the west porch of Chartres, which are still very rigid, to the supple figures of the neighbouring porches, we can see Gothic statuary taking on the aspect of the forms of life; the figures of Christian art gain a new power of expression. We cannot imagine more gracious majesty than that of the "Vierge Dorée" of Amiens, nor a more noble and more divine Christ than the "Beau Dieu" of Amiens. The sculptors fixed new types and without doubt modified the religious sentiment by creating stirring and beautiful figures close to common humanity.

REIMS: THE VISITATION. *(Photo by Neurdein.)*

NOTRE DAME, PARIS: CORONATION OF THE VIRGIN. *(Photo by Hachette.)*

REIMS: ANNUNCIATION. *(Photo by Neurdein.)*

These figures already so alive in themselves were often associated by the sculptors in a common action. The movement does not destroy the tranquil rhythm of their attitudes. The figures have kept from their monumental origin the discipline of straight lines, and yet how much life there is in these bodies of stone. They would have been the unequalled masterpiece of Christian inspiration if painting had not reserved for us the Madonnas of Fra Angelico.

BOURGES: THE ELECT. *(Photo by Neurdein.)*

BOURGES: LAST JUDGMENT (DETAIL). *(Photo by Neurdein.)*

BOURGES: THE DAMNED. *(Photo by Neurdein.)*

The sculptors of the thirteenth century continued the tradition of the "Last Judgments" of the Romanesque epoch. All the cathedrals show this grandiose scene where the sculptor instructs the faithful as to the joys of Paradise and torments of Hell. The most complete is that of the cathedral of Bourges. This Gothic sculpture finally became separate from the cathedral and numerous saints were given a typical face and a personal attitude. It was statuary that regained naturalism and rendered possible an entirely new popular iconography.

# SCULPTURE AT THE END OF THE MIDDLE AGES

In the *evolution of all schools of sculpture we observe the same phases. After a period of archaic rigidity the statuary reaches an idealistic period during which a balance is established between the liberty of life and the tranquil rhythm. Then the plastic art becomes more supple and more agitated, at the same time the sculpture becomes more hollowed out and shows a more naturalistic expression and more characteristic types. So at the end of the Middle Ages in the fourteenth and fifteenth centuries sculpture arrived at the portrait and in the religious art it expressed more pathetic sentiments than in the thirteenth century.*

CHARLES V. LOUVRE.

JEANNE DE BOURBON. LOUVRE.

ST. MICHAEL. MUSEUM OF THE AUGUSTINES, TOULOUSE. *(Photo by Hachette.)*

VIRGIN AND CHILD. MUSEUM OF THE AUGUSTINES, TOULOUSE.

JEANNE DE BOULOGNE. POITIERS. *(Photo by Hachette.)*

VIRGIN. CHATEAUDUN. *(Photo from Mts. Hist.)*

## Portrait Sculpture

During the fourteenth century the idealistic statuary of the thirteenth century was applied to the representation of individual types. Among typical statues, we admire the King Charles V and the Queen Jeanne de Bourbon who were in the church of the Celestines as donors. The types of the Virgins and saints are characterised enough to permit us to recognise the regional facial differences.

TOMB OF PHILIPPE LE HARDI. DIJON.

MOURNERS. DIJON. *(Photo by Neurdein.)*

TOMB OF PHILIPPE POT. LOUVRE.

## Funeral Sculpture

An important part of plastic activity was devoted to funeral statuary after the thirteenth century. Especially in the fifteenth century the tombs of kings and great nobles at St. Denis, at Dijon, at Souvigny, were present in their typical form: a sarcophagus having walls decorated with mourners on which repose the bodies of the effigies. The richest of the tombs are those of the Dukes of Burgundy; the most pathetic is that of Philippe Pot where the mourners cease to be decoration and become active figures carrying the corpse on their shoulders.

CLAUS SLUTER: VIRGIN. CHAMPMOL. *(Photo by Neurdein.)*

CLAUS SLUTER: KING DAVID. DIJON.

CLAUS SLUTER: THE WELL OF MOSES. DIJON.

CLAUS SLUTER: ZECHARIAH AND DANIEL. DIJON.

APOSTLES FROM THE ABBEY OF RIEUX. MUSEUM, TOULOUSE.

## Claus Sluter

One of the wealthiest groups of sculptors at the end of the Middle Ages was in Burgundy. These artists from different regions, assembled for the service of the dukes, worked especially at the Carthusian convent of Champmol near Dijon. The most famous was Claus Sluter. His most powerful work is the Well of Moses. Long before the Renaissance, this Gothic art foreshadowed Donatello and Michelangelo.

tradition of Lycippus was not forgotten appears in such a work as the *Boxer* (in the Terme Museum, Rome), or in various portrait statues.

*The Asiatic Schools.—Pergamon.*—Important groups from the great altar at Pergamon are in Berlin. The frieze, representing the struggle between the gods and giants, shows that sculpture has become more restless and emotional in character. (See Pergamon.)

*Tralles.*—The group known as the *Farnese Bull*; and probably also the original group of the *Niobides* (see) belong to this school.

*Rhodes.*—The famous statue group of *Laocoön* was probably the work of Rhodian sculptors.

*Alexandria.*—The city of Alexandria, founded by Alexander, soon became an important metropolis. Its intermediary situation between Africa and Asia, favoured the development of wealth. There had been an official art at the court of the Ptolemies, the splendour of which we can only imagine. Among the monuments which must be associated with the school of Alexandria, are certain works which combine the Egyptian style with the Greek style, such as some portraits with Egyptian costumes and Hellenic technique.

Julius Caesar, called Germanicus. (Louvre.)

Other Alexandrian works include: *Statue of the Nile* (Vatican); the *Old Fisherman*, and the *Old Peasant Woman Carrying a Lamp* (both in the Palazzo dei Conservatori, Rome); *Boy with a Goose* (Munich).

See Pl. 25, Vol. I.

The triple-headed Typhon. (Limestone group from a pediment found on the Acropolis of Athens.)

*The Greco-Roman Period.*—In the second half of the 2nd century B.C., Greek sculpture was adopted by the Roman world. The penetration of Greek art in the Latin world goes back further, however; for already, in the 3rd century, the victories of Rome in the East, and in Sicily, were accompanied by the pillage of works of art and their transport to Rome. Even Etruscan art of the 6th century was influenced by the Greeks. When Greece was conquered, its art was immediately adopted, and from this time the production of Greek sculpture must often be followed in Rome.

Athens, in default of political power, had preserved her intellectual prestige.

Tablet. (Fragment of an ancient illustration for the *Iliad*.)

The Tower of the Winds, decorated with comparatively poor reliefs representing the winds, dates from the 1st century B.C.

The name "Neo-Classical" is given to a school of sculptors who, in the 2nd and 1st century B.C., imitated the most famous types of previous sculpture, and thus made them known to the Roman world. This school is less remarkable for originality than for technical skill.

Among the most remarkable works of this class are: the *Belvedere Torso*, the *Venus di Medici*, and the so-called *Germanicus*, in the Louvre.

See Pl. 32, Vol. I.

Bibliography: Brunn, *Geschichte der griechischen Künstler.*—M. Collignon, *Histoire de la Sculpture Grecque.*—Murray, *History of Greek Sculpture.* — Ernest Gardner, *A Handbook of Greek Sculpture.* London, 1920.

terra cottas.—The art of modelling in terra-cotta was always much practised in Greece. The material was used for temple ornaments such as acroteria, engraved plaques, and statuettes. The terra cotta industry was largely concerned with the latter, and it produced some charming works which express the skill and delicacy of the modellers.

It is very difficult to indicate exactly the date when many of these statuettes were made, because even after they had acquired real ability, artists continued to reproduce certain very crude figures, the type of which had been fixed by religion and popular belief. In many cases, however, the style allows us to say approximately when they were made.

About 3000 B.C. terra cotta statuettes were made in the Troad and in Cyprus; between 2000 and 1000 B.C., in Crete and Mycenæ. Between 1000 and 700 B.C. is the Geometric period, which followed the Dorian invasion. In the 7th and 6th centuries, the finest works are those of Rhodes and Cyprus. The 5th and

The lyre player. (Figurine from Tanagra.)

4th centuries are (as in the case of sculpture, painting and the other arts) the classical period, with Attic predominance. This was followed in the 3rd and 2nd centuries by the Alexandrine period. Then came the Roman period, until about the 5th century A.D.

Most of the terra cottas have been discovered in tombs, where rites demanded that they should accompany the dead. Often they were broken when the body was placed in the coffin. Others have been found in the temples, treasuries and houses. It must not be supposed, however, that the terra cotta statuettes were always destined for the dead, or as votive offerings in the temples.

Grotesque figure. (Statuette from Tanagra.)

This prosperous industry was supported by a very varied "clientèle," who bought its products for many purposes: as clay divinities to adorn their houses and family altars; as fetishes or charms; or as toys for their children. This explains the quantity of the production and the variety of the types. All countries in antiquity produced statuettes of very varied types, which can best be grouped according to where they were found.

(1) *Troad and Cyprus.*—The oldest Greek terra cotta figures were executed about 300 B.C., in Cyprus and in ancient Troy or Hissarlik. This industry was already very prosperous among the Egyptians and Chaldeans. The earliest attempts were modelled by hand with pieces of clay. They frequently represent figures of animals made into the form of a vase. There was also an attempt to reproduce nude figures of women and children. These figures are of no artistic value. This art never developed in Troy, from the time it was destroyed by the Greeks; but in Cyprus the case was otherwise. Gradually the xoana (primitive idols) lost their shapelessness, and modellers even came to represent scenes of daily life, such as sailors in their ship, women at their toilet, etc.

Figurine. (Terra cotta from Tanagra.)

About the 9th century B.C. animals and xoana gave place to statuettes of divinities, such as Aphrodite. The Cyprian modellers of the 5th century also produced some fine figures of Demeter, and graceful figures of women, and of Nikè.

In spite of the progress made in Cyprus during this long period of 25 centuries, the art never attained to the perfection of Attic work of the 4th and 3rd centuries.

(2) *Mycenæ.*—The earliest works are crudely fashioned idols. Statuettes of Mycenaean women are always clothed, and the details indicated by means of colour. Figures of animals were also produced. All these works were much influenced by Egyptian art.

(3) *Rhodes.*—The early work of Rhodes was also influenced by Egyptian art. The first statuettes are small nude figures, which became, in the 6th century, amiable, smiling divinities—Aphrodites and statuettes of graceful young girls; grave, noble goddesses, and fierce armed warriors.

(4) *Greece proper* (*Attica,* and the studios of *Tanagra*).—The great centre of the terra cotta industry in Greece was Tanagra. In the necropolis of this town there was discovered a great quantity of statuettes dating from all periods.

The earliest figures of Tanagra, Attica and of continental Greece in general, in which real progress is seen, date from the 7th and 6th centuries. They represent figures of women, warriors, scenes of daily life, slaves, servants, bakers and peasants, in their various occupations. The figures are coloured, sometimes with bright enamel.

MYRINA: BACCHANALE. (Terra cotta, Louvre.)

The work of the 6th and 5th century is characterised by nobility of attitude, graceful simplicity of drapery, and health and beauty of body. The terra cotta modellers were inspired by the works of the great Greek sculptors — Calamis, Onatas, Phidias—and their small statuettes reproduce the majestic, serene attitudes of the gods and heroes which peopled the temples.

Gradually, in the course of the 5th century, the figures lost their severity. The favourite divinities were Aphrodite, Apollo and Dionysos. Grace and suppleness replaced majesty. Drapery became lighter, and gradually slid from shoulders and arms. Religious sentiment weakened.

In the 4th century, the art of terra cotta statuettes reached its highest point of perfection. Olympus gave place to mortals, and the modellers favoured familiar subjects. Most of the statuettes are of charming young women, but youths, old men and children were also represented. Nothing could be more gracious and lively than some of these delightful figures of young women—walking, sitting, in conversation, or leaning against each other.

(5) *Southern Greece.*—Other studios opened in the Peloponnesus,

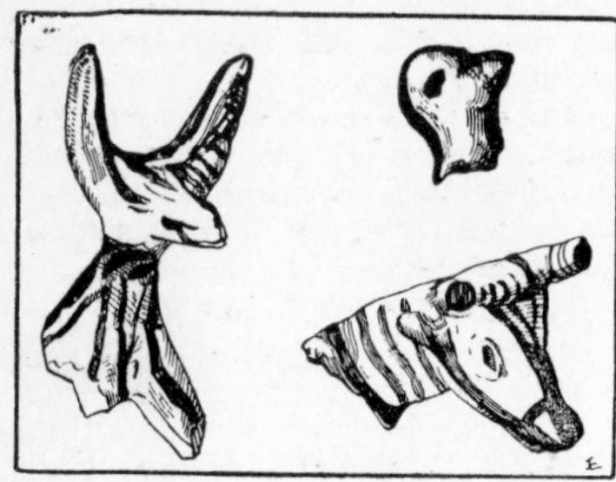

MYCENÆ: TERRA COTTA IDOLS.

Ægina, and Megara. Without attaining to the perfection of the celebrated artists of Tanagra, they nevertheless produced charming statuettes. While they continued to execute graceful feminine figures, the artists tried to render little scenes with several figures, or "subject" pieces—*Aphrodite at Her Toilet,* kneeling in a shell, *Tyro on the Rock,* with his children, etc. Sometimes also the modellers amused themselves by making comic or grotesque figures —actors with a grimacing masque and emphatic gesture, merchants, slaves, old women, the caricatures of which are most amusing.

(6) *Asia Minor.*—Of all the terra cotta factories which flourished from the 3rd to the 1st century, the most celebrated are those of Alexandrian Egypt, of Smyrna. Tarsus, and particularly of Myrina. The Tanagran models are copied with the greatest exactitude. In Egypt, in Alexandria, the types offer the greatest variety, and Oriental subjects mingle with the others, often with very curious results.

Next to Tanagra, the most celebrated studios are those of Myrina. An admirable series of figures which decorated the tombs of the necropolis have been brought to light. They date from the 3rd, 2nd and 1st centuries B.C. Some recall the figures of Tanagra, but on the whole the taste seems to have been for mythological scenes, athletes, and for subjects that could give play to a graceful fantasy—such as groups of winged Victories, Cupids, or Satyrs dancing.

The modellers of Myrina, like most others of the same period, were inspired by the great works of sculpture and painting. It is remarkable that, unlike the ceramists who frequently signed their works, the statuette-makers never signed theirs. Among all those who, during a period of thirty centuries, worked on Greek soil, very few have come down to us, and all these names appear to be of modellers of Myrina or of Priene. The best known is Diphilos, who made a nude Youth (Louvre), several Aphrodites and other works.

(7) *Italy and Sicily.*—The Greek colonies of Italy and Sicily were influenced by the art of their native soil, in the industry of terra cottas as in other branches of art.

The production of terra cotta statuettes gradually died out about the 1st century, probably under the influence of Christianity which forbade the worship of idols. But the time of the great flowering was over. Here, as in sculpture and painting, there was decadence, as may be judged from the Gallo-Roman statuettes.

See Pl. 26, Vol. I.

BIBLIOGRAPHY: Panopka, *Terracotten des königlichen museums zu Berlin,* 1842.—J. Martha, *Catalogue des figurines en terre cuite du musée d'Athènes.*—Pottier, *Les statuettes de terre cuite dans l'antiquité; Diphilos et les modeleurs des terres cuites Grecques.*

PAINTING.—The Greeks appear to have been as proud of their painters as they were of their sculptors. To gain an idea of the great Greek paintings, we must have recourse to ancient writers, to the painted stelae of the 6th and 5th centuries—(although rather rare), to the frescoes of Pompeii, and to the numerous vases, cups and funeral plaques found in European museums.

The earliest paintings of which important specimens have been found, in Greece, were discovered at Mycenæ — hence the name "Mycenæn painting," which is given to early Greek painting. The palace of Mycenæ was decorated with friezes of geometrical drawings, and frescoes which show considerable skill in composition—animals, warriors, and monsters. A Mycenaean tombstone also has a whole series of animals and figures. The palace of Tiryns contained frescoes, one of which is famous—the Bull fresco—showing a hunting or acrobatic scene.

The finest paintings come from Crete, from the palace of Cnossus. One is the fresco of the *Cup-bearer* which decorated a corridor of the Palace. It is remarkable for the precision of its drawing, and ability of execution. (See Crete.)

The technique was of the simplest. The palette included only a few bright colours—blue, red, yellow—and a bluish grey and black. They were used in a very conventional way—animals were painted red with a blue leg, or blue with a red. The human body was painted reddish brown.

In the 5th century, Athens became the artistic centre of Greece. Head of the Attic school of painting was a Polygnotus, one of the most glorious painters of Greece.

The names of painters from many other schools have also come down to us; but unfortunately their works have not survived.

BIBLIOGRAPHY: Paul Girard. *La Peinture antique.*

ENGRAVED GEMS (Glyptology).—Glyptology is the study of engraved gems. These little jewels were in great demand among the Greeks and Romans. From the remotest times, the Greeks believed that the stones possessed certain healing virtues, and accordingly they used them as talismans to protect the wearer from illness.

Many precious and semi-precious stones were used. Among the most common were various agates, amethyst, cat's-eye, beryl, garnet chalcedony (of a dull white sometimes bluish colour)—one of the most frequently engraved—hematite, jasper of various colours—black, green, red and azure blue. Malachite was used (chiefly for seals), onyx and sadonyx (chiefly used for cameos) and seals.

The chief classes of engraved gems are: (1) *Intaglios,* which have the design sunk below the surface, and were used as seals. (2) *Cameos,* which have the design carved in relief and were intended for ornaments; and (3) *Scarabs* (beetles) which combine the characteristics of both the others, as the back is carved in relief, in imitation of a beetle, while the base has a design in intaglio.

Gems had to be cut with a very hard material. Often they were rubbed with powder of diamonds, or with emery mixed with oil, either by means of a hand tool, or with a revolving wheel.

The earliest engraved gems of Greece date from the Cretan and Mycenaean epoch. These were largely intaglios. In shape they were chiefly lenticular (i.e., in the form of a broad bean). The subjects consist of flowers, birds, fishes, animals —all engraved with astonishing mastery. Later the Egyptian scarab was copied, and sphinxs and lions were added to the list.

The Cretan-Mycenaean civilisation was destroyed by the Dorian invaders, and the newcomers borrowed from all the Asiatic arts. Their engraved gems reproduced not only the subjects but also the form of Egyptian, Chaldean, Assyrian and Phœnician gems. But soon original figures came to be added—fantastic animals, mythological scenes, etc.

In the 6th century, Ionian Greece was particularly advanced in the art of glyptology, as in sculpture.

In the 5th century, all forms were produced, and engraved with the utmost perfection both of design and technique. The influence of sculpture is often apparent. Thus two beautiful intaglios in the British Museum have subjects recalling the caryatids of the Erechtheum, and some figures from the frieze of the Parthenon. A gem in the Cabinet des Médailles reproduces the *Amazon* of Polyclitus.

For several centuries, until the 2nd century A.D. the production of fine cameos continued. We possess, for instance, a series of portraits of the Emperors and Empresses after the Roman conquest.

Under the Romans, the glyptic art fell into decadence. It flourished again, throughout the Middle Ages, in Byzantium.

BIBLIOGRAPHY: King, *Antique Gems, their origin, uses, etc.* London, 1872.—Billing, *The Science of Gems, Jewels, etc.* London, 1867.—E. Babelon, *La gravure en pierre's fines.*—S. Reinach, *Pierres Gravées.* —Furtwängler, *Antike Gemmen.* Leipzig, 1900.

**GREENOUGH (Horatio).**—American sculptor (1805-1852), of Boston, studied first under Thorvaldsen in Rome and subsequently under Bartolini in Florence, where he lived for many years. He is a typical exponent of the tendencies of the Neo-Classical movement, nowhere more so than in his famous colossal statue of Washington (1843) in the Smithsonian Institution, seated semi-nude and draped like a Greek deity.

**GRENOBLE (Isère, France).**—The most interesting buildings are: —the *Palais de Justice* (the oldest parts are the entrance-door, and the vaulted passage of the courtyard; the façade is later, and was built in the 16th century); the *Church of St. André* (13th century); the *Cathedral* (the tower dates from the 12th century; also the Choir, which is the finest and oldest part of the building); the *Chapelle Saint Laurent*—this is the oldest Christian building in France, and dates from the 6th century. It is chiefly interesting for its carved capitals, which show classical and Byzantine influence.

**GRÈS.**—See Ceramic.

**GREUZE (Jean Baptiste).**—French painter, 1725-1805. He had

GREUZE (J. B.).

his first artistic education at Lyon, with a mediocre painter; but he went to Paris fairly early and became a student at the Académie Royale.

He painted scenes of domestic life which were intended to teach moral lessons. Thus filial respect provides the theme in the *Malédiction Paternelle* and the *Fils Puni* (Louvre). These lessons take the form of a little romance in action, like Hogarth's compositions. It must be admitted that nowadays the narrative of these paintings leaves us indifferent, and his fame rests on his skilful painting of certain parts of his pictures, especially of children and young girls. His portraits are not profound, but his painting of flesh is often exquisitely delicate.

The vogue for Greuze in his own day was immense. His art, which was a surprising mingling of moral preaching and sensuousness, appealed alike to the licentious taste inherited from the preceding age, and to the ideal of virtue set on foot by philosophers of the period.

GREUZE: THE BROKEN PITCHER. (Louvre.)

Later, taste turned against him, and he died almost forgotten.

See Pl. 46, Vol. II.

BIBLIOGRAPHY: Goncourt, *L'Art au XVIII^e^ siècle*. Vol. II. 1887.—Charles Normand, *J. B. Greuze*. Collections des artistes célèbres. C. Mauclair. *Jean-Baptiste Greuze*. Paris, 1905.

**GRIMMER (J.).**—Flemish painter (1526-1590). Painter of charming landscapes.

**GRIMOU (Alexis).**—Swiss painter, 1678-1740. Born in Romont. Son of one of the Hundred Swiss Guards of Versailles. He had a passion for Rembrandt, and imitated his style in some of his portraits (Louvre).

BIBLIOGRAPHY: L. Dimier, *Les peintres français du XVIII^e^ siècle*, Vol. II.

**GRISAILLE.**—Decorative painting in grey monotone; applied especially to such painting on glass.

**GROPIUS (Walter), 1883-.**—German architect and leader in the post-War phase of the modern movement in architecture, the so-called International style whose other chief exponents are Le Corbusier in France and Oud in Holland. The Bauhaus at Dessau, which he designed in 1926 to replace the Grand Ducal Art School previously at Weimar, was, until its suppression in 1933, the propagating center for the new mode as well as its most celebrated example. Only less celebrated have been his Hausing Project, Dessau, 1928, and Dammerstock-Seidlung, Karlsruhe, 1929. His Fagerswerk at Anbeld am den Lahn, 1911, is astonishingly advanced for its period. Gropius was in England, 1934-1936, and in the latter year accepted the post of Professor of Architecture, Harvard University, U.S.A.

**GROS (Antoine Jean).**—French painter, 1771-1835. He studied under David for a time, and then went to Italy. On his return to Paris, he was commissioned to perpetuate the memory of the Battle of Nazareth, but was stopped in this work by the jealousy of Bonaparte, who was disturbed to see the imperious Junot glorified. A compensation was due to the artist, and the first Consul ordered him to paint the *Pest*

GROS (BARON A. J.)

*House of Jaffa* (Louvre). The interest of the picture is concentrated on the group around Bonaparte, who touches the breast of one of the plague-stricken. Strange to say, considering the contemporary craze for the antique, the *Pest House* was an immediate success.

In 1807, there was an open competition for a vast composition: *Napoleon Visiting the Field of the Battle of Eylau*. Gros's sketch easily won it; and the picture (shown in 1808) produced a great sensation.

Among his paintings are the following: *The Taking of Madrid* (Versailles), which is unpleasantly monotonous; *The Battle of the Pyramids* (theatrical); *Francis I and Charles V in St. Denis* (Louvre); *The Departure of the Duchess of Angoulême;* and various portraits.

GROS: PORTRAIT OF THE COUNT FOURNIER-SARLOVÈZE. (Louvre.)

The Empire made Gros, and its downfall destroyed him. Contemporary history having no longer any interest for him, he returned to the antique. His submission was deplorable, and criticism did not spare him.

Charles X asked him to contribute to the decoration of an Egyptian Museum he was about to form, and Gros painted a kind of allegory on the fame of the Prince (which was destroyed in 1830), and a series of other allegories, of which *Valour, Virtue, Wisdom, Temperance* and *Victory* are the principal subjects.

Attacks against him increased, and his *Hercules and Diomede* (Salon of 1835) hastened his downfall. He drowned himself the same year.

See Pl. 50, Vol. II.

BIBLIOGRAPHY: J. B. Delestre. *Gros, sa Vie et ses Œuvres*. Paris, 1845.—Eugène Delacroix, *Notice sur Gros*, Revue des Deux-Mondes," 1848.—J. Tripier le Franc, *Histoire de la Vie et de la Mort du Baron Gros*. Paris, 1880.—H. Lemonnier, *Gros*. Paris.—G. Barnaud and Y. Sjöberg, *Gros-ses amis, ses élèves*. Paris, cat. of exhib., 1936.

**GROSVENOR GALLERY.**—See Burne-Jones.

**GROTESQUE.**—This word, which denotes an ornamental subject, comes from the word "grotto." When the soil of Rome was excavated, in the 15th century, to discover antique monuments, it was found that the holes thus hollowed were in the form of grottos. Many of the buildings brought to light were decorated with paintings formed of arabesque, of sinuous lines, the curling ends of which were composed of figures of men, realistic or fantastic animals, flowers, and objects of all kinds. This type of ornament has been given the name of "grotesque." Grotesques were much used during the Renaissance, by Perugino (in the Sala del Cambio, Perugia), by Raphael, and by Giovanni d'Undine in the Loggia of the Vatican; and in France, by Jean Bérain and others.

**GRÜNEWALD (Mathias).**—German painter, birth date unknown (possibly between 1470-80); died 1528 in Halle. Probably a pupil of Holbein the Elder. He worked in Mayence, Aschaffenburg, Isenheim (Alsace), and Halle. He was a citizen of Seligenstadt, near Würzburg. The oldest known picture by him is the *Mocking of Christ*, Munich (after 1503). In 1505 he painted a *Crucifixion* (Basle). The *Isenheim Altarpiece* (1510 to 1514, now in Colmar Museum) is his most important work. It was originally an altarpiece with a double pair of shutters and two fixed wings. One compartment shows Christ crucified, with grief-stricken figures at his feet. Another panel reveals the Joys of Mary—the Virgin, holding the Child in her arms, is seated in a smiling landscape; in the background, God the Father sends down upon her golden rays which animate a dancing shower of angels. Finally, the Legend of St. Anthony supplies a fantastic scene with devils, and a reposeful scene with St. Anthony and St. Paul conversing in a strange, poetic landscape.

Other paintings by Grünewald are in Karlsruhe, Freiburg, in the Breisgau, Stuppach, and Munich. The Stuppach *Madonna* dates from 1519, the Munich *St. Erasmus and St. Maurice* from c. 1524-25.

See Pl. 3, Vol. II.

BIBLIOGRAPHY: H. A. Schmid, *Mathias Grünewald, Gemälde und Zeichnungen*. Strasbourg, 1907.—Friedländer, *M. Grünewald, der Isenheimer Altar*. Munich, 1908.—Réau, *Mathias Grünewald*. Paris, 1921.

**GRUNTHUNSE (Hôtel).**—See Bruges.

**GUADALAJARA (Spain).**—*Casa de los Infantados*. 15th century palace of the Dukes of Infantado, in the mingled Mudéjar, Gothic, and Renaissance style of the plateresque.

**GUARDI (Francesco).**—Venetian painter, 1712-1793. Guardi is the painter of a great many charming Venetian landscapes, which are somewhat in the style of Canaletto, but more lively and more pearly: the golden sunshine strikes his buildings more brightly; and the silver reflections play more happily on the green water. Sometimes clouds threaten a storm; sometimes lights dance amid the joys of Carnival. Guardi's art is almost impressionistic.

BIBLIOGRAPHY: G. H. Simonson, *Francesco Guardi*. London, 1905.—G. Fiocco, *Francisco Guardi*.

**GUARIENTO.**—Painter from Padua or Verona, active in Padua from 1338.

In 1365 Guariento was called to Venice to do paintings in the Doge's Palace; and between 1368 and 1370 he died, and was buried in Padua. His works, which show the influence of Giotto upon the northern Byzantine tradition, include the following:

Padua, Museo Civico, *Madonna, St. Mark and Twenty-eight angels*, a fragment of the ceiling from the destroyed Cappella del Capitanio; Padua, R. Accad. di Lettere ed Arti, frescoes from the same chapel (1340-50), much ruined; Padua, Eremitani, *Coronation of the Virgin*, remains of a frescoes from S. Agostino, and frescoes in the choir with scenes from the *Legends of SS. Augustin and Philip*, which have been overpainted; Bassano, Museo Civico, signed *Crucifix*; Venice, Doge's Palace, remains of Paradise with *Coronation* in Grand Council Hall (1365-68).

BIBLIOGRAPHY: Vasari-Milanesi, III.—Crowe and Cavalcaselle, Douglas ed., III.—Schubring, *Altichiero und seine Schule*. Leipzig, 1898.—A. Venturi, *Storia d. arte ital.*, V, 1907.—L. Venturi, *Le origini della pitt. venez.*, 1907.—Testi, *Storia della pitt. venez.*, I, 1909.—Moschetti, *Padova*, 1927.

**GUASPRE (Le).**—See Dughet.

**GUARINI (Guarino), 1624-1683.**—Italian architect of the School of Turin and one of the boldest and most fanciful designers of the 17th century. He was the author of the *Chapel of the Santissima Sindone*, c. 1668; the Jesuit *Academy of Sciences*, 1679; the *Palazzo Carignano*, c. 1680; and the church of *S. Lorenzo*, 1687. All these buildings are in Turin.

**GUDE (Hans).**—Norwegian painter, 1825-1903. He was professor at Düsseldorf, Karlsruhe and Berlin, successively. He painted romantic landscapes.

**GUÉPIÈRE (P.L. de la).**—German architect, designer of the Neues Schloss, Stuttgart, in collaboration with Retti. He was the sole author of Mon Repos and Schloss Solitude.

**GUERCINO (Francesco Barbieri, known as).**—Bolognese painter, 1591-1666. He was known as "Guercino" because he was blind in one eye. Born at Cento, near Ferrara. He went to Bologna, where he became the pupil of Ludovico Carracci, and he worked a good deal in Rome.

Guercino was among those who contributed to a type of religious painting which has survived until the present day in many pious images—conventional, sentimental scenes, lacking all simplicity but having studied grace or pathos, and exaggerated naturalism. How moving his *St. Sebastian* (Pitti Palace) tries to be! Classical subjects also attracted him: *Venus, Mars and Cupid* (Modena), the *Death of Dido* (Palazzo Spada, Rome), *Cleo-*

*patra* (Palazza Brignole, Genoa), etc.

Among Guercino's chief works may be mentioned: the *Madonna with two Monks* (Bologna), *the*

Guercino: Martyrdom of St. Peter. (Modena.)

*Resurrection* (Vatican), the *Martyrdom of St. Peter* (Modena), *Christ Crowned with Thorns* (Munich). See Pl. 22, Vol. II.

Guercino: Venus, Cupid and Mars. (Museum, Modena.)

**GUÉRIN (Pierre Narcisse).**—French painter, 1774-1833 (Rome). From his master, Regnault, Guérin acquired a taste for the antique, as it was conceived at that period.

His picture of *Marcus Sextus* (Louvre) was received with acclamation when it was exhibited at the Salon of 1799. He then went to Rome and Naples. On his return to Paris, far from turning to the study of nature, his source of inspiration was the most artificial—that of the theatre.

Nevertheless, in 1802, the success of *Phædra Accusing Hippolytus before Theseus* (Louvre) was not less than that obtained by *Marcus Sextus.* But eight years later, at the Salon of 1810, his *Andromache* did not receive the same praise. *Æneas*

Guérin: Aeneas and Dido. (Louvre.)

*and Dido* and *Clytemnestra,* two of Guérin's most important pictures, were exhibited in 1817.

After being nominated Director of the School in Rome, Guérin painted little else. He had ceased to be Director when he died in Rome in July, 1833. He was buried in the Church of Santa Trinità del Monte, beside Claude Lorrain.

See Pl. 50, Vol. II.

**GUIDINI (Guidici).**—See Franciabigio.

**GUIDO PAGANINO.**—See Mazzoni.

— **RENI.**—Bolognese painter, 1574, or '75-1642. After studying in Calvaert's studio, he became one of the most gifted pupils of the Carracci. It was not long before he was entering into rivalry with one of his masters, Ludovico Carracci, for the decoration of the Palazzo Pubblico of Bologna.

Like other artists of his school, he went to Rome, where he devoted a good deal of time to copying Apollos and Venuses, and other antique statues, which he greatly admired. In his paintings he aimed rather at achieving plastic beauty than merely dramatic or realistic effects. His figures always have an air of distinction, which sometimes verges on coquettishness. Their intense fervour is characteristic.

Nevertheless, Guido Reni sometimes imitated Caravaggio, as in two large paintings, the *Crucifixion of St. Peter* (Vatican), and *St. Paul and St. Anthony in the Desert* (Berlin). His paintings in the Chapels of St. Gregorio, Rome, are more truly characteristic.

In 1609, he painted the *Annunciation,* the *Transfiguration,* and the *Ascension* (Vatican), and the *History of Simeon,* in the apartments of Cardinal Borghese. The same year he finished his famous ceiling of *Aurora,* in the Casino Rospigliosi.

In 1610, Guido Reni decorated the dome of the Quirinal Palace, collaborating with Antonio Carracci and others. He also painted some frescoes in the Borghese Chapel of Santa Maria Maggiore. He worked in Ravenna, and in Naples.

Guido Reni: Head of Christ. (Pinakothek, Dresden.)

The paintings of St. Sebastian, in the Bologna Gallery and in the Louvre, are among the best examples of his art. A few of his best known religious works are: the *Crucifixion* (in Bologna, and in San Lorenzo, Rome), the *Assumption* (in Sant'Ambrogio, Genoa), the *Glory of Domenico* (in San Domenico, Bologna), the *Trinity* (in the Trinità dei Pellegrini, Rome). Among his other works may be mentioned: *Atalanta* (Naples), *Samson Victorious* (Bologna), *Judith* (Palazzo Adorno, Genoa), a fine portrait of his mother, and the so-called portrait of Beatrice Cenci, in the Palazzo Barberini, Rome.

See Pl. 22, Vol. II.

Bibliography: Max von Boehn, *Guido Reni,* 1912.

**GUIDO DA SIENA.**—Painter of the dugento in Siena, known by one panel in the Palazzo Pubblico, Siena, first mentioned as being in S. Gregorio in Campo Regio and later in S. Domenico. This panel was repainted in part by a follower of Duccio who evidently altered the original inscription with the date,

Guido Reni: Virgin in contemplation.

which now reads 1221, and which Milanesi has attempted to prove should be 1271.

Bibliography: Milanesi, *Della vera età di Guido pittore senese, etc.,* Giornale degli archivi toscani, III, 1859; and *Scritti varii.* Siena, 1873, p. 89.—Wickhoff, *Über die Zeit des Guido von Siena,* Mittheil. des Öster. Inst. f. Gesch.—forsch., X, 1889, p. 244.—Crowe and Cavalcaselle, Douglas ed., I, p. 161.—R. Davidsohn, *Guido da Siena,* Repert. f. Kstw., XXIX; and Rivista d'arte, 1907, p. 29.—Weigelt, *Duccio di Buoninsegna.* Leipzig, 1911, p. 211.—Van Marle, *La pitt. Senese prima di Duccio,* Rassegna d'arte antica e moderna, VII, 1920, p. 265; and *Italian Schools, etc.,* I, 1923, p. 364ff.

**GUILDHALL.**—See London.

**GUILANO DI ARRIGO.**—See Pesello.

**GUILLAUME SULPICE CHEVALIER.**—See Gavarni.

**GWALIOR.**—See India; also Pl. 35, Vol. I.

**GYNÆCEUM.**—In antiquity, the women's quarters in a house or establishment.

# H

**HADDON HALL (Derbyshire, England).**—English manor house of irregular plan arranged about two interior courts. Parts of the building are Norman, dating from the 11th century. The Gothic banqueting-hall, 14th century, is between the two courts. The long gallery is Elizabethan, 1567-1584, and is over 100 ft. long.

**HADRIAN.**—See Athens; Rome; also Pls. 19, 30, Vol. I.

**HALICARNASSUS.**—See Mausoleum of Halicarnassus.

**HALL (Peter Adolphus).**—Swedish miniature painter (1739-1793). About 1760, he went to Paris. His artistic talent, combined with the fact that he was a musician, and fond of dancing, gained him admittance to the "salons" of the aristocracy. He was one of the most brilliant miniaturists of the 18th century, and attacked vellum or ivory with a freedom of handling that seemed well-nigh impossible on such a restricted field.

**HALS (Frans).**—Famous Dutch painter (born 1580-81 in Antwerp; died 1666). He lived in Haarlem where he was the pupil of Karel van Mander until 1602. He led rather a disorderly life and was often in debt. Frans Hals' first work of outstanding importance, the *Banquet of the Officers of the Archers of St. George* (Haarlem Museum), was painted when Hals was about thirty-six years of age (1616). About 1621 he painted the superb portrait group of a *Married Couple* (Amsterdam) which has perhaps mistakenly been identified with the painter and his second wife. From 1627 dates the *Banquet of the Officers of St. George's Shooting Company* (Haarlem) with eleven officers assembled in front of a large draped curtain. They are richly dressed with bright scarves, and a flag adds colour to the scene. Their positions are free and natural and the faces admirably drawn. Another banqueting scene, that of the *Officers of the St. Andreas Shooting Company* in 1622 (?) has not the mastery of that painted in 1633, which represents the Officers of the same Company. The latter picture is more lively and picturesque. The jovial heads, the magnificent clothes, the scarves and flags—all make a splendid composition against the dark background. This picture is a masterpiece among those large "corporation pictures" which were so much in demand in Holland at that time. In 1641 Hals painted the *Governors of the St. Elizabeth Hospital* (Haarlem). Like Rembrandt's *Syndics* — painted twenty years later—the Governors are seated round a table with serious expressions, dressed in black and wearing large black hats. In 1664 he painted a portrait group of the five Governors of the almshouse and another of the four lady Governors (Haarlem)—both masterpieces. His pictures are very sombre in colour, only lightened by the white collars of the sitters. But in none of his works did the painter show more skill in the use of colour: there are the rarest tones in these blacks, and greys and whites.

Hals (Frans).

Hals (Frans): Portrait of René Descartes. (Louvre.)

Besides his large compositions the best-known of which we have mentioned, Frans Hals painted numerous portraits and *genre* scenes. He excelled in portraying laughter—from a subtle smile to an outburst of merriment which brightens the eyes, wrinkles the face and shows the teeth. Among Frans Hals' most famous works may be mentioned the *Children Laughing* (Glasgow, Dijon, etc.), the *Youthful Singers* (Cassel), the *Lute Player* (Paris, Robert de Rothschild collection), the *Merry Drinker* (Amsterdam), the *Fisherboy* (Antwerp), the *Laughing Cavalier* (Wallace Collection).

Hals' able and decided brush animated and gave character to the most ordinary face. Every touch is vivacious, and makes the technique itself attractive. Hals had many pupils, amongst whom were his sons.

See Pl. 36, Vol. II.

Bibliography: E. W. Moes, *Frans Hals.* Brussels, 1909.—Hofstede de Groot, *A Catalogue Raisonné,* Vol. III, 1910.—W. von Bode and J. Binder, *Frans Hals.* Berlin, 1914.—Klassiker der Kunst, ed. Valentiner, 1923.—Martin, Wilhelm, *Frans Hals en zijn tijd.* Amsterdam, 1935.

**— (sons of Frans).**—Dutch painters seventeenth century. Little is known about their lives. The eldest, Herman, was chiefly a painter of "conversation pictures," and perhaps of the *Drinker*, in the Haarlem Museum.

Frans the younger, the best known of Frans Hals' sons, was supposed to have been one whose style was most akin to that of his father, although no definite proof of this assumption has come to light.

Jan and Reynier are feeble artists. Nicholas—or Claes—is the author of a charming landscape (Haarlem) and of the *Young Woman Reading* (The Hague), an able painting.

**HAMPTON COURT (England).**—A palace begun for Cardinal Wolsey in 1515 but taken over by Henry VIII, who made additions, building the great north wing with the hammer-beam roofed Great Hall. Sir Christopher Wren built the Fountain Court circa 1690 in a restrained baroque design of red brick based with white trim and interrupted by white stone pavilions.

**HAN KAN.**—Chinese painter, middle of 8th century. Known for his paintings of horses.

See China—Art.

**HANGING GARDENS.**—See Babylon.

**HARDING (Chester).**—American painter (1792-1866). He was born at Conway, Massachusetts, 1st September 1792, but in 1806 the family moved to Madison County, New York. During the excitement of the War of 1812 young Harding joined the service as a drummer boy, but the novelty soon wore off. Soon he was a cabinet-maker, at first in Caledonia, New York, and later in Pittsburgh. Then he tried painting signs and became an itinerant portrait painter. Encouraged by several commissions he went to Philadelphia and studied for a few months at the Pennsylvania Academy of Fine Arts. Although he wished to go to Europe to study he did not find the opportunity then. Instead he pursued his successful career, painting the portraits of famous people in Washington, Northampton and Boston. From 1823 to 1826 he travelled in Europe, but then he returned to the United States because of financial worries. For a few years he stayed in Boston, but in 1830 he settled permanently at Springfield, Massachusetts. His last years were spent painting the notable men of that time, including Daniel Webster, John C. Calhoun, John Marshall, William T. Sherman. In 1828 he became a member of the National Academy of Design. He died in Boston 1st April 1866. His portraits are sincere representations of his sitters, but are not examples of psychological analysis to any degree.

Bibliography: Margaret E. White, ed., *A Sketch of Chester Harding, Artist,* 1929.

**HARDOUIN (Jules).**—See Mansart.

**HARLOT'S PROGRESS (The).**—See Hogarth.

**HARPIGNIES (Henri).**—French painter, 1819-1916. Pupil of Jean Achard, a painter of Grenoble. Harpignies travelled in Italy, but France was his real field of study. He painted the country round Fontainebleau, the Nivernaise, and the Auvergne, but he ended by settling on the banks of the Allier during the fine season,—a charming and secluded spot, where he could work in peace. His many pictures may be seen in the Museums of Lille, Orléans, Grenoble, in the Luxembourg, and in other French and foreign collections. He interpreted nature sincerely, with quiet colours and very simple drawing. His painting has an air of profound serenity. He loved big sweeps of earth and tall trees, preferring to paint them in the mysterious light of evening, against a twilight sky.

Harpignies: The banks of the Allier.

He has not the tender sweetness of Corot, nor his grace and colour, but he has the gravity and majesty of the masters of landscape painting. He also painted water-colours, which are valued by connoisseurs.

**HARPSICHORD.** — The oldest harpsichords are of Italian or Flemish make. In the 17th century they were often without feet, and were simply placed on the table. That is why one finds them with the case bearing a decoration in the Louis XIV style; while the feet, added later, are in the style of Louis XV or of Louis XVI. They are decorated on the exterior, and on the inside of the cover, with inlay-work, in the style of Boulle, or with paintings on a gold background. They had already, on a small scale, the ungraceful form of our grand-pianos, which made it very difficult to give them any beauty of line.

**HARPY TOMB.**—See Greece (Sculpture); Lycia.

**HARRISON (Birge).**—American painter, born 1854, pupil of Cabanel and Carolus-Duran in Paris, noted for his figure subjects in the open air and (later) landscapes.

**HART (George Overbury "Pop").**—American painter (1868-1933). He was born in Cairo, Illinois, 10th May 1868 and early in life manifested an interest in drawing. He drew even while in charge of the vats in his father's glue factory and thereupon was dismissed for the neglect of his duties. Then began a long life of wandering which carried him to the far corners of the earth. He worked his way to London on a cattle boat and then returned to study at the Chicago Art Institute for a while. He engaged in sign painting on a trip down tne Mississippi to New Orleans and in 1900 made his way to Italy and Egypt, visiting museums and making sketches everywhere of people singly or in groups, engaged in their usual pastimes, which held for him a strange fascination. In 1903 he left San Francisco for Tahiti and Samoa, where natives, treated as common people instead of the exotic personalities of Gauguin's art, were sketched and painted. In 1905 he returned to the United States and in a short time left for Copenhagen and Iceland. Two years later he was in Paris, where for three months he studied at the Académie Julian, his only really long period of instruction. He was not in sympathy with the academic standards and so left to sketch vistas along the Seine and the Oise. That same year, 1907, he had a picture accepted for the Carnegie International Exhibition and he then returned to the United States to settle down. He lived in Coytesville, New Jersey, and for the next five years he painted signs for amusement parks in New York and New Jersey. From 1912 to 1920 he painted movie sets in the summers and spent his winters in the south in the West Indies, Paraguay, or New Orleans. After that he devoted himself exclusively to his art and began to make etchings and lithographs. He sold a print to the Metropolitan Museum of Art in 1924 and soon his fame became more assured. In 1925 and 1926 he was President of the Brooklyn Society of Etchers. He made a sketching trip to Mexico in 1926, when he made many studies around Oaxaca of the "humor and beauty of everyday life." He died in New York City 9th September 1933.

Bibliography: Holger Cahill, *George O. "Pop" Hart,* 1928.

— **(William).**—American painter (1823-1894). He was born 31st March 1923 in Paisley, Scotland, but came to the United States when he was a young boy. The family made its home in Albany, New York, and there he became an apprentice to a carriage manufacturer. It was at that time the custom to decorate the carriages with decorative panels, and from his proficiency in this art young Hart turned to the painting of portraits. He also tried landscapes, for which he showed a greater aptitude, and developed his ability in that field. With the help of some friends he was able to visit his native Scotland and there he roamed about the countryside, absorbing the beauties of nature and trying in his own way to transfer them to canvas. Upon his return to the United States he opened a studio in New York City and there painted landscapes in the traditional manner of the Hudson River School. Some of his scenes show cattle in the midst of rolling valleys, with the details of the vegetation and trees clearly brought out, causing lack of unity of the whole. In 1858 he became a member of the National Academy of Design. He was the first president of the Brooklyn Academy of Design and helped to organise the American Society of Water Colorists, acting as its president for some years. He died at his home in Mt. Vernon, New York, 17th June 1894 and was buried in Brooklyn.

Bibliography: C. H. Caffin, *Story of American Painting,* 1907.—G. W. Sheldon, *American Painters,* 1881. —H. T. Tuckerman, *Book of the Artists,* 1867.

**HARUNOBU (Suzuki).**—Japanese painter and printer. Born at Yedo, 1725 to 1770. Pupil of Shigenaga. He is believed to have begun his career in the style of the early masters; but the influence which endured longest was that of Masanobu. From him he learned to acquire a gracious familiarity with his subjects, even when interpreting scenes from mythology or history; then, like him, he surrounded his principal subject with details, and

Harunobu: The basin of red fish. (Color print, British Museum.)

gave it a foreground and middle-distance to make it more life-like. Finally, he adopted Masanobu's most up-to-date manner of interpreting backgrounds.

Harunobu: Horseman on a bridge talking to a woman. (Color print, Vever Collection.)

Harunobu was the inventor of true polychrome printing, which he gradually brought to perfection, passing from two or three blocks to six, seven or more.

Among his many prints may be mentioned: *Woman on the Stairs of a Temple; Woman on a Snow-covered Bridge; Two Women by the Sea-shore* (one with a crab attached to her sandal), etc.

In his last years, c. 1764, Harunobu published the first books in polychrome printing, which were called, probably on account of their bright appearance, *nishiki-e* (brocades). He usually used scenes of everyday life for these polychrome prints, eschewing portraits of actors and courtesans. His style, which had a great delicacy, had an overwhelming influence on his contemporaries.

Harunobu had a number of pupils, among them Isoda Koriusai.

See Pl. 40, Vol. I. and see Japan —Art, Prints.

Bibliography: J. Kurth, *Harunobu* (Suzuki), 1910.

**HASENAUER (Karl F. von).**—Viennese architect, 1833-1894. A collaborator with Semper in the design of the Heldenplatz, Vienna, and the single author of, in the same city, the museums of Art History and of Natural History.

**HASSAM (Childe).**—American painter and etcher (1859-1935). He was born in Boston, Massachusetts, 17th October 1859, the descendant of old Colonial stock. He was fond of painting as a boy and began to study at the Boston Art School. He made some illustrations for magazines and about 1883 he went to Paris. There he worked under the guidance of Boulanger and Lefebvre, but the tenets of Monet were more inspiring than the old academic standards and soon he became definitely connected with the Impressionist movement. He came back to the United States and began to paint the long series of New England scenes which have made him famous: village streets, the little white wooden churches of the Colonial period, particularly the one at Old Lyme, the flaming tints of an autumn landscape, and figure studies in sunlit interiors or in the open air. All were treated from a very personal viewpoint with a lightness of touch and an extremely decorative sense. He attempted to express the vibrating rays of sunlight on objects by a technique of short brush strokes of clear bright colour carefully disposed on the canvas in close juxtaposition, which gave an air of coherence when viewed from a distance. At the close of the World War he was inspired by the flag-decked streets of New York in honour of the return of peace and managed to impart to his work some of the festive air and joyful spirit of the atmosphere of those stirring times. He won a prize in the Paris Exposition of 1889 and the gold medal of the Munich Exhibition in 1892 and after that time many awards in the United States and abroad. He was a member of the Ten American Painters and in 1906 was elected to full membership in the National Academy of Design. In his later years he devoted quite a lot of his time to making etchings of landscape studies and figure subjects, done in a crisp manner yet light as the strokes of his brush, suggesting the thinness of the atmosphere surrounding his models. He died after a year's illness 27th August 1935 at his home in East Hampton, Long Island. Although his impressionistic technique and subject matter seem very close to the work of Monet, still it was Childe Hassam's belief that the Impressionist movement began in England in the 18th century with the work of Constable, following the tradition of Bonington, who influenced the French Barbizon school of the next century.

See Pl. 62, Vol. II.

Bibliography: A. E. Gallatin, *Childe Hassam, a Note,* 1907.—Nathaniel Pousette-Dart, *Childe Hassam,* Distinguished American Artists Series, 1922.—F. T. Robinson, *Living New England Artists,* 1888.—*Catalogue of the Etchings and Drypoints of Childe Hassam,* with an introduction by Royal Cortissoz, 1925.—*Childe Hassam,* with an appreciation by James C. McGuire, American Etchers Series, Vol. 3, 1929.—*Handbook of the Complete Set of Etchings and Drypoints of Childe Hassam, N. A.,* Leonard Clayton Gallery, New York, 1933.

**HASTINGS (Thomas).**—American architect (1860-1929). He was born in New York City 11th March 1860, the descendant of a family which included both doctors and ministers. He studied for a time at Columbia University and then went to Paris to study architecture at the École des Beaux-Arts. There he worked under Jules André and received his diplôme from the French government in 1884. Back in New York City he entered the employ of McKim, Mead and White and there met again John Carrère. Two years later he entered into partnership with Carrère and the firm of Carrère and Hastings continued in existence for a long period of time, planning structures based mostly on French classic models. The firm was responsible for, among other buildings, the New York Public Library. After Carrère's death in 1911, Hastings developed a more eclectic style though always in the classic tradition. Among his chief works should be mentioned the Tower of Jewels for the Panama-Pacific Exposition at San Francisco in 1915, the Henry C. Frick home, the chapel of St. Ambrose in the Cathedral of St. John the Divine, and the Standard Oil Building on lower Broadway, all in New York City. He wrote many articles for periodicals and in 1917, with the assistance of Ralph Adams Cram and Claude Bragdon, published *Six Lectures on Architecture.* He was a Chevalier of the Legion of Honour and one of the founders of the Federal Art Commission. In 1922 he received a medal from the Royal Institute of British Architects in recognition of his work. He died 22d October 1929 in New York City after an operation.

Bibliography: *Thomas Hastings, Architect,* collected writings, together with a memoir by David Gray, 1933.

**HAWKSMOOR (Nicholas).**—British architect, 1661-1736. One of the foremost architects of the Georgian Period, Hawksmoor is known for his grandiose designs for Castle Howard, 1702; the Clarendon Press, Oxford; Queen's College, Oxford, 1710; and St. Mary's Woolnoth, 1713-1719.

**HAYDON (Benjamin Robert).**—English historical painter, 1786-1846. In 1809 he exhibited for the first time and won a great success with his picture of *Dentatus Killed by His Soldiers*, but he was dissatisfied with the way his work was exhibited, and afterwards only showed his paintings in private. The *Entry of Christ into Jerusalem*, which is now in America, is one of his best works. Among his other paintings may be mentioned: the *Raising of Lazarus* (1823), *Xenophon* (1832), and *Nero Watching Rome Burn*.

**HAYEZ (Francesco).**—Italian painter (1791-1882), the author of "genre" pictures, reminiscent of Dutch painting, especially of Terburg. His best known work is *The Kiss*, now in the Brera Gallery.

**HEALY (George Peter Alexander).**—American painter (1808-1894) a much-patronised portrait painter, who produced likenesses of a large number of celebrities of his time, American and European.

**HÉBERT (Ernest).**—French painter, 1817-1908. After studying under David d'Angers, then under Delaroche, he won the Prix de Rome in 1840. He had already exhibited an early picture, *Tasso in Prison* (1839, Grenoble). In Italy he acquired a very personal style, and a taste for a rather sickly and melancholy type of Italian beauty. Nevertheless, the last picture he sent from Rome and finished in Paris—the *Kiss of Judas* (1854, Luxembourg) is a fine picture in its way. His favourite subjects were Italian, following on the great success of his picture *Malaria* (1850, Louvre).

Hébert was director of the Académie de France, in Rome, from 1867 to 1873. In accordance with a vow which he made during the war of 1870, he there painted a picture (the *Virgin of the Deliverance*) for the Church of la Tronche, his native village. Inspired by Byzantine Madonnas, this Virgin, tragic, with enormous eyes, was popularised by

HÉBERT: MALARIA. (Louvre.)

a fine engraving by Huet. He repeated this subject several times, with variations. His best pictures of this kind are the *Madonna Addolorata* (1873) and the *Sleep of the Infant Christ* (1895). Hébert returned to Paris in 1882, and died at a ripe old age, painting till his last day.

He designed mosaics for the Panthéon and for the Louvre (Escalier Daru).

His graceful, supple style is that of a gifted painter, skilful in his use of light and shade. His colour is deep and warm. He may be criticised for the abuse of certain greenish tones, and for his obsession for a certain feminine type, rather sickly and melancholy, which too often led him into repeating a mere formula.

**HEDA (Willem Claasz).**—Dutch painter (about 1594-about 1680-82) of Haarlem. He was influenced by P. Claesz and painted still-life groups in neutral colours, with effects of light and shade, and reflections of silver and glass on his grey background such as one may admire in his *Still Life* in the Louvre.

HEDA: STILL LIFE. (M. Labouret Collection.)

**HEEM (Jan Davidsz de).**—Dutch painter (1606-1683/4). Worked at Leyden, Utrecht and Antwerp. He was a brilliant painter of still-life, flowers, fruits and animals. His pictures have a brightness and a vivacity of colour which give them a jewel-like quality. He had a son, Cornelis (1631-1695), who imitated him ably.

**HEEMSKERCK (Martin van).**—Dutch painter, 1498-1574. His real name was Martin van Veen. He was a pupil of Jan van Scorel, and imitated his style in the picture of *St. Luke Painting the Portrait of the Virgin* (1532). He then went to Rome, where he imitated Michelangelo. Recently some interesting portraits have been attributed to him.

BIBLIOGRAPHY: Preibisz, Leon, *Martin von Heemskerck*. Halle, 1910.—Friedländer, M. J., *Altniederländische Malerei*, Vol. 13.

**HEERE (Lucas de).**—Flemish painter (1534-1584) of Ghent, worked also in France and England; exiled for a while from his native country as a Protestant. He painted numerous portraits.

**HEIDELBERG (Baden, Germany).**—The *Castle*, or the Heinrichsbau, was destroyed by lightning in 1764, so that only the splendid 16th-century façade remains.

The *Friedrichsbau* (1601-1607), in the German Renaissance style, is adorned with sixteen statues of the Electors Palatine and their forefathers.

**HELIOPOLIS.**—See Baalbek.

**HELST (Bartholomeus van der).**—Dutch portrait painter (about 1613-1670). Very little is known of

HELST (VAN DER): PORTRAIT OF PAUL POTTER. (Museum, The Hague.)

his life, but so great was his reputation in his own time that he was preferred to Rembrandt. He painted a great many portraits of rich citizens of Amsterdam: the Burgomaster Bicker, the Lieutenant Admiral Kortenaar, and the four heads of the Confraternity of St. Sebastian. All these pictures are in the Museum of Amsterdam. At The Hague is a fine portrait of Paul Potter; in Leningrad, the portrait of Govart Flinck; in Munich, that of Admiral Tromp.

Besides these portraits, which were painted in a broad style with fine colour and rich accessories, Van der Helst painted some large Corporation pictures, and banquet scenes—such as: the *Civic Guards of Captain Roelos Bicker* (Amsterdam, 1639), and the *Banquet for the Peace of Westphalia* (1648), his masterpiece.

It shows twenty-five people sitting round a table. The heads are full of life and expression. The hands have always aroused so much admiration that it has been said that, if they were put in a heap, one could recognise to whom they belonged. The rich dresses, bright scarves, and numerous accessories give this painting an appearance of great richness. It does not reveal the genius of a Hals; but it shows the equality of workmanship, the ability in staging a scene, and the brilliant colour which characterises official pictures.

BIBLIOGRAPHY: J. J. de Gelder, *Bartholomeus von der Helst*. Rotterdam, 1921.

**HEMESSEN (Jan Sanders, called Van).**—Painter of the Flemish school of Antwerp, 16th century. Born about 1500 in Hemessen, near Antwerp. He became a member of the guild in 1524; and he may have lived in Haarlem after 1551. He probably died before 1566. He was greatly influenced by the painting of Matsys and Jan Gossart, and he made several copies after them of popular scenes. His drawing is hard; his colour, vigorous, and sometimes strange, with many brown tones.

In 1536, he painted a *Calling of St. Matthew* (Munich); in 1541, a *St. Jerome* (Prague, and a copy in the Brussels Gallery); in 1556, a *Christ Driving the Money Lenders from the Temple* (Nancy); in 1556, the *Prodigal Son* (Brussels). His best picture is the *Village Surgeon* (Prado).

BIBLIOGRAPHY: Graefe, F.; *Jan Sanders v. Heemessen u. s. Identification mit dem Braunschweiger Monogrammisten*. Leipzig, 1909.—Friedländer, M. J., *Altniederländische Malerei*, Vol. 13.

**HENNER (Jean Jacques).**—French painter (Alsace, 1829-1905). After studying in Strasbourg, he went to Basle, where he studied Holbein, who influenced him for some time (see, in the Luxembourg, his Portrait of the Curé Hugard). In 1857 he returned to Paris and the same year he won the Prix de Rome with his picture of *Adam and Eve Finding the Body of Abel*. In Rome, where he became acquainted with Carpeaux and Chapu, he worked hard, studied old masters, and travelled. The last work he sent from Rome, *Suzanna* (1863, Luxembourg), was exhibited at the Salon. He returned to Paris, which he only left for short visits to Holland, Spain and to his native village in Alsace where he spent two months every year. Soon his style changed. He fell under the influence of Correggio and of Prud'hon, painting supple luminous figures against dark backgrounds. In this type of painting he evolved an individuality independent of models, and he produced some pieces of exquisite colour and modelling. Unfortunately, success induced him to

HENNER: IDYL. (Musée du Luxembourg.)

repeat himself and his technique became slipshod. Some of his best works are already spoiled by cracks and restorations necessitated by this negligence. Perhaps the use of bitumen may have caused this deterioration. He painted numerous portraits; the painter Schnetz (1863), who was his director at the Villa Medici; General Chanzy (1873); but his best and most characteristic pictures are of nude women, which he painted under different titles. A few of them are: the *Woman Reading*, the *Nymph* (Luxembourg), *Idyl* (Luxembourg). Henner's range was narrow, but within his limits he is distinguished, and no painter in the 19th century surpassed him in painting the human body bathed in a nocturnal atmosphere.

**HENRI (Robert).**—American painter (1865-1929). He was born 25th June 1865 in Cincinnati, Ohio. His early ambition for a writing career was given up in favour of studying painting. At the age of twenty he entered the Pennsylvania Academy of Fine Arts, where he worked under Thomas P. Anschutz for the next two years. In 1888 he went to Paris to study at the École des Beaux-Arts and also at the Académie Julian under Bouguereau and Fleury. Later he travelled through Holland, Brittany, Italy and Spain and was much impressed with the work of Hals, Manet and Velazquez. Three years later he took a position as instructor at the Women's School of Design in Philadelphia. But in 1894 he returned again to Paris to teach an international class of students. The summer of 1899 was spent at Concarneau and then he returned to New York to open a studio which became the headquarters of the so-called pre-War realists. He passed the next years teaching his methods of painting at the Veltin School, the Chase School, the Ferrar School, and the Art Students' League. In 1908 he became a member of the "Eight," which society included A. B. Davies, William J. Glackens, Ernest Lawson, George Luks, Maurice Prendergast, Everett Shinn and John Sloan. After 1906 Henri spent much of his time travelling to Spain, Holland, France, Italy, England, Ireland and Mexico, that he might make character studies of the natives in their picturesque garb. He also enjoyed making sketches of childhood, preferably poor urchins with expressions of eagerness or joy lighting up their thin faces. In 1923 there was published *The Art Spirit*, a curious collection of pithy and epigrammatic sayings compiled from the class notes of his pupils, advice on specific problems and general criticism of the system of close copying of the work and methods of any one artist. Henri's last few summers were passed in County Mayo, Ireland, where his keen delight in racial studies was allowed full play. On the way back from Ireland in 1929 he was taken ill and died in New York 12th July of that year. His ability to create a mood, whether in portraiture or a phase of nature, through the employment of vivid colouring neatly disposed in a harmonious blending of tones is the characteristic motif of his work. His racial studies reveal his keen observation and the translation of the facial peculiarities of the region by the use of a few simple strokes cleverly placed and set off by the bright colours and the suggestion of chiaroscuro.

BIBLIOGRAPHY: Nathaniel Pousette-Dart, *Robert Henri*, Distinguished American Artists Series, 1922.—Helen Appleton Read, *Robert Henri*, American Artists Series, 1931. —William Yarrow and Louis Bouché, ed., *Robert Henri, His Life and Works*, 1921.—For a more complete bibliography see *The Index of Twentieth Century Artists* for January, 1935.

**HEREFORD (England).**—*Cathedral*, 1099-1352. An archiepiscopal cross church terminating in a Lady Chapel. The nave and choir are Norman with Loucet vaults. The rest of Hereford is Loucet, except for the Decorated lantern.

**HERKOMER (Sir Hubert Von).** —English painter of Bavarian origin (1849-1914). He was a much employed portrait painter during the Victorian era, while among his noted subject pictures are *The Charterhouse Chapel, My Village, Souvenir of Rembrandt.* He was Slade Professor at Oxford from 1885 to 1894.

**HERMES OF PRAXITELES.**— See Greece (Sculpture); also Pl. 24, Vol. I.

**HERLIN (Friedrich).**—German painter, about 1435-1500. School of Nördlingen. His chief works are the high-altar of the Church of St. George (Nördlingen, 1462); the altarpiece of St. James of Rothenburg (1466); the votive triptych (1488), and some *Nativities* and *Annunciations*. He imitated Flemish painters.

BIBLIOGRAPHY: F. Haack, *Friedrich Herlin.* Strasbourg, 1900.

**HERNÁNDEZ or FERNÁNDEZ (Gregorio).**—(Born c. 1576 in Galicia; died 1636 in Valladolid.) J. Agàpito y Revilla states that the national art of sculpture crystallizes in this carver and painter of wooden images. The German art historian G. Weise points out that Hernández is the representative of the third phase in the development of Castilian sculpture, a phase of naturalism following upon a classicistic current which in turn was preceded by the ecstatic style of the early baroque of the first half of the 16th century as represented by Alonso de Berrugute and Juan de Juni. "Instead of heroic pathos and representations of an idealized world rendered by conventional and classicistic formulas ("Romanismus"), we witness now the appearance of a creative urge imbued with feelings in conformity with the national character striving after reality. . . . Zurbarán represents in painting the new style of an objectivity without pretense . . . and at Valladolid Gregorio Hernández is the trailblazer of the new tendency." Maria Elena Gómez-Moreno states the reasons why Gregorio should be called the only really great sculptor of XVIIth century Castile: "the predominant note is derived from his religious feelings which are profoundly sincere. He endeavours to transmit them by means of an interpretation which, perhaps, is too human but none the less very efficacious." "His interpretation of form is sober and naturalistic . . . his nudes are exclusively masculine and not, as so often as those by others, a demonstration of anatomical learning. . . . The principal interest is almost always centered in the heads which carry a tremendous emotional force. . . . On the other hand his treatment of clothes resembles pleated paper doubled in rigid folds which stand out from the body. . ."

A. L. Mayer emphasizes the fact that whereas Alonso de Berrugute, Juan de Juni and Becerra decorated their statues with rich gilding and enameled the flesh-tones, Gregorio prefers subdued color-tones allowing for a frank naturalistic effect. This naturalism is still further heightened by the insertion of glass eyes and sometimes by the application of glass tears.

We are uncertain about the facts of his life until 1605 when, upon order of Philip IV, he sets up a workshop at Valladolid. A contract for an altar for the Church of San Miguel at Valladolid dates from 1606. His great predilection for the scenes of the Passion can be seen in the *pasos* (processional figures) at the Museum of Valladolid (1614). He executed a great number of statues and altars, among them the *Holy Family* for the Church of San Lorenzo of Valladolid (1621); the High altar as well as the two lateral altars for the Franciscan monastery of Eibar (1624-29); the altar for San Miguel at Vitoria (1632), etc. The altars and some of the choir-stalls of the Franciscan monastery at Aranzaza, begun in 1627, were finished in 1635 shortly before his death. A portrait of Gregorio Hernández, probably by Valentín Diaz, is preserved at the Museum of Valladolid.

BIBLIOGRAPHY: *Thieme-Becker*, Vol. XI. Leipzig, 1915; art. *Fernández (Hernández), Gregorio* by A. L. Mayer.—M. Dieulafoy, *La statuaire polychrome en Espagne*. Paris, 1928. —*Museo provincial de bellas artes de Valladolid. Catal. secciòn de escultura.* Valladolid, 1916. (By Juan Agàpito y Revilla).—A. L. Mayer, *Spanische barock-plastik.* Munich, 1923.—R. de Orueta, *Gregorio Hernández.* Colección Popular.—*Enciclop. universal ilustrad. europeo-americana*, Vol. XXIII. Barcelona 1924. Art. *Fernández (Gregorio)*.—G. Weise, *Spanische Plastik aus sieben Jahrhunderten.* Reutlingen, 1927.—*Junta superior de estudios é investigaciones scientificas, Centro de estudios historicos,* El museo nacional de escultura de Valladolid. Valladolid, 1933.—Maria Elena Gómez-Moreno. *Breve historia de la escultura española.* Madrid, Misiones de arte, 1935.

**HERRERA (or HERRERA HINESTROSA) FRANCISCO, also called el Mozo (the younger).** —Spanish painter and architect who was born in Seville in 1622 and died at Madrid in 1685. The tyrannical character of his father Francisco Herrera, *el Viejo* may be one of the reasons why he left for Rome where, it is supposed, he remained until 1656, date of the latter's death. His predilection for painting fish earned him the by-name "lo Spagnuolo degli pesci." (The *Fish-Vendor*—Berlin, Block coll.; *Boy with Fish* at Städelsche Institut, Frankfurt is, according to Mayer, by him and not by Murillo; etc.) Upon his return to Seville he painted the *Triunfo del Santisimo Sacramento* (Cathedral, *Capilla Sacramental*) and a year later (1657) the *Ascension of St. Francis* (Cathedral, Chapel of St. Francis). Concurrently with the foundation of the Seville Academy (1660) he became its sub-director. Ten Spanish artists who in the same year submitted to the King the plan for foundation of a Spanish academy in Rome suggested him as president. He became instructor in drawing to Charles II and in 1672 he was given the position of Pintor del Rey. In 1677 he became Maestro mayor de las Obras de Palacio. Many of his frescoes executed at Madrid are partly destroyed or poorly preserved. The finest quality of many of his paintings is the color, the glow of which recalls the great Venetians. Some of these works are: *Ecce Homo* and *Christ Bearing the Cross*, Madrid, Cerralbo Coll.; *St. Leo, Pope*, Madrid, Prado Mus. As an architect he created the first important Baroque Cathedral, provided the plans for *Nuestra Sra. del Pilar at Saragossa* are his (A. L. Mayer, passim).

BIBLIOGRAPHY: A. L. Mayer, *Geschichte der span. Malerei.* Leipzig, 1922.—Id. in *Thieme-Becker*, Vol. XVI. Leipzig, 1923; art. *Herrera, Francisco.*—Sentenach, *La pintura en Madrid*, 1907.—Schubert, *Gesch. des Barock in Spanien*, 1908.—*Encicloped. univers. ilustrad. europeo-amer.* Vol. XXVII. Barcelona (Espasa) 1925. Art. *Herrera el Mozo.*

**— (Francisco de).**—Called "el Viejo" ("the Old") to distinguish him from his youngest son Herrera "el Mozo" ("the Younger"). Spanish painter (Seville, 1576-Madrid, 1656).

HERRERA: ST. BASIL PREACHING HIS DOCTRINE. (Museum, Seville.)

Herrera had a strange, intensely passionate nature, and his art resembles the man. He painted emotional and dramatic subjects—martyrdoms, tortures of the damned, apocalyptic visions. His execution has a certain force which, while it disconcerts, commands admiration. Moreover, his drawing is very correct and true; and his colour, strongly contrasted, is always harmonious. He knew how to render the Monks and Priests of Spain. The choice of types, the composition, his lighting effects, and the energy of his painting, are very personal, although his early works show the influence of Juan de las Ruelas, who was (with Herrera) the creator of the new indigenous school of Seville. From his early period dates the *Last Judgment*, which adorns the Church of San Bernardo—an enormous painting, somewhat pedantic, in which Herrera already shows his powers of composition, anatomical knowledge, and fine colour. More interesting is his *Pentecost* (1617), probably from the church of St. Inés. Now in the Greco Museum at Toledo.

Herrera's personality expresses itself still more strongly in the *St. Basil Dictating his Doctrine*, painted for the Church of that saint in Seville, and now in the Louvre. Another powerful canvas dedicated to St. Basil, and representing the saint with Christ and the Apostles, is in the provincial museum of Seville (another version in the Louvre), which also possesses his very impressive *St. Hermenegild* (painted before 1624). Likewise in Seville is one of his most important works—the fresco which decorates the dome of the Church of St. Bonaventura; for which the artist, in 1629, painted four pictures (other paintings for this cycle were done by Zurbaran), the subjects of which were taken from the life of the doctor saint, and which formed part of the collection of the Earl of Clarendon; two are now in the collection of Dr. Carvalho (France); the third was donated to the Prado Museum; the fourth is lost.

Herrera was an excellent etcher, and he also produced medals. This work, which the artist enveloped in mystery, caused him to be denounced as a false-coiner, and threatened with the galleys. He had to take refuge in the Jesuit Monastery of St. Hermenegild. He only obtained his pardon and recovered his liberty in 1624, on the occasion of Philip IV's visit to Seville, when the king greatly admired and praised the superb *Triumph of St. Hermenegild* which Herrera had, in testimony of his gratitude, painted for an altarpiece. Also "His genre pictures (called Bodegones) contributed greatly to his fame." (Coll. Czernin, Vienna; Mus. Nantes; Mus. Avignon.)

On resuming his work he became still more bitter and fierce. His wife left him; his daughter entered a convent; and his youngest son, Herrera el Mozo, fled to Italy. His pupils had deserted his studio. His eldest son, Herrera el Rubio, died in the flower of manhood, having given rise to great hopes as a painter. Herrera's mood became darker and darker. He left Seville in 1650, and died in Madrid in 1656. During his stay in Madrid he was subjected to the influence of the Venetians (*Christ Bearing the Cross*) Madrid, University.

Besides his two sons, Herrera had among his pupils Francesco de Reina, Ignacio Iriarte, and, most famous of all, Diego Velázquez, who, however, only stayed a few months with this tyrannical master.

# IVORY

*Ivory is a rare material which since ancient times has been dedicated to the making of little carved objects. Ivories are among the works which have from antiquity served to spread the ornamental or iconographical themes; they give valuable documents for epochs which have left no monumental sculptor or painting. On the transition from the ancient to the Christian world, on the relations of the Orient and the Occident, ivories carry unique evidence.*

LID OF THE CASKET OF VEROLI. VICTORIA AND ALBERT MUSEUM.

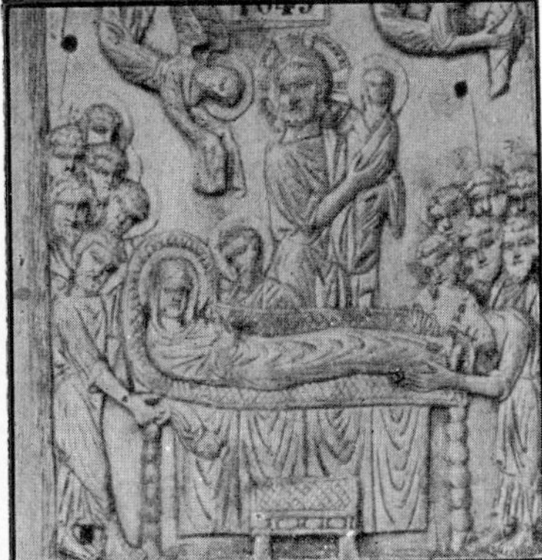

BOOK COVER. CAROLINGIAN ART. MUSÉE DE CLUNY. *(Photo by Hachette.)*

CHRIST ON THE CROSS. CAROLINGIAN ART. MUSÉE DE CLUNY. *(Photo by Hachette.)*

CAROLINGIAN IVORY. EVANGELISTARY COVER. BIBL. NAT. *(Photo by Giraudon.)*

TRIPTYCH. FRENCH ART, FOURTEENTH CENTURY. MUSÉE DE CLUNY. *(Photo by Hachette.)*

DETAIL OF THE COVER OF THE PSALTER OF CHARLES THE BALD, BIBL. NAT. *(Photo by Giraudon.)*

VIRGIN AND CHILD. FRENCH ART, FOURTEENTH CENTURY. LOUVRE.

CORONATION OF THE VIRGIN. IVORY, FRENCH ART, THIRTEENTH CENTURY. LOUVRE. *(Photo by Hachette.)*

DESCENT FROM THE CROSS. FRENCH ART, TWELFTH CENTURY. LOUVRE.

## Gothic Ivories

When the Gothic sculpture had developed a plastic system independent of the Byzantine iconography, the little ivory figures also changed in style and reproduced in miniature the elegance of the great monumental statuary. It is not difficult to recognise the source which unites most of the ivory Virgins in the Vierge Dorée of Amiens. The little tableaux of the triptychs are designed and composed exactly like the contemporary miniatures of the psalters which they imitate.

# GIOTTO AND THE GIOTTESQUE PAINTERS

*There are two particularly important moments in the pictorial arts of the Middle Ages: the end of the twelfth century when for the first time the French sculptors worked statues in stone; and the beginning of the fourteenth century when the Tuscan painters rediscovered the secret of the living form. The two inventions are otherwise joined, and Giotto, in his frescoes with figures strongly constructed, transposed into painting the essentials of sculpture. Painting deprived of its usual partner, sculpture, during the long Byzantine period, had lost the sense of relief, until Giotto found it again.*

GIOTTO: NATIVITY. PADUA.
*(Photo by Alinari.)*

GIOTTO: JOACHIM AND THE SHEPHERDS. PADUA.
*(Photo by Alinari.)*

GIOTTO: PIETÀ. PADUA.
*(Photo by Alinari.)*

## Giotto

Giotto is a Florentine painter of the beginning of the fourteenth century whose best authenticated work is the frescoes in the Arena Chapel in Padua. These represent the traditional episodes of the life of the Virgin and Christ. But the composition is so happy, the forms so true, the attitudes so expressive, the colour so beautiful that the stories seem to have been encountered for the first time. Giotto is one of the most beautiful inventors of forms and expressive compositions; for inspiration there is only Fra Angelico who has been as moving.

SCHOOL OF GIOTTO: ST. FRANCIS ESPOUSING POVERTY. ASSISI.
*(Photo by Alinari.)*

GIOTTO: DEATH OF ST. FRANCIS. FLORENCE.
*(Photo by Anderson.)*

SCHOOL OF GIOTTO: ST. FRANCIS RENOUNCING HIS FAMILY. ASSISI.
*(Photo by Anderson.)*

## Giotto

We have acquired the habit of attributing to Giotto numerous frescoes in the church at Assisi, and this attribution seems to justify itself so much that a comparison is often made between the action of Giotto in art and that of St. Francis in the religious life. In reality, the frescoes of Assisi as a whole do not appear to be by the same hand that painted the Arena Chapel at Padua. Another group of frescoes at Santa Croce in Florence seems to be worthy of the hand of the master of Padua. They have a very rare beauty, in spite of damage and restorations.

ANDREA DA FIRENZE: ROAD TO CALVARY. FLORENCE.
*(Photo by Alinari.)*

ANDREA ORCAGNA: LAST JUDGMENT. FLORENCE.
*(Photo by Alinari.)*

TADDEO GADDI: PRESENTATION IN THE TEMPLE. FLORENCE.
*(Photo by Alinari.)*

## The Followers of Giotto

We call "Giottesque" innumerable painters who in the course of the fourteenth century covered with frescoes the walls of the churches and monasteries of Tuscany. They scarcely attained the power of composition and expressive spirit of Giotto. They are in general very puzzled as to the disposition of their figures in space. The most striking defect of the period is a total ignorance of the laws of perspective. But the colour is always clear and light and the decoration has a pure gaiety.

Some of his engravings are: Title page for *Comentarios sobre S. Tomás* (1625); a large leaf with SS. Justa and Rufina, King Philip IV, Conde-Duque de olivares and their wives (1627); St. Ferdinand (document of payment 1637).

See Pl. 32, Vol. II.

BIBLIOGRAPHY: J. Gestoso y Perez, *Guia artistica de Sevilla,* 1886.—J. Gestoso y Perez, *Artif. Sevillanos,* 1899.—A. L. Mayer, *Sevillaner Malerschule,* 1911.—Id., *Geschichte der span. malerei.* Leipzig, 1922.—Id., art. *Herrera, Francisco, gen. el Viejo* in *Thieme-Becker.,* Vol. XVI. Leipzig, 1923.—*Enciclop. univers. ilustrad. europeo-americana,* Vol. XXVII. Barcelona (Espasa) 1925. Art. *Herrera el Viejo.*

**— (Juan de).**—Spanish architect, 1530-1597. Favorite architect of Philip II and the personality most closely connected with the austere and gloomy Manneristic architecture of late 16th century Spain. He succeeded Juan Bautista as architect of the Escorial, which is substantially his design. He also designed, in the same style, the Cathedral of Valladolid, begun 1585, and La Lonja, Seville, 1584-1588.

**HEXASTYLE.**—See Greece (Architecture).

**HIERON.**—See Greece (Vases).

**HIGHMORE (Joseph).**—English painter (1692-1780), pupil of Kneller. Principally known for his portraits, though he occasionally treated *genre* subjects (e.g., the charming *Pamela* series, now divided between the National Gallery, Millbank, the Fitzwilliam Museum, Cambridge, and the National Gallery of Victoria, Melbourne).

**HILDEBRAND (Adolf).**—German sculptor, born in 1847. He preached a return to the antique.

"His theories of art, as set forth in a book which had a great influence, *The Problem of Form,* marks the beginning of a renaissance founded on better-understood tradition."

**HILDESHEIM (Germany).**—*St. Michael,* 1001-1033. Rebuilt 1186. An important monument for the study of Ottonian architecture, St. Michael has inside heavy piers alternating with columns and is covered by a timber roof. The complication of the west end, here seen to so great an extent for the first time, effects a profound transformation of the basilican tradition. There are eastern and western lanterns, transepts and apses.

*St. Godehard,* 1133-1172. A Romanesque church, St. Godehard shows the persistence in Germany of Ottonian principles in its obvious dependence upon the earlier church of St. Michael.

**HINDU ART.**—See India; also Pl. 35, Vol. I.

**HIROSHIGE (Ando).**—Japanese painter and printer, 1797-1858. Son of a pump-maker of Yedo, he was the pupil of Toyohiro. He is as realistic as Hokusai, but less lyrical, and more poetic and tender. He expressed better than any, and with amazing skill in rendering atmospheric effects, the idyllic and true Japan, and this with a harmony of colour and a perfection of workmanship which derives from the best eighteenth century masters.

He painted series of flowers, birds, fishes, and, above all, a famous series of landscapes:—the *Eight Views of Omi,* the *Kinko hakkei,* the *Toto Meisho,* the *Kyoto Meisho,* for which Kunisada appears to have painted the figures; the *Tokaido* (one of the most remarkable); and the *Houcho Meisho.* By Hiroshige also are the *Hundred Views of Yedo,* and the *Thirty-six Views of Fuji*—landscapes remarkable for their grandeur. With the simplest means—a few flat colours—the artist rendered a thousand delicate and fleeting aspects of nature.

Pl. 40, Vol. I. See Japan—Art.

HIROSHIGE: MOONLIT LANDSCAPE.

**HIROSHIGE II.**—Japanese painter and printer, whose very existence is not certain. He produced works so close in style to those of his master that it is difficult to know whether one or two personalities existed under the name of Hiroshige.

Hiroshige II is sometimes credited with the following series of landscapes:—the *Little Tokaido,* the *Kisokaido,* the *Hundred Provinces,* and the *Thirty-six Views of Yedo,* which show, rather more slightly, the remarkable qualities of the master.

**HIROTAKA.**—Japanese painter, 10th century. Grandson of the celebrated Kanoaka. He is said to have painted the first Japanese picture of "Hell," a vast composition, kept in a temple of the province of Oumi.

**HITTITE ART.**—Hittite is a term now applied to a wide cultural and ethnical area of ancient Asia Minor, bordering on Mesopotamia. Strictly speaking, it should apply only to the original Nasi whose dominance over the Hittite Empire was terminated about 1800 B.C. when they were conquered by the Khatti. In the western portion of this region the artistic style was dominated by Khatti, Hittite influence, while in the east the Khurri-Mitani strain held sway. In Syria both these streams mingled with the Aramaic. The most important finds have been made at Karkemish, Malatia, Boghazkoi, Euyuk, Yasili Kaya, Zenzurli, and Tell Halaf. The excavations at Tell Halaf have raised the very important problem of the dating of the earlier Hittite monuments. Herzfeld has placed the earliest pieces even prior to 2000 B.C. The inscribed reliefs of the Palace of Capar would seem to indicate a date of about 1200 B.C. but since they are obviously not all in the same style this date must be taken as the point ante quem. These stone sculptures were certainly taken from earlier buildings, inscribed and reused by Capar. Hittite art differs from Sumerian in that the former is always in large scale. However, there are connections in iconography and style. The earlier Hittite works are crude but extremely powerful and inventive. The later sculpture is much closer to Assyrian art, and although the former has often been considered a provincial copy of the latter, it is quite possible that the origins of Assyrian art are to be found in the earlier Hittite style.

**HITTORFF (Jacques Ignace).**—French architect (1792-1867). He built:—the Church St. Vincent-de-Paul (in collaboration with Le Père), 1824-1844; the Circus of the Champs Elysées; the *Gare du Nord* (1861-1865), in which Hittorff tackled new problems with great boldness.

BIBLIOGRAPHY: A. Normand, *Notice sur la vie et les ouvrages de J. I. Hittorff.*

**HOBBEMA (Meindert).**—Dutch painter, 1638-1709. Next to Ruisdael, he is the most famous of the Dutch landscape painters. Little is known of his life. He was probably born in Amsterdam. He married, in 1668, and had a son and two daughters. He died in poverty.

HOBBEMA: THE MILL. (Louvre.)

Hobbema is the painter of the pleasant, familiar Dutch countryside. He loved to represent little red-roofed houses, canals, tree-shadowed streams, and, above all, water-mills which appear in nearly all his paintings. His drawing is precise, minute, able. His rendering of trees, feathery or thickly branched, and of reflections of the sky in water, are very happy; but his colour is often dull, and his compositions are monotonous.

At the age of nineteen, he painted *The Water-Mill* (1657) of the Bridgewater Gallery. Among his best works are the following:—*The Water-Mill* (Wallace Collection); *The Village* (National Gallery); *The Edge of the Forest* (Dutuit Collection); *Dutch Village,* and *The Old Oak Trees* (both in the Louvre); two landscapes in Buckingham Palace; *The Water-Mill,* of the Rothschild Collection. But the two most celebrated pictures by Hobbema are *The Water-Mill,* in the Louvre, and *The Avenue at Middelharnis,* in the National Gallery. The Louvre picture shows a little mill, great trees, and a sky which is reflected in the water; it is well composed, and harmonious; and the colour is gayer than in most of the painter's works. In *The Avenue* the picture is, as it were, cut in two by a straight road bordered with tall, slender trees, which are bare of foliage except for tufts at the top, like a plume. Some shrubs, rose trees, two or three houses, a village lightly indicated in the distance, and a fine sky, form a picturesque and delightful whole.

See Pl. 37, Vol. II.

BIBLIOGRAPHY: E. Michel, *Hobbema et les paysagistes de son temps en Hollande.* Paris, 1890.—Hofstede de Groot, *Catalogue raisonné,* Vol. IV, 1911.

**HODLER (Ferdinand).**—Swiss painter, born 1853. Considered as one of the leaders of the modern school in his country.

**HOFER (Karl).**—Contemporary German painter. He was born at Karlsruhe 11th October 1878. He studied art at the Karlsruhe Academy under Poetzelberger and Kalckreuth from 1896 to 1900. That year he went to Paris to work and from there he went to attend classes at the Academy of Stuttgart, and later entered the atelier of Hans Thoma in Zurich. From 1903 to 1908 he was in Rome in the studio of Herm and then from that time until 1913 he was working in Paris. He made other trips to Zurich and Berlin and settled permanently in the latter city in 1919. The next year he was named a professor in the School of Applied Arts in Berlin and in 1925 he became a member of the Prussian Academy of Fine Arts. Hofer early was influenced by the style of Puvis de Chavannes, Cézanne, Picasso and Derain, but after the war his tendencies changed and he became more interested in abstractions and expressionism. His figures are stylised to such an extent that they resemble cut-out bits of wood that have come alive. Among his favourite subjects are circuses, intimate home scenes, nudes, portraits and still lifes. The compositions are arranged in a classical manner with the centre of interest made up of simplified elements which are yet capable of expressing the desired symbolism. Occasionally there are pictures which recall the compositions of Dirk Bouts and van Oostsanen, but others are peculiarly modern in their subject matter and treatment. His *Kartenspieler* is very close in subject to the *Card Players* of Cézanne, but the figures are as flat caricatures rather than living people engrossed in the problems of the game. Examples of Hofer's work may be seen in the museums of Berlin, Cologne, Detroit, Dresden, Hamburg, Munich, Rome and Vienna.

BIBLIOGRAPHY: Benno Reifenberg, *Karl Hofer,* 1924.

**HOFFMAN (Josef)** 1870.—Viennese architect and pupil of Otto

Wagner, instrumental in effecting the change from "art nouveau" to the modern style. In 1903 he founded the Viennese Workshops, a spiritual successor to the Arts and Crafts Exhibition in England and forerunner of the Bauhaus at Dessau. He designed, in 1898, the Exhibition Rooms of the Vienna Secession. Other designs include the Stoclet House, Brussels, and exhibition pavilions at the expositions at Cologne, 1914, and Paris, 1925.

**HOFFMAN (Malvina).**—Contemporary American sculptor. She was born in New York City 15th June 1887. Her father was Richard Hoffman, a pianist of note. While still a child she became interested in painting and spent six years under the tutelage of John W. Alexander. At the age of twenty-two her interest turned to sculpture when she made a bust of her father. He died soon after it was completed and Malvina, accompanied by her mother, left for Europe to study. In Paris she worked at the Academy and took anatomy lessons. After some time spent with Herbert Adams and Gutzon Borglum she became the pupil of Auguste Rodin. In his studio she strove to emulate his great work, trying to understand the method back of his expression. Her own style developed, at once alive and reflective, imaginative and realistic, imbued with a strong vitality. Her subject matter varied, including portrait busts, large groups for memorials, animal and garden pieces. Her early fame was based on studies of the dance personified by Pavlowa, one of her intimate friends. She also had some outside interests and in 1919 became director of the National and Foreign Information of the Red Cross in New York City. She founded the Appui aux Artistes in Paris and served on the Relief Administration in Jugoslavia under Herbert Hoover. In 1920 she received a commission for a memorial to the Harvard men who lost their lives in the World War and for them she created *Sacrifice,* showing the sorrow of a mother left with the body of her son. More recently the Field Museum in Chicago gave her the commission of making figures to decorate their anthropological section to perpetuate the various "Races of Man." Accompanied by her husband, Samuel Grimson, and a British anthropologist, Sir Arthur Keith, she travelled around the world to little-known parts of Asia, Africa and Australia, gathering new material and modelling the figures in the native homes of her subjects. In the fall of 1932 she returned to New York with almost all of the required one hundred bronze figures and portrait busts, each distinguished by a strong expression of the racial characteristics of the subject. Some of these bronzes are in the form of groups where families are shown engaged in some typical employment of their region, while others are portrait heads of individuals chosen as typical examples of their race or tribe.

See Pl. 64, Vol. II.

BIBLIOGRAPHY: Arsène Alexandre, *Malvina Hoffman.* Paris, 1930.—For a complete bibliography see *The Index of Twentieth Century Artists* for October, 1934.

**HOGARTH (William).**—English painter and engraver, 1697-1764.

The child acquired his first notions of drawing from the goldsmith, Ellis Gamble. He soon learned engraving, and, in 1724, he produced the *Taste of the Town* and *Buckingham Gate,* which are

HOGARTH.

already violent satires. He engraved for his publishers scenes from Milton's *Paradise Lost,* from Butler's *Hudibras,* and from Beaver's *Military Punishments.* He became acquainted with Sir James Thornhill, painter to the king, and married his daughter, after having eloped with her.

It was not until 1734 that he began to execute those paintings which made him more than ever famous. In 1757, he was appointed serjeant-painter to the king, succeeding, in that capacity, his brother-in-law, son of Sir James Thornhill. He died at Leicester Fields.

Hogarth was an intensely individual painter. His work is so personal that no trace of any influence, ancient or modern, can be found in it. His early humorous and satirical works were regarded with horror by contemporary painters; they were none the less enthusiastically received among the English public. The brutalities, corruption and coarseness of the 18th century could not fail to interest such an observer as Hogarth. With him, drawing, colour and composition had to serve an end—to expound ideas, and those ideas had to point a moral, and to be intelligible to all. Indeed, his works are documents on the life of his age. Horace Walpole, who, incidentally, did not like him at all, said of him: "Hogarth's pictures are the most faithful criticisms on our way of life that we have had for a hundred years."

It was in 1734, by a first series of pictures, entitled *The Harlot's Progress,* that he became known. Other series followed: in 1735, *The Rake's Progress;* and, in 1745, *Marriage à la Mode,* which is in the Tate Gallery (London). It shows astonishing qualities of technique, and proves that Hogarth was a painter in every sense of the word, in spite of the fact that his pictures are also sermons. His satire is biting, acid, and animated by a spirit of revenge that can only be seen elsewhere in the works of Goya and Daumier.

The series entitled *Work and Idleness* comprises twelve engravings.

Hogarth also painted several good portraits, including those of: Captain Coram, Wilkes, Fielding, Garrick, and the delightful *Shrimp Girl,* in the National Gallery.

See Pl. 48, Vol. II.

BIBLIOGRAPHY: Austin Dobson and Sir W. Armstrong, *William Hogarth,* 1902.—G. Baldwin Brown, *Hogarth.*

**HOITSU (Sakai).**—Japanese painter (1761-1828). He belonged to the highest aristocracy. He based his style on that of Ogata Korin. Hoitsu is a delightfully sensuous colourist. His watercolours are of a brilliance and lightness because of the extreme purity of the pigments. His subjects, moreover, are always very original.

To Hoitsu we owe the collecting and publishing of Korin's work for lacquer decoration. This collection contains several thousand designs, some of which bear the signature of Hoitsu himself.

See Japan—Art.

**HOKKEI.**—Japanese colour printer. The best pupil of Hokusai, with whom he is sometimes confused. He was an excellent colourist. Two very fine prints by him are the *Carp leaping a Water-Fall,* and the *Pheasant.*

**HOKUBA.**—Japanese printer. Pupil of Hokusai. Chiefly known for his surimonos.

**HOKUJU.**—Japanese printer. Pupil of Hokusai. He made landscapes in the European style.

**HOKUSAI (Katsushika).**—Japanese painter and printer. At the beginning of his career, he also signed himself Shunro and Sori. Born at Yedo (about 1760-1849), son of Nakajima Ice, a maker of mirrors. Hokusai was first employed in a library; then, between the ages of fourteen and eighteen, he was apprenticed to a wood engraver. Desirous to become a designer, he next joined the studio of Shunsho. There, he began by illustrating cheap novels. He was sometimes responsible for the text as well. The best known are: *The Story of Nichiren* (1782); *The Little Violet of Yedo; The Diplomacy of General Fourneau,* etc. He also produced a number of separate blocks, in the style of the Katsugawa, and which, signed "Shunro," as pupil of Shunsho, imitate this master, without always having his vigour of drawing and freshness of colour. Some of them even show a curious mixture of Shunsho's style, with the exaggerated physiognomies so characteristic of Sharaku.

HOKUSAI: THE WAVE. (Louvre.)

However, Hokusai soon renounced these imitations, and, in 1786, he left the studio, and set about illustrating fashionable novels, legends, and fairy tales. These early volumes are generally in black and white, sometimes lightly touched with colour. He no longer owes anything to Shunsho, but shows a personal style—although he, too, succumbed a little to the grace of Utamaro's mannerism. This influence is specially apparent in a number of surimonos which he executed between about 1795 and 1806, among which are: *Invitation to a Cock Fight; Visit to the Temple of Shinobazu; Travellers arriving at an Inn,* and a *Dance of the Shietus.* In the two last, Utamaro's influence is declining. The artist has found his own style, which was precise and supple, and if his types are less refined, they are much more lifelike. It is impossible to enumerate the illustrated works, or albums of prints, which were published about this time. We can only mention: *The Fifty-three Stations of the Tokaido* (the coast-road between Yedo and Kyoto), about 1800; the *Views of the Sumida,* 1800; the *Yehon assobi* (Walks in Yedo), 1802; and the delightful *Yehon Yama mata Yama* (*Mountains and Mountains*), 1804. He shows extraordinary invention in the novel way he arranges his crowds of little figures, but his treatment is rather dry, and his colour, alternately dull or too crude, prevents his obtaining atmospheric effects.

HOKUSAI: TRAVELLERS.

Hokusai had evidently learned, from a European source, something of perspective, which he rarely used, as well as some notions of anatomy, and a leaning towards the study of muscular action, and violent gesture. But, after all, if Hokusai was a wonderful and powerful designer, with a passion for life and movement, a sensitive landscapist, a caricaturist, often vulgar, doubtless, but full of life and humour, he was not essentially a colour printer. For him, line, colour and decorative harmonies were not an end in themselves; rather they were the means, exact and quick, of interpreting and spreading his illustrations. This appears chiefly in the wonderful *Mangwa.* The publication of his thirteen volumes, begun in 1813, lasted no less than thirty-six years, until Hokusai's death.

He published also a number of series of colour-prints, in which the colour is often apt to be heavy and harsh. Some of these series which contain the finest examples are: *The Thirty-six Views of Fuji* (1823-29); *Large Flowers;* the five pieces of the *Apparitions; Tortoises;* the *Falcon;* the *Hundred Poems.* And next: *Bridges; Waterfalls;* and the *Hundred Views of Fuji.*

Hokusai died, almost ninety years of age, in 1849, unhappy at not having brought his art to greater perfection, and saying regretfully: "If heaven had granted me another ten years, or even five years, of life, I could have become a really great painter. . . ."

Hokusai had a great many pupils. Noteworthy are Gakutei, Hakuba, Hokuju and Hokkei.

See Japan—Art, and Pls. 39, 40, Vol. I.

Bibliography: Edmond de Goncourt, *Hokusai.* Paris, 1896.—E. F. Strange, *Hokusai.* London, 1906.—H. Focillon, *Hokusai.* Paris, 1914.

**HOLBEIN the Elder (Hans).**—German painter. Date of birth unknown—probably about 1460; died in 1524 in Isenheim. He belonged to the Swabian school of Augsburg, where he worked from 1493 to 1517. It is not known where he learned painting.

One of Holbein's first dated works is the altarpiece from the convent of Weingarten (Augsburg Cathedral), painted in 1493. He next painted, for the convent of St. Catherine of Augsburg, the *Basilica of Santa Maria Maggiore,* in 1499, above which he represented the *Coronation of the Virgin,* the *Adoration.* and the *Martyrdom of St. Dorothy.* Several *Passion* series (Munich, Frankfort, and the Donaueschnigen Gallery) have hideous, grimacing figures, painted in violent colours.

In 1516, Holbein painted his finest work, the *Altarpiece of St. Sebastian.* The figures of St. Barbara and of St. Elizabeth (Munich Gallery) which adorn the wings are famous. The Gothic decorations have given place to graceful Renaissance architecture; the two saints, in garments which hang in harmonious folds, recall the noble figures of Italian art. One is tempted to attribute them to the son of Holbein the Elder—Hans Holbein the Younger. The figure of the beggar kneeling behind the one who is holding out his bowl to St. Elizabeth is that of the painter.

*The Fountain of Life* (Museum, Lisbon) was painted in 1519. Although it is signed by the painter, the authenticity has often been disputed. It is a kind of "Holy Conversation," in the Italian style.

Besides these pictures, we possess a series of portraits, drawn in silverpoint (most of which are in the Museums of Basle and Berlin) representing monks, priests and scribes, in an amusing and expressive way.

The Elder Holbein who, at the beginning of his career, followed the Gothic tradition, was gradually swept away by the current of the Renaissance, of which he was the first representative in Augsburg.

See Pl. 3, Vol. II.

Bibliography: C. Glaser, *Hans Holbein der ältere.* Leipzig, 1908.—H. Woltmann, *Holbeiri der ältere Silberstiftzeichnungen im kgl. Museum zu Berlin.* Leipzig, 1910.

**— the Younger (Hans).**—German painter, born in 1497, in Augsburg. Son of Hans Holbein, the Elder. Early in life, he settled in Basle, and entered the studio of the painter, Hans Herbster.

Holbein's early works include drawings for a copy of Erasmus' *In Praise of Folly.* These drawings, full of life, and made by a young artist, who was a sophisticated and gay companion, greatly pleased Erasmus, and from that time the humanist remained on very friendly terms with the painter.

In 1516, Hans Holbein painted

Holbein the Younger, self-portrait. (Florence, Uffizi.)

the Portrait of Hans Herbster, that of Meyer, and of his wife. Before carrying out his painted portraits, the artist made a preparatory drawing in pencil, silver-point or red chalk. The Museum of Basle possesses a magnificent collection of these drawings. In his portraits, Holbein reveals himself above everything else as a draughtsman. He combines precision with a keen sense of beauty and elegance. One does not find, in his work, those hard, bony faces, beloved of Dürer; nor yet the generalised types of the Italians. While sacrificing no essential characteristic, forms and colours are not emphasised, and the portraits owe most to Holbein's exquisitely delicate sense of line.

In 1517, he went to Lucerne, where he decorated the façade and interior of Hertenstein's house with pictures, which have been destroyed. From there, he may have gone to Italy. It is not known where or how he spent the years 1518 and 1519, until the end of September, 1519, when he returned to Basle. The same year he painted the portrait of Boniface Amerbach, the

Holbein: John the Goldsmith, from Antwerp.

head of an energetic thinker. Then he designed façades for houses, and armorial bearings for stained-glass windows. The walls of houses which he painted, he covered with the most varied figures—citizens, merchants, princesses, knights, and peasants.

In 1521, Holbein painted his celebrated *Dead Christ* (Basle), which, according to tradition, was painted from the body of a drowned man, taken from the Rhine.

The decoration for the Town Hall of Basle—three large frescoes, painted in 1521—have disappeared, in spite of restorations.

In 1522, Holbein painted the *Madonna of Solothurn;* the *St. Ursula,* and *St. George,* of Karlsruhe; and made several illustrations for books. In 1523 comes the famous portrait of Erasmus (Louvre, and Basle Museum).

About this time, he made a journey to France—to Avignon, and Marseilles—during which he made crayon drawings of the statues of the Duc de Berry and of his wife.

On his return, he painted the *Passion of Christ,* in eight panels (Basle Museum), for the Town Hall of Basle. Then he executed the famous compositions of the *Old Testament* and the *Dance of Death,* which were cut in wood by Hans Lützelburger. The latter are really little genre pictures, showing Death attacking all classes of society, from the peasant to the King and Pope. They are varied and lively.

*The Madonna of the Bourgomaster Meyer* (Darmstadt; copy in Dresden, by a Flemish painter) was painted in 1526, for the bourgomaster of Basle, who wanted to protest against the Reformation, and to draw divine protection on himself and on the town. In vain, for religious controversies soon absorbed all vital forces, and painters no longer found the means to exercise their art. "The arts are dead in this country," said Erasmus. Holbein, threatened with starvation, accepted the offer of Sir Thomas More, ambassador of Henry VIII, and in 1528 he went to London where he remained until his death, except for two journeys to Basle, in 1528 and 1538.

In England, Holbein painted the most famous people of the day:—Sir Thomas More and his family (unfortunately lost, but the sketch for it is in the Museum of Basle); the Archbishop of Canterbury (Louvre, and Lambeth Palace); the Bishop of Rochester Sir Bryan Luke (Munich), etc.

In 1528, he paid a short visit to Basle, during which he painted the portrait of his wife and his two children. He modelled with great delicacy the tired, and not very attractive face of Elizabeth Schmid, his wife, who was no more able than was the town of Basle to keep the artist, who was in a hurry to return to England.

There, he resumed his series of portraits, that of Jörg Gisze (1532, Berlin); the *Ambassadors* (National Gallery); Morette (Dresden).

In 1536, Holbein entered the service of Henry VIII, and painted the portrait of King Henry VIII, and that of his successive wives. His portrait of Christine of Denmark is another notable painting in the National Gallery.

In the midst of an easy life, while his talent was appreciated by the English court, the artist suddenly died of the plague (1543).

See Pl. 26, Vol. II.

Bibliography: Stein, H., *Bibliographie des publications relatives au peintre Holbein.* Besancon, 1897.—Woltmann, A. *Holbein und seine Zeit.* Leipzig, 1874-76.—Chamberlain, Arthur B., *Hans Holbein the Younger.* London, 1913.—Ganz, P., *Hans Holbein,* Klassiker der Kunst, Vol. 20.—Zoege v. Manteuffel, K. *Hans Holbein der Maler.* Munich, 1920.—Zoege v. Manteuffel, K., *Hans Holbein der Zeichner f. Holzschnitt und Kunstgewerbe.* Munich, 1920.

**HOLT (Thomas Z.).**—British architect, 1578-1624, who worked in the hybrid Gothic and Renaissance style of the Jacobean Period. He was particularly active at Oxford, where he designed the entrance to Merton College; the Merton College Library, 1610-1624; the Gateway of the Schools, 1612; Wadham College, 1610-1613; and the Bodleian Library, 1613-1618.

**HOMER (Winslow).**—American painter (1836-1910). He was born in Boston, Massachusetts, 24th February 1836. From his artistic mother doubtless he inherited some of his talent for drawing, which early manifested itself. At the age of nineteen he became the apprentice of a lithographer and two years later he was making illustrations for *Ballou's Pictorial* and *Harper's Weekly.* He attended evening sessions at the National Academy of Design at the same time. In 1861 he was named artist correspondent at the front for *Harper's Weekly.* He made some brilliant sketches and some oil paintings of the war of which *Prisoners at the Front* is perhaps the best known. Two years after the close of the Civil War, Homer went to Europe, where he spent ten months in France, visiting museums but apparently gaining little if any new artistic influences. Upon his return to the United States he worked at Gloucester, Massachusetts, and later at Petersburg, Virginia, where he made some Negro studies. He continued his drawings for *Harper's Weekly* until 1875, but after that time gave up doing magazine illustrations. In 1881 and 1882 he was again in England, at Tynemouth, painting marine scenes and subject pictures of coast guards busy at their task of saving ships, which type of work constituted his favorite material. Two years later he settled permanently in a cottage at Prout's Neck off Scarboro, Maine, where he spent the summers for the rest of his life. Winters he went to Nassau or Bermuda to sketch tropical scenes of marine interest, bringing home vivid watercolours which reflected the brightness of sea and sky under the hot sun of the tropics. It was during this period that *Fog Warning* and *Eight Bells* were executed, pictures remarkable for the realistic treatment of such everyday occurrences along the coast of Maine. Honours began to come to this hermit-like painter; a gold medal at the Columbian Exposition of Chicago in 1893, and another gold medal from the Pan-American Exposition at Buffalo in 1901. Winslow Homer died 29th September 1910 at a time when his work was more popular than it has been since his death. His artistic style shows almost no European influence, while the technique and subject matter used are predominately American, reflecting the genre interest of the past century at its best and close to the impressionistic methods of John Singer Sargent in the tropical watercolours, as in the *Gulf Stream,* where the vivid sea seems a poor imitation of the brilliant sky overhead.

See Pls. 58, 62, Vol. II.

Bibliography: Kenyon Cox, *Winslow Homer,* 1914.—William Howe

Downes, *The Life and Works of Winslow Homer*, 1911.—Nathaniel Pousette-Dart, *Winslow Homer*, Distinguished American Artists Series, 1922.—For other biographical material see *The Index of Twentieth Century Artists* for November, 1933.

**HONTHORST (Gerard van).**—Dutch painter of Utrecht (1590 to 1656), who introduced into his country the dark colours of Caravaggio. He painted so many night effects that in Italy he came to be known as "Gerard of the Night" (*Gherardo della notte*).

Bibliography: A. V. Scheider, *Die Niederlärudischen Caravaggisten*. Marburg, 1933.

**HOOCH (Pieter de).**—Dutch painter. Born in Rotterdam, in

Hooch (Pieter de): Dutch Interior.

1629; died after 1677. Little is known about his life. He was probably the pupil of Berchem, in Amsterdam. About 1653, he went to Delft, where he knew Vermeer. He seems to have had an early struggle, for, unable to earn his living only by painting, he became a domestic servant to a certain Justus de la Grange, who gave him the opportunity to paint. These pictures were apparently not much valued by his contemporaries to judge from the low prices which they gave for them. In 1654, he married and settled in Delft, where he lived until his wife's death in 1667, when he went to Amsterdam. It was during this Delft period that he produced his finest works.

De Hooch delighted in painting spotless Dutch rooms, with brick chimney-pieces, and furniture and utensils glistening with cleanliness, while a soft light enters by an open door, or little window. The figures are calm and composed. De Hooch was no painter of human passions, and we are hardly more interested in the expression on the face of the young mother, servant or cavalier than in the painting of a cushioned chair, on which the household cat is sleeping, the fine copper casserole, or the bed in an alcove. Details are pleasing but not overemphasised; the colour is warm and soft; but, above all, it is the fair, gentle light which, caressing figures and objects alike, makes these peaceful interiors so wholly delightful. Equally charming are De Hooch's pictures of little red brick courtyards.

In the latter part of his life, De Hooch, who then lived in Amsterdam, in a less tranquil environment, painted scenes in which the figures are given more importance—"concerts" and "visits." These are not his best works. Like Chardin, he is essentially a painter of silent intimacies.

Among De Hooch's most celebrated pictures must be mentioned: *Courtyard of a Dutch House, Interior of a Dutch House, Refusing the Glass* (all in the National Gallery); *The Linen-Cupboard, Woman tending her Child's Hair, Interior* (all in Amsterdam—the two last with double lighting effects); *Interior* (Louvre), etc.

The titles of the pictures differ, the figures vary a little; but always we see a few figures in a little courtyard, or in a spotless room with an open door or window, through which the light enters, and through which we can often catch a glimpse of a courtyard or street. Nothing disturbs the peaceful life of these well-managed households.

See Pl. 36, Vol. II.

Bibliography: A. de Rudder, *Pieter de Hooch*. Antwerp, 1914.—Hofstede de Groot, *A Catalogue Raisonné*, Vol. I, 1908.—W. R. Valentiner, *Pieter de Hooch*. London, 1930.

**HOOD (Raymond Mathewson).**—American architect (1881-1934). He was born at Pawtucket, Rhode Island, 29th March 1881. After his graduation from the Massachusetts Institute of Technology in 1903 he entered the employ of Cram, Goodhue and Ferguson as a draftsman. The next year he went to Paris to continue his study of architecture. He entered the École des Beaux-Arts and won his government diplôme there in 1911. Upon his return to the United States he was connected with Palmer, Hornbostel and Jones in New York City and later with Henry Hornbostel in Philadelphia. From 1914 to 1927 he practised alone in New York. In association with John Mead Howells, Hood in 1922 won the competition for the new home of the *Chicago Tribune*. It was a Gothic tower they planned and saw executed in stone suitable for the decorative carving of the sides. The American Radiator Building in New York City was made striking by reason of the use of colour—black bricks and the top covered with gold-leaf decoration. Other buildings of a more modern cast followed: the Beaux Arts Apartment, the News Building, and the McGraw-Hill Building—all in New York City. Though the exteriors were embellished by the use of metal, glass and terra cotta blocks in polychromatic effects, the underlying structure was of firm construction with an eye to its practical value and appropriateness for its function. Simple masses with an emphasis on height and pleasing exterior appearance were also taken into consideration. From 1927 till the time of his death Raymond Hood was a member of the firm of Hood and Fouilhoux, which before 1931 was known as Hood, Godley and Fouilhoux. Mr. Hood was called into consultation at the time of the rebuilding of the University of Brussels, and was connected with the designing of Rockefeller Center and the Century of Progress Exposition buildings at Chicago in 1933. He received the medal of honour of the Architectural League of New York in 1926 and served as President of that society from 1929 to 1931. He was a member of the American Institute of Architects and a Chevalier of the Crown of Belgium. He died at his home in Stamford, Connecticut, 14th August 1934, after a year's illness. His buildings have been termed realistic structures, practical and appropriate without being extreme in their design.

See Pl. 64, Vol. II.

Bibliography: A. H. North, ed., *Raymond M. Hood*, Contemporary American Architects Series, 1931.

**HOOGSTRATEN (Samuel van).**—Dutch painter, 1626-1678. Painter of little scenes, such as the *Sick Woman* (Amsterdam). He was a pupil of Rembrandt, for whom he kept a faithful admiration, although towards the end of his life, he changed his style of painting.

Hoogstraten was the author of the *Inleyding tot de hooge schoole der schilderkonst* (Rotterdam, 1678), an important book on Dutch art and artists of the 17th century.

**HOPKINS (James R.).**—American painter, born 1877, one of the most prominent American figure painters of his generation, noted for his delicately observed interiors.

**HOPPER (Edward).**—Contemporary American painter and graver. He was born at Nyack, New York, 22d July 1882. As a boy he was fascinated by the boats in the Hudson River and liked to watch them go up and down, and he also liked to see the clear-cut outlines of buildings against the sky. He attended the Chase School in New York, where he worked under Robert Henri and Kenneth Hayes Miller. From Henri he learned to admire the work of Manet, Velázquez, Goya and Hals. After completing his work there he went to Paris to work and there came in contact with the art of Renoir, Sisley and Pissarro whose impressionistic tendencies influenced him for a short time. He returned to the United States in 1907 and began exhibiting works in oil, water-colour and some etchings. Today he is best known for his oils, mostly landscapes done from a purely objective viewpoint. The emphasis is laid on the contrasting masses of light and dark and the interesting shapes of buildings silhouetted against the sky. In *Lighthouse at Two Lights* sunlight pours down on a gleaming lighthouse which stands out bright and clear under a cloudless sky. Less numerous are some interior scenes which in the precise technique and drawing recall the work of the Dutch Little Masters. His etchings, too, exhibit a clear-cut quality akin to his paintings, without blurred or shadowy effects often noticed in the work of other graphic artists. Examples of his work may be seen at the Fogg Art Museum in Cambridge, the Wadsworth Athenaeum in Hartford and the Phillips Memorial Gallery in Washington, D. C.

See Pl. 63, Vol. II.

Bibliography: Guy Pène du Bois, *Edward Hopper*, American Artists Series, 1931.—Forbes Watson, *Edward Hopper*, The Arts Portfolio Series, c. 1931.—For other articles see *The Index of Twentieth Century Artists* for July, 1934.

**HOPPNER (John).** — English portrait painter, born 1758. He had a talent for music, but, having lost his voice following an illness, he devoted himself to painting. In 1780, he married the daughter of Mrs. Patience Wright, a celebrated sculptress of the day. Thanks to the favour of the Prince of Wales, Hoppner soon became one of the most esteemed society painters, and the rival of Sir Thomas Lawrence. These two artists divided the honours for over twenty years. Hoppner also acquired a certain fame as a writer, and, in 1806, he published some Eastern poems, translated into English verse. His life was easy and brilliant; but towards the end of it, he showed signs of mental derangement, and he died, nearly insane, in 1810.

Hoppner (John): Princess Sophia.

Hoppner's paintings often have exaggerated contrasts of light and shade; but, in spite of some reserves, his works are at once elegant and simple. Above all, he was a refined and harmonious colourist. His best works are in private collections.

See Pl. 48, Vol. II.

Bibliography: W. MacKay and W. Roberts, *The Works of John Hoppner*. London, 1903.

**HOROLOGIUM (of Andronikos).**—See Athens.

**HOSMER (Harriet).**—American sculptress (1830-1908), worked for some time in Rome, practising a style of gentle charm. Among her works are *Oenone* (Museum of Fine Arts, St. Louis), *Beatrice Cenci* (Mercantile Library, St. Louis), *Zenobia* (Metropolitan Museum of Art, New York).

**HÔTEL DES INVALIDES.**—See Paris.

**— DE VILLE.**—Town hall. See Paris; Poitiers; etc.

**HOUDON (Jean Antoine).**—French sculptor, 1741-1828. Son of a domestic servant of Versailles, where he was born. He first studied in the rather poor school of Michel-Ange Slodtz, and then with Pigalle. At the age of twenty, he won the Rome prize for sculpture, and went to Italy, where he spent eight years, just at the time when antiques were being dug up in great numbers from the soil of Herculaneum and Pompeii. Two of his most famous works date from this period —the large statue of St. Bruno, which is now in Santa Maria degli Angeli, Rome; and a study for a St. John the Baptist which was to have been associated with the St. Bruno. This figure of St. Bruno is extremely simple and majestic, and already shows Houdon's reaction from the teaching of Michel-Ange Slodtz, who treated the same subject in the mannered tradition of Bernini.

Houdon returned to Paris about 1769, and was "accepted" by the Académie Royale, with a plaster figure of Morpheus, which he exhibited at the Salon of 1771, and of which he made a marble copy four years later. This *Morpheus* was represented by a young man stretched on the ground. Its simplicity was new. He also exhibited some busts, among others that of Diderot, which reveal already his brilliant qualities as a portrait sculptor. His fertility was amaz-

HOUDON.

ing. He made a bust of Franklin, during one of the appearances in Paris of the popular American hero; he resurrected Molière in marble (in the foyer of the Comédie Française); he did the same for La Fontaine.

HOUDON: DIANA. (Louvre.)

In 1781, he exhibited his marvellous statue of Voltaire, which is in the Comédie Française, and the *Diana*—which was first made in plaster, and then copied in marble, and in bronze (Louvre). Another famous work is his *Shivering Woman*, of which there are also several copies. His head of the little four-year-old Louise Brongniart (1777) is one of the happiest pieces of French sculpture in the Louvre. In 1785, he was commissioned by the United States Congress to make a bust of General Washington.

After the Revolution, Houdon was held in less high esteem. The new order seemed to bear him a grudge because of the important position he had occupied in the time of the fallen régime. The Society of Friends of the Constitution ordered a bust of Mirabeau, and then refused it, on the pretext that the work lacked idealism. A competition was opened, in which Houdon refused to compete. He then offered the bust to the National Assembly. It is a work worthy of his "Glück," and shows scrupulous observation, but, in this very quality, it contradicted the theories of the "beau idéal," which the school of David was beginning to make fashionable. The bust now belongs to M. Delagrave. It bears the date: 10th April, 1791, which reminds us that it was executed the week following Mirabeau's death, which occurred on the 2nd.

With the Empire, Houdon returned to favour. He modelled a bust of Napoleon and of the Empress Marie-Louise. While the allies were in France in 1814, he made a bust of the Tsar Alexander.

Houdon was a member of the Institut, and a professor in the École des Beaux Arts. His most frequent advice to his students was: "Copy! Copy constantly; and, above all, copy just what you see." This he urged while the cold statuary of the new school was appearing around him. He died in 1828.

See Pl. 45, Vol. II.

BIBLIOGRAPHY: C. H. Hart and E. Biddle, *Memoirs of the Life and Works of Jean Antoine Houdon.* Philadelphia, 1911.

**HSIA KUEI.**—Chinese landscape painter c. 1180-1230. He was one of the great monochrome landscape painters of the Sung period. Several versions of his famous scroll *Ten Thousand li of the Yangtze* exist which, if not originals, reflect his style.

See China—Art.

**HSIEH HO.**—Chinese painter and critic 479-510, who formulated the *Six Principles of Painting.*

See China—Art.

**HUANG KUNG-WANG.**—Chinese painter, 1269-1354. One of the "Four Masters" of Yuan. He had two styles of painting; monochrome, with thick strokes; and a faint purple-brown coloring with delicate strokes.

See China—Art.

**HUDSON RIVER SCHOOL.**—A group of nineteenth century American painters who frequently chose landscapes along the Hudson River for the subjects of their paintings. See Doughty (T.); Hart (W.); Inness (G.); Martin (H.D.). See also Pl. 61, Vol. II.

**HUET (Christophe).**—Born ?—Died 1757. French decorator. He decorated rooms with light, fantastic designs, in which monkeys, and Chinese and Turkish subjects, play the chief part. This kind of decoration was much in vogue in the first half of the eighteenth century. Huet's work is graceful, ingenious and amusing. He is credited with the paintings known as the "grande singerie" ("singerie" means "monkey trick"), in the Château of Chantilly, and those which adorn the Château of Champs (between Chelles and Noisiel). In Paris, in the old Hôtel de Rohan (now the National Printing Office), may be seen a room entirely decorated by him with Mandarins, Chinese women, and children with shaved heads. The latter disport themselves with all the frolics of youth, in the midst of a varied fauna, in which baboons and monkeys indulge in the most absurd antics.

Christophe Huet was a professor in the Académie de Saint Luc. He was the uncle of J. B. Huet.

**— (Jean Baptiste Marie).**—French engraver and designer, chiefly known as an animal painter (1745-1811). He received his first lessons from a member of the Académie de Saint Luc, of the name of Dagommer, who was a successful animal painter; and he next studied in the studio of Le Prince. He first fell under the influence of Boucher; and later, of Prud'hon.

J. B. Huet was a painter particularly of domestic animals. The Louvre possesses his "Morceau de réception" at the Académie—*A Mastiff Attacking some Geese*—but this painting does not do him justice. His touch was broad; his lighting, just. Some of his paintings are marred by an unpleasant reddish colouring. His drawings are particularly able. He composed several series of animals, for the purpose of teaching drawing; and made several etchings after his own work.

His three sons were also artists. The eldest, Nicolas, was attached as draughtsman to the Museum of the Jardin des Plantes, which possesses over two hundred watercolours by him, representing animals, birds, and insects. The second son, François Huet, known as Villiers Huet (from the name Villiers-Sur-Orge, where he was born) painted miniatures. He went to England, where he became painter to the Duke of York. The third son, who lost an arm in the cause of the Revolution, engraved the works of his father and eldest brother.

BIBLIOGRAPHY: C. Gabillot, *Les Huet (Jean Baptiste et ses trois fils)*, Collection des Artistes célèbres.

**HUNT (W. Holman).**—English painter. London, 1827-1910. His work is a faithful application of the doctrines and principles of the Pre-Raphaelite Brotherhood. He tried to copy nature in its smallest details. This carefulness often detracted from the beauty of his pictures as a whole. His colour is bright and crude. The first religious picture, which he exhibited in 1854, *The Light of the World,* represents Christ, lantern in hand, knocking at a door (Keble College, Oxford). In 1856, he painted a strange picture, entitled *The Scape-Goat.* Then, to satisfy his passion for local detail, he spent several years in Palestine, to study the character of the country, its inhabitants, and its buildings. He tried to represent Biblical incidents in their true setting. These pictures include the following:—*Christ with the Doctors; After Sunset in Egypt; The Triumph of the Innocents; The Virgin Finding Jesus in the Temple; The Shadow of Death.*

BIBLIOGRAPHY: W. Holman Hunt, *Pre-Raphaelitism and the Pre-Raphaelite Brotherhood.* London, 1905.

**— (Richard Morris).**—American architect (1828-1895). He was born at Brattleboro, Vermont, 31st October 1827, a young brother of William M. Hunt, the painter, and exerted quite a bit of influence on contemporary architecture. He was educated at the Boston Latin School, where he graduated in 1843. He was the first of an army of American architects who studied at the Beaux-Arts in Paris and who were responsible for the triumph of eclecticism in America in the late 19th and early 20th century. He studied first with Samuel Davies in Geneva and then with Hector M. Lefuel in Paris. In 1846 he entered the École des Beaux-Arts. For the next nine years he studied and worked at his chosen profession, travelling to the Near East and Egypt as well as on the mainland of Europe. In 1854 he was an assistant to Lefuel, then engaged in the remodelling of the Louvre and the Tuileries, and the following year he returned to the United States. He acted as a draftsman for Thomas Walter who was enlarging the United States Capitol, and soon opened his own place of business in New York City. During the 1860's, however, he went back to France to work and on his return to the United States began drawing plans for his best-known structures. He designed among others in New York the Tribune Building, the J. J. Astor and Wm. K. Vanderbilt homes and a large part of the Metropolitan Museum of Art. He also planned and saw carried out the summer homes of New York society at Newport, including those of Ogden Goelet, Cornelius Vanderbilt and Oliver H. P. Belmont. The Vanderbilt home on Fifth Avenue, New York, in the style of the French Renaissance, was widely copied in many sections of the East. He was a Chevalier of the Legion of Honor and received an award from the Royal Institute of British Architects. He died 31st July 1895, leaving behind him such pupils as William R. Ware and Frank Furness.

BIBLIOGRAPHY: J. V. Van Pelt, *A Monograph of the William K. Vanderbilt House,* 1925.—Barr Ferree, *Richard Morris Hunt; His Art and Work,* 1895.

**— (William Morris).**—American painter (1824-1879). He was born 31st March 1824 in Brattleboro, Vermont, and was the older brother of Richard M. Hunt, the architect. His first teacher was Gambadella, an Italian painter friend of the family. He was far more interested in drawing than in his school work and succeeded in getting himself suspended from Harvard College. Since he was not very healthy at that time his mother took him abroad to live in Italy. There in Rome he met Henry K. Brown, the sculptor, and became interested enough in that branch of the fine arts to try his hand at some modelling. Some reports say that he then studied for a while with Antoine Barye, the animal sculptor, in Paris, but in 1845 he entered the classes of the Royal Academy at Düsseldorf. He resented the strict discipline and rules of technique that they laid down there and soon departed again for Paris. The next few years were spent in the studio of Thomas Couture, where he was content. It was at this time that he became acquainted with Jean François Millet and from him absorbed some of the tenets of the Barbizon school. Hunt bought such pictures done by the Barbizon masters as he could afford and in after years was influential in gaining recognition for that landscape school in the United States. He returned to America in 1855, settling first at Newport, Rhode Island, and later at Boston, Massachusetts. There he was very popular and had some artistic influence in the Boston society, trying to gain some acclaim for the works of Millet, Corot and Rousseau at a time when they were only names to the general public. His own work progressed slowly, as always, and its character was very uneven due to his impetuous methods. The *Bathers,* now in the Worcester Art Museum, one of his best works, was done at this period, showing one youth standing on the shoulders of another preparatory to the plunge in the dark waters which show dimly behind the large light figures of the boys.

In 1875 he received a commission for two mural panels in the new State Capitol at Albany, New York. For this he did the *Discoverer* and the *Flight of Night,* painted in oil directly on the stone ceiling of the Assembly Chamber. It was a job done in a hurry and from sketches and reproductions now available, it must have been very effective in both composition and colouring. Unfortunately it did not harmonise with the rest of the decoration of the room and when the dampness seeped in through the stone the pictures became ruined and the whole was subsequently covered by a wooden ceiling. However, the murals were well received at the outset, in 1878, and plans were made for other decorations in that building. This plan was vetoed by the governor, which action probably contributed to Hunt's subsequent breakdown. The next year 8th September 1879 he was drowned in a pool on the Isle of Shoals off the New Hampshire coast.

Bibliography: H. C. Angell, *Records of William M. Hunt,* 1881.—Helen M. Knowlton, *The Art and Life of William Morris Hunt,* 1899.—Helen M. Knowlton, *William Morris Hunt, Artist,* 1913.—Martha A. S. Shannon, *Boston Days of William Morris Hunt,* 1923.—*William Morris Hunt,* Masters in Art Series, August, 1908.—*William M. Hunt's Talks on Art,* compiled by Helen M. Knowlton, 1896-1898.

**HUNTINGDON (Daniel).**—American painter (1816-1906), at one time much noted for his pictures of historical subjects; also a prolific portrait painter.

**HUNTINGTON (Anna Vaughn Hyatt).**—Contemporary American sculptor. She was born in Cambridge, Massachusetts, 10th March 1876. Her first interest was in music, but soon she turned to modelling and sculpture. She studied in the Boston studio of Henry H. Kitson and later went to New York where she worked with Hermon A. MacNeil and Gutzon Borglum. From Borglum she learned how to model horses and through raising them on her place in Maryland she came to have an intimate knowledge of their anatomical structure and the flex of their great muscles at times of strain. Some of her early work was done in collaboration with Abastenia St. Leger Eberle, the woman sculptor of delightful child figures. Miss Hyatt learned to work directly in the stone and gained much proficiency in her method of expression. During the early years of the 20th century she was in Europe, studying and working. She exhibited in the Paris Salon of 1907 and the next year was in Naples, working on the lion which is now the property of the Dayton, Ohio, High School. In 1910 she was in Paris, busy with her equestrian statue of *Joan of Arc* for Riverside Drive, New York City, and in 1921 she made a replica of that statue which was erected in Blois, France. About 1917 she was appointed head of the department of sculpture of the Museum of the French Art Institute in the United States. She became a full member of the National Academy of Design in 1923 and the same year she married Archer M. Huntington, the founder of the Hispanic Society of America. In 1933 she became an Officer of the French Legion of Honor. Some of her small bronzes are in the Metropolitan Museum of Art, the Cleveland Museum of Art and the Musée du Luxembourg in Paris.

Bibliography: Grace Humphries, *Anna Vaughn Hyatt's Statue of Jeanne d'Arc,* International Studio, Vol. 57, 1915, pp. xlvii-l.—Mrs. A. C. Ladd, *Anna V. Hyatt—Animal Sculptor,* Art and Progress, Vol. 4, 1912, pp. 773-776.—Cecilia Morrow, *An Artist-Patriot: A Sketch of Anna Vaughn Hyatt,* Touchstone Magazine, Vol. 5, July, 1919, pp. 286-293.—F. N. Price, *Anna Hyatt Huntington—Animal Sculptor,* International Studio, Vol. 79, 1924, pp. 319-393.—B. H. Smith, *Two Women Who Collaborate in Sculpture,* Craftsman, Vol. 8, 1905, pp. 623-663.

**HUYSMANS (Corneille).**—Flemish painter (1648-1727). A good landscape painter, with a taste for grand sites, rocks, ravines, and clumps of old oak-trees.

**HUYSUM (Jan van).**—Dutch flower painter, 1682-1749.

**HYATT (Anna Vaughan).**—See Huntington (A.V.).

**HURTAULT TOWER.**—See Amboise.

**HYDRIA.**—See Greece (Vases).

**HYPOGÆUM.**—In ancient architecture, the subterranean portion of a building.

**HYPOSTYLE.**—With a roof supported by rows of columns.

# I

**ICONOCLASTS.**—See Byzantine Art (First Golden Age, et seq.); Ivory.

**ICONOGRAPHY.**—That branch of study which concerns itself with the subject matter or content of works of art.

**ICONOSTASIS.**—See Byzantine Art.

**ICON.**—This word is borrowed from the Russian language (ikona), and implies a religious picture with figures painted, generally, on wood, and in the Byzantine style. These pictures, usually of small size, are scattered profusely throughout Russia. No dwelling, however humble, was (before the Revolution) without its icon. The churches were full of them.

**ICTINOS.**—See Acropolis of Athens.

**ILICE.**—See Elche.

**ILLUMINATIONS.**—See Miniature.

**IMOLA (Innocenzo Francucci da).**—Bolognese painter, 1494-1550. Pupil of Francia, then, in Florence, of Albertinelli. His best known pictures are a *Madonna with St. Francis and St. Clare* (Museum of Bologna), and a *Marriage of St. Catherine* (in San Giacomo Maggiore, Bologna).

**IMPASTO.**—The use of thick layers of paint to give an effect of solidity and relief; also applied in general to the layers of pigment on the surface of a painting.

**IMPRESSIONIST MOVEMENT.**—This was a school of painting formed at the end of the 19th century, under the influence of the realistic movement, and in reaction against historical and "genre" painting and its methods.

In 1871, several young French painters, among them Claude Monet, Camille Pissarro, and Sisley, who were greatly interested in Manet's struggles against the methods of the classical school, were in London. They, too, wanted to break with the formulae of the school, with its academic drawing and colour, and its artificial lighting. They observed the attempts of their English colleagues of the Pre-Raphaelite Brotherhood, who endeavoured to use bright colours. They saw Turner's paintings, and were struck with the brilliant results which he obtained by using pigments variously juxtaposed, which, though multicoloured, blended when seen at a little distance. They noticed that this division of touch gave the colours a vivacity and sparkle which the same colours mixed on the palette no longer possessed.

On their return to France, these young painters continued their researches. They simplified their palettes, rejecting all earth colours, and keeping only seven or eight colours—yellows, oranges, vermilions, reds, blues and greens. They painted with multicoloured little strokes, or commas, of pure colour, which were juxtaposed, and entangled, and which, at a distance, reconstituted the colours, by what is known as "optical blending." On the theory that black does not exist, they aimed at giving distinct colouring to every shadow, and avoided all neutral tones. Pushing their theories still further, they considered nature simply as colour, and not as a series of lines, planes, and values, as was taught in the schools. The very basis of painting according to the accepted formula was reversed. A picture was no longer to be a work slowly composed and elaborated, and set up with the help of a previous scaffolding of drawing. It became instead the expression of an aspect of light seen in nature. The artist abandoned himself to his subject. He no longer tried to paint it as it "existed" (in a solid, or three dimensional sense), but as it appeared at the chosen moment, and in the lighting of that moment. The importance of this lighting was such that local colour, that is to say, the particular colour of any object, no longer existed. What exists to the eyes of the Impressionist painter is the colour of that object in the surroundings in which it is placed.

When the first pictures of this kind were exhibited, they were not understood, but were derided. They were looked upon as eccentric fantasies, or as attempts merely to astonish people. But when the "jest" lasted, and a Parisian picture dealer, Durand-Ruel, opened, in 1877, an exhibition of the works of these young revolutionaries, amusement turned to horror. Claude Monet, Pissarro, Sisley, Renoir, Degas, Jongkind and their partisans were labelled "Impressionists." This word, borrowed from the title of Monet's painting *Sunrise, an Impression,* and hurled at them as an insult, they adopted. The school, thus baptised, lived, fought, and, little by little, established itself. A general and undeniable influence of the Impressionist school is apparent in the painting of the end of the century, although the public continued not to understand it, and to protest. When the painter Caillebotte bequeathed a series of Impressionist paintings to the Luxembourg, outcries increased. Nevertheless, the gift was accepted, and placed in a room in the Museum. Soon amateurs began to join the early defenders and Impressionist pictures began to sell. Sisley died in 1899; Pissarro, in 1903. Their work fetched high prices. The little town of Moret, where Sisley lived, erected a memorial to him (1911). At a sale in 1912, a picture by Degas, *Dancers in the Bar,* attained a price of 435,000 francs, a sum which no picture by any living artist had ever approached. Impressionism was established. The Louvre received the Camondo Collection, in 1914. It is still too soon to judge this school, but it has certainly rendered a service to art in giving an honourable place to "open-air" painting, and has produced some charming landscapes. It excelled in the painting of sunlight effects.

The Impressionist theory of division of tone, which was not systematically observed, was re-stated in 1886, by the young artists, Seurat (1859-1891), and Signac. Impressionism gave birth to Neo-Impressionism. Chromatic theories were pushed to their limits. Pure, separated tints, balanced according to a scientific method, were used to depict some visual impression. Impressionism had no rules. Neo-Impressionism harmonised its composition, and tried to make its work an artistic creation. A *View of Notre Dame,* by Signac, in the Caillebotte Collection (in the Luxembourg) is a good example of this original and decorative style. It shows the colours grouped by contrasts, in small, equal touches, according to the rules of complementary colours. Owing to the scientific strictness of this system, Neo-Impressionism has not many adepts.

See Pl. 56, Vol. II.

Bibliography: Fénéon, *Les Impressionists,* 1886.—Mauclair, *L'Impressionnisme.*—Mellerio, *L'Exposition de 1900 et L'Impressionnisme.*—Paul Signac, *D'Eugène Delacroix au Néo-impressionnisme.*

**INCA.**—See America (Andean Civilizations).

**INDIA-ART.**—Indus Valley Civilization.—Within the last decade knowledge of Indian art has been extended by over two thousand years. Excavations at Mohenjo-daro in the Indus Valley region and in neighboring Harappa have revealed a civilization that existed in the third millennium B.C. and probably earlier. Seven strata have been discovered at the site of Mohenjo-daro but because little stylistic difference is found among the artifacts from the various strata and because of flood conditions that may have created the different strata at comparatively frequent intervals, the excavator, Sir John Marshall, estimates a duration of only about five hundred years for the site. Since seals of the type found at Mohenjo-daro have been found in comparatively well dated excavations at Elam (c. 2800 B.C.), the Mohenjo-daro finds can reasonably be considered to extend from c. 3000 B.C. to 2500 B.C.

*Seals.*—Among the most numerous artifacts were seals which bore inscriptions in a still undeciphered script and representations of animals including the zebu, the elephant, the tiger, fantastic animals and demonic figures. Most of the representations are not only organically convincing but exhibit a naturalism that is fully able to depict the subject recognizably and which already is in the process of selecting and eliminating fortuitous detail. Animals are uniformly portrayed in profile although the horns are sometimes shown from the front view.

*Sculpture.*—Important finds of sculpture from these sites show a variety of styles. One type is distinctly reminiscent of contemporaneous styles in the Near East. The most important piece of this group is a stone figure of a bearded man carved in simplified naturalism. Large eyes, a band around the hair as in Greek archaic heads of about 700 B.C., and a trefoil pattern on the robe all point to contacts with Sumerian civilization. Another type of sculpture is exemplified by a male torso found at Harappa. The naturalism of this piece at first glance is almost as exaggerated as a Greek work of the fourth century B.C., but closer observation betrays more fluidity of form and less naturalism. The suppleness of this piece seems to represent the beginning of a primary characteristic of Indian sculpture which has persisted until our own time. Even more developed from the point of view of Indian aesthetic is a bronze figure of a dancing girl. It has the same sinuous rhythms that are found in representations of Dancing Siva as late as the sixteenth and seventeenth centuries A.D.

A large group of pottery figures and heads were also discovered at these sites. Most of these are crudely modelled and probably represent the folk art of the time. Made of clay the noses are merely pointed pellets attached to the face, as are the eyes. The prominent breasts which have led these figures to be identified with a mother goddess, are another feature which remained characteristic of all Indian sculpture.

The relationships of these different styles and their chronological evolution is still unknown. It is unlikely that, with the slight evidence at present available, any sound deductions can be drawn concerning their development.

*Pottery.*—Large quantities of painted pottery vessels have been found at the Mohenjo-daro and Harappa sites. The designs on the vessels sometimes are composed of stylized animals which closely resemble those on pottery from Susa. In other instances the decoration has parallels with neolithic Chinese pottery of the Yang-Shao period which probably was contemporary with it.

VEDIC PERIOD (1500 B.C.-800 B.C.) and SAISUNAGA-NANDA DYNASTY (643 B.C.-322 B.C.). Between the fall of the Indus Valley civilization in the middle of the third millennium B.C. and the fourth century B.C., little is known of the arts of India. Surviving artifacts are small clay figurines of the mother goddess type, which show a technical advance over their rather crude prototypes at Mohenjo-daro. An indigenous and true archaic style is found in these pieces. Instead of the facial features being represented merely by pellets of clay, the nose and the eyes are modelled according to definite formulae. If, however, we know little of the art of this period, there is no question about the importance of this age which codified the religions and philosophies that the arts were to interpret during the following generations.

The Aryans who conquered northern India about 1500 B.C. brought with them a nature worship which was soon codified into a religion. This involved a pantheon of friendly and antagonistic deities, most important of whom were Indra, the supreme deity, and Brahma, the creator. In the Hymns of the *Rig-Veda* the ceremonies for dealing with these deities are prescribed. The main features of this religion were: (1) that all existence comes from the "Sea of Life" (*Samsara*) and everyone and everything, including the gods, return to it in order to be born again, (2) that the condition in rebirth is dependent upon the type of life spent in previous existences and that merit is gained or lost according to individual acts (*Karma*), (3) that the only release from existence is in the destruction of personality, and its union with the absolute (*Moksa*). In the *Upanishads* written about 800 B.C. this philosophy is centralized in the theory of the Atman or the Brahman (not to be confused with Brahma).

To achieve a oneness with this all-comprehending and impersonal existence was the aim of all beings. This state could be attained only through the various stages of rebirth depending upon the *Karma* of the individual.

Out of this religion came Buddhism, not as an opponent, but as an heresy. According to the philosophy of Prince Siddhartha (Gautama Buddha), who lived in the sixth century B.C., one could escape his *Karma* by attaining release from all earthly desires through enlightenment. This state of release is called *Nirvana*. The methods of attaining *Nirvana* have been varied by different sects of Buddhists many of which have wandered far from the original teachings. After the seventh century A.D., Buddhism in India itself was lost in an amalgam with later Brahmanism, but to its strength may be credited most of the fine monuments of early India.

MAURYA PERIOD (325 B.C.-185 B.C.).—The earliest of the Buddhist monuments date from the Maurya period. It was at this time that Alexander the Great invaded India, possibly even penetrating into the Indus Valley. The expedition had little effect on Indian art as a whole, however, although Greek satraps dominated parts of the Punjab. At the end of the fourth century B.C., Chandragupta Maurya united most of India under his rule, and from that time to the reign of Asoka (274-236 B.C.) the arts flourished. Many of the specimens reflect the old Hindu divinities. Buddhist art also appears fully developed, based mainly on the indigenous style. The characteristics of this style which were to remain basically unchanged for more than a millennium were: (1) in sculpture an all-pervading sensuousness of surface treatment, (2) the inextricable relationship of sculpture and architecture, (3) the elaborate profusion of sculpture on buildings.

*Sculpture.*—Wood was probably the first medium for sculpture and architecture in India as is shown by surviving forms in stone which simulate wooden constructions. The tropical climate of India has not preserved any of the work done in this perishable material and our knowledge of the art during the first millennium B.C. derives mainly from a series of columns erected in the reign of Asoka the great sponsor of Buddhism. These columns are closely related to the Achaemenid columns of Persepolis dating from about the fifth century B.C.—(See Persian—Art). Since the Maurya rulers maintained contact with their Persian neighbors it is not strange to find the commercial intercourse reflected in the art. The

AJANTA (INDIA): FAÇADE OF A CHAITYA.

earliest of these columns is dated 243 B.C. and is a single polished stone 32 feet high rising without a base and surmounted by a capital decorated with a lion. Other capitals at Sarnath and Sanchi also have lion capitals while at Rampurva bulls are used as a part of the ornament. The sculpture often gives a heraldic effect, often because of the position of the animals addorsed. Important as these objects are, they really do not follow the main current of Indian sculpture. Except in the minor decorations in bas-relief they betray little of the indigenous flavor of other contemporaneous remains.

Other early sculptures are representations of *Yakshas* found at Parkham, Baroda, and Besnager. These have completely developed the vegetative sensuousness and voluptuousness that was inherent in the primitive work from Mohenjo-daro. The typical figure of the female with full breasts and the swaying "S" curve of the body was to dominate most of later Indian sculpture.

SUNGA-ANDHRA PERIOD (c. 185 B.C.-50 B.C.).

*Architecture.*—The following centuries codified this style and brought it to new perfections in Buddhist architecture. One of the important forms taken by architecture was the *stupa*. This was essentially a mound built to mark a sacred spot or to hold Buddhist relics. In its developed form it consisted of a flattened dome placed on a terrace. At the top of the dome was placed the triple umbrella of sovereignty, while around the dome was a balustrade with *toranas* (gateways) at the north, south, east and west. It is the construction of these *toranas* that shows us that the stone architecture of this time derived from an earlier type in wood. It is also interesting to note that the *toranas* are similar to the *tori* in Japan to which they are stylistically as well as linguistically related. The most important of these early *stupas* is at Sanchi. The railings and *toranas* of this building are covered with an exuberant profusion of figures which symbolically represent the Buddha. Other important sites dating from the same period are the similar *stupa* at Bharut and the ruins at Amaravati. At Sanchi, the most important site, the *toranas* date from about the end of the first century B.C. The sculpture, both in round and in relief, is eminently pictorial and is used to narrate tales from the lives of the Buddha. However, the Buddha himself is never portrayed by an image at this period, but is represented only by symbols such as the wheel or the lotus.

KUSHAN PERIOD.—In northern India by 128-29 Kanishka became Maharaja of the Kushans and consolidated a dynasty which was to last for about two centuries.

*Sculpture.*—Many of the sculptures from Amaravati (mentioned above), although not under Kushan rule, date from this period. They still retain the pictorial characteristics noted at Sanchi and were, in fact, probably originally painted. At Mathura much material has been uncovered by excavations. One of the innovations of sculpture from this site seems to be the convention of indicating drapery by incised lines, and by thus reducing it, giving to the figure an effect of nudity. The first dated image of Buddha also belongs to this period and is inscribed with the third year of the Kushan era. Especially fine in quality and typically Indian in its voluptuous and "Bacchanalian" treatment of a religious theme is a series of reliefs now in the Mathura Museum. Still pictorial in treatment, these sculptures are in high relief and perpetuate the sensuous contours and flowing rhythms that distinguish the best of Indian statuary.

*Gandhara.*—Recent studies indicate that the Graeco-Buddhist sculpture from Gandhara in northwestern India probably dates from the second and third centuries A.D. The style of these sculptures is closely related to the style of another site, Taxila, and, less closely, to that of Hadda in Afghanistan. Although the subject matter is purely Buddhist, the style of the sculptures is based on the late Hellenistic art of the West. Drapery is modelled with the same full folds found in late Antique statuary. The indigenous vegetative quality of Indian art rarely appears. Instead, the body is patterned on the form of debased Greek sculpture. Few sculptures from these sites attain great aesthetic qualities, but their importance in the history of Far Eastern sculpture is primary, for it was the style and iconography of these Graeco-Buddhist statues that spread with Buddhism across Central Asia and formed the art of that region from whence it spread to China where it formed the basis of the splendid sculptures of the fifth and sixth centuries.

GUPTA PERIOD (A.D. 320-600).—The Gupta age is often considered the classical age of Indian art. Strong rulers established the capital at Pataliputra (Patna) and their power was interrupted only for a brief interlude toward the end of the fifth century by invasions of the Huns who were finally subdued in 528.

*Sculpture.*—Sculpture continued to be the dominant art of India. The representation of the Buddha reached the final stage of its development at this time. The type evolved in this period is well exemplified by the frequently illustrated representation of Buddha preaching in the Deer Park (Archaeological Museum, Sarnath). The figure has lost the sensual quality of the earlier periods and, in keeping with Buddhist philosophy, has acquired a more spiritual appearance. The body is more elongated than the earlier types and frequently is nude or covered with drapery so tightly drawn that it can hardly be differentiated from the flesh.

Brahman (or Hindu) sculpture reflects the same changes that are found in Buddhist statues, although there is, because of the difference in philosophy between the two religions, a greater sensuousness. Examples of Hindu sculpture are found at the Saiva temples at Ellora and Elephanta. The representation of Siva as an ascetic (at Deogarh) shows how the pictorial style of the earlier periods lingered in the Hindu sculpture although the figures have lost the voluptuous mass of preceding eras.

*Painting.*—The earliest painting that we have any real knowledge of in India dates from Gupta times. The greatest monument of this art are the frescoes in the cave temples of Ajanta. Earlier paintings in the Jogimara Cave (near Mirzapur District) and in some of the Ajanta caves may date as early as the first or second century B.C., but the largest group and the finest date from the sixth and early seventh centuries A.D. Other examples of early Indian painting are found in Bamiyan in Afghanistan and date from the third and fourth centuries A.D. These are decidedly provincial in character and by the fourth century are strongly influenced by the art of Sassanian Persia.

The paintings of Ajanta which represent the climax of early Indian painting are painted in red outline and colored with purple-browns, white, green, and red. The compositions are of Buddhist subjects and are frequently overcrowded and confused in the manner of some early sculpture, but the individual figures themselves have the same charm of supple contours that is found in the contemporaneous statuary. One of the finest individual figures is the so-called *Benevolent Bodhisattva.* This divinity expresses the same calm spirituality that has been noted in the Buddhist sculpture of the period, while the calligraphic contours add a lyrical note not often found in early Indian painting. Another series of caves at Bagh in Gwalior State contains paintings similar to those of Ajanta but the condition of these paintings is so bad that little judgment can be made of their quality.

At Sigiriya in Ceylon there is another group of cave paintings dating from the last quarter of the fifth century. Their style has much in common with the later paintings at Ajanta. The pictures represent a religious procession of females. The figures are cut off at the waist by clouds. This has been interpreted by some scholars as signifying that the women are divinities, while other scholars have explained the phenomenon as an artistic treatment of the uneven wall space. Other paintings of the same date in Ceylon are at Anuradhapura.

MEDIEVAL PERIOD (A.D. 600-1200).—It has already been noted that sculpture in India is almost always closely integrated with architecture. In this summary the fragmentary condition of early buildings, however, precludes a discussion of that integration. But many excellently preserved temples of the medieval period remain which show the relationship of sculpture to architecture.

DELHI: THE GREAT MOSQUE JAMI MASJID.

*Architecture.*—The Northern style of architecture generally has a steeple with swelling curves which is placed over the sanctuary. The earliest forms have low steeples which in appearance resemble domes (*Muktevesvara Shrine,* Orissa). The Great Temple at Orissa has a high tower which curves only at the top. Perhaps the finest example of this type of temple is the temple of the Sun at Konorak.

The Southern style of architecture is differentiated from the Northern mainly by the towers which instead of being curved are either pyramidal or vertical and are covered with barrel vaults or domes. High gates (*gopuram*) form the entrance to a quadrangle in which the shrine and subordinate buildings are placed. In later times the *gopuram* becomes the dominating feature of the architecture and supersedes the shrine itself as the point of architectural interest. Examples of this type of building are the great temple of Tanjore and the "Seven Pagodas" at Mamallapuram.

*Sculpture.*—Although quantities of sculpture dating from the medieval period have survived, little of the work shows the creative power of the earlier periods. Themes and style were already greatly codified. In general the figures become more slender and the sensuous contours and fluid surfaces that had given the sculpture of the preceding centuries their greatest charm begin to disappear. Nevertheless, despite a certain hardness of treatment the tradition in which the statuary was made was so strong that almost all the sculpture maintains a high technical quality and many monuments attain real importance.

Some of the best of this sculpture is found in the cave temples of Ajanta and Ellora (Ramesvaram Cave and Kailasanatha Temple), and the Sivaite sculpture at Elephanta ranks with the best of the period. The change from the early sculpture is, perhaps, best observed in the erotic sculpture of Konerak and the "dancing girls" at Bhuvanesvar. Although these monuments were consciously attempting to reproduce the sensuous abandon of the past they lack the vitality of the earlier examples. Interesting sculptures of this period are the bronzes, best represented by the graceful but vigorous statue of Siva as Nataraja (c. 10th-12th centuries) in the Madras Museum.

*Painting.*—Painting in medieval India is known almost entirely from the frescoes in the Kailasanatha Temple at Ellora. These date from about the eighth century, and show even more clearly than the sculpture of the same period how frozen the stream of creative art had become. Contrasted to the paintings at Ajanta, these works are stiff and uninspired, merely repeating formulae of a once vital art.

MOSLEM INVASIONS.—The north of India began to be harried by Moslem invaders as early as the eleventh century and at the beginning of the sixteenth century the territory was consolidated under the rule of the conquering Moguls, as these emperors styled themselves. Northern India was ruled by various Moslem dynasties until the art of the country became essentially the Mohammedan art of the Near East. Southern India, however, remained under the rule of native princes and, with little change, perpetuated the older art forms.

SACRED BULL OF MYSORE.

*Architecture.*—The peak and essence of Mogul architecture is embodied in the Taj Mahall, Agra, built from 1632 to 1653 by Shah Jehan as a memorial for his wife Mumtaz-i-Mahall. Built of white marble, the design conforms to the purity of the medium. The palace is almost square and is surmounted by a central dome, while smaller domes decorate the corners. The domes contract at the base, swell slightly, and then terminate in slender spires. Four minarets around the palace recapitulate the rhythms of the domes. Although the building depends for its beauty upon the simplification of line and perfection of proportion, floral ornament in delicate carvings and inlaid stones add to the architect's achievement.

*Painting.*—Like architecture, the painting of the Mogul court was derived from the Near East. The earliest extant paintings date from the sixteenth century. At that time one of the sovereigns, Humayum, engaged Mir Sayyid Ali and Abdus Samad of Shiraz to paint illustrations for the Persian legend, *Amir Hamsa.* These paintings are larger than the usual Persian miniatures and less refined. The color is usually less delicate than that of the Persian prototypes. There is, however, a virile quality and direct characterization that raise these illustrations to the class of the creative arts.

Toward the end of the 16th century the indigenous Indian quality began to reassert itself. At this time, also, the Indian artists came in contact with European art through the activities of Jesuit missionaries. As Dr. Dimand has pointed out, it is the mixture of Persian Hindu and European elements that is characteristic of the school at the end of the 16th century.

In the Punjab the so-called Rajput School carried on the native tradition even more closely. For its subject matter it went to old Indian legends. The colors are vivid, and there is no shading. Another school of miniature paintings is that of the Jain sect. Some of these paintings date as early as the 15th century and are of interest more because of their historical than their artistic value. They are religious subjects and their technique is crude, showing a degeneration from the classic models of the Gupta period.

BIBLIOGRAPHY: A. Coomaraswamy, *History of Indian and Indonesian Art.*—A. Coomaraswamy, *The Dance of Siva,* 1918.—V. A. Smith, *A History of Fine Art in India and Ceylon.* Oxford, 1930.—B. Rowlandson, *A Revised Chronology of Gandhara Scultpure.* The Art Bulletin, September 1936.—L. Bachhofer, *Early Indian Sculpture.*—J. Marshall, *Mohenjo-Daro.*—M. Dimand, *Islamic Miniature Painting,* 1933.—J. Ferguson, *History of Indian and Eastern Architecture,* 1910.

**INDIAN MOUNDS.**—See America (Archæology).

**INDO-CHINA.**—The art of Indo-China can be divided into three sections, Siam, Cambodia, and Annam. In each of these countries the existing monuments of art are in a large measure dependent upon the arts of the neighboring countries, India and China. The influence of these two conflicting civilizations is in almost direct ratio to their distance from the various countries of Indo-China. Thus the civilization of Annam shows a great many Chinese characteristics while the civilizations of Siam and Cambodia are basically Indian.

CAMBODIA.—The greatest of these civilizations was that of Cambodia. The first civilization which we can

# SIENESE PAINTERS

*While at Florence a new painting was developing born of the genius of Giotto, in the lofty and gracious city of Siena, the painters since the beginning of the fourteenth century had softened and animated the Byzantine icons. These Sienese masters, Duccio, Simone Martini, the Lorenzettis, did not have the sculptural vigour of the Tuscans; with them the figures of Byzantine art retained their slenderness, and as a whole the Sienese school stayed more faithful to its religious origin; it did not lapse into naturalism. It is a precious art that died too soon—the school scarcely survived the fourteenth century.*

DUCCIO: MADONNA AND CHILD. FLORENCE.
*(Photo by Anderson.)*

SIMONE MARTINI: THE ANNUNCIATION TO THE VIRGIN. FLORENCE.
*(Photo by Anderson.)*

SIMONE MARTINI: ST. CLARA AND ST. ELIZABETH. ASSISI.
*(Photo by Alinari.)*

## Duccio and Simone Martini

Duccio rewakened life in the dead faces of the Byzantine icons; the expression of tenderness followed the warmth of life. Simone Martini was the most beautiful master of Italian painting in the fourteenth century, along with Giotto; he was very celebrated. Some frescoes by him are preserved at Siena, Assisi and even at Avignon. He was a designer of exquisite lines.

A. LORENZETTI: ALLEGORY OF GOOD GOVERNMENT. SIENA.
*(Photo by Alinari.)*

A. LORENZETTI: PEACE. SIENA.
*(Photo by Anderson.)*

A. LORENZETTI: A VIEW OF SIENA. SIENA.
*(Photo by Alinari.)*

## The Lorenzettis

The two brothers, Ambrogio and Pietro Lorenzetti, painted in the Palazzo Pubblico of Siena great allegorical compositions representing good and bad government. But the allegory is mixed with real faces, portraits and landscapes so well done that we now recognize the bourgeoisie of this time, the city and the country; the comparison between the reality of today and these frescoes of the fourteenth century adds a new attractiveness to these old paintings. The painters of Siena had many imitators; the city was as influential a centre as Florence.

THE TRIUMPH OF DEATH. CAMPO SANTO, PISA.
*(Photo by Brogi.)*

This famous fresco has for a long time been attributed to Andrea Orcagna because of a confusing statement by Vasari. It is probably the work of some master of the school of Siena. The Sermon on the Mount which it develops in very clear pictures was a frequent subject in the Middle Ages, and it is also suited to its place in a cemetery. Some young hunters come upon some corpses in their coffins, and at one side, Death, with a scythe in his hand, passes scornfully over the miserable ones who call him, to strike down the happy ones in their youth. Like many of the works of the end of the fourteenth century, this painting allies a curious realism of detail with an ignorance of perspective.

# MINIATURES

*This is a very old art, as ancient as the writing on papyrus. The Egyptian manuscripts are illustrated with miniatures. The Gospels that passed from monastery to monastery during the height of the Middle Ages brought to the whole of Christianity some oriental images. The miniature was the principal method of transporting the Christian iconography.*

LETTERING OF THE SACRAMENTARY OF GELLONE. BIBL. NAT.

PSALTER OF ST. LOUIS. BIBL. NAT. *(Photo by Catala.)*

CHRIST ON THE CROSS. BRITISH MUSEUM, LONDON.

REGISTRUM GREGORII. MUSÉE CONDÉ. CHANTILLY.

SATAN DIRECTING THE TORTURES. BIBL. NAT. *(Photo by Catala.)*

BANQUET GIVEN TO THE EMPEROR CHARLES V. BIBL. NAT.

JEAN DE VAUDELAR PRESENTING HIS BOOK TO CHARLES V. THE HAGUE.

JACQUEMART DE HESDIN: THE MARRIAGE AT CANA. BIBL. NAT.

CHARLES V RECEIVING A BOOK BIBL. NAT. *(Photo by Catala.)*

## The Miniature up to the Fourteenth Century

This is one of the richest and most instructive of arts because we find in these little pictures evidences of ages from which we have no other monuments; in them we possess Merovingian and Carolingian images. In the Romanesque and Gothic periods, the miniature was comparable to many of the compositions in stained glass. In the fourteenth century it became naturalistic and introduced the contemporary world in the traditional compositions.

THE DUKE OF HAINAUT AND JACQUELINE OF BAVARIA. *(Photo by Catala.)*

FEBRUARY. GRIMANI BREVIARY, VENICE. LIBRARY OF ST. MARK'S. *(Photo by Hermans.)*

THE HUNT AT VINCENNES. TRÈS RICHES HEURES DU DUC DE BERRY.

THE SOWERS. CHANTILLY. *(Photo by Hachette.)*

FOUQUET: THE FALL OF JERICHO. BIBL. NAT. *(Photo by Catala.)*

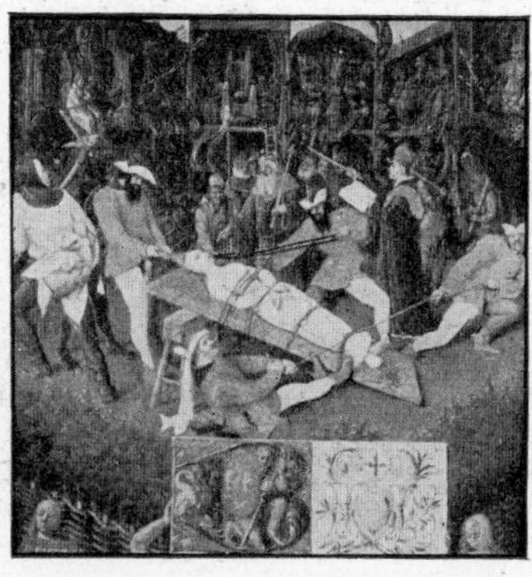

FOUQUET: THE MARTYRDOM OF ST. APOLLONIA. CHANTILLY.

FOUQUET: THE BIRTH OF ST. JOHN THE BAPTIST. CHANTILLY.

FOUQUET: THE BEARING OF THE CROSS. CHANTILLY.

## The Limbourg Brothers and Jean Fouquet

In the fifteenth century the miniature had its most beautiful flowering. Its precious examples include the *Très Riches Heures du Duc de Berry*, illuminated by three artists from Limbourg and the miniatures by Jean Fouquet. In these little paintings we recognise the France of Joan of Arc and Louis XI.

judge artistically is known generally as Pre-Khmer. We know that in the 4th century a dynasty was founded by a Brahman but the natives soon overthrew it and established their own government. In the 17th century this civilization was superseded by the Khmer culture. The art of this Pre-Khmer civilization is essentially Indian and is based on

BANGKOK: THE VAT CHENG.

the classical Gupta style. However, the sculpture, the only art which comes down from this period, is rather archaic in appearance and, opposed to the gentle and suave Gupta style, there is a latent strength that lends it great dignity.

From the 8th to the 14th century we have the true Cambodian Art, known also as Khmer. Large quantities of sculptures and many magnificent buildings testify to the wealth of this civilization. The huge temples of Angkor Thom, Angkor-Vat and Phnom Penh are still in good condition and covered with an exuberance of architecture. These sculptures represent a mixture of Hindu divinities, which include Buddhist as well as Brahman deities.

turies is almost indistinguishable from it. It is only from the 10th to the 14th century that the figures are more subtly modelled and the abstract appearance of the features supplanted by a greater liveliness. At this period too the contours of the figures become more fluid and especially in the bas-reliefs the sculpture becomes definitely pictorial. Examples of this type are found in the ground floor of The Bayon in Angkor-Thom and a bas-relief of dancing girls now in the Musée Guimet in Paris. There is a voluptuous rhythm in many of these works which is entirely Cambodian and which in its lyricism has no relation to the sensuousnes of early Indian Sculpture.

In the beginning of the 14th century the civilization was destroyed by the conquering Thais who had come from south China and who afterward established themselves in Siam. The disappearance of the Cambodian civilization was so rapid that although descriptions of a Chinese traveller in 1295 give very clear pictures of the culture, three hundred years later when the ruins were first seen by Europeans even the tradition of the civilization had been lost and the monuments were ascribed to Greek or Roman conquerors.

SIAM.—Siamese art never reached the heights achieved by its neighbor. The only art of world importance in Siam is that of sculpture which flourished for only a brief span from about the 12th to the 14th century. During this period the sculpture is characterized by restraint and intensity. The figures are usually tall and thin and drapery is subordinated to the rhythm of the figure. The features are usually sharp and have an aloof expression. After the 14th century there is a general softening of the figure style. Accompanying this change is a greater elaboration of ornament. By the 16th century an almost complete decadence pervaded the art and caused its decline.

ANNAM.—A close proximity to China has prevented Annam from ever creating a strong national art.

PNOM-PENH: PALACE OF KING NORODOM.

The buildings are usually of sandstone which is often coated with lime mortar in order to simplify decoration. The interiors were decorated with wood carvings some of which still exist. A great feature of these buildings however is their size and the enormous amount of sculpture which decorates them.

The sculpture derives directly from the earlier Pre-Khmer sculpture and in the 9th and 10th cen-

Excavations which are now going on show that as early as the Han period (B.C. 221-206 A.D.) the art of Annam was basically Chinese. However, one important group of objects—bronze drums—that has been found in Annam is of great interest because it shows a possible connection with Japan at an early period. The pattern on these drums is formed by a narrow thread-like line and depicts scenes of boats, houses, and animals. In Japan *dotoku* are found which are made with the same technique and have the same motifs. Since the motifs are essentially Indo-Chinese (compare House on Piles) it is possible that this relationship may help to explain one of the sources of early Japanese culture (see Japan—Art).

BIBLIOGRAPHY: H. Marchal, *Archaeological Guide to Angkor,* 1933. —A. Coomaraswamy, *A History of Indian and Indonesian Art.*— V. A. Smith, *History of Fine Arts in India and Ceylon,* Oxford, 1930.

**INGEGNO (L').**—Andrea di Luigi, of Assisi, called l'Ingegno. A painter of the end of the 15th and the beginning of the 16th century. He was one of Perugino's best and most devoted assistants, and to him may be attributed many of the works which resemble those of the master without being by his hand. He is mentioned in some documents about 1509, and at the end of his life he was probably blind. Perhaps he painted in the Sistine the *Baptism of Christ,* designed by Perugino. Similarly, he might have been responsible for the *Scipio* and the *Temperance,* in the Sala del Cambio in Perugia, for the *Combat of Love and Chastity* (Louvre), and the *Sporzaligio* (Caen). From 1508 to 1512, he probably worked again for his master, painting the *"Assumption"* of Santa Maria of Corciano, near Perugia.

**INGHAM (Charles C.).**—Irish-American painter (1796-1863) born and trained in Dublin, settled in America in 1816, much patronized as a portrait painter in New York.

**INGRES (Jean Auguste Dominique).**—French painter. Born in

INGRES.

Montauban, 1780; died in Paris, 1867. His father, Joseph Ingres, was a painter, sculptor and architect, originally from Toulouse. Dominique Ingres himself said: "I was brought up on red chalk. My father, who was both a musician and a painter, destined me for painting, and taught me music as a pastime. This excellent man . . . sent me to study with M. Rogues, a pupil of Vien, in Toulouse. In the theatre of this town I performed a violin concerto by Viotti, in 1793, at the time of the king's death. I made rapid progress in drawing. A copy of the *Madonna dell' Sedia,* which my master brought back with him from Italy, reduced me to tears. This impression of Raphael had a great effect on my vocation and filled my life. Ingres today is the same as Ingres was at twelve years old."

In 1806, Ingres' dream was fulfilled, and he went to Rome. Italy absorbed him entirely, and he remained there for twenty-eight consecutive years.

Among his previous works are the Portrait of his Father (Montauban, 1804), a Self-Portrait (Chantilly, 1806), and the fine portraits of the Rivière family (all three in the Louvre, 1805).

From the earliest pictures which he painted in Rome, Ingres shows a leaning towards ideal, decorative compositions, with contrasted harmony of lines, and considered balance of masses.

This preoccupation is apparent in his *Œdipus and the Sphinx* (1808, Louvre), and his *Thetis and Jupiter* (1811, Aix). David's influence is still evident in the former work. The figure of Œdipus is a fine, academic painting, but the attitude lacks emotion and nobility. Very different in feeling and technique is the *Seated Woman,* or the *Bathing Woman,* painted in the same year, and also in the Louvre. This is one of Ingres' masterpieces. David gave his forms the roundness of sculpture; Ingres, despite the purity of his draughtsmanship, remained faithful to his model. Thus, at the beginning of his long career, appears the truth of the statement which Baudelaire made in 1846: "One of the things which chiefly distinguishes M. Ingres' talent is love of women."

His pictures of *Virgil Reading the Aeneid to Augustus* (1812, Museum of Toulouse), the *Dream of Ossian* (1812, Montauban), and *Romulus Overcoming Acron* (1812, École des Beaux Arts) are still feeble and academic. But another influence soon came to the fore—that of Raphael. In the Vatican, Ingres constantly studied and copied the master's great works. Such pictures as *Raphael and la Fornarina, Francesco da Rimini, Raphael and Cardinal Bibbiena,* and *Christ Giving the Keys to St. Peter* were the result. But owing to his respect for

INGRES: ODALISQUE. (Louvre.)

the model, and to the long series of portraits which he designed or painted, Ingres never lost touch with life.

A compatriot, Joachim Murat, King of Naples, became interested in the young artist, and commissioned the *Sleeping Woman* of Naples, and the *Odalisque* (Louvre). He invited him to his court to paint members of his family. Ingres began by that of Caroline Murat; but the events of 1814 upset these plans. The new régime destroyed the *Sleeping Woman* and the portrait of Caroline Murat.

For five years, Ingres struggled against poverty, painting some historical pictures—*The Duke of Alba at St. Gudule* (1815); *Aretino at the House of Tintoretto* (1816); *Henry IV Playing with His Children* (1817); the *Death of Leonardo da Vinci* (1818)—and some portraits, such as those of Cortot, and of Maltedo, not to mention innumerable pencil portraits. Nevertheless, his resources diminished so much that Rome no longer became favourable to him, and the artist went and settled near his friend Bartolini, in Florence, accompanied by his wife, Magdeleine Chapelle, whom he had married in 1813.

After settling in Florence, Ingres painted one of his most curious compositions, *Renaud Delivering Angelica* (Louvre), which shows his strong sympathy with Perugino and the painters of the Quattrocento. The influence of his friend Granet, the painter of monastic life, inspired him to paint scenes of Vatican ceremonies. In 1821, the state commissioned him to paint *The Vow of Louis XIII*, for the Cathedral of Montauban. He worked at this picture for three years. The arrangement of the subject between curtains recalls Raphael's *Sistine Madonna*. The Virgin, also, is too directly borrowed from this picture. Only the figure of Louis XIII, in the tradition of Philippe de Champaigne, relieves this work, which is wanting in individuality.

In 1824, Ingres left Italy for Paris, where he soon became head of a school. He now painted his *Apotheosis of Homer* (1827, Louvre), which has several very fine figures, such as the Iliad and the Odyssey; but the colour is, on the whole, unpleasant, and the architecture of the classical temple is poor and cardboard-like. Nevertheless, the picture is important. It created a style of decorative painting which was developed throughout the nineteenth century. It showed the effect that could be produced by the use of flat, bright pigments, of almost equal value, with but slight modelling, and no artificial effects of light and shade.

In 1832, Ingres painted one of the most typical of his portraits, that of Bertin (Louvre). It is masterly in its penetration, and suggestion of power in repose.

*The Martyrdom of St. Symphorien* (Autun Cathedral) dates from 1834. At the end of the same year, he returned to Rome.

Among Ingres's most important works must be included: *Odalisque with a Slave* (1839); *Stratonice* (1840, Chantilly); *Venus Anadyomene* (1848); *La Source* (1856, Louvre); the *Harem* or *Turkish Bath* (1864, Louvre); and many fine portraits of women.

Ingres had returned again to Paris in 1841. In 1849, his wife died; and he married again three years later. He died in 1867, in the pride of a long, well-filled life.

See Pl. 54, Vol. II.

BIBLIOGRAPHY: H. Delaborde, *Ingres*, 1870.—Amaury Duval, *L'atelier d'Ingres*.—H. Lapauze, *Portraits dessinés d'Ingres*.—H. Lapauze, *J. A. D. Ingres*, 1911.—Fröhlich-Bum, *Ingres, sein Leben u. sein Stil*, 1924.

**INMAN (Henry).**—American painter (1801-1846). He was born near Utica, New York, 28th October 1801. When he was twelve the family moved to New York City and there he became very much interested in painting. He had earlier considered going to West Point and had been accepted, when he decided to waive the opportunity and study with John Wesley Jarvis, the portrait painter. He became Jarvis' apprentice and for seven years travelled with him around the country, doing the backgrounds and accessories for portraits. In 1823 he opened his own studio in New York City and was fairly successful for some time. He was instrumental in the founding of the National Academy of Design in 1825 and was the vice-president of that society for a number of years. During the 1830's he moved to Philadelphia and there became a director of the Pennsylvania Academy of Fine Arts. But around 1835 his health began to fail, some investments that he had made proved worthless and his creditors made life miserable for him. Back in New York City his luck was no better and his attacks of asthma continued. In 1844 he received a commission from some friends to go to England to paint the portraits of Wordsworth, Macaulay and Dr. Chalmers. The trip was in part beneficial to his health, his spirits revived temporarily and the portraits turned out well. But the next year he was forced to return to the United States and there his health grew worse. A commission from Congress for some historical pictures came and he began work on the first of the series. But the strain was too great and he died 17th January 1846. His work was able but not extraordinary. Among the men whose portraits he executed were Chief Justice John Marshall, Martin Van Buren, William H. Seward, Nathaniel Hawthorne and DeWitt Clinton.

BIBLIOGRAPHY: C. H. Caffin, *Story of American Painting*, 1907.—William Dunlap, *History of the Rise and Progress of the Arts of Design in the United States*, 1918.—C. E. Lester, *The Artists of America*, 1846.—Samuel Isham, *History of American Painting*, 1927.—H. T. Tuckerman, *Book of the Artists*, 1867.

**INNESS (George).**—American landscape painter (1825-1894). He was born near Newburgh, New York, 1st May 1825, but his boyhood was spent in Newark, New Jersey. He did not take kindly to school work but began to take drawing lessons early after an unsuccessful period in a grocery store. At the age of sixteen he began to work for a firm of map makers in New York and then studied with Regis Gignoux, a French landscape painter living in New York. In 1845 he opened his own studio, but two years later with the financial aid of a friend he went to Italy to paint the scenery around Rome. Six years later he again went to Italy, this time accompanied by his second wife, Elizabeth Hart. In 1854 they went to live in the Latin Quarter of Paris, at which time he absorbed some influences from the Barbizon school. Five years later they were in Boston and Medfield, Massachusetts, where he painted many delightful bits of landscape. In 1871 Inness again went to Rome to stay there for about four years and in 1878 he finally settled down in Montclair, New Jersey, where he spent the rest of his life except for brief trips to other parts of the country. During these last years he was an established artist, successful in selling his pictures and happy in his comfortable circumstances. However, the lure of travel still beckoned and he died abroad of heart disease at the Bridge of Allan in Scotland 3d August 1894.

His early works were stiff and mannered in the style of the Hudson River school, depicting vast expanses of landscape in the detailed manner with the brownish cast of the atmosphere. Typical of this period are *Delaware Water Gap* and *Peace and Plenty*. After his various trips to Italy and France he changed his style to a softer rendering of the forms of nature as seen in small intimate views and bathed in the warm glow of the atmosphere. He painted all types of landscapes in the flush of early spring or the last brilliant touches of autumn, early in the cool of the morning or lying hot under the noonday sun, wrapped in the calm of a perfect day or just before the outbreak of a rainstorm when thick black clouds scud across the sky. Inness was a man who was strongly stirred by his religious beliefs and sought to express the fundamental truths of the universe as they are found in the phases of nature.

See Pl. 61, Vol. II.

BIBLIOGRAPHY: George Inness, Jr., *The Life, Art and Letters of* George Inness, 1917.—Alfred Trumble, *George Inness, N.A., A Memorial*, 1895.—*George Inness*, Masters in Art Series, June, 1908.—W. H. Downes, *Twelve Great Artists*, 1900.—Elliott Daingerfield, *Fifty Paintings by George Inness*, American Artists Series, 1913.—Elliott Daingerfield, *George Inness, the Man and His Art*, American Artists Series, 1911.

**INTAGLIO.**—See Greece.

**— (ENGRAVING).**—See Engraving.

**INTERNATIONAL STYLE.**—See Gentile da Fabriano.

**IONIA.**—See Greece.

**IONIC ORDER.**—See Capital; Greece (Architecture).

**IRAN.**—See Persia.

**IRON AGE.**—See Prehistoric Archæology.

**IRONWORK.**—Iron does not appear to have been used for decoration in ancient times. It was only used as a substitute for wood or bronze. One of the oldest uses to which iron was put seems to have been locksmith's work. The earliest locks were made by the Romans. The box is generally of metal repoussé, of a single piece and without any decoration. The key is often bent and the wards are often arranged in a very complicated way. For caskets and small pieces of furniture, "ring keys" were made, in which the shank, perpendicular to the ring, lay along the finger, so that the key could be carried without inconvenience as a ring. Padlocks were also made, little boxes provided with a bent and hinged shank, one end of which was able to penetrate the box. A spring kept it there, and the action of a simple key on this spring caused the shank to open. None of these locks, however, have any artistic value. Nevertheless a beautiful key has been found at Tartare (Rhône). It represents Silenus sitting on a wine-skin, and pressing a bunch of grapes.

IRONWORK OF A DOOR OF NOTRE DAME, PARIS.

LAMOUR: IRON-BARRED GATE OF THE PLACE STANISLAS, NANCY.

The barbarian invasions resulted in the extinction of all artistic effort in Europe. It is not until the Middle Ages that we find ironwork again. In the 12th century, it begins to rank as a fine art. The fine choir-screens of the Church of Conques (Avignon); the screens and hinges of Reims Cathedral, of Saint Martin, Angers, of Saint Saturnin—all date from this period. All the screens or grilles are made in the same way: a rectangular body, forming the frame, receives the bars, which are connected with others by means of square or rectangular pieces of iron, soldered together at the shoulders. These shoulders and pieces of iron were twisted into volutes, and constituted the entire decoration. But about the end of the century, ornamental subjects, such as flowers, fruit, and thistles, were soldered on to the ends of these volutes, which until then had been simply terminated in a point. St. Denis, St. Germer, and Westminster offer examples.

In the 13th century the method became more general. Also, ornaments were now not only inset between the bars, but were applied on to one side of the grille. In this way the iron volutes could be extended freely, and spread out in the most graceful and complicated curves. The four folding doors of the rood-screen of Rouen Cathedral were made like this (now in the Departmental Museum of Rouen).

Church doors owed to the ironworkers a new form of decoration. Originally, braces were only strengthening cross-pieces, rendered necessary by the size of the doors and the imperfect adjustment of their joists. They ended in a strong, flat bar, terminated at one extremity by a hinge, and at the other by a rudimentary flower. The thirteenth century, however, produced marvels of grace and strength.

On the right and left doors of the façade of Notre Dame, Paris, are splendid braces, dating from this period, skilfully restored by Viollet-le-Duc.

Ironwork reached its highest level at the end of the 13th century. The ironworkers then achieved a perfection and suppleness, simply by the use of the hammer, which has never since been equalled. Indeed this very technical ability and facility led, as was the case with so many other arts, to decadence; for craftsmen were tempted to overload their work with useless ornament, simply to show off their skill. Then the demand for decorated grilles and braces grew to such an extent that, from the 14th century, there was an endeavour to produce them more quickly and easily. Thin, flat iron which was easy to work was more and more used. The example of the armourers led the ironworkers to beat the iron into thin plates and work it with a hammer. The use of beaten iron came from Germany, and soon became general. Fine grilles were still made, of a new pattern, the upright and transverse bars being equidistant, and thus forming squares which filled with "twigs," often in very complicated curves (e.g., in the Church of Langeac, and Siena and Orvieto Cathedrals).

The file seems to have been invented about the end of the 14th century. This new instrument allowed the work to be finished easily, seams to disappear, and more regular and more delicate curves to be obtained; but its appearance hastened still more the decadence of fine ironwork. At the beginning of the 15th century, little was made but wrought-iron work, worked with a hammer and finished with a file. This was applied to the door, by interposing layers of copper or canvas, painted red, the remains of which are visible in many places. Gradually the progress of carpentry, the invention of stronger tenons and of planed joists, gave doors enough solidity so that braces became purely ornamental, and were finally abolished.

Although the file was fatal to the finest ironwork, its use gave to locksmith's work a precision and finish hitherto unknown. Beautiful locks were made in the 14th century, and were generally put in a projecting position on the door, without being let in to the wood. They were decorated with designs of foliage and flowers; and almost always the key-hole is masked by a spring guard, decorated with the figure of an animal, and controlled by a button. Other locks call to mind those coarse fastenings which one sees nowadays on barn doors: a round iron bolt is handled by means of a hinged flap, the hasp, which carries a ring, the catch. When the hasp is lowered, this ring gets stuck in an opening of the lock, and is held there by a bolt which functions the key. All these pieces were decorated first with the hammer, then with the file and chisel. These kinds of locks were much used for shutters, windows and furniture.

All metalwork in the 15th century was attractively decorated—hand-guards, little hinges on the doors of furniture, etc. Locks with a double turn came into use. A very fine lock dating from this period may be seen on a door of the Sacristy of Rouen Cathedral.

Of all the iron accessories used for dwellings, one of the most interesting is the door-knocker. It seems to date from the 11th century (Cathedral of Le Puy, in Velay). It was then a simple, heavy ring. Its presence on church doors was of special significance: the mere seizing it sufficed to give right of sanctuary. About the 15th century, the door-knocker became a veritable "objet d'art." It was made in the form of an animal's head, a winged monster, a lizard, etc. The following century saw the return of the ring, but much ornamented; and then the appearance of a singular apparatus, the handle-scraper. A twisted iron handle is fixed horizontally on the door. A large ring is attached to it, and by making it slide along the handle, a grating noise was made. The handle-scraper remained in favour until the end of the 16th century. It was the earliest mechanical warning. It was succeeded by the bell.

About the end of the 16th century, there appeared in France a new kind of grille, which originated in Germany, made of twisted shafts of iron. It was succeeded, in France, by grilles of sheet-iron, cut and soldered, or even riveted (St. Ouen, Rouen; St. Sernin, Toulouse), and was used until the end of the seventeenth century. The whole of Europe soon adopted it, and one of the finest examples may be seen in the Cathedral of Roskilde, in Denmark. The grilles of the "Galerie d'Apollon" and those of the hall of Gallo-Roman antiquities (Louvre) belong to the same period. They were designed by Daniel Marot for the Château de Maisons, and are among the finest examples of late French ironwork.

The 18th century was the century of fountains, and these allowed scope for the ironworker, in the making of railings, which were often decorated with complicated ornaments. Railings were sometimes used to enclose statues. The most famous of these are those of Versailles, of the hospital of Troyes, and, above all, of the Place Stanislas, Nancy,—the work of Lamour.

Nearer our own day forged iron was often successfully applied to the decoration of houses, and pieces of furniture were often decorated with iron rails.

See Pls. 11, 34, Vol. I.

BIBLIOGRAPHY: *Fidelle ouverture de l'art du Serrurier,* by Mathurin Jousse. Rouen, 1627.—R. Davesne, *Plauches de serrurerie et ferronnerie.* 1676.—Hoyan, *L'art du serrurier.* Paris, 1826.—R. Bordeaux, *La serrurerie du moyen âge.* Paris, 1858.—J. Labarte, *Histoire des arts industriels au moyen âge et à l'époque de la Renaissance.*—A. Pergin, *Recueil des modèles de serrurerie et de ferronnerie.*—Loquet, *Aperçu historique de la serrurerie et de la ferronnerie.* Rouen, 1886.

**ISABEY (Jean Baptiste).**—French painter (1767-1855). He

ISABEY: THE FIRST CONSUL IN THE PARK AT MALMAISON. (Museum, Versailles.)

learned the elements of his art in his native town of Nancy, at the studio of Girardet, the painter of history, and with Claudot, a landscape painter. In 1786, Isabey went to Paris. Eventually he became the pupil of David, who had returned from Rome. His solid lessons did much to make Isabey a master in the lighter style which he had already chosen.

In 1789, Isabey was commissioned to paint a certain number of portraits for a library, and, on the strength of a remark by Mirabeau, he decided to give up historical painting for portraiture. The portraits of David and of Madame de Stael were done in pencil.

Many of his compositions were reproduced in engraving, among them two pictures known as *Departure for the Army* and *The Return.* But his chief success was won by a more intimate subject, *The Barque of Isabey* (Louvre). Here the painter has represented himself steering a boat in which his three children are grouped round their mother, who is seated under a rustic pavilion.

The large composition of the *Revue of the First Consul* is, perhaps, still better known. No painting is more interesting and in the best sense of the word historical, than that simple Revue, for which Carle Vernet drew the horses.

According to contemporaries Isabey painted better likenesses of Napoleon, at various periods of his life, than anyone else. The painter had known Bonaparte after his return from his first campaign in Italy. He had already been acquainted with Madame Bonaparte, and had taught drawing to her daughter. Isabey was so greatly in favour that he was ordered to direct the ceremony of the Coronation. According to custom, the memory of it was to be consecrated by a magnificent series of engravings. Isabey had control of it and made drawings of all the standing figures. The work was not finished in 1814, when Napoleon was forced to abdicate.

After condoling with the fallen Emperor, Isabey painted a fine portrait of Louis XVIII (Louvre). He followed Marie-Louise to Vienna, where he profited from his sojourn in the capital by making many drawings of Viennese actors. The same day that Napoleon re-entered the Tuileries, Isabey returned to Paris. After Waterloo, he went to England, whence, however, he soon returned to resume his artistic life. He died in 1855, at the age of eighty-eight.

**ISENBRANDT (Adriaen).**—Flemish painter, of the beginning of the 16th century. He was probably born at Haarlem about 1485. Nothing is known of him until 1510, when he settled in Bruges and became a master of the Guild of Saint Luke. He died in 1551. If he was not the pupil of Gerard David, he at any rate imitated him, and was probably his assistant, notably in *The Marriage of Cana* (Louvre), a great part of which he seems to have painted.

Sweetness of facial expression, careful workmanship, and brilliant, transparent colour are his characteristics. No document or signature allows any work to be attributed to him with absolute certainty. He is, however, considered to be the painter of a beautiful diptych, painted between 1528 and 1534, for Barbara de la Meere, widow of a burgomaster of Bruges, representing the *Madonna of the Seven Sorrows* (one panel is now in Notre Dame of Bruges, the other, representing the donors, is in the Brussels Gallery). This work reveals a strong influence of Gerard David. By analogy, he is also credited with the *Adoration of the Magi* (Lubeck Cathedral), *The Presentation of Christ at the Temple* (Bruges, Saint Sauveur), the *Appearance of the Virgin to St. Ildefonse* (late Northbrook Collection, London), *Saint Luke Painting the Virgin,* and other pictures.

BIBLIOGRAPHY: Fierens Gevaert, *Les Primitifs flamands.* Vol. II. Brussels.—Friedländer, M. J., *Altniederländische Kunst,* Vol. II.

**ISIDORE OF MILETUS.**—See Byzantine Art (First Golden Age); Constantinople; Saint Sophia.

**ISPAHAN (Persia).**—*Mosque.* See Moslem Architecture, Persian School, also Moslem Art.

**ISRAELS (Josef).**—Dutch painter, 1824-1911. His parents wanted to make him a rabbi, and early in life he studied and became familiar with the Talmud. He then worked in his father's little bank. In 1870, Israels went to Amsterdam, and entered the studio of Jan Kruseman, who was a fashionable painter at that time. He lived there for seven years, his parents placing him with a very pious family who lived in the Ghetto of Amsterdam. He was enchanted with the quaintness of this part of the town, with its narrow streets and old market-place, still touched with oriental charm. Like Rembrandt, he watched the merchants of all kinds—sellers of fish, oranges and various fruits—and observed the Jewish housewives going about their daily tasks.

Under the influence of his master he painted some large historical pictures. In 1845 he visited Paris and saw the exhibition of Ary Scheffer, and he resolved, for a time at least, also to become "a painter of sentiment." He joined Picot's studio and competed for admission to the École des Beaux Arts. Then he entered the studio of Paul Delaroche, just when Millet was leaving it. He stayed there for three years, and then returned to his own country, and painted Biblical and historical scenes, according to the Academic receipts which he had learned in Paris—paintings which are poor in workmanship, and crude in colour. It was not until he was about forty years old that Israels discovered himself. Staying with some fisher-folk, he became enthusiastic for the life of the sea, and interested in the simple and tragic lives of its toilers. His first success, the *Wrecked*, was immense. It shows a marked tendency to anecdotal pathos, and an excessive use of bituminous colour. Unfortunately, these two faults persisted in Israels' art. In 1871 he settled in The Hague, where he painted what are probably his best works, *The Sacristan, A Son of the People,* and *Old Age.* These pictures, which are quiet in tone, belong, nevertheless, to that great modern movement which was interested, above all else, in problems of light.

See Pl. 59, Vol. II.

Bibliography: Veth, Jan., *J. Israels en zijn Kunst.* Arnhem, 1904.—Plasschaert, A., *J. Israels.* Amsterdam, 1924.—Dake, C. L., *J. Israels.* Berlin, 1911.

**ITCHÔ (Hanabusa).**—Japanese painter and poet (Osaka, 1653—Yedo, 1724). Although a pupil of Yasunobu he broke away from the Kano School, keeping, however, its technique. One of the masters of humorous and realistic art in the following of Matahei, with whom he has more than one point of resemblance. His realistic works are much sought after for no artist has shown more fantasy in the rendering of peasants' costumes, or more humour than in his pictures of the Seven Gods of Happiness and of the Buddhist gods. In 1698 he was exiled to Ôshima in Izu where he remained for twelve years.

Hokusaï and more especially Hiroshige owed much to him. His influence is seen chiefly in their landscapes. Among Itchô's best works may be mentioned the *Twelve Months,* in the Gierke Collection, and *Summer Shower* in Baron Kuki Shûzô's Collection, in Tokyo.

**IVÁNYI-GRÜNWALD (Béla).**—Contemporary Hungarian painter and illustrator, born in 1867 in Somogy. He was a pupil of Székely and Lotz, and studied at Munich and the Academie Julian in Paris. He painted large religious compositions which received public recognition. In 1896 we find him among the founders of the Nagybánya art colony in Hungary. In 1904, as the recipient of the Prix de Rome he left for Italy for two years. In 1911 he founded the second Hungarian art colony at Kecskemét, where he taught until 1918. Although this artist never rid himself of the Germanic influences as seen in his preference for painting the individual rather than the type, he has nevertheless worked with a strong nationalistic spirit. In his later years he turned to Hungarian landscape and rural life as represented by Munkácsy and Paál. He may be called the connecting link between the past and present art in Hungary, in his combination of pathos and sonority with sparkle and imagination. He illustrated several books and designed gobelins.

Bibliography: Genthon, *Uj magyar festömüvészet,* 1935.

**IVORY.**—Under this heading we shall consider statues and bas-reliefs which have come down to us

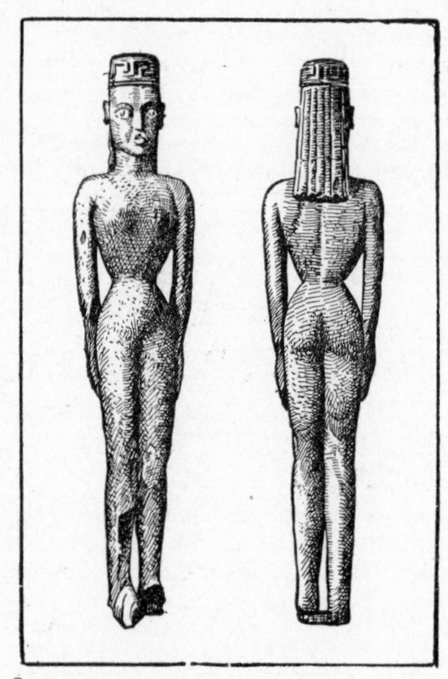

Small ivory statue found in a tomb, Athens.

from ancient and mediæval times, and which are designated under the general name of "Ivories." From the most remote times, artists cut little blocks or plaques from the trunks of elephants and carved them into little figures and reliefs. This hard material with its very fine grain, which gives an admirable surface, lends itself to the execution of carvings which are often veritable masterpieces. The Greeks practised Chryselephantine sculpture, that is to say, ivory carving associated with gold, silver and precious stones. The famous statue of Pallas Athena, which Phidias made for the Parthenon, was in ivory, inlaid with precious metal and stones. The Romans used ivory for their diptychs, which were leaves of ivory covered with wax to make a surface for writing; the consular diptychs are the most interesting, because they are generally decorated with sculptured bas-reliefs. After the downfall of the Roman Empire, the centre of civilisation shifted to the East, with Byzantium as its capital. The art of ivory carving occupies a very important place in Greco-Byzantine art. The most famous schools in the fourth to the sixth centuries of our era, were in Alexandria (Egypt). Artists made chiefly diptychs, caskets and pyxes (little boxes with a lid). Among the most remarkable works of this period and of this region must be mentioned the ivory plaques, discovered in a necropolis of Alexandria and which adorn the Bishop's Throne of Aix-la-Chapelle; the Brescia casket, dating from about the fifth century on which are carved scenes from the Miracles and Passion of Christ, in an interesting architectural setting; the *Angel,* in the British Museum, which dates from the sixth century and the famous Barberini Diptych of the Louvre. In all these works the grace of the drapery, the noble attitudes of the figures and the regularity of the features, evoke the memory of Greek art. But soon oriental influence predominated, and it is well seen in two monuments of Ravenna—the famous throne of Maximian, decorated with ivory bas-reliefs, and the diptych of Murano (Museum of Ravenna), which is decorated with those long angular figures which are so often

Diptych of the Muses (ivory in the antique style of the sixth century). (Louvre.)

found in Byzantine art. The plaquette of the Treasury of Trèves which represents a Translation of Relics is also a fine Byzantine work of the sixth century. One could name quantities of caskets and boxes now scattered in museums throughout Europe. In the eighth century, in Byzantium, we come to the Iconoclastic period, that is to say a reaction, at once religious and political, against works of art—frescoes, mosaics, ivories—with representations of Christ, the Virgin, saints and prophets. Many works were destroyed, and on those which were still made, religious subjects disappeared. In the eighth and ninth centuries, Byzantine ivories consisted of magnificent caskets, decorated with pagan subjects—scenes from the chase, mythology, and history — surrounded with delicate borders of rosettes and foliage, such as may be admired in the Pirano casket (Vienna) and the Veroli casket (Victoria and Albert Museum). When the quarrel of the Iconoclasts had died down, and the Church had again authorised the representation of sacred figures, the art of the ivory carvers took on a new lease of life. It spread with such profusion that the quality of the work often suffered, and articles became merely industrial objects.

Nevertheless, genuine artists continued to make caskets, diptychs and triptychs, with religious and pagan subjects. To the tenth and eleventh centuries belong such remarkable works as the casket in the Treasury of Troyes, a fine casket in the Cluny Museum, the Harbaville triptych (Louvre), with an Apotheosis of Christ, which is a masterpiece of observation and delicacy (eleventh century), the reliquary of Cortona, the coffer of the Treasury of Sens (between the tenth and twelfth centuries), etc. During the twelfth and thirteenth centuries, the art of carving on

Evangelistary cover (Ivory of the fifth century). (Bibl. Nat.)

ivory was still practised in Byzantium, but it gradually disappeared at the time of the Renaissance. The Byzantine Empire, a prey to political agitations, weakened; poverty succeeded the opulence of the Imperial court, and luxury arts, such as ivory carving and jewelry, died out, as the demand for them ceased.

The countries of the West, however, after troubled times and barbarian invasions, resumed their old splendour. In Italy and France,

Evangelistary cover (Ivory plaque of the eleventh century). (Bibl. Nat.)

Romanesque art produced marvels of beauty. The art of the ivory sculptor revived. Certainly there had been, from the fifth or sixth century, attempts at carving on ivory; from Merovingian times, articles such as combs and caskets, have come down to us, but their interest is rather historical than artistic. It was not until the Carolingian period that we find really interesting ivories. In the ninth and tenth centuries, able workers, inspired by Eastern models, revived this art. One of the earliest works is a book cover of the Psalter of Charles the Bald (Bibliothèque Nationale), executed between 842 and 859. One of the leaves shows "Christ Blessing with the Apostles," and the other, "Nathan reproaching David for the murder of Uriah." The Monastery of Saint Gall possesses a Bible of which the ivory cover is the work of the monk Tuotilo (ninth century), the only artist of that period whose name we know. Other Carolingian ivories, made either in France or in Germany, are to be found in various Church Treasuries or Museums.

SADDLE-BOW (Italian ivory of the thirteenth century). (Louvre.)

One of the most remarkable ivory caskets dating from the Romanesque period is the Bamberg reliquary (Munich). The best Romanesque ivories were made in France, Germany and Spain. One of the finest is the Crucifix of Leon Cathedral, which dates from the middle of the eleventh century; the Almogueira casket (Louvre), a fine casket in the Museum of Madrid, and others, in various Church Treasuries, show the influence of Arabic art. At this time (eleventh century) the countries of northern Europe were also working in ivory. Great Britain and Scandinavia carved sets of chess-men, often inspired by Eastern art, caskets and plaques. Romanesque Italy has left us only one ivory, the altar-front of Salerno Cathedral, on which are represented, in more than thirteen panels, scenes taken from the Bible. The composition, much influenced by Byzantine art, is, from an iconographical point of view, of great interest.

Finally, the Arabs were excellent workers in ivory and left some wonderful examples of their art. The finest ivories belonged to the Gothic period. This precious material, imported from Africa, was thrown on European markets in great abundance and amateurs, princes, courtiers and rich citizens all wanted ivory carvings of religious or secular objects—combs, tablets, boxes, book-covers, crucifixes—but it would be impossible to mention here the innumerable articles which were sculptured in ivory during the 13th and 14th centuries. Some names have come down to us, but we cannot connect them with any particular works; Jean le Scelleur, who worked for Philippe le Long in Paris, and for the Comtesse d' Artois, about 1320; Bertrand; Jean le Braellier; and Jean de Marville, ivory worker of the Duc de Bourgoyne in the second half of the 14th century. It will be noticed that all these names, and many others mentioned in the registers, are French. Indeed, many workshops of the ivory makers were situated in the Ile-de-France, and many in Paris itself. Certainly there were, in the Gothic period, ivory carvers in Italy, in the countries of the Rhine, in England and in Flanders, but in many cases they copied French models, and in this art French influence was supreme. Among works having an original style and character may be mentioned the Virgin of the Treasury of Pisa, attributed to Pisano, the Grandison diptych (British Museum), a Virgin in Berlin, the chalices of the Münster Treasury, and various pieces from the famous studio of the Embriachi in Venice,—Virgins, triptychs, caskets,—and still others—too many to enumerate. On the whole, however, the great mass of magnificent ivories is of French inspiration and workmanship.

Foreign princes who visited Paris purchased ivories, and left important orders. These Gothic ivories differ very much from the Romanesque ivories, both in style and technique.

For half a century, from the beginning of the 13th century, it seemed that the art of ivory carving was partly lost, for no work of that period has come down to us; and when, in the last thirty years of the 13th century, artists set to work, it was to create a new art, that of statuettes. Instead of plaques, diptychs, caskets, decorated with bas-reliefs in the old manner of the Byzantine and the Romanesque artists, we now have isolated figures or groups. It seems as though the ivory workers tried to reproduce the wonderful statues which adorned the porches and altars of the great Cathedrals, and sometimes even scenes with several figures. A little later, they used the old forms as well, while continuing to make statuettes. Among the most beautiful Gothic ivories are, the Virgin, rather archaic in type, of the Hamburg Museum, the *Virgin* of the Cluny Museum, and the *Deposition*, and the very lovely *Coronation of the Virgin* (both in the Louvre). All these works were made in the last thirty years of the 13th century.

From about the end of the same century dates a group of charming diptychs, which M. Molinier thinks came from a work-shop in Soissons. "The characteristic feature of this School is its architectural decoration." None of these works remains in France. They are now scattered in the Hermitage in Leningrad, in the Vatican, and in the Victoria and Albert Museum and Wallace Collection (London). On most of them are represented scenes from the Life of Christ, especially of the Passion. At the beginning of the 14th century, the art of ivory carving attained its highest degree of perfection. From this time, date those exquisite Virgins, with smiling faces, who hold the child on one hip, a position which is very graceful in its movement, when not exaggerated, as it sometimes is in statues carved in stone. The most famous is the *Virgin* of the Sainte Chapelle (Louvre), which dates from the first quarter of the 14th century. During this century, the ivory workers made chiefly *Virgins*, and little portable altars, which were kind of altar-screens or triptychs, divided into compartments. These were generally carved with subjects taken from the life of the Virgin—the Nativity, the Presentation at the Temple, the Death and Assumption of the Virgin. Often, the middle compartment is occupied by a statue of the Madonna in relief. The finest of these altar-screens, or triptychs are in European Museums (Cluny, Victoria and Albert Museum, Vienna), and in the Treasuries of the Cathedrals.

Throughout the 14th century, a great quantity of these ivories were made, but there was a gradual decadence, although artists such as those who carved the diptychs of the Passion (Louvre, Museums of Madrid, Copenhagen, Berlin, Dijon, Victoria and Albert Museum), continued to work in ivory, and often showed remarkable ability in carving scenes with many figures, and perspective effects. But signs of affectation began to appear, and easily lapsed into mannerism: elegance tended to usurp sincerity. One must, however, call attention to certain charming ivories, decorated with subjects taken from the chase, tournaments, and mythology.

After the 14th century, there came an end to the beautiful art of ivory carving, which had been practised, in ancient times and throughout the Middle Ages. There were still some artists who, in addition to more ambitious works, carved some charming statuette or bas-relief, but these things are of much less interest.

See Pls. 43, 55, Vol. I.

BIBLIOGRAPHY: E. Molinier, *Les Ivoires*. 1896.—A. Maskell, *Ivories*. 1905.—E. Scherer, *Elfenbeinplastik seit der Renaissance*. 1903.—A. Goldschmidt, *Die Elfenbeinskulpturn aus der Zeit der karolingischen und sächischen Kaiser*.—R. Koechlin, *Les Ivoires Gothiques Françaises*. 1924. 3 Vols.—M. H. Longhurst, *English Ivories*. London, 1926.

# J

**JACKSON (John).**—English portrait painter, 1778-1831. He went to London in 1804, and entered the Academy in the following year. He became an R.A. in 1817, and two years later went to Italy. In Rome he painted the portrait of Canova, his best work, and that of John Flaxman, and of Lady Dover.

**JACOB OF AMSTERDAM.**—See Cornelisz van Oostsanen.

**JACOBELLO DEL FIORE.**—Venetian painter, about 1370-1439. He was inspired by Guariento, whose *Paradise* he copied, and by Gentile da Fabriano. He painted the figure of Justice and two Archangels (1421, Venice), the *Lion of St. Mark*, with the Doges Palace in the background (1415). Other panels by him are well scattered.

**JACOMART BAÇÓ.**—Spanish painter, died in 1461. "His works though betraying a knowledge of the art and techniques of Jan van Eyck, show nevertheless characteristic motifs of distinct Valencian tradition." In 1440 Jacomart went to Valencia, as the king's painter. He was certainly acquainted with a painter from Bruges, Louis Alimbrot, who was living at Valencia at that time; but he never went to Flanders. He only made one journey to Italy, called by King Alphonse to Naples (1440). In 1451 he was again at Valencia.

To Jacomart is attributed a panel, with a gold background, in the Church of San Lorenzo, representing St. Francis giving the Rule of his Order. The *St. Jerome* (Naples) formerly attributed to Hubert van Eyck, was originally part of the altarpiece of San Lorenzo. It must be recognised, however, that none of the pictures which Jacomart painted in Spain approach Flemish models so nearly as do these panels of San Lorenzo.

Also attributed to him is a triptych which Cardinal Alfonso Borgia gave to the Collegiate Church of Jativa, and which still adorns that Church. In the middle of the altarpiece is the seated figure of St. Anne, holding on her knees the young Virgin, richly attired, who is herself holding the child Christ. On the side panels, on either side of the saint, are figures of two bishops—St. Augustine, before whom is kneeling his mother, St. Monica, and St. Ildefonso, before whom the donor, Cardinal Alfonso Borgia, is kneeling. Against the preciously worked backgrounds, shining brocades, and jewelled stuffs are painted with such finish as almost to deceive the eye. Two panels of the predella of the triptych are preserved in the Church of Jatavia. One of them represents the Baptism of St. Augustine, the other, the Virgin handing to St. Ildefonso the Miraculous Chasuble.

In 1457, Jacomart finished a large altarpiece depicting the legend of St. Martin, and probably destined for the Monastery of Val de Cristo (now in the Sacristy of the Church of San Martin de las Monjas at Segorbe). Jacomart Baçó died in 1461, shortly after having finished the altarpiece for the church of the village of Cati (signed contract of Jan. 1st, 1460), part of which is identified as his work. In the pictures which have been restored to his authorship, it is easy to see how the weighty magnificence of the materials, inspired by the Van Eycks, strengthened the rather soft elegance of the Valencian painter. The use of oil and varnish in the glazes gave his colour a new richness. Nevertheless, Jacomart, owing to his naïveté and freshness, remains the direct descendant of the Trecento masters. By the very abundance of his work, he must have exercised a lively influence on the artists of his day. A triptych, in the Church of Santa Catalina, in Saragossa, dating from 1454, shows clearly the influence of Jacomart, but the author is still unknown.

Bibliography: D. S. Sampere y Miguel, *Los Quatrocentistas.* Barcelona. 1905-1906.—E. Bertaux, *Peinture espagnole au XIV<sup>e</sup> et au XV<sup>e</sup> siècle.* Paris, 1908.—*Thieme-Becker,* vol. II., 1908; art. *Baçó, Jacomart* by M. v. B.—R. Ch. Post, *Hist. Span. Painting;* vol. VI, part i.

**JACOPO del CASENTINO.**—Florentine painter, c. 1300-c. 1358.

In 1339 Jacopo is mentioned as "chonsigliere" of the Compagnia di San Luca (Horne in Rivista d'Arte, VI, 1909); and he is also mentioned in the archives between 1339 and 1358 (see Horne, op. cit.). A provincial painter, eclectic and archaistic, Jacopo was probably formed in Arezzo under mingled Florentine and Sienese influence, and was later profoundly affected by the painting of Bernardo Daddi. His works, as given by Dr. Richard Offner in his *Corpus of Florentine Painting,* are the following:

Arezzo, Ospedale, the *Virgin,* two representations of the Savior, three scenes below; Berlin, Kaiser-Friedrich, *Madonna and Child, Saints and Angels;* Berlin, Herr Paul Bottenweiser, *Madonna del Latte;* Berne, Museum, tabernacle, *Coronation,* four scenes in shutters; Bonn, Museum, *Madonna and Child, Saints, Angels, Donors;* Brussels, Musée, *Madonna and Child;* Flechtingen, Baron von Schenk, fragments of a tabernacle; Florence, S. Miniato al Monte, altarpiece, *S. Miniato and Scenes from His Life;* Florence, Palazzo dell'Arte della Lana, tabernacle, *Madonna and Child, Saints and Angels;* Florence, Academy, three panels, St. John Evangelist, St. Nicholas, St. John Baptist; Florence, Fondazione Horne, *Madonna and Child;* Florence, Uffizi, *St. Bartholomew Enthroned with Eight Angels;* Florence, Loeser Collection, *Annunciation, Dormition, Madonna and Child with Saints and Angels;* Frankfurt, *Madonna and Child, Saints and Angels;* Göttingen, Museum, wings of a tabernacle; Herefordshire, Lord Somers, wings of an altarpiece; Milan, Don Guido Cagnola, small tabernacle (signed); Mulin del Piano (near Florence), Castello, *St. Peter Enthroned;* Pavia, Museo Civico, two wings of small triptych; Pozzolatico, Sto. Stefano, *Madonna and Child;* Princeton, Marquand Collection, *Crucifixion;* Rome, Vatican, *Madonna and Child;* Scarperia, Oratorio della Madonna di Piazza, *Madonna and Child, Two Angels;* Vienna, Herr Oscar Bondy, tabernacle, *Madonna and Child, Nativity, Crucifixion.*

Bibliography: H. P. Horne, *A Commentary upon Vasari's Life of Jacopo del Casentino,* Rivista d'Arte, 1909.—G. G. Goretti-Miniati, *Vita di Jacopo di Casentino* (Vasari-Occhini-Cozzani). Florence, 1913.—Richard Offner, A Corpus of Florentine Painting, Section III, Vol. II, Part II, 1930.

**— di CIONE.**—Florentine painter, brother and follower of Andrea Orcagna.

The earliest documentary evidence regarding Jacopo is of 1368 when he was commissioned to finish the panel of *St. Matthew* begun by Andrea. In 1368-69 he matriculated in the corporation of Medici, Speziali e Merciai. Between 1370 and 1373 he collaborates with Niccolò di Pietro Gerini, executing within that period the *Coronation* for S. Pietro Maggiore (1370-71) now in the National Gallery, London; and the *Coronation* for the Zecca Vecchia, now in the Uffizi. In 1387 he is mentioned as among the six consuls of the guild of Medici e Speziali, and in 1388 is a member of the S. Luca guild. In 1389 Jacopo colors and ornaments four marble statues for the Cathedral; and in 1390 pays for marble ordered by his brother Matteo and received after the latter's death. He is mentioned for the last time in 1394.

Authenticated works by Jacopo included the *Matthew and Four Scenes from His Life,* of 1367-68, now in the Uffizi, and the *Coronation* of 1373. For this latter work, executed in collaboration with Niccolò di Pietro Gerini and a helper, Jacopo received by far the largest payment, hence it is to be assumed that he did the larger part of the work. The 1370-71 large *Coronation* in the National Gallery, documented as a production of the shop of Gerini, was said by Vasari to be by Jacopo. Little as Vasari's attributions are to be trusted the polyptych is stylistically allied to the School of Orcagna, and has been attributed to Jacopo on these grounds.

Bibliography: See literature on Orcagna.

**— della QUERCIA (Jacopo di Pietro d'Angelo).**—Sienese sculptor and architect born in Quercia Grossa near Siena, probably in 1367; died in Siena 1438.

In 1401, Jacopo della Quercia competed with Ghiberti, Brunelleschi and other sculptors (see Ghiberti) in the competition for the doors of the Baptisty in Florence. In 1406 he executed the tomb of Ilaria del Caretto (died 1405) in the Duomo at Lucca; in 1408 the *Seated Madonna* in the Museum of the Duomo in Ferrara; at the end of this latter year he was back in Siena. In 1412 he was given the commission, by the Concistoro of Siena for the Fonte Gaia in the Piazza del Campo (sculptures now in the Palazzo Pubblico). In 1413 he was charged with decorating the Duomo, Lucca, with statues of the twelve Apostles; at the same time he offered to finish the sculptural ornament of the tabernacle, columns and window of the north side of the Cathedral. His helper was Giovanni Francesco da Imola. In this same year he returned once more to Siena, and in 1414 there were certain negotiations with Sano di Matteo, Nanni di Jacopo da Lucca, and Jacopo del Corso da Firenze about the marble reliefs for the Fonte Gaia. In 1416 he began the gravestone for the Trenta family in Lucca, but his presence was demanded in Siena and he went back to complete his plan for the Fonte Gaia. Finished in 1419, this received such approval that,

Jacopo della Quercia: Charity. (Palazzo Pubblico, Siena.)

according to Vasari, Jacopo was given the name of "della Fonte." In 1421 he received payment for the group, in wood, of the *Annunciation* in the Pieve in S. Gimignano; and the next year the Trenta altar in S. Frediano, Lucca, was finished. From 1423 dates the Intelminelli Tomb. In 1425 Jacopo was commissioned to design the great portal of S. Petronio, Bologna, and made trips to Verona, Venice, and Milan to acquire stone. Two years later he was still in Bologna and appointed Giovanni da Siena to substitute for him in Siena in directing further work on the Fonte Gaia. In 1428 he was requested to return to Siena where, in 1430, he received the commission for the bronze relief of *Zaccharias Driven from the Temple,* for the font (S. Giovanni, Siena). In 1429 he had been again in Bologna and had again travelled to Venice, Vicenza, Verona, and Ferrara in search of stone. Negotiations for the ornamentation of the Cappella di Sta. Maria e di S. Sebastiano in the Duomo of Siena probably began in Bologna through the Cardinal Casini who was there as Papal Legate. In 1436 Jacopo was named master architect of the Duomo in Siena; and the next year the quarrel between Siena and Bologna as to which city should enjoy his services came to a focus when the Signoria of Siena intervened between Jacopo and the Bolognese, who claimed that he had not kept his promise to them. After a trip to Bologna in this year he became ill and died in Siena in 1438.

Bibliography: Vasari-Milanesi, II.—Carl Cornelius, *Jacopo della Quercia.* Halle, 1896.—Landsberger, *Jacopo della Quercia* (Biblioth. d. Kstgesch., Vol. 74). Leipzig, 1924.—J. B. Supino, *Jacopo della Quercia.* 1926.—Pèleo Bacci, *Jacopo della Quercia, Nuovi doc. e commenti.* Siena, 1929.

**— da VALENZA.**—Venetian painter of the end of the 15th and the beginning of the 16th century, his signed works dating from 1485 to 1509; follower and assistant of Alvise Vivarini.

**JACQUE (Charles).**—French engraver, 1813-1894. He was a great admirer of Rembrandt and of Van Ostade. The influence of the latter is very definite in all his engravings, which are generally very remarkable, and among which may be mentioned the *Pig-stickers,* and the *Rat-trap.* Charles Jacque also made some coloured engravings.

**JACQUET (Mathieu).**—French sculptor, born about the middle of the 16th century, died in 1609. His father came from Grenoble, and he worked under the direction of Primaticcio on the tomb of Henry II, in Paris.

Mathieu's chief work is the fine model chimney-piece in the Château of Fontainebleau, which was destroyed in 1725, to make room for the theatre of Louis XV. The marble carvings remained in a shop until the reign of Louis-Philippe, when the most important piece, the equestrian statue of Henri IV, was used for a modern chimney-piece. The Louvre received bas-reliefs representing the Battle of Ivry, and the Surrender of Mantes, four figures of children holding the initial letter of Henri's name and the royal insignia, and two Victories. These are very charming works, refined in workmanship, and of a restraint which seems particularly admirable at this period of Italian influence. Mathieu's three sons were also sculptors.

Bibliography: St. Lami, *Dictionnaire des sculpteurs de l'école française du moyen âge au règne de Louis XIV.* Pp. 289-292.

**JADE.**—See China—Art.

**JAEN (Spain).**—*Cathedral,* 16th century. A church in the Griego-Romano style inaugurated by Diego de Siloé in the Cathedral of Granada, 1523-1528. Jean is more advanced than Granada in possessing Renaissance domes instead of late Gothic ribbed vaults.

**JAMNITZER.**—Family of German goldsmiths—Wenzel and Albrecht, two brothers, and Christopher, the grand-son of Wenzel. The best known is Wenzel (1508-1575), who worked at Nuremberg for Charles V. He made vases, coffers, and especially tables, decorated with figures of men and animals. Examples of his work may be seen in the Museums of Dresden, Munich, and Vienna.

Bibliography: Rosenberg, M., *W. Jamnitzer.* Frankfurt am Main, 1920.—Habich, G., *Die deutschen Medailleure des 16 Jahrh.* Halle, 1916.

**JANMOT (Louis François).**—French painter. Born in Lyon, 1814; died 1892. The rather sickly mysticism of this pupil of Ingres pleased Delacroix. Baudelaire found "his drawing refined, and his colour rather crude, recalling the old German masters." His best works are the *Last Supper* in the Hospice de l'Antiquaille in Lyon, and in the Church of St. François-de-Sales, in the same town. Janmot published, in 1881, a curious *Poème de l'Ame,* and, in 1887, the *Thoughts of an Artist on Art.*

**JAPAN — ART.** — Prehistory. — Little is known of the beginnings of Japanese art. The earliest artifacts belong to a neolithic culture of which pottery vessels and figurines, incised, pressed and carved, are the most important objects. Attempts to link the people or peoples of that age with the modern Japanese have been and still are unconvincing. Some scholars have claimed that the neolithic peoples were the ancestors of the modern Ainu. While others claim that they were a proto-Japanese race, still others claim that they were an unidentified race which had a circum-Pacific distribution. Absolute dates for the age have been as difficult to determine. But the end of the neolithic period is no later than the beginning of the Christian era when another culture appears which can be dated by finds of Chinese objects of the Han period (221 B.C.-A.D. 206).

*Pottery.*—The repertoire of the pottery includes bowls, bottles shaped like flasks, jars and figurines. The last are peculiar for their curving limbs and for the treatment of their eyes which are surrounded by a ridge-like circumference. Attempts to group the vessels by a study of motifs or material have been as unsuccessful as the search for their creators since a conglomeration of types has been found in the same tombs. The designs in one group consist mainly of a rope pattern, in another of a spiral which may be a conventionalized eye.

*Mirror.*—Chinese mirrors of the Han dynasty appear in tombs of the next civilization which flourished in Japan, a civilization which was acquainted with metal. Copies of the cast bronze mirrors of China are so fine that it is difficult to determine which were imported and which were made in Japan. A type of mirror peculiar to Japan and to this period is an adaptation of the Chinese mirror to which is added a series of bells around the circumference. The most typical object of the culture, however, is the *haniwa.* These are cylindrical pottery tubes, made of a reddish clay, which were set, like a fence, around important tombs. The earliest of these merely have perforations to indicate the eyes and mouth of the human face. Later, however, the forms develop into recognizable busts of men and women, and in the most advanced types, completely costumed figures and animals are represented. Because of similarities with Chinese costumes of the Wei period these advanced types can be dated in the sixth century A.D. It can further be presumed that these most advanced *haniwa* figures date from this time because their development was suddenly arrested by Buddhist art which appeared in the middle of the sixth century.

*Dotaku.*—Unique in this culture too is the *dotaku* which resembles, in general shape, a bell without a clapper. It is not known whether it actually was used as a bell or whether it had some entirely different use. Designs on the surface of the *dotaku* are distributed in rectangular panels and rendered in a thin raised line. The subject matter of the designs consists of scenes from daily life, houses, boats, and sometimes representations of animals. The motifs as well as the manner of rendering them are sometimes very similar to those found on bronze drums from Annam which date from the beginning of the Christian era. The shape of the *dotaku,* on the other hand, recalls that of bells found in Korea. Other relationships to Korea at this time are evident in the gray pottery vessels with conical foot and the *magatama,* crescent shaped stones which were extensively used for decoration (possibly with symbolic meaning) in both cultures. (See Korea—Art.)

ASUKA (552-646) OR SUIKO PERIOD (592-628).—The first historic period of Japan is known either as the Asuka period after the location of the capital, or as the Suiko period after the powerful Empress of that name. Tradition tells that the Chinese written language had been introduced into Japan as early as 400 A.D., but Japanese civilization had remained basically indigenous until 552 when, also according to tradition, the first Buddhist image was brought to Japan.

*Sculpture.*—The styles of the earliest Japanese sculptures corroborate this legend for they have such close resemblances to Chinese and Korean statuary of the middle of the sixth century that the provenance of certain pieces is still a matter of question. The earliest dated sculpture existing is a statue of the Buddha of Healing, which bears an inscription with a date that corresponds to 607 and indicates that the sculptor was *Tori Bushi,* a personage known from other sources. A Buddhist trinity by the same hand, dated 623, is in the same style, a style which still carried on the formulae popular in China seventy-five years before. (See China—Art.) In the Yumedono of the Temple of Horyuji there is a large wooden statue of Kwannon (Chinese Kuan Yin) which by tradition and style still belongs to this early period. The sculptor of this statue translated the technique of bronze casting into wood. As in most of the statues of this period the figure preserves a strict frontality, accentuated by wing-like draperies which militate against three-quarter or profile views. The elongation of the figure bears testimony of Korean, rather than direct Chinese influence. This is to be expected, for traditions emphasize the importance of the immigration of Korean workers at that time. A large group of smaller statues contain the same elements found in the sculptures described above, the great masterpieces of the earliest group.

A change from the two dimensional character of the earliest statues appears in the representations of the Four Guardian Kings (dating from 645-654) in the Kondo of Horyuji. Contrasted to the flat frontality of the types already discussed, a new understanding of the full-round treatment indicates an advance in technique.

*Painting.*—Painting in the Asuka period is known only from two existing monuments. One of these is the painting in litharge on the doors and sides of the Tamamushi Shrine, so-called because of the iridescent wings of the beetle (*tamamushi*) which were used as decoration beneath the grille work. The paintings on the sides and doors of the shrine which dates from the end of the sixth century include figures of the Guardian Kings and stories from the former lives of the Buddhas (*Jatakas*). The style with its fleeting rhythms resembles Wei painting in China while the stylization of some of the elements are reminiscent of the earlier styles of the Han period. A cinematographic progression which depicts a Buddha, first at the top of a cliff, then jumping, and finally at the bottom of the cliff being eaten by a tiger, is found in one panel.

*Embroidery.*—The same figure style is found in the remnants of an embroidered textile made about 623 in memory of the great protector of Buddhism in Japan, Prince Shotoku Daishi.

HAKUHO PERIOD (646-710).—The Hakuho period was a period of transition. During that time the Japanese began to assimilate and modify Chinese art which they had taken over in the preceding century.

*Sculpture.*—The angular frontality of the sculptures became more rounded and the stiff folds soften, losing the stony quality of the preceding style. The finest example of this phase is the Miroku (Maitreya) in the Chuguji Monastery. In wood, the lacquered figure still gives the effect of its bronze prototypes, but the modelling is far more subtle and a human quality begins to replace archaic aloofness, and sensuous surfaces begin to supplant conventionalized planes. While many Hakuho sculptures follow this tradition, a new wave of Chinese influence brought in the full-blown T'ang style and again Japanese sculpture became involved in assimilating the art of foreign China instead of developing along its own line of creation. The climax of this movement is found in the Yakushiji Trinity made in 686 or 710. The figures adopt the baroque fulness of T'ang statues, and a distinct "S" curve appears in the bodies of the standing Bosatsu (Bodhisattva), a mannerism which was to be even further elaborated in the following Nara period. An archaistic tendency is visible in a few sculptural groups, the most important of which are the Shrine of the Lady Tachibana and the statue of Yakushiji Niorai in Shin-Yakushiji. These maintain much of the earlier repose and simplified formulae which are combined with the naturalism that was introduced towards the end of the period.

*Painting.*—The only painting remaining from the period is on the base of the Tachibana Shrine. More natural than the Asuka style it shows the beginning of shading used, as it was in the contemporaneous paintings of Tun Huang, for decorative rather than illusionistic purposes. (See China—Art.) A painting of Shotoku Daishi with his son and younger brother has been ascribed to the period 663-696, but is considered by many authorities to be a close copy of a later period. There is no doubt, however, that the painting reproduces the style of the period. The shading, the simplicity, the hieratic composition, and the treatment of the drapery all have many features in common with the *Emperor Scroll* attributed to Yen Li Pen (in the Museum of Fine Arts, Boston).

TEMPYO OR NARA PERIOD (710-794).—In 710 the Imperial capitol was moved to Nara. The period which dates from this time to 794 when the capital was again moved to the Heian district of Kyoto, is known either as Nara or Tempyo.

*Painting.*—The powerful art of T'ang China found a receptive atmosphere in the sumptuous court at Nara. In the Kondo of Horyuji a series of mural paintings representing hieratic groups of Buddhist divinities (c. 710) brings to a climax the type of painting which has been observed in the Asuka and Hakuho periods. The style is at this time so purely Chinese that some authorities consider the Horyuji paintings to be the work of imported artists. The scenes represent a Buddha flanked on each side by a Bodhisattva. The compositions preserve the same hieratic formality that is present in the T'ang painting at Tun Huang in westernmost China. The supple curves of the bodies represent as well the Indian influence which China passed on to Japan, but the technique is entirely Far Eastern. An archaistic trend is observable in an illustrated manuscript, the *Inga-kyo* (Sutra of Cause and Effect). The painting is evidently a copy of a sixth century Chinese work, and bears close resemblances to the few paintings and to the bas-reliefs that remain from that time.

The art of the Nara period is especially well known because in 754, following the death of the Emperor Shomu, his widow, the Empress Komyo, dedicated his belongings to the Daibutsu, the great Buddha (see below). A series of inventories show that, with few additions, this bequest has remained almost intact until today, in the original building in which it was stored, the Shosoin at Nara. Important for our knowledge of the figure style of the eighth century is a group of screens which represent on each panel a court lady standing beside a tree. Only the outlines and the faces of these paintings remain, for originally the pictures were completed by filling in the body with kingfisher feathers which have since disappeared. The figures carry on the same rather heavy type known in eighth century China from pottery figurines. A representation of Kichijoten belonging to the Yakushiji Temple still preserves the splendor of the style so palely reflected by the screen paintings. More like a court lady than a divinity the figure shows the artist's interest in rich raiment and human beauty. Even the organic movement of the body recalls little of the stylized grace of the preceding century.

The Shosoin contains other objects of importance. Literature of the time shows how thoroughly the Chinese civilization had penetrated the courtly circles, but in the Shosoin there are objects of material culture that speak even more strongly than the descriptions of contemporaneous writers. Little sketches on the backs of paper made by scribes to pass the time evince such a free calligraphic brushwork that, were it not for the complete lack of artistic consciousness inherent in these fragments, one would assume a virtuoso quality in painting at that early date.

Extremely fine lacquers also were deposited in the Shosoin. Some inlaid with mother-of-pearl or ingeniously decorated with gold and silver are finer artistically as well as superior technically than the best lacquers of later periods. A large group of textiles shows the same care in execution and sumptousness of decoration. Many of the designs on the objects show the influence of Sassanian art which probably reached Japan by way of T'ang China where strong Near Eastern influences were also felt at the same time.

Very important for the study of Chinese landscape painting is a series of paintings on the face of several *biwa,* musical instruments similar to a lute. Some of these may be the work of Chinese artists, but all reflect the style of continental painting. Other articles in the Shosoin are mirrors (including Chinese), bows and arrows, swords, and innumerable different objects of the courtly life. All have this in common, that they show the overwhelming influence of China.

Motonobu (Kano): Painting in black and white.

*Sculpture.*—Sculpture was also influenced by China. The Yakushiji trinity which is either late Hakuho or early Nara has already been noted. This trinity exemplifies one trend of the Nara period, namely the baroque. Another trend appears in sculpture at this period, that is, the development of naturalistic sculpture. The climax of this naturalism was reached in a series of priest portraits. In these the only trace of the hieratic tradition is noticeable in the slight formalism of the draperies, and the somewhat generalized treatment of personalities.

Although most of the deities have the baroque characteristics of T'ang sculpture, a definite restraint is manifest in the clay representations of Four Heavenly Kings in the Todaiji at Nara. Perhaps it was the material which led the sculptor to create these highly compressed forms, narrow waists, and arrested gestures which embody a latent strength more terrifying than the violent representations of later periods. Both wood and dry lacquer were popular media for sculpture at this period. In 752 a gigantic bronze statue, The Daibutsu, was built at Nara. It so depleted the bronze reserves of the country that for the succeeding centuries little work was done in that medium. Most of the statue has since been destroyed by fire but some of the petals from the lotus pedestal remain. These bear engravings of the period which reproduce the same baroque and sensuous style found in contemporaneous sculpture and painting.

*Architecture.*—Architecture of this age is known from a series of existing buildings at Horyuji and Nara. Like the other arts of the period, architecture carries on Chinese traditions with the emphasis on an overhanging roof supported by intricate bracketing systems and terminated by upturned corners (see China—Art). Another type of building which has existed in Japan for centuries is the indigenous Shinto type. This follows the form of a thatched hut frequently raised on piles. The most distinguished feature is the continuation of the end roof beams so that they cross, forming a "V" over the ridge pole. Since Shinto traditions require that a building be torn down and completely rebuilt every twenty years,

Japanese saber guards. (Musée des Arts Décoratifs.)

no actual building dates from an early period. However the Shrine of Ise has always been rebuilt just as the previous building and thus probably differs very little from the form of its early prototype.

The Ninth Century Konin or Jogan Period (Early Heian) (794-897).—The ninth century is known variously as the Konin or Jogan period after eras of those names, or as Early Heian after the transfer of the court in 794 to the Heian district of Kyoto. In general the artistic styles of the time are developments of Nara traditions. An increasing heaviness noted towards the end of the eighth century is supplanted in the next hundred years by a clumsy formality. Coincidental with the heavier forms,

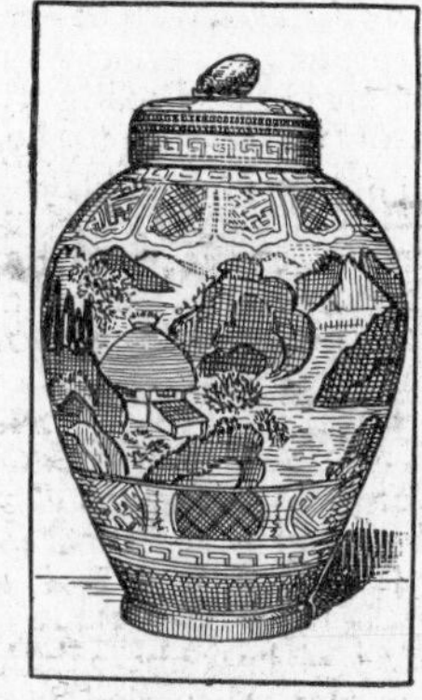

Vase of Kutani ware. (Musée Cernuschi.)

a new iconography appeared based on the mystical Buddhist sects, Shingon and Tendai, which enjoyed great popularity at that time. Figures with multiple arms and heads become more common, while a deeply sensuous feeling pervades the sculpture. A greater elaboration is found also in the exploded power of the figures. Contrasted with the latent force of eighth century figures those of the ninth century have additive cumulations that are only bombastic reflections of the real strength of Nara. The formalism of the age can be observed in the heavy rather unpleasant features which lack the calm serenity of the past century. A formula known as the "rolling wave" pattern is another evidence of a growth towards conventionalism in an art that has passed its peak. This pattern consists of an alternation of sharp with round ridges to represent the folds of drapery. Beginning about 800, it ceases to be used by the end of the century and is a distinctive mark of this age.

*Painting.*—Painting follows the same aesthetic found in sculpture. Figures are painted in the so-called expansive style. The bodies fill out the surface, something projecting, beyond the edge of the picture, as in the well known *Red Fudo* in Myo-O-in. The same effect is carried out in the paintings of *Mandaras,* mystical and symbolical representations of assembled deities which became popular with the growth of esoteric Buddhism.

Later Heian or Fujiwara Period (897-1184).—During the tenth century the imperial power was gradually superseded by that of the Fujiwara clan who followed a policy of intermarrying with the imperial family and allowing the emperor to be the theoretical head of the government although deprived of all important power. Towards the end of the period in 1156 the Fujiwara were displaced by the Taira clan who in their turn were overthrown in 1184 by the Minamoto. At that time the capital was once more moved and the Heian period ended. The period is artistically important for the development of an indigenous style in Japan. The disturbed condition of China during the Five Dynasties materially weakened China's influence on Japanese art. Literature in the Japanese language takes the place of Chinese poems written by the *literati,* just as in the sixteenth century the English vernacular finally superseded Latin as the literary language. The *Tale of Genji* written by Lady Murasaki at the beginning of the tenth century describes the court of the period, a court that is also portrayed in the painting of the period.

*Painting.*—Indeed, illustrations to this story become one of the standard themes of later Fujiwara painting as well as that of following periods. Besides the traditional Buddhist painting which continued to be perpetuated, other types appeared. Most important is the school of *Eshin Sozu* (d. 1017). Innumerable representations of Amida Buddha accompanied by Kwannon and Dai Seshi reflect the sweetness of the "Pure Land" sects whose tenets in some instances held that the believer had only to call on Amida when dying to attain salvation. Painting of these sects has a human and decorative quality which takes the place of the traditional hieratic types that coexisted with them.

Secular painting becomes important at this time. Two main types appear. The first is decorative, with bright colors, silver and gold, and conventionalized figures seeming more like puppets than people. This type makes use of certain formulae. The conventional bird's-eye view was adopted and combined with roofless houses for the purpose of more easy narration, as well as for the decorative possibilities of the diagonals of the houses which were used to vary the compositions. Faces were drawn in the "single stroke" technique with a single line for the nose, each eye, and the mouth. Opposed to this almost purely decorative illustrational type was the lively, dramatic type, depending more upon line than color for its effects, and emphasizing personality almost to the point of caricature. Examples of the first decorative school are the many versions of the *Tale of Genji,* and even some illustrated Buddhist sutras which, although of religious inspiration, are purely secular in treatment. The *Heike Nokyo,* painted about 1164 and now in the Itsukushima Shrine, belongs in this category as does a series of fans which bear parts of sutras painted over illustrations. These and many paintings of the decorative school are painted in the *tsukuri-e* technique. This method was first to sketch (or print as in the case of the fans) the outline then to cover the surface with a sizing (gofun) after which the picture was colored and the outline retouched. Such a method naturally led to more and more decorative work, and also permitted amateur painters to carry out the designs of masters. Many of these paintings took the form of the hand scroll or *makimono,* but up to the end of the Fujiwara period the continuous composition was not used. Instead the pictures were isolated units separated from each other by sections of text. The first scroll to show the continuous composition is also one to show the linear style of the Yamato-e style. It illustrates the *Shigisan Engi,* the story of the *Flying Granary,* and has often been attributed to *Toba Sojo Kakuyu* but there seems to be no basis for the attribution. In sharp contrast to the other paintings noted, this scroll is painted in light colors and achieves its effect by vivid characterization and free calligraphy.

*Sculpture.*—Sculpture of the Fujiwara follows the same trends that have been observed in the paintings. Since sculpture was confined almost entirely to Buddhist subjects the clash between the religious symbolism and the decorative treatment was more obvious. The dangers that were inherent in the period that produced sutras on fans led sculpture towards a decline. Sweetness of expression and elaboration of carving too often take the place of true sculptural qualities. The statues become flat and a greater elaboration of drapery creates a pictorial form. Yet in the best of these statues there is a warm humanity that expresses the easy going Buddhism of the time which contrasts sharply with the forbidding features of the Early Heian religion. Technical advances were great at this time. Chief among these was the manner of piecing together a wooden statue rather than cutting it out of one block as had been done previously. This method served two purposes; it tended to prevent the wood from cracking and it greatly facilitated the carving. It is pertinent to notice here that the Japanese wood sculptor always showed decided respect for the grain of his material. Even when the statue was to be painted the same skill was expended to bring out the beauties of the wood. One reason for this may be that the sculptor frequently did not paint his figures, but that specialists were used for that work. Thus the sculptor, with the pride of the true craftsman, probably aimed at perfection in his own work irrespective of the changes to be made by others. Another innovation of the period was the use of inlaid glass eyes, a technique that was the forerunner of the realism that developed during the following period. Although Fujiwara was not a great sculptural period, many fine sculptors carried on their work and formed schools that served to train the masters of the thirteenth century. Chief among these leaders were *Jocho* (d. 1057), his pupil *Chosei* (d. 1091), and *Inkaku* (middle of the twelfth century).

Kamakura Period (1184-1392).—In 1184 the Minamoto clan defeated

# THE VAN EYCKS

*The two brothers, Hubert and Jan van Eyck, who worked at Ghent and Bruges, in the first half of the fifteenth century, revealed the power of oil painting. This revelation changed the whole of modern painting. They fixed for all time the aim of the art of the Netherlands which is to give an exact portrait of things. While remaining a religious art, busy reworking the themes of Christian iconography, Flemish painting showed before long that it would always be an art of portraits, landscapes and still lifes. The van Eycks were the first great men of the movement; later masters include Rubens and Rembrandt.*

The famous Ghent altarpiece is the work of Hubert and Jan van Eyck. On the central panel and the two wings, the painter shows God the Father between the Virgin and St. John the Baptist, angels who sing and play music, and Adam and Eve recalling the fall of man. Below the lamb of the sacrifice is the goal of the processions of martyrs, saints, prophets and doctors; on the wings are the soldiers of Christ, the good judges, the pilgrims and the hermits.

This work is full of symbolism and Christian thought, and it shows the best qualities of Flemish painting. There we find all that characterises this art, a wonderful landscape of the springtime with flowers in the grass, Adam and Eve, the two most truly academic figures in painting, the tiara of God the Father, the robes of the angels, the precision and the truth of the portraits. The colour has remained as bright as it was when new. On the exterior wings are portraits of the donors.

HUBERT AND JAN VAN EYCK: ALTARPIECE OF THE SACRED LAMB (CATHEDRAL OF GHENT) (1424-1432).
*(Photo from Société photo. de Berlin.)*

MAN WITH THE PINK. BERLIN.
*(Photo by Hanfstaengl.)*

VIRGIN OF CANON VAN DER PAELE. BRUGES.
*(Photo by Bruckmann.)*

VIRGIN OF THE CHANCELLOR ROLIN. LOUVRE.
*(Photo by Hachette.)*

WIFE OF THE ARTIST. BRUGES.
*(Photo by Bruckmann.)*

## Jan van Eyck

Hubert van Eyck is known to us only by his collaboration in the Altarpiece of the Sacred Lamb where his part is difficult to distinguish. Jan is the author of pictures where the naturalism of the new painting reconciles itself with religious sentiment. His portraits are of a merciless frankness. It is impossible to concentrate more truth on a little wooden panel.

MASTER OF FLÉMALLE: ADORATION OF THE SHEPHERDS. DIJON.
*(Photo by Hachette.)*

MASTER OF FLÉMALLE (JACQUES DARET OR ROBERT CAMPIN): ANNUNCIATION. BRUSSELS.
*(Photo by Van Oed.)*

PETRUS CHRISTUS: ST. ELIGIUS. UNITED STATES.
*(Photo by Bruckmann.)*

## The Contemporaries of the van Eycks

We do not know the names of all the painters to whom we owe these little masterpieces. The *Master of Flémalle* was perhaps Jacques Daret or Robert Campin. *Petrus Christus* was a pupil of Jan van Eyck who, using as a pretext the story of St. Eligius, actually painted for us the portrait of a shopkeeper.

# FLEMISH PRIMITIVES

*Flemish painting as it had been started with the technique of the van Eycks was practiced during the whole of the fifteenth century by minute and impeccable masters. Their works are both religious pictures destined for altars and at the same time naturalistic paintings where it is easy for us to recognise the men and objects of that time. We can admire in them the exactitude of observation and an infinite application. On the other hand we can find some awkwardnesses in the disposition of the people; the Flemish masters kept certain habits of their predecessors, the miniaturists, when they piled up their figures in compositions often very confused. In comparison with the Italians who knew how to distribute their actors in a large scene, the Flemish artists encumbered their settings with persons. Also they found more charm in showing beautiful textiles than in drawing elegant poses. When compared with Italian painting, Flemish painting seems to be searching for richness of detail and precision of colour rather than beauty of line and majesty of composition.*

ADORATION OF THE MAGI. MUNICH.
*(Photo by Hachette.)*

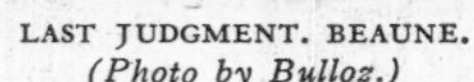

LAST JUDGMENT. BEAUNE.
*(Photo by Bulloz.)*

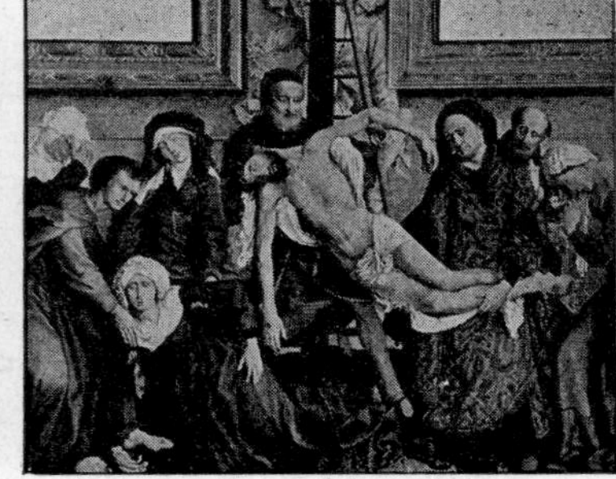

DESCENT FROM THE CROSS. ESCORIAL.
*(Photo by Anderson.)*

## Roger van der Weyden

Roger van der Weyden, or Roger de la Pasture, from Tournai was one of the most illustrious masters of the fifteenth century. There is sometimes in his figures an intensity not common to the Flemish. No painter has given a more pathetic expression to the face of the Virgin fainting on Mount Calvary, or to the grimaces of the damned. The *Last Judgment* of Beaune, which is attributed to him, is one of the most important works of the primitive Flemish school; the beautiful *Descent from the Cross*, which he painted in two other versions, seems to have been modelled after a wooden altarpiece. In the *Adoration of the Magi* he is more gracious.

THE LAST SUPPER. LOUVAIN.
*(Photo by Bruckmann.)*

CONDEMNATION OF AN INNOCENT MAN AND HIS REHABILITATION. BRUSSELS.
*(Photo by Hanfstaengl.)*

GEERTGEN TOT SINT JANS: RESURRECTION OF LAZARUS. LOUVRE.
*(Photo by Hachette.)*

## Dirk Bouts

Dirk Bouts is admired for his precise and sparkling execution. The details of the costumes and the still life are always magnificent, but the faces which are lifelike portraits seem motionless and the attitudes have the stiffness of mannequins. Geertgen tot sint Jans, like Bouts, is from Haarlem.

THE ADORATION OF THE SHEPHERDS. FLORENCE.
*(Photo by Alinari.)*

THE DEATH OF THE VIRGIN. BRUGES.
*(Photo by Daled.)*

JUSTUS OF GHENT: THE LAST SUPPER. URBINO.
*(Photo by Anderson.)*

## Hugo van der Goes and Justus of Ghent

In the middle of the fifteenth century, Flemish painting was in contact with the Italian painting. This junction is not very evident at this date, but we see already the art of Hugo van der Goes penetrate into Italy; his *Adoration of the Shepherds* was painted for the Portinari family of Florence. Justus of Ghent passed an important part of his life at the court of the dukes of Urbino. For the moment, Flemish art gives more than it receives in the exchanges with Italy.

the dominant Taira clan, seized the power, and moved the capital from Kyoto to Kamakura. The sophisticated Fujiwara court had become so degenerated that it was able to offer little resistance to its hardy opponents. Purged of the elaborate and artificial restraints of the Fujiwara nobility a new art developed, stronger, more of the earth, and more materialistic. To the parvenu rulers naturalism probably seemed the most difficult artistic problem to solve and therefore the most important.

*Sculpture.*—In sculpture especially, the new approach is most manifest. The greatest sculptor of the age, *Unkei* (d. 1223), set the standard for this art early in the thirteenth century. In his work there is a much greater monumentality than was generally recognizable in Fujiwara sculpture. Naturalism appears, but always subordinated to sculptural means. The power of his art can be seen in a statue of one of the Ni-o in the Todaiji at Nara. The gigantic figure, twenty-six feet high, is convincing organically despite some exaggerations, and expresses a tremendous vigor which almost seems to symbolize the art of the age. The naturalistic style of the period was not without its dangers. Unkei is credited with having perfected the technique of constructing the wooden sculpture so that in his time it became a complicated and formulated process in which the figure was built up in innumerable pieces according to set formulae. The head was made in three pieces so that the face could be carved like a mask. Such a technique could lead to nothing but virtuosity and even in this period some of the statues are decidedly manneristic. Zen Buddhism, with its insistence on individualism appealed to the hardy nobles of this period who were more accustomed to the battle field than the court, also led to naturalism in sculpture. Relying on inspiration rather than on ritual the Zen sect preferred the representation of their priests to the conventionalized icons of the other sects. The artistic influence of this sect, of course, extended beyond the bounds of its own artists and we find a statue of Kuya Shonin, a leader of one of the Amida sects, extremely realistic, not content merely to represent movement, but in addition startling the observer by attempting to recreate speech by means of a series of small statues of Amida symbolizing the prayer which issues from the mouth. More successful, according to our western taste, is a lantern bearer made by *Koben* in 1215. Its amusing grotesquerie is based on a sure knowledge of the principles of naturalistic art and is surpassed only by some of the finest portrait sculpture of the period which it reflects in its worldly lack of deep religious feeling.

*Painting.*—In painting of the Kamakura period, as in sculpture, portraiture becomes a common theme. Scrolls depicting the Thirty-six Poets, each as an individual picture having no respect for the continuity of the scroll form, represent one phase of this trend. More typical of the Kamakura individualism and interest in personality than these rather formal characterizations are larger portraits painted as *kakemonos.* A portrait of the poetess Abutsuni owned by Mr. Kinta Muto which was shown at the important Japanese Exhibition at the Museum of Fine Arts, Boston in 1936 (#46) embodies the same characteristics that were present in the finest of the naturalistic sculpture of the period. More important in the history of painting is the full development of the Yamato-e style. The *Shigisan Engi* painted at the end of the Fujiwara period had already utilized the horizontal space afforded by the *makimono* (hand scroll) to develop a continuous composition, and although the *makimono* with individual illustrations persisted (e.g. the scrolls of the *Diary of Murasaki Shikibu* attributed to Fujiwara Nobuzane), the tendency was towards perfecting the continuous scroll. The finest example of this type to be found outside of Japan and one of the most excellent in existence is the *Heiji Monogatari* scroll in the Museum of Fine Arts, Boston. In this painting which depicts the burning of the Sanjo Palace, the artist has combined the whole spirit of Kamakura art. Instead of the quiet and decorative scenes of Fujiwara, there is the tumult of a virile society. The gold and silver decorative patches have been subordinated to the driving line which was evinced in the *Shigisan Engi.* The stylized faces of the Fujiwara courtiers are forgotten in the incisive characterizations of the hurrying populace. Especially important, however, is the manner in which the composition has been adapted to the scroll. Just as in Chinese painting the artist has composed his subject so that although only one part of the picture is seen at one time the whole picture maintains a temporal as well as a spatial unity. In western art the best comparison would be to a symphony, with its central theme, its variations on the theme, its crescendos and diminuendos. In some paintings as in this the ending can be compared to a deceptive cadence in music. It is a narrative art, but a narrative told in terms of the brush stroke and composition, a narrative that needs no explanation to be understood. If we never know the references to the story in this painting, we should still understand the artist's intent, so universal is his language. This painting may be considered typical of the best Yamato-e painting of the period. The style was to be perpetuated in less powerful forms for the next four hundred years, until it succumbed to its legitimate successor—the art of Ukiyo-e.

Traditional Buddhist painting maintained a high level in the Kamakura period. Its designs and iconography remained to a large extent based on Chinese models, but distinctive Japanese characteristics were always maintained. *Kirigana,* gold leaf intricately cut and laid upon the painting as a decorative appliqué, becomes popular. Contemporary China, however, had a strong attraction for the painters of the Takuma school, as is shown by a set of *The Twelve Devas* painted by Takuma Shoga in 1191. One has only to compare these figures with some of the tenth century panels from Tun Huang (see China—Art) to see their continental prototypes. At the end of the Kamakura period the *suijaku* art appears, an art that is based upon the older Buddhist styles but that combines a Shinto iconography.

*The Art of the Sword.*—The minor arts flourished at this time, but it was the art of the sword that began to assume proportions that were to make it one of the dominant arts of later periods. The soldier nobles of Kamakura living by their swords naturally developed a great respect for their weapons and the men who made them. The result was that the armorers became the recipients of great honor. Before he would forge a sword the armorer would spend appropriate time in praying and fasting in order to insure the success of his work. Sword blades of this time are among the finest ever made and in some respects surpass the Toledo blade of Western fame. Although the blade was most venerated, admiration for the sword included the accessories. The guard (*tsuba*) was designed with care as were other accoutrements (*minuki*), and the sheath which was usually made of lacquer. The early *tsuba* were mainly of iron and ornamented functionally so that by decorative reticulation the weight of the metal was decreased. Good blades continued to be made into the seventeenth century at which time the peaceful condition of the country precluded a large demand for actual fighting weapons and the art degenerated, to be carried on in the manufacture of court weapons for display with elaborate *tsuba* that show great ingenuity and technical skill but that lose all the power of the early types.

Ashikaga Period (1392-1570).—In 1333 the Kamakura period proper came to an end. For the next half century civil war disturbed the country until in 1392 the Ashikaga Shoguns gained control of the government which they held despite insurrections, until 1570 when their power was finally ended. During all this period with its continuous warfare the arts attained new peaks and new arts developed. In contrast to the preceding period which had witnessed the growth of indigenous arts, the Ashikaga period again turned to China as a model. One reason for the turn to the continent was that intercourse with China—which had been interrupted because of the Mongol attempts to invade Japan during the Yuan dynasty—commenced again after the native Ming dynasty had overthrown the foreign rulers in 1368. Another reason was that Zen Buddhism, which had spread during the Kamakura period, attained great importance under the Ashikaga Shoguns. The art of the Zen Buddhists had no tradition in Japan and was dependent on the monochrome ink paintings of the Sung dynasty in China (see China—Art). Sculpture which was little used by the Zen sect declined and persisted only in weak adaptations of old styles which were combined with a pictorial technique carried over from painting.

*Painting.* — Painting, however, flourished. Although the traditional Buddhist painting of the Amidist and other cults were perpetuated with little change, the Zen painters turned to their predecessors in China. There they found two types of painting that appealed to them. One was the portraits of priests (which were sometimes given as diplomas to superior students); the other was the suggestive ink monochrome which the Ch'an (Zen) priests in China had used so successfully for their portraits of patriarchs and for the representations of legends. One of the earliest painters to use the Chinese method of ink painting was Josetsu (c. 1400) who painted Zen themes in the manner that swept the country at that time. The style which became known as *suibokugwa* is also represented by the paintings of Kao who worked in the style of Liang K'ai. (See China-Art.) But the major step in the naturalization of this art was made by Shubun during the fifteenth century. By that time monochrome painting had ceased to be purely Zen in inspiration, and although the chief practitioners were still Zen priests, themes were taken from the more academic Sung masters. The influence of Ma Yuan and Hsia Kuei (see China—Art, Sung) is easily observed in the paintings attributed to Shubun. The compositions are almost identical but a peculiar use of mist distinguishes the Japanese works from the Chinese. However, the general belief that there is an obvious difference between Japanese and Chinese painting is by no means correct. It is quite likely that many of the paintings attributed to Chinese masters may be copies by Japanese artists, although the difference is usually perceptible.

The style was carried on by other painters: Soga Jasoku (d. 1483), Geiami (1431-1485), his pupil Kei Shoki, and others. Soami, the son of Geiami, brought a new spirit into the art that by 1500 already showed a tendency towards conventionalization. Influenced by the Chinese painter Mu Ch'i, he popularized the soft tonalities that are so typical of later Japanese monochromes. The greatest painter of this period and perhaps the greatest of all Far Eastern painters was Sesshu (1419-1506). Trained to be a Zen priest, he specialized in painting and in 1467 went to China to study painting. In China he was received more as a master than as a student and was little influenced by the contemporaneous Ming painting. His early style was based on the Sung styles of Hsia Kuei and Ma Yuan, but has a clarity and rugged strength not found in the surviving works of those masters. His masterpiece in this style, the famous landscape scroll in the collection of Prince Mori Motoaki, is certainly the finest landscape scroll in existence. About fifty feet long it does not falter as it passes through quiet panoramas to turbulent scenes. Another style which Sesshu employed is the "ink-splash" in which the subject is barely suggested by the broad and powerful stroke of the brush.

Although Sesshu had a large number of pupils his closest follower, Sesson, seems not to have come in personal contact with the master. Sesson, a master in his own right, adopted both of Sesshu's styles but in the "ink-splash" technique he introduced subtle variations that make his work entirely individual.

At this time a new school made its appearance in Japan. This was the Kano school which was to be the leading school for the next three hundred years. The first master of this school was Kano Masanobu (1453-1490). The school did not attain importance until his son, Kano Motonobu (1476-1559), became one of Japan's leading painters. The style of this school differed only in emphasis from the style of the Sesshu school. Both specialized in black monochrome painting, but the Japanese innovations that had been apparent in the work of Soami and other painters of the late fifteenth century, were intensified in the work of the Kano artists. A genre and decorative element was added to the remote and austere beauty of the Chinese landscape, while the typical "Kano line" that was to assume a virtuoso quality in later painters was already noticeable. The school was carried on during the Ashikaga period by Motonobu's younger brother, Yukinobu (1513-1575).

At the same time another school became prominent. The old Yamato-e style had continued to coexist alongside the Chinese schools. Workmanship, however, was not as fine in the Ashikaga period as it had been in the Fujiwara or Kamakura periods. A gifted family of artists, the Tosa, created a renascence of the indigenous style about 1500. The school claimed to descend from the great painters of the Kamakura period, but for this contention there is no proofs. The name Tosa, probably was not acquired by the family until the beginning of the fifteenth century, and the fame of the family itself did not reach its zenith until the time of Tosa Mitsunobu (1434-1525). The Tosa style, in addition to pure Yamato-e qualities, reveals the assimilation of certain elements derived from Chinese schools. Among the later followers of this school two directions are apparent. One emphasized the genre elements while the other preferred the decorative elements characteristic of the school.

*The Tea Ceremony.*—In the Ashikaga period the Tea Ceremony became a definite feature of cultured Japanese life. Okakura Kakuzo's *Book of Tea* has treated this phase of Japanese life so perfectly that it requires temerity to do more than mention the bare essentials of this rite. Ultimately derived from Zen Buddhism the tea drinking ceremony soon became a formal occasion at which almost every gesture and topic of conversation was prescribed. Special houses were built in which to hold the rite. Simplicity was rigorously maintained, but perfection of that simplicity was attained through the use of expensive materials and the employment of superb craftsmanship. The pottery tea bowl used in the ceremony gave the appearance of crudity, but its marvelous tactile qualities, its subtle tonalities, and its honest form have endeared it to the Westerner who can appreciate its aesthetic merits without the associations which win the affection of the Japanese. The potters' art at this time, like painting, was influenced by China although the forms and glazes are less dependent on the continent.

MOMOYAMA PERIOD (1570-1603).—The contending forces which had torn the Ashikaga power during the sixteenth century were united in 1570 and the Ashikaga Shogunate destroyed. The men who accomplished this feat were first Nobunaga and then Hideyoshi, the so-called Napoleon of Japan. Of comparatively low birth, the new rulers embarked on a typical *nouveau riche* program of unprecedented magnificence.

*Painting.*—The huge palace of Momoyama, from which the period derives its name, surpassed previous buildings in size and elaboration. For this and for other buildings of grand scale huge quantities of furnishings were needed. Chief among these was the large six-fold screen which, brilliantly colored with large areas of gold leaf serving as a background, offered the greatest opportunities for painting at that time. Most of the leading painters of the period were Kano artists, but intermarriage with the Tosa family which began in the sixteenth century caused the two styles to coalesce. The Kano painters adopted the bright coloring of the Tosa school and the genre subject matter. The leading themes were the historical legends which had remained standard since the days of the Yamato-e artists. Landscape screens were also common but instead of the suggestive monochromes of the Ashikaga painters the Momoyama masters preferred the decorative color and pattern offered by a group of trees against a gold background. The leading painters of this school were Kano Eitoku (1548-1590), Kano Sanraku (1559-1635), and Kano Naizen (1570-1660). Hasegawa Tohaku (1539-1610), although not a follower of the Kano school, painted in a similar style. His ink monochrome paintings adapt the style of the Sung master Mu Ch'i, but he also painted decorative screens with gold backgrounds in the contemporaneous taste. Another painter who specialized in monochrome painting was Miyamoto Niten (1582-1645) who was equally famous as a swordsman. The sweeping line of his brush stroke has frequently been identified with the swinging blade of a sword and in the often illustrated picture, the *Shrike on a Branch*, the comparison is striking.

A new style dominated by the two masters, Honnami Koetsu (1556-1637) and Tawaraya Sotatsu (flourished c. 1615-1635), arose to meet the requirements of this age of splendor. The roots of this new decorative style had always been latent in the branch of Yamato-e painting that stressed pattern and in the Tosa style. Although these painters used the same themes as their Kano contemporaries, they are especially famous for their purely decorative patterns which are composed of a few sprays of flowers arranged in a simple but bold pattern. A *makimono* in the collection of Mr. Kinto Muto, which was exhibited in 1936 in the *Special Loan Exhibition of Art Treasures from Japan* at the Museum of Fine Arts, Boston, is a splendid example of the calligraphy of Koetsu and the painting of Sotatsu. The style of the two masters blend to form a perfect unity. Sotatsu is supposed to have created a new technique which is called the *tarashikomi*. By painting one color over another which had not thoroughly dried he partially fused his hues, thus obtaining soft tones and an attractive surface texture.

The Tosa school continued its traditional decorative and highly detailed painting throughout the period but its influence continued to decline. The leading member of the family at that time was Tosa Mitsuyoshi (d. 1613).

*Sculpture.*—Sculpture ceased to show any creative characteristics during the Momoyama period. Confined either to conventionalized repetitions of Buddhist images or to the decorations of sumptuous palaces belonging to the nobles, it fell into the sphere of craftsmanship and showed its excellence only in virtuoso displays of carving.

TOKUGAWA OR EDO PERIOD (1603-1867).—In 1603 the dominance of the Tokugawa Shoguns was complete and the period from that date until the rise of the Meiji power in 1867 is known as Tokugawa. Sometimes, however, it is called Edo (Tokyo) after the new capital. For at least half a century the art forms continued to perpetuate and refine the styles of the preceding period. Untroubled by serious civil or foreign wars a wealthy and prosperous bourgeoisie began to supplant the nobles as consumers of art, and to satisfy the requirements of this class a new art arose—the Ukiyo-e.

*Painting.*—Painting was the only major art to remain progressive during this time. The Kano artists maintained their popularity during the seventeenth century. Among these were several fine painters: Kano Koi (d. 1636), Naonobu (1607-1680), Tsunenobu (1636-1713), and Sansetsu (1589-1651). These all followed in the Kano tradition which they varied but with little creative inspiration. Another painter of this school, Kano Tannyu (1602-1674) who is also known as Morinobu, is representative of the decline of the style during the seventeenth century. A rather dull brush work is felt as an end in itself rather than as one of the component parts of the picture. Strokes become formularized and derivative.

The decorative school of Koetsu and Sotatsu found brilliant exponents in Ogata Korin (1658-1716) and his brother, Ogata Kenzan (1663-1743). Korin was a universal artist equally famous as a master of the Tea Ceremony and as a lacquerer. His style of painting is closely related to that of Sotatsu but his brush work is more fluid and his compositions more stylized. Kenzan, like his brother, was a versatile artist and is even better known as a potter than as a painter. Sometimes his style is close to Korin's but frequently his bold brush work and free designs are obviously derived from painting on pottery. Both of these artists had followers who continued their methods of painting during succeeding generations.

The Tosa school, under the leadership of Tosa Mitsuoki (1671-1719) passed through a brief renascence. Mitsuoki was the first of the Tosa painters to completely absorb the Chinese manner of painting which the Kano artists had accepted for generations, so that his success must be attributed to his personal genius rather than to the Tosa tradition from which he derived.

More important from the point of view of art history was the rise of the school of Ukiyo-e (pictures of the passing world). The subjects of this school were mainly genre scenes which in time became predominantly pictures of actors and actresses. The founder of this school was Matabei (or Matahei). According to H. Minamoto the full name of this painter was Iwasa Matabei, also known as Shoi, who died in 1650 at the age of seventy-two. However, no indisputable works of his hand are known. Nevertheless, many which are attributed to him, permit us to define his style. This betrays a Tosa training mixed, as all Tosa work was at that time, with Kano elements chief among which was the powerful brush stroke. His figures are heavier than the usual Tosa types and, more than anything else, his homely interpretation of even classical themes distinguishes him from his predecessors. The genre elements appealed to the growing merchant and petty bourgeois classes and to satisfy the growing demand a low priced medium was necessary. The print, because of its reproductive nature, was comparatively cheap and available in great quantities, and thus answered the needs of a new society. Most of Matabei's followers were print makers as well as painters (see below).

Another important school which arose somewhat later was the naturalistic school of Maruyama Okyo (1732-1795). Okyo had studied not only the various Japanese and Chinese methods of painting but also those of Western painting (probably through engraved copies of paintings). The fusion of these styles is evident in his work, for while he adhered strictly to the methods of Far Eastern painting, he produced work that was more naturalistic than any that had been created up to that time in Japan. His most important follower was Mori Tessan (1775-1841) whose father-in-law, Mori Sosen (1747-1821), is said to have influenced Okyo. Sosen, famous mainly as a painter of monkeys, used a naturalistic style similar to that of Okyo.

Towards the end of the eighteenth century the coexistence of numerous schools enabled many painters to develop individual styles by combining their own tastes with eclectic borrowings from the various schools. One of the most individual was Ito Jakuchu (1713-1800) who is particularly well known for his paintings of roosters. Ganku (1749-1835), also a naturalistic painter, found his inspiration in the realistic schools of contemporaneous China. A large group of landscape painters at this time were greatly influenced by the "ink flinging" landscapes of the "literary man's" style in China. A few artists like Hoitsu (1761-1828) perpetuated early styles, but the latter half of the eighteenth century and the early nineteenth century belonged to the masters of the print who were developing a true creative style to meet the requirements of their age.

*Japanese Prints.*—The Japanese print is a far less mechanical art than the usual Western print. The artist first draws his picture on paper which the woodcutter places on a block and cuts so that the black lines of the painting will be in relief on the block. Using this as a master block the wood cutter prints as many copies as there are colors in the picture and makes a separate block for each color. The actual printing is done by painting each block in colors (usually noted by the painter) and then placing a slightly dampened paper upon the block and rubbing the paper carefully so that it absorbs the colors. A perfect register is obtained by fitting the paper into a right angled corner at one end and against a horizontal block at the other. Infinite variations can be made in the coloring of the blocks, the manner of painting the blocks, and the number of blocks used.

Although wood-block printing had been known in Japan as early as the eighth century it had never been used as an independent artistic medium until the seventeenth century. At that time Moronobu (1645-1715) recognized the usefulness of the wood block for book illustrations (*yehon*) and for single sheets (*ichimai-e*). He is the first of the primitives, so-called because they were the pioneers in the popular use of the wood-block print. These early prints were entirely in black and white, although sometimes colored by hand. In Moronobu's work we recognize a characteristic strength of line and composition which exploits the striking juxtaposition of solid black masses with areas of white. Another of these early print masters was Torii Kiyonobu (1664-1729). First a maker of theatrical posters, he adapted the bold style of brush work to pictures of actors and courtesans. Many of his powerful figure studies were later colored by hand in red, yellow, and blue. The red, a lead oxide (*tan*) which now has become orange, has caused this type of print to be called *tan-e*. The Torii school with its powerful brush strokes and monumental figures remained, under the leadership of Kiyomasu, Kiyotada, Kiyohiro and Kiyomitsu, the chief group of print artists until the middle of the eighteenth century. Closely related to the Torii painters was the Kwaigetsudo family. The few surviving prints of this group are more sophisticated although still strong in design. Prints by artists of this group such as Kwaigetsudo Dohan (c. 1704-1716) and Kwaigetsudo Anchi (c. 1704-1716) are among the finest prints ever produced. It is significant to note that even at this early date the painter made his designs especially for his prints and did not merely adapt them from paintings.

About 1740 printing in color took the place of hand colored prints. Until 1760 two colors were preferred: rose (*beni* from which the prints are called *beni-e*) and green. The artistic concept alters, the print becomes smaller in size, the compositional elements break up, and the stately figure is superseded by one smaller in size. Okamura Masanobu (1691?-1768) was one of the first to use this method. Harunobu (1725-1770), inspired by the rich and variegated color print of China, employed the polychrome print (*nishiki-e*, brocade picture) about 1760. An exquisite delicacy creeps into his diminutive figures, into his color, and into his almost square compositions.

After the death of Harunobu the next step was to exaggerate the subject matter already almost exhausted. In the prints of Kiyonaga (1752-1815), Utamaro (1753-1806), Toyokuni (1769-1825), and their numerous contemporaries, are to be seen the tall slender figures with the female heads extraordinarily if effectively elongated. Interest runs towards prints of two and three sheets in which the design is continuous. Even six sheets are not unusual, and scenes of festive delight take the place of small groups.

A reaction to the sentimentality of these artists is apparent in the almost fierce power seen in the prints by Sharaku (worked 1790-1795), the actor artist whose caricature portraits so horrified the populace accustomed to the idyllic beauty of his contemporaries, that he had to abandon painting and return to the stage.

Landscape scenes as a new subject matter saved the art from further exaggerations and multiplications of enfeebled themes. Hokusai (1760-1849) and Hiroshige (1797-1858) added vigor to the art which already was showing signs of decline. Both of these painters painted similar scenes but in Hokusai there is a largeness of concept which contrasts with the intimacy of Hiroshige's style. These artists began to assimilate Western methods and at their death with the introduction of badly understood Western theories and chemical dyes the great period of Japanese prints was over.

*Pottery.*—The pottery traditions established in the Ashikaga period persisted into the Tokugawa period. Innovations were made by Kenzan whose bold patterns and colors reflected the decorative spirit of the period in contrast to the suggestive subtlety of Ashikaga. Another well known ware of the period was Satsuma which was made in the dark *temmoku* glazes for use in the Tea Ceremony and in a creamy crackled glaze with floral motifs in enamel decoration. In the nineteenth century the decoration on this ware was supplemented by human figures. Imari ware colored with blue and an orange red became popular especially as an export ware in the nineteenth century. For a time Imbe or Bizen ware received a temporary popularity because of its glazes which reproduced the appearance of metal. Other important kilns were at Seto and Iwari where simple pottery painted in free bold brush strokes were made as well as other types.

*Lacquer.*—The technical perfection of the age was expressed in the almost virtuoso triumphs of the lacquerers. Korin carried over the patterned style of painting to lacquer decoration and works by his school (frequently signed with his name) are often too elaborately ornamented with inlay or carving. One of the common utensils at that time was the *inro* a small box carried by a cord at the girdle. On this object the lacquerer exercised his ingenuity.

*Netsuke.*—Related to the *inro* was the *netsuke*, the button-like toggle used to catch the *inro* cord around the girdle. Sometimes of lacquer or wood the typical material of this object was ivory. The *netsuke* took almost every conceivable form and often represented human and animal figures in miniature size. Usually portrayed with much humor and imagination these minute carvings were the most creative sculpture of the period.

*Otsu-e.*—Closely related to *Ukiyo-e* are the *Otsu-e*. These were paintings made in the village of Otsu, near Lake Biwa, and sold at the roadside as votive offerings or souvenirs to pilgrims at the shrine. Crudely painted they have a vitality and unpretentious beauty that ranks them with the finest folk art ever produced. A limited selection of subject matter released the craftsman from any speculations and permitted him to produce these sketches in quantity production for the less favored classes.

Modern Japan.—Since 1868 little important art has been created in Japan. For a time an indiscriminative acceptance of Western methods completely destroyed all but the most traditional work. For the past few years, however, a return to old methods with modern applications and the gradual assimilation of some of the better Western theories has been leading towards a finer and more indigenous art.

Bibliography: Tajima, *Selected Relics of Japanese Art*. Tokyo, 1900ff.—Okakura Kakuzo, *The Book of Tea; The Ideals of the East*. London, 1905.—H. P. Bowie, *On the Laws of Japanese Painting*. San Francisco, 1911.—E. F. Fenolossa, *Epochs of Chinese and Japanese Art*. New York, 1912.—*Horyuji Okami* (Temple Treasures at Horyuji Temple), 1913.—L. Binyon, *A Cat. of Japanese and Chinese woodcuts preserved in the sub-dep't of Oriental prints and drawings*. London, 1916.—K. With, *Buddhistische Plastik in Japan*. Vienna, 1919.—V. F. Weber, *Koji Hoten*. Paris, 1923.—L. Warner, *Japanese Sculpture of the Suiko Period*. New Haven, 1923; *The Craft of the Japanese Sculptor*, 1936.—H. Minamoto, *Illustrated History of Japanese Art* (trans. by H. G. Henderson). Kyoto, 1935.—Sir G. B. Samson, *Japan, A Cultural History*. London, 1931.—J. Harada, *English Cat. of Treasures in the Imperial Household Museum*. Tokyo, 1932.—M. Anesaki, *Art, Life, and Nature in Japan*. Boston, 1933.—N. Tsuda, *Handbook of Japanese Art*. Tokyo, 1935.—K. Toda, *Japanese Scroll Painting*. Chicago, 1935.—Periodicals: *Kokka; Bijutsu Kenkyu*.

**JARDINIÈRE (La Belle).**—See Ghirlandaio (Ridolfo); Raphael; also Pl. 19, Vol. II.

**JEAN DE JUNI.**—See Pl. 23, Vol. II.

**JEANNERET-GRIS (Charles Edouard), known as LE CORBUSIER.**—Contemporary Swiss architect and painter. The son of a watchmaker and a musically gifted mother, Jeanneret was born in 1887 in La Chaux-de-Fonds, Switzerland. Between the ages of thirteen and seventeen he attended the local school of Arts and Crafts to study engraving with L'Epplatennier, an ardent follower of naturalism and the Art Nouveau. Chosen in a competition to design his teacher's house, he employed the corner window for the first time. The following years he travelled in Italy and Austria, and finally reaching Paris he worked with Auguste Perret for two years, at the same time studying mathematics, physics and sketching the primitives in the Trocadero. In 1910 he went to Berlin to exchange ideas with Peter Behrens, to be followed by a trip to Greece, Asia Minor and Italy. During the World War he managed a factory in France. Through his friendship with Amédée Ozenfant he became interested in purism and experimented in that field. In 1922 he became the partner of his cousin, the architect Pierre Jeanneret, and consequently adopted the name of his maternal grandfather, Le Corbusier. Besides being a painter and an architect, Le Corbusier is a lecturer of note and the author of *Vers une Architecture* (1923), *Peinture Moderne* (1924), *Urbanisme* (1925) and innumerable articles in the *Architectural Record, Journal of Architectural Association, Art d'Aujourd'hui, Architect and Building News* and many others. Le Corbusier rejected all architectural laws achieved by age and time and believes in attacking each problem from an individual point of view, taking into great consideration the landscape, geological qualities, light and similar factors. He is logical, clear and economic. He was the first to give an architectural character to ferro-concrete, to combine polychromy with architecture and to use glass for the whole southern façade of a building. Some of his structures are resting on pillars of concrete which rise several feet above the ground, thus utilising every inch of space by permitting vehicular and pedestrian traffic to pass underneath the building. Elevated traffic passages are also among his inventions. Besides individual dwellings, Le Corbusier is extremely concerned with sociological housing projects and urbanisation. In all cases the results are aesthetic, comfortable and supremely functional. Some of his chef d'œuvres include Domino Project (1914), Citrohan Project (1921), Pavillon de l'Esprit Nouveau (1925), Salvation Army Project in Paris (1931), Fondation Suisse in Paris (1932), Villa Ozenfant, Villa à Vaucresson, Villa des Garches and many others.

Bibliography: Museum of Modern Art, *Modern Architects*, New York, 1932.—Le Corbusier, *Towards a New Architecture*. N. Y., 1927.

**JEAURAT (Étienne).**—French painter, 1699-1789. He is known chiefly for his "genre" pictures of scenes taken from Parisian streets and market-places.

**JEFFERSON (Thomas).**—American statesman and architect (1743-1826). Although better known for his statesmanship and his prominent position in the political world of the young American republic still it must be conceded that Thomas Jefferson was also an eminent student of architecture and one who tried to apply the principles that he learned to the business at hand. He began with the erection of his own home, *Monticello*, on a wooded mount near Charlottesville, Virginia. It was a period when men of culture were expected to be conversant with the various branches of the arts, an age before the advent of trained architects. House plans and layouts for public buildings were adapted from the designs used in Europe at a slightly earlier period. Jefferson was the owner of a book of designs by the Italian architect, Andrea Palladio, who had worked in the 16th century, and the design for *Monticello* was taken directly from that book with some necessary revisions and adaptations to contemporary conditions. A great admirer of Roman architecture, Jefferson kept his eyes open while minister to France and in 1789 brought back to America the idea for the dome of the present *Monticello* from the Temple of Vesta in Rome. At the same time during his incumbency in France he was asked to get the advice of French architects regarding a new building for the State Capitol of Virginia. It was his own plan based on the Maison Carrée at Nîmes and adapted with the aid of Clérisseau, the French architect and authority on Roman remains, that was finally used with but slight changes. And finally in his later years Jefferson was able to bring about the germination of an old idea, the beginning of the University of Virginia located at Charlottesville within sight of his home. He planned the great Rotunda after the Roman Pantheon, and the colonnaded walks with the student quarters and separate pavilions for the professors. Drawings in his own hand with detailed specifications for this undertaking are still in existence. He was also the designer of several private residences in that section of the state, alone or in collaboration with others, and his designs are especially distinguished by the seclusion of the stairways, and large airy rooms opening from a main entrance hall.

See Pl. 64, Vol. II.

BIBLIOGRAPHY: John S. Patton, *Jefferson, Cabell and the University of Virginia,* 1906.—John S. Patton, Sallie J. Doswell, Lewis D. Crenshaw, *Jefferson's University,* 1915.—Fiske Kimball, *Thomas Jefferson and the First Monument of the Classic Revival in America,* 1915.—Paul Wilstach, *Jefferson and Monticello,* 1931.—I. T. Frary, *Thomas Jefferson, Architect and Builder,* 1931.—*Thomas Jefferson, Architect —Original Designs in the Collection of Thomas Jefferson Coolidge, Jr.,* with essay and notes by Fiske Kimball, 1916.

**JERUSALEM (Temple of).**—The old Temple of Jerusalem was built by Solomon on the hill of Moria. It was pillaged and destroyed by the Sumerians, and then rebuilt on the same site. It lasted thus for five centuries, until Herod transformed it.

Solomon had great works carried on inside the rock—walls, vaultings, and embankments, to support the temple, its annexes, and the palace. These under-buildings have allowed the site of the temple and of the palace to be discovered, and defined.

JERUSALEM: SIDE VIEW OF THE TEMPLE AND THE ENCLOSURE OF THE COURT OF THE PRIESTS, TAKEN FROM THE NORTHWEST. (Restoration by Ch. Chipiez.)

To have an idea of what this temple was like, one must read the description in the first Book of Kings, chapters V to VIII, the best and most detailed text; Chapters XL to XLIII of Ezekiel; and chapters IV and V of the book of Chronicles.

MM. Georges Perrot and Chipiez made a reconstruction of the temple of Jerusalem from the description of Ezekiel.

A large pylon preceded the entrance, which faced east. The temple was divided into two parts—the Holy Place (or Hecal), and the Holy of Holies (or Debir). The general arrangement resembled a Greek temple. Numerous buildings surrounded the sanctuary—sacristies, refectories, shops, priests' dwellings, porticoes, courtyards, corridors, stables, slaughter houses, and, finally, the Palace of the Kings of Judah. The sacred wall which enclosed the temple and its dependences was a square, each side of which measured 500 cubits. Thus the temple itself occupied only a very limited area compared with the whole of the sacred buildings.

The temple did not contain many statues—merely, perhaps, colossal statues of fantastic beasts, with the wings of a bird, and the body of a bull. The decoration of the sanctuary was derived from plant forms. It contained very rich furniture, made by the Phœnician Hiram-abi, or under his direction—the high-altar, in stone covered with bronze plaques (it was in two storeys, and was approached by a staircase); bronze tables; seven-branched candlesticks; and the two famous bronze columns, known as Iakin and Boaz, placed in front of the altar. In the principal courtyard was a large bronze recipient, known as the Bronze Sea, the work of Hiram-abi: twelve bronze oxen, larger than life-size, supported the basin, with which water for ablutions was poured every day. Hiram-abi also made ten large mobile basins, mounted on wheels, which distributed water in various parts of the temple. All this work, like the temple decoration, was of Phœnician inspiration and workmanship.

*Church of the Holy Sepulchre.* Erected by Constantine 312-337, the church underwent considerable change at the hands of the Saracens and such complete rebuilding under the Crusaders in the 12th century and under modern hands after its partial demolition in 1808 that the original design is completely drowned within subsequent accretion. The 12th century entrance, of Romanesque design under Saracenic influence, leads into the transept, before which is the domed crossing, to the west of which is the domed rotunda of the Sepulchre, which is partially surrounded by a semicircular ambulatory with three semicircular chapels. To the east is the Crusaders' Church, which has an apse with an ambulatory and radiating chapels. The church influenced hospice churches of the Templar Order elsewhere.

*Dome of the Rock* (Mosque of Omar). See Moslem Architecture, Syro-Egyptian school. See Pl. 33, Vol. I.

*Mosque-el-Akbah.* See Moslem Architecture, Syro-Egyptian school.

**JESUIT STYLE (Churches).**—See Pl. 43, Vol. II.

**JEWISH ART.**—A general consideration of Jewish art must be prefaced by a reference to the fact that the study of the subject is in its infancy, that much of the basic research has yet to be done. Therefore it is not possible to go very far in any attempt to define its aesthetic character or relationships with other art movements. However, from what has been done to date, it is evident that the subject has a very broad scope, and has probably exerted important influences upon some phases of art history.

Jewish art considered as a whole is unique in that it was produced by a nation whose communities were scattered throughout the civilized world, rather than confined to a single locality. These communities existed each within the framework of a larger non-Jewish community, and were completely integrated within themselves as cultural and national entities. There were also times when distinctive regional groups also developed, such as in Spain and southern France, or Germany and northern France.

It must also be noted that from the material available, it is necessary to carry the study of Jewish art history as far back as Roman Empire times. It is evident that any accurate study must give due consideration to the historical period and the region in which a particular group of art works were produced.

A word must also be said about the popular misconception that there have ever been religious prohibitions against Jewish production of works of art, or of representational art. It is common in this connection to refer to the second of the Ten Commandments, "Thou shalt make no graven image . . ." This single verse is supposed to have checked or stifled the natural artistic expression of the Jew.

Read within the context of the Old Testament, this prohibition cannot be interpreted as anything more than a prohibition against idolatry. Moreover, since Roman Empire times at least, the religious guidance of the Jew was embodied, not in the Old Testament, which is a very primitive legal and religious code suitable only for a primitive society, but in the Talmud and the later writings. And the Talmud and these later writings contain no general condemnation of art, either decorative or representational.

*The Art of the Jews During the Roman Empire and Middle Ages.*—The remains of Jewish art in ancient times are very meagre. But this poverty can be accounted for by the political history of Palestine. The art of the other ancient nations, Babylon, Nineveh, Egypt, and Greece, have been spared, either because they fell into neglect and were buried when the civilizations that produced them declined, or because they were admired and preserved by their conquerors.

But Jerusalem, between the time it was established as the capital of the Jewish nation by King David, and its final destruction by the Roman Emperor Hadrian, suffered no less than twenty-three sieges, and three of these ended in complete devastation. The other important cities of Palestine were swallowed in similar ruin. After the fall of Rome, Palestine was the scene of successive waves of conquest and reconquest by the Byzantines, Persians, Arabs, Franks and Turks.

What can be known of ancient Jewish art and architecture must be reconstructed from the remains of about 40 synagogues dating from Roman and early Christian times. Documents and excavations have also brought to light Jewish architectural and artistic activities at such places as Heliopolis, Alexandria, and Hamman-Lif, in north Africa; Malta, Delos, Miletus, Aegina, Priene, Dura-Europos, and Rome.

Jewish communities were established in northern Africa at least as early as the 5th century B.C., as is shown for example by legal and other documents from the Elephantine Island, in the Nile, near Assuan. Other documents tell of their communities in Alexandria from the time of Ptolemy III.

Alexandria had a large and important Jewish community, carrying on a very active commercial life. An active intellectual life was also carried on and many contributions were made by writers, philosophers, and scientists. The Septuagint translation of the Bible, for instance, was made in Alexandria. Two of the five parts of the city were Jewish, and they had forty-two synagogues, besides the chief synagogue whose size and splendor have been described by contemporary writers in almost fabulous terms.

Important finds have also been excavated at Hamman-Lif, near Carthage, where a 4th century synagogue, very elaborately designed has been brought to light, with a very beautiful mosaic floor in an unusual state of preservation.

In and around Rome itself a rich artistic life is indicated. A relatively large body of Jewish catacomb painting, sarcophagi, lamps, and pictorial gilt glass has already been brought to light. The iconography bears a strong resemblance in spirit and approach to the contemporary Christian iconography. Its emphasis is upon the representation of cult symbols and objects, such as the seven branched candelabra, the closet containing the holy scripts, instruments used in the religious festivals, and certain symbolical animals and birds.

With the rise of Christianity to complete domination of the Mediterranean lands, the Jewish communities declined under systematic persecution, until the Moslems seized northern Africa and they were able to regain some of their freedom. A curious situation is recorded in some 7th century documents which tell how Christian churches in Füstat were seized by the ruling Moslems for non-payment of taxes and sold to Jews. Another interesting story is sketched in an 11th century court record, which tells of a litigation in Cairo, in which certain Mohammedan citizens charged that the Jews were building a new synagogue, contrary to law. But the defendant Rabbi proved that he was simply rebuilding an old synagogue since the location was an ancient synagogue site, and the decision was rendered in favor of the Rabbi.

There is also a very important group of signed and dated 10th century illuminated manuscripts, now in the Leningrad Library, which were found during the excavation of the abandoned storeroom of a Cairo synagogue. The style and delicacy of the ornament show a marked kinship to that of the Moslems. The iconography is a continuation of the "Roman" tradition of the representation of cult symbols and objects.

*Art of the Jews in Spain (including Portugal and southern France)*.—Spain was the scene of one of the great periods of Jewish history and culture. Here the Jews made a brilliant contribution in literature, philosophy and science, not only to Spain but also to western civilization as a whole. The history of the Jews in Spain covers a period from at least as early as the 2nd and 3rd century A.D., to 1492 when they were expelled by Ferdinand and Isabella.

Architectural examples which have survived in such centers as Seville, Cordoba, and Toledo can only suggest the brilliance that once characterized the Jewish community of Spain. Other synagogues and ritual baths have been discovered at Lorca, Brihuega, Segovia, and Bembibre. Documents tell of no less than 12 synagogues in Toledo itself, of which two have survived as unique and exquisite types of mudejar architecture in Spain. Santa Maria la Blanca, dating most probably from the end of the 12th century, and El Transito de Nuestra Señora, dated 1366 (the synagogues were rededicated as churches after the Jews had been driven out), exhibit many features which have no parallel in any other examples of mudejar architecture. Future study may reveal them to be part of a genuine national tradition of Jewish architecture in Spain.

The art of manuscript illumination was apparently highly developed among the Jews. The 13th to 15th centuries have provided us with the largest number of examples, though no exhaustive study of the collections have been made as yet. One very interesting item is a treatise on the art of manuscript illumination written by one Abraham ben Judah ibn Hayyim, in 1262, at Laulé, Portugal (Parma, cod. de-Rossi 945). The language is Portuguese, but it is written in Hebrew characters.

Jewish painters followed a variety of local schools, working for both Jewish and Christian patrons. They do not seem to have developed a national school in either iconography or style. The text most frequently illuminated was the Haggadah, the book of ritual and prayers for the Passover holy days, although Bibles and prayer books were also illuminated. The subject matter was usually the Old Testament narrative series, rather than a continuation of tradition of cult symbolism. The narrative series was similar to the familiar Bible Histoire type of illumination, with two or four scenes on a page in adjacent rectangles. Some of the illustrations depict national and religious customs, but the iconography for this type of subject matter seems to have been developed by the Jews of Germany.

The studies have not yet been undertaken, but it is very probable that the Jews contributed to the iconography of Bible illustration in Spain. It is well known that the services of Jewish scholars and translators were in great demand by Spanish churchmen and noblemen. Most striking examples of this have to do with the production of the famous Alba Bible, and the Escorial Bible.

The *Alba Bible*, dated 1422 to 1433, is a Castilian translation from the Hebrew, made by Rabbi Moses Arragel upon commission of Don Luis Guzman, Grand Master of the Knights of Callatrava, and Lord of Algaba. The documentation on the execution of this book is unusually complete, mainly in the form of a lengthy correspondence between the Christian nobleman and the Jewish scholar. It describes not only the writing of the text, but also the painting of the very complete set of illustrations. There are three hundred and forty-four illustrations which were painted by Toledo artists, under the supervision of Rabbi Moses.

The *Bible of the Escorial* (Ms. I. j.3.) was probably executed for Don Diego Hurtado de Mendoza, first Duke of Infantado. The unusual character of its text and 65 illustrations has been commented upon by scholars who have apparently had no knowledge of the literature on Jewish art. Samuel Berger pointed out (Histoire de la Vulgate, Paris, 1893) that the text follows the Hebrew canon rather than the Vulgate canon, and has many other characteristics which seem to indicate conclusively that the text is a direct translation from the Hebrew, probably by a Jewish scholar. Berger also made this comment: "The miniatures are alien in style and subject matter and details to Christian tradition. If it is possible that the Jews practiced the arts, we may recognize here a produce of Hebrew art."

From the studies and documents published to date, it is evident that Jewish artists and architects were active in localities throughout the length and breadth of Spain, Portugal, and southern France, and their work was highly regarded by Christian as well as Jewish patrons. Under pressure of the Inquisition, steps were taken to deprive them of their Christian patronage, such as the appointment of Francisco Chacon as royal censor to see that no Jew or Mussulman paint the figure of Christ, Mary, or any of the Saints (Letter of Isabella, Dec. 20, 1480).

*Art of the Jews in Germany (and northern France)*.—In Germany the Jews produced an art with a greater individual national orientation apparently than in any other region. This is probably due to two factors: (1) the intensive development of popular art in Germany, and (2) the consistent policy of segregation of Jews in their ghettos practiced in Germany more thoroughly than in any other land. Both in style and subject-matter their art was akin to German popular art, especially as developed in the early phase of the arts of woodcut and engraving.

Though the Jews sponsored other forms of representational art, such as mural painting, the most characteristic development is to be found in their book illumination. They developed a very rich and individual iconography, based upon their own experience, both secular and religious. This iconography mirrors not only their religious and social mores, but is also quite unique in that it depicts quite frankly and in a very lively fashion the persecution to which they were from time to time subjected.

This tradition began to be developed at least as early as the 13th century, and was developed to its richest expression in the 15th century. It is characterized in form by miniatures placed in the margins of the manuscript page next to the text or idea referred to. Interestingly enough, this form of illustration is to be found in a Syro-Palestinian monastic art tradition, originating there about the 5th century A.D., and spreading throughout the Byzantine-Orthodox west. This so-called monkish-theological psalter illustration tradition was productive until at least the 17th century.

With the coming of the 16th and 17th centuries, the indigenous Jewish art tradition was affected by the current Baroque styles and mannerisms, and it broke down. With the "emancipation" of the Jews from the ghettos, the tradition was lost, and with the coming of modern times, Jewish artists, individually followed the trends of western European art, some with considerable success.

*Poland and Eastern Europe*.—It was in this region that a creative folk art was carried on by the Jews into the 20th century, after the west European Jews became deliberately Europeanized, after the Spanish Jewish communities had been wiped out, and after the Mediterranean communities had become poverty stricken and declined.

A unique wooden architecture has been created, designed very expressively, showing a fine instinct for the development of forms and spaces. The ceilings are elaborately painted.

Bibliography: David Kaufman, *Sens et l'origine des symboles tumulaires de l'Ancien Testament dans l'art chretien primitif*, in Revue des Études Juives, Vol. 14. Paris, 1887.—D. H. Mueller and J. v. Schlosser, *Die Haggadah von Sarajevo*. Vienna, 1898.—Guenzberg and Strassoff, *l'Ornament Hebreu*. Berlin, 1905.—H. Kohl and C. Watzinger, *Antike Synagogen in Galilaea*. Leipzig, 1916.—Bruno Italiener (editor), *Die Darmstaädter Pessachhaggadah*. Leipzig, 1927.—Richard Krautheimer, *Mittelalterliche Synagogen*. Berlin, 1927. —E. L. Sukenik, *Ancient Synagogues in Palestine and Greece*. London, 1934.—G. K. Lukomski, *The Wooden Synagogues of Eastern Europe*, in The Burlington Magazine. London, Jan. 1935.—Rahel Wischnitzer - Bernstein, *Gestalten und Symbole der jüdichen Kunst*. Berlin, 1935.—Michael Fooner, *Notes on Jewish Art*, in Opinion. New York, December, 1936.

**JOHN (Augustus Edwin)**.—Contemporary British painter and graver. He was born 4th January 1879 in Tenby, England. Showing artistic talents at an early age he was sent to the Slade School in 1894, where he studied under Brown and Tonks up to 1898. Throughout his school-days he was an outstanding pupil, winning prizes frequently. In 1901 he married Ida Nettleton and moved to Liverpool, where he instructed in the department of art of the University. About this time he began to develop an interest for print-making and soon the oil technique was replaced exclusively by etching and lithography. In 1904 he collaborated in founding the Society of Twelve; two years later he held his first large exhibition at the Chenil Gallery. Having sojourned in Paris and travelled in Normandy and Brittany, John became influenced by the Post-Impressionist way of painting and this new tendency was manifested in his oil and watercolour. In 1915 Bliss purchased thirty-two of his etchings and presented them to the Fitzwilliam Museum in Cambridge. After several successful exhibits John returned to the continent and lived in Spain for some time, to return to England and receive his nomination as Associate of the R. A.; he was finally elected a member in 1928. Not being bothered by the activities of his contemporaries, Watts and Whistler, John painted in his own unrestrained and vigorous way, his original conceptions often shocking the conservative English audience. His artistic output is a synthesis of all that went before him, showing his great fondness for the art of Rembrandt, Rubens and Goya, his knowledge of the Quattrocentists as well as Whistler's colour theories. John was a thinker as well as a craftsman; his paintings and etchings, which include landscape, figure compositions, gypsy scenes, narratives, etc., show his splendid capacity to organise on a large scale; his intense personality is brought forth in the spirit as well as in the substance of his paintings. His work may be divided into three groups, the first being portraits, etched or in oil. Of these the single sitters are more fortunate than the group pictures; he catches their personality, giving even to the vulgar types a classic pose and tone. The colour is predominantly brilliant, used in large masses and the technique sketchy. Among those portrayed are W. B. Yeats, G. B. Shaw, Epstein, Charles McEvoy, etc. To the second group belong the gypsy scenes, which are among the best liked and most popular works of the artist. Having led a gypsy life in the deserts of Dartmoor he had an inherent flare for, and comprehension of, their spirit; he painted and etched all their activities in their natural surroundings; the colour is again strong and bold and the technique vigorous. His last group is that of etchings. His technique is dexterous, showing a direct influence of the engravings of Rembrandt, and his expressive calligraphy is reminiscent of oriental brushwork. These etchings, frequently based on early sketches, are architectural in composition and are dominated by a smooth, flowing rhythm. There are four examples engraved on glass. He has also done cartoons and a mural design for the Museum at Johannesburg, South Africa. In 1906 Campbell Dodgson began to collect his etchings; a comprehensive catalogue was published in 1920. His works may be seen in the museums of London, Liverpool, Cambridge, New York, Paris and in private collections.

Bibliography: Anthony Bertram, *Augustus John*, 1923.—Charles Marriott, *Augustus John*, Masters of Modern Art Series, 1917.

**JOHNSON (Cornelius)**.—Anglo-Dutch painter (1593-1667), born in London, worked as a successful portrait painter first in England and then in Holland.

**JONES (Inigo)**.—British architect, 1573-1662, who was responsible for the change in style of 17th century British architecture from Transitional Renaissance to the Palladian style. He spent many years in

Italy, chiefly studying the monuments of Palladio. He was a protegé of James I and rival for royal favor with Ben Jonson, his arch enemy with whom he was frequently forced to cooperate in the presentation of masques and pageants. His most important architectural commissions were never completed because of the advent of the Commonwealth. The *Banqueting Hall, Whitehall,* was all that was built of a grand conception on a large scale. *St. Paul's Covent Garden,* London, was a simple and dignified church united by arcades to the adjoining market. *Greenwich Hospital,* completed by Wren, is another great scheme, of which the Queen's House was carried out according to Jones' designs. His many houses, derived from the palaces of Palladio, set the style for the manor house architecture of the succeeding Georgian Period. Among them may be mentioned *Stoke Park* and *Wilton House.* His foremost disciple and the connecting link between him and later British architects was his nephew John Webb.

Bibliography: J. A. Gotch, *Inigo Jones.* London.

**JONGKIND (Johan, B.)**.—Dutch painter, 1819-1891. He was the greatest Dutch painter of the 19th century. Jongkind left his native land for the first time in 1846 to work with Isabey in Paris. He soon enjoyed very high esteem among certain discerning spirits. The brothers Goncourt eagerly seized upon the newcomer and spread his name in the best artistic circles. Jongkind joined the school of Fontainebleau, and it is almost impossible to write a history of landscape painting in France without recalling the exquisite and charming works of this Dutchman. Diaz was the first who fell under his influence. Jongkind was essentially the initiator of contemporary Impressionism, and it is assuredly in him that the real awakening of the Dutch feeling for light finds its highest expression. He used the technique of division of tones, keeping his colours at their greatest intensity and transparence. He was the true master of Monet, Sisley, and Pissarro. Every year he returned to his own country, revisiting for choice Rotterdam and Dordrecht. "There, in the pride of summer nights, he learned to paint moonlight on the water in a way that no one has surpassed." He died in France (Côte-Saint-André Isère).

See Pl. 59, Vol. II.

Bibliography: Muther, *The History of modern Painting.*

**JORDAENS (Jacob)**.—Flemish painter, 1593-1678. Jordaens was born in Antwerp. His father was a draper, and was unable to give his son the brilliant education which other artists of the time, such as Rubens and Van Dyck, received. In 1607 he entered the studio of Van Noort, becoming his favourite pupil and, after eight years of apprenticeship, his son-in-law. Thus in 1616 began a happy, hard-working family life which was enlivened by feasts and drinking parties, at which the family assembled to be entertained by good cheer and merry songs. Jordaens had three children, and lived in the Rue Haute, not far from the house where he was born. Twenty years later he rebuilt his house, and turned it into a magnificent richly furnished dwelling, which he decorated himself. His early marriage prevented him from visiting Italy, like the other great artists of his time. But he studied and copied the pictures by Italian masters, which were to be found in Flanders, all the more assiduously. As soon as he was married, he became a member of the Guild of St. Luke, as a "Water-schilder" (a water-colour painter), probably because he made, especially at the beginning of his career, large decorations and cartoons for tapestry, in distemper. In 1621, he became leader of the Guild. He worked with a great many pupils, and with them he was able to carry out vast decorative works which he could not have undertaken alone. Sometimes, however, their collaboration was excessive. In the 1650's Jordaens turned Calvinist and was fined once for the distribution of heretical writings. After Rubens, Jordaens was the greatest Flemish painter of his day. Perhaps even better than Rubens (who, however, influenced him strongly), he personifies the genius of the Flemish race—with his pictures of robust, placid youths, and fat, contented women, loving good living, endless feasts, and riotous merry-making. His colour is bright and sensuous—his whites luminous, his browns reddish and deep, and his reds have provoked the saying that "if Rubens painted with blood, Jordaens painted with fire." In Jordaens' pictures colour is more important than line; but this is not to say that he was an incorrect or inadequate draughtsman. Many drawings, in various galleries, proved that he drew firmly and precisely. But the full expression of his genius is found only in his painting. His production was abundant and varied. He soon became famous, and was overwhelmed with commissions. One of his earliest pictures is the *Crucifixion,* in the Church of St. Paul (Antwerp) painted in 1617, which does not yet show his finest qualities. The following year he painted the *Adoration of the Shepherds* (Stockholm), in which they are already discernible—the contrast of light and shade, which is one of Jordaens' characteristics, is here very lively. This was one of his favourite subjects, for there are other versions of it (Frankfort, Lyon, etc.). The *Martyrdom of St. Apollonia* (Antwerp, Church of the Augustin monks) was painted in 1627. In 1630, Jordaens painted for the High Altar of the Church of St. Martin, Tournai, the *St. Martin Healing a Man* (now in the Brussels Gallery), which is well composed, and vigorously modelled. In the same gallery is his painting called *Fecundity,* a subject which he repeated with variations, on the canvas in the Wallace Collection (London). In these pictures Jordaens could give free play to his delight in painting opulent nudes bathed in warm light. The drawing and modelling are firmer and more precise than in most of his works. Jordaens did not care much for portrait painting as it did not give free rein to his fantasy, and so he only painted a few. The one believed to be of Admiral de Ruyter (Louvre), painted about 1642, is the most celebrated. His self-portraits are among his best. The one in the Prado, with his wife, is full of charm; but the *Family of Jordaens* (Hermitage) is more lively, alert and amusing. *The Four Evangelists* (Louvre) is perhaps the best of Jordaens' religious pictures. After 1630, he frequently painted subjects which especially suited his bent—proverbs, banquets and "genre" pieces. The old Flemish proverb *"Soo d' oude songen, soo pepen de jongen"* (*"as the old folk sing, the youngsters pipe"*) was wonderfully illustrated by him in five pictures (Antwerp, Paris, Berlin, Dresden, Munich). The seniors are singing an old tune, while the children are blowing into musettes, and all have the satisfied air of prosperous, well-nourished people. The best of these proverbs is the one in Antwerp, painted in 1638. It is perhaps to his "Feasts" that Jordaens owes the greatest part of his fame. In them he reveals all the richness of his Flemish genius. The subject does not allow for sentiment, delicacy or pathos, but what abundant vivacity, striking colour, and fancy! Once more we see the artist's family—his wife, sisters-in-law, nieces, laughing boisterously at the gallantries of ruddy faced young men, full of wine. Probably the family meals were quieter than in Jordaens' paintings! The subjects which he represents in his banquets illustrate an old Flemish custom, the "rite of the Bean," by which the feast of the Epiphany was celebrated, with great feasting. It is impossible to say how many times the artist painted the subject called *The King Drinks.* The best known versions are in the Brussels Gallery, the Louvre, the Museums of Cassel, Lille, Vienna, etc. Among his religious and mythological paintings may be mentioned: *Christ Driving the Money Lenders from the Temple* (Louvre); the *Miraculous Draught of Fishes,* a very fine sketch in the Museum of Marseille; and the *Adoration of the Magi,* formerly in Dixmuiden, destroyed in the war, 1914-18. In 1641, Charles I of England commissioned the artist to paint twenty-two pictures for the apartments of Henrietta Maria, at Greenwich. What has become of them is not known. About the same time, Jordaens finished a series of twelve paintings which had been ordered by the King of Spain from Rubens, who died before the work was finished. These paintings, which represented the *Metamorphoses* of Ovid, were partly destroyed by fire in 1710. Some fragments remain in the Prado. Perhaps Jordaens' finest work is the decoration of the Orange Room of the House-in-the-Wood, near The Hague. This house was built for Henry of Nassau, but was not finished until after his death. His widow commissioned several artists to decorate the walls. Jordaens painted the *Triumph of Henry of Nassau.* He had several sketches ready by 1651 (three remain—in Brussels, Antwerp and Varsovia), and he set to work at once. In the centre, a statue of Victory crowns the Prince of Nassau and his son; Mercury, Athena, nymphs, and cupids surround them; while Science, Peace, the Arts, Death and Fame all contemplate the scene. After finishing the paintings in the House-in-the-Wood, Jordaens set about decorating his own house with large compositions, eight of which now adorn the residence of M. Van der Linden (Antwerp), the owner of Jordaens' own house. In 1665, Jordaens painted three ceilings (Antwerp) for the Guild of Painters, representing *Pegasus, Commerce and Industry Protecting the Fine Arts, and Human Law Humbling Itself before the Divine Law*—mediocre compositions, which have none of Jordaens' old zest. The artist still continued to paint for some years, but before long he became feeble-minded. He died in 1678, at the age of eighty-five.

Jordaens. (Uffizi, Florence.)

Jordaens: Portrait of Admiral de Ruyter (?). (Louvre.)

Jordaens: The Four Evangelists. (Louvre.)

See Pl. 35, Vol. II.

Bibliography: Max Rooses, *Jordaens,* Antwerp, 1907.—P. Buschmann, *Jac. Jordaens.* Brussels, 1905.

**JORGE INGLÉS**.—*Spanish* painter, perhaps of English origin. From a document of 1455 we know that in that year he was commissioned with an altarpiece, four panels of which are now in Madrid, in the palace of the present Marquis of Santillana Duque del Infantado (the first Marquis of Santillana, Inigo Lopez de Mendoza, had commissioned the altarpiece, and he is represented kneeling, in one of the panels). The painting is extremely vigorous.

F. J. Sánchez Cantón attributes a number of miniatures to him.

BIBLIOGRAPHY: *Thieme - Becker,* Vol. XIX, 1926; art. *Jorge Inglés,* by A. L. Mayer.—A. L. Mayer, *Geschichte der Span. Malerei,* 2nd. ed. 1922.—Ch. R. Post, *Hist of Span. Ptg.,* 1933; vol. IV.—T. Borenius and E. W. Tristram, *English Medieval Painting.* Florence (Pantheon), 1927.

**JOSETSU.**—Japanese painter and priest during the Oei period (1393-1411). He represents, not the founder of the coloristic black and white painting, but one of its earliest exponents. His work has the combined simplicity and strength of Zen art.

**JOSÈS (Jehan).**—See "Dinanderie."

**— (Nicolas).**—See "Dinanderie."

**JOUVENET (Jean).**—French painter (Rouen, 1644-Paris, 1717).

JOUVENET: DESCENT FROM THE CROSS. (Louvre.)

The most famous of a family of painters whose ancestry was perhaps Italian; the name may have been changed from Giovinetti to Jouvenet, when the family settled in Rouen. Jouvenet was sent to study in Paris in 1661. There he received the Academic instruction of Le Brun; but these narrow doctrines made little appeal to his free, Norman nature. Nevertheless, Le Brun, while employing him at Versailles for about twenty years, taught him to construct the most complicated compositions. In 1675, Jouvenet became a member of the Académie on the presentation of his picture, *Esther before Ahasuerus;* in 1681, he became professor. Until this time he appeared merely as a facile, correct follower of Poussin and of Le Brun. It was only after the death of the latter (1690) that Jouvenet revealed his originality. His self-portrait, already very personal (Rouen) belongs to this time. Louis XIV wished in vain to send Jouvenet to Italy at the expense of the State. The South did not attract him, and it is doubtless to this that we owe his robust, if defective, personality. At the end of the century he was fully master of himself, and to this period belong some of his finest works. In their dramatic feeling, they are akin to Rubens. His colour is sumptuous, and were it not for a certain coarseness of handling, his paintings would recall the Venetian school. If his *Resurrection of Lazarus* (Louvre) seems somewhat insincere and declamatory, his *Descent from the Cross* (Louvre) after Rubens, is a masterpiece. The design is moving and majestic, the attitudes natural and vigorous, and light and shade are used with very powerful effect.

How charming and intimate an artist the penetrating portrait painter of Fagon (Louvre), could be, when he wished, is seen in his *View of the High Altar of Notre Dame* (Louvre). This time his realism is delicate and refined. In 1709 Jouvenet was still working in the Chapels of the Invalides and Versailles; but in 1713 he was taken with complete paralysis of the right side of his body. Like Holbein, he then painted with his left hand. In this way he finished, for Notre Dame, his paintings of the Magnificat and the Visitation. He died in 1717. One of his best pupils was his nephew, Jean Restout (See this name).

**JUÁN DE JUNI.**—Also known under Jony, Juani, c. 1507-77. French sculptor, painter and architect who spent the greater part of his life in Spain where he also died (Valladolid). See Pl. 23, Vol. II.

BIBLIOGRAPHY: *Thieme - Becker,* Vol. XIX, 1926. Art. *Juni. Juán* by A. L. Mayer.—See also Bibliography listed under Berruguete, Alonso.

**JUANES (Juan de).**—Spanish painter (c. 1500-1579). Son of Vicente Mesip. He was, through his father, influenced by Llanos, Yañez and others. The Spanish critic Allende-Salazár states that it is difficult to distinguish between the early works of the son and the late ones by the father. The same critic believes that Juanes must have been to Italy, judging from the influence of Florentine and Milanese painters then not represented in Spain but discernible in his works.

BIBLIOGRAPHY: *Thieme - Becker,* Vol. XXIV, 1930; art. *Masip, Vicente Juan* (gen. Juan de Juanes) by J. Allende-Salazár (with an excellent list of the painter's oeuvre). —A. L. Mayer, *Gesch. span. Malerei,* 2nd ed., 1922.

**JUMIÈGES (France).**—*Abbey Church* (1048-1067). A ruined church of the earlier Romanesque of Normandy. The west front has the paired towers and salient porch of Carolingian Germany. The interior, now open to the sky, had a system similar to that of S. Zeno, Verona: alternate piers carried a vertical strip which was continued to the top of the clerestory wall. This system, here employed in conjunction with a timbered roof, was prophetic of the later use of the groined vault implied in the alternate system.

**JUSTINIAN.**—See Byzantine Art.

**JUSTUS OF GHENT.**—Flemish painter of the 15th century. Very little is known of the life and works of this artist. It is only known that, in 1460, he became a member of the Guild of St. Luke, of Antwerp; and, in 1464, of that of Ghent. In 1474, he went to Italy, at the request of the Duke of Urbino. There he painted, for the Brotherhood of the Corpus Domini, a *Last Supper,* in which the grouping of the figures is bold and original (Urbino). To him are also attributed, with some probability, twenty-eight portraits of scholars, artists and ancient poets, some of which are in the Louvre, and others in the Barberini Palace. From these portraits, the young Raphael drew some sketches, which are kept in the Accademia of Venice.

The date and place of Justus' death are unknown.

See Pl. 60, Vol. I.

BIBLIOGRAPHY: Fierens Gevaert, *Les Primitifs flamands.* Brussels, 1909.—M. J. Friedländer, *Altniederländische Malerei,* III, 1925.

**JUVARA (Filippo).**—Italian abbot and architect; born in Messina (1676-1736), where Vittore Amedeo met him, and persuaded him to go to Turin. There, Juvara soon made headway among the other architects, bringing a classical repose to their baroque extravagances. The fine peristyle of the famous Church of Superga, on the outskirts of Turin, recalls those of ancient temples. The dome, and the whole design, has grandeur of conception. The double staircase of the Madamo Palace (1718) ascends with a fine sweep. He also built the Church of the Carmine; the façade of Santa Cristina; the dome of San Sebastiano, in Mantua; that of Como Cathedral, and many other works, including La Granja, Madrid, 1721, the royal palace.

BIBLIOGRAPHY: Chavet and Grossi, Alfredo Melani, *L'Abate detto Filippo Juvara.* Vita d'Arte, 1909.

# K

**KAKEMONO.**—"Hanging thing," Japanese term, now commonly used for a scroll painting vertical in shape. See Japan—Art (Painting).

**KAL'AT SIM'ÂN (Syria).**—*Convent of St. Simeon Stylites,* 459. An outstanding monument of early Christian architecture, now in ruins. All the artistic endeavor of Antioch was poured on Kal'at Sim'ân in the 2nd half of the 5th century, on the church and the monastery buildings to the southeast. Kal'at Sim'ân was a pilgrimage center for all northern and northeastern Syria, for it was there that St. Simeon had perched on his final and highest column. The church is an octagon with four niches bringing it to a square, the octagon being open to the sky, with four basilican arms changing the complete plan to a Greek cross. Only the east arm has apses, and so formed the choir. The main entrance was on the south, and the façade there consists of three arches separated by piers, in a design prophetic of the French Romanesque church of St. Gilles-en-Provence.

**KALB LAUZEH (Northern Syria).**—*Church,* c. 480 A.D. An important monument of Early Christian architecture, Kalb Lauzeh's façade, like that at Dêr Termânîn, is an arched narthex flanked by chambers becoming dwarf towers in the clerestory. The salient apse has two stories of applied columns and a corbeled cornice surprising for its early date.

**KAMAKURA.**—See Japan—Art.

**KANAOKA (Kosé).**—Japanese painter and poet (850-931); founder of the Kosé school. The greatest early Japanese artist, and the earliest painter of whom we have any precise record. He was famous for his portraits of sages, his landscapes, and his animal paintings. He is said to have decorated the walls of the Imperial palaces. Practically all of his work has disappeared.

**KANO (School of).**—See Japan—Art, *Ashikaga Period;* Motonobu.

**KARFIOL (Bernard).**—Contemporary American painter. He was born in Budapest 6th May 1886 of American parentage. The family soon returned to the United States, where his boyhood was spent in Brooklyn and on Long Island. In 1900 he entered the art school of the National Academy of Design and four years later he was attending sessions at the Académie Julian in Paris. In 1904 and 1905 he exhibited in the Paris Salon and the next year he returned to New York. From 1908 to 1913 he painted and taught, gaining self-confidence and improving his technical ability. Hamilton Easter Field showed some of his paintings along with work by John Marin in 1917, which exhibition was the turning point in his career. Many of the subjects of his outdoor studies are made in the region of New York City and Ridgefield, New Jersey, while others are painted at Ogunquit, Maine, his summer home. His style is particularly individual in character and does not seem directly connected with any previous art movements. However, the aloof quality of his work, as well as the simplification of the human form, is to a certain extent connected with archaic art which has inspired so many of our younger artists. A strong feeling for form and sensuous colours characterise his work, of which an outstanding example is the *Babette* of the Detroit Institute of Arts. He is a member of the American Society of Painters, Sculptors and Gravers and in 1928 won the Corcoran Gold Medal and first William A. Clark prize in the eleventh biennial exhibition of the Corcoran Gallery of Art in Washington, D. C.

BIBLIOGRAPHY: Jean Paul Slusser, *Bernard Karfiol,* The Arts Portfolio Series, c. 1930.—Jean Paul Slusser, *Bernard Karfiol,* American Artists

Series, 1931.—For other articles see *The Index of Twentieth Century Artists* for March, 1934.

**KARNAK.**—See Egypt (Architecture).

**KASR IBN WARDAN (East Syria).**—*Church,* 564 A.D., in basalt and burned brick. Not a genuine Syrian expression but built under influence from First Golden Age Constantinople. It is now ruined. It had a domed central square block with a groin-vaulted aisle surrounding it on the north, south and West. At the east wall an apse and two pastophoria, all contained within the exterior square boundary of the plan.

**KAUFFMANN (Angelica).**—German painter, 1741-1807, very celebrated in her day. Her father was her first master. He sent her to Como and Milan, where she painted the portrait of the Duke and Duchess of Modena. Returning to her native village of Schwanzerberg, she painted pictures for the church. Then she returned to Italy, and went to Florence and Rome, where she became the pupil of Winckelmann. She was influenced by his theories, and painted classical allegories. Famous throughout Europe, she visited many cities, and settled in London in 1765. She married an adventurer, who passed for the Count of Horn. The day after the wedding she learned that her husband was only the footman of him whose name he had taken. The marriage was annulled, and she retired to Rome, where she married the painter, A. Zucchi. She often exhibited her work. From this period date *The Return of Arminius*; the *Funeral of Pallas*; portrait of herself as a nurse or a bacchante; portrait of herself as a Vestal Virgin (Dresden).

Angelica Kauffmann's painting is bright, insipid and sentimental; her drawing, inadequate.

Bibliography: Frances A. Gerard, *Angelica Kauffmann,* 1892.

**KAULBACH (Wilhelm von).**—German painter, 1805-1874, of the school of Munich. His large compositions, the *Destruction of Jerusalem,* the *Defeat of the Huns,* etc., on the staircase of the new Museum in Berlin, and his satirical decoration in the new Art Gallery in Munich, are of secondary importance, in spite of their reputation. Kaulbach is also known for his illustrations to Reinecke Fuchs, and other works by Klopstock, Wieland and Goethe.

**KEENE (Charles Samuel).**—English draughtsman (1823-1891), contributed abundantly to the pages of *Punch,* displaying qualities of excellent draughtsmanship and incisive characterisation.

**KEEP.**—In the Middle Ages, the keep was the chief tower of a castle, the redoubt protected by enclosing walls where, in case of attack, the garrison and the inhabitants of the castle retired. The keep was to the castle what the castle was to the town (Viollet-le-Duc). The earliest keeps were simple, wooden towers, soon replaced, from the end of the tenth century, by stone towers. The keep was square or round, and was often flanked with buttresses or angle turrets. In the interior were rooms, staircases, and storerooms for provisions and arms. One of the most celebrated French keeps, or "donjons," was that of Coucy, destroyed by the Germans. There are a great many in the Loire region.

**KEIRINCX (Alexander).**—Flemish landscape painter (1600-1652). Worked for some time in England.

**KEISAI YEISEN.**—Japanese painter and printer, 1792-1848, born at Yedo. A Ukiyo-e artist specializing in portraits of beautiful women and of courtesans, he was profoundly influenced by Hokusai. See Japan—Art.

**KELMSCOTT PRESS.**—See Morris.

**KENT (Rockwell).**—Contemporary American painter and graver. He was born in Tarrytown, New York, 21st June 1882. In 1898 he entered the summer art school of William Merritt Chase and in 1903 went to Dublin, New Hampshire, to study with Abbott H. Thayer. He also studied under Robert Henri and Kenneth Hayes Miller, but his greatest inspiration came from Thayer. He studied for a time at the Columbia University School of Architecture, but the desire to travel proved stronger. From 1905 to the present time he has alternated trips to different parts of the Americas with periods of painting and exhibiting in New York. His trips provided opportunities to paint scenes of life in the different regions that he touched. During that time he has travelled and painted at Monhegan Island, Maine, the White Mountains of New Hampshire, Winona, Minnesota, Newfoundland, Fox Island near Seward, Alaska, and around Cape Horn and Tierra del Fuego. More recently he has made his permanent home at Ausable Forks, New York, and from there has made two trips to Greenland to paint and gather information for his books. For not only is he well known as a painter but also as an illustrator of magazine articles and books, including his own books, which tell of his travels to the places above mentioned. His writings include *Wilderness, A Journal of Quiet Adventure in Alaska, Voyaging Southward from the Strait of Magellan, N by E,* the last one relating some of his Greenland adventures.

In the intervals of his travels he has exhibited his pictures, at first with but little comment but now well received, paintings of large simple masses of colour nicely harmonised and arranged for effectiveness, as is the *Winter* in the Metropolitan Museum of Art. He has also done a good many advertisements, where his ability in the graphic arts is well shown. A very representative collection of his prints is to be found in the book *Rockwellkentiana.* Examples of his work are in the Columbus, Ohio, Gallery of Fine Arts, the Whitney Museum of American Art in New York City and Phillips Memorial Gallery in Washington.

Bibliography: Rockwell Kent and Carl Zigrosser, *Rockwellkentiana,* 1933.—For other bibliography see *The Index of Twentieth Century Artists* for April, 1934.

**KENZAN (Ogata).**—Japanese painter, lacquerer, ceramist (Kyoto, 1663-Yedo, 1743). Younger brother of Korin, whom he imitated in his paintings and lacquers, but he is considered one of the most original of Japanese ceramists, and his faience is as famous as his brother's lacquer. The decoration, which he lavished on his pottery, is extremely able and fresh and free in comparison to his brother's work; the colour is unequalled, especially in his choice of enamels with which he obtained effects of colour previously unknown. See Japan—Art.

**KERAMIC.**—See Ceramic.

**KERNSTOCK (Károly, or Charles).**—Contemporary Hungarian painter, born in Budapest, 1873. A pupil of Hollósy and of Bouguereau, in Munich and Paris respectively, he became interested in 1908 in Post-Impressionism and Fauvism. The founder of the *Nyolcak* (The Eight), the Post-Impressionist group in Hungary, he introduced the new French doctrines in his native land. A forceful painter, his most frequently used themes are athletic young men and horses arranged in vertical compositions. In these studies, as *Nude* or *Horsemen,* we find the same interest in architectonic organization as in Cézanne's landscapes or *Bathers.* These men with their dynamic countenances appear with the whole weight of their bodies within a fixed plan as the highest and worthiest mass that painting can produce. Kernstock has a powerful and often brutally frank vision as well as clarity and logic. He is not interested in atmosphere, but in the evolution of form and constructive power. He is in search of rhythm and motion; the function of colour is merely to bring out form. As a result he has a very personal style which is achieved through thought and effort. He has done some fine stained glass for the *County House* in Debrecen.

Bibliography: Krucken and Parlagi, *Das geist. Ungarn,* 1918.

**KESSEL (Jan van).**—Flemish painter, 1626-1679. Grandson of Velvet Breughel. He painted animals and flowers. His *Four Continents* (Schleissheim Gallery) are very well done.

**— (Jan van).**—Dutch landscape painter, 1641/42-1680, Amsterdam. He was a close follower of Jacob v. Ruisdael.

**KETEL (Cornelis).**—Dutch painter and architect, 1548-1616. In 1566, he went to work at the Château of Fontainebleau. Then he went to England, where he painted portraits of Elizabeth's court. He returned to Holland, and settled in Amsterdam, where he painted portraits and Corporation pictures.

In his last years, Ketel often painted without a paint brush, with his fingers, and even with his feet.

**KEY (William).**—Flemish painter, 1520-1568. Formerly celebrated as painter of portraits. His work has been properly identified only very recently.

Bibliography: Friedländer, M. J., *Altniederländische Kunst,* Vol. 13.

**KEYSER (Nicaise de).**—Belgian painter, 1813-1887, of the Romantic school. His *Battle of Woeringen* (Brussels, 1839), one of his best works, shows that he was wanting in power.

**— (Thomas de).**—Dutch painter, 1596-1667, author of an *Anatomy Lesson* (Amsterdam), the *Assembly of the Bourgomasters of Amsterdam on the Arrival of Marie de Medici* (The Hague), etc. Keyser was the leading portrait painter in Amsterdam before the arrival of Rembrandt v. Rijn.

Bibliography: Oldenburg, R., *Thomas de Keyser.* Leipzig, 1911.

**KHORSABAD.**—See Assyria and Sumerian Art; also Pl. 18, Vol. I.

**KIEV.**—See Byzantine Art—Russia.

**KIKUMARO (after 1796 called Kitagawa Tsukimaro).**—Japanese colour-printer (died in 1829) pupil of Utamaro.

**KILIAN.**—Augsburg family, which produced many copper engravers. The following (in chronological order) are of interest:

**— Lucas** (1579-1637), pupil of D. Custos. He engraved, in Venice, reproductions of pictures by the Italian masters.

**— Wolfgang** (1581-1662), brother of Lucas, whom he accompanied in Italy. He also worked after the Italian masters.

**— Philipp** (1628-1693), son of Wolfgang. He painted some good portraits.

**— Bartholomœus** (1630-1696), brother of Philipp, the best-known of this family of artists. Among his very numerous engravings may be mentioned the portrait of the Emperor Joseph I on horseback.

**— Philipp Andreas** (1714-1759), grand-nephew of Bartholomœus.

Bibliography: Lützow, *Geschichte des deutschen Kupperstiches.* Berlin, 1891.

**KINKAKUJI (The Kinkakuji, or Golden Pavilion).**—Built in Kyoto (Japan), by the Emperor Yoshimitsu, in 1397. It is perfectly preserved, and is considered by the Japanese as typical of the national architecture.

**KIRKSTALL ABBEY.**—One of the four English abbeys of the Cistercian order, built between 1152 and 1182 in the austere Cistercian style.

**KISS (A.).**—German animal sculptor, 1802-1865. His best work is the admirable *Amazon,* placed in front of the Berlin Museum.

**KIYOHIDE.**—Japanese painter and printer. Pupil of Kiyonaga.

**KIYOHIRO (Torii).**—Japanese painter and printer. Began to produce about 1738, died in 1776. He was influenced by Kiyomitsu, and then by Toyonobu.

**KIYOMASA.**—Japanese painter and printer. Son and pupil of Kiyonaga.

**KIYOMASU (Torii).**—Japanese painter and printer, about 1702 to 1763. Probably brother of Kiyonobu, whose pupil he was. He was strongly influenced at the beginning of his career by Masanobu, in his prints of women; then by Kiyonobu, especially in his prints of actors. He also illustrated books.

**KIYOMINE.**—Japanese painter and printer; pupil of Kiyonaga, he directed the school of Torii after him, and died about 1840.

**KIYOMITSU (Torii).**—Japanese painter and printer, about 1735-1785. Son and pupil of Torii Kiyomasu, he began to produce about 1750, in two colours, a process which he helped to perfect, and which he seems to have preferred, although he must certainly have been acquainted with polychrome printing.

**KIYONAGA (Torii).**—Japanese painter and printer (1752-1815), brilliant innovator of the artistically guided realism of Ukiyo-e. From his real name, Seki, it is believed that he was the son of a tobacco merchant. Like most artists, Kiyonaga went through a tentative period when he was inspired by first one and then another of his predecessors whom he seems to have understood fully. Thus he painted pictures which might be mistaken for the work of Moronobu, and made a number of prints, inspired by Harunobu.

He also made some portraits of actors in the style of Shunsho; but it was Masanobu whose influence he felt most strongly. Among Kiyonaga's first really personal works is a triptych showing the interior of a tea-house, painted in a harmony of rosy yellows and greenish greys, beautifully set off by the blacks in the men's costumes.

KIYONAGA: PROMENADE AT NIGHT.

Kiyonaga's work shows extreme simplicity of means, and profound observation of anatomical proportions, of unusual gestures, and of attitudes which, for all their naturalness, have the grace and nobility of bearing of former days. He gives a delightful balance to his figures by means of linear rhythm and contrast. The following works will serve to illustrate this: *Fête in a Temple; Crouching Woman Suckling her Child; Woman Standing under some Red Lanterns; Two Geishas Accompanied by a Servant, Struggling against a Wind;* and some of his admirable triptychs, such as the *Terrace by the Sea-shore*; the *Farewell*; the *Nocturnal Walk*; *Boating Party on the Sumida; Women Bathing,* etc.

KIYONAGA: STREET SCENE (color print). (Louvre.)

Kiyonaga is an admirable colourist. Skilfully he contrasts his whites and grey-greens with browns, pinks and brick reds and discreetly he uses deep, soft blacks on parts of garments. It is no wonder he had such a strong influence on Utamaro, who was chiefly inspired by Kiyonaga's last period, when the master considerably elongated his types. With Kiyonaga, this elongation always remained graceful, stately, and faithful to life. The heads of his figures were still moderately oval, and the bodies in proportion. He set the standard for a new feminine type.

When Kiyonaga used landscape backgrounds he painted them in a new spirit, which only Masanobu had suggested. No more strange rocks and little trees; but the high piles of a bridge, and the river with all its come-and-go.

Although Kiyonaga had a profound influence on the following generation, he does not seem to have had many imitators.

See Pl. 40, Vol. I.

**KIYONOBU (Torii).**—Japanese painter and early print master, 1664-1729. He began as a painter of theatrical posters, then adapted his bold style to pictures of actors and courtesans, many of which were colored by hand in red, yellow, and blue (*tan-e*). He was the first to devote himself to depicting actors and the Japanese theatre, and thus it was he who founded the remarkable school of the Torii which devoted itself almost exclusively to that kind of painting.

KIYONOBU: BIJIN IN A DRESS DECORATED WITH CHARACTERS AND FLOWERS OF PAULOWNIA.

Kiyonobu's actors are full of life and energy in their expressive mimicry.

**KLEE (Paul).**—Contemporary Swiss painter who is often considered a member of the modern German school of which he is a product. He was born in a little town near Berne, Switzerland, 18th December 1879, the son of a musical family. He took violin lessons as a small boy, but at the age of ten began to copy pictures and to create his own ideas in pictorial compositions after nature. He studied with Knirr in Munich and in 1898 entered the Munich Academy, working under Stuck, where he learned to perfect his designs. About 1901 together with the sculptor B. Haller he went to Italy. There he visited Rome, Naples and Florence and was much impressed by the examples of Byzantine art that he saw. Four years later he made a short trip to Paris and the next year, 1906, moved to Munich, where he lived until 1920. At that time he became a professor in the Bauhaus in Weimar and moved with that school in 1926 to Dessau. In 1930 he was named professor in the Academy of Düsseldorf, which position he still retains. His early style was satirical, but later he came under the influence of Cézanne and Picasso. The colour became brighter and the subjects more fantastic and to a certain extent abstract. His most important work has been done on the order of Surrealism with a strange world of fantasy as his setting, inhabited by peculiar creatures of his own imagination. They are expressions of his subconscious mind, evolved without any regard for naturalism and linked together in an incoherent manner. About 1912 Klee was connected with Kandinsky and Marc in the foundation of the movement known as the *Blaue Reiter*, and in 1926 along with Jawlensky he helped found the *Blaue Vier.* Beside his painting Klee has made a number of prints and in 1912 did the illustrations for Voltaire's *Candide.* His pictures may be seen in the Gallery of Living Art in New York City, and in the museums of Berlin, Detroit, the Hague, the Barnes Foundation in Merion, Pennsylvania, and the Phillips Memorial Gallery in Washington, D. C.

BIBLIOGRAPHY: René Crevel, *Paul Klee,* 1930.—W. Grohmann, *Paul Klee,* 1929.—W. Grohmann, *Paul Klee Handzeichnungen, 1921-1930,* 1934.—H. von Wedderkop, *Paul Klee,* 1920.—L. Zahn, *Paul Klee,* 1920.

**KLENZE (L. von).**—1784-1864, German architect and leader in the Greek phase of Neo-Classicism in the early 19th century. In that mode he designed the *Glyptotek, Altapinakotek, Neue Königsbau,* and *Propylaia,* Munich; the *Walhalla,* Regensburg; and the *Hermitage,* Leningrad.

**KLINGER (Max).**—Of Leipzig. German painter, engraver and sculptor, born in 1857, died in 1920. He is considered in Germany to be one of the most gifted and individual German artists of the second half of the 19th century. In 1891, his book, *Malerei und Zeichnung* (Painting and Drawing), was published. It had at least as great an influence as the *Problem of Form* by the sculptor Hildebrand. Klinger was chiefly a painter of mythology and allegory, a seeker after new symbols, which he felt impelled to express by the most modern methods. As a result of this preoccupation, Klinger's works lack unity, and are often uneven and restless. His paintings include the *Judgment of Paris, Pietà* (Dresden), *Crucifixion, Christ on Olympus,* Leipzig. Perhaps even more as an engraver, he gave way to his creative genius—*Eve and the Future; Cupid and Psyche; Intermezzi; Four Landscapes; A Life,* etc. Several of his compositions were inspired by the Fantasies of Brahms.

Klinger next took up sculpture. His *Salome*, a restless figure; his *Cassandra*; his *Bathing Woman*; and, above all, his most important work, the *Beethoven*, in marble, ivory, gold, bronze and platinum (Leipzig Museum), exemplify very well the sumptuous and expressive style of this original genius.

**KLOSTERNEUBURG (Austria).**—The chief fame of this Danubian town near Vienna rests upon an ancient monastery, founded here in 1108 by Leopold, margrave of Austria. The altarpiece in the chapel is by Nicholas de Verdun.

**KNELLER (Sir Godfrey).**—Anglo-German painter (1646-1723). A native of Lübeck, he studied in Amsterdam under Ferdinand Bol and possibly Rembrandt, and came to England in 1674. He soon won considerable fame as a portrait painter, being successively patronized by Charles II, James II, William and Mary, Queen Anne and George I; in 1715 he was made a Baronet. He may be studied particularly well at Hampton Court (The Court of William and Mary), at Greenwich Hospital and in the National Portrait Gallery.

BIBLIOGRAPHY: C. H. Collins Baker, *Lely and the Stuart Portrait Painters.* London, 1912.

**KNIGHT (Laura Johnson).**—Contemporary English painter. Laura Johnson was born in Long Eaton, England and brought up in Nottingham where her mother painted and gave lessons in art. For a time she was in school in Saint Quentin, France but soon returned to England and entered the Nottingham Art School. She drew and painted from early childhood making her sketches in broad strongly conceived lines which caused her work to be characterised as masculine. As a young woman she spent a holiday at Staithes on the Yorkshire coast where she was impressed by the colour and life of that fishing village. In 1903 she was married to Harold Knight, an artist who is famous in his own right as a portrait painter. They travelled to Holland and worked for some time at Laren near Amsterdam. Later they lived in England and painted the bleak landscape to be found around Newlyn in Cornwall. Mrs. Knight then turned her attention to the travelling troupes of dancers including the members of Diaghileff's company, Pavlova, Nijinsky and many others. She and her husband made other trips to the Tyrol, Czechoslovakia and the United States. In 1927 she was elected an associate member of the Royal Academy and in 1929 received from the King the honorary title of Dame Commander of the Civil Division of the British Empire. Since that time the majority of her pictures have dealt with the life of the circus as seen both from the viewpoint of the audience and from behind the scenes. For a season she travelled with a circus round England sketching various phases of the life of the performers, the members of the menagerie and any subject which she fancied. In this latest period of her development she has broken away from the low tonality of her earlier pictures and has made interesting experiments in the use of brilliant sunlight and the contrasting artificial lighting of the theatre or a circus tent. Aside from her work in oil she has done some etchings and aquatints learning the technique from books. She won a prize at the exhibition of the Carnegie Institute in Pittsburgh in 1912, and a gold medal at the Panama-Pacific Exposition in San Francisco in 1915. Examples of her work are to be found in London, Nottingham, Ottawa and various places throughout the British Empire.

Bibliography: Ernest G. Halton, *The Work of Laura and Harold Knight,* 1921.—Laura Knight, *Oil Paint and Grease Paint, an Autobiography,* 1936.—*Laura Knight, a Book of Drawings,* with a Foreword by Charles Marriott, 1923.—*Twenty-one Drawings of the Russian Ballet by Laura Knight,* 1920.

**KNOBELSDORFF (G. von).**—1699-1753, German rococo architect who designed the *Neues Schloss,* Charlottenburg; *Sans Souci,* Potsdam; and the *Royal Opera House,* Berlin.

**KNOSSOS or CNOSSUS.**—See Crete.

**KNOTT (Ralph).**—British architect and designer of the London County Council Building, 1922.

**KODJA-KALESSI (Anatolia).**—The site of a ruined early Christian church in stone masonry. It is clear from the remains that the church was vaulted and possibly domed. The church dates from the 5th century.

**KOETSU (Honnami).**—Japanese painter, lacquerer, connoisseur of swords, Tea master, and calligrapher, 1556-1637. He was the most celebrated of the lacquer artists. He, together with Sotatsu, dominated the decorative school which sprang up during the Momoyama period of great splendor, and from which emerged one of the masters of Japanese art—Korin.

**KOLBE (Georg).**—Contemporary German sculptor. He was born 15th April 1877 in Waldheim, Saxony. He studied painting and drawing in the Dresden Academy and later worked in Munich and Paris. From 1898 to 1900 he was in Rome, studying with Louis Tuaillon, and it was at this time that he decided to give up his painting and devote his entire time to sculpture. He was strongly influenced by the art of the classic civilisations and upon his return to Paris worked for a while under the guidance of Auguste Rodin. His single figures and groups are characterised by a feeling for the important moment in an action cleverly handled, or the quiet repose of a calm interlude. He is the author of some charming portrait heads which are extremely plastic and show the careful delineation of the features which impart the personality of his models. In his figures, which are usually individual in feeling and movement even when combined with others in a group, there is an expression of balance and monumentality enriched by overtones of sentiment. His early work showed the influence of Rodin, and some features were borrowed from archaic Greek sculpture, as well as certain traits which had their origin in the Romanesque carvings of the Rhine valley, but since the war the figures are cloaked in restraint mingled with touches of sadness. Among his best-known pieces are the *Dancer* in the National Gallery in Berlin and the group for the Heine Memorial. Other examples of his work, which is essentially German in spite of the classic elements, may be found in the museums of Chicago, Denver, Detroit, Hamburg, Munich, Rome and Vienna.

Bibliography: Ernst Benkard, *Das Ewige Antlitz, eine Sammlung von Totenmasken mit einem geleitwort von Georg Kolbe,* 1927.—Ludwig Justi, *Georg Kolbe,* 1931.—Richard Scheibe, *Georg Kolbe,* 1931.—W. R. Valentiner, *Georg Kolbe, Plastik und zeichnun,* 1922.

**KOLLWITZ (Käthe Schmidt).**—Contemporary German painter, graver and sculptor. Käthe Schmidt was born 8th July 1867 in Königsberg. Her father, a student of law, was a mason by profession; her mother, an artistic person, was the daughter of a socialistic minister, Dr. Julius Rupp. While she was still a very young girl her brother, Conrad, later the editor of the *Vorwaerts,* aroused in her a great appreciation for the works of Goethe, Ibsen, Zola and the Russian novelists. It was a volume of Hogarth's satirical drawings that served as the incentive for her artistic career. Her first teachers were the engraver Maler G. Naujok and Rudolf Mauer; at eighteen she was sent to Berlin to study painting, and she showed an especially keen sense for line as well as for light and shadow. Returning to Königsberg she studied classical art under Emil Neide, which was followed by a year of hard work in Munich. After her schooling was completed she began to develop her own style, mastering all the techniques of etching and being guided by the engravings of Goya, Rembrandt and Klinger as well as by the aphorisms of Ruskin. In 1891 she married Dr. Karl Kollwitz, a physician, and they moved to Berlin, where they settled in the poor workers' quarters. A mother, wife and assistant to her husband, she did not neglect her art. In 1898 she exhibited at the Berlin Academy and was nominated for an award which she did not receive. However, she caught the public's attention with her illustrations to Hauptmann's *Weber,* in which she grasped the drama and tragedy with more intensity than the poet. This *Weberaufstand* also marked the beginning of the mother and child and death motives, the dominating themes of her work. In 1899 Kollwitz exhibited in Dresden and received a medal. Her next series of illustrations were for Zola's *Germinal.* Through heritage as well as through the inevitable influence of her environment—living in constant contact with misery—Kollwitz became an ardent socialist, dedicating her art and life to the working masses. Degenerate and miserable creatures served as her models, her keen eye discovering their suffering and their soul. She comprehended their despair and worry as well as their fears of pregnancy and starvation, and shows her great compassion for her fellow beings. Her fantasies on the Grim Reaper and despondent mothers were intensified by the loss of one of her sons in the World War. Her style is creative and truly stirring. Like Rembrandt she too began by etching self-portraits and studies of hands, the interest being limited to spotlight effects and chiaroscuro. In all her etchings she recreated the expressive movement of figures and masses in a rather soulful and sympathetic way. From etching she turned to lithography, which proved a more plastic medium of expression. Besides war scenes and mother and child topics she has done Pietàs, inn-scenes, peasants at work, etc. She is a skillful sculptor and wood carver. Her works may be seen in the museums of Berlin, Hamburg, Dresden and Chemnitz.

Bibliography: E. Bechts, *Käthe Kollwitz, en de techniek in Haarlemsche Kunstboekjes,* 1916.—Ludwig Kaemmerer, *Käthe Kollwitz,* 1923.—Alfred Kuhn, *Käthe Kollwitz,* 1921.—H. W. Singer, *Käthe Kollwitz,* 1908.

**KONINCK (Philip de).**—Dutch painter, 1619-1688. Pupil of Rembrandt. A landscape painter of much power.

Bibliography: Gerson, H., *P. Koninck.* Berlin, 1936.

**KOREA—ART.**—Korea, although so close to China of which it is geographically a peninsular appendage, is racially different from China as it is from Japan; its people, a mixed group, probably stem from the northern Manchurians or Tungus peoples, with, perhaps, some Malayan infiltration. As a cultural group in the Far East it emerges into a historic period at a relatively late date. While the great Chou dynasty (B.C. 1122-B.C. 250) flourished in China, Korea was beginning to experiment with metal which, however, was not used extensively. According to both Chinese and Korean records the kingdom of Chosen (the "Land of Morning Cool"; or Korai, the "Land of Beautiful Mountains") was founded in B.C. 2317 by Tankun (Dan Koon) whose dynasty is reputed to have lasted over a thousand years. Chinese and Korean records also relate how, in B.C. 1122 Ki-tze (considered, according to tradition, to be the author of the Chinese classic, the *Shu-King*) led thousands of Chinese into the territory around Heijo in northern Korea; established a kingdom called *Ch'ao-Hsien* which ruled until the 4th century B.C.; and introduced Chinese civilization into Korea. Thus, probably as early as the Chou period, there was a slow Chinese penetration of Korea. During the Han period (B.C. 221-206 A.D.) trade relations were extensively carried on between the two countries. However, the historic age in Korea has a reliable beginning only with the establishment of the Silla kingdom, said to be in the year B.C. 57.

*Pre-History.*—Dolmens, found in Japan but not in China, are numerous in Korea, but always unadorned. As in Japan there is no trace of the great painted pottery that was produced in Neolithic China. There is some pottery which, however, is never painted, only combed or decorated with an impressed, striated line. Thousands of *magatama* have been found in the graves of Korea and Japan, but never in those of China. These are bean shaped beans made of stone. jade, semi-precious materials, and later of glass paste. The main weapons were the chisel and the socketted celt. Unique are daggers —probably ceremonial weapons—made of stone but simulating bronze. These have even been found in Silla.

*Lo-lang* (1st century A.D.—313).—During the Han period in China several Chinese perfectures were established in Korea, most important of which, politically and culturally, was Lo-lang (Rakuro). Functioning as a Chinese colony in Korea it brought with it the great civilization of Han, the path having probably been prepared for it by the Chou settlers. Recent excavations at the tombs of Lo-lang in northern Korea have revealed Han artifacts of unexpected magnificence. The tombs of Seliganri and Wang Hsu have yielded various types of lacquered vessels similar to those found west of China, in Noin-Ula, Mongolia. Red, black and green in color there are: large open trays; cups with ears; square trays frequently with quatrefoil bronze inlay, sometimes with glass paste inlay; deep bowls with ears, usually red in the interior; trays or boxes containing mirrors, occasionally consisting of a whole set of lacquer boxes similar to a make-up kit. Inscriptions corresponding to the dates B.C. 85 to 69 A.D. have been found. The lacquer is applied with a brush and consequently is a form of painting. The motifs, mainly abstract, are drawn with a remarkable freedom and energy of line, undulating rhythm, and asymmetric balance. Ornament is made to move lightly over the surface of the vessels but always in architectonic relation to their frames. One round tray bearing an inscription dating it 69 A.D. and indicating Ssuchuan, an industrial center in China at that time, as the place of production, is decorated with a painting of the Queen Mother of the West, her attendant, and the animal symbols of the Four Quarters of the Earth. The same fleeting rhythm of the abstract decoration characterizes these representations.

That the art of painting was in an advanced stage of development is evidenced by a tortoise shell box painted in black with celestial sprites, and, especially, by a painted lacquer basket of Naneiri, Lo-lang (2nd century A.D.). On it are painted a series of seated and standing figures in foreshortened positions drawn in fluid calligraphic lines. Decorative borders agree stylistically with the other painted lacquers of Lo-lang. The thoroughly advanced character of this painting has altered the art historian's conception of the nature of Han painting. There is neither Han painting nor engraving left in China that so perfectly expresses the basic laws of all Chinese painting.

Bronze vessels of Lo-lang are engraved, not cast as in China. In comparison to the Chinese vessels they are heavy in outline and organic in shape. They are utensils, not ceremonial objects or symbols of religious piety or secular power (see China—Art, Chou Bronzes). Consequently many are simple and unpretentious (jar, amalgam of copper and gold, Gov't Mus., Seoul). There are bronze ornaments and shallow bowls with ears in répoussé work. There are Han mirrors and coins, and for the first time in the Far East there is the long sword (made of cast iron). Especially important and particularly beautiful is a gold filigree buckle decorated with one large dragon and seven small dragons and inlaid with turquoise. In technique and shape it is curiously similar to the buckles and gold work made by the Scythians in the 6th century B.C. and later by the Sarmatians, around the Black Sea. It is, perhaps, of Scythian origin.

Pottery vessels include: incense burners or hill jars of the Han type with representations of Yi the killer and tamer of animals (according to

Hentze's interpretation of the hunting scene); funeral statuettes of columnar mass; models of houses, etc., in the green-glazed ware of Han. Little jade was found and whatever there is, was used for dressing the dead. Small pendants of amber and objects of jet and realgar, all in the shape of animals, are also unmistakably Han in character. The presence of glass in lacquer, in *magatamas*, and in beads of cobalt blue proves (contrary to Laufer's theory that glass was only introduced into China in the 5th century A.D. through contact with the peoples of the Steppes) that it was known in Han times. Blown glass vessels with the conic foot and general shape of Syrian glass must have been imported from Syria.

*The Three Kingdoms: Silla* (B.C. 57?-935 A.D.), *Kudara* (B.C. 37-663 A.D.), *Kokurai* (B.C. 17-668 A.D.).—In the southeast, with Keishu as its capital, one of the Three Kingdoms, Silla, reputedly founded in 57 B.C., flourished from the 3rd century on. Certain characteristics of the artifacts (3rd-7th centuries) indicate a culture built on an intermixture of Chinese with Steppe elements.

During the 4th century Korea became an important cultural center. Having adopted from China its script, its literature, its political and social philosophy, in 372 Buddhism was adopted from China by the Kokurai kingdom from whence it spread all over the country. It was through Korea that Japan became acquainted with Chinese art which was to revolutionize her indigenous culture.

Silla is particularly important for its ceramics, its gold crown, and its temple of Buddhist sculpture. Pottery vessels are impressed, incised, never painted, and only occasionally glazed. A bowl with two handles and a large conic base, as well as pendants of pointed oval shape, reflect the art of the Siberian Steppes. Funeral statuettes, unpainted and unglazed, appear to be provincial Han invested with an individual dramatic force. There are "praying mourners," simple and expressive in their general shape, and two men on horse modeled in the form of pouring vessels. The latter are covered with ornamentation. The men seem to be of the Tungus tribe. They wear pointed caps.

Among the objects of gold from Silla a rare gold crown in filigree work appears to be a Shamanistic funeral object. It is composed of stylized antlers and trees and profusely decorated with pendants of pointed oval shape. The crown should be compared with the Sarmatian Treasure of Novocherkask.

In the southeastern country of Silla there is a Buddhist cave temple, called *Sokkulam* (Temple of the Rock Cave), which contains some of the finest sculpture in the Far East. It was founded in 752 and the slender proportions and melodic sequence of line that characterizes the Bodhisattva representations shows a fifty year lag between these and the more ponderous and muscular art of T'ang China. More of the T'ang spirit is present in the Lohans (ten), and the Four Kings of Heaven which stand in the corridor leading to the chamber of Sakyamuni. The colossal statue of the Buddha is comparatively poor in its expressionless austerity.

During the Suiko period in Japan (580-650) the Three Kingdoms in Korea transmitted their Chinese culture to the Island. According to historical documents the first Buddhist image was sent to Japan by the King of Kudara in 552 or 538. Thus the archaic art (Buddhist-Romanesque) of Wei was transformed by Japanese as well as by Korean artists who left their imprint on the famous Tori group of Japanese sculptors. It is impossible to determine whether many of the early bronze and wood sculptures preserved in Japan were made in Korea or in Japan by Korean artists or by Japanese artists. In 607 the great temple of Horyuji was built and many Korean artists and priests emigrated to Japan. The renowned *Kudara Kwannon* (Horyuji) is traditionally of Korean importation and the painting of Shotoku Taishi (Imperial Household, Tokyo) is considered the work of the Korean Prince, Asa, although scholars now prefer to regard it as a copy of the original (see Japan—Art).

In Silla country there are also funeral statuettes (human figures with animal heads) corresponding to the Six Dynasties in China, Ganddharva (guardians with animal heads), stelae resting on the tortoise and surmounted with interlaced dragons, and stone reliefs of the 8th and 9th centuries. There was a rich production of Kokurai roof tiles whose motifs and vegetative exuberance show a strong Indian influence.

Korea has its important early monuments of painting as well as of sculpture—the royal tombs of Kokurai. Among the most impressive are: The Great Tomb (559) whose truncated vaulting is the same that is found at Tun Huang (See China—Art); the Tomb of the Two Pillars (6th century) in which are represented a king and queen sitting on a platform, their shoes placed before them, a flame halo behind their heads to denote their importance, and a procession of figures in short jackets and pleated skirts, probably the Korean court dress; the Great or Royal Tomb (c. 565) which has the symbols of the Four Quarters painted (as is the decorative elements of flower, plant, and cloud motifs) with the lively, rhythmic movement, calligraphic energy, and brilliant color that typify the Wei painting of Tun Huang.

*Korai or Wang Dynasty* (918-1392).—From the beginning of the 8th to the beginning of the 10th century Silla, which spread its boundaries, was the only stable rule in Korea. The northern province of Korai, lead by Wang the Founder, rebelled and united all of Korea and part of southern Manchuria under its rule. Kaijo was its capital. There is some small stone sculpture, many mirrors of which there are two types, the courtly and the primitive. While the latter are poor in technique and comparatively scarce, the former are of refined workmanship based on T'ang models, and abundant; they have a silvery patina and are decorated with flowers, plant tendrils, animals and birds, especially the phoenix. But Korai is most famous for its pottery, particularly for its celadon glaze (never the light "pea green" of Chinese celadons, but more grey or brown in tone) and its inlay of white and black pottery which was imitated in Japan but never equalled for its beauty of ordered design and its perfection of technique.

*I Dynasty* (1392-1910).—After the ravages of Jenghiz and Kublai Khan in the 13th century, Ni Taijo (Li Tan) founded the I Dynasty with Keijo as its capital. Korea in reality paid allegiance to the Mings of China and renounced Buddhism for Confucianism. The former high culture of Korea is lost. Korai pottery is still manufactured but pottery inlay is abandoned. Sculpture is crude. Painting, although at times gracious and charming, is greatly dependent upon China. Lacquered objects are simple, frequently inlaid with large tesserae of mother-of-pearl; textiles are woven in bright hues; and furniture is embellished with metal ornaments.

Bibliography: *Chosen Koseki Zufu* (Cat. of Korean hist. remains). Keijo, 1915.—Eckardt, *A History of Korean Art*. London, 1929.—Y. Harada, *Lo-lang*. Tokyo, 1930.—Koizumi and Hamada, *The Tomb of the Painted Basket of Lo-lang*. Keijo, 1934.—A. Salmony, *Statuettes Funeraires de Corée,* Cahiers d'Art, 1935, p. 375.—Lorraine Warner, *Korai Celadon in America,* Eastern Art, Vol. II, 1930.

**KORIN (Ogata).**—Japanese painter, lacquerer, and Tea master. Born at Kyoto, in 1658; died in 1716. He studied under the Kano masters but turned to the decorative and sumptuous art of Sotatsu

Korin (1660-1716): Stags and Doe (Hoitsu Edition, 1802).

and Koetsu. Like the latter he emphasized pattern, giving to his designs less of the vigor of Sotatsu's paintings and more of grace and loveliness. His brush stroke had great variety in width. He is "the most Japanese of the Japanese." He is a very interesting colourist. He painted all kinds of subjects, but he seems to have excelled in the study of flowers, used in decorative compositions. As for Korin's lacquers, they seem to have been "cut in a block of gold." They are often enhanced with mother-of-pearl, silver, or bronze. One of Korin's most celebrated works is the large screen, in the Boston Museum, on which the artist represented a tempest.

Korin (Ogata): Lacquered screen with a design of waves. (Museum, Boston.)

**KORIUSAI (Isoda).**—Japanese painter and printer, worked c. 1760-1780. He entered Shigenaga's studio, in Yedo, where he was probably the fellow pupil of Harunobu, and perhaps subsequently his pupil. In any case, the latter completely dominated the beginning of his career, and there is a whole series of works by Koriusai which, without the sig-

Koriusai: Heron and crow on a branch blossoming in the snow.

nature, might at once be attributed to Harunobu. Among them: *A Couple in the Snow under a Big Umbrella; Two Children Playing with a Wooden Horse; Two Young Girls Washing Their Hands,* etc.

A series of realistic animals is the strongest expression of Koriusai's art. Indeed, it is difficult to recognise the same hand in the two vigorous *Cock Fights*; the *Heron and Crow,* perched on the branch of a flowering tree, covered with snow; the *White Falcon*; and the magnificent kakemono, also representing a "Sacred Falcon" on a rock, near which are growing chrysanthemums and a banana tree.

Next we come to his many series of courtesans; about 1770-1780, his long *Hashira-ye* (pillar print), a delightful art, well proportioned, able in composition, and in which the figures have extraordinary slimness and grace. Very different are his albums, in which the figures are short and rather thick-set.

The whole of this series of courtesans had a very great influence, not only on the master Kiyonaga, but also, in the type of faces, on Utamaro.

**KORVEY (Germany).**—*Abbey Church,* 9th-12th century, a Saxon Carolingian and Romanesque church with the typical feature of the gallery connecting the two western towers, the gallery being higher than the nave roof. In the center of the façade is a slightly projecting porch. There is a western choir tribune above the entrance.

**KRAFFT (Adam).**—German sculptor, about 1455/60-1509. Swabian school. He worked in Nuremberg, where all his carvings may be seen. His style is robust and picturesque, and borders on pathetic and popular realism.

The oldest known work by Adam Krafft is the Tomb of the Schreyer family (1490-1492), in the Church of St. Sebald. It is decorated with four bas-reliefs representing the Bearing of the Cross, the Crucifixion, the Entombment, and the Resurrection, The cemetery of St. John possesses another very pathetic work by Krafft—the Entombment of the Holzschuher Chapel. He did not, however, only carve tragic scenes.

KRAFFT (ADAM): DETAIL FROM THE EPITAPH OF THE PERGENSTÖRFFER FAMILY. (Frauenkirche, Nuremberg.)

There is plenty of popular good fellowship in the bas-relief which, in 1497, he executed for the gate of the Stadtwage as well as in the rustic group of the two spies, Joshua and Caleb, carrying a colossal bunch of grapes, 1495-97. In his work, generally, naturalism abounds. The scenes are set in stony landscape, with rocks, mountains and trees. The scene of the Bearing of the Cross is especially moving.

From 1493 to 1496, Krafft executed, for the Church of St. Lawrence, the famous Tabernacle of the Holy Sacrament, at the base of which he represented himself and his two assistants, kneeling in the manner of caryatides. He is an original type, with his massive, square head framed by a beard, which gives him the appearance of an old sailor. A series of figures and bas-reliefs, recalling different incidents of the Passion are distributed over the monument, which rises in pyramidal form, like a Gothic pinnacle, to the vaulting of the church. This tabernacle won Adam Krafft considerable fame.

One of the most moving works which he made afterwards (about 1505) is the *Way of the Cross* of the cemetery of St. Jean. The rather rough and strong style which is characteristic of such pieces became softer and more refined when he essayed to represent the Virgin. His work includes some charming Madonnas, such as the *Madonna of the Bindergasse*, and those which appear on the epitaphs of the Pergenstörffer and Rebeck families (between 1498 and 1501, in the Frauenkirche of Nuremberg), and in the Church of St. Giles, on the bas-relief executed in 1503, for the tomb of Landauer (which is in the Church of St. Egide).

To Adam Krafft or his school is attributed a series of tabernacles derived from the one in the Church of St. Lawrence. These are in: Kalckreuth, Heilsbronn, Fürth, Schwabach, Katzwang, and Krailsheim.

See Pl. 25, Vol. II.

BIBLIOGRAPHY: B. Daun, *Adam Krafft und die Künstler seiner Zeit.* Berlin, 1897.—D. Stern, *Der Nürnberger Bildhauer A. Krafft.* Strassburg 1916.

— **(J. P.)**—Austrian painter 1780-1856. Famous for his portraits of the Viennese aristocracy; and author of popular scenes.

**KRATER.**—See Crater.

**KREMLIN.**—See Moscow.

**KRITIOS.**—See Antenor.

**KROLL (Leon).**—Contemporary American painter. He was born 6th December 1884 in New York City. He was taught the rudiments of drawing by John H. Twachtman and later studied at the Art Students' League and the National Academy of Design. From 1919 to to Paris to study with Jean Paul Laurens and upon his return to the United States became an instructor in the art school of the National Academy of Design. From 1919 to 1923 he was a visiting critic for the Maryland Institute of Arts. He also served in the same capacity for the Art Institute of Chicago in 1924 and 1925, and in 1929 and 1930 at the Pennsylvania Academy of Fine Arts. He has been the recipient of numerous awards, including a bronze medal at the Panama-Pacific Exposition at San Francisco in 1915, the Potter Palmer Gold Medal at the Art Institute of Chicago in 1924, the Beck Gold Medal at the Pennsylvania Academy of Fine Arts in 1930, and the first Altman prize at the National Academy of Design in 1932. Much of his work is done in New York City, although his summers are spent in Maine and Massachusetts. His subjects are varied, including landscapes, figure studies and some portraits. He has been successful in his paintings of women perhaps because of a great understanding of female intuition. The modelling is excellent and plastic and the figures stand apart from the setting whether in landscape or interiors, as may be seen in *Cape Ann* at the Metropolitan Museum of Art. Other examples of his work are in the Art Institute of Chicago, the Los Angeles Museum of History, Science and Art, and the California Palace of the Legion of Honor in San Francisco.

BIBLIOGRAPHY: For a complete bibliography see *The Index of Twentieth Century Artists* for January, 1934.

**KU K'AI-CHIH.**—Chinese painter c. 350-412. A painting which is possibly an original by Ku is in the British Museum. It consists of a series of didactic scenes under the title *Admonitions of the Instructress in the Palace.* An appended scene representing an archer shooting at a host of animals on a distant mountain may portray Yu, the legendary hero archer of China.

See China-Art.

**KULMBACH (Hans Suess von).**—German painter and graver, about 1480-1522. Probably a pupil of Jacopo de' Barbari and assumedly apprentice to Dürer. He was active in Nürnberg where he painted the altar-predella of *St. Nicholas* for the church of St. Lorenzo in 1505-07, this early style reflects the Gothic tradition. His first mature work is the wings for the altar at Krakau (1511), depicting scenes from the *Life of the Virgin;* although dominated by the spirit of Barbari and Dürer, the lively and harmonious colors are typically Kulmbach's. The most impressive work, the *Tucheraltar*, for the Sebaldus church dates from 1513. It is known that in 1511 Dürer submitted the first sketches for this. To Kulmbach's mature period also belong the *St. Katherine* altar (1514-15), and the *St. John* altar (1516) both ordered by the Boner family of Krakau. Other stories of the *Life of the Virgin* are in Bamberg, Leipzig, Munich. The most important work of his late period is the *Coronation of the Virgin with St. Sebastian and St. Roch* (Vienna), dated 1518. After this year the artist's powers rapidly declined. He was also court painter for Kaiser Maximilian. Many fine portraits and designs for stained glass, of religious and allegorical topics, are attributed to him.

BIBLIOGRAPHY: Glaser, C., *Die altdeutsche Malerei.* München, 1924. —Sokolowski, *H.S.v.K.* Krakau, 1883.—Thode, *Malerschule von Nürenberg,* 1891.—Zldanowski, *H.S. v.K., Leben u. Werke,* 1927.

**KUNISADA (Utagawa).**—Japanese painter and printer, 1786-1865. Pupil of Toyokuni, he worked with his master on some albums of actors as well as with Hiroshige in several series, in which he did the figures. Among others, he made two illustrations of the Gengi Monogatari, some landscapes, and some works on actors and the occupations of women. Unfortunately he introduced crude colours, which came to characterise the school of Osaka. In 1845 he adopted the name of his master, Toyokuni.

KUNISADA: HORSE LYING DOWN.

**KUNIYOSHI (Yasuo).**—Contemporary American painter. He was born in Okayama, Japan, 1st September 1893 and spent his early youth in that city. When he was thirteen he came to the United States and the next year entered the Los Angeles School of Art and Design. He was also a student at the Art Students' League where he worked under Kenneth Hayes Miller. Later he attended the art school of the National Academy of Design, the Independent School of Art and the Woodstock, New York, Summer School. He has made two trips to Europe, in 1925 and again in 1928, travelling in England, Spain, Italy and France. He became influenced by the plastic forms of Delacroix and the subjective conceptions of studies by Daumier, and sought to add these elements to his own art. That he was successful in this way may be learned from the fact that his work when shown in Japan in 1932 aroused comments that it had a Parisian character. Oriental designs and lingering traces of the refinement of the East are to be found in the work of this artist in combination with Occidental introspection and realism of appearance. His palette is composed of sombre colours, which lend an air of fascination to his pictures by reason of their individual character and intrinsic harmony. He received an honourable mention at Carnegie Institute, Pittsburgh, in 1931 and the Temple Gold Medal at the Pennsylvania Academy of Fine Arts in Philadelphia in 1934. Examples of his work are in the Columbus, Ohio, Gallery of Fine Arts, the Gallery of Living Art and the Whitney Museum of American Art in New York City.

BIBLIOGRAPHY: William Murrell, *Yasuo Kuniyoshi,* Younger Artists Series, 1922.—For further information on this artist see *The Index of Twentieth Century Artists* for April, 1934.

**KUO HSI.**—Chinese painter, c. 1020-1090, famous for majestic landscapes with "mountains like cumulous clouds." Author of a famous treatise on landscape painting.

See China-Art.

**KUYUNJIK.**—See Assyria and Sumerian Art.

**KWAIGETSUDO (The).**—Group of 18th century Japanese painters and print masters, closely related to the Torii school. Kwaigetsudo Anchi and Kwaigetsudo Dohan worked about 1704-1716 and are renowned for their prints (*tan-ye*) of monumental figures drawn with bold sweeping lines of calligraphic splendor. Hardly more than a dozen of their highly prized prints are extant, five of which are in the collection of Mr. Louis V. Ledoux, New York. A painting of a *Courtesan in Red and White Kimono* in the William Rockhill Nelson Gallery of Art, Kansas City, identical in style to the Kwaigetsudo prints, is signed Nihon Giga Kwaigetsudo (1710). Kwaigetsudo Ando appears to be the first of these artists.

**KYLIX.**—See Cylix.

**KYOSAI (Kawanabe).**—Japanese painter (1831-1889). He was a pupil of Kuniyoshi and at eleven worked in the studio of Tohaku. He had a keen sense of caricature and his work is lively. Until the middle of 1863 he signed his work "Chikamaro."

# THE NEW STANDARD
# ENCYCLOPEDIA
# OF ART

VOLUME TWO

# L

**LAACH (Germany).** — *Abbey Church,* 1095-1156. A smaller version of Mainz, Laach Abbey shows the persistence in German Romanesque architecture of Ottonian duplication of elements east and west. There are eastern and western towers, lanterns, and apses.

**LABROUSTE (F. M. T.).**—French architect of the nineteenth century (1799-1875), best known for his Bibliothèque Ste. Geneviève, Paris, in the Renaissance Revival style.

**LABYRINTH.**—A complex path of some kind, generally a complicated series of rooms and columns. The earliest labyrinth is in ancient Egypt, built in the year 2900 B.C. by Amenhemat III, in the middle of Lake Moeris. It has entirely disappeared. According to Herodotus, it was one of the finest proportioned Egyptian buildings. It was said to be composed of 3000 chambers, of which 150 were subterranean. There were hidden the religious treasures of Egypt and the tombs of the kings.

The early Christians used a subterranean labyrinth as a place for worship and safety.

Term also applied to a system of decoration consisting of colored stones forming intercrossed lines at right angles to one another (pavement at Chartres).

**LACHAISE (Gaston).**—Contemporary American sculptor (1882-1935). He was born in Paris, France, 19th March 1882. He studied under Bernard Palissy and later at the École des Beaux-Arts under Gabriel Jules Thomas. Even at that time he was not satisfied with the academic training and standards then prevalent in the art schools. He wanted to work from the living model in preference to the customary work from casts. He studied a while in the studio of Lalique and exhibited a few times in the annual Salon. About 1906 he came to the United States and for the next six years made his home in Boston. There he worked in the studio of Henry H. Kitson, improving his technique and general ability. Then in 1912 he came to New York City, where he entered the studio of Paul Manship to continue his studies. Soon he opened his own studio and began to work out his ideas of the modelling of the human figure. Like the sculptors of the Italian Renaissance he worked directly in the stone and created many variations of the female nude. All are characterised by ample proportions of the torso combined with slender legs and arms, the whole treated in large simple masses and closed contours not far from the work of certain students of abstract form. Aside from the many statues of Woman he has also done panels in low relief for building decorations, including a frieze for the American Telephone and Telegraph Building in New York City, a few portrait heads and some typical male figures. In every product of his the psychological aspect of the subject is subordinated to the charm of the rhythmical flow of the surfaces whether of stone or bronze. One of his latest creations is *La Montagne*, a half-reclining female figure executed in cement with admirable results, though of course lacking beauty of surface treatment. Lachaise, a naturalised American citizen, stands alone in the field of modern sculpture, owing his style to no one school of the past and confident of the appeal of his work. He died 19th October 1935 in New York City.

BIBLIOGRAPHY: A. E. Gallatin, *Gaston Lachaise*, 1924.

**LACQUER.**—Lacquer is a varnish which the Chinese and Japanese make with the gum of the "rhus vernificera," a tree cultivated in China for this purpose. This gum blackens on exposure to air. With it all kinds of objects, big and little, are covered, and these are often marvels of taste and delicacy. The process of lacquer work is very long, and very minute, and, therefore, very expensive. Nowadays it is almost impossible to find as perfect works as formerly. To obtain the lacquer, a certain number of chemical operations must be gone through, to give the desired consistency, and then the colour—black, red, gold, blue, green, etc.—obtained by means of various chemical products. Then the wood, cardboard, or metal that is to receive the lacquer must be polished, and covered with a special glaze to make it dry. Next the lacquer must be added in very thin layers (at least three, up to eighteen or even more), great care being taken that each layer dries before the next is added. Lacquer objects are generally decorated with drawings which demand great ability on the part of the artist, since no correction is possible. Lacquer articles are often inlaid with mother-of-pearl, ivory and fine stones; and the finest objects are often strewn with a quantity of little particles of gold, which give them incomparable richness.

The invention of the art of lacquer work is due to the Chinese, but it is impossible to tell how far back the process dates, or how it was developed. It is certainly very old. During Han times the Koreans and Chinese in Lo-lang and the people in Noin-Ula, Mongolia, imported Chinese lacquers of superb craftsmanship from the province of Ssuchuan.

See China—Art. Korea—Art.—Lo-lang; and Japan—Art.

**LADBROOKE (Robert).**—English landscape painter, 1769-1824. The same age as Old Crome, of whom he was an intimate friend; the two artists married two sisters. Ladbrooke was, with Old Crome, the founder of the Norwich School. He painted minutely and conscientiously, his technique recalling that of the Pre-Raphaelites. He shows a passionate love of nature. *The Great Oak* is his finest work.

**LAFARGE (John).**—American painter and decorator (1835-1910). He was born of French parentage in New York City 31st March 1835. His maternal grandfather, Binsse de St. Victor, was a miniature painter and gave the boy lessons as soon as he was old enough. In 1856 he went to Paris to stay with relatives and there came in contact with Théophile Gautier, Puvis de Chavannes, Dante Gabriel Rossetti, John E. Millais and many other prominent names of the younger generation. He was not particularly interested in painting as a vocation but on the advice of his father entered the studio of Couture. The master advised him to prepare himself for painting by observing and copying the drawings of the old masters in the museums of Europe. During the next two years he absorbed much of the draftsmanship of the old masters and was strongly impressed by the work of Rembrandt, Rubens, Velázquez and Titian. Then he returned to the United States and began again to study law, which he had taken up before. Some influence from William Morris Hunt urged him to give up the legal profession and he accompanied Hunt to Newport, Rhode Island, to do figure and landscape painting for the next few years. In the period immediately following the Civil War he became interested in problems of light relationships, rather foreshadowing the French impressionistic movement. He had always been interested in colour and now he became more aware of its potentialities. He was invited in 1876 by the architect, Henry Hobson Richardson, to do some mural decoration for Trinity Church, Boston. Under very difficult circumstances when the building was still unfinished and with inexperienced assistants he executed those murals which add to the charm of that structure and seem to fulfill the promise of the architectural setting. The following year he did some murals for St. Thomas'

Church in New York City, since destroyed by fire, but these were not so successful as the early ones.

A trip to England made in 1873 had shown him the stained glass used at that time, which he considered of inferior quality. He now turned all his attention to the problem of making better coloured glass which should benefit by the sunlight cast on it. After much experimentation he developed a kind of opalescent glass which lent itself to compositions admirably and even gave the effect of shadow on some pieces. Among his best-known windows made of this glass are the Watson Memorial Window, which won for him a first-class medal at the Paris Exposition of 1889 and the Legion of Honor decoration from the French government, the Peacock Window in the Worcester Art Museum and the windows in Trinity Church, Buffalo.

Because of ill health he took a trip to Japan, Samoa and the South Seas in 1886 and was much impressed by the art of Japan. His earlier work of magazine illustrations, flower pieces, landscape and figure pieces has been lost sight of in the number of mural commissions that he did in later years. Perhaps his most important one is the *Ascension* for the Church of the Ascension in New York City, an admirable and commendable composition but not very happy in its architectural setting.

He wrote and lectured on the fine arts and was very influential in forming the style of his young assistants. Though his early work was detailed and stiff the influence of William M. Hunt induced him to spend more time on generalised figures and simplified compositions, thereby adding to their grandeur and dignity. He died at the age of seventy-five in New York City 14th November 1910.

BIBLIOGRAPHY: Royal Cortissoz, *John LaFarge, a Memoir and a Study,* 1911.—Cecilia Waern, *John LaFarge, Artist and Writer,* 1896.

**LAGRENÉE (Louis Jean François).**—French painter, 1724-1805. Pupil of Carle Van Loo. He painted a quantity of historical and mythological pictures, in correct style, but they are very cold in colour.

**LA HIRE (Laurent de).**—French painter, 1606-1656. Pupil of the school of Primaticcio, he maintained the influence of Vouet. His work is varied, and uneven. The *Nicholas V before the Body of St. Francis* shows his personal gifts; whereas paintings such as the *Virgin and Child* and *Christ Appearing before the Holy Women* (both in the Louvre) are in the conventional style.

LA HIRE: POPE NICHOLAS V AND ST. FRANCIS. (Louvre.)

**LAIRESSE (Gerard de).**—Dutch painter, born 1641 in Liège, died 1711 in Amsterdam. He studied in his father's studio, painted portraits from the age of fifteen, and lived in poverty until he went to Amsterdam to decorate houses and palaces. His compositions are generally very large. He was also an engraver (*The Story of Dido*), and wrote books of art criticism (*The Principles of Drawing* and the *Art of Painting*).

Three brothers and two sons were also painters.

**LAKE DWELLINGS.**—See Neolithic (Period).

**LAMI (Eugène Louis).**—French painter, 1800-1890. Pupil of Horace Vernet and of Gros. He began by painting scenes of the Wars of the Republic and Empire. Pictures at Versailles show him as a painter of battle scenes.

LAMI: THE DANCING FOYER AT THE OLD OPERA HOUSE. (Maurice Lecomte Collection.)

Lami's best work is undoubtedly in scenes of four or five figures, such as the *Loge aux Italiens.*

He was also an accomplished water-colour painter.

BIBLIOGRAPHY: Paul André Lemoisne, *Eugène Lami.* Paris, 1912.

**LANCRET (Nicolas).**—French painter, 1690-1743. Pupil of Watteau, whose style he imitated so well that his works were taken for those of his master. But beside Watteau, his colour is cold and his drawing weak, and none of his pictures have the delightful feeling of the *Embarkation for Cytherea.* But he had a gift for observation and a facility of invention which enabled him to bring new life to such themes as the well-worn seasons.

LANCRET: WINTER. (Louvre.)

See Pl. 47, Vol. II.

BIBLIOGRAPHY: Ed. Pilon, *Watteau et son temps.* Brussels, 1912.—E. Dacier, *La Gravure de Genre et des Mœurs.* Paris, 1925.—G. Wildenstein, *Lancret.* Paris, 1924.

**LANDOWSKI (Paul).**—French sculptor. Born in Paris, 1875. His chief works are: *David Fighting;* the *Sons of Cain* (bronze; court of the Carrousel). *Architecture* (in stone; court of the Carrousel); *Hymn to Aurora* (bronze; Petit Palace); *Monument to Unknown Artists* (Panthéon); equestrian statue of Edward VII (Place Edouard VII, Paris); *Monument to the Reformation* (Geneva); *Monument to Victory* (at Casablanca, 1924); and numerous busts. To sculpturesque qualities this artist adds rare decorative feeling, and his works always express nobility of thought.

**LANDSEER (Sir Edwin).**—English painter (1802-1873). One of the most popular animal painters in England. He was very prolific and very successful.

All the dogs, horses and stags which won him so much favour with the general public are painted in their "Sunday best," with shining coats. He added something of human nature to their animal nature; and painted man in the guise of the beast. His stags have appealing attitudes, and his dogs seem over-endowed with reason and almost seem to have the power of speech.

**LANGHANS (K. G.).**—German architect, 1733(?)-1808. An exponent of neo-classicism, Langhans finished Gontard's Marble Palace, Potsdam, 1786-1796, and designed the Schloss Theater, Charlottenburg, 1788, and the Brandenburger Tor, Berlin, 1788-1791.

**LANGUEDAC (Churches of).**—See Pl. 44, Vol. I.

**LANINI (Bernardino).** — Lombard painter (1512?-1583?). Pupil of Gaudenzio Ferrari. There are pictures by him in the Milan and Turin Galleries, and frescoes in the churches of Milan, Vercelli, Legnano, Novara, and Saronno.

**LANZIANI (Polidoro), more correctly Polidoro da Lanciano.**—Italian painter (1515-1565). Pupil of Titian and painter of numerous pictures of the Madonna and Child in the manner of his master, his only authenticated work being a *Pentecost* of 1546 in the Venice Academy.

**LAOCOÖN (The).** — Marble group which was discovered in Rome in 1506. The work is due to three sculptors of the school of Rhodes,—Agisandros, Polydoros and Athenodoros. It has been restored, copied and commented upon, especially by Winckelmann and by Gotthold Lessing in *Laokoön.* The group represents the priest of Apollo and his two sons being entwined by serpents sent from Neptune. The father's body is contorted by pain and effort. Its tension is shown by the swelling of the muscles and the stiffness of the tendons.

The date of the *Laocoön* is a matter of debate, but it is probably a century earlier than the frieze of Pergamon.

See Pl. 25, Vol. I.

BIBLIOGRAPHY: Collignon, *Histoire de la sculpture grecque.* Vol. II, pp. 550-556.

**LAON (Aisne).**—The old Cathedral of Notre Dame is a fine Gothic building, begun shortly after 1150, finished about 1225. The cathedral has five towers, one on each transept, two on the façade, and a lantern tower at the crossing. The colossal bulls on the façade towers were, it is said, put there in commemoration of the animals who dragged up the building materials to the plateau on which the town stands. The interior is in four storeys, a treatment characteristic of transitional Gothic churches. The square sanctuary and the lancet openings and ring capitals show the influence of the English bishop who held the see late in the 12th century.

LAON: THE CATHEDRAL.

BIBLIOGRAPHY: R. C. Lasteyrie de Saillant. *L'architecture réligieuse en France à l'époque gothique.* Paris, 1926.

THE LAOCOÖN. (Vatican, Rome.)

**L'ARGENTA.**—See Aleotti.

**LARGILLIÈRE (Nicolas de).**—French painter. Paris, 1656-1746. He lived in London for four years, where he became intimate with several Flemish painters. Brought up, like them, in the tradition of Rubens, he had already a feeling for the portrayal of physical life, and pearly skins. In rendering, and even idealising, feminine graces, he showed a tenderness which Rigaud lacked. None was more successful than he in revealing exquisite complexions, delicate reflections of materials, and autumnal skies. His freshness of colour, and light, spirited touch must have delighted his charming sitters. The "historical" portraits then in fashion suited Largillière's talents, and his good taste is revealed in his restrained use of accessories.

All his gifts appear in his finest work—a portrait of the painter, with his wife and daughter (Louvre).

See Pl. 41, Vol. II.

LARGILLIÈRE: PORTRAIT OF MME. DE GUEYDAN. (Museum of Aix.)

BIBLIOGRAPHY: Pierre Marcel, *La peinture en France au début du XVIII^e siècle*. Paris, 1905.

**LARSSON (Carl).**—Swedish painter (1853-1919). He painted subjects taken from Swedish history of the 18th century, for the Stockholm National Museum. They are frescoes in bright fresh colours; and show delicate feeling. Notable also as a water-colour painter and illustrator.

**LAST JUDGMENT (The).**—The judging of the blessed and the damned, a subject widely represented from the Romanesque period onward.

**LASTMAN (Pieter).**—Dutch painter, 1583-1633. His chief claim to fame is that he was Rembrandt's master. He imitated Caravaggio and Elsheimer. His influence upon Rembrandt was more important than is usually conceded. Pictures are preserved in Berlin, Augsburg, Amsterdam, Brunswick, Leningrad, etc.

BIBLIOGRAPHY: K. Freise, *Pieter Lastman*. Leipzig, 1911.

**LAST SUPPER (The).**—Supper shared by Christ and His disciples on the night of His betrayal. Famous representations in art include those of Leonardo da Vinci (See Pl. 17, Vol. II), Thierry Bouts, Andrea del Castagno, and Ghirlandaio.

**LATERAN.**—See Vatican.

**LA TOUR (Georges de).**—French painter, 1593-1652. La Tour, one of the greatest French painters of the 17th Century remained in complete obscurity until 1863 when a pamphlet was written on his life by Alexandre Joly. However, none of his works were known until 1914 when Dr. Hermann Voss discovered several of his paintings. Since then other works have been found which can definitely be assigned to La Tour. The quality of his painting is attested to by the fact that many of his paintings had been attributed to other great painters such as Zurbaran and Velásquez. Most of the paintings by La Tour are night scenes in which the artist was able to use the heavy chiaroscuro of Caravaggio. His subject matter is usually religious and he achieves great luminosity through the strong contrast of light and dark. A dull red often occupies an important place in his pictures. The only painting by this artist which is not a night scene is *The Sharper* (Coll. Landry, Paris) which is signed "Georgius Delatour fecit."

LA TOUR: THE MARQUISE OF RUMILLY. (Doucet Collection.)

BIBLIOGRAPHY: H. Voss *Tableaux a eclairage dirune de G. de la Tour,* Formes. June, 1931.—Louis Carré *Loan Exhibition of Paintings by Georges de la Tour and the Brothers Le Nain,* 1936.

**— (Maurice Quentin de).**—French pastel portrait artist. Born in Saint Quentin, 1704; died in the same town, 1788. Pastel, set in fashion by Rosalba, was then at the height of its popularity. La Tour, by his unwearying taste for analysis, is typical of the age of rational scepticism in which he lived. His art has

LA TOUR: PORTRAIT OF RESTOUT. (Museum of St. Quentin.)

not the lightness of touch of Perronneau, nor does he pander, in the same way, to his sitters' vanity. La Tour, the satirist, played the moralist, and was no respecter of persons in his penetrating reading of character. Among the numerous "stars"

LA TOUR: L'ABBÉ HUBERT. (Museum of St. Quentin.)

who had their portraits painted by La Tour was the opera singer Mademoiselle Fel (who created the part of Colette in the "Devin de Village" of Jean Jacques Rousseau). This, and many of his finest pastels, are in the Musée Saint Quentin.

See Pl. 46, Vol. II.

BIBLIOGRAPHY: Goncourt, *L'art au XVIII^e siècle*. Vol. II.—M. Tourneux, *La Tour*. "Collection des grands artistes."—G. Brière and Elie Fleury, *Catalogue des pastels de Maurice Quentin de Latour*. Paris, 1920.

**LATROBE (Benjamin H.)**—See Thornton.

**LATTANZIO DA RIMINI.**—Venetian painter, active end of the 15th century; pupil of Giovanni Bellini. His principal work is a composite altarpiece in the Church of San Martino at Piazza Brembana near Bergamo. A Madonna signed by him is in the Schloss museum in Berlin.

BIBLIOGRAPHY: Crowe and Cavalcaselle, *History of Painting in North Italy,* ed. Tancred Borenius. Vol. I. London, 1912.

**LAUGHING CAVALIER (The).**—See Hals.

**LAURANA (Francesco da).**—Sculptor and medalist, of Dalmatian origin, who worked in Italy and in central France in the second half of the 15th century. By his art and education he belongs to that complex Neapolitan school in which south Gothic and realistic Flemish influences combine with the tendencies of the Renaissance.

LAURANA: UNKNOWN WOMAN. (Louvre.)

After 1468 he was in Sicily where he executed a statue of the Madonna in S. Maria della Neve, signed and dated 1471.

In 1474 he was in Naples, and in 1477 again in France, which he had visited in 1464.

The most important and most authentic works by Laurana belong to about the same period: the decoration of the Chapel of St. Lazarus in the old Cathedral (or Church of the Major, Marseille); and the high-altar of the Church of the Celestines—now the Church of St. Dédier,—Avignon. Both works date from 1479-81.

BIBLIOGRAPHY: Heiss, *Médailleurs de la Renaissance; Laurana et Pietro da Milano*. Paris, 1882.—P. Vitry, *Michel Colombe et la sculpture française de son temps*. 1901.—L. Courajod, *Leçons*. Vol. II. 1907.—W. Rolfs, *Laurana*. 1907. 2 Vols.

**— (Luciano da.)**—Architect, of Dalmatian origin. Flourishing from 1468 to 1479. According to Egidio Calzini, he ought to be called Urana and not Laurana, Urana being the name of his native town near Zara. He owes his fame to his work on the fine Ducal Palace of Urbino, commanded by Federigo da Montefelto, who summoned Laurana there in 1465. Bramante may have been a pupil of Laurana.

BIBLIOGRAPHY: Egidio Calzini, *Urbino e i suoi monumenti*.—Rocca San Casciano. 1897.—A. Colasanti, *Luciano Laurana*. Rome, 1922.—Fiske Kimball, *Luciano Laurana and the High Renaissance,* Art Bulletin, Vol. X, 1928.

**LAURENCIN (Marie).**—Contemporary French painter and graver. She was born in Paris 31st October 1885. Her first instruction in painting was at the Lycée Lamartine and then she studied design with Ferdinand Humbert. She met and became the friend of Braque and Picasso and showed her pictures in the Salon des Indépendants in 1907. One-man shows of her art were held at the Galerie Barbazanges in 1912 and at the gallery of P. Rosenberg in 1920. From 1914 to 1920 she travelled on the continent, visiting Spain and the Rhenish district of Germany, and then returned to Paris to make her home. Her work both in painting and in lithography is marked by a very distinct original quality. The most frequent colours are pink and blue in the lightest of pastel shades, and the figures dressed in these tints are endowed with fragility of physique and sweetness of countenance. Some have compared them to the creatures of fairyland, which is not far from the truth. Dainty maidens sing to while away the hours or loll in chairs while their faithful dogs stand watch at their feet. There is a resemblance to old Persian miniatures and a fragrance of the rococo period in an atmosphere which is charged with "sweetness and light." Her early attempts at etching and wood cuts contain some elements related to Negro sculpture which must be the result of her contact with the art of Picasso and his school. About 1913 her prints had an air of the theatre about them, but it was because she was doing some stage decorations at that time, including work for the Comédie-Française and the Ballet Russe of Serge de Diaghilev. Her first lithographs did not appear until 1920, but they contained the germs of her art as shown in her earlier productions, consisting of fanciful persons engaged in trivial pastimes in an Utopian atmosphere. Some of her work includes portraits of persons which seem but pale reflexions of humanity, coloured as they are by the personality and objective approach of this artist.

BIBLIOGRAPHY: Roger Allard, *Marie Laurencin,* 1921.—Marcel Jouhandeau, *Marie Laurencin,* 1928.—Helmud Kolle, *Marie Laurencin,* n. d. André de Ridder, *Marie Laurencin,* n. d.—H. von Wedderkop, *Marie Laurencin,* 1921.

**LAUTREC.**—See Toulouse-Lautrec.

**LAWRENCE (Sir Thomas).**—English painter (1769-1830).

He was most successful in his portraits of women. His art often lacks simplicity and adequate draughtsmanship, but he was a brilliant painter and his work has considerable distinction.

The portrait of Mrs. Siddons, which he exhibited in 1797, established his reputation. He became highly successful as a portrait painter, his sitters including many of the celebrated persons of the time ("Waterloo Room," Windsor Castle,

etc.). He became President of the Royal Academy in 1820.
See Pl. 48, Vol. II.

LAWRENCE (THOMAS).

BIBLIOGRAPHY: Sir Walter Armstrong, *Lawrence*. London, 1913.

LAWRENCE: CHILD WITH A LAMB. (National Gallery, London.)

**LAZZARINI (Gregorio).**—Venetian painter, 1654-1740. One of the best painters who mark the revival

LAWRENCE: MRS. SIDDONS. (National Gallery, London.)

of Venetian painting in the 18th century, after the years of decadence which followed the period of Titian and Veronese. His works include a vast composition representing the Charity of St. Laurence Giustiniani, which is rich in architectural subjects and crowds of people. He has been compared with Raphael owing to the solidity of his compositions, but it is a cold perfection. He may have been one of Tiepolo's masters.

**LEANING TOWER.**—See Pisa.

**— Towers Asinelli and Garisenda.**—See Bologna (It.).

**LE BLOND (Jacques Christophe).**—French engraver, born in Frankfort, of French parents, in 1670, died in 1741. He was the inventor of a process of engraving in colours.

BIBLIOGRAPHY: H. W. Singer in *Nittisbengen der Geschschift für vervielfültigende Kunst*. 1901.

**LE BRUN (Charles).**—French painter, 1619-1690. Son of a master painter of Paris, Le Brun received his first lessons from his father. Then he entered the studio of Vouet. In 1642, he went to Rome, where he stayed three years, and then returned to Paris, whither his reputation had preceded him. Keen to advance in the world, he became acquainted with rich and influential people. In 1657, Fouquet entrusted him with the decoration of the Château of Vaux, and a kind of artistic directorship, thus anticipating Colbert and Louis XIV. From this time no kind of painting embarrassed Le Brun—he painted mythological, religious and historical scenes, and portraits.

After the downfall of Fouquet, Le Brun united his fortune to that of

LE BRUN (CHARLES). (After Largillière.)

Colbert. In 1663, he became director of the Gobelins.

From 1664 to 1683, he attained the height of his authority and of his glory. From 1660 to 1668, he painted

LE BRUN: TAPESTRY OF THE SEASONS: WINTER.

the *History of Alexander* (Louvre). In 1662, he undertook the decoration of the "Galerie d'Apollon" in the Louvre. In 1667, he decorated a part of the rooms of the new Château of Saint Germain, and decorated the grand staircase of Versailles, as well as the "Galerie des Glaces," and the Salons of War and of Peace.

At the same time he directed almost all the ornamentation of the Park. The statues and groups executed by the Le Hongres and others are almost all "according to the design of Monsieur Le Brun."

From the time of his nomination as Director of the Manufacture of the Gobelins in 1663, he is the great inspirer of all the decorative arts.

Besides painters and sculptors a great many artisans of all kinds were under his orders. Le Brun furnished the cartoons of magnificent tapestries which are more appreciated nowadays than are his paintings.
See Pl. 41, Vol. II.

**LE CORBUSIER.**—See Jeanneret-Gris.

**LECYTHOS.**—See Greece (Vases); also Pl. 27, Vol. I.

**LEGENDRE (Tomb of Robert.)**—See Pl. 4, Vol. I.

**LÉGER (Fernand).**—Contemporary French painter. He was born at Argentan in l'Orne in February, 1881. He was a free student at the École des Beaux-Arts in Paris, working under Gérôme and Gabriel Ferrier for the three years from 1902 to 1905. He tried his hand at making some designs and did some work as an architect, but soon turned to painting. In 1910 he exhibited his pictures with the Independents and became an active member of that group. His compositions are characterised by the violent contrasts of objects and colours, by which means the artist endeavours to achieve the harmony of the whole. It is a northern variety of cubism aiming at the plastic organisation of space and the suggestion of the third dimension by contrasts of colour and line in the volumes therein represented. His first style was strongly influenced by the work of the Italian primitives and the patterns seen in Byzantine mosaics, but later his pictures became more naturalistic in theme and consequently more lyrical in the method of treatment. From an early plastic period he passed to a static stage, when the figures were treated in a strictly objective manner without any attempt to suggest movement. His present compositions are dynamic representations of objects done in clear colours juxtaposed without any real reason other than the combination of a variety of solids. The art of Léger has been very influential in other European countries and may be recognised in the neoplasticism of Holland, the constructivism of Russia, the abstractionism of Germany and the movements of objectivism and purism. He made stage sets for the Swedish ballet, helped in the production of a film entitled the *Ballet Mécanique* and has illustrated several books including *La Fin du Monde* by Blaise Cendrars and *Lunes en Papier* by André Mabraux. He is today connected with Amédée Ozenfant in the direction of the Académie Moderne in Paris.

BIBLIOGRAPHY: Waldemar George, *Fernand Léger*, 1929.—Maurice Reynal, *Fernand Léger*, n. d.—E. Teriade, *Fernand Léger*, 1928.

**LEGROS (Alphonse).** — French painter and engraver, 1837-1899.

LEGROS: CHARITY.

After studying in Dijon, he went to Paris. In 1857, he exhibited the *Portrait of his Father* (Tours Gallery), which is charmingly fresh. Unable to make his name in France, he went to London, where he married, and became Professor at University College. He continued to paint: *Women Praying* (1860, Tate Gallery), *The Blessing of the Sea* (1872), *The Stoning of St. Stephen*, etc. He also devoted himself to etching.

Legros shows a conviction which sometimes recalls the primitives. As an artist, he is severe and vigorous. His painting is grave, sometimes very dramatic. His drawing is refined and precise, and shows great technical ability but it is a little monotonous and cold.

**LEHMBRUCK (Wilhelm).**—German sculptor, painter and graver (1881-1919). One of eight children he was born 4th January 1881 in Duisburg-Meiderich, of peasant ancestry. Due to his father's death he had to go to work at an early age in a metal concern, where he developed a feeling for the medium. He managed to attend art school from 1895 to 1899. Two years later he received a stipend and was accepted at the Academy of Düsseldorf, where he studied for five years under the guidance of Janssen. After a trip to Italy he went to Paris, where he exhibited in the Salon of the Société Nationale of 1907. In 1912 he went to Italy again, and from 1914 to 1917 he was active in Berlin. He committed suicide at the prime of his life, 25th March 1919, in Berlin. Lehmbruck's favourite form of expression was the female figure; the mother-and-child subjects are the dominant themes of his output. The essence of his sculpture is always in the spiritual aspects; he is seldom preoccupied with the realism of physical form. Lehmbruck was a thinker as well as a craftsman; his figures reflect the mental rather than the physical state of his subjects, they are sensitive, idealistic, the mood is most frequently reflective or dreamily melancholic. A romantic flavour characterises his sculpture as well as his painting, although his early style tended towards neo-classicism. The change was brought about by the influence of Maillol's artistic canons. The marble, stone, bronze and terra cotta figures are equally dominated by tactile values and subtle rhythmic line. His best work is the *Knieende*, 1911, while the *Emporsteigende Jüngling* is considered to be his self-portrait. It expresses the young artist's aspiration for higher and spiritual things and the doubt and hardship that confront him in his strivings. It is only in his drawings that he breaks away from the reflective mood; in these his subjects are often Biblical scenes and other figures. His objective is to search for the purely feminine in woman or to solve the characters' psychological problems. His drawings are done with a few rapid strokes suggesting form and silhouette. Although a solitary figure in life as well as in art, Lehmbruck's influence on the successive generation is of great importance. His works may be seen in the museums of Berlin, Dresden, Duisburg, Cologne and Munich as well as in Buffalo, Detroit and New York.

BIBLIOGRAPHY: August Hoff, *Wilhelm Lehmbruck*, 1933.—P. Westheim, *Das Werk Lehmbrucks*, 1919 and 1922.

**LEIGHTON (Frederick, Lord).**—English painter (1830-1896), studied in London and in various Continental centres (Rome, Dresden, Berlin, Florence, Paris, Frankfort); treated at first subjects from Italian mediæval history, but afterwards mainly subjects from Greek mythology in a style of pseudo-classical academism. He was elected a full member of the Royal Academy in 1868, and held the post of President of that institution from 1878 to his death; he was raised to the peerage in 1896.

**LE LORRAIN (Robert).**—French sculptor, 1666-1743, born in Paris; pupil of Girardon; influenced Jean Baptiste Le Moyne.

See Pl. 45, Vol. II.

**LELY (Peter van der Faes, called Lely or Lilly).**—Painter, born in Westphalia, naturalised English, 1618-1680. He lived in London, where he painted numerous portraits of the courtiers and great dignitaries of the courts of Charles I and Charles II. He was very successful in his time. To posterity he seems somewhat lacking in power and originality. A gallery of his portraits may be seen in Hampton Court Palace.

Bibliography: C. H. Collins Baker, *Lely and the Stuart Portrait Painters.* London, 1912.

**LE MANS (France).**—*The Cathedral of St. Julian,* begun

Le Mans: Doorway of the Cathedral.

about 1060, in the Romanesque style, by Vulgrin, who was both bishop and architect. Much damaged by fire, it was restored and consecrated in 1158; covered with a Gothic vault, and definitely finished, from 1217 to 1254, by the building of a magnificent choir. The choir was separated from the nave by the construction of a stone rood-screen, decorated with statues and bas-reliefs, in the 15th century, and destroyed by the Protestants. The façade, which turns towards the East, is Romanesque, and pierced by three doorways. The central one, much larger than the other two, is surmounted by carvings, representing two signs of the Zodiac. The interior is vast and imposing. Several stained glass windows in the side aisles are among the oldest in France (12th century). The choir, one of the largest and finest in France, is lighted by remarkable 13th century windows, and buttressed by the most elaborate system of flying buttresses in all Europe.

The baptismal chapel contains the tombs of Charles of Anjou, by the Italian sculptor Francesco da Laurana (15th century), and of Guillaume du Bellay (16th century).

See Pl. 48, Vol. I.

Bibliography: R. C. Lasteyrie de Saillant, *L'architecture religieuse en France à l'epoque gothique.* Paris, 1926.

**LE MOYNE or LEMOINE (François).**—French historical and decorative painter, 1688-1737. His well known works include the ceiling of St. Sulpice in Paris and the *Marriage at Cana* in the Montpellier Museum.

See Pl. 47, Vol. II.

**LEMOYNE (Jean Baptiste).**—French sculptor, 1704-1778. Pupil of his father Jean Louis and also of Le Lorrain. His most important works were his three statues of Louis XV—one, equestrian, in Bordeaux, another in Rennes, showing the King standing between Brittany and Health (an allusion to the famous cure of illness contracted in

Lemoyne (J. B.).

Metz), and a third in the École Militaire.

Bibliography: D'Argenville, *Vies des plus fameux arch. et sculpteurs.* Vol. II. 1787.—St. Lami, *Dictionnaire des Sculpteurs.* Vol. II. 1911.

Lemoyne (J. B.): Model of the Monument of Louis XV. (Louvre.)

**LE NAIN (The brothers).**—French painters: Antoine (1588-1648), Louis (1593-1648), and Mathieu (1607-1677). The Le Nains were born in Laon. They painted realistic, familiar scenes of peasants and workmen, with the same enjoyment with which they painted court portraits. The Portrait of a member of the Pérussy Family (Avignon) shows us how these painters of rustic life rendered the cavalier grace of the costume of the period with its sumptuous lace collar. Their religious paintings are of secondary importance; the large shadows and brutal lighting effects borrowed from Caravaggio tend to vulgarise these pious scenes, which are wanting in sincerity. The Le Nains are chiefly interesting in their pictures of peasants, which are solidly constructed, and painted in a greyish brown harmony, rather sad, or sometimes brightened with a crude red.

See Pl. 39, Vol. II.

Le Nain: Portrait of a member of the Perussy family. (Museum of Avignon.)

Bibliography: A. Valabrèque, *Les frèses Le Nain.* Paris, 1904.—P. Jamot, *Les Lenain.* Paris, 1929.

**LENBACH (Franz von).**—German painter, 1836-1904. He began by painting genre scenes, of which the best are the *Arch of Titus* and the *Little Herdsman,* one in the Museum of Pressburg, and the other in the Schack Gallery, in Munich. He then became the finest portrait painter of Germany in the 19th century. Lenbach's merit lies chiefly in the vigorous way in which he evokes the personality of his sitters. Among his portraits may be mentioned those of Bismarck, of Count von Moltke, of Gladstone, of Döllinger, and of Mommsen.

See Pl. 59, Vol. II.

Bibliography: Rosenberg, A., *Frans Lenbach.* Bielefeld, 1898.

**LENDINARA (Cristoforo da).**—Italian painter and worker in intarsia, Modena, of the end of the 15th century. His best work is the *Virgin Enthroned* (Modena Gallery) of 1482.

**LE NOTRE (André).**—French garden architect (1613-1700). Of

Le Notre (André).

humble extraction, Le Notre was at first destined to follow the career of his father and grandfather, who had been engaged, in their day, in tending the royal gardens. Soon the varied teaching he had received would have allowed him to find other employment than reversion to the capacity of gardener of the Tuileries.—For he had studied painting with Simon Vernet, beside Le Brun; and learned the elements of applied architecture, which was to be so valuable to him in the future.—But he conformed to paternal wishes in accepting this modest position. Thus, he was placed under the direction of Claude Mollet, head gardener to the king, and in 1637, at the age of 24, Le Notre became gardener in chief of the Tuileries. Six years later he became the designer of all the layouts and walks of His Majesty's gardens.

His work was considerable, and there exists scarcely a park that does not owe something to him—not only Versailles, but Trianon, Saint Cloud, Chaville, Saint Germain, etc.,—not counting gardens in England, Germany, and even in Italy.

Le Notre aimed at achieving wide views; and the fine perspective effects at Versailles magnificently justified the theories of this creator of the French garden.

Bibliography: L. Corpechot, *André Le Notre.* Paris, 1912.

**LENZ (P.).**—German sculptor (1822-1928) who founded, about 1880, the Benedictine school of religious art of Beuron, which is connected with the neo-classic movement. The fault of this art is that it relied too often on formula, and remained a stranger to nature and life.

**LEOCHARES.**—Athenian sculptor of the 4th century B.C. He made numerous portraits. That of Isocrates is one of his most famous works. An example of a realistic work is the *Portrait of a Slave-merchant.* Many other votive portraits by him have disappeared. He executed the sculptures of the east side of the Mausoleum of Halicarnassus, according to Pliny. It is generally considered that the *Rape of Ganymede,* in the Vatican Museum, is the copy of a bronze work of Leochares, which was no doubt transported to Rome, where Pliny described it. In this group, the sculptor ably expressed the upward motion of the figure. The *Apollo Belvedere* is sometimes attributed to Leochares.

Bibliography: Collignon, *Histoire de la sculpture grecque.* Vol. II. Paris, 1896.

**LEON (Spain).**—The *Church of St. Isidoro* was founded in the 11th

Leon: The Cathedral.

century, and enlarged in the 12th. The church was consecrated in 1147. Its heavy pillars, doors and windows, in which the semi-circular arch reigns supreme, give the building a monastic character. The Romanesque capitals are decorated with rich carvings; and in the crypt are frescoes, in a remarkable state of preservation.

*Leon Cathedral* is one of the three Spanish cathedrals in a pure Gothic style. It is light and graceful. The stained glass windows of the nave are the most precious ornament of the Cathedral, and are unique. It was begun in 1249.

See Pls. 45, 49, Vol. I; Pl. 2, Vol. II.

Bibliography: Gade, J. A., *Cathedrals of Spain*. Boston, 1911.

**LEONARD LIMOSIN.**—Limosean enameller. Born about 1505, died between 1575 and 1577, in Limoges. He is the great artist of that fine period of limosean enamel, which dates from 1500 to 1580, and includes, besides Leonard Limosin, such artists as Jean II Pénicaud, Pierre Raymond, Martin Didier and the two Couley Noylier. Leonard

Limosin (Leonard): The Hunt. (Enamel, Louvre.)

Limosin was the first of a family of enamellers. In 1532, he painted eighteen plaques representing the scenes of the Passion, after Albrecht Dürer, which is the first work we have by him, and which equals all that followed it.

In 1545, he was in Paris, and painted for Francis I, after cartoons of Primaticcio, the *Twelve Apostles,* which are in the Church of St. Pierre, Chartres. In Paris, Leonard

Limosin (Leonard): Portrait of Claude de Lorraine. (Soltikoff Collection.)

Limosin came into contact with the Italian artists whom Francis I had called about him, and he absorbed something of the encyclopædic spirit of the Renaissance. He took to mythological subjects. His best known work is a plate representing the *Feast of the Gods,* inspired by an engraving of Marcantonio Raimondi, after Raphael. Here are Henry II, in the guise of Jupiter, Catherine de' Medici and Diane de Poitiers. In the same way, a cup representing the *Combat of Lapiths and Centaurs,* has portraits of Francis I and Charles V.

The two most important pictures of this painter on enamel are in the Louvre: Henry II ordered them for the Sainte Chapelle. They are more than a metre high, and formed a collection of forty-six plaques, representing scenes from the life of Jesus Christ. In the Louvre, again, are two plaques: Francis I and Galiot de Genouilhac, in the guise of St. Thomas and St. Paul.

Leonard also executed a great many portraits about thirty of which have come down to us.

He did not hesitate to exploit his success, and put his name to all the pieces which came out of his studio, some of which he probably never touched.

See Pl. 30, Vol. II.

Bibliography: Bourdery, *Leonard Limousin et son œuvre.* Limoges, 1895.—Bourdery and Lachenard, *Leonard Limosin, peintre de portraits.* Paris. H. May, 1897.—René Jean, *Les Arts de la terre,* 3rd part, l'Emaillerie. Paris, 1911.—P. Lavedan, *Leonard Limosin et les Emailleurs français.* Paris, 1913.

**LEONARDO DA VINCI.**—Italian painter, sculptor, architect, mu-

Leonardo da Vinci: Self-portrait. (Royal Library, Turin.)

sician, engineer and scientist—1452-1519. He lived in Florence, Milan, and France. Leonardo was an exquisite, intellectual painter—a thinker, and one deeply interested in the researches of his art. He studied facial expression with a view to expressing the mind. "La pittura è cosa mentale"—"painting is a thing of the spirit," he said. He was a great worker. He drew constantly, sketching the people he saw in the movements of daily life. There are quantities of little note-books with his sketches, notes and calculations. He studied folds of drapery as he studied the human body. He studied the sea, in its infinite variety. He made extraordinary caricatures, of which there are examples in many museums.

His researches were universal. Besides painting, he was a sculptor, architect, a composer of music. He sang extremely well, and accompanied himself on the lyre. He studied all branches of science—mathematics, geometry, mechanics, geology, anatomy, etc. He designed cannons and other offensive machines, optical instruments, even flying machines. He divined modern science, and anticipated Bacon, always going forward and trying to surpass himself. At the same time, he organised splendid fêtes. When old, he made, to amuse Francis I, an automatic lion which opened out a little and covered the king's feet with lilies. He filled volumes, wrote a treatise on painting, left numerous manuscripts. J. P. Richter published two volumes in 1883, and Charles Ravaisson twelve manuscripts of the Institute Library in 1891. In the Ambrosian Library at Milan, there is the *Codex Atlanticus,* a volume of 804 pages, with drawings, and autographs.

In painting, Vinci was a great initiator by reason of his efforts to reproduce the volume of objects by the play of light and shade. Instead of painting with dry lines, and with flat shadows marking off the lights, like the primitives, his caressing touch enveloped forms in a subtle "atmosphere" (sfumato). As he drew very correctly, the shapes are not obscured by this vaporous handling. He lost only the decorative character of the 15th century, and the rich colour is hidden by the deepness of the shadows and the brightness of the lights. Thus he did not care for fresco, which is incomparable for rendering soft, flat effects; and he experimented with new techniques, usually disastrously, chiefly with a view to making oil paint adhere to wall surfaces.

Leonardo da Vinci was born in 1452, at the house of Vinci, between Florence and Pisa. His father, Pietro, a notary, perceiving his abilities, sent him, in 1470, to work at Verrocchio's studio in Florence, where, as companion, he found Perugino and Lorenzo di Credi, who, younger than he, was much influenced by him.

In Verrocchio's *Baptism of Christ* (after 1475) which was ordered by the monks of Vallombrosa, and is now in the Uffizi Gallery, the angel at the left, by Leonardo, informs us concerning his development during his apprenticeship.

Vasari tells us of many other works, now lost, painted by Leonardo in this first period,—works which already showed (according to the descriptions) the characteristics which we find in him later. For instance, there was a cartoon for a tapestry, representing the Fall of Man, in which the trees are represented with the learned minuteness of a naturalist. It seems that one day he collected all the most various kinds of animals that he could find, lizards, serpents, grasshoppers, bats, etc., in order to create a monster out of their various parts—"molto orribile e spaventoso"—to put on the wooden shield of a peasant.

*The Annunciation,* of the Uffizi, is one of those works the authenticity of which has been discussed. It was probably painted by him at the beginning of his career (1472). It is very delicate and charming. Kneeling in the open air upon a carpet of flowers, in front of a row of black cypresses, the angel is seen in profile, bowing. The Virgin, noble and gentle, is at some distance, behind a rich marble desk, resembling a sarcophagus. She raises her hand, but hears the divine message without timidity. This *Annunciation* resembles one in the Louvre, where Leonardo's personality is more marked, no doubt because he painted it afterwards.

The *Adoration of the Magi* in the Uffizi, was ordered in 1481, for the monks of San Donato at Scopeto and never finished. It has a dreamlike quality, all in subdued browns and blues, and the expressive heads of the shepherds look wonderingly through the mist, at the chubby child in the Virgin's arms; they seem dazed by the light of God. Behind, amid the fantastic architecture of ancient ruins, are horses and a preparation for the massacre of the Innocents.

One of the most discussed problems has been that of the *Virgin of the Rocks.* There is one version of this picture in the Louvre, and another (almost the same) in the National Gallery. Very probably the original work of the master is the one in Paris. It is finer, and more expressive, especially in the Angel who, with a movement of the finger which is most difficult to render, resembles many drawings (at Turin, at Windsor, and at Paris, in the École des Beaux Arts, and in the Louvre). A document, published in 1893, shows that Leonardo

Leonardo da Vinci: Adoration of the Kings. (Drawing, Louvre.)

and his pupil, Ambrogio da Predis, were engaged in painting an altarpiece, with the Virgin in the middle and two angels on the sides, for the Brotherhood of the Conception at San Francesco in Milan. Ambrogio painted the two angels (they are in London). Leonardo should have received 200 ducats for the Virgin; but when the picture was finished, the experts only offered him 25, and possibly he was so dissatisfied that he reclaimed his Virgin, and put in its place a copy painted by Ambrogio da Predis. The authentic Virgin came to the Louvre with the collection of Francis I. It was once thought that it was painted in Florence. But according to a document, which seems to refer to this painting, it belongs to about the time of Leonardo's visit to Milan.

He went to Milan in 1484, in the service of Ludovico il Moro. Vasari relates that he took there a marvellous lute, which he had made himself, in the shape of a horse's head, and that, when playing on this instrument, he surpassed all the other musicians.

Some historians have supposed that he went to the East, from 1482-1486 (according to a letter to a lieutenant of the Holy Sultan of Babylon), but this is hardly probable.

He must have stayed at Milan, glad to have the chance of exerting his genius in the midst of the court which was at that time, the most brilliant in Europe. In a letter of the "Codex Atlanticus" (Charles Ravaisson has proved that this is not by his hand, but was perhaps dictated by him, or copied) one sees the wonderful schemes that he offered to Ludovico: plans for building movable bridges, for protecting fortresses, for making cannons, catapults, underground passages, sculpture, etc., and, finally, the equestrian statue of the Duke's father, Francesco Sforza. He was very well received. "Not to mention his physical beauty which cannot be praised enough," says Vasari, "he performed every act with infinite grace." Ludovico must have been delighted to have so complete and rare an artist at his court, and Leonardo, on his side, must have enjoyed all the refined pleasures of this luxurious life and the honours that were paid him. He became acquainted with poets and artists, and with Bramante in particular. He was commissioned to paint a *Nativity* for the Emperor Maximilian—a painting now lost. But above all he was concerned with the equestrian statue of Francesco Sforza. For sixteen years he worked in a studio, installed in the palace. But in spite of the large number of drawings at Windsor, we know little of the result. Descriptions of fêtes, given in honour of the marriage of Maria Bianca (1493) mention the exhibition of an equestrian statue by Leonardo on a triumphal arch. It has been stated that it was destroyed by the French, in 1499, but in 1501, the Duke of Ferrara wrote to reclaim it from the King of France, as though it still existed.

Other works have likewise perished: portraits of Ludovico il Moro, of his son, Maximilian, of the duchess, Beatrice.

His most important work during his stay in Milan was, however, the *Last Supper,* painted in the refectory of the Dominican Convent of Santa Maria delle Grazie, between 1495 and 1498. It is one of the most famous pictures in the world, and one of those that has been most widely circulated in copies, drawings, engravings and descriptions. Leonardo painted it on the wall, in oil paint by a process which he invented. Even, in 1560, Lomazzo, in his *Treatise on Painting,* said that it was "rovinata tutta," "totally ruined." It was further spoiled in attempts to restore it; and, finally, the occupation of the refectory as a barracks did not improve matters. It is pale and phantom-like now. In the large dining-room, Christ eats with his disciples for the last time. Behind, the open windows let in the pure air of wide spaces. They have all been happy together, enjoying the evening hour; when suddenly Jesus says: "One of you shall betray me." His beautiful face does not change: it is full of an infinite acceptance, framed in fine hair, with the eyelids lowered, and the mouth half open. He realises that the moment is a grave one. An immediate stir moves the disciples, like a tempestuous wind. Each one feels the drama in his heart and is moved according to his nature. A sketch in the Louvre shows us five persons (nude, as was his wont) round a table which he certainly copied for his *Last Supper.* He sought long for the facial expressions which would respond to his thought. The most celebrated engravings and reproductions of the *Last Supper* are those of Raphael Morghen (1800), of Castellozo, attributed also to Marco d'Oggiono, and of Theodore Matteini.

But the sumptuous reign of Ludovico il Moro came an end. The French drove him out of Milan, and set fire to his palace, and all the great works of Leonardo da Vinci were stopped.

Then in 1503, at nearly fifty years of age, he returned to Florence. He passed through Venice and Mantua, where he made a charcoal portrait of Isabella d'Este. This great lady endeavoured to keep him as her artist, and he must have painted some pictures for her (perhaps, *Christ among the Doctors*).

In Florence, Leonardo worked for the Servite monks, at the *Virgin with St. Anne,* of which there is a cartoon in Burlington House, London. The painting is in the Louvre. The landscape, derived from that of Verrocchio, fades into a faery distance, where waters wander among strange rocks, veiled in blue mist.

In 1502, Leonardo da Vinci was in the service of Cesare Borgia, as military engineer. In 1503, he was ordered, together with Michelangelo, to decorate the Council Chamber of the Palazzo dei Signori in Florence, and he represented the Battle of Anghiari. He took the Pope's room in Santa Maria Novella, as a studio, and there made the cartoon. But when he wished to carry it out on the wall, it took badly, and he only succeeded in painting certain figures (the episode of the Standard) which disappeared almost immediately afterwards, so defective was his method. Unfortunately, the cartoon, too, has disappeared, having for long been the admiration of the world, by the side of Michelangelo's. We have only reproductions. The oldest is an engraving by Lorenzo Zacchia of Lucca, dating from 1558, but it was not necessarily made from the picture itself. At the Louvre there is a drawing by Rubens, and at Oxford, another drawing. At Windsor, in a drawing attributed to Leonardo, we find the same horse. As far as may be judged, it was a realistic battle scene—the cruel and horrible confusion of combat to the death. Leonardo was supreme in his power of representing horses (*"stupendissimo in far cavalli,"* said Ludovico Dolci).

In 1505, he painted *La Gioconda* (Louvre), bought by Francis I, which is the portrait of Mona Lisa, a Neapolitan, third wife of Zanobi del Giocondo. Everything that it is possible to say has been said of her smile and less of the extraordinary development of the portrait form, particularly in the rendering of space. The figure in harmonious coordination with the background of vanishing blue distance is an evolution of the Florentine form first implied in Castagno's Mellon portrait and its successors and further explored in Baldovinetti's Louvre Madonna.

The *Saint John,* in the Louvre, a later work, has the same smile, but it has become still more enigmatic, at once ironical and flattering.

About the same time, he painted a *Leda,* which must have been for some time a neighbour of *La Gioconda,* at Fontainebleau. But it has disappeared, and now we have only copies and drawings to give us an idea of the composition. He painted the *St. Jerome* (Vatican), a bald old man, whose inner being is expressed in a well-constructed and well-modelled body.

In 1506, Leonardo went to Milan, called there by the French Governor, Charles d'Amboise. The French king was already wanting to attach Leonardo to his court, and he painted two pictures for him: the *Virgin of the Balances* (which he painted with pupils), and the *Holy Family,* of the Hermitage Museum.

Maximilian Sforza, returning to Milan after having turned out the French, Leonardo da Vinci went to Rome in 1513, to be near Leo X. There, Michelangelo, Raphael and Bramante were in all their glory. They received him badly. He was an unwanted rival. The Pope was chiefly interested in his alchemy, and the way in which he distilled herbs in a crucible to make a varnish.

But he was soon presented to the king of France, Francis I, and immediately obtained his favour. He ended by agreeing (1516) to follow him to France in the capacity of royal painter, with a salary of 700 écus a year. He lived in the Château of Cloux, near Amboise, always much admired and patronised, and he organised fêtes and planned numerous works. But he became weak, and paralysed in his right hand. In the end the illness proved mortal, and he died in his Château of Cloux, on the 2nd May, 1519.

Leonardo da Vinci left a great reputation. His most important pupils, who followed him religiously, were Marco d'Oggiono, Cesare da Sesto, Giovanni Antonio Boltraffio, Andrea Solario, and Ambrogio da Predis. Luini and Sodoma were much influenced by him. Leonardo sought, above everything else, to express the moral life, and to reveal the secret emotions of the soul by the fleeting tremors of facial expression. His pupils, who had not his searching genius, retained only his thick, enveloping style, and the softness of his touch.

See Pl. 9, Vol. I; Pl. 17, Vol. II.

Bibliography: G. Séailles, *Léonard de Vinci, l'artiste et le Savant.* Paris, 1892.—A. Rosenberg, *Leonardo da Vinci.* Bielefeld, 1898.—Müntz, *Léonard de Vinci.* Paris, 1899.—Selwyn Brinton, *Leonardo.* Florence, 1900.—G. Gronau, *Leonardo da Vinci.* London, 1902.—E. McCurdy, *Leonardo da Vinci.* London, 1904.—G. Carotti, *Le Opere di Leonardo, Bramante e Raffaello.* Florence, 1900.—G. Gronau, *Leonardo da Vinci.* London, 1901.—R. Horne, and H. Cust, *Leonardo da Vinci.* London, 1908.—O. Sirèn, *Leonardo da Vinci.* Yale, 1916.

**LEONI (Leone).**—Milanese sculptor. 1509-1590, the most important of his day. As famous for his medals as for his bronze statues and his busts. He worked chiefly in Milan, where he constructed in 1565 the Palazzo dei Omenoni (big men), because of the giants which decorate the façade. His best known work is the rich tomb of the Margrave of Marignano (in the Cathedral), with his figures in bronze (1560-1564).

Leone Leoni visited Spain in 1559 with his son Pompeo, who continued his work for Philip II. Most of his works are in Spain, a number of them in the Prado.

Bibliography: E. Plon, *Leone Leoni.* Paris. 1887.

**— (Pompeo).**—Sculptor, son of Leone Leoni. Died in 1608. He worked in Spain where he made statues of Charles V, Philip II, etc.

**LEOPARDI (Alessandro).**—Venetian sculptor of the end of the 15th and of the beginning of the 16th century. He died in Venice 1522 or 1523. He began his career as a goldsmith. It was he who finished Verrocchio's *Colleone.*

**LEPICIÉ (Nicolas Bernard).**—French painter and engraver, 1735-1784. Pupil of Carle Van Loo. Besides large historical pictures, he painted little "genre" scenes, to which he finally devoted himself. In engraving, he interpreted some of Chardin's paintings, successfully.

**LE PRINCE (Jean Baptiste).**—French painter and engraver, 1733-1781. A pupil of Boucher.

**LE PUY (France).**—The town, which is very old and picturesque, lies on a hill, at the top of which stands a splendid Romanesque Cathedral, *Notre Dame du Puy,* built about the middle of the 12th century, in a style which recalls the architecture of L'Auvergne, Périgord, Burgundy, and also betrays Arabic influences. The Cathedral has fine Romanesque cloisters.

In a suburb of Le Puy, on a conical rock, 85 metres high, stands the ancient chapel of *Saint Michel d'Aiguille* (10th and 11th centuries).

**LERIDA (Spain).**—*Cathedral.* Catalan Gothic Cathedral, 1203-1490. The façade and tower are 14th century, the spire early 15th.

**LESCOT (Pierre).**—French architect, 1510-1578. He enjoyed the favour of Francis I and Henry II, who entrusted him with important works. He often worked in conjunction with the sculptor, Jean Goujon. Together they built the magnificent rood-screen of St. Germain d'Auxerrois, which was destroyed in 1750; then the *Fontaine des Innocents,* (transferred and restored in the 19th century by Davioud), and a part of the Louvre courtyard. This last work was the great task of his life. He devoted eighteen years to it, from 1546 to 1564. He built half of the western wing, which touches the Pavillon de l'Horloge, and half of the south part, the Salle des Caryatides. Pierre Lescot also worked at the Château of Fontainebleau.

Lescot (Pierre): Louvre. (Left wing of the Pavillion de l'Horloge.)

Bibliography: A. Berty, *Les grands architectes français de la Renaissance.* Paris, 1860.—R. T. Blomfield, *History of French architecture from the reign of Charles VIII till the death of Mazarin.* London, 1911.—W. H. Ward, *Architecture of the Renaissance in France.* London, 1926.

**LESSING (Karl Friedrich).**—German painter, 1808-1880. The most virile and representative of the school of Düsseldorf (which arose in reaction against the austere teaching of Munich) which included such artists as Hildebrand, Hübner, Bendemann, Schrödter, etc. Lessing was one of the first German artists to represent the beauties of his country.

**LE SUEUR (Eustache).**—French painter. Born in Paris in 1616. A pupil of Vouet, whose manner he retained for a long time. His *St. Paul at Ephesus* (Louvre), which was considered as his masterpiece, shows the artist influenced by Raphael and Poussin, and one looks in vain for any personal feeling in this learned composition. But Le Sueur was essentially a religious painter, and his best work has individual grace and simple feeling. His work has suffered greatly from clumsy restorations, but the *Life of St. Bruno* (Louvre) shows something of his tendencies.

See Pl. 39, Vol. II.

BIBLIOGRAPHY: Dussieux, *Nouvelles recherches sur la vie et les œuvres du peintre Le Sueur,* 1852.—Vitet, *Eustache le Sueur,* 1853.

LE SUEUR: THE APPEARANCE OF ST. SCHOLASTICA TO ST. BENEDICT. (Louvre.)

**LEUTZE (Emanuel).**—American painter (1816-1868). He was born in Gmünd in the Württemberg district of Germany 24th May 1816, but the family moved to the United States soon after his birth. They settled in Fredericksburg, Virginia, but later moved to Philadelphia. There young Leutze had his first instruction in drawing and soon was doing portraits and figure pieces. From the sale of his work and the help of some local patrons he was enabled to go to Europe to study. In 1841 he entered the academy of Düsseldorf and there worked under Karl Friedrich Lessing. He began to paint historical compositions and his first, *Columbus before the Council of Salamanca,* was purchased by the Art Union of Düsseldorf. He made a trip through the Tyrol and Italy and then returned to Düsseldorf, where he married and spent the next twenty years. He became interested in painting pictures which dealt with important events in the history of the United States. Probably his best known of these, *Washington Crossing the Delaware,* was begun while he was still in Germany and the floes of ice were inspired by his view of the Rhine river in the winter. Leutze returned to the United States in 1859 and the following year was commissioned by Congress to decorate a stairway in the Capitol at Washington. For this he chose the subject, *Westward the Course of Empire Takes Its Way,* combining both historical and allegorical figures in a pyramidal composition. All of his works are characterised by the accurate technique of the German school, but present a rather theatrical and unreal appearance which is alien to true American painting. He was elected to full membership in the National Academy of Design in 1860 and died in Washington, D. C., 18th July 1868.

BIBLIOGRAPHY: Lorinda M. Bryant, *American Pictures and Their Painters,* 1920.—C. H. Caffin, *Story of American Painting,* 1907.—Charles E. Fairman, *Art and Artists of the Capitol of the United States of America,* 1927.—Helen W. Henderson, *The Art Treasures of Washington,* 1912.—Samuel Isham, *History of American Painting,* 1927.—H. T. Tuckerman, *Book of the Artists,* 1867.

**LE VAU (Louis).**—1612-1670, French architect of the age of Louis XVI, known chiefly for his work at Versailles.

**LEVITSKY (Dimitri).**—Russian painter, 1735-1822. He is, with Rocotof, the best portrait painter of the 18th century in Russia. In colour, his paintings often recall Greuze and Perronneau, and sometimes, by their caustic humour, the French pastelist, La Tour.

**LHERMITTE (Léon Augustin).**—French painter (1844-1925). His painting is rather slight and delicate, but he renders open-air lighting effects admirably.

Among his pictures may be mentioned: — *The Reapers' Reward* (Luxembourg Gallery); *Harvest* (1883); *The Vintage* (Metropolitan Museum); *Haymaking* (1887, Museum of Buffalo); *The Friend of the Humble* (1892, Boston Museum).

**LIANG K'AI.**—Chinese painter active c. 1203. Resigned from the Imperial Academy and became one of the founders of the expressionistic painting adopted by the Ch'an Buddhist painters.

**LIBERALE da VERONA.**—Veronese painter, born probably in 1445; died in 1529. Perhaps a pupil of Vincenzo di Stefano, influenced by Mantegna and the Bellini.

**LIBERI (Pietro).**—Venetian painter, born in Padua, 1605-1687. He travelled a great deal, and studied Michelangelo and Raphael in Rome, Correggio in Parma, and other masters in Germany. He returned and settled in Venice. His masterpiece is the large *Battle of the Dardanelles,* in the Doge's Palace. He also painted religious scenes for the churches of Venice, and mythological subjects (notably figures of Venus after the manner of Titian).

**LIBERTY LIGHTING THE WORLD (Statue of Liberty).**—See Bartholdi.

**LICHFIELD (England).**—*Cathedral,* in the Lancet style except for the unique group of three spires. The spires are Decorated.

**LICINIO (Bernardino).**—Venetian painter. Worked between 1520 and 1544. Born at Poscante, near Bergamo. Pupil of Pordonone. He specialised in portraits, especially family groups. Their serious and powerful simplicity recall Holbein. *The Family of His Brother, Arrigo Licinio,* in the Borghese Gallery of Rome, is composed in the rather cold, solemn manner of the famous Basle picture, the *Wife and Children of Holbein. The Painter's Family* (1524, in Hampton Court) is of the same kind, and so is the portrait of his wife, in the Prado Gallery.

His best religious picture is the *Madonna with Saints,* in the Church of the Frari, Venice.

BIBLIOGRAPHY: Crowe and Cavalcaselle, *History of Painting in North Italy,* ed. Tancred Borenius, Vol. III. London, 1912.

**LIE (Jonas).**—Contemporary American painter. He was born in Norway 29th April 1880, the namesake of an uncle famous as a short-story writer in the last century. His paternal aunt was a famous pianist and as a boy he too wanted to become a musician. However, he began to study drawing under Christian Skredsvig and gradually found himself more interested in the pictorial arts. His father died when the boy was only twelve and he then went to live with his famous uncle in Paris, where he met such noted Norwegians as Bjornson, Ibsen, and Grieg. He attended a small art school there for a time, but the next year joined his mother and sisters in New York. After his graduation from the Ethical Culture School in 1897 he secured a position as a designer of textiles, continuing in that profession for the next nine years. During that time he attended evening sessions at Cooper Union Institute, the National Academy of Design and later at the Art Students' League. He had a picture accepted for the annual exhibition of the National Academy in 1901 and soon the public began to recognise and approve his work. In 1906 he made a trip back to Norway and followed it with a visit to Paris, where he came under the influence of the brilliant palette of Claude Monet. Upon his return to the United States a greater breadth of style was apparent. Vistas of city streets framed by tall skyscrapers appealed to him, as did views of small boats buffeted by the wind, or the colour of autumn foliage, subjects inspired by trips to the Adirondacks and the Maine coast. In 1913 he visited the Panama Canal, then under course of construction, and brought back bright canvases of the men at work, akin in spirit to the lithographs of Joseph Pennell of the same subject made the previous year. A trip to Utah some years later was made to record the artist's impressions of the industry of a copper mine. Gradually Jonas Lie's status in the field of modern American landscape painting has advanced until today he is in the first rank of those who portray the natural beauties of this country. In 1932 he was appointed to the Art Commission of the City of New York and in 1934 he was elected President of the National Academy of Design. His work is represented in the collections of the Art Institute of Chicago, the Metropolitan Museum of Art and the Musée du Luxembourg in Paris.

BIBLIOGRAPHY: For a complete bibliography see *The Index of Twentieth Century Artists* for August, 1934.

**LIEBERMANN (Max).**—German painter of Berlin, 1847-1936. The chief representative of the modern school which was initiated by Menzel and Leibl. Besides these masters, he was strongly influenced by the French Impressionist paintings in the Munich exhibition of 1879. He later went to Holland, and studied under Degas in Paris. His chief works are: *A Village Street in Holland, Woman with Goats* (Munich), *Bathing Children,* and numerous portraits, which show sincere observation and a faithful rendering of atmosphere and light.

BIBLIOGRAPHY: Hancke, E., *Max Liebermann, sein Leben und seine Werke.* Berlin, 1923.—Scheffler, K., *Max Liebermann.* München, 1923.—Friedländer, M. J., *Max Liebermann.* Berlin, 1924.

**LIÉGE (Belgium).**—The *Cathedral of St. Paul,* founded in 968, was rebuilt in 1280 in the Gothic style. The nave was not finished until 1528. Originally, an abbey church, it only became a Cathedral in 1802.

The *Church of St. Barthélémy* contains an early bronze baptismal font with remarkable reliefs.

*St. Jacques* is a splendid building in the flamboyant Gothic style, with three aisles, built in 1016, but transformed about 1522-28. The west front dates from the 12th century.

**LIESBORN (Master of).**—German painter of the second half of the 15th century, whose chief work was the high-altar of the Abbey of Liesborn (one part in London, and the other part in Münster). The artist shows a tender idealism, and a precise technique in the rendering of details. School of Westphalia.

LIÉGE: BAPTISMAL FONT OF THE CHURCH OF ST. BARTHÉLÉMY.

BIBLIOGRAPHY: Ehrenberger, *Beiträge zur Westphaelischen Kunstgeschichte.* Münster.

**LIGORIO (Pietro).**—Italian architect, born in Naples, and worked chiefly in Rome. Died 1580. He built the charming Casino of Pope Pius IV, called the Villa Pia (1560), in the middle of the Vatican Gardens. He there used Greek and Roman reliefs. His chief work was the creation of the *Villa d'Este* at Tivoli, for Cardinal Ippolito d'Este (1549).

See Pl. 7, Vol. II.

**LIGOZZI (Jacopo).**—Venetian painter, 1543-1627. Called to Florence by the Grand Duke Ferdinand II, he adopted the Tuscan style.

**LI KUNG-LIN, also known as LI LUNG-MIEN (c. 1040-1106).**—One of the leading Chinese painters of the early Sung period. Famous for his early horse paintings and paintings of Buddhist subjects.

See China—Art.

**LIMBOURG (Pol, Hermann and Hannequin de).**—Three brothers, originally from Limbourg. Miniaturists, of the 15th century. They worked for the Duc de Berry. It appears that, of the three brothers, Pol de Limbourg was the most gifted. The chief work of the brothers is the famous manuscript known as *Les Très Riches Heures du Duc de Berry* (Chantilly), the finest of those illustrated calendars which were so popular in the 15th century. There they painted snow scenes, springtime meadows, harvests, and in all these landscapes are seen little figures of peasants, lords, and huntsmen. They are painted with a strong sense of the picturesque and of reality. *Les Très Riches Heures* were not finished by the Limbourgs. The death of the Duc de Berry (1416) interrupted the work, which was finished later by Jean Colombe.

See Pl. 58, Vol. I.

BIBLIOGRAPHY: P. Durrieux, Chantilly, *Les Très Riches Heures du Duc de Berry.* Paris, 1904.—G. Hulin, *Les Très Riches Heures de Jean de France, Duc de Berry par Pol*

# LATE FLEMISH PRIMITIVES

*Before it died out in the second half of the fifteenth century, the school of Bruges brought forth two painters of Gothic mysticism, Memling and his pupil Gerard David. Memling left charming pictures in which we see the charm and elegance of the city of Bruges. David was also an ambitious and stirring portraitist; he, however, was in the habit of painting more dramatic compositions.*

MEMLING: PAINTINGS FROM THE SHRINE OF ST. URSULA. HOSPITAL OF ST. JOHN, BRUGES.

THE ARRIVAL AT COLOGNE. THE ARRIVAL AT BASEL. THE ARRIVAL AT ROME. THE RETURN, THE EMBARKATION AT BASEL. THE MASSACRE OF ST. URSULA'S COMPANIONS. THE DEATH OF ST. URSULA. *(Photo by Bruckmann.)*

H. MEMLING: THE VIRGIN. BRUGES. *(Photo by Hachette.)*

H. MEMLING: THE MYSTIC MARRIAGE OF ST. CATHERINE. BRUGES. *(Photo by Hanfstaengl.)*

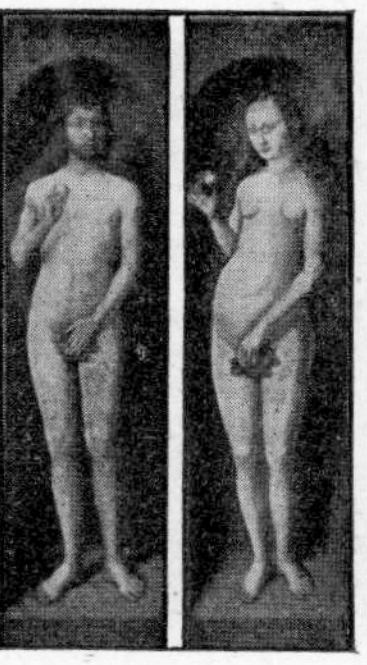

MEMLING: ADAM AND EVE. VIENNA. *(Photo by Löwy.)*

MEMLING: THE MADONNA OF SIR JOHN DONNE. *(Photo by Bruckmann.)*

H. MEMLING: PORTRAIT OF MARTIN VAN NIEUWENHOVE. *(Photo by Hachette.)*

GERARD DAVID: CAMBYSES AND SEMIRAMIS. BRUGES. *(Photo by Daled.)*

GERARD DAVID: MADONNA AND SAINTS. MUSEUM OF ROUEN. *(Photo by Leniept.)*

GERARD DAVID: THE BAPTISM OF CHRIST. BRUGES. *(Photo by Bruckmann.)*

MATSYS: THE FAMILY OF THE VIRGIN. BRUSSELS. *(Photo by Hanfstaengl.)*

MATSYS: THE BANKER AND HIS WIFE. LOUVRE. *(Photo by Hachette.)*

MATSYS: THE ENTOMBMENT. MUSEUM OF ANTWERP. *(Photo by G. Hermans.)*

## Quentin Matsys

At the beginning of the sixteenth century, the school of Bruges began to decline and Antwerp which inherited its prosperity became the principal centre of Flemish painting. Quentin Matsys started this school which was to last to the time of Rubens.

# SPANISH PRIMITIVES

*Under Arab domination Spain for a long time remained an oriental province. Christianity, while repulsing Islam, introduced there her own art in its successive forms. From the twelfth to the sixteenth century in the peninsula, Romanesque art, Gothic art, realism, flamboyance and finally the Renaissance styles followed one another. The Spanish accent always persisted, easily recognisable in these successive art forms which Christian Europe gave to the kingdom wrested from the control of the Arabs.*

AVILA: DETAIL OF THE WEST PORTAL OF SAN VICENTE. *(Photo by Lévy.)*

SANTIAGO DE COMPOSTELA: STATUES OF THE PORCH OF THE CATHEDRAL. *(Photo by Dieulafoy.)*

CATHEDRAL OF LEÓN: PARADISE. *(Photo by Dieulafoy.)*

LEÓN CATHEDRAL: ROYAL FIGURE. *(Photo by Dieulafoy.)*

TARRAGONA CATHEDRAL: THE VIRGIN. *(Photo by Dieulafoy.)*

## Romanesque and Gothic Sculpture

The same evolution is followed in Spanish sculpture as in French art; the same archaic rigidity during the Romanesque period and the same influence of Byzantine painting upon the first statues. During the Middle Ages, the arts reveal an extraordinary association of style between the two countries.

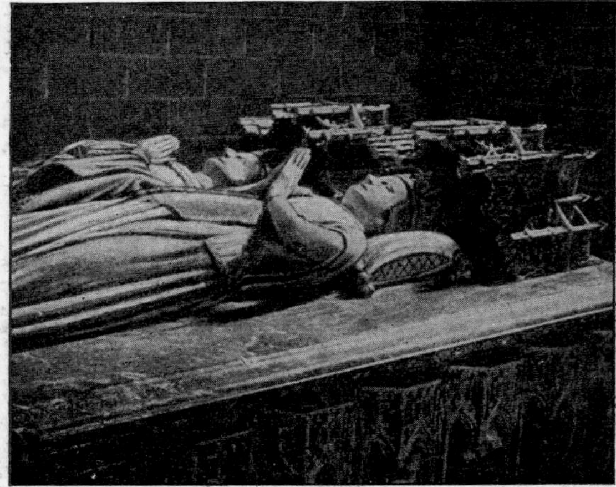

TOMB OF DON CARLOS THE NOBLE (DETAIL). PAMPLONA. *(Photo by Dieulafoy.)*

GIL DE SILOÉ: TOMB OF DON JUAN DE PADILLA. MUSEUM OF BURGOS. *(Photo by Lévy.)*

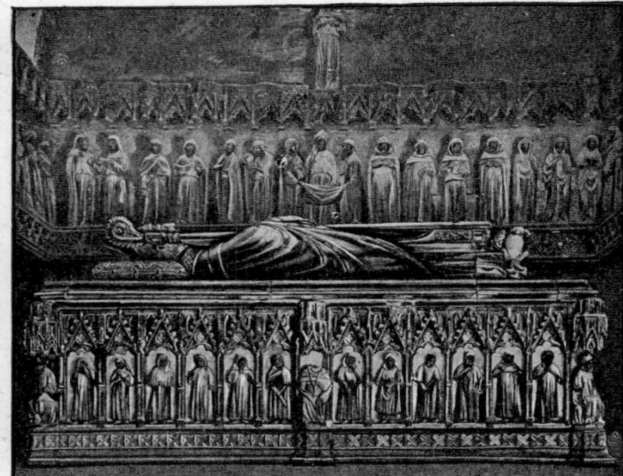

TOMB OF LOPE DE LUNA. LA SEO OF SARAGOSSA. *(Photo by Lacoste.)*

## Gothic Tombs

The great Spanish churches have preserved in their chapels a large number of beautiful tombs from the fifteenth and the sixteenth centuries. These monuments always show parallelism with those of the northern countries. Furthermore, documents show that Flemish sculptors went to Spain, and in return, Spanish names are encountered among the stone carvers who worked in France, particularly in Burgundy.

VERGÓS: DETAIL OF A DESTROYED RETABLE OF BARCELONA. *(Photo by Thomas.)*

LUIS DALMAU: RETABLE OF THE COUNCILORS. MUSEUM OF FINE ARTS, BARCELONA. *(Photo by Institut d'Estudis catalans.)*

NUNO GONÇALVES: TRIPTYCH OF ST. VINCENT. LISBON.

## Painters of the Fifteenth Century

Spain has also preserved a large number of retables of the fifteenth century, painted in oil on wood panels. The most beautiful show a curious resemblance to Flemish painting, particularly to that of Jan van Eyck. It is known that van Eyck made a journey to Portugal. Other Flemish artists may have established themselves in Spain. The Prado contains a number of panels in the Flemish style. The celebrated retable by Dalmau, at Barcelona, shows Flemish traces.

*de Limbourg et ses frères.* Ghent, 1903.

**LIMBURG (Germany).**—*Cathedral,* built 1881-1230. On a plan of the early 11th century, Limburg-on-the-Lahn is transitional from Romanesque to Gothic. The clerestory openings are round-headed, as in Romanesque, and the sex-partite vaults are also Romanesque in character, having heavy transverse ribs and no wall ribs. The four storey interior recalls Novon, in France. There are seven towers on the exterior.

**LIMOGES.**—See Enamel; Monvaerni.

**LIMOSIN.**—See Leonard Limosin.

**LIMOUSIN.**—Former province of France, corresponding roughly to the present arrondissements of Limoges and Saint Yrien in Haute-Vienne and part of the arrondissements of Brive, Tulle, and Ussel in Corrèze.

**LINCOLN (England).**—One of the most distinguished of English cathedrals, 1185-1314. Begun in the Lancet style, it is an archiepiscopal cross in plan, and is like Canterbury, save in its possession of a rectangular choir. The façade is a screen cutting off the lower half of the two western towers. The lantern, 270 feet high, is the tallest in England. Inside, the "Angel Choir" (1256) is perhaps the best known example of the Decorated style of English Gothic architecture.

Bibliography: F. Bond, *Cathedrals of England and Wales.* England, 1912.

Lincoln: The Cathedral.

**LINDSAY (Sir Coutts).**—See Burne-Jones.

**LINTEL.**—Horizontal beam spanning an opening (as a door) and supporting a superstructure.

**LION GATE.**—See Mycenæ.

**LINTOTT (Edward Barnard).**—Contemporary English painter. He was born in London, England, on December 11, 1875. He studied art at the Académie Julian in Paris under Jean Paul Laurens and Benjamin Constant. He was also a pupil at the École des Beaux-Arts and received some instruction from M. E. Cuyer, the anatomy teacher. During the World War he acted as secretary to the British Ambassador to Russia, Sir George Buchanan, and was afterward connected with other political posts. For several years he was the librarian of the Royal Academy and he was the Art Adviser of the *London Times* in which capacity he was instrumental in the formation of the Commission of Art. At the time of the war he helped to raise a fund to assist Belgian refugee artists and later for seven years was the Examiner in Art to the English Board of Education. For the last six years Mr. Lintott has been a resident of the United States, living and painting in and around New York City.

The subjects of his paintings include portraits, flower studies, figure pieces, landscapes and several examples of still life. His portraits are characterized by a harmony of color, well planned designs, and an excellent rendering of the physical features with some attempt at psychological analysis. Among the notables whom he has painted are Leslie Howard, Lady Diana Duff Cooper, Chester Dale and Mrs. Cornelius V. Whitney. He has been particularly successful in his flower compositions. His subject matter covers a wide range. All is treated with a simplicity and clarity in which the harmony of composition plays a leading rôle. Examples of his work are to be found in the British Museum, the Victoria and Albert Museum, the Tate Gallery, London, and in the museums of Ghent, Aberdeen, Brooklyn, Boston and Sydney, Australia.

Bibliography: E. Barnard Lintott, *The Art of Water Colour Painting,* 1926.—E. Barnard Lintott, *Tools and Materials: Water Color Painting, American Magazine of Art,* April, 1935.

**LIPPI (Filippino).** — Florentine painter, son of Fra Filippo Lippi and pupil of Botticelli; born in 1457, he was but twelve years old when his father died, and was brought up at Prato.

In the register of the Compagnia di S. Luca of 1472, Filippino is listed as working with Botticelli. In 1478, on attaining his majority, he had to defend himself against the dishonest pretensions of Fra Diamante to a house Filippino had inherited. His famous early picture, the *Apparition of the Virgin to St. Bernard,* in the Badia in Florence, was painted in 1480; in 1482 he was working in the Priors' Room, Palazzo della Signoria, on a fresco the commission for which had originally been given to Perugino. Filippino's masterpiece was begun in 1484, in which year he was entrusted with the completion of the fresco decoration of the Brancacci Chapel, left unfinished over half a century before by Masolino and Masaccio. In this chapel Filippino executed part of the fresco of the *Raising of the King's Son;* the *Angel Delivering Peter; Paul Visiting Peter in Prison; Peter and Paul before the Proconsul;* the *Martyrdom of Peter.* From 1485-86 dates the large *Virgin and Saints* for the Palazzo della Signoria, now in the Uffizi (this order had been given first to Piero Pollaiuolo, then to Leonardo, who made a drawing for it). In 1487, Filippino received the commission for the frescoes in the Strozzi Chapel, Sta. Maria Novella; and in 1489 he wrote Filippo Strozzi asking him to have patience with him for his slow progress. Filippo Strozzi, who died in 1491, made arrangements for the continuance of the decoration in his will; and the frescoes were completed and signed in 1502. The delay for which Filippino apologized was probably due to his having under way at the same time another important fresco commission, the decorations (1489-1493) of the Caraffa Chapel (commission from Cardinal Oliviero Caraffa) in Sta. Maria sopra Minerva, Rome. In 1496 he painted the *Adoration of the Magi* from S. Donato, now in the Uffizi; and in 1497 the dated *Meeting of Joachim and Anne* in Copenhagen. In the latter year Filippino was requested to estimate the value of a fresco by Baldovinetti in Sta. Trinità. The frescoed tabernacle on a street corner in Prato was made in 1498; in the same year Filippino received the order for a large panel for the council room of the Palazzo Pubblico, which he did not undertake, and was appointed a member of a council to discuss the restoration of the cupola of the Duomo of Florence, which had been struck by lightning. *The Mystic Marriage of St. Catherine* in S. Domenico, Bologna, was painted in 1501. In 1503 Filippino received an invitation from the King of Hungary to visit him but did not accept it, sending instead two panels, one of which he refers to in his will of this year as a Madonna. Also in 1503 he painted the *Sebastian and Saints* in the Palazzo Bianco, Genoa; and the *Madonna* in Prato which had been ordered in 1501. He died in 1504.

Lippi (Filippino): Study for two prophets. (Facsimile of a drawing, École des Beaux-Arts, Paris.)

Bibliography: Vasari-Milanesi, III.—Guasti, *I quadri d. Gall. d. Prato,* 1888.—Horne, *Sandro Botticelli,* 31, 107, 346.—E. Müntz, Arch. stor. dell'arte, 1889, p. 484.—Mesnil, Rivista d'arte, 1906.—Crowe and Cavalcaselle, Douglas ed., IV; Italian ed., VII.—J. B. Supino, *Les deux Lippi,* 1904.—P. G. Konody, *Filippino Lippi,* 1908.—A. Venturi, *Storia d. arte ital.,* VII, I, 1911.—Berenson, *Drawings of Florentine Painters,* 1903, I, 70ff, 75ff.—Van Marle, *Italian Schools,* XII, 1931, 291ff.

**LIPPI (Fra Filippo).**—Florentine painter, born c. 1406; died 1469. A pupil of Lorenzo Monaco, influenced by Masaccio and Fra Angelico.

Fra Filippo took his monastic vows in 1421, and in 1430 he is listed in the convent registers as a painter. A document of 1434 indicates that at that time he was in Padua, and the Anonimo Morelliano states that he executed pictures in S. Antonio, Padua, and collaborated with Niccolò Pizzolo and Ansuino da Forlì in the Chapel of the Podestà, information which is not substantiated by further evidence. In 1437 he is back in Florence and is commissioned by the corporation of Or San Michele to paint a *Madonna* for the Barbadori Chapel in Sto. Spirito. Also of 1437 is the extant *Madonna* of Corneto Tarquinia. In 1438 Lippi writes to Piero de' Medici complaining about the smallness of his income and mentioning that he has six nieces to marry—a plaint which evidently produced results for in 1442 he receives from the Pope, with the influence of the Medici, the "Commenda" from the parish church of S. Quirico at Legnaia, for life. The *Coronation of the Virgin* now in the Uffizi was commissioned for Sant'Ambrogio in 1441 and was paid for in 1447; and between 1446 and 1447 Fra Filippo also executed two panels, the *Annunciation* and *St. Bernard,* for the Palazzo Pubblico. In 1450 he became chaplain at S. Niccolò de' Frieri, Florence, but in the same year he forges the signature of his assistant, Giovanni di Francesco della Cervelliera, on a receipt for money which he, Lippi, owed him, and was imprisoned and tortured.

Charged to execute a painting for a chapel in S. Domenico, Perugia, in 1451, Fra Filippo was sued when it was found that he had turned this work over to a pupil. The next year he was busy at frescoes in the Pieve at Prato, where he was assisted by Fra Diamante; at this same time Leonardo di Bartolommeo Bartolini demands an indemnity if the picture he had ordered, a tondo, is not finished within four months. In 1453, Lippi receives payment for the *Madonna* now in the Prato Gallery, from the Ospedale del Ceppo, and is sued by Lorenzo de' Manetti over the non-execution of a *St. Jerome* he had ordered. In 1454 he is mentioned as one of three experts who give opinions on the frescoes of Bonfigli at Perugia; and he buys a house in Prato. Retribution overtakes Fra Filippo for the irregularity of his life when in 1455 he is deprived of his ecclesiastical benefices; and is followed by his crowning irregularity when in 1456 he abducts the nun, Lucrezia Buti, from the Convent of Sta. Margherita of Prato. Of this union two children were born: Filippino, 1461, and Alessandra, 1465. Protracted delays in the execution of the Prato frescoes called down upon him reproaches, protests, and threats. They were finally finished before 1464. In 1457 Lippi executed for Giovanni de' Medici a picture intended for the King of Naples. The two lateral panels are now in the Cook Collection, Richmond. In the same year he was back in Prato to do an altarpiece for the Servi Convent, completed in 1468. The frescoes at Spoleto, Fra Filippo's last commission, in the execution of which he was assisted by Fra Diamante, were left unfinished at the time of his death in 1469.

Fra Filippo was the master of a large group of painters and exercised a profound influence upon the development of the Florentine school. Having been trained in the lineal and lyrical style of Lorenzo Monaco, he early came under the influence of Masaccio whose frescoes decorated the church of the monastery in which he grew up. The overwhelming impact of Masaccio's forms upon a painter related by nature and schooling to another tradition is very obvious in the *Corneto Madonna.* This influence, however, wanes as Fra Filippo develops his own way of seeing, and the strained plasticity and squatness of form of the early pictures gives way to the attenuated delicacy of his Nativities and the interweaving line that was to be used so exquisitely by his pupil, Botticelli. In the Prato frescoes Lippi makes his last effort to attain Masaccio's monumentality, but it was a tradition imposed upon him, not the outgrowth of his own conviction. His designs for the frescoes at Spoleto, and those parts actually executed by him, indicate that he had discarded it, as antipathetic to his style.

Bibliography: Vasari-Milanesi, II.—G. Milanesi, *Fra Filippo Lippi*, L'Arte, 1877, Dec., 1878, Jan.—Crowe and Cavalcaselle, Douglas, ed., IV.—J. B. Supino, *Les deux Lippi*. Florence, 1904.—H. Mendelssohn, *Fra Filippo Lippi*, Berlin, 1909 (with documents).—Venturi, *Storia d. arte ital.*, VII, I, 1911.—Van Marle, *Italian Schools*, etc., X, 1928.—Berenson, *Fra Angelico, Fra Filippo e la cronologia*, Bollettino d'arte, July, August, 1932.

**LIPPO di DALMASIO (Dalmasio Scannabecchi).**—Painter of Bologna, born 1352; active until 1410. Formed by Vitale and Andrea da Bologna.

In 1376 Lippo painted two polyptychs, one in the parish church of Borgo Panicale, the other in that of Castel S. Pietro dell' Emilia; in 1388 the signed *Madonna of the Casa Binarini*. A signed *Madonna and Child* is in the National Gallery, London, from the Palazzo Ercolani in Bologna, and a small *Coronation* is in the Bologna Pinateca.

Bibliography: Vasari-Milanesi, II.—Crowe and Cavalcaselle, Douglas ed., III.—Venturi, *Storia, etc.* V, 1906.—L. Frati, *Dalmasio e Lippo de Scannabecchi* (Atti e Mem. della R. Dep. di St. P. per le prov. di Romagna, 3 Serie, Vol. 27). Bologna, 1910.—E. Manceri, *Lippo Dalmasio* (Il commune di Bologna, Feb. 1933, No. 2, 4).

**LIPPO MEMMI.**—See Memmi.

**LIPPO VANNI.**—See Vanni.

**LISBON.**—The *Cathedral of Santa Maria* is the oldest religious building in Lisbon. It was an old mosque, transformed in 1150. After an earthquake in 1344, most of the edifice was rebuilt. The existing west front was built in 1380. The dome was destroyed by an earthquake in 1755.

Lisbon: The Arsenal.

The *Castello de Sâo Jorge* (Fortress of St. George), formerly the *Castello dos Mouros*, was transformed into a royal residence by Alphonse III (died 1279). There still remains from the time of the Moors, a part of the walls, and the three towers of Ulysses, Menagem and Albaram.

*Cintra* (28 kilometres from Lisbon).—The finest building in Portugal, which still retains features recalling the distant Moslem domination, is the Palace of Cintra, which was begun about the end of the 14th century and finished at the beginning of the 16th. Externally, the two conical chimneys of the kitchen, visible from far off, the Moorish horseshoe arches, and the crenellated Arabic cornice, are especially striking. The rich adornment of the walls with ceramic, and the concave wooden ceilings of the interior are a heritage from the Moorish period.

Bibliography: Brito Aranha, *Bibliographie des Ouvrages portugais pour servir à l'étude des villes et monuments du Portugal*. Lisbon, 1900.—Walter Crum Watson, *Portuguese Architecture*. London, 1908.—E. Bertaux, *L'Art en Espagne et au Portugal* (in *l'Histoire générale de l'Art publiée*, by André Michel).—M. Dieulafoy, *Spain and Portugal*. Ars Una Series.

**LISIEUX (France).** — The *Church of St. Pierre*, the old Cathedral, is an imposing building of the 12th and 13th centuries.

The town, with its curious old Norman houses, is very picturesque.

See Pl. 52, Vol. I.

**LI SSU-HSUN.**—Chinese painter, born c. 650, died 716 or 720. One of the most important landscape painters of China, he is considered the founder of the Northern School of landscape painting. He created panoramic landscapes filled with lyrical detail and drawn in a fine line and with bright colors of green, blue, and gold. None of his works is extant and his style is known through copies and descriptions. One of the best copies is *Landscape with Sages* (Freer Gallery of Art, Washington, D. C.).

**LITHOGRAPHY.** — Lithography is the art of reproducing on paper a drawing executed on special stone, called "lithographic stone," which is a very fine, close limestone. After the stone has been prepared to make its surface quite smooth, the drawing is traced on it with a pencil or with a pen dipped in specially prepared ink. Then the stone is washed with a liquid which attacks it, except in those parts which have been touched with the pencil or special ink. These parts are then left in slight relief. The stone is then placed in a press, damped with ink, which spreads on the drawing in relief. Then, by placing successively sheets of paper on this stone, as many proofs can be taken as are desired. The stone wears, however, and will hardly yield more than 600 to 800 good proofs. The later ones are less precise. Lithography in colour, or chromolithography, is much used. Lithography was invented by the German, Aloys Senefelder, of Munich, who discovered this process in 1793. Among the most famous lithographers are Charlet, Raffet, Gavarni, and Daumier.

**LOCHES (Indre-et-Loire).**—Old 11th century château, built, it is said, by Foulque Nerra, count of Anjou. It has a formidable square keep. Under Henri II Plantagenet and Philippe Auguste it was surrounded by a rampart with bastions, which were reinforced under Louis XI. The "Tour du Martelet," now a prison, has deep dungeons in which Ludovico il Moro was imprisoned. In the 15th century, the French kings left this gloomy feudal castle for the charming Gothic building, known as the Logis du Roi. In the tower of the façade is the tomb of Agnes Sorel, and in another part of the Logis is the oratory of Anne de Bretagne, with charming 15th century carvings.

Loches: The Château and the Collegiate Church of St. Ours.

**LOCHNER (Stephan).**—German painter, of Swabian origin, who painted in Cologne after about 1440. He painted a large altarpiece for the Church of St. Lawrence, of which the central panel represents a Last Judgment (Cologne Museum); the wings are in the Museums of Frankfort (*Martyrdom of the Apostles*) and Munich (groups of *Saints*). His other works are: *The Virgin with a Violet* (Cologne Seminary), painted for Elsa de Reichenstein, foundress of the Convent of St. Cecilia; the *Nativity* (Saxe-Altenburg Collection); the *Dombild* (Cologne Cathedral), his masterpiece, painted between 1430 and 1440 for the Chapel of the Town Hall. The central part of this altarpiece represents the Adoration of the Magi; on the left wing, St. Ursula, her companions and her betrothed; on the right wing, St. Gereon and the Theban legion; on the exterior of the wings is a charming *Annunciation*. He also painted the *Madonna of the Rosebush* (Cologne Museum), a charming idyll, in the midst of roses and angel musicians; the *Presentation at the Temple*, 1447 (Darmstadt Museum); and two altar wings representing the Apostles and the Fathers of the Church (National Gallery, and Cologne Museum). Lochner died in 1451, probably of the plague.

His Madonnas are the tenderest of the Cologne school, with soft complexions, and slender virginal figures. His colour is at once soft and brilliant. But through this idealism, one feels already the influence of Netherlandish realism in the careful rendering of details, materials and embroideries. Certain figures might almost be portraits.

See Pl. 8, Vol. I; Pl. 3, Vol. II.

Bibliography: Aldenhoven, *Geschichte der Kölner Malerschule*. Lübeck, 1902.—Förster, Otto H., *Die Kölnische Malerei von Meister Wilhelm bis Stefan Lochner*. Köln, 1923.—Reiners, H., *Die Kölner Malerschule*. München-Gladbach, 1925.

**LOMAZZO (Giovanni Paolo).**—Milanese painter, 1538-1600. His style was mannered, but rather lively. At the end of his life he became blind, and he then wrote books on the art of painting—in 1584, *Trattato dell'Arte della pittura, scultura ed architettura*, and, in 1590, *L'Idea del Tempio della pittura*. He studied the proportions of the human body, and facial expression under the influence of different passions; also colours, considered from a moral and philosophic point of view, etc.

**LOMBARD (Lambert).**—Flemish painter, 1506-1566. Born in Liége, worked first in Antwerp, then in Middelbourg and in Italy. He touched many branches of study—letters, archæology, painting, engraving. The only one of his paintings that has come down to us is the *Sacrifice of the Pascal Lamb* (Liége) (an elegant but cold work) and a certain number of ink drawings.

Bibliography: Goldschmidt, A., *Jahrbuch der preuss. Kunstsammlungen*, XL. 1919.—Friedländer, M. J., *Altniederländische Malerei*, Vol. 13.

**— (Pierre).**—French engraver, 1612-1682. Pupil of Simon Vouet. He made engravings from the pictures of Raphael, Titian and Poussin.

**LOMBARDI (Alfonso Cittadella).**—Italian sculptor, 1497-1537. He was the son of one Lucca, who settled in Ferrara in 1496. He came with his father to Bologna while still young and passed there the greater part of his life.

His *Pietà* in S. Giovanni Battista, Ferrara, exists only in fragments. A large group of the *Death of the Virgin*, 1419-22, is in Santa Maria della Vita, Bologna. His bust of *St. Hyacinth* is in San Domenico, in Ferrara. For the doors of San Petronio, Bologna, he made a *Resurrection of Christ* (1526), in the lunette of the left doorway.

**LOMBARDO (Antonio and Tullio).**—Venetian architects and sculptors of the end of the 15th century and beginning of the 16th. Sons of Pietro Lombardo, with whom they worked from their childhood. Together they continued his style, and made some fine tombs in Venice. They also worked in the Church of the Santo, Padua, and in the Cathedral of Treviso. Antonio died young probably in 1516. Tullio continued, alone, to carry out vast architectural works, the interior of San Salvatore, the Palazzo Dario and Manzoni with delightful pilasters, and a great many carvings.

**— (Pietro).**—Italian architect and sculptor of Carona, born c. 1435, died 1515. One of the chief Venetian architects and sculptors of his period. In spite of his name and origin, there are hardly any works by him in Lombardy.

In Venice, where he worked from 1474, the Palaces of Vendramin Calergi and Gussoni, at San Leo, the Church of San Giobbio, the interior courtyard of the Scuola di San Giovanni Evangelista, the tombs of the Doges Pietro Mocenigo and Marcello, in the Church of San Giovanni e Paolo, sufficed to make him famous. He built the little Church of Santa Maria dei Miracoli—one of the most charming works of the Renaissance.

In 1482, Pietro Lombardo was called to Ravenna by Bernardo Bembo. In 1485, he worked in the Cathedral of Treviso, and in 1490 for the Scuola di San Marco, in Venice. He was summoned to Mantua in 1495 by Francesco Gonzaga to make a chapel there. It was not finished in spite of the numerous statues that he made for it. In 1498, he became chief of the building of the Doge's Palace, Venice. He had not time to carry out his elaborate plans himself, and was assisted by his sons, Antonio and Tullio, and by numerous pupils.

**LONDON.**—Temple Church, 1185. A typical Anglo-Norman Templar church with a round nave surrounded by an arcade. The type was due to the Crusades, for the prototype was the Church of the Holy Sepulchre, Jerusalem. Tombs of knights of the order are in the church.

*Westminster Abbey.* Founded 960 by St. Dunstan and rebuilt in the middle of the eleventh century, the Abbey underwent so many successive demolitions and reconstructions that the present church is now largely 13th century Gothic. It is the most French of English churches of Cathedral size, being tall in proportion and possessing a complete system of flying buttresses and the only fully developed chevet in England. The north transept has three portals with a rose window above and is clearly derived from Reims, the coronation church of France. Of the many tombs and chapels which the Abbey has accreted through the centuries the most notable is the Chapel of Henry VII on the extreme east, built 1502-1513 in the Perpendicular Gothic style. It has extraordinary pendant vaults and great elaboration of decoration. The chapel exterior has buttresses with traceried panels. Wren did the towers in the 17th century.

*Whitehall.* See Inigo Jones.

*Parish Churches.* See Sir Christopher Wren.

*St. Paul's Cathedral,* 1672-1710. One of the great cathedrals of Europe and Sir Christopher Wren's masterpiece. He originally intended St. Paul's to be a Greek cross in plan but was forced by the clergy to change to a Latin cross. The Cathedral has a colonnaded two storey pedimented front between towers of baroque design. The nave is covered by a succession of domical vaults. At the crossing is a huge dome in two shells, the outer shell being of wood covered with lead; the huge stone lantern is carried not on this outer dome but on a hidden brick cone a hundred feet in height built between the two shells. Equally deceptive is the treatment of the exterior flank, which apparently is in two storeys; actually the second storey is a screen concealing the flying buttresses used to abut the vaults. The exterior dome is paneled and gains added monumentality through being imposed on a colonnaded drum, a treatment planned for St. Peter's by Bramante, but never executed. (See Sir Christopher Wren.)

*British Museum.* See Smirke.

*Buckingham Palace.* See John Nash.

*Houses of Parliament.* See Sir Charles Barry and A. W. N. Pugin.

*Crystal Palace.* See Paxton.

LONDON: BRIDGE ON THE THAMES.

BIBLIOGRAPHY: F. Bond. *Westminster Abbey.* London, 1909.

**LONGHENA (Baldassare).**—Venetian architect, 1604-1682, author of the triumphantly baroque. *S. Maria della Salute,* a church central in plan with a large dome buttressed by huge consoles with statues atop.

**LONGHI (Alessandro).**—Italian painter and engraver. Born in Venice in 1733, died in 1813. He was the son of the painter Pietro Longhi, and was a pupil of Nogari. He wrote a *Compendio delle vite dei famosi pittori Veneziani di questo secolo* (1763).

**— (Luca).**—Of Ravenna. Painter (1507-1580), who spread the influence of Raphael. *Virgin between Saints* (Brera Gallery).

**— (Pietro).**—Venetian painter (1702-1785). Pupil of Balestra and of Crespi. He painted the everyday life of well-to-do Venetians—in the street, at the barber's, at the dancing class. These people play, eat, and show off their satin clothes and their good manners, with no thought of the sadness and tragedy of life. They call to mind the vivacity and spirit of Goldoni's characters. These pictures are to be found chiefly in Venice, in Bergano and in London. One picture shows The Dentist, in his spectacles and cotton cap, solemnly torturing his pretty little patient; an old man with a splendid white beard takes notes, and on shelves are arrayed the finest of chemist's jars. Another picture shows the painter Longhi himself painting the portrait of a delicate person lost in the finery of her immense crinoline.

BIBLIOGRAPHY: Aldo Ravà, *Pietro Longhi.* Florence, 1923.—O. Uzanni, *Pietro Longhi.* Paris, 1925.

**LONGPONT (Aisne, France).**—Ruins of a Cistercian monastery, of which parts of the church remain.

**LORENZETTI (Ambrogio).**—Sienese painter, the brother, perhaps younger, of Pietro Lorenzetti.

The discovery of the *Madonna Enthroned* of 1319 at S. Angiolo at Vico l'Abate, near Florence, confirms the supposition that Ambrogio's earliest activity was in Florence. In 1324, he sells property at Siena. The chronicler Tizio states that the frescoes in S. Francesco, Siena, were executed by Ambrogio in 1331. Ghiberti mentions a signed and dated panel of 1332 in S. Procolo, Florence, also scenes from the *Life of St. Nicholas.* In 1335 Ambrogio decorated Sta. Margherita, Cortona, of which nothing remains; in the same year he restored a *Madonna* in the Duomo of Siena and worked with Pietro on the façade of the Ospedale della Scala. From 1337 to 1339 there are records of ten payments, perhaps for the extant frescoes in the Palazzo Pubblico, representing *Good and Bad Government.* In the last year he was paid for an *Angel* and candlesticks to stand in front of the Virgin's altar in the Duomo. In 1340 he receives payment for an altarpiece. From 1342 is the signed and dated *Presentation in the Temple* in the Uffizi, painted for the Spedaletto of Monna Agnesa; and from 1344 the *Annunciation* in the Academy, painted for the Palazzo Pubblico. In this year he was asked to execute a cosmographical chart in the Palazzo Pubblico. In 1345 he is paid for work in the Camera dei Signori Nove, which is not preserved. He is last mentioned in 1347 as speaking in the Council in Siena.

BIBLIOGRAPHY: Vasari-Milanesi, I. —Milanesi, *Doc. . . . senese.*—A. L. von Meyenberg, *Ambrogio Lorenzetti.* Zurich, 1903.—L. Gielly, *Les trécentistes siennois: Ambrogio Lorenzetti,* Revue de l'art ancien et moderne, 1912.—De Nicola, *Il soggiorno fiorentino di Ambrogio Lorenzetti,* Bollettino d'Arte del Ministero della Pubbl. Istr., 1922.—Van Marle, *Italian Schools, etc.* II, 1924.

**— (Pietro).**—Sienese painter and brother of Ambrogio; active 1305, in which year he was an artist of established reputation, until 1348.

In the year 1305 is recorded a document of payment for a painting made for the Council of Nine, Siena; and in 1320 a contract with Guido Tarlati, Bishop of Arezzo for an altarpiece for the Pieve at Arezzo, still extant. The document of payment for the *Madonna and Saints* now in the Opera del Duomo of Siena is of 1326, and the signed *Madonna and Two Saints* at Sant' Ansano in Dofana of 1328. Two parts of the predella of this last mentioned altarpiece are in the Academy, Siena, representing scenes from the *History of the Carmelites.* In 1329 mention is made of a panel for the monks of Sta. Maria del Carmine in Siena, a *Madonna, St. Nicholas, Apostles, Saints,* etc., and of an altarpiece for the Church of the Umiliati at Siena. In 1333 is recorded the document of payment for a fresco in the portal of the Duomo of Siena, which was repainted by Luca di Tommè, and of which nothing remains. In 1335 Pietro received an advance on the payment for a panel of *St. Savinus,* with scenes; and of this year were the lost frescoes, scenes from the *Life of the Virgin,* in the Ospedale della Scala, probably destroyed in 1720. In 1337 he executed an altarpiece for the Church of S. Martino at Siena. The *Madonna* for San Francesco at Pistoia, now in the Uffizi, is signed and dated 1340. The *Birth of the Virgin* in the Opera del Duomo, Siena, is signed and dated 1342, and in this year Pietro is mentioned as buying property. In 1344 his wife sells property.

The diptych at Altenburg is signed by Pietro but not dated. No further exact information is recorded about Pietro's works; a chronology has been prepared by E. T. DeWald in his monograph, cited below, on the basis of style. The most notable of the works generally attributed to him are the frescoes in the Lower Church of St. Francis at Assisi.

BIBLIOGRAPHY: Vasari-Milanesi, I. —Milanesi, *Doc. . . . senese,* I.—Thode, *Studien zur Geschichte der Ital. Kunst des XIV Jahrh.,* Repert. f. Kunstwiss., 1888.—Schubring, Repert. f. Kunstwiss., 1899.—O. Wolff, *Zur Stilbildung der Trecento Malerei.*—Van Marle, *Italian Schools, etc.* II, 1924.—E. T. DeWald, *Pietro Lorenzetti,* 1930.

**LORENZO d'ALESSANDRO da SAN SEVERINO (called Lorenzo da San Severino the Younger to distinguish him from Lorenzo Salimbeni da San Severino—see Salimbeni).**—Umbrian painter, mentioned between 1468 and 1503, influenced by Niccolò da Foligno and by Crivelli. Many works by him are still to be found in Umbria and the Marches.

**LORENZO di CIONE.**—See Ghiberti.

**— di CREDI.**—See Credi.

**— MAITANI (Da Vitale di Lorenzo).**—Sienese sculptor. Born about 1275, died in 1330. One of the chief forerunners of the Renaissance, whose work is both original and beautiful. He worked at Orvieto until his death, except for two chief absences—one to go to Perugia, in 1319, to work on the fountain of the Piazza, and another to go to Siena to give his opinion on the solidity of the Duomo. The bas-reliefs on the façade of Orvieto Cathedral are his masterpiece. He must have directed and designed the whole. On pilasters between the doorways scenes from the Old and New Testaments are represented among leaves and branches. He also carved the *Madonna and Angels* on the lunette of the door, and one other *Madonna* in the Opera del Duomo.

BIBLIOGRAPHY: Luigi Fumi, *Il Duomo d'Orvieto e i suoi restauri.* Rome, 1891.

**— MONACO (Piero di Giovanni before he became a Camaldolese monk).**—Florentine miniature, panel and fresco painter from Siena (according to a document of 1414); born c. 1370; died 1425.

Lorenzo Monaco became underdeacon in the degli Angeli Monastery in 1392, to fill which position he would have had to be at least twenty-one. In 1398-1400 he executed an altar for the Church of Sta. Maria del Carmine. In 1406 he was living outside the Monastery near the Church of S. Bartolo; in 1420 and 1422 he is mentioned as receiving payments for the altarpiece for S. Egidio. In 1421 two of his pupils are mentioned: Giovanni di Bernardo and Giovanni di Francesco.

Lorenzo Monaco exercised a profound influence upon the development of Florentine painting, having introduced into it an art which certainly had its origin in Siena, the musical, lineal Gothic style, with flowing drapery that does not mould the forms, a disregard for plastic space, and an exquisite refinement of physical types. He transmitted this style through Fra Angelico and Fra Filippo to Botticelli and Filippino. The following works by him are authenticated and dated: the 1400 Berlin *Madonna Enthroned* (the inscription may be later); the 1404 Florence, Academy, *Pietà* and the *Empoli triptych*; the 1405 Florence, Berenson Collection, *Humility Madonna;* the triptych of 1406-10 in the Uffizi, a *Madonna and Saints* executed for Monte Oliveto, Benedictine Monastery; the 1408 wings from an altar in the Louvre; the 1409 miniatures in the Codex of that date in the Laurenziana Library; and the 1413 Uffizi *Coronation.* Frescoes by Lorenzo Monaco are in Sta. Trinità, scenes from the *Life of the Virgin;* and in the Chiostro dell' Oblate, Pietà and scenes from the *Passion.* There are additional miniatures by him in the Laurenziana and the Bargello.

BIBLIOGRAPHY: Vasari-Milanesi, II. —Poggi, Supino, Ricci, *Il Bigallo*. Florence, 1905, p. 48.—O. Sirèn, *Don Lorenzo Monaco*. Strassburg, 1905. —D'Ancona, *Miniat. fior.; La miniatura italiana*.

**— di NICCOLÒ GERINI.**—Florentine painter, son of Niccolò di Pietro Gerini.

Lorenzo di Niccolò is mentioned in 1392 as the helper of his father in the work he was executing for Datini in Prato; in 1399-1401 he collaborated with Niccolò di Pietro and Spinello Aretino in the altarpiece of the *Coronation of the Virgin,* now in the Academy, Florence. From 1401 dates the altarpiece at S. Gimignano, signed and dated, with *St. Bartholomew* and scenes; from 1402 the Cortona, S. Domenico, polyptych, painted for S. Marco, Florence, signed and dated; and the *Terenzano altarpiece,* a signed and dated triptych. In 1408, Lorenzo di Niccolò matriculated in the guild of Medici e Speziali and in 1410 in the Compagnia di S. Luca. In 1411 he is last mentioned when he receives payment for repainting frescoes in S. Pietro Maggiore, now lost.

BIBLIOGRAPHY: Vasari-Milanesi, II. —O. Sirèn, *Lorenzo di Niccolò,* L'Arte, VII, 1904; *Don Lorenzo Monaco*. Strassburg, 1905; *Gli affreschi nel Paradiso degli Alberti, Lorenzo di Niccolò e Mariotto di Nardo,* L'Arte, XI, 1908.—Khvoshinsky e Salmi, *I pittori toscani dal XIII al XVI secolo,* II, 1914.

**— DI PIETRO.**—See Vecchietta.

**— and JACOPO da SAN SEVERINO.**—See Salimbeni.

**— VENEZIANO.**—Venetian painter, 1356-79, pupil of Maestro Paolo.

His work includes: Berlin, two fragments of an altarpiece, *SS. Mark and John Baptist;* Bologna, S. Giacomo Maggiore, Cari Chapel, lower half of an ancona, the upper half being by Jacopo di Paolo; Milan, Brera, *Coronation of the Virgin,* of 1368, from the above altarpiece in Bologna; Padua, Pinacoteca, *Madonna Enthroned,* 1372; Venice, Academy, two fragments of an altarpiece, *SS. Peter and Lawrence,* signed; also, altarpiece with eighteen parts in two rows, 1357, from the Church of S. Antonio Abbate in Venice; also, five panels of an altarpiece with, in the middle, the Annunciation and God the Father, 1371, on the sides SS. Gregory, John Baptist, James and Stephen. Attributed to Lorenzo is the *Marriage of St. Catherine* in the Museo Civico Correr, and *Christ Giving the Keys to Peter,* of 1368. In the Vicenza Duomo, Cappella del Parto, is his 1366 *Dormition of the Virgin.*

BIBLIOGRAPHY: Crowe and Cavalcaselle, Douglas ed., III.—A. Venturi, *Storia d. arte ital.,* V, 1907.—Testi, *Storia d. pitt. venez.,* I, 1909. —L. Venturi, *Le origini d. pitt. venez.* I, 1909, II, 1915.

**LORRAIN (Claude Gellée, called).**—French painter, born in 1600. An orphan from the age of twelve, he lived with his elder brother, who was a wood engraver, and resided in Freiburg in Bresgau. He spent a year designing arabesques and grotesques, and then a relation sent him to Rome, where he lived for three or four years. After which, at the end of his resources, Claude went to Naples, where he received lessons from Godefroi Walss, a painter of Cologne, who taught him perspective and architecture. He returned to Rome so poor that he had to join the household of the landscape painter, Augustino Tassi, a pupil of Paul Bril, as much in the capacity of servant as that of pupil. There he lived until the spring of the year

LORRAIN (CLAUDE): SEAPORT AT SUNSET. (Louvre.)

1625, when he went back to his native Lorrain, passing through Venice, Tyrol, Bavaria and Swabia. In Nancy, Claude worked under the direction of De Ruet, until he met with an accident and fell from some scaffolding—a mishap which led to his return to Rome, in 1627. He soon became acquainted with Nicholas Poussin, who had a noble influence on his development. The two artists were neighbours, and foregathered with Valentin, le Guaspre and Jacques Stella.

Lorrain's real master was the sun. He was the first painter who dared to look it in the face and try to paint it as he saw it. He went out into the country at daybreak to see the wonders of the dawn and, in the evening, he returned to watch the twilight. Generally without pencil or paint-box, he simply observed the gradations of shades—yellows passing from orange to vermilion, from vermilion to crimson and violet. His memory retained impressions of light effects and reproduced them faithfully on the canvas. Details of landscape, rocks, humble buildings, etc., drawn with the pen, with washes of Chinese ink or sepia, he generally did from nature. As for the palaces, the colonnades of which make a majestic frame to his harbour scenes, he borrowed their architecture from Vignola and Palladio. His visits to Naples and Venice had given him an opportunity to study the imposing and picturesque ships of his day.

The figures in Lorrain's pictures were rarely painted by him. One of the most remarkable characteristics of Claude's pictures is the extraordinary feeling of distance which they suggest.

Claude soon became exposed to copyists and plagiarists, and so he kept a sketch of all the paintings which came out of his studio. This admirable collection he entitled *Livre d'Invention* or *Livre de Vérité*. It is now in the Duke of Devonshire's Collection.

He also made some fine etchings, among them the *Campo Vaccino* which strongly recalls the picture in the Louvre.

Lorrain had a wide influence until the rise of the Impressionist school, which had other methods of representing the luminous appearance of objects bathed in sunlight.

See Pl. 40, Vol. II.

BIBLIOGRAPHY: Mrs. Mark Pattison, *Claude Lorrain*. Paris, 1884.—Edward Dillon, *Claude*. London, 1905.—Walter Friedländer, *Claude Lorrain*. Berlin, 1921.

**LORSCH (France).**—An important center for the study of Carolingian architecture. *The Chapel,* founded 764, burned down 1090. *The Gateway* (c. 800) has, on the ground storey, a triple arch of triumph motif in a debased classical style. The arches spring from impost blocks on piers to which half-columns are attached. The attic storey above has small windows framed in mitred arches. The façade is enriched with a complete repertoire of Carolingian decorative motifs: billet-mould, dogtooth, chequer, etc.

**LOTTO (Lorenzo).**—Venetian painter, 1480?-1556. Born in Venice, and not in Bergamo or Treviso, as is sometimes stated. He was a pupil of Alvise Vivarini, and developed under the influences of Giorgione, Palma Vecchio and Titian. But he remained original. He was of a restless, dreamy disposition, loving solitude. His independence prevented him from being attached strictly to a school. He had something of the precision of the Florentines, combined with the warmth of the Venetians. But his extraordinary fantasy and his feeling for nature are definitely northern in quality and incline one to suspect that he was familiar with contemporary German painting. In spite of his charm, some of his works show a tendency to bitter characterisation, as in the *Pietà* (Brera Gallery), and in the *Woman Taken in Adultery* (Louvre).

He painted some wonderful portraits, which are distinguished and severe in style—for instance, the *Man with a Red Beard* (Brera); the *Bishop Bernardo di Rossi* (1505, Naples); the *Portrait of a Man,* in the Borghese Gallery, Rome, and those in Vienna; the *Prothonotary Giuliano,* in the National Gallery.

LOUVAIN: CITY HALL.

He sometimes painted the nude, as the *Triumph of Chastity,* in the Rospigliosi Gallery, Rome, testifies.

His landscapes are sometimes very fine, and modern in treatment, as that in the *St. Jerome,* of the Louvre (1500), or that of the Doria Gallery, Rome.

Lorenzo Lotto lived in Venice. He also travelled. He stayed for a long time in Bergamo, where there are fine altarpieces by him in San Bartolommeo (1516), in San Bernardino (1521), and in Santo Spirito (1521). He painted frescoes in S. Michele del Pozzo and in Treviso, in the Church of San Niccolò. He is supposed to have visited Rome, but he lived chiefly in the Marches, and died in Loreto.

BIBLIOGRAPHY: B. Berenson, *Lorenzo Lotto*. London, 1901.

**LOUIS XIII STYLE.**—See Furniture (France); also Pl. 42, Vol. II.

**— XIV STYLE.**—See Furniture (France); also Pls. 41, 42, Vol. II.

**— XV STYLE.**—See Furniture (France); also Pls. 43, 44, Vol. II.

**— XVI STYLE.**—See Furniture (France); also Pl. 44, Vol. II.

**LOUVAIN.**—Town in Flanders. It was very prosperous in the 14th century. It possesses a splendid *Hôtel de Ville* (town-hall), in the flamboyant style, built 1444-1458, by Mathieu de Layens. It is very richly decorated with sculpture.

THE LOUVRE AT THE TIME OF CHARLES V. (Miniature from the *Très Riches Heures* of the Duc de Berry, Chantilly.)

The *Church of St. Pierre,* begun in 1423, is of very pleasing proportions.

The artistic treasures of Louvain suffered severely in the war; and the rich *University Library* was destroyed, but has recently been rebuilt by Whitney Warren.

**LOUVIERS (Eure).**—The Gothic Church of Notre Dame dates from the 15th century. It has stained glass of the 15th and 16th centuries.

See Pl. 50, Vol. I.

**LOUVRE.**—The Louvre is the most beautiful and varied art museum in the world. It is first mentioned under its present name in 1204 during the reign of Philip Augustus, but it is probable that the site had already been occupied by a fortified palace, perhaps for two or three centuries. Because of the name, presumably derived from *loup,* it is believed originally to have been the rendezvous of wolf hunters. The palace was augmented during the reign of Charles V, 1364-1380, but of this building nothing remains. We have an idea of its appearance from a miniature in the *Très Riches Heures* of the Duc de Berry. The King lived here part of the time and kept his treasure and manuscripts here, but after his death the place was allowed to fall to ruin.

In 1527 Francis I ordered repairs, and it is to his interest in art that the Louvre owes a number of its masterpieces, including paintings by Raphael, Leonardo da Vinci and Titian. He planned to reconstruct the entire edifice, but died before the work was well under way. However, his architect, Pierre Lescot, with Jean Goujon (see these two names) in charge of the sculptural decorations, was able to carry on during the reign of Henry II. Henry's widow, Catherine de' Medici, in 1563 began the construction of the château of the Tuileries, confiding the work first to Philibert de l'Orme, then to Jean Bullant and Du Cer-

The Petite Gallery of the Louvre. (Apollo Gallery.) (From an engraving by Israël Silvestre.)

ceau, but it was not until the time of Napoleon III that her dream of connecting it with the Louvre was realised. The Tuileries were burned in 1871 and have not been rebuilt.

The Grand Gallery was finished under Henry IV. The Pavilion of Sully, known also as the *Pavillon d'Horloge*, was constructed under Louis XIII by Le Mercier who fol-

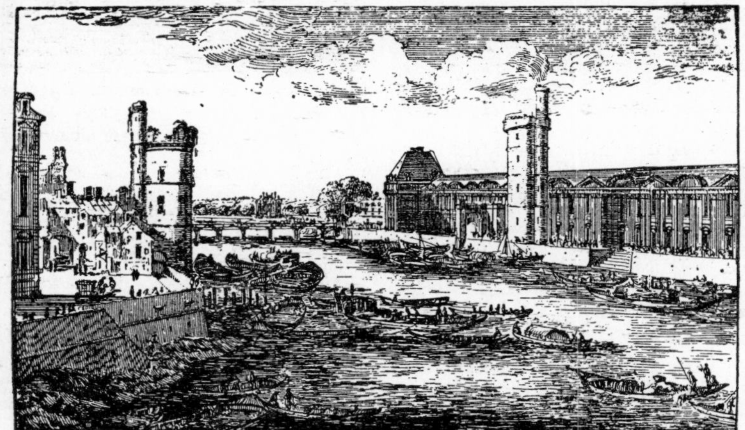

The Grand Gallery of the Louvre. (From an engraving by Israël Silvestre.)

lowed the style of Pierre Lescot. In 1661 the Petite Gallery (now the Apollo Gallery) was destroyed and rebuilt by Le Vau. The decorations were by Le Brun who celebrated the Roi-Soleil, Louis XIV, in his allegory, *Apollo Directing the Chariot*

The Louvre: Colonnade by Perrault.

*of the Sun*. It was also during the reign of Louis XIV that Claude Perrault (see this name) built the famous Colonnade. After this the Louvre once more fell upon sad days and was again on its way to ruin when Napoleon I in 1803 ordered the work resumed. His architects were Percier and Fontaine. But Napoleon's greatest contribution was not in building; it was in the enrichment of the galleries with masterpieces from the countries he had conquered. The final additions to the structure were made under Napoleon III.

All arts and all countries are represented at the Louvre. Here one finds the *Virgin of the Rocks* and the *Mona Lisa* as well as many of the most celebrated productions of the Flemish, Dutch, English, German, Spanish, and other schools—forming altogether the most comprehensive collection of paintings in the world. The sculpture is hardly less notable. It includes the Venus of Milo and the Victory of Samothrace along with many other excellent pieces from the ancient world and much that is best from the Renaissance and modern times. In addition there are fine collections of tapestry, ivory, porcelain, terra cotta, gems, jewels, and numerous other objets d'art.

See Pl. 27, Vol. II.

**LÜBECK (Germany).**—*Cathedral,* 1173-1335. A Baltic Romanesque church in the brick architecture common to the region, with 14th century Gothic aisles and choir.

The Louvre: Apollo Gallery.

*Marienkirche,* 1251-1310. A Gothic church in the elaborate brick style of North Germany.

**LUCARNE.**—A dormer window.

**LUCA di TOMMÈ di NUTO.**—Sienese painter, first mentioned in 1355 as a member of the painters' guild in Siena.

In 1357 Luca, with Cristoforo di Stefano, restores a *Madonna* above the door of the Siena Cathedral. From 1366 dates his *Crucifixion* in the Pisa Gallery; from 1367 his polyptych in the Academy, Siena, a *Madonna and St. Anne with Four Saints;* and from 1370 his altarpiece in the Gallery at Rieti in Umbria, a *Madonna and Saints.* In 1373, Luca is mentioned as a member of the city government, Siena, and paints a picture commemorating the victory of Sienese troops over the troops of the Condottiere Cappelucci. In 1374 he appears in Orvieto. In 1379 he is again a councillor of Siena and from 1388-89 a member of the Cathedral committee. In the last year he is paid for assistance to Bartolo di Fredi and Andrea di Bartolo on an altarpiece for the Cathedral.

Bibliography: Vasari-Milanesi,—Milanesi, *Doc. . . . senese,* I, Crowe and Cavalcaselle, III.—R. Van Marle, *Simone Martini,* etc., 1920; and *Italian Schools,* etc. II, 1924.

**LUCAS van LEYDEN.**—Dutch painter and engraver, who was born in Leyden in 1494, and who died in 1533. His earliest works suggest that he was preoccupied with technical questions: such are the *Abigail,* and the *Resurrection of Lazarus.* His masterpiece, *Mahomet and the Monk Sergius* (1508) shows great knowledge, and especially a remarkable and new understanding of aerial perspective.

The series of the *Passion* (1509) shows the artist in possession of all his powers.

The theme of his engravings is generally a religious scene, but to Lucas van Leyden the subject was not of great importance. What interested him was the composition of figures and landscape, and the superposition of planes. The landscapes are lightly indicated, but the figures are very closely studied. Historical truth is not attempted: all that matters is that the costume is beautiful, and adapts itself to the movement of the figures. Nor did van Leyden aim at effects of light, and strong contrasts of light and shade, but at a more even distribution of tone. Among his very numerous engravings may be mentioned: the *Conversion of St. Paul, Calvary, Ecce Homo*—vast compositions, with a great many figures—the *Return of the Prodigal Son,* the *Adoration of the Magi, David Playing before Saul,* and the *Temptation of St. Anthony.*

In 1520, Lucas van Leyden and Albrecht Dürer met in Antwerp. From this time on, his modelling becomes accentuated, the opposition of tones more energetic, and his compositions become more closed in, so that his fine backgrounds are lost. *The Passion* (1521), *St. Jerome* (1521), *St. Peter and St. Paul* (1527), mark this new tendency. "Genre" subjects are becoming more frequent (*Musicians, The Surgeon,* etc.), and some fine portraits were executed in these years.

During his last years, from 1528, van Leyden escaped from the influence of Dürer, and fell under that of Marcantonio. He recovered his taste for large, monumental compositions. He also took to engraving the nude: *Venus,* allegorical figures of *Virtues, Adam and Eve Chased from Paradise,* etc.

Lucas van Leyden: The Temptation of St. Anthony. (Engraving.)

Lucas van Leyden made a certain number of wood-engravings, but they are not the most interesting part of his work—*Samson and Dalila,* etc.

The surviving paintings by Lucas van Leyden are not very numerous: the most important are a triptych in the Hermitage, representing, in the central panel, *Christ Healing the Blind,* and another one with the *Last Judgment,* in his native town, Leyden.

Bibliography: L. Baldass, *Die Gemälde des Lucas van Leyden,* Vienna, 1923.—M. J. Friedländer, *Lucas van Leyden.* Leipzig, 1924.—M. J. Friedländer, *Altniederländische Malerei,* Vol. 10.

**LUCCA (Italy).**—A girdle of ramparts—not, however, very picturesque—surrounds this little mediæval town, with its narrow streets, on either side of which are massive palaces, dominated by high towers.

The oldest of its buildings is *San Frediano,* founded in the 7th century by the kings of Lombardy, and rebuilt from 1112 to 1147, in the Romanesque style. On the façade, a mosaic of the 12th or beginning of the 13th century (much restored) represents Christ and the Apostles. The church contains an altar decorated with bas-reliefs by Jacopo della Quercia.

*San Michele,* a very old church,

was rebuilt in the 12th, 14th and 16th centuries. It has a very rich façade added on to a much lower church, built in the 8th century.

The *Cathedral* is a fine Romanesque edifice, built from 1060 to 1070, decorated about the year 1200 with a façade, with porticoes and richly carved galleries, by Guido da Como and his son: the subjects are taken from the life of St. Martin—they are stiff and archaic. Two bas-reliefs below the left-hand portal (the *Nativity*, and the *Deposition*) are the earliest carvings of Niccolò Pisano. The Cathedral contains the *Tempietto*, a little marble chapel built in 1484 at Civitali to shelter the famous Volto Santo (crucifix).

LUCCA: THE CATHEDRAL.

*Santa Maria della Rosa,* built in 1309, is a delicate Gothic chapel.

The *Palazzo Guinigi,* built about 1380, is a red brick fortress in the Gothic style.

The *Palazzo Mansi* was built at the beginning of the 17th century in the Baroque style. It contains a picture gallery.

BIBLIOGRAPHY: J. de Foville, *Pise et Lucques,* Collection des Villes d'art célèbres.

**LUDOVISI THRONE.**—See Pl. 22, Vol. I.

**LUINI (Bernardino).**—Lombard painter, born c. 1475; died 1531-32. Probably pupil of Borgognone, profoundly influenced by Leonardo.

A great many of Luini's works are in the Brera Gallery, Milan, coming from Santa Maria Brera, from the old Santa Maria della Pace, and from the Casa Pelucca. There are paintings by him in the Ambrosiana, Castello, Poldi-Pezzoli, and Borromeo Galleries, and in various Milanese churches and collections.

LUINI (BERNARDO): FRANCESCO BENOZZI AND HIS PATRON SAINT. (Detail from the *Flagellation of Christ*, MONASTERO MAGGIORE, Milan.)

In 1522, Luini painted a *Crowning with Thorns* (now in the Ambrosian Library).

In 1525, Luini began more important frescoes in the celebrated pilgrimage church of the Madonna, in Saronno. Unfortunately, these are now in a very bad condition, having been over-cleaned. In the Choir he painted the *Presentation of Christ at the Temple,* and the *Adoration of the Magi*; above, Sibyls, Evangelists and Fathers of the Church.

The many frescoes in the Convento Maggiore must have been executed from 1525-1530, commissioned by Alessandro Bentivoglio, who was banished from Bologna by Julius II, and who married Hippolyto Sforza. His daughter, Alessandra, had taken the veil at the convent. Luini represented the Bentivoglio, the Sforza and the Besoppi kneeling in groups, in front of saints which have their daughters' features: thus St. Agnes represents Alessandra, and the beautiful St. Catherine, who inclines her pensive head to receive the blow of the scimitar, represents Bianca Maria, who was condemned to be beheaded (1526). Beside a representation of God the Father surrounded by angels on the chapel vaulting, is the date—11th August, 1530. In this great undertaking, Luini was helped by his two sons, and this may account for the inferiority of some details.

There are several pictures by Luini in Como Cathedral.

The most celebrated and perhaps the last work of Luini is the decoration of Santa Maria degli Angeli, of Lugano (1529). *The Passion* entirely covers the rood-screen, which divides the church in two, and is represented in two stages, with a crowd of episodes, and figures. On the left hand wall, the *Last Supper*, now much damaged, is a striking composition. A beautiful Virgin, in one of the chapels is of 1530.

Luini had a real gift for decoration with his skilled use of pale colours. His oil paintings may sometimes be feeble reminders of Leonardo da Vinci, but his facile, exquisite frescoes are always charming.

See Pl. 17, Vol. II.

BIBLIOGRAPHY: Pierre Gauthiez, *Luini*. Paris.—G. Williamson, *Bernardino Luini*. London, 1900.—L. Bertrami, *Luini*. Milan, 1911.

**LUKS (George Benjamin).**—American painter (1867-1933). He was born in Williamsport, Pennsylvania, 13th August 1867, the son of a doctor who drew for amusement and a mother with some artistic ability. He studied at the Pennsylvania Academy of Fine Arts and later at the Düsseldorf Academy, as well as in Paris and London. But in spite of all his academic training he formed a style which is not related to any contemporary movement but rather reflects the genre subjects painted by the Dutch Little Masters. In 1895 and 1896 Luks was in Cuba, the war correspondent and artist for the *Philadelphia Bulletin*. He was arrested by the authorities and deported shortly before the outbreak of the Spanish-American War. Back in New York he got a job drawing cartoons for the *New York Herald*, which included the series of *McFadden's Flats*. He fitted up his own studio, where he commenced painting the bits of human life that appealed to his jovial nature. These included coal miners, recalling his early vocation as a breaker-boy, and prize-fights, with the knowledge gained from his own fistic career as "Lusty" Luks. Other pictures showed the life and people of the lower East Side of New York, the market folk, the pawnbroker's daughter, newspaper vendors and the tattered street urchins. Especially in such a study as the *Spielers* he reached a climax with this representation of carefree childhood swept along by the emotion of the music of a battered street organ. Pictures such as these were coldly received by the academic circles and some of them refused by the National Academy which were later seen in the exhibitions of the "Eight." Luks was for many years an instructor at the Art Students' League until he founded a school of his own. He died suddenly 30th October 1933 at a time when he was still at the height of his artistic ability. Although not always acceptable to the general public his pictures have been widely circulated and admired for the breadth of treatment and vividness of the life portrayed there.

See Pl. 63, Vol. II.

BIBLIOGRAPHY: Elisabeth Luther Cary, *George Luks,* American Artists Series, 1931.—Guy Pène du Bois, *George B. Luks,* The Arts Portfolio Series, 1931.—For other information see *The Index of Twentieth Century Artists* for April, 1934.

**LUNDBERG (Gustavus).**—Swedish pastel artist, 1694-1786. After being the pupil of Rosalba, in Venice, he settled in Paris, where he was received by the Académie Royale on the presentation of portraits of Boucher and Natoire (1741). These portraits are in the Louvre.

**LUNETTE.**—Space or object in the shape of a crescent moon; generally refers to the space above an arched door or window. When decorated with a painting the painting itself is referred to by this name.

**LUNGHI (Martino) the Elder.**—Milanese architect, about 1570. After studying under Giacomo della Porta, he worked chiefly in Rome. He became one of the best representatives of the Baroque style. Its characteristic type is the façade, with pilasters or engaged columns combined with projecting columns. He united the two storeys which are of different width, by enormous volutes, or buttresses, in concave arch form, which give the building its graceful appearance—rather strange, but sometimes very harmonious.

He built the façades of San Girolamo degli Schiavoni and of San't Anastasio, began the fine Palazzo Desia (later Borghese), and built the Chiesa Nuova in Rome.

His grandiose staircase in the Palazzo Lancellotti (now Avellino), in Velletri, is one of his most famous works.

**LU T'AN-WEI.**—Important Chinese painter c. 440-500, painted portraits and Buddhist subjects. No extant works are known which reproduce his style.

**LUTERI (Giovanni).**—See Dosso Dossi.

**LUTYENS (Sir Edwin L., R.A.).**—British architect, born 1869, of classical tendencies. Designer, among other monuments, of the Government Buildings, New Delhi, India, 1912-1929; the Art Gallery, Johannesburg; the Cenotaph, London; Britannic House, London, 1923; the British Embassy, Washington, U.S.A., 1929.

**LUXEMBOURG (Palace).**—Built between 1615 and 1624 for Marie de Medicis, this imposing edifice brought great honour to its architect, Salomon de Brosse. It is the great monument of the baroque style of Louis XIII.

PALAIS DU LUXEMBOURG, PARIS: HALL OF THE LIVRE D'OR.

It is a mistake to consider it a copy of the Pitti Palace. No doubt the Florentine queen desired her "Medici palace" to recall the residence of the grand dukes of Tuscany. But if its central dome and wooden construction were borrowed from Italy, the plan is quite French. Nevertheless, De Brosse and his "palais Médicis" did not have much influence on building in the time of Mazarin and Colbert.

The architectural decoration of the Palace, either on the side which faces the road or in the large courtyard, was the same outside as it is today, but behind the existing courtyard, between the two chief pavilions, existed a second court of honour. This was a terrace, raised about one yard from the exterior ground level of the palace.

De Brosse planned splendid gardens, but only the fountain, known as the Medici Fountain, remains to recall their magnificence.

Great restoration works were undertaken, under Louis-Philippe.

BIBLIOGRAPHY: Scellier de Gisors, *Le Palais du Luxembourg*. Paris, 1847.

**LUXOR.**—A village near Thebes, in Upper Egypt, famous for its temple dedicated to Ammon, which is one of the most remarkable buildings of ancient times. It was built fifteen centuries before our era, on the same plan as the temple of Karnak. Sesostres (Rameses II) there set up two celebrated obelisks on either side of the façade of the temple. One of them was given to France by Mehemet Ali, and is set up in the Place de la Concorde, in Paris. They were covered with commemorative inscriptions, and preceded by an avenue of sphinxes.

The pylons are still covered with painted bas-reliefs, representing battle scenes.

**LUZZI (Lorenzo).**—Italian painter (died 1526), a native of Feltre, influenced by the Venetian artists. A signed example of his work, dated 1511, is a *Madonna with Saints* in the Berlin Museum.

**LYCIA.**—Lycia is situated in Asia Minor, between the Gulf of Macri and the Bay of Adalia, opposite the Island of Rhodes. From the 6th century B.C., the Persians subdued it, and later the Macedonians. But, before this period, it possessed an original civilisation of which scarcely more than the funeral monuments have come down to us. The old temples, completely destroyed, were rebuilt by the Greeks, and even of these temples only some ruins remain.

Frieze from the Harpy tomb, Lycia. (British Museum.)

Although built of stone, the Lycian tomb recalls the form of a wooden house, with its plinths, beams and heavy panels forming the walls (tombs of Xanthos, Pinara, Phellos, Myra, etc.). Generally, it is cut into the rock, and only the façade is made to represent the front of a house. Sometimes the two sides are also detached from the rock. It is very rare for the entire building to be isolated. The roofs of these tombs are flat, in the form of a terrace, or sometimes in the form of a pointed arch—this arched form being usually employed for sarcophagi, of which there are still many examples. The Lycians also built some funeral monuments affecting the form of a tower. Such is the "Harpy tomb," so called from its bas-reliefs of human-headed birds. (British Museum.)

Funeral tower of Xanthos.

The Lycians seem to have had more aptitude for sculpture than most of their neighbours in Asia Minor. They produced fairly vivacious figures of men and animals, particularly of lions. The oldest of these carvings, which are previous to the Persian conquest, are from tombs of the town of Xanthos. The British Museum possesses a rich collection. Sometimes the sculptures and bas-reliefs were painted in bright colours, only faint traces of which remain.

See Nereid Monument.

Bibliography: Perrot and Chipiez, *Histoire de l'Art*. Vol. V.

**LYONS.**—*The Cathedral* replaces a Carolingian church, and a Romanesque church of the 11th century. The apse was built between 1165 and 1180, while the façade, begun later, was only finished in 1480. In spite of these various periods of construction, the Cathedral is far from lacking architectural beauty. It contains some very fine stained glass windows.

Lyons: The Cathedral.

The *Basilica of St. Martin d'Ainay* was rebuilt in the 10th and 11th centuries. Two side aisles were added in the 12th and 13th centuries. The building is surmounted by two square towers—one on the centre of the façade, and the other between the nave and the choir.

The *Church of St. Nizier*, the original Cathedral of Lyons, dates from the 15th century. The central doorway is sometimes attributed to Philibert de l'Orme.

The Palais du Commerce houses the richest *Textile Museum* in the world. It possesses over 500,000 specimens, of all periods and all countries.

See Pl. 52, Vol. I; Pl. 29, Vol. II.

Bibliography: L. Bégule, *La Cathédrale de Lyon*. Paris.—d'Hennezel, *Lyon*, Collection des Villes d'art célèbres. Paris.—A. Kleinclausz, *Lyon*. Lyon, 1925.

**LYSICRATES (Choragic Monument of), in Athens.**—A small circular building which is the oldest example of the Corinthian order in Athens. It was built in 335 B.C. on the eastern slope of the Acropolis, in honour of Lysicrates. Such monuments were erected to support a tripod, as a prize for athletic exercises, or musical competitions, in Greek festivals.

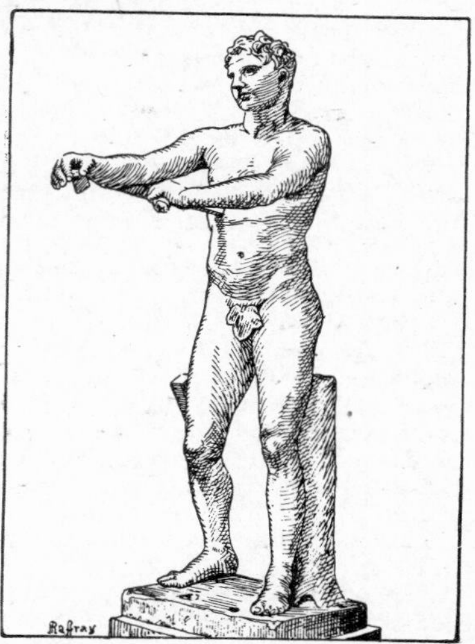

Lysippus: Athlete Apoxyomenos. (Museum of the Vatican, Rome.)

A podium, 4 metres high, supports six Corinthian half-columns, which are attached to curved panels. On the architrave is an inscription in honour of the winner. The conical marble roof supported the bronze tripod which was handed to the victor. The monument, and the ground on which it stands, were bought by some French capuchins, in 1669, and France has retained the charge of it.

**LYSIPPUS.**—Greek sculptor, who flourished in the second half of the 4th century B.C. His great predecessors, Praxiteles and Scopas, worked in the first half of the century. He heralded the period which historians call "the Hellenistic Age," and which corresponds to the spreading of the Greek spirit, after the conquests of Alexander the Great.

Lysippus: Hercules Epitrapezios. (Louvre.)

According to ancient texts, Lysippus came from Sicyonia. He was working from about 350 to 300 B.C. Lysippus is said to have modified the proportions of the Polyclitan type by making the body more slender, the head smaller and the muscles more sinewy. He was a very prolific sculptor. Of his extant works, first place must be given to the statue of Agias, a marble replica of which was found by French excavators at Delphi. The original was probably in bronze. The replica probably bears a close relation to the work of Lysippus himself. It is above all the treatment and expression of the face of the *Agias* which gives us a new conception of Lysippus' art. The eyes are deep-set, and have the same intensity of expression as do the heads of Scopas, but here the gaze is fixed upon some nearer object.

Lysippus: Farnese Hercules. (National Museum, Naples.)

It is uncertain whether the famous statue, known as the *Apoxyomenos*, is by Lysippus, or not. it differs considerably in style and physical type from the *Agias*.

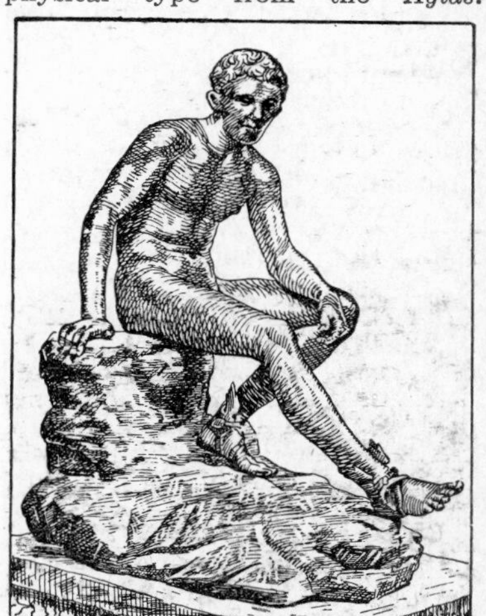

Lysippus: Mercury. (National Museum, Naples.)

On the whole, it seems safer, in considering the attribution of other statues to Lysippus, to refer them to the standard of the *Agias* rather than, as formerly, to that of the *Apoxyomenos*.

Lysippus' portraits of Alexander were, in ancient times, among his most famous works; and the portrait head of Alexander in the British Museum may well be by this artist.

Lysippus heralded many of the tendencies of later art.

See Pl. 25, Vol. I.

Bibliography: Franklin Johnson, *Lysippos*. 1928.

# M

**MABUSE (Jan Gossaert, called).**—Flemish painter (about 1478-1533), who worked in Antwerp and Holland. Born at Maubeuge (from which he took his name); master of the Guild of Antwerp in 1505; entered the service of Philip of Burgundy, who sent him to Rome (1503), where he studied monuments of classical antiquity; worked in Middelburg, then in Utrecht, always following his patron, Philip of Burgundy.

His most famous works are: The *Adoration of the Magi* (National Gallery); *St. Donatian* (Tournai); Portrait of a Knight (Rome, Doria Palace); a triptych of the Virgin (Palermo); Portrait of Philip of Burgundy, painted about 1510 (Amsterdam); *St. Luke Painting the Virgin* (Vienna and Prague); *Danaë* (Munich); *Adam and Eve* (Hampton Court and Berlin); portrait of a Monk (Louvre), *Neptune and Amphitrite* (Berlin).

Mabuse was one of the first painters to bring influences from the Italian Renaissance into Flanders. In his work, Italian and Flemish details mingle.

Bibliography: Maurice Gossart, *Jan Gossart, sa vie et ses œuvres.* Lille, 1902.—Sir Martin Conway, *The Van Eycks and Their Followers.* London, 1921.—E. Weiss, *Jan Gossart genannt Mabuse.* Parchim, 1913.—M. J. Friedländer, *Altniederländ. Malerei,* Vol. VIII.

**MACCHIAVELLI (Zanobi).**—Florentine painter, follower of Angelico, influenced by Benozzo, Lippi and Pesellino; born 1418 in Florence; died 1479, perhaps in Pisa, not in Florence.

Cadastral declarations for Macchiavelli are listed in 1457 and 1469; in 1472 he appears on the register of the Compagnia di S. Marco. In 1473 he was active in Pisa (his *Coronation of the Virgin* of 1473 in Dijon comes from this period). In 1475-76 he is again, or still, mentioned in Pisa. From 1463 is his *St. James* in Berlin, signed and dated. Another signed, but not dated, picture by Macchiavelli is the *Madonna and Saints* in Dublin, the National Gallery.

Bibliography: Vasari-Milanesi, III.—G. Poggi, *Zanobi di Macchiavelli,* Rivista d'Arte, IX, 1916.—P. Bacci, *Zanobi Macchiavelli in Pisa,* Rivista d'Arte, X, 1917.—Van Marle, *Italian Schools, etc.,* XI, 1929.

**MACHICOLATION.**—Opening between the corbels of a parapet through which missiles can be shot or thrown upon an enemy below; also applied to a parapet, etc., with such openings.

**MACHUCA (Pedro).**—Spanish architect, died 1550. He designed the Palace of Charles II at Granada, 1527, in a style based upon that of the Veronese architect of the Italian High Renaissance, Michele Sanmicheli, The interior court of the Palace is round and is erroneously called a bull-ring.

**McBEY (James).**—Contemporary Scotch etcher. He was born 23d December 1883 in Newburgh in Aberdeenshire. At the age of fifteen he was working in the North of Scotland Bank in Aberdeen, making drawings and paintings in his spare time. He copied the illustrations of books in the Aberdeen Free Library and learned to sketch directly from nature. An English translation of Lalanne's *Gravure à l'Eau-Forte* came to his attention and soon he was trying to make etchings, aided by a homemade press for printing the plates. In the winter of 1902 he was in the Edinburgh branch of the bank and made a number of etchings of the scenery around that region. In the summer of 1910 McBey left the employ of the bank and sailed for Holland, where he proceeded to do a series of landscapes which have been compared not unfavourably with those by Rembrandt. Soon he returned to Scotland, working at Fintray and in the region of the Dow River and the next year he went to London. That summer he travelled to Spain, where he executed a series of plates, including some studies of the bull fights. The next few months were spent in Wales and Sandwich, capturing the glamour of landscapes bathed in sunlight or veiled in mists of driving rain. In 1912 he went to Morocco, where in Tetuan he glimpsed and set down his impressions of the life in the native bazaars, as may be seen in the picture of the *Story-Teller* who holds the attention of the crowd by the magic of his words. Another trip to Holland followed and this time he made some watercolour studies in addition to his etchings. In the campaigns of 1917-1918 James McBey was named the official artist of the Palestine division and to that period belong his studies of the camel corps, the capture of Jerusalem and scenes of army activities in the Sinai Desert. After the close of the war McBey returned to his London studio and continued recording his impressions of the life along the Thames as well as some portrait studies of his friends. Later in the middle years of the 1920's came more etchings of Holland and some watercolour paintings of Venice—all seen and characterised by a freshness of vision and a strong sense of construction enlivened by his touches of imagination in portraying the romantic aspects of the scene. Particularly noteworthy is his study entitled *Night in Ely Cathedral,* which preserves an air of mystery and the silence of a vast interior but yet suggests a perfect understanding of the architectural setting on the part of the artist.

Bibliography: *Etchings and Dry Points from 1902 to 1924 by James McBey,* a Catalogue by Martin Hardie, 1925.—Malcolm C. Salaman, *The Etchings of James McBey,* 1929.—Malcolm C. Salaman, *James McBey,* 1924.

**McKIM (Charles Follen).**—American architect (1847-1909). He was born at Chester City, Pennsylvania, 24th August 1847. He went to the Lawrence Scientific School at Harvard University with the intention of becoming a mining engineer. Then he became interested more in architecture and entered the office of Russell Sturgis in New York City as a draftsman. From 1867 to 1870 he was in Paris studying with Daumet in the École des Beaux-Arts, and then at the threat of the impending Franco-Prussian War he left for the United States. He entered the employ of Charles D. Gambrill and Henry Hobson Richardson in Orange, New Jersey, but soon opened his own office. In 1878 he formed a partnership with William R. Mead and William B. Bigelow. The next year Stanford White took the place of Bigelow and then began the long career of the famous firm of McKim, Mead and White. The members of the firm made a trip through the region of Boston, Salem and Portsmouth, noting the effectiveness of the early Colonial architecture. Basing their style on the work of Sir Christopher Wren and Charles Bulfinch this group of collaborators began executing their long line of successful enterprises. Later the style of the firm changed more to the manner of the Italian Renaissance and it was in this mode that their greatest successes were made. In 1887 the firm received the commission for the new public library in Boston. They demanded the best materials and also planned for the mural decorations by Edwin Abbey, John Singer Sargent and Puvis de Chavannes. While too elaborate and ornate from present standards this building was perhaps the most famous one executed by that firm. During the early years of the twentieth century they were engaged in planning for the new government buildings in Washington, which included a restoration of the White House and some new structures for the Army War College. Other large projects carried out by this firm were for Columbia University, the Pierpont Morgan Library and the Pennsylvania Railroad Station. Early in 1908 McKim retired from an active interest in the firm and he died at St. James, Long Island, 14th September, 1909.

See Pl. 64, Vol. II.

Bibliography: Charles Moore, *The Life and Times of Charles Follen McKim,* 1929.—A. H. Granger, *Charles Follen McKim; A Study of His Life and Work,* 1913.—C. H. Reilly, *McKim, Mead and White,* 1924.

**MacMONNIES (Frederick William).**—Contemporary American sculptor. He was born in Brooklyn, New York, 28th September 1863, the son of a Scotch father and a mother who was the niece of Benjamin West, the early American painter. He worked for a while as a clerk in a jewelry store and then at the age of sixteen became an apprentice to Augustus St.-Gaudens. For the next five years he remained in his studio, studying in the evenings at the National Academy of Design and the Art Students' League. In 1884 he went to Paris, where for a short time he worked at the École des Beaux-Arts and then went on to Munich to do some painting. After another brief period in the studio of St.-Gaudens he returned to the École des Beaux-Arts, where he worked under Falguière, and for two successive years he won the *prix d'atelier,* which is the highest award offered to foreign students. For a time he was in the private workshop of Antonin Mercié, but soon he opened his own studio in Paris. He won a mention in the Salon of 1889 and at the same time received a commission for some angels for St. Paul's Church in New York. He returned to New York City and in 1891 his *Nathan Hale* was erected in City Hall Park. He designed the *Columbia Fountain* for the Columbian Exposition in Chicago in 1893, a colossal undertaking with many figures disposed as if riding in a great barge on the surface of the lagoon. The next year he executed the *Bacchante,* which is now in the Metropolitan Museum of Art, a sprightly group of mother and child, joyous and carefree, characterised by a simplicity and lightness of treatment. Other commissions which followed include the *Victory* at West Point, New York, the group of the *Horse Tamers* in Prospect Park, Brooklyn, and statues of Theodore Roosevelt and General McClellan in Washington. He also did the Princeton *Battle Monument,* statues for the Marne Battlefield, and *Civic Virtue* for New York City. This last figure created a furor like that raised by the *Bacchante.* It is splendidly modelled and vigorous in conception, but not quite attaining the idealism demanded of such a subject. MacMonnies has received many awards, including the Order of St. Michael of Bavaria and the French Legion of Honor. His strength of conception and boldness of technique have caused him to be likened to Donatello or Michelangelo, with the pure delight in the plastic surfaces overriding the intellectual side of his work. One of his most recent works is a portrait bust of Thomas Hastings, the architect of the New York Public Library, placed in the entrance hall of that structure. Here is an excellent representation of facial expression combined with a skillful character analysis of the subject in a delightful plastic composition.

Bibliography: Charles H. Caffin, *American Masters of Sculpture,* 1903.—George Henry Chase and Chandler Rathfon Post, *A History of Sculpture,* 1925.—Kineton Parkes, *Sculpture of To-day,* 1921.—Chandler Rathfon Post, *A History of European and American Sculpture,* Vol. 2, 1921.—Lorado Taft, *The History of American Sculpture,* 1930.—Lorado Taft, *Modern Tendencies in Sculpture,* 1921.

**MACNEIL (Herman A.).**—American sculptor, born in 1866, among whose many renderings of subjects from Indian Life the *Sun Vow* (Metropolitan Museum of Art, New York) may be singled out for mention.

# RHENISH PRIMITIVES

*Flemish painting of the style of van Eyck, Dirk Bouts and Roger van der Weyden spread toward the east; it penetrated the Rhine valley and conquered southern Germany, Suabia and Franconia. There were as many artistic centres and schools of painting as there were towns. In each of them the work takes on a different accent; the pictures show personalities sufficiently defined so that one may classify them and recognise the common author of an entire group of paintings even when one is unable to identify the author by name.*

MASTER WILHELM: ST. VERONICA.
*(Photo by Hachette.)*

STEPHAN LOCHNER: ADORATION OF THE MAGI. COLOGNE CATHEDRAL.
*(Photo by Hanfstaengl.)*

CONRAD WITZ: ST. MARY MAGDALENE AND ST. CATHERINE. STRASBOURG.
*(Photo by Bruckmann.)*

## School of Cologne

This school is dated prior to the blossoming of the great school of Bruges, that of the van Eycks and that of oil painting. It flourished at the end of the fourteenth century when painting was being executed by means of tempera with soft, clear colours upon a background of gold. The manner is still very near to that of miniature painting.

SCHONGAUER: THE VIRGIN IN THE ROSE ARBOR. COLMAR.
*(Photo by Bruckmann.)*

THE MASTER OF THE LIFE OF MARY: BIRTH OF THE VIRGIN. PINAKOTHEK, MUNICH.
*(Photo by Hachette.)*

ZEITBLOM: THE ANNUNCIATION. STUTTGART.
*(Photo by Schaller.)*

## Flemish Influence

Toward the middle of the fifteenth century, the mystics of Cologne began to copy reality in the manner of the painters of Bruges. Thus a second school of Cologne, much more naturalistic than the first, was born. The influence of Dirk Bouts and Roger van der Weyden may be noticed in the dry silhouettes and stiff attitudes. Zeitblom and Schongauer preserve the tenderness of the primitive school.

HOLBEIN THE ELDER: ST. BARBARA AND ST. ELIZABETH. PINAKOTHEK, MUNICH.
*(Photo by Hachette.)*

GRÜNEWALD: THE CRUCIFIXION. COLMAR.
*(Photo by Bruckmann.)*

MICHAEL PACHER: WINGS OF THE ALTARPIECE. CHURCH OF ST. WOLFGANG, AUGSBOURG.
*(Photo by Hanfstaengl.)*

## Italian Influence

At the beginning of the sixteenth century, the Italian style already exerts its influence upon these Germanic masters as it does upon French or Flemish art. One may even notice it in the tortured forms and the strange colours of Mathias Grünewald, the powerful master of Colmar. But one finds it again still better shown in the regal elegance of the saints by Holbein the Elder, as in the bold attempts at perspective that Michael Pacher shows us. At this period, Gothic and Italian art are reunited by the narrow passages of the Alps and one observes how the Renaissance is gradually changing the points of view of the northern masters.

# FRENCH PRIMITIVES

*French paintings prior to the Renaissance are known as primitives. Under this title there are groups rather remote from one another which cannot be said to easily fall within the same classification. The three principal schools are the Burgundian, the school of Provence and the school of the Loire. It must not be forgotten that French painting was particularly stained glass painting, tapestry, or miniature rather than panel painting in tempera or oil.*

BELLECHOSE: MARTYRDOM OF ST. DENIS. LOUVRE. *(Photo by Hachette.)*

MELCHIOR BROEDERLAM: SCENES FROM THE LIFE OF THE VIRGIN. DIJON. *(Photo by Neurdein.)*

MALOUEL: THE DEAD CHRIST. LOUVRE. *(Photo by Hachette.)*

## The Burgundian School

The duchy of Burgundy at the beginning of the fifteenth century was a brilliant art centre. The dukes, lords of the Flemish provinces, attracted the best artists of Bruges and Ghent to their court at Dijon. They had Jan van Eyck in their service. Before this time Bellechose, Broederlam and Jean Malouel painted with sparkling colours in tempera on gold backgrounds, a method which is very close to that of the illuminators of manuscripts.

PIETÀ. SCHOOL OF AVIGNON. LOUVRE. *(Photo by Hachette.)*

NICOLAS FROMENT: THE BURNING BUSH. AIX. *(Photo by Neurdein.)*

ENGUERRAND CHARONTON: THE CORONATION OF THE VIRGIN. VILLENEUVE-LÈS-AVIGNON. *(Photo by Langlois.)*

## The School of Provence

During the fifteenth century, there were painters at Avignon, the old city of the popes and at Aix with good king René. We even know the names of some of them: Nicolas Froment d'Uzès, Enguerrand Charonton de Laon. What one notices most particularly among them is the naturalistic genius, and the diligent and minute style of the Northern masters; they used oil painting.

FOUQUET: ÉTIENNE CHEVALIER. BERLIN. *(Photo by Hanfstaengl.)*

FOUQUET: CALVARY. CHANTILLY. *(Photo by Hachette.)*

FOUQUET: CHARLES VII. LOUVRE. *(Photo by Hachette.)*

FOUQUET: JOB ON HIS DUNGHILL. CHANTILLY. *(Photo by Berthaud.)*

FOUQUET: JUVÉNAL DES URSINS. LOUVRE. *(Photo by Hachette.)*

J. BOURDICHON: NATIVITY. BIBL. NAT. *(Photo by Berthaud.)*

THE MASTER OF MOULINS: THE VIRGIN IN GLORY. MOULINS. *(Photo by Neurdein.)*

THE MASTER OF MOULINS: ADORATION OF THE SHEPHERDS. AUTUN. *(Photo by Langlois.)*

THE MASTER OF MOULINS: ST. MARY MAGDALENE AND A DONOR. LOUVRE.

## The School of Tours

It is the painters of central France, from the Loire and the Bourbonnais region who at this date best represent the national genius. One of them, Fouquet, is above all else an illuminator who has left some portraits of notable personalities. The other is called "The Master of Moulins" because his principal work is in the Cathedral of Moulins. Jean Bourdichon is an illuminator, a pupil of Fouquet.

**MACRINO D' ALBA.**—Painter of the school of Vercelli (1470-1528?). His real name was Macrino da Alladio. He developed under the influence of Foppa and the Milanese school. Particularly well represented at Turin.

**MADELEINE (Grotte de la).**—This grotto, situated in the department of Dordogne, France, is celebrated because it gives its name to a prehistoric epoch—the Magdalenian period. A quantity of objects were found there—articles of gold and of ivory, jewellery, and engraved stones.

See illus., p. 205.

**MADERNA (Carlo).**—Roman architect (1556-1629). Nephew of

MADERNA (CARLO): PORCH OF THE FAÇADE OF ST. PETER'S, ROME.

Fontana. One of the chief representatives of the Baroque style. With Vignola, Borromini and several others, he helped to transform parts of Rome with his sumptuous buildings. The complicated, worldly churches which were being built at this time are not without a certain grandeur. Unfortunately, they sometimes trespass too much on ancient beauties, smothering the pure lines of old buildings and even destroying the past to give their fancies freer play.

Maderna directed the works of St. Peter's, from 1605, under Pope Paul V. He decided to add three bays to the nave and, in its plan, the Latin cross definitely triumphed over the Greek cross. The altar was no longer placed in the middle of the church—it seemed almost lost in the vast reception hall. Pomp and magnificence was attained at the expense of architectural harmony. To complete his work, Maderna made a colossal façade, surmounting the pediment with large declamatory statues. This completely hides the fine drum of Michelangelo's dome, which can only be seen at some distance away.

Among Maderna's other important works are: the façade of Santa Susanna (1603); Sant'Andrea della Valle (except the façade which is by Carlo Rainaldi); Santa Maria della Vittoria; and the famous Barberini Palace (begun in 1624; finished by Bernini). He may have designed the Garden of the Quirinal Palace.

BIBLIOGRAPHY: A. Muñoz, *Carlo Maderno*. Rome, 1921.

**— (Stefano).**—Roman sculptor (1571-1636). He is the creator of the *Saint Cecilia* in Santa Cecilia in Trastevere. The moving realism of this work is such that it is said to have been copied from nature. In 1599, the saint's coffin was opened, and her body appeared to be miraculously preserved.

**MADONNA DEL GRANDUCA.**—See Raphael; also Pl. 19, Vol. II.

**— DI FOLIGNO.**—See Raphael; also Pl. 19, Vol. II.

**— OF THE CHAIR.**—See Raphael; also Pl. 19, Vol. II.

**MADRAZO (Jose de).**—Spanish painter, 1781-1859. Pupil of David, he soon became the head of the academic school in Spain. In the Prado is a frigid allegory by this painter—*Sacred and Profane Love.*

**MADRID.**—*The Royal Palace.*—On Christmas night of the year 1734

MADRID: ARCADE OF THE ALJAFERÍA OF SARAGOSSA. (Museum of Madrid.)

fire destroyed the Royal Palace of Madrid, and Philip V entrusted its rebuilding to the Turin architect, Filippo del Juvara, pupil of Bernini and Fontana. The building was finished in 1764 by Charles III. The construction of this palace had a decided influence on Spanish art, which tended to become simpler.

The collection of royal tapestries, one of the finest in the world, includes over two thousand pieces, mostly Flemish or Spanish.

*Prado.*—This is one of the finest museums in Europe. It is housed in a building which was begun in 1785, under Charles III, by Juan de Villanueva, and finished under Ferdinand VII, from 1819 to 1830. The magnificent collection of pictures owes its origin to the fine collections formed by the Kings of Spain. In 1818, Ferdinand VII brought together the pictures which until then had been scattered in the palaces and royal residences of Madrid, to form the "Real Museo de pintura del Prado," to which he later added new acquisitions. The Prado Museum possesses over two thousand pictures, a great many of which are of the highest order. It gives a complete idea of the history of Spanish painting, especially of its golden age, and of the greatest of its masters—Velázquez. There is also an admirable collection of Venetian pictures; including over twenty paintings by Titian, most of which are late works.

**MAES (Nicolaes).**—Dutch painter (1632-93), one of the best pupils of Rembrandt. He worked in Dordrecht, and was in Rembrandt's studio between 1648 and 1653.

BIBLIOGRAPHY: Hofstede de Groot, *Catalogue of Dutch Painters,* Vol. VI.—W. R. Valentiner, *Nicolaes Maes*. Stuttgart, 1924.

**MA FEN.**—Chinese painter, end of the 11th century. An extremely fine painting, *Hundred Wild Geese* (Honolulu Acad. of Arts), may be his work. He is the first painter of

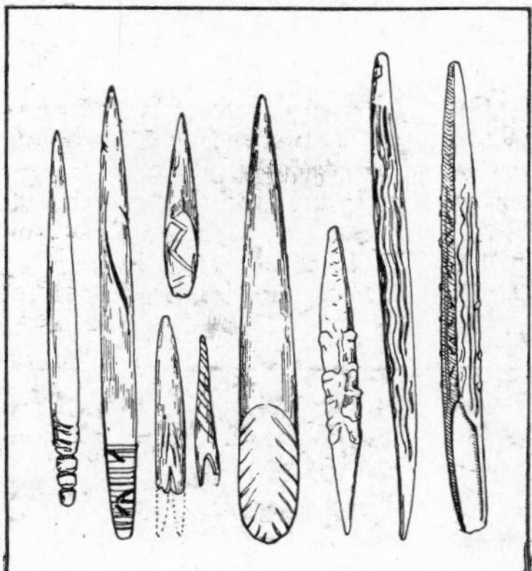

POINTS, PINS, ARROWHEADS AND DARTS OF IVORY, REINDEER ANTLERS AND BONE. (After J. Déchelette, *Manuel d'Archéologie préhistorique,* A. Picard, edit.)

the Ma family which was to introduce the academic landscape style that dominated Chinese painting.

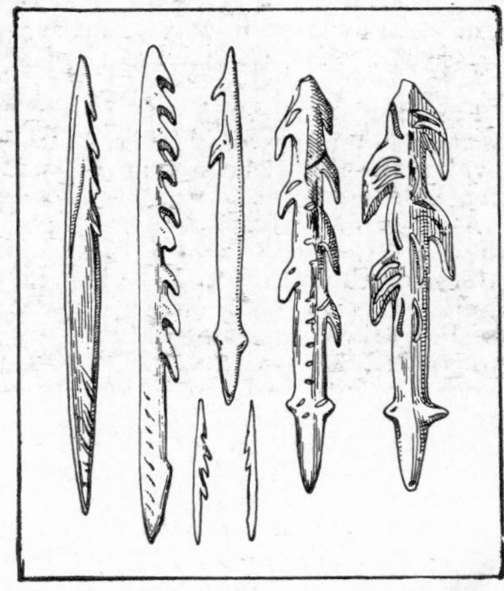

MAGDALENIAN DARTS OF REINDEER ANTLERS. (After J. Déchelette, *Manuel d'Archéologie préhistorique,* A. Picard, edit.)

**MAGDALENIAN PERIOD.**—See Madeleine (Grotte de la); Prehistoric Archæology.

IVORY REINDEER, MAGDALENIAN PERIOD. (After J. Déchelette, *Manuel d'Archéologie préhistorique,* A. Picard, edit.)

**MAGHRIL SCHOOL.**—See Moslem Art.

**MAHOMETAN ART.**—See Moslem Art.

**MAILLOL (Aristide Joseph Bonaventure).**—Contemporary French sculptor and painter. Maillol was born 25th December 1861 in Banyuls-sur-Mer, Roussillon. His ancestors were fishermen who recently had shifted to wine culture. At the age of twenty-one Maillol won a scholarship to the École des Beaux-Arts, where he studied painting with Cabanel for five years. He went on painting in an academic way until he came in contact with the works of Gauguin, which aroused in him an interest in decorative problems and a simplified method of approach. Dissatisfied with the Gobelins which were produced in Paris at that time,

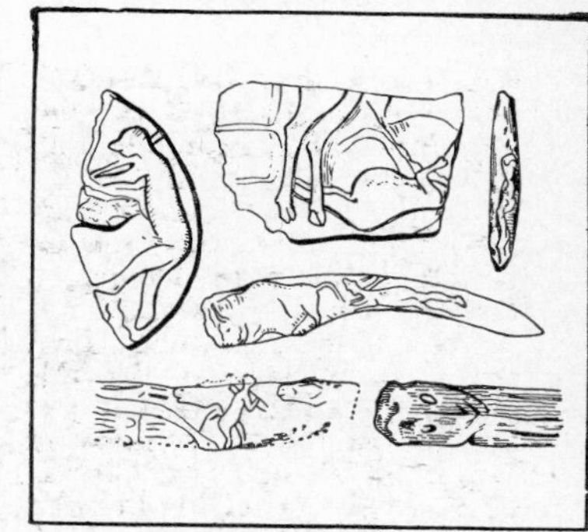

ENGRAVINGS WITH HUMAN REPRESENTATIONS, MAGDALENIAN PERIOD. (After J. Déchelette, *Manuel d'Archéologie préhistorique,* A. Picard, edit.)

Maillol turned to tapestry making, even manufacturing his own materials and experimenting with plants and roots to obtain more vivid colours for his dyes. It was only later in his career that he began to do sculpture, first with wood, then in wax and clay; metal work, stone

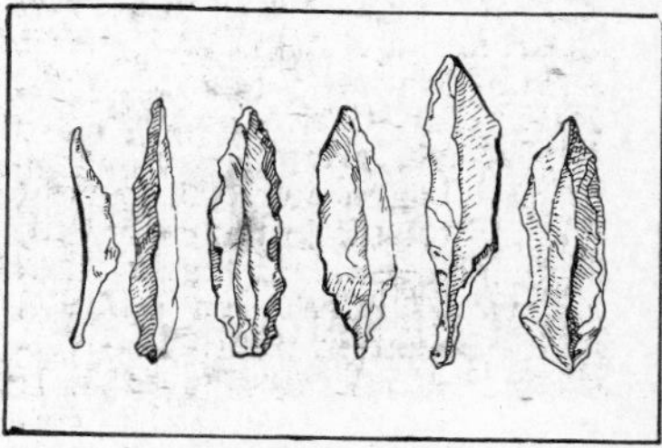

MAGDALENIAN FLINTS. (After J. Déchelette, *Manuel d'Archéologie préhistorique,* A. Picard, edit.)

cutting and casting were his final media. His themes with few exceptions are focussed on the feminine nude, although there are a few fine busts and other figures. His first sculpture was exhibited in 1896 at the Salons, and again in 1903. Art to Maillol is a question of suitability and economy of materials to express most appropriately the different forms. In his sculpture he aims throughout to get effects of floating lightness, which he achieves through the simplest of movements. Maillol fills out the forms instead of the customary hollowing out. All his compositions are marked primarily by tactile values; the figures are closed up and linked together in a way to emphasise this. The smooth continuity is never broken or disturbed by an arabesque. Maybe the fact that Maillol comes from the Provence accounts for his love of classical figures; he is the first Frenchman since the Gothic age who shows no trace of the Baroque in his art, but has the greatness of antiquity.

His works are represented in the museums of Berlin, the Luxembourg and Swiss private collections. His son Lucien is an able painter.

BIBLIOGRAPHY: Julius Meier-Graefe, *Modern Art,* Vol. 2, G. P. Putnam's ed., 1908.—Catalogue, *Sculpture by Maillol,* Brummer Gallery, New York, 1933.

**MAINARDI (Sebastiano or Bastiano).**—Florentine painter, brother-in-law and follower of Domenico Ghirlandaio, for whom we do not possess one document or signed work. His reconstruction depends upon Vasari's statement that it was he who painted the *Assumption* in the Baroncelli Chapel, Sta. Croce.

In 1474-75 he worked at San Gimignano with Domenico; in 1494, with Granacci, collaborated with Domenico in the execution of paintings in the Duomo, Pisa; and in the same year Mainardi himself did a painting for the town hall, Pisa. He died in 1515.

Most of the anecdotes of Mainardi's life are merest speculation or fable, and his artistic personality is highly indefinite. Compilations of work to be attributed to him have been made by various art historians.

BIBLIOGRAPHY: Vasari-Milanesi.—C. de Francovich, *Sebastiano Mainardi,* Cronache d'Arte, 1927, fascs. 3, 4.—Van Marle, *Italian Schools, etc.* XIII, 1931, 186ff.

**MAINZ (Germany).**—*Cathedral.* Mainz was begun in 1036, burned in 1081, and rebuilt in the early 12th century. The original early 12th century vaults have been replaced by vaults begun in 1191. The Cathedral was consecrated in 1239. It is a representative Rhenish Romanesque church, in pink limestone, with persistent Ottonian doubled apses, transepts, towers, and lanterns. The solidity of the interior construction, with the square piers and heavy walls, is also reminiscent of Ottonian architecture. The terminal decoration of the eastern lantern and towers is 14th century Gothic. Much of the western part of the Cathedral is modern.

**MAISON CARRÉE.**—See Nîmes; also Pl. 30, Vol. I.

**MAJANO (Benedetto) da.**—Florentine sculptor and architect, 1442-1497. One of the most distin-

BENEDETTO DA MAJANO. (After Vasari.)

guished of his time. At the beginning of his life he studied engraving with his brother Guiliano.

His bust of Pietro Mellini (1474), in the Museo Nationale, Florence, is very striking in its intense realism. The tomb of St. Savinus, in the Cathedral of Faenza, with incidents of St. Savinus (1471-72?), has the same richness as Antonio Rossellino's monuments, but less gentle roundness, and more character and sense of tragic truth.

The pulpit in Santa Croce has often been called the most beautiful Italian pulpit, but in its perfection it is a little lacking in individuality. Here, Benedetto da Majano tells stories from the life of St. Francis.

About the same time (1481), Benedetto made a beautiful decoration for the door of the Audience Chamber of the Palazzo dei Signori. Of this there remain (Museo Nationale) a figure of *Justice* in ample draperies, two candelabra and a *St. John.*

BENEDETTO DA MAJANO: BUST OF FILIPPO STROZZI. (Louvre.)

For the Cathedral of Loreto, Benedetto made two angels round a lavabo in the Sacristy, and four Evangelists over a door.

At San Gimignano he made an altar to St. Fina (about 1475), and later an altar to St. Bartolda in Sant' Agostino (1494-95). He also finished the tomb of Maria of Aragon, at Monte Oliveto, Naples, begun by Antonio Rossellino on the model of his monument to the Cardinal of Portugal, in San Miniato, and (by order of the Duke of Terranuova, husband of Maria of Aragon) he made, for the same Church, an altar with an *Annunciation,*

BENEDETTO DA MAJANO: PULPIT OF SANTA CROCE, FLORENCE.

*St. John the Baptist and St. Jerome;* and six small bas-reliefs.

From the same time, date the portrait of Giotto in a medallion, and that of the musician Squarcialupi (1490) in the Duomo of Florence (ordered by Lorenzo de' Medici), the black marble tomb of Filippo Strozzi, and a round bas-relief in Santa Maria Novella.

He is also the author of a ciborium in San Domenico, Siena; and of the *Madonna dell'Ulivo* in Prato Cathedral; of the large wooden Crucifix in Florence Cathedral; and of a *Madonna* and a *St. Sebastian* in the Church of the *Misericordia.* The Louvre has his bust of Filippo Strozzi.

Towards the end of his life, Benedetto da Majano was sought after and patronised by Filippo Strozzi, for whom he began the beautiful palace in Florence. He executed in Santa Maria Novella the splendid black and white marble tomb of his patron.

BIBLIOGRAPHY: L. Düssler, *Benedetto da Majano.* Munich, 1923.

**MAJANO (Giuliano da).**—Florentine architect and designer of decoration in woodwork (1432-1490), brother of Benedetto (see: Benedetto da Majano). He worked in Florence, in Siena, but chiefly in Naples.

**MAJOLICA.**—This word signifies pottery with an opaque tin glaze. It was first produced in Spain and then in Italy, where the term "Majolica" (derived from the Balearic Island,

CUP FROM CASTEL-DURANTE REPRESENTING APOLLO AND MARSYAS. (Louvre.)

Majorca) was applied to it. No doubt the art originated in Spain. Probably the Moors introduced the

VASE FROM PESARO WITH METALLIC REFLECTIONS. (Louvre.)

use of metallic lustre, which characterises Hispano-Moresque pottery, and the chief workshops were in

SALT CELLAR WITH GROTESQUE ORNAMENTS FROM URBINO. (Baron G. de Rothschild Collection.)

Malaga and Valencia. Majorca was the centre whence the wares of Valencia were transpòrted to Italy: hence the term "maiolica."

The technique consists of covering the half-fired biscuit clay with a glaze. When this is dry the design is painted over it, and the vessel is replaced in the kiln, where the colour becomes incorporated in the enamel. The earlier ware of mezza-majolica (half majolica) was covered with a lead glaze over the white slip, with the decoration partly painted and partly scratched (sgraffito) through the slip. True majolica is covered with a stanniferous glaze (tin enamel), which, when fired, produces a milky white surface. The invention of this enamel used to be attributed to Luca della Robbia, but it was known in Italy before, although he was the first to apply it to sculpture. It was afterwards used for pavements, and for vessels destined rather for the decoration of the sideboard than for the table. The art of majolica reached its highest development in Italy during the 15th and 16th centuries. A treatise written by the potter Picolpasso, about 1550, gives an account of the technique. The earliest workshop was that of Faenza, near Bologna, founded in 1387. Little remains of its productions, save the pavement of San Petronio, in Bologna. One of the most celebrated workshops of this school was "Casa Pirota" (1520-1536). In the works of Faenza, the colour blue predominates; then orange, and yellow.

CUP FROM GUBBIO. (Louvre.)

The Caffagiolo workshop produced its finest ware about 1530. Its decoration is borrowed from Florentine art, with figures and grotesques.

At Deruta in Umbria, mother-of-pearl lustre was employed, but this was soon eclipsed by the work produced in Gubbio. The greatness of this school was probably due to Giorgio Andreoli, who was probably born in Pavia, and settled in Gubbio in 1498. He first used lustre like

COMFIT-DISH FROM DERUTA. (Louvre.)

that of Deruta, but, not content with perfecting its quality, he invented ruby lustre. The advantage of this new lustre was that it was possible to add it to finished vessels, and, as Maestro Giorgio never revealed the secret of its manufacture, pieces, already painted, were often sent to him from neighbouring towns, to receive the lustre. He died about the middle of the 16th century and the prosperity of the Gubbio workshops did not outlive him.

Urbino and Castel Durante (today Urbania) produced some of the finest pieces of majolica. The latter factory flourished from 1361 till the middle of the 18th century and is characterised by the use of musical instruments ond trophies, as ornamental motifs. Isabella d'Este who always employed the best artists, ordered a service from Castel Durante during the first third of the 16th century. Pieces of it are now scattered in various museums. They are attributed to Nicolo Pellipario, who afterwards established himself in Urbino and took the name of Nicolo Urbino, and with him the prosperity of Castel Durante workshops passed away. The most prosperous ateliers at Urbino were those directed by Francesco Xanto Civelli da Rovigo (who worked from 1529 to 1542), and by the Fontanas—Guido, son of Nicolo Pellipario and his three sons, Orazio, Camillo and Nicolo. (There is a dish by Orazio Fontana, the most famous of the three, in the Berlin Museum.) The Fontanas introduced the fashion for grotesques in ornamentation.

Many other cities in Italy produced majolica, but without much originality. In the 17th century, the majolica produced at Castelli, near Naples, was highly prized, particularly the works of the potters Grue and Gentili.

See Ceramic.

Bibliography: E. Molinier, *Les majoliques italiennes en Italie*. Paris, 1883.—Picolpasso, *Les Trois livres de l'art du potier* (translated from Italian into French by Popelin). Paris, 1860.—René Jean, *Les Arts de la terre*. Paris.—E. Hannover, *Pottery and Porcelain*, ed. B. Rackham. London, 1925.—D. Fortmun, *Catalogue of the Maiolica in the South Kensington Museum*. London, 1873.

**MAJORCA (Château of the Kings of).**—See Perpignan.

**MAKART (Hans).**—Austrian painter, 1840-1884. He distinguished himself as a painter of history. Influenced by Rubens and the Venetians. His best known pictures are in Vienna: *Catarina Cornaro, The Seven Deadly Sins, Entry of Charles V into Antwerp, Romeo and Juliet*, etc. Hans Makart had an unprecedented success in Austria. But his glory was as ephemeral as it was bright; for most of his compositions, executed hastily and without technical knowledge, have blackened.

Bibliography: Hevesi, L., *Österreichische Kunst im 19 Jahr*. Leipzig, 1903.

**MAKIMONO.** A scroll painting that unrolls horizontally.

See Japan—Art.

**MA K'UEI.**—Chinese painter of the 13th century. Grandson of Ma Fei and brother of Ma Yuan.

**MALAGO (Spain).**—*Cathedral*, begun 1534. Diego de Siloé, architect. A Griego-Romano church of the type inaugurated by the same architect in the Cathedral of Granada.

**MA LIN.**—Chinese painter of the 13th century, son of Ma Yuan and follower of his style.

**MALMAISON (Seine et Oise, France).**—This château, which has no particular beauty, was built by Josephine de la Pagerie, the future Empress Josephine, shortly before her marriage, on the site of a thirteenth century château. Josephine lived there after her divorce, and Napoleon there paid her a last visit before leaving for England in 1815. It now contains a Napoleonic museum.

Château of Malmaison, from the park (1799).

**MALOUEL (Jean).**—Flemish painter, beginning of the fifteenth century. He worked for Philip the Bold, Duke of Burgundy. About 1398, he executed five paintings for the Chartreuse de Champmol, near Dijon; and a triptych representing the Virgin between the two Saint Johns, St. Peter and St. Anthony. These works are lost. He painted the statues of the *Well of Moses* of the Chartreuse de Champmol, but no trace of this painting remains; and in 1412 he did a portrait of Jean sans Peur. He began the picture, now in the Louvre of the *Last Communion and Martyrdom of St. Denis*, which was finished after his death (1416) by Bellechose. He is also credited with a *Virgin and Child* (Louvre), and the Louvre panel representing God the Father, the Dead Christ and the Holy Ghost, in the form of a dove, with the Virgin, St. John and six angels.

Bibliography: Bouchot, H., *Les Primitifs Français*. Paris, 1904.

See Pl. 4, Vol. II.

**MANASSIJA (Serbia).**—See Byzantine Architecture, Late Period.

**MANDER (Carel van).**—Dutch painter, 1548-1606. He painted some worthless pictures, and was the master of Frans Hals. He owes his fame to his *Book of Painters*, which appeared in 1604. Mander had travelled a good deal, and knew many of the painters of whom he writes—in general, these are Netherlandish artists. In spite of the fictions and errors of the book, his testimony has great historical value. Carel van Mander's book has been reedited, with a learned commentary by P. Hymans, in Brussels, in two volumes. A part of his work has been translated into English by C. v. de Wall, New York, 1936.

Bibliography: Greve, H. E., *De bronnen van C. van Mander*, 1903.—E. Valentiner, *Karel van Mander als Maler*. Strasbourg, 1919.

**MANDORLA.**—Term used for the representation in art of the aureole surrounding a sacred figure, usually of Christ but occasionally of the Virgin, God the Father, or the Trinity. The word is derived from the almond shape of this glory, as generally depicted in Western art. In Byzantine iconography, however, the mandorla is usually elliptic. The earliest occurrence in Christian art is that in Sta. Maria Maggiore in Rome, of the 4th century.

**MANET (Edouard).**—French painter, 1832-1883. Son of a magistrate, he began his career as a cabin-boy. On his return from a voyage to Brazil, his parents yielded to his desire to be a painter. He worked for six months in the studio of Couture, and copied the masters in the Louvre. He visited Holland, Germany and Italy, and especially admired the paintings of Hals, El Greco, Velázquez, and Goya. In 1859, he exhibited the *Child with Cherries* (private collection), while his *Absinthe Drinker* (private collection) was rejected. These works show the influence of his study in the art galleries.

Manet: The Fifer. (Louvre.)

In 1863, he began to attract attention and to achieve popular notoriety with his *Dejeuner sur l'herbe* (Collection Moreau Nélaton, Musée des Arts décoratifs), then called *The Bath*. The picture was refused at the Salon. The rejections that year were so numerous, and seemed to some so little justified that the protests of the victims decided the Emperor Napoleon III to command the opening of a "Salon of the Rejected," near the official Salon. There artists exhibited, who were afterwards to become famous—Vollon, Whistler, Pissarro, J. P. Laurens, Legros, Harpignies, and others. The *Dejeuner sur l'herbe* had a "succès de scandale." Artists thought the work was revolutionary, others judged it improper. Nowadays it is amazing to think that it could have evoked so much anger. One must, however, go back to the date of its appearance. The picture did not fall into any known category, and it treated a simple study in the dimensions of an historical painting. It represents some young men in contemporary dress sitting on the grass near a nude woman, while another woman, clad only in a chemise, is bathing in the background. While the ignorant public were shocked, certain artists admired a painter who could thus overthrow all academic rules and the perceptive saw that new doors were opening to sincere painters. It was the dawn of a revolution.

Manet (E.). (His portrait, by Fantin-Latour.)

The following year (1864), *The Angels at the Tomb* and *Incident at a Bull-Fight* were received at the Salon without raising a storm. But in 1865, the *Olympia* (Louvre) brought forth a torrent of abuse. Manet had dared to represent a nude woman, painted in light tones, without obvious modelling, reclining on a white bed, and, by her side, a negress holding a bouquet, and at her feet a black cat! The freshness of touch and delicacy of some of the colour escaped most of his critics. So great was the outcry that Manet, not discouraged but heartened, went to Spain to work and to see the old masters he loved.

The following year the judges did not dare to accept the *Fife-Player* (Louvre), and the *Tragic Actor* (portrait of Rouvière in the part of Hamlet; in the Vanderbilt Collection, New York), even although the subjects could not shock the public, and their pictorial qualities are considerable. The harmony of blacks on the grey background, in the portrait of Rouvière; the white shoulder-belt and yellow cap of the *Fife-Player*, and the freshness of treatment of both these paintings must now be apparent to everyone.

Zola—who was at that time writing for *Figaro*, as critic of the Salon—urged by his friend, the painter Cézanne, took up the defence of Manet in an enthusiastic article. Public indignation affected Villemessant himself. To calm his subscribers and keep their confidence, he sacrificed his contributor, and hastened to announce that Zola had left *Figaro*.

In 1867, being again excluded from the Salon, Manet opened an exhibition on the Quai de l'Alma, which attracted a laughing, ignorant crowd. Fortunately, his defenders became more numerous. Some friends understood him and surrounded him. A group was formed of artists and men of letters, among them Pissarro, Monet, Sisley, Renoir, and Degas, encouraged by Zola, Antonin Proust and others. They often met in the Café Guerbois, Avenue de Clichy. In 1868 and 1869 things began to calm down.

The Salon accepted the portrait of Emile Zola (private collection), *The Balcony* (Luxembourg), and *Le Déjeuner* (Collection of A. Pellerin).

When the Franco-German war broke out in 1870, Manet fulfilled his duties as a citizen during the siege of Paris. As soon as peace came, he again took up the struggle which he had to maintain till the end of his life.

At this time his friends, the "Impressionists," began to influence him. He became a painter of the open air. While producing *Le Bon Bock* (1873, private collection), in which his previous style, proceeding from the old masters, especially Frans Hals, reappeared, he painted the *Chemin de fer* (private collection), which shows a little girl looking at a passing train through a railing—a picture which, owing to the vivacity of its colour, revived public hostility. Nevertheless, a dealer, M. Durand-Ruel, bought, for 40,000 francs, one of Manet's most daringly experimental paintings. *Argenteuil* (1875, private collection), representing a boatman and his wife on a bank.

In 1881, a sympathetic manifestation of a certain number of artists, members of the jury, won him a second medal at the Salon. Antonin Proust, his old comrade at Couture's studio, who had become "Ministre des Beaux Arts," hastened to confer on him the Legion of Honour, in 1882. But Manet was exhausted. He exhibited *The Bar at the Folies-Bergère* 1882, private collection), and died in 1883.

Manet played a very important part in renewing the art of painting. He destroyed the old sacred formulas. He broke down barriers which separated people. He painted scenes of real life in dimensions previously reserved for historical painting. Manet was not a thinker, but a seer. He was not always sure of himself, not always distinguished —but his hesitations and errors were those of an explorer and he had the rare merit of opening up new paths. The Impressionists went further, but he was their forerunner.

See Pl. 56, Vol. II.

Bibliography: E. Bazire, *Manet*, 1884.—Th. Duret, *Histoire d'Edouard Manet et de ses œuvres*. 1902. —C. Mauclair, *L'Impressionisme*.— A. J. Meier-Graefe, *Edouard Manet*. Munich, 1912.—J. E. Blanche, *Manet*. London, 1925.

**MANGLARD (Adrien).**—French painter of marine pictures, and engraver, 1695-1760. He spent most of his life in Italy, where he was the master of Joseph Vernet.

**"MANNERISM."**—See Pl. 24, Vol. II.

**MANNI (Giannicola).** — Italian painter of the beginning of the 16th century, of the school of Perugino. He worked in the Chapel of the Cambio, in Perugia, from 1515 to 1519, imitating the *Sibyls* of the Church of S. Maria della Pace, in Rome.

Bibliography: Crowe and Cavalcaselle, *History of Painting in Italy*. Vol. V, ed. T. Borenius.

**MANSART or MANSARD (François).** — French architect of Paris (1598-1666). Son of Absalon Mansart, a master carpenter.

In 1632, François Mansart built the Church of the Visitation (rue Saint Antoine, Paris); in 1635, the Hôtel de la Vrillière; and the same year, he undertook improvements in Blois, for Gaston d'Orléans; in 1642 (and until 1650) Mansart built for René de Longueil, the magnificent Château of Maisons. His rapid rise won him many enemies. He had to renounce the building of the Church of the Val de Grace, for which he had furnished all the plans. This half religious, half worldly building shows François Mansart imbued with classical doctrines. He built many private houses, in Paris and in the country. He modified the Hôtel Carnavalet, and built the Hôtels Conti, de Bouillon, Fieubet and d'Aumont; and at the gates of Paris, the Châteaux of Bercy and of Choisy-le-Roi. The mansard roof, a hip roof designed to make attics available for rooms, was invented by him.

Mansart (F.).

See Pl. 39, Vol. II.

**— (Jules Hardouin).**—French architect, grand-nephew of the above. Born in Paris, in 1646; died at Marly in 1708. Son of a painter named Jules Hardouin, he took the name of his uncle, whose pupil he was, when he became an architect. His career was even more brilliant than that of Le Brun. In 1674, he was charged by Louis IV with the building of the Château of Clagny; and in 1675, at the age of twenty-nine, he became an academician and architect by appointment to the king. The following year, he went to Versailles, and there reigned as master until his death. Honours were heaped upon him.

Works of Versailles after 1676, the Grand Trianon and Marly, are by him, as well as the Place des Victoires, and the Place Louis le Grand. He also began, after 1677, the Church of the Invalides, his chief work—even more so perhaps than Versailles.

He also executed numerous works at Chantilly; and in one year (1685-1686) built the Maison Royale of Saint Cyr.

Mansart was a man of affairs, as well as an artist. His high qualities justified his good fortune, possessing, as he did, a spirit of enterprise, an aptitude for managing men, self-knowledge, and ability to control his affairs. Moreover, he was an architect of genius. Not that the Versailles of Louis XIV can be attributed to him but, at Versailles, the new Orangery, the chapel, the colonnade, the stables and the Grand Trianon belong to him, and these are first rate works, which, in their variety and perfect appropriateness, reveal a profound understanding of æsthetics and of architectural technique.

See Pl. 43, Vol. II.

**MANSHIP (Paul).** — Contemporary American sculptor. He was born 25th December 1885 at St. Paul, Minnesota. He attended the local art school to learn drawing but soon realised that better opportunities for him lay in the field of sculpture. When he was twenty he came to New York to study under Solon Borglum, the animal sculptor, and there he began the training for his life work. He also studied at the Pennsylvania Academy of Fine Arts under Charles Grafly and Isadore Konti. He showed such ability that in 1909 he won a scholarship for the American Academy in Rome. For the next three years he studied in Rome, feeling the strong influence of the classical era, whose monuments were to be found in that region. He became interested in Greek and Egyptian art and also showed some appreciation of the sculpture of ancient India and China. His first work was done in a strong classical manner which he applied to some garden sculpture for a commission he received soon after his return to the United States in 1912. From neo-classicism he turned to realism, revealing a strong Renaissance feeling in the relief of his baby daughter Pauline, which is now in the Metropolitan Museum of Art. He served during the World War with a Red Cross division on the Italian front and then returned to the United States and his sculpture. Some war memorials came first and then more animal studies, tending more toward naturalistic rendition than the archaistic leanings of his early work. One of his most recent commissions is the gate in memory of Paul J. Rainey at the Bronx Zoo. There are represented lifelike renditions of some of the animals of the zoo, arranged in a decorative manner in an architectural framework. Other examples of his work may be found at the Addison Gallery of American Art in Andover, the Detroit Institute of Arts and the Metropolitan Museum of Art.

Bibliography: A. E. Gallatin, *Paul Manship, a Critical Essay on His Sculpture and Iconography*, 1917.—Paul Vitry, *Paul Manship, Sculpteur Américan*, Paris, 1927.—Also see *The Index of Twentieth Century Artists* for December, 1933.

**MANSUETI (Giovanni).**—Venetian painter of the end of the 15th century, and beginning of the 16th (1470?-1530). Pupil of Gentile Bellini.

Bibliography: Crowe and Cavalcaselle, *History of Painting in North Italy*, ed. T. Borenius. Vol. I.

**MANTEGAZZA (Cristoforo).**—Lombard sculptor, of the 15th century (died 1482). He had first been a goldsmith, and the habit of minute workmanship remained with him even when he made large architectural decorations. He is chiefly known for his work at the Certosa of Pavia.

**MANTEGNA (Andrea).**—Italian painter of Padua. One of the greatest of his period, both on account of the strength and beauty of his work, and because of his influence, which stretched as far as the south of Italy, and, to the north, as far as Germany. According to documents published by Vittorio Lazzarini, he was born in Isola di Sopra or Isola di Carturo on the territory of Vicenza. This island being a dependence of Padua, he signed himself "Andrea Mantegna Patavinus." While quite young, he became the adopted son and pupil of the celebrated scholar Squarcione. From the age of ten the little Mantegna lived in the studio frequented by the best artists, surrounded by antique marbles, the rich collection of his master. Painters such as Bono da Ferrara, Ansuino da Forli, Marco Zoppo of Bologna, came from all parts of Italy to listen to the same teaching. The great Donatello arrived in the town in 1443, and Filippo Lippi and Paolo Uccello further deepened the influence of Tuscany.

Mantegna: St. James on his way to torture (detail). (Padua, Church of the Eremitani.)

Mantegna soon showed his independence. In 1455, he went to Venice to get his contract with Squarcione annulled, alleging that he was a minor at the time of the engagement. He was now chiefly attracted by the Venetians. His connection with Jacopo Bellini began in 1450 and 1454, and he married his daughter, Nicolosia.

Mantegna: The Baptism of Hermogenes (detail). (Padua, Church of the Eremitani.)

Mantegna, formed in the Paduan School and highly sensitive to the influence of his great Venetian and Florentine contemporaries, nevertheless evolved his style out of the urgency of his own genius and according to the dictates of his temperament. The intensity of his vision, the lack of atmosphere in his pictures, the hard, flinty quality of his painting are characteristically North-Italian. He loved foreshortening, plastic and sculptural anatomy. The very tension of such draughtsmanship created a kind of beauty, as the impressive and uncompromising realism of the *Dead Christ* (in the Brera Gallery) proves. It is often said that, in Mantegna's art, intellect smothered feeling; but the result is profoundly moving. He realised that precision and realism could increase intensity of feeling, and he made use of his knowledge not to display his ability, but to intensify the emotional effect of his pictures.

His realism and his treatment of space make his works most striking. His very archæological interests—reconstructions of antique buildings, triumphal arches or pilastered porticoes, his clean-shaven Roman faces, his attempts at historically accurate local colour—all these contribute to the impression of serious and intense solidity which he gives us.

From the beginning, he showed his genius in the frescoes of the Eremitani Chapel, Padua, which are among his most famous works. Antonio Ovetari had bequeathed the chapel to Jacopo Leone, in 1443, to be decorated with scenes from the *Life of St. James* and the *Life of St. Christopher*. The works were commissioned from Squarcione, and in 1446, they were still not begun. In 1452, the history of *St. James* was almost finished. Six subjects are certainly by Mantegna: to the left, the *Baptism of Hermogenes, St. James before the Praetor, St. James Led to His Martyrdom,* the *Martyrdom of St. James;* and, to the right, the *Martyrdom of St. Christopher,* and the *Bearing away the Body of St. Christopher*. The other frescoes were executed by Bono da Ferrara, Ansuino da Forli and Niccolo Pizzolo. But the whole decoration is united in conception, and Mantegna must have directed the work of the rest. His style is splendidly revealed in the parts by his hand, in bold effects of perspective, in the height of the horizon (which is sometimes above the frame), in the drawing of the figures.

There are numerous works belonging to Mantegna's youth. Vasari mentions an altarpiece painted for the Altar of Santa Sofia of Padua, signed and dated 1448. There are fine pictures of the Virgin and Child: the *Madonna* of the Berlin Gallery, those of the Gallery of Bergamo and of the Museo Poldi Pezzoli in Milan.

About 1452, Mantegna made a painting of *St. Anthony of Padua*, representing St. Anthony and St. Bernard, kneeling and holding a crown.

On the 10th August, 1453, the Benedictines of Santa Giustina, Padua, ordered the decoration of a chapel dedicated to St. Luke. Mantegna painted the large polyptych, divided into twelve compartments and into two tiers which is now in the Brera Gallery.

About 1454, he painted the *St. Euphemia* (Naples Museum)—the painting is dated, but this date is, nevertheless, disputed—and the *St. Sebastian* (Louvre) must date from the same period. The saint is bound to the column of a ruined temple, like a statue. The numerous arrows from which he endures martyrdom do not seem to enter into human flesh but into a magnificent piece of marble, gleaming coldly beside the ruins of pagan statues.

Mantegna's *St. Sebastian* in Vienna, recalls that of the Louvre.

The *Mount of Olives* is also one of Mantegna's finest works, and intensely dramatic. Giovanni Bellini's *Mount of Olives,* is to be seen in the National Gallery, alongside Mantegna's work. Both are inspired by drawings in Jacopo Bellini's sketch book.

Mantegna was soon in demand at the rich court of Mantua. The Marquis Ludovico Gonzaga wrote to him for the first time in 1457, to ask him to come to him, and he continued to urge him. In 1459 the triptych of San Zeno was still unfinished, but it must have been a little after this date that he made the journey to Mantua.

Mantegna: Portrait of Cardinal Ludovico Mezzarota (1460). (Kaiser Friedrich Museum, Berlin.)

The altarpiece of San Zeno, in Verona, is Mantegna's last important work before his departure for Mantua. It was ordered by Gregorio Correrro, and is a triptych with the Virgin between Saints (still in the choir of San Zeno). Of the three predelle, two are in Tours: the *Prayer on the Mount of Olives,* and the *Resurrection of Christ*; and one is in the Louvre—the *Crucifixion.* To right and left, below abrupt mountain peaks, the thieves on their crosses are grimacing with suffering, but the cross of Christ stands darkly against the sky, between sombre rocks, on which are perched, like eyries, the towns of unhappy men. The group of women clasping each other forms a single block of tearful figures, round the fainting Virgin. Feverish colours, abrupt rocks seen against the sky, twisted garments, glimmers of light, the dying head of Christ—the whole is a human and eternal drama on a small panel.

Mantegna: The Mount of Olives (detail). (National Gallery, London.)

In Mantua, Mantegna found himself in a society where art and letters flourished, where the famous Vittorino Rambaldoni di Feltro founded his educational Institute of the Casa Gioconda, to hold discussions in the woods on Plato, where Alberti was erecting his classical buildings, and where Poliziano's "Orfeo" was played at rich weddings. Mantegna was charged with the decoration of the Chapel of the Castello Vecchio, whence, probably, comes the triptych, now in the Uffizi, with the rich *Adoration of the Magi* in the middle, and the *Ascension* and *Circumcision* on either side. From the same period date, probably: the *Death of the Virgin* (Prado Gallery, Madrid—the attribution to Mantegna is disputed by Morelli); *St. George* (Accademia, Venice); and the *Madonna of the Quarries,* in the Uffizi.

Mantegna's most important work was the decoration of the Camera degli Sposi, in the Castello di Corte. The work was finished in 1474. All Mantegna's qualities as a painter may be seen there—bold, perspective effects, striking and serious realism, wealth of decoration, and fair landscapes. The scenes are framed by the fall of the arches of the building, surrounded with garlands of flowers, fruit and emblems, portraits of emperors, imitation bas-reliefs, etc. Amid all this decoration are magnificent portraits of the Gonzaga family—sturdy, thick-set figures, richly dressed, and powerfully grouped. The variety of character portrayed is remarkable; but this variety is harmonised by the qualities all the figures possess in common—stately bearing and gravity. The scenes (which are sadly repainted in parts) represent: *The Reception of an Ambassador by Ludovico* (left wall on entering); *Horses and Dogs of Ludovico in a Landscape* (right of entrance); *Meeting of Ludovico with Cardinal Francesco* (left of entrance); and (on the ceiling) *Ladies Leaning over a Balustrade.*

Mantegna: Judith. (Pen drawing, Print Room of the Uffizi, Florence.)

Another of Mantegna's masterpieces is the *Triumph of Julius Cæsar* (begun 1484, finished 1492) in nine cartoons. They remained in the Pusterla Palace until 1525, when they were removed to the Castello Vecchio, and bought, in 1627, for Charles I of England. They are still to be seen in the Orangery at Hampton Court. These paintings show very clearly Mantegna's debt to the antique. The scenes represent the "Triumph" passing. Musicians playing the lyre and tambourine, follow soldier trumpeters. The second composition shows the gods of the vanquished country borne on chariots—battering-rams and all kinds of instruments of war follow—then come a mass of trophies of arms, drawn by small oxen, guarded by a youth with a pike—now come young priests bearing the sacred treasure from the temples—another blast of trumpets, and the sacrificial beasts draw near—and now the elephants, bearing the sacred fires. More trophies follow—a procession of prisoners—and, finally, Julius Cæsar himself, the conqueror, before whom goes a youth bearing the device, "Veni, Vidi, Vici."

In 1488, Mantegna went to Rome in the service of Pope Innocent VIII, to decorate the Belvedere Chapel. This work was, unfortunately, destroyed by Pius VI, in the course of enlargements of the Vatican, and we only know from Vasari that it included four frescoes, representing the *Baptism of Christ*, the *Nativity*, the *Adoration of the Magi* and the *Virgin Enthroned.*

The most important works of Mantegna's later years include: the *Virgin* of the Uffizi Gallery; the *Madonna* (Brera Gallery, Milan); the *Madonna of Victory* (Louvre), which was an offering of Francesco Gonzaga to the Virgin (1496); the *Madonna* of Santa Maria in Organo, a tempera painting, begun in 1496; *Virgin and Child* (National Gallery); the *Holy Family* (Dresden); the *Madonna* of the Museo Civico, Verona (authenticity doubtful); the *Man of Sorrows* (Copenhagen). We may also mention the religious scenes which decorate the Chapel of Sant'Andrea, in Mantua, and which were carried out by pupils, from his drawings.

Mantegna's portraits are admirable. The *Cardinal Ludovico Mezzarota* (1459), Roman in its direct force, is in Berlin; and the *Cardinal Francesco Gonzaga* in Naples.

Finally, Mantegna made two very light and graceful works, for Isabella d'Este—*Virtue Triumphing over the Vices*, and *Parnassus*. These panels were bought by Richelieu, and are in the Louvre.

In spite of the adulation he received, Mantegna remained aloof and harsh in his life. He was constantly in need of money to carry out his artistic schemes.

Mantegna was also a prolific engraver. Among his many fine and energetic works in this field, we mention seven in the British Museum: the *Seated Virgin*; *Bacchanalian Group with Silenus; Bacchanalian Group with a Wine-press;* the *Entombment*; the *Risen Christ between St. Andrew and St. Longinius*; the *Combat of Tritons*; and the *Combat of Marine Gods.* He is also credited with the splendid drawing of *Judith*, in the Uffizi.

The *Triumph of Scipio*, in the National Gallery (ordered in 1505, by Francesco Cornaro Cornelia), was finished by Lorenzo Costa.

None of Mantegna's pupils possessed his power, but his influence throughout the whole of Italy was considerable.

See Pl. 15, Vol. II.

BIBLIOGRAPHY: Thode, *Mantegna*. Bielefeld, 1897.—Charles Yriate, *Mantegna*. Paris, 1901.—Maud Cruttwell, *Mantegna*. London, 1901. —P. Kristeller, *Mantegna*. London, 1901.—F. Knapp, *Mantegna, Klassiker der Kunst*. Vol. XVI. 1910.—Crowe and Cavalcaselle, *History of Painting in North Italy,* ed. T. Borenius. Vol. II.

**MANTUA (Italy).**—The finest church in Mantua is *Sant'Andrea*, begun in 1472 by L. B. Alberti, and

MANTUA: CASTELLO DI SAN GIORGIO.

continued by Viani. The dome dates only from the 18th century. (See Alberti.)

The *Reggia* is the old palace of the Bonacoisi family. Embellished by the Dukes of Mantua, and especially by Isabella d'Este. Afterwards decorated by Giulio Romano (1525).

The *Castello di Corte* is also an old castle of the Gonzaga family. Built by Novara from 1395 to 1406, it contains famous frescoes by Mantegna in the Camera degli Sposi (1474).

**MANUEL (Nicolas).**—Swiss painter, 1484-1550, called "Deutsch." Author of a *Dance of Death* for the cloister of the Dominicans of Berne (1515); a *Judgment of Paris*; and a *Beheading of St. John the Baptist*.

**MANUELIAN (Style).**—In Portugal, Dieulafoy says: "The Manuelian style was probably a hypertrophy of the Gothic, 'Mudejar' (see) and Plateresque (see) styles of the last half of the 15th century, determined by the too rapid influx of gold."

The Monastery of Belem is the most famous of the Manuelian buildings, and shows the extraordinary richness and complexity of the style.

BIBLIOGRAPHY: Walter Crum Watson, *Portuguese Architecture*. London, 1908.

**MANUSCRIPTS (Illuminated).** —See Byzantine Art—Miniatures.

**MAN WITH A HOE (The).**—See Millet (J. F.); also Pl. 55, Vol. II.

**MAN WITH THE PINK.**—See Van Eyck; also Pl. 59, Vol. I.

**MAO I.**—Chinese painter of the 12th century, member of the Imperial Academy, known for paintings of animals.

See China—Art.

**MARATTA (Carlo).**—Roman painter, 1625-1713. Pupil of Andrea Sacchi. He was a learned, able and cold imitator of Guido Reni, and a restorer of Raphael's frescoes. The *Virgin with the Sleeping Child* (Palazzo Doria, Rome) is in the style of Guido Reni; his *Martyrdom of St. Blaise* (in Santa Maria di Carignano, Genoa) recalls Domenichino; and his *Virgin*, of the Pitti Palace, Florence, is academic art "par excellence."

**MARBURG (Germany).**—*St. Elizabeth*, 1233-1283. A typical High Gothic German *hallenkirche,* a type of church in which the nave and aisles are the same height and, flying buttresses being unnecessary, pier buttresses oppose the vaults. The interior has the appearance of a large hall. The towers of St. Elizabeth were executed in 1360.

**MARCANTONIO RAIMONDI.** —See Raimondi.

**MARCHES (The).**—A division of east-central Italy.

**MARCO D'OGGIONO.** — Lombard painter, died c. 1530. Pupil of Leonardo da Vinci, whom he imitated in rather a heavy manner. The picture of three Archangels, in the Brera Gallery, is his best-known work.

**MARCONI (Rocco).** — Venetian painter (died in 1529). Pupil of Palma Vecchio, and influenced by Giovanni Bellini. His best pictures are: *The Descent from the Cross* and the *Woman Taken in Adultery,* in the Accademia of Venice, and the *Christ between the Apostles Peter and Andrew*, in the Church of San Giovanni e Paolo.

**MAREES (Hans von).**—German painter, 1837-1887. He is, in a sense, the Puvis de Chavannes of Germany. His best-known compositions, most of which are to be found in the New Pinacothek, Munich, are *The Hesperides, St. Martin, St. George* and the *Three Ages of Life*. Among his best works must be mentioned the allegorical frescoes of the Zoological Station of Naples. Marees settled in Rome. His influence on contemporary artists was very great, especially on the Swiss Böcklin and the sculptor Hildebrand.

BIBLIOGRAPHY: Meier-Graefe, J., *Hans von Marees, sein Leben und sein Werk*. München (3rd edition), 1920.—Meier-Graefe, J., *Der Zeichner Hans von Marees*. München, 1925.

**MARESCALCO (Il).**—See Buonconsiglio.

**MARGARITONE d'AREZZO.** —Dugento painter, mentioned as renting a house in Arezzo in 1262. A signed altarpiece in the Sanctuary delle Vertighe at Monte San Savino, with the Madonna and Child, Annunciation, Nativity, Adoration of the Magi, Assumption of the Virgin and six figures in side compartments is the work about which Margaritone's paintings have been grouped. It is associated with the altarpiece in the National Gallery, which shows the Madonna and Child in a mandorla, with small scenes; and with various other panels.

BIBLIOGRAPHY: Vasari-Milanesi, I. —A. Del Vita, *La vita di Margaritone commentata, Lettere Vasariane*. Arezzo, 1910; and *Notizie e documenti sui antichi artisti aretini,* L'Arte, XVI, 1913, p. 228.—U. Pasqui, *Pittori aretini vissuti dalla metà del sec. XII al 1527,* Rivista d'arte, X, 1917-18, p. 36.—Van Marle, *Italian Schools, etc.* I, 1923, p. 329 ff.

**MARIETTE (Pierre Jean).**—French engraver and writer on art, 1694-1774. He was known not so much for his engravings as for the taste with which he enriched the fine collection of engravings and drawings which his family had left him, and by his writings: *Architecture française* (1727), *Le Cabinet Crozat* (1729), *Notice sur Léonard de Vinci* (1730), etc.

**MARIN (John).**—Contemporary American painter. He was born in Rutherford, New Jersey, in 1870, a descendant of English, Dutch and French stock. After a year spent at Stevens Institute he went into some architects' offices to act as draftsman, spending four years at that occupation. The next three years were spent in study, two at the Pennsylvania Academy of Fine Arts and one at the Art Students' League. Then he spent four years abroad in study in Paris, working in the various media of oil, watercolour and some etchings. In 1909 he became a protege of Alfred Stieglitz, who exhibits his work at An American Place now and believes in the genius and worth of this artist. Marin's early work was tinged with a relationship to the delicate colours used by Whistler, but gradually he broke away from old traditions and entered into the abstract expressionism which has since been his forte. His colours are brilliant and kaleidoscopic, enhancing greatly the decorative quality of his work. His is a most personal reaction and an attempt to suggest the nervous tenor of life in the city and the country. All his pictures are arranged with the emphasis on a central effect, an object around which all interest and movement take place. To some, his paintings are unintelligible because of the distortion of the figures and natural objects to strengthen the central point and draw the attention to it at once. He is best known for his paintings in watercolour and examples of his work may be seen in the Fogg Art Museum at Cambridge, the Columbus Gallery of Fine Arts, and the Phillips Memorial Gallery in Washington, D. C.

In 1936. the Museum of Modern Art held a retrospective exhibition of his works and Marin was acclaimed one of America's greatest watercolorists.

See Pl. 63, Vol. II.

BIBLIOGRAPHY: Herbert Seligman, Jr., ed., *Letters of John Marin*, 1931. —E. M. Benson, *John Marin*. Washington, 1935.—For other articles see *The Index of Twentieth Century Artists* for October, 1933.

**MARIOTTO ALBERTINELLI.** —See Albertinelli.

**MARIOTTO di NARDO.**—Florentine painter, School of Orcagna, influenced by the Gerini Shop.

In 1394-5 Mariotto executed the extant altarpiece for the Church of S. Donnino in Villamagna; in 1394 and 1398 altarpieces for the Duomo in Florence. He designed a window for the Duomo in 1402, and in 1404-5 worked in a chapel of the Cathedral. In 1404 he signed one of the figures in a window of S. Domenico, Perugia (the whole window has been much restored). He appears on the list of the guild of painters in Florence in 1408. In 1412 Mariotto was commissioned with Francesco di Jacopo Arrighetti to paint a panel for the Tolomei Chapel in Sto. Stefano a Ponte, the commission having come through the Confraternity of Sta. Maria in Or San Michele. In 1413 he contracted to execute a fresco of the *Madonna with Saints* over the door of Sta. Maria Primerana in Fiesole and a *St. Matthew* and a *Madonna* in the Hospital of St. Matthew. The Arte della Lana commissioned him in 1414 to paint an altarpiece for the Church of S. Lorenzo, Chapel of St. Jerome. In 1415 authorities of the above-mentioned hospital requested another representation of St. Matthew. In 1416 the Confraternity of Sta. Maria del Bigallo ordered an altarpiece from Mariotto; and in 1417 he estimates, with the Frate degli Angeli, frescoes by Ambrogio di Baldese in the Oratory where one of his own pictures was placed. He made his will in 1417.

There are no signed paintings by Mariotto; his artistic reconstruction has been built up on the identification of the S. Donnino a Villamagna (near Florence) altarpiece, a *Virgin and Child with Two Angels and Saints* and a predella. Dates upon works attributed to Mariotto range between that of the Fontelucente *Assumption* (environs of Fiesole), of 1398, and the polyptych in the Serristori Collection, Florence, of 1424.

BIBLIOGRAPHY: Vasari-Milanesi, I. —Crowe and Cavalcaselle, Douglas ed., II.—O. Sirén, *Gli affreschi nel Paradiso degli Alberti, Lorenzo di Niccolo e Mariotto di Nardo,* L'Arte, VII, 1904.—O. H. Giglioli, *Mariotto di Nardo e la sua tavola d'altare per la Pieve di Villamagna,* Osservatore Fiorentino, 1906.—Khvoshinsky e Salmi, *I pittori toscani dal XIII al XVI secolo,* II, 1914.

**MARIS (Jacob).**—Dutch painter. Born at The Hague in 1837, pupil of Van Hove, died in 1899. One of the most gifted colourists of The Hague school. He painted views of towns and meadows, ferry-boats crossing canals, and especially windmills seen against great moving clouds.

BIBLIOGRAPHY: Thomson, D. C., *The Brothers Maris*. London and Paris, 1907.

**MARLY (Horses of).**—See Coustou (Guillaume and Guillaume II); Coysevox.

**MARMION (Simon).** — Flemish painter, born in Antwerp or Valenciennes, about 1420; died in 1489. His chief work was an altarpiece, now lost, finished in 1459 for the Abbey of Saint Omer, and representing the *Life of St. Bertin* in twelve panels. It is believed that two wings of it have been found—parts are in the Berlin Museum and parts in the National Gallery. It is the only work we possess by this painter, who also painted: a figure of *St. Luke*; a portrait of Charles the Bold and of Isabella of Bourbon; several church pictures; and the illuminations of a Book of Hours, for Charles the Bold. It is just possible that the *Bishop Preaching* and *St. Francis Preaching*, in the Brussels Gallery, may be by Marmion. However, his chief fame lies in his excellent miniatures.

BIBLIOGRAPHY: Fiérens Gevaert, *Primitifs flamands*. Brussels.

**MAROCHETTI (Baron).**—French sculptor. Born in Turin, 1805; died in London, 1868. Of Italian origin, Marochetti became a naturalised Frenchman in 1841. His works include:—an equestrian statue of Emmanuel Philibert, Duke of Savoy (in the Piazza San Carlo, Turin); a bas-relief on the Arc de Triomphe de l'Etoile, Paris, representing the *Battle of Jemmapes;* and the *Tomb of Napoleon*, in the Invalides.

**MARRIAGE À LA MODE.**—See Hogarth.

**MARS BORGHESE.**—See Alcamenes.

**MARSH (Reginald).**—Contemporary American painter. He was born in Paris, France, 14th March 1898 of American parentage. While a student at Yale University he drew cartoons for the *Yale Record,* the humorous magazine published by the students. After his graduation in 1920 he went to New York and there engaged in newspaper work. In 1922 he did illustrations for *Vanity Fair* and from 1922 to 1925 he was staff cartoonist for the *Daily News.* He studied for a time at the Art Students' League under Kenneth Hayes Miller and then went abroad, where he copied the works of the old masters in Paris, Florence and London. He made cartoons for curtains for the "Greenwich Village Follies" in 1922 and 1923, for "Sancho Panza" with Otis Skinner in 1924, also for "Jack and Jill," "Dearest Enemy" and the "Almanac of 1929." He has also done many illustrations for the *New Yorker* magazine since its beginning some years ago. The subjects of his many oils are street scenes or interior views of the East Side, at work and at play in its stores and the burlesque houses. They are complicated subjects involving the use of many figures, but all are handled with ease and dexterity and present a sympathetic viewpoint. Some are almost caricatures with the well-rounded figures and vivid colours which add to the sense of reality. In the subject matter and technique his works resemble similar studies done by Forain, John Sloan and Boardman Robinson. One of his pictures, *Tattoo and Haircut,* in the Wanamaker collection shows the exterior of a shop under the "el" with the hustle and bustle of a street scene and the different physical types to be seen along any street in that district. Examples of Marsh's work are in the Metropolitan Museum of Art and the Whitney Museum of American Art in New York City.

BIBLIOGRAPHY: *Art*: *U. S. Scene, Time,* Vol. 24, December 24, 1934, p. 25.—Alan Burroughs, *Reginald Marsh, Creative Art,* Vol. 9, October, 1931, pp. 301-305.—Holger Cahill and Alfred H. Barr, Jr., *Art in America in Modern Times.* 1934.—Katherine G. Sterne, *On View in the New York Galleries,* Parnassus, Vol. 3, October, 1931, pp. 8, 34.

**MARSHALL (Benjamin).**—English painter (1767-1835), especially noted for his hunting and racing subjects.

BIBLIOGRAPHY: Walter Shaw Sparrow, *George Stubbs and Ben Marshall.* London, 1929.

**MARTIN (Henri).**—French painter, born in Toulouse, 1860. Martin was influenced by the Impressionists, and by Puvis de Chavannes. He had a kindred feeling for decoration, and, in spite of the naturalism of his figures, his paintings have the beauty of grace and breadth, and a feeling for the poetry of light.

**— DIDIER-PAPE.**—Limoges enameller, of whom it is only known that he was living in 1539, and to whom are attributed all the works signed MP, MD, MDPAPE, MDPP. The most important are an *Adoration of the Magi* and a *Christ Washing the Feet of the Apostles.* It is, however, obvious that the works attributed to Martin Didier may be divided into two series with quite distinct characteristics, and they are certainly due to two different masters.

BIBLIOGRAPHY: René Jean, *Les arts de la terre,* 3rd part: l'Emaillerie (Paris, 1911).—P. Lavedan, *Léonard Limousin et les émailleurs français.* Paris, 1913.

**MARTIN (Homer Dodge).**—American painter (1836-1897). He was born in Albany, New York, 28th October 1836, the son of a carpenter. He worked in his father's store and acted as a draftsman for an architect before taking some drawing lessons from James MacDougal Hart, the landscape painter. Other than that he had little instruction in drawing and painting. From the time he was sixteen he was trying to sell his landscapes to earn a living. They were lonely scenes of a wild romantic character accurate in detail but extremely dry in treatment. In 1862 he was working in the New York studio of James Smillie and three years later he moved to New York to open his own studio. He was still painting landscapes but of a more experimental character in soft greens and greys like nature rather than the prescribed brown tint of the Hudson River school. They no longer had a minute treatment of the foliage and the subject matter was of a more rural and quiet aspect. On a trip to England in 1876 Martin came in contact with the work of Whistler and profited by a modified tonal character. In 1882 he was sent by *Scribner's Monthly* to England to make some illustrations for an article and that winter he went to Normandy to stay. With his family he settled in Villervilie near Honfleur and stayed there for the next four years. The rustic charm of the scenery delighted him and he caught some of the impressionistic traits of the Barbizon school. During the time he spent there he was painting or storing up in his memory for future use intimate glimpses of the countryside. His eyesight was much weakened, but on his return to the United States in 1887 he continued to paint. Such scenes as the *View on the Seine,* now in the Metropolitan Museum of Art, which dates from this period are numbered among his best works painted from his memories of the Normandy country. In 1892 he went to live with his son, Ralph, in St. Paul, Minnesota, and there he died 12th February 1897 after a long illness. He died in poverty but only a few years later his pictures were selling widely, their quietude and gentle melancholy making an appeal to all.

BIBLIOGRAPHY: *Fifty-eight Paintings by Homer D. Martin,* described by D. H. Carroll, American Artists Series, 1913.—Mrs. Elizabeth Gilbert Martin, *Homer Martin, a Reminiscence,* 1904.—Frank Jewett Mather, Jr., *Homer Martin, Poet in Landscape,* American Artists Series, 1912.

**— (Robert).**—See Furniture (Eighteenth Century).

**MARTINI (Simone).**—See Simone.

**MARTINO di BARTOLOMMEO di BIAGIO.**—Sienese fresco and panel painter, influenced by Andrea Vanni and Taddeo di Bartolo, son of a goldsmith; died 1434-35.

MARTIN (HENRI): THE REAPERS. (Capitole, Toulouse.)

Martino is mentioned on the guild rolls in Siena beginning in 1389. From 1398 is his signed fresco cycle in the Church of S. Giovanni Battista at Cascina near Pisa, much ruined and restored. In 1402 he worked in partnership with Giovanni di Pietro da Napoli, executing a polyptych for the high altar of S. Chiara in Pisa, a *Madonna Enthroned with Saints* (now Museo Civico, Pisa). The document for the work specifies that Martino is to do the figures, Giovanni the rest. From 1403 is the dated and signed (by Martino alone) polyptych with half-figures in the Museo Civico, Pisa, from the Ospedale dei Trovatelli, Pisa. In 1404 he was paid for thirty figures executed for the same hospital; the dated *Marriage of St. Catherine* in the Museo Civico, Pisa, is of this year; in 1405 was active in the Crescentius Chapel in the Duomo of Siena; in 1406-7 painted in the Savinus Chapel and the Chapel of S. Niccolò. In 1407 he was paid for restoring a painting on the altar of the "Maestri de la Pietra," and was paid for paintings in the arches between the Chapel of the Palazzo Pubblico and the Sala del Concistoro. In the same year he was commissioned to paint the ceiling of the Sala dei Nove (or di Balia), Palazzo Pubblico (extant), where Spinello Aretino was also working; and he appraised Taddeo di Bartolo's frescoes in the Palazzo Pubblico. In 1408 is recorded the payment for the Palazzo Pubblico work. Andrea di Bartolo, in 1419, appraises Martino's painting in the Concistoro. Of 1425 was the signed and dated polyptych formerly in S. Antonio Abbate in Siena, now lost. In 1432 he estimated a picture of Sassetta's. A number of documents refer to minor activity of Martino's —painting the dial of the clock of the Ospedale della Scala, painting and repainting statues, etc.

BIBLIOGRAPHY: Vasari-Milanesi, I. —Della Valle, Lettere Sanesei, II, 1785.—Milanesi, Doc. . . . senese, 1854, I, II.—Borghesi e Banchi, Nuovi doc. ecc. 1898.—Crowe and Cavalcaselle, Douglas ed., III, 1908. —E. Jacobsen, *Quattrocento in Siena,* Strassburg, 1908.

**MARVILLE (Jean de).**—See Champmol; Sluter (Claus).

**MARZIALE (Marco).**—Venetian painter (flourished about 1489-1507). He shows in a striking way the influence that Northern painters, especially Dürer, had on certain Venetians—e.g., his *Supper at Emmaus* (Venice, Accademia). His *Circumcision* (London)—1500. *Circumcision* (Museo Civico, Venice—1499), and *Madonna* (Gallery of Bergamo 1504), also recall Carpaccio. He was a pupil of Gentile Bellini.

**MASACCIO (Tommaso di Giovanni Guidi).**—Florentine painter, born at Castello di S. Giovanni Valdarno in 1401; died in Rome between July, 1427, and the end of 1429, probably in 1428 (Landini and the Codex Magliabechiano both state that he died at the age of twenty-six). A pupil of Masolino.

Few records exist for the brief period of Masaccio's artistic activity. In 1421 he matriculated as a painter; in 1423 his name is found again in the register of the painters' guild. In 1426 he was active in Pisa, where he executed an altarpiece for the Church of the Carmine. Contact with Donatello is mentioned in the documents referring to this commission, and Andrea di Giusto is named as his helper. A tax declaration of 1427 gives his age as twenty-five.

The limited number of Masaccio's works is counter-balanced by their epochal importance in the development of Florentine painting. The Pisa altar of 1426 is now widely scattered: in Berlin, predella panels of the *Adoration of the Magi,* and the *Martyrdom of St. Peter and the Baptist;* and *Four Saints;* in London the central *Madonna,* and a small roundel of *God the Father;* in Vienna, the Lanckoronski Collection, *St. Andrew;* in the Pisa Gallery, *St. Paul;* and in Naples, the *Crucifixion.* Masaccio's fame rests primarily upon the frescoes in the Brancacci Chapel in the Church of Sta. Maria del Carmine, Florence, in which fresco-cycle he executed the *Expulsion from Paradise;* the *Tribute Money; Peter and John Healing the Sick with Their Shadows; Peter Baptising; Peter and John Distributing Alms;* and part of the fresco of the *Raising of the King's Son,* the rest of which is by Filippino Lippi. The other frescoes in this chapel are divided between Masolino and Filippino Lippi, and are listed under these painters. In Sta. Maria Novella the fresco of the *Trinity with Two Donors* is by Masaccio; the panel of the *Virgin and St. Anne* in the Uffizi by Masaccio and Masolino, Masaccio having executed the Madonna and Child.

Two male portraits, one in the Gardner Collection, Boston, the other in the Mellon Collection, Washington, are by Masaccio's school.

Vasari states that the Brancacci Chapel became the school of the Florentine painters of succeeding generations, and the fact is only too obvious in the strength of their influence reflected in the works which have come down to us. Masaccio did not give a new direction to the painting of Florence; he created a quattrocento form in which was expressed the spirit that had produced the trecento painting of Giotto; with him the central tendency of Florentine art entered its second great phase. Masaccio's figures are plastic, substantive, generalized as Giotto's had been, but his are moulded in light, a light which reveals, isolates and gives actuality to the forms. Like Giotto's, their weight and bulk are stated with extraordinary force, and they are articulated in relation to a limited space, thus giving to the whole composition a sense of controlled power, but in a more rational perspective and with a developed knowledge of the physical world. In them the indomitable will of Florence finds one of its most highly realized expressions.

BIBLIOGRAGHY: Vasari-Milanesi, II.—Schmarsow, *Masaccio-Studien.* —Berenson, *Flor. Painters of the Ren.*—Mario Salmi, *Masaccio.* Rome, 1930.

**MASANOBU (Kano).**—Japanese painter, 1453-1490, first master of the Kano school which was to be more fully established by his son, Kano Motonobu, after which it flourished for over three hundred years.

**MASANOBU (Okumura).**—Japanese print master, pivotal figure in the development of Ukiyo-ye (1691?-1768). He is credited with having first used printed color and *urishi-e* or lacquer prints in which a glossy surface was given to the print by an overlay of glue. He experimented with western perspective and drew many realistic scenes of the theatre, among the best of which is *Interior of a Theatre.*

**MASO di BANCO.**—Florentine Giottesque painter.

Maso is first mentioned in 1341 when his belongings in the shop of Sandro di Giovanni were sequestered on the demand of Rodolfo dei Bardi, among them an altar with the Madonna, Baptist, and St. Francis. In 1343, 1346 and 1350 he is listed on the guild rolls in Florence. Villani tells us that he was a student of Giotto; Ghiberti that he executed a story of the Holy Ghost over the entrance of Sto. Spirito and a tabernacle of the Madonna on the Piazza outside the church, also the story of St. Sylvester and the Emperor Constantine in Sta. Croce, and a marble figure on Giotto's tower. Antonio Billi mentions frescoes in the tower of the Palace of the Podestà; and the Anonimo Gaddiano repeats Ghiberti's list and Billi's attribution and, with Vasari, adds that he painted "many things" in Sto. Spirito.

The only existing works among those mentioned are the Sta. Croce frescoes, about which Maso's personality has been reconstructed on stylistic grounds. The problem has been made more difficult by his having been confused with Giottino, a painter mentioned in documents but who has left no substantiated work.

BIBLIOGRAPHY: Vasari-Milanesi, I. —Manzoni, *Statue e Matricole,* etc. —Gualandi, *Memorie,* VI.—G. Poggi, *Nuovi documenti su Maso di Banco,* Rivista d'Arte, 1910.

**MASOLINO da PANICALE.**—Florentine painter, born in 1384; probably died in 1447.

Masolino enrolled in the guild of Medici e Speziali in 1423, and of the same year is his earliest dated picture, the *Madonna* in Bremen. In 1424 he is recorded as working for the Confraternity of Sta. Croce, and it was probably in that year that he painted the fresco in Empoli, Sto. Stefano, of the *Madonna and Child and Angels.* In 1427 he was in Hungary, working for Pippo Spanno. The fresco of the *Madonna* in the Church of S. Fortunato at Todi is of 1432.

Masolino's great fresco series, those of the Brancacci Chapel in Sta. Maria del Carmine, Florence; of the Collegiata at Castiglione d'Olona; and of S. Clemente in Rome, are undated. In the Brancacci Chapel, where he painted the *Preaching of Peter;* the *Raising of Tabitha* and the *Healing of the Cripple;* and the *Fall of Adam and Eve,* his style can be contrasted with that of his great pupil, Masaccio. They reveal him as a master of an older tradition, softer, more Gothic, more two-dimensional and more sensuously graceful, without Masaccio's forceful creative energy. This impression is borne out by Masolino's other frescoes, and by his panel pictures, which include, in addition to the Bremen Madonna mentioned above, a *Madonna* at Munich; a *St. Julian* in the Uffizi (from Settimo); a predella panel of *Julian Killing His Parents* at Montauban; an *Annunciation* formerly in the Henry Goldman Collection, New York; and now in the possession of the Mellon Foundation; and the figures of St. Anne and Angels in Masaccio's *Madonna with St. Anne* in the Uffizi.

BIBLIOGRAPHY: Vasari-Milanesi, II. —Schmarsow, *Masaccio-Studien,* I. —G. Poggi, *Masolino e la Compagnia della Croce in Empoli,* Rivista d' Arte, III, 1905.—P. Toesca, *Masolino da Panicale,* 1908.—Berenson, *Study and Criticism of Italian Art,* II, 1914.—R. Offner, *A St. Jerome by Masolino,* Art in America, 1920.

**MASSON (Antoine).**—French engraver, 1636-1700. The influence of G. Audran is apparent in his portraits of the Comte d'Harcourt, of the painter Dupuis, and of Gaspard Charrier. Masson engraved the *Pilgrims of Emmaus,* by Titian; *The Assumption,* by Rubens, etc.

He had many pupils, among them Pierre Drevet.

**MASTABA.**—Pyramidal building, in stone or brick, erected over the vault where the Egyptian mummies were placed. The Mastaba served as a chapel, contained offerings, and was decorated with paintings. The relatives of the deceased could go there when they wished to visit his "double." It communicated, by means of a shaft, with the vault where the mummy rested, but this shaft was carefully filled in, and made impassable, once the mummy had been laid there.

**MASTER of the ALTAR of ST. BARTOLOMEW.** — German painter, 15th and beginning of 16th century,—so-called from one of his works (in Munich) which is both naïve and precious. He also painted a *Crucifixion* (Cologne), and a *St. Thomas* (Cologne). His pictures are rather awkward, but expressive. He shows a definite influence from the works of early Flemish and Dutch masters. His best work is the *Descent from the Cross,* in the Louvre. It lacks simplicity, certain attitudes are affected, but the colour has a richness and warm brightness which is uncommon at this period.

BIBLIOGRAPHY: Aldenhoven, *Geschichte der Kölner Malerschule.* Lübeck, 1902.—Escherich, M., *Die Schule von Köln.* Strassburg, 1907. —Huppertz, A., *Die altkölnische Malerschule.* München, 1914.

**— of the BAMBINO VISPO.**—An anonymous Florentine painter of the school of Lorenzo Monaco, called thus by Osvald Sirén, whose works have been gathered together through their stylistic affinity.

BIBLIOGRAPHY: O. Sirén, *Di alcuni pittori fiorentini che subirono l'influenza di Lorenzo Monaco,* L'Arte, IV, 1907, p. 337; and *Don Lorenzo Monaco,* p. 171; and *A Late Gothic Poet of Line,* Burlington Magazine, 1913-1914, XXIV, p. 323.

**— of the CABINET of AMSTERDAM (also known as the "Master of the Hausbuch").**—German engraver, so named because of a series of his works found in the Cabinet of Engravings in Amsterdam.

He probably lived in the middelrhenish region in the last quarter of the 15th century. His engravings are chiefly of genre scenes, allegories and pastorals. His work is able and refined and executed in the so-called dry point manner.

The master seems to have been the head of a large shop in which many paintings were executed. No agreement has been reached in regard to which of these paintings were executed by the master himself. The most likely are a triptych in Freiburg, some single panels in Frankfort and Berlin, and the *Lovers* in Gotha. Other pictures in Dresden, Mainz, Karlsruhe, St. Louis, Basle, and elsewhere. The name "Master of the Hausbuch" was given to him from a large book with illustrations in pen drawing, preserved in the collection of Count Waldburg-Wolfegg.

BIBLIOGRAPHY: Bossert und Storck, *Das mittelalterliche Hausbuch.* Leipzig, 1912.—Flechsig, E., *Der Meister des Hausbuchs als Maler,* Zeitschrift für bild. Kunst. VIII. 1897.—Geisberg, *Die Anfänge des deutschen Kupferstichs und der Meister E. S.* Leipzig, 1909.—Lehrs, M., *Bilder und Zeichnungen vom Meister des Hausbuchs.* Johrbuch der preuss. Kunstsaml., XX.—Storck, *Der Meister des Amsterdamer Kabinetts,* 1912.

**— of the CASTELLO NATIVITY.**—Florentine master of the 15th century, who gets his name from the *Nativity with God the Father and Angels* in the Uffizi (from the Villa Reale di Castello). An eclectic and rather slight little master, he was evidently influenced by a succession of painters, including Lippi, Angelico, Botticelli and Benozzo. His style has been recognized in a number of pictures, mainly Madonnas and Nativities, and in three female profile portraits, in the Bache and Lehman Collections, New York, and the Gardner Museum in Boston.

**— of the DEATH OF MARY.** —See Cleve.

**— E. S. (or "The Master of 1466").**—German engraver, whose name is unknown, 15th century. His works are very numerous. Like most of his successors, his work is skillful, though still timid, and he had the characteristically German delight in careful workmanship. He made an alphabet, in which each letter is formed of a group of figures, animals, or plants: one represents a tournament; others, saints.

The modelling is indicated so lightly and delicately that they suggest pencil sketches. One of his most charming works is the *Infant Christ Being Bathed.* The Virgin, seated under a curtained dais, is absorbed in reading, while a kneeling servant bathes the smiling infant in a tub, through the naïve architecture in the background may be seen a simple landscape—a tree, and a castle on a hill. The execution is free, without stiffness, and shows that the artist was master of his means.

Perhaps better known is the *Madonna of Einsiedeln,* which represents the interior of a Gothic Cathedral, in which a number of people are assembled. Of the works of this master deserve to be mentioned:—*The Sibyl Announcing the Nativity to Augustus;* the *Virgin Surrounded by Eight Saints;* the *Stable at Bethlehem,* and many others.

The influence of Master E. S. was very great, and was felt as far as Italy, where it is not impossible to find it in the work of Baccio Baldini. In Germany itself he had numerous followers and imitators.

BIBLIOGRAPHY: Cust, L., *The Master E. S. and the ars moriendi.* Oxford, 1898.—Hind, A. M., *History of Engraving and Etching,* 1923.—Lehrs, M., *Die Spielkarten des Meisters E. S.,* Chalk Ges. 1891.

**— of the HOLY BLOOD.**—Flemish painter, whose name is unknown, and who flourished in the first third of the 16th century. His name comes from the Chapel of the Holy Blood, in Bruges, where is his chief work—the *Deposition from the Cross,* offered in 1519 by J. Van der Straeten. Other works by this master appear to be the *Deipara Virgo* of the Church of Saint Jacques, in Bruges; *Lucretia* (Budapest Museum); and *Holy Family between St. Barbara and St. Catherine* (Weber Collection, Hamburg). The artist was influenced not only by Gerard David, but also by Quentin Matsys and the Antwerp school.

**— of the HOLY KINSHIP.**—Cologne painter, 15th century. Author of a great number of pictures in various German galleries. His main work, rendering the *Holy Kinship,* from which his name was derived, is preserved in the Wallraf Richartz Museum in Cologne. He was influenced by Flemish artists.

Less mystical than his contemporaries of the Cologne school, the painter aimed at rendering familiar attitudes and expressing the character of his figures, rather than idealising them. His colour is bright and pleasant.

BIBLIOGRAPHY: Aldenhoven, *Geschichte des Kölner Malerschule.* Lübeck, 1902.—Huppertz, A., *Die altkölnische Malerschule.* München, 1914.

**— K. I. P.**—Limoges enameller, 16th century, whose existence is hypothetical. A certain number of important works are grouped under this designation, almost all "grisailles," which are certainly by the same hand, and bear the monograms KIP, IP, IPK, KI, or a lion and the initials IK.

BIBLIOGRAPHY: P. Lavedan, *Léonard Limosin et les Emailleurs Français.* Paris, 1913.

**— of the LEGEND of ST. LUCY.**—Flemish painter of the end of the 15th century, whose identity is unknown. His chief work is the *Martyrdom of St. Lucy* (Church of Saint Jacques, Bruges), which bears the date 1480. He worked in Bruges and was strongly influenced by works of D. Bouts and H. Memling.

# FLORENTINE ARCHITECTURE

*During the course of the fifteenth century, Florentine architecture changes from the Gothic style to that of the Renaissance. The forms of ancient art are adopted to replace those of the Middle Ages; the Roman column is substituted for the Gothic pillar, the semi-circular arch succeeds the pointed arch. The introduction of ancient architecture begins with the use of decorative details, but gradually there appears an interest in the essential parts of construction. The column carries the entablature, the pediment, all the ancient orders, and finally modern architecture accepts the law of proportions laid down by Greek art.*

ARNOLFO DI CAMBIO AND BRUNELLESCHI: DUOMO OF FLORENCE. *(Photo by Alinari.)*

ARNOLFO DI CAMBIO: NAVE OF SANTA CROCE, FLORENCE. *(Photo by Brogi.)*

ALBERTI: FAÇADE OF SANTA MARIA NOVELLA, FLORENCE. *(Photo by Alinari.)*

## Florentine Churches

The famous cupola of the Cathedral of Florence, constructed by Brunelleschi in the first half of the fifteenth century, was anticipated in its general arrangement by the architect of the cathedral, Arnolfo di Cambio. The beautiful façade of Santa Maria Novella by Alberti is only a veneer of marble, prefiguring the innumerable Jesuit churches of the sixteenth and seventeenth centuries; but it also presents many similarities to Romanesque churches. In the fifteenth century, the Renaissance manifests itself only in ornamentation.

ALBERTI: RUCELLAI PALACE, FLORENCE. *(Photo by Brogi.)*

PITTI PALACE, FLORENCE. *(Photo by Brogi.)*

MICHELOZZO: RICCARDI PALACE, FLORENCE. *(Photo by Brogi.)*

## Florentine Palaces

In the Middle Ages there were fortresses placed right in the town with only a few windows opening on the street. In the fifteenth century architecture became more open in aspect, while preserving the general arrangement of the original building. The projections of rusticated stones persist sometimes, especially on the ground floor. Soon the ancient orders make their appearance and begin to frame the windows.

BRUNELLESCHI: PAZZI CHAPEL, FLORENCE. *(Photo by Brogi.)*

MATTEO CIVITALI: TEMPIETTO, CATHEDRAL OF LUCCA. *(Photo by Brogi.)*

DESIDERIO DA SETTIGNANO: TOMB OF MARSUPPINI. SANTA CROCE. FLORENCE. *(Photo by Brogi.)*

BRUNELLESCHI AND MANETTI: NAVE OF SAN LORENZO, FLORENCE. *(Photo by Alinari.)*

## Imitation of the Antique

The architects first borrowed from ancient art decorative elements, but when they adopted the column, which is not only an ornamental agent but also a useful and active unit, the system of the buildings was transformed. On the columns they were not able to support pointed arches as they had on Gothic pillars. Gradually Greco-Roman architecture returned and churches began to resemble the first Christian basilicas.

# VENETIAN ARCHITECTURE

*The Republic of Venice has always occupied a place apart in the history of Italy. It belongs to the continent, but its empire is in the eastern Mediterranean; it is an Asiatic power. Its architecture manifests this diversity of the empire; it is Romanesque and Byzantine, it is Gothic, it is Arabic, and finally it is classical. All these elements exist and mingle together to make up the most varied and the most picturesque architectural decoration in the world. In the eastern manner the Venetians have always loved decorative polychromy, and in the Gothic and Arabic manner, they have multiplied linear fantasies; finally they show a classical elegance.*

INTERIOR. SAINT MARK'S.
*(Photo by Martin and Michieli.)*

PIAZZA AND BASILICA OF SAINT MARK'S.
*(Photo by Alinari.)*

DUCAL PALACE: PORTA DELLA CARTA.
*(Photo by Anderson.)*

## St. Mark's

The church of St. Mark's is one of the richest buildings in the world. It is a church of Byzantine plan—a Greek cross, covered by five domes. Flamboyant embellishments are placed upon its roofs, but its decoration in the eastern manner results particularly from its covering of marbles and mosaics. There is no surface which is not adorned with precious material. In the interior, walls and vaults scintillate with gold, and upon this gleaming background Byzantine figures appear accompanied by inscriptions. The taste for mosaic was preserved in the many restorations of this monument, and one may see mosaics there after compositions by Tintoretto.

## Venetian Palaces

Since the public square is lacking in Venice, these square palaces enclose a narrow court and they present upon one side a richly adorned façade. The other façades show an unprepared masonry, generally of brick. The visible façades are of different periods and styles; some are in the Romanesque style, others are Gothic; the Renaissance and the classical styles are also found in Venetian palaces. Certain buildings—including the Palace of the Doges—show the influence of Mohammedan architecture. Whatever the style of these buildings may be, it is very remarkable that the transformations are much more in the decorative elements than in the fundamental arrangement of the structure. One may substitute flamboyant arches for Romanesque, and the ancient orders for Gothic columns transforming the appearance of the palace without changing the placing of the windows and the loggias. At the end of the Grand Canal upon the piazzetta the most beautiful types of architecture of this city are found; St. Mark's, the Palace of the Doges, and the Library constructed by Sansovino. The jewels of polychrome marble are rendered still more precious by the patina of time.

ENTRANCE OF THE GRAND CANAL: IN THE BACKGROUND, SANTA MARIA DELLA SALUTE, AT THE RIGHT, THE LIBRARY CONSTRUCTED BY SANSOVINO.
*(Photo by Michieli.)*

CORNER OF THE PALACE OF THE DOGES.
*(Photo by Martin and Michieli.)*

VENDRAMINI PALACE.
*(Photo by Martin and Michieli.)*

COURT OF THE PALACE OF THE DOGES.
*(Photo by Michieli.)*

FARSETTI PALACE.
*(Photo by Alinari.)*

THE CA D'ORO.
*(Photo by Michieli.)*

BIBLIOGRAPHY: Fierens Gevaert, *Les Primitifs Flamands.* Brussels, 1909.—Friedländer, M. J., *Altniederl. Malerei,* Vol. VI.

**— of the LEGEND of ST. URSULA.**—Anonymous Flemish painter, whose works date from the second half of the 15th century. He is named after a series of eight pictures from the life of St. Ursula (Convent des Sœurs noires, Bruges). The work is a little anterior to the *Shrine of St. Ursula* (by Memling), and the colour is less brilliant. Other paintings are in Aix-la-Chapelle (*Madonna*), New York (*Madonna,* and diptych), Philadelphia (Johnson Coll.), Bergamo, and in many private collections.

BIBLIOGRAPHY: Sir Martin Conway, *The Van Eycks and their Followers.* London, 1921.

**— of the LIFE of MARY.**—German painter, of the second half of the 15th century, whose name is unknown. He painted chiefly scenes from the Life of the Virgin and from the Passion.

It is supposed that he was the pupil of Dirk Bouts. He combines the composition, types and colour of the Flemings, with the gentle sweetness of the school of Cologne.

There is a *Crucifixion* by this artist in the Museum of Cologne, and another in the gallery of Munich. The latter also possesses an altarpiece of the Virgin, in eight panels (except one, which is in London) representing scenes from her life. In 1463, his studio produced the *Seven Joys of Mary* for the altar of Linz, on the Rhine; then a *St. Catherine and St. Barbara* (Cologne); a *Virgin with St. Bernard* (Cologne); the *Virgin in a Garden* (Berlin); and a *Descent from the Cross* which is his finest work.

See Pl. 3, Vol. II.

BIBLIOGRAPHY: Aldenhoven, *Geschichte der Kölner Malerschule.* Lübeck, 1902.

**— MATEO.**—See Mateo (Master).

**— M. D.**—French enameller, 16th century. Author of several triptychs, representing the *Life of St. John the Baptist* (Lyon, Bologne, etc.).

**—of MOULINS.**—French painter, 15th century, whose name is unknown. It has been suggested that he may be identified with Jean Perréal. In any case, under the name "Maître de Moulins" have been grouped certain works, which seem to be by the same hand. The most famous of these is a fine altarpiece in Moulins Cathedral, painted about 1498, representing the Virgin and Child, her feet on a crescent moon. The figure of the Virgin is sweet and tender, the colour is both bright and refined; and the angels surrounding the Madonna are graceful and charming.

*The Nativity,* in Autun, is earlier, and was probably painted in 1483.

The Louvre possesses two "wings," which have been attributed to the Master of Moulins. They represent Pierre de Bourbon with St. Peter, and Anne de Beaujeu with St. John in a fresh-coloured landscape, in which the Castle of the Bourbons may be distinguished (about 1488). In another painting (Collection of Madame Yturbe) one sees the portrait of Suzanne de Bourbon, daughter of Anne de Beaujeu, which is attributed to the Master of Moulins, and which was painted about 1488. The artist is also given:—a Portrait (Glasgow), *Magdelen and Donor* (Louvre), *Veronica,* the style of which recalls the Louvre picture, and a *Virgin* (Brussels).

MASTER OF MOULINS: ANNE DE BEAUJEU AND ST. JOHN. (Louvre.)

The personality of the Master of Moulins, and the works which must be ascribed to him and his school are naturally the cause of many controversies.

See Pl. 4, Vol. II.

BIBLIOGRAPHY: H. Bouchot, *L'exposition des primitifs français.* Paris, 1904.—P. Durrieu, *La peinture à l'exposition des primitifs français.* Paris, 1904.

**— of the ST. CECILIA ALTARPIECE.**—Identifying name for an anonymous Florentine painter, contemporary with Giotto and the third well-defined master, with Giotto and Pacino di Bonaguida, of his period. More lyrical and narrative than Giotto, and more a miniature painter, the St. Cecilia Master exercised a considerable influence upon the development of the trecento Florentine school. His style is related to that of Roman painting. He is so called from the altarpiece by him in the Uffizi, representing *St. Cecilia and Scenes from Her Life.* In addition his hand has been recognized in the following works: Assisi, San Francesco, Upper Church, *Life of St. Francis,* Scenes 1, 26-28; Florence, S. Giorgio sulla Costa, *Madonna and Child;* Florence, S. Simone, *St. Peter and Angels;* Montici, Sta. Margherita, *St. Margaret and Six Scenes from Her Life.*

BIBLIOGRAPHY: A reconstruction of and complete bibliography for the St. Cecilia Master are given in R. Offner, *A Corpus of Florentine Painting.* New York, Section III, Vol. I, 1930.

**—of SAINT SEVERINO.**—German painter, end of the 15th century. School of Cologne, but the artist is less idealistic than the other painters who surrounded him. His figures are more realistic, often deliberately made ugly—faces wrinkled, nose and cheek-bones made too prominent, complexions reddened. His best known pictures are the *Adoration of the Magi* (Cologne) and the *Legend of St. Ursula.*

BIBLIOGRAPHY: Huppertz. A., *Die altkölnische Malerschule.* München, 1914.—Scheibler and Aldenhoven, *Geschichte der Kölner Malerschule.* Lübeck, 1902.

**—of the UNICORN.**—See Duvet.

**— WILHELM.**—See Wilhelm.

**MATAHEI (Ionasa).**—Japanese painter of the 17th century, who broke with tradition and, disdaining the "noble" art of the Tosa school, devoted himself to the representation of popular scenes.

See Japan—Art.

**MATEJKO (Jan).**—Polish painter (1838-1893). He was an ardent patriot, and painted a great many historical pictures.

**MATEO (Master).**—Spanish sculptor and architect, probably of French origin. In the last quarter of the 12th century, he built the celebrated narthex of the Cathedral of Santiago de Compostela, the "Portico de la Gloria," which in the amplitude of its proportions rivals the great French porches, surpassing them in power of expression and grandeur of execution. This porch is raised, like a church, over a crypt. Only the interior decoration is intact. Against the pier of the great bay is a small marble column, which forms a pedestal for the statue of St. James. Its shaft is a tree of Jesse. Its capital has a strange representation of the Trinity. On the columns of the embrasures of the three doorways are figures of St. James and prophets (right), and of the Apostles (left). In front of them are statues, less numerous, with their backs to the external pillars of the porch. These are four prophets and a crowned woman—possibly the prophetess Judith—and a veiled woman, the Sibyl of the Last Judgment. In the four corners of the doorway are four angels sounding trumpets to awaken the dead. Between the tympana of the three portals, angels gather in their robes the souls of the resurrected. On one side, on the curve of the arch, angels and elect form couples of the blessed; on the other side, devils torture the damned. In the tympanum of the middle doorway, the Christ (a gigantic figure, over five metres high) is surrounded by Evangelists and angels. On the immense archivolt are the twenty-four Kings of the Apocalypse, playing divers instruments in honour of the Heavenly King. In Christian Spain, before the era of the great cathedrals of the 13th century, there is no monument comparable with the narthex of Santiago de Compostela—the work of an expressive master, who was as perfect a poet as he was a great sculptor and a learned architect. This "Portico de la Gloria" is the more remarkable when one considers the date, which is carved under the lintel, on the right and left of the figure of St. James, in an inscription in which the master himself is proudly mentioned: "In the year of the Incarnation 1183, of the Spanish era 1226, 1st April, the lintels of the great doorway of the Church of St. James have been placed in position by Master Mateo, who has been master-builder since the foundation of the narthex." A donation from the King of Leon, Ferdinand II, to Master Mateo, which is preserved in the archives of the Cathedral of Compostela, proves that the artist was master builder at the beginning of the year 1168. The works undertaken at that date were probably those of the lower chapel, which was to extend the foundations of the Church and serve as a crypt to the great narthex.

Everything points to the belief that this bold architect, this vigorous yet delicate sculptor, was of French origin. However that may be, neither the Romanesque sculptors of France, nor those of Bruges had the dramatic power, or the epic quality of the master who, in 1183, placed in position the lintels of the great doorway of Compostela. He is one of the few mediæval artists whose name is known to us.

**MATISSE (Henri).**—Contemporary French painter, graver and sculptor. He was born 31st December 1869 in Cateau (Nord). As a youth he attended the art school of Maurice la Tour in St. Quentin, but began his career as a barrister. He went to Paris in 1892 to obtain his degree, but his great love for art made him change his profession and he enrolled in the Académie des Beaux-Arts as the pupil of Bouguereau, Gérôme and Gustave Moreau, showing remarkable ability in draftsmanship. In his frequent wanderings through the Louvre Chardin's style seemed to appeal to him most. He travelled considerably and had the opportunity to study the art of Giotto and other Italian primitives as well as Negro and oriental art, and was especially impressed with the latter's expressive simplicity. Back in Paris he went through all the phases of Impressionism. In 1896 he exhibited at the Salon of the Champs de Mars, 1901 at the Salon des Indépendants and from 1903 regularly at the Salon d'Automne. After a brief stay in St. Tropez he spent two years in Morocco, and returning to Paris in 1908 he opened an art school for a short time; students from all over the world came to study with him. One of the leaders of the Fauves, Matisse expressed his aims as: simplification, organisation and expression. His style is a reaction against the methods of copying old masters in the Louvre, a position which he held as a young man through the French government. His passion for order and simplicity made him render the maximum expression with the minimum of means. Keen observer that he is, he catches the salient and vital significance of objects and perpetuates these truths with a few logical and symbolic strokes. He was especially successful in his expressive distortions, which have probably been affected by the paintings of El Greco, Oceanic and Negro art; his abstractions are the culmination of his intellectual conception of form. Matisse is primarily a designer and decorator and is more interested in pattern than in rendering tactile values of objects. He paints with verve—large flat areas of bright colour spots are juxtaposed in great order, applying only pure colour and not seldom white and black. He is not in sympathy with the accepted colour traditions of the Impressionists. His subject matter includes portraits, nudes, landscape, interiors and still life; his lithographs are considered as fine as his paintings. Since 1916 his work has achieved a mellow maturity, a melodiousness which delights the eye rather than torments the spirit. He illustrated Mallarmé's *Poésies.* The Luxembourg owns his *Odalisque* and *Le Buffet*; other works may be seen in the museums of Moscow, London, Oslo, Copenhagen, Paris, Berlin, Chicago, New York and Philadelphia.

BIBLIOGRAPHY: A. Basler, *Henri Matisse,* 1924.—Élie Faure, *Henri Matisse,* 1920.—Marcel Sembat, *Henri Matisse, et son Œuvre,* 1920.

**MATSYS (Cornelius).**—Flemish painter (before 1508-about 1580).

MATSYS (QUENTIN).

Son of Quentin Matsys. His paintings include: *The Return of the Prodigal Son* (Amsterdam), and *St. Jerome in a Landscape* (Antwerp). He is known better as creator of a number of drawings and engravings, in which landscape plays an important part.

**— (Jan).**—Flemish painter (1509-1575). Son of Quentin Matsys. Besides many copies of his father's works, he painted:—*Judith with the Head of Holophernes* (Boston); *Hospitality Refused to the Virgin and St. Joseph* (Antwerp); *David and Bethsabe* (Louvre); the *Prophet Elias* (Karlsruhe), etc.

**— (Quentin).**—Flemish painter. Born in Louvain in 1466. Died, 1530. Son of a locksmith, Joos Matsys, he began by learning ironmongery, and some attribute to him the beautiful well-cover which adorns the Cathedral Square in Antwerp. In any case, he studied painting at the same time, for in 1491 he became a master of the Guild of St. Luke. It is uncertain whether he visited Italy, but this is unlikely.

MATSYS (QUENTIN): PORTRAIT OF A CANON. (Lichtenstein Gallery, Vienna.)

It is difficult to define the genius of this first great painter of the Antwerp school. He painted religious pictures, portraits, "genre" scenes, decorations. He rendered with equal success the gentle faces of Madonnas and saints, faces in which all human passions left their mark, and the peaceful, homely features of good citizens. His colour is at once rich and soft. His style of painting recalls that of Gerard David and Dirk Bouts, with more liveliness and fancy. He unites the qualities of the old school of Bruges with those of the new school of Antwerp, of which he is the first representative. The influence of Italian Renaissance art characterises this school. This is apparent in the architectural setting of many of Matsys' pictures (particularly of his religious pictures), in which Renaissance forms (round arches, and little ornamental columns) mingle strangely, but not inharmoniously, with Gothic forms. A knowledge of the works of Leonardo da Vinci must also be assumed, for reasons of his subtle shading of flesh tints and his interest in the physiognomic character studies.

MATSYS (QUENTIN): MADONNA. (Berlin.)

Matsys' earliest works were religious pictures, such as: the *Face of Christ*, and *Face of the Virgin* (Antwerp), *Madonna* (Berlin), *St. Luke Painting the Virgin* (preserved only in a later engraving). One of the most charming works of this period is the *Virgin and Child*, in the Brussels Gallery. Shortly after, about 1502, the artist must have painted a large altarpiece found in Spain, at Valladolid, representing, in the interior, the *Nativity* and the *Adoration of the Magi*; and, on the exterior, the *Mass of St. Gregory*.

The oldest dated work of Quentin Matsys is the *Legend of St. Anne*, painted in 1509, for the Confraternity of St. Anne, in Louvain (Brussels Gallery). In the middle panel, the Virgin with the Child is seated near St. Anne, surrounded by Mary Salome, Mary Cleophas and their family. On the left wing, an angel announced to St. Joachim the forthcoming birth of the Virgin. On the right wing, we see the *Death of St. Anne*. The colour is delightful—warm and harmonious; bright in the foreground, and fading softly into the distance.

Quentin Matsys' masterpiece is perhaps the *Lamentation of Christ* (Antwerp Gallery), which was finished in 1511. The bright colours of the dresses contrast with the body of Christ. The left-hand wing shows *Salome*, presenting the head of St. John the Baptist to Herod and his wife; and, on the right, the *Martyrdom of St. John the Evangelist*.

The works of this time show, more and more strongly, Italian influence. There is the *Portrait of a Man* (Musée Jacquemart André, Paris), painted in 1513, from a medal which probably represents Cosimo di Medici; then a charming and delicate little *Magdalen*, (Antwerp Gallery); the *Virgin and Child Playing with a Lamb* (Posen Museum); and various "Calvaries."

Of Matsys' "genre" pictures, one of the finest is in the Louvre, *The Money Changer and his Wife*, painted in 1514. The faces are admirably observed.

Matsys' portraits include:—Portrait of Erasmus (Pal. Corsini, Rome); *Head of a Canon* (Vienna); portrait in the Uffizi Gallery, etc.

It is thought that Matsys also furnished cartoons for tapestries—notably for the one representing the *Life of the Virgin*, in the Cathedral of Aix.

See Pl. 2, Vol. I; Pl. 1, Vol. II.

BIBLIOGRAPHY: Boschere, J. de, *Quentin Massys*. Brüssel, 1907.—Brising, H., *Quentin Massys*. Uppsala, 1909.—Cohen, W., *Studien zu Quentin Massays*. Bonn, 1904.—Conway, Sir Martin, *The Van Eycks and their Followers*. London, 1921.—Friedländer, M. J., *Altniederl. Malerei*. Vol. VII.

**MATTEO da CAMPIONE.**—Italian sculptor, of the end of the 14th century, who worked at Monza, on the façade and pulpit of the Duomo, and on the Baptistery. He introduced Tuscan forms into his work.

**— di GIOVANNI di BARTOLO (called Matteo da Siena).**—Sienese Painter, born c. 1430 in Borgo S. Sepolcro; died 1495 in Siena. Active from 1452-53 until his death; influenced by Domenico di Bartolo, Vecchietta, and the school of Florence, particularly Antonio Pollaiuolo.

There are many extant pictures by Matteo di Giovanni, among them: the 1470, Siena Academy *Madonna Enthroned*; the 1477, S. Eugenia, Siena, *Madonna and Child;* the 1479, S. Domenico, Siena, *Pietà*, lunette; *Barbara Enthroned;* and *Adoration of the Magi*, lunette; the 1482, Cambridge, Fogg Art Museum, *St. Jerome;* the 1483, Siena, Duomo, *Samian Sibyl;* the 1487, Borgo San Sepolcro, Sta. Maria dei Servi, *Assumption of the Virgin, Annunciation and Saints;* the 1488, Naples, Museo Nazionale, *Massacre of the Innocents;* the 1491, Siena, Sta. Maria dei Servi, *Massacre of the Innocents*.

BIBIOGRAPHY: Crowe and Cavalcaselle, Hutton ed.—Borghese e Banchi, *Nuovi doc., etc.,* 1898.—Jacobsen, *Das Quattrocento in Siena,* 1908.—Berenson, *Central Italian Painters,* 1909.—G. F. Hartlaub, *Matteo da Siena u. s. Zeit* (Zur Kstgesch. des Auslandes). Strassburg, 1910.

**— da GUALDO.**—Umbrian painter, active from 1460; died 1503, a pupil of Giovanni Boccati da Camerino. His work is hardly to be seen outside of Italy and is concentrated in Umbria and the Marches.

**MAUBERGEON TOWER.**—See Poitiers.

**MAUSOLEUM of HALICARNASSUS.**—Mausolous, satrap of Caria, died in 353 B.C. Although under Persian authority, he had an intense admiration for Hellenic culture. His sister, Artemisia, whom he married, according to Carian custom, was overcome with grief at his death. His obsequies were celebrated with competitions of poetry and eloquence in which Theopocupus and his master, Isocratus, took part. His widow, Artemisia, built a gigantic tomb, the *Mausoleum,* which the Greeks counted among the Seven Wonders of the World. It was built at Halicarnassus, on the coast of Asia Minor. The architects were Pythios and Satyros; and the sculptures were executed by Timotheos, Bryaxis, Leochares and their master, Scopas. When Artemisia died, in 351 B.C., the work was not yet finished. The very foundations of the Mausoleum had almost disappeared when, in 1856, an English mission made excavations and discovered important remains. The sculptures were transported to the British Museum. The reconstruction of the whole building still left many doubts. (Various drawings of reconstructions, in the British Museum.)

ARTEMISIA. (Figure from the Mausoleum of King Mausolus, British Museum.)

Among the fragments of sculpture in the British Museum, the most important and best preserved are the figures of Mausolus himself, and Artemisia, his wife, which were placed side by side on the chariot which crowned the monument. The head of Mausolus is fairly well preserved. It presents all the characteristics of a portrait, with its low forehead, deep-set eyes, bearded and rather heavy face, and the hair thrown back. The clothing is carved with consummate skill. The face of the Queen has been entirely destroyed. These figures are very important in the history of art. They show the way in which Greek sculpture developed after the Parthenon figures. One is tempted to see the hand of Scopas in these figures, but Pliny tells us that they are the work of the architect of the monument, Pythios. The British Museum also possesses fragments of three sculptured friezes. One very beautiful piece represents an eager charioteer.

See Pl. 24, Vol. I.

BIBLIOGRAPHY: The scholar who discovered the ruins of the Mausoleum published the result of his discoveries: C. T. Newton, *History of Discoveries at Halicarnassus, Cnidus and Branchidae.* 2 vols. London, 1862-63.—Chr: Petersen, *Das Maussoleum oder das Grabmal des Kœnigs Maussolos von Karien.* Hamburg, 1867.

**MAUVE (Anton).**—Dutch painter, 1838-1888.

**MAYA.**—See America (Archæology).

**MAYER (Constance).** — French painter, 1778-1821. Pupil of Suvée and of Greuze, then of Prud'hon. There are three pictures by her in the Louvre:—*The Happy Mother, The Abandoned Mother,* and *Le Rêve du bonheur*.

**MA YUAN.**—Chinese painter, c. 1190-1224, great-grandson of Ma Fen. With Hsia Kuei, Ma Yuan developed a style of landscape painting which was to become the predominant style for later academicians.

See China—Art.

**MAZO (Juan Bautista Martinez del).**—Spanish painter, c. 1612-1667. When quite young he entered Velázquez's studio. He showed such great ability that Velázquez soon allowed him to assist in the preparation of his own work. He married one of Velázquez's daughters. Mazo became an excellent painter. It has been accepted that he painted jointly with Velázquez the *View of Saragossa,* 1647 (Prado, Madrid), and the portrait of Queen Mariana, 1666 (Natl. Gallery, London). J. Allende-Salazar assigns to his middle period the portraits of the Infante Balthasar Carlos (Budapest,—Coll. Baron Herzog)—that of the Infanta Maria Teresa (N. Y.,—J. Pierpont Morgan Coll.)—the *Duel in the Pardo* (London,—Natl. Gallery); etc.—Not only as a portraitist but also as a painter of landscapes and city-views he deserves fame. On the death of his father-in-law, del Mazo became "Pintor de Camara" (1661).

Bibliography: A. de Beruete y Moret, *The School of Madrid,* 2nd ed. London, 1911.—Id. *Retratos de Pulido Pareja.* Madrid, 1916.—Id. *Conferencias de Arte.* Madrid, 1924. —A. L. Mayer, *Gesch. de span. Malerei,* 2nd ed. 1922.—*Thieme-Becker,* Vol. XXIV, 1930. Art. *Mazo, Juan Bautista Martinez del.* by J. Allendez-Salazar.

**MAZZOLA (Filippo).**—Painter of Parma, c. 1460-1505. Influenced by Giovanni Bellini and Antonello da Messina.

**— (Francesco).**—See Parmegiano.

**— (Girolamo).**—Painter of Parma, 1500-1569 (about). Pupil of Correggio. He decorated the nave of the Duomo of Parma with medallions, cherubim and garlands of fruit.

**MAZZOLI (Ludovico) (Called MAZZOLINO).**—Ferrarese painter, c. 1478-1528. He continued the style of Lorenzo Costa and of Ercole de' Roberti. Among his numerous works are:

*Adoration of the Shepherds,* and *Massacre of the Innocents* (Uffizi); *Christ Among the Doctors* (Berlin); *The Miraculous Draught of Fishes* (Louvre).

**MAZZONI (Guido).**—Often called *Guido Paganino* or *Modanino.*—Italian sculptor (15th-16th century). Born in Modena. He made carnival masks, organised public fêtes, and made a certain number of life-size groups, in polychrome terra cotta (such as the *Lamentation,* in San Giovanni, Modena).

Mazzoni: Deposition. (San Giovanni, Modena.)

He worked in Naples, and (from 1495 to 1516) in France. Mazzoni was a facile worker, and his output during the twenty years in France must have been considerable, but we only know for certain of two works—the *Tomb of Charles VIII,* and the *Equestrian Statue of Louis XII* for the entrance doorway of the Chateau of Blois—both of which have disappeared.

In 1516, Mazzoni returned to Italy. He died there in 1518.

**MAZZUCCHELLI (Pier Francesco), called Il Morazzone.**—Lombard painter, born at Varese (1571-1626). Influenced by Camillo Procaccini.

**MEAUX (France).**—Fine Gothic Cathedral, begun in the 12th century, finished in the 16th. Remarkable façade, with two towers, one of which is unfinished.

**MECKENEM (Israel van).**—Engraver, of the end of the 15th century. Active in Bocholt, in a border region between Germany and Holland. Only a part of his work represents original inventions, the rest being copies of various other masters such as E. S., Schongauer, Dürer, etc.

Bibliography: Geisberg, *Der Meister der Berliner Passion und Israhel von Meckenem.* Strasbourg, 1903.—Geisberg, *Verzeichniss der Kupferstiche Israhel von Meckenem.* Strasbourg, 1905.—Warburg, Anni, *Israhel van Meckenem.* Bonn, 1930.

**MEER.**—Prominent Dutch family of painters.

**— (Jan van der, the older).**—Landscape painter of Haarlem, 1628-1691. It is assumed that he worked with Rembrandt; he is often called the Vermeer of Haarlem because he used similar color schemes to those of the master of Delft. He painted dunes, water and forest scenes.

**— (Jan v.d., the younger).**—Landscape painter and graver of Haarlem, 1656-1705. Son and pupil of the above, he also studied with Berchem. He travelled in Italy and worked in the style of the Italian mannerists, his paintings are rather cold and lack the charm of his father's work.

**— (Jan. v.d., III.).**—Historic and portrait painter of Utrecht, 1630/5-1688. He lived in Rome for a while and was court painter in the Northern countries.

**MEGALITH.**—A huge stone or boulder used in prehistoric monuments.

See Pl. 14, Vol. I.

**MEGARA.**—See Greece (Terra cottas).

**MEISSONIER (Ernest).**—French painter (Lyon, 1815-Paris, 1890). As a young man, Meissonier had a hard struggle. He illustrated a number of books—*Paul et Virginie, The Vicar of Wakefield, Roland furieux,* etc.—and constantly sent "genre" paintings to the Salon. In 1834, he exhibited the *Flemish Citizen* (now in the Wallace Collection). *The Chess Players* (1836), *The Reader* (1840), and *The Chess Party* (1841) followed. While Ingres and Delacroix were painting their large pictures, Meissonier painted simple, old-fashioned scenes, copying old furniture and old costumes so well, and giving his figures such easy, natural ways that they seem to live in their frames. His conscientious love of detail naturally attracted him to the Dutch school. He realized the life of each of his figures, and each one acts so appropriately that the least detail of his belongings, as well as of his gestures, expresses his personal character. This scrupulous care of detail is apt to detract from the main action, and ends by wearying the attention. Intelligent enough to realize the danger of his method, Meissonier painted some scenes of violent action. *The Skirmish* (Windsor) shows a violent battle scene. The composition is perfect, but the deliberateness of its execution is such that the work leaves one cold. He was more at home with his smokers, and drinkers, and print-collectors!

Meissonier: The sign-painter. (Wallace Collection, London.)

Meissonier: Flute-player. (Louvre.)

Bibliography: O. Gréard, *Meissonier.* London, 1897.

**MEIT (Konrat).**—German sculptor, 15th and 16th century. Author of bas-reliefs of the Chapel of the Cathedral of Worms; and of statuettes, the finest of which are: *Adam and Eve* (Vienna, and Gallery of Gotha), in wood; *Judith and Holophernes* (Munich, about 1530), in alabaster; and *Strength* (Cluny). He worked at the decoration of the Church of Brou (in France), and on the tombs of Margaret of Austria and Philibert le Beau, in Brou.

Bibliography: Vöge, *Konrat Meit und die Grabdenmäler in Brou.* Jahrbuch. d. pr. ks. 1910.

**MELCHERS (Gari).**—American painter (1860-1932). He was born 11th August 1860 in Detroit, Michigan. His father was a sculptor and woodcarver and the son naturally became interested in artistic expression. At the age of seventeen he went to Düsseldorf to study in the Royal Academy, where he worked under Professor Von Gebhart. He visited Paris long enough to see the Exposition of 1878, but then returned to Düsseldorf for three more years of study. In 1881 he entered the École des Beaux-Arts in Paris, working there with Boulanger and Lefebvre. He then took a trip to Italy before returning to the United States. In 1884 he went back to Europe and opened studios both in Paris and Egmond, Holland. Soon his fame became widespread and he was known as a painter of religious and secular scenes, some portraits, landscapes and flower pieces. He received a medal of honour at the Paris Exposition of 1889 and another at Berlin in 1891. In 1893 he did some mural decorations for the Columbian Exposition in Chicago, which were later transferred to the University of Michigan Library at Ann Arbor. He also did murals in the Library of Congress at Washington and the Detroit Public Library. In 1909 Melchers was invited by the Grand Duke of Saxe-Weimar to make his home in Weimar and there he held the post of Professor of Painting at the State Academy of Art until 1914. At that time he returned to the United States and soon moved from New York to Fredericksburg, Virginia. He was elected to the National Academy of Design in 1906 and received awards abroad in France, England and Bavaria. He received a gold medal from the National Institute of Arts and Letters in 1932. That same year 30th November he died at his home, Belmont, near Fredericksburg, Virginia. His early training in draftsmanship and design stood him in good stead all through his life. Some of his most characteristic works are the studies of Dutch girls and boys in their quaint costumes, engaged in their daily tasks or dressed in their Sunday best attending church services.

Bibliography: Henriette Lewis-Hind, *Gari Melchers, Painter,* 1928. —For a more complete bibliography see *The Index of Twentieth Century Artists* for October, 1933.

**MELDOLLA (Andrea).**—See Schiavone.

**MELIORE TOSCANO.**—Dugento Tuscan painter, known from a signed and dated (1271) panel with five half-length figures, the *Christ,*

*Virgin and Saints,* in the Parma Gallery, with which several works have been grouped.

Bibliography: A. Venturi, *Di un dipinto di Meliore Toscano nella Galleria di Parma,* L'Arte, VIII, 1910; and *Storia d. arte ital.,* V.—P. Bacci, *Coppo di Marcovaldo,* p. 12. —Van Marle, *Italian Schools, etc.* I, 1923.

**MELLAN (Claude).**—French engraver, 1598-1688. He spent many years in Rome, where he was an intimate friend of Simon Vouet, and executed a great many engravings and portraits, notably a *St. Peter,* one of his best works.

See **Pl. 12, Vol. I.**

**MELONE (Altobello da), or Antobello Ferrari.**—Painter, of Cremona, of the beginning of the 16th century. Co-worker with Boccaccio Boccaccini. He painted some frescoes in Cremona Cathedral.

**MELONI da CARPI (Marco).**—Italian painter, of the beginning of the 16th century. Imitated Perugino.

**MELOZZO da FORLÌ.**—Italian painter. Born at Forlì in 1438. Pupil of Piero della Francesca. There is nothing archaic about his work, and little sentiment or emotion; but he had vigorous, almost Flemish, powers of observation, combined with Italian breadth of style.

He painted his most important works in Rome, between 1477 and 1481. In the Vatican Library, he made a vigorous portrait of Sixtus IV, surrounded by various grand personages. In the apse of the Santi Apostoli, he represented the *Ascension.* The central part of it is in the Quirinal; and some *Musical Angels* are in the Sacristy of the Vatican. He died in 1494.

Bibliography: Corrado Ricci, *Melozzo da Forlì,* L'Opera dei grandi artisti italiani, raccolta da Corrado Ricci. Vol. II. Rome, 1911. —O. Okkonen, *Melozzo da Forlì.* Helsingfors, 1910.

**MELROSE (Scotland).** — The Abbey of Melrose was founded in the 12th century, rebuilt in the 14th and 15th centuries, and is now a magnificent ruin. Choir and transept remain; also part of the nave and tower, the south aisle and a part of the north aisle.

**MELZI (Francesco).**—Lombard painter (1492-1570?). Favourite pupil of Leonardo da Vinci, and inheritor of part of his goods.

Memling: The two St. Johns. (Imperial Museum, Vienna.)

**MEMLING (or MEMLINC).**—Flemish painter. Probably born near Mayence, in the village of Mömling (hence his name), about 1430.

Hans Memling is one of the most delightful painters of the 15th century. His Germanic origin, allied to the Flemish training of his genius, make him an original artist, in whom sweetness and gentleness unite with precision, and richness of colour. Without having the vigour of a Van Eyck, or the power and pathos of a Van der Weyden, he possesses a tender mysticism, an unaffected gracefulness, and dreamy charm, which make him one of the most appealing of 15th century artists. He is a painter of charming Madonnas, exquisite saints, smiling children, and peaceful, meditative apostles.

Memling: Calvary (detail): Dice throwers. (Cathedral of Lübeck.)

To his first period belongs the famous triptych of Sir John Donne of Kidwelly (Duke of Devonshire's Collection, Chatsworth). The central panel represents the Madonna and Child between two angels, at the feet of whom are kneeling the donor with his wife and daughter, presented by St. Barbara and St. Catherine. On the left wing is St. John the Baptist, behind whom is a man who, according to the tradition, may be Memling himself. The right-hand wing represents John the Evangelist.

Memling: Wing of St. Christopher Altarpiece, representing William Moreel, his sons and his patron Saint. (Museum, Bruges.)

*The Martyrdom of St. Sebastian* (Brussels) was probably painted in 1470. The figure of the saint is unusually elegant.

In 1473, the artist painted a large altarpiece representing the *Last Judgment.* The work was probably commissioned by Jacopo and Catterina Tani, of Florence. It had to be transported to Italy, and was sent on a Dutch boat, which was captured by a captain of Danzig, Peter Beneke. He presented the picture to the Church of Saint Mary, Danzig, whence it was taken to Paris, then to Berlin, and finally returned to Danzig. The work was certainly inspired by the Beaune altarpiece by Roger van der Weyden.

The little picture in the Museum of Turin—*The Passion,* or *The Seven Sorrows of the Virgin*—contains two hundred figures and is treated with great delicacy and finish.

Memling worked for four years on his *Marriage of St. Catherine* (Hôpital de Saint Jean, Bruges), which was finished in 1479. The diptych in the Louvre dates from the same period.

The *Adoration of the Magi* (1479, Bruges) is a little marvel of colour.

Among Memling's best works is the *Triptych,* painted in 1484, for the Church of St. Jacques (Bruges, Museum).

The *Diptych of Martin van Niewenhoven* (Bruges, Hôpital de Saint Jean) was finished in 1487. On one panel is the Virgin offering an apple to the child Jesus; on the other, the figure of the donor, Martin van Niewenhoven, an excellent portrait of an intelligent, energetic young man.

Memling's most famous work is the *Shrine of St. Ursula,* which belongs to the Hospital of St. John, Bruges. This reliquary is in the form of a Gothic chapel—87 centimetres high, by 91 centimetres long. It has a gilded architectural framework, into which are set eight panels, and six medallions on the sloping roof. The panels are painted with a delicacy and brilliance of colour which recalls miniatures. The panels at the two extremities represent, one, the Virgin and Child protecting two nuns of the Hôpital; and the other, St. Ursula sheltering two of her companions under her mantle. The scenes at the sides show: (1.) *Ursula Embarking at Cologne;* (2.) *Ursula Arriving at Basle;* (3.) the *Arrival in Rome;* (4.) the *Return to Basle with the Pope;* (5.) the *Return to Cologne and the Martyrdom of Virgins:* (6.) the *Death of Ursula.* The four little medallions on the "roof" represent angels, the two larger ones, the Virgin and Saint Ursula and her companions. The medallions are inferior to the rest of the work, and may be by pupils. In spite of the tragic history they relate, the scenes have the unreality of a fairy-tale. We do not believe that the maidens are harmed by those arrows! But the panels illustrate Memling's delightful, naïve way of telling a story, and they are gems of bright, fresh colour.

Memling's favourite subject was certainly the Madonna and Child. His Virgins are unfailingly sweet and gentle and unperturbed, and generally accompanied by delightful angels. He often painted them seated on a dais, with a brocade panel behind them, while in the background we catch glimpses of fresh green meadows, and a little mediæval town, or a church tower.

Memling's last dated work is the *Passion,* in Lübeck, a large altarpiece painted in 1491.

See Pl. I, Vol. II.

Bibliography: Sir Martin Conway, *The Van Eycks and Their Followers.* London, 1921.—M. J. Friedländer, *Die altniederländische Malerei.* Vol. VI.—Grete, Ring, *Niederl. Bildnismalerei.* Leipzig, 1913.

**MEMMI (Lippo).** — Sienese painter, close follower of Simone Martini. Lippo worked in collaboration with his father, Memmo di Filipuccio, at S. Gimignano in 1317 on a fresco of the *Madonna, Saints, Angels and a Donor* which is still extant. In 1333 he assisted Simone Martini, his brother-in-law, on the *Annunciation* now in the Uffizi. He is mentioned in 1341 as making wooden models for the spires of the town hall in Siena (which proves that he did not go to Avignon at the time Simone went there, although a document of 1347 in Avignon may refer to him).

His works include: the signed *Madonna della Misericordia* in Orvieto, in the Opera del Duomo; the signed *Madonna* (half-length) in Berlin, on the back of which is "Insegni Campo Santo di Pisa", which indicates that Lippo may have accompanied Simone to Pisa in 1320; the signed *Madonna of the People* in the Church of the Servi, Siena; and the signed *Madonna* at Altenburg.

Bibliography: Van Marle, *Simone Martini et les peintres de son école.* Strassburg, 1920; *Italian Schools, etc.,* II, 1924.

**MEMMI (Simone).**—See Simone Martini.

**MEMNON (Colossi of).**—See Egypt (Sculpture); Thebes.

**MEMPHITE ART.**—See Egypt.

**MENARD (René).**—French painter, born 1862. Some of his pictures may be seen in the Luxembourg.

**MENDELSOHN (Erich).**—German architect and leader in post-War modernism, 1887-. His Einstein Tower, Potsdam, 1922, an apparently monolithic concrete structure gashed with wide openings represents a phase of his development succeeded by the more open and rectilinear style observable in the work of Gropius and the Bauhaus group. This second style may be seen in the Rudolf-Messe Store, Berlin, 1923, and the Schöcken Building, Stuttgart, 1927. Mendelsohn left Germany for England after the succession of the Third Reich, 1933.

**MENGS (Raphael).**—German painter, 1728-1779. His development shows the change from late Baroque to Classicism (after c. 1760). He worked first for the court of Saxony; later he spent most of his life in Italy and Spain.

Bibliography: Schmidt, Paul F., In Thieme-Becker, Künstlerlexikon.

**MENHIR.**—An upright stone forming a prehistoric monument, or, with other stones, part of such a monument.

See Pl. 14, Vol. I.

**MENZEL (Adolph von).**—German painter (1815-1905). He painted a series of pictures of the *Life of Frederick the Great.* But Menzel is seen at his best in his paintings of daily life. About 1845, under the influence of Constable, who had revealed to him the charm of fresh and sincere interpretation of nature, he painted the admirable *Sunny Interior,* in the National Gallery of Berlin, which in its freedom of handling, delicacy of values, and sensitiveness to light and atmosphere, recalls the Impressionist school. Menzel did many drawings and greatly inspired the art of wood engraving.

BIBLIOGRAPHY: Knackfuss, H., *Menzel,* Bielefeld and Leipzig, 1900. —Tschudi, H. von, *Adolph von Menzel.* Munich, 1905.—Jordan, M., *Das Werk Adolf Menzels.* München, 1905.—Meier-Graefe, J., *Der junge Menzel.* Leipzig, 1906.—Kurth, W., *Adolf Menzels graph. Kunst.* Dresden, 1921.

**MEO da SIENA.**—Painter mentioned on the tax lists in Perugia as a citizen of Perugia in 1319. He is still active in 1333. A signed polyptych with half-figures of the *Madonna and Child between Saints* in the Perugia Pinacoteca from the Abbey of Montelabate, near Perugia, shows stylistic relation to the school of Duccio. Another altarpiece with half-length *Virgin and Saints and a Holy Bishop* is in the same gallery, as well as two other works in a ruined state. Various attributions have been made to Meo, who had a profound influence upon the development of Umbrian painting.

BIBLIOGRAPHY: L. Manzoni, *Di un pittore del secolo 14mo non conosciuto in patria,* Nozze Hermanin-Hausmann. Perugia, 1904.—Vavasour-Elder, *La pittura senese nella Galleria di Perugia,* Rassegna d'arte senese, 1909.—C. Weigelt, *Duccio di Buoninsegna,* 1911, p. 181.—M. Salmi, *Note sulla Galleria di Perugia,* L'Arte, XXIV, 1921.—Van Marle, *Italian Schools, etc.,* V, 1925.

**MERCIÉ (Antonin).**—French sculptor and painter (1845 to 1916).

MERCIÉ (A.): MEMORY. (Musée du Luxembourg.)

He began his studies as a painter, but, urged by a friend, he finally joined the studio of the sculptor, Jauffray. He became a sculptor, but did not give up painting. He won the Prix de Rome with *Theseus Thanking the Gods after Overcoming the Minotaur.* In Rome, he made the *David* (1872, Luxembourg) and the *Gloria Victis* (1874, Hôtel de Ville, Paris), a patriotic group which was very popular.

Mercié worked in the classic tradition of Jean Goujon, and his work is characterised by an elegant style, and moral and patriotic sentiment. To mention a few of his numerous works:—*Le Souvenir* (Luxembourg); *Tombs of Baudry,* and of *Michelet* (Père Lachaise, Paris); *Monument to Gournod* (Parc Monceau, Paris); *Arago* (Perpignan).

As a painter, Mercié has a delicate charm, but his colour is rather anemic (e.g., *La Vénus au Bain*)—Luxembourg.

**MERCIER (Philippe).**—French painter, pupil of Watteau (1689-1760). He travelled much, but stayed chiefly in England, where he painted, generally in the style of his master, numerous "genre" subjects, many of which have been engraved. His *Juggler* is in the Louvre (Salle La Caze).

**MERSON (Luc Olivier).**—French painter (1846-1920). Pupil of

MERSON (L. O.): DETAIL OF A PAINTING IN THE OPÉRA-COMIQUE. (Paris.)

Pils. From his earliest work he shows a facile and charming imagination. He had a good knowledge of drawing at his service, but his palette was rather restricted, and does not reveal the temperament of a painter. As a result, his mural decorations are not his best works: *St. Louis Opening the Prisons; St. Louis Condemning Enguerrand de Coucy* (in the Court of Appeal); *The Song of the Middle Ages; Poetry* (staircase of the Opéra Comique); Decoration of the House of Silvie (Chantilly). On the other hand, he painted some very charming anecdotal scenes, ingenious and delicate, in the size of easel pictures: *The Wolf of Agubbio* (1878, Lille); *St. Francis Preaching to the Fish* (1881, Nantes); *The Sleep of Fra Angelico;* the *Arrival at Bethlehem;* the *Annunciation;* and, above all, *Rest on the Flight into Egypt* (1879), one of the most popular pictures of the end of the 19th century, showing the Virgin asleep between the paws of a statue of the Sphinx. Merson also made illustrations (*Notre Dame de Paris, Le Misset de Jeanne d'Arc,* etc., and two cartoons for tapestries for the Gobelins: *Le Sacrifice à la Patrie* and *St. Michael.*

**MÉRYON (Charles).**—French engraver, 1821-1868. He began his career as a naval officer. Then he studied engraving, especially the Dutch school. He left about a hundred engravings, among them reproductions and ocean views, of scant interest. But about twenty views of Paris are remarkable:—*Le Pont Neuf, The Apse of Notre Dame,* etc.

BIBLIOGRAPHY: H. Focillon, *Méryon,* L'Art et les Artistes, 1907. —L. Delteil, *Le Peintre-Graveur illustré,* Vol. II. *Charles Méryon.* Paris, 1907.—A. M. Hind, *A History of Engraving and Etching.* London, 1923.

**MESDAG (H. W.).**—Dutch painter, born in 1831 at Groningue; died 1902. Belonged to the school of The Hague. He was the founder of the Mesdag Museum, at The Hague. He lived for a long time in Brussels, in company with his friend Alma Tadema.

In the Luxembourg Museum, Paris, is a painting by him called *Sunset on the Sea.*

See Pl. 59, Vol. II.

**MESSEL (Alfred).**—German architect, 1853-1907. An early exponent of modernism, Messel is chiefly known for his Wertheim department store, Berlin, 1896-1907.

**MESSKIRCH (Master of).**—German painter of the 16th century, Swabian school, whose name is not yet known (some critics have proposed Jörg Ziegler). Painter of several altarpieces in Donaueschingen, Berlin and other places. His chief work is the *Adoration of the Magi,* in the Church of Messkirch. An elegant but cold painter, strongly influenced by H. Baldung Grien.

**MEŠTROVIČ (Ivan).**—Contemporary Serbian sculptor-architect, painter and graver. He was born 15th August 1883 of poor peasant parents. To the age of eighteen he tended sheep in the mountains and passed his time by carving bits of stone and wood he could find. His father recognised the youth's talent and took him to Spalato, where he became an apprentice to a marble carver. The academic style of his master did not curb the young peasant boy's technique of imagination. In 1902 he was recommended to Vienna, where after much futile wandering he found a Czech patron who introduced him to Hellmer. Meštrovič's talent impressed him so much that he helped the ambitious youth to enter the Academy and receive a stipend. Participating in the new style of the Secessionists, the sculptor exhibited in their show of 1902. In 1906 we find him in England presenting his work at Earl's Court, the following year in Paris, where he formed an intimate friendship with Rodin. This year he also exhibited at the Salons. In 1911 he went to Rome, where he stayed for three years, studying the sculpture of Michelangelo and the style of the archaic Greeks. In 1912 he participated in the International Show at Rome; in the Venice exhibition of 1914 he presented twenty-six pieces of sculpture. Since the World War he has been living in Zagreb, where in 1922 he was appointed rector of the Academy. The foremost chronicler of the Slav spirit, he imbues his art with an intense patriotism and religious fervor. His subjects for the most part are religious themes, mythological figures and others representative of Slav folklore. However, he made some fine busts catching the psychological importance of his sitters; these include beside the members of his family *Rodin, Lady Cunard* and others. Although wood is his pronounced medium, he carves marble, stone, granite and also casts with skill. Meštrovič's productivity is divided into three stylistic periods: from 1901-1906, in Vienna, formal compositions showing the influence of the Secession, as seen in the *Well of Life;* 1907-1914, in Paris and Rome, inspiration derived from the art of archaic Greece, the sculpture of Phidias and this combined with his racial heritage is the essence of his chef d'œuvre, *The Temple of Kossovo.* This simple and noble monument includes the *Sphinx* and a row of graceful caryatides. The third period is from 1914 to 1918, in London, Rome, Geneva, Cannes, when his work shows a conscious and planned leaning towards the Cinquecento and the high art of the Byzantine civilisation, as seen in *Crucifixion, Pietà,* busts. In 1918, arriving at full maturity precipitated by experiences of the World War, his art becomes dominantly glyptic, as in *The Račič Mortuary Chapel* near Ragusa (1922). In this masterpiece the whole structure is richly carved, the walls are decorated with small angels and caryatides support the porch. Besides these monuments he has done medals in relief and vases reminiscent of the Greek ones. All his sculpture is characterised by a marvellous flow of rhythmic line, large plastic masses carved with a degree of vehemence, the decorative pattern always in harmony with the inherent quality of the material. He always seems to strike the correct balance between the static and the dynamic. His sculpture can be seen in the museums of Vienna, Zagreb, Budapest, London, Paris and Rome in Europe and in the Art Institute of Chicago in the United States.

BIBLIOGRAPHY: G. Jean-Aubrey, *Un Artiste Serbe, Revue de Paris,* 1915, Vol. 6.—M. Ćurčin, *Ivan Meštrovič,* 1919.—A. Yusuf Ali, *Meštrovič and Serbian Sculpture,* 1916.

**METOPE.**—The space between two triglyphs in a Doric frieze.

**METSU (Gabriel).**—Dutch painter, 1630-1667. Born at Leyden. He was a pupil of Gerard Dou, and a member of the Leyden guild in 1648. He then went to Amsterdam, where he lived until his death.

METSU: THE MUSIC LOVERS. (The Hague.)

His works are not very numerous, for he died young, but they are sensitive and individual. He painted the well-to-do Dutch citizens with their wives, in gallant conversation; and some delightful *Music Lessons,* etc.

To mention a few of his works which are charming in feeling, and in the finish of their technique:—*The Sick Child* (Antwerp); *The Visit* (Louvre and New York); *Music Lovers* (The Hague); *The Music Lesson* (National Gallery, London); *An Old Woman Asleep*, etc. (Wallace Collection, London).

See Pl. 36, Vol. II.

BIBLIOGRAPHY. Hoftede de Groot, *Catalogue of Dutch Painters*, Vol I.

**METSYS**—See Matsys.

**METZ.**—The Cathedral of St. Étienne (14th and 15th centuries) is a fine Gothic building, very light in character. The interior is lit by some magnificent windows, those of the south aisle dating from the 13th century.

**MEULEN (Adam Frans Van der).**—Flemish painter, 1632-1690, born at Brussels; noted for his representations of battles and sieges.

See Blarenberghe.

**MEUNIER (Constantin Emile).**—Belgian sculptor, painter and graver (1831-1905). The son of an impecunious tax collector, Meunier was born in Etterbeek, a suburb of Brussels, 12th April 1831. He was still a small child when his father left his wife and six children. Young Constantin, however, received a fair education and began his artistic studies with his brother Jean-Baptiste Meunier, the well-known painter and etcher. Later on he learned the fundamentals of sculpture from Charles A. Faikin and at the Academy he studied painting with F. J. Navez. His style at this time was rather conventional, until 1857, when realism first began to appear in his art. His technique was broad and severe, influenced by the old masters and by the religious painters of Belgium. Around 1880 his gloomy palette became lighter, dominated by a silvery tonality, as he let himself be guided by the doctrines of the Impressionists. For the topics

MEUNIER (CONSTANTIN): THE FORGE.

on monks and the Bible he substituted historic scenes, landscape and incidents from the labourers' lives. Together with his friend De Groux he became a member of the Académie Libre. In 1882-1883 he was commissioned by the Government to go to Spain and copy Kempeneer's *Descent from the Cross*. On his return to his native land he devoted most of his time to sculpture, the medium through which he attained his masterpieces. In 1886 he finished one of his most powerful pieces, the *Hammerschmied*. From 1887 to 1895 he was professor of painting at the Art School of Löwen. After a short stay in Brussels he went to Paris, where he exhibited at Bing's. This was followed by further successes in Dresden and Vienna, but especially in Berlin. It was only in the late '90s that he attained public recognition and understanding. He died in Ixelles 3d April 1905 as a result of a prolonged cardiac ailment. A pensive and religious man, he did not realise his own significance and achievements. The height of his early religious and naturalistic style reached its culmination in

MEUNIER (CONSTANTIN): THE SOWER. (Botanical Gardens, Brussels.)

his *Peasants' War* of 1875; but slowly he forsook the heroes and martyrs of the faith for the victims of economic pressure and distress. His objectives were those of the Greek sculptors whom he admired, and he interpreted these in the forms of all types of workers, miners, puddlers, etc. He has also done some bronze busts of children, and reliefs as well. Although essentially social and fraternal, his work does not aim to reform or have a mission. He is represented in the museums of Brussels, Antwerp, Paris, Berlin, Vienna, Budapest, Dresden, Munich and Venice.

See Pl. 59, Vol. II.

BIBLIOGRAPHY: Christian Brinton, *Constantin Meunier*, 1914.—Eugene Demoeder, *Constantin Meunier*, 1901.—A. Fontaine, *Constantin Meunier*, 1923.—Walter Gensel, *Constantin Meunier*, 1905.—A. Heilmeyer, *Constantin Meunier*, 1909.—Camille Lemonnier, *L'Œuvre de Constantin Meunier*, 1896.—Ibid., *Constantin Meunier*, 1904.—M. C. Poinsot, *Constantin Meunier*, 1910.—G. Treu, *Constantin Meunier*, 1898.—A. Vermeylen, *L'Œuvre de Constantin Meunier*, 1904.

**MEUSE (School of the).**—See Enamel.

**MEXICAN ART.**—See America (Archæology); also Orozco; Rivera.

**MEXICO CITY.**—*Cathedral*, 1573-1804. A huge cathedral church begun in the Renaissance style in 1573, and continued in the 17th century by the Spanish architect Juan Gomez de Mora. The baroque façade dates from 1672 and the grandiose baroque towers from 1791 to 1804.

**MEZZOTINT.**—See Engraving (Black Manner).

**MICHAUX STONE.**—See Assyrian Art and Sumerian Art.

**MICHEL (Georges).**—French painter, 1763-1843. He is seen at his best in his scenes of Paris and neighbourhood.

See *Environs de Montmartre* (Louvre).

BIBLIOGRAPHY: Alfred Sensier, *Etude sur Georges Michel*. Paris.

**MICHELANGELO BUONARROTI.**—Florentine sculptor, painter, architect and poet (1475-1564).

Scientific researches, treatises on perspective anatomical studies had, in the course of the 15th century, greatly enlarged the scope of Italian art. What was still a difficulty and an effort with Paolo Uccello had become almost second nature to later painters. Perspective was no longer a mystery, and the body could be painted correctly in any position. All resources seemed to be at the disposal of artists of the late 15th and early 16th centuries. At the top of this mountain of achievement is the Olympian, Michelangelo, the creator. He moulded the human body at will—distorting it, if need be, but making it suggest an intense inner power of mind and of suffering. No inability of hand hampered his creative passion. He let slip some of the traditions of elegance and decorative rhythm that existed before in Florence; but his amazing knowledge was not merely a cold, learned lesson. It was not through mere acquired knowledge that he solved the most complicated problems of movement; but because his very soul was haunted by immense visions.

Michelangelo was born at Caprese, on the 6th of March, 1475. From his infancy he would do nothing but draw, and his father sent him to the studio of Domenico Ghirlandaio, where he received solid teaching. Then he took to sculpture and joined the school of Bertoldo, where he worked in an atmosphere of admiration for the antique, and for Donatello. He very soon earned the patronage of the Medici. Lorenzo took him into his household, and put him in touch with poets and humanists; and very soon he found himself in the midst

MICHELANGELO: CUPID. (Victoria and Albert Museum, London.)

of the brilliant life of the Renaissance. He worked amidst Lorenzo's fine collection of antiques. He sculptured antique subjects, infusing them with his own passionate spirit: *The Combat of Centaurs and Lapiths* (in the Casa Buonarroti—1490-1492); *Laughing Satyr*, in the Bargello of Florence (1490-1492); the relief of *Apollo and Marsyas*; the colossal *Hercules* (1492), which disappeared during the 17th century; the *Cupid*, of the Victoria and Albert Museum, London.

It was the time when Savonarola was delivering his sermons, full of threatening visions. Michelangelo perhaps heard them, and when Charles VIII appeared, as though in fulfilment of prophecy, he was seized with fear, like the whole of Florence, and fled to Venice (1494),—then to Bologna (where he made an Angel for the Arca di San Domenico). He returned to Florence in 1495, in spite of the strife which always reigned there, and it must have been about this time that he painted the *Deposition*, which is now in the National Gallery. In 1496, he went to Rome. In 1498, the year of Savonarola's death, he began the *Pietà* (St. Peter's, Rome), one of his most beautiful works. The Virgin, supporting the relaxed body

MICHELANGELO: THE PROPHET JOEL. (Sistine Chapel, Rome.)

of her dead son on her knees, gazes down piteously but with restrained grief. In 1501, Michelangelo returned to Florence where Cardinal Francesco Piccolomini commissioned him to make fifteen figures for the altar of Siena Cathedral. Some three years later (1504), he produced the *David*. Agostino di Duccio had spoiled a block of marble in trying to make the figure of a prophet. Out of this unformed, interrupted work, Michelangelo made the colossal young *David*, which was placed triumphantly in front of the Palazzo della Signoria. It is now in the Accademia, but a copy was put in its old position. Another copy, in bronze, dominates the hill of San Miniato. Michelangelo made another *David*, also in bronze, of which

MICHELANGELO: CHRIST AND THE MADONNA. (Detail from the Last Judgment, Sistine Chapel, Rome.)

only a drawing in the Louvre remains. In 1503, he received the order for twelve apostles for the Duomo of Florence: he only carried out the *St. Matthew*. In 1504, the Gonfaloniere, Soderini, put him into rivalry with Leonardo da Vinci, and ordered them both to decorate the Council Room of the Palazzo della Signoria. Leonardo made a cartoon of the *Battle of Anghiari*; Michelangelo, one of the *Battle of Cascine*. We can no longer compare them: they were destroyed, and we have only descriptions, and fragments of copies or interpretations. But we know how much they were admired, and imitated, and we know that Michelangelo's manner of treating the subject was characteristic—in so far as he represented nude figures bathing, instead of warriors fighting.

During the same period (1501-1505), he made several Madonnas: a round bas-relief which is in the Bargello in Florence; the *Holy Family*, in Burlington House, London; the *Holy Family*, in the Uffizi, painted for Agnolo Doni, which is very careful, very sculptural, a little cold, and crude in colour; and the sculptured *Madonna and Child* in Bruges.

The life of Michelangelo has something of the impetuosity and grandeur of his works. He passed some time among the mountains of Carrara, and one can picture the artist, among the shining whiteness of marble quarries, longing to change the whole mountain into living forms. The history of the tomb of Julius II was a tragedy for Michelangelo. When, in 1505, he had been commissioned by the Pope to make his tomb, and had conceived his great project (involving a considerable number of statues) he went himself to choose the most beautiful blocks of marble which were carried away only with great difficulty. Suddenly Julius II abandoned the project. In January, 1506, he began the rebuilding of St. Peter's. He had no further need of Michelangelo who was ruined, with so much marble on his hands. Distracted and enraged, Michelangelo fled on horseback to Florence (17th April, 1506). Then Julius II recalled him: all the Popes who succeeded him became Michelangelo's patrons and almost implored him to work for them. But the scheme for the great tomb, which failed almost from the moment of its birth, pursued him as an infinite regret. After the Pope's death, his successors persecuted him with their commands, reproaches and criticisms. In the end, the tomb, much reduced, was finished in 1545, and then only by dint of protests, and chiefly by the hands of pupils. The great *Moses* (1513-1516), with a sad, grave countenance, framed in flowing hair and beard, should have been only a detail, but it became the most important statue. It is now in San Pietro in Vincoli. Other precious remains are the despairing *Slaves*, in the Louvre, who suffer in chains which bind them as cruelly as the grip of earthly life.

MICHELANGELO: TOMB OF POPE JULIUS II. (San Pietro in Vincoli, Rome.)

In spite of his disappointments, Michelangelo always returned to the deserts of marble, and always transported in advance immense provisions for his too vast projects.

When Julius II recalled him, Michelangelo made many difficulties in yielding. However, he had to consent and obey all the wishes of the Pope, who now wanted him to make a bronze statue in Bologna, although Michelangelo declared that he understood nothing of casting in bronze. He fell out with his assistants, and made himself ill by this distasteful task: the statue, finished with difficulty, was destroyed and made into a cannon.

Next, Julius charged him with the ceiling of the Sistine Chapel. He knew nothing of the technique of fresco painting: he came, however, to rival Raphael. He began on the 10th May, 1508. He refused all the assistants who were sent to him. He shut himself up alone in the Chapel, and on top of the immense scaffolding, put up by Bramante, lying on his back, with his face to the bare ceiling, he began the dizzy task of creation. He formed the Creator himself, in a skilful foreshortening, stretching out his arms in the void to give birth to light—the source of so many dramas to come. Again, he stretches his divine hand towards the human hand held out to him, and the two hands almost touch across the whiteness of the sky, as though they had need of one another, while the beautiful new body, lying lightly on the bare mountain, looks with resigned and weary sadness at him who had the severity to give him life. Eve, newly created, joins her hands and bows before her unknown future. He painted the terror of the relentlessly rising waters of the Deluge, the despair of men, who could only stay crouching and trembling on the tops of bare mountains.

Thus he painted scenes from Genesis: *God Dividing Light from Darkness:* the *Creation of Sun and Moon; God Dividing the Waters;* the *Creation of Man and Woman;* the *Temptation*, and *Expulsion*; *Cain and Abel;* the *Deluge*; and the *Drunkenness of Noah.*

In the angles of the cornices are beautiful nude figures; and in the twelve pendentives he painted twelve *Prophets and Sibyls*—Daniel, Isaiah, Ezekiel, Jeremiah, Jonah, Joel, Zachariah, Lybica, Persica, Cumæa, Erithrea, Delphica—great figures in whom thought is always more ponderous than the body is powerful. In foreseeing the Christ to come, they dream of the immense and mysterious history of the world. Jeremiah's heavy head is supported on his rugged hand, and his closed eyes seem to behold eternal things.

Above the windows, the forerunners and ancestors of Christ await in poignant silence the heavy and inevitable future. At the four angles are represented the conflicts which saved the people of God: *David Killing Goliath, Judith Carrying the Head of Holophernes,* the *Brazen Serpent,* the *Sacrifice of Aman.* (There are some drawings for the Sistine at the University of Oxford.)

The work on the ceiling had been a terrific labour. Michelangelo's letters reveal how often he had almost lost heart. Finally on the 1st September, 1510, Michelangelo consented regretfully to allow the Pope to see the masterpiece. In 1512, all was finished. And the year after, Julius II died.

The new Pope, Leo X, ordered Michelangelo to make a façade for San Lorenzo, the Church of the Medici in Florence. The contract was signed in 1518. But the work was not accomplished. Michelangelo again found himself a prey to all sorts of difficulties. He quarrelled with the architect, Baccio d'Agnolo, and with all those who could have helped him. Then Cardinal Giuliano dei Medici, who became Clement VII, ordered the building of the new Sacristy of San Lorenzo, and with the Medici tombs (1520), and from the time that he became Pope (1523), he protected him, and gave him a house and a pension. Unfortunately, in 1527, the Florentine revolution interrupted everything. Michelangelo had to work for the Republic, and was made responsible for citadels and fortifications. He ended by fleeing from Florence, and the Signoria brought him back (1529). After the days of the siege, which he spent on top of San Miniato, or in the dome of the Cathedral which he wanted to protect against the bombardments, he was able at last, in 1530, to give himself up to work for the glory of the Medici, whom he had come to fight.

In the Sacristy of the Chapel of San Lorenzo, on the *Tomb of Lorenzo di Medici*, under his statue, which symbolizes Thought, Dawn is weary and desolate even before awaking, and can with difficulty raise her heavy limbs. Dusk is dreaming. On the tomb of Giuliano di Medici, under his statue which symbolizes Action, Day, at once proud and afraid, looks over his shoulder, perhaps at the light which may be too cruel. But Night has collapsed, and holds her head, for she is without hope and can only abandon herself to her dark dreams. Against another wall is a sorrowful Virgin, nursing her Child.

The work remained unfinished. Michelangelo painted for the Duke of Ferrara (doubtless about this period, 1531) a *Leda and the Swan* (which was destroyed in 1643). He also left the Laurentian Library unfinished.

In 1534, Michelangelo returned to Rome. He had friendships and quarrels. It is chiefly at this time that he wrote his poems. (Frey: *Die Dichtungen des Michelangiolo Buonarroti*—Berlin, 1897), and that his friendship began with the noble Vittoria Colonna, who was a descendant of the great Federigo d' Urbino, and who lived a retired life in a convent.

The new Pope, Paul III Farnese, nominated him architect, painter and sculptor of the Apostolic Palace, in April, 1535. He agreed to paint the *Last Judgment* behind the altar of the Sistine, and had no scruples about painting over the fresco of Perugino, whom he considered "an old blockhead." Once more he painted with feverish passion. He fell from the scaffolding (about 1535), and hurt himself seriously, but he continued, and on the wall where formerly saints had prayed in a luminous landscape, the bodies of the resurrected reeled and fell, amidst the dark blue clouds to the feet of God the Judge. The spectator is overwhelmed on seeing, for the first time, this strange metallic sky through which an avalanche of livid bodies is falling. The fresco has been subject to many trials: it has been marred by damp, blackened by fire, and spoiled by restorers who, under the pretext of morality, clothed the nude figures in shapeless drapery. Where it has grown mouldy by the penetration of stagnant water, it is about the colour of ploughed earth. But this feverish gloom evokes indeed the nightmare of the *Last Judgment.* The figures are anxious and panting. The extraordinary power of foreshortening and vigorous drawing of all these limbs, intermingled like the tortured branches of a gale-swept forest, impressed generations, who copied and recopied them.

The figures of the dead suddenly reawakening to life were inspired no doubt by those of Signorelli, on the walls of Orvieto Cathedral, who lift their wondering gaze on coming out of the deep night. But, this time, they crawl in pain. No joy lightens the realization that again they feel, think, and awake to suffer.

The Almighty is there, surrounded by large figures of Apostles and Saints, who look at him with questioning eyes. At his side, the Virgin is crouching like a bird. He is not beautiful; nor gentle. Thickset and solid, he raises his hand to condemn. And everywhere in the frozen sky, demons carry off their prey, while below, on the side opposite to the awakening, the barque of Charon, ever rowing on the horrible waters, bears away the new dead, who crush one another in the terror.

Not only did the Master of Ceremonies, Biagio da Cescena, (who Michelangelo, in revenge, represented in the form of Minos) and Aretino protest, but a crowd of enemies rose up against it, and, in spite of all the artists who came from all parts of the world to copy it, it was flouted, meddled with, spoilt. In spite of all this, it remains a superhuman vision.

Michelangelo painted the *Conversion of St. Paul*, and the *Crucifixion of St. Peter*, in the Pauline Chapel in 1542. But only fragments remain of these frescoes, which suffered damage by fire.

He was old. But he worked always, and above all for the glory of

God, he said. Although Michelangelo had not the suave piety usual with Tuscan painters, he was far from lacking religious feeling, and more than once he wrote that he would give up his work if he did not feel called to it by God.

Paul III now commissioned him not only to attend to the fortifications of Rome, but also to improve the Farnese Palace (where he made some fine cornices), the Porta Pia, Santa Maria degli Angeli, and San Giovanni dei Florentini (where money was lacking to carry out these plans). He entered into rivalry with San Gallo, all of whose schemes he overthrew. Each had his partisans, and the struggle was bitter and malicious. In spite of everything Michelangelo succeeded in making the wooden model of the beautiful and harmonious dome of St. Peter's. He united memories of Brunelleschi with schemes of Bramante.

He showed himself to be as great an architect as he had been a great sculptor, and a great painter. But he was most essentially a sculptor. He said that painting seemed to him so much the better when it most resembled sculpture, and sculpture so much the worse when it most resembled painting. His drawings are marvellous. He scorned oil painting, which he said was good for women.

Towards the end of his life, he could paint no longer. He made the moving *Deposition*, which is in the Duomo of Florence. The marble was rough-hewn with difficulty when Michelangelo himself broke it, and his friends had to restore it as best they could. But it is not less beautiful thus, the figures seeming to emerge with difficulty from the material, like a feeling too intimate to reveal. The sorrowful figures are intermingled like the branches of an old tree. Mary, and the Magdelen, are united in their great love; while St. Joseph of Arimathea, the old man muffled up in a hood, bends his sad gaze towards them.

Michelangelo had always been an untamed spirit. He lamented being lame, and having been "deprived of a beautiful human face" by a blow on the nose from the fist of a comrade. More and more, he lived alone, in spite of his famous acquaintances, and shut himself up in his thoughts, and his pride. Within him burned an intense mingling of revolt and of mysticism, of hate and of love. When he had been brutal, he busied himself with kindness to his nephew, Leonardo, and to his niece, Francesca, or to his old servants. He had always been sickly. He became very weak, but he worked to his last day. He died in Rome on the 18th February, 1564. His body was taken to Florence. The grandeur of his spirit departed with him; and his tomb in San Lorenzo is merely pompous and theatrical. His influence upon later artists was unfortunate. The imitation of his mannerisms, his scale and monumentality, without his informing spirit, produced a school of exaggerated pompousness and monotony.

Thus it was that the grandeur of Michelangelo, and of Raphael, led to the downfall of Italian art.

See Pl. 4, Vol. I; Pls. 7, 18, Vol. II.

Bibliography: Corrado Ricci, *Michelangelo*. Florence, 1901.—Henry Thode, *Michel-Angelo und das Ende der Renaissance*. Berlin, 1902-1903.—Romain Rolland, *Michel-Ange*. Les Maîtres de l'Art, Paris.—Sir Charles Holroyd, *Michael Angelo Buonarroti*. London, 1911.—F. Knapp, *Michelangelo* (*Klassiker der Kunst*. Vol. VII).

**MICHELE GIAMBONO.** — See Giambono.

**MICHELE di MATTEO.**—Painter of Bologna (15th century) who has been confused with a painter of the same name, belonging to Bergamo. He painted an altarpiece, now in the Gallery of Venice, with the *Legend of the Cross* in the predella. He was evidently influenced by Gentile da Fabriano.

**MICHELE da VERONA.**—Venetian painter, early 16th century—died after 1536. Pupil of Domenico Morone, his chief works are in Verona.

**MICHELI (Andrea).**—Called Il Vicentino. Venetian painter, 1539-1614. Pupil of Palma Giovane. His principal pictures (the *Disembarcation of Henry III*, and the *Battle of Cuzzola*) are in the Doges Palace. Vast, declamatory paintings. Fine in colour.

**MICHELINO da BESOZZO.**—Painter of Pavia, influenced by German painting. He is first mentioned in 1388, at which time he painted frescoes in the Cloister of S. Pietro in Ciel d'Oro in Pavia. In 1394 he is recorded as working in the Church of S. Mustiola in Pavia; and he was active on the Duomo of Milan between 1418 and 1442.

There is no documented work of Michelino's extant, but a signed panel of the *Mystic Marriage of St. Catherine* in the Academy at Siena has enabled art historians to identify his style.

Bibliography: P. Durrieu, *Michelino da Besozzo et les rélations entre l'art italien et l'art français*, Mem. de l'Acc. des Insc. et Belles Lett., XXXVII, 2, 1911, p. 365.—Toesca, *Michelino da Besozzo, Pitt. e min. nella Lombardia,* 1912.

**MICHELINO (Domenico).**—See Domenico.

Micheli (Andrea). (His portrait, after Vasari.)

**MICHELOZZO MICHELOZZI.**—Florentine architect and sculptor, 1396?-1472. One of the most important artists of the Tuscan Renaissance. He was trained as a goldsmith, and this influence shows in the refinement and delicacy of his work. He co-operated with Ghiberti in the statue of *St. Michael* for Or San Michele, and this decided his vocation. He also worked with Donatello on the Tomb of Pope John XXII, in the Baptistery of Florence; on that of *Cardinal Brancacci* in Naples; and on that of the poet *Aragazzi*, in Montepulciano (1427). The latter has been dismembered. The very beautiful angels, which are both grave and charming, and which are probably by Michelozzo Michelozzi, are in the Victoria and Albert Museum, London. Other fragments remain in the Cathedral of Montepulciano. The inert hands of the deceased are very expressive, as are nearly all those which Michelozzo sculptured.

About the same period, he also made the lunette over the principal doorway of the Duomo of Montepulciano; and in Florence, a *St. John* for the cloister of the "Annunziata," another for Santa Maria del Fiore, and a charming tabernacle in San Miniato.

Michelozzo. (His portrait, after Vasari.)

As an architect, Michelozzo built the Riccardi Palace for Cosimo di Medici (1444). The success which this won for him encouraged him to produce a great number of plans for palaces, churches and cloisters. Nevertheless, he did not desert sculpture. He assisted Ghiberti in the third door of the Baptistery; made, with Luca della Robbia and Maso di Bartolommeo, that of the Sacristy of the Duomo; and added charming garlands and masks round that of the Noviziato of Santa Croce.

It was Michelozzo who introduced the Tuscan style of architecture into Lombardy. Towards the end of his life he went to Milan to reconstruct the palace given by Francesco Sforza to Cosimo di Medici. He gave the Milanese an exquisite example of the Florentine style in the Portinari Chapel of Sant'Eustorgio (1462-1466).

See Pl. 5, Vol. I.

**MICHELSEN (Hans).**—Norwegian sculptor, 1789-1859. His wood carvings deserve notice.

**MICHETTI (Paolo)** —Italian painter. Born in 1851. Morelli's most celebrated pupil.

**MICON.**—Greek painter and sculptor of the 5th century B.C.

**MIDAS (Tomb of).**—See Phrygia.

**MIEL (Jan).**—Flemish painter, 1599-1663. Spent his life in Italy. He painted scenes from the chase, pastorals, etc., and occasionally executed the figures in Claude Lorraine's pictures. The Museums of the Louvre, the Hermitage, the Prado, and Turin, have a number of his works.

**MIELICH or MÜELICH (Hans).**—German painter of Munich, 1516-1573. The most important of the Munich painters, he was influenced by Altdorfer, and in 1541 by Italian art, during his stay in Rome. He was the official court painter of the Bavarian princes, such as Wilhelmus IV and later Albert V. He was the leader and most influential member of the Renaissance movement in southern Germany. Mielich was the leading portrait painter and set a definite style for his followers. He also did some historic paintings, miniatures and woodcuts.

Bibliography: Röttger, *Der Maler Hans Mielich,* 1925.

**MIEREVELD (Michiel van).**—Dutch painter, 1567-1641. Born in Delft; studied in Utrecht; worked in his own country without ever travelling. He was the painter of rich citizens and the Dutch aristocracy and is particularly famous for his portrait of members of the house of Orange.

He painted a great number of portraits (*e.g.*, "The Prince of Orange," "Portrait of a Woman"—both in Amsterdam).

**MIERIS (Franz).**—Dutch genre painter and etcher, Leiden 1635-1681. A pupil of Dou, he was patronized by Heemskerk and later was under the patronage of nobility. He was invited to Vienna as court painter, but refused it. A member of Steen's circle, Mieris was the most outstanding member of the Leiden group of portrait painters; his elegant style, miniature like rendering of lace and other detail, and his glowing deep color were unsurpassed by any of his contemporaries. His use of light effects is reminiscent of Dou. Mieris's best works are in Munich; his *chef d'œuvre* called *La Dormeuse* is in the Uffizi.

**MI FEI.**—Chinese landscape painter (1051-1107), founder of an impressionistic manner of painting with large blobs of ink.

See China-Art.

**MIGNARD (Pierre)**—French painter, 1610-1695. Studied under Vouet. In 1635, went to Rome, where he stayed for twenty-two years.

Mignard (Pierre). (His self-portrait.)

Mignard: Catherine Mignard. (Museum of Versailles.)

Mignard was not an original artist, and his work easily became commonplace. Nevertheless, at his best, he was an able, delicate painter, whose fashionable portraits of women have considerable charm. One of the best is that of his daughter, the Comtesse de Feuquières (Versailles). She is represented as "Fame," and is presenting her father's portrait.

# ROME OF THE RENAISSANCE

*At the beginning of the sixteenth century, artistic activity was concentrated at Rome. Hitherto, during the fifteenth century, Florence had been a much more spirited center. It was during the brief pontificates of Julius II and Leo X that Rome again took the lead in the great movement of the Renaissance. Florentine art, becoming installed at Rome,—as it had already approached ancient Greek art—took on a broader character and a sort of majestic authority; it benefited from the papal power. Moreover, being introduced into a city where ancient memories remained alive amidst the ruins, the Renaissance was affected by archæology.*

ST. PETER'S, ROME, FAÇADE.
*(Photo by Maurel.)*

ST. PETER'S, ROME, INTERIOR.
*(Photo by Alinari.)*

## St. Peter's

Julius II had Bramante begin the construction of the Basilica of St. Peter. The plan was that of a Greek cross with a dome in the middle and apses at the ends. But the supports of the dome were found insufficient and the successors of Bramante continued to strengthen them. Among those who continued the work one must consider Michelangelo, who followed most closely the original plan. The architect Maderna at the beginning of the seventeenth century constructed the nave which transformed the Greek cross into a Latin cross. Finally, in the seventeenth century, Bernini erected the baldachin of the altar as well as the majestic colonnade in a double hemicycle, which encircles the open space in front of the church.

SANGALLO: FARNESE PALACE.

MICHELANGELO: PIAZZA, CAPITOLINE HILL.
*(Photo by Maurel.)*

PERUZZI. VILLA FARNESINA.

## Roman Palaces

In the sixteenth century, the work of the Roman architects, Michelangelo, Peruzzi, the San Gallos, etc., represented the decorative principles of the Florentine architects of the fifteenth century, the palace retaining its square plan with an interior court. But there came a time when the architects rejected the decoration of façades by the superposition of the ancient orders. They suppressed the pilasters only to preserve the frieze which separated the stories. The upper cornice assumed importance. But these Roman palaces, in order to attain majesty, often fell into a monotonous and colourless style. The architecture of Peruzzi, at the Farnesina, was much more charming and colorful.

ANNIBALE LIPPI: VILLA MEDICI.
*(Photo by Boyer.)*

GARDENS OF TIVOLI.

PIRRO LIGORIO: VILLA D'ESTE.
*(Photo by Alinari.)*

## Roman Villas

Florentine and Roman palaces were set up in the city as square fortresses. But the constructions outside the city, the villas, were surrounded by gardens, whose plan was complementary to that of the building. Laid out most often on uneven ground, they added to the geometrical decoration of the flower beds and the terraces, the picturesque quality of the belvederes, the combination of trees and of sculptures, and particularly, the large number of fountains. The Renaissance captured the antique tradition of the Romans who also loved beautiful country homes.

# GHIBERTI AND DONATELLO

*It was in sculpture that the genius of Florence attained its most complete expression. Workers in marble and bronze developed the expressive power of the forms and the flexibility of the material much further than did the Gothic sculptors. In general the work of the sculptors preceded that of the painters. During the course of the fifteenth century, one may very often find the influence of ancient statuary in Florentine works; this influence is not preponderant until later, after Michelangelo. Hitherto Florentine sculpture, ignoring antique examples which were excavated, remained faithful to Gothic naturalism.*

BRUNELLESCHI: SACRIFICE OF ABRAHAM. BARGELLO, FLORENCE. *(Photo by Brogi.)*

GHIBERTI: STORY OF ABRAHAM. BAPTISTERY, FLORENCE. *(Photo by Brogi.)*

GHIBERTI: STORY OF JOSEPH. BAPTISTERY, FLORENCE. *(Photo by Brogi.)*

JACOPO DELLA QUERCIA: THE CREATION OF EVE. BOLOGNA CATHEDRAL. *(Photo by Brogi.)*

## Ghiberti

After he had carried off the prize in the competition in which Brunelleschi had taken part, with the bronze bas-relief above, Ghiberti, during the first half of the fifteenth century, executed the famous doors of the Baptistery of Florence concerning which Michelangelo said that they were worthy of being the gates of paradise. These doors present bronze pictures which are conceived as veritable paintings. By means of the height of the relief, more or less accentuated, by means of the effect of perspective and the representation of landscape, Ghiberti, in bronze, gave the modelling much the appearance of Florentine paintings. Jacopo della Quercia likewise took part in the competition for the doors of the Baptistery.

DONATELLO: THE ANNUNCIATION. SANTA CROCE, FLORENCE. *(Photo by Brogi.)*

DONATELLO: DAVID. BARGELLO, FLORENCE. *(Photo by Brogi.)*

DONATELLO: "IL ZUCCONE." CAMPANILE, FLORENCE. *(Photo by Brogi.)*

DONATELLO: ST. GEORGE. BARGELLO, FLORENCE. *(Photo by Brogi.)*

## Donatello

Donatello is a powerful creator, a versatile artist, never indifferent, one of the boldest and most expressive personalities in history. He belongs to the art of the Middle Ages, with his figures of prophets roughly hewn whose heads sometimes arise startlingly from garments with twisted folds; moreover, he likes to hollow out the stone in order to disengage emaciated figures such as St. John the Baptist or the Magdalene. Other works, on the contrary, show him an admirer of antique elegance hewing in marble or casting in bronze feminine beauty or adolescent grace.

DONATELLO: GATTAMELATA. PADUA. *(Photo by Anderson.)*

DONATELLO: MADONNA AND CHILD. SAN ANTONIO, PADUA. *(Photo by Alinari.)*

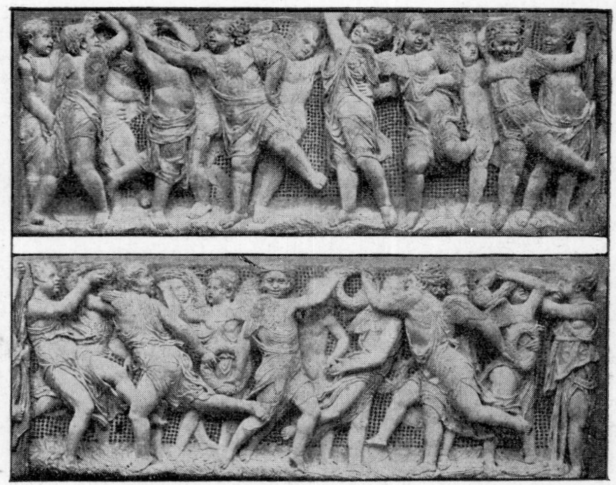

DONATELLO: DANCING CHILDREN. MUSEUM OF THE DUOMO, FLORENCE. *(Photo by Brogi.)*

## Donatello

Donatello was the first artist since antiquity to cast in bronze a colossal equestrian statue. It is the famous statue of a Venetian condottiere, Gattamelata, which today still stands in the open square before the Cathedral of Padua. At the same time, the great Florentine executed many statuettes or bas-reliefs in bronze for the great altar of this cathedral, but this altar, left unfinished, has only recently been reconstructed.

Among his other most important works may be mentioned: *The Circumcision* and *The Baptism of Christ* (in St. Eustache, 1669); *The Birth of Apollo, Apollo on Parnassus, Apollo and Aurora*, the *Olympus of Homer* (at St. Cloud, 1678); and (in the small apartments of Versailles) the *Genius of France between Apollo and Minerva, Prometheus* and *Pandora in Olympus.* Almost all these have disappeared.

Bibliography: A. Babeau, *Nicolas Mignard, sa vie et ses œuvres*, 1895. —L. Hourticq, *De Poussin à Watteau.* 1921.

— **(Pierre).**— French architect, 1640-1725. Son of Nicolas Mignard and nephew of Pierre. He built the Porte Saint Michel and the façade of the College of Saint Nicolas (both in Paris). The Abbey of Montmajour, near Arles, is his chief work.

See Pl. 41, Vol. II.

**MIHRAB.**—See Moslem Art (Syro-Egyptian School).

Milan: Santa Maria presso San Satiro.

**MILAN (Italy).**—*S. Lorenzo.* The oldest church in Milan, a peri-apsidal structure with an octagonal dome.

Milan: Santa Maria delle Grazie.

*S. Ambrogio.* A Lombard Romanesque church dating chiefly from

Milan: Basilica of Sant'Ambrogio.

the 11th and 12th centuries. The date of the vaults is controversial. S. Ambrogio is in plan an atrium; a narthex; three quadripartite square nave bays in the alternate system, so that there are six aisle compartments on either side; a lantern bay; and a triapsidal east end. There are no transepts. The church is vaulted in quadripartite ribbed groin vaults, a daring construction for its time, and one which necessitated the omission of the clerestory. The easternmost compartment is covered by an octagonal lantern. The exterior, of brick, is decorated with open and blind arcades, pilaster strips, and arched corbel tables. The campanile has similar decoration.

*S. Eustorgio.* A 13th century Gothic church, rebuilt in the 17th century. It contains the handsome Early Renaissance Portinari Chapel, built by the Florentine Michelozzo 1462-1466.

*Cathedral,* 1385-1485. One of the largest churches in the world, Milan has five aisles, the triforium and clerestory being suppressed because of the height of the lateral aisles, as in the contemporaneous architecture of Germany. Most of the scores of master builders who directed the works were Germans. The choir is very Germanic, with its polygonal apse. The apsidal windows have extaordinary Flamboyant tracery. The transepts are French in character, and the crossing dome natively Italian. The flat roofs are concealed by the flying buttresses and the wealth of intricate, vertical, and lace-like Flamboyant decoration of pinnacles, tracery, panelling, and sculpture. There are no western towers. The façade is largely Renaissance.

*S. Maria presso S. Satiro.* See Bramante.

*S. Maria delle Grazie.* See Bramante.

*Brera.* Picture gallery, built 1651 as a Jesuit college.

Bibliography: T. F. Bumpus. *Cathedrals and Churches of Italy.* New York, 1926.—A. K. Porter. *Lombard Architecture.* New Haven, 1915-1917.

**MILLAIS (John Everett).**—English painter, 1829-1896. At the age of eleven, he entered the Royal Academy School, where he was probably the youngest student. At seventeen, he was exhibiting his paintings. He was not out of his teens when he painted *Lorenzo and Isabella*, which bears the letters "P.R.B." ("Pre-Raphaelite Brotherhood"). All the persons represented were friends of the artist, among them Dante Gabriel Rossetti. The picture shows a party of young thirteenth century Florentines seated at a dinner table. The care with which the details are painted is amazing; and it is in every way a remarkable work for so young an artist.

*The Carpenter's Shop* (Tate Gallery, London) appeared in 1850. In its careful draughtsmanship, and bright colour, the influence of the Quattrocento painters is again evident.

He continued to take his subjects from the Bible or from mediæval poems. Among his paintings are the following: *The Death of Ophelia* (1852, Tate Gallery); *The Huguenot* (1852); *The Valley of Rest; The Eve of St. Agnes* (1863), illustrating Keats' poem· *The Boyhood of Sir Walter Raleigh* (1869).

Careful study of nature, minuteness of execution, and brilliant colour, give these works an extraordinary feeling of life.

Millais was a fine portrait painter. His simple, virile nature was especially successful in this kind of painting, which demanded more observation and exactitude than imagination. The poses of his figures, whether in portraits or "subject" pictures, are always serious, dignified and serene.

See Pl. 58, Vol. II.

Bibliography: J. G. Millais, *Life of Sir John Everett Millais, Baronet.*

**MILLET (Aimé).**—French sculptor, 1819-1891. Pupil of David

Millet: The Sweeper.

d'Angers. He was greatly influenced by his master, and retained his classical manner. Like him, Millet executed many statues of famous men. The *Ariana* (1857, Luxembourg Museum) was his greatest success; and another very popular work was *Vercingetorix*, a colossal statue (1865, Alise-Sainte-Reine) which stands on top of a hill.

— **(Jean François).** — French painter, 1814-1875. His people were farmers, near Cherbourg. When he was twelve years old, the

Millet: Peasant cow-herder.

vicar of Gréville gave him Latin lessons. The lad was enraptured by the *Bucolics* and *Georgics* of Virgil, which opened his eyes to the nobility of work on the land, in which, as eldest son, he was beginning to help his father. In the evening, after the day's work, he read. Then he began to draw, copying what he saw around him—peasants, animals, houses, trees and flowers. His father encouraged him; and, when he was eighteen, took him to Cherbourg to have lessons.

A few years later, the Municipal Council of Cherbourg granted him a small pension, and he was able to go to Paris to study. He arrived there in January, 1837. Finally, he joined the studio of Paul Delaroche. His pension arrived irregularly, and he had a hard struggle to make ends meet.

Millet: Young mother cradling her child in her arms.

Millet is the painter of peasant life. His men—hardy, primitive types—work in the open fields, intent on their labour. They are one with the earth. His women, too, work in the fields, or sit indoors, occupied with their young children. Millet brings home the dignity of common things. He expresses, too, a certain sense of tragedy that

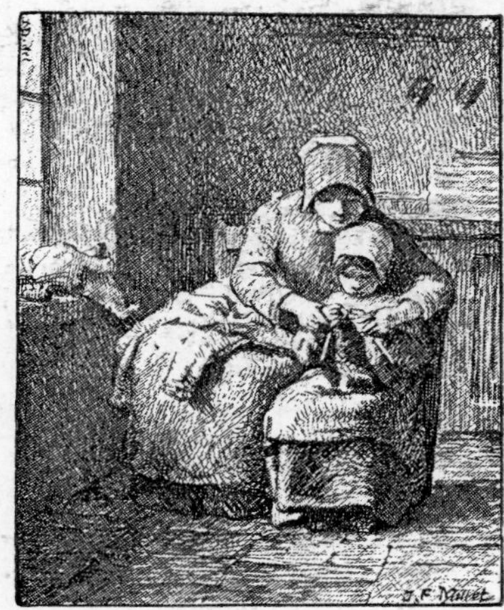

Millet: The knitting lesson. (Staats Forbes Collection.)

hovers over the hard life of the French peasant, without breaking it. His pictures are numerous. Among the best known is *The Gleaners* (1857, Louvre), which shows admirable economy in the means of expression, simplified drawing, and power of selection. The incidental is left out, that what is enduring in human life and nature may be more forcibly expressed. And this is characteristic of Millet's best work. The poses of some of his figures have the simple dignity of an antique bas-relief. *The Angelus* (Louvre) followed. The silhouettes of the man and the woman, in the solemn beauty of the landscape, are full of dignity.

The *Man with a Hoe; The Lacemaker; the Shepherdess with Her Flock;* the *Potato Gatherer;* the *Knitting Lesson; Young Mother with Her Baby*—these are but a few of Millet's many pictures.

As an artist, Millet owed much to Flemish and Dutch painters. He was influenced, too, by Le Nain, Chardin, and, above all, Poussin. It should be noted that Millet painted entirely from memory. He was a patient, steady observer of nature.

See Pl. 55, Vol. II.

BIBLIOGRAPHY: Alfred Sensier, *La vie et l'œuvre de J. F. Millet*. Paris. —Romain Rolland, *J. F. Millet*. London.—Henry Marcel, *J. F. Millet*. Paris, 1903.—Etienne Moreau-Nélaton, *Jean François Millet raconté par lui-même*. Paris, 1922.

**MILLS (Clark).**—American sculptor (1815-1833), whose monument to Andrew Jackson in Lafayette Square, Washington, is notable as being the first equestrian statue produced by an American (1853).

**MINBAR.**—See Moslem Art (Syro-Egyptian School).

**MINDEN (Meister Bertram von).**—German painter who lived at Hamburg, from 1367 to 1415. His best known work is an altar-screen formerly in the Church of Saint Peter at Hamburg (now Kunsthalle, Hamburg). This is also called the *Grabow altar-screen* (1379), and is composed of twenty-four pictures representing the *Creation of the World, The Story of Adam and Eve, The Life of the Virgin*. The figures, badly drawn and clumsy, are nevertheless full of life, and the style of painting executed in dotted lines, is extremely curious.

BIBLIOGRAPHY: Lichtwark, *Meister Bertram*. Hamburg, 1905.—C. G. Heise, *Norddeutsche Malerei*. Leipzig, 1918.

**MINELLO (Antonio Minello de Bardi).**—Paduan sculptor at the end of the 15th and the beginning of the 16th century, to whom is attributed the first bas-relief representing *Saint Anthony Donning Monastic Garb*, in the famous series on the walls of the chapel of the "Santo" at Padua.

**— (Giovanni).**—Paduan architect and sculptor of the 15th century. He began, with his son Antonio, the construction and the decoration of the chapel of the "Santo," at Sant'Antonio, Padua.

**MING (Tombs of the).**—See Peiping.

**MINIATURE (Illuminations).**—Miniature has been defined as a kind of delicate painting, done with very fine colours, diluted with water mixed with gum. The term comes from the Latin "miniare," to write with red-lead—the red oxide from lead. In the Middle Ages, the name "miniator" was given to the calligraphist who either used or prepared this substance. The red-lead was almost replaced by cinnabar or vermilion, and then one spoke of a "writer in vermilion." The first period, purely calligraphic, is limited to the beautifying of writing, and the ornamentation of the initial letters of chapters, and paragraphs. Gold and silver are soon introduced with brilliant effect. The art has now become the new "ars illuminandi," which is a Parisian name according to the authority of Dante, who speaks of "L'onor di quell'arte ch'alluminare, è chiamata in Parisi." The Latin word becomes the word "illuminate." Later on, the workers colouring drawings are called "illuminators," and the present-day illustrators are the successors of the miniaturists and illuminators.

It is in *Egypt* that we find the oldest miniature, in the form of a mixture of drawing and writing, which composes the *Book of the Dead*, a compilation of prayers which used to be interred with the mummy. The copy of a type of one of these has been published by

THE SOURCE OF LIFE. (Painting from the Evangelistary of Charlemagne. Bibl. Nat.)

Lepsius, after a Turin manuscript. It is composed of rolls of canvas and papyrus, on which is writing which is extremely careless, but in which each chapter has its title writ-

BINDING OF THE BOOK OF HOURS OF CATHERINE DE' MEDICI. (Louvre.)

ten in red ink, illustrated by a vignette which indicates the subject matter. The pictures serve as a commentary on the belief in a future life.

*Persia* has always excelled in manuscript art. (See Persian Miniatures.)

*Byzantium.*—It is in Byzantium that the Oriental miniature develops most fully. (See Byzantine Art—*Miniatures.*)

In the 14th century there was a second renaissance, in which the miniature, although inferior in technique, gains in fancy and in picturesqueness. Nevertheless the art approached decadence. This period saw an abundant output of secular manuscripts. The most celebrated ones, like the *Theocritus* (middle of the 14th century. Paris, Bibliothèque Nationale), and the story of *Balaam and Jehoshaphat*, are inspired by antique tradition, and are also under the decided influence of contemporary conditions.

The importance with which the portrait was invested is seen in *Hippocratus* (1350, Paris, Bibliothèque Nationale).

The inferior qualities of the technique are very apparent in the *Saint Denis the Areopagite* of 1408 (in the Louvre), and in the famous *Skylitzes* of the 14th century (National Library of Madrid). Religious manuscripts are far less nu-

THE MAGDALENE. (Painting from the Grimani Breviary.)

merous; the tendencies towards a free and familiar art are shown as well in the *Commentaries on Job* (Bibliothèque Nationale, Paris) of 1368, as in the well-known *Serbian Psalter* (in Munich) of the end of the 14th century. After this date there are no more works worth mentioning. In *Greece* the painting of manuscripts was a very flourishing art, but no trace of it remains to us. Only written witnesses give us the authority to assert that, in this respect, the Greeks were the direct pupils of the Egyptians.

In *Rome*, miniature art was as much cultivated as in Greece. Even one century B.C. a Greek artist, Lala de Cyzique was painting on vellum and on ivory, real miniatures. The manuscripts were embellished by calligraphic designs and paintings. Here again are found in the luxury volumes the purple parchment and the gold and silver letters of the East. Of pagan Rome we now have nothing but the manuscripts of the decadent period. Two *Virgils* in the Vatican (the oldest of the 4th century), a *Roman calendar* of the 4th century (Vienna Library), and an *Iliad* of the 5th century (Ambrosiana). The manuscripts of the 8th to the 10th centuries are only copies of ancient manuscripts.

In the West the miniature develops parallel with painting. Like all arts it was eclipsed after the fall of the Roman Empire, and only reappeared under the influence of Christianity. Manuscripts were then almost exclusively the monopoly of the monks, and, above all, of the Benedictines. Illumination remains at first purely calligraphic, in spite of the persistence of ancient traditions. In the famous *Pentateuch* of Tours (6th or 7th century), an artist of the decadent Roman school copied the process of the *Virgil* of the Vatican, but this is an exception.

Ornamentation proper begins then by an initial letter drawn with the pen, and then coloured. It is formed by fanciful designs, geometrical and interlaced lines which persistently follow the motifs of Gallo-Roman decoration. Simultaneously new decorative elements are introduced. These come from the North and are brought from the East by the barbarians, and represent fishes, birds, reptiles and all imaginable fanciful conceptions of animals. Gradually one can see the development of a subject; first it is only inside an initial; then the design itself grows in importance, and becomes at times a real picture. At the latter stage it is what we today call a "miniature." In France, in the Middle Ages it was called a "story," to distinguish it from the illumination which was merely ornamental.

The history of the miniature has two successive phases; from the 6th to the 8th centuries, it is the exclusive concomitant of the church, and is produced by the monks alone. The religious compositions only show the conventional traditional types. The aim, which was essentially religious, precluded any inspiration from real life. This is what is called the "Hieratic phase." In the "Naturalist phase," miniature art is inspired by secular literature, and gains new acquisitions outside the scope of the church. It is in this period that the portrait appears, and also landscape and all the artistic or satirical representations of contemporary life. These subjects even penetrated the church books.

After the dissolution of the Roman Empire, a new style is created; mixture of degenerate antique art, and northern art, Germanic in origin. This fusion takes place first in *Ireland*, then the new art passes into Great Britain, about the 7th century. Thence the missionaries spread it into Burgundy, eastern Switzerland and western Germany. Real schools of art now spring up in the monasteries. We shall follow their evolution in each country.

Up to the 13th century, the most beautiful manuscripts come from England, Rhenish countries and also the district north of the Loire. But the pen drawings, set off by illumination in flat colour washes, are the only successful ones. In the middle of the 13th century we reach the realistic phase, when miniature reaches its culmination which is maintained during the classical Renaissance. Already in the 16th century the art declined, killed by the new invention of printing. Illuminated manuscripts became more and more rare, and finally the production of them ceased.

*France.*—In France miniature was introduced in the 6th and 7th centuries by English missionaries. Nevertheless in spite of the influence of antiquity, miniature remained, till the time of Charlemagne, simply an art of calligraphy.

The fusion of Anglo-Saxon tendencies with those of antiquity and the Gallo-Roman art resulted in a style known as "Carolingian." Attention was given to the creation of independent figures, especially of Christ and his disciples, surrounded by geometrical designs. An example of the most important manuscripts is: *Charlemagne's psalter* (781, Bibliothèque Nationale, Paris). By the 11th century, France possessed several schools of calligraphy. Of the Northern school there still exists the *Psalter* (Vienna); of the school of Tours, there remains *Alcuin's Bible* (British Museum). There were other schools at Orléans, Lyons, etc. Throughout the 11th century, the influence of antiquity was considerable, as is shown by the *Psalter of Charles the Bald* (Bibliothèque Nationale).

During the 10th to the 13th centuries, the influence of monastic schools (especially the Benedictines) was supreme. It was a time of riotous fancy in linear design, and in the representation of animal and plant life, and of "grotesques." The human figure also now appeared, and though at first they were too heavy and massive, they acquired grace after the 11th century, though their pose and gesture was often clumsy and exaggerated. The Bibliothèque Nationale in Paris is rich in examples of this period (*e.g., The Life of Christ* from Limoges, etc., etc.). Byzantine influence can still be easily traced in the work of this time.

In the 13th century began the realistic Gothic phase, when illumination was no longer limited to religious subjects, monks and knights too, being sometimes treated in a satiric spirit. Figures gained elegance and were often represented in costumes of the period, and amid contemporary furniture and decoration. Examples are, the ***Psalter of St. Louis,*** and the ***Credo of Joinville*** **(1290)**.

In the 14th century the outside world itself was depicted, and miniature art freed itself from the monastic influence. Genre scenes, and Paris in the 14th century can be seen in the work of this century, though the mixture of traditional types with realistic ones, was often clumsy, as in the *Life and Miracles of St. Denis*. Landscape was only introduced in the 14th century. It is first found in the Books of Hours, in the representations of the twelve months of the year.

In the 15th century the classical Renaissance was represented in France by the greatest of miniaturists—*Jean Fouquet*, or *Jehan Foucquet*, who founded the school of Touraine. Paris was now, too, a great centre for production of Books of Hours.

In the 16th century, the art declined, and printing superseded manuscript work. The famous *Hours of Anne of Brittany* (1508) were almost the last productions of miniature art. Manuscripts became rare and valuable. Italian influence predominated. Examples are *The Book of Noble Women* (Boccaccio); *The Book of Hours* of Catherine de' Medici (now in the Louvre).

In the beginning of the 17th century, manuscripts became still rarer. Portraits of Louis XIII, and Anne of Austria, etc., illustrate the *Heures satiriques* of Bussy Rabutin. In the reign of Louis XIV the Account of his Campaigns during the Dutch War must be mentioned. (Bibliothèque Nationale.)

By the 19th century, attempts to revive the art only led to copies of old models.

In other countries, miniature had a very similar development and decline to that of France. Mention can only be made of periods which show any distinct originality.

*In England and Ireland,* miniature was first introduced in the 6th and 7th centuries. From this time, schools of the art were founded in the monasteries, where an interesting and original decoration was formed (*e.g., Psalter* of the 8th century; now in Utrecht). Anglo-Saxon art continued on its own lines up to the 13th century, and examples may be found in the British Museum, and in the Museums of Rouen and Boulogne.

*Germany,* in the 9th century, was famous for its great schools, such as that of Metz; and the Abbey of St. Gall, founded by Irish monks; Salzbourg; etc.

The 14th century in Germany is important historically, *e.g., Wolfram of Eschenbach,* and *Parzival* (Munich); and *William Tell* (1334, in Cassel, etc.).

In the 15th century, the school of Bohemia produced work now in Prague and Vienna.

In *Flanders,* in the 14th century, began the truly realistic school, which was largely influenced by that of France.

In the beginning of the 15th century began the Franco-Flemish school, which borrowed largely from Italy, and combined realism with imitation of the antique (*e.g., The Book of Hours* of Philip the Good; in The Hague; and the famous *Breviary* of the Cardinal Grimani; now in Venice).

*In Italy,* in the 14th century, miniature acquired an originality of its own, and its progress was largely due to Giotto. The drawing was good, but the decoration apt to be heavy. From Siena came a frontispiece to a *Virgil*, by Simone Martini (now in Milan). There was a Franco-Italian school in Naples also. The 15th century also marks in Italy the highest point of miniature art. Florence was the centre of activity, and produced, for instance: *Missal* (1456-1487; in Brussels); and a *Roman History*, etc. Some work was also done at this time in Milan and Rome.

The name "miniature" has also been given—wrongly—to those little pictures which are delicately executed. This art, however, began in France in the 15th century, in the decoration of furniture. The taste for it developed in the 17th century, perhaps under the influence of Henrietta of England. About 1660 other countries (Italy, Switzerland, Germany) took up the art, and it has still, at the present time, many representatives.

See Moslem Art; also Pl. 58, Vol. I.

Bibliography: A. de Bastard, *Peinture et ornements des Manuscrits du IVe au XVIe siècle*. Paris, 1835.—A. Molinier, *Les Manuscrits et les miniatures*. Paris, 1892.—J. A. Herbert, *Illuminated Manuscripts*. London, 1911.

**MINIO (Tiziano).**—Sculptor of the Venetian school, from Padua. 16th century. Pupil of Jacopo Sansovino. He made rich decorations, particularly on the ceiling of the Chapel Antonio, in the Santo (from Sansovino's drawings, about 1540).

**MINOAN CIVILISATION.**—See Crete.

Mino da Fiesole. (His portrait, after Vasari.)

**MINO da FIESOLE.**—Florentine sculptor. Born at Poppi, in the Casentino (1430 or 1431-1484). Pupil of Desiderio da Settignano. He executed a great many works—Madonnas, busts, tombs. He worked chiefly in Florence, but he also went to Rome—first in 1463, to make a Benediction pulpit, which Pope Pius II wished to erect in front of St. Peter's (unfinished due to the Pope's death); and then again from 1473 to 1480.

The principal works previous to his long sojourn in Rome are: the Altar and tomb of Salutati in the Cathedral of Fiesole (1464); the tomb of Bernardo Guigni, in the Badia (1468); the tomb of Count Ugo and the Altar of Diotisalvi, also in the Badia (1469); the Ciborium of the Baptistery of Volterra (with his pupils); the Altar of the Baglione Chapel, in San Pietro of Perugia (1473); the Tabernacle of Santa Croce (1473); the Altar of Diotisalvi Neroni is specially fine.

From his Roman period his chief works are: the Altar of San Marco (now in the Sacristy); the tomb of Paul II (Vatican); the tomb of Cardinal Forteguerra (died 1473), in Santa Cecilia; the tomb of Francesco Tornabuoni (died 1480), in Santa Maria Minore; the charming Madonna of the tomb of Cristoforo della Rovere, in Santa Maria del Popolo (1479), and that of San Spirito. Many works signed "Opus Mini," as, for instance, the rich bas-reliefs of the Choir of Santa Maria Maggiore, may be by the Neapolitan sculptor, Mino del Reame.

After his return to Florence, Mino da Fiesole finished the tomb of Count Ugo, in the Badia (1481). Then he made a Tabernacle for the Chapel of the Miracle in Sant'Ambrogio.

See Pl. 9, Vol. II.

Bibliography: Angeli, *Mino da Fiesole*. Florence, 1904.

**— del REAME.**—Italian sculptor, of the 15th century. He may have come from Naples. He is often confused with Mino da Fiesole, both on account of his name and of his style. He lived chiefly in Rome, and because of this, there is now a tendency to attribute to him the Roman works signed "Opus Mini," which, though they are charming and very decorative, are less refined than most of the works by the elegant sculptor of Fiesole. It was he who in all probability signed the tympanum of the Church of San Giacomo degli Spagnuoli, in Rome, beside the signature of Paolo Romano. He was probably the author of the four bas-reliefs from the ciborium executed for Cardinal d'Estouteville, which are now built into the walls of the choir of Santa Maria Maggiore. They represent the Life of the Virgin.

Numerous other works could be attributed to Mino del Reame, in Rome, among them the Tabernacle of Santa Maria in Trastevere.

**MIRBEL (Lisinka Rüe, Madame de).**—French miniature painter, 1796-1849. When she married, about 1823, Monsieur de Mirbel, Mademoiselle Lisinka Rüe was already known as the painter of numerous portraits, among them those of the king, of the Marquis de Lauriston and of Lord Fitz James.

From 1830, Madame de Mirbel's house was open to artists, and she sometimes used her influence on their behalf. The able miniature painters who worked in the reign of Louis-Philippe never surpassed some of her portraits. The Louvre possesses several miniatures by Madame de Mirbel, among which are excellent portraits of Ingres and Baron Gérard.

**MIRÓ (Joan).**—Contemporary Spanish painter and sculptor. He was born 20th April 1893 at Montroig, of Catalan parents. Already before his fifteenth birthday he was enrolled at the École des Beaux-Arts, but gave up his artistic studies for two years to join his father in business. He soon discovered that he was not meant to spend his days in an office and at the age of eighteen he entered the Academy of Gali in Barcelona. Gali made him feel objects in a dark room, then model them in clay and finally paint them from memory. It was as a result of this experience that Miró gained his great plastic understanding. In 1919 he moved to Paris, where he found a patron in Dalmau, who sponsored some of his exhibitions. Influenced by his French contemporaries, Miró remained objective only for a short time; he became esoteric turning towards Surrealism. In 1921 he exhibited his *Dog Barking at the Moon,* which was hailed by French critics as one of the finest examples of Surrealism. The artist shows his sense of humour and a vast conception of space, a sort of mental field in which objects are permitted to roam about freely. He preserves a personal freshness of the eye in all his works. His early style is dominated by the purification of formal realisation; the details are concrete although the whole gives an abstract point of view. The technique is that of the miniaturists and the general atmosphere is romantic. In 1926 a change in his style and interpretation took place. The paintings became functional, dynamic and irrational, avoiding the static, coherent and rational. Freudian psychology of the subconscious, and spiritual processes are employed in accumulating objects on the canvas without logical order or sequence, just like in a dream. However, Miró remains fundamentally a Catalan. His colour is always fresh and clear and is applied in broad expanses of tempera paint. Together with Max Ernst he designed the set for *Romeo et Juliette* for Diaghilev's Ballet, and for the Monte Carlo Ballet Russe he originated a setting for the *Jeux d'Enfants*. Among the many books he illustrated are: Péret's *Et les Seins Mouraient,* Hirtz's *Il Etait Une Petite Pie,* Hugnet's *Enfances* and Tzara's *L'Arbre des Voyageurs*. His works are represented in the Museums of Moscow, New York, Grenoble and Stockholm.

Bibliography: *Joan Miró,* Cahiers d'Art, 1934.

**MISTRA.**—See Byzantine Art (Last Evolution); also Pls. 2, 42, Vol. I.

**MITSUOKI (Tosa).**—Japanese painter, considered, with Mitsunobu, as the most famous master of the school of Tosa, which he helped to formulate. He was born in 1616 and died in 1691. His decorative compositions—flowers, birds, landscapes—were adapted by the 17th century lacquer workers. His paintings are often relieved with touches of gold. Those of his best known paintings represent quail in millet (*Quail and Millet Screen*, Coll. Viscount Fukuoka Takaaki, Tokyo.)

**MNESICLES.**—Greek architect of the 5th century B.C. He built the Propylea of the Acropolis of Athens (437-432). At the foot of the Propylea was discovered an inscription with the name of Mnesicles, son of Epicrates. This is all that is known of the architect of this famous monument.

BIBLIOGRAPHY: Brunn, *Geschichte der Griech. Künstler*. Vol. II.

**MOCETTO (Girolamo).**—Italian engraver, 16th century. He came from Verona, and settled in Venice. He was a pupil of Giovanni Bellini, and made engravings of compositions by his master, Mantegna, and Cima da Conegliano. His work has an almost brutal vigour, combined with a delicate feeling for beauty of form and decoration. Examples are: *St. John the Baptist, The Roman Sacrifice* (with the Doges' Palace and Campanile in the background), and the *Calumny of Apelles* (which shows San Zanipolo, and the Colleoni statue.

BIBLIOGRAPHY: Crowe and Cavalcaselle, *History of Painting in North Italy,* ed. T. Borenius. Vol. II.

**MODANINO.**—See Mazzoni.

**MODENA (Italy).**—*Cathedral,* 1099-1184. The best known of Emilian Romanesque churches, closely connected with, but still distinct from, the contemporary architecture of Lombardy. Master Lanfranco was the designer. It is a triapsidal basilica in plan, and in elevation has a ground storey, triforium, and clerestorey, a treatment radically different from the Lombard and probably derivative from the earlier Apulian church of S. Nicola, Bari, Modena has originally its alternate system, but girder arches under a timber roof were projected instead of the Lombard domical ribbed groin vaults which now cover the structure.

**MODIGLIANI (Amedeo).**—Italian painter and sculptor (1884-1920). An Italian of Jewish origin, Modigliani was born in Livorno 12th July 1884. He received his early training at the local gymnasium, where he showed particular fondness for the works of Dante. The young student, whose face recalled to his friends the type Bellini painted so often, went to Florence to study at the Accademia delle Belle Arti, to be followed by short trips to Venice and Rome; it was here that he began his careful study of the drawings of Michelangelo. In 1906 he went to Paris and settled in the Montmarte district in a studio which was formerly inhabited by Émile Zola. Modigliani began at that time to do sculpture. At Haviland's he came into contact for the first time with Negro sculpture, in which he found great satisfaction and inspiration, contrary to the spirit of the Academy against which he revolted openly. Modigliani was very popular among his contemporaries: Derain, Utrillo, Vlaminck, Kisling and Cocteau with whom he visited the Rotonde and the Famous Dôme; they all admired the brilliant young man despite his constant state of drunkenness. Modigliani lived in extreme poverty and seemed to find consolation and refuge only in the use of narcotics. His brother Emanuel, the political leader, sent him money sometimes, but this was barely enough to keep him alive. So Modigliani began to sketch; he drew the portraits of passersby and when he earned a few sous he spent them again on drugs. He was entangled in several unhappy alliances; his patroness was a well-known English poetess. It was only towards the end of his career that he started to paint with oil; his first exhibition at the Salon des Indépendants was in 1909. The constant indulgence in hashish and other narcotics hastened his end. Modigliani died of tuberculosis at a Charity Hospital 25th January 1920, with these last words: "Cara Italia." His brother wired Kisling: "Bury him like a prince," and Modigliani was put to rest among other immortals in the cemetery of Père Lachaise. From the destructive effects of drugs there emerged a genius imbued with all the dramatic force and poetry of his age and race. In spite of the life he led, Modigliani's art showed no trace of the vulgar or banal. The bodies and faces of the women, especially, are done with an eager, flowing brush or a sinuous line retaining some of the delicate, elongated proportions derived from the Negro art of which he was so fond. His restrained colour and energetic grace are purely Italian in character. Modigliani was a sensitive and intelligent observer, and although acquainted with and somewhat influenced by Picasso's cubism, he was too great a personality to accept it. Almost immediately after his death, his paintings, up to this time in obscurity, suddenly began to claim a market. Among his most admirable portraits are those of Zborowska, Cocteau, Soutine and Bakst. He is represented in the museums of Berlin, Moscow, Detroit, London, Zurich, as well as in private collections.

BIBLIOGRAPHY: Adolph Basler, *Modigliani,* 1931.—André Salmon, *Modigliani, Sa Vie et Son Œuvre.*—Giovanni Scheiviller, *Amedeo Modigliani,* 1927.—Lamberto Vitali, *Disegno di Modigliani,* 1929.

**MOHAMMEDAN ART.**—See Moslem Art.

**MOHOLY-NAGY (László, or Ladislas).**—Hungarian painter and graver. Born in 1895, he is active in Germany and England. From 1923-28 he was professor at the Bauhaus in Weimar. One of the founders of the new constructivism, he experimented with painting, drawing, photography, stage-sets, sculpture and a number of other arts. Architectonic organization and the investigation of materials are his fundamental principles. Unlike his contemporaries, he stresses the diagonal rather than the vertical or horizontal movement in space. Many of his space-stage sets with modern lighting effects brought him fame.

BIBLIOGRAPHY: L. Moholy-Nagy, *Von Malerei zur Architectur,* 1929.—Sweeney, *Plastic Redirections in 20th Century Painting,* 1934.

**MOISSAC (Church and Cloisters).**—In about the 7th century, St. Amand founded at Moissac an abbey which, in 1047, was affiliated to the congregation of Cluny, and became a rich and powerful monastery. In the second half of the 11th century, Durand began a Romanesque church, which was replaced by a domed church (of which practically nothing remains), and then by the present church, which dates from the 15th century. The remains of the Abbey buildings have disappeared, with the exception of the famous cloisters. The principal doorway is remarkable for its Romanesque carvings. In the tympanum is represented the Christ of the Apocalypse seated on a throne, surrounded by symbolic animals, and the twenty-four Elders. The doorway is also decorated with fantastic, intertwined beasts, and delicately carved rosettes. The arcades in the cloisters are adorned

MOISSAC: TRUMEAU OF THE PORTAL.

with little columns, with rich and varied capitals.

See Pl. 46, Vol. I.

MOISSAC: THE CLOISTER.

**MOLENAER (Jan Mienze, or Johannes Molenaer).**—Dutch genre painter of Haarlem, about 1605-1668. He was strongly influenced by Frans and Dirk Hals; he married Judith Leyster, Hals's most talented woman pupil. In 1636 he moved to Amsterdam. He led a debauched existence and was in many financially embarrassing situations. His pictures depict Dutch folk-scenes in a free and mischievous manner. In 1637 he painted 37 portraits of the patriarchs of Amsterdam. He is represented in all important museums.

**MOLINARI (Antonio).**—Venetian painter (1665-after 1727). He painted the *Triumph of the Holy Army* in the hall of the Libreria.

**MOLNÁR (C. Pál, or Paul).**—Hungarian painter, born in 1894-. He studied at the Hungarian Academy at Rome and was particularly impressed by the works of Lorenzo di Credi; many of his paintings of *The Infancy Cicle* are done in the style of the Florentine master. Most of Molnár's work, although depicting religious topics, is expressed in a decorative and typically Hungarian setting, with crisp line and unbroken color, the composition is laconic and tends towards monumentality. His portraits are executed in the so-called New Gothic style. There are some excellent woodcuts, showing the artist from a more realistic and poetic angle.

**— (Josef).**—Hungarian painter, 1821-1899. Not a relation of the aforementioned. Studied in Venice, Rome and Munich. Outstanding painter of historic subjects, *Capture of Buda,* as well as of religious paintings and landscapes.

BIBLIOGRAPHY: Boetticher, *Malerwerke des 19. Jahrh.,* 1898.

**MOMPER.**—Family of Flemish artists, who painted a great many pictures. It is difficult to differentiate their work. The family included one Francis de Momper, and Joos de Momper (see below), who was the most famous.

**— (Joos de).**—Flemish painter; about 1564-1635. He painted a great many landscapes which form an important link in connecting Breughel's landscape conception with that of the Dutch 17th century masters. Paintings by Momper are found in most of the larger galleries in Europe.

BIBLIOGRAPHY: R. Grosse, *Die hollandische Landschafts Kunst* 1600-50, 1925.—*Teutoonstelling Joost de Momper.* Amsterdam, 1930.

**MONA LISA.**—See Leonardo da Vinci; also Pl. 17, Vol. II.

**MONACO.**—See Lorenzo Monaco.

**MONET (Claude).**—French painter, 1840-1927. Devoting himself to painting against the wishes of his family, Monet was soon reduced to poverty. His early pictures were conceived in the traditional style, and painted in the grey, sombre colours favoured by Courbet and Corot. He went to London, in 1871, and there studied the English masters, especially Turner and certain Pre-Raphaelites. He noticed that the Pre-Raphaelites aimed at vivacity of tone, and at producing the colour of shadows, repudiating the neutral shades which certain painters reserved for all tones which were difficult to note. He observed that Turner obtained great freshness by the use of almost pure colours which harmonised at a distance. He pursued his studies in company with his friend, the painter, Pissarro. They observed that these touches of pure colour, placed on the canvas in thin lines, appeared to blend in the distance. Henceforth Monet and

MOISSAC, PORTAL: THE FLIGHT INTO EGYPT AND THE PRESENTATION IN THE TEMPLE.

his friend banished neutral and earthy colours from their palettes, and retained only the bright colours of the spectrum. Next, observing that bright colours became duller by mixing, they obtained violet, for instance, not by mixing blue and red on the palette, but by the juxtaposition on the canvas of a touch of blue and a touch of red. This theory was not strictly adhered to in practice. Monet did not paint exclusively in bright colours, but he enlivened a tendency to monochrome by varied tints. Later, he composed some delightful pictures on a grey base, without bright colours, but still relieved by varied shades.

The first landscapes which Monet painted under the influence of his theories are such luminous and charming pictures as *Breakfast on the Grass* (Cassirer Collection, Berlin) or *The Marsh*. He soon attached still further importance to the treatment of light, and gave up painting figures. To this period belong his pictures of the *Cliff*, and the *Avenue of Poplars*, and he painted them successively at all hours of the day, without changing his position, but finding infinite variety in effects of light. Then he painted the porch of Rouen Cathedral, finding a fairy-like world of colour in the grey stones. He went to London, and painted its streets and bridges, the River Thames and the Houses of Parliament, which, through mist and fog, assumed a gigantic appearance. Monet had now acquired a dignified simplicity of style. Since the basis of his theory was that there is no such thing as "local colour," but only colour given to an object by light, at a precise moment, his colour is never "exact" in a descriptive sense, but it is intensely vital. In Monet's pictures the inanimate seems to live. He found beauty and colour even in the smoke and grime of noisy railway stations; and, as a decorator, was filled with a sense of poetry and harmony.

Among many other works, may be mentioned: *Portrait of a Woman* (Berlin); London *Bridge* (Durand-Ruel Collection); *Gare Saint Lazare* (Luxembourg Museum); *Rouen Cathedral* (Luxembourg Museum), etc.

After an exhibition in Paris in 1877, Monet and his friends came to be known as "Impressionists." They accepted the name, and added lustre to it. Of all the Impressionists, Monet was the most characteristic, and the most influential. He lived in the country and never exhibited at the salon.

See Pl. 56, Vol. II.

Bibliography: T. Duret, *Manet and the French Impressionists*. London, 1910.—A. Alexandre, *Claude Monet*. Paris, 1921.—L. Werth, *Claude Monet*. Paris, 1928.

**MONKWEARMOUTH (England).**—*Monastery*. The vault of the Anglo-Saxon porch, c. 675, is the only remaining vault of its time and place which is not part of a crypt and is based upon the previous Roman architecture of England.

**MONNOYER (Jean Baptiste), called Baptiste.**—French painter; born, 1634; died, in London, 1699. One of the best flower painters of the seventeenth century. The Louvre possesses three of his pictures.

**MONOLITH.**—A single stone or block of stone, usually of great size, shaped into a pillar, monument, or similar structure.

**MONREALE (Cathedral of), Sicily.**—Built by William II, the Norman King of Sicily, 1174-1189. The general conception of this colossal work is the same as in all the Byzantine designs of the 10th and the 11th centuries, but there are Norman and Arabic elements as well as Byzantine. Although the plan is according to the Christian tradition, it does not follow that the execution has the same artistic values as Cefalù or the Palatine Chapel. There, indeed, one feels the hand of the Greek masters; at Monreale, the Byzantine motifs are executed by indigenous pupils, and although, at first glance, the eye is dazzled by incomparable richness of effect, a detailed study reveals the coming decadence of Norman-Byzantine art, in Sicily.

**MONSIAU (Nicolas André).**—French painter, 1754-1837. He painted scenes of history and of the theatre, which are preserved in the Museums of Versailles and of Marseilles.

**MONTAGNA (Bartolommeo).**—Painter of Vicenza. Born 1450, in Orzinovi, near Brescia; died in Vicenza in 1523. He was formed by Giovanni Bellini, and was influenced by Antonello, Alvise Vivarini and by the sculptor, Bellano. Pictures by him may be seen in the Brera Gallery, Milan, in Venice, Vicenza, Padua, Verona, and elsewhere. There is a *Pietà* in Monteberico. Montagna had great influence, not only in Vicenza but throughout Northern Italy. See Pl. 14, Vol. II.

Bibliography: T. Borenius, *The Painters of Vicenza*. London, 1909.

— **(Benedetto).**—Engraver and painter of Vicenza of the end of first half of the 16th century, Son of Bartolommeo Montagna.

Bibliography: T. Borenius, *The Painters of Vicenza*. London, 1909.

**MONTAIGNE (Dordogue, France).**—Château, made famous by Montaigne, author of the *Essays*, who was born, lived, and died there. The château was destroyed by fire, and has been rebuilt on the same plan, in a richer style. The entrance tower, which was not destroyed, was the residence of Montaigne.

**MONTAÑÉS (Juan Martinez).**—Spanish sculptor and architect.

Montañés: Crucifix. (Cathedral of Seville.)

(Baptized in 1568, died, 1649). School of Seville. Pupil of Pablo de Rojas. He raised polychrome sculpture to a high degree of splendour and beauty. In 1609 he signed the contract for the altarpiece and statues ordered by the Hieronimites for their monastery of San Isidoro del Campo, at Santiponce, near Seville. The bas-reliefs tell the story of the Life of Christ, and of the Virgin. The sculptural decoration includes statues of *St. Jerome, St. John the Baptist,* the four *Theological Virtues* and of *Christ Crucified*. The *St. Jerome,* which equals Torrigiano's masterpiece in plastic beauty, is relieved against a background of subdued tones. The flesh tints look as though they had been painted on old ivory, the golden patina of which had been retained here and there. The *Crucifix de los Cálices* (1614) established his fame. Montañés made this figure of *Christ Crucified,* of natural size, for Vázquez de Leca, archdeacon of Carmona, who gave it to the Monastery of Santa Maria de las Cuevas, on the condition (since transgressed, for it is now in the Cathedral of Seville) that it was never to be taken away. This *Crucifix* is perhaps the supreme rendering of the divine Victim. In the extended arms, in the bent head, in all the sorrowful humanity of the Crucified, there is mingled a resignation and nobility which are more than human. The painting of this figure was entrusted to Pacheco, who executed it in the non-lustrous tones he affected. It is harmonious, and does honour to the painter.

Montañés: Immaculate Conception. (Cathedral of Seville.)

Maria E. Gomez-Moreno says that he created here the Andalusian type of Christ. Perhaps among the most outstanding of his statues are those at the *Mus. Prov.* of Seville, namely those of *San Bruno, St. John the Baptist,* the *Virgen de las Cuevas* and *San Domingo de Guzmán el Penitente*.

It was reserved for Montañés to give an ideal representation of the miraculously conceived Virgin. His first *Concepción* (Immaculate Conception; Seville Cathedral, Capilla de los Alabastros, (1628-31). The Virgin, clad in a voluminous mantle, stands, with her hands joined in prayer. The face, noble and grave, has a withdrawn expression, and the eyelids are lowered in meditation. Montañés, although he does not emphasize feminine contours after the manner of Torrigiano, nevertheless chose for his model a young Andalusian in the flower of her beauty. Though the lines of the body are attenuated, they give a peculiar grace to the folds of the robe and mantle. Such was the theme which the master varied in its details, but to which he remained faithful, the theme which so many painters and sculptors reproduced after him. "Innumerable works left the shop of Montañés. He received many commissions for altars and images destined for America, especially for Lima. Seville and its environs did not stand behind ordering *retablos,* those of the Convents of San Leandro (1622) and Santa Clara (1623) being among the best". One of Montañés' works which stands apart from the religious statues characteristic of the artist, is the design for a statue of Philip IV which served as a model for an equestrian statue of that monarch made at Florence by Pietro Tacca (1640).

Montañés, of whom Velázquez painted an admirable portrait (Prado Gallery, Madrid), died in Seville in 1649, at a great age. His passionate art, which is essentially Spanish, is never wanting in nobility. It is generally restrained and even when he abandons himself completely to the ardour of his faith, as in the *Santo Domingo de Guzmán,* he still created, by reason of his wholehearted sincerity, a masterpiece of sculpture. Under the appearance of realism, Montañés aspired to spirituality. He is one of the finest representatives of 17th century Christian art. He had numerous assistants and pupils among them Juan de Mesa and the great Alonso Cano.

Bibliography: F. Araujo Gomez. *Historia de la escultura en España,* 1885.—M. Dieulafoy. *La statuaire polychr. en Espagne*. Paris, 1908.—V. V. Loga. *Span Plastik,* 1923.—*Enc. Un. il. europ-am.* (Espasa). Barcelona. Vol. XXXIII, art. *Martinez Montañés.*—C. López Martinez. *Testimonios para la biografia de Juan Martinez Montañés*. Univ. de Sevilla. Laboratorio de Arte, Sevilla, 1931.—*Thieme-Becker;* Vol. XXV, 1931.—Art. *Martinez Montañés* by A. L. Mayer.—Maria Elena Gomez-Moreno. *Breve historia de la escultura española*. Madrid (misiones de Arte), 1935.

**MONTANO D'AREZZO.**—Tuscan painter, died after 1313. The only existing painting by him is a *Madonna* painted for the Church of Montevergina, in Naples, of 1310.

**MONTELUPO (Baccio da).**—Florentine painter and sculptor, 1469-1535? His style recalls the preceding century. Thus his statue of *St. John the Evangelist* (1515), at Or San Michele, is near enough in style to the other Corporation statues, carved in the "Quattrocento," for it not to stand out from the rest. The Church of San Paolino, Lucca, which is attributed to him (about 1530) recalls the Badia, by Brunelleschi, at Fiesole, and has the virtue of simplicity. His statue of *Mars,* in the Frari of Venice (1503), is more academic.

— **(Raffaello da).**—Florentine sculptor, 1505-1567. Son of Baccio da Montelupo. One of the chief pupils of Michelangelo, with whom he worked. His work lacks power and originality.

**MONTEVERDE (Giulio).**—Italian sculptor (1837-1917). He won considerable success in France and central Europe. His chief works are: *Jenner Inoculating His Son; Architecture; Child Chasing a Cock.*

**MONTFERRAND.**—See Clermont-Ferrand.

**MONTICELLI (Adolphe).**—French painter, 1824-1886. Living unknown, and dying almost in want, this artist is today much esteemed; and pictures which he was glad to sell for a few francs now fetch high prices. His work is very individual. His little dream-like figures, dressed in bright colours, move in enchanted landscapes. He painted thickly, with strokes which appear confused, until seen at a distance, when the whole assumes depth, brilliance and poetry. He greatly influenced Van Gogh who admired his work. Examples of his work may be seen in the Museum of Lille, in the Glasgow Art Gallery, in Paris, and, above all, in Marseilles (Collection André).

**MONTORSOLI (Fra Giovanni Angelo).**—Florentine sculptor and architect, 1507-1563. This monk began by being a passionate imitator of Michelangelo, with whom he worked, in 1533, on the statue of *Giuliano di Medici.* He himself made the statue of *Saint Coso,* which was never to adorn the tomb for which it was designed, and which now stands in front of a wall of the Medici Chapel.

Montorsoli travelled a great deal. He went to France in the service of Francis I, to Venice, Padua, Verona, Mantua, Arezzo, Naples, etc. On his return to Florence he began a group of *Hercules and Anteus,* for the gardens of the Villa di Castello, which was later destroyed by the jealous and brutal Bandinelli.

He achieved his chief fame in Genoa as architect of Andrea Doria. He transformed for him the Palazzo Doria in Fasolo (1529), which was afterwards splendidly decorated by Perino del Vaga. He made of it a simple, elegant building with open porticoes giving on to gardens filled with fountains. He himself made the bas-reliefs for the vestibule.

His decoration of the interior of the Church of San Matteo, Genoa, is rich and harmonious (1530).

Montorsoli's figures of the *Risen Christ,* the *Virgin* and *St. John, Adam* and *Moses,* on the high-altar of the Church of the Servi in Bologna (finished 1561) are over large and declamatory.

From 1547 to 1551, he worked in Messina on the magnificent black and white marble fountain which was in the Cathedral square.

Montorsoli returned to Florence in 1561, and shut himself up in his monastery from which he emerged only to undertake religious works.

**MONTPELLIER (France).**—*Promenade du Peyrou,* begun by d'Aviler in 1689; finished in 1785 by Giral and Dounat. The reservoir, with Corinthian columns, joins the aqueduct (*Aqueduc Saint Clément*), a fine construction in two tiers of arches (1753-1766), due to Pitot.

**MONT SAINT MICHEL (La Manche, France).**—Granite island surmounted by a Benedictine Abbey founded in 708 by St. Aubert of Avranches. The church which was built from 1022-1094 in the Romanesque style has a 15th century Gothic choir, tower and spire. The group of buildings known as La Merveille, 1203-1228, includes the almonry and cellar, the Hall of Knights, the refectory, the dormitory, and the cloister.

**MONVAERNI.**—Under this name are grouped the earliest painted Limoges enamels, of which nothing is known except that their date is previous to 1503 (the date of the *Crucifixion* by Nardon Pénicaud, the earliest signed and dated enamel we possess). Some pieces do, in fact, bear signatures, or rather inscriptions such as Monvaer or Monvaerni; and all the pieces, about forty, which show similarity of workmanship, are united under this name. It is, however, merely a convenient designation, and to "Monvaerni" must not be attributed a real existence; there is no trace of it in the archives. One can merely give this group of work to the end of the fifteenth century.

Examples of this mysterious Monvaerni may be seen in Limoges Museum (an *Entombment,* and an *Adoration of the Magi*), in the Cluny Museum, in Paris (*Virgin and Child,* and a *Pietà*), and in the Louvre (scenes from the Passion, and another relating an incident in the life of St. Christopher). In all these works blue and gold predominate.

See Pl. 30, Vol. II.

Bibliography: Demartial, *Les émaux peints. Les Primitifs, L'École de Monvaërni.* Limoges. 1910.—P. Lavedan, *Léonard Limousin, et les émailleurs français.* Paris, 1913.—J. J. Marguet de Vasselot, *Les émaux limousins.*

**MOORISH ART.**—See Moslem Art; Mudejar.

**MOR (Antonio van).**—See Moro (Antonio).

**MORALES (Luis de).**—Born in Badajoz (Extremadura) where he died in 1586, supposedly in his 77th year. "We are in the dark as to the beginning of the career of this most characteristic and most national of Spanish painters. In some instances related to Juan de Juanes—though more harsh than that Valencian master, he seems to have studied the paintings of Northern Italy and the Low-Countries with equal zeal. We do not know where nor from whom he received his artistic education" (A. L. Mayer). Because Morales painted almost exclusively religious paintings which are inspired by a fervent sense of devotion his contemporaries gave him the surname "El Divino" (The Divine) under which he is still known. Documents of payment tend to indicate that the greater number of his paintings had been ordered for his home-town. (See *Thieme-Becker*). ". . . In spite of the soft modelling of his figures and a characterization sometimes bordering on caricature, Morales is the most important of Spanish 'Devotional' painters of the 16th century. His paintings are imbued with a sense of genuinely Spanish, somehow harsh melancholy. . . . Because of their appeal to all classes of people they were copied and imitated again and again. . . . Though a Renaissance painter, in more than one of his pictures can be felt traces of the Gothic." The *Ecce Homo* and the *Pietá* in the Acad. de Bellas Artes of Madrid as well as the *Virgin and Child* in the Prado (ex. coll. Bosch) may be numbered among the best and most typical of his works.

Bibliography: *Museum,* Vol. V. Barcelona, 1916-17.—E. Tormo y Monzó, *El Divino Morales.*—A. L. Mayer, *Gesch. der span. Malerei,* 2nd ed., 1922.—Id. in Thieme-Becker, Vol. XXV, 1931; art. *Morales, Luis de.*—Ibid. *Morales, glorias del "manierismo" español,* Arte Español. Madrid, 1913.—W. Goldschmidt, *El problema del arte de L. Morales,* Rev. española de arte. Madrid, 1935.—Morales in the Hisp. Soc. of Am. N. Y., 1922.

**MORBIDEZZA.**—In painting, colouring the flesh to express its natural delicacy and softness.

**MOREAU (Jean Michel), called Moreau the Younger.**—French draughtsman and engraver, 1741-1814. He spent some time in Russia, but returned to France in 1759. He visited Italy in 1785, and spent the rest of his life in Paris. He made several vignettes for an edition of the comedies of Molière, and for the works of Rousseau and Voltaire. The marriage of Louis XVI, in 1770, and the fêtes held in 1782, in honour of the birth of the Dauphin, inspired several engravings, such as the *Masked-Ball,* and the *Queen's Arrival at the Hôtel de Ville.* One of the most important collections of his work is due to his contribution to the *Monument du costume,* which first appeared in 1777. His drawing is refined and careful, and he interpreted contemporary life in a very lively way.

Moreau the Younger: Engraving for the illustration of the "Précieuses Ridicules" by Molière.

Moreau (Gustave): Orpheus. (Musée du Luxembourg.)

See Pl. 47, Vol. II.

Bibliography: E. Boucher, *Catalogue raisonné des œuvres de Moreau le Jeune,* 1882.—Adrien Moreau, *Les Moreau,* Collection des Artistes célèbres.

— **(Gustave).**—French painter, 1826-1898. As an artist, Moreau's ideal was rather literary than plastic, and he tended to express himself by means of symbolism, and to combine the aims of Ingres and Delacroix, rather in the manner of Chassériau. He cared little for the appearance of things, and his mythological scenes are often vague and artificial, but his colour is rich and splendid.

Moreau was a great and indulgent teacher. One of his illustrious pupils was Henri Matisse.

Examples of his pictures are: *Jason and Medea, Death and the Young Man, Prometheus, Salome, Orpheus,* etc.

**MOREELSE (Paulus).**—Dutch portrait and historic painter and architect of Utrecht, 1571-1638. He was a pupil of Mierevelt, and spent some time in Italy about 1604. His favorite themes were blond young girls dressed up as shepherdesses, done in the style of the first Utrecht school. He is responsible for a number of public buildings and city gates in Utrecht.

**MORELLI (Giovanni).**—Italian art critic, 1816-1891. It was he who secured the act which prohibits selling works of art from public and religious institutions in Italy. His researches into Italian art were published in three volumes under the title, *Critical Studies.*

**MORETTO da BRESCIA (Alessandro Bonvicino).**—C. 1498-1554. Influenced by Venetian School. His immense religious pictures fill the churches of that town: in San Clemente (5 pictures), San Giovanni Evangelista, San Francesco, Santa Maria delle Grazie, SS. Nazaro e Celso (where there is one of his finest works, the *Coronation of the Virgin*), and in the Museo Martinengo. They are striking chiefly for their cold silvery colour, which is not without beauty, the more so because it is combined with quiet, harmonious design.

Venice (in Santa Maria della Pieta, and in the Academy), Bergamo (in Sant'Andrea), Milan (in the Brera), Verona, Trent, and the Vatican, also possess fine works of Moretto, showing generally the same characteristic of a rather cold nobility. Sometimes, however, as in the *Madonna* of Sant'Andrea, in Bergamo, the colour is warm and deep.

He painted some distinguished portraits, and there shows his debt to the great portrait painter, Moroni. The most important are the Lecturer, of the Palazzo Rosso, in Genoa (1553), a *Portrait of a Man* in the Museum of Brescia, two portraits, in the National Gallery, London, and a *Portrait of a Man on Horseback* in the Palazzo Donà delle Rose, Venice.

**MORGHEN (Raphael).**—Italian engraver, 1758-1833. Pupil of Volpato. He left some burin engravings, the best of which are: the *Virgin of the Chair,* after Raphael; the *Portrait of the Marquis of Moncade,* after Van Dyck; *The Last Supper,* after Leonardo da Vinci; the *Dance of the Seasons,* after Poussin, etc. His reputation was considerable, but he owed it chiefly to his technical ability.

See Pl. 17, Vol. II.

Bibliography: N. Palmerini, *Opere d'intaglio del cav. R. Morghen.* Florence, 1824.—Hasley, *R.*

*Morghen: engraved work.* New York, 1885.

**MORIENVAL (France).**—*Abbey Church* (1080-1230): The chief importance of this small Romanesque church of the Île de France with a Gothic choir is the employment, about 1120, in the ambulatory vaulting, of the structurally pointed rib in order to raise the crown of the tranverse arch almost to the height of the crown of the vault. This treatment is a landmark in the transition from Romanesque to Gothic architecture.

**MORLAND (George).**—English painter, 1763-1804. He is known chiefly as a painter of "genre" scenes, and of animals. His pictures show great delicacy of handling; and recall the old Flemish masters.

During his lifetime, Morland achieved amazing popularity. Coloured engravings of his pictures were found everywhere in England. His pictures include: *Reckoning at the Inn* (Victoria and Albert Museum); *The Bull's Head Inn;* the *Halting-Place* (Louvre); *Off to the Fair, Return from Market, Interior of a Stable* (National Gallery); etc.

Bibliography: Sir W. Gilbey and E. W. D. Cuming, George Morland. London, 1907.

**MORO (Antonio).**—Dutch portrait and historic painter, about 1512-1575. Very little is known about his family or early life, he studied with Scorel prior to 1540. Around 1552 he was called by Charles V of Spain to paint the portraits of the royal family, as well as the rulers of Portugal. A document regarding the payment is dated 1552. He painted several portraits of

Moro (Antonio).

*Mary Tudor* of England; the best of these is in Madrid. After completing a number of portraits in England, he returned once more to Spain. Moro is the most outstanding portrait painter of the Rubens-Van Dyck school. Although a naturalist, he avoids the mannerisms of the Italian school. Due to his psychological insight he gives a characteristic individuality to all of his sitters; he is equally skilled in rendering lace and the play of reflecting light on costume. He was seldom surpassed in technique. His style is related to that of Sebastiano del Piombo and Morone.

Bibliography: M. J. Friedländer, *Altniederländische Malerei,* Vol. XIII.—V. H. Hymans, *Antonio Moro.* Brussels, 1910.

**— DI VERONA (Il).**—See Francesco Torbido.

**— (Guilio dal).**—Venetian sculptor, 15th-16th century. Pupil of Jacopo Sansovino.

**MOROCCO.**—See Moslem Art.

**MORONE (Domenico).**—Veronese painter (1442 after 1517). He was a pupil of Benaglio and was influenced by Gentile Bellini and Mantegna.

**— (Francesco).**—Veronese painter (c. 1471-1529). Son and pupil of Domenico Morone.

**MORONI (Giovanni Battista).**—Painter of Brescia (about 1520-1578). Pupil of Moretto, he became one of the best portrait painters of the Renaissance. His figures, well drawn and calm, are painted in cold colours, and have considerable distinction and vigour. His portraits, of a serious and noble beauty, were great enough to have attracted the admiration of Titian, and to have inspired him. Among the most important are: *Man in Black* (1563) and the *Scholar* (of the Uffizi); Portrait of the Podestà of Bergamo (Brera, 1565); the *Old Gentleman* and other portraits in the Museum of Brescia that of Bergamo and the Academy of Venice.

**MORONOBU (Hishikawa).**—Japanese painter (1645-1715). The father of Japanese prints, he designed for black and white single sheets. The real formation of his art, he owes to the school of Matahei or the early Ukiyo-e.

Moronobu perfected the still rudimentary methods of engraving on wood, so that he was able to draw his host of little figures easily, and precisely. He made albums of en-

Moronobu: Amazons riding. (H. Vever Collection, Paris.)

gravings, representing for the first time, scenes of daily life, such as *Yamato no Oyosé* (a veritable mine of information concerning Japanese customs, about 1680). These albums were drawn in black.

**MORAZZONE (Il).**—See Mazzucchelli.

**MORRIS (William).**—English decorator and designer (1834-1896), also a notable poet and social reformer. From 1865 onwards he, with a number of associates, kept a workshop in Queen Square, Bloomsbury; in 1881, he founded a tapestry factory in Merton, Surrey and in 1891 a private printing press, "The Kelmscott Press." He is one of the originators of what has become known as the "arts and crafts" movement in England.

Bibliography: J. W. Mackail, *The Life of William Morris.* London, 1901.

**MOSAIC.**—The invention of Mosaic may perhaps be attributed to the Romans. They used it to pave their buildings and cover their walls. The Byzantines, however, made popular, under the name of "opus Grœcum," or "Grœnicum," a kind of mosaic composed of little cubes in clay and in coloured and gold glass. This process must have been used at Cordova, for the ceiling of the mosque, for instance; it prevailed in the early stages of Arabic art. It is presumed that these mosaics are the work of several Andalusian artists, although originally

Virgil: Mosaic from Sousse.

they were executed in old buildings by Greek workmen, steeped in Byzantine traditions. In the same sense may be considered the marvellous mosaics of the Koubbet-es-Sakhra, in Jerusalem.

In Egypt, in the Arabic period, mosaic was made in two ways. It consisted of small marble cubes applied to a mortar bed, or of various pieces of marble fixed in a single piece which formed the background of the work. The latter method resembles inlay work. The marbles which were most frequently used in the mosaics of Cairo were red, yellow, black and white.

See Byzantine Art; Early Christian Art; Torcello; also Pls. 10, 41, 43, Vol. I.

Bibliography: Gaston Migeon, *Manuel d'art Musulman.*—Stanley Lane-Poole, *Saracenic Arts,* Ch. III, Stone and Plaster.

**MOSCOW (Russia).**—The heart of old Russia, Moscow, was originally a humble village, founded in the 12th century by Dolgorouki, on the Moskova. In those times of constant insecurity, the most necessary building to a city was the fortress, or Kremlin, to defend it. At the top of the hill on which it stood, the Kremlin, or, more exactly, the Kremi, a kind of Acropolis, was gradually surrounded by other buildings. The use of the Kremlin was for a long time pacific, and Moscow replaced Vladimir as the capital and sacred city, uniting in the interior of her Kremi, the principal public buildings, several churches, two cathedrals (both de-

Moscow: Church of St. Basil.

stroyed) and the little church of the *Saviour in the Forest,* surmounted by domes.

The Moscovite princes whose power increased soon judged that the buildings of the Kremlin were too simple and too small, and they decided to replace them by more grandiose buildings. For this, they summoned Italian architects—A. Fioraventi, P. A. Salario, M. Ruffo and A. Novi. Their buildings were naturally in the Italian Renaissance style. (The churches, however, kept to the Byzantine tradition.) They were begun in the reign of Ivan III, in the second half of the 15th century. The Kremi is surrounded by

Moscow: The Kremlin.

a strong fortified wall, the work of Italian builders (1495-1508). It is triangular in shape, surrounded by water, and flanked by 18 strong towers.

The Kitai Gorod, or commercial quarter of Moscow, possesses the strangest building—the Church of

Vassili Blajennoy (St. Basil), built by Ivan IV, in 1560, in recognition of the taking of Kazan (1552). This building, which is both one and many, is composed of a central stone church dedicated to the Virgin, surrounded by eight brick chapels. The central church is surmounted by a pyramid; each chapel is covered by a bulbous dome, and these eight domes are all different. One is like a melon, another resembles a pine-cone, a third has facets, a fourth is honey-combed. To add to the strange effect, they are covered with brightly-coloured tiles. The interior is composed of separate chapels, low and dark, decorated with paintings and full of icons. The church is the work of two Russians, Postnik and Barna. See Russia.

BIBLIOGRAPHY: Léger, *Moscow.* Collection des villes d'art célèbres.

**MOSER (Lucas).**—German painter, 15th century. Moser's painting recalls, in its freshness, that of Malouel and the miniature painters. The one work certainly by him is the *Altarpiece of St. Mary Magdalen* in Tiefenbronn (near Pforzheim).

**MOSLEM ART.**—Sometimes called Muhammadan (*Mahometan*) or *Saracenic* art.

ARCHITECTURE.—Muhammadan architecture "differs from other styles in being the product of a religion rather than of a country . . . and though the style exhibited local divergences in treatment and detail, it prevailed in all countries brought under Mahometan influence" (Banister Fletcher).

The study of Moslem architecture extends to the buildings of North Africa, Sicily, Turkey in Europe, Asia Minor, Syria and Egypt, Arabia, Mesopotamia, Persia, Turkestan, and Moslem India.

In accordance with the grouping of M. Saladin, we will study this architecture under the following headings:—

(1) The Syro-Egyptian school.
(2) The Maghril school.
(3) The Persian school.
(4) The Ottoman school.
(5) The Indian school.

(1) *The Syro-Egyptian School.*—It will be useful to give some preliminary information, gathered from M. Saladin, on the general arrangement of the Mosque. "The embryo of it is the mihrab or Kibla, a niche cut in the wall which indicates to the faithful the direction of Mecca, towards which they ought to turn in their prayer. This wall is enclosed by an open courtyard, and thus was obtained the primitive arrangement of the Msalla of Northern Africa.

"The earliest type of mosque is that of the mosque with portico. It is formed of a square central courtyard (salon), in the middle of which is a fountain for ablutions. This courtyard is closed by porticoes (liwans), the deepest of which is the one to the east. At the back of this eastern portico is the Mihrab. This portico constitutes an oratory with five parallel aisles. Beside the mihrab is the minbar (preacher's pulpit), the dikkas (platforms on which stood readers of the Koran) and the Koursis (massive pulpits where the sacred book was kept).

"This is the plan of all the mosques of Cairo, as far as the Ayoubites. From this period, the small mosques and even the large ones were often built in the cruciform plan of the Medresses, or religious academies. Finally, later on the Ottoman conquest brought to Cairo the plan of the great domed Turkish mosques."

Practically all the early mosques were made on this logical plan.

The mosques of *Egypt* were, on the whole, built of coarse materials, such as the mosque of Tulun in Cairo, made of bricks, with a coat of plaster. The decoration consisted of paintings, and was especially rich in its gildings and sumptuous stuffs. The mosques of *Syria*, on the contrary, and particularly those of Jerusalem and Damascus, were built of precious materials, covered with mosaics, metal-work, marble, and even enamels. The decoration thus formed an integral part of the work, constructed according to Byzantine and Romanesque methods. The bronze doors, the gilding of the roof, the veneers of marble, the capitals and the columns were, thus, as much a part of the building as they were decoration. In theory, all the decorative subjects were of vegetable, floral or geometric character; actually, there were many exceptions, and here and there, contrary to canonical rules, the human figure appears in the ornamentation.

It is only from documents that we learn anything of the arrangement of these early mosques. Not until the rule of the Fatimids did an architectural style develop, the evolution of which we will follow later, because it already contains strong elements of the Arabic art of Cairo, of the 13th and 14th centuries. The cruciform plan appeared in Cairo in the 13th century. It seems to have originated in Mesopotamia.

Oriental influences disappeared about the middle of the 12th century when the Ayoubite dynasty dethroned the Fatimite dynasty of Cairo. Assyrian methods are seen in religious and civil buildings, in the use of coloured stones and polychrome marbles. Later, buildings in Syria were built largely according to Egyptian methods. This influence is especially noticeable under the Mameluke Sultan, Vaharites, and it attained its full flowering from 1382 to 1515, under the Mamelukes. About the same period, also, the great civil buildings of Cairo, and of the big centres of Syria and Egypt were built. In A.D. 1517, Egypt became part of the Ottoman Empire, and was ruled by Pashas from Constantinople until 1707.

On the whole, architecture changed very little under Turkish rule, although the type of cupolas used by Ottoman mosques was introduced and occasionally employed.

The Mosque of Sultan Berkuk, Cairo (A.D. 1384) "is famous for its graceful domes over tomb-chambers and for its minarets."

Many of the civil and religious buildings of Palestine and Syria were destroyed from the 13th to the 14th century by the Mongols.

We will now examine, in rough chronological order, some of the Moslem buildings of Egypt and Syria:—

DAMASCUS: COURT OF THE GREAT MOSQUE.

*The Mosque of Amr, Cairo,* was founded in 642. It was restored in the 15th century and rebuilt several times until the 18th.

*The Dome of the Rock* (so-called, *Mosque of Omar*), *Jerusalem,* was founded in 688 A.D., but it suffered various transformations, and in 707 A.D. it was rebuilt, and covered with a bronze dome from a church of Baalbek. It was again restored many times, until 1561, when Suleiman the Magnificent reconstructed the dome, and the whole building was covered externally with brilliant Persian tiles and internally with marble slabs. The Dome of the Rock "occupies a spot on the temple platform sacred from time immemorial; for there had stood successively the Altar of David, the Temple of Solomon . . . and Hadrian's Temple of Jupiter (A.D. 70). . . . Tradition has it that from this rock Mahomet ascended to heaven, and the building probably intended to enshrine this sacred spot was certainly not a mosque, and was not built by Omar." Although the building is similar in some ways to certain monuments of central Syria, it remains none the less a Byzantine work. The central dome, which covers the sacred rock, is supported by columns and arches. This central part is surrounded by a double octagonal portico which bounds the external walls.

EL-AKSA: DOORWAY OF THE MOSQUE.

*The Mosque-el-Aksah, Jerusalem,* rivals the "Mosque of Omar" in magnificence. It was several times injured by earthquakes and frequently restored.

*The Great Mosque, Damascus,* stands on the site of a Roman temple, which was converted into a Christian church by Theodosius (A.D. 349), and rebuilt as a mosque by the Muhammadans (A.D. 705). All that remains of the original mosque are the external doorways, the façades of the mosque and of the transept, and the arcades of the portico.

*The Mosque of Ibn-Tulun, Cairo,* was built from 872-879.

*The Mosque of Sultan Hassan, Cairo* (1356-1359), is the most important and most admirable of the mosques built on a cruciform plan. From the central, uncovered courtyard with the fountain for ablutions, four rectangular arms project. "They are covered with pointed barrel vaults, which had been introduced into Egypt at the time of the foundation of Cairo in A.D. 971." The eastern arm forms the sanctuary; behind the wall at the back is the tomb chamber. Three other "liwans" complete the plan, and between the arms of the cross are colleges of the four orthodox rites, each possessing a courtyard with one liwan and rooms for

JERUSALEM: MOSQUE OF OMAR.

# FLORENTINE SCULPTURE

*This Florentine sculpture of the fifteenth century furnishes one of the most attractive chapters in the history of art. One of the most exquisite museums in the world is the Bargello at Florence, where some of the masterpieces of this school are assembled. Antique marbles present more majesty and a more regular beauty but they do not have the nervous quality, the vitality and the charm that one almost always recognises in Florentine marbles and bronzes.*

AGOSTINO DI DUCCIO: MADONNA. LOUVRE. *(Photo by Hachette.)*

LUCA DELLA ROBBIA: MADONNA. BARGELLO, FLORENCE. *(Photo by Brogi.)*

ROSSELLINO: MADONNA. SAN MINIATO. *(Photo by Brogi.)*

## Luca della Robbia

Luca della Robbia was a very simple artist, even ingenuous, who depicted a great deal of sentiment in his art; he was one of those to whom faith was most essential. It was he who had the idea of multiplying the figures of the Virgin or of Jesus using terra cotta covered with enamel. This was an economical method of sculpture. Luca della Robbia originally only used white enamel for his figures and blue enamel for the background. His nephew Andrea and other workers in enamel of his school employed a richer palette, but with a more questionable harmony.

ANDREA DELLA ROBBIA: THE VISITATION. SAN GIOVANNI, PISTOIA.

MATTEO CIVITALI: THE MADONNA NURSING HER SON. CHIESA DELLA TRINITÀ, LUCCA. *(Photo by Brogi.)*

DESIDERIO DA SETTIGNANO: ST. JOHN THE BAPTIST. MARTELLI COLLECTION, FLORENCE. *(Photo by Alinari.)*

MINO DA FIESOLE: BISHOP SALUTATI. CATHEDRAL OF FIESOLE. *(Photo by Brogi.)*

## The Little Masters

The school of Florentine sculpture of the fifteenth century is as fruitful as the school of painting. Each of the masters has his own individuality; some specialize in portraiture; others are fond of carving adorable Madonnas in marble relief. The figures of children have always greatly inspired these artists because they know how to render vivacity, movement and grace.

VERROCCHIO: DAVID. BARGELLO, FLORENCE. *(Photo by Brogi.)*

VERROCCHIO: COLLEONE. VENICE. *(Photo by Brogi.)*

A. POLLAIUOLO: HERCULES AND ANTAEUS. BARGELLO, FLORENCE. *(Photo by Brogi.)*

## Verrocchio

Verrocchio is one of the most engaging masters of the Florentine art of the fifteenth century because of his own work and because of his influence upon Leonardo da Vinci. He seems to have taken up the most famous subjects of his master Donatello in order to excel him in elegance and power. One may compare the David of Verrocchio and his Colleone at Venice with Donatello's David and Gattamelata. The Pollaiuoli, like Verrocchio, were painters and sculptors.

# MASACCIO AND FILIPPO LIPPI

*During the first half of the fifteenth century, painting at Florence boldly freed itself from the Giottesque point of view; it rejected the large number of charming conventions, replacing them with the observation of nature. At the same time, Flemish art with the van Eycks was inaugurating naturalistic painting. But Flemish naturalism was direct, immediate; the painter copied his model just as he saw it. Florentine naturalism had higher ambitions. It analysed nature first in order to become acquainted with it and then in order to reorganize it. Its art relied upon science.*

MASACCIO: ADAM AND EVE. CHURCH OF THE CARMINE, FLORENCE. *(Photo by Anderson.)*

MASACCIO: JESUS AND THE APOSTLES. CHURCH OF THE CARMINE, FLORENCE. *(Photo by Anderson.)*

MASOLINO: SALOME. CASTIGLIONE D'OLONA. *(Photo by Alinari.)*

## Masaccio

In the Church of the Carmine at Florence, one may admire an ensemble of frescoes begun by Masolino, continued by his pupil Masaccio and finished very much later by Filippino Lippi. It is especially before the masterpiece of Masaccio, Jesus ordering St. Peter to pay the tax collector, that one is conscious of the growing naturalism of the Florentine painters. Compared to the Giottesque figures, the personages of Masaccio are more real; they stand more firmly on the ground, strongly modelled by light and shade; the postures recall Giotto and prefigure the *Acts of the Apostles* by Raphael.

PAOLO UCCELLO: BATTLE OF SANT'EGIDIO. NATIONAL GALLERY, LONDON. *(Photo by Hachette.)*

ANDREA DEL CASTAGNO: THE LAST SUPPER. FLORENCE. *(Photo by Alinari.)*

## Paolo Uccello and Andrea del Castagno

These painters are among the powerful precursors who established Florentine naturalism relying upon the laws of perspective, the knowledge of anatomy and the precedents of sculpture. The figures of Castagno reveal an apparent relationship to the sullen prophets of Donatello. As for Paolo Uccello, he was famous because of his passion for perspective. He arranged his figures in space as a geometrician who works out a descriptive problem.

FILIPPO LIPPI: THE DANCE OF SALOME. CATHEDRAL OF PRATO. *(Photo by Brogi.)*

FILIPPO LIPPI: THE VIRGIN AND CHILD. UFFIZI, FLORENCE. *(Photo by Anderson.)*

FILIPPO LIPPI: THE ANNUNCIATION. NATIONAL GALLERY, LONDON. *(Photo by Hachette.)*

## Filippo Lippi

This painter, who was a monk before he renounced monastic garb, followed the naturalistic movement in painting, inaugurated by Masaccio. He was in touch with the research of his contemporaries in the science of perspective, and he placed his figures in realistic decorations. He even introduced into the subjects of religious painting contemporary personalities and architecture. However, this realist preserved a beauty and an expression of charming ingenuousness, in particular, in the countenance and the gestures of the Virgin.

the students. The Mosque of Sultan Hassan has two minarets—originally there were four. The interior is extremely rich, and yet severe, with its bronze door, its lights, its chains, its dikka, and marble minbar. The delightful buildings of the *Mosque of Kait Bey* (1472-76, near Cairo) were inspired by the Mosque of Sultan Hassan. They form an "ensemble" of all the foreign elements found in this mosque, combined

KAIRWAN: MINARET OF THE GREAT MOSQUE.

with local characteristics. With the Mosque of Kait Bey, the great Saracenic building age in Egypt ended.

(2) *Maghril School.*—The earliest mosques of Morocco, Tunis and Algiers had, like those of Ibn-Tulun (872-879, Cairo) and of Amron, parallel aisles, which allowed of lateral extension by the addition of several aisles. Until the 10th century, they were built of antique materials. It was not until about four centuries later that an original style came to be established. The Maghril mosque differs from the Egyptian mosque, in that the central aisle is always very much wider. Many buildings were erected in Morocco up until the 16th century, especially mosques which always kept the same arrangement. But after this date, the plans varied. Most of the buildings were square in plan with round towers at each corner, and in the middle of each front. In the inner courtyard

TUNIS: MAIN ENTRANCE OF THE GREAT ZITOUNA MOSQUE.

was a little mosque with a minaret. Tombs were associated with the mosque and decorated only internally. They consisted, in the cemeteries, of a single domed chamber. The most interesting, covered with ornamentations and inscriptions, are those of Kairwan and Tunis. Military architecture is Byzantine in origin, and did not evolve. Arabic towers are square or polygonal, with interior arches. The most important are those of Sfax in Tunisia, of Tlemcen in Algeria and of Chella and Fez in Morocco. As for the Arabian castles, they were built in the style of fortified convents. Civic buildings are, on the contrary, much more varied in character; these consist of aqueducts, fountains, reservoirs, bridges and bazaars. Some buildings, such as public cisterns and hydraulic works, show Roman influence.

The Maghril houses were a combination of the Byzantine house and the Roman house—to judge from the representations that have come

VERANIM: SELEUCID MOSQUE.

down to us in mosaics, and in the miniatures of manuscripts. Nevertheless, there was discovered at El-Alia, the remains of a villa with very thick walls, and narrow windows, and covered with paintings. As to the royal palaces, for any knowledge of those earlier than the 13th century, we can only refer to historians. But from the 13th century onwards there are palaces still standing which surpass in general conception, in richness and in elegance, all that can still be seen of

TAURIS: THE BLUE MOSQUE.

their kind in Syria, in Egypt and in Turkey. There were aqueducts, fountains, pavilions covered with mosaics of ceramic and marble. The ceilings were carved and covered with arabesques. The palace of El-Bedi, in Marrakech, was among the most precious. It was surrounded with gardens, where silver statues adorned basins and fountains. This astonishing luxury is still reflected in some of the old Arabic houses of Tunis. Nevertheless, it is only in Morocco, with its sculptured plaster decorations, its painted ceilings, woodwork and mosaics, that we can form a fair idea of this extraordinary wealth.

Among the chief Moslem buildings of the Maghril may be mentioned one of the oldest—the Djama Zitouna, of Tunis. Its plan is like that of all the Tunisian mosques prior to the 11th century. (Sfax, Beja, Gafsa, etc.). Its aisles are arranged parallel to the wall of the mihrab with a central aisle wider than the others, which continues to form a T. The central aisle is covered at each end with a cupola on a polygonal drum, one over the entrance, and one over the mihrab. Its minaret is built at the side of the courtyard, parallel to the entrance façade, and is square in plan. The decoration appears to have been inspired by certain churches of Central Syria.

"After the Moorish conquest of *Spain* in the 8th century and the establishment of the Western Caliphate at Cordova, many mosques were erected on the Peninsular, with the usual open court and rectangular prayer chamber of numerous arcades. . . . These mosques were devoid of a dome which in the East usually indicated the presence of a tomb chamber, but they displayed the same elaboration of geometrical design with bright colours in decoration which characterise Saracenic Architecture of all countries" (Banister Fletcher).

*The Great Mosque, Cordova* (A.D. 786), the glory of the Western Caliphate, was the centre of Islam in the West. "The enclosed portion alone occupies a larger area than any Christian Cathedral." It has 19 aisles, with 33 bays to each aisle, and is approached by 19 bronze doors. At the back of the great central aisle is the mihrab. The interior is richly adorned with semi-precious stones and coloured marble columns.

Arabic architecture had a great influence in *Sicily* for at least three centuries—as may be seen in the Capella Palatina, Palermo (A.D. 1132), which served as a model for Monreale Cathedral.

After the 15th century Maghril art lost its character. The decadence was less rapid in Tunis than in Morocco.

Morocco and Persia are the only countries in which the tradition of Moslem art survives.

(3) *The Persian School.*—Very important monuments enable us to study Persian architecture from the earliest times. The general characteristics are: (1) Lintel over columns, the construction being of wood, and the walls of unbaked brick. (2) Vaulted construction, resting on square, octagonal or circular pieces of brick. Owing to the scarcity of wood, the Persians perfected this system of constructing vaults to such an extent that these works can only be rivalled by mediæval buildings. Generally these monuments are in unbaked brick, preserved on the exterior by burned brick. Stalactites may be considered as a "decorative expression locally deduced from the method of construction." They were made of terra cotta and served to clothe the body of the building, and were used in the voussoirs, cornices and corbelling, etc.

Nearly all Persian buildings were decorated with enamelled earthenware, and in the 14th and 15th centuries the Persian potters began to produce work of the highest merit. In the 16th century, all the resources of this art were already known, and it was applied to bands, friezes, walls, domes and cornices. Window-panes also formed an essential element in the decoration, with their marquetry of wood, rare metal, gilding, friezes of plaster or stucco, moulded and sculptured, and, later on, Venetian glass.

The *Mosque at Samarra* is one of the most important monuments of mediæval Moslem art in Persia. The mosque was built on a square plan; the interior still contains arches and columns.

*Bagdad* became the capital of the Eastern Caliphate under the Abbasides dynasty. Nothing remains of the glorious monuments built there in the days of Haroun-al-Raschid. They were mostly of unbaked clay, and consequently not very durable, and were destroyed when Bagdad was taken by Hulagu, in 1250. The most important Persian mosque of the time of the Abbasides is the *Great Mosque of Ispahan* (760-770). It consists of a large courtyard, in the centre of which is a great square pavilion. In the interior square piers carry the vaults, engaged columns support the dome, which is covered externally with enamelled tiles. The two minarets are also entirely covered with tiles.

The Mongols had at first, after their invasion, no influence on Persian architecture. The most perfect building is the *Mosque of Veranim* (1322). It is placed at the

FOUNTAIN OF THE SERAGLIO OF SOLYMAN.

far end of a court. The mihrab faces the entrance door. It is an ogival niche with a lace-like vault resting on a small frieze terminating in a cubic inscription very richly ornamented. The façade is decorated with a mosaic of tiles in two shades of blue, and its plan is one of the simplest. Despite the richness of its decoration in carved plaster and stucco, its general lines are severe.

Construction with enamelled tiles is an important feature of some of the monuments of Samarcand, the Mosque of *Shar Sindah* (1392) being one of the most typical examples. The façade and porch are covered with a mosaic of tiles, producing a very rich effect. Carpets were probably hung on the walls.

The Mausoleum of Timur or Tamerlane (Gur Emir, 1485) is composed of a group of tombs, the most important of which is that of Timur and which is placed at the end of a court, entered through a great doorway. Unfortunately, this doorway, once decorated with tiles, is partly destroyed, but even in its present condition it is very beautiful.

The madrasa of Shir-dar (1620) is very interesting on account of its dome, with sides ending in stalactites superimposed in three successive tiers. The interior is decorated with tiles recalling the colours of Chinese porcelain. This combination of Persian and Chinese elements occurs again in the balustrades of the arches of the Kodjit Mosque. In the blue mosque of Tauris we see the evolution of enamelled decoration which takes the form of foliage, stems, scrolls and floral motifs in place of geometric ornament. The Mosque of Tauris was built with very thick walls, to resist earthquakes.

The modern period of the Persian school comprises all the monuments built from the 16th century until the present day. A renaissance took place under the Safavid Dynasty, when architecture underwent an

Ahmedabad: The mosque Jama Masjid. (Jaino-Moslem type.)

extraordinary development. This style continued until the 18th century. Unfortunately, it seems to have lost all expression at the present time. The tomb of Sheikh-Safi (1642) at Ardebil is one of the most admirable monuments of the modern Persian school. It was begun in the 16th century and consists of two courts, the second one lead ing into an octagonal chamber surmounted by a dome, and containing the tomb. The door leading from the court to the oratory, and the two smaller doors leading to the tombs of the princes of the reigning house, are composed entirely of silver. The dominant note of the whole decoration is the employment of enamelled pottery, producing an effect of great richness.

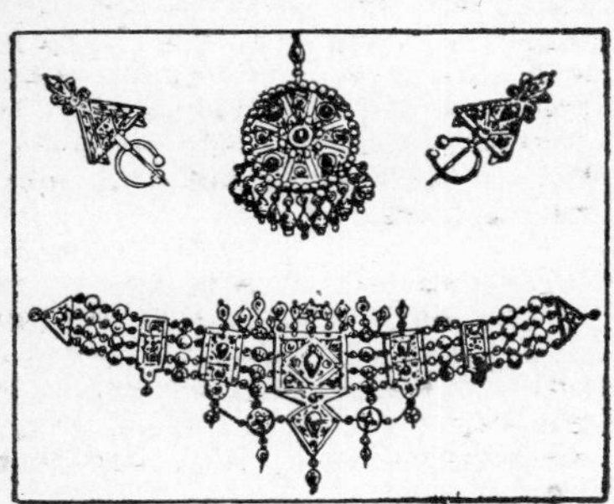

Kabylic jewels. (Beni Yenni, Algiers.)

Shah Abbas (17th century), one of the greatest Persian sovereigns, conceived the idea of making Ispahan the most beautiful city in the East, and he fully succeeded. Chardin's descriptions enable us to form some idea of its gardens, promenades, and principal buildings, among which mention must be made of the Promenade and the Char-bag canals. This avenue is flanked by sumptuous buildings, with a canal flowing down the centre, and the king's pleasure-house occupying one end. In front of the admirable porphyry gate, Aali-Kapu, rises the great royal mosque, the Masjid-i-shah of Ispahan, admirable alike in plan and execution. It is fully described by Chardin. The exterior is composed of brick and enamelled tiles, producing an effect of unique splendour.

The public buildings in Persia, such as bazaars and baths, are often very luxurious. The most interesting baths are those of Kashan.

Mention must also be made of certain bridges, such as the one over the Daliki (on the road from Shiraz to Bender Bushir), and to a number of dove-cotes near Ispahan.

The military architecture was nearly all built of brick with the result that practically nothing now remains of it.

(4) *Ottoman School.*—It was not until the 14th century, when the Mongols had conquered Alahed-in-III that the Osmantis Turks began to play a part in politics. The germs of Ottoman art must be sought in the Seljuk monuments. Seljuk

Ivory coffer. (Cathedral of Bayeux.)

art also shows a strong Byzantine influence, as well as that of certain Greek buildings. The essential elements of Ottoman art are seen at Konia. Yet in spite of the Ottoman invasion of Anatolia, local traditions of building continued to be employed by architects. Later on, Byzantine architecture exercised a great influence on the Turkish empire, and created a very original style—though, curiously enough, Arab and Persian elements always served as decorative motives in Ottoman art, up to the period when a mock-Italian rococo poisoned the taste of the Turks.

*Armenia* was also influenced by the art of the Seljuks and Turks. It has always been famous for its builders, and it was Armenian architects who were called to repair

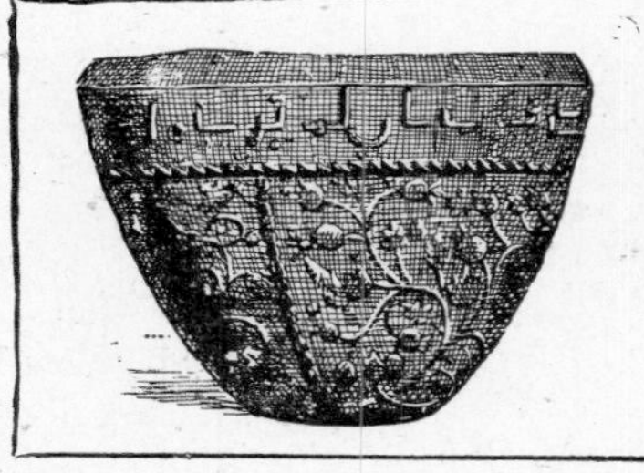

Terra cotta bowl. (Decoration in low relief. Louvre.)

Saint Sophia, in 989, when an earthquake had damaged it.

We shall now consider the Ottoman buildings of Turkish art from the 16th to the 18th centuries. Immediately after the conquest of Constantinople by the Turks (in 1453) the plan of the mosque was completely transformed and remodelled after the domed churches of Constantinople, especially St. Sophia. Ottoman architecture evolved towards the conception of the Turkish mosque—that is, towards a Byzantine plan, with Persian and Syro-Egyptian decoration. Its characteristic is the square hall covered with a dome on spherical pendentives. The number of domes varies according to the size of the mosque. The minbars are very high and all of marble. The mihrab keeps the form of an arched niche. Minarets affected cylindrical form, and were covered by a roof in the form of a cone.

Among the chief Ottoman buildings must be mentioned: the Mosque of Sultan Murad, the Mosque of Yechil-Damji, or the Green Mosque, the baths of Yeni-Kaplidja.

The oldest mosque in Constantinople is the Mosque of the Sultan Bayezid. In plan it resembles St. Sophia and it became the type of Ottoman mosque, and other mosques repeated its general arrangement. The "Suleimaniyeh," or Mosque of Suleiman I (1550-1556), was built on the same principles. The "Ahmediyeh" (1608-1614), or Mosque of Ahmed I, is the largest mosque in Constantinople. Its plan is extremely simple. It has a central dome, on massive circular pillars surrounded by semi-domes, while at the four angles are smaller domes bringing the plan to a square. It has six minarets of great lightness.

Lamp of a mosque. (Musée des Arts Décoratifs.)

(5) *The Indian School.*—"Moslem architecture passed into India from Persia, where it had been influenced by the old Sassanian Empire (A.D. 226-642). The *Pathan Dynasty* (A.D. 1193-1554), and the *Mogul Dynasty* (1526-1857) include the two main periods of Saracenic architecture—covering the whole time since the Mahometan conquest of Delhi, in A.D. 1193."

The Muhammadan conquerors adopted Jaina temples to their use, by removing the Jaina shrine, and adding the mihrab.

Moslem buildings in India are of marble and sandstone, and thus show more genius in solving constructional problems than those of other countries.

From among the multitude of Muhammadan buildings in India, only a few can be mentioned:

*The Kutub, Delhi* (1193), is almost entirely in ruins. It is celebrated chiefly for its immense minaret, which remains almost intact. It is built of red sandstone and white marble.

*The Tomb of Sher Shar, Sahsarâm* (1539), rises from a platform in the middle of a sheet of water. It is octagonal in plan; and more austere.

Minbar of the Mosque of Kait Bey, fifteenth century. (Kensington Museum.)

*The Tomb of Malmûd, Bijapur,* has eight Persian arches bearing an immense dome. The imposing character of this tomb is accentuated by the simplicity of its internal and external decoration.

Fountain of the Lions. (Alhambra of Granada.)

The Jâmi Masjid, Jaunpur (1438); the Atala Masjid, Jaunpur (1408); and the Jâmi Masjid Champanir (1500) are other remarkable buildings.

"It has been said that while the great Moguls designed like Titans, they finished like jewellers. This unusual combination gives the special character to these palace-tombs."

*The Tâj-Mahal,* Agra, is one of the most famous buildings in the world. It is of incomparable richness. It was built by Shah Jehan, as a tomb for his wife. Twenty thousand workmen were employed on it from 1630 to 1647, and materials for its construction were sent from all countries. The monument, which is octagonal in plan, rises from a square terrace. The angles are flanked by four minarets. The hall is of white marble with inscriptions of black marble. The silver doors, unfortunately, exist no longer. The entrance in the centre of each face is of the usual recessed type. The beautiful marble work was covered with inlays of jewels.

"As a palace of pleasure it enchants alike by its perfection of symmetry, beauty of design, and delicacy of decoration. It stands by the waters of the Jamna, amidst marble terraces, fountains and lakes, and is invested with the solemnity suitable to a mausoleum by the dark sentinel cypresses which stand around" (Banister Fletcher).

STAR OF SCULPTURED STUCCO, THIRTEENTH CENTURY. (Louvre.)

BIBLIOGRAPHY: H. Saladin, *Manuel d'art Musulman.*—Gayet, *L'Art Arabe,* 1900.

(1) Syro-Egyptian School: Bourgoin, *Précis de l'art arabe.* Paris, 1873.—Gayet, *L'art arabe.* 1900.

(2) Maghril School: Doutté, *Merrakeck, comité de Maroc.* 1906.—Ricard, *Pour comprendre l'art Musulman dans l'Afrique du nord et en Espagne.* Paris, 1924.

(3) Persian School: M. Dieulafoy, *L'Art antique de la Perse.*—Murdoch Smith, *Persian Art.*

(4) Ottoman School: Moatani, *L'Architecture Ottomane.* Constantinople, 1873.

(5) Indian School: A. Cunningham, *Archæological survey of India.* London, 1871.—J. Furgusson, *History of Indian and Eastern Architecture.* London, 1899.

*Mesopotamian Glass.* This consists of vases, ewers, and especially of bottles with long necks, gilded or greenish, generally, with foliage decoration, figures, animal friezes, and designs which are decidedly Chinese in type. Examples: the vases of the Rothschild collection (Victoria and Albert Museum, London); those in the British Museum and in the Museo Civico of Bologna. The most beautiful bottle is that belonging to Mr. Sigismond Bardac.

*Goblets.* A whole series of these exist. They are of enamelled glass, and many have been in Europe for centuries. The best 13th century examples are in Chartres; the 14th century ones in Dresden, Cassel, and the British Museum.

*Glass Industry in Spain.* This was a flourishing industry, but no examples have come down to us.

*In Persia; 17th and 18th centuries.* Long-necked bottles were made to hold rose water or perfumes. These were varied in shape and the workmanship of great delicacy.

*Stained Glass in Egypt.* Glass was much used for enclosing bays, and, set in open plaster work, often showed delightful originality. Example: the stained glass window with plaster work (Karamiah), of Cairo (14th and 15th centuries).

BIBLIOGRAPHY: Gerspadi, *La Verrerie.*—Migeon, *Manuel d'art Musulman.*

*Stucco and Stonework.* According to some authorities, stucco was used from the time of its origin, in Egypt, and the mosques of Ibn Tulun (which dates from 872-9); of el-Azhar (971); el-Hakem (1012)—all have still some of their original primitive stucco decoration. This is generally in the form of geometrical designs or leaf patterns. In the 13th century the technique was masterly, as is shown by the mosque-tomb of the Sultan Ralaoun, or that of Mahomet el Nassir, the decoration of which has some similarity to the early Moorish art in Spain. Even at the time when stone was much used, stucco was still employed for a long time, as in the frieze in the Mosque of Sultan Hassan, etc.

Stone was not used till comparatively late, in the Arabic buildings of Egypt, in, for instance, the cupolas of the funeral mosque of Berkuk (1384), etc. The work was very simple—the decoration floral. The most remarkable examples of sculptured stone work were to be found in the buildings of the Sultan Kait Bey (1472-1476). Some of the arabesques from these are in the Cairo Museum.

MIHRAB OF WOOD, TWELFTH CENTURY. (Chapel of Sitta Rukayah, Museum of Cairo.)

Stone was not only used in large buildings, but also for pulpits of mosques, in tribunes, cenotaphs, etc. The minbar, or pulpit, of the mosque of the Sultan Berkuk (Cairo Museum), which belongs to the end of the 15th century, is one of the most typical examples of Arabic decoration. There were also many tombstones (châhid) generally in serpentine, and sculptured in relief. In Cairo, many large jars were made. These had decorative ornamentation, and supports to keep them upright. The white marble plaques of fountains were also sculptured, and count among the works of art. The best example of Arabic sculpture in marble is the large octagonal basin in the Victoria and Albert Museum. This is the type of Syro-Egyptian sculpture of the 13th century. In Venice, the white marble seat in San Pietro di Castello, shows the influence, in the Middle Ages, of Eastern art upon Western. The "copper" from Medinet ez-Zahra (10th century) is a magnificent example of sculpture in Spain, as is also the marble basin (pila) in the Alhambra in Granada, which has reliefs representing lions devouring stags. The sculptured capitals (in stone or marble) in Spain can, in their bold execution, give us an idea of the genius of the anonymous artists of this time. They are to be found in most Spanish museums, especially in Saragossa. On the whole, however, the sculptured decoration of Spanish buildings was more mechanical in workmanship, and cannot rival stone carved as one sees it in Cairo, or in the Mosque of the Sultan Hassan. Moreover, the buildings of the Sultans Seleucids of Konieh show that Moslem art did represent living creatures in spite of the old assertion that Islamic peoples were forbidden by their religion to do so. The Museum of Constantinople has fragments of friezes representing animals chasing each other, and the Konieh Museum has three important bas-reliefs showing sculptures of human forms—the rarest of all Arabic art—riders, lance in hand, spearing lions and dragons. They are finely done, and remind one of Renaissance sculpture. Another bas-relief represents two winged figures.

CHURCH SEAT. (Museum of Madrid.)

*Sculptured Wood* was very widely used in Arab art in spite of the scarcity of suitable wood in Egypt. It is probable that Syria and Asia Minor, rich in fine trees (pines and cedars), imported their production. Sculpture on wood, however, was little used for mosque decoration, except for decorative friezes in the pulpits, ceilings, cupboard doors, and for doors and furniture of private houses. The oldest known Arab woodwork (in Cairo Museum) dates from the 8th or 9th century. In the same museum, the great wooden doors include one with the name of the Caliph el-Hakem bi amr Illah (996-1020), which came from the Mosque el-Azhar, and whose leaf decoration in high relief, and rhythmic arabesque-like decoration, make it a superb work of art. Art reached a high level at the Court of the Fatimids (Arabs of the Shiite sect). The Fatimid work is epitomised in the three wood mihrabs in the Cairo Museum. The first, with simple, archaic foliage decoration, came from the Mosque el-Azhar. The second, formed of little sculptured panels, dates from the 12th century, and came from the Mosque of Sitta Nefisa. The third and most important came from the Chapel Sitta Rukayah, in Cairo, and the frieze ornaments, panels with flowers and fruit—a type of decoration peculiar to the 12th century—form a magnificent work of art. In the 13th century, panels became smaller, and forms more varied. An example is the cenotaph from a neighbouring tomb of the Mosque of Imam el Chafey, of which three sides are in the Arabic Museum of Cairo, and the fourth in the Victoria and Albert Museum in London. The method of adorning tombs with panels of sculptured wood was general in the 13th century, and the tomb of Salih Ayoub (1249) is the oldest example of a whole set of panels. So far there had been no infringement of the rule that no living creature should be represented. This, however, was not henceforward strictly adhered to, and there are now examples of wood sculpture representing hunts, games, etc., as in the doors of the Moristan of Kalaoun, which is an important work in the history of woodwork in Egypt. The origin of this type of decoration is to be found in Persia or Mesopotamia, whose influence on Cairo workers was considerable, especially in the 13th century.

Animal decoration was no longer considered a profanation, though, in the reign of Mohammed en-Nassir, arabic decoration returned to geometrical patterns and arabesques. Minbars, especially, were decorated with wonderful sculptured panels, the typical example of the minbar of the Egyptian mosque, being that of the Sultan Kait Bey, in the London Victoria and Albert Museum. This is in perfect preservation, and shows wonderfully delicate, varied work.

The Cairo Museum has good examples of the wonderful woodwork done for the Koursi, a kind of pulpit where the Koran was placed. The moucharabiehs (enclosures which, in mosques, served to cut off the tombs, and also, in private houses, served as a sort of grill, overlooking the street, and allowing the inhabitants of the houses to look out, without being seen themselves) were also elaborately decorated. Ceilings, too, were adorned with wood carving.

A minbar and a maksoura were also sculptured, in the first years of Islam, at Cairo, the geometrical designs showing Byzantine influence. It is the oldest extant example of Arab woodwork of the end of the 9th century. The Palermo Museum has a part of a wood ceiling of the Palatine Chapel (12th century), which is similar to the Egyptian work, and represents leaves and animals. As for the Mosque at Cordova, one can only rely on descriptions of this wonderful work, as it was destroyed in 1713.

BIBLIOGRAPHY: Stanley Lane-Poole, *Saracenic Arts.* London, 1886.

*Moslem Carpets.*—Those dealt with will be the knotted carpets, or the large pieces, woven on looms, with their close, pliable surface of wool or silk.

(1) *Archaic carpets with stylised decoration.* Example: a large carpet acquired by the Kaiser Friederich Museum of Berlin is decorated with dragons, lions, panthers, borders of foliage or flowers of Chinese type. It was made in the north of Syria in the early 13th century.

(2) *Carpets with hunting scenes or animal fights.* They are sometimes woven with silk, with threads of gold and silver, but most often with very fine and bright wools mixed with silk. The most famous is the

famous "hunting" carpet in the palace of Schönbrunn near Vienna. Among other examples is the wonderful wool carpet in the Victoria and Albert Museum, London, those in the Poldi Pezzoli Museum (Milan) and in the Stieglitz Museum (Leningrad). The two latter are of silk. There is also a carpet in the Sarre collection, which is perhaps the finest texture in existence, as there are 650 knots in a square inch. It came from the Mosque of Ardebil in Persia. The Louvre has a series of Persian carpets which show Chinese influence to the extent that one is led to believe that they are of the time when Persia and China were united under one ruler—Jenghis Khan and his successors.

SMALL CARPET OF SILK VELOURS. (Persian art, sixteenth century. Musée des Arts Décoratifs.)

3. *Carpets with large flowers, lamps and vases.* The stylised flower decorations were derived from the lily or the sun. Examples may be found in the Kunstgewerbe Museum in Berlin; in the Commercial Museum in Vienna; but the chief example is the huge carpet in the Victoria and Albert Museum, which, dated 1535, forms an important document in the history of Persian textile art.

4. *Carpets with stiff floral designs.* Example: in the Kunstgewerbe Museum, Berlin, etc.

5. *Carpets with geometrical designs.* These carpets, in wool, smaller in size, are more numerous. They may have been Persian in origin, or from Asia Minor.

6. *Carpets called Polish.* These usually have floral designs, of a kind more stiff and cold than in Persian carpets with floral patterns. These are always silk, with a ground threaded with gold and silver. They have been attributed to the time of Sobieski, King of Poland (1629-1696). The making of carpets has not ceased in the East and Ouschak in Asia Minor, where Smyrna carpets are made. Turkish carpets are coarser and less delicately finished than the Persian ones which the women of Kurdistan and Meched make.

BIBLIOGRAPHY: Griggs, *Asiatic Carpets Design.* London.—Sulbelkian, *Fabrication des tapis en Orient.*—M. S. Dimand, *A Guide to an Exhibition of Oriental Rugs and Textiles* (The Metropolitan Museum of Art). New York, 1935.

*Painting and Miniature.* The Arabs were famous painters, who founded schools in certain towns in the East. The Fatimids encouraged animated painting. Two artists' names have come down to us; that of Ibn el-Aziz, and Kasir, who did the mural decorations in the Sultan's palace. Nothing of their work remains.

PERSIAN RUG, SIXTEENTH CENTURY.

On the other hand, many miniatures still exist, for Moslem art excelled in water-colour ornamentation of manuscripts. These, instead of being done directly on a page of the book, were generally done on a leaf lightly covered with a layer of gesso mixed with Arabic gum. Sometimes the layer of paint is so thick that it looks like relief work.

Most of these paintings are unsigned; or else the name and date are difficult to decipher. The written text, however, is always signed and dated, as though the art of calligraphy were held in greater esteem than that of miniature.

Animal forms were represented, in spite of the law, and curiously, Eastern painters rendered the human figure better in miniature than in any other branch of art. Some of their hunting scenes, heroic in character, exact in realism of pose, and with a rare beauty of poetical conception and of colour—equal the best work of the West.

ASSEMBLAGE OF HARIRI, THIRTEENTH CENTURY. (Bibl. Nat.)

Manuscripts are naturally divided into three groups; Arab, Persian and Turkish.

1. "The Arabs observed more strictly than Turks or Persians the law of Mahomet, and their manuscripts are seldom illuminated with miniatures." In any case none of the extant ones can be dated earlier than the 13th century. In the Bibliothèque Nationale is a copy of the Ma-Kamat (1237) which contains 101 miniatures, many of which are military scenes in the Byzantine manner. This museum has other examples, as does the British Museum. Something of the customs of the Arabs can be gathered from these. There is also a Makamat in the Imperial Library in Vienna (1334), and this shows a procession of riders, a school group, and some acrobatic feats.

JENGHIS KHAN RECEIVING HOMAGE FROM HIS TWO SONS, SIXTEENTH CENTURY. (Bibl. Nat.)

It was chiefly in the Koran that the beauty of ornament and design, in Egypt, attained its highest perfection. The 13th century Koran in the British Museum shows wonderful colour and geometric designs, though the most important ones are in the Khedive's Library in Cairo.

THE STORY OF THE PROPHETS: THE SEVEN SLEEPERS. (Bibl. Nat.)

2. For Islamic miniature painting see Persian Miniatures.

Indo-Persian art produced miniatures, some of which were masterpieces. These are not to be found in books, but on isolated pages, as though they were little pictures, representing scenes of private life, or jousts, or combats. There are also landscapes, which show a lovely sense of colour and poetry.

There are also portraits whose power of conveying character, whose drawing and observation, equal the best work of Western art from Giotto to Velázquez.

For Indian miniature painting see India—Art, Pls. 33, 34, Vol. I.

BIBLIOGRAPHY: E. Blochet, *Les Écoles de peinture en Perse.* (Revue Archéologique. July and August, 1905.)—Gaston Migeon, *Manuel d'art Musulman,* 1907.

**MOSQUE.**—See Moslem Art.

**MOSTAERT (Jan).**—Dutch painter, c. 1474-1555. For 18 years he was court painter to Margaret of Austria. His best known works are an *Altarpiece* (Amsterdam); *Portrait of a Man* (Brussels); the *Adoration of the Magi* (Amsterdam). Jan Mostaert was one of the first of his countrymen to be influenced by Italian Renaissance painting.

BIBLIOGRAPHY: Sander Pierron, *Les Mostaert. . . .* Brussels, 1912. —M. S. Friedländer, *Die altniederländische Malerei,* vol. X.

**MOTONOBU (Kano).**—Japanese painter, 1476-1559, son of Kano Masanobu whose style he developed so that it became established as the Kano School. He was influenced by Chinese paintings of the Yuan and early Ming periods and he introduced into the Chinese style the indigenous characteristics of Yamato-e.

**MOUNT ATHOS (Group of Monastic Churches of), or the Sacred Mountain.**—Begun, at the beginning of the 11th century, with the Churches of Lavra, Iviron, and Vatopedi, building was continued in the 13th century with Chilandari, in the 14th century with Pantocrator, in the 15th century with Saint Paul, in the 16th century with Xenophon, Caracallou, etc., etc. All these churches are built on the plan of a Greek cross: their dome is supported on four pendentives, and buttressed by four arches. The Catholicon of Lavra (1004) merits special attention. One of the peculiarities of the churches of Athos is the ending of the transept by two semicircular apses, in which the monks' seats were placed—an arrangement which, in the 14th and 15th centuries, spread throughout the west. Athos was an important centre of artistic activity. The Catholicon of Vatopedi contains mosaics dating from the 11th century. Many of the Churches of Athos have frescoes, all of which were restored in the 16th and 18th centuries. They dated from the 14th and 15th centuries. One name seems to be especially famous—Manuel Panselino, author of the *Guide to Painting,* which was discovered in 1839. It is unknown which part of the work should be attributed to him, also the exact period when he lived. The figures and scenes in all these churches have remarkable uniformity. The best preserved paintings are those in the Chapel of St. George, in the Convent of St. Paul.

Bibliography: G. Millet, *Monuments de l'Athos*. I. *Les peintures*. Paris, 1927.

**MOUSTERIAN EPOCH.**—See Prehistoric Archæology.

**MOYA (Pedro de).**—Spanish painter, 1610-1666. He studied under Van Dyck in London. Some months after the death of his master he returned to Spain. Even his best paintings show too much the influence of Van Dyck, Rubens and Murillo.

**MOZARAB.**—Congregation of Spanish Christians which existed under the Moors.

**MOZO (El).**—See Herrara.

**MSCHATTA.**—See Byzantine Architecture.

**MU CH'I.**—Chinese painter and Ch'an Buddhist priest of the 13th century. One of the founders of the expressionistic painting of the Ch'an sect.

See China—Art.

Toledo: Santa Maria La Blanca.

**MUDEJAR (Style).**—The word Mudejar is derived from Mudeddjan = "authorised to remain." After the reconquest of Spain, the Moorish subjects of the Christian kings continued during the centuries to work in their style, the forms of which they adapted to the buildings of the new kingdoms. The Spaniards gave this Moorish-Christian style the name of *Mudejar*.

Toledo is still full of examples of "Mudejar" art, which may be followed from the 12th to the 16th centuries, from the arches of the *Puerta del Sol* to the gilt stuccoes of the *Casa de Mesa*. Segovia also offers examples of this singular architecture.

Toledo: El Tránsito, modelled stucco.

Mudejar art in Spain was at its best in the 14th century. The infidels decorated religious buildings. Very remarkable is the large cloister of the Monastery of Guadalupe, with its Moorish arches and fountains decorated with ceramic.

Even after the expulsion of the Moors by Philip III, some Moslem influence remained with the Christian craftsman.

Bibliography: M. Dieulafoy. *Spain*. 1912.—P. Ricard, *Pour comprendre l'art Musulman*. Paris, 1924.

**MULTSCHER (Hans).**—Painter and sculptor, of the 15th century, founder of the Swabian School of Ulm. As a sculptor, he worked at the decoration of the cathedral. His main work as a painter is the Altarpiece in the Berlin Museum (1437), with scenes from the Life of the Virgin and the Passion. It is violent and dramatic, with bright, crude colours. The paintings of the Altarpiece in Sterzing, Tirol (1458), which occasionally are attributed to Multscher, probably were executed by a younger artist under strong Flemish influence; the sculptured parts of the same altar, however, are by Multscher himself.

Bibliography: K. Gerstenberg, *Hans Multscher*. Leipzig, 1928.—W. Pinder, *Die deutsche Plastik*, Handbuch der Kunstwissenschaft, 1924-28.—Reber, *Hans Multscher von Ulm*. Munich, 1898.—Stadlier, *Hans Multscher und seine Werrkstatt*. Strasbourg, 1907.

**MUNARI (Pellegrino).**—Italian painter of the school of Modena, 1460?-1523. Pupil of Francia. According to Vasari "the ornament of his century."

He is chiefly represented by gentle Madonnas on thrones with calm, pious saints and little angel musicians. (*Virgin* of the Church of San Pietro at Modena; *Virgin*, in Ferrara Gallery.)

**MUNCH (Edvard).**—Contemporary Norwegian painter. Descending from cultured parents he was born 12th December 1863 in Loeiten. His father was a physician and Jacob Munch (1776-1839), the painter, was one of his ancestors. As his mother died when he was still an infant, he was brought up by his sister who encouraged his early artistic endeavours and even posed for him. In 1882 he attended art school at Christiania, studying under Midelthun, Heyerdahl and Krogh. In 1885 he went to Paris and receiving a stipend he attended the life class of Léon Bonnat, to be followed by travel in Italy and Germany. He was a member of the internationally known group of Norsemen that included, among others, Ibsen, Hamsun and Sibelius. Gauguin was one of his best friends and claimed to discover a similarity between his work and that of Leonardo. Due to illness he returned home and settled in Kragerö in 1912. In 1915 he designed the murals for the University of Oslo and in 1926 another set for the chocolate factory in the same city. Munch's style underwent several changes. His early works in light blues and greys show him as a realist. Around the '90s he broke with the academicians and his art reflects the influence of French impressionism; however, his strong native flavour never left his art. Around 1907 another change appears; he paints in large masses with the broken colour of the Neo-Impressionists. His last works show a freedom in movement and relaxed contours, the sombre colour which dominated his works during his illness is replaced by light tonality. All his works reflect his philosophy of life; the beauty in nature as well as the inevitable northern atmosphere and the symbolism and mysticism of the literature of his country are prevalent. Besides his outstanding woodcuts he has done portraits of Sandberg, Max Linde, Strindberg, Ibsen and Meier-Graefe. His best-known symbolical pictures are *Puberty, Sick Girl, Jealousy, Death of Marat*. He is represented in the museums of Oslo, Berlin, Detroit, Moscow, Tokio, Munich and others.

Bibliography: Paul Gauguin, *Edvard Munch*, 1933.—Kurt Glaser, *Edvard Munch*, 1918.—Jens Thiis, *Edvard Munch and His Age*, 1934.

**MUNICH.**—Famous buildings include the 12th century church of

Munich: The Propylaea.

*St. Peter*, the *Frauenkirche*, and *St. Boniface*, a copy of an early Christian basilica. Many of the fine buildings are copies of celebrated struc-

Munich: The Alte Pinakothek.

tures of an earlier day. The museums, which make the city one of the richest storehouses in the world for art, include the *Glyptothek* (sculptures), the *Pinakothek* (paintings), the *New Art Gallery*, and the *Lenbach House*. The greatest science museum in the world, the *Deutsches Museum*, is also in Munich.

**MUNKÁCSY (Mihály, or Michael).**—Hungarian painter, 1844-1909. This internationally prominent artist descends from a Bavarian family called *Lieb*, who settled in Munkács in the early 17th century. He studied in Budapest, and with Rahl in Vienna. In 1866 he worked in Munich, followed by a short stay in Paris, 1867; in 1870 he studied with Knaus in Düsseldorf, and in 1872 he settled in Neuilly, near Paris. A frequent contributor to the Salons, his *Milton Dictating to his Daughters*, 1878 (N. Y. Publ. Libr. 42 Str.), won the gold medal and international acclaim. One of the leading naturalists, his style was conditioned by the doctrines of Courbet, but Munkácsy retained an unmistakably native temperament and interpretation throughout. His large and dramatic compositions are those of religious themes as *Christ before Pilate*, 1881; the genre scenes are drawn from the local life of Hungary. A heavy impasto applied with a dynamic and free brushwork, fiery colors mingled with brilliant whites, identify most of his works. Some consider his oil sketches of landscape and genre as his superior contribution. He is represented in the Louvre, Metropolitan Museum, as well as in many other institutions in Europe and the U.S.A.

Bibliography: Ilges, *Michael v. Munkácsy*, 1899.—Malonyay, *Michael v. Munkácsy*, 1907.—Sedelmeyer, *Michael v. Munkácsy*, 1914.

**MUNTHE (Ludvig).**—Norwegian painter, 1841-1896. He lived chiefly in Germany, but he was influenced by the French "open air" painters and had considerable influence on the landscape painting of his country.

**MURANO.**—See Quirizio da Murano.

**MURANO.**—Island in the Venetian lagoon about a mile north of Venice; especially famous in the fifteenth and sixteenth centuries. The fifteenth century school of painting (see Vivarini) played an important part in the development of the Venetian school.

**MURILLO (Bartolome Esteban).**—Spanish painter, baptized at Seville on January 1, 1618; died there on April 3, 1682. When an orphan ten years old, he was tenderly brought up by an uncle who entrusted his artistic education to Juan de Castillo. It has been recently argued that he did not make a trip to Madrid in 1642, as formerly believed, nor that he ever left Seville. At least he declared in 1645 that he was never absent from his native town where he can be traced

MURILLO: BOYS WITH GRAPES. (Munich.)

since 1641. In the collections of the aristocracy of Seville, he had the opportunity to study those masters

MURILLO: THE ANNUNCIATION. (Prado.)

who should make the greatest impression on him: Reubens, Van Dyck, Raphael, Correggio. Also engravings after important Italian and Dutch paintings must have been available to him. He was the first President of the Seville Academy of Painting,—founded in 1660, but renounced this office five years later. From his testament we know that he was prosperous. (A. L. Mayer).

His early works, "somewhat dry, but nevertheless superior to the output of contemporary Sevillian painters," give no hint as to his future evolution. (*Madonna,*—Seville, Palace of Archbishop; *Madonna of the Mercenarios,* Seville Museum, 1641; *Fray Lauterio before the Virgin and SS. Francis and Dominic,*—Cambridge, Fitzwilliams Museum, bef. 1642). The eleven scenes (1645-46) from the lives of SS. Francis, San Diego de Alcalá, Gil, formerly in the Churchyard of San Francisco of Seville and now distributed in the gallaries of Europe and America established his fame. The *San Diego Feeding the Poor* (Madrid, Academy) is justly considered the most prominent of the series. "The wholesome freshness of observation as noticed in the rendering of the natural and sensitive humor of the Saint accepting the thanks of the poor was never again shown by Murillo. Also influences derived from Ruelas, Ribera and Zurbaran are noticeable in these paintings. In 1665, in celebration of Pope Alexander VII's new Breve or ordinance in favour of the Immaculate Conception, he is said to have executed the six paintings for the Church of Sta. Maria la Blanca. "These pictures belong to the most beautiful accomplishments of the painter and have always been acknowledged as such." (The *Purisima with Worshipers* is in the Louvre,—*The Dream of the Roman Patrician* is in the Prado at Madrid,—etc.). In 1667 and 1668 he was mainly active for Seville Cathedral, (*Immaculate*

MURILLO: ST. ANTHONY OF PADUA AND THE INFANT JESUS. (Museum of Seville.)

*Conception, SS. Leander, Isidore, Ferdinand, Justa* and *Rufina,* etc., all for the Chapter Room).—The greater part of the paintings formerly adorning the High Altar and other altars of the Church of the Capuchin Convent are now in the Seville Museum. According to Mayer this series consisting originally of 22 pictures was begun toward the end of 1665, interrupted in and finished after 1668. In 1671, on occasion of the canonization of King Ferdinand III of Castile, he and Valdés Leal were engaged in the decorations ordered by the Cathedral for the celebrations of this event. (Etching by M. Arteaga of Murillo's decoration of the *Sagrario*). Between 1671-74, he painted eleven pictures for the Church of the Confraternity (*Hermandad*) *de la Caridad* to which he had been admitted as a member in 1645. (Some still in situ; lost is the *Tobias Burning the Corpses of the Condemned.* The rest are in Leningrad, Madrid, London, Stafford House, etc.). "The joy of activity during these years increased in astonishing measure, and Murillo's imagination produced again and again new creations." In 1678, he was executing commissions for the Church of the Augustine Convent and for the Hospital of the Confraternity of the *Venerables Sacerdotes.* While working in 1682 on a Painting for the High Altar of the Capuchin Church of Cadiz, representing the *Mystic Marriage of St. Catherine,* he fell from the scaffold,—an accident which was to hasten his death.

The appreciation of the œuvre of very few artists has been subject to such violent changes as that of Murillo. In increasing degrees his art was the object of admiration by his contemporaries and the generations, culminating in the 19th century. Today the very same pictures enjoy esteem only among small circles. More commonly they meet with indifference or have become subject to irony, if not frank contempt. Perhaps more so than with other artists, it seems desirable to examine this painter's merits in the light of objectivity. Criticism of

MURILLO: DICE PLAYERS. (Munich.)

such kind has been furnished, in his various writings by A. L. Mayer: "The great and certainly justified success which came early to Murillo made him somehow indolent, and there arises the question whether he could not have done better, given his rich artistic qualifications. Indisputably, his later activity shows an entirely clear evolution, and certainly he did progress. But he took his tasks somewhat easily and only rarely did he attack at their source the artistic problems which he approached. Indolence and the love to indulge are Andalusian traits, and in many instances Murillo is the artist in whom the Andalusian character is most clearly and brilliantly revealed.

"But, unfortunately, in representations of the Madonna and of children he is somehow monotonous and sweetish. Though he has brought down to earth for his Andalusian compatriots their beloved Saints, he did not succeed in carrying them into the celestial regions of a truly great art as was that of Ribera or Zurbaran. Yet it must be said that because of composition, conception, and pictorial excellence, the *Dream of the Roman Patrician* and the *Foundation of Santa Maria Maggiore* (from the cycle decorating formerly Sta. Maria la Blanca, Seville) belong to the best creations of Spanish art.

"Murillo is the most Sevillian among Sevillian painters. He is so in the very conception of his art, in his religious feeling, in his style and in the treatment of his works. It is quite in keeping that due to the cheerful character of that blessed country, things are rendered here less seriously and dramatically than for instance at Valencia. There. people and painters were somehow always imbued with the sinister cruelty of the Iberian native settlers. . . . There would then be the danger to become sentimental, and Murillo did not always escape this danger. This may explain that he would have succeeded less in rendering scenes of profound emotions and that it would have been difficult for him to do justice to tasks of a more monumental character. We, therefore, find only few authentic representations from the Passion of the Lord. Dear to him were themes such as the bliss of parenthood as seen in his *Holy Families* and *Madonnas*; his faith in God is revealed in his *Saints,* or the *Immaculate Conception.* In these *Imaculadas* becomes newly manifest the genuinely Andalusian character which found its finest expression of chivalry in the worship of the Virgin Mary" (for instance the three *Immaculate Conceptions*: Prado, Madrid 1665-1670; Prado, Madrid 1655-1665; Museum, Seville 1652-1665).

"He is fortunate when endowing his religious paintings with a genre-like character. (*The Holy Family with the Bird,* Prado, Madrid 1645-1650; *Holy Family with the Infant St. John,* Budapest 1660-1670; *St. Anne Teaching the Virgin,* Prado, Madrid 1655-1665; *The Virgin of Seville,* Louvre, Paris 1670).

Mendicant monks served as models, it seems, for the representations of Saints: (*San Francisco de Paula,* Prado, Madrid, 1665-1675; another version also at the Prado, 1670-1680; *San Felix de Cantalicio,* Museum, Seville 1672-1676).

"Murillo used the same popular types for his purely genre pictures depicting the ragged children of Seville whom one still finds there today. But their representations are not so satisfactory and refreshing as for instance those by Brower. We do not complain that he did not give us photographic views of life nor that he molded an incidental scene into an artful composition, but that he consciously beautified and, as one would like to say, dressed up these scenes for parlor use. (*Street Boys,* Munich 1670-1682; *The Poor Negro Boy,* Dulwich Gallery 1660-1670; *The Meal of the Old Woman,* Carstanjen Coll., Munich 1650-1660.)

"His portraits probably belong to the best among his artistic productivity. Although sometimes of uneven quality, one encounters portraits which for a long time passed as Velázquez and would by no means be unworthy to carry this great name. (*Madre Dorotea de Villalda,* Seville Cathedral, 1674; *Portrait of a Nobleman,* heirs of Sir William van Horne, Montreal; *Self-Portrait,* Lord Spencer, Althorp Park, c. 1675; *Don Andrés de Andrade y Col,* Metropolitan Museum, New York.)

"Among Murillo's pupils, his slave Sebastian Gomez, who because of his race was called *el Mulato,* takes the most prominent place. (*Concepcion,* Mus. Seville etc.)."

BIBLIOGRAPHY: Villaamil, Gregorio Cruzada. *Nuevas noticias de la vida y obras de Murillo* in El Arte en España. VI, p. 5, 1867.—C. Justi. *Murillo.* Leipzig, 1904.—A. L. Mayer. *Murillo.* Stuttgart, 1912.—Ibid. *Gesch. der span. Malerei,* 2nd ed. 1922.—Ibid. in Thieme-Becker, Vol. XXV, 1931; art. *Murillo, Bartolomé Esteban.*—Ibid. *Anotaciones al arte y á las obras de Murillo* in Rev. esp. de arte, 1936.—P. Lafond, *Murillo*—Les Grands Artistes. Paris, 1930.—*Enc. il. un. europ. am.* Barcelona (Espasa); Art, *Murillo.*

**MUSI (Agostino).**—See Veneziano.

**MYCENÆ.**—The town of Mycenæ played an important part in the history of archaic Greece. According to tradition it was founded by Perseus, the descendant of Danaos. The town was destroyed by

Argos in 468 B.C. Pausanias, who visited the town in the second century A.D. found only ruins. He wrote: "Part of the enclosing wall and the chief doorway, surmounted by lions, may still be seen. . . . In the midst of the ruins is a fountain, and subterranean chambers of Atreus and his sons—treasuries, where they deposited their riches." The excavations of Mycenæ were begun in 1876 by Schliemann and Stamatahis.

MYCENÆ. THE TREASURY OF ATREUS.

The acropolis of Mycenæ occupies an approximately triangular plain, and is larger than that of Troy, Tiryns, or even of Athens. The walls recall those of the neighbouring fortress of Tiryns, with their huge blocks of stone surmounted by smaller stones. Elsewhere the work is more finished. Cyclopean and polygonal work appears. The surrounding walls have two doors, the chief one being towards the West. This famous one is known as the *Lion Gate* dating about 1400 B.C. It is reached by going between two bastions; it is formed of four monoliths; a triangular slab of stone surmounts it, over the lintel. It has bas-reliefs (two lionesses face each other), but the sculpture has deteriorated. These symbolic lions—standing as the sign of force—the protecting spirits of the palace—play a part in the architecture, similar to that of the bulls on the doors of Assyrian palaces. The column between the two lions shows us what the wood columns of the primitive *megaron* must have been like.

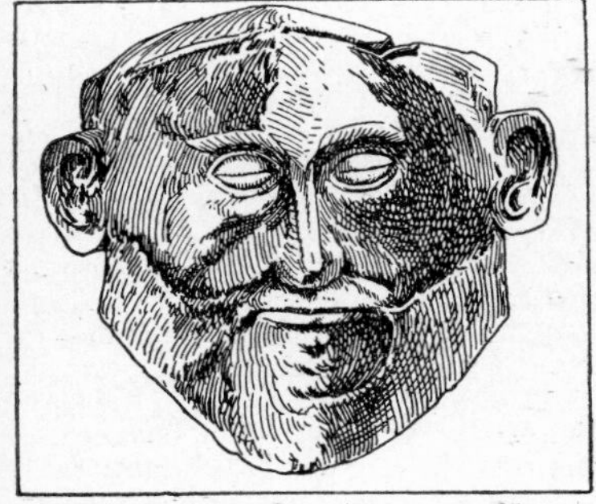

SOLID GOLD MASK. (Mycenæ, fifth grave.)

See Pl. 1, Vol. I.

Near the Lion Gate, inside the Acropolis, is a circular enclosure, where Schliemann, in 1876, discovered the tombs and their treasures (now in the Athens Museum).

According to Pausanias, in Mycenæ were buried Agamemnon, Cassandra, Electra, and Atreus. This ancient writer mentions six tombs, five of which were in all probability, those which Schliemann discovered.

These tombs are generally considered to be older than the Lion Gate, and to date from 1650-1450 B.C. Other tombs, outside the acropolis, are more recent, probably of the same period as the Lion Gate, and belong to the times of the Achæans and Pelopians. This civilization, which was a reflection of that of Crete, dating from c. 1650-1450 B.C., may be assigned to the Early Mycenæan period.

GOLD CROWN FOUND ON THE HEAD OF ONE OF THE THREE PERSONAGES BURIED IN THE THIRD GRAVE AT MYCENÆ.

The excavations also brought to light groups of dwellings; some apparently having been the modest habitations of men in service, or of soldiers; another building, however, being a veritable palace, with courtyard, vestibule, antichamber and megaron. The plan of this building is identical with that of Tiryns. A Doric temple of the 6th century was superimposed on the site of the palace. Several cisterns were discovered, one of which was a reservoir in the form of a well, so that the fortress did not lack water in the event of a siege.

FIRST FUNERAL STELE FOUND AT THE GRAVES OF THE ACROPOLIS, MYCENÆ.

Outside the citadel was the lower town which was also surrounded by a rampart. Several funeral monuments indicated its site. The most famous is the tomb known as the *Treasure of Atreus*, or the *Tomb of Agamemnon*, excavated in 1876. This tomb was hollowed out of the side of a hill. Tombs of this sort (some exist in Asia) consist of a corridor, or *dromos*, which leads to a rotunda covered by a cupola. The upper lintel was surmounted by a triangular slab, the fragments of which show it was of red porphyry. The rotunda had a door leading to the funeral chamber which was hollowed out of the rock. The chief member of the family was laid there, while the others were in the rotunda, which, built on the form of a hut, recalls primitive dwellings. This tomb, like all the neighbouring ones, dates from the end of the 15th to the end of the 14th century, B.C.

Not far from this tomb is a similar one, sometimes called the *Tomb of Clytemnestra.*

Among the things found in the Mycenæan tombs, the most interesting were the five gold masks which used to cover the heads of the dead, having been put over their faces at the time of burial. Only the men had masks; the women were simply adorned with jewels. The masks are too thick to have been moulded directly on the face. These masks are of very unequal workmanship. One of them is very archaic, and was doubtless done long before the others. They must have been done by a gold worker, before burial, and from nature, being, indeed, actual portraits, which fact gives them great interest, apart from some crudities of execution. Representation of the human figure is also found on the sides of a silver vase. The profiles, in relief, have, in spite of their archaic character, something modern about them.

SILVER BULL'S HEAD WITH GOLD HORNS. (Mycenæ, fourth grave.)

The excavations of Mycenæ, Tiryns, and Troy also brought to light numbers of fragments of ceramics, silver and gold vases, and plaques of ivory and jewels. Among them were the *Golden Goblets of Vaphio* in a bronze dagger with gold and silver incrustation, representing hunting scenes. This work is an example of that which Homer describes as being used on the shield of Achilles. There were also found a gold diadem; rings with stones showing representations of religious sacrifices, etc. Among the vases was a beautiful ewer, representing an octopus among sea plants; and also showing a building from which modern archæologists have gained their knowledge of the upper parts of the Mycenæan palaces.

LARGE ALABASTER VASE WITH THREE HANDLES. RESTORED WITH THE HELP OF FRAGMENTS (Mycenæ, fourth grave.)

The excavations also revealed a certain number of fragments of wall paintings, one of which represents preparations for a race or chariot procession. A fresco from Tiryns shows a bull hunt, and owing to his ignorance of perspective the artist has, according to the usual convention, placed the hunter above the bull. Another painting (less clear) shows women sacrificing at an altar. Their costume is similar to that of the little terra cotta figures, and to those found in Crete. It was the costume of women of the time of Cretan and Mycenæan civilisation —fifteen centuries before our era. The excavations of Schliemann, Dörpfeld, etc., prove that the old primitive Greek legends had a historical foundation. It is now supposed that the Homeric poems date from the 8th century B.C.—that is, after many centuries of civilisation. The cities mentioned in the Homeric poems as being the centres of civilisation are the very ones in which archæologists have found the most—in Troy, Mycenæ, Tiryns, Orchomenus (to whose treasures Achilles alludes); Amyelae (the dwelling place of Priam, Agamemnon, Menelaus). The questions raised by modern discoveries have not yet been answered. It is not known to what race to attribute this civilisation, nor from whence it came. At least, however, it is known that between the 20th and the 10th centuries B.C., a brilliant civilisation flourished in Greece and in the islands, the centre of which was doubtless Crete. Then the Dorian invasion destroyed this first civilisation, and Greece entered into a period of barbarism, only to begin later a new civilisation—that of classical Greece.

See Ceramic; Greece.

BIBLIOGRAPHY: G. Perrot, *Histoire de l'art*. Vol. VI. *La Grèce primitive*.—Schliemann, *Mycènes*. 1879.

VAPHIO CUP (detail). (Museum, Athens.)

**MYRINA.**—See Ceramic; Greece (Terra cottas).

**MYRON.**—Greek sculptor of the 5th century. Pausanias called him an Athenian, and pupil of Ageladas, a sculptor of Argos. Actually Myron was born in Bœotia. Pliny states that his period of greatest activity was in 420. It is now supposed, however, that he was born about 490; was working about 470 in the studio of Ageladas, and that the time of his maturity was about 450.

For Ægina he did a *Hecate*; for the Ephesians, an *Apollo*; for the Samians a group of the three figures of Zeus, Athena and Heracles. Pausanias describes a group on the Acropolis, representing *Athena Striking Silenus Marsyas*, who had offended her by picking up a double flute. This recalls the myth of Athena who, upon inventing the double flute, threw it away after discovering how it distorted her face. It was then picked up by Marsyas who incurred the disdain of Athena. This group served as a model for several ancient works of art, even perhaps for the *Marsyas* in the Lateran, whom a modern restorer has turned into a dancing faun by adding arms and castanets.

Ancient texts also refer to the statue of an athlete, the *Ladas*, who won a long-distance race at the Olympic games, but died from it. Myron also did many other groups of athletes.

A faithful copy of one of Myron's bronze statues is the famous *Discobolus* (bending to throw the disc), which was one of his best-known works.

In ancient times, Myron had the reputation of being an incomparable animal sculptor. Nothing now remains, however, of his bronze cow, which was then famous.

Myron was generally considered an innovator, especially in his treatment of new, rapid, spontaneous attitudes. He was certainly an artist who contributed greatly to the Greek sculptor's knowledge of the limitless resources of the human body.

See Pl. 20, Vol. I.

BIBLIOGRAPHY: Collignon, *Histoire de la sculpture grecque*. Vol. I. Paris, 1892.—Ernest Gardner, *Six Greek Sculptors*. London, 1923.

# N

**NANCY.**—Nancy is an eighteenth century town. From this period date a whole collection of buildings, and the planning of squares and colonnades, such as those which were made by the dukes of Lorraine, above all, Stanislas, with the help of such excellent artists as Boffrand, Héré, de Corny, Guibal, Cyfflé, Girardet, and Lamour. They preserved the old "cité," and built a large new town with regular streets which were united with the old cité by the Place Stanislas and the triumphal arch. This square is surrounded with buildings conceived in the same style: the town-hall, the old bishop's palace, the theatre (destroyed by fire in 1901), pavilions and fountains. At the four corners of the Place Stanislas are fine wrought-iron screens, ornamented with gold. Two of these angle screens frame two monumental fountains, with statues of Amphritrite and Neptune, accompanied by allegorical figures. These screens, which were executed by Lamour, are one of the wonders of the Place Stanislas. Their richness contrasts with the simple and noble lines of the façades by Héré.

NANCY: GATES OF THE PLACE STANISLAS, BY LAMOUR.

NANCY: PLACE STANISLAS.

The Église des Cordeliers, begun about 1482, by the Duc René, in gratitude for the deliverance of Nancy, is composed of a single nave. Its rich interior decoration is lost.

See Pl. 11, Vol. I; Pl. 43, Vol. II.

BIBLIOGRAPHY: W. H. Ward, *Architecture of the Renaissance in France*. N. Y., 1926.

**NANKING (Tower of).**—Famous Chinese pagoda (see China: Architecture) entirely covered with porcelain. Built in the 4th century by the T'sin; then destroyed, and rebuilt in the 15th century, it was completely destroyed in 1853, during a revolt.

**NANNI d'ANTONIO di BANCO.**—Florentine sculptor, born c. 1373; died by 1421, a pupil of Niccolò d'Arezzo, influenced by Donatello.

In 1405 Nanni di Banco matriculated in the stone-masons' guild; in 1407-09, with his father and his teacher, he executed wreaths and a frieze with angels for the north side-portal of the Duomo; in 1408 with Niccolò d'Arezzo, Donatello and Ciuffagni he was commissioned to execute the Evangelist statues for the façade of the Duomo (now in side chapel). Of this commission, Nanni's statue was of St. Luke. Also of this date are his early statues for Or San Michele, St. Philip and four Saints in a niche. In 1515 he made the S. Eligio for Or San Michele. Nanni's last work is the Madonna in a mandorla with Angels, giving her girdle to St. Thomas, over the north entrance of the Duomo.

BIBLIOGRAPHY: Vasari-Milanesi, II. —M. Reymond, Gazette des Beaux Arts, 1895, I.

**NANNI (Giovanni di).**—See Giovanni da Udine.

**NANTES (France).**—The *Cathedral* was begun in 1437, by the architect Mathelin Rodier. The choir was not finished until the 19th century. The south transept contains the celebrated Tomb of Francis II of Brittany and of his wife, Marguerite de Foix, which was made by Michel Colombe. The effigies of the duke and his wife are dying on a wide, black marble slab; at their feet, a lion and a dog. Four statues at the angles represent Prudence, Temperance, Justice and Courage. In the sixteen upper niches are statuettes representing the apostles; and in the sixteen lower niches are weepers, in green marble.

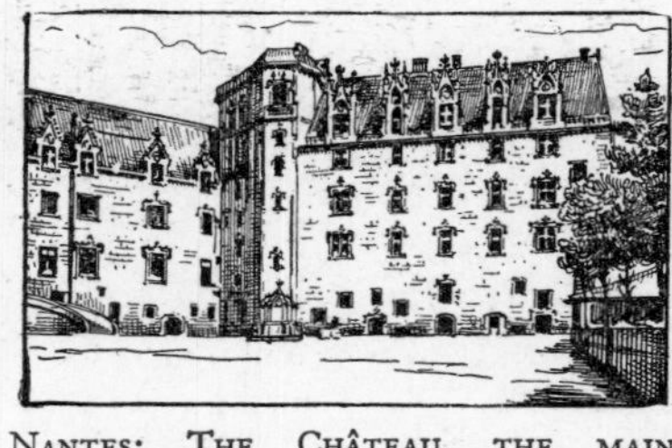

NANTES: THE CHÂTEAU, THE MAIN BUILDING AND THE DUCAL PALACE.

The *Château*, begun in 1466, was finished in the 16th century. It is composed of a main block, with a tower, and of a smaller building, dating from the time of Louis XII. The tower dates from the 12th or 13th century.

**NANTEUIL (Robert).**—French draughtsman and engraver, 1623-1678. He was destined for the bar; but he soon showed a taste for drawing. At the age of nineteen, he engraved the frontispiece of his treatise in philosophy.

In Paris, he executed some portraits in the Sorbonne world; and he was soon commissioned to reproduce on copper the drawings which had been commissioned from him by members of Parliament and courtiers. Finally, the king, whose portrait he had engraved about eleven times, gave him several audiences, as the result of which Nanteuil received the title of draughtsman to the Cabinet.

Most of Nanteuil's drawings were executed with three crayons. Their colour is quiet and refined. He probably drew a great number of portraits which were not engraved afterwards; but he probably engraved very little that he had not drawn.

NANTEUIL: PORTRAIT OF TURENNE.

At the Gobelins, Nanteuil formed a large following of portrait-engravers, but no one surpassed him in this special art. In his portraits, individual characteristics are so clearly defined, and the features are rendered so justly that one cannot doubt their truth to life. Lacking in artifice, Nanteuil's portraits appear almost devoid of art. But on considering them attentively, one discovers a very rare ability—that which hides itself under an appearance of simplicity.

His portraits of Turenne, of Van Steenberghen, and of Loret are among his best. They exemplify his refinement of drawing, and of ex-

# FRA ANGELICO

*P*AINTING *was born and developed in order to place before us Christian thought. Then, in the fifteenth century at Florence, it lost a little of the recollection of its religious origin in order to devote itself thoroughly to reproducing the aspects of nature. There is, however, a painter who was at the same time naturalistic and mystical; he is Fra Angelico. His painting is devoted to religious subjects and the colours and forms are always adapted to the expression of the sentiment. The figures and the landscapes of this master are as true as the most naturalistic pictures of his day and yet they resemble celestial visions. Legend states that angels painted his panels while he slept; this is the best explanation of his work. It is, moreover, probable that the legend was inspired by his luminous frescoes.*

FRA ANGELICO: THE CORONATION OF THE VIRGIN. LOUVRE.
*(Photo by Hachette.)*

FRA ANGELICO: THE ANNUNCIATION. FLORENCE.
*(Photo by Anderson.)*

FRA ANGELICO: DEPOSITION. FLORENCE.
*(Photo by Anderson.)*

FRA ANGELICO: ST. STEPHEN PREACHING. ROME.
*(Photo by Anderson.)*

FRA ANGELICO: CALVARY. ROOM IN THE CHAPTER HOUSE OF SAN MARCO, FLORENCE.
*(Photo by Brogi.)*

FRA ANGELICO: ST. STEPHEN GIVING ALMS. ROME.
*(Photo by Anderson.)*

## Fra Angelico

THE figures of Fra Angelico are celestial because his drawing, characterised by very simple but very flexible lines, retains only those forms which are essential to endow them with moral life. His colour is pure and of such a brilliancy that shadows scarcely darken it; the pictures are luminous and radiant as the figures of illuminated manuscripts or of stained glass. But this painter above all puts into his work a sentiment so ardent, a faith and a tenderness so passionate, that one forgets the painting; the pleasure of the eye is dominated by a higher emotion.

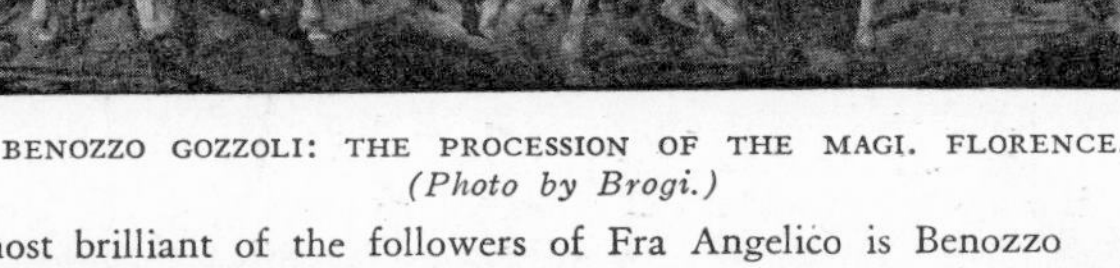

BENOZZO GOZZOLI: THE PROCESSION OF THE MAGI. FLORENCE.
*(Photo by Brogi.)*

BENOZZO GOZZOLI: THE VINTAGE OF NOAH. PISA.
*(Photo by Alinari.)*

## Benozzo Gozzoli

THE most brilliant of the followers of Fra Angelico is Benozzo Gozzoli; he has preserved the clear colours of his master and his ingenuous drawing, but he has not remained the painter of purely religious sentiment. He is diverted by reality. As with all painters who seek the picturesque element more than emotional value, Benozzo Gozzoli has given us a record of his own times.

# GHIRLANDAJO AND BOTTICELLI

*During the second half of the fifteenth century Florentine painters have as examples the works of the sculptors and in imitating them have often made their style flexible; never does the art of painting show more vigour, more expression.*

DEATH OF SANTA FINA. SAN GIMIGNANO.
*(Photo by Alinari.)*

ADORATION OF THE MAGI. SANTA TRINITÀ.
*(Photo by Brogi.)*

THE VISITATION. SANTA MARIA NOVELLA, FLORENCE.
*(Photo by Anderson.)*

## Domenico Ghirlandajo

This prolific painter is one of the most representative masters of Florentine genius. He was a fine portraitist and he has peopled his compositions with figures which are the living images of his friends and patrons. Even the landscapes recall Florence, town and country.

MADONNA OF THE MAGNIFICAT. UFFIZI, FLORENCE.
*(Photo by Brogi.)*

ADORATION OF THE MAGI. UFFIZI, FLORENCE.
*(Photo by Brogi.)*

MADONNA ENTHRONED. ACADEMY, FLORENCE.
*(Photo by Anderson.)*

THE VIRGIN WITH THE POMEGRANATE. UFFIZI, FLORENCE.
*(Photo by Anderson.)*

THE BIRTH OF VENUS. UFFIZI, FLORENCE.
*(Photo by Giraudon.)*

PALLAS. PITTI PALACE.
*(Photo by Anderson.)*

SPRING. ACADEMY, FLORENCE.
*(Photo by Anderson.)*

## Sandro Botticelli

Botticelli's work shows, in the highest degree, the characteristics of Florentine painting in the second half of the fifteenth century. The refined elegance of line, the acuteness of drawing a little overstressed, the sickly character of the faces and the gestures, the meticulous analysis of the varieties of form, the linear expression dominating the covering of light and shade—these are the traits of all Florentine art whether it be primitive or pre-Raphaelite. In Botticelli's work, mythology begins to appear; he gives the same mournful restlessness to a Venus that he gives to a Madonna.

VERROCCHIO: BAPTISM OF CHRIST. UFFIZI, FLORENCE.
*(Photo by Anderson.)*

A. BALDOVINETTI: MADONNA AND CHILD. LOUVRE.
*(Photo by Hachette.)*

FILIPPINO LIPPI: THE LIBERATION OF ST. PETER. CARMINE.
*(Photo by Anderson.)*

A. POLLAIUOLO: MARTYRDOM OF ST. SEBASTIAN. NAT. GALLERY, LONDON.
*(Photo by Anderson.)*

FILIPPINO LIPPI: APPARITION OF THE VIRGIN TO ST. BERNARD BADIA, FLORENCE.
*(Photo by Anderson.)*

## Florentine Primitives

In the second half of the Florentine fifteenth century, the painters are numerous and they are rarely commonplace. Baldovinetti, the Pollaiuoli, and Verrocchio are inquiring technicians whose works are sometimes harsh and laborious but always individual. Because of their dry and sharp style these primitives experienced a renewal of success when contemporary taste grew tired of classic perfection. Filippino Lippi is between the two manners.

# UMBRIAN PAINTING

*The painters of Umbria constitute a well-defined group although their school was not inclosed within the precincts of a city as was the Florentine school. The two principal centres were Urbino and Perugia. The Umbrians are distinguished by their landscapes. Almost always, the picturesque quality of the atmosphere compels us to believe that their art was nurtured in the open air, and not between the walls of the studio.*

GENTILE DA FABRIANO: THE ADORATION OF THE MAGI. UFFIZI, FLORENCE.
*(Photo by Brogi.)*

MELOZZO DA FORLI: THE ASCENSION. QUIRINAL, ROME.
*(Photo by Alinari.)*

PIERO DELLA FRANCESCA: THE QUEEN OF SHEBA. AREZZO.
*(Photo by Alinari.)*

Gentile da Fabriano is an Umbrian master who worked at Venice and in his delicate art one finds again the gracefulness of southern illuminators of manuscripts. Melozzo da Forli is known to us only by some fragments of his work; they are admirable for their grandeur and the boldness of the drawing and the brilliance of the colour. The frescoes of Piero della Francesca in Arezzo are one of the most grandiose monuments in fifteenth century Italian art.

LUCA SIGNORELLI: THE RESURRECTION. ORVIETO.
*(Photo by Anderson.)*

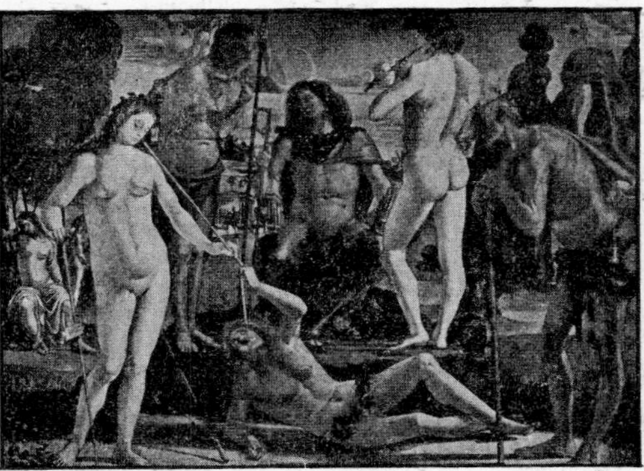

LUCA SIGNORELLI: PAN AND NYMPHS. BERLIN.
*(Photo by Hanfstaengl.)*

LUCA SIGNORELLI: PREACHING OF THE ANTI-CHRIST. ORVIETO.
*(Photo by Anderson.)*

## Luca Signorelli

Luca Signorelli, before the time of Michelangelo, is the painter who was most obsessed with muscular beauty and athletic elegance. In his decoration of the church at Orvieto he found an opportunity to disclose the resources of this human plastic art which, for the time being, was much less an imitation of antique sculpture than a copy of the living model. Michelangelo was aware of these frescoes in which one already sees the damned struggling against acrobatic devils but Signorelli did not yet know of the violent foreshortenings of the Florentine.

PERUGINO: TOBIAS AND THE ARCHANGEL RAPHAEL. LONDON.
*(Photo by Hachette.)*

PERUGINO: JESUS DELIVERING THE KEYS TO ST. PETER. SISTINE CHAPEL, ROME.
*(Photo by Anderson.)*

PINTURICCHIO: AENEAS SYLVIUS AND ELEANOR OF PORTUGAL. SIENA.
*(Photo by Alinari.)*

## Perugino

Perugino during his life experienced a great popularity. This Umbrian studied in the Florentine workshop of Verrocchio where he knew the young Leonardo da Vinci. It was there that he learned to use those lovely shadows which soften the austerity of his archaic drawing. His colour also is sweet and winning; his gracious attitudes, and his ecstatic visages appear to be the most sincere expression of religious tenderness. It is by virtue of his luminous landscapes that he appears to us to be a fine painter. Pinturicchio is a charming, facile decorator.

# PAINTING IN VENICE IN THE FIFTEENTH CENTURY

*The school of Venetian painting in the fifteenth century combines elements of different origins. To begin with, there is the inheritance of Byzantine art. Furthermore, the Venetians early learned the technique of oil painting and its evolution among them was determined by conditions entirely different from those which determined the Florentine style; in the latter, it was the* fresco *which imposed a grand manner with a predominance of form over the colour. At Venice colour dominated the compositions.*

BARTOLOMMEO VIVARINI: MADONNA AND SAINTS. VENICE. *(Photo by Alinari.)*

CRIVELLI: MADONNA AND CHILD. MILAN. *(Photo by Anderson.)*

ANTONELLO DA MESSINA: JESUS BOUND TO THE COLUMN. VENICE. *(Photo by Alinari.)*

ANTONELLO DA MESSINA: THE CONDOTTIERE. LOUVRE. *(Photo by Hachette.)*

## From the Icon to the Portrait

In the Venetian school of the fifteenth century, the masters of Murano (the Vivarini and Crivelli) represent the Byzantine heritage: hieratic attitudes, bright colour, the use of gold; a brilliant *icon* rather than a living portrait. When naturalism begins to animate these pictures it appears in rare and dazzling tones. Antonello da Messina left some intensely alive figures.

CARPACCIO: AMBASSADORS OF THE MARRIAGE OF ST. URSULA. VENICE. *(Photo by Hachette.)*

CARPACCIO: ST. URSULA TAKING LEAVE OF HER PARENTS. VENICE. *(Photo by Anderson.)*

CARPACCIO: THE FUNERAL OF ST. URSULA. VENICE. *(Photo by Anderson.)*

## Carpaccio

Among the Venetians at the end of the fifteenth century, Carpaccio is one of those who charms us most; in his work there is everything to entertain the eye: the great number of figures, the abundance of episodes, the luxury of the costumes, the richness of the architecture, the picturesque quality of the landscape. In the work of this primitive one notices in advance everything which will magnificently be unfolded by the great decorators of the following century. The most brilliant ensemble of this painter is preserved in the Academy at Venice in his *Life of St. Ursula.*

CATENA: ST. CHRISTINA. VENICE. *(Photo by Alinari.)*

BARTOLOMMEO MONTAGNA: PIETÀ. MONTE BERICO, NEAR VICENZA. *(Photo by Alinari.)*

BASAITI: THE SONS OF ZEBEDEE. VENICE. *(Photo by Alinari.)*

CIMA DA CONEGLIANO: MADONNA AND SAINTS. LOUVRE. *(Photo by Hachette.)*

## Venetians Outside of Venice

We have been accustomed to give first place to Venice among the schools of northern Italy, but many of the towns had local schools. The physiognomy of each remains characteristic. At the same time, there are common traits. The influence of Mantegna, the great Paduan master, is apparent in the construction of the figures. The importance of landscape is common to all. Sky and horizon lend new life to religious themes and Byzantine figures awake from their lethargy.

pression, and his admirable dexterity.

Bibliography: Charles Loriquet, *Robert Nanteuil, sa vie et ses œuvres.* Paris, 1885.

**NAPLES (Italy).**—Naples is perhaps interesting chiefly on account of its wonderful collection of objects found at Pompeii and at Herculaneum.

Of its Greek and Roman buildings, Naples retains the ruins of a large theatre. The town was several times taken by barbarians, and sacked, and no buildings have come down to us previous to the 13th century. The *Castel Nuovo* was built for King Charles I of Anjou, from 1279 to 1283. It is preceded by the *Arch of Alfonso the Magnanimous* (1451-1470). The *Castel Capuano* was built about 1231 by the architect Fuccio.

Naples: Castel Nuovo.

Religious edifices of the 13th century are: *Santa Maria la Nuova,* built by Giovanni da Pisa; *San Domenico Maggiore,* a large building, built in 1289; the *Cathedral,* built from 1272 to 1323, in the Gothic style, destroyed in 1456, and rebuilt partly in the same style. The Cathedral communicates with *Santa Restituta,* a Gothic building which was the original Cathedral. *San Lorenzo,* built in 1284, was transformed in the 16th century.

Naples possesses very many other churches—nearly three hundred—but the beauty of the town is due to its marvellous site.

**NARDI (Angelo).**—Florentine painter, 1601 to 1660, who spent his life in Spain. In 1625, he became painter to Philip IV. He worked for the Archbishop of Toledo, for several convents, painting religious pictures in oil and fresco. (*Adoration of the Shepherds, Circumcision, Crucifixion.*)

**NARDO di CIONE.**—Florentine painter and sculptor, brother of Andrea Orcagna. Nardo's style, with his brother's, evolves out of the Giottesque tradition, but is more intimately related to that of Siena.

In 1345 he matriculated in the guild of painters, as Nardus Cionis; and in 1355 is accepted in the corporation of wood and stone sculptors, where he is mentioned as Lionardus Cionis. In 1363 Nardo is charged by the captains of the Company of Sta. Maria del Bigallo to execute decorations on the ceiling of the Oratorium. In the next year his name appears as Nardo Cioni on the rolls of the S. Luca guild. In 1365, Nardo, very ill, makes his will, naming his brothers, Andrea, Jacopo, and Matteo as his heirs. His brothers receive their heritage in 1366.

Ghiberti's statement that the frescoes in the Strozzi Chapel of Sta. Maria Novella are by Nardo is the basis for the reconstruction of his artistic personality. His works as gathered together by Richard Offner are: Florence, Sta. Maria Novella, Cloisters, four scenes from the *Life of the Virgin,* two *Saints* (very largely assisted); Florence, Badia, Cappella Giochi e Bastari, frescoes, *Scenes of the Passion* (assisted); Ponte a Mensola (Florence), Berenson Collection, *Scene from the Life of St. Benedict* (fragment of predella); New York Historical Society, large *Virgin and Saints;* London, Victoria and Albert Museum, *Coronation of the Virgin;* Fiesole, Museo Bandini, *Crucifixion;* Munich, Alte Pinakotek, two panels, five *Saints* each; New Haven, Jarves Collection, *SS. John Baptist and Peter;* London, National Gallery, *SS. John Evangelist, John Baptist, and James;* Minneapolis, Herschel V. Jones Collection, *Standing Madonna;* New York, Goldman Collection, small triptych, *Virgin and Saints;* Frankfurt-a.-M., Rudolph Bauer Collection, *Crucifixion.*

Bibliography: For general literature, see Orcagna.—Also: Richard Offner, *Studies in Florentine Painting,* 1927, p. 97ff.

**NARTHEX.**—The narthex is a gallery or porch at the entrance to a church. It must not be confused with the porch open to the outside (as in many Gothic churches). This arrangement dates from Early Christian times, when the catechumens were not allowed to enter the church with the faithful, and so a sheltered place had to be reserved for them. Narthices were very numerous until the 13th century, and then gradually disappeared.

**NASH (John).**—English architect, 1752-1835. An exponent of the classic style, Nash designed a city plan for London, a plan represented now by Regent Street, 1813-1821; the Marble Arch, London, 1825; and Buckingham, London, begun 1825.

**— (Paul).**—Contemporary English painter. He was born in London in May, 1889, and is the brother of John Nash, who is also a painter. At first he studied architecture and then turned his thoughts to the practice of painting. He studied painting in 1908 at the Chelsea Polytechnic and later worked in the London County Council School of Art in Fleet Street. His art education was completed at the Slade School of Art, where he was a fellow pupil of Wadsworth, Nevinson and Stanley Spencer. His early painting showed a definite influence of the work of William Blake and Dante Rossetti in its visionary character and romantic interpretation of the scene with poetic allusions. During the war he became one of the official artists on the western front and his painting of the *Menin Road* is in the Imperial War Museum. His landscapes of that period were still romantic with rich colourful patterns of the scenery as they appeared after the destruction of war, portrayed not in a realistic manner but rather as symphonies of colour and graceful shapes of the trees and countryside. In 1920 Nash was designing stage sets, textiles, and trying his hand at lithography and wood engravings. He made the sets for Barrie's *Truth about the Russian Dancers,* which was produced in that year, and has illustrated many books, including John Drinkwater's *Cotswold Characters,* Ford Madox Ford's *Mister Bosphorus and the Muses* and *Welchman's Hose.* Since that time his compositions have showed more restraint and the elimination of details with a greater use of rectilinear lines than heretofore. His trees have a very individual character and suggest a mood for the scene more than the attempt to show any particular species. The structure of his pictures is carefully considered and any figures that have been introduced are mere accessories and not of primary interest to the artist. From 1924 to 1925 Nash was a professor of design in the Royal College of Art and examples of his art may be seen in the British Museum, the Tate Gallery, the Art Gallery in Manchester and the Musée de la Guerre in Paris.

See Pl. 65, Vol. II.

Bibliography: Anthony Bertram, *Paul Nash,* Contemporary British Artists, 1923.—Anthony Bertram, *Paul Nash,* 1927.

**NASMYTH (Patrick).**—Scottish painter (1787-1831), son and pupil of the landscape painter Alexander Nasmyth. One of the best of the minor British landscape masters of the early 19th century.

**NATIONAL GALLERY.**—See London.

**NATOIRE (Charles Joseph).**—French painter, 1700 to 1777. Born at Nîmes. He inherited from his master, François Lemoine, a facile manner, which he weakened still more by lighter and softer colour. He excelled at decorating apartments with figures of women and children.

Bibliography: Charles Blanc, *Histoire des peintres, École française.* Vol. II.

**NATTIER (Jean Marc).**—French painter, 1685-1766. After the death of Raoux, Nattier replaced him in the labour of the fashionable world. The Louvre and the Château of Chantilly possess two pictures dating from the beginning of his vogue. These are *Mademoiselle de Lambesc as Bellona, with Her brother,* and *Mademoiselle de Clermont as the Goddess of the Waters of Health* (both painted in 1729). It was the period when women wanted their portraits painted in the guise of Flora, Iris, Aurora, or of other mythological goddesses, or nymphs, etc. Thus, Nattier painted *Madame Henriette as: Flora, Reclining beside a Brook* (Versailles), *Madame Adéloïde as Diana,* and *Madame de Chateauroux as Dawn* (Marseille).

Nattier: Mme. Henriette as Flora. (Museum of Versailles.)

He painted many portraits of the royal family, and portraits of Madame de Pompadour. Portraits of the Princess de Rohan (Rothschild Collection), and of Madame Adélaïde Tatting (Versailles) are characteristic examples of his art.

Nattier: The Princess de Rohan. (Rothschild Collection.)

Nattier's portraits are graceful and tactful, rather than closely observed. They characterise rather the collective type of a period than an individual. He favoured light colours (especially a certain shade of bright blue), pink-cheeked faces under powdered hair, and soft rounded lines.

See Pl. 46, Vol. II.

Bibliography: P. De Nolhac, *Nattier.* 1905.—Dimier, *Les peintres français du XVIIIe siècle.* Vol. II.

**NAVE.**—From the Latin *navis* (ship), meaning the vessel or body of the church—the part between the choir, or crossing of the transept, and the entrance. It may be single or divided into several parallel aisles separated by rows of columns or pillars. In this case the middle aisle is known as the *nave*, and the lateral divisions as the *side aisles* or simply *aisles*.

**NAXOS.**—See Paros.

**— (School of).**—See Greece (Sculpture).

**NAZARENES (The).**—At the end of the 18th century in Germany, when religion seemed to be the preoccupation of all the finest spirits, there appeared a work in which were found summaries of all the religious and artistic aspirations of the new generation. In all the book-shops was to be found a little book, without the author's name, bearing the title "Effusions of a Convert to the Arts," with a frontispiece decorated with a head in the manner of Raphael; the face is enthusiastic, with prominent eyes and thick lips. It was the portrait of the author, Wrackenroder.

When scarcely twenty, Wrackenroder, in company with his great friend Treik, proceeding to the University of Erlangen and passing by Nuremberg, became fired with enthusiasm for the buildings of old Germany. The two friends could hardly leave the churches: a whole religious world was re-created for them in Dürer's city. They then went to Dresden, and visited the picture galleries; through the influence of art, they gave themselves to the worship of the Madonna. To Wrackenroder, the old masters appeared, above all, as servants of the faith; art was an object of devotion: picture galleries were temples; and his admiration expressed itself through prayer. In a word, he confused the adoration of God with a passion for works of art. His enthusiasm was, however, limited. Thus, in his eyes, the 16th century was a pagan age and therefore inartistic. Wrackenroder's doctrine was presented with such simplicity, warmth and sincerity, that very soon the whole of Germany was captivated by it. He founded a review, the "Atheneum" (1800), directed by the brothers Schlegel who were recent converts to Catholicism, to draw attention to the German "primitives," that is, to the old religious masters. Christianity was substituted for antiquity as the source of inspiration. Frederick Schlegel was the mouthpiece of the new school. The articles which he published in his paper, "Europe," contain all the doctrines of this little group of artists, which was known as the "Nazarenes." German painting was henceforth to be like the Primitives—faithful, innocent, sensitive and reflective, and striving for no technical ability. The programme was followed to the letter. The leader of this little group of artists, Friedrich Overbeck, and his friends, went to Italy, where they studied, not the classics, but works of purely Christian inspiration. They were all converted to Catholicism, and lived on the Pincio, in Rome, a life of work and meditation, persuaded that the artist must live a pure and noble existence, in accordance with his artistic ideal. Their mornings were reserved for household tasks, which they performed themselves; reserving the afternoons for art.

The ardour which the Nazarenes showed for putting religion at the base of all artistic activity, their way of only understanding art as an expression of faith, must have irritated Goethe considerably. According to him, religion no longer sufficed for art, which was developed by taste, and he remarked ironically that "if some monks were artists, it does not follow that all artists must become monks." He called the life of the Nazarenes "a kind of masquerade opposed to modern life." In "Art and Antiquity" he wrote his famous article: "The New German Patriotico-Religious Art," or "The History of the New and False Religious Art Since the 18th Century," which must have wounded the feelings of the young fraternity. It does not appear to us just on Goethe's part to have reproached his contemporaries for seeking their inspiration in the Middle Ages, while he praised unreservedly the followers of Winckelmann, and their insipid productions.

Indeed, the Nazarenes, like Goethe himself when he applied himself to classic art, created but stale compositions. Nevertheless, the Nazarenes are to be thanked for having reacted against the doctrine of Carteno, for whom colour was something negligible, and, in fact, they were the first painters worthy of the name after the period of this artist.

The Nazarene school was, like the classical school, never more than an imitation. It gave birth to no new, vital form. They gave up the living model, on principle. Cornelius alone ventured to copy feminine forms. Overbeck refused to represent the Virgin Mary, whom he thought should not be represented as an earthly being. Occasionally the Nazarenes posed for one another, for a study of drapery or costume. Their compositions were painted from imagination in the solitude of their cells. There is a nobility in the pose and line of their figures, but they are wanting in life. Their two principal works are the frescoes of the Casa Bartholdi and of the Villa Massini. These six large mural paintings represent the History of Joseph in Egypt. Cornelius, Overbeck, Veit and Schadow collaborated in them. They are now in the National Gallery of Berlin. The frescoes of the Villa Messini represent scenes taken from the work of Dante and Tasso. The Nazarenes were engaged on these works for several years, in the midst of innumerable difficulties. Despite their imperfections, they reveal such sincerity of feeling, and nobility of conception that the like can only be found among the greatest artists. A group of young men, caring only for religion and art, with no ambition for fame, fortune or success could not but produce works which, if they cannot always force admiration, command constant respect.

Bibliography: W. Neuse, *Das Wesen der Nazarenerkunst und ihre Bedeutung für die deutsche Kunst des 19 Jahr-hunderts*. Bonn. Gesellschaft Kunstwissenschaftliches Jahrbuch. I, 62, 1928.

**NEAGLE (John).**—American painter (1796-1865) of Philadelphia, a much employed portrait painter whose best known work is his full length of Patrick Lyon, the blacksmith (Pennsylvania Academy of the Fine Arts).

**NEEFFS (Peeter).**—Flemish painter of Antwerp, about 1578-1656. He painted the interiors of churches, especially Notre Dame of Antwerp, which he reproduced admirably. His son, Peter the Younger, assisted him so well that it is often difficult to distinguish the works of father and son. He is represented in all important museums.

**NEER (Aart, or Aert v. d.).**—Dutch landscape painter of Amsterdam; about 1603-1677. Probably a pupil of Camphuysen, influenced by Buytewegh. Painted river and canal scenes, and winter landscapes with many small figures skating or playing golf. His compositions were quite original in concept and clever in treatment of light effects. His moonlit marines, and sunsets over canals are his best works. Only the paintings of his later period are dated, among these are *Landscape*, 1639 (Amsterdam), *Moon-marine-scape*, 1643 (Brussels). Van der Neer has often been faked.

**— (Eglon Hendrik).**—Probably 1634 to 1703. Son of Aart, pupil of Jacob van Loo. He travelled a great deal in France and Holland and finally settled in Düsseldorf, where he died. His activities may be divided into two periods: 1. The heroic landscapes, influenced by Elsheimer; 2. genre scenes, influenced by Terborgh and Metsu. Many of his works have been confused with those of Netscher. One of the leading mannerists, he studied nature carefully and shows interest in group composition, although the results often tend towards stiffness. He was court painter in Düsseldorf.

Bibliography: C. Hofstede de Groot, *A Catalogue Raisonné of the Works of the Most Eminent Dutch Painters of the Seventeenth Century*. Vol. VII. London, 1923.

**NEGRO ART—AFRICA.**—The chief forms of recent West African art are masks, used at the initiation rites of secret societies, at agricultural ceremonies, and at other religious ceremonies; and statuettes which serve as dwelling places for the souls of the dead, as temporary houses for local natural divinities, or as special "fetishes" which come into existence upon the carving of the figure. The chief present day material is wood, but brass, gold, and iron are occasionally employed.

The most important artistic tradition in West Africa was that of Ife-Benin (British Nigeria; city of Benin razed in 1897), whose main medium was bronze produced by the lost-wax process and close to European standards in its composition, but considerable carving was also done in ivory. If we except the solid clay heads found at Ife, which are of the first millennium, Benin art seems to go back to the thirteenth century, its golden age falling ca. 1575-1650, and the style petering out in the eighteenth and nineteenth centuries. Some 2500 Benin objects are known, mostly bronze portrait heads and carved ivory tusks used on altars in connection with blood sacrifices, and bronze plaques which decorated the courtyard of the kings' palace. At its best Benin art achieves a great naturalism within the confines of a strong tradition. In the later productions of Benin wood is substituted for metal, and the facial formula and decorative motives are carried on in the nineteenth century work in wood of Dahomey (last king 1911), which uses bright earth colors for decoration.

The Benin influences may be seen in the small brass weights of the Ashanti of the Gold Coast, and of certain Ivory Coast tribes, as well as in the metal castings of the Cameroon grasslands. The art of this latter region, reflecting its culture, is the least dominated by religion of any in Africa, concentrating on house decoration and the adornment of utilitarian objects. There is regional specialisation dependent on greater trading than is usual, although here as elsewhere the artists are not exclusive professionals.

The sculpture of the Ivory Coast tribes is the best known in Europe. That of the Baulé consists of statues for the dead, intended as accurate portraits since the spirit must be able to find its home, and apparently recognizable as such by the natives though to modern eyes they have the typical quality common to all African art. The skill and care with which the tribal marks are rendered are good examples of African realism in detail. Baulé masks (human with occasional animal decoration) are used in dances formerly religious but now largely secular. The Guro make no statues, and their masks are stylisations of the more naturalistic Baulé pattern, while their combination of animal with human forms indicates an influence from the Sudan. The masks of the Dan show all degrees of stylisation, the most extreme being the form known as the "gorilla-mask."

The art of Guinea and the Sudan is the most stylised of any in Africa. Baga figures were connected with the secret societies, important before Islam, and they also made maternity figures. The Bambara carved ancestral and fecundity figures of vertical emphasis, and highly stylised animal forms worn as headdresses in connection with agricultural ceremonies. Only seven Dogo funerary figures are known, but they also made fecundity figures and masks in various animal forms. The Malinke, Mossi, and Senufo should also be mentioned.

In the Gabun the most people artistically are the Pangwe and Osyeba tribes of the Fang, recent immigrants and so unaffected by Benin art. Fang sculpture is entirely mortuary, and is typical rather than individual in character. Its degree of stylisation varies greatly but no developmental sequence has yet been established. Fang art is entirely in wood; that of the Bakota uses brass hammered over wood, with the body reduced to schematic bent legs. The "ghost-masks" of certain Ogowe River tribes, though seemingly oriental in affiliation, can be shown to be a development of purely African forms.

Excepting the northern region, where there is almost no art, the styles of the Belgian Congo may be divided into three large groups: 1. The Lower Congo (Mayumbe, Bakongo) producing maternity fetishes, magic figures, and masks, all showing some influence of European materials and techniques. 2. The Kasai-Sankuru region (Bushongo, Bayaka, Bena-Lulua, Bateke) all under the influence of the Bushongo style. Bushongo art is mainly decorative, excelling in weaving (raphia "velvets") and the decoration of wooden utensils; predominant in both are various forms of the interlace, which derives originally from the technique of the former and is combined in the latter with naturalistic motives such as the hand, sun-disk, and lizard. Only five Bushongo statues (going back to the seventeenth century) are known, but these are of extremely high order, while the statuettes of the Bena-Lulua show strong Bushongo influence. 3. The Eastern region (Baluba, Warua, Warega) producing wooden "mendiant figures" and stools supported by crouching figures, both naturalistic and highly stylised masks, and small ivory maternity charms and ivory head-rests which indicate the influence of pastoral peoples further to the east.

The medieval Zimbabwe culture of Rhodesia, whose monuments are now known to have been Bantu in production, should also be mentioned.

BIBLIOGRAPHY: Guillaume, Paul, and Munro, Thomas, *Primitive Negro Sculpture*. New York, 1926.—Maes, J., and H. Lavacherv, *L'Art nègre*. Brussels, 1930.—Sydow, Eckart von *Die Kunst der Naturvölker und der Vorzeit*. Berlin, 1923.—Vatter, Ernst, *Religiose Plastik der Naturvölker*. Frankfurt, 1926.

**NELLI (Ottaviano).**—Umbrian painter of Gubbio, documents of whose activity run from 1400 to 1444. He is dead by 1450.

In 1400 Nelli is consul for the S. Andrea quarter of Gubbio and in the same year the Priors of Perugia charge him to paint the coat-of-arms of Gian Galeazzo Visconti, with the assistance of Francesco d'Antonio and Cristoforo di Nicoluccio of Perugia. In 1403 he is again consul, and in this year his name appears on the Madonna del Belvedere at Gubbio and on the Pietralunga polyptych. In 1410 and 1415 he is once more consul at Gubbio and is further mentioned there in 1405 and 1411. In 1417 and 1420 he is recorded as at Urbino; and in 1424 he paints the extant frescoes of the Trinci Palace in Foligno. Between 1428 and 1432 he is again at Urbino, working for the Brotherhood of Sta. Croce; a *Madonna Crowned by Angels* in the Oratorio di Sta. Croce dates from this period. In 1426 he is at Borgo San Sepolcro. From 1437-44 documents prove his continuous residence in Gubbio. In 1441 he takes Domenico di Cecco di Baldo as pupil.

Ottaviano Nelli's works are to be found chiefly in Gubbio, Urbino, Assisi, Foligno, etc.

BIBLIOGRAPHY: L. Bonfalti, *Mem. stor. di Ottaviano Nelli*. Gubbio, 1843.—Scatassa, *Per Ottaviano Nelli di Gubbio*, Rassegna bibl. dell' arte ital., 1908, p. 105.—W. Rothes, *Anfänge u. Entwickelungsgänge der alt Umbrische Malerschulen*. Strassburg, 1908, p. 29.—E. Jacobsen, *Umbrische Malerei*. Strassburg, 1914.—U. Gnoli, *Pittori e miniatori*, p. 227.—Van Marle, *Italian Schools, etc.*, VIII, 1927.

**NEO-CLASSICAL SCHOOL.**—See Greece (Sculpture).

**— STYLE.**—See Adam (Robert).

**NEO-CLASSICISM.**—See David (J. L.).

**N E O - IMPRESSIONISM.**—Founded by Georges Seurat, c. 1885, who considered line and color the fundamentals of painting. He worked out a system of applying pigment in measured strokes of calculated values (Pointillism), thus making the theories of Impressionism more intellectual, more scientific. He mastered formal design and, instead of the evanescent character of the Impressionists' work, his is stable and classical in definition. Signac and Cross were his followers. Cubism based its theories on those of Neo-Impressionism.

See Impressionism.

**NEOLITHIC (Period).**—"Neolithic" is the name given to the age of polished stone, as opposed to the "paleolithic" age or age of cut stone. During this period, a warm, very damp climate succeeded the period of dry cold of Magdalenian times. The reindeer disappeared, and was replaced by the stag. Man, after living by hunting, came to cultivate the earth. He left caves, and lived in huts. It is the period of the Megalithic structures (menhirs, dolmens), and lacustrine (lake) dwellings. Archæologists have not explained the long interruption which exists between the Magdalenian civilisation and the neolithic period. What is certain is that among the conquests of man at this period was the domestication of animals, and the cultivation of cereals. Important remains of neolithic villages allow us to imagine something of human existence of the period. On the site of huts, bone instruments have been found, and pieces of ceramic. An enumeration of stations of this kind is found in Dechelette's *Manuel*. One of the most important stations is the camp of Chassey, on the boundary which separates the departments of Saône-et-Loire and the Côte d'Or (France).

See Pl. 14, Vol. I.

BIBLIOGRAPHY: *Dechelette, Manuel d'archéologie préhistorique*. 1912.

**NEOLITHIC (Sculpture).**—The period of polished stone is far from presenting us with work of an artistic interest comparable to the rock engravings and paintings of the Magdalenian period. Nevertheless, it represents a less imperfect civilisation. The tombs reveal a more advanced religion—the worship of the dead; the cutting of flint is much more skillful, and the instruments are more varied. Although sculpture is not entirely absent, its forms are crude and barbaric. It represents men, or various objects, or is simply ornamental.

The very crude representations of the human figure, discovered principally in Gaul, should, according to Dechelette, be connected with Greek art: a similar type of divinity was produced from Asia Minor to the British Isles. This divinity may be a prototype of the goddess-mothers which were so frequent in the ancient religions.

BIBLIOGRAPHY: Dechelette, *Manuel d'archéologie préhistorique*. Paris, 1912.

**NEPTUNE (Fountain of).**—See Gian da Bologna; also Bologna (It.).

**— (Temple of).**—See Paestum; also Pl. 19, Vol. I.

**NEREID MONUMENT.**—This monument was discovered in Lycia, near Xanthos, in 1838, by an English delegation which brought important fragments of it to London. It is called the *Nereid Monument* because figures of nereids, or marine nymphs, with their attributes, originally stood between the columns. It is generally considered to have been a sepulchral monument; and it probably dates from the first quarter of the 4th century. The model in the British Museum was designed from important fragments discovered by Sir Charles Fellows. The monument consisted of a central chamber surrounded by an Ionic colonnade on a podium. The figures of Nereides which stood between the columns expressed variety of movement, and their garments were rendered as though blown about them by the wind.

MONUMENT OF THE NEREIDS: BAS-RELIEF REPRESENTING A LYCIAN TOWN.

BIBLIOGRAPHY: Collignon, *Histoire de la sculpture grecque*. Vol. II. Paris, 1896.—The sculptures of the Nereid Monument are reproduced in the *Denkmäler* of Brunn and Bruckmann.

**NERI di BICCI.** — Florentine painter, son of Bicci di Lorenzo, born 1419; died 1491. Neri di Bicci's career is fully documented from a journal which he kept from 1453 to 1475, and which is now in the Uffizi. He was enormously productive, his shop a veritable factory, producing carved objects, tapestries, shop signs, crucifixes, and many other objects besides paintings. He had, consequently, a large number of pupils and collaborators, the most important of whom was Cosimo Rosselli.

Neri di Bicci's style is easily recognizable, and his works are to be found in collections and museums all over the world. Many of them are dated.

BIBLIOGRAPHY: Vasari-Milanesi, II.—Van Marle, *Italian Schools, etc.* X, 1928, p. 523ff.

**NEROCCIO di BARTOLOMMEO di BENEDETTO de' LANDI.**—Sienese painter and sculptor, born 1447; died 1500, a pupil of Sassetta and Vecchietta.

In 1467 Neroccio already had his own atelier, which he maintained in collaboration with Francesco di Giorgio, perhaps his brother-in-law, certainly related to him in some way, until 1475. In 1467 the Compagnia di S. Girolamo paid him for an altarpiece; and in 1468 he was paid by the same company for a terra cotta statue of *St. Jerome*. In 1470 he was commissioned to execute the extant wood sculpture of *St. Catherine of Siena* in the Casa di Sta. Caterina, Siena. In 1472 he painted an *Assumption* for Monte Oliveto Maggiore, the predella of which is now in the Uffizi. His first dated altarpiece is the triptych in the Siena Academy of 1476, a *Standing Madonna with Michael and Bernardino*. In the same year he painted for Bernardino Nini an altarpiece, two cassoni and a lettuccio, work estimated by Francesco di Giorgio. Perhaps the altarpiece mentioned in the document is identical with that now in the Academy. In 1483 the *Helespontine Sibyl* on the pavement of the Duomo was executed from his design. His tomb of Tomaso Testa Piccolomini was done a few years after (the Bishop died in 1485). In 1485 he was charged by the authorities of the Duomo to make a marble statue of *St. Catherine of Alexandria* for the newly built Baptismal Chapel of the Duomo. The frieze over the portal of Fontegiusta is of 1489; from 1492 the *Madonna with Six Saints* in the Siena Academy; and from 1496 the lost altarpiece for Sarteano.

BIBLIOGRAPHY: Milanesi, Doc. . . . *senese*, II, III; and *Sulla storia dell'arte toscana*, 1873.—Borghese e Banchi, *Nuovi doc., etc.*, 1898.—P. Schubring, *Die Plastik Sienas im Quattrocento*, 1907.—E. Jacobsen, *Die Malerei des Quattrocento in Siena*, 1908.—Berenson, *Central Italian Painters*, 1909.—Crowe and Cavalcaselle, Douglas ed., V, 1914.—Venturi, *Storia d. arte ital.*, VI, 1908, VIII, I, 1923.

**NESIOTES.**—See Antenor.

**NETSCHER (Caspar).**—Dutch portrait and genre painter, 1639-1684. Pupil of Koster and of Terborch. Member of the Guild of The Hague in 1662. He painted conversation pieces and mythological scenes, and late in his career mostly portraits. He was clever in rendering costume; the early works are dominated by a golden tonality while the latter ones tend to be more silvery. He must have gone to France, since he painted two portraits of Madame de Montespan (Dresden, 1670 and 1671). Most European galleries possess some of his works.

BIBLIOGRAPHY: C. Hofstede de Groot, *A Catalogue Raisonné of the Works of the Most Eminent Dutch Painters of the 17th Century*. Vol. V. London, 1913.

**NETSUKÉ.**—The netsuké is a Japanese button or toggle. Netsukés are made of lacquer, coral, china, but the finest are in ivory, or sometimes in wood. In these little articles the Japanese artist had scope for his delicacy, love of detail, and bent for caricature. The finest netsukés date from the 17th century. Some, of larger size, have a certain æsthetic affinity with the gargoyles of European cathedrals.

**NEUFCHATEL (Nicholas), or Lucidel.**—Flemish painter, 16th century. He painted some good portraits, the best of which are in Munich.

**NEUMANN (J. Balthasar).**—German architect, 1687-1753, Premier exponent of the magnificent and grandiose rococo of Germany, a style essentially different from French rococo in being applied to exterior as well as interior design and in being a structural system rather than purely decorative; it is, therefore, more akin to the previous baroque. His buildings represent the most complete fusion ever achieved of turbulent and wildly undulating elements of architecture, sculpture and painting. His masterpiece is the Wallfahrtskirche, Vierzehnheiligen. He also designed the Residenz and the Käpelle, Würzburg.

**N E V E R S (France).**—The *Church of St. Étienne* was built in the 11th century (restored, 1850). It contains one of the earliest choirs of the Pilgrimage Romanesque style, with an ambulatory with radiating chapels surrounding the apse.

The *Cathedral* (St. Cyr) dates from the 13th and 14th centuries. In the Romanesque apse is a large fresco of *Christ in Glory*.

The *Palais ducal* was probably built at the end of the 15th century.

**NICCOLÒ dell'ARCA.**—Bolognese sculptor, died in 1494. He worked chiefly in Bologna, but he was of South Italian origin. It may be because of this, or because of his study of northern art (it has even been suggested that he worked in France) that his figures are very contorted, and reveal an intense, almost grimacing realism.

The *Pietà* of Santa Maria della Vita in Bologna (1463) resembles a dance of maniacs round a corpse. Having seen this work, it is difficult to attribute to Niccolò dell'Arca the *Tomb of Annibale Bentivoglio* in San Giacomo of Bologna. It is, however, certain that he worked, in 1469, on the Arca di San Domenico (begun by Fra Guglielmo of Pisa in the 13th century), for which he made a fine *Coronation* with the figures and heavy garlands supported by angels. We no longer find the forced violence of the *Pietà*. The Saints still have a certain rudeness, however; they are carved in simplified planes, and recall figures of the vigorous Claus Sluter, just as the *Pietà* recalls certain northern works.

The tomb-stone of Domenico Garganelli in the Museo Civico of Bologna is much ruined.

The *Madonna di Piazza*, on the façade of the Palazzo dei Anziani (Bologna), is more graceful and gentle, but the figure is still rather contorted.

Niccolò dell'Arca had a great influence. His *Pietà* was the source of a whole school of popular, dramatic art.

BIBLIOGRAPHY: Schubring, *Niccolo da Bari, Zeitschrift für bild. Kunst.* 1904.

**— da BOLOGNA.**—Miniaturist of Bologna; middle of the 14th century.

**— BUONACCORSO.** — Sienese painter; died 1388. Follower of Lippo Memmi. He signed a picture representing the *Marriage of the Virgin* (National Gallery). There is a *Madonna Enthroned* in the Venice Academy.

**— da FOLIGNO.**—Umbrian painter, c. 1430-1502, pupil of Benozzo Gozzoli.

**— di PIETRO.**—Venetian painter, of the end of the 14th century and beginning of the 15th. He freed art from the shackles of Byzantine tradition by his *Madonna* (1394, Venice).

BIBLIOGRAPHY: Crowe and Cavalcaselle, *A History of Painting in North Italy.* Vol. III. London, 1908.

**— di PIETRO GERINI.**—Florentine painter, follower of Taddeo Gaddi and master of a large and very productive school, which tended to prolong the dependence upon trecento Giottesque and Orcagnesque forms into the quattrocento.

The earliest date recorded for Niccolò is 1368, at which time he is mentioned on the rolls of the Medici e Speziali. In 1370 he contracted to execute the *Coronation of the Virgin* for S. Pietro Maggiore, now in the National Gallery. Finished in 1371 it was probably painted by Jacopo di Cione, with whom Niccolò di Pietro was collaborating at the time. In 1373 he and Jacopo produced the *Coronation* of the Zecca Vecchia, now in the Uffizi, Jacopo executing, as is proved by the document of payment, the major part of the work. In 1386 Niccolò di Pietro collaborated with Ambrogio di Baldese on frescoes for the façade of the Bigallo, which are still extant. In 1391 he was employed by Datini in Prato; and from 1392 date the frescoes in S. Francesco, Pisa. Niccolò was working for Datini again in 1394. In 1401 he finished, with his son, Lorenzo di Niccolò and Spinello Aretino, the triptych for the altar of Sta. Felicità, now in the Academy, Florence. In 1408 he was once more in Prato, working on the frescoes in the Church of S. Francesco which are still extant. In the next year he was paid for a figure of *St. Nicholas* on a pillar of Or San Michele, Florence, which still exists, and two years later, in 1411, he had returned to Prato and was decorating the façade of the Palazzo del Ceppo. In 1414 he received payment for the decoration of a chapel in Sta. Maria Nuova. He died in 1415.

BIBLIOGRAPHY: Vasari-Milanesi, II.—Crowe and Cavalcaselle, II.—Van Marle, *Italian Schools, etc.,* III, 1924.—R. Offner, *Studies in Florentine Painting,* 1927, 83ff.

**— di SEGNA.**—Sienese painter, Mentioned 1331-45; pupil of his father, Segna di Bonaventura. A *Crucifix,* dated 1345, in the Siena Gallery bears his name.

BIBLIOGRAPHY: Crowe and Cavalcaselle, *A History of Painting in Italy.* Vol. III. London, 1908.

**— PISANO.**—See Pisano.

**— di TOMMASO.**—Florentine painter, follower of Nardo di Cione.

In 1365, he is a witness to the will of Nardo di Cione. In 1366 he advises on the construction of the Cathedral of Florence. The date 1371 appears on a triptych in S. Antonio, Naples.

The discovery of this 1371 triptych establishes the name of a personality which had been recognized in a number of works, notably the frescoes of the Convento del T in Pistoia, representations of the *Creation and Fall, Episodes from the Old Testament,* and a fragment of a *Paradise.* With these frescoes and the Naples triptych, Dr. Richard Offner, in his reconstruction of the master (op. cit. below) has associated: a *Coronation* in the Academy, Florence; a triptych in the Walters Gallery, Baltimore; a *St. James* and a small *Nativity* in the Griggs Collection, New York; *Two Saints* in the Fondazione Horne, Florence; *Four Saints* at the Vatican; and a tabernacle, with a *Nativity,* in the Johnson Collection, Philadelphia.

BIBLIOGRAPHY: Vasari-Milanesi, I.—R. Offner, *Studies in Florentine Painting,* 1927, 109ff.

**NICHOLAS de VERDUN.**—French goldsmith, 12th century, whose principal work was the great enamelled altar frontal at Klosterneuburg near Vienna, dating from 1181.

**NICIAS.**—See Acropolis of Athens (Erechtheum).

**NICOLA PISANO.**—See Pisano.

**NICOLAO FLORENTINO (or Dello di Nicola).**—Spanish painter, born in Florence, 1402. In 1432, he went to Castille, where he settled. He only returned to his native land once, in 1446. Dello was still living in Castille about 1460. D. M. Gomez seems to have proved that Nicolao Florentino and Dello di Nicola were but one person, and author of a very important collection of Florentine paintings, preserved in Salamanca, where they decorate the apse of the old Romanesque Cathedral.

The contract of 1445 reveals that when he was commissioned for the frescoes, the altarpiece had already been painted some time. In the enormous altarpiece, which is entirely Spanish in conception, one is surprised to find that the painting of the little panels is still more purely Florentine than the *Last Judgment.* The artist appears to have been influenced sometimes by Masolino and sometimes by Pesellino. He was evidently assisted in his work either by his brother Samson, or by a young man of Avila, whom the Florentine engaged, in 1466, as apprentice.

BIBLIOGRAPHY: M. Gomez Moreno, *Salamanca el retablo de la Catedral vieja y Nicolao Florentino.* Bol. de la Soc. Castellana de Excurs. Valladolid. June, 1905.—R. van Marle, *The Development of the Italian Schools of Painting.* Vol. IX.

**NIEHAUS (Charles Henry).**—American sculptor, born 1855, creator of numerous public monuments (Garfield, Washington and Cincinnati, Hahnemann, Washington, etc.), statues in the manner of the Antique, bas-reliefs of historical and allegorical subjects (*e.g.,* one pair of Astor Memorial doors, Trinity Church, New York, Tympana in State House, Hartford, etc.), etc.

**NIELLO.**—See Silver.

**NIGHT WATCH (The).**—See Rembrandt; also Pl. 38, Vol. II.

**NIKE.**—The goddess of victory. See Acropolis of Athens.

**NÎMES (France).**—Old Roman town, which preserves numerous Romanesque and mediæval buildings.

NÎMES: THE TEMPLE OF DIANA.

The *Arena,* built by the Romans, is formed of large stones placed one on another, without mortar, and is in the shape of an ellipse. Four gateways give access to the interior, which could hold 24,000 spectators. The wall separating the track from the steps is low, and from this it is concluded that the arena of Nîmes was not used for combats of wild beasts, but for gladiatorial contests, chariot and horse races, and bull fights.

The *Maison Carrée* is one of the most famous Roman buildings in France. Of small and harmonious dimensions, well situated and detached, this temple has been admired at all times. Colbert even wanted to remove it stone by stone to Versailles. The temple was dedicated, in the first year of our era, to Caius and Lucius Cæsar, adopted sons of Augustus. According to certain archæologists, it was the annex to a forum; but more probably it was a "capitol," or temple consecrated to Jupiter, Juno and Minerva. The temple stands on a stylobate, and is approached by steps. The entablature is supported by thirty fluted columns of the Corinthian order, twenty of which are attached to the walls. The other ten support the peristyle, under which opens the

NÎMES: THE PRADIER FOUNTAIN.

large doorway, crowned by a cornice, which is supported by consoles. The roof is modern. The Maison Carrée contains a museum of Gallo-Roman antiquities, mostly discovered in the region.

The ribbed barrel-vaulted *Temple of Diana* was probably the Nympheum of the Roman thermæ (baths) which have disappeared. The building itself is in ruins, restored in the 18th century, and surrounded by a railing.

The *Arch of Augustus* was, according to the inscription on the cornice, built in 16 B.C.

The *Tour Magne* was the highest of ninety towers which defended the ramparts of Nîmes.

Besides these Roman buildings, Nîmes possesses a Romanesque *Cathedral*—rebuilt in the 16th and 17th centuries.

See Pl. 30, Vol. I.

BIBLIOGRAPHY: Roger Peyre, *Nîmes, Arles et Orange.* Collection des Villes d'art célèbres.

**NIMRUD.**—Excavations at Nimrud, twenty miles south of Nineveh, were begun in 1845 by the English archæologist Layard. Nimrud was the seat of the Assyrian monarchy before the Sargonides transported the seat to Nineveh. Of all the buildings of which traces have been found, the oldest is the Palace of Assurnasirpal (885-860 B.C.); from which there are remarkable wall slabs in the British Museum. These low reliefs represent King Assurnasirpal surrounded by court officials; presenting offerings to the gods; hunting, or in battle. Some of these reliefs are the masterpieces of Assyrian sculpture. The ruins of Nimrud have revealed the existence of later palaces, notably that of King Esarhaddon.

See Assyria—Art.

**NINEVEH.**—Nineveh is situated on the right bank of the upper Tigris. It was the favourite place of residence of the Assyrian monarchy from the 8th to the end of the 7th century B.C. It has the remains of three palaces built by Sennacherib (B.C. 705-681), Esarhaddon (B.C. 681-668), and Assurbanipal (B.C. 668-626). The bas-reliefs in the British Museum show not only warlike pursuits, but building operations, and traces of the action of the fire which destroyed Nineveh in B.C. 612.

See Assyria—Art.

**NINO PISANO.**—See Pisano.

**NIOBIDES.**—Series of antique statues in the Uffizi Gallery. Nine of them were discovered in Rome, in 1583. Other figures have been added to this initial group. The statues recall the myth of Niobe's children, who were killed by the arrows of Apollo and Artemis, to satisfy the jealousy of their mother, Latona. The finest of these figures is the one representing the mother herself. She is endeavouring to protect her daughter by holding part of her garment over her, and gazing imploringly towards heaven. The

NIOBID. ANTIQUE SCULPTURE, FLORENCE. (Uffizi.)

other figures of the children all express grief and terror. In their subject these statues are unique. They must all be copies of a series of statues which were in the Temple of Apollo, Rome, in the time of Pliny. Their original arrangement is a matter of conjecture. They were evidently not intended for a pediment. It is more likely that they were placed at different heights on a rock, and thus formed a garden or park decoration.

See Pl. 25, Vol. I.

BIBLIOGRAPHY: Collignon, *Histoire de la sculpture grecque.* Vol. II.

**NI TSAN.** — Chinese painter, 1301-1374. One of the "Four Masters" of the Yuan dynasty, his quiet scenes are closer to the academic Sung models than those of his great contemporaries.

**NITTIS (Giuseppe de).**—Italian painter, born in 1846, near Naples, of a very poor family. He died in 1884. In 1868, he went to Paris, where Gérôme and Meissonnier became interested in him. In the Salons of 1875 and 1876, he exhibited: *La Place des Pyramides,* and *Le Pont Royal.* In 1876, Claretie wrote: "De Nittis paints modern Parisian life for us, as the Abbé Galiani spoke French—that is, much better than we do it ourselves." His last pictures of England are unusually able.

**NOEL (Alexandre Jean).**—French painter of sea-pieces, 1752-1834. In the Musée Carnavalet (Paris) there are some views of the Seine by him, which are painted in the manner of Joseph Vernet, his master.

**NONNOTTE (Donat).**—French painter, 1708-1785. Pupil of Le Moyne, with whom he collaborated in the decoration of the Chapel of the Virgin, in St. Sulpice. He painted chiefly portraits.

**NOORT (Adam van).**—Flemish painter, 1562-1641. He travelled in Italy and in 1587 settled in Antwerp. He is primarily famous as a teacher; among his pupils were the young Rubens, and Jordaens who later became his son-in-law.

**NORBLIN de la GOURDAINE (Jean Pierre).**—French painter and draughtsman, 1745-1830. Pupil of Casanova.

**NORTHCOTE (James).**—English painter, 1746-1831. In 1771, he entered Reynolds' studio. In 1787, he became a R.A. Northcote was not only a painter. He was also a poet and art critic. He left remarkable biographies of Titian and Reynolds. Together with Fuseli, Opie, Stothard and Haydon, Northcote belonged to that school of historical painters who endeavoured to treat their subject freshly, and showed skill in draughtsmanship and colour. These painters were all influenced by Reynolds' *"Discourses."*

Northcote painted vast historical compositions for the Shakespeare Gallery of Boydell.

BIBLIOGRAPHY: W. Hazlitt, *Conversations of James Northcote, A.R.A.,* 1813, 1894.

**NORWICH (England).**—*Cathedral.* A 12th century Norman structure with 14th century Gothic vaults.

**— SCHOOL.**—See Crome; Ladbrooke.

**NOTRE DAME (Cathedral of).** —See under the name of the city where it is located, *e.g.,* Amiens, Paris, Reims, Rouen, etc.

**NOYON (France).**—*Cathedral of Notre Dame,* 1149-1200. Early Gothic cathedral similar to Senlis, but on a larger scale. The vaults are 13th century.

**NUREMBERG (Bavaria).** — In the 15th and 16th centuries, Nuremberg was a flourishing artistic centre. Michael Wolgemut, Albrecht Dürer, Adam Krafft, Peter Vischer, etc., lived there. To a great extent, the town has kept its mediæval aspect.

NUREMBERG: FOUNTAIN OF THE MAN WITH THE GEESE.

The mediæval fortifications have been partly destroyed, but numerous towers which belonged to them remain.

The *Church of St. Lawrence* was built from the 13th to the 15th centuries (restored in the 19th century). It contains the famous *Imhof Tabernacle* by Adam Krafft (see this name), the *Annunciation,* by Veit Stoss (see). The *Cathedral* was built from 1355 to 1361, on an almost square plan, with choir and aisleless nave. It contains the epitaph of the Pergetstorfer family, by Krafft, and the Tucher altarpiece (15th century).

The *Church of St. Sebald* was begun in the 11th century, and rebuilt in the 13th and 16th centuries. It has a charming doorway, known as the "bride's doorway"; on the south doorway is a *Last Judgment.* The church contains the celebrated *Shrine of St. Sebald* by Peter Vischer (see Vischer), and some high reliefs by Veit Stoss. The fountain of the *Man with Geese* has a pleasing statue, by Labenwolf (1530).

See Pl. 25, Vol. II.

The *Guildhall* is largely a Renaissance building.

The streets of Nuremberg are very picturesque, bordered with old, uneven houses. The most curious is the *Bratwurstglöcklein Inn* (Bell of the Roast Sausage); it is said to have been built in 1400. The *Imhof House* was probably built in the 15th century by Beheim. Its "historic courtyard" possesses a graceful stone balustrade with armorial bearings and figures by Adam Krafft. *Dürer's House* is one of several interesting wooden constructions of the 15th century. Statues of the Virgin are often found at the corners of old houses in Nuremberg. Several houses date from the 16th century.

NUREMBERG: THE GERMAN NATIONAL MUSEUM.

The *Germanic Museum* is very rich in works of the German schools of the 15th and 16th centuries. The principal artists there represented are: Albrecht Dürer (by several pictures), the Elder Holbein, Burgkmair, Altdorfer, Zeitblom, the Elder Cranach, Pleydenwurff, Dünwegge, Wolgemut, the Master of the Passion of Liversberg, etc.

The Museum also contains very interesting sculptures by Veit Stoss, Reimenschneider, and the fine *Virgin of Nuremberg,* by Peter Vischer. All these works are picturesquely situated in an old Gothic convent (14th century).

Outside the town, on a rock, is the *Castle,* which was begun in the 11th century, and enlarged in the 12th century by Frederick Barbarossa. Restored in 1854.

BIBLIOGRAPHY: P. J. Rée, *Nuremberg.* Les Villes d'art célèbres. Paris.

# O

**OBELISKS.**—Ancient Egyptian monuments, generally cut from a single block of granite with their four faces covered with hieroglyphic inscriptions. Owing to their elongated form they are also known as "needles" (the name "obelisk" signifies, in Greek, "needle"). They were usually placed on either side of the pylon, or entrance, to Egyptian temples, and measure from 20 to 30

Obelisk of Luxor. (Paris.)

metres. The tremendous weight of these monuments made their erection extremely difficult, and the Pharaohs employed thousands of slaves for the task.

**OCEANIC ART.**—Oceanic art may be divided along geographical lines into Melanesian and Polynesian. Of the former that of New Guinea is the most important: The art of the Papuan gulf and Massim areas of the southeast is chiefly ornamental, the main motives used for decorating planks, shields, and spatula being small stylised human figures or adaptations of the frigate bird. The chief masks and statues come from the Sepik River area and the islands to the north of this coast. Features are painted on rather than truly carved in the round; the main colors used are red and white. Masks are often of bird character, due to the conception of the soul as a bird, and human and bird combinations are common. A variety of dissimilar media is used in the same object, with no underlying structural principle visible. From the Bismarck Archipelago come great open work headdresses of bird and snake motives connected with sun and moon cults; from New Caledonia large bulbous-nosed wooden masks with leaf decoration and ornamented house posts; and from the New Hebrides masks and crude figures made of tree roots. Pottery is produced only in Melanesia (none in Polynesia), the best in Fiji and New Guinea.

The wooden sculpture of the New Zealand Maoris was of three kinds: decoration of the ridge-pole, uprights, door, and window of the communal and store houses; decoration of the stern and bow pieces of the war canoes; and the carving of clubs, adzes, and boxes. Characteristic of all these designs is the use of the double spiral (often in pierced work), and the separation and geometrisation of the parts of the human figure, which are then treated as independent units. Patterns painted in red, black, and white were used in the houses in connection with this carving. Weapons, tools, and ornaments were made of nephrite (greenstone), also in geometrical forms. Tattooing was elaborate and important. In its use of curved designs and in its combination of human and animal forms Maori art is connected with New Guinea rather than with the rest of Polynesia.

Marquesan art is allied with the Maori in its emphasis on the head, due in both to a religious head cult, and in the similarity of the facial formula (especially the broad mouth with protruding tongue and the large eyes). Marquesan stone statues are found against the house walls with bases sunk in the open house platform, and also in open worshipping places, thus showing affinities with Easter Island. Objects decorated in wood include club ends, foot-rests, and bowls. The figure is stylised in the same way as in stone, but often the head only is shown, or single features alone, or these multiplied as geometrical patterns with a tendency towards angular rather than curved designs. Tattooing reached a development comparable to that in New Zealand.

The only Samoan art was that of tapa cloth, common to and important in all Polynesia. Tapa is made from the inner bark of the paper-mulberry tree, strips being softened, beaten smooth, and joined together by water percolation. It was decorated by dyeing, painting in various designs, stamping, or stencilling; the patterns were generally based on a small unit freely repeated, and were angular, geometric, and fairly simple.

Hawaiian art also shows connections with that of the Marquesas and New Zealand in the large figure-8 mouths, button noses, and flaring eyes of both wooden figures, found in temple enclosures, and those covered with feathers. Featherwork (which also produced helmets and cloaks) was done over a wicker frame of fig-tree roots; the colors—red and yellow—are those of the feathers and not due to dyeing.

The monolithic statues of Easter Island, half-figures twenty feet high, were placed facing out to sea on terraces where the dead were exposed. Their exact significance is not known. Wooden figures about two feet high, elongated and with the ribs showing, are common, either separate or decorating staffs and pendants. Various stylised bird forms are found in wood, and these, like the bird-headed men carved and colored on rock, were connected with a bird cult. The "hieroglyphics" of Easter Island have not yet been deciphered.

Bibliography: Chauvet, Stephan, *Les Arts indigènes en Nouvelle-Guinée*. Paris, 1930.—Mead, Margaret, *The Maoris and their Arts*. New York, 1928.—Sydow, Eckart von, *Die Kunst der Naturvölker und der Vorzeit*. Berlin, 1923. Vatter, Ernst, *Religioese Plastik der Naturvölker*. Frankfurt, 1926.

**OCHTERVELT (Jacob).**—Dutch genre painter, about 1635-1708/10. Together with de Hooch he was a pupil of Berchem, and a member of the Guild of Rotterdam about 1665. In 1674, he painted, in Amsterdam, the *Directors of the Leper Hospital*, a well conceived work, in which the portraits reveal fine precise draughtsmanship. He is also the author of many interiors, original in composition and colour scheme. His style is very close to that of Terborch, but the quality of his paintings is inferior.

**ODERISI (Roberto).**—Neapolitan painter, active middle of 14th century, formed under Roman school, influenced by Giotto and Simone Martini. His chief works are frescoes in Naples.

**ODERISIO DI GUBBIO.**—Bolognese miniaturist of the 13th century. He retained Byzantine characteristics.

**OGEE.**—Moulding with a double or S-shaped curve; also an arch formed by such curves.

**OGIVE.**—Salient arch or rib crossing a Gothic vault; also applied to the pointed arch.

**OGNISSANTI.**—See Florence.

**OINOCHOË.**—See Greece (Vases).

**O'KEEFFE (Georgia).**—Contemporary American painter. She was born in Sun Prairie, Wisconsin, 15th November 1887. She began to draw as a child and at seventeen spent one year at the Art Institute of Chicago, working under John Vanderpoel. The next year she studied in New York at the Art Students' League under William Merritt Chase, F. Luis Mora and Kenyon Cox. During 1908 and 1909 she was doing some advertising art in Chicago. From 1912 to 1914 she attended the classes of Alon Bement at the University of Virginia. Then for the next two years she worked with Bement and Professor Arthur Dow at Teachers College in New York. In 1916 and 1917 she was the supervisor of public schools in Amarillo, Texas, and the following year she was the head of the art department of West Texas State Normal College. About 1916 she began to exhibit her flower pieces and city scenes and in 1917 Alfred Stieglitz, later her husband, held a one-man show of her work at his famous "291" Fifth Avenue.

Her early studies of flowers and her later studies of the sun-bleached skulls of the New Mexican desert were characterised by simplicity and directness of approach in pure tones of luminous colour. Some of the forms had hard outlines, but there were others with very delicate contours visible and embodying sinuous shapes and tender sentiment. They were feminine in character, but as her work grew in breadth of treatment and force of strongly contrasted colour schemes it became more abstract. All is symbolic although not always in a manner which is clearly understandable to the general public. She also does studies of barns, skyscrapers and some landscapes—all in the same definite and clear technique which is at once precise and stiff, and yet fascinating primarily by the colours used and the harmony of the design. Examples of her work are found in the Phillips Memorial Gallery in Washington, the Whitney Museum of American Art and the Metropolitan Museum of Art in New York City.

See Pl. 63, Vol. II.

Bibliography: C. J. Bulliet, *Apples and Madonnas*, 1927.—Sheldon Cheney, *A Primer of Modern Art*, 1924.—Marsden Hartley, *Adventures in the Arts*, 1921.—Samuel Kootz, *Modern American Painters*, 1930.—Duncan Phillips, *A Collection in the Making*, 1926.—Paul Rosenfeld, *The Port of New York*, 1924.

**OLBRICH (Josef Maria).**—Austrian architect, 1867-1908. A pupil of Wagner, the pioneer continental modernist, and an organizer of the Vienna "Secession" of 1897. He designed the Exhibition Building for the movement, 1898. Other exhibition buildings he designed include that for Darmstadt, 1906. In 1907 he designed the Tietze Warehouse, Düsseldorf.

**OLYMPIA.**—I. *Architecture.*—Olympia was not a town. Rather, it was a collection of temples, owned

Head of Heracles: Metope of the Temple of Olympia. (Museum of Olympia.)

successively by the neighbouring towns of Pisa and Elis. Olympia was, with Delphi, the most important religious centre in Greece.

From earliest times, the possession of Olympia was sharply disputed, and it suffered many invasions. Each group of invaders which settled there built an altar to its deity, and introduced a new worship. According to tradition the first Olympic games must have been organised well before the Dorian Invasion. After several wars between the Dorians, the Ætolians and the Achæns, an agreement was made between all the states by which Olympia was to remain a neutral place, where each had their altars and their treasuries, the finest being reserved for the supreme god, Zeus.

Nearly all the buildings of Olympia were grouped within an enclosed space known as the Altis, or sacred grove, the boundaries of which were, according to tradition, laid out by Heracles. This enclosure was, however, often enlarged as the number of buildings increased. The Altis, as defined by Heracles, was a square, surrounded by pale olive and shady plane trees. The earliest building, now existing, was the temple of Hera or the Heræum built c. 700 B.C. Originally it was probably a joint temple of Zeus and Hera. It was a Doric temple, the columns of which were originally of wood. The stylobate rested on a base 50 metres long by 18 metres 75 wide. As the steps were very high, there were two staircases of lower steps on the southwest side. The façades had six columns, and the sides, sixteen. Close to the spot where Pausanias had seen it in the Heræum, was found the famous Hermes of Praxiteles, during the excavations of 1877 (Museum of Olympia). Statues of Zeus and Hera stood probably against the west wall of the cella (*Head of Hera* in the Museum of Olympia may probably belong to this group).

OLYMPIA: METOPE FROM THE TEMPLE OF ZEUS.

The most celebrated of the temples of Olympia was the *Temple of Zeus*. An architect from Elis, named Libon, must have made the designs for it about 468 B.C. The temple was fully completed by 456 B.C. It is of the Doric peripteral, hexastyle type. The peristyle was approached by a ramp and two side stairways. The façade had six columns, and there were thirteen at the side. The entablature was strongly proportioned, and the pediments were surmounted by acroteria, the works of Pæeonius. The pediments are celebrated for the sculpture which adorned them. These acroteria were probably figures of victory similar to the one which he later executed for the Messenians in Naupactus.

Statues and votive offerings decorated the spaces between the columns.

The interior of the temple was divided into three parts. The pronaos was closed by a grille, and the floor was paved with a mosaic, a fragment of which remains. The cella communicated with the pronaos by a great bronze door. Two tiers of seven Doric columns divided it into three parts, and supported a storey with two galleries. The upper columns held the roof which may have been built of wood. The entrance door served as the sole means of light for the cella.

The famous statue of Zeus, by Phidias, stood at the end of the cella. This majestic bearded figure was seated upon a magnificently ornamented throne supported by a pedestal nearly 10 metres long and nearly 7 metres wide. All trace of the statue is unfortunately lost, save small copies on coins of Elis, which give us a general notion of the pose of this great ivory and gold statue.

To the north of the Temple of Zeus was the inetroum, the temple

HEAD OF A LAPITH WOMAN: PEDIMENT OF THE TEMPLE OF OLYMPIA. (Museum of Olympia.)

of the mother of the gods. It was smaller than the Heræum. It was built on 3 steps and had 6 columns on the east and west and 11 on the north and south. Its cella had piodomos and opisthodomos. The temple was probably built in the 4th century and later underwent a Roman restoration. Behind the place originally occupied by this temple are the remains of a very ancient altar, perhaps dedicated to Rhea-Cybele, mother of the gods. Further, to the west is another altar, and the ruins of the exedra of Herodotus Atticus, a noble Athenian who lived in the second century A.D. The walls were of brick, covered with marble, and decorated with Corinthian pilasters. Between these pilasters were statues in niches.

To the east of the exedra is a slope with steps reaching to the stadium. This is the Terrace of Treasuries. It has been seen that almost all the Greek towns built monuments at Olympia, and the treasuries, or little temples containing offerings, occupied most of the terrace. The ruins of thirteen of these buildings have been brought to light. They were built in the 6th and 5th centuries B.C., on the same plan: a pronaos preceding a cella without a peristyle. These buildings include: the Treasury of Sicyon, built in the 5th century; the Treasury of Carthage, which was rather, according to Pausanias, a Treasury of Syracuse, built by three architects, Pothaios, Megacles and Antiphilos. It dates from the early 5th century. The Treasury of the Selinutines, which recalls, on a small scale, the architecture of the large temples of Selinus; the Treasury of Megara (early 6th century), which was the most richly decorated of all the Olympian treasuries and contained splendid offerings. There remain several Doric columns belonging to it, as well as fragments of a small sculptured pediment, and some bits of painted decoration.

Outside of the Altis, the stadium occupied a hollow, bordered by a bank. The lowest slopes of Mount Kronos formed the northern bank, and the others were artificial. The steps could hold 45,000 people. The track measured 212 metres long by 30 metres wide. Near the northwest corner of the Altis was located the Philippeum, dedicated by Philip of Macedon after his victory at Chæronea (338 B.C.). The building possessed a circular Ionic colonnade about 15 metres in diameter which was raised on 3 steps enclosing a circular cella, with 14 Corinthian half-columns. In the stadium there took place wrestling, foot racing, javelin- and discus-throwing competitions, and the like.

The Hippodrome, situated behind the south bank, was used for chariot races. Later it was destroyed by the river Alpheus. It extended for a length of 770 metres (4 stadia) and a width of 192 metres.

The stadium was separated from the Altis by two large parallel porticoes which bordered the sacred enclosure at the east. Also outside the Altis was the Bouleuterion, or Palace of the Olympic Council, which comprised an Ionic portico, and a central space (14 metres square), in the middle of which may have been a statue of Zeus Horkios, and where the competitors came to take their oath before the judges. From this central space issued two aisles ending in apses (6th and 7th centuries), which contained documents and material. A Roman road, bordered with statues, the bases of which are in position, led to the largest building of Olympia, the Leonidaion, which was probably used to house important guests who were invited to the Olympian games. The building was composed of an atrium surrounded by a peristyle of 44 Doric columns. The rooms were arranged round this peristyle. The building contained some fine statues, among which was discovered a *Head of Aphrodite* (Museum of Olympia).

To the north of the Leonidaion was a group of buildings of which the studio of Phidias occupied, according to Pausanias, the greater part. The studio had the same proportions as the Temple of Zeus, where the master's famous statue was placed. Later, the studio was changed into a Christian church.

The German excavations have uncovered almost all the buildings described by Pausanias. The Museum of Olympia contains objects found in the ruins.

See Pl. 19, Vol. I.

BIBLIOGRAPHY: Curtius, *Adler Dörpfeld Olympia, Ergebnisse der Ausgrabungen,* 1890-1897. 3 vols.—Monceaux and Laloux, *Olympia restauration et histoire*. Paris, 1889. —E. Norman Gardiner, *Olympia, its History and Remains.* Oxford, 1925.

**OLYMPIA (Sculptures of).**—We know that the temple of Zeus was built to its full height in 456, because in that year the crowning acroterium of the east pediment already consisted of the golden shield dedicated by the Spartan allies (the victory statues of Pæonius were not erected until later in the century. Thus the sculptures on the metopes were probably carved before this date. The temple had twelve metopes, arranged in two groups of six—one group at the entrance of the pronaos, the other on the opisthodomos. Of these metopes, three are in the Louvre, and the remainder in the Museum of Olympia. The scenes represented are taken from the life of Heracles.

The pedimental sculptures were discovered by German excavators, and they have been reconstructed in the Museum of Olympia. The subject of the eastern pediment was taken from the Iliad. It represents the preparation for a chariot race, which cost King Oinomaos his life, and gave the victory to Pelops, who married the king's daughter, and inherited the kingdom. According to the description of Pausanias, the pediment must have comprised thirteen figures, and thirteen figures have been found. In the middle is the tall, standing figure of Zeus, his limbs enveloped in drapery, and holding a sceptre in his left hand. To the right is the bearded Oinomaos, wearing a helmet, his left

OLYMPIA: MOSAIC IN THE MUSEUM.

hand leaning on his lance, and a chlamys thrown over his shoulders. Near him is his wife, Sterope. On the other side of Zeus is Pelops, armed with shield and lance, and the graceful and robust figure of the young Hippodamia. These five central figures are standing in erect attitudes, which are not quite free from archaic stiffness. The arrangement of the angle figures and chariots is a matter of controversy. Only the placing of the central figures is certain.

The sculptures on the western pediment represent the fight between the Lapiths and Centaurs at the wedding of Pirithous. Here a series of contorted and struggling figures stands in contrast to the almost lifeless repose of the eastern group, but there is the same strict symmetry of composition, and the same even gradation in the size and height of the figures. The execution of this lively group is unequal, but, on the whole, admirable. The pedimental sculptures were calculated to be very decorative when seen from a distance.

See Pl. 22, Vol. I.

BIBLIOGRAPHY: G. Treu, *Die Bildwerke von Olympia in Stein und*

*Thon*. Berlin, 1897.—V. Laloux and P. Monceaux, *Restauration d'Olympia*. Paris, 1889.—Ernest A. Gardner, *A Handbook of Greek Sculpture*. London, 1923.—E. Norman Gardiner, *Olympia, its History and its Remains*. Oxford, 1925.

**OMODEO.**—See Amadeo.

**ONATAS.**—Greek sculptor. The most famous representative of the sculptors of the school of Ægina. He probably worked between the years 490 and 460 B.C. One of his works, mentioned by Pausanias, was a bronze chariot, commemorating at Olympia a victory of Hieron of Syracuse. Among other works by Onatas, Pausanias also mentions a *Demeter*, and votive statues.

**ONESIMOS.**—See Greece (Vases).

**OOST (Van)**—Family of Flemish painters, of which the best known is Jacob Van Oost. Four other painters of this name worked in Flanders in the 17th century. Jacob the Younger (1639-1713) son of Jacob Van Oost, lived chiefly in Lille, where most of his works are to be seen.

**— (Jacob Van).**—Flemish painter, 1601-1671. Worked in Bruges. He spent several years in Rome copying the works of Carracci, and was influenced by Rubens. His paintings are characterised by vigorous realism, and warm colour. He executed a great many portraits and religious pictures. Among the best may be mentioned: *Ecclesiastic Dictating an Epistle* (Bruges), and *Philosopher Meditating* (Bruges, Hospital of St. John).

**OPIE (John).**—English painter, 1761-1807. John Opie began his career as a painter of historical and "genre" scenes. He exhibited at the Royal Academy, for the first time, in 1782; but it was really not until 1786 that he became known with three pictures: the *Assassination of James I of Scotland, Sleeping Nymph*, and *Cupid Stealing a Kiss*. In 1787, he won a new success with the *Murder of David Rizzio*, and entered the Academy. He was also an able portrait painter. From 1790 he gave himself up entirely to this branch of art, and he became very successful. Among his best works may be mentioned: *Portrait of the Actor, William Siddons* (National Gallery), *Self-portrait* (Royal Academy), and *David Rizzio* (Guildhall).

Bibliography: A. Earland, *John Opie and his Circle*. London, 1912.

**OPISTHODOMOS.**—See Greece (Architecture).

**OPPENORD (Gilles Marie).**—French architect and decorator, 1672-1742. Like his rivals, Robert de Cotte and Germain Boffrand, he was a pupil of Mansart. He spent eight years in Rome, where he acquired a taste for Borromini's fantastic buildings. On his return to France, he divested the French style of the heaviness which it had derived from the "grand siècle," and (without, however, breaking the rules of symmetry established by Charles Le Brun) replaced them by complicated arrangement of graceful and elegant lines. His art heralded the Rococo. In 1704, he built the high-altar of the Church of Saint-Germain-des-Près and that of Saint Sulpice. Among his other works are the little château of Montmorency, and the enlargement of the house of Pierre Crozat (Rue de Richelieu, Paris).

Bibliography: L. Dimier, *Les peintres français du XVIII<sup>e</sup> siècle*. Vol. I (1928).

**ORANGE (Vaucluse).**—The town of Orange, which flourished under Roman rule, has kept from that period monuments of which the most remarkable is the *Theatre*. It is composed of a façade of 103 metres in length, and 36 metres in height. The wall, which is 4 metres thick, is pierced with three doors, and decorated with a blind arcade, and a cornice. The theatre could seat 40,000 spectators. The *Arch of Triumph* has three openings. The façades (except the western one) have retained their carvings. It was probably erected under Tiberius.

See Pl. 30, Vol. I.

Bibliography: Roger Peyre, *Nîmes, Arles et Orange*, Collection des villes d'art célèbres.

**ORANS.**—See Early Christian Art (Painting).

**ORCAGNA (Andrea di Cione).**—Florentine painter, sculptor, mosaicist and architect, one of the most influential masters of the post-Giottesque period.

Orcagna is mentioned in a document discovered by Romohr as "Andrea di Cione Arcagnuolo." In 1343 he matriculated in the guild of Medici e Speziali; and in 1347 his name occurs on a list of the five best painters of Florence, one of whom was to be chosen to paint an altarpiece for S. Giovanni fuorcivitas in Pistoia. The commission was given to Taddeo Gaddi. In 1352, Orcagna received payment for a *Madonna*; in 1354 and 1356, he vouches for artists who are entering the corporation of sculptors; in 1355 he is capomaestro of Or San Michele; and in 1356 he makes a plan for the façade of the Duomo, which is accepted, and is a member of a committee for its interior decoration. In 1357 the altarpiece for the Strozzi Chapel in Sta. Maria Novella, a *Christ Enthroned with Saints*, Orcagna's only authenticated extant painting, is ordered by Tommaso di Rossello Strozzi. (The predella is not by Orcagna but by a Daddesque painter.) The same year finds him still busy with the Duomo; and in 1358 he is occupied on the sculptured tabernacle for Or San Michele (extant) but leaves this work to go to Orvieto for five years to direct the construction of the Cathedral. Later in 1358 he is back in Florence, at work on the tabernacle, and the next year he goes again to Orvieto, accompanied by his brother Matteo, returns to Florence to complete the tabernacle, and departs for Orvieto again. However when in 1360 he again leaves Orvieto for Florence he is forced to resign the Orvieto commission, with which his brother is entrusted in his stead and which ocupies him (Matteo) until 1367. In 1361, Orcagna visits Orvieto once more to finish a mosaic, which is approved in this year. In 1364, 1366, and 1367 he is working on the construction of the Cathedral of Florence, and in 1368 is commissioned to execute a *St. Matthew* for one of the pillars of Or San Michele, which, owing to his ill-health, was finished by Jacopo, his brother. The exact date of Orcagna's death is not known, but took place before 1376.

Numerous works have been attributed to Orcagna, both in early literature, by Ghiberti, Vasari, and so forth, and in later critical literature.

Bibliography: Vasari-Milanesi,—G. Orsini, *Vita di Andrea Orcagna* (Vasari), 1914.—Milanesi, *Nuovi documenti*.—Baldinucci.—K. Frey, *Loggia dei Lanzi*, p. 101.—L. Luzi, *Il Duomo di Orvieto*. Florence, 1860.—L. Fumi, *Il Duomo di Orvieto e i suoi restauri*. Rome, 1891.—Suida, *Florentinische Maler*, etc., p. 4.—Sirén, *Giotto and Some of His Followers*.

**ORCHARDSON (Sir William Quiller).**—Scottish painter (1835-1910), one of the most distinguished representatives of the British School of his generation, frequently expressing himself in a vein of social or historical anecdote (*Her Mother's Voice*, 1888, *Napoleon on Board the "Bellerophon,"* 1880, both in the National Gallery, Millbank). Elected A.R.A. 1868, R.A., 1877.

Bibliography: Hilda O. Gray, *The Life of Sir William Quiller Orchardson*. London, 1930.

**ORLEY (Bernard Van).**—Flemish painter, of Brussels. Born in Brussels about 1493, of noble family. He visited Italy about 1514 and about 1526. He died in 1542. He painted a portrait of Charles V, and of several princes and princesses, all of which have disappeared. The only existing portrait by Bernard Van Orley is that of Dr. Zelles (1519, Brussels Gallery). His work shows diverse influences, caused by the study of the various schools of Antwerp, Haarlem, Florence, and especially of Michelangelo and Raphael. He is thus singularly varied. His drawing is careful. His figures are supple, elegant and animated.

Orley (van): Portrait of Dr. Zelles. (Museum of Brussels.)

In 1515, he painted a triptych, the *Entry of Christ into Jerusalem*, one of the wings of which is in Leningrad. In 1518, he painted the *Adoration of the Trinity by all the Saints*, for Notre Dame of Lübeck. In 1521, he executed the *Trials of Job* for Margaret of Austria, who offered it to Count Antoine de Lalaing. Here Michelangelo's influence was strongly felt in the bold, violent attitudes, sometimes exaggerated. Michelangelo's influence is seen again in Van Orley's chief work, the *Last Judgment* and the *Seven Works of Mercy* (Antwerp Gallery).

Besides altarpieces and portraits, Bernard Van Orley designed a great many cartoons for tapestries, and stained glass windows. Among others, are the *Life of Abraham* (Hampton Court), the *Battle of Pavia* (Naples), and, finest of the three, *Hunting Scenes* (Paris), which have charming landscapes of the environs of Brussels.

Bibliography: A. Wauters, *Bernard Van Orley*. Paris, 1893.

**OROZCO (José Clemente).**—Contemporary Mexican painter. He was born in Zapotlan in the state of Jalisco 23d November 1883, the descendant of early Spanish settlers. In 1900 he graduated from the National Agricultural School of Mexico and spent the next four years at the National University, specialising in mathematics and also studying drawing in the School of Fine Arts of the University. He was connected with the architect Carlos Herrera for a time and then in 1909 he decided to become a painter. He studied painting until 1915 and then two years later came to the United States, where he stayed in California, working and improving his technique. Then about 1922 he returned to Mexico and became one of the leaders of the Syndicate of Painters and Sculptors which was interested in reviving the old art of murals and fresco painting under the patronage of the Mexican government, through the agency of the Ministry of Education. Orozco did frescoes in the Casa de los Azulejos, the National Preparatory School in Mexico, the Art School of Orizaba, and in the United States at Pomona College in Claremont, California, and the New School for Social Research in New York City. His most recent commission was for a series of mural panels in the Baker Library at Dartmouth College, Hanover, New Hampshire, in which he traced the history of America by the *Coming of Quetzalcoatl*, the *Return of Quetzalcoatl*, and *Modern Industrial Man*. These panels testify to his early training in architecture by their well-balanced compositions logically tied together to form the story, each episode made vivid by the vigorous personalities depicted and the strong colours used to emphasise the importance of the human beings as contrasted with the necessary background elements. The fact remains that Orozco is one of the most important mural painters in Mexico and one who has done much to revive the interest in that craft on the American continent.

Bibliography: Albert I. Dickerson, *The Orozco Frescoes at Dartmouth*, 1934.—*José Clemente Orozco*, ed. by the Palace of Fine Arts, Mexico, 1934.—Alma Reed, *José Clemente Orozco*, 1932.—Hans Tietze, *José Clemente Orozco, Als Zeichner*, 1933.

**ORPEN (Sir William).**—Irish painter (1878-1931). He was born in Stillorgan (County Dublin), 27th November 1878. Deciding to become a painter he enrolled in the Metropolitan School of Art in Dublin. From 1897 to 1899 he studied at the Slade School in London. In 1910 he became an associate of the Royal Academy and in 1919 he was elected R.A. Sir William was the favourite

# MANTEGNA

*THE schools of painting of northern Italy in the fifteenth century cannot easily be brought together into a united whole. Each city gave birth to a family of painters: Verona, Ferrara, Bologna, Parma. But a master, the Paduan Mantegna, dominates all these schools in the second half of the fifteenth century. In his work, one may observe a rigorous progression toward a picturesque naturalism which, just as at Florence, depends upon science, perspective and anatomy; the art of Mantegna manifests this intellectualism, which always distinguishes Italian naturalism from that of the northern masters; thought always dominates observation.*

PISANELLO: ST. GEORGE, LIBERATOR OF TREBIZOND. SANT'ANASTASIA, VERONA. *(Photo by Anderson.)*

SQUARCIONE (ATTRIBUTED TO): MADONNA AND CHILD. BERLIN. *(Photo by Hanfstaengl.)*

PISANELLO: THE VISION OF ST. EUSTACE. NATIONAL GALLERY, LONDON. *(Photo by Hachette.)*

## Pisanello

NORTHERN ITALY is brought into relationship with Germanic Europe by way of the Alps. The northern schools likewise appear allied to the masters of France, Flanders and Germany. Thus Genoa, Piedmont, Milan, Verona and Venice welcomed painters on their arrival in Italy and the art of these cities felt the effect of these importations. Pisanello of Verona often reminds us of the Gothic miniaturists.

MANTEGNA: ST. SEBASTIAN. LOUVRE. *(Photo by Hachette.)*

MANTEGNA: CALVARY. LOUVRE. *(Photo by Hachette.)*

MANTEGNA: PARNASSUS. LOUVRE. *(Photo by Hachette.)*

MANTEGNA: ST. JAMES ON HIS WAY TO EXECUTION. EREMITANI, PADUA. *(Photo by Alinari.)*

## Mantegna

THIS Paduan painter who worked particularly at Mantua is well represented at the Louvre where one may observe his chief preoccupations, and the dependence of his imagination upon the study of anatomy, perspective and archæology. In the *Parnassus*, done toward the end of his life, a commission from Isabella d'Este, his severe genius is relaxed and his usual harshness softened.

COSIMO TURA: ST. GEORGE OVERCOMING THE DRAGON. FERRARA. *(Photo by Anderson.)*

L. COSTA: ST. CECILIA GIVING ALMS TO THE POOR. BOLOGNA. *(Photo by Anderson.)*

FRANCESCO COSSA: THE TRIUMPH OF MINERVA. FERRARA. *(Photo by Anderson.)*

FRANCIA: ADORATION OF THE SHEPHERDS. BOLOGNA. *(Photo by Alinari.)*

## Ferrara and Bologna

IN THESE two cities, the painters seem to have willingly accepted the influence of Mantegna. At Ferrara, Cosimo Tura and Francesco Cossa owe him their vigorous drawing. At Bologna, the harshness of the Paduan style is softened in the compositions of Lorenzo Costa and Francia. The latter already belongs to the modern age. Bologna is, from his time, predestined to become the centre of eclecticism and to display in a composite art the influences of Venice and of Florence.

# FROM BELLINI TO TITIAN

*It is at the beginning of the sixteenth century that the change in Venetian painting is observed which brings us from the primitive to the modern style. This was the result of a normal evolution which in all the schools of Europe led from sharp precision and dryness of treatment to more flexible drawing and the play of light and shade. At Florence, this transformation appears to be the work of Leonardo da Vinci. At Venice, it seems a natural consequence of the use of oil painting.*

GIOVANNI BELLINI: MADONNA OF THE FRARI. VENICE.
*(Photo by Anderson.)*

GIOVANNI BELLINI: PIETÀ. MUSEUM, MILAN.
*(Photo by Anderson.)*

GIOVANNI BELLINI: ALLEGORY OF FORTUNE. VENICE.
*(Photo by Anderson.)*

## Giovanni Bellini

This painter lived a long and fruitful existence. He began as a primitive; he learned a great deal from his brother-in-law, Mantegna, whose exact drawing and whose brittle draperies he imitated. But at Venice he was a painter with vivid and delicate colours; in his paintings Byzantine madonnas are transformed into charming and dreamy virgins. Sometimes he attains Christian pathos; elsewhere he is gracious and pagan. In his workshop the entire Venetian school which is to blossom in the sixteenth century is developed.

GENTILE BELLINI: ST. MARK PREACHING AT ALEXANDRIA. MILAN.
*(Photo by Anderson.)*

GENTILE BELLINI: THE MIRACLE OF THE HOLY CROSS. VENICE.
*(Photo by Anderson.)*

## Gentile Bellini

Gentile Bellini was the brother of Giovanni. They were the sons of Jacopo Bellini of whose work little is known. Gentile appears to have been a facile painter and a brilliant narrator in the manner of Carpaccio; his compositions reveal the Venice of his day. The decorations and even sometimes the actors in the scenes may be recognised. Even when he wishes to suggest scenes abroad, he still portrays vistas in his own city.

GIORGIONE: THE TEMPEST. VENICE.
*(Photo by Anderson.)*

TITIAN: CONCERT CHAMPÊTRE. LOUVRE.
*(Photo by Hachette.)*

GIORGIONE: MADONNA. CASTELFRANCO.
*(Photo by Mayer.)*

## Giorgione and Titian

It is to Giorgione, according to Vasari, that one must attribute the glory of having transformed the Venetian school at the beginning of the sixteenth century. Vasari, who knew Venice only slightly, appears to have greatly exaggerated his role. His pictures are not those of a revolutionary. Some, admired as his, must be rightfully restored to their true authors.

# LEONARDO DA VINCI

*LEONARDO DA VINCI is the most representative genius of the Renaissance, primarily because of the universality of his curiosity. He was a savant as well as an artist; he studied the secrets of nature before reorganising it in its reality. And he even did not consider his skill as a painter as the first of his talents. This attitude of a spirit at the same time turned toward knowledge and creation very well characterises the Italian Renaissance in its entirety. In the history of art and of thought, Leonardo is the first of the moderns because he established his art upon the knowledge of nature and not upon tradition.*

DA VINCI: THE VIRGIN OF THE ROCKS. LOUVRE.
*(Photo by Hachette.)*

DA VINCI: ST. JOHN THE BAPTIST. LOUVRE.
*(Photo by Hachette.)*

DA VINCI: LA GIOCONDA. LOUVRE.
*(Photo by Hachette.)*

DA VINCI: ST. ANNE. LOUVRE.
*(Photo by Hachette.)*

DA VINCI: THE LAST SUPPER (MILAN). AFTER THE ENGRAVING BY RAPHAEL MORGHEN.

LEONARDO DA VINCI renewed the Florentine style and transformed the visual habits, replacing the dry and linear style with the softened manner—the *sfumato*; thus he infinitely stretched the possibilities of refinement in modelling, and he introduced into his painting a new element, that of atmosphere. Finally, thanks to his distinctive drawing, he was able to render the finest expressions of the countenance; his paintings seem to attain the purpose that he proposed for such a long time, which was to show the life of the soul in the movements of the body, and particularly the play of faces. The famous composition of the *Last Supper* is a drama in which the painter has introduced as much of psychology as plastic language can express.

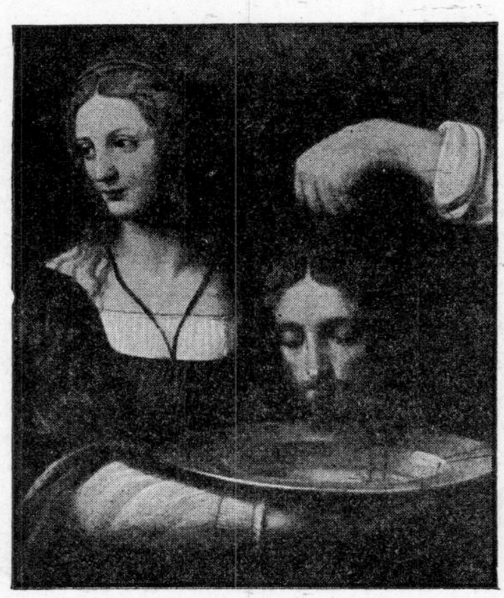

LUINI: SALOME. LOUVRE.
*(Photo by Hachette.)*

LUINI: THE BATHERS. MILAN.
*(Photo by Brogi.)*

SODOMA: EVE, SIENA. ST. SEBASTIAN. UFFIZI, FLORENCE.
*(Photos by Alinari and Anderson.)*

## The Followers of da Vinci

THE Florentine master lived at Milan for a long time, in which city he gathered about him many students. His manner of painting with large caressing shadows and with delicate modelling was suitable to the indolent Lombard beauty. Among those painters who have shown the most individuality while continuing his style, one must reckon Luini and Sodoma.

# MICHELANGELO

*Michelangelo is a sculptor of marble who was forced by circumstances to become a painter of frescoes. But in his stone statues, as in his paintings in the Sistine Chapel, he represented only the human body, its suppleness and its force. The picturesqueness of nature, of costumes, light and colour, held no interest for him; he retained from reality only the muscular play of great figures thrilling with effort or distorted by despair. His genius, of an indomitable strength, twisted the human form into attitudes which infinitely go beyond the possibilities of a body posed in a studio. Michelangelo is the last word in Florentine science.*

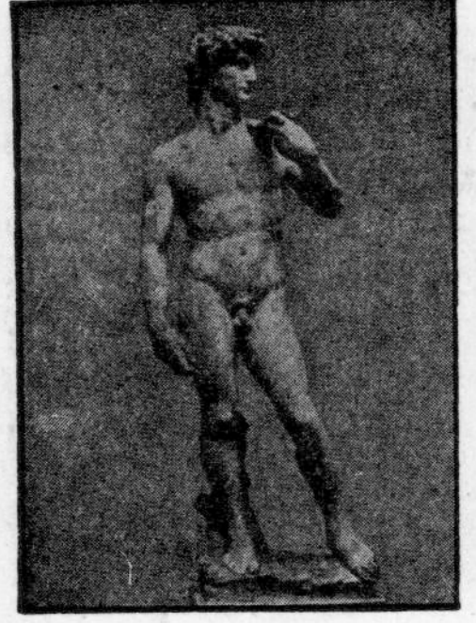

DAVID. ACADEMY, FLORENCE.

PIETÀ. ST. PETER'S, ROME.

BACCHUS. NATIONAL MUS., FLORENCE.

JEREMIAH. SISTINE CHAPEL, ROME.

LIBYAN SIBYL. SISTINE CHAPEL, ROME.

SLAVE. LOUVRE.

MOSES. ROME.

SLAVE. LOUVRE.

CREATION OF ADAM. SISTINE CHAPEL, ROME.

After the first works which still recall the fifteenth century, and the antique influence, the *Slaves* in the Louvre destined for the tomb of Julius II indicate the two themes dear to Michelangelo, the struggling body and the resigned; Moses is one of the most extraordinary figures in the history of sculpture.

Upon the Sistine ceiling, Michelangelo employed his sublime drawing to narrate the first verses of Genesis and to fix in unforgettable attitudes the meditations of Prophets and of Sibyls. Floating through the elements He has just created, Jehovah transfers the spark of life into the marvellous body of Adam.

TOMBS OF GIULIANO AND LORENZO DE' MEDICI. FLORENCE.

NUDE FIGURE. SISTINE CHAPEL, ROME.

NUDE FIGURE. SISTINE CHAPEL, ROME.

BENVENUTO CELLINI: PERSEUS. FLORENCE.

MICHELANGELO: PIETÀ. DUOMO, FLORENCE.

GIOVANNI DA BOLOGNA: MERCURY.

LAST JUDGMENT (DETAILS). SISTINE CHAPEL, ROME.

The tombs of the Medicis under two figures of Meditation and Action show us great bodies crushed by despair or trembling with rage. It is the vehement soul of the artist breathes life into these tormented figures. Michelangelo's followers were able only to imitate his plastic beauty.

In his paintings in the Sistine Chapel, Michelangelo was compelled to show the bodies in attitudes at the same time magnificent and yet impossible. He was thus compelled to invent foreshortenings of an unforeseen violence, which gave to his elect as well as to his damned the same passionate agitation.

portraitist of the English social world as well as of the big American financiers. With a catholic eye for paintable detail he caught the significant features of his sitters, although his portraits show little comprehension of the inner meaning of his subjects. The paintings of men, which are more penetrating than those of women, render the dignity of rank or office of the people portrayed. Among his non-British sitters are President Wilson, Otto Kahn, Paul D. Cravath, the Danforths and other leading industrialists. His early canvases show a decided influence of old Dutch genre paintings. Orpen uses their setting of interiors, not omitting any of the incidental paraphernalia, and focussing artificial light on the figures or permitting rays of sunlight to pass through the open windows. His next phase is done in the traditional Sargent and Raeburn manner. Maybe the most personal and appealing examples of his productivity are the Irish folk tales such as *Irish Wedding*, which show a sense of humour and fine value pattern, and his self-portraits *Myself and Venus*, and *Leading the Life in the West*. His technique has always been commendable for its even, clean-cut surface and the crisp rendering of detail. Orpen has also done battle pieces and landscapes. His paintings may be seen in the museums of Belfast, Durban, Oxford, London, Liverpool, Paris, New York, Pittsburgh and Worcester. He is the author of: *An Onlooker in France*, 1917-1919, *Stories of Old Ireland and Myself*, 1924. He died 29th September 1931.

Bibliography: *Sir William Orpen*, in *Contemporary British Art* (ed. by Albert Rutherston, 1923).—Edited by Sir William Orpen, *The Outline of Art*, 2 Vols., 1923.

**ORRENTE (Pedro).**—Spanish painter. About 1570-1644. When he was very young Orrente was sent to Toledo, where he probably received lessons from El Greco. In Valencia, he trained able pupils, such as Pablo Poutons and Esteban March. The Prado Gallery possesses seven works by this artist, among them *The Adoration of the Shepherds*, the *Crucifixion*, *Christ Appearing to the Magdalen*, and the *Family of Abraham*.

**OR SAN MICHELE.**—See Florence.

**ORVIETO (Italy).**—Orvieto is a little town built on the site of Volsini, an old Etruscan town which the Romans pillaged and destroyed in 280 B.C. From this period there remains an Etruscan necropolis, the tombs of which date from the 5th century B.C. They contained painted Grecian vases and pottery (in the Museum).

The Cathedral of Orvieto is a magnificent Gothic building begun before 1285 in honour of the miracle of Bolsena and of the institution, by Urban IV, of Corpus Christi. Arnolfo di Cambio may have made the plans for it. The Cathedral is built in black basalt and grey limestone, alternating in horizontal stripes. The most famous artists of the day worked on it. Lorenzo Maitani, the Sienese architect, began the façade, which is decorated with three gables (which were finished in the 16th century), and with a profusion of mosaics and carvings. The pillars are decorated with fine bas-reliefs. The interior possesses frescoes by Gentile da Fabriano, Pietro di Paccio, and, above all, the mural paintings of the Cappella Nuova. These were begun in 1447 by Fra Angelico da Fiesole and Benozzo Gozzoli, his pupil, who painted, on the ceiling *Christ Judging the World*, and some figures of prophets. They were finished, from 1499 to 1502, by Luca Signorelli, who also painted the *Downfall of Antichrist*, the *Resurrection*, and the *Last Judgment*. In another chapel is a precious shrine of gilded silver, in the form of the Cathedral façade. It is the work of Ugolino di Maestro Vieri. The *Miracle of Bolsena* is in translucent enamels.

**OSTADE (Adriaen Van).**—Dutch painter and graver, 1610-1685. Born in Haarlem, where he frequented Frans Hals' studio and where he spent most of his life. Like a true Dutchman, Ostade painted what he saw around him—his family, the townsfolk in their spic-and-span houses, peasants, and many "genre" scenes, with people laughing, drinking, smoking and playing music. One of the greatest masters of light and shade effects, he evoked a supreme harmony of hues and tonalities. His color is always pure and scintillating, even in his pinks and lavenders. He much admired Rembrandt, and was influenced by him.

Among his numerous works may be mentioned, at The Hague: *Peasants in an Inn, The Wandering Violinist Before a House* (1673). The Louvre possesses, among others, *Fishmarket*, a *Man Drinking*, the *Painter's Family*, and the *Schoolmaster* (1662). Many trades provided subjects for the painter; these are: the *Cobbler*, the *Knife-Grinder*, the *Weaver*, etc.

**— (Izaack Van).**—Dutch painter of Haarlem, 1621-1649. Brother of Adriaen, whose pupil he was. He began by painting tavern scenes, but his most successful paintings are his winter landscapes, showing Dutch villages under a mantle of snow, with frozen canals, and skaters. Most of the European galleries—notably, the National Gallery—possess pictures by Izaack Van Ostade.

Bibliography: A. Rosenberg, *Adrian und Izaack Van Ostade*. Leipzig, 1909.—M. Van der Wiele, *Les frères Van Ostade. Paris*, 1893.—Hofstede de Groot, *Catalogue of Dutch Painters*. Vol. III.

**ÖSTBERG (Ragnor).**—Contemporary Swedish architect, born 1866. He is best known for the City Hall, Stockholm, an attempt to compromise modern and classical architecture, as may be seen in the attenuated shafts which form a colonnade along the front.

**OSTIA (Italy).**—Now a small, unimportant town, Ostia was formerly a large trading port. The port and the town have lost their prosperity. Ostia possesses numerous antique ruins—tombs, a Roman gateway, a theatre (perhaps built under Agrippa), a little sanctuary of Mithra, a temple (the cella of which is still in a good state of preservation), and a Sanctuary of the Magna Mater, with colonnades. A little further on, where the Tiber turns out of its old course, are the ruins of old warehouses. One of them contains great earthenware jars, in which wine and oil were kept. Then there is a fine house, decorated with columns, and containing baths, and an altar.

**OSUNA (Bas-reliefs of).**—In the town of Osuna, the ancient Urso or Gemina Urbanorum of the Romans, some curious bas-reliefs, which possibly date from the 5th century B.C. have been discovered. The Louvre possesses a *Warrior of Osuna*, who is taking cover behind a huge shield, and preparing to strike with his sword. This figure must be the work of a native sculptor, under Greco-Phœnician influence.

**OTIS (Bass).**—American painter and engraver (1784-1861), chiefly notable as having been the person to introduce the technique of lithography into the United States (1819).

**OTTAVIANO NELLI.** — See Nelli.

**OTTOMAN ART.**—See Moslem Art.

**OUDRY (Jean Baptiste).**—French painter, 1686-1755. Son of a picture dealer, he was, first, the pupil of his father, then of a painter of the name of Serre; and, finally, of Largillière. He became a sufficiently able portrait painter to be commissioned to paint Peter the Great, when he visited Paris in 1717. Largillière often set his pupil to paint landscapes, animals, and still-life groups, and he observed, even in these secondary works, much sensitiveness and a very subtle feeling for light. "Get along!" exclaimed his master one day, "you will never be anything but a painter of hounds!" And, indeed, Oudry became chiefly a painter of hunting scenes.

Oudry: Louis XV hunting. (Tapestry.)

Louis XV made him recorder of the scenes of his great hunts, just as Desportes had been to Louis XIV.

Oudry had a genuine talent for landscape—not in the Poussin tradition, but inspired by his admiration for Berchem.

After being head of the Gobelins factory, he became director of that of Beauvais.

Bibliography: Jean Locquin, *Catalogue raisonné de l'œuvre de J. B. Oudry*. 1912.

**OUWATER (Albert Van).**—Dutch painter, probably born at Ouwater, near Haarlem. Contemporary of Jan van Eyck. He worked in Haarlem about 1430 to 1460, and was probably the master of Geertgen van Sint Jans. He painted with oils and is known for his accurate draughtsmanship, and for rendering short, stubby hands. The pictures we have by him are the *Resurrection of Lazarus* (Berlin), and the altar in the St. Baro Church (Haarlem).

**OVERBECK (Friedrich).**—German painter, 1789-1869. He belonged to the group known as the "Nazarenes." (See.) In 1810, Overbeck broke with the Academy of Vienna, and went to Rome. There he met two painters, the brothers Franz and Johannes Riepenhausen, who had recently been converted to Roman Catholicism, and who had passed through a phase of neo-classicism to the devotion of Early Christian art. Overbeck also became a Catholic, and lived a life of work and meditation in an old monastery on the Pincio. Schlegel exhorted the artist to be, like the "primitives," "faithful in heart, meditative, innocent, and even a little inexperienced in the technique of his art." Owing to his scruples, Overbeck refused, all his life, to work from the living model. His work, which is inspired, lacks solid groundwork, and is often very poor in drawing and colour. Although his earliest works show exceptional qualities of execution, he yet, under the influence of the Quattrocento masters, lapsed into a very narrow formalism. The composition of his *Triumph of Religion in the Arts* (1846), painted for the Städel Institute of Frankfort, is borrowed partly from the *Disputà del Sacramento* and partly from the *School of Athens*. His *Holy Family* (1825, Munich) is inspired entirely by Raphael. Other paintings recall Perugino.

Overbeck's best work is undoubtedly to be found among his drawings, and his portraits, some of which show what expressive character he could attain when he observed nature faithfully.

He had a share in the fresco decoration of the Casa Bartholdi, and the chief work is certainly Overbeck's representation of *Joseph Sold by His Brothers* (now in the National Gallery of Berlin). He also decorated the Villa Massima, painting compositions inspired by Dante, Tasso and Ariosto.

Bibliography: Atkinson, *Overbeck*, 1882.—Howitt, *F. Overbeck, sein werk u. s. Schaffen*, 1886.

**OVIEDO, SPAIN (Cathedral of).**—The foundation of the existing Gothic building was not laid until 1388, on the site of the church erected by Froila I, and rebuilt in 830 by Alonso II. The Bishop Mendoza consecrated the tower in 1528. The decoration was not completed until the end of the 17th century. The tower, with its well-arranged ornaments and four elegant turrets, is one of the finest in Spain.

**OXFORD (England).** — Oxford was several times burned down—so entirely, by the Normans, in the 11th century, that no buildings survive previous to that date. *St. Peter's in the East*, one of the oldest churches (12th century), is fortified. The two apsidal turrets probably served as watch-towers. *St. Aldate* dates from 1318 (enlarged in

Oxford: Interior of the Cathedral.

the 19th century), and has a graceful belfry. The Church of *St. Mary Magdalen* (14th century) is adorned with an open gallery. *St. Michael and All Angels* is in the Saxon style, with an old 4th century tower (restored in the 19th century). But the churches are of less interest than the famous Oxford colleges. Among the colleges, those which possess the finest buildings are: *Merton College,* which was founded in 1270 by Walter of Merton. His muniment room is one of the oldest parts of the college. The chapel, finished about 1300, is a charming Gothic building, and contains fine stained glass dating from 1283. The library is very curious, and retains its old wooden ceiling, its 16th century German glass, and its desks to which, formerly, manuscripts were chained. *New College,* built in 1386, is very imposing. The cloisters with their wooden ceiling, the chapel (with its massive flying buttresses and fine stained glass windows), and the quadrangles form a pleasing "ensemble." *Magdalen College,* founded in 1456, is formed of four quadrangles, surmounted by three towers. The large tower dominates the town. *Christ Church,* the largest of the Oxford colleges, dates from 1532. The gateway of the large quadrangle is surmounted by a tower (the "Tom Tower"). Then a magnificent hall, with a timbered roof, carved with armorial bearings, is preceded by a staircase (17th century), the fan vaulting of which is supported by a single pillar. The Chapel of Christ Church is the old Cathedral of St. Frideswyde (12th and 13th centuries).

Among many other interesting buildings may be mentioned: *Balliol College* (17th century Gothic); *St. John's College* (interesting 17th century façade); *Jesus College* (17th century Gothic). The *Bodleian Library* has a fine courtyard, and a square tower in four storeys. The *Sheldonian Theatre,* surrounded by busts, and surmounted by a dome, was built on the plan of the theatre of Marcellus in Rome (1664-1669).

See Pl. 50, Vol. I.

Bibliography: R. T. Blomfield, *History of Renaissance Architecture in England.* London, 1897.—E. S. Prior, *Medieval Architecture in England.* Cambridge, 1922.

# P

**PAÁL (László, or Ladislas).**—Hungarian landscape painter, 1846-1879. He studied in Vienna, Munich and Düsseldorf and travelled in Holland. In 1872 he joined the Barbizon painters and became a follower of Rousseau and Diaz. Most of his paintings are forest scenes, the transparent dusk being interrupted by a burst of light through the foliage. A touch of melancholy may be felt in many of his works,—the foreboding note of his illness which brought him to an insane asylum, where he also died. He was the leader of the romantic realists in Hungary. *Woods of Fontainebleau* (Budapest) is a characteristic work.

Bibliography: Genthon, *Uj Magyar Festömüvészet Története,* 1935. —Lázár, *Ladislas de Paál, un peintre hongrois de l'école de Barbizon,* 1904.

**PACCHIA (Girolamo del).**—School of Siena, 1477-1535. Pupil of Fungai, influenced by Raphael, Signorelli and the Florentines.

**PACCHIAROTTO (Giacomo).**—Sienese painter, 1474-1540. Pupil of Matteo di Giovanni.

**PACHECO (Francisco).**—Spanish painter and writer. Baptized on March 11th, 1564, at Sanlucár de Barameda; died at Seville in 1654. In 1611 he travelled to Toledo (where he visited El Greco) and to Madrid. He was named "Pintor Real" in 1619. Four years later he accompanied his son-in-law Velázquez to Madrid and remained in the capital until 1625. There he made friendship with Vicente Carducho. On the 23rd of April, 1618, Pacheco married his daughter to Velázquez, whose genius he had the discernment to see. The master's studio was a rendezvous for all the finest spirits of Seville. Quevedo and Cervantes visited Pacheco. Artists, poets, writers and orators held it an honor to be received in that "golden prison of art", as Palomino called it. Pacheco left a valuable collection of portrait drawings of the celebrities of his own time in his unfinished manuscript entitled *Libro de Descripción de verdaderos Retratos de ilustres e memorables Varones* (Coll. D. José Lázaro, Madrid). Besides the portrait drawings, the manuscript also contains biographical notices. His book *El Arte de la Pintura, su Antiguedad y Grandeza* appeared in 1649 at Seville. His philosophy of art leaves nothing to the inspiration of the painter, trying to impose orthodox formulae for all sacred subjects. "Art," wrote Palomino, "has no other mission than to inspire men with piety, and to lead them to God." This theologian of painting tried to regulate everything, regarding the poses, expressions, and costumes, belonging to persons of sacred history. In 1618, the Inquisition appointed him to supervise the maintenance of orthodoxy and decency in paintings.

His early works are rather dry as for instance the two scenes from the *Life of St. Peter Nolasco* (1601, 1602) in the Seville Museum. One of his most important paintings is that of *St. Sebastian* in the Church of Alcalá de Guadeira (1616)—not only so because of its chiaroscuro but also on account of the inherent realism manifest in conception as well as in rendering. (For instance St. Irene is seen brushing off, with her olive branch, the flies which otherwise would molest the Saint resting in his bed). In his representations of the *Immaculate Virgin* the introduction of landscapes, city-views and portraits is often very felicitous in effect. (For instance: *Purisma* with Miguel Cid in Seville Cathedral). His best, however, he produced in portraiture. (Portrait of a Caballero de Santiago, Coll. Cook, Richmond; 1625).—(A. L. Mayer, passim).

Bibliography: J. M. Asensio, *El libro de descripción de verdaderos retratos de ilustres varones . . . .* Seville, 1870.—Id., *Francisco Pacheco.* Seville, 1886.—C. Cruzada Villaamil, Re-edition of Pacheco's *Arte de la Pintura,* etc., 2 vs. Madrid, 1866.—A. L. Mayer, *Die Sevillaner Malerschule,* 1911.—Id., *Gesch. der span. Malerei;* 2nd ed., 1922.—Ibid. in Thieme-Becker, Vol. XXVI, 1932. Art. *Pacheco, Francisco.—Enc. un. il. europ. am.* Barcelona (Espasa); Vol. XC, 1920; Art. *Pacheco del Rio,* Francisco.—*Archivo Esp. Art y Arqueol.,* 1926; 1928; 1929.

**PACHER (Michael).** — German painter and sculptor, of the 15th century (about 1435-1498), of the Tyrolese school. He was both a painter and a sculptor, though some critics have attributed the carvings of his altarpieces to Veit Stoss. His chief work is the *Altarpiece of St. Wolfgang* (Austria, 1481), with scenes from the life of Christ, and the Virgin, and the death of the Virgin. On the outside of the wings is the legend of St. Wolfgang. His affinities to the circle of Bellini, Donatello and Mantegna, as seen in this work, prove the supposition that he worked in Northern Italy. About 1490, he painted the *Altarpiece* for the church in Salzburg.

In all these works, Pacher introduced the types and attitudes of the Northern Gothic painters; but his composition is more learned, and his essays at perspective often successful. The height of altar-painting in the northern schools was achieved by him.

See Pl. 3, Vol. II.

Bibliography: Allesch, *M. Pacher,* 1931.—Hempel, *M. Pacher,* 1931.—Wolff, *Michael Pacher.* Berlin, 1910.

**PACINO di BONAGUIDA.**—Florentine painter, contemporary of Giotto, but representing a fundamentally different stylistic tendency.

Pacino is mentioned in the Archivio dei Contratti in 1303 (Milanesi, *Nuovi documenti,* 1901). The signed polyptych in the Academy, Florence is probably of 1315, not later than 1330. He matriculated in the Arte de' Medici Speziali e Merciai in the period between 1320 and 1339 (Frey, *Loggia,* 331).

His works are as follows: Florence, Academy, *Tree of Life,* and polyptych, *Crucifixion and Four Saints;* Florence, Fondazione Horne, *Madonna and Child and Two Saints;* Florence, Sta. Felicità Sacristy, *Crucifix;* New York, Mrs. Jesse Straus, diptych.

A widely productive painter, Pacino had many assistants and worked largely in book, miniature and panel painting, to which he was naturally disposed. His group clings to the Roman tradition, influenced by the St. Cecilia Master. His manner is brisk, whimsical and narrative. A considerable number of miniatures and book-illuminations from the school of Pacino exist, some of them in the Biblioteca Laurenziana, Florence.

Bibliography: Milanesi, *Nuovi doc.,* 1901.—Crowe and Cavalcaselle, Douglas ed., II, 1903.—H. Thode, *Franz. v. Assisi,* 1904.—W. Suida, Jahrb. d. preuss. Kstslgn, XXVI, 1905, 106ff.—Offner, Art in America, XI, 1923.—Van Marle, *Italian Schools,* etc., III, 1924; V, 1925.—Offner, *A Corpus of Florentine Painting,* Section III, Vol. II, Part I, 1930.

**PADOVANINO (Alessandro Varotari, known as).**—Venetian painter, 1590-1650. Son of Dario Varotari, and originally of Padua, hence his name. Padovanino had considerable influence on painting owing to his reaction from the murky shadows, which were the fashion in his day, to the luminosity of Titian, whom he studied and copied unceasingly. He acquired a boldness of style which enabled him to paint figures in learned perspective, and to design complicated buildings, without losing breadth of modelling. His best work is, perhaps, the *Marriage at Cana* (in the Academy of Venice), in which cypress trees, growing in front of the Temple, beside colossal columns, accentuate a decorative rhythm in the grand manner, while a splendid crowd animates the wedding feast. *St. Liberale Saving the Condemned* (Church of the Carmini), *The Martyrdom of St. John the Evangelist* (San Pietro di Castello), and *The Triumph of Venus* (Bergamo) are powerful examples of his style.

**PADUA (Italy).**—According to the legend, Padua was founded by

Padua: Piazza and Sant' Antonio

Antenor, brother of Priam. The town was very prosperous under Roman domination, but it was sacked by the barbarians, and its buildings were destroyed. In the 13th century St. Anthony of Padua visited the town, and died in the neighbouring village of Arcella in 1231, whence his body was taken to Padua. The inhabitants built a splendid basilica over his remains.

*S. Antonio* (1232-1307) was an important pilgrimage church and, accordingly, has many chapels. Seven domes cover the square compartments of the nave, crossing, choir and transept arms, a treatment reminiscent of S. Marco at Venice. The façade has a Gothic arcading and the domes are crowned with Oriental-like turrets. This building demonstrates the persistence of Byzantine feeling in North Italian Gothic architecture.

It was damaged by an explosion, in 1616; by a fire, in 1749; restored, and whitewashed. The three-aisled interior contains many chapels. The Chapel of the Saint is a rich, Renaissance construction, built on the plans of Riccio by Minello, Sansovino and Falconetto and decorated with reliefs and statuary which relate the life of St. Anthony. The Chapel of St. Felix is decorated with 14th century frescoes by Altichiero and Avanzo. The high altar, executed by Donatello and his pupils (1444-1449), was remade in 1895, the sculptures of the Florentine master being retained.

Outside the basilica is Donatello's famous equestrian statue of *Gattamelata* (finished in 1453), leader of the Venetian army.

The *Scuola del Santo,* built for re-unions of the Confraternity of St. Anthony, is decorated with frescoes, three of which are works of Titian's youth (1511).

The *Madonna dell'Arena,* built in 1303, by Scrovegni, contains precious frescoes by Giotto (see Giotto). These frescoes completely cover the walls and the vaulting.

The 13th century, *Church of the Eremitani,* is famous for the frescoes by Mantegna, in the Chapel of St. Christopher (painted, 1453-1459). They represent the *Life of St. James,* and the *Execution and Burial of St. Christopher* (see Mantegna).

The *Chapel of St. George* contains frescoes by Altichiero and Avanzo.

The high altar of the vast Renaissance *Church of St. Justine* is decorated with a fine picture of Veronese, the *Martyrdom of St. Justine.*

The *Cathedral* (built 1551-1577), in the Renaissance style, has an unfinished façade.

The *Palazzo della Ragione* is a fine building, built from 1172 to 1219, according to the plans of Pietro Cozzo di Limena.

BIBLIOGRAPHY: Roger Peyre, *Padoue et Vérone,* Collection des Villes d'art célèbres.

**PAEONIUS of MENDE, THRACE.**—Greek sculptor, to whom Pausanias attributes the eastern pediment of the temple of Zeus, at Olympia. This sculptor is now known by a work which was discovered during the German excavations at Olympia. This is a marble *Victory,* bearing the following inscription on its base: "The Messenians and the Naupactians consecrated this statue to Olympian Zeus, as tithe of the spoils taken in the neighbourhood. Paeonius of Mende made it; and, for the acroteria placed on the temple, he won the prize." The victory of the Messenians happened in 424 B.C., that is, of the temple of Olympia, which thirty years after the completion was finished in 456 B.C. Thus it is unlikely that the pediment sculptures are by the same artist. Moreover, the *Victory* of Paeonius, in the Museum of Olympia, is in a very different style. The figure is represented as floating through the air. The rough block on which she is supported may have been painted blue, so as to keep up the illusion, and be barely distinguishable from the sky. The drapery is a very beautiful study of the effect of wind, as it clings to the girlish form, and floats in wide folds behind. In spite of Pausanias's statement, it certainly seems unlikely that this can be by the same artist who carved the rather stiffly posed figures on the pediment of the Temple of Zeus.

**PAESTUM (Sicily).**—The town of Paestum, now completely deserted, was founded by the Greeks in the 7th century B.C. It did not flourish for very long, the unhealthfulness of the climate having early scared the population.

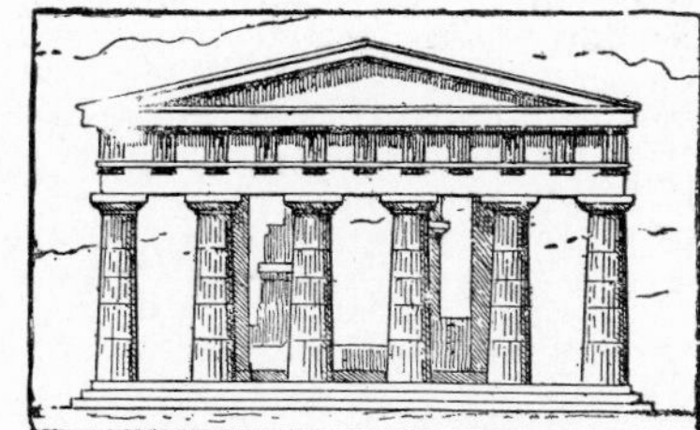

PAESTUM: TEMPLE OF NEPTUNE.

In the 11th century, it was pillaged by Robert Guiscard, who carried off a number of columns and statues. In the 5th century B.C. the Greeks had built there several temples of imposing beauty, in the pure Doric style. There they stand proudly, in a solitary landscape.

The *Temple of Neptune,* built in B.C., c. 460, is one of the finest temples in the Doric style which the art of Greece produced. Its effect of power is very striking. It is a triumph of pure architecture, the severity of which is no longer relieved by sculpture or colour. It is simply by the nobility and sober ordinance of its lines, and by the beauty of its proportions that this work of Greek genius commands admiration. The façades have six Doric columns, and there are fourteen each side. The cella is divided into three aisles by a double row of smaller columns, of which eight are still entire. The Temple of Neptune is the only one of all the Greek temples which still possesses its two tiers of columns standing. The exterior columns support an entablature of surprising height —three-sevenths of the height of the whole.

See Pl. 19, Vol. I.

The so-called *Basilica* is an older building than the Temple of Neptune, having been built c. 540 B.C. Each façade has nine columns, and the sides eighteen. In the middle of the building, a row of columns divides it into two parts longways. This peculiarity has led to many discussions. The hypothesis that the so-called basilica was a portico with two galleries is a likely one, since the forum spread out at the foot of the two temples, and a shelter for pedestrians would have been a natural provision. About ten yards from the western façade is an altar, and on the site of the forum are still to be found traces of altars and statues.

*The Temple of Ceres* stands at some distance from the other two buildings. It is much smaller than them, but very happily proportioned. It was built c. 520.

**PAGODA.**—The pagoda is a religious monument of India and the Far East, which often shelters a reliquary. Pagodas were often elaborately decorated with bas-reliefs. Chinese pagodas are towers in several storeys, each one slightly smaller than the one below, with curved roofs. Sometimes there is a balcony round the base of each storey. Some believe that this Chinese type (the oldest extant is the octagonal reliquary at She Shan, c. 600 A.D.) derives from the Indian stupa. In India, the name pagoda is often given to a collection of buildings, palaces, temples and gardens, within an enclosure.

**PAJOU (Augustin).**—French sculptor, 1730-1809. He had lessons from J. B. Lemoyne, who was considered to be one of the most enlightened teachers, and who also taught Pigalle, Houdon and Falconet. In 1748, Pajou won the Grand Prix for sculpture, in the second competition, established to form the school of students patronised by the king. He went to Rome for three years. Some years after his return he was made an Academician (1760), on the presentation of a statue of *Pluto Holding the Chained Cerberus* (Louvre), a work which is correct, learnedly composed, but rather lacking in individuality. Not power, but delicacy, and even a certain liveliness, when his theme suited him, are characteristic of Pajou. He made some imaginative works, such as his *Bacchante* (1774, Louvre), or decorative subjects, of remarkable taste and variety, such as those which he made in the "foyer" of the opera, built at Versailles, where they may still be admired. But his most remarkable production is the collection of portraits which he left of his contemporaries. These include those of: his master, Lemoyne (1759, Louvre), Hubert Robert (in the École des Beaux-Arts, and in private collections), Madame Dubarry (Louvre—in the space of three or four years, 1770-1774, he made four busts of this model, who perhaps inspired his best work), Descartes, and Bossuet (now in the Institut).

PAJOU: MME. DUBARRY. (Louvre.)

It was Pajou who had charge of the work of transferring Jean Goujon's fountain when, in 1788, it was removed from a corner of the Rue Saint Denis to the position it occupies now. He must have added some figures of nymphs, for which he seems to have been inspired by the old master who decorated the "bull's-eyes" of the Louvre courtyard. To the Salon of 1802, he sent a bust of Cæsar, in the manner of the day.

BIBLIOGRAPHY: H. Stein, *Auguste Pajou.* 1912.

**PALA D'ORO.**—See Enamel (Origins); Saint Mark's.

**PALAIS DE JUSTICE.**—See under the name of the city where it is located, e.g., Paris, Poitiers, Rouen.

— **DES THERMES.**—See Paris.
— **ROYAL.**—See Paris.

**PALAMEDESZ (Anthonie, called Stevers).**—Dutch genre and portrait painter, 1601-1673. He was a pupil of Frans and Dirk Hals in Haarlem, his portraits reflect Hals' influence. Palamedesz was one of the best chroniclers of his time, depicting society in an elegant manner. His ability to render material and his bright colors may be seen in *The Party,* 1633 (Amsterdam).

**PALATINE CHAPEL.**—See Palermo and Aix-la-Chapelle.

**PALAZZO BARBERINI.**—See Rome.

— **DEI DIAMANTI.**—See Ferrara.
— **DELLA PODESTA.**—See Bologna (It.).
— **DELLA RAGIONE.**—See Milan; Padua.
— **DEL MUNICIPIO.**—See Perugia.
— **DORIA.**—See Genoa; Rome.
— **MEDICI.**—See Florence.
— **PICCOLOMINI.**—See Siena.
— **PUBBLICO.**—See Siena.
— **QUARATESI.**—See Florence.
— **RUCELLAI.**—See Alberti; Florence.
— **RUSSO.**—See Genoa.
— **SFORZA.**—See Milan.
— **STROZZI.**—See Florence.
— **VECCHIO.**—See Florence.

**PALEOLITHIC (Period).**—See Neolithic (Period).

**PALERMO (Sicily).** — Palermo was founded by the Phœnicians, and conquered successively by the Romans, Goths, Arabs, and Normans, who left several buildings there.

PALERMO: INTERIOR OF THE PALATINE CHAPEL.

The royal Palace, begun by the Arabs for a fortress, was finished by the Normans.

The *Palatine Chapel,* built about 1130, half Arab, half Byzantine, is decorated with magnificent mosaics on a gold background, the oldest of which date from the 12th century.

From the same period dates *San Giovanni degli Eremiti,* now in ruins. Its plan is original, being in the form of an Egyptian cross, with three apses. Its arrangement of domes and its decoration show a fusion of Saracenic and Byzantine points of view, the Saracenic remaining uppermost.

The *Martorana,* which has a dome, and three apses, and was built in 1143 is similar. The *Church of the Magione* was founded in 1161. The *Cathedral,* consecrated in 1185, has suffered many unfortunate restorations. The eastern façade has a fine portal, and two towers built from 1300 to 1359. The interior contains tombs of kings, of the 12th and 13th centuries, in rich porphery sarcophagi.

The *Palazzo Sciafani,* built in 1330 (now a barracks), possesses a fine 15th century fresco by a Flemish artist, representing the *Triumph of Death.*

*Santa Maria della Catena* is a charming 16th century church of the early Renaissance.

The *Palazzo Chiaramonti,* built after 1307, still possesses a room with a ceiling of wood, painted in a half Byzantine, half Arabic style.

See Pl. 10, Vol. I.

BIBLIOGRAPHY: Charles Diehl, *Palerme et Syracuse.*

**PALISSY (Bernard).**—French maker of ceramics (about 1510-1590). Bernard Palissy started his career as a painter on glass. He then became a surveyor, and settled at Saintes, where he became converted to Protestantism and married. About 1543, someone showed him an enamelled cup which he greatly admired, and he determined to discover the secret of making such beautiful things. After many fruitless efforts, he found the secret of those fine glazes, and joined the front rank of French ceramists. So great was his prestige that, having been imprisoned as a heretic, he was set free almost immediately; and in 1565 he went to Paris, where he worked for Catherine de' Medici. Unfortunately, his prosperity did not last. He was betrayed by one of his co-religionists, and imprisoned in the Bastille, in 1588, when he was nearly eighty years of age. He died there two years later.

Bernard Palissy has been praised as the greatest of French ceramists. Nowadays he is less highly thought of: his work seems overloaded with detail, and lacking in design.

See Pl. 31, Vol. II.

BIBLIOGRAPHY: E. Dupuy, *Bernard Palissy: l'homme, l'artiste, le savant, l'écrivain.* Paris, 1902.

PALLADIO: OLYMPIC THEATRE. VICENZA.

**PALLADIO (Andrea).**—One of the most famous Italian architects of the Renaissance. Born in Vicenza, 1508; died, 1580. He was the son of a miner, and was given the name of Palladio, derived from Pallas, the patron goddess of that science. His influence was so important that he has been called the founder of modern architecture.

No architect was more devoted than Palladio to antiquity, but he studied classical art in Rome, and not in Greece. Nevertheless, he felt it in all its grandeur and beauty, appreciating rather the harmony of the whole than particular details. He realised that excessive decoration diminished the effect, and in the rarity of his ornamental details, and in the extreme simplicity of his capitals, he remained detached from the movement which was then tending towards the Baroque. He still followed the precepts of Bramante, but with more strictness. He differed from the other artists of his day in not attempting to add to the style of ancient Rome. He favoured brick rather than marble. His art is serious and pure in style, but it is coldly correct, and wanting in great imagination.

Classical Rome could not provide Palladio with examples of churches and palaces, but it was in this very application of the principles of antiquity to these new buildings that Palladio's originality lay. To the houses of Vicenza he applied the lessons he learned in the Roman baths, and the town, which he hardly ever left, was enriched with many fine houses.

The *Basilica of Vicenza* is a grandiose reconstruction of the mediæval Palazzo della Ragione. It was begun in 1549, and in it are those arcades, framed by attached columns of one of the great orders, and supported by free columns of a smaller order, which are characteristic of Palladio. Each bay, accordingly has a round-headed opening flanked by two square-headed openings, the treatment being known as the "Palladian motif." Palladio did not invent it but was responsible for its great popularity.

The chief palaces which Palladio built in Vicenza after this Basilica were the *Palazzo Giulio Porto* (unfinished, formerly the *Casa del Diavolo*), and the Palazzo Chiericati (restored, now houses the Museo Civico). He built the *Ponte San Michele,* the *Loggia del Capitano,* and a great many villas in the neighbourhood, among them the *Villa Capra* (Villa Rotonda, 1570), which has a circular room, with a dome in the centre, and a portico with an Ionic pediment at each corner of the square building. The little house which passes as his own residence was built by him in 1566 for Pietro Cogolo.

The *Teatro Olympico,* which he also built in Vicenza, was finished after his death by Scamozzi. It is a remarkable attempt at a theatre in the ancient style, according to the rules of Vitruvius, with steps for the spectators, and a curious stage forming, in perspective, streets of a town.

Palladio's style spread, and superseded the Gothic style of the old palaces. Happily, in spite of his numerous buildings in Venice, he did not destroy the city's older character. Nevertheless he thought the Ducal Palace was badly designed, and constantly criticised Sansovino.

Palladio was the architect of *San Giorgio Maggiore,* which stands in the middle of a lagoon, and is one of the features of Venice. The interior, the monks' choir and the refectory were much admired by authorities. On the whole, his religious buildings in Venice are reminiscent of Bramante, and of the plans of Antonio da Sangallo for the façade of St. Peter's, but with the proportions much reduced.

He is the architect of the Church of Il Redentore (1577); of the Convent of the Carità (1561), now the Academy, which he left unfinished, and which was much admired by Goethe; of the façade of San Francesco della Vigna (1568), and of the little Church of the Nuns of the Zitelle which was built after his death, from his designs.

Palladio's influence on Renaissance architecture was probably not so great as was that of some of his successors, but it is true, nevertheless, that (after an eclipse during Borromini's ascendancy, and the fashion for the Baroque) his noble and simple style of architecture became the model. He has remained the master of the classic school in Italy.

BIBLIOGRAPHY: Palladio, *I quattro libri dell'Architettura.* Venice, 1570. —*Les bâtiments et dessins d'André Palladio recueillis et illustrés par O. B. Scamozzi.* Vicenza, 1776-1781. 4 Vols.—Zanella, *Vita d'Andrea Palladio.* Milan, 1880.—G. Lukomski, *Andrea Palladio.* 1924.

**PALMA (Antonio).**—Venetian painter of the 16th century, who flourished about 1555 to 1575. A nephew of Palma Vecchio. He has been called Bonifazio Veneziano, and confused with Bonifazio del Pitati, his helper, whose niece he married. He was a mediocre artist.

**— (Jacopo, called the Younger).** —Venetian painter, 1544 to 1628, grand nephew of Palma Vecchio and son of Antonio Palma, who had married the niece of Bonifazio di Verona. After studying under various masters, and copying Titian in particular, he went to Urbino and Rome, where, in addition to the influence of rich Venetian colourings, he fell under the inspiration of Roman grandeur. When he returned to Venice his art was enslaved by theories. He was commissioned to paint a great *Last Judgment* in the hall of the Doges' Palace, and other scenes in the Great Council Hall.

After the death of Titian and Veronese, he was without a rival, and was sure of the success of his pictures. He painted some fine portraits of the doges, and sometimes he succeeded in recapturing pure rich colour, and in achieving harmonious decorations. He painted rapidly, and his drawing is often negligent. He became more and more addicted to dramatic gestures, and violent movements which became theatrical, and irritating.

He had a great many pupils.

**— (Jacopo Negretti), known as PALMA VECCHIO.**—Venetian painter, about 1480 to 1528. Born at Serina, near Bergamo, and called Palma Vecchio to distinguish him from his nephew, Palma the Younger, a pupil of Titian. He was one of the great painters of his period, when ample forms and warm colours were the order of the day, and, if he lacked the genius and emotion of Titian, he at least created pictures which are a feast for the eyes. He died in his forties, leaving some vigorous, unfinished canvases as witnesses of a tranquil youth. There is a *Virgin between St. George and St. Lucy,* in San Stefano of Vicenza; a *St. Peter between Six Saints,* and an *Assumption,* in the Academy of Venice; the *Adoration of the Magi,* in the Brera Gallery; the *Visitation,* in the Belvedere Gallery of Vienna (finished by Cariani). He excelled in *Holy Conversations,* in which calm, beautiful figures converse peacefully in a serene landscape. Examples may be seen in Leningrad, Milan, Vienna, and in the Uffizi Palace, Florence. The finest and perhaps the latest since it has many points in common with Titian's *Madonna del Pesaro,* which was put in position in 1526, is the one which was added recently to the Academy of Venice. There we see St. Joseph, St. John the Baptist, the Virgin, and the beautiful Violante, daughter of Palma, in the character of St. Lucy.

The *Meeting of Jacob and Rachel* (Dresden) shows his feeling for nature.

Palma Vecchio especially loved to paint women in all the radiant beauty of health. The robust *St. Barbara between St. Anthony and St. Sebastian,* in Santa Maria Formosa, is neither praying nor meditating. Her face is a little heavy, but she has breadth and dignity.

The *Three Sisters,* in the Dresden Gallery, are a repetition of the same type of beauty. In Vienna there is the beautiful and charming *Violante.* In Rome, in the Villa Borghese, there is a *Lucretia* brandishing a dagger, and apparently thinking more of the æsthetic impression she is producing than feeling the horror of the drama she is enacting.

Palma Vecchio's portraits of men include that of Francesco Querini (in the Querini Stampalia Gallery of Venice); an Unknown Man, in Berlin; and *The Poet,* in the National Gallery.

Palma's chief lack is that distinction which arises from depths of thought, and intensity of emotion.

BIBLIOGRAPHY: Elia Fornari, *Notizie biografiche su Palma il Vecchio.* Bergamo, 1886.—Pasino Locatelli, *Notizie intorno a Giacomo Palma il Vecchio.* Bergamo, 1890.—E. Fornari, *Palma il Vecchio.* Bergamo, 1901.—M. Boehm, *Giorgione und Palma Vecchio.* Leipzig, 1908.—Crowe and Cavalcaselle, *History of Painting in North Italy,* ed. T. Borenius. Vol. III.

**PALMER (Erastus D.).**—American sculptor (1817-1904), of Albany, of whose many works the *White Captive* in the Metropolitan Museum and the *Angel at the Sepulchre* in Albany Cemetery may be singled out for mention.

**— (Samuel).**—English painter and etcher (1805-1881), specialized in landscapes and pastoral scenes, evincing a charming sense of harmonious composition.

**PALMERUCCI (Guido).**—Central Italian painter of Gubbio, active 1315-49. Follower of Meo da Siena and the Lorenzetti.

**PALMEZZANO (Marco).**—Italian painter, c. 1456-after 1543, born at Forlì. Pupil of Melozzo da Forlì. About 1493 he painted, from Melozzo's cartoons, the decoration of the Chapel of the Treasury of Santa Maria of Loreto, and in his hands the design became heavier, and more conventional. The decoration of the Feo Chapel, in San Biagio, Forlì, was carried out under the same conditions. He himself appears to have designed the painting of the lunette, and the *Martyrdom of San Giacomo* (before 1495). He called himself Marcus of Melotius as may be seen in the inscription of a picture in San Francesco of Matelica (1501), and of another representing *St. Anthony,* in the Gallery of Forlì. He lived to be very old, and in the Forlì Gallery may be seen his portrait at the age of eighty, dated 1536.

Palmezzano left a considerable number of rather cold, monotonous works—*Madonnas* (Bologna, Faenza, Milan, Munich, etc.); a *Coronation* and a *Nativity* in the Brera; two paintings of the *Annunciation* (Forlì); a *Crucifixion* (Uffizi), etc.

**PANATHENAIC PROCESSION.**—See Acropolis of Athens.

**— STADIUM.**—See Athens.

**PANDROSEION.**—See Acropolis of Athens.

**PANNINI (Giovanni Paolo).**—Italian painter, 1691-1764. He was an able painter of buildings and ruins, and also of contemporary ceremonies and pageants in Rome.

**PANTHEON of AGRIPPA, ROME.**—This is one of the most famous and best preserved of the old Roman temples. It was built in the reign of Augustus by his stepson Agrippa, in the year 27 B.C., in honour of all the gods who protected the family of Augustus. In the reign of Trajan it was almost demolished by lightning. The portico alone remained intact. Hadrian built the rotunda and the dome. In fact, it is practically certain, as proven by the stamps on the bricks, that all of the work, with the exception of the columnar porch, is that of Hadrian, dating from the first quarter of the 2nd century A.D. When Christianity succeeded paganism, the temple was unused, until, in the 7th century, it was transformed into a church under the name of Santa Maria Rotunda.

The Pantheon is preceded by a portico (formerly approached by five steps) 33½ metres wide. It is supported by sixteen granite Corinthian columns. The old dedication on the architrave has been replaced by a modern one. Below, an inscription mentions a restoration under Septimius Severus and Caracalla. The bas-reliefs on the pediment have disappeared. Eight columns adorn the façade. The portico was originally covered with a bronze roof which Pope Urban VIII had melted down to make cannons, and columns for the high-altar of St. Peter's.

The Pantheon of Agrippa was rather different from the building we see today. It was not circular, but rectangular, and, according to Pliny, divided into three aisles. The façade of the portico had eight columns instead of the ten which were placed there under Hadrian. The interior is lighted only by the magnificent dome (43½ metres in height and in diameter). It is paved with marble and porphyry. Statues of the gods formerly adorned the niches, which are framed by the fluted columns which support the architrave. The upper part of the building has lost its rich marble decoration.

The Pantheon covers the tombs of many artists, among others, that of Raphael.

See Pl. 29, Vol. I.

**PANTHEON.**—See Paris.

**PANTOJA de la CRUZ (Juan).**—Spanish painter, Madrid, 1551-1609. He was a pupil of Sánchez Coello, but his works sometimes also show the influence of Titian and Antonio Moro. He had obtained the favor of Philip II, and Philip III held him in high esteem and commanded a great number of family portraits from him. Unfortunately most of these works which decorated various royal residences were destroyed by fire. Nevertheless the Prado still contains fine portraits by this master (For instance *Philip II with Rosary; Queen Margarita de Austria,* 1607). Other portraits in or near Madrid are in the Escorial (Philip II, 1608); in the Convent de las Descalzas Reales; in private houses of the aristocracy; etc. Also the Pinakothek at Munich as well as the Vienna Museum own portraits by Pantoja depicting royal personages. In the portraits of Philip II, Pantoja has represented his restless, subtle and sickly master with singular insight. Of his religious paintings may be cited the *Birth of the Virgin* and the *Birth of Christ* dating from

Pantoja de la Cruz (Juan): Philip II. (Prado.)

1604 (Prado, formerly in the Chapel of the *Casa del Tesoro* adjoining the Royal Alcázar). Other religious compositions are in the Cathedrals of Toledo, Segovia and elsewhere.

Bibliography: A. L. Mayer, *Gesch. der span. Malerei;* 2nd ed., 1922.—Id. in Thieme-Becker, Vol. XXVI; 1932. Art. *Pantoja de la Cruz, Juan.*—C. Juste, *Velázquez u. sein Jahrhundert,* 1922-23.—E. Tormo y Monzó, *Las iglesias del antiguo Madrid,* Madrid, 1927.—*Hisp. Soc. of Am.,* N. Y. (*P. C. in the Collection of . . .* ), 1927.

**PAOLO ROMANO.**—Roman sculptor, beginning 15th century. He made a great many tombs in Rome. The deceased are generally represented lying under a canopy supported by angels. Examples are: the tomb of Bartolommeo Carafa (in Santa Maria del Priorato), that of Cardinal Stefaneschi (in Santa Maria in Trastevere), and that of the brothers Anguillara (in San Francesco di Capranica).

This sculptor must not be confused with Paolo di Mariano di Tuccio Taccone, called "Romano," to the end of the century.

**PAOLO di STEFANO BADALONI (called Schiavo).**—Florentine painter, born 1397 in Florence; died 1478 at Pisa.

In 1429 Paolo di Stefano appears on the rolls of the Medici e Speziali; in 1436 is named in connection with windows for the cupola of the Duomo. His destroyed frescoes in the Cappella della Vergine Assunta in Pistoia were probably of 1448. After this time he is mentioned as buying a house in Pisa; and a document of 1462 indicates that he is at work on a panel or a "colmo" for the Church of S. Domenico, Pisa, on contract from the goldsmith Raniero di Antonio. In 1472, Paolo di Stefano is mentioned in Florence.

Among his works are: the fresco of the *Madonna with Four Saints,* San Miniato, Florence, probably of 1436 (date almost illegible); the Florence, Sant' Apollonia *Crucifixion,* 1440; the *Assumption of the Virgin,* altarpiece, at the Oratorio of S. Maria delle Querce, near Florence, 1460.

**PAOLO VENEZIANO.**—Venetian painter, mentioned in Venice 1333-58, died probably before 1362; chief representative of the Byzantine tradition in the Venetian trecento.

In 1345 Paolo, with his sons Luca and Giovanni, executed the extant altar-frontal covering the *pala d'oro* in S. Marco, Venice. The next year he was paid for an altarpiece for the Cappella S. Niccolò in the Doge's Palace, now lost.

Two pictures remain, signed by Paolo alone: the 1333 *Dormition of the Virgin with Saints* in Vicenza; and the 1347 *Madonna Enthroned with Angels,* at Carpineta, near Cesena. One is signed in collaboration with his son Giovanni, the 1358 *Coronation of the Virgin,* in the Frick Collection, New York.

Bibliography: Crowe and Cavalcaselle, Italian ed., IV, 1900.—Testi, *Storia d. pitt. venez.,* I, 1909.

**PARAY-LE-MONIAL (Saône-et-Loire).**—The Basilica of St. Peter is a remarkable 12th century building, in the Burgundian Romanesque style. It may be regarded as a smaller version of the great Third Abbey Church of Cluny, and affords us some notion of the original appearance of the latter. The two square towers date from the 12th century, but that at the crossing is modern.

**PARENTINO (Bernardino),** or **Parenzano.**—Italian painter of Modena and of the Paduan school, 1437-1531. A follower of Mantegna, he was afterwards very strongly influenced by Ercole Roberti and several of the pictures generally attributed to this master are now restored to him.

**PARENZO (Italy).**—*Cathedral,* 535-543. Early Christian basilica of Istria, Ravennate in design.

See Grado.

**PARIS.**—Paris was originally a little town situated in the Ile de la Cité. It was there, in 53 B.C., that Julius Cæsar, after conquering Gaul,

Notre Dame, Paris: The Virgin.

assembled the envoys of the vanquished tribes. Gradually, the town expanded. The oldest remains is an *Arena,* built in the 1st or 2nd century A.D., at the foot of Mount Sainte Geneviève, restored in the 6th century, and largely ruined since. In the Roman period, a palace, surrounded with gardens, was built on the left bank of the Seine, on the present site of the Cluny Museum. Of this old palace, deserted by the French kings, about the 9th century, then given over in 1340 to the Abbey of Cluny, there remains the *Palais des Thermes,* probably the old Roman baths. This large vaulted chamber now shelters a collection of statues, and sculptural fragments.

The next oldest remains in Paris date from the 11th century. The oldest of the Parisian churches, *St.*

Paris: St. Germain-de-Prés.

*Germain-des-Près,* was begun at the opening of the 11th century. The Romanesque tower dates from that period; the nave and choir were

Notre Dame, Paris: Christ as a gardener.

begun in 1163, and a 17th century doorway covers the jambs of the old Romanesque entrance. The importance of the church rests in its status as a monument which is transitional

Paris: The Arena of Lutetia.

from Romanesque to Gothic. Its external flying buttresses are among the earliest known.

The reign of Philip Augustus (1180-1223) was prosperous. Buildings of all kinds—churches, convents, market-places, hospitals, and fountains—were erected. It was surrounded by a wall, traces of which remain (Rue Clovis). The king undertook the rebuilding of the Louvre, about 1204; he built two wooden bridges, and worked at the construction of *Notre Dame*. The present church replaced a Merovingian cathedral, and a second cathedral, built in the 9th century, and decorated in the 10th and 11th centuries. In the 12th century, the Bishop of Paris, Maurice de Sully, undertook the rebuilding of this cathedral, which had become too small. The choir, consecrated in 1163, was used for worship in 1185. The nave was finished in the 13th century, as well as the façade and towers. About 1240, the new cathedral was built. At once, modifications were introduced. Side chapels were built, and the high nave windows were added. Bold flying-buttresses replaced the older ones. About 1258, the master of the works, Jean de Chelles, added a bay to the transepts. Finally, at the end of the 13th, or the beginning of the 14th, century, Pierre de Chelles built the choir chapels. By about 1315, the cathedral had assumed its present appearance. After remaining intact for centuries, Notre Dame suffered greatly during the Revolution when many objects were melted, and again in 1793 when by order of the Paris Commune other objects were destroyed. The restoration by Viollet-le-Duc (1845-1864) effaced signs of the damage it had sustained. The plan of the cathedral is a Latin cross. The vaulting is sexpartite. The double ambulatory of the choir is surrounded by fifteen chapels. Externally, the imposing façade, divided into three parts by the tower buttresses, has three doorways, which are decorated with carvings, celebrated in the history of mediæval art. Most of the sculptures of the South doorway (the St. Anne doorway) date from the 12th century. In the tympanum, the Virgin, seated in the midst of angels, is worshipped by the kneeling Louis VII and Maurice de Sully. The sculptures on the other two doorways must have been carved about 1220. The north doorway (*Portail de la Vierge*) celebrates, on its tympanum, the resurrection and coronation of the Virgin. In delicacy of expression, and purity of touch, this piece is one of the most remarkable works of the Middle Ages. A rich leafy decoration, naturalistically treated, adds to the impression of freshness. Finally, on the middle doorway, the *Last Judgment* is represented (much restored). Below, the modern carvings of the medallions are devoted to the Virtues and Vices. These three are surmounted by a gallery of kings (28 modern statues). The stage above contains the central rose-window. The doorway of the South transept is dedicated to St. Stephen. The rather enigmatical reliefs on the base of the doorway show the transformations of Gothic sculpture from 1220 to 1258. The same evolution is manifest on the contemporary doorway of the North transept ("porte du Cloître"). Over the side chapels of the ambulatory, flying-buttresses spring to meet the high windows of the choir. The grace of these arches, and the harmonious elevation of the apse, make this part of the cathedral one of the most moving creations of Gothic architecture.

See Pls. 11, 47, 53, Vol. I.

Paris: Musée de Cluny.

Paris: Musée de Cluny. The Baths.

Paris: Sainte Chapelle.

Paris: St. Germain l'Auxerrois.

Paris: Detail of Notre Dame.

Bibliography: R. C. Lasteyrie de Saillant, *L'architecture religieuse en France à l'époque gothique*. Paris, 1926.

The *Church of Saint Julien-le-Pauvre* was built in the same period (about 1160). It is now consecrated to the Greek cult.

*Saint Séverin* is a charming Gothic church, begun at the opening of the 13th century. From this period date the porch under the tower, the side doorway, the lower part of the façade, and a part of the nave. The side aisles and apse date from the 15th and 16th centuries. The 13th century doorway comes from Saint Pierre-aux-Bœufs. The tower belongs to the 13th and 14th centuries; and the church contains windows dating from the 15th and 16th centuries.

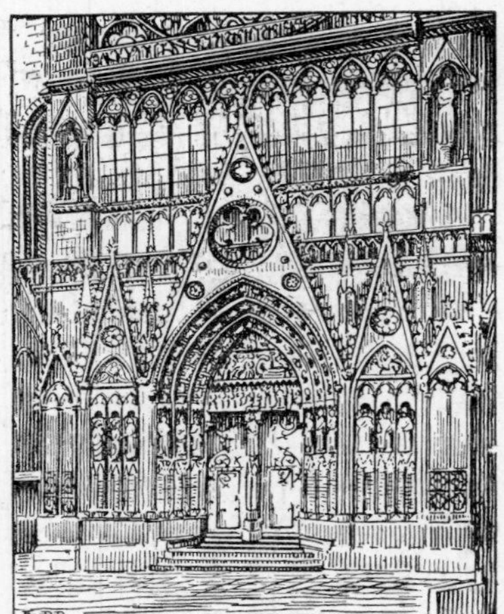

Paris: Notre Dame, Doorway of the cloister.

Paris: Hôtel Carnavalet.

The reign of Saint Louis enriched Paris with several beautiful churches. He built *Sainte Chapelle* to hold the Corwn of Thorns, and a piece of the True Cross. It was built between 1242 and 1247, and not according to the plans of Pierre de Montereau, as tradition has it. It was restored in the 19th century by Viollet-le-Duc and others. This charming edifice is composed of two superimposed chapels; and the portal is formed of two superimposed porches, above which is a large rose window (15th century). The sculptures in the tympana are modern. The fifteen high windows are filled with marvellous stained glass (restored by Lusson), representing scenes from the two testaments, and the *Legend of the Holy Cross*. The Sainte Chapelle is enclosed in the buildings of the *Palais de Justice*, which cover a large area. These buildings date from different periods. The clock tower, and the César, Argent and Boubec towers, date from the 13th and 14th centuries; while the large buildings date from the 18th and 19th centuries.

Paris: Hôtel Sully.

The rebuilding of the *Church of Saint-Germain-l'Auxerrois* belongs to the same period as the Sainte Chapelle. It was founded in 560, and destroyed in the 10th and 12th centuries. The tower at the right of the choir is a remains of the old church. The principal doorway, the choir, and the apse, date from the 13th century; the north side chapels, from the 14th century; and the nave, façade, porch, transepts, and choir chapels, from the 15th and 16th centuries. The church was restored in the 19th century.

Paris: The Porte St. Denis.

In the 14th century, Paris, already with a population of 272,000 was concentrated in three main districts: the Cité (the heart of the town), the University and its dependencies, on the left bank, and the town round the Hôtel de Ville. Then the *Bastille*, a castle, flanked by eight strong towers, was built, at the Porte Saint Antoine. Old engravings of the Bastille exist. It was used as a prison until the 14th July, 1789.

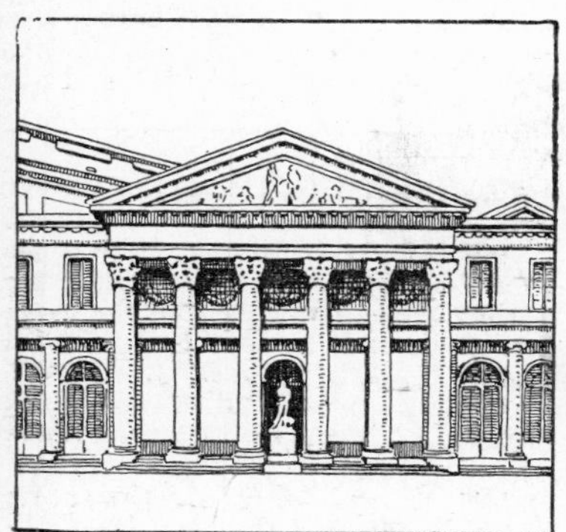

Paris: The School of Medicine.

During the 15th century, under Charles VI, Louis XI, Charles VIII and Louis XII, several new buildings came into existence. Imitating the king, who enlarged and embellished his Louvre, the great lords and bishops built themselves private houses (hôtels). The *Hôtel de Cluny* is a charming Gothic construction, built at the end of the 15th century by Jacques d'Amboise, abbé of Cluny. The Hôtel de Cluny was acquired by the State in 1844, and contains a most interesting museum of mediæval and Renaissance objects. The *Tour Saint Jacques* was built from 1508 to 1522, at the end of Louis XII's reign. It is the graceful remnant of a church which exists no longer.

The reign of Francis I (1515-1547) saw the beginnings of several churches, of which the finest is

Paris: Chapel of the Val de Grâce, the high altar.

*Saint Étienne du Mont*. In 1517, the work was begun, on the site of a 13th century church. The Gothic choir was finished in 1537, at the same time as the south part of the nave. The rest is in the Renaissance style. The *Church of St. Eustache* was begun in 1532, on the plans of Pierre Lemercier, and finished in 1654. The principal doorway was rebuilt in 1755. The tomb of Colbert, by Coysevox and Tuby, from designs by Le Brun, is in a chapel of the choir. Both St. Etienne du Mont and St. Eustache appear Gothic from even a short distance, but close examination reveals that Renaissance ornament has been applied to structures still essentially Gothic.

The *Fontaine des Innocents*, which was originally built on the site formerly occupied by the cemetery of the Innocents, was reconstructed, in 1550, by Pierre Lescot and Jean Goujon, on another site. It is remarkable for the fine bas-relief figures of nymphs, by Jean Goujon, and three others, by Pajou.

The *Hôtel Carnavalet*, also, is the work of Pierre Lescot and Jean Goujon. It was inhabited from 1677 to 1692, by Madame de Sévigné. The building is decorated with four bas-reliefs, probably by Jean Goujon, representing the seasons. On the carriage-entrance, three figures by the same artist: Authority, between two genii, representing Fame. In 1660, Mansart added a storey to each of the three blocks of the building, which had only possessed a ground-floor, and added the façade which faces the Rue de Sévigné, keeping, however, the old door which Jean Goujon had decorated with two bas-reliefs—the Submissive Lions, and a figure of Abundance, on the key-stone. A statue of Louis XIV, by Coysevox, stands in the courtyard. The Hôtel Carnavalet now houses the historical Museum of Paris.

In 1578, under Henri II, Androuet du Cerceau began the construction of the *Pont Neuf*, the oldest of the bridges of Paris. It was finished in the reign of Henri IV.

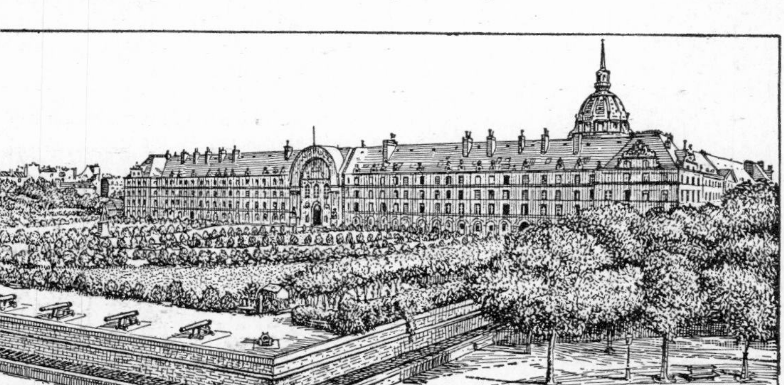

Paris: Façade of the Hôtel des Invalides.

By establishing the monarchy definitely in Paris, Henri IV brought about the creation of the modern town, which was better planned than the Gothic one, and adapted to the needs of politicians and financiers, whose sway was now beginning. During the reigns of Henry IV and Louis XIII there was strong influence from the early baroque of the Low Countries. Brick, stone and slate were used in building, as in the *Place Royale* (now *Place des Vosges*), by Claude Chastillon (1604). This building still preserves its harmonious character, at once dignified and gay. Four rows of pavilions, of uniform design, are built round a square courtyard. These pavilions are three storeys high and in front of the ground-floor is a series of arcades, forming a long corridor. The walls and tall chimneys are made of brick; and stone, ingeniously fluted, is used for the Doric pilasters of the colonnade, and for decoration; the roofs are of slate. There is formed a tricoloured mass, in which grey slate harmonises pleasantly with red brick, and white stone. The Place Royale was finished under the minority of Louis XIII, in 1612, and it became a favoured quarter of residence with the nobility, while the new promenade attracted the youth and fashion of Paris. In 1639, Richelieu set up an equestrian statue of Louis XIII in the middle of the Place. After 1660, the glory of the Place Royale began to fade, and the 18th century hastened its downfall.

See Pl. 2, Vol. I.

Paris: The Sacré Coeur, Montmartre.

It has been said that the importance of the work which he undertook at Versailles made Louis XIV desert and neglect his capital. Certainly, Louis XIV did not enjoy Paris. Nevertheless, the town was not neglected. The king had an important part in the works of the Louvre, in the building of the *Observatory* (1667-1672, on the plans of Perrault), of the *Arc de Triomphe* (unfinished) in the St. Antoine neighbourhood, and of the *Invalides*. The Invalides, and the Colonnade of the Louvre, have done nearly as much for his fame as his Versailles.

The official creation of the *Hôtel des Invalides* dates from the edicts of 1670 and of 1674. By this time, work on the building was already far advanced. The plan of the hôtel, which has not changed, comprises a vast quadrangle of buildings and gardens, enclosed by a moat. The work is due to Liberal Bruand. With Mansart, from 1677, the architects' schemes became more grandiose. Over Bruand's low church, Mansart raised the gilded dome of the royal chapel. The interior, which is strong and harmonious, makes a magnificent setting for Napoleon's tomb, which is surrounded by figures of Victories (by Pradier), and trophies of Austerlitz. The church is a classicized version of the contemporary Italian baroque.

In spite of the residence of the Court at Versailles, Paris grew every day, and new bridges were being built to bind together the newly-built quarters of the city. The *Pont Royal*, the most important of these bridges, is due to the Dominican friar, Jean Romain (1685).

In the 18th century, the king was decidedly more king of Versailles and of Trianon than of Paris; and comparatively little official building was carried out. Nevertheless, Paris developed, and many elegant private houses were built.

Louis XV's reign saw the creation of one of the finest squares in Paris, the Place Louis XV, now the *Place de la Concorde*, finished in the reign of Louis XVI by the refined and classical architect, J. A. Gabriel. (See Gabriel.)

The *Palais Royal* is one of the finest group of buildings dating from Louis XVI's reign. It was the last effort of Parisian architecture under the old monarchy.

In the 17th century many churches were built in Paris—such as the *Church of the Sorbonne* (which contains the dignified tomb of Cardinal Richelieu, by Girardon); *St. Sulpice;* and *St. Roch*, which contains many works of 17th and 18th century art. All these churches owe a debt to the Jesuit style of Italy.

Religious buildings of the 18th century are much less numerous.

Paris: Chapel of the Val de Grâce, the choir.

The most important are *Saint Philippe-du-Roule*; *La Madeleine* (begun in 1764, and transformed, in 1806, by order of Napoleon, into the guise of a Roman temple), and the *Panthéon* (which was built in accordance with a vow made by Louis XV to obtain his cure). It was begun in 1757. Soufflot conceived the idea of his building from St. Peter's, Rome; but he placed his dome, not on the great piers to which Michelangelo had recourse, but only on four columns. The plan is a Greek cross. The imposing portico is formed by columns which are the same height as the temple. The Panthéon is used as the last resting place of France's great men. The interior is vast and almost bare, except for the large frescoes which cover the walls. The best of these is a series by Puvis de Chavannes, representing the Life of St. Geneviève, the patron saint of Paris.

Napoleon I completed the *Champs Elysées*, built bridges, the *Bourse*, and began erecting triumphal arches. The Cemetery of *Père Lachaise*, created by Brogniart in

1804, is the largest in Paris. The magnificent "Monument aux Morts" by Bartholomé, is among its most notable tombs.

The *Arc de triomphe du Carrousel*, begun in 1806, recalls the proportions of the Arch of Septimius Severus, in Rome. The façades are decorated with bas-reliefs representing historical events of Napoleon I's reign.

The *Arc de triomphe de l'Étoile* is much larger. It was begun in the same year, 1806, abandoned, and then completed under Louis-Philippe. The two façades are decorated with bas-reliefs, much the most interesting of which is the "Depart de 1792," generally known as "La Marseillaise," by Rude. Under the arch is the tomb of the Unknown Soldier. Louis-Philippe enlarged the Hôtel de Ville, placed the obelisk from Luxor on the Place de la Concorde, and the July Column on the Place de la Bastille.

Under the Second Empire, Paris was transformed by the energies of the Prefect Haussmann: dark, narrow streets were replaced by wide avenues (the *Boulevards* Strasbourg, Saint-Michel, Haussmann, Saint Germain, etc.), the Louvre was finished, fountains were built (such as the Molière fountain), and gardens embellished.

The *Opera House* was built, from 1861 to 1875, by Garnier in the style of the Baroque Revival. Its pleasing façade is decorated with coloured marbles, and graceful statues —of which the most remarkable is Carpeaux's lively group of the Dance. The building is surmounted by a dome. The grand staircase is celebrated for the elegance of its conception, and for its happy proportions.

The Third Republic restored or rebuilt monuments which had fallen into disrepair or been destroyed by war or revolution, it created new "quartiers," and finished the big avenues. The Universal exhibitions of 1878, 1889 and 1900 were the occasion of vast buildings, several of which have been preserved—such as the *Trocadero*, built for the Exhibition of 1878. It now contains an interesting museum of comparative sculpture.

The *Church of the Sacré Cœur*, Montmartre, was begun, as the result of a national vow, in 1873. It is built in the Romanesque-Byzantine style of the 12th century.

The *Hôtel de Ville* was rebuilt on the site of the one which had been destroyed by fire in 1871.

From the Exhibition of 1900, date three monuments—the Pont Alexandre III, the Grand Palais, and the Petit Palais, which possesses a charming inner courtyard, and contains the Musée des Beaux-Arts, of Paris.

See Louvre; also Pls. 29, 39, 43, Vol. II.

Bibliography: R. T. Blomfield, *History of French Architecture from the death of Mazarin till the death of Louis XV*. London, 1921.—Same author, *History of French Architecture from the Reign of Charles VIII till the death of Mazarin*. London, 1911.—J. F. Blondel, *Réimpression de l'architecture française*. Paris, 1904-05.—W. H. Ward, *Architecture of the Renaissance in France*. New York, 1926.

Paris: The Mint.

**PARIS BORDONE.**—See Bordone.

**PARIS (Jean de).**—See Perréal.

**PARMA.**—The *Cathedral* and the *Baptistery* are 12th century buildings in the Lombard Romanesque style.

See Pl. 45, Vol. I.

**PARMA (Lodovico da).**—Italian painter of Parma, 1470?-1540?. A picture in the Parma Gallery is attributed to him.

**PARMIGIANINO (known as), Francesco Mazzola, Parmese painter, 1503-1540.**—He was taught by his uncles, Mario Mazzola (died, 1545), and Michele Mazzola (died, 1520), who were mediocre painters. But when Correggio came to Parma he followed the great master. He is one of Correggio's best pupils, and the one who resembles him most closely. Nevertheless, his figures are less exquisite, and sometimes more commonplace than those of Correggio. The thoughtful heads are supported on very long necks which often give a strange effect which is not without charm. Il Parmigianino did not attain to his master's delicacy of chiaroscuro. He had ability, and treated soft, brightly coloured draperies lightly, but he is an enfeebled Correggio, lacking lyrical inspiration.

This graceful, gentle painter had an agitated life. He spent some years in Rome, but the sack of 1527 compelled him to flee to Bologna, where he painted one of his finest pictures, which is now in the picture gallery there. The charming profile of St. Margaret, which is both keen and gentle, draws near to the child Christ, regarding him fixedly. The Virgin is more commonplace and affected.

After the coronation of Charles V, Parmigianino returned to Parma, where he undertook the decoration of the Church of the Steccata. But, as the result of quarrels, he had to take refuge in the fortress of Fontanellato. There he painted *Diana and Acteon*. He was then able to return to Parma and continue his work there. This did not last long. He had to take flight again, and he died at Casal Maggiore, at scarcely thirty-seven years of age.

His most important pictures, apart from the one in the Bologna Gallery, are the *Madonna* of the Pitti Palace, and the *St. Catherine* of the Borghese Palace. He is especially distinguished as a portrait painter where he shows himself as a serious master, as in such paintings as those of Columbus and Vespucci, and in that of Antea.

Bibliography: L. Fröhlich-Bum, *Parmigianino und der Manierismus*. Vienna, 1921.

**PAROS (Marble of).**—The island of Paros is one block of marble, which, from ancient times, has been considered as the finest material for sculpture. It is estimated that 30,000 cubic metres of marble were taken from the quarry known as Marpessa. This was the only one that was open to the sky; thus, the Greeks called this marble "luchnites lithos," from the word "luchnos," which signifies lamp. In its fracture, Parian marble resembles cane sugar; whereas Pentelic marble resembles beet sugar. They are both pure white, although in the Parian marble it tends a little towards a grey-blue tint. It is more transparent than any other, for the light penetrates it to a depth of 35 millimetres, whereas it does not penetrate Pentelic marble for more than 15 millimetres. Thus this material gives to figures sculptured in it a transparence which suggests warm, living flesh. It never splits into strata, as some other marbles do to the great annoyance of sculptors. The island of Naxos furnishes a similar marble.

Bibliography: G. Richard Lepsius, *Griechische Marmorstudien*. Berlin, 1890.

**PARRASIO (Michele).**—Venetian painter of the 17th century. Pupil of Veronese. Author of a large picture in the Church of San Giuseppe, where he represented himself praying before the dead Christ.

**PARRHASIOS.**—Greek painter of the end of the 5th century B.C. He was a contemporary of Zeuxis, and enjoyed a great reputation which was only equalled by his pride. He believed that he was descended from Apollo, and said that the gods visited him in dreams. He led a princely life, and charged enormous sums for his pictures. Like Zeuxis, he seems to have exercised a great influence, not only on painters, but on all artists, potters and ceramists. None of his work remains.

**PARRI SPINELLI.**—Florentine-Aretine painter, son and assistant of Spinello Aretino, influenced by Lorenzo Monaco; born 1387; died 1453.

In 1407 Parri collaborated with his father in the Palazzo Pubblico, Siena; in 1434 the Confraternità dei Laici order from him a painting for their church with *SS. Lorentinus and Pergentinus*; in 1435-37 several payments are listed from the above society for the *Madonna della Misericordia*, now in the Gallery, Arezzo; in 1448 there is a small payment for work for the Confraternità; and in 1444, he executes the *Crucifixion* for the Oratory of S. Cristoforo, now the Chapel of the Convent of Sta. Caterina (date given in the inscription).

Bibliography: Vasari-Milanesi, II. —Vasari-Salmi (Vita di Parri Spinelli), Florence, 1914.—Crowe and Cavalcaselle, Douglas ed.—Sirén, *Don Lorenzo Monaco*.—A. del Vita, *Documenti indici pitturi di Parri di Spinello*, Rassegna d'Arte, 1913.—U. Pasqui, *Pitt. aretini vissuti dalla meta del sec. XII al 1527*, Rivista d'Arte, X, 1917, p. 76.—A. Aretini, *Note psichiatriche su Parri Spinelli*.

**PARRISH (Maxfield).**—American painter, born 1870, cultivating a romantic style and perhaps best known through his paintings illustrating the story of *Old King Cole* (St. Regis Hotel, New York).

**PARROCEL (Charles).**—French painter, born and died in Paris (1688-1752), son of Joseph Parrocel, the painter of skirmishes and "pistol shots." In 1745, the King ordered him to paint, for his Château of Choisy, the Battle of Fontenoy. Parrocel's touch is less bold than that of Bourguignon, and less delicate than that of Van der Meulen, but his manner of drawing horses seemed to his age the most skillful that had ever been seen.

**— (Joseph).**—French painter and engraver, 1646-1704. Early in life, he went to Rome, where he worked under the guidance of Bourguignon. On his return to France, he settled in Paris, from 1675. Le Brun did not wish to employ Joseph Parrocel at the *Gobelins*, for the *Battles of Louis XIV*. But Louvois, informed of Parrocel's talent, commissioned him to represent the *Conquests of Louis XIV* in one of the four refectories of the Hôtel des Invalides. "Some time after the death of Louvois (1691), Parrocel delivered the *Crossing the Rhine*, which had been ordered from him for the Gallery of Marly, and it pleased the King so much that he had it placed in the Council Chamber at Versailles." This fine *Crossing of the Rhine*, which is lively and vigorous, and is thus mentioned in the records of the Académie Royale, is now in the Louvre. The Galleries of Florence and Copenhagen also possess pictures by this good painter of battle scenes, who himself engraved ninety of his compositions.

**PARTHENON.**—See Acropolis of Athens.

**PASITELES.**—Greek sculptor of the first century B.C. He was a Roman citizen. In default of any work by him, we can perhaps glean some idea of his style from the statue signed by Stephanos, one of his pupils. It is the statue of a standing youth, which is in the Villa Albani, Rome. Pasiteles does not seem to have created an original style, for the works which are signed by Stephanos, his pupil, and Menelaos, the pupil of Stephanos are very far from being in the same manner.

Bibliography: Collignon, *Histoire de la sculpture grecque*, Vol. II; p. 659 et seq.—Brunn, *Griech. Künstler*, Vol. I. p. 595.

**PASTEL.**—This is the simplest of all methods of painting, but it is also the most delicate. The powdered colour is used almost pure, and is held together by a slight addition of gum-arabic, to which a little pipe-clay is added in powders which have too little resistance.

There are three kinds of pastels—hard, medium, and soft. Soft pastel contains less gum, and leaves the powder purer and brighter.

Owing to its fragile nature, pastel must be carefully protected and framed. Fixatives have been tried, but all of them more or less de-

# RAPHAEL

In the *history of art Raphael occupies a predominant position not only because of his own genius but also because of the time at which he appeared and the city in which he achieved his work. He arrived on the scene at the moment when the Renaissance had reached a state of maturity; what the primitives had for a long time sought was now attained by the sixteenth century masters, flexible modelling, light and shade, and a knowledge of anatomy, perspective, and archæology. Furthermore, it was at Rome in the Vatican, that is to say at the very centre of the Catholic world, that his work was introduced. When Europe came to Rome to search for examples of ancient art, she was able to study architectural ruins and marble sculptures but paintings were lacking. It was Raphael who took the place of the absent Apelles. In his* Apotheosis of Homer, *Ingres placed Raphael among the ancients.*

LA BELLE JARDINIÈRE. LOUVRE.
*(Photo by Hachette.)*

MARRIAGE OF THE VIRGIN. BRERA, MILAN.
*(Photo by Anderson.)*

THE THREE GRACES. MUSÉE CONDÉ, CHANTILLY.
*(Photo by Hachette.)*

SISTINE MADONNA. DRESDEN.

MADONNA DEL GRANDUCA. FLORENCE.
*(Photo by Anderson.)*

MADONNA DI FOLIGNO. VATICAN LIBRARY.
*(Photo by Anderson.)*

DISPUTÀ. VATICAN.
*(Photo by Anderson.)*

SCHOOL OF ATHENS. VATICAN.
*(Photo by Anderson.)*

HELIODORUS DRIVEN FROM THE TEMPLE. VATICAN.
*(Photo by Anderson.)*

FIRE IN THE BORGO. VATICAN.
*(Photo by Anderson.)*

BALTHAZAR CASTIGLIONE. LOUVRE.
*(Photo by Neurdein.)*

MADONNA OF THE CHAIR. PITTI.
*(Photo by Anderson.)*

THE TRANSFIGURATION. VATICAN.
*(Photo by Anderson.)*

POPE LEO X. PITTI.
*(Photo by Brogi.)*

CARDINAL ALIDOSI. PRADO, MADRID.
*(Photo by Anderson.)*

The work of Raphael, although it fills only a brief span of years, is of great variety. He died at thirty-seven and until his death his manner was in a state of evolution. In his youth he painted charming figures in luminous landscapes. Then, at Florence, he perfected his drawing. After he arrived at Rome for the decoration of the Vatican chambers, his style suddenly took on an unexpected grandeur. It is there that his finest claim to glory is found.

# TITIAN

*Titian appeared in the Venetian school at the very beginning of the sixteenth century. It was he who showed the decorative power of oil painting, which, until that time, was employed only for panels of small dimensions and slender figures. Thus the inherent naturalism in this technique chanced to lend to the decoration the beauty and poetry of nature and life. Titian brought to Venice the majesty and the freshness of his native Alps; he gave to figures of the traditional subjects an intensity of life and consequently an expressive power altogether new to Venetian painting.*

TITIAN: SACRED AND PROFANE LOVE. BORGHESE GALLERY, ROME.
*(Photo by Anderson.)*

TITIAN: THE PRESENTATION IN THE TEMPLE. ACADEMY, VENICE.
*(Photo by Brogi.)*

TITIAN: ASSUMPTION OF THE VIRGIN. VENICE.
*(Photo by Anderson.)*

TITIAN: BACCHANAL. MADRID. *(Photo by Hachette.)*

TITIAN: THE ENTOMBMENT. LOUVRE.
*(Photo by Hachette.)*

TITIAN: MADONNA OF THE PESARO FAMILY. CHURCH OF THE FRARI, VENICE.
*(Photo by Naya.)*

## Christian and Pagan Inspiration

The naturalism and the poetry of this painting have at the same time transformed Christian themes and revealed the beauty of pagan themes. The art of Titian treats with the same gravity and the same serene sensuality a bacchanal or a "sacra conversazione." No painter has ever given more beauty and more nobility to Christ or to the Virgin and it is with the same caressing brush, the same luminous and glowing colour, that he painted Venus and the nymphs. And always the softness of the light adds the supreme touch.

TITIAN: CHARLES V. PRADO, MADRID.
*(Photo by Hachette.)*

TITIAN: ALLEGORY. LOUVRE.
*(Photo by Hachette.)*

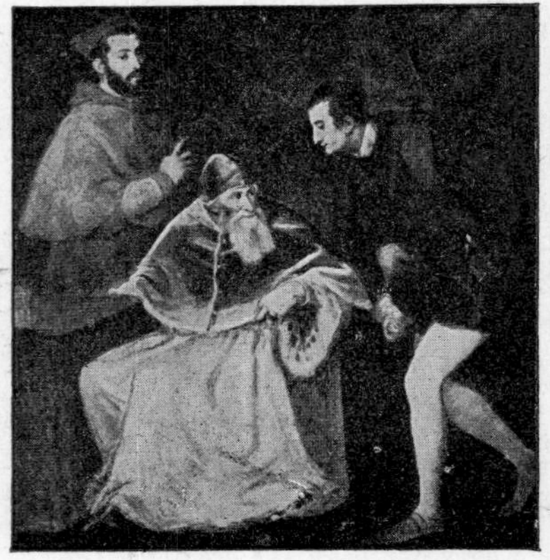

TITIAN: PAUL III AND CARDINAL FARNESE. NAPLES.
*(Photo by Alinari.)*

## Portraits

Titian is one of the finest portraitists in history; his profound naturalism realises the very depths of character by means of the intensity with which he seizes upon the essentials of the physical temperament. He painted the most illustrious personalities of his own day, princes, kings, emperors and popes. He depicted himself in the *Allegory* of the Louvre, painted on the occasion of the death of his wife Cecilia.

# VERONESE AND TINTORETTO

*When he felt old age coming upon him, Titian designated Veronese as his successor and heir. However, Veronese was not his pupil, while Tintoretto, who was a member of his atelier, took the manner of Titian for a point of departure. But there is in the art of Tintoretto a violent and sombre romanticism and especially a boldness of execution which could well have shocked a master as zealous of perfection as Titian. On the other hand, the painting of Veronese radiates from a serene clarity. It appears to us to express miraculously the poetry of Venice. There are some visions in the manner of Veronese and not in that of Tintoretto, which we carry away from the city of St. Mark's and yet, for all that, Tintoretto alone is Venetian.*

VERONESE: MARTYRDOM OF ST. GIUSTINA. PADUA.
(*Photo by Anderson.*)

VERONESE: THE FEAST IN THE HOUSE OF LEVI. VENICE.

VERONESE. THE MARRIAGE AT CANA. LOUVRE.
(*Photo by Hachette.*)

VERONESE: THE GLORY OF VENICE. DUCAL PALACE, VENICE.
(*Photo by Alinari.*)

## Veronese

There is no decorator more radiant than this artist. Veronese, in contrast to Titian and Tintoretto, floods his vast compositions with splendour. The sky acts as a foil for the figures; the painter, even when he is not decorating a ceiling, sets up silhouettes against a green sky and white clouds. Architecture plays an important role; palaces of Sansovino and of Palladio frame the throngs of great lords. One admires these pictures, but dramatic feeling is almost always absent; these are festivals for the eye; the heart and mind cannot be interested.

TINTORETTO: THE PRESENTATION IN THE TEMPLE. MADONNA DELL'ORTO, VENICE.
(*Photo by Noya.*)

TINTORETTO: MIRACLE OF ST. MARK. ACADEMY, VENICE.
(*Photo by Alinari.*)

TINTORETTO: VENUS AND MERCURY. DUCAL PALACE, VENICE.
(*Photo by Anderson.*)

## Tintoretto

Tintoretto primarily took his palette from Titian: the glowing light, the tones of purple and gold. But Titian's harmony of colours was obtained by laborious work and Tintoretto was a rapid improviser. He has greatly simplified and reduced by means of sharp contrasts many of the delicate nuances. Furthermore, this painter is a draftsman of violent postures and of movement. He was inspired by the vehement gesticulations invented by Michelangelo. He had, it appears, written over the doorway of his studio: "the colour of Titian and the drawing of Michelangelo." That is to say that he wished to unite the best that Italian art had to offer. He is more dramatic than decorative.

TINTORETTO: PARADISE. DUCAL PALACE, VENICE.
(*Photo by Anderson.*)

TINTORETTO: CALVARY. SCUOLA DI SAN ROCCO, VENICE.
(*Photo by Alinari.*)

## Tintoretto

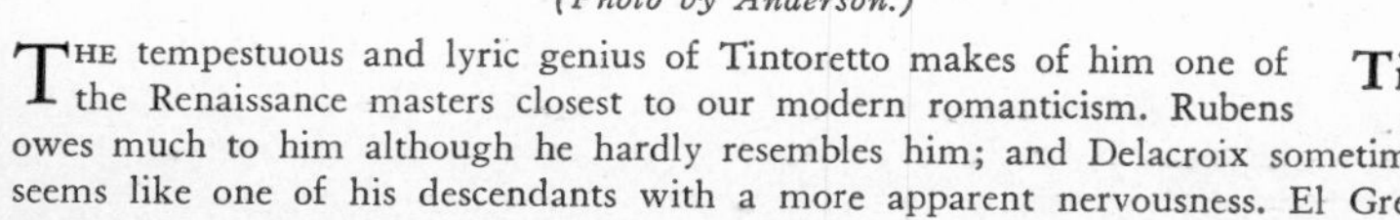

The tempestuous and lyric genius of Tintoretto makes of him one of the Renaissance masters closest to our modern romanticism. Rubens owes much to him although he hardly resembles him; and Delacroix sometimes seems like one of his descendants with a more apparent nervousness. El Greco pushes to absurdity his boldness in distortion. Some of the compositions of Tintoretto as, for example, the *Paradise* and the *Calvary*, are together with the works of Michelangelo the most formidable pictures designed by the human mind.

# CORREGGIO AND THE SCHOOL OF BOLOGNA

*During the Renaissance, the two principal centres of Italian painting were the school of Florence (including the Umbrian and the Roman masters) and the school of Venice (with the numerous northern schools issuing from it). But there was an intermediate region, that of Emilia, which always accepted the influences of both the North and the South, those of Venice and Florence. At Parma lived Correggio, one of the most original masters of Italian art. At Bologna, eclecticism was born.*

CORREGGIO: THE MADONNA OF ST. JEROME. PINACOTECA, PARMA.
*(Photo by Anderson.)*

CORREGGIO: DANAE. BORGHESE GALLERY, ROME.
*(Photo by Anderson.)*

CORREGGIO: THE MYSTIC MARRIAGE OF ST. CATHERINE. LOUVRE.
*(Photo by Hachette.)*

## Correggio

The great museums of Europe contain paintings by Correggio which appear as among the most seductive works in Italian art. But it is at Parma only that we learn that Correggio was one of the most prolific decorators, the most powerful of the Renaissance. He is, in short, the inventor of beautiful ceiling perspectives which transform the interiors of domes into pictures of heaven. There the postures reveal an admirer of Michelangelo. This painter is not only a student of da Vinci whose soft modelling he has adopted, but also his colour has retained Venetian warmth of colouring.

A. CARRACCI: VIRGIN AND SAINTS. PINACOTECA, BOLOGNA.
*(Photo by Anderson.)*

A. CARRACCI: LAST COMMUNION OF ST. JEROME. PINACOTECA, BOLOGNA.
*(Photo by Alinari.)*

DOMENICHINO: LAST COMMUNION OF ST. JEROME. VATICAN, ROME.
*(Photo by Anderson.)*

L. CARRACCI: VIRGIN AND SAINTS. PINACOTECA, BOLOGNA.
*(Photo by Anderson.)*

## The Bolognese School

During the last quarter of the sixteenth century, when the activity of the great schools of the Renaissance, Florence and Rome, and even Venice, was about finished, some painters believed that art could find a new life and they established a method of instruction whose essence consisted in using the best of the great schools which had just shone forth during the Renaissance. This was the first of the eclectic schools. The Carracci, of Bologna, were thus the founders of Catholic painting in the seventeenth century.

GUIDO RENI: SAMSON. PINACOTECA, BOLOGNA.
*(Photo by Anderson.)*

CARAVAGGIO: ENTOMBMENT. MUSEUM OF THE VATICAN.
*(Photo by Anderson.)*

CARAVAGGIO: DEATH OF THE VIRGIN. LOUVRE.
*(Photo by Hachette.)*

GUERCINO: ST. BRUNO. PINACOTECA, BOLOGNA.
*(Photo by Anderson.)*

## Caravaggio

The academic quality of the Bolognese clashed with the naturalism of Caravaggio. There were two camps among the painters: those who, like the Carracci, preserved the traditions of Florence and Venice, to which may be added the cult of antique sculpture, and those like Caravaggio who acknowledge no master but nature. This naturalism did not show all its strength until the time of the Spanish school.

tract from the freshness and brilliance which are the chief charms of this medium.

Pastels should be kept in a dry place, for dampness is their greatest destroyer.

See Pl. 8, Vol. I.

**PASTURE (Roger de la).**—See Van der Weyden.

**PATEL (Pierre).**—French painter (1620-1676), pupil of Vouet. Contemporary of Le Sueur and Le Brun, Patel had a good reputation as a landscape painter. He worked at the decoration of the Hôtel Lambert.

— **(Pierre Antoine).**—French painter (1648 or 1654 to 1708). Son of the above. The Louvre possesses the *Four Months* and a *Landscape* by this painter.

Pater: Conversation in a park. (Louvre.)

**PATER (Jean Baptiste).**—French painter, 1695-1736. Like Watteau, he was a native of Valenciennes, and he received lessons from his compatriots, but their incompatibility of temperament brought about a separation. His production was abundant and hasty; and he imitated his old master. He had neither Watteau's genius, nor the elegant refinement of Lancret, who pleased the aristocracy. The subjects which pleased him most were those taken from scenes of romantic comedy, such as *The Arrival of Comedians in the Town of Le Mans.* In spite of the hastiness of his execution, and the incorrectness of his drawing, his work often has considerable liveliness.

Bibliography: Florence Ingersoll-Sinouse, *Pater.* Paris, 1928.

**PATINIR** or **PATENIER (Joachim).**—Flemish painter. About 1485-1524. In 1515, received into the Guild of St. Luke, in Antwerp, together with Gerard David, whose pupil he may have been in Bruges. He was the friend of Albrecht Dürer who, in his journal, describes him as an excellent landscape painter. The two artists exchanged several paintings. His importance, however, was overrated. Most of his landscapes are painted in a characteristic blue-green tonality, with cliffs, villages and small figures in the distance. His technique is that of a miniaturist. Pictures which may be attributed to him with certainty are: the *Baptism of Christ* (Vienna), inspired by that of Gerard David, to which it is inferior; *Rest on the Flight into Egypt* (Antwerp); the *Temptation of St. Anthony* (Prado), in which he collaborated with Quentin Massys in Madrid, and *St. Jerome* (Karlsruhe).

Bibliography: Friedländer, *Altniederl, Malerei,* IX, 1931.

**PAUSANIAS.**—Greek geographer and historian of the second century A.D., author of a description of Greece which is one of the chief sources of our knowledge of ancient Greek buildings and monuments.

Pavia: The Certosa.

**PAVIA (Certosa of).**—The *Certosa* (Carthusian Monastery) was begun, in 1396, by Giovanni Galeazzo Visconti. In plan it is a Latin cross and similar to many German crosses in the triapsidal endings to sanctuary and transepts, but the nave is in square, and the aisles in oblong bays, in the Italian manner. On the south are two cloisters. The exterior is a fascinating and perplexing compound of styles. The most remarkable part is the façade of the church, in the most sumptuous Renaissance style. The architecture is elegant, and well-conceived, and serves as a frame for a profusion of sculptures, bas-reliefs, medallions, and various kinds of decorative work, and is by Amadeo, 1491. (See Certosa).

The church contains the remains of a pictorial decoration by Borgognone, some 15th century glass, an iron and bronze rood-screen (1660), recumbent statues of Ludovico il Moro and his wife, Beatrice d'Este, and the tomb of Giovanni Galeazzo Visconti.

The *Fountain Cloister* is decorated with little marble columns, and terra cotta ornaments.

See Pl. 2, Vol. I.

— **(Italy).—S. Michele.** A Lombard Romanesque Church burned in 1004 and rebuilt c. 1180-1125. The vaulting system is like that at S. Ambrogio, Milan.

**PAXTON (Sir Joseph).**—1803-1865. Author of the Crystal Palace, London, 1851, the first building to be constructed of glass and steel.

**PEALE (Charles Willson).**—Early American painter (1741-1827). He was born in St. Paul's Parish, Queen Anne County, Maryland, 15th April 1741. He was brought up in Chestertown, but moved to Annapolis in 1750 when his father died. When he was thirteen years old he was apprenticed to a saddler and when his term of apprenticeship was over he set up in business for himself. During the agitation roused by the Stamp Act of 1764 he joined the organisation of the Sons of Freedom and was put out of business by his Loyalist creditors. He had always been fond of painting and now he decided to take it up as his profession. He made a short trip to Boston in 1765, where he met and came under the influence of John Singleton Copley. The following year some of his townspeople raised enough money to send him abroad to study with Benjamin West in London. There he learned about miniature painting and mezzotint engraving and painted a few miniatures. In 1769 he returned to Annapolis and began painting the prominent persons around that vicinity. Some years later he moved to Philadelphia, where he spent the rest of his life. He acted on political committees including the General Assembly of Philadelphia, and served through part of the Revolutionary War. He was also interested in natural science and was instrumental in the founding of the Pennsylvania Museum and the Pennsylvania Academy of Fine Arts. He died 22d February 1827 and was buried in St. Peter's Churchyard in Philadelphia.

His portraits were done in the English tradition with the figure placed in landscape with some accessories pertaining to his social or political position. In 1772 he made a portrait of George Washington which is now in the New York Public Library and he did six other studies of him from life, about sixty portraits of the man in all. It is these portraits as well as those of other celebrities that have established his reputation.

Bibliography: W. S. Baker, *The History of a Rare Washington Print,* 1889.—William Dunlap, *The History of the Rise and Progress of the Arts of Design in the United States,* 1918. —C. H. Hart, *Charles Willson Peale's Allegory of William Pitt, Earl of Chatham and the Pitt Statues in Cork, Ireland and Charleston, South Carolina,* 1915.—Cuthbert Lee, *Early American Portrait Painters,* 1929.—A. C. Peale, *Charles Willson Peale and His Services during the American Revolution,* n.d.—H. W. Sellers, *Engravings by Charles Willson Peale, Limner,* 1933.—*Catalogue of an Exhibition of Portraits by Charles Willson Peale and James Peale and Rembrandt Peale,* Pennsylvania Academy of Fine Arts, Philadelphia, 1923.

— **(Rembrandt).**—American painter (1778-1860), son of C. W. Peale. A noted portrait painter in Philadelphia; won much praise while making a stay in Paris during the reign of Napoleon I, when he painted the portraits of several eminent Frenchmen. David, we are told, ranked him as high as Gerard.

**PECORI (Domenico).** — Italian painter. Died of plague in 1527. Pupil of Don Pietro Dei. He was the author of a *Madonna* in the Church of Campriano, of a *Madonna della Misericordia,* in the Museum of Arezzo, and of a *Circumcision* in the Sant'Agostino of Arezzo, painted in collaboration with Lo Spagna and Niccolò Soggi.

Bibliography: Crowe and Cavalcaselle, *A History of Painting in Italy,* Vol. V. London, 1914.

**PEDIMENT.**—The triangular gable formed by the sloping roof of a building; also applied to a similar form used as decoration over doors, etc.

**PEETERS.**—Family of Flemish painters: Gilles (1612-1653) landscape painter; Bonaventura (1614-1652), the most famous of them, a marine painter. Jan Peeters (1624-1677) also a marine-painter is far from equaling Bonaventura.

The youngest of these three brothers, Gilles, had three sons, who were mediocre artists.

**PEIPING** or **PEKING.**—The *Temple of Heaven* was built in Peiping under the Emperor Yung-lo (third sovereign of the Ming Dynasty) in 1420 to celebrate the ceremonies of the official worship (the religion of Confucius). The building is composed of several altars: the High-Altar of Heaven (T'ien-T'an) built of white marble, formed of three superimposed terraces, 25 feet high, of which the first is 120 feet in diameter, surrounded by marble balustrades, supporting a stone table on which animals were sacrificed. Both it and the Temple of the Imperial Tablets have a gilt dome; the latter, of the t'ing type, has a roof covered with blue enamelled bricks.

Peiping: Temple of Confucius.

To the north of the High-Altar of Heaven is a marble altar in three tiers, "the Altar of Prayer for the Grain," and then "the Altar of Prayer for the Year," which is 35 metres high and has three superimposed roofs resting on twelve cedar pillars. During the ceremonies, "everything is blue inside the temple. The utensils for sacrifice are of blue porcelain, the faithful are dressed in blue brocade, and the very light is blue, for daylight only penetrates through thin rods of blue glass." In 1531, the Emperor Kia-Tsing built the Altar of the Earth (Ti t'an) to the north of the enclosure, and then the Temples of the Sun and the Moon to the east and west. These three are identical with the Temple of Heaven, but smaller in size.

*The Imperial Palace* is surrounded by a fortified enclosing wall, consisting of forty-eight vast palaces which are built in the middle of rectangular courts and symmetrical gardens. In the centre is the largest palace, the T'ai-ho-Tien, or Hall of the Highest Peace, covered with three enormous projecting roofs, covered with enamelled bricks, and supported by eight pillars on each side. All the other palaces are built on the same plan. Only the dimensions vary. The whole is grandiose and imposing, although monotonous.

*Tombs of the Ming.* The funeral monuments built by the Ming dynasty (1368-1643), in the neighbourhood of Peiping, are often known as the "Tombs of the Emperors." Thirteen emperors are buried there. The most famous and important is that of the Emperor Yung-lo (1403-1424). An avenue of colossal statues leads to a triple portico, opening on to a court. Crossing a little chamber, one arrives at the principal courtyard where the great hall of sacrifices is situated. It is placed on the top of a terrace, and surrounded by three carved marble balustrades and an immense vertical slab, resting on a tortoise, and bearing the posthumous inscription, "Tomb of the Emperor Jen Tsung" (erected in 1424). The tumulus is more than 800 metres round. An underground passage, 40 metres long, leads to the tumulus, the door of which is closed by masonry. But the east and west staircases give access to the terrace which covers the tomb. There, before the hillock and immediately above the passage which leads to the coffin, is the stone tomb-stone.

*The Temple of Confucius* is a faithful reproduction of ancient buildings dedicated to Confucianism. It is composed of several one-storeyed buildings, of the t'ing type, arranged on the same axle and separated by courtyards. The principal building is placed at the end of an avenue of cypress-trees. Neither paintings nor statues adorn the interior. In the middle of the altar of the main building is an ancestral tablet in ebony, bearing, in golden letters, the following inscription: "Tablet of the Spirit of the very holy Ancestor and Master, Confucius." On the walls other tablets bear, also in letters of gold, the names of seventy disciples of the master.

See Pl. 3, Vol. I.

**PELLEGRINO da SAN DANIELE.**—Italian painter, about 1467-1547. His real name is Martino da Udine. His early works, the still naïve frescoes in Sant'Antonio of San Daniele, and altarpiece of Udine Cathedral, do not distinguish him from other painters of the local school. But he went to Venice in 1508-1512, and was strongly influenced by Giorgione. The last frescoes of the mural decoration of Sant'Antonio in San Daniele (1497-1522) have a richness of colour characteristically Venetian, and charming figures in the manner of Palma. He painted an *Annunciation,* now in the Academy of Venice, and a pleasing *Madonna* in Santa Maria dei Battuti at Cividale.

BIBLIOGRAPHY: Crowe and Cavalcaselle, *History of Painting in North Italy,* ed. T. Borenius, Vol. III.

**PELOPONNESUS.**—See Greece.

**PENCZ (George).**—German engraver. About 1500-1550. Influenced by Dürer; Italian characteristics a result from a probable trip to Italy. His oils of religious topics and ceiling decorations recall the subject matter, plastic treatment and color schemes of Palma, Bronzino and Giulio Romano respectively. His etchings, mostly of mythological and allegorical topics, show an affinity to Raphael. His wood-cuts illustrate the writings of Hans Sachs, and Rivius' notes on architecture. Pencz was active mostly in Nürnberg.

BIBLIOGRAPHY: Nagler, Monogr., III.—Waldmann, *Die Nürnberger Kleinmeister,* 1910.

**PENDENTIVE.**—Triangular, curved, overhanging masonry which helps to support a circular dome over a square or polygonal area.

**PÉNICAUD (The).**—Family of Limoges enamellers, 16th century.

Nardon Pénicaud.—He is the earliest enamel worker of whom we possess a signed and dated work—the *Crucifixion,* 1503. This piece

PÉNICAUD (NARDON): CRUCIFIXION AND DESCENT FROM THE CROSS. (Louvre.)

reveals an art that has almost reached its perfection, and an artist who was master of his art. The background is blue adorned with gold fleurs-de-lys, and the garments are deep blue and violet, leaving no strong contrast to the white body of Christ. The colours are not very varied, but they are deep, and the gold touches are added with discretion. Most of Nardon Pénicaud's work is in the form of the triptych, *e.g.,* the *Virgin of Pity* and the *Coronation of the Virgin* (both in the Louvre), the *Crucifixion* (Bourges), and the *Coronation of the Virgin* (in the Victoria and Albert Museum).

Jean I Pénicaud.—We possess certain pieces signed Johan Penicault, or Johannes Penicaudi, or Johan-P., or simply bearing the initials IP. It is supposed that this Jean Pénicaud might well be the brother of Nardon. The similarity of their conceptions does indeed lead to the conclusion that the two artists were contemporaries. Some of Jean I Pénicaud's enamels were made after Dürer's engravings (the *Flagellation,* and the *Crown of Thorns,* in the Victoria and Albert Museum), after the *Hours* of Simon Vostre (an *Adoration of the Magi*). The Berlin Gallery possesses one of his finest works—a triptych representing the *Crucifixion, Calvary* and the *Descent from the Cross.*

Jean I's colour is richer than that of Nardon in whose work blue predominated. Jean favoured bright colours—greens, yellows, reds—which he enhanced by means of thin gold leaf imprisoned under a coat of translucent coloured enamel. A slightly excessive attention to detail connects Jean I Pénicaud with the primitives of the end of the preceding century.

Jean II Pénicaud.—We possess some pieces of enamel signed "Penicaudus junior," or "Johannes Penicaudi junior," or P. I. It is thought that he may have been a son or nephew of Nardon. His earliest works date from 1530, and it seems that he died about 1588. He

PÉNICAUD (JEAN): LID FOR A CUP. (Louvre.)

was a very fine artist, and cannot be ranked below Léonard Limousin. His inspiration was both Flemish and Italian. After Parmigianino, he made the cup (in the Victoria and Albert Museum), dated 1539, and representing the *Story of Samson;* after Lucus van Leyden, the *Adoration of the Magi.*

He sometimes superimposed coats of white enamel on a black ground, and attained great refinement of modelling by freeing, with a needle, the black ground under the white coat.

Jean II Pénicaud spent all his life in Limoges.

Two other enamellers, less well known, belong to the same family—Jean III (son or nephew of Jean II), and Pierre (possibly the son of Jean III). There is a moving *Crucifixion* by Jean III, in the Louvre. It has a dark green background. Pierre's work has no interest.

See Monvaerni; also Pl. 30, Vol. II.

BIBLIOGRAPHY: René Jean, *Les Art de la Terre,* 3rd part: L'Emaillerie. Paris, 1911.—P. Lavedan, *Léonard Limosin et ses émailleurs français.* Paris, 1913.

**PENNACCHI (Girolamo).**—Of Udine or of Treviso. Painter of the Venetian school (1497-1544), son of Piero Maria. He has been credited with the charming painted and gilded chests in Santa Maria dei Miracoli, in Venice, and, in the Sacristy of Santa Maria della Salute, a *St. Roch between St. Jerome and St. Sebastian.* He worked in Bologna, and in the Romagna, entering eventually the service of Henry VIII of England as an engineer; he was killed at the siege of Boulogne.

**— (Piero Maria).**—Venetian painter (1464-1515), of Trevisian origin. Pupil of the Vivarini and of Giovanni Bellini. To him have been attributed an *Assumption of the Virgin* in the Cathedral of Treviso, and several pictures in the Accademia of Venice.

**PENNELL (Joseph).**—American author, illustrator and graver (1857-1926). This artist was born in Philadelphia, Pennsylvania, 4th July 1857. Although brought up as a Quaker and educated in their schools he was more interested in art than his other studies. When he graduated from school he tried to enter the Pennsylvania Academy of Fine Arts, but was rejected. Though disappointed he did not give up that ambition. Working by day for the Philadelphia and Reading Coal and Iron Company, he studied evenings at the Pennsylvania School of Industrial Art. About this time he learned the technique of etching and came into contact with the illustrations of contemporary Spanish artists, including Fortuny and Rico. He soon gave up his business and finally was able to enter the class of Thomas Eakins at the Pennsylvania Academy of Fine Arts. In 1880 he opened his own studio and soon entered the employ of the Century Book Company as an illustrator. A great many sketches were made for their magazine for articles on such widely differing subjects as English Cathedrals and the Louisiana Creoles. This work entailed trips to the exact location of the articles and so led to his wide travelling in the United States and Europe.

In 1884 he married Miss Elizabeth Robins of Philadelphia with whom he had worked. and together they visited foreign countries and sent back to the *Century Magazine* articles written by Mrs. Pennell and illustrated by Mr. Pennell. Their permanent home was in London, where Mr. Pennell acted as art critic for the *London Star* and other newspapers and lectured at Slade School, University College, and in different parts of the country. His early illustrations dealt with quaint bits of architecture or picturesque landscapes, but in his later years the progress of industry or the *Wonder of Work,* as he called it, was his all absorbing interest. In 1912 he made a trip to the Panama Canal which was then in the course of construction and made a memorable set of lithographs of his impressions of the various scenes of industry along the length of the canal. The following year he went to Greece to make a record of the condition of the ancient temples as they were at that time. During the war with the special permission of the British government he went into the munition plants and shipyards to set down the modern way of preparing for hostilities. Later he made a similar series of the American industrial plants during war time. He returned to the United States to live in 1917 and soon settled in Brooklyn. He travelled to the Middle West and South, lecturing, and he also taught the arts of etching and lithography at the Art Students' League. The strain of such unceasing activity finally wore down his resistance and he died of pneumonia after a short illness 23rd April 1926. He was the author of a number of books, including *The Adventures of An Illustrator,* and magazine articles and made illustrations for about fifty books by other authors as well as innumerable sketches for current periodicals. Clear linear patterns distinguish his work throughout his long career. He was the recipient of many prizes both here and abroad and examples of his work can be found in the large cities of Europe and the United States.

BIBLIOGRAPHY: Elizabeth Robins Pennell, *The Life and Letters of Joseph Pennell,* 1929.—Louis A. Wuerth, compiler, *Catalogue of the Etchings of Joseph Pennell,* 1928.—Louis A. Wuerth, compiler, *Catalogue of the Lithographs of Joseph Pennell,* 1931.—For a complete bibliography see *The Index of Twentieth Century Artists* for June, 1935.

**PENNI (Francesco).**—Known as "il Fattore." Florentine painter, 1488-1528. Pupil of Raphael. His best work is his contribution to the charming decorations of the Loggie of the Vatican, and of the Farnese Palace. His next pictures—the *Coronation of the Virgin*, painted in 1525, from sketches by Raphael, for the convent of Monte Luce, near Perugia, now in the Vatican Museum, and the *Madonna with Saints*, in the Sacristia dei Canonici—already show signs of decadence.

**PENTELICUS (Marble of).**—Attica is rich in marbles. The most famous is that of Pentelicus. This marble mountain furnishes a material which, in whiteness and purity, compares with the marble of Paros. Nevertheless, the Athenians made use chiefly of the latter, until the day when the great works ordered by Cimon and above all by Pericles caused the opening of quarries in the Attic Mountain.

Bibliography: G. Richard Lepsius, *Grieschische Marmorstudien*. Berlin, 1890.

**PERCIER.**—See Fontaine (Pierre François Léonard).

**PÈRE LACHAISE (Cemetery of).**—See Paris.

**PERGAMON.**—This town on the east coast of Asia Minor was

Gaul killing himself after having slain his wife. (Group from Pergamon, Terme Museum, Rome.)

the capital of Alexander's successors. In the 3rd century of our era it was an important artistic centre.

Excavations carried out by Germans, from 1869 to 1880, led to the discovery of important monuments.

Pliny gives a list of the sculptors who were employed by Attalus on the monuments in commemoration of his Gallic Wars—Isigonos, Phyromachos, Stratonikos, Antigonos. Inscriptions on some of the monuments bear the names of Xenocrates, a pupil of Lysippus; Myron, a Theban; Praxiteles, and others. The subjects most often represented were: the battle of the Pergamenes against the Galatians; of the Athenians against the Persians; of the Athenians against the Amazons; of the Gods against the Giants. It is thought that the two celebrated statue groups representing the *Dying Gaul*, and the so-called *Death of Arria and Paetus* may be copies of votive statues of Attalus. The statues are treated with a realism which was new to Greek art.

The group representing a *Gaul Stabbing Himself after Killing His Wife*, is in the Boncompagni Museum, in Rome.

Attalus I, in 201 B.C., had placed on the Acropolis of Athens a votive offering recalling his victories over the Galatians. It includes a great many figures. Brunn recognises copies of this offering in a certain number of statues which are scattered in the Galleries of Naples, the Vatican, the Doges' Palace, the Louvre, and the Museum of Aix (*Dead Giant and Amazon*—Naples; *Wounded Gaul*—Louvre).

The German excavators discovered a great marble altar, forty feet high, with large sculptures. It is known as the *Altar of Zeus and of Athene Nikephoros.* It is composed of an enormous base, forming a slightly irregular square. This base is itself raised on steps, and round it runs a sculptured frieze, over two yards high. The important remains of this frieze are in the Berlin Museum. The subject is the old theme of the Gigantomachy (Battle of the Giants), but the sculptors have here represented a confusion of battle which was only made possible by casting aside all the canons of previous art. They showed great freedom of imagination in the expression of brutal force and disorder. It is impossible not to see a common inspiration in the work; but it could not have been executed by only one artist. Several mutilated signatures have been deciphered.

These bas-reliefs of Pergamon show how sculpture had been transformed since the classical period. It was now conceived as a picture, with accessories and perspective effects. It became narrative and picturesque.

Bibliography: Brunn, *Jahrb. der K. preuss-Kunstsammlungen*. Vol. V, 1884, pp. 231-291.—Ernest Gardner, *A Handbook of Greek Sculpture*. London, 1920.—Rayet, *Études d'archéologie et d'art*, p. 261.

**PERICLES.**—See Acropolis of Athens.

**PERICOLI (Niccolò).**—See Tribolo.

**PERIGARD (Churches of).**—See Pl. 44, Vol. I.

**PERIGUEUX.**—The town of Perigueux contains several Roman ruins: the *Tower of Vesone*, the remains of a temple dedicated to the goddess Vesone, patroness of the town (Perigueux was originally called Vesuna); the *Norman Gateway*, which formed part of the Roman Wall; the *Arena*, which held 20,000 people, and which was later transformed into a citadel.

The Romanesque Church of *St. Étienne*, formerly the Cathedral, is surmounted with domes.

The most famous church is that of *St. Front*, in the Romanesque-Byzantine style, rebuilt in 1120. Its form is that of a Greek cross of which the crossing and the four equal arms are surmounted with Byzantine domes. A tower, 60 metres high, supported by six pillars, dominates the building. The restoration of St. Front was begun in 1853 by the architect Abadie. The liberty he took provoked much protest.

See Pl. 44, Vol. I.

Bibliography: R. C. Lasteyrie Saillant, *L'architecture réligieuse en France à l'époque romane*. Paris, 1912.

**PERIPTERAL.**—Surrounded by a colonnade.

**PERISTASIS.**—See Greece (Architecture).

**PERPENDICULAR STYLE.**—Term applied to the latest (fifteenth century) English Gothic style. It is characterised by rectilinear lines and horizontal transoms.

See Pl. 50, Vol. I.

**PERPIGNAN (France).**—The *Château of the Kings of Majorca* (begun 1270) stands in the centre of a citadel. In the course of centuries, both have suffered many changes.

Perrault: The Louvre. (Two-storied pavilion between the gallery along the river and "the Charles IX window.")

**PERRAULT (Claude).**—French architect, 1613-1688. He studied medicine, and until nearly the end of his life he employed his title of

Perrault: The Louvre. (Entrance to the pavilion facing the Pont des Arts.)

"Doctor" for official use. He was anatomist of the "Académie des Sciences," from its foundation, in 1666. He had already proposed a plan for the completion of the Louvre, and this was accepted.

The translation of Vitruvius, which he had undertaken at the request of Colbert, had inspired Perrault with an enthusiasm for architecture. His *Vitruvius*, on which he was engaged for ten years, only appeared in 1673. He was praised by the Academy of Architecture for having elucidated, in remarkably erudite notes, the obscurities of Vitruvius's text.

The East front of the Louvre (1666-1670), to which Perrault owes his fame, tends to obscure the fact that he also built the greater part of the existing Louvre. The façade which overlooks the Seine is entirely by him. Here, Perrault realised the dignified, rather bare, rather monotonous forms which, as a theorist, he loved. The southern façade, perhaps the most original, is more French in taste. It has a happy proportion of plain surfaces and openings, and has a robust simplicity.

In his designs for other buildings, Perrault varied his style. In the *Observatory* (1667-1671), he conceived an austere, massive building without borrowings from the architectural orders.

The *Arc de Triomphe* of the Faubourg Saint Antoine (du Trône) was, on the contrary, a most graceful design. It was richly decorated with sculpture.

He was concerned with technical researches, and he followed the example of the ancients in placing the stones in position without mortar.

Claude Perrault's aesthetic theories present themselves under almost contradictory aspects. If the patient translator of Vitruvius keeps much of the doctrinal conception of his day, and if for him barbarism reigned in art from the downfall of the Roman Empire until the time of François I, he, nevertheless, took singular liberties in the full tide of academic despotism. "The beauty of a building," he wrote, "has this in common with the human body—that it consists not so much in exactness of proportion as in grace of form." He declared, at the very beginning of his translation, that the conception of beauty was allied to a kind of prejudice. Thus were aesthetic dogmas called in question.

Claude Perrault carried his tendency to organise into other spheres. He submitted to the Académie des Sciences a plan for the study of natural history, especially of comparative anatomy. When he built the Observatory he desired to create a kind of Faculty of Astronomy.

He held discussions on Animism, and dissected strange animals which furnished the Menagerie of Versailles. It was this which caused his death, at the age of seventy-five. He had been infected while assisting at the dissection of a camel.

Bibliography: P. Bonnefon, *Charles Perrault*, Revue d'histoire littéraire, 1905 ff.—Charles Perrault, *Mémoires de ma Vie*. Edited, P. Bonnefon, 1909.

**PERRÉAL (Jean), also known as Jean de Paris.**—French painter, born about 1460, died in 1530. No authentic work has come down to us. It is known that he painted portraits, and made drawings for the tomb of François de Bretagne (at Nantes), and for the decoration of the Church at Brou. It has been suggested that Perréal may have been the author of those works which are grouped together under the name of the "Master of Moulins."

Bibliography: E. Baucel, *Jehan Perréal*. Paris, 1885.—R. de Maulde de la Clavière, *Jean Perréal, dit Jean de Paris*. Paris, 1896.

**PERSEPOLIS.**—This capital of Persia was situated on the plane of the Polvar, before Lake Niris, on the site now called Mery-Dacht. Remains of several buildings are disposed at different levels on an artificially constructed terrace at the foot of a mountain.

There lived the Persian sovereigns after Darius. They cut themselves tombs deep in the side of this mountain.

See Persia.

**PERSEUS.**—See Cellini; also Pl. 18, Vol. II.

**PERSIA.**—Persia includes the immense tracts of country which geographers now call the plateau of Iran. The inhabitants of this plateau were partly conquered by the Assyrians, at least those of the southern part, or Media. Then, from the height of their plateau, the armed Medes and Persians descended into the plain of Mesopotamia, and vanquished, in their turn, ancient Assyria. From that time, after the short interlude of the Macedonian Empire, the Persian princes, Arsacides and Sassanides, reigned on the plain, and even the Romans were never able to dislodge them.

Persepolis: Façade of the Palace of Darius.

Under Darius (521-485 B.C.) Persian rule attained its height. It extended over more than half Europe. Darius divided his empire into twenty satrapies, which provided a heavy tribute in soldiers and money to the central power. He fixed his capital at Susa, whence great roads radiated over the empire. Persepolis was the place of the tombs of the dynasty. This empire was arrested in its expansion eastwards by the Scythians, and westwards by Greece. It succumbed in 330 by the conquest of Alexander, after lasting 230 years.

*Architecture.*—The Persian Kings expended much of their enormous resources in building palaces in the country which was the cradle of their dynasty. Every prince endeavoured to build a palace bearing his name, and decorated with his image. To hasten construction, brick was used as well as stone. The buildings were light, spacious, and covered with wooden roofs. The forests of Taurus and Lebanon probably furnished the gigantic cedar trunks for the roofs of the palaces of Susa and Persepolis. Persia is, in fact, destitute of forests. This wooden architecture was the result of a royal caprice. Side by side with this architecture, which could not endure longer than the power of the Persian Kings, a popular style of building, more in conformity with the country's resources, was developed. It is characterised by the use of brick, and the arch, and recalls Assyrian architecture. This style of building survived the power of the Achæmenians, spread under the Sassanian dynasty; influenced Byzantine architecture, and subsists in modern Persia.

Palace of Sarvistan.

It is in Persia that the oldest examples of domes are found. As the dome generally had to cover square buildings, roughly formed angle semi-domes enabled the circular dome to be applied to a square compartment, as at Sarvistan, and Firouz-Abad. To counterbalance the lateral thrust of these arches, external buttresses were not used. The partitions of the building itself were used as buttresses, and the abutment was carried to the interior. These principles were adopted in Byzantine architecture.

The palaces of the Persian Kings were covered with wooden roofs. These roofs were supported on columns, the capitals of which were carved to represent crouching bulls. The columns were fluted, and often rested on a base which sometimes takes the form of a bull and sometimes of a reversed bell. The capitals of Persepolis have many superimposed elements—first, a bell form (which recalls the capitals of the porch of Thotmes, at Karnak), then a corolla (resembling the Egyptian lotus-flower capital), volutes are superimposed, and, finally, crouching bulls. This capital is perhaps the most characteristic part of Persian architecture. It appeared in the reign of Darius, and persisted until the last days of the monarchy. In the Palace of Xerxes, at Persepolis, the bulls were replaced by a mythical animal, the unicorn with the paws of a lion. In all its manifestations, the function of this complicated capital is to make a transition between the slender column and the horizontal entablature which it supports.

Persian architecture, like that of Assyria, made constant use of polychrome decoration. Coloured enamel bricks were used. Bricks found in the excavations of Persepolis and Susa allow the reconstruction of rich, harmonious decorations. A favourite ornamental subject was the rosette, perhaps inspired by the flowers of the countryside. Decorative fauna included especially the bull and the lion. Sometimes the lion appears wrestling with a hero, sometimes files of lions walk one after another. The bull is still more frequent. Metal was also used for architectural decoration. Plaques of bronze, silver or gold were sometimes fixed to the wall. Precious metals, thinned down to leaves, were applied to the bricks to disguise them. The descriptions which the ancient Greeks have left of these palaces say that the king lived in a dwelling gleaming throughout with gold and ivory.

*Tombs.*—Funeral architecture, so important in Egypt, hardly existed, one might say, in Assyria and Chaldea. In Persia it resumed importance. It sometimes helps us to reconstruct domestic building. The tomb is often cut in the side of a rock. The face of this rock is frequently cut to resemble a palace chamber. But tombs were also built on the surface of the soil.

*Temples.*—To the worship of the stars which belonged to the Chaldeans, the Persians added the worship of fire. Essential to this worship was the altar. In Persia may be seen several monuments which the people of the country call "fire places." Among these old sanctuaries of the sacred fire are those of Naksh-i-Rustum. Two altars stand on a pedestal cut in the natural rock. In some places the altars have disappeared but the pedestals remain.

*Palaces.*—It is above all in the architecture of the royal palaces that the power and originality of Persian art are expressed. "At Susa," said Polyclitus, quoted by Strabo (XV, III, 21), "on the top of the hillock, each king constructed a separate building, with treasuries and store-rooms, to receive the tributes levied during his reign. The buildings remained as a memorial to his government." This text agrees with extent of territory which, at Susa, seems to have been occupied by successive palaces of the Persian kings. As to Persepolis, its ruins include those of four monarchs. These kings, following a custom which survives to our own day with the Shahs of Persia, concerned themselves very little with the buildings left by their predecessors. They sometimes even left them unfinished, or falling in ruins, and gave all their attention to the new buildings which were being constructed in their name.

Persepolis: Ruins of the Palace of Darius.

From the time of Darius, Persepolis was the capital of the Empire, and there are still to be found very important ruins. These ruins are enclosed by a rectangular space, and the terrace which carries all the buildings bears four inscriptions of Darius, in three languages—Persian, Susian, and Assyrian. From this it is concluded that these buildings are the work of this prince.

There were two ways of approaching this terrace. One made a long detour and allowed chariots to ascend to the top of the terrace; but the finest and shortest way is the one by which the visitor mounts a wide staircase. The first buildings one encounters at the top of the staircase are the Propylæa of Xerxes. The remains consist of two enormous pillars, 11 metres high, carved with huge figures representing the forepart of the bodies of two quadrupeds, with wings and human heads.

The remains of the hypostyle hall of Xerxes—thirteen standing columns, and the bases of others—allow of the reconstruction of this hall, which is the most important building on the plateau of Persepolis, and is believed to have been the throne-room (or apadana) of Xerxes. The capitals of the columns are not alike. Those of the side doors are composed of figures of unicorns; those of the central hall present that superimposition of elements we have analysed higher up —lotus-shaped capital, the bell-shaped capital, the capital with volutes, and, finally, bulls.

Persepolis: The Propylæa of Xerxes.

Near this apadana was built the Hall of a Hundred Columns, in which the columns are ranged in rows of ten, bearing the roof of the square hall. Nothing remains. It is supposed to have been burned down by the soldiers of Alexander; and, indeed, microscopic analysis reveals the presence of cinders of burned cedar wood, the remains of the roof which must have collapsed suddenly, dragging down the columns in its fall. These halls were the halls of state. The king lived in a less open palace. The Palace of Darius is placed on a terrace which dominates by three metres that on which the apadana of Xerxes stands. This palace was built according to the plan which dominates all ancient habitations of the East. It was closed, and the rooms were ranged

Persepolis: Hypostyle hall of Xerxes. (Restoration, by Ch. Chipiez.)

round a large inner hall, into which they opened.

There remain traces of other palaces in other sites. The most important are at Susa.

See Pl. 33, Vol. I.

*Sculpture.*—The civilisation of the Medes left no sculpture. In Susa, however, an Elamite art had long been in existence when the Persians came there.

PERSEPOLIS: BAS-RELIEF FROM A DOOR JAMB OF THE PALACE.

Persian sculpture took the form of bas-reliefs. Apart from the sculptures of Persepolis, the most important that have come down to us are a bas-relief from Pasargadæ,

BAS-RELIEF FROM PASARGADÆ.

which may represent Cyrus, though some authorities think it dates from the early years of Darius' reign. The king (if it is he) is represented in profile, winged like the genii of Assyrian art, the head covered with ornaments which recall Egyptian art.

The bas-relief of Tak-i-Bostan is one of the most famous works of Persian art. It is sculptured in the side of a rock, at a great height. It represents the Triumph of Darius. In its arrangement and narrative character the work recalls the Assyrian reliefs; but in the detail of the costumes and execution the work is very different.

Most of the remains of Persian sculpture are found in the ruins of Persepolis. They represent episodes in the life of the king. We see the costumes and types of the Persians at the court of Darius or Xerxes; and subject races bearing tribute. One relief represents the king enthroned, and the throne is held up by figures symbolising the countries conquered by Darius. It is easy to recognise the different nationalities. Over the figure of the king is the figure of Ahura Mazda with outspread wings. Sometimes the king is represented fighting against monsters, especially the griffon; or walking, while a servant holds over his head a parasol. A frequent subject is a fight between a lion and a bull—probably symbolising the king, and his enemies. It is, indeed, to be noted that this Persian art is not as purely naturalistic as Assyrian art. It has symbolic pretensions.

At Susa, the Dieulafoy mission discovered a great number of enamelled bricks with reliefs, which allow of the reconstruction of an extremely brilliant mural decoration. They compose a frieze of lions walking in line, and a frieze of archers (Louvre).

In spite of differences, Persian sculpture, in its technique and style, derives from that of Assyria. The figures are dressed in similar costumes, and the nude rarely appears. When it does, it has not the hardness of modelling of the Assyrian relief. Its fault is, on the contrary, a certain softness in the rendering

SUSA: THE FRIEZE OF THE ARCHERS. (Louvre.)

of details. The forms are rounder and fuller. The drapery is less rigid. The Persian sculptor was able to represent different types of physiognomy, without analysing them very closely. He was not, however, as successful as the Assyrian sculptor in rendering movement.

Persian sculpture was not the spontaneous creation of a people using the language of form, as well as of words, to express emotions and ideas. Figures and poses were chosen less on account of their intrinsic beauty, than for their import; and this was to increase the respect in which the king was held by his subjects. To this end, each group, each figure, each attitude, was subservient.

See Persian Miniatures; also Pl. 5, Vol. I.

BIBLIOGRAPHY: Ker Porter, *Travels in Georgia, Persia, Armenia, Ancient Babylonia, etc.* 1821-22.—Marcel Dieulafoy, *L'Art Antique de la Persie, Achemenides, Perses, Sassanides* (5 parts). 1884-89.—J. Dieulafoy, *La Perse, la Susiane et la Chaldée.* 1887.—G. Perrot, *Histoire de l'art dans l'antiquité.* Vol. V. *La Perse.*—Arthur Upham Pope, *An Introduction to Persian Art since the Seventeenth Century* A.D. London, 1930.—Sir E. Denison Ross, *The Persians.* London, 1931.

**PERSIAN MINIATURES.**—The flight, called the Hegira, of Muhammad in 622 from Mecca to Medina marked the beginning of Islam, a new and great civilization. In 632, on the death of the Muhammad, the Arabs, converted and inflamed by the new religion, swept through Mesopotamia. Syria, Persia, Egypt, North Africa, and Spain. In these countries the Arabs found flourishing arts. With the aid of local artists and craftsmen, whom the conquerors patronized because they had few artists of their own, local traditions were fostered. In Mesopotamia and Persia the Arabs found the advanced art of the Sassanians (226-637) which was to have formative influence on the art of Islam.

Little is known about Persian painting before the Mesopotamian school of the 12th and 13th centuries. Recently, however, Arabic frescoes have been discovered at Kusair Amra (built by Al-Walid I, 712-715), in Syria, and at Samarra (9th century), near Baghdad. While the former show East Hellenic, Indian, and Sassanian influence, the latter unmistakably evolved from Sassanian models. Fragments of Egypto-Arabic frescoes of the 10th century and fragments of manuscripts of the 9th and 10th centuries have been found (Archduke Rainer Coll., Vienna), and literary evidence substantiates the belief that there was a school of miniature painting in Egypt during the Fatimid period (969-1171).

*Mesopotamian School (12th-13th century).*—The earliest Arabic miniatures belong to the period of the Seljuk Turks who came frim Central Asia, conquered the Islamic countries, and gave renewed vigor to their arts. The school of painting which had its most important center in Baghdad, produced miniatures whose style, fused with East Christian or indigenous elements and with pre-Islamic or Persian elements, derives from the international character of the Islamic civilization.

Most of these 12th and 13th century miniatures are illustrations of the *Fables* of Bidpai, the Hindu poet, the *Materia Medica* of the Greek, Dioscorides (copy written and illustrated by Abdullah ibn al-Fadl, 1222-23, pages widely distributed), the *Makamat* or "Entertainments" by Hariri (1237 copy in the Bibliothèque Nationale; 1250 copy in the Asiatic Museum, Leningrad). They are vivid in their contrasting colors of red, blue, green, and purple, in their firm and direct line, their simple narrative, their conventionalized perspective which depends on successive levels for the creation of tridimensional space, and their decorative interchange of stylized and naturalistic motifs.

Another artistic center of the Mesopotamian school flourished in the north where al-Jazari, inventor of mechanical contrivances, such as water clocks and wine dispensers, was commissioned by Prince Nur ad-Din Muhammad in 1181-82 to write a treatise on his inventions. His book, known as the *Automata,* was completed in 1206. Only recently a manuscript has been found which bears this date and seems to be the original copy (in the library of the Top Kapu Serai, Istanbul). Most important among the numerous later copies are one dated 1315 (pages distributed); and one written for Nasir al-Muhammad ibn Tulak, dated 1354 (in the library of Santa Sophia).

*Seljuk Period (12th-13th century).*—Persian painting of the Seljuk period survives only in some fragments depicting figures in bold colors, and in the painted decoration on Rhages pottery. The decoration, which is pictorial, both continues the ancient Persian traditions and becomes the prototype for the miniature painting of the later Mongol period.

*Mongol Period (13th-14th century).*—Persia, under the Mongols, nomads from Central Asia who conquered the whole of the Asiatic mainland, was ruled by Hulagu, founder of the Il-khan dynasty whose capital was Tabriz. Hulagu brought with him from Yuan China not only Chinese books which were placed in his library in Maragha, but Chinese architects and painters. The Mongols, after the holocaust of their invasion, adopted Persian culture and, like the Arabs before them, cultivated the native arts. The manuscripts of this period are characterized by their brilliant color, monumental and realistic style, and large page size. Several styles coexisted: Mesopotamian, Central Asian (sometimes called Sino-Mongolian), Chinese and Persian.

The earliest known manuscript of this period is the Persian copy of Ibn Bakhtishu's *Manafi al-Hayawan* (Description of Animals), now in the Morgan Library. It was completed between 1295-1300 for Ghazan Khan of the Il-khan dynasty and is the product of several collaborators, probably three, each with his individual style. Most of the miniatures, particularly those with landscapes, reflect the black and white paintings of the Sung and Yuan dynasties. Some, like the unusual representation of Adam and Eve draped in Indian garments, are reminiscent of Central Asian and Indian (post-Ajanta) painting. Others are so Chinese in character that the theory has been projected that they were painted by Chinese artists working in the court of Ghazan Khan. In comparison with the miniatures of the Mesopotamian school, the style of which persists in several of these illustrations, those of the Mongol period are more naturalistic. The influence of China is especially evident in the treatment of landscape, plants, and personages.

Invaders and conquerors, the Mongols, originally a war-like people, showed marked preference for the *Shah-nama* (Book of Kings), an epic relating the heroic wars and exploits of the Iranian kings, written by the poet Firdausi in 1009-10. The most famous copy is the *Demotte Shah-nama,* so-called after the name of its former owner (pages now distributed). This manuscript was also illustrated by several artists. The colors, composed of blue, red, gray and green, are striking. There is a great deal of movement, especially in the battle scenes, and the figures begin to move in organic space and natural surroundings. Chinese landscape elements, drawn in black and white and slightly tinted, are so combined with polychromed Persian figures and buildings that it has been thought that the figures were executed by one artist while the backgrounds were painted by another.

Another famous manuscript of the Mongol school is the *Jami at-Tawarikh*, or "Universal History," written by Rashid ad-Din, dated 1307-1314 (now divided between the Royal Asiatic Society, London, and Edinburgh University). An important later copy, c. 1400, is in the Bibliothèque Nationale. The first, the work of several artists, clearly illustrates the Chinese style while an early 14th century copy of the *Shah-nama* (pages in the A. Chester Beatty collection) exemplifies the more lavish color and more refined drawing of the earlier Persian style of the Seljuk period, 12th and 13th centuries, which was to become the model for the later school of Persian miniatures.

*Timurid Period (late 14th-15th century).*—A Turkish tribe, under the leadership of Timur or Tamerlane (1369-1404) conquered Persia at the end of the 14th century and established a new center at Samarkand. No abrupt change was reflected in the miniature art of the Timurids but with the disintegration of the warrior class and its rugged vitality, there arose a culture more refined, more subtle, and more consciously artistic. There developed the great art of the book comprised of calligraphy which was prized most highly, of painted illustrations, of decorative illuminations (e.g., *tughra* or monograms, ornamented titles, and marginal embellishments), and of precious bindings. Under the active patronage of Shah Rukh (1404-17, the Son of Timur), and Prince Baisunkur Mirza (1397-1433, the grandson of the conqueror), the great calligraphers of the period (Ja'far Baisunkur and Sultan Ali Mashhadi) were employed to make copies of the popular books of the period. At Herat, which became the center of Persian culture after Timur, Ja'far was placed in charge of an academy of forty calligraphers and miniaturists. The *Shah-nama* continued to attract the attention of calligrapher and painter but a new school of Persian literature which had developed presented the miniaturist with idyllic material for his illustrations and an exquisite harmony was achieved between the text and its pictorial accompaniment. Most popular were the writings of the poets Nizami (1140-1203) and Sa'di (1184-1292).

The new style of miniature painting that evolved manifests little Chinese influence. It is characterized by its delicacy, its predilection for illustrations of small scale and figures of small size, its insistence on the elegant silhouette, its interest in detail and multifarious colors of enamelled appearance, its harmonious and lyrical interplay of all compositional elements: figures, architecture, and landscape. Spongy mountains and low bound turbans are emblematic of this school. Though the costumes and customs depicted are so realistic as to be accurate historically, yet the style of portrayal is such that the figures move as imagined beings in an imaginary and romantic world.

Among the most famous manuscripts of this period are: pages from the *Shah-nama*, dated 1397, divided between the A. Chester Beatty Coll. and the British Museum, a magnificent example of the combined arts of the book; a *Shah-nama* of 1393 in the Egyptian Library, Cairo, copied in Shiraz which has been considered as the probable cradle of the Timurid style; a Herat copy of Nizami's *Khamsa* (Quintet), 1405-47, in the Louis Cartier Coll.; Ja'far Baisunkuri's copy of Sa'di's *Gulistan* (Rose Garden), dated 1426; and the same famous calligrapher's copy of the *Shah-nama*, dated 1429-30, in the Gulistan Museum, Teheran. The continuation of the Mongol style with its greater freedom and use of Chinese elements is exemplified by: several pages of the *Shah-nama* of 1397, mentioned above; copy of the *Shah-nama*, 1430, divided between the Metropolitan Museum and Paul J. Sachs Coll.; the *Mi'raj-nama* (Book of the Prophet), Herat 1436, in the Bibliothèque Nationale. The Mesopotamian style also had expression during the Timurid period, e.g. Kazwini's *Wonders of Creation* (A. Chester Beatty Coll.).

Towards the end of the 15th century miniature painting was dominated by one figure, the artist Behzad, born c. 1440, died 1525. Only very few miniatures can definitely be assigned to his hand although many not only are ascribed to him but bear his frequently forged signature. Behzad brought the Timurid style to a magnificent fulfillment. In his works and those of his followers the miniature became an even more sumptuous art. As a subtle colorist and master of harmonious tints he is unrivalled. His fame also rests on his exquisite line drawing and his remarkable ability to characterize his figures by their lineaments and their gestures. His is admired for his use of space, his knowledge of nature, and his genius for illustration. His style and his method of working is made clear in the unfinished miniature in the Philip Hofer Collection. Three of the most important manuscripts by Behzad are: copy of Sa'di's *Bustan*, 1478-1479,—"Painted by the slave, the singer. Behzad—may evil better his condition" (colophon written by the calligrapher, Mir Shaikh Muhammad and quoted here from Dr. Dimand); *Khamsa*, 1442 and later, British Museum; *Bustan*, 1488, Egyptian Library, Cairo, considered to be Behzad's masterpiece.

*Early Safavid Period (16th century).*—It was in the 16th century, under the early Safavid rule (1502-1736), that miniature painting, in accordance with the luxurious and gay court, reached its most sumptuous stage of development. Under the rule of Shah Tahmasp (1524-1576), himself a painter and student of Behzad and the court painter, Sultan Muhammad, painting reached its climax with the work of Behzad and his followers. Behzad was protected and encouraged by the Safavid Shahs. Although Tabriz was made the capital, Herat remained active as an art center. Important manuscripts copied at Herat during this time are the *Khamesa*, 1524-25, the Metropolitan Museum, and the works of Mir Ali Shir Nawa'i, 1526-27, Bibliothèque Nationale. The greatest work of this period is a copy of *Khamsa*, made for Shah Tahmasp between 1539-1543 (Louis Cartier Coll.). It contains paintings by Sultan Muhammad, Mirak, and other illustrious miniaturists of this time.

In the latter part of the century, portrait painting became popular, representing the best work of the period, and many single portrait miniatures and separate figure studies were executed. Especially characteristic of these miniatures is the representation of the Safavid high turban (*kulah*). During the Timurid period independent portraits were painted for albums (*muraqqa*), not for the book. The outstanding artists were Ustad Muhammadi, Sultan Muhammad's son and pupil, admired for his slim elegant figures, and Sadiki Beg, known for his portraiture and draughtsmanship.

*School of Bukhara (16th century).*—While the schools of painting at Herat and Tabriz were active, Bukhara in the third decade of the 16th century began to draw the artists from Herat. Among the leaders were Mahmud Muzahhib, whose love scenes established the style of this school which closely followed the Timurid style of Behzad. These miniatures can be distinguished by the low cap turban and the predilection for brilliant colors, especially vermilion.

*Period of Shah Abbas (1587-1628).*—At Isfahan, where Shah Abbas patronized the arts, there flourished the last period of miniature painting in Persia. Miniatures of this period are less inventive and vital than before. The perfect cooperation between the book arts disappears and the illustrations become mannered and stereotyped. The turban of this time is plain, loosely tied, and frequently surmounted with a flower or feather.

The great painter of this period was Riza-i-Abbasi (worked 1598-1643). The majority of his paintings deal with single figures or groups of realistic figures—dervishes, pilgrims, and other genre subjects—drawn with a strong and sensitive calligraphy based on the hatched stroke. His characters are expressive, even caricatured.

Instead of the lavish color of earlier miniatures the paintings of the late 16th and 17th centuries are mostly monochrome ink drawings in the Chinese manner, touched with some mulberry red and gold. The pigment is thinner and as a result the jewel-like quality of the polychromy begins to disappear.

After a period of over four centuries the great school of Persian miniature painting came to an end with the introduction of incompatible European methods which resulted from open commerce with the west.

**PERU.**—See America (Archæology).

**PERUGIA (Italy).**—Umbrian town, picturesquely situated on a

PERUGIA: PALAZZO DEL MUNICIPIO.

hill dominating the Umbrian plain. It has kept the appearance it had in the 14th and 15th centuries, the period when it was most flourishing.

From the Roman period there remains a gateway, known as the *Arch of Augustus*, the foundations of which were laid down by the Etruscans, and a portion of the Etruscan walls.

The oldest church is *San Pietro dei Cassinensi*, built about the year 1000, a three-aisled basilica, with a gilded roof. It contains many pictures by Perugino, Sassoferrato, etc.

In the 13th century, Perugia began to adorn herself with fine buildings. One of the first is the *Fonte Maggiore*, built from 1277 to 1280. It is composed of two basins, and a bronze vase in the shape of a chalice. The lower basin is decorated with fifty-four bas-reliefs, representing the labours of the months and Biblical scenes, sculptured by Niccolò and Giovanni Pisano, and Arnolfo di Cambio. The second basin is decorated with statuettes.

The *Palazzo del Municipio* is a large building begun in 1281. It needed more than a century to finish this imposing building which is more like a fortress than a palace, with its rough walls. The interior was decorated with frescoes, of which only those painted by Bonfigli in the Priors' Chapel and by Fiorenzo di Lorenzo, remain, besides those in the Sala dei Notari painted about 1297. The palace contains a picture gallery.

*San Domenico,* built in 1304, perhaps by G. Pisano, was rebuilt in 1604 by Maderna. It possesses a fine glass window, made in 1441, from designs by Fra Bartolommeo of Perugia.

The *Cathedral of San Lorenzo* was built in the 15th century, in the Gothic style.

The Oratory of San Bernardino possesses a remarkable façade, the polychrome marble decoration of which, as well as the charming painted sculpture, was executed from 1457 to 1461, by Agostino di Duccio. The sculptures represent the *Glory of San Bernardino*, the *Franciscan Virtues,* and *Angel Musicians.*

The *Collegio del Cambio* possesses a fresco decoration painted in 1499-1500, by Perugino, for the Guild of Merchants. The figures represent the four cardinal virtues, the three theological virtues, Greek heroes and philosophers, and scenes from the Bible. It is sometimes said that Raphael had a hand in this work, and it is very likely. He is also the author of a fresco in *San Severo*. This fresco, the first which he painted entirely alone, in 1504, when he had left Perugino's studio, represents the *Trinity and Saints.* It is not without analogy with the upper part of the *Disputà*, in the Vatican (see Raphael).

BIBLIOGRAPHY: R. Schneider, *Pérouse,* Collection des Villes d'art célèbres.—William Heywood, *A History of Perugia,* 1910.

**PERUGINO (Pier della Pieve; known as Il).**—Son of Cristoforo di Vannuccio; born at Città di Pieve in 1445; died in 1523. He was called "Perugino" because he worked

PERUGINO: MADONNA AND CHILD. (Louvre.)

chiefly in Perugia. He went to Florence, where he studied in Verrocchio's studio where Leonardo da Vinci was a pupil. He was also influenced by Melozzo da Forlì.

He excelled in composition. His art expands in calm and serenity, and he places his figures in the pure atmosphere of wide spaces, with the horizon veiled in misty blue distance, lower in the center, rising toward the edges of his compositions. This exploitation of an infinite atmospheric space is characteristically Umbrian, and appears throughout the painting of Perugino's followers.

His earliest remaining work is the *Crucifixion with SS. Christopher and Jerome* in the Borghese Gallery, Rome. In 1454, Perugino began an *Assumption* (Museo Civico, of Borgo San Sepolcro), which was finished only about 1469. In 1481, he went to Rome, to work in the Sistine Chapel of the Vatican. Part of his decoration was destroyed to make room for Michelangelo's *Last Judgment*. But we can still admire his *Christ Giving the Keys to St. Peter*. It is perhaps here that his genius for composition may be best appreciated. In the frescoes of *Moses in Egypt, The Last Days of Moses,* and the *Baptism of Christ*, also in the Sistine, Perugino was assisted by pupils.

During the following years, documents are often wanting, which would allow us to follow his movements, but his hand can be recognised in a great number of works. There are the *Madonnas*, in the National Gallery, in the Hofmuseum (1493—Vienna); and in the Louvre; the Uffizi (1493); *Apollo and Marsyas,* in the Louvre; a triptych in the Villa Albani, Rome; a *St. Sebastian*, in the Louvre; the *Madonna with Michael, Raphael and Tobias* (1499), in the National Gallery, etc.

The chief *Crucifixions* are those of the Borghese Gallery (mentioned above), of Leningrad, of the Uffizi in Florence. The finest is that of Santa Maria Maddelena dei Pazzi in Florence (1493-96).

The frescoes of the Cambio, Perugia, were made for Agostino Chigi (c. 1500).

In 1505, he was invited by Isabella d'Este—at the same time as Costa and Mantegna—to decorate her little boudoir with a mythological picture. This commission resulted in the *Combat of Love and Chastity* (Louvre).

In 1521, Perugino painted six saints in San Severo, Perugia, under the *Trinity* by Raphael, his great pupil. He painted frescoes in Santa Maria Maggiore of Spello and in Sta. Maria delle Lagrime, Trevi. These two fresco-cycles are also of 1521.

Perugino died two years later.

See Pl. 13, Vol. II.

BIBLIOGRAPHY: W. Bombe, *Perugino,* Klassiker der Kunst. Vol. XXV. 1914.—Williamson, *Perugino.* London, 1900.—Crowe and Cavalcaselle, *A New History of Painting in Italy*. Vol. V. 1914.—Bernhard Berenson, *The Italian Painters of the Renaissance.* Book III. Oxford, 1930 (revised edition).

**PERUZZI (Baldassare).**—Sienese architect, sculptor and painter, 1481-1536. He founded a school of classical decoration of the kind of that of Giovanni de'Udine. One of Bramante's most important pupils, he carried on his noble and severe style, but he began, with his rich decorations, to foreshadow the Baroque. In painting, he imitated Raphael in the Academic way of the Mannerists.

Peruzzi is known chiefly for his work in Rome. He was entrusted by Agostino Chigi to make his beautiful house on the banks of the Tiber —later known as the *Farnesina.*

PERUZZI: CLOISTER OF THE ORATORY OF ST. CATHERINE, AT SIENA.

Here the artist realised an exquisite work—"non murato, ma veramente nato," as Vasari says, "not built, but truly born," and seeming to emerge from the earth like the flowers in the beautiful garden which surrounds it, rather than constructed of heavy materials. Peruzzi devoted all his care and ability to it, and when the building was accomplished, with its wings and charming loggia, he painted the interior, and adorned a sumptuous ceiling with the constellations of heaven (1511). But the brilliance of this ambitious painting was eclipsed by the simple and delightful *Galatea* of Raphael.

The *Palazzo Massimi* (1535), with its convex façade, quite new at the time, and often recalled by baroque artists, also added to Peruzzi's fame.

Such an artist could not have failed to be called to give his contribution to the great work of the period, the rebuilding of St. Peter's. His part was not, in the long run, very important here.

Peruzzi's talent was universal. He was an adept at wood decoration, at the carving of organs or fine consoles; at painting in perspective, to deceive the eye.

See Pl. 7, Vol. II.

BIBLIOGRAPHY: Weese, *Baldassare Peruzzi.* 1894.—Crowe and Cavalcaselle, *A New History of Painting in Italy.* Vol. VI. 1914.—W. W. Kent, *Life and Works of Baldassare Peruzzi.* London, 1925.

**PESARESE (Il).**—See Cantarini.

**PESELLINO (Francesco).**—Florentine painter, grandson of Giuliano d'Arrigo di Giuocolo Giuochi, called Giuliano Pesello, a painter known only through documentary references. Pesellino was born in 1422; died in 1457. He is mentioned as a child in his grandfather's house in 1427 and 1433.

In 1447 he enrolled in the Compagnia di S. Luca (Gualandi, *Memorie,* VI, p. 181); in 1452 he is mentioned as in collaboration with a certain Zanobi and Piero di Lorenzo Pratese. In 1452 he undertook an altarpiece for Sta. Trinità in Pistoia, which was left unfinished at his death in 1457. His wife later had a lawsuit with Piero di Lorenzo, who was Pesellino's assistant, regarding payment (Vasari-Milanesi, III; Weisbach, p. 127). The existing portions of this altarpiece are at present in the National Gallery and include panels of the *Trinity and Two Angels*; *SS. Zeno and Jerome; SS. James and Mammas* (the last being lent by H. M. the King). The predella of this altarpiece, which was not executed by Pesellino but by Fra Filippo and assistants, is on loan to the National Gallery from the Collection of Felix Warburg, New York.

According to tradition Pesellino did the predella for an altarpiece which Fra Filippo Lippi executed for Sta. Croce, with the *Madonna and SS. Damian, Cosmo, Francis* and *Anthony of Padua*, now in the Uffizi. These predella panels include: three scenes in the Uffizi (8355) and two in the Louvre (1414). Little documentary evidence exists as a basis for the attribution of pictures to Pesellino. Among those given to him are the predella-panels illustrating the *Life of Pope Sylvester*, of which two are in the Doria Gallery, Rome, and the third in the Worcester Museum, Massachusetts. Pesellino is also credited with the Louvre drawing of the *Nativity* and a drawing of a single saint in the Uffizi.

BIBLIOGRAPHY: Vasari - Milanesi, III.—Gualandi, *Memorie,* VI, p. 181 ff.—Crowe and Cavalcaselle, Douglas ed, IV.—Morelli, *Gal. Borghese u. Doria-Pamfili,* 332 ff.—Weisbach, *Francesco Pesellino und die Romantik der Renaissance,* 1901. —P. Bacci, Rivista d'Arte, II, 1904, p. 8.—Chiappelli, Rivista d'Arte, VI, 1909, p. 314.—Cust and Fry, Burlington Magazine, XVI, 1909, p. 124; Borenius, Burlington Magazine, LIV, 1929, p. 140; LV, 1929, p. 145.

**PESELLO (Guiliano d'Arrigo; called Pesello).**—Florentine painter, 1367-1446. The grandfather and teacher of Pesellino. See Pesellino.

**PETERBOROUGH (England).** —Magnificent cathedral, built from 1116 to 1200, in the Norman style. The West front (14th century), one of the largest in Europe, is decorated with statues.

**PETITOT (Jean).**—French painter and miniaturist, 1607-1691. As he was a Calvinist, he lived chiefly in Switzerland and England. Nevertheless, he spent some years at the French court, and he painted miniature portraits of Louis XIV and the royal family. We have very few of his works. The Louvre, however, possesses a charming portrait of Madame de Maintenon; and one of his best works, Portrait of the Duchess of Southampton, is in the Duke of Devonshire's collection.

BIBLIOGRAPHY: C. J. H. Davonport, *Jean Petitot.* 1909.

**PHAESTOS.**—See Crete.

**PHIDIAS.** — Although he was closely associated with the public history of Athens during its most glorious period, nothing definite is known about the most famous of all Greek sculptors. He was the friend of Pericles, and his right hand in matters of art.

The date of Phidias' birth is unknown; but it may be supposed that, when he undertook the great works commanded by Pericles in 447 B.C., he was already renowned, and in the full flowering of his genius. Thus he was probably born about 490-485 B.C.

His first master in Athens was the sculptor Hegias. According to ancient writings, Phidias worked afterwards in the studio of the sculptor Ageladas of Argos. This tradition is far from being proved. Nevertheless, we know that Phidias was not only an able worker in marble, but also an excellent toreuticien and it is not at all unlikely that he had learned the secrets of the art of bronze in one of his masters' schools. The first-mentioned work by Phidias is a chryselephantine statue, consecrated to Athena. He next worked for Cimon of Athens, who ordered from him (between the years 465 and 460) a votive group, in bronze, dedicated by the Athenians, at Delphi, in commemoration of the Victory of Marathon. Pausanias tells us that the figures included

HEAD OF ZEUS, STYLE OF PHIDIAS.

Athena, Apollo, Miltiades, Theseus, Phyleus, mythical ancestor of the house of Cimon, etc. In this work, Phidias conformed to the style of the Æginetan bronze sculptors, who grouped separate figures in this way.

About 459, Phidias was entrusted by the Platæans with the execution of an Athena Areia. Pausanias informs us that this statue, which was doubtless intended to be made in ivory and gold, was executed in the most modest materials, gilded wood and Pentelic marble. Collignon attributes also to Phidias' youth a certain number of works mentioned by the ancients.

About 450, the Lemnians, who were colonists of the Athenians, desired to dedicate an image to Athena. They ordered from Phidias a bronze statue which was called by the ancients, the *Lemnian Woman.* Her young, fresh beauty enchanted all who went to the acropolis to contemplate the two more famous statues of Athena. The figure was several times copied in marble, and Furtwängler believes that he has reconstructed one of these copies by uniting a head, which is in the Bologna Gallery, to a body, in the Dresden Gallery. The head is especially admirable. The body, with its slightly rigid draperies, is rather more archaic. But "that adorable head, virginal and proud, seems less the issue of an expert knowledge, which reasons and calculates, than the spontaneous blossoming of an entirely fresh inspiration. She is the rare and perfect flower, such as an artist may gather but once in the morning of his days" (Lechat).

Cimon had asked Phidias not only for the monument at Delphi to commemorate the Battle of Marathon. He also ordered, at the expense of the public treasury, a colossal statue of Athena, for the

Acropolis. This statue was to recall the part taken by the Athenians in the recent struggle against the Persians. It was placed on the road which led from the Propylæa to the Erechtheum. Pausanias relates (I, 28, 2), possibly with some exaggeration, that from the high seas after doubling Cape Sunium, the plume of her helmet and the point of her lance could be seen flashing in the sun. On coins, the image of this Athena is represented as exceeding the height of the Parthenon. Actually, the statue being 9 metres high, including the pedestal, was considerably less elevated than the Parthenon, which was 21 metres high. The statue represented the helmeted Athena standing, a statue of Victory in her left hand, her right hand holding a lance. It was ordered before 449 B.C., the date of Cimon's death.

When Cimon died, Pericles was not content to follow his plans for the embellishment of Athens. He conceived more ambitious schemes. "The Parthenon of Ictinos, built on the old foundations, the entrance to the Acropolis adorned with the magnificent Propylæa of Mnesicles, the temple of the Goddess Polias entirely rebuilt, were to make the Acropolis unique in the world, and a perfect architectural jewel" (Collignon).

The works began before 447 B.C. They were probably incomplete at the beginning of the Peloponnesian war (432). Petrarch tells us that Phidias was the friend of Pericles, and that, with the great statesman, he directed everything, having under his command the greatest architects and artists. A whole army of workers were engaged on the Acropolis—"carpenters, sculptors, bronze casters, masons, artisans skilled in dying gold, and softening leaves of ivory, painters, inlay workers, and engravers."

The chryselephantine statue of Athena Parthenos was solemnly dedicated in the summer of 438. It was made of plaques of gold and ivory on an armature of wood. Such statues were probably not of great solidity; and the richness of their material would tempt robbers. This work of Phidias still existed in the year 375 of our era, after which a text, of dubious authenticity, says that it was transported to Constantinople. But probably the precious metal was already melted down.

Pausanias thus describes the statue (I, 24, 5): "The statue of Athena is made of ivory and gold. In the middle of her helmet is set a sphinx, and gryphons on either side of it. The figure is standing, clothed in a chiton which falls to the feet; and on her breast is wrought a head of Medusa. The Victory, which she holds, is four cubits high. The goddess' other hand rests on her shield, and also holds a lance. . . . On the base of the statue is represented the birth of Pandora." Pliny adds: "On the convex surface of her shield was embossed the battle of the Amazons, on its concave side was the fight of the gods and giants. On her sandals were Lapithæ and Centaurs. Phidias indeed regarded every available field as suited to the exercise of his art."

We possess a good many more or less direct copies from the statue. Unfortunately, these are poor, and give no idea of what the majesty of the original must have been. "At the back of the Parthenon, in the twilight of the Greek temples . . . the Athena of Phidias presented a vision of unearthly splendour."

According to the judgment of the ancients, Phidias' statue of Zeus at Olympia was the work of even loftier inspiration. It was executed between 437 and 432, the probable date of the artist's death. Pausanias tells us that Zeus was represented seated on a throne, his head crowned with gold olive leaves. On his right hand rested a figure of Victory in ivory and gold; in his left hand he held a sceptre on which was placed an eagle.

Writers of antiquity all agree in placing Phidias in the first rank of artists. "It has only been given to one man to realise with such mastery the perfect expression of beauty, at one of those moments—so rare in the history of humanity—when everything helped to create the most favourable conditions for the work of a powerful and many-sided genius: strength of national feeling, and religious sense; great works to accomplish; an art already formed, young, vigorous, but still awaiting the master capable of interpreting, in a complete form, the pure beauty of which there was, as it were, a confused vision" (Collignon).

Phidias was a genius powerful enough to give concrete and visible form to an ideal. The ancients recognised in him a philosophical genius capable of conceiving and realising a divine figure. It was because of this that he surpassed his contemporaries Polyclitus and Myron, whose chief concern was to render the perfect human body. It was said of Phidias and his Olympian Zeus: "Either the god descended to earth to show you his image, O Phidias, or you mounted to heaven to behold the God."

For the Parthenon sculptures which were executed under the direction of Phidias, see the article on the Acropolis of Athens.

See Pl. 23, Vol. I.

Bibliography: Collignon, *Phidias*. Paris, 1886.—Ernest Gardner. *Six Greek Sculptors*. London, 1925 (3rd impression). Lechat, *Phidias*. Paris, 1906.

**PHIGALEIA (Sculptures of).**—The Phigaleians, a tribe of Arcadia, having been spared from the plague from which Greece suffered sometime in the latter part of the first half of the 5th century, rendered thanks to Apollo by building a great temple to the god—the Temple of Apollo Epicurius, of which Ictinus was the architect. The temple dates from about 450 B. C. The building is of hard, grey limestone, which is now covered with a pink lichen which gives it a mellow appearance.

Fragments of sculptured metopes, and twenty-three slabs from the frieze are in the British Museum. It is thought that the sculptures, as well as the building itself, may have been executed by Attic artists. The sculptures represent the battle of the Greeks and Amazons, and the contest between Centaurs and Lapiths. They are rendered with great vivacity, and show much invention in the variety of the attitudes. But there is also considerable inequality in the workmanship; and it would appear that, while some of the reliefs are the work of Attic sculptors, others are only the work of Peloponnesian assistants.

Bibliography: Anderson, Spiers and Dinsmoor, *The Architecture of Ancient Greece*. London, 1927.—Collignon, *Histoire de la sculpture grecque*. Vol. II. Paris, 1896.—Ernest Gardner, *A Handbook of Greek Sculpture*. London, 1920.

**PHILÆ (Upper Egypt).**—Here the Ptolemies built one of the most celebrated of Egyptian temples (600 B.C.). It shows the influence of the Romans, who worked there after them.

See Egypt: Architecture.

**PHOCIS (Greece).**—St. Luke of Stiris.

See Byzantine Architecture, Middle Period.

Phœnician Art: Statuette of a warrior. (Louvre.)

**PHŒNICIAN (Art).**—The Phœnicians, a people of practical traders and navigators, occupied a narrow strip of territory, between Lybia and the Mediterranean. Situated with one side near Egypt, and the other side near Assyria and Chaldea, they borrowed from these countries elements of their civilisation. In architecture as in sculpture they merely copied. Their buildings were of medium size, often very coarsely worked. They built hastily wherever they went. Phœnician towns were incapable of growth, since, wedged in between the sea and the mountain, as they were, there was no space for very large buildings. They were chiefly concerned with well-being and utility. The chief works of Phœnician art were ports, vast quays for unloading, fortresses, aqueducts and cisterns. The fortifications of Carthage are perhaps the largest of their constructions.

Very little indeed is known of Phœnician civil architecture, which has entirely disappeared. We are better informed about their religious architecture, though there are no remains in the country that we can study.

The oldest Phœnician works are the tombs. The Phœnicians interred their dead in subterranean tombs cut in caves, and, later, in the soil. The general shape of these tombs is a rectangular hollow, composed of one or many chambers. When the body was not put simply into the niche, it was enclosed in a sarcophagus of stone, lead or wood. The most curious of these coffins are the sarcophagi known as "anthropoidës" ("in human form"), which were coloured all over, and generally without an inscription. The Louvre possesses the richest collection of these sarcophagi (the *Echmounazar* sarcophagus). The Phœnician tombs, whose hollows were cut deeply in the soil, were generally surmounted by a monument in the form of a cone or pyramid. They have almost all disappeared; but some remain at Amrith.

The Phœnicians originally worshipped in the open air. They only built temples after seeing those of Egypt, which they copied on a smaller scale. The most famous were those of Idalium, Golgoi, Athieno, Paphos, Hagiar, Kim, Echmoun (in Carthage), Cytherea, and Byblos. They were roughly built with irregular blocks of limestone.

Their sculpture shows to what an extent the Phœnicians were a race of imitators. First Assyrian, and then Egyptian, influence predominated.

Phœnician ceramics have no artistic value. Their glass industry, on the contrary, produced objects, remarkable for their grace of form and beauty of colour, and they were much esteemed in ancient times. The Phœnicians kept the monopoly for a long time, as well as that of woven and dyed materials. To them is owing the discovery of purple.

See Cyprus.

Bibliography: Ernest Gardner, *A Handbook of Greek Sculpture*. London, 1920.

**PHRYGIA.**—The population of Phrygia was originally "Asianic." The persistence of the native "Asianic" cults lasted long after the so-called Phrygian immigration into Asia Minor. Tradition would lead us to believe that the Phrygians entered Asia Minor from Thrace some time before 1200 B. C. Homer states that the Phrygians rendered aid to King Priam in the Trojan War because of the fact that he had previously protected them against the Amazons (probably the Hittite forces) on the banks of the Sangarius River.

The oldest monuments are those which the Phrygians built in the Mount Sipylus district, to the north of the Gulf of Smyrna. Here, there have been found the remains of walls, an acropolis, and a necropolis, the chief monument of which is the tomb of Tantalus, spoken of by Pausanias. It is impossible to date this tomb, which has been much damaged.

Phrygia: Tomb of Midas.

On another side of Mount Sipylus is a colossal statue of *Cybele*. Not far from this are the remains of buildings. The most famous monument remaining is the *Tomb of Midas*, which probably dates from

# SPANISH SCULPTURE IN THE SIXTEENTH AND SEVENTEENTH CENTURIES

*In the great museums of Europe Spanish painting makes a fine showing but it is only in Spain that one can see many examples of Spanish sculpture. At the beginning of the sixteenth century, it came under Italian influence. Italians had set themselves up in Spain but, above all, Spanish artists were working in Italy; one finds mention of them even in the studio of Michelangelo. It was the imitators of Michelangelo who introduced the Renaissance into Spain.*

DIEGO DE SILOÉ: MARIA MANRIQUE. GRANADA.
*(Photo by Dieulafoy.)*

A. BERRUGUETE: ST. SEBASTIAN. VALLADOLID.

JUAN DE JUNI: DEPOSITION. SEGOVIA.
*(Photo by Dieulafoy.)*

HERNANDEZ: BAPTISM OF CHRIST. MUSEUM OF VALLADOLID.
*(Photo by Lacoste.)*

## Berruguete and Hernandez

Alonso Berruguete must be reckoned among the sculptors who knew how to assimilate Italian instruction without sacrificing any of the Spanish genius. Juan de Juni is an artist of whose origin little is known, to whom we are indebted for several works of dramatic realism. Gregorio Hernandez is considered one of the most perfect masters of Spanish sculpture. He knew how to employ colour with skill and taste. Spanish sculpture never renounced the coloured richness of painting.

MONTAÑÉS: ST. JEROME. SAINTIPONCE.
*(Photo by Dieulafoy.)*

MONTAÑÉS: CHRIST CROWNED WITH THORNS. SEVILLE.
*(Photo by Dieulafoy.)*

ALONSO CANO: HEAD OF ST. JOHN THE BAPTIST. GRANADA.
*(Photo by Alinari.)*

MONTAÑÉS: ST. BRUNO. CADIZ.
*(Photo by Lacoste.)*

## Juan Martinez Montañés

Juan Martinez Montañés was a follower of Hernandez. Monsieur Dieulafoy wrote of him: "No one else had the respect for truth nor a more lively feeling for propriety, for nobility and for the aesthetic, which the association of Christian idealism demands in the reproduction of human forms. He is a credit to the school; he lifts Spanish polychrome sculpture to a high degree of splendour; he looks down from the same heights as Velazquez and Murillo, his admirers and brothers in genius."

PEDRO ROLDAN: HOLY SEPULCHRE. GRANADA.
*(Photo by E. Beauchy.)*

ALONSO CANO: SOLEDAD. GRANADA.
*(Photo by Dieulafoy.)*

PEDRO MENA: MAGDALENE. VISITATION, MADRID.
*(Photo by Dieulafoy.)*

J. A. GIXON: DYING CHRIST. SEVILLE.
*(Photo by Dieulafoy.)*

## The Pupils of Montañés

Alonso Cano was a seventeenth century master who continued the work of Martinez Montañés. He was a painter as well as a sculptor. His *Soledad* at Granada has been one of the most popular works in Spain.

# FLEMISH PAINTING IN THE SIXTEENTH CENTURY

DURING *the fifteenth century, the Flemish painters after the van Eycks employed their qualities of observation and their prodigious technical skill in introducing the picture of their society into the sacred themes of religious painting. Their art had no ambition other than that of absolute likeness and impeccable execution. But, from the end of the fifteenth century, the Flemish allowed themselves to be influenced by Italian art which had just created a broader style at Florence, and during the entire sixteenth century they aimed to animate their exact studies after nature with the new Renaissance spirit of the Italians.*

BREUGHEL THE ELDER: THE MASSACRE OF THE INNOCENTS. KUNSTHISTORISCHES MUSEUM, VIENNA.
*(Photo by Bruckmann.)*

JEROME BOSCH: ADORATION OF THE MAGI. MADRID.
*(Photo by Anderson.)*

BREUGHEL THE ELDER: PEASANT WEDDING. KUNSTHISTORISCHES MUSEUM, VIENNA.
*(Photo by Bruckmann.)*

## Breughel the Elder

WHILE the majority of Flemish painters forgot their native style and poetry in Italy, Breughel the Elder, although he may also have crossed the Alps, never ceased to be true to his northern ideals. The faithful follower of the fifteenth century masters he remained the portraitist of his own region. No one has ever been more spirited and picturesque in painting the peasant, villages in the snow and the blustering banquets. Sometimes a bit of the Gospels serves this painter of joyous naturalism as a pretext. Jerome Bosch, of the same family, displays a taste for deviltries which continues the mediaeval inspiration into the High Renaissance.

VAN COXCYEN: MARTYRDOM OF ST. SEBASTIAN. ANTWERP.
*(Photo by Hermans.)*

FRANS FLORIS: FALL OF THE ANGELS. ANTWERP.
*(Photo by Hermans.)*

OTTO VAENIUS: CALLING OF ST. MATTHEW. ANTWERP.
*(Photo by Hermans.)*

MARTIN DE VOS: INCREDULITY OF ST. THOMAS. ANTWERP.
*(Photo by Hermans.)*

## The Mannerists

IT is at Antwerp especially that the new school of Flemish Mannerists was developed. They renounced the somewhat narrow naturalism of the fifteenth century. They compelled themselves, in the Italian manner, to depict vividly great athletic bodies, powerful muscles, violent attitudes, and bold foreshortenings. Michelangelo and Raphael were the models that they spurred themselves on to equal. They did not succeed immediately, but after a century they had assimilated the best of the Italian school; then Rubens was born.

AD. KEY: THE SCHMIDT FAMILY. ANTWERP.
*(Photo by Hermans.)*

ANTONIO MORO: THE DUKE OF ALBA. BRUSSELS.
*(Photo by Bruckmann.)*

ANTONIO MORO: MAXIMILIAN II. MADRID.
*(Photo by Anderson.)*

ANTONIO MORO: MARY TUDOR. MADRID.
*(Photo by Anderson.)*

## Antonio Moro

BUT while the Mannerists were losing their best qualities in wishing to attain to the grand style of the Italians there is a type of painting which these master observers did not relinquish—that of the portrait. Imitating the Venetians, and particularly Titian, they acquired more breadth without ceasing to be truthful. Antonio Moro is one of the most eloquent witnesses of the end of the sixteenth century. He painted at both the Spanish and English courts.

# GERMAN RENAISSANCE SCULPTURE

*This art remains Gothic even to the high point of the Renaissance; it belongs to the Middle Ages, and is only slightly touched by Italian influence. Its character is to a great extent determined by its favourite medium: wood. Wood tends to give sculpture a hollowed out and rugged character; furthermore, it is finished off with a covering of colour. The Vischers also cast and modelled bronze. Krafft and Riemenschneider also worked in stone.*

VEIT STOSS: RETABLE OF THE VIRGIN. CHURCH OF OUR LADY, CRACOW.

VEIT STOSS: ANGELIC SALUTATION. CHURCH OF ST. LAWRENCE, NUREMBERG. *(Photo by Stich.)*

ADAM KRAFFT: TABERNACLE. CHURCH OF ST. LAWRENCE, NUREMBERG. *(Photo by Stich.)*

ADAM KRAFFT: EPITAPH OF THE PERGENSTÖRFFER FAMILY. NUREMBERG.

## Veit Stoss and Adam Krafft

Nuremberg is, together with Augsbourg, and even more than Augsbourg, the city of the German Renaissance. It is in its churches and its museum that the majority of characteristic works of German art on the eve of the Reformation are found. Veit Stoss is the master of wood carving, an art which is very close to painting. In Flanders triptychs were executed in which the center panel was of carved wood while the wings were only painted; thus the two arts complemented and influenced one another.

TILMANN RIEMENSCHNEIDER: ANNUNCIATION. THE ABOVE SHOWS HOW SCULPTURE COPIES THE TWISTED STYLE OF PAINTING. NUREMBERG. *(Photo by Bruckmann.)*

THE "BEAUTIFUL MADONNA" WOODEN FIGURE. GERMANIC MUSEUM, NUREMBERG. *(Photo by Stich.)*

SHRINE OF ST. SEBALD. CHURCH OF ST. SEBALD, NUREMBERG. *(Photo by Stich.)*

TILMANN RIEMENSCHNEIDER: TOMB OF THE BISHOP RUDOLPH VON SCHERENBERG, CATHEDRAL OF WÜRZBURG. *(Photo by Hachette.)*

PANCRAZ LABENWOLF: FOUNTAIN OF THE MAN WITH THE GEESE. SMALL FIGURE OF PICTURESQUE SIMPLICITY. NUREMBERG. *(Photo by Stich.)*

PORTRAIT OF PETER VISCHER. SHRINE OF ST. SEBALD, NUREMBERG. *(Photo by Stich.)*

THE APOSTLE PAUL. SHRINE OF ST. SEBALD, NUREMBERG. *(Photo by Stich.)*

DETAIL FROM THE SHRINE OF ST. SEBALD: APOSTLE. NUREMBERG. *(Photo by Stich.)*

PETER VISCHER: KING ARTHUR. CHURCH OF THE FRANCISCANS. INNSBRUCK. *(Photo by Stich.)*

## Peter Vischer

Peter Vischer, the founder and sculptor in bronze, is together with Albrecht Dürer, the great master of the German Renaissance. He has represented himself, among the figures of his masterpiece—the tomb of St. Sebald—in a workman's costume, his tools in his hands.

# ALBRECHT DÜRER AND HOLBEIN

*The technique of Flemish painting rather than its style, spread into southern Germany. The Suabian and Franconian painters have always shown a severity which is far removed from the picturesque style of the masters of Bruges. It was in the second half of the fifteenth century that these schools flourished; they became extinct in the following century; a late and short time of flourishing. The German genius is more spontaneously manifest in the art of engraving. Before passing away, the school contributed Dürer and Holbein to the art of the sixteenth century.*

A. DÜRER: MELANCHOLIA. ENGRAVING ON COPPER.

A. DÜRER: ADORATION OF THE MAGI. UFFIZI, FLORENCE.
*(Photo by Alinari.)*

A. DÜRER: ST. JOHN AND ST. PETER, ST. PAUL AND ST. MARK. PINAKOTHEK, MUNICH.
*(Photo by Hanfstaengl.)*

## Albrecht Dürer

This Nuremberg master is one of the most original of draftsmen and one of the keenest of painters. His pen, his burin and even his brush definitely fasten upon and model forms with an acute touch, a little involved and scrawled, but so exact and so expressive that he introduces a forceful feeling even into the infinitesimally small object. In some of his paintings and engravings he reveals a curious and bold intelligence, an inexhaustible imagination and a powerful naturalism. Dürer lacked only a sense of beauty to have become one of the greatest masters of the Renaissance.

LUCAS CRANACH: THE FLIGHT INTO EGYPT. MUSEUM, BERLIN.
*(Photo by Hanfstaengl.)*

H. BALDUNG GRÜN: CORONATION OF THE VIRGIN. CATHEDRAL OF FREIBURG.
*(Photo by Köbeke.)*

LUCAS CRANACH: SELF-PORTRAIT. UFFIZI, FLORENCE.
*(Photo by Brogi.)*

## Hans Baldung Grün and Lucas Cranach

The other German masters of the sixteenth century naturally submitted to the influence of Albrecht Dürer. They imitated his tortuous sharp-edged drawings. Some, like Baldung Grün, by the selection of the subjects and the slightly sharp freshness of colour, still show the tender and softening inspiration of Cologne to which is added a slightly vulgar and fairly sympathetic good humour. Others, like Lucas Cranach, remind us that German art is far from the Italian type and in the confines of barbarism.

H. HOLBEIN: GEORGE GISZE. MUSEUM, BERLIN.
*(Photo by Hanfstaengl.)*

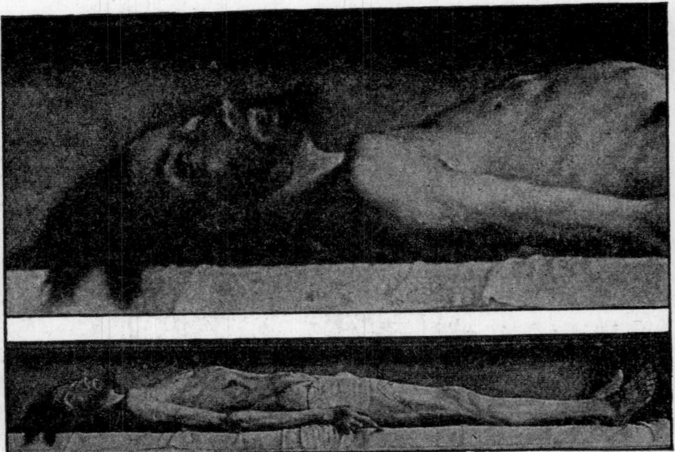

H. HOLBEIN: THE DEAD CHRIST. MUSEUM, BASEL.
*(Photo by Hanfstaengl.)*

H. HOLBEIN: ERASMUS. LOUVRE.
*(Photo by Hachette.)*

## Holbein the Younger

Hans Holbein the Younger, son of a master of Augsbourg, is only partly a member of the German family. He is of all these masters the one who best assimilated the lesson of Italian art. His drawing is nervous and sharp, but it is of an exquisite and impeccable elegance, which adorns the worst vulgarities with beauty. Holbein defines the forms with a free touch and models them with light shadows. What he reveals, countenances, hands, flowers, tapestries, is put forward by this flexible and decisive art with a supreme degree of clarity.

the 8th century B.C. The face of it is cut in the rock and covered with sculptural ornamentation. Over the façade, following the line of the pediment, is an inscription which informs us that this monument was consecrated to Midas.

The Phrygians do not appear to have built temples. The sanctuaries of their gods were cut in the rock, or in the earth. Sculpture had little place in their art. It is almost limited to some low reliefs crudely cut on the tombs and sanctuaries.

BIBLIOGRAPHY: Ernest Gardner, *A Handbook of Greek Sculpture.* London, 1920.—G. Perrot, *Histoire de l'art dans l'Antiquité.* Vol. V.—Wm. Ramsay, *Studies in Asia Minor.*—Charles Texier, *Description de l'Asie Mineure.*

**PIACENZA (Italy).**—*Cathedral,* 1122—13th century. An Emilian Romanesque church, cruciform in plan with transept terminating in apses, and with the three-storey interior elevation derived from the Apulian church of S. Nicola, Bari.

**PIAZZA DELLA SIGNORIA.**—See Florence.

**PIAZZETTA (Giovanni Battista).**—Italian painter (1682-1754). Born in Venice, he followed rather the Bolognese school. He had a taste for effects of chiaroscuro, and dark shadows. He greatly admired Guercino's painting. He has not, however, the cold correctness of the Bolognese painters; but shows a more vigorous temperament in his *Beheading of St. John* (Padua); *David and Goliath* (Dresden), etc. His religious paintings are, however, less attractive than his portraits and naturalistic scenes, such as the *Fortune-teller* (Accademia, Venice).

BIBLIOGRAPHY: A. Ravà, *Giovanni Battista Piazzetta.* 1921.

**PICASSO (Pablo Ruiz).**—Contemporary Spanish-French painter, graver and sculptor. The son of Basque parents, Picasso was born in Malaga, Spain, 23d October 1881. He spent his youth in Barcelona, where his father was professor at the Academy of Arts. Young Pablo entered this school in 1896 and received his first lessons in art from his father. The following year he was enrolled in the École des Beaux-Arts in Madrid, where he received a prize for draftsmanship. He visited Paris in 1900 and settled there in 1903, after having travelled through Spain. In Paris he immediately attracted attention for his wit, intelligence and fine artistic ability. Among his friends were Braque, Derain, van Dongen; Apollinaire, A. Salmon and Max Jacob were his sponsors. About 1908 the Stein family began to collect his paintings, this tradition being carried on by Gertrude Stein as well as Vollard. Picasso's work may be divided into several very definite periods: from 1895-1901, the Realistic Period, influenced by Degas and Toulouse-Lautrec and marked by carefully planned plastic arrangements and fine draftsmanship; 1901-1904, the Blue Period, rendering in a rather morbid and melancholy manner harlequins, circus dancers, etc., with the style still naturalistic and the colour almost monochromatic; 1905-1906, the Rose Period, somewhat reminiscent of the works of Cézanne and Van Gogh, painting of the *Saltimbanques*; 1907-1908, the Negro Period, when Picasso was beginning to be influenced by the Fauvist doctrines gradually leading to his cubist formulae. The paintings were done in delicate browns and greys, displaying constructive design and representing mainly the human figure. From 1909 to 1914 was the period of cubism, during which period the artist did not render form but tried to achieve it by painting those simple geometric shapes which, when combined, constituted the body to be interpreted. Creating form in this manner the artist has to discard resemblance and work with *abstractions;* he must be acquainted with the simultaneous rendering of surfaces and functional line and colour. Picasso also combined pieces of wood, sand and other matter with the oils. In 1917 he joined Diaghilev and his Ballet Russe in Rome; he travelled with them and designed the decors for the *Three Cornered Hat, Pulcinella* and other ballets. After 1918 Picasso returned to natural form and to classical painting, due to the influence that antique sculpture had on him in Rome. This new phase was preceded by a period of sketching and gradually lead up to the ensuing extremely plastic and gigantic paintings. Besides being the founder of cubism together with Braque, some consider Picasso the only great modern innovator besides Cézanne. Among his illustrations are those for Salmon's book: *Le Manuscrit Trouvé Dans Un Chapeau.* His best-known portraits include those of Stravinsky, Cocteau, Jacob and others. Picasso is represented in the museums of Berlin, Barcelona, Moscow, Dresden, New York, and the private collections of Paul Rosenberg, Paris, and Reber, Lausanne.

BIBLIOGRAPHY: André Level, *Picasso,* 1928.—Eugenio d'Ors y Rovira, *Pablo Picasso,* 1930.—Maurice Raynal, *Picasso,* 1921.—André Salmon, *Picasso,* 1920.

**PICCONI.**—See Sangallo (Antonio da, the Younger).

**PIER FRANCESCO FIORENTINO.**—Florentine painter, follower of Benozzo Gozzoli.

In a cadastral declaration of 1469-70, a painter, one Bartolommeo di Donato, mentions his son, Ser Pier Francesco, a priest of twenty-five, who may be identified with our painter. The will of Antonio di Matteo di Ricci, filed in Empoli in 1474, specifies that a picture after the design of "Ser Piero Francesco pittore" is to be placed on the altar of the Church of S. Andrea. This picture is still in the Gallery at Empoli. The same year Pier Francesco di Bartolommeo is mentioned as working in the Collegiata of S. Gimignano with Domenico of Florence (Ghirlandaio) and Mainardi.

His dated works include the following: 1477, *Madonna and Saints* from Barbiano now in the Gallery at San Gimignano; 1485-95, frescoes in the Palazzo dei Priori, Certaldo, near San Gimignano; 1490, large altar of the Cappella di Monte, near S. Gimignano; 1494, S. Agostino, San Gimignano, large altar; 1497, fresco, *Trinity,* Municipio, San Gimignano; 1497, the altar at Montefortino.

BIBLIOGRAPHY: L. Peccori, *Storia della terra di San Gimignano,* 1853. —*Di alcuni quadri sconosciuti di Pier Francesco Fiorentino,* Rassegna d'Arte, VI, 1906.—G. Poggi, *Una tavola di Pier Francesco Fiorentino nella Coll. d'Empoli,* Riv. d'Arte, VI, 1909.—P. Soulier, *Pier Francesco Fiorentino, Pittore di Madonne,* Dedalo, VII, 1926.

**PIERINO del VAGA (called Piero Buonaccorsi, of Florence).**—Florentine painter, 1501-1547. Pupil of Raphael, after having had several other masters who influenced him less strongly. He owed his development and his reputation to his collaboration in the charming decorations of the Loggia of the Vatican. Under the eye of the great master, he painted from his cartoons the *Crossing of the Jordan,* the *Taking of Jericho, Joshua Stopping the Sun,* and he contributed a great many ornaments, especially in the Hall of Planets.

He also worked in Genoa.

**PIERO di COSIMO.**—Florentine painter, born 1462, son of Lorenzo, a goldsmith. In 1480, he became a pupil of Cosimo Rosselli, whose name he assumed, according to a quite prevalent practice. In 1482, he accompanied Cosimo Rosselli to Rome, on work on frescoes in the Sistine Chapel. In 1504 he was the member of a commission to decide on the placing of Michelangelo's David. He died in 1521.

The sparse facts known of Piero's life caused Vasari to depart into a mass of fable concerning the peculiarities of his character, but he is more circumstantial in his discussion of his pictures. An eclectic and yet original genius. Piero was influenced by a whole succession of painters, including Verrocchio, Signorelli, Filippino and Credi. His fanciful imagination expressed itself with greater effect in his mythological panels than in his more conventional altarpieces, which tend to monotony. Of the former there are fine examples in Berlin, Dalkeith (Scotland), London, the Uffizi, the Collection of Prince Paul of Jugoslavia, and, very recently, in the Worcester Art Museum.

A notable portraitist, Piero is the painter of the *Simonetta Vespucci* in the Musée Condé at Chantilly; the *Portrait of a Lady as Magdalen* in the Museo Nazionale, Rome; the *Lady with a Rabbit* in the Jarves Collection, New Haven; the Portrait of Giuliano de San Gallo and that of his father, at the Hague; and the *Man in Armor,* London, National Gallery (after 1505, since the David by Michelangelo is seen erected in the view of Florence in the background). Among Piero's Madonnas and Holy Families are: the tondo in Dresden; the *Madonna and Child* in Stockholm, belonging to the King of Sweden; the *Madonna in a Landscape* in the Liechtenstein, Vienna; the *Madonna with Saints* in the Innocenti, Florence; the *Immaculate Conception* in the Uffizi; the *Adoration of the Shepherds* in Berlin; and the tondo that has recently become the property of the Toledo Museum, Ohio.

BIBLIOGRAPHY: Vasari - Milanesi, IV.—H. Ulmann, *Piero di Cosimo,* Jahrb. der K. preuss. Kunstsamml., XVII, 1896.—F. Knapp, *Piero di Cosimo.* Halle, 1899.—H. Haberfeld, *Piero di Cosimo.* Breslau, 1901.

**PIERO della FRANCESCA (dei Franceschi).** — Umbro - Florentine painter, born in Borgo San Sepolcro, between 1410 and 1420, probably matured in Florence.

The first record of Piero's activity is that of his assisting Domenico Veneziano in 1439 in the execution of the frescoes for the choir of S. Egidio (destroyed). In 1442 Piero was appointed councillor of his native Borgo San Sepolcro; in 1445 was charged with the execution of an altarpiece with the *Madonna della Misericordia* for the Confraternità della Misericordia (still in the Gallery of Borgo S. Sepolcro). Between 1440 and 1450 he was active at the court of the Duke of Urbino. Toward the end of this period he went to Ferrara where he did frescoes in the Este Castle and in S. Andrea (now lost). In 1451 he executed the extant fresco for Sigismondo Malatesta at Rimini. Between 1452 and 1466 dates the famous Arezzo cycle (Bicci di Lorenzo, who had previously been given the commission, died in 1452). In 1450 Piero was commissioned to paint a *Resurrection* for S. Agostino in Borgo San Sepolcro, for which he was paid in 1469 and which is now in the Gallery in the same town. In 1459 he did paintings in the Vatican for Pius II (lost). In 1462, the Confraternity of the Misericordia in Borgo San Sepolcro gave money owed Piero to his brother, indicating that the painter was then absent. The two portraits of Federigo da Montefeltre and his wife Battista Sforza, with allegories on the backs of the panels, now in the Uffizi, were painted in 1465-66, according to a contemporary sonnet by Ferrabò, which cites them.

In 1466 Piero is back in Arezzo; the Confraternity of the Annunciation order from him a gonfalcon with an *Annunciation.* In 1467 he is once more in Borgo; and in the next year he finishes a standard at Bastia, near Borgo, where he had fled to escape the plague. Piero is again at Urbino in 1469; in 1471-73 he is mentioned in fiscal documents in Borgo San Sepolcro; in 1474 he is paid for frescoes in the Madonna of the Badia; in 1477 is elected member of the people's council in Borgo; in 1478 painted a lost *Madonna* in the Church of the Hospital of the Misericordia; in 1480 he is appointed chief of the priors of the Brotherhood of S. Bartolommeo.

Piero was in Rimini in 1482, where he rented a house with a kitchen garden. In 1487 he made his will, and his death is recorded in 1492.

The first treatise on perspective was presented to his patron, Federigo of Urbino between 1474 and 1478; the second was finished after the Duke's death in 1482. Apart from the works mentioned above which still exist the following works are by Piero: three pictures in the National Gallery, London, the *Baptism, Nativity,* and *St. Michael;* the Milan, Poldi-Pezzoli, *St. Thomas Aquinas;* the *St. Peter* in the Frick Collection, New York; the Urbino *Flagellation;* and the Venice, Academy, *St. Jerome and Donor.*

One of the greatest geniuses of the Renaissance, Piero was one of the few painters capable of realizing to the full the portentous innovations of Masaccio, and of using them as a point of departure for his own researches. His achievements in space composition were so in advance of his age as to be beyond the imitation of the vast majority of his contemporaries and followers, who contented themselves, where they felt his influence, with borrowing from his types and style-formulae. Few painters have ever used space with the confidence, knowledge and exquisite subtlety of Piero; and few have created figures, which, like his, seem to come from a more-than-human world, of god-like dignity and nobility.

BIBLIOGRAPHY: Piero della Francesca, *De Prospectiva Pingendi,* ed. Janitschek in Kunstchronik, XIII, 1878. — Vasari-Milanesi, II. — Milanesi, Giornale stor. d. archivi toscani, VI, 1862, II; Il Buonarroti, III, ser. t. II, 1885; *Nuovi doc. per la stor. d. arte toscana,* 1893.—Pini-Milanesi, *La scritt. d. artisti ital.,* I.—Crowe and Cavalcaselle.—G. F. Pietri, *La vita e le opere di Piero della Francesca.* Borgo San Sepolcro, 1892.—Witting, *Piero dei Franceschi.* Strassburg, 1898.—W. G. Waters, *Piero della Francesca.* London, 1901.—C. Ricci, *Piero della Francesca.* Rome, 1910.—Roberto Longhi, *Piero della Francesca* (English ed.) 1930.

**— FRANCESCO DEI.**—See Bartolommeo della Gatta.

**— di LORENZO PRATESE.**—Italian painter, 15th century. Assistant of Pesellino in Pistoia (1453). A *Nativity* in the Louvre is attributed to him.

**PIERREFONDS (France).**—The famous Château of Pierrefonds, built in 1400 by Louis d'Orléans, was reduced to ruins by Louis XIII in 1617, and restored—one might almost say rebuilt—by Viollet-le-Duc, who replaced the ancient ruins by a new feudal castle, learnedly conceived and executed.

See Pl. 51, Vol. I.

PIERREFONDS: THE CHÂTEAU.

**PIETÀ.**—Representation of the Virgin grieving over the dead Christ taken from the cross, or of any group of the holy women at the Deposition. Famous *pietàs* include those by Fra Angelico, G. Bellini, Correggio, Quentin Matsys, Rubens, etc.

**PIETRO da CORTONA.**—Pietro Berettini of Cortona: Italian architect and painter, 1596-1669. He was born at Cortona, but he studied in Florence and Rome, copying the works of Raphael and Michelangelo, and antique reliefs. The *Rape of the Sabines* and the *Battles of Alexander* which he painted for Cardinal Sacchetti established his reputation, and soon afterwards Pope Urban VIII set him to work in the Church of Santa Bibiena, with Ciampelli.

His gifts as a decorator showed themselves on the large ceiling of the Palazzo Barberini, which is his most celebrated work. He there presented an allegory of the Barberini family.

He was commissioned for several ceiling paintings, among them those of the Pitti Palace. That of the sacristy of the Chiesa Nuova in Rome, on which angels hold instruments of martyrdom, is also by him.

There are several easel-pictures by him in the galleries of Vienna, Dresden, Paris, Milan, etc.

**PIETRO di DOMENICO.**—Sienese painter (1457-1506), influenced by Matteo di Giovanni and Francesco di Giorgio.

**PIETRO di DOMENICO da RECANOTI.**—Painter active during the first half of the 15th century in the Italian Marches; follower of Gentile da Fabriano, influenced by the Sienese school, particularly Simone Martini.

**PIETRO di GIOVANNI AMBROSI.**—Sienese painter, active 1428-50, assistant and follower of Sassetta.

**PIGALLE (Jean Baptiste).**—French sculptor. He studied under the sculptor Robert Le Lorrain, where he was a fellow-pupil of Lemoyne, his elder by some years. Lemoyne became his friend, and he afterwards studied with him. At his studio he met Falconet, a jealous rival. Pigalle made slow progress, and his comrades are said to have called him the "mule of sculpture." He failed to win the Prix de Rome. Nothing daunted, he went to Italy all the same—on foot, it is said. There he was saved from extreme poverty by Guillaume Coustou, to whom he showed lifelong gratitude.

PIGALLE: TOMB OF MARÉCHAL D'HARCOURT. (Notre Dame, Paris.)

He remained in Rome for three years. After spending some months in Lyon, he returned to Paris, bringing back a work which immediately established his reputation—*Mercury Tying His Sandal* (Louvre), a figure which expresses great lightness of motion.

Pigalle worked for Madame de Pompadour, for whom he made statues destined for the gardens of her Châteaux of Crécy (near Dreux) and Bellevue—*e.g.,* the group of *Love and Friendship.*

Graceful and brilliant as was his art, Pigalle also undertook such monumental tasks as the tomb of the Duke of Harcourt (1764), in Notre Dame, Paris, and of Marshal Saxe, in the Temple of St. Thomas, Strassburg. The latter shows the marshal descending with a firm step into the tomb which Death holds open to receive him. France, in the distracted attitude of a tragedy queen, tries to keep him back, and intercedes with Death. The whole conception is a little theatrical, but still imposing.

Pigalle's growing taste for realism led him to make a nude statue of the seventy-year-old Voltaire (1776). The figure is now in the Bibliothèque of the Institut.

In his later years, Pigalle returned to the graceful type of work which in his youth had inspired his *Child with a Cage.* From this time dates his *Child with a Bird* (Louvre), and the *Young Girl with a Thorn.*

See Pl. 45, Vol. II.

BIBLIOGRAPHY: P. Tarbé, *Jean Baptiste Pigalle.* 1859.—Stanislas Lami, *Dictionnaire des sculpteurs français.*—S. Rocheblave, *Jean Baptiste Pigalle.* 1919.

**PILASTER.**—A flat columnar structure partly sunk in a wall.

**PILLEMENT (Jean).** — French painter, engraver, and draughtsman, 1727-1808. The best part of his work is represented by his flower drawings, which were in the Chinese fashion of the day, and intended for silk factories.

**PILON (Germain).**—French sculptor, 1535-1590. Pilon, while influenced by the Renaissance, combined classical forms with the simpler, more naturalistic art of the preceding century.

PILON (GERMAIN): BUST OF HENRY III. (Louvre.)

Pilon was employed in making the various tombs of Henri II. As the sepulchre for the heart, he sculptured the *Three Graces* bearing a bronze urn. Until the Revolution, it was kept in the Church of the Célestins, Paris. It is now in the Louvre. He worked at the tomb of Henri II, from 1564 to 1570, under the direction of Primaticcio, who gave him the general design, and took part in casting some of the bronzes. He called other sculptors as well, but Pilon had the principal share in the work, and finally it was left to him. Like the tombs of Louis XII and Francis I, it is in two storeys. Below, on a marble bed, are the reclining figures of the king and queen. On a platform are kneeling bronze figures of the king and queen praying. At the corners are four bronze statues of Virtues, which are more Italian in their inspiration than the other parts of the tomb, which are simpler and more realistic.

Pilon sculptured in marble, stone, wood, terra cotta and bronze. He made monuments. bas-reliefs, busts. He was not solely occupied with form, and his bronzes have an incomparable patina.

He worked for the churches, in which many of his works are to be seen. For instance: the four wooden statues of *Virtues* supporting the shrine of St. Geneviève, in the church of this name; the three bas-reliefs of the preacher's chair of the Church of the Grands Augustins (the *Preaching of St. Paul*; *Christ and the Samaritan Woman*; the *Preaching of St. John the Baptist*); the *Entombment* in bronze, from the rood-screen of St. Germain l'Auxerrois; and the *Christ on the Mount of Olives* of St. Étienne du Mont. The two most important are the tombs of the Chancellor de Birague and of his wife. Of the latter, in marble, there remain but the two statues of the deceased, one seated, the other lying down, and two genii. The kneeling statue of the Chancellor (the finest bronze of the 16th century; it was probably painted) is perhaps Pilon's masterpiece. In its intensely lifelike quality, it may be compared with bust of Jean de Morvillier (Orléans), of Henri III (Louvre), and of Charles IX (Wallace Collection).

Pilon was also a decorator. The monumental chimney-piece from the Château de Villeroy (Louvre) is traditionally attributed to him.

In 1573, Pilon was made Controller General of the Mint. He made the finest medallions of his time, medals, and coins.

Germain Pilon died in 1590. His chief pupil, Barthélemy Prieur, forms the transition between his art and that of the sculptors of the age of Louis XIII. Unfortunately nothing is known about his son, Raphael Pilon (born about 1560), who was a sculptor, and worked with his father on the tomb of Cardinal Birague.

See Pl. 28, Vol. II.

BIBLIOGRAPHY: L. Palustre, *Germain Pilon.* Gazette des Beaux Arts. 1894-95.—P. Vitry and G. Brière, *L'église abbatiale de Saint Denis et ses tombeaux.* Paris, 1908. —L. Gonse, *La sculpture française.* Paris, 1895.

**PINE (Robert Edge).**—Early American painter (1730-1788). He was born in London about 1730, the son of John Pine, a well-known engraver, and the brother of Simon Pine, a miniaturist of some repute. He was trained by his father and in 1760 exhibited with the Society for the Encouragement of Arts, which is now the Royal Society of Arts. In that year and again in 1763 he won the prize offered for the best historical picture by that organisation. His main interest was in the people of the theatre and he made four portraits of David Garrick beside a series illustrating famous scenes from the plays of Shakespeare.

In 1784 he came to the United States, where he settled with his wife and two daughters in Philadelphia. He had been in accord with the colonies in their struggle for independence and was desirous of making a series of pictures showing important episodes in the Revolutionary War. In preparation he executed many portraits of the prominent persons of that era, including George Washington, General Gates, Baron von Steuben, Benjamin Franklin and Charles Carroll of Carrollton. Only one historical composition was ever painted, that of *Congress Voting Independence,* now in the possession of the Pennsylvania Historical Society, which was finished after Pine's death by Edward Savage. Robert Pine died suddenly 19th November 1788 and many of his pictures found their way to the Columbia Museum in Boston, which was later destroyed by fire with their loss. In consequence but few of his portraits remain to bear witness to the ability of this early painter and the majority of these are in private collections.

Bibliography: W. S. Baker, *The Engraved Portraits of Washington,* 1880.—William Dunlap, *The History of the Rise and Progress of the Arts of Design in the United States,* 1918. —C. H. Hart, *The Congress Voting Independence, Pennsylvania Magazine of History and Biography,* January, 1905.—J. H. Morgan and Mantle Fielding, *The Life Portraits of Washington,* 1931.

**PINTORICCHIO.**—Italian painter. Bernardino di Betto (born in 1454, died in 1513) was called "il Pintoricchio," the "painter in bright colours"; or "il Sordicchio," because he was "deaf, small, and of insignificant appearance."

Pintoricchio was trained in the Umbrian school, perhaps as a pupil of Fiorenzo, and was a close follower of Perugino.

In 1481 he joined the guild of painters of Perugia, and was associated with Perugino in the Sistine Chapel. He painted some figures in the *Testament of Moses,* and executed the *Circumcision of the Sons of Moses,* from a cartoon by Perugino.

At about the same period he did the paintings of the Bufalini Chapel, Sta. Maria in Aracoeli, Rome, where he represented the *History of San Bernardino,* with charming angels playing music.

From 1485 to 1489, Pintoricchio was once more in Perugia. In 1490, he returned to Rome, where he worked in the Palazzo dei Santi Apostoli, now Colonna, with Perugino (1492).

He also painted the charming blue and white *Nativity* of Santa Maria del Popolo, and the *Madonna della Pace* for the Sacristy of the Cathedral of San Severino.

Pintoricchio shows himself at his brightest in the Borgia apartments of the Vatican. He painted this decoration for Pope Alexander VI, with a great many assistants (1492-94), and the walls shine like precious enamels. In one room, he painted the prophets in medallions on the ceiling. On the walls, he and his assistants painted scenes from the Life of Mary—the *Annunciation,* the *Nativity,* and the *Adoration of the Magi.* In the *Resurrection of Christ,* Pintoricchio represented Alexander VI kneeling. The Room of the *Lives of Saints* was painted almost entirely by Pintoricchio himself. Over the door is the Virgin in a round frame. On the walls, *Susanna* encounters the elders by a richly gilded fountain, round which little monkeys and rabbits are playing. Even the fleeing *St. Barbara* is surrounded with riches, and her fear is not very great. The finest scene is that of *St. Catherine* (Lucrezia Borgia) *Disputing with the Emperor Maximilian.* Fair and pale, she stands before him, counting the syllogisms on her fingers. The spectators wear the richest embroideries, and jewels, and multicoloured turbans. On the other walls are *St. Paul the Hermit, St. Anthony in the Desert,* the *Visitation,* and a fine *St. Sebastian* whose martyrdom is taking place before the Coliseum. In the *Hall of the Liberal Arts and Sciences,* the *Allegories* (chiefly the work of pupils) preside on marble thrones in front of mosaic backgrounds. In the last room, the decoration on the vaulting represents Prophets and Sibyls, and has been a good deal retouched.

Pintoricchio was called to Orvieto in 1492, but he soon returned to Rome to work for Alexander VI, and only returned to Orvieto four years later, where he painted two doctors in a chapel of the Duomo.

He next painted for the Pope in the Castle of Sant'Angelo (1495), frescoes of the coming of Charles VIII to Rome. In 1495, he painted an altarpiece for Santa Maria dei Fossi, and, in 1500, a *St. Augustine*—both are now in the Gallery of Perugia. From 1501 to 1508, he worked in Santa Maria Maggiore of Spello, for which he painted a *Madonna* and frescoes in the Baglioni Chapel.

In June, 1502, Cardinal Francesco Piccolomini ordered him to paint four historical pictures in the Libreria of the Duomo of Siena. He worked there until 1509. These paintings are admirably preserved and represent, in ten scenes, the *Life of Enea Silvio Piccolomini,* who became Pope under the name of Pius II. His frescoes of the life of St. John Baptist are in the Chapel of St. John, Siena Cathedral (1504).

See Pl. 13, Vol. II.

Bibliography: Evelyn March Philips, *Pinturicchio.* London, Bell, 1908.—C. Ricci, *Pintoricchio.* Perugia, 1912.—Crowe and Cavalcaselle, *A New History of Painting in Italy.* Vol. V. 1914.

**PIOMBO.**—See Sebastiano del Piombo.

**PIRANESI (Giovanni Battista).** —Italian engraver, 1720-1778. He had a passion for ancient Roman buildings, old arches, broken columns, etc. He had a very skillful way of opposing deep blacks and strong effects of light. Not content with reproducing ancient ruins, he imagined still more colossal arches, gigantic stairways and fantastic *Prisons,* peopled with dreamlike figures.

Gian Battista Piranesi had a son, Francesco (1756-1810), who continued his work. He re-edited his father's series of views of Rome, and added some of his own. He engraved plates of the *Antiquities of Greece.* He was turn about engraver, archæologist, and minister of the Roman Republic in Paris, where he took his father's collection. He was assisted by his brother Pietro and his sister Laura.

Bibliography: H. Focillon, *Giovanni Battista Piranesi.* Paris.—A. M. Hind, *Giovanni Battista Piranesi.* London, 1922.

**PISA (Italy).**—On a vast grass-covered space at the end of the town are three marvels of architecture: the Duomo, the Baptistery and the Campo Santo, dominated by the Campanile.

The *Duomo* was begun in 1063, by the architects Busketus and Rainaldus. The history of its construction has been the subject of much discussion. Several critics suggest that the edifice was built as it exists now, between 1063 and 1121; and it certainly shows a unity of conception, and harmony of line, which seems to characterise a work sprung from a single inspiration. Other critics (Fontana, Venturi) distinguish several periods in the construction: from 1063 to 1118, the old Church of Santa Reparata was completely transformed to make the new Cathedral; at the beginning of the 13th century, the building was enlarged, the façade begun after 1204, and finished about 1270, by Giovanni Pisano; in the 16th and 17th centuries details of decoration were added. However that may be, the Duomo is characterised by unity of style, and magnificent simplicity. Its plan is that of a Latin cross, divided into five aisles, and ending in an apse. The aisles are divided by strong columns of red granite and of porphyry, several of which are antique, supporting arches of black and white marble. Above these arches is a gallery with marble columns. The central nave is covered with a Renaissance ceiling, richly decorated with gold. The whole building is in black and white marble. The magnificent façade is pierced with three doorways and adorned with arcades; above this are four tiers of arcaded galleries (copied by the neighbouring towns of Lucca and Pistoia). Over the crossing is an elliptical dome. The old bronze doors were destroyed by a fire, with the exception of that of the south transept, which has twenty-four scenes from the Bible, executed by Bonannus of Pisa in an uncouth style.

Pisa: The Campo Santo. (Cloister.)

The *Baptistery,* facing the Duomo, is a circular marble building, surmounted by a dome. It was begun in 1153, by Diotisalvi; finished about 1200; remodelled externally between 1250 and 1260, and then about 1278. Niccolò Pisano and his son Giovanni executed part of the work, in the second half of the 13th century. It is a beautiful building, in the Romanesque and Gothic styles. The bottom storey is decorated with a wall arcade with semi-circular arches, and is pierced by four doorways. Above is another circle of arcades, with pinnacles; and then a conical dome.

Pisa: The Baptistery and the Cathedral.

See Pl. 45, Vol. I.

The Baptistery contains Niccolò Pisano's famous hexagonal pulpit, sculptured in 1260, and decorated with bas-reliefs representing the *Annunciation,* the *Nativity,* the *Adoration of the Magi,* the *Presentation at the Temple,* the *Crucifixion,* the *Last Judgment,* and, at the angles, statues of Prophets and the Evangelists.

The Romanesque *Campanile* is famous under its name of the *Leaning Tower of Pisa.* It was begun in 1174, by Bonannus of Pisa and William of Innsbruck. It was not finished until 1350. The ground floor is a wall of circular marble, decorated arcades; above are six storeys with round arches on columns forming open external galleries. The tower is 179 feet high, and leans 13 feet out of the perpendicular. It has sometimes been held that this inclination was intentional. This is unlikely. It is more probable that a subsidence of the soil caused a sinking of the foundations.

The *Campo Santo* was begun in 1270, from the plans of Giovanni Pisano, to surround the cemetery, founded by Ubaldo dei Lanfranchi. It was finished in the 14th century. The burial-ground is surrounded by a cloister or covered way, which has traceried arcades giving on to the cemetery, and a plain wall enclosing it all round. The inner side of this wall is covered with frescoes, dating from the 14th and 15th centuries, which are the glory of the Campo Santo, and including those by Andrea da Firenze, Antonio Veneziano, Traini, and Benozzo Gozzoli. The galleries of the Campo Santo also shelter many tombs and pieces of sculpture, including a *Virgin,* by Giovanni Pisano.

Other buildings in Pisa are of less interest. *San Paolo in Ripa d'Arno* dates from the 13th century, and has a fine façade with three tiers of columns; *Santa Maria della Spina* (1230) is decorated with sculptures by pupils of Giovanni Pisano; *San Francesco* is a Gothic church dating from the 13th and 14th centuries.

Bibliography: Jean de Foville, *Pise et Lucques.* Collection des villes d'art célèbres.—C. A. Cummings, *History of architecture in Italy from the time of Constantine to the dawn of the Renaissance.* Boston, 1927.

**PISANELLO (Antonio Pisano).** —Veronese medallist and painter, born 1397 (from a Veronese document of 1433, which states his age as thirty-six and that he was then living in Verona).

In 1431 Pisanello is mentioned as active in Verona, and in the same year he starts work in Rome, in the Lateran, receiving payment for paintings done there in 1431-32. In 1432 Pope Eugenius IV grants him a passport to enable him to leave Rome, and he appears the next year in his native city, as indicated by the document mentioned above. In 1435 Pisanello sends to Lionello d'Este of Ferrara a portrait of Caesar. From 1438 dates his first medal, the John Palaeologus at Ferrara; in the same year he is exiled from Verona. Between 1438 and 1442 Pisanello's name appears among the adherents of the Marquess of Mantua. In 1439 he executes the medal of Gianfrancesco I

Gonzaga, and in this year he visits Verona. He is in Milan in 1440. In 1441 he is in Venice (it was probably in that year that he competed with Jacopo Bellini for the portrait of Lionello, which commission was won by Jacopo); he goes from Ferrara by boat to Mantua, where a debt is recorded against him; and he is mentioned as at Milan and Pavia. From 1441 date the medals of F. M. Visconti, N. Piccinino and Francesco Sforza. In 1442 he is brought before the tribunal of Venice on a charge of calumniating the republic while at the court of Lodovico Gonzaga; he is allowed to leave Venice for Verona.

PISANELLO: PORTRAIT OF GINEVRA D'ESTE. (Louvre.)

In 1443-44 Pisanello is chiefly at Ferrara, where he executes some of the smaller medals of Lionello and the medal commemorative of his marriage, with his portrait on one side and *Love Taming the Lion* on the other. In 1443 he writes to Gianfrancesco Gonzaga requesting money due him. In the same year Gonzaga writes that he is sending a messenger for a painting of the Savior, on canvas, that Pisanello has taken away without permission. In the next year he is requested to come to Mantua, where he undertakes various works, decorates a chapel, the hall of the Ducal Palace, and several pictures on panel (none of which have been preserved). Payments are recorded from Lionello d'Este in 1444 and 1447. In 1444-45 Pisanello executes the small and large medals of Sigismondo Malatesta and that of Domenico Malatesta. In 1445-46 he pays taxes in Verona. In 1446-47 he does the medal of Vittorino da Feltre and those of Cecilia Gonzaga and Belloto Cumano; in 1447-48 that of Lodovico III Gonzaga. In the latter year the medal of Decembrio is finished at Ferrara, and Pisanello goes to Naples where he receives a regular salary as a member of the household of King Alfonso. From 1449-50 date the Liberalitas and Venator medals of Alfonso, other medals of Alfonso and of Iñigo d'Avalos. Documents of payment for work done by him for the Marquess of Mantua date from 1449. The date of Pisanello's death is not certain; it may have occurred in 1455.

With the exception of Pisanello's medals, the number of works by him which still exist is remarkably small in comparison with his evident constant activity, much of which concerned painting. His remaining frescoes are at Verona: that of *St. George and the Princess* on the wall of S. Anastasia and the *Annunciation with George and Michael* at S. Fermo. There is a profile portrait of Lionello d'Este at Bergamo; and one of Ginevra d'Este in the Louvre. In the National Gallery, London, are Pisanello's *St. Hubert and the Madonna Appearing to George and Anthony Abbot.*

One of the finest medallists of all time, it is perhaps in this field that Pisanello's influence was strongest, not only upon other creation in the same medium but upon the development of the painted profile portrait. His style as a painter is characteristically northern, develops out of the tradition of Altichiero, and is related to the miniature illumination of France. His love of exquisitely rendered naturalistic detail is evident not only in his paintings but in the series of drawings, many of them of animals, which are to be seen in the Louvre, the British Museum, and elsewhere.

BIBLIOGRAPHY: Vasari - Milanesi, III.—Vasari-Venturi, I, 1896 (Lives of Gentile da Fabriano and Pisanello).—G. F. Hill, *Pisanello.* London, 1903 (with older literature).—L. Testi, *Storia d. pitt. venez.,* I, 1909.—A. Calabi e G. Cornaggia, *Pisanello.* Milan, 1928.—A. H. Martinie, *Pisanello.* Paris, 1930.—G. F. Hill, *Drawings by Pisanello, A Selection, with Introduction and Notes by G. F. H.,* 1929.—Same author. *A Corpus of Italian Medals of the Renaissance.* London, 1930.—J. Babelon, *Pisanello.* Paris, 1931.

**PISANO (Andrea).** — Goldsmith, sculptor and architect; born at Pontedera, near Pisa, date unknown; died 1348-49.

Andrea's activity before 1330 is undocumented and the subject has provoked endless discussion and produced a number of theories which purport to explain the origins of his style, which appeared fully developed at the time of his first great recorded commission.

In 1330 he begins work on the bronze doors of the Baptistery, Florence; where he was to do goldsmith's work alone, that is, he was to design the doors and model the reliefs, but not cast them. On goldsmith's work he had various helpers: Piero di Jacopo, from the beginning of the work until 1332; Piero di Donato, from 1331-35; Lippo Dini, from 1331, last mentioned 1332. A Venetian caster is mentioned and two helpers. In 1333 Andrea undertook to finish twenty-four lions' heads for the second wing of the doors; in 1335 he agreed to straighten the doors which had warped; in 1337 they were gilded and set in place; and in 1338 occurred the final installation.

In 1340 Andrea is mentioned as "major magister" of the Opera del Duomo, and the Canonica of the Duomo, then being planned, is referred to. It was destroyed in 1826. The contemporary chronicle of Pucci states that Andrea was made capomaestro of the Cathedral on the death of Giotto in 1336. His second master-work in Florence is his work upon the Campanile, for which exact dates do not exist but which he continued, probably varying Giotto's designs. His part in the decoration is difficult to determine, since there is no way of proving which, if any, of the reliefs were actually carried out by Giotto, how far Andrea was bound by Giotto's designs, and what part of the execution is by Andrea's own hand as distinguished from those of his pupils.

ANDREA PISANO: DETAIL FROM THE DOOR OF THE BAPTISTERY, FLORENCE.

In 1347-48 he is mentioned as capomaestro of the new ecclesiastical works at Orvieto; where the documents refer exclusively to his activity as a sculptor, referring specifically to the coloring of a Madonna Enthroned with Angels. In this same period references are made to trips by Andrea to Siena, and to Pisa to fetch finished sculptured works in marble and marble-blocks, so that it is evident he kept a workshop in Pisa in the interval between his Florentine and Orvietan activity. With him in Orvieta was his son, Nino. No documented work by him is left from Orvieto, although a number of works have been attributed to this, and preceding, stages in his career.

BIBLIOGRAPHY: Vasari-Milanesi, I.—Kallab, *Vasaristudien.* Vienna, 1908. — Crowe and Cavalcaselle, Douglas ed., II.—Bode, *Ital. Bildhauer der Ren.*—V. Schlosser, Jahrb. d. Ksthst. Slgn. d. ah. Kaiserh., XVII, 1896, 53 ff.—Reymond, *La sculp. flor.,* 1897, I.—A. G. Mayer, *Oberitalien. Frühren.,* 1897-1900, I.—Bode, *Florent. Bildhauer d. Ren.* Berlin, 1902.—Brach, *Nic. u. Giov. Pisano.* Strassburg, 1904.—Perkins, *Tuscan Sculptors,* I.—Biehl, *Das toskan. Relief.* Leipzig. 1910.—V. Schlosser, Jahrb. d. K. K. Zentralkomm., IV, 1910.

**— (Antonio).**—See Pisanello.

**— (Giovanni).**—Sculptor and architect; born probably 1245, son of Nicola d'Apulia or Niccolò Pisano, sculptor.

In 1266 Giovanni's father Nicola made the contract for the pulpit in the Cathedral of Siena, specifying the wages of his pupils Arnolfo and Lapo and those of Giovanni, his son, if the latter really wanted to come to Siena and promised to stay at his work and be persevering.

GIOVANNI PISANO: THE MASSACRE OF THE INNOCENTS. (Civic Museum, Pisa.)

Giovanni's payment was less than that of the other two; he was apparently still a youth. Giovanni worked on the Siena pulpit until 1268, the number of assistants having been augmented by the addition of Donato. In 1277 he worked with his father on the fountain at Perugia, which was completed in 1278. Between 1278 and 1283 he was in Pisa, active on the Campo Santo, Baptistry, and Cathedral. In 1284 he was made a citizen of Siena and was exempted from taxes because of his work on the Cathedral there. Between 1284 and 1298 he designed the southern portal of the Cathedral at S. Quirico d'Orcia. In 1285 he was directing the works at the Cathedral of Siena; in 1287 he is mentioned in an inscription concerning the enlargement of the Cathedral at Massa Marittima. A document of 1288 clearly indicates that the Grand Council of Siena considered him supreme arbiter of all works for the Cathedral. In 1295 he worked at San Giovanni in Pisa; the next year a sum owed him was paid in Pisa; in 1298 he inspected the slant of the Campanile at Pisa. In the same year he was appointed by Arnoldo degli Arnoldi to construct the pulpit of St. Andrew, Pistoia. In 1299 he left Siena for Pisa, and pledged himself to carve ivory figures of the utmost perfection. He is mentioned as capomaestro of the Cathedral of Pisa between 1299 and 1302. In 1301 he completed the pulpit of St. Andrew at Pistoia and began the new pulpit for the Cathedral of Pisa. He went to Carrara in 1302 to get marble for the above. In the next year he took as pupil Andreuccio, son of Master Simone. In 1304-06 he submitted to an inquiry about the Pisan pulpit; c. 1306 he carved statues for the chapel of the Madonna dell'Arena, Padua; in 1310 the Pisan pulpit was finished. In 1313 Giovanni was appointed by Henry VII to execute a monument to his wife Margaret of Luxembourg. It was probably in 1317 that he carved the statuette of the *Madonna della Cintola,* in the Duomo, Prato.

Departing from the art of his father, based upon the Romanesque and antique, Giovanni evolved a style of specifically Italian inspiration, which had enormous influence upon both sculptors and painters throughout the whole of Italy. The documents refer chiefly to Giovanni as a sculptor and but slightly to his activity as an architect, which was of the highest importance, and which was concentrated in two centers: Pisa, where he worked on the Duomo, the Baptistry, and planned the Campo Santo; and Siena, where he made important architectural contributions to the Cathedral.

BIBLIOGRAPHY: See Nicola Pisano. A chronological bibliography given in Adolfo Venturi, *Giovanni Pisano, His Life and Work,* Pegasus Press, New York, 193? (undated).

**— (Nicola or Niccolò).**—Sculptor, born probably in Apulia, c. 1220-25; died after 1278 and before 1287.

In 1258 Nicola is already at Pisa, where he completes the Baptistry pulpit in 1259, his first signed work. In 1266 he lays down specifications for his work on the pulpit of the Duomo in Siena, arranging for the payment of his helpers, Arnolfo and Lapo, and his son, Giovanni. In 1267 Lapo's brother Donato is added to the assistants. The pulpit is finished in 1268. In 1273 Nicola was active on a marble altar for the Duomo in Pistoia, now lost.

The Perugia fountain, on which he worked with his son Giovanni, was finished in 1278. The exact date of Nicola's death is not known.

The Chronicle of the Cloister of Sta. Caterina in Pisa names Nicola as the sculptor of the Arco di S. Domenico in Bologna, a work which shows a relationship with the Siena pulpit.

Nicola Pisano occupies a very important position as a sculptor who enriched the existing Romanesque tradition through the study of Classic Sculpture, whose spirit he attempted to recapture, but whose significance for the future development of Italian art is less than that of his son Giovanni, who was a great innovator and a creator of new **forms.**

BIBLIOGRAPHY: Vasari-Supino, *Vita di Nicola e Giovanni Pisano*. Florence, 1911.—Vasari-Frey, I, 1911.—Milanesi, *Doc. . . . senese,* I.—Tanfani Centofanti, *Notizie . . . pisani,* 1897.—Bacci, *Doc. toscani*. Florence, I, 1910.—Crowe and Cavalcaselle, Douglas, I.—Brach, *Niccolò und Giovanni Pisano*. Strassburg, 1904.—G. Swarzenski, *Nicola Pisano*. Frankfurt, 1926.—Venturi, *Storia d. arte ital.,* III, IV.—Toesca, *Storia d. arte ital.,* I, 1927.

**— (Nicola).**—Italian painter, 1499-1538. Pupil of L. Costa.

**— (Nino).**—Sculptor, goldsmith, and architect of Pisa, son of Andrea Pisano; died before 1368.

In 1349 Nino is active with his father at Orvieto. Documents of 1358-59 refer to goldsmith's work executed by him in Pisa. A signed *Madonna* now in the niche over the tomb of Fra Aldobrandino Cavalcanti in Sta. Maria Novella, Florence, is mentioned by Vasari. Close stylistically is the *Madonna* in the Opera del Duomo of Orvieto, perhaps begun by Andrea and finished by Nino. The latter's chief work is the *Tomb of Archbishop Saltarelli* in Sta. Caterina in Pisa, which is not in its original form. His *Tomb of Archbishop Scarlatti,* of 1362, originally in the Duomo of Pisa, now in the Campo Santo, has likewise suffered changes in the course of time. Certain of the reliefs from this tomb have been exchanged with those of the neighboring *Tomb of the Archbishop Moricotti* (died 1394), probably at the time the two tombs were moved to their present position. The subject-matter of the reliefs for the Scarlatti Tomb is specified in the original documents of commission to Nino Pisano, and tallies closely with that of the reliefs on the tomb of Moricotti.

Nino collaborated on the execution of the *Tomb of Doge Marco Cornaro* in SS. Giovanni e Paolo in Venice; the Madonna is signed by him; the rest is shop work. In 1368 there is record of a document of payment to Andrea, son of the late Nino Pisano, for the Tomb of Doge Agnello, executed by his father and formerly in S. Francesco, Pisa, now lost. A statue of a *Bishop* in S. Francesco, Oristano, Sardinia, is signed by Nino.

BIBLIOGRAPHY: Vasari-Milanesi, I.—Tanfani Centofanti, *Notizie . . . pisani*. Pisa, 1897.—Brach, *Niccolò und Giovanni Pisano*. Strassburg, 1904.—Supino, *Arte pisana,* 1904.—A. Venturi, *Storia d. arte ital.,* IV, 1906.—Bode, *Florent. Bildhauer der Ren.,* 1910; *Ital. Plastik* (Handbk. of the Berlin Museum), 1910.

**PISSARRO (Camille).** — French painter, 1830-1903. In 1852, he went to Venezuela, and brought back a number of sketches. On his return to France (1855) he became acquainted with Corot, and fell under his influence. He painted the environs from Paris, Montmorency, La-Varenne-Saint-Hilaire to Pontoise. He was living in Louveciennes when the War of 1870 broke out. Pissarro took refuge in London, leaving his studio, which was pillaged by the Germans. This accounts for the rarity of his early work. He was familiar with the Impressionists, and, like them, he studied Turner when he was in London. He simplified his palette, and used only pure colours. Together with his friend Monet he helped develop more fully the theories of Impressionism. At one period he even practised the methods of the Neo-Impressionists (1886), created by Seurat, which consisted of carrying the Impressionist method of division of tone still further, and of painting by means of equal, minute spots of colour. But he grew tired of this method. He aimed not at brilliance by contrast, but at softness by harmony. He was a great teacher who had important influence over many of his contempories, such as Cézanne, who spent a great deal of time with him during the years 1872-73, and Gauguin. His last works are his best: broad, vigorous, concise and expressive, they represent scenes of street life in London, Paris, Rouen, Le Havre, Dieppe, etc. His other pictures include: a portrait of Cézanne; *Jardin de Poitoise; Pathway through the Cabbages; Le Père Melon Sawing Timber* (1879); *Woman Breaking Timber; Apple Gathering* (1886); *The Chat* (1892); *Woman Bathing* (1896), etc. Pissarro left numerous series of pastels, water-colours, etchings and lithographs. Several of his pictures are in the Luxembourg Gallery. They may also be seen in the Galleries of Berlin, Dublin, Le Havre, Dieppe; in the Louvre, and in the Tate Gallery.

BIBLIOGRAPHY: A. Tabarant, *Pissarro,* 1925.—T. Duet, *Histoire des peintres impressionnistes,* 1905.

**PISTOIA (Italy).**—This little town was a very prosperous artistic centre in the 11th, 12th and 13th centuries.

The oldest of its monuments is the 12th century *Church of Sant'Andrea*. On the entrance architrave are sculptures executed in 1166 by Gruamono and Adeodat. It contains a remarkable pulpit, sculptured by Giovanni Pisano, from 1298 to 1301, on the model of that of Pisa, sculptured by his father, Niccolò Pisano. It is supported on seven red marble columns; and is adorned with bas-reliefs representing *Aaron,* the *Nativity, David,* the *Adoration of the Magi, Jeremiah,* the *Massacre of the Innocents,* the *Crucifixion,* and the *Last Judgment*. Below are sibyls and prophets.

The *Cathedral,* built in the 12th century, was restored in the 13th. The apse, built by Lafri, dates only from 1599. The façade is preceded by a porch surmounted by a medallion by Andrea della Robbia. The *Campanile* once formed part of the fortifications. The arcaded galleries were added when, from being a fortified tower, it became a bell-tower.

Vasari attributes the plan of the *Baptistery* to Andrea della Robbia. Whoever may have been the original architect, the building was transformed in 1337, in the Gothic style, by Cellino di Nese.

The *Ospedale del Ceppo,* built in 1277, was restored later. It is decorated with a frieze of bas-reliefs by Giovanni della Robbia.

*San Francesco al Prato* (1295) is in the Gothic style. It is decorated with the works of fine pupils of Giotto (14th century).

The *Palazzo Pretorio* was rebuilt in the 14th century in the Gothic style (the top storey is modern). It possesses a very fine courtyard surrounded with arcades with semicircular arches, and decorated with paintings representing the armorial bearings of magistrates.

The *Palazzo del Comune,* finished in 1385, is in the Gothic style.

The *Madonna dell' Umilità* was built from 1495 to 1509, by a pupil of Bramante, Ventura Vitoni. The façade is unfinished. There is a fine narthex. The dome was added by Vasari.

**PITTI PALACE.**—See Florence; also Pl. 5, Vol. II.

**PITTONI (Gian Battista).**—Venetian painter, 1687-1767. Pupil of Lazzarini. An elegant and facile painter. His principal work is the *Miracle of the Loaves and Fishes,* in the Sacristy of San Stefano.

BIBLIOGRAPHY: Laura Pittoni, *Dei Pittoni artisti Veneti*. Bergamo, 1907.

**PIZZOLO (Niccolò).** — Paduan painter and sculptor, 1421-1453. Born at Villa Ganzerla, near Vicenza. He belonged to the school of Squarcione, and he collaborated with Mantegna in the Eremitani. He may also have worked on the bronzes for the altar of the Santo, with Donatello.

BIBLIOGRAPHY: Crowe and Cavalcaselle, *History of Painting in North Italy,* ed. T. Borenius, Vol. II.

**PLACE DE LA CONCORDE.**—See Paris; also Pl. 43, Vol. II.

**PLACE DES VOSGES (Place Royale).**—See Paris; also Pl. 2, Vol. I; Pl. 39, Vol. II.

**PLANTIN (Musée).**—Christopher Plantin, a celebrated French printer, born about 1515, near Tours, went and settled in Antwerp, and there founded, about 1555, a press which was unrivalled in Europe. In 1576, he moved his workshops into his private house, which remains as it was then. This is the Musée Plantin, which was bought, in 1877, by the State, together with its furniture and pictures (fifteen by Rubens, portraits, etc.). It is interesting because it has preserved its appearance of an old Flemish house.

**PLATERESQUE (Style).**—After the death of Calixtus III, a famous Catalanian goldsmith, Pedro Diez, returned to Spain and settled in Toledo. He was allowed to take part in work on the Cathedral, and there he acquired such ascendancy that Enrico de Egas, son of the chief master of the work, fell under his influence. Although he had been educated by his father in the pure traditions of the Flemish Gothic style, he nevertheless built at Valladolid the College of Santa Cruz (1480-1492), which shows the influence of the Italian Renaissance. From this time onward, the goldsmith (the *platero*), is closely associated with the evolution of architecture. Hence the name *plateresque* is given to that elegant and singular style, which is the brilliant expression of the Spanish genius in the time of the Catholic Kings and Charles V. This plateresque style is but a metamorphosis of the picturesque forms which characterise the flowery Gothic style, just as this latter may be considered in its turn as a transformation from the style of the Alhambra and of *Mudejar* architecture. The three forms are as different as possible, but the principle of covering plain surfaces with the richest, most refined and fantastic ornaments, is the same in all three. The transformation was very slow.

After the first tentative efforts of Enrique de Egas, at Valladolid, another combination of the Germanic tradition with Italian motifs was attempted in 1516, in a high doorway at Burgos, in the chevet of the old cathedral, by Francisco de Colonia, son of Simon.

DETAIL FROM THE TOMB OF BISHOP FERNANDO DE ARCE. (Cathedral of Sigüenza.)

Spanish religious architecture hardly paused at the plateresque stage. It generally passed from Gothic to the Griego-Romano style which was so sumptuously heralded at Granada.

In civil architecture, the characteristics of plateresque are curves and counter-curves, and braces introduced by the Moslems; twisted columns, sometimes slender, sometimes decorated with sculpture; medallions, open balustrades, etc. About 1530, plateresque became (especially at Burgos and Salamanca) most elaborate. Extraordinary fantasy, rhythm of movement, general unity of impression combine with variety of motifs, exuberance, and

VALLADOLID: LOWER PART OF THE FAÇADE OF SAN PABLO.

elements borrowed from nature, to give these works a charm which disconcerts reason.

The plateresque arts did not remain confined to Spain. From the end of the 15th century, Portugal adopted them (see Manuelian Style); and Charles V transported them to his Germanic domains. Their influence may be seen in the Castles of Heidelberg and Schalburg. In France, plateresque influence may be seen at Besançon, Toulouse, and elsewhere.

The plateresque style died a violent death, condemned by Philip II who wanted an architecture in accord with his morose and sombre humour.

BIBLIOGRAPHY: E. Bertaux, *Les Arts en Espagne*. Paris, 1911.—M. Dieulafoy, *Spain*. Paris, 1912.

**PLEINAIRISM.**—The painting of pictures in the open air.

**PLINTH.**—Sub-base, as of a pier or column; base for a statue, vase, pedestal, etc.

**POBLET (Spain).**—A huge Cistercian abbey built for Ramon Berenger in 1150.

**POCCETTI (Bernardino).**—Florentine painter, 1542-1612. He belonged to the decadence which followed after Michelangelo. There are numerous frescoes by him in Florentine convents, especially in the large cloister of Santa Maria Novella.

**POELENBURGH (Cornelisz van).**—(Sometimes called *Brusco* or *Satyr.*) Dutch historic and landscape painter of Utrecht, 1586-1667. He was a pupil of Abraham Bloemart; in the years 1617-1622 we find him in Rome studying the works of Raphael, but especially the antiques. Soon he went to Florence where for a short time he was court painter, then he returned to Utrecht. Poelenburgh was a close friend of Rubens whom he also painted. In 1637 he went to London, where he did many portraits. Most of Poelenburgh's paintings are small idyllic landscapes done in the Italian tradition depicting forest scenes or ruins with nude female figures used as *staffage*. His graceful figures were often compared to bits of porcelain in their smoothness of texture, and in coloring and tonality. He had many pupils and followers. His best religious compositions are in the Hermitage: *Expulsion of Adam and Eve*; *Flight to Egypt*. Other paintings may be seen in all important museums.

**POINTILLISM.**—See Neo-Impressionism, Seurat, and Signac.

**POITIERS.**—The oldest existing building in Poitiers is the *"Temple Saint Jean"*—a baptistery built in the Gallo-Roman period (4th century), and rebuilt in the 7th century. The porch was done away with, the piscina replaced by baptismal fonts, and the walls pierced with windows. It is a rectangular building, the upper portion decorated with pediments and pilasters. The apse has six sides. The narthex was built in the 11th or 12th century. The Baptistery contains frescoes, the oldest of which date from the 12th century.

POITIERS: ST. RADEGONDE.

The *Church of St. Hilaire* was built in the 11th century, and seriously damaged in 1562, by the Protestants. The nave and part of the vaulting which had collapsed were rebuilt according to the original pattern, after 1869. The nave has three aisles on either side, and the choi has an ambulatory out of which open four chapels.

See Pl. 1, Vol. I.

The *Church of Sainte Radegonde*, originally called Notre-Dame-Hors-les-Murs, was founded in the 6th century by St. Radegonde, Queen of France. It was destroyed by fire in 1083, and rebuilt almost immediately. The apse and base of the tower are Romanesque of the 9th century, and the nave dates from the 12th century. In the crypt is the black marble tomb of St. Radegonde, which is very old, and a white marble statue of the saint by Nicolas le Gendre.

The *Church of St. Porchaire*. built at the end of the 11th century or at the beginning of the 12th century, has a Romanesque tower as its façade, decorated with arcades. The rest of the building is Gothic.

The finest Romanesque Church in Poitiers is *Notre Dame la Grande*, celebrated for its wonderful façade (12th century), which is crowded with carving and sculpture. The nave of Notre Dame is older than the façade, and probably dates from the end of the 11th century. It is covered with mediocre paintings, executed in 1857. There are no transepts. There is a barrel-vault. The choir is surrounded with an ambulatory, on which open chapels. The apse is decorated with a fresco (about 12th century), representing the Virgin and Child with six saints.

See Pl. 44, Vol. I.

The *Cathedral Saint Pierre* was begun after 1150, under Henry II Plantagenet, and was consecrated in 1379. The façade is flanked with two square towers. It has three doorways, richly decorated with carving. The choir ends by a high, straight wall, pierced with three windows—a type of architecture which is rare in France; where a round apse is characteristic. (The square-ended choir is typical of English cathedrals.) The interior is simple and imposing. Of old glass, little remains save the magnificent *Window of the Crucifixion*, at the east end, executed in the 13th century. There is no triforium and the aisles are nearly the height of the nave. This is characteristic of the Plantagenet Gothic style.

In the 13th century, Poitiers possessed a Château, which was destroyed by the English, and rebuilt by the Duc de Berry, about 1378. Only two towers of it remain, and the reproduction on one of the miniatures of the Grandes Heures of the Duc de Berry.

The *Palais de Justice*, formerly the royal palace, and then the palace of the counts of Poitou, was partly rebuilt in the 12th century, by the counts of Poitou, and restored at the end of the 14th century, and the beginning of the 15th century, for the Duc de Berry. Before the reconstruction of the large hall of the palace, the Duke built the *Tour Maubergeon*, the annex of the Palais de Justice, about 1388. This tower is a keep, which has no longer the sombre appearance of the old feudal keeps; it is a large building, each angle of which is flanked by a large round tower. It is pierced with wide, tall windows, and is in two storeys, the second of which is decorated with statuettes. The building seems unfinished, as though cut short at the second storey. It is uncertain whether it was ever finished, or whether the upper part was destroyed. The Palais de Justice contains a fine Gothic hall, which has a magnificent chimney-piece. The external wall of this "salle," which adjoins the Maubergeon tower, is gable-ended, with pinnacled buttresses, and turrets.

Poitiers possesses some fine Gothic houses of the 15th and early 16th centuries.

The *Hôtel de Ville* is modern, and possesses two frescoes by Puvis de Chavannes: *The Entry of Charles Martel into Poitiers,* and *Fortunat Reading His Poems to St. Radegonde, in the Convent of Sainte Croix.*

BIBLIOGRAPHY: L'Abbé Auber, *Histoire de la Cathédrale de Poitiers*, 1849.—Lucien Maque, *Le Palais de Justice de Poitiers.*—H. Labbé de la Mauvinière, *Poitiers et Angoulême* (Collections des Villes d'art célèbres).

**POITOU (Churches of).**—See Pl. 44, Vol. I.

**POL de LENA (Spain).** —*Sta. Cristina,* early 10th century. A tiny hall-church with four portici. Sta. Cristina de Lena shows the amazing precocity of pre-Romanesque Asturian builders in its possession of a ribbed barrel-vaulted system and external buttresses, a system cognate with that of Sta. Maria de Naraneo.

**POLIDORO CALDARA (da Caravaggiò).** — Lombard painter, 1492-1543. Pupil of Raphael, he owed his reputation to the decoration of numerous façades in Rome.

See Pl. 44, Vol. I.

**POLLAIUOLO (Antonio).**—Florentine painter, sculptor, engraver, and goldsmith; brother of Piero Pollaiuolo. Born 1433; died 1498.

The greater part of the documents which inform us about Antonio Pollaiuolo refer to his activity as a goldsmith, in which trade he was evidently trained, and from which he graduated, as did so many other Italian artists, to the so-called major arts. In 1457 he was commissioned to make a silver cross for S. Giovanni, now in the Opera del Duomo, for which payment was made two years later. In 1460 he executed, with Piero, the *Labors of Hercules* for Lorenzo Magnifico, according to a letter which Antonio himself wrote in 1494. In 1461 he did a reliquary for the prior of S. Pancrazio; in 1461-62 receives payments for a silver belt and chain for Filippo di Cino Rinuccini; in 1465 is commissioned to make two candelabra for San Giovanni; in 1466 undertook the designs for two tunics, a chasuble and a cope for S. Giovanni (embroideries now in the Opera del Duomo), for which the last payment was of 1473. From 1466 dates the commission for an altarpiece for the Portuguese Chapel, S. Miniato, which was executed by Piero. In 1468 Antonio buys property near Pistoia at Quarata; estimates the value of the metal ball on Brunelleschi's cupola of the Duomo; decorates the coat of armor and fittings worn by Benedetto Salutate at a joust. In 1472 he adorns the helmet of the Duke of Urbino; and in this year his name appears in the register of the guild of Florentine painters. Between 1473 and 1478 there are documents referring to various metal works including a *Crucifix* for the Carmine and reliefs for the silver altar of S. Giovanni, also a reliquary for the finger of St. John the Baptist. The *St. Sebastian* in the National Gallery is of 1475. In 1480 a cadastral declaration indicates that Antonio's shop was separate from that of Piero; in 1481 he buys more property in S. Michele and in Florence; and in 1483 still more property in Bacchereto. In this latter year is recorded the last payment for the altar reliefs. In 1484 Antonio and Piero go to Rome, where Antonio executes the *Tomb of Innocent VIII* and the *Tomb of Sixtus IV* (finished in 1493). He apparently returns to Florence during this period, however, for in 1491 he takes part in a competition for the façade of the Duomo. In 1494 he is commissioned to make a bronze bust of Condottiere Gentile Virginio Orsini. He dies in 1498.

Various sculptures are attributed to Antonio, in addition to those already mentioned (his magnificent bronze of *Hercules and Antæus* is in the Bargello); and the following paintings: the Berlin *David*, and *Profile Portrait of a Lady*; the Uffizi *Hercules and Hydra*, and *Hercules and Antæus*; the *Flying Angels* in the Church of S. Miniato, near Florence; the frescoes of the *Dancing Nudes* in the Torre del Gallo, near Florence; the London *Sebastian* (in which he was assisted by pupils), and *Apollo and Daphne*; and the Milan, Poldi-Pezzoli, *Profile Portrait of a Lady*. Among his most famous works is the print of the *Battle of the Nudes*. Several drawings are attributed to Antonio, among them the cartoon for Piero's *Charity*, on the back of the panel in the Uffizi.

Most Florentine of artists, Antonio's sculptural and anatomical knowledge is obvious in his painting, but did not cause him to produce paintings which imitate sculpture. The figures in his fresco of the *Dancing Nudes* are supremely decorative, rendered with the immediacy of a drawing, and with the searching, functional, electric line of a great anatomist. The concentrated muscular energy of the two Hercules panels in the Uffizi relates them closely to his sculptures; but the little *Apollo and Daphne* in London is brilliantly pictorial; and his two female portraits among the most exquisite of the quattrocento.

BIBLIOGRAPHY: See Piero Pollaiuolo.

**— (Piero).**—Florentine painter and sculptor, younger brother and assistant of Antonio Pollaiuolo, who worked mainly on his designs; born 1443; died 1496.

In 1460 Piero assisted Antonio on the *Labors of Hercules* mentioned above under Antonio Pollaiuolo; and in 1466 executed the altarpiece for the Portuguese Chapel at San Miniato, with the figures of *SS. Eustace, James, and Vincent*. The panel is now in the Uffizi, its place at S. Miniato having been taken by a copy. In 1469 he called out a commission for allegorical figures for the Mercatanzia of Florence, which are now in the Uffizi. (The *Fortitude* in this series is by Botticelli.) One cartoon, that of *Charity*, is the work of Antonio and is to be found on the back of Piero's panel. In 1477 he presented a model for the tomb of Forteguerri, Pistoia, in competition with Verrocchio, and his model was accepted over that of Verrocchio by the Operai, a decision which was instantly reversed by Lorenzo de' Medici, who ordered Verrocchio's model executed. In a competition of 1478 for an altarpiece for the Cappella di S. Bernardino in the Palazzo Vecchio, Piero lost to Leonardo. Between 1484 and 1496, Piero collaborated with Antonio in Rome.

The following paintings are by Piero: Berlin, *Annunciation;* Uffizi, Allegorical figures of Hope, Justice, Temperance, Faith, Charity (by Piero and pupils); Portrait of Galeazzo Sforza; Profile Portrait of a Lady; Miniature Profile of a Lady; and the three Saints from S. Miniato, mentioned above; San Gimignano, *Coronation of the Virgin,* 1483 (painted for S. Agostino); Strassburg, *Madonna.*

Bibliography: Pollaiuoli: Vasari-Milanesi, III.—Borghini, Il Riposo.—Gaye, *Carteggio.*—Gualandi, *Mem. orig.,* V, 1840.—Baldinucci, *Not. d. prof. etc.,* 1845-47, I.—B. Cellini, *Trattati dell' orificeria e d. scult.,* Milanesi ed., 1857.—Berenson, *Drawings of Florentine Painters,* 1903.—Cruttwell, *Antonio and Piero Pollaiuolo,* 1907.—Venturi, *Storia d. arte ital.,* VI, 1908.—Crowe and Cavalcaselle, Douglas, ed., 1911.—Van Marle, *Italian Schools, etc.,* XI, 1929.

**POLYCLITUS.**—Greek sculptor of the fifth century. We know very

Polyclitus: Amazon. (Museum of the Vatican, Rome.)

little of his life. His dated statues belong to the second half of the fifth century. He must have been born about 470. It is doubtful whether there is truth in the story that he was a pupil of Ageladas, though his work continued the tradition of this master's school.

The most famous of the statues of Polyclitus was the *Doryphorus,* or Lance-Bearer, a young, virile, strong and athletic figure. Copies of this work have been recognised in a series of statues, of which the best is a marble statue, found at Pompeii, now in the Naples Museum. It represents a young athlete, slowly and carelessly advancing, who gives an impression of restrained strength. The original was in bronze, but it is not known where it was intended to be placed. The ancients considered this statue as a model, or canon. Certainly, Greek artists strove to give proportion to human beauty, and the sculptors of the School of Argos aimed at establishing the exact proportions of the perfect human form whose beauty lies in its harmony. Polyclitus is one of those who have fixed one such canon of measurement in detail. The statues of Polyclitus are characterised by rather square proportions. The torso in the copies of the Doryphorus illustrate this. If his figures are slightly heavy in the rendering, the ease and suppleness shown in their attitudes corrects this impression. The Doryphorus, for instance, has his weight thrown onto the right leg, and in this way Polyclitus modifies the stiffness of the figure itself. This turn of the body was not invented by Polyclitus, but it was he who has made the best use of it.

Another of Polyclitus' statues, the *Diadumenus,* is very famous. There have been many copies of it. There are well-known figures of the Diadumenus—a young man tying round his head the band which was the sign of victory—in the British Museum, in Naples, and in Roman collections. Their very number shows the popularity of this subject. The Diadumenus is very similar to the Doryphorus. It too showed a young man in the act of walking indolently, slightly dragging the left foot. The ancients said that Polyclitus repeated his model in nearly all his statues.

Another athletic figure represented a man using a strigil (or scraper for the skin). Among the Olympian statues of athletes which have been attributed to Polyclitus, only a few bases now remain.

According to Pliny, there were, in the Temple of Artemis at Ephesus, statues of Amazons, of which one had been done by Cresilas, another by Phidias, and a third by Polyclitus. He adds the following anecdote: the Ephesians, having left to the artists the decision as to which was the most beautiful, each of them gave himself the first prize, but the second to Polyclitus.

Museums preserve statues of Amazons whose types modern archæologists often feel go back to the statues of Amazons in the temple of Ephesus. All of them seem to be copies of originals in bronze (in the Capitoline, Vatican and Berlin Museums). The Berlin one seems to reproduce well the characteristics of Polyclitus.

Finally the ancients lauded the beauty of the chryselephantine statue which Polyclitus did for Argos. According to the description of Pausanias, we can imagine this goddess seated on a throne, her head circled by a crown. The ancient writers do not hesitate to compare this with the masterpieces of Phidias.

Summing up the judgment of ancient writers on Polyclitus, he was represented as an artist whose perfection equals that of the greatest. He is the perfect sculptor in bronze, while Phidias is the perfect sculptor in marble. All agree in their praise of his technique. Polyclitus was not carried away by a daring imagination; he holds to certain types which he perfects. In comparing him with Phidias, he was found lacking in a certain majesty and authority which was not wanting in the divine types created by the Athenian sculptor. Polyclitus was preoccupied rather with the perfection of form than depth of thought. Thus he came to create the image of the perfect human body.

See Pl. 20, Vol. I.

Bibliography: Collignon, *Histoire de la Sculpture Grecque.* Paris, 1892.—A. Furtwängler, *Meisterwerke der Griechischen Plastik.* Leipzig, 1893.—Ernest Gardner, *Six Greek Sculptors.* London, 1925 (3rd imp.)—A. Mapler, *Polyklet und Seine Schule.* Athens and Leipzig, 1902.—P. Paris, *Polyclète.* Paris, 1895.

**— the Younger.**—Greek sculptor, who worked at the beginning of the 4th Century B.C. He is often confused with his famous namesake. He was also an architect. According to Pausanias, he built a theatre at Epidaurus, which still exists.

Bibliography: Defrasse and Lechat, *Epidure.* Paris, 1895.

**POLYDOROS.**—See Laocoön.

**POLYEUCTOS.**—Attic sculptor, who, in 280 B.C., executed a bronze statue of Demosthenes. He represented the orator standing, the arms down, and hands crossed. On the base were engraved the words, "Had thy power, O Demosthenes, equalled thy genius, the Macedonian Ares would never have commanded the Greeks." It is thought that this statue served as a model for the statues which have come down to us under this name, one of which is in the Vatican.

Bibliography: Collignon, *Histoire de la Sculpture Grecque.* Vol. II.

**POLYGNOTUS.**—Greek painter, beginning of the 5th century B.C. Little is known of his life, except that he was the lover of Elpiniké, Cimon's sister. Records speak of the many public buildings in Athens which Polygnotus decorated. The most notable was probably the Stoa Poikile and the Pinacotheca.

The most famous of his masterpieces was the decoration of the Lesché of Delphi, a gateway, built near the temple of Apollo, by the town of Cnidus. In two paintings on the same panel, Polygnotus represented the *Taking of Troy,* and *Ulysses in Hades.*

He painted many other works—none of which has survived. He was greatly admired in his day, and we learn that he was one of the first to free his figures from archaic stiffness, and to give his faces varied expressions.

Bibliography: O. Jahn, *Die Gemälde des Polygnotos in der Lesche zu Delphi.*—Charles Lenormaut, *Mémoire sur les peintures que Polygnote aurait exécutées dans la Lesche de Delphes.* Brussels, 1864.—Mary H. Swindler, *Ancient Painting.* New Haven, 1929.

**POLYPTYCH.**—From the Greek polyptychon (that which has many folds). This word signifies painted or sculptured panels divided into several compartments which can be folded. They served as portable altars, or as decoration over an altar (altarpieces).

**POMERANCIO (Cristoforo Circignani; known as Il).**—Roman painter, end of 16th century. He had a predilection for the colossal and terrible.

**— (Niccolo Circignani; known as Il).**—Italian painter, born in Pomerancio (1520-1593). Pupil of Titian. A gifted painter, but he had little originality, and contented himself with copying the great masters.

**POMPEII (Italy).**—Ancient Pompeii was a very prosperous town, whose inhabitants numbered between twenty and thirty thousand. Built by the Osci at the mouth of the Sarno, it was later dominated by the Samnites, and subsequently by the Romans. After a period of wars, a long era of peace followed, till a violent earthquake almost entirely destroyed the town in 63 A.D. The inhabitants at once set to work to rebuild their dwellings and raise their monuments afresh, when, sixteen years later, a far more terrible catastrophe overwhelmed the unfortunate city, and ruined it for ever. The famous eruption of Vesuvius in 79 A.D. destroyed the towns of Pompeii, Herculaneum, Stabiæ, Torre del Greco, and several villages of the neighbourhood. Thousands of inhabitants were buried in their houses, in the streets and in the fields. A thick layer of dust, cinders, and lava covered the dead cities. Nothing was done, except to enter some of the buildings, and to take away precious things; oblivion came to reign in the abandoned towns, which gradually became covered over with earth, and overgrown with vegetation.

It was not till 1748 that excavations were begun, without order—excavations which aimed at the discovery of statues and objects of antiquity, rather than at laying bare the buildings. Since that time, the work has been several times continued and then again abandoned.

In 1860 Fiorelli undertook to direct the work methodically. It was he who thought of making a plaster mould of the bodies discovered in the town. (The ashes had preserved their exact shape.) Most of the objects found at Pompeii are in the Museum of Naples. More than half the town is now excavated, and thanks to the catastrophe of the year 79, we can gain a good idea of ancient life in the first century B.C.

The roads are paved with blocks

Pompeii: House of the Dancing Satyr.

of lava, with narrow pavements on each side. Here and there huge stones project upwards in the road, so that the walker can cross without getting wet when the roads themselves are damp. Along the streets can be seen the shops with their signs; electoral bills, and scrawls can be seen on the walls. The brick houses were hastily reconstructed between the two catastrophes. They sometimes had two or even three floors, but the top storeys have disappeared. They were built on the plan of Latin and Roman houses; the important part is the atrium, a wide courtyard, in the middle of which a basin (the impluvium) receives rainwater. Covered galleries surround the atrium—at the end of the atrium opens out a large open hall, the tablinum, a sort of drawing-room. To the right and left are the bedrooms. Close by these are the alœ,—open rooms. The dining-room and other rooms were on the first floor. Later, under Greek influence, new refinements were introduced, the peristyle, the exedra or drawing-room, corridors, gardens adorned with basins and

Pompeii: House of the Vettii.

statues. According to the wealth of the owner, the size and decoration of the houses varied, but the plan was the same. Most Pompeians possessed in their atrium a little altar raised to the Lares (household gods) and adorned with paintings and bronze statuettes.

Several important *houses* have been excavated. The house of the *Vettii* is one of the most remarkable. The atrium is ornamented with a charming frieze on a black ground, representing Cupids at their various tasks, and groups of children. The great hall near the peristyle is the most luxuriously adorned. Groups of Cupids on the wall, play amid scenes of mythology. Almost every room is decorated with paintings—a charming garden is full of statuettes and marble tables, while in the kitchen, household utensils are still in their place.

The *cemeteries* of the Pompeians are to be found, as in all Latin cities, outside the town. The tombs border the roads which lead from Pompeii. The most ancient date from the third century B.C. Some have the form of a small altar, raised above the urn which contains the ashes. Others have the form of a temple, and are often adorned with statuettes.

Pompeii, which was a flourishing city, possessed numerous public buildings, the majority of which were destroyed by the earthquake in 63 A. D., and rebuilt later.

It is the *triangular Forum* which contains the most ancient monuments of Pompeii. This Forum, surrounded on three sides by a portico, contains ruins of a temple which dates from the sixth century B.C. It had eight fluted Doric columns on the façade, but there only remain two fragments of columns, four capitals, altars, and a staircase. This temple was probably dedicated to Minerva.

The *ramparts* of Pompeii were begun shortly after the foundation of the town—repaired in the course of centuries, often in haste, when danger threatened the town. They

Pompeii: The Temple of Apollo.

were formed of two parallel walls, with battlements, buttresses and twelve towers placed at unequal distances apart. These ramparts were pierced by eight doors, of which three are now uncovered, the gates of Herculaneum, Nola and Stabiæ. They were of brick and blocks of stone without cement, and were arched.

It was in the second century B.C., that Vibius Popidius, Quæstor of Pompeii, surrounded the square which formed the Forum, on three of its sides, by a portico in two storeys (Doric order below; Ionic above), with spaced columns supporting a solid wooden beam on which the architrave rested. In the year 80 B.C., Sulla sent Roman colonists to Pompeii. One of their first works was to transform the Forum, or rather to enlarge it on the North side, and to give it a magnificent entrance by building there a Temple of Jupiter, flanked by two triumphal arches. A monumental staircase is formed at the back, by a platform on which the altar was placed; then came the hall, the cella ornamented with pictures on stucco, and decorated with Ionic columns. At the back, too, three rooms held the statues of the three Capitoline gods: Jupiter, Juno, Minerva. Of the two triumphal arches, the left one still exists. A curious bas-relief, discovered in one of the altars, shows us the plan of the Temple and the triumphal arches. The Forum was surrounded by several monuments. One of the most ancient was the basilica, built on the plan of Greek basilicas, and surrounded in the interior by thirty Ionic columns. The wall was pierced by five doors. The portico was roofed; it is thought that the central nave was not covered. M. Thédenat, however, thinks it was covered by a roof which was higher than that of the aisles. At one end, a platform decorated with columns served as a tribunal. The basilica was destroyed in 63 A.D. by the earthquake. The Temple of Apollo was an ancient building, destroyed in 63 A.D. and rebuilt with modifications. The triglyphs, covered with a layer of stucco, were decorated with

Pompeii: General view of the Forum.

Pompeii: The Temple of Jupiter and the Triumphal Arch.

griffins and garlands, and the forty-eight columns of the court became more Corinthian than Doric in the same way. In the middle of this court existed a building with a Corinthian peristyle, and columns. In front, of this building there remain only the foundation and the bases of six columns which used to support statues, and two small altars.

Before it served for civil and political meetings, the Forum was used by merchants, who, little by little, were refused admittance. It was then necessary to build a market for them. This *market* was situated at the North-East corner of the Forum. At the base of the portico-

Pompeii: The House of Lucretia.

columns which served as a hall, were seventeen statues. The present market of Macellum which belongs to the first century A.D. occupies the site of an earlier structure used for a similar purpose. The Macellum consisted of a rectangular courtyard surrounded by a colonnade. In the centre was a tholos composed of twelve columns supporting a roof. This tholos served as a fish stall. Behind the colonnade on the south was a row of shops opening directly on to the colonnade. At the far end, wide halls served as sanctuary for the religion of the Emperors, for banqueting-halls, for slaughter-houses. On the right eleven rooms were used as shops. The market was decorated with works of art, with beautiful pictures, representing, besides scenes such as Argos and Io, Ulysses and Penelope, vases of oil and wine, fruit and vegetables.

The building of Eumachia, near the Forum, was built by the Priestess of that name, perhaps to serve as a cloth-hall. A little further on is the tiny temple of Vespasian, and then a temple of the Household Gods ("Lares").

Beside the monuments which surround the Forum, many others had been built in different parts of the town, such buildings as the Temple of Fortuna Augusta; the Temple of Isis; etc. Of the latter (rebuilt after 63 A.D., important ruins remain—Doric columns in brick covered with stucco; a beautiful statue of Isis; an altar on which used to lie the remains of the last sacrifice; an elegant sanctuary with a triangular pediment; the purgatorium where ablutions took place. Many objects were found in this temple.

Pompeii possessed *two theatres. The Great Theatre*, near the triangular Forum, was founded before Roman colonisation, several times reconstructed, and finally rebuilt at the beginning of the first century B.C. The semicircular arena which contains the seats, is divided into three parts: the lower part, composed of four rows, for the important people; the middle, which has twenty rows of seats; the upper with four rows.

There was seating room for five thousand spectators. The stage, long and narrow, was decorated with statues, and three doors gave access to it. Above the seats was a wall, surmounted by posts to which an awning was attached. In one of the angles, a square tower served as a reservoir for the water, which was lightly sprinkled to refresh the spectators.

*The Little Theatre* is built in the same way, and is better preserved. It was covered with a roof, so we learn from an inscription. The seats were moulded; behind each place there was a slight hollow intended for the feet of the spectator sitting above. This building served for musical gatherings. At the entrance to the Great Theatre and to the triangular Forum, is an elegant portico with six fluted columns of the Ionic order. The triangular Forum is surrounded on three sides by a magnificent and very long portico which communicated with the upper seats of the great theatre, while another portico communicated with the lower seats of the great theatre,

# CHATEAUX OF THE RENAISSANCE

*The art which best expresses the genius of France during the Renaissance is the architecture of the château. These monuments, very numerous, are of great variety both in their plan and their decoration. They continue feudal architecture which was of a military character. They preserve the general arrangement of towers at the corners joined by the main part of the building. The mediaeval fortress has been disarmed; this new phase of architecture corresponds to a moment of feudal life when the monarchy, becoming all powerful, forbade and rendered useless the entire system of defence in the interior of the kingdom.*

CHAUMONT.
*(Photo by Hachette.)*

BLOIS: WING OF THE TIME OF LOUIS XII.
*(Photo by Neurdein.)*

USSÉ.
*(Photo by Neurdein.)*

## Style of Louis XII

Several generations of châteaux followed one another at the end of the fifteenth century to the middle of the following century. The oldest already reveal a renovation in style, the beginning of the Renaissance, without one being able to notice the slightest intervention of Italian art. They present at their corners the powerful round towers of the strong old châteaux in which there rarely were window openings. On top of the walls, the crenellations and the machicolations remained, memories of a defensive arrangement which is now only a picturesque decoration.

BLOIS: STAIRCASE.
*(Photo by Hachette.)*

CHAMBORD.
*(Photo by Neurdein.)*

CHENONCEAUX.
*(Photo by Hachette.)*

## Style of Francis I

The majority of French Renaissance châteaux are composed of parts differing in age and style; the manner in which a pavilion of the time of Charles VII or Louis XII is attached to a castle-keep of the twelfth or thirteenth century is one of the picturesque elements of this architecture. But, when, toward the first third of the sixteenth century, the Renaissance château is definitely set apart, the builders begin to place more unity in the plan and more regularity in the decoration. The château of Chambord is a marvel of ingenuity and construction. It is the supreme flower of feudal architecture.

LOUVRE. FAÇADE DESIGNED BY J. GOUJON.
*(Photo by Hachette.)*

FONTAINEBLEAU: GALLERY OF THE TIME OF HENRY II.
*(Photo by Hachette.)*

ANET: FAÇADE NOW PLACED IN THE COURT OF THE ÉCOLE DES BEAUX-ARTS, PARIS.
*(Photo by Hachette.)*

## Style of Henry II

During the course of the sixteenth century, the influence of Italian architecture upon that of France increases. The characteristics of the French château (turret, crenellations, machicolations, roof-timbers, etc.) tend to disappear and at the same time the Italian decorative system is introduced which strengthens and transforms the appearance of the façades. It brings with it classic regularity. Finally, one may see the antique orders superposed upon the French façades, as at Florence and at Rome. After that time, the great problem of all architecture was to adjust nicely these columns or pilasters to the arrangement of the palaces. Church façades also used the classical orders.

# FRENCH SCULPTURE IN THE SIXTEENTH CENTURY

*The transformation of French sculpture during the sixteenth century is at once spiritual and plastic; it depends upon thought and form. The Christian themes invented since the thirteenth century continue to live, but soon the Renaissance style transforms the spirit of them. Furthermore, an entirely new world appears, that of the ancient gods and pagan allegories. And, with the introduction of this mythology comes a conception opposed to Christian inspiration. After spiritual expression plastic beauty dominates art; it is like a revenge of paganism upon Christianity, an evolution begun in the twelfth century.*

COLOMBE: TOMB OF FRANCIS OF BRITTANY. NANTES CATHEDRAL. *(Photo by Hachette.)*

THE VIERGE D'OLIVET. LOUVRE. *(Photo by Hachette.)*

SEPULCHRE OF THE ABBEY OF SOLESMES. *(Photo by Hachette.)*

## Michel Colombe

The name of Michel Colombe dominates the period which marks the transition between the Gothic style and the Renaissance. *The Tomb of Francis of Brittany* is still Gothic in its general arrangement and the naturalism of the figures; but the ornamentation is already borrowed from Italy and the allegorical virtues, although dressed in the French manner, are of an almost pagan inspiration. The *Vierge d'Olivet* and the *Sepulchre of Solesmes* are also of the period in which French art tends toward a calm beauty, without, however, renouncing Christian feeling.

JEAN GOUJON (ATTRIBUTED TO): DIANA THE HUNTRESS. LOUVRE. *(Photo by Hachette.)*

LIGIER RICHIER: SEPULCHRE OF THE CHURCH OF ST. ETIENNE AT SAINT-MIHIEL. *(Photo from Mon. hist.)*

JEAN GOUJON: FOUNTAIN OF THE INNOCENTS. PARIS. *(Photo by Hachette.)*

## Jean Goujon

Jean Goujon is a master of radiant purity; the influence of Italian art upon his style is undeniable: the elongated forms in the manner of Primaticcio, the fluid suppleness of the draperies, the delicate qualities of the bas-relief. But this student of the Florentines displays a freshness which is lacking in the masters he imitates. Ligier Richier, however, although he is also influenced by Italian art, appears more faithful to Christian inspiration.

PHILIBERT DELORME AND PIERRE BONTEMPS: TOMB OF FRANCIS I. ST. DENIS. *(Photo by Hachette.)*

GERMAIN PILON: CHRIST. CHURCH OF ST. PAUL, PARIS.

GERMAIN PILON: THE THREE GRACES. LOUVRE. *(Photo by Hachette.)*

GERMAIN PILON: TOMB OF HENRY II. ST. DENIS. *(Photo by Neurdein.)*

## Germain Pilon

Germain Pilon is one of the loveliest masters of the French school; he gives an intense life to his figures; from marble and from bronze he obtains admirable and varied effects of grace and force. At some moments one might suppose him to be of the Middle Ages, at others he resembles the eighteenth century. He was the favourite artist of Catherine de' Medici and the misfortunes of the period prevented him from making at Saint-Denis the great things of which he had dreamed. The tombs of the sixteenth century more and more take on the appearance of triumphal monuments. The lowly sarcophagi of the thirteenth century are now triumphal arches to the glory of death, with Virtues which recall his rewards.

# FRENCH CITY HALLS

*Mediaeval civil architecture has not the broadness and beauty of religious architecture. The old châteaux were for a long time only fortresses too exclusively adapted to one regime to have been able to survive succeeding ones. In the French towns, the architecture of the houses and of the town halls, in the face of magnificent cathedrals and the powerful châteaux, remained very modest. This was because the form of rural French society, feudal and monarchical, scarcely favoured urban civilisation. The communes, so active during the time of Philippe Auguste, were not so advanced in freedom as the Flemish or Italian cities.*

SAINT-ANTONIN.
*(Photo by Boulanger.)*

HOSPITAL AT BEAUNE.
*(Photo by Hachette.)*

SAINT-QUENTIN.
*(Photo by Hachette.)*

## Gothic Civil Monuments

In the period of the Middle Ages, there were no town halls in the French cities. Even at Paris, the most important city of the realm, the *parloir aux bourgeois* was only a very modest building, a symbol of the weakness of municipal power. In the thirteenth century, authority was much more in the hands of the bishop than in those of the mayor. Furthermore, the municipal building par excellence was at that time the cathedral. In the fourteenth and fifteenth centuries, municipal power appeared only to enter immediately in the struggle against the monarchy. There were no city halls.

ARRAS.
*(Photo by Boulanger.)*

CITY HALL, PARIS, FROM A SEVENTEENTH CENTURY ENGRAVING.
*(Photo by Hachette.)*

COMPIÈGNE.
*(Photo by Hachette.)*

## City Halls of the Renaissance

It is only in the sixteenth century, during the reign of Francis I, that Paris began the construction of its town hall. The architecture is always so closely allied to the political life that the story of this monument is really that of the greatest events of French history, and in particular of the revolutions. The modern political history is the history of the rivalry between this town hall and the Louvre, the Tuileries and Versailles. The other French cities which have beautiful town halls dating from the sixteenth century, are cities which participated in the urban civilisation of the north.

LYON.
*(Photo by Hachette.)*

REIMS.
*(Photo by Neurdein.)*

LA ROCHELLE.
*(Photo by Hachette.)*

## The Classic Period

Nevertheless, the great provincial cities, in the seventeenth century, when they were built in modern architecture, raised town houses of Renaissance style, and particularly of the style set by Salomon de Brosse and Mansard, altogether adapted to the elegant simplicity of the bourgeois society: a very modest campanile a very sober decoration, bearing only a correct delineation of the orders; these façades have a charming appearance facing on the great square and present the expressive countenance of the city. Naturally, these façades followed, even to the end of the old regime, the transformations of the architectonic styles under Louis XV and Louis XVI.

# ENAMEL

*E*NAMEL *is obtained by the fusion of mineral materials which are coloured with metallic oxides. The substance thus obtained is a veritable coloured crystal which is used in the composition of small pictures. As with all the precious metal techniques, the art of enamelling came to us from the Orient. At Byzantium, especially, it flourished; it is there that this technique, which certainly had its origin in the land of enamelled terra cotta (Assyria and Persia) was adapted to the Christian iconography. Byzantine enamel work produced its most beautiful works in the tenth and eleventh centuries; they were the models for the Limosin and Rhenish ateliers which worked at a later date.*

RELIQUARY FIGURE OF STE. FOY. CONQUES.
*(Photo by Hachette.)*

SHRINE OF PEPIN OF AQUITAINE. CONQUES.
*(Photo by Moreau.)*

THE DEATH OF THE VIRGIN. LOUVRE.
*(Photo by Hachette.)*

CHRIST IN GLORY. MUSÉE DE CLUNY.
*(Photo by Hachette.)*

## The Romanesque and Gothic Periods

ENAMEL has, from its first appearance in the West, always been associated with jewelry. This painting of costly material is laid upon gold, silver and sometimes copper plates. The metal serves as a supporting panel; it is a ground for sculpture, cast, engraved or pricked in. The reliquaries contain precious metals and stones and enamel.

MONVAERNI: ST. CHRISTOPHER. LOUVRE.
*(Photo by Giraudon.)*

JEAN PENICAUD: ENAMELLED CUP. LOUVRE.
*(Photo by Hachette.)*

N. PENICAUD: THE CRUCIFIXION. LOUVRE.
*(Photo from Mon. hist.)*

## Renaissance Enamels

IN THE thirteenth century, the finest enamel workers belonged to the ateliers at Limoges. Toward the end of the fifteenth century, a new style, one much closer to painting appeared. In this manner, the enamel colours are no longer placed in separate compartments on the metallic plate; they blend with each other in imitation of the colors of oil painting. At the same time, the enamel workers were no longer satisfied to take as their model the work of the manuscript illuminators. The most beautiful enamels treated are still those of the Limosin ateliers.

LÉONARD LIMOSIN: ENTRANCE OF JESUS INTO JERUSALEM. LOUVRE.
*(Photo from Mon. hist.)*

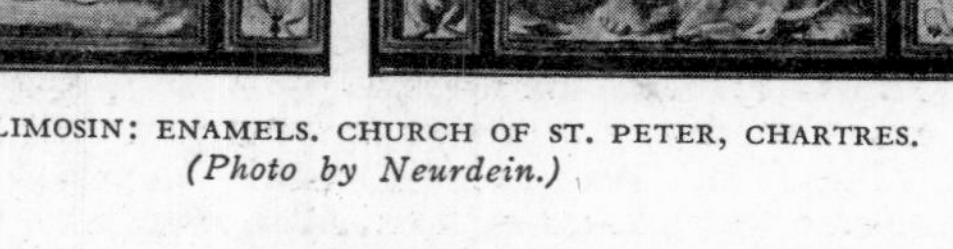

LÉONARD LIMOSIN: ENAMELS. CHURCH OF ST. PETER, CHARTRES.
*(Photo by Neurdein.)*

CONSTABLE OF MONTMORENCY. LOUVRE.
*(Photo by Hachette.)*

## Léonard Limosin

LÉONARD LIMOSIN is the most popular name in the history of enamel painting. He lived in the sixteenth century. In his work, the art of enamelling becomes a fairly faithful transcription of great painting. He translates into his precious material the compositions of the school of Fontainebleau or the portraits in the style of Clouet. There is nothing more learned and more clever. But it must be observed that in this attempt to imitate both portraitists and historical painters, enamel work lost much of its original qualities. Soon, in fact, this art began to descend to a rather vulgar commercialism. Toward the end of the sixteenth century, enamelling died along with the arts of the miniatures and stained glass.

and with the little theatre. In the event of sudden rain, the spectators could take refuge under its galleries. It was formed of 74 Doric columns, surrounding a court. In the time of the Empire, it was turned into barracks for gladiators. Boxes on two tiers were built all round. Those in this building suffered greatly at the time of the catastrophe. It was here that the greatest number of bodies was found.

The *Amphitheatre*, built in the first century B.C., is the oldest of its kind known. It could contain 20,000 spectators. At the two ends are two monumental doors. The arena is surrounded by a wall which was once adorned with pictures (now destroyed), representing fights of men and animals. The first rows of seats were placed on the slope of the soil, which was hollowed out for this purpose; the others were built by degrees, the public having been obliged at the beginning, to sit on the grassy slopes. These seats were divided into three parts, like those of the theatre. The highest ones rested against a wall upheld by arcades.

The Pompeians, following the example of the Greeks, soon built public *thermæ* (*baths*). They had them long before the Romans. The thermæ of Stabiæ were erected in the second century B.C., during the Samnite period, and reconstructed in the following century.

Having crossed the threshold, one finds oneself in the hall (decorated with paintings on a red ground) which overlooks a vast courtyard—the palæstra. All round are the different halls of these thermæ which were excellently fitted up;—men's baths; women's baths; frigidarium, caldarium, tepidarium, piscines. The walls of the palæstra and the rooms, were covered with vivid paintings. The Romans, as soon as they had settled in Pompeii, built the thermæ of the forum. These had no palæstra; they had the same room-plan as the baths of Stabies. The tepidarium is particularly well preserved.

The country around about Pompeii was scattered with splendid villas which disappeared in the catastrophe of the year 79. None except the villa of Boscoreale has been excavated.

See Pl. 31, Vol. I.

BIBLIOGRAPHY: H. Thédenat, *Pompéi.* 2 vols.—E. Mazois. *Les ruines de Pompéi.* Paris, 1824.—P. Gusman, *Pompéi: la ville, ses mœurs, les arts.* Paris, 1899.—M. Della Corte, *Pompeii, The New Excavations* (*Houses and Inhabitants*). 1925.—A. Maiuri, *Pompeii*, 1929.—A. J. Rusconi, *Pompeii*. 1929. VII.

*Pompeian Painting.* — Painting played a very important part in the life of Pompeians. Not only public buildings, but also private dwellings, sometimes very modest ones, are decorated with frescoes or tempera paintings. There are imitations of coloured marble which often surround a central picture executed by a more skilled artist; friezes imitating colonnades; pediments, canopies, flowers and people. A vein of most amusing fantasy runs through the fresco painting of Pompeian houses. The themes, introduced by the Greeks, and often executed by them, recall Greek mythology to the Latin race. It is not the mythology of heroic legends, but an amusing mythology, which shows us the gods sharing human weakness. Jupiter, Mars, Venus, Hercules, Adonis, Perseus are among the favourites. Their adventures are displayed among plump cupids, graceful little figures who frolic and laugh, standing out clearly against a black background. The most famous of these cupids are those in the house of the Vettii, who are occupied with various games or tasks; sometimes they are goldsmiths, blacksmiths, harvesters or merchants. It is rare to find a trace of serious feeling on Pompeian walls. Certainly there is Ariadne abandoned by Theseus: Io as captive of Argos; but the painter's light, fantastic touch, makes us admire their elegance and grace, rather than think of their misfortunes. "At Pompeii we see the old Greek mythology die in laughter. In it there has survived no feeling of depth or seriousness."

The decorators have also painted landscapes, rivers, hills, porticos, villas, gardens, through which little people wander. Interiors of inns, of shops, and workmen at their labour, are also represented. These paintings are not imitated from Greek masterpieces, but owe their existence to the invention of artists skilled in depicting the small scene with amusing virtuosity. Among the best decorated houses are, besides the house of the Vettii,—the house of the tragic Poet, and the house of Cecelio Giocondo. The paintings in the market too, are among the most famous.

Another form of decoration which was in great repute among the Pompeians, was mosaic. First used for the paving of buildings, it ended by becoming the medium for pictures, such as the *Battle of Issus*, found in the House of the Faun, and now in the Museum of Naples. It is a vast composition in which the armies of Darius and Alexander meet and clash. Many private and public buildings had mosaic pictures on their floors or walls.

See Pl. 28, Vol. I.

BIBLIOGRAPHY: W. Helbig, *Wandergemälde der von Vesuv. Verschütteten Städte Campaniens*, 1868.—Aug. Mau, *Geschichte der decorativen Wandermaterei in Pompéi.* Berlin, 1882.

**PONT du GARD (France).**—Part of a magnificent Roman aqueduct, 25 miles long, built by order of Agrippa, son-in-law of Augustus, to lead to Nîmes the waters of the source of the Evre. It is in good preservation, about 900 feet long, and is formed of three tiers of arches crossing the valley 180 feet above the River Gard. The masonry is laid dry, without mortar. The stone is a beautiful golden colour.

See Pl. 30. Vol. I.

**PONT NEUF.**—See Paris.

**PONTE VECCHIO.**—See Florence.

**PONTIUS (Paul).**—Flemish engraver, 1603-1658. Pupil of Rubens and friend of Brouwer, he is the most important etcher of the Rubens—Van Dyck School. A brilliant technician, he developed his own unique style. For *Van Dyck's Iconography* he etched 38 plates.

BIBLIOGRAPHY: Hymans, *Hist. de la grav. dans l'école de Rubens,* 1879.

**PONTORMO (Jacopo Carrucci; known as).**—Florentine painter, 1494-1556. Pupil of Andrea del Sarto. Pontormo was a notable portraitist and fine canvases by him are to be found in Florence in the Uffizi and the Pitti; in Rome, in the Borghese Gallery and the Galleria Nazionale; in the Louvre; in Berlin, and elsewhere.

In the cloisters of the Annunziata (Florence), he painted a quite pleasing *Visitation* (1516); and there are frescoes by him in Certòsa di Galuzzo (1523) and Poggio a Cajano (1521).

BIBLIOGRAPHY: F. Goldschmidt, *Pontormo, Rosso und Bronzino.* 1911.—F. M. Clapp, *Jacopo Carrucci da Pontormo.* New Haven, Yale University Press, 1916.

**POPES (Palace of the).**—See Avignon.

**PÖPPELMAN (Matthäus Daniel).**—German architect, 1662-1736, and exponent of the grandiose late baroque of Germany. The Zwinger, Dresden, shows the turbulence of the style and its attempt at complete fusion of architecture, sculpture, and painting.

**PORCELAIN.**—See Ceramic; China.

**PORDENONE (Giovanni Antonio; known as Il).**—Italian painter, of Friuli—1483-1539. Developed under the influence of the Bellini, and later of Giorgione and Titian.

PORDENONE (G.A.): ST. LAWRENCE THE JUST AND OTHER SAINTS. (Academy of Venice.)

In the Cathedral of Cremona he painted colossal and dramatic frescoes of the *Passion* (1521-22), and an altarpiece representing the *Virgin between Saints.*

For the Cathedral of Pordenone (his native town) he painted a *Madonna of Misericordia* before a landscape (1515); *St. Erasmus and St. Roch* (1525) and a large *Glorification of St. Mark* (1535).

After 1535, he settled in Venice, where he did some of his best work. We mention: the *St. Catherine of* San Giovanni Elemosinario; the remains of frescoes painted in the courtyard of the convent of San Stefano; frescoes of the Madonna di Campagna of Piacenza (representing scenes from the *Life of the Virgin*, and the *Legend of St. Catherine*): *Lorenzo Giustiniani and other saints* (Accademia, Venice) (1532).

Pordenone died in Ferrara in 1539.

BIBLIOGRAPHY: Crowe and Cavalcaselle, *History of Painting in North Italy*, ed. T. Borenius, Vol. III.

**PORTA (Giacomo della).**—Lombard sculptor and architect, 1541-1604. He may have been Michelangelo's pupil. In any case, he was strongly influenced by the great master, and rebuilt Michelangelo's dome for St. Peter's after it fell.

He planned the fine terraced gardens of the Villa Aldobrandini, mingling grottos and fountains with noble and tranquil decoration.

His chief work in sculpture is the tomb of the parents of Clement VIII in the Aldobrandini Chapel, in Santa Maria Sopra Minerva.

His greatest architectual achievement was the early Baroque façade of Il Gesù, Rome, c. 1573.

**PORTAIL (Jacques André).**—French painter and draughtsman. (Died, 1759.)

**PORTE NOIRE (Porte de Mars).**—See Besançon.

**— ST. DENIS.**—See Blondel (F).

**PORTO (Guglielmo della).**—Lombard sculptor (about 1510 to about 1577). He was greatly influenced by Michelangelo. His chief work is the tomb of Paul III, in the choir of St. Peter's, a grandiose, original work, which shows a tendency to the baroque, though still restrained.

**POT (Hendrick Gerritsz).** — Dutch historic and portrait painter, about 1585-1657. He was probably a pupil of van Mander, and worked under the influence of Frans Hals. In 1631 he was in London painting the portrait of Charles I. and members of his family. In the famous *Officers of the Arquebussiers*, which Hals painted in 1633, we find Pot as one of the younger members. He was supposedly included in another group painting by the famous master. Pot's early works are gay group-scenes done in the Hals tradition; to his middle period belong the large allegorical pieces; his late works are portraits and conversation pieces done in a more formal manner with set types, but not even in these works does he lose the witty, sharp characterization of his sitters. Kalf and Palamedesz were his most famous pupils. Pot's paintings may be seen in Berlin, London, Amsterdam, Dresden, etc.

BIBLIOGRAPHY: Philippi, *Blüte der Malerei in Holland*, 1901.

**POTTER (Paulus).** — Dutch painter and graver, 1625-1654. At the age of fifteen he painted the *Boarhunt* in the Frankfurt a.M. Museum. He nearly always painted animals and shepherds, trying to reproduce faithfully their attitudes and characteristics, and often glorifying them. He observed every minute detail and was never surpassed in rendering them. However, in composition he could not compete with Rubens or Fyt. His earlier group compositions were replaced in his late period by paintings of single animals and scenes of typical Dutch lowlands. He is represented in all leading Museums.

See Pl. 37, Vol. II.

BIBLIOGRAPHY: C. Hofstede de Groot, *A Catalogue Raisonné of the Most Eminent Dutch Painters of the Seventeenth Century.* Vol. IV, 1912. London.

**POTTERY.**—See Ceramic; Greece (Vases); America (Archæology); China—Art; etc.

**POURBUS (Frans).**—Flemish painter (1545-1581), son of Pieter Pourbus. Most important pupil of Franz Floris of Antwerp; especially well known for portraits, his historical paintings are less brilliant than those by his father.

**— (Frans II, or the Younger).** —Flemish painter, son of Frans Pourbus, 1569 or 1570-1622. He worked for the Court of the Archdukes of Brussels, when the Duke of Mantua took him into his service in 1599. He painted his famous *Chamber of Beauties*, composed of portraits of fine ladies of the period including many of Neapolitan and Florentine nobility. He was in Paris twice as court painter. He painted portraits of *Henry IV* (Louvre), and *Marie de Médicis*; of *Anne of Austria;* and *Louis XIII as a Child* (Uffizi), etc.

POTTER (PAUL): THE PASTURE. (Museum of Dresden.)

**— (Pieter)**; known as Pourbus the Elder. Flemish painter, 1510-1584. He worked chiefly in Bruges where most of his works are to be seen. He painted religious pictures, the most celebrated of which is the *Last Judgment* (Bruges Museum); and many portraits of local celebrities. He occupied himself not only with painting, but also with architecture and topography. He made a large map of Bruges and its environs for the provosts.

BIBLIOGRAPHY: Kervyn de Volkaersbeke, *Les Pourbus,* 1870.

**POUSSIN (Nicolas).** — French painter. Born 1594; died 1665. In 1610, Quentin Varin, on his way to

POUSSIN: THE CHILDHOOD OF BACCHUS. (Musée Condé, Chantilly.)

Grand-Andely, became interested in the young scholar, looked at the pictures which he drew all over his books, and gave him his first lessons. Six years later he took him with him to Paris.

From the studio of Quentin Varin, Poussin went to that of Ferdinand Van Elle, of Malines, a portrait-painter, and then to another unnamed painter. Finally he went to Rome, but neither the realism of Caravaggio, nor the mannerisms of the Carracci school, satisfied him.

In fact, what the young painter sought in Rome was the teaching of the dead rather than that of the living. His protector, Varin, went to Naples where he died; the Cardinal Barberini, to whom he had letters of introduction, left Rome on diplomatic work with the result that Poussin remained unknown, and sold his pictures for a mere nothing. But his needs were few, and he lodged modestly with two sculptors.

As these two were studying antique sculpture, Poussin took the opportunity to do some modelling, and to do some figures in relief. With his friends he carefully measured the Niobe, the Laocoön, etc. This time he had found a school to which he always remained faithful—that of ancient Greece and Rome. In all the serious work of Poussin, one can trace the attitudes, lines, volumes and proportions, of Greek and Roman sculpture.

It has been said that, in introducing into his pictures the forms and gestures of classical sculpture, the artist had lost his sense of life—that he had forgotten nature only to become a servile copier of marble—and above all, that he was wrong to try to express in his figures feeling which painting cannot render.

These critics cannot confine themselves to the years during which Poussin produced his best work; that is from 1630 to 1640—in other words from the first work undertaken for the Cardinal Barberini, up to the time of his departure for Paris where Louis XIII claimed him. Deeply impressed by Titian, the painter of the *Triumph of Flora* fell under the spell of colour. This canvas tells us more than all the commentaries on the various influences which at this time, affected the artist—the influence of Titian who was chiefly responsible for making Poussin the "creator" as he has been called, "of the laws of landscape painting." The influence of Raphael in whom he saw the follower of the ancients, several times suggested to him the attitudes we see in Poussin's Muses. The influence of antiquity guided his genius, and that of nature played its part.

POUSSIN: SHEPHERDS OF ARCADY. (Louvre.)

The Poussin of this stage, was a young man. In the human form, as in landscape, he is attracted by the outward and plastic. We even see this tendency, in several *Bacchanals* and in the *Leda*, dominating moral points of view.

His *Ballo della Vita umana* in the Wallace Collection; his *Rule of Flora* in Dresden; *The Triumph of Galatea* in the Hermitage; the *Parnassus* of the Prado, the *Inspiration of the Poet* in the Louvre; *Bacchus and Midas* in Munich—all these show qualities which engage realists and idealists alike.

But, if this period is that of the Bacchanals, it has also produced the *Death of Germanicus*, the *Saint Erasmus* (ordered for St. Peter's at Rome), the *Israelites Gathering Manna in the Desert* (1639) and several others.

Poussin saw his reputation growing not only in Rome, but also in France. By order of Louis XIII and Richelieu the painter was offered in the king's name, in 1639, a paid appointment, apartments in the Tuileries, and the walls of the great gallery in the Louvre, to cover with paintings. Some days later, a letter from the king insisted on the painter's appearance at court. Two years passed, however, before the artist could decide to leave his quiet Roman retreat. Finally, in 1640, a friend sought him out, and obliged him to go with him to Paris. The reception which awaited him there the dazzled Poussin describes himself in a letter in 1641.

The enchantment was of short duration. Vouet and his pupils adapted themselves compliantly, executing most varied and thankless tasks. But Poussin was of different calibre. Art, for him, meant long and unremitting effort. Besides, the religious painting which he was at first expected to do, could not add greatly to his reputation. The *Last Supper* and the *Miracle of Saint Francis Xavier* show us the lack of harmony which exists between the art inspired by antiquity and that springing from the religious sense.

In these pictures of Poussin's, in which the Almighty appears in the likeness of Jupiter, there is no trace of the feeling of a devoutly religious kind, as there is in Le Sueur.

But Poussin failed chiefly in purely decorative painting. Appointed in 1641 the "King's Chief Painter," he had to undertake, besides huge cartoons for tapestry, the decoration of the great gallery in the Louvre. Perpetually at variance with the architect Le Mercier, with Vouet who was jealous of him, and the Baron of Fouquiers, the independent artist decided to return to Rome, not, however, without being bound to return. The sketches which remain of these *Labours of Hercules,* intended for the ornamentation of the gallery, show that Poussin's genius did not lend itself to this task. Henceforward, art is for him, but a means of expressing an idea. It has been said of him; "he was not content to know things through the senses alone, nor to base his knowledge on the examples of the greatest masters; he strove to know the reason of the different kinds of beauty found in works of art." It was no longer enough to examine the remains of ancient sculpture and architecture. Like Corneille, he sought in the books of the ancients, to discover the moral beauty which he worshipped. More fortunate than Corneille, however, his days passed in the land of gods and heroes, so that, in him, more than in any other French painter, is the feeling for ancient times, which comes out in *Shepherds of Arcady*.

The more Poussin identified himself with his absolute ideal, the more his art becomes dissociated from the underlying ideas of nature and life. Contrary to the realists, he is not interested in movement in so far as it is picturesque; he simply enquires if it is significant. The various attitudes of his figures should express different feelings.

His theories, literary by nature, will not go far. As in Greek music, which had different modes (Lydian, Doric, Phrygian) for different subjects, so Poussin considered that painting too, should have its modes. The treatment, for instance, of the *Rape of the Sabines* differs considerably from that of the *Shepherds of Arcady*, painted about the same time. While, to express the disorder and violence of the *Rape,* the colour is dry and hard, the brush seeming to beat out the modelling of muscles like a hammer—the treatment of the Virgilian scene of the three shepherds and the girl grouped before the sad epitaph, is, on the contrary, softer and more tender.

As the artist aged, he considered less and less the human model which he thought imperfect. At this time he was not averse to finding inspiration in nature. Only to see the drawings made along the banks of the Tiber, in a few pen-strokes or pencil, is to understand what an admirable realist Poussin could have been, had his proud ideal permitted him.

Nobody has understood better than he, the massive construction of Italian skies—none has surpassed him in treatment of winding distances, or of leafy banks. In the *Four Seasons*; in *Apollo and Daphne* which is unfinished, the painter's genius comes out most clearly in the landscape.

In 1665, Poussin, already famous and considered a classic, died at the age of seventy-one.

It is significant, that the 17th century with Le Brun; the 18th with Boucher; the Empire with David; in 1830, Ingres and Delacroix; and in modern times, Puvis de Chavannes, the neo-classic group—all subsequent French schools of painting have recognised Poussin to be one of the most representative of French painters. No other painter has had more scorn for easy execution than Poussin. None clung more firmly to the triple ideal of plastic, moral and intellectual beauty. Above all, Poussin's work possesses in the highest degree, the qualities of proportion, reason, clarity, and in these he represents not only the spirit of his century, but the most characteristic qualities of French genius.

See Pl. 40, Vol. II.

Bibliography: W. Friedländer, *Nicolas Poussin.* 1914.—E. Magne, Paris, 1914.—O. Grautoff, *Nicolas Poussin.* Munich and Leipzig, 1914.

**POWERS (Hiram).**—American sculptor (1805-1873). He was born near Woodstock, Vermont, 29th July 1805. He had to work as a boy and tried his hand as a bill collector, errand boy and library worker. The family had moved to Ohio when he was young and he got a job in a waxworks museum in Cincinnati. There he was able to show his talent for modelling new figures and soon he was receiving commissions for portrait busts. For a time he had instruction from Eckstein along with Henry Kirke Brown and then about 1835 he moved to Washington, D. C. There he made busts of Chief Justice John Marshall, John C. Calhoun, Daniel Webster and many others, all well characterised. Two years later with the financial assistance of some friends he was able to go abroad to study. A short time was spent in Paris and then he moved on to Florence. There he settled permanently and got a start with the assistance of Horatio Greenough, who had lived in that city over a long period of time. His early interest in portraiture changed gradually as he became influenced by the neo-classic style then popular in sculpture. In 1843 his famous *Greek Slave* was produced in marble. It represented a nude female in chains, purporting to represent a Greek prisoner of the Turks in the Greek Revolution. Modern standards of criticism are not quite so inclined to call it a masterpiece. The modelling of the form is negligible, whereas the main stress is laid on the details of the chains and the draped pillar against which she is leaning. Other ideal figures and busts followed, which have the same type of modelling. But in his own time Hiram Powers was acclaimed as a great sculptor and his home in Florence was visited by many notables of the literary and artistic circles, including Henry W. Longfellow, Robert Browning, Charles Dickens and Thomas Ball. He exerted a wide influence on contemporary American sculpture although he never returned to the United States. He died after a long illness, resulting from a fall, 27th June 1873 and was buried in Florence.

Bibliography: William J. Clark, Jr., *Great American Sculptures,* 1878. —Edward Everett, *A Defence of Powers' Statue of Webster,* 1859.—C. E. Fairman, *Art and Artists of the Capitol,* 1927.—Miner Kilbourne Kellogg, *Justice to Hiram Powers,* 1848.—*Powers' Statue of the Greek Slave,* 1848.—Lorado Taft, *The History of American Sculpture,* 1903.—H. T. Tuckerman, *The Book of the Artists,* 1867.—*Vindication of Hiram Powers in the "Greek Slave" Controversy,* 1849.

**POYNTER (Sir Edward).**—English painter (1836-1919), studied in London and in Paris where he was the pupil of Charles Gleyre. Elected full member of the Royal Academy in 1877, he held the post of President of that Institution from 1896 to 1918, and was also Director of the National Gallery between 1894 and 1904. A much employed painter and a great power in the English art world of his time, Poynter was a typical representative of the more conservative, academical tendency in painting during the second half of the nineteenth century: his most famous work is perhaps the *Visit to Æsculapius* (1880) in the National Gallery, Millbank.

**POZZO (Father Andrea).**—Italian Jesuit painter and architect, 1642-1709. He was the master of illusions and "trompe-l'œil" (pièces painted stereoscopically to deceive the spectator). His best work is probably the ceiling of Sant'-Ignazio, in Rome, which, though heavy, shows Father Pozzo's amazing brilliance and his gift of rendering perspective effects.

**PRADIER (Charles Simon).**—French engraver, 1786-1848. He engraved after Gérard and Ingres. *"Tu Marcellus eris"* (1833) is his chief work.

**— (Jean-Jacques; called James).**—French sculptor, 1790-1848. Brother of the above.

**PRADO.**—See Madrid.

**PRAGUE.** — The *Cathedral* is composed of a Gothic choir (14th century). Towers finished in the 19th century. The Cathedral shelters a statue of St. Wenceslas, by Pieter Vischer.

The Castle was begun in the 13th century; restored at the end of the 15th century; and finished in the 18th century, by Maria-Theresa.

**PRAIRIE ARCHITECTURE.**—See Wright (F. L.).

**PRATT (Bela Lyon).**—American sculptor (1867-1917), much employed on monumental sculpture notably in Boston (State House, Library, Opera House, etc.).

**PRAXITELES.**—Athenian sculptor of the fourth century.

Judging from the little which is known about Praxiteles, the date of his birth must have been about 390 B.C. About 360 B.C. he was already working at Athens. According to Pausanias, it is during this time (360-350) that the statue of a Satyr and one of *Eros* were created.

About 350, Praxiteles must have journeyed into Asia Minor, for he made for the new temple of Artemis at Ephesus, an altar decorated with bas-reliefs (the old temple had been destroyed in 356). During this voyage the *Aphrodite of Cos* and that of *Cnidus,* were executed. An *Eros* for the town of Parium was doubtless also made during this time in Asia Minor.

It seems that Praxiteles passed the last years of his life at Athens. The *Hermes* of Olympia, which is the only authentic work, doubtless belongs to the end of his life. It is supposed that he died rather before 332, the date of the coming of Alexander. He left two sculptor sons, who worked at Athens during the last part of the fourth century.

It remains to consider the works which can recall to us the original statues which the ancient writers mention.

Firstly, there are the bas-reliefs made for Mantinea, shown in the museum at Athens. Mantinea was rebuilt in 370 and in 362. Praxiteles made a group of Latona and Apollo for the temple consecrated to Latona in this town. The group has been lost, but the bas-reliefs which decorated the base and which Pausanias mentions, were discovered by M. Fougères in 1887. They represent the Muses and the *Contest of Apollo and Marsyas.* It is not certain that they were the work of Praxiteles, but their soft grace leads to the conclusion that they were inspired by him.

According to Pausanias, there was in the "Street of the Tripods" at Athens, a statue of a Satyr, of which Praxiteles was very proud. This satyr, pouring wine, no doubt served as a model to a certain number of statues which have come down to us in a more or less mutilated condition. The best of these is a satyr in the Boncompagni Museum at Rome. It is quite a new type of satyr, with no trace of the primitive, bestial type.

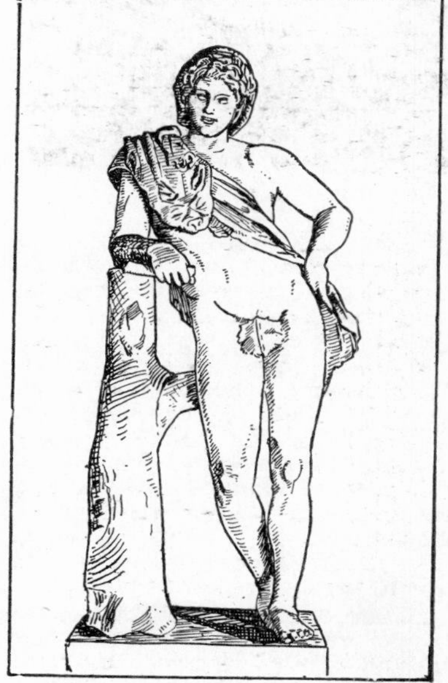

Praxiteles: The Faun. (Capitoline Museum, Rome.)

Praxiteles had made several statues of *Eros*; one at Thespiæ and one at Parium, and a third, whose existence is mentioned, but whose situation is unknown. The *Eros of Thespiæ* was taken to Rome, and was replaced by an Athenian's copy. It was a much-praised work, which had been copied several times by ancient sculptors. Among several extant copies, those at Naples and the Vatican seem to correspond to the descriptions in old writings. They each have the lowered eyes, and strained look, and the feminine arrangement of the hair, which characterised the original.

In the Thespian Temple, near the Eros, was a statue of Aphrodite which had been chosen and dedicated by Phryne. It is thought to have been taken to Athens, where a torso of Aphrodite was discovered near the theatre of Dionysos. It probably was after some celebrated original, because it is the same which served as model for the famous *Venus of Arles,* discovered in the theatre of that town in the seventeenth century. The face of the Venus of Arles is almost exactly similar to that of the *Venus of Cnidus* by Praxiteles. "The face of this Arles Venus is turned towards the mirror with a charming expression of grave coquetry, and the hair, caught by the double bandeau, has the same elegant and simple arrangement as in the *Venus of Cnidus.*" (Collignon.) An important innovation should be noticed in this statue; the form of the goddess is half draped, half nude. This daring was unknown in the art of the fifth century. It is in the fourth century that, with such sculptors as Scopas and Praxiteles, the figure of Aphrodite was by degrees represented without draperies.

The *Venus of Cnidus* was very famous, and has been frequently praised by ancient writers, but unfortunately they laud it rather than describe it, but one account suggests the same attitude as that stamped on the coins of Cnidus. These show the goddess standing, with the garment which she has just taken off, falling over a vase. These coins and the one brief description enable us to recognise, among the innumerable Aphrodites of our Museums, the type which conforms most nearly to that created by Praxiteles. The most beautiful is certainly that in the Vatican, which is shown with some drapery which has been added, but it has been possible to photograph the statue without this. The ancients particularly admired the face of the Venus of Cnidus. This statue, transported to Constantinople, was destroyed there by fire, but M. Furtwängler thinks he recognises a work by Praxiteles in a head of Aphrodite in the Leconfield collection in England.

Praxiteles: Hermes. (Detail.)

It was after 350 that Praxiteles must have made in Asia Minor for the city of Parium, his statue of *Eros* which was equally famous in classical times, but which has since disappeared. A coin of Parium suggests the general attitude. Eros must have been standing, the left leg slightly bent, the left arm touching the hip and holding some drapery. A figure in the Louvre, known as the "Borghese Spirit" is the statue which corresponds most nearly to this attitude.

Praxiteles had also sculptured the figure of *Artemis* which was in the temple of Artemis Brauronia. An archæologist, M. Studniczka, recognises a copy in the famous statue known by the name of "Diana of the Gabii." This Diana is clothed in a garment with wide sleeves, which she has lifted with two girdles, so that it only falls to her knees. The goddess is in the act of clasping a cloak on her right shoulder. M.

Studniczka explains this gesture by saying that the action recalls the gift which Athenian Matrons used to give to the goddess. They used to bring her a cloak which Artemis accepted, and which she herself placed on her shoulders. It is also noteworthy that the face of this goddess recalls that of the Aphrodite of Cnidus, though the former is somewhat more severe.

One of the favourite subjects of Praxiteles was that of a young man leaning on an elbow in a careless attitude, and showing in the calm, free-and-easy pose, a harmony of rhythmic lines. One of the most charming figures of this type is the *Apollo Sauroctonus*, one of the best reproductions of which is in the Louvre. The original was in bronze; the Louvre figure is in marble. It shows a youth, leaning against a tree-trunk, looking at a climbing lizard. This prop gives a better opportunity to show the rounded, youthful suppleness, than the movement shown in the figure of Polyclitus, who leans on one leg.

It is similarity of attitude which connects to Praxiteles with the famous *Satyr in Repose* in the Vatican.

It is quite probable that the statue of *Hermes*, discovered in Olympia in 1877, is an authentic work by Praxiteles. It was found buried under layers of earth, in the place where such a statue was said by Pausanias to be. This Hermes, similar in attitude to the Apollo Sauroctonus, and the Satyr in repose, is leaning on the left elbow, and holding with his left arm the infant Dionysos, who is holding out his arms towards the object which Hermes is holding in his raised right hand. The right arm is missing, but Hermes was probably holding a bunch of grapes. This Hermes has extraordinary excellence of technique, and the drapery, when photographed, could be mistaken for real. The modelling of the eyes has so much delicacy that Praxiteles was said to be able to render almost the luminous softness of life. The figure of the child is the least careful part of the group.

Many other works of which no trace remains, were attributed to Praxiteles.

Praxiteles, judged by ancient writers and by his extant works, seems to have been the sculptor of grace; of feminine beauty and of adolescence; the creator of the type of Eros and of Aphrodite. He gave up bronze for marble, and marble enabled him the better to render the qualities of flesh.

His influence was considerable, and can be traced in a number of works of the fourth century. None are more attractive than the little terra cotta Tanagra figurines (see under Greece: Terra cottas).

In his own times, and today, the name of Praxiteles stands for Greek genius in its most pleasing and attractive form.

See Pl. 24, Vol. I.

BIBLIOGRAPHY: Collignon, *Histoire de la sculpture grecque*. Vol. II. Paris, 1896.—G. Perrot, *Praxitèle*. Paris, 1905.—Collignon, *Scopas et Praxitèle*. Paris, 1907 (this contains a fairly complete bibliography on works of Praxiteles).—Ernest Gardner. *Six Greek Sculptors*. London, 1925 (3rd imp.).

**PREDELLA.**—The step or platform upon which an altar rests; also the series of small painted panels below the main panels of an altar-piece.

**PREHISTORIC (Archæology).**—Archæology is the study of antiquities which are older than the most ancient historical documents that humanity has bequeathed us. Prehistoric archæology is the study of remains which have been lost and recovered. The beginning of the historic period varies greatly according to the country. In Egypt, history begins about 5000 B.C.; for Gaul, it begins some centuries before our era; for the Scandinavian countries, ten centuries after our era. In prehistoric archæology, chronologies are always approximate.

Prehistoric times are generally divided into three parts, according to the remains of implements which have been found—the Stone Age, the Bronze Age, the Iron Age. All these three periods belong to the Quaternary epoch, the three earlier epochs being previous to the appearance of humanity. Archæologists also distinguish epochs within the Quaternary epoch. They generally count four, based on the fauna, and on human industry, and they have named them after the most important archæological stations. These are:—

| | Divisions of the Quaternary era | Fauna | Products | |
|---|---|---|---|---|
| Old Quaternary or Pleistocene | Chellian era | Hippopotamus | Worked flint | Paleolithic |
| | Acheulian era | | | |
| | Mousterian | Mammoth | | |
| | Solutrean Magdalenian | Reindeer | Paintings and Sculpture | |
| Actual Quaternary or Holocene | Actual Quaternary | Present Varieties | | Neolithic |

CHART SHOWING PREHISTORIC PERIODS.

(i) Chellian epoch (station of Chelle)—hippopotami; flint instruments.

(ii) Acheulian epoch (station of St. Acheul, near Amiens)—tools similar, but more careful.

(iii) Mousterian epoch (station of Moustier, Dordogne)—mammoths; flint generally cut on one surface only.

(iv) Solutrian and Magdalenian epoch (Solutré, Saône-et-Loire; La Madeleine, Dordogne)—Reindeer, carvings and paintings.

**PREHISTORIC (Art).**—See Pl. 13, Vol. I.

**PRENDERGAST (Maurice Brazil).**—American painter (1859-1924). He was born in St. Johns, Newfoundland, in 1859, but the family soon moved to Boston, Massachusetts, where he passed his youth. While in his teens he began to paint show cards for a living. His week-ends were spent in excursions into the country that he might see and sketch herds of cattle grazing in the meadows. A minister's wife in Roxbury was impressed by his drawings and urged him to go abroad to study. In 1884, accompanied by his brother Charles, he worked his way to France on a cattle boat. His brother returned to the United States, but he stayed to study at the Académie Julian under Jean Paul Laurens and he also worked at the Académie Colarossi. He was in France for five years and then returned to settle in Winchester, Massachusetts. There he assisted his brother with the carving of picture frames, as was then the fashion. Sometimes he was free to go and paint at Revere Beach nearby, recording his impressions of the throngs there in vivid water-colours. Early in the 1890's he again went to France to paint in Paris and in Normandy and in 1898 he visited Venice and St. Malo. Two years later, back in the United States, he made some trips to New York City and there sketched the crowds in Central Park. Other tours of Italy were made in 1909 and 1912, where he created compositions in his typically mannered style. In 1913 he went to New Hampshire and his studies of the New England countryside showed a simplification and clarifying of his style. After another short trip abroad he and his brother Charles settled in New York. Maurice was growing deaf and in 1922 his health broke down. Unable to do further painting directly from nature he had to be content with pieces done in his studio. He died 1st February 1924 shortly after receiving one of the few prizes of his lifetime. His art is peculiarly characteristic in the pointillistic technique that he employed in the majority of his works. Never a detailed style he yet gave a sense of space and bulk to the figures of his scenes as in the *Ponte della Paglia*.

BIBLIOGRAPHY: Margaret Breuning, *Maurice Prendergast*, American Artists Series, 1931.—For other material see *The Index of Twentieth Century Artists* for March, 1935.

**PRE-RAPHAELITE BROTHERHOOD (The).**—About 1848, a school of painting was founded, in England, which took the name of the Pre-Raphaelite Brotherhood. It was a reaction against the anecdotal and sentimental art of the day. Four young men—the three painters, Holman Hunt, Millais, Rossetti, and the sculptor, Thomas Woolner,—who were soon followed by the art critics, Stephens and James Collinson,—inspired by the same ideal, resolved to save English art from a materialism, "which they feared would soon degenerate into a false and superficial convention." One day, at Millais' house, they were looking at an album of engravings reproducing the frescoes of the Campo Santo of Pisa, and Hunt tells us that it was probably meeting with this book at that particular moment which determined the foundation of the Pre-Raphaelite Brotherhood. On the whole the spirit of this art was, as Ruskin said later, essentially true. The Pre-Raphaelites did not say that there had been no good art since Raphael, but it seemed to them that later art was often corrupted, and that it was only in the work of the Primitives that they were sure of finding perfect health. Thus Hunt, Millais and Rossetti studied the Italian painters of the 14th and 15th century, and were inspired to re-create, in their own school, a spirit of purity and a chaste imagination which could again feel, and revive, the heroisms, the holiness, and the grace of legend, of history, and of the Gospels. Art, according to them, should serve a moral end. Their love of nature led them to represent everything very precisely and minutely. In their desire to realise truth, "the principle and end of all morality," this system resulted in almost microscopic analysis. They were feeling this ideal in a confused way, when Hunt discovered the *Modern Painters* of Ruskin, the first volume of which had appeared in 1843, and the second in 1846. In Ruskin, the Pre-Raphaelites found their champion and their æsthete. According to him, they had but one ideal: absolute truth in all their work. This they achieved by working from nature down to the smallest detail. Every figure is a faithful portrait of a living person. Every detail, even the smallest is painted with the same care. All this naturalism is exterior, and reveals but the execution. In 1850, the Pre-Raphaelite Brotherhood founded a review, the *Germ*, to spread and defend their ideas, and also to explain their works. This review only had a short life. The influence of the Pre-Raphaelites in England, during the second half of the 19th century was extraordinary, and it spread to France. Among the best known artists who adopted their ideals were James Collinson, George Wilson, Arthur Hughes, F. Sandys, Noel Paton, Charles Collins, Fairfax Murray, Cayley Robinson, Walter Crane, etc. In 1861, Rossetti wrote: "Each of us (Madox Brown, Burne-Jones; Phillip Webb, the architect, and William Morris) is going to make at his own expense, an object or two of furniture. Rest assured we have no intention of adding to the expensive rubbish which has so much success, but simply of providing something in good taste at current prices." A little shop, in Red Lion Square, was opened where the artists exhibited their work. The most interesting results seem to have been obtained by William Morris and Walter Crane. Their activity was

BURNE-JONES: KING COPHETUA.

ROSSETTI: ASTARTE SYRIACA.

engaged in the arts of woodwork, metal work, pottery, and, in fact, in all the "arts of life," which they entirely regenerated.

BIBLIOGRAPHY: Percy H. Bate, *The English Pre-Raphaelite Painters*. London, 1901.

**PREVITALI (Andrea).**—Italian painter of Bergamo, active 1502; died 1528. He worked in Venice, and was influenced by Giovanni Bellini. He painted small pictures with charming landscapes. His large compositions were less successful. He is also well known for his portraits.

His principal works are: the *Madonna Enthroned* (Bergamo Museum); *St. John the Baptist Surrounded by Four Saints*, with a fine landscape (Santo Spirito, same town, 1515); and the *Betrothal of St. Catherine* (in the Sacristy of San Giobbe, Venice).

BIBLIOGRAPHY: Crowe & Cavalcaselle, *History of Painting in North Italy*, ed. T. Borenius, Vol. I.

**PREVOST or PROVOST (Jan).**—Flemish painter, 1465-1529.

Many influences may be noticed in the work of Jan Prevost—that of the school of Bruges, and that of the school of Antwerp. Probably the influence of Bosch gave him a taste for strange, sometimes diabolical details. Between 1490 and 1520, he painted several pictures of which the most important are: A *Virgin in Glory*, for the Abbey of St. Flines (near Douai); a *Last Judgment* (Douai Museum); the *Martyrdom of St. Catherine* (Antwerp); etc. The only documented work is the *Last Judgment*, 1524 (Bruges), which, artistically is not his best work, and it is by comparison with this that the others are attributed to him.

BIBLIOGRAPHY: W. H. J. Weale, *Peintres brugeois: les Prévost*. 1912.

**PRIAMO della QUERCIA.**—Sienese painter and sculptor, brother of Jacopo della Quercia.

In 1438-39 Priamo is requested by the authorities of Bologna to finish the Vari monument and the doors of the Church of S. Petronio, Bologna, left unfinished by Jacopo. Priamo is too occupied. An argument over Jacopo's property follows; and the whole matter fills a long correspondence. In 1442 Priamo is commissioned to paint an altarpiece for S. Michele, Volterra; and is paid for the fresco of the *Blessed Agostino Novello Investing the Rector of the Hospital*, which is still in the Pellegrinaio of the Ospedale della Scala, Siena; it belongs to the series executed by Domenico di Bartolo and may have been after his design. In 1444 he is back in Volterra, where he is paid for a panel of *St. Anthony*. In 1453 he makes a property declaration in Siena; in 1467 he is mentioned among the foreign debtors of Volterra.

Priamo's only authenticated work is the fresco mentioned above; but certain pictures at Volterra are attributed to him.

BIBLIOGRAPHY: Milanesi, *Doc. . . . senese*, II.—G. de Nicola, *Priamo della Quercia*, Rassegna d'arte, XVIII, 1918.—M. Battistini, *Maestro Priamo della Quercia e il quadro di S. Antonio di Volterra*, Rass. d'arte, XIX, 1919.

**PRIEUR (Barthélemy).**—One of the principal French sculptors of the end of the 16th century, born about 1540. Died 1611. He was, almost certainly, the pupil of Germain Pilon, whose influence on the sculpture of the day was considerable. There is good reason to compare the *Graces* and *Virtues* of Pilon with the three large figures of *Peace, Justice* and *Abundance* (of a classicism, however, already heavy in the types and draperies) which made part of the tomb for the heart of Anne de Montmorency.

The three statues are placed on a coloured marble base, at the foot of a twisted column, which once supported a bronze urn (Louvre). Prieur had previously executed the Tomb of the Constable, for the Church St. Martin-de-Montmorency. Of it there remain two statues of the Duke and Duchess (Louvre).

He is also the author of the tomb of Christophe de Thon (after 1582), for the Church of St. André des Arcs. The Louvre possesses the polychrome marble bust, and two bronze figures. He made the kneeling statue of Marie de Barbançon-Cani, the first wife of the President of Tron, which figures in the Mausoleum of the latter, by François Anguier (Louvre). Like all the sculptors of the 15th century, Prieur was employed on the decoration of

PRIEUR: MARIE DE BARBANÇON-CANI. (Museum of Versailles.)

Châteaux—first at Ecouen, for the Montmorency family; next, in the Louvre (two charming figures of *Fame*, and *Genii* in the Petite Galerie, are by his hand); finally, at Fontainebleau. Prieur also made the two tombs for the heart of Henri III (formerly at St. Cloud; now in St. Denis). Like many artists in the 16th century, Prieur was a Protestant; a fact which may partly explain the favour which Henri IV accorded him, in making him "sculpteur du roi" in 1590. He was, however, the most notable sculptor of his day. He marks the transition from the school of Germain Pilon to the school of sculptors of the reign of Louis XIII. With Pierre Biard, he was one of the few to resist the invasion of Italianism.

BIBLIOGRAPHY: L. Gonse, *La sculpture française*, 1895.—L. Courajod, *Leçons de l'École du Louvre*, Vol. III.

**PRIMATICCIO (Francesco).**—Italian painter (1504-1570). Pupil of Giulio Romano, with whom he painted in Mantua. His stucco decorations and friezes of the Palazzo de Tè, with the *Fall of Phaeton*, the *Entry of the Emperor Sigismund into Mantua*, and many other subjects, after the master's designs, show great magnificence, and research into decorative devices.

It was, however, chiefly in France that Primaticcio revealed his qualities as a decorator. He worked at Fontainebleau, in the service of Francis I and Henri II. He was there assisted by Niccolò dell'Abbate of Modena, and formed many pupils. He had a great influence in spreading the Italian style.

BIBLIOGRAPHY: Dimier, *Le Primatice*, 1900.

**PROCACCINI (Camillo).**—Milanese painter, 1546-1629. Son of Ercole Procaccini.

**— (Ercole, also known as the Elder).**—Milanese painter, 1520?-1591. The chief of a family of painters who represent the mannerism of the period.

**— (Ercole, the Younger).**—Milanese painter, 1596-about 1679. Descendant of above.

**— (Giulio Cæsare).**—Milanese painter, 1560-1626. Son of Ercole Procaccini. He was also a sculptor, in which capacity he worked for Milan Cathedral.

**PROCTOR (A. Phimister).**—American sculptor, born 1862, noted for his renderings of animals (*Puma*, Metropolitan Museum of Art, New York, *Tigers*, Nassau Hall, Princeton, etc.).

**PRODOMOS.**—See Greece (Architecture).

**PRONAOS.**—See Greece (Architecture).

**PROPYLÆUM.**—Architecturally important vestibule or entrance to a building or enclosure. Often in plural, *propylœa*.

See Acropolis of Athens.

**PROTOGENES.**—Greek painter of the 4th century. Contemporary of Apelles who helped to make him known and appreciated. His best work was the *Ialysos*, portrait of the founder of Rhodes, which he took seven years to paint. To combat the ravages of time, he superimposed four coats of paint on this picture.

**PROVENCE (Churches of).**—See Pl. 44, Vol. I.

**— (School of).**—See Pl. 4. Vol. II.

**PROVINS (France).**—The town owes its character to its strong girdle of ramparts which surround the city for a length of 5 kilometres. Begun in the 12th century, the ramparts are fortified about every 30 metres with large, thick-walled towers. The

PROVINS: TOWER OF CAESAR. (Constructed in the twelfth century, since rebuilt.)

*Tour de César*, or Grosse Tour, dates from the 12th century, but it has suffered many changes. It is a strong, massive construction, with a square base, the angles of which are flanked with turrets. The upper part is octagonal, and is surmounted by a roof in eight planes.

The *Grange aux Dîmes* is a 12th century monument.

BIBLIOGRAPHY: Bourquelot, *Histoire de Provins*. 1839.—L. Morel-Payen, *Troyes et Provins*. Histoire des villes d'art célèbres.

**PROVOST (Jan).**—See Prevost.

**PRUD'HON (Pierre Paul).**—French painter, 1758-1823. After a

PRUD'HON: ANDROMACHE EMBRACING ASTYANAX. (Louvre.)

journey to Parma, Milan and Florence, Prud'hon was strongly influenced by Correggio and Leonardo da Vinci. While an admirer of antique forms, the chief charm of his

PRUD'HON: MME. JARRE. (Louvre.)

work lies in the tender seduction of colour and light. The graceful forms of his nymphs bathe in an atmosphere which they illuminate with

PRUD'HON: PSYCHE. (Musée Condé, Chantilly.)

their own whiteness. He painted historical and mythological pictures (an early work is *Andromache Embracing Astyanax*—Louvre); portraits, and many versions of his favourite subject of *Psyche*—whom he often depicted being carried through the air by Cupids and Zephyrs.

Two characteristic portraits (in the Louvre) are those of Madame Jarre, and the Empress Josephine. The latter sits dreaming in a melancholy landscape, beneath a pale sky which glimmers through the foliage of the trees.

One of Prud'hon's most famous pictures is *Justice and Vengeance Pursuing Crime* (Louvre), which was originally painted for the Hall of Assizes of the Palais de Justice.

See Pl. 50, Vol. II.

BIBLIOGRAPHY: Pierre Gauthier, *Prud'hon.* 1886.—E. Bricon, *Prud'hon,* Paris. 1907.

**PUCCIO di SIMONE.**—Florentine painter, registered 1343, 1345, 1346 in the guild of Medici e Speziali; and toward the end of the register of 1320-52 and in 1357 as a member of the Compagnia di S. Luca. A signed polyptych by Puccio di Simone is in the Academy, Florence; and a panel is recorded which was formerly in the Artaud de Montor Collection, signed and dated 1350.

BIBLIOGRAPHY: Frey, *Loggia dei Lanzi,* pp. 323, 333, 337.—W. Suida, *Florentinische Maler,* etc., 1905, p. 42.

**PUGET (François).** — French painter (?-1707). He was the pupil

PUGET: ATLANTES. DOORWAY OF THE CITY HALL OF TOULON.

of his father, Pierre Puget. The Louvre possesses a curious portrait by him, of *Pierre Puget;* and a painting (rather a weak one) representing *Portraits of Artists.*

**— (Pierre).** — French sculptor. (Marseilles, 1622-1694.)

The son of a mason, his father apprenticed him to a shipbuilder. He was not yet sixteen, when a ship was launched, on which he had made all the sculpture. At seventeen, he started for Italy on foot. In Rome he did some decorations for the Barberini Palace, and for the Pitti. In 1644 he returned to Marseilles, and was later called to Paris by Fouquet, and finally began some work for the king (decoration of Vaux) in 1667. One has only to look at the muscular arms of the wooden figures for ships (now in the Louvre) to see with what vigorous ornamentation he had hitherto adorned Colbert's ships.

In 1667, when Puget was 47, his production had comprised sculpture and painting, and works of his are to be found in Genoa, Marseilles and Toulon, where he had built his famous door of the Hôtel de Ville, and modelled his gloomy Atlantes, athletes who are struggling desperately so as not to be crushed by the weight of the balcony.

In 1672, Puget received from Colbert a command for the *Milo of Crotona* (Louvre); and for *Alexander and Diogenes* (Louvre). The first was sent to Versailles in 1682; the group of *Perseus and Andromeda* in 1684; the *Diogenes,* made later, was not taken to Versailles.

The following works must also be mentioned: *The Gallic Hercules* (Louvre); the *Louis XIV;* The *Plague of Milan.*

This disciple of Michelangelo and of Bernini was not fitted to mix easily with the peaceful decorators whom Charles Le Brun directed. His forceful genius would have spoiled the harmony of the whole. The high-relief, crowded and turgid, in the *Diogenes and Alexander,* in which the muscles strain almost to breaking point, show us the spirited sculptor ignoring the limits of the architectural frame, and disdaining all linear constraint. This tumultuous work could not have found a place amid the majestic and calm setting of Versailles.

Doubtless, the *Perseus and Andromeda* (Louvre) was better suited to the gardens of Le Nôtre. However, besides the startling but intentional disproportion which exists between the hero and the freed Princess, one must admit that Puget's genius is not at its best in subjects demanding grace and feeling in their treatment. When he forces himself to attempt these qualities, as in the *Conception of the Virgin* (Genoa) he simply reminds us of Bernini. The fact is, that his genius is more powerful than original, and his conceptions not so far removed from those of his own times, as one might at first think. He imagines or accepts academic theories; represents the king in a semi-antique costume, accompanied by Neptune and two sailors. In tragic subjects, which he affected, Puget was not sufficiently restrained. In the bas-relief of the *Plague of Milan,* for instance, all his figures have exaggerated forced attitudes.

However, Puget attains genius when he succeeds in expressing his ideal of force: force in repose, in the Gallic *Hercules* (Louvre); force in action, in the *Milo of Crotona;* or, in the *Caryatides* of Toulon, force of pathos evoked by virile grief.

See Pl. 4, Vol. I; Pl. 41, Vol. II.

BIBLIOGRAPHY: Philippe Auquier, *Pierre Puget,* 1904.—*Pierre Puget décorateur naval et mariniste,* 1906.

**PUGIN (Arthur W. N.).**—English architect, 1812-1852. As a pamphleteer he was instrumental in furthering the popularity of the Gothic Revival. He assisted Barry with the Houses of Parliament, London, and designed many churches in the Gothic style, including the Cathedral, Southwark, 1845.

**PULIGO (Domenico).**—Florentine painter, 1475-1527. Pupil of Ridolfo Ghirlandaio, influenced by Andrea del Sarto.

**PULZONE (Scipione Gaetano).**—1560-1600?. Italian painter, known from his birthplace Gasta as il Gastano. Chiefly noted as a portrait painter.

**PUTTO.**—A young boy (plural, *putti*).

**PUVIS DE CHAVANNES (Pierre).**—French painter. 1824-1898.

His father, a chief mining engineer, wanted to see his son enter the Polytechnic. A long and serious illness which the young student had at the time of his entrance examinations, changed the plans of his family. After two years rest, he took a journey of pleasure, to Italy, and returned with the desire to study painting. A short stay in the studio of Henri Scheffer, brother of Ary Scheffer, gave him the opportunity of seeing Italy again. This visit, made for the purpose of study, lasted a year. On his return to Paris, Puvis de Chavannes asked the advice of Delacroix. But hardly had he become the great artist's pupil, than the studio was closed. After fifteen days in the studio of Delacroix, Puvis de Chavannes passed three months in that of Couture, then took complete liberty and first he set up alone, and then with a group of friends, in whose company he worked, chattered and experimented. In 1852 he settled in the Pigalle square, where he passed the rest of his life.

Up to 1861, the young painter produced numerous works, hesitating and contradictory though they yet were, and showing the results of very varied influences. The public and the press mocked at his work, though a very few critics (Delécluze, Théophile Gautier, Thédore de Banville) noticed, defended and encouraged him.

Rejected by the Salons, laughed at by the majority, Puvis retired to a proud and silent isolation, and worked only for himself. In 1861 a first success encouraged him. He

PUVIS DE CHAVANNES: CHILDHOOD OF ST. GENEVIÈVE. (Panthéon, Paris.)

sent to the Salon *War* and *Peace,* gained a medal, and had *Peace* bought by the State. But he was not yet understood, and it was to an indifferent public that the Salon, in 1863, showed *Work* and *Rest.* A few admired him, and *War* and *Peace* were bought for the gallery at Amiens, and when hung, won a success.

Puvis, pleased and grateful, gave *Work* and *Rest* to the same museum. He was then asked to paint for the museum's staircase walls. The composition chosen for this purpose, *Ave Picardia Nutrix,* was hung in the Salon of 1865. In this work, the painter gave a new treatment to old themes. He no longer symbolised general ideas, such as War and Peace; he depicted the whole life of a province and showed in an allegory, the precise and plastic image of fruitful Picardy. And above all, he suggested the close unity between the figures and their landscape. This marked the painter's originality, and showed a characteristic he was to develop as years went on. Landscape was no longer merely some kind of vague background just introduced to throw up the figures; the soil of Picardy, its rivers and vegetation, are recognisable in this *Ave Picardia Nutrix.* Now the details are subservient to the whole, and henceforward Puvis de Chavannes disciplines himself to the strict method which rules out virtuosity. A single figure contributes to the expression of the group to which it belongs, and the group in its turn harmonises with the whole composition. Starting from a general idea, he expresses it plastically, restrainedly, till the idea is co-ordinated, condensed and given life in nature and in types of humanity, whose simple and calm movements express the essential idea of the whole composition. It is by the effort of thinking, that he attains the unconscious simplicity of the primitives.

These calm landscapes and these crowds of simple folk, with their imperfect, even awkward forms, were not pleasing to a public who found his poetic painting faded and uncouth compared with that of Meissonier, Gérôme or Laurens. Actually the art of Puvis de Chavannes was not suited to the surroundings of a salon; its serenity needed the serenity of architecture to set it off. Success came to him when, as in the case of Amiens, his painting was seen surrounded by wide wall-spaces.

In 1867 Marseilles requested two mural paintings to decorate the staircase of Longchamp, and in *Marseilles, a Greek Colony* and *Marseilles Port of the West* the qualities of decorative unity which he had shown in the Amiens paintings, reappeared. Poitiers (1872) followed the example of Marseilles, and asked for its Town Hall two pictures; *Radegonde, in Retreat at the Convent of Sainte-Croix, Gives Shelter to Poets, and Protects Literature;* and *Charles Martel in 732 Saves Christianity by His Victory over the Saracens, near Poitiers.* In spite of these orders, Puvis was still the object of ridicule and protest. And yet, in the Salon of 1876, there appeared the *Childhood of Saint Geneviève,* which should have finally and definitely won the admiration of all. But, in spite of the praise of friends, the critics remained unfavourable, and in 1881, when he had just done the *Ludus pro Patria* which completed the Amiens decoration, the *Poor Fisherman* in the Salon had very violent attacks levelled against it.

Happily the painter's energy was proof against all insults. Unmoved, he worked on unwaveringly. In 1883, for Lyons, his native town, he painted *The Wood Sacred to the Arts and to the Muses.* In 1884 he decorated the Sorbonne; from 1889 to 1893 the Guildhall of Paris, (the Hôtel de Ville), with *Summer; Winter; Victor Hugo Offering His Lyre to Paris.* From 1890 to 1892 he painted for Rouen the *Inter Artes et Naturam;* from 1895 to 1898, the Boston Library. Finally, in 1898, a few months before his death, he put the finishing touches to the decorations of the Panthéon, and finished *Saint Geneviève Supplying Paris with Provisions,* and *Saint Geneviève Watching over Paris,* both to take their place beside the *Youth of Saint Geneviève.*

If, till his death, Puvis de Chavannes was discussed, he had, from the middle of his career a general influence on the art of his generation. He revolutionised mural painting which now, for instance, included landscape. Imitators exaggerated his manner, and sometimes only copied his faults, of which the most striking is the intended awkwardness of the drawing which sometimes reaches the point of being incorrect, but his influence as a decorator was fortunate, coming too at a time when art was suffering from too much manual skill, and execution devoid of feeling.

Puvis de Chavannes asserted that art is not merely skill, and above all he proved that mural painting has not the same requirements as easel pictures. This is, perhaps, the greatest of his services to art.

His chief works, besides those already mentioned are: *Sleep* (Lille), *Autumn* (Lyons), and the *Poor Fisherman* (in the Luxembourg, Paris).

See Pl. 57, Vol. II.

Bibliography: Marius Vachon, *Puvis de Chavannes.* Paris, 1896.—A. Michel, *Puvis de Chavannes.* 1912.

**PYLON.**—Gateway, especially a gateway in the form of a truncated pyramid, e.g., one forming the entrance to an Egyptian temple.

See Pl. 15, Vol. I.

**PYNAS (Jan Symonsz).**—Dutch painter, 1583/4-1631. He left Amsterdam about 1605 to travel in Italy with his brother Jacob and with Pieter Lastman; after living in Rome for a while he returned to Amsterdam where he opened his art school. Rembrandt was one of his more famous pupils. Influenced by Elsheimer and the Venetian painters of 1600, Pynas was an extreme realist, and the most important of the Pre-Rembrandt painters. His religious paintings show his strong use of chiaroscuro, the placement of dark figures in the foreground (as used later by Rembrandt), but their rendering was less plastic than the paintings of Lastman. He is represented in the important museums.

Bibliography: Hofstede, *Urkunden über Rembrandt,* 1906.

**PYRAMIDS.**—See Egypt.

**PYRRHOS.**—See Acropolis of Athens.

# Q

**QUATRE - NATIONS (Collège des, Paris).**—The building was finished in 1672. Now, the Institut de France.

**QUELLINUS (Artus or Quellien, the elder).**—Flemish sculptor, 1609-1668, Antwerpen. Pupil of Duquesnoy, related to Lucas van Uhden and Verbruggen. Most outstanding baroque sculptor in the Rubens tradition of his time. Did busts of many notables, also grave reliefs, terra cotta and ivory figurines. Of his architectural decorations, the allegorical and mythological figures of the Hôtel de Ville (now Royal Palace) of Amsterdam are most famous, 1650-1663.

Bibliography: J. Gabriels, *Artus Quellien de Oude.* Antw., 1930.

**— (Erasmus, the younger).**—Flemish painter, 1607-1678. Pupil of Rubens. Known for his large religious and historical paintings. The churches of Northern France and of Belgium possess a great many pictures by him; *e.g. Rest on the Flight into Egypt* (Ghent, St. Sauveur), *St. Roch* (Antwerp, St. Jacques), etc.

**— (Jan-Erasmus).**—Flemish painter, son of Erasmus Quellinus, 1634-1715. Married daughter of David Teniers. He visited Rome and returned to Antwerp in 1660. Became court painter of Leopold I and Joseph I. From 1680 on he signed his canvases with "Pict. Caes. Ma." Was strongly influenced by the style of Veronese. *Pool of Bethsaida* (Antwerp); the *Coronation of Charles V* (Vienna); and the fifteen ceilings of the Palace of Vienna.

**QUERCIA.** — (see Jacopo della Quercia).

**QUESNOY (François du).**—Flemish sculptor, 1594-1642. Son of Jerome du Quesnoy. François worked chiefly in Italy for popes and cardinals. He made the colossal statue of *St. Andrew,* which ornaments one of the piers supporting the dome of St. Peter's, Rome. It is powerfully and broadly sculptured. He also made the tomb of the Bishop de Triest (Ghent, St. Bavon), which was finished by his brother, Jerome the Younger.

**QUIRIZIO DA MURANO.**—Venetian painter collaborator, or pupil, of Giovanni d'Alemagna and Antonio Vivarini, mentioned in two documents of 1461 and 1478 as a witness. His *Scenes from the Life of St. Lucy* are in the Gallery of Rovigo and are signed and dated 1462. In Venice, Academy: *Madonna Adoring the Sleeping Child,* signed; and *Christ Giving the Communion to a Nun,* signed.

Bibliography: Testi, *Storia d. pitt. venez.,* II, 1915.

# R

**RAEBURN (Sir Henry).**—Scottish painter. Born at Stockbridge, 1756; died in Edinburgh, 1823. His master was David Martin, and he began by painting miniatures. Having married, at the age of twenty-two, a young lady with money, he was able to visit Italy. After a sojourn of two years, he settled in Edinburgh, where, for more than a generation, no one disputed his title as the leading painter of Scotland. Wilkie, in one of his letters from Madrid, wrote that in front of Velázquez's paintings, he could not help thinking of Raeburn; and, indeed, some of the works of the great Scottish painter (such as a portrait of Lord Newton), are such powerful compositions that there is no profanation in comparing them with those of the Spanish master. The 325 portraits by Raeburn which were exhibited at the Royal Academy of Scotland in 1876, allow us to form a precise idea of Edinburgh society, just as the works of Sir Joshua Reynolds describe London society. In fact, all the Scottish celebrities of the day—Robertson, Hume, Ferguson, Walter Scott, etc.—served him as models. Raeburn painted more than 600 portraits, a modest production if one compares it with Reynolds' 2,000 portraits.

Raeburn: Mrs. Scott Moncrieff.

Raeburn: William Ferguson of Kilrie.

He painted his models in full light, giving only necessary importance to the dress, for he was chiefly attracted by the character and expression of the face.

The different phases of his art may be followed very well in the chief galleries of Scotland.

See Pl. 48, Vol. II.

Bibliography: Sir Walter Armstrong, *Raeburn.* 1901.

**RAFFAELLI (Jean François).**—French painter, sculptor and designer, 1850-1923. After hesitating beginnings, during which he studied both poetry and painting, Raffaelli decided for painting. A stay in the outskirts of Paris made him "a Parisian Millet," according to the description of Huysmans. He became the painter of landscapes, and of the miserable population of the surroundings of the capital, of its quays, and of its crowded districts. Because of his technique he is sometimes placed among the Impressionists; but he shared only their dislike of studio work, and their habit of painting directly from nature without selection or stylisation. He did not use division of tone with a view to obtaining lively colouring. His palette was grey and sad: he built up his pictures with touches of elementary colours, on a concise and hasty design. His portraits are direct and vigorous, and include such incisive studies as those of Clemenceau (Luxembourg), and of de Goncourt (Museum of Nancy). His pictures of the outskirts of Paris are his most characteristic works.

Raffaelli: Guests attending a wedding. (Musée du Luxembourg.)

Bibliography: A. Alexandre, *J. F. Raffaelli,* 1909.

**RAFFAELLINO del GARBO (dei Carli, di Crolli, di Capponi).**—Florentine painter, a most confused personality, due to the plurality of his names. Vasari mentions but one Raffaellino; Berenson distinguishes two; and Milanesi, three.

Raffaello dei Carli was born in Florence, c. 1470. His father, Bartolommeo di Giovanni died in 1479, and Raffaello was cared for by Pasquine di Carlo, but was later adopted by the Capponi family (records of 1505, 1517), adding its name to his own. In 1499 he matriculated in the corporation of painters as "Raphael Bartolommei Nicola Capponi pictor nel Garbo"—the last name being that of the street in which his shop was located. A painter called Raffaellino offered his services in 1508 to Michelangelo as assistant in the Sistine Chapel, mentioning that he was apprenticed to Piermatteo d'Amelia, an Umbrian painter. If this record refers to the same personality which is of course highly doubtful, it would explain the strong Umbrian influence apparent in his later work. In 1513-15 he is mentioned as a tenant of the Badia. Vasari says that he died in 1524, but the date is not substantiated.

Raffaellino's various signatures appear on the following works: 1500, Uffizi, *Madonna with Two Saints and Two Donors;* 1501, Sarasota, Florida, Ringling Museum, *Mass of Gregory;* 1502, Florence, Corsini, *Madonna Enthroned with Saints and Angels;* 1503, Florence, Scuola Elementare, Via della Colonna, *Miracle of the Loaves and Fishes.*

Bibliography: Vasari-Milanesi, IV.—Morelli, *Critical Studies of Italian Painters,* I.—Crowe and Cavalcaselle, III.—Frizzoni, Arch. stor. dell'Arte, VII, 1894, p. 163; II a, series I, 1895, pp. 202-205.—Berenson, *Florentine Painters of the Ren.,* III, pp. 126, 135; and *Drawings of Florentine Painters,* I, pp. 80, 86, 95, 98; II, 32, 39.—C. Gamba, *Dipinti ignoti di Raff. dei Carli,* Rassegna d'Arte, VII, 1907, p. 104.—Van Marle, *Italian Schools, etc.,* XII, 1931, p. 417.

**RAFFET (Denis Auguste Marie).**—French painter and lithographer. Paris, 1804—Genoa, 1860. He attended the Académie de Suisse and was introduced to Charlet, who gave him drawing lessons, while Rudder taught him the elements of lithography, In 1824, he was admitted to the École royale des Beaux-Arts, and Gros became his master. Raffet, however, thought more about lithography than painting, and, inspired by the example of Horace Vernet and of Chalet, the "Grande Armée" became a favourite theme.

Raffet: "Attention! The Emperor is watching us."

Raffet: The Reveille. (Bibl. Nat.)

In fact, the example of Chalet decided his bent, and he took to lithography, almost exclusively.

He travelled to Asia. On his return, he made admirable pictures of the Napoleonic wars, which stirred his sense of romance, but he was still more interested in contemporary events. Raffet was an accomplished artist, a master of coloured lithography, and he was well able to express the sentiments of a nation essentially military, and to represent its patriotic ideal in a popular form.

Bibliography: A. Giacomelli, *Raffet, son œuvre lithographique et ses eaux-fortes.* Paris, 1868.—August Bry, *Raffet, sa vie et ses œuvres.* Paris, 1861.—F. L'homme, *Raffet.* Paris.—Armand Dayot. *Raffet.* Paris.

**RAFT OF THE MEDUSA (The).**—See Géricault; also Pl. 53, Vol. II.

**RAIBOLINI (Francesco).**—See Francia.

**RAIMONDI (Marcantonio or Marc Antonio).**—Italian engraver, born near Bologna about 1480, died between 1527 and 1534. He had lessons from Francesco Francia, who taught him *niello. The Triumph of Neptune* is the only work in this medium universally ascribed to him. A rather poor engraving, *Pyramus and Thisbe,* dating from 1505, is the first print we have by him. From studying the works of Albrecht Dürer, when visiting Venice, Marcantonio realised how expressive the art, of which he had so far learned only the technique, could be. His admiration for Dürer made him copy some of the engravings of the Nuremberg master, but not, apparently, without some forethought of monetary gain, for he imitated them scrupulously, down to the signature. Vasari tells that Albrecht Dürer was much irritated by this, and that he

Raimondi (Marcantonio).

came to Venice to complain of it to the Signory, with the result that Marcantonio was forbidden to add Dürer's monogram to his copies. The *Life of the Virgin* (after Dürer) bears the German artist's signature, whereas the engravings of the *Passion* have no trace of a monogram.

About 1510, Marcantonio settled in Rome, where Raphael commissioned him to engrave one of his drawings—the *Death of Lucrezia.* Marcantonio's work pleased Raphael, who gave him more work to do. No other engraver has expressed Raphael's ideas more happily, and no one has so perfectly understood his harmonious art. There is nothing original about Marcantonio's work, but one is compelled to admiration by its distinction and restraint.

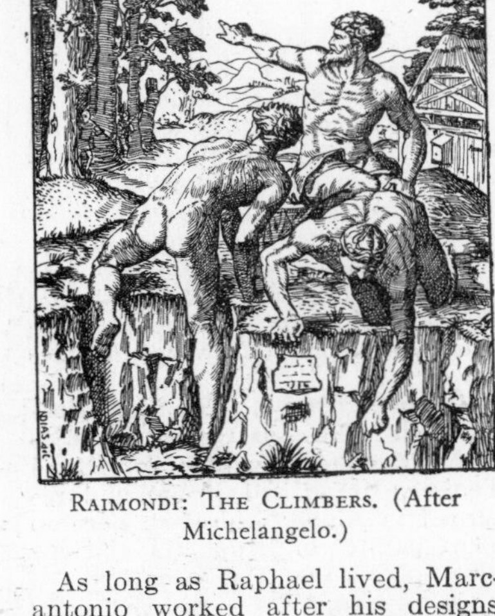

Raimondi: The Climbers. (After Michelangelo.)

As long as Raphael lived, Marcantonio worked after his designs. He engraved his *Judgment of Paris, The Massacre of the Innocents,* the *Plague of Phrygia, St. Cecilia, Parnassus,* and *Poetry.* It should be observed that some of these engravings differ notably from the pictures by Raphael. The reason is that they were made, not from the pictures themselves, but from drawings or cartoons which Raphael himself modified when he came to paint them on canvas, or on the wall.

When, after ten years of working together, Raphael died, Marcantonio refused to continue, alone and undirected, to interpret his master's work in his own medium, and he joined his favourite pupil, Giulio Romano. From this time, date some fine works, of which the most remarkable is *Hercules and Antæus.* Other pupils of Raphael, Pierino del Vaga, or Francesco Penni, supplied him with models, but there seems to have been a general indifference to engraving at this time, and Marcantonio became hard up, if not actually in want. His misfortune led him to regrettable compromises, and he engraved some obscene drawings of Giulio Romano for a book by Aretino. Both artists were quickly recognised. Pope Clement VI had the book destroyed, and ordered the arrest of its authors. Aretino and Giulio Romano escaped, but Marcantonio was imprisoned, and it was not for some months, and on the earnest entreaties of Cardinal Guiliano dei Medici and of the sculptor Baccio Bandinelli, that the Pope set him at liberty. To show Baccio Bandinelli his gratitude, Marcantonio engraved after him the *Martyrdom of San Lorenzo*—his most important work.

From this time onward practically nothing is known of Marcantonio's life. It is said that he was seriously wounded in the sack of Rome by the Spaniards, in 1527, and that he had to pay a ransom which completed his ruin. This is the last that is heard of him, and it is only known that he was already dead in 1534.

Marcantonio's influence was considerable, and he still has fervent admirers. Dürer himself, who had complained about him, had the highest opinion of his ability, and even gave some of his engravings to his pupils, as models. Some of them (*e.g.* Bartholomaeus Beham, and J. Binck) left Dürer and went to Rome, to study under Marcantonio. They, in their turn, founded a school there, and taught other German engravers, and it was these who afterwards brought back to Germany Italian traditions. In Italy itself, Marcantonio had many pupils, but they were of less importance. Among his followers was Diana Scultori, who seems to have been the first woman engraver.

The absence of original work places Marcantonio on his true level. He was, however, the most able and intelligent of interpreters, and this suffices to assure his fame.

Bibliography: (See Bibliography under Engraving).—H. Delaborde, *La gravure en Italie avant Marc-Antonio.* Paris. 1883.—H. Delaborde, *Marc-antonio Raimondi.* Paris, 1887.—Thode, *Die Antiken in den Stichen Marcantonio's.* Leipzig, 1881.—A. M. Hind, *A History of Engraving and Etching.* London.

**RAINALDI (Carlo).**—Italian architect, 1611-1691. One of the outstanding Baroque architects, he is best known for his Roman churches in the Jesuit style, notably *S. Maria in Campitelli,* 1659. He collaborated with Barromini in the design of *Sant'Agnese.*

**RAINERI D'UGOLINO (or Ranieri).**—Dugento Pisan painter, who signed a *Crucifix* in the Museo Civico, Pisa, close in style to Giunta Pisano.

**RAKE'S PROGRESS (The).**—See Hogarth.

**RAKKA.**—A town on the Euphrates, between Aleppo and Bagdad, celebrated in the 9th century for its ceramics.

**RAMBERG (Johann Heinrich).**—German painter and etcher, 1763-1840, Hanover. Was patronized and financed by George III of England. Travelled extensively throughout Europe; his oil-portraits show the resulting various influences on his art. His personal style is achieved in his humorous and satirical drawings, and many book illustrations.

Bibliography: J. L. Neumann, *Über R.'s Kunst u. Kunstwerk.* Dresden, 1792.—F. Stuttmann, *J. H. R.* Munich, 1929.

**RAMBOUILLET.**—The Château of Rambouillet was originally a feudal residence, of which only one large tower remains. It was rebuilt after 1450, by Jean d'Angennes, and surrounded by a magnificent park. Francis I died there. It was also inhabited by Francis II, Catherine de Médicis, and Henri III. It was then bought by Louis XIV for his son, the Comte de Toulouse, who added two wings.

**RAMENGHI (Bartolommeo).**—See Bagnacavallo.

**RAMSAY (Allan).**—Scottish painter, 1713-1784. His father was a publisher and a poet. In 1734, Allan Ramsay came to London, where he spent two years. Then he went to Italy, and returned to Edinburgh in 1739. He married the niece of Lord

# DECORATIVE STYLE OF THE RENAISSANCE

*The period called the Renaissance, which fills the entire interval between the end of the Gothic world and the classic epoch of the seventeenth century, was a time of extremely rich and varied decorative development. The forms of flamboyant Gothic, those which come from Italy and even those borrowed from antiquity, are mixed in the architecture and the decorative art. Then order and regularity are imposed and the decorative fantasies appear very sophisticated.*

FAÏENCE PLATE FROM ROUEN. MUSEUM OF ROUEN. *(Photo by Hachette.)*

FAÏENCE LONG-LIPPED CRUET FROM OIRON. PETIT PALAIS. *(Photo by Hachette.)*

BERNARD PALISSY: LARGE COARSE PLATTER. LOUVRE. *(Photo by Hachette.)*

FAÏENCE CUP FROM OIRON. MUSÉE DE CLUNY. *(Photo by Hachette.)*

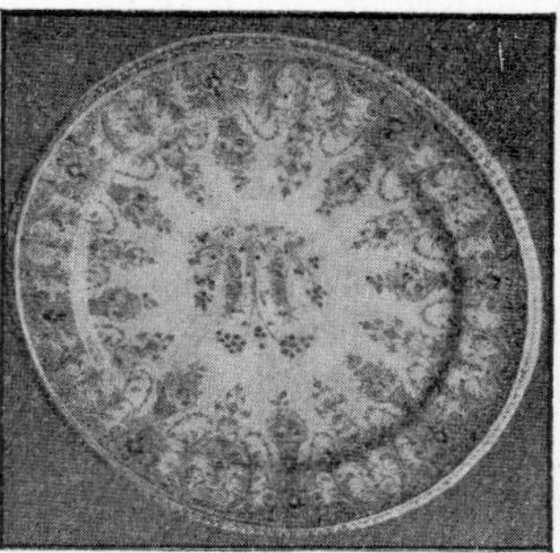

FAÏENCE PLATE FROM ROUEN. MUSEUM OF ROUEN. *(Photo by Hachette.)*

## Ceramics

The faïences of the sixteenth century in Italy and France are among the most characteristic objects of the Renaissance. In the celebrated potteries of Bernard Palissy, the so-called "rustic figures" of animals and modelled plants receive a covering of enamel which the baking colours, making strange combinations. The potter to whom one owes these effects, has lengthily related for us his researches, his disappointments and his pertinacity. The faïences from Oiron and from Saint-Porchaire are of fine material and of a complicated and scholarly execution and the small number of them makes them very rare and much sought after objects. The ateliers of Rouen and Nevers manufactured beautiful plates generally with blue decoration.

SO-CALLED HOUSE OF FRANCIS I, MOVED FROM MORET TO PARIS. *(Photo by Hachette.)*

## Ornamental Sculpture under Francis I

At Blois, at Chambord and in the châteaux of this period, one may follow the invasion of the ornamental Gothic style by the Italian modes. As in flamboyant architecture, the taste for decorative richness and ornate façades is preserved. But in the above façade Gothic supports have become pilasters, colonettes balusters, pointed arches semicircular; the sharp lines of the cornices bring back the strong horizontals which correspond to the courses of the stories on the façades.

JEAN GOUJON AND JEAN BULLANT: THE EVANGELISTS AND THE DIVINE VIRTUES FROM THE CHÂTEAU OF ÉCOUEN. CHAPEL OF THE CHÂTEAU OF CHANTILLY. *(Photo by Hachette.)*

## The Style of Henry II

After the ornate exuberance of Francis I, the Renaissance became sophisticated; the forms take on a more regular simplicity and sometimes even a little geometric dryness. It was the moment when, on the façades of the palaces, the pure elegance of the antique orders was adapted to the arrangement of the stories and of the windows. Ornamentation followed architecture. The most perfectly executed art was undoubtedly the decorations in bas-relief; one of the greatest names of the French Renaissance is that of Jean Goujon.

# VELAZQUEZ

*In the first half of the seventeenth century one of the most powerful schools of painting is that of the Spaniards. As with all the European schools at this time, it derives in part from Italian painting, the Bolognese school and especially the naturalistic painting of Caravaggio. But that which is transplanted into Spain there swiftly displays a strong zest for humble subjects. A harsh, ardent genius which one might already anticipate from the sculpture of the sixteenth century was more forcibly revealed when painting entered into the full possession of its naturalistic means.*

HERRERA THE ELDER: ST. BASIL DICTATING HIS DOCTRINE. LOUVRE. *(Photo by Hachette.)*

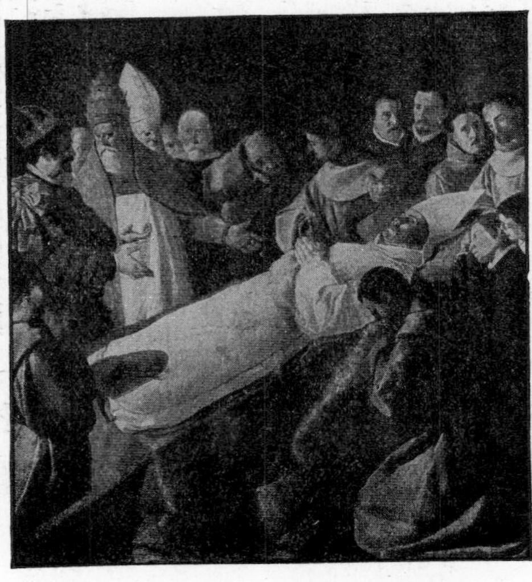

ZURBARAN: THE FUNERAL OF ST. BONAVENTURE. LOUVRE. *(Photo by Hachette.)*

EL GRECO: THE BURIAL OF THE COUNT OF ORGAZ. SANTO TOMÉ (DETAIL), TOLEDO. *(Photo by Hachette.)*

## Greco and Herrera

Before coming to Velazquez, one must pass over the generation of predecessors. El Greco is the strangest and the most attractive of these painters. He brings to Toledo, into the most Spanish of cities, memories of his Greek origin and his Venetian schooling. His painting often foretells the saner, more flexible and more soothing art of Velazquez. The master of the latter was Herrera the Elder.

VELAZQUEZ: PHILIP IV. PRADO, MADRID. *(Photo by Hachette.)*

VELAZQUEZ: MENIPPUS. PRADO, MADRID. *(Photo by Hachette.)*

VELAZQUEZ: THE ENFANT DON CARLOS BALTHAZAR. PRADO. *(Photo by Hachette.)*

VELAZQUEZ: OLIVARES. PRADO, MADRID. *(Photo by Hachette.)*

## Velazquez

Velazquez carried further than anyone else the naturalistic power of painting. Because of the exactness of his values, the freshness and the nicety of his tones, the flexibility of his touch and the exactitude of his vision, he is the king of performers. He paints what he sees; he never invents. His work is the triumph of following nature. He is the born portraitist of the human countenance, also of animals and things.

VELAZQUEZ: THE SURRENDER OF BREDA OR "LAS LANZAS." PRADO, MADRID. *(Photo by Hachette.)*

VELAZQUEZ: LAS MENIÑAS. PRADO, MADRID. *(Photo by Hachette.)*

VELAZQUEZ: THE SPINNERS. PRADO, MADRID. *(Photo by Hachette.)*

## Velazquez

This painter who was employed almost exclusively by King Philip IV remains the most truthful historian of the Spanish court. Sometimes his portraits compose historical tableaux and, a very rare thing at this date, contemporary history, as in the three masterpieces above in which one may see various aspects of old Spain: the army of the siege of Breda which was destroyed some years later at Rocroy; a Madrid studio, and finally, in *Las Meniñas*, Velazquez himself painting the king and queen whose reflections may be seen in the mirror at the back.

# RIBERA AND MURILLO

*Velazquez dominates the entire Spanish school; however, he left an unexploited field, that of the imagination and of mythological and Christian history. He only painted after nature and rarely used nature in a fictitious manner. The other Spanish masters remained faithful to the tradition of religious art; in no other European country were there as many fine painters to furnish pictures for the purposes of devotion.*

RIBERA: MARTYRDOM OF ST. BARTHOLOMEW. PRADO, MADRID.
*(Photo by Anderson.)*

RIBERA: ADORATION OF THE SHEPHERDS. LOUVRE.
*(Photo by Hachette.)*

RIBERA: CHRIST IN THE TOMB. LOUVRE.
*(Photo by Hachette.)*

## Ribera

Ribera is one of the masters who served to bring together Italy and Spain. He worked close to Caravaggio and borrowed some of his methods: opaque shadows, the study of relief, the taste for violent effects. Ribera is the painter of tortures and of martyrdoms; but in his somber dramas he sometimes includes the freshness of a young countenance. He touches the two chords of tenderness and brutality.

MURILLO: ST. JOHN THE BAPTIST. PINAKOTHEK, MUNICH.
*(Photo by Hachette.)*

MURILLO: MADONNA OF THE ROSARY. PRADO, MADRID.
*(Photo by Anderson.)*

MURILLO: THE IMMACULATE CONCEPTION. LOUVRE.
*(Photo by Hachette.)*

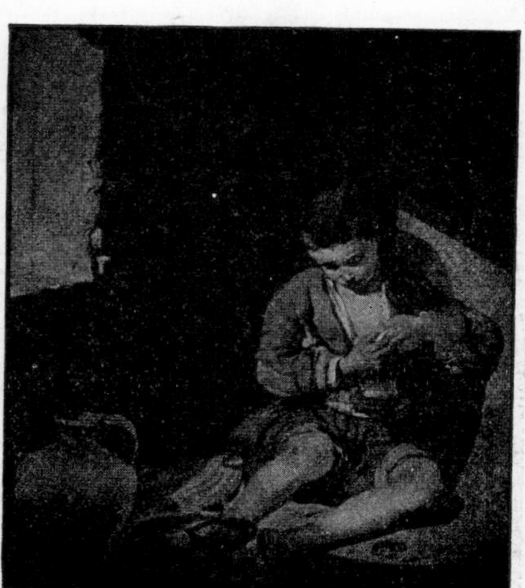

MURILLO: THE YOUNG BEGGAR. LOUVRE.
*(Photo by Hachette.)*

## Murillo

If Ribera is the painter of martyrs, Murillo is the painter of celestial visions; his most popular works show Madonnas on rosy clouds with little cherubs. More than with any other painter, one finds in his work the influence of foreign schools, Italy and Flanders, Raphael and Van Dyck. However, he remains inherently Spanish by reason of his naturalism, the choice of his types—his Virgin is a young woman of Seville. In all his work there is an admirable mixture of both the natural and supernatural.

GOYA: PORTRAIT OF A WOMAN. NATIONAL GALLERY, LONDON.
*(Photo by Hachette.)*

GOYA: THE ROYAL FAMILY. PRADO, MADRID.
*(Photo by Hachette.)*

LOPEZ: PORTRAIT OF GOYA. PRADO, MADRID.
*(Photo by Lacoste.)*

## Goya

At the end of the seventeenth century the Spanish school suddenly became worn out. What painters there were came from France with the Bourbon king and, in the eighteenth century, held the role of official portrait painters at the court. But Spain remained a country of fine painters. Sometimes they flourished in an unexpected manner; Goya at the end of the eighteenth century was one of these dazzling and inexplicable meteors.

# RUBENS

*R*UBENS *almost entirely dominates the Flemish school of the seventeenth century. His pupils or his imitators can only exploit aspects of his genius. During the sixteenth century, the Flemings had applied themselves to penetrating the secrets of the great decorative painting of the Italians. This was not without some vulgarity, at first, but by the time Rubens appeared they had learned to speak this oratorical language smoothly.*

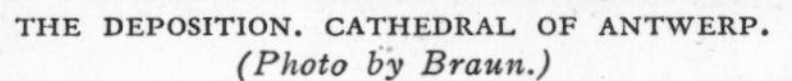

THE DEPOSITION. CATHEDRAL OF ANTWERP.
*(Photo by Braun.)*

THE ADORATION OF THE MAGI. MUSEUM OF ANTWERP.
*(Photo by Braun.)*

LE COUP DE LANCE. MUSEUM OF ANTWERP.
*(Photo by Braun.)*

## Religious Compositions

RUBENS practiced all kinds of painting, and treated all sorts of themes. First of all he executed great religious compositions for the churches of his own country. In these one finds something of the theatrical setting of the Bolognese, but Flemish naturalism lends a new life to the traditional themes and the brilliant palette of Rubens transforms them into gorgeous decorative pieces. The inspiration of the painter, the joy which he finds in playing with colour sometimes makes him forget the gravity of the subject that he treats.

THE DISEMBARKATION OF MARIE DE MÉDICIS. LOUVRE.
*(Photo by Hachette.)*

SILENUS WITH HIS FOLLOWING. PINAKOTHEK, MUNICH.
*(Photo by Hachette.)*

CASTOR AND POLLUX ABDUCTING THE DAUGHTERS OF LEUCIPPUS. PINAKOTHEK, MUNICH.
*(Photo by Hachette.)*

THE GARDEN OF LOVE. PRADO, MADRID.
*(Photo by Anderson.)*

HOLY FAMILY. ST. JAMES. ANTWERP.
*(Photo by Braun.)*

THE KERMIS. LOUVRE.
*(Photo by Hachette.)*

## Secular Themes

RUBENS went back to paganism for his naturalistic divinities. The gods of Olympus are for him a chance to paint the nude; they are not marble figures, but beings of flesh and blood. At the end of his life, he often abandoned great decorative compositions to treat for his own pleasure themes of an entirely personal inspiration: "gardens of love," landscapes and kermisses, family portraits and in particular portraits of his second wife, Helena Fourment. Never has his art been more tender or more sensitive than in these.

Mansfield, and settled in London in 1762. In 1767, he became painter to George III. Reynolds was his successor in that capacity. Ramsay's portraits have great distinction and a delicacy which verges on timidity.

Rambouillet: The Château.

**RAOUX (Jean).**—French painter, 1677-1734. After spending five years in Rome, as in Venice, he returned to France in 1714. In 1720, he went to England, where he painted numerous portraits. He died in Paris in 1734. His reputation does not rest on his historical pictures (*e.g. Pygmalion*, in the Louvre), but on his faces of *Vestal Virgins* (in the Galleries of Versailles, and of Montpellier).

**RAPHAEL (Raffaello Sanzio).**—Italian painter, son of Giovanni Santi, born: 28th March 1483, in Urbino; died: 6th April 1520.

Vasari says that Giovanni Santi took his son to Perugino in Perugia. But the boy was only twelve years old when his father died, in 1494, and Perugino was not in Perugia at that time. He was probably first entrusted to a pupil of Giovanni Santi, Evangelista di Pian di Meleto, and then to a pupil of Francia in Urbino, the gay and charming Timoteo Viti. His painting was, however, unquestionably formed by Perugino.

The earliest picture that we have by Raphael, the *Knight's Dream* (about 1498—in the National Gallery) is delightfully fresh and graceful. On either side of the sleeping knight stand Pleasure and Virtue. Pleasure is a pure, gentle maiden, and there is nothing forbidding in the aspect of Virtue, nor does the young knight appear to be disturbed by the problem of his dream.

The little *Saint Michael* and *St. George*, of the Louvre, painted about 1502-1503, when he was only twenty years old, are charming fairy-tales. *The Three Hesperides*, of Chantilly, are also early.

About 1499, he must have gone to Perugia to study under Perugino, who was then engaged upon the decoration of the Cambio, and he immediately assimilated his master's style. The *Way to Calvary*, 1505, in the National Gallery, and the *Coronation of the Virgin*, 1503, painted for the Cathedral of Perugia (now in the Vatican Gallery), are very Peruginesque in character. "If they were not signed," says Vasari, "one would think they were by Perugino." The young Raphael must have helped his master in the decoration of the Cambio, and painted especially the prophets and Sibyls. Gradually he surpassed the elder man in breadth and power and grace. He became less naïve and more human. He was intimate with Bernardino Betti and Pintoricchio. The *Sposalizio* (signed and dated 1507) of the Brera Gallery, was inspired by Perugino's picture of *Christ Entrusting the Keys to St. Peter.*

Raphael: The Vision of the Knight. (National Gallery, London.)

Raphael then returned to Urbino, but he was immediately attracted to Florence (1505-1508). There he found Michelangelo, Leonardo da Vinci, Fra Bartolommeo, etc. He joined Baccio d'Agnolo's studio, and set to work, copying chiefly Donatello and Leonardo. His original works were mainly Madonnas. They are gentle and lovely, more human than pious, yet more ideal than realistic. They are all harmoniously balanced. They have pure, oval faces, with refined regular features. Their figures are well-proportioned, supple and graceful.

Raphael: The Entombment. (Borghese Gallery, Rome.)

Among the best known of Raphael's Madonnas are:—The large *Cowper Madonna* (1508), Mellon Collection, Washington, D. C.; and the small *Cowper Madonna*, Widener Collection, Philadelphia; *La Belle Jardinière* (1507, Louvre); the *Virgin with a Lamb* (1507, Madrid); the *Madonna of the Goldfinch* (about 1506, Uffizi); the *Madonna del Granduca* (about 1505, Pitti Palace); the *Bridgewater Madonna* (Lord Ellesmere's Collection, London); the *Madonna of the Meadow* (1505, Vienna); the *Esterhazy Madonna* (1507-1508, unfinished, Budapest); the *Aldobrandini Madonna* (1508, National Gallery); the *Tempi Madonna* (1505, Munich); the *Colonna Madonna* (1507, Berlin), and the *Ansidei Madonna* (1507, National Gallery, London).

Raphael: The Madonna del Pesce. (Madrid.)

Raphael's Roman period embraces such Madonnas as:—the *Virgin with the Diadem* (1510, Louvre); the *Madonna of the Curtain* (1513-1514, Munich); the *Madonna del Foligno* (1512, Vatican Gallery); *Holy Family under the Oak-tree* (executed chiefly by Giulio Romano); the *Madonna of the Fish* (1513), in the Prado Gallery, Madrid; and the *Virgin of the Divine Love*, in Naples. We may also mention the *Holy Family*, of the Hermitage, Leningrad; and the *Holy Family* of Francis I (execution Giulio Romano), in the Louvre (1518).

Raphael: Portrait of Pope Julius II (detail). (Pitti Palace, Florence.)

In the course of years, Raphael's Madonnas became graver, and more noble. The last, the *Sistine Madonna*, of the Dresden Gallery (about 1515-1519), is a wonderful vision behind a raised curtain. The Virgin appears in the clouds, serious and serene. Her bare feet rest on the globe of the earth, and in her arms she carries the divine child. Two little angels lean over the frame, gazing in rapture, and Pope Sixtus, below, gazes in rapture.

While Raphael was painting this infinite variety of exquisite maternal scenes, he was commissioned for a *Deposition* for a chapel of the Perugia Cathedral (1507), now in the Borghese Gallery, in Rome. That he worked much at it, drawings in the Louvre, in the Uffizi, in Vienna, and elsewhere, prove.

Raphael was in Florence when Julius II decided that he could not inhabit the Borgia apartments, in the Vatican, which were decorated with frescoes by Pintoricchio, but full of odious associations. He had the storey above arranged by Bramante, and the old quattrocento frescoes were destroyed (with the exception of those by Fra Angelico in the Chapel of Nicholas V). He summoned a great many painters to make new decorations. Among them was Raphael, who had been recommended by the Duke of Urbino, and presented by Bramante. When the Pope saw Raphael's sketches, he commissioned him at once.

In November 1508, while Michelangelo was still shut up by himself in the Sistine Chapel, Raphael was installed in the Apartment of Julius II, where he, who had previously painted only small pictures, realised a mighty work. The first room he decorated was the Stanza della Segnatura. Passing by the rectangles and medallions of the ceiling, we will consider his first wall painting—the *Disputà del Sacramento.* This is designed in concentric zones (suggestive of Early Christian apsidal mosaics), with contrasting celestial and earthly groups, centering in the Mystery of the Altar. Above, seated on clouds, on either side of the central figure of Christ, are noble figures of the Apostles and heroes of the Old Testament. Below, are archbishops, monks and saints. The pointing hand of a prophet seems to unite the earthly scene with the heavenly vision. The whole composition opens out a new world of imaginative design.

Perhaps even more masterly is the great *School of Athens*, in which he introduces portraits of contemporaries. The whole movement of the composition is towards the two philosophers, Plato and Aristotle, who stand at the top of the steps under the vaulting of the vast building in which the scene is represented.

The *Parnassus* (the last picture in the room—finished 1511) shows less inventive power. On the summit of the sacred hill, amid silvery olive trees, are the muses and poets. Apollo is in the midst of them, and we can recognise Dante, Virgil and Petrarch in the throng.

In the Stanza d'Eliodoro, the second treated (representing the triumphs of the Church) portions of every fresco are by pupils. In the *Expulsion of Heliodorus from the Temple*, the figures on the left form a magnificent portrait group. It is a scene of contrasts and violent effects. The *Mass of Bolsena* (1511-14) succeeds in uniting the new fulness of form with old decorative beauty. *The Deliverance of St. Peter from Prison* (1514), is chiefly interesting for its chiaroscuro. *The Repulse of Attila* is an allusion to political events. The group of portraits, of Leo X and his Cardinals, are in part by Raphael, the rest by pupils. (When this fresco was painted Julius II had died—January 1513—and Leo X had succeeded.)

The third room—the Stanza dell'Incendio (1514-17)—bears no evidence of Raphael's hand, but the design was his conception. *The Incendio del Borgo,* which gives its name to the Stanza, is the only fresco we need consider. It represents Pope Leo IV staying by his prayers the progress of a devouring fire. In the background appears the façade of old St. Peter's. The execution is largely that of Giulio Romano.

The fourth room was painted by pupils.

Leo X now ordered a new work from Raphael—tapestries, this time, to adorn the Sistine Chapel. He designed the cartoons, which were executed in Brussels. These were stolen during the sack of Rome—were taken to Constantinople—to Paris—back to Rome, where their faded colours now adorn a dark corridor in the Vatican. The splendid Cartoons (executed by pupils from Raphael's designs) for these tapestries may be seen in the Victoria and Albert Museum, London. They illustrate the acts of the apostles.

Other works of these years should be mentioned: the Farnesina, a villa of the Sienese banker, Chigi, was built and decorated by Raphael. The central hall is illustrated with the *Story of Psyche* (1517—badly repainted) and the *Banquet of the Gods.* The last important decorative commission (1517 to 1519) was the building of the Loggie opening beyond the Vatican rooms and their decoration with scenes from Old Testament stories. His most distinguished achievement as an architect is the *Palazzo Pandolfini,* Rome, 1520.

While Raphael worked at these large decorations, he continued to paint his Madonnas and Holy Families. He made sketches for the Magliana, the hunting-box of Leo X, and plans for the charming Villa Madama. He was engaged on work for St. Peter's, and diverse restorations of classical Rome. He painted some admirable portraits—Julius II, portraits of Angelo and Maddalena Doni (Pitti Palace), Leo X (Pitti Palace, 1518), Baldassare Castiglione (Louvre, 1515).

Raphael's late work shows an over-taxed phase. His last painting, the *Transfiguration* (1519, Vatican) is vehement and forced. The later pictures, left to pupils for execution, appeal little, save in design.

Raphael died on Good Friday, 6th April 1520; and was buried in the Pantheon.

See Pls. 7, 12, Vol. I; Pl. 19, Vol. II.

BIBLIOGRAPHY: J. D. Passavant, *Raphael d'Urbin.* Paris, 1860.—Crowe and Cavalcaselle, *Raphael.* London, 1882.—Klassiker der Kunst, Vol. I.—O. Fischel, *Raphael's Zeichnungen.* Berlin, 1913.

**RATISBON (Bavaria).**—*Cathedral,* begun in 1275. Façade dates from the 15th century; spires, modern. It contains a great many tombs, the most famous of which is that of Marguerite Tucher, by Peter Vischer. The *Town Hall* was begun in the 14th century and finished in the 15th and 16th centuries.

**RAUCH (Christian Daniel).**—German sculptor, 1777-1857. His activities may be divided into 4 phases, his 3 Italian periods, and under German royal patronage. Collaborated with Canova and Tieck. Known for his tomb-sculpture, superb portrait-busts catching invariably the sitter's personality, and for restoration of antique sculpture. Best known work: *Monument of Frederick the Great,* from his last period, 1840-57.

BIBLIOGRAPHY: Eggers, *Ch. D. R.* Berlin, 1873-87.

See Pl. 59, Vol. II.

**RAVENNA.**—One of the oldest Italian towns. It flourished during ancient times and in the Middle Ages, and owed to its strong situation the double advantage of not having been destroyed by the barbarians, and of having very profitable relations with the East. It is rich in buildings of the 5th, 6th, 7th and 8th centuries from which may be studied the Early Christian and Romano-Byzantine styles. The most interesting are:—

RAVENNA: SANT'APOLLINARE NUOVO.

*Sant'Agata,* a 5th century basilica, which underwent great modifications in the 15th century, but was restored to its original form in 1893. The campanile dates from the 15th century.

The *Baptistery of the Orthodox* may have been originally a thermal establishment, built in the 2nd or 3rd century. It is an octagonal building, covered with a pottery roof. The interior is formed in two tiers of arcades, those of the upper tier framing windows. The dome is covered with mosaics dating from the 5th century (partly restored in 1902). These, and those of the *Tomb of Galla Placidia,* are the oldest, and are on a deep blue background. (The gold background was not used until a century later.) They represent the Baptism of Christ. The simplicity of the design, and the gravity of the faces, suggest Roman influence: Byzantine mosaics are generally brighter and richer. Below the vaulting is a frieze, and then decorated arcades, with sixteen figures on a gold background.

RAVENNA: PALACE OF THEODORIC.

The *Tomb of Galla Placidia* is a chapel erected 449-452 by Galla Placidia, sister of the Emperor Honorius. The interior (restored in 1898) is decorated with mosaics, dating from the 5th century, on a deep blue background. The most celebrated represents *Christ as the Good Shepherd,* with the disciples as his flock. The composition is formed of large cubes which recall the pavement, the origin of mosaic work. The building contains the marble sarcophagus in which the Empress was buried.

*San Giovanni Evangelista* was founded about 427, in accordance with a vow made by Galla Placidia during a storm. It was almost entirely transformed in 1747. The Campanile dates from the 11th century. One of the chapels is decorated with frescoes by Giotto, executed between 1317 and 1320. They represent the Evangelists with their symbols, and the Fathers of the Church.

RAVENNA: TOMB OF THEODORIC.

*Sant'Apollinare Nuovo* was built by Theodoric in 526, for the Arian worship, under the name of San Salvatore, and became a Catholic church in 560, under the name of San Martino in Cœlo aureo. It received its present name in the 8th century. The Campanile is old, the narthex and apse were transformed in the 16th and 17th centuries, but the nave has retained its magnificent interior decoration of 6th century mosaics: the two long lines of virgins and martyrs in glowing mosaic, are wonderfully impressive.

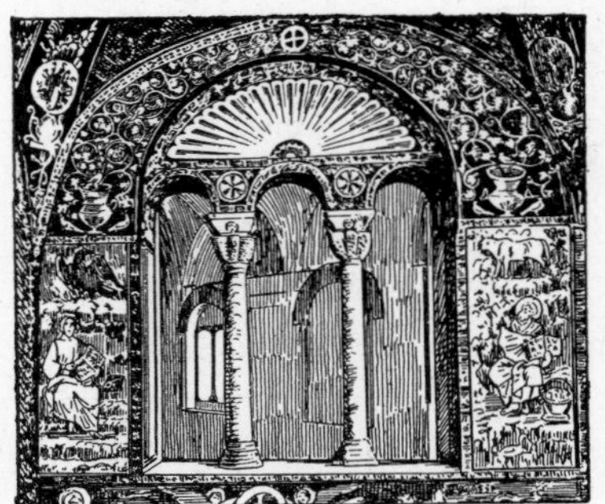
RAVENNA: SAN VITALE, WINDOW OF THE UPPER GALLERY.

The *Mausoleum of Theodoric* (later called Santa Maria della Rotunda) was probably built by Theodoric about 520. It is built of blocks of square stone, carefully cut and superimposed without mortar.

*San Vitale* (begun about 525) is an octagonal building, with an apse —which is decorated with famous mosaics, representing Christ with angels and saints; the Emperor Justinian and his suite, and the Empress Theodora with her court, bearing offerings.

See Pl. 10, Vol. I.

The so-called *Palace of Theodoric* was built in 520.

A few miles from Ravenna is the port of Classe, near which was built the basilica of *Sant'Apollinare in Classe,* which is Ravenna's largest church (built c. 549). It is flanked by an 8th century round campanile. The apse is decorated with mosaics dating from the 6th and 7th centuries (restored), representing a large cross on a blue and starry background, the Transfiguration, Moses and Elias, etc.

Besides these buildings, Ravenna possesses a Cathedral, built in the 18th century.

BIBLIOGRAPHY: Charles Diehl, *Ravenna.* Collection des villes d'art célèbres.—Corrado Ricci, *Raccolte artistiche di Ravenna.* Bergamo, 1908.—Barbier de Montault, *Les mosaïques des églises de Ravenne.* Paris, 1897.

**RAVESTEYN (Jan Anthonisz van).**—Dutch painter, 1570-1657. Worked in the Hague. One of the founders of the so-called *Pictura.* Associated with the group of Delft, mentioned in a document of Oct. 23, 1597. He represented assemblies, civic guards, banquets, etc., with some fine realistic portraiture, reminiscent of the style of Hals. After 1630 his typical red-brown skin-tones become more subdued. Many paintings have been wrongly attributed to him. Several works are signed in full.

**REALISM.**—See Pl. 56, Vol. II.

**REDON (Odilon Bertrand).**—French painter and engraver (1842-1916). He was born in Bordeaux 20th April 1842, the son of a French father and Creole mother. He spent his childhood in Le Médoc and at the age of seven he moved to Paris, where he frequented the Louvre. It was the impression he got from the works of Delacroix which made him decide to pursue an artistic career. He was influenced by the botanist Armand Chavaud and the graver Bresdin, as well as by the writings of Baudelaire, Poe, and Hindu poetry. His first teacher was Gorin; later he came under the influence of his friend Corot and the teachings of Courbet and Gustave Moreau. He exhibited in 1867 at the Salons; the following year he wrote an article on art for *La Gironde.* In 1870 he was ordered by the architect Albert Carré to decorate the chapel at Arras. The Franco-Prussian war interrupted his artistic career for two years while he served in the army. Then he went to live in the country, leading a leisurely life and painting for the sheer joy of it, and travelling considerably in Italy, Belgium, Holland and Spain. It was in 1878 that Fantin-Latour acquainted him with the possibilities of lithography, and this became his preferred medium until 1900. In 1889 he participated in the famous showing at the Durand-Ruel Gallery and exhibited frequently after that time. Redon died in Paris 6th July 1916. Among his friends were A. Vollard, Huysmans, Mallarmé, Bonnard and Sérusier. Of a romantic spirit, and not having to worry about the reality and hardships of everyday life, Redon could freely dream, live and paint in his realm of fantasies and oriental mysticism. His work reflects his subjection to the fear of the unknown and the secrets of the beyond; this is manifested in the dramatic and tragic vein of his death scenes and mythological and religious pieces. His fantasies and religious paintings are carried out in a logical way, the forms are purely classic, there is nothing hackneyed or trite about them, even though he is sometimes hampered by an amateurish technique. Catching the spiritual significance of his varied subject matter he shows a new conception of Christ and Buddha, imbuing them with a deep religious feeling and utter sincerity. The same ethereal and evanescent effects are carried over to his later period, becoming the spiritual essence of his delicate and fragrant flower pieces. Redon's span of activity may be divided into three periods: his early style, influenced by the Barbizon painters, when he worked in pastels and oils, painting landscapes, figures and narratives; from 1878 to 1900, when he worked chiefly with charcoal and lithography, and which, according to some critics is his most outstanding period; and finally his last phase, which showed the influence of post-impressionistic canons, the outstanding subjects being the brilliant floral compositions. Among his portraits are Vuillard, Roger-Marx, Armand Parent and Mme. Redon. He also illustrated the *Apocalypse de St. Jean* and Flaubert's *Tentation de St. Antoine*, which is merely a pictorial rendering of the text. Redon is the author of *Confidences d'Artistes*, 1894, *Rodolphe Bresdin*, 1908, *Letters* (ed. 1923) and *A Soi-Même* (1922 ed.). His works may be seen in the museums of Amsterdam, Berlin, Haarlem, Detroit, Worcester, the Luxembourg, Metropolitan Museum of Art and many famous private collections.

BIBLIOGRAPHY: Jules Destrée, *L'Œuvre Lithographique d'Odilon Redon,* 1891.—Charles Fegdal, *Odilon Redon,* 1929.—André Mellerio, *Odilon Redon,* 1923.—Walter Pach, *Odilon Redon,* 1913.—Claude Roger-Marx, *Odilon Redon,* 1920.

**REGNAULT (Jean Baptiste).**—French painter, 1754-1829. His paintings include *The Education of Achilles* and the *Three Graces*, both of which are in the Louvre.

**— (Henri).** — French painter, 1843-1871. After several attempts, he won the Prix de Rome, in 1866,

HENRI REGNAULT: SALOME. (Metropolitan.)

with a picture of *Achilles Weeping over the Body of Patroclus.* He afterwards visited Spain, where he arrived at a time of revolution, and continued his journey to Morocco. He returned to France to take his part in the War of 1870, and, in 1871, he was killed, at the age of twenty-seven. Among his most notable paintings are *Salome,* and the *Execution in Tangiers.*

BIBLIOGRAPHY: Duparc, *Correspondance de Regnault.* Paris, 1890.

**REIMS.**—The *Porte de Mars* is an antique triumphal arch in three bays, built, it has been said, in hon-

HENRI REGNAULT: GENERAL PRIM. (Louvre.)

our of Augustus, but more probably in the 3rd century. It was damaged in the Middle Ages, and has been recently restored. Under the central arch are carved the months of the year.

*St. Rémy.* The oldest church in Reims, and almost as large as the Cathedral. The Church was begun in 1039, and by 1049 the Romanesque nave and a transept were built. In the 12th century, the choir was built according to the new principles of Gothic art. The nave and transept were altered, and the façade reconstructed. The spire was built in 1400, and was destroyed in 1825. The northern tower was rebuilt, but the Southern tower dates from the 11th century. The façade of the South transept dates from the 16th century. The Choir contains—or, rather, contained, before the War — thirty-eight stained glass windows, dating from the 12th century, representing the Blessed and,

REIMS: ST. RÉMY.

underneath, the archbishops of Reims. The bombardment, during the war, caused the collapse of the vaulting of St. Rémy and the destruction of its art treasures. The building is in course of reconstruction.

The *Cathedral of Notre Dame.* The National Cathedral of France, because it was the old coronation church. It was also one of the finest of Gothic cathedrals, but the War left it in a state of ruin. It is being restored. The building was begun in 1211, on the site of a church, dating from the 9th, 10th and 11th centuries, which was burned in 1210. The west towers, and the spire over the crossing were finished about 1430. In 1481, a terrible fire destroyed part of the town, and the whole roof of the Cathedral, and damaged the towers.

REIMS: THE HOUSE OF THE MUSICIANS.

This disaster was repaired, and restorations were carried out in the 17th, 18th, and 19th centuries.

Of all French Gothic Cathedrals, that of Reims presents, with that of Paris, the greatest unity of plan. The façade has the same arrangement of windows and galleries, and the same division into three main parts, but Notre Dame of Reims is the more ornate in style, and has a lacework of stone under which the horizontal lines are lost. The western façade had a wealth of statues, all famous for their beauty and character. Over the main doorway, there was a lovely rose-window, and above that a "Gallery of Kings,"

REIMS: STATUES FROM THE MAIN PORTAL OF THE CATHEDRAL.

the statues of which date from the end of the 14th century. The façades were, indeed, wonderful in proportion, and in decoration. Before the war the high windows gloried in their original glass: "Grisailles" of the 13th century, in the transept, figures of the kings of France and of the archbishops of Reims in two tiers, in the nave windows; the rose-window in the north transept traced the story of the creation, and the large "rose" in the west front glorified the Virgin.

The old *Archbishop's Palace* was entirely destroyed in the war.

See Pls. 30, 47, 53, Vol. I.

BIBLIOGRAPHY: Anthyme Saint Paul, *La cathédrale de Reims au XIIIe siècle.* 1906.—Abbé Tourneur, *Histoire et description des vitraux et des statues de l'intérieur de la cathédrale de Reims* (in the Works of the Académie de Reims, Vol. IV, 1846). — Gosset, *Cathédrale de Reims, histoire et monographie,* 1895.—Louis Demaison, *La Cathédrale de Reims.* Paris.—Bréhier, *La Cathédrale de Reims.* Paris, 1916.

**REMBRANDT (Harmensz van Rijn).**—Dutch painter and etcher. Born on July 15, 1606 at Leyden, died Oct. 4, 1669 at the Rosengracht. There is a vast amount of extant documentary data concerning his life and activities. The son of a well-to-do miller, he was enrolled in Latin school and later attended the University of Leyden for a short time. From 1620-23 he worked in the atelier of Jacob Isaacsz Swanenburgh, leaving at the age of 17 to go to Pieter Lastman in Amsterdam; he was also a pupil of Jan Pynas. In 1626 he settled in Leyden and remained there until 1632 when he moved to Amsterdam. Two years later Rembrandt married Saskia van Uylenburch; she died in 1642. Of her 4 children only Titus remained alive. After her death, Geertghe Dircx lived with Rembrandt as housekeeper (1642-49), leaving him for supposed breach of promise. Another servant, Hendrickje Stoffels, who probably entered the household in 1645 (first documentary mention in 1649), became his common-law wife. Increasing financial difficulties were confronting the aging artist. In 1639 he bought a house in Breestraat, but all his property including many of his own paintings were auctioned off in 1657, when he filed bankruptcy. Hendrickje and Titus set up an art dealers' shop in 1660 where they employed the old Rembrandt. Hendrickje died in 1662-63.

Rembrandt's activity may be divided into 5 general phases as follows: the Leyden period, 1626-32, characterized by realism and romanticism; the late '30's, a period of highest tension and wildest movement which may be attributed to his happy marriage and artistic success, the origin of light and shadow which become functions of a special lighting system; the '40's saw a series of small canvases, great softness in construction of form and a variety of movements, intimate atmosphere, and a mysterious lighting used for compositional or psychological emphasis; the '50's show Rembrandt's interest in classicism, especially in Titian's color and composition, larger canvases are done in a monumental style, there is a new rigidity, larger and dignified figures, a Caravaggesque lighting of a definite source, light and shadow becoming the function of a color system; and finally the '60's bring geometric tendencies in large units and broad brushwork, yet these late paintings are sensitive, the figures are isolated but remain within a spatial "ambiente," the source of light is indeterminable.

There are three definite influences on Rembrandt's early style. Although he refused to go to Italy, he nevertheless was influenced by Italian art through the works of Lastman; dramatic action and composition, bright colors, an interest in *chiaroscuro,* rendering of detail in strong sweeping lines, may be noticed in his early Biblical paintings as *Baalam and His Ass,* 1626 (Cognac Jay, Paris), *Tobias and His Wife,* 1626 (Amsterdam), and the genre scenes as *Musical Party,* 1626

(Dieren), which represents the artist's family. From Pynas he took over a new feeling for space and the use of dark figures in the foreground, as well as pictorial lighting, *Presentation in the Temple,* 1627-28. A more dramatic lighting appears in the *Supper at Emmaus,* 1629, with more contrast in composition, movement and *chiaroscuro,* as influenced by the Second Utrecht School. Careful painting of details and use of cool colors is also a characteristic of this period. While in Leyden, the artist signed his works with his initials; later on he used his full name.

To his early Amsterdam period belong a number of mythological scenes, still retaining some of the youthful realism, but with the appearance of a new vitality and dramatic tension; the landscape backgrounds are reminiscent of Elsheimer. To this period belong several versions of *Minerva,* and the *Rape of Europa,* 1632 (Berlin). The culmination of small figure composition was achieved in the *Preaching of St. John in the Wilderness,* 1635 (Berlin), which also shows traces of the master's etching technique. In 1633-36 he did a series of religious scenes for Prince Frederick Hendrick of Orange. Other religious paintings were the famous *Deposition, Entombment* and *Resurrection,* all of 1633, now in Munich. Rembrandt's *chef d'oeuvre* of this period, was however a composition of portraits: the *Anatomy of Dr. Tulip,* 1632 (Hague), ordered by the Surgeons' Guild. The treatment of the heads is expressive, emphasizing the dramatic concentration on the cadaver; the problem of grouping is solved masterfully, the lighting is in the direct line of vision. From this period date also a number of portraits of *Saskia,* in a flattering, yet ruthful style, retaining some of the romantic realism of his youth. Another traditional type of group portrait was his famous *Night Watch,* 1642 (Amsterdam), ordered by Captain Frans Banning Cocq for the Riflemen's Guild. It is not a night scene. Full with romantic and dramatic animation, it shows full length figures in commotion. As Rembrandt's interest lay in rendering deep space, movement of light, and not in individual portraiture, the company was highly displeased with the artist's results.

REMBRANDT: OLD WOMAN. (Museum, Vienna.)

After the public failure of this painting, and the various personal difficulties that confronted him, Rembrandt's further development rooted mainly in his inner experience; and to the same degree that he became personally isolated, his art became also isolated in the sequence of Dutch painting. He refused to compromise and did not care for social success, which would require the adoption of Flemish culture and the French language. About this time dates his first period of landscape painting, which shows the influence of Seghers whom Rembrandt admired, and many of whose works he owned. The fantastic element dominates buildings and waterfalls. Dramatic lighting may also be seen in *River Landscape,* 1641 (Cassel). Despite the many blows, the artist's most fruitful period and most mature phase begins. A glowing mellowness appears in his colors and light adds to the rendering of atmosphere. He projects his thorough understanding and sympathy with the poor peasant class into various religious paintings which underneath are pure Dutch genre scenes. *Holy Family* (Louvre), shows the Virgin as a poor peasant woman caressing her infant, with all the paraphernalia of a modest home in the background. The 50's were also Rembrandt's best years at portraiture. The early influence of Thomas de Keyser has gone; there is an unfailing grasp of the salient features, expression, and a mature insight into life and human psychology. With this he combined a masterful play of light on the drapery and the glitter of jewels: *Selfportrait,* 1658 (Frick, N. Y.), *Titus,* 1658-59 (Vienna). In the latter there is a tender light transfiguring the youth. There are a number of portraits of *Hendrickje,* and she probably posed for many of the allegories as well. Approaching his late period one notices a freedom and regularity; the compositions are based on triangles and freely swinging curves instead of on verticals and horizontals. The narrative as a whole becomes widened beyond its literal meaning and becomes a symbol of human relationships in their most fundamental aspects. The figures sometimes seem frozen in their gestures. Whatever stories Rembrandt tells, they are interpreted with the most simple, human understanding, and are removed from reality by means of mysterious light. The light parts of the painting are usually of heavy impasto so that the color often forms a relief and casts its own shadow. He painted with glazes, never used pure color planes. Much coloristic movement may be seen in *Potiphar's Wife Accusing Joseph,* 1655?, (Berlin).

REMBRANDT: PORTRAIT OF ELIZABETH BAS. (Ryksmuseum, Amsterdam.)

A new Town Hall was built in Amsterdam, begun after the Peace of Westphalia by Joseph van Campen and done in the baroque and classic style. The decorations were started by Bol and Flick, and Rembrandt was to do the *Julius Civilis Giving Oath to the Batavians.* It was his largest work, 7/6 metres. There were some objections to it, so Rembrandt took it home in 1660 and never returned it; he cut it up, and fragments are in Berlin and Stockholm today. In 1661-62 he received another commission from the Drapers' Guild; the result was the *Staalmeesters* (Amsterdam, dated 1652 by some). It is a restful composition of a group of men seated high and looking down; there is no more of the physical action, instead there is psychological animation. Each face is a vivid portrait.—Late portraits are subjective and reflect immediate expression of his state of mind, they are serious and often melancholy. There are a number of *Monks* reflecting the artist's own moods. *Jewish Bride,* 1668, is one of these series. *The Prodigal Son* (Leningrad), is probably his last work. There is no dramatic concentration; the gestures are spellbound but without tension. It is endowed with the splendor of his late color. It is said that this painting of forgiveness and pity is Rembrandt's last artistic confession; it shows the resolution of his conflicts with the world.

Rembrandt was also the greatest etcher of all times. He avoids straight lines, uses broken outline and loose spatial arrangement, *Raising of Lazarus,* 1642. His style crystallized about 1648; space is rendered by sequence of planes; the forms become simplified and architectonic; gesture is restrained (*Synagogue*). In the *Ecce Homo,* 1665, the figures are subordinated to architecture and become architectural themselves. His late etchings are done with a heavy line, little attention is paid to detail. His drawings and etchings were influenced by Italian art and by Indian miniatures. Rembrandt painted over 600 pictures, there are more than 1500 etchings and drawings. He is represented in museums and collections all over the world.

BIBLIOGRAPHY: E. Michel, *Rembrandt, sa vie, son œuvre, et son temps.* Paris, 1893.—Bode, *The Complete Work of Rembrandt.* Paris, 1897-1906.—*Rembrandt,* Klassiker der Kunst, Vol. II.—Hofstede de Groot, *Catalogue of Dutch Painters,* Vol. VI.—A. M. Hind, *Rembrandt's Etchings.* London, 1912.—Bredius, *Rembrandt,* 1936.

**RENAISSANCE.** — The unfortunate, but inextinguishable and universally used term which describes the artistic outpouring in 14th, 15th and 16th century Europe. Called a "rebirth" of Classical art and learning, it was in reality simply the birth of a great Western art, entirely un-Classical in spirit, which adapted the lessons of the past to its own use. The aesthetic development of the Renaissance period (covering the 14th, 15th and 16th centuries in Italy, the 15th and 16th in the North) is discussed under the various artists who gave to it its unique glory.

**RENAN (Ary).**—French painter, **1858-1902.** Son of the great French writer, pupil of Puvis de Chavannes and of Delaunay, his painting is soft in colour, recalling his first master. But he only painted easel pictures. He exhibited for the first time in 1880. *Aphrodite* (1883); *Christ Preaching on the Lake* (1887); the *Banks of Jordan* (1888). These works were painted after a journey to the Holy Land. Later paintings include: *Scylla,* 1894; *Sappho* (Luxembourg); *Voices of the Sea,* etc. Ary Renan wrote critical articles and accounts of travel in the "Gazette des Beaux-Arts," "Le Temps," etc.

**RENI (Guido).**—See Guido.

**RENOIR (Pierre Auguste).**—French painter, graver and sculptor (1841-1919). The son of a tailor, he was born 25th February 1841 in Limoges. When he was four years old the family moved to Paris. Gounod, who was aware of his artistic powers, advised him to become a musician, but Renoir chose a pictorial career. At thirteen he was an apprentice in a ceramic shop, where he painted flowers on porcelain; later on he made a living by painting fans and window shades. In 1861 he was admitted to the studio of Gleyre, where he got acquainted with Sisley, Monet and Bazille. His frequent visits to the Louvre made him appreciate the works of Boucher, Fragonard and Watteau; he was also attracted to and influenced by Goujon's *Fountain of the Innocents.* It was while sketching in the forests of Fontainebleau that he met Diaz, and in 1863 he made the acquaintance of Cézanne. His first public appearance was in 1868 when he exhibited the *Esmeralda* in the Salons. Besides his participation in the Salons, he exposed at the Impressionist show of Nadar in 1874. Although his fame was increasing, the only means of livelihood he could find was painting portraits; finally the auctions of his works at the Hôtel Drouot in 1875 and 1877 bettered his pecuniary state. In 1879 he travelled to Algiers and in 1881-1882 in Italy. He also visited Spain, Holland, Belgium and England. From 1892 on he lived at the art colony in Pont-Aven. In 1910 he went to Germany and then settled on his estate at Essoyes, Burgundy, which he purchased in 1898. His last years were spent in the Provence, still painting, although his hand was useless due to arthritis, and his brush had to be strapped to his wrist. Renoir died in Cagnes 3rd December 1919. His love for the commonplace as seen in his early style, until 1868, shows the influence of Courbet's art on the young painter. After studying Delacroix's theories on colour he became interested in impressionism about 1870, but refused to acknowledge its pragmatic approach. From his early interest in tone he put the emphasis on colour without the sacrifice of light. His hues were brilliant and his paintings reflected his *joie de vivre.* To this period belong the *Odalisque* and *La Loge.* After the Nadar exhibition his interest turned towards rendering texture, and the sensual approach in painting nudes makes its appearance, as seen in *Baigneuse* and *Moulin de la Galette.* By 1883 he derived all that he found satisfactory from the Impressionists, and being against the *faire du premier coup,* he turned to closed forms with emphasis on the contour, volume and tactile values. Influenced by the art of Pompeii while in Italy, his paintings reflect a contemplative classic style and more conservatism. Towards the end of his activity he returned to the painting of sumptuous nudes rendered in luscious colours, reaching the monumentality of Rubens through the art of Watteau. Renoir produced about 6000 paintings, 155 lithographs, several pieces of sculpture and bronze medals of Corot, Delacroix, Ingres, Monet, Cézanne and Rodin. His art throughout is impetuous and spontaneous, there is no theorising; his life and art were completely one. His works are conserved in the museums of London, Berlin, Dresden, Tokio, Philadelphia, Chicago, New York, Paris, Oslo, Moscow and Zurich.

BIBLIOGRAPHY: Albert André, *Renoir,* 1919, 1923, 1928.—Adolphe Basler, *Pierre Auguste Renoir,* 1928.—Albert C. Barnes and Violette de Mazia, *The Art of Renoir,* 1935.—Georges Besson, *Renoir,* 1932.—Gustave Coquiot, *Renoir,* 1925.—Théodore Duret, *Renoir,* 1924.—Georges Duthuit, *Renoir,* 1923.—Élie Faure, *Renoir,* n. d.—François Fosca, *Renoir,* 1924.—Julius Meier-Graefe, *Renoir,* 1929.—Octave Mirbeau, *Renoir,* 1913.—*Renoir, Peintre du Nu,* 1923.—Georges Rivière, *Renoir et ses Amis,* 1921.—Claude Roger-Marx, *Renoir,* 1933.—Léo Stein, *Renoir,* 1928.—Ambroise Vollard, *La Vie et Les Œuvres de P. A. Renoir,* 1919.—Ambroise Vollard, *Intimate Record of Renoir,* 1925.

**REPOUSSÉ.**—Formed in relief, as by beating metal into relief from the back, thus impressing the pattern on the reverse side.

**REREDOS.**—A screen or wall facing behind an altar; of stone or wood, usually ornamented.

**RESTOUT (Jean).**—French painter, 1692-1768. He never freed his figures from a certain vulgarity, and their attitudes tend to be theatrical. Most of his pictures were intended for churches. They show freedom of handling, skill in their lighting effects, and a sense of harmonious composition.

RESTOUT: CHRIST HEALING A PARALYTIC.

His painting of *Christ Healing a Paralytic* is in the Louvre.

**RETABLE.** — A shelf, ledge, screen, or wall covering behind an altar; usually decorated with painting, carving, sculpture, or other ornamentation.

**REYMOND.**—Family of Limoges enamel workers, of which one Pierre Reymond, who lived in the 16th century, deserves special mention. He was born about 1513 and died about 1584. His enamels are signed P. R., or P. Reymon, or Reymond. The Louvre possesses a cup by him, dated 1544. He probably controlled an important workshop, for a great many pieces bear his signature, and it is difficult to tell which were really by his own hand. In the Louvre is a series of plates which tell the story of Suzanna; and in the Cluny Museum are plaques representing the *Annunciation* and episodes from the life of Christ. Pierre Reymond's work is very uneven, but some of his enamels are very fine.

BIBLIOGRAPHY: René Jean, *Les Arts de la Terre,* (3rd part), *L'émaillerie.* Paris, 1911.—P. Lavedan, *Léonard Limosin et les Emailleurs français.* Paris, 1913.

**REYNOLDS (Joshua).**—English painter, 1723-1792. Born at Plympton, near Plymouth. He was a precocious child. At the age of about fifteen, he was seized with such a passion for Raphael that he decided to follow in the master's footsteps, and, without further ado, he told his father he wished to be a painter. His father sent him to London, to one of his friends, Thomas Hudson, who was a well-known portrait painter. Reynolds soon became known. His father having died in 1746, he (the youngest of ten children) settled, with his two sisters, in Plymouth. There he opened a studio, which, thanks to his influential friends, was frequented by the neighbouring aristocracy. There he made the acquaintance of a painter, William Gaudy, whose father had been a pupil of Van Dyck, and who had a considerable influence on the forming talent of Reynolds. In 1749, he had the opportunity of going to Italy by sea. His impressions were rather cold; his enthusiasm for Raphael died down. Nevertheless, he discovered, in the Vatican, that all he had learned about painting, in England, must be put aside. He must, he said, become a small child again. During the three years he spent in Rome, he made numerous copies of the old masters. He left Rome in May 1752, and, passing through Florence, Venice, and Paris, where he spent a month, he returned to Plymouth about the end of the year, and in 1753, settled in London with one of his sisters. He made his début with the portrait of Captain Keppel, which was a success. Commissions came to him, and, thanks to his modest prices, which he later increased, he soon acquired independence. He sometimes received six orders a day. He then rented a comfortable residence on Newport Street, and cut a fashionable figure. He had made the acquaintance of Dr. Samuel Johnson, to whose influence we shall return. But Reynolds' success was so great, that he again changed his abode. In 1760, we find him installed in a princely residence in Leicester Square. His studio became a fashionable rendezvous. In 1764, he founded the Literary Club where the most eminent men of the day foregathered—Johnson, Oliver Goldsmith, and Edmund Burke were among the members. In 1765, he founded the Society of British Artists, which became, in 1768, the Royal Academy. Reynolds was elected President, and, in 1769, was knighted. His unquestioned supremacy only lasted a time. The rising fame of Gainsborough and of Romney must sometimes have disquieted Sir Joshua. There even came a period when London was divided into two factions—the Reynolds faction and the Romney faction—and Reynolds' commissions dwindled.

SIR JOSHUA REYNOLDS: Self-Portrait.

REYNOLDS: LORD AND LADY BONINGTON.

Reynolds, who had made his début in art criticism under the auspices of Samuel Johnson, and who, in 1765, had assisted him in an annotation of Shakespeare's works, now attempted history. Nevertheless, his contributions to the Royal Academy were regular and brilliant until the end of his life. His studio was never deserted, and his prices rose. In 1776, he was made a member of the Academy of Florence. In 1784, on the death of Ramsay, he became first painter to the King. In 1786, Catherine II requested a picture from him, and an example of his discourses. She rewarded him with fifteen hundred guineas, a gold box, enriched with pearls, and a most complimentary letter. Reynolds was at the height of his fame. Then, in 1789, he had trouble with his eyesight, and had to give up his work. Gradually, his liver became seriously disordered, and he died on the 23rd February, 1792.

REYNOLDS: ANN BINGHAM.

Reynolds was a great worker, well-balanced, master of himself, extremely prudent, upright, and free from envy of rising young artists who, at the end of his life, he saw preferred before him. He was a refined and accomplished gentleman, and by no means wanting in a sense of humour.

Reynolds himself said: "In any career success depends, not on an inner aptitude for that special career, but on the general vigour of the spirit, and on its strength and constant tension towards one specific end. Ambition is the cause of all superiority; hazard is the means. Feeling for æsthetic excellence is an acquired taste which no one possesses without prolonged culture, hard work, and great care." Reynolds went to work with the quiet assurance of a man of affairs. He was a hard worker. "He always did his best."

"I am never tired," he said, "of trying new methods and new effects. I always have some idea in my head, and a constant desire to progress." By nature and education, Reynolds was a realistic painter. He was not at home with the "grand manner" of painting, which he saw in Rome. Apart from an understanding of the human physiognomy, Reynolds expressed the character of his sitters by their attitudes and accessories. Thus, a scholar is represented in his library: a sailor, on his ship, and a soldier in front of his troops.

REYNOLDS: FRANCES HARRIS WITH HER DOG.

Reynolds was, as he says himself "very sensitive to impressions of light, and to curious effects of chiaroscuro." He tried to express his subject "not by lines, but by effects of light and shade." In this he was strongly influenced by Rembrandt, and perhaps still more by Correggio. Reynolds had a charming sense of fresh colour. "Avoid clay, and brick, and carbon," he said, "seek out the pearl, and the ripe peach." All his life he studied and searched, endeavouring to give to his works those qualities which were lacking in the productions of his own day. He had to make many experiments on his own account, since, as he said, he never had the chance of learning about principals of colour, early in life, for there was no one able to teach him. Consequently, many of Reynolds' portraits have deteriorated, fading, blackening, or

REYNOLDS: THE DUCHESS OF DEVONSHIRE WITH HER DAUGHTER.

clouding over, as the result of incompetent preparations, and the use of colours of which he had not the secret. Fortunately, many works remain (especially among his portraits of children and young women) in which we can still see in their pure brightness, those exquisite colours, which belong to "the pearl and the ripe peach."

Reynolds had considerable influence on the painters of his generation, and on the generations which followed. His writings are of the greatest interest. They may be divided into two parts: first, the literary work, which consists of some annotations for Samuel Johnson's edition of Shakespeare, two dialogues which put the great writer on the scene, and also an elegy consecrated to his memory. The second part of Reynolds' writings includes several letters on Art, published in "The Idler," and very important notes on Du Fresnoy's work, "The Art of Painting." He also wrote accounts of travels in Flanders, containing interesting observations on the painters he saw there. Finally, there are the famous discourses, which he delivered at the Royal Academy, and which contain appreciations of the art of Gainsborough, of some other contemporaries, and of Michelangelo.

Reynolds' chief paintings are as follows:—

In the National Gallery: Self-portrait; portraits of Lord Heathfield, of Samuel Johnson, of Lord Ligonier, of Le Banni; a *Holy Family; Heads of Angels;* the *Graces Decorating a Statue of Hymen:* the *Age of Innocence*; etc.—in all, twenty-three pictures.

In Huntington Collection, California: *Mrs. Siddons as the Tragic Muse.*

And there are many pictures by Reynolds, in private collections, in England and America.

See Pl. 48, Vol. II.

BIBLIOGRAPHY: Sir William Armstrong, *Sir Joshua Reynolds.*

**RHEIMS.**—See Reims.

**RHINE SCHOOL.**—See Enamel.

**RHODES.**—See Greece (Sculpture; Terra Cottas).

**RIBALTA (Francisco).**—Spanish painter. Date and place of his birth are unknown; he was buried in Valencia on Jan. 14th, 1628. "Ribalta belongs to the founders of the national school of Spanish painting of the 17th century and stands at the head of the School of Valencia. The problems of his evolution and of the relationship of his art with that of Caravaggio are still unsolved. Although the supposition that he made his studies in Italy lacks evidence, some of his paintings, for instance the *Martyr-death Suffered by Santiago de Compostela in the Battle of Clavijo,* painted in 1603 for the parish-church of Algemesí, indicate that he must have studied Caravaggio before that year. . . . He knew how to liberate himself from the influence of the school of Rome and stimulated by Sebastiano del Piombo, and later by Correggio, he created independently a *light and dark style* ('Tenebroso') which is a genuinely Spanish counterpart to that of Caravaggio. . . . By his use of light and shadow he achieved eminently plastic and dramatic effects." (A. L. Mayer, passim.) The *Last Supper* from the High-altar of the Church of the Colegio del Patriarca of Valencia (paid for in 1606) and now in the Museum there is regarded to be his masterpiece. His last works were for the Cartuja de Porta Coeli, near Valencia. Among the paintings for the High-altar (Mus. Valencia) his rendering of San Bruno is especially impressive. Characteristic of his later art are also the *Vision of St. Francis* (Madrid, Prado), and *St. Francis Crowned by Christ* (Mus. Valencia), which he painted for the Capuchin Convent of Valencia. He also was active and esteemed as a portrait painter (portraits of his patron Juan de Ribera, Archbishop of Valencia and founder of the aforementioned Colegio del Patriarca; of Sor Angullona, and of San Tomás de Villanueva, all at Valencia; double portrait of a knight of Santiago and his wife in coll. of Sir William Eden in England). His outstanding pupil was Jusepe de Ribera. (Id., passim.)

BIBLIOGRAPHY: *Archivo de Arte Valenciano,* 1917. Art. by Tramoyeres.—A. L. Mayer. *Gesch. der span. Malerei,* 2nd ed., 1922.—Id. in *Thieme-Becker,* Vol. XXVIII, 1934. Art. *Ribalta, Francisco.*—M. Gonzalez Marti. *Los grandes maestros del Renacimiento.* Valencia, 1928.

**— (Juan de).**—Spanish painter, 1596-1628. Son and pupil of the preceding. He soon became an able painter. His picture, in the Museum of Valencia (formerly church of S. Miguel de los Reyes), representing the *Crucifixion,* reveals a still bolder and more personal style than that of Francisco de Ribalta. This picture which bears signature and date, 1615, is the only one to be assigned to the painter on basis of evidence.

BIBLIOGRAPHY: See Ribalta, Francisco.

**RIBERA (Jusepe de).**—Spanish painter, c. 1590-1652. Because of Ribera's nationality and small stature he was nicknamed, in Italy, *Le Spagnoletto.* Ribera was the descendant of a noble Spanish family, and though the date of his birth is not known, we know that he was born at Játiva, near Valencia. He studied at Valencia under Francisco Ribalta and left later for Italy. An interesting contemporary letter by Mancini dealing with the painter's life in Rome still awaits publication. We know that he was at Parma as attested by his *St. Martin* in the Church at San Andrea, and, judging from his copy of Veronese's *Christ and the Doctors* which before

RIBERA: DIOGENES AND HIS LANTERN.

1616 was at Padua we may assume that he was also at that city. We have evidence that he settled at Naples in 1616. There he enjoyed the patronage of the Spanish viceroy, Don Pedro Girón y Téllez, Duque de Osuna, who made him his court painter. Also the successors of Osuna favoured him, especially the Conde de Monterey. His fame quickly spread, and in order to keep up with all the commissions given him by private persons, convents, etc., he was obliged to engage numerous assistants whose works now often pass as his. In 1626 he was made a member of the Academia di San Luca of Rome, and in 1646 the Pope decorated him with the Order of Christ. Velázquez visited him in 1629 and 1649. The last years of the artist's life were upset by failing health and domestic grief. Don Juan de Austria, bastard son of Philip IV of Spain, seduced one of his daughters. Desirous of ending his days in retreat, Ribera left his ostentatious residence in Naples and retired to Posilippo where he died on September 2nd, 1652.

". . . The concept of his early art betrays a close relationship to his master Ribalta. . . . The study of Titian, Veronese, and mainly of Correggio, however, produced results which were entirely different from those produced by Ribalta. This accounts for his long struggle between his strongly avowed style affecting dark colors and heavy shadows—*Tenebroso*—and his predilection for light which is so pronounced that one is tempted to speak of *Pleinairismus.* Were it not for the fact that most of his paintings are dated one would be prone to establish a rather different chronology of his works,—an instructive lesson teaching us to be on guard against the common belief that the evolution of an artist has always to develop along a straight line.

"His earlier works such as the *Cristo de la Expiración* (1616-1620) in the Collegiate Church of Osuna and the scenes from the *Life of St. Ignatius of S. Gesú,* Naples, are strong with Venetian reminiscences." In his paintings of the twenties "an attempt at external effect is noticeable, attenuated however by exceedingly skilful compositions, by monumentality and quality of drawing and execution." (*St. Jerome Listening to the Trumpet of the Last Judgment,* Naples Museum; etching of the same subject.) ". . . Contrasting with a group of highly dramatic and somehow gruesome pictures (*Martyrdom of St. Andrew,* 1628, Budapest, Museum; *Ixion* and *Prometheus,* Prado, Madrid; etc.) are such lyrically conceived canvases as the *San Sebastian Nursed by Women* (1626, Leningrad, Hermitage) and the *Ecstasy of St. Magdalen* (1626? Madrid, Ac. de S. Fernando). . . . The humorous *Silen* in the Naples Mus. (1626) forms a curious link between these two groups.

"Ribera's keen interest in everything characteristic becomes chiefly manifest in portraits (the bearded *Magdalena Ventura,* 1631—Madrid, Duque de Lerma; the sculptor *Gambazo,* 1632,—Prado) as well as in his *Philosophers* and *Apostles* which earned him great popularity having been imitated by the hundreds. (*Alchimedes,* 1630, Prado; twelve half-length representations of the *Apostles,* also at Prado.) In the course of the thirties he succeeds in eliminating the disagreeable and violent notes of his art. His representations become more profound and his heroes more sublime. Around 1635 he begins to prefer cool silvery tones, . . . and later on his flesh colours obtain a magnificent amber-like luminosity. The treatment of light gains more and more importance. The grandiose and sparkling *Concepción Imaculada* at Salamanca, 1635, and the *Saint Agnes,* bathed in golden light, in the Dresden Gallery represent the two poles in this period. . . . The dramatic effect of all the miracle scenes is in the first place brought about by the miracle itself being symbolized by the power of light, the concrete incarnation of which are the Christ Child or angels. For his silvery manner, are especially characteristic the *Concepción* and *St. Januarius* at Salamanca, c. 1636; *St. Anthony and the Infant Jesus,* 1636 at the Madrid Academy; the *Marsyas* in the museums of Naples and Brussels, 1637. Ranking in importance with his mythological scenes and representations from the Old Testament (for instance *Jacob's Dream,* 1633,—Prado) are Ribera's subjects taken from the New Testament (the *Mystic Marriage of St. Catherine,* 1643, formerly London, Earl of Northbrook; *Pietà,* 1637, Capella del Tesoro of the Convent Church of San Martino of Naples; the *Trinity,* 1632, Escorial; etc.). . . . Vigorous manhood is rendered in the representation of *St. Francis with the Angel* (Prado), *St. Joseph with the Infant Jesus* (Palazzo Pitti), etc.

"Of great monumentality are the representations of the *Twelve Prophets, Moses* and *Elias* 1638-43, filling the spandrels of lunettes of the arcades in the Church of San Martino at Naples. The figures are not intended, as is usual in baroque, to break up space but to fill it in a dignified manner. The difficult problem of integrating the figures into their allotted space has been solved here by means as perfect as they are noble. . . . These figures constitute without doubt the most important spandrel-fillings of baroque art. . . . The ground is kept in dark, and the colours are deep. The artist has availed himself of effectual contrasts by rendering these powerful figures either in an attitude of repose or in animated movement. Ribera preferred to represent them as 'The Wise Men of the People' with features rather sublimated than 'beautiful.' . . . Neither do we miss in this period character-heads which are supposed to represent personages of the antique (the *Blind Homer,*—original lost, best copy at Turino; *Diogenes,* 1637, Dresden; etc.). . . . Only few portraits are preserved of this time (*Portrait of a Missionary,* Milan, Mus. Poldi Pezzoli; portrait of a Spanish youth of noble descent with his Patron Saint, 1637, Gallery Schwerin; etc.). . . .

". . . The *Concepción* of the High Altar of the Convent Church of Sta. Isabel of Madrid, 1646, represents the beginning of the last stage of Ribera's art. . . . It is significant for the painter that the stove in this picture does not play a main role but is only rendered as light in light. His technique is now broad and tender, the light glimmers and scintillates and no obtrustive gesticulations are seen any more. . . . In 1649 he painted his *Paul the Ermite* (Prado), probably his most perfect nude. The famous *Adoration of the Shepherds* in the Louvre is of the following year, and his greatest artistic achievement, the *Communion of the Apostles* for the Church of S. Martino of Naples was, after many years of labour finished in 1651. The *St. Sebastian and St. Jerome in Meditation*, transferred from the Certosa of Naples to the Museum; the *St. Jerome* of the Heritage of Leningrad, another *St. Jerome* in the Naples Mus. (1652, one of his last works); and other paintings of this his last period show a great profoundness in their soulful expressions. . . . The luminosity of the flesh colours has been raised to the highest level, the bodies of these Saints are shining forth in their warm amber tones of gold. . . .

"His etchings are throughout productions of highest quality. . . . Besides study-heads and larger compositions Ribera also did facial detail-studies (mostly towards 1622). Of his later period only the portrait of D. Juan de Austria is known. His etchings have been repeatedly published (Louis Ferdinand, Paris, 1650; G. Valk—after Ribera—Madrid, 1774). Here also he showed how much he cared for the treatment of light and sometimes succeeded even to a greater degree in his efforts than his paintings. . . . "His drawings are an eloquent proof of his most careful draughtsmanship. . . ." (Mus. of Cordova, Uffizi, Brit. Mus., etc.).

"Ribera took pride in his Spanish nationality; to his signature he added the word "español." . . . His deep religious feeling, his naturalism and colours are thoroughly Spanish; his dramatic temperament is Valencian. . . . Ribera is not only one of the most brilliant among Spanish 17th century painters but represents one of the strongest artistic personalities of his century. He exerted a lasting influence on almost all of his native fellow-painters as well as on those of Naples, which was his second country. . . ." (A. L. Mayer, passim).

BIBLIOGRAPHY: C. Justi, *Velázquez u. sein Jahrhundert,* 1903.—A. L. Mayer, *Gesch. der span. Malerei,* 2nd ed., 1922.—Id., *Jusepe de Ribera* (Kunstgesch. Monographien) 1908; 2nd ed. 1923.—Ibid. in Thieme-Becker, Vol. XXVIII, 1934, art. *Ribera, Jusepe de.*—E. Tormo y Monzó, *Ribera en el Museo del Prado* (El Arte en España, no. 21). —*Ribera in the Collection of the Hisp. Soc.,* Hisp. Soc. of Am., 1928. —G. Pillement, *Ribera.* Paris (*Maîtres de l'art ancien*) 1929.

**RIBOT (Théodule).** — French painter and engraver, 1823-1891. Ribot is a magnificent craftsman. He began his artistic career late in 1861. In spite of his desire to devote himself to painting, and after studying for a short time under the painter Glaize, he worked for manufacturers, went to Algiers to direct building operations, and lived as a commercial designer. The success of the first pictures he exhibited decided him, and he exhibited regularly. His work is remarkably able, but of wearying uniformity. His subjects, however, are varied: he painted still-life groups, kitchen scenes, and historical pictures. Examples of his work include the following, which are in the Luxembourg Gallery: *The Martyrdom of St. Sebastian* (1865); *The Good Samaritan* (1870), and *Jesus among the Doctors.*

**RICARD (Gustave).** — French painter, 1823-1872. When quite young he was a comrade of Monticelli at the art school of Marseille. In Paris he became the pupil of Cogniet, and he gave a great deal of time to studying the old masters in the Louvre—copying, notably, Rembrandt, Correggio and Van Dyck. After travelling in Italy, he visited London in 1848, where he studied Van Dyck, Reynolds, Gainsborough and other English painters. Finally, in 1850, he returned to Paris, where he exhibited eight portraits, among them one of Madame Sabatier which created a sensation. After being a great success at the Salon, he gave up exhibiting in public. He lived a very simple and solitary life in a modest studio in the Rue Duperré, which he only left to go from time to time to London or Venice. He went once to Belgium and Holland. He painted admirable portraits, among them those of Mesdames Arnavon, Baignières, d'Heilbuth (Louvre); of Paul de Musset (Louvre), Lanone (Versailles), etc. His work recalls the masters he studied so much, and his preference for Titian, Rembrandt and Van Dyck is evident.

RICARD: PORTRAIT OF HEILBUTH. (Louvre.)

Like his masters, he had recourse to striking effects of light, which accentuated the physiognomy of his sitters. Imitation of the old masters did not, however, prevent his work from possessing an individual character, but his preoccupation with technique was, unfortunately, excessive, and most of his portraits have yellowed and darkened.

RICARD: PORTRAIT OF MME. A.

**RICCARDI PALACE.**—See Florence; also Pl. 5, Vol. II.

**RICCI (Marco).** — Venetian painter (1676-1729). Landscape and marine painter.

— **(Sebastiano).** — Venetian painter (1660-1734), of Bellano. He is facile and attractive, and represents the transitional art, which was inspired by Correggio, Titian, or Veronese, and which prepared the way for Tiepolo. His large compositions of Venice are almost all lost. His picture of Pius V between saints and angels is in the Jesuit Church. He designed the cartoon for the fine mosaic, representing Venetian magistrates venerating the body of St. Mark, which is on the façade of San Marco. Large decorations by him are in Hampton Court Palace.

**RICCIARELLI (Daniels).**—See Volterra.

**RICCIO (Andrea Briosco, called).** — Paduan architect and sculptor (1470-1532). Pupil of Bellano. He contributed to the decoration of the fine chapel of the Santo, in Sant'Antonio of Padua. He excelled in bronze casting. His large bronze candelabra in the Santo, Padua, decorated with many Christian and pagan subjects (1507-1517), is among the most famous works of the Renaissance. Riccio also made two bas-reliefs (1506-07) in the marble cloisters, besides those of Bellano—*David,* and *Judith and Holophernes.*

Also by Riccio are: the Della Torre monument in S. Fermo Maggiore in Verona; and the wall-tomb of the Abbot Antonio Trombetta in the Santo at Padua.

— **(Domenico).**—See Brusasorsi.

**RICHARDSON (Henry Hobson).** —American architect (1838-1886). He was born on the Priestley plantation in St. James' Parish, Louisiana, 29th September 1838. His mother was a Priestley, granddaughter of Joseph Priestley the famous American chemist. He was graduated from Harvard in 1859 and the next year entered the École des Beaux-Arts in Paris. While he studied he was employed by Théodore Labrouste and J. I. Hittorf, who worked in the neo-classic manner. In 1865 he returned to New York to open his own office and at first was associated with a Mr. Roberts in Brooklyn. Two years later he entered into a partnership with Charles D. Gambrill which lasted until 1878. In 1872 he won the competition for a design for Trinity Church, Boston. With the completion of that building his future was assured. In character it is French Romanesque, like the churches of the region of Auvergne, although the lantern is adapted from that of the Old Cathedral of Salamanca. It was the foundation for a Romanesque revival in civil buildings and private dwellings. Sever Hall at Harvard University and the Marshall Field Building in Chicago were further examples of this French Romanesque type which became the vogue. About 1876 he was engaged in the completion of the State Capitol at Albany, New York, whose architectural style he changed from the Victorian to the Romanesque but not with any measure of success. In 1882 he made a trip abroad for his health, when he travelled through Auvergne and northern Spain, absorbing the elements of the Romanesque style and estimating how best to adapt them to present-day requirements of American building. He was a Fellow of the American Institute of Architects, and a member of the American Academy of Arts and Sciences. He suffered a bad heart attack in the fall of 1885 and another in the spring of 1886, from which he did not recover, and died 27th April of that year.

The transformation of his early style in his late period became the foundation for the development of the modern style by Louis Sullivan. Accordingly, Richardson may be regarded as one of the fathers of the new architecture.

See Pl. 64, Vol. II.

BIBLIOGRAPHY: Mariana G. Van Rensselaer, *Henry Hobson Richardson and His Works,* 1888.—Fiske Kimball, *American Architecture.* Indianapolis, 1928.

**RICHIER.**—Family of sculptors of Lorraine, of the 16th, and beginning of the 17th century. The most celebrated is Ligier (1500 or 1506-1567), and works of the school (which lasted from about 1530 to 1640) are often attributed to him.

— **(Ligier).**—French sculptor, born at Saint-Michel, about 1500. Died in Geneva about 1567. He lived and worked in Lorraine, where most of his works are still to be found. He was strongly influenced by the Italian sculptors, especially Michelangelo.

His chief works are: the altarpiece in the Church of Hattonchâtel (1523); *Christ and the Two Thieves,* in the Church of St. Pierre, of Bar-le-Duc; the *Pietà* in the Church of Etain (1528) of which there is a terra cotta, on a smaller scale, in the Church of Clermont-en-Argonne (1530); the *Child in the Manger,* in the Louvre; the powerfully realistic skeleton (1547), which forms part of the tomb of René de Châlon, Count of Nassau (Church of Saint Pierre of Bar-le-Duc); the funeral statue of Philippe de Gueldre, second wife of René II of Lorraine (Eglise des Cordeliers, Nancy). Richier's last and most notable work is the *Tomb of Saint Mihiel* (Church of St. Etienne), which was begun in 1553, and which is composed of thirteen life-size figures. Richier, who was of the reformed religion, had to take refuge in Geneva in 1560.

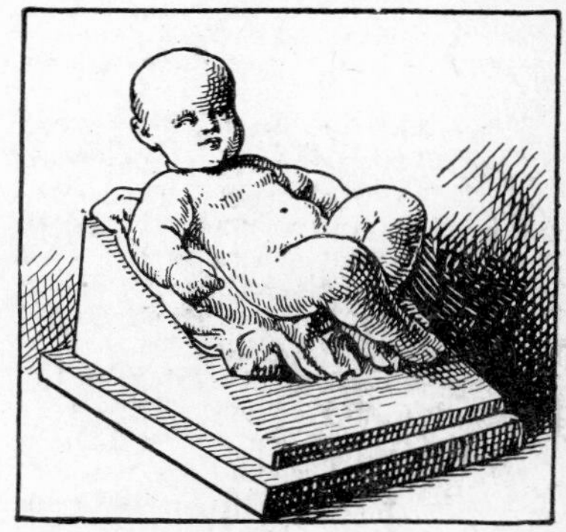

RICHIER (LIGIER): THE INFANT JESUS.

BIBLIOGRAPHY: P. Denis, *Ligier Richier.* Nancy 1911.

**RICHTER (Ludwig).**—German painter and graver, 1823-1884. Richter was a sensitive painter, with a great understanding of nature, especially fond of the surroundings of Dresden. He began by trying to paint classical landscapes, but he was far more successful with peaceful scenes of his native countryside, which are fresh in color and sincere. He also illustrated children's books. This painter represents a simple, nationalistic art in the spirit of German late Romanticism.

BIBLIOGRAPHY: Jahn, *Mitteil. über L. R.,* 1855.—Golz, *L. R. der Mann u. sein Werk,* 1920.

**RIEMENSCHNEIDER (Tillmann).** — German sculptor, 1468-1531. He came from Saxony and settled in Würzburg in 1483. The productive period of his life was between 1490 and 1525, when he was compromised in a peasants' revolt against their bishop, and thrown into prison, where he died six years later. Like his contemporaries at Nuremberg, he endeavoured to combine realism with picturesqueness. His groups are crowded, and the folds of their dresses are deep and stiff; but his work reveals a certain high-pitched sensibility and an intense seriousness, which are very individual. His figures affect ungainly attitudes, but their expression is colder and calmer than are those of Veit Stoss and Adam Krafft. His chief works are the wooden altarpiece of Münnerstadt (1490), now walled up, in the centre of which appeared the Magdalen, clothed in her long hair, and being caught up to heaven; *Adam and Eve* (1490-93), in stone, the two earliest known nude statues, of the 15th century, in Germany (door of the Marienkapelle, in the Marienkirche, of Würzburg); and the *Madonna of the Neumünsterkirche*, represented standing on a crescent moon (1493).

The period of his best work was between 1495 and 1520. In this interval of time he made the Creglingen altarpiece, representing the *Assumption of the Virgin*; the tomb of Bishop Rudolf von Scherenberg, in the Cathedral of Würzburg; in coloured marble and stone, carved with admirable skill; the Altar of the Holy Blood, in the Church of St. James, Rotenbourg (1495-1505), one of the works most characteristic of Tillmann Riemenschneider's manner: In the centre is the *Last Supper*, and on the wings, the *Entry of Christ into Jerusalem* and *Christ on the Mount of Olives*.

His masterpiece is certainly the Tomb of Henry II and of his wife Cunegonde (between 1499-1513), in Bamberg Cathedral. The statues of the reclining figures are treated with majestic amplitude. On the sides are carved scenes in the lives of the deceased. One of the most remarkable is the relief representing Henry II on his death-bed. The care which the artist has bestowed on beauty of line and grace of pose is very sensitive; and his idealism is again manifest in the statues of *St. Dorothy* and *St. Margaret*, in the Marienkapelle of Würzburg; whereas the types, although very fine, of the *Pietà* of Maïdbronn recall rather those of Claus Sluter on the doorway of Champmol (see Sluter).

BIBLIOGRAPHY: Tönnies, *Leben und Werke der Würzburger Bildschnitzers T. Riemenschneider*, Strasbourg. 1900.

**RIESENER (Jean Henri).**—See Furniture (Eighteenth Century).

RIGAUD (HYACINTHE): SELF-PORTRAIT.

**RIGAUD (or RIGAU) Y ROS (Hyacinthe François, and Honorat Mathias Pierre André Jean).**—French painter, 1659-1743. Son and grandson of an obscure painter. Hyacinthe Rigaud came to Paris in 1681, at the age of twenty-two, and was fortunate in pleasing Charles le Brun. Although Rigaud won the Prix de Rome in 1685, Le Brun advised him to stay in Paris, where his ability as a portrait painter would have ample scope.

His portraits include those of Girardon, Coysevox, Nicolas Coustou, the painters Sébastien Bourdon, Claude Hallé, La Fosse, Joseph Parrocel, the architects Robert de Cotte, Mansart, and such interesting people as La Fontaine, Boileau, Jean Racine and Santeul.

His portrait of Mignard, at Versailles, shows that this prolific painter was capable of psychological penetration. Here, there is no splendour of stuffs and accessories, but the very image of Le Brun's rival. What passion in the withered face! And what agitation is expressed in those refined hands! This emotion, rare with Rigaud, we find again in the Portrait of his Mother (Louvre), a most admirable painting. The careful modelling, the fresh colour, the fineness of the skin beneath which one can almost see the blood, the brightness of the eyes, the subtlety of the flesh tones—all these qualities make this filial painting one of the most beautiful portraits in French art.

RIGAUD (HYACINTHE): PORTRAIT OF J. F. P. DE CRÉQUI AS A CHILD. (Louvre.)

Rigaud was never more himself than when he was painting his courtier models—great periwigged lords, attired in rich cloaks and flowery laces, posing for the future, in a gorgeous setting of brilliant stuffs and ornaments. In spite of his preoccupation with these things, Rigaud was none the less interested in character. In his portrait of Bossuet, all are admirable—the nobility of pose, the minute study of the episcopal robes, the distinguished hands, and the proud, shrewd face, illuminated by a sovereign intelligence.

His portrait of Louis XIV shows the ageing king, as Saint Simon describes him, wrinkled in his majesty.

The portrait of Cardinal Polignac (Louvre), painted in 1715, betrays the literary vanity of the author of *Anti-Lucretia*, under the Cardinal's robe.

From the beginning of the 18th century Hyacinthe Rigaud's reputation stood high, and he painted most of the important people of his time. He died on the 27th December 1743, at the age of eighty-four, without posterity. See Pl. 41, Vol. II.

BIBLIOGRAPHY: Pierre Marcel, *La Peinture en France au début du XVIII^e siècle*. Paris, 1905.

**RIMINI (Italy).**—*S. Francesco.* See Alberti.

**RINEHART (William H.).**—American sculptor (1825-1874), a prolific worker in a graceful vein, one of his most famous performances being the *Clytie* in the Peabody Institute, Baltimore (where practically the whole of the artist's productions may be studied in casts).

**RIPOLL (Spain).**—*Abbey Church,* 9th-10th century. A five-aisled basilica of the First Romanesque style brought into Catalonia from Lombardy. It is a T-cross in plan with six absidioles as well as the main apse. The tower and octagonal lantern are modern. The richly carved façade is 12th century and shows obvious Lombard inspiration. The construction is brick.

**RIPPL-RÓNAI (Josef).**—Hungarian painter and graver, 1861-1927. The most important exponent of modern Hungarian painting. He studied in Munich and then with Munkácsy in Paris. Through his personal charm and ability he was accepted midst the artistic "élite" of Paris; among his closest friends were Bonnard, Vuillard, Denis and Gauguin. He knew Cézanne and Puvis well. For a while he worked with Maillol, and then he was active at Pont-Aven. In 1892 was his first important exhibition which brought him immediate fame. He painted in the typical French manner; simplicity, decorative flat surfaces and coherence were his motives. He thought in terms of abstract structure underlying form, and aimed to create a mood and retain a spiritual quality. His colors were somewhat influenced by Japanese prints. After he returned to his native Kaposvár his art underwent a great change. The French character of his work, which was not appreciated at home, was soon replaced by a native flavor; the gray tonality of many of his early paintings vanished and a brighter, daring colorscheme took its place. In this period he painted mostly peasant interiors emphasizing their charming simplicity. His late works, mostly pastels, are toned down in intensity and are more subtle and philosophic in content. Among his best known works is *My Mother*, often compared to that of Whistler. *Portrait of Vuillard*, and *Janitor's Daughter* also show his power to analyze personalities. His *Self-portrait* is in the Uffizi.

BIBLIOGRAPHY: Malonyay, *A Fiatalok*, 1906.—Kállai, *Neue Malerei in Ungarn*, 1925.—Petrovich, *Ujakról és Régiekröl*, 1923.

**RISTORO (Fra).** — Florentine architect of the 13th century (died in 1283). He and Fra Sisto built the beautiful church of Santa Maria Novella.

**RIVERA (Diego Maria Concepción Juan Nepomuceno Estanislao de la Rivera y Barrientos Acosta y Rodriguez).**—Contemporary Mexican painter. He was born in 1886 in the mountain town of Guanajuato; on his father's side his grandfather was a Spanish nobleman and his grandmother a well-to-do Portuguese Jewess; from his maternal side he had Spanish and Indian blood. His father, a mining engineer, was aware of the child's ability and equipped his son with a drawing room where he could experiment freely in a number of media. From 1898 to 1904 he attended the National Preparatory School and later studied at the Academy of Fine Arts in Mexico City. He began by copying nature, but this procedure seemed unsatisfactory to him; consequently he approached the classical art of Mexico, in the study of which he was more content. He seemed to discover for himself the divine basis of art, that something which is hidden within the visible spectacles of the world. After exhausting the possibilities of Mexican art he went to Paris, where he studied with Picasso and became interested in the problems of cubism. However, this approach was too intellectual for him so he turned to the doctrines of classical art. To achieve plastic purity became the aim of his painting. In 1915 he contributed to the Salon of the Independents. After having sampled the different trends of French painting he spent two years in Spain, concentrating on the problems and effects of chiaroscuro. He also devoted a great deal of time to the *cuisine* of painting, that is, to its chemistry. After having travelled and profited in Italy he returned to France. His canvases up to this time reflect the whole history of modern painting; the subsequent influences of Seurat, El Greco, Cézanne, Renoir and Zuloaga can be traced in his work. By 1912 Rivera was ready to forget and unlearn everything he had mastered and to evolve his own very personal style of expression, which was most adaptable to mural painting. His compositions are primarily architectonic and only secondarily decorative; they are characterised by the rhythmic continuity of modern industry. He finds beauty in the shapes of modern machines and other mechanical devices as well as in the activities of every type of labourer. He renders them in large simple masses of forceful pattern and with luminous colours, the warm hues dominating. His liberal spirit, resulting from his rather complex ancestry, as well as his sympathy with the working classes is the theme of all his later works, which, not infrequently, has caused political controversy. Diego is married to a half-German half-Mexican woman. His first acclaimed painting was *Los Viejos* (1912). The following buildings are decorated with his murals: Amphitheatre of the Preparatory School, Mexico, University of Education, National Palace in Mexico City, Stock Exchange, School of Fine Arts in San Francisco, Institute of Arts, Detroit, and the New Workers' School. His murals for Rockefeller Center in New York City were removed after a controversy concerning the political import of their subject matter. He has written *A Portrait of America* (1934), several magazine articles and has, together with Bertram Wolfe, published *Portrait of Mexico* (1936).

BIBLIOGRAPHY: Anne Merriman Peck, *Young Mexico*, 1934.—George F. Pierrot and Edgar P. Richardson, *The Diego Rivera Frescoes*. Detroit, 1934.—Diego Rivera and Bertram Wolfe, *Portrait of America*, 1934; *Portrait of Mexico*. New York, 1936.

**RIZZO (Antonio).**—Veronese architect, sculptor, and marine engineer, active 1465-1498, formerly confused with Antonio Bregno. He worked chiefly in Venice. He executed the tomb of *Niccolò Trono* (died, 1473), in Santa Maria dei

# THE SCHOOL OF RUBENS

RUBENS *directed a large atelier of well-trained students who worked under his inspiration on his great decorations; each one had his special study in the collaboration: Snyders, Fyt, van Thulden painted the animals and the landscapes. Among these collaborators the most famous was Anthony Van Dyck who, while very young, left the studio of Rubens to find fortune and glory at the court of Charles I of England. This Flemish artist became the official portraitist to the royal family and the English lords. In his work the strong healthy Flemish vigour was refined. Gainsborough took his inspiration from Van Dyck.*

VAN DYCK: CHARLES I. LOUVRE.
*(Photo by Hachette.)*

VAN DYCK: ST. MARTIN SHARING HIS CLOAK. CHURCH OF SAVENTHEM.
*(Photo by Pardon.)*

VAN DYCK: PORTRAIT OF HENRIETTA OF FRANCE. WINDSOR CASTLE.
*(Photo by Braun.)*

JORDAENS: FECUNDITY. MUSEUM OF BRUSSELS.
*(Photo by Pardon.)*

JORDAENS: THE KING DRINKS. MUSEUM OF BRUSSELS.
*(Photo by Hermans.)*

DAVID TENIERS: THE PRODIGAL SON. LOUVRE.
*(Photo by Neurdein.)*

DAVID TENIERS: THE TEMPTATION OF ST. ANTHONY. LOUVRE.
*(Photo by Neurdein.)*

A. BROUWER: THE BRAWL. MUSEUM OF DRESDEN.
*(Photo by Bruckmann.)*

## Jordaens and Teniers

JORDAENS was not a student of Rubens; he did not, like the other Flemings, make the voyage to Italy. But what a painter! His overflow of vulgarity is compensated for by his picturesque qualities. His unbridled liveliness animates his craft. On the other hand, Teniers, although he willingly paints feasts and ribald scenes, is a little master with a delicate brush giving a fine and spiritual touch appropriate to the medium. Brouwer is also a painter of peasants but his craft, like his models, is less sophisticated.

# HOLLAND: PAINTERS OF THE PEOPLE

*The Dutch school of the seventeenth century forms a separate chapter in the general artistic history of Europe. Circumstances had in fact separated this group of painters from the rest of the great European family, with no trips to Italy, and no more Christian motifs. Religion and politics hemmed in these Protestant painters in their own cities and compelled them to be self-sufficient. Then they rediscovered the qualities of their fifteenth century predecessors: a love for all things even the smallest, and careful application in making life-like portraits. It is a country where art is in harmony with life.*

FRANS HALS: THE JESTER. MUSEUM OF AMSTERDAM.
*(Photo by Hanfstaengl.)*

FRANS HALS: THE REGENTS OF ST. ELIZABETH'S HOSPITAL. MUSEUM OF HAARLEM.
*(Photo by Dewald.)*

FRANS HALS: THE OLD WOMAN OF HAARLEM. BERLIN.
*(Photo by Hanfstaengl.)*

## Frans Hals

All the Dutch painters with the exception of landscape painters were portraitists. Many of them became specialists in the art of portraiture. But the most brilliant of these masters is without doubt Frans Hals. The most important of his pictures, group portraits of the guilds, remain at Haarlem, the city in which he lived and worked. This artist is one of the most skilled technicians and one of the liveliest of painters.

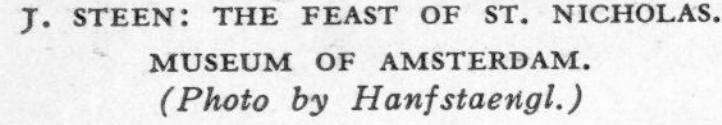

J. STEEN: THE FEAST OF ST. NICHOLAS. MUSEUM OF AMSTERDAM.
*(Photo by Hanfstaengl.)*

METSU: SOLDIER RECEIVING A LADY. LOUVRE.
*(Photo by Hachette.)*

TERBORCH: THE MILITARY LOVER. LOUVRE.
*(Photo by Hachette.)*

PIETER DE HOOCH: THE STOREROOM. MUSEUM OF AMSTERDAM.
*(Photo by Lévy.)*

## Genre Painters

The Dutch have translated into exquisite small pictures the poetry of intimacy; they show us the bourgeoisie, the people and the peasant in the ordinary course of their existence. Their pleasure in painting, their extraordinary accuracy of execution, and their sympathetic vision cause them to discover an entire world which one ordinarily considers beyond the province of art. The merit of these charming works is in the perfection of the method; but each painter brings forth his own genius and the series of these intimate scenes is as varied as life iself.

PIETER DE HOOCH: THE MESSENGER. MUSEUM OF AMSTERDAM.
*(Photo by Hanfstaengl.)*

VERMEER OF DELFT: WOMAN RECEIVING A LETTER. AMSTERDAM.
*(Photo by Hanfstaengl.)*

VERMEER OF DELFT: WOMAN READING A LETTER. AMSTERDAM.
*(Photo by Hanfstaengl.)*

GERARD DOU: THE DROPSICAL WOMAN. LOUVRE.
*(Photo by Hachette.)*

## Genre Painters

Jan Steen is the most literal and least artistic of these little masters. Metsu and Terborch are equals in expressing the details of an interior; Pieter de Hooch applies himself to rendering the effects of light, a golden light which sometimes seems to radiate from the work of Rembrandt; the light of Vermeer of Delft is, on the other hand, cool and limpid like enamel. Practically the only great defect in the Dutch manner is in its attention to minute details. With Gerard Dou the exactness of this technique is meticulous to excess. Dutch painting died for this reason.

# DUTCH LANDSCAPE PAINTERS

*DUTCH civilisation is above all urbane like that of Flanders of which it is only a branch. If the Dutch had been a peasant people only, they might have become architects or even sculptors, but they could not have made painting the favourite method of expression for their genius. It is characteristic for natives to admire the countryside. Therefore, the Dutch masters practiced landscape. Moreover, in this small republic the town is never far off; on the horizon one may always see the steeples of Dordrecht or of Haarlem. The countryside of Holland almost as much as the city is a creation of human industry.*

VAN GOYEN: VIEW OF DORDRECHT. MUSEUM OF THE HAGUE.
*(Photo by Hachette.)*

RUYSDAEL: THE JEWISH CEMETERY.
PINAKOTHEK, DRESDEN.
*(Photo by Alinari.)*

RUYSDAEL: THE BLOCKADE. LOUVRE.
*(Photo by Hachette.)*

## van Goyen and Ruysdael

J. VAN GOYEN astonishes and charms because of the simplicity of his methods: some earthy tones more or less thinned out by oil which are sufficient to render the transparency of the atmosphere, and the lightness of great clouds. Among the landscape painters the sky is always dramatic, observed and rendered with the same precision as a countenance. The clouds of Ruysdael have a majestic sadness; they foretell the storm. Ruysdael was a romantic poet; he loved the sadness and tumult of the elements.

HOBBEMA: THE MILL. PINAKOTHEK, DRESDEN.
*(Photo by Alinari.)*

PAUL POTTER: THE BULL. BUCKINGHAM PALACE, LONDON.
*(Photo by Hanfstaengl.)*

HOBBEMA: MIDDLEHARNIS AVENUE. NATIONAL GALLERY, LONDON.
*(Photo by Hachette.)*

## Hobbema and Paul Potter

HOBBEMA, quite unlike Ruysdael, paints nature as friendly and receptive. His mills and his approaches to the village do not have the majestic melancholy of Ruysdael's works; they are more truly Dutch. His delicate brush carefully details the leaves of the trees without ever falling into broad synthesis. Paul Potter died young, but not before he had proved by several masterpieces that one could paint a portrait of cattle. His power of rendition and the sincerity of his observation are astonishing.

BERCKHEYDE: THE TOWN HALL OF HAARLEM.
*(Photo by Hachette.)*

CUYP: THE COW (DETAIL).
NATIONAL GALLERY, LONDON.
*(Photo by Anderson.)*

J. VERMEER OF DELFT: VIEW OF DELFT. MUSEUM OF THE HAGUE.
*(Photo by Hachette.)*

## Vermeer of Delft and Cuyp

THE Dutch also exploited the picturesque qualities of their cities. In the background of landscapes by Cuyp and van Goyen one may often see the heavy silhouette of the church of Dordrecht standing erect. Berckheyde applied himself to representing the picturesque architecture of Haarlem with a minute exactitude. But the finest portrait of a city—one of the finest paintings in the world—is the *View of Delft* by Vermeer. Houses have their portraitists as well as animals and trees.

# REMBRANDT

*Dutch painting was purely naturalistic; these masters were almost entirely faultless technicians who possessed but little imagination. However, there is one exception: Rembrandt, the greatest Dutch painter and one of the most powerful geniuses in history. With him naturalism develops into a touching poetry. He was too far advanced to be fully understood by his contemporaries. It was necessary for human sensibility to become enriched by modern romanticism before Rembrandt could take his place finally in the pantheon of painting. Rembrandt understood only his own art; but he increased the expressive power of it.*

PORTRAIT OF REMBRANDT. NATIONAL GALLERY, LONDON.
*(Photo by Hachette.)*

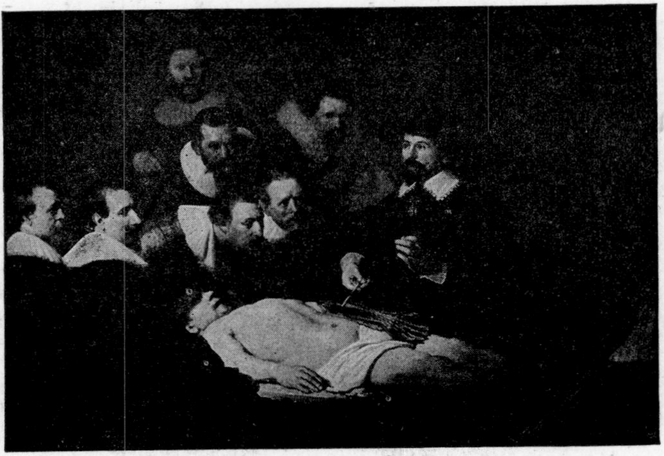

THE ANATOMY LESSON. MUSEUM OF THE HAGUE.
*(Photo by Hanfstaengl.)*

THE PRESENTATION IN THE TEMPLE. MUSEUM OF THE HAGUE.
*(Photo by Hanfstaengl.)*

## The Young Rembrandt

Rembrandt achieved success early. This was the time when he painted, according to the Dutch taste, exact careful pictures; one of the notable works of this first manner is *The Anatomy Lesson* of The Hague, beautiful because of the precision and the propriety of the method. At the same time, Rembrandt was already haunted by the effects of light and shade; he wanted to give to figures and objects such a luminous intensity that they might stand out clear against the surrounding shadows. He employed etching as well as colour to achieve this light which was sufficient to transform the truest images into fantastic visions.

DETAIL FROM "THE PRAYER OF MANOAH." MUSEUM OF DRESDEN.
*(Photo by Braun.)*

THE NIGHT WATCH. MUSEUM OF AMSTERDAM.

THE PILGRIMS AT EMMAUS. LOUVRE.
*(Photo by Hachette.)*

## The Period of Maturity

But Rembrandt did not stop with the painting of likenesses. He tried to express the hidden soul; he rises above the world of appearances; he makes one feel the emotion of the men portrayed much less by the play of the countenances than by the strangeness and mystery of his illumination. He knew how to bring forth the humanity as well as the divinity of the Scriptures.

REMBRANDT AS AN OLD MAN. LOUVRE.
*(Photo by Hachette.)*

THE SYNDICS OF THE CLOTH GUILD. MUSEUM OF AMSTERDAM.
*(Photo by Hanfstaengl.)*

HENDRICKJE STOFFELS.
*(Photo by Hachette.)*

## The Late Years of Rembrandt

In the last part of his life, Rembrandt lived alone, deprived of his wealth and surrounded by misfortune. But in the midst of these disasters and sorrows, he continued to paint more profoundly and more movingly. This group of honest drapers looks at the spectator with a strange intensity. At the time, Rembrandt often took for his models the persons of his household, his son and his servant who became his wife. He himself appears in working costume, ravaged by age but still full of inspiration, despite his misfortunes.

Frari, masterpiece of Venetian sculpture and tomb-architecture, and the *Tomb of Vittore Cappello* (died, 1467), in Sant'Aponal. From 1483, all his energies were devoted to the Doges' Palace, which had been partly destroyed by fire. A document of 1491 may refer to work on the figures of Adam and Eve.

**ROBBIA (Andrea della).**—Florentine sculptor, 1435-1525. Son of Marco di Simone della Robbia, nephew and heir of Luca della Robbia, under whom he studied. His work is less simple than that of his uncle, his drapery more complicated,

Robbia (Andrea della): The Visitation. (San Giovanni, Pistoia.)

and his figures larger. The process of enamelled terra cotta is the same; he limited himself, as did Luca in his late work, to the use of white and blue, but his white is not the milky, warm tone of Luca, but a bluish, cold one.

Andrea della Robbia probably assisted his uncle in several works, particularly in the Chapel of the Cardinal of Portugal at San Miniato.

About 1463-1466, he executed the work by which he is perhaps best known—the decoration of the Loggia dei Innocenti, in Florence.

Robbia (Luca della): The Singing Children.

The Madonna with two angels in the Opera del Duomo is of 1489. In 1491 he did the frieze and medallions of the Madonna delle Carceri in Prato, and the portal-lunette of the Duomo there.

Of his very abundant work, we may mention: several terra cottas in the Church of La Verna (1479); the lunette of the loggia of San Paolo, Florence, representing *The Meeting of St. Francis and St. Dominic* (late); the lunettes of the three doors of Santa Maria della Quercia, near Viterbo (1508); the *Madonna* in the Bargello, Florence; a terra cotta altar in triptych-form, with the *Coronation of the Virgin*, in Sta. Maria degli Angeli, near Arezzo; a *Coronation of the Virgin* in the Monastery of the Osservanza, near Siena; an *Adoration of the Magi* (Victoria and Albert Museum). The *Visitation*, in the Church of San Giovanni Fuorcivitas, Pistoia, variously attributed to Andrea and to Luca, is now attributed to Andrea.

His later works tend to over-facility.

Andrea della Robbia had many sons, Antonio (1467), Marco (1468), Giovanni (1469), Paolo (1470), and other descendants who contributed to the spreading of the graceful art of enamelled terra cotta in Tuscany, in the Marches, in Umbria, and as far South as Naples and Sicily.

See Pl. 6, Vol. I; Pl. 9, Vol. II.

For Bibliography, see Luca della Robbia.

**— (Giovanni della).** — Florentine sculptor, 1469-1529. Son of Andrea della Robbia. He imitated his father in the charming fountain of Santa Maria Novella (1497), in the *Pietà* in the Berlin Museum c. 1500; the altar in S. Medardo at Arcevia (1513); *The Bearing of the Cross* in the Museo Nazionale, Florence, and in many other works in enamelled terra cotta. But he represents the late period of the school, which is characterised by an ever increasing richness both in ornament and colour. With strong colours and heavy garlands of fruit and flowers, the material became less beautiful. The round faces, less well modelled and less expressive, are, on the other hand, sometimes not enamelled at all. Sometimes the whole relief is in white glaze. This searching after overloaded effects, combined with the use of mediocre materials, shows that the art invented by Luca della Robbia was nearing its death.

**— (Girolamo della).** — Sculptor, and architect. Born in Florence, 1488; died in Paris, 1566. He was the son of Andrea, who died in 1525, and grandnephew of Luca. He was one of the architects of the Château de Madrid, in the Bois de Boulogne, and he worked at Fontainebleau about 1537. He made a reclining figure of Catherine de Médicis for the tomb of Henri II. The one which was placed on the tomb was the work of Germain Pilon. Della Robbia's statue is in the École des Beaux-Arts.

**— (Luca della).** — Florentine sculptor, and founder of the Della Robbia shop, 1400-1482. Like many of the best Florentine artists, he began his education as a goldsmith. He must have been much appreciated by 1431, for in that year he was commissioned to make a "cantoria" (or singing gallery) for the Cathedral, even before Donatello, who was given the order for a second gallery. They are now both in the Museo dell'Opera, facing one another. The charming children which adorn Luca's cantoria sing in unison, play on instruments, or dance. They are all vigorously modelled, and clearly grouped. The work reveals Luca della Robbia's sincerity of expression, his gentleness, his freshness, his sense of rhythm.

In his numerous Madonnas, we find the same round faces, sweet and childlike, free of trouble. Three are in the Louvre, and there are several in Florence, in Berlin, and in many other collections.

Luca della Robbia discovered a method of enamelling terra cotta with a milky white glaze, to which he generally added a lovely blue. The glazed reliefs of the *Resurrection* and the *Ascension* (1446-50) in the Duomo of Florence, are in his finest style. About 1448, Luca made some exquisite medallions for the roof of the Portuguese Chapel in San Miniato.

Another work by Luca della Robbia—in marble with terra cotta decorations—is his Tomb of Bishop Federighi, now in Santa Trinità in Florence. Behind it, in three panels, are bas-reliefs of Christ, the Virgin and St. John. The tomb is framed by a garland of coloured flowers and leaves.

Luca della Robbia was a prolific artist, and it is impossible to enumerate all his works. Of his many Madonnas, one of the loveliest is the *Madonna of the Roses* in the Bargello, Florence.

In most of his glazed terra cottas Luca generally confined himself to blue and white. Occasionally, he introduced other colours as well, but always with a discretion which was often lacking in his followers.

See Pl. 9, Vol. II.

Bibliography: Reymond, *Les della Robbia*, 1897.—Burlmacchi, *Luca della Robbia*. London, 1900.—Allan Marquand, *Luca della Robbia*, Princeton, 1914. *Giovanni della Robbia*, Princeton, 1920.

**ROBERT (Hubert).**—French painter, 1733-1808. After spending eleven years in Italy, Robert returned to Paris, and contributed architectural pictures to the Salons. He painted souvenirs of Italy, and Parisian buildings, new or in ruins, and pictures of great fires, such as the one which devastated the Opera du Palais Royal, in 1781. He had a taste for the art of gardens, and he was charged, by the court of Ver-

Robert (Hubert): The Maison Carrée at Nîmes.

sailles, with the transforming of the arrangement of the Baths of Apollo (1777), the appearance of which has not been altered since.

In 1784, he became director of the Académie; and in the same year he was nominated "garde des tableaux" of the Louvre.

At the time of the Revolution, his relations with the old court and the aristocracy caused him to be imprisoned during the Terror. The story goes that a prisoner, bearing the same name as he, perished in his place on the scaffold. It is always said that he was liberated after the fall of Robespierre.

During the Dictatorship, he was re-established in his former post of Curator of the Louvre.

Hubert Robert was famous for his versatility, for his extraordinary adventures in Italy and for his skill at games. His painting was brilliant, facile and decorative. From his sojourn in Italy he acquired a taste for colonnades and marble steps; from his stay at Tivoli, in the Villa d'Este, he kept also a love of greenery, and of silvery cascades and fountains.

See Pl. 43, Vol. II.

Bibliography: Gabillot, *Hubert Robert et son temps*, Collection des Grands artistes.—P. de Nolhac, *Hubert Robert*, 1910.

**— (Léopold Louis).** — French painter (1794-1835). The engraver Charles Girardet sent him to Paris, and taught him his craft, while he also followed the teaching of David. After the Hundred Days, David went into exile; and later Léopold Robert went to Italy to finish his studies.

In Rome the young artist was so taken with the charm of Italian models that he almost forgot to transform them into Madonnas and heroes.

The *Return of the Pilgrimage to the Madonna dell'Arco* (Louvre) made an impression at the Salon of 1827. The picture represented Naples and the Springtime. Another painting (also in the Louvre)—*Arrival of Harvesters in the Pontine Marshes*—represented Rome and summer. The country round Florence staged a *Vintage* scene, which symbolised Autumn and Tuscany; while *Venetian Carnival* served to represent the Venetian people, and Winter.

*The Harvesters* was enthusiastically received at the 1831 Salon; but Robert's weaknesses are apparent in this composition: the too-obvious arrangement, dryness of modelling, hard shadows and opaque colour. Nevertheless, this kind of painting was so successful that very soon Robert's imitators were innumerable.

Bibliography: Feuillet de Conches, *Léopold Robert*. Paris, 1848.—J. B. Delécluze, *Léopold Robert*. Paris.

**ROBERT-FLEURY (Joseph Nicolas).**—Born in Cologne of French parents, 1797-1890. Robert-Fleury was the pupil of Girodet, Gros and Horace Vernet. His long career as a painter of history was full of official honours. Such pictures as *Christopher Columbus Being Received by Ferdinand and Isabella the Catholic* (Louvre), and *Jane Shore* (Fontainebleau) are fine documents, studied in the smallest detail; but this application becomes wearisome.

**ROBERTI (Ercole).**—Ferrarese painter, born c. 1456; died 1496; a pupil of Tura, he studied at Padua, was influenced by Mantegna and the Bellini.

Ercole is first mentioned in Ferrara in 1479, at which time he was in partnership with his brother Polidoro and a goldsmith. From 1480-81 dates the large altarpiece for S Maria in Porto, Ravenna, now in the Brera, Milan. After this commission Ercole probably left for Bologna, where he was active for several years, finishing the work left by Cossa on his death in 1477. In 1482 Ercole was godfather for the son of Bartolommeo Garganelli and painted for Domenico Garganelli the chapel in S. Pietro, Bologna, left unfinished by Cossa, which was destroyed in the 17th century. Copies exist of some of Ercole's frescoes for this chapel; one, a copy of the *Crucifixion* is in the Sacristy of S. Pietro; one of the *Dormition of the Virgin* is in Sarasota, Florida, the Ringling Museum; and a copy of a fragment, four male figures, is in the Louvre. In this period Roberti painted for the high altar of S. Giovanni in Monte the predella now divided among the Dresden (*Bearing of the Cross* and *Betrayal*) and Liverpool (*Pietà*) Galleries. From 1486 until his death he was in the service of the Este family in Ferrara. He probably went to Hungary with Cardinal Ippolito d'Este in 1487; in 1490 he accompanied the newly married Isabella d'Este to Mantua; in 1492 he was sent to Rome as companion to Prince Alfonso, and visited Florence.

The number of accepted pictures by Ercole is small: a group of small Saints, all from the pilasters of the frame of a large altarpiece, are distributed among the Louvre (*Michael and Apollonia*); Vienna (*Anthony Abbot*); and the Benson Collection in London (*Catherine and Jerome*). The *St. Michael* in the Bologna Pinacoteca is from the Santini Collection, Ferrara. Other works are: the *John Baptist* and the *St. Jerome* both in Berlin; the Uffizi *Sebastian*; the *Gathering of Manna*, London; the Rome, Count Blumenstihl, *Pietà with Two Donors* (from S. Domenico, Ferrara); the *Deposition*, Bologna Pinacoteca, from S. Benedetto, Ferrara, and the Santini Collection, left unfinished by Ercole, completed in the 16th century. Other attributions to Ercole Roberti are highly controversial.

Bibliography: Vasari-Milanesi, III.—A. Venturi, Archivio storico dell' arte, II, 1889; also, *Storia d. arte ital.*, VII, III, 1914; also, *North Italian Painting, Emilia.*—C. Gamba, in *l'Esposizione d. pitt. ferr. d. rin ascim.*, Ferrara, 1933.—Roberto Longhi, *Officina Ferrarese*, 1936.

**ROBETTA (Cristoforo di Michele).**—Florentine engraver, born 1462, still active 1522. About fifty of his prints remain.

Bibliography: A. M. Hind, *Cristoforo Robetta*, Print Collectors Quarterly, X, 1923.

**ROBINSON (Boardman).**—Contemporary American painter. He was born 6th September 1876 at Somerset, Nova Scotia. His art training started at the Massachusetts Normal Art School. Later he went to Paris and there studied at the Académie Colarossi and the École des Beaux-Arts. He was strongly attracted by the work of Jean Louis Forain and was to a certain extent influenced by his technique. Being unsuccessful in his attempt to exhibit his work in Paris he returned to the United States. After an interval of four years in San Francisco he came east to New York and there soon became recognised as an illustrator. From 1907 to 1910 he was connected with the *Morning Telegraph* and then until 1914 he worked for the *New York Tribune*. A trip in 1914 to Russia with John Reed resulted in a large number of sketches for the *Metropolitan Magazine* the next year. From 1915 through 1922 he was connected with *The Masses*, the *Liberator* and *Harper's Weekly*, and the following year he drew cartoons for the *London Outlook*. All the drawings are characterised by careful draftsmanship a few necessary lines conveying the gist of his meaning, whether humorous, political or satirical. He then turned to book illustration, which branch of his work includes drawings for John Reed's *The War in Eastern Europe*, Betty Sage's *Rhymes of If and Why* and Constance Garnett's translation of Dostoyevsky's *Brothers Karamazov*. In 1925 he became an instructor at the Art Students' League and in 1934 he was a teacher in the Fountain Valley School in Colorado. He was commissioned in 1929 to do a set of mural panels for the Kaufmann Department Store in Pittsburgh portraying the *History of Commerce*. These panels are notable for the solid masses of the forms and the vivid colouring of the whole, as well as for the distinctive medium used, a kind of automobile paint specially treated. Since then he has also executed a mural, *Man and His Toys*, for the R. C. A. Building in Rockefeller Center, which further strengthens his position in the field of modern American mural painting.

Bibliography: For a complete bibliography see *The Index of Twentieth Century Artists* for April, 1935.

**ROBUSTI (Jacopo).**—See Tintoretto.

**ROCOCO.**—The term Rococo, used in the 18th century, is found mentioned, for the first time, in 1842, to designate a style which flourished under the Regency and during the reign of Louis XV.

Banquet hall of the Palace of Potsdam.

An elaboration and deterioration of the Baroque, Rococo ornamentation was inspired by the shapes of shells, varied with great fantasy, and mingled with garlands of flowers, volutes and spirals. This precious, refined and often mannered style was responsible for charming pieces of furniture and goldsmiths' work. But in architecture the Rococo was essentially a decorative, nonstructural style, and, accordingly, was in France confined to interiors. Germans used the style in exteriors.

Already at the end of the reign of Louis XIV, taste in architecture and decoration tended towards a less serious and more capricious art. The growing interest in Chinese art was not without its influence. The nobility of straight lines was replaced by the grace of undulating ones. Angles were transformed into volutes. Nevertheless, the new art at first respected the laws of balance and symmetry. It was only later that it developed its characteristic caprice and deliberate lack of symmetry.

**RODEZ (Aveyron).**—The Cathedral, 1277-1535, has a famous Flamboyant rose-window in the main façade.

See Pl. 48, Vol. I.

**RODIN (Auguste).**—French sculptor, 1840-1917. He went to school at Beauvais until he was fourteen, and then returned to Paris. After making three vain attempts to enter the École des Beaux Arts, and following courses by Barye, he (in 1864) sent an admirable bust to the Salon, the *Man with a Broken Nose*, which was rejected. From 1871 to 1877, Rodin assisted with the interior decoration of the Bourse, in Brussels. In 1876, the marble of the *Man with a Broken Nose* was accepted. The following year, appeared the *Age of Bronze* (Luxembourg), also known as the *Awaking of Man*. This figure raised a scandal among artists. Rodin was accused of exhibiting a figure actually cast from the model. In 1879, Rodin's statue of *St. John the Baptist* (Luxembourg) won a third prize medal at the Salon; and in 1880, the *Age of Bronze* reappeared cast in bronze, in the Salon. If the artist was now recognized as a master, he nevertheless gave rise to passionate discussions for many years. From 1879 to 1880, he worked for some months at the Sèvres factory. Then he produced his *Eve* (1881), and a magnificent series of busts: *J. P. Laurens* (1882); *Carrier-Belleuse* (1882); *Legros* (1883); *Victor Hugo* and *Dalou* (1884); *Antonin Proust* (1885); *Falquière* (1899); *Eugène Guillaume* (1904), etc. During this period he modelled the group of the *Burghers of Calais* (1889) for the town of Calais. This work was not generally understood. The movement of the figures, their expressions and their costumes were discussed; and, finally, the group was badly placed on a high pedestal and not at all as the artist intended it should be.

Rodin (Auguste).

Rodin: Monument of the Burghers of Calais.

The Claude Lorrain, in Nancy, aroused similar criticism (1898), but all these differences were as nothing compared with those to which his statue of Balzac gave rise. It suffered a storm of sarcasms. The committee of the "Société des Gens de Lettres" informed Rodin that by 11 votes to 4 the Society "did not recognise Balzac." Rodin, without disputing the matter, replied in writing to the newspapers: "Out of consideration to my dignity as an artist, I beg you to make known that I withdraw my statue from the Champ du Mars (the Salon), and that it shall be erected nowhere." But this caused a protest on the part of the younger men, artists and amateurs, who gave the artist all the sympathy and encouragement they could. This movement was led by an amateur, Monsieur Pellerin, who acquired the much discussed work.

Rodin: Bellona. (Musée Rodin.)

In the same year Rodin had exhibited the *Kiss* (Luxembourg), a work which the public accepted without a murmur, and which was acquired by the State. Other works of about this time were also bought for the Luxembourg: *Bust of a Woman, Thought*, the *Hand of God*—a huge hand in which are two small figures, representing humanity in the hand of the Creator. These official recognitions did not reassure public opinion, but Rodin did not trouble himself about it. He said: "If one's preoccupation were to please that million-headed monster, the public, one would soon lose one's personality and independence." And he continued to produce work which shocked most people. His statue of *The Thinker* was set up in front of the Panthéon, and the contorted figure aroused immediate protests.

During this active, disturbed life, Rodin passed an isolated existence. For ten years he lived at Sèvres; and then he settled in a small house in Meudon in the Val-Fleuri. But he worked in Paris, finally in the hôtel Biron (now converted into a museum of Rodin's works).

The movement created by Rodin was a revolt against official art. Rodin venerated antique art, but he admired it without slavish imitation, and retained his own individuality. He said: "The artist should have knowledge and patience. He should leave nothing to chance. Everything he does should be done willingly." To those who reproached him with breaking with tradition, he replied: "I am in the tradition.

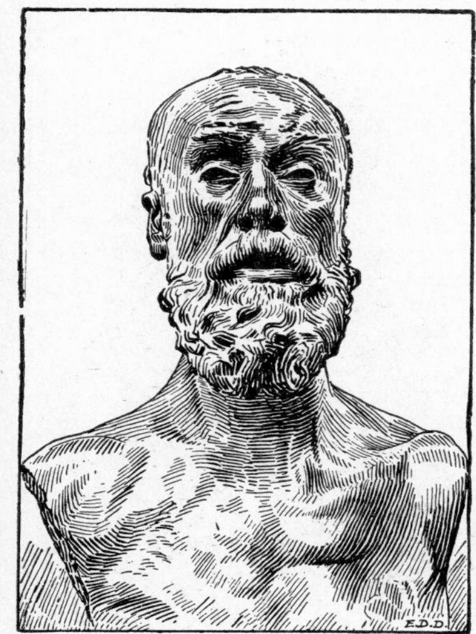

RODIN: J. P. LAURENS. (Musée du Luxembourg.)

It is the École des Beaux-Arts that has broken with it. I am in the tradition of the Primitives, of the Egyptians, of the Greeks and of the Romans. I have studied the sculpture of antiquity and of the Middle Ages, and I have gone to healthy and life-giving nature. I interpret nature as I see it, according to my temperament, and the feelings which it evokes in me. I have not striven to arrange it, or to apply laws of composition. I simply observe Nature, and seize upon her in the fulness of her life and harmony." An examination of the master's work proves the truth of his words. His *Bust of a Woman* (Luxembourg), the *Kiss*, or many other statues, prove that Rodin was capable of the utmost grace and deli-

RODIN: BUST OF A WOMAN. (Musée du Luxembourg.)

cacy when he wished. These contrast with the more "revolutionary" pieces, such as the *Burghers of Calais, Balzac, Le Penseur, L'Homme qui Marche* (Farnese Palace, Rome), and many other statues, which he was accused of leaving unfinished, incomplete and incomprehensible. Another group of work is comprised of those blocks of marble which are roughed out with the chisel so that a mask, or a limb, or a torso seems to be emerging out of the very block.

Rodin formed his works by planes of light and of shade. He used his thumb like a paint-brush for deepening a shadow, smoothing a light, or lengthening a half-tone. Thus, he has been called an Impressionist in sculpture. Rodin, like Delacroix, looked upon Nature as a dictionary, and art as the passionate exaggeration of Nature. In this, he is not only an Impressionist, he is also a Romantic. The proud, dreamy expression of *Balzac* dominates the heaviness of the body. The *Man of the Bronze Age*, and the *Thinker* express the effort of growth, and of thought. In his desire for emphasis Rodin is not hindered by laws of anatomy. One is reminded of Delacroix's reply to a friend who pointed out an error of construction: "I could easily correct it, but I should risk losing the expression, which is good."

Rodin's drawings are mostly studies for the Porte de l'Enfer, the project for the Musée des Arts Décoratifs, which was never completely realised, but for which he made a good many figures, such as *Le Penseur*, the *Kiss, Ugolino*, etc. The drawings are mostly summary sketches, expressing much in a few lines, and many of them have a wash of water-colour. Rodin also made a series of etchings of various subjects. Most of the artist's work is in the Musée Rodin, Paris. Finally, he wrote an important work on the French Cathedrals, illustrated with his own drawings.

See Pl. 52, Vol. II.

BIBLIOGRAPHY: L. Maillard, *Rodin*. Paris, 1898.—Judith Cladel, *Auguste Rodin, L'œuvre et l'homme*. Paris, 1908.—Coquiot, *Le Vrai Rodin*.

**ROGERS (John).**—American sculptor (1829-1904), exponent of a definitely realistic tendency and best known through his numerous little bronze or green clay groups of scenes from contemporary American life (including episodes from the Civil War) which have enjoyed a great popularity.

**— (Randolph).**—American sculptor (1825-1892), whose principal performance is the pair of bronze doors of the Rotunda of the Capitol, Washington. He is also the author of some statues of much popular fame (*Nydia, The Lost Pleiad,* etc.).

**ROMANESQUE ARCHITECTURE.**—The style which characterized most Western art between 1050 and 1200, roughly, persisting, during the last half-century of its existence, in the face of the rising tide of Gothic. The loose integration of the feudal society which produced Romanesque art resulted in great variation from country to country and section to section. Romanesque was a local synthesis, but there are international elements in the styles because of the Crusades, the pilgrimages, and the internationalism of the great monastic orders. Romanesque architecture was essentially monastic. The architecture is in general heavy and solid, and represents an attempt to transform the light and airy Early Christian basilica into a fireproof, vaulted structure with Roman weight and monumentality. The Romanesque churches of Italy, the most important center of the style next to France (including Norman England), remained closer to Early Christian architecture and, except for a pioneering group of churches in Lombardy and Piedmont, were largely unvaulted.

As an inclusive term Romanesque is sometimes used to refer to all Western European architecture between Early Christian and Gothic times. It then includes what is more generally styled pre-Romanesque, the crude and tiny buildings of Italy under the Lombards, Merovingian France, and Visigothic, Asturian, and Mozarabic Spain. The Carolingian period (c. 775-950) saw the revival of monumental architecture; and Carolingian architecture, with the important Ottonian (c. 950-1050) of Germany, led directly into the Romanesque. Señor Puig has distinguished an international style of architecture of about the same duration as Ottonian and interpenetrating with Ottonian. He calls it the First Romanesque style and derives it from Lombard architecture of the 9th and 10th centuries. Germany continued Ottonian architecture into the Romanesque period.

See Pls. 44, 45, Vol. I.

BIBLIOGRAPHY: A. W. Clapham. *Romanesque architecture in western Europe*. Oxford, 1936.—G. G. Dehio and G. v. Bezold. *Die kirchliche Baukunst des Abendlandes*. Stuttgart, 1892-1901.—R. C. Lasteyrie de Saillant. *L'architecture religieuse en France à l'époque romane*. Paris, 1912.—A. K. Porter. *Medieval architecture*. N. Y., 1909.—J. Puig y Cadafalch. *Le premier art roman*. Paris, 1928.

**— ENAMEL.**—See Pl. 30, Vol. II.

**— SCULPTURE.**—See Pl. 46, Vol. I; Pl. 2, Vol. II.

**ROMANINO (Girolamo).**—Painter of Brescia (1485/6-1566). With Moretto, one of the most important painters of this school. Like him, he was influenced by Savoldo and the Venetians.

His chief works include: *Virgin Enthroned with Six Saints* (the masterpiece of his youth, finished in 1511; in San Francisco of Brescia); *Madonna Enthroned* (1513), a *Last Supper* (both in Padua); and innumerable works in the galleries and churches of Brescia, Trent, Rome, Milan, Verona, and other cities of Italy and elsewhere.

BIBLIOGRAPHY: Crowe & Cavalcaselle. *History of Painting in North Italy*, ed. Borenius. Vol. III.

**ROMANTICISM.**—See Pl. 53, Vol. II.

**ROMBOUTS (Theodoor).**—Flemish painter, 1597-1637, sometimes erroneously called Roelands. Contemporary with Rubens, he travelled in Italy and then opened his shop in Antwerp. A prolific painter, he did many large conversation pieces reminiscent of the style of Rubens and Caravaggio. *Descent from the Cross* (St. Bavo, Ghent) and *The Five Senses* (Ghent. Mus.) are his most important works. His genre pieces and gravings are represented in most museums.

**ROME.**—*Note:* This article is arranged under three main headings:

A. Ancient Rome.

B. Early Christian and Mediæval Rome.

C. Renaissance Rome.

It should be understood that this arrangement is purely arbitrary; since under A, reference may be found, for instance, to Renaissance paintings adorning an ancient building. However, most of the buildings, etc., are mentioned in a rough chronological sequence.

(A) ANCIENT ROME.—The city which from the earliest times was called the "Eternal City," the capital of a vast empire, was founded by shepherds who came down from the Albanian hills. They settled on one of the seven hills, on which the City of Rome was afterwards built, and gave it the name of *Mount Palatine*, in honour of Pales, the god of shepherds. Of this primitive

ROME: AQUEDUCT OF CLAUDIUS.

period, excavations have brought to light tombs which date from about the 8th century B.C. (Museum of the Palazzo dei Conservatori), and terra cotta pottery and bronze rings of the same period.

On the Palatine Hill the oldest sanctuaries of "Roma quadrata" were built, the palaces of the patricians of the republic, and then those of the emperors. These build-

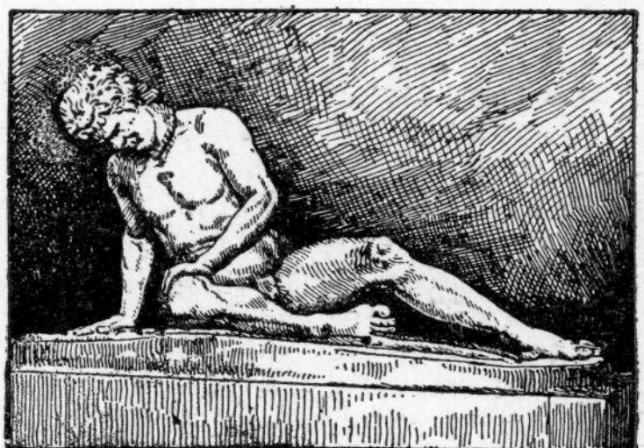

DYING GAUL. (Capitoline Museum, Rome.)

ings, covered in the Middle Ages, by gardens, convents, and fortresses, were brought to light by excavations in the 18th century. The work of excavating began seriously in 1870

ROME: COLUMN OF TRAJAN.

and has been steadily continued since that time. To the North of the hill some very old buildings were discovered. It was on this spot that the "tugurium Faustuli," preserved until the 4th century, stood. This "tugurium" is often identified with the house of Romulus. Under this house, excavations, undertaken in 1907, revealed stone walls and a tomb containing vases of the 5th century B.C. Next to it are the ruins of the *Temple of Jupiter Victor*, built by Fabius Maximus, about 295 B.C.; of the *Temple of Cybele* or of the *Magna Mater*, dedicated in 191 B.C. only the foundations, and some remains of columns are left. The *House of Livia* (covered with a modern roof) is composed of several parts, which open on to a square courtyard. Three of these rooms are decorated with mural paintings, representing *Io guarded by Argos, Galatea* and *Polyphemus*, scenes of sacrifices, landscapes, and garlands of fruit and flowers. The other rooms are not entirely cleared. The *Palace of Augustus* occupies a large part of the hill. The parts brought to light are the reception rooms and the throne room, with its apse in which the throne was found. In front of the palace of Augustus, stretches the *Stadium*. It was formerly surrounded by doors, with a portico. Some of its half-columns still remain.

At the other side of the Palatine are the ruins of the *Palace of Tiberius*, which was enlarged by Caligula, and then by Septimius Severus (only the plan remains), and the ruins of a temple of Apollo. All these buildings were supplied with

Rome: Ruins of the Clivus Victoriae on the Palatine Hill.

water by an immense aqueduct, the *Aqua Claudia* (built in the year 52 A.D. by the Emperor Claudius), the enormous arches of which stretch across the Roman compagna.

The *Capitol* hill, less extensive than that of the Palatine, was of still greater importance in the life of ancient Rome. According to the legend, the first buildings were erected by Romulus. In the year 509 B.C., which saw the birth of the Republic, the *Temple of Jupiter Capitolinus* was probably dedicated. It was burned down in 85 A.D.; rebuilt by Domitian, and destroyed in the 6th century. The Capitol also possesses a temple of Juno Moneta, on the site of which is built the Church of *Santa Maria in Aracœli*, a very old building, the date of which is unknown. Eighth century documents refer to it under the name of Santa Maria di Capitolio. The façade is unfinished. The interior is divided into three aisles by ancient granite columns; frescoes by Pintoricchio tell the story of San Bernardino of Siena, and there is a fresco by Benozzo Gozzoli representing St. Anthony of Padua; also magnificent tombs of the Savelli family (13th and 14th centuries).

The Piazza Aracœli is united to that of the Capitol by a great stairway, built in 1348. The Piazza of the Capitol was planned by Michel-

Rome: The Catacombs.

angelo, who also designed the façades of the three palaces and had an admirable *Equestrian Statue of Marcus Aurelius*, in bronze, placed in the centre.

The *Museum of the Capitol* has an incomparable collection of antique works.

Between the Palatine and the Capitol is a small valley which became the centre of the Roman world when it was occupied by the *Forum*, and covered with magnificent buildings, of which nothing is left but the ruins.

The Palatine is joined to the *Esquiline* hill by a slight elevation,

Rome: San Giorgio in Velabro.

the *Velia*, on which are several monuments—the *Arch of Titus*.

Maxentius built the basilica which bears the name of the *Basilica of Constantine*. Constantine, who vanquished Maxentius, had it rebuilt. The forum is dominated by its three enormous arches of barrel vaulting. Four colossal pillars divide the three aisles of this vast edifice. Near the Basilica are the remains of old Roman houses which bordered the Via Sacra (Sacred Way), in the time of Hadrian. Following the Via Sacra, one arrives at the site of the famous *Golden House* which Nero built for himself after the fire of Rome (64 A.D.), and where the most extravagant luxury abounded. It was destroyed after his death. The remains of the base of a colossal statue of Nero, which stood in the vestibule of the Golden House, may still be seen. The house possessed a superb park, in the middle of which was a lake. It was on the site of this lake that the Flavians were to build the greatest amphitheatre in the world, the *Colosseum* A.D. c. 70-82. On the site of the Golden House, they built also the *Baths of Titus* 80 A.D. To the south-west of the Colosseum is the *Arch of Constantine* 315 A.D.

Although the Forum of the Republic was the most important in Rome, it was not the only one. The emperors built several of them, and covered them with splendid buildings. The earliest was begun by Julius Cæsar and finished by Augustus. The latter built a new forum,

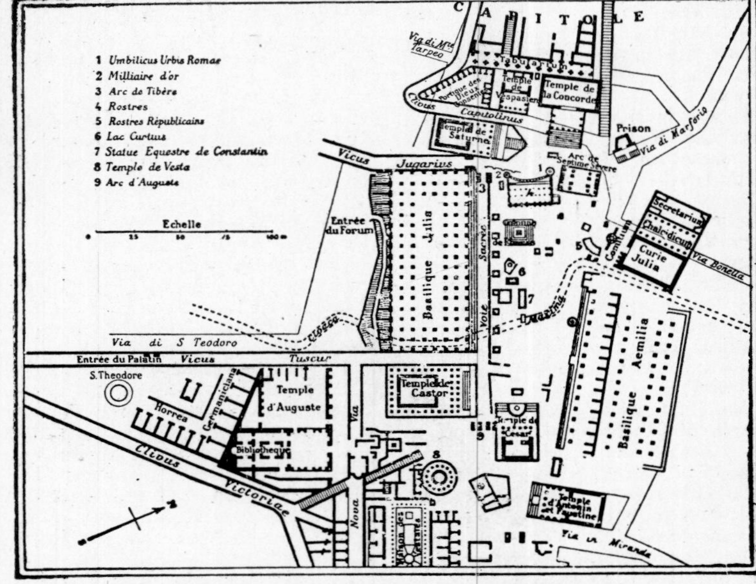


Rome: Plan of the Roman Forum under the Empire.

which contained the *Temple of Mars Ultor*. The Roman fora were neglected by the successors of Augustus. It was Vespasian who resumed work on them, and built a new forum. Domitian united the Forum of Vespasian to that of Augustus, thus forming the *Forum transitorium* (of passage), also known as the *Forum de Nerva* 98 A.D.

The vast *Forum of Trajan* contained the most sumptuous buildings. The story goes that Pope Gregory the Great, having greatly admired them, was full of grief at the thought that this good and generous monarch must be damned, because he was a pagan; and, by his

Rome: The Appian Way, Tomb of Cecilia Metella.

prayers he won the deliverance of Trajan's soul. The famous *Trajan Column* is the best preserved monument of ancient Rome 112 A.D. It is decorated with a series of bas-reliefs in a spiral formation around the column.

On the other side of the Palatine is the *forum boarium*, or beef market. Between the Aventine and the Tiber is the *Temple of Vesta*, a small circular building, with Corinthian columns (roof modern).

The Romans were not content to build on the Forum, the Palatine, the Aventine and the Caelius. No doubt these quarters, which form the south of the town, possess the greatest number of ancient buildings, but the rest of the town also possesses many. One of the oldest is the *Tomb of Scipio*. Most of the ancient tombs are found along the Via Appia, or the roads leading from Rome to the outskirts of the city.

The *Theatre of Marcellus*, begun by Cæsar, was finished by Augustus.

The famous *Pantheon* of Agrippa, was built under Augustus, by his son-in-law, Agrippa. Behind this splendid building are the *Baths of Agrippa*, now in ruins. Augustus built eighty-two temples. It might truly be said that when he died he left behind him a city of marble, in place of the city of brick which he had found.

Hadrian built, for himself and his successors, a colossal *Mausoleum*, and a bridge, the *Pons Aelius*, now the Bridge of Sant'Angelo (134), to connect his Mausoleum with the city. The statues which adorn the bridge date from the 15th and 17th centuries (ten statues of angels from

Rome: On the Palatine.

designs by Bernini). The *Baths of Caracalla* contained great halls—the frigidarium (for cold baths), the tepidarium (for warm baths) and the caldarium (for steam baths). The *Baths of Diocletian* were still larger. The tradition is that they were built by Christians condemned to death. An early church was built there (5th century); then a second, *Santa Maria dei Angeli* (by Michelangelo, in the 16th century). The old Baths now house a magnificent collection of sculpture (the *Thermae Museum*).

Bibliography: Giuseppe Lugli, *The Classical Monuments of Rome and its Vicinity*. Rome, 1929.—Platner and Ashby, *A Topographical*

*Dictionary of Ancient Rome*. London, 1929.

(B) EARLY CHRISTIAN AND MEDIÆVAL ROME.—With the reign of Constantine, a new era began for Rome. Christianity became the state religion; and Constantine moved his residence to Constantinople.

After the Edict of 313, which placed the Christian religion on the same rank as the pagan religions, the first Christian churches were built. The *Catacombs* had existed from the 1st century of our era. There the early Christians buried their dead, and perhaps worshipped in secret.

It was in the age of Constantine that the Early Christian style of art seems definitely to have been formulated. Unfortunately, there is left not one original Constantinian basilica in Rome. We know 4th century Roman basilicas only by their plans.

*Old St. Peter's*, destroyed to make way for the present cathedral, was built in 330. It was a huge five-aisled basilica with a slightly projecting bema and was preceded by a narthex and atrium.

*Sta. Costanza* (c. 337) is a round church of Constantinian vintage. It has a heavy dome carried on a colonnade of paired columns. The annular aisle retains much of the original vault mosaic. The building may be considered a translation of a basilica into a centralized type of building. Sta. Costanza was remodeled in the 13th century.

The *Baptistery of S. Giovanni in Laterano* (330), another Constantinian structure, is also round, and, therefore represents the central type of building as opposed to the basilican. The central type was preferred for baptisteries.

*S. Clemente*, a small basilica, was built in 385 and rebuilt 1085.

*S. Paolo f.l.m.* (386) was a great five-aisled structure. The present basilica is a 19th century reconstruction after a disastrous fire.

*Sta. Sabina* (425-35) is a small and well preserved basilica.

*Sta. Maria Maggiore* (431) is a great three-aisled basilica with a flat classical entablature instead of arches above the columns.

*S. Lorenzo f.l.m.* consists of two basilicas originally with conjoined apses which were, in the 13th century, thrown into one church. The earlier and easternmost church is now the choir. It was built in 432. The western church was built in 578.

*S. Stefano Rotondo* (468-482) is a huge round church covered by a timber roof.

*Sant'Agnese f.l.m.* (625-38) shows Byzantine influence in having aisles in two storeys and columns with pulvin blocks above the capitols.

Many of the early Christian churches contain beautiful mosaics, especially in their apses, and remains of frescoes. The columns and capitals used in their construction, were often taken from the ruins of ancient buildings.

During the Middle Ages Rome suffered much from invasions of barbarians. Decimated by war, the plague, poverty, and surrounded by an unhealthy campagna, crowds of Romans left the city which had in the days of its glory controlled the world. However, a power was growing which was to save the city and restore it to new prestige. The Eternal City, after being the capital of the Roman Empire, became the centre of Christendom. In the domain of the arts, the Popes were the successors of the Emperors.

In 476, the Roman Empire, already divided in 395, ceased to exist in the west. From the 5th century, the Popes built churches, convents, towers and fortresses, for they had to struggle constantly against the nobles, the peoples, and neighbouring states. It was a period of trouble and vandalism. Magnificent ancient buildings were despoiled of their treasures, destroyed, transformed. Their columns and sculptured friezes were used to adorn new buildings. Many of these were destroyed or transformed in their turn.

*Santa Maria in Trastevere* was rebuilt in 1140. The portico dates from 1702. The building was restored in 1866. On the façade are some 12th century mosaics. One of the *Annunciations* on the portico is attributed to Pietro Cavallini. The mosaics in the apse are also attributed to him.

Most medieval building in Rome consisted of modification of already existing structures. The only Gothic church in Rome is *Santa Maria sopra Minerva*.

During the greater part of the 14th century (1309-1377) the Popes transferred the seat of the Papacy to Avignon, to escape the incessant warfare between the Guelphs and Ghibellines. The city knew the greatest distress, and was deserted by a great part of the population. Prosperity returned with the Popes in 1377.

(C) RENAISSANCE AND MODERN ROME.—In the 15th century, under Popes Nicholas V, Sixtus IV and Alexander VI, churches were built, and palaces richly decorated. The *Church of St. Peter* was begun in 1450. *Santa Maria della Pace* was built in 1484. The interior is decorated with fine paintings by Raphael, representing Sibyls (1514) *Santa Trinità de' Monti* was built in 1495, by the French king, Charles VIII. Splendid palaces were erected. The *Vatican* (see this word) is the most remarkable.

The 16th century saw the magnificent flowering of the Italian Renaissance. It is the period of Michelangelo, Raphael, Bramante, and a host of artists who, under the patronage of Popes Julius II, Leo X and Sixtus V, enriched Rome with artistic treasures. The city suffered dreadful ravages in 1527, when Rome was sacked by the troops of Charles V, who pillaged all they could. But the damage was repaired. Churches and palaces were built, and enriched with sumptuous decorations.

BIBLIOGRAPHY: A. L. Frothingham, *Monuments of Christian Rome from Constantine to the Renaissance*. New York, 1925.

*Il Tempietto, S. Pietro in Montorio* (1501-03). See Bramante.

*S. Pietro*. See Saint Peter's.

*Palazzo Cancellaria* (c. 1495). See Bramante.

*Court of the Vatican* (1506). See Bramante.

*Palazzo Farnese* (1514-46) Begun by the younger Antonio da San Gallo and finished by Michelangelo. Inside is a magnificent court with heavy arcades on piers with applied columns. Frescoes by Agostino and Annibale Carracci decorate the first floor. The exterior is developed from the 15th century Florentine type of palace but now has quoins at the corners and tabernacle windows, which alternate curved and triangular pediments, in addition to the great cornice.

*Palazzo Farnesina* (1515) is by Peruzzi. It has a central arcaded loggia and two wing pavilions. The frieze has windows. Inside is a cycle of paintings by Raphael (*The Story of Psyche*). Also known as the Palazzo Chigi.

*Palazzo Massimi* (c. 1531) Also by Peruzzi, it shows Bramantesque refinement in the court, which is trabeated instead of arcuated.

*Campodoglio Group* (1538-92) By Michelangelo. Three buildings, the "Palazzo dei Conservatori," the "Palazzo del Senatore," and the "Museo Capitolino" are arranged in a rhomboidal plan about an open piazza. The nervous architecture prophesies the Baroque.

*Villa di Papa Giulio* (1550) By Vignola. The palace has a semi-circular open court about which curves the rear façade. The garden architecture is notable.

The later 16th and the 17th centuries saw a great decoration of Rome with grandiose Baroque churches and palaces. St. Peter's was finished in the Baroque style by Della Porta, Maderna, Bernini and Vannitelli.

*The Gesù* was begun by Vignola in the Mannerist style in 1568 and finished by Della Porta in the Baroque, 1573-80. The turbulent Baroque façade, with the nave and aisle divisions united by consoles, was influential in spreading the Jesuit style all over the Catholic world. The Gesù is the mother church of the Jesuits.

*S. Carlo alle Quattro Fontane* (1638-1665) A magnificent swirling baroque church cleverly composed on a corner. Borromini was the architect. The church is curvilinear in plan as well as in elevation, and seems to change in appearance as the observer shifts his vantage point.

*Sant' Agnese* (1645-50) By Borromini and Rainaldi.

*S. Maria in Campitelli* (1659) By Rainaldi.

*S. Giovanni in Laterano, façade* (1734) By Galililei. Here the Baroque calms down and approaches the neo-classic. The façade has a pediment carried on a huge paired colossal order.

*S. Maria Maggiore, façade* (1743) By Fuga. Here also can be seen the relaxation of the Baroque.

*Palazzo Barberini* (1630) Begun by Maderna, finished by Bernini and Borromini.

*Palazzo Spada*. Remodelling by Borromini 1632.

*Palazzo Pamphili* (1650) By Rainaldi.

*Palazzo Corsini* (1732-1735) by Fuga, in the relaxed Baroque style.

*Villa Albani* (1760) By Marchionne and Winckelmann, in the neo-classic style.

*Monument of Vittore Emmanuele* (1884-1929) By Sacconi. A huge monument, consisting of a great colonnade and steps, in a conglomerate style reminiscent of both the classical and the Baroque.

See Pls. 28, 29, 30, 32, Vol. I; Pl. 7, Vol. II.

BIBLIOGRAPHY: E. Bertaux, *Rome*, 3 vols.—Homo. *Rome antique*. 1921 A.D.—Tani, *Chiese di Roma*. Turin, 1922.

**ROMNEY (George).**— English painter, born at Dalton-in-Furness, in 1734. Died in 1802. In 1762 he went to London, leaving his wife and two children. Then in 1773 he went to Italy, where he stayed for two years. On his return to London, he shared the public favour with Reynolds and Gainsborough, and built himself a studio in Hampstead, which is now part of the local Conservative Club. In 1799, he returned to Kendal, where three years later he died in the arms of his wife whom he had left for fourteen years.

As a portrait painter, Romney had the gift of idealising his sitters without losing the likeness. Celebrated beauties, court ladies and actresses sat for him, and he represented them in many allegorical pictures, such as were made fashionable by Reynolds. Thus he painted the famous Lady Hamilton as Joan of Arc, as a Bacchante and in many other guises.

ROMNEY: MISTRESS MARK CURRIE. (National Gallery, London.)

The National Portrait Gallery (London) possesses a fine Self-Portrait of the artist; and his lovely portrait of Perdita Robinson is in the Wallace Collection.

See Pl. 48, Vol. II.

BIBLIOGRAPHY: T. H. Ward and W. Roberts. *Romney*, London, 1904.

**RONDINELLO (Niccolò),** of Ravenna. Painter of the Venetian school of the end of the 15th century. Pupil of Giovanni Bellini.

**ROOD.**—A cross or crucifix. In mediæval churches it is usually the large crucifix at the entrance to the chancel, often supported on a beam or screen.

**ROOS (Johann, Heinrich).**—German painter and graver, 1631-1685. After studying in Holland and Italy, he settled in Frankfurt a.M. and became court painter in 1673. Especially a portrait painter, he was also known for his Italian landscapes, gypsy camp scenes and animal pictures.

**ROPS (Félicien).**—Belgian painter and engraver. Strongly influenced by Gavarni and Daumier, his extensive output centered around political and social satire. He was a regular contributor to "Uylenspiegel" and the "Charivari belge." Experimented with, and developed every technique of the graver and etcher; he also worked with heliography. Most of his works are in French private collections.

BIBLIOGRAPHY: Péladan, *F.R.*, 1885. Lemonier, *F.R., l'homme et l'art* 1908.

**ROQUEPLAN (Camille Joseph Etienne).**—French painter and lithographer, 1802-1855. He chose pretty women for his models, and rejoiced in effects of light, and the beauty of materials. His little landscapes and seascapes, and "genre" pictures have no other aim than to give pleasure.

**ROSA (Salvator).** — Neapolitan painter, 1615-1673. Pupil of Ribera. He excelled in painting tempestuous landscapes, revelling in dark clouds with silvery gleams, and dishevelled trees. His paintings may

Rosa (Salvator).

be seen in the Corsini and Colonna Palaces (Rome); in the Uffizi and Pitti galleries (Florence), and in many European galleries, especially in England.

Bibliography: L. Ozzolo, *Vita e opere di Salvator Rosa*. Strasbourg, 1908.

**ROSALES (Eduardo).**—Spanish painter, 1837-1873.

**ROSLIN (Alexandre Charles).**—Swedish portrait painter, 1718-1793. After staying for ten years in Germany and Italy, he went to France in 1752. His success in the reign of Louis XVI equalled that of Madame Vigée Lebrun and Madame Labille-Guyard. His treatment of materials is especially noteworthy.

**ROSSELLI (Cosimo).**—Florentine painter, born 1439 in Florence; died 1507. In 1453, Cosimo was a pupil of Neri di Bicci; in 1456 he left that master, perhaps became the pupil of Benozzo Gozzoli. His earliest dated work is of 1471, the *St. Anne Enthroned* in Berlin. In 1482 he worked with Botticelli, Ghirlandaio, and Perugino in Rome in the Sistine Chapel, which was consecrated in 1483. In 1485 he works in Sant' Ambrogio, Florence; in 1491 is a member of a commission to decide on the restoration of the façade of the Duomo; in 1496 estimates Baldovinetti's fresco in Sta. Trinità; and in 1497 is appointed executor for the will of his friend Benedetto da Maiano. In 1506 he makes his own will, and he dies in 1507.

Among Cosimo's dated works are: the fresco of St. Filippo Benizzi in the Cloister of the SS. Annunziata, of 1476; the Sto. Spirito *Madonna* of 1482; the Academy *Madonna* of 1492; the *Madonna in Glory* in Sant' Ambrogio of 1498; the *Coronation of the Virgin* in Sta. Maria Maddalena dei Pazzi of 1505. All these works are in Florence.

He was the master of Piero di Cosimo.

Bibliography: Vasari-Milanesi, III.—Gaye, *Carteggio,* II.—F. Knapp. *Piero di Cosimo,* 1897.—G. Gronau, *Über die frühere Tätigkeit des Cosimo Rosselli*, Repert. f. Kunstwiss., 1897.—Van Marle, *Italian Schools, etc.*, XI, 1929.

**ROSSELLINO (Antonio).**—Florentine sculptor, 1427-1479. Pupil of his brother Bernardo, with whom he worked at the beginning of his activity.

One of his most important works is the Tomb of the Cardinal of Portugal (d. 1459), in San Miniato, which shows considerable skill in composition and modelling. The tomb of Maria of Aragon (d. 1460), in the church of Monte Oliveto, at Naples, is of similar design (this tomb was completed after Antonio's death, by Benedetto da Majano).

Rossellino: Monument of the Cardinal of Portugal. (Detail.) (San Miniato, Florence.)

The other principal works by Antonio Rossellino include: the tomb of Filippo Lazzari for San Domenico of Pistoia (1467); three bas-reliefs on Mino da Fiesole's pulpit, at Prato (1473); the *Madonna del Latte*, a relief over the tomb of Francesco Nori (d. 1478); in Santa Croce, the portrait bust of Matteo

Rossellino: Saint Sebastian. (Empoli.)

Palimeri (Museo Nazionale, Florence); and many others.

See Pl. 9, Vol. II.

**— (Bernardo).**—Florentine architect and sculptor, 1409-1464. Master of Antonio Rossellino, his brother, who was 18 years younger than he. His sculptural masterpiece is the *Tomb of Leonardo Bruni* (d. 1444), in Santa Croce, Florence. Among Bernardo's other works are: the high-relief of the *Annunciation*, in Santo Stefano, Empoli (1447); the *Tomb of the Beata Villana*, a fourteenth-century saint, in Santa Maria Novella (1451); the tomb of Filippo Lazzari (d. 1462) in San Domenico, at Pistoia (finished by his brother, after his death). He designed a group of buildings in Pienza for the Piccolomini family and did much work in Siena. His architectural activity was wide and included the building of the Palazzo Rucellai (c. 1451) after Alberti's designs.

**ROSSELLO di JACOPO FRANCHI.** — Florentine painter, 1376-1457; follower of Lorenzo Monaco. There is by him a *Madonna and Saints*; a *Coronation* (1420), an *Annunciation*, in the Accademia of Florence; and a picture of 1439, in the Siena Magazine.

**ROSSETTI (Biagio).**—Architect of Ferrara (15th and beginning of the 16th centuries) where he worked.

**— (Dante Gabriel).** — English painter, 1828-1882. Born in London; but he was of Italian origin, and he retained characteristics of the Latin race.

When quite young he became a devotee of the mysticism of Dante, whose work he knew by heart. At the age of 18, he entered the Royal Academy schools, and studied under Madox Brown, who was not much older than himself. In 1849, when he exhibited his first picture, he had already published numerous poems. After his painting, *Ecce Ancilla Domini* (Tate Gallery, London), Rossetti exhibited only once in public, in 1856. He worked only for his friends, and "his friends' friends." In 1850 he became acquainted with Miss Eleanor Siddal, a young dressmaker. "She was tall and slim," said Arthur Hughes, "with copper-red hair, and the too bright complexion of the consumptive. She had the unnatural simplicity and purity of aspect which Rossetti has so well noted in the drawings he has made of her." They did not marry until 1860, and it was during this ten years that Rossetti painted his best works: *Beata Beatrix, Monna Vanna, Venus Vesticordia, Lady Lilith,* and *The Belovèd.* Two years after their marriage, Eleanor died. In his intense grief, Rossetti placed in her coffin a whole volume of poems, in manuscript, for which his well-beloved had inspired him. Seven years later, urged by his friends, he had the tomb opened, and recovered the poems, which were published in 1870. In 1881, he published a second volume of poems. In 1882, he died after an attack of paralysis.

Although Dante Gabriel Rossetti was the soul of the young movement, his temperament differed entirely from that of Millais and Holman Hunt who, with him, founded the "Pre-Raphaelite Brotherhood," in 1848. In spite of their romantic subjects, the early works of Hunt and Millais are always obvious; whereas Rossetti was already a dreamy mystic, and his apparent simplicity has subtlety, and even

Rossetti: Beata Beatrix. (Tate Gallery, London.)

something of affectation, behind it; but Rossetti was the true innovator of lyrical painting.

These distinctions only became more decided, and, from about 1858, Rossetti fell away from his comrades, for Brown, Hunt and especially Millais tended more and more to choose realistic subjects, which allowed them to copy nature. About 1868, Rossetti accepted the offer to execute, in Oxford, mural paintings, drawn from the Legends of Arthur. He was assisted by students, especially by Burne-Jones, whom he brought back to London with him. These two friends became the most famous representatives of that idealist school in which the purity and grace of early Italian art was allied to the Romanticism of early English poetry. After two or three Biblical subjects, Rossetti gave himself up to painting purely imaginative and romantic subjects, often inspired by the work of Dante, such as: *Giotto Painting Dante's Portrait, The Greeting of Beatrice,* and *Dante's Dream* (1870), which is his finest work.

*Proserpine, Fiammetta, The Dreamer, Le Ghirlandate* are isolated figures, painted in memory of his wife, who continued to inspire his paintings and poems. She always appeared to him sublimely beautiful, clad in rich Venetian dress, and surrounded by roses and lilies. Rossetti's drawing and anatomical knowledge leave much to be desired. He borrowed much from poetry; and the artist's work cannot be fully understood unless one is also acquainted with his poetry.

See Pl. 58, Vol. II.

Bibliography: H. C. Marillier. *Rossetti.* London, 1901.

**ROSSO (Giovanni Battista dei Rossi, called "Il" or "Rosso Fiorentino").**—Florentine painter (1494-1540). He painted first in Florence; then went to Rome, whence he fled after the sack of that city. In 1531, he was called to France by Francis I to decorate the Château of Fontainebleau. He, Primaticcio, and many of their compatriots, together with French artists, formed the famous School of Fontainebleau (not to be confused with that of the landscape painters in the 19th century) which worked largely in the Château.

Rosso excelled in painting large mythological scenes, and allegories. His frescoes at Fontainebleau are still to be seen in the Salle François Premier. The paintings have been much retouched. Rosso is best represented at the Uffizi.

The Louvre possesses two canvases by Rosso—a *Pietà*, rather devoid of feeling, and the *Pierides*. Both are the work of a draughtsman who had given much attention to the study of Michelangelo's drawings. Rosso was a pupil of Andrea del Sarto.

**ROTTENHAMMER (Johan).**—German painter, 1564-1625. Active in Rome until about 1595. 1596-1606 in Venice, influenced by Tintoretto's frescoes in S. Rocco, and by Veronese. Friend of Palma Giovane, and several Italian dukes. Latter part of life spent in Augsburg. He was the painter of numerous mythological and religious pictures. His style is mannered, and influenced by Italian cinquecento painting; besides many predelle, he painted frescoes for chapels as well as for ducal palaces.

**ROUAULT (Georges).**—Contemporary French painter. Georges Rouault was born in Paris 27th May 1871. He was the son of a Parisian mother and a Breton ivory worker. While still a child his maternal grandfather, a patron of the arts, paid particular attention to him and saw to it that he should develop a liking for pictures. He was still a young boy when he became apprentice to a stained-glass painter, and, showing unusual ability in handling the brush, he was sent to the École Supérieur des Beaux-Arts to study with Gustave Moreau. The talented youth soon became the favourite of his master, who urged him to compete for the Prix de Rome at the age of eighteen, but he failed; however, in 1894 he received the Prix Chenavard for his *Enfant Jesus Chez les Docteurs*, later on winning a bronze medal for the same work at the Exposition Universelle. He exhibited at the Salons d'Automne and in 1924 at Druet's. His most fruitful period was between 1905 and 1913. At the present he is conservateur of the Musée Gustave Moreau; he is married and has four children. Rouault is not only one of the most versatile of contemporary French artists, but he is one of the innovators, and a master without actual pupils. His media include oil, watercolour, pastel, sepia, gouache; he also does etchings, lithographs and ceramics. Rouault also writes forceful prose and lyric poetry imbued with stoic philosophy. Among the many books which he illustrated are *Ubi Roi, Danse Macabre, Les Fleurs de Mal, Ubu aux Colonies,* and his own *Miserere et Guerre*. He paints clowns, judges, nudes and religious figures for the most part, his themes always carrying the spirit of vice, desolation and death, expressing his religious hatred of this world and his grief for mankind. The intensely tragic tone combined with romanticism, and the total absence of satire or moral implications put Rouault in a class all by himself, although some have compared him to Jerome Bosch. His technique is equally original; he uses clear blues and reds with audacious strokes of black edges; he strives for plastic expression. Ambroise Vollard is his promoter.

Bibliography: Georges Charensol, *Georges Rouault,* 1926.—Charles Terrasse, *Georges Rouault, Art d'Aujourd'hui,* 1928.—Michel Puy, *Georges Rouault et Son Œuvre,* 1921.

**ROUBLEW (André)**.—Russian monk (1370?-about 1430), painter of icons. His frescoes in Moscow and Vladimir are so much restored that it is difficult to see his hand in them. His chief remaining work represents the *Trinity* (Monastery of the Trinity St. Serge, near Moscow).

**ROUEN (France)**.—Rouen has many interesting old churches.

The *Cathedral of Notre Dame* is a fine 13th century Gothic building; the Flamboyant façade dates from the 16th century. This façade is flanked by two towers of unequal proportions. The tower on the left is comparatively plain; that on the right, much more ornate, is known as the Butter Tower (Tour de Beurre), because it was built with the money of the faithful who paid for permission to use butter during Lent. The Cathedral shelters many interesting tombs, among them that of Richard Cœur de Lion's heart.

The *Church of St. Ouen*, 1318-1339, is even larger than the Cathedral.

*St. Maclou* is a little gem of the flamboyant Gothic style (begun, 1432; finished 1520). The façade is a lace work of stone. The interior with its light vaulting, its lantern and slender pillars, is very graceful. See Pl. 50, Vol. I.

The *Palais de Justice*—15th and 16th centuries—has been recently restored. It is one of the finest civil Gothic buildings in France. The central block is wonderfully decorated. The left wing contains the vast hall of the Pas-Perdus, with its timbered ceiling. The right wing is modern. See Pl. 52, Vol. I.

Rouen: The Cathedral.

Rouen: Portail de la Calende.

The *Hôtel Bourgthéroulde* is an interesting 15th century building. The most curious part is that which opens on to the courtyard.

Rouen: The Grosse Horloge.

The *Tour de la Grosse Horloge* dates from 1385.

The memory of Jeanne d'Arc, whose deeds and suffering shed lustre on the town, is felt everywhere in Rouen, though no old work of art remains to recall them.

**ROUSSEAU (Henri Julien)**.—French painter (1844-1910), pseudonym *Le Douanier*. Rousseau was born at Laval 21st May 1844. He received a general education but no art training whatsoever. During the Mexican War (1861-1867) he became an army musician; during the Franco-German War in 1870-1871 he served in the capacity of sergeant. Later on he settled in Paris, earning his livelihood as a customs officer, hence his pseudonym Le Douanier. It was in 1880 that he first began to paint merely for pleasure and self-expression. He opened a stationery store, where among other items he sold his own works of art. His naïve paintings drew the attention of his famous contemporaries and he was first hailed in 1888 by Odilon Redon and Gustave Coquiot; he was accepted in the circles of Remy de Gourmont and A. Jarry; the poet Apollinaire was also among his friends. Rousseau opened a school in Paris where he taught painting, music, dramatics and diction. He exhibited from 1886 to 1910 at the Salons des Indépendants; in 1905 and 1907 at the Salons d'Automne; in 1912 at Bernheim-Jeune, and had memorial shows in 1926 and 1933. He died in Paris 9th September 1910. A simple bourgeois, Rousseau painted for the sheer love of it. Not having had any art training he went back to nature, working without the critical and methodical restraint of his Impressionist and Cubist contemporaries. He was one of the few who saved the actual object for painting, restoring to the tactile elements all their former prestige. He painted landscapes, jungle scenes, animals and portraits in a genial, unsophisticated way delighting in fine, decorative detail and employing refreshing local colours. His shapes are primitive and he never outgrew the stage of *frontality*. He is classical in a popular way. Rousseau is represented in the museums of Prague, Moscow, Frankfort, the Louvre, and the Luxembourg as well as in several famous private collections.

Bibliography: Roch Grey, *Henri Rousseau,* Les Artistes Nouveaux, ser. 1, 1924.—Philippe Soupault, *Henri Rousseau,* 1927.—William Uhde, *Henri Rousseau,* 1914.

— **(Jacques)**.—French painter, architect and engraver, 1630-1693 (died in London). He worked for Versailles, Saint Cloud and Saint Germain. In 1690, he went to London to collaborate with La Fosse and Monnoyer in the decoration of Montague House (now the *British Museum*), and he furnished the plans for part of the building. He made 19 etchings, which have become very rare.

Rousseau (Théodore).

Rousseau (Th.): The Hut of the Charcoal Burners. (Gould Collection.)

— **(Théodore)**.—French painter (Paris, 1812-Barbizon, 1867). A visit to a Jura forest when he was quite a boy, decided Rousseau's vocation as a landscape painter.

Rousseau (Th.): The Pool.

When he was not yet nineteen, he exhibited at the Salon a view of "a valley enclosed by the Cantal mountains, with a ruined bridge over a stream." The gorges and steep places of the Auvergne, its rocky and strange formations, provided the artist with romantic subjects, and he was strongly influenced by scenery.

Rousseau studied landscape with La Berge, on the outskirts of Paris, but he soon thirsted for wider horizons, and wearied of his master's minute observations.

Following the Salon of 1833 (at which he exhibited a painting)

Rousseau became acquainted with the wildest parts of the forest of Fontainebleau. At the following Salon (1834) it was not, however, his picture of the forest that was accepted, but the *Edge of a Wood in the Forest of Compiègne*, which gained a third class medal. The following year, his picture of *Cows descending from the Jura* (The Hague—Mesdag Museum) was rejected. A rejection by the Salon was then a serious matter for an artist. Public favour dropped away from Rousseau, and he ceased to sell his pictures. He found ease from his troubles in the great forest of Fontainebleau; and in 1835, he took "pension" at Barbizon with the famous "père Ganne" who had Diaz and d'Aligny among his guests.

Two years later, saddened by his mother's death, he accepted the invitation of the young landscape painter, Charles Leroux, to join him at Vendée, to study the sleeping waters of the Loire. Later, he visited the Landes. Finally he returned to Barbizon; and his work came to be in great demand. Rousseau became more and more attracted to unambitious landscape, loving, above all, the old oaks of the forest of Fontainebleau. All his works show a grave, almost a religious, application. In his passionate desire for exactitude, he seized upon too many small details—when he painted a tree, he endeavoured to explain it—to show its age, the grain of the wood, the gnarled branches, the dense foliage. He was more intent on getting "likeness," that is, stating permanent characteristics, than on exploring effects of light, or even of telling us the season. The influence of Ruysdaël and Hobbema is evident.

Rousseau's pictures are to be found in many galleries—notably in the Louvre and in the Wallace Collection.

See Pl. 55, Vol. II.

BIBLIOGRAPHY: E. Michel, *Les Maîtres du paysage*. Paris, 1906.—P. Dorbec, *Théodore Rousseau*. Paris, 1911.

**ROWLANDSON (Thomas).** — English draughtsman and engraver, 1756-1827. He drew chiefly caricatures and political satires, lively in execution.

**ROYAT (Puy-de-Dôme, France).** —Royat possesses a very curious fortified church—Romanesque, 11th century.

**ROYMERSWALEN (or Roemerswaelen, Marinus Claeszoon).**—Flemish painter, born about 1497, died after 1567. Painted exclusively life-sized half-figures, the elongated and bony limbs recalling Martin Schongauer. Many of his works have been wrongly attributed to Quentin Matsys, whom the artist copied. Clean-shaven faces and fantastic costumes are characteristic of his work. Vasari mentions him, as he was widely known in Italy and Spain.

BIBLIOGRAPHY: H. Hymans, *Martin de Zélandais*, Bulletin de l'Academie royale de Belgique, 1844.—A. Michel, *Histoire de l'art*, Vol. V., p. 295.

**RUBENS (Peter Paul).**—Flemish painter. Born June 28, 1577 in Siegen, Westphalia, where his family was in exile. Lived in Cologne from 1578 to 1589, then moved to Antwerp. He attended Latin school, was a court page, and finally apprenticed with three rather unimportant masters: Tobias Verhaecht, Adam van Noort and Otto Vaenius. In 1600 he went to Florence, Rome and Mantua; in 1603 he was in Spain; later alternately in Genoa, Mantua, and Rome, 1606-08. In 1608 he returned to Antwerp and became court painter. In the same year he married Isabella Brant. He established his studio and had a large number of pupils. Between 1620 and 1625 he received a number of commissions for the French court. After the death of his wife in 1626

RUBENS: HELENA FOURMENT, RUBENS AND THEIR SON. (Collection of Baron A. de Rothschild.)

Rubens entered the diplomatic service and made several trips to England and Spain. In 1630 he married Helena Fourment, with whom he had five children. He had had three with his previous marriage. Rubens spent his later years at his castle Steen near Brussels where he died in 1640 from gout.

Rubens' activity may be divided into five general periods as follows: 1600-08, period of study; 1609-1614, establishment of workshop and formation of individual style; 1615-22, period of full mastership and demonstration of artistic self-confidence; 1622-32, transition from plastic to pictorial style, execution of large, international commissions; 1632-40, late period, creations of greatest dissolution of tactile values in favor of coloristic lightness and fluency.

The comparison of an early work, *Venus, Bacchus and Ceres*, 1613 with a late work, *Three Graces* (late 30's, Prado), shows the general trend of his development from sculptural, isolated bodies in statuary poses, with simple unbroken outline and either vague or strained expressions, towards figures in transitory, loosened and rhythmical movement, with delicate modelling of surface, sensitive outlines, and differentiated and animated expression. In his later works groups are formed by common impulse, and these groups are bound together with movement which is carried on in, or taken up by, their environment. In early works the environment is hardly more than a casual foil. Coloristically there is a development from strong contrasts of dark and light colors of unbroken simplicity (in flesh tints a schematic use of bluish shadows and rosy reflections of light), to a lightness and subtler variety of color (in flesh tints a mother-of-pearl effect in carnation red). While in Italy, Rubens studied the paintings of the great masters as well as the monuments of classical antiquity. There are many extant copies, the selection of which was probably due to commissions. The first large commission he received was three paintings for *Santa Croce in Gerusalemme* (now in Grasse, France), from the Archduke Albert. To his early group belong the *St. Helena with Cross, Raising of Cross, Crowning with Thorns*, 1602, which are characterized by conventional expression and awkward overcrowded composition; the strong chiaroscuro is probably due to Caravaggesque prototypes. In 1603, while in Spain, Rubens did a series of *Twelve Apostles and Christ* for the Duke of Lerma; these half-

RUBENS: HELENA FOURMENT IN HER WEDDING GOWN. (Pinakothek, Munich.)

length figures show the development towards a more dignified gesticulation and individual characterization. *Trinity*, 1604-05, painted for the Jesuit Church in Mantua, was unfortunately cut up in 1797; two big fragments have been preserved in the Palazzo Ducale, Mantua, other pieces are in Vienna and elsewhere. It is most interesting to note in these fragments the influence of Veronese, as merged with the compositional patterns and figural types of Michelangelo and Raphael. Thus Rubens attempted to combine the styles of Venice and Rome according to the traditional aesthetic postulates. His last big commission in Rome was the altarpiece of *Santa Maria* in Vallicella (Chiesa Nuova), at present in Grenoble. A style of luxuriant abundance and display, together with motifs of ancient statuary, characterize this work.

RUBENS: THE FOUR PHILOSOPHERS. (Capitoline Museum, Rome.)

The years following 1608 are dominated by problems of evolving a narrative style, in which all figures are bound up with the main theme, and the subject is visualized in striking clarity; and by creating figural types which have unity and are suited to bring about the clarity desired. To achieve these ends, Rubens turned for a while to simple subjects with less violent action and a smaller number of figures. He also intensified his study of classical figural types, many of which now enter his paintings. It was in these years (1614-15) that he created types, such as The Man, The Child, The Woman, The Aged Man. In *Deposition from the Cross*, 1611-14 (Antwerp) the composition is emphasized by the physical activity of descending; the isolation of the group as a sculptural unit is contained in its entity, within the picture. This is repeated in the large simple color units. Re-creation of gods of classic antiquity as happy beings, unconscious of worldly worries, enjoying life in harmony with nature, appear in compositions around 1614-15, as *Drunken Herakles* (Dresden). *Abduction of the Daughters of Leukippus*, 1615 (Munich) marks the beginning of the new period. Although one still may find the statuary isolation of groups with figures seen as separate bodies, yet there is noticeable a striking advance in regard to formal relationship of movements. But these movements lack transitory character; however, this problem is attacked with more success during the following years, in compositions of numerous battle scenes, hunting scenes, etc. The frequently used abduction scene is best represented in *Boreas and Orythia*, 1619-20 (Vienna); the expression of resistance of the young woman, the general feeling of the whole seems more convincing; one may also notice an increase in transitory character.

The experimentations with grouping bodies leads to garlands of figures as in his famous *Last Judgment*, 1616 (Munich); another circular composition it may be compared to is the *Battle of Amazons*, 1617, or the *Virgin with Garland of Putti*, for circular movement around an empty center. The climax of conglomerated bodies is attained in the *Fall of the Damned*, 1618-20 (Munich); there are rendered the utmost possibilities of interlacing figures for the sake of visualization of movement, which extends beyond the limits of a single body. A parallel development occurs in battle and hunting scenes. The *Hunt of Crocodile and Hippopotamus*, 1615-16 (Augsburg) shows the formation of single sculptural bodies into a group, as compared to the *Lion Hunt*, 1617-18 (Munich) of a more transitory character, and chain of bodies in a looser arrangement in space.

The large commissions in Rubens' career were: 1616-17, designs for *Tapestries* (Decius Mus.); 1616-20, decorations for his own house; 1620, the famous decorations for the church of the Jesuits in Antwerp (36 paintings burned in the 18th century, copies by De Wit are still extant); 1622-25, decorations for the Luxembourg Palace for Marie de Médicis; 1630-34, ceiling in Whitehall; 1635, triumphal entrance of Ferdinand and several others. One of the galleries in the Luxembourg Palace was to contain twenty-one large paintings, illustrating the life of Marie de Médicis. He set to work in Antwerp (1621-1625). In this gigantic task, he was assisted by his pupils. Snyders undertook details and animals. Van Thulden executed the landscapes and backgrounds. The master himself designed the whole, painted the principal figures, advised, and retouched.

The subject presented many difficulties. He had to represent

# FRENCH ART UNDER LOUIS XIII

*At the beginning of the seventeenth century, the return of the monarchy to Paris inaugurated a new era in the history of French art. During the Renaissance, the king lived in the country; it is in Touraine and at Fontainebleau rather than at Paris that one must study the French Renaissance. When Henry IV recovered his capital the Renaissance was at a close; the new art was much less brilliant but more reasoned; it marked the reign of the bourgeoisie.*

PARIS. PLACE DES VOSGES, FORMERLY PLACE ROYALE.
*(Photo by Hachette.)*

PARIS. HOUSES OF THE PONT-NEUF.
*(Photo by Hachette.)*

S. DE BROSSE: PALACE OF THE LUXEMBOURG. PARIS.
*(Photo by Hachette.)*

LE VAU: CHÂTEAU OF VAUX-LE-VICOMTE.
*(Photo by Hachette.)*

FR. MANSART: CHÂTEAU OF MAISONS-LAFFITTE.
*(Photo by Lévy.)*

## Urban Architecture and Country Homes

France is the only European country which at the same time was bound to the southern Latin civilization and that of northern and Germanic Europe. The constructions of brick and stone with high roofs remind one that Paris is a northern city, but alongside these are buildings in which the ancient orders are utilized.

LE NAIN: GROUP OF PEASANTS. LOUVRE.
*(Photo by Hachette.)*

LE NAIN: PEASANTS EATING. LOUVRE.
*(Photo by Hachette.)*

PHILIPPE DE CHAMPAIGNE: PORTRAIT OF THE MOTHER SUPERIOR CATHERINE AGNÈS ARNAULD AND SISTER CATHERINE OF ST. SUZANNE. LOUVRE.
*(Photo by Hachette.)*

PHILIPPE DE CHAMPAIGNE: RICHELIEU. LOUVRE.
*(Photo by Hachette.)*

LE SUEUR: THE MUSES. LOUVRE.
*(Photo by Hachette.)*

SIMON GUILLAIN: LOUIS XIII. LOUVRE.
*(Photo by Hachette.)*

SÉBASTIEN BOURDON: FOUQUET. VERSAILLES.
*(Photo by Hachette.)*

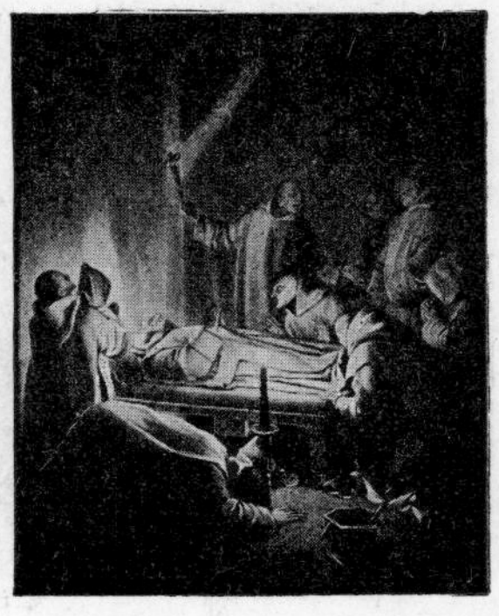

LE SUEUR: THE DEATH OF ST. BRUNO. LOUVRE.
*(Photo by Hachette.)*

## Painting and Sculpture

Parisian society at the time of Louis XIII demanded paintings for the churches which were being constructed. Simon Vouet and his pupil Eustache Le Sueur were prolific painters of holy personages; they were likewise decorators of houses. What is most interesting in this art is the sincerity of its naturalism: truthful portraits are not restrained by pretensions to a grand style.

# NICOLAS POUSSIN AND CLAUDE LORRAIN

*In the first half of the seventeenth century, the finest painters of the French school did not live in France. Paris was not yet the art capital of Europe. Almost all of the French artists went to Rome for their training. More than one remained there. It was thus that Nicolas Poussin of Normandy and Claude Gellée of Lorraine spent the greatest part of their existence in Italy as Italians. They are none the less members of the French family, especially Poussin, because of their spirit and especially because of the training which they gave to French artists.*

POUSSIN: THE TRIUMPH OF FLORA. LOUVRE.
*(Photo by Giraudon.)*

POUSSIN: THE BLIND MEN OF JERICHO. LOUVRE.
*(Photo by Hachette.)*

## Poussin, Historical Painter

Poussin is primarily a historical painter; this type has played in French art somewhat the same role as tragedy in French literature. The artist according to the nature of the theme of mythology, religious history or pagan history, reconstructs the human drama by means of painting, expressing sentiments in plastic language. This language is expressive first of all because of the rhythm of the lines and the beauty of the attitudes; still more so because of the adaptation of mimicry to express the intentions of the actors. In the *Triumph of Flora*, it is the rhythm which dominates and in the *Blind Men of Jericho*, it is the physical gestures.

POUSSIN: POLYPHEMUS. PETROGRAD.
*(Photo by Hanfstaengl.)*

POUSSIN: ORPHEUS AND EURYDICE. LOUVRE.
*(Photo by Hachette.)*

POUSSIN: THE DELUGE. LOUVRE.
*(Photo by Hachette.)*

## Poussin, Landscape Painter

Finally, in every composition of Poussin the landscape itself plays a rôle which surpasses that of simple decoration. By means of its lines, the mass of the buildings, land and clouds, it participates in the rhythm of the composition. It also happens that as the figures become less important, the landscape reveals its majesty better; Poussin even demands of it that it express thought as it does in the *Deluge* in which one sees humanity hemmed in by nature. The landscape of Poussin is not that of the moderns, it is nature organised having in view a picturesque and poetic effect. Many of the elements in it are borrowed from the natural surroundings of Rome.

CLAUDE LORRAIN: CHRYSEIS RETURNED TO HER FATHER. LOUVRE.
*(Photo by Hachette.)*

CLAUDE LORRAIN: THE CAMPO VACCINO. LOUVRE.
*(Photo by Hachette.)*

## Claude Lorrain

As with Poussin, Lorrain lived in Italy but much more than Poussin, he readily gave himself up to the contemplation of charming or grandiose sights and especially the radiant Mediterranean light. Unlike Poussin, he did not organise his landscape for the figures in it; the figures here have scarcely any importance; Lorrain did not always paint them himself. It is solely with light that he composes his pictures. The *Port at Sunset* shows the effect which he considers most important: the glow of the horizon and the thousand rays which the sun casts upon the architecture and the waves. The *Campo Vaccino* has the sincerity of a sketch after nature.

# SCULPTORS AND PAINTERS UNDER LOUIS XIV

*During the second half of the seventeenth century, the greatest part of French artistic activity was devoted to the construction and the decoration of Versailles. The sculptors Girardon, Coysevox, Tuby, Desjardins and Demarsy, and even Puget carved marble nymphs and cast bronze divinities for the walks of the park and its water basins. The painters of the school of Le Brun painted the ceilings of the apartments and designed the cartoons which the Gobelins factory translated into tapestry. The work was carried out under the direction of Charles Le Brun, whence comes the admirable unity of the Louis XIV style.*

COYSEVOX: BUST OF MIGNARD. LOUVRE.
*(Photo by Hachette.)*

GIRARDON: NYMPHS BATHING. VERSAILLES.

THE PUGET ROOM IN THE LOUVRE. FROM LEFT TO RIGHT: ALEXANDER AND DIOGENES, MILO OF CROTONA, HERCULES, PERSEUS AND ANDROMEDA.

COYSEVOX: BUST OF CONDÉ. LOUVRE.
*(Photo by Hachette.)*

## The Sculptors

Sculpture in the seventeenth century is torn between two tendencies: the naturalism which manifests itself in the portraits and funeral statuary and the idealistic and decorative tendency, allegorical and mythological figures. From the sculptors at Versailles, allegories and pagan divinities were particularly in demand. Coysevox, frankly a realistic genius, understood how to adapt himself to the rhetorical majesty of monarchical art. Girardon is perhaps the one who shows the greatest flexibility in carrying out the program of Le Brun. Puget is an independent genius who lived apart.

LE BRUN: THE FAMILY OF DARIUS AT THE FEET OF ALEXANDER.
*(Photo by Hachette.)*

PIERRE MIGNARD: LOUIS XIV. VERSAILLES.
*(Photo by Hachette.)*

LE BRUN: CONQUEST OF THE FRANCHE-COMTÉ. VERSAILLES.
*(Photo by Hachette.)*

## Charles Le Brun

The painter Charles Le Brun had the complete direction of the art activities, with the exception of architecture, during the creation of Versailles. With this title he made many of the sketches for the sculptors and the decorators. He reserved for himself the execution of paintings or tapestry cartoons representing the noble deeds of the king in allegorical form. His masterpiece, the ceiling of the Hall of Mirrors, is the epic poem of the reign. Mignard, who led the opposition against Le Brun, was the stylish portraitist of the period.

HYACINTHE RIGAUD: BOSSUET. LOUVRE.
*(Photo by Hachette.)*

LARGILLIÈRE: THE PAINTER AND HIS FAMILY. LOUVRE.
*(Photo by Hachette.)*

HYACINTHE RIGAUD: LOUIS XIV. LOUVRE.
*(Photo by Hachette.)*

## Largillière and Rigaud

In the last years of the seventeenth century, at the time when Versailles was being completed, a style of painting opposed to the instruction of Le Brun and to the Royal Academy obtained public favour. This style, more colourful and more florid, patterned itself in the Flemish manner after the art of Rubens and Van Dyck while the school of Le Brun extolled above all the correctness of the drawing and the psychological expression. These neo-Flemings prepared the way for Watteau. Among the most famous one must include Desportes, Rigaud and Largillière.

# VERSAILLES

*The Château of Versailles, constructed by Louis XIV, was not conceived and executed by a single architect. It was originally a gracious country house built by Jacques Lemercier for Louis XIII. Le Vau and Mansart enlarged the wings, gradually extending them while always preserving the central construction. The château thus kept the plan of the French town house which was always laid out between a court and a garden. It was immeasurably amplified. The house of the king became the seat of the government and in the wings the servants of the monarchy were installed.*

THE MARBLE COURT.
*(Photo by Hachette.)*

THE CHÂTEAU, EAST FAÇADE.
*(Photo by Hachette.)*

THE CHAPEL.
*(Photo by Hachette.)*

## The Entrance Courts

From this side the original château of Louis XIII is visible; and again when one drives into the marble court. This charming façade impressed its simple and picturesque style upon all the façades facing east: red brick framed by white stone, topped with blue slate. In the eighteenth century, Gabriel unluckily began to reface them with classic colonnades.

THE STAIRWAY OF THE QUEEN.
*(Photo by Hachette.)*

THE HALL OF MIRRORS.
*(Photo by Hachette.)*

INTERIOR OF THE CHAPEL.
*(Photo by Hachette.)*

THE KING'S BEDCHAMBER.
*(Photo by Hachette.)*

## The Decoration of the Interior

The interior decoration of the château, like the plan of the building itself, is related to the person of the king. The "Stairway of the Ambassadors," destroyed in the eighteenth century, was much admired; the Stairway of the Queen gives a diminished idea of it. The decoration of the salons is the work of Le Brun and his school.

THE ORANGERY.
*(Photo by Hachette.)*

THE FAÇADE LOOKING UPON THE PARK.
*(Photo by Hachette.)*

THE GRAND TRIANON.
*(Photo by Hachette.)*

## The Park Façade

The garden of Louis XIII grew into a park just as the house became a château. From this side, the palace presents a gala façade. No trace of the simplicity of Louis XIII remains. There is an order continued in simple fashion from north to south between a basement and an attic; there are columns disengaged at various points and trophies along the roof without interrupting the majesty of the horizontal lines. This façade was constructed upon an uncultivated embankment as if the very vegetation had withdrawn to refrain from eclipsing its lofty simplicity.

THE BASIN OF APOLLO.
*(Photo by Hachette.)*

THE "TAPIS VERT" AND THE PERSPECTIVE OF THE GRAND CANAL.
*(Photo by Hachette.)*

THE COLONNADE OF MANSART.
*(Photo by Hachette.)*

## The Park

With embankments, trees and fountains, Le Nôtre composed a park whose plan, because of its grandiose simplicity, corresponds to the majestic unity of the château. The long avenue of the "Tapis Vert" continued by the view of the grand canal, divides it in the middle. Along each side are placed groves in varying arrangements. The paths wind among the trees about the basins where bronze divinities throw forth jets of water. These basins themselves are grouped about the central Basin of Apollo, since the Sun God reigns in the park as the Sun King did in the château.

contemporary events which were quite inglorious, with the life of an elderly, rather uninspiring heroine as the chief theme. The painter tackled it by mingling mythology with history. Marie de Médicis was clothed as a Pallas or Juno, surrounded by the goddesses of Peace, Fruitfulness and Power—Envy, Pride and Disorder are put to flight.

RUBENS: CHILDREN CARRYING A GARLAND OF FRUIT. (Munich.)

Historical truth is not sacrificed, only embellished. These paintings now adorn a special gallery in the Louvre. A warm, golden light plays over bright stuffs, shining armour, and fair nude bodies. The subjects of a few of the twenty-one paintings are:—(1.) The fates spinning the destiny of Marie de Médicis. (2.) Her birth. (No. 7) Her marriage in Lyon. (No. 11.) The Coronation of Henry IV., etc.

RUBENS: PORTRAIT OF HIS TWO SONS. (Liechtenstein Gallery.)

In the Marie de Médicis and Henry IV cycles there is a blend of Greek mythology with the 17th century cavalier tradition. Gods and men are interchangeable in an ideal world; this theme was an original creation of Rubens. While in Spain in 1628-29, Rubens made a number of copies of Titian's paintings; the Venetian color influence was henceforth noticeable in his work, especially in the increasing lightness and softness of tones, and in the constant use of glazes. Despite the many commissions, he found time, in his late period, to work for himself. This was made possible by his employing pupils and apprentices to finish parts of the paintings. *Het Pelsken* (Vienna) is a lovely painting of his second wife. There are many works based on love between man and wife, or just love festivals, as *Venus Festival* (Vienna) (probably inspired by Titian), and *Offering to Venus. Flemish Kermess* (Louvre) shows a graceful interpretation of peasant festival. Love themes are also found in his allegorical paintings of the play between sexes, as *Venus and Adonis* (N. Y. Metropolitan), *Judgment of Paris,* 1638. (Coll. of Mr. Edward Robinson), etc.

Rubens' landscapes may be classed in two periods, those done between 1615-22, and 1635-40. The first period is characterized by strong contrasting movements and large bodies as *Landscape with Cart* (Hermitage), while in his second period one may find the idyllic type as *Tournament before the Castle Steen* (Louvre). He also painted many portraits of himself, of his wives and of nobility.

BIBLIOGRAPHY: Oldenbourg, Klassiker der Kunst (1904).—Vischer, *P. P. Rubens,* 1904.—Rooses, *Rubens' leven en werken,* 1901.

**RUCELLAI MADONNA.**—See Duccio.

**RUCELLAI PALACE.**—See Florence; also Pl. 5, Vol. II.

RUDE (FRANÇOIS).

**RUDE (François).**—French sculptor, 1784-1855. Rude's father was one of the first to embrace the cause of the French Revolution. From his earliest years he received an intensely republican and patriotic education. This may account for the spirit of one of his most characteristic works—the *Marseillaise*—which adorns the Arc de Triomphe, Paris. Rude made numerous drawings—now lost and scattered—for the whole decoration of this Arch; but the only remaining relief of the original composition is this *Marseillaise.* It shows Rude's characteristic passion for movement, and is a strange combination of classicism and violent impetuosity.

One of the first works to bring him success was the *Mercury Tying His Sandals* (Louvre) which is delightfully expressive of lightness and movement. The *Neapolitan Fisherboy Playing with a Tortoise* (Louvre) is another charming work. The *Joan of Arc Listening to the Voices* (Louvre, 1852) is somewhat devoid of character, and unlike most of Rude's work, which is generally realistic, and vigorous. The figure of *Christ* (Louvre) is restrained. More characteristic of his revolutionary tendencies is the extraordinary work, *Napoleon Awaking to Immortality,* which represents Napoleon, crowned with a laurel wreath, emerging from his shroud. The *Tomb of Godefroy Cavaignac* (Montmartre Cemetery, Paris) belongs to the same period, and shows the influence of the tombs of the Dukes of Burgundy and of Philippe Pot, which he had seen in Dijon. Nothing could be more simple and less theatrical than this figure lying in its shroud. Only the head and chest are visible, and the drapery is treated very realistically.

See Pl. 51, Vol. II.

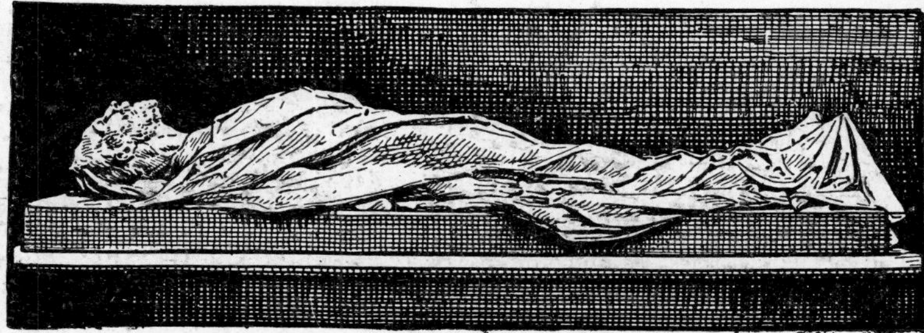

RUDE: TOMB OF GODEFROY CAVAIGNAC. (Montmartre Cemetery, Paris.)

RUDE: NEAPOLITAN FISHER BOY. (Louvre.)

RUDE: NAPOLEON AWAKING TO IMMORTALITY. (Fixin, Côte d'Or.)

BIBLIOGRAPHY: Théophile Sylvestre, *Histoire des artistes vivants.*—Alexis Bertrand, *François Rude.* Paris, 1888.—L. de Fourcaud. *Rude.* Paris, 1903.

RUDE: THE CHRIST. (Louvre.)

**RÜE (Lisinka).**—See Mirbel.

**RUELAS (Juan de, also Ruela, Roela, Roelas).**—Spanish painter, born c. 1558-60; died at Olivares in 1625.—"Juan de Ruelas is to be regarded as the ancestor of the School of Seville of the 17th century. His is the great merit to have freed this school from the paralyzing spell of the cold and dreary school of Rome. Introducing new treatments of pictorial problems as well as following determinedly in the wake of the art of Tintoretto he steered it onto new and fertile paths . . ." (A. L. Mayer).

From documents we know that from 1598 to 1602 he was a citizen of Valladolid, and also that in 1603 he was a priest at Olivares, near Seville. The years 1606-1609 he probably spent at Venice. Ruelas' first documented extant paintings are the *Sweet Name of Jesus* and the *Birth of Christ* of the High-altar of the Jesuit church of Seville University. According to José Hernández Diaz other documented works of his are the *Santiago in the Battle of Clavijo,* 1609, Seville Cathedral; *Vision of St. Bernard,* 1611, Hospital de San Bernardo el Viejo, Seville; the *Man of Sorrows* and *St. Ignatius of Loyola,* 1612, Jesuit Church of Cordova; also from 1612 are the *Flagellation* in the Church of San Salvador at Seville, the *Deliverance of Peter* in the Church of San Pedro and the *Death of San Isidoro* in the Church of

S. Isidoro in the same city. Important among the paintings which may be safely attributed to the painter is his *Pentecost* in the Seville Museum (1605), which aroused the admiration of the German scholar, C. Justi.

BIBLIOGRAPHY: A. L. Mayer, *Sevillaner Malerschule,* 1911.—Id., *Gesch. span. Malerei,* 2nd ed., 1922. —*Archivo español de Arte,* 1925; 1926; 1928; 1929.—Thieme-Becker, Vol. XXIX, 1935. Art. *Ruela, Juan de,* by José Hernández Diaz.

**RUISDAEL (Jacob Izaakszoon).** —Dutch landscape painter and etcher. Born and died in Haarlem, 1628/9-1682. Belongs to a family of painters. Was obviously inspired by Everdingen. He is undoubtedly the most important landscape painter of his time, breaking away from the traditional schools of landscape painting and anticipating Constable, Corot, Rousseau, etc. He painted by power of his imagination rather than through observation; nature with him seems to be filled with latent energy. His waterfalls and forest-scenes show the new principles in landscape painting: tension, dramatic interpretation, special unity and characterization of materials. In many of his landscapes there is a strong moralizing element, or an underlying philosophy. He seldom painted figures. It is difficult to establish the chronology of his work. Most paintings done between 1645-1653 are dated, but after he moved to Amsterdam in 1657, he seldom dated any ceasing to date them altogether after 1663. The romantic scenes were done in the 50's: *Bentheim Castle* (Dresden); the dynamic and dramatic phase falls in the late 60's: *Mill Near Wijk* (Amsterdam); *Swamp* (Hermitage); in the 70's we find poor repetitions of older motifs.

BIBLIOGRAPHY: E. Michel, *Jacob van Ruysdael.* Paris, 1890.—G. Riat, *Ruysdael.* Collection des grands artistes. Paris, 1905.—Hofstede de Groot, *Catalogue of Dutch Painters,* Vol. IV.

**— (Salomon van).**—Dutch landscape painter. Born and died in Haarlem, 1600-1670. Pupil of Van Goyen and Esaias van de Velde, he was already prominent in 1628. One of the most outstanding members of the naturalistic school of landscape painting, he was undoubtedly a forerunner of Jacob Izaakszoon. He painted village, river and canal scenes in the traditional vein. He is represented in all important museums.

**RUNEBERG (Walter).**—Finnish sculptor (1838-1921); son of the celebrated poet Runeberg. He studied widely. His work, however, shows the influence that Thorwalden exercised on his education, and he attached great importance to the classic tradition. He is known chiefly for a statue symbolising *Finland.*

**RUNGE (Philipp Otto).**—German painter and æsthete (1777-1810). His early work is in the Neo-Classic style; but his originality was too strong to be subjected to formulæ, well-defended though they might be, by Winckelmann, Goethe and others. He came to study directly from nature.

**RUPERT (Prince).**—English engraver, nephew of King Charles I, 1619-1682. He learned, in Holland, the "black manner" (see Engraving) the secret of which was revealed to him by its inventor, L. de Siegen, and introduced into England. He made some good engravings, among them one of the *Executioner's Head,* after Ribera.

BIBLIOGRAPHY: H. Delaborde, *La Gravure en manière noire.* Paris, 1839.—A. Whitman, *The Masters of Mezzotint.* London, 1898.—Fred. Wedmore, *British Mezzotints.* London, 1902-1904.

**RUSCONI (Benedetto).**—See Diana (Benedetto).

**RUSH (William).** — American sculptor (1756-1833), of Philadelphia, known as the Father of American sculpture. He rose from the craft of wood carving and the production of ships' figureheads to sculpture properly speaking; the most notable examnle of his work is the statue of Washington in Independence Hall, Philadelphia.

**RUSKIN (John).**—See Pre-Raphaelite Brotherhood.

**RUSSELL (John).** — English painter and pastel worker, 1754-1806. In 1776 his *Study on the Elements of Painting* had a certain vogue.

Towards the end of his life he abandoned painting for astronomical studies.

He is known chiefly for his pastels. His portraits have freshness, but they reveal a certain lack of observation. They include portraits of King George III, the Queen, and the Prince and Princess of Wales.

**RUSSIA.**—Russian art has had no brilliant development or expansion. It has existed on importations of Byzantine art, then of the Italian Renaissance and finally of French art, adapting them to the needs and character of the Russian people. Throughout the centuries this immense territory has not produced a single great artistic personality.

Civilization penetrated Russia from the South, the earliest Russian Byzantine buildings having been erected at Kiev. Most of them have disappeared. Those which remain—*St. Sophia, St. Michael* and *St. Cyril*—have suffered so many restorations that it is difficult to recognise the 11th century buildings. They are built of brick and decorated with Byzantine mosaics, and frescoes. The plan is very simple: a square nave with three apses, surmounted with domes.

Kiev was demolished by the Mongols, in the 13th century; and Novgorod became the artistic centre of Russia—the *Cathedral of Santa Sophia; Church of St. George* (12th century); and *St. Nicholas* (12th century). The form is very simple; and the Byzantine dome is flattened into a bulbous shape. Civil buildings were in wood, and none have come down to us.

About the 11th century, the population of the valley of the Dnieper began to spread towards the eastern regions of the valley of the Volga. New cities were built at Souzdal, Jaroslav, Vladimir and Moscow. Churches were built from the 12th century. In plan, they resemble the Churches of Kiev, but stone was substituted for brick, and this allowed of a sculptured decoration which was new in Russia. The Old Testament forbids all representation of the human figure: "Evil be to him who makes a carved image, for it is the abomination of the Lord." In Russia, this interdict was regarded until the 18th century. The soft stone of this Volga region was very tempting to artists, though the interdicts of the Church were too formal for sculptors to risk representing the human figure otherwise than in very low relief—a kind of incised drawing on stone which could not tend to idolatry. Some churches are covered with these reliefs, the subjects of which were borrowed from Byzantine art. The finest churches of this region are: *St. Dimitri* (Vladimir), the *Cathedral of the Dormition* (Vladimir); the *Cathedral of Souzdal,* the *Church of the Transfiguration* (Pereialavi).

The prosperity of these towns did not last. In 1238, they fell under the Tartar invasion, and Moscow became the capital of Russia. Founded in the 12th century, she prospered and grew, gradually enclosing in her walls the fortress of the Kremlin, which, from the top of its hill, defended the town, and thus became the heart of the city. The new capital suffered not so much from Mongolian invasions as from its distance in the interior of the country. Following the taking of Constantinople by the Turks (1453), the Muscovites were free from the religious bondage of Byzantium, and the head of the Russian Orthodox religion was installed in Moscow.

PETROGRAD: CHURCH OF ST. ISAAC.

The capital was thus free to create a national art. The chief change in the construction of churches was the substitution of the pyramid for the dome, inspired by wooden architecture (*Church of the Decollation,* near Moscow; *Church of Kolomenskoe*). Sometimes the two elements are combined.

The Baroque style was first introduced at Kiev, but it was in Moscow, Rostov and Iaroslav that it acquired originality. Churches were built in storeys. One of the most remarkable models is that of Fili. However, this new style of architecture did not last long in the Muscovite region; for in 1714 Peter the Great issued a decree forbiding the building of any large churches in Russia, except in St. Petersburg.

PETROGRAD: THE WINTER PALACE.

The finest 17th century building is, perhaps, the *Cathedral of the Resurrection,* at Borisoglebsk. It is surrounded by galleries decorated with frescoes.

Some of the finest frescoes are to be found in the Church of the Saviour (12th century) at Nereditsa. The composition is generally very simple with few figures, and in an almost uniform ochre colour. Recently, since 1910, good frescoes were discovered in Volotova, in St. Theodore Stratilate (Novgorod), in the Church of the Transfiguration, of the Saviour, and of the Dormition, in Vladimir. But the most famous old Russian frescoes are those already mentioned.

Sculpture—except for such basreliefs as we have mentioned—did not exist in Russia before the 18th century. Fine paintings were, however, made especially at Novgorod. They were chiefly church frescoes and icons. Many of the frescoes are seriously damaged and badly restored. They are the work of Greek or Byzantine artists, assisted by native artists. One of the finest series is that of the Monastery of Theraponte, near Novgorod, one of the most celebrated sanctuaries of Mediæval Russia. They were executed in the 15th century by Master Denis.

Besides these mural decorations, Russian painting left us numerous icons, or holy images. The first flourishing school of painting was in Novgorod.

The technique of icon painting is almost the same as that of tempera, and consists of painting, with colours mixed with yoke of egg, on a wooden panel covered with a layer of plaster. The oldest icons show the influence of Greece, then of Byzantine art. The colours are generally bright; the background is often red. Until the 16th century these works were never signed. We know the name of but one painter, that of the monk Roublev.

The Byzantine tradition was gradually lost in a new school of painting which was developed in Moscow. The icons which came from the studios of Moscow were more realistic. The inspiration is less ideal, the colour, harsher, and the use of gold too liberal.

In the 17th century, under Ivan the Terrible, painting ceased to be reserved for religious subjects. The palaces were adorned with allegories, nude figures, and historical scenes.

It was about this time that Russia came into closer relationship with the Western nations. Especially in the reign of Peter the Great, works of art, and Polish, German, Dutch and Italian artists, found their way into Russia. In spite of the opposition of the clergy, artists began to take more and more liberty in the way of treating old themes, and did not always conform to the precepts laid down in manuals, often illustrated, which imposed on religious painters iconographical subjects and traditional interpretation. The 17th century is full of these struggles. They are apparent in the work of Ouchakov: his icons are a compromise between orthodox Byzantine inspiration, and imitation of Western Art.

After the 17th century, Russian art fell completely under the influence of Western art, especially that of Italy.

*Minor Arts.*—In the minor arts, also, Russia was under the influence of Byzantine art. The principal centres were, in the Middle Ages, Kiev and Novgorod, which were unfortunately pillaged by the Mongols. Some Psalters enriched with miniatures escaped, such as the Ostomir Gospel. Scarcely any objects in precious metal have come down to us from the Middle Ages. Such as remain bear witness to an imperfect art, lacking in originality. Enamels and mosaics are purely Byzantine.

Bibliography: Grabar, *Istoria rousskavo iskousstva.* — Viollet-le-Duc, *L'art russe.* Paris, 1877.—Réau, *L'Art russe.* 1921.

Petrograd: Cathedral of Kazan.

**RUSTICI (Giovanni Francesco).** —Florentine sculptor, 1474-1554. One of the chief representatives of the 16th century style. Pupil of Verrocchio and of Leonardo da Vinci. His best work is the *Preaching of St. John the Baptist,* over Ghiberti's first door of the Baptistery of Florence. He went to France in 1527, and died there in 1554.

**RUSUTI (Filippo).**—Roman painter and mosaicist of the late dugento and early trecento, follower of Torriti.

The mosaic on the façade of Sta. Maria Maggiore in Rome is signed by Rusuti. Later he went to Poitiers to work for Philippe le Bel, is mentioned there in 1308, together with his son Giovanni and one Nicholas Desmarz. In 1309 they receive payment for restorations in the palace; and in 1317 the three are mentioned in documents as painters to the King. In 1322 only Giovanni's name appears.

Vasari states that Rusuti's mosaic on Sta. Maria Maggiore was completed by Gaddo Gaddi shortly after 1308. Rusuti probably worked at Assisi, where certain frescoes in the Upper Church reveal his style.

Bibliography: Vasari-Milanesi, I, p. 347.—H. Moranville, *Peintres romains pensionnaires de Philippe le Bel,* Bibliot. de l'Ec. des Chartes, XLIII, 1887, p. 631.—B. Prost, *Quelques documents sur l'histoire des arts en France,* Gazette des Beaux Arts, XXXV, p. 358.

**RUWÊHA (Syria).** — *Bizzos Church.* A large 6th century Early Christian basilica of North Syria, with a façade consisting of a great horseshoe portal between west towers. There are horseshoe relieving arches at either entrance beside the great portal.

**RUYSDAEL.**—See Ruisdael.

**RYCKAERT (David).** — Flemish painter. Antwerp, about 1612 to 1661. His subjects and way of painting recall Jordaens, Teniers and Ostade. He painted peaceful citizens at work and at home; his colouring is very brilliant; he used the same model throughout. His best pictures are in Vienna: *Dancing Peasants* (Mus.); *Musical Party,* 1650 (Lichtenstein); other paintings are in Dresden, Antwerp, etc.

**RYDER (Albert Pinkham).**— American painter (1847-1917). He was born 19th March 1847 in New Bedford, Massachusetts. He tried his hand at drawing and painting as a young boy, copying engravings after the old masters under the guidance of a Mr. Sherman. When the family moved to New York about 1868 Ryder took up the serious study of painting with William E. Marshall. In 1871 he went to classes at the National Academy of Design but was not content to draw from antique casts. He had always been interested in the sea in its different moods and from that time on devoted himself almost exclusively to the reproduction of it on canvas. He was a poor business manager and there were many times when he had scarcely enough to eat. His studio was an accumulation of dust and disorder, where he turned out his few canvases after long hours of experimentation with the medium, trying to gain transparent effects of surface and depth. He was never satisfied with the results but reworked his canvases many times, and at his death left only about one hundred and fifty pictures. In 1893 he went abroad with Cottier and Olin Warner, the sculptor, but aside from his ever-present interest in the ocean did not find much to interest him. Because of his weak eyes, which had been injured in youth by impure vaccine, he was accustomed to take long walks in the moonlight, reflecting on the mysterious effects it produced on the landscapes and the water. His most familiar picture, *Toilers of the Sea,* represents an attempt to capture this lonely mood which harmonised so well with the lonely spirit of the man. He did not care for human contacts, preferring rather to devote his entire existence to painting. In 1915 he had a serious illness and it was after that that he went to live with friends at Elmhurst, Long Island, and there he died 28th March 1917. He had not produced a great quantity of work but the mysterious poetic quality of his pictures has not been equalled by any other American painter. Self-taught though he was and crude though his technique, yet he was very successful in capturing the romantic melancholy mood of the sea on a moonlit night.

Ruisdael (Jacob van): The Stag Hunt. (Pinakothek, Munich.)

See Pl. 62, Vol. II.

Bibliography: Frederick Newlin Price, *Ryder (1847-1917), A Study of Appreciation,* 1932.—Frederic Fairchild Sherman, *Albert Pinkham Ryder,* 1920.—For other articles see *The Index of Twentieth Century Artists* for February, 1934.

# S

**SAARINEN (Eliel Gottlieb).**—Contemporary Finnish architect. He was born 20th August 1873 in Rantasalmi and received his art training at the Polytechnikum of Helsingfors. Together with A. Lindgren and H. Gesellius he founded an architectural office in 1897, which became the most progressive and influential of its kind in the country. In 1904 he participated in a competition for a new Railroad Station of Helsingfors and his extremely functional and imposing model won the first prize. In 1907 he severed his connexion with his associates and has worked independently ever since; his wife has been his constant collaborator, she executes his models to the last intricate details. In 1911 another of his designs won first prize: the *Railroad Station of Wiborg*. The same year he designed the *Rathaus* in Lahti, to be followed by the *Estobank* in Reval in 1912, and the *City Hall* in Joensuu in 1913. In 1922 Saarinen participated in the competition for a new building for the *Chicago Tribune*; although the public, critics and architects as a whole acclaimed his model as far superior to the others, the jury accorded him only second prize, preferring the design of Hood and Howell. However, his subtle and functional steel structure had considerable effect on the surface expression of subsequent skyscrapers. The same year he came to America, where he immediately became a leader of the new movement in architecture. He designed the buildings for the Cranbrook School, Bloomfield Hills, Michigan, and for a while was lecturer on design at the University of Michigan. Of a progressive and creative mind, Saarinen applies his native norms in a modified way to suit American conditions and demands. His structures are based on sound engineering, with the vertical line dominating. Despite the versatile design the structures are extremely simple, large geometric masses are prevalent, free from ornamentation. His love and understanding for texture can be traced to his intimate contact with materials while he worked as a practical builder. He is also known for his design for the League of Nations Building at Geneva, and for scientific city planning, as for Chicago and Detroit. In these he tries to get away from the right-angle corners, thus increasing the rate of traffic and circulation. Saarinen believes in creating a new architectural form essentially its own set by modern conditions and combining functional expression with the attitudes of independent and historic forms.

Bibliography: Donnell Tilghman, *Eliel Saarinen, Architectural Record*, Vol. 63, May, 1928.

**SABATINI (Andrea).**—Neapolitan painter, 16th century. Died in 1545. Chief of the Neapolitan school of his period.

Chief works: *The History of San Gennaro* (in San Gennaro dei Poveri), and an *Adoration of the Magi*, in Naples Museum.

**SACCHI (Andrea).**—Roman painter, 1599?-1661. Pupil of Francesco Albani. One of the most important representatives of the 17th century school, who reacted against the careless facility of Pietro da Cortona by surer drawing and more vigorous colour. His most admired work is the *Vision of St. Romuald* (c. 1640), in the Vatican Gallery.

**— (Piero Francesco).**—Painter of Pavia, 16th century. He worked chiefly in Genoa. He was especially successful with landscape backgrounds. *Three Saints in a Landscape,* in Santa Maria di Castello (1526) is his best work.

**SADELER.**—Family of Flemish engravers. The best known is Egidius Sadeler (1570-1629), who worked in Prague.

**SAENREDAM (Jan Pietersz).**—Dutch engraver, 1565-1607. He was a pupil of Goltius. Careful technique and silvery tonality are characteristic of his work, which belongs stylistically to late Mannerism.

Bibliography: Bartsch, *Le peintre graveur*. Vol. III.—J. Ph. Van der Kellers, *Le peintre graveur, hollandais et flamand*. Utrecht, 1866.

**— (Pieter, Jansz).**—Dutch painter, 1597-1665. Pupil of his father and of Pieter de Grebber, he lived in Haarlem, where he became a member of the Lucas guild in 1623. Considered as the founder of the realistic school of church painting, his rendering of structural details in a precise and pictorial manner make his church interiors documents of archeological importance. The canvases of the 30's were done in pale yellow tonalities and bring out the study of contrast between the wide naves and other spatial elements, and the small details of architectural ornamentation. From 1641 on his paintings became more colorful, but his last works return to the subtle schemes once more. One of his best known works is the *Church of St. Bavo of Haarlem*, 1636 (Amsterdam).

**SAFTLEVEN (Cornelis).**—Dutch painter and graver, 1608-1681. Painted "genre" scenes often with a satirical flavor.

**ST. ALBANS (England).**—*Cathedral,* old Abbey—has a Norman nave (the longest in England), choir and transepts. The west end of the nave is Early English. It was built partly of Roman brick, from the neighbouring ruins of Verulamium.

**SAINT AMBROSE OR SAINT AMBROGIO (Milan).**—See Milan and Pl. 45, Vol. I.

**SAINT-AUBIN (The).**—Family of French draughtsmen and engravers. They were sons and brothers of embroiderers to the king.

*Gabriel Jacques de Saint-Aubin* was born in 1724. Winning only second prize in the Rome competition Saint-Aubin gave up all academic ambition. He is said by contemporaries to have been always drawing.

His brother *Germain* was of a caustic, spirited temperament. Author of *Papillonneries humaines*, and of sketches of theatrical representations. His drawings are spontaneous and varied in method.

*Gabriel* worked in etching, a medium which suited his lightness and precision of touch. *The Salon of 1765* and the *Bal d'Auteuil* are examples.

*Augustin de Saint-Aubin* was twelve years younger than Gabriel, and was born in 1737. A very fine etcher; in this medium he made portraits, and illustrated books. His original work includes: *The Concert, Promenade on the Ramparts, Unveiling of the Statue of Louis XV,* etc. Almost all of Augustin de Saint-Aubin's work is in the possession of the Cabinet des Estampes, at the Bibliothèque Nationale, Paris.

Augustin de Saint-Aubin: L'Abbé Mauroy.

St. Denis: Crypt of the Abbey.

Bibliography: Goncourt, *L'art au XVIII^e^ siècle*. Vol. I.—E. Bocher, *Catalogue descriptif et raisonné des estampes d'Augustin de Saint Aubin,* 1879.—Adrien Moureau, *Les Saint Aubin*. Collection des Artistes Célèbres.—E. Dacier, *Gabriel de Saint-Aubin*. Paris, 1929.

Augustin de Saint-Aubin: The Promenade on the Ramparts.

**SAINT BRIEUC (France).**—The *Cathedral* is a Gothic building. The 13th century porch (restored) is framed by two heavy towers.

**SAINT DENIS (Abbey of).**—The Abbey Church of Saint Denis, near Paris, was built by the Abbot Suger between 1132 and 1144, in the first synthesis of the Gothic style, which, heretofore, had merely been prophesied in buildings still essentially Romanesque. The definite ideation of Gothic we find here spread rapidly, and, from about 1150, all the new churches of the Île de France, Champagne, and Normandy are Gothic in their rationale. All that remains of Suger's St. Denis is part of the choir, built above the Romanesque crypt. The nave and most of the choir are High Gothic and date from 1231-1281. The reason that Suger's St. Denis was so influential in spreading the style is that St. Denis was a great pilgrimage center, being the church of the patron saint of France.

The Abbey of St. Denis is not only of great architectural interest. It is interesting as the burial-place of the French kings. The oldest tombs now in St. Denis are the tomb-stone of Fredegonde, mosaic of the 11th century, and two statues (12th century) of Clovis and Childebert. About 1263, Saint Louis built a vast tomb-chantry in memory of his ancestors, and from his reign the kings of France had their own images and those of their ancestors carved on their tombs.

Among the many royal tombs in St. Denis are those of Charles V and Francis I.

See Pl. 54, Vol. I.

Bibliography: P. Vitry and G. Brière, *L'Église Abbatiale de Saint Denis et des ses tombeaux*. Paris, 1908.

**SAINT FOY.**—See Enamel.

**SAINT FRANCIS OF ASSISI.**—See Assisi.

**SAINT GALL (Switzerland).**—*Monastery:* Built 820, destroyed in the French Revolution, St. Gall was one of the largest and most important Benedictine monasteries in Christendom. We know Carolingian St. Gall only through a schematic plan in a medieval manuscript and through literary sources. The buildings were extremely elaborate and complex but it is the monastery church which really excites interest. It appears to have had apses and towers east and west, the doubling and repetition of elements later characteristic of Ottonian and German Romanesque architecture. The western apse first appeared in the Early Christian architecture of North Africa. How it appeared in German architecture is conjectural.

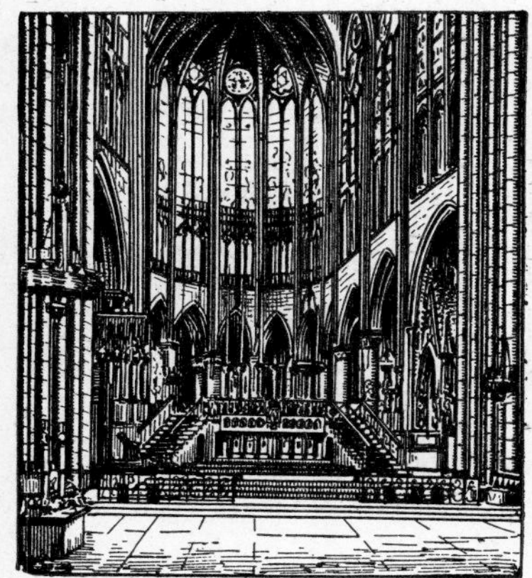

St. Denis: The Choir.

**SAINT-GAUDENS (Augustus).**—American sculptor (1848-1907). He was born in Ireland 1st March 1848, the son of a French father and an Irish mother. His youth was spent in New York City, where he was apprenticed to a cameo-cutter when he reached the age of thirteen. In the evenings he studied at Cooper Union Institute and later at the National Academy of Design. In

St. Denis: Isabel of Bavaria.

1867 he went to Paris to study at the École des Beaux-Arts, remaining there for the next three years. From 1870 until 1873 he was at work in Rome, cutting cameos and copying the ancient sculpture in the museums. He returned to New York to set up his own studio, but in 1877 he sailed again for Europe with his bride, Augusta F. Homer. During their stay in Paris Saint-Gaudens exhibited his model for the *Farragut Monument* in the Salon of 1880. It was one of the first of the many great public monuments which he executed during his long career. He and his wife returned to the United States a short time after that and took up their residence in New York. Their summers were spent at Cornish, New Hampshire, and it was there that Augustus Saint-Gaudens died after a short illness 3d August 1907.

St. Denis: Du Guesclin.

His works include commemorative monuments, equestrian statues, decorative groups attesting great charm and delicacy of execution, portraits of children in bas-relief, medals and designs for coinage. He received many prizes both here and in Europe and his work is to be found in cities of America and Europe in the public places as well as the museums. Among his most celebrated works must be mentioned his *Puritan* in Springfield, Massachusetts, the *Monument to Mrs. Adams* in Washington, D. C., the *Seated Lincoln* in Chicago and the *Memorial to Colonel Robert Gould Shaw* in Boston, Massachusetts.

See Pl. 64, Vol. II.

Bibliography: Royal Cortissoz, *Augustus Saint-Gaudens,* 1907.—William Howe Downes, *Twelve Great Artists,* 1900.—C. Lewis Hind, *Augustus Saint-Gaudens,* 1908.—Homer Saint-Gaudens, *The Reminiscenses of Augustus Saint-Gaudens,* 1913.—For other articles see *The Index of Twentieth Century Artists* for May, 1934.

**SAINT GERMER DE FLY.**—A Parisian church (c. 1130), transitional in style from Romanesque to Gothic. Hidden flying buttresses are under the aisle roofs. In the 13th century the High Gothic Ste. Chapelle, similar in appearance to the more famous Parisian church of the same name, was joined to its choir.

**SAINT GILLES (Gard, France).**—This little town possesses the celebrated *Church of St. Gilles,* begun 1116. The Romanesque building is chiefly interesting on account of its three semi-circular doorways with rich sculptural decoration—figures of apostles, and a frieze with scenes from the New Testament. An interesting feature of these doorways is the classical influence, clearly seen in medallions with pagan subjects, acanthus leaf mouldings, Corinthian capitals, etc. The temples and theatres which the Romans built in the South of France left their mark on the architecture of this part of the country.

See Pls. 44, 52, Vol. I.

**SAINT JOHN LATERAN.**—See San Giovanni in Laterano.

**— JOHN THE DIVINE (Cathedral of).**—See Cram (R. A.); Hastings (T.).

**SAINT MARCEAUX (Charles Reus' de).**—French sculptor, 1845-1915. His works include: *Genius Guarding the Secret of the Tomb* (Luxembourg Museum); *Harlequin;* the *First Communion* (Lyon);

St. Gilles: Detail of the façade of the church.

*Dawn;* and some fine figures for tombs, such as that of Alexandre Dumas, fils.

**SAINT MARK'S (San Marco).**—Venice. This church, which is in plan a Greek cross, is the masterpiece of Byzantine art in Venice. The building was rebuilt 1047-1071, and consecrated on the 11th October 1111. The façade, which screens the true character of the building, is more Romanesque and Gothic than Byzantine. Although a Second Golden Age building in point of time, S. Marco preserves a First Golden Age scheme.

The mosaics which cover the floor of the sanctuary, the domes and arches date from the 11th century. They represent: the *Descent of the Holy Spirit* (west dome); the *Ascension,* with sixteen figures of women, *Virtues and Beatitudes* (central dome); the *Christ Emmanuel* surrounded by sixteen prophets (dome of the sanctuary); and, on the arches, the great feasts, the *Miracles of Christ,* and the *Life of St. Mark.* The mosaics in the narthex date from the 13th century (Genesis). The Mosaics of the Baptistery date from the 14th century, and show the *Death of St. John the Baptist* in "genre" scenes, from which all religious feeling is absent. The realistic details of interiors are animated, and have great documentary value.

St. Mark's possesses one of the finest pieces of Byzantine enameller's goldsmiths' work—the *Pala d'Oro,* formed of eighty-three plaques of gold, on which are represented the principal subjects of Byzantine iconography. It probably dates from the 12th century.

See Venice and Pl. 6, Vol. II.

**SAINT NON (Jean Claude Richard).**—Born in Paris, 1727; died, 1791. French engraver and archæologist, he travelled in Italy with Fragonard, and published a *Voyage pittoresque dans les royaumes de Naples et de Sicile* (5 vols.), which contained 417 engravings by the best contemporary artists (1781-1786).

Bibliography: Robert Dumesnil, *Le Peintre graveur français.*—Portalis, *Les Graveur amateurs de XVIII<sup>e</sup> siècle.* Paris, 1882.

**SAINT PAUL'S CATHEDRAL.**—See London.

**SAINT PETER'S (San Pietro), Rome.**—The present Cathedral, on the site of an earlier building, was the outcome of the work of many architects. It owes its origin to the

St. Peter's, Rome: Loggia of Longinus by Lorenzo Bernini.

ambition of Pope Julius II. A competition in 1506 produced a number of designs and that of Bramante was selected. His church was planned in the form of a Greek cross, and each arm was to be surmounted by a dome. After the death of Julius II, Bramante was superseded by Giuliano da Sangallo, Fra Giocondo, and Raphael, but the two former died in 1515. Raphael proposed a plan in the shape of a Latin cross, but he died in 1520, and Baldassare Peruzzi, who was then appointed architect, reverted to the Greek cross plan. Finally, in 1547, Michelangelo (then in his seventy-second year) succeeded him. He held to Bramante's Greek cross plan, strengthened the

St. Peter's, Rome: Colonnade of St. Peter's erected by Lorenzo Bernini.

piers of the dome, and redesigned the surrounding chapels and apses. He planned the great dome, which was completed by Giacomo della Porta and Domenico Fontana. In 1564 Vignola added side cupolas; but these became ineffective when Carlo Maderna followed Pope Paul V's unfortunate idea of lengthening the nave to form a Latin cross, and added the gigantic façade. Finally, Bernini erected (1656-1663) the splendid colonnade round the piazza. The Basilica, therefore, is more Baroque than Renaissance.

St. Peter's is the largest church in the world. It is almost impossible to gauge its vast proportions, and there is disagreement as to its exact dimensions. The total length is about half as much again as that of Salisbury Cathedral.

Over the entrance doorway is a mosaic, *la Navicella* (St. Peter's Ship) by Giotto (restored). Five doorways give access to St. Peter's. The central bronze door has reliefs by Filarete.

The interior is remarkable for the grandeur and harmony of its proportions.

The famous bronze statue of St. Peter probably dates from the 5th century. Among the numerous monuments in the church must be mentioned Michelangelo's *Pietà* (1498); the tomb of Innocent VIII by the Pollaiuolo brothers; the tomb of Sixtus IV by Antonio Pollaiuolo. The vast nave is decorated with inlays of coloured marble, statues, altars and canopies by Bernini, who made the tombs of Urban VIII, Alexander VII and Clement IX, and the Throne of St. Peter—monuments remarkable for their magnificence and virtuosity.

See Pl. 7, Vol. II.

Bibliography: A. D. Tani, *Chiese di Roma*. Turin, 1922.

**SAINT-PORCHAIRE.** — This name of a French village, not far from Bressuire, is used to designate certain 15th century pottery, of rather mysterious origin. This pottery (it was doubtless made in the neighbourhood) is precious on account of its rarity, and the delicacy of its workmanship. The oldest pieces were decorated in black or red, and often reproduce little buildings, with ornaments in relief. The latest are more decorated, and have the addition of coloured enamels. (See Museums of Louvre, Cluny, Victoria and Albert, etc.)

Bibliography: B. Fillon, *Les Faïences d'Oiron*, Fontenay, 1882.—E. Bonnaffé, *Faïences de Saint Porchaire*. Gazette des Beaux Art. April, 1888; April, 1895.

**SAINT SAVIN (Vienne, France).**—The Church of St. Savin, 11th century, is divided into three aisles of equal height, a high barrel vault, and lacks a triforium. It is decorated with famous frescoes, which date from the 12th century

St. Savin: Scene from the Apocalypse. (After the monograph by Mérimée.)

and are the oldest in France. These frescoes are in the porch, on the roof of the nave, in the choir, and in the crypt. In the porch, are scenes from the Apocalypse, faint in outline and colour, but of beautiful design, recalling manuscripts of the period.

The roof is decorated with some thirty scenes from the Old Testament. The frescoes in the choir have almost disappeared. Those in the chapels still possess figures of angels, saints and prophets. In the crypt, frescoes in a better state of preservation trace the judgment and death of St. Savin and St. Cyprian.

All these paintings were inspired by Byzantine art, but not slavishly imitated. The drawing of the dresses, and the varied attitudes are partly derived from nature. Moreover, they are represented on a light background, whereas the Byzantines painted on a dark ground. It is the most important series of French Romanesque paintings that has come down to us.

**SAINT SEBALD (Church of).**—See Nuremberg; also Pl. 25, Vol. II.

**SAINT SOPHIA (Hagia Sophia-divine wisdom), of Constantinople.**—(532-537). This Cathedral was built by order of Justinian, on the site of two earlier basilican churches of the same name. The Emperor resolved to build a church surpassing in splendour all existing churches. Egypt sent him columns of granite and porphyry; the most famous quarries gave marbles—white, light green, white and red, and streaked rose colour; gold, silver, ivory and precious stones—nothing was spared to increase its richness and splendour. The Cathedral was built by the architects Anthemius of Tralles and Isidoros of Miletus. The plan of the church proper consists of a great central space, with four massive stone piers pierced by arches for aisles and gallery, supporting four semi-circular arches upon which rests the dome (107 feet in diameter, and 180 feet above the ground). East and west of this central area are great hemicycles, crowned with semi-domes—the whole area thus forming a great oval nave. The interior gives the impression of one vast domed space, but the detailed effect is of extreme delicacy. The high nave columns and galleries are surmounted by white marble impost capitals, finely carved with foliage, especially with acanthus leaf decoration.

St. Sophia owes much of its character and splendour to its many-coloured decoration—its skilful combination of marbles of all kinds, jasper, alabaster and porphyry. Moreover, under Justinian, the whole of the interior was covered with mosaics with a gold background, which disappeared under the Turks. The effect must have been glorious beyond words. "On entering this church to pray," wrote Procopius, "one feels that it is no work of human industry, but the creation of the Almighty himself; and the soul lifts up itself to God, knowing he is near, and well pleased with his dwelling-place."

St. Sophia is unique. As the Parthenon is the masterpiece of Greek architecture, and the Pantheon of Rome, so it remains the crowning glory of Byzantium.

See Pl. 42, Vol. I.

Bibliography: W. R. Lethaby & H. Swanson, *Church of Santa Sophia, Constantinople*. London, 1916.

**SAINT TROPHÎME (Church of).**—See Arles.

**SAINT URSULA (Shrine of).**—See Bruges; Memling.

**SAINTE CHAPELLE.**—See Paris.

**SAINTES (Charente-Inférieure, France).**—The *Church of St. Eutrope* is a fine Romanesque building, although the nave has been destroyed. The crypt (11th and 13th century) is richly decorated with carving. Tower and spire, 15th century.

The *Church of Sainte Marie des Dames* possesses a 12th century façade and an elaborately sculptured doorway.

**SAITIC ART.**—See Egypt.

**SALAMANCA (Spain).** — *Catedral Vieja* (old Cathedral), or *Santa Maria de la Sede*.—Founded about 1120 by Count Raymond of Burgundy, but only finished a century

Salamanca: Patio of the University.

later. The Romanesque building, which seems to have been influenced by the churches of Aquitaine and Anjou, is especially famous for its dome, which is treated internally with great originality. It has plain pendentives, supporting a high drum

Salamanca: Patio of the Casa de las Conchas. (1514)

pierced with two-storey windows and crowned with a stone ribbed cupola. The exterior is effective, with high drum, semi-circular windows, angle turrets and an octagonal spire.

The *Catedral Nueva* (new Cathedral) was begun in 1513 by Anequin de Egas and is in the late Gothic style on the Moorish type of plan found in the earlier Cathedral of Seville.

The *Church of San Esteban* (more commonly called *Santo Domingo*) was built from 1524 to 1610. The plateresque (see this word) façade is decorated with sculptures.

**SALERNO (Italy).**—One part of the town has retained its mediæval appearance. The *Cathedral* was built in 1270 by Robert Guiscard. The courtyard is surrounded with antique columns, brought from Paestum.

**SALIBA (Antonio de).**—Venetian painter, active 1480-1535. A pupil of his cousin Jacobello and follower of Jacobello's father, Antonello da Messina, as well as of Giovanni Bellini.

**SALIMBENI DA SAN SEVERINO (Lorenzo and Jacopo).**—Painters of the Marches, followers of Alegretto Nuzi.

Lorenzo was born in 1374 (from an inscription of 1400 on a triptych in San Severino). In 1404 he executed frescoes in the Church of the Misericordia, fragments of which still exist. In 1416, with Jacopo, he painted frescoes in S. Giovanni Battista in Urbino (extant). In 1420 he was dead. There is no additional documentary evidence for Jacopo's artistic activity; it is recorded that in 1427 he was a member of the town council of San Severino. Other frescoes in the old cathedral of San Severino are works of collaboration between Lorenzo, Jacopo and one Oliviero, according to an inscription which was once visible. Various attributions have been made to the Salimbeni brothers.

Bibliography: A. Ricci, *Mem. stor. dell' arte e degli artisti della Marca d'Ancona*.—G. B. Cavalcaselle e Morelli, *Catalogo delle opere d'arte nelle Marche,* Gallerie Nazionali, II, 1896, p. 191.—A. Colasanti, *Lorenzo e Jacopo Salimbeni da Sanseverino,* Bollettino d'Arte del Minist. della Pubbl. Istruz., IV, 1910, p. 409.—U. Gnoli, *Lorenzo e Jacopo Salimbeni,* Rassegna d'Arte Umbra, II, 1911.—A. Colasanti. *Italian Painters of the Marches.*

Salisbury: The Cathedral.

**SALISBURY (England).**—Magnificent *Cathedral* in pure Early English style, built from 1220-1284, by the architect Elias of Durham.

**SALONICA.**—See Thessalonika.

**SALVI (Giovanni Battista).**—See Sassoferrato.

**— (Niccolò).**—Roman sculptor of the 18th century. Author of the "Trevi" Fountain in Rome, one of the most famous of the monumental fountains in the Baroque style (from designs by Bernini).

**SALVIATI (Francesco de' Rossi; known as).**—Florentine painter (1510-1563).—Imitator of Michelangelo. His declamatory and violent pictures won him success in his own day.

**SAMARCAND.**—See Moslem Art.

**SAMOS.**—See Greece (Sculpture).

**SAMOTHRACE.**—See Victory of Samothrace.

**SANCHEZ (Juan).** — Spanish painter. He was working in Seville about 1480. In a chapel of the Cathedral he painted a large picture of the *Crucifixion*, and a *Descent from the Cross* (Bilbao).

**SÁNCHEZ COELLO (Alonso).**—Spanish painter born at Benifayo (prov. of Valencia), 1531-32; died at Madrid, 1588. He was the descendant of a noble Spanish family which had been in Portuguese service. When a child he was taken to Lisbon, where he received his first instruction in the arts. There he met Antonio Moro, with whom he formed an intimate friendship, which was only interrupted by the master's hurried departure for the Netherlands. In 1557 we find him at the Spanish court at Valladolid, perhaps through recommendation of D. Juan de Portugal, brother-in-law of Philip II of Spain. He became a favourite of this King who, though usually observing a rigid reserve toward his entourage, called him "his much beloved son." "Though in portraiture he does not take the place of a first rate painter, yet occasionally he did highly creditable work approaching in most cases the paintings of his master Antonio Moro. . . . In these paintings, which are of greatest historical and cultural interest, it is evident that besides Moro the great Venetians, especially Titian, also made an impression of great consequence. But his portraits have a note of their own, namely restraint and balanced objectivity, arrangement of forms in space, concentration upon essentials, a use of a new proportion of color values such as should find later an ideal expression in Velázquez. As the art historian Dvořak observed, there is a straight line leading from Sánchez Coello over Pantoja de la Cruz to Velázquez." Among the many portraits that earned him the admiration of his King and the Spanish aristocracy some are preserved at the Convent de las Descalzas Reales at Madrid, in private collections (Duque del Infantado, Duque de Montellano) and at the Madrid Museum (Prado). Also the State Museum of Vienna owns a full-length portrait of a lady in black attire, etc.

"Coello's religious paintings, in the great majority, are dry and too much under the influence of great Italian art." Of these we cite the paintings of the High Altar of the Parish Church of Espinar (1574-77), the signed and dated *Mystic Marriage of St. Catherine* (1578), formerly of the Escorial and now at the Prado Museum, Madrid, the altar paintings still preserved at the Monastery of El Escorial and a representation of the *Doubting Thomas* (signed and dated Alfonsus Santius, 1585) in the Cathedral of Segovia.

BIBLIOGRAPHY: Aureliano de Beruete y Moret, *The school of Madrid*. London, 1909.—A. L. Mayer, *Geschichte der spanischen malerei*. Leipzig, 1922.—Thieme Becker, Vol. XXIX. Leipzig, 1935; art. *Sánchez Coello* by A. L. Mayer.

**SANDRART (Joachim van).**—German painter and engraver, 1606-1688. After completing his studies in Nuremberg, he became a pupil of Aegidius Sadeler in Prague, and of Honthorst in Utrecht. He travelled a great deal in Italy and in England, and knew personally all the great French, Italian and English artists of his day; Rubens was also among his friends. He is chiefly known as a portrait painter who received commissions from royalty of different nations; he was, however, overrated in his time. Sandrart's main importance lies in his collection, and in his archæological activities. In 1675 he wrote a German art history: *Teutsche Akademie der edlen Bau- Bild- und Mahlereikünste*. He is represented in all important museums.

**SANGALLO or SAN GALLO (Antonio da), the Elder.**—Florentine architect, 1455-1534. He is known chiefly for the construction of the *Madonna di San Biagio*, in Montepulciano (1518-1537), a large edifice in the form of a Greek cross.

He lived also in Monte San Savino, where he built the *Municipal Palace*, the *Loggia de' Mercanti*, and several palaces and churches. In Arezzo, he partly built the *Church of the Annunziata*. In Florence, he and Baccio d' Agnolo built the house of the *Confraternity of the Servi di Maria*. The fortress of *Città Castellana* was built from his plans.

BIBLIOGRAPHY: Gustave Clausse, *Les San Gallo*. 3 vols: 1900.

**— (Antonio da); the Younger: Antonio Cordiani (Vasari calls him Picconi).**—Nephew of Antonio da Sangallo the Elder. Florentine architect, 1485-1546.

One of Bramante's most important pupils, he spread his style in Rome. He was also influenced by Raphael. Some of his works are:—*Chapel in the Church of San Giacomo degli Spagnuoli*, in Rome; *octagonal chapel in the Cathedral of Foligno* (1527), *Palazzo Sacchetti* (which he built for his own use, in 1543), etc.

Antonio da Sangallo is, however, chiefly known as one of the architects of *St. Peter's*, of the *Pauline Chapel*, and the *Chapel Royal*; and the principal architect of the *Farnese Palace*. The *Theatre of Marcellus* was his model, and he took materials from this and from the Coliseum for his work.

See Pl. 75, Vol. II.

BIBLIOGRAPHY: Gustave Clausse, *Les San Gallo*. 3 vols· 1900.

**— (Francesco).**—Florentine sculptor, 1494-1576; son of Giuliano, the architect. Pupil of Sansovino. His work is not very interesting.

**— (Giuliano da).**—Florentine architect and sculptor, 1445-1516. Brother of Antonio da Sangallo, the Elder.

One of the architects who at one time had charge of the work on St. Peter's, Rome (see Saint Peter's). It is to this that he chiefly owes his fame. His other work includes: the *Villa of Poggio a Caiano* (for Lorenzo the Magnificent); and the *Madonna delle Carceri*, at Prato, one of the most beautiful of Renaissance churches. He made it in the form of a Greek cross, and himself designed the medallions of the pendentives and the terra cotta frieze, which Andrea della Robbia carried out (1491). He added the high altar later (1512). He also designed the *Palazzo Strozzi*. He may have built the graceful octagonal Sacristy of Santo Spirito.

In Rome, the splendid roof of Santa Maria Maggiore is attributed to him. The gilding was made with the first gold that came from America.

Together with Baccio Pontelli, he built the fortress of Ostia (1483-1486).

BIBLIOGRAPHY: J. de Laurière, *Giuliano da San Gallo et les Monuments antiques du midi de la France*. Paris, 1885.—Gustave Clausse. *Les San Gallo*. 3 vols: 1900.

**SAN GIMIGNANO (Italy).**—Little town in Tuscany. Very interesting because it keeps its mediæval appearance—its old walls and towers. The *Cathedral* dates from the 12th century. It was enlarged in the second half of the 15th century by Giuliano da Majano, and decorated with frescoes in the 14th and 15th centuries. The finest of these frescoes are the *Martyrdom of Saint Sebastian* and the *Virgin and Saints*, by Benozzo Gozzoli; the *Last Judgment*, by Taddeo di Bartoldo, and above all the *Vision and Funeral of St. Fina*, painted by Ghirlandaio, about 1475.

SAN GIMIGNANO: THE TOWERS.

Sant' Agostino (1280-1298) is decorated with frescoes by Benozzo Gozzoli, representing, in seventeen compositions, scenes from the *Life of Saint Augustine*. The altar of the chapel of San Bartolo is one of the masterpieces of Benedetto da Majano.

SAN GIOVANNI IN LATERANO: THE FAÇADE.

**SAN GIOVANNI IN LATERANO (St. John Lateran), Rome.**—Basilica in the time of Constantine 330. Entirely rebuilt by Innocent X (1644-1655), without any primitive elements. It is now the metropolitan church of Rome. Galilei designed the façade in 1734.

**SAN JULIÁN DE LOS PRADOS (Near Oviedo, Spain).**—A pre-Romanesque Spanish church of the Asturian period, Santullano, as it is known, dates from 792-842. The scale, as in all barbarian structures, is small, and the design precocious. Buttresses appear here, for opposition to the thrust of the barrel vaults. The narthex has mural decorations in late classical style.

**SAN LORENZO.**—See Escorial.

**SAN LORENZO (Church).**—See Genoa; Perugia, Florence.

**SAN LORENZO FUORI LE MURA.**—See Rome.

**SANMICHELI (Michele).**—The chief Veronese architect, 1484-1559, of the Renaissance. The grateful town has erected a statue to his memory, bearing the inscription "grande nella architettura civile e religiosa, massimo nella militare." One of his greatest triumphs was, in fact, the construction of fortifications which were not only solid and severe, but also beautiful. He was born at San Michele, in the environs of Verona, and his talent was developed under Bramante's influence. One of his earliest works was the *Cathedral of Monte Fiascone* (1519), which is on the plan of a Grecian cross. At Orvieto, he made the crypt of *San Domenico* (1519 to 1523).

Sanmicheli's finest work is, however, in Verona. He built the *Palazzo Canossa*, the *Palazzo Pompei alla Vittoria* (about 1530), and others. He generally left the lower part of the building simple and massive, and the first storey, which was lighter, rested on a gallery of columns.

SANMICHELI: GATE OF SAN ZENO AT VERONA.

He also made numerous doorways: the *Porta Nuova*, the *Porta San Zeno* (1540), the *Porta Struppa*. He made the unfinished *Campanile* of the Duomo. He transformed the *Church of Santa Maria in Organo*, and later that of *San Giorgio in Braida*.

One of his most admired works, on account of its decorative richness is the *Pellegrini Chapel*, in the Church of San Bernardino, built in 1557, with a dome which recalls the Bramante's unexecuted design made for St. Peter's.

In Venice, he built the Palazzo Grimani (1549), one of the most finely proportioned and varied of Renaissance palaces.

BIBLIOGRAPHY: Salva, *Elogio di Michele San Micheli*. Rome, 1814.—Ronzani and Luciolli, *Le fabbriche civile, ecclesiastiche e militare di Michele San Micheli*. Venice, 1832.

**SAN MIGUEL DE LIÑO (Near Oviedo, Spain),** 842-850.—A completely barrel-vaulted church of the precocious pre-Romanesque Asturian style. The plan has definite equations with Armenian churches of the 7th century.

**SAN MINIATO AL MONTE.**—The basilican Church of San Miniato al Monte was built in the 11th century on a hill in the environs of Florence. The façade is of white marble, decorated with inlays, and 13th century mosaics. The campanile was built by Baccio Agnolo, in 1519. The interior is divided into three aisles, without a transept. Some of the marble columns are antique. The chapel of San Giacomo, built by Rossellino, from 1461 to 1467, contains the beautiful tomb of the Cardinal of Portugal, also by Rossellino.

**SANO di PIETRO (Ansano di Pietro di Mencio).**—Sienese painter, pupil of Sassetta.

In 1428 Sano is listed in the guild of painters in Siena and is paid for a painted model of a baptismal font for the Baptistry. In 1432 he judges a picture by Sassetta in the Duomo; in 1439 collaborates with Vecchietta in the execution of an *Annunciation* for the Duomo and is elected captain of the Contrada di S. Donato; in 1440, 1443, and 1446 he receives payments for various works in Siena. In 1445 Sano is commissioned to portray *S. Bernardino* (who died the year before) for the Confraternity of Sta. Maria degli Angeli; and in 1448 the Confraternity of the Madonna sotto l'Ospedale orders a portrait of Bernardino. In 1448 and 1450 Sano does decorations for the Duomo and Palazzo Pubblico; and in 1450 a portrait of Bernardino for the Palazzo Pubblico, ordered by the Biccherna (extant). In 1452 he, with Vecchietta, estimates the unfinished fresco by Sassetta on the Porta Romana; in 1459 illuminates a psalter for the Convent of Monte Oliveto; and in 1460 is commissioned to finish the above Sassetta fresco (extant). In 1464-65 Santo acts as arbiter in a dispute between Antonio di Maestro Simone and his patron; in 1465 is paid for a picture made for the Confraternity of St. Jerome; in 1469 for an altarpiece in S. Domenico (further payment in 1475); and in 1471 for illuminations in an antiphonary for the Duomo. In 1473 he receives payments from the Ospedale della Scala; and in 1475-6 arbitrates a dispute which concerns Neroccio and Francesco di Giorgio. He dies in 1481.

Sano di Pietro was enormously prolific, as might be assumed from the above record of his activity. Among his authenticated works are the following: 1444. signed and dated polyptych in the Siena Academy (No. 246), a *Madonna Enthroned with Saints, Angels and a Donor*; 1445, fresco, *Coronation*, in the Hall of the Biccherna, ground floor of the Palazzo Pubblico, signed and dated by Sano, in part by Domenico di Bartolo; 1446, fresco of *St. Peter as Patron of Siena and Two Saints*, outside the above-mentioned room; 1447, triptych (No. 232) in the Academy, Siena, *Madonna Enthroned with Bartholomew and Lucy*, signed and dated; 1449, triptych (No. 255) in the Academy, Siena, *Madonna Enthroned with SS. Blaise, the Baptist, Lawrence, and Martha*, and predella, signed and dated; 1450, fresco of S. Bernardino in the Sala di Biccherna, documented and dated; 1456, *Vision of Pope Calixtus III* (No. 241), Siena Academy, signed, the date formerly visible; 1458, polyptych, signed and dated, at S. Giorgio at Montemerano; 1465, *Coronation with Jerome*, S. Girolamo, Siena; 1470, eighteen miniatures in an antiphonary in the Duomo of Siena; 1471, altarpiece, Badia a Isola Church, near Monteriggioni; 1479, polyptych (Nos. 259, 260), Academy, Siena, from the church of S. Petronilla.

Numerous smaller works, book bindings, miniatures and the like, are dated, and a large number of other paintings are attributed to Sano.

Bibliography: E. Gaillard, *Sano di Pietro*, Chambéry, 1923 (with a summary of all documents cited by Milanesi and Borghese-Banchi).—J. Trübner, *Die Stilistische Entwickelung der Tafelbilder des Sano di Pietro*.

**SAN PAOLO FUORI LE MURA (St. Paul's outside the Walls), Rome.**—Founded in 386; destroyed in 1823 but rebuilt on the original design. It is the largest and most impressive of all basilican churches. Precious frescoes were destroyed in the fire of 1823. The mosaic on the triumphal arch represented a vision of the Apocalypse. (This was restored after the rebuilding, but the effect is deplorable.)

See Rome.

**SAN SALVADOR DE VALDEDIOS.**—A Spanish pre-Romanesque church of the Asturian period, dedicated 892.

**SAN SEVERINO.**—See Lorenzo and Jacopo da San Severino.

**SANSOVINO (Andrea Contucci, called), born at Monte Sansovino.**—Florentine sculptor, 1460-1529, and one of the most celebrated of his day. Sansovino spent eight years (1491-99) in Spain and Portugal; returned to Florence, and in 1505 went to Rome and won the favour of Pope Julius II.

In Santo Spirito, Florence, is a marble altar of the Holy Sacrament, which may have also been a youthful work. In the same church he constructed the vaulting of the vestibule leading to the Sacristy of Giulio da San Gallo and of the Cronaca.

Andrea Sansovino is chiefly known as the creator of the sculpture on Bramante's tombs of the Cardinals Girolamo Basso della Rovere and Ascanio Sforza, in Santa Maria del Popolo, in Rome. These, he made in 1505-1507, by order of Julius II.

The Baptism of Christ, by Andrea Sansovino. (Baptistery, Florence.)

A marble group of *St. Anne, the Virgin and Christ*, is in Sant' Agostino, Rome (1512). The group of the *Baptism of Christ*, which he had executed earlier (begun 1502), in Florence, was finished by Vincenzo Danti.

Sansovino (Andrea): Tomb of Cardinal Ascanio Sforza. (Santa Maria del Popolo, Rome.)

During the last years of his life (1513-1529) he was engaged on the decoration of Santa Casa, in Loreto. Among other works, he made a magnificent marble balustrade, from Bramante's designs. He was assisted by a great many other sculptors (such as Bandinelli, Tribolo, etc.) in the execution of numerous statues and high reliefs. Of the reliefs, the *Annunciation* and the *Nativity* may be by his hand.

Bibliography: Schönfeld, *Andrea Sansovino und seine Schule*. Stuttgart, 1881.—Huntley, G. H., *Sansovino, sculptor and architect of the Italian Renaissance*. Cambridge, 1935.

Sansovino (Jacopo): The Entombment and the Resurrection. (Detail from the bronze door of St. Mark's, Venice.)

**— (Jacopo Tatti, called).**—Florentine architect and sculptor (1486?-1570). Pupil of Andrea Sansovino, whose surname he adopted. One of the principal Renaissance masters, to whom we owe a great many works, and the finest Venetian buildings of the 16th century. He was strongly influenced by Bramante during his sojourn in Rome, but his work had a vigorous, personal character. He sought new combinations of architectural lines, leaving his fantasy and his taste for pomp and richness, to expand in the Venetian sunshine. This distinguishes him from Palladio, who always remained rather cold.

He settled in Venice in 1527, after the sack of Rome, and in Venice he remained. There he finished the *Scuola della Misericordia*, built the fine *Palazzo della Ca Grande* (1532), with arches between double colonnades on the two upper storeys; the nave of San Francesco; the *Scala d' Oro*, in the Doges' Palace (1538); the *Scala dei Giganti* (1554); and the *Fabbriche Nuove*, at the Rialto (1555). His most celebrated work was the *Libreria Vecchia* on the Piazzetta (1536-1553), one of the most brilliant of Renaissance buildings, with a splendid colonnade, the metopes of which are exaggerated at the expense of the triglyphs and architrave. The very high reliefs afford strong contrasts of light and shade. The building excited the greatest admiration. Scamozzi imitated it, but the new Procuratis have lost all the harmony of the model. Palladio criticised all the liberties which Sansovino allowed himself, but his criticism was perhaps tainted with envy.

Sansovino also built the *Loggetta* at the base of the Campanile (1540), which was destroyed by an earthquake and rebuilt in 1905.

The latter part of his life was chiefly occupied with sculpture. Although he was influenced by Michelangelo, his own natural elegance prevailed, and his *Bacchus*, in the Museo Nazionale, shows all his smiling grace. He contributed to the large reliefs of the Chapel of St. Anthony, in Padua. But his *Resurrection of the Suicidal Woman* is one of the least successful, and most affected scenes.

He made a *St. James* in the Duomo of Florence; a *Madonna*, in Sant'Agostino, Rome; and a *St. Anthony of Padua* in San Petronio of Bologna.

His finest statue in Venice is the figure of *Hope*, belonging to the tomb of Doge Venier in San Salvatore (the Doge died in 1556), which has a beautiful serenity. The *Charity* is less good.

Mention may also be made of the statues which belonged to the Loggetta of the Campanile, *Peace, Apollo, Mercury, Pallas*, the colossal statues of *Mars* and *Neptune* which have given its name to the Scala dei Giganti; the celebrated bronze door leading to the Sacristy of San Marco, with its bas-reliefs of the *Death and Resurrection of Christ*. He is said to have worked for twenty years on this door. Other works in St. Mark's: and the *Madonna* in gilded terra cotta, from the interior of the Campanile.

Sansovino (Jacopo): Loggetta of the Campanile. Piazza San Marco, Venice.

See Pl. 6, Vol. II.

**SANT' ANGELO (Castle), in Rome.**—This strong monument was built by the Emperor Adrian, for his tomb and that of his successors. It was finished in 139 by Anthony the Pious. It is composed of a square base on which rests a round building, 64 metres in diameter.

# FRENCH ARCHITECTURE IN THE EIGHTEENTH CENTURY

*The eighteenth century was a period of great activity for architecture. The previous century had been largely occupied by the construction of Versailles, and the Versailles style was carried over in the following century at Paris, in provincial cities and abroad. Paris and the provincial cities took on their modern appearance. They were elegantly arranged; and majestic quality, sometimes slightly emphatic because of Italian influence, was adapted to the spiritual tone of the age.*

PLACE DE LA CONCORDE, PARIS (FORMERLY PLACE LOUIS XV).
*(Photo by Hachette.)*

## The Architecture of Gabriel

Gabriel is a great architect of the Louis XV epoch. He is the successor of Perrault, of the Mansarts, and Robert de Cotte, the builders of the Louvre and Versailles. In short, he is their pupil, and one finds again in his manner the best habits of his predecessors. But he disposes the colonnade with more freedom than the architect of the Louvre. All the same, in all parts of the building, he displays an elegant skill. The two palaces of the Place de la Concorde are incomparable models of urban architecture.

GABRIEL: THE PETIT TRIANON. VERSAILLES.
*(Photo by Hachette.)*

HÉRÉ: PLACE STANISLAS. NANCY.
*(Photo by Hachette.)*

HUBERT ROBERT: THE HAMLET OF THE PETIT TRIANON. VERSAILLES.
*(Photo by Hachette.)*

## Provincial Cities

During the eighteenth century the great civic classical architecture spread into the provincial cities and also into the towns of northern Europe (Germany and Russia). Nantes, Bordeaux, Reims, Montpellier and especially Nancy owe much of their elegance to the fact that these cities were laid out anew during the finest period of French architecture. At this time, architects were not satisfied with constructing gracious palaces, hotels or theatres; they brought together an ensemble of monuments whose façades formed a beautiful urban decoration.

J. H. MANSART: CHURCH OF THE INVALIDES. PARIS.
*(Photo by Hachette.)*

P. VIGNON: CHURCH OF THE MADELEINE. PARIS.
*(Photo by Hachette.)*

SERVANDONI: CHURCH OF ST. SULPICE. PARIS.
*(Photo by Hachette.)*

## Religious Architecture

The church architecture during the two classical centuries shows very well the gradually complete taking over of antique styles. In the churches known as the Jesuit type which, in the seventeenth century, are always more or less derived from St. Peter's in Rome, the ancient orders are cleverly adjusted to the building and are subordinate to its general arrangement. In the eighteenth century, they are no longer only a façade ornamentation; at the Panthéon or at the Madeleine they have changed the appearance of the building relating it more and more to the ancient type. Thus, the Madeleine is an enlarged edition of the Maison Carrée of Nîmes.

# DECORATIVE ART IN THE EIGHTEENTH CENTURY

*It was in the eighteenth century that decorative art, both that of furniture and of interiors, attained its independence and perfection. It is first at this time that it is altogether disengaged from the general architecture in order to adapt itself to the spaciousness and conveniences of civilization. Up until this period it was always more or less the architectural façades which determined the ornamentation of the interiors. However, the use of carved wood and bronze and tapestry led to the setting forth of a special style which was no longer derived from marble and the classic orders. The factory of the Gobelins played an important role in the history of French furniture.*

CHÂTEAU OF FONTAINEBLEAU; THE COUNCIL HALL.

## Louis XV Style, the Council Hall at Fontainebleau

This room of the château of Fontainebleau was constructed at the time of Francis I and decorated during the reigns of Louis XIV and Louis XV. On the ceiling whose compartments recall the Renaissance, it is the style of Louis XV which is particularly dominant, also in the furniture covered in Beauvais tapestry as in the decoration of the panels which were painted by Boucher and Van Loo. The decoration of the Louis XV style is distinguished from that of Versailles primarily because wood has almost everywhere replaced marble or bronze.

CHÂTEAU OF VERSAILLES: ROOM IN THE SMALL APARTMENT OF MARIE ANTOINETTE. *(Photo by Gruyer.)*

VERSAILLES: GRAND TRIANON, EMPIRE ROOM. *(Photo by Gruyer.)*

## The Styles of Louis XVI and the Empire

As early as the second half of the eighteenth century, there was a general reaction in architecture and all the decorative arts against the capricious fantasies of the Rococo. In the Louis XVI style the curves of the Louis XV style were straightened and the forms returned to simplicity. Soon elements borrowed from ancient art appeared and presently this influence became dominant; decorators at the end of the eighteenth century sometimes believed they were remaking Roman furniture.

# SCULPTURE FROM BOUCHARDON TO HOUDON

*F*RENCH *sculpture, in the eighteenth century, participates in the intellectual movement and the trend toward sensibility and displays those qualities with the same vivacity as painting. Moreover, it appears not to have escaped the influence of painting from which it sometimes borrows a little of its spirit and sensuality. The great works such as the decoration of Versailles no longer engage the activity of the artists; the latter may disperse their talents according to their own predilections or the opportunities of patronage. The technical skill of all these sculptors is very superior to that of their predecessors.*

COUSTOU: GROUP FROM MARLY. PARIS.
*(Photo by Hachette.)*

BOUCHARDON: FOUNTAIN OF THE RUE DE GRENELLE, PARIS.
*(Photo by Hachette.)*

LE LORRAIN: HORSES OF THE SUN. HÔTEL DE ROHAN, PARIS.
*(Photo by Neurdein.)*

## Bouchardon

AT THE beginning of the eighteenth century, sculptors in imitation of the Italian style and of Puget were fond of the twisted, agitated form, rugged and picturesque in bearing. Working in this manner were Coustou and Robert Le Lorrain who in their modelling disclosed quite a bit of shading. It was in reaction to this style that Bouchardon advocated a simplified manner with pure lines. He represents a majestic art, somewhat sophisticated, in the midst of artists more disposed toward relaxation. His equestrian statue of Louis XV was admired by contemporaries.

FALCONET: BATHER. LOUVRE.
*(Photo by Hachette.)*

PIGALLE: MONUMENT OF THE MARÉCHAL DE SAXE. STRASBOURG.
*(Photo by Soc. phot. Berlin.)*

FALCONET: PETER THE GREAT. PETROGRAD.

PIGALLE: MERCURY ATTACHING HIS SANDALS. LOUVRE.

## Pigalle and Falconet

THERE is no sculpture as different in style as the work of these two masters. Pigalle was a prolific sculptor as spiritual as he was eloquent. Falconet is especially admired for some graceful works, nymphs and Venuses and some trinkets which the Sèvres factory reproduced. However, he cast a gigantic equestrian statue of Peter the Great.

CAFFIERI: BUST OF ROTROU. THÉÂTRE FRANÇAIS, PARIS.
*(Photo by Hachette.)*

HOUDON: BUST OF LOUISE BRONGNIART. LOUVRE.
*(Photo by Hachette.)*

CLODION: FEMALE SATYR. MUSÉE DE CLUNY.
*(Photo by Hachette.)*

HOUDON: VOLTAIRE. THÉÂTRE FRANÇAIS, PARIS.
*(Photo by Hachette.)*

## Clodion and Houdon

AT THE end of the century during the reign of Louis XVI sculpture becomes sufficiently supple to attempt to rival painting in its nervousness and softness; Clodion in sculpture corresponds to Fragonard in painting. But the great sculptor of this period and one of the greatest in the French school is Houdon. He was the portraitist of his day, animated, keen, nervous. His gallery of busts makes the France of Louis XVI and the Revolution live again. But his unequalled masterpiece is the *Voltaire* in his old age.

# FRENCH PAINTING IN THE EIGHTEENTH CENTURY

*One of the liveliest attractions of eighteenth century French painting, besides its decorative charm, is in the truthfulness and the lifelike quality of the portrait which it has left us of contemporary Parisian society. The very finest nuances of intellectuality of this highly intelligent society are found in the pictures of the portraitists and the paintings of the "moralist" artists. In a school of painting, the influence of the public upon art sometimes assumes more importance than that of instruction; the spirit of the salons at that time had precedence over the aesthetic dicta of the Royal Academy.*

LA TOUR: SELF-PORTRAIT. AMIENS. *(Photo by Hachette.)*

LA TOUR: MLLE. FEL. SAINT-QUENTIN. *(Photo by Hachette.)*

LA TOUR: D'ALEMBERT. SAINT-QUENTIN. *(Photo by Hachette.)*

NATTIER: MME. ADELAIDE. VERSAILLES. *(Photo by Hachette.)*

## The Portraitists

All the painters of the eighteenth century were more or less portraitists. Some of them are closely associated with the picture of their times. Nattier was the official portraitist of the ladies of the Court and in particular the daughters of Louis XV; it is he who fixed the type of elegance and of beauty in the Louis XV style. But La Tour, with his pastels, left us much more characteristic figures; they are animated by an intellectual flame visible in the warmth of the glance and the spiritual nervousness of the mouth. These figures belong to the world of literature, the theatre, finance, the great rôles of contemporary history.

CHARDIN: THE BLESSING. LOUVRE. *(Photo by Hachette.)*

CHARDIN: BOY WITH A TOP. LOUVRE. *(Photo by Hachette.)*

CHARDIN: MME. CHARDIN. LOUVRE. *(Photo by Hachette.)*

## Chardin

Painter of a penetrating charm, a discreet sentimentality, and impeccable honesty, historian of the *petite bourgeoisie*, he progressed from the painting of still life to such subjects as the servant, the mistress and her children, a tranquil silent atmosphere in which the poetry of the hearth reigns. Chardin paints with a robust and loving craftsmanship which lends an interest even to vulgar things. He enchants both poets and painters yet he does not seek to move or to amuse us. Under its modest exterior the work of Chardin is one of the rarest successes in the history of art.

MME. VIGÉE-LEBRUN: THE ARTIST AND HER DAUGHTER. LOUVRE. *(Photo by Hachette.)*

GREUZE: THE VILLAGE BRIDE. LOUVRE. *(Photo by Hachette.)*

GREUZE: THE MORNING PRAYER. MONTPELLIER. *(Photo by Hachette.)*

## Greuze

The generation of Boucher in painting concerned itself with sensitive and honest decoration. The following generation was governed by a more moving inspiration. The style of Greuze corresponds to the pathetic comedy and the sentimental romance. His compositions are scenes from comic operas and melodramas. His contemporaries were fond of weeping after they had so often smiled. But if they were fond of Greuze it was because his moral preaching did not extinguish his sensuality. In the portraits of Madame Vigée Lebrun, deep feeling has replaced shrewd irony.

Probably above this there was a round construction with a column which supported the colossal statue of Hadrian mounted in his chariot. The mausoleum sheltered the remains of Hadrian, Anthony, Marcus Aurelius, Septimus Severus and Caracalla. In the 6th century it was used as a fortress against the Goths who laid siege to Rome. In 590, Gregory the Great, during a procession, saw St. Michael in the clouds, sheathing his sword. In memory of this apparition Gregory built, in the beginning of the 7th century, a Chapel dedicated to "St. Michael in the Clouds," at the top of the building, which henceforward kept the name of the Castello di Sant'Angelo ("the Castle of the Holy Angel"). Throughout the Middle Ages it served as a fortress. In the 14th century, it became the property of the Popes, who joined it to the Vatican by a covered gallery, and rebuilt the parts which had been destroyed in divers sieges. That the Castle became the property of the Popes did not save it from new and redoubled assaults. In 1527, Clement VII was besieged there, and the Constable of Bourbon was killed in the tumult, perhaps by Benvenuto Cellini. Urban VIII added external defense works. In 1752 a statue of Saint Michael (by the Fleming, Verschaffelt) was placed at the top of the building. Restoration work was begun at the beginning of the 20th century. Inside, may still be seen the sepulchral chambers, with niches which contained the urns; the Pope's hall of justice; and a chapel, the façade of which was executed from Michelangelo's designs. On the first floor are the apartments of the Popes, decorated with frescoes by Perino del Vaga, pupil of Raphael, and representing the History of Alexander the Great, and the story of Psyche.

**— in FORMIS.**—Church near Capua, S. Italy. Famous for its remarkable mural paintings, which show a curious mingling of Byzantine style with Latin influence, characteristic of Benedictine art. In the tympanum of the door of the narthex is the Virgin Queen in a medallion upheld by two angels, with an inscription in Greek. In the apse, Christ Enthroned is surrounded by symbols of the evangelists. The aisles are decorated with scenes from the Old and New Testament, and conform to the traditions of Early Christian art.

At Sant'Angelo in Formis it may be seen to what extent the Italians, although profoundly impregnated with Byzantine methods, were able to free themselves from it, and to give their figures the attitudes and gestures of life.

**SANT'APOLLINARE-IN-CLASSE.**—Basilica of Ravenna, built c. 549 in cruciform plan. The outside walls are bare. There is strong Byzantine influence, noticeable particularly in the use of dosserets and the character of the carved detail. Syrian influence may be seen in the open western porch flanked by dwarf towers. The campanile is 8th century. The interior is covered with rich mosaics which present a curious mixture of mystical symbolism and historical fact. High on the raised apse, in the middle, is a jewelled cross, in a blue medallion, strewn with golden stars. To the right and left are two symbolical figures, all in white. At the bottom of the apse, St. Apollinaris surrounded by twelve sheep, raises his arms towards the cross. The figure of the saint is astonishingly realistic.

**— NUOVO (c. 1526).**—Basilica in Ravenna. A Christian Roman basilica under strong Byzantine influence, seen particularly in the detail and the use of dosseret.

Five columns, which support semi-circular arches, divide the building into three aisles. Over the arches are three superimposed bands of mosaics. Below, Christ and the Virgin, seated on thrones, amid angels, receive saints who are represented emerging from the walls of Ravenna and Classe. In the middle are figures of saints, prophets and apostles. Above, the Miracles and Passion of Christ. These mosaics are not only of great historical interest, but of the highest artistic importance. (See Ravenna.)

**SANTA CROCE (Girolamo da).**—Painter of Bergamo, 16th century (active from 1503; died 1556). Follower of the Bellini, influenced by numerous other Venetian painters.

**SANTA MARIA MAGGIORE (Rome).**—One of the most typical of the basilican churches of Rome, built 431 A.D. The portico dates from 1743, and was designed by Ferdinand Fuga.

See Rome.

**SANTA MARIA DE NARANCO (near Oviedo, Spain).**—A tiny church of the precocious pre-Romanesque of Spain under the Asturian kings. It was dedicated in 848. In plan it is a narrow hall with an open arcaded portico at either end and a lateral porch at either side. The interior has lateral arcading and a banded barrel vault. Medal-like ornaments of barbaric design fill the spandrels.

**SANTA SOPHIA.**—See Saint Sophia.

**SANTERRE (Jean Baptiste).**—French painter, 1658-1717. This artist was a pupil of François Lemaire and of the elder Boullogne, and represents admirably the evolution of painting between the end of Louis XIV's reign and the first years of the Regency. As a portrait painter, he never rose above fantasy; as painter of history, he only succeeded in expressing the daintiness of his Parisian models. His charming *Suzanna Bathing* (Louvre) heralds the pleasant insipidity of Nattier.

Bibliography: Pierre Marcel, *La peinture en France au début du XVIII^e siècle*. Paris, 1905.

**SANTI (Giovanni).**—Italian painter of the 15th century (about 1435-1494). Father of Raphael. Son of a grain merchant from the neighbourhood of Urbino. He was a pupil of Melozzo da Forlì in Urbino, and was influenced by Perugino and Justus van Ghent. He aspired to poetry, and made a rhymed chronicle in which he speaks of all the painters he admired from Masaccio to Leonardo da Vinci. One of his earliest pictures must have been the *St. Jerome* in the Vatican Gallery. Among his *Madonnas* are those of the Palazzo Communale of Gradara (1484), of the Kaiser Friedrich Museum, of the Church of Santa Croce, in Fano, of the Ducal Palace of Urbino. The most attractive is the one in the National Gallery, London.

In San Domenico of Cagli, Santi painted some frescoes which are among his best work, a *Madonna* (1481), a *Resurrection*, and a *Pietà* with St. Jerome and St. Bonaventura. The *St. Sebastian*, in the Urbino Gallery, is one of his most charming works.

Giovanni Santi had the patronage of Guidobaldo di Montefeltro and of Elizabeta Gonzaga.

His son Raffaello was born in 1483 and was still young when his father died in 1494.

Bibliography: Passavant, *Raffaello d'Urbino e il padre suo Giovanni Santi*, Vol. I. Florence, 1882. —A. Schmarsow, *Giovanni Santi, der Vater Raphaels*. Berlin, 1887.—G. Natali, *Pittori marchigiani anteriori a Raffaello, Rivista Moderna politica e letteraria*. 15th July 1902. —Crowe and Cavalcaselle, *A New History of Painting in Italy*. Vol. V. London.

**SANTI di TITO.** — Florentine painter, 1537-1603. He continued the Florentine tradition and remained comparatively simple in the midst of the exaggerated imitators of Michelangelo.

**SANTIAGO de COMPOSTELA.**—The basilican *Cathedral of Santiago de Compostela*, the oldest, largest, and most imposing of the Spanish Romanesque churches, is in its chevet, and in the proportions of its transepts, identical with Saint Sernin of Toulouse. The two churches are contemporary, and both descend from a prototype of the Auvergne, or Limoges country. The Cathedral of Santiago de Compostela was finished about 1128. The work had taken 53 to 54 years.

The three aisles are preceded by a magnificent portal, known as the "Portico de la Gloria," the masterpiece of Master Matthew, who had charge of the Cathedral works from 1168. The portal is decorated with numerous figures, full of expression and life, and dominated by a statue of the Saviour. A seated figure of *St. James* is supported on an onyx column. Juan d'Avila (1606) made the choir stalls. The Capilla Mayor was completely rebuilt in the 17th century. The two bronze pulpits were made by J. B. Celma (1563).

On the south side of the Cathedral are the cloisters, among the finest and largest in Spain.

See Pl. 45, Vol. I; Pl. 2, Vol. II.

Bibliography: K. J. Conant, *The Early Architectural History of the Cathedral of Santiago de Compostela*. Cambridge (Mass.), 1926.

**SANTULLANO.**—See S. Julián de los Prados.

**SANTVOORT (Dirck Dircksz van, called Bontepaert).** — Dutch painter, 1610-1680. Strongly influenced by Rembrandt, he is chiefly known for his portraits. In the Rotterdam Gallery are two pictures by him, representing a *Flute Player*, and a *Young Shepherd*. *Four Regents of the Spinhuis* is in Amsterdam.

**SAN VITALE (Ravenna).**—One of the most beautiful of Byzantine basilicas, built in the 6th century. An octagonal construction, surmounted by a dome which is supported by eight thick pillars, united by exedras with two tiers of columns. The roof is extremely light, being formed of long hollow tubes of terra cotta, one fitted into another.

San Vitale derives directly from the oriental Martyrion, the type of which owes its origin to Asia Minor and Syria.

The walls and arches are covered with mosaics. The two most famous represent the Emperor Justinian (who founded the church) with high officials and clergy of Ravenna; and the Empress Theodora with ladies of the court.

**SARACENIC ART.**—See Moslem Art.

**SARAGOSSA.**—The *Aljaferia* of Saragossa was built in the last years of the Moslem occupation (between 1039 and 1081). The fantastic character of the architecture has still freer play here than in the "maksoura" of the mosque of Cordova. The many-lobed arches interlace, twist into knots, and unroll with the suppleness of a ribbon; and delicate ornaments refine the salient features of the architecture. The decoration of this palace, which was built by the Beni Hud outside the ramparts of Saragossa, and which preserves an important fragment of its little mosque, hardly differs from that of the mosque of Tlemcen, which was built about the same time. Two very richly ornamented doors from this palace, have been placed in the Archæological Museum of Madrid.

Saragossa: Multifoil arcade from the Aljaferia.

*La Seo* was founded in 1119. Almost square, it is divided into five aisles, by four rows of Gothic pillars, which rest on bases of yellow marble. It was restored and modified in 1490. See Pl. 2, Vol. II.

*Nuestra Señora del Pilar:* Originally a little chapel built to receive a miraculous image of the Virgin. In 1681, the first stone of the present church was laid. It was built according to the plans of Herrera in the style of the Cathedral of Valladolid, and continued in 1753 by Ventura Rodriguez. It has a rather monotonous appearance, with ten cupolas, a large central dome, and four towers at the angles, two of which were only finished quite recently. The interior is indescribably rich; everything is of marble, bronze or silver.

**SARCOPHAGUS.** — This word comes from a Greek one which signifies "that which devours the flesh." The earliest sarcophagi had, in fact, been made of a stone which had the property of consuming the bodies. The term came to be extended to chests, in wood, stone, lead or terra cotta, in which corpses were laid. The Greeks made great use of terra cotta sarcophagi, which were sometimes decorated with paintings or carvings, such as the sarcophagi from Clazomene and from Sidon. The Phœnicians made sarcophagi in human shape, with head, body and limbs. Etruscan sarcophagi, either in stone or terra cotta, are decorated with bas-reliefs, and the lid is often surmounted with one or two reclining, or half-raised, figures. The Romans have bequeathed us a large quantity of carved sarcophagi, most of which date from the Empire. These are generally decorated with bas-reliefs of mythological or historical subjects. Examples of them are to be seen in most European museums. The carvings are naturally of very unequal value. Those on the earliest Christian sarcophagi are of a rudimentary character; a little later, they show a curious adaptation of pagan legends to Christian scenes. With the coming of the barbarian invasions, sculpture virtually disappeared, and, on the sides of the heavy stone sarcophagi one finds only clumsily traced outlines. In the Romanesque and Gothic periods sculptured tombs reappeared; but these are no longer, properly speaking, sarcophagi, for they do not as a rule contain the body, which is interred elsewhere in a coffin. However, they often have the same form.

Bibliography: Martha, *L'Art étrusque*.—Le Blaut, *Les sarcophages chrétiens de la Gaule*.—Reinach, *Les sarcophages de Clazomene*. Revue archéologique, 1883.

**SARGENT (John Singer).**—American painter (1856-1925). He was born in Florence, Italy, the son of American parents, 12th January 1856. His mother had some talent in watercolour painting and she encouraged him to copy the works of the old masters in the great museums of Europe. In 1874 accompanied by his father he went to Paris and there entered the salon of Carolus-Duran, the celebrated portrait painter. He worked there for the next two years and then made his first trip to the United States. Next he went to Spain, where he saw the work of Velázquez, and then on to North Africa, doing some brilliant sketches of the natives. After that he returned to Paris to open his own studio and soon commissions began to come in in a steady and unceasing flow. His portraits, though in general swiftly executed, gave a vivid impression of his models subtly characterised. Indeed, the portrait of *Madame Gautreau,* perhaps better known as *Mme. X.*, was so realistic and true to life that it caused much criticism of his methods. Sargent, disliking any disturbance of the sort, left for England in 1884 and made his home there for the rest of his life. In 1890 he received the commission to do a set of murals for the new Public Library in Boston. For the preparation of these he made a trip to Egypt to get an idea of the proper accessories and then in company with Edwin A. Abbey took a studio outside London. Abbey was then engaged in the Grail series of murals for the same building. Sargent's murals consisted of the *Frieze of the Prophets, the Dogma of Redemption* and some lunettes, the whole not completed until 1916. He also did a series of mural decorations for the Boston Museum of Fine Arts, which were finished shortly before his death. In England as in France he enjoyed steady patronage of the noble families seeking to have their likenesses painted for posterity by his brush in the mould of veracity. After 1910 Sargent was less interested in portraiture and returned to the use of watercolours, which he had relinquished. He worked around Venice and in the Austrian Tyrol and behind the lines during the World War, getting striking results from his impressionistic method of handling that medium. Afterward he returned to England to resume his portraits, continuing his work until the very end. He died in his sleep 15th April 1925, just as he was preparing to visit the United States.

Sargent (John): Carmencita.

John Sargent is especially noted for his portraits in oil. Men, women and children, all were transferred to canvas by his magic touch, their faces sketched in an accurate description, though the paintings were not great psychological analyses of his models. The resulting pictures, though often the product of long hours of work, always give the final impression of the tireless and effortless output of genius. His watercolours, on the other hand, were mainly figure pieces and landscapes done in an impressionistic style with great suggestive patches of the paper left exposed. The murals in the Boston Public Library are monumental in conception, simple colour harmonies carefully strengthened to suggest solidity and flatness suitable for such decoration. He was a creative and prolific artist whose main forte was the delineation of the first families of England and America.

See Pl. 58, Vol. II.

Bibliography: The Honorable Evan Charteris, *John Sargent,* 1927.—William Howe Downes, *John S. Sargent, His Life and Work,* 1926.—Martin Hardie, *J. S. Sargent, R. A., R. W. S.,* Famous Water Colour Painters, No. VII, 1930.—J. B. Manson and Mrs. Meynell, *The Work of John S. Sargent,* 1927.—Nathaniel Pousette-Dart, *John Singer Sargent,* Distinguished American Artists Series, 1924.—T. Martin Wood, *Sargent,* 1909.—For a complete bibliography see *The Index of Twentieth Century Artists* for February, 1935.

**SARRAZIN (Jacques).**—French sculptor, 1588-1660. Early in life, he studied in Paris, under Nicholas Giullain. About 1610, he went to Rome, where he stayed till 1628. He returned to Paris in 1629, and lived there until his death. Jacques Sarrazin was an important artist in his day, and figured as head of a school of sculpture. Thibaut Poissant, Louis Lerambert, Le Hongre, and the two Marsy, passed through his studio. Buyster, Guérin, Van Opstal and Le Gendre, worked on his models. Almost all the churches of Paris wanted sculpture from him—Notre Dame, Saint Gervais, Saint-Paul, Saint-Louis, and Saint Nicholas-des-Champs, where one may still see his four statues for the high-altar. Employed at Chilly, Rueil and Maisons he was, above all, the official sculptor of the monarchy. He decorated the central pavilion of the Louvre, and furnished models which were carried out by Van Opstal, Gilles Guérin and Buyster: caryatides supporting the dome, and figures of Fame placed over the pediment. He sculptured the tomb of Bérulle, and that of Henry II de Condé, his masterpiece, at Chantilly. It is one of the first, and not the least, examples of academic funeral art.

Sarrazin (Jacques): Tomb of Henry II of Condé. (Chantilly.)

Sarto (Andrea del): Madonna del Sacco. (Santa Annunziata, Florence.)

Sarto (Andrea del).

Again, in the tomb for the heart of Louis XIII (Louvre), one finds a certain nobility and delicacy which are Sarrazin's essential qualities. Though he submitted too slavishly to Italian influence and did not sufficiently study nature for himself, it must be admitted that his work has a certain dignity and moral tone.

— **(Pierre).**—French sculptor, 1602-1679. He assisted his brother Jacques in most of his work. He was a member of the Académie royale.

**SARTO (Andrea d'Agnolo di Francesco di Luca Vanucci, known as del).**—Florentine painter, 1486-1531. A pupil of Piero di Cosimo, influenced by Michelangelo. His self-portrait in the Uffizi reveals a graceful young Florentine with long hair and a serious expression. His work has an attractive facility, and charming colour. The soft, velvety grace of his figures sometimes ends by smothering the expression, which is apt to be commonplace. But, at the same time, this tendency towards the envelopment of form leads to an advance in chiaroscuro which was not without an important influence on painting. While he was not afraid of large expanses of shadow, del Sarto realised the need of light to give relief to his figures. The energy and passion of soul of a Michelangelo, and even the feeling in the fine "Sfumato" of a Leonardo da Vinci, are replaced by a joyous facility, and the artist gives pleasure by the sheer skill of his painting. Later generations threw themselves wholeheartedly into this chiaroscuro, but they lost all formal distinction, and fell into mere mannerism.

Andrea del Sarto began his training with a goldsmith. He continued it with the painter Piero di Cosimo. In 1508, he was entered into the Guild of Painters.

Sarto (Andrea del): Charity. (Louvre.)

In the *History of Filippo Benizzi,* a youthful work (before 1510), which he painted in fresco, at the entrance of the Annunziata, he already shows his ability. But it is rather the *Journey of the Magi,* and above all the *Nativity of the Virgin* (1514), that attract the admiration of visitors. The *Madonna del Sacco* (1525), over the doorway leading from the cloisters to the church, is also in fresco.

The monochrome frescoes representing incidents from the Life of St. John the Baptist, in the cloisters of the Scalzo, cover the period 1512-25.

In 1521, he painted a large fresco at the Villa Poggio at Caiano, representing Cæsar receiving tribute

SARTO (ANDREA DEL): THE HOLY FAMILY. (Louvre.)

(continued by Alessandro Allori). He painted a *Last Supper,* begun 1519, in the Convent of San Salvi. The arrangement of figures and draperies seems to have interested the painter more than the moment of Christ's terrible revelation.

Among his numerous work, may also be mentioned the following:

In the Pitti Palace, Florence: the *Annunciation,* the *History of St. Joseph* (1517), *the Deposition from the Cross,* the *Disputà.*

In the Uffizi Gallery, Florence: the *Madonna delle Arpie* (1517).

In the Dresden Gallery: the *Sacrifice of Isaac,* and the *Marriage of St. Catherine.*

SARTO (ANDREA DEL): MADONNA OF THE HARPIES. (Uffizi, Florence.)

In the Vienna Gallery: the *Pietà.*

In the Louvre, Paris: *Charity,* and the *Holy Family.*

In Berlin: the *Madonna and Saints* (1528).

Andrea del Sarto was summoned to the court of Francis I in France, but he embezzled money which had been entrusted to him by the king for the acquisition of works of art. He ended by dying of the plague in Florence, in 1531, at the age of forty-five.

BIBLIOGRAPHY: Crowe and Cavalcaselle. *A History of Painting in Italy,* Vol. VI. ed. T. Borenius.

**SARVISTAN (Mesopotamia).**—*Palace.* A Sassanian building of the 4th or 5th century with a triple arched façade with a *kubbeh* dome on squinches behind. The domed compartment was flanked by barrel-vaulted rooms and succeeded by a court. Construction was very crude.

**SASSETTA (Stefano di Giovanni).**—Sienese painter, pupil of Paolo di Giovanni Fei, born 1392; died 1450.

Sassetta's earliest known work is the altarpiece he executed, 1423-26, for the Arte della Lana in Siena. In 1424 there is a mention of a document of payment for a sketch of a baptismal font; in 1428 he is included in the list of the corporation of painters in Siena; and in 1430 is charged to execute a panel for the Cathedral. The Chiusdino altarpiece is of 1430-32. In 1432 the panel for the Duomo mentioned above is estimated by Martino di Bartolommeo; and in 1433 is recorded the document of payment. In the same year Sassetta executes a Crucifix for S. Martino, which was cut to pieces in 1820, and of which certain fragments are in the Academy, Siena. From 1436 dates the triptych at Osservanza, near Siena. The next year Sassetta is commissioned to paint an altarpiece for S. Francesco in Borgo San Sepolcro, which is paid for in 1440. Also in 1440 he is paid for sketches made by him for a window which was never carried out. In 1442 he executed banners for the Cathedral; in 1444 was paid by the Ospedale della Scala for a picture of S. Bernardino; and in 1445 made sketches of liturgical vestments for the Cathedral. In 1447 Sassetta was commissioned to paint a fresco on the Porta Nuova or Porta Romana but died before finishing the task (completed by Sano di Pietro).

The 1423-26 altarpiece for the Arte della Lana mentioned above is dispersed among the following collections: Budapest, *St. Thomas Aquinas in Prayer;* Rome, Vatican, *Christ Thanking St. Thomas Aquinas;* Barnard Castle, Bowes Museum, *Miracle of the Sacrament;* Siena, Academy, *Last Supper, Temptation of Anthony, Four Saints;* New Haven, Jarves Collection, *Temptations of Anthony Abbott.* Next in date come the Chiusdino (1430-32) and Osservanza (1436) altarpieces; and last that of Borgo San Sepolcro, which is also divided: Florence, Berenson Collection, *St. Francis in Ecstasy,* the *Baptist, Beato Ranieri;* New York, Clarence Mackay Collection. seven scenes from the *Legend of Francis;* Chantilly. Musée Condé. *Marriage of Francis with Poverty.* Sassetta's style has been recognized in a number of other panels.

BIBLIOGRAPHY: G. Milanesi, *Doc . . . senese,* I, 1854, p. 48; II, pp. 198, 242, 243, 244, 245, 276.—Borghesi e Banchi, *Nuovi doc. senesi,* 1898, pp. 119, 142, 145, 166.—Langton Douglas, *A Forgotten Painter,* Burlington Magazine, I, 1900, p. 306; *A Note on Recent Criticism of the Art of Sassetta,* Burlington Magazine, IV, 1903, p. 265.—Berenson, *A Sienese Painter of the Franciscan Legend.* London, 1910.—G. De Nicola, *Sassetta between 1423 and 1433,* Burlington Magazine, XXIII, 1913, pp. 207, 276, 332; XXIV. 1913, p. 232.

**SASSOFERRATO (Giovanni Battista Salvi da).**—Italian painter (1605-1685), born at Sassoferrato, where, in the church of San Pietro, there is a Madonna by him. He was a pupil of Domenichino. Sassoferrato has little originality, but he is conscientious and sentimental. He is represented by a *Holy Family* (in the Doria Palace, Rome), *St. Joseph's Workshop,* and an *Adoration of the Shepherds* (Naples Gallery), and a *Madonna of the Rosary* in Santa Sabina, Rome. He greatly admired Raphael, and made a copy of *La Fornarina,* which is in the Borghese Palace.

**SAVERY (Roelant Jacobsz).**—Flemish painter, 1576-1639. He was a meticulous landscape painter, who chiefly painted views of Switzerland and of the Tyrol. He preferred to paint mythological scenes in which he cleverly used groups of animals. Most of his pictures are in the galleries of Vienna: the *Earthly Paradise,* and Dresden: *Noah's Ark. Orpheus Charming the Animals* is at The Hague.

**SAVOLDO (Girolamo).**—Brescian painter, who died at a great age, after 1548. He studied in Venice, and was influenced chiefly by Palma. He had a predilection for painting sunsets, evening landscapes, and night scenes, in which a Holy Family very often figures. But his tones are apt to be too cold and blackish. Nevertheless, his cool colour must have had a charm for his celebrated pupil, Moretto.

His chief works are a *Nativity* (Brescia Gallery), a large *Madonna Appearing to Saints* (in the Brera Gallery, Milan); another *Madonna* in Santa Maria in Organo (Verona); a *Transfiguration* (in the Uffizi); a *Holy Family,* and an *Adoration of the Shepherds* (Turin).

BIBLIOGRAPHY: Crowe and Cavalcaselle, *A History of Painting in North Italy,* ed. T. Borenius, Vol. III.

**SCAMOZZI (Vincenzo).**—Architect of Vicenza and of Venice (1552-1616). Pupil and successor of Palladio, he built the *Trissino Palace* (*Palazzo del Municipio*), and the *Trento Palace* (Valmarana), and he finished Palladio's *Teatro Olympico,* for which he made the interior decoration. Scamozzi was very popular and was employed in Genoa, Rome, etc. He wrote a large volume—*L'Architettura Universale.*

**SCEAUX (Seine).**—The Château of Sceaux is famous for the name of those who inhabited it, and for the brilliance of the fêtes and literary gatherings which were given there. It was sold to Colbert in 1670, who had a luxurious residence reconstructed. Le Brun arranged the decoration. Only two buildings remain —the Orangery, and the famous "Pavillon de l'Aurore," decorated by Le Brun and Audran (a remarkable painting on the dome, representing the *Rising of Aurora*). From Colbert, the château passed to the Duc du Maine. This opened a splendid period for Sceaux, which became the rendezvous of the court and of literary society. In 1793, this magnificence was destroyed. A new château was built on the site of the old one. It was burned down in 1871. In the park there remain some of the sculptures which formerly adorned it—two fine groups by Coysevox, and a *Rape of Proserpine,* by Giradon.

**SCHALCKEN (Godfried).**—Flemish painter and graver of portraits and "genre" scenes, 1643-1706. He was a pupil of Gerard Dou, and spent most of his life in Dordrecht and in The Hague. In 1692 he went to England where his popularity brought him a considerable amount of wealth. Influenced by Dou, he too liked to paint light effects produced by candles; but unlike Dou, some of his compositions tend to become unappealingly large in size. The *Self-portrait* (Uffizi), is similar to most of his portrait studies: the figure holds a lighted candle in his hand, the red light reflecting on his face. As a portrait painter he was overrated, however his "genre" scenes are charming with a sense of humor and appealing satire. His *chef d'œuvre, Vrouwtje Kom Ten Hoog,* is in Buckingham Palace.

BIBLIOGRAPHY: Hofstede, *Holl. Maler,* v. 5.

**SCHEFFER (Ary).**—Painter. Born at Dordrecht, 1795; died at Argenteuil, in 1858. His father, a talented painter, died very young, leaving a widow and three children. His mother settled in Paris, and placed her son under Guérin, in whose studio he became acquainted with Géricault, Champmartin. Sigalon and Delacroix.

At the Salon of 1831, two paintings which made a considerable sensation — *Faust* and *Marguerite* — inaugurated the series of scenes inspired by Goethe. Dante also inspired him. His *Francesca da Rimini* is one of his most touching works.

A leader of the romantic movement, he was famous for his portraits and historical scenes.

**SCHIAVONE (Andrea Meldolla, known as).**—North Italian painter, c. 1515-1563. Born at Sebenico. He was a pupil of Titian, and was, towards the end of his life, influenced by Parmigianino.

Tintoretto said that every painter ought to have a picture by Schiavone in his studio, so that he could constantly study his beautiful colours. Unfortunately, a good deal of his work, such as the frescoes which he painted on the façades of Venetian palaces, has been lost. There exist by him a *Christ before Pilate,* a *Circumcision,* and some *Allegories,* in the Academy; a *Christ at Emmaus,* in San Giacomo dell'Orio; several paintings in Santa Maria del Carmine; a *Madonna* and *St. Catherine,* in Querini-Stampalia Collection; the *Samson Killing a Philistine, Adam and Eve,* and the *Adoration of the Shepherds,* in the Pitti Palace, Florence; and works in Vienna, London, Hampton Court, Berlin, etc.

**— (Giorgio, misnamed Gregorio, real name Giorgio Chiulinović).**—School of Padua, born 1436-37 in Scadrin, Dalmatia; died 1504 in Sebenico.

In 1456, Schiavone, in Venice, becomes the pupil of Squarcione, and in 1458 is still Squarcione's pupil. His period of activity in Padua was short; in 1462 he is in Zara, where Squarcione, through the mediation of the cancelliere civico, requests that he return certain drawings and money owed him. In 1463, Schiavone settles in Sebenico. where he marries the daughter of an architect and which he leaves afterward only for brief trips. 1464 brings another reference to the money and the drawings, which Squarcione is still trying to collect; in 1467 part of the money is paid, and presumably the rest of it soon after, for in 1474 Squarcione transfers his attack to one Marinello who was supposed to have transmitted the money to Squarcione but who kept it for himself. In 1476 Schiavone is for a short time in Padua. Nearly three hundred documents in Sebenico apply to Schiavone; only two of which have reference to any artistic activity. In 1489 he is commissioned to paint an altarpiece for S. Giacomo in Sebenico. A quittance payment to his heirs for an altarpiece in this church is registered in 1536. The other documents have to do with Schiavone's activity as a merchant. He evidently all but abandoned painting in Dalmatia, since no works by him have been found there.

None of his paintings are dated; the *Madonna* in the Kaiser-Friedrich Museum, Berlin, from S. Francesco in Padua, is signed; and the London polyptych, *Madonna and Child, Saints,* and *Pietà,* is also signed. In Padua, in the Museum, is a fresco-fragment of the *Madonna and Child*; in the Sacristy of the Duomo, two panels with *Saints*; and in the Eremitani, a *Dead Christ with Angels.* In Paris, Musée Jacquemart-André, is a *Madonna Enthroned with Two Saints and Angels*; and a *Bust Portrait of a Man,* signed; in Turin, Pinacoteca, a signed *Madonna, Child, and Angel;* and in Venice, Museo Correr, a *Madonna and Child,* restored.

BIBLIOGRAPHY: L. Venturi, *Le origini d. pitt. venez.,* 1907.—Testi, *Storia d. pitt. venez.,* I, 1909.—Crowe and Cavalcaselle, *Hist. of Painting in North Italy,* Borenius ed., II, 1912.—A. Venturi, *Storia d. arte ital.,* VII, III, 1914.—A. Moschetti, *Padova,* 1927.—P. Kolendić, *Slikar Juraj Ćiulinović in Sibenicu* in Vjesnikaza Archeologiju i hist. dalmat., 1930 (all Dalmatian documents recorded).—A Moschetti, *Il Museo di Padova,* 1936.

**SCHINKEL (Karl Friedrich).**—German architect and painter, 1781-1841, who, in addition to working in the Greek phase of neo-classicism, as in the Royal Theatre and Old Museum, Berlin, inaugurated the Gothic Revival in Germany with his never-executed design for the Cathedral of Berlin, 1819.

BIBLIOGRAPHY: A. Grisebach, *Carl Friedrich Schinkel.* 1924.

**SCHLEGEL (Frederick).**—See Nazarenes.

**SCHLIEMANN (Heinrich).**—See Mycenæ; Troy.

**SCHMIDT (Georg Friedrich).**—German engraver, 1712-1775. He was trained in Paris by his compatriot, Wille, and then he became the pupil of Larmessin, who introduced him to the art of Lancret, which became a life long influence on Schmidt. Under the patronage of Rigaud and La Tour, he was one of the court favorites. Later he was called to St. Petersburg where he founded a school. His work consists chiefly of engraved portraits and some etchings.

BIBLIOGRAPHY: Crayen, *Catalogue raisonné de l'œuvre de G. F. Schmidt.* Leipzig, 1789.—L. D. Jacoby, *Schmidt's Werke.* Berlin, 1815.

**SCHMIDT-ROTTLUFF (Karl).**—Contemporary German painter, sculptor and graver, 1844—. One of the most outstanding members of the "Brücke," he studied with Max Pechstein and Nolde. His early, rather monumental works were done in the style of the impressionists, but he soon found himself involved with the problems of expressionism. From this period dates his *Self-portrait* (1910), and several landscapes, characterized by sweeping strokes, an architectonic structure, and often violent color. His recent landscapes and portraits are more in the imaginative vein tending towards realism.

BIBLIOGRAPHY: Valentiner, M. R., *Schmidt-Rottluff,* Junge Kunst, 1920.

**SCHMITZ (Bruno).**—German architect, 1856-. Designer of the Monument of the Nations, Leipzig, 1898-1913, and the Soldiers and Sailors Monument, Indianapolis, U.S.A.

**SCHŒNBRUNN (Austria).**—Château built in 1774 under the reign of Maria Theresa. It has artistically and historically important rooms, an interesting chapel, and a park in the French style. The son of Napoleon I, the King of Rome, lived there after the abdication, and died there. It was the summer palace of the Hapsburg emperors.

**SCHONGAUER (Martin).**—German painter and engraver of the 15th century, born in Kolmar about 1430—died 1491, son of a goldsmith of Augsburg, probably a pupil of Gaspard Isenmann (author of a *Passion,* painted in 1462, for the Church of St. Martin). The earliest authentic works are two drawings, which Dürer signed with the initial S, and dated 1469. His known works are rare: the *Madonna of the Rosebush* (Kolmar, Church of St. Martin, 1473); the *Adoration of the Shepherds* (Berlin); and two wings of an altarpiece (Berlin), representing the Virgin and Child, St. Anthony, and a donor. Schongauer was strongly influenced by Roger van der Weyden. We find in his work the same long, angular forms, and broken folds. He retains the bright colour of the primitives, and reveals a delicate sensibility.

Schongauer is, however, more essentially an engraver than a painter. There are fifteen engravings by him, most of which represent scenes from the Passion, and some "diableries," of which the *Temptation of St. Anthony* is one of the best. Schongauer enjoyed a great reputation, not only in his own country but also in Italy.

See Pl. 3, Vol. II.

BIBLIOGRAPHY: Girodie, *Martin Schongauer,* Collection des maitres de l'Art. Paris, 1900.—Wendland, *Martin Schongauer als Kupferstechr.* Berlin, 1907.—C. Champion, *Schongauer,* 1925.—Wurzbach, *M.S.,* 1880.

**SCHÜCHLIN (Hans).**—German painter of the 15th century, died about 1505. Swabian School of Ulm. His most important and only authentic work is the altarpiece of Tiefenbronn, painted in 1469. In the centre, is a *Descent from the Cross* and a *Pietà*; on the wings, scenes from the *Life of the Virgin,* and from the *Passion.* His style is derived from the Flemish and Nürenberg schools.

BIBLIOGRAPHY: Haack, *Hans Schüchlin.* Strasbourg, 1905.

**SCHUT (Cornelis).**—Flemish painter and graver, born in Antwerp (1597-1655.) Pupil and imitator of Rubens, who often entrusted him with work. His colour is less warm and less luxurious than that of the master. Besides other works, he was responsible for one of the four pictures in the Jesuit Church of Antwerp, *St. George* (Antwerp); the *Assumption of the Virgin,* (Amsterdam), and the *Triumph of Time* (Vienna).

**SCHWARZRHEINDORF (Germany).**—*Doppel-Kirche,* 1150-1170. An elaborate example of a Byzantine type of church used for palatine chapels in Romanesque Germany: a two-storeyed building, square in plan, divided into nine equal compartments by four columns, the central compartment being in two storeys and roofed by a lantern, the other compartments being in one storey with a tribune above forming a gallery about the central compartment.

**SCHWIND (Moritz von).**—Austrian painter and graver, 1804-1871. Of noble descent he studied philosophy at the university, when in 1821 he decided on an artistic career. He was prominent with the intellectuals, listing among his close friends Schubert, Lenau and others. At first he was an illustrator and lithographer (*Robinson Crusoe illustrations*), working in a sentimental style. His etchings to Goethe's works were published in Leipzig in 1827-30. In 1827 was painted his

SCHWIND (MORITZ VON): THE WEDDING TRIP. (Schack Gallery, Munich.)

first oil *The Promenade* (Vienna), in the typical Biedermeier fashion. This soon was followed by *Dante and Cupid,* and other mythological and literary subjects, all done in vivid colors, in the romantic and narrative manner. He received several commissions to paint frescoes for ceilings in royal residences, among which was an offer in 1832 for the Munich palace of the king. He traveled in Italy and England and spent much time in Frankfort a.M., where he developed a liking for water colors. In 1863 we find him decorating the lobby of the Vienna Opera House with scenes of Mozart's *Zauberflöte.* He was a typical exponent of the very patriotic movement in Germany, expressing the spirit and literary achievements of his country through his art.

BIBLIOGRAPHY: Holland. *M. v. S.,* 1873.—Pastor, *M. v. S.,* 1910.—O. A. Weigmann, *Schwind,* Klassiker der Kunst (Vol. IX); 1906.

**SCOPAS.**—Greek sculptor of the 4th century B.C. Almost nothing is known of his life, except that he came from Paros. According to Pliny, Scopas was, in 320 B.C., in his period of full activity. He probably went early to Greece, in the Peloponnesus and in Attica. before returning to Asia Minor, where he seems to have ended his career. His Statue of *Aphrodite Pandemos* was probably a youthful work. On a coin of Elis, this Aphrodite is represented seated on a running bull, a design which may have been conceived by Scopas. After 395, the date of the destruction of the temple of Athena Alea at Tegea, Scopas rebuilt and decorated it. Excavations on the site of this old temple have led to the discovery of the foundations and some remains of sculpture which originally belonged to the pediments, and which are now in the Athens Museum. These pediments represented the hunt of the wild boar of Calydon. Certain Argine influences still linger on, such as the square shape and massive proportions of the heads of the combatants.

Scopas probably settled in Athens about 380. At this time the Attic city had recovered a little of her prestige which had suffered through the disasters of the Peloponnesian War. We know through the historians that Scopas made two "Furies" for their temple on the Acropolis. There is also mention of a statue of Hestia, which was transported to Rome.

From Athens, Scopas probably went to Asia Minor. There is mention of statues by him in Cnidus, at Ephesus, at Samothrace, etc. In the temple of Mars, in Rome, there was a statue of Ares seated, which probably came from Pergamum. It is sometimes suggested that the Ludovisi *Ares* may be a copy. There was also in Rome a statue of Aphrodite which was much appreciated; archæologists have wondered whether the Venus of Milos is not a reproduction of the type. Again in Rome, an important group, including Poseidon, Thetis and Achilles, was set up in the temple of Neptune.

SCOPAS: BACCHANTE. (Albertinum, Dresden.)

Scopas seems to have spent his last years in Asia Minor. About 350 B.C., he was in Halicarnassus, employed on the work of the mausoleum.

No authentic work by Scopas remains, and it is therefore difficult to represent his style very exactly. Judging from the very mutilated Tegean figures, from descriptions by ancient authors, and from the subjects he chose it is concluded that Scopas excelled in the expression of passion. He has been credited with the groups of Niobides (see) and the Victory of Samothrace, in the Louvre. He was the head of that artistic movement which ended in the vehement and dramatic art of the school of Pergamon.

Bibliography: Collignon, *Scopas et Praxiteles*. Paris, 1907. (This gives a fairly complete bibliography).—Ernest Gardner, *Six Greek Sculptors*. London, 1925 (3rd imp.).

**SCOREL (Jan van).**—Dutch painter, born at Scorel, 1495-1562. He was the pupil of W. Cornelisz of Haarlem, of Jacob Cornelisz, of Amsterdam, and of Mabuse. He visited Germany, Jerusalem, and was the first Dutch painter to go to Italy. In 1525, he painted a series of *Portraits of Pilgrims* returning from the Holy Land, including himself. These portraits are in Utrecht, where he worked during the greater part of his life. He also painted a *Family Group* (Cassil Gallery); *Portrait of a Boy* (Rotterdam); the *Last Judgment* (Rijks Museum, Amsterdam); *Adam and Eve* (Haarlem); the *Baptism of Christ*, *Magdalen*, the *Queen of Sheba* (all in Amsterdam); and the triptych of the Vischer van der Gheer family (Utrecht Museum). The colouring and light effect reveal the influence of Venetian art on Scorel. Scorel was the master of Martin van Heemskerck and of Antonio Moro.

See Pl. 24, Vol. I.

Bibliography: G. J. Hoogewerff, *Jan van Scorel, peintre de la Renaissance hollandaise*. 1923.

**SCOTT (Sir Gilbert).**—English architect, 1810-1877. An exponent of Gothic, Scott designed in that style among other buildings St. Nicholas, Hamburg, 1846-1863; the Albert Memorial, 1851; the Government Offices, Whitehall, 1860-1875; and Glasgow University, 1860-1870.

**— (Giles G.).**—Contemporary English architect, born 1880. He is the designer of the huge Gothic Liverpool Cathedral, begun 1903 and still building.

**— (Samuel).**—English painter (1710-1772), specialized in topographical subjects, notably views of London. Many pictures which are really copies after Canaletto have been assigned to him.

**SCUOLE.**—See Carpaccio (V.).

**SEBASTIANO DEL PIOMBO (Sebastiano Luciani).**—Venetian painter, 1485-1547. He began as a pupil of Giovanni Bellini and Giorgione. He probably painted the *Incredulity of St. Thomas* for San Niccolò of Treviso (1505-06). The altarpiece of San Giovanni Crisostomo, in Venice, which has been attributed to Giorgione, shows a growth of his powers (before 1510).

Sebastiano del Piombo: The Resurrection of Lazarus. (National Gallery, London.)

About 1509, he was called to Rome to decorate the Villa Farnesina. He painted the *Metamorphoses* of Ovid, and a colossal *Polyphemus*, in warm, Venetian colours. The *Portrait of a Woman* (Uffizi), long supposed to be by Raphael, is now generally ascribed to Sebastiano.

Sebastiano soon fell under the sway of Michelangelo. He retained something of the rich colouring of Venice, which was as well, for, though he imitated the Florentine master, he possessed nothing of Michelangelo's power.

His principal pictures, in the rather pompous style he adopted in Rome, are: *The Resurrection of Lazarus* (National Gallery—1519); the striking *Pietà* (in San Francesco of Viterbo—c. 1517); an unfinished *Madonna* (Naples); the *Martyrdom of St. Agatha* (Pitti Palace—1520); blackened frescoes in a chapel of San Pietro in Montorio, in Rome (1525); a *Birth of the Virgin*, in the Chigi Chapel of Santa Maria del Popolo, Rome.

Sebastiano del Piombo: Portrait of La Fornarina. (Museum of Berlin.)

His portraits remained more strongly Venetian in character. The pale, cold figure of Andrea Doria (in the Doria Gallery, Rome) is a masterpiece. Other striking portraits are: *Man with a Beard* (Pitti Palace); *Portrait of Young Roman Woman* (Berlin), and two male portraits in the Uffizi.

To Sebastiano is sometimes attributed the *Death of Adonis*, in the Uffizi, which is supposed to be a work of Moretto.

His last years were sad. He quarrelled with Michelangelo, who had been his god, and died in Rome in 1547, almost forgotten.

Bibliography: G. Bernardini, *Sebastiano del Piombo*. Rome, 1908. —P. d'Achiardi, *Sebastiano del Piombo*. Rome, 1908.

**SECOS.**—See Greece (Architecture).

**SEGANTINI (Giovanni).**—Italian painter, 1858-1899. He was born at Arco in the Tyrol. He became an orphan early in life, and was abandoned to the charge of a relative in Milan. He decided to make his fortune, and set out on foot for France, but he did not go very far, and became a swineherd: he was seven years old. For a year he lived alone in the mountains. Then he worked in the fields. His story is that of Giotto. Like him, his earliest drawings were of the animals he tended, drawn on walls and stones. One day he drew, with a piece of charcoal on a rock, one of his pigs. The peasants carried it in triumph to the village. After this, he found patrons, and was able to go and study in the Academy of Milan, but his extreme independence of character shortened his time there, and from then onwards he carved out his own artistic career. His early work is entirely romantic in character, and, curiously enough, shows division of tone at a time when Segantini could have had no acquaintance with the Impressionists, then misunderstood, and could hardly have known about their methods. The painter then went and settled in a village perched up in the Swiss Alps, Val d'Albola, far from the world of artists. He painted a series of works which are remarkable for their simple intensity of feeling, and for the sincerity of their naturalism.

Segantini acquired a still bolder technique, as may be seen in such works as *Spring in the Alps, Winter in Savogino*, etc. At this time the artist was living in retirement in the Engadine. Besides these more realistic paintings, others reveal a mystic strain, such as: *Grief Comforted by Faith, The Angel of Life*, and *Love at the Spring of Life*.

There is a seriousness and purity in Segantini's work, which places him among the best of 19th century Italian artists.

See Pl. 59, Vol. II.

Bibliography: Gottardo Segantini, *Giovanni Segantini*. Zurich, 1919.

**SEGESTA.**—The town of Segesta, in Sicily, was very early influenced by Greece. It possesses one of the best preserved Greek temples in Sicily. The parts which are lacking, such as the cella, were never built. The columns were never fluted. The temple of Segesta, which was built in the second half of the 5th century B.C., is in the Doric style, peripteral hexastyle. The temple, with its majestic architecture, and solitary landscape setting, produces an impression similar to that given by the temple of Neptune, at Paestum.

Temple of Segesta.

See Pl. 19, Vol. I.

**SEGHERS, or SEGERS (Hercules Pietersz).**—Dutch landscape painter and etcher. Born in Haarlem 1590, died in Amsterdam 1640. He was a pupil of Coninxloo and was influenced by Elsheimer. Through his earlier works it may be inferred that he travelled in Italy and Switzerland. His style reflects the general tendencies between Breughel and the 17th century concept of landscape painting. However he was a singlar personality in the field of etching: each proof was an entirely original and different copy from any previous one; this was achieved through the experimentation and addition of new color to the plate before each printing. His later etchings, as well as his mellow, brown tonality anticipate the style of Rembrandt. He never signed nor dated his paintings. Seghers died in great poverty without having achieved much fame in his days. *Ruin of the Abbey of Rijnsberg*, and *View of Rhenen* (Berlin), are typical examples of his work.

Bibliography: Hoogstraten, *Inleyding*.

**SEGNA di BONAVENTURA.**—Sienese painter, pupil of Duccio, mentioned 1298-1326.

In 1305-06 Segna was working for the Bicherna at Siena; in 1317 he executed a *Madonna* for the high altar at Lecceta, near Siena; in 1319 he was at Arezzo. He died before 1331.

Two signed works are extant: an *Enthroned Madonna* in the Collegiata, Castiglione Fiorentino; and *Four Saints* in the Academy at Siena. Documents which prove his acquaintance with the Abbot of SS. Fiora e Lucilla, Arezzo, virtually document the *Crucifix* in that Church, already attributed to him, and place it in 1319. Many additional works are grouped around these three on grounds of stylistic affinity.

Bibliography: Vasari-Milanesi, I. —Crowe and Cavalcaselle, Douglas ed.—M. Salmi, *Il Crocifisso di Segna di Bonaventura in Arezzo*, L'Arte, 1912.

**SEGONZAC (André Dunoyer de).**—Contemporary French painter and graver. Segonzac was born at Boussy-Saint-Antoine (Quercy) 6th July 1884. His youth was spent in La Brie, the château country; he attended the Lycée Henri IV and then began his artistic studies at the École des Beaux-Arts under the guidance of Luc-Olivier Merson. The young student scandalised his professor with his atmospheric drawings instead of working in the required academic tradition. He changed teachers, but received an equally unappreciative reaction from J. P. Laurens and Jacques Emile Blanche. Not being able to force himself to draw in the classical vein, Segonzac devoted the next two years to obtaining a degree at the École des Langues Orientales, making a special study of the dialects of Sudan. Although an excellent student, his love for art eventually brought him back to brush and paint. In 1906 he rented a studio and continued his studies at the Académie Julian and the Palette, with Guérin. He travelled in Italy, Spain and Africa and in 1908 we find him among the notable artists at the colony of Saint-Tropez. His first exhibition in 1914 was received indifferently. The following year he served as an officer at the front; after the war he resumed his work in Montparnasse. In 1922 he contributed to the Salon d'Automne. Segonzac had a great fondness for Flemish masters; he was also influenced by the art of Courbet and Cézanne as well as by Roman sculpture. His etchings and drawings, especially his fine war sketches, show a subtle arabesque and sensitive line, but Segonzac excels primarily as a painter of nudes, still life and landscapes done in oils and watercolour. He has a straightforward manner and senses the logical and vital shapes in nature. His early works are characterised by a heavy impasto often applied with the palette-knife, giving solidity and energy to his canvases. After 1922 his style ripens and becomes more sonorous;

the former richness is replaced by a lighter touch and thinner surface, a more spiritual and discreet quality and delicate colour. The objects are always reduced to their pictorial elements and the attention is concentrated on the narrow joining of horizontal planes. His characteristic colours are greys, greens and earth tones. Segonzac has designed theatrical costumes and illustrated Tristan Bernard's *Tableau de la Boxe,* Roland Dorgélès' *Les Croix de Bois* and Gustave Flaubert's *Education Sentimentale.* His albums include *Boxers, Ballets Russes, Isadora Duncan.*

BIBLIOGRAPHY: Jacques Guenne, *Dunoyer de Segonzac,* n. d.—Claude Roger-Marx, *André Dunoyer de Segonzac,* 1925.—Christian Zervos, *Dunoyer de Segonzac,* L'Art d'Aujourd'hui, 1924.

**SEGOVIA.**—The might of Rome is still expressed in the aqueduct of Segovia, which is built of fine blocks of granite, so perfectly cut that for centuries they have remained in position without mortar or cement. Several arches were destroyed by the Moors in the 11th century, and were rebuilt at the end of the 15th century. In 1520, figures of the *Madonna* and *St. Sebastian*

SEGOVIA: ROMAN AQUEDUCT.

replaced that of Hercules, which was found high up in a niche. The aqueduct is formed of a series of 118 arches, over a stretch of 818 metres. The direction of the aqueduct, and its height, vary according to the ground. The arcades are from 7 metres to 28 metres high. They are arranged in two storeys, with remarkable daring and lightness.

**SELINONTE or SELINUS (Temples of).**—The town of Selionte (Sicily), founded in 628 B.C. by a Greek colony, possesses important ruins of Greek temples. Here was the triumph of Doric art, and, although not a column remains standing, its development may be followed perfectly by studying the numerous temples, which have been distinguished by the letters A, B, C, D, E, F, G. Some are situated in the town itself, others on the Acropolis, which was the original town.

The oldest temple of Selinonte is the temple C, on the Acropolis, probably dedicated to Heracles (some say to Apollo) and built at the end of the 7th century B.C. or the beginning of the 6th century. The temples D and F were built shortly after the temple C, and, like it, are hexastyle peripteral. Both seem very long in proportion to their width. (Temple D is situated on the Acropolis; temple F on a hill to the east.) Temple G is one of the largest Greek temples. It was apparently unfinished, and most of the columns are still unfluted. According to an inscription, temple G was dedicated to Apollo.

Most of the Selinonte temples (C, E, F, G) have large dimensions, and it must have taken many years to build them. It is this very length of time which makes it possible to follow the development of Greek art in Sicily, and the formation of the pure Doric style.

BIBLIOGRAPHY: Serradifalco, *Le Antichità della Sicilia,* 5 vol., Florence, 1834-1842.—Hittorf and Zanth, *Architecture antique de la Sicile,* 1 vol. Paris, 1870—Koldeway and Puchstein, *Die Griechicher Tempel in Unteritalien und Sicilien,* 2 vol., Berlin, 1899.—Benndorf, *Die Metopen von Selinunt,* 1 vol. Berlin, 1873. —Salinas, *Nuove metope arcaïsche Selinuntine.* Rome, 1892.

**SELJUK ART.**—See Moslem Art (Ottoman School).

**SELLAIO (Jacopo del).**—Florentine painter, born in 1442, son of a saddler, pupil of Fra Filippo Lippi.

In 1460, 1472, and 1473, Sellaio's name is to be found on the rolls of the Compagnia di S. Luca; in 1480 he is still living with his family but has a workshop with Filippo di Giuliano in Piazza San Miniato fra le Torri. He died in 1492 at the age of fifty-one.

Vasari mentions Sellaio as a pupil of Lippi. He was influenced by Botticelli.

In 1472 he executed the *Annunciation* in San Giovanni Valdarno, Sta. Maria delle Grazie; in 1473 the *Annunciation* in S. Lucia de' Magnoli, Florence; in 1479 the *Sebastian* in the Jarves Collection, Yale University; and in 1483, for the Compagnia of S. Frediano, the *Pietà* now in the storeroom of the Berlin Museum.

BIBLIOGRAPHY: Vasari-Milanesi, II.—Crowe and Cavalcaselle, IV.—H. Mackowsky, *Jacopo del Sellaio,* Jahrb. der K. preuss. Kunstsamml., XX, 1899.—Mary Logan, Revue archéologique, 1899.—O. H. Giglioli, *L'antica cappella Nenti nella Chiesa di S. Lucia dei Magnoli a Firenze, etc.,* Rivista d'Arte, IV, 1906.—H. Horne, *Jacopo del Sellaio,* Burlington Magazine, 1908.

**SEMPER (Gottfried).** — German architect and esthetician, 1804-1879. Although an eclectic designer in baroque and Renaissance manners, Semper, in his writings, was instrumental in freeing architecture from the bondage of tradition and in laying down a theoretical rationale for the modern style. His buildings include the Festspielhaus, Bayreuth, 1872, and the Burg-Theater, Vienna 1880-1886. Previously, he had designed the Hoftheater, Dresden (rebuilt as the Opera, 1871) 1838-1841, and the Synagog, Dresden, 1838-1840.

BIBLIOGRAPHY: M. G. Mustterlein, *Gottfried Semper und Dessen Monument—albauten am Dresdener Theaterplatz.*

**SENLIS (Oise).**—This little town, which is so picturesquely situated, is rich in monuments from its prosperous past. The Silvanectum of the Romans has kept a great part of its ramparts, with thick walls, 7 metres high. The arena probably dates from the third century.

The *Cathedral,* begun in 1145, was not completed until 1556. Despite its lack of unity of style, the building is harmonious. It was begun in Romanesque, and has a Gothic vault. The Romanesque portal has three doorways, decorated with statues and bas-reliefs. The towers are Romanesque at the base, and end in Gothic. The southwest tower has an octagonal spire, one of the finest in Northern France (13th century). The side façades, especially the southern façade, are richly decorated.

*St. Frambourg* is composed of an

SENLIS: THE CATHEDRAL.

aisle-less nave and choir, without transepts, built from the end of the 12th century to the end of the 13th. After being used as a riding-school, the church is now a workshop.

*St. Pierre* (choir and transept date from the 13th century) serves as a covered market.

BIBLIOGRAPHY: M. Aubert, *La Cathédrale de Senlis.*

**SENS (William of).**—See Canterbury.

**SENS.**—The *Cathedral of St. Étienne, in Sens,* is one of the oldest Gothic cathedrals. It was begun in 1124, under the archbishop Sanglier, probably according to the plans of Guillaume de Sens, and was rebuilt in the following centuries. The oldest parts are the ambulatory and one of the absidioles. On the façade, below a wide window, is a doorway with sculptures representing the Wise and Foolish virgins.

SENS: THE CATHEDRAL.

The south portal of the west façade is decorated with statuettes of prophets (the heads of which are broken), and in the tympanum are bas-reliefs, representing the Death, Burial, Assumption and Coronation of the Virgin. Over this doorway is a tower, with niches containing ten large statues of archbishops of Sens. The left-hand doorway has two bas-reliefs.

The two large transept doorways were executed between 1490 and 1513. The Northern one is the most remarkable. It is decorated with a profusion of statuettes in niches.

BIBLIOGRAPHY: Chartraire, *La Cathédrale de Sens.* Paris, 1921.—*Le Trésor de la Cathédrale de Sens.* Paris, 1924.

**SERLIO (Sebastiano).**—Bolognese architect, 1475-1552. He was a contemporary of Vignola and may have influenced him. With him, he studied the principles of Vitruvius in the ancient buildings of Rome, and he owes his reputation as much to his architectural books as to his buildings. Patronised by Francis I, he must have worked at Fontainebleau, and perhaps on the Louvre.

**SERVANDONI (Jean Nicolas).** —Architect and painter, born in Florence, and died in Paris (1695-1766). After studying painting and architecture under Pannini and Rossi, and travelling in various countries, he settled in Paris in 1724. His first works were devoted to the Opera House for which he designed the decorations. He had a real genius for this art—much more than Boucher, who succeeded him in the same task. His work shows a break-away from monotonous regularity, and a bold attempt to give an impression of reality and space. At one time, he was official organiser of all public fêtes. Such was his fame that between 1740 and 1760 he was called to various European courts where he

SERVANDONI: ST. SULPICE, SOUTHWEST CORNER OF THE LOWER PART.

furnished plans and designs for entertainments. When he returned to Paris, he found himself supplanted by the brothers Slodtz and the architect Gabriel.

See Pl. 43, Vol. II.

**SESSHU (or Toyo).**—One of the greatest painters of Japan and the Far East, Sesshu, also a Zen priest, lived 1419-1506. He was a pupil of Shubun. In 1467 he was in China where he was honored by the Ming court. Not satisfied with Ming painting he fashioned his style after the masters of Sung and he brilliantly captured the spirit of Sung pantheism in his landscapes. He painted in two styles using in the one a dry brush and a carefully and precisely organized stroke which was at the same time bold, rugged and expressive of a vigorous hand. In the other he employed the "ink splash" method of the impressionists. The greatest of his paintings, and one of the greatest landscape paintings of the Far East, is the makimono in the Prince Mori Motoaki Collection, Tokyo.

See Japan—Art.

**SEURAT (Georges Pierre).**—French painter (1859-1891). Born in Paris in 1859 of well-to-do parents, Seurat entered the École des Beaux-Arts at the age of sixteen and worked for four years with Henri Lehmann, a former pupil of Ingres. As a boy he spent all his free time haunting the Louvre and the art galleries, studying Delacroix with great interest and being utterly unaware of the growing influence of the Impressionists. After spending a year in military service Seurat happened to read Ogden Rood's book on *Colour* which led him to the theory of the division of light and its reaction upon surface texture. Keeping these theories in mind Seurat went around Paris making random colour-notes of most everything about him, and experimenting with these. In 1884 he presented his *Baignade* at the Independents' after it was previously rejected by the Salons. Two years later he brought forth his chef d'œuvre: *Un Dimanche à la Grande Jatte,* the first canvas to be done entirely in the pointillist technique of the Neo-Impressionists. From this date on he contributed annually to the Salon des Indépendants; in 1913 he was represented in the International Exhibition and he also had several memorial shows. Seurat died in Paris of an infection at the same time as his young child. As a painter he achieved the highest degree of atmospheric vibration of any of his contemporaries. He derived the initial idea of the division of colour from Delacroix and supplemented this theory by reading extensively treatises on science, and by naturalistic observations which he separated into abstract visions and then reassembled in his compositions. Besides being a great colourist, Seurat was a first-rate designer, emphasising the horizontal aspect and extremely fine value patterns in his paintings. His technique, called *pointillism,* is achieved by applying small dots of pure colour juxtaposed to each other; the pigment is mixed optically in the spectator's eyes, thus producing the effect of diffused light and vibrating atmosphere. Besides painting Seurat has done fine illustrations and drawings inspired by the dock scenes of Brittany. He is represented in the Luxembourg, Art Institute of Chicago, Barnes Foundation, Tate Gallery and in The Hague.

See Post-Impressionism.

BIBLIOGRAPHY: Walter Pach, *Georges Seurat,* 1923.—Lucie Cousturier, Seurat, Cahiers d'Aujourd'hui, 1926.—André Lhote, *G. Seurat,* Les Artistes Nouveaux, 1922.

**SEVILLE (Spain).**—*Alcazar* (el kasr = the Castle).—The existing building dates for the most part, from the reign of Don Pedro I (the Cruel), 1350-1369 and is Mudejar in style. The new Alcazar was built by architects from Toledo, who were joined by Moslems from Granada, sent by Yusuf I on command of the king. In the 15th century, under the Catholic rulers, Ferdinand and Isabella, various converted Moorish architects worked there. In 1526, works of enlargement were executed in the Renaissance style on the occasion of the marriage of Charles V. In 1624, Philip IV entirely restored the Palace. In 1733, Philip V built the Apeadero.

The plan of the Alcazar is very simple. The most interesting remains are the principal façade, and the "Patio de las Doncellas," surrounded by the Hall of the Ambassadors, and other apartments.

SEVILLE: CASA DEL ATUNTAMIENTO.

See Pls. 33, 34, Vol. I.

*Cathedral.*—After the taking of Seville (1248), the great Mosque, begun in 1173 by Abu Yakub Yusuf was utilised as a Cathedral under the name of Santa Maria de la Sede. But, in 1401, its solidity being impaired, the Chapter decided to rebuild it in the late Gothic style on the mosque plan. The masters of the work preserved the minaret, the famous Giralda, and the courtyard known as the "Patio de los Naranjos." A forest of columns divides the Cathedral into five aisles. Seville Cathedral is one of the greatest Christian fanes. Its area (124,000 feet) is three-quarters that of St. Peter's. Its nave arches rise to 165 feet. The interior is dark, the windows being small. There is no triforium, the aisles being nearly the height of the nave. See Pl. 49, Vol. I.

The *Church of Santa Ana* (in the neighbourhood of Triana), built in the "Mudejar" style, and consecrated in 1280, contains precious works of art, among them a *Virgen de la Rosa,* by Alejo Fernandez, and numerous paintings by Pedro Campaña.

BIBLIOGRAPHY: A. F. Calvert, *Seville.*

**SGRAFFITO.**—See Majolica.

**SHANNON (James Jebusa).**—American painter (1862-1923). He was born in Auburn, New York, 3d February 1862. The family moved to many places in the United States and then settled in St. Catherine's, Ontario, where his boyhood was spent. He played truant from the local school to paint and ran away when placed in a boarding school. He began to study art under a teacher named Wright and in 1878 went to England for further instruction. In London he entered the South Kensington School and was a fellow pupil of Menpes and Clausen. Sir Edward Poynter encouraged him and persuaded him to stay longer than Shannon had at first intended. He had to work for his living and it was not too easy to get along. When he was only eighteen he was given a commission to paint one of the ladies-in-waiting of Queen Victoria and from such a start his fame grew. He opened his own studio and was soon busy painting the portraits of English nobility in his characteristic manner. He also made studies of the members of his own family, including *Miss Kitty,* which won a prize at the Carnegie Institute in Pittsburgh in 1897 and was then purchased by that institution. He travelled in Scotland and Holland in the summers and in 1905 made a trip to the United States, painting portraits in New York, Boston and many other places. He became an associate member of the National Academy of Design in 1908 and a full member of the Royal Academy in 1909. In his last years he was confined to a wheel chair with paralysis resulting from a fall, but continued painting as long as he was able. He was knighted by the King in 1922 and died in February, 1923, after a long illness. His work is characterised by good draftsmanship and character analysis and compares favorably with other English work of the period.

BIBLIOGRAPHY: Christian Brinton, *Modern Artists,* 1908.—Kitty Shannon, *For My Children,* London, 1933.

**SHARAKU (Toshusai).** — Japanese engraver, of the 18th century. His master is unknown, and his life is wrapt in mystery, but it seems to have been brief. All his known works were created during two years, 1794 and 1795. The story goes that after having been a dancer, he began making portraits of actors, and which were, from the very outset, collected by the best publisher of engravings, Tsutaya Juzabro. His first portraits are in the traditional style, and hardly give promise of the rare qualities which blossomed suddenly, first in the little pages with representations of an actor (bust) on a yellow background; and then in the magnificent series on a background of silver or of mica.

Sharaku is an admirable colourist, and very original. Some of his tones, which are rather dull in themselves, are so fine in quality, and placed so exquisitely that they give value to the whole work.

These early works of Sharaku seem to have been a great success. Unfortunately the jealousy between the dancers of No (where Sharaku had been one of them) and the newer actors (whom he may have trained) irritated him into emphasising his tendency to caricature, and he then published the series of two busts of actors, the biting irony of which was badly (or too well) understood, and excited a general outcry. So bitter was it that Sharaku, deserted by his buyers and even by his publisher, seems to have had to give up engraving. What he did then—whether he died, or whether he sought for a less treacherous and more lucrative career, are questions which, despite all the ingenious guesses which have been made, remain unanswered to this day.

See Pl. 40, Vol. I.

BIBLIOGRAPHY: Kurth, Dr. Julius, *Sharaku.* Munich, 1910.

**SHEELER (Charles).**—Contemporary American painter. He was born in July, 1883, at Philadelphia, Pennsylvania. He studied applied design at the School of Industrial Art in that city. After completing a three-year course there he went to the Pennsylvania Museum of Fine Arts School to work under William Merritt Chase. During the three years that he was there he made two trips abroad with Chase to see the galleries in England, France, Spain and Italy. In 1909 he made another trip abroad, this time to Paris, where he became interested in the work of the French modernists: Picasso, Matisse, and Braque. He was influenced by their pictures, and upon his return to the United States began to paint studies of still life, landscapes and interiors with the main idea of predominating design. From realism he began to experiment with abstract art and soon his work developed its present status of the extreme simplification of natural forms, with enough of their real appearance left to make them easily identified, linked together in designs enhanced by various shades of colours which are not necessarily naturalistic tints, but expressive and harmonious to the whole arrangement. He seeks to express the essential character of things by the relation of planes and the outline of their contours with a total lack of literal meaning. Mr. Sheeler is an excellent photographer, which may account for his methods of selection and synthesis with the emphasis laid on colour tones and the interrelation of planes. Examples of his work are to be found in the Art Institute of Chicago, the Cleveland Museum of Art, and the Phillips Memorial Gallery in Washington, D. C.

See Pl. 63, Vol. II.

BIBLIOGRAPHY: Ernest Brace, *Charles Sheeler,* Creative Art, Vol. 11, October, 1932, pp. 97-104.—C. J. Bulliet, *Apples and Madonnas,* 1927. —Samuel Kootz, *Modern American Painters,* 1930.—Eugen Neuhaus, *The History and Ideals of American Art,* 1931.—Duncan Phillips, *A Collection in the Making,* 1926.

**SHENG MOU.**—Chinese painter of the Yuan dynasty. He followed the style of the early Sung painters.

**SHERATON (Thomas).**—English cabinet-maker and furniture designer (c. 1751-1806), worked in London where, in 1791, he published a book of designs entitled *The Cabinet-Maker and Upholsterer's Drawing Book,* followed in 1802 by *The Cabinet Dictionary* and in 1804 by *The Cabinet Maker.*

**SHIGEMASA (Kitao).**—Japanese painter and print master. He was born in 1739 and lived, it is believed, until 1819, but he seems to have given up engraving long before that date. He was the pupil of Shigenaga, but was chiefly influenced by Shunsho in some series of actors. His engravings are rare, and he seems to have been chiefly an illustrator of books, and also, it is believed, a publisher. The two finest are *The Mirror of the Beauties of the Green Houses* (1776) and *Silkworm Culture* (1786), both in collaboration with Shunsho, and among the masterpieces of Japanese illustration.

His pupils included his son, Massayoshi, Kita, Masanobu, and Kondo Shunman.

**SHIGENAGA (Nishimura).** — Japanese painter and print master. Born in 1697, he was first a teahouse keeper in Yedo. He made his début as an engraver about 1716, with a series of little hand-coloured landscapes. He then became a pupil of Kiyonobu, and imitated his master in portraits of actors and pictures of birds of prey, but rigour of expression is lacking. Under the influence of his fellow-pupil, Masanobu, he gave up actors for feminine subjects. Although these are painted with charming distinction, they show the first traces of that softness of drawing and rather contorted grace which so much influenced Harunobu and his generation. Shigenaga's engravings are rather rare. He died in 1756, leaving a son, Shigenobu, who followed in his footsteps, and several pupils, among whom the most famous were: Toyonobu, Harunobu and Shigemasa.

**SHIR-DAR (Madrasa of).**—See Moslem Art.

**SHUNCHO (Kichizaemon).**—Japanese painter and print master, c. 1780-1800. First a pupil of Shunsho, then of Kiyonaga, by whom he was perhaps too much influenced. He retained, however, a certain sharpness of line, from his first master.

**SHUNKO (Katsugawa).** — Japanese painter and engraver; pupil of Shunsho. He was active chiefly between 1765 and 1775, when he produced work in the style of the Katsugawa. He made some extremely good portraits of actors.

— II.—Japanese engraver, pupil of Shunyei.

**SHUNMAN.** — Japanese painter and print master, working from 1789 to about 1820. He was first a pupil of Shigemasa, then of Shunsho, and finally of Kiyonaga. He made a certain number of engravings, besides illustrating books. The fine work of the *Fifty-one Poets* appeared in 1801.

**SHUNRO.**—See Hokusai.

**SHUNSEN.**—Japanese print master, pupil of Shunyei.

**SHUNSHO (Katsugawa).**—Japanese painter and engraver; born in Yedo in 1726, died in 1792. He was the pupil of Shunsu who founded the school of the Katsugawa, who made some rare wood blocks.

SHUNSHO (KATSUGAWA): AN ACTOR.

It is difficult to trace influences in Shunsho's art. Although his work has a bearing on the theatre, and he revived the tradition of Torii, he does not appear to have been much indebted to that school. His drawing is more angular and more vigorous than that of Harunobu, but he has not the breadth and nobility and calligraphic style of the Torii. Shunsho seems to have been the first to substitute characteristic and different features for the rigid and conventional faces which had been usual until then.

Among his most remarkable engravings must be mentioned the actor Segawa Kikunojo in some of his feminine parts; and a series of fat wrestlers, in which Shunsho evidently enjoyed caricaturing their ungainly bodies. In this he was a forerunner of Sharaku. He used rather bright colours, in a decorative way.

He had many pupils, the most celebrated being Hokusai.

**SHUNYEI.** — Japanese painter and print master, 1761-1819. Pupil of Shunsho, this original artist sometimes surpassed his master in his heads of actors, with their lips and chins curiously shaved.

**SICILY.**—See Greece (Terra cottas); Moslem Art.

**SICKERT (Walter Richard).**—Contemporary English painter. He was born in Munich in 1860, the son of a Danish painter whose parent had worked in the service of the King of Denmark. His family moved to England when the boy was nine years old and his first art training came at the Slade School under Legros. Later he attended Heatherley's School and for a time was a pupil and collaborator of James Abbott McNeill Whistler. The paintings of his early period reflected this study depicting scenes in the music halls of the East End of London in dark colours giving a feeling of the dreariness of human life even in the midst of its garish pleasures. In the early 1880's he went to France and there came into contact with the art of Degas which made a profound impression on him and influenced all his subsequent work. From Degas he learned the importance of correct drawing and the habit of painting canvases from a series of small sketches of details rather than directly from nature. He acquired also an interest in contemporary experimentation with the methods of painting and soon developed his own type of impressionism blending the colours on his palette and then placing them on the canvas in small patches. A trip to the region around Dieppe resulted in some pictures of landscapes and interesting bits of architecture. He also tried etching the views in the Norman towns and parts of Venice. His present style is based largely upon the tenets of Degas, Monet and Toulouse-Lautrec and reflects their interests in the landscapes and the studies of domestic interiors as well as those of the public houses. His paintings are built up by laborious and careful work with the result of a feeling of great artistic capacity veiled by the impersonal attitude of the artist. He is a member of the Royal Academy, the International Society of Sculptors, Painters and Gravers, the Société du Salon d'Automne and the Allied Artists Association. Examples of his art are in the British Museum, the Tate Gallery, the Luxembourg and the museums of Manchester and Johannesburg.

See Pl. 65, Vol. II.

BIBLIOGRAPHY: François Fosca, *Walter-Richard Sickert,* L'Amour de l'Art, Nov., 1930.—John Rothenstein, *A Pot of Paint,* 1929.—*Sickert, Reproductions of Paintings and Drawings,* with Preface by Clive Bell, 1919.—Alfred Thornton, *Walter Richard Sickert,* Artwork, Spring, 1930.—Sir Frederick Wedmore, *Some of the Moderns,* 1909.—Virginia Woolf, *Walter Sickert,* 1934.

**SIEGEN (Ludwig von).**—Dutch engraver, 1609-1680. Inventor of the mezzotint, which he used for the first time to engrave the portrait of the regent Amelia Elizabeth. He kept the secret of his invention for a long time, but finally revealed it to Prince Rupert, who made it known in England.

BIBLIOGRAPHY: A. M. Hind, *A History of Engraving and Etching.* London, 1923.

**SIENA (Italy).**—*S. Galgano,* c. 1217. A Cistercian abbey church now in ruins. It was the austere and arid Cistercian style, with high bare arches, suppressed triforium, and doming vaults, which determined the character of Italian Gothic.

*Palazzo Pubblico,* a large brick and travertine edifice (built from 1289-1305), except the upper storey which dates from the 17th century. It is dominated by a high tower, the Torre di Mangia. The interior is adorned with frescoes by Simone Martini and many other painters, above all with the celebrated frescoes by Ambrogio Lorenzetti, which are especially interesting in revealing to us, in allegorical form, the political ideas of the Sienese in the 14th century.

SIENA: THE CATHEDRAL.

See Pl. 2, Vol. I.

*Cathedral.*—Begun in 1245. In 1322, the Sienese decided to change its plan, and make it the largest church in Italy. This too-ambitious scheme could not be realised. The façade, in black, white and red marble, is decorated with three pediments, a large rose window, a cornice, and a great many sculptures (mostly modern). There is no roof behind the gable, and the façade is just a screen. The crossing of the transept is covered by a dome. The interior is covered with black and white marble, in stripes, and the marble pavement is decorated with celebrated graffiti, representing scenes from the Old Testament. The famous pulpit has bas-reliefs by Niccolò Pisano and his son, Giovanni (see Pisano).

The *Cathedral Library* was built in 1495 by Cardinal Piccolomini. On the doorway are remarkable carvings by Lorenzo di Mariano (1497); and the interior is decorated with bright frescoes by Pintoricchio and his pupils (1505-1507). representing events in the life of Archbishop Piccolomini. It contains a fine antique group—the *Three Graces.*

The Church of *San Francesco,* built from 1250 to 1326 in the Gothic style, was rebuilt after 1655.

*San Domenico* is more like a castle than a church. It was built from 1293-1391. Campanile, 1340. The Chapel of St. Catherine is decorated with frescoes by Sodoma, representing scenes from the life of the saint.

The old *Baptistery of San Giovanni* (14th century) possesses a fine, but unfinished façade. The interior contains magnificent baptismal fonts (1425-1432) by Jacopo della Quercia. The reliefs which adorn it are by various celebrated artists, and are interesting to compare.

Siena possesses many interesting palaces and old houses, such as the *Palazzo Piccolomini* (by B. Rossellino, in the Renaissance style 1469), and *St. Catherine's House.*

BIBLIOGRAPHY: Robert Langton Douglas, *A History of Siena.* London, 1902.

— **(School of).**—See Pl. 57, Vol. I.

**SIGALON (Xavier).** — French painter, 1788-1837. His first picture made his reputation. This was *The Young Courtesan* (Louvre), which portrays a beautiful young girl receiving a bank-note in one hand, and a box full of jewels in the other.

SIGALON: THE YOUNG COURTESAN. (Louvre.)

It was a great success in the Salon of 1822. The picture has fine Venetian qualities.

The Theatre of Racine inspired Sigalon with a dreadful picture—*Locusta and Narcissus Experimenting with Poisons* (Nîmes). The "Romantics" claimed Sigalon as one of themselves.

The *Vision of St. Jerome* (Louvre) is another characteristic picture.

**SIGNAC (Paul).**—French painter and critic (1863-1935). Signac was born in Paris 11th November 1863. His parents desired him to become an architect, but already in his teens the boy showed a great talent for painting. In 1883 he entered the Académie Libre de Bing; through his master Guillaumin he became acquainted with the teachings of the Impressionists and developed a special fondness for the art of van Gogh, Gauguin and Cézanne. Signac was well read and considered a thinker; he was also greatly impressed by the teachings of the socialists of his time. In 1886 he took a trip to Italy, Holland and Switzerland; his fondness for the ocean made him spend considerable time at the sea-ports of France where he sketched boats, docks and the fishermen. In 1887 he was seen in southern France in the company of his good friends Pissarro and Seurat. With them he experimented and developed the theories and technique of the so-called Neo-Impressionist school; he also assisted Charles Henry, the physicist, in his experiments of the "Cercle Chromatique" (1890). Signac was elected member of the Salon des Vingt of Brussels, he was one of the founders of the Independents and became their president in 1908. Being very fond of sports, especially yachting, Signac participated in several regattas, his *Olympia* coming in first in 1891. He travelled constantly and went as far east as Constantinople. Signac painted and sketched with a keen

# FRENCH PAINTING IN THE EIGHTEENTH CENTURY

*Instead of working for the King and for the Church as in the previous century, the artists made contacts with Parisian society which naturally inspired them with its own tastes and preoccupations: wit, love, irony, and emotion. Mythology and history are not entirely excluded but they are adapted to the whim of society. As for the style, it is transformed primarily by the influence of the Flemish colourists; the school of Rubens has conquered the Italian domination. Painting in light tones has replaced the sombre manner and the spiritual vivacity of the worldly taste has driven out the pedantry of the academies.*

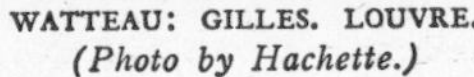

WATTEAU: GILLES. LOUVRE.
*(Photo by Hachette.)*

WATTEAU: THE EMBARKATION FOR CYTHERA. LOUVRE.
*(Photo by Hachette.)*

LANCRET: ITALIAN COMEDY. LOUVRE.
*(Photo by Hachette.)*

## Watteau

Watteau came from Valenciennes to Paris at the beginning of the eighteenth century bringing with him his Flemish inheritance, a sense of painting and a taste for brilliant colour. A kinsman of Teniers, he received his education in the city and readily forgot the peasants of his own country for the gracious cavaliers and spritely Parisian ladies. He created a world half real and half fictitious, with subjects borrowed from every-day life and from the theatre, countenances which are portraits and costumes which are disguises, decorations from the opera and the parks, a world uniting reality with the dream world. The "fêtes galantes" of Watteau, manifest in his *Embarkation for Cythera*, express the poetry of Paris during the Regency.

LE MOYNE: HERCULES AND OMPHALE. LOUVRE.
*(Photo by Hachette.)*

BOUCHER: VENUS AND VULCAN. LOUVRE.
*(Photo by Hachette.)*

BOUCHER: A PASTORAL. LOUVRE.
*(Photo by Hachette.)*

## Boucher

Boucher is the most characteristic decorator of the eighteenth century. Beneath his brush, colours and forms are softened, becoming only ornamental fantasies. The divinities, still a trifle heavy at Versailles, show considerably more refinement in the panels of the Louis XV era. Of all these divinities, there is only one for which the century has preserved some piety, Venus the blonde goddess of love. When Boucher is unfaithful to her, it is to show us gallant idyls. But, whatever the theme, figures and accessories are secondary elements in the fantasies of the decorator.

FRAGONARD: THE SYMBOL OF LOVE. WALLACE COLLECTION, LONDON.
*(Photo by Spooned.)*

MOREAU LE JEUNE: THE BILLET DOUX.
*(Photo by Hachette.)*

FRAGONARD: THE PURSUIT. PIERPONT MORGAN COLLECTION.
*(Photo by Giraudon.)*

## Fragonard

At the end of the eighteenth century, in the reign of Louis XVI, a delightful painter, Fragonard, again took up the themes of gallant painting; he is of a period which was fond of sentiment and his "petites femmes" show a passionate ardour which was lacking to their elders, the heroines of Boucher and Watteau. The art of Fragonard is completed by delightful landscapes, without doubt those of the Isle of Cytherea, balustrades, thick foliage and roses. His friend, Hubert Robert, was also fond of decorating his panels with roses delicately curled, and fantastic ruins.

# ENGLISH PAINTING IN THE EIGHTEENTH CENTURY

*One of the peculiarities in the history of England is the extraordinarily late appearance of painting in its art, nor does sculpture follow a normal course. In the Middle Ages, the monastic civilisation of England and of Ireland brought forth a brilliant profusion of illuminated manuscripts; this art was not followed as on the Continent by a production of panel painting. This isolation kept England aloof from the artistic life of Europe. The monarchy and even the aristocracy were able to admire painting sufficiently to demand portraits, but there were no English painters.*

HOGARTH: THE SHRIMP GIRL. NATIONAL GALLERY, LONDON.

REYNOLDS: THE AGE OF INNOCENCE. NATIONAL GALLERY, LONDON.

REYNOLDS: NELLY O'BRIEN. WALLACE COLLECTION, LONDON.

REYNOLDS: TWO GENTLEMEN. NATIONAL GALLERY, LONDON.

## Hogarth and Reynolds

Until the middle of the eighteenth century, England patronized the artists of the Continent giving them commissions for decorative painting and more often still for portraits: Holbein, Antonio Moro, Van Dyck. At the beginning of the eighteenth century there were French masters who went to London. Finally, national painters evolved a British style. It is to Hogarth that one must rightly attribute the honour of having won for his country artistic independence. But it is Reynolds who set forth the English style with authority.

GAINSBOROUGH: THE MORNING PROMENADE. ROTHSCHILD COLLECTION, LONDON.

GAINSBOROUGH: MISTRESS GRAHAM. NATIONAL GALLERY, EDINBURGH.

GAINSBOROUGH: THE BLUE BOY. HUNTINGTON COLLECTION.

GAINSBOROUGH: MISTRESS ROBINSON. WALLACE COLLECTION, LONDON.

## Gainsborough

Gainsborough and Reynolds are rivals and practically contemporaries. Reynolds is a magnificent practitioner, very skilled and very versatile, who was educated to a great extent in the galleries of Italian or Flemish art. Sometimes he makes one think of Correggio and at others of Rubens. He is very capable in rendering the luminous freshness of the skin and the elegance of the silhouette. Gainsborough is more spontaneous and his painting more sensitive. Gainsborough, who was a landscapist, places his models in a setting of nature which adds its dreamy poetry to their beauty. The two painters, who were not very fond of one another, were reconciled later, thanks to Van Dyck.

RAEBURN: LORD NEWTON. EDINBURGH GALLERY. *(Photo by Giraudon.)*

ROMNEY: LADY ARABELLA WARD. COLLECTION OF VISCOUNT BANGOR.

HOPPNER: PORTRAIT OF AN UNKNOWN WOMAN. FLEISCHMANN COLLECTION.

LAWRENCE: JULIUS ANGERSTEIN. NATIONAL GALLERY. *(Photo by Hanfstaengl.)*

## Portraitists of the Eighteenth Century

This school of painting was exclusively a school of portraitists. It was to have their portraits painted that English kings previously called upon masters of the Continent. The English school, flourishing at a late date, did not participate in the play of imagination of the Renaissance; it ignored the Gospel and Olympus; it was also not interested in naturalism of the Dutch or Spanish variety. It yielded to landscape, but was especially devoted to the portrait, seeking decorative effect rather than psychological analysis.

# THE PAINTER LOUIS DAVID

*This artist occupies a particularly important place in the history of art, because his work brought about a great revolution in style and in taste. He was the leader of a school; it was he who led the attack against the worldly art of the eighteenth century in order to bring back the severity of academic art and archæology. He taught the ideal in art, and this ideal he thought he could find in the best examples of ancient sculpture. This return of modern art to the Greek and Roman ideals is not exclusively confined to French art. It is a general movement in European art as was the great revolution of the Renaissance.*

THE SABINES. LOUVRE.
*(Photo by Hachette.)*

THE DEATH OF SOCRATES. BIANCHI COLLECTION.
*(Photo by Hachette.)*

## David and Antiquity

This increased interest in antiquity had many causes; among these one must include the interest aroused in Europe at that time by the discoveries at Pompeii. This archæological interest was impractical since it offered marble statues as models; ancient painting offered only secondary works. It was on the basis of Greco-Roman statuary that Louis David and his school substituted a new plastic system for that of the painters and decorators of the eighteenth century; drawing found firmness and correctness, but painting lost much of its decorative quality.

MADAME RÉCAMIER. LOUVRE.
*(Photo by Hachette.)*

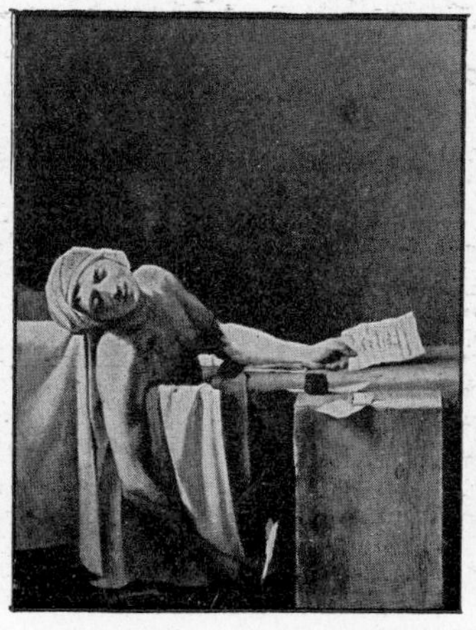

THE DEATH OF MARAT. MUSEUM OF BRUSSELS.
*(Photo by Neurdein.)*

THE DEATH OF BARA. MUSEUM OF AVIGNON.
*(Photo by Hachette.)*

## David and the Revolution

If David had consistently followed his doctrine, he would have confined his art to historical restorations, drawing his documentation from the texts and monuments of antiquity. But he lived at a troubled time and events compelled him to sometimes abandon Greek and Roman models for contemporary events. Thus the powerful realist in him sometimes manifested itself in lifelike portraits such as the charming painting of *Madame Récamier*, or even in compositions of violent cruelty like the unforgettable figure of the corpse of Marat in his bath.

THE DISTRIBUTION OF THE EAGLES. VERSAILLES.
*(Photo by Hachette.)*

THE CORONATION OF NAPOLEON I. LOUVRE.
*(Photo by Hachette.)*

## David and Napoleon

Napoleon who knew how to exploit the talents of men understood how to make use of David's talent. Two great works remain of his vast project: the *Coronation of Napoleon* and the *Distribution of the Eagles*. In each the idealism of the "historical painting" adds thought to simple realism. David, not satisfied with placing beneath our eyes living images of a contemporary scene, understood how to show profound thought and to make visible the idea which distinguishes an historical scene from the daily commonplace.

# THE SCHOOL OF DAVID

*L*ouis David *so imperiously dominated the art of his own time that even the painters who were not his pupils were influenced by him. The doctrine which he represented seriously hampered originality and especially spontaneity. He professed an excessive admiration for antique sculpture and this admiration was not the sort of thing to develop truly picturesque qualities. However, these doctrines rarely completely extinguish genius and among David's contemporaries the most gifted, such as Gros and Prud'hon, were not harmed by his influence.*

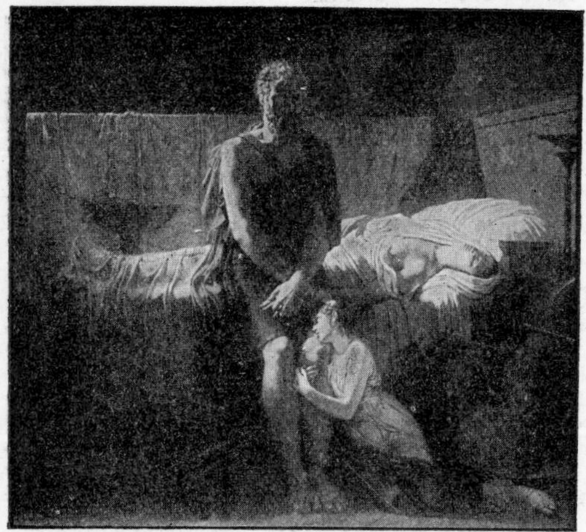

GUÉRIN: THE RETURN OF MARCUS SEXTUS. LOUVRE.
*(Photo by Hachette.)*

GÉRARD: PORTRAIT OF ISABEY AND HIS DAUGHTER. LOUVRE.
*(Photo by Hachette.)*

GIRODET: THE FUNERAL OF ATALA. LOUVRE.
*(Photo by Hachette.)*

## The Pupils of David

Guérin, without being a pupil of David, is nevertheless one of those who applied most freely the principles of that archæological painter. Girodet, who is also a draftsman of cold, academic figures, nevertheless experienced the romantic thrill. But this poetry, borrowed from Chateaubriand, remained frozen under the hand of a dull craftsman. On the other hand, Gérard, allowing himself to be governed by his own facile talent, was a charming portraitist; he left us a gallery of figures in which one may admire the lifelike quality of the models.

GROS: THE PLAGUE-STRICKEN AT JAFFA. LOUVRE.
*(Photo by H. Mauvais.)*

GROS: THE BATTLEFIELD AT EYLAU. LOUVRE.
*(Photo by Hachette.)*

## Gros

Gros is the painter of the imperial epoch. From nature he took the qualities of movement, colour, life in picturesque aspects. He admired Rubens and for a time engaged in the life of the army camps. It is to be observed that the great official painters do not represent battles in the blind fury of slaughter but rather after the struggle. Napoleon is presented not as the genius of war but as the benevolent hero who comes to dress wounds and to comfort the victims. These two masterpieces are admirable not only for the picturesque value but for the nobility of thought. Delacroix studied this master.

PRUD'HON: THE ABDUCTION OF PSYCHE. LOUVRE.
*(Photo by Hachette.)*

PRUD'HON: JUSTICE AND VENGEANCE PURSUING CRIME. LOUVRE.
*(Photo by Hachette.)*

PRUD'HON: JOSEPHINE AT MALMAISON. LOUVRE.
*(Photo by Hachette.)*

## Prud'hon

Prud'hon is one of the most charming painters in the French school. He preserves a little of the eighteenth century sensuality ennobling it, however, with the honesty of his drawing. His figures make one think simultaneously of Correggio and Praxiteles. They have the purity of form and the softness of the antique. His brilliant flesh tones beneath a soft lighting are bathed in a vaporous atmosphere. This art easily passes from amorous allegories to tragic symbolism and there was scarcely a more grandiose and more moving composition ever conceived than his *Justice Pursuing Crime.* His portraits have a dreamy grace which already anticipates the melancholy of the *Méditations* of Lamartine.

eye on nature always; he mastered skillfully every medium of pictorial expression. His work is dominated by a keen sense for the laws of contrast and the principle of their application. His technique is the logical consequence of Monet's impressionism and the further development of Seurat's pointillism. Signac breaks up one of Seurat's value surfaces into ten more gradations, and instead of the dots he applies pigment in small rectangles, giving his canvases the appearance of mosaics. His oils especially are superbly decorative; the vibrating colour and the rendering of shimmering water have not been surpassed by others. Signac's work is generally divided into two classes: the primitive group characterised by straight lines and the more plastic compositions dominated by richer and rounder forms. Signac is the author of *De Delacroix au Néo-Impressionism*, 1899, and *Jongkind*, 1927.

Bibliography: Lucie Cousturier, *Paul Signac*, 1934.—Jacques Guenne, *Entretien avec Paul Signac*, L'Art Vivant, March, 1925.—Georges Besson, *Paul Signac*, 1922.

**SIGNORELLI (Luca di Egidio).** —Italian painter, born at Cortona, about 1441-1523. Pupil of Piero della Francesca (See). He is first mentioned as a painter in 1470. Like his master, this great painter made research in the science of perspective, and the analysis of form. His great knowledge of anatomy did not cramp his sense of the beauty of supple, vigorous bodies. Signorelli loved best to paint pale nude flesh. His drapery tends to become complicated and heavy.

Signorelli was greatly admired and respected. Vasari refers to him as "il buon Vecchio." He travelled in Umbria and Tuscany and many of his paintings may be seen scattered in the museums and churches of Italy.

Signorelli: The Education of Pan. (Museum, Berlin.)

About 1479, he was commissioned by Cardinal Girolamo delle Rovere to decorate the Sagrestia della Cura of the Dom at Loreto, assisted by Perugino and Antomio Dei. *St. John the Evangelist, St. Augustine,* and the *Fall of St. Paul*, especially seem to be by his hand.

The frescoes of Monte Oliveto (1497-1501), which represent the *Life of St. Benedict* show an increase in life and movement. The white robes of the monks spread out against a complexity of landscapes and buildings, while black demons set about demolishing the churches.

In the *Education of Pan* (1490, Berlin) we see Signorelli's broad way of grouping simple, strong bodies.

The other most important early pictures are: a *Crucifixion* and a *Flagellation* (San Crescentino, of Morra); a *Flagellation* (Brera, Milan); to the middle period belong: *Circumcision* (National Gallery); *Annunciation* (Palazzo dei Priori, Volterra); the *Birth of St. John* (Louvre); a *Crucifixion* and a *Pentecost* (Santo Spirito, Urbino), etc.

In the Cathedral of Cortona, the *Last Supper* (1512), is an original work, but the *Nativity* in the Lunette of the sacristy is doubtfully attributed.

In 1481, Signorelli went to Rome to work in the Sistine Chapel, but he only made the drawing for the *Law of Moses* which was executed by Piero Antonio Dei and Pintoricchio.

His masterpiece is in the Dom of Orvieto (1499-1504). The decoration of the Brizio Chapel, in the Cathedral, had been begun by Fra Angelico Benozzo Gozzoli and Perugino. Signorelli continued the interrupted work, and painted some magnificent frescoes. There, in the scene of the *Preaching of Anti-Christ*, in front, are his own portrait and that of Fra Angelico; it shows the artist's mastery of handling throngs and the application of his knowledge of perspective. The scene in *Hell* shows muscles strained and twisted under the tortures inflicted by devils; while in *Paradise* the blessed rejoice. In the *Resurrection* graceful human figures emerge from the earth. Some, still half buried, are dazzled by the light; others, already delivered, raise their heads in ecstasy to the heavenly trumpeters who call them to the feast of life. Certainly, when Michelangelo went to Orvieto he found there the powerful elements which must have helped him in creating his gigantic work of the Sistine Chapel.

Under these great frescoes at Orvieto there are little medallions in "grisaille" representing the future life according to the poets, especially Dante. He has also done very fine portraits, as that of *A Lawyer* (Berlin).

Signorelli: The Condemned. (Detail of the large fresco in the Cathedral of Orvieto.)

See Pl. 13, Vol. II.

Bibliography: Manni, *Vita di L. S., pittore Cortonese,* 1756.—Venturi, *L. S.,* 1923. London, 1864.—Crowe and Cavalcaselle, *A New History of Painting in Italy*. Vol. V.—M. Salmi, *L. S.,* 1924.—L. Dussler, *Signorelli* (Klassiker der Kunst, Vol. XXXIV). 1927.

**SIGÜENZA (Spain).** — *Cathedral.* Romanesque and Transitional Gothic, 11th and 13th centuries. Although it belongs to the period of Cistercian churches, the Cathedral of Sigüenza escapes, perhaps because of its situation, the direct influence of the order.

Dieulafoy has noted striking similarities between this Cathedral and St. Nazaire of Carcassonne.

**SILANION.**—Athenian sculptor, contemporary with Praxiteles. He was the author of a bronze statue of Plato, which Mithridates offered to Athens and consecrated to the Muses. Among various works mentioned by the ancients, is a portrait of Sappho, which may be the one in the Villa Albani.

Bibliography: Collignon, *Histoire de la sculpture grecque.* Vol. II, p. 345 seq.

**SILOÉ (Diego de).**—See Pl. 23, Vol. II.

**— (Gil de).**—Sculptor active in North Castile from c. 1475 to c. 1505. "The problem of the origin of Gil de Siloe has never been solved, and so far it concerns the exact school from which he sprang; only a document, yet to be discovered, will speak with finality.—According to a document in the *Archivo Historico Nacional* at Madrid he is to be identified with a Maestre Guilles who with Diego de la Cruz executed a retable which once existed in the chapel of San Gregorio at Valladolid."—We have mainly to rely on documentary evidence as gathered by the two 18th century writers Cean Bermudez and Antonio Ponz as well as on a few notes which, at the Cartuja de Miraflores had been copied around 1800 from earlier entries. From contemporary documents we only know that in 1496 he rented and that in 1498 he bought houses at Burgos. Documented works of his are the tombs in the church of the Cartuja de Miraflores, near Burgos (in 1486 he executed the designs for the tombs of John II and Da. Isabel of Portugal, parents of Queen Isabel of Castile, and the Infante Alonso, her brother; he was paid for these in 1489 and 1493), and two destroyed angels in the *Reja* also of the Cartuja. Documented works of his and Diego de la Cruz are the *Tree of Jesse* Retable, in the chapel of St. Anne in Burgos Cathedral (c. 1486-92); the destroyed retable of the Church of San Gregorio at Valladolid; and the high altar of the Cartuja de Miraflores (1496-99). Attributed to him in conjunction with Diego de la Cruz as well as with the Cartagena Master are several sculptural works in Burgos,—chiefly in the Cathedral. (H. E. Wethey, passim).

Siloé (Gil de): Funeral Monument of Don Juan II and Doña Isabella. (Certosa of Miraflores.)

"The alabaster tomb of John II and his Queen is a free-standing monument in the form of an eight-pointed star, a reminiscence of Moorish civilization. . . . Its size (15½ ft. x 12 ft. x 6 ft.) and glamorous richness almost startle the spectator. . . . He is bewildered in the presence of such fascinating opulence, whether to look first at the base, partly veiled in solemn shadow, with its figures seated and standing under intricate canopies, its snarling lions, its deeply cut mouldings, or above at the colorful saints and luxuriously robed effigies. . . . The King and Queen lie side by side in elaborate architectural niches, . . . a delicate alabaster grille separates the widely spaced effigies and above the heads are canopies infinitesimal in detail . . . with tiny saints and undercut foliage.—The surface of the tomb is also adorned with the figures of the four Evangelists and eight standing statuettes (out of the original twelve) representing Apostles.—Due to the ground-plan the base consists of 16 sides against which, and under and amidst Gothic architectural motifs, are placed the statues of the Seven Virtues of seven Old Testament figures, a Pietà, a Nursing Madonna, etc., etc."—Wethey, from whose description the information given here has been borrowed, recalls G. E. Street's comment on this funerary monument: ". . . for beauty of execution, vigor and animation of design it is finer than any other work of the period."

The tomb of the Infante Alonso represents a richly decorated Gothic niche with the deceased kneeling in prayer before a prière-Dieu.

"The last documented work of Gil de Siloe is the high altar in the church of Miraflores (undertaken in partnership with Diego de la Cruz). A tremendous structure, approximately thirty feet broad and but a trifle greater in height. . . . The first impression of the retable is a blaze of gold in which the colossal body of Christ stands out relieved against the great aureole. . . . Upon closer inspection the composition is seen to be based upon repeated geometric forms. The great (central) circle is echoed in four small medallions within it and in others in the same diminished form without. The intervening vertical spaces are closed by statues of St. Peter and St. Paul. . . . All critics of the retable have stressed the Mudejar influence in the repetition of geometric forms in a tapestry-like scheme. . . . The polychromy has not been retouched, and it retains its original richness and splendor only slightly dimmed by time." Wethey reproduces a plan of this altar including the predella with indications of the various subjects represented such as scenes from the Life of the Lord, the four Evangelists, the statue of John II and Isabel as donors, etc.

Bibliography: H. E. Wethey, *Gil de Siloe and his school.* Cambridge, Mass. (Univ. Press) 1936. (Bibliography, p. 141).

**SILVER.**—For many reasons, silver is one of the most beautiful materials employed by artists. It is bright, yet slightly mat, and takes on a new mellowness with age; its ductility makes it adaptable to all kinds of work; it is comparatively hard (and its hardness greatly increases under hammer and chisel);

and, finally, it resists oxidation. But it is hardly workable except in a state of alloy with a small proportion of copper, especially for objects of a certain size, which would be put out of shape in use if they were of refined metal. The different standards of silver used by silversmiths vary between 950 and 800 parts in 1000.

Silver-gilt is only silver gilded or, more exactly, gilded with red gold by means of mercury.

After iron and copper, silver is the metal most used in the art of furniture. The techniques to which it gives rise are innumerable; the chief are sculpture in the block, casting, embossing, chiseling and engraving.

A special silver technique is "niello." To make a niello, the metal is first pressed in with a graver following a traced design; a hollow is thus made there into which a paste is introduced, composed of sulphur, copper, lead, silver and borax, previously melted together, then finely ground and dissolved in gummed water. It goes through a furnace, and a kind of champlevé enamel of a beautiful black is obtained, which only needs to be polished.

**SILVESTRE (Israel).**—French engraver, 1621-1691. His work is composed of nearly a thousand pieces, and is very valuable from a documentary point of view. He represented the life of the 17th century—its houses and streets—in a spirited way, and with a lightness of execution which makes one think of pen-and-ink sketches. His minute views are always well composed, and have none of the dryness which is often seen in architectural drawing.

SILVESTRE (ISRAEL): THE TOWER OF NESLE.

**— (Louis de).**—French painter, 1675-1760. The third son of Israel Silvestre. For twenty-four years he was director of the Academy of Dresden, in which city he decorated princely residences in bright fresh colours, which recall Lemoyne. Some of his mythological paintings may be seen in the gallery there.

**SIMON (Lucien).**—French painter, born in Paris, 1861. After having some lessons in his youth from the painter Jules Didier, he worked chiefly among comrades, such as Desvallières, Cottet and Jacques Blanche, and developed a concise, energetic and very personal style. In his earliest pictures he sought his models among his friends and his family. (Portrait of his Mother, 1883; Reading in his Studio, 1887.) After a journey to Brittany in 1890, he devoted himself to Breton subjects, but his work continued to have a feeling of intimacy. His Breton pictures were very successful. To mention a few of his paintings: *The Procession* (1901, Luxembourg Museum), his best-known work; *The Ball* (1902); *Low Mass* (Chicago Gallery); *Evening Conversation* (Stockholm); *Tea in the Studio* (Pittsburgh Gallery).

Then Simon took to painting figures of bathing girls. His work, which reveals an intelligent, reflective and sensitive artist, is at once realistic and synthetic. He represents the appearance of human beings and of things with a certain rough frankness, simplifying them in a realistic sense, and not in the classical sense of following an ideal of preconceived beauty.

**SIMONE dei CROCIFISSI.**—Bolognese trecento painter, whose name appears for the first time in a document of 1355.

In 1359 he married, his wife being a relative of the painter Vitale and sister of Lippo Dalmasio. In 1366 are recorded contracts to execute five frescoes of *Old Testament* scenes in the Church of Mezzaratta. In 1380 he was elected Magistrate. In 1397 and 1399 there are two wills, the executor in each case being the miniaturist Niccolò di Giacomo.

The only signed and dated work by Simone dei Crocifissi is the *Crucifix* in the Church of S. Giacomo Maggiore, of 1370. Other pictures are signed only: the Bologna, Pinacoteca, polyptych (No. 474), *Coronation of the Virgin with Donor, Saints, Crucifixion* and *Resurrection*; Bologna, Pinacoteca, *Coronation* (No. 164); and the Pope Urban V (Pope between 1362 and 1370), in the same Gallery; the Davia Bargellini Gallery picture representing *Giovanni di Eithinl*, who died in 1368; the Bologna, Pinacoteca, *Virgin and Christ among Kneeling Apostles and Donors*, with the Crucifixion above; the Rieti, Villa of Prince Potenziani, *Madonna della Misericordia;* and the Pesaro, Museum, *Coronation of the Virgin* (on canvas).

BIBLIOGRAPHY: Baldani, *Doc. e studi pubbl. per cura della R. Deput. di Stor. Patr. per la Romagna*, III.—L. Frati, *Dalmasio e Lippo de' Scannabechi e Simone dei Crocifissi*, Atti e Mem. della R. Deput. di Stor. Patr. per la Romagna, Serie III, Vol. XXVII, 1909.—Van Marle, *Italian Schools*, etc., IV, 1924.

**SIMONE MARTINI.**—Sienese painter, pupil of Duccio, and leader, after Duccio, of the Sienese school; born perhaps in 1285, which date is given by Vasari and is unsubstantiated; died 1344 in Avignon.

In 1315 Simone signed the extant fresco *Maestà* in the city hall of Siena. Two years later he is in Naples, where a payment to the Knight Simone Martini is ordered by King Robert. Of this date is the *Louis of Toulouse Crowning His Brother Robert of Naples*, still in Naples. Of 1320 are the signed extant polyptych for the Church of Sta. Caterina, Pisa; and the signed and dated extant altarpiece for the Dominican monastery in Orvieto (Orvieto, Opera del Duomo), for which a document of payment exists in the monastery archives. From 1321 to 1322 Simone is busy in Siena, where he restores his 1315 fresco; executes a *Madonna* for the Council of Nine; is paid for a painting in the Loggia of the Palazzo Pubblico and for a *St. Christopher* with the coat of arms of the Podestà in the Biccherna. None of these paintings exist. In 1324 he married Giovanna, daughter of Memmo di Filipuccio, which made him the brother-in-law of Lippo Memmi. The next year he painted for the Capitano del Popolo; and in 1326 was employed as architect to inspect houses. In 1327 he was paid for ornamental work; in 1328 executed the Guidoriccio da Fogliano, equestrian portrait in fresco on the wall of the Palazzo Pubblico (extant); in 1329 did two angels for the altar of the Council of Nine and decorated certain houses with Neri Mancini; in 1330 painted a figure of *Marcus Regulus* for the Council of Nine and was active at Arcidossa. In 1332, Simone, with Lippo, made a pedestal for a cross for the Council; and in the next year, also with Lippo, signed and dated the *Annunciation* for the altar of S. Ansano, now in the Uffizi (Lippo is responsible for decorative details alone). In 1339 Simone left for Avignon, on the suggestion of Cardinal Jacopo Stefaneschi who was his patron there. Traces of frescoes by Simone still remain in Avignon in the Cathedral porch. He died there in 1344.

Frescoes by him are in the Chapel of St. Martin, Lower Church of Assisi, but are not dated. A number of other attributions have been made to him on the basis of style.

It is difficult to overstress the extent of Simone Martini's influence. He conditioned the style of the school of Siena for generations; his forms affect the painting of North Italy, of Central and South Italy as far as Sicily appearing with particular emphasis in Naples where he worked in person, and even modify the strong tendency of the Florentines. More than any other Italian painter he contributed to the development of the painting of North Europe, and even before his trip to Avignon his compositions are copied and adapted in France. Great master of the Gothic line, his gift was one of the most exquisitely poetic in the history of painting.

BIBLIOGRAPHY: Milanesi, *Documenti per la storia dell' arte senese*, I.—Crowe and Cavalcaselle, III.—A. Gosche, *Simone Martini*. Leipzig, 1899.—M. L. Gielly, *Les trécentistes Siennois, Simone Martini et Lippo Memmi*, Revue de l'Art Ancien et Moderne, 1913.—R. Van Marle, *Simone Martini et les peintres de son école*. Strassburg, 1920.

**SINDING (Stefan).**—Norwegian sculptor, born 1846; of the symbolic school of sculpture. His best works are busts, among them those of Ibsen and of Björnson.

**SISLEY (Alfred).**—French painter, 1840-1899. A delicate artist, who adopted the theories of the Impressionists and was one of the best painters of that school. He lived on the outskirts of Paris—at Marly; then at Moret, and afterwards at Fontainebleau—and painted its country and streets. His chief care was to reproduce first effects of light—effects of light on snow, and the delicacy of morning sunshine in spring.

SISLEY: SNOW SCENE.

His paintings include: *River Bank* (Luxembourg Museum); a *Flood* (Chouanard Collection); *Loing Canal; Effect of Snow;* etc.

See Pl. 56, Vol. II.

**SISTINE CHAPEL.**—See Michelangelo; Vatican; also Pl. 18, Vol. II.

**— MADONNA.**—See Raphael; also Pl. 19, Vol. II.

**SLOAN (John).**—Contemporary American painter and graver. He was born 2d August 1871 in Lock Haven, Pennsylvania. The family soon moved to Philadelphia, where he was educated and began to study art at the Spring Garden Institute. Later he worked at the Pennsylvania Academy of Fine Arts under Thomas P. Anschutz. He then acted as staff illustrator on the *Philadelphia Inquirer* and *Philadelphia Press*, improving his draftsmanship. He was interested in posters and made several, gaining inspiration from Japanese prints and the work of Aubrey Beardsley. In 1905 he moved to New York and there made illustrations for such periodicals as *The Masses, Everybody's, Collier's* and *Harper's Weekly*. He became a member of the "Eight," a group of young artists working for new breadth and freedom from old academic traditions. In 1913 he was one of the sponsors of the famous Armory Show and in 1917 he helped with the establishment of the Society of Independent Artists. Since 1918 he has been the president of this organisation, which believes in "no jury and no prizes." From 1914 to 1928 Sloan was an instructor at the Art Students' League and in 1930 he was the president of the League. For many years he spent his summers at Gloucester, Massachusetts, but for the last fifteen years he has spent his vacations at Santa Fe, New Mexico. With Miss Amelia E. White he was one of the sponsors of the travelling exhibition of Indian Tribal Arts that was shown in New York City in 1931. His compositions are realistic and intimately connected with human life even in outdoor scenes. The life on the roof-tops of New York, Indian festivals in New Mexico, some portraits—all furnish material for his brush. And the same is true of the subject matter of his etchings—nudes, figure pieces of New York life and portraiture. His recent work in oil partakes of a certain experimentation in cross-hatching lines which tend to disrupt the continuity of the composition. He received a gold medal at the Sesqui-Centennial Exposition in Philadelphia in 1926 and the Carol H. Beck Gold Medal at the Pennsylvania Academy of Fine Arts exhibition in 1931. His pictures may be seen in the Detroit Institute of Arts and the Phillips Memorial Gallery in Washington, D. C.

See Pl. 62, Vol. II.

BIBLIOGRAPHY: Guy Pène du Bois, *John Sloan*, American Artists Series, 1931.—A. E. Gallatin, *John Sloan*, 1925.—For a more complete bibliography see *The Index of Twentieth Century Artists* for August, 1934.

**SLUTER (Claus, sometimes called Claes Sluyter).**—Sculptor of Dutch origin, whose activity centred round the Carthusian Monastery of Champmol, built in 1385, for Philip the Bold, Duke of Burgundy. The sculptor appointed by the Duke was at that time, Jean de Marville, a former collaborator of Hennequin of Liége. The door of the church of the Chartreuse (monastery) in which Philip the Bold wanted to have his tomb, was adorned with five statues; on the pier the *Virgin and Infant Christ*; on the left, the *Kneeling Duke Presented by Saint John the Baptist*; on the right, the *Duchess and Saint Catherine*. The statue of the Virgin is generally attributed to Jean de Marville, the folds of the robe falling in the stiff pointed clusters which are characteristic of the School of Paris. When Jean de Marville died in 1389, the direction of the studio was given to Claus Sluter, who, between 1389 and 1400, made the four other statues, which show genius of quite another order. These statues show remarkable strength both in conception and treatment. That of Philip the Bold in particular, praying in his ample cloak with ermine collar, is admirable. The figure is solidly modelled, the flesh rounded, the expression thoughtful, showing both good nature and energy. The drapery forms wide straight and simple folds.

At the same time that he was finishing these statues, Sluter undertook another work, the *Well of the Prophets* (known as the *Well of Moses*), which he began in 1395, and at which he worked till his death in 1406. This well, which was to spread far and wide his reputation as a great sculptor, was very original in idea. In the middle, on a pile of stonework, rises a little hexagonal erection, round which stand the six prophets; Moses, David, Jeremiah, Zechariah, Daniel and Isaiah. Above, a platform upheld by angels, supports a Calvary, of which only the head of Christ remains. The figures were originally painted. In order to understand fully the meaning of this work, it must be compared to the mystery of the *Judgment of Christ*, which used then to be played, and of which this is a powerful plastic representation. The Virgin used to come to plead the cause of her son before the Prophets, but these were unmoved, and one after another,

SLUTER (CLAUS): PHILIP THE BOLD AND ST. JOHN THE BAPTIST. (Dijon.)

pronounced sentence of death. This is explained by the inscribed verses from the Bible which the Prophets are holding, and also by the crucifixion above. The beauty of the work lies in the intensity of expression shown both in the faces and attitudes of the figures, and in the treatment of the drapery. Each Prophet, true to his own physical and moral type, is rendered with ruthless realism. The Moses, haughty and imposing, with long patriarchal beard, is not inferior to the Moses of Michelangelo.

From 1384 to 1411, Jean de Marville, Claus Sluter and Claus de Werwe, made the *Tomb of Philip the Bold*, now in the Museum of Dijon, and one of its most famous possessions. This work, in black and white marble is composed of a rectangular pedestal, covered with a projecting slab on which lies the effigy of the Duke. In the niches round the base, forty little figures, dressed in the costume of "mourners" or "weepers," symbolise the funeral procession. The theme was not new. The originality lies in the treatment. Sluter has given to each of his figures, an expression and an attitude which are alive and expressive. Even the drapery is individual, and each mourner has his own way of showing his grief.

This magnificent tomb served as a model for a whole series of others, notably for that which Jean de la Huerta of Aragon, and Antoine le Moiturier of Avignon did between 1443 and 1469 for Jean Sans Peur and his wife Margaret of Bavaria, and which is also in the Dijon Museum.

The followers of Claus Sluter, who constitute the Burgundian school, spread throughout France his vigorous style which is characterised by the squat proportions of the figures, the rendering of character rather than beauty, and the weight, and importance of the drapery. In Burgundy itself works of this kind, done in the 15th century, are numerous. Some of the most interesting are the old apostle in the church of Rouvre; a bust of Saint Anthony in the Dijon Museum; a St. John the Baptist in the Rolin Museum at Autun, etc.

Outside Burgundy, the influence of Sluter and his school is to be found in a series of monuments, of which some of the most important are; the statues of *Charles and Agnes of Burgundy*, done in 1453 at Souvigny, by the great sculptor, Jacques Morel; in the South, the *Entombments* in Saint-Pierre (Avignon) and in St. Trophîme (Arles), and others in Aix, Toulouse, Albi, Fécamp, Lisieux, etc.

See Pl. 54, Vol. I.

BIBLIOGRAPHY: A. Kleinclausz, *Claus Sluter et la sculpture bourguignonne au XVe siècle*. Paris, 1906.

**SMIBERT (John).**—Early American painter (1688-1751). This artist, whose name is sometimes spelled Smybert, was born in Edinburgh, Scotland, in April, 1688. As a youth he was apprenticed to a house painter and then went to London where he worked as a coach painter and copied paintings for art dealers. From 1717 till 1720 he was in Italy copying the art of Titian, Raphael and the pictures of Rubens and Van Dyck improving his technique and artistic ability. Upon his return to England he settled in London and spent some years in filling portrait commissions. In 1728 he accepted the invitation of Reverend George Berkeley to go to America as a professor of painting and drawing for a college of arts and sciences which Berkeley was planning to open in Bermuda for the benefit of the American Indians. The party arrived in Newport, Rhode Island, in January, 1729, and there they remained waiting the arrival of funds to finance the new college. The money never came and Berkeley soon returned to England while Smibert stayed behind to establish himself in a studio in Boston. In connection with his studio he also managed a shop which sold artists' supplies and copies and prints of the work of the old masters. He was successful in filling portrait commissions for the prominent people of Boston and also showed an interest in civic affairs. In 1740 he formulated the plan for Faneuil Hall which burned soon after his death but was rebuilt in a plan very close to the original. His eyesight failed about 1748 and he was forced to give up his painting but he did not die until April 2, 1751. Among the paintings from his hand that have survived perhaps the most famous is the group picture of Bishop Berkeley and his family which is now in the Yale School of Fine Arts in New Haven. Other portraits include those of Sir William Pepperell in the Essex Institute in Salem, Sir Peter Warren, and one of his wife, Mary Williams. All are characterised by an honesty of execution, a keen insight into character despite the occasionally awkward and inadequate representation. He was influential in bringing the art of the old world to the new by his copies of the old masters which served as inspiration for Vanderlyn and Copley among others.

See Pl. 61, Vol. II.

BIBLIOGRAPHY: Frank W. Bayley, *Five Colonial Artists of New England*, 1929.—Frederick W. Coburn, *John Smibert, Art in America*, XVII (1929), 175-187.—William Dunlap, *A History of the Rise and Progress of the Arts of Design in the United States*, 1918.—Horace Walpole, *Anecdotes of Painting in England*, IV, 1765-1771.

**SMIRKE (Sir Robert).**—English architect, 1780-1867, and exponent of neo-classicism. He designed the Grecian Ionic British Museum, 1822-1847; the Union Club, 1822; and King's College, London, 1828.

**SMITH (John).** — English engraver, c. 1652-1742. He was successful in using mezzotint to reproduce the works of the Italian masters, and especially portraits after Kneller. He made over three hundred engravings of Kneller's works, among them *Locke, Newton, The Duchess of Marlborough*, and *Lady Howard*.

BIBLIOGRAPHY: A. M. Hind, *A History of Engraving and Etching*. London, 1923.

**— (John Raphael).**—English engraver, 1752-1812. He engraved in mezzotint and left some engravings of great delicacy, among them the *Prince of Wales*, after Gainsborough; and *Miss Stanhope*, after Reynolds. He also engraved plates in colour, according to the method invented by Le Blond.

His best work of this kind is a fine portrait of *Lady Hamilton as Bacchante*.

The grace and precision of his modelling, and his knowledge of draughtsmanship place John Raphael Smith in the first rank of engravers of the English school.

BIBLIOGRAPHY: Julia Frankan, *John Raphael Smith*. London, 1902.

**SNAYERS (Pieter).** — Flemish painter (Antwerp, 1512—Brussels, 1667). Pupil of Vranx, the most celebrated battle painter of the time, and a painter appointed by the Archduke Albert and the Cardinal-Infant Ferdinand. He painted with brilliancy and animation, episodes of the Thirty Years' War. The backgrounds of his huge canvases show a faithful reproduction of the country of Flanders. His battle scenes may be found in several European museums (five in Dresden, five in Brussels, fifteen in Madrid, seventeen in Vienna). He was the master of Van der Meulen.

**SNYDERS (Frans).** — Flemish painter, 1579-1657. Pupil of Breughel, and of Van Balen. He travelled in Italy and on his return to Antwerp, he married the sister of de Vos. He was a friend of Van Dyck and collaborator of Rubens. Snyders is, with Fyt, the greatest animal painter of Flanders. He excels in painting wild beasts, dogs, birds, fish, reptiles, etc. His ease and spirit, and his fresh luminous colour made him one of the most valued of Ruben's collaborators. He painted the animals in Rubens' hunting scenes, as well as the flowers and fruit (*Diana Returning from the Hunt; Silenus and His Followers*, etc.). Between 1635-40 he worked together with Rubens on the 18 paintings designated by the Spanish King for the *Palace de la Torre de la Parada* near Madrid.

He did a great many pictures alone, and these show his vigour of treatment and powerful colour harmonies. His fiery inspiration has free rein in his hunting scenes; *Stag Hunt* (The Hague); *Bear Hunt* (Berlin); *Tiger Hunt* (Rennes); *Fox Hunting* (Vienna); *Hippopotamus Hunt*, and *Crocodile* (Amsterdam); *Fight between Buffaloes and Wolves, Cock-Fight* (Berlin), etc. More peaceful are the *Birds Singing; Monkeys Playing;* and innumerable pictures of *Game* (Brussels, Valenciennes, Munich, Caen).

Snyders had admirers and pupils, among whom the most famous are Fyt and Paul de Vos.

BIBLIOGRAPHY: P. Buschmann, *François Snyders*. 1921.

**SOANE (Sir John).**—English architect (1753-1837). He collaborated in the building of several London buildings; Saint James' Palace; Houses of Parliament; Westminster, the Bank of England, etc. He was Professor of Architecture in the Royal Academy (1809) and chief royal architect (1815).

BIBLIOGRAPHY: H. J. Birnstingl, *Sir John Soane*. 1925.

**SOCLE.**—Projecting member at the foot of a wall or under the base of a column, pedestal, etc.; usually moulded.

**SODOMA (Giovanni Antonio Bazzi).**—Piedmontese painter, born in 1477 at Vercelli, surnamed Sodoma. His father, Giacomo, was a shoemaker. He sent him, in 1490, to study painting under a certain Martino Spanzotti, who had settled in Vercelli. He may also have studied with a pupil of Vicenzo Foppa—Macrino d'Alba. Finally, it has been suggested that he was a pupil of Leonardo da Vinci at Milan.

In 1501 Sodoma was in Siena. His patron was Pandolfi Petrucci, who prided himself on imitating Florentine princes, by cultivating art and letters. Sodoma painted his portrait, which was unfortunately lost. He worked especially for the churches and monasteries which were still imbued with the cult of St. Catherine and St. Bernardino.

He found at Siena, two innovators who must have influenced him;

Pintoricchio who, from 1502, began the gay lively decoration of the Library of the Duomo; Jacopo della Quercia who was working at the marvellous Fonte Gaia. Vasari says that Sodoma began to copy Jacopo from the time of his arrival at Siena, and a document proves that he himself did sculpture, for in 1515 he was ordered to make a statue in bronze for the Cathedral.

SODOMA. (After Vasari.)

The tondo of the *Nativity* and the great *Descent from the Cross* in the Academy of Siena, are works of his youth, but already, with the detail of the schools of Umbria and Tuscany, have something of Sodoma's sensual exaltation. The group showing the Virgin drooping, and white with grief, in the arms of women, is the forerunner of the famous picture of the Swoon of Saint Catherine.

In 1503, he was entrusted with the decoration of the Convent of Santa Anna in Camprena, near Pienza. There he depicted the *Miracle of the Loaves*; *St. Benedict among the Monks; St. Anne, the Virgin and Child,* and above the door a representation of the *Pietà*. Unfortunately these frescoes have greatly deteriorated.

SODOMA: CHRIST TIED TO THE COLUMN. (Academy of Fine Arts, Siena.)

But in the Monastery of Monte Oliveto Maggiore, standing in the surroundings of Siena, in a comparatively unpopulated, hilly district, we can see a whole poem in painting by Sodoma (1505-1508). It continues a series of paintings by Signorelli, and stands beside it. The Monks called him "Mattacio," or the great Madman, and he must indeed have seemed a little mad, for he had brought with him a menagerie in which he took great pleasure, and here and there in these frescoes we see horses, donkeys, monkeys, squirrels, chickens, etc. whose originals the monastery must have had to feed. On the walls of the Cloisters, Sodoma painted those scenes from the *Life of Saint Benedict* which Signorelli had not done; the departure of the young Saint; his preaching; the saint presiding over the building of the Monastery; the miracle of the excommunicated nuns; etc.

SODOMA: ST. CATHERINE RECEIVING THE STIGMATA (DETAIL). (San Domenico, Siena.)

He gave his monks a realistic setting, often putting the chief scene in the background, so as to show them at their daily tasks. One can see peasants, dreaming shepherds, workmen, painters or masons; the young Saint on a fine horse, leaving his parents, his nurse on a mule.

SODOMA: ST. VICTOR. (Palazzo Pubblico, Siena.)

The *Christ Bearing the Cross* of Monte Oliveto, is beautiful in its resigned weariness, and in its expression still tender in spite of suffering. The *Christ at the Column* is less successful, but it shows the same emotion as that in the Museum of Siena.

Pagan fables suited Sodoma as well as mystic scenes. It was fortunate that, thanks to the protection of Agostino Chigi, the great banker of Siena, he was called to Rome. In 1508 he began by painting in the Vatican some decorations on the ceiling of the Segnatura room, afterwards entrusted to Raphael. In the charming Farnese Villa Sodoma painted the *Family of Darius before Alexander, Vulcan in His Forge,* etc.

The best-known and best preserved scene is the *Marriage of Alexander and Roxana,* inspired by Lucian's description of a celebrated picture of Aetion, painter to the King of Macedonia.

The Oratory of Saint Bernardino, Siena, was decorated by Sodoma (1518), who was helped by Girolamo del Pacchia and Domenico Beccafumi. The *Presentation of Mary in the Temple*; the *Visitation*; the *Coronation of the Virgin,* show facility and feeling.

Sodoma also painted a *Last Supper* in the Convent of Monte Oliveto, near Florence, probably about 1527, the year he was ill in the hospital of Santa Maria Nuova.

Sodoma was married in 1510, to Beatrice, daughter of Luca de Galli. He called his children Apelle and Faustine. He painted Beatrice in the *Judith* in the Siena Academy; and in the *Lucretia* of Turin which was offered to Leo X in Florence, in 1515.

In the Academy of Siena are two beautiful fragments of pictures executed for the company of Santa Croce; the *Christ in the Garden of Olives*, and the *Descent to Limbo*, in which there is a magnificent study of the nude, in the group of Adam and Eve.

The decoration of the little Chapel of Saint Catherine, in San Domenico of Siena, is the masterpiece which is always connected with the name of Sodoma. It was painted about 1525-1526. He delighted in paintings of fantastic crowded architecture, realistic relief, numbers of little cupids perched on capitals, and a profusion of garlands which verges on the excess of the baroque style.

His works are numerous. He also painted a *Saint Victor*, and a *Saint Ansanus* and a *Blessed Bernardo Tolomei*, founder of the monastery of Monte Oliveto Maggiore. (All in Palazzo Pubblico, Siena.) These pictures again show the effects of the baroque style, in the crowds of figures placed on sham cornices, their limbs in strong relief appearing to hang in space (1529-33).

He did an *Adoration of the Magi* (before 1533) for the Piccolomini altar, in Sant'Agostino, with the traditional treatment and rather strident colour; also a beautiful *Resurrection* (about 1535) in one of the ground floor rooms of the Palazzo Pubblico. He decorated the Spanish Chapel of Sto. Spirito, with frescoes and panels dating from 1530.

He did a *Madonna* (1539) in the Capella di Piazza del Campo; did a *Birth of the Virgin* for the Church of the Carmine; a *Madonna* for a Church of Colle di Val d'Elsa, now in Turin; and restored a *Circumcision* by Luca Signorelli. For the Pisa Cathedral (1540-1542) he did an *Entombment* (1540), and a *Sacrifice of Isaac* (1542).

One of his last pictures is a *Madonna* painted for Santa Maria della Spina, now in the Museum of Pisa (1542).

Sodoma's last years were passed in obscurity, but we know that he died on February 15th, 1549.

See Pl. 17, Vol. II.

BIBLIOGRAPHY: R. Hobart Cust, *G. A. Bazzi; Il Sodoma*. London, 1906.—E. von Kupffer, *Der Maler der Schönheit, G. A. il Sodoma*. Leipzig, 1908.—Lilian Priuli Bon, *Sodoma*. London, 1908.—E. Jacobsen, *Sodoma und das Cinquecento in Siena*. Strassburg, 1910.—Henri Hauvette, *Le Sodome*. Paris.—M. L. Gielly, *Le Sodome*. Paris, 1911.

**SŒST (Conrad de).** — German painter, of the beginning of the 15th century. School of Westphalia. Author of a *Crucifixion* (1404—Church of St. Paul, Sœst), and a large triptych of Bad Wildungen.

BIBLIOGRAPHY: Schmitz, *Die mittelalterliche Malerei in Sœst*. Munster, 1906.

**SOFIA (Bulgaria).** — *Hagia Sophia*, c. 550-575. A First Golden Age Byzantine church transitional between the domed basilica type represented by St. Sophia, Constantinople, and the Greek cross type of the Middle Byzantine period.

**SOGLIANI (Giovanni Antonio).** —Florentine painter (1492-1544). Pupil of Lorenzo di Credi. Most of his works are in Florence, among them the *Saint Dominic Fed by Angels* (1536), much discoloured, in the Refectory of San Marco, in Florence.

**SOHAG (Egypt).**—The site of two Early Christian Coptic basilicas of the 4th century: the monastery church of the White Monastery (Dêr el Abiad), and the church of the Red Monastery (Dêr el Aḥmar). Both have trefoil east ends within a straight east wall, and, from the ruins, appear to have had a west return of the colonnade.

**SOJARO (Il).**—See Gatti.

**SOLARI (Cristoforo), called il Gobbo.**—Lombard sculptor of the end of the 15th century (died about 1527). He was the author of the *Tomb of Ludovico il Moro and Beatrice d'Este*, in the Certosa of Pavia. Solari's journey to Venice and especially that to Rome, developed him, and when he returned, he was appointed official sculptor of the Milan Cathedral. In his search for sumptuous and theatrical effects, he prepared the way for the 16th century movement.

**— (Giovanni).**—Milanese architect of the 15th century, architect of the Cathedral of Milan, and of the Certosa of Pavia (1450), he represents the transitional style between Gothic and Renaissance. His work is elegant, with its lavish rondo decorations of children among flowers and leaves.

**— (Guiniforte).**—Lombard architect of the 15th century. Son of Giovanni Solari, he continued his father's work in the Cathedral of Milan, and in the Certosa of Pavia, and finally succeeded Filarete in the Ospedale Maggiore of Milan, where he made some beautiful windows with pointed arches. He died in 1481.

**SOLARIO (Andrea).**—Lombard painter, active 1493—c. 1515, of the family of architects of the same name. Formed under Alvise Vivarini

SOLARIO (ANDREA): THE VIRGIN OF THE GREEN CUSHION. (Louvre.)

in Venice, he was strongly influenced by the Bellini, Antonello, and, like all Milanese painters, by Leonardo. He was called to France, in 1507 by Charles of Amboise.

BIBLIOGRAPHY: K. Badt, *Andrea Solario*. 1914.

**— (Antonio da), called the Zingaro.**—Venetian painter, active early 16th century, follower of the Bellini, later of Carpaccio and Umbrian painters. He painted frescoes in the Cloister of San Severino, in Naples, representing the *Life of Saint Benedict*.

**SOLIS (Virgil).**—German painter and engraver, born in 1514; died in 1562. He worked at Nuremberg and he was influenced mostly by Italians. His engravings are numerous, though probably he was the head of a studio, and merely directed the work, retouching and signing the work of his pupils. He was not without talent and an engraving after Aldegrever, *The Bath of the Anabaptists*, shows great skill. He left many little engravings, which were often grouped in a series according to their allegorical, mythological or other subject-matter, such as *The Muses, The Planets*, etc. He also did the *Beheading of John the Baptist* and some illustrations of the *Metamorphoses* of Ovid, the value of which lies in the finish and clarity of the composition.

BIBLIOGRAPHY: A. Racinet, *Virgile Solis*. Gazette des Beaux Arts. 1876.

**SOLOMON'S TEMPLE.**—See Jerusalem (Temple of).

**SOLUTRIAN EPOCH.**—See Prehistoric Archæology.

**SOMER (Paul van).**—Flemish painter (1576-1621), who worked chiefly in London and Brussels, where he painted many portraits of princes and nobles of the court.

**SORI.**—See Hokusai.

**SORBONNE (Church of the).**—See Paris.

**SOROLLA Y BASTIDA (Joaquín).**—Spanish painter (1863-1923). The son of poor parents he was born 27th February 1863 in Valencia. His father, a Catalan and his mother, an Aragonese, both died before he reached the age of three and he was cared for by his aunt Isabel Bastida and her husband. As he preferred to sketch rather than to do his school work, he was put to work as an apprentice in his uncle's locksmith shop. In his free time he attended the local artisans' school where he carried off all the first prizes. At the age of fifteen he was accepted at the San Carlos Academia de las Bellas Artes; his early style of academic formalism was soon replaced by a more naturalistic expression. He was known to the art patrons and became the favourite of Señora Estruch. Among his sponsors was Don Antonio García, whose daughter Clotilde later became his wife. In 1880 he exhibited at the Academy and won a scholarship to Rome. During his travels in Italy he copied some of the frescoes in Assisi and painted religious topics such as *El Entierro de Cristo*, which shows the influence of Morelli. However, the impressions he gathered in Italy were not fertile as a whole. In 1884 he exhibited *El 2 de Mayo* in Madrid, which increased his already growing popularity. The following years he travelled to Paris, London, Belgium and Holland and was influenced by the art of Bastien-Lepage and Menzel; he studied the art of the old masters as well as that of the Impressionists. He exhibited in Munich and Vienna, and in 1900 he won the Grand Prix at the Paris exposition; this was followed by other successes in European centres and was capped by the exhibition of 350 of his paintings at the Hispanic Society in New York in 1909. Sorolla belongs to the Impressionists but not to the school of Monet. He is extremely interested in light, sunshine and the out-of-doors. He sees nature with a very personal vision modulated by the subtle experiences in which he has steeped his brain, and by a native tact of omission. Employing watercolour or oil he paints landscapes, seascapes, fishermen, cattle, common people, carefree children, etc., seizing the fleeting and momentary aspects and bringing out his great love and understanding for humanity. His brilliant palette consists of six to seven crisp colours and white, which he applies with virile, broad brush strokes. There is never any overpainting or blending of tones, each colour is separate and free, placed on the canvas with assured finality, but not giving the aspect of divisionism as used by the French Impressionists. He never thinks of line by itself but merges it with colour and tactile values. Frank charm, lyricism, carefreeness and a lack of philosophical thought characterise most of his paintings. He has done the portraits of Blasco Ibañez, statesmen and members of the Spanish royal family. What Sorolla achieved was through his native genius and his stubborn will to succeed. His paintings may be seen in the museums of St. Louis, Berlin, Madrid, Venice, the Metropolitan Museum of Art and the Hispanic Society in New York, and in many private collections.

See Pl. 59, Vol. II.

BIBLIOGRAPHY: Aureliano de Beruete, *Joaquín Sorolla*, n. d.—Raphaël Doménech, *Sorolla, Sa Vie et Ses Œuvres*, 1910.—Camille Mauclair, *Sorolla y Bastida*, 1906.—*Eight Essays on Joaquín Sorolla Y Bastida*, by a number of authors (incl. E. L. Cary, Ch. Brinton, J. Huneker, etc.), 1909.

**SOTADES.**—See Greece (Vases).

**SOTATSU.** — Japanese painter of the 17th century, pupil of Yosunobu, he became, towards the end of his life, a brilliant follower of the school of Tosa. His paintings, which are dated between 1624 and 1643, are often remarkable on account of their skilful combination of gold dust and Chinese ink, which was then a new process, but one which has been often imitated since. He was the precursor of Korin, and some of his works even rival those of this great artist.

**SOUFFLOT (Jacques-Germain).**—French architect (1709-1780). He spent three years in Italy, after which he went to Lyons and designed, for the Carthusian Friars of the town, a building with cupolas which he always looked upon as one of his best. He was kept at Lyons to carry out the *Loge du Change* (1745), (which has since been converted into a Protestant Church), and also the façade and cupola of the Hospital. Admitted in 1749 to the Royal Academy of Architecture, he undertook fresh work for Lyons, designing for instance a large theatre. His chief work is the *Panthéon* built by order of Louis XV, and which, begun in 1757, was not finished until over ten years later. A fountain in Paris (in the rue de l'Arbe Sec) is also of his design.

SOUILLAC (LOT): APSE OF THE CHURCH.

**SOUILLAC (France).**—A beautiful Romanesque Church of the 12th century covered by a succession of domes on pendatives. The interior wall of the façade is adorned with bas-reliefs representing, doubtless, a scene in Hell, and a Prophet.

See Pl. 46, Vol. I.

**SOUTMAN (Pieter Claesz).**—Dutch painter and engraver, born in Haarlem about 1580, died about 1657. He was in Antwerp and was probably the pupil of Rubens, after whose early works he made 15 engravings, among which are the *Miraculous Draught of Fishes* and some *Hunting Scenes*. He was court painter to the King of Poland. Later he published the first prints of C. Visscher and J. Suyderhoef. The tonality of some of his pictures recalls the style of Frans Hals.

BIBLIOGRAPHY: J. Ph. van der Kellon, *Le peintre graveur hollandais et flamand*. Utrecht, 1866.—H. Hymans, *Histoire de la gravure dans l'école de Rubens*. Brussels, 1870.

**SOUVIGNY.**—See Pl. 54, Vol. I.

**SPADA (Lionello).**—Painter of Bologna (1576-1622). Pupil of the Carracci. He belonged to the Naturalistic school and aimed at violent contrasts of hard light, and dark shadows, and effective realistic details. His chief pictures are in the Museums of Parma and Modena, though the *Slaying of Abel* is in the Naples Museum.

**SPAGNA (Giovanni di Pietro).**—Italian painter (c. 1450-1528), he is called Lo Spagna because he was born in Spain, but he lived chiefly in Umbria and the Marches and was a pupil of Perugino.

In 1507-1508 Lo Spagna was at Todi, and 1508-1510, at Macerata, then again at Todi, and at Spoleto where he died shortly after 1528. His first known work, the *Madonna della Spineta*, painted for the Spineta Cloisters (near Todi), is now in the Vatican. It is an imitation of Perugino, who again inspired him in the *Coronation of the Virgin* of Todi (1511); in the *Assumption* of San Martino; near Trevi (1512). Later, however, his admiration for Raphael led him to give his pictures greater force and more relief, and his figures greater movement. In spite of this, he remained a little cold and lifeless and lacking in originality. This is evident in the *Madonna* of San Francesco of Assisi (1516); in that of the Spoleto Museum and the allegorical figures in the same gallery, in the frescoes of San Giacomo of Spoleto, and in the *Saints* of Santa Maria degli Angeli of Assisi. His best work is *The Entombment* (1520) in the Church of Sta. Maria delle Lagrime in Trevi.

BIBLIOGRAPHY: Crowe and Cavalcaselle, *History of Painting in Italy*, Douglas ed.

**SPAGNOLETTO (Lo).** — See Ribera.

**SPAGNUOLO (Lo).**—See Crespi (Guiseppe Maria).

**SPALATO (Palace of Diocletian, in Dalmatia).**—A vast building of the 6th century, of great importance in the development of Byzantine art, it repeats the type of the great Syrian palaces of Antioch. It is enclosed in a great rectangular space bounded by solid ramparts, flanked by massive towers, and having on the north the Golden Gate and a great relieving arch above the lintel of the entrance. Within the walls are two great avenues, both with porticoes, and where they cross, a court of honour which is one of the purest remains of architecture of the 3rd century. The entrance to the rooms was by a circular hall surmounted by a cupola, and fronted by a vestibule with four red granite columns. On the west was the palace chapel; on the east, the Mausoleum of the Emperor—octagonal in shape, with a cupola on the top. According to ancient texts, the decoration both inside and out, of astounding magnificence, was purely oriental; with its vases, lions, griffins, gleaming mosaics, granite columns, and porphyry brought from Egypt.

**SPANDREL.**—Triangular space between the exterior curve of an arch and the inclosing rectangle; usually decorated.

**SPANZOTTI (Gian Martino).**—Italian painter who worked from 1481-1524. Born at Casale in Montferrat, he settled in Vercelli, and developed under the influence of Macrino d'Alba, Foppa, and Leonardo. He had as pupils, Defendente de Ferrari and Sodoma, from 1490. The frescoes in the Monastery of San Bernardino near Ivrea have been attributed to him.

**SPEICHER (Eugene).**—Contemporary American painter. He was born in Buffalo, New York, 5th April 1883. He began studying art at the Buffalo Fine Arts Academy and in 1906 won the Albright General Scholarship to study at the Art Students' League in New York. For the next two years he worked with Frank Vincent DuMond and William Merritt Chase. In 1909 he became a friend of Robert Henri and through him met George Bellows and the other leaders of the modern art movement. In 1911 he received the Thomas R. Proctor prize of the National Academy of Design and the following year was elected to associate membership in that distinguished group. He made some trips to Europe, coming back with a wider vision and greatly improved technique. He divides his time between his New York studio and Woodstock, New York, painting portraits, figure pieces, landscapes and some still lifes. He is particularly well known for his portraits, all characterised by remarkable fidelity to outward appearances plus a certain amount of introspective analysis of the personality of the subject. He was elected to full membership in the National Academy of Design in 1927 and is also a member of the International Society of Painters, Gravers and Sculptors, and the National Institute of Arts and Letters. Examples of his work are in the Detroit Institute of Arts, the Whitney Museum of American Art in New York, and Carnegie Institute, Pittsburgh. See Pl. 63, Vol. II.

BIBLIOGRAPHY: Frank J. Mather, Jr., *Eugene Speicher,* American Artists Series, 1931.—Mildred Palmer, *Eugene Speicher,* The Arts Portfolio Series, 1930.—For other articles see *The Index of Twentieth Century Artists* for December, 1933.

**SPERANDIO OF MANTUA.**—Medallist and sculptor, son of a Roman goldsmith, born c. 1425.

Sperandio is first mentioned in the goldsmiths' guild in Mantua in 1433. He probably went to Ferrara with his father about 1437, and is mentioned as a medallist in Ferrara in 1445, again in 1447. He returned to Mantua in 1451, was in Ferrara in 1463 and 1466. The latter city was his domicile until 1477. A document of payment from the Duke of Milan is recorded in his household accounts of 1460-66, but there is no proof that Sperandio visited Milan. In 1475 he was paid for two marble busts of the Duke of Ferrara; in 1476 for "imagines depinctas" (colored statues?). A document of this year may refer to painting activity. In 1477 he was in Faenza working for Carlo II Manfredi, and signed a five-year contract. The revolution of 1477 stopped work on the Cathedral of Faenza and Sperandio left for Bologna which he reached in 1478 and inhabited for ten years, working on medals, sculptures, such as the monument to Alexander V which was finished in 1482, and terra cottas of the façade of the Santa. He was, in spite of all this activity, very poor, and received alms in 1486 and 1488. In 1491 he returned to Ferrara, and in 1494 left for Padua. The next year Lodovico Gonzaga, Bishop of Mantua, recommended him to his nephew Francesco II Gonzaga as architect and cannon-founder. In commemoration of the battle of Fornovo he made medals of the Doge Barbarigo and Francesco. In 1496 he was in Venice, making a *pax* for the Scuola di S. Marco, which was not finished by 1498 (the plaquette of the Resurrection at Berlin has been identified with this). By 1504 he was too feeble to work.

SPERANDIO: MEDALLION OF AGOSTINO BUONFRANCESCO.

Sperandio was one of the most prolific medallists of the 15th century and a master of portraiture, tending, however, to coarseness, and very careless about his reverse designs. His stylistic development is imperceptible and it is almost impossible to date his medals on stylistic grounds. There are certain dated medals: the 1472 medals of Pietro Albani and Carlo Quirini, both of Venice; the 1473 medal of Prisciano de' Prisciani of Ferrara; those of 1474 of Bartolommeo della Rovere, Bishop of Ferrara and of Giacomo del Giglio of Bologna; the 1479 medal of Virgilio Malvezzi of Bologna.

Sperandio's huge production includes the following notable medal portraits: From 1462-77: Giovanni II Bentivoglio, Prince of Bologna; Francesco Sforza, Duke of Milan; Marino Caracciolo of Naples; Ercole I d'Este, Duke of Ferrara; From 1477-78: Carlo Manfredi, Lord of Faenza; Galeotto Manfredi; From 1478-90: Giovanni II Bentivoglio; Federigo da Montefeltre of Urbino; Francesco Gonzaga of Mantua; From 1495-96: Francesco II Gonzaga, Marquess of Mantua.

BIBLIOGRAPHY: G. F. Hill, *Corpus of Italian Medals of the Renaissance,* 1930 (with bibliography).

**SPERANZA (Giovanni).**—Painter of Vicenza (1480-1536). Pupil and close follower of Bartolommeo Montagna.

**SPHINX (The Great).** — The Egyptians made numbers of statues with the head of a man or a woman, on a lion's body. These were generally placed at the entrances to temples, which it looked as though they were guarding. The most famous is the great Sphinx near the pyramid of Gizeh. Its body is now buried in the sand, so that only the head emerges. It has been several times unearthed, and its measurements taken (20 metres high; 55 metres long). It was certainly sculptured on the spot, from a rock. Thotmes IV had built between its paws, a temple, which was reached by a flight of 32 steps. The head is damaged.

**— (Temple of).**—So called on account of its proximity to the colossus of the same name, this building, the oldest in the world, is situated on the road to Thebes (Egypt). Of limestone and blocks of polished granite, it is built on a very simple plan in the form of a T. In the centre, a long hall, divided in the middle by six thick pillars, five metres high; on the left a long transversal hall, with two rows of six pillars, getting light from air-holes high up in the walls; on the right a gallery terminated by a rectangular hall containing six superimposed niches. As it is decorated neither on the exterior nor the interior, its beauty lies in the purity of its lines and the perfection of its proportions.

**SPINELLO ARETINO.**—Painter, born in Arezzo c. 1346, into a family of goldsmiths.

In 1373, Spinello is mentioned as buying property; in 1375 is commissioned by the Confraternity of Sta. Maria with the execution of frescoes in the Chapel of Francesco degli Accettanti, Arezzo. From 1385 is his first dated extant work, the altarpiece painted for Monte Oliveto (reconstruction given below). In the next year he appeared as witness in an act in Arezzo. The extant frescoes at San Miniato al Monte were ordered by Benedetto degli Alberti and painted before 1387; from about the same date are the extant frescoes at Sta. Caterina, Antella, near Florence. In 1391 Spinello was called to Pisa to execute frescoes in the Camposanto, and in 1392 was paid for them. A signed triptych of 1391, *Madonna and Angel and Saints,* is in the Academy, Florence. From 1395-96, Spinello was again in Arezzo, where he did a much damaged fresco of the *Pietà* above the door of the Fraternity and two figures in the "Udienza." In 1399-1401 he executed the *Coronation of the Virgin* for Sta. Felicità, Florence, now in the Academy, with the assistance of Niccolò di Pietro Gerini and his son, Lorenzo di Niccolò. In 1401 he was commissioned to decorate two chapels in the Pieve, Arezzo; the last payment for these frescoes is of 1404. In 1405 he went with his son Parri to Siena and worked for seven and a half months in the Duomo; of this activity nothing remains. Two years later, with Parri, he contracted for the extant frescoes in the Palazzo Pubblico, Siena, which were begun in 1408. He died in 1410, in Arezzo.

Since Spinello's style is influenced profoundly by Florentine painting, Gaddesque and Orcagnesque, he must have received his early training in Florence before he is first mentioned there in 1387.

The reconstruction by Perkins of the Monte Oliveto polyptych of 1384 is as follows: the central *Madonna Enthroned and Angels,* signed; right panel, figures of *SS. Benedict and Lucilla*; and predella, Fogg Art Museum, Cambridge, Massachusetts; the other lateral panel, *SS. John Baptist and Nemesius;* part of the predella with their legends, in the Budapest Museum; the middle part of the predella, *Death of the Virgin and Coronation,* in the Academy, Siena; two small *Saints,* which formerly separated predella panels, in the Wallraf-Richartz Museum, Cologne.

BIBLIOGRAPHY: Vasari-Milanesi, I. —O. Pasqui, *Pittori aretini vissuti della metà del sec. XII al 1527,* Rivista d'Arte, 1907.—G. F. Gamurrini, *I pittori aretini da 1150 al 1527,* Rivista d'Arte, 1917.—F. Mason Perkins, *Una tavola d'altare di Spinello Aretino,* Rassegna d'Arte, XVIII, 1918.—Van Marle, *Italian Schools,* etc., IX, 1924.

**SPIRES (Germany).**—*Cathedral,* 1030-1200. One of the outstanding Romanesque cathedrals in Europe. Spires was begun in 1030 by Conrad II, and was rebuilt 1080-1103 under Henry IV, and rebuilt again 1106-1200. The church still rests on its original foundations, and marks a departure from the customary German Romanesque treatment in displaying merely a narthex in place of the west transept and in having no western apse and choir. Domical groined vaults of Lombard inspiration and disputed date, though probably 12th century, cover the eastern part of the nave. The westernmost vaults are modern. The tower ornamentation of pilaster strips and arched corbel tables also show Lombard inspiration.

**SQUARCIONE (Francesco).**—Italian painter, 1394-1474. He founded a school in Padua. He had travelled a great deal, particularly in Greece, and brought back a rich collection of antiques which he used to teach drawing. Thus pictures by his pupils are often crowded with motifs taken from the antique, and have a certain hardness, the result of this archæological training. Squarcione's most famous pupil was Andrea Mantegna (see Mantegna), and, chiefly through him, the school had considerable influence on the Venetians.

Very few of Squarcione's own paintings have come down to us. One is the altarpiece, in five compartments, now in the Museum of Padua (1452); another a *Madonna and Child* in the Berlin Museum. See Pl. 15, Vol. II.

BIBLIOGRAPHY: Crowe and Cavalcaselle, *A History of Painting in North Italy,* ed. T. Borenius, Vol. II.

**STAINED GLASS.**—I. *Method and Processes through the Centuries.*—In Gothic buildings the unpleasing appearance of uncoloured windows gave rise to a new method of decoration, which consisted of replacing opaque mosaic by a transparent kind let into the window openings. This new tendency was apparent towards the end of the 11th century and the beginning of the 12th century, only to be neglected later. It was only during the last years of the 19th century that there was a recrudescence of the art of stained glass, and an attempt to improve.

BASILICA OF ST. DENIS: MARTYRDOM OF ST. LAWRENCE. (Twelfth century stained glass.)

The technique of stained glass has not changed since the 11th century. Glass coloured in the mass by means of various metals (oxides, gold, copper, etc.), is used, and while molten, it is "blown," being either worked into cylindrical form (and later unrolled)—or turned into a flat tray. After making a coloured sketch of the glass window, a model on strong paper is then made, in the actual dimensions the window is to be; then this large plan is placed on the sheets of glass which are chosen according to the colours in the tinted sketch. Today glass is cut with a diamond; formerly a hot iron was used.

CATHEDRAL OF CHARTRES: THE STORY OF CHARLEMAGNE.

At the time when glass was made

by the method of turning it into a flat disc, the discs of glass thus obtained, varied very much in thickness. As these were coloured in a mass, the variety in thickness was matched by a corresponding difference in tone-values, so that one piece of glass might show greatly varied shades of one colour. Glass-

Cathedral of Chartres: The Nativity.

makers made good use of this peculiarity, turning to advantage what was really only the result of imperfect making. They put the thinnest pieces on the lighter side, and the thickest on the side which was in shadow, and so did not need to use "grisaille." Unfortunately glass prepared in this way has an uneven surface, catches the dust, etc., and after some time, loses its transparency.

If the material and making of glass has not changed during eight centuries, the use to which it can be put has varied. From the 12th to the 14th century, stained glass was really considered as a transparent mosaic,

Cathedral of Chartres: The Annunciation to the Shepherds (above). The Visitation (below).

and its function was then supposed to be the breaking up, softening and colouring, of light, while the subject on the glass was of very little importance. One of the most characteristic examples of the glass of this time, are the windows in the choir of Saint-Denis. They show medallions and little figures, divided by floral or geometrical designs, and a large border surrounds the whole. From a distance one can only see a glowing combination of reds and soft blues, and a symmetrical design in which the figures are not at once apparent. The masterpiece of the school of Aquitaine (whose development is contempo-

Poitiers Cathedral: Stained glass.

rary with that of the Ile de France) is the window of the *Passion* in the Cathedral of Poitiers. A Christ, on a red cross edged with blue is in the centre of the composition; round him are the Madonna, apostles, soldiers and St. John, in red. In the

Poitiers Cathedral: Stained glass from the apse.

upper part is the Ascension. The Christ ascends with hands outstretched in the middle of an oval medallion (a "Mandorla") with an angel on each side. The general effect of the colour is luminous, and the different values have been arranged in such a way that they bring out the strong contrasts.

Stained glass in grisaille. (After Viollet-le-Duc.)

With the development of Gothic art, the space given to stained glass increased, and the thirteenth century was the period of slender pillars and large clerestories. There still exist many of the windows of this time. They do not differ very greatly in idea from those of the earlier age. So intense at that time was the desire to build that glass workers, dealing always with the practical and executive aspect of their art, had no time for experimental work. They mostly applied traditional methods, and the work of this time

Cathedral of Bourges: Stained glass.

often shows gross carelessness. As for the use of colour, it was limited to blue, red and mauve (for large surfaces); green and yellow (only used with great moderation), a whitish shade and an opaque brown, which was used to indicate the out-

St. Lô. Notre Dame: Stained glass.

lines of the design and the shading lines of the shadows. These colours vary in different windows, but, on the whole, they were less clear and pure than those of the preceding century, and this alone distinguishes the glass of the two epochs. The iron lattice-work which supported the glass was, however, improved. Originally these formed simple bars in vertical or horizontal lines, which cut up the figures in an unpleasing way. In the 13th century artists thought of making this lattice-work follow the general lines of the de-

Notre Dame, Paris: Symbolic stained glass "Multi vocati electi pauci."

sign, and hence-forward they no longer crossed it. Designs and colours could now be combined in an elaborate and effective way, as in the window of St. Joseph in Bourges, and in those of the Sainte-Chapelle in Paris.

In the 13th century, the figures in lofty upper windows were often tall, and frequently surrounded by simple architecture. The little medallions, kept for the lower windows, would in fact have been invisible higher up. In some cases, the question of economy appears to have been a consideration, and in certain of the upper windows of Chartres, for instance, two large figures of apostles are repeated four times, the colour and the name only being different in each case. In Le Mans Cathedral, on the contrary, by a strange error, the medallions have

Cathedral of Bourges: Moses.

been put in some of the higher windows, and the effect is confused and incomprehensible.

In the second half of the 13th century, grisaille was more generally used, and here again, considerations of economy must have influenced the work. Grisaille developed a great deal during the 14th century and produced some very decorative results, as in some windows of Chartres, Le Mans, Troyes. It was also employed for public buildings, and private houses, but today only the church grisaille remains.

Bourges, St. Bonnet: Story of St. Claudius.

Little by little, during the 14th century, the art of stained glass followed the evolution of other decorative arts. The study of human form became the chief concern of painters, and portraiture, of workers in glass. The figures were placed amid architecture in grisaille which was easier to execute after the discovery (made at the end of the century) of a "silver stain" (a prepara-

Cathedral of Auch: Stained glass of the choir.

tion of silver) which stains the parts painted a yellow, which, when the light is behind it, gives an appearance of engraving on wood. Nevertheless there was soon a reaction against this process, as one can see by the upper windows in Saint-Severin in Paris, and the late 15th century windows of Bourges, whose figures, surrounded by grisaille, are themselves highly coloured. These show a return to the tall 13th century figures, though the difference in design, drawing and modelling is so great as to allow of no confusion between the work of the earlier period, and that which was due to that renaissance in the art of stained glass, which began towards the end of the 15th century, and continued during the 16th.

After this time comes the period of decadence. The very adaptability which glass painting had acquired was, to some extent, the cause of its decline. Artists on glass soon aimed solely at obtaining the effects of painting. Veritable pictures were attempted, by the use of enamels, but this medium produces heavy, dense tones. In window designs treated in this way, adjacent tones mingle and become indistinct, and the whole conception loses its power and brilliance. Thenceforward the art of stained glass steadily declined, so

Cathedral of Auch: Stained glass.

that at the end of the 18th century and the beginning of the 19th, even its technique was forgotten, and it was seriously believed that windows were coloured by the use of tempera or glaze, on white glass.

II. *Origins.*—The actual origin of the art of stained glass is not known. There is no connection between stained glass as used in France (for instance), and the pieces of coloured glass which, in the mosques, were set in plaster tracery or in marble. There were certainly no window designs representing people. It is merely known that between 969 and 988, Reims Cathedral had storied windows.

In fact the oldest known stained windows are those of Reims and Dijon.

III. *Historical Summary.* — No stained glass of the 11th century now exists.

(a) *12th century windows.*—The oldest are those of St.-Denis (1140-1144), which show such perfection that it has been supposed work and experiment in the art had been going on throughout the previous century. The reconstruction of St.-Denis, at this time, brought artists from far and wide, to assist in the work, and one window (the tree of Jesse) in Chartres is similar to that in St.-Denis, of which only fragments remain. In fact, it has been

J. Gruber: Eucharist window. (Executed for a church of the Meuse.)

thought that York Cathedral shows the widespread influence of the St.-Denis work, though the most lasting effect was made in France itself (Chartres, Bourges, Le Mans, etc.). A group of stained glass artists also furthered the art generally in the West. The Eastern churches more frequently derived their type of window from other sources.

All 12th century glass, however, was similar in execution; all the fittings and accessories being stiff; orthogonal iron bars too often cutting across the medallions; the drapery clinging closely to the figures. On the other hand, the ornamentation (often floral in design) had a beauty which no later centuries ever re-

Magne (Marcel): Stained glass.

captured. The colour too (in spite of the comparative technical ignorance as to its properties, etc.)—is magnificent. The background is nearly always a deep restful blue—in the rest of the composition blues and orange-yellows—reds and greens—were used in close and harmonious proximity. These colours, with black and white, formed almost the entire range of the artist's colours.

(b) *13th century glass.*—The art was widely practised in this century and a considerable amount of glass, made then, still exists.

Notre Dame of Paris provided the link between the two centuries, but its glass was destroyed.

At Chartres (begun in 1210) there grew up a school of glass painters, whose influence may even be traced in Sens, Rouen, Lincoln and Canterbury.

Later, a similar school came into existence at Lyons.

Stained glass production dwindled towards the middle of the century when many important works had been finished. Many glass painters went to Paris, where, by 1248, the Saint Chapelle windows were completed, and those of many other buildings. Among the changes of this time, was the introduction of large rose windows in transepts; the abandonment of the hitherto invariably blue background; and the formation of sort of regular (often circular) tracery designs.

With the development of Gothic art, windows were enlarged, and became, too, more costly. The decoration, therefore, had to be simplified, and grisaille began to be widely used, though the process itself was not a new one. There are examples at Bourges, Auxerre, Lyons, etc.

Thirteenth-century window designs and settings are less stiff, drapery more flowing, attitudes more natural

Stained glass of St. Etienne du Mont, Paris.

and easy. Accessories, however, were neglected; ornamentation tended to be repeated too often; backgrounds were often mauve, and the 12th century's glowing colour became colder.

Subjects were of two kinds—biblical and legendary, the latter being more numerous (examples: Bourges, Chartres).

(c) *14th-century windows.*—Stained glass now began to be used in private houses, public buildings, etc. This led to the decadence of the art, which finally gave place to the industry of coloured glass. Horizontal and vertical bars returned to general use, and grisaille, with some yellow at times, was almost exclusively employed.

(d) *15th-century windows.*—The windows of this century were calculated to play their part in the architectural effect of the whole build-

# SCULPTURE OF THE ROMANTIC PERIOD

*Modern sculpture has naturally felt the influence of ancient art since antique art is particularly represented by its statuary. Also, after Houdon, the sculptors began to abandon the impressionistic verve of the eighteenth century to seek classic majesty. Then in the nineteenth century, in the romantic era, the artists continued to express modern sentiments and to glorify the great men of the present or the past; thus they were faced with the problem of costume and statuary had to abandon heroic nudity or ancient drapery. Modern costume brings forth a picturesque quality of a new sort, but it is a great sacrifice for the sculptor as compared with that of nudity.*

DAVID D'ANGERS: STATUE OF GUTENBERG. STRASBOURG. *(Photo by Neurdein.)*

DAVID D'ANGERS: TO THE GREAT MEN FROM A GRATEFUL FATHERLAND. PEDIMENT OF THE PANTHEON, PARIS. *(Photo by Hachette.)*

DAVID D'ANGERS: STATUE OF DROUOT, NANCY. *(Photo by Neurdein.)*

RUDE: STATUE OF MARÉCHAL NEY. PARIS. *(Photo by Hachette.)*

RUDE: THE SONG OF DEPARTURE. ARC DE TRIOMPHE DE L'ÉTOILE. PARIS. *(Photo by Hachette.)*

RUDE: LOUIS XIII AS A BOY. CHÂTEAU OF DAMPIERRE. *(Photo by Hachette.)*

BARYE: TIGER ATTACKING A HORSE. LOUVRE. *(Photo by Giraudon.)*

DAVID D'ANGERS: MEDALLION OF MME. RÉCAMIER. MEDALLION OF VICTOR HUGO. *(Photo by Hachette.)*

BARYE: ELEPHANT. LOUVRE. *(Photo by Hachette.)*

## The Romantic Sculptors

Sculptors such as David d'Angers are already modern in inspiration, but in style they are still classical. Rude is the most powerful of these artists who inject a new sentiment into a traditional form. His relief from the Arc de Triomphe conforms to the precept of Chénier who expressed new thoughts in ancient verse forms. Barye found a practically unexploited field in the sculpturing of animals. He represents them not in decorative and hieratic attitudes but in the confusion or violence of life in the desert or the jungle.

# FRENCH SCULPTURE AT THE END OF THE NINETEENTH CENTURY

*In the second half of the nineteenth century, sculpture followed the same movement as painting; it tended to free itself from the idealism of classicism tending toward a more accentuated realism. Furthermore, romanticism, although it did not find as great a facility in sculptural technique as in painting, nevertheless made the plastic language a great deal more flexible. During the second half of the century, two tendencies may be observed: that of bold or restless sculptors limiting themselves to an expressive art, sacrificing beauty for character, and that of masters who are attached above all to purity of form and nobility of style.*

CARPEAUX: UGOLINO. LOUVRE.
*(Photo by Hachette.)*

CARPEAUX: FOUNTAIN OF THE FOUR CORNERS OF THE WORLD. PARIS.
*(Photo by Hachette.)*

CARPEAUX: THE DANCE. OPERA HOUSE, PARIS.
*(Photo by Hachette.)*

## Carpeaux

Carpeaux is a contemporary of Courbet, and without resembling him represents nevertheless the naturalistic tendency, the effort to express movement and life. Contemporaries were sometimes shocked by the freedom of his figures; they were not accustomed to such vivacity in large statuary. Carpeaux expands the figurines of Clodion but the bacchanals which are tolerated in such trifles appear shocking in monumental sculpture. Carpeaux understood how to adapt his materials to the movements of passion and life. By the sensitiveness of his modelling, he added colour to sculptural qualities.

DUBOIS: JEANNE D'ARC. REIMS.
*(Photo by Hachette.)*

FALGUIÈRE: DIANA.
*(Photo by Hachette.)*

CHAPU: YOUTH. PARIS. (ÉCOLE DES BEAUX-ARTS.)
*(Photo by Hachette.)*

FRÉMIET: JEANNE D'ARC. PARIS.
*(Photo by Hachette.)*

## Classic Statuary

Sculpture is an art too much attached to material conditions as well as monumental uses to have the sculptor treat forms with the same freedom as the draftsman or the painter. It is in recognition of these internal laws that sculptors contrast the classical tradition with the daring of naturalistic or romantic sculpture. Dubois and Chapu restore the Greek or Florentine aesthetic principles; Falguière and Frémiet are indebted to the inspiration of modern naturalism. All these artists continue to multiply the historical effigies which are the "Saints" of modern patriotism.

RODIN: THE KISS. MUSÉE DU LUXEMBOURG.
*(Photo by Hachette.)*

BARTHOLOMÉ: MONUMENT TO THE DEAD. PARIS. (PÈRE LACHAISE.)
*(Photo by Hachette.)*

RODIN: THE THINKER. MUSÉE RODIN.
*(Photo by Hachette.)*

## Rodin

The powerful originality of Rodin lies in the fact that he pursued his research of character in modelling further than any other artist. Although he constructs figures which possess perfect anatomical mechanism, he sometimes treats the human form with the daring of a romantic who values expression before correctness. His twisted modelling equally suitable for representing tenderness or violence appears to restrain, with difficulty, a tumultuous life. The sculpture of Bartholomé, on the contrary, appears to return to the simplicity of the Gothic style.

# ROMANTIC PAINTING

*During the Restoration, while a gradual lull in politics became apparent, the revolution in the world of literature and of art burst forth: this was Romanticism. In painting, romanticism was primarily a violent reaction against the aesthetic theories of David and in particular against the cult of ancient art and impersonal idealism. Already during the lifetime of David there were painters who did not accept without a struggle the austere discipline of classicism; but after his death, a new generation made itself known in the brilliant and feverish works of Eugène Delacroix. This was the beginning of the romantic battle.*

GÉRICAULT: THE RAFT OF THE MEDUSA. LOUVRE.
*(Photo by Hachette.)*

GÉRICAULT: THE LIGHT CAVALRY OFFICER. LOUVRE.
*(Photo by Neurdein.)*

GÉRICAULT: RACE AT EPSOM. LOUVRE.
*(Photo by Hachette.)*

## Géricault

This painter, who died at an early age, did not have sufficient time to play out the important rôle in the French school to which his talent destined him. He was singled out by an impetuous painting, *The Light Cavalry Officer*, and, when the imperial period was over, he executed the powerful and tragic composition of *The Raft of the Medusa*, in which, as with Michelangelo, physical or moral suffering is expressed by muscular violence. He ended his brief career painting admirable horses whose silky coats and movements he lovingly rendered.

DELACROIX: ENTRANCE OF THE CRUSADERS INTO CONSTANTINOPLE. LOUVRE.
*(Photo by Hachette.)*

DELACROIX: THE MASSACRE OF SCIO. LOUVRE.
*(Photo by Hachette.)*

DELACROIX: THE BARRICADE. LOUVRE.
*(Photo by Hachette.)*

## Delacroix

Delacroix contains in his style the best that romanticism had to offer; he had scarcely an imitator or a pupil and he taught that the artist ought to invent and not to imitate. He is in all points opposed to the classical school. He sought themes in the Middle Ages, in contemporary history, in the Orient, and even in Greco-Roman antiquity; but he was never inspired to translate ancient sculpture into painting. His preferences drew him toward the impetuous colouring of Rubens and sometimes the decorative pomp of Veronese. But he manifested a romantic restlessness, not robust certainty.

DELACROIX: MEDEA. LILLE.
*(Photo by Hachette.)*

DELACROIX: ARABIAN FANTASY. MONTPELLIER.
*(Photo by Hachette.)*

DELACROIX: THE JUSTICE OF TRAJAN. ROUEN.
*(Photo by Hachette.)*

## Delacroix

It is not only by the choice of his subjects, it is especially by his new conception of drawing and of colour that Delacroix is opposed to the classical school. His violent and twisted drawing always expresses movement and effort. But it is also by means of colour that he accentuates the pathetic in painting. He depicts it brilliant and ostentatious, sometimes tragic and even morbid; there was never before such power of emotion. But Delacroix is not entirely obsessed by this preoccupation. Colour, drawing and composition, all participate in the same passionate lyricism.

# INGRES AND HIS SCHOOL

*R*OMANTICISM *was not completely the winner in the plastic arts. It tended to break with too traditional customs whose conditions governing painting and sculpture were the same: the imitation of nature, and correctness and purity of form. Delacroix sacrificed these qualities in his research into character and in the heat of inspiration. It was Ingres who took up the defence of classical principles against the romantic revolt. He represents them with a steadfastness which is slightly pedantic, since his culture and intelligence were not equal to his talent; as almost always happens, the artist in him was worth more than the theorist.*

INGRES: THE VOW OF LOUIS XIII. CATHEDRAL OF MONTAUBAN.
*(Photo by Neurdein.)*

INGRES: APOTHEOSIS OF HOMER. LOUVRE.
*(Photo by Hachette.)*

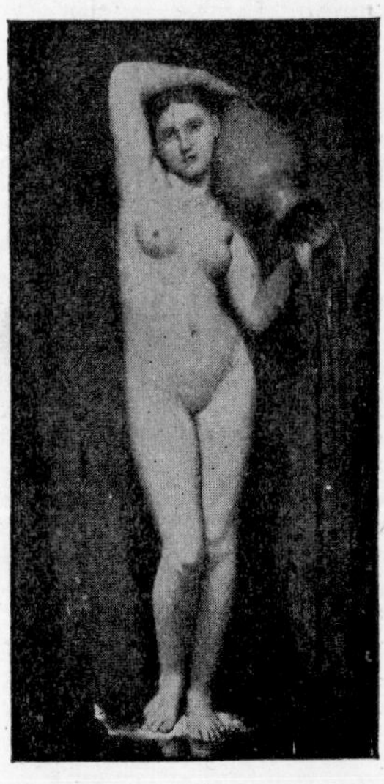

INGRES: LA SOURCE. LOUVRE.
*(Photo by Hachette.)*

## The Drawing of Ingres

IT IS customary to sum up the quarrel between Ingres and Delacroix by making the former the representative of drawing and the latter the champion of colour. The real explanation rests in the fact that the dynamic drawing of Delacroix seeks to render effort and movement while Ingres stabilizes the living form in contours of incomparable purity.

INGRES: PORTRAIT OF M. BERTIN. LOUVRE.
*(Photo by Hachette.)*

INGRES: THE GOLDEN AGE. CHÂTEAU OF DAMPIERRE.
*(Photo by Bulloz.)*

INGRES: MME. DEVAUÇAY. MUSÉE CONDÉ, CHANTILLY.
*(Photo by Hachette.)*

## Ingres the Portraitist and Decorator

INGRES, by nature, was especially inclined to paint odalisques and Venuses. But a painter as attentive in observing nature should become a fine portraitist. His portraits exhibit a very rare quality in the harmony between reality and the classic style. He handles feminine figures with refined elegance; masculine portraits are elevated to the majesty of historic types. The choice of attitudes, the drawing of the draperies, the linear combinations add to the lifelike faces the definitive quality which is "style."

FLANDRIN: THE NATIVITY. ST. GERMAIN DES PRÉS, PARIS
*(Photo by Hachette.)*

FLANDRIN: NAPOLEON III. MUSEUM OF VERSAILLES.
*(Photo by Hachette.)*

DELAROCHE: PAINTING FROM THE HEMICYCLE OF THE ÉCOLE DES BEAUX-ARTS.
*(Photo by Hachette.)*

## The Decorative School of Ingres

IT IS perhaps in the title of painter-decorator that Ingres played a particularly important rôle in the art of the nineteenth century. To the brilliant and impulsive decoration of Delacroix he contrasted serene figures with tranquil lines in discreet colours which seem to revive the style of the Florentine fresco artists. Thus the *Apotheosis of Homer* gave rise to a school which decorated the churches, constructed or restored at Paris under the Second Empire. The most famous of these Neo-Giottesque masters is Hippolyte Flandrin.

ing, so that, for instance, the figures were planned to resemble, in type, the statues round the doors. Various stages in this period of stained glass may be seen at Bourges, Quimper, Le Mans. There was also glass work done in Provence, especially in Avignon, though little of it now remains.

(e) *16th-century windows.*—There was a revival of stained glass art, so that the productive activity of this century equalled that of the 13th century. The work now definitely assumed the type of a picture on glass. The divisions of the bays were no longer an obstacle, and the pictures would continue from one lancet to another. Copies of paintings or engravings were now done on glass (Dürer's, or Schongauer's, etc.). Beauvais, Normandy and Champagne were centres of the art, all of which showed great activity in production. There were also many windows made in Brittany, etc., during this century.

From this time the art of stained glass rapidly declined. Lamentable copies of master painters were made; there was a straining after subtlety, and too lavish a use of detail and of varied colour. The application of enamel, which had been looked upon as an advance, really resulted in heaviness, confusion, and lack of transparency.

(f) *17th- and 18th-century windows.*—During these centuries, the art did not develop, and only a few windows are worth mentioning. (Sainte-Gudule in Brussels; Sainte-Eustache, Paris, etc.)

(g) *19th-century glass.*—Towards the end of this century tentative efforts were made to revive this dead art, and nowadays the excellence of the old methods is recognised.

See Pl. 10, Vol. I.

BIBLIOGRAPHY: E. Didron, *Le Vitrail depuis leuts ans et à l'Exposition de 1809*. Coulommiers, 1889.—L. Magne, *L'œuvre des peintres verriers français*, Paris.—E. Mâle, Articles on *La Peinture sur verre*, in *l'Histoire de l'art*, published under the direction of André Michel; Vol. I, 2nd part; Vol. II, 1st part; and Vol. IV, 2nd part.—E. Mâle, *L'art religieux du XIIIe siècle*. Paris.—Ottin, *Le vitrail*. Paris.—Westlake, *History of Stained Glass*. London, 4 vols.—Hugh Arnold, *Stained Glass in the Middle Ages in France and England*. Illustrated by Lawrence B. Saint. London, 1913.

**STANFIELD (William Clarkson).**—English painter (1793-1867), achieved great vogue as a painter of seascapes and lake scenes in oil and water colour. Elected A.R.A. 1832, R.A. 1835.

**STARK (Arthur James).**—English painter (1794-1859). Pupil of old Crome, he was one of the most brilliant of the Norwich School, and exhibited regularly at the Academy. He did remarkable landscapes which, in spite of their apparent simplicity, show a real knowledge of technique. Two examples of his work are in the National Gallery, Millbank.

BIBLIOGRAPHY: A. P. Nicholson, *The Norwich School and their last Exponent*. 1907.

**STARNINA (Gherardo).**—Florentine painter, mentioned 1387 in the Guild of S. Luca; commissioned in 1408 to decorate a chapel in the Church of S. Stefano at Empoli. Vasari identifies this painter with the follower of Agnolo Gaddi who did the frescoes in the Castellani Chapel of Sta. Croce (after 1383) and gives various facts about his life. Further attributions have been made on the basis of these frescoes, for whose authorship we have only Vasari's word.

BIBLIOGRAPHY: Vasari-Milanesi, II.—O. H. Giglioli, *Su alcuni affreschi perduti dello Starnina*, Rivista d'Arte, III, 1905; same author, *Empoli artistica*. Florence, 1906.—Schmarsow, *Wer ist Gherardo Starnina?* Abhandl. der K. Sächs. Gesellsch. der Wissensch., XXIX, V. Leipzig, 1912.

**STAUROTECHE.**—See Byzantine Art (Enamels).

**STEEN (Jan Haviksz).**—Dutch genre painter, born and died in Leyden, 1626-1679. He was a pupil of Ostade and van Goyen, and married the daughter of the latter.

STEEN: THE FAMILY MEAL. (Louvre.)

He was active in The Hague for a while, until in 1654 he moved to Delft where he managed a brewery. In 1657 we find him returning to Leyden as an innkeeper. One of the great Dutch masters, he is unsurpassed as a humorist and painter of customs and characters. The very free life Steen led brought him in contact with every class of people: gamblers, courtesans, noblemen and the village drunkards. He depicts them faithfully in their respective settings, among their characteristic activities; a keen observer and somewhat a psychologist, each figure is a bit of portraiture in itself, and the composition as a whole reflects and perpetuates the significance of the moment perfectly. The superiority in handling group scenes may be seen especially well in the various wedding festivals. Steen was often assisted by Metsu, and some of his works are reminiscent of the style of Mieris. The quality of his paintings is very inconsistent, often becoming loose and muddy in color, a result of the baneful effects of his debauched life. Even paintings like the *Marriage of Cana* (Brussels), and *Treason of Delilah* (Antwerp) are treated as inn-scenes. His *Self-portrait* is in Amsterdam; other works may be seen in large numbers in London, Paris, Leningrad, and elsewhere.

BIBLIOGRAPHY: J. Van Westrheene, *Jan Steen*. The Hague, 1856.—C. Hofstede de Groot, *A Catalogue Raisonné of the Works of the most Eminent Dutch Painters of the Seventeenth Century*. Vol. I. London. 1907.

**STEER (Philip Wilson).**—Contemporary English painter. He was born at Birkenhead on December 28, 1860, the son of a painter and teacher of art. His youth was spent in Whitchurch, Monmouthshire, and when he was about sixteen years of age he attended the School of Art at Gloucester studying under John Kemp. In 1882 he went to Paris and at first enrolled in the Académie Julian where he worked under Bouguereau and later went to the Ecole des Beaux-Arts receiving instruction from Cabanel. He was much impressed by the Manet Memorial Exhibition held in Paris in 1883 and turned from the purely academic training to some experiments in impressionism. In 1885 he returned to England to live and there saw some of the work of James Abbott McNeill Whistler whose style influenced him for a time. Gradually he turned away from the theories he had gained in France and went back to the impressionistic formulae composed by Constable and Turner. Although most of his work consists of wide spreading landscapes, he has done some nudes, figure pieces and interiors. His work is done directly from nature and shows the results obtained from his great powers of concentration coupled with hard work and a vivid imagination. His subjects treat exclusively of the English countryside occasionally adorned by some bit of architecture. As he himself has said so fittingly of his work: "all that one has to go on are nature and tradition." He was one of the first members of the New English Art Club which broke away from the academic standards of the Royal Academy. His work is to be seen in the British Museum, the Imperial War Museum, the Tate Gallery, galleries in Manchester, Dublin, Cambridge and Johannesburg and his self-portrait hangs in the famous collection in the Uffizi in Florence.

See Pl. 65, Vol. II.

BIBLIOGRAPHY: D. S. MacColl, *Steer*, Artwork, Spring, 1929.—John Rothenstein, *A Pot of Paint*, 1929.—Sir Frederick Wedmore, *Some of the Moderns*, 1909.

**STEFANO.**—Florentine painter of the beginning of the 14th century; follower of Giotto; praised by Ghiberti for a *Saint Thomas Aquinas* in Santa Maria Novella, for the paintings in the cloisters of Sant'Agostino in Florence, and for a *Gloria* in Assisi. He was called "Nature's monkey" by Villani and he was often quoted and much renowned, but there are now no paintings which can definitely be attributed to him.

BIBLIOGRAPHY: R. van Marle, *The Development of the Italian Schools of Painting*, Vol. III.

**STEFANO da ZEVIO (da Verona).**—Painter of the Altichiero tradition in Verona, influenced by Tyrolese art; born c. 1375; died 1451.

In 1434 Stefano is recorded as a witness; he lived at this time in the region of Trent; from 1435 dates his signed *Adoration of the Magi*, painted for the Ottolini family, Verona, now in the Brera. In 1438 his will mentions an altarpiece for Sta. Anastasia, Chapel of Nicholas, which was left unfinished. His signature was once visible on a fresco over the side door of Sta. Eufemia, Verona, but has since disappeared. His painting is best to be studied in Verona, where there are frescoes and panels by him.

BIBLIOGRAPHY: Vasari-Milanesi.—V. Cavazzocco Marzanti, *Stefano da Zevio*, Arch. stor. Ver., XXIV, 1886, *fasc.* 72.—Crowe and Cavalcaselle, *History of Painting in North Italy*, ed. T. Borenius, Vol. II.—A Pomello, *Stefano da Zevio*. Verona, 1899.—E. Langer, *Über einen alter Maler, Meister Stephan*, Kunstfreund, 1900.—Gerola, *Questioni storiche d'arte veronese*. Verona, 1908.—G. Cervellini, *Quando nacque Stefano da Verona?* Verona, 1909.—L. Testi, *Questioni d'arte veronese*. Verona, 1909; same author, *Storia della pitt. venez.*, II, 1915.— Van Marle, *Italian Schools, etc.*, VII.

**— DI GIOVANNI.**—See Sassetta.

**STELE.**—Stone slab or pillar used to mark a grave or for some other commemorative purpose.

**STELLA (Jacques).**—French painter (about 1596-1657). Arriving in Rome about 1623, he became the friend and disciple of Poussin. The soft religiosity which the Jesuits had set in fashion, and which so mars the painter of the *Miracle of St. Francis Xavier*, Jacques Stella had in a high degree. One has only to look at his little picture, painted on marble, of *Christ Receiving His Mother in Heaven* (Louvre), with its insipid colours and sickly sentiment, to understand how this feeble talent must have seduced the devotees of the period. On his return to France, in 1634, he was, thanks to the favour of Richelieu, made King's painter, and lodged in the Louvre. Stella was a good second-rate painter, sometimes crude like Perrier, sometimes pale like Le Sueur.

FRAGMENT OF A STELE FROM TELLO. (Louvre.)

**STEREOBATE.**—The lower part of a building or pedestal.

**STERNE (Maurice).**—Contemporary American painter and sculptor. He was born at Libau in 1878. His early youth was spent in Moscow, but he came to New York City when he was eleven. In 1894 he entered the National Academy of Design where he studied anatomy under Thomas Eakins. For the next ten years he studied at art schools in this country and in 1904 he won a travelling fellowship from the National Academy of Design. He then went to Paris, where he was influenced by the work of Cézanne and then to Italy, where he came under the spell of Piero della Francesca. He absorbed from that Italian Renaissance master the method of modelling figures in light and shade in a composition dignified and unified by a harmonious use of colour. His next years were spent in Greece, drawing and studying the sculpture of the 4th and 5th centuries B.C. His own attempts in sculpture, including the Rogers-Kennedy Memorial at Worcester and smaller pieces, show the influence of that study in their broad plain surfaces and the largeness of the modelled forms. From 1911 to 1914 Sterne stayed in Bali, absorbing the artistic trends of the natives and borrowing their knowledge of the use of colour, which now served to enhance his work already dignified by a sense of form and design. After that he returned to Italy, to Anticoli near Rome, where he could express himself in colourful compositions filled with the warm glowing spirit of that country. At present he works in the United States, spending some of his time in Anticoli. Examples of his work may be found in the Art Institute of Chicago, the California Palace of the Legion of Honor in San Francisco and the Phillips Memorial Gallery in Washington.

BIBLIOGRAPHY: Italo Tavolato, *Maurice Sterne,* Rome, 1925.—For other information see *The Index of Twentieth Century Artists* for February, 1934.

**STIMMER (Tobias).** — Swiss painter, 1539-1583. Author of the fresco decoration of the House of the Knight (Schaffhausen) and two fine portraits of Jacob Schwytzer and his wife (1564; Basle Museum).

**STIPPLING.**—See Engraving.

**STOCKHOLM.**—*Town Hall.* See Östberg.

*Concert Hall.*—See Tengbom.

*Law Court.*—See Westman.

**STONE AGE.**—See Prehistoric Archæology.

**STONEHENGE (England).** — Stone circle, possibly an ancient necropolis and sanctuary.

See Pl. 14, Vol. I.

**STORY (William Wetmore).**— American sculptor (1819-1895), a prolific artist who in his lifetime enjoyed a great popularity, especially noted for his female figures from the domain of classical history or mythology (e.g. *Cleopatra,* 1862, Metropolitan Museum of Art).

**STOSS (Veit).**—German sculptor, about 1445-1533. Probably born at Nuremberg, but worked in Kracow, Poland, from 1477 to 1496. He began as a pupil of Michael Wolgemut. His earliest work dates from 1477-49. In Kracow he made two important works—a model for the *Tomb of the King of Poland, Casimir IV Jagellon* (1492); and the *Altar of Mary* (1477-1486) in the Church of Our Lady. Veit Stoss returned to Nuremberg in 1496, and remained there until his death, the highly pathetic nature of his early style giving way to a more tranquil development. At the end of the century, Veit Stoss made for the Church of Our Lady, the *Virgin,* 1500 (now in the Germanic Museum, Nuremberg). Three stone reliefs of the choir of St. Sebald (*The Last Supper, Christ on the Mount of Olives,* and the *Arrest of Christ*), dating from 1499, are attributed to him. It has been noted that the soldiers are dressed in Polish fashion.

The year 1503 was an unfortunate one for Veit Stoss. He was accused of having made a false receipt, arrested, and condemned to death. Then he was reprieved, but branded on the cheeks with hot irons. In spite of this, he continued to live and work in Nuremberg.

In 1507, he made for the Church of St. Lawrence, the famous *Angelic Salutation* (or *Great Rosary*)—a wooden chaplet of carved roses, and medallions representing the Seven Joys of Mary. In 1508, he made for the Church of Schwabach, an altarpiece, which shows the *Coronation of the Virgin with St. John and St. Martin,* and, on the wings, the *Holy Family,* the *Descent of the Holy Spirit to the Virgin, Her Death, and Assumption.* In 1520-1523, he made for the Church of Bamberg, another altarpiece, the *Adoration of the Shepherds,* showing Dürer's influence. Another important work is *St. Roch,* 1510, in Sta. Annunciata (Florence). Although one of the important sculptors of the Gothic period, his altars mark the beginning in Renaissance feeling; less Gothic decorations, round arches framing the composition. Flat relief background, linear hardness of types of faces, show the influence of Roger v. d. Weyden's paintings. His favorite medium was wood.

The atelier created by Veit Stoss in Kracow, was continued after his departure, under the direction of his son Stanislas (born in 1464).

See Pl. 25, Vol. II.

BIBLIOGRAPHY: Daun, *Veit Stoss und Seine Schule in Deutschland, Polen, Ungarn und Siebenbürgen.* Leipzig, 1916. — Lossnitzer, *Veit Stoss, die Herkunft seiner Kunst, seine Werk v. Sein Leben,* 1912.

**STOTHARD (Thomas).** — English painter (1755-1834), a prolific painter of mythological and romantic subjects, a long series of which may be seen in the National Gallery, Millbank. Elected A.R.A. 1791, R.A. 1794.

**STRANGE (Sir Robert).**—English engraver, 1721-1792. Pupil of Le Bas; did many reproductions from the Italian masters.

BIBLIOGRAPHY: Charles Le Blanc, *Catalogue of the work of R. Strange.* Leipzig, 1848.

**STRASBOURG.**—The finest building in Strasbourg is the *Cathedral,* which was built in the 11th and 12th centuries. The Gothic nave and façade were rebuilt in the 13th century. The tower dates from the 15th century. Crypt and choir are Romanesque. The architecture is essentially French, but German elements are commingled. The sculpture is more Teutonic than the architecture. The Cathedral possesses old glass, and a remarkable stone pulpit (15th century).

In the Cathedral square are old wooden houses, the most famous of which is the Maison Kammerzeil (15th and 16th centuries).

See Pl. 48, Vol. I.

BIBLIOGRAPHY: Welshinger, *Strasbourg.* Collection les villes d'art célèbres.

**STRIGEL (Bernhard).**—German painter, 1461-1528. School of Swabia. Court painter of the Emperor Maximilian. His paintings reveal the new found interest in personality in portrait painting, and a capacity for powerful group characterization. Painting with his left hand, his colors and treatment are often reminiscent of Van der Weyden. Strigel's chief works are the *Sippenbilder* (pictures of the family of the Virgin), *Conrad Rechingen and His Eight Children* (1517; Munich), the *Family of Councillor Cuspinian* (Berlin); *the Emperor Maximilian and His Family* (Vienna).

**STROBL (Alajos or Alois, de Lipôtujvár).**—Hungarian sculptor, 1856-1937. Born on June 21 at Királylehota, he received his first artistic education at a Hungarian tile factory. Strobl's serious studies began in Vienna with König and later he spent four years at the Academie Julian in Paris. A prolific artist, he completed several notebooks of lifelike sketches of soldiers; and his first monumental sculpture *Persée,* caused a sensation in Berlin, and Vienna as well. Although somewhat influenced by the new Cinquecento Renaissance in Europe, he nevertheless felt in the trend the lack of originality, profundity and truth; he liberated his sculpture just in time, and it was his sincerity throughout which saved his art and brought it to its high standard. A true genius, in his works is reconciliated the art

STRASBOURG: CHÂTEAU DE ROHAN.

of the present and the past, the traditional beauty and a truth to life. He was a great admirer of Michelangelo and tried to achieve some of his force and power. In 1882 he returned to Budapest and executed a number of svelte nudes in marble. He received the commission to do the sculpture for the Royal Opera House which was designed by Ybl. Subsequently he did the two *Sphinx,* the statues of *Cherubini, Spontini, Erkel* and *Liszt*; the two latter ones placed in niches and reminiscent in composition, pensiveness and depth, of Michelangelo's *Moses.* In 1906 he created the seated *Liszt* before the Academy of Music. His portraits are a fusion of realism and nobility of character, the *Prince—Primate Simor* (Esztergom) and the tragic actress *Maria Jászi* are among the most expressive ones. Expression of grief is admirably rendered in the *Kossuth* monument, 1909; the *Deák Mausoleum,* 1885, shows his ability in architectural sculpture. Later portraits are characterized by more pathos and sustained passion. He also did a number of fountains, caryatids and public monuments.

**— (Zsigmond or Sigismund, de Kisfaludi).** — Contemporary Hungarian sculptor. Born in Budapest in 1884, he received his artistic education in Budapest, Vienna, the Academie Julian in Paris, and in Italy. While in Rome, he absorbed the ideals of the classicists, as reflected in his *Morning* (Hearst Coll.), the *Bather* (Amsterdam) and *Woman with Lizard* (Budapest), all done in marble and characterized by a plastic but static mood. While in Florence, his appreciation of Renaissance sculpture may be seen in *Kurucz Rider* and the seated statue of *Peter Pázmány.* In his middle period we find a combination of naturalism and classicism, motion and repose. A series of bronze boxers date from this time, as well as the famous *Archer* which calls to mind Bourdelles's *Herakles* in vigour and action, although Strobl's work tends more towards realism, while the French prototype is decorative. A perfect equilibrium combined with dynamic movement may be studied in *Adastra,* his genius and active imagination are at their height in the *Birth of Venus.* Other dramatic works, however, show the influence of Michelangelo and Rodin. Strobl was foremost as a portrait sculptor; fidelity, plastic beauty and insight, characterize all these busts. He works in clean-cut planes, yet modelling the vital nuances, thus bringing out all the personal irregularities. He did the portraits of many famous statesmen and artists, among these the best are *Count Apponyi,* and *Perczel.* While in England he modelled *Lord Rothemere,* the *Duke of York, Randolph,* grasping the racial characteristics of the British admirably, in contrast to the Hungarian type. It is interesting to note, that the male portraits are done in bronze, while those of ladies and children are of marble. These marble busts are melodies in classic beauty, and have seldom been surpassed by any modern sculptor (*Actress Paulay, Mrs. Paul Konody* and others).

**STRONGYLION.**—See Acropolis of Athens.

STRASBOURG: PULPIT OF THE CATHEDRAL.

**STROZZI (Bernardo).**—Genoese painter, 1581-1644. Pupil of Pietro Sorri. He was influenced chiefly by the harsh, gloomy naturalism of Carravaggio, as may be seen in his vigorous painting of a beggar in the Museo Nationale, Rome.

The end of his life was agitated, for he endeavoured to forsake the cloister. He was put in prison, escaped, and died in Venice.

BIBLIOGRAPHY: G. Fiocco, *Bernardo Strozzi.* 1921.

**— (Zanobi de').**—Florentine panel and miniature painter, of noted family, born 1412; died 1468; a pupil of Fra Angelico.

In 1436 Strozzi was paid for a panel for Sta. Maria Nuova; in 1446-53 decorated nineteen antiphonaries for S. Marco, on the order of Cosimo de' Medici (with Filippo di Matteo Torelli; Strozzi painting the figures); in 1457 he worked for the Church of S. Pancrazio; in 1463 ornamented two antiphonaries for the Duomo of Florence (with Francesco d'Antonio del Cherico). In 1466, with Baldovinetti, he estimated a picture by Neri di Bicci.

BIBLIOGRAPHY: Vasari - Milanesi, II.—Milanesi, *Storia della miniatura italiana,* 1850.—D'Ancona, *Un ignoto collaboratore del Beato Angelico,* L'Arte, 1908; same author *La miniatura fiorentina,* 1914; *La miniature italienne,* 1924. — Van Marle, *Italian Schools, etc.* X, 1928.

**STUART (Gilbert).**—Early American painter (1755-1828). He was born at Narragansett, Rhode Island, 3d December 1755. He was educated at Bishop Berkeley's school in Newport and when a boy of fourteen he received several portrait commissions. About 1770 he had some instruction from a Scotch artist, Cosmo Alexander, and accompanied him on his return to Scotland. There Alexander died, as did shortly afterward a Sir George Chambers to whom Alexander had commended the boy. It was a hard and arduous journey back to the United States, since he had scarcely any money. About 1775 he sailed for England and there lived and worked with Benjamin West for about eight years. He also listened to lectures by Sir Joshua Reynolds and some anatomy talks given by Dr. Cruikshank. He exhibited his pictures at the Royal Academy and the Incorporated Society of Artists. In 1783 he set up his own studio and painted for Mr. Boydell a portrait of Sir Joshua Reynolds. He was a poor manager of his finances and came near to being jailed for debt. From 1787 to 1793 presumably he was painting in Ireland where he did some portraits of prominent men, but apparently continued to live extravagantly, as was his custom. About 1793 he returned to the United States, where he lived in New York for a while. In 1795 he had his first sitting with Washington. It was an event to which he had looked forward for many years and the results of his first portrait (the Vaughan type) were not altogether pleasing to him. He made later studies of Washington known as the Athenaeum type, and the Lansdowne type, which is a full length portrait. At that time he was residing in Philadelphia, which was then the national capital, but when Congress moved to Washington about 1803 he went to that city to live. A few years later he moved to Boston and there spent the rest of his life. His health failed and he suffered a stroke of paralysis. He died 9th July 1828 and was buried on Boston Common. His work is generally done in thin tones of delicate colours with the main emphasis on the head of the subject of the portrait. In general the likenesses are capably rendered with some attempt at character analysis. Less successful are the full-length portraits, where the figure and accessories are clumsily handled. This fault was common in the work of all the early American painters who followed the contemporary English tradition of portraiture. Since his death his fame as a portrait painter has declined, but his face of Washington as idealised in the Athenaeum portrait has become the one accepted by the American public as the most faithful likeness of the father of his country.

See Pl. 61, Vol. II.

BIBLIOGRAPHY: S. P. Avery, *Some Account of the "Gibbs-Channing" Portrait of George Washington Painted by Gilbert Stuart,* 1900.—Mantle Fielding, *Gilbert Stuart's Portraits of George Washington,* 1923.—Mantle Fielding, *The Life and Works of Gilbert Stuart,* 1923.—*Gilbert Stuart,* Masters in Art Series, January, 1906.—Hannah R. London, *Portraits of Jews by Gilbert Stuart and Other Early American Artists,* 1927.—G. G. Mason, *The Life and Works of Gilbert Stuart,* 1879.—Lawrence Parke, *Gilbert Stuart,* 1926.—William T. Whitley, *Gilbert Stuart,* 1932.

**STUBBS (George).** — English painter (1724-1806), one of the most talented among the English eighteenth-century painters of sporting subjects, noted for his rendering of horses, a subject to which he devoted close study, publishing a work on *The Anatomy of a Horse* in 1766. Elected A.R.A. in 1780, R.A. in 1781.

BIBLIOGRAPHY: Walter Shaw Sparrow, *George Stubbs and Ben Marshall.* London, 1929.

**STUCK (Franz).**—German painter, born in 1863. An admirer of the antique. More interested in plasticity, than in psychology. *The Sphinx* and *War* (Munich) show that he was capable of attaining grandeur.

**STÜLER (Friedrich August).**—German architect, 1800-1865. Author of the New Museum, Berlin, 1843-1855, and the National Museum, Stockholm, 1850-1866.

**STUPA.**—See India art.

**STYLOBATE.**—The continucus flat coping or pavement at the base of a building, serving to support a row of columns.

**SUBLEYRAS (Pierre).**—French painter, 1699-1749. He spent most of his life in Italy, where he enjoyed a big reputation, and where he worked for the Pope. His vast painting of *The Swoon of Emperor Valens While Assisting at a Mass Celebrated by St. Basil,* pleased the Pope so much that he gave the order for it to be reproduced in mosaic and placed above the high altar in St. Peter's.

**SUESS (Hans).**—See Kulmbach.

**SUKENOBU (Nishigawa).**—Japanese illustrator, 1674-1754. He illustrated scenes of the Occupations of Women; and only produced works in black and white.

**SULLIVAN (Louis Henry).**—American architect (1856-1924). He was born in Boston, Massachusetts, 3d September 1856. His youth was spent there and on his grandparents' farm at South Reading nearby. He was a very impressionable child and early became interested in buildings and the men who conceived their designs. He decided to become an architect and studied at the Massachusetts Institute of Technology under Professor William R. Ware and Eugene Letang, who was a graduate of the École des Beaux-Arts. Then he worked for a while as a draftsman for the firm of Furness and Hewitt in Philadelphia, but was discharged during the depression of 1873. At that time he went west to Chicago and there did some architectural drawing for Major William Jenney, but the next year he left to go to Paris. There he began studying at the École des Beaux-Arts in the Atelier Vaudremer, but did not feel that the courses offered there gave much chance for individual expression. He left the school and travelled south to Florence and Rome before returning to Chicago. There he worked independently for some time, but in 1880 joined the firm of D. Adler and Company. The following year it became known as Adler and Sullivan and rivalled the other Chicago firm of Burnham and Root. In 1885 Adler and Sullivan received the contract for the Auditorium to house the Chicago opera. It was a long exhaustive task and Sullivan's health broke down when it was completed. He took a trip to California to recuperate, returning by the way of New Orleans.

The development of steel frames for buildings was in its infancy and the Wainwright Building in St. Louis designed bv Sullivan in 1890 was one of the first steel frame skyscrapers. The Transportation Building which he built for the Columbian Exposition of 1893 attracted wide attention as much by its colourful decoration as by the new functional method of construction. Other structures by Sullivan include the Guaranty Building in Buffalo and the Trust and Savings Building in St. Louis. While the early structures show the influence of Richardson he later developed new methods of vertical accents to give height to the buildings as well as adequate support by the steel framework. He died 14th April 1924 in Chicago.

See Pl. 64, Vol. II.

BIBLIOGRAPHY: Louis Henry Sullivan, *The Autobiography of an Idea,* 1924.—Hugh Morrison, *Louis Sullivan,* 1936.

**SULLY (Loiret).**—The château was built by the La Tremoille, in the 15th and 16th centuries, and granted by them to Sully (minister of Henri IV), who took the name of his new domain. Situated on an islet of the Loire, it includes three blocks of buildings flanked by numerous towers.

SULLY-SUR-LOIRE: THE CHÂTEAU, SOUTH SIDE.

**— (Thomas).** — Early American painter (1783-1872). He was born at Horncastle, Lincolnshire, England, 8th June 1783. His parents were actors and brought their family to America in 1792. They settled in Charleston, South Carolina, and there the boy entered the office of an insurance broker. His brother-in-law, Mr. Belzons, was a French miniature painter and instructed young Sully, who seemed more interested in painting than in business. But they quarrelled and Thomas Sully at the age of sixteen went to live with his older brother, Lawrence, who was also a miniature painter in Richmond, Virginia. In 1801 they moved to Norfolk, and there Lawrence died. Young Thomas worked at his profession as a portrait painter to support his brother's family and soon married the widow. In 1806 they moved to New York City and there he received some instruction from John Trumbull and for a time acted as assistant to John Wesley Jarvis. The next year he went to Boston to work under the able direction of Gilbert Stuart. Early in 1809 he became an American citizen and later that same year sailed to England for further study. He studied with C. B. King and later with Benjamin West and absorbed some influence of the style of Sir Thomas Lawrence. In his spare moments he copied the works of the old masters represented in West's collection in fulfilment of an agreement made with the men who sponsored his European trip. In 1810 he returned to the United States and began the best period of his work. He did portraits of some actors, including *Cooke as "Richard III,"* now in the Pennsylvania Academy, and others of prominent men, including *Stephen Decatur* for the city of New York and in 1824 a full-length portrait of the *Marquis de Lafayette.* The St. George Society of Philadelphia sent him abroad in 1837 to do a portrait of the young Queen Victoria. It was a hard commission, but he managed to make quite an imposing composition of the short and not very beautiful young woman who was then on the threshold of her long and eventful reign. He returned to the United States the following year and continued his painting even when he was over seventy-five years of age. It has been estimated that he did about two thousand portraits and miniatures in all, beside about five hundred subject paintings. Most of these were mentioned in his carefully kept diary, often with some notations regarding the price and a description of the works. He died 5th November 1872 after a long and fruitful career. Perhaps the most famous of his subject paintings is the *Boy with a Torn Hat,* where remarkably transparent shadows obscure the face of the sitter without obliterating the masses or contour with the thick black shadows generally associated with that period.

See Pl. 61, Vol. II.

BIBLIOGRAPHY: Edward Biddle and Mantle Fielding, *The Life and Works of Thomas Sully,* 1921.—*A Register of Portraits Painted by Thomas Sully,* introduction and notes by Charles Henry Hart, 1909. —*Catalogue of the Memorial Exhibition of Portraits by Thomas Sully,* Pennsylvania Academy of Fine Arts, Philadelphia, 1922.

**SULTANIEH.**—Town of Persia, founded in the 13th century and entirely destroyed, with the exception of a very fine mausoleum of the King Euldjaïton Khoda-Bendé, built from 1303-1316. It is octagonal in shape, and covered with a dome of turquoise blue tiles.

**SUMERIAN ART.**—Sumer or, as it has been called, Chaldea or Babylonia, covers the region between the Tigris and Euphrates rivers and was inhabited from the fourth millennium by a non-Semitic people only recently established as the Sumerians. Their exact origin, history, and even composition, are still highly controversial. Evidences of human habitation are to be found as early as palaeolithic times in the Syrian desert. Although no trace of mesolithic or neolithic culture exists in Sumer, there are neolithic finds in the region east of the Tigris.

From the earliest stages of the aeneolithic culture (fourth millennium) there are small figurines, flints and burnt-clay implements. The earliest pottery is hand-made and crude but with the introduction of the wheel it soon became quite refined. The pottery of this period is thin and hard; green in color because of bad firing; and decorated with black animal and abstract forms. Architecture of early aëneolithic times was limited to reed, clay and sun-dried brick huts. In the middle stage there is already a developed decorated architecture of the courtyard type. The late aëneolithic period which is characterized by pictographic script has left us a number of interesting small pieces including religious idols in clay and small carved-pebble representations of animals and humans of high artistic quality. There is one stone relief known as the "Figure aux Plumes" which is really a forerunner of the historic period of Sumerian art.

The historic era of Sumerian civilization begins at about 3000 B.C. and is characterized by rectilinear script and a wide use of bronze. The building material was a curious small oblong brick with a flat top and a concave lower surface. The architecture was decorated with terra cotta mosaic work and in some cases metal. Pottery is unimportant at this stage and the painted ware was imported.

Sumerian Head found at Tello. (Louvre.)

The earliest works of the historic period are attributable to Mesilim (about 3000), King of Kish, and consist of a mace-head, a lance-blade, the "Monument circulaire" and two stone plaques. From the time of the first king of Lagash, Ur-Nanse (Nina) (about 2900) we have three genealogical tables crudely carved, with squat, heavily-clothed figures depicting the king together with the members of the royal family at various religious or civic functions. An alabaster statue of Ur-Nanse's daughter and one inscribed Korlil are short, neckless masses dominated by the original stone block. Under the succeeding Eannatum (about 2830) the Stele of Vultures was produced. This two-faced stone slab depicts the victory of Eannatum over his enemies. The king is shown gathering his conquered opponents into a net surmounted by the Eagle of Lagash; another section contains his marching army trampling the fallen enemy dead. The figures are more advanced both in conception and carving than the earlier Ur-Nanse plaques. Also from this period are eighty female statues, found at Assur, of remarkable execution, which give the first definite evidence of facial expression. The famous silver vase from the time of Entemena (about 2780) has a very finely encised surface design of the triumphant Eagle of Lagash. Most of the evidence of the Dynasty of Lagash derives from the excavations of de Sarzec at Tello.

Excavation at Al Ubaid covering the First and Second Dynasties of Ur in the tombs of A-Anne-Padda, Meskalum-Dug and Sub-Ad revealed works of a different Sumerian sphere which because of stylistic reasons must be contemporary with Eannatum and Entemena. Among the more important finds are an enameled-mosaic pastoral frieze which covered the building walls. The metal work of thin beaten copper upon a bitumen base is of exceptional beauty. A now restored over-porch metal decoration depicted a tiger-headed eagle grasping two deer.

Fragment of a Stele from Tello. (Louvre.)

During the declining years of both the Lagash and Ur Dynasties, Sumerian history is vague. The question of whether the Guti invasion is prior and anterior to the Empire of Akkad (2772-2549 or 2429) is still doubtful, but artistically there seems to be no break between the last Lagash rulers, Lugal-Anda and Uru-Kagina, and the early Akkadian kings, Sargon and Manistusu. The Empire of Akkad is the height of Sumerian art and may be divided into three major phases—Sargon, Naram-Sin and Gudea. There was in these periods a progressive flowering and fruition of art comparable to the great stages of the Italian Renaissance.

The Stele of Sargon is the major work of the first period. It shows Sargon, King of Akkad, with bare right shoulder, long hair knotted in the back, accompanied by a servant carrying an umbrella, a sign of royalty in the East even down to modern times. Vultures are feeding on the dead enemies. The figures are slimmer than those of the previous style of Lagash and Ur and closer to the early Kish style; which would seem to point toward a double tradition, one Semitic and northern with thin figures and the other Sumerian and southern with short, squat figures. This conception of the Akkadians as Semites is further strengthened by the fact that the warriors carry specifically Semitic weapons.

The sandstone Stele of Naram-Sin six feet in height was discovered at Susa. On it the conquering Naram-Sin with his cohorts are trampling their fallen foes. For the first time in Sumerian reliefs there is an attempt at a coherent landscape, with the hills, trees, sun and moon represented as still more or less abstract symbols. The great bareness and apparent scattering of figures would indicate that the stele was originally painted in greater detail. Although the action is still symbolic, it already has in single elements the beginning of a naturalistic treatment. A similar relief, probably antedating that of Naram-Sin, has been found carved on the mountain rock near Sippurla. One of the finest individual pieces of this time is a small, fragmentary woman's head done with great freedom and expressiveness, and spiritually related to Greek art of the fifth century B.C.

Of the Gudea period we have a number of statues in the round which are the most famous examples of Sumerian art. These pieces are not all Gudean, but, more likely, belong to the entire Sargonic era. They are generally quite small although giving the impression of great monumentality. In all these works, of which Gudea as architect is the most famous, we are faced with the absolute lack of a formal canon; some are short, others tall, in conformity with the original shape of the stone block. They were executed in very hard stone which enforced a certain simplicity of form, a rigidity and frontality. But in spite of the prismatic character, they do show a forceful and robust realism. The modelling of the nude parts, the feet, hands and right shoulder, has virility as well as refinement. The drapery is either a simple undifferentiated mass with incised pattern lines, or a thin veil revealing the underlying musculature. The whole figure gives the impression of monumentality, of powerful but contained force. The isolated heads have this same quality. The artist has modelled in large planes, while carving certain details, such as the long arched eyebrows, very minutely. The general head-shape is square, the lower jaw solid, the cheek-bones prominent, the lips finely moulded. In the bearded heads, both the beard and hair are done with exquisite delicacy and formal decorative restraint.

All work after Gudea under the Empire of Sumer and Akkad (about 2400-2300) or the dissolution of Sumerian culture under the respective dynasties of Isin, Larsa and Babylon (about 2400-1870), as well as the possibly contemporary third dynasty of Ur, is really a devitalized or degenerate form of the great Sargonic art of the Empire of Akkad. Subsequent examples all show a greater massiveness, but a disintegration of the vital quality inherent in all Sargonic art.

*Seal-Cylinders.* The seal-cylinders, which in their early button-form date back to prehistoric times, were used either as amulets or most frequently as property-markings. The cylinder seal was a small, circular, stone drum carved with a drill. This drum was then rolled on wet clay producing thereby a sort of bas-relief strip of isocephalic figures together with inscriptions. The very earliest examples consist of a series of simple, drilled holes which later develop into a recognizable pattern. From these early forms they further develop into very complicated ribbon-scenes with many figures. The major subject matter was concerned with the legendary exploits of the hero, Gilgamesh, or with religious scenes involving the worship of specific gods. No two are alike in all elements, each being peculiar to its owner and serving as his brand or coat of arms. The early historic seals are composed of an endless succession of related animals and men, but during the period of Lugal-Anda and the Sargonic era, this endless pattern disintegrates into a series of composed units. Some of these Sumerian seals are of exquisite beauty and as a class they are superior to any other group of seal-cylinders.

Bibliography: De Sarzec, E. and Hèuzey, L. A., *Découvertes en Chaldée.* Paris, 1884-1912.—Peters, J. P., *Nippur.* New York, 1897.—Hèuzey, L. A., *Origines Orientales de l'Art.* Paris, 1891-1915.—Meyer, E., *Sumeren und Semiten,* Abhandlung der Preussischen Akademie d. Wissenschaften, 1906.—Ward, W. H., *The Seal Cylinders of Western Asia.* Washington, 1910.—Cros, G., *Nouvelles fouilles de Tello.* Paris, 1910-14.—Meissner, B., *Babylonien et Assyrien.* Heidelberg, 1920-25.—Langdon, S. H., *Excavations at Kish.* Paris, 1924, Vol. 1.—De Genouillac, H., *Fouilles francaises d' el-Akhymer.* Paris, 1924-25.—Schaefer, H. and Andrae, W., *Die Kunst des Alten Orient:,* Propyläen Kunstgeschichte, Vol. 2. Berlin, 1925.—Mackay, E., *Excavations of the "A" Cemetery at Kish.* Field Museum of the Oxford University Joint Expedition. Chicago, 1925, Vol. 1.—Hall, H. R. and Woolley, C. L., *Ur Excavations,* Joint Expedition of the British Museum and the Museum and the University of Pennsylvania (Al Ubaid, Vol. 1). Oxford, 1927.—Contenau, G., *Manuel d'Archéologie Orientale depuis les origines jusqu'a l'époque d'Alexandre.* Paris, 1927-31.—Jordon, J., *Uruk-Warka.* Leipzig, 1928.—Childe, V. D., *New Light on the Most Ancient East.* London, 1934.—*Oriental Institute of Chicago, Communications.* Khafadja and Tell Asmar.

**SURREALISM.**—Modern French art movement aiming at the presentation of dream states and the unconscious on the theory, derived from Freud, that these are the true indices of the whole personality.

See Chirico; Dali; Miró.

**SUSA.**—Town of Persia which was successively the capital of several empires and different civilisations. The oldest was that of the Kingdom of Elam, which dates from about the twenty-third century B.C. It is also the one which was discovered the last—by J. de Morgan, in 1897. He discovered two vast brick buildings, an obelisk and various objects bearing inscriptions. About 645 B.C. Susa fell into the hands of the Assyrians, who sacked the city and scattered its riches. Then it passed under the domination of Persia, and knew a new era of splendour. Darius made it his capital, and built a magnificent palace, the Apadana, which was destroyed by fire, and rebuilt by Artaxerxes II. Monsieur Dieulafoy, who directed the excavations of Susa in 1884, discovered the remains of this palace. From there came the famous friezes of Arches and Lions, which is in the Louvre.

See Persia.

**SUTTERMANS or SUSTERMANS (Justus).**—Flemish painter, 1597-1681; pupil of Guillaume de Vos, then of Pourbus the Younger. He soon went to Florence where he enjoyed a great reputation as a portrait painter for Cosimo II. He painted the Emperor Ferdinand II, Pope Urban VIII, cardinals, princes, dukes, etc. His portraits have the executive finish of Pourbus, the elegance of Van Dyck.

A great many of his paintings are in the Italian galleries. E.g. *Christian of Denmark* (Pitti).

Bibliography: P. Bautier, *Juste Suttermans, peintre des médicis.* 1912.

**SWAN (John Macallan).**—English painter and sculptor (1847-1910), studied in Worcester, London and Paris, being very much influenced by the work of Barye, and devoting himself to the portrayal of wild animals, the forms and movements of which he interprets with much expressive power. Elected A.R.A. 1894, R.A. 1905.

SUTTERMANS: CHRISTIAN OF DENMARK. (Florence, Pitti Gallery.)

**SWEBACH - DESFONTAINE (called Fontaine; Jacques José).**—French painter and lithographer (Metz, 1769—Paris, 1823). Like Carle Vernet, this little master is dry, precise and nervous. His drawings and engravings are not unpleasing, but his paintings are cold and inharmonious. After a visit to Russia, his compositions acquired a certain strangeness and "local colour." They show facility, and sold easily. The Musée Carnavalet possesses several of Swebach's works, which are very precious from a documentary point of view.

**SYMMACHI.**—See Byzantine Art (Sculpture).

**SYNDICS OF THE DRAPERS.**—See Rembrandt; also Pl. 38, Vol. II.

**SYRACUSE.**—The town of Syracuse, in Sicily, was founded in 734 by a colony of Carthaginians, in the islet of Ortygia, and it soon became the most flourishing town in Sicily. Successive governments, aristocrats, and tyrants, helped to cover the city with magnificent buildings, temples, theatres and civil edifices. Almost nothing is left of all these wonders. The rich city, which contained 18,000 metres within its walls, is now a little town of 40,000 inhabitants. One finds there the remains of many civilisations. The various peoples who possessed the town—Greeks, Romans and Normans, among others—erected buildings of which scarcely more than the ruins remain.

SYRACUSE: GREEK THEATRE.

Of the splendid Greek buildings, there remain the ruins of two temples, and a theatre. Both temples date from the very beginning of the 6th century, B.C. The *Theatre* of Syracuse dates from the 5th century. It was one of the largest of the Greek world. It is placed high and embraces a marvellous view.

The Romans also built at Syracuse. There remain the ruins of a Roman *amphitheatre* and baths.

Syracuse is very rich in its collection of Greek coins. The finest pieces are signed by Evaenetos and Cimon, and are very firm and pure in drawing.

BIBLIOGRAPHY: Serrdifalco, *Le antichità della Sicilia,* 5 vols.: Palermo, 1834-1842.—Hittorf and Zanth. *Architecture antique de la Sicile,* 1 vol.: Paris, 1870.

**SYRIA.** — See Byzantine Art (Syria); Moslem Art.

**SZÉKELY (Bertalan).** — Hungarian painter, 1835-1910. The greatest figure of Hungarian academic painting, he descended from an old noble family. He studied with Rahl in Vienna and with Piloty in Munich. His monumental paintings are endowed with a patriotic spirit; his broad, epic style and philosophical interpretation of current and past historical occurrences were replaced, in his last years, by a free, impressionistic approach, visualizing rustic and peasant scenes. A superb draughtsman and fresco painter, Székely was commissioned to decorate several churches and public buildings with frescoes of religious topics. The *Battle of Mohács* (1866), *Louis V. and Cillei* (1870), *Japanese Girl* (about 1900), are among his famous works.

BIBLIOGRAPHY: Genthon, *Uj Magyar Festömüvészet Története,* 1935.

**SZINYEI-MERSE (Paul).**—Hungarian painter, 1845-1920. Son of a well-to-do family, he studied with Piloty and Böcklin, and was acquainted with the works of Bastien-Lepage and Courbet; however he was never in France, nor did he see the paintings of Manet, Monet, or the other leading exponents of French Impressionism. Quite apart from the French experiments, Szinyei-Merse freed himself from all academic traditions and evolved the doctrines of the decomposition of light while working in his studio. Painting indoors was also contrary to the French procedure. His *chef d'œuvre, Majális* ("Picnic in May") (1873), marks a new era in Hungarian painting. This picture has been compared to Manet's *Dejeuner Sur L'Herbe,* not merely because of its similarity of subject matter and treatment, but also because of the reception it received from the public. Like Manet's work, this picture too was painted indoors, but gives more the impression of *pleinair* and atmosphere than the French parallel. It is an organic composition, quite original and not dependent on any academic predecessor, as was Manet's work; it is done in brilliant colors with bold shadows. Due to the very adverse reception that this painting received, the artist discarded his brush and paint for many years. Later in his life he resumed painting but the works of this date lack the freshness and spontaneity of his early creations. Szinyei-Merse's importance lies not merely in the fact that he discovered impressionism apart from the French, but that unlike the French, he retained and gave dominant importance to form, line and volume.

BIBLIOGRAPHY: Genthon, *Uj Magyar Festömüvészet Története,* 1935. —Kallai, *Neue Malerei in Ungarn,* 1925.

# T

**TACCA (Pietro).**—Florentine sculptor, died about 1650. Pupil of Giovanni da Bologna.

**TACCONI (Filippo).**—Painter of Cremona, late 15th century. He was influenced by the school of Lombardy, and the school of Verona.

**— (Francesco).**—Painter of Cremona, end of 15th century. Pupil of Giovanni Bellini.

**TADDEO di BARTOLO.**—Sienese painter, born c. 1362-63; died in 1422.

In 1389 Taddeo, elected to the Cathedral Council in Siena, must, in order to receive this post, have been well known. According to Baldinucci, Taddeo made an altarpiece for S. Paolo a Collegarli in 1389. In 1393, in Lucca, he contracted for the altarpiece for the Church of S. Luca; and in the same year executed the extant frescoes in the Collegiata of San Gimignano. In 1395 he painted in Pisa the lost altarpiece for the Sardi and Campigli Chapel, S. Francesco, also the extant frescoes, hidden under whitewash for centuries, in the same church. In 1400 he was active at Montieri and signed the *Madonna between SS. John Baptist and Andrew* for the Compagnia di Sta. Caterina della Notte, still in the Ospedale of Siena. The next year he received an order to paint in the Chapel of S. Antonio in the Duomo of Siena, on the wall above the sacristy and in the choir; also a predella for an altarpiece in the Palazzo Pubblico. From the same year dates the polyptych at Montepulciano. A polyptych in the Gallery at Perugia, *Madonna and Saints,* from S. Francesco; and a panel of the *Descent of the Holy Spirit* from S. Agostino, are both of 1403. In 1404 Taddeo returned to Perugia, after having executed frescoes in the Siena Cathedral, and an extant *Nativity* for the Chiesa dei Servi. In 1405 he executed four frescoes in the Duomo and decorated two doors of the organ. The next year he designed an *Assumption* window for the Cathedral. From 1407 date the extant frescoes in the Palazzo Pubblico, the *Life of the Virgin*; from 1409 the Polyptych, signed and dated, in the Academy, with the *Annunciation, Trinity, Saints, Dormition.* In 1411 Taddeo was employed in Volterra; a polyptych by him is in the gallery there. In the same year he contracted to paint the façade above the entrance to the Consistory, Siena. In 1412, 1416, and 1420 he was a member of the City Council, and in 1418 was Capitano del Popolo. The decoration of a chapel in the Palazzo Pubblico with allegorical frescoes, which still exist, was finished in 1413; frescoes in a room between the Consistory and the chapel in 1414; and in 1416 he was charged to decorate the Porta San Viene; and was asked for advice about Jacopo della Quercia's fountain "del Campo." The *Madonna and Saints* in the Fogg Art Museum, Cambridge, is of 1418. In 1422 Taddeo died.

As will be seen from the above account, we are unusually well supplied with evidence and existing authentic works, about which Taddeo di Bartolo's numerous works may be grouped.

BIBLIOGRAPHY: Vasari-Milanesi.—Milanesi, *Doc . . . senese,* I.—Borghese e Banchi, *Nuovi documenti, etc.*—Crowe and Cavalcaselle, Douglas ed., III.—Van Marle, *Italian Schools, etc.,* II, 1924.

**TADEMA (Sir Lawrence Alma).**—English painter, born in Friesland in 1836; naturalised English in 1871; died in 1912. He lived in Brussels. He was a pupil of Wappers and De Leys, and very intimate with Mesdag. His instinct was archæological, and his work revives scenes of antiquity and the Middle Ages. E.g. the *Education of the Grandsons of Clothilde* (1861); *Catullus at the House of Lestia; Roman Dance* (1866); *Tarquinus Superbus* (1867), etc.

**TAFḤA (Syria).**—*Basilica.* A 4th century South Syrian church entirely in stone, as was customary in that treeless region. Girder arches with flat tops line the interior. Stone slabs for roofing were laid longitudinally across the flat tops of the arches, which ran transversely.

**TAFT (Lorado).**—American sculptor (1860-1936). He was born at Elmwood, Illinois, 29th April 1860. The family soon moved to Champaign, Illinois, where his father was a professor in the state university. Young Taft entered the modelling class at the university before he was old enough to be admitted as a regular student. He graduated from the University of Illinois in 1879 and the next year went to Paris to study. He entered the École des Beaux-Arts, working there for three years under Dumont, Bonnassieux and Thomas. After a short trip back to the United States he went again to Paris to work for two more years, perfecting his technique and increasing his sculptural ability. In 1886 he returned to Chicago to live and there took charge of modelling classes at the Art Institute of Chicago. He remained as a teacher there until 1929. He also had lecture courses at the University of Chicago and the University of Illinois. At the close of the World War he gave lectures in YMCA camps in France. He is the author of *A History of American Sculpture* and *Modern*

*Tendencies in Sculpture.* He modelled the *Fountain of the Great Lakes* outside the Art Institute of Chicago, *Blackhawk,* a colossal figure of an American Indian at Oregon, Illinois, and the *Columbus Fountain* in Washington, D. C. For many years he was developing his great idea for a *Fountain of Time* and finally in 1920 it took permanent form in concrete on the Midway in Chicago. This represents an arched bridge over which about one hundred colossal figures plod while Time watches their slow progress, unceasing and inevitable. All degrees of joy and sorrow, youth and age, hope and despair are portrayed and even a self-portrait of the artist is included in this procession which typifies the passing of all that is human before the unchanging face of Time. Mr. Taft died in Chicago 30th October 1936.

BIBLIOGRAPHY: George Henry Chase and Chandler Rathfon Post, *A History of Sculpture,* 1925.—Frank J. Mather, Jr., Charles R. Morey, and William J. Henderson, *The American Spirit in Art,* Pageant of America, Vol. 12, 1927.—Robert H. Moulton, *Lorado Taft, Dean of Chicago Sculptors,* Art and Archaeology, Vol. 12, December, 1921, pp. 243-250.—Kineton Parkes, *Sculpture of To-day,* 1921.

**TAJ MAHAL.**—See India (Hindu-Moslem Architecture); Moslem Art (Indian School).

**TAMAGNI (Vincenzo).**—Umbro-Florentine painter, 1492—after 1537, a pupil of Mainardi, follower of Sodoma, influenced by Pintoricchio.

**TAMERLANE (Mausoleum of).**—See Moslem Art.

**TANAGRA FIGURES.**—See Ceramic; Greece (Terra cottas); also Pl. 26, Vol. I.

**T'ANG YIN.**—Noted Chinese painter (1466-1524) of the Ming dynasty. Paintings attributed to him include figures, landscapes and genre scenes.

See China—Art.

**TANNER (Henry O.).**—American painter (Negro), born 1859, pupil in Paris of Benjamin Constant and J. P. Laurens, specialising in religious subjects (e.g. *The Resurrection of Lazarus,* Luxembourg, Paris).

**TANNYU (Kano).**—One of the most popular painters of Japan, and one of the most famous representatives of the great school of Kano, during the 17th century decline. Born in 1602, died in 1674. Tannyu died at Yedo, after exercising considerable influence on his contemporaries. He studied the old masters and made many small copies of their paintings ("Tannyu small-scale copies"). His brush work was modeled after Sesshu, but retained the precision and stiff order of his own time.

**TAORMINA (Sicily).**—The most interesting monument in this little town is the celebrated Greek Theatre, which was partly cut in the rock. It was restored by the Romans, who added a high brick gallery, and stage buildings which are still in a good state of preservation, and include rooms for the actors and dressers.

**TAPESTRY.**—*The Technique.*—**This is the name given to a textile which is obtained by the hand-weaving of threads of various colours (called** *woof*) **among other threads of uniform colour (generally white),** stretched parallel to one another, and of which the whole constitutes the *warp.*

Throughout the Middle Ages, and even at a time much nearer our own day, the word *tapestry* has been wrongly applied to textiles of all kinds, which are often simply embroideries. It is by such an extension of meaning that one speaks of the *Bayeux Tapestry,* a celebrated work which depicts the conquest of England by the Normans, and is really embroidery on canvas, and not tapestry at all.

Thus, to avoid confusing it, the name tapestry should be reserved for textiles made by means of interlaced threads, on looms, known as "haute lisse" and "basse lisse," which we are going to describe briefly.

OUDRY: THE HUNT OF LOUIS XV: RECALLING THE HOUNDS.

The "haute lisse" loom is composed of two upright pieces between which are placed above and below, two horizontal cylinders, capable of turning about their axes, and called "beams." On the beams are placed the warp-threads, formerly of silk or wool, now of cotton, and white in colour. Crossbars, made of glass, separate the even and uneven threads, and divide them into two parallel strips. The name of *lisse* is given to the cord rings which are fixed to the threads of the cloth from behind, and passing on a pole placed above the weaver and his reach, allow him to bring these threads from the front to the back, and to cross the two cloths at the moment of the passing of the spindle which carries the thread of woof. The tapestry worker first places the warp on the loom, then on the white surface traces, in ink, the design, to guide him; then by crossing the cloths and passing threads of the required colour, he covers it entirely, going from bottom to top. As he is behind his work, he makes use of an inclined mirror placed on the other side of the warp. He can only work with one hand, the other being occupied with finding, separating, and crossing the threads of the warp. Such work is delicate and extremely slow. An excellent tapestry worker cannot cover more than 28 square centimetres a day, which corresponds to an annual production of about one square metre. This explains the high cost of "haute lisse" tapestries.

SCENE FROM THE LIFE OF THE VIRGIN. (Tapestry, Royal Palace, Madrid.)

DE LA FOSSE: TAPESTRY OF THE METAMORPHOSES. DIANA RETURNING FROM THE CHASE.

In the "basse lisse" looms, the beams are arranged in a horizontal way. The "lisses" (warp) are functioned by pedals, and the worker can use both hands. The cartoon is placed under the horizontal cloth formed by the warp, and sees it by the intervals which separate his threads. "Basse lisse" work is more rapid and therefore less costly than that of "haute lisse," but the worker sees the cartoon and the work obliquely and this makes mistakes easier. It is, however, often difficult to tell the difference in a finished piece.

*Tapestry in antiquity.*—The invention of tapestry takes us back to a very early epoch. Babylon and Assyria had a great reputation for the practice of this art, especially in the 8th century B.C. These peoples invented the strange animals, unicorns, and griffins which later recur so often in the works of the East, and in those done by peoples of the West, during the Middle Ages. Babylonian tapestries were very expensive. The Bible refers to the Veil of the Temple of Jerusalem, but it is not known if this was a Hebraic work, or one imported from Babylon.

DAVID WATCHING BATHSHEBA. (Tapestry, Royal Palace, Madrid.)

ROGER VAN DER WEYDEN: DETAIL. (Tapestry, Museum of Berne.)

In Greece, the Iliad and the Odyssey frequently refer to tapestry work. This seems too, to have played an important part in the decoration of Greek temples, the Parthenon, for instance, being hung with tapestries inside. They might have been designed by Phidias. During the contact with the East, in the time of Alexander, many tapestries were imported into Greece, where there were several centres for the practice of the craft.

Rome produced hardly any tapestry, but bought from the East.

The Barbarian invasions resulted, as far as tapestry was concerned, in the introduction of brighter colour, and a preference for elaboration of subject, rather than perfection of work. Gaul and Great Britain now began to make tapestry, with conventional designs, flowers and ani-

Tapestry of the Apocalypse from Angers. (Detail.)

mals, and often with calligraphic ornamentation.

Abraham pursuing Hagar and Ishmael. (Italian tapestry of the sixteenth century. M. Bellenot Collection.)

*Tapestry of the 10th to the end of the 13th century.*—There were small

Christ fallen beneath the weight of the Cross. (Tapestry from the Vatican.)

workshops at Poitiers and Limoges. Some oriental tapestries were introduced after the first crusade. Gradually the use of "haute lisse" became general, and tapestries were much in demand to cover bare wall spaces in castles and churches, or to display at tournaments. Few tapestries of this time exist, though there are fragments at Lyons, Nuremberg, and the Victoria and Albert Museum in London.

The Hunt of Maximilian. (Tapestry, Louvre.)

*Tapestry in the 14th century.*—In the beginning of the 14th century, there was a remarkable development in tapestry work, particularly in the north of France and in Flanders.

Tapestry from Flanders: subject taken from a romance of chivalry, end of the fifteenth century. (M. Dubouché Collection.)

Paris, Brussels and Arras were the great centres of production, and from Angers came the famous tapestry of the Apocalypse.

The "Unicorn" Tapestry. (Musée de Cluny.)

Little is known of the Brussels art before the next century.

Paris, in 1292, had twenty-four master tapestry workers, and more by 1302. By 1375 we hear of *Nicolas*

Interior showing the costume and furniture of the period of Louis XII. (Tapestry of Flemish manufacture.)

*Battaille* who was attached to the Duke of Anjou, brother of Charles V, and for whom he executed the *Apocalypse* tapestry, which was the chief work of the 14th century. It has come down to us damaged, and in the form of sixty-nine complete pictures, now in the cathedral at Angers. Originally each part had a figure seated under a canopy of Gothic architecture. There were also two friezes, each containing seven pictures, beneath each of which was a legend. Above the friezes were the sky, stars and angels, and below, a

Tapestry: Panel of the series of Royal Houses. (Fontainebleau.)

field with little animals. The miniatures of the contemporary manuscripts show remarkable similarities to this tapestry.

The Arras workshops also produced many tapestries, some dealing with scenes of chivalry, others being biblical or mythological. Few tapestries of the time are still in existence, and it has been suggested that their great size may have been the reason for their loss. Moreover tapestries were not yet regarded as decorative works of art, but rather as belonging to the more worthless part of furnishings, and little care was taken of them.

However the Cinquantenaire Park Museum, in Brussels, has a "Presentation in the Temple" which was probably done about 1340.

Germany did not come under the influence of Flanders either in this century or the next, though there are some German tapestries in Fribourg, Ratisbon, and Nuremberg.

As for Italy, the fabrication of tapestry did not exist.

Tapestry after Teniers: The Fortune. Panel of a screen, Gobelin. (Collection of M. L. Gauchez.)

England, at the beginning of the 14th century, founded workshops at Romsay, London, etc. One of the best known tapestries was the "Story of Guy of Warwick."

*The 15th century.*—At the beginning of this century the "haute lisse" tapestry spread throughout Europe. The English Wars which had impoverished France, were nearly fatal to the Parisian produc-

The Château of Monceaux, from the Series of the Months, after van der Meulen. (Gobelin tapestry. Collection of M. L. Gauchez.)

tions. Arras, on the contrary, which was allied with England, bought English wools, and became the most important tapestry centre during almost the whole century, till the death of Charles the Bold in 1477.

Only one 15th century tapestry (in Tournai) was signed. On the whole the work of this period is as rare as that of the preceding century. Actuality began to take its place in the art of tapestry, whereas in the 14th century there was only one work (the Battle of Rosebecke) which dealt with recent events.

The Arras work was not essentially different from the Parisian, except in the beauty of the famous "fine thread of Arras," and by a more frequent use of gold and silver thread.

Of the Flemish tapestry, the Berne Museum has nine remarkable pieces; the *Adoration of the Magi*; the *Justice of Trajan*; *History of Cæsar*; etc. There are others at Nancy (*Ahasuerus*, etc.) and at Reims (The *Crowning of Clovis.*) Only two pieces of the six of which this coronation tapestry was composed, now remain, but these two are of great beauty.

PASTORAL SCENE, AFTER F. BOUCHER. (Beauvais tapestry. Collection of M. L. Double.)

These pieces and some others have characteristics in common; the general tone is rather grey and dull; the people extraordinarily ugly; a lack of perspective, and no blank spaces. All these points are illustrated in the *Miracle of the Loaves* in the Louvre.

Other centres were almost equal to Arras, those of Brussels, and Tournai, for instance, being important. The Tournai production began in 1449. It was ended in 1513 (after falling into the hands of the English) by a plague which exterminated part of the population. There were tapestries made at Lille, Valenciennes, Courtrai, Bruges, etc., but

AUDRAN: THE GROTESQUE MONTHS. (Gobelin tapestry.)

it is not known which works to attribute to each particular town, except in the case of a tournament scene done by Valenciennes, and *The Life of St. Anatole* by Bruges. There is a famous tapestry in the form of an altar-screen (in the Louvre) of *Moses Striking the Rock*; *Virgin and Child*, etc., but though obviously the work of a master, it is not known from which town he came.

After the ruin of Arras, in 1477, the fortune of Brussels began, and was to occupy almost the whole of the 16th century. The town had previously attempted production, thanks to Van der Weyden who seems to have done cartoons for a certain number of tapestries. Berne has what are supposed to be reproductions of these, the originals having been destroyed. Under Flemish influence, tapestry underwent a very important development, and henceforward it was no longer composed of crowds of figures, grouped without regard to perspective, but treated rather as a picture.

*Tapestry in the 16th century.*—The decorative aspect of tapestry made it widely used at this time, for instance, in the display on the Field of the Cloth of Gold. The development of the art is evident in the choice of subject; sometimes scientific; sometimes dealing with contemporary events, etc. Great painters (Raphael, Titian, etc., etc.,) were asked to make cartoons for tapestry. It was, on the whole, Italians who did the cartoons; Brussels workers who carried them out in tapestry.

During the 16th century Brussels produced her masterpieces in tapestry (*Petrarch's Triumphs* (1507); *Struggles between Virtues and Vices*, etc.). Several series of tapestries dealing with one subject were made, and some of these were sold to Spain in the time of Charles V. These were used for formal ceremonies, such as Charles V's abdication, and later, for Philip II on state occasions. An example is the series dealing with the *Apocalypse*.

CHARLES COPYEL: DON QUIXOTE, THE BALL. (Gobelin tapestry.)

In the Cinquantenaire Park in Brussels are some large tapestries (*Glorification of Christ, Story of Jeptha;* etc.) which are similar in conception and treatment to those in Madrid.

In 1515, by command of the Pope Leo X, the workers of Brussels did the famous *Acts of the Apostles*, after Raphael's cartoons. These introduced new elements into the art. It was the first time Flemings had exactly carried out an Italian design. Raphael's cartoons, as a matter of fact, were better adapted to fresco than to tapestry. Their execution, as tapestry, led to the imitation of paintings in this medium, and thereby marked the first step towards its decadence. Many copies were made of these famous compositions.

Leo X commanded many other tapestries after Italian cartoons, but there were also some tapestries purely Flemish in composition as well as in execution. The *Maximilian's Hunting Scenes* (Louvre) were designed by Bernard Van Orly.

Italy, on the whole, did very little actual tapestry work.

France did not at this time produce as much as Brussels, but a royal industry was begun at Fontainebleau. The famous *Lady with the Unicorn* (Cluny), belongs to no school. There are several series of tapestry compositions to be found in French cathedrals—in Angers; Le Mans; and above all, in Reims (*Life and Death of the Virgin*, etc.), and in Beauvais, etc., while several of the productions of the studios of Fontainebleau and of Paris, still exist. Henry II helped the Paris workers financially, and Henry IV also showed great interest in the craft.

*The Gobelins.*—A well-known manufactory of tapestry was established in Paris by a family which gave it its name. This was eventually bought in 1662 by Louis XIV, who constituted it a royal industry. Colbert was ambitious that its superiority over other centres should add to the prestige of the king, so he arranged a kind of garden-city for the workers, and himself exercised great authority over their productions. Artists, such as Charles Le Brun, did a large number of cartoons for the Gobelins. A great deal of tapestry work (e.g. 16 pieces in gold and silk, of *The King's Reign*, etc., etc.) was done at this time. The death both of Colbert and Le Brun was a great blow to the activity of the Gobelins. Under Mignard and then Mansart reproduction tended to replace originality.

GOBELIN TAPESTRY: MELEAGER HUNTING. (After Le Brun.)

During the second half of the 18th century, however, remarkable works were once more produced. (*Sunrise and Sunset*, after Boucher; *Vulcan's Forge*; *Portrait of the King* (1769) after Van Loo; and *Portrait of the Queen*, after Nattier, etc., etc.)

Louis XVI's reign saw the return to classicism—the Revolution period marks the time of decadence.

The *Beauvais* manufactory was founded in 1664. It was noted for its representation of turf, and green undergrowth, etc. The Revolution spared this industry, which has continued to this day, but is at present without renown.

*Floor tapestries.* — These are closely connected with tapestry proper, and some, especially the Eastern ones, are often remarkable. A group dealing with hunting scenes or animal fights were of Persian origin (the best belonged to the House of Austria, and some to the Museum of Decorative Arts and the Friedrichs Museum, Berlin). A second group, introducing flowered carpets, or designs with lamps or vases, are also Persian. The carpet with stiff floral decoration dates from the 16th and 17th centuries. Finally the geometrical designs come (through the Venetians) from Asia Minor. These are often reproduced in 17th century Dutch pictures. French carpets of the time of Henry IV, with their garlands and attempts at modelling, are very different from the oriental ones.

BIBLIOGRAPHY: G. L. Hunter, *The Practical book of Tapestries.* 1925.—G. L. Hunter, *Tapestries, their origin, history and Renaissance,* 1912.—W. G. Thompson, *A History of Tapestry.* London, 1930.

**TARRAGONA (Spain).**—The extensive Roman remains include a monument known as the Sepulcro de los Escipiones (believed to be the tomb of the Scipios) and a temple built by Augustus around 26 B.C. and restored by Hadrian, 117-138 A.D.

The *Cathedral*, which dates from the late 12th century, is one of the finest examples of early Spanish architecture. The portal is Gothic.

See Pl. 2, Vol. II.

**TARSIA.**—See Furniture (Renaissance).

**TASSAERT (Nicolas François Octave).**—French painter, 1800-1874. Pupil of Lethière, he was more influenced by Fragonard than by the lessons of his master. Nevertheless, his earliest paintings are of historical subjects. But he was essentially a painter of sentimental scenes—the *Unhappy Family* (1849—Louvre); *Young Girl Dying* (1853); *Ariadne Forsaken*, etc.

In the taste of the 18th century, Tassaert tried to combine edification with sensuality. Mary Magdalen and various "tempted" saints provided him with pretexts. His paintings have remarkable transparence and refinement of colour.

BIBLIOGRAPHY: Bernard Proet, *Tassaert.* Paris.

**TATE GALLERY.**—See London.

**TATTI (Jacopo).**—See Sansovino (Jacopo Tatti).

**TEDESCO (Adamo).**—See Elsheimer.

**TELAMON.**—See Atlante.

**TELLO.**—See Assyrian and Sumerian Art; also Pl. 18, Vol. I.

**TEMPEL (Abraham van den).**—Dutch painter, 1622-1672. We possess very few of his works. He is the author of a Portrait of Abraham Vischer, and a *Family Gathering* (both in Amsterdam).

**TEMPERA.**—This method is one of the simplest as well as one of the oldest of the art of painting. The colour, previously ground with water, is at the moment of painting, tempered with size, kept liquid in a water-bath. The quantity of size mixed with the colour depends upon the powder used: some colours require more size than others. The tones become brighter when dry, and this has to be taken into consideration, as the difference is very great in the deep tones. The result is a dull, pleasant surface. If the mixing

# THE SCHOOL OF FONTAINEBLEAU

*One of the happiest discoveries of nineteenth-century painting was that of nature. Landscape took on a highly poetic value, a great sentimental and picturesque richness and it went further than the preceding schools—even that of the seventeenth-century Dutch—in the analysis and the reproduction of nature. This devotion to nature is not confined to painters alone; it is one of the aspects of the great romantic revolution. But it is in painting that its most far-reaching consequences were experienced. Landscape at first appeared a subject apart by itself; then gradually it became the principal theme in painting. By the end of the nineteenth century, the landscape painters had suppressed completely or changed all other subjects.*

COROT: DANCING NYMPHS. LOUVRE.
*(Photo by Hachette.)*

COROT: CATHEDRAL OF CHARTRES. MUSÉE DES ARTS DÉCORATIFS.
*(Photo by Hachette.)*

COROT: THE ROAD TO ARRAS. LOUVRE.
*(Photo by Hachette.)*

## Corot

His long and prolific career led him from "historical landscapes" to "impressionism"; that is to say, the notation of the effects of light. His first training taught him "style," but by his sincere study of nature, he set up a new vision and he accustomed himself particularly to seeing the play of light and shade. He is, par excellence, the painter of "values." He loves slanting rays of sunlight and great shadows; it is atmosphere more than any other thing which fascinates him. This vision is fused with revery and the wraiths of mist which arise from the meadows become pale dancing nymphs.

ROUSSEAU: THE EDGE OF THE FOREST. LOUVRE.
*(Photo by Hachette.)*

DUPRÉ: MORNING. LOUVRE.
*(Photo by Hachette.)*

DAUBIGNY: THE DAM AT OPTEVOZ. ROUEN.
*(Photo by Hachette.)*

## The Barbizon School

Rousseau, established at Barbizon, on the edge of the forest of Fontainebleau, was the portraitist of old oaks. He does not linger long over the charms of light; he sets forth vegetable "personalities." His trees have a character and a history of their own. The painter's eye and his craftsmanship are equally painstaking, applied to rendering the roughness of the trunks and branches and the detail of the foliage and grass. Dupré, furthermore, seeks a decorative effect by means of great masses, and his effects are more deliberate; he is less the slave of his model. Daubigny is the painter of quiet water reflecting the trees along the river bank.

MILLET: THE SHEPHERDESS. LOUVRE.
*(Photo by Hachette.)*

MILLET: THE MAN WITH A HOE.
*(Photo by Kuhn.)*

MILLET: THE ANGELUS. LOUVRE.
*(Photo by Hachette.)*

## J. F. Millet

Millet, installed at Barbizon, near his friend Rousseau, did not lose himself in the forest; he sought out the plain where he found peasants working the land. This was his favourite theme. Some silhouettes against the sky express stubborn effort, weariness or even revery and piety. Millet is above all, a fine draftsman of expressive attitudes. His realism is not a copy of nature. There is mingled with it a poetry of grandiose melancholy; he has found a hidden beauty in the harsh law of humanity: "by the sweat of thy brow shalt thou earn thy bread."

# REALISM AND IMPRESSIONISM

*After the romantic movement, art, like all other forms of intellectual activity, entered into a period of certainty. After the greatest lyrical outburst, there was attentive observation. And while the romantic Delacroix held that the artist is a poet who invents and sings his sentiments and his passions; while the classical Ingres thought that beauty must be sought in the reconciliation of truth with exact and perfect form, realism which was about to succeed these doctrines, laid down its principles: that the painter and sculptor must above all imitate nature, without care for style or poetry, literal truth being his only consideration.*

COURBET: THE BURIAL AT ORNANS. LOUVRE.
*(Photo by Hachette.)*

## Courbet

The characteristic painter of the realistic generation of 1850 is Courbet. His masterpiece is the *Burial at Ornans.* The picture is by a master craftsman who studied Spanish and Bolognese realists. It was not favourably received by all his contemporaries; and it certainly appears that Courbet went out of his way to appear aggressive. He belonged to the first realists who quite often found grotesque qualities in their models.

MANET: LE BON BOCK. (PRIVATE COLLECTION.)
*(Photo by Durand-Ruel.)*

MANET: BREAKFAST ON THE GRASS. MUSÉE DES ARTS DÉCORATIFS.
*(Photo by Hachette.)*

MANET: THE LAUNDRY. (PRIVATE COLLECTION.)
*(Photo by Hachette.)*

MONET: THE REGATTA AT ARGENTEUIL. MUSÉE DU LUXEMBOURG.
*(Photo by Hachette.)*

MONET: DANCING WOMEN. MUSÉE DU LUXEMBOURG.
*(Photo by Hachette.)*

SISLEY: ROAD IN THE SUBURBS OF PARIS. MUSÉE DU LUXEMBOURG.
*(Photo by Hachette.)*

## Impressionism

The realism of Courbet was slightly limited by his inability to render outdoor atmosphere. It is quite apparent that the personalities in the *Burial at Ornans* were painted in the studio. The followers of Courbet attempted the effects of open air replacing the strong contrasts of light and shade which modelled the forms in the studio with the diffused light and the play of reflections in broad daylight. They are called "Impressionists" because they express the fleeting aspects of nature. From landscapes, they turned to the study of the human figure.

is satisfactory, the colour will resist rubbing; but it always remains soluble in water.

This is the principle of the method of tempera painting, but it lends itself to many combinations. Size may be replaced by egg. The white and yolk mixed are used, or the yolk only, and a little vinegar is added to hasten corruption of the egg.

This process was perfected by Vibert. His method does not require the manipulations which the old painters used, and which are indicated in the *Trattato* of Cennino Cennini. Gum, honey, and the milk of the fig tree, etc., may also be used as media.

A distemper is obtainable which shows almost the same colour wet as it will have when dry. Colour merchants make numerous media of this kind which resemble pure tempera.

See Pl. 8, Vol. I.

**TEMPLE CHURCH.**—See London.

**TEMPLE OF HEAVEN.**—See Peiping.

**TENGBOM (Ivor Justus).**—Contemporary Swedish architect, born 1878, and author of the Högalidskirke, Stockholm, 1923; the International March Company; and the Concert Hall, 1926.

**TENIERS (David—known as "the Elder").**—Flemish painter, 1582-1649. Father of the famous

Teniers: Peasant Wedding. (Pinakothek, Munich.)

David Teniers. A pupil of Rubens, and Elsheimer, he lived in Rome for a while. It is difficult to attribute paintings to him definitely, as many of his son's early works and those of Elsheimer have been credited to him.

— **(David).**—Flemish painter; son of Teniers the Elder, born in Antwerp, in 1610. From the age of fourteen, he helped in his father's work. During his early life, he lived quietly, sometimes paying with a picture for a meal at an inn, but he soon became known to his contemporaries, and he gained the protection of the Court of Flanders. In 1637 he married the beautiful Anne Breughel, daughter of "Velvet" Breughel, and Rubens' ward. He had seven children. This marriage put Teniers into closer relation with Rubens. He used to live in Antwerp for part of the year, and during the other part, in the domain of Dry Torens near Rubens' Steen Castle, which he introduced into several of his pictures. In 1646, Leopold, governor of the Netherlands, made Teniers come to Brussels, and appointed him artist of his court, and curator of his picture gallery. He became a widower in 1656, and married, the same year, Isabella of Fren. His successes gained him the protection, not only of the governors of the Netherlands, but also that of the King of Spain, Philip IV, and of the Stadtholder, William II. It was at the French Court that he was least appreciated, as Louis XIV had little taste for "Tenier's grotesque figures." In 1663, he founded, at Antwerp, an Academy for the teaching of painting. Teniers led a hard-working life, which would have been very happy, had it not been for quarrels and divisions among the members of his family. After the death of his second wife, he was left alone, and passed his last years sadly. It has even been suggested that he committed suicide, but actually nothing is known

Teniers: The Alchemist. (Museum of Dresden.)

of the end of his life, or even the date of his death, which must have been about 1690.

Teniers was a talented, original artist, painting with wonderful skill his little pictures which are so full of life. His favourite subjects were tavern scenes, and scenes of peasant life. His drinkers and smokers are not, like those of Jordaens, Flemings who are always drunk, eating and drinking amid noisy brawls—Teniers' characters are healthy, hearty folk who make merry peacefully. He, in fact, portrays the serious, hardworking type of Flemish peasant. Teniers never liked sober, dull colours; his technique was a little heavy. Rubens, and later Brouwer, influenced him greatly, with the result that his colour became more silvery and transparent, and he produced effects of light and shade with considerable success. He handled his brush with ease, working rapidly, though his speed was in no way detrimental to his admirably composed and drawn, compositions. His perspective was well done, and so was the rendering of shadow, it was sufficiently transparent to allow the smallest detail to be visible in a dark interior. Teniers' work is very varied; he did religious and mythological pictures, though his fame and his originality are due to his "genre" painting, to his cabaret and peasant scenes. He did numerous paintings —52 in Madrid—48 in Leningrad—43 in Vienna, etc. The best known are: *The Money Changer and His Wife* (National Gallery); *The Five Senses* (Brussels); *The Dentist* (Cassel); *The Smoker* (Louvre), etc. *The Painter's Family* (Berlin, Madrid, Brussels, Paris); *The Great Kitchen* (The Hague) in which he painted his wife. After 1640 Teniers preferred to paint peasants out of doors than in taverns, and he also painted large pictures, such as *The Prodigal Son* (Louvre); *The Entry of the Archduchess Isabella to Brussels; The Kermesse* (Louvre), etc., etc. His *Temptations of Saint Anthony* (which he painted several times), remind one of those by Breughel and Bosch.

In the hands of this artist, Flemish painting became an art of "genre" scenes, rather than of great decorative compositions. The "genre" painting thus inaugurated was to be very successful in the 18th century. Teniers' art answered new needs and the taste of his own time.

See Pl. 35, Vol. II.

Bibliography: Vermælden, *Teniers le Jeune*. Antwerp, 1895.—Smith, *Catalogue raisonné of the Most Eminent Dutch, Flemish and French Painters*.—Royer Peyre, *Téniers*. Collection des grands artistes. Paris.

**TERBORCH (Gerard), or TERBURG.**—Dutch painter born at Zwolle (1617-1681). He is, with Pieter de Hooch, the greatest of the

Terborch: The Guitar Lesson. (Louvre.)

Dutch "little-masters." He was the pupil of Pieter Molyn, at Haarlem. While quite young, he drew views of Haarlem and of the surrounding country, and scenes of military life. He travelled widely, going to London (1635); probably to Italy; to Amsterdam; Munster (1645); and supposedly to Spain. He returned,

Terborch: The Letter. (Buckingham Palace, London.)

in 1650, to Holland, and he married in Deventer. He painted the life around him—soldiers; young and charming women in beautiful satin dresses. A very personal artist, his pictures give information about the customs and life of his contemporaries, whom he observed impartially and portrayed with truth. He was equally skilful in compositions containing numbers of figures, as he was in treating an episode of violence, or again, in a small, lively picture such as those of military officers. His drawing is correct and vigorous; he used his colour sparingly and afterwards glazed them by degrees to a substance sufficient to produce that melting impasto, so marvellous in his work. Among his most famous works, are: *Self-Portrait* (The Hague); *The Telegram* (The Hague); *The Van Moerkerken Family* (The Hague); *The Visit* (Amsterdam); *The Toilet* (late Steengracht Collection, The Hague), which is also called *Maternal Care* (as it depicts a mother combing her little daughter's hair); *The Music Lesson* (Louvre), again showing Terborch's skill in painting satin; and *The Concert* (Louvre).

See Pl. 36, Vol. II.

Bibliography: E. Michel, *Gérard Terburg*. Paris, 1887.—A Rosenberg, *Terborch und Jan Steen*. Leipzig, 1897.—F. Hellens, *Gérard Terborch*. Brussels, 1911.—Hofstede de Groot, *Catalogue of Dutch Painters*, Vol. V.

**TERRA COTTAS.**—See Ceramic; Greece; also Pl. 6, Vol. I; Pl. 26, Vol. II.

**TERRES DE LORRAINE.**—See Biscuit; Ceramic.

**TESSERÆ.**—Small square pieces of glass or stone used in mosaic work.

**TESSIN (Nicholas).**—Swedish architect, 1654-1760. Royal architect for Charles XII, for whom he designed the Royal Palace, Stockholm, in the contemporary style of Louis XIV of France. He spent much of his life in Paris, and prepared unexecuted designs for Versailles and for the Louvre.

**TEXTILE MUSEUM.**—See Lyon.

**THAULOW (Fritz).**—Norwegian painter, 1847-1906. He was the pupil of Gude at Carlsruhe; but he soon went to Paris where he fell under the influence of certain Impressionists.

He had remarkable skill in seizing upon the fugitive and changing appearance of things—smoke blown by the wind and mingling with the moving clouds—water beaten by storms. His work is attractive by reason of its boldness, combined with minute observation, and charm of colour.

**THEBES.**—A town of ancient Egypt, the ruins of which are near Luxor and Karnak. Thebes followed Memphis as capital of Egypt, and had, since the time of the 10th dynasty, incomparable prosperity which lasted for ten centuries. By virtue of its situation, it became an exceptionally noted commercial centre. The kings, after victorious wars, peopled it with prisoners who built many magnificent monuments. In its turn, however, Thebes suffered the fate of conquered towns. In the 7th century B.C. it was taken and sacked by the Assyrians; then by the Persians. An earthquake finished its destruction in the year 27. The chief buildings whose imposing ruins still stand on the Egyptian plain, are the temples of Luxor and Karnak, of Ammon, of Seti II, of Phtah, and Khouson; also chapels, pylons, the avenues of the Sphinx; Necropoles, the Rameseum; the Colossi of Memnon; and

several ruined temples, on the opposite bank of the Nile.
See Egypt.

Bibliography: M. Pillet, *Thèbes, Karnak et Louxor*. 1928.

**THEMISTOCLES.**—See Acropolis of Athens.

**THEODORA.**—See Byzantine Art; Constantinople.

**THEOTOCOPULI (Domenico).**—See Greco, El.

**—(Jorge Manuel).**—Spanish painter, sculptor and architect (died, 1631). Son of the above. As a painter he closely followed the style of his father. Between 1606 and 1616, he worked under the direction of Juan Bautistà Monegro, on the sculptures of the altarpiece of the Chapel del Sagrario (Toledo Cathedral). His chief merit is as an architect.

Bibliography: M. B. Cossio, *El Greco*. Madrid, 1908.—A. L. Mayer, *Dominico Theotocopuli,* El Greco, 1926.—A. F. Calvert, *El Greco*. London, 1909.—*Archivo Esp. Arte y Argueol.,* 1927; F. de B.—San Román. *De la vida del Greco,* Nueva série de documentos inéditos.

**THESSALONIKA (Greece).**—*St. George*. A pagan periapsidal round structure on the principle of the Pantheon transformed *circa* 400 into a domed Christian church.

*Eski-Djuma*. A 5th century basilica with early impost blocks.

*St. Demetrius*. See Byzantine architecture, Early Period.

*Hagia Sophia,* 495-530. A domed basilica of the First Golden Age.

*St. Elias,* 1012-1054. A typical church of the Greek School of the Middle Byzantine Period.

**THINKER (The).**—See Rodin; also Pl. 53, Vol. II.

**THOMA (Hans).**—German painter, born, 1839. His best-known works, popularised in Germany through engraving and lithography are: *Summer, Grandmother and Grandson, The Village Violinist*. He is one of the most sincere exponents of German sentimentality.

Bibliography: K. Sommerlatt, *Hans Thoma*. 1910.

**THOMAR (Portugal).**—*Convento de Christo*.—This convent, a veritable fortress of the Order of Christ, gives an idea of the different phases of Portuguese architecture in the 12th and 13th centuries. To the epoch of the Templars, belong small cloisters and the old church at the top of the hill, an attempted reproduction of the Church of the Holy Sepulchre, in Jerusalem. Two other cloisters and a chapter-house were founded by Henry the Navigator (1418-1460). King Manuel built the new Church of the order of Christ, with a chapter house under the "Coro alto," the little Claustro de Santa Barbara, and the new chapter house (unfinished).

Thomar: The Church.

The reform of Juan III turned knights into monks (1523), and rendered necessary the creation of four new cloisters, with large dormitories and other buildings, which were only finished under Spanish domination.

**THOMASSIN.**—Family of French engravers of the 16th and 18th centuries. Philippe Thomassin (about 1556-about 1635) was the master of Callot.

**THOMIRE (Pierre Philippe).**—French metal worker, 1757-1843, who, in the royal manufactories, cast several pieces of French sculpture, as well as various articles of furniture.

**THON (C.).**—Russian architect, 1793-1851. He was imbued with classic formulæ, of the Empire style, which found their best expression in the reign of Nicholas I.

**THORNHILL (James).**—English painter, 1676-1734. He was chiefly a historical painter, and a decorator. Thanks to the patronage of Queen Anne, he obtained numerous commissions, among which must be mentioned the decoration of the large hall of Greenwich, that of some of the apartments in Hampton Court Palace, and the staircase of Easton Newton. His most important works are the decorative paintings in the dome of St. Paul's Cathedral, London, and the eight frescoes representing the principal events in the life of St. Paul. His technique is not very experienced, but he had a sense of composition.

Thomar: The Cathedral.

Bibliography: O. Brackett, Architectural Review. XXIII, 152. 1908.

**THORNTON (W.).**—American architect (1761-1828), studied in France; his plans for the Capitol at Washington were given the prize at the competition in 1792, and he directed the work of construction until 1803, when he was succeeded by Benjamin H. Latrobe, who completed the edifice.

**THORPE (John).**—English architect of the Jacobean period, active 1570-1618. He was the author of Kirby House and, perhaps, of Burghley House and Wollaton House. His architecture shows influence from Germany and the Low Countries.

**THORWALDSEN (Bertal).**—Danish sculptor, 1779-1844. He lived for some forty years in Italy, where he produced the greater part of his work. He made his début in 1803, with a Jason, which was enthusiastically admired by Canova. His work was widely appreciated. A greater knowledge of antique art makes us see how superficial was the imitation he attempted; but it must be admitted that he owed one quality to the ancients—his attempt to give rhythm to his work.

Of his immense production, possibly the *Young Dancer* is his freshest work. It has an easy, healthy grace which contrasts happily with Canova's affectations.

Thorwaldsen's works are in the Museum at Copenhagen, which bears his name.

Bibliography: A. Rosenberg. *Thorwaldsen* (Künsller-Monographism, No. 16). 1896.

**THULDEN (Theodore Van).**—Flemish painter, 1606-1676. He lived in Paris where he painted religious subjects. In Antwerp he collaborated with Rubens, his master, on a number of portraits. Many of his original paintings are attributed to Rubens. The Huisten Bosch at The Hague and the Vienna Gallery contain several examples of his work.

**TIARINI (Alessandro).**—Painter of Bologna, 1577-1668. One of the best pupils of the Carracci. His large religious pictures are rather declamatory. *San Domenico Raising a Dead Child* (in San Domenico, Bologna); *Marriage of St. Catherine,* and *Descent from the Cross* (in the Gallery of Bologna); and *Rinaldo in an Enchanted Forest* (Munich), a work which is very Venetian in character.

**TIBERIO D'ASSISI.**—Umbrian painter, c. 1470-1524. He helped Pintoricchio in the Borgia apartments, in Santa Maria del Popolo, and in the decoration of the Piccolomini Library in Siena. Numerous frescoes by him are to be found in Assisi, and in Montefalco and Trevi.

Bibliography: Crowe and Cavalcaselle, *A New History of Painting in Italy,* Vol. V. London.

**TIBERIUS (Palace of).**—See Rome.

**TIEPOLO (Giovanni Battista).**—Venetian painter (1693-1770). The most important painter of the 18th century, he belongs to the end of the history of Venetian painting.

He owed his inspiration chiefly to Veronese, being influenced by his splendid skies, majestic colonnades and figures clothed in gorgeous silk. The satins Tiepolo painted were even more brilliant than Veronese's, his chiaroscuro more pronounced, and his color scheme lighter and less rich.

Ephemeral skies, of a clear pale blue give an impression of transitoriness, while his clouds, often touched with rosy and golden reflections, seem to be floating away. He liked to paint bold effects of perspective, and also became a great ceiling painter. His scenes were bright and luminous, and he painted such subjects as Miracles, Triumphs, Apotheoses. They were less powerful, splendid and solid than those of Veronese, because his drawing is more mannered, his compositions less balanced, and his colour less strong. Nevertheless he was an original painter, who, just at a time when it seemed as though everything had been done, found new forms of expression. His ethereal treatment distinguishes his work from the splendour of the earlier Venetians.

Tiepolo: The Immaculate Conception. (Prado, Madrid.)

His output was enormous, and his works were to be found in Venice, Bergamo, Vicenza, Milan, Verona, Padua. He even went to Würtzburg in Germany, and he worked in Spain, where he must have influenced Goya. His ceiling paintings may be found in many Venetian churches; in, for instance, San Giovanni e Paolo; in Santa Maria della Pietà; in the Scalzi; and the Carmine. He also decorated many palaces. He painted *Neptune and Venice* in the Sala delle Quattro Porte of the Ducal Palace;

Tiepolo: St. Catherine of Siena. (Museum, Vienna.)

*Anthony and Cleopatra* in the Labia Palace; he decorated the Pisani Palace at Strà; the Clerici Palace, in Milan; the Canossa Palace, in Verona. He painted the *Marriage of Frederick Barbarossa* in the Castle of Würtzburg. He did a *Christ at Emmaus*, in the Frari; a *St. Rose*, in the Santi Apostoli; a *Miracle of St. Anthony* in the Church at Murano, etc. In the Musée André in Paris, is his *Reception of Henry III*; in the Accademia in Venice, the *Discovery of the Holy Cross by St. Helena*. To these may be added very many other scenes, large and small, as well as the drawings now to be found in many museums.

He did many allegorical, as well as religious subjects, painting for instance, the *Chariot of the Sun* soaring heavenwards amid light-floating clouds. A background of over-ornamented white buildings is the setting for the banquet of *Anthony and Cleopatra*, and musicians, stationed on balconies, twang their guitars. The *Finding of Moses in the Bulrushes* in the Edinburgh Gallery, is set in a magnificent park.

This prolific, refined painter had nine children as the result of his marriage to Cecilia, sister of Francesco Guardi. He taught his art to two of his sons, Domenico and Lorenzo. His life was spent peacefully among his family. He died at Madrid on March 27th, 1770, while he was engaged in decorating the king's palace.

See Pl. 7, Vol. I.

Bibliography: H. Modern, *Giovanni Battista Tiepolo*. Vienna, 1902.—E. Sack, *Giambattista und Domenico Tiepolo*. Hamburg, 1903. —P. Molmenti, *G. B. Tiepolo*, Milan, 1909.

**TILBORCH (Gillis van).**—Flemish painter, born in Brussels about 1626. Died, 1678. Pupil of Teniers. His best pictures are: *Flemish Wedding* (Dresden), *The Five Senses* (Dijon); *The Village Fête* (Lille); *The Feast* (The Hague).

**TIMGAD (Algiers).**—In the 1st century of our era, the Romans founded a small military outpost at Timgad. In the year 100, the Emperor Trajan enlarged it, and surrounded it with ramparts. Inside the walls several monuments were built. Timgad became a prosperous city, until the Byzantines endeavoured to take possession of it, and, to prevent this, the neighbouring peoples destroyed the town. Excavations have brought the ruins to light. The town is divided into four quarters by two principal streets crossing at right angles. At the approach to one of the roads is the *Arch of Trajan*, with three bays, and fluted columns. The monument probably dates from the end of the 2nd century. Nearer the centre of the town is the *Forum*, and ruins of houses, temples and a theatre (on the side of a small hill) which could once hold 3500 spectators.

The houses of Timgad do not seem to have been adorned with paintings. This "African Pompeii" loved comfort and solidity more than grace, and it always retained something of its character as a military city, bastion of Rome in Africa.

See Pl. 31, Vol. I.

**TINO da CAMAINO (di Crescenzio di Diotisalvi).** — Sienese sculptor, 14th century. We first hear of him in Pisa in 1311, where he no doubt followed Giovanni Pisano, and where he became his successor as Capo Maestro of the Duomo. From this time must date the baptismal fonts (now destroyed) and the altar of the Chapel of San Ranieri, now in the Ammanati Chapel of the Campo Santo. Here one sees the influence of Giovanni Pisano. Tino began the tomb of the Emperor Henry VII which was finished by Lupo di Francesco and his pupils. He made some graceful *Madonnas*, which were much imitated. Those in the Museo Civico of Turin, of the Museum of Berlin, and of the Böhler Collection, in Munich, are probably by him. He next went to Siena (1318), where he made the tomb of Cardinal Petroni in the Cathedral; then to Florence, where he made the tombs of Gaston de la Tour, in Santa Croce, of Tedice Aliotti in Santa Maria Novella, and of Bishop Orso in the Cathedral.

In 1325, he went to Naples, where Bertaux attributes to him the tomb of Catherine of Austria, in San Lorenzo Maggiore. The tombs of Mary of Hungary (in Santa Maria di Donna Regina), of Carlo di Calabria (in Santa Chiara), of Marie de Valois and of Marie de Calabria are surely by him. His bas-reliefs of the *Life of St. Catherine*, in Santa Chiara (also attributed to Giovanni and Pacio da Firenze), depict simple, well-composed scenes. He was the official sculptor of King Robert.

Bibliography: Supino, *Arte Pisana*. Florence, 1904.—Bertaux, *Le Mausolée de l'Empereur Henri VII, à Pise*. Paris, 1902.

**TINTORETTO (Jacopo Robusti; called Il Tintoretto).**—He was one of the greatest painters of the Venetian School (1518-1594). His father, Battista Robusti, lived in Venice where he was a dyer, and this occupation gave the child his nickname, "little dyer," or "Tintoretto." He seems to have shown his gifts at an early age, and may have been a pupil of Bonifazio Veronese, much influenced later by Titian.

In any case, Tintoretto, still quite young, found himself on his own feet, with the single aim of developing his work alone. He had been initiated into the mysteries of colour. He had also discovered the genius of Michelangelo. He got from Florence, models of the marbles of San Lorenzo. The lessons he gave himself, consisted in copying them, together with the antiques which he was beginning to collect. As his own aims grew clear, he wrote them up on the walls of his studio, as "the drawing of Michelangelo and the colour of Titian." He was already seeking above all, to portray energy. He used to draw in the evenings by the light of a lantern, so as to obtain strong shadows. He worked in clay or wax, draping his figures, so as to gain an insight into the study of relief.

From his youth, Tintoretto showed himself independent and impassioned. In his pictures, calm white clouds change into storm clouds, and there are contrasts of black and white; of force and serenity; of night and day. Before Pilate, Christ appears among sombre Jews, like a shining white flower on the dark rocks of a craggy mountain (in the Scuola di San Rocco, Venice).

In certain works, especially in the earlier ones, we still find beautiful warm tones. The *Miracle of Saint Mark*, in the Academy of Venice, shows reds, golds, and whites which glow even more than Titian's. When he painted *Adam and Eve* and even the *Slaying of Abel* for the Trinità, (now in the Academy; the other pictures of this series have disappeared) and the *Vulcan*, and *Venus and Cupid* (now in the Pitti; Florence), and later (1578), mythological scenes in the Doge's Palace (*Bacchus and Ariadne; Mercury and the Graces, Vulcan's Forge*, etc.)—Tintoretto felt a sensuous delight in the opportunity of treating the nude which these subjects gave him. In these pictures he renders, like Titian himself, the splendour of warm flesh tints, the very pulse of life in the lights which are impregnated with shadow, and the sensuousness of the Venetians.

Tintoretto's output was prodigious and his pictures provoke a strong reaction on the beholder. They are always dramatic. He did not fear lack of proportion, or of balance, if these things served to increase the effect of movement, or when these inexactitudes were the inevitable result of an impetuous imagination. Thus he achieves a great design with the vivacity of a sketch. If he was asked to submit a sketch, he insisted upon doing it in the dimensions of the finished product. He was the winner of a

Tintoretto: Portrait of a man. (Louvre.)

competition to decorate the ceiling of the Scuola di San Rocco, the subject being the *Glorification of Saint Roch* (1560). Tintoretto must have laughed at the surprise he was preparing with this work, for when his turn came, he unveiled his huge canvas, already in its place in secret. Scandalised and jealous, but filled with admiration for such rapidity, the members of the "Scuola" could not do otherwise than commission him to paint other pictures. They got one of the most wonderful series of pictures representing the Passion, in the world.

In his composition, Tintoretto aimed more at force and the element of surprise, than at rhythm. He loved perspectives which attract the eye to the shadows in a large hall. In the *Wedding at Cana* (Uffizi), the Christ, who is at the end of the table in a composition of this sort, almost disappears, because he is shorter than the figures in the foreground, who cluster round the great jars of the story of the miracle. In the background, right in the distance, appears a stormy sky. The *Last Supper* in San Rocco, appears almost to be painted stereoscopically, so greatly is the depth accentuated. What perspectives there are, too, in the *Discovery of the Body of Saint Mark in the Basilica of Saint Euphemia of Alexandria*, which we see in the Brera, and in the *Transportation of the Body of St. Mark* in the Ducal Palace in Venice. Here the depth greatly accentuates the sense of drama, while lightning rends the skies, and the terrified crowd rushes towards the doorways like a storm-stricken man. And when the little Virgin mounts the great staircase for her *Presentation in the Temple*, in Santa Maria dell'Orto, the composition is arranged in such a way that her silhouette stands out clearly in relief against the sky. The feeling in this picture is more intense than in Titian's fine rendering of the same subject.

When his subject allows of crowds, a contest, or a drama, Tintoretto's fire and passion know no bounds. Few treatments of the *Massacre of the Innocents* is as tumultuous as that in the *Scuola di San Rocco*. A hurtling, terrified crowd of mothers suggests an avalanche of stones rolling into water. In the *Last Judgment* (Madonna dell'Orto), Tintoretto has really painted a sinister torrent of water falling amid a billowing crowd of naked figures. Charon's barque has capsized, and the pale, drowned bodies are being swept in a flood down to the abyss, caught in the vortex of the torrent, and cast into Hell above the weir.

In 1556, the Senate asked him to contribute some paintings to the Doges' Palace, but the work was lost in a fire in 1577.

He painted some pictures for the Church of San Rocco, but it is for the Hospice of the Scuola di San Rocco, after his triumph in the competition for the ceiling painting, that he created his masterpieces. The whole was begun about 1560, but was not finished before 1587.

The Passion was a theme deeply appealing to the passionate imagination of Tintoretto. He had painted a *Crucifixion* at San Cassiano, and for San Severo, he had painted the great *Crucifixion* of the Academy, and already sounded the note of pathos in the tumult of the crowd and in the women at the foot of the cross. In the Scuola di San Rocco, he could portray the whole of the Passion. He painted Christ, a tall, white figure before Pilate; an *Ecce-homo* over the door; the *Carrying of the Cross*; and then in 1565, the *Crucifixion*. In this picture, the sky is leaden, the trees twisted, the crowd struggles, pale gleams light the scene. Men contort their limbs in their efforts to raise the crosses of the thieves, beside the cross of Christ. He, crucified, looks intently at the group of women and saints crouching at his feet.

In the great hall, Tintoretto painted the scenes which led up to the terrible climax. First, on the ceiling, are Old Testament scenes; the *Original Sin; Moses Striking the Rock; The Brazen Serpent; The Manna*; and in less important places, *The Sacrifice of Abraham*; etc.

On the walls, he told the life of Christ; *The Adoration of the Shepherds; The Baptism; The Last Supper; The Washing of Feet*; etc.

On the ground floor, he continued with the *Annunciation*, the *Assumption*, scenes of the childhood of Christ; the *Massacre of the Innocents*; the *Flight into Egypt*; etc.

These paintings in the Scuola di San Rocco had considerable influence. Painters such as the Carracci and more modern artists, did engravings from them.

Requests for pictures flowed in to the now-famous artist, and he painted the *Wedding at Cana* (1561, now in the Church of the Salute); the *Descent from the Cross* (in the Academy in Venice. A small copy is in the Pitti at Florence) and several other pictures.

Tintoretto also worked outside Venice. He went to Milan, Bologna, Brescia, Vicenza, etc. For the Emperor Rudolph II he painted four pictures, among which was probably the *Concert of Muses* now in the Dresden Museum. For Philip II, of Spain, he did some Old Testament scenes which are in the Prado Museum. For the King of England he did the *Washing of the Feet* in the National Gallery, while he probably did this gallery's *St. George* for the Senator Pietro Cornaro.

Tintoretto also painted portraits. A Self-portrait is in the Louvre. Portraits of Doges and other statesmen and eminent citizens are to be found in the Ducal Palace; in the Academy (Venice); also in the Pitti and the Uffizi (in Florence); many in the Prado; a woman in mourning, in the Dresden Gallery. All these portraits are grave, distinguished, realistic, somewhat in the tradition of Titian, but still more subdued, and executed with a rapidity which gives them greater intensity.

In 1574 or 1575, he began his beautiful mythological paintings for the Ante-Collegio.

After the fire of 1577, the whole decoration of the Council Hall had to be done afresh. In the middle of the ceiling, beside *The Triumph of Venice* by Veronese, Tintoretto painted *The Doge Niccolo da Ponte Receiving the Homage of Subject Towns.* Then he did battle scenes, such as *The Defense of Brescia*; *The Battle of Riva*, etc.

On the walls he painted the Ambassadors of Pope and Doge before Frederick Barbarossa, and transformed this twelfth century event into a sixteenth century Venetian scene.

In the Sala dello Scrutino he painted his largest battle picture, in which the air is thick with arrows.

Now, when he was 77, he still worked enthusiastically, and hoped to carry out the plan of painting a huge "Paradise" with 500 figures, on the ceiling of the great Council Hall. Tintoretto made many sketches for this, representing a Paradise which was as dramatic as a Hell, and colossal in size and composition.

He died in 1594, and was buried in Santa Maria dell'Orto. It is impossible to indicate the extent of his influence, which has persisted down to the present.

See Pl. 2, Vol. II.

BIBLIOGRAPHY: H. Thode, *Tintoretto.*—J. B. Stoughton Holborn, *Jacopo Robusti.* London, 1903.—F. P. B. Osmarton, *The Art and Genius of Tintoret.* London, 1915.

**TIRYNS OR TIRYNTHE.**—See Mycenæ.

**TISSOT (James).**—French painter and engraver, 1836-1902. Pupil of Flandrin and of Lamothe. A conscientious artist, but restless and easily influenced, he produced works which were very different from each other, though always governed by a kind of Lutheran pedantry.

In 1859, he produced two religious pictures, two portraits and a *Walk in the Snow*, which shows a very modern tendency. Two years later he exhibited, on the contrary, *The Meeting of Faust and Marguerite* (Luxembourg), a scrupulous composition, dry in drawing, and a feat of archæology as much as of painting. However, he returned to modern scenes, and, during a long sojourn in London, he painted a *Story of the Prodigal Son*; the *Departure*; the *Return*, and the *Fatted Calf* (1883—Luxembourg Museum) which recalls the literary and laborious works of the Pre-Raphaelite school. An important work of Tissot's includes 350 watercolours (1894), which disclose the painter's intense way of rendering facial expression, and the exactitude with which he treated landscape and figures. But this scrupulous exactitude was obtained by equality of execution, and hardness of colour; and a tiresome monotony detracts from the rare merits of his work.

TISSOT: THE MAGI. (Collection of M. de Brunhoff.)

**TITIAN (Tiziano Vecellio, known as).**—One of the greatest masters of painting, and the head of the brilliant Venetian school.

He was born at Pieve di Cadore, at the foot of the Dolomites—one of the most beautiful sites in the world. He passed the first ten years of his life amid this grand and radiant scenery, and he was always attracted to the landscapes of his childhood. When he became famous and was living in a beautiful Venetian palace, he gladly returned to spend the summer months in these mountains. One finds them in some of his compositions. The peaks of Marmolata may be recognised in the background of his famous *Presentation of the Virgin at the Temple.* And in his early pictures it is impossible not to recognise the places which were familiar to him, and of which he had made numerous pen-and-ink sketches.

TITIAN. (His portrait after Vasari.)

The date of his birth has been a matter of controversy. It is believed to this day, as Titian himself said, that he was born in 1477. And as he died in 1576, he then lived nearly a century.

He came to Venice with his elder brother, Francesco Vecellio, who was also a painter, in the first years of the 16th century. After a short time in the studio of a mosaic worker, he became a "garzone" in the studio of Giovanni Bellini, who was then the most illustrious master of the Venetian school. He likewise studied with Gentile Bellini.

It was at this time, about the year 1507, that Giorgione had inaugurated his "modern manner," that is to say, painting with a bold naturalism and in a large, supple design. It seems that the young Titian profited by the innovations of his elder. But he does not appear to have been long in his studio, as has been said, because, in 1508, when Giorgione painted his frescoes in the Fondaco dei Tedeschi, Titian was no longer a pupil; he took part in this decoration. And even contemporaries found that the figures painted by Titian excelled those by Giorgione. From 1508, Titian was famous in Venice.

TITIAN: THE VIRGIN OF SORROWS. (Prado, Madrid.)

TITIAN: VENUS AND ADONIS. (Prado, Madrid.)

After this, we find Titian at Padua (1501-11) where the results of his visit, a collection of frescoes, are to be seen at the Scuola del Santo (three frescoes representing the *Miracles of St. Anthony of Padua*, all begun 1511).

By 1510 to 1515, Titian, in spite of his youth, had become the great master of the Venetian school. Giovanni Bellini was very old and his influence declining; Giorgione died in 1510; a little later, Sebastiano, Titian's comrade, departed for Rome, where he spent the whole of his career.

TITIAN: CHRIST WITH THE TRIBUTE MONEY. (Royal Gallery, Dresden.)

Titian was then without a rival. Also, after the death of Giovanni Bellini in 1516, he obtained the post of agent of the salt mart, a sinecure, accompanied by a salary, which made him the official painter of the Doges, appointed by the Republic. For this salary, he had to paint portraits and receptions of the Doges, and had besides to continue the decoration of the Great Council Room. Unfortunately, a fire in 1577 destroyed the paintings which Titian made for the Doges' Palace; they included a composition representing the *Meeting of Pope Innocent III and Frederick Barbarossa*, and a *Battle* (said to be of Cadore), which was only finished long after it was commissioned, in 1537.

TITIAN: ST. MARGARET. (Prado, Madrid.)

It was during these years, between 1510 and 1518, that most of Titian's freshest works were painted: works of a young and tender inspiration, and of an already refined skill. The first were portraits and some *Madonnas Surrounded by Saints.* The *St. Mark, between Saints Cosmo and Damiano,* and *St. Roch and St. Sebastian* (now in the Sacristy of the Salute, at Venice), show at what point (from 1512) the young artist was freed from the minute application, taught in Bellini's school. The *Baffo Presented to St. Peter by Alexander VI* (now in the Antwerp Gallery) shows the influence of the old forms very well, in a certain smallness of handling.

TITIAN: NYMPHS OF DIANA AND SATYRS OR THE HUNT OF ACTAEON. (Louvre.)

The *Christ and the Tribute Money* (Dresden) is another early picture of great beauty; and the *Noli Me Tangere* of the National Gallery, London, owes its poetry to an incomparable evening light, and a landscape which may well have been a recollection of his native Cadore.

But the masterpiece of this youthful period is the famous picture known as *Sacred and Profane Love,* which is the glory of the old Borghese Gallery of Rome. The significance of this work has given a great deal of trouble to archæologists. It is a recollection of the *Dream of Poliphile,* where Poliphile and Polia approach the tomb of Adonis, on which Venus weeps, whilst Cupid catches his blood which dyes the flowers red. This is the moment for lovers to implore the favour of the goddess. This wonderful and mysterious picture is like a prayer to Love, drawn by a painter-poet, who shows us Venus and Violante, Palma's daughter, of whom the artist was enamoured. Other works of this time show us a personal and sentimental inspiration in Titian's art, that remained, however, throughout his long life of production.

From this time, Titian became likewise an admirable portraitist, one of those who knew how to sum up the complexity of a living face into a grand painting. It always seems as though the models who posed for him were personalities of exceptional grandeur. At this time, he did not yet associate with the great lords and princes who were soon to be his clients. It was his friends, the young men like himself, whom he painted at this period, and whom we now admire, in the Uffizi and Louvre Galleries, with energetic, ardent faces. The powerful simplicity of this art evokes an intense feeling of life.

From 1516, Titian's biography is better known. On the 20th March 1518, the *Assumption* was unveiled, —Titian's first great religious picture, painted for the Church of Santa Maria dei Frari where it is still to be found. The monks who had commissioned it were surprised by it and did not understand its value until the ambassador of Charles V wished to buy it from them. This is the first oil painting, of which the figures are as large as those of the biggest frescoes (the apostles measure nearly three yards); the colours are vigorous, and placed with the boldness for which Gentile Bellini reproached his pupil. This powerful style, which aims at grand effects is seen again in the *Annunciation* (at Treviso) which dates from the same time; and in the famous *Resurrection,* at Brescia (Saints Nazzaro and Celso, 1520-22), enframed by an *Annunciation* and a *Saint Sebastian and Donor;* Titian here shows what is almost a sculptor's interest in the turn of the muscles, and the pose of athletic bodies. The *Madonna* at Ancona (1520) is also painted in large, expressive masses as is the *Virgin with Six Saints* (1523—Vatican), known as the *Virgin with Saint Nicholas.*

At this time, Titian, who had been acquainted with the Duke of Ferrara, Alfonso, since 1516, was commissioned by this prince for several pictures for his "studio": one in praise of Love, and the other in praise of Wine. Titian painted the *Offering to Love* (Prado Museum) according to an extremely exact programme, drawn from a text of Philostrates. In front of a statue of Venus, to whom nymphs come, bringing their gifts, is a crowd of Cupids, playing and gamboling—those plump, radiant infants, who frolic joyfully throughout the work of Titian, angels or cupids, just as full of mischief in the glory which encircles a Madonna, as when tumbling in the paths of Venus. The *Bacchanal* (Prado Museum) is likewise taken from a text of Philostrates, which inspired the attitudes. The third picture of the Duke of Ferrara, *Bacchus and Ariadne* (National Gallery—1523) shows Ariadne fleeing from Bacchus who is leaping out of his chariot with a charming, but impossible movement. Here again, Titian followed faithfully a text of Catullus in the *Marriage of Peleus and Thetis.*

From this period also date the famous *Madonna del Pesaro,* finished in 1526 (Santa Maria dei Frari), and the *Entombment* (Louvre). The former depicts the Madonna, a simple, noble figure, at the foot of immense columns, graciously receiving members of the Pesaro family.

Titian's relations with the Duke of Ferrara were sometimes stormy. The Duke was exacting, and threats succeeded entreaties when commissions were slow in forthcoming. The painter found a new patron, of more amiable character, but not less exacting, in the young Federigo II Gonzaga, who later became Duke of Mantua.

Titian worked a great deal for the Duke of Mantua and many of these paintings are in the Louvre. Then the relation was dropped for several years, until, wishing to come again to the Duke's notice, he listened to the advice of his friend Aretino, who recommended him to send a present. This present took the form of two marvellous portraits—that of Aretino (Louvre—under the title of *Unknown Man*), and that of Girolano Adorno, the *Man with the Glove* (Louvre), which shows us a dreamy, ardent-looking young man, dressed in black, against a dark background. The Duke was enraptured, and very soon commissions came showering upon the artist. (The *Virgin with a Rabbit* [Louvre] was painted in 1530.) The Duke of Mantua engaged Titian to paint pictures, which he sent to the Emperor, or gave to favourites; but he could never resign himself to losing completely the artists' work, and he made him make copies of them. This accounts for the copies we find in various galleries. The *Allegory* of the Louvre, which portrays Titian and his wife Cecilia, was painted in 1531, shortly after her death, which explains the serious tone of the picture.

Throughout his life Titian desired riches for himself and his children, and he was always besieging his patrons for money and privileges. Desirous of obtaining for his son, Pomponio, ecclesiastical benefices, Titian managed to enter into relations with Pope Paul III. The Pope offered him a position already occupied by Sebastiano Luciani, a friend of Titian, who for that reason refused, while asking compensation. He painted the Portrait of Paul III (1543, Naples Museum), which shows astonishing insight into character, and is equally remarkable in its satisfying composition, and lovely colour. He also painted *Paul II between Cardinal Alessandro and Ottavio Farnese* (Naples, 1545), which depicts the old man, with restless, suspicious look, and the young one, with easy, obsequious charm and the treachery of a tiger concealing its claws.

Titian also painted for the Pope an *Ecce Homo;* and a wonderful *Danaë* (1546, Naples) for the Pope's grandson. Several copies were made. Titian thus won the honourable title of Citizen of Rome, and the much-coveted benefice for his son Pomponio.

In 1537, Titian painted the famous *Battle of Cadore* for the Doges, which his contemporaries considered to be his masterpiece. It was destroyed by fire in 1577. There exists only a copy of a portion of this picture, in the Uffizi; a charming head of a young girl (mentioned by Vasari), and an engraving by Fontana. From about the same period, dates the enormous canvas of the *Presentation of the Virgin at the Temple* (Accademia, Venice).

In the middle-distance to the right, are great buildings; in the far distance, to the left, a mountainous landscape, which transports us to the open spaces of Cadore. In the foreground is a crowd of people, and a high monumental staircase which the little Virgin goes up, while the high priest waits for her at the top. Four pictures in the Church of the Salute, Venice, show violent, dramatic attitudes, foreshortenings, and contrast of light and shade—the *Descent of the Holy Spirit, Cain and Abel,* the *Sacrifice of Abraham, David and Goliath.* The *Christ Crowned with Thorns* (Louvre), painted about 1540, shows the unfortunate result to art of Titian's researches into muscular effects, in the manner of Michelangelo. The same might be said of *The Resurrection* and the *Ecce Homo* (both in Vienna). The *Martyrdom of St. Lawrence* (Gesuiti Church, Venice) is a confused picture, with a strange effect of light, calling to mind Tintoretto's tumultuous compositions.

Besides his large pictures, Titian painted a great many portraits. Not the least fine are those of the *Man with a Glove* and of *Aretino,* to which reference has been made. The latter, who was his friend, he painted again in 1545. The sensuality and assurance of the man are so ruthlessly portrayed that Aretino was shocked by them (Pitti Palace, Florence). The portrait known as *Ariosto* (National Gallery) and the *Catarina Cornaro,* Uffizi, are early works. The subject of the famous portrait of *La Bella* (1536, Florence, Pitti) is unknown. The same face appears in the *Girl in a Fur Cloak* (Vienna). He painted the Duke and Duchess of Urbino (both in the Uffizi, Florence, 1537); Andrea Gritti, who was Doge of Venice, and his friend (Czernin Gallery, Vienna); the very fine *Portrait of a Young Englishman* (Florence, Pitti). Titian painted several portraits of his daughter, Lavinia—one is in Berlin; another, Lavinia in the guise of *Salome,* is in the Prado; *Lavinia as a Young Bride* is in Dresden (1555).

We have so far spoken of Titian's religious and allegorical pictures, and of his portraits. There remain his paintings of nudes, of which he did a great many. His wonderful Venuses are usually in one of three poses—that of the Dresden Venus; or the Uffizi Venus; or the Danaë of Naples. The first nude figures that he painted are the *Dresden Venus* (which was begun by Giorgione), and the young sleeping woman in the Bacchanal. Next came the *Venus of Urbino* (in the Uffizi; about 1538), which shows us, in the same attitude as the Dresden Venus—not the Duchess of Urbino —but some beautiful Venetian. The Danaë series is still more beautiful. The first (Naples Museum) was done in 1546, for the grandson of Paul III. This *Danaë* roused so much admiration, that Titian had to repeat her several times. In the Prado (1553) she is accompanied by an old woman who replaces the Cupid in the Naples picture. Other copies are in Vienna, and the Hermitage.

*Venus and Cupid* (Uffizi) was painted about 1545. The pale flesh tints are thrown up by a drapery of brown velvet, and a red curtain. In the background is a beautiful mountainous landscape. The *Venus and Organ Player* (Prado) reproduces the attitude of this Uffizi picture, exactly, and, except for the arm thrown behind the head, these two Venuses repeat the pose of the sleeping woman in the foreground of the Bacchanal. The two pictures of *Diana and Actaeon* (in the Bridgewater Collection, London, and the collection of the Earl of Harewood) were painted in 1559. The same year, Titian painted *Diana and Callisto* (Bridgewater Collection), done (as were the two Dianas and Actaeon) for the King of Spain.

Titian did a great deal of work for Charles V and for his son, Philip II. The Emperor's first command was for his own portrait, *Charles V with His Dog* (Prado), painted in 1532. This won for Titian several titles, but did not cause him to change his way of life. The Emperor, after fighting the Protestants, at Mühlberg, sent for Titian to come to him at Augsburg. Charles V, in armour, posed for the magnificent picture (in the Prado)—*Charles V at the Battle of Mühlberg* (1548). This realistic painting shows the Emperor, old already and tired, but sitting proudly upright on his richly caparisonned horse. The *Portrait of Charles V* in Munich, painted the same year, represents the Emperor in his private capacity, sitting heavily in a chair, with a careworn expression. His admiration for Titian was unbounded. He one day picked up the painter's brush, saying "Titian is worthy to be served by Caesar." The courtiers, jealous at first, came to imitate the Emperor in demanding their portraits. Most of these were lost in a fire at the Prado, but a few scattered ones remain in private collections. Charles V granted Titian a pension, but this was never paid. Philip II when he ascended the throne was forgetful about money, but continued to command new pictures. In 1550, Titian painted the full-length portrait of Philip II which is now in the Prado; in 1553, another (Naples Museum); in 1552 he sent the King of Spain a *Saint Margaret* (Prado); then a *Danaë* (Prado)—a copy of the one at Naples; a *Holy Trinity* (Prado); *Venus and Adonis* (Prado); *The Martyrdom of St. Lawrence*. The very titles of these pictures throw light on the strange character of the gloomy Philip II, a mingling of the religious and devout and the love of sensuous pleasure and art. Charles V had requested only religious pictures or portraits. When the latter abdicated, he took with him to the monastery two of Titian's paintings—the *Our Lady of Sorrows* (Prado), and the *Trinity*. In 1558, Titian wrote to Philip II to announce the completion of a *Diana and Actaeon* and *Diana and Callisto* (now in the Bridgewater Collection), both of which greatly pleased the king, as did the next pictures—*Europa on the Bull* (Gardner Museum, Boston); an *Entombment* (Prado); and *Actaeon Torn to Pieces by His Dogs*. The latter is wonderfully painted, and is also remarkable for the introduction of several avatars. In the Louvre, it is wrongly called *Jupiter and Antiope*. The details have become so important (the sleeping nymph—the satyrs, etc.) that it detracts from the actual scene of Actaeon, who, changed into a stag by the wrath of Diana, is seized by his own dogs. Titian never painted an Antiope for the King of Spain. The *Actaeon* (which was later called the *Venus of the Prado*) was given by Philip IV to Charles I of England, whence it later went to the Louvre. From 1562 to 1567, Titian worked at the *Last Supper* (Escorial), which is much restored. About the same time he did the *Adoration of the Magi* (Prado); *Christ in the Garden of Olives* (Prado); *Christ on the Cross* (Escorial); *Saint Jerome* (Escorial). *Religion Aided by Spain* (Prado) was described by Vasari as "the nude figure of a girl, making obeisance to Minerva." As this picture lay in Titian's studio for many years, it happened that Minerva's olive tree was changed to a Spanish standard, and the king's arms were added to her shield. Neptune, in his chariot, was given a turban, and like a Turk, fled before the Spanish fleet, as had actually just happened, in 1571, at the battle of Lepanto.

Titian's last years were spent in the service of the king, whom he painted once more; *Philip Presenting His Son to Victory* (Prado; 1571-75). Titian died while he was working at a *Pietà* which he intended for his tomb. It is a tragic scene, in a strange light. Titian painted himself as the Joseph of Arimathea. This work was finished by Palma the Younger, and is in the Academy of Venice.

See Pl. 9, Vol. I; Pls. 16, 20, Vol. II.

BIBLIOGRAPHY: Crowe and Cavalcaselle, *Titian: His Life and Times*. London, 1877.—Gronau, *Tizian*. London, 1900.—L. Hourticq, *La Jeunesse du Titien*. 1919.—O. Fischel, *Tizian*. Klassiker der Kunst, Vol. III.

**TIVOLI.**—Little town near Rome. The Roman patricians built beautiful villas there, which were destroyed during the Middle Ages. From Roman times, there remains the *Temple of Vesta*—a round building, with Corinthian columns —and a still smaller *Temple of the Sibyl*.

The beautiful *Villa d'Este* was built in 1549, by Piero Ligorio, for Cardinal Ippolito d'Este.

**TOBA SOJO.**—Great Japanese painter and priest, 1053-1114. He had considerable influence on the character of later Japanese art by creating a humorous kind of painting, known as toba-yé. He is most famous for his satires in which he employs the animal kingdom in the role of human activity. Humorous scenes attributed to Toba Sojo are preserved in the Kozanji.

See Japan—Art.

**TOCQUÉ (Louis).**—French portrait painter, 1696-1772. A delicate

TOCQUÉ (LOUIS): PORTRAIT OF THE DAUPHIN LOUIS OF FRANCE. (Louvre.)

painter, who used light, transparent colours. The tendency of his art was towards greater naturalism.

An example of his style may be seen in the Portrait of the Dauphin, Louis of France, in the Louvre.

BIBLIOGRAPHY: Comte A. Doria, *Louis Tocqué*. Paris, 1929.

**TOLEDO (Spain).**—The *Cathedral*, begun in 1227, under the reign of Fernando III, almost at the same time as the Cathedral of Burgos, is the largest and most solemn of the 13th century Gothic Cathedrals in Spain. There are five aisles (recalling Bourges). The aisles are high and the triforiums suppressed.

*The Church of San Juan de los Reyes.*—This church made part of a convent erected in 1477 by the Catholic Kings. The first architect was a Fleming, Jan Guas. Enrique de Egas finished the church, endowing it with a raised western choir.

*Church of Santo Tomé.*—14th century Mudejar church, with a graceful clock-minaret and engrailing in

TOLEDO: INTERIOR OF THE CATHEDRAL.

brick and tile, in the Moorish style. The church contains El Greco's masterpiece—the *Burial of Count Orgaz*.

The *Puerta del Sol* is a very old gateway, in the Moorish style. It was built about 1200.

*S. Maria la Blanca,* 14th century. —A Mudejar synagogue adapted to Catholic worship.

*El Transito,* 14th century.—Also known as S. Benito. A Mudejar synagogue built for Samuel Levi, treasurer of Peter the Cruel. It is now a church.

**TOLSTOI (Theodore).**—Russian sculptor (also painter). He made busts, medallions and high reliefs.

**TOMMASO da MODENA.**—Modenese painter, born in Modena 1325, son of a painter.

In 1342, 1344, and 1346 Tommaso is mentioned in documents in Modena, and in 1349 he appears in Treviso, where he is again referred to in 1358. In 1366-68 he is once more in Modena; and in 1379, when he died, he was away from that city; his children certifying his decease.

Evidences of Tommaso da Modena's activity having been found in the Castle of Karlstein in Bohemia, it has been assumed that he went there at the request of the Emperor Charles IV during one of the periods when he is not mentioned in Modena and vicinity. Probably this sojourn was late in the master's career, since records of painting operations in Karlstein, referring to other artists, date from 1365 to 1367.

The earliest work by Tommaso is probably the frescoes in the Chapter House of S. Niccolò, Treviso, signed and dated 1352 and consisting of forty figures of *Dominican Monks*. Other frescoes in S. Niccolò are by Tommaso's school; and also by his school are frescoes in San Francesco and Sta. Lucia, Treviso. A signed altarpiece, a triptych; and two wings of a triptych with the *Madonna* and an *Ecce Homo* are in Karlstein. The Modena Gallery possesses a *Madonna* with a signature and an arguable date, which has been interpreted as 1355.

BIBLIOGRAPHY: J. v. Schlosser, *Tommaso da Modena und die Altere Malerei in Treviso,* Jahrb. der Kunsthist. Samml. des allerh. Kaiserh., XIX. Vienna, 1898.—G. Bertoni e E. P. Vicini, *Tommaso da Modena, pittore modenese del secolo XIV,* Mem. della R. Deput. di Stor. Patr. per la prov. di Modena, ser. V, Vol. III; same authors, *Tommaso da Modena a Treviso,* L'Arte, 1916.—Testi, *Storia d. pitt. venez.,* I.—Van Marle, *Italian Schools, etc.,* IV, 1924.

**TOMMÈ (Luca).**—See Luca di Tommè.

**TORBIDO (Francesco).**—Veronese painter, c. 1486-1561; a pupil of Liberale, he was influenced by Giorgione and Titian.

**TORCELLO (Italy).**—*S. Fosca,* 975-1000. A Venetian Romanesque church of marked Byzantine quality.

*Campanile.*—A great tower of the 11th century windowless from ground to belfry and decorated by pilaster strips. Since the fall of the campanile of S. Marco, Venice, it has been the finest of its type.

**— (mosaics of).**—They belong to the 11th and 12th centuries, and are among the best of Byzantine mosaics. They form a vast series of compositions conceived after the dogmatic tradition of the 6th century, but with the technique of a new style. The oldest are those in the apse; the Madonna and the twelve apostles; with white draperies, uniform attitudes; and austere faces. Above the entrance, on the interior façade, is the *Last Judgment*, rich in detail—symbolic figures of *Earth* and *Sea*—familiar episodes from the Apocrypha—and a huge Hades holding Antichrist in his hands.

**TOREUTICS.**—Art of working in metal (sometimes in other materials) by embossing, chasing, etc.

**TORII (School of).**—See Japan—Art (prints).

**TORRIGIANI (Pietro).**—Spanish sculptor (Florence, 1470; Seville about 1528). According to Vasari, this over-strong pupil, employing violence against a fellow-student, deprived Michelangelo for ever of his looks. The scene took place in

TORRIGIANI: ST. JEROME. (Painted terra cotta. Church of Santa Ana, Granada.)

1492. Torrigiani, who belonged to a noble family, but whose action had angered Laurana Medici, had to leave Florence, only returning once to it, in 1519, for a short time. He first became a soldier under Cesare Borgia. After ten years of warfare, Torrigiani went to live in England. The Tudor Chapel in Westminster Abbey, contains the tombs he made in bronze, for Henry VII, his wife and mother; austere, realistic works which have nothing of the forms of antiquity, nor of Italian classicism. It is not known why Torrigiani left England for Andalusia. In 1526 he was in Seville at the time of the marriage between Charles V and Isabella of Portugal. He did a bust of the young Empress, in terra cotta.

Once more, fortune did not favour the Florentine exile. Charles V did not take him to Granada. He was thrown into prison by the Inquisition (on the charge of having broken, in a fit of anger, a marble Virgin for which the Duke of Arcos had paid an absurd price) and died of hunger.

The Monastery of the Hieronymites had several of his works, two of which are now in the Seville Museum. They are large painted figures in terra cotta. The *Virgin and Child* shows a beautiful peasant woman, strongly built, her robe falling in simple natural folds.

The *Saint Jerome* which Goya considered the "best piece of modern sculpture in Spain" is a realistic study of the nude.

Torrigiani, who was so unjustly forgotten in the 17th century, is, by virtue of his realism, truth and noble simplicity, the direct forerunner of Montañes.

**TORRITI (Jacopo).**—13th century Roman mosaicist and painter.

Two important mosaic decorations, both signed, are by Torriti: the apsidal mosaic in S. Giovanni in Laterano (restoration of preexisting mosaics with new additions, signed "Jacobus Torriti pictor hoc opus fecit"); and the apsides of Sta. Maria Maggiore, *Coronation of the Virgin.* Torriti's hand has been recognized in the fresco decoration of the Church of St. Francis at Assisi.

Bibliography: E. Müntz, *Des éléments antiques dans les mosaïques romaines du Moyen âge,* Revue archéologique, 1879.—J. de Laurière, *L'Abside de St. Jean de Latran,* Bull. Monum., V Serie, VII, 1879. —T. Armellini, *L'abside della basilica Lateranese,* 1880.—De Rossi, *Mosaici cristiani.* — Morey, *Lost Mosaics and Frescoes of Rome.*

**TORO (Spain).** — *Colegiata.* A 12th century Romanesque church of the same type as the Old Cathedral, Salamanca, having a similar decorative ribbed dome.

**TOSA (School of).**—See Japan—Art (Painting).

**TOULOUSE (France).** — The most interesting building in Toulouse is the *St. Sernin,* the largest Romanesque Church in France. It was begun in the middle of the 11th century and consecrated in 1096. The building has five aisles, and a large transept. The apse is surrounded by five chapels; and the octagonal central tower, in five storeys, is both harmonious and grandiose.

See Pls. 44, 46, Vol. I.

The *Church of the Jacobins* (built from 1260-1292) is of brick supported by strong buttresses, and the nave is divided into two by a row of columns.

Among many other old buildings, reference must be made to such civil edifices as the *Collège de Foix* (15th century); the *Hôtel de Bernuy* (1470 to 1530), half Gothic, half Renaissance; and the *Capitole,* or Hôtel de Ville, which possesses a 17th century courtyard, and a wide façade, the windows of which are separated by eight red marble columns.

Bibliography: J. de Malafosse, *Étude et notes d'archéologie,* 1898.—J. de Lahondès, *L'église Saint Étienne, l'Hôtel d'Assézat et l'Hôtel de Pierre.*

Toulouse: The Capitole, Court of Henry IV.

**TOULOUSE - LAUTREC - MONFA (Count Henri Marie Raymond de).**—French painter and graver (1864-1901). Born 24th November 1864 at the estate of his father, the Count Alphonse de Toulouse-Lautrec-Monfa, at Albi. As a young boy he broke both his legs, this accident retarding his growth and giving him the appearance of a cripple. The unfortunate youth was shortsighted and of a homely physiognomy. He received a first-rate education and was a brilliant student in every field; but owing to his physical appearance he was not welcome at home and had to seek solace in the friendship of the horse painter René Princeteau, who first stirred in him an interest in art. His first real teacher was Léon Bonnat, soon to be succeeded by Cormon; in the latter's studio he made the acquaintance of van Gogh. In 1885 Lautrec met Degas, through whom he found his true path in the realm of art. Humiliated and despised by society, the young man sought refuge in the cafés of Montmartre, becoming a steady patron of the Moulin Rouge and the Moulin de la Galette. His brilliance and his wealth drew a large crowd of intelligentsia around him; Lautrec sketched them all: Yvette Guilbert, van Gogh, Oscar Wilde, as well as his night club favourites: Jane Avril, La Goulue and others. He had various residences, all famous for the bars they contained and the colourful parties that the host held for every one he knew, regardless of title and profession. In 1889 he became a member of the Independents. He travelled considerably in England and the Netherlands. In 1899 he had his first severe attack from overindulgence and was confined to a sanatorium. He recovered for a short time, but died 6th September 1901 at the family estate at Malarmé from a paralytic stroke. Lautrec was continually at work, producing uncanny amounts of drawings, posters, etchings, lithographs and paintings in all media, often done on ordinary cardboard. He also illustrated several contemporary newspapers. He assisted his printer, M. Stein, personally. Due to his own misfortune he had an unusual insight into human nature, invariably grasping the salient characteristics and subtle expressions of his sitters. His infallible judgment in the psychology of mankind was due to his association with every class of human being from aristocrat to prostitute; his keen observation of the ugly and destructive side of life and his fascination for the antediluvian vigour of vice surrounding him are apparent in most of his drawings; it is impossible to separate in them art from life. In his technique one may detect his enthusiasm for Degas, as well as a knowledge of Japanese prints and the paintings of Puvis. His brilliant brushwork, crisp line and sparing use of dabs of unadulterated colour have not been surpassed. Most of his sketches are conserved in the Musée d'Albi; he is also represented in the Luxembourg, the Metropolitan Museum of Art, Museum of Hamburg and many private collections. His best-known works are *La Goulue et sa Soeur, Messalina, Femme au Chien, A la Mie.*

Bibliography: Gotthard Jedlicka, *Henri de Toulouse-Lautrec,* 1929.—Maurice Joyant, *Henri de Toulouse-Lautrec,* 1926.—L'Amour de l'Art, Special Toulouse-Lautrec number in Vol. 12, April, 1931 (by a number of authors).

**TOURAINE (School of).**—See Miniature.

**TOUR MAGNE.**—See Nîmes.

**— MAUBERGEON.**—See Poitiers.

**— ST. JACQUES.**—See Paris.

Tournai: Transept of the Cathedral.

**TOURMANIN.**—See Dêr Termânîn.

**TOURNAI (Belgium).**—One of the oldest towns in Flanders, containing several fine churches. The Cathedral of Notre Dame is a magnificent Romanesque and Gothic building. The great nave (1146-1213) is purely Romanesque; the transept, the apses and the chapels, built in the 13th century by French architects, are Gothic, and so is the choir. The porch, with Gothic arcades, is in front of a great Romanesque doorway on which is some good sculpture of the 13th century and later. The capitals of the pillars are remarkable; and also a marble rood-screen attributed to Cornelis de Vriendt; and some 14th century stained glass windows.

See Pl. 45, Vol. I.

*Saint-Quentin, Saint-Jacques,* and *la Madeleine* are all Transitional Gothic.

*Saint-Brice* (12th century) contained the tomb of Chilperic, in which a number of Merovingian objects were found. There is a 12th century *belfry.* The *Pont des Trous* was built in the 13th century.

Tournai has many very interesting old houses.

Tournai: The "Porte Mantile of the Cathedral."

**TOURS (France).**—This pleasing town possesses numerous interesting monuments. The *Cathedral of Saint Gatien* was begun in 1170, and finished in the middle of the 16th century. It is graceful, light, and rather narrow for its height. The 15th century façade is ornate, and the towers are crowned with Renaissance lanterns. The interior shelters Michel Colombe's tomb of the children of Charles VIII. Next to the Cathedral are cloisters.

Tours: The Cathedral of St. Gatien.

The *Basilica of St. Martin* was rebuilt in the 19th century.

Tours possesses numerous old houses, from the 12th to 15th centuries. The Museum contains two famous pictures by Mantegna, *The Mount of Olives* and the *Resurrection,* which come from the predella of the altarpiece of San Zeno.

Bibliography: Henry James, *A Little Tour in France.* Leipzig, 1885.

**— (School of).**—See Pl. 4, Vol. II.

**TOWER.**—A high construction, intended to hold clocks, bells, or used for purposes of fortification. The oldest that have come down to us are those of Verona and Ravenna, and date from the 9th century. Two Roman Churches, the Lateran and St. Peter's had 8th century towers, but they have been destroyed. Towers are sometimes isolated, especially in Italy and in the South of France. Sometimes they served purposes of defense. Sometimes they were built near a church or, more often, on the church. In the latter case, their position, like their form, is very various: they are either built on the front of the façade, or above the crossing of the transept (and these were frequently lantern towers, with windows, to light the building), or in the axis of the side-aisles. Some churches have several towers, three, five, seven (Reims Cathedral), nine (Laon Cathedral). As to their form, this naturally varies according to country, period, and the fancy of the architect. They are seldom round, more often octagonal, and still more often square. A very widespread form has a square base, surmounted by octagonal stages which frequently recede into pyramidal form. More massive at the base, pierced with a few straight openings, they sometimes become a lacework of stone (Strasbourg Cathedral). Some are finished by a crenelated terrace (Elne); others, by a gable (Brantôme), or by square or octagonal spires, sometimes very high; yet others, by domes (Renaissance and modern churches); and each country transforms these principal types with characteristics of its own. In the Ile de France, stone and brick are often substituted by a wooden flèche (spire) covered with lead, to finish the tower. Languedoc has octagonal towers, without spires, scarcely becoming thinner towards the top. Brittany has square towers with balconies and spires. Finally, it often happens that architects cannot finish the building of their tower, either owing to lack of resources, or through having planned too ambitiously, too daringly, this part of the building, which best expresses their ideal or their ability.

Bibliography: Viollet-le-Duc, *Dictionnaire de l'archit.*

**TOWNSEND (C. Harrison).**—Contemporary British architect and the first British modernist. In the Bishopsgate Institution, London, 1893-1894, and in the Horniman Museum, London, 1900-1901, can be seen his style developed from that of the American, H. H. Richardson.

**TOYOHARU (Utagawa).**—Japanese painter and print master, 1733-1814. Pupil of Shigenaga, or of Toyonobu, to whose style his own is analogous; he was the founder of the Utagawa school. He made, in the style of Harunobu, some prints, the subjects of which disclose, however, a very different personality: street scenes in which he makes use of European perspective, crowds in the theatres, and especially realistic landscapes, which are already under western influence. Owing to the success of Kiyonaga, he seems to have given up wood-cutting.

Among his pupils were Toyohiro, Toyohisa, and above all Toyokuni.

**TOYOKUNI (Utagawa).**—Japanese painter and print master, 1769-1825. He was the pupil of Toyoharu. In his youth he imitated in turn, Kiyonaga, Shunman, Yeishi, Choki; but, above all, he was influenced by Utamaro. In this style may be mentioned, among others, the triptych representing a princess watching her companions make a snow-ball, and the diptych which shows two women watching some children who are gazing at the reflections of their own faces in lacquer panels.

However, Toyokuni soon created a very individual type, which recalls, a little, the rounded faces of Hokusai's women. This type is found in most of his beautiful triptychs, in which he reveals ingenuity, and very graceful composition. (E.g. *Women Cutting Bamboos; Women Fishing.*)

In this style, too, Toyokuni illustrated some novels, notably those of Kiyoden and of Bakin. Then, under the influence of Sharaku, he took to delineating the theatre and the actors of his day, representing, in this, the tradition of Shunsho, whose pupil he may even have been.

It was Sharaku, however, who had the greatest influence on Toyokuni. He copied his types, his figures, his colour. His colour which, to begin with was harmonious, became more and more strident. He did not, however, employ analine colours which his pupils abused, and which hastened the decadence of wood-cutting.

Toyokuni died in 1825—that is, he saw the beginning of this decadence, and could not entirely resist its effect himself, and his last works show the repetition of mere factory production, devoid of his earlier inspiration.

**TOYONOBU.**—Japanese painter and print master, 1711-1785. He was a pupil of Shigenaga, and after his master's death he took over the direction of the school of Okomura, which had been founded by Masanobu and continued by Shigenaga. He appears to have been profoundly influenced by these two artists. He has the same distinction—the same supple elegance in his studies of women. The bodies, however, being more slender, are apt to make the heads seem bigger, and the attitudes tend to be more contorted. Toyonobu was also a delicate colourist.

**TRAINI (Francesco).**—Pisan painter, active second quarter of the 14th century.

In 1323 Traini is mentioned as receiving payment for paintings in the Town Hall, Pisa, and for other works for the city. In 1337 he takes a brother of Cristofano di Piestrasanta as his pupil; in 1341 paints a standard for the Landi Company; in 1344 begins the extant altarpiece of St. Dominic, ordered by Giovanni Coco, finished in 1345 and signed. The central panel is now in the Gallery at Pisa, the side panels in the Seminario. Attributed to Traini are the panel of *St. Thomas Aquinas in Glory* in the Church of Sta. Caterina, Pisa, and the frescoes of the *Triumph of Death* and the *Last Judgment* in the Campo Santo.

Bibliography: Vasari-Milanesi, I. —Crowe and Cavalcaselle, Douglas ed.—Bonaini, *Memorie inedite intorno alla vita e di dipinti di Francesco Traini.* Pisa, 1846.—Simoneschi, *Notizie e questione intorno a Francesco Traini.* Pisa, 1898.—Supino, *Il trionfo della morte e il giudizio universale nel Campo Santo di Pisa,* Arch, stor. dell' arte, 1899, p. 32; same author, *Arte pisana,* p. 268.—Kurzwelly, *Buffalmacco—Traini Frage,* Repert. f. Kunstwiss., 1912, p. 337.

**TRAJAN (Arch of).**—See Timgad.

**— (Forum of).**—See Rome; also Pl. 29, Vol. I.

**TRAJAN'S COLUMN.**—See Rome.

**TRANI (Italy).**—*Cathedral,* 1090-1143. A great Apulian Romanesque basilica based upon the slightly earlier church of S. Nicola, Bari.

**TRANSEPT.**—The arm of a cruciform church lying at right angles with the nave.

**TRÈVES OR TRIER.**—Ancient city on the Moselle River in Rhenish Prussia. It has Roman remains, including an amphitheatre and a fortified gate, the Porta Nigra. The Cathedral, which dates from 1021-1047, contains the famous "Holy Coat of Trèves" which is believed by the devout to be the seamless robe of Christ.

See Pl. 30, Vol. I.

**TRIANONS.**—See Versailles.

**TRIBOLO (Niccolò Pericoli, known as).**—Florentine sculptor (1485-1550). Pupil of Andrea Sansovino with whom he worked in Loreto. He was powerfully influenced by Michelangelo, as may be seen by his statue of *St. James,* in the Duomo of Florence, and more especially in his decorations for the doors of San Petronio, in Bologna (1528), where the prophets and sibyls recall the Sistine figures.

It was, however, as an organiser of fêtes and a designer of beautiful gardens, that he excelled. Every time he wanted to celebrate a marriage, a baptism or a triumphal entry, Cosimo I called upon Tribolo. He created the beautiful Boboli Gardens (Florence), at the request of the Duchess Eleanor of Toledo.

**TRIER.**—See Trèves.

**TRIFORIUM.**—Gallery in a church above the side aisles of the nave.

**TRIPTYCH.**—A sequence of three panels, painted or sculptured. Generally the two side wings can be closed, by means of hinges; the exterior of these wings is often painted. Triptychs were generally used as portable altars, or as altarpieces above the altar. They were also made in carved ivory, in enamel, and in gold-work.

**TRISTAN (Luis).**—Spanish painter, 1586-1640. He was the most distinguished of El Greco's pupils, whose style he adopted to such an extent that the following work (though signed "Luys Tristan faciebat, Toleti, 1629") was attributed to El Greco—namely, *The Holy Trinity,* which is in the Cathedral of Seville.

At the age of thirty, about 1616, Tristan did his masterpieces, the paintings of Yepes.

In 1619, he did the portrait of the Archbishop of Toledo, Cardinal D. Bernado de Sandoval, for the Cathedral Chapter House. About the same time, he painted the portrait of Lope de Vega (in the Hermitage).

The Prado possesses Tristan's *Portrait of an Old Gentleman,* quiet and assured in execution; and the Academy of San Fernando has a *St. Jerome* which reminds one of Titian's compositions.

Velázquez, at the beginning of his career, admired Tristan, and for a short time was influenced by him.

A link between El Greco and Velázquez he was, in a way, a forerunner of the brilliant Spanish school of the 17th century.

What really gained for him the admiration of Velázquez was his fidelity to the tradition of realism which characterises Spanish painting.

Bibliography: Pelayo Quintero Atauri, *Luis Tristan.* Boletin de la Soc. esp. Excur (Madrid, 1909).

**TROAD.**—See Greece (Terra cottas).

**TROCADERO.**—See Paris.

**TROUBETSKOI (Paolo, Prince).**—Russian sculptor, born in 1866. The creator of Impressionist sculpture. He made the equestrian statuette of Count Leo Tolstoi, which is in the Luxembourg. His chief work is an equestrian statue of Alexander III which, in 1910, was set up in front of the station at Moscow.

**TROY.**—The ancients called the plain of Troy the lower valley of the Menderez (the ancient Scamander) in the north-west corner of Asia Minor, opposite the peninsula of the Dardanelles (Chersonesus Thracica). The formation of the places, rivers, hills, all indicate the site of ancient Troy, the town of the Homeric poems. It was in 1875 that Schliemann, a German, began the excavations which only ended with his death in 1890. He explored the mound called Hissarlik, and his work was continued by Dörpfeld, an engineer and architect.

The first explorations exposed the remains of a town which must have been built after the reign of Alexander. In one of the buildings were the remains of the sanctuary of a deity, Athena of Illium, who was celebrated in Macedonian and Roman times. The lower settlement led Schliemann to believe that he had found the remains of seven superimposed towns. Actually, archæologists only recognise four strata of civilization.

Troy: West postern. (After a photograph by Dörpfeld.)

The most ancient town was only a village, where many arms carved in silex (or flint) and monochrome pottery, were found. It was an acropolis, or citadel. The second town showed changes which indicated that it had been in existence two or three centuries. This town changed and grew several times, having suffered by fire, but it was reinstated and protected by three successive walls all round. Here were found the remains of a palace, or at least of a dwelling, a very simple one, which is very similar in plan, to those discovered at Mycenæ and Tiryns. Everywhere were signs of fire; in the brick walls, places had been kept by the builder, for wooden beams. These had all been burned. So entire a destruction cannot be attributed to a simple accident. It must have resulted from pillaging or from deliberate destruction. The objects found in the

# DECORATIVE PAINTING

*When a painter such as Courbet is preoccupied with making an exact and powerful copy of reality, he composes pictures which do not harmoniously fit in with the architecture. The very much emphasised realism of oil painting is not always adaptable to the demands of decorative painting. Paintings of this sort compel one's admiration because of the realism they present and not for the way they harmonise with their background. When naturalism is emphasised in the pictorial arts, it is necessary to distinguish a "decorative" style from a "realistic" style. But painting paused before it found what it was seeking.*

COUTURE: ROMANS OF THE DECADENCE. LOUVRE.
*(Photo by Neurdein.)*

CHASSÉRIAU: PEACE. LOUVRE.
*(Photo by Hachette.)*

## The Forerunners of Puvis

In the nineteenth century painting was often puzzled to find a decorative system which could adapt itself to modern architecture. In constructions which were copies of the Renaissance style, imitation of the painting of this period seemed logical. Thus Couture, influenced by colourful romanticism and the classical style, did not hesitate to fall back upon Veronese in his famous composition of the *Romans of the Decadence*. Chassériau who was more original maintained a balance between Ingres and Delacroix in his work which was partly destroyed.

PUVIS DE CHAVANNES: "LUDUS PRO PATRIA." MUSEUM OF AMIENS.
*(Photo by Hachette.)*

## Puvis de Chavannes

It was Puvis de Chavannes who best understood the needs of decorative painting in modern palaces. His painting has no need of stucco or gilt wood frames. His pale colours, light as those of fresco—although he always painted in oil—harmonise with the paleness of the bare stone. As for the lines of the compositions, by the dominant horizontals and verticals they recall an architectural framework. Thus, movement and the stir of life are harmonised on the wall surface by means of the quiet geometry of the lines and the sobriety of the colour.

PUVIS DE CHAVANNES: CHRISTIAN INSPIRATION. MUSEUM OF LYON.
*(Photo by Bulloz.)*

PUVIS DE CHAVANNES: ST. GENEVIÈVE WATCHING OVER PARIS. PANTHÉON.
*(Photo by Hachette.)*

PUVIS DE CHAVANNES: THE SACRED GROVE. MUSEUM OF LYON.
*(Photo by Hachette.)*

## Puvis de Chavannes

Decoration is not confined to ornamentation. A picture, especially one on a grand scale, should interest the intellect while it charms the vision. Puvis de Chavannes was not satisfied with finding a world of new aspects; he created a modern poetry giving life to the allegories which were generally stiff and cold in contemporary art. Their charm is in their plastic expression and the extraordinary beauty of the landscape in which they exist. Puvis' sentiment for nature is very modern; light is the music which lends supreme harmony to his sacred groves.

# MODERN PAINTING, ENGLAND AND AMERICA

*In European art, England always plays a conservative rôle; she remains insular even in painting. She does not follow the large movements of continental art. However, she maintains a relationship with Europe; she only chooses what best appears to suit her own genius. Thus, English art, although its origin was on the Continent, does not always harmonise with the latter. In the nineteenth century, two groups of artists are particularly important: first, the landscapists who were contemporaries of the French Romanticists, then the Pre-Raphaelites, contemporaries of continental naturalists.*

CONSTABLE: THATCHED COTTAGE IN A WHEAT FIELD. VICTORIA AND ALBERT MUSEUM, LONDON.

TURNER: THE PILGRIMAGE OF CHILDE HAROLD. NATIONAL GALLERY, LONDON. *(Photo by Hanfstaengl.)*

CONSTABLE: THE FARM IN THE VALLEY. NATIONAL GALLERY, LONDON.

## English Landscapes

Already in the eighteenth century, Gainsborough was a very sensitive landscape painter and understood how to use nature as the setting for his beautiful models. At the beginning of the nineteenth century, two very fine landscape painters represent the English school. One of them, Constable, is purely English; he is the painter of fresh green grass beneath grey clouds; very often he reveals a kinship with Ruysdael and Hobbema, but romantic nervousness has taken the place of Dutch calmness. Turner is less faithful to English landscapes. He has a longing for the Mediterranean light, which Claude Lorrain revealed to him, whose radiant brilliance he seeks for in the mists of his own country.

ROSSETTI: REGINA CORDIUM.

MADOX BROWN: ELIJAH AND THE SON OF THE WIDOW. VICTORIA AND ALBERT MUSEUM, LONDON.

BURNE-JONES: THE DEPTHS OF THE SEA. (BENSON COLLECTION.)

MILLAIS: YEOMAN OF THE GUARD. TATE GALLERY, LONDON.

## The Pre-Raphaelite School

This was a somewhat artificial but rather curious movement. These painters in their reaction against the too facile skill of their predecessors sought in the Florentine primitives of the fifteenth century the secret of naturalism and analytical art. These masters were sometimes poets rather than painters and they often appear rather as distinguished amateurs than professionals.

WINSLOW HOMER: A SUMMER NIGHT. LOUVRE. *(Photo by Bulloz.)*

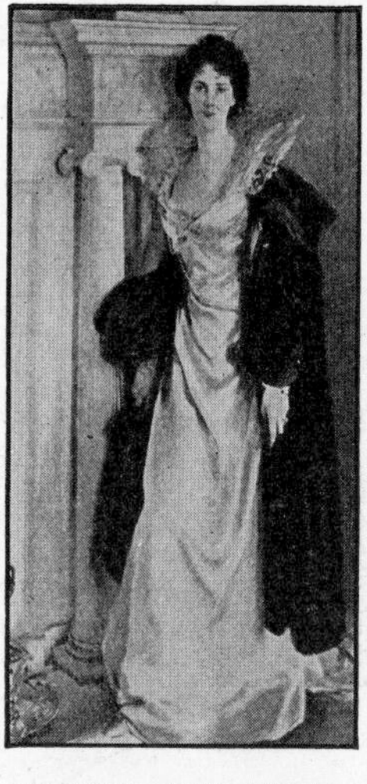

SARGENT: THE DUCHESS OF PORTLAND.

WHISTLER: THE ARTIST'S MOTHER. MUSÉE DU LUXEMBOURG. *(Photo by Hachette.)*

## American Painters

During the 19th century, American artists broke away from the English and Dutch traditions, and sought their training in Düsseldorf, Munich, Barbizon and especially Paris. Some remained abroad and were virtual expatriates for years. Whistler, and later Sargent, lived in London; Duveneck taught in Munich. Homer leads the home-staying group, beginning, like many, as lithographer and illustrator, and finally devoting himself in oil and watercolour to the search for truth in nature as he saw it.

second town show great progress, in comparison with those of the first town. Metal had, in many cases, replaced stone—gold, silver, lead, bronze and copper were used, and there were even some iron implements. Among the bronze objects, was a statuette having a curiously modern grace. The attitude, the silhouette, the dress caught in at the waist, the frilled skirt, all show an art that had something modern and "European" about it. Ceramic art had also reached a high point of perfection; vases were beautifully shaped, instead of merely having decorations added round the sides near the top. Some of these vases were adorned to represent eyes, or a nose, etc. There were also earthenware objects, some of which had marks on them which might have been letters.

Above these primitive towns were layers of debris, which Schliemann and Dörpfeld thought were the remains of seven towns. Perhaps this debris was merely the accumulation resulting from new houses having replaced those which had crumbled. The ruins of the upper layer, by their more regular construction, show that they probably belonged to the Macedonian and Roman town.

In this third town were found the remains of another palace. Schliemann thought it was the palace of King Priam. It might, however, have been the temple of that Illium Athena which was visited by many pilgrims, in Graeco-Roman times.

Modern archæologists seem to agree in thinking the site of ancient Troy was on the mound of Hissarlik which Schliemann excavated. Dörpfeld thought the town of Priam had been completely destroyed by the magisterial works of the Romans. One cannot hope to find the palace of Priam. It was obliterated by later buildings just as the earlier structures of the Athenian Acropolis were obliterated by the 5th century buildings.

Bibliography: H. Schliemann, *Bericht über die Ausgrabungen in Troja im Jahre 1890:* mit einem Vorwort von Sophie Schliemann und Beiträgen von Dr. Wilhelm Dörpfeld. Leipzig, 1891.—W. Dörpfeld, *Troja und Ilion,* 2 vols. Athens, 1902.—G. Perrot and C. Chipiez, *Histoire de l'art dans l'antiquité,* Vol. VI. Paris, 1895.—René Dussand, *Les civilisations préhelléniques.* Paris, 1910.

**TROY (Jean-François de).**—French painter (1679-1752). He was the son of the portrait painter, rival of Lagillière, Rigaud and François de Troy. He studied the works of Rubens and Veronese, often borrowing from the latter his spacious backgrounds and ornate architecture. One of his chief pictures, the *Plague of Marseilles* (in the Marseilles Museum) is painted with the enthusiasm and picturesqueness which are fairly characteristic of his style.

He was a spontaneous artist, who generally spoiled his sketches when he developed them.

His love of pleasure and dissipation was harmful to his artistic development. He had among his friends several important financiers, some of whom asked him to decorate their houses. Towards the middle of his life, he saw his fame being eclipsed by that of François Lemoine, and the result was a rivalry between them. He sought and found success in "conversation pictures" of scenes of gallantry, like those which Lancret did so well, but Troy did not attain Lancret's lightness and charm. One of his chief works was the series of cartoons on the *Story of Esther,* which he did for the Gobelins. These compositions had no Biblical character, but were charming in their modern grace. Troy was, in 1738, appointed Director of the French School in Rome.

Bibliography: Dimier. *Les peintres français du XVIIIe Siècle,* Vol. II.

**TROYES.**—The church of *St. Magdalen* is the oldest building in Troyes. It has been altered several times. The choir, enlarged from 1495 to 1508, had its absidioles added at this time. On the right of the chief entrance is a beautiful Renaissance

Troyes: The Cathedral.

tower. The church contains some remarkable sculpture. It is divided into a nave and four aisles, whose heavy pillars have fine capitals. The magnificent rood-screen was made 1508-1517 by Jean Gaide or Gualde. It is formed of three broken arches adorned with festoons. Each is surmounted by a sculptured group of seated figures, surrounded by flowers and leaves. Above, an open gallery upholds statues. By a pillar of a transept is a famous 16th century statue of St. Martha. In the Chapels are magnificent stained glass windows of the 15th and 16th centuries.

The *Cathedral of St. Pierre* was begun in 1208, and finished at the end of the 15th century. The façade is very fine (beginning of the 16th century to 1638), and has three richly carved doors which have unfortunately lost many of their statues. Many windows still have glass of the 12th, 13th and 15th centuries, representing lives and legends of saints, gospel stories, etc., and the renowned press of Linard Gontier (1625).

The Gothic *Collegiate Church of Saint Urbain* (begun 1262), has good 13th, 14th and 15th century stained glass.

*Saint-Rémy* has a high tower (14th century) and on the tabernacle, an admirable Christ in bronze, by Girardon.

The large *Church of Saint-Jean* (end of the 14th century) contains the famous group of the Visitation, and a chevet altar in white marble by Girardon.

*Saint Pantaléon* (16th century) contains various works of art.

Troyes is also interesting for its many Renaissance houses. The *Hôtel de Ville* was built in the 17th century.

Bibliography: Lucien Morel Payen, *Troyes et Provins,* Collection des Villes d'art célèbres.

**TROYON (Constant).**—French painter, 1810-1865. He painted open-air life—cattle and farm-yard scenes

Troyon: Cows at the watering place. (Louvre.)

—with great freshness. His colour often surpasses his draughtsmanship, as in his remarkable *Feeding the Chickens,* in which the very colours seem alive. He realised the importance of sky in a landscape. *Cows Drinking* (Louvre); *a Bull under a Stormy Sky; Huntsmen and dogs*—such were the subjects of his paintings.

Bibliography: Henri Dumesnil, *Troyen.* Paris, 1888.

Troyon: Feeding the poultry. (Louvre.)

**TRUMBULL (John).**—Early American painter (1756-1843). He was born at Lebanon, Connecticut, 6th June 1756, the son of Jonathan Trumbull, who was the Governor of Connecticut during the Revolutionary War. He enjoyed drawing when a boy and tried copying all available pictures and prints. He graduated from Harvard College in 1773 and after teaching a short while began drilling some friends for the war with England which was then threatening. He was an adjutant in the Connecticut troops and became an aide-de-camp on General Washington's staff after drawing a plan of some British fortifications on Boston Neck. In 1776 he went with General Gates' expedition as a deputy adjutant-general with the rank of colonel and two years later he accompanied General Sullivan in an unsuccessful attempt to regain control of Rhode Island. He then left the army to take up painting again and the winter of 1778 he spent in Boston working under Smibert's direction. Friends urged him to go abroad to study with Benjamin West, so in 1780 he set sail for France and from there he went to London, bearing a letter to West from Benjamin Franklin. He had not been in England long when he was arrested and put into prison as an American officer and when his release was effected by West he was deported for the duration of the war. After a short trip to Holland he returned to the United States and there became interested in contracting supplies for the U. S. army. But in 1784 Trumbull returned to England to study with West and also at the Royal Academy. He became interested in historical compositions and was encouraged to continue along those lines. While in West's studio he executed the *Battle of Bunker Hill,* the *Death of General Montgomery* during the attack upon Quebec, and the *Declaration of Independence.* This last picture was enlivened by the introduction of heads drawn from life as he was able to find the men who had participated upon that occasion. He went to Paris then and painted some of the French officers for his projected *Surrender of Lord Cornwallis,* before returning to the United States in 1789. Back at home he painted some portraits of George Washington and some studies of prominent people for his large historical canvases. In 1794 he accepted the post of secretary to John Jay, then ambassador extraordinary to Great Britain. While in London he served on a commission to settle damage claims against Great Britain for the impressment of seamen, but when that broke up he returned home in 1804. Settled in New York he painted a portrait of John Jay and another of Alexander Hamilton, from a portrait bust, among many others. He made another trip to England in 1808 and got caught there until the close of the War of 1812. Soon after he had returned to New York he received the commission to make four pictures for the Capitol at Washington, D. C. For the next eight years he worked and in 1824 they were installed in the rotunda, the subjects being: the *Declaration of Independence,* the *Surrender of General Burgoyne,* the *Surrender of Lord Cornwallis* and *Washington Resigning His Commission.* He gave some instruction at the American Academy of Fine Arts and was president of that organisation for several years. About that time he made an arrangement with Yale College whereby in return for an annuity for the duration of his life he gave to the college his collection of pictures and sketches to which he added as he continued his painting. He made some replicas of his earlier work, including the panels done for the U. S. Capitol. In 1841 he published his autobiography in New Haven but shortly afterward went to New York City to live. There he died 10th November 1843 and was buried beneath the Trumbull gallery in the Yale School of Fine Arts in New Haven, Connecticut.

See Pl. 61, Vol. II.

BIBLIOGRAPHY: *Autobiography, Reminiscences and Letters of John Trumbull,* 1841.—J. H. Morgan, *Paintings by John Trumbull at Yale University,* 1926.—John F. Weir, *John Trumbull, a Brief Sketch of His Life,* 1901.

**TUBULURE.**—A short tubular opening.

**TUDELA (Spain).**—*Cathedral.*—This basilica (12th century) belongs to a group of large and robust Cathedrals built in the East of Spain—in Tarragona, Lerida, and Sigüenza: buildings strongly influenced by the architecture of the Cistercians in France, covered with solid pointed vaulting; and externally severe as fortresses.

**TUILERIES.**—Former royal palace in Paris between the Louvre and the Place de la Concorde. It was begun for Catherine de' Medici in 1564 by Philibert de l'Orme. Jean Bullant succeeded him as architect. The palace was burned by the Commune in 1871, but the garden remains as a public park.

THE TUILERIES BEFORE THE FIRE OF 1871.

**TUNG CH'I-CHANG.**—Chinese painter and critic, 1555-1636, who formulated much of the philosophy for the literary man's paintings.

See China-art.

**TUNG YUAN.**—Chinese painter of the 10th century. His landscapes were important as influence on Yuan and China painters.

See China-art.

**TUNIS.**—See Moslem Art.

**TURA (Cosimo or Cosmé).**—Painter of Ferrara and founder of the Ferrarese school, born 1429-1430; died 1495.

Tura is recorded in documents in 1451, when he estimated, with Galasso, painted pennons; and in 1452 when he painted a *cimiero* with the unicorn for the winner of the "Palio," also for having decorated boxes with miniatures and reliefs. From 1452 to 1456 he was probably absent from Ferrara, perhaps at Padua where he may have worked with Mantegna, and at Venice. In 1457 he is again mentioned in Ferrara; and in 1458 he painted a *Nativity* for the Duomo. Between 1460 and 1463 he worked on the decoration of the Studio di Belfiore begun by Angelo da Siena and perhaps continued by Michele Pannonio; and executed other minor works. In 1465-67 he was probably at the Mirandola where he decorated the Biblioteca del Pico with allegorical and mythological figures, of which decoration nothing remains. Tura is mentioned again in Ferrara in 1468, as having finished the decoration of the Sacrati Chapel with scenes from the New Testament and with a panel of the *Adoration of the Magi.* From 1469 date the small doors of the organ painted for the Duomo and now in the Opera del Duomo, Ferrara; and in this same year was charged by Duke Borso to decorate a chapel at Belriguardo; in the spring he went to Venice to get colors and gold, and in November to Brescia to see the chapel painted there by Gentile da Fabriano. In 1472 his work in the Belriguardo Chapel was estimated by Baldassare d'Este and Antonio Orsini da Venezia. The paintings included representations of *God the Father, Seraphim, Evangelists,* and *Fathers of the Church.*

Tura was official portraitist to the Este family, executing in 1472 a portrait of Ercole II, and Lucrezia, his natural daughter; in 1477 three portraits of Alfonso I; in 1479 a portrait of Lucrezia, fiancée of Annibale Bentivoglio; in 1480 one of Isabella, fiancée of Francesco Gonzaga; and in 1485, Beatrice, fiancée of Lodovico il Moro.

In 1475 he painted for Ercole d'Este a *Madonna and Child with Saints* to be placed in a carved ancona; between 1477 and 1481 he executed three panels with allegorical figures of female nudes, and received payment for these and other works in 1483. According to a contemporary chronicle, Tura died in Ferrara in 1495.

Few documented works by Tura exist and the extensive works mentioned in the records are all lost. The two panels for the organ doors referred to above as being in the Opera del Duomo, Ferrara, depict the *Annunciation* and *St. George and the Dragon.* Works by his hand are to be found in a number of museums and private collections. In them his style can be studied, a lapidary style, reflecting a positive passion for defining the substance of things, as hard and sharp as diamond or basalt, rendered in a design of extraordinary fantasy and imaginative power.

BIBLIOGRAPHY: Berenson, North Italian Painters. — *Catalogo della Esposizione della pitt. ferrarese del Rinascimento.* Ferrara, 1933.—Roberto Longhi, *Officina Ferrarese,* 1936.

**TURKISH ART.**—See Moslem Art.

**TURNER (Joseph Mallord William).**—English painter (1775-1851)

TURNER (J.).

was born in a dark little house in a narrow street of old London, in a neighbourhood of monotonous dingy houses. At fifteen he exhibited in the Academy; at eighteen engravings were done after his designs; at twenty he was known; at twenty-seven he was a member of the Academy. He first earned money by doing little clear precise views of English country or castles, and in so doing, he travelled about a large part of England. It is said that during one of these wanderings, he had a love affair, and that he was so much hurt and saddened by its result, that he determined never to marry. In 1808 he was appointed Professor of Perspective. His father then gave up his trade as barber, and came to live with him. For economy's sake he always refused to have a proper studio, and lived in a miserable lodging, receiving nobody, and often bringing home his meals in paper bags. His energy was boundless. Every morning he got up at six, shut his door, and worked till evening, always with the same regularity. He was one of the most original characters of our time. He was far from being as refined as his pictures would lead one to expect; he was clumsy, heavy, uncultivated and prosaic, with a thick-set figure, wide shoulders, and prominent muscles. He was economical to the point of avarice, silent, reserved and unapproachable. It was at Chelsea in a little furnished room, more miserable than the one in which he was born, that he died. He left a great number of pictures, and several thousands of pounds. He left to the country, three hundred and sixty-two oil paintings, and nineteen thousand drawings, and two thousand pounds to the Academy, stipulating that his two best pictures should be hung in the National Gallery between two by Claude Lorrain; a thousand pounds for the purpose of erecting a monument in St. Paul's, where he lies beside Reynolds.

TURNER: BURIAL OF SIR DAVID WILKIE. (National Gallery, London.)

Turner's life is generally divided into three parts; his beginnings; then the time when he was inspired by Claude Lorrain, and finally the time when he really expressed himself. In the first period he was obviously influenced by the Dutch and by Wilson; during the second (that is, up to 1819) he was obsessed by the genius of Claude Lorrain, and the two pictures he wished to be hung beside Claude's, were *The Sun Rising in Mist* (1807) and the *Foundation of Carthage* (1815). One of the most characteristic works of this time is *Dido building Carthage.* The colour of this is splendid, though a little heavy; otherwise the works of this period are rather chaotic and confused. He had not yet harmonized purely classical ideas of design, and the modern conception and treatment of atmosphere. In Italy (1819), his point of view was profoundly changed, so that he was able to say on his return "Now I am going to begin to be Turner." He aimed at rendering atmospheric effects of misty scenes; then, when these everlasting greys had finally exasperated him, he went to sunny countries to try to attain his ideal of suggesting light. Typical subjects

TURNER: THE "TÉMÉRAIRE." (National Gallery, London.)

painted at this time, and showing a new aspect of his genius, are ships in a warm haze, or the sun shining through mist and making everything glow with golden light, etc. Soon his composition became freer and more facile. He was entirely concerned with light, which suffuses his scenes, so that the reality of objects is absorbed in the warm, colourful calm or tragic brightness. At this time when he was fully expressing his own personality, many of his earlier admirers left him. The fate of all innovators overtook him; his work provoked hostility, and it was even rumoured that Turner had gone mad.

In 1872, a Doctor Liebreich stated in an article the medical explanation of the morbid affection from which the great painter suffered. Scornful amusement greeted the exhibition of a picture he had just given to the Pinakotek of Munich. Typical pictures of this period are, *Gulf of Baia* (1823), and *Ulysses and Polyphemus* (1829). Little by little, however, a few people were won back to admiration of his painting, and during the last twenty years of his life he studied more and more ardently, light and colour, producing extraordinary compositions in which form is indicated only by the often vague melting shapes of shadow and colour, sometimes subtle, in shade, though sometimes striking and brilliant, but always caused by the iridescence of the solar prism. Examples of this tendency are: *Rain, Steam and Speed* (1844), or the *Approach to Venice* (1843). Some of Turner's best work belongs to this period, notably the *Childe-Harold's Pilgrimage*; and *The Fighting Temeraire; Storm at Sea; Venetian Sun; Apollo Victorious; Castle Kilgarren; Guildhall Banquet.*

Turner was very well read and knew contemporary poetry; he illustrated a great many well-known works. Turner had no pupils, no school, no imitators, but he invented, or at least foresaw, that particular technique by the use of which, the first Impressionists founded a new school. Turner must be accounted one of the most original of artists who freed art from the principles of the Renaissance.

See Pl. 58, Vol. II.

Bibliography: Sir Walter Armstrong, *Turner,* 1902.—Muther, *Painting in the Nineteenth Century.*

**TWACHTMAN (John Henry).**—American painter (1853-1902). He was born 4th August 1853 at Cincinnati, Ohio. His German father painted floral designs on window shades and he began his art career working at that profession. Evenings he went to the Mechanical Institute and after a while to the Cincinnati School of Design, where he studied with Frank Duveneck. In 1876 these two, Duveneck and Twachtman, went abroad to study at Munich. There they worked under Ludwig Loefftz for two years, absorbing the characteristic dark brown tonality practised by that school. At that time Twachtman returned to the United States to paint in New York and Cincinnati, but the following year he went back to Europe and joined Duveneck and Chase in Venice. He made other trips to Europe with his wife in 1881, travelling in England, Holland, and Germany and again in 1883, when he stayed for two years in Paris, working at the Académie Julian under Boulanger and Lefebvre. When he returned to the United States he could find no employment except as caretaker for his father-in-law's farm. Soon, however, he went to Chicago to paint some of the sky for a cyclorama of the Battle of Gettysburg. After that Twachtman moved his family to Branchville, Connecticut. He grew absorbed in his study of the waterfront at Bridgeport nearby and made some delightful etchings of it. About 1890 he purchased a large farm at Greenwich, where his last years were spent. He had summer classes at Newport and in the winter taught at Cooper Union Institute and the Art Students' League. He was one of the founders of the "Ten American Painters," whose members were DeCamp, Benson, Dewing, Hassam, Metcalf, Reid, Simmons, Tarbell and Weir. He spent a few summers at Gloucester and there he died 8th August 1902. His first work was done under the strong influence of the Munich school, but gradually he was able to break away toward the lighter tones used by the French Impressionists. His subjects were generally secluded bits of woodland often done in winter so he might use blue shadows on the snow, as in the *Hemlock Pool,* where the ice on the margin of the water stands out against the drab tones of the winter landscape. Examples of his work are to be found in museums in Andover, Cincinnati, Providence and Washington.

Bibliography: Eliot C. Clark, *John Twachtman,* American Artists Series, 1924.—Allen Tucker, *John H. Twachtman,* American Artists Series, 1931.—For other articles see *The Index of Twentieth Century Artists* for March, 1935.

Tympanum: Abbey of Charlieu, Loire.

**TYMPANUM.**—The space inclosed by an arch and a lintel, as over a doorway or the center of a pediment; frequently decorated with painting, sculpture, or mosaic.

# U

**UCCELLO (Paolo di Dono).**—Florentine painter, born probably in 1397; died 1475.

Uccello is first mentioned as one of Ghiberti's helpers in the execution of the second doors of the Baptistery, Florence (Vasari-Milanese, II, p. 256). In 1425 he files a testament, in which he states that he is the owner of a house (Gaye, I, 147). His name is mentioned in the cadastral registers of Florence in 1427, 1430, 1433, 1434, 1442, and 1446, but he was not continuously in Florence during this time. In 1427 his wife makes a declaration that he had left for Venice two years before; and in 1432 the directors of the works on the Duomo of Florence write to the representatives of the Republic of Venice asking concerning the artistic merits of Paolo di Dono who had executed mosaics on the façade of S. Pietro in Venice (Poggi, *Italienische Forschungen,* II, 1909, No. 773). He had already left this work to undertake mosaics in S. Marco (Gaye). In 1434 the operai of the Duomo write to him in Venice, asking him to order stained glass, and promising him work if he will return to Florence. His equestrian fresco of *John Hawkwood* in the Duomo of Florence was finished in 1436, having been done over for the second time because the first version did not prove satisfactory. The repainting occupied Paolo from the 6th of July to the 31st of August of this year. In 1443 Uccello was working on windows for the Cathedral, where he executed a *Resurrection, Ascension, Nativity,* and *Annunciation.* The existing Resurrection window is certainly by him (Poggi, op. cit., nos. 746, 747, 749, 750, 754, 761, 770). In 1451 he estimates the value of a tabernacle painted by Stefano d'Antonio for the Church of Sta. Maria a Montici; in 1452 a figure of the *Blessed Andrea Corsini* for the Cathedral Library. In 1465 Uccello is mentioned in Urbino (Calzini, 1899, p. 143); and in 1467-68 he executes in Urbino an altarpiece for the Confraternity of Corpus Christi (Pungileoni, 1822, p. 75). A year later, in 1469, he declares himself seventy-three years old, and feeble, incapable of work. He died in 1475.

Uccello's works are few in number, but of the highest possible importance for Florentine painting of the quattrocento. In Florence, Uffizi, is one of his three extant battle pieces, the *Battle of San Romano*; in the Duomo, on the wall above the entrance, four heads of Prophets, and to one side, the Hawkwood equestrian; also the Resurrection window. In Sta. Maria Novella, in the Cloister, are his ruined frescoes of the *Flood,* the *Sacrifice of Noah, Creation of Adam, Creation of the Animals,* and *Creation and Temptation of Eve.* In London, the second *Battle of S. Romano*; in Oxford, the Ashmolean Museum, *A Hunt;* in Paris, Louvre, five portraits, *Giotto, Uccello, Donatello, Brunelleschi* and *Antonio Manetti*; and the third *Battle of San Romano.* In Urbino is the predella-series of the *Miracle of the Host* (1467-68).

Bibliography: Vasari-Milanesi.—Gaye, *Carteggio.*—Poggi, *Il Duomo di Firenze.*—Calzini, *Urbino e i suoi monumenti.*—Crowe and Cavalcaselle, *History of Painting in Italy,* 1903-14, vol. 4.—Van Marle, *Development of Italian schools of painting,* 1928, vol. 10.—P. Soupault, *Paolo Uccello,* 1929.

**UDEN (Lucas van).**—Flemish painter, 1595-1672. Pupil and collaborator of Rubens. His work so closely resembles that of this master that it is difficult to distinguish one from the other. He also painted some pleasing little pictures in the style of "Velvet" Breughel.

**UFFIZI PALACE.**—See Florence.

**UGO da CARPI.**—Italian engraver, 16th century, who seems to have popularized in Italy the process of wood engraving in cameo, by means of two or more plates.

One of his earliest attempts was *Hercules and Antæus,* after Raphael, made from two plates. It was so successful that it occurred to him to experiment with three and even four plates, e.g. *Aeneas and Anchises* (1518), after Raphael; and the *Miraculous Draught of Fishes.*

Bibliography: Gualandi, *Ugo da Carpi.* Bologna, 1854.—L. Rosenthal, *La gravure.* Paris, 1909.

**UGOLINO di NERI da SIENA.**—Sienese trecento painter, a pupil of Duccio, for whom no dates or documents are available. An altarpiece for Sta. Croce, the inscription on which was seen by Padre delle Valle, is his authentic work. It originally consisted of a *Madonna and Child,* three half-length *Saints* in either wing, seven predella panels, four half-length *Saints* above and seven others in the pinnacles. The central piece which bore the inscription has disappeared. The other panels are distributed as follows: Berlin, three figures of *Saints* which formed the left wing, *SS. Peter, Paul and John Baptist;* and the *Flagellation* and *Entombment* from the predella; London, National Gallery, the *Betrayal of Judas* and the *Calvary* from the predella. Three other scenes were some years ago in private hands in England.

Also attributed to Ugolino are a polyptych in Brolio, Chianti; a *Madonna between Saints* in the Academy, Siena; and an *Apostle* in the Lehman Collection, New York.

Bibliography: Vasari-Milanesi, I.—Crowe and Cavalcaselle.—F. M. Perkins, *Alcuni appunti sulla Galleria delle Belle Arti di Siena,* Rassegna d'Arte Senese, 1908.—G. De Nicola, *Ugolino e Simone a San Casciano,* L'Arte, 1916, p. 13.—Van Marle, *Italian Schools, etc.,* II, 1924.

**— di VIERI.**—Sienese goldsmith, 14th century, whose principal work is the silver reliquary of Orvieto Cathedral, decorated on the back and front with translucent enamels (1338).

**UHDE (Fritz von).**—Contemporary German painter, belonging to the Neo-religious school of which Gebhardt was the leader (about 1880).

Until 1877, Uhde was an officer then he went to Holland, where there awoke in him a tenderness for humble folk, and he began to paint incidents from sacred history in the everyday dress of his contemporaries, just as Rembrandt and the Primitives had done before him. His influence was considerable, even abroad. His chief works are: *Christ among the Peasants, Holy Night; The Sermon on the Mount.* (They are in the Museum of Frankfort).

Bibliography: H. Rosenhagen, *Uhde: des Meisters Gemälde in Abbildungen,* 1908.

**ULM (Germany).**—The *Cathedral* of Ulm is the largest Cathedral in Germany, after Cologne. It dates from the 14th and 16th centuries, but was not finished until the 19th century. It contains a high-altar, painted in 1521 by Martin Schaffner, and the portrait of Eitel Besserer, also by Schaffner.

See Pl. 49, Vol. I.

**UMBRIA (School of).**—See Pl. 13, Vol. II.

**URANA.**—See Laurana (Luciano da).

**URBANIA.**—See Majolica.

**URBANO da CORTONA.**—Italian sculptor of the 15th century. Assistant of Donatello in Padua, he spread his influence to Siena and Perugia; but Urbano's work is heavy and ungraceful. His principal works in Siena are the tomb of Cristoforo Felice in San Francesco, and a symbolical *Angel* and a *St. Bernard Surrounded by Angels,* in the Museo dell'Opera.

Bibliography: Schubring, *Die Plastik Sienas in Quattrocento.* Berlin, 1907.

**URBINO (Italy).**—Small town, very flourishing in the 15th century under the rule of the Montefeltre; who drew the best artists to their court. It was they who ordered Luciano del Laurana to build the *Ducal Palace* in 1468—an original edifice, of irregular charm. The doors and windows were decorated with sculptures by D. Roselli, Ambrogio da Milano, etc.

The Ducal Palace contains fine paintings by Piero della Francesca (*The Flagellation*), Baroccio (*Martyrdom of St. Sebastian*), Timoteo Viti, and others.

**URN.**—In ancient times, urns were vessels in which the ashes of the dead were placed. These vessels were of various shapes—egg-shaped, round, with or without handles, and often mounted on a foot.

The Etruscans often used sculptured urns, evoking the idea of a miniature tomb.

Urbino: Ducal Palace.

Christianity, by forbidding the cremation of the dead, almost suppressed the use of urns. They were rarely used in the Middle Ages. (There is one, in the Cluny Museum, which was intended for the heart of St. Hughes.) The Renaissance revived the use of urns: some were used to contain the heart of a king (e.g. urn of Francis I in St. Denis) or other famous person; others were used as motifs of decoration in architecture, or tomb sculpture.

Ussé (Indre-et-Loire): The Château.

**USSÉ (Indre-et-Loire, France).**—Splendid château, built 1522 to 1538. The buildings occupy three sides of a square courtyard. The sides which open on to this courtyard are pierced with pretty windows, both pediments and balconies. On the exterior side, however, the strong walls are protected with machicolated towers.

See Pl. 27, Vol. II.

**UTAMARO (Kitagawa).**—Japanese painter and print master. His real name was Yusuké, and he was born in Kwagoye, in the province of Musachi, in 1754, but, when he was very young, he went to Yedo, where he became the pupil of Toriyama Sekiyen. About 1776, he left Sekiyen's studio, and worked chiefly at engraving. His first productions lack individuality, and show, in turn, the influence of Shunsho, Masanobu, Harunobu, and especially of Kiyonaga, whose influence may be traced in several engravings, such as those representing the comic dances of the Niwaka, the procession of the King of Korea, a young prince lying on a terrace, and two crouching women, the one in the background in a white dress, and the one in the foreground in a transparent black dress, with a red undergarment showing through.

The artist soon became successful, and from 1785 he was surrounded by a group of pupils. His forms became elongated in face and figure. By 1790, his style was practically formed, and he soon reached the height of his ability. In spite of the exaggerated proportion of his figures, he retained something of Kiyonaga's feeling for graceful and appropriate line, but the suppleness of his drawing sometimes degenerates into virtuosity and distortion. His engravings show a study of facial expression, and of nature.

Utamaro's colour is always subtle, but he rarely attains to the sumptuous decorative effects of Kiyonaga. He is chiefly distinguished for his delicate tones, for the value of his beautiful blacks, and for his effects of transparence.

He painted some charming scenes of motherhood, of courtesans writing or playing, of women weaving, cooking, bathing, etc. He painted larger compositions of walks on the banks of the Sumida, of the Kiogoku bridge, etc. These works, which are, rather unjustly, more celebrated in Europe than are the works of his best period, unfortunately became more and more exaggerated.

About 1880-1801, Utamaro, pressed by commissions, fell into mannerism—his drawing became feebler, and his types of figures inexpressive, and sometimes, in their elongation, untrue to life. But it must be remembered that Utamaro played only a small part in the enormous output of his studio.

See Pls. 12, 40, Vol. I.

Bibliography: Goncourt (E. de), *Outamaro, le peintre des Maisons Vertes.* Paris, 1891.—Kurth (Dr. Julius), *Utamaro.* Leipzig, 1907.

Utamaro: Women on the great bridge of the Sumida on a summer evening.

**UTILE da FAENZA (Giovanni Battista).**—Florentine painter, active until 1515 and very prolific; follower of Ghirlandaio and Verrocchio.

**UTRECHT (Holland).**—*Cathedral,* 1251-1267. A Dutch Gothic church in brick, bare internally. The interior whitewash was applied in the 17th century because of Protestant dislike of ornamental display. The nave is rebuilt, having fallen in 1674.

**UYTEWAEL (Joachim Antionisz, sometimes called Wttewael).** Dutch painter of Utrecht, 1566-1638. A follower of Goltzius, he is one of the leading Dutch mannerists. After having travelled two years in Italy and two in France, he settled in Utrecht in 1592. He is known especially for the historical and mythological paintings which are to be found in most leading museums. There is a *Self-Portrait* in Utrecht, representing himself with the affected virtuosity so common in portrait painting of that time.

# V

**VAENIUS or VAN VEEN (Otto).**—Flemish painter, born at Leyden, 1556. Died 1629. A popular court painter, his painting is devoid of great power and originality but it is luminous and pleasant. His pictures are of less importance than is the fact that at one time he taught Rubens.

The following will serve as examples of his many works: *The Calling of St. Matthew* (Antwerp); *The Raising of Lazarus* (St. Bavon, Ghent); and the *Life of the Virgin* (Schleissheim), in fifteen pictures.

See Pl. 24, Vol. II.

**VALDÉS LEAL (Juan de).**—Spanish painter (1630-1691). He was born at Seville as proven by Romero de Torres. He studied his art at the studio of Antonio del Castillo.

VALDÉS LEAL: THE SPOILS OF LIFE. (Hospital of Charity, Seville.)

"His temperamental character is responsible for his works, full of gripping passion—something uncommon for Seville. Remarkable is his realism. His tremendous gift as a colourist is revealed in many canvasses—veritable colour symphonies of deepest glow and greatest beauty. Without doubt, he is the greatest colourist of 17th century Spain." (Mayer.)

Soon, as in the *Assumption* (of the National Gallery), the *Immaculate Conception* (Seville Gallery), *The Virgin of the Goldsmiths* (Cordova Museum), he shows definitely that he was inspired by Murillo. He sometimes indulged in a gruesome realism often bordering on violence and horror. Valdés Leal's output was considerable. His first works (now in Cordova) are simpler and more vigorous, and their colour recalls the earlier work of Velázquez. Examples are: *Portrait of D. Enrique de Alfaro* (his brother) and a *Saint Andrew.*

It was in Seville that he left his chief paintings. Many churches and chapels contain pictures by him.

When D. Miguel de Mañara founded the Hospice of the Caridad, he gave the decoration of it to Murillo and Valdés Leal. Besides the *Exaltation of the Cross,* of which there is a sketch in the palace of San Telmo, in Seville, Valdés Leal did for the crypt two pictures on which, with a mixture of mysticism and ruthless realism, he expressed the fatality of death, and the nothingness of earthly greatness. (Their titles are: *The Spoils of Life,* and *Two Corpses Gnawed by Worms.*) In the Cathedral of Seville is a *Flagellation,* and *St. Ildefonso Receiving the Host.* In 1671 he was appointed to superintend all the Cathedral decoration.

In 1682, after the death of Murillo, Valdés Leal was considered the best painter of Andalusia. In 1690, while doing several compositions intended for the Church of *Los Venerables,* he became paralysed. His son no doubt finished his father's compositions alone, for in 1691, Valdés Leal died.

In the provincial Museum of Seville, his most striking pictures are to be found, notably: *The Baptism of St. Jerome; The Temptation of St. Jerome;* and *St. Jerome Flagellated by Angels.* In the Prado, where he is not well represented are only the *Presentation of the Virgin in the Temple,* and *Christ Disputing with the Doctors.*

BIBLIOGRAPHY: A. de Beruete y Moret, *Valdés Leal,* Madrid, 1911. —E. Romero de Torres, *Documentos inéditos* in *Museum* (Barcelona), 1911.—J. Gestoso Pérez, *Juan de Valdés Leal,* Seville, 1916.—A. L. Mayer, *Gesch. der span. Malerei* 2nd ed., 1922.—*Enc. un. il. europ. am.,* Vol. LXVI; Barcelona (Espasa) 1929.—Art. *Valdés Leal, Juan.* Exhibitions: *Catálogo exposición J. Valdés Leal,* Cordoba, 1916.—*Catálogo expos. Valdés Leal y de arte retrospectiro,* Seville, 1923.

**VALENTIN (Jean de Boullongne; known as Le).**—French painter, 1600-1634. He was most strongly influenced by the example of Caravaggio's art. His realistic instinct caused him to search out strong effects of light and shade, at the expense of unity. His *Suzanna* and his *Judgment of Solomon* (Louvre) are very ill-composed; but the powerful modelling of the old men, in the semi-darkness, the lighting of a sleeve, and the brutal gesture of the guard who restrains the aged accuser are admirable.

VALENTIN (LE): THE CONCERT. (Louvre.)

The most characteristic part of Valentin's work are his Smoking Room scenes, which he turns into scenes of musical festivity (e.g. the *Family Concerts,* in the Louvre).

At a time when, with Poussin, idea and sentiment meant so much in French painting, the case of Valentin is an anomaly. He cared nothing for pure and noble forms. Everything in nature interested him equally. He is the first French painter for whom the value of the work resides largely in beauty of execution.

**— (Simon François).**—French painter, 1606-1671. He knew Guido Reni in Italy, and was influenced by him. He painted chiefly religious pictures, which are monotonous and cold.

**VALKENBORCH (Frederik van).**—Flemish painter, about 1570-1623, son of Lukas (below), but less talented.

**— (Lukas van).**—Flemish painter, 1540-1625(?). Exiled in Frankfurt a. M. and Nürnberg as he was a Protestant. He painted landscapes, which recall Patenir; and "genre" scenes, reminiscent of Breughel, such as *Winter Landscape* (Vienna) and the *Village Inn.*

**— (Martin van).**—Flemish painter, about 1542-1604, brother of Lukas (above). Travelled to Venice and Rome, painted landscapes and "genre" scenes and experimented with "bird's-eye" perspective.

**VAN CLEVE (Corneille).**—French sculptor, 1645-1732. Pupil of François Anguier. He made the large marble group representing the *Loire and the Loiret,* which is in the Jardin des Tuileries. His work at Versailles was considerable (e.g. the High Altar in the Chapel).

BIBLIOGRAPHY: Stanislas Lami, *Dictionnaire des sculpteurs français,* Vol. II.

**VAN DER BECKE (Joos).**—See Cleve.

**VAN DER GOES (Hugo).**—See Goes.

**VAN DER HELST.**—See Helst.

**VANDERLYN (John).**—Early American painter (1776-1852). He was born in Kingston, New York, 15th October 1776, and at the age of sixteen entered the employ of Thomas Barton, an English importer of engravings, in New York City. In the evenings he received some instruction from Archibald Robertson at the Columbian Academy. With the patronage of Aaron Burr he was enabled to go to Philadelphia to study some months under Gilbert Stuart. Burr also financed his trip to France in 1796 and there he worked in Paris under Vincent for the next five years. From 1801 to 1803 he was in the United States, where he did for the second time portraits of Aaron Burr and his daughter Theodosia, and he also made a trip to Niagara Falls to record his impression of that great natural wonder. In 1803 he sailed again to Europe, passing some time in London before going on to Paris. Two years later with Washington Allston he visited Rome and there was much impressed by the classical ruins. While under that influence he painted *Marius Amid the Ruins of Carthage,* which received a medal at the Paris Salon of 1808 with the personal commendation of the Emperor. Four years later his *Ariadne* was displayed in the Salon, a nude study which won acclaim and is one of the few painted by an American artist at that early period. Vanderlyn was famous for his work and able to help his old patron Burr when the latter fled in poverty to France. In 1815 Vanderlyn returned to the United States and there in New York set up a Rotunda in City Hall Park to show panoramas of Paris, Athens, Versailles and Geneva as well as battle scenes of Lodi, Waterloo and the siege of Paris. It was not a financial success and he soon retired to his old home at Kingston, where he spent the rest of his life. He had but few portrait commissions because of the slowness of his methods but in 1842 he was commissioned by Congress to paint a panel in the United States Capitol. For this space he created *The Landing of Columbus,* but left the execution to his young assistants so that it bears but little resemblance to his youthful work. While his work was academic and in the case of the *Marius* closely allied to the pictures by Gerard David, it was solid and firm in construction and a faithful representation of his interpretation of the facts. He died in poverty in Kingston 23d September 1852.

BIBLIOGRAPHY: Charles Henry Hart, *Portrait of Abraham Hasbrouck Painted by John Vanderlyn,* Art in America, Vol. 5, 1917, pp. 105-110.—Frank Hayward Severance, *John Vanderlyn's Visit to Niagara Falls in 1802,* Buffalo Historical Society Publications, Vol. 15, 1911, pp. 159-173.—John Edwin Stillwell, *The History of the Burr Portraits,* 1928. —*Vanderlyn,* Art Digest, Vol. 4, January 1, 1930, p. 8.

**VAN DYCK (Anthony).**—Born in Antwerp, 22nd March 1599. He received an excellent education, and learned several languages. He possessed a lively, amiable character; the grace and charm of his manners exercised a great attraction

VAN DYCK: THE VIRGIN OF SORROWS. (Prado, Madrid.)

on everyone he met. In 1609, he joined Van Balen's studio, which he left in 1612, and entered that of Rubens about 1617, whose favoured pupil he soon became. At the age of twenty, he was already famous and, some say, almost as much admired as Rubens. The two artists often worked together, and Rubens' influence on the younger painter was considerable. About the end of 1620, Van Dyck, by the wish of Charles I, was invited to settle in England. He spent three months there, during which time he executed numerous portraits, and then he took eight months' leave to visit Italy. He returned to Antwerp in 1622, and left the following year for Italy, where he stayed until 1627. He then returned to his native town; and, in 1632, settled in London as painter-in-ordinary to the king. He lived luxuriously and entertained lavishly. He was much sought after by the highest society. Commissions poured in upon him from all sides, and he executed them with astounding rapidity. About 1640, the artist married a young girl of noble family, Mary Ruthven. Worn out by overwork and fatigue, he died in December 1641, and was buried in the old Church of St. Paul's.

Despite the influence of Rubens, Van Dyck kept his originality. The career of this brilliantly gifted painter was a continuous transformation and ascension. Van Dyck's dreamy, tender genius reveals itself in religious themes. He loved to paint melancholy figures of weeping saints and martyrs; and he soon used warm, deep colours, instead of the brighter colours he had favoured when studying the Italian masters. It was, however, chiefly as a portrait painter that Van Dyck displayed all the resources of his rich colour; he ended by devoting himself exclusively to this branch of art. His innate refinement and nobility impelled him to bring out the moral grandeur and physical distinction of his models; but he idealised them only to an extent compatible with truth.

An indefatigable worker, endowed with astonishing fecundity, Van Dyck left a great many pictures that are impossible to enumerate. The earliest work we possess by him is a *Portrait of an Old Man* (1613). From 1617 to 1621, date two heads of *St. John* (Berlin Museum); a *Christ Carrying the Cross*, some heads of apostles (Munich); a *Drunken Silenus* (Brussels), and the *Martyrdom of St. Peter* (Brussels), both powerful, but rather crude.

From about 1620 dates his famous picture of *St. Martin Dividing His Cloak* (in the Church of Saventhem), which betrays various influences. The beggar crouching in the road is in the manner of Rubens; another, with a piece of linen tied round his head, recalls Raphael; while the figure of the saint himself is inspired by one of Titian's pictures which Van Dyck copied, and which we find in his sketch-book, belonging to the Duke of Devonshire.

The town of Genoa possesses some fifty portraits which Van Dyck executed there between 1621 and 1624—a whole series of ladies, nobles and warriors; e.g. *Lady Seated* (Palazzo Durazzo). A fine portrait of *Cardinal Bentivoglio* is in the Pitti Palace, Florence. From 1624, date some religious pictures which show the influence of the Italian masters, especially of the Venetians—two *Holy Families* (Palazzo Balbi Piovera); *Holy Family* (Turin); *Martyrdom of St. Lawrence* (Venice, Santa Maria dell'Orto); *Entombment* (Borghese Palace, Rome), etc.

In 1627, Van Dyck was back in Antwerp. After the "Italian period," comes the "Flemish period," during which he painted chiefly religious pictures. They are not among his best works, although owing to their sentiment of tender devotion they excited great admiration in his own day. . . . In the many portraits he executed at this period, we see a modification of his style. The colours are still warm, but less glowing and more restrained than in his Italian works. The modelling becomes more precise. Among these admirable portraits may be mentioned those of *Cornelis van der Geest*, Rubens' great friend, in the National Gallery; *Portrait of Henry, Count de Bergh* (Prado); an exquisite *Young Lady* (Antwerp); a happy group of *Frans Snyders and His Family* (Hermitage), and another portrait of *Snyders and his Wife* (Cassel). Some mythological pictures complete the series of works of the Flemish period—e.g. *Danaë* (Dresden). Then there is a fine series of twenty-three etchings (Louvre), representing famous people of his day—artists, poets, writers.

Attractive as Van Dyck's work had been, it had not yet reached its highest development. It was during the English period, from 1632 until his death, that he did his finest work. In these twelve years he painted about three hundred and fifty portraits—including thirty-eight of *King Charles I*; thirty-five of *Queen Henrietta Maria*; and many of their children. One of the most famous is *Charles I in Hunting Attire* (Louvre), painted in 1635, which reveals so perfectly the dignity and elegance of the king. Among so many masterpieces, only a few can be mentioned: *Lord Digby and Lord William* (Spencer Althorp Collection); the poet *Carew* (Windsor); some delightful groups of the children of Charles I, the best of which is certainly that of the Turin Museum (painted in 1636); *Lords John and Bernard Stuart* (1638—Cobham Hall); *William of Orange and His Betrothed,* which is exquisitely delicate in sentiment and handling (Amsterdam).

Sir Anthony van Dyck founded, in London, a kind of Corporation of Painters, not unlike the Flemish Guilds. Besides the Flemish painters whom he employed in his studio to work on the backgrounds of his pictures, he soon had many English imitators who maintained his tradition until his true successors appeared in the persons of Reynolds and Gainsborough.

See Pl. 35, Vol. II.

BIBLIOGRAPHY: Sir Lionel Cust, *Anthony van Dyck*. London, 1900.—E. Schaeffer, *Van Dyck,* Klassiker der Kunst, Vol. XIII, 1909.

**VAN EYCK.**—Family of Flemish painters. The brothers Van Eyck came originally from Maaseyck.

**Hubert van Eyck** was probably born about 1366, and he died in 1426. There are several extant documents of 1425, 1426 regarding payments for paintings; little else is known about his life.

**Jan van Eyck** (1380-1441).—Together with Hubert, he was the founder of Flemish panel painting. Born around 1390, died in 1441. After working between 1422 to 1425, for the Duke of Bavaria, he entered the service of Philip the Good, Duke of Burgundy, as painter and valet de chambre. In 1426 and 1427 he lived in Lille, and afterwards made various journeys, and went on

JAN VAN EYCK. (His portrait after Vasari.)

a secret mission. In 1428, he took part in an embassy to Portugal, to paint the portrait of the Infanta Isabella whom his master sought in marriage. On his return in 1429 he settled in Bruges, and there enjoyed the highest esteem and admiration of his patron, the Duke of Burgundy.

The Van Eycks were not, as was long believed, the inventors of oil-painting. This method was already known in the 10th century, and is often mentioned in some contemporary writings. But nothing remains of the work of the artists who used it. It was left to the Van Eycks to renew this method entirely.

VAN EYCK (HUBERT AND JAN): JODOCUS VYDT AND HIS WIFE. (St. Bavon, Ghent.)

Of the authentic works of the Van Eycks, the *Altarpiece of Ghent* is one of the most important ones. (San Bavon, wings in Brussels and Berlin). It was started by Hubert, and was finished by Jan in 1432; it is impossible positively to divide the work of the two brothers. It is only known that Hubert, who worked at the altarpiece for many years, received the commission from Jodocus Vydt, that he conceived the whole composition, and painted the principal figures, while Jan did both sides of the wings. It was exhibited in the Church of St. Bavon on 6th May 1432.

The subject of this altarpiece is taken from the Apocalypse and from the Golden Legend, and is the *Glorification of the Mystic Lamb*, come down to earth for the redemption of mankind. On the closed altarpiece the artists painted, on the

VAN EYCK (HUBERT AND JAN): THE KNIGHTS OF CHRIST AND THE JUST JUDGES MARCHING TOWARD THE LAMB. (St. Bavon, Ghent.)

upper part, the *Annunciation*, the prophet *Zachariah* and the *Sibyl of Erythrea*, the *Cumean Sibyl*, and the prophet *Michael*, and, on the lower part, portraits of the donor

VAN EYCK (HUBERT AND JAN): MUSICAL ANGELS. (St. Bavon, Ghent.)

and his wife, and monochrome figures of *St. John the Baptist*, and *St. John the Evangelist*. "When the triptych is opened the effect is dazzling; the immense jewel is marvellously enamelled, and its ten compartments reveal the philosophy, and whole universe of a 15th century Christian."

The grandeur of the conception of this work is in no wise diminished by the realism and exactitude of the execution. In all these people we recognise the types of the worthy citizens of Bruges and Ghent. From the time it was exhibited, the picture of the Van Eycks was unceasingly admired and studied by painters, and for more than a century Flemish, Dutch, French and German artists flocked to see it.

The *Adoration of the Lamb* is the only signed work which can be attributed to Hubert van Eyck.

Jan van Eyck, on the contrary, is the undoubted author of several other masterpieces, authentic among which are *Portrait of a Young Man, "Tymotheos"* (London), signed and dated Oct. 10, 1432; *Madonna and Child,* 1433; *Portrait of an Older Man* (London), signed and dated 1433.

In 1434 he painted the famous picture of *Giovanni Arnolfini and His Wife* (National Gallery). The pair are standing in their room, hand in hand. The husband, dressed in a long, dark cloak edged with fur, and a high felt hat with a wide brim, looks in front of him, with his right hand slightly raised. His wife has a resemblance to Jan van Eyck's wife, and it has been supposed that they were sisters, but the resemblance is in a great measure due to the arrangement of the hair and head-dress. The picture has an intimate charm. The couple, full of quiet happiness, are painted in the midst of familiar objects, furniture, and well-polished brass. Behind them a convex mirror reflects part of the scene. Another very remarkable portrait by Jan van Eyck is *A Man with a Pink,* in the Berlin Gallery.

In 1436, Jan van Eyck finished one of his most famous religious pictures, the *Madonna with Child, St. Donatus, St. George and the Donor: Canon van der Paele* (Bruges), which was commissioned by George van der Paele, Canon of St. Donatus. In the apse of a Romanesque Church, the Virgin is seated under a dais. Kneeling on the left of the Virgin, robed in a white surplus, the Canon is holding an open missal, his spectacles and gloves. Van Eyck painted this old, wrinkled face, the two thin tufts of hair, the chin embedded in rings of flesh, and the pendulous cheeks, with relentless sincerity.

The *St. Barbara* (Antwerp), painted in 1437, is another celebrated work, no less important for being unfinished, for it shows us something of Jan van Eyck's method. The little panel depicts the saint seated, the ample folds of her dress filling most of the lower part of the picture. Behind her is a magnificent tower, on which a crowd of labourers are working.

One of the most charming and poetic of Jan van Eyck's works is the little *Virgin of the Fountain* (Antwerp), painted in 1439. The Madonna, dressed all in blue and holding the infant Jesus in her arms, stands by a copper fountain from which flow four jets of water. Behind her two angels are holding up a piece of rich brocade, which forms a carpet under the Madonna's feet.

In 1439, Van Eyck painted the portrait of his wife, *Margaret* (Bruges), a remarkable work, which reveals the face of a youngish woman, with a cold, vigilant expression, and thin, dry lips. It is the face of one who must have been a good, precise manager, and have ordered her household with more authority than softness. It is one of Van Eyck's finest portraits.

There are several other definitely known, and a list of merely presumed paintings, attributed to the master. In technique as well as in pictorial qualities the Van Eycks had a tremendous influence on all subsequent paintings. Not only did they develop oil technique to a hitherto unknown, and never surpassed perfection, but they were the first to paint real portraits, in three-quarter view reflecting the sitter's personality. They were also innovators in rendering light effects, and the appearance of objects at a distance.

See Pls. 9, 59, Vol. I.

Bibliography: Weale (James H.), *Hubert and John van Eyck: their life and work.* London, 1908.—Sir Martin Conway, *The Van Eycks and their Followers.* London, 1921.—M. J. Friedländer, *Altniederländische Malerei,* Vol. I.

**VANLOO or VAN LOO (The).** —French painters of Dutch origin.

Van Loo (Carle): Halt During the Hunt. (Louvre.)

The first known in France is *Jacques Van Loo* (1614-1670), painter of the Portrait of Michel Corneille père (Louvre), and *Italian Sunset.*

*Jeane-Baptiste* was grandson of Jacques; born in Aix, he died in Paris (1648-1745). His portrait of Louis XV, done from memory, made him known at court. He also painted the king's fiancée, Marie Leczinska, and her parents. On the strength of his *Diana and Endymion,* eleven years later, he was received as member of the Academy. As historical painter, he submitted to the mannered taste of the age, but his colour is not unpleasing, and he had decided skill in rendering flesh tints. His portraits are the most interesting part of his work. In London, where he went in 1736, he enjoyed extraordinary popularity, and did portraits of Colley Cibber, Sir Robert Walpole, and many others. He also painted some frescoes.

*Carle Van Loo* (1705-1765) was the younger brother of Jean-Baptiste. In his own time he was held in great repute, but to us today he seems only a mechanical improvisor. In his *Halt during a Hunt* (Louvre), however, he appears at his best. He was chiefly a decorative artist, like most other 18th century painters, and his production was inexhaustible, and his sketches sometimes brilliant. So completely did he reflect the mannerisms of his times, that during the First Empire, the word "vanlootage" was coined to express this kind of treatment. *Louis Michel* (1707-1771); son of Jean-Baptiste and nephew of Carle. He was the least ambitious of the Vanloo family, but the one who seems at the present time to have done the most interesting work. He was chiefly a portrait painter. His own Self-portrait in the Louvre is very well done. His contemporaries admired his skill in rendering materials, and also many of them expressed their liking for him as an unassuming and good-natured character. While in Spain, he painted Philip V and Elisabeth Farnese, whom he also portrayed among their children. A large picture by him in Versailles, shows him, near his sister, engaged in painting his father. He did many other portraits.

See Pl. 44, Vol. II.

*Charles-Philippe-Armédée,* third son of Jean-Baptiste (1715-1795?). He was painter to Frederick II, who employed him, with Pesne, to decorate his castles of Potsdam and Sans Souci. A facile executionist, designer of cartoons for tapestry, he continued in the tradition of artificial art which characterises the art of the Vanloo family. His work was apt to be devoid of interest except when he was dealing

Vanloo (J. B.): Louis XV. (Museum, Versailles.)

with reality, that is, in his case, the modelling in portraiture.

*Jules-César-Denis,* son of Carle (1743-1821) was a landscape painter, chiefly distinguished for his rendering of the effects of snow.

Bibliography: Daudré Bardon, *Carle Vanloo.* 1920.

**VAN LOO (Jakob).**—See above, Jacques Vanloo.

**VANNI (Andrea).**—Sienese painter, born c. 1332 (his father married in 1329).

From 1368 to 1380 he is mentioned repeatedly in the city government of Siena; in 1379 he was Capitano del Popolo. In 1372 he was sent as ambassador to the Papal Court at Avignon; in 1373 on a mission to Florence, and in 1383-85 as envoy to Naples, from whence he went to Sicily.

Fairly complete documentation exists as to his artistic activity: in 1353, with Bartolo di Fredi, he opens a workshop; in 1355 his name appears on the rolls of the painters' guild; in 1363 it is listed in the "Libro delle Capitudini dell' Arte." In 1370 he and Francesco Vanni, his brother, are paid for painting three chapels in the Cathedral at Siena, and for painting a façade near the Crocifisso Church and the vault of the dome (with Francesco da Venezia). In 1375 Andrea, while at Naples, was commissioned by Count Raimondo del Balzo with decorations in the Church of Castello di Casaluce, which are still extant. In 1376 he was again in Siena and four years later was paid for repainting a *Madonna and Child* on the façade of the Cathedral. In 1379 he executed a picture for the altar of St. Sebastian in S. Martino. In 1398 he receives a small sum for an *Annunciation;* and the next year is paid for painting the over doors of the Cathedral and decorations in the chapel of S. Giacomo Interciso inside the Cathedral. Cristofano Guidini, godfather of a son of Andrea, commissioned him to paint in this chapel a portrait of *S. Catherine* and scenes from the *Life of St. James.* In 1400 he received payment for the extant altar in S. Stefano, now in the sacristy. There is no document for Andrea's death; Milanesi puts it at 1414 without giving his reasons for arriving at the date.

The Casaluce frescoes of 1375 at Aversa, near Naples, and the 1400 S. Stefano polyptych are thus the only certain works of Andrea. His personality has been reconstructed around them.

Bibliography: Milanesi, *Doc. . . . senese,* I.—S. Borghesi e L. Banchi, *Nuovi doc. . . . senese,* 1898.—F. M. Perkins, *Andrea Vanni,* Burlington, 1903.—Van Marle, *Italian Schools,* II, 1924.

**— (Lippo).**—Sienese painter, follower of Simone Martini and the Lorenzetti.

The first document recorded for Lippo, of 1341, refers to his activity as a miniaturist. In 1344 he is called *miniatore,* and illuminates a liturgical book; the next year he is paid for miniatures which are those of Corale 4 in the Cathedral Library in Siena. From 1352 dates the *Coronation of the Virgin* in the Biccherna, entirely repainted in 1445 by Sano di Pietro. The old signature still exists, also the document of payment. Lippo is entered in the list of the guild of painters in 1355 and in 1358 signed the triptych in the Monastery of SS. Domenico e Sisto at Rome. In 1360 and 1373 he was a member of the Republican government. From 1372 date the fragments of frescoes in S. Domenico, Siena.

Lippo Vanni was a most prolific painter; many works are identified with his style.

Bibliography: Milanesi, *Doc . . . senese,* I.—Crowe and Cavalcaselle.—*Arte inedita in Siena,* p. 12.—Van Marle, *Simone Martini et les peintres de son école,* 1920; same author, *Italian Schools, etc.,* II, 1924.

**— (Turino).**—Pisan painter, second of two painters by that name; born Rigoli, near Pisa, in 1349; died 1438; deeply influenced by the school of Siena.

In 1330, 1392, and 1395, Turino is recorded as executing minor decorative work. A fragmentary inscription of a *Madonna, Fourteen Angels and Saints,* from S. Martino near Palermo, now in the Palermo Gallery, refers to him; and there is a signed and dated (1397) panel in the Church of S. Paolo a Ripa. The signed *Madonna* in the Pieve at Rigoli is considerably repainted. A *Madonna* in the Louvre (No. 1563) is also by Turino.

Bibliography: Crowe and Cavalcaselle, Douglas ed., III.—Van Marle, *Italian Schools,* V, 1925.

**VAN ORLEY (Bernard).**—See Orley.

**VANVITELLI (Luigi).**—Neapolitan architect, 1700-1773. He designed the Royal Palace, Caserta, in 1752; SS. Annunziata, Naples, 1757-82; and the clocks, St. Peter's, Rome.

**VAO (Lorenzo de).**—Spanish sculptor. In 1554, he made images of kings for the royal Chapel of Seville.

**VAPHIO (Golden Goblets of).**—See Mycenæ.

**VARLEY (John).** — English painter (1778-1842), chiefly noted for his watercolours: several of the most prominent English watercolour painters of the 19th century were taught by him.

**VAROTARI (Alessandro).**—See Padovanino.

**— (Dario).** — Veronese painter, 1539-1596. Father of Padovanino. He worked chiefly in Padua, and made some facile, graceful works, such as the altarpiece of San Barnaba, in Venice, and the *Visitation* in the Accademia.

**VASARI (Giorgio).**—Florentine biographer, architect, and painter (1511-1574). He is known chiefly for his *Lives of the Most Famous Architects, Painters, and Sculptors, etc.,* a work which is not only enormously useful for the student of Italian art and society but is in itself an historical landmark, earliest attempt in European culture to historicize, describe and appraise a whole school of artists.

Vasari drew upon earlier writings, such as the *Libro di Antonio Billi* and the *Codice Magliabecchiano* and personal accounts such as Ghiberti's *Commentarii,* adding to the information there furnished that which he himself could garner through personal investigation and a wide correspondence. If he occasionally gave to legend the same respect accorded sober fact, in doing so he merely reflected the tendency of his age, which thought more of glory than of historical accuracy.

The surprising thing about Vasari's *Lives* is not that they contain a huge number of errors but that there is so much in them that is true, and that has been substantiated by archivistic research. They still provide the framework upon which Italian art history is based.

In addition to Vasari's inevitable inaccuracy, it is necessary to discount his Florentine bias. Convinced as he was that the mainspring of Italian culture was Florence, he tended to give a Florentine origin to every important innovation, to claim for Florence every available masterpiece, and to minimize the gifts and quality of other schools.

This work (*Vite de' più eccellenti Architetti, Pittori e Scultori ecc.*) appeared first in 1550; then in 1568—a more complete edition, with engraved portraits by Cristofano Coriolano.

Some eighteen editions of Vasari have been published since 1568, of which the most valuable is that edited and annotated by Gaetano Milanesi (Florence, 1878-81). The most recent English edition is that of A. B. Hinds (London, 1927).

Vasari was himself a painter, but, as such, of no particular importance.

In his capacity as architect, he built the *Uffizi Palace,* in Florence (1560-1574).

Bibliography: R. W. Carden, *The Life of Giorgio Vasari.* 1910.

**VASCO FERNANDEZ.**—Portuguese painter. He died between 1541 and 1543. Pupil of Velasco. Vasco Fernandez is represented in the Sacristy of the Cathedral of Vizcu by four large altarpieces. The first is the famous *St. Peter*—a pope sitting on a wide Renaissance throne, before a gallery, through the arches of which one sees a wild landscape, with, on one side, the calling of the Fisherman, and on the other a group of *Domine, quo Vadis?*

Bibliography: V. Correia, *Vasco Fernandez, mastro do retábulo da sé de Lemego.* 1924.

**VASNETSOF (Victor).** — Born 1848, he was the best artist of the reign of Alexander III. An excellent historical painter, the *Stone-Age* is his finest work. About the same time, he executed certain cartoons for mosaics for the walls and ceiling of the Cathedral of Kazan, and his *Fathers of the Russian Church*—mural paintings of the Church of Saint Vladimir—show his talent as a religious painter. Nevertheless Vasnetsof was most at home in painting scenes from old Russian tales.

**VATICAN.**—In classical times, the part of Rome between the Mario hill and the Janiculus, was called Ager Vaticanus. There was built the Church of St. Peter, near which the Popes possessed, since the end of the 5th century, a modest dwelling. Soon the papal church and house were surrounded by many buildings, convents, churches, chapels and hospitals, which Leo IV encircled by walls and towers (9th century). The Popes lived in the Lateran until the seat of the Papacy was transferred to Avignon. Gregory IX, returning from Avignon, settled in the Vatican in 1377. In the middle of the 15th century, Nicholas V began to build a magnificent palace, for himself, his cardinals and retinue. At the time of his death, the building was almost finished; his successors completed and adorned it.

The buildings covered an enormous ground space, and contained over a thousand apartments. Bramante was the architect of the great Court of the Belvedere, with the huge exedra. Raphael designed the Loggia of the Vatican, and decorated it with the arabesque orna-

Vatican: The Library Fontana Gallery.

ment of the Baths of Caracalla. The most famous are those painted by Michelangelo and Raphael.

The *Sistine Chapel* was built between 1473 and 1481, in the time of Sixtus IV. It is adorned with fres-

Vatican: The Scala Regia, by Bernini.

coes, the most famous of which are those which Michelangelo painted on the ceiling, the pendentives and the altar wall. This—one of the world's most splendid decorative schemes—took him four years to paint (1508-1512). He represented the Creation; Temptation; Flood; Drunkenness of Noah; in the pendentives, the Prophets and Sibyls; on the altar wall the Last Judgment, etc. (See Michelangelo.)

The wall frescoes of the Sistine were painted between 1481 and 1483, under Sixtus IV, by the great Florentine and Umbrian artists, to whom the Popes and Cardinals had extended protection and given commissions. Botticelli painted *Moses before the Burning Bush; The Temptation,* etc. Perugino, *The Baptism; Christ Giving the Keys to St. Peter.* Cosimo Rosselli painted *Moses on Mount Sinai; The Golden Calf; The Sermon on the Mount,* etc.

Behind the Sistine Chapel is the *Royal Apartment;* the *Ducal Hall;* etc., most of which rooms are decorated or built by famous artists, architects and sculptors.

Like Michelangelo, Raphael is excellently represented in the Vatican. Julius II, wishing the reception rooms, or *Stanze,* to be decorated, gave the work to several Sienese or Umbrian artists, among them Perugino, who brought with him his young pupil, Raphael. The Pope was so much pleased with Raphael, that he finally gave him complete charge of the decoration. The following are some of Raphael's Vatican compositions:—(in Stanza della Segnatura; 1508-1511): *Parnassus; School of Athens;* (on the ceiling) *Theology, Poetry, Justice,* etc.; (in Stanza d'Eliodoro): *Heliodorus Chased out of the Temple; The Deliverance of St. Peter,* etc. The frescoes in some of the other apartments, were done by Raphael's pupils.

The *Chapel of Nicholas V* possesses frescoes by Fra Angelico, which depict stories of St. Lawrence and St. Stephen. They were painted with the assistance of Benozzo Gozzoli between 1447 and 1449.

The *Borgia* rooms were inhabited by Alexander VI Borgia and his family. Several of the rooms in this suite contain frescoes by Pintoricchio and his pupils. The Galleria degli Arazzi has a fine collection of tapestries for which Raphael did the cartoons (1515, 1516) representing scenes from the life of Christ and the Apostles. The Vatican has a very good picture gallery and a wonderful collection of antiques, the richest, perhaps, in the world. It was founded by Julius II, Leo X, Clement VII, and Paul III.

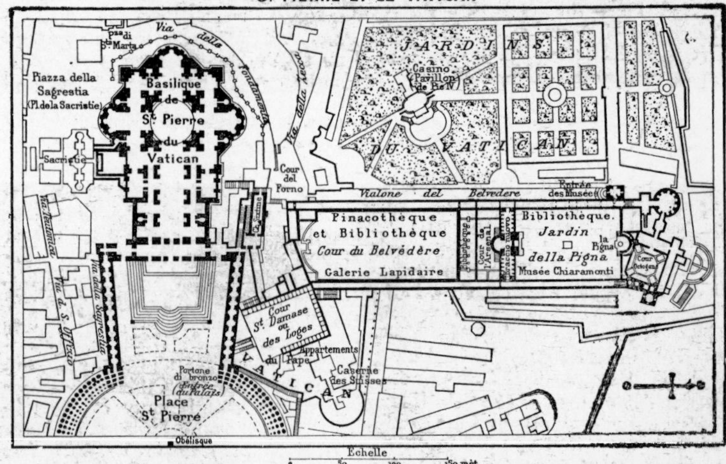


Plan of St. Peter's and the Vatican.

**VAULT.**—Arched structure, usually a ceiling or roof, built of masonry. A *barrel vault* is continuous. A *groined* or *cross vault* consists of two barrel vaults intersecting at right angles. A *ribbed vault*

# EUROPEAN ART IN THE NINETEENTH CENTURY

*Although the artistic schools may be conveniently limited within the frontiers of each state in the nineteenth century, there is an intimate connection between the arts of the great European countries. All passed from classicism to naturalism by way of a romantic phase. Yet one may recognise in each national school the faithfulness with which it preserves its historic traditions.*

H. DE BRAEKELEER: THE PRINTER OF ENGRAVINGS. MUSEUM OF ANTWERP.
*(Photo by Hermans.)*

A. STEVENS: THE LOVE LYRIC. MUSÉE DU LUXEMBOURG.
*(Photo by Neurdein.)*

MEUNIER: THE LABORER. MUSÉE DU LUXEMBOURG.
*(Photo by Hachette.)*

CONSTANTIN MEUNIER: INDUSTRY. MUSÉE DU LUXEMBOURG.
*(Photo by Hachette.)*

MESDAG: THE BEACH. RIJKSMUSEUM, AMSTERDAM.
*(Photo by Abrahamson.)*

JONGKIND: MARINE.

JOSEPH ISRAELS: THE BRIC-A-BRAC MERCHANT. RIJKSMUSEUM, AMSTERDAM.
*(Photo by Abrahamson.)*

SOROLLA Y BASTIDA: THE RETURNING FISHERMAN. MUSÉE DU LUXEMBOURG.
*(Photo by Neurdein.)*

SEGANTINI: AT THE BAR. NATIONAL GALLERY OF MODERN ART, ROME.
*(Photo by Alinari.)*

LENBACH: BISMARCK.

BÖCKLIN: THE NAIADS. MUSEUM OF BASEL.

RAUCH: MONUMENT OF FREDERICK THE GREAT. BERLIN.

The Belgians are worthy heirs of their ancestral naturalists: the van Eycks and Rubens. The Dutch have remained observing landscapists. The Spaniards carry out a brilliant lyricism in their painting of light. The Italians show virtuoso qualities and several of them have discovered hitherto hidden aspects in nature. The Scandinavians have followed impressionism. Among the Russians, the Byzantine inheritance remains apparent. The Germans are skillful observers in portraiture.

# THE EXPOSITION OF DECORATIVE ARTS OF 1925

*It is not only in painting or sculpture that the modern age drives itself to creating pictures. Architecture and the decorative arts which are natural complements have long sought to create new forms. The use of new materials—in particular iron and reinforced concrete—the necessity of constructing vast shelters for stations or exposition palaces has profoundly modified public architecture; there was a time, when in this metallic architecture, iron came into use. Today the union of iron with cement makes it possible to combine the resistance of metal with the appearance of stone.*

PORTE D'HONNEUR OF THE EXPOSITION OF DECORATIVE ARTS. (HENRY FAVIER AND ANDRÉ VENTRE, ARCHITECTS. EDGAR BRANDT, CHIEF IRONWORKER.) *(Photo by Hachette.)*

INTERIOR OF THE GRAND PALAIS: THE MONUMENTAL STAIRCASE. (CHARLES LETROSNE, ARCHITECT.) *(Photo by Hachette.)*

ROOM BY RUHLMANN. *(Photo by Hachette.)*

DINING ROOM BY LALIQUE. *(Photo by Hachette.)*

PAVILION OF THE CITY OF PARIS. *(Photo by Hachette.)*

The Paris Exposition of 1925 laid down a novel program in excluding every work related to ancient styles. Daring construction made possible by the use of iron enclosed in cement; silhouettes and especially proportions which appeared paradoxical have proved that they were reasonable and logical and that they thus had every opportunity of being judged beautiful. In the decorative arts, the influence of architecture is felt; it is architecture which shows the decorators simplified forms and freely treated masses which they give to even the most precious materials.

is one in which the masonry is supported by a framework of ribs.

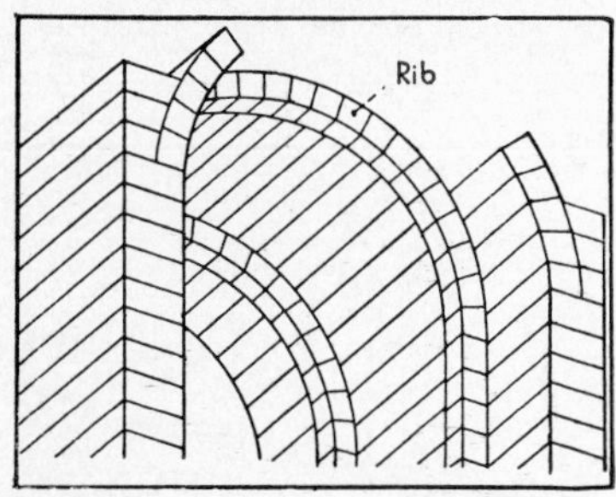


RIBBED VAULT.

**VECCHIETTA (Lorenzo di Pietro; called).**—Sienese sculptor and painter (about 1412-1480). More sculptor than painter, and pupil of Jacopo della Quercia and Donatello; as a painter, pupil of Sassetta. In 1441, he made a fresco in the Pellegrinaio of the Hospital of the Scala. In 1450-53, he did frescoes in the Baptistery; in 1457, an altarpiece which is in the Uffizi; in 1461, the *Madonna of Mercy*, in the Palazzo Pubblico, as well as a *St. Catherine*. He painted an *Assumption* in the Cathedral of Pienza (1461). As sculptor, there is by him, in the Cathedral of Siena, a bronze tabernacle (1465-72).

**VECELLI (Tiziano).**—See Titian.

**VEDDER (Elihu).** — American painter (1836-1923), author of a famous series of illustrations of Omar Khayyam's Rubaiyat, and also of a number of paintings in the Library of Congress in Washington. He died in Rome where he had been settled for over half a century.

**VEEN (Martin van).**—See Heemskerck.

**VEII (Italy).**—Formerly a rich Etruscan city, which the Romans conquered in 396 B.C. Excavations have discovered a cave which contains the oldest Etruscan paintings. These are frescoes on a greyish background, with figures arranged in horizontal bands. They represent the demons of death leading to Hades a man mounted on a horse, led by Charon.

**VEIT (Philipp).**—German painter, 1793-1877. He painted, in the Staedel Institute the *Introduction of Christianity into Germany*, which is one of the best productions of the Nazarene school (*V. v.*).

**VELA (Vincenzo).**—Italian sculptor, 1822-1891, who, reacting against the pseudo-academic school, turned to realism. His most famous work is the *Napoleon Dying*, which is now in the Museum of Versailles.

**VELASCO.**—Portuguese painter, first half of the 16th century. This robust artist was for a long time confused with Vasco Fernandez, who was probably Velasco's pupil. The name of Velascus is written on a parchment, thrown in the foreground of the picture of the *Pentecost* which hangs in the Sacristy of Santa Cruz of Coïmbra and of which the elegance proclaims the influence of the master of the *Paraïso*. But the fingers are more nervous, the features more tender, and the expressions more intense than in the picture of the *Crucifixion*, which was painted facing the *Pentecost* by the master of the *Paraïso*. The artist came from the school of Lisbon, but broke away from it by reason of his powerful temperament. The Cathedral of Sâo Joâo of Taronca, between Vizeu and Lamego, contains two fine, proud figures, a *St. Peter* which Vasco Fernandez copied, and a *St. Michael*, which may be restored to Velasco.

The "Great Vasco" really lived under the name of Vasco Fernandez; but he was only an able, facile copier. It is Velasco, master of Vasco Fernandez, who is the greatest, if not "the great."

**VELÁZQUEZ (D. Diego Rodriguez de Silva).**—Spanish painter.

VELÁZQUEZ: SELF-PORTRAIT

(Christened at Seville, June 6th, 1599—died at Madrid, August 6th, 1660.)

He was thirteen when he was sent as a pupil to the painter Francisco Herrera the Elder, a strange and impetuous man. From 1613 to 1618, he studied under Francisco Pacheco. In contrast to the studio

VELÁZQUEZ: AESOP. (Prado, Madrid.)

of Herrera, the house of the author of *El Arte de la Pintura* was rather like a distinguished academy, where the wits, nobles, poets, and artists of Andalusia used to meet.

It is difficult to say what he owed to either of these masters. "The originality which distinguished Velázquez from his youth was noticed in its early stages by the sagacity of Pacheco. Velázquez freely followed his leaning towards the study of nature and its representation just as he saw it, without idealizing. The faithful representation of nature was always the end to which he devoted himself with the strictest severity, guided at first by natural instinct, and impelled afterwards by deep-rooted conviction."

*The Old Woman Frying Eggs* (Cook Coll., Richmond, 1620-1622) and the *Water Carrier* (Apsley House, Duke of Wellington, London, c. 1618) were painted in "the dry and harsh manner characteristic of Velázquez during this period, with a somewhat thick impasto in the bright parts, and even in the shadows, which appear but little less transparent. Warm tones predominate in the colouring, an effect due in part to the pronounced brown shade of the heads and hands."

"The most important religious picture of this period is undoubtedly the *Adoration of the Magi*, in the Prado, which is dated 1619, at which time the artist was only twenty years of age.

"Like all those which Velázquez executed at that period, this picture is painted in an exceedingly sombre tone, and with an exaggerated hardness, but one is struck by its lustre and by the sculptural relief of many of the details. . . ." (Beruete, passim.)

Lefort and others believe that at that time Velázquez was under the influence of Ribera. This theory has been rejected by Justi and Beruete. The latter explains the characteristics common to both painters on the ground that "the instinct which guided both towards the realistic interpretation was the same, but the progressive development of their tastes caused an increasing divergence between their respective manners of painting."

VELÁZQUEZ: PORTRAIT OF MARIANA OF AUSTRIA, WIFE OF PHILIP IV. (Prado, Madrid.)

Other prominent paintings of his early style are: *Christ in the House of Martha* (National Gallery, London, 1619-1621); *Christ at Emmaus* (Met. Mus., Altman Coll., N. Y., 1619-1623); *St. John the Baptist in the Wilderness* (Chicago Art Institute, c. 1620-1622); *St. Ildefonso Receiving the Chasuble* (Seville, Palace of the Archbishop, c. 1623); *Servant* (Chicago Art Institute, c. 1619-1620); etc.

Highly important is the discovery made in 1927 of a full-length portrait signed and dated by Velázquez in 1620. This painting was found in the Convent of Santa Isabel de los Reyes in Toledo and represents Doña Geronima de la Fuente, a Franciscan nun, who was the founder of the Convent of Santa Clara at Manila. Also this painting unites all the characteristics of the early style of the young Velázquez as summed by Señor Beruete.

In 1618 he married Pacheco's daughter, Juana, their two daughters were born in 1619 and 1620. Equipped with letters of introduction given to him by his father-in-law, he journeyed in 1622 to Madrid. There, however, he did not succeed in his main aim, which was to be presented to the king. Yet the portrait of D. Juan Fonseca, gentleman usher to the monarch, established his fame in the capital. It was due to this painting that a year later his countryman the Count, Duke of Olivares, recalled him to Madrid to paint the portrait of Philip IV.

We know from Pacheco, who had accompanied his son-in-law to Madrid, that Velázquez "made the first portrait of the king on August 30, 1623, as well as a sketch of the Prince of Wales, who paid him 100 crowns for it." This portrait, as well as the equestrian portrait for which it served as a study, are lost, and so is the sketch of the English prince (afterwards Charles II.).

". . . The keystone of his success, according to Pacheco, was the

VELÁZQUEZ: PORTRAIT OF QUEEN ISABELLA OF BOURBON. (Prado, Madrid.)

approbation of the Count—Duke of Olivares, who maintained that no painter had ever succeeded so well in painting the king. . . . The monarch, too, ordered his favourite to have all his portraits which were in the palace removed, and added that in the future only Velázquez should paint his portrait. . . ." On October 6, 1623, Velázquez was admitted into the king's service. He was given lodgings in the city, a studio in the palace, and a salary of 20 ducats a month, "a paltry reward, but one which was in conformity with the customs of the time. . . ." (Beruete.)

Critics place Velázquez' second period from 1623 to 1629, that is from the time he settled at Madrid until his first Italian journey. It has much of the character of the first, but there is already greater simplicity of treatment. The artist is less interested in minor detail; the shadows become rather more transparent; the painter's aims become simpler and larger; and the '*Borrachos*' already hint at impressionism to come. (Mayer.)

"In spite of the grievous loss of the equestrian portrait of Philip IV, we have in . . . two superb paintings, specimens of the talent of Velázquez when he became known at court. They are the first of that long series of portraits of the king which Velázquez painted in the course of his life: the full-length portrait of Philip IV, then eighteen years of age, standing in front of a table and dressed entirely in black, and the bust-portrait of the king in armour and with a scarf. Another picture even more interesting from an artistic point of view than the full-length portrait of Philip IV is that which Velázquez painted of the Infante Don Carlos (c. 1627). This picture where the figure, painted without any accessories, stands out from an uniform grey background, is perhaps, on account of its perfect sobriety and distinction, the finest of the portraits of this period. Nothing could be happier than the silhouette of the young Prince, a type of the gentlemen of his Court, dressed in a magnificent black costume. . . ." (Beruete, passim.)

The dates of the portrait of Philip IV and that of the Count-Duke of Olivares in the Met. Mus. of New York are known from a receipt signed by Velázquez on December 4, 1624. From this receipt, preserved in the same museum, we learn that the painter had executed these two paintings and a third one which has disappeared for Da. Antonia de Ipoñarrieta. (A portrait of Da. Antonia herself with her little son is in the Prado Mus.) As regards the portrait of Olivares, Mayer points out that "Velázquez must certainly have painted another version of this picture, earlier, for the Conde-Duque himself." (Conde-Duque is the customary abbreviation of the full name of Philip IV's all-powerful Minister Don Gaspar de Guzmán, Conde de Olivares, Duque de San-Lucár.)

In 1628 Velázquez began the magnificent equestrian portrait of Philip IV (Prado, No. 1178) which was "mainly executed about 1634, when all the earlier parts were repainted by the master. Very probably it was enlarged and altered again by Velázquez after the fire of 1640. . . ." Mayer believes that the *Christ After the Flagellation* in the National Gallery in London was painted about 1629. The drawing for this painting in the Jovellanos Collection at Gijon has probably been destroyed by fire during the present civil war.

VELÁZQUEZ: CHRIST ON THE CROSS. (Prado, Madrid.)

But most famous of all the paintings by Velázquez of this period is the *Borrachos* (The Drinkers) in the Prado Museum. It was paid for on July 22, 1629, but finished most probably in 1626, at latest in 1628. (Mayer.) C. Justi says: "During the first chapter of his Court life the royal painter probably devoted himself entirely to portraiture. Through portraiture he obtained his appointment, and he must doubtless have sought to retain it by perfecting himself in this department. But towards the close of this first lustrum he resumed the old studies, even breaking new ground by entering the field of mythology. Here we are introduced to a rural bacchanalian revel, in which the young god, enthroned on a cask between two of his rotaries, entertains and crowns a narrow circle of fellow-tipplers. . . . Although the scene takes place in the open, it is nevertheless depicted in the light of the studio. . . . The brightest light is concentrated on the chief figure, reflecting his white flesh tints, and contrasting with the four weather-beaten swarthy heads in their sharply chiselled modelling, their light-absorbing worn-out brown and yellow cloaks and vests. Lastly come four figures in the shade, from which emerge some light nose tips and frontal bosses. . . . The weak sides of the picture are the shading and the dark element. The crouching tapster on the left is little more than a silhouette, while the foliage of the vine is reduced to thick brown masses. . . . This work . . . marks a certain eminence in the master's art. Strictly speaking it was never surpassed in vigour, firmness, and *morbidezza*. . . ."

The *Expulsion of the Moriscos* was probably destroyed in the fire of the Madrid Alcazar (Royal Castle) in 1734. The story of this picture is re-told by Beruete. "The king, having become aware of criticisms, by the Court painters, told Velázquez that it was said of him that 'he could only paint heads,' to which the artist calmly replied: 'These gentlemen do me a great honour, for personally I do not think anyone is capable of painting them well!' . . . Desirous of proving that . . . he was not incapable of producing other works of a character generally considered more elevated, Velázquez begged the king to give him an opportunity of rendering this power potent to the eyes of everyone. Philip IV chose an historical subject of recent date—the expulsion of the Moriscos in 1609 by Philip III." Carducho, Caxes, Nardi, and Velázquez were ordered to paint this subject. A tribunal composed of the Italian painter and architect, Cresconcio, and of Mayno, who was a pupil of El Greco, awarded the prize to Velázquez.

In 1625 Velázquez received a gift of 300 ducats and in the following year a pension of the same amount. The post of a gentleman usher was conceded to him in 1627.

In the fall of 1628 Rubens had arrived at Madrid, staying nine months in the capital. The two painters shared the same studio, and Pacheco informs us that Rubens "did not make friends with many artists, with the exception of (his) son-in-law (who was already his correspondent), whose modesty and talent he greatly praised, and with whom he went to visit the Escorial." It is believed that Velázquez undertook his Italian trip largely upon the advice of Rubens.

On August 10, 1629, Velázquez sailed from Barcelona for Genoa. From there he went to Milan and thence via Ferrara, to Rome. At Venice he copied the *Crucifixion* and *Last Supper* by Tintoretto (both copies lost). Cardinal Barberini offered him lodgings at the Vatican, but the artist preferred to stay at the Villa Medici, which was the property of the Duke of Tuscany. Opinion is divided as to whether Velázquez painted the two *Views of the Gardens of the Villa* (Prado) during his first or second stay (1650) in Rome. "These works are views of the gardens with buildings in the Rennaissance style, and some figures sketched in which give life to the scene. . . . The execution is free, but firm and sure, and relief is given in a masterly manner by a few decisive touches." Fevers compelled Velázquez to move into town, where he stayed with Count Monterey. Beruete believes that though he doubtlessly studied and admired the works of Rafael and Michelangelo, it does not follow that he copied them. The *Forge of Vulcan* (Prado) and *Joseph's Coat* (Escorial, Lala Capitular) were painted at that time.

In the *Forge of Vulcan* "Apollo is seen relating the story of the infidelities of Venus with Mars. Vulcan, aided by his cyclops, is engaged in forging a mass of iron on an anvil, and listens, full of surprise, to Apollo's tale; this surprise is shared by all those who are working in the forge. With the exception of the figure of Apollo, nothing in this composition recalls the mythological types which had been, and still were, in vogue. Velázquez has admirably solved the difficult problem of successfully treating a work where the nude is the principal feature. . . . The light which bathes the scene is more diffused than that which illuminates the preceding pictures of the master; the general touch is greyer; in fact, if we compare it with the *Borrachos* there is more atmosphere, more freedom in the figures, and more transparency in the shadows." (Beruete.) Critics are not quite sure whether the self-portrait in the Capitoline Museum is to be assigned to 1630 or to a later date. Before returning to Madrid, Velázquez was ordered to proceed to Naples to paint the portrait of Philip IV's beautiful sister, the Infanta Maria Anna. The Infanta having been married by proxy to the King of Hungary, afterwards Emperor Ferdinand III, was then at Naples en route to her new country.

VELÁZQUEZ: ST. ANTHONY VISITING ST. PAUL. (Prado, Madrid.)

In the beginning of 1631 Velázquez was back at Madrid. Beruete is opposed to the opinions of other critics, claiming that the artist, during his stay in Italy, had come, in varying degrees, under the influence of Tintoretto, Guido, and even Poussin. He rather agrees with Wyzeva that Velázquez "learnt from the Italians all that he could, without in any way losing any of his own characteristics: the art of painting all the elements of a picture, and also the art of combining tones to obtain clearly defined effects."

Mayer expresses his views thus on the cause as well as the nature of the artist's third style: "The journey to Italy, the study of Venetian colouring and of classic art in Rome, lead the painter into new ways; his colour becomes much brighter and more brilliant, and the heavy shadows begin to disappear. The first important step in the new impressionism seems to date from about 1635, from the beginning of the 'forties onwards, he becomes freer and freer, and the water-colour-like technique, . . . as already apparent towards the end of the 'thirties, becomes more and more an essential factor in his work."

In contrast to other critics who date the famous *Christ on the Cross* in the Prado as early as 1628 and as late as 1638, Gomez Moreno believes it to have been painted in 1632. The *Coronation of the Virgin* in the same museum antedates the year 1644, when, as emphasized by Mayer, Jusepe Martinez painted a free replica of this composition for the Sea of Saragossa. Allende Salazar assigns the *SS. Anthony Abbot and Paul the Hermit in the Wilderness* (Prado) to 1634, whereas it is dated by Mayer as "not before 1642" and by Beruete even of a period as advanced as 1651-1660.

Well known among the portraits painted during the decade following the return from Italy is that of Philip IV in the National Gallery, London (1631-1632); so are, too, the three portraits in the Prado depicting the monarch (1634-1635), his brother, the Infante Don Ferdinand (1635-1636), and his little son, Don Balthasar (1637), all three in hunting costume with gun and hounds; the equestrian picture of Olivares (1634) in the same museum, etc.

Beruete points out that the three *Portraits of the Hunters* are characteristic of the artist's manner when painting human figures against a landscape background. Their "originality constitutes one of the individual peculiarities of the artist. Indeed, the numerous landscape backgrounds in question up till that time, which may be observed in so many portraits, although in detail inspired by nature, were purely conventional in treatment, and placed there only with the intention of diversifying the work. . . . We may say that most of the landscapes represent evening effects, with flame-coloured skies and very dark vegetation for the sake of dramatic effect. In the landscape backgrounds of Velázquez the tones are always cold bluish greys. They are painted from nature, and inspired by the views which he saw from the windows of the palace itself, or which he noted either in the neighbourhood of the palace, the Prado, or the Escorial. . . . All who know the varying aspect of the country round Madrid . . . and have observed the tints of the slopes of the Prado with its evergreen oaks planted in the grey and reddish soil, and in the distance the brilliant yet delicate blue of the snow-capped Guadarrama, will understand how Velázquez, impressed by these effects, saw in them a background at once artistic and novel, for the austere originals of his portraits."

The much-beloved painting of the Infante Don Balthasar Carlos on horseback (Prado) dates from 1635 to 1636. Mayer recalls in his *Catalogue* Palomino's description of a large composition representing this prince on horseback in the riding-school, which has been lost. According to various critics the two paintings in the Wallace Coll., London, and in the Coll. of the Duke of Westminster, which depict the same subject, are not by Velázquez' hand.

Mayer suggests that the noteworthy half-length portrait of Cardinal D. Gaspar de Borja y Velasco, owned by Lord Duveen of Milbank, may date from 1643 to 1644.

The *Surrender of Breda* or *Las Lanzas* (Prado) was painted about 1634-1635, the years from which, onward, according to Mayer, Velázquez' new impressionism seems to date. In this picture, which commemorates the surrender of the fortress (June, 2, 1625), the main protagonists are the defender, Justin of Nassau, and the victorious Count Spinola. "The governor, at the head of the infantry, which formed the center of the march out, had reached the quarters at Tetteringen, where Spinola was expecting him. . . . Here both dismount, and the throng stands back, silently doffing their hats. Justin approaches, but Spinola advances to meet him, bending forward and laying his hand on the shoulder of the governor, who addresses him and holds out the keys. . . . In Spinola's face and jesture are blended an aristocratic elegance and natural kindliness with Italian refinement. The victorious captain has a fellow-feeling for the brave man who is reduced to his sad extremity. . . . The choice of a purely human and noble sentiment, as the most prominent motive is a feature which would not have occurred to everybody. . . . The composition is determined by that principle of unity, that simplicity of nature, which lay in the very nature of the man. He gives us nothing but the central movement of the delivery of the keys, and the accessories immediately associated with that action. . . . On the other hand, the two commanders are conspicuous, both with a crowded following, which, in the observer's imagination, stretch away in thousands beyond the frame of the picture. . . . A somewhat peculiar effect is produced by the twenty-nine almost vertical ashwood lances, which give an alternative name to the picture, and which cut off over a third of sky and landscape. . . . Horses, costumes and arms are reproduced in colour and texture with the unerring touch of the expert. . . . Notwithstanding the fulness of the foreground, the artist has contrived to make room for a far-reaching perspective. . . . The distant objects somewhat clouded in the misty atmosphere of these watery lowlands are disposed with topographical accuracy. . . ." (Justi.)

"From the beginning of the 'forties onward Velázquez becomes freer and freer and the water-colour-like technique . . . as already apparent toward the end of the 'thirties becomes more and more an essential factor in his work." (Mayer.) In 1643, Velázquez was appointed gentleman-in-waiting to the King and in 1647 inspector of buildings. In 1644 he accompanied the King on his journey through Aragon, and at Traga he painted several pictures, among them the portrait of the King now in the Frick Coll. of New York. "Even the best reproduction can give a very faint idea of the beauty of the original. . . . Nor will any contrast of tone give an idea of the sparkle that is produced in the original by the rapid scribbling of silver lace upon the marvelous rose coral of the King's coat. . . . Silver and coral and black form the basis of this harmony, the glimpse of the doublet beneath the coat shows a dull yellow which underlines, as it were, the slightly warmer tones of the flesh." As regards the well-known *View of Saragossa* in the Prado (1647) by Velázquez' son-in-law, del Mazo, Mayer emphasizes the fact that the often-claimed "collaboration of Velázquez is quite hypothetical." The portrait by Velázquez, called *The Lady with the Fan* in the Wallace Coll., London, is believed to represent his daughter, Doña Francisca, who was married to del Mazo. Beruete places it between the years 1644 and 1649.

"The question of creating a Royal Academy of Fine Art at Madrid had been considered in the time of Philip III; the reopening of this question principally, and the necessity of procuring works of art to adorn the new buildings of the Alcazar, of which . . . Velázquez was the inspector, led our painter to beg of the King the permission and the means to return to Italy. . . . He embarked at Málaza on January 2, 1649, and landed at Genoa on February 11. He stopped at Milan and Padua on his way to Venice, where he bought several paintings, as, for instance, Veronese's *Venus and Adonis*, Tintoretto's *Purification of the Midianite Virgins* as well as a sketch for the celebrated *Paradise* by the same master (all these works now in the Prado). . . . He then went to Rome—and left almost at once—for Naples, where he chose a number of marbles and antique bronzes, and ordered some casts to be sent to Spain. . . . He returned to Rome, where the Pope commissioned him to paint his portrait. . . . It was then, doubtless, in order to get his hand accustomed to work again, that he painted the *Bust Portrait of his Servant Juan Pareja* (Longford Castle; Earl of Radnor). . . . The portrait of Innocent (Rome, Pal. Doria Pamphilli) is one of the largest works of the master. . . . The scrutinizing gaze, which has an irresistible fascination, the face, one of the most living which Velázquez ever modelled, on which even the perspiration is visible, the robust and ample body, the rich harmony of the reds and whites, the magic of the whole, in short, impress the spectator, who is mute with admiration." (Beruete.) The study-bust for this portrait, formerly in the Hermitage at Leningrad, is now in the A. Mellon Collection in Washington. It is not improbable that the portrait in the His. Soc. of Am. N. Y., supposed to represent Cardinal Camillo Pamphilli, had been painted during Velázquez' second stay at Rome.

The letters of Philip IV to his ambassador at Rome, recalling Velázquez to Madrid, bespeak of the pressure which had to be brought on the painter to return to Spain. He left Italy embarking at Genova and arrived in Barcelona in June, 1651.

It was in the last ten years of his life (1650-1660) "that Velázquez, a complete master of his art, taught by a life of serious and thoughtful labor, executed his most surprising works. Simplicity of artistic means, a harmonious synthesis of conception and interpretation, are the elements of what is called his 'summary' style. . . . The transition from the second to the third manner was, in the case of Velázquez, as imperceptible as had been that from the first to the second. There was nothing sudden in his evolution. Each of the canvases which left his studio summed up all the qualities of his earlier works, together with the progress made since. . . ." (Beruete.)

In 1652 Philip IV raised Velázquez to the rank of a grand marshal of the palace. It has been justly said that the award of this distinction deprived posterity of many masterpieces by the artist whose freedom had become further curtailed by the many obligations imposed by his new office. In spite of this Velázquez, during the last decade of his life, produced many great works, and among them those which established his fame as the chronicler of the life at the Court of Madrid. The full-length portrait of Philip's second wife, Queen Maria Ana (1652), in the Prado (No. 1191) is regarded one of the finest works of the artist. "The delicate color of the head and hands, the silver of the ornaments fastened on the very dark robe, the reds of the knots of the sleeves, . . . the refined white of the handkerchief and the carmine of the curtain, are the elements which go to compose one of the most harmonious pictures ever painted by Velázquez." A delightful subject for the master was Philip's and Maria Ana's daughter, the Infanta Margareta (born in 1651). "The earliest portrait, and likewise the most beautiful, which exists of this charming Princess is the one in the Vienna Museum (No. 615). The Infanta appears to be three years old; she is standing and wears a pink-and-silver dress. . . . The delightful colour of her flaxen hair blends brilliantly with the delicate pink of her dress and the blue of the background." . . . (Beruete.) The Vienna Museum also contains a painting of the Infanta which was discovered not long ago (No. 609b), painted in 1659, and which, with the portrait of the Infante Philip Prosper (Vienna Museum), had been sent to Emperor Leopold I. The much-admired half-length picture in the Louvre belongs, according to Mayer, to a series probably painted by Mazo. A full-length life-size portrait in the Prado, 1659-1660 (No. 1192) is as suggested in the *Catalogue* of the Prado the "last work of Velázquez which he left unfinished; . . . Mazo finished not only the head, but probably the hands as well"—"It is an effective work in which the reds, ranging from light pink to carmine, dominate and blend with the silvery grey of the ornaments and the delicate white of the handkerchief which the Infanta holds in her right hand. . . . All must admire the marvelous genius of Velázquez, who, thanks to this rich harmony, was able to counterbalance the unpleasant effect produced by the most gigantic crinoline ever painted by him." (Beruete.) Almost all of Velázquez' portraits of the Infanta Maria Teresa, the sister of Philip IV, who in 1660 was married to Louis XIV of France, were executed in the years following the return from Italy. The portraits in the Vienna and Boston museums—the latter "painted with the aid of a studio assistant" were finished before February 22, 1653, when they were sent as presents by Philip to his relatives at Vienna (the picture in the Vienna Museum was a gift to Emperor Leopold I and that at Boston to the Archduke Leopold Wilhelm.) . . . A study-bust for the above-mentioned portraits is in the Victoria and Albert Museum. Another bust portrait is owned by Mr. Philip Lehman, New York. The head in the Jules Baches Coll., N. Y., is a fragment of a larger picture painted in 1653-1654.

"In no other place was the extravagant and inexplicable fashion of adding to the retinue of princes deformed and often insane people . . . more in vogue than at Madrid. . . . One is struck, on examining official documents by the large number of these individuals, as well as by the picturesque nicknames by which they were called. . . . In spite of all this, it is to the relative importance of these buffoons that we owe the series of portraits whose diversity reveals a fresh side of the talent of Velázquez. . . . The magic power of the art which was able to move the beholder as deeply by means of what was ugly and even repugnant, as by what was pleasing and beautiful." (Beruete.) The earliest of these portraits, according to Mayer, is the *Court-fool holding a glass of wine* (1623-1624; Mus. Toledo, Ohio), the same model being represented in the so-called *Geographer* in the Museum of Rouen (1624-1628). The portrait of Don Juan de Calabazas (Sir Herbert Cook Coll., Richmond), of *Pablillos de Valladolid* (Prado) and Pernia, called *Barbarossa* (Prado) date from 1626 to 1636. To the late period of the artist belong, among others, the pictures of *Calabazillas, Sebastian de Morra, D. Juan de Austria, El Inglés, El Nino de Valluecas,* all in the Prado Museum.

Of a number of paintings representing mythological subjects executed by Velázquez during the last years of his life only three are known to be extant—the *Mars* (1653-1658) and *Mercury and Argus* (1659) in the Prado, and the *Venus and Cupid* (1658) in the Nat'l Gallery, London. . . . "The *Mars* was painted for the Torre de la Parada of the Pardo Castle, where it was placed between the *Aesop* and *Monippus* (critics vary on date of these two paintings, Ed.), the rather doubtful philosophers to whom Mars' repellent mien renders him a worthy companion, in spite of the mythological name by which he is dignified. . . . Velázquez never restrained his realistic instincts, not even in the mythological scenes painted at the end of his life. . . . Seated facing the spectator, and almost nude, the god's head is covered by a helmet, the shadow of which strongly accentuates every rascally trait in his features. . . . The general disposition of the figure, notably the gesture of his left hand, reminds both Professor Justi and M. Michel of the statue of the *Pensieroso* by Michelangelo for the monument of Lorenzo de'Medici. It is a splendid piece of flesh painting, of great strength, and treated in the broadest manner. . . . The *Venus and Cupid,* also called the *Venus with the Mirror,* was purchased by the Nat'l Galley in 1906 for the sum of 45,000 pounds sterling. . . . Venus, entirely undraped, and lying on a bed, turns her **back** to the spectator. She contemplates herself in an ebony-mounted mirror which is held by a cupid kneeling on her bed. . . . The principal part of the work is the body of Venus, which Velázquez has interpreted with the conscientiousness and regard of truth which he put into all his work. . . ." (Beruete, passim.)

"Among the most characteristic and individual works of Velázquez there are none which are so celebrated as the *Hilanderas* or Spinners and the *Meninas*." Both are in the Prado Museum, the former was executed about 1657, and the latter in 1656. "These canvases are representations of everyday life. . . . The subjects which struck the painter's attention were not transposed, as was the usual custom, for, instead of reproducing the scenes in his studio with illumination *ad hoc*, and by means of professional models, Velázquez painted them on the spot after the manner of an instantaneous photograph. The light in the picture was the real light which bathed the scene, and the models were the real actors in it. This innovation in the art of painting, to which for a long time the critics paid no attention, is one of the reasons which nowadays lead us to consider Velázquez as the greatest of innovators. . . ."

"The picture of the *Hilanderas* represents the interior of one of those workshops for the manufacture of tapestry, which existed in those days, in the Calle de Santa Isabel. . . . The workshop communicates by means of an archway with another small room the floor of which is raised like the stage of a theatre."

"In the first room are five figures which form various groups. . . . The chief interest is centered on two of them in the foreground, an old woman, who is spinning at a wheel, and a young girl busy disentangling a skein, with her back towards the spectator. This charming spinner, the finest and most pleasing figure in the work, is in the high light of the picture, which is almost entirely in half-light. In the small room in the background a scene presents itself which bears no relation to that in the foreground. Brightly lighted by the rays of sunshine which penetrate through an unseen side window, three ladies are examining a piece of tapestry with a mythological subject depicted on it, hung from the ceiling of the room, which also contains a violoncello leaning against a stool. . . . Senor P. de Madrazo thus sums up the observations which he devotes to the atmospheric effects in this canvas. 'In virtue of I know not what law of optics, unknown to other painters the surrounding atmosphere interposed between the spectator and the canvas combines with the work of the artist, and finishes off so wonderfully the strokes of the brush left unfinished by him in an unfinished state, that the confusion which seems to reign when the surface of this picture is viewed near at hand, disappears and all becomes plain as the spectator retires from the picture. Then space opens out before your eyes, the canvas deepens; and there, where there was but a single smudged and confused plane, you perceive the different distances of a vast scene; the uncertain and opaque colour of the first mist changes into atmosphere; life begins.'

"The *Meninas* represents a scene at court, the principal figure being that of the Infanta Margareta at the age of five or six. . . . She is accompanied by her two *Meninas* or maids of honour. One of them, Doña Augustina Sarmiento, kneeling before the Infanta, offers her a flagon, while the other, Doña Isabel de Velasco, stands at her left side. On the right of the table, in the foreground, is a group composed of two of the Court dwarfs, Mari Barbola, a perfect monster, one of the most repugnant types of the whole collection, and Nicolasico Pertusato, a dwarf with hydrocephalic head and stunted body who is teasing with his foot a huge mastiff. . . . The opposite end of the picture is occupied by a large canvas placed on an easel in front of which is Velázquez himself with his palette, brushes, and mahl-stick; the artist is looking at his models, whose features are reflected in a mirror at the end of the room, and who are those of Philip IV and Queen Mariana. . . . In the middle distance, in shadow, Doña Marcela de Ulloa, a lady-in-waiting wearing a mantle, is engaged in conversation with a *guardadamas*, . . . finally, quite in the background on the threshold of a large open door brightly illuminated by a concentrated light, which contrasts with the subdued daylight of the rest of the scene, appears the Aposentador of the queen, D. José Nieto. . . . In the first scene . . . Velázquez managed to arrange in the most harmonious fashion the different parts of the composition, disposing his colour in the most ingenious way, varying his light so as to concentrate the interest on the figure of the Infanta standing out from the halftones which fill the room, and to quicken the obscurity in which the studio is plunged by means of the two luminous spots in the background—the mirror and the light which enters by the door. Last of all, what gives such a great air of faithfulness to the picture is the unusual disproportion which exists between the figures and the height of the canvas. The empty space above their heads is sufficient to allow us to see the ceiling, of which the lines and the surprising modelling help to give the illusion of depth and atmosphere. . . . The work is exceedingly skilful; confused when viewed close at hand, but most striking in effect when seen from a distance, etc. It would be tedious to enumerate all the eulogies of this picture which Luca Giordano called the theology of painting, and Sir Thomas Lawrence, in his letter to Wilkie (XI-27-1827) 'the true philosophy of art, the collection of essentials. . . .' (Beruete). It is assumed that the cross of a Knight of Santiago, which in this painting appears on Velázquez' coat has been painted in after the artist's death. Velázquez received the robes of the order in 1659. The various difficulties which not only he, but also his royal patron, had to overcome in order that Velázquez should be admitted to this order has been retold by Sr. Beruete.

"Velázquez' last performance was one connected with the office, not of court painter, but of palace marshal." On April 8, 1660, he departed for Fuenterrabia with the purpose of arranging for the impending journey of the king as well as for the festivities which were to take place on the small *Island of the Pheasants*, situated in the Bidasoa River. There on June 7, the Infanta Maria Teresa was given away by her brother Philip IV to young Louis XIV of France, a betrothal that was meant to fasten the ties between the two nations, who had concluded the treaty of the Pyrenees in the previous year.

In a letter dated July 3 Velázquez wrote the painter Diego Valentin Diaz at Valladolid that "he had returned to Madrid on June 26, tired with travelling by night and working by day, but that he was in good health . . . and that so were also his family." Yet on July 31 he was taken ill, and on August 6 he died. His wife, Doña Juana Pacheco survived him by only seven days.

Juan Bautista del Mazo ranks amongst Velázquez' pupils and next to him the Mulatto Juan de Pareja. Many of the works associated with Velázquez' name are studio replicas or works by his numerous assistants, and it is often difficult to assign some of them to any given artist. (Mayer, passim.)

BIBLIOGRAPHY: G. Cruzado Villaamil, *Anales de la vida y de las obras de Velázquez es critos con ayuda de nuevos documentos*. Madrid, 1885.—C. Justi, *Diego Velázquez and his times* (transl.), London, 1889. Id., *Diego Velázquez u sein Jahrhundert* (4th ed.). Zürich, 1933.—A. de Beruete, *Velázquez*. London, 1906. Id., *El Velázquez de Parma; retrato de Felipe IV pintado en Fraga*. Madrid, 1911—Sir W. Stirling Maxwell, *Annals of the Artists of Spain*, Vols. 2 and 4. London, 1891.—A. Calvert and C. G. Hartley, *Velázquez, an Account of His Life and Works*. London, 1908. —A. de Beruete y Moret, *School of Madrid*. London. Id. in *The Connoisseur*, Vol. 58, 1920, pp. 187-197. —A. L. Mayer, *Geschichte der span, Malerei*. Leipzig, 1922. Id., *Diego Velázquez*. Berlin, 1924. Id., *Velázquez; a Catalogue raisonné*. London, 1936. (The same author in: *Belvedere*, Vol. 3, Nos. 7, 8, 1922; *Art in America*, April, 1926; *Burlington Magazine*, July, 1926; June, 1927; *Pantheon*, July, 1929; May, 1930; *International Studio*, April, 1930.)—J. Allende-Salasar. *Valázquez des meisters gemälde. Klassiker der Kunst*. Vol. 6. Stuttgart, 1925. (Introd. by W. Gensel.)—L. Justi. In *Repertorium f Kunstwissenschaft*. Vol. 48. No. 2, 1927; Vol. 50, No. 6, 1929—R. Cortissoz, in *International Studio*, June, 1928—F. Howard. "The Silver Philip," in *The Connoisseur*, March. 1937.

**VELDE (Adriaen van de).**—Dutch painter (about 1635 or 1639-1672); son of Van de Velde the Elder. Travelled in Italy and was active in Amsterdam. Painted landscapes with figures and animals as *staffage*, which mark the height of that type of painting in Holland. He also did religious and mythological scenes. He painted the *staffage* for Hobbema, Ruysdael and many others.

BIBLIOGRAPHY: C. Hofstede de Groot, *A Catalogue Raisonné of the Works of the Most Eminent Dutch Painters of the 17th century*, Vol. IV, 1912.

**— (Essaias van de).**—Dutch painter (about 1590-1630); brother of Adriaen, probably a pupil of Coninxloo. Painted sporting pictures, landscapes and carnivals. A sense of humour dominates his work.

**— (Willem van de) senior.**—Dutch painter (1611-1693). Primarily a draughtsman, he took up oil painting only late in his life. He took part in the naval war between Holland and Sweden in 1656. His works are mainly marines and a number of sketches of sea-battles.

**— (Willem van de) called the Younger.**—Dutch painter (1633-1707). He chiefly painted ships, boats, warships with their large sails, armed with cannons. Among his best pictures, is the *Cannon Shot* (Amsterdam). A pupil of Simon de Vlieger, he was court painter in England.

BIBLIOGRAPHY: C. Hofstede de Groot, *Catalogue of Dutch Painters*, Vol. VII, 1923.

**VENDOME (Loir-et-Cher).**—The Abbey of the Trinity was founded about 1030.

See Pl. 50, Vol. I.

**VENICE (Italy).**—*Cathedral of St. Mark* was begun in 830, to house the relics of St. Mark, and

VENICE: STA. MARIA DEI FRARI.

was transformed in the middle of the 11th century in the Byzantine style. In the 15th and 16th centuries Gothic and Renaissance details were added, without ruining the Byzantine harmony of the whole. The

VENICE: PALAZZO LOREDAN.

architects were probably Byzantines assisted by Venetians and Lombards. The building is in the form of a Greek cross, and on each end of the cross is a cupola, while in the centre is a fifth and larger cupola.

VENICE: THE PIAZZETTA.

The façade has a peristyle, whose arcades are decorated with mosaics. The oldest of these, dating from the 13th century, represent Old Testament subjects; others belong to the 17th and 18th centuries. The interior of the church, with three naves, and lighted by little windows, is incomparable in splendour owing to the mosaics on a gold ground which cover the walls and vaulting. The oldest part of these mosaics, over the great door, shows Christ, the Virgin and St. John, and was done in the 10th century. Above the high altar is the "pala d'oro" (an ornament in gold, and silver; and enriched with enamels and precious stones) which was made in Constantinople in 1105.

The four famous horses of St. Mark, in gilded bronze, which are above the chief doorway originally came, no doubt, from Nero's triumphal arch. They had adorned that of Trajan. Then they were sent to Constantinople; then brought back to Venice by Dandolo in 1204; taken to Paris by Napoleon; and finally given definitely to Venice in 1815.

*Campanile* (98 metres high) fell into ruins in 1902. It dated from the 11th century. It has been replaced by a reconstruction.

In the Piazzetta, which runs from the square to the lagoon, are two magnificent buildings—the Palace of the Doges, and the Library.

The *Doges' Palace* was founded in 814; rebuilt in 976; then in 1105, and several times altered during the following centuries. The building is Gothic in style. The entrance (near St. Mark) has fine sculpture, near which are two porphyry bas-reliefs which may come from the Ptolemies. The court of the palace is magnificent; the "Giant's Staircase," adorned with huge statues of *Mars and Neptune* (by Sansovino and *Adam and Eve*, by Rizzo, is at one end. In fact, the greatest Venetian masters worked at the decoration of the interior. A fire in 1577 destroyed a great many of the pictures while others were taken to France by Napoleon in 1797. Among the most famous works which still exist, is Tintoretto's *Paradise* (the biggest oil painting in the world); his pictures of Venetian history, and ceiling decoration;—also Veronese's well-known *Glorification of Venice*; *Neptune* and *Mars*, etc. There are also Titian's *Doge Grimani kneeling before Religion*; and pictures by the younger Palma, etc.

The Doges' Palace is connected with the Prisons by the *Bridge of Sighs*, built between 1595 and 1605.

*Libreria Vecchia.* (Old Library) begun by Sansovino in 1536.

There are many churches in Venice:

*Madonna del Orto* has a fine Gothic façade and a curious tower.

*Santa Maria Formosa* contains Palma Vecchio's famous picture of *St. Barbara.*

*S.S. Giovanni e Paolo* contains the Doges' tombs, and many works of art. Titian's *Martyrdom of St. Peter* was done for this church, but was destroyed by fire, and replaced by a copy. Near this building is the famous equestrian statue of *Bartolomeo Colleoni*, by Verrocchio.

The Church of the *Frari*, built between 1250-1280 for the Franciscans, is one of the most beautiful in Venice and one of the richest in works of art. It contains, for instance, two of Titian's masterpieces, the *Pesaro Madonna*, painted in 1526, and the *Assumption*—also a triptych by Giovanni Bellini, painted in 1488, *The Virgin Surrounded by Saints and Angels.* Titian's tomb is in the Frari, and bas-reliefs on the wall reproduce his masterpieces.

*San Stefano* is a Gothic 14th century Church with a brick façade; *San Zaccharia* has Giovanni Bellini's *Madonna with Four Saints*; etc.

*San Rocco,* begun in 1490, finished in 1725, contains many of Tintoretto's pictures (episodes in the life of St. Roch). *The Scuola di San Rocco* (1524-1550) has mural paintings by Tintoretto, and an *Ecce Homo* by Titian.

*San Salvatore,* one of the most remarkable churches in Venice (1506-1534) has a Baroque façade added later. In the interior are an *Annunciation* and a *Transfiguration* by Titian, and *Christ at Emmaus* by Carpaccio.

*San Giorgio degli Schiavoni* contains paintings by Carpaccio. *San Sebastiano* has several pictures by Veronese. The Church of the *Redentore*, on the island of the Giudecca, begun by Palladio in 1577, was finished in 1592.

*Santa Maria della Salute* was built after the plague of 1630. It is surmounted by a lofty cupola. One of Titian's earlier works is in the interior. The *Gesuiti* has some of Tiepolo's frescoes, and so has the *Chiesa dei Scalzi.* (See Longhena.)

Most of the magnificent Venetian palaces are on the banks of the Grand Canal.

The *Fondaco dei Turchi*, built in the 11th century, was a Turkish warehouse in the 17th, and now houses the Correr collection. The *Contarini Fasan* palace is of the 14th century; the *Foscari*, of the 15th; the *Cà d'Oro* (Golden House), so called because its façade was, it is said, once gilded, is the most charming of all the Gothic palaces. It was built between 1424 and 1430. The *Giovanelli* palace contains *The Storm* which is one of the few authentic pictures by Giorgione. Besides these and other Gothic palaces, there are also many Renaissance ones, such as the *Vendramin*, the *Grimani* (one of the finest), the work of Sanmichele (1549), etc., etc.

Over the Grand Canal is the *Bridge of the Rialto*, built by G. da Ponte (1588-1592).

See Pl. 6, Vol. II.

BIBLIOGRAPHY: P. Gusman, *Venise.* Paris, 1913.—John Ruskin, *The Stones of Venice.* New York and London, 1851-53.

**— (Fifteenth Century Painting).** —See Pl. 14, Vol. II.

**VENUS ANADYOMENE.**—See Apelles.

**— de' MEDICI.** — This famous statue is in the Uffizi, Florence, and bears the name of the sculptor Cleomenes, son of Apollodoros. The work belongs to the first century before our era. In pose and type, it was inspired by Praxiteles' Venus, and it is the best of many similar reproductions.

See Pl. 25, Vol. I.

BIBLIOGRAPHY: M. Collignon, *Histoire de la sculpture grecque*, Vol. II.

**— OF MILO.** — Famous Greek statue in the Louvre, discovered in 1820, in the Isle of Milo, by a peasant who was digging his field near the theatre of the old town.

Opinions differ as to the date of its execution. Collignon considers that it was made shortly after the death of Alexander.

The arms are missing, and the question of their attitude has given rise to much discussion among archæologists.

See Pl. 25, Vol. I.

BIBLIOGRAPHY: Ernest Gardner, *Handbook of Greek Sculpture.* London, 1923.

**VENUSTI (Marcello).**—Roman painter, 1515-1579. Pupil of Michelangelo. One of his best works is a portrait he made of his master, in the Gallery of the Capitol in Rome.

**VERESTCHAGIN (V. V.).**—Russian painter, 1842-1904. His work is not of great value as art, but it has historical and documental interest. He painted chiefly realistic battle scenes.

VERESTCHAGIN: THE ATTACK.

**VERMEER (of Delft or Jan van der Meer).**—Dutch painter (1632-1675). He was born in Delft, married there, had ten children, and died at the age of forty-three. He was a pupil of Fabritius, and probably was employed in the faience factory of Delft. He was not greatly appreciated in his own day, and still less in the century after his death. Today he has been given the place he deserves among the greatest of Dutch painters. The number of pictures known to be his is small. He painted chiefly portraits and genre-like compositions of two or three figures and an occasional landscape. Not brilliant in composing a picture, his great fame lay in his unsurpassed coloristic achievements. Bright reds, blues, white, yellow and black are combined in an inimitable manner producing the effect as if the setting sun were illuminating the whole canvas. This glowing effect was achieved through his invention of underpainting: probably a coat of tempera on all water color covered by a thin layer of varnish, on top of which the oil color was applied. His early works are characterized by deep shadows next to bright highlights as *Self-Portrait* (Brussels) and *Girl with Flute*, showing a definite Caravaggesque influence; while in works after 1656 there is a more even and subdued chiaroscuro, as in *Milkmaid* and *Girl with Letter* (Amsterdam). His figures show little movement, and their gestures are the calm expression of their tranquil lives. Vermeer shows deep feeling, and can convey the charm of domestic life, though he never depicts passionate or dramatic situations.

VERMEER OF DELFT (JAN): THE ARTIST IN HIS STUDIO. (Czernin Collection, Vienna.)

See Pls. 36, 37, Vol. II.

BIBLIOGRAPHY: G. Vanzype, *Vermeer de Delft.* Brussels, 1908.—C. Hofstede de Groot, *A Catalogue Raisonné of the works of the most eminent Dutch painters of the 17th century.* Vol. I, 1907.—E. Plietzsch, *Vermeer van Delft*, 1911.

**VERMEJO (Bartolomé).**—Spanish painter, of the late fifteenth century, born at Cordova, working at Barcelona. His *Lamentation over the Dead Christ* in the Cathedral of Barcelona (1490), his *Ecce Homo* in the Vich Museum and his *St. Michael* in the collection of Lady Ludlow in London entitle him to a most distinguished rank among the Spanish painters of his period.

**VERMEYEN (Jan Cornelisz).**—Dutch painter and graver, about 1500-1559. One of the most outstanding portrait painters of the period, he was called to Augsburg in 1530 by Margaret of Austria, to paint the portraits of *Charles V* and of *Maria of Hungary.* He became court painter of Charles V, whom he also accompanied on his campaign to Tunis in 1535. Twelve large paintings, finished in 1547, commemorate this *Tunis Campaign* (Vienna). Vermeyen was also an original and outstanding etcher. His personality and his beard to his waist are a source of many historical anecdotes.

**VERNET (Antoine - Charles; called Carle).**—French painter and lithographer (Bordeaux, 1758; Paris, 1836). Pupil of his father and of Lépicé, he gained the Prix de Rome in 1782, with the *Prodigal Son.* He showed surprising facility at an early age. His historical painting he considered merely as an opportunity to paint horses. During the Revolution, he was wounded by the Republicans. His talent suffered, and was not exercised again till the time of the Directory (Directoire).

VERNET (CARLE): THE ROAD FROM ST. CLOUD. Lithograph. (Bibl. Nat.)

His *Death of Hippolytus* and *Chariot Races* were spirited drawings from which many engravings were made. He also caricatured contemporary fashions and customs, as in the *Incroyables* and the *Merveilleuses* which are amusing if malicious, and were renowned both then and now.

He was also a painter of battles, and was the first to give importance to the strategic element of war scenes. (Battle of *Marengo*: *Austerlitz;* in the Museum of Versailles.) Unfortunately the colour is cold and dull. As painter of dogs, races, etc., he is unequalled, and he also frequently painted horses, in his pictures of ladies in carriages, huntsmen, etc.

During the Restoration period he gave up painting for crayon. He was one of the first to use the lithographic process, which suited his type of spontaneous talent well. The invasions gave him the opportunity to caricature the Cossacks, English, Prussians, etc. He also depicted many types of Parisian life.

**— (Claude - Joseph).** — French painter of sea pieces and landscapes; born at Avignon, and died at Paris (1714-1789). He was the son of a painter of figures and armorial bearings. When only seventeen he was sent to Rome and there entered the studio of two seascape painters. He spent most of his time observing the country round about, and trying to reproduce the exact colours of the sky at different times of day. He even invented an alphabet consisting of signs, which represented variations of colour, however subtle and fleeting, and which enabled Vernet to recapture, in his studio, changing lights and colours. Vernet had renown in Europe in his own day, but what his contemporaries chiefly appreciated was that aspect of his work which is thought less of today. They liked his tempests, ships on fire, and scenes showing man in danger. Today we prefer his calm seas, delicate rendering of atmosphere, etc., which show his lightness of touch and subtlety of vision.

BIBLIOGRAPHY: L. Lagrange, *Les Vernet.* 1864.

**— (Emile Jean Horace).**—French painter (Paris, 1789-1863). He was

VERNET (HORACE): NAPOLEON I AT THE BATTLE OF JENA. (Museum, Versailles.)

the son of Carle Vernet, and grandson of Joseph. In his father's studio he encountered many witnesses of the wars of the Republic and the Empire, so when in 1810 he exhibited his first picture, the *Taking of an Entrenched Camp,* he showed skill in painting uniforms. Two years later, he won official recognition by his portrait of Jerome Bonaparte, King of Westphalia.

In 1814 he took part in the defense of Paris, which gave him the idea for one of his best military scenes, *The Barrier of Clichy* (Louvre).

In the Salon of 1822 none of Vernet's pictures were hung, as the *Battle of Jemmapes* and the *Barrier of Clichy* had been refused. As these were patriotic pictures, there was general indignation, and when Vernet had a private show of his refused pictures, everybody went to see them. This included, besides the two above-mentioned pictures, *The Soldier of Waterloo; The Death of Poniatowski; Horace's Studio.*

The government favoured him and for this reason he was twice commissioned to paint the portrait of Charles X, and then became Director of the French School at Rome, for which, however, he was

DETAIL OF THE LITHOGRAPH BY JAZET AFTER H. VERNET: THE FAREWELL AT FONTAINEBLEAU. Lithograph. (Bibl. Nat.)

not suitable. The antique and nature meant little to him. His *Judith* is a theatrical attempt at a subject he could not do.

Replaced in Rome by Ingres, he returned to France when Louis-Philippe was restoring Versailles, and Vernet decorated the Constantine apartment with his battle scenes. These vast compositions show an almost photographic exactitude. Detailed as these are, however, they are somewhat disconnected. Truth to tell, his vast, facile paintings are not the works of an artist. He simply invented a kind of military panorama.

BIBLIOGRAPHY: Armand Dayot, *Les Vernet.* Paris.

**VERNIS MARTIN.**—See Furniture (Eighteenth Century).

**VERONA (Italy).**—A town which has been important since ancient

VERONA: THE CATHEDRAL.

times. It has some Roman buildings, such as the *Porta Leoni* and the *Porta Borsari,* and the *Arena,* which may have been built about 290 A.D., and was restored by Napoleon. There are also ruins of a Roman Theatre. The Emperor Theodoric, and later, Pepin, son of Charlemagne, further added to the town, though in Pepin's time, a violent earthquake destroyed many buildings.

*San Zeno Maggiore*—the oldest Romanesque Church of Verona, and also the most remarkable of its kind in Northern Italy. It dates from the 11th century—the choir (since restored) belongs to the 13th. The nave is divided into bays articulated by diaphragm arches carrying

VERONA: SAN ZENO MAGGIORE.

gables which support the roof timbers. The choir is raised above the large vaulted crypt. The façade is very simple. The columns of the porch rest on two red marble lions; the door is decorated with bas-re-

VERONA: THE ARENA.

liefs of the 12th century; one of them represents Theodoric fleeing from the devil. The interior has three aisles. Behind the high altar is a beautiful *Madonna* by Mantegna.

The *Cathedral* has a Romanesque façade with Gothic windows; a 12th century choir; a 14th century Gothic nave. There is sculpture round the door. Behind one of the altars is an *Assumption* by Titian. The choir communicates with the *Baptistery San Giovanni in Fonte* (12th century) which has good Romanesque reliefs.

*Santa Maria Antica,* a little Romanesque church has, outside it, the famous *Tombs of the Scaligers,* the work of Lombard sculptors.

See Pl. 50, Vol. I.

The *Palazzo della Ragione* begun in 1183, is an austere building with Romanesque windows; the *Loggia,* or *Palazzo del Consiglio* is Renaissance in style.

*Santa Anastasia* is a Gothic church with a brick façade and marble doorway with reliefs and a 14th century fresco. There are frescoes in the interior, by Altichiero and Pisanello, among others.

The *Piazza delle Erbe,* formerly a forum, is surrounded by interesting buildings; the *Maffei Palace* (Baroque style); the *Casa dei Mercanti,* etc.

The *Bridge of the Scaligers* (1354) leads to the *Castello Vecchio* (built in 1355 by Can Grande II)—a dull red brick fortress.

**VERONESE (Paolo Caliari, known as).**—Venetian painter, 1528-

VERONESE, SELF-PORTRAIT (from the Marriage at Cana).

1588; called "Veronese" because he was born in Verona. It was also in Verona that he received his training as a painter. He began by learning sculpture with his father Gabriele Caliari, who was himself a sculptor. But, attracted by colour, he ended by joining the studio of Antonio Badile, who had a certain reputation as a painter. There, his marvellous gifts soon became manifest. Early works, which he already painted with considerable mastery and brilliance, is the Berilacqua Altarpiece of 1548, now in the Gallery at Verona, in bad state. He went to Castelfranco, where he decorated

VERONESE: THE PILGRIMS AT EMMAUS. (Louvre.)

the Sacristy of San Liberale with frescoes in 1551. In 1553, he made the decoration of the Villa Emo, at Fanzolo, near Treviso.

Veronese had not yet been to Venice, that paradise of painters. But one of his compatriots, Father Bernardo Taliani, Prior of the Gerolamini of San Sebastiano, called him there, and he arrived at the end of 1554, or the beginning of 1555. There he found many painters who must have heightened his enthusiasm—Tintoretto—Paris Bordone—and, above all, Titian.

He was not able to paint profoundly moving scenes, such as Titian's *Entombment* (Louvre). He is the great painter of Venetian pomp and ceremony, which he emphasised, making marble porticoes higher and whiter, jewels brighter, people more brilliant, even than those he saw in that luxurious city. He discovered the decorative beauty of well-drawn silhouettes, seen on a rich balcony, against a blue sky. He was influenced by the best artists of Verona.

His first works in Venice were for the Church of San Sebastiano: a ceiling, with the *Story of Esther*; another, in the Sacristy, with the *Coronation of the Virgin*; several altarpieces, a *Virgin with Saints* and a *Crucifixion* (all between 1555 and 1560). This church is a veritable museum of his paintings, and later (c. 1565), he painted there one of his most dramatic compositions—the *Martyrdom of St. Mark and of St. Marcilian*, beside the *Martyrdom of St. Sebastian.*

VERONESE: JUDITH. (Museum, Vienna.)

In 1561, Titian chose Veronese to assist him, with other painters, in the decoration of the Libreria; and he painted there three allegorical medallions, representing *Music*, *Mathematics* and *Honor*, and he won the gold chain offered as a prize for the best painting.

He covered the ceilings of the Doge's Palace with magnificent compositions, working there intermittently from 1553 to 1587.

In 1563, he painted, for the refectory of the Convent of San Giorgio Maggiore, the celebrated *Marriage of Cana*, of the Louvre. The subject was made for him. He amplified it, and enriched it, and gave it all possible brilliance. It was nothing to his purpose that in the simple times of the Gospel, the scene would not have been thus, and that its splendour was to be contemplated by monks, while they eat in silence. Among the guests who take part in the marriage feast, he represented well-known people of his time. The bride is Eleanor of Austria, wife of Don Alphonso d'Avalos; Francis I, the Emperor Charles V; Queen Mary of England and the Sultan Soliman I are seen with Christ. The painter himself, and Titian, are playing music. Behind the actual scene of the feast, runs a balcony, with figures silhouetted against the blue sky. Beyond, are the towers of great buildings.

Veronese often painted banquet scenes—*Christ at Emmaus* (Louvre); *Feast at the House of Levi* (Accademia, Venice, versions in the Louvre and at Turin). He was not the first to introduce fantastic wealth and contemporary figures into religious scenes; but he certainly went further in this direction than any previous artist had done—so far, that he was finally called before the Holy Office, owing to his painting of *Christ in the House of Simon*, which he painted for the Domenicans of San Zanipolo. The licence he allowed himself had become dangerous. He was allowed three months to alter his picture at his own expense

Veronese's temperament was admirably suited to paint mythological scenes. Two pictures of the *Rape of Europa* are in the Doge's Palace, and in the Capitol, Rome.

About 1566, he painted the *Family of Darius at the Feet of Alexander* (National Gallery). His luminous gold and silvery colour is admirably seen in his painting of *Venice, Queen of the Adriatic*, in the Doge's Palace.

Veronese's work is so abundant that only a fraction of it can be mentioned. Besides the paintings already noted, there are: *Ceres Offering Her Gifts to Venice* (Accademia); *St. George* (Verona); *The Martyrdom of St. Justina* (Padua); *St. Anthony* (Brera); *Portrait of Daniele Barbaro* (Pitti, Florence); and many fine paintings in the National Gallery, in the Prado, in Dresden, Leningrad, Paris, and, above all, in Venice.

Veronese died in Venice in 1588, and was buried in the Church of San Sebastiano, all decorated with his works.

See Pl. 21, Vol. II.

BIBLIOGRAPHY: P. H. Osmond, *Paolo Veronese*. London, 1927.—G. Fiocco, *Paolo Veronese*. 1929.

**VERROCCHIO (Andrea del).**—Florentine sculptor, painter, architect and goldsmith; born 1435, died 1488.

VERROCCHIO (ANDREA): CHRIST AND ST. THOMAS. (Or San Michele, Florence.)

In 1452 Verrocchio is mentioned as having unintentionally killed a friend with a stone; in the next year he is acquitted of the charge of homicide. In 1457 his cadastral declaration states that he had temporarily given up his trade as a goldsmith because of lack of orders. In 1461 he competes for a commission to design a chapel in the Duomo of Orvieto; and in 1465 he is commissioned to execute a bronze group of Christ and St. Thomas still on the exterior of Or San Michele. The first document of payment for the above is of 1467. In 1468 Verrocchio is paid for a bronze candlestick for the audience hall of the Palazzo Vecchio; and in the next year his drawing for Faith, one of the personifications painted by Piero Pollaiuolo for the Mercatanzia, is rejected. In 1471 a copper globe, cast by Verrocchio, is put into place on the top of Brunelleschi's dome (destroyed by lightning in 1600). From 1465 dated the commission to execute a tomb for Cosimo de' Medici; and two years later Cosimo's body is buried in the tomb. In 1471 the tomb of Giovanni and Piero de' Medici in San Lorenzo was finished. The bronze David, executed for the Medici villa at Careggi, was bought by the Signoria

VERROCCHIO (ANDREA): FOUNTAIN OF THE PALAZZO VECCHIO. (Florence.)

of Florence in 1476. (The putto by Verrocchio now in the Palazzo Vecchio was also made for Careggi.) Other Medici commissions filled by Verrocchio are listed in an inventory of 1496, including a bust of Giuliano de' Medici from Verrocchio's own hand (Mellon Collection, Washington). Giovanni Rucellai mentions in his journal that Verrocchio worked for his family.

In 1473 Verrocchio estimates the value of a pulpit by Mino da Fiesole and Rossellino at Prato. Leonardo is mentioned as living with Verrocchio in 1476. In 1477 competes for the Forteguerri monument, Pistoia, with Piero Pollaiuolo. Piero's design was accepted by the operai, but Andrea's was ordered executed by Lorenzo de' Medici, a decision in which the operai concur, admitting that they are incompetent to judge. In the same year he presents two models for reliefs for the altar of S. Giovanni, and one, the Beheading of St. John, is accepted. This relief is finished in 1840. The commission for the Colleoni equestrian statue in Venice was awarded in 1479, the model to be executed in Florence. It was sent to Venice two years later. From 1485 there is a document of payment for an altar painting of the *Virgin between Saints* for the Duomo of Pistoia, mentioned as being almost finished. In 1488 Verrocchio's will requests that Credi, his pupil, be entrusted with the casting of the Colleoni (it was actually cast by Leopardi, who had assisted Verrocchio in its execution; the casting was begun in 1490 and the monument erected in 1496). In this same year Verrocchio was charged to execute a fountain to be erected in Florence by the King of Hungary. Marble had been bought for this work when the sculptor died.

Not one absolutely certain (documented) painting exists by Verrocchio, who must have been a painter of note, because of his evident influence upon contemporary and succeeding painters. The *Baptism* in the Uffizi is universally accepted as by his hand (the angel at the left by Leonardo); and there are *Madonnas* in Berlin, Frankfurt, and the Metropolitan Museum attributed to him.

BIBLIOGRAPHY: Vasari-Milanesi.—Gaye, *Carteggio*, I.—C. von Fabriczy, *Andrea del Verrocchio al servizio dei Medici*, Arch. stor. dell' arte, 2nd series, I, 1895, p. 163; *Verrocchio und das Altarbild der Sacraments Kapelle im Dom zu Pistoia*, Repert. f. Kunstwiss., XXII, 1899, p. 338; *Neues zum Werke Andrea Verrocchios*, Repert. f. Kunstwiss., 1904.—Cruttwell, *Verrocchio*, 1904.

**VERSAILLES (France).**—The palace of Versailles, built for Louis XIII, shows to perfection the art of the reign of Louis XIV, and contains work by Mansart, Le Nôtre, Le Brun, and Le Vau.

VERSAILLES: FORECOURT OF THE CHÂTEAU.

In the interior, the apartments, in spite of the restorations of Louis

CHÂTEAU OF VERSAILLES: UPPER VESTIBULE OF THE CHAPEL.

Philippe's time, also show the sumptuous decoration which reflected the character of the time of absolute monarchy under Louis

XIV. Le Brun's decoration, for instance, of the great gallery (1679), was the culmination of his life as an artist. Gobelin tapestries were ordered for the Palace; marble, glass, gold work, etc., adorned the walls.

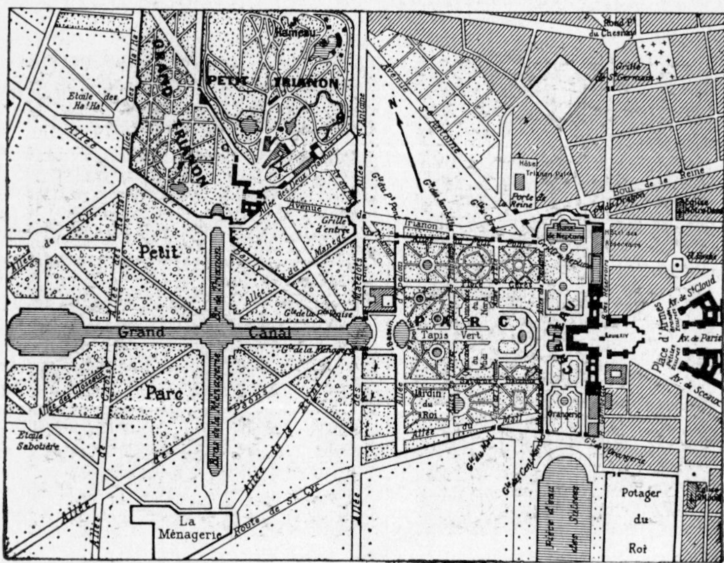


VERSAILLES: PLAN OF THE CHÂTEAU AND ITS OUTBUILDINGS.

The castle was enlarged to meet the needs of the whole court. The chapel took ten years to build (1700-1710). J. H. Mansart, who had played so large a part in the construction of the palace, died before the chapel was finished.

PARK OF VERSAILLES: THE ONE HUNDRED STEPS.

Under Louis XV, Versailles showed something of the paganism which was the spirit of the age, even in the introduction of little sculptured cherubs in the chapel, and in the type of ceiling painting (the *Apotheosis of Hercules*) in the new "Salon d'Hercule."

CHÂTEAU OF VERSAILLES: SALON OF VENUS AND THE STATUE OF LOUIS XIV BY JEAN WARIN.

In the time of Louis XVI, Marie Antoinette (later to face at Versailles the outraged people during the French Revolution) gave new character to the small rooms, sometimes showing a liking for the classical style which the recent excavations of Pompeii, etc., had brought into fashion.

VERSAILLES: THE CHÂTEAU FROM THE PARK AFTER THE FIRST WORK BY LE VAU. Engraving by Pérelle.

Napoleon, fortunately, had no time to harm Versailles, while Louis Philippe, in his turn, turned Louis XIV's castle into a National Museum.

The grounds of Versailles shared the fate of the castle. They gave great pleasure to Louis XIV, while enlargements or alterations of their formal arrangements were frequently made. The *Trianons* (the large and small) again show the dominant court style of architecture. They became, from being places for refreshment, small marble palaces—retreats and pleasure places for the court. The *Petit Trianon*, built by Louis XV in 1759, won the approval of Madame de Pompadour, and was later where Marie Antoinette played her pastoral games on the very eve of the Revolution.

See Gabriel, Mansart, Le Nôtre, and Le Vau. Also Pls. 42, 43, 44, Vol. II.

**VESTIER (Antoine).** — French miniature painter, 1740-1824. His works may be seen in the Louvre, and in the Museum of Tours.

BIBLIOGRAPHY: H. Bouchot, *La Miniature en France*. 1910.

**VÉZELAY (Yonne).**—*Church of the Madeleine*. One of the finest Burgundian Romanesque churches in France. It was built on the site of a ninth century church, and retains the choir of the early building. In 1096, the Abbé Artaud enlarged the edifice to meet the needs of the great throngs of pilgrims who flocked to Vézelay. The construction of the nave was accomplished from 1096 to 1104, and the narthex probably between 1120 and 1135. The choir was probably destroyed by fire, in the 12th century, and was rebuilt at the end of it at the same time as the transept. The façade, tower and gable are later, by some years. The church, spared by the Revolution, suffered much from the ravages of time. It was in a very dilapidated state in 1840, when Viollet-le-Duc undertook its restoration.

VÉZELAY: CAPITAL FROM THE NAVE.

Behind the façade opens a magnificent narthex, 22 metres long, composed of three aisles, which forms a kind of introductory nave, or little church preceding the large nave, with which it communicates by three doors, over which are wonderful carvings. In the tympanum over the middle doorway Christ is represented sending down the Holy Spirit on the Apostles. Above this scene are eight little square compositions with figures. Some think these represent the seven churches of Asia, and St. John; others, that they are scenes from the life of the apostles. On the lintel is a series of little figures (shepherds, archers, knights, men, women, dwarfs, and monsters), which admit of various interpretations. Mâle thinks it shows a kind of map of the world, representing the different peoples. Others think it represents the Israelites going to the land of Canaan. The tympanum of the south (left) portal of the narthex is divided in two parts: below is the *Annunciation*, and *Birth of Christ*, and above is the *Adoration of the Magi*. The right-hand tympanum is also divided into two, and represents the last scenes of the *Life of Christ* (pilgrims of Emmaus), and, above, the *Ascension*. All the capitals of the narthex pillars are decorated with charming carvings representing little scenes (*David and Bathsheba*, *St. Peter* and *St. Paul*, the *Dream of Pharaoh*, the *Sacrifice of Abraham*, etc.).

VÉZELAY (YONNE): PORTAL OF THE NARTHEX OF THE CHURCH OF THE MADELEINE.

The nave of the Madeleine is a magnificent construction, 62 metres long by 14 metres wide, in ten groin vaulted bays without diagonal ribs, and arcades with semi-circular arches. The capitals of the pillars are carved (in the first thirty years of the 12th century). The choir dates from the end of the 12th century, and has a sexpartite vault. The same for the transept. The ambulatory has nine chapels leading out of it, with Gothic vaultings, separated by Romanesque arcades.

Nothing remains of the old dwelling places of this once powerful Abbey. The town retains only a part of its mediæval wall, the Porte Neuve, and its two solid, round, battlemented towers.

At the foot of the hill of Vézelay is a charming Gothic church, *Saint-Pierre-sous-Vézelay*. On the façade, is a gable decorated with statues recalling those of the Madeleine.

See Pls. 44, 46, Vol. I.

**VICENTINO (Il).**—See Michelí (Andrea).

**VICENZA (Italy).**—Vicenza possesses some fine buildings, such as the *Basilica Palladiana* built in two

# AMERICAN ART: EIGHTEENTH AND NINETEENTH CENTURIES

*The development of an art tradition in America was singularly dependent on the accumulated traditions adopted from the older countries. The native Indian art has had only a relatively minor influence upon the truly American tradition, even in the present time when the art efforts of the American Indian are better known. Early in the history of the Colonies, sheer living conditions were sufficiently precarious and all-absorbing of time and effort to provide little opportunity for artistic activity, and that little was first applied to the arts related to beautification of the homes: furniture, woodwork, metal work, glass.*

JOHN TRUMBULL: FISHER AMES.
*(Courtesy of the Detroit Institute of Arts.)*

JOHN SMIBERT: FAMILY OF BISHOP BERKELEY.
*(Courtesy Raymond and Raymond.)*

RALPH EARLE: WILLIAM CARPENTER.
*(Courtesy of the Worcester Art Museum.)*

The English tradition is the predominant tradition upon which American art is founded, and most 17th and 18th century artists were trained in England. West opened his atelier and taught and painted for years in London. Trumbull, Earle, Peale, and many more were his pupils, while Stuart later came strongly under his influence. Smibert, an early 18th century artist, introduces elements of the Dutch tradition, at least in his technique, for he builds on a slate-blue ground of underpainting rather than in the traditional red-ochre of the English school. By his fusion of Dutch and English elements, in addition to his own personal point of view, he is among the first really American painters.

GILBERT STUART: GEORGE WASHINGTON.
*(Courtesy of Frick Art Reference Library.)*

BENJAMIN WEST: MRS. WEST AND HER SON RAPHAEL.
*(Courtesy of the Cleveland Museum of Art.)*

JOHN SINGLETON COPLEY: ELIZABETH GOLDTHWAITE.
*(Collections of the Brooklyn Museum—Gift of Walter H. Crittenden.)*

THOMAS SULLY: BOY WITH THE TORN HAT.
*(Courtesy Raymond and Raymond.)*

Portraiture, monumental battle-scenes, and depiction of great memorable public occasions were the characteristic subjects, executed for the most part in stilted and conventional fashion. With few exceptions, the work of this period is capable and faithful depiction of contemporary figures and the important events involving their activities, subjects which today would be relegated largely to the photographer. Such men as Stuart and Sully bring originality to their interpretation of the English tradition. Interest in character and personality, in individual form and artistic conception becomes apparent.

JAMES A. MCNEILL WHISTLER: RIVA (NO. 2).
*(New York Public Library.)*

FRANK DUVENECK: COBBLER'S APPRENTICE.
*(Courtesy Taft Museum.)*

GEORGE INNESS: PEACE AND PLENTY.
*(Metropolitan Museum of Art.)*

Whistler makes a doubly important contribution to American painting tradition in his impressionism, and in his virtual introduction of Japanese art to the West. In America after the Civil War, there was new interest in painting, and opportunities for education and production in the arts were more favourable. The idea of working from direct observation gave rise to an ever more important landscape school, so interestingly launched by the Hudson River School in the first half of the century, with Inness, Martin and Wyant carrying on the tradition later. Duveneck brought back the Munich technique based on direct drawing with the brush.

# AMERICAN ART: NINETEENTH AND TWENTIETH CENTURIES

*Until some security, some leisure were assured in the lives of the colonists, almost every article of beautification for the home or the community was imported from the mother country. It is small wonder then that the Colonial artists, with not only the memory of the old artistic traditions, but also with the imported examples before their eyes, should at first have been little more than copyists. With new means at their disposal, with new conditions to work in, the old methods and designs soon develop from pure imitations into new designs and methods.*

ARTHUR B. DAVIES: UNICORNS.
*(Metropolitan Museum of Art.)*

ALBERT P. RYDER: TOILERS OF THE SEA.
*(Addison Gallery of American Art, Phillips Academy, Andover, Mass.)*

Davies and Ryder are two artists of the type which appears in every period: lone workers, withdrawn from any group though often working in various groups, seeking always for solutions to their own problems. They retire in their own worlds: Ryder with his emotionalism, his drama, his search for harmonious tone and shape; Davies in love with charm and youth depicted with sentiment and delicate idealism.

CHILDE HASSAM: SUMMER AFTERNOON, OREGON.
*(Raymond and Raymond.)*

MARY CASSATT:
GIRL COMBING HER HAIR.
*(From the Chester Dale Collection.)*

GEORGE BELLOWS: STAG AT SHARKEY'S (LITHOGRAPH).
*(Courtesy of Mrs. George Bellows—Photo, McKillop.)*

## Impressionism

Impressionism was to be an influence for more than a generation in America. The searching nature schools of Barbizon and Düsseldorf, the doctrine of *plein-airism* beginning as revolutionary, were to find their echo for years in the academies not only of Paris but also in the studios of America. The Impressionism of Manet as well as Monet finds sympathetic response in varied groups. Manet's belief in the supreme importance of light, viewing nature as a collection of areas seen in varying degrees of light and colour, Monet's broken colour and interest in fleeting effects influenced the vision and technique of many groups, at the head of which Hassam, Prendergast, Twachtman, Cassatt, and others stand as strong influences and disciples.

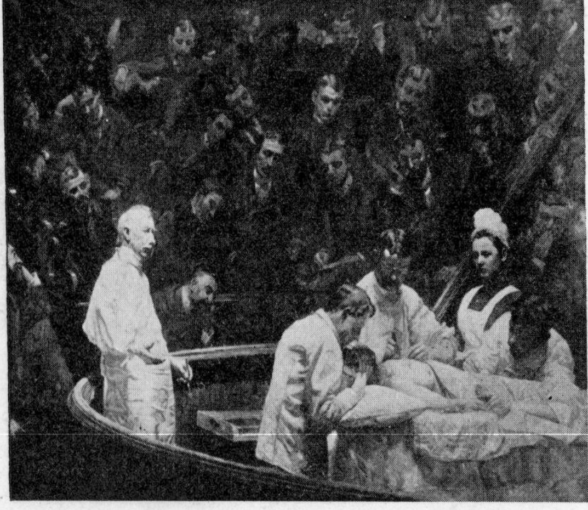

THOMAS EAKINS:
PORTRAIT OF DAVID HAYES AGNEW AND HIS CLINIC.
*(Courtesy George H. Nitzche, University of Pennsylvania.)*

WINSLOW HOMER: PALM TREE
(WATERCOLOUR).
*(Metropolitan Museum of Art.)*

JOHN SLOAN: MCSORLEY'S BAR.
*(Courtesy of the Detroit Institute of Arts.)*

Following Homer's precept of direct nature observation comes the scientific, painstaking absorption in an ever widening range of subject-matter, a sincere and objective search for realistic form, and a detestation for shallow prettiness. Eakins stands as early example of this group, with his medical and anatomical research and conscientious rendering of local and particular scenes. Bellows later was of this important group to which Luks, Henri and Sloan are a few of the members, absorbed in finding inspiration for their art in the contemporary American scene.

storeys of arcades, Doric and Ionic. It was constructed from 1549 to 1614 according to the plans of Palladio. The *Museo Civico* is also the work of Palladio, and so is the *Teatro Olympico*. The Villa Rotonda is a square building with four Ionic porticoes. In the centre is a large circular chamber, covered with a dome, 1570.

**VICTORIA AND ALBERT MUSEUM.**—See London.

**VICTORY of SAMOTHRACE.** —This famous statue of Victory, now in the Louvre, was discovered on the island of Samothrace in 1863. Later, in 1879, the blocks which formed the pedestal were also transported to the Louvre, so that the monument has been restored in its entirety. This pedestal consists of an oblong base. The statue was a votive offering, following the victory of Demetrios Poliorcetes over Ptolemy in 306 B.C., and it must have been made immediately after this date. The Victory is represented as standing on the forecastle with outspread wings. In her right hand she holds a trumpet to her lips. The head and arms have not been recovered. The wind blows against the body, and the delicate material of the garment, which streams out behind the goddess. The drapery is wonderfully treated. Belonging to the date which it does, such a work as this may be related quite naturally to the school of Scopas.

See Pl. 25, Vol. I.

Bibliography: Collignon, *Histoire de la sculpture grecque,* Vol. II, p. 464, *et seq.*—Ernest Gardner, *A Handbook of Greek Sculpture*. London, 1923.

**VIEN (Marie Joseph).**—French painter, 1716-1809. Born at Montpellier, pupil of Natoire. He won the "grand prix," and went to Rome in 1744. Reacting against the conventional and affected art of his day, he was inspired by the realism of Caravaggio, as his *Sleeping Hermit* (Louvre) shows. But on seeing the recently discovered antiquities of Herculaneum, he tried to combine the study of nature with that of the antique. He achieved only a coldly calculated art, which degenerated into a feeble Hellenism. His chief interest lies in the fact that he was the master of David, whom he influenced to the study of the antique, but who kept his own strength and virility. Vien's cold, correct painting is well seen in his picture of the *Preaching of St. Denis,* in the Church of Saint Roch, Paris.

**VIENNA (Austria).**—*Cathedral of St. Stephen.* Built from 1300 to 1519, on the site of a Romanesque church, of which some parts remain. It is a late Gothic building, in the form of a Latin cross, with three naves (108 metres long). Large pillars, decorated with statues, support the vaulting. There are two small west towers. There are larger towers above the transept portals. The north transept tower shows East European influence in its onion dome. The south transept tower has a huge steeple. The nave and aisles are nearly the same height and there is neither triforium nor clerestorey. The roof is very high.

The *Palace* (until 1918, the Imperial Palace) was begun in the 13th century, but has many modern buildings.

Most Viennese buildings date from the 19th century.

**VIERGE DORÉE.**—See Amiens; Also Pl. 53, Vol. I.

**VIERZEHNHEILIGEN.** — See Neumann, J. Balthasar.

**VIGÉE - LEBRUN (Elizabeth Louise).**—French painter, 1755-1842. Daughter of Louis Vigée, a portrait painter, she had her first lessons from her father, then from the

Mme. Vigée-Lebrun (Elisabeth Louise). Self-portrait. (Louvre.)

Academicians Briard and Doyen, and she was also helped by Greuze. She worked a great deal in the studio of the expert painter, Lebrun, who allowed her to copy pictures there, and ended by marrying her. Owing to her husband's dissipated habits, she separated from him, and became the favoured portrait painter of Marie Antoinette. The Academy opened its doors to Madame Vigée-Lebrun in 1783. The list of her works made by herself in her Memoirs, includes all the people known at Court, and in Parisian society, whom she had to paint under Louis XVI. Her salon was one of the most elegant and lively "rendez-vous" in Paris. The first events of the Revolution sent Madame Vigée-Lebrun abroad. (Her

Vigée-Lebrun (Mme.): The Dauphin and the Duchess of Angoulême. (Museum, Versailles.)

rival, Madame Labille-Guyard, stayed in Paris). She went to Turin, Florence (where her own portrait by herself joined the famous collection of self-portraits in the Pitti Palace), Rome (where she painted more portraits, including one of Hubert Robert), and Naples—where she painted all the royal family, and Lady Hamilton "as a Bacchante, lying by the sea-shore." She stayed in Parma, Venice, Vienna (for three years), and St. Petersburg, where she lived for six years, painting for the Empress Catherine, then for Paul I and Alexander I. Berlin was one of the last cities she visited before returning to Paris, which she did in the winter of 1801. This was only to leave again for another three years, which she spent in England. She painted portraits of the Prince of Wales, and Lord Byron, and was a great success. She paid two visits to Holland and Switzerland before finally settling in Paris.

Madame Vigée-Lebrun concludes her memoirs with certain advice about painting. She seems to have chosen Rubens, Van Dyck and Greuze for her masters.

If her drawing is often uncertain and betrays the mannerisms which were the fashion in her youth, if she exaggerates expressions of affection into sentimentality, there is still a freshness about her figures which attracts. Her colour is bright. There is a charming variety and delicacy in her flesh tints, and in her stuffs. In her arrangements there is a certain unexpectedness, which seems to owe something to English engravings, and gives to her work the charm of diversity.

See Pl. 46, Vol. II.

Bibliography: *Memoires de Mme. Vigée-Lebrun,* 2 vols.—P. de Nolhac, *Madame Vigée-Lebrun.* 1910.

**VIGNOLA (Jacopo Barozzi, known as).**—Architect (Italian), 1507-1573. Called Vignola from his native place, near Modena. A theorist, he aspired to be a second Vitruvius. He was a leader of the academic group of Mannerist architects who clung to the antiquarians of the High Renaissance and shunned the turbulence of the proto-Baroque. He wrote a *Treatise on the Orders,* which became a handbook for architects. With the example of his works as well as his writings, his influence was felt for centuries.

He began as a painter in Bologna, but architecture soon drew him, and, after studying in Rome, he went as assistant to Primaticcio, at Fontainebleau, to arrange the settings of pictures. He then returned to Bologna, where he built the *Palazzo Bocchi* and the tower of the *Palazzo Isolani.*

Then he went to Rome, and became the architect of Julius III, and of the whole Farnese family. The *Casino* and the *Villa di Papa Giulio* (1550-1555), in which Michelangelo and Vasari also had a part, were chiefly executed by Vignola. He was, above all, the architect of the famous *Castle of Caprarola,* built in 1547 for Alexander Farnese, nephew of Julius III. This was splendid in its elevation, its staircases, and its wings, but simple and harmonious at the same time. Then Vignola built the little *Oratory of Sant'Andrea* outside the Porta del Popolo; the external façade of this gateway (1561); and the porticoed stairways which lead to Santa Maria Aracœli and to the Tarpeian Rock. In the building of the Mother Church of the Jesuits (1568) he created a type which was to be repeated in a crowd of churches far and wide. It appealed to the taste for elegance and worldliness. Jesuit churches became salons. Vignola aimed at having as much space as possible. He, therefore, suppressed side aisles, and erected the altar at the back of the apse. He respected the Latin cross. But on either side of the big nave—which was built as high as possible, and seemed like a ballroom—the chapels were hardly more than little niches to give the illusion of more space. In spite of its richness and gilding, the Gesà was still harmonious, but the Baroque style was created, and even researches into the illusion of perspective, which were so much the fashion in the succeeding century, appeared, already, in the midst of correct arrangements. It only wanted architects to push these innovations to their logical conclusion, and they were not wanting. The façade of the Gesà and much interior decoration is by Della Porta.

Bibliography: O. Raschdorff, *Memorie e Studi intorno a Jacopo Barozzi. Vignola,* 1908.—A Ricci, *Storia dell'Architettura italiana.*—Vignola's works: *Regola dei cinque ordini d'architettura* (1563); *Due regole della prospettiva pratica.*

**VIGNON (Barthélemy).**—French architect, 1762-1829. He worked at the Château St. Leu and in Paris, for Louis Bonaparte. The Empress Josephine entrusted him and his friend Thibaud with various works at Malmaison.

**VILLA BORGHESE.**—See Rome.

— **d'ESTE.**—See Pl. 7, Vol. II.

— **MEDICI.**—See Rome; also Pl. 7, Vol. II.

**VILLARD de HONNECOURT.** —French architect of the middle of the 13th century, famous for his sketch-book, which is kept in the Bibliothèque Nationale (Manuscrits français, No. 19093, 33 pages). This document, which is infinitely valuable to the study of mediæval art, tells us of his travels in France, Switzerland, and Hungary, whither his reputation had preceded him, and it tells us, too, a good deal about the methods of the Gothic builders. Villard de Honnecourt

Villard de Honnecourt: The Falcon. (Bibl. Nat.)

made a series of very varied sketches—of Reims Cathedral, designs of cloisters and rose-windows, battles, religious scenes taken from the *Golden Legend,* animals, conversations, geometric figures for the construction of buildings. All these drawings prove how wide were his interests.

Some have given to Villard the glory of Reims Cathedral, but this attribution cannot be maintained. It has been shown that he very probably worked at the building of the church of Vaucelles, and of the collegiate church of Saint-Quentin, and that he was very likely called to Hungary by the monks of Citeaux, the architectural methods of which he must have observed.

Bibliography: Quicherat, *Mélanges d'archéologie et d'histoire.* Paris, 1886, Vol. II, pp. 238-298.—Bibliothèque Nationale, Manuscript Department: *Album de Villard de Honnecourt, architecte du XIIIe siècle.* Paris (Berthaud). This is an entire reproduction of the album in phototype, and a complete bibliography. H. R. Hahnloser, *Villard de Honnecourt.* Vienna, 1935.

**VINCI.**—See Leonardo da Vinci.

**VIOLLET - LE - DUC (Eugène Emmanuel).** — French architect. Paris, 1814—Lausanne, 1879. He travelled from the North to the South of France on foot, studying all the buildings he saw, making sketches and notes. From 1836-1838 he visited Italy. In 1840, he became inspector of the restoration works of the Sainte Chapelle, under the direction of Duban and Lassus. For forty years, he gave his services, as architect, inspector general, and writer, to the restoration of mediæval buildings. In 1842, he obtained, in competition with Lassus, the restoration of Notre Dame. They worked there together from 1845 to 1856. The sacristy, which has been so strongly criticised, is their joint work. In 1857, on the death of his collaborator, Viollet-le-Duc had sole charge of the restoration of the Cathedral. The central spire, the high-altar, and the chapels are by him.

Viollet-le-Duc: Entrance to the Château of Pierrefonds (Oise).

To mention only a few of the many restorations for which he was responsible: the old fortified town of Carcassonne (1852), the Château of Pierrefonds (1858—his masterpiece), the Church of St. Sernin, Toulouse, the ramparts of Avignon, the Porte Saint André, at Autun, the cloisters of the Church of Moissac.

Viollet-le-Duc left many writings describing his numerous restorations.

Nowadays, Viollet-le-Duc is much criticised for his bold restorations. But, it may be asked, if the Viollet-le-Ducs, and the Lassuses had not completed ruins and re-established wholes, what idea should we have left of the Middle Ages? Without 19th century "Gothic," which did not scruple to add to the restored charms of mediæval works, such things as the porches of Notre Dame and of Vézelay would be nothing but ruins and museum scraps.

**VIRGIN OF THE ROCKS.**—See Leonardo da Vinci; also Pl. 17, Vol. II.

**VISCHER (Peter the Elder).**—The most famous German sculptor, about 1450-1529, born at Nuremberg. His work marks the transition between the Gothic and Renaissance styles. In this respect, Vischer may be said to have played a part in the evolution of German sculpture analogous to that of Albrecht Dürer in painting. He belonged to a family of artists. His father, Hermann, was a famous bronze caster. (He made the *Baptismal Fonts of St. Sebald*, in Nuremberg; those of Wittenberg (1457), and the *Tombstone of Bishop Georg,* in Bamberg.) From 1488, we find Peter's name on the guild register, in which he was described as "master sculptor and founder."

Peter Vischer's first known work, the *Tomb of Archbishop Ernst of Saxony*, 1496, in Magdeburg Cathedral, is still Gothic in conception. Surrounded by a profusion of ornaments, are statues of apostles, striking in their distinction and dignity. The statuette of *St. Maurice* is similar in angular outline and spatial feeling to Florentine sculpture of 30 years before (Verrocchio).

Peter Vischer: The Apostles St. Paul and St. John. (St. Sebald, Nuremberg.)

Peter Vischer: Saint Sebald healing a blind man. (St. Sebald, Nuremberg.)

About 1503-1504, Peter Vischer seems to have been called to Wittenberg and Torgau, by Frederick the Wise, and he must have made the acquaintance of Albrecht Dürer and Jacopo de' Barberi. It was, in fact, the latter who provided Peter Vischer with a drawing for the figure of the Duchess Sophia (died 1503), whose tomb is at Torgau (1504). From 1504 to 1508, Vischer was in Poland, where he left a series of important works, chiefly tombs. About 1508, he made, for the Church of Römhild, the *Tombstone of Hermann VIII von Henneberg* and of *Elizabeth of Brandenburg*.

On leaving Poland, Peter Vischer undertook, in collaboration with his five sons, Hermann, Peter, Hans, Jacob and Paul, the magnificent *Shrine of St. Sebald*, which is the pride of Nuremberg. Done between 1508-19, it is chiefly the work of his sons. In its main lines, it resembles the tomb of Casimir Jagellon, made in 1492, by Veit Stoss, in Kracow Cathedral. At each end of the two short sides is a statue—that of St. Sebald as a pilgrim, and that of Peter Vischer himself, beaming with good nature, and enveloped in a large leather apron. The Apostles can be divided into two groups: one taking up the idealistic style of the late 14th century, as opposed to the symbolic realism of the "crumpled" style; the other based on Venetian Renaissance and Lombard bronze sculpture. While the St. Sebaldus legend shows Dürer's influence, the use of household implements was taken from the Paduans.

While working on this Shrine, Peter Vischer carried out other orders aided by different artists, notably the two fine, life-sized figures of *Theodoric* and *King Arthur*, for the *Tomb of Maximilian*, at Innsbruck, 1512-13, together with some twenty statues representing the emperor's legendary ancestors, characterized by hardness of modelling and sharp precision of line.

After 1520, it is difficult to follow Vischer's works. Many other statues are attributed to him such as the celebrated *Madonna of Nuremberg*, a slender figure, carved in wood.

See Pl. 5, Vol. I; Pl. 25, Vol. II.

Bibliography: Autenrieth, *Das Sebaldusgrab P. Vischers.* Ausbach, 1887.—Headlam, *Peter Vischer.* London, 1901.—*Peter Vischer,* Collection des maîtres de l'Art. Paris.

**— (The Sons of Peter).**—Peter Vischer the elder had five sons, who worked in the paternal studio. It is difficult to say precisely what part each of them had in the works which came out of the Vischer Foundry. Peter the Younger (1487-1528) made the *Tomb of the Elector Frederick the Wise*, in 1527 (Castle of Wittenberg). Hans Vischer (died 1550) finished the double *Monument of Elector Joachim I and Johann Cicero of Brandenburg* (Berlin, Protestant Cathedral), in 1530. After this date, the Vischer foundry produced no longer tombs, but little decorative pieces, and a general decline was evident.

Bibliography: Meller, *Peter Vischer der Ältere u. seine Werkstatt,* 1925:—Seeger, *Peter Vischer der Jüngere.* Leipzig, 1897.

**VISCONTI (Louis Tullius Joachim).**—French (naturalised) architect. Born in Rome, 1791. Died in Paris, 1853. Son of Ennius Visconti, the famous archæologist, Louis Visconti went to Paris with his father in 1798, and was naturalised the following year.

Louis Visconti built various fountains in Paris (such as the Louvois, and Molière fountains), and organised many public fêtes. He built Napoleon's tomb in the Invalides.

**VITI (or della Vite, Timoteo).**—Umbrian painter, born in Ferrara, 1467-1523. He began by studying goldsmith's work in Bologna, and was a pupil of Francia. Then he went to Urbino where he spent the greater part of his life, and where he was the master of Raphael. His *St. Mary of Egypt* is in the Bologna Gallery. The altarpiece in the Sacristy of Urbino Cathedral—*St. Martin and St. Thomas à Becket*—is considered to be his best work.

Mention might also be made of: the *Virgin between Saints Crescenzio and Vitale*, and an *Annunciation*, in the Brera Gallery, Milan, and the *Noli me Tangere* of Cagli.

Bibliography: Crowe and Cavalcaselle, *History of Painting in North Italy,* ed. T. Borenius, Vol. II.

**VITRUVIUS.**—Roman architect. of the first century A.D. What one knows of him is taken from his treatise, *De Architectura.* This work is divided into ten books which deal with methods of constructing and decorating private and public buildings, as well as engines for war, various instruments, such as sundials, etc. The treatise is particularly valuable in that it is the only one of its kind that has come down to us from antiquity. Vitruvius was not only a scholar, strongly versed in the arts of Greece, Asia Minor, and Italy, but he was also a good technician, for he was the architect of the basilica of Fanum in Umbria, and was commissioned to reorganize war machines.

**VITTORIA (Alessandro).**—Venetian architect and sculptor, 1525-1608. Pupil of Jacopo Sansovino. His most important work in architecture is the *Balbi Palace*, in Venice (now Guggenheim). He was still more admired as a sculptor. Among his chief works are: his own tomb, in San Zaccaria; the *St. Jerome* of the Frari, with its much-studied anatomy; *St. Sebastian* of San Salvatore; and *St. Catherine* and *Daniel on the Lion*, in San Giuliano. He made some very lively busts, which have been compared with portraits by Titian and Tintoretto.

**VIVARINI (Alvise).**—Venetian painter, son of Antonio Vivarini, nephew of Bartolommeo; born 1446; died 1505.

Alvise is first active in 1475 when he paints a polyptych at Montefiorentino. In 1483 he executed the *Madonna* at Barletta, and in 1485 the triptych at Naples. These two pictures, with some undated panels at Bari, have caused it to be assumed that Alvise made a trip during this period to the south of Italy. In 1484 he shared in an inheritance; and four years later he is certainly in Venice, for he offers to paint a picture for the Large Council Hall, to show his ability, free of charge except for payment for his materials. His offer is accepted, and in 1492 he is at work on it. In 1494, 1497 and 1498 he works for the Church of S. Giovanni in Bragora; in 1501 paints a banner for the Scuola Grande di S. Marco; in 1503 promises to pay a debt to Federico Morosini, but the debt is still unpaid in 1505 after Alvise's death. His picture for the Church of the Frari was begun in 1503, and finished by Basaiti.

Dated works by Alvise include: the 1480 Venice Academy altarpiece from S. Francesco, Treviso; the 1483 panel of the *Madonna Enthroned*, S. Andrea, in Barletta; the 1485 Naples triptych; the 1489 Capodistria *Madonna Enthroned*; the 1497 male portrait in the National Gallery (a signed but undated *Madonna* is also in the National Gallery); the 1498 *Resurrection* for S. Giovanni in Bragora, Venice. A signed but not dated large altarpiece from S. Maria dei Battuti in Belluno is now in Berlin; and another signed painting is in the town hall of Cherso.

Bibliography: Berenson, *The Study and Criticism of Italian Art;* same author, *Venetian Painting in America.*—Van Marle, Italian Schools, XVIII, 1936.

**— (Antonio).**—Venetian painter, the date of whose birth is uncertain, perhaps c. 1415. The brother of Bartolommeo, father of Alvise Vivarini.

From 1444 on, Antonio worked in collaboration with Giovanni d'Alemagna. In 1446 his son Alvise is born; in 1453 his name appears as a witness; in 1461 he remarries; and in 1465-66 he is mentioned as heir of a widow Simeone di Ludovico. He dies c. 1470.

There are two works extant signed by Antonio Vivarini alone: the polyptych of 1443-45 at Parenzo; and the triptych of 1464 in the Vatican Gallery. Signed by both Antonio and Giovanni d'Alemagna is the altarpiece in the Vienna Gallery, *Madonna and Saints*, painted for the Church of S. Stefano in Venice in 1441; the Sta. Zaccaria, Venice, polyptych, *Sabina and Saints*, of 1443; the *Coronation of the Virgin* in S. Pantaleone, Venice, 1444; the Venice Academy *Madonna Enthroned* from the Scuola Grande della Carità (on canvas) of 1446; the polyptych formerly in S. Francesco, Padua, lost for over a century and discovered in the Castle of Konopischt in Czecho-Slovakia, a *Nativity with Saints* of 1447. In 1448 Antonio and Giovanni d'Alemagna were engaged for the decoration of the ceiling of the Eremitani in Padua. Giovanni died in 1450 and Antonio took as partner his younger brother Bartolommeo. Together they executed: in 1450 the polyptych in the Bologna Pinacoteca, given by Pope Nicholas V to the Certosa of Bologna, signed and dated; the signed altarpiece of 1452 in the Collection of Don Guido Cagnola, Milan; the 1458 polyptych in the convent of St. Eufemia on the Island of Arbe off the coast of Dalmatia.

Bibliography: Vasari - Milanesi, III.—L. Venturi, *Le origini della pitt. venez.*, 1907.—Testi, *Storia della pitt. venez.*, 1909.—Berenson, *Venetian Painting in America*, 1916.—Van Marle, XVII, 1935.

**— (Bartolommeo).** — Venetian painter, brother of Antonio, born 1432; date of death unknown, probably c. 1491.

Bartolommeo collaborated with his father during his first activity and signed with him the 1450 polyptych in the Bologna Pinacoteca; the 1452 Cagnola Collection, Milan, altarpiece; the 1458 polyptych in Arbe. (See Antonio Vivarini.) From 1459 when Bartolommeo's individual activity starts with the signed and dated picture of Beato Giovanni da Capestrano, now in the Louvre, and the half-length *Madonna* in the Museum at Murano, dated and signed paintings by him are very frequent.

In 1467 he with Andrea da Murano receives an order for two panels for the Scuola di S. Marco; if successful they are to receive the same payment as Jacopo Bellini. In 1473 he is mentioned as executing the extant triptych for Sta. Maria Formosa.

Among his authenticated and dated paintings are the following: the 1464 polyptych in the Academy, Venice, from S. Andrea della Certosa; the 1465 altarpiece in the Gallery, Naples; the 1468 *Madonna* in the Davia Bargelini Gallery, Bologna; the 1470 Sassari (Sardinia) *Madonna*; the 1471 *Madonna Enthroned* in the Colonna Gallery, Rome; the 1472 *Annunciation* in the Cathedral of Modugno; the 1473 Sta. Maria Formosa, Venice, triptych with the *Madonna della Misericordia*; and the altarpiece in SS. Giovanni e Paolo; the 1474 triptych in the Frari, Venice; the 1475 *Madonna* in the Church of S. Antonio at Lussingrande (Istria); and the polyptych with the *Madonna Adoring the Child* in the Venice Academy (assisted); the 1476 altarpiece in the Church of S. Nicola at Bari; the 1477 polyptych in the Church of S. Bernardino at Morano Calabro; and the Venice Academy altarpiece from the Scuola di Taglia Pietra (probably assisted; Bartolommeo's style in this period begins to be pompous and heavy); the 1482 triptych in the Frari, the *Madonna Enthroned*; the *Five Saints* at Bari, of 1483; the 1485 Boston polyptych; and the *St. George Slaying the Dragon* in Berlin (largely shop executed); the 1488 *Madonna Enthroned* in the Gallery at Bergamo; the 1490 Venice Academy *Magdalen and Barbara*.

Bibliography: Vasari - Milanesi, III.—E. Sinigaglia, *De' Vivarini pittori da Murano*, 1905.—Berenson, *Venetian Pictures in America*, 1916. — Moschini, *Rivedendo alcune opere di Bartolommeo Vivarini*, L'Arte, 1935.—Van Marle, *Italian Schools*, XVIII, 1936.

**VLAMINCK (Maurice Edmond de).**—Contemporary Flemish-French painter. Son of musically gifted parents, Vlaminck was born in Paris 4th April 1876. His father was Flemish and his mother came from Lorraine. His childhood was spent near Le Vesinet, where he received a general education and was known as the bad boy of his school. From his father he learned to play the violin and he earned his livelihood as a musician to the age of thirty-five. When eighteen he won a championship as a professional bicyclist. Vlaminck then enlisted for military service and it was at this time that he discovered an aptitude for writing popular novels and verse. Returning home he married and is now the father of three daughters. Around the age of twenty-five he formed an intimate friendship with Derain and from this time on Vlaminck became seriously interested in painting. He sketched the boats and docks on the shores of the Seine merely for the pleasure of it; the only training he has received was in a Sèvres factory painting china. One day Vollard visited his studio and bought every canvas there. Vlaminck was so surprised that he presented his first patron with a hand-carved table, and thus started his career as an artist. In 1905 he exhibited eight paintings at the Salon des Indépendants. Although at heart a pacifist, Vlaminck was obliged to participate in the World War; in 1914 he was stationed with the 74th Infantry at Rouen, but returned to Paris six months later as an industrial designer. Up to 1919 his paintings showed the influence of the smoky atmosphere of the smithies and the colour harmonies were dominated by reds and black. The last year of the war he served with the aviation division at Le Bourget, but continued to paint in his spare moments. An impatient, aggressive man by nature, Vlaminck is known to be a wit as well as an exacting pantheist. He paints still life, portraits and landscape; he detests the vulgar things in life and shows his fondness for nature, especially for snow scenes. The watercolours as well as the oils are characterised by a feeling of space and the infinite, his canvases all seem to breathe air. He is imaginative as well as critical in his selection and rejection of plastic elements; his art is essentially popular and romantic in quality, the technique is broad and vigorous. Together with Derain, Vlaminck is considered as the leader of the Fauvists in their reactions against certain aspects of Post-Impressionism. Vlaminck illustrated his own *Communications* (1921), *Histoire de Mon Époque* (1927), as well as G. Duhamel's *Les Trois Journées de la Tribu* (1923) and *Voyages* by Vanderpyl (1920). He also designed a tapestry and has made a quantity of prints. Vlaminck is represented in the museums of Paris, Hamburg, Brussels, New York, Los Angeles, Moscow and in Japan.

Bibliography: Georges Duhamel, *Maurice Vlaminck*, Art d'Aujourd'hui, 1926.—Florent Fels, *Vlaminck*, 1928.

**VLIEGER (Simon, Jacobsz de).**—Dutch painter, 1600-1653. Pupil of Willem van de Welde the Elder, he was active in Delft and Amsterdam. One of the most important marine painters, he was a good portraitist and etcher besides. His most important painting, *The Beach*, 1643, is in The Hague.

**VOLLARD (Ambrose).**—See Cézanne; Rouault; Vlaminck.

**VOLLON (Antoine).**—French painter, 1833-1900. He came of a family of Lyonese ironworkers. After studying in Lyon, he went to Paris, where he had all he could do to gain a livelihood, although the first picture he sent to the Salon (*Art et Gourmandise*) was accepted in 1865. A picture, the *Monkey at the Accordion* (1866, Lyon Museum) attracted the attention of the Superintendent of the Beaux-Arts, who ordered a still life from him (*Curiosities*, 1868, Luxembourg). From that time, success began to come to him, and paintings, admirable in their assurance and virtuosity of execution, followed. Most of his paintings are of still-life groups. He often contrived to give a kind of heroic beauty to the most common objects.

**VOLTERRA (Daniele da).**—Daniele Ricciarelli, known as Il Volterra, because he was born at Volterra. Roman painter, 1509-1566. He began by imitating Sodoma. Then, in the studio of Pierino del Vaga, he felt Raphael's influence. He soon fell under the sway of Michelangelo, and was seized with a passion for dramatic gestures and athletic muscles. Nevertheless, it was he who agreed, no doubt through envy, to clothe the splendid nudes in Michelangelo's *Last Judgment*, in shapeless draperies.

Volterra (Daniele da): The Massacre of the Innocents. (Uffizi, Florence.)

The *Descent from the Cross* in Santa Trinità de' Monti, in Rome, is one of his best known works, and shows his attempt to be imperious and dramatic, while he only succeeds in being studied and cold. The colour is heavy, and laboured.

The *Massacre of the Innocents* (Uffizi), and *David Overcoming Goliath* (Louvre) show the same faults, due to the imitation of Michelangelo, faults which lead to the decadence of art.

**VOLUTE.**—Spiral scroll-shaped ornament, especially characteristic of the Ionic capital.

**VORSTERMAN (Lucas).**—Dutch engraver, 1595-1676. He began by publishing engravings after Breughel, Elsheimer and Goltzius, and thus became a practician of the first order. He met Rubens, about 1617, and engraved some of his compositions. Rubens was so pleased with them that he installed Vorsterman in his own house, and tried to gather a company of engravers to work under his direction. Rubens never found another such perfect interpreter. He himself had not patience for the laborious work of copper engraving, but Vorsterman understood his directions perfectly.

Vorsterman's principal engravings include *St. Francis Receiving the Stigmata*, the *Adoration of the Shepherds*, the *Adoration of the Magi*, and the *Battle of Thermodon*, which appeared in 1623 when he had already broken with Rubens. In fact, the engraver, who does not seem to have been too easy-going, left Rubens in 1622. In 1624, he settled in England, where he engraved the *St. George of Raphael*, portraits by Holbein, a *Pietà*, by Van Dyck, and portraits of the Duke and Duchess of Arundel.

Bibliography: Basan, *Catalogue des Estampes Gravées d'après Rubens*. Paris, 1867.—H. Hymans, *Histoire de la gravure dans l'École de Rubens*. Brussels, 1879.—A. Rosenberg, *Der Kupferstich unter dem Einfluss der Schule des Rubens*. Vienna, 1893.—H. Hymans, *Lucas Vorsterman*. Brussels, 1893.

**VOS (Cornelis de).**—Flemish painter, 1585-1651. He was a contemporary of Rubens, and was influenced by that master as well as by Van Dyck. He is a realistic and very individual artist. His colour is soft and quiet, and has none of Rubens' brightness and warmth. Nevertheless, his peaceful figures are full of expression and life. He excelled in portraiture. Rubens, who was unable to carry out all the commissions for portraits which

Vos (Cornelis): Messenger of the Company of St. Luke. (Museum, Antwerp.)

came his way, sent his sitters to Vos, whose portraits are worthy of our admiration. To mention a few of his paintings—there is a very fine group of the *Artist, His Wife and His Two Daughters* (Brussels), painted in soft, brown tones and pleasantly lighted; the *Portrait of the Artist's Daughters* (Berlin); Portrait of *Albert and Isabella* (Mérode Collection); a *Couple Seated on a Porch* (Berlin); *A Young Woman and Two Children* (Brunswick). His best portrait, after the one in Brussels, is that of *Abraham Grapheus*, messenger of the Guild of St. Luke (Antwerp), a life-like figure, with large medals covering his chest.

De Vos' historical and mythological pictures are inferior to his portraits. De Vos has scarcely received the admiration which is due to him. After Rubens, Van Dyck and Jordaens, he is the best artist of that brilliant epoch.

— **(Marten de).**—Flemish painter, 1531-1603. He studied under Tintoretto, in whose paintings he often did the background. In Rome (S. Francesco a Ripa) is his *Immaculate Conception*, and in the Palazzo Colonna the *Four Seasons*. Active mostly in Antwerp he lacks originality and the best qualities of pictorial art, retaining little of Tintoretto's influence or of Venetian color.

Vos (Marten de): Portrait of the Anselmo Family. (Museum, Brussels.)

His best works include: The *Incredulity of St. Thomas* (Antwerp Cathedral) and the *Triumph of Christ* (Antwerp Museum). His portraits—such as the *Portrait of the Anselmo Family* (Brussels)—are superior to his religious pictures.

See Pl. 24, Vol. II.

— **(Paul de).**—Flemish painter, 1590-1678. Brother of Cornelis de Vos; brother-in-law of Snyders whose pupil he was. His paintings of animals and hunting scenes brightly coloured—may be seen in many European galleries (e.g. *Hunting Scenes*, and *Noah's Arks*).

**VOUET (Aubin).**—French painter, 1599-1641. Brother and pupil of Simon Vouet. There are paintings by him in the Palais de Justice, of Versailles; and in St. Thomas d'Aquin, Paris.

— **(Simon).** — French painter, 1590-1649. After a visit to England, and a journey to Constantinople, the young artist spent a year in Venice, where he copied the paintings of Veronese, and became inspired with a taste for vast, slightly theatrical compositions. In 1613, he went to Rome, where he stayed, until he was called to Paris by Louis XIII in 1627. The king made him his chief painter, and took lessons in pastel from him. His pupils included Charles Le Brun, Pierre Mignard, Eustache Le Sueur, etc. Too often, overwhelmed by commissions, Vouet contented himself with making a sketch for his work, and leaving the execution of it to pupils.

Vouet (Simon): Wealth. (Louvre.)

Vouet (Simon): Portrait of Louis XIII between France and Navarre. (Louvre.)

Simon Vouet's reputation is today considerably reduced. We judge this brilliant, facile decorator by his pictures in the Louvre. His religious paintings have no sincerity of feeling. Nothing could be more mannered and vulgar than his *Entombment*; nothing more repulsive than the false attempt at realism, and feebly drawn, of the *Crucifixion* (Louvre). *Riches* and *Faith* are other works in the Gallery. His colour is generally superficial and strident.

The *Presentation at the Temple* (Louvre) is rather a decorative panel than a religious picture. It was long considered to be his masterpiece; and, indeed, some of his most durable qualities are manifest here—the architecture is clever, theatrically adequate, of the pure Jesuit style. The light in the background is pleasantly repeated.

To be just to Vouet, one should have seen his big decorations in the Châteaux of Richelieu, Rueil, Chilly; of the Hôtel Séguier, of the Palais Royal, etc. But these have all disappeared, and can only be judged from engravings by his sons-in-law.

**VOUSSOIR.**—Any wedge-shaped piece in an arch or vault. The central voussoir in an arch is the keystone.

**VRANCKX (Sebastian).**—Flemish painter, 1573-1647. Pupil of Van Noort. He was in Italy about 1597 and then became master of Antwerp. His work is very varied: he painted kermesses, landscapes, and military scenes. Among his best work may be mentioned: *View of the Interior of the Jesuit Church of Antwerp* (Vienna), and *View of the Medici Villa in Rome*, with several figures (Naples).

**VRELANT (Willem).** — Dutch painter, 1430-1481/2. A friend of Memling, he was one of the most important illuminators and miniaturists of the time. Among the mss. he illuminated are *Chronicle of Hennegau*, 1467, and *Les Chroniques de Jherusalem abregies*, etc. Miniatures of the *Ursula Legend* are also among his authentic works. There has been some controversy among art historians, whether, and how much, of these works may have been done by Memling himself.

**VROOM (Hendrik Cornelisz).**—Dutch painter, c. 1566-1640, of Haarlem, painted chiefly seapieces (notably naval battles) of which several may be seen in the Museum of Amsterdam and Haarlem. His paintings are not of the high calibre as those of de Vlieger or W. v. d. Velde.

# W

**WAEL (Cornelis de).**—Flemish painter of battle scenes on land and sea, 1592-1662. He was born in Genoa where he spent most of his life.

**WAGNER (Otto).**—Austrian architect, 1841-1918. Early exponent of modernism, as in his stations for the Metropolitan Railway, Vienna, 1894-1897, and the Postal Savings Bank, also in Vienna, 1905. Through his pupils, Olbrich and Hoffman, he has been effective in shaping the character of all recent Central European architecture.

**WALARSHAPAT (Armenia).**—See Byzantine Architecture, Early Period, Armenia.

**WALCH (Jacob).**—See Barbari (Jacopo de').

**WALDMÜLLER (Ferdinand Georg).**—Austrian painter, 1793-1865. One of the greatest Austrian painters. He was a pupil of Mauser and Lampi in the Academy of Vienna. He lived in Italy, and then in Paris. He studied the Dutch masters, to whom he owed his solid technical qualities. There is a modern accent in his landscapes and popular scenes, owing to his fresh, sometimes rather crude, colour, and to his study of open-air effects. His most characteristic works are: *Hütteneck, Kermesse at Petersdorf, Convent Supper*. Waldmüller was, however, chiefly remarkable as a portrait painter. The intense truthfulness of his portraits recalls Holbein. His masterpiece is the *Portrait of Prince André Rasumoffski*.

**WALKER (Frederick).**—English painter (1840-1875), a leading figure in the English school of the third quarter of the 19th century, among his most famous works being *The Vagrants* (1868), *The Plough* (1870), *The Harbour of Refuge* (1872), all now in the National Gallery, Millbank.

— **(Horatio).**—Contemporary American painter. He was born in Lisfowel, Ontario, in 1858. He studied under J. A. Fraser, a miniature painter, in Toronto and then spent some years at Rochester, New York. About 1880 he went on a walking trip from L'Epiphanie, near Montreal, all the way to Quebec, studying the peasants on their small farms with the cows, chickens and pigs in their farmyards. He sketched all these and also some of the wild fowl, including turkeys and ducks, and hares. In 1882 he went to Europe, travelling in England, Spain, Normandy and Holland. The following year he returned to America and settled permanently at a small place on the Ile d'Orléans, an island in the St. Lawrence River near Quebec, inhabited by peasants who live much as their French ancestors did when they first arrived in this country. There Mr. Walker has found most of his subjects in the quaint thatched-roof cottages, the cattle and hogs of the farmyards, the rolling meadows and thick woodlands. He came to New York in 1885 for some study and in 1891 was elected to full membership in the National Academy of Design. He won an award at the Paris Exposition of 1889 and gold medals at various expositions including the Columbian Exposition in Chicago in 1893, the Pan-American Exposition in Buffalo in 1901, the St. Louis Exposition in 1904 and the Panama Pacific Exposition in San Francisco in 1915. His work very definitely shows the influence of Millet and the Barbizon school in the choice of subject matter, but is different in that the artist is more attracted to the animal life than human activities. There is no intimate relationship, but the scenes are treated sympathetically and with a feeling for simplicity.

Bibliography: F. Newlin Price, *Horatio Walker,* 1928.

— **(Ralph).**—American Architect, designer of the building of the *Chicago Tribune*, Chicago (1928), the Telephone Building, New York and other remarkable edifices typical of the tendencies of modern architecture in America.

**WALLACE COLLECTION.**—See London.

**WALLOT (Paul).**—German architect, 1841-1912. Designer of the Reichstag, Berlin, 1882-1894.

**WALTER (T. Ustick).**—American architect (1804-1887) designer of the extension of the Capitol at Washington (retired from this work, 1865).

**WALTON (Henry).**—English painter (1746-1813), pupil of Zoffany; a talented artist whose works now are very scarce: one, the charming *genre* scene *Plucking the Turkey* (1776) in the National Gallery, displays a certain affinity to the art of Chardin.

**WANG MÊNG.**—Chinese painter, d. 1385. One of the "Four Masters" of the Yuan dynasty. He painted rugged landscapes.

**WANG WEI.**—699-759, Chinese painter considered to be the founder of the monochrome landscape tradition.

See China—Art.

**WARD (James).**—English painter and engraver (1769-1859), trained at first as a mezzotint engraver under his brother William Ward; worked subsequently as a painter, and achieved much fame through his subjects from animal life. He was elected a full member of the Royal Academy in 1811.

BIBLIOGRAPHY: Julia Frankau, *William and James Ward,* London, 1903.

**— (John Quincy Adams).**—American sculptor (1830-1910). He was born in Urbana, Ohio, in 1830 and his early years were spent on a farm there, where he modelled tiny figures in the native clay. When he was nineteen he made a trip to Brooklyn to visit a sister and while there came in contact with the work of Henry Kirke Brown. He entered the studio of that sculptor as a pupil and during the six years that he stayed there made such remarkable progress that he was able to call himself an independent artist at the close of that period. In 1859 he made a trip to Washington to execute some portrait busts and two years later he opened his own studio in New York City. In 1863 he was elected to membership in the National Academy of Design and the following year his *Indian Hunter* was accepted for its present location in Central Park. He was much interested in sculptural technique and learned to do his own cutting directly in the stone and bronze casting with excellent results. He was an admirer of the French methods of training, but was not in accord with the pseudo-classic models of the earlier part of the century. Among his best-known works are the *Washington* in front of the Sub-Treasury in New York City, *Henry Ward Beecher* in Brooklyn, *President Garfield* in Washington and *Horace Greeley* in New York City. In 1874 he was president of the National Academy of Design and in 1893 president of the newly established National Sculpture Society. One of his last works was the pediment of the New York Stock Exchange done in collaboration with Paul W. Bartlett. He died 1st May 1910, active up to the time of his last illness. His portraits were faithful likenesses, but there was a certain amount of classicism apparent in his work which may be traced back to the influence of Houdon. He encouraged the work of younger men and also women, urging them not to forget the precepts of ancient Greece but to base their art on American ideals and ground them by a firm understanding of technique and workmanship.

See Pl. 64, Vol. II.

BIBLIOGRAPHY: Adeline Adams, *John Quincy Adams Ward, An Appreciation,* 1912.

**— (William).**—English engraver (1766?-1826), pupil of John Raphael Smith and one of the leading mezzotint engravers of his time.

BIBLIOGRAPHY: Julia Frankau, *William and James Ward,* London, 1903.

**WARNER (Olin Levi).**—American sculptor (1844-1896), studied in Paris under Jouffroy and Carpeaux, becoming one of the most notable American sculptors of his generation. Apart from numerous statues, busts and medallions he did one pair of bronze doors for the Congressional Library, Washington (another pair begun by him, was completed after Warner's death by Herbert Adams).

**WARREN (Whitney).**—Contemporary American architect. He was born in New York City in 1864. From 1885 to 1894 he studied at the École des Beaux-Arts in Paris under Daumet and Girault. When he returned to the United States he joined in partnership with Mr. Wetmore in the firm of Warren and Wetmore. This firm designed the new Grand Central Terminal, which is modelled after the style of the Italian Renaissance and incorporates an elaborate substructure as well as space for the waiting rooms, stores and offices. They also designed the hotels Belmont, Vanderbilt, and Biltmore in New York. In 1905 Warren became affiliated with the Institut de France and in 1909 became an associate member of the Académie des Beaux-Arts. At the close of the World War he was chosen by a committee of the Académie des Beaux-Arts and the Institut de France to take charge of the rebuilding of the Library of Louvain, which had been destroyed during the hostilities. Quite a controversy ensued when in accordance with Cardinal Mercier's wishes he added the inscription: "Furore Teutonico diruta, dono Americano restituta." The rector of the university objected and another balustrade without the plaque was finally substituted. Mr. Warren was elected to the Académie Royale of Belgium and given the Cordon of the Order of the Belgian Crown.

BIBLIOGRAPHY: *Larousse du XX<sup>e</sup> Siècle,* Paris, Vol. 6, 1933.—Pierre de Soete, *The Louvain Library Controversy,* 1929.—Whitney Warren, *État de la Cathédrale de Reims après le Bombardement par les Allemands,* Paris, 1914.

**WATER-COLOUR.**—A process in which the powdered colour is crushed in water and mixed with gum arabic, in quantities varying according to the nature of the colour, in such a way that it gives the same tone wet as after having dried. In water colour, the colour ought to be applied very liquid. The choice of paper is very important, and it is prudent to keep it in a dry place. The best water-colourists seem to prefer coarse-grained paper. A water colour, because of its delicacy, and tendency to fade and discolour, should be strong in tone and colour. Certain water-colourists make use of a medium, of clear appearance, which seems to be a base of wax; it allows of a use of thickness of tones which one wishes to emphasise. Salesmen, with a view to preserving the moisture of the colours longer, use the slime of the snail, the milk of the fig-tree, glycerine, and gum arabic. Water-colours thus treated are softened by the least humidity in the atmosphere. It seems best to use only the simplest products. For some years fixatives have been manufactured, which protect the water-colour like a varnish.

**WATSON (Thomas).**—English engraver (1743 or 1750-1781), specially noted for his mezzotints of which his *Lady Bampfylde* after Reynolds is one of the finest.

BIBLIOGRAPHY: G. Goodwin, *Thomas Watson,* etc. London, 1904.

**WATTEAU (Antoine).**—French painter, 1684-1721. He was born at Valenciennes, in Flanders. His first master was an obscure local painter of the name of Jacques Albert

WATTEAU: FÊTE CHAMPÊTRE. (Museum, Edinburgh.)

Gérin, who died in 1702. Watteau then joined an able theatre decorator who took him to Paris, with a view to working for the opera. But shortly after this his master left him in the capital, and returned to Valenciennes. This brief new application of his gifts doubtless cultivated in him the art of fantastic staging of a scene.

Left alone in Paris, necessity soon reduced Watteau to provide figures of *St. Nicholas* to an image-maker of the Pont Notre Dame, who sold such devotional images by the dozen. Some of Watteau's drawings or paintings fell under the eyes of Gillot, who took an interest in the young man, and invited him to travel, and even to live in his house. Watteau could not have had better fortune, for Gillot, the inventor of fantastic decorative allegories, worked at precisely the same art of scenic figuration that had already influenced Watteau at the studio of the painter in Valenciennes. A quarrel, the cause of which is uncertain, interrupted this new arrangement.

He next spent some time with Claude Audran, painter of arabesques and grotesques, who worked in the Luxembourg Palace. He nat-

WATTEAU: THE PLEASURES OF LIFE. (Wallace Collection, London.)

urally developed Watteau's sense of ornamentation. Watteau became acquainted with the great financier Crozat, and later went to live with him, as his painter, in his residence (at the corner of the Rue de Richelieu) with its large and lovely garden. Crozat also possessed at Montmorency a superb villa with gardens designed by Le Notre. Although Watteau must have found much to delight his eyes, his was an untamed nature, and he soon wearied of the agitation of a fashionable life, and he ended by regaining his independence.

He fell into a consumption which darkened his spirits, and reduced him to melancholy. His efforts to regain his health were unsuccessful. In 1720, being advised to go and consult a great London doctor, he crossed the channel. In England, he painted several pictures, but his illness grew worse. Shortly afterwards he died, near Paris, at the age of thirty-seven.

In spite of the shortness of his life, Watteau accomplished a considerable amount of work—halts and encampments of armies (early), pictures of "fêtes galantes," landscapes, decorative compositions, etc.

Watteau's wild and restless nature was united to an exquisite sensitiveness which was exceptional in his day. He anticipated that modern instinct which leads the soul to associate nature with its own feelings. His little panels show some reflection of the great Venetian masters—the russet colours of Titian, the silvery satins of Veronese. Watteau worked for operatic decorators, and his most delicate reveries seem to have been evoked by a graceful minuet in some fairy play. His actors sometimes wear the dress of the actors of the Italian theatre, but more often dresses invented by the painter, which display the charming ease of his little figures. The men, dressed in gay satins, like the ladies, seem ready to drop on their knees or perform a pirouette. The ladies meet their advances, half consenting, half resisting. Fans flutter, and among the folds of their silken dresses, the light gleams, darts and glances, shifting with their dainty, rhythmic gestures. All this is relieved against dark trees, or the faint blue of distant horizons. The flashes of satin are somewhat subdued by the mystery of the landscape, as are the whisperings of lovers by the majestic silence of the evening.

In his *Embarkation for Cythera* (Louvre), Watteau brought together all the groups of lovers scattered throughout his works. The couples in this exquisite gathering show a certain hesitation, but the journey to the island of love is so alluring!

The Louvre possesses many of Watteau's paintings, and albums of exquisite drawings in red chalk. There we find: the *Actors of the Italian Theatre; Gilles; Pastoral,* etc.

The Wallace Collection (London) possesses: *Fête in a Park; the Music Party*; the *Champs Elysées*; the *Music Lesson,* etc. In the National Gallery, we find: *Perfect Harmony* and *La Gamme d'Amour.* The National Gallery of Scotland possesses a charming *fête champêtre.*

See Pl. 47, Vol. II.

BIBLIOGRAPHY: G. Dargenty. *Watteau,* Collection des Artistes Célèbres.—E. Pilon, *Watteau,* 1912.—C. Mauclair, *Watteau,* 1906.—S. Sitwell, *Watteau.* 1925.

**WATTS (George Frederick).**—English painter, 1817-1904. Born in London. He studied at the Royal Academy, and then in the studio of the sculptor, William Behnes. He became a passionate admirer of the Parthenon sculptures. In 1837 he exhibited for the first time at the Royal Academy, and, in 1842, a scholarship enabled him to go to Italy where he spent four years. There he painted a great many portraits. The best-known are those of Lord Holland, English Minister at the Court of the Duke of Tuscany, of the Countess of Castiglione, and of the Countess Walewska. On this return to England he won a second prize of five hundred pounds, this time for a decoration of the Houses of Parliament. In 1853, he took part

WATTS: SELF-PORTRAIT. (Uffizi, Florence.)

in the expedition to find the site of Halicarnassus. His life, entirely devoted to work, was uneventful. His output was immense. Watts drew his subjects from all sources, interpreting antique symbols, and mystic and mediaeval legends, and painting Biblical themes. To mention the subjects of a few of his paintings: *Endymion, Daphne, Psyche, Orpheus and Eurydice*; then *Chaos*, the *Story of Eve*, the *Building of the Arc*, the *Good Samaritan*. His allegories include: *Love and Life, Love and Death, Hope, Time, Love Triumphant, Death Crowning Innocence, Mammon.* In the abstract character of his subjects and in his way of treating them, he shows himself an idealist. In such paintings as *Paolo and Francesca, Fata Morgana*, and the *Creation of Eve*, he attains, in symbolism, to a rare loftiness of thought. "Watts's ideal," said one of the most eminent English critics "was to make English art worthy of English literature. He believed that art was only the means to an end, and that end was to ennoble humanity not only in moving it by means of aesthetic beauty, but by pointing a moral." These are the principles of the Pre-Raphaelite Brotherhood. Watts, speaking of certain painters, said: "They have not respected great ideas and intellectual problems, which are alone capable of making art truly great." This shows the significance that Watts wished to impose on art. In his portraits, Watts considered that he had far more to do than to give a merely material representation, feature by feature, of his model, especially when his sitter was such a one as Matthew Arnold, Swinburne, Robert Browning, Rossetti, Tennyson, John Stuart Mill, William Morris, Gladstone, Carlyle, or Walter Crane. What he was really trying to portray was, in Browning, speculation; in Taylor, reason; in Swinburne, passion; in William Morris, taste.

Watts often failed to realise his conceptions. His skill was uncertain, and often unequal to expressing the dream and thought which were in his mind.

BIBLIOGRAPHY: Mary S. Watts, *George Frederic Watts. The Annals of an Artist's Life*. London, 1912.

**WEBB (John).**—English architect, 1611-1672. A nephew and pupil of Inigo Jones, he was instrumental in popularizing the Palladian style of his uncle, with whom he was associated in plans for Greenwich. He was the sole author of Ashburnham House, 1640.

**WEDGWOOD (Josiah).** — See Ceramic.

**WEENIX (Jan Baptist).**—(Called *Ratel*). Dutch painter and engraver, 1621-1660. Pupil of Abraham Bloemart and Moeyaert. In 1643 he was in Rome where he painted for Cardinal Pamfili. In 1647 he returned to Amsterdam, two years later joining the Guild of Utrecht. He painted still-life, landscapes, genre scenes in the manner of Dou; his social compositions have architectural background. His brilliant coloring was influenced by the art of Italy.

— **(Jan).**—Dutch painter, 1640-1719. Pupil of his father and of d'Hondekoeter. In 1714 he decorated the palace of the Count of Pfalz (near Düsseldorf) with paintings rivalling those of the Italian masters. These are today in a number of museums. Although he painted every type of subject matter, he was especially popular for animal compositions.

**WEERTS (French painter).**—Born in 1847. Pupil of Cabanel. He has painted numerous portraits, and some pictures, of which one of the best known is *The Death of Bara.*

**WELL OF MOSES.**—See Sluter; also Pl. 54, Vol. I.

**WELLS (England).**—Wells Cathedral was rebuilt in the 12th and 13th centuries. Some details of the 12th century Norman building remain. The most famous part is the west front, which is very broad, and enriched with arcades, carvings and six hundred statues. The Northern porch is older (1189) and is in the Norman style. The Choir, in the Norman and Early English styles, is very fine, with 14th century glass windows.

**WERFF (Adriaen van der).**—Dutch painter, 1659-1722. One of the outstanding academic painters, his strongly naturalistic works include historical, mythological and harbour scenes. He was active in Rotterdam, and was well paid for numerous portraits of nobility.

**WERTMÜLLER (Adolphus Ulric).**—Swedish painter, 1749-1812. He settled in France in the reign of Louis XVI, became a member of the Academy, and painted portraits and genre scenes. One of his pictures is in the National Museum in Stockholm: *Marie Antoinette Walking with Her Children in the Alleys of the Trianon.*

**WERWE (Claus de).** — See Sluter.

**WEST (Benjamin).**—Early American painter (1738-1820). He was born in the present town of Swarthmore, then Springfield Township, Pennsylvania, 10th October 1738. His parents belonged to the Society of Friends and he was brought up in the beliefs of that religious sect. Some of the Indians in the neighbourhood showed the boy how to use their paints and it is said that he took hairs from the family cat to make his first brushes. After a particularly good drawing of his young niece he was given regular paints and stayed away from school at times to enjoy them. At the age of sixteen he announced to his parents that he wanted to become an artist. A special meeting of the Friends was called and it was finally decided that he could go ahead with his studying although painting was not in accord with the tenets of their religion. Young West opened a studio in Philadelphia and in 1760 with the help of some friends was able to go to Italy. There he stayed three years, copying the old masters and striving after their colour schemes, particularly that of Titian. In 1763 he removed to England and there he settled permanently, never again returning to his native country. He married Miss Elizabeth Shewell, who sailed to join him despite her brother's strong opposition, and they made their home in London. Through contact with the Archbishop of York he met King George III who was so impressed by his work that he appointed him his historical painter. In 1768 under the patronage of the King the Royal Academy was started with Sir Joshua Reynolds as its first president. After his death in 1792, West became president, which office he retained for many years.

When he painted the *Death of General Wolfe* he was strongly criticised for using contemporary costumes by all but Reynolds. However, he retaliated by saying that the people in Canada were not clad in Greek and Roman dress and he saw no good reason for not representing the true state of affairs. In 1801 he painted *Christ Healing the Sick* for a hospital in Philadelphia, but sent them a copy, the original being preserved in the National Gallery in London. He also executed a number of portraits including one of King George III, another of Queen Charlotte and her children, and a self-portrait which is in the Pennsylvania Museum in Philadelphia. According to some estimates he is credited with about three thousand pictures, historical and religious subjects besides portraits, and in doing work in such large quantities it is not to be wondered at that much is mediocre and detailed, with a lack of concentration of the main interest. He began the decoration of the Royal Chapel at Windsor, but the work was stopped when the King's madness became evident and other hands took up the business of governing. West's wife died in 1817 and after that his health failed and he gave up working. He died 11th March 1820 and was buried in St. Paul's Cathedral in London. He painted after the Italian manner with the academic poses and patterns then popular, and although he modelled his colours upon Titian he did not achieve very good results. He was influential upon later American art due to the great number of pupils he had, including Charles Willson Peale, Gilbert Stuart, Thomas Sully, Robert Fulton, Washington Allston, John Trumbull and Samuel F. B. Morse. See Pl. 61, Vol. II.

BIBLIOGRAPHY: John Galt, *Life, Studies and Works of Benjamin West*, 1820.—Henry E. Jackson, *Benjamin West, His Life and Work*, 1900.

**WESTMAN (Carl).** — Contemporary Swedish architect, born 1866, and author of the Law Courts, Stockholm, 1915.

**WESTMINSTER ABBEY.**—See London.

**WEYDEN (Roger Van der).—or Roger de la Pasture.**—Flemish painter; born in Tournai, in 1399. Very little is known of his early years. He was a pupil in the studio of Robert Campin, in 1427 and was received as master painter in 1432 in the Guild of Tournai.

On the death of Van Eyck, he became the leader of the Flemish school. He was in Italy in 1449-50,

ROGER VAN DER WEYDEN: BLADELIN ALTARPIECE, THE NATIVITY. (Museum, Berlin.)

probably at the court of Lionello d'Este at Ferrara.

None of his paintings were signed and their attributions to the master are to some extent uncertain even today. The earliest of his paintings is the *Altarpiece of the Virgin*, or the triptych of *Miraflores* (Berlin). Of about the same date (about 1431), is the *Altarpiece of St. John*, with the *Baptism of Christ* in the centre; the *Birth of St. John* on the left; *The Beheading* on the right. The varied backgrounds of these three scenes have picturesque details.

As chief painter of the town of Brussels, he had to decorate the Hôtel de Ville, and did four pictures representing examples of Justice.

Van der Weyden's masterpiece is the *Descent from the Cross* (Escorial). In this he shows his gift for pathos, which did not, however, exclude restraint and good composition.

Between 1443 and 1450 he did the famous *polyptych* in the Hospital of Beaune. This large painting, in seven panels, is, after Van Eyck's

ROGER VAN DER WEYDEN: THE CRUCIFIXION. (Prado, Madrid.)

*Adoration of the Lamb*, the most important work of Flemish painting. It represents *The Last Judgment*; Christ as Judge, is seated on a rainbow; St. Michael; the Virgin, etc.

The authenticity of the magnificent *Seven Sacraments* (Antwerp) (1455) has been questioned, but without sufficient grounds. The painting shows the *Sacrament of the Eucharist* (in the centre); *Baptism, Confirmation, Confession* (on the left); *Order, Marriage, Extreme Unction* (on the right). This picture shows a hitherto undeveloped tendency towards greater realism.

In Brussels there is a little *Pietà* attributed to Van der Weyden.

About 1460 he painted the beautiful *Altarpiece of the Magi* (Pinakotek, Munich). This wonderful work shows the influence of Gentile da Fabriano. The little town in the background is probably Middelburg. On the wings are a *Presentation*, and an *Annunciation*.

The last of his works is in Berlin. It is a *triptych*, with a *Nativity* in the middle, and paintings on the wings. His modelling has become softer, and the colour, though bright, is harmonious. In Berlin there is also the portrait of a woman, attributed to Van der Weyden.

The Louvre has had (since 1913) a fine altarpiece representing *Christ the Redeemer*, in which the types are similar to those in the Beaune work.

The life-like portrait of *Philip the Good* (Antwerp) is probably a copy of an earlier picture by Van der Weyden, which was lost. In the same way, there are several copies (evidently done from a lost original) of *St. Luke Painting the Virgin*.

It is very difficult to authenticate the works of Van der Weyden and of his followers. His influence, both during and after, his lifetime, was even greater than that of the Van Eycks. The varied work done in his studio (miniatures, sculpture and engraving) influenced the development of many artists, among whom were Memling and Dirk Bouts.

See Pl. 60, Vol. I.

BIBLIOGRAPHY: Sir Martin Conway, *The Van Eycks and their Followers*. London, 1921.—M. J. Friedländer, *Altniederländische Malerei*, Vol. II.—Wauters, *R. v. d. Weyden, ses oeuvres, ses élèves et ses descendants*, 1855.—Hasse, *R. v. Weyden u. R. van Brügge mit Ihren Schulen*, 1905.

**WHISTLER (James Abbott McNeill).**—American painter and graver (1834-1903). He was born in Lowell, Massachusetts, 10th July 1834, the son of a railroad constructor. In 1843 the family moved to St. Petersburg, Russia, where his father was to build a railroad from St. Petersburg to Moscow. There young Jimmy Whistler took drawing lessons at the Academy of Fine Arts, but soon went to live in England with a sister who had married Seymour Haden, later known as a famous etcher. His father died suddenly in Russia in 1849 and the family returned to the United States. Young Whistler studied at a school in Pomfret, Connecticut, and soon entered the United States Military Academy at West Point. After three years he was dismissed for a failure in chemistry and for a while worked for the United States Coastal and Geodetic Survey. In 1856 he went to Paris to study art and there entered the atelier of Gabriel Charles Gleyre, a follower of Ingres, and became associated with the younger artists there including Courbet, Fantin-Latour, Manet, Monet and Degas. His pictures were rejected by the Salons of 1859 and 1863 but in the latter year his *White Girl* was exhibited at the Salon des Refusés, causing quite a sensation. His French Set of etchings was brought out about the same time and soon after came his removal to London.

WHISTLER (JAMES MCNEILL): PORTRAIT OF CARLYLE.

He settled in the Chelsea district and became friendly with the members of the Pre-Raphaelite Brotherhood, including the Rossettis, Oscar Wilde and Algernon Swinburne. With his quick wit and sharp criticisms and his striking dress Whistler soon became one of the outstanding personalities of the city. His pictures were entitled after musical arrangements: nocturnes, harmonies, notes and symphonies. All were framed in colours designed to set them off to the best advantage and the whole colour scheme of the exhibition gallery was in harmony, even to the livery of the attendants. The pictures partook of the impressionism of Velázquez and the fantasy of Japanese art, but were undoubtedly individual, with human shapes faintly seen against dark backgrounds. He was opposed to the strongly realistic tendencies of the Pre-Raphaelite school and was the object of an attack by the critic Ruskin in 1877 because of his nonconforming to the current standards of art.

About 1865 he had painted the famous *Portrait of the Artist's Mother* under the title of *An Arrangement in Grey and Black*. In this as in his other portraits he was more intent upon the tonality of the whole rather than a detailed study of the individual person. Because of his strong sense of colour values he was asked by F. R. Leyland to decorate the dining room of his home at Prince's Gate. It was a success as far as the artist was concerned, but the patron did not approve of the painting over of all the Spanish leather panels to harmonise with the picture of the *Princess of the Land of Porcelain*, which was the chief decorative motif. The whole room is now in the National Gallery in Washington, D. C.

In the fall of 1879 Whistler went to Venice to fill an order for some etchings for a publication of the Fine Art Society. They are perhaps his best work in that medium, catching in some measure the mysterious aspect of the old buildings and the hazy atmosphere surrounding the architecture along the canals. At the same time he made some charming pastels of the region around there characterised by a few lines cleverly woven together. Whistler tried his hand at writing too, bringing out an account of the attack by Ruskin and the subsequent lawsuit and following it up in 1890 by *The Gentle Art of Making Enemies*. He was fond of pitting his wits against others in order to show his individual approach to art and its criticism, but he was not always the victor in these encounters.

He married in 1888 Mrs. Beatrix Godwin and from that time until her death eight years later he was at the peak of his fame. His *Portrait of the Artist's Mother* was bought by the French government and the *Portrait of Thomas Carlyle* was purchased by the Corporation of Glasgow, Scotland. His health began to fail about 1900 and he travelled south to Italy and later to Holland, but it did not improve. He returned to England and tried to go on painting but without much success. His illness recurred and he died 17th July 1903 and was buried at Chiswick beside his wife.

See Pls. 58, 61, Vol. II.

BIBLIOGRAPHY: Joseph Pennell and Elizabeth Robins Pennell, *The Life of James McNeill Whistler*, sixth edition, 1919.—Hans W. Singer, *James McNeill Whistler*, Langham Series of Art Monographs, London, 1905.—For a complete bibliography see *The Index of Twentieth Century Artists* for June, 1934.

**WHITE (Stanford).**—American architect (1853-1906). He was born in New York City 9th November 1853, the son of a literary and music critic. As a lad he was fond of sketching and in 1872 became a draftsman in the office of Henry H. Richardson in Boston, where he remained for the next seven years. During the construction of Trinity Church in Boston he came into contact with Augustus St.-Gaudens who was engaged in some decorations for that structure. White assisted St.-Gaudens in his work, designing the bases for the General Farragut Monument, the Morgan tomb, which was destroyed by fire, and the Robert D. Randall statue at Sailors' Snug Harbor on Staten Island. In 1878 White with McKim, another employee of Richardson's firm, set out for Europe. They took a trip to the south of France, sketching architectural details and making notations which later they were to use in their plans. The next year, back in New York, White joined the firm of McKim, Mead and Bigelow which soon became McKim, Mead and White. The firm specialised in structures after Italian Renaissance patterns, showing its adaptability to present-day conditions. During the late 1880's White was busy designing the new chancel of the Church of the Ascension in New York, and soon came commissions for the Boston Public Library, Washington Arch and Madison Square Garden. These buildings were followed in 1892 by the Herald Building, patterned after a Renaissance structure in Verona, Italy. In 1895 Stanford White was entrusted with the job of restoring the Rotunda at the University of Virginia which had been partially burned. He was very successful in this, following closely the original plans of Thomas Jefferson. He was largely responsible for the buildings of New York University at Harlem Heights, and also designed the Century Club, the Colony Club, the Tiffany and Gorham buildings. One of his last structures was the Madison Square Presbyterian Church, designed in an East Christian pattern, since torn down and replaced by other structures. He also designed some magazine covers for *Scribner's* and the *Century*, but they were not used very long in their original form. White was killed by Harry Thaw, 3d June 1906.

See Pl. 64, Vol. II.

BIBLIOGRAPHY: Charles C. Baldwin, *Stanford White*, 1931.—*Sketches and Designs by Stanford White*, with an outline of his career by his son, Lawrence Grant White, 1920.

**WHITEHALL PALACE.**—See London.

**WIERIX.**—Family of Antwerp, of which three members are known as engravers: Jan (1549-1615?), Jérôme (1553-1619), and Antoine (1552-1624). Profound technicians, they had little feeling for color. They were employed by the Jesuits, and did many religious pictures as well as portraits of many of the important people of their day.

BIBLIOGRAPHY: A. Alorin, *Catalogue raisonné de l'œuvre de Jean, Jérôme et Antoine Wiertz* Brussels, 1899.

**WIERTZ (Antoine).** — Belgian painter, 1806-1865. His work is ambitious and theatrical. He painted antique scenes, and complicated philosophical and social subjects. In execution, he emulated Rubens.

**WILDENS (Jan).** — Flemish painter, 1586-1653. Pupil and assistant of Rubens. He painted landscapes, and still-life groups in the master's pictures and also assisted Jordaens, Snyders, Rombouts and others. He does not seem to have had great individuality, and rarely painted a picture of his own. Among the few works entirely by him are: *View of Antwerp*, 1636 (Amsterdam); *Hunting Scene in Winter*, 1624 (Dresden).

**WILHELM VON HERLE (Master).**—German painter of the school of Cologne, died 1378, the probable author of some wall paintings in the "Hansasaal" of the Cologne Town Hall, of which some fragments now exist in the Cologne Museum.

See Pl. 3, Vol. II.

**WILKIE (David).** — Scottish painter (1785-1841), was one of the greatest "genre" painters of Britain. When he was 14, he entered the Edinburgh school of art, where he worked for four years under the historical painter, John Graham. On his return to Cults, a fair he saw, gave him the idea for his first painting of rural life, *The Fair of Pitlessie*. In London he exhibited in 1805 *The Village Politicians*. From that time, his name was made, and each new work made a sensation. He produced in succession; *The Card Player; The Blind Fiddler* (National Gallery); *The Cut Finger; Village Fête* (National Gallery). In 1814 he went to Paris to study the Dutch masters, and on his return, painted his masterpieces; *The Reading of the Will; The Rabbit on the Wall; Rent-Day*. In 1809 he became an associate of the Royal Academy, and in 1811, Academician. Up to 1825, art, for him, meant the representation of family life, and he painted domestic scenes, village types, all aspects of peasant life, fêtes, games and dances. He had a great gift of observation, and humour, and a feeling for the picturesque. Unfortunately, he undertook, in 1825, a journey across Europe, which was fatal to his talents. He visited Spain, Italy, France, and Flanders, and thereupon gave up the manner which had, quite rightly, made him famous. Among the pictures he exhibited on his return are: *Two Scenes of Italian Life;* and *Three of Spanish Life.* His success was tremendous, but posterity would doubtless have given him a more important place in the history of British painting if he had continued in his earlier manner. In 1830 he was nominated painter-in-ordinary to the king, and after the death of Sir Thomas Lawrence there is but one interesting picture to his credit; *John Knox Preaching before the Lords of the Congregation* (National Gallery). In spite of the real qualities of this work, it cannot be compared with the village scenes, and the colour lacks harmony and warmth. In 1840 Wilkie went on a journey to the East, and died during his return. It might be said of Wilkie as of Hogarth; "this artist sees more with his mind than with his eyes."

His chief works can today be seen at South Kensington (where there are 8); and in the Wallace Collection which possesses *The Scottish Toilet.*

Bibliography: D. Laing, *Etchings by Sir David Wilkie, R.A.*—C. Dodgson, *The Etchings of Sir David Wilkie*. London. Walpole Society XI, 73, 1923.—Lord R. Gower, *Sir David Wilkie*. London, 1902.—W. Bayne, *Sir David Wilkie*. London, 1903.

**WILLE (Jean-Georges).** — German engraver on gold (1715-1808), who went while quite young to Paris, where he lived all his life. He had little originality, but what he liked was to reproduce paintings, patiently and exactly, especially those of Mieris, Metzer, and Gerard Dou.

Bibliography: Charles Le Blanc, *Catalogue de L'œuvre de J. G. Wille.* Leipzig, 1847.—Delaborde, *La Gravure.*—L. Rosenthal, *La Gravure*. Paris, 1909.

**WILSON (Richard).** — English painter (1714-1782). Having amassed a small sum of money by painting portraits. Wilson's dream of seeing Italy could at last come true. He went to Venice in 1749, and entered into communication with Zuccarelli, a famous Italian landscape painter. In Rome, he met Joseph Vernet with whom he became friends. He returned to London in 1755, and it is possible that his works had a certain vogue, for, in 1760, he had a real success with his landscape in *Niobe*, which shows his delicate feeling for composition, though the influence of Claude Lorrain is still too apparent. Unfortunately this success did not last long. The English public preferred the naturalism of Gainsborough, to Wilson's decided taste for ruins and Greek temples. He had the misfortune to be contemporary with Hogarth and Gainsborough, both essentially English artists, and the public did not forgive him for what was called his "lack of patriotism." Wilson, in fact, preferred all his life, the idealistic landscapes, and the poetical lands of Italy, to those of England. He lived miserably in Tottenham Court Road, passing his days in taverns. He finally retired to Wales where he died of an attack of delirium. Today his works are very valuable, and he is called "the English Claude." Certainly he was greatly influenced by Claude Lorrain, Lucatelli and Zuccarelli, but he added his own characteristic qualities in the drawing; in the composition; in the poetic imagination and the (often remarkable) execution.

The figures in his landscapes were not all painted by him. He was often helped by John Hamilton Mortimer, an historical painter, and member of the Royal Academy.

Bibliography: B. Fletcher, *Richard Wilson, R.A.* London, 1908.

**WINCHESTER (England).** — The *Cathedral* was begun in 1070. Norman transepts and tower. The Norman nave and choir were transformed by William of Wykeham and his successors (1394-1486) by a veneer of Perpendicular architecture and a vaulted roof.

Winchester has the greatest total length of any English Mediæval Cathedral.

**WINCKELMANN (Johann Joachim).**—German archæologist, 1717-1768, whose knowledge of ancient art exceeded that of any of his contemporaries. His chief work is a *History of Ancient Art*, 1764, Paris.

**WINDSOR.**—*St. George's Chapel*, 1481-1537. A royal palatine chapel in the Perpendicular Gothic style with impressive fan-vaulting.

**WINT (Peter de).** — English landscape painter, 1784-1849. A painstaking water-colour painter of the Surrey hills, and plains of Lincolnshire.

**WINTERHALTER (Franz Xavier).**—German painter, 1806-1873, of the second empire. He painted chiefly the sovereigns of Europe, and the most illustrious persons of their courts. Perhaps his most famous work is the *Empress Eugénie with Her Ladies-in-Waiting.*

Winterhalter: The Empress Eugénie. (Museum, Versailles.)

**WIT (Jacob de).**—Dutch painter and graver, Amsterdam, 1695-1754. While in Antwerp from 1711 to 1712, he copied 36 of the Rubens paintings in the Jesuit church there, and made many sketches of others. These proved especially valuable after a fire in the 18th century destroyed a number of these original paintings. After 1751 he settled in his native town. De Wit designed a number of tapestries and decorated many rooms for the aristocracy, among these also several for the Royal Palace. He was an excellent draughtsman, acquiring his spontaneity and freedom from copying Rubens' paintings.

**WITTE (Emanuel de).**—Dutch painter, 1618-1692. He spent most of his life in Delft and led a very unstable existence. His early works were portraits and genre scenes, until he discovered a special aptitude and liking for a hitherto unexplored field in Holland, namely painting church interiors. It is through these paintings that he achieved fame and began a precedent. Rendering architectural detail and perspective with great skill, he was a master in bringing about effects in chiaroscuro. The light usually penetrates through the clerestory, focusing on a column or part of the central apse, leaving the rest of the church in obscurity. The early brown and muddy colors later on became a charming silvery tonality. A number of small figures and dogs are used as *staffage*, and a red cloaked gentleman is usually present in the gathering.

Represented in the museums of Amsterdam, Berlin, Detroit, etc.

**— (Gaspard de).** — Flemish painter, 1624-1681. Travelled in Italy and France. He painted mostly landscapes in a theatrical style.

**— (Pieter de).**—See Candido.

**WITZ (Konrad).**—Painter (1348-1447), by origin belonging to the Upper Rhine (Swabian School), but working chiefly at Basle. Son of Hans Witz, a painter whose work is unknown, and who was in the service of the Duke of Burgundy. Konrad Witz followed his father to France and Flanders where he studied the masters of the time. He settled in Constance from 1412 to 1427, then at Rottweil, and then at Basle, and Geneva from 1434 till his death. There is in the Basle Museum, a great altarpiece of his, representing *David* and three of his servants; *Esther and Ahasuerus, Melchizedek Offering Bread and Wine to Abraham*, etc. On the panels, a *Levite, Saint Christopher*, the *Synagogue*.

There is also the Altarpiece of the archæological museum of Geneva (the *Adoration of the Magi*; the *Miraculous Draught of Fishes*, the *Deliverance of Saint Peter*, the *Virgin with a Cardinal*, 1444)—and the *Meeting at the Golden Gate* (Basle Museum); and *Saint Catherine and Saint Magdalen* (Strassburg).

Konrad Witz's painting underwent the influence of Burgundian art; his figures are vigorously modelled, the costumes and armour luxurious, the landscape and the play of light, carefully studied and rendered.

See Pl. 3, Vol. II.

Bibliography: Mela Escherich, *Konrad Witz*. Strasbourg, 1916.—H. Graber, *Konrad Witz*. Basle, 1922-24.

**WOLGEMUT (Michael).**—German painter, 1434-1519, born in Nuremberg. He directed a large atelier in which he and his assistants executed sacred paintings, wood carvings, and wood engravings. His famous pieces include several retables, e.g., that for the Austin friars of his native city (now in the museum there). Dürer was one of his pupils.

**WOOD (John the Elder).**—English architect, 1704-1754. Wood is best known for his effective work in city planning on a large scale, example of which may be seen in his work at Bath.

**WOOLLETT (William).**—English engraver, 1735-1785. His best engraving is *Diana and Actaeon*, after P. Lauri; and the best known, the *Death of General Wolfe*, after B. West. He was influenced by French engravers.

Bibliography: L. Fagan, *A Catalogue Raisonné of the Engraved Work of William Woollett*. London, 1885.

**WOOLNER (Thomas).**—See Brown (F. M.); Pre-Raphaelite Brotherhood.

**WORMS (Germany).**—*Cathedral*, reconstructed 1181-1230 on plan of 1000-1025. A representative Rhenish Romanesque cathedral with eastern and western apse, towers, and lantern. There is no western transept. The entrances are in the aisles. The arched corbel tables and the pilaster strips found in Germany first at Speyer constitute the external decoration.

**WOUWERMAN (Philips).** — Dutch painter of Haarlem, 1619-1668. He painted chiefly hunting scenes, encampments and battle charges in which he was never surpassed by anyone. A brilliant colorist and draughtsman, his compositions are inexhaustible variations about the same theme. His early works may be detected through the clumsy horses and brown tonality. In his late style the silvery tones dominate and the horses possess an inimitable grace and movement. The Louvre possesses his *Cavalry Skirmish, Cavaliers,* and *Pilgrims.* An able painter, and extraordinarily prolific, he painted over 800 canvases, not counting the numberless figures he painted in the pictures of his fellow artists.

Wouwerman: Cavalry Engagement. (Museum, The Hague.)

Bibliography: C. Hofstede de Groot, *A Catalogue Raisonné of the Works of the Most Eminent Dutch Painters of the Seventeenth Century*, Vol. II. 1909.

**WREN (Christopher).**—English architect, 1632-1723. He also studied mathematics and astronomy. In 1661, he became associated with Sir John Denham, Inspector General of Works, and began his career as an architect (*Pembroke Chapel*, Cambridge; *Sheldonian Theatre*, and *Trinity College*, Oxford).

After the great fire of London in 1666, he elaborated a remarkable plan, which was not adopted, for rebuilding the city. He built over fifty churches, one of the finest of which is *St. Stephen's*, Walbrook. His masterpiece is *St. Paul's Cathedral* (1675-1710), for which he made several plans, all remarkable.

This tremendous undertaking did not, however, absorb all his time. He made plans for more than fifty other buildings—palaces, colleges, the towers of Westminster Abbey, and the eastern part of Hampton Court, the design of which is very elegant and pure in style.

Wren had a great admiration for

# AMERICAN ART: CONTEMPORARY

*G*ROWING *luxury and security increased the demand for beauty, and the years up into the nineteenth century produced more and more artists, trained in old traditions, but gradually branching out with innovations and styles all their own. The nineteenth century gives evidence of the growth of new styles, both native and foreign, individual and national, responding to the increasing and varied interests of both artist and patron. Truly American style and tradition was laid down in this century, although much of the inspiration and training, of necessity, still came from abroad.*

EDWARD HOPPER: LIGHTHOUSE AT TWO LIGHTS.
*(Collection, Mrs. Samuel A. Tucker, N. Y.)*

EUGENE SPEICHER: TORSO OF HILDA.
*(Courtesy of the Detroit Institute of Arts.)*

JOHN MARIN: MAINE ISLANDS (WATERCOLOUR).
*(Phillips Memorial Gallery, Washington, D. C.)*

## Modernism

BETWEEN 1910 and 1920 the clash of the old tradition with modernism came into prominence. The impressionistic creed of "back to nature" disputed ground with the new group who sought the solution of art problems by delving into the methods and sources of the past. The intellectual and abstract qualities of art were probed by this younger group who stressed such elements as organisation, structure and design, frequently to the point of ignoring subject-matter entirely. In this decade Post-Impressionism, Cubism, Futurism and Expressionism were spread out before the public eye, sounding the battle-cry against academicism.

CHARLES SHEELER: BUCKS COUNTY BARN
(WATERCOLOUR WITH PENCIL).
*(Courtesy Whitney Museum of American Art.)*

CHARLES BURCHFIELD: PROMENADE (WATERCOLOUR).
*(Collection of A. C. Goodyear—Courtesy the Museum of Modern Art.)*

## Watercolour

THE brilliant heritage of watercolour, which Homer left to his successors, finds varying expressions in the 20th century. Sheeler's lucid draughtsmanship and selective realism stand in contrast to Burchfield's romantic emotionalism, and Marin's mastery of medium and arbitrary freedom expressed through his own very personal shorthand. Whether in watercolour or other media, each contemporary artist illustrates in his own way the extraordinary variety and range of interest and conception finding expression today.

GEORGE B. LUKS: THE SPIELERS.
*(Addison Gallery of American Art, Phillips Academy, Andover.)*

THOMAS BENTON: ARTS OF THE WEST (MURAL).
*(Courtesy of Whitney Museum of American Art Photo Juley.)*

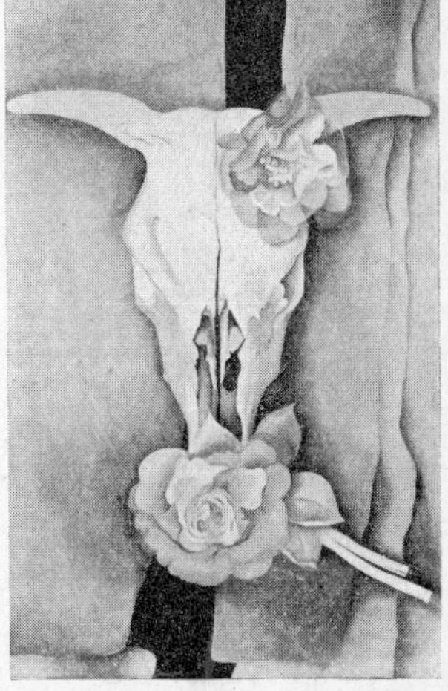

GEORGIA O'KEEFFE:
COW'S SKULL AND WHITE ROSES.
*(Collection An American Place, New York.)*

## Mural

THE progress of mural painting in the last years leads many to believe in its potential development into a medium peculiarly sympathetic as a means of American art expression. The decorative function of art, a significant aspect of modernism, is especially applicable to mural painting. Men like Benton and Robinson have definitely revealed their power in this field, while the Mexicans, Ribera and Orozco, have in their work given tremendous impetus to a reviving interest in wall-painting.

# AMERICAN SCULPTURE AND ARCHITECTURE

*With the foundations for an American art tradition laid down in the nineteenth century, there has been an increasingly awakening interest in art on the part of the American public. The result is a solidification of the foundations, with promise in the future for artistic accomplishment which will be a truly American contribution to the accumulation of art works of all countries throughout the ages.*

J. Q. A. WARD:
GEORGE WASHINGTON.
*(Photo Bogart.)*

AUGUSTUS ST. GAUDENS:
ADAMS MEMORIAL.
*(Photo Leet Brothers, Washington, D. C.)*

JACOB EPSTEIN:
MADONNA AND CHILD.
*(Collection the artist.)*

MALVINA HOFFMAN:
BLACKFOOT INDIAN MAN.
*(Courtesy Field Museum of Natural History, Chicago—Photo copyright.)*

WILLIAM ZORACH:
MOTHER AND CHILD.
*(Courtesy The Downtown Gallery, New York.)*

## Sculpture

American sculpture before the latter half of the 19th century adds a little to the significance of American art. After the Civil War, men like Ward, St. Gaudens, French and Barnard begin the history of American sculpture as such. Notable modern figures include Epstein, Zorach, Hoffman, Lachaise, Manship and Mahonri Young.

THOMAS JEFFERSON: MONTICELLO.
*(Photo Ewing Galloway, N. Y.)*

HENRY H. RICHARDSON:
MARSHALL FIELD WAREHOUSE, CHICAGO.
*(Courtesy The Museum of Modern Art.)*

## Architecture

Thomas Jefferson stands as father of the Classic Revival which seized the new American Republic at the end of the Revolution, and which constituted the first break from the English tradition. The tradition endured until the Gothic Revival which was followed by the Renaissance Revival during the last twenty years of the century. Richardson's modified Romanesque and Byzantine, and personal style affected American architecture long after his death.

LOUIS SULLIVAN:
GUARANTY BUILDING, BUFFALO.
*(Courtesy Hugh Morrison—Photo Fuermann, Chicago.)*

MCKIM, MEAD AND WHITE:
UNIVERSITY CLUB, NEW YORK.
*(Courtesy of McKim, Mead and White.)*

FRANK LLOYD WRIGHT:
MILLARD HOUSE, PASADENA.
*(Courtesy Museum of Modern Art.)*

RAYMOND HOOD:
DAILY NEWS BLDG., N. Y.
*(Courtesy Museum of Modern Art.)*

Growing wealth and expansion fostered architecture at the end of the century, and numerous styles developed: McKim, Mead and White used Italian and French Renaissance and free styles; Hunt, neo-Greek and Francis I; others, Victorian Gothic. Business centralisation brought the "skyscraper." Sullivan's innovations in tall-building design, expressing the underlying steel construction, are further developed by Gilbert, Goodhue, Hood, etc. Wright, a great innovator of this century, conceives his designs in terms of the skeleton structure, walls becoming interesting planes, and interiors complex single spaces.

# English Art: Survey

A grouping of English art works covering several centuries will be of value as showing the range of interests which has attracted English artists since the Middle Ages. The history of English art development in the last centuries has been the history of national absorption and interpretation of the movements in art which penetrated every country in Europe at one time or another. The manuscript tradition is translated into both monumental painting and sculpture, the influence of both Gothic and Renaissance styles travelled over from France and Italy, as did the varied influences of French schools of painting from the end of the Renaissance up to the present time. Not least of the English heritage lies in their extraordinary gift for embroidery, and in the development of Celtic manuscript illumination with its geometric conventionality reaching an astounding degree of skill.

MOSES, YORK CATHEDRAL.
*(Copyright York Museum—Copyright Victoria and Albert Museum.)*

ANGEL GABRIEL.
*(Courtesy H. M. Office of Works—Copyright Victoria and Albert Museum.)*

CENTRE OF ALABASTER RETABLE.
*(Courtesy and Copyright Victoria and Albert Museum.)*

PORTRAIT OF RICHARD II, WESTMINSTER ABBEY.
*(Courtesy Alfieri Picture Service.)*

## Medieval Sculpture

The history of English medieval sculpture is analogous to the development of Gothic architecture: it interprets the principles laid down by the French, in terms of English national genius. As in the French, English sculpture of this period is to a preponderant degree architectural, the stone-carver intending his work to be seen in relation to the architectural background which it was to adorn. Many characteristics of the French schools may be identified in such details as the ropy beard of Moses, the swirling drapery and hipshot pose of Gabriel. Painting of the period follows the traditions of manuscript illumination.

MONTACUTE HOUSE (WEST FRONT).
*(Courtesy Valentine & Sons, Ltd.)*

BANQUETING HALL, WHITEHALL.
*(Courtesy Valentine & Sons, Ltd.)*

ADELAIDE HOUSE.
*(Courtesy Topical Press Agency, London.)*

## Architecture

The development of domestic architecture is like the development of architecture in public and ecclesiastical building in that the blending of styles and the transition from one style to another is of slow growth. The Gothic castle, designed primarily for defense and protection, slowly gives way to the manor house making its appearance in less troublous times. Growth of wealth makes possible greater comfort and richness, with fewer restrictive conditions. Gothic detail is succeeded by the Renaissance tradition redolent of Classical forms imported from Italy through France. Modern developments follow the same sort of growth dependent on new conditions, new means, and new interpretation in terms of national and individual character.

P. W. STEER: RICHMOND CASTLE.
*(Copyright National Gallery.)*

PAUL NASH: WOODS ON THE DOWNS.
*(Courtesy Raymond and Raymond.)*

W. R. SICKERT: PRIVATE VIEW OF THE R.A.
*(Courtesy College Art Association, and Leicester Galleries, London.)*

## Modern Painting

The juxtaposition of two landscapes such as these by Steer and Nash provides a stimulating example of contrast in contemporary points of view. English Impressionism is the welding of two strong influences: the Impressionism of Turner and Constable blending with the Impressionism of Monet and Manet. Steer, with his interest in atmospheric effects combined with the gusto inspired by Constable, is in direct contrast to the more "modern" Paul Nash, interested as he is, entirely in the basic inner organisation of his landscapes to the exclusion of interest in superficial or accidental detail. Walter Sickert and Augustus John provide an analogously interesting contrast in genre and portrait painting.

the antique, which he adapted to the needs of his day, with restrained elegance, sometimes a little cold. He had a fine sense of noble proportion, and contributed lavishly to the architecture of London.

See London, St. Paul's Cathedral.

BIBLIOGRAPHY: James Elmes, *Life and Works of Sir C. Wren,* 1823.—Sir Lawrence Weaver, *Sir Christopher Wren.* London, 1923.

**WRIGHT (Frank Lloyd).**—Contemporary American architect. He was born 8th June 1869 in Richland Center, Wisconsin. About 1880 the family settled at Madison, Wisconsin, and as soon as he was old enough he entered the University of Wisconsin, studying engineering under Dean Allen D. Conover. He did some practical work with Dean Conover, who was entrusted with the plans of the college buildings. In 1887 he went to Chicago and there entered the office of J. L. Silsbee, the architect of All Souls' Church in Chicago. The following spring he became a designer for the firm of Adler and Sullivan and because Sullivan was busy with the Auditorium Building it fell to Wright to design plans for private houses. In 1894 he opened his own office and proceeded to develop his own particular Prairie Architecture, which he considered well suited for private dwellings. In this style he emphasised the long horizontal bands of the eaves and large windows, stressing long low lines so as to make the dwelling conform to the contours of the landscape where it was located. As his reputation grew he became more radical and made long rows of windows with great overhanging eaves and the general subordination or elimination of any decoration to the plastic lines of the whole. Of this type the Robie House is perhaps most characteristic. The Administration building in Buffalo for the Larkin Soap Company placed its emphasis on simple surfaces with the predominance of horizontal lines and the grouping of the elevator shafts in one end of the building. Next came the monolithic poured cement Unity Temple for Oak Park, Illinois, of striking appearance but rather gloomy. From 1916 to 1920 he was engaged in building the Imperial Hotel in Tokyo, Japan. In this he used the floating cantilever construction and added local characteristics of style whenever possible. It was an architectural success, withstanding perfectly the heavy earthquake of 1923. Since then he has devoted himself largely to innovations in the designs of small houses with roof terraces, large windows, etc., planning them for the appearance of mass with concrete blocks alternating with much window space. He is the author of authoritative writings on modern American architecture, including *Modern Architecture* and *Two Lectures on Architecture.*

See Pl. 64, Vol. II.

BIBLIOGRAPHY: Heinrich DeFries, ed., *Frank Lloyd Wright,* Berlin, 1926.—*Frank Lloyd Wright,* Les Maîtres de l'Architecture contemporaine, No. 1, Paris, 1928.—*The Lifework of the American Architect, Frank Lloyd Wright,* introduction by H. Th. Wijdeveld, Holland, 1925.—Frank Lloyd Wright, *An Autobiography,* 1932.—Catalogue, *Modern Architects,* by Alfred H. Barr, Jr., Henry-Russell Hitchcock, Jr., Philip Johnson, and Lewis Mumford, Museum of Modern Art, New York, 1932.

**— (Joseph).**—Early American painter (1756-1793). This son of the gifted sculptor of wax figures, Mrs. Patience Wright, was born in Bordentown, New Jersey, 16th July 1756. Soon afterward his father died and when Joseph was sixteen the family moved to London. There his mother's work had a great vogue and his sister married John Hoppner, the artist. Young Wright began to develop his own ability as a portrait painter by study with Hoppner and the celebrated American, Benjamin West. According to one report he was said to have painted the Prince of Wales, later George IV, before his departure for France in 1782. He carried with him letters to Franklin and Pierre, the painter. While in Paris he painted the portrait of Franklin of which the original is in the Royal Society, London. Wright soon afterward set sail for America and the next year painted General and Mrs. Washington at Rocky Hill, New Jersey. At the same time he modelled a life mask and worked on a small bust of Washington for an order of Congress. Apparently the portrait pleased Washington, as two copies of it by Wright were sent abroad, one as a gift to a friend in Saxony and the other taken by Jefferson to France, where it was retouched by Trumbull, for the purpose of finding someone to make a statue of the great American leader. During 1786 Wright removed to New York and kept a studio there until Congress moved to Philadelphia, where he followed for the purpose of painting Madison. In 1790 he made an etching of Washington based, according to legend, upon a sketch made in church. Washington appointed Wright as first die-sinker and engraver of the United States Mint and he is said to have created a design for a one-cent piece which was never used. He also made dies for a Washington medal based on the bust by Houdon, and a congressional medal for Major Lee. He died during the yellow fever epidemic in Philadelphia in the fall of 1793. Several of his copies of the 1783 portrait of Washington exist, a copy of the Franklin portrait is in the Corcoran Gallery of Art in Washington, and his own family portrait is in the Pennsylvania Academy of Fine Arts in Philadelphia. He was the teacher of William Rush, one of the earliest of the well-known sculptors, and Wright's etching of Washington was an inspiration for some copies in oil and sculpture by later artists.

BIBLIOGRAPHY: William Dunlap, *The History of the Rise and Progress of the Arts of Design in the United States,* 1918.—Charles Henry Hart, *An Original Portrait of Doctor Franklin, Painted by Joseph Wright, Belonging to the Royal Society, London, Pennsylvania Magazine of History and Biography,* Vol. 32, 1908, pp. 17, 320-334.—Fiske Kimball, *Joseph Wright and His Portraits of Washington, Antiques,* Vol. 15, May, 1929, pp. 377-382; Vol. 17, January, 1930, pp. 35-39.

**— (Mrs. Patience Lovell).**—American sculptress (1725-1785), of Bordentown, N. J., the first American on record to practice sculpture. In 1769 she settled in London, where she died. She specialised in small portrait heads in wax; an example of her work (bust of Thomas Penn) may be seen in Independence Hall, Philadelphia.

**WU CHEN.**—Chinese painter, 1280-1354. One of the "Four Masters" of the Yuan dynasty. He painted with extremely broad brush strokes.

**WU TAO-TZU.**—Chinese painter of the 8th century. The most famous of all Chinese painters.

See China—Art.

**WYANT (Alexander Helwig).**—American painter (1836-1892). He was born in Evans Creek, Tuscarawas County, Ohio, 11th January 1836, but soon the family moved to Defiance, Ohio, where his boyhood was spent. There he was apprenticed to a harness maker and at odd times did some sign painting. He was interested in becoming an artist and was much impressed by an exhibition of landscapes in Cincinnati. He admired especially the work of George Inness, which reflected the Barbizon tradition, and made a long trip to New York to get his advice. With some help from friends in Cincinnati he was able in 1865 to go abroad to study. He worked for a time with Hans Gude in Carlsruhe, Germany, working in the Düsseldorf tradition and then made a trip to England and Ireland before returning home. He was interested in the work of the English landscape school as done by Constable and Turner and from them came his desire to draw directly from nature. Back in New York he followed that practice and his *Mohawk Valley* at the Metropolitan Museum of Art shows his work of that time. It is well balanced and the eye is carried logically to the objects in the far distance and the whole scene is wrapped in a soft diffused light. In 1873 Wyant joined a government exploring expedition to Arizona and New Mexico but the physical hardships broke his strength and he was forced to return east by train. Ill as he was he would not admit defeat, but continued past his Ohio home to New York, where he had a paralytic stroke which rendered his right side helpless. Thereafter he was forced to paint with his left hand. His pictures grew more personal and more naturalistic, though endowed with neutral sunny tones of colour. Instead of the large compositions of his early period he depicted small wooded glens and rolling meadows. After 1880 his summers were spent at Keene Valley in the Adirondacks and later at Arkville in the Catskills. He would sit on the porch of his cabin for hours at a time and gaze over the valley below, watching the cloud effects and the lights and shadows of the hills and dales. His later pictures were painted from memory in the studio, although he had in his youth been a firm believer in work done directly from nature. He died 29th November 1892, interested almost to the last in his art and the beauties of nature around him.

BIBLIOGRAPHY: Elliott Clark, *Alexander Wyant,* American Artists Series, 1916.—Elliott Clark, *Sixty Paintings by Alexander H. Wyant,* American Artists Series, 1920.

**WYNANTS (Jan).**—Dutch landscape painter (about 1620-1682). He painted dunes, and forest clearings with old oak trees somewhat in the manner of Ruysdael.

The Louvre possesses a *Forest Glade* by him. He painted a large number of pictures, interesting himself only in landscape, and generally trusting others—Wouwermans, Adriaen van de Velde, his pupils,—to execute the figures.

BIBLIOGRAPHY: C. Hofstede de Groot, *Catalogue of Dutch Painters,* Vol. VIII.

# X

**XANTHOS (Funeral Tower of).** —See Lycia.

**XERXES.**—See Persia.

**XOANON.**—Primitive image made of wood, usually an idol.

**XYLOGRAPH.**—See Engraving (History).

# Y

**YEN LI-PÊN.**—Chinese painter of the 7th century. A painting of thirteen emperors now in the Museum of Fine Arts, Boston, may be by his hand.

See China—Art.

**YORK (England).**—Magnificent Gothic *Cathedral*, which replaced a

YORK: TRANSEPT OF THE CATHEDRAL.

Norman Cathedral begun about 1070. Built from 1171 to 1472. It possesses a remarkable façade with towers. The south transept has a row of long narrow pointed windows, celebrated as the "Five Sisters." The nave and choir are one of the finest specimens of "decorated" Gothic architecture. The Chapter House is one of the finest in England.

See Pl. 49, Vol. I; Pl. 65, Vol. II.

**YOUNG (Mahonri Mackintosh).** —Contemporary American sculptor. This artist, a grandson of the famous Mormon leader Brigham Young, was born at Salt Lake City, Utah, 9th August 1877. He tried modelling figures in the native adobe soil and later in clay, after seeing that material used by Cyrus Dallin in a model for his statue of Brigham Young. In 1899 Mahonri Young came to New York City to study at the Art Students' League and the next year he went to Paris. There he worked at the Académie Julian and other schools, but soon returned to the United States. He went back to his native state of Utah and there continued his modelling and sketching. About 1912 there began to appear his studies of Navajo Indians in their picturesque garb, engaged in herding the flocks of sheep. Many other phases of their existence were shown in boldly conceived etchings, delicate bronze bas-reliefs, and vivid pastels.

The next step in his development followed the love of industry which had been his since childhood. He moved to New York City and began to turn out statuettes of labouring men engaged in different jobs and yet all helping to create some monument of man's invention. Stevedores, boxers, men with shovels, labourers worn out by the day's toil—all were faithfully represented. He has also made some fine portrait busts, studies of animal life and, recently, charming pastel sketches of the nude and boldly conceived oils. All attest to his versatility in media and subject matter, which is rather exceptional in this day of specialisation. He taught at the American School of Sculpture and is still an instructor at the Art Students' League. Representative examples of his work may be found in Salt Lake City, the Metropolitan Museum of Art and the Phillips Memorial Gallery in Washington.

BIBLIOGRAPHY: For a complete bibliography see *The Index of Twentieth Century Artists* for December, 1934.

**YPRES (Belgium).**—Old Flemish town, once prosperous and busy. The *Cathedral* is a fine thirteenth century building.

On the grand place stood the famous *Cloth Hall* (1200-1304), an imposing building, quietly deco-

YPRES: THE CLOTH-HALL.

rated with a turret at each end of the façade, in the middle of which was a fine belfry tower. This magnificent building was destroyed by German artillery, during the war.

**YSENBRANT.**—See Isenbrant.

# Z

**ZAGANELLI da COTIGNOLA (Francesco).**—Romagnole-Ferrarese painter, c. 1460-1531. Pupil of Palmezzano, influenced by Ercole Roberti and Fra Bartolommeo. Worked with his brother Bernardino.

**ZAMORA (Spain).**—*Cathedral.* Built from 1151 to 1176, this is a Romanesque building of remarkable purity and simplicity of style. The domed lantern is similar to that of the nearly Old Cathedral of Salamanca. Unfortunately it was altered by later additions.

See Pl. 45, Vol. I.

**ZAMPIERI (Domenico).** — See Domenichino.

**ZANCHI (Antonio d'Este).**—Venetian painter, 1639-1722, of the decadence. He executed the *Martyrdom of St. Anthony*; and the *Prodigal Son* (Venice, Academy).

**ZANOBI di BARTOLO.**—Florentine sculptor, 14th century. He worked in the Duomo.

**— MACCHIAVELLI.**—See Macchiavelli (Zanobi).

**ZAVATTARI.**—Gothic Lombard painters, of which the family included: Cristoforo, active 1404; Franceschino, active 1414 and 1417; Ambrogio, active 1456, 1459; and Gregorio, who decorated in 1475 a sanctuary at Corbetta.

Frescoes in the Chapel of the Queen Teodolinda in the Cathedral of Monza, are signed by an inscription with the family name and the date 1444, but there is no indication as to which of the family is responsible for their execution. These frescoes are most important for their number and extent and are the only authenticated work by the Zavattari.

BIBLIOGRAPHY: C. Fumagalli e L. Beltrami, *Le cappella della Regina Teodolinda nella basilica di S. Giovanni.*—Toesca. *Pittura e miniatura nella Lombardia,* 1912.

**ZEGHERS (Gerard).** — Flemish painter, born in Antwerp, 1591-1651. Pupil of Rubens. Greatly influenced by his master.

His chief works include: *Joseph's Dream, Virgin and Child* (St. Michel, Antwerp), *The Adoration of St. Francis* (Louvre).

**ZEITBLOM (Bartholomaeus).**—German painter (about 1450-1520), of the Swabian school of Ulm. He painted a triptych of the Church of Heeberg (1498—Stuttgart Gallery), and the Altarpiece of Eschuch (1498).

Zeitblom was a talented artist who designed calm, simple, pictures, with tall, rather stiff figures. His colour has a tender freshness.

See Pl. 3, Vol. II.

BIBLIOGRAPHY: Bach, *Bartto Zeitblom.* 1881.

**ZENALE (Bernardino).**—Milanese painter and architect from Treviglio. Pupil of Foppa, influenced by Bramante. Worked in close partnership with Butinone, from whom it is difficult to distinguish him, and with whom he executed the 1485 polyptych in S. Martino, Treviglio.

**ZEUXIS.**—Greek painter of the period between the end of the 5th century and the beginning of the 4th century B.C. None of his paintings have come down to us. The most celebrated of them are known to us from the descriptions of ancient writers. Many of them represented scenes from mythology, such as *Menelaus Praying at the Tomb of Agamemnon*; *Pan*; a *Family of Centaurs.* One of his most admired pictures was the *Child with a Bunch of Grapes,* in which the painting of the fruit attracted the birds. One of his most celebrated pictures was *Helen at the Bath.*

**ZIEGLER (Jörg).**—See Messkirch.

**ZIEM (Felix).**—French painter, 1821-1911. He won a prize at the School of Architecture of his native town (Beaune), which enabled him to go to Paris and Rome. He accomplished the journey to Rome on foot. He travelled widely, in Europe, and in the East, and finally returned to Venice.

His pictures include: *Sunrise in Constantinople* (1859—called by Théophile Gautier, the finest painting of the modern school); *Venice* (Wallace Collection); *Dutch Landscape* (Rouen); *Santa Sophia, Morning,* and *The Old Port of Marseille, Evening* (Petit Palais), etc. His water colours are numerous, and much esteemed.

Ziem was a gifted painter, and at his best a brilliant colourist. His later paintings show a falling off of his qualities of restraint.

**ZIGGURAT.**—The Ziggurat was a Sumerian or Assyrian building, formed of several superimposed towers, the size of which diminishes as they are placed higher. Sometimes they were quadrangular. Mesopotamia was covered with this form of building which recalls slightly that of the Egyptian pyramids.

ZIEM: VENICE. (Musée du Luxembourg.)

**ZINGARO (Lo).**—See Solario (Antonio da).

**ZOAN ANDREA.** — Italian engraver of the end of the 15th and beginning of the 16th century. Very little known, he has given rise to many controversies. An engraver of the name of Zouâ Andrea signed an engraved plate, after the Apocalypse of Dürer, which appeared in Venice in 1516. Plates signed Z. A., I. A., i. a. have been attributed to him.

BIBLIOGRAPHY: Bartch, *Le Peintre-graveur,* Vol. XIII. Passavent, *Le Peintre-graveur,* Vol. I.

**ZOFFANY (Johann).** — Anglo-German painter (1735-1810), born probably at Frankfort, he settled in England about 1758, and soon established for himself a considerable position, being elected a foundation member of the Royal Academy in 1768. He stayed in India from 1783 to 1790. A facile and pleasing artist whose "conversation pieces" (group portraits) have lately come in for a considerable vogue.

BIBLIOGRAPHY: Lady Victoria Manners and G. C. Williamson, *John Zoffany.* London, 1920.

**ZOPPO (Marco).**—Ferrarese painter, assistant and imitator of Cosimo Tura, influenced by the Bellini. Born 1433 at Bologna, pupil of Squarcione at Padua, went to Venice in 1462, then to Bologna. In 1471 he was again in Venice. The last notice referring to him is in Bologna in 1489. The polyptych in the chapel of the Collegio di Spagna, Bologna, is signed; and a number of other works are attributed to Marco Zoppo.

BIBLIOGRAPHY: Berenson, *North Italian Painters of the Renaissance.* —*Catalogue dell' Esposizione Ferrarese.* Ferrara, 1933.—Roberto Longhi, *Officina Ferrarese,* 1936.

**ZORACH (William).**—Contemporary American painter and sculptor. He was born in Russia in 1887 but came to the United States as a small child. His people made their home in Ohio and when he was twelve he became an apprentice in a lithograph plant at Cleveland, Ohio. He began to take an interest in painting and went to night sessions of the Cleveland Art School. A short time later he came east and studied at the National Academy of Design in New York City. In 1910 he went to Paris for further instruction and had some work exhibited at the Salon d'Automne of 1911. The following year he returned to New York and with his wife, Marguerite Zorach, who is well known for her paintings and tapestries, settled in the Greenwich Village section. His paintings of a cubistic nature were shown in the Armory Show of 1913 and at the Panama-Pacific Exposition in San Francisco in 1915. But he was not satisfied with his progress and in 1922 turned to the carving of wood. At first it was just a pastime, but soon it became his whole interest. From modified abstractions of the human figure in wood it was only a step to a similar treatment of stone. He learned to carve directly in the stone and sought to find the figure hidden in each block, using the rough form to its best advantage. It was a tenet that would have appealed to the archaic Greek sculptors and to Michelangelo. His heroic group of *Mother and Child* in Spanish granite is a typical example of his method of work. Despite his preoccupation with sculpture Zorach has not entirely given up his painting. During his vacations in Maine he paints landscapes, clear and simple in the treatment of the watercolour medium. It is seldom that one meets today an artist so proficient in these two fields of the pictorial arts. Examples of his work are in the Art Institute of Chicago, the Columbus, Ohio, Gallery of Fine Arts, the Whitney Museum of American Art and the Phillips Memorial Gallery in Washington, D. C.

See Pl. 64, Vol. II.

BIBLIOGRAPHY: Dorothy Lefferts Moore, *William Zorach,* The Arts Portfolio Series, 1931.—For a complete bibliography see *The Index of Twentieth Century Artists* for May, 1934.

**ZOR'AH (Syria).** — *St. George,* 515. A central type South Syrian church based on the nearby Cathedral of Bosia. It is a square succeeded in the east by two pastophoria and a salient polygonal apse. Corner niches bring the square to an interior octagon divided into a central area and an annular aisle by eight piers also arranged in an octagon. The church has a modern *kubbeh* dome in scoriac, but it is doubtful whether or not it was originally domed.

**ZORN (Anders Leonhard).**—Swedish painter, engraver and sculptor (1860-1920). He was born 18th February 1860 in Gruddgarden. His father was a German master-brewer, his mother came from an old Swedish middle-class family. As a youngster he drove cattle in the pastures of the neighbouring hills until he was sent to the Infant School at Mora. Already at the age of eight he was known to be a skilled wood carver, and while in grammar school at Enköping, from 1872 to 1875, he carved away rather than absorbed the teachings of his school master. At Stockholm he studied sculpture at the Technical School and it was through his fine pencil portraits that, in 1875, he was admitted to the Preparatory School of the Academy of Art. He received an academic training and studied portrait painting with Georg v. Rosen, but being bored with the procedure and requirements he left in 1881. The following years were spent in travel, including visits to Paris, London, Spain, Portugal and Tangiers. In 1881 he returned to his native land to marry Emma Lamm and on his honeymoon he visited Hungary and Constantinople, Italy and Greece. He opened a fashionable studio in London, which he kept until 1885, painting the portraits of many prominent socialites. After a short visit to Sweden in 1887 he went to Algiers and Spain. After that he settled in Paris, where he contributed frequently to the various Salons and exhibitions up to 1911. He came to America in 1903 and lived in Chicago with his friends. By this time his fame was established all over the world. His last years were spent in Mora, his home and circle being considered as one of the culture centres of Sweden. He died in September, 1920. His early and rather sentimental watercolours showed the influence of Lundgren; the clever portrait pieces were characterised by cool elegance done in fresh colours with greens dominating. *Our Daily Bread* is the best example of this period. His later style is more restless and alive. It shows the artist as an acute observer of detail and a master of his technique. His favourite subject matter became water studies combined with bathing feminine nudes. It was his stay in Paris in 1888 that made him develop an appreciation for oil as a possible medium. He painted mostly portraits and scenes from peasant life. It was in 1890 that he first experimented with landscapes, but these were never as successful as his other subjects. *Omnibus* may be called his chef d'œuvre of this class. His style slowly became cosmopolitan, although the roots of his art always remained in Mora. In 1893 another change took place due to his sojourn in the United States. He again turned to portraiture and to painting nudes, glorifying healthy womanhood in warm golden tones and with a flying brush technique. *Mona* is representative of this stage. However, he never ceased to paint the Dalecarlia peasant types and now added the new subject of genre. During his last years, although his mastery of rendering air and the play of light was superb, his way of interpreting nudes became brutal and indiscreet. Zorn always considered etching a form of recreation, limiting himself to the pure needle technique on a soft ground, using the burin only occasionally. His topics were dominated by figure pieces and scenes from Sweden. He strove for plastic effects, which he achieved with the use of line and handscraping of the plate. The plates which were adaptations of his earlier oil paintings are specially fine in value relationship. He also did very fine sculpture in bronze.

BIBLIOGRAPHY: Karl Asplund, *Anders Zorn,* 1921.—Albert Engström, *Anders Zorn,* 1928.— Franz Gervaes, *Anders Zorn,* 1910.—Tor Hedberg, *Anders Zorn,* 1926.

**ZUCCARELLI (Francesco).** — Venetian painter, of Tuscan origin (1704-1788). He is known for his luminous landscapes, filled with elegant personages. He painted a great deal in London, where he became a foundation member of the Royal Academy.

**ZUCCARO (or ZUCCHERO, Federigo).** — Florentine painter, 1542-1609. One of the chief representatives of "mannerism," the pompous and affected imitation of Michelangelo, Raphael and Correggio. Like other painters of his day, he was bound by technical ability and a striving after sensational subjects and effects. He travelled widely—in Italy, Flanders and England. He went to Spain, where he worked in the Escorial, in the service of Philip II. He spent the latter part of his life in Rome. He wrote works on æsthetics and founded an Academy of Drawing. With Taddeo Zuccaro, he did the Decoration of the Caprarola Palace. His last important works were frescoes in the Ascoli Chapel, Santa Sabina.

**— (Taddeo).** — Italian painter (1529?-1569?). Imitator of Michelangelo. One of his most important works is the decoration of the Caprarola Palace, done in collaboration with Federigo Zuccaro, his brother.

**ZUCCONE (Il).**—See Donatello; also Pl. 8, Vol. II.

**ZULOAGA Y ZABALESA (Ignacio).**—Contemporary Spanish painter. He was born at Eibar near Bilbao 26th July 1870, the son of a sculptor and the descendant of a line of ceramic manufacturers. His father tried to make him study engineering and also architecture, but the boy was more interested in drawing. He became an apprentice in his father's factory and there learned the art of damascening of metal for arms and armour. He made a trip to Madrid, where he saw the work of El Greco, which exercised a strong influence over his art. When Ignacio Zuloaga was eighteen he obtained the reluctant permission of his family to study art and departed for Rome. There he found the academic tradition prevailing in the studios and soon left for Paris. He tried his hand at painting impressionistic pictures but without much success. After a short trip to England he returned to his native Spain and from 1892 to 1899 he tried to find his own individual means of artistic expression. In order to earn his living he acted as an art critic and in the intervals sent his paintings to the exhibitions in France and Spain, but without raising much comment in the world of art. Then he settled near his uncle in Segovia and began to paint in earnest, drawing upon his many experiences for his material. Gradually he became known in the Salons of Paris but it was a long time before he was recognised as a great artist in Spain. He did studies of bull fighters, old women in the markets, vivacious young women, dwarfs, sheep herders, dancers and portraits of society persons. With the revenue from the sale of his pictures Zuloaga bought pictures by the old Spanish masters, including El Greco, Goya, Velázquez and many others. It became fashionable to have one's portrait painted by this master and almost always the model was dressed in a variety of Spanish costume. All of these studies displayed the artist's ability to portray character through an intensive study of the features with the figure and background acting merely as accessories to set off the person or persons. His art is essentially Spanish with the combination of dreaminess and mysticism, pride and strength of character shown in the faces of the people of that country, all marked by a richness of colour and directness of delineation. Occasionally there is a note of satire which seems to have been borrowed from the work of Goya, and the strength of the chiaroscuro is closely related to that found in the paintings of Ribera. Zuloaga now lives in Zamoya near St. Sebastian, where he maintains his studio and still retains his collection of the masterpieces of the old Spanish tradition, of which his art is but the natural continuation.

BIBLIOGRAPHY: Léonce Bénédite, *Ignacio Zuloaga,* n. d.—Giulio de Frenzi, *Ignacio Zuloaga,* 1912.—*Ignacio Zuloaga,* Coll. Monographias d'arte, 1920.—Gregorio Martinez, *Ignacio Zuloaga,* n. d.

**ZURBARÁN (Francisco de).**—Spanish painter, 1598-c. 1664. He was born at Fuente de Cantos (Prov. of Badajos; Extremadura). His parents were humble peasants. When sixteen years old Zurbarán entered the studio of Pedro Diaz de Villanueva at Seville. The contract for

ZURBARÁN: ST. CASILDA. (Prado, Madrid.)

the artist's apprenticeship, covering a period of three years, is preserved and has been translated into English by N. S. Evans (See Bibliography). The hypothesis that he studied later in Italy has been refuted by modern critics.

ZURBARÁN: THE ANNUNCIATION. (San Telmo Gallery, Seville.)

From 1616, when the artist was only eighteen, we possess a signed and dated work—an *Immaculate Conception*—represented by a little girl borne up to heaven on clouds. "The influence of Herrera the Elder is visible in works such as in the seven full-length figures representing Apostles in the Lisbonne Museum (1624) as well as in the altar executed for the Marqués de Malagón" (1625. Chapel of St. Peter, Seville Cathedral). The series of paintings in the Cathedral of Seville representing scenes from the life of St. Peter Nolasco, which were formerly attributed to Zurbarán, have been recently ascribed by Sr. Sánchez Cantón to Francisco Reina.

The four paintings executed for the Church of St. Bonaventura of Seville are now scattered in the galleries of Berlin (*St. Bonaventura visited by St. Thomas*), Dresden (*St. Bonaventura visited by an Angel who points out to him which Cardinal should be elected Pope*), —and of the Louvre (*St. Bonaventura Presiding over a Chapter of Minor Friars,* and the *Saint on his Death-bed*). Of the above picture the one at Berlin bears the date 1629.

In 1631 Zurbarán finished his *Apotheosis of St. Thomas of Aquinas.* It was originally ordered for the chapel of the College of St. Thomas of Seville and is now in the Museum of that city. This picture can pass as one of the noblest productions of the Spanish school of painting.

In the same year Zurbarán painted the Blessed Alonso Rodriguez (Ac. de San Fernando, Madrid).

It is supposed that in 1633 he began to work on the series of paintings of the Carthusian Monastery of Jerez de la Frontera. On the high altar he represented the *Annunciation,* the *Adoration of the Shepherds,* the *Four Evangelists,* and other *Saints*; in the passage leading to the sanctuary, *Saints* belonging to the order; in the Sacristy, *St. Christopher and St. Bruno;* on the altarpiece in the Choir, the lay brothers, two large canvases which tell the history of the Chartreuse Monasteries; on the walls of the Choir, the *Virgin and Child* surrounded by kneeling brothers, and *Our Lady* coming, in a battle to the succour of the inhabitants of Jerez. Still other pictures adorned the monastery. Some of them are now in the provincial Museum of Cadiz; and four of these magnificent paintings belong to the Museum of Grenoble: the *Adoration of the Magi,* the *Adoration of the Shepherds,* the *Nativity,* and the *Circumcision.*

The Church of the Hieronymite Monastery of Guadalupe, in the wild region which separates the North of Estremadura from Castile, contains what is probably Zurbarán's most important work. It consists of thirteen (only eleven mentioned by Kehrer) pictures. Two, *St. Ildefonso* and *St. Nicholas of Bari,* are placed on two side altars at the entrance to the Choir; eight, representing *Incidents from the life of*

ZURBARÁN: ST. CATHERINE. (Cathedral of Palencia.)

*St. Jerome* decorate the walls of the second sacristy; two others, likewise devoted to the life of the founder of the order, are found in a neighbouring apartment, which also contains the *Triumph of St. Jerome.* These large paintings are in a deplorable state of preservation. This is a great loss to art, for these simple and dignified compositions are the most complete expression of Zurbarán's genius.

About 1650, he went to Cordova where he had several commissions to fulfill.

In 1650, at the instigation of Velázquez, who greatly admired him, Zurbarán was called to Madrid and charged by Philip IV to take part in the decoration of the Buen Retiro Palace. He painted mythological compositions. His ten paintings of the *Labours of Hercules* are now in the Prado. However, they do not count as the best among his oeuvre.

In the same year the Marquésa de Campo Alange commissioned him to paint, for the Capucine Monastery of Castellón, where they are still preserved, a series of paintings representing the great founders of religious orders (St. Basil, St. Benedict, St. Elias, St. Augustin, St. Dominick, St. Peter Nolasco, St. Bruno, St. Jerome, St. Ignacio de Loyola).

A *St. Francis of Assisi in Meditation,* formerly in the Coll. of Sr. Beruete at Madrid, and a *Virgin with the Holy Infant,* are dated 1659. "Were it not for the signature, nobody would recognize the latter as a painting by Zurbarán as in drawing, colouring, and character it is very different from his other works." The *Immaculate Conception* in the Budapest Museum, and the *Christ despoiled of his Raiments,* in the Parish Church of San Juan Bautista of Jadraque, both dated 1661, are the last pictures known to have been executed by the artist: "They terminate for us his large artistic output." We do not know the date of his death. The last documentary mention we have is of the year 1664 when, on February 28th, he appraised, with the painter Francisco Rici, the paintings of the estate of D. Francisco Jacinto de Salcedo of Madrid.

"The Spanish clergy of his period is alive in the work of Zurbarán, from the eloquent and erudite theologian to the simple saintly brother with poorly trimmed beard; from the prince of the Church, smiling and well treated by life, to the poor liverish monk, corroded by fears of after-life; and, finally, to the essential mystic weakened by penitence, and imbued, almost with a touch of magic as, for instance the stupendous *San Luis Beltrán* in the Museum of Seville." Enc. Espasa). The foregoing analysis recalls paintings with single figures such as those of *Father Jeromino Pere* and *Father Pedro Machado* in the Accademia de Bellas Artes of Madrid,—of a *Reading Carthusian Monk* in the Hisp. Soc. of Am—of the *Mystic Enrique Suso* and *Pope Gregory the Great* in the Seville Museum, of St. Thomas Apostle and St. Cyril in the Coll. of the Duke of Sutherland, Stafford House, London, etc.

ZURBARÁN: ST. THOMAS AQUINAS. (Museum, Seville.)

On the other hand "a very singular conception is that of the holy women he pictured, attired in a magnificence quite archaic, of demure carriage, strong and youthful, beautiful and haughty, none would say they are the Virgins of the legends, but rather titled ladies contemporaries of the artist. If they had not the attributes of the saints, one might think, when seeing the pearls and jewels they display, that they belonged to the Court of Philip III, and that, far from being images of women who were canonized for their virtues, they are portraits of worldly realities, of wealthy dames looking fixedly at us in an imposing air of nobility and attractiveness" (Cascales y Muñoz). Fitting this description are such of his paintings as the *Santa Rufina* (N. Y. Coll. of Mr. Archer Huntington)—*St. Margaret* (London, Natl. Gallery)—*St. Casilda* (Madrid, Prado)—*St. Elizabeth* (Montreal, Heirs of Sir William van Horne) — *St. Apollonia* (Paris, Louvre).

"Zurbarán's artistic endowment is not only revealed in his paintings